Elements of Land Law

Fourth edition

Kevin Gray   LLD (Cantab), DCL (Oxon), FBA
Of the Middle Temple, Barrister
Professor of Law and Fellow of Trinity College, University of Cambridge

and

Susan Francis Gray   MA (Cantab), F Land I
Solicitor of the Supreme Court
Sometime Assistant Land Registrar, HM Land Registry

OXFORD
UNIVERSITY PRESS

OXFORD
UNIVERSITY PRESS

Great Clarendon Street, Oxford OX2 6DP

Oxford University Press is a department of the University of Oxford.
It furthers the University's objective of excellence in research, scholarship,
and education by publishing worldwide in

Oxford New York

Auckland Cape Town Dar es Salaam Hong Kong Karachi Kuala Lumpur
Madrid Melbourne Mexico City Nairobi New Delhi Shanghai Taipei Toronto

With offices in
Argentina Austria Brazil Chile Czech Republic France Greece
Guatemala Hungary Italy Japan South Korea Poland Portugal
Singapore Switzerland Thailand Turkey Ukraine Vietnam

Oxford is a registered trade mark of Oxford University Press
in the UK and in certain other countries

Published in the United States
by Oxford University Press Inc., New York

© Oxford University Press 2005

A catalogue record for this title is available from the British Library

Library of Congress Cataloging in Publication Data
Data available

First edition 1987
Second edition 1993
Third edition 2000
Fourth edition 2005

0-406-97577-9

Typeset by Columns Design Ltd, Reading
Printed in Great Britain
on acid-free paper by
Ashford Colour Press Ltd, Gosport, Hampshire

For our friend

SUE PLEDGER

Preface

This fourth edition of our *Elements of Land Law* has been rewritten and restructured in order to accommodate the new legal landscape created, with effect from 13 October 2003, by the enactment of the Land Registration Act 2002 and the introduction of the Land Registration Rules 2003. Other legislative developments have followed apace, not least the recreational access provisions of the Countryside and Rights of Way Act 2000 (effective 19 September 2004), the 'commonhold' provisions of the Commonhold and Leasehold Reform Act 2002 (effective 27 September 2004) and the new 'regulated mortgage contract' regime brought into being by the Financial Services and Markets Act 2000 (effective 31 October 2004). We have also incorporated an account of the Planning and Compulsory Purchase Act 2004 and the likely effect of the Housing Bill 2004. These statutory initiatives, together with the need to monitor the onward march of case law in this jurisdiction and in other parts of the common law world, have ensured that the production of this fourth edition has been no easy matter (*'tantae molis erat ...* ').

Our task has been made possible by the intellectual and practical support provided by many friends. We owe thanks, in particular, to Tim Bonyhady, Peter Butt, David L Callies, Hansa Chauhan, Laura Pieters Cordy, Brendan Edgeworth, Margaret Francis, Scott Grattan, Iain McMorrin, Kenneth Reid, Craig Rotherham, Geoffrey Samuel, Nicholas Seddon, Helene Shapo, Michael Taggart, Patrick Troy, Laura Underkuffler, André van der Walt, Bruce Ziff, Leslie Zines and Justices Bryan Beaumont and Paul Finn of the Federal Court of Australia. A Freehills Research Fellowship at the University of New South Wales in 2003 enabled us to maintain a lively contact not only with many colleagues throughout Australia, but also with some of the most insightful property jurisprudence of the common law world. Back in England invaluable help was given, as always, by the magnificent staff of the Squire Law Library (and, in particular, by Lesley Dingle, David Wills and Peter Zawada). The white heat of technology was fired (and sometimes doused) by Max Hacking of Hacking Network Solutions of Cambridge.

We must express our gratitude to our former publishers, who have assumed sole responsibility for drawing up lists, tables and the index for this edition. We owe particular thanks to Isabel Isaacson and Julian Roskams (who have overseen successive editions of this book) and to our new publishers, the ever helpful staff of Oxford University Press. We must also pay tribute to the amazing team at Columns Design Limited of Reading, without whose superlative efforts this book would not have seen the light of day.

Last, but by no means least, we must thank Antony Gormley and Jay Jopling / White Cube for allowing us to use, as our cover image, the haunting sculptures ('Inside Australia') which Antony has installed at Lake Ballard in Western Australia. It seems to us that, in the shimmering haze of the desert landscape, these figures superbly capture the elemental nature of the association between humans and the land on which they live.

Kevin Gray

Susan Francis Gray

18 October 2004

Contents

Abbreviations

Legislation:

AEA 1925	Administration of Estates Act 1925
AHA 1986	Agricultural Holdings Act 1986
AJA 1970	Administration of Justice Act 1970
AJA 1973	Administration of Justice Act 1973
ANLA 1992	Access to Neighbouring Land Act 1992
ASBA 2003	Anti-social Behaviour Act 2003
C(RTP)A 1999	Contracts (Rights of Third Parties) Act 1999
CCA 1974	Consumer Credit Act 1974
CCA 1984	County Courts Act 1984
CJ&POA 1994	Criminal Justice and Public Order Act 1994
CLA 1977	Criminal Law Act 1977
CLPA 1852	Common Law Procedure Act 1852
CALRA 2002	Commonhold and Leasehold Reform Act 2002
COA 1979	Charging Orders Act 1979
CPR	Civil Procedure Rules 1998 (SI 1998/3132)
CROWA 2000	Countryside and Rights of Way Act 2000
CTA 1987	Channel Tunnel Act 1987
DPA 1972	Defective Premises Act 1972
ECHR	European Convention for the Protection of Human Rights and Fundamental Freedoms
EPA 1990	Environmental Protection Act 1990
FLA 1996	Family Law Act 1996
FS&MA 2000	Financial Services and Markets Act 2000
HA 1985	Housing Act 1985
HA 1988	Housing Act 1988
HA 1996	Housing Act 1996
HB 2004	Housing Bill 2004
HRA 1998	Human Rights Act 1998
IA 1986	Insolvency Act 1986
LA 1980	Limitation Act 1980
LCA 1925	Land Charges Act 1925
LCA 1972	Land Charges Act 1972
LPA 1922	Law of Property Act 1922
LPA 1925	Law of Property Act 1925
LPA 1969	Law of Property Act 1969
LP(MP)A 1989	Law of Property (Miscellaneous Provisions) Act 1989
LP(R)A 1938	Leasehold Property (Repairs) Act 1938
LRA 1925	Land Registration Act 1925

LRA 1967	Leasehold Reform Act 1967
LRA 2002	Land Registration Act 2002
LRH&UDA 1993	Leasehold Reform, Housing and Urban Development Act 1993
LRR 2003	Land Registration Rules 2003 (SI 2003/1417)
LR(S)A 2003	Land Reform (Scotland) Act 2003
L&TA 1927	Landlord and Tenant Act 1927
L&TA 1954	Landlord and Tenant Act 1954
L&TA 1985	Landlord and Tenant Act 1985
L&TA 1987	Landlord and Tenant Act 1987
L&TA 1988	Landlord and Tenant Act 1988
L&T(C)A 1995	Landlord and Tenant (Covenants) Act 1995
MHA 1983	Matrimonial Homes Act 1983
PA 1832	Prescription Act 1832
PEA 1977	Protection from Eviction Act 1977
P&CPA 2004	Planning and Compulsory Purchase Act 2004
RA 1977	Rent Act 1977
SCA 1981	Supreme Court Act 1981
SLA 1925	Settled Land Act 1925
T&CPA 1990	Town and Country Planning Act 1990
TA 1925	Trustee Act 1925
TA 1996	Treasure Act 1996
TA 2000	Trustee Act 2000
TOLATA 1996	Trusts of Land and Appointment of Trustees Act 1996
UCTA 1977	Unfair Contract Terms Act 1977

Law Commission Publications:

Law Com No 127	*Transfer of Land: The Law of Positive and Restrictive Covenants* (January 1984)
Law Com No 142	*Codification of the Law of Landlord and Tenant: Forfeiture of Tenancies* (March 1985)
Law Com No 158	*Property Law: Third Report on Land Registration* (March 1987)
Law Com No 174	*Landlord and Tenant: Privity of Contract and Estate* (November 1988)
Law Com No 188	*Transfer of Land: Overreaching: Beneficiaries in Occupation* (December 1989)
Law Com No 194	*Landlord and Tenant: Distress for Rent* (February 1991)
Law Com No 201	*Transfer of Land: Obsolete Restrictive Covenants* (July 1991)
Law Com No 221	*Landlord and Tenant Law: Termination of Tenancies Bill* (February 1994)
Law Com No 238	*Landlord and Tenant: Responsibility for State and Condition of Property* (March 1996)
Law Com No 254	*Land Registration for the Twenty-First Century: A Consultative Document* (September 1998)
Law Com No 270	*Limitation of Actions* (July 2001)
Law Com No 271	*Land Registration for the Twenty-First Century: A Conveyancing Revolution* (July 2001)
Law Com No 284	*Renting Homes* (November 2003)
Law Com CP No 174	*Termination of Tenancies for Tenant Default* (January 2004)

Other:

Bl Comm	W Blackstone, *Commentaries on the Laws of England* (1st edn London 1765–1769)
BPR	Butterworths Property Reports
Challis	*Law of Real Property* (3rd edn London 1911)
Co Litt	E Coke, *The First Part of the Institutes of the Laws of England* or *A Commentary upon Littleton* (11th edn London 1719)
Jiro	Journal of the Institute of Rent Officers
Litt	*Littleton's Tenures* (ed E Wambaugh, Washington DC 1903)
Ruoff & Roper	*Ruoff & Roper on the Law and Practice of Registered Conveyancing* (looseleaf edn)
Sheppard's Touchstone	W Sheppard, *The Touchstone of Common Assurances* (London 1651)

Table of statutes

Paragraph number in **bold** type indicates where the legislation is set out in part or in full.

Land Charges Act 1972 – *contd*
s7 (1), (2).. 12.336
8.............................. 12.333, 12.334, 12.336
9 (1)... 12.325
10 (1).................................. 12.277, 12.325
(2)... 12.325
(4), (6)... 12.326
11 (1)–(3)............................... 12.51, 12.326
(5), (6)............................... 12.51, 12.326
s 17 (1) 1.23, 1.117, 9.121, 12.281, 12.293,
12.294, 12.332, 12.368,
14.136, 15.246

Land Compensation Act 1961
s 5–6... 13.169

Land Compensation Act 1973...... 7.307, 14.201
s 33A–33C... 13.169
33D... 13.169
33D (3)–(4)... 13.166
33E–33K.. 13.169

Land Reform (Scotland) Act 2003............. 5.46
s 1 (1)–(5)... 5.50
s 2 (1), (3)... 5.48
s 3 (1)–(3)... 5.48
s 6... 5.50
s 9... 5.50
s 10... 5.48

Land Registration Act 1925 ... 1.7, 2.101, 2.109,
2.136, 2.163, 6.24, 12.61,
12.84, 12.130, 12.140,
12.156, 12.176, 12.234,
12.237, 12.250, 13.114
s 3 (xi)... 2.128
(xv), (xvi)... 12.61
s 8 (1) (a)... 7.228
s 8 (1A).. 7.228
20 (1).. 12.159
s 21.. 7.228
23 (1).. 12.159
54 (1)... 12.85
55, 56.. 12.85
57 (1)... 12.85
s 66... 9.113
70 (1).............................. 12.61, 12.130
(a)................... 9.100, 12.135, 12.237
(c).. 12.243
(f).. 12.135
s 70 (1) (g) 3.11, 11.212, 12.135, 12.147,
12.154, 12.159, 12.173,
12.182, 12.222
(i).. 12.242
(k)....... 12.140, 12.143, 12.144, 12.145
75 (1)–(2).. 6.54
82 (1).. 12.245
(3)... 3.11
(a), (c)..................................... 12.254
101–103.. 12.61
112 (1).. 6.20
s 123 (1)... 2.114
s 123A... 2.114

Land Registration Act 1988
s 1 (1)... 6.20

Land Registration Act 1997..................... 2.101
s 1.. 8.249
5 (4)... 8.249

Land Registration Act 2002 .... 1.2, 1.8, 2.48,
2.76, 2.101, 2.103, 2.104,
2.110, 2.113, 2.116, 2.117,
2.118, 2.122, 2.134, 2.136,
2.137, 2.142, 2.151, 2.155,
2.156, 2.162, 2.164, 2.167,
2.173, 2.174, 2.191, 3.34,
6.3, 6.8, 6.24, 6.25, 6.26,
6.27, 6.30, 6.53, 6.54, 6.56,
6.57, 6.64, 6.65, 6.68, 6.71,
6.134, 7.30, 7.62, 7.217,
8.115, 8.206, 9.159, 11.136,
11.145, 11.222, 11.223,
11.224, 12.7, 12.60, 12.61,
12.63, 12.64, 12.75, 12.76,
12.83, 12.107, 12.113,
12.133, 12.135, 12.140,
12.150, 12.161, 12.163,
12.177, 12.179, 12.180,
12.205, 12.221, 12.232,
12.239, 12.240, 12.247,
12.276, 12.277, 13.113,
14.236, 15.177, 15.237
s 1 (1)... 6.9
2 (a)................................ 1.135, 2.143, 6.26
s 2 (b).. 2.144
s 3... 2.143
s 3 (1)............................... 1.135, 7.39, 7.229
s 3 (1) (a)... 3.26
(b).. 8.227
s 3 (1) (c)... 2.149
(d).. 8.116
s 3 (2) 1.135, 2.115, 6.26, 7.39, 7.229, 8.116,
8.227
s 3 (2) (a)..................................... 3.26, 7.39
s 3 (2) (b).. 7.39
s 3 (3)..................... 2.149, 7.229, 8.116, 8.227
s 3 (4)... 7.229
s 3 (5)... 7.228
s 3 (6)... 7.39, 7.229
s 4... 2.143
s 4 (1)............................... 1.135, 2.115, 7.40
s 4 (1) (a)..................................... 2.175, 7.242
s 4 (1) (c) (ii).. 7.237
s 4 (1) (d), (e)....................................... 7.237
s 4 (1) (g)................. 7.40, 7.242, 8.252, 15.246
s 4 (2)........................... 1.135, 2.115, 7.40, 7.237
s 4 (2) (b)... 7.241
s 4 (3)... 7.40, 7.242
s 4 (5)... 7.228, 8.251
s 4 (7) (a), (b)... 7.40
s 4 (8)................................. 7.40, 7.242, 8.252
s 4 (9)... 7.40
s 5 (1)... 2.175, 7.239
s 5 (1) (a)... 7.40
s 5 (2)... 7.239
s 6 (1) 2.115, 6.26, 7.40, 7.41, 7.237, 7.242,
7.243, 15.245
s 6 (2)... 2.115, 8.253
s 6 (2) (a).......................... 7.40, 7.242, 8.252
s 6 (2) (b)............................... 7.40, 7.242
s 6 (3)... 2.115, 7.243
s 6 (3) (a)... 7.239
s 6 (3) (b)... 7.242
s 6 (4) 7.41, 7.237, 7.243, 8.253, 12.52,
15.245
s 6 (5)... 7.41
s 6 (6).. 7.40, 7.242

Table of cases

A

C

D

G

H

I

J

K

L

M

O

P

Q

R

S

T

V

W

X

Y

Z

Chapter 1

Land

THE SIGNIFICANCE OF LAND

1.1 Land is elemental: it is where life begins and it is where life ends. Land provides the physical substratum for all human activity; it is the essential base of all social and commercial interaction. We spend scarcely a moment out of contact with terra firma and our very existence is constantly sustained and shaped by the natural and constructed world around us. The significance of land in human affairs is therefore incalculable, although it is only in an era of global environmental threat that we slowly begin to realise how fragile and irreplaceable is the rich resource on which we so utterly depend. In the case of real property, as was once observed, 'there is a defined and limited supply of the commodity.'[1]

1   *Linden Gardens Trust Ltd v Lenesta Sludge Disposals Ltd* [1994] 1 AC 85 at 107D per Lord Browne-Wilkinson.

The construction of a legal regime for land

1.2 The construction of a coherent legal regime for land has not been a simple or instant process. Indeed, it is not easy to imagine, *tabula rasa*, how best to fashion a systematic body of rules governing rights in and over land. The evolution of our present system of land law has taken most of a millennium, resulting in the remarkable corpus of legislation found largely in the property statutes of 1925,[1] as now supplemented by the Land Registration Act 2002 and the Commonhold and Leasehold Reform Act 2002. In general this framework of rules functions today with admirable success, but it is far from obvious that, if the task of construction were begun again, the end result would necessarily resemble the law of real property in its present form. The conceptual points of departure which lie at the back of the English law of land contain little, if anything, of a particularly compelling or *a priori* nature. There was nothing inevitable about the eventual shape of modern land law, but it remains true that the law of today is still heavily impressed with the form of ancient legal and intellectual constructs.

1   For reference to 'Lord Birkenhead's great scheme for the reform of English real property law embodied in the 1925 legislation', see *Abbey National Building Society v Cann* [1991] 1 AC 56 at 76B–C per Lord Bridge of Harwich.

Changing perceptions of land

1.3   Modern awareness of the phenomenon of land has been considerably sharpened by environmental concerns. More than a century ago the American environmentalist John Muir recorded, in a strangely haunting journal entry, that one day he 'only went out for a walk, and finally concluded to stay out till sundown, for going out, I found, was really going in.'[1] In its distinctive way, Muir's understanding of the receptive quality of the physical world mirrored the centrality of land in the thinking of an earlier age of the common law. Four centuries ago Coke spoke of the 'precedent dignity' of land, the 'element of the earth' being 'preferred before the other elements: first and principally, because it is for the habitation and resting-place of man.'[2] But while Coke believed, for this reason, that 'land builded is more worthy than other land', it is today increasingly recognised, amidst the turmoil of crowded urban life, that recreational access to undeveloped land is a precondition for the flourishing of the human spirit. A powerful perception of the social importance of land is nowadays incorporated in various legislative guarantees of access to the regenerative influence of wild country.[3] For example, the Countryside and Rights of Way Act 2000, with its reinforcement of a qualified 'right to roam' over open country, was aimed quite explicitly at promoting the salutary, democratic and educative effects imparted by contact with the natural environment.[4] Each successive generation formulates its own, slightly different, understanding of the importance of land as a primary resource.

1   R Engberg and D Wesling, John Muir: *To Yosemite And Beyond – Writings from the Years 1863 to 1875* (Univ of Wisconsin Press, Madison 1980), p 23.
2   *Co Litt*, p 4a.
3   Justice William Douglas of the United States Supreme Court once wrote of the 'citizenship of the mountains', where '[p]overty, wealth, accidents of birth, social standing, race [are] immaterial' (W O Douglas, *Of Men And Mountains* (London 1951), pp 211, 293). See Gray, 'Equitable Property' (1994) 47(2) CLP 157 at 200–202.
4   **[Para 5.46]**. See *Access to the Open Countryside in England and Wales: A Consultation Paper* (DETR, February 1998), paras 3.50, 3.66–3.67.

The pervasive reach of land law

1.4   In a world of limited goods and attenuated altruism, the commodity of land always requires regulation. Land law is, accordingly, that part of the general law which governs the allocation of rights and obligations in relation to 'real' or 'immovable' property. There is no moment of any day in which we stand beyond its pervasive reach. No matter what we are doing, the law of land has something to say to us, since it constantly describes our jural status in relation to terra firma (whether as owner-occupiers, tenants, licensees, members of the general public, or even simply as trespassers). Largely unnoticed, land law provides a running commentary on every single action of every day.[1] Not only does it supplement or reinforce our instinctive labelling of the things of the external world as *meum* and *tuum*; it also plays a deeply instrumental role in facilitating and regulating the efficient use of all land resources.

1   'To go to sleep in one's bed is as much and as little of a legal act per se as signing a deed' (Max Radin, 'The Permanent Problems of the Law' 15 Cornell LQ 1 at 3 (1929–30)).

The pivotal function of land law

1.5   Not all, of course, have shared this purposive vision of the regime of land law. Some social theorists have regarded the initial demarcation of property rights in land as a cause of profound regret.[1] For others it has provided a stimulus to radical change of the social order.[2] Nevertheless the consensus view is that the idea of property – particularly in relation to the all-important commodity of land – plays an indispensable role in the organisation of our social and business life.[3] We can no more contemplate a society without some notion of property than we can imagine a society which has yet to discover the device of contract.[4] Some theorists have gone even further in underscoring the link between the phenomenon of property and the endorsement of the individual's sense of personal integrity.[5] For such writers the idea of property in land is closely associated with a concept of personal and territorial inviolability which remains deeply embedded in the history of the common law. This powerful connection is reflected in the way in which trespass (both to person and to land) emerged as the earliest and most important action at common law. It may even be that the notion of trespass itself derives from yet older Anglo-Saxon and Norse concepts of 'seisin', which some have claimed to underlie the ideal of democratic government developed in Northwestern Europe during the last thousand years.[6]

1   See eg J-J Rousseau, 'Discourse on the Origin of Inequality', in *The Social Contract and Discourses* (Everyman's Library edn, London 1913), p 76.

2   'Property is theft' (J Proudhon, *Qu'est-ce que la propriété? Premier Memoir* (Paris 1840), p 131).

3   Some philosophers have indeed perceived in the institution of property the vital prerequisite of civilised co-existence. David Hume was able to say that '[n]o one can doubt that the convention for the distinction of property, and for the stability of possession, is of all circumstances the most necessary to the establishment of human society, and that after the agreement for the fixing and observing of this rule, there remains little or nothing to be done towards settling a perfect harmony and concord' (*A Treatise of Human Nature* (Everyman's Library edn, London 1911), Vol II, pp 196–197 (Book III, Part II)).

4   It was John Locke who argued that the 'great and chief end ... of men's uniting into commonwealths, and putting themselves under government, is the preservation of their property' (*Two Treatises of Government* (2nd critical edn by T P R Laslett, Cambridge 1967), *The Second Treatise*, s 124 (pp 368–369)). More recently it has been said that '[n]ext to constitutional rights, property rights are the strongest interests recognised by our law' (*White v Chandler* [2001] 1 NZLR 28 at [67] per Hammond J).

5   This association is a commonplace in literature. See, for instance, John Galsworthy, *The Forsyte Saga, Vol 1: The Man of Property* (London 1906), pp 44–45: 'In his great chair with the book-rest sat Jolyon, the figurehead of his family and class and creed, with his white head and dome-like forehead, the representative of moderation, and order, and love of property.' See also M J Radin, 'Property and Personhood' 34 Stan L Rev 957 (1981–82).

6   For an elaboration of this argument, see Alice Tay, 'Law, the citizen and the state', in E
      Kamenka, R Brown and A E-S Tay (ed), *Law and Society: The Crisis in Legal Ideals* (London
      1978), p 10. On the significance of 'seisin', see Chapter 3 [**para 3.1**].

The function of this book

1.6   This book contains an account of the basic elements of the English law of
land. Land law has acquired a reputation as a highly technical area which many
students find difficult and unrewarding. However, none of this need be so and
this book seeks to show that even quite complex problems of modern land law
can be explained in simple terms which start from underlying 'elements' or first
principles. Part of the aim is also to use these elements of land law to pinpoint
fundamental features of the more general phenomenon of property. In the
process it will become obvious that the law of property is not really about *things*
but rather about *people*, and that the study of land law is ultimately an inquiry
into an important range of socially defined relationships and morally conditioned obligations. Indeed, as Alice Tay once said,[1] the 'concept of property,
the way in which it is legally defined and the extent to which it is legally, socially
and politically protected raise immediately the most fundamental problems of
political philosophy and social life – the relationship between the individual and
his social environment, between the citizen and the State and – in modern
society – between the personal and the commercial.'

1   A E-S Tay, 'Property and Law in the Society of Mass Production, Mass Consumption and
      Mass Allocation' (1977) 10 ARSP (New Series) 87 at 97-98.

Stasis and change

1.7   This relational view of land law highlights certain characteristics of
property which are essential to any genuine understanding of the subject. The
law of land comprises a crystallised expression of values, obligations and
ideologies, all cast in sharp relief against the landscape of the law. Although
this branch of the law often seems to have a strangely durable quality, it should
not be assumed that the narrative of land law is a history of stasis. Throughout
most of the 20th century the real property law of England and Wales was
dominated by a vast corpus of statute law (the '1925 legislation') which came
into effect on 1 January 1926.[1] This legislation was itself the summation of
steady progress towards reform which had been set in motion some 80 years
earlier; and it was perhaps inevitable that the structural features of English land
law, so painstakingly gathered together in the 1925 legislation, should have been
destined to survive relatively intact until recent times.

1   Foremost in this body of legislation were the Law of Property Act 1925, the Settled Land
      Act 1925 and the Trustee Act 1925, with the Land Registration Act 1925 tacked on as an
      ill-drafted piece of legislation relating to a little used form of title registration.

1.8   But '[r]adical change has … been a part of the development of property
law.'[1] Social values and legal directions change, sometimes quite dramatically,

and the impact of these changes inevitably makes the law of land as exciting and fast-moving as any other area of contemporary English law. Many of the familiar features of 20th century land law have now been removed, sidelined or transformed beyond recognition. Unregistered land law, which formed the core of the 1925 legislation, is virtually a thing of the past. During the last ten years there has been an explosion of new legislation. We are now entering an era of almost universal registration of title and must prepare rapidly for the brave new world of electronic conveyancing. The Land Registration Act 2002, most of which came into effect on 13 October 2003, promises to alter the legal landscape in hugely significant ways. Modern land law is also being reshaped by the impact of the Human Rights Act 1998, European Union law and the law of environmental regulation. Far-reaching reformulations of the law of easements and the codes regulating domestic lettings and mortgages are now well within view. Suddenly the land law of the immediately foreseeable future appears markedly different from the law we have known in the past.

1   *Western Australia v Ward* (2000) 170 ALR 159 at 362 per North J.

Property law as a network of jural relationships

1.9 This book sets out to explore some of the broader connotations of property within the constantly changing context of English land law. It examines the way in which the land lawyer uses and manipulates technical concepts in order to describe the accumulation of wealth and security. It discusses the way in which the underlying ideology of property law interacts with key issues of priority and efficiency. Above all, it depicts property law as a network of jural relationships between individuals in respect of valued resources, and land law as a body of rules which ultimately governs the distribution of utility in the particularly significant resource of realty.

THE COMMON LAW CONCEPT OF 'LAND'

1.10 The world of the common lawyer has always been a curious blend of the physical and the abstract, a commixture of the earthily pragmatic and the deeply conceptual.[1] Having broken away from the Romanist legal tradition, the common lawyer devised a distinctive regime of property rules which – notwithstanding the extensive statutory consolidation of the early 20th century – is still piecemeal and full of internal ambivalence. This alternative to the *dominium* of civilian jurisprudence remains a collocation of organic adaptations, the common lawyer's crudely empirical outlook being encapsulated in a general reluctance to embrace any grand or overarching model of the phenomenon of ownership.[2] In consequence the common lawyer's understanding of land still oscillates between a purely material conception of the physical stuff of land and a more cerebral image of land as comprising a co-ordinated set of abstract rights.

1   For a discussion of the tension between these various elements, see Gray and Gray, 'The Idea of Property in Land', in S Bright and J K Dewar (ed), *Land Law: Themes and Perspectives* (OUP 1998), pp 18–39.

2   See e g *Commissioner for Railways et al v Valuer-General* [1974] AC 328 at 351H–352A per Lord Wilberforce **[para 2.77]**. Compare the dominium of Roman law, which treated as conceptually inseparable the owner's right to use, dispose of, and exclude others from, his property. Dominium was an indivisible unity and the idea that it might be fragmented between a number of owners, each with a separate proprietary right to different aspects of dominium, was and still is unacceptable to civilian legal thought.

The tension between the empirical and the conceptual

1.11   At one level, the common lawyer's primary concern is with the observable phenomenon of de facto possessory control as exercised over physically identifiable terrain or premises.[1] What actually happens on the ground – whether rightly or wrongly – has always constituted a powerful determinant of entitlement in English land law. The normative tug of sheer physical fact should never be underestimated. Yet, at another level, the common law perception of property embodies an obsession with the rational manipulation of abstract concepts and with the careful outworking of axiomatic truths. Nowhere is this fascination with the naked force of reason more apparent than in the law of land, with its remorseless taxonomy of estates and interests,[2] its subclassifications of legal and equitable right,[3] and with its multiple applications of propositional dogma.[4] In the hands of the common lawyer, land law became a field of highly artificial concepts, each defined with meticulous – almost mathematical – precision.[5]

1   **[Para 3.1]**.
2   **[Para 1.120]**.
3   **[Para 1.155]**.
4   **[Para 2.178]**.
5   See *Wright v Gibbons* (1949) 78 CLR 313 at 330 per Dixon J (confirming that central features of modern property law bear 'many traces of the scholasticism of the times in which its principles were developed').

The creative product

1.12   The outcome of this creative tension between the physical and the abstract has been the elaboration of a pragmatic, but highly operational, law of land. A vigorous preoccupation with earthy reality, coupled with the constant subjection of the inner workings of property to logical ordering, has for centuries rendered it unnecessary for the common law to construct any large or systematic theory of ownership.[1] The conceptual purity of a regime of individually ordered estates and interests in land seemed to provide a perfectly functional substitute for more holistic ideas of *dominium*. It was, however, the characteristic interplay of empirical and conceptual concerns which has made modern land law what it is, although the interaction has also served to infuse land law with a structural ambiguity which goes to the root of even the definition of such basic terms as 'land' itself.[2]

1   See Gray, 'Property in Common Law Systems', in G E van Maanen and A J van der Walt (ed), *Property Law on the Threshold of the 21st Century* (MAKLU, Antwerp, 1996), pp 277–278.
2   See, for example, the fusion of the material and the abstract which is evident in various statutory definitions [**paras 1.24, 1.117**].

The multiple dimensions of 'land' in English law

1.13   The underlying tension between the material and the conceptual has imparted a multi-dimensional complexity to the understanding of the term 'land' in English law. The first three dimensions of land as a physical reality are perfectly consistent with the rough and ready empiricism which characterises so much of our land law. To these crudely factual dimensions the common law was to add a fourth, more cerebral, dimension of *time*.[1] In this way the common law gave a chronological significance to the raw pragmatic notion of possession and, in the process, introduced the transformative concept of time-related 'estates' in the land. A fifth dimension of land emerged when the common law was required to accommodate an interpenetrating system of conscience-driven rules of equity,[2] with the consequent recognition that 'estates' in land could be held either *at law* or *in equity*. The multiple dimensions inherent within the concept of 'land' must now be explored in greater detail.

1   [**Para 1.123**].
2   [**Para 1.155**].

THE FIRST TWO DIMENSIONS OF 'LAND'

1.14   The first two dimensions of land lend themselves easily, and most usefully, to graphic representation in the form of maps and plans which depict the boundaries and other salient topographical features of specific areas of 'land'.[1]

1   See A Pottage, 'The Measure of Land' (1994) 57 MLR 361.

Mapping

1.15   One attempt at a definition of 'land' might focus, quite reasonably, upon the way in which the surface area of England and Wales has been meticulously mapped by the Ordnance Survey, a task which began in 1791 and continues to the present day. The mapping tools may have changed from theodolite and chain to digital imaging by satellite, but the product remains the same – a remarkably detailed two-dimensional representation of the defining contours, features and limits of the 'land' comprised in England and Wales.[1] Such maps are essential to the activities of conveyancers, land registrars, surveyors and ramblers alike, but their usefulness in determining the boundaries of estate ownership is inevitably somewhat restricted. For instance, the Ordnance Survey can mark the position of a hedge or wall only by a solid line drawn along the centre of the topographical feature in question, but such marking provides no conclusive indication whether that feature is itself owned by one or other adjacent occupier (or is indeed shared by both).

1   The 'land' comprised within England and Wales clearly includes some territory beyond the low water mark at the coastline. Thus, for instance, Channel Tunnel Act 1987, s 10(1) provides that the space of the Channel Tunnel and its immediately surrounding subsoil extending to the mid-point of the English Channel are 'incorporated into England' and form part of the county of Kent (see now the registration of 'The Seaward Section of the Channel Tunnel' under Land Registry Title No K655621). It is also arguable that the sea bed underlying an encircling three-mile belt of territorial waters constitutes part of England and Wales (see generally G Marston, *The Marginal Seabed* (Clarendon 1981), pp 286–298). See also *Commonwealth of Australia v Yarmirr* (2001) 208 CLR 1 at [34]; *Attorney-General v Ngati Apa* [2002] 2 NZLR 661 at [19]–[22].

Imprecision of boundaries

1.16   The Ordnance Survey does not (and cannot) fix private boundaries.[1] Where a conveyance of land is accompanied by a plan of the area conveyed (usually derived from the Ordnance Survey map), the purpose of the plan is normally specified as being that of general identification only. In such cases the exact boundary requires to be established by inference from existing or historic topographical features such as walls, hedges and fences or from other evidence.[2] In the rules which govern registered conveyancing, the imprecision of maps and plans is explicitly acknowledged in the so-called 'general boundaries rule'. This rule recognises that the filed plan or General Map relevant to any registered title normally demarcates only a 'general boundary' and 'does not determine the exact line of the boundary.'[3]

1   *Wibberley (Alan) Building Ltd v Insley* [1999] 1 WLR 894 at 901H per Lord Hope of Craighead ('The purpose of the survey is topographical, not taxative').
2   *Wibberley (Alan) Building Ltd v Insley* [1999] 1 WLR 894 at 896A–B, 897B–C per Lord Hoffmann.
3   LRA 2002, s 60(1)–(2). The general boundaries rule, previously buried in LRR 1925, r 278(1)–(2), is now promoted to a position of prominence in the 2002 Act, thereby 'reflecting its importance' (see *Land Registration Rules 2003 – A Land Registry Consultation* (2002), para 8.1 (p 73)).

1.17   The more precise delineation of boundaries is usually left to be ascertained from other evidence, supplemented by a number of rebuttable common law presumptions, of which the 'hedge and ditch' and *ad medium filum* presumptions are perhaps best known. The venerable 'hedge and ditch' presumption provides that, where a hedge and ditch are found along a boundary between two parcels of land, the boundary is presumed to lie along the edge of the ditch on the far side from the hedge.[1] According to the *ad medium filum* rule, a conveyance of land abutting upon a highway presumptively includes the soil of the adjoining highway to its midway point,[2] a similar 'ad medium' presumption applying to the subjacent soil of any adjoining non-tidal river or waterway.[3] So conscious are the courts that boundary disputes are 'a particularly painful form of litigation', that a modern premium has been placed on ensuring that 'the law on boundaries should be as clear as possible.'[4] This concern is further met by the provision of a statutory procedure under which the proprietor of a registered estate may apply to Land Registry[5] for the determination of the exact line of a boundary where evidence of such exists.[6]

1   See *Vowles v Miller* (1810) 3 Taunt 137 at 138, 128 ER 54 at 55 per Lawrence J. The presumption envisages that the ditch maker will normally cut to the extremity of his own soil, thereafter depositing the excavated earth upon his own land and, typically, planting a hedge on top of it. The 'hedge and ditch' presumption even overrides the boundary as located on an Ordnance Survey map, where the two parcels have never been in common ownership and there is no evidence that the ditch was dug before the boundary was drawn (see *Wibberley (Alan) Building Ltd v Insley* [1999] 1 WLR 894 at 900H–901A; [2000] Conv 61 (J Cross and G Broadbent)). See also *Hall v Dorling* (1996) 74 P & CR 400 at 406.

2   *Berridge v Ward* (1861) 10 CB (NS) 400 at 415, 142 ER 507 at 513; *Pryor v Petre* [1894] 2 Ch 11 at 18; *Commissioners for Land Tax for the City of London v Central London Railway Co* [1913] AC 364 at 384; *Bellevue Crescent Pty Ltd v Marland Holdings Pty Ltd* (1998) 43 NSWLR 364 at 373A–B. See also *Pardoe v Pennington* (1998) 75 P & CR 264 at 270–271; *Commission for New Towns v J J Gallagher Ltd* [2003] 2 P & CR 24 at [25].

3   See *Micklethwait v Newlay Bridge Co* (1886) 33 Ch D 133 at 145, 152, 155.

4   *Wibberley (Alan) Building Ltd v Insley* [1999] 1 WLR 894 at 895G per Lord Hoffmann ('Feelings run high and disproportionate amounts of money are spent. Claims to small and valueless pieces of land are pressed with the zeal of Fortinbras's army'). See also *Clarke v O'Keefe* (2000) 80 P & CR 126 per Peter Gibson LJ.

5   The corporate name of HM Land Registry is now simply 'Land Registry' (see *Land Registry, Annual Report and Accounts 2002–03* (HC891, July 2003), p 29).

6   LRA 2002, s 60(3); LRR 2003, rr 118–120. In the absence of objection from adjoining owners, the registrar must accede to the application if otherwise satisfied as to the identification of the exact boundary line (LRR 2003, r 119(1), (6)–(7)). Cross-relating entries are then made in the relevant registers of title to the effect that an exact line has been determined (LRR 2003, r 120(1)). On a subdivision of land the registrar has certain powers to determine, of his own motion, an exact boundary line (LRR 2003, r 122).

Boundary disputes

1.18   In the vast majority of instances neighbours are content to accept that absolute precision in the location of mutual boundaries is unattainable[1] and that a 'certain amount of vagueness' or 'latitude' inevitably attends the definition of the exact line.[2] Nevertheless conflict over land boundaries tends to be a fertile source of litigation,[3] usually triggered by (and providing a focus for) other forms of unneighbourly discord or unhappiness.[4] It remains notorious that boundary disputes provide the easiest means of burning money.[5]

1   Land surveying 'is not an exact science' (see *National Trustees, Executors and Agency Co of Australia Ltd v Hassett* [1907] VLR 404 at 412; *Boyton v Clancy* (1998) 9 BPR 16585 at 16589).

2   *Wibberley (Alan) Building Ltd v Insley* [1999] 1 WLR 894 at 901E–F per Lord Hope of Craighead. For reference to a Heisenberg-like principle of uncertainty in the law of boundaries, see Gray and Gray, 'The rhetoric of realty', in J Getzler (ed), *Rationalizing Property, Equity and Trusts: Essays in Honour of Edward Burn* (Butterworths 2003), p 228.

3   The courts issue frequent admonitions about 'sloppy conveyancing' which results in 'imprecise boundaries' (see e g *Joyce v Rigolli* [2004] 1 P & CR D55 at D56 (Transcript at [23]) per Arden LJ).

4   For an extreme instance, see *Times*, 7 July 2000 ('Man shot dead after garden hedge dispute'). See also *Addison v Chief Constable of West Midlands Police* [2004] 1 WLR 29 (Note) (breach of the peace).

5   See e g *Segaram v Grant* (1997) 73 P & CR D35 (where a disagreement between neighbours
    over six inches of land had already cost £12,000 even before the matter reached the Court of
    Appeal) and *Targett and Targett v Ferguson and Driver* (1996) 72 P & CR 106 (where the equity
    in the relevant home was clearly insufficient to meet the eventual order for costs). See also
    Jones v Stones [1999] 1 WLR 1739 (where the casus belli concerned, inter alia, six flower pots
    on a dividing wall); *Rimmer v Pearson* (2000) 79 P & CR D21 (22 day county court trial over
    three-inch boundary strip).

Alluvion and diluvion

1.19   The delineation of an area of 'land' is sometimes affected, albeit in
relatively rare cases, by the physical processes of *alluvion* (which causes an
addition or accretion to title) and *diluvion* (which brings about a subtraction
from title).[1] The common law recognises, as a matter both of fairness and of
convenience, that where land is bounded by water the forces of nature are likely
to cause changes in the boundary between the land and the water. Consistently
with a perception of property in land as largely constituted by empirical
reality,[2] the common law on this occasion follows Roman law[3] in acknowledging that the 'long-term ownership of property' is 'inherently subject to gradual
processes of change.'[4] So long as these geophysical changes are indeed gradual
and imperceptible,[5] the law considers the title to land as applicable to the land
as it may be changed from time to time.[6] This is so even if there still remains
some means of identifying the original boundaries of the estate in question[7]
and even though these boundaries have been recorded in the Land Register.[8] In
effect, land is transferred prima facie subject to and with the benefit of such
additions and subtractions as may take place over the course of time.[9]

1   Compare the case where catastrophic sea erosion cuts into cliffs and ultimately causes cliff-top
    buildings to collapse on to the foreshore, thereby altering the configuration of land (*Holbeck
    Hall Hotel Ltd v Scarborough BC* [2000] QB 836 (hotel 65 metres above sea level)). Climate
    change and higher tides are beginning to weaken sea defences in certain parts of England (see
    Times, 5 November 1999 ('Three homes to vanish in futile battle with sea')). See also *Times*,
    12 January 1999 (p 1) for an account of the collapse into the sea of a 50ft wide slab of some
    200 yards of cliff at Beachy Head.
2   **[Paras 1.11, 2.77]**.
3   See Inst 2.1.20; *Attorney-General of Southern Nigeria v John Holt & Co* (*Liverpool*) *Ltd* [1915]
    AC 599 at 613–614.
4   *Southern Centre of Theosophy Inc v State of South Australia* [1982] AC 706 at 716E per
    Lord Wilberforce, who attributed the doctrine of accretion to 'the nature of land ownership'.
5   The requirement that the relevant change be gradual and imperceptible is widely accepted (see
    Bl Comm, Vol II, p 262; *Attorney-General v McCarthy* [1911] 2 IR 260 at 276, 293 per Palles
    CB; *Southern Centre of Theosophy Inc v State of South Australia* [1982] AC 706 at 716C;
    Clarke v City of Edmonton [1929] 4 DLR 1010 at 1015; *Port Franks Properties Ltd v The
    Queen* (1980) 99 DLR (3d) 28 at 36; *Lawrence v Kempsey Shire Council* (1995) 6 BPR 14111 at
    14115).
6   Any change caused by the deliberate action of the claimant falls outside the doctrine of
    accretion (*Brighton and Hove General Gas Co v Hove Bungalows Ltd* [1924] 1 Ch 372 at 390;
    Southern Centre of Theosophy Inc v State of South Australia [1982] AC 706 at 720A).
7   *Hazlett v Presnell* (1982) 149 CLR 107 at 116.
8   LRA 2002, s 61(1). Contrast the tendency in other jurisdictions to regard the boundaries of a
    Torrens title as definitive (see e g *Johnson v Alberta* (2001) 203 DLR (4th) 476 at [39]). The
    English rule reflects the long held belief that the mere fact that a grant of land is accompanied

by a map delineating the boundary is not conclusive against the operation of either alluvion or diluvion (see *Southern Centre of Theosophy Inc v State of South Australia* [1982] AC 706 at 716F–G; *Attorney-General v McCarthy* [1911] 2 IR 260 at 284).

9　In relation to unregistered land, the prima facie consequences of alluvion and diluvion can be displaced by clear evidence of a contrary intention, but an agreement about the operation of alluvion or diluvion affecting a registered estate is effective only if registered in accordance with LRR 2003, r 123 (see LRA 2002, s 61(2)).

Alluvion

1.20 If an addition is made to land by wind-blown or water-borne deposit,[1] the landowner's territory is regarded as having been extended by alluvion into the area which was previously water.[2] This doctrine of accretion applies equally to lakes and rivers,[3] and in the case of rivers may reposition the boundary between two parcels of land by relocating the *medium filum* of the river bed.[4] The doctrine of accretion has no application to substantial and recognisable changes in the boundary between land and water which take place suddenly.[5] However, in the case of wind-blown deposit, the mere fact that the leading edge of a sand dune may move forward two or three feet in a perceptible jump over a 24 hour period in conditions of strong winds does not disqualify such an advance as an allowable accretion to the land, if in the long term the movement is imperceptible.[6]

1　The distinction between these forms of deposit, even if possible, is irrelevant (*Southern Centre of Theosophy Inc v State of South Australia* [1982] AC 706 at 719H–720A, 720D).

2　*R v Lord Yarborough* (1824) 3 B & C 91 at 105, 107 ER 668 at 673, affd sub nom *Gifford v Lord Yarborough* (1828) 5 Bing 163, 130 ER 1023; *Stirling v Bartlett* 1993 SLT 763 at 767I; *Dunstan v Hell's Gate Enterprises Ltd* (1986) 22 DLR (4th) 568 at 584; *Sunlea Investments Pty Ltd v State of New South Wales* (1998) 9 BPR 16707 at 16709. The title extended by accretion also confers a right to any minerals situated below the newly claimed land (*Re Eliason and Registrar, Northern Alberta Land Registration District* (1981) 115 DLR (3d) 360 at 364).

3　*Southern Centre of Theosophy Inc v State of South Australia* [1982] AC 706 at 715F; *State of Hawaii by Kobayashi v Zimring*, 566 P2d 725 at 734 (1977). See (1983) 99 LQR 412 (P Jackson).

4　[Paras 1.17, 1.108–1.109]. See eg *Stirling v Bartlett* 1993 SLT 763 at 768K, 769D–G.

5　See *Nebraska v Iowa*, 143 US 359 at 361, 370, 36 L ed 186 at 188, 190 (1892); *Stirling v Bartlett* 1993 SLT 763 at 767I–J, 768J–K, 769C. The Supreme Court of Hawaii has held that extensions of land created by catastrophic lava flows should inure, not for the windfall gain of a limited segment of the population of an overcrowded island, but for the public as a whole. The added land is held by the government in public trust (*State of Hawaii by Kobayashi v Zimring*, 566 P2d 725 at 735 (1977)).

6　*Southern Centre of Theosophy Inc v State of South Australia* [1982] AC 706 at 722F, 723B. It is sufficient that the transfer of sand or soil cannot be seen to happen before the eyes of the observer (see *Stirling v Bartlett* 1993 SLT 763 at 768D).

Diluvion

1.21 Again, if part of a landowner's land is removed by diluvion or gradual erosion caused by water-based advance or attrition, the landowner is simply treated as losing a portion of his 'land'.[1] In the lottery of life, the landowner 'may lose as well as gain from changes in the water boundary or level.'[2] However, no subtraction from title occurs in the case of rapid, easily perceived and violent shifts of land.[3] Such emergence of 'large changes'[4] is regarded not as diluvion, but as 'avulsion', and does not affect pre-existing legal boundaries.[5]

1   *Southern Centre of Theosophy Inc v State of South Australia* [1982] AC 706 at 716D. See also *Fellowes v Rother DC* [1983] 1 All ER 513 at 515a; *Environment Protection Authority v Saunders and Leaghur Holdings Pty Ltd* (1995) 6 BPR 13655 at 13659.
2   *Southern Centre of Theosophy Inc v State of South Australia* [1982] AC 706 at 721D per Lord Wilberforce.
3   Thus a river which suddenly alters course, by cutting through the neck of a bend, causes no change in land boundary (*Nebraska v Iowa*, 143 US 359 at 370, 36 L ed 186 at 190 (1892) per Brewer J).
4   *Southern Centre of Theosophy Inc v State of South Australia* [1982] AC 706 at 721E per Lord Wilberforce.
5   See *State of Hawaii by Kobayashi v Zimring*, 566 P2d 725 at 734 (1977); *Stirling v Bartlett* 1993 SLT 763 at 767J, 768J.

Mobile estates in land

1.22   It is possible that land, the ultimate immovable, may in fact 'move', even though this can bring about the improbable result that someone holds title to a constantly mobile piece of land. It is quite feasible, for instance, that the pattern of tide levels on a coastline may vary over time, with the result that the foreshore extending between the high- and low-tide marks shifts position. The foreshore is normally vested in the crown,[1] but if a portion of the foreshore has been conveyed to an individual (or more usually a local authority), the title conveyed may well, in the absence of a contrary intention, relate to a moving strip of foreshore.[2]

1   See *Blundell v Catterall* (1821) 5 B & Ald 268 at 293, 304, 106 ER 1190 at 1199, 1203.
2   See *Baxendale v Instow Parish Council* [1982] Ch 14 at 23B–C (contrary intention shown). See also *Re Monashee Enterprises Ltd and Minister of Recreation and Conservation for British Columbia* (1979) 90 DLR (3d) 521 at 531. A movable fee simple seems not to be a fee simple absolute in possession and can therefore take effect only pursuant to the Settled Land Act 1925 or under a trust of land (see R E Annand, [1982] Conv 208 at 211). See also *Scratton v Brown* (1825) 4 B & C 485 at 498, 107 ER 1140 at 1145.

STATUTORY DEFINITIONS OF 'LAND'

1.23   More than two centuries ago Blackstone declared 'land' to be a word of 'a very extensive signification'.[1] Something of its amplitude is captured in a number of statutory definitions which, although not uniform or consistent, point to 'land' as having a fairly complex meaning in English law. For instance, the Law of Property Act 1925, the primary statute contained within the corpus of English property legislation of 1925, describes 'land' as including

land of any tenure, and mines and minerals, whether or not held apart from the surface, buildings or parts of buildings (whether the division is horizontal, vertical or made in any other way) and other corporeal hereditaments; also a manor, an advowson, and a rent and other incorporeal hereditaments, and an easement, right, privilege, or benefit in, over, or derived from land ...[2]

1 *Bl Comm*, Vol II, p 16.
2 LPA 1925, s 205(1)(ix). This definition is replicated, with variations, in many other interpretation sections (see e g SLA 1925, s 117(1)(ix); LCA 1972, s 17(1); Limitation Act 1980, s 38(1); TOLATA 1996, s 23(2); LRA 2002, s 132(1)). See also 'land' as defined by Interpretation Act 1978, s 5, Sch 1.

1.24 For the purpose of the Law of Property Act 1925, 'land' thus includes both 'corporeal' and 'incorporeal' components (or 'hereditaments'[1]). In broad terms *corporeal hereditaments* refer to the physical and tangible characteristics of land, whereas *incorporeal hereditaments* refer to certain intangible rights which may be enjoyed in, over or in respect of land.[2] This collocation of corporeal and incorporeal aspects within the definition of 'land' highlights a central tension in English land law: there remains a deep indeterminacy as to whether property in land is essentially a matter of physical fact or of abstract right.[3] Together, however, corporeal and incorporeal hereditaments are known as 'realty' – in order to distinguish them from 'personalty' (ie *personal* or *movable* property).

1 The term 'hereditament' is defined in LPA 1925, s 205(1)(ix) as 'any real property which on an intestacy occurring before the commencement of this Act [1 January 1926] might have devolved upon an heir'.
2 **[Para 1.116]**. Distinct corporeal and incorporeal property rights in relation to one object may exist concurrently and be held by different parties (*Yanner v Eaton* (1999) 201 CLR 351 at [85] per Gummow J).
3 **[Paras 1.11, 2.76]**.

CORPOREAL HEREDITAMENTS

1.25 Corporeal hereditaments comprise those 'substantial and permanent objects' which 'affect the senses',[1] the only objects which are truly 'permanent' being those constituted by or connected with immovable property. Corporeal hereditaments thus include not merely the clods of earth or rock outcrops which make up the surface layer of land (ie the *solum*), but also many physical things which are attached to or are inherent in the ground.[2] Subject to a few specific exceptions, corporeal hereditaments extend to cover such things as buildings, trees, subjacent minerals, and even some portion of the superjacent airspace.[3]

1 *Bl Comm*, Vol II, p 17.
2 **[Paras 1.52–1.104]**. Corporeal hereditaments do not include flowing water. 'No ordinary users of the language will be surprised by the conclusion that water is not land' (*Thames Heliports Plc v LB of Tower Hamlets* (1997) 74 P & CR 164 at 177 per Ward LJ).
3 *Mitchell v Mosley* [1914] 1 Ch 438 at 450 **[para 1.37]**.

THE THIRD DIMENSION OF 'LAND'

1.26   It will be obvious from the foregoing that any elucidation of the concept of 'land' must inevitably grapple with the quantification of not just two, but three, measures of territorial or jurisdictional control. 'Land' must have at least *some* three-dimensional significance: a transfer of a merely two-dimensional plot of land would have little meaning and even less utility.[1] So much is already conceded by the standard statutory definitions of 'land', which recognise that 'land' may be 'held apart from the surface' and that it may be subject to horizontal division.[2] In the result it is quite clear that the 'land' comprised within any specified map co-ordinates must include at least limited portions of the subjacent and superjacent domains. It follows moreover that, to this extent, titles to 'land' can be stratified and vested in various owners simultaneously, each holding a different portion or stratum of cubic space either below or above the surface layer of the ground.

1   '[L]and, for proprietary purposes, cannot be two-dimensional' (*Central London Commercial Estates Ltd v Kato Kagaku Co Ltd* [1998] 4 All ER 948 at 950j per Sedley J). See also *Taylor v Hamer* [2002] EWCA Civ 1130, [2002] 1 P & CR D9 (Transcript at [84]) per Sedley LJ; *Lacroix v The Queen* [1954] 4 DLR 470 at 475.
2   [**Para 1.23**].

Cuius est solum eius est usque ad coelum et ad inferos

1.27   The extended significance of the term 'land' is more eloquently than accurately expressed in the Latin maxim, *cuius est solum eius est usque ad coelum et ad inferos*: he who owns the land owns everything reaching up to the very heavens and down to the depths of the earth. Although in many ways discordant with the conceptual apparatus of the common law, this maxim has often been invoked in support of some notion of the sacrosanct nature of property rights.[1] Nowadays the maxim generally serves a more limited function in reinforcing the landowner's exercise of all the rights required for reasonable enjoyment of his property.

1   See e g *Lewvest Ltd v Scotia Towers Ltd* (1982) 126 DLR (3d) 239 at 240.

Origin of the maxim

1.28   The *cuius est solum* maxim cannot be traced back to Roman law[1] and seems to be a brocard of medieval origin.[2] It contains a certain measure of truth as far as English law is concerned, for there is doubtless a general sense in which common lawyers have often conceptualised 'land' as having an extended three-dimensional quality.[3]

1   See Lord McNair, *The Law of the Air* (3rd edn, London 1964), p 393; J C Cooper, 'Roman Law and the Maxim "Cuius est Solum" in International Air Law' (1952) 1 McGill LJ 23 at 26.
2   Its first recognised appearance seems to be in the 13th Century Glossa Ordinaria on the Corpus Iuris (Digest, VIII.2.1) by Accursius of Bologna (see H Guibé, *Essai sur la navigation*

aérienne en droit interne et en droit international (Paris 1912), p 35). It has been suggested that the maxim may have derived from even earlier Jewish origins (see (1931) 47 LQR 14; Deuteronomy, xxx: 11–14, Isaiah, vii: 11), but see D E Smith, 'The Origins of Trespass to Airspace and the Maxim "Cujus est solum ejus est usque ad coelum" ' (1982) 6 Trent Law Journal 33 at 38. For the earliest English reference, see the terminal note in *Bury v Pope* (1588) Cro Eliz 118, 78 ER 375, where the maxim is said to have been known from the time of Edward I (1239–1307). (It has been pointed out that Franciscus, the son of Accursius, travelled to England in 1274 at the invitation of Edward I (see McNair, op cit, p 397)). The maxim was later incorporated in Co Litt, p 4a ('the earth hath in law a great extent upwards'); *Bl Comm*, Vol II, p 18.

3   Thus the mere superaddition of a quantity of dumped soil on the surface layer of Greenacre does not in itself increase the 'land' owned by the proprietor of Greenacre or mark any increase in his interest in that 'land' (see *McClure v Petre* [1988] 1 WLR 1386 at 1390D, 1393E).

Limited definitional value

1.29   The original Latin maxim is now subject to so many qualifications that it has become virtually worthless as a statement of contemporary law.[1] In no sense can it be understood to mean that 'land' in English law comprises a limitless cubic domain from the centre of the earth to the heavens, not least since 'so sweeping, unscientific and unpractical a doctrine is unlikely to appeal to the common law mind.'[2] The common lawyer has no intellectual predisposition to propound large abstract declarations of ownership, but relies instead upon substantial reserves of common sense as applied, on a case-specific basis, to the raw facts of human behaviour. At most the maxim serves nowadays as a crude approximation of the extent of the rights pertaining to owners of land[3] and of the extent of the ownership which is transferred by conveyance.[4]

1   In *Bernstein of Leigh (Baron) v Skyviews & General Ltd* [1978] QB 479 at 485C, Griffiths J dismissed the maxim as merely 'a colourful phrase'. The formula has been said to be 'imprecise' and 'mainly serviceable as dispensing with analysis' (*Commissioner for Railways et al v Valuer-General* [1974] AC 328 at 351G), and to have 'no place in the modern world' (*United States v Causby*, 328 US 256 at 261, 90 L ed 1206 at 1210 (1946)). See also *Re The Queen in Right of Manitoba and Air Canada* (1978) 86 DLR (3d) 631 at 635, 637; *Didow v Alberta Power Ltd* [1988] 5 WWR 606 at 610, 613–615.
2   *Commissioner for Railways et al v Valuer-General* [1974] AC 328 at 351H–352A per Lord Wilberforce.
3   See e g *Pountney v Clayton* (1883) 11 QBD 820 at 838 per Bowen LJ.
4   See e g *National Carriers Ltd v Panalpina (Northern) Ltd* [1981] AC 675 at 708C, where Lord Russell of Killowen noted that a grant of an estate in fee simple passes the land 'as to its surface and below its surface, and the airspace above, subject to exclusions'.

Stratified ownership

1.30   That there can be a horizontal stratification of 'land' is not a new idea.[1] The possibility of horizontal division follows almost necessarily from the maxim *cuius est solum eius est usque ad coelum et ad inferos*. However attenuated the force of this maxim today, it is recognised that, at least to some limited extent, the landowner is competent to convey away separate estates in horizontal strata of his 'land'.[2] These strata may be subterranean. It is quite feasible, for instance, that one person should own the freehold estate in the surface layer of the ground,[3] while another person owns the freehold in the subsoil[4] or in a subjacent cavern,[5] layer of minerals,[6] underground cellar[7] or embedded pipe or cable duct[8] or even in fixtures situated on and unsevered from the land.[9] A common example of stratified ownership is nowadays found in the case of any highway which is maintainable by a highway authority at public expense. Here, although the subjacent soil of the highway is owned by the adjoining landowners,[10] the highway authority is statutorily invested with a determinable fee simple interest in the surface of the highway and in so much of the subjacent land and superjacent airspace as is required for the discharge of its statutory duties.[11] If the highway ever ceases to be a highway, the highway authority's interest presumptively reverts to the owner or owners of the adjoining land.[12]

1   See *Williams v Usherwood* (1983) 45 P & CR 235 at 253. LPA 1925, s 205(1)(ix) establishes beyond doubt that 'land' is capable of horizontal as well as vertical division, and that a land title can therefore relate to a slice of defined area or cubic space which is not grounded on the surface layer of the earth. A modern example of such an area is an upper-storey flat.

2   The strata need not even be horizontal. There is nothing impossible about the creation or transfer of an estate in a sloping subterranean area (e g a cave or mineral bed) or in a sloping 'flying freehold' (e g an enclosed walkway across a street between different levels of adjacent buildings).

3   **[Paras 1.125, 7.2]** (meaning of 'freehold estate').

4   See e g *Taylor v North West Water* (1995) 70 P & CR 94 at 107 (underground sewer owned by water company **[para 3.19]**). See also *Commissioners for Land Tax for the City of London v Central London Railway Co* [1913] AC 364 at 384.

5   *Cox v Colossal Cavern Co*, 276 SW 540 at 542–543 (1925).

6   *Harris v Ryding* (1839) 5 M & W 60 at 69–71, 76, 151 ER 27 at 31, 33; *Cox v Glue* (1848) 5 CB 533 at 549, 136 ER 987 at 993; *Batten Pooll v Kennedy* [1907] 1 Ch 256 at 264–265; *Williams v Usherwood* (1983) 45 P & CR 235 at 253.

7   The possibility that there can, in this sense, be such a thing as a 'subterranean flying freehold' was conceded in *Grigsby v Melville* [1974] 1 WLR 80 at 83D–E. See also *Metropolitan Railway Co v Fowler* [1893] AC 416 at 420, 422.

8   *Corpn of City of Toronto v Consumers' Gas Co of Toronto* [1916] 2 AC 618 at 624 per Lord Shaw of Dunfermline; *North Shore Gas Co Ltd v Commissioner of Stamp Duties (NSW)* (1940) 63 CLR 52 at 69–70 per Dixon J; *Telecom Auckland Ltd v Auckland CC* [1999] 1 NZLR 426 at 440.

9   See *Commissioner of Taxation v Metal Manufactures Ltd* [2001] FCA 365; *Eastern Nitrogen Ltd v Commissioner of Taxation* [2001] FCA 366; (2001) 75 ALJ 405 (P Butt).

10   See *Norman and Norman v Department of Transport* (1996) 72 P & CR 210 at 221–222.

11   Highways Act 1980, s 263 **[paras 5.12, 7.7]**. See *Coverdale v Charlton* (1878) 4 QBD 104 at 116–118, 121, 126; *Mayor etc of Tunbridge Wells v Baird* [1896] AC 434 at 442; *Foley's Charity Trustees v Dudley Corpn* [1910] 1 KB 317 at 322, 324; *Tithe Redemption Commission v Runcorn UDC* [1954] Ch 383 at 398, 403; *Wiltshire CC v Frazer* (1984) 47 P & CR 69 at 72; *Sheffield CC v Yorkshire Water Services Ltd* [1991] 1 WLR 58 at 66E–F, 67B–H; *Overseas Investment Ltd v Simcobuild Construction Ltd and Swansea CC* (1995) 70 P & CR 322 at 329; *Secretary of State for the Environment, Transport and the Regions v Baylis (Gloucester) Ltd and Bennett Construction (UK) Ltd* (2000) 80 P & CR 324 at 335–336 per Deputy Judge Kim Lewison QC.

12   *Rolls v St George the Martyr Southwark Vestry* (1880) 14 Ch D 785 at 797–798.

Flying freeholds

1.31 Although there has always been something controversial in the suggestion that separate freehold estates can be created above ground level,[1] the idea is
by no means novel. Coke allowed that '[a] man may have an inheritance in an
upper chamber though the lower buildings and soil be in another, and seeing it
is an inheritance corporeal it shall pass by livery.'[2] The horizontal stratification
of land has more often been achieved through the creation of leasehold estates[3]
rather than the transfer of freehold estates, but there is in principle nothing
impossible in the idea that a landowner may carve out of his own estate a
'flying freehold' which is not contiguous with ground level.[4] Although somewhat unusual in England, such titles do exist in certain parts of London, most
notably in parts of Lincoln's Inn. The principal objection to the 'flying
freehold' has always been practical rather than conceptual.[5] Planning considerations apart,[6] a freeholder has an inherent right to destroy his land or allow it
to fall into disrepair. A flying freehold is therefore extremely vulnerable to the
possibility that a subjacent freeholder may damage or prejudice the structure
on which the 'flying freehold' physically rests. Of course, the answer to this
dilemma lies in fastening upon the subjacent owner the required positive duties
of physical support and repair in relation to superior freeholders,[7] but such a
solution has, historically, been fraught with further difficulty. English law has
never made it easy for the burden of positive freehold covenants to run with the
land so as to affect successors in title.[8]

1 Some have doubted whether it is possible to convey a freehold of an entire building separate
  from the freehold of the subjacent land (see *Hardy v Wardy* (2001) 10 BPR 18577 at [37] per
  Bryson J). However, as a matter of principle, there seems to be no fundamental objection.
2 *Co Litt*, p 48b. The Law Commission has noted that conveyances of freehold flats are drafted
  on the assumption that the freehold estate conferred is capable of lasting beyond the life of
  the building itself, i e 'an estate can exist in what has become mere airspace' (Law Commission,
  Transfer of Land: The Law of Positive and Restrictive Covenants (Law Com No 127, January
  1984), para 4.6).
3 **[Paras 1.141, 7.69]** (meaning of 'leasehold estate').
4 See S M Tolson, '"Land" without earth: Freehold Flats in English Law' (1950) 14 Conv (NS)
  350.
5 See *Bursill Enterprises Pty Ltd v Berger Bros Trading Co Pty Ltd* (1971) 124 CLR 73 at 92 per
  Windeyer J.
6 **[Para 13.155]**.
7 See *Harris v Ryding* (1839) 5 M & W 60 at 70–76, 151 ER 27 at 31–33.
8 See *Rhone v Stephens* [1994] 2 AC 310 **[para 13.51]**; Law Com No 127 (1984), para 4.6. This
  difficulty is now alleviated, but not altogether dispelled, by the advent of commonhold
  legislation **[paras 1.33, 7.356]**.

Condominiums and strata titles

1.32 In other parts of the common law world the difficulties inherent in the
transmission of covenanted burdens relating to stratified ownership have been
resolved by the adoption of more sophisticated devices of landholding. Something akin to the flying freehold is made possible by resort to the North
American phenomenon of the 'condominium' and the concept of 'strata title'

successfully pioneered in Australia in the early 1960s.[1] Such devices have proved to be extremely flexible, even to the extent that it is possible to convey lots within a 'strata plan' which comprise separate and geographically distinct cubic spaces of thin air.[2]

1   See Conveyancing (Strata) Titles Act 1961 (New South Wales), now replaced by Strata Titles Act 1973 (New South Wales).
2   See Strata Titles Act 1973 (New South Wales), s 8(1)(f)(iii); *Burgchard v Holroyd Municipal Council* [1984] 2 NSWLR 164 at 169F.

Commonhold ownership

1.33   A statutory form of stratified freehold ownership has now become available in England and Wales with the introduction of freehold ownership of 'commonhold land'.[1] The Commonhold and Leasehold Reform Act 2002 draws upon the parallel of condominium and strata title legislation in facilitating a novel form of tenure for blocks of flats and other multi-unit properties.[2] Commonhold ownership schemes represent a significant innovation in English law, combining the legal and psychological benefits of freehold ownership with a new scope for democratic self-management of co-operatively held premises.[3] Commonhold ownership adapts the notion of freehold ownership as a means of regulating relations between owners of separate, but interdependent, properties which lie in close proximity to each other. Under the commonhold scheme each 'unit-holder' (e g a flat-owner) takes a freehold estate by way of exclusive ownership of his own unit[4] and also becomes a member of a management company or 'commonhold association' which owns the common parts of the building and its grounds.[5] Each unit-holder is governed by a body of standard rights and obligations defined by a 'commonhold community statement', which effectively operates as a binding constitutional document for the entire commonhold development.[6] These rights and obligations thereafter attach automatically by force of statute to each unit, irrespective of subsequent changes in the ownership of the unit.[7]

1   [Para 7.356].
2   See *Commonhold and Leasehold Reform: Draft Bill and Consultation Paper* (Lord Chancellor's Department, Cm 4843, August 2000), Part I, para 1.1.5 (p 79).
3   For further discussion of commonhold schemes, see Chapter 7 [**para 7.357**] and Chapter 13 [**para 13.57**].
4   CALRA 2002, s 9(3)(b)–(c).
5   CALRA 2002, Sch 3, Pt 2, para 7.
6   CALRA 2002, ss 14, 31.
7   CALRA 2002, s 16(1).

SUBTERRANEAN ZONES

1.34   English law recognises that a landowner (or, more accurately, one who has a right to possession of land[1]) is entitled to at least some quantum of the underlying soil or void encapsulated within the two-dimensional co-ordinates of his or her surface boundaries. The *cuius est solum* maxim has a qualified application to the subterranean zone,[2] with the result that a transfer of an estate in land (whether freehold or leasehold) is normally effective to convey the void space contained within an immediately subjacent cellar,[3] most subjacent minerals,[4] and even the vacant underground spaces from which minerals have been worked out.[5] In general, however, it is unlikely that a landowner's rights extend much further than some 200 metres below the surface.[6]

1   For the coincidence of possession of land and estate ownership, see Chapter 2 [**para 2.77**] and Chapter 3 [**para 3.13**].
2   See *Grigsby v Melville* [1974] 1 WLR 80 at 83F–G, 85G. The claim to possession of 'everything ... down to the centre of the earth' (see *Elwes v Brigg Gas Company* (1886) 33 Ch D 562 at 568) is extravagant.
3   *Grigsby v Melville* [1974] 1 WLR 80 at 84F–G, 86G–H.
4   The subterranean limits of the landowner's rights may sometimes be curtailed by legislation. See e g *Goldblatt v Town of Hempstead*, 369 US 590 at 595–596, 8 L Ed 2d 130 at 135 (1962) (prohibition on excavation below the water table).
5   See *Mitchell v Mosley* [1914] 1 Ch 438 at 450.
6   See A J Bradbrook, 'The Ownership of Geothermal Resources' 1987 AMPLA Yearbook 353 at 365.

Minerals and other inorganic substances

1.35   Minerals and other inorganic substances present in the ground comprise part of the realty and, unless reserved from the transfer of land to a surface owner or severed altogether from the realty, are regarded as annexed to his estate.[1] Thus substances ranging from stone and mineral ores to gravel, sand and china clay comprise 'land' for legal purposes. To this principle there exist certain exceptions relating to hydrocarbons. Most notably the ownership of all unworked coal is vested by statute in the Coal Authority[2] and all rights in petroleum (inclusive of mineral oil and natural gas) existing in its natural condition in strata are vested in the crown.[3] The crown also has a prerogative right to mines of gold and silver.[4]

1   *Bl Comm*, Vol II, p 18.
2   Coal Industry Act 1994, ss 1(1), 7(3).
3   Petroleum Act 1998, ss 1(a), 2(1). The crown may grant exploration and exploitation licences (see Petroleum Act 1998, s 3(1)).
4   *Case of Mines* (1568) 1 Plowd 310 at 336, 75 ER 472 at 510; *Bl Comm*, Vol I, p 284.

Trespass

1.36   The *cuius est solum* principle carries the implication that those entitled to possession of the *solum* may sue in trespass in the event of subterranean invasions of their land. Thus, for example, a trespass is committed where one landowner, by means of an access situated on his own land, gains entry to a cave[1] or coal seam[2] located beneath the surface of his neighbour's land.[3] Likewise the unauthorised installation of a sewer pipe in the ground plainly constitutes an actionable trespass to land.[4]

1   *Edwards v Sims*, 24 SW2d 619 at 629 (1930); *Edwards v Lee's Administrator*, 96 SW2d 1028 at 1029 (1936) (the 'Great Onyx Cave' in Kentucky).
2   *Bulli Coal Mining Co v Osborne* [1899] AC 351 at 362–365.
3   No trespass is occasioned by spreading tree roots (see *Lemmon v Webb* [1894] 3 Ch 1 at 11, 24), although any damage caused may be actionable in nuisance (see *Delaware Mansions Ltd v Westminster CC* [2002] 1 AC 321).
4   *Roberts v Rodney DC* [2001] 2 NZLR 402 at [2].

SUPERJACENT SPACE

1.37   The *cuius est solum* maxim – however imprecise its scope[1] – confirms in the estate owner certain rights over a limited portion of the airspace situated above the relevant solum. It is trite law that a pragmatic distinction must be drawn between two different strata of airspace.[2]

1   [Para **1.29**].
2   *Bernstein of Leigh (Baron) v Skyviews & General Ltd* [1978] QB 479 at 488A–B.

The lower stratum

1.38   The lower stratum of airspace comprises that portion of the immediately superjacent airspace whose effective control is necessary for the landowner's reasonable enjoyment of his land at ground level.[1] There is no doubt that the surface owner's rights (whether analysed in terms of ownership or as mere possession[2]) must extend to this stratum, since he would otherwise commit a trespass in that airspace as soon as he set foot on his own land. As Justice Douglas once said in the Supreme Court of the United States, the landowner must have 'exclusive control of the immediate reaches of the enveloping atmosphere' since otherwise 'buildings could not be erected, trees could not be planted, and even fences could not be run.'[3]

1   *Bernstein of Leigh (Baron) v Skyviews & General Ltd* [1978] QB 479 at 488A [para **1.50**].
2   See generally C L Bouvé, 'Private Ownership of Airspace' 1 Air L Rev 232 (1930); H H Hackley, 'Trespassers in the Sky' 21 Minn L Rev 773 (1936–37).
3   *United States v Causby*, 328 US 256 at 264, 90 L ed 1206 at 1212 (1946). It is this territorial sovereignty which, in the absence of contrary easements or covenants, underpins the unrestricted common law freedom of the landowner to construct tall buildings on his land (see *Hunter v Canary Wharf Ltd* [1997] AC 655 at 685C–G per Lord Goff of Chieveley, 709G–710G per Lord Hoffmann, 721C–E per Lord Cooke of Thorndon).

Vertical extent

1.39   Courts are notoriously unwilling to quantify the extent of the airspace which falls within the control or dominion of the landowner, but it seems unlikely in most cases to reach beyond an altitude of much more than 150 or 200 metres above roof level.[1] Even within this lower stratum the landowner may not enjoy unqualified dominion.[2] He is subject to such restrictions as may be imposed by a local authority or state agency by way of planning or zoning regulation.[3]

1   In Britain some guidance is provided by the rule that no aircraft may normally fly 'closer than 500 feet to any person, vessel, vehicle or structure' (Rules of the Air Regulations 1996 (SI 1996/1393), Sch 1, r 5(1)(e)). Exceptions are made for aircraft while landing or taking off (r 5(2)(d)(i)) and for gliders while hill-soaring (r 5(2)(d)(ii)), but not for evangelists who use motorised paragliders to preach to the local populace from the air (see *Times*, 13 March 1998 (p 3) ('The heavenly host is fined for low flying')). The US Court of Claims has confirmed a 'general rule that 500 feet above ground level in uncongested areas is the dividing line' (*Powell v United States*, 17 Avi Cas (CCH) p 17,988 at 17991 (1983)). It may also be relevant that the subterranean range of a landowner's rights probably extends no further than 200 metres below the surface [**para 1.34**].

2   See *Hunter v Canary Wharf Ltd* [1997] AC 655 at 721D per Lord Cooke of Thorndon (modern controls on building height make it 'inadequate to say that at the present day owners of the soil generally enjoy their rights usque ad coelum').

3   [**Para 13.155**]. The United States Supreme Court has upheld the constitutional validity of various restrictions imposed for aesthetic or practical reasons on the 'air rights' of the landowner (see e g *Welch v Swasey*, 214 US 91 at 107, 53 L ed 923 at 930 (1909); *Penn Central Transport Company v City of New York*, 438 US 104 at 130–131, 57 L Ed 2d 631 at 652–653 (1978)). See also *Cheyenne Airport Board and City of Cheyenne v Rogers*, 707 P2d 717 at 727–729 (1985) (Supreme Court of Wyoming).

Ownership of thin air

1.40   As a matter of strict definition[1] 'land' may include a cubic quantum of airspace which is separate from the physical solum.[2] From this there follows the initially improbable notion that an individual can literally own an estate in thin air – a proposition which neatly gives the lie to any assumption that land is necessarily a tangible resource. A three-dimensional quantum of airspace can exist as an 'independent unit of real property'.[3] Such airspace can be conveyed in fee simple[4]; it can be leased[5]; it can be subdivided[6]; and it can even be subjected to land taxes.[7] The exploitability of airspace as a commerciable resource nowadays ensures that a transfer or lease of airspace in a crowded down-town location often operates as an efficient means of urban development. New buildings and walkways can be suspended above street level, thus maximising the utility of existing resources and reconciling otherwise incompatible forms of land user.

1   [**Paras 1.26, 1.30**].

2   Gray, 'Property in Thin Air' [1991] CLJ 252 at 258–259. See *Tileska v Bevelon* (1989) 4 BPR 9601 at 9606 per Waddell CJ.

3   *Macht v Department of Assessments of Baltimore City*, 296 A2d 162 at 168 (1972); *Re Trizec Manitoba Ltd and City Assessor for the City of Winnipeg* (1986) 25 DLR (4th) 444 at 450. See also *Ports of Auckland Ltd v Auckland CC* [2000] 3 NZLR 614 at [81]–[82].

4   *Reilly v Booth* (1890) 44 Ch D 12 at 23 per Cotton LJ, 26–27 per Lopes LJ; *Tileska v Bevelon* (1989) 4 BPR 9601 at 9606. See also *Melluish v BMI (No 3) Ltd* [1996] AC 454 at 474D–E per Lord Browne-Wilkinson.

5   *Macht v Department of Assessments of Baltimore City*, 296 A2d 162 at 168 (1972); *Re Trizec Manitoba Ltd and City Assessor for the City of Winnipeg* (1986) 25 DLR (4th) 444 at 452.

6   *Bursill Enterprises Pty Ltd v Berger Bros Trading Co Pty Ltd* (1971) 124 CLR 73 at 91 per Windeyer J; *Ratto v Trifid Pty Ltd* [1987] WAR 237 at 255 per Brinsden J.

7   *Re Trizec Manitoba Ltd and City Assessor for the City of Winnipeg* (1986) 25 DLR (4th) 444.

Aerial trespass

1.41   Almost any lateral invasion of lower stratum airspace is prima facie actionable in trespass.[1] Remedies range from declaratory relief to the award of money damages and/or the granting of injunctive relief.[2]

1   See *Anchor Brewhouse Developments Ltd v Berkley House* (*Docklands Developments*) *Ltd* (1987) 38 BLR 82 at 94; *Savva and Savva v Hussein* (1996) 73 P & CR 150 at 155.
2   See Chapter 3 [**para 3.80**].

Access to sunlight

1.42   The question sometimes arises whether the deprivation of access to sunlight constitutes any wrong actionable at law.[1] The problem can emerge in various contexts.

1   Similar questions arise in relation to the obstruction of access to a current of wind for a windmill or wind generator (see *Webb v Bird* (1861) 10 CB (NS) 268 at 284, 142 ER 455 at 461 (affd (1863) 13 CB (NS) 841, 143 ER 332)). See also A J Bradbrook, 'The Access of Wind to Wind Generators' 1984 AMPLA Yearbook 433.

BUILDINGS

1.43   The shadow cast by a neighbouring building cannot found any action in either trespass or nuisance. A natural right to lateral light is not a common law incident of ownership of land[1] and no wrong is committed at common law merely because a neighbour builds so as to overshadow a much prized garden.[2] Rights to light can be created or acquired only in limited circumstances and only as easements.[3] It remains the case in English law that no easement of light can be claimed in respect of vacant land as distinct from a building.[4]

1   *Earl Putnam Organisation Ltd v Macdonald* (1979) 91 DLR (3d) 714 at 717–718.
2   See, however, A Bradbrook, 'Nuisance and the Right of Solar Access' (1983) 15 Western Australian L Rev 148. Solar access may, of course, be protected in many instances through the sensitive application of planning controls [**para 13.155**].
3   On easements of light, see Chapter 8 [**para 8.103**]. It is possible that a freedom from overshadowing – as distinct from a right to light – may be secured indirectly through the negotiation of a restrictive covenant which prohibits development of adjoining land.
4   See also *Earl Putnam Organisation Ltd v Macdonald* (1979) 91 DLR (3d) 714 at 718.

TREES

1.44   In one context the overshadowing effect of a neighbour's land[1] can give rise to a legal remedy. In recent times the aggressive use of fast-growing leylandii trees as a weapon of boundary warfare[2] has led to so many disputes that the Anti-social Behaviour Act 2003 contains a procedure for the imposition of height restrictions on such features.

1   'Land' includes trees growing on the land [**para 1.104**].

2   See e g *Jones v Stones* [1999] 1 WLR 1739 at 1741H; *Burns v Morton* [2000] 1 WLR 347 at
    349H–350A.

HIGH HEDGES

1.45   The Anti-social Behaviour Act 2003 provides that the owner or occupier
of a 'domestic property'[1] may complain to his local authority that his 'reasonable enjoyment' of that property (or any part of it) is being 'adversely affected
by the height of a high hedge situated on land owned or occupied by another
person.'[2] For present purposes a 'high hedge' comprises so much of a barrier to
light or access as is formed wholly or predominantly by a line of two or more
evergreen or semi-evergreen trees or shrubs and rises to a height of more than
two metres above ground level.[3] Complaint to the local authority is envisaged
as a last resort following the failure of all attempts at amicable settlement
between neighbours. The local authority may reject the complaint if it considers that the complaint is 'frivolous or vexatious' or that the complainant has not
'taken all reasonable steps to resolve the matters complained of' without
recourse to the authority.[4] However, if otherwise satisfied that the complaint is
made out,[5] the authority has power to issue to all relevant parties a 'remedial
notice' (together with reasons for the authority's decision).[6] This remedial
notice may require certain 'initial' or 'preventative' action to be undertaken
(including a reduction in the height of the offending hedge to two metres above
ground level).[7] Failure to comply with a remedial notice within the stipulated
compliance period is generally a criminal offence.[8] The remedial notice, while in
force,[9] constitutes a local land charge[10] and is binding on all persons (including
successors in title) who are for the time being owners or occupiers of the land
concerned.[11] The local authority ultimately has power to enter land subject to a
remedial notice[12] and, in default of appropriate action by the owner or
occupier, to carry out the required action at his expense.[13]

1   'Domestic property' includes a building and any garden or yard which is used and enjoyed
    wholly or mainly in connection with a dwelling (ASBA 2003, s 67(1)).
2   ASBA 2003, ss 65(1), 67(3). A complaint may be made in respect of a domestic property
    which is for the time being unoccupied (ASBA 2003, s 65(2)), but in no case can the complaint
    relate to the effect of the roots of a high hedge (ASBA 2003, s 65(4)).
3   ASBA 2003, s 66(1). Significant gaps in the hedge may take the hedge outside the statutory
    definition of a 'high hedge' (ASBA 2003, s 66(2)). The Secretary of State and the National
    Assembly for Wales have power by regulation to amend ASBA 2003, ss 65–66 to extend the
    scope of complaints relating to high hedges and to alter the definition of a 'high hedge'
    (ASBA 2003, s 83(1)).
4   ASBA 2003, s 68(2).
5   The local authority has statutory rights of entry for the purpose of determining whether a
    remedial notice is appropriate or has been complied with (ASBA 2003, s 74(1)).
6   ASBA 2003, s 68(4). There is a process of appeal (in England) to the Secretary of State and (in
    Wales) to the National Assembly for Wales (ASBA 2003, s 71). See also ASBA 2003, s 80(1).
7   ASBA 2003, s 69(2). The remedial notice cannot require the removal of the hedge (ASBA
    2003, s 69(3)).
8   ASBA 2003, s 75(1) (see, however, ASBA 2003, s 75(3)–(4)).
9   The notice may later be withdrawn or its requirements relaxed (ASBA 2003, s 70).
10 ASBA 2003, s 69(8)(a) [**paras 12.7, 12.242**].
11 ASBA 2003, s 69(8)(b).

12   Entry may be made with a vehicle and any necessary persons, equipment or materials (ASBA 2003, s 77(7)).

13   ASBA 2003, s 77(1)–(2). Expenses reasonably incurred by the local authority again constitute a local land charge and bind successive owners and occupiers of the land (ASBA 2003, s 77(3)).

The higher stratum

1.46   Whatever its application to lower stratum airspace, the *cuius est solum* maxim has no relevance at all to the higher stratum of airspace which lies beyond any reasonable possibility of purposeful exploitation by the landowner below.[1] This upper stratum is left as an unpropertised commons,[2] owned by no state or individual,[3] but available for use by all.[4] Inevitably the borderline between the upper and lower zones of airspace is somewhat imprecise,[5] but the landowner's rights in superjacent airspace seem to be restricted to 'such height as is necessary for the ordinary use and enjoyment of his land and the structures upon it.'[6] Above this height the landowner 'has no greater rights in the air space than any other member of the public.'[7] Any other view would lead to 'the absurdity of a trespass at common law being committed by a satellite every time it passes over a suburban garden.'[8]

1   See the distinction indicated by Griffiths J in *Bernstein of Leigh (Baron) v Skyviews & General Ltd* [1978] QB 479 at 486D, 487F.

2   See Gray, 'Property in Thin Air' [1991] CLJ 252 at 256.

3   See *Re The Queen in Right of Manitoba and Air Canada* (1978) 86 DLR (3d) 631 at 635 per Monnin JA, where this classification of airspace as res omnium communis devastated Manitoba's attempt to tax sales on board aircraft flying over the province: the sales did not take place 'within the province'.

4   The upper stratum of airspace 'belongs to the world' (*Hinman v Pacific Air Transport*, 84 F2d 755 at 758 (1936), affd 300 US 655, 81 L ed 865 (1936)) and comprises 'free territory ... a sort of "no-man's land" ' (*Thrasher v City of Atlanta*, 173 SE 817 at 826 (1934)). See also *Lacroix v The Queen* [1954] 4 DLR 470 at 476.

5   [**Para 1.39**]. See S S Ball, 'The Vertical Extent of Ownership in Land' 76 U of Penn L Rev 631 (1928).

6   *Bernstein of Leigh (Baron) v Skyviews & General Ltd* [1978] QB 479 at 488A per Griffiths J. See likewise *Staden v Tarjanyi* (1980) 78 LGR 614 at 621–622; *Swetland v Curtiss Airports Corporation*, 55 F2d 201 at 203 (1932); *Lacroix v The Queen* [1954] 4 DLR 470 at 476; *Griggs v Allegheny County*, 369 US 84 at 88–89, 7 L Ed 2d 585 at 588 (1962); *Laird v Nelms*, 406 US 797 at 799–800, 32 L Ed 2d 499 at 503 (1972); *Didow v Alberta Power Ltd* [1988] 5 WWR 606 at 614–616; *Kim Beng Lee Pte Ltd v Kosion Enterprise (S) Pte Ltd* [1994] 1 SLR 700 at 702H.

7   *Bernstein of Leigh (Baron) v Skyviews & General Ltd* [1978] QB 479 at 488B.

8   *Bernstein of Leigh (Baron) v Skyviews & General Ltd* [1978] QB 479 at 487G per Griffiths J. For example, local authority byelaws cannot simply prohibit hang-gliding at any height above prescribed areas. In order to be valid, the relevant byelaw must specify a level above which the hang-glider is free to fly (*Staden v Tarjanyi* (1980) 78 LGR 614 at 623). See also Rules of the Air Regulations 1996 (SI 1996/1393), Sch 1, r 5(2)(d)(ii) [**para 1.39**].

Civil immunity of overflying aircraft

1.47   It follows that overflying aircraft commit no trespass when flying at a height of hundreds or thousands of feet.[1] The mere intrusion of such aircraft into superjacent airspace normally causes no interference with any reasonable use to which the landowner may wish to put his land.

1   This was first recognised in relation to overflight by hot air balloons (see e g *Pickering v Rudd* (1815) 4 Camp 219 at 220–221, 171 ER 70 at 71), but is now more generally acknowledged in relation to harmless traffic in navigable airspace. See also *Didow v Alberta Power Ltd* [1988] 5 WWR 606 at 611–612.

Statutory immunity

1.48   Section 76(1) of the Civil Aviation Act 1982 provides accordingly that no action can lie in trespass or nuisance in respect of the flight of an aircraft over any land 'at a height above the ground, which, having regard to wind, weather and all the circumstances of the case is reasonable',[1] provided that the aircraft complies with all relevant regulatory legislation.[2] However, recent years have thrown a new focus on the question whether the noise pollution caused by night flights in and out of major airports constitutes a violation of a surface dweller's right to respect for his private and family life and home pursuant to Article 8 of the European Convention on Human Rights.[3] In *Hatton v United Kingdom*[4] the Grand Chamber of the European Court of Human Rights, although declining to find on the instant facts that night flights at Heathrow Airport breached Article 8,[5] held that the general statutory prohibition of any action in trespass and nuisance, taken in conjunction with the inadequacy of judicial review, meant that English domestic law is now failing to provide an effective remedy for an arguable violation of Convention rights.[6]

1   The Civil Aviation Act 1982, s 76(2) imposes on the owner of the aircraft an absolute liability for any material damage or loss caused by the aircraft in flight. See *Weedair (NZ) Ltd v Walker* [1961] NZLR 153 at 157; *Southgate v Commonwealth of Australia* (1987) 13 NSWLR 188 at 191E–F (rider thrown by horse when frightened by helicopter flying at 50 to 100 feet above ground). See also *Bernstein of Leigh (Baron) v Skyviews & General Ltd* [1978] QB 479 at 489H.
2   See e g Rules of the Air Regulations 1996 (SI 1996/1393), Sch 1.
3   **[Paras 2.60, 2.61]**.
4   (2003) 37 EHRR 28 (reversing *Hatton v United Kingdom* (2002) 34 EHRR 1 at [95]–[107]).
5   (2003) 37 EHRR 28 at [118]–[130]. A majority in the Court considered that, in the context of the strong national economic interest in air travel, it had not been demonstrated that the state had failed to strike a fair balance between the Art 8 rights of affected individuals and the conflicting interests of the community as a whole. A stern (and particularly articulate) minority in the Court dissented on the ground that the majority's view marked 'a step backwards', ECHR Art 8 being sufficiently wide to protect a newly emerging category of 'environmental human rights' (Joint Dissenting Opinion at [2]–[5] **[para 2.64]**).
6   (2003) 37 EHRR 28 at [139]–[142] (see ECHR Art 13).

Limits of the immunity

1.49   The immunity provided by the Civil Aviation Act 1982 does not necessarily cover all forms of overflight. It applies only to 'innocent passage'[1] and does not, for instance, confer any tort immunity in respect of an aerobatic display above another's land.[2]

1   Shawcross and Beaumont, *Air Law* (4th edn, London 2000), Vol I, V/133.
2   J E Richardson, 'Private Property Rights in the Air Space at Common Law' (1953) 31 Can Bar Rev 117 at 120. See also Rules of the Air Regulations 1996 (SI 1996/1393), Sch 1, r 5(2)(c)(ii).

Aerial photography and surveillance

1.50   More difficult is the use of overflight for the purpose of aerial photography and surveillance. In *Bernstein v Skyviews & General Ltd*[1] Griffiths J firmly rejected trespass and nuisance claims arising from mere overflight for the purpose of commercial aerial photography.[2] Such overflight within the upper domain of airspace had not interfered with the claimant's use of his land, although different consequences might have attached to the 'harassment of constant surveillance of [the claimant's] house from the air, accompanied by the photographing of his every activity'.[3] In itself reasonable commercial overflight involves no tortious activity or unlawful invasion of privacy.[4]

1   [1978] QB 479. See (1977) 93 LQR 491 (R Wacks).
2   It did not help that the television company of which the claimant was chairman had recently made a series of films involving substantial aerial photography over wide areas of privately held land.
3   [1978] QB 479 at 489G.
4   Contrast the non-innocent passage evident in *E I du Pont de Nemours & Co v Christopher*, 431 F2d 1012 at 1015 (1970); affd 400 US 1024, 27 L Ed 2d 637 (1971) (aerial photography used as an unlawful means of obtaining a trade secret).

1.51   While surface dwellers may indeed 'have to put up with the occasional downward glance of a passing pilot or passenger',[1] more substantial concerns are raised by the increasingly frequent employment of aerial surveillance as a means of law enforcement.[2] Overflight by police helicopters and the device of thermal imaging are used nowadays not only for the purpose of traffic control, but also for the detection of crime and for the searching of areas which would otherwise be inaccessible in the absence of a properly obtained warrant.[3] In this context no English court has yet addressed the balance which requires to be maintained between the individual's legitimate interest in his own freedom and privacy and the general public interest in the detection and due prosecution of crime.[4] After intense judicial debate American courts, doubtless in response to the exigencies of modern law enforcement, came to accept that both 'the public and police lawfully may survey lands from the air',[5] but this concession has not been allowed to validate the more invasive forms of aerial police surveillance.[6] It remains to be seen whether English courts will be happy to accept that aerial surveillance by the police is 'but a form of routine "street patrol" to which the modern public must be deemed to be resigned.'[7] The question is now given a sharper edge by the advent of a supra-national Convention guarantee of the 'right to respect' for one's private and family life and for one's home.[8]

1   *People v Cook*, 221 Cal Rptr 499 at 501 (1985) (Supreme Court of California).
2   Police overflight is exempt from many of the strictures of the Rules of the Air Regulations 1996 (see Rules of the Air Regulations 1996 (SI 1996/1393), Sch 1, r 5(2)(b)).

3   Overflight provides an ideal means of detecting the cultivation of prohibited substances. See e g *Dean v Superior Court for County of Nevada*, 110 Cal Rptr 585 (1973); *People v Cook*, 221 Cal Rptr 499 (1985) (aerial observation of marijuana field).

4   Compare *People v Cook*, 221 Cal Rptr 499 (1985), where the Supreme Court of California held by a majority that a warrantless aerial police search conducted with a telephoto lens from a height of 1,600 feet had frustrated the individual's 'reasonable expectation of privacy from purposeful police surveillance of his backyard from the air.'

5   *Oliver v United States*, 466 US 170 at 179, 80 L Ed 2d 214 at 224 (1984). In *California v Ciraolo*, 476 US 207 at 213–215, 90 L Ed 2d 210 at 217–218 (1986), a bare majority in the United States Supreme Court held that the Fourth Amendment protection of privacy is not violated by 'warrantless naked-eye observation' from an altitude of 1000 feet. See also *Dow Chemical Co v United States*, 476 US 227 at 239, 90 L Ed 2d 226 at 238 (1986).

6   See e g *People v Deutsch*, 52 Cal Rptr 2d 366 at 369–370 (1996) (private home scanned by thermal imager); *State v Siegal*, 934 P2d 176 at 191–192 (1997).

7   See *People v Cook*, 221 Cal Rptr 499 at 504 (1985).

8   ECHR Art 8(1). This right is, of course, expressly limited by the need to promote the 'prevention of disorder or crime' (ECHR Art 8(2)).

BUILDINGS AND OTHER CONSTRUCTIONS

1.52 English law adopts an ancient rule of accession to realty, derived from Roman law,[1] under which buildings and other constructions integrally or irreversibly linked with land merge with, and become part and parcel of, the land.[2] This general principle is expressed in yet another Latin maxim: *superficies solo cedit* (a building becomes part of the ground). Most durable and substantial features of the built environment are therefore viewed, not so much as 'fixtures',[3] but simply as having melded with, and become part of, the freehold.[4] In this way buildings constructed on foundations placed in the soil become part of the realty[5] or 'immovable property'.[6] The top floor of a high-rise block of flats comprises 'land'. A garage[7] or garden shed or fence wall[8] likewise qualifies as 'land', provided that in each case it is firmly attached to the ground. Once incorporated within the realty, all such constructions pass presumptively on any subsequent transfer of an estate in the land.[9]

1   See Gaius, 2.73; Inst 2.1.29. See also S S Ball, 'The Jural Nature of Land' 23 Illinois L Rev 45 at 48 (1928–29).

2   Buildings and other annexed objects thus become 'incorporated with the soil' (*Lancaster v Eve* (1859) 5 CB (NS) 717 at 728, 141 ER 288 at 293) or partes soli (*Bain v Brand* (1876) 1 App Cas 762 at 769).

3   The terminology of 'fixtures' [**para 1.64**] seems strangely inappropriate for a man-made building construction, the recent case law preferring its more intrinsic characterisation as 'part and parcel' of the land or simply as 'real property in its own right' (see e g *Elitestone Ltd v Morris* [1997] 1 WLR 687 at 690G–691H, 693C per Lord Lloyd of Berwick, 694H, 697A per Lord Clyde). See also *Ports of Auckland Ltd v Auckland CC* [2000] 3 NZLR 614 at [72].

4   For reference to the test of incorporation into the 'freehold', see *Reid v Smith* (1905) 3 CLR 656 at 659 per Griffith CJ; *Elitestone Ltd v Morris* [1997] 1 WLR 687 at 693F per Lord Lloyd of Berwick.

5   *Mitchell v Mosley* [1914] 1 Ch 438 at 450.

6   The civilian terminology of 'immovable property' has transplanted itself into English law through EC Directives. See e g *Mechanical Engineering Consultants Ltd v Commissioners of Customs and Excise* (Unreported, VAT and Duties Tribunal, 18 May 1995), where it was

accepted that 'immovable property' comprises land in the full common law sense inclusive of accessions and fixtures. See also *Staatssecretaris van Financiën v Shipping and Forwarding Enterprise Safe BV* [1990] 1 ECR 285.

7   See e g *Harrow LBC v Donohue* [1995] 1 EGLR 257 at 259F.

8   *Moody v Steggles* (1879) 12 Ch D 261 at 267.

9   Subject to any contrary intention expressed in the conveyance, every conveyance of land is deemed to include all 'buildings' and 'erections' on the land (LPA 1925, s 62(1)) and, in the case of land with houses or other buildings on it, likewise operates to convey all 'outhouses, ... cellars, areas, courts, courtyards, cisterns, sewers, gutters, drains, ways, passages, lights, [and] watercourses' appertaining to the land (LPA 1925, s 62(2) [**paras 8.153–8.154**]). See *Cadogan v McGirk* [1996] 4 All ER 643 at 652e.

Criteria of accession to realty

1.53   In *Elitestone Ltd v Morris*[1] the House of Lords highlighted certain criteria as relevant to the identification of those chattel items and structures which, by virtue of their use for construction purposes, provide instances of real accession. Special significance is attached to the nature of any physical bonding between a particular structure and the subjacent land,[2] to the practical feasibility of removing or reassembling the constituent elements of the construction in any intact form,[3] and, more dubiously, to the generic character of the building in question.[4] However, all such factors merely subserve or illuminate the primary analysis,[5] which relates to the objectively demonstrable intention or purpose which underlies the construction.[6] In the case of large constructions such as dwelling-houses, annexation to the realty 'goes without saying',[7] essentially because of 'the uses and purposes for which they were erected and designed.'[8] A like analysis establishes the annexation of a bridge fixed on either side of a river[9]; and gas mains and service pipes embedded in the soil similarly lose their chattel character.[10]

1   [1997] 1 WLR 687. See (1997) 141 Sol Jo 565 (G Webber); (1997) 147 NLJ 1031 (H W Wilkinson); [1997] CLJ 498 (S Bridge); [1998] Conv 418 (H Conway).

2   [1997] 1 WLR 687 at 692A–B per Lord Lloyd of Berwick, 696F per Lord Clyde.

3   [1997] 1 WLR 687 at 690B per Lord Lloyd of Berwick, 696G–H per Lord Clyde. See also *Chelsea Yacht & Boat Co Ltd v Pope* [2000] 1 WLR 1941 at 1945G–1946A per Tuckey LJ (moored houseboat with plug-in or snap-on service connections easily removable); [2001] CLJ 40 (D Gibbs). Compare *Ports of Auckland Ltd v Auckland CC* [2000] 3 NZLR 614 at [75]–[76] (floating pontoons attached to jetty by rings).

4   [1997] 1 WLR 687 at 697A–G per Lord Clyde. Reference to the 'genus of the alleged chattel' is vulnerable to the objection of circularity, as in Lord Clyde's declaration (at 697F) that 'dwelling houses are generally of the nature of real property.'

5   See [1997] 1 WLR 687 at 693A, E per Lord Lloyd of Berwick.

6   [1997] 1 WLR 687 at 698E–H per Lord Clyde. The mere fact that the occupant of a construction pays council tax or poll tax is irrelevant to the question of accession to the realty (see e g *Chelsea Yacht & Boat Co Ltd v Pope* [2000] 1 WLR 1941 at 1947C–D (council tax); *Stubbs v Hartnell* (1997) 74 P & CR D36 (poll tax)).

7   [1997] 1 WLR 687 at 692B per Lord Lloyd of Berwick. The issue is 'as much a matter of common sense as precise analysis' (at 692H). See also *Chelsea Yacht & Boat Co Ltd v Pope* [2000] 1 WLR 1941 at 1946C–D per Tuckey LJ ('[I]t is common sense that a boat on a river is not part of the land. A boat, albeit used as a home, is not of the same genus as real property').

8   *Goff v O'Conner* (1855) 16 Ill 421 at 423, cited [1997] 1 WLR 687 at 692F–G per Lord Lloyd of Berwick.

9   *Montague v Long* (1972) 24 P & CR 240 at 246; *Attorney-General* (*ex rel Yorkshire Derwent Trust Ltd*) *v Brotherton* [1992] 1 AC 425 at 441E (although query a rope bridge). Compare also *Tate & Lyle Food and Distribution Ltd v GLC* [1983] 2 AC 509 at 534F (jetty).
10   *North Shore Gas Co Ltd v Commissioner of Stamp Duties* (*NSW*) (1940) 63 CLR 52 at 67–68, 70.

The objectivity of the realty classification

1.54   Classifications of realty do not fluctuate in accordance with the subjectively held intentions of the builder.[1] Nor can the general status of a structure be dictated arbitrarily either by simple declaration[2] or by express contractual stipulation.[3] The definitive test of accession centres on the objectively understood purpose of the construction or installation as inferred from all the circumstances of the case. Thus, for instance, even if a person erects a brick-built construction on land with the subjective intention, after a brief occupancy, of demolishing it and perhaps rebuilding on the same location, he cannot thereby maintain that the first building is a mere chattel.[4] The building retains its original character as an integral part of the land even though, on demolition, the disassembled parts of the building revert to the status of personalty[5] and even though the miracles of modern engineering often permit buildings to be jacked up intact and transported elsewhere.[6]

1   Accession occurs regardless of whether the relevant construction was erected in innocent mistake of title (see *Pull v Barnes*, 350 P 828 (1960) (mountain cabin built in error on another's land)) or was quite deliberately put up by a knowing trespasser (see *Harrow LBC v Donohue* [1995] 1 EGLR 257 at 259F). See also *Elwes v Brigg Gas Company* (1886) 33 Ch D 562 at 567.
2   No person 'can make his property real or personal by merely thinking it so' (*Dixon v Fisher* (1843) 5 D 775 at 793 per Lord Cockburn).
3   *Elitestone Ltd v Morris* [1997] 1 WLR 687 at 690D–F, 693E–F per Lord Lloyd of Berwick, citing *Melluish v BMI* (*No 3*) *Ltd* [1996] 1 AC 454 at 473D–G per Lord Browne-Wilkinson. Here, as so often in the ascertainment of legal status, contractual autonomy is overridden by objective legal reality: see Lord Lloyd's direct analogy with the distinction between lease and licence (*Street v Mountford* [1985] AC 809 [**para 7.177**]). See also *Potton Developments Ltd v Thompson* [1998] NPC 49; *Chelsea Yacht & Boat Co Ltd v Pope* [2000] 1 WLR 1941 at 1947H per Morritt LJ (lease of houseboat as a private residence was irrelevant to the classification of the boat as realty or otherwise).
4   See *State Savings Bank v Kircheval* (1877) 27 Am Rep 310 at 311; *Reid v Smith* (1905) 3 CLR 656 at 667, 681; *N H Dunn Pty Ltd v L M Ericsson Pty Ltd* (1979) 2 BPR 9241 at 9244.
5   *R v Leominster DC, ex p Antique Country Buildings Ltd* (1988) 56 P & CR 240 at 247.
6   In *Elitestone Ltd v Morris* [1997] 1 WLR 687 at 692H–693A, Lord Lloyd conceded that a house 'constructed in such a way as to be removable, whether as a unit, or in sections, may well remain a chattel, even though it is connected temporarily to mains services such as water and electricity.' See also *Lichty v Voigt* (1978) 80 DLR (3d) 757 at 761–762.

Structures which rest merely by force of gravity

1.55   Because of the overriding significance of objectively determined intention, accession to realty can occur even in the absence of any physical bonding between a construction and the underlying *solum*. Annexation may occur where a highly purposive juxtaposition of materials and land indicates a self-evident understanding that such materials should constitute realty. A venerable instance is provided by the dry stone wall or dyke, which inheres in the landscape in such a way as to 'become part of the land',[1] even though the same stones, 'if deposited in a builder's yard and for convenience sake stacked on top of each other in the form of a wall', would remain chattels.[2] In *Elitestone Ltd v Morris*[3] a wooden bungalow or chalet resting on concrete pillars attached to land was held, by inevitable inference from the circumstances, to have been intended to merge with the realty.[4] The structure could be used only in situ and could not have been removed to another location without demolition and destruction. Every case turns, however, on its own facts,[5] and the accession principle may not extend to structures such as 'Dutch barns',[6] mobile homes,[7] transportable motel units,[8] and movable greenhouses,[9] where the relevant structure can be, and is demonstrably intended to be, removable to other locations.

1   *Holland v Hodgson* (1872) LR 7 CP 328 at 335 per Blackburn J.
2   See similarly *Vaudeville Electric Cinema Ltd v Muriset* [1923] 2 Ch 74 at 83 per Sargant J; *Taylor v Hamer* [2003] 1 P & CR D9 (Transcript at [34], [37]) per Arden LJ.
3   [1997] 1 WLR 687.
4   A house which is 'constructed in such a way that it cannot be removed at all, save by destruction, cannot have been intended to remain as a chattel. It must have been intended to form part of the realty' ([1997] 1 WLR 687 at 693A per Lord Lloyd of Berwick).
5   *Elitestone Ltd v Morris* [1997] 1 WLR 687 at 696D per Lord Clyde.
6   See *Culling v Tufnal* (1694) Bull NP (5th ed) 34.
7   See *Lichty v Voigt* (1978) 80 DLR (3d) 757 at 761–762; *Royal Bank of Canada v Beyak* (1981) 119 DLR (3d) 505 at 508–509. See also the chattel classifications upheld in *Neylon v Dickens* [1979] 2 NZLR 714 at 720–722 (prefabricated dwelling on permanent foundations and connected to mains services); *Permanent Trustee Australia Ltd v Esanda Corporation Ltd* (1991) 6 BPR 13420 at 13427 (prefabricated 'transportable' home).
8   See *Potton Developments Ltd v Thompson* [1998] NPC 49.
9   See *H E Dibble Ltd v Moore* [1970] 2 QB 181 at 189A; *Deen v Andrews* [1986] 1 EGLR 262 at 264G.

NATURAL RIGHT TO SUPPORT FOR LAND

1.56   Landowners have certain 'natural rights', protected by the law of torts,[1] which come into being automatically and are not the subject of any grant.[2] One such natural right is the right to support for land.[3] Every landowner has a right to enjoy his own land in its natural state and is therefore entitled to have his land physically supported by the lateral thrust provided by his neighbour's land.[4] Interference with this 'right of property'[5] gives rise to a form of strict or no-fault liability in the neighbour. The natural right to support is quite distinct in nature and origin from any easement,[6] although, as the House of Lords decided in *Dalton v Angus & Co*,[7] it is quite possible that a building sited on land may acquire an *easement* of support from the soil of adjoining land after the effluxion of a prescriptive period of 20 years following the construction of that building.[8]

1   [Paras 1.110–1.113]. Violation of a natural right is actionable in the law of nuisance.
2   Not least for this reason natural rights are distinguishable from easements [para 8.14].
3   See generally J F Garner, (1948) 12 Conv (NS) 280. This natural right is an incident of ownership which passes without express provision on transfer of the land (*Dalton v Angus & Co* (1881) 6 App Cas 740 at 791 per Lord Selborne LC; *MCA Camilleri Building & Constructions Pty Ltd v H R Walters Pty Ltd* (1981) 2 BPR 9277 at 9279).

4   *Backhouse v Bonomi* (1861) 9 HL Cas 503 at 512–513, 11 ER 825 at 829; *Bognuda v Upton &
     Shearer Ltd* [1972] NZLR 741 at 760; *MCA Camilleri Building & Constructions Pty Ltd v H R
     Walters Pty Ltd* (1981) 2 BPR 9277 at 9279. The natural right to support for land is
     supplemented by a duty on the part of a private adjoining owner to take reasonable care to
     prevent a landslip on that adjoining land from causing injury or damage to a neighbour's land
     (see *Leakey v National Trust for Places of Historical Interest or Natural Beauty* [1980] QB 485
     at 524A–D; *Yared v Glenhurst Gardens Pty Ltd* (2002) 10 BPR 19485 at [99]).
5   *Dalton v Angus & Co* (1881) 6 App Cas 740 at 808 per Lord Blackburn.
6   *Dalton v Angus & Co* (1881) 6 App Cas 740 at 791 per Lord Selborne LC.
7   (1881) 6 App Cas 740.
8   **[Para 8.190]**.

Extent of the right

1.57   Every landowner has a natural right that the lateral thrust exerted on his
soil by his neighbour's land should not be removed (e g by mining or excavating
operations on the neighbour's land which cause subsidence).[1] The neighbour's
duty in this regard is non-delegable and it is no defence that damage is caused
by the wrongful acts of the neighbour's contractors.[2] The natural right to
support clearly includes an entitlement to support from a neighbour's subjacent
minerals and from any adjacent bed of wet sand or running silt.[3] But the
natural right of support does not extend to any claim that land should be
supported by subterranean water present in adjoining land, with the result that
no action lies in respect of a neighbour's extraction of such water and
consequent subsidence.[4] Nor does the natural right imply any obligation on the
neighbour to preserve his own land untouched in its natural state.[5]

1   *Dalton v Angus & Co* (1881) 6 App Cas 740 at 808; *Byrne v Judd* (1908) 27 NZLR 1106 at
     1118–1120. In certain cases of subsidence damage the Coal Authority may be liable to
     undertake remedial works or to compensate for diminished property values (see Coal Mining
     (Subsidence) Act 1957, ss 1(2), 13; *Wilkes v Coal Authority* [1998] LS Gaz R 33; *McAreavey v
     Coal Authority* (2000) 80 P & CR 41 at 48, 54, 58).
2   See *Bower v Peate* (1876) 1 QBD 321 at 326–327 per Cockburn CJ.
3   *Stephens v Anglian Water Authority* [1987] 1 WLR 1381 at 1384H.
4   *Stephens v Anglian Water Authority* [1987] 1 WLR 1381 at 1385A; *LJP Investments Pty Ltd v
     Howard Chia Investments Pty Ltd* (1988) 4 BPR 9640 at 9643.
5   *Bullock Holdings Ltd v Jerema* (1998) 77 ACWS (3d) 207 at [12].

Requirement of actual damage

1.58   The natural right to support is violated only where the excavation of the
adjacent or subjacent land of a neighbour causes actual disturbance of or
damage to the surface of the claimant's land.[1] Thus there is no interference with
the natural right where the claimant's land suffers a mere 'apprehension of
future damage'[2] or a mere loss of stability as distinct from actual physical
damage.[3] There can be no recovery in respect of a purely prospective loss.[4]

1   *Dalton v Angus & Co* (1881) 6 App Cas 740 at 808 per Lord Blackburn; *Darley Main
     Colliery Co v Mitchell* (1886) 11 App Cas 127 at 151; *West Leigh Colliery Co v Tunnicliffe &
     Hampson Ltd* [1908] AC 27 at 31–32; *Taylor v Auto Trade Supply Ltd* [1972] NZLR 102 at 108;

Bognuda v Upton & Shearer Ltd [1972] NZLR 741 at 760; *Xpress Print Pte Ltd v Monocrafts Pte Ltd and L & B Engineering (S) Pte Ltd* [2000] 3 SLR 545 at 563B.

2   *West Leigh Colliery Co v Tunnicliffe & Hampson Ltd* [1908] AC 27 at 29 per Lord Macnaghten.

3   *Lamb v Walker* (1878) 3 QBD 389 at 400; *Midland Bank Plc v Bardgrove Property Services Ltd* [1991] 2 EGLR 283 at 286F–G; *Martin v Butcher* (Unreported, Court of Appeal, 15 July 1997).

4   See *Benzie v Happy Eater Ltd* (Unreported, Queen's Bench Division, 18 May 1990).

No requirement of positive action by the adjoining owner

1.59   The natural right of support cannot obligate a neighbour to take any active steps to maintain lateral support. In reality the right of support entails no positive right at all, but merely a right not to have lateral support withdrawn by a neighbour's direct action.[1] What is prohibited is 'an *active interference* with the support which causes damage.'[2] In consequence a fortuitous slippage of land on a neighbouring tenement constitutes no breach of the natural right,[3] although the neighbour may be liable on alternative grounds of negligence and nuisance.[4]

1   *Morgan v Lake Macquarie CC* (Unreported, New South Wales Court of Appeal, 2 September 1993, BPR Casenote 96792).

2   *Xpress Print Pte Ltd v Monocrafts Pte Ltd and L & B Engineering (S) Pte Ltd* [2000] 3 SLR 545 at 563B per Yong Pung How CJ.

3   See *Xpress Print Pte Ltd v Monocrafts Pte Ltd and L & B Engineering (S) Pte Ltd* [2000] 3 SLR 545 at 563C, where the Court of Appeal of Singapore inclined towards the view that no liability can arise in connection with an Act of God (e g landslide or earthquake).

4   A duty of care to prevent danger to higher land from lack of support caused by natural erosion arises, however, only where the owner or occupier of the lower land knows or is presumed to know of a patent defect in his land which could reasonably foreseeably cause damage to the higher land (see *Holbeck Hall Hotel Ltd v Scarborough BC* [2000] QB 836 at [39]–[42], [54] per Stuart-Smith LJ).

Remedies

1.60   Violation of a landowner's natural right to support gives rise to a liability in damages and may even be the subject of a mandatory injunction.[1] However, the natural right to support is not infringed if the land which has been excavated and the adjacent land from which lateral support has thereby been removed are both, at the date of excavation, within the common ownership of one person.[2] A subsequent purchaser of the portion of land from which lateral support has been removed cannot claim any violation of his natural right in the event of a later collapse of his land,[3] but may be able to sue in negligence.[4]

1   See *Redland Bricks Ltd v Morris* [1969] 2 All ER 576 at 579H–580F; *Economy Shipping Pty Ltd v A D C Buildings Pty Ltd and Fischer Constructions Pty Ltd* [1969] 2 NSWR 97 at 106; *Grocott v Ayson* [1975] 2 NZLR 586 at 590.

2   *Blewman v Wilkinson* [1979] 2 NZLR 208 at 211–212, 215–217. See also *Jennings v Sylvania Waters Pty Ltd* [1972] 2 NSWLR 4 at 14C–D; *Soich v Sutherland SC* (1980) 2 BPR 9273 at 9275.

3   *MCA Camilleri Building & Constructions Pty Ltd v H R Walters Pty Ltd* (1981) 2 BPR 9277 at
     9281. See also *Soich v Sutherland SC* (1980) 2 BPR 9273 at 9275 per McLelland J.
4   *Blewman v Wilkinson* [1979] 2 NZLR 208 at 212, 215, 217. See also *Bognuda v Upton &
     Shearer Ltd* [1972] NZLR 741 at 757–758. An action for loss of support may lie against the
     person withdrawing support even though he has since ceased to own the land adjoining that
     from which support was withdrawn (*Thynne v Petrie* [1975] Qd R 260 at 262F–G). The
     successor in title of the person who withdrew the support is not liable for the acts of his
     predecessor (*Greenwell v Low Beechburn Coal Co* [1897] 2 QB 165 at 177–179; *Hall v Duke of
     Norfolk* [1900] 2 Ch 493 at 502–503).

Protection for buildings situated upon land

1.61   The decision of the House of Lords in *Dalton v Angus & Co*[1] has always
been viewed as providing venerable authority for the proposition that the
natural right of support avails land only in its original state unencumbered by
buildings or other constructions.[2] On this basis the landowner's natural right
strictly comprises no right to support for his buildings[3] and if excavation or
demolition on a neighbour's land causes a landowner's house to collapse, the
landowner normally has no remedy in the absence of either nuisance, negligence or a duly acquired easement of support.[4] If, however, the neighbour's
activities on his land would have caused the subsidence of land in any event –
irrespective of the presence of buildings thereon – the damages recoverable for
the violation of the natural right of support for land may include damages in
respect of any buildings which have been affected.[5]

1   (1881) 6 App Cas 740.
2   It is possible that if a vendor sells part of his land, knowing that the purchaser intends to erect
     a building, the vendor may be taken as having impliedly covenanted not to use his own
     adjoining land so as to injure or interfere with the purchaser's new building (*Siddons v Short,
     Harley & Co* (1877) 2 CPD 572 at 577). See *Kebewar Pty Ltd v Harkin* (1987) 9 NSWLR 738
     at 741B–742A **[para 8.131]**.
3   See *Midland Bank Plc v Bardgrove Property Services Ltd* [1991] 2 EGLR 283 at 286B; *Latimer
     v Official Co-operative Society* (1885) 16 LR Ir 305 at 308; *Public Trustee v Hermann* [1968] 3
     NSWR 94 at 108; *LJP Investments Pty Ltd v Howard Chia Investments Pty Ltd* (1988) 4 BPR
     9640 at 9642; *Fyvie v Anand* (1994) 6 BPR 13743 at 13747 per Young J.
4   *Peyton v London Corpn* (1829) 9 B & C 725 at 735–737, 109 ER 269 at 273–274; *Ray v Fairway
     Motors (Barnstaple) Ltd* (1968) 20 P & CR 261 at 264; *Benzie v Happy Eater Ltd* (Unreported,
     Queen's Bench Division, 18 May 1990); *Thurston v Hancock* (1815) 12 Mass 220, 7 Am Dec 57
     at 61–62; *Green v Belfast Tramways Co* (1887) 20 LR Ir 35 at 40–43; *Gateley v H & J
     Martin Ltd* [1900] 2 IR 269 at 272–273.
5   *Stroyan v Knowles* (1861) 6 H & N 454 at 465, 158 ER 186 at 191; *Hunt v Peake* (1860) 29 LJ
     Ch 785 at 787; *Attorney General v Conduit Colliery Co* [1895] 1 QB 301 at 312; *Ray v Fairway
     Motors (Barnstaple) Ltd* (1968) 20 P & CR 261 at 268; *Midland Bank Plc v Bardgrove Property
     Services Ltd* [1991] 2 EGLR 283 at 286F; *Public Trustee v Hermann* [1968] 3 NSWR 94 at
     108–109. See also *Brace v South East Regional Housing Association* (1984) 270 EG 1286; *Fyvie
     v Anand* (1994) 6 BPR 13743 at 13747. See generally E H Bodkin, (1962) 26 Conv (NS) 210.

Growing criticism of the exclusion of buildings

1.62   In recent years the confinement of the natural right of support to
undeveloped land has been increasingly criticised as incompatible with the high

intensity user of land in crowded urban areas.[1] Moreover, the dogmatic restriction of the ancient rule leaves uncomfortable anomalies in its wake. A landowner's land, if left undeveloped, commands a strict duty of support from his neighbour's soil, but if the landowner invests in construction on his own land, the neighbour may immediately excavate with impunity on his side of the boundary, thereby causing the landowner's new building to crumble to the ground.[2] Furthermore, the neighbour's liberty to ignore the landowner's need for support is rather incongruously transformed, after the effluxion of the 20 year prescription period, into a positive duty of support in respect of the landowner's building.[3]

1   The doctrinal limitation has been said to be 'catastrophic' under modern urban conditions (see *MCA Camilleri Building & Constructions Pty Ltd v H R Walters Pty Ltd* (1981) 2 BPR 9277 at 9280 per Needham J). See also *Kebewar Pty Ltd v Harkin* (1987) 9 NSWLR 738 at 740G–741A (Court of Appeal of New South Wales); *LJP Investments Pty Ltd v Howard Chia Investments Pty Ltd* (1988) 4 BPR 9640 at 9642.

2   *Dalton v Angus & Co* (1881) 6 App Cas 740 at 804 per Lord Penzance. Some jurisdictions have left open the possibility that, if and to the extent that any claim of natural right is defeated by the ancient rule, cases of loss may still find a remedy in damages for negligence or nuisance (see e g *Bognuda v Upton & Shearer Ltd* [1972] NZLR 741 at 756–758; *Stoneman v Lyons* (1975) 133 CLR 550 at 567 per Stephen J; *Kebewar Pty Ltd v Harkin* (1987) 9 NSWLR 738 at 743E–G; *LJP Investments Pty Ltd v Howard Chia Investments Pty Ltd* (1988) 4 BPR 9640 at 9643).

3   A further irony is that the decision in *Dalton v Angus & Co* is as well known for the proposition which it did not decide (i e that a neighbour may excavate his land with reckless abandon prior to the effluxion of the prescriptive period) as for the proposition which it did decide (i e that a prescriptive right of support for a building may be acquired after 20 years). See *Xpress Print Pte Ltd v Monocrafts Pte Ltd and L & B Engineering (S) Pte Ltd* [2000] 3 SLR 545 at 552F per Yong Pung How CJ. In fact several judges in *Dalton v Angus & Co* indicated that the natural right of support ought to confer protection, ab initio, on 'all those burthens which man is accustomed to lay upon the soil' (see (1881) 6 App Cas 740 at 772 per Fry J, 803–804 per Lord Penzance).

Reversal of the rule

1.63 Many common law jurisdictions have indicated that the doctrinaire limitation on the natural right of support is now over-ripe for reversal by supreme appellate tribunals.[1] The lead has finally been taken by the Court of Appeal of Singapore in *Xpress Print Pte Ltd v Monocrafts Pte Ltd and L & B Engineering (S) Pte Ltd*.[2] Here the Court condemned as 'anachronistic' the rule supposedly enshrined in *Dalton v Angus & Co*, declaring that in a modern context of high density urban development there is 'scant justification' for the 20 year gestation period for a right of support in respect of a building. The Court considered it 'inimical to a society which respects each citizen's property rights' that, within the prescriptive period, a landowner could 'excavate his land with impunity, sending his neighbour's building and everything in it crashing to the ground.'[3] Instead the Court appealed to the principle, *sic utere tuo ut alienum non laedas*,[4] to uphold, on behalf of an injured party, a 'right of support in respect of his buildings by neighbouring lands from the time such buildings are erected.' It is likely that this enlightened approach, imposing a strict and non-delegable duty on landowners, will now be followed by other final appellate courts.[5]

1   See e g *Kebewar Pty Ltd v Harkin* (1987) 9 NSWLR 738 at 740G–741A per McHugh JA; *LJP Investments Pty Ltd v Howard Chia Investments Pty Ltd* (1988) 4 BPR 9640 at 9642; *Fyvie v Anand* (1994) 6 BPR 13743 at 13747 per Young J.
2   [2000] 3 SLR 545. See P W Young, (2000) 74 ALJ 727; P Pillai, 'The Primacy of the Principle of Reciprocity in the Singapore Land Regime' (2001) 13 SAcLJ 198; Tang Hang Wu, 'The Right of Lateral Support of Buildings from the Adjoining Land' [2002] Conv 237.
3   'The damage that might be caused ... could be astronomical, not to mention the cost in human lives or injury to property' ([2000] 3 SLR 545 at 562E per Yong Pung How CJ).
4   'Use your own property in such a manner as not to injure that of another'. The Latin maxim expressly underlays the statement of principle adumbrated by Lord Penzance in *Dalton v Angus & Co* (1881) 6 App Cas 740 at 804. For further reference to the maxim in this context, see *Walker v Strosnider*, 67 SE 1087 at 1090 (1910); *Wilton v Hansen* (1969) 4 DLR (3d) 167 at 171 per Freedman JA; *Bognuda v Upton & Shearer Ltd* [1972] NZLR 741 at 757 per North P.
5   The stance adopted by the Court of Appeal of Singapore, if accepted in English law, would render redundant the prescriptive acquisition of rights of support after 20 years: the 'natural right' to support would include the support of buildings from the date of their construction.

FIXTURES

1.64   The demarcation of realty remains problematical in other contexts.[1] As indicated in section 62 of the Law of Property Act 1925, the statutory definition of 'land' includes 'fixtures' attached to the land. English law has effectively adopted the maxim *quicquid plantatur solo, solo cedit* (whatever is attached to the ground becomes a part of it),[2] but in so doing has had to fashion an uneasy distinction between 'fixtures' and 'chattels'.

1   It can even be said that certain kinds of earth are not 'land'. In *R v Parker, ex p Mullavey* [1989] WAR 233 at 237–238, the Full Court of Western Australia's Supreme Court held that 'tailings' (ie waste residue or leavings of earlier mining operations) constitute chattel property and thus a species of personal property. Brinsden J indicated (at 238) that if the tailings were later to be 'spread upon and ... mingled with the earth upon which they rest' they might revert to the status of realty. This approach mirrors the old common law rule that a heap of dung is a mere chattel but can, if spread on the ground, merge with the realty (*Yearworth v Pierce* (1647) Aleyn 31 at 32, 82 ER 900, sub nom *Carver v Pierce*, Sty 66 at 73, 82 ER 534, 539).
2   *Lancaster v Eve* (1859) 5 CB (NS) 717 at 727, 141 ER 288 at 293 per Williams J. Thus the freeholder 'has exactly the same interest in everything attached to the freehold as he has in the bricks and mortar' (*Ex p Daglish. Re Wilde* (1873) LR 8 Ch App 1072 at 1080 per James LJ).

The relevance of classification

1.65   'Fixtures' comprise that category of material objects which, when physically attached to land, are regarded as becoming annexed to the realty.[1] By contrast, the category of 'chattels' consists of physical objects which never lose their independent character as mere personalty, even though placed in some close relation with realty.[2]

1   *New Zealand Government Property Corpn v H M & S Ltd* [1982] QB 1145 at 1160H–1161A.

'The land and the fixtures are one' (*Emanuel* (*Rundle Mall*) *Pty Ltd v Commissioner of Stamps* (1986) 39 SASR 582 at 592). As in the case of buildings [**para 1.52**], fixtures become 'incorporated with the soil' (*Lancaster v Eve* (1859) 5 CB (NS) 717 at 728, 141 ER 288 at 293). See also *Telecom Auckland Ltd v Auckland CC* [1999] 1 NZLR 426 at 440.

2   Thus a mortgagee of realty normally obtains no security over chattels (e g furniture) in or on the mortgaged property (see *Deutsche Genossenschafts Hypothekenbank v Amstad* (Unreported, Chancery Division, 22 January 1997)).

Effect on title

1.66 Irrespective of its previous ownership, title to a fixture vests automatically and exclusively in the owner of the realty (whether freeholder or leaseholder[1]). As a fixture the annexed object is regarded, by virtue of some legal metamorphosis,[2] as having merged with the land.

1   See *Melluish v BMI* (*No 3*) *Ltd* [1996] 1 AC 454 at 477B–C per Lord Browne-Wilkinson.
2   In *Deutsche Genossenschafts Hypothekenbank v Amstad* (Unreported, Chancery Division, 22 January 1997), Harman J discussed the homely example of the bath which, on the builder's merchant's lorry was a chattel, but which is converted by installation into a fixture.

Expropriation of chattel owner

1.67 This merger of chattel with realty automatically extinguishes any separate title formerly held in the relevant object.[1] The process of annexation thus expropriates the owner of the affixed chattel[2] – if he is not also the freehold owner – whilst simultaneously disabling the landowner from claiming any independent title in the fixture which is distinct from his general title in the 'land'.[3] In stark contrast, objects which retain their chattel status are never included within the realty, undergo no change of title, and do not automatically pass with subsequent conveyances or transfers of the land.

1   The owner of the affixed object loses title even if the attachment to the realty is carried out by someone else (*Reynolds v Ashby & Son* [1904] AC 466 at 472–473, 475), but may have a remedy for the tort of conversion. See also the related discussion of proprietary estoppel [**para 10.168**].
2   The provider of the object is immediately expropriated, even though he has attempted to protect himself by means of a retention of title clause (see *Aircool Installations v British Telecommunications* [1995] CLY 821; *F & M Horwood Nominees* (*NSW*) *Pty Ltd v Mark Building Enterprises Pty Ltd SC* (*NSW*) (Unreported, Supreme Court of New South Wales, 17 July 1981); *Sanwa Australia Leasing Ltd v National Westminster Finance Australia Ltd* (1988) 4 BPR 9514 at 9515). Moreover, the mere fact that providers of equipment may retain some equitable rights relating to such objects (in the form of a right to enter and remove the equipment [**para 1.87**]) does not mean that 'the equipment itself belongs to them', even if their equitable rights are enforceable against subsequent takers of the land (*Melluish v BMI* (*No 3*) *Ltd* [1996] 1 AC 454 at 475H–476A per Lord Browne-Wilkinson).
3   See *Emanuel* (*Rundle Mall*) *Pty Ltd v Commissioner of Stamps* (1986) 39 SASR 582 at 587 per White J.

Transactions with the land

1.68 It also follows from the fact of annexation that a fixture passes presumptively with all subsequent conveyances or transfers[1] of the realty unless and until lawfully severed from the land.[2] It has long been accepted that, in the absence of contrary stipulation,[3] a purchaser is entitled to all fixtures attached to the land at the date of exchange of contracts.[4] Recently, in the interests of promoting '[c]ommon sense and common decency' in the handling of ordinary house purchases, a majority of the Court of Appeal has indicated that this entitlement extends to all fixtures which, to the knowledge of the purchaser, attached to the land at the earlier point in time when offers of purchase were invited and the land was inspected by potential purchasers.[5] Only thus can the law deal appropriately with the surreptitious removal of fixtures during the interval which almost inevitably occurs between the purchaser's inspection of the premises and the date of contract.

1   LPA 1925, s 62(1)–(2).
2   *North Shore Gas Co Ltd v Commissioner of Stamp Duties* (*NSW*) (1940) 63 CLR 52 at 68; *Emanuel* (*Rundle Mall*) *Pty Ltd v Commissioner of Stamps* (1986) 39 SASR 582 at 590. It has been held that a purchaser's pre-contract knowledge that certain fixtures are not intended to be included (e g because they have already been sold to another) can rebut the presumption that fixtures pass (see *Meehan v The New Zealand Agricultural Co* (*Ltd*) (1907) 26 NZLR 766 at 768; *Murphy v Hudson* (1995) 6 BPR 14061 at 14068–14069). In English law such a conclusion is probably supportable only by reference to some form of estoppel **[para 10.168]**.
3   LPA 1925, s 62 can be excluded by contrary intention expressed in the conveyance (see LPA 1925, s 62(4)).
4   **[Paras 1.83, 9.18, 12.26]**. However, much of the heat has now been removed from what used to be a vexed aspect of conveyancing. In modern domestic conveyancing practice the widespread use of 'tick lists' of items to be retained by a vendor has tended, in most cases, to clarify the contractual position beyond all doubt (see *Taylor v Hamer* [2002] EWCA Civ 1130, [2002] 1 P & CR D9 (Transcript at [52]) per Arden LJ).
5   See *Taylor v Hamer* [2002] EWCA Civ 1120, [2002] 1 P & CR D9 (Transcript at [82], [93]) per Sedley LJ ('simple morality suggests that [the seller] cannot remove [fixtures] without telling the buyer that they are no longer for sale') (see likewise Wall J at [76]).

Effect on mortgage securities

1.69   The elusive distinction between fixtures and chattels used to be primarily relevant at the point when land came to be sold. Nowadays the spotlight has moved away from transactions of sale to those of mortgage, where the mortgagee is only too anxious in circumstances of default to maximise the value of the land over which his security has been taken.[1] A mortgage ranks as a 'conveyance' of land,[2] with the result that the mortgagee presumptively takes a security over the land inclusive of all fixtures.[3] The value of the security is effectively inflated by any genuine accretions to the realty paid for by the borrower during the currency of the mortgage loan, the mortgagee's security covering all fixtures irrespective of the date of their annexation, ie whether before or after the creation of the mortgage.[4]

1   As a sociological aside, the items so often at stake in today's case law are no longer the statuary, stuffed birds and tapestries of the late Victorian era but rather the sophisticated household appliances and artefacts associated with a more recent culture of aggressive domestic consumption (see e g the attempt in *Botham v TSB Bank plc* (1996) 73 P & CR D1 to attach the value of an expensively installed Neff kitchen). See also [1998] Conv 137 (M Haley).

2   **[Para 2.42]**.
3   *Ex p Daglish. Re Wilde* (1873) LR 8 Ch App 1072 at 1080 per James LJ; *Re Yates* (1888)
      38 Ch D 112 at 120 per Cotton LJ, 124–125 per Lindley LJ; *Re Rogerstone Brick &
      Stone Co Ltd* [1919] 1 Ch 110 at 124; *Melluish v BMI (No 3) Ltd* [1996] 1 AC 454 at
      474H–475A per Lord Browne-Wilkinson; *Re Penning; Ex p State Bank of South Australia*
      (1989) 89 ALR 417 at 427.
4   *Kay's Leasing Corp Pty Ltd v CSR Provident Fund Nominees Pty Ltd* [1962] VR 429 at
      436–438; *Sanwa Australia Leasing Ltd v National Westminster Finance Australia Ltd* (1988) 4
      BPR 9514 at 9519 per Powell J.

Other implications

1.70   The distinction between fixtures and chattels is important for several
other legal purposes. For instance, fixtures can be the subject of theft only if
severed from the land.[1] An equitable charge over fixtures can be created only by
writing, since fixtures constitute an interest in land.[2] The borderline between
fixture and chattel is increasingly important not only in the law of taxation[3] but
also in the protection of the environment[4] and of the national heritage.[5] But
perhaps the most significant difference between fixtures and chattels relates to
the circumstances in which they can be removed from the land.[6]

1   Theft Act 1968, s 4(2)(b)–(c). See also *R v Dowsey* (1903) 29 VLR 453 at 456.
2   *Jarvis v Jarvis* (1893) 9 TLR 631 at 632; *North Shore Gas Co Ltd v Commissioner of Stamp
      Duties (NSW)* (1940) 63 CLR 52 at 68.
3   See e g *Melluish v BMI (No 3) Ltd* [1996] 1 AC 454 at 473B–C.
4   Planning permission is required only in respect of material changes **[para 13.163]** in the use of
      'land' (see e g *Thames Heliports Plc v LB of Tower Hamlets* (1997) 74 P & CR 164 at 168,
      176–177).
5   See Planning (Listed Buildings and Conservation Areas) Act 1990, s 1(5); *Debenhams Plc v
      Westminster CC* [1987] AC 396 at 408H–409B per Lord Mackay of Clashfern. Listed building
      protection covers fixtures (see *Corthorn Land and Timber Co Ltd v Minister of Housing* (1965)
      17 P & CR 210 at 217) and has been extended to such objects as a heavy carillon clock in a
      stately home (*R v Secretary of State for Wales, ex p Kennedy* [1996] JPL 645 at 649), but not to
      Canova's 'The Three Graces' ([1991] JPL 401). See [1991] Conv 251 (H W Wilkinson). 'The
      Three Graces' was subsequently sold to the J Paul Getty Museum in California (*Times*,
      29 September 1993).
6   **[Para 1.82]**.

The distinction between fixtures and chattels

1.71   The distinction between fixtures and chattels has often been said to turn
on two separate but related tests as to the intention of the original owner of an
object in bringing it into close association with the realty. As Blackburn J
indicated in *Holland v Hodgson*,[1] these tests relate, *first*, to the degree or mode
of annexation present in the given circumstances and, *second*, to the general
purpose of the annexation. The intention of the annexor himself is material
only in so far as it can be presumed from either the degree or the overall
purpose of the annexation.[2] In reality, however, the differentiation of fixtures
and chattels may now depend so heavily upon the circumstances of each

individual case that relatively few guidelines remain in the modern law which are capable of unambiguous application to particular facts.[3] Almost the only immutable principle is the idea that some degree of physical connection is necessary before a chattel can be said to have become part of the realty.[4]

1   (1872) LR 7 CP 328 at 334.
2   *Hobson v Gorringe* [1897] 1 Ch 182 at 193; *Stack v T Eaton Co* (1902) 4 OLR 335 at 338; *Royal Bank of Canada v Beyak* (1981) 119 DLR (3d) 505 at 509. As in the case of buildings constructed on the land [**para 1.54**], the element of intention or purpose must be assessed not subjectively but objectively (see *Elitestone Ltd v Morris* [1997] 1 WLR 687 at 698E–H per Lord Clyde). Even an express agreement between the fixer of a chattel and the landowner as to the ownership of the object serves merely to govern their contractual rights inter se to sever the object from the realty (see *Melluish v BMI (No 3) Ltd* [1996] AC 454 at 473D–G per Lord Browne-Wilkinson).
3   See L Griggs, 'The doctrine of fixtures: questionable origin, debatable history, and a future that is past!' (2001) 9 APLJ 51.
4   *Berkley v Poulett* [1977] 1 EGLR 86 at 88M–89A per Scarman LJ; *Botham v TSB Bank plc* (1996) 73 P & CR D1 at D2 per Roch LJ. See, however, *Moody v Steggles* (1879) 12 Ch D 261 at 267 per Fry J ('Everybody knows that a key, although in its nature a chattel, belongs to the house, and passes with the freehold').

The physical degree of annexation

1.72   The older of the two traditional tests takes the more primitive form of an enquiry into the degree of the physical attachment between the object and the pre-existing realty. The more firmly, permanently or irreversibly an object is affixed to the earth or to a building thereon, the more likely is the object to be classified as a fixture.[1] Conversely, in the absence of a durable physical connection with land, a crude sort of gravity test points towards a prima facie chattel classification. As Blackburn J observed in *Holland v Hodgson*,[2] when 'the article in question is no further attached to the land than by its own weight it is generally considered to be a mere chattel.'[3]

1   Even if the physical attachment of an object is only slight and the object can be fairly easily removed, its character is prima facie that of a fixture (see *Holland v Hodgson* (1872) LR 7 CP 328 at 335; *Stack v T Eaton Co* (1902) 4 OLR 335 at 338; *Royal Bank of Canada and Saskatchewan Telecommunications* (1985) 20 DLR (4th) 415 at 417–418). As soon as physical attachment is established, the onus of proof rests on the party who asserts the continuing chattel status of the object in question (see *Vaudeville Electric Cinema Ltd v Muriset* [1923] 2 Ch 74 at 83; *National Australia Bank Ltd v Blacker* (2000) 179 ALR 97 at [17]). Ease of removal may reverse the prima facie characterisation (*National Australia Bank Ltd v Blacker*, supra at [28]).
2   (1872) LR 7 CP 328 at 335.
3   See e g *Deen v Andrews* [1986] 1 EGLR 262 at 264G. There has been wide acceptance of the gravity test. See *Wiltshear v Cottrell* (1853) 1 E & B 674 at 689, 118 ER 589 at 595; *Vaudeville Electric Cinema Ltd v Muriset* [1923] 2 Ch 74 at 83; *Berkley v Poulett* [1977] 1 EGLR 86 at 88M per Scarman LJ; *Stack v T Eaton Co* (1902) 4 OLR 335 at 338; *Plaza Equities Ltd v Bank of Nova Scotia* (1978) 84 DLR (3d) 609 at 631; *Palumberi v Palumberi* (1986) 4 BPR 9106 at 9109; *National Australia Bank Ltd v Blacker* (2000) 179 ALR 97 at [17].

Fixture classifications

1.73 On this basis the courts have been able to assign the status of fixture to such objects as spinning looms bolted to the floor of a mill,[1] an automatic car wash machine bolted to the ground,[2] petrol pumps installed on a station forecourt,[3] central heating, elevators, video/alarm systems and swimming pool filtration plant,[4] rails and sleepers embedded in stone,[5] and air conditioning equipment cut into, bolted on to, or ducted into, the walls of a building.[6] Fixtures can thus include anything attached to any part of the land by bolts, screws or nails. Perhaps to the surprise of the lay person, even such objects as a bathroom cabinet, towel rail[7] or overhead heater, if attached to a wall, become prima facie part of the 'land'. The more difficult it is to remove or disconnect an item from the realty without serious damage, the more likely it is that the item was objectively intended to comprise a permanent enhancement of the realty.[8]

1 *Holland v Hodgson* (1872) LR 7 CP 328 at 340.
2 *Lombard and Ulster Banking Ltd v Kennedy* [1974] NI 20 at 23.
3 *Smith v City Petroleum Co Ltd* [1940] 1 All ER 260 at 261G–H; *Costa Investments Pty Ltd v Mobil Oil Australia Ltd* [1979] 1 SR (WA) 137 at 148.
4 *Melluish v BMI (No 3) Ltd* [1996] 1 AC 454 at 476C–D.
5 *Herbert v British Railways Board* (Unreported, Court of Appeal, 15 October 1999).
6 *Aircool Installations v British Telecommunications* [1995] CLY 821; *Famous Makers Confectionery Pty Ltd v Sengos* (1993) 6 BPR 13222 at 13224.
7 See e g *Botham v TSB Bank plc* (1996) 73 P & CR D1 at D3.
8 The fact that kitchen units are carefully surrounded by tiling may indicate an intention to annex such units permanently to the realty (see e g *Botham v TSB Bank plc* (1996) 73 P & CR D1 at D3 per Roch LJ, who contrasted the case of the freestanding cooker with that of the split level cooker set into a work surface). See also *Berkley v Poulett* [1977] 1 EGLR 86 at 88L–M, 89B–C per Scarman LJ; *Chelsea Yacht & Boat Co Ltd v Pope* [2000] 1 WLR 1941 at 1944C–E per Tuckey LJ, 198C–D per Morritt LJ.

Chattel classifications

1.74 Consistently with the classic rule of thumb, courts have tended to regard as mere 'chattels' those objects which rest by their own weight, such as heavy printing machinery otherwise unattached to a floor[1] and fitted and integrated kitchen appliances which, although connected electrically, remain in position by their own weight.[2] Where connection to a mains supply involves no more substantial attachment to the land than is strictly necessary for their effective use, freestanding domestic appliances will generally rank as personalty only.[3]

1 *Hulme v Brigham* [1943] KB 152 at 157. See similarly *National Australia Bank Ltd v Blacker* (2000) 179 ALR 97 at [25] (electric pumps resting by own weight).
2 *Aircool Installations v British Telecommunications* [1995] CLY 821; *Botham v TSB Bank plc* (1996) 73 P & CR D1 at D4.
3 *Botham v TSB Bank plc* (1996) 73 P & CR D1 at D4 per Roch LJ (equating refrigerators and dishwashers with electric kettles, food mixers and microwave ovens). See also *Northern Press & Engineering Co v Shepherd* (1908) 52 Sol Jo 715 (connection to motor or power supply irrelevant).

The deemed purpose of the annexation

1.75 The degree of annexation is not in itself a conclusive test of the status of an object as a fixture or chattel.[1] At most it provides a prima facie characterisation, which may be reversed by evidence of some contrary purpose or scheme behind the positioning of a given object in relation to the realty. Modern case law strongly suggests that the relative significance of the degree of annexation has declined and that considerations of purpose are 'now of first importance.'[2] Generally the tests of degree and purpose coincide in result,[3] but this is not always or necessarily the case. Inferences drawn from the physical mode of annexation may well be overridden by more subtle considerations relating to the objectively understood motivation underlying the annexation in question.

1   *Palumberi v Palumberi* (1986) 4 BPR 9106 at 9109. In the modern case law the 'mere fact of screwing down or bolting down' is not ultimately conclusive of annexation (see *Potton Developments Ltd v Thompson* [1998] NPC 49).
2   *Hamp v Bygrave* (1983) 266 EG 720 at 724 per Boreham J. See also *Leigh v Taylor* [1902] AC 157 at 162 per Lord Macnaghten ('its relative importance is probably not what it was in ruder or simpler times'); *Re Hulse* [1905] 1 Ch 406 at 411; *Berkley v Poulett* [1977] 1 EGLR 86 at 88K–L; *Botham v TSB Bank plc* (1996) 73 P & CR D1 at D2 per Roch LJ; *Commonwealth of Australia v New South Wales* (1923) 33 CLR 1 at 34; *Palumberi v Palumberi* (1986) 4 BPR 9106 at 9110; *Famous Makers Confectionery Pty Ltd v Sengos* (1993) 6 BPR 13222 at 13223 per McLelland CJ in Eq (objectively imputed intention is now 'the fundamental principle').
3   See e g *Royal Bank of Canada v Beyak* (1981) 119 DLR (3d) 505 at 509–510.

Objectively understood purpose

1.76 Relevant intention is not to be assessed on a purely subjective basis.[1] The subjective intentions of the fixer of an object may have some persuasive value,[2] but much greater relevance attaches to the objective intention or underlying purpose of the annexation as disclosed by surrounding circumstances,[3] by the duration of the annexation[4] and, in particular, by shared or communal understandings of the function to be served by the annexation.[5] Ultimately the question is whether, viewed objectively, the item in dispute was intended to constitute a permanent accretion to, or lasting improvement of, the realty[6] or was attached to the land merely temporarily and for the purpose of the more convenient use or enjoyment of the object itself.[7]

1   *Re De Falbe; Ward v Taylor* [1901] 1 Ch 523 at 535; *Elitestone Ltd v Morris* [1997] 1 WLR 687 at 698E–H per Lord Clyde; *Palumberi v Palumberi* (1986) 4 BPR 9106 at 9109. The status of the affixed object cannot be arbitrarily defined by the simple declaration of the proprietor [**para 1.71**].
2   See P Butt, (1997) 71 ALJ 816 at 821; *National Australia Bank Ltd v Blacker* (2000) 179 ALR 97 at [12].
3   The 'type of person' who installs an item may be significant. Items installed by a builder will tend to be fixtures, whereas those installed by a carpet contractor or curtain supplier may well not be (see *Botham v TSB Bank plc* (1996) 73 P & CR D1 at D3). Likewise an article bought on hire purchase is not to be regarded as a fixture unless the intention to effect a permanent improvement is 'incontrovertible' (ibid).
4   Built-in obsolescence may be highly relevant. Thus, for example, the fact that even fitted and integrated kitchen appliances (such as refrigerators, freezers, washing machines, extractor fans

and gas hobs) have a relatively limited lifespan and require periodic replacement may point towards a chattel classification – an indication intensified where each item can be bought and installed separately (see e g *Botham v TSB Bank plc* (1996) 73 P & CR D1 at D4).

5   See *N H Dunn Pty Ltd v L M Ericsson Pty Ltd* (1979) 2 BPR 9241 at 9244–9245 per Mahoney JA.

6   If the purpose of affixing a chattel was to improve the freehold, then the object – even if only tenuously affixed – is more readily regarded as a fixture (*Holland v Hodgson* (1872) LR 7 CP 328 at 339; *Re Davis* [1954] OWN 187 at 190).

7   *Berkley v Poulett* [1977] 1 EGLR 86 at 88L per Scarman LJ; *Botham v TSB Bank plc* (1996) 73 P & CR D1 at D2 per Roch LJ. See also *Elitestone Ltd v Morris* [1997] 1 WLR 687 at 692G–H per Lord Lloyd of Berwick.

Objects integral to landscape or interior design

1.77   Certain objects which rest on the ground by their own weight may still be regarded as fixtures if the circumstances are such as to show that they must have been intended to become part of the land.[1] Sometimes an item is simply 'so heavy that there is no need to tie it into a foundation.'[2] Accordingly fixtures can include heavy marble statues of lions[3] and substantial garden ornaments,[4] if the presence of these objects was integral to a permanent architectural design or if they were part of a general scheme for the improvement of the realty.[5]

1   *Berkley v Poulett* [1977] 1 EGLR 86 at 88M; *Reid v Smith* (1905) 3 CLR 656 at 669; *N H Dunn Pty Ltd v L M Ericsson Pty Ltd* (1979) 2 BPR 9241 at 9243; *McIntosh v Goulburn CC* (1985) 3 BPR 9367 at 9374.4. The onus of proof that the items were intended to annex to the realty lies on those who assert that they have ceased to be chattels (see *Holland v Hodgson* (1872) LR 7 CP 328 at 335; *Haggert v Town of Brampton* (1897) 28 SCR 174 at 180–181).

2   *Berkley v Poulett* [1977] 1 EGLR 86 at 88M per Scarman LJ.

3   *D'Eyncourt v Gregory* (1866) LR 3 Eq 382 at 397 (ornamental statuary resting in strategic locations held to have been intended to meld permanently with the land). Compare, however, *Berkley v Poulett* [1977] 1 EGLR 86 at 89F–H.

4   Thus, while a freestanding garden gnome in a suburban garden mercifully constitutes a mere chattel, a substantial collection of carefully co-ordinated garden ornaments may well comprise a group of fixtures (see *Hamp v Bygrave* (1983) 266 EG 720 at 726 (large urns, a statue and a lead trough)).

5   See *D'Eyncourt v Gregory* (1866) LR 3 Eq 382 at 396.

Objects of intrinsic enjoyment

1.78   Conversely, items which are firmly fixed to the realty may yet remain chattels if the objectively detectable purpose of their annexation was merely to facilitate their enjoyment as chattels and if the degree of connection was no more than was necessary for the achieving of that purpose.[1] In some instances attachment to the realty affords the only realistic way in which an object can be enjoyed in its own right. The category of affixed objects which thus persist as chattels has been held to include such items as tapestries,[2] display cases of stuffed birds,[3] pelmets and venetian blinds[4] and a private automatic branch telephone exchange switchboard.[5] The chattel character of such items survives if there was no self-evident intention that they should attach indefinitely and gratis to the realty.[6]

1   This reasoning covers wide categories of ornamental objects (*Berkley v Poulett* [1977] 1 EGLR 86 at 89E–F; *Botham v TSB Bank plc* (1996) 73 P & CR D1 at D2–D3). See *Hamp v Bygrave* (1983) 266 EG 720 at 724; *Re Royal Bank of Canada and Saskatchewan Telecommunications* (1985) 20 DLR (4th) 415 at 417–418.

2   *Leigh v Taylor* [1902] AC 157 at 161. Compare, however, *Re Whaley* [1908] 1 Ch 615 at 619–620, where a fixture classification was accorded to a picture and tapestry displayed in a house which had been rebuilt as a 'complete specimen of an Elizabethan dwelling-house'. See also *Re Lord Chesterfield's Settled Estates* [1911] 1 Ch 237 at 245 (Grinling Gibbons carvings held to be fixtures).

3   *Viscount Hill v Bullock* [1897] 2 Ch 482 at 483–486.

4   *Palumberi v Palumberi* (1986) 4 BPR 9106 at 9111 ('essentially a form of furnishing installed for the greater comfort and convenience of the occupants of the premises').

5   *N H Dunn Pty Ltd v L M Ericsson Pty Ltd* (1979) 2 BPR 9241 at 9245–9247 (Court of Appeal of New South Wales). See also *McIntosh v Goulburn CC* (1985) 3 BPR 9367 at 9273.

6   *Leigh v Taylor* [1902] AC 157 at 159.

Improvement of the realty or enhancement of the chattel?

1.79   An important element in the 'purpose test' is said to turn on whether the demonstrable purpose of an attachment is more heavily directed towards maximising the use which can be made of the land or towards promoting enjoyment of the object itself.[1] This can, however, prove an extremely elusive distinction[2] since '[i]n a sense every chattel affixed to a building could be said to improve the building or else it would not be affixed'.[3] In this respect, as elsewhere in land law, an element of ambiguity flows from the fact that benefit to land does not have 'any rational or, indeed, any human significance, apart from its enjoyment by human beings.'[4]

1   *Hellawell v Eastwood* (1851) 6 Ex 295 at 312, 155 ER 554 at 561 per Parke B. The fact that an object is attached to the land in order to increase the commercial value of the realty for mortgage purposes may point irresistibly towards a fixture characterisation (see *Haggert v Town of Brampton* (1897) 28 SCR 174 at 182; *Bank of Nova Scotia v Mitz* (1980) 106 DLR (3d) 534 at 539–540).

2   'These considerations tend to overlap' (*Macrocom Pty Ltd v City West Centre Pty Ltd* (2001) 10 BPR 18631 at [20] per Windeyer J).

3   *Credit Valley Cable TV/FM Ltd v Peel Condominium Corp No 95* (1980) 107 DLR (3d) 266 at 275. See also *Holland v Hodgson* (1872) LR 7 CP 328 at 339–340.

4   *Stilwell v Blackman* [1968] Ch 508 at 524G–525A per Ungoed-Thomas J **[para 9.165]**.

1.80   The case law is neither uniform nor consistent. Whilst bathroom fittings may be classified as fixtures (on the ground that they are necessary for a room which is used as a bathroom[1]), similar status is often denied to light fittings, chandeliers and integrated kitchen appliances (on the ground that some connection with the realty is an essential precondition of their use[2]). Wall-to-wall carpeting may be categorised ambiguously as intended for the better use of a building (and therefore a fixture[3]) or as merely a removable chattel whose annexation to the land is insubstantial.[4] Is the installation of a bowling alley intended to promote the better use of a building or to facilitate more efficient bowling?[5] Can it really be said that the attachment of a mobile home to the ground is intended to enhance only the enjoyment of a chattel rather than the enjoyment of the land?[6] Does the installation of a television antenna or television cabling and equipment improve a building or merely make it possible for its occupiers to receive a television signal?[7]

1   *Botham v TSB Bank plc* (1996) 73 P & CR D1 at D3.
2   *Botham v TSB Bank plc* (1996) 73 P & CR D1 at D4. Compare *Palumberi v Palumberi* (1986) 4 BPR 9106 at 9111 (freestanding gas stove regarded as 'an essential and integral element' of a kitchen and thus 'properly characterised as being for the benefit of the premises').
3   *La Salle Recreations Ltd v Canadian Camdex Investments Ltd* (1969) 4 DLR (3d) 549 at 556 (hotel). See also *Young v Dalgety plc* [1987] 1 EGLR 116 at 117K–L. A similar conclusion may be reached in respect of domestic carpeting affixed to grips or runners (see *Palumberi v Palumberi* (1986) 4 BPR 9106 at 9111) and carpet tiles which are glued to a floor (see *Botham v TSB Bank plc* (1996) 73 P & CR D1 at D4).
4   *Botham v TSB Bank plc* (1996) 73 P & CR D1 at D4 (gripper rods insufficient connection). See also *Holland v Hodgson* (1872) LR 7 CP 328 at 335.
5   *Re Davis* [1954] OWN 187 at 190 (held not to be realty).
6   See *Lichty v Voigt* (1978) 80 DLR (3d) 757 at 761–762 (chattel only). See also *Turismo Industries Ltd v Kovacs* (1977) 72 DLR (3d) 710 at 715.
7   See the chattel classification upheld in *Credit Valley Cable TV/FM Ltd v Peel Condominium Corp No 95* (1980) 107 DLR (3d) 266 at 275; *Palumberi v Palumberi* (1986) 4 BPR 9106 at 9111. Yet exactly the opposite conclusion could have been drawn. Such is the modern citizen's cultural dependence on televisual images that the presence of reception apparatus may nowadays be a vital factor in facilitating the enjoyment of many kinds of land (see *Bridlington Relay Ltd v Yorkshire Electricity Board* [1965] Ch 436 at 446C–F per Buckley J; *Hunter v Canary Wharf Ltd* [1997] AC 655 at 684E–685A per Lord Goff of Chieveley, 719F–H per Lord Cooke of Thorndon; *Nor-Video Services Ltd v Ontario Hydro* (1978) 84 DLR (3d) 221 at 231 per Robins J).

The relative indeterminacy of fixture status

1.81   The contemporary borderline between fixtures and chattels may now be more case-specific and more context-dependent than was once believed.[1] The ultimate test of fixture character rests on informed, but objectively based, intuitions as to the likelihood that the annexor, if questioned by some officious bystander,[2] would realistically have reserved the right to remove the disputed object from the realty in the event of a future sale of the land.[3] In this way the day-to-day practice of the marketplace effectively defines the classification of fixtures and chattels.[4]

1   See *Palumberi v Palumberi* (1986) 4 BPR 9106 at 9110 per Kearney J; *National Australia Bank Ltd v Blacker* (2000) 179 ALR 97 at [16].
2   See the test of the 'outside observer' employed by Windeyer J in *Macrocom Pty Ltd v City West Centre Pty Ltd* (2001) 10 BPR 18631 at [22].
3   On this basis a satellite dish might easily appear to retain its chattel character, whereas the same may not be true of an ordinary television aerial. Compare, however, *Macrocom Pty Ltd v City West Centre Pty Ltd* (2001) 10 BPR 18631 at [22].
4   Something close to a 'normally removable' test was applied by Roch LJ in dealing with fitted carpets and curtains in *Botham v TSB Bank plc* (1996) 73 P & CR D1 at D4.

Common law and statutory rights to remove fixtures

1.82   The legal differentiation of fixtures and chattels has long been beguiled by issues relating to removability.[1] A chattel may be removed from the land at any time by the owner of the chattel, subject to any contractual commitment (e g a television hire or hire-purchase agreement) which regulates the location and use of the chattel. The right to remove fixtures is more complex. A fixture, once attached to land, is in principle irremovable except by the freehold owner or by another pursuant to agreement with the freehold owner.[2] In some circumstances, however, the common law permits tenants, on the termination of their interest in the land, to sever from the realty certain kinds of fixture attached during the course of their tenancy. A clear distinction must be drawn between the principle of accession and the rules of removability,[3] since otherwise there arises a potential confusion between those objects which rank as fixtures but are nonetheless removable and those objects which are removable precisely because they never constituted fixtures in the first place.[4]

1   See *Elitestone Ltd v Morris* [1997] 1 WLR 687 at 691B–C per Lord Lloyd of Berwick, 694H–695D per Lord Clyde.
2   Unauthorised removal by a limited owner is prima facie an act of 'waste' **[para 1.133]**. See *Bain v Brand* (1876) 1 App Cas 762 at 767.
3   *Elitestone Ltd v Morris* [1997] 1 WLR 687 at 695D per Lord Clyde.
4   See *Elitestone Ltd v Morris* [1997] 1 WLR 687 at 691C per Lord Lloyd of Berwick.

Removal by the freehold owner

1.83   The freehold owner who attaches fixtures to his own land may, of course, remove those fixtures at any time before he starts to sell his estate to a stranger.[1] The removal of his own fixtures is simply part and parcel of his rights of ownership.[2] However, if the freeholder enters into a contract to dispose of his estate to another, the disposition operates, unless otherwise agreed,[3] to pass to the purchaser all fixtures which were attached to the land at the date of the contract.[4]

1   See *Taylor v Hamer* [2002] EWCA Civ 1130, [2002] 1 P & CR D9 (Transcript at [82], [93]) per Sedley LJ **[para 1.68]**.
2   *Re Whaley* [1908] 1 Ch 615 at 620; *Taylor v Hamer* [2002] EWCA Civ 1130, [2002] 1 P & CR D9 (Transcript at [93]) per Sedley LJ. In certain circumstances removal of a fixture even by the freehold owner may require planning permission or listed building consent (see eg *R v Secretary of State for Wales, ex p Kennedy* [1996] JPL 645 at 649 **[para 1.70]**).
3   LPA 1925, s 62(4) **[para 8.153]**. See (1986) 136 NLJ 652 (J E Adams). The doctrine of proprietary estoppel may confer upon the purchaser the right to claim any chattels which were advertised in an estate agent's particulars of sale as being included in the sale of a house **[para 10.239]**.
4   LPA 1925, s 62(1)–(2) **[para 1.68]**; *Phillips v Lamdin* [1949] 2 KB 33 at 41–42; *Hamp v Bygrave* (1983) 266 EG 720 at 726. Between contract and conveyance the vendor is, in some sense, a trustee for the purchaser **[paras 9.24–9.34]**.

Removal by a leaseholder

1.84   All fixtures attached by a tenant or lessee accede prima facie to the realty, thus representing an uncompensated benefit for the landlord at the expense of the tenant.[1] In order to mitigate the harshness of this rule,[2] the law has conceded certain exceptions from the strict effect of annexation to the realty.[3] Although a tenant is normally under no obligation to remove fixtures,[4] he has a right to remove any fixtures which he has attached for trade[5] or ornamental and domestic[6] purposes and more limited rights to remove objects attached to realty during a tenancy of an agricultural holding[7] or during a farm business tenancy.[8] However, such fixtures remain the property of the landlord unless and until the tenant severs them from the realty,[9] which he must do (if at all) before or on the expiry of his tenancy or within a reasonable time thereafter.[10] Fixtures not removed are effectively forfeited to the landlord.[11] However, if a lease expires or is surrendered and is followed immediately by the grant of another term to the same tenant in possession, the tenant does not lose his right to remove fixtures installed during the first term. His right of removal is preserved to the end of the new term.[12]

1   See *North Shore Gas Co Ltd v Commissioner of Stamp Duties (NSW)* (1940) 63 CLR 52 at 68; *D'Arcy v Burelli Investments Pty Ltd* (1987) 8 NSWLR 317 at 320D.

2   See *Lombard and Ulster Banking Ltd v Kennedy* [1974] NI 20 at 23–24; *Mancetter Developments Ltd v Garmanson Ltd* [1986] QB 1212 at 1218G–1219A.

3   The proliferation of exceptions has been attributed to the need, during the years following the Industrial Revolution, to provide incentives for recoverable investments and improvements made by tenants (see *Penton v Robart* (1801) 2 East 88 at 90, 102 ER 302 at 303 per Lord Kenyon). See also *Concept Projects Ltd v McKay* [1984] 1 NZLR 560 at 567–568; *D'Arcy v Burelli Investments Pty Ltd* (1987) 8 NSWLR 317 at 320D–E.

4   See *Never-Stop Railway (Wembley) Ltd v British Empire Exhibition (1924) Incorporated* [1926] Ch 877 at 886–887 (licensee's fixtures, but the same principle seems applicable to a lessee).

5   *Climie v Wood* (1869) LR 4 Ex 328 at 329–330; *New Zealand Government Property Corpn v H M & S Ltd* [1982] QB 1145 at 1157A–B, 1161E–F. The tenant's right to remove trade fixtures may be excluded by clear terms in the lease (see *Re British Red Ash Collieries Ltd* [1920] 1 Ch 326 at 333; *Lombard and Ulster Banking Ltd v Kennedy* [1974] NI 20 at 26–27). An action may lie for the tort of waste in respect of failure to make good any damage done by the removal of the tenant's fixtures, at least where the building is left no longer weather-proof (see *Mancetter Developments Ltd v Garmanson Ltd* [1986] QB 1212 at 1219D–1220A, 1224D–E).

6   *Spyer v Phillipson* [1931] 2 Ch 183 at 199–201, 208–210 (ornamental panelling and fireplaces held to be removable provided no substantial or irreparable damage was done).

7   Agricultural Holdings Act 1986, s 10 (post, **[para 14.361]**). Written notice must be given to the landlord, who enjoys an option to retain any fixtures on payment of fair value (s 10(4)).

8   Agricultural Tenancies Act 1995, s 8(1)–(2) **[para 14.362]**. The landlord may resort instead to a scheme of compensation for tenants' improvements (Agricultural Tenancies Act 1995, ss 2(2)(d), 16(1), 17(1)).

9   See *Holland v Hodgson* (1872) LR 7 CP 328 at 336–337; *Hobson v Gorringe* [1897] 1 Ch 182 at 191–192; *Crossley Brothers Ltd v Lee* [1908] 1 KB 86 at 90; *North Shore Gas Co Ltd v Commissioner of Stamp Duties (NSW)* (1940) 63 CLR 52 at 70. Compare, however, *Re Hulse* [1905] 1 Ch 406 at 411. Unusually, a tenant under an agricultural holding retains ownership of his fixture so long as he is entitled to remove it (Agricultural Holdings Act 1986, s 10(1)).

10 *Ex p Stephens. Re Lavies* (1877) 7 Ch D 127 at 130. The allowance of a reasonable time for removal following the termination of a lease applies only in the case of a periodic tenancy or tenancy at will (see *D'Arcy v Burelli Investments Pty Ltd* (1987) 8 NSWLR 317 at 323A). The tenant under a fixed term of years has no common law right of removal after termination unless there is some new lease or the tenant remains in possession under a genuine colour of right (*Concept Projects Ltd v McKay* [1984] 1 NZLR 560 at 568) or there are circumstances, amounting to an estoppel, in which there arose a reasonable expectation that the time limit would not be strictly enforced (see *Reader v Christian*, 234 SW 155 at 158–159 (1921)). Tenants of agricultural holdings may remove fixtures up to two months after the termination of their tenancy (Agricultural Holdings Act 1986, s 10(1)).

11   See *Carabin v Offman* (1989) 55 DLR (4th) 135 at 150.
12   *New Zealand Government Property Corpn v H M & S Ltd* [1982] QB 1145 at 1160A. The prolongation of the right of removal applies also where, after the expiry of a contractual tenancy, the tenant remains in possession pursuant to some statutory or periodic tenancy [**para 14.317, 14.336**].

1.85   There is occasional judicial ambivalence as to whether the treatment of 'tenant's fixtures' truly represents an exception to a general rule of accession to the realty. It is sometimes argued that the case law concerning 'tenant's fixtures' merely comprises instances where the courts, by engaging in a more benevolent interpretation of the purpose of the annexation, have been more difficult to convince that the object attached to the land has lost its chattel character.[1]

1   For the suggestion that more exacting standards of annexation are applied as between landlord and tenant (thereby favouring the tenant), see *Fisher v Dixon* (1845) 12 Cl & Fin 312 at 328, 8 ER 1426 at 1433; *Webb v Frank Bevis Ltd* [1940] 1 All ER 247 at 251G–H; *Doran v Willard* (1873) 14 NBR 358 at 360; *Bank of Nova Scotia v Mitz* (1980) 106 DLR (3d) 534 at 538; *Royal Bank of Canada v Beyak* (1981) 119 DLR (3d) 505 at 506–507.

Removal by a tenant for life

1.86   Any fixtures attached by a tenant for life likewise become part of the realty.[1] As such they must be left for the person next entitled (ie the remainder-man), with the exception of trade and ornamental and domestic fixtures, which the tenant for life is entitled to remove if he wishes.[2]

1   On the role of the tenant for life under a strict settlement, see Chapter 9 [**para 9.214**].
2   *Lawton v Lawton* (1743) 3 Atk 13 at 15–16, 26 ER 811 at 812. See also *Re Hulse* [1905] 1 Ch 406 at 410–411; *Registrar of Titles v Spencer* (1909) 9 CLR 641 at 645–646.

Contractual rights to remove fixtures

1.87   Some persons may acquire a contractual right to enter another's land for the purpose of removing chattels which have been affixed to the realty and which have therefore assumed the character of fixtures. Equipment or machinery may, for instance, be the subject of a contract for hire or hire-purchase. If this equipment or machinery has been attached to the land of the hirer, it becomes annexed to his realty. The former chattel owner loses his title,[1] but may well have reserved a contractual 'right of entry' in order to sever the equipment or machinery in the event of default in the payment of the relevant hire charges or hire-purchase instalments.

1   [**Para 1.67**]. See also *Lombard and Ulster Banking Ltd v Kennedy* [1974] NI 20 at 27–28.

1.88   If the land is transferred or mortgaged to a third party during the currency of the hire or hire-purchase, there emerges a potential collision between rights of contract and rights of property. Can a contractual right of recovery prevail against the new owner of proprietary rights in the land? English law seeks to resolve this conundrum by recognising that title to the equipment or machinery has merged in the title to the realty,[1] but that the former chattel owner has, in relation to that land, an equitable 'right of entry'[2] which can bind third parties to whom the land is later conveyed. In registered land a contractual right to enter and remove hired fixtures is protectable by the entry of a 'notice' in the hirer's register of title.[3] In unregistered land the right to remove hired fixtures is enforceable against all third parties other than a bona fide purchaser of a legal estate for value without notice.[4]

1　*Melluish v BMI (No 3) Ltd* [1996] AC 454 at 475H–476A per Lord Browne-Wilkinson **[para 1.69]**.
2　**[Para 8.265]**. See also *Re Morrison, Jones & Taylor Ltd* [1914] 1 Ch 50 at 58. The contractual right to repossess on default 'confers ... a species of equitable interest which entitles [the former chattel owner], as against the hirer, to enter upon the premises and sever and remove the chattels which have become fixtures' (*Kay's Leasing Corp Pty Ltd v CSR Provident Fund Nominees Pty Ltd* [1962] VR 429 at 436 per Adam J).
3　**[Para 12.84]**.
4　See *Poster v Slough Estates Ltd* [1968] 1 WLR 1515 at 1520G–1521C **[para 12.319]**. A right of entry therefore binds a subsequent equitable mortgagee of the land (*Re Samuel Allen & Sons Ltd* [1907] 1 Ch 575 at 582; *Melluish v BMI (No 3) Ltd* [1996] 1 AC 454 at 475D–F per Lord Browne-Wilkinson).

OTHER THINGS IN OR ON LAND

1.89　Quite apart from the allocation of fixture status, difficult questions may arise as to the ownership of other assets or things which have been brought into close association with land.

Lost and hidden objects

1.90　In certain circumstances a landowner may be entitled to lost or hidden things found in or on his land where the true owner's identity is unknown and the only other claimant is the actual finder.[1] The law in this area provides another vivid demonstration of the infinitely gradable character of the common law concept of property.[2] Property in resources is never absolute, but only relative.[3] As so often, the English law of ownership and possession identifies not absolute entitlement, but merely 'priority of entitlement.'[4] Consistently with this approach, the law relies heavily upon operative concepts of possessory title.[5] In the present context a primary distinction is drawn[6] between those things which are hidden *under* the surface of the land (where the landowner's claim to be the 'substitute owner' emerges as stronger) and those things which are found merely resting *on* the land surface (where, in the absence of clear possessory intent on the landowner's part, the finder's claim seems more compelling).[7]

1　The law relating to claims of ownership and possession of goods found on someone else's land has been said to be 'in an unsatisfactory state' (*R v Hancock* [1990] 2 QB 242 at 251H–252A per Auld J). For an excellent discussion of the relevant problems, see Tim Bonyhady, *The Law of the Countryside: the Rights of the Public* (Abingdon 1987), pp 268–285.
2　**[Para 2.13]**.

3   [**Para 2.12**]. See Gray, [1991] CLJ 252 at 295–296.
4   *Waverley BC v Fletcher* [1996] QB 334 at 345C per Auld LJ.
5   Compare the law of adverse possession [**para 6.28**].
6   See *Hannah v Peel* [1945] 1 KB 509 at 520. See also Joycey Tooher, 'Jubilant Jamie and the Elephant Egg: Acquisition of Title by Finding' (1998) 6 APLJ 117.
7   This distinction may prove difficult in borderline cases (eg that of the lost watch which is slowly incorporated into the surface layer of a muddy path), but for recent confirmation of its importance, see *Waverley BC v Fletcher* [1996] QB 334 at 344H–346B.

Objects found within the ground or attached to land

1.91   Someone who has ownership or possession of land is also regarded as enjoying possession of, and therefore being entitled to, all things embedded or concealed within the ground or attached to it.[1] This follows notwithstanding that, before the date of discovery, he was unaware of the presence of the object[2] and even though he is not the actual finder[3] and has never previously manifested any intention to control the land.[4]

1   *Elwes v Brigg Gas Company* (1886) 33 Ch D 562 at 568–569 (prehistoric longboat); *Hannah v Peel* [1945] 1 KB 509 at 520; *Attorney-General of the Duchy of Lancaster v G E Overton (Farms) Ltd* [1981] Ch 333 at 338C; *Flack v National Crime Authority* (1997) 150 ALR 153 at 160–161. *South Staffordshire Water Co v Sharman* [1896] 2 QB 44 is supportable on the ground that the rings found by the employee in this case were embedded in mud at the bottom of a pool of water (see *Hannah v Peel*, supra at 517–518; *Parker v British Airways Board* [1982] QB 1004 at 1010E, 1013A).
2   There is 'nothing unusual' in a person having property in an object of which he or she is unaware (see *Yanner v Eaton* (1999) 201 CLR 351 at [56] per McHugh J). See also *Flack v National Crime Authority* (1997) 150 ALR 153 at 161.
3   See eg *Elwes v Brigg Gas Company* (1886) 33 Ch D 562 at 569; *Waverley BC v Fletcher* [1996] QB 334.
4   *Waverley BC v Fletcher* [1996] QB 334 at 350C.

1.92   This outcome, although sometimes supported by reference to the *cuius est solum* maxim,[1] owes more to the simple idea that an embedded or attached chattel 'is to be treated as an integral part of the realty as against all but the true owner.'[2] For want of the true owner of the chattel,[3] the person in lawful possession of the land (whether as freeholder or leaseholder) has a right superior to that of any finder who locates the previously unknown item,[4] even if the finder is not a trespasser, but a licensee, on the land.[5] In any event no trespasser can assert a lawful title to things found by him within the ground.[6] Indeed the finder's act of excavation or detachment of the object is almost inevitably an act of trespass to the soil itself. Accordingly in *Waverley BC v Fletcher*[7] the Court of Appeal recognised the superior entitlement of a local authority landowner in respect of a medieval brooch found with the aid of a metal detector nine inches below the surface of a public park. The actions of the finder in the 'digging and removal of property in the land' were, in the absence of specific authority, acts of trespass.[8]

1   *Elwes v Brigg Gas Company* (1886) 33 Ch D 562 at 568.
2   *Parker v British Airways Board* [1982] QB 1004 at 1010C per Donaldson LJ. Thus title to a buried box of bank notes remains in its original owner (if identifiable). In some rare

circumstances the original owner may have little interest in asserting his title, but may be held to retain it in spite of his attempt at abandonment. See e g *Vincent v State Bank of NSW Ltd* (Unreported, Supreme Court of New South Wales, 30 July 1993), where Young J proffered the instance of drums of toxic waste dumped illicitly on someone else's land. Irrespective of strict title, however, the innocent occupier of the land may still be responsible for the removal of such waste (see Environmental Protection Act 1990, s 59(1), (6); Water Resources Act 1991, s 161(3)).

3   See Limitation Act 1980, ss 2, 3(2).
4   *Waverley BC v Fletcher* [1996] QB 334 at 346A–B, 350A–B; *Tamworth Industries Ltd v Attorney-General* [1991] 3 NZLR 616 at 621. As between a freehold owner and a leasehold finder, the freeholder takes priority if the object was embedded in the realty at the commencement of the lease and the lease does not otherwise provide (*Elwes v Brigg Gas Company* (1886) 33 Ch D 562 at 569).
5   See *Elwes v Brigg Gas Company* (1886) 33 Ch D 562 at 568.
6   The finder may even be liable to prosecution if his find was facilitated by the use of a metal detector in a 'protected place' of archaeological importance (Ancient Monuments and Archaeological Areas Act 1979, s 42(1)).
7   [1996] QB 334; [1996] Conv 216 (J Stevens).
8   [1996] QB 334 at 350C.

Objects found on the ground

1.93   In relation to an object of unknown provenance which a stranger finds unattached on the surface of land,[1] there is far less compelling reason to recognise any superior claim on behalf of the person allegedly in possession of the land.[2] Here the title of the finder is subject to any 'prior possessory title' which may be asserted by the owner/occupier of the premises,[3] but everything turns on whether such a title can be set up. The cases demonstrate that mere nominal or 'metaphysical'[4] possession of the land by an owner/occupier is an insufficient ground of claim to the chattel and must be reinforced by some clear evidence of territorial sovereignty.[5]

1   Here the case law has always been a shambles (see *Hannah v Peel* [1945] 1 KB 509 at 513–520; *Parker v British Airways Board* [1982] QB 1004 at 1008B). The difficulties are allegedly 'enhanced by reading articles ... and textbooks' (see *White v Alton-Lewis* (1974) 49 DLR (3d) 189 at 195), doubtless because it is often the task of professors and text writers 'to attempt to reconcile the irreconcilable' (*Hibbert v McKiernan* [1948] 2 KB 142 at 149 per Lord Goddard CJ).
2   The police, albeit significant finders of property, enjoy no greater civil claim than any other category of finder of goods (*Tamworth Industries Ltd v Attorney-General* [1991] 3 NZLR 616 at 620).
3   *Flack v National Crime Authority* (1997) 150 ALR 153 at 159 per Hill J.
4   *Kowal v Ellis* (1977) 76 DLR (3d) 546 at 549.
5   According to Hill J in *Flack v National Crime Authority* (1997) 150 ALR 153 at 162, the outcome of the case law is effectively to require evidence on the part of an owner/occupier of an 'intention ... to exclude others from the premises and the things in it'.

'Special property' vested in the owner or possessor of land

1.94   In default of an identifiable owner of a chattel found on the land surface,[1] the owner/occupier of the land takes priority over the actual finder if, but only if, before the chattel was found, that owner/occupier had 'made plain his intention to control the land and anything that might be found on it.'[2] This element of *animus* is an essential component of the prior possessory title needed to defeat the finder's claim,[3] but it is not fatal that the owner/occupier cannot demonstrate an intention to exercise control over the *particular* chattel which is the subject of that claim.[4] It is sufficient that control was intended to be asserted generally over a building and the things in it.[5] The requisite intention may be manifested either expressly or impliedly,[6] and the title to the discovered chattel depends on the individual facts of each case. To the extent that an owner/occupier can demonstrate a pre-existing intention to assert effective territorial control,[7] he acquires a 'special property' in any chattels which have been lost[8] or abandoned[9] on that land by persons unknown. This qualified form of property not only defeats the competing proprietary claim of a later finder, but is also sufficient to support an allegation of theft[10] (or, in former days, larceny[11]) against any finder who removes the relevant objects without authority.

1   Title would, of course, remain in an identifiable owner (see *Bridges v Hawkesworth* (1851) 21 LJ QB 75 at 78; but compare Limitation Act 1980, s 2).
2   *Waverley BC v Fletcher* [1996] QB 334 at 339H–340A, 346B per Auld LJ. See also *South Staffordshire Water Co v Sharman* [1896] 2 QB 44 at 47; *Ebner v Official Trustee* (2003) 196 ALR 533 at [33]. 'There is no difference in principle between a chattel in a building and one on land' (*R v Ellerm* [1997] 1 NZLR 200 at 207). See e g *Tamworth Industries Ltd v Attorney-General* [1991] 3 NZLR 616 at 618–619 (money bags on ground under floorboards). In relation to things found in a building, the priority of a landowner's claim depends on his having 'manifested an intention to exercise control over the building and the things which may be upon it or in it' (*Parker v British Airways Board* [1982] QB 1004 at 1018A; *Tamworth Industries Ltd v Attorney-General*, supra at 621). See also *Canada (Attorney-General) v Brock* (1993) 83 CCC (3d) 200 at 209.
3   *Flack v National Crime Authority* (1997) 150 ALR 153 at 159. See generally O W Holmes, *The Common Law* (Boston 1881), pp 221–224.
4   Indeed the owner/occupier may not even know of the existence of the specific chattel in question.
5   *Flack v National Crime Authority* (1997) 150 ALR 153 at 161–162.
6   *Parker v British Airways Board* [1982] QB 1004 at 1018B–C. Whereas there used to be a presumption that the landowner owned all chattels found on the land (see *Re Cohen, Decd* [1953] 1 WLR 303 at 306), the tendency nowadays is to require an affirmative demonstration by the owner or possessor of the intention to exercise control.
7   This element of intention may be particularly difficult to establish on behalf of someone who was never at any material time physically in possession of the premises (see *Hannah v Peel* [1945] 1 KB 509 at 521).
8   *R v Ellerm* [1997] 1 NZLR 200 at 208 (effective possession demonstrated by conservancy regime).
9   **[Para 1.98].** See *Hibbert v McKiernan* [1948] 2 KB 142 at 149–150 per Lord Goddard CJ (golf club mounted police patrol to warn off trespassers seeking to harvest lost golf balls).
10   See *R v Ellerm* [1997] 1 NZLR 200 at 208.
11   See *R v Rowe* (1859) 8 Cox CC 139 at 140, Bell 93 at 94–95, 169 ER 1180 at 1181. In *Hibbert v McKiernan* [1948] 2 KB 142 at 151, Humphreys J thought it 'fantastic' to suggest that the unauthorised taker of misdirected golf balls had 'acquired any sort of property in the balls'. Property in golf balls abandoned by individual members rested instead in the members of the golf club as an unincorporated association.

Effective possessory control

1.95   In ascertaining whether a landowner or occupier has asserted the required possessory control over the location of a find, the degree to which the public enjoys free or relatively unregulated access may be heavily determinative.[1] Finders' claims will fail in relation to articles discovered in premises where extremely restricted access indicates an overwhelming *animus possidendi* (or intention to possess).[2] Thus the owner/occupier retains a 'special property' or 'prior possessory title' in relation to chattels found in a private residence[3] or in the basement or cellar of a shop,[4] although not in relation to articles discovered in the public areas of that shop[5] or in an airline passenger lounge.[6] Likewise a valuable chattel found by a stranger on the floor of a bank vault[7] or bank reception area[8] belongs to the bank, whereas the same chattel found in a public park[9] or in derelict or unattended premises[10] belongs prima facie to the finder. An owner/occupier's effective control of premises may also be reinforced by the duties implicit in a relationship of employment or agency. For instance, a find made in the course of employment by an employee of the owner/occupier is deemed to be made on the latter's behalf, not least since the employee has a duty to account for money or property received by reason of his or her employment. 'Property' in the find is accordingly attributed to the employer.[11]

1   See *Grafstein v Holme and Freeman* (1957) 9 DLR (2d) 444 at 447; *Flack v National Crime Authority* (1997) 150 ALR 153 at 158–159.
2   *Parker v British Airways Board* [1982] QB 1004 at 1020B–C.
3   *Parker v British Airways Board* [1982] QB 1004 at 1020B–C per Eveleigh LJ ('the occupier of a house will almost invariably possess any lost article on the premises'). In *Flack v National Crime Authority* (1997) 150 ALR 153 at 163, the Federal Court of Australia was prepared to presume the relevant intention to control in relation to 'residential premises of which the owner/occupier has exclusive possession'. See also *South Staffordshire Water Co v Sharman* [1896] 2 QB 44 at 47 per Lord Russell of Killowen CJ; *Bird v Fort Frances* [1949] 2 DLR 791 at 798; *Tamworth Industries Ltd v Attorney-General* [1991] 3 NZLR 616 at 624.
4   *Grafstein v Holme and Freeman* (1957) 9 DLR (2d) 444 at 447, (1958) 12 DLR (2d) 727 at 738–740.
5   *Bridges v Hawkesworth* (1851) 21 LJ QB 75 at 78 (money found by a commercial traveller held to belong to the finder rather than the shopkeeper). The decision in *Bridges v Hawkesworth* has been subjected to much undeserved criticism over the years, but was followed by the Court of Appeal in *Parker v British Airways Board* [1982] QB 1004. For further emphasis on the relevance of a de facto regime of unrestricted access to commercial areas, see also *Parker v British Airways Board*, supra at 1019C, 1021B–C; *Flack v National Crime Authority* (1997) 150 ALR 153 at 158–159.
6   *Parker v British Airways Board* [1982] QB 1004 at 1019C–D, 1020B–C **[para 1.96]**. See *Flack v National Crime Authority* (1997) 150 ALR 153 at 159–160, 162.
7   See *Parker v British Airways Board* [1982] QB 1004 at 1019B, 1020C; *Customs and Excise Commrs v Sinclair Collis Ltd* [2001] STC 989 at [77] per Lord Scott of Foscote.
8   *Heddle v Bank of Hamilton* (1912) 5 DLR 11 at 12–13 (the more so because the finder was an employee of the bank: see *M'Dowell v Ulster Bank* (1899) 33 Ir LT Jo 223 at 226).
9   *Parker v British Airways Board* [1982] QB 1004 at 1019B–C.
10   *Tamworth Industries Ltd v Attorney-General* [1991] 3 NZLR 616 at 623–624.
11   *M'Dowell v Ulster Bank* (1899) 33 Ir LT Jo 223 at 226 per Palles CB; *Hannah v Peel* [1945] 1 KB 509 at 519; *Corporation of London v Appleyard* [1963] 1 WLR 982 at 988; *Parker v British Airways Board* [1982] QB 1004 at 1017F–G; *Grafstein v Holme and Freeman* (1957) 9 DLR (2d) 444 at 447; *White v Alton-Lewis* (1974) 49 DLR (3d) 189 at 195. The employment-based rationale provides a better explanation of *South Staffordshire Water Co v Sharman* [1896]

2 QB 44 [**para 1.91**]. See also *Willey v Synan* (1937) 57 CLR 200 at 217, 219 per Dixon J; but compare *Haynen v Mundle* (1902) 22 Can LT 152 at 153.

'Special property' for the non-trespassing finder

1.96 Where the owner/occupier of land cannot demonstrate the requisite intent to control the locus of a find, there may be unsuspected legal force in the lay person's maxim 'finders keepers'.[1] Although no 'absolute property' is acquired in chattels found on the surface of another's land,[2] it is now the finder who may claim a 'special property'[3] or 'possessory title'[4] in the subject matter of his discovery. This qualified form of property gives him a 'perfect right against all others'[5] with the exception of the true owner of the chattel. Thus, for example, in *Parker v British Airways Board*[6] a gold bracelet found by a passenger on the floor of an executive lounge at Heathrow Airport was held to belong to that passenger when attempts to locate the true owner ultimately proved fruitless.[7]

1   Intriguing questions arise, however, where two or more persons simultaneously notice an article irretrievably lost, say, on the floor of a shopping mall. For want of evidence of its true ownership, the law is driven back to primitive notions of first occupancy, although it is generally assumed that bare sight of the object confers no title (see *Bridges v Hawkesworth* (1851) 21 LJ QB 75 at 76).
2   *Armory v Delamirie* (1722) 1 Str 505, 93 ER 664; *Parker v British Airways Board* [1982] QB 1004 at 1017E.
3   The finder has a 'special property ... arising out of his relationship to the unknown owner' (*Kowal v Ellis* (1977) 76 DLR (3d) 546 at 548). The finder – unless perhaps an employed cleaner (see *M'Dowell v Ulster Bank* (1899) 33 Ir LT Jo 223 at 226) – has, of course, no duty to pick up a discovered object. But if he does so, he has been said to become a gratuitous bailee and to be obliged to make reasonable efforts to locate the true owner (see *Kowal v Ellis*, supra at 547–548). This duty will usually involve informing the occupier on whose land the object was found (see *Parker v British Airways Board* [1982] QB 1004 at 1017B–G).
4   See *Flack v National Crime Authority* (1997) 150 ALR 153 at 156.
5   *Wood v Pierson* (1881) 7 NW 888 at 889. The finder has been said to be a 'quasi depositary, invested with such possessory interest as will entitle him to hold [the object] against all the world except the rightful owner' (*Tancil v Seaton* (1877) 26 Am Rep 380 at 382, 28 Gratt 601). See *Armory v Delamirie* (1722) 1 Str 505, 93 ER 664 (jewel found by chimney sweep's boy); *Bridges v Hawkesworth* (1851) 21 LJ QB 75 at 78.
6   *Parker v British Airways Board* [1982] QB 1004 at 1019D, 1020G–H, 1021E.
7   The decision was supported by the argument that if 'finders had no prospect of any reward, they would be tempted to pass by without taking any action or to become concealed keepers of articles which they found' ([1982] QB 1004 at 1017B). See also *Tamworth Industries Ltd v Attorney-General* [1991] 3 NZLR 616 at 621–624.

Trespassing finders

1.97 The rights of a trespassing finder are 'frail' but not wholly non-existent.[1] Although he cannot resist the claim of the owner/occupier on whose land the property was found,[2] the common law gives him 'very limited rights' to retain the chattel – if only in order to prevent a 'free-for-all situation ... in that anyone could take the article from the trespassing finder.'[3]

1   *Parker v British Airways Board* [1982] QB 1004 at 1009D.
2   'Wrongdoers should not benefit from their wrongdoing' (*Parker v British Airways Board* [1982] QB 1004 at 1009D per Donaldson LJ). See also *Munday v Australian Capital Territory* (Unreported, Supreme Court, ACT, 8 July 1998).
3   *Parker v British Airways Board* [1982] QB 1004 at 1009D–E per Donaldson LJ.

Abandoned objects

1.98   The foregoing rules concerning lost and hidden objects come into play only where the identity of their original owner is currently unknown, since otherwise title to all such objects, whether present *within* or *on* land, remains in that owner. Questions of priority between an owner/occupier of land and a finder of chattels arise only in default of a better title; and the existence of a superior title vested in an original owner may sometimes depend on the doctrine of abandonment.[1]

1   Treasure represents a special case [**para 1.101**], as does the abandonment of waifs (stolen goods discarded by a thief in flight), which likewise vest in the crown (see *Foxley's Case* (1601) 5 Co Rep 109a, 77 ER 224 at 225; *Provincial Treasurer of Manitoba v Minister of Finance for Canada* (1943) 3 DLR 673 at 681; *Vincent v State Bank of NSW Ltd* (Unreported, Supreme Court of New South Wales, 30 July 1993)). In the latter case the crown's claim is justified historically 'as a punishment upon the owner, for not himself pursuing the felon, and taking away his goods from him' (*Bl Comm*, Vol I, pp 286–287).

The legal mechanics of abandonment

1.99   The doctrine of abandonment has for centuries been mired in contro-versy.[1] The better view is that ownership of a chattel may be divested by abandonment provided that the original owner intends[2] to renounce his title and provided that the chattel is received or reduced into the lawful possession of another person.[3] Unless and until this happens, title to the chattel remains in the would-be abandoner.[4] Abandonment of a chattel is therefore successful only if and when it generates at least a possessory title in someone else:[5] no chattel ever comprises a *res nullius*.[6] The inception of a new possession in the owner/occupier of the locus of the abandoned chattel requires, in its turn, that this person should have manifested an intention to control that land and to exclude trespassers, thereby acquiring for himself a 'special property'[7] in the abandoned object.[8] In relation to goods unsuccessfully 'abandoned'[9] on uncon-trolled or derelict land (there being, therefore, no inception of a new possessory title), a subsequent finder stands 'in the same position as the finder of a lost chattel who does not know who the owner of it is.'[10]

1   See T J Bonyhady, *The Law of the Countryside: the Rights of the Public* (Abingdon 1987), pp 269–272; A H Hudson, 'Is Divesting Abandonment Possible at Common Law?' (1984) 100 LQR 110; L Aitken, 'The Abandonment and Recaption of Chattels' (1994) 68 ALJ 263.
2   The case law provides no definitive guidance as to whether intention should be assessed subjectively or objectively (see *Moorhouse v Angus and Robertson (No 1) Pty Ltd* [1981] 1 NSWLR 700 at 713A; *Cook v Saroukos* (1989) 97 FLR 33 at 41; *Australian Olympic Committee Inc v The Big Fights Inc* (Unreported, Federal Court of Australia, 3 August 1999)).
3   *Haynes' Case* (1614) 12 Co Rep 113, 77 ER 1389. See *R v Edwards and Stacey* (1877) 13 Cox

CC 384 at 385; *Tancil v Seaton* (1877) 26 Am Rep 380 at 382, 28 Gratt 601; *Vincent v State Bank of NSW Ltd* (Unreported, Supreme Court of New South Wales, 30 July 1993). Thus one cannot abandon a chattel which remains on one's own land (*Steel v Houghton* (1788) 1 H Bl 51 at 63, 126 ER 32 at 39 per Wilson J; *Williams v Phillips* (1957) 41 Cr App R 5 at 8). See Bonyhady, op cit, p 270.

4   *Munday v Australian Capital Territory* (Unreported, Supreme Court, ACT, 8 July 1998). Views on this point differ: compare *Cook v Saroukos* (1989) 97 FLR 33 at 40–41; *Re Jigrose Pty Ltd* [1994] 1 Qd R 382 at 386; *Keene v Carter* (1994) 12 WAR 20 at 24–25, 27.

5   For the view that even intentional abandonment does not, in itself, divest the chattel owner of his ownership, see *Wilmot Pty Ltd v Kaine* (1928) 23 Tas LR 43 at 58 per Inglis Clark J.

6   Bonyhady, op cit, p 272. See also F Pollock, (1894) 10 LQR 293. It was Oliver Wendell Holmes who observed that the common law 'abhors the absence of proprietary or possessory rights as a kind of vacuum' (*The Common Law* (Boston 1881), p 231).

7   See *Hibbert v McKiernan* [1948] 2 KB 142 at 149 per Lord Goddard CJ.

8   The indictment in *Hibbert v McKiernan* [1948] 2 KB 142 **[para 1.94]** named the golf club members collectively as having held the property in the lost golf balls. In order to uphold the larceny conviction of the trespassing scavenger, the Divisional Court was forced to emphasise the degree of control exercised by the club over the golf course (by way of police patrol). In this way it became feasible to treat the property in the balls as having been divested by abandonment, although the Court was clearly less than comfortable with such terminology (see e g [1948] 2 KB 142 at 151 per Humphreys J, 152 per Pritchard J). See also *Parker v British Airways Board* [1982] QB 1004 at 1009F–G per Donaldson LJ; *Kowal v Ellis* (1977) 76 DLR (3d) 546 at 549.

9   In *Vincent v State Bank of NSW Ltd* (Unreported, Supreme Court of New South Wales, 30 July 1993), Young J hypothesised that 'one could not get rid of a liability for radioactive waste merely by renouncing one's property in it.'

10   *Wilmot Pty Ltd v Kaine* (1928) 23 Tas LR 43 at 58 per Inglis Clark J.

The rubbish tip

1.100   The best testing ground for these propositions is nowadays the municipal rubbish tip or the privatised waste disposal centre. The householder who dumps his rubbish at either location divests himself of title by abandonment when he throws his goods into the communal bin and departs from the tipping area.[1] At this point his intention to renounce title is clearly completed by his parting with actual or constructive possession. Simultaneously the operator of the tip acquires a possessory title over the goods by reason of the characteristically strict control exerted by such persons over the waste disposal site.[2] It is not thereafter open to another member of the public, who notices a discarded Monet or Stradivarius in the communal bin, to claim finder's rights over such objects. The owner/occupier of the site now enjoys possessory rights which are superior to the claims of all subsequent visitors and even to the claim of the hapless former owner who attempts, a day later, to retrieve his precious abandoned goods.[3] However, unless the public's invitation to enter the waste disposal site is expressly so limited, there is no reason why a watchful scavenger at the site should not, an instant before the act of abandonment, intercept the careless chattel owner, solicit from him a gift of the chattel by manual delivery, and thereby acquire a title good against the whole world.[4]

1   *Munday v Australian Capital Territory* (Unreported, Supreme Court, ACT, 8 July 1998) per Higgins J. See also *Australian Capital Territory v Munday* (2000) 173 ALR 1.

2   **[Para 1.94]**.

3   The intending dumper of goods does not complete his act of abandonment by mere entry to the waste disposal site or even by placing objects temporarily on the ground within that site (*Munday v Australian Capital Territory* (Unreported, Supreme Court, ACT, 8 July 1998)).

4   See *Munday v Australian Capital Territory* (Unreported, Supreme Court, ACT, 8 July 1998) per Higgins J.

Treasure

1.101   Until 1997 the law relating to treasure hidden by an unknown owner was governed by the principles of 'treasure trove'.[1] At common law all treasure trove vested in the crown by prerogatival right, irrespective of whose land concealed the treasure.[2] Treasure trove comprised only objects containing a 'substantial' amount of gold or silver[3] and only those goods hidden with the intention of later discovery.[4] The capriciously restrictive definition of treasure trove unfortunately excluded a vast range of other antiquarian finds from protection as part of the national heritage. Calls for a more effective and coherent regime of conservation[5] finally led to the enactment of the Treasure Act 1996.

1   For a more detailed account of these principles, see *Elements of Land Law* (2nd edn 1993), pp 31–32.

2   Co Inst, Part III, p 132; *Bl Comm*, Vol I, p 285.

3   *Attorney-General of the Duchy of Lancaster v G E Overton (Farms) Ltd* [1982] Ch 277 at 291H, 294A; [1981] Ch 333 at 343B.

4   Treasure trove did not include lost or abandoned goods (*Bl Comm*, Vol I, p 285; *R v Hancock* [1990] 2 QB 242 at 247C–E). This distinction was sufficient, for instance, to disqualify the Sutton Hoo burial find of 1939, which was in fact donated to the nation by the relevant landowner (see [1980] CLJ 281 (D E C Yale); N E Palmer, (1981) 44 MLR 178 at 182).

5   See *Attorney-General of the Duchy of Lancaster v G E Overton (Farms) Ltd* [1982] Ch 277 at 293B–D. See also *Webb v Ireland* [1988] IR 353 at 390–391, where, in dealing with the Derrynaflan hoard found in 1980, Walsh J suggested that a modern sovereign state, concerned to emphasise its historical origins, may claim rights of ownership in all antiquities of national importance even though not comprising items of gold and silver.

Scope

1.102   The Treasure Act 1996[1] displaces the old law of treasure trove,[2] introducing a new, and wider, definition of 'treasure', which, when found, will normally vest in the crown.[3] 'Treasure' comprises objects (other than single coins) at least 300 years old bearing 10 per cent precious metal;[4] finds of 10 or more coins of any metal which are at least 300 years old;[5] and other objects which are at least 200 years old and fall within categories designated by the Secretary of State as having 'outstanding historical, archaeological or cultural importance.'[6] Treasure also includes other objects which are part of the same find as objects within the primary definition of 'treasure'.[7] The 1996 Act applies to all treasure irrespective of the nature of the place in which it was found[8] and regardless of whether the goods were hidden, lost or merely abandoned with no intention of recovery.[9]

1   The 1996 Act is now accompanied by a Code of Practice (The Treasure Act 1996 Code of Practice (Department of National Heritage 1997)). See Treasure Act 1996, s 11(1); [1998] Conv 252 (J Marston and L Ross).
2   The Act applies the new term 'treasure' to anything which would have constituted 'treasure trove' (Treasure Act 1996, s 1(1)(c)).
3   Treasure Act 1996, s 4(1)(b). The only exception to crown ownership occurs where the crown has granted a franchise to receive treasure found in a particular place (Treasure Act 1996, ss 4(1)(b), 5(1)). See also *Attorney-General v Trustees of the British Museum* [1903] 2 Ch 598 at 608.
4   Treasure Act 1996, s 1(1)(a)(ii).
5   Treasure Act 1996, s 1(1)(a)(iii).
6   Treasure Act 1996, ss 1(1)(b), 2(1).
7   Treasure Act 1996, s 1(1)(d).
8   Treasure Act 1996, s 4(4)(a).
9   Treasure Act 1996, s 4(4)(b).

Duties and rewards of finders

1.103   The purpose of the Treasure Act 1996 is clearly to enhance the preservation of the national heritage. Accordingly a criminal offence is committed by any person who, after finding an object which he 'believes or has reasonable grounds for believing is treasure', fails within the following 14 days to report his find to the local coroner.[1] Even before the commencement of the 1996 Act, it had long been established practice to make ex gratia payments to finders who immediately reported their discovery.[2] Under the 1996 Act the Secretary of State may always disclaim discovered treasure,[3] but if instead the treasure is transferred to a museum the Secretary of State has full discretion to allocate an ex gratia 'reward'[4] to the finder and/or the occupier or other persons interested in the land where the treasure was found.[5]

1   Treasure Act 1996, s 8(1)–(3).
2   Such payments provide an incentive to finders to reveal their recovery of objects of archaeological interest and, for this reason, are made even to those who were trespassers at the time of the find (see Bonyhady, op cit, p 277). See the £1.75 million award made by the Treasure Trove Committee to the finder of the Hoxne hoard near Eye, Suffolk (*Times*, 16 August 1997, p 2).
3   Treasure Act 1996, s 6(3)–(4). The allocation of the treasure, subject to any rights which otherwise exist at law, is then governed by the Code of Practice (Treasure Act 1996, s 6(4)(b)).
4   The Secretary of State may determine the amount of the reward, the total reward not to exceed the treasure's market value (Treasure Act 1996, s 10(3)(b), (4)).
5   The Code of Practice suggests that, in the case of a chance find by a non-trespasser, any reward is likely to be shared equally by the finder and the owner/occupier of the land. Deliberate search by a non-trespasser may justify an allocation of the full reward to the finder. Depending on the nature of their trespass, trespassers are not entirely excluded from benefit. See [1998] Conv 252 at 259–263 (J Marston and L Ross).

TREES, PLANTS AND FLOWERS

1.104   'Land' includes for legal purposes all trees, shrubs, hedges, plants and flowers growing thereon, whether cultivated or wild.[1] Such forms of growth attach to the realty and are thus part of the estate owned by the landowner.[2]

However, realty is capable of horizontal division and it is, in this sense, feasible to own and to convey a freehold or leasehold estate in a tree which is separate from estate ownership of the subjacent soil, provided that the tree has not yet been severed from the realty.[3] It is likewise possible that the soil and growing crops may be vested in different ownerships.[4] Although ownership of living vegetable matter thus vests prima facie in the owner of the soil, no theft is committed by a stranger who, for non-commercial purposes, picks wild mushrooms, or flowers, fruit or foliage from a plant growing wild upon the land.[5] Such actions do not constitute criminal damage either,[6] even if the motive is commercial, but may comprise the torts of trespass and conversion.[7]

1   See *Monsanto plc v Tilly* [2000] Env LR 313 at 322 per Stuart-Smith LJ.
2   *Bl Comm*, Vol II, p 18. See *Stukeley v Butler* (1615) Hob 168 at 170, 80 ER 316 at 317.
3   See *Liford's Case* (1614) 11 Co Rep 46b at 49a, 77 ER 1206 at 1211; *Stukeley v Butler* (1615) Hob 168 at 173, 80 ER 316 at 320; *John Austin & Sons Ltd v Smith* (1982) 132 DLR (3d) 311 at 319. The largest estate which can exist in a growing tree is presumably a fee simple conditional upon the life of the tree (see *Smith v Daly* [1949] 4 DLR 45 at 48). The characterisation of a forest as realty means that the fee simple or a term of years in the trees may be owned by one person whilst an estate in the surface soil is owned by someone else (see e g *Herlakenden's Case* (1589) 4 Co Rep 62a at 63b, 76 ER 1025 at 1029–1030; *Eastern Construction Co Ltd v National Trust Co Ltd* [1914] AC 197 at 208; *Southwestern Lumber Co v Evans*, 275 SW 1078 at 1082 (1925); *McDonell Estate v Scott World Wide Inc* (1997) 149 DLR (4th) 645 at 649–650). See also *Commonwealth of Australia v New South Wales* (1923) 33 CLR 1 at 34.
4   *Back v Daniels* [1925] 1 KB 526 at 542 per Scrutton LJ; *Monsanto plc v Tilly* [2000] Env LR 313 at 322 per Stuart-Smith LJ.
5   Theft Act 1968, s 4(3). However, theft is committed if the entire plant is uprooted (see Theft Act 1968, s 4(1)). See also Wildlife and Countryside Act 1981, ss 13(1), 21(3).
6   Criminal Damage Act 1971, s 10(1)(b).
7   *Mills v Brooker* [1919] 1 KB 555 at 558 [**para 3.55**].

WILD ANIMALS AND BIRDS

1.105   Wild animals[1] and birds cannot, whilst alive, be the subject of absolute ownership in English law.[2] The migratory tendency of such creatures renders proprietary analysis at least problematical.[3] However, the person in possession[4] of the land which they temporarily inhabit has a 'qualified property'[5] which arises *ratione soli*.[6] He has a common law right to hunt and catch wild creatures,[7] thereby reducing them into his possession.[8] This 'qualified property' in wild animals and birds persists only so long as the hunter 'can keep them in sight' and has 'power to pursue them'.[9] Provided that the pursuit is lawful,[10] it may be that no stranger is entitled to frustrate the pursuit (e g by intercepting an animal and capturing it himself).[11] Attempted disruption of the chase may, moreover, constitute the crime of aggravated trespass.[12] If and when the wild creatures finally escape to the land of a neighbour, it is the latter who takes over the 'qualified property' in them.[13]

1   There is no definition of a 'wild animal' for this purpose, but in its common law usage the phrase is sufficiently narrow to exclude fish and sufficiently broad to encompass birds, insects and reptiles. The criterion of 'wildness' connotes that the animal does not by habit or training live with or in association with or in the service of man (see *McQuaker v Goddard* [1940] 1 KB

687 at 696). The distinction between domesticated and undomesticated species is not entirely satisfactory (see generally Tim Bonyhady, The Law of the Countryside: the Rights of the Public (Abingdon 1987), pp 215–239).

2   *Bl Comm*, Vol II, p 391. See *Case of Swans* (1592) 7 Co Rep 15b at 17b, 77 ER 435 at 438; *Blades v Higgs* (1865) 11 HL Cas 621 at 638, 11 ER 1474 at 1481 per Lord Chelmsford; *Yanner v Eaton* (1999) 201 CLR 351 at [24].

3   See e g *Yanner v Eaton* (1999) 201 CLR 351 at [22], where the High Court of Australia was perplexed by the question whether state legislation could give the crown ownership of 'every bird that has ever crossed the Queensland border' or confer ownership of migratory birds 'only as they pass through Queensland' (compare McHugh J at [55]). See also *McKee v Gratz*, 260 US 127 at 135, 67 L Ed 167 at 170 (1922) per Justice Holmes.

4   See *Yanner v Eaton* (1999) 201 CLR 351 at [46] per McHugh J.

5   *Bl Comm*, Vol II, p 391.

6   That is, 'in consideration of the property of the soil whereon they are found' (*Bl Comm*, Vol II, p 393). See also *Blades v Higgs* (1865) 11 HL Cas 621 at 634, 11 ER 1474 at 1480 per Lord Westbury LC ('ownership of the game is considered as incident to the property in the land'); *Kearry v Pattinson* [1939] 1 KB 471 at 479; *Yanner v Eaton* (1999) 201 CLR 351 at [80] per Gummow J.

7   This right can be extended to any person to whom the freehold or leasehold owner gives consent (*Walden v Hensler* (1987) 163 CLR 561 at 565), but is otherwise exclusive (*Yanner v Eaton* (1999) 201 CLR 351 at [24]).

8   *Blades v Higgs* (1865) 11 HL Cas 621 at 631, 11 ER 1474 at 1478–1479; *Walden v Hensler* (1987) 163 CLR 561 at 566 per Brennan J. This common law right is nowadays curtailed by conservationist legislation aimed at the protection of rare or endangered species, although such legislation still grants substantial immunity to the landowner or occupier (see e g Wildlife and Countryside Act 1981, ss 2(2), 4(3), 10(4), 27(1)). There are also anomalous exceptions to the landowner's rights which include the little known, but much flouted, provision contained in Game Act 1831, s 3, which still prohibits hunting for game on Sundays and Christmas Day!

9   *Bl Comm*, Vol II, p 393 (swarm of bees). See also (1939) 17 Can Bar Rev 130; G W Paton, 'Bees and the Law' (1939–41) 2 Res Judicata 22.

10   'Power to pursue' was construed in *Kearry v Pattinson* [1939] 1 KB 471 at 479 to mean 'lawful power' to pursue without committing trespass.

11   *Kearry v Pattinson* [1939] 1 KB 471 at 481 per Goddard LJ. (Compare, however, *Young v Hichens* (1844) 6 QB 606 at 611, 115 ER 228 at 230). Interception of an animal which is in the course of being reduced into possession may now be theft (see Theft Act 1968, s 4(4)). There is a vivid literature on qualified proprietary claims to fugitive wild creatures (see *Littledale v Scaith* (1788) 1 Taunt 243(n), 127 ER 826; *Pierson v Post*, 2 Am Dec 264 at 265–267, 3 Caines 175 (1805); *Hogarth v Jackson* (1827) Moo & M 58, 173 ER 1080; *Skinner v Chapman (ex rel Alderson)* (1827) Mood & M 59(n), 173 ER 1081; *Baldick v Jackson* (1911) 30 NZLR 343 at 345). See Gray, 'Equitable Property' (1994) 47(2) CLP 157 at 158–159.

12   [*Para 3.96*]. See e g *Nelder v DPP* (1998) Times, 11 June (although the Court of Appeal opined that no aggravated trespass could arise if the disrupted hunter was himself trespassing on another's land). In these liberated days even the act of filming a hunt may generate a criminal liability on failure to comply with a direction given by a senior police officer who 'reasonably believes', albeit in error, that an aggravated trespass has occurred (see *Capon v DPP* (Queen's Bench Division, 4 March 1998) per Lord Bingham CJ).

13   *Sutton v Moody* (1697) 1 Ld Raym 250 at 251, 91 ER 1063 at 1064; *Kearry v Pattinson* [1939] 1 KB 471 at 480–481 (swarm of bees). It has been suggested that certain distinctive or exotic animals (e g a tiger which has escaped from a zoo) must represent an exception to this rule (see T Beven, 22 Harv L Rev 465 at 481–482 (1908–09)). There used to be an ancient doctrine of 'hot pursuit' which gave a hunter immunity from trespass when pursuing vermin from his own land on to a neighbour's land if the purpose of the incursion was merely the destruction of the vermin (see *Earl of Essex v Capel*, Hertford Assizes 1809, cited in *Locke on the Game Laws of England and Wales* (5th edn, London 1866), p 45), but this immunity cannot now survive (see *Paul v Summerhayes* (1878) 4 QBD 9 at 11). See Tim Bonyhady, op cit, p 224.

1.106   As soon as wild creatures are killed, they become personalty and therefore proper objects of absolute ownership by the owner of the soil.[1] Thus if A kills a wild animal found on his own land, it belongs to him absolutely.[2] Likewise, if A trespasses on the land of B and there kills a wild animal, the absolute property vests in B, both *ratione soli*[3] and because the trespasser may not profit by his wrong.[4] Anomalously, however, if A starts the chase on the land of B and hunts the animal into the land of C, where he eventually kills it, it seems that the absolute property in the animal vests inexplicably in A,[5] although A may well be liable in trespass to both B and C.[6]

1   *Blades v Higgs* (1865) 11 HL Cas 621 at 631, 11 ER 1474 at 1478–1479.
2   *Blades v Higgs* (1865) 11 HL Cas 621 at 638, 11 ER 1474 at 1481 per Lord Chelmsford.
3   *Sutton v Moody* (1697) 1 Ld Raym 250 at 251, 91 ER 1063 at 1064, 5 Mod 375 at 376, 87 ER 715; *Earl of Lonsdale v Rigg* (1856) 11 Ex 654 at 675, 679, 682, 156 ER 992 at 1001–1003, 1 Hurl & N 923 at 937, 156 ER 1475 at 1481; *Blades v Higgs* (1865) 11 HLCas 621 at 634, 11 ER 1474 at 1480.
4   *Blades v Higgs* (1865) 11 HLCas 621 at 632–633, 11 ER 1474 at 1479.
5   *Sutton v Moody* (1697) 1 Ld Raym 250 at 251, 91 ER 1063 at 1064; *Churchward v Studdy* (1811) 14 East 249 at 251, 104 ER 596 at 597; *Blades v Higgs* (1865) 11 HLCas 621 at 633, 11 ER 1474 at 1479, but see the doubts expressed by Lord Chelmsford at 639–640, 1482. In any event, A's ownership in this example holds good only so long as B's original entitlement arose merely ratione soli. If B were the owner of some special franchise, his rights would persist even if the animal were killed in the land of C (*Blades v Higgs* (1865) 11 HLCas 621 at 632–633, 11 ER 1474 at 1479).
6   *Sutton v Moody* (1697) 1 Ld Raym 250 at 251, 91 ER 1063 at 1064.

WATER

1.107   It is perhaps surprising that English property law remains relatively uncertain or incoherent in its conceptual treatment of the increasingly vital resource of water.[1] Although the ownership of water promises to become one of the critical questions of the 21st century, English law persists in regarding water as incapable of being owned.[2] It may be that, since water is a supremely fugitive substance, hidden dangers have seemed to trammel any attempt to subject it to the rigour of proprietary analysis: the natural flow of water across the landscape might give rise to allegations of theft or misappropriation. Accordingly, water has always proved to be a matter of some doctrinal embarrassment. In English law inland water (whether a river or lake) is generally considered to be merely 'a species of land',[3] in that lawyers treat such areas of water as simply areas of 'land covered with water.'[4]

1   Compare Eric Freyfogle, 'Context and Accommodation in Modern Property Law' 41 Stan L Rev 1529 at 1530 (1988–89) ('water is the most thoroughly advanced form of property, and its model should prove particularly influential ... property law future will be a version of water law present').
2   *Alfred F Beckett Ltd v Lyons* [1967] Ch 449 at 481G–482A; *Attorney-General ex rel Yorkshire Derwent Trust Ltd v Brotherton* [1992] 1 AC 425 at 441A per Lord Goff of Chieveley, 445G–446A per Lord Jauncey of Tullichettle; *Thames Heliports Plc v LB of Tower Hamlets* (1997) 74 P & CR 164 at 177. See Chapter 8 [**para 8.18**].
3   *Bl Comm*, Vol II, p 18 ('which may seem a kind of solecism; but such is the language of the law'). See e g *Thames Heliports Plc v LB of Tower Hamlets* (1997) 74 P & CR 164 at 169, 177.

4   *Bl Comm*, Vol II, p 18. See e g *East London Waterworks v Leyton Sewer Authority* (1871) LR
     6 QB 669 at 673 per Cockburn CJ; *Hampton UDC v Southwark and Vauxhall Water Co* [1900]
     AC 3 at 4; *Attorney-General for British Columbia v Attorney-General for Canada* [1914] AC 153
     at 167 per Viscount Haldane LC. See also Channel Tunnel Act 1987, s 49(1); Interpretation
     Act 1978, s 5, Sch 1 (definition of 'land').

Conveyancing implications

1.108   Although English law can contemplate with equanimity the conveyance
of an estate in thin air,[1] it has substantially more difficulty in relation to a
conveyance of water. A conveyance of an estate in the land carries with it
certain rights over the superjacent water,[2] whereas a grant of the water itself
without reference to the land passes merely a right of fishing.[3] In the absence of
contrary evidence,[4] a conveyance of riparian land bounded by a non-tidal river
carries with it the soil *ad medium filum* (or to the middle point of the river),
whether the conveyance be of a freehold or leasehold estate.[5]

1   [Para 1.40].
2   *Bl Comm*, Vol II, p 18. See *Thames Heliports Plc v LB of Tower Hamlets* (1997) 74 P & CR 164
     at 180, where Beldam LJ endorsed the proposition that 'the water of an enclosed lake, though
     fed by stream at either end, would be regarded as included in a hereditament.'
3   *Bl Comm*, Vol II, p 19.
4   *Tait-Jamieson v G C Smith Metal Contractors Ltd* [1984] 2 NZLR 513 at 514.
5   *Tilbury v Silva* (1890) 45 Ch D 98 at 108–109; *City of London Land Tax Commissioners v
     Central London Railway Co* [1913] AC 364 at 371, 379; *Southern Centre of Theosophy Inc v
     State of South Australia* [1982] AC 706 at 715G; *Tait-Jamieson v G C Smith Metal Contrac-
     tors Ltd* [1984] 2 NZLR 513 at 514; *Lawrence v Kempsey Shire Council* (1995) 6 BPR 14111 at
     14115.

Limits of the landowner's rights

1.109   The mere fact that rights over water are attributed to the owner of the
underlying land does not confer upon that owner any absolute title to the water
itself.[1] The landowner has no property or proprietary right either in water
which flows across his land in a defined channel (e g a river)[2] or in water which
percolates through his land.[3] His right to abstract such water is strictly
controlled by the requirement that he should obtain a licence to do so.[4]
However, the landowner does have an exclusive right to fish in any non-tidal
river which runs through his land.[5] If he owns only one of the banks of the
river, he owns the subjacent land out to the *medium filum*,[6] and each riparian
owner may fish as far across the river as he can reach by normal casting or
spinning.[7]

1   However, the owner of the bed and soil of a lake or river, if he enjoys a corporeal right to
     fishing, is entitled to restrain canoeing on the water (*Wills' Trustees v Cairngorm Canoeing and
     Sailing School Ltd* 1976 SC 30 at 63; *Tennent v Clancy* [1987] IR 15 at 20, 22).
2   *Mason v Hill* (1833) 5 B & Ad 1 at 24–25, 110 ER 692 at 701; *Thames Heliports Plc v LB of
     Tower Hamlets* (1997) 74 P & CR 164 at 177, 179.
3   *Ballard v Tomlinson* (1885) 29 Ch D 115 at 120–121, 126.
4   Water Resources Act 1991, ss 24(1), 24A (as supplemented by Water Act 2003, s 1(1)). No

licence is required if the water is abstracted merely for the domestic purposes of the occupier's household or for agricultural purposes other than spray irrigation (Water Resources Act 1991, s 27(4)(b)).

5   *Attorney-General for British Columbia v Attorney-General for Canada* [1914] AC 153 at 167. See also *Ecroyd v Coulthard* [1898] 2 Ch 358 at 366, 374; *Jones v Llanrwst UDC* [1911] 1 Ch 393 at 401. If the right to fish is severed from the solum, it becomes a profit à prendre [**para 8.18**]. The public has no general right of fishing except in the open sea and in tidal waters [**para 5.27**].

6   *Micklethwait v Newlay Bridge Co* (1886) 33 Ch D 133 at 145, 152, 155; *Tait-Jamieson v G C Smith Metal Contractors Ltd* [1984] 2 NZLR 513 at 515–516.

7   So long as he stands on his own bank or wades out no further than the medium filum, each riparian owner may cast beyond the medium filum (*Fothringham v Kerr* (1984) 48 P & CR 173 at 186–187).

Natural rights to water

1.110   Since water is incapable of ownership, the rights of landowners are more properly described in terms of certain 'natural rights' to the enjoyment of water present on their land. Here a distinction turns on whether the water flows in a defined watercourse or merely percolates through the land in an undefined channel.

Water flowing in a defined channel

1.111   Every owner and occupier of land has a natural right to water where it flows naturally in a defined channel on to, through or past his land.[1] This right, being part of the fee simple estate in the land, passes without any express provision on the conveyance of that estate.[2] The right is heavily qualified. The riparian owner is entitled to the 'flow of the water, and the enjoyment of it' subject to the similar rights of all other riparian owners to 'the reasonable enjoyment of the same gift of Providence.'[3] Thus the riparian owner has a natural right to receive and is bound to accept the undiminished flow of water past or through his land.[4] He is not entitled to deprive those lower down the stream of its flow,[5] nor to pen it back upon the land of his upstream neighbour,[6] but he is entitled to receive the flow of water 'in its natural state of purity'.[7] Any unauthorised pollution of this flow is actionable as an infringement of the riparian owner's natural right.[8]

1   *Chasemore v Richards* (1859) 7 HLCas 349 at 382, 11 ER 140 at 153; *Swindon Waterworks Co Ltd v Wilts and Berks Canal Navigation Co* (1875) LR 7 HL 697 at 703–704, 708–709; *Jennings v Sylvania Waters Pty Ltd* [1972] 2 NSWLR 4 at 10E.

2   *Jennings v Sylvania Waters Pty Ltd* [1972] 2 NSWLR 4 at 12B–D.

3   *Embrey v Owen* (1851) 6 Ex 353 at 369, 155 ER 579 at 586 per Parke V-C, who indicated that any 'unreasonable and unauthorised use of this common benefit' would constitute an actionable wrong. See similarly *John Young & Co v Bankier Distillery Co* [1893] AC 691 at 698 per Lord Macnaghten. The common law concept of 'reasonable' use was generally understood to include the abstraction of water for certain ordinary domestic and agricultural purposes (see *Kensit v Great Eastern Railway* (1883) 23 Ch D 566 at 574; *McCartney v Londonderry and Lough Swilly Railway Co Ltd* [1904] AC 301 at 306), but it is doubtful whether, in more recent times, the common law right could have extended much further.

4   *John Young & Co v Bankier Distillery Co* [1893] AC 691 at 698 per Lord Macnaghten; *Scott-Whitehead v National Coal Board* (1985) 53 P & CR 263 at 270; *Thames Heliports Plc v LB of Tower Hamlets* (1997) 74 P & CR 164 at 179. Statutory water undertakers have, however, no implied power to discharge surface water into a landowner's watercourses without his consent (*British Waterways Board v Severn Trent Water Ltd* [2001] EWCA Civ 276, [2002] Ch 25 at [45]).

5   Having no property in the water of the stream, the riparian owner has no right to appropriate any of that water to himself for extraordinary purposes without restoring that water to the flow undiminished in quantity and quality (*McCartney v Londonderry and Lough Swilly Railway Co Ltd* [1904] AC 301 at 307; *Attwood v Llay Main Collieries Ltd* [1926] Ch 444 at 458; *Rugby Joint Water Board v Walters* [1967] Ch 397 at 422F–423B). For a pivotal American decision to this effect, see *Herminghaus v Southern California Edison Co*, 252 P 607 at 619–621 (Supreme Court of California 1926) (power company not entitled to divert water for production of electricity).

6   *Home Brewery Co Ltd v William Davis & Co (Leicester) Ltd* [1987] QB 339 at 345B–D.

7   *Scott-Whitehead v National Coal Board* (1985) 53 P & CR 263 at 270.

8   *Scott-Whitehead v National Coal Board* (1985) 53 P & CR 263 at 270. Licence to pollute may effectively be granted in the form of discharge consents purchased pursuant to the Water Resources Act 1991 (see Water Resources Act 1991, s 88(1), Sch 10, as substituted by Environment Act 1995, s 120(1), Sch 22, para 183) or obtained under Environmental Protection Act 1990, s 6. Increasing statutory regulation of pollution has now rendered largely irrelevant the law relating to prescriptive and other rights to pollute rivers and waterways (see e g *Scott-Whitehead v National Coal Board* (1985) 53 P & CR 263 at 272–276).

Water percolating in an undefined channel

1.112   There exists, by contrast, no natural right to water which percolates in an undefined channel.[1] Such percolating water is regarded as 'a common reservoir or source in which nobody has any property, but of which everybody has, as far as he can, the right of appropriating the whole.'[2] The common law effectively allows a free-for-all in this portion of the unpropertised commons.[3]

1   *Cambridge Water Co v Eastern Counties Leather Plc* [1994] 2 AC 264 at 296H–297A per Lord Goff of Chieveley. See *Bradford Corpn v Pickles* [1895] AC 587 at 592, 595, 600; *Stephens v Anglian Water Authority* [1987] 1 WLR 1381 at 1385B; *LJP Investments Pty Ltd v Howard Chia Investments Pty Ltd* (1988) 4 BPR 9640 at 9643.

2   *Ballard v Tomlinson* (1885) 29 Ch D 115 at 121 per Brett MR. See also *Steadman v Erickson Gold Mining Corp* (1989) 56 DLR (4th) 577 at 579–580.

3   See Gray, [1991] CLJ 252 at 256–257.

Unwanted invasion of percolating water

1.113   A lower occupier has no cause of action if a higher occupier, acting reasonably, permits water to percolate into, and flood, the lower occupier's land.[1] The natural drainage of water to lower ground comprises, in itself, a natural right annexed to ownership of the higher ground,[2] being incapable of grant or reservation by easement.[3] The lower occupier's remedy at common law is to erect his own defences and repel or pen the water back,[4] even at the cost of damage to the higher occupier, provided that he acts reasonably for the protection of his own land and with no intention of injuring his neighbour.[5] The lower occupier has no right to divert the flow unnaturally so as to damage the land of some adjacent third party.[6] The foregoing principles are subject, however, to the increasingly pervasive influence of 'reasonableness between neighbours' as a foundational precept of the law of nuisance.[7] It is therefore possible that, if a higher occupier acts *unreasonably* in allowing floodwater to escape on to a neighbour's land, he may be liable in nuisance for the foreseeable consequences of his failure to control the hazard present on his land.[8]

1   *Palmer v Bowman* [2000] 1 WLR 842 at 850D, 855F per Rattee J ('authority is scarcely needed ... it is nature, not the law, that imposes the burden of receiving such drainage on the lower land').

2   See *Gibbons v Lenfestey* (1915) 84 LJPC 158 at 160 per Lord Dunedin ('a natural right inherent in property'). It is different if the higher occupier (as distinct from some third party for whose actions he is not responsible) causes water to flow in a more concentrated form than is natural (see *Gartner v Kidman* (1962) 108 CLR 12 at 48 per Windeyer J).

3   *Palmer v Bowman* [2000] 1 WLR 842 at 850A–B, 856A–B **[para 8.14]**.

4   The critical question is whether the water was flowing in a defined channel at the point when it left the higher occupier's land or whether it simply drained into the lower occupier's land by a process of percolation (*Palmer v Bowman* [2000] 1 WLR 842 at 852C–F). In the former case the lower occupier must accept the flow of water; in the latter case he may be entitled to resist it.

5   *Home Brewery Co Ltd v William Davis & Co (Leicester) Ltd* [1987] QB 339 at 351H–352H. See similarly *Gartner v Kidman* (1962) 108 CLR 12 at 49 per Windeyer J. In *Palmer v Bowman* [2000] 1 WLR 842 at 855G–H, the Court of Appeal was less clear that the lower occupier is entitled to take reasonable physical action to repel the flow. The right may be lost if the lower occupier effects a major change to his own land, as distinct from merely acting in protection thereof (see *Comserv (No 1877) Pty Ltd v Wollongong CC* (2001) 10 BPR 18791 at [42] per Hodgson CJ in Eq).

6   *Gartner v Kidman* (1962) 108 CLR 12 at 49 per Windeyer J. See e g *Comserv (No 1877) Pty Ltd v Wollongong CC* (2001) 10 BPR 18791 at [42].

7   *Delaware Mansions Ltd v Westminster CC* [2001] UKHL 55, [2002] 1 AC 321 at [29], [34] per Lord Cooke of Thorndon; *Abbahall Ltd v Smee* [2002] EWCA Civ 1831, [2003] 1 WLR 1472 at [36]–[38] per Munby J. See also *Southwark London Borough Council v Mills* [2001] 1 AC 1 at 20D–E per Lord Millett; Gray and Gray, 'The rhetoric of realty', in J Getzler (ed), *Rationalizing Property, Equity and Trusts: Essays in Honour of Edward Burn* (Butterworths 2003), pp 256–257.

8   See *Green v Lord Somerleyton* [2003] EWCA Civ 198, [2004] 1 P & CR 520 at [83]–[86], [100]–[102] (applying the principle in *Leakey v National Trust for Places of Historical Interest or Natural Beauty* [1980] QB 485).

Selfish exploitation of percolating water

1.114   Consistently with the common law regime of free-for-all, every occupier is entitled (subject nowadays to statutory controls) to sink wells and so obtain a water supply, but is vulnerable to the truncation of that supply by a neighbour's exercise of the same right on his own land.[1] Likewise a higher occupier owes no common law duty to lower occupiers to preserve the flow of water which passes or percolates freely above or below ground level in undefined channels.[2] Deprivation of that supply affords the lower occupier no remedy even though he has hitherto enjoyed long user of an undiminished flow,[3] and even though the abstraction by the higher occupier may have been motivated entirely by malice.[4] Moreover, it has now been clarified that pollution of percolating water is actionable in nuisance or under *Rylands v Fletcher*[5] only if harm of the relevant type was foreseeable by the polluting occupier. In *Cambridge Water Co v Eastern Counties Leather Plc*,[6] one of the most significant environmental law cases to arise in England in recent decades, the House of Lords rejected a pure principle of strict liability. The House decided unanimously in favour of a corporate polluter who for years had caused an industrial solvent to leak into groundwater, thereby contaminating the plaintiff's borehole over a mile away.[7]

1 *Chasemore v Richards* (1859) 7 HLCas 349 at 386–390, 11 ER 140 at 155–156; *Stephens v Anglian Water Authority* [1987] 1 WLR 1381 at 1385B.
2 *Chasemore v Richards* (1859) 7 HLCas 349 at 382, 11 ER 140 at 153; *Home Brewery Co Ltd v William Davis & Co (Leicester) Ltd* [1987] QB 339 at 345D–G.
3 *Broadbent v Ramsbotham* (1856) 11 Ex 602 at 615–617, 156 ER 971 at 976–977.
4 *Bradford Corpn v Pickles* [1895] AC 587 at 592, 595, 600 [**para 13.4**]. See *Home Brewery Co Ltd v William Davis & Co (Leicester) Ltd* [1987] QB 339 at 345F–G.
5 (1866) LR 1 Exch 265.
6 [1994] 2 AC 264 at 306A–B per Lord Goff of Chieveley.
7 For criticism of this decision as retrograde and buried in an excess of textual technicality, see Gray, 'Property in Common Law Systems', in G E van Maanen and A J van der Walt (ed), *Property Law on the Threshold of the 21st Century* (MAKLU, Antwerp, 1996), p 282. See also (1994) 110 LQR 185 (R F V Heuston); G Samuel, 'Property Notions in the Law of Obligations' [1994] CLJ 524 at 539. Compare the strict liability imposed in respect of the criminal offence, under Water Resources Act 1991, s 85(1), of causing poisonous matter to enter controlled waters (*Environment Agency v Empress Car Co (Abertillery) Ltd* [1999] 2 AC 22 at 33D; *Environment Agency v Brock* (1998) Times, 26 March), but see also *Express Ltd v Environment Agency* [2003] EWCA 448 (Admin), [2004] 1 WLR 579 (emergency).

FISH

1.115 A landowner who by reason of the ownership of land owns also a right to fish in superjacent water[1] is regarded as having a 'qualified property' in fish found within the limits of his 'fishery'.[2] The fish become his absolute property only when he catches and kills them. If those fish are caught by some unauthorised person, the absolute property in the fish vests – on the analogy of wild animals – not in the trespasser but in the owner of the fishing rights.[3]

1 [**Para 1.108**]. See *Gannon v Walsh* [1998] 3 IR 245 at 273. Correspondingly, it is assumed that a person entitled to a several fishery in non-tidal waters owns the river bed over which the right is exercised (*Gannon v Walsh*, supra at 272–275).
2 *Nicholls v Ely Beet Sugar Factory Ltd* [1936] Ch 343 at 347.
3 *Nicholls v Ely Beet Sugar Factory Ltd* [1936] Ch 343 at 347. The unlawful taking of the fish is not theft as such but may constitute an offence under Theft Act 1968, s 32(1), Sch 1, para 2(1).

INCORPOREAL HEREDITAMENTS

1.116 Most statutory definitions of 'land' include, within this term, the notion of 'incorporeal hereditaments'.[1] In contradistinction to 'corporeal hereditaments', which are tangible, 'incorporeal hereditaments' are not 'the object of sensation, can neither be seen nor handled, are creatures of the mind, and exist only in contemplation.'[2] Incorporeal hereditaments comprise, in effect, a range of intangible rights which may be held over land as a physical resource. Such rights proliferated in medieval law and were closely associated with the needs of a rural and agricultural economy. The significance of many of these entitlements has almost disappeared in modern times, but surviving examples of incorporeal hereditament include rentcharges,[3] franchises,[4] profits *à prendre*,[5] and easements.[6] Of these examples the most important is nowadays the easement, perhaps best typified in the right of way which one landowner, A, may enjoy over the land of another, B.

1   [**Para 1.23**].
2   *Bl Comm*, Vol II, p 17.
3   [**Para 8.225**].
4   An example is the relatively rare franchise to receive treasure found in a particular place [**para 1.102**].
5   [**Para 8.19**].
6   [**Para 8.24**]. See *Willies-Williams v National Trust* (1993) 65 P & CR 359 at 361 per Hoffmann LJ.

1.117   A consistent theme in the history of English land law has been the tendency to blend physical and abstract perceptions of 'land'.[1] This conflation of property as *fact* with property as *right* is supremely evidenced in the manner in which, as a matter of statutory definition, the term 'land' is made to include 'an easement, right, privilege, or benefit in, over, or derived from land.'[2] This reification of intangible entitlement – a frequent feature of the common law mind-set[3] – brings about the result that the benefit of A's abstract right over B's land is treated as an integral component of A's 'land' – just as much as the soil on which A's house is built.[4] This abstract benefit being notionally annexed to A's land,[5] it follows that any future conveyance or transfer of A's land to C will effectively pass to C not merely A's corporeal hereditaments, but also his incorporeal hereditaments, including the benefit of his right of way.[6]

1   [**Para 1.10**].
2   See LPA 1925, s 205(1)(ix); SLA 1925, s 117(1)(ix); LCA 1972, s 17(1); TOLATA 1996, s 23(2). Likewise 'land' is defined by Interpretation Act 1978, s 5, Sch 1, as presumptively inclusive of 'any estate, interest, easement, servitude or right in or over land.'
3   See Duncan Kennedy, 'The Structure of Blackstone's Commentaries' 28 Buffalo L Rev 205 at 342–350 (1979).
4   'An easement is ... an estate or interest carved out of a larger estate or interest ... but also itself "land" vested in the proprietor of the dominant tenement' (*Willies-Williams v National Trust* (1993) 65 P & CR 359 at 361 per Hoffmann LJ).
5   See LPA 1925, s 187(1).
6   See LPA 1925, s 62(1) [**para 8.207**].

THE FOURTH DIMENSION OF 'LAND'

1.118   The first three dimensions of land in English law relate essentially (although not entirely) to the world of physical reality. From the early medieval period onwards, however, the intermittent temptation towards abstraction in the definition of land found a new and significant form of expression. The idea of land was taken into a fourth, more cerebral, dimension with the introduction of a theory of notional *estates* in land. In effect, English law invented an entire intellectual apparatus of artificial constructs in order to explain various forms of entitlement to land.

1.119   The device of the 'estate' in land articulated the jural relationship between the landholder (ie the 'tenant'[1]) and his land, but it also did rather more. The inspired evolution of the 'estate' came eventually to provide a functional alternative to the holistic idea of *dominium* (or direct ownership of the land itself) which was part of the European heritage derived from Roman law.[2] Indeed, perhaps the single most striking feature of English land law is the absence, within its conceptual scheme, of any overarching notion of *ownership*.[3] English law cannot be properly understood except in the light of its history,[4] and it is in the distinctively English doctrines relating to estates and tenures that the roots of modern land law are to be located. Whereas the doctrine of tenures served to describe the relationship existing between a tenant and his *lord*,[5] it was the doctrine of estates which mediated the relationship between the tenant and the *land*. The latter doctrine still plays a fundamental role in the classification of interests in land.

1   Here the word 'tenant' was used in its original and deepest sense as connoting one who 'held' land from another.
2   Following Roman law, the great codes of civilian law still define 'property' in terms of the right to enjoy a thing and to dispose of it in the most absolute manner (see e g Code civil, art 544; Bürgerliches Gesetzbuch, para 903; Swiss Civil Code, art 641).
3   [Paras 1.10, 6.4].
4   See generally A W B Simpson, *A History of the Land Law* (2nd edn, Oxford 1986); S F C Milsom, *Historical Foundations of the Common Law* (2nd edn, London 1981).
5   [Para 1.142].

THE DOCTRINE OF ESTATES

1.120   The origins of the medieval theory of English land law lay in the Norman invasion of 1066. By virtue of an act of conquest the king acquired an ultimate or 'radical' title to all land in England.[1] This radical title was simply 'a concomitant of sovereignty'[2] – a brute emanation of territorial power acquired and sustained through physical force.[3] It denoted the political authority of the crown both to grant interests in the land to be held of the crown and also to prescribe the residue of unalienated land as the sovereign's beneficial demesne.[4] It followed that the king's subjects – be they ever so great – occupied their lands on the terms of some grant derived ultimately from the largesse of the crown. It was not initially clear what (if anything at all) the individual tenant could say he 'owned', but an answer was eventually found in the doctrine of estates.

1   *Mabo v Queensland (No 2)* (1993) 175 CLR 1 at 48 per Brennan J, 80 per Deane and Gaudron JJ. (The *Mabo* case, involving the land rights of the Meriam people of the Murray Islands, provided an unusual – indeed almost unprecedented – forum for the critical examination in the High Court of Australia of the most fundamental concepts of English land law.) See also *Lax Kw'Alaams Band of Indians v Hudson's Bay Co* (1998) 159 DLR (4th) 526 at 535.
2   *Mabo v Queensland (No 2)* (1993) 175 CLR 1 at 48 per Brennan J.

3   'Radical title links international and constitutional law notions with those which support the private law of proprietary rights and interests in land' (*Wik Peoples v Queensland* (1996) 187 CLR 1 at 186 per Gummow J). For reference to the uncannily parallel notions of state sovereignty and private property, see Gray, [1991] CLJ 252 at 304; 'The Ambivalence of Property', in G Prins (ed), *Threats without Enemies* (Earthscan Publications 1993), p 169.
4   *Mabo v Queensland* (*No 2*) (1993) 175 CLR 1 at 48 per Brennan J.

The interposed abstraction of the estate

1.121   The doctrine of estates carefully avoided the absolutist dogma that a person could have any direct relation of ownership with physical land. At the heart of medieval theory lay the proposition that there could be no ownership of land, as such, outside the *allodium* – or prerogatival title – of the crown. The object of each tenant's ownership was instead an artificial proprietary construct called an 'estate'.[1] The notional entity of the estate was interposed between the tenant and the land,[2] with the consequence that each tenant owned (and still owns) not land itself but an *estate* in land,[3] each estate being graded with reference to its temporal duration.[4] Consonantly with the feudal theory of ultimate sovereign title, some form of abstract estate constitutes the maximum interest which any subject – we should nowadays say *citizen* – may ever hold in respect of land.[5] All proprietary relationships with land thus fall to be analysed at one remove – through the intermediacy of an *estate* – the tenant always having ownership of an intangible right (ie an *estate*)[6] rather than ownership of a tangible thing (ie the *land*). At this point the law of real property becomes distanced from the physical reality of land and enters a world of considerable conceptual abstraction.[7] But in the process the doctrine of estates effectively provides an invaluable means by which the three-dimensional phenomenon of realty can be carved up in a fourth dimension of time.[8]

1   'In English law no subject can own lands allodially – he can own only an estate in land' (*Minister of State for the Army v Dalziel* (1944) 68 CLR 261 at 277 per Latham CJ). See also *Stokes v Costain Property Investments Ltd* [1983] 1 WLR 907 at 909E–F.
2   See F H Lawson, *The Rational Strength of the English Law* (London 1951), pp 66–67.
3   See *Lowe v J W Ashmore Ltd* [1971] Ch 545 at 554F per Megarry J.
4   [**Para 1.123**].
5   See *Mabo v Queensland* (*No 2*) (1993) 175 CLR 1 at 80 per Deane and Gaudron JJ.
6   See Gray and Gray, 'The Idea of Property in Land', in S Bright and J K Dewar (ed), *Land Law: Themes and Perspectives* (OUP 1998), pp 27–29. See also *Western Australia v Ward* (2000) 170 ALR 159 at 360 per North J.
7   As the late Professor F H Lawson once wrote, the intellectual constructs of land law often appear to move 'in a world of pure ideas from which everything physical or material is entirely excluded' (*The Rational Strength of the English Law* (London 1951), p 79). Indeed there appears to be a level at which all common law-derived systems of property are not only highly ordered but consist, in Lawson's terms, of systematic abstractions which 'seem to move among themselves according to the rules of a game which exists for its own purposes.'
8   See *Newlon Housing Trust v Alsulaimen* [1999] 1 AC 313 at 317C–D per Lord Hoffmann; *Fraser v Canterbury Diocesan Board of Finance* [2001] Ch 669 at [42] per Mummery LJ.

The radical title of the crown

1.122 An important distinction must be drawn between the crown's ultimate or 'radical' title to all land and the proprietary 'estates' which may be parcelled out amongst the subjects of the crown. There is a danger that the location of radical title in the crown may prompt the inaccurate suggestion that 'ownership' of all physical land reposes in the crown[1] or that the crown is the only true 'owner' of land in England and Wales.[2] This extrapolation from radical title to a concept of crown 'ownership' is almost certainly a more modern innovation, dating (significantly) only from the era of colonial or imperial expansion in the 17th and 18th centuries.[3] The crown's radical title is, in truth, no proprietary title at all,[4] but merely an expression of the *Realpolitik* which served historically to hold together the medieval theory of land tenure. The empirical fact of territorial sovereignty[5] should not be equated with any more modern notion of absolute beneficial ownership of the land.[6] Such a concept was probably quite alien to the medieval cast of mind.[7]

1 See T C Williams, (1931) 75 Sol Jo 843 at 844.
2 See e g *Bl Comm*, Vol II, p 51; *Lowe v J W Ashmore Ltd* [1971] Ch 545 at 554F per Megarry J ('it is a fundamental of English land law that nobody save the Crown owns any land').
3 See *Wik Peoples v Queensland* (1996) 187 CLR 1 at 186–187 per Gummow J.
4 See *Sandhurst Trustees Ltd v 72 Seventh Street Nominees Pty Ltd (In Liq)* (1998) 45 NSWLR 556 at 563D. Historically there was no 'estate' in crown land capable of registration as a freehold title (see *Scmlla Properties Ltd v Gesso Properties (BVI) Ltd* [1995] BCC 793 at 798). See now LRA 2002, ss 79(1), 80(1) **[para 7.24]**.
5 See Stephen CJ's reference to the sovereign as the 'universal occupant' of all his or her land – a 'fiction [which] ... is adopted by the Constitution to answer the ends of government, for the good of the people' (*Attorney-General v Brown* (1847) 1 Legge 312 at 316).
6 It is the recognition of precisely this distinction which enabled a majority in the High Court of Australia to rule in the Mabo case that the colonial appropriation of Australia did not extinguish existing proprietary rights based on native title. On this view, the doctrine of terra nullius caused the crown to acquire absolute beneficial ownership of land only where such land was truly desert and uninhabited (see *Mabo v Queensland (No 2)* (1993) 175 CLR 1 at 48–51 per Brennan J). To his credit Blackstone had already observed, more than two centuries earlier, that the question how far the 'driving out or massacring [of] ... innocent and defenceless natives ... was consonant to nature, to reason, or to christianity, deserved well to be considered by those, who have rendered their names immortal by thus civilising mankind' (*Bl Comm*, Vol II, p 7).
7 See A W B Simpson, *A History of the Land Law* (2nd edn, Oxford 1986), pp 47–48; *Lansen v Olney* (1999) 169 ALR 49 at [44] per French J.

ESTATES AS SLICES OF TIME

1.123 The doctrine of estates gave expression to the idea that each landholder owned not land but a *slice of time* in the land.[1] By identifying a number of conceptual 'estates' as potential objects of ownership,[2] the doctrine of estates effectively quantified the abstract entitlement which might be enjoyed by any particular tenant within the tenurial framework. The careful calibration of these estates injected a crucial dimension of time into the phenomenon of landholding, each estate comprising a time-related segment – a temporal slice –

of the rights and powers exercisable over the land.[3] As Pollock and Maitland so aptly put it, the doctrine of estates enabled proprietary rights in land to be 'projected upon the plane of time.'[4]

1   As was argued so elegantly in *Walsingham's Case* (1573) 2 Plowd 547 at 555, 75 ER 805 at 816–817, 'the land itself is one thing, and the estate in the land is another thing, for an estate in the land is a time in the land, or land for a time, and there are diversities of estates, which are no more than diversities of time ... '.
2   See B Rudden, 'Economic Theory v Property Law: The Numerus Clausus Problem', in J Eekelaar and J S Bell (ed), *Oxford Essays in Jurisprudence* (*Third Series*) (Clarendon 1987), p 239.
3   'By virtue of its durability, land invites an intricate layering of rights over time. Lawyers have never bothered to create an elaborate doctrine of, say, "estates in automobiles" ... because after only a limited number of years, any given automobile will end up in the junk heap' (Carol Rose, 'Canons of Property Talk, or, Blackstone's Anxiety' 108 Yale LJ 601 at 614 (1998–99)).
4   *The History of English Law* (2nd edn, London 1968), Vol 2, p 10.

THE OLD FREEHOLD ESTATES OF THE COMMON LAW

1.124   The rich taxonomy of estates in medieval land law provided for a number of 'freehold' estates which were distinguished by gradations of time. The three freehold estates known to the common law were the *fee simple*, the *fee tail* and the *life estate*.[1] Of these estates only one (the fee simple) enjoys any modern significance, the entailed interest and the life interest existing nowadays (if at all) only behind some form of trust.[2]

1   See *Re Walker's Application* [1999] NI 84 at 89a per Girvan J.
2   [**Paras 1.139, 1.140**].

The estate in fee simple

1.125   The estate in fee simple has long been the primary estate in land.[1] As an estate of potentially unlimited duration, it represents the amplest estate which any tenant can hold.[2] As was said in *Walsingham's Case*,[3] 'he who has a fee-simple in land has a time in the land without end, or the land for time without end.'[4] In so far as real property represents a 'bundle of rights' exercisable with respect to the land, '[t]he tenant of an unencumbered estate in fee simple in possession has the largest possible bundle.'[5] The fee simple estate connotes, moreover, a vital exclusivity of entitlement[6] and, although the terminology is strictly inappropriate to the common law conceptualism of estates, the fee simple is 'for almost all practical purposes, equivalent to full ownership of the land itself.'[7]

1   For further examination of the fee simple estate, see Chapter 7 [**para 7.2**].
2   See *Commonwealth of Australia v State of New South Wales* (1923) 33 CLR 1 at 42 per Isaacs J; *Miller v Ameri-Cana Motel Ltd* (1983) 143 DLR (3d) 1 at 7 per Wilson J.
3   (1573) 2 Plowd 547 at 555, 75 ER 805 at 817.
4   See *Co Litt*, p 4a ('the most highest and absolute estate that a man can have').
5   *Minister of State for the Army v Dalziel* (1944) 68 CLR 261 at 285 per Rich J. The fee simple

confers 'the widest powers of enjoyment in respect of all the advantages to be derived from the land itself and from anything found on it' (*Wik Peoples v Queensland* (1996) 187 CLR 1 at 176 per Gummow J). See similarly *Commonwealth of Australia v New South Wales* (1923) 33 CLR 1 at 42 per Isaacs J; *Fejo v Northern Territory* (1998) 195 CLR 96 at 126 per Gleeson CJ, Gaudron, McHugh, Gummow, Hayne and Callinan JJ.

6   **[Para 7.3]**. 'Exclusivity is a common law principle derived from the notion of fee simple ownership' (*Delgamuukw v British Columbia* (1997) 153 DLR (4th) 193 at [156] per Lamer CJC).

7   *Mabo v Queensland* (*No 2*) (1993) 175 CLR 1 at 80 per Deane and Gaudron JJ. See also *Nullagine Investments Pty Ltd v Western Australian Club Inc* (1993) 177 CLR 635 at 656 per Deane, Dawson and Gaudron JJ; *Wik Peoples v Queensland* (1996) 187 CLR 1 at 250 per Kirby J; *Mogo Local Aboriginal Land Council v Eurobodalla SC* (2002) 10 BPR 19473 at [22] (New South Wales Court of Appeal).

Infinite transferability of the fee simple estate

1.126   Although in theory each tenant in fee simple merely holds a notional estate in land as a 'tenant in chief' of the crown,[1] the plenary rights of the fee simple endure for ever.[2] The fee simple estate is capable, more or less indefinitely, of transfer inter vivos or of devolution on death. The owners of the fee simple estate may come and go but the estate remains, since it is of potentially infinite duration.[3] Each new owner simply steps into the shoes of his predecessor – the modern effect of the Statute *Quia Emptores* of 1290.[4]

1   **[Para 1.149]**.
2   See *Standard Life Assurance Co v British Columbia* (*Assessor of Area #01*) (1997) 146 DLR (4th) 247 at 252 ('an absolute estate in perpetuity').
3   Crown forfeiture of estates for high treason was terminated by the Forfeiture Act 1870.
4   **[Para 1.148]**.

Policy of unrestricted alienability

1.127   The tenant of an estate in fee simple is sometimes called a 'freeholder' – the owner of a freehold estate. Although modern legislation often curtails the fee simple owner's rights of use and enjoyment (for environmental and planning purposes[1]), there are relatively few limitations on his power to dispose of an estate in the land whether by will or by alienation inter vivos.[2] Important public policy considerations require that the fee simple estate in land should remain freely alienable, since unrestricted transferability is a vital precondition of a healthy and vibrant economy.[3] Any grant or conveyance of an estate in fee simple subject to some condition which completely prohibits alienation by the grantee conflicts with this public policy. The offending condition is liable to be declared void at common law,[4] in which case the conveyance takes effect unconditionally.[5]

1   **[Para 13.8]**.
2   See, however, Inheritance (Provision for Family and Dependants) Act 1975, s 2; Race Relations Act 1976, ss 21–22.

3   **[Para 2.39]**. See *Linden Gardens Trust Ltd v Lenesta Sludge Disposals Ltd* [1994] 1 AC 85 at
    107D per Lord Browne-Wilkinson.
4   *Co Litt*, p 223a.
5   **[Para 7.13]**. See e g *Kirby v Allen* (1997) 9 BPR 17445 at 17447.

The entailed interest

1.128   The 'fee tail' or 'entailed interest' was an estate in land which endured
so long as the original grantee (the 'tenant in tail') or any of his lineal
descendants remained alive.[1] Historically the entail provided a form of landholding designed to retain land within the family.[2] However, from the 16th
century onwards, this purpose was commonly frustrated by the 'barring' of the
entail by the tenant in possession – which usually had the effect of converting
the entail into some form of fee simple.[3] The grantor's expressed intention was
of course subverted by the barring of an entail,[4] but few tears were shed on this
account, partly because it came to be widely accepted that the 'dead hand' of
the grantor should not prevail for ever, and partly because entailed interests
generated an especially onerous liability to taxation.[5]

1   As was said arguendo in *Walsingham's Case* (1573) 2 Plowd 547 at 555, 75 ER 805 at 817, 'he
    who has land in tail has a time in the land or the land for time as long as he has issues of his
    body.' An entailed interest in land created prior to 1997 could take effect only under a 'strict
    settlement' governed by the complex machinery of the Settled Land Act 1925 **[para 9.206]**. It
    has been impossible since 1996 to create new entailed interests **[para 1.139]**.
2   The fee tail frequently provided a means of giving effect to intricate patterns of landholding
    within an aristocratic dynastic family setting (see A W B Simpson, 'Introduction' to W
    Blackstone, *Commentaries on the Laws of England* (Facsimile edn, Chicago and London,
    1979), Vol 2, pp x–xi). Entails, said Samuel Johnson, 'are good, because it is good to preserve
    in a country, series of men, whom the people are accustomed to look up to as their leaders'
    (see A W B Simpson, (1979) 24 Jur Rev (NS) 1).
3   The 'barring' of an entail may generally be achieved either by will (see LPA 1925, s 176) or by
    means of a disentailing assurance, which comprises a declaration by deed executed by the
    tenant in tail that he henceforth holds a fee simple rather than an entailed interest.
4   Entails may occasionally be rendered unbarrable by statute. Examples are the entails
    conferred for public services upon the first Duke of Marlborough and the Duke of Wellington
    (6 Anne, c 6 (1706), s 5; 6 Anne c 7 (1706), s 4; 54 Geo 3, c 161 (1814), s 28). See *Hambro v
    Duke of Marlborough* [1994] Ch 158 at 161E.
5   The enlargement of the interest of the tenant in tail immediately takes the land outside the
    clutches of the Settled Land Act 1925 (see *Re Alefounder's Will Trusts* [1927] 1 Ch 360 at 364
    [para 9.209]) and operates to simplify title by sweeping all limited interests off the land. There
    has never been much sympathy for any grievance felt by the remainderman who, but for the
    barring of the entail, would have taken the fee simple in possession. No great injustice is
    worked against the latter if a right which was initially almost worthless (in view of the
    possibility of the barring of the entail) is in fact rendered completely worthless (when that
    possibility materialises).

The life interest

1.129   A life interest in land is plainly coextensive and coterminous with the
life of its grantee.[1] Following the commencement of the 1925 property legislation and until 1997 life interests could be created only behind a trust for sale[2] or

under a strict settlement of land (in which case the owner of the life interest became the 'tenant for life').[3] A life interest comprises a transferable asset but, if conveyed to a stranger, ranks merely as an interest *pur autre vie*: it still endures only for the lifetime of the original grantee.[4] Unlike an entailed interest, a life interest cannot be unilaterally transformed into any interest of greater duration.

1   '[H]e who has an estate in land for life has no time in it longer than for his own life' (see *Walsingham's Case* (1573) 2 Plowd 547 at 555, 75 ER 805 at 817). See also *Newlon Housing Trust v Alsulaimen* [1999] 1 AC 313 at 317D per Lord Hoffmann. A right of occupation for so long as the grantee wishes is classified as a life interest (see *Charles v Barzey* [2002] UKPC 68, [2003] 1 WLR 437 at [7] per Lord Hoffmann [**para 10.302**]).
2   [**Para 9.221**].
3   [**Para 9.211**].
4   See *Re Wharfe* [1981] 2 NZLR 700 at 706–707.

A functional form of land ownership

1.130   The substitution of an abstract estate in land (in place of land itself) as the object of proprietary rights has had the most profound influence on English law. The ingenious compromise of the doctrine of estates resolved at a stroke the apparent contradiction between theory and reality in the ownership of land. At one level the 'estate' in the land merely demarcated the temporal extent of the grant to a tenant within the vertical power structure emanating from the crown. In practice the conceptualism of interlocking estates facilitated a functional scheme of landholding which obviated any holistic theory about the wider phenomenon of ownership. Indeed, it was the concentration on the rights and powers appertaining to different kinds of 'estate' which so sharply distinguished the common law view of real property from the continental emphasis on full ownership in the sense of *dominium*.[1]

1   [**Paras 1.10, 1.119**]. It was Otto Kahn-Freund who pointed out that '[o]wing to its habit of looking at the powers and rights arising from ownership rather than at ownership in the abstract, English law has been able to introduce the time element into the property concept. The continental notion of property, like the dominium of Roman law, contains, as a matter of principle, the element of eternity' ('Introduction' to Karl Renner, *The Institutions of Private Law and Their Social Functions* (London and Boston 1949), p 23).

Flexibility in the management of wealth

1.131   From the earliest times the doctrine of estates equipped English land law with a range of highly manipulable constructs which conferred enormous convenience in the management of wealth. Through the doctrine of estates the common law was able to organise the allocation of certain powers of administration, enjoyment and disposition over land in respect of particular periods or 'slices' of time. The conceptual legerdemain of estate ownership facilitated almost endless disaggregations of title through differentially graded grants of land. Proprietary rights over land could be fragmented and distributed in myriad ways: Greenacre could be allocated, say, to A for life, thereafter to B in tail, and then to C in fee simple. Such temporal distribution of fragments of title connoted a flexibility and versatility largely unknown to civilian systems of property law.

The immediate jural reality of successive estates

1.132   It was possible, moreover, to accord an immediate conceptual reality to each 'slice' of time represented by an 'estate'. In other words, any particular 'slice' of entitlement in the land could be viewed as having a present existence, notwithstanding that its owner was not entitled to *possession* of the land until some future date.[1] In a world of jural abstractions it was quite easy to conceive of rights to successive holdings of the land as 'present estates coexisting at the same time',[2] albeit that the actual enjoyment of some was postponed. It was ultimately this feature of the time-related aspect of the 'estate' in land which made it possible for the common lawyer to comprehend the feasibility of *current* dispositions of, and dealings with, *future* interests in land. Each successive interest had an immediate jural existence as of the date of grant; each was freely commerciable (ie mortgageable) long before the estate in question came to vest 'in possession'.[3]

1   See *Ingram v IRC* [2000] 1 AC 293 at 300B–C per Lord Hoffmann; *Western Australia v Ward* (2000) 170 ALR 159 at 359–360 per North J.
2   F H Lawson, *The Rational Strength of the English Law* (London 1951), p 67.
3   **[Para 7.21]**.

The doctrine of 'waste'

1.133   Precisely because the doctrine of estates recognised the possibility of successive estates in the same land, rules were developed both at common law and in equity in order to restrain the current estate owner (usually the 'tenant for life'[1]) from prejudicing the value of the land in the hands of any successor (or 'remainderman'). These rules took the form of a doctrine relating to waste, 'waste' being defined as any action or inaction on the part of the estate owner which permanently altered the physical character of the land. The unauthorised commission of waste operates implicitly as a compulsory transfer of wealth from the remainderman to the limited owner, and for this reason the law relating to waste was designed 'primarily to police the temporal boundary' between the two.[2]

1   **[Para 9.211]**.
2   R A Epstein, 'Past and Future: The Temporal Dimension in the Law of Property' 64 Wash ULQ 667 at 707 (1986).

1.134   Waste can be committed in several ways, although not all forms of waste lead to any legal remedy. The courts have been unwilling, for instance, to restrain the commission by a tenant for life of *ameliorating waste*, which merely has the effect of improving the land and of enhancing its value.[1] Only if the terms of his grant so stipulate can a tenant for life be made liable for *permissive waste*, which comprises defaults of maintenance and repair leading to the dilapidation of buildings situated on the land.[2] More serious is *voluntary waste*, which includes any positive diminution of the value of the land (for instance, by quarrying or by the cutting of timber). A tenant for life is liable for such waste unless the terms of his grant give him specific exemption by declaring him 'unimpeachable for waste'.[3] Even if a tenant for life is at common law unimpeachable for waste, in equity he can be restrained from the commission of *equitable waste* in the form of wanton destruction of the land to the prejudice of any remainderman.[4]

1   See e g *Doherty v Allman* (1878) 3 App Cas 709 at 722–723 (conversion of dilapidated premises into dwelling-houses).
2   See eg *Re Cartwright* (1889) 41 Ch D 532 at 535–536.
3   *Woodhouse v Walker* (1880) 5 QBD 404 at 406–407.
4   See e g *Vane v Lord Barnard* (1716) 2 Vern 738 at 739, 23 ER 1082. The concept of equitable waste has more recently been used in explanation of the inherent limits of aboriginal or native title (see *Delgamuukw v British Columbia* (1997) 153 DLR (4th) 193 at [130] per Lamer CJC).

THE MODERN IMPACT OF THE DOCTRINE OF ESTATES

1.135   The old common law estates were preserved, with modifications and additions, in the property legislation of 1925. Indeed the scheme of title registration now contained in the Land Registration Act 2002 is actually premised on the intellectual construct of the 'estate'.[1] Modern property legislation thus faithfully maintains the ancient theory that land ownership and use are mediated, not by the attribution to individuals of any direct ownership of or *dominium* over the land itself, but rather by the distribution of intangible jural entitlements which are interposed *between* persons and land. In this respect at least, the perspective embraced by the statutory scheme is, essentially, of property as an *abstract right* rather than as a *physical resource*, precisely on the footing that the only property in land which one can have is necessarily property in the form of a *right*.[2]

1   First registration of title applies only to 'estates' in 'land' (see LRA 2002, ss 2(a), 3(1)–(2), 4(1)–(2), 132(1); LRR 2003, r 2(2) **[para 2.115]**).
2   **[Para 2.82]**.

The primacy of the fee simple estate

1.136   Long before 1925 it had become clear that the fee simple estate was the primary estate in English law and that the grant of the other former freehold estates had been rendered – for reasons both social and fiscal – really rather rare. The significance of the 'fee simple absolute' as the major legal estate in land was expressly confirmed by the 1925 legislation,[1] the pre-eminence of the fee simple estate now being underscored by its new role as the conceptual base of commonhold ownership.[2]

1   LPA 1925, s 1(1)(a) **[para 7.21]**.
2   See Commonhold and Leasehold Reform Act 2002, ss 1(1)(a), 2(1) **[paras 1.33, 7.356]**.

Words of limitation

1.137   The primacy of the fee simple estate is also reinforced by the provision in the Law of Property Act 1925 that all conveyances of freehold land now presumptively invest the grantee with a fee simple estate.[1] The grant of any limited estate in land must, accordingly, be cut back by express 'words of limitation'. A conveyance of freehold land without further reference to the estate or interest intended to be granted (eg Greenacre 'to X') is nowadays effective to invest the grantee with a fee simple estate in the land.[2] If the grantor wishes to dispose of some lesser estate in the land, he must actually employ words of limitation in his grant (eg Greenacre 'to X for life').

1   Pursuant to LPA 1925, s 60(1), a conveyance of freehold land to any person 'without words of limitation, or any equivalent expression' is effective to pass to the grantee 'the fee simple or other the whole interest which the grantor had power to convey in such land, unless a contrary intention appears in the conveyance.' An exactly parallel provision governs testamentary dispositions (see Wills Act 1837, s 28).
2   Before 1882 a grant in fee simple required the use of the formula 'to X and his heirs' (but see now LPA 1925, s 60(4)). In this formula the phrase 'to X' comprised words of purchase indicating the identity of the grantee. The phrase 'and his heirs' comprised the words of limitation which defined the nature of the estate granted, thereby removing any ambiguity between the grant intended and the grant of a life interest.

Decline of the lesser freehold estates

1.138   In recognising the pre-eminence of the fee simple estate, the 1925 legislation also confirmed the relegation of almost all limited forms of estate ownership to equitable status only.[1] The old qualified freehold estates (ie the fee tail and the life estate) became capable of creation only under the shadow of a statutorily regulated trust or settlement.[2] The rules relating to these limited types of entitlement took a new and different turn under the Trusts of Land and Appointment of Trustees Act 1996, which came into effect on 1 January 1997.

1   The significance of equitable status is discussed shortly **[para 1.159]**.
2   **[Paras 9.206, 9.221]**.

Entailed interests

1.139   By the later years of the 20th century it was quite clear that the entail had become archaic and the prospective abolition of this phenomenon was recommended by the Law Commission.[1] Accordingly no new entails may be created after 1996. As of 1 January 1997 any purported grant of an entailed interest takes effect, not as a grant in tail, but as a declaration that the land is held in trust for the grantee absolutely.[2] Thus a purported settlement of Greenacre upon X in tail now confers on X an equitable interest in *fee simple* under the aegis of a 'trust of land'.[3]

1   See Law Commission, *Transfer of Land: Trusts of Land* (Law Com No 181, June 1989), para 16.1.
2   TOLATA 1996, Sch 1, para 5(1). See, however, E Bennet Histed, 'Finally Barring the Entail?' (2000) 116 LQR 445.
3   **[Para 9.172]**.

Life interests

1.140   Whereas life interests created prior to 1997 took effect under either a 'strict settlement' or a 'trust for sale' of land,[1] the grant of a life interest on or after 1 January 1997 gives rise to a statutorily regulated 'trust of land'.[2]

1   **[Para 10.302]**.
2   TOLATA 1996, s 2(1) **[para 10.308]**.

Emergence of the leasehold estate

1.141   During the last three centuries the gradual decline of the lesser freehold estates has been accompanied by the increasing prominence of the *leasehold* estate.[1] This estate – more properly known as a 'term of years absolute' – denotes exclusive possession of land for a term certain. Although leases were viewed, in the early days of the common law, as conferring rights of a merely personal or contractual nature, the leasehold device later came to be recognised as giving rise to entitlements of a distinctly proprietary character. The 1925 legislation duly confirmed that the fee simple absolute had been joined as an estate in land by the 'term of years absolute'.[2] The leasehold estate, comprising by definition a slice of time of fixed maximum duration,[3] can be granted either out of the allodium of the crown (by way of crown lease), or by the owner of a fee simple estate, or indeed by a leaseholder by way of sublease (for any period shorter than the duration of his own leasehold estate).[4]

1   For further examination of the leasehold estate, see Chapter 7 **[para 7.68]**.
2   LPA 1925, s 1(1)(b).
3   **[Para 7.100]**.
4   **[Para 7.195]**.

THE THEORY OF TENURE

1.142   It follows from the pre-eminence of the estate concept as the vehicle of modern land ownership that relatively little now remains of the medieval theory of tenure.[1] Under the tenurial system of tiered or hierarchical landholding, all land in England (save unalienated crown land) was held, in pyramidal relationships of reciprocal obligation,[2] either mediately or immediately of the crown.

Whereas the concept of the estate systematised the relationship between the tenant and the physical land, the concept of tenure characterised more closely the relationship between tenant and lord,[3] it being 'implicit in the relationship of tenure that both lord and tenant have an interest in the land.'[4] Under the original feudal principle the lord *seised* his tenant of his tenement.[5] Unless the tenant failed in his service, the lord owed him enjoyment of his tenement as long as he lived.[6]

1   'Tenure is already, to some extent, a fiction in England' (*Wik Peoples v Queensland* (1996) 187 CLR 1 at 244 per Kirby J).

2   'In an understanding of these relationships ... "proprietary language is out of place" ' (see *Wik Peoples v Queensland* (1996) 187 CLR 1 at 186 per Gummow J, quoting S F C Milsom, *The Legal Framework of English Feudalism* (Cambridge University Press 1976), p 39).

3   *Attorney-General of Ontario v Mercer* (1883) 8 App Cas 767 at 771–772 per Earl of Selbourne LC.

4   *Mabo v Queensland (No 2)* (1993) 175 CLR 1 at 46 per Brennan J.

5   The concept of 'seisin' is discussed in Chapter 3 [**para 3.5**].

6   In this context, as Toby Milsom (op cit, p 40) has memorably pointed out, 'to seise is as much a transitive verb as to disseise': protection was the correlative of fealty.

Origins of tenure

1.143   The theory of tenure ultimately identified the 'radical' title[1] at the back of all relationships in respect of land – the sovereign title of the king as paramount lord, achieved by conquest in 1066 and sustained by strong political control thereafter. Since the Normans had brought with them no written law of land, they initiated in their new territory what was effectively a system of landholding in return for the performance of services to a feudal superior.[2] The fact of territorial subjugation provided the foundation for the theory that all lands were ultimately held of the king[3] and could be granted to subjects of the crown only upon the continued fulfilment of certain conditions.[4] Each land-holder (or 'tenant') therefore held his land in return for services to be rendered either to the king himself or to some intermediate *baron* or lord within a complex structure of lordship which had the king at its apex.[5]

1   [**Para 1.120**].

2   Pollock and Maitland remarked that this 'extensive application' of the feudal formula 'perhaps was possible only in a conquered country' (*The History of English Law* (2nd edn, London 1968), Vol 1, p 236). See also *Attorney-General v Brown* (1847) 1 Legge 312 at 316 per Stephen CJ.

3   Pollock and Maitland (op cit, Vol 2, p 3) explained quite simply that all land in England 'must be held of the king of England, otherwise he would not be the king of all England.' In their view, to have wished in medieval times for an ownership of land which was not subject to royal rights was 'to wish for the state of nature'.

4   It seems that, in reality, the tenurial relationship was one of deeply reciprocal obligation. Milsom has described how 'it is the lord rather than the tenant who should be imagined as the buyer in some initial transaction.' The lord 'buys services and pays directly in land. But of course the land is not transferred out-and-out: the basic purchase is of a life's service for a life tenure. He buys a man' (S F C Milsom, op cit, p 39). See also *Sandhurst Trustees Ltd v 72 Seventh Street Nominees Pty Ltd (In Liq)* (1998) 45 NSWLR 556 at 563A–B per Bryson J; M A Heller, 'The Boundaries of Private Property' 108 Yale LJ 1163 at 1170–1171 (1998–99).

5   In this pyramid of free tenants the actual occupiers of the land (the 'tenants in demesne')

formed the base, their overlords ('mesne lords') stood in the middle, and the king ultimately received services from his immediate tenants ('tenants in chief') (see *Mabo v Queensland (No 2)* (1993) 175 CLR 1 at 80 per Deane and Gaudron JJ).

Classification of tenures

1.144   It was left to the doctrine of tenures not only to spell out the complex tariff of services and duties owed within the network of feudal relationships, but also to delineate the valuable 'incidents' or privileges which attached to tenure.[1] The feudal services rendered by tenants were an integral part of early English land law, and in time became standardised and identifiable by the type of service exacted and performed. The different methods of landholding (differentiated according to the form of service required) were known as 'tenures', each tenure indicating the precise terms on which the land was held. The tenures were themselves subdivided into those tenures which were 'free' (and therefore formed part of the strict feudal framework) and those tenures which were 'unfree' (and appertained to tenants of lowly status, some of whom were *adscripti glebae* – effectively little better than slaves).

1   See Pollock and Maitland, *The History of English Law* (2nd edn, London 1968), Vol 1, pp 229–406.

Free tenures

1.145   The kinds of service provided by those who enjoyed free tenure included, for instance, the provision of armed horsemen for battle (the tenure of 'knight's service') or the performance of some personal service such as the bearing of high office at the king's court (the tenure of 'grand sergeanty'). These tenures were known as 'tenures in chivalry', and were distinct from the 'spiritual tenures' of 'frankalmoign' and 'divine service' (by which ecclesiastical lands were held in return for the performance of some sacred office) and the somewhat humbler 'tenures in socage' (which obliged the tenant to render agricultural service to his lord). With the passage of time, military and socage tenures were commuted for money payments, but all tenures carried with them incidents (or privileges enjoyed by the lord) which were often more valuable than the services themselves.

Unfree tenures

1.146   The common labourer or 'villein tenant' originally had no place on the feudal ladder at all. He merely occupied land on behalf of his lord, and it was the latter who was deemed by the common law to have 'seisin'[1] of the land thus occupied. Villeinage (later called 'copyhold tenure'), although of an unfree nature, came in practice to enjoy increasing protection. This form of tenure retained its existence in law until the enactment of the property legislation of 1922–1925.

1   [**Para 3.1**].

The Statute Quia Emptores 1290

1.147   Pollock and Maitland described the system of tenures in terms of a series of 'feudal ladders', noting that 'theoretically there is no limit to the possible number of rungs, and … men have enjoyed a large power, not merely of adding new rungs to the bottom of the ladder, but of inserting new rungs in the middle of it.'[1] This process of potentially infinite extension of the feudal ladder was known as *subinfeudation*. However, subinfeudation carried the disadvantage that it tended to make the feudal ladder long and cumbersome, and in time the process of alienating land by *substitution* became more common. Under the latter device the alienee of land simply assumed the rung on the feudal ladder previously occupied by the alienor, and the creation of a new and inferior rung was no longer necessary.

1   Op cit, Vol 1, p 233. In one of the authentic examples provided by Pollock and Maitland, it could be said that '[i]n Edward I's day Roger of St German holds land at Paxton in Huntingdonshire of Robert of Bedford, who holds of Richard of Ilchester, who holds of Alan of Chartres, who holds of William le Boteler, who holds of Gilbert Neville, who holds of Devorguil Balliol, who holds of the king of Scotland, who holds of the king of England'.

Prohibition of subinfeudation

1.148   By the end of the 13th century a new concept of land as a freely alienable asset was beginning to displace the restrictive feudal order, and this evolution culminated in the enactment of *Quia Emptores* in 1290. The Statute *Quia Emptores* constituted a pre-eminent expression of a new preference for freedom of alienation as a principle of public policy. The major innovation contained in the Statute was the prohibition for the future of alienation by subinfeudation.[1] Following the enactment of 1290 only the crown could grant new tenures, and the existing network of tenures could only contract with the passage of time. Every conveyance of land thenceforth had the effect of substituting the grantee in the tenurial position formerly occupied by his grantor: no new relationship of lord and tenant was created by the transfer.

1   The participants in the 17th and 18th century plantations of Ulster were commonly dispensed from the impact of the Statute Quia Emptores 1290 and thus had power to subinfeudate by way of 'fee farm grants' [**para 7.11**]. The surviving effects of the subinfeudation which then took place are obvious in the complexity of the 'pyramid titles' which, even in relatively recent times, have created acute difficulties in the conveyancing of urban land (see *Report of the Committee on Registration of Title to Land in Northern Ireland* (Cmd 512, 1967), para 116).

The levelling of the feudal pyramid

1.149   It is the Statute *Quia Emptores* which – quite unnoticed – still regulates fee simple transfers of land today.[1] Each transfer is merely a process of substitution of the transferee in the shoes of the transferor. The operation of the Statute during the last seven centuries has tended towards a gradual levelling of the feudal pyramid so that all tenants in fee simple are today presumed (in the absence of contrary evidence) to hold directly of the crown as 'tenants in chief'.

1   Quia Emptores remains effective in many parts of the common law world (see eg Imperial Acts Application Act 1969 (New South Wales), s 36; Property Law Act 1974 (Queensland), s 21). See also Bruce Ziff, *Principles of Property Law* (3rd edn, Carswell, Ontario 2000), pp 55–60.

The demise of the theory of tenure

1.150   The doctrine of tenures lost most of its practical importance after the dismantling of the feudal system. Already the tenant had been guaranteed by *Quia Emptores* the right to alienate land without the consent of his lord. The suppression of the feudal order was later accelerated by more direct measures aimed at a reduction of the forms of tenure. Under the Tenures Abolition Act 1660, almost all free tenures were converted into 'free and common socage' or 'freehold tenure'. By 1925 the only remaining tenures which enjoyed any importance were socage tenure and copyhold tenure. The Law of Property Act 1922[1] enfranchised all copyhold tenure, converting it automatically into freehold (ie socage) tenure, with the result that all tenures have now been commuted to a uniform socage tenure directly from the crown.[2]

1   Effective 1 January 1926.
2   Law of Property Act 1922, s 128, Sch 12, para 1.

Vestiges of tenurial consequence

1.151   Although never entirely abolished in English law, only the most marginal features of tenurial theory remain today. In some extremely notional sense, therefore, every parcel of land in England and Wales is held of some lord – almost invariably the crown. It is still technically the case that the crown holds the ultimate or radical title in all land; that no citizen can own allodially; and that all occupiers of land are merely – in the feudal sense – 'tenants'. Moreover, Land Registry is empowered to grant first registration of title only to 'estates' in 'land', and the latter term is statutorily defined as requiring the existence of 'tenure'.[1] Otherwise, however, the last lingering implications of tenurial orthodoxy have all but disappeared.[2] Tenure of land for an estate in fee simple is tantamount to absolute ownership of the land – or as close to total control of land as is nowadays possible.

1   See LRA 2002, s 132(1), incorporating by reference LPA 1925, s 205(1)(ix)–(x).
2   Only in the context of the landlord-tenant relationship does the notion of tenure have much contemporary meaning [**para 7.68**]. See also *Warner v Sampson* [1959] 1 QB 297 at 312–313; (1959) 75 LQR 310 (P V Baker).

Reversion to the crown as tenurial overlord

1.152   A vestigial trace of tenurial theory is found in the law of escheat. Tenure requires a *tenant*, with the result that where, for some reason, there ceases to be a competent tenant in relation to any estate in land, that land reverts (or 'escheats') to the superior lord.[1] Thus, for example, a freeholder's estate passes automatically to the crown as bona vacantia in the event of death without any competent successor.[2] In recent times an increasingly common application of the same residual principle occurs in the context of corporate and personal insolvency. Where a freehold estate held by an insolvent entity or person is subject to substantial financial burdens, it is open to a company liquidator or trustee in bankruptcy to disclaim the estate.[3] The effect of such disclaimer is the termination of the estate and the automatic escheat of the land to the crown.[4] Thus the implosion of the largest common law estate simply revests the land within the allodium of the crown,[5] in rather the same way in which a lease for years falls in for the landlord on the expiration of the term granted.[6] A recent and dramatic index of the modern irrelevance of tenurial theory is evident in the fact that the rule of automatic reversion to the crown has been gravely modified in relation to registered estates. The Land Registration Act 2002 now provides for rules which, notwithstanding the destruction of the tenurial relationship, will prevent the automatic closure of registered titles to escheated land.[7]

1   See *Attorney-General of Ontario v Mercer* (1883) 8 App Cas 767 at 772 per Earl of Selbourne LC. Nowadays it is generally safe to assume that the escheat will be to the crown rather than to some mesne lord (see *Scmlla Properties Ltd v Gesso Properties (BVI) Ltd* [1995] BCC 793 at 799).
2   Administration of Estates Act 1925, s 46(1)(vi) **[para 7.66]** (the modern equivalent of 'escheat propter defectum sanguinis').
3   See Insolvency Act 1986, ss 178(2), 315(1)–(2) **[paras 7.27, 7.67]**.
4   See e g *Scmlla Properties Ltd v Gesso Properties (BVI) Ltd* [1995] BCC 793 at 805F.
5   See *Re Mercer and Moore* (1880) 14 Ch D 287 at 295 per Jessel MR **[para 7.65]**.
6   See *Wik Peoples v Queensland* (1996) 187 CLR 1 at 91 per Brennan CJ.
7   LRA 2002, s 82; LRR 2003, rr 79(3), 173 **[para 7.66]**.

Link with environmental theory

1.153   Tenurial theory has one further, indirect, significance for 21st century land law. In positing a mutuality of obligation, tenurial theory did at least reinforce the notion that right and responsibility are inseparable components of the deep theory of property.[1] To the American property scholar, John Cribbet, we owe the ironic reflection that the abolition of the incidents of feudal tenure, in freeing land from archaic and obsolete obligations, contributed towards a more general dissociation of entitlement and obligation in landholding.[2] It is only in modern times that some element of the protective stewardship implicit within tenure has resurfaced as a basis for suggesting that, for environmental reasons, ownership of land is inherently qualified by social or community-oriented obligation.[3]

1   See Gray, 'Equitable Property' (1994) 47(2) CLP 157 at 183–189, 198, 208–214.

2   See J E Cribbet, 'Concepts in Transition: The Search for a New Definition of Property' (1986) U Ill L Rev 1 at 39.
3   See Gray, 'Property in Common Law Systems', in G E van Maanen and A J van der Walt (ed), *Property Law on the Threshold of the 21st Century* (MAKLU, Antwerp, 1996), pp 244–245. On the modern resurgence of ideas of environmental stewardship, see Chapter 2 [**para 2.87**] and Chapter 13 [**para 13.156**].

THE FIFTH DIMENSION OF 'LAND'

1.154 If land is capable of description in *three* physical dimensions, and of extension into a *fourth* dimension by the component of time, English law soon added a further dimension of analysis. This extra dimension turned on the 'legal' or 'equitable' quality accorded to the various abstract rights which had emerged from the medieval conceptualism of estates. It came to be recognised that each estate could itself be 'the subject of "ownership" both in law and in equity.'[1] Although for historical reasons 'legal estates and equitable estates have differing incidents', it is truly the case that 'the person owning either type of estate has a right of property.'[2] Indeed, much of the rich complexity of today's law of property results from the potential duality of estate ownership, for amidst other consequences it makes possible that most significant of English contributions to jurisprudence, the institution of the *trust*.[3]

1   *Mabo v Queensland (No 2)* (1993) 175 CLR 1 at 80 per Deane and Gaudron JJ. See *Yanner v Eaton* (1999) 201 CLR 351 at [85] per Gummow J ('Equity brings particular sophistications to the subject'). On the existence of 'equitable estates corresponding to ... legal estates', see *R v Tower Hamlets LB, ex p Von Goetz* [1999] QB 1019 at 1024C–1025A per Mummery LJ, 1026F–G per Peter Gibson LJ.
2   *Tinsley v Milligan* [1994] 1 AC 340 at 371A–B per Lord Browne-Wilkinson.
3   [**Paras 1.163, 9.175**].

LEGAL AND EQUITABLE RIGHTS

1.155 Within the field of proprietary rights in land, English law still draws a fundamental distinction between *legal* and *equitable* rights. Historically this distinction was grounded on the fact that *legal* rights were enforceable only in the common law courts of the king, whereas *equitable* rights fell within the exclusive and conscience-based jurisdiction, initially of the king's Chancellor, and later of the Court of Chancery.[1] In Chancery the ultimate value was the faithful discharge of moral obligation and the equity dispensed in Chancery was conceived as a corrective system of justice, designed to supplement the common law by responding more flexibly and sensitively to the need for fair dealing and just outcomes.[2] Equity therefore addressed, on an instance-specific basis, the hard cases for which the generalised actions and dogmas of the common law afforded no adequate remedy.[3] In time equity hardened into a system of rules which proved, in many ways, to be just as rigid as the common law it was intended to ameliorate.

1   See Pollock and Maitland, *The History of English Law* (2nd edn, London 1968), Vol 1, pp 193–197; Maitland, *Equity* (2nd edn revd by J Brunyate, London 1936), pp 2–11.

2   See *R Griggs Group Ltd v Evans (No 2)* [2004] EWHC 1088 (Ch) at [39] ('a kind of supplementary jurisprudence which was intended to fill up the gaps in the common law').
3   '[I]t is not possible to make any general rule of law, but that it shall fail in some case … Wherefore … equity is ordained … to temper and mitigate the rigour of the law' (Christopher St Germain, *Doctor And Student* (17th edn 1787), p 45). See also *Midland Bank plc v Cooke* [1995] 4 All ER 562 at 575a per Waite LJ ('Equity has traditionally been a system which matches established principle to the demands of social change').

Conflict between the jurisdictions of law and equity

1.156 Inevitably the jurisdictions of common law and equity came into conflict, in so far as they frequently recognised different forms of entitlement and provided different forms of remedy for the litigant.[1] The supremacy of the Court of Chancery became settled by the 17th century, but the mutual antagonism of the courts of common law and equity was not resolved until late in the 19th century. The Supreme Court of Judicature Act 1873 finally established that the rules of law and equity should be administered by all courts of the land, so that the remedy obtained should no longer depend upon the precise court in which the claimant brought his action. In view of this fusion of administration, it can nowadays be said that 'English law has one single law of property made up of legal and equitable interests.'[2] Rights and remedies, whether legal or equitable, are now recognised and enforced in all courts, albeit subject to the overriding statutory principle that, in cases of conflict between law and equity, the rules of equity should prevail.[3] Significant differences nevertheless persist between the remedies available at law and in equity. The range of potential remedy extends much more widely in equity than at law, embracing forms of relief which operate *in personam* (eg decrees of specific performance, injunctions and orders for rectification).[4] However, whereas the characteristic common law remedy of damages is available as of right once the claimant's case has been proved, equitable remedies are always discretionary.

1   An example is provided by the fundamentally divergent responses of common law and equity to the phenomenon of the trust **[para 1.174]**.
2   *Tinsley v Milligan* [1994] 1 AC 340 at 371A per Lord Browne-Wilkinson.
3   Supreme Court of Judicature Act 1873, s 25(11) **[para 9.65]**, now incorporated in Supreme Court Act 1981, s 49(1). See eg *Muscat v Smith* [2003] EWCA 962, [2003] 1 WLR 2853 at [33], [38] per Buxton LJ **[para 14.62]**.
4   **[Para 9.8]**.

The borderline between legal and equitable rights

1.157 Legal and equitable proprietary rights, although today acknowledged by all courts alike, are quite different from each other. It is difficult to summarise these points of distinction here, since they constitute much of the substance of this book. Moreover, the borderline between legal and equitable rights in land has now been artificially, and somewhat arbitrarily, redefined by the property legislation of 1925.[1] Under this statutory categorisation of rights some sorts of entitlement may now exist *either* at law *or* in equity; yet others may exist *only* in equity. But there remains considerable truth in the idea that legal rights are normally created by compliance with various statutory requirements of documentary formality or bureaucratic registration,[2] whereas equitable rights tend to be generated, in a more diffuse fashion, by informal transactions,[3] by implications from circumstance,[4] and by obligations of conscience.[5]

1   See LPA 1925, s 1(1)–(3) **[para 2.123]**.
2   **[Paras 2.126, 2.136]**.
3   **[Paras 9.42, 10.61]**.
4   **[Paras 9.115, 10.8]**.
5   **[Paras 9.176, 10.64]**.

Differences between form and substance

1.158   In some important sense – particularly in the context of the trust[1] – legal rights can often be said to represent *form*, whereas equitable rights represent *substance*.[2] It is frequently the case that legal rights comprise merely a nominal or paper title, as evidenced in some superficial record, and therefore carry more of a connotation of responsibility than of entitlement. Equitable rights, on the other hand, reflect more clearly the *inner reality* (as distinct from the *outer form*) of a transaction and generally locate rather more accurately the substance of intended beneficial enjoyment.

1   **[Para 1.163]**.
2   See *Sussman v AGC Advances Ltd* (1995) 37 NSWLR 37 at 45B, where Kirby P referred to the 'rule of equity that substance is given priority over form.' See also *Hewitt v Court* (1983) 149 CLR 639 at 668 per Deane J **[para 9.5]**; *Corin v Patton* (1990) 169 CLR 540 at 579 per Deane J.

Differences of binding impact

1.159   At the level of raw common law principle, legal rights are automatically binding upon the world. In practice the enhanced publicity inherent in the formal or documentary derivation of most legal rights has tended to ease the impact of legal rights upon strangers.[1] Equitable rights frequently arise in less formal circumstances, with the consequence that, although the recent extension of title registration has eroded some of the practical distinction between legal and equitable rights, the enforcement of equitable entitlements against strangers often requires the assistance of various mechanisms of registration[2] or even the application of conscience-based doctrines of equity such as the 'doctrine of notice'.[3]

1   **[Paras 2.179, 12.274]**.
2   **[Paras 2.157, 2.185]**.
3   **[Paras 2.191, 12.337]**.

DIFFERENTIATION OF LEGAL AND EQUITABLE OWNERSHIP

1.160   Quantum developments of the law of property have tended, historically, to coincide with the emergence of distinct kinds of 'equitable' entitlement.

Quite often the differentiation of legal and equitable components of entitlement has generated a chain reaction of profound jurisprudential consequence. The recognition of the potentiality of separate legal and equitable estates in land provides an important demonstration.

Totality of estate ownership

1.161 Where the 'whole right of property' vests in one person, there is of course 'no need to suppose the separate and concurrent existence of two different kinds of estate or interest, ie the legal and the equitable'.[1] The sole owner of Greenacre need not see himself as owning both the *legal* and the *equitable* estate in that land.[2] Merger in one owner of the totality of entitlement is said to render such a distinction unnecessary and even impossible:[3] the owner of the whole has no separate equitable estate since this is 'absorbed in the legal estate.'[4] But the moment this totality of ownership is split between two or more persons, the device of the trust becomes virtually unavoidable,[5] ownership of the formal or documentary estate being a phenomenon recognised *at law* and ownership of the beneficial estate being recognised only *in equity*.

1 *Commissioner of Stamp Duties (Queensland) v Livingston* [1965] AC 694 at 712C–D per Viscount Radcliffe. See also *Grey v IRC* [1958] Ch 690 at 708 per Evershed MR; *Westdeutsche Landesbank Girozentrale v Islington LB* [1996] AC 669 at 706E per Lord Browne-Wilkinson; *DKLR Holding Co (No 2) Pty Ltd v Commissioner of Stamp Duties* [1978] 1 NSWLR 268 at 278B–E per Sheppard J, (1982) 149 CLR 431 at 463 per Aickin J; *Wollondilly Shire Council v Picton Power Lines Pty Ltd* (1991) 5 BPR 11503 at 11508 per Young J; *Chief Commr of Stamp Duties v ISPT Pty Ltd* (1997) 45 NSWLR 639 at 658B per Fitzgerald A-JA.
2 See *Re Transphere Pty Ltd* (1986) 5 NSWLR 309 at 311E, where McLelland J spoke of 'the imprecision of the notion that absolute ownership of property can properly be divided up into a legal estate and an equitable estate.'
3 *Corin v Patton* (1990) 169 CLR 540 at 579 per Deane J. For this reason an absolute owner is often said to be incompetent to transfer a bare legal estate whilst purporting to retain the absolute beneficial interest (see *DKLR Holding Co (No 2) Pty Ltd v Commissioner of Stamp Duties (NSW)* (1982) 149 CLR 431 at 442 per Gibbs CJ, 463–464 per Aickin J, 473–474 per Brennan J).
4 *DKLR Holding Co (No 2) Pty Ltd v Commissioner of Stamp Duties (NSW)* (1982) 149 CLR 431 at 442 per Gibbs CJ.
5 **[Para 9.175]**. See, however, *Westdeutsche Landesbank Girozentrale v Islington LB* [1996] AC 669 at 706H–707A per Lord Browne-Wilkinson.

Enforcement of a conscientious obligation

1.162 There are indeed certain significant circumstances where the otherwise undifferentiated totality of estate ownership may require to be bifurcated between two or more owners, one owning the *legal estate* and the other or others owning the *equitable estate*. Such separations of legal and equitable entitlement are always doctrinally motivated.[1] Equitable rights of property are generated by the judicial recognition of conscience-driven obligations which bind an estate owner to deal with an asset or resource in a certain way.[2] The process represents the practical realisation of equity's central contribution to common law jurisprudence – the idea that conscientious obligation takes priority over strict legal right.[3] In many contexts, therefore, the controlled conscience of equity causes new rights to become impressed upon pre-existing estates. Such rights, as and when they arise in response to the mandate of equitable doctrine, are not so much 'carved out of' the legal estate as 'engrafted' upon it[4] and, by virtue of their origin, rank thereafter as 'equitable' proprietary rights. In the process, the application of equitable principle has generated a new variety of estate ownership – recognised only in equity – which coexists with, and heavily qualifies, the estate ownership upheld at law.

1   Here as elsewhere, equity 'calls into existence and protects equitable rights and interests in property only where their recognition has been found to be required in order to give effect to its doctrines' (*Commissioner of Stamp Duties (Queensland) v Livingston* [1965] AC 694 at 712E per Viscount Radcliffe). See also *DKLR Holding Co (No 2) Pty Ltd v Commissioner of Stamp Duties* [1978] 1 NSWLR 268 at 278D–E.
2   See Patrick Parkinson, 'Reconceptualising the Express Trust' [2002] CLJ 657.
3   See Gray, 'Equitable Property' (1994) 47(2) CLP 157 at 163, 207–214. See also *Legione v Hately* (1983) 152 CLR 406 at 444 per Mason and Deane JJ **[para 9.1]**. 'Every law student knows that equity may mitigate the rigour of the common law in circumstances where (according to developed principles) it is held that it would be unconscionable for an individual to rest on his strict legal rights' (*Mountney v Treharne* [2002] EWCA Civ 1174, [2003] Ch 135 at [84] per Laws LJ).
4   *DKLR Holding Co (No 2) Pty Ltd v Commissioner of Stamp Duties (NSW)* (1982) 149 CLR 431 at 474 per Brennan J. See also *Re Transphere Pty Ltd* (1986) 5 NSWLR 309 at 311E–F per McLelland J.

THE INSTITUTION OF THE TRUST

1.163   The institution of the trust provides the classic circumstance where equitable ownership necessarily diverges from legal ownership. Nowhere is the potential duality of estate ownership more clearly demonstrated.[1] The extended enforcement of the conscientious obligations undertaken by the trustee has evolved, over time, into a recognition that the beneficiary's right to compel due performance of the trust 'constitutes an equitable estate in the property.'[2] Equity answers its primary call of conscience by engrafting a corrective image of entitlement – a species of equitable ownership – upon the legal estate of the trustee.[3] But some idea of what this really means can be gained only by examining, at least in outline, the essential nature of the trust device.[4]

1   **[Para 1.154]**.
2   *Re Transphere Pty Ltd* (1986) 5 NSWLR 309 at 311E–F per McLelland J; *Mills v Ruthol* (2002) 10 BPR 19381 at [122] per Palmer J.
3   See *Western Australia v Ward* (2000) 170 ALR 159 at 362 per North J ('a concurrent system to take account of the demands of conscience'); W Markby, *Elements of Law considered with reference to Principles of General Jurisprudence* (6th edn, Clarendon 1905), p 171 ('double ownership'). See also *Westdeutsche Landesbank Girozentrale v Islington LB* [1996] AC 669 at 709C, where Lord Browne-Wilkinson referred to 'the basic premise on which all trust law is built, viz that the conscience of the trustee is affected.'
4   See generally Roger Cotterrell, 'Trusting in Law: Legal and Moral Concepts of Trust' (1993) 46(2) CLP 75; Carol M Rose, 'Trust in the Mirror of Betrayal' 75 Boston U L Rev 531 (1995).

The essential structure of the trust

1.164   The core of every trust is the idea that the formal or titular interest in some asset (eg the legal estate in fee simple) is vested, in a nominal capacity, in one or more persons *as trustee*.[1] The strict duty of such persons is to deflect all beneficial enjoyment of the trust asset to the *beneficiaries* or *cestuis que trust*, who are together entitled to the equitable interests (eg the equitable estate in fee simple).[2] It is, in short, the *beneficiaries* who *benefit* under a trust (see *Fig.* 1).

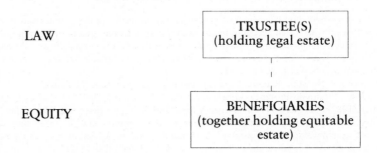

LAW

EQUITY

Fig. 1

1   See W G Hart, 'What is a Trust?' (1899) 15 LQR 294.
2   See *Thorpe v Bristile Ltd* (1996) 16 WAR 500 at 505C–D per Malcolm CJ.

The express trust

1.165   In its classical form the trust is a device created expressly for a specific purpose, the author of the trust (or 'settlor') quite explicitly nominating both the trustees and the desired range of beneficiaries and stipulating the precise terms of the trust.[1] The simplest kind of trust arises where S, the owner of a legal estate in land, transfers that estate to A as trustee, on the undertaking that A shall thereafter hold the estate at law 'on trust for' B, a named beneficiary (see *Fig.* 2).[2] In view of the confidence which S (the settlor) has placed in A, the trust gives rise to a conscientious obligation in A to apply the trust asset faithfully in accordance with S's instructions.[3] All beneficiaries or 'cestuis que trust' have an essentially personal right against their trustee to ensure that the latter carries out the terms of his trust[4] – a right which is enforceable by court order or through the recovery of damages in respect of any breach of trust which has already occurred.

1   The creation of express trusts of land is necessarily marked by a certain degree of documentary formality. It is one of the venerable rules of trust law that a declaration of trust respecting land must be 'manifested and proved by some writing' signed by the author of the trust (LPA 1925, s 53(1)(b) [**para 9.188**]).
2   Alternatively, S may declare himself to be a trustee of his own legal title on behalf of B. It could even be that S himself owns merely an equitable interest and can therefore create only a sub-trust of his equitable interest for B (see *Chief Commr of Stamp Duties v ISPT Pty Ltd* (1997) 45 NSWLR 639 at 650F–G per Mason P). Such cases are, however, merely more sophisticated variants of the trust model portrayed in *Fig.* 2.

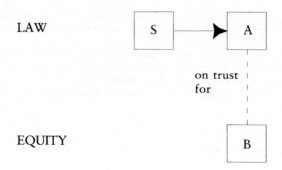

Fig. 2

3   In an expressly created trust it is the trustee, after all, who has consented to undertake the
function of trusteeship and in conscience he cannot later be heard to disavow his trust. For the
view that the trustee's liability is almost certainly of contractual origin, see Maitland, *Equity*,
pp 110–111.
4   See *Re Transphere Pty Ltd* (1986) 5 NSWLR 309 at 311E per McLelland J.

1.166   Once an express trust has been created, its author (ie the settlor)
normally has no further part to play. Unless he has, by explicit declaration,
constituted *himself* a trustee of the legal estate,[1] he has divested himself of the
'whole right of property' in the land.[2] The legal estate in the trust property is
held thereafter by the nominated trustee, who as estate owner is invested with
administrative powers of management and disposition.

1   **[Para 9.184]**.
2   See *Commissioner of Stamp Duties* (*Queensland*) *v Livingston* [1965] AC 694 at 712C–D per
Viscount Radcliffe **[para 1.161]**.

Duties of the trustee

1.167   In the example illustrated in *Fig.* 2, the trustee, A, is charged with
fiduciary responsibility for the management of the trust property in such a way
as to render it productive of income or other use value, subject always to the
duty to divert the benefit (whether in the form of income or actual enjoyment)
to the beneficiary, B.[1] It is a cardinal principle of trust law that A must never
derive any unauthorised personal profit from his office of trust.[2] A's task is
simply one of decision-making in the performance of the administrative duties
connected with the trust. He manages the trust property and ultimately
exercises powers of disposition (ie sale, lease or mortgage) in relation to that
property.[3] Even the latter function is, however, purely administrative. Any sale
of the trust property simply converts that asset into cash, which is still governed
by the terms of the trust and requires to be reinvested in some form or other for
the benefit of B.

1   The principles outlined here are exactly the same whether there is one trustee alone or several
persons acting together as trustees, and whether the beneficiary is one person or many persons
collectively.

2   See e g *Keech v Sandford* (1726) 2 Eq Cas Abr 741, 22 ER 629, Sel Cas T King 61 at 62, 25 ER
      223. A may, of course, benefit from the trust if he also happens to be one of its designated
      beneficiaries.
3   See Thomas W Merrill and Henry E Smith, 'The Property/Contract Interface' 101 Col L
      Rev 773 at 844 (2001) ('The trustee exercises managerial authority over the trust corpus ...
      [but] ... is subject to a complicated set of duties, tantamount to a third-party beneficiary
      contract, that requires that the beneficial value of the property be devoted to the welfare of
      the beneficiary').

The trust as a management device

1.168   The expressly created trust is, in effect, a sophisticated form of management device. It depends fundamentally on a functional separation of *administration* and *enjoyment*. The trustee is invested with a purely nominal title and is a mere
'paper owner'.[1] The practical benefit derived from the land held on trust – whether
by way of occupation, rental exploitation or sale – is reserved at all times for the
nominated beneficiary or beneficiaries. It is, indeed, this fragmentation of title,
management, use and enjoyment which makes the trust so alien to the stolid
notion of *dominium* in civilian systems of property law.[2] For Maitland, the
invention and development of the trust represented 'the most distinctive achievement of English lawyers. It seems to us almost essential to civilisation, and yet
there is nothing quite like it in foreign law.'[3] The major historic consequence of the
trust was undoubtedly the final dismantling of the feudal system and its replacement by a new and much more flexible mechanism for the distribution of family
wealth. In more recent times, however, the divorce between administration and
beneficial enjoyment within the trust device has ensured its utility as one of the
most potent instruments of the capitalist economy.[4]

1   'If we have regard to the essence of the matter rather than to the form of it, a trustee is not an
      owner at all, but a mere agent, upon whom the law has conferred the power and imposed the
      duty of administering the property of another person' (Salmond, *Jurisprudence* (12th edn by P
      J Fitzgerald, London 1966), p 256).
2   **[Para 6.4]**. Otto Kahn-Freund observed that, in creating the trust, the English legal mind has
      made it 'unnecessary and impossible for itself to search for a definition of property in the
      continental sense' ('Introduction' to K Renner, *The Institutions of Private Law and Their
      Social Functions* (London and Boston 1949), p 23).
3   *Equity*, p 23. See also A Nussbaum, 'Sociological and Comparative Aspects of the Trust' 38
      Columbia L Rev 408 (1938); V Bolgár, 'Why No Trusts in the Civil Law?' (1953) 2 AJCL 204.
4   The trust was once described as 'a device of an individualistic character, conforming to the
      Anglo-Saxon system of economic liberalism' (see A Nussbaum, 38 Columbia L Rev 408 at
      412 (1938)).

The implied trust

1.169   Although many trusts arise by express creation, probably even more
trusts are created by implication (particularly in the family context).[1] It falls within
the general remit of any court, in the exercise of its equitable jurisdiction, to
recognise or *construct* equitable entitlement on behalf of any claimant who can
demonstrate that another has incurred a conscientious obligation to hold a legal

title on trust for him or her as beneficiary.[2] Implied trusts fall into two broad categories – the *resulting trust*[3] and the *constructive trust*[4] – and it is not impossible that a valid resulting or constructive trust may emerge from circumstances where a purported express trust of land has failed for want of formality.[5]

1   [**Para 9.180**].
2   In relation to implied trusts, the requirement of formal creation is necessarily abrogated (LPA 1925, s 53(2) [**para 9.192**]), although the standard of evidence required in order to make good a claim of implied trust may still be disconcertingly demanding [**paras 10.94, 10.128**].
3   [**Para 10.8**].
4   [**Para 10.58**].
5   [**Para 9.192**].

Beneficial interests under the trust

1.170   Trusts come in many shapes and sizes: there may be more than one trustee; there may be a multiplicity of beneficiaries.[1] Where there exists more than one cestui que trust, the beneficial interests under the trust are usually – although not always – quantifiable as fractional shares in the assets of the trust. Thus, in an example which recurs in many forms throughout land law, the legal estate in a dwelling-house may be held by a trustee or by trustees, who hold on trust for two beneficiaries who take equitable shares of, say, 75 per cent and 25 per cent respectively, or 50 per cent each, or indeed any other percentages which add up to a unity (see *Fig.* 3).

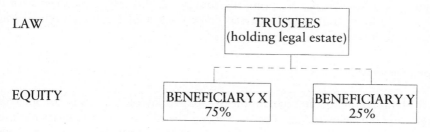

Fig. 3

1   There is nothing, in principle, to prevent (some or all of) the trustees and beneficiaries from being the same people [**para 11.128**].

Enforcement of the obligation of the trust

1.171   The evolving recognition of the obligation of the trust is no easy story. The slow emergence of the modern trust is one of the more complex domains of legal history and can be described here only in crudest summary.[1]

1   On the history of the trust, see Maitland, *Equity*, pp 43–56.

The device of the 'use'

1.172   The enforcement of trust obligations finds its historical origins in the development, during the 13th and 14th centuries, of the institution of the 'use'.[1] Partly because the feudal law of the 13th century ruthlessly curtailed the power to leave land by will,[2] the 'feoffment to uses' came to provide an effective testamentary substitute.[3] An inter vivos conveyance (or 'feoffment') of land could be made to a 'feoffee', who undertook to hold land to various 'uses' indicated by the 'feoffor' (which characteristically included the conferment of benefits on nominated persons living after the feoffor's death). By the 14th century the Chancellor had begun, on grounds of conscience, to enforce 'uses' on behalf of their beneficiaries (or 'cestuis que use'). When, in the 16th century, the 'use' was subjected in its turn to severe restrictions,[4] the foundations were laid for the alternative device of the 'trust', which was to perform most of the functions earlier discharged by the use.

1   See generally A W B Simpson, *A History of The Land Law* (2nd edn, Oxford 1986), pp 173–207.
2   See *The Collected Papers of Frederic William Maitland* (ed H A L Fisher, Cambridge 1911), Vol III, p 335.
3   See W F Fratcher, 'Uses of Uses' 34 Missouri L Rev 39 (1969).
4   The Statute of Uses 1535 effectively abolished the power to create a use by will.

The development of the trust

1.173   From the 17th century onwards the Court of Chancery began to fashion the principles which were to harden into the body of rules known as 'equity' – rules which were primarily (but not exclusively) concerned with the internal administration and external consequences of trusts of both real and personal property.

Form and substance

1.174   Integral to the recognition of obligations of trust was the idea that legal title is a mere matter of *form*, whereas the rights of beneficiaries represent *substance*. From its earliest days the common law was concerned only with form,[1] and the common law courts accordingly afforded a remedy only to the formal owner of the legal estate, the trustee. If asked to determine the ownership of a disputed parcel of land, a court of common law simply declared that full rights of ownership were as indicated by the paper title, ie vested in the person whose name appeared as transferee on the most recent deed of conveyance. The common law took no account of any moral obligation which the author of a trust had, by agreement, fixed on the conscience of the transferee of that paper title. The formal record of the title was regarded as exclusive of any rights in the supposed trust beneficiaries and as conclusive of any question relating to use, benefit or enjoyment.

1   See Alice Tay, 'The sense of justice in the Common Law', in E Kamenka and A E-S Tay (ed), *Justice* (London 1979), p 79.

The jurisdiction of conscience

1.175 Equity has always been more deeply impressed by substance than by form[1] and it was, accordingly, left to a jurisdiction founded upon conscience to remedy the deficiencies of the common law.[2] It was in the court of the Chancellor, and only in his court, that the moral obligations imposed on, and accepted by, trustees came to be enforceable. It was by virtue of the Chancellor's 'equity' that the beneficiary of a trust could vindicate his entitlement under the trust. Although never denying that the trustee was the owner of the *legal* estate in the trust property,[3] the Court of Chancery afforded to trust beneficiaries the remedies denied them by the courts of common law. The Court of Chancery insisted that the terms of trusts be observed and that trust property be dealt with for the benefit of those persons named as beneficiaries or, as it came to be said, for the benefit of those persons 'entitled in equity'.[4] The pre-eminence of this equitable perspective was finally confirmed when the administration of law and equity was fused in the late 19th century under the overarching instruction that, in cases of conflict, the rules of equity should prevail.[5]

1 See e g *Chung Ping Kwan v Lam Island Co Ltd* [1997] AC 38 at 48G per Lord Nicholls of Birkenhead.
2 [**Para 1.155**].
3 Maitland fought, perhaps unnecessarily, against the 'absurdity' of supposing that before 1875 there were two courts of co-ordinate jurisdiction, one of which maintained that A was the owner, the other that B was the owner, of Greenacre. 'That means civil war and utter anarchy ... Equity did not say that the cestui que trust was the owner of the land, it said that the trustee was the owner of the land, but added that he was bound to hold the land for the benefit of the cestui que trust. There was no conflict here ... Equity without common law would have been a castle in the air, an impossibility' (*Equity*, pp 17, 19).
4 '[E]quity traditionally fastens on the conscience of one party to enforce equitable duties which arise out of his relationship with the other' (*Campbell v MGN Ltd* [2004] UKHL 22, [2004] 2 WLR 1232 at [44] per Lord Hoffmann).
5 [**Para 1.156**].

Extended impact of the trust on third parties

1.176 Although the obligation of the trust began as a personal obligation owed by the trustee to his beneficiary, the phenomenon of the trust would have enjoyed only limited significance if this obligation had remained enforceable merely against the original trustee. The fiduciary responsibility implicit in the trust would have been frustrated by any subsequent change of legal title, whether occurring on the death or insolvency of the trustee or on his transfer of the legal estate in the trust property to some third party. The impact of the trust was accordingly extended to affect many categories of person other than the original trustee and cestui que trust. Equity, as a jurisdiction of conscience, expanded the reach of the beneficiary's rights so that these rights came to bind any third party who could be regarded as implicated in the conscientious obligation of the trust.[1] The rule which emerged from this development of equitable doctrine was known as the *bona fide purchaser rule* or the *equitable doctrine of notice* and ultimately governed even those equitable rights which arose outside the context of a trust.[2]

1   For an excellent historical account, see A W B Simpson, 'The Equitable Doctrine of Consideration and the Law of Uses' (1965–66) 16 U of Toronto LJ 1 at 24–28.
2   **[Para 2.181]**.

1.177   The gradual diffusion of trust liability beyond the nexus of trustee and cestui occurred with the transmission of the trustee's legal estate to various kinds of third party. Trusts came to be enforced against the following categories of person (see *Fig. 4*).

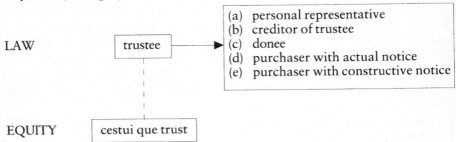

Fig. 4
Persons who succeed to the estate of the trustee

1.178   It was but a short step for equity to declare that the cestui que trust may enforce the terms of the trust against any person who, on the trustee's death, takes the trustee's legal estate by succession. The beneficiary thus becomes entitled to enforce the trust against the trustee's personal representatives (ie his executors in the case where the trustee dies testate, and his administrators in the case of death intestate).[1] Clearly the trustee's successors cannot claim to stand in any better position than the trustee himself.

1   These persons are regarded as 'sustaining wholly or partially the persona of the original trustee and being bound by his obligations as regards the proprietary rights to which they have succeeded' (Maitland, *Equity*, p 112).

Creditors of the trustee

1.179   The next step was to allow the cestui que trust to enforce the trust against personal creditors of the trustee.[1] These creditors may not claim the trust property in satisfaction of personal debts owed by the trustee,[2] for the trust property is that to which the trustee is only nominally entitled as a paper owner. The underpinning ethos of the trust is the idea that the benefit derived from the trust property belongs exclusively to the cestui que trust.[3]

1   *Finch v Earl of Winchelsea* (1715) 1 P Wms 277 at 282, 24 ER 387 at 389.
2   See *Worrall v Harford* (1802) 8 Ves 4 at 8, 32 ER 250 at 252; *Re Morgan* (1881) 18 Ch D 93 at 104.

3   **[Para 1.164]**. This principle is currently preserved in Insolvency Act 1986, ss 283(1)(a), (3)(a), 306 **[para 11.251]**.

Donees of the trustee

1.180   A difficult question of ethical and economic priority arises if a trustee, acting in breach of his trust, gratuitously transfers the legal estate in the trust property to an innocent third party.[1] Both the donee and the cestui que trust are entirely blameless, but from early times equity declared that the cestui is entitled to enforce the trust against the donee (or 'volunteer').[2] The donee takes the gifted property subject to subsisting equitable claims: he cannot be heard to disavow the trust attached to the estate which he has received. Equity operates upon conscience, and the conscience of the donee is sufficiently affected by the fact that he has received something to which, strictly, he had no prior entitlement.[3] It would be 'against conscience' that he should retain the gift in its unqualified form after he comes to know that it was made in breach of trust.

1   It cannot be doubted that legal title has been validly transferred by the gift.
2   'Equity will not assist a volunteer' **[para 9.6]**.
3   See e g *Burgess v Wheate* (1759) 1 Eden 177 at 195, 28 ER 652 at 659; *Re Diplock* [1948] Ch 465 at 503. The donee's liability may rest on a theory of unjust enrichment (see J B Ames, *Lectures on Legal History* (Cambridge Mass 1913), p 255).

Purchasers from the trustee with actual notice of the trust

1.181   At a very early stage in the development of equity it was also decided that the beneficiary of a trust may enforce his rights against any stranger who purchases the trust estate with actual knowledge of the existence of the trust.[1] The ground of the third party's liability is something akin to fraud.[2] The basis for this conclusion was beautifully rendered in the law-French of 1471:

> Si mon feoffee de trust etc enfeoffe un autre, que conust bien que le feoffor rien ad forsque a mon use, subpoena girra vers ambideux: scil auxibien vers le feoffee come vers le feoffor ... pur ceo que en conscience il purchase ma terre.[3]

Thus the claims of equity operate upon conscience. If a stranger knowingly buys land held on trust, he does what is unconscientious. He must therefore be regarded as holding on trust since, 'in conscience' (and with perhaps only a slight rhetorical flourish), it can be said that he has purchased the land of the beneficiary.

1   **[Para 12.345]**.
2   The purchaser is liable ex delicto vel quasi (Maitland, *Equity*, p 113). A W Scott attributed the liability of the purchaser with actual notice to the fact that he was 'colluding with the trustee in a breach of trust' (see 'The Nature of the Rights of the Cestui Que Trust' 17 Columbia L Rev 269 at 281 (1917)). See also *R Griggs Group Ltd v Evans* (*No 2*) [2004] EWHC 1088 (Ch) at [44], [47].
3   YB 11 Edw IV, fol 8: 'If my trustee conveys the land to a third person who knows well that the

trustee holds for my use, I shall have a remedy in the Chancery against both of them: as well against the buyer as against the trustee: for in conscience he buys my land' (Maitland, *Collected Papers*, Vol III, p 345).

Purchasers from the trustee with constructive notice of the trust

1.182   If equity had stopped there and gone no further, purchasers could have taken good care to ensure that their consciences were unaffected by actual notice of any trust. They would simply have 'shut their eyes' to the possible existence of a trust and would have relied on the absence of actual notice as their ground of immunity from the obligation of the trust. Accordingly equity developed the further rule that, in order to take a legal estate free of trust, the purchaser must be not only honest but also diligent. He must make all such investigation of the vendor's title and land as a prudent purchaser would have made, and he is affected with 'constructive notice' of all equitable rights of which he would have acquired actual notice had he made the proper enquiries.[1] The trust is therefore enforceable against any purchaser who would have known of the trust had he behaved as prudent purchasers behave in the conduct of their affairs.[2] In effect the courts elaborated a standard of diligence in order to fasten upon the conscience of the unreasonable or disingenuous purchaser. If not actually guilty of *dolus*, such a purchaser is at least 'guilty of that sort of negligence which is equivalent to *dolus*. He had shut his eyes in order that he might not see.'[3]

1   [**Para 12.346**].
2   'When the facts at [the purchaser's] command beckoned him to look and inquire further, and he refrained from doing so, equity fixed him with constructive notice of what he would have ascertained if he had pursued the further investigation which a person of reasonable care and skill would have felt proper to make in the circumstances' (*Somers v W* [1979] IR 94 at 108 per Henchy J).
3   Maitland, *Collected Papers*, Vol III, p 346.

The defence of the bona fide purchaser

1.183   At this point the long arm of equity stopped. Equity recognised that if the purchaser who acquires a legal estate from the trustee is excusably ignorant of the rights of the cestui que trust, then he must be left to enjoy the estate unencumbered by any equitable claim.[1] Since his conscience is unaffected, the Chancellor's equity has no hold upon him.[2] In *Pilcher v Rawlins*[3] James LJ regarded it as 'established law' that a plea of 'purchase for valuable consideration without notice is an absolute, unqualified, unanswerable defence, and an unanswerable plea to the jurisdiction of this Court.'

1   *Burgess v Wheate* (1759) 1 Eden 177 at 195, 28 ER 652 at 659 ('A conveyance with consideration without notice bars a trust').
2   'Equity cannot touch him, because ... his conscience is unaffected by the trust' (Maitland, *Equity*, p 115). See also *Royal Bank of Scotland plc v Etridge (No 2)* [2001] UKHL 44, [2002] 2 AC 773 at [145] per Lord Scott of Foscote.

3   (1872) 7 Ch App 259 at 268–269.

The 'equitable doctrine of notice'

1.184   This limitation on the invasive reach of equity became enshrined in a more general formula known as the 'equitable doctrine of notice' (or, sometimes, the 'bona fide purchaser rule').[1]

1   'The doctrine of notice lies at the heart of equity' (*Barclays Bank Plc v O'Brien* [1994] 1 AC 180 at 195G per Lord Browne-Wilkinson).

The equitable rule

1.185   Prior to the commencement of the 1925 property legislation, the equitable doctrine of notice ensured that all equitable rights – including, by analogy, even those equitable rights arising outside the context of the trust[1] – were enforceable against all persons *other than*

a bona fide purchaser of a legal estate for valuable consideration without notice (whether actual or constructive).[2]

Immunity from prior equitable rights was thus guaranteed only in the case of the purchaser of a legal estate whose conscience was wholly unaffected.[3] Such a purchaser was sometimes known simply as 'Equity's Darling' – one who had found favour in the eyes of equity.

1   As Lord Browne-Wilkinson pointed out in *Westdeutsche Landesbank Girozentrale v Islington LB* [1996] AC 669 at 706H–707A, certain equitable rights may be enforceable against the owner of a legal title without, in any sense, rendering the legal owner a trustee (e g equitable easements [**para 9.87**] and restrictive covenants [**para 9.138**]).
2   For further examination of the bona fide purchaser rule, see Chapter 2 [**para 2.191**] and Chapter 12 [**para 12.337**].
3   See *R Griggs Group Ltd v Evans (No 2)* [2004] EWHC 1088 (Ch) at [37]–[39] per Deputy Judge Peter Prescott QC.

Modern displacement of the notice doctrine

1.186   The doctrine of notice, whilst undoubtedly encapsulating a primary rule of fairness or good conscience, later came to be seen as productive of uncertain and unpredictable outcomes.[1] As will become apparent in subsequent chapters of this book, the application of this doctrine was severely cut back by the statutory rearrangement of English land law which occurred during the 20th century.[2] Nowadays the bona fide purchaser rule has, in the strictest sense, no relevance at all to land titles registered under the Land Registration Act[3] and only a residual relevance in the law of unregistered estates in land.[4] The historic role of the doctrine of notice has thus been largely displaced, but the inspirational force of the doctrine lives on in various substitute mechanisms[5] which ensure that the publicity secured by the registration of rights now operates as a form of mandatory notice to the world at large.[6]

1   [Para **12.275**].
2   [Paras **2.193**, **12.264**].
3   [Paras **2.121**, **12.105**].
4   [Paras **2.191**, **12.355**].
5   See e g LRA 2002, s 29(2)(a)(i) [paras **2.163**, **12.84**]; LPA 1925, s 198(1) [para **2.187**].
6   See e g the reference to 'statutory notice' in *Kemmis v Kemmis* [1988] 1 WLR 1307 at 1332E per Nourse LJ [para **12.84**].

Ownership of an equitable estate in land

1.187   Writers of a century ago were accustomed to inveigh against references to the beneficiary under a trust of land as the 'equitable owner of the land.'[1] They were indeed correct in regarding such assertions as only a lazy shorthand or convenient rhetoric. The idea that the cestui is the equitable owner of land plainly cuts across the orthodoxy that conceptual 'estates' constitute the only object of ownership known in English land law.[2] The primary object of the cestui's ownership is, in fact, the obligation of the trustee. But, as Dean Ames himself once noted, 'an obligation is as truly the subject-matter of property as any physical *res*.'[3] And what began as the beneficiary's purely personal right to compel the trustee's due performance of his trust[4] evolved into an ownership, not of *land*, but of the *equitable estate* in the land held on trust.[5]

1   See e g J B Ames, 'Purchase for Value without Notice' 1 Harv L Rev 1 at 9 (1887–88). Maitland similarly insisted, at least in his early writings, that the cestui's rights were merely rights *in personam*, not rights *in rem* (see *Equity*, p 47).
2   [Para **1.135**]. Much of the early debate as to whether the trust beneficiary enjoys rights *in rem* or rights *in personam* would have been clarified if the participants had focused on ownership of the estate rather than ownership of land. Maitland expended enormous energy in seeking to rebut the view that 'whereas the common law said that the trustee was the owner of the land, equity said that the cestui que trust was the owner' (*Equity*, p 17).
3   J B Ames, 1 Harv L Rev 1 at 9 (1887–88).
4   [Para **1.163**].
5   See *Re Transphere Pty Ltd* (1986) 5 NSWLR 309 at 311E–F per McLelland J; *Mills v Ruthol* (2002) 10 BPR 19381 at [122] per Palmer J. See also *Swiss Bank Corpn v Lloyds Bank Ltd* [1979] Ch 548 at 565F–H per Browne-Wilkinson J; *Mountney v Treharne* [2002] EWCA Civ 1174, [2003] Ch 135 at [71] per Jonathan Parker LJ.

Estate ownership good against almost the entire world

1.188   The trust beneficiary's equitable estate in land results, almost inevitably, from the extended enforcement of the moral obligation which is fastened upon the conscience of the trustee. The steady expansion of trust liability to an extremely broad range of third parties serves powerfully to reinforce the perception that equitable rights are akin to proprietary rights. In effect, the benefit of the fiduciary obligation of the trust has enlarged into an equitable ownership good against *almost* the entire world. As even Maitland admitted, 'the benefit of an obligation has been so treated that it has come to look rather like a true proprietary right'.[1]

1   *Equity*, p 115. See now *Westdeutsche Landesbank Girozentrale v Islington LB* [1996] AC 669 at
     705F per Lord Browne-Wilkinson ('Once a trust is established, as from the date of its
     establishment the beneficiary has, in equity, a proprietary interest in the trust property').

The 'equitable owner' of land

1.189   Technically, of course, it remains inaccurate to refer to the trust
beneficiary as the 'equitable owner of the land' held on trust. Yet the phrase is
often irresistible[1] and conveys something of the reality of proprietary relations
within a trust.[2] This over-statement of the equitable rights of the trust
beneficiary merely recognises that the legal estate of the trustee is in most cases
a mere 'shadow' following the equitable estate 'which is the substance'.[3] The
case law and commentary on equity are redolent with assertions that equity
'regards the cestui que trust of property as the true owner of the property
itself.'[4] Salmond spoke of the trustee as a 'nominal owner' who merely held his
estate 'on behalf of the real owner.'[5] For Maitland, '[s]upposing that a man is in
equity the owner ("tenant in fee simple") of a piece of land, it makes very little
difference to him that he is not also "owner at law" and that, as we say, "the
legal ownership is outstanding in trustees".'[6] The point remains that the
ownership of the cestui – more accurately his ownership of an abstract estate in
equity – is an indelible part of the scheme of systematically ordered estates
which provides the intellectual base for the propositional logic of English land
law.

1   In his later writings Maitland seemed more reconciled to the terminology of 'equitable
     ownership' or 'ownership in equity' as descriptions of the entitlement of the trust beneficiary
     (see *Collected Papers*, Vol III, pp 349–350).
2   The beneficiary has 'an equitable interest in the land because an equity court, acting upon the
     conscience of the trustee, will compel the trustee to deal with the land in a certain way for the
     benefit of the cestui que trust' (*Mills v Ruthol* (2002) 10 BPR 19381 at [122] per Palmer J).
3   *Title Insurance and Trust Co v Duffill*, 218 P 14 at 21 (1923) (Supreme Court of California);
     Town of Cascade v Cascade County, 243 P 806 at 808 (1926) (Supreme Court of Montana).
     This was also the view espoused, typically, by Lord Mansfield CJ in *Burgess v Wheate* (1759)
     1 Eden 177 at 217, 28 ER 652 at 668 ('trusts are considered as real estates, as the real
     ownership of the land'). See also *Attorney General v Lady Downing* (1767) Wilm 1 at 22, 97
     ER 1 at 9 per Wilmot CJ ('the legal estate is nothing but the shadow which always follows the
     trust estate, in the eye of a Court of Equity').
4   *Hoysted v Federal Commissioner of Taxation* (1920) 27 CLR 400 at 422 per Isaacs J. It is this
     perception of the cestui's true rights that ultimately underlies the rule in *Saunders v Vautier*
     [para 11.155], which allows the beneficiary or beneficiaries of a trust, if sui iuris (of full age
     and sound mind), to terminate the trust and direct the trustee or trustees as to the disposition
     of the trust property (see *Saunders v Vautier* (1841) 4 Beav 115 at 116, 49 ER 282; affd Cr & Ph
     240 at 249, 41 ER 482 at 485).
5   Salmond, *Jurisprudence* (12th edn by P J Fitzgerald, London 1966), p 256.
6   *Collected Papers*, Vol III, p 349.

CHAPTER 2

Property

THE ELUSIVE CONCEPT OF PROPERTY

2.1 Few concepts are quite so fragile, so elusive and so frequently misused as the notion of property. There is a pervasive element of shared deception in our normal property talk: property is not theft, but *fraud*.[1] We commonly speak of property as if its meaning were entirely clear and logical, but property is a conceptual mirage which slips tantalisingly from view just when it seems most solidly attainable.[2] Amongst the misperceptions which dominate the conventional analysis of both lay persons and lawyers is the lazy myth that property is a 'monolithic notion of standard content and invariable intensity.'[3] Our daily references to property therefore tend to comprise a mutual conspiracy of unsophisticated semantic allusions and confusions, which we tolerate – frequently, indeed, do not notice – largely because our linguistic shorthand commands a certain low-level communicative efficiency.

1   See Gray, 'Property in Thin Air' [1991] CLJ 252 at 305 (property 'comprises, in large part, a category of illusory reference').
2   The High Court of Australia has confirmed that '[t]he concept of property may be elusive ... and it may be ... that "the ultimate fact about property is that it does not really exist: it is mere illusion" ' (*Yanner v Eaton* (1999) 201 CLR 351 at [17] per Gleeson CJ, Gaudron, Kirby and Hayne JJ). See similarly *Donovan v Secretary, Department of Family and Community Services* (Federal Court of Australia, 9 May 2003) per Finn J.
3   See *Yanner v Eaton* (1999) 201 CLR 351 at [19].

2.2 Part of the present task is, accordingly, to jolt ourselves out of our traditional, reassuringly three-dimensional, imagery about property.[1] As Bruce Ackerman once said, one of the main purposes of a property course is to disabuse law students of their 'primitive lay notions regarding ownership.'[2] Not the least significant aspect of this process is the abandonment of the 'absolutist' view of property with which most of us begin – the passionate and instinctive belief that ownership is unqualified, sacrosanct and inviolable – and the adoption of a more 'relativist' perception that entitlements of property are constantly defined and redefined by competing user rights, by social context and by community-directed obligation. Accordingly, the present chapter seeks to explore the inner meaning of 'property', to examine the borderline between proprietary and non-proprietary rights, and finally to outline the way in which proprietary rights in land are accommodated within the complex structure of English property legislation.

1   For an insightful examination of the notion of property, see Craig Rotherham, 'Conceptions of property in common law discourse' (1998) 18 Legal Studies 41.
2   *Private Property and the Constitution* (Yale UP 1977), pp 26–27 ('[O]nly the ignorant think it meaningful to talk about owning things free and clear of further obligation ... [and] it risks serious confusion to identify any single individual as *the* owner of any particular thing ... Once one begins to think sloppily, it is all too easy to start thinking that "the" property owner, by virtue of being "the" property owner, must *necessarily* own a particular bundle of rights over a thing').

Limitations of the property reference

2.3   It remains painfully true that most of our everyday references to property are unreflective, naive and relatively meaningless. In our crude way we are seldom concerned to look behind the immediately practical or functional sense in which we employ the term 'property' in relation to land. What does it really mean to say that Julian Bishop 'owns' 25 Mountfield Gardens or that these premises are his 'property'? It certainly does not mean that he is entitled to exercise an unlimited range of rights over this land. He is not automatically entitled to alter his 'property', build on it or extend it,[1] paint it whatever colour he likes, or even destroy it if he so chooses.[2] His land may be subject to a multitude of rights vested simultaneously in a number of strangers.[3] Furthermore, his land remains vulnerable to compulsory acquisition by the state, on usually less than satisfactory terms, if such unconsented transfer is ever deemed to serve a higher public or social purpose.[4] What then of the lofty assertion that this is Julian Bishop's 'property'?

1   See Town and Country Planning Act 1990, Part III; Planning (Listed Buildings and Conservation Areas) Act 1990, Part I, Ch III **[para 13.160]**.
2   Planning permission is required even for the demolition of buildings **[para 13.161]**.
3   **[Para 2.18]**.
4   **[Para 13.8]**.

The mistaken reification of property

2.4   As the High Court of Australia acknowledged in *Yanner v Eaton*,[1] much of our false thinking about property 'stems from the residual perception that "property" is itself a thing or resource rather than a legally endorsed concentration of power over things and resources.'[2] The root of the difficulty lies in the fact that non-lawyers (and often lawyers) tend to speak rather loosely of 'property' as the *thing* which is owned (eg 'that book / car / house is my property').[3] Whilst this reification of property is harmless enough in casual conversation, it has the effect of obscuring important features of property as a legal and social institution.

1   (1999) 201 CLR 351 at [18] per Gleeson CJ, Gaudron, Kirby and Hayne JJ. See also *Kanak v Minister for Land and Water Conservation* (*NSW*) (2000) 180 ALR 489 at [31].

2   As Hernando de Soto puts it, '[p]roperty is not the [asset] itself but an economic concept *about* the [asset], embodied in a legal representation' (de Soto, *The Mystery of Capital: Why Capitalism Triumphs in the West and Fails Everywhere Else* (Bantam Press 2000), pp 42–43).

3   It was C B Macpherson who drew attention to the way in which, in the transition from the pre-capitalist world to the world of the exchange economy, the distinction between a right to a thing (ie the legal relation) and the thing itself, became blurred. 'The thing itself became, in common parlance, the property' ('Capitalism and the Changing Concept of Property', in E Kamenka and R S Neale (ed), *Feudalism, Capitalism and Beyond* (Canberra 1975), p 111).

Property is not a thing but a power relationship

2.5   Deep at the heart of the phenomenon of property is the semantic reality that 'property' is not a thing, but rather the condition of being 'proper' to a particular person (eg 'That book / car / house is *proper* to me').[1] For serious students of property, the beginning of truth is the recognition that property is not a thing but a *power relationship* – a relationship of social and legal legitimacy existing between a person and a valued resource (whether tangible or intangible). To claim 'property' in a resource is, in effect, to assert a significant degree of control over that resource.[2] Moreover, as Karl Renner once said, '[p]ower over matter begets personal power.'[3] 'Property' ultimately articulates a political relationship between persons. Land – the physical substratum of all human interaction – becomes a vital component of all social and economic engineering.

1   In archaic English, the word 'proper' served to indicate relationships of proprietary significance. Thus the poor were described as not 'hauyng ony thynge proper'; and a very early 15th century reference describes someone as having been slain 'with his own propre swerd' (*Oxford English Dictionary* (Clarendon 1933), Vol VIII, p 1469 ('Proper', I, 1)).

2   See *Commonwealth of Australia v Yarmirr* (2001) 208 CLR 1 at [286] per Kirby J ('the right to exclude others from, and to control access to, a resource produces a proprietary relationship'). The identification of property as residing in control is now a consistent theme in High Court jurisprudence (see the joint judgments of Gleeson CJ, Gaudron, Gummow and Hayne JJ in *Yarmirr*, supra at [13], and *Western Australia v Ward* (2002) 191 ALR 1 at [88]).

3   *The Institutions of Private Law and Their Social Functions* (ed O Kahn-Freund, London and Boston, 1949), p 107.

ALL PROPERTY TALK IS VALUE-LADEN

2.6   All property references are, at some level, a statement about the social legitimacy attaching to the claim in question. The etymological links between such terms as 'property', 'proper', 'appropriate', and 'propriety' underscore the value-laden complexity of inter-relating nuances of property talk. Genuine property discourse thinly conceals a subtext of social propriety.[1] The law of property incorporates a series of critical value judgments, reflecting the cultural norms, the social ethics and the political economy prevalent in any given community. It is inevitable that property law should serve in this way as a vehicle for ideology, for 'property' has commonly been the epithet used to identify that which people most greatly value. The terminology of 'property' also points more subtly to relationships of dependence, for dependence is the inescapable outcome of unequal distributions of that which is valued. The terms 'property' and 'dependence' are merely positive and negative descriptions of existing distributions of control over socially valued resources.

1   Gray and Gray, 'Private Property and Public Propriety', in J McLean (ed), *Property and the Constitution* (Hart Publishing 1999), p 13.

The limits of property

2.7   The limits of property, it has been said, 'are the interfaces between accepted and unaccepted social claims.'[1] This proposition may easily be tested by transmuting the proposition, 'That slave is Robert's property', into the more revealing assertions that 'Robert has property in that slave', and 'That slave is proper to Robert'. It becomes more immediately apparent why the institution of slavery came to be viewed as abhorrent and (eventually) worthy of legal repression. The possibility of having property in other human beings was repudiated when it became socially accepted that human beings could never be described as exhibiting the condition of being 'proper' to fellow human beings.[2] A similar (albeit less extreme) evolution of proprietary morality is more recently to be found in the insistence, on the part of proponents of a 'right to roam',[3] that no individual may ever claim exclusive property in a mountain or any other extensive tract of wild country.[4] The modern expansion of rights of recreational access over privately held land articulates one increasingly important component of the liberal democratic ideal, a virtue which some have called 'pedestrian democracy'.

1   *Dorman v Rodgers* (1982) 148 CLR 365 at 372 per Murphy J.
2   See *Somerset v Stewart* (1772) Lofft 1 at 19, 98 ER 499 at 510 per Lord Mansfield ('The state of slavery is of such a nature, that it is incapable of being introduced on any reasons, moral or political … it's so odious, that nothing can be suffered to support it').
3   **[Paras 2.16, 5.46]**.
4   See Gray, 'The Ambivalence of Property', in G Prins (ed), *Threats Without Enemies* (Earthscan Publications 1993), pp 153–154.

Property and human rights

2.8   It has long been one of the fundamental features of a civilised society that exclusory claims of property stop where the infringement of more basic human freedoms begins. Indeed the law of property has always said much more than is commonly supposed about the subject of human rights, which is one of the reasons why the English law of realty is now so heavily implicated in the assimilation of European human rights standards brought about by the Human Rights Act 1998.[1]

1   The House of Lords has indicated, however, that the Human Rights Act 1998 has no application to events occurring before its commencement on 2 October 2000 if retrospective

application would produce an unfair result for one or other party (see *Wilson v First County Trust Ltd (No 2)* [2004] UKHL 40, [2004] 1 AC 816). See also *National Westminster Bank Plc v Malhan* [2004] EWHC 847 (Ch) at [52] per Morritt V-C **[para 11.216]**.

Excessive claims of property

2.9 Ultimately the language of property collapses back into communal perceptions of the boundary to be drawn between liberty and privacy. Property talk is reducible to a dialogue about moral and personal space, about the mutual frontier between autonomy and vulnerability, between social accommodation and immunity from predation.[1] Excessive claims of exclusive ownership always threaten, in John Locke's well known phrase, to bring about a world in which there is not 'enough, and as good left in common for others.'[2] It was Henry George who more darkly imagined that if one claimant could concentrate in himself 'the individual rights to the whole surface of the globe, he alone of all the teeming population of the earth would have the right to live.'[3] And, as Lord Bingham of Cornhill has more recently declared, 'few things are more central to the enjoyment of human life than having somewhere to live.'[4]

1   Gray, 'Equitable Property' (1994) 47(2) CLP 157 at 160. See also Loren E Lomasky, *Persons, Rights, and the Moral Community* (Oxford 1987), p 121.
2   Locke, *Two Treatises of Government* (2nd critical edn by T P R Laslett, Cambridge 1967), *The Second Treatise*, s 27 (p 306).
3   H George, *Poverty And Progress* (New York 1981 (first published 1879)), p 345 ('he ... could expel therefrom all the rest of its inhabitants'). On the question whether the indigenous inhabitants of Australia could 'lawfully have been driven into the sea at any time after annexation', see *Mabo v Queensland (No 2)* (1992) 175 CLR 1 at 66 per Brennan J.
4   *Harrow London Borough Council v Qazi* [2003] UKHL 43, [2004] 1 AC 983 at [8].

The ambivalence of the human rights interface

2.10 The interplay between human rights and property rights has today a profoundly ambivalent character. On the one hand, an extremely important feature of contemporary human rights culture is constituted by the intensified recognition and protection of private rights of ownership and enjoyment. This trend is most clearly apparent in the ever-expanding reach of various supra-national guarantees of 'peaceful enjoyment' of possessions[1] and of respect for 'private and family life' and the 'home'.[2] In contrast, another facet of the same human rights culture involves a countervailing movement towards the 'democratisation' of property – a process which entails not the classic Marxist reduction of economically pivotal goods to collective ownership, but rather the provision of various rights of communal access to socially desired facilities.[3] As Professor C B Macpherson once pointed out, the idea of property is being gradually broadened to include a 'right to a kind of society or set of power relations which will enable the individual to live a fully human life.'[4]

1   **[Para 2.29]**.
2   **[Para 2.60]**.

3   The sharp point of the modern transformation of property may thus turn out to be, not the resumption of title by the state, but the recognition of various sorts of communal easement on behalf of the people.

4   'Capitalism and the Changing Concept of Property', in E Kamenka and R S Neale (ed), *Feudalism, Capitalism and Beyond* (Canberra 1975), p 120. It is this feature of property which helps to make sense of Macpherson's famous tension between property as comprising a right to exclude and property as constituted by a right of access (loc cit, pp 116–124).

PROPERTY IS A QUANTUM OF SOCIALLY APPROVED CONTROL

2.11   Once property is recognised as a relationship of socially permissible control, it becomes infinitely more accurate to say that one has property in a thing than to declare that something is one's property.[1] 'Property' is what we have in things, not the things that we think we have.[2] 'Property' is simply the word used to describe particular concentrations of power over things; and every claim of 'property' comprises the assertion of some quantum of socially approved power as exercisable in respect of some socially valued resource. For these reasons so-called 'private property' is seldom 'property' in the authentic sense of the term; it is never truly private[3]; and it is rarely (if indeed ever) truly absolute.[4] Several consequences follow.

1   'In legal usage property is not the land or thing, but is *in* the land or thing' (*Dorman v Rodgers* (1982) 148 CLR 365 at 372 per Murphy J).

2   See also Jeremy Bentham, *An Introduction to the Principles of Morals and Legislation* (ed by W Harrison, Oxford, 1948), p 337, note 1 (Chapter XVI, section 26).

3   Gray, 'Property in Thin Air' [1991] CLJ 252 at 303–304.

4   'A man's right in his real property of course is not absolute. It was a maxim of the common law that one should so use his property as not to injure the rights of others … [T]he maxim [expresses] the inevitable proposition that rights are relative and there must be an accommodation when they meet' (*State v Shack*, 277 A2d 369 at 373 (1971)). See also *Marsh v Alabama*, 326 US 501 at 506, 90 L Ed 265 at 268 (1946) per Justice Black.

Property is relative

2.12   The power relationship implicit in property is not an absolute but a *relative* phenomenon. The lay perception of 'property' is that it comprises a unitary phenomenon, monolithic in stature and unqualified in scope. The common law has, however, no concept of absolute title, property or ownership.[1] All title in land remains relative and, even in its statutory form, essentially defeasible.[2]

1   [Paras **2.86**, **6.4**].

2   [Paras **6.4**, **12.245**]. See eg LRA 2002, s 65, Sch 4.

Property has gradations

2.13   There can, moreover, be *gradations* of property in a resource; and these gradations may even vary over time.[1] The quantum of property which a specified individual may claim in any piece of land is capable of calibration – along some sort of sliding scale – between a maximum value and a minimum value. A maximal property value is, of course, provided by ownership of the fee simple estate.[2] But where a property value tends towards zero (as, say, in the claim of a bare licensee[3]), it is normally a misuse of language to assert that the claimant has any property at all in the land in question. Other kinds of property claim lie straddled at some intermediate point across a spectrum of 'propertiness', exhibiting either stronger or weaker degrees of proprietary content.[4] Thus, far from being a notion of standard content and invariable intensity, property turns out to have an almost infinitely gradable quality. Indeed, much of English land law is concerned with the identification and measurement of the quantum of property which someone has in a particular land resource at any particular time. Upon this often depends the capacity of a specific entitlement to survive onward transfers of an estate in the land concerned or even to qualify for protection under the European Convention on Human Rights.

1   For a classic demonstration of this proposition in the law of adverse possession, see Chapter 6. The variable nature of property is also increasingly evident in the law of proprietary estoppel (see e g *Sledmore v Dalby* (1996) 72 P & CR 196 [**para 10.280**]).
2   [**Paras 1.125, 7.2**].
3   [**Para 4.6**].
4   [**Para 2.52**].

Property in land can be variously 'bundled'

2.14   In the absence of any generalised concept of *dominium* or direct ownership of land,[1] the historic technique of the common law has been to parcel up various degrees of socially approved control over the resource of realty, describing each parcel (or quantum) of control in terms of some artificially defined conceptual entitlement in respect of the land.[2] The precise quantum of control which any individual has over a particular block of land – or, as one might just as easily say, the amount of 'property' which he or she has in that land – is demarcated by the size of the 'estate' or 'interest' (if any) which he or she holds. Some abstract bundles of entitlement connote the allocation to the right-holder of a large element of socially permitted control over the use and exploitation of the land in question. For instance, those who own a fee simple estate (or even a term of years) in Greenacre can accurately assert that they have a great deal of 'property' in that land.[3] Other bundles of entitlement connote that the right-holder enjoys significantly less control over – i e has only a limited quantum of 'property' in – the land concerned. For example, the person who owns an easement to use another's land as a communal garden can certainly claim to have *some* 'property' in that land, but not to the extent of having a right to dictate such matters as that a particular flower bed be maintained for ever in a particular location within the garden.[4] The arrogation of this more intense degree of control over terrain is inconsistent with the 'estate' actually owned (i e an easement) and is, instead, an illicit assertion of some rather larger quantum of 'property' in the land such as that denoted by a fee simple estate.[5]

1   [**Paras 1.119, 2.86**].

2   [**Para 1.121**].
3   [**Para 1.125**].
4   See e g *Jackson v Mulvaney* [2002] EWCA Civ 1078, [2003] 1 WLR 360 at [25] [**para 8.71**].
5   See e g *Copeland v Greenhalf* [1952] Ch 488 at 498 [**para 8.75**].

Property is socially constructed

2.15   Property is a socially constructed concept, indirectly reflecting and
reinforcing an extensive range of the power relations permitted within society.
Land-based claims cover a broad spectrum, but the recognition of proprietary
control over land is liable to be curtailed at either end of that spectrum. Some
user-claims in respect of land simply lack gravamen: they do not exhibit a
sufficient quantum of 'property' in land to constitute a true proprietary right of
any kind.[1] Other claims of 'property' in land are subject to severe restriction in
the public interest. The exaggerated emphasis of former times upon property as
a monopolistic right of control and exploitation has long since been eroded by
extended conceptions of the public good.[2] Even maximal claims of property in
land are far from *absolute* entitlements of property. The purchase of a 'bundle
of rights' in land, it has been aptly said, 'necessarily includes the acquisition of
a bundle of limitations.'[3]

1   An example is provided by the entitlement conferred on the invitee by a casual party invitation
     [**para 2.51**].
2   'At one time private property owners exercised virtually unfettered control over property. As
     social standards changed, the law changed to recognise the primacy of certain public interests
     over the rights of private property owners' (*Green Party of New Jersey v Hartz Mountain
     Industries, Inc*, 752 A2d 315 at 322 (2000) per O'Hern J (Supreme Court of New Jersey)).
3   *Gazza v New York State Department of Environmental Conservation*, 679 NE2d 1035 at 1039
     (NY 1997). See also *Aston Cantlow and Wilmcote with Billesley PCC v Wallbank* [2003]
     UKHL 37, [2003] 3 WLR 283 at [72] per Lord Hope of Craighead ('The peaceful enjoyment
     of land involves the discharge of burdens which are attached to it as well as the enjoyment of
     its rights and privileges').

Impermissible arrogations of proprietary power

2.16   Some kinds of claim constitute excessive, and therefore impermissible,
arrogations of property in the resource of land.[1] The estate owner who bars the
way to those who would rescue the child from the mad axeman on his premises
is doubtless claiming a quantum of property in excess of our collective social
tolerances.[2] His assertion, in these circumstances, of an otherwise fairly standard exclusory privilege[3] takes him beyond the limits of the property which we
are nowadays prepared to recognise in any piece of realty.[4] Certain claims of
proprietary power are therefore disallowed simply because they involve a degree
of control over land which, if unchecked, would operate in an oppressive or
anti-social manner. In a further demonstration of this principle of constraint,
Parliament has legislated in favour of enhanced recreational access and greater
'social equity'[5] by limiting the powers of estate owners to exclude the general
public from substantial tracts of wild and scenic country.[6]

1   There are distinct limits, practical, moral and social, upon the amount of property which may be claimed (Gray, 'Equitable Property' (1994) 47(2) CLP 157 at 160).
2   See *McGowan v Chief Constable of Kingston upon Hull* [1967] Crim LR 34 at 35.
3   **[Para 4.33]**.
4   **[Para 4.34]**.
5   *Access to the Open Countryside in England and Wales* (DETR Consultation Paper, February 1998), para 3.67.
6   The Countryside and Rights of Way Act 2000 confers on members of the public a right to 'enter and remain ... for the purposes of open-air recreation' on 'access land' as statutorily defined (see CROWA 2000, s 2(1) **[para 5.47]**). There is also nowadays a large question whether landowners may properly exclude the individual citizen for no good reason from various sorts of socially valuable 'quasi-public' space which function as attractive venues for a range of recreational, educational and associational uses **[para 4.38]**.

Public interest controls on property in land

2.17   In these and many similar ways it is increasingly acknowledged that the quantum of property which any person may claim in land is limited by certain overriding rights and responsibilities.[1] Property in land is cut back both by human rights considerations[2] and by the impact of an extensive range of planning and environmental constraints which, on behalf of the community, regulate the development of the urban and rural landscape.[3] Even the maximal claim of property asserted by the fee simple owner is crucially bounded by a broader social interest. The estate owner cannot, for instance, demand as of right to build a skyscraper or a factory or a supermarket on 'his' suburban block of land. Proprietary rights are nowadays curtailed by proprietary duties – that is, by a whole series of social accommodations and compromises which operate mandatorily for the benefit of the community at large.[4]

1   See the seminal pronouncement of the Supreme Court of New Jersey in *State v Shack*, 277 A2d 369 at 372–373 (1971) that '[p]roperty rights serve human values. They are recognised to that end, and are limited by it ... [A]n owner must expect to find the absoluteness of his property rights curtailed by the organs of society, for the promotion of the best interests of others for whom these organs also operate as protective agencies.'
2   **[Paras 2.8, 4.55]**.
3   **[Paras 2.89, 13.10]**. See generally *Robins v Prune Yard Shopping Center*, 592 P2d 341 at 344 (1979).
4   This is a deeply European theme (see e g Art 14(2) of the German *Grundgesetz* **[para 2.92]**). See also *R (Reprotech (Pebsham) Ltd v East Sussex County Council* [2003] UKHL 8, [2003] 1 WLR 348 at [34] per Lord Hoffmann.

PROPERTY IS CAPABLE OF FRAGMENTATION AND DISTRIBUTION

2.18   It follows from the gradable quality of 'property' that, even in relation to the same parcel of land, the law often oversees the simultaneous distribution to a number of persons of distinct allocations of 'property', each of a different form of intensity. One person's claim of property in a particular parcel of land is wholly consistent with the acquisition or retention by *others* of different quantums of property in the same resource. Thus, on a relativist analysis of property, casual lay concepts of 'ownership' dissolve into differently constituted aggregations or bundles of power exercisable over land. Popular ascriptions of 'ownership' serve at best to indicate merely the current allocation of a predominating or strategic quantum of property in the resource in question.[1]

1   Gray, 'Equitable Property' (1994) 47(2) CLP 157 at 161.

Multiple claims of property in the same land

2.19   Consider, for a moment, a hypothetical block of land, Greenacre, the fee simple estate in which is owned by X.

Landlord-tenant relationship

2.20   X's claim to own a fee simple estate in Greenacre is perfectly compatible with Y's assertion of a term of years (or lease) in the same land (X is simply Y's landlord).[1] Both X and Y may correctly claim to have 'property' in Greenacre, albeit that the quantum of each property claim is different – X's is larger because unlimited by time – and even though their respective claims are mediated through the language of different estates in the land.

1   [**Para 7.68**].

Restrictive covenants

2.21   Suppose that one of X's neighbours, N, acquires from X the benefit of some restrictive undertaking respecting the user of Greenacre (eg an agreement that no building of more than one storey will be constructed there). An agreement of this kind confers on N a degree of control over the use and exploitation of Greenacre which, although markedly less extensive than the control implicit in ownership of (say) the fee simple estate, is nevertheless of some significance. For over 150 years English law has recognised that such adjustments of the balance of power in respect of land connote the allocation of a distinct quantum of 'property' to the beneficiary of the arrangement.[1] For this reason N is acknowledged to be the owner of an equitable proprietary interest in Greenacre – an entitlement which is known as a *restrictive covenant*.[2]

1   [**Para 9.151**]. See *Commonwealth of Australia v Western Australia* (1999) 196 CLR 392 at [281] per Callinan J ('To be able to prevent or restrict the usage of property in a certain way is just as much an incident of ownership as is an ability to use it without restriction'). See also *A-G v Blake* [2001] 1 AC 268 at 298E per Lord Hobhouse of Woodborough.
2   See *Tulk v Moxhay* (1848) 2 Ph 774, 41 ER 1143 [**paras 9.147, 13.108**].

Easements

2.22   If another neighbour, Q, simultaneously enjoys a right of way over Greenacre (eg shared use of a driveway or garden path), this entitlement denotes that a further sliver or quantum of property in Greenacre has been severed off and transferred to Q.[1] This particular marginal shift in the balance of control over Greenacre is described as the grant of an *easement*.[2]

1   See *Simpson v Fergus* (1999) 79 P & CR 398 at 401 per Robert Walker LJ; *Gallagher v Rainbow* (1994) 179 CLR 624 at 640 per McHugh J.
2   [**Paras 8.24, 9.87**].

Other proprietary claims

2.23   The taxonomy of claims affecting Greenacre is readily expandable: a bank may hold a legal charge (or mortgage) over Greenacre as security for a loan of money made to X,[1] whilst X's partner or ageing parent or business associate may have rights in respect of Greenacre which are based on co-ownership[2] or estoppel.[3] Likewise, the supplier of industrial plant to Greenacre may have a right of entry, entitling him (in the event of default) to come and remove machinery which has been hired for use in a factory sited on that land.[4] Alternatively a property developer may hold an option to purchase either the fee simple estate or a long lease in Greenacre, a right of option being considered in English law to confer a substantial form of 'property' in the subject land. Examples could proliferate.

1   [**Paras 8.232, 8.249**].
2   [**Paras 10.11, 11.1**].
3   [**Para 10.168**].
4   [**Paras 8.263, 8.265**].

Parasitic (or dependent) forms of property in land

2.24   It is already abundantly clear that Greenacre may be the subject of multiple, and wholly reconcilable, claims of property vested in a number of different persons. Each quantum of property is capable of independent alloca- tion, although in a narrow category of cases (e g the property comprised in the restrictive covenant or easement) the holding of 'property' in the subject land, Greenacre, is parasitic or dependent upon some larger form of 'property' in *other* land – let us say, Redacre – which receives the benefit of the arrangement. This means, in practice, that the benefit of restrictive covenants and easements over Greenacre must be 'annexed' or attached to an estate in fee simple or a term of years in Redacre[1] and that the person who seeks to enforce the restrictive covenant or easement against *Greenacre* must be the freeholder or leaseholder of *Redacre*. It also follows that the benefit of such a restrictive covenant or easement cannot be independently transferred to some third party, but only in conjunction with the disposition to that third party of an estate in Redacre.[2]

1   [**Paras 8.33, 9.164**].
2   [**Paras 8.52, 13.69**].

IRREDUCIBLE FEATURES OF PROPERTY

2.25 Although the definition of 'proprietary' entitlement comprises a notorious conundrum of the law, it becomes possible to isolate at least three key features which lie irreducibly at the core of property as a social and semantic phenomenon:
- immunity from summary cancellation or extinguishment
- presumptive entitlement to exclude others
- entitlement to prioritise resource values.

IMMUNITY FROM SUMMARY CANCELLATION OR EXTINGUISHMENT

2.26 As Morris Cohen once said, there are certain 'first or fundamental principles of the law which may be regarded as practically or *quasi a priori*.'[1] Amongst these 'axioms or fundamental assumptions' he included the postulate that 'property should be protected.' Firmly embedded in the very notion of *proprietary* entitlement is the idea that property is not arbitrarily terminable at the will of others.[2] Were it otherwise, the game which property lawyers play would disintegrate into some sort of lottery – the juristic equivalent of a game of musical chairs – in which claims to desired resources would be constantly liable to be swept aside by random, unilateral and unappealable fiat. By contrast, 'property' implies some element of indefeasibility or absence of term[3]; and property rights necessarily have the character of at least a qualified promise of secure or non-precarious enjoyment.[4] Revocable enjoyment and fragility of tenure are the antithesis of proprietary entitlement; and rights which are liable to summary, unconsented and uncompensated cancellation – whether by the state or by some other party[5] – cannot comprise 'property' in the generally accepted sense of the term.[6]

1 'The Place of Logic in the Law' 29 Harv L Rev 622 at 631 (1916).
2 'A core idea in the liberal concept of ownership is that the interest of an owner is terminable only by his own decision' (Andrew Reeve, *Property* (Macmillan 1986), p 163). See *R v Toohey; Ex parte Meneling Station Pty Ltd* (1982) 158 CLR 327 at 353 per Wilson J ('[i]rrevocability is an important feature of an estate or interest in land').
3 See eg *National Provincial Bank Ltd v Ainsworth* [1965] AC 1175 at 1247G–1248A per Lord Wilberforce. An estate or interest in land must be 'something much more substantial' than a 'relatively ephemeral' claim (*R v Toohey; Ex parte Meneling Station Pty Ltd* (1982) 158 CLR 327 at 345 per Murphy J).
4 See Lawrence C Becker, 'The Moral Basis of Property Rights', in J R Pennock and J W Chapman (ed), *Nomos XXII: Property* (New York 1980), p 213. See also A M Honoré, 'Ownership', in A G Guest (ed), *Oxford Essays in Jurisprudence* (Oxford UP 1961), pp 119–120.
5 See eg *Saeed v Plustrade Ltd* [2002] 2 P & CR 266 at [17]–[18], where the Chancery Division pointed out that a right extinguishable at will was incompatible with the status of a proprietary right (here an easement).
6 See eg *R v Toohey; Ex parte Meneling Station Pty Ltd* (1982) 158 CLR 327 at 342–343, 345, 353 (High Court of Australia).

Historic protection

2.27   The prohibition against the arbitrary deprivation of property 'expresses an essential idea which is both basic and virtually uniform in civilised legal systems.'[1] As Justice Kirby has emphasised in the High Court of Australia, this premise underlying property holdings is quite 'fundamental'.[2] The instinct against summary dispossession is at least as old as Magna Carta[3] and later animated the great 18th century declarations of social and civil liberties.[4] For Blackstone, writing in 1765, it was inconceivable, 'even for the general good of the whole community', that 'sacred and inviolable rights of private property' should be stripped away 'in an arbitrary manner.'[5] This principled approach to the institution of property has since found its way into a range of national[6] and international[7] prohibitions on the taking of property by the state except for justifiable public purposes and on payment of fair value.

1   *Newcrest Mining (WA) Ltd v Commonwealth of Australia* (1997) 190 CLR 513 at 659 per Kirby J.
2   *Malika Holdings Pty Ltd v Stretton* (2001) 178 ALR 218 at [121]. See also *Wilson v Anderson* (2002) 190 ALR 313 at [140] per Kirby J (referring to the 'basic human right ... to be immune from arbitrary dispossession of property').
3   Magna Carta 1215, Arts 39, 52 **[para 3.1]**. See also *Mabo v Queensland (No 1)* (1988) 166 CLR 186 at 226 per Deane J.
4   See e g Declaration of the Rights of Man and of the Citizen (1789), Art 17.
5   *Bl Comm*, Vol I, p 135.
6   The sentiment against capricious takings finds perhaps its most famous expression in the guarantee of the Fifth Amendment of the United States Constitution that '[n]o person shall be ... deprived of ... property, without due process of law; nor shall private property be taken for public use, without just compensation' **[para 13.174]**. Likewise section 51(xxxi) of the Constitution of the Commonwealth of Australia operates as a 'constitutional guarantee ... against acquisition without just terms' (*Commonwealth of Australia v State of Tasmania* (1983) 158 CLR 1 at 282 per Deane J). See Tom Allen, *The Right to Property in Commonwealth Constitutions* (Cambridge University Press 2000), pp 36–82.
7   See e g United Nations Universal Declaration of Human Rights (1948), Art 17(2).

2.28   In the common law tradition the bias against uncompensated expropriation came to have the status of a strong presumptive principle in the definition of both legislative[1] and prerogatival[2] powers. It has been readily accepted as a 'principle' of the unwritten constitution of the United Kingdom 'that no citizen is to be deprived of his land by any public authority against his will.'[3] Privately held land may be compulsorily taken by the state only if 'the public interest decisively so demands: and then only on the condition that proper compensation is paid.'[4] But when rights in or over land are eventually outweighed by a 'substantial public interest',[5] a consensus throughout the common law world holds that the economic impact of the dislocation of private interests must not be 'disproportionately concentrated on a few persons.'[6] On any taking of property from the citizen for the benefit of the wider community, as Lord Hoffmann emphasised in *Grape Bay Ltd v A-G of Bermuda*,[7] 'the loss should not fall upon the individual whose property has been taken but should be borne by the public as a whole.'[8] It would be wrong, in effect, that an individual citizen should be 'singled out to bear a burden which ought to be paid for by society as a whole.'[9]

1   *Western Counties Railway Co v Windsor and Annapolis Railway Co* (1882) 7 App Cas 178 at 188 per Lord Watson; *A-G v De Keyser's Royal Hotel Ltd* [1920] AC 508 at 542 per Lord Atkinson; *Belfast Corpn v O D Cars Ltd* [1960] AC 490 at 517–518 per Viscount Simonds, 523 per Lord Radcliffe; *A-G v Blake* [2001] 1 AC 268 at 289G per Lord Nicholls of Birkenhead. See also *The Queen v Tener* (1985) 17 DLR (4th) 1 at 8 per Estey J (Supreme Court of Canada); *Newcrest Mining (WA) Ltd v Commonwealth of Australia* (1997) 190 CLR 513 at 657–661 per Kirby J (High Court of Australia).
2   *Burmah Oil Co Ltd v Lord Advocate* [1965] AC 75 at 112–113 per Lord Reid, 162–163 per Lord Pearce, 169–170 per Lord Upjohn.
3   *Prest v Secretary of State for Wales* (1983) 81 LGR 193 at 198 per Lord Denning MR. See also *St Marylebone Property Co Ltd v Fairweather* [1963] AC 510 at 539 per Lord Radcliffe. It would be wrong to suppose that the United Kingdom has never had experience of a constitutionally entrenched prohibition of uncompensated appropriation (see Government of Ireland Act 1920, s 5(1); Gray, 'Land Law and Human Rights', in Louise Tee (ed), *Land Law: Issues, Debates, Policy* (Willan Publishing 2002), p 217).
4   *Prest v Secretary of State for Wales* (1983) 81 LGR 193 at 198. See likewise *Belfast Corpn v O D Cars Ltd* [1960] AC 490 at 517–518 per Viscount Simonds, 523 per Lord Radcliffe; *Westminster Bank Ltd v Minister of Housing and Local Government* [1971] AC 508 at 535B per Viscount Dilhorne.
5   *Chesterfield Properties plc v Secretary of State for the Environment* (1998) 76 P & CR 117 at 131 per Laws J.
6   *Penn Central Transportation Co v New York City*, 438 US 104 at 124, 57 L Ed 2d 631 at 648 (1978) per Justice Brennan.
7   [2000] 1 WLR 574 at 583D.
8   Lord Hoffmann's formulation closely followed the classic rationale of the 'Takings Clause' enshrined in the Fifth Amendment of the United States Constitution (see *Armstrong v United States*, 364 US 40 at 49, 4 L Ed 2d 1554 at 1561 (1960) per Justice Black).
9   *Florida Rock Industries, Inc v United States* (1999) 45 Fed Cl 21 at 23 per Smith CJ.

European protection against takings of property

2.29   The human right to protection from arbitrary dispossession is nowadays encapsulated in Protocol No 1, Article 1 of the European Convention on Human Rights.[1] This pivotal provision proclaims that

Every natural or legal person is entitled to the peaceful enjoyment of his possessions. No one shall be deprived of his possessions except in the public interest and subject to the conditions provided for by law and by the general principles of international law.

The preceding provisions shall not, however, in any way impair the right of a State to enforce such laws as it deems necessary to control the use of property in accordance with the general interest or to secure the payment of taxes or other contributions or penalties.[2]

1   See Human Rights Act 1998, s 1(1), Sch I, Part II. See also Constitution of the European Union, Part II (Charter of Fundamental Rights), Title II, Art II-17 (approved 18 June 2004).
2   It is a constant refrain of European Court jurisprudence that the overarching principle of 'peaceful enjoyment' of possessions colours the interpretation of the remaining rules in

Article 1 relating to 'deprivation' and 'control of use' (see *James v United Kingdom*, Series A No 98 (1986) at [37]; *Tre Traktörer Aktiebolag v Sweden*, Series A No 159 (1989) at [54]; *Allan Jacobsson v Sweden*, Series A No 163 (1989) at [53]; *Mellacher v Austria*, Series A No 169 (1989) at [42]; *Fredin v Sweden*, Series A No 192 (1991) at [41]; *Former King of Greece v Greece* (2001) 33 EHRR 516 at [50]; *Jahn and Others v Germany* [2004] ECHR 36 at [62]). See also *Aston Cantlow and Wilmcote with Billesley PCC v Wallbank* [2003] 3 WLR 283 at [67] per Lord Hope of Craighead.

2.30   Despite its slightly awkward reference to 'possessions',[1] Article 1 of Protocol No 1 has been broadly understood in human rights jurisprudence as 'in substance guaranteeing the right of property.'[2] Although this property guarantee is not absolute and permanent deprivations of property are sometimes justifiable,[3] Article 1 affords an important safeguard against the summary expropriation or extinguishment of rights.[4] Interference with property will breach the overarching promise of 'peaceful enjoyment' unless certain rigorous conditions are met.[5]

1   The term 'possessions' has been said to have an 'autonomous meaning which ... is independent from the formal classification in domestic law' (*Beyeler v Italy* (2001) 33 EHRR 1224 at [100]). The term may even include certain 'legitimate expectations' generated by the representations or dealings of a public body (see e g *Stretch v United Kingdom* (2004) 38 EHRR 196 at [35]–[36]; *Rowland v Environment Agency* [2003] EWCA Civ 1885 at [85], [92] per Peter Gibson LJ, [104] per May LJ) **[para 10.284]**.
2   *Marckx v Belgium*, Series A No 31 (1979) at [63]. See also *Sporrung and Lönnroth v Sweden*, Series A No 52 (1982) at [57]; *James v United Kingdom*, Series A No 98 (1986) at [37]; *Banér v Sweden* (1989) 60 DR 128 at 138.
3   See *R (Fuller) v Chief Constable of Dorset Police* [2003] QB 480 at [62].
4   See e g *Papachelas v Greece* (1999) 30 EHRR 923 (expropriation of land for road building); *Jahn and Others v Germany* [2004] ECHR 36 at [93] (compulsory reassignment of land redistributed under earlier land reform). See also *Wilson v First County Trust Ltd (No 2)* [2004] 1 AC 816 at [42] per Lord Nicholls of Birkenhead.
5   See Jean Howell, 'Land and Human Rights' [1999] Conv 287.

Requirement of 'legality'

2.31   The rule of law, being 'one of the fundamental principles of a democratic society', is inherent in all of the Articles of the European Convention.[1] It is, accordingly, a major premise of Article 1 of Protocol No 1 that state intervention be 'lawful',[2] a precept which excludes any provision that operates erratically, over-selectively or in a wholly arbitrary manner.[3] Interference with rights of property can be justified only in accordance with a law which satisfies criteria of 'accessibility, precision and foreseeability.'[4] It is of the essence of justice that laws should function at a certain level of generality,[5] with the consequence that any randomness of application undermines the 'legality' of the provisions concerned.[6] The excessively 'individualised' targeting of state action in respect of land begins to smack of a 'bill of attainder'[7] and, by denying equal protection under the law,[8] is also likely to breach the anti-discrimination provision contained in Article 14 of the Convention.[9]

1   *Jahn and Others v Germany* [2004] ECHR 36 at [71]. See likewise *Former King of Greece v Greece* (2001) 33 EHRR 21 at [79].

2   See *Banér v Sweden* (1989) 60 DR 128 at 141.
3   See the precisely similar analysis of ECHR Art 8 **[para 2.60]** in *Harrow London Borough Council v Qazi* [2004] 1 AC 983 at [120] per Lord Scott of Foscote.
4   *Jahn and Others v Germany* [2004] ECHR 36 at [73].
5   See *Bl Comm*, Vol I, p 44; *Buckley & Others* (*Sinn Féin*) *v A-G* [1950] IR 67 at 70 per Gavan Duffy P; *Liyanage v The Queen* [1967] 1 AC 259 at 291 per Lord Pearce. See also Lon L Fuller, *The Morality of Law* (Yale UP, New Haven and London 1964), pp 46–49 (referring to generality as an intrinsic component of the inner morality of law).
6   See *Hentrich v France*, Series A No 296-A (1994) at [42]; *Aston Cantlow and Wilmcote with Billesley PCC v Wallbank* [2002] Ch 51 at [44].
7   *An Blascaod Mór Teoranta v Commissioners of Public Works in Ireland* (Irish High Court, 27 February 1998), per Budd J (affd *An Blascaod Mór Teoranta v Minister for Arts* [2000] 1 ILRM 401 at 409).
8   See *Aston Cantlow and Wilmcote with Billesley PCC v Wallbank* [2002] Ch 51 at [45], [51]–[53] (later reversed by the House of Lords on substantially different grounds ([2003] 3 WLR 283)).
9   ECHR Art 14.

Requirement of 'public interest'

2.32   No deprivation of property can be justified in terms of Article 1 of Protocol No 1 unless it serves the 'public interest'.[1] The European Court of Human Rights has long recognised that, for current purposes, the identification of the 'public interest' commonly involves a complex consideration of political, economic and social issues and that national authorities must inevitably enjoy a wide 'margin of appreciation' in determining the content of the relevant 'public interest'.[2] It follows that the 'public interest' test under the Protocol is failed only if a national legislature's judgement as to 'public interest' is 'manifestly without reasonable foundation.'[3]

1   See *Aston Cantlow and Wilmcote with Billesley PCC v Wallbank* [2002] Ch 51 at [36]; [2003] 3 WLR 283 at [134] per Lord Scott of Foscote.
2   *James v United Kingdom*, Series A No 98 (1986) at [46]; *Former King of Greece v Greece* (2001) 33 EHRR 21 at [87]; *Aston Cantlow and Wilmcote with Billesley PCC v Wallbank* [2002] Ch 51 at [44]; *Sheffield CC v Smart* [2002] LGR 467 at [42] per Laws LJ. See also *Hatton v United Kingdom* (2003) 37 EHRR 611 at [97]–[101].
3   *Mellacher v Austria*, Series A No 169 (1989) at [45]; *Jahn and Others v Germany* [2004] ECHR 36 at [80]; *Connors v United Kingdom* (ECtHR decision, Application No 66746/01, 27 May 2004) at [82].

Requirement of 'fair balance'

2.33   In determining whether any particular state intervention in respect of land has violated the guarantee of 'peaceful enjoyment' of possessions, the European Court of Human Rights has consistently set itself the task of examining whether a 'fair balance' has been struck between 'the demands of the general interest of the community and the requirements of the protection of the individual's fundamental rights.'[1] The 'fair balance' test thus seeks to weigh the private interest of the affected citizen against the collective interest: the property guarantee is breached only where one landowner has been singled out to bear an 'individual and excessive burden' in relation to some community-directed obligation or sacrifice which should have been shared more broadly.[2]

1   *Sporrung and Lönnroth v Sweden*, Series A No 52 (1982) at [69]; *James v United Kingdom*, Series A No 98 (1986) at [50]; *Fredin v Sweden*, Series A No 192 (1991) at [51]; *Holy Monasteries v Greece*, Series A No 301 (1994) at [70]; *Air Canada v United Kingdom*, Series A No 316-A (1995) at [36]; *Matos e Silva, LDA and others v Portugal* (1997) 24 EHRR 573 at [106]; *Jahn and Others v Germany* [2004] ECHR 36 at [82]. See also *Former King of Greece v Greece* (2001) 33 EHRR 21 at [89].

2   *Sporrung and Lönnroth v Sweden*, Series A No 52 (1982) at [73]; *James v United Kingdom*, Series A No 98 (1986) at [50]; *Håkansson and Sturesson v Sweden*, Series A No 121 (1990) at [51]; *Aston Cantlow and Wilmcote with Billesley PCC v Wallbank* [2002] Ch 51 at [43].

2.34   The 'fair balance' test requires, in particular, that all instances of state interference with rights of property should display a 'reasonable relationship of proportionality between the means employed and the aim sought to be realised by any measure depriving a person of his possessions.'[1] In this context the European Court of Human Rights has indicated that the 'fair balance' test turns significantly on whether state-funded compensation is available for those affected by state-directed intervention. Failure to provide for compensation terms in expropriatory legislation points heavily towards the imposition of a disproportionate burden. Accordingly, there is universal agreement in European jurisprudence that the required 'fair balance' is almost inevitably lacking unless 'deprivations' of property (ie outright confiscations of title)[2] are accompanied by payment to the expropriated owner of an amount reasonably related to the value of the asset taken.[3] Uncompensated deprivation normally constitutes a 'disproportionate interference'; and, as the European Court recently confirmed in *Jahn and Others v Germany*,[4] a total lack of compensation can be justified under Article 1 of Protocol No 1 'only in exceptional circumstances.'

1   *Jahn and Others v Germany* [2004] ECHR 36 at [82]. See similarly *James v United Kingdom*, Series A No 98 (1986) at [50]; *Allan Jacobsson v Sweden*, Series A No 163 (1989) at [55]; *Banér v Sweden* (1989) 60 DR 128 at 141–142; *Mellacher v Austria*, Series A No 169 (1989) at [48], [57]; *Fredin v Sweden*, Series A No 192 (1991) at [51]. 'The means chosen to cure the social mischief must be appropriate and not disproportionate in its adverse impact' (*Wilson v First County Trust Ltd (No 2)* [2004] 1 AC 816 at [69] per Lord Nicholls of Birkenhead).

2   Contrast instances of mere 'control of use' of property (eg through the imposition of environmental or planning restrictions), which fall to be considered, not as a species of 'deprivation', but as a presumptively legitimate form of community-directed intervention which carries no 'inherent' right to compensation (see *Banér v Sweden* (1989) 60 DR 128 at 142 **[para 13.182]**). See generally Gray, 'Land Law and Human Rights', in Tee (ed), *Land Law: Issues and Debates* (Willan Publishing 2002), pp 227–228.

3   *James v United Kingdom*, Series A No 98 (1986) at [54]; *Lithgow v United Kingdom*, Series A, No 102 (1986) at [122]; *Banér v Sweden* (1989) 60 DR 128 at 142; *The Holy Monasteries v Greece*, Series A No 301 (1994) at [71]; *Former King of Greece v Greece* (2001) 33 EHRR 516 at [89].

4   [2004] ECHR 36 at [82], [93].

PRESUMPTIVE RIGHT TO EXCLUDE OTHERS

2.35   Another irreducible component of proprietary right is a general entitlement to exclude others from enjoyment of, or from interfering with one's own enjoyment of, a designated resource.[1] The 'propertiness' of property depends heavily on some concept of defensible monopoly[2]; and it is this notion of 'excludability' which gets us closest to the essence of proprietary institutions.[3] Property is constituted, at least in large part, by the facility of excluding the world from a particular resource[4] – is, indeed, characterised by the exercise of regulatory control over the access of strangers to the various benefits inherent in that resource.[5] Were things otherwise, the property game would dissolve into the chaos of the commons, in which all assets are constantly up for grabs and in which the process of trading with assets is neither meaningful nor necessary.[6] It is for reasons such as these, deeply rooted in the phenomenology of property, that the courts of the common law world have united behind iconic descriptions of the right to exclude strangers as a 'fundamental element of the property right'[7] and as 'one of the essential sticks in the bundle of property rights.'[8] Thus, in conventional analysis, proprietary entitlement has been widely understood as conferring a prerogative – however arbitrary, selective or capricious – to determine who may enjoy the resource of land and on what terms.[9] In one extreme – and almost certainly untenable – formulation, the proprietary owner may be said to have purchased (or otherwise acquired) the right to be utterly unreasonable in shutting his doors against all comers.[10]

1   On the 'logical primacy' of the right to exclude, see Thomas W Merrill, 'Property and the Right to Exclude' 77 Neb L Rev 730 at 740–745 (1998). See also David L Callies and J David Breemer, 'The Right to Exclude Others From Private Property: A Fundamental Constitutional Right' 3 Wash J of Law and Policy 39 (2000).

2   *Anchor Brewhouse Developments Ltd v Berkley House (Docklands Developments) Ltd* (1987) 38 BLR 82 at 96 per Scott J. See similarly *South Staffordshire Water Co v Sharman* [1896] 2 QB 44 at 46 per Lord Russell of Killowen CJ; *Entick v Carrington* (1765) 19 Howell's State Trials 1029 at 1066 per Lord Camden CJ [**para 4.2**].

3   Gray, 'Property in Thin Air' [1991] CLJ 252 at 268, 294–295. See also Felix S Cohen, 'Dialogue on Private Property' 9 Rutgers L Rev 357 at 373, 378 (1954–55).

4   For Blackstone the 'right of property' was 'that sole or despotic dominion which one man claims and exercises over the external things of the world, in total exclusion of the right of any other individual in the universe' (*Bl Comm*, Vol II, p 2).

5   See *Yanner v Eaton* (1999) 201 CLR 351 at [18] per Gleeson CJ, Gaudron, Kirby and Hayne JJ; *Commonwealth of Australia v Yarmirr* (2001) 208 CLR 1 at [13] per Gleeson CJ, Gaudron, Gummow and Hayne JJ, [286] per Kirby J; *Australian Capital Territory v Pinter* (Federal Court of Australia, A27 of 2001, 26 June 2002) at [241] per Finn J; *Western Australia v Ward* (2002) 191 ALR 1 at [88], [95] per Gleeson CJ, Gaudron, Gummow and Hayne JJ, [624] per Callinan J. In strict terms, the facility of control over access is an emanation of *possession* (see *Western Australia v Ward*, supra at [52]), but, at least historically, the notions of property and possession have been inseparably intertwined.

6   A world in which resources were not excludable, but were used by all comers at will and then abandoned – ready for the next user – at the terminus of such use, would simply comprise a regime in which private property no longer had any meaning (see Gray, [1991] CLJ 252 at 270–271).

7   *Kaiser Aetna v United States*, 444 US 164 at 179–180, 62 L Ed 2d 332 at 346 (1979) per Justice Rehnquist. See also *Loretto v Teleprompter Manhattan CATV Corp*, 458 US 419 at 435, 73 L Ed 2d 868 at 882 (1982) per Justice Marshall ('traditionally ... one of the most treasured strands in an owner's bundle of property rights').

8   *Prune Yard Shopping Center v Robins*, 447 US 74 at 82, 64 L Ed 2d 741 at 752 (1980) per Justice Rehnquist. See also *Colet v The Queen* (1981) 119 DLR (3d) 521 at 526 per Ritchie J; *Gerhardy v Brown* (1985) 159 CLR 70 at 150 per Deane J; *Newbury DC v Russell* (1997) 95 LGR 705 at 715 per Rattee J.

9   See Gray and Gray, 'Civil Rights, Civil Wrongs and Quasi-Public Space' (1999) 4 EHRLR 46 at 52–55 [**para 4.33**].

10   See e g *CIN Properties Ltd v Rawlins* [1995] 2 EGLR 130 [**para 4.56**].

RIGHT TO PRIORITISE RESOURCE VALUES

2.36   Not only does the notion of proprietary entitlement connote some basic exclusionary privilege exercisable against the rest of the world. The concept of property also implies, on behalf of the proprietor, a vital discretion over the priority to be accorded to the various forms of value inherent in a particular asset.[1] For the proprietor the resource of land holds not only a 'use value' (ie a privilege of non-exhaustive consumption); it also carries an 'exploitation value' (ie a privilege of exhaustive consumption) and a 'non-survival value' (ie a privilege of destruction[2]). Perhaps even more important, land offers the proprietor various forms of 'exchange value' (ie a privilege of lucrative disposal), 'endowment value' (ie a privilege of gift) and 'non-commodity value' (ie privileges of aesthetic or recreational or cultural appreciation). The owner is, by definition, entitled to prioritise the relevant values which the land holds for him, that is, to determine whether at any given moment to devote his interest in the land toward the objective of use, sale, endowment or recreational or cultural enjoyment, and so forth. It is this element of decisional control – of functional discretion – which helps to explicate the proprietary phenomenon and demarcate some of its essential features.[3] Indeed it is this plenitude of administrative authority in the governance of resources which goes far to distinguish proprietary entitlements from other species of right recognised by law.

1   See Gray, 'Equitable Property' (1994) 47(2) CLP 157 at 193, 199.
2   See e g *Phipps v Pears* [1965] 1 QB 76 at 83E–F per Lord Denning MR; *R v Denton* [1981] 1 WLR 1446 at 1148G, 1149C per Lord Lane CJ.
3   See *Western Australia v Ward* (2002) 191 ALR 1 at [52] per Gleeson CJ, Gaudron, Gummow and Hayne JJ (describing, as an essential indicium of possession, the right to 'make binding decisions about the use to which [land] is put'). See also *Rhone v Stephens* [1994] 2 AC 310 at 317D–E per Lord Templeman; *Hunter v Canary Wharf Ltd* [1997] AC 655 at 726D per Lord Hope of Craighead.

THE RATIONAL CO-ORDINATION OF PROPERTY IN LAND

2.37   In separating off land as a subject of especial legal concern, English law merely follows the practice of most developed systems in regarding land as having enhanced qualities of utility and indestructibility which justify its distinction from other, more perishable, forms of resource.[1] We have already seen how it is possible for a number of people to acquire different, but potentially compatible, rights in respect of the same land resource.[2] Somehow land law must co-ordinate the many property claims which proliferate around the modern freehold estate; and indeed the inter-relation of these multiple gradations of property comprises the stuff of much contemporary land law.

1   See *National Carriers Ltd v Panalpina (Northern) Ltd* [1981] AC 675 at 691A–B per Lord Hailsham of St Marylebone, 700B–E per Lord Russell of Killowen.

The versatility of land

2.38   In so far as land law governs the expectations and life-chances of an entire community, the orderly accommodation of competing claims of property in land assumes enormous importance. The complexity of land law is intensified by the fact that the physical asset of land can simultaneously support an almost infinite variety of purposeful modes of exploitation – social, recreational, residential, commercial, industrial and agricultural. There is, moreover, a significant social interest in enabling realty to be used as a means of sharing out wealth and of allocating other kinds of benefit or advantage incidental to land. It is, in many ways, vital that estate owners should be able to carve various forms of distributable benefit out of their land. The fragmentability of 'property' in land is as intrinsic to co-ownership of the family home as it is to the inter-generational transfer of wealth or the rational ordering of land use between neighbouring owners. The owner of a legal estate may wish to share the equitable ownership of the family home with her partner or their children. Equally it may make enormous sense for her to maximise the practical or environmental utility of the land by trading away to adjoining owners such rights as easements or restrictive covenants. The sheer multiplicity of uses sustained by a particular block of land need not, in itself, generate conflict. It is the task of the law of real property to organise a sensible structuring of all land-related claims, to regulate the allocation and transfer of such claims amongst a diverse range of potential resource users, and ultimately to determine questions of priority should conflict between these resource users prove inevitable.

The importance of commerciability

2.39   The difficulty of the task facing the land lawyer is greatly accentuated by the significance of land as a commerciable resource. A key premise of our regime of land law has long been the perception that a healthily functioning economy requires that land should remain permanently open to efficient processes of sale, lease, mortgage or other disposition.[1] It is important, so to speak, that land should be kept on the move.[2] One of the central truisms of market economics is the idea that the free alienability of property rights 'in practice make[s] it less likely that they will fall into disuse: market forces will tend to bring the rights into the ownership of those who will make best use of them.'[3] In particular, the borrowing of money secured by mortgages of land operates as an extremely powerful engine of wealth creation, housing provision, commercial investment and industrial expansion. Yet the existence of a marketplace for property rights is also, in its turn, vitally dependent on the formalisation of a limited range of standardised proprietary entitlements which are capable of serving as the subject matter of frequent low-cost exchange.[4]

1   '[E]xperience hath shewn, that property best answers the purposes of civil life, especially in commercial countries, when it's transfer and circulation are totally free and unrestrained' (*Bl Comm*, Vol II, p 288).

2   'In the case of real property ... it has been held contrary to public policy to restrict the free market' (*Linden Gardens Trust Ltd v Lenesta Sludge Disposals Ltd* [1994] 1 AC 85 at 107D per Lord Browne-Wilkinson).

3   *Bettison v Langton* [2000] Ch 54 at 71G–H per Robert Walker LJ. This thesis is closely associated with the influential Coase Theorem, which decrees that, if certain rigorous assumptions are met, initial assignments of property rights are ultimately irrelevant: the parties will simply exchange or modify these rights until they achieve the allocation of resources which maximises their joint welfare (see Ronald Coase, 'The Problem of Social Cost' 3 J Law & Econ 1 (1960)).

4   [**Paras 2.95–2.97**]. For a general thesis that civilised living in market economies is due not simply to greater prosperity, but rather to the order brought by a system of formalised property rights, see Hernando de Soto, *The Mystery of Capital: Why Capitalism Triumphs in the West and Fails Everywhere Else* (Bantam Press 2000). See also Land Registry, *Annual Report and Accounts 1996–97* (1997), p 54.

Bias towards alienability

2.40   English land law is accordingly pervaded by a strong bias in favour of alienability,[1] the common law long regarding commerciability as being of the essence of property.[2] In *National Provincial Bank Ltd v Ainsworth*,[3] Lord Upjohn observed that '[i]t has been the policy of the law for over a hundred years to simplify and facilitate transactions in real property.'[4] Lord Upjohn added, significantly, that it is 'of great importance that persons should be able freely and easily to raise money on the security of their property.' Indeed, a central feature of the English property legislation of 1925 was the desire to provide adequate conveyancing machinery for the sale of the great settled estates[5] and to assimilate all co-ownership of land within statutorily regulated 'trusts for sale'.[6] A key focus of the Land Registration Act 2002 is similarly placed upon the process and consequence of registered dispositions of estates in land.[7]

1   See Robert Walker LJ's reference in *Bettison v Langton* [2000] Ch 54 at 71H, to 'the law's general policy of favouring alienability over inalienability, where it can.'

2   See e g *Re Ridley* (1879) 11 Ch D 645 at 648–649 per Jessel MR; *Hall v Busst* (1960) 104 CLR 206 at 218 per Dixon CJ; *Clos Farming Estates Pty Ltd v Easton* (2001) 10 BPR 18845 at [15] per Bryson J.

3   [1965] AC 1175 at 1233G.

4   See also *State Bank of India v Sood* [1997] Ch 276 at 281F per Peter Gibson LJ.

5   Settled Land Act 1925. See now, however, TOLATA 1996, s 2(1) [**para 9.205**].

6   [**Para 11.124**]. The 'trust for sale' created a highly artificial trust form which incorporated a predisposition towards sale (see *Re Mayo* [1943] Ch 302 at 304; *Mortgage Corporation v Shaire* [2001] Ch 743 at 758H per Neuberger J). The 'trust for sale' has now been largely replaced by the 'trust of land' governed by the Trusts of Land and Appointment of Trustees Act 1996 [**para 9.240**].

7   LRA 2002, ss 28–29.

Tension with long-term security of entitlement

2.41   The powerful policy motivation in favour of free marketability inevitably throws up a huge tension between the commerciability of estates in land and the need to afford long-term security to a slather of rights which may have already been created in or over the land concerned. Free transferability of title seems incompatible with the durable creation of lesser entitlements in real property capable of surviving dispositions of the land. When the estate owner of Greenacre sells or mortgages his land to a stranger, what happens to the assortment of subsidiary rights which have already been generated in or over that land? What happens now to the rights of co-ownership or estoppel acquired by the estate owner's partner or parents, or to the term of years held by his tenant, or to the rights of way or restrictive covenants which have long been enjoyed by his neighbours? Are these various interests simply destroyed by the dealing with Greenacre or do they somehow survive the act of alienation? These were always questions to which the 1925 legislation (and its successor enactments) would have to provide a definitive and satisfactory response.

Wide definitions of the conveyancing process

2.42   Land is kept on the move by the processes of 'registered disposition' and 'conveyance', these terms generally referring to dealings with *registered* and *unregistered* estates respectively.[1] It is important, moreover, to note that English property legislation defines the terms 'registrable disposition'[2] and 'conveyance'[3] extremely broadly so as to include not merely the outright transfer of an estate in land, but also the creation of any legal charge or mortgage over such an estate, together with the grant of many kinds of leasehold term out of an estate.[4] A 'purchaser' is likewise defined as including 'a lessee, mortgagee or other person who for valuable consideration acquires an interest in land.'[5] In practice, the term 'disponee' – now a statutory term of art[6] – is accorded a similar ambit except in so far as a 'disponee' can also include a donee or a trustee in bankruptcy.

1   See also LPA 1925, s 205(1)(ii) (definition of 'disposition').
2   LRA 2002, ss 27(2), 132(1).
3   LPA 1925, s 205(1)(ii).
4   'Conveyance' also includes an 'assent, vesting declaration, vesting instrument, disclaimer, release and every other assurance of property or of an interest therein by any instrument, except a will' (LPA 1925, s 205(1)(ii)).
5   LPA 1925, s 205(1)(xxi).
6   See LRA 2002, ss 26(3), 52(2).

2.43   It is, in particular, the inclusion of mortgage transactions as a relevant form of disposition which dramatically intensifies the practical difficulty of co-ordinating a myriad of property claims in land. As Lord Diplock famously pointed out in *Pettitt v Pettitt*,[1] Britain has evolved into 'a property-owning, particularly a real-property-mortgaged-to-a-building-society-owning, democracy.' Any excessive disadvantage imposed by the rules of land law on institutional lenders such as banks and building societies has the potential to exert a damaging impact both on business life and on the living patterns of millions.[2]

1   [1970] AC 777 at 824C.
2   See, for instance, the widely expressed fear that an unsympathetic stance towards mortgage lenders may jeopardise an 'important public interest', namely that the substantial wealth tied up in land should not be rendered 'economically sterile' (*Barclays Bank Plc v O'Brien* [1994] 1 AC 180 at 188G–H per Lord Browne-Wilkinson). See similarly *Royal Bank of Scotland plc v Etridge (No 2)* [2002] 2 AC 773 at [35] per Lord Nicholls of Birkenhead; *Buhr v Barclays Bank plc* [2002] BPIR 25 at [55] per Arden LJ.

THE CENTRAL PROBLEM OF CONVEYANCING

2.44   Every working day in England and Wales sees the completion of over 18,000 transactions falling within the statutory concept of 'registered disposition' or 'conveyance'.[1] There is, quite simply, a lot of land on the move.[2] Land is constantly being sold, leased and mortgaged.[3] Given both the sheer volume of land transactions and the importance of the policy of commerciability, it is plain that the operation of an efficient conveyancing system calls imperatively for a high degree of clarity in determining the fate of any land-related claim following a disposition of the estate to which it relates.[4]

1   See Land Registry, *Annual Report and Accounts 2002–03* (HC891, July 2003), Appendix 2 (p 93).
2   It has been estimated, for example, that on average one in ten adults in Great Britain moves house in any one year (*Social Trends 29* (1999 edn London), p 171).
3   Land Registry claims to process approximately £1 million worth of property every minute, ie one property sale every nine seconds (Land Registry Press Notice LRP03/03, issued 4 February 2003).
4   See *Wik Peoples v Queensland* (1996) 187 CLR 1 at 221, where Kirby J opined that '[c]onformably with the legal rights of those involved, the avoidance of unnecessary doubt and confusion is a proper objective of land law.' See also *Tanwar Enterprises Pty Ltd v Cauchi* (2003) 201 ALR 359 at [83] per Kirby J.

The problem of durability

2.45   The central problem of conveyancing is therefore the question whether various subsidiary claims relating to land survive transactions with the major estates, thereby remaining valid and enforceable against the land in the hands of another (see *Fig.* 5). The twin objectives of commerciability of title and fragmentation of benefit are, in the first analysis, set against each other in irreconcilable opposition. The concern of the disponee to take title free of conflicting rights and burdens militates directly against the social and commercial purposes which commonly underlie the fragmentation of the benefits of realty.

2.46   The key dilemma of land law is how best to accommodate the effective protection of subsidiary rights of enjoyment within a scheme which places a

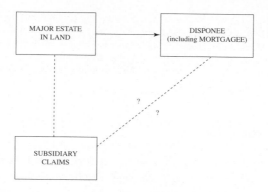

Fig. 5

heavy premium upon the unrestricted commerciability of land titles. The fate of these fragments of entitlement following a disposition of land is a matter of some significance for *both* the disponee of title *and* the claimant of the subsidiary rights in question. People tend, one way or another, to make the largest investment of their lifetime in realty.[1] It is, for them, a matter of substantial concern that rights for which they have given value should not be taken away, superseded or destroyed without proper compensation – a concern which usually applies just as much to the claimant of some subsidiary interest in the land as to the disponee of one of the major estates. Every purchaser of an estate in land (including a lender or 'chargee') has a legitimate interest in knowing precisely which rights will remain binding on him in the aftermath of the transaction. It is therefore important for all concerned that there be transparency and predictability in the outcome of dealings.

1   See *Newham London Borough Council v Khatun* [2004] EWCA Civ 55 at [77] per Laws LJ.

The value of certainty

2.47   The English law of real property accordingly confirms, in a mantra-like formula, that '[i]n matters relating to the title to land, certainty is of prime importance.'[1] To permit any uncertainty as to the impact of land transactions on various subsidiary claims is to place an intolerable burden on the process of land transfer and the long-term planning of land use. Uncertainty inhibits purchasers, destabilises expectations, and ultimately stultifies dealings in land.[2] No purchaser (again including, for this purpose, a mortgagee) will wish to risk his money if there is any danger that the land may be subject to adverse claims vested in others which prejudice the value of the estate: no one really wants to buy a law suit. It is equally the case that rational decision-making about land use becomes pointless if co-ordinated strategies (whether for sharing a home, taking a tenancy or obtaining a right of way) are liable to be swept aside or defeated by any subsequent dealing with the legal estate in the land concerned.

1   *Ashburn Anstalt v Arnold* [1989] Ch 1 at 26D per Fox LJ. See similarly *Bernstein of Leigh (Baron) v Skyviews & General Ltd* [1978] QB 479 at 486G–H; *Anchor Brewhouse Developments Ltd v Berkley House (Docklands Developments) Ltd* (1987) 38 BLR 82 at 94; *London &*

Blenheim Estates Ltd v Ladbroke Retail Parks Ltd [1994] 1 WLR 31 at 37F–G per Peter Gibson LJ; *Wibberley (Alan) Building Ltd v Insley* [1999] 1 WLR 894 at 895G per Lord Hoffmann; *Ferrishurst Ltd v Wallcite Ltd* [1999] Ch 355 at 370H per Robert Walker LJ; *Lloyd v Dugdale* [2002] 2 P & CR 167 at [52(5)] per Sir Christopher Slade.

2   See also Carol M Rose, 'Property and Expropriation: Themes and Variations in American Law' (2000) Utah L Rev 1 at 2.

The role of rationality

2.48   A large part of the narrative of modern English land law recounts the way in which stable and predictable legal mechanisms have been introduced to reconcile the durability of rights with the facility of commerce. There has always been an instinctive bias in favour of transactional certainty in the land market[1] and this perceived imperative has now acquired a heightened emphasis with the enactment of the Land Registration Act 2002. By various means this legislation infuses a new quality of rationality into dealings with land. Consistently with the preoccupations of a materialistic and increasingly affluent age, stability of title has become an ever more central focus of social (and therefore legal) concern. Security in the enjoyment of accumulated wealth has become essential to individualist visions of the good life. The 2002 Act accordingly oversees an intensified system of almost universal recordation of property rights in the Land Register, thereby sharpening up the effects of dealings between strangers and reducing potential threats to any title taken by a transferee or mortgagee. In the process the registered estate in English law has inevitably been nudged rather closer towards the civilian concept of *dominium*.[2]

1   See eg *Royal Bank of Scotland plc v Etridge (No 2)* [2002] 2 AC 773 at [2] per Lord Bingham of Cornhill.

2   See Gray and Gray, 'The rhetoric of realty', in J Getzler (ed), *Rationalizing Property, Equity and Trusts: Essays in Honour of Edward Burn* (Butterworths 2003), p 244.

PROPRIETARY AND NON-PROPRIETARY RIGHTS IN LAND

2.49   For the purpose of determining which kinds of entitlement survive a dealing and remain binding on a new estate owner or purchaser, English land law draws a conventional distinction between 'personal' and 'proprietary' rights in respect of land.

Differential effects

2.50   Only those rights which are classified as *proprietary* have the potential to bind a purchaser of the land; personal rights can never do so, although they may sometimes retain a limited enforceability (usually by way of a remedy in damages) against their grantor, the former owner of the estate now transferred. In effect, those claims or interests which appear low in the calibrated scale of 'property' value described earlier[1] will simply not make the grade. Even though they relate in some way to the land, they lack a sufficient intensity of 'property' content to merit general or long-term protection. Consequently they do not rank, in the relevant conveyancing sense, as *proprietary* rights in land and cannot survive dispositions of the estate to which they refer.

1   [Para 2.13].

2.51   A few practical examples may help to illustrate the way in which certain kinds of claim relating to land are recognised, almost intuitively, as having either proprietary or non-proprietary quality. For instance, the recipient of an invitation to a dinner party in someone's private home could never claim any legally significant quantum of 'property' in the location of the planned dinner party.[1] The entitlement of such an invitee to be present on the land is entirely personal in quality. His or her rights are merely those of a bare licensee[2] – the rights of one who has no 'stake' at all in the land.[3] A very different analysis applies, however, to the rights of someone whose entitlement takes the form of, say, a two-year lease or tenancy of a house on the land concerned. Here the rights of the occupier have recognisably crossed a vital threshold of proprietary character, thereby acquiring the potential to bind all comers.[4] Somewhere in between these examples fall the entitlements of such persons as the cinema-goer or the football fan or the closely regulated occupant of the student bed-sit. It is almost instinctively apparent that the rights of these persons somehow lack the critical mass required to qualify as claims of 'property' in land.[5] The cinema ticket confers no 'property' in the cinema.[6] As the Chief Justice of Australia once tersely remarked, '[f]ifty thousand people who pay to see a football match do not obtain fifty thousand interests in the football ground.'[7] These categories of claim, although perhaps more substantial than that of the dinner party invitee, amount to no more than instances of personal contractual licence as distinct from true proprietary right.

1   In the unlikely event that, say, the dinner party host abruptly sold his home during the week preceding the party, the invitee would have no rights which could conceivably survive the transfer of the land. The invitee could scarcely turn up at the premises on the appointed evening and demand to be entertained by the new estate owner. Moreover, since the invitee's licence was created gratuitously, the invitee would have no remedy even as against the original grantor.
2   [Para 4.6].
3   [Paras 2.80, 3.21].
4   If the land were suddenly sold, the sitting tenant would have a sufficient quantum of 'property' in the land to sustain his entitlement as against the new estate owner. The new owner would be required to suffer the tenant's continuing presence on the land for the remainder of the contracted period.
5   There has always been some uncertainty as to whether various kinds of long-term contractual licence – particularly those which most closely resemble the (indubitably proprietary) term of years – have themselves acquired a sufficient quantum of property to cross the borderline and assume the potential of binding impact upon purchasers of the relevant estate [**para 7.139**].
6   [Para 4.62].
7   *Cowell v Rosehill Racecourse Co Ltd* (1937) 56 CLR 605 at 616 per Latham CJ [**para 4.6**]. This non-proprietary analysis is liable to conflict with popular perceptions of the status of the season-ticket holder. See, for instance, *Duffy v Newcastle United Football Club Ltd* (Unreported, Court of Appeal, 29 June 2000), where irate bondholders, who thought that they had purchased a 10 year entitlement to a particular seat in the stadium, sued unsuccessfully to

enforce their supposed rights. Over 9,000 supporters had bought £500 bonds, many in response to statements that the designated seat could be passed on to their son or grandson, but the small print in the bond offer was held to reserve a right for the Football Club to move bondholders to less advantageous seats as part of an overall renovation scheme aimed at providing corporate hospitality suites.

The proprietary threshold

2.52   Binding impact on third parties is therefore made to depend upon a threshold criterion of proprietary quality. Somewhere across the spectrum of 'property' in land there comes a point at which certain rights gather sufficient gravamen to qualify, for conveyancing purposes, as *proprietary* rights in the land. It is even possible that, in large historic processes of evolutionary development, some kinds of claim affecting land can actually alter their status,[1] moving backwards or forwards across this threshold of proprietary character,[2] thereby losing[3] or gaining[4] that vital conventional attribute of potential third party impact. The most famous example of such movement, almost too familiar to attract attention, is the term of years,[5] which began as a personal contractual relationship only to evolve into one of the most significant proprietary estates in land.[6] Another example is provided by the restrictive covenant,[7] which 150 years ago shifted significantly across the spectrum of propertiness to assume a proprietary (as distinct from purely personal) dimension. A contemporary instance involves the licence supported by contract[8] or estoppel,[9] the suggestion emerging increasingly frequently (in both statute and judge-made law) that such entitlements have now acquired certain important proprietary characteristics.[10]

1   Property is not static, but dynamic. Property is not absolute but conditional (see Gray, 'Equitable Property' (1994) 47(2) CLP 157 at 160).
2   See eg *Western Australia v Ward* (2000) 170 ALR 159 at [109] per Beaumont and von Doussa JJ.
3   See eg *National Provincial Bank Ltd v Ainsworth* [1965] AC 1175 (deserted wife's 'equity' **[para 12.92]**).
4   For reference to the 'policy issues ... that arise whenever the courts are required to consider whether they should recognise (or create) novel proprietary interests', see *Wily v St George Partnership Banking Ltd* (1999) 161 ALR 1 at 3–4 per Sackville J.
5   **[Para 7.68]**.
6   See *Western Australia v Ward* (2000) 170 ALR 159 at [816] per North J.
7   **[Para 9.146]**.
8   **[Para 4.60]**.
9   **[Para 10.168]**.
10   **[Paras 4.95, 12.222]**.

Imperfect definitions

2.53   Nowhere, perhaps, is the imperfect logic of English land law more clearly apparent than in its attempt to demarcate proprietary rights in land from those rights which are non-proprietary (or merely personal). The outcome is a philosophical shambles, but English law has never been overly concerned with philosophical propriety. Although the way in which the law identifies the categories of proprietary right is deeply unsatisfactory, the difficulties (albeit irksome) should not be over-estimated.[1] Somehow English law blunders its way towards roughly the correct conclusions and there is usually little doubt, except perhaps at the perimeters of the field, as to whether a particular entitlement is or is not proprietary in the relevant conveyancing sense.

1   See Martin Dixon, 'Proprietary and non-proprietary rights in modern land law', in Louise Tee (ed), *Land Law: Issues, Debates, Policy* (Willan Publishing 2002), p 8.

The conventional understanding

2.54   Conventional wisdom dictates that, in order to enjoy a proprietary as distinct from merely personal character, rights in land must be capable of third party impact.[1] In other words, their benefit must be inherently transferable to strangers by way of onward sale or gift and their burden must also have the potential to bind new owners of the relevant estate in land. These twin indicia of assignability of benefit and enforceability of burden – of commerciability and durability – are deeply embedded in one of the classic statements of English property law. In *National Provincial Bank Ltd v Ainsworth*,[2] Lord Wilberforce declared that before a right or interest can be admitted into the 'category of property, or of a right affecting property', it must be 'definable, identifiable by third parties, capable in its nature of assumption by third parties, and have some degree of permanence or stability.' Personal rights in respect of land seldom enjoy any of these characteristics.[3]

1   See e g *Bruton v London & Quadrant Housing Trust* [1998] QB at 845E per Millett LJ; *Wily v St George Partnership Banking Ltd* (1999) 161 ALR 1 at 3 per Sackville J, 10 per Finkelstein J.
2   [1965] AC 1175 at 1247G–1248A. See likewise Russell LJ's reference in *National Provincial Bank Ltd v Hastings Car Mart Ltd* [1964] Ch 665 at 696, to 'rights in reference to land which have the quality of being capable of enduring through different ownerships of the land, according to normal conceptions of title to real property.'
3   Thus, for instance, the informal dinner party invitation – to an occasion of ill-defined content and uncertain duration – is neither transferable to others nor apt to endure through a change of ownership of the freehold estate in the land [**para 2.51**].

The vice of circuity

2.55   The difficulty with this orthodox understanding of proprietary quality is, of course, that it is riddled with circularity: the definition of proprietary character becomes entirely self-fulfilling.[1] If naively we ask which entitlements are 'proprietary', we are told that they are those rights which are assignable to and enforceable against third parties. When we then ask which rights these may be, we are told that they comprise, of course, the entitlements which are traditionally identified as 'proprietary'.[2] It is radical and obscurantist nonsense to formulate a test of proprietary quality in this way.[3] There is, moreover, an irreversible tautology in supposing that proprietary status emanates from some criterion of 'permanence' or 'stability'. Quite often, as for instance in *National Provincial Bank Ltd v Ainsworth*[4] itself, the reason for asking whether a particular claim is *proprietary* is precisely in order to determine whether the claim is capable of binding purchasers of the land, thereby attaining the relevantly critical qualities of permanence and stability. The question whether an interest is 'proprietary' (and therefore enforceable against third parties) cannot be sensibly addressed in terms of a definition which uses enforcement against third parties as a criterion of 'propertiness'. Durability of entitlement cannot be both the *cause* and the *effect* of proprietary quality.[5] The truth is that rights are not enforced against third parties because they are 'proprietary'; they are 'proprietary' precisely because they are enforced. It is the 'degree of protection afforded' which makes it appropriate to describe particular rights as 'property'.[6] Proprietary character is not 'the basis upon which that protection is given', but is simply a term descriptive of the 'effect of that protection.'[7]

1   This 'apparent circularity of reasoning ... may illustrate some of the limits to the use of "property" as an analytical tool' (*Yanner v Eaton* (1999) 201 CLR 351 at [17] per Gleeson CJ, Gaudron, Kirby and Hayne JJ). See also *Colbeam Palmer Ltd v Stock Affiliates Pty Ltd* (1968) 122 CLR 25 at 34 per Windeyer J; *Mills v Ruthol* (2002) 10 BPR 19381 at [124]–[125] per Palmer J.

2   Property is property because it is property: property status and proprietary consequence confuse each other in a deadening embrace of cause and effect (see Gray, 'Property in Thin Air' [1991] CLJ 252 at 293).

3   Lord Wilberforce's definition 'is too broad ... [and] does not suggest a mechanism by which a proprietary interest is to be distinguished from a personal right' (*Wily v St George Partnership Banking Ltd* (1999) 161 ALR 1 at 9 per Finkelstein J). See also *Mills v Ruthol* (2002) 10 BPR 19381 at [125] ('found wanting').

4   [1965] AC 1175 [**paras 2.54, 12.92**].

5   The problem is 'to isolate as the initiating factor the proprietary interest or the right to enforce the interest ... This problem is almost of jurisprudential mystery' (*Burns Philp Trustee Co Ltd v Viney* [1981] 2 NSWLR 216 at 223E per Kearney J).

6   *Smith Kline & French Laboratories (Australia) Ltd v Secretary, Department of Community Services and Health* (1990) 95 ALR 87 at 135 per Gummow J. This approach is consistent with the view, frequently expressed long ago in the High Court of Australia by Isaacs J, that equitable property is commensurate with equitable relief (see *Glenn v Federal Commissioner of Land Tax* (1915) 20 CLR 490 at 503; *Trustees, Executors and Agency Co Ltd v Acting Federal Commissioner of Taxation* (1917) 23 CLR 576 at 583; *Hoystead v Federal Commissioner of Taxation* (1920) 27 CLR 400 at 423). See also *Re Cunliffe-Owen* [1953] Ch 545 at 557 per Evershed MR; *Stern v McArthur* (1988) 165 CLR 489 at 522–523 per Deane and Dawson JJ.

7   *Yanner v Eaton* (1999) 201 CLR 351 at [85] per Gummow J. See also *Victoria Park Racing and Recreation Grounds Co Ltd v Taylor* (1937) 58 CLR 479 at 509 per Dixon J; *Moorgate Tobacco Co Ltd v Philip Morris Ltd (No 2)* (1984) 156 CLR 414 at 438 per Deane J; *Breen v Williams* (1996) 186 CLR 71 at 90 per Dawson and Toohey JJ.

Proprietary quality does not require transferability

2.56   A further difficulty with Lord Wilberforce's definition of proprietary quality in *National Provincial Bank Ltd v Ainsworth* is that it is now widely acknowledged that alienability or transferability is not an essential qualifying characteristic of a right of 'property'.[1] To be sure, transmissibility is often an important incident of proprietary entitlement, but it is far from being an indispensable or invariable index of proprietary character.[2] Indeed it was a stubborn adherence to the view that 'property ... generally implies ... the right to alienate'[3] which, for two centuries, prevented recognition of the proprietary nature of traditional or native land rights in many parts of the common law world.[4]

1   *Dorman v Rodgers* (1982) 148 CLR 365 at 374 per Murphy J; *R v Toohey; Ex parte Meneling Station Pty Ltd* (1982) 158 CLR 327 at 342–343 per Mason J; *Delgamuukw v British Columbia* (1997) 153 DLR (4th) 193 at [113] per Lamer CJC. See also *National Trustees Executors and Agency Co of Australasia Ltd v Federal Commissioner of Taxation* (1954) 91 CLR 540 at 583 per Kitto J; *Georgiadis v Australian and Overseas Telecommunications Corp* (1994) 179 CLR 297 at 311–312 per Brennan J; *Commonwealth of Australia v Western Australia* (1999) 196 CLR 392 at [282] per Callinan J.

2   Some well recognised rights of 'property' are clearly non-transferable (see *Dorman v Rodgers* (1982) 148 CLR 365 at 374 per Murphy J). For example, most entitlements to a pension are strictly non-assignable, yet undoubtedly comprise 'property' (*Ex parte Huggins. Re Huggins* (1882) 21 Ch D 85 at 91 per Jessel MR; *Hollinshead v Hazleton* [1916] 1 AC 428 at 447 per Lord Atkinson). See Gray, 'Property, Divorce and Retirement Pension Rights', in *Cambridge-Tilburg Law Lectures 1982* (Kluwer 1986), pp 41–51.

3   *Milirrpum v Nabalco Pty Ltd* (1971) 17 FLR 141 at 272–273 per Blackburn J.

4   It was only with the controversial decision in *Mabo v Queensland (No 2)* (1992) 175 CLR 1 that it was finally accepted that Australia's native peoples had not lost all 'proprietary interest' in their traditional homelands (see (1992) 175 CLR 1 at 40 per Brennan J). See also *Western Australia v Ward* (2000) 170 ALR 159 at [97] per Beaumont and von Doussa JJ.

The snare of market psychology

2.57   In present respects English property thinking has become locked into a preoccupation with commerciability which impedes deeper understanding of the third party impact of 'property'. At the core of the property lawyer's instincts is the crude belief that if something is property, one can buy and sell it in the market; if one can buy and sell it, it must be property.[1] Now, in order to be commerciable, rights must of course have a sufficient stability of definition to enable ready identification of the entitlement which is being traded. But in a lazy confusion of thought it has often been assumed that those *descriptive* qualities of certainty and stability (which serve most usefully to mark out the benefits to be traded to others) also operate as *prescriptive* hallmarks of the kinds of claim which, in the context of transfer, ought to bind third parties. Beguiled by the heavily formative pragmatics of the 19th century marketplace, the common lawyer started to believe that the only rights which could *burden* third parties were those rights sufficiently hard-edged to *benefit* third parties. In this way the judgment whether a particular claim is sufficiently identifiable to confer a commerciable benefit has also tended, rather irrationally, to predetermine the question of binding impact on strangers.

1   There are, here, hidden traces of the mindset which mistakenly reifies 'property' as a *thing* [**para 2.5**].

HUMAN PROPERTY RIGHTS

2.58   The fundamental, if philosophically inexact, distinction between proprietary and personal rights marks out the field of operation of the English law of
realty. Proprietary rights remain the authentic concern of the land lawyer since,
at least in conventional theory, only these rights can exert any enduring impact
on strangers. Personal rights in respect of land can, on this view, be safely left
to the contract lawyer, since most personal rights originate in contract and
generally sound only in money damages against the other contracting party.
Personal rights thus remain outside the realm of real property. It is now
beginning to emerge, however, that this relatively simple analysis takes no
account of the modern phenomenon of human rights jurisprudence. Almost by
accident the 'new landscape created by the Human Rights Act 1998'[1] threatens
to transcend the traditional divide between proprietary and personal rights. The
process has evoked a distinct measure of judicial apprehension lest orthodox
forms of proprietary entitlement be weakened or even obliterated from the 'new
landscape'.

1   See *Harrow London Borough Council v Qazi* [2004] 1 AC 983 at [27], [32] per Lord Steyn. See
also *Rowland v Environment Agency* [2003] EWCA Civ 1885 at [101] per May LJ (referring to
the Human Rights Act 1998 as a 'fundamental watershed in the development of both
substantive and procedural law').

Human rights as a bridge between personal and proprietary entitlement

2.59   The European Convention on Human Rights identifies a number of rights
and freedoms, both substantive and procedural, which are considered to be 'most
central to the enjoyment of human life in civil society.'[1] Domestic legislation must
now be read and given effect 'in a way which is compatible with Convention
rights'[2]; and it has become unlawful for any public authority to act 'in a way which
is incompatible with a Convention right.'[3] One of the Convention guarantees is
directly aimed at protecting the citizen from interference with 'the peaceful
enjoyment of his possessions'[4] and is therefore a provision of obvious relevance to
the delineation of proprietary entitlements. But other guarantees contained in the
European Convention, whilst appearing to have a purely personal significance,
can also be seen – in so far as they regulate what can and cannot be done with realty
– as creative of new forms of positive or negative proprietary right. As Justice
Stewart recognised long ago in the Supreme Court of the United States, 'the
dichotomy between personal liberties and property rights is a false one.'[5] A key
question under the Human Rights Act 1998 therefore concerns the degree to
which certain human rights now bridge the divide between the personal and the
proprietary. Has English land law, by incorporating the human rights standards
proclaimed by the European Convention, fashioned a novel category of hybrid
rights – 'human property rights' – which hover ambiguously somewhere between
the personal and the real?

1   *Harrow London Borough Council v Qazi* [2004] 1 AC 983 at [8] per Lord Bingham of Cornhill.

2   HRA 1998, s 3(1). This obligation may require the court to 'read in words which change the meaning of the enacted legislation, so as to make it Convention-compliant', provided that the imported meaning is not 'inconsistent with a fundamental feature' of the legislation (*Ghaidan v Godin-Mendoza* [2004] UKHL 30 at [32]–[33] per Lord Nicholls of Birkenhead).
3   HRA 1998, s 6(1). The 1998 Act 'does not create any new cause of action between private persons. But if there is a relevant cause of action applicable, the court as a public authority must act compatibly with both parties' Convention rights' (*Campbell v MGN Ltd* [2004] 2 WLR 1232 at [132] per Baroness Hale of Richmond).
4   ECHR Protocol No 1, Art 1 [**paras 2.29, 13.182**].
5   *Lynch v Household Finance Corp*, 405 US 538 at 552, 31 L Ed 2d 424 at 434–435 (1972).

Respect for private and family life and the home

2.60   The interaction between personal and proprietary entitlements is most controversially highlighted by Article 8 of the European Convention on Human Rights, which confirms that

(1)   Everyone has the right to respect for his private and family life, his home and his correspondence.

(2)   There shall be no interference by a public authority with the exercise of this right except such as is in accordance with the law and is necessary in a democratic society in the interests of national security, public safety or the economic well-being of the country, for the prevention of disorder or crime, for the protection of health or morals, or for the protection of the rights and freedoms of others.[1]

1   The progenitor of ECHR Art 8 is United Nations Universal Declaration of Human Rights (1948), Art 12. See also Constitution of the European Union, Part II (Charter of Fundamental Rights), Title II, Art II-7 (approved 18 June 2004).

A right to well-being

2.61   Article 8, although conferring no positive right to be provided with a home,[1] has nevertheless been understood to import a composite entitlement to what is now fashionably termed 'well-being'. Thus Article 8 proclaims a 'right to live one's personal life without unjustified interference',[2] a guarantee which serves to safeguard 'an important aspect of [one's] dignity as a human being.'[3] Article 8 similarly provides a measure of protection, not only for the citizen's right of continuing enjoyment of his residence, but also for his right to 'personal development' and the formation and furtherance of 'relationships with other human beings and the outside world.'[4] Article 8 has recently been described as underpinning rights of central importance to the individual's 'identity, self-determination, physical and moral integrity ... and a settled and secure place in the community.'[5] As the new European Constitution declares, '[h]uman dignity is inviolable.'[6]

1   *Chapman v United Kingdom* (2001) 33 EHRR 399 at [99]; *Harrow London Borough Council v Qazi* [2004] 1 AC 983 at [6] per Lord Bingham of Cornhill, [69] per Lord Hope of Craighead, [89], [100] per Lord Millett; *Anufrijeva v Southwark London Borough Council* [2004] 2 WLR 603 at [19] per Lord Woolf CJ; *Ghaidan v Godin-Mendoza* [2004] UKHL 30 at [6] per Lord Nicholls of Birkenhead, [135] per Baroness Hale of Richmond.

2   *Anufrijeva v Southwark London Borough Council* [2004] 2 WLR 603 at [10] per Lord Woolf CJ
     ('the right to one's personal integrity'). See also *Pretty v United Kingdom* (2002) 12 BHRC 149
     at [61] (European Court of Human Rights).
3   *Harrow London Borough Council v Qazi* [2004] 1 AC 983 at [89] per Lord Millett. See also
     Ghaidan v Godin-Mendoza [2004] UKHL 30 at [132] per Baroness Hale of Richmond. ECHR
     Art 8 thus embodies the European equivalent of the American 'right to be let alone' – an
     entitlement once described by Justice Brandeis as 'the most comprehensive of rights and the
     right most valued by civilized men' (*Olmstead v United States*, 277 US 438 at 478, 72 L Ed 944
     at 956 (1928)).
4   *Pretty v United Kingdom* (2002) 12 BHRC at [61]. See also *Marckx v Belgium*, Series A No 31
     (1979) at [31]. There is, accordingly, a 'zone of interaction of a person with others, even in a
     public context, which may fall within the scope of "private life" ' (*Peck v United Kingdom*
     (2003) 36 EHRR 719 at [57]).
5   *Connors v United Kingdom* (ECtHR decision, Application No 66746/01, 27 May 2004) at [82].
6   Constitution of the European Union, Part II (Charter of Fundamental Rights), Title I, Art
     II-1 (approved 18 June 2004). This provision reiterates verbatim Art 1(1) of the German
     Grundgesetz.

A 'new equity' in property relationships?

2.62   In the present context it becomes vital to ascertain whether the rights
incorporated in Article 8 – and particularly the requirement of 'respect' for
one's 'home'[1] – mean that the citizen has acquired some new form of proprietary protection which, subject only to issues of 'proportionality',[2] ranks
alongside and potentially overrides the proprietary rights of others. For
instance, can a residential occupier assert his Article 8 rights as a defence to a
possession claim brought against him by a bank which alleges that he has
defaulted on his mortgage repayments[3] or by a landlord who seeks to forfeit his
lease on grounds of breach of covenant[4]? The courts have broadly accepted
that the strict enforcement of the rights of a mortgagee or landlord under
municipal law may well result in a derogation from the respect to which the
home is prima facie entitled.[5] The critical question is, however, whether the
engagement of Article 8 confers on the court a new discretionary jurisdiction to
vary or moderate the application of the ordinary domestic laws regulating the
rights of the parties. Have the human rights recognised by Article 8 effectively
engrafted a 'new equity' on to the property relationships of citizens?

1   The term 'home' is an autonomous concept in Strasbourg jurisprudence (*Buckley v United
     Kingdom* (1997) 23 EHRR 101 at [63]; *Khatun v United Kingdom* (1998) 26 EHRR CD 212 at
     215). Whether a habitation comprises a 'home' does not depend on the resident being able to
     claim that he owns any proprietary interest in the premises (*Sheffield CC v Smart* [2002] LGR
     467 at [26] per Laws LJ; *Harrow London Borough Council v Qazi* [2004] 1 AC 983 at [97] per
     Lord Millett; [2002] HLR 276 at [26] per Arden LJ, [65] per Peter Gibson LJ) or even that his
     presence there is lawful (*Buckley*, supra at [63]; *Qazi*, supra at [11] per Lord Bingham of
     Cornhill). The test is essentially a factual test, ie whether the claimant of Art 8 rights can
     show sufficient and continuous links with the place (*Gillow v United Kingdom*, Series A No 109
     (1986) at [46]; *Qazi*, supra at [68] per Lord Hope of Craighead).
2   **[Para 2.34]**.
3   **[Para 15.147]**.
4   **[Para 14.115]**.
5   In particular, the removal of a residential occupier from his premises is bound to interfere with
     his enjoyment of the right to respect for his 'home' pursuant to Art 8(1) (see *Lambeth London*

Borough Council v Howard (2001) 33 HLR 636 at [30] per Sedley LJ; *Sheffield CC v Smart* [2002] LGR 467 at [26] per Laws LJ; *Harrow London Borough Council v Qazi* [2004] 1 AC 983 at [70], [78] per Lord Hope of Craighead).

Freedom of expression, assembly and association

2.63 Subject to limited exceptions in favour of the public interest, Articles 10 and 11 of the European Convention on Human Rights guarantee certain rights to freedom of speech, assembly and association.[1] A large question likewise opens up as to whether these freedoms indirectly alter the balance of existing proprietary rights in or over land, thereby creating new entitlements for the citizen, in appropriate circumstances, to enjoy unconsented access to the land of others for the purpose of exercising the guaranteed rights of expressional and associational freedom. It is salutary to remember that democracy remains a futile ideal without assured access to the space or terrain within which to exercise supposed democratic rights. Does the European Convention, in relevant respects, generate on behalf of the citizen what American jurists have called 'a kind of First-Amendment easement'[2] over the land of strangers?

1 **[Para 4.58]**. See also Constitution of the European Union, Part II (Charter of Fundamental Rights), Title II, Arts II-11, II-12 (approved 18 June 2004).
2 See Harry Kalven, 'The Concept of a Public Forum' 1965 Sup Ct Rev 1 at 13 **[para 5.3]**.

Environmental human rights

2.64 A further point of coalescence between personal and proprietary entitlement appears in the emerging concept of civic rights to environmental welfare.[1] A number of Convention rights have the potential to impose severe restrictions on various forms of land use which are inimical to the public interest. Thus, for example, the Convention guarantee that '[e]veryone's right to life shall be protected by law'[2] is beginning to be used in support of claims to be shielded from environmental dangers which pose a risk of injury to health.[3] Similarly the protection afforded to 'family life' and the 'home'[4] is increasingly employed, even in the absence of danger to health, to combat environmental pollution which 'may affect individuals' well-being and prevent them from enjoying their homes in such a way as to affect their private and family life adversely.'[5] By way of broader generalisation such developments have been said to demonstrate that a 'deterioration in the quality of life' can result in an infringement of Convention rights.[6] An inevitable effect of the European Convention has therefore been some redefinition of existing proprietary rights so as to accord with significant objectives of environmental policy. It is no accident that in *Hatton v United Kingdom*[7] the European Court of Human Rights recently coined the phrase 'environmental human rights', thereby positing, albeit in tentative terms, a new jurisprudential category of ecologically sensitive entitlements which straddle the boundary between personal and proprietary rights.[8]

1 See Gray, 'Equitable Property' (1994) 47(2) CLP 157 at 188–206; L Zarsky (ed), *Human Rights and the Environment: Conflicts and Norms in a Globalizing World* (Earthscan Publications 2002).

2   ECHR Art 2(1).
3   See e g *Guerra v Italy* (1998) 26 EHRR 357 at [45]–[52], [61]–[62] [**para 13.167**].
4   ECHR Art 8 [**para 2.60**].
5   See e g *Lopez Ostra v Spain* (1994) 20 EHRR 277 at [51] (emission of noise, fumes and smells from waste treatment plant). See also *Hatton v United Kingdom* (2003) 37 EHRR 611 at [96], [98], Dissenting Opinion at [2]–[4].
6   *Anufrijeva v Southwark London Borough Council* [2004] 2 WLR 603 at [19] per Lord Woolf CJ. This approach has resulted in the creation of a very basic platform of rights to residential amenity for the tenants of local authority housing (see e g *Lee v Leeds CC* [2002] 1 WLR 1488 at [48]–[49] per Chadwick LJ [**para 14.24**]).
7   (2003) 37 EHRR 611 at [122] and Dissenting Opinion at [1]–[2].
8   See M DeMerieux, 'Deriving Environmental Rights from the European Convention for the Protection of Human Rights and Fundamental Freedoms' (2001) 21 OJLS 521.

Right to a 'fair and public hearing'

2.65   The 'key procedural provision'[1] of the European Convention on Human Rights is the requirement that any determination of a person's civil rights and obligations be accompanied within a reasonable time by a 'fair and public hearing' conducted by an independent and impartial tribunal established by law.[2] This entitlement to due process and adjudication places a substantial question mark over a range of extra-curial mechanisms of recovery and relief which have been longstanding features of English land law. It becomes highly arguable that the procedural guarantee provided by the Convention has now imposed significant human rights limitations on a number of self-help remedies (such as the mortgagee's paramount right to possession[3] or the landlord's right of peaceable re-entry[4]) which have hitherto seemed natural incidents of proprietary ownership.

1   See *Harrow London Borough Council v Qazi* [2004] 1 AC 983 at [52] per Lord Hope of Craighead.
2   ECHR Art 6(1). See also Constitution of the European Union, Part II (Charter of Fundamental Rights), Title VI, Art II-47 (approved 18 June 2004).
3   [**Para 15.111**].
4   [**Para 14.123**].

A sharp division of judicial philosophy

2.66   One of the more intriguing questions of modern land law is whether (and if so, to what extent) the Human Rights Act 1998 has changed the nature of property in land. With the incorporation of a supra-national charter of rights it becomes immediately arguable that the European Convention 'constitutes a supplementation and development of the legal sources appropriate to the performance of the judicial function in addressing contemporary problems.'[1] On this view, the 1998 Act has altered the force field of proprietary rights under domestic law by creating new dimensions of property entitlement which draw their existence purely from the text of the Convention.[2] If this is true, the Convention has, in effect, generated novel forms of entitlement which modify or even override the proprietary rights and obligations of parties under pre-existing English law. On this analysis, all municipal law regulating propri-etary relationships now requires to pass through the prism of the European Convention, with the result that the enforcement of orthodox English law entitlements may be significantly deflected by the rights and freedoms enshrined within the Convention.

1   See *Commonwealth of Australia v Yarmirr* (2001) 208 CLR 1 at [318] per Kirby J (referring to the analogous impact on the common law of the infiltration of European Convention norms and the Australian recognition of native title).
2   This outcome accords with the long held view that the Convention is a living instrument (*Airey v Ireland*, Series A, No 32 (1979) at [26]) and that the jurisprudence of the Strasbourg organs is 'evolutive, that is it develops in accordance with the demands of changing social conditions' (*Qazi v Harrow London Borough Council* [2002] HLR 276 at [47] per Arden LJ).

A liberal view

2.67   Early indications emerging from the evolving jurisprudence of the Human Rights Act 1998 appeared to suggest that English courts were prepared to accord a fairly expansive scope to the provisions of the Act. It seemed that any enforcement of proprietary rights under domestic law which interfered with the 'peaceful enjoyment' of possessions or with 'family life' or the 'home' would henceforth require objective justification as both necessary and proportionate in relation to the overall social goals sought to be achieved.[1] Thus, for example, a court order endorsing an estate owner's strict legal right to recover possession from a home occupier could be made only after a curial investigation of the broader social merits and demerits of evicting the person concerned. Of course, the interposition of such judicial scrutiny might well result in a conclusion that the proposed interference with Convention entitlements was, on the particular facts, entirely justified and proportionate.[2] Nevertheless the superaddition of this merit-based form of inquiry appeared to equip the courts with an unprec-edented layer of discretionary control over the enforcement of rights even in those cases where, under domestic law apart from the Human Rights Act 1998, the estate owner enjoyed an automatic and absolute right to recover posses-sion.[3]

1   See *Aston Cantlow and Wilmcote with Billesley PCC v Wallbank* [2002] Ch 51 at [51].
2   See *Sheffield CC v Smart* [2002] LGR 467 at [28] per Laws LJ. In *Harrow London Borough Council v Qazi* [2004] 1 AC 983 at [25] even Lord Bingham of Cornhill (who was in the minority) thought it likely to be 'very highly exceptional' that, following such judicial scrutiny, a court would be justified in declining to make a possession order.
3   See *Harrow London Borough Council v Qazi* [2004] 1 AC 983 at [36] per Lord Hope of Craighead.

2.68   It was small wonder that, in *R (on application of Gangera) v Hounslow London Borough Council*,[1] Moses J expressed the fear that such an approach 'would fundamentally transform our law as to enforcement of property rights.'[2] It also became obvious that, if the courts had indeed acquired a discretion to refuse to enforce orthodox proprietary entitlements on grounds of supposed disproportionality, the overall effect was the creation, on behalf of home occupiers, of novel rights to security of tenure in derogation of the existing proprietary rights of others. As Mummery LJ saw clearly in the Court of Appeal in *Newham London Borough Council v Kibata*,[3] the Human Rights Act 1998 would, on this view, have brought about 'a new species of property right in a "home".' Yet, as Peter Gibson LJ opined in the Court of Appeal in *Qazi v Harrow London Borough Council*,[4] 'the fact that the Convention now confers new enforceable rights on persons in the United Kingdom' is simply 'a consequence of the Human Rights Act 1998.'

1   [2003] EWHC (Admin) 794 at [49] (cited with approval in *Harrow London Borough Council v Qazi* [2004] 1 AC 983 at [109] per Lord Millett).
2   See likewise *R (on application of Gangera) v Hounslow London Borough Council* [2003] EWHC (Admin) 794 at [49] per Moses J; *Hounslow London Borough Council v Adjei* [2004] EWHC 207 (Ch) at [35] per Pumfrey J.
3   [2003] 3 FCR 724 at [2].
4   [2002] HLR 276 at [66].

A conservative reaction

2.69   The liberal stance outlined above was destined to provoke a controversy in English law which has yet to reach any definitive resolution. In a series of recent developments the House of Lords has attempted to foreclose the argument that the Human Rights Act 1998 gives rise to parallel proprietary rights which, in given cases, can derogate from the proprietary entitlements recognised, apart from the Act, under domestic law. The first indication of this judicial backlash occurred in *Aston Cantlow and Wilmcote with Billesley PCC v Wallbank*.[1] Here the Court of Appeal had struck down, as non-compliant with Article 1 of Protocol No 1, a chancel repair liability[2] which had improperly 'singled out' certain persons, as the current proprietors of former rectorial glebe land associated with a parish church, for an archaic and 'arbitrary' form of local taxation.[3] The House of Lords unanimously reversed this ruling on a number of grounds, but one leading theme in the law lords' speeches was the contention that the Convention guarantee of 'peaceful enjoyment' of possessions could not be used to deflect the enforcement of a private law obligation created by the common law as an incident of ownership of particular land.[4] To hold that the Convention granted relief from liabilities voluntarily incurred in accordance with the civil law would be, said Lord Rodger of Earlsferry, 'a momentous step.'[5]

1   [2002] Ch 51 (CA); [2004] 1 AC 546 (HL).
2   This liability, usually of medieval origin, imposes burdens relating to probably one third of all parish churches in England and Wales (see *Property Law: Liability for Chancel Repairs* (Law Com No 152, November 1985), para 1.2) and can expose registered proprietors to an onerous and sometimes unexpected form of financial levy (see e g *Chivers & Sons Ltd v Air Ministry* [1955] Ch 585 at 594–595).
3   [2002] Ch 51 at [45]–[46], [51]–[53] (elderly couple confronted with liability of £96,000 (*Times*, 29 March 2000)). See *Elements of Land Law* (3rd edn, Butterworths, London 2001), p 974. The levy was also declared 'unjustifiably discriminatory' in terms of ECHR Art 14.
4   [2003] 3 WLR 283 at [72] per Lord Hope of Craighead, [91]–[92] per Lord Hobhouse of Woodborough, [134] per Lord Scott of Foscote (who regarded chancel repair liability as a public law obligation).

5   [2003] 3 WLR 283 at [142]. See also *Wilson v First County Trust Ltd (No 2)* [2004] 1 AC 816 at [108] per Lord Hope of Craighead.

The Qazi ruling

2.70   The same broad issue of principle arose in an even starker form in *Harrow London Borough Council v Qazi*.[1] Here HLBC, a local housing authority, claimed possession of a council house from Q, a former joint tenant whose tenancy had been terminated by his wife's unilateral notice to quit the premises.[2] Q was left with no legal or equitable right in the house under the municipal law of property, but nevertheless continued to live there together with his new partner. HLBC was unquestionably entitled to possession of the premises, but was precluded by a 'basic rule' of statute law[3] from taking possession without a court order. Q argued that the Human Rights Act 1998 had now interposed a requirement that any court hearing the possession claim against him must consider the proportionality of his eviction in the light of the Article 8 guarantee of 'respect' for his 'home'. On this basis, HLBC would have to demonstrate pursuant to Article 8(2) that a possession order against Q was necessary 'in the interests of national security, public safety or the economic well-being of the country, for the prevention of disorder or crime, for the protection of health or morals, or for the protection of the rights and freedoms of others.'

1   [2002] HLR 276 (CA); [2004] 1 AC 983 (HL). See M Davis and D Hughes, 'An End of the Affair – Social Housing, Relationship Breakdown, and the Human Rights Act 1998' [2004] Conv 19.
2   [**Para 7.298**].
3   Protection from Eviction Act 1977, s 3 [**para 14.109**]. See [2004] 1 AC 983 at [36] per Lord Hope of Craighead.

The majority approach in Qazi

2.71   By the barest of majorities, the House of Lords rejected Q's contention, holding the test of proportionality under Article 8(2) to be entirely irrelevant in the context of a claim by a party who, like HLBC, was already entitled under domestic law to an automatic possession order against a former tenant. There is, said Lord Millett 'nothing further to investigate' in terms of proportionality,[1] precisely because the court has, in these circumstances, no 'discretion to refuse an order for possession.'[2] As Lord Scott of Foscote emphasised, the Human Rights Act 1998 affords no authority for the idea that a landlord's proprietary entitlements 'under the ordinary law' can be deflected by some additional exercise of discretionary judgment based on 'the degree of impact on the tenant's home life of the eviction.'[3] To hold otherwise would be to 'engage in social engineering in the housing field'[4] and to effect a significant judicial 'amendment of the domestic social housing legislation.'[5] Article 8, declared the majority in the House of Lords, is concerned with the protection of privacy not property,[6] with the result that this Article can never be invoked to defeat contractual or proprietary rights to possession which, apart from the Convention, have already crystallised under municipal law.[7] Article 8 cannot be said to have 'conferred some countervailing property rights'[8] on otherwise disentitled persons or to have altered the balance of proprietary relations under ordinary domestic law. Any contrary construction, indicated Lord Scott in *Qazi*, would hold that Article 8 'can vest property rights in the tenant and diminish the landlord's contractual and property rights ... an effect that [Article 8] was never intended to have.'[9] The European Convention, on this view, imprints no 'new equity' upon the standard principles of English property law.

1   [2004] 1 AC 983 at [108]. No balancing exercise need be conducted 'where its outcome is a foregone conclusion' (at [103] per Lord Millett). See likewise Lord Hope of Craighead at [78].
2   [2004] 1 AC 983 at [85]. Any impropriety in the enforcement of strict legal entitlements would, of course, be challengeable in proceedings for judicial review ([2004] 1 AC 983 at [79] per Lord Hope of Craighead, [91], [109] per Lord Millett; *Wandsworth London Borough Council v Michalak* [2003] 1 WLR 617 at [78]; *Hounslow London Borough Council v Adjei* [2004] EWHC 207 (Ch) at [34]).
3   [2004] 1 AC 983 at [146].
4   [2004] 1 AC 983 at [123].
5   [2004] 1 AC 983 at [151] (see likewise at [125], [127]).
6   [2004] 1 AC 983 at [50]–[53], [82] per Lord Hope of Craighead, [89] per Lord Millett, [125] per Lord Scott of Foscote. See likewise *Marckx v Belgium*, Series A No 31 (1979) at [7] (Dissenting Opinion of Sir Gerald Fitzmaurice).
7   [2004] 1 AC 983 at [84] per Lord Hope of Craighead, [108]–[109] per Lord Millett, [125], [149], [151]–[152] per Lord Scott of Foscote. The majority's approach has since been faithfully followed in *Newham London Borough Council v Kibata* [2003] 3 FCR 724 at [25], [31], [39] per Mummery LJ, [52] per Holman J; *Royal Borough of Kensington v O'Sullivan* [2003] EWCA Civ 371 at [82]; *Birmingham CC v Bradney* [2003] EWCA Civ 1783 at [15].
8   [2004] 1 AC 983 at [127] per Lord Scott of Foscote.
9   [2004] 1 AC 983 at [125] (see likewise at [146]).

The minority approach in Qazi

2.72   In *Qazi* a majority in the House of Lords thus decided that the Article 8 guarantee of 'respect' for the citizen's 'home' does not 'vest in the home-occupier any contractual or proprietary right that he would not otherwise have.'[1] The majority took the view that the enforcement of legal and equitable proprietary rights as already established under municipal law does not necessitate any further scrutiny in terms of a supra-national charter of rights.[2] This stance was fiercely challenged by the minority in the Appellate Committee. In forceful dissenting speeches Lord Bingham of Cornhill and Lord Steyn maintained that the process of scrutiny against an overriding European standard – with its associated requirement of proportionality – was exactly what was mandated in the 'new landscape created by the Human Rights Act 1998.'[3] Lord Steyn condemned the majority ruling as 'contrary to a purposive interpretation of article 8' and as 'inconsistent with the general thrust of the decisions' of the European Court of Human Rights and the now defunct European Human Rights Commission.[4] For him, the majority's approach 'emptie[d] article 8(1) of any or virtually any meaningful content' and exhibited 'the basic fallacy ... that it allows domestic notions of title, legal and equitable rights, and interests, to colour the interpretation of article 8(1).'[5] Lord Steyn[6] joined with Lord Bingham[7] in applauding the much broader acceptance of evolving European jurisprudence evident in *Sheffield CC v Smart*[8] where, on behalf of a united Court of Appeal, Laws LJ had declared that to exclude domestic law procedures from judicial scrutiny for conformity with the European Convention would cause the Convention to be 'much more remotely engaged in the fabric of our domestic law' and, thereby, to fail to provide a process which is now 'demanded by the fullness of our municipal law of human rights.'

1   [2004] 1 AC 983 at [144] per Lord Scott of Foscote.
2   The court is not, in other words, obliged to consider in every case whether a possession order would be disproportionate (*R (on application of Gangera) v Hounslow London Borough Council* [2003] EWHC (Admin) 794 at [43]–[44] per Moses J). It has been said that entire statutory schemes could be 'undermined' if regard was required to be had, in particular cases, to the 'general or particular merits of possession being retaken' (*Wandsworth London Borough Council v Michalak* [2003] 1 WLR 617 at [78] per Mance LJ). See likewise *Sheffield CC v Smart* [2002] LGR 467 at [40] per Laws LJ; *Gangera*, supra at [45].
3   See *Harrow London Borough Council v Qazi* [2004] 1 AC 983 at [27], [32].
4   [2004] 1 AC 983 at [27]. The majority speeches in *Qazi* somewhat uncomfortably required that the conclusion of the European Human Rights Commission in *S v United Kingdom* (1986) 47 DR 274 be 're-worded' in support of the actual decision in *Qazi* (see [2004] 1 AC 983 at [97] per Lord Millett, [127], [134] per Lord Scott of Foscote).
5   It was noticeable in *Qazi* that Lord Scott of Foscote consistently addressed the central issue in terms of whether ECHR Art 8 had authorised an assault on, or diminution of, the proprietary or contractual rights of owners (see [2004] 1 AC 983 at [125], [128], [135]–[136], [139]–[141], [144]–[146], [151]). In response to this arguably prejudicial form of question it seemed instinctively correct to affirm that 'Article 8 does not attack the owner's legal right to possession' ([2004] 1 AC 983 at [137] per Lord Scott).
6   [2004] 1 AC 983 at [32].
7   [2004] 1 AC 983 at [23].
8   [2002] LGR 467 at [27].

The future?

2.73   The debate engendered by the House of Lords' decision in *Qazi*, which is as much about the proper role of the European Convention on Human Rights in English law as it is about the definition of proprietary rights, is bound to continue. The *Qazi* decision marks only an initial stage in the discourse. There are already indications of deep ideological resistance in the Court of Appeal to the strictures of the majority ruling in *Qazi*[1] and it remains to be seen whether that majority ruling can itself withstand further reference to the European Court of Human Rights at Strasbourg. Some immediate indication of the European Court's likely stance can be derived from its decision in *Connors v United Kingdom*,[2] a case which concerned the eviction of a gypsy applicant and his family following the due revocation of their licence to occupy a local authority-provided caravan site.[3]

1   See e g *Rowland v Environment Agency* [2003] EWCA Civ 1885 at [90]–[91] per Peter Gibson LJ (a member of the Court of Appeal in *Qazi* [2002] HLR 276, whose decision was overturned by the House of Lords).
2   Application No 66746/01 (27 May 2004).

3   There had been an uncontested allegation that the applicant's sons and their visitors were
     responsible for anti-social behaviour on the site (Transcript at [77]).

2.74   In *Connors* the European Court proved remarkably unmoved by the fact
that, having terminated the occupiers' licence and rendered the family trespassers, the local authority was clearly entitled under domestic law to summary
possession without any independent court review as to the reasonableness of or
justification for the eviction.[1] Instead the Court proceeded to examine, at
length, the question whether the family's eviction was a proportionate response,
under Article 8(2), to the need 'in a democratic society' to protect the rights of
other occupiers of the site and the rights of the local authority as owner and
manager of the site. The Court concluded that Article 8 *had* been violated
because the legal framework regulating the applicant's occupancy had failed to
ensure 'sufficient procedural protection of his rights.'[2] In particular, in sharp
contrast to the procedural protection enjoyed by other residents of publicly
provided accommodation (such as secure tenants of council housing),[3] the local
authority's supposed power of summary eviction 'without the burden of giving
reasons liable to be examined as to their merits by an independent tribunal' was
thought to serve no 'pressing social need' and to be disproportionate to the
legitimate aim being pursued.[4]

1   **[Para 4.20]**.
2   Transcript at [85], [95]. The decision-making process leading to the applicant's eviction had
     not been 'fair and such as to afford due respect to the interests safeguarded to the individual
     by Article 8' (Transcript at [82]).
3   Transcript at [73], [89].
4   Transcript at [94]–[95], [114] (damages of EUR 14,000 were awarded).

2.75   The approach adopted in *Connors* by the European Court of Human
Rights carries the strongest implication that *Qazi* was wrongly decided by the
majority of the House of Lords. The *Connors* decision also demonstrates the
difficulty inherent in any attempt to argue that Article 8 is concerned only with
privacy and not with property. The distinction between these notions is readily
blurred by the modern expansive interpretation of Article 8 as a guarantor of
personal autonomy, dignity and self-determination.[1] Such claims coalesce very
substantially with the sense of belonging, control and domain which characterises claims of 'property' in land,[2] a link which is explicitly embedded in much
European jurisprudence. Indeed, in some national jurisdictions the test of
eligibility for constitutional protection as 'property' has been said to turn
precisely on whether a claimed entitlement provides 'a secure area of freedom
where the [claimant] can take responsibility for control over his or her life.'[3]

1   **[Para 2.61]**.
2   **[Para 2.79]**.
3   89 BVerfGE 1 at 6 (1993) (*Besitzrecht des Mieters* Case) (German Constitutional Court). See
     likewise 24 BVerfGE 367 at 389, 400 (1968) (*Hamburg Flood Control* Case). See also A J van
     der Walt, 'Property Theory and the Transformation of Property Law', in E Cooke (ed),
     Modern Studies in Property Law: Vol 3: Property 2004 (forthcoming).

FLUCTUATING PERSPECTIVES ON PROPERTY IN LAND

2.76 Quite apart from the uncertainties generated by the Human Rights Act 1998, the conventional identifiers of 'property' in land have never proved particularly successful in isolating or distilling the essence of proprietary character.[1] Undoubtedly some of this imprecision flows from the circumstance that in English law the dominant models of 'property' in land fluctuate inconsistently between three rather different perspectives.[2] The common law world has never really resolved whether 'property' in land is to be conceived in terms of socially constituted fact, of abstractly defined entitlement or of some kind of stewardship of a community resource. Although these three perspectives sometimes interact and overlap, it remains ultimately unclear whether the substance of 'property' resides in the raw empirical data of human conduct or in artificially constructed claims of jural entitlement or in the socially directed control of land use.[3] Our idea of 'property' in land oscillates between the behavioural, the conceptual and the obligational, between competing models of property as a *fact*, property as a *right* and property as a *responsibility*.[4]

1   [Para **2.54**].
2   See Gray and Gray, 'The idea of property in land', in S Bright and J K Dewar (ed), *Law and Land: Themes and Perspectives* (Clarendon Press, Oxford, 1998), p 18.
3   See *Western Australia v Ward* (2000) 170 ALR 159 at [789]–[791] per North J.
4   Something of the tension between these various images of property in modern land law is already apparent in the way in which the protection of the European Convention on Human Rights focuses, sometimes controversially, on the organic connections surrounding the 'home' [para **2.61**] and on the socialised sense of community-oriented duty which is assumed to constrain the use of land [para **2.92**]. Meanwhile, by contrast, domestic property legislation such as the Land Registration Act 2002 firmly characterises property in land in terms of a series of tightly defined conceptual abstractions [para **2.107**].

PROPERTY AS SOCIALLY CONSTITUTED FACT

2.77 Much of the genius of the common law derives from a rough-and-ready grasp of the empirical realities of life. According to this perspective the identification of 'property' in land is an earthily pragmatic affair. There is a deeply anti-intellectual streak in the common law tradition which cares little for large abstract theories of ownership,[1] preferring to fasten instead upon the raw organic facts of human behaviour. Being heavily preoccupied with what happens on the ground, the crude empiricism of this outlook leaves the recognition of property to rest upon 'essentially intuitive perceptions of the degree to which a claimant successfully asserts de facto possessory control over land.'[2] On this view 'property' in land is more about *fact* than about *right*; it derives ultimately not from 'words upon parchment'[3] but from the elemental primacy of sustained possession.[4] 'Property' in land is thus measurable with reference to essentially behavioural data; it expresses a visceral insight into the current balance of power-relationships in respect of land.[5] The phenomenon of 'property' in land is simply a product of behavioural reality or socially constituted fact.[6] It is, indeed, at this point that it becomes most clearly apparent that effective possession comprises the basis of most claims of 'property' in land.[7]

1   See e g *Commissioner for Railways et al v Valuer-General* [1974] AC 328 at 351H–352A per Lord Wilberforce [**para 1.10**].
2   *Western Australia v Ward* (2000) 170 ALR 159 at [100] per Beaumont and von Doussa JJ, [790] per North J.
3   *Bl Comm*, Vol II, p 2.
4   In some deep sense the sustained exercise of exclusory power is perhaps all there really is to the grand claim of proprietary ownership (Gray, 'Property in Common Law Systems', in G E van Maanen and A J van der Walt (ed), *Property Law on the Threshold of the 21st Century* (MAKLU, Antwerp, 1996), p 265).
5   [**Para 2.5**].
6   On the constitutive effect of empirical fact, see Gray and Gray, 'The Idea of Property in Land', in S Bright and J K Dewar (ed), *Land Law: Themes and Perspectives* (Oxford UP 1998), pp 18–27. It is significant that perceptions of 'property' in land as resting on 'socially constituted fact' have recently played a vital role in Australia in securing the recognition of native land claims as a form of proprietary entitlement (see e g *Yanner v Eaton* (1999) 201 CLR 351 at [38] per Gleeson CJ, Gaudron, Kirby and Hayne JJ, [86] per Gummow J; *Western Australia v Ward* (2000) 170 ALR 159 at [99]–[111] per Beaumont and von Doussa JJ, [786]–[792] per North J, (2002) 191 ALR 1 at [580] per Kirby J; *Rubibi Community v Western Australia* (2001) 6 AILR 42 at [31]–[32]; *Members of the Yorta Yorta Aboriginal Community v Victoria* (2001) 180 ALR 655 at [39] per Black CJ; *Commonwealth of Australia v Yarmirr* (2001) 208 CLR 1 at [304] per Kirby J).
7   [**Para 3.13**].

The territorial imperative

2.78   If 'property' in land is no more and no less than a socially accepted *fait accompli*, the quantum of property which a person has in land is measured by his ability to vindicate his sovereign control over territorial space.[1] It is this pragmatic perception of property which underpins the historic proposition that possession (even if initially wrongful) is ultimately the root of all common law title.[2] It also links private law notions of property with international and constitutional law concepts of sovereignty.[3] Property 'consists primarily in control over access'[4] and describes 'a relationship between owner and object by reference to the power of the owner to deal with the object to the exclusion of all others, except a joint owner.'[5] On this basis 'property' is ultimately constituted by the social reality of excludability or defensibility – the degree to which the claimant is prepared to resist the incursion of others upon the land.[6]

1   'If we defend the title to our land ... we do it for reasons no different, no less innate, no less eradicable, than do lower animals. The dog barking at you from behind his master's fence acts for a motive indistinguishable from that of his master when the fence was built' (Robert Ardrey, *The Territorial Imperative* (Collins, London 1967), p 16). An 'owner' of land has, at common law, an 'unquestionable right to erect a boundary fence' upon his or her land (see *Lewis v Wakeling* (1923) 54 OLR 647 at 653 per Middleton J; *MacKenzie v Matthews* (2000) 180 DLR (4th) 674 at 681).
2   Adverse possession of land ripens eventually into unassailable estate ownership [**para 6.29**]. Likewise the law of finding is heavily determined by factors of effective possessory control of land [**para 1.94**]. The constitutive effect of empirical fact is also evident in the demarcation of

the borderline between the lease and the licence [**para 7.184**]. Examples could be multiplied (see Gray and Gray, 'The idea of property in land', in S Bright and J K Dewar (ed), op cit, pp 23–24).

3   [**Para 1.120**]. See *Wik Peoples v Queensland* (1996) 187 CLR 1 at 186 per Gummow J.
4   *Yanner v Eaton* (1999) 201 CLR 351 at [18] per Gleeson CJ, Gaudron, Kirby and Hayne JJ [**para 2.35**]. See e g *South Staffordshire Water Co v Sharman* [1896] 2 QB 44 at 46 per Lord Russell of Killowen CJ (freeholders 'have the right to forbid anybody coming on their land or in any way interfering with it'). See Gray, 'Property in Thin Air' [1991] CLJ 252 at 299.
5   *Yanner v Eaton* (1999) 201 CLR 351 at [49] per McHugh J.
6   [**Para 2.35**].

The propriety of property

2.79   Concealed within this view of territorial behaviour as constitutive of property is, inevitably, some 'primal perception of the *propriety* of one's nexus with land.'[1] To have 'property' in land is not merely to allege some casual physical affinity with a particular piece of land, but rather to stake out a claim to the legitimacy of one's personal space in this land.[2] It is to assert that the land is 'proper' to one; that one has 'some significant self-constituting, self-realising, self-identifying connection with the land; that the land is, in some measure, an embodiment of one's personality and autonomy.'[3] To claim 'property' in land is to arrogate at least a limited form of sovereignty over the land and to allege that the land provides for the claimant a significant source of psychological, cultural, religious or investment-backed security.[4] To have 'property' in land connotes, ultimately, a deeply instinctive self-affirming sense of belonging, control and domain.[5]

1   See *Western Australia v Ward* (2000) 170 ALR 159 at [101] per Beaumont and von Doussa JJ, [790] per North J.
2   This inner awareness of 'property' in land is essentially pre-legal in character. No matter how elusive and inexpressible the nature of the psychological link, its absence is recognisably familiar. The obverse of 'property' in land is found in the lurking unease experienced by the bare trespasser and in the diffidently self-conscious demeanour evinced by those who do not feel quite 'at home' in a stranger's territory (see e g *Caradon DC v Paton* (2000) *Times*, 17 May, where Latham LJ pointed out that a person who occupies a holiday cottage for a week or two is not 'at home'). In some degree the obverse of 'property' is disempowerment, disorientation and alienation – the uncomfortable realisation that one's presence on land is either improper or crucially dependent on the sufferance of another (see Gray and Gray, 'The Idea of Property in Land', in S Bright and J K Dewar (ed), op cit, p 20).
3   See *Western Australia v Ward* (2000) 170 ALR 159 at [101] per Beaumont and von Doussa JJ, [790] per North J.
4   So profound is this idea of spiritual connection with the land that, in the context of native title, it may be 'easier ...to say that the clan belongs to the land than that the land belongs to the clan' (*Milirrpum v Nabalco Pty Ltd* (1971) 17 FLR 141 at 270–271 per Blackburn J).
5   See e g Lorna Fox, 'The Meaning of Home: A Chimerical Concept or a Legal Challenge?' (2002) 29 J Law & Soc 580. Although property in land is not, of course, confined to residential premises, it was to this same idea of organic connection that Lord Millett alluded in *Uratemp Ventures Ltd v Collins* [2002] 1 AC 301 at [31], when he defined a 'dwelling' as the place where a person 'lives and to which he returns and which forms the centre of his existence.' See also *Harrow London Borough Council v Qazi* [2004] 1 AC 983 at [8] per Lord Bingham of Cornhill.

Stakeholder status

2.80   It is precisely this psycho-spatial understanding of property which helps to identify the two pre-eminent proprietary estates of modern law, the fee simple and the term of years.[1] The 'property' enjoyed by freeholder and leaseholder alike is indelibly associated with the claim to hold a 'stake' in the premises and to be able to call the land one's own.[2] This 'stake' in the land is sufficiently substantial to be both transferable to and defensible against strangers. The same could not be said, however, in respect of many other kinds of occupancy of land. It would generally be conceded, for example, that the occupant of the average student bed-sit lacks the overall territorial control, the general immunity from supervisory regulation and the ultimate self-assurance which together mark out significant claims of 'property' in land.[3] The student lodger is almost certainly no more than a mere contractual licensee[4]; his entitlement is personal rather than proprietary in quality. The lodger's rights afford him a money remedy against his licensor in the event of premature and wrongful termination of his occupancy, but comprise no 'property' in the land which could possibly affect a third party who purchased the land occupied.

1   See LPA 1925, s 1(1) [**paras 1.136, 1.141**].
2   [**Para 3.20**].
3   [**Paras 2.80, 3.21**].
4   See *R v Tao* [1977] QB 141 at 146F–G [**para 3.21**].

2.81   This classification of the student lodger's rights rests, admittedly, more upon intuitive perception than upon rational analysis, but it tends closely to mirror the balance of power inherent within the relationship in issue. Thus, for instance, the student lodger will feel instinctively (and quite regardless of any agreement entered into) that he is precluded from any unilateral transfer of his room to another person.[1] Likewise, in the event of unconsented entry by the licensor into the student lodger's premises, the latter is highly unlikely to respond by issuing a claim in the local county court for damages and an injunction to restrain further trespass. But it is entirely consistent with much of the common law tradition of realty that the raw data of possessory behaviour should be definitive of 'property' in land. The student lodger, by his supine acquiescence in someone else's overriding territorial control, merely demonstrates that he lacks any significant quantum of property in the land.

1   The average student will not assume that it is inherently permissible for him to rent his room out for a few weeks to another student or to an American tourist, even if to do so would enable him to repay his entire student loan.

PROPERTY AS CONCEPTUAL ENTITLEMENT

2.82   A rather different focus is provided by the perception that 'property' in land is not an emanation of socially constituted fact, but comprises 'various assortments of artificially defined jural right.'[1] In sharp contrast to the crudely empirical foundations of property as a fact, the vision of property as a right rests upon a complex calculus of carefully calibrated estates and interests in land, all underpinned by the political theory implicit in the doctrine of tenure.[2] All property relationships with land are, accordingly, analysed through the intermediacy of artificial conceptual abstractions.[3] No citizen can claim that he or she owns the physical *solum*, merely that he or she owns some composite jural right in or over that *solum*. One has 'property' in the form of an abstract right rather than 'property' in a physical thing.[4] Each right is itself a pre-packaged bundle of tightly defined entitlement, the precise content of the bundle depending on the right involved.[5] On this view the conceptual or cerebral aspect of 'property' in land takes over from the factual or pragmatic.

1   *Western Australia v Ward* (2000) 170 ALR 159 at [105] per Beaumont and von Doussa JJ, [791] per North J.
2   [**Para 1.142**]. See *Western Australia v Ward* (2000) 170 ALR 159 at [791] per North J.
3   In this sense, as Laskin J once said, 'all legal interests are incorporeal' (*Saskatchewan Minerals v Keyes* (1972) 23 DLR (3d) 573 at 586).
4   [**Para 1.135**].
5   'Property, in relation to land, is a bundle of rights exercisable with respect to the land' (*Minister of State for the Army v Dalziel* (1944) 68 CLR 261 at 285 per Rich J). See also *Western Australia v Ward* (2000) 170 ALR 159 at [97] per Beaumont and von Doussa JJ.

Sharply defined intellectual constructs

2.83   A concentration upon 'property' as an artificial jural abstraction imme-diately places a premium on the maintenance of strict definitional boundaries around the various intellectual constructs which form part of the overall scheme.[1] The intangible character of property entitlements dramatically inten-sifies the need for conceptual discreteness. On this more abstract analysis, 'property' in land is constituted by a limited number of cleanly hewn blocks of entitlement whose parameters require, at all times, careful delineation.[2] Each discrete block of entitlement – each estate or interest in land – must have a clear-cut or crystalline quality which admits of no doubt either as to the presence of 'property' or, just as important, as to its absence or infringement.[3] This formalisation of proprietary entitlement is an essential precondition of any successful market economy.[4] The rights which comprise 'property' must therefore have a hard-edged integrity conducive to the intellectual orderliness of the regime as a whole. 'Property' must come in neat conceptual compartments, immune from capricious tampering or even well-intentioned amplification.[5]

1   See Gray and Gray, 'The idea of property in land', in S Bright and J K Dewar (ed), op cit, pp 31–34.
2   The principle of the *numerus clausus* is discussed later [**para 2.95**].
3   See e g *Webb v Bird* (1861) 10 CB (NS) 268 at 282, 142 ER 455 at 460 per Erle CJ [**para 8.57**].
4   A good legal property system provides 'a way to represent reality that lets us transcend the limitations of our senses. Well-crafted property representations enable us to pinpoint the economic potential of resources so as to enhance what we can do with them' (Hernando de Soto, *The Mystery of Capital: Why Capitalism Triumphs in the West and Fails Everywhere Else* (Bantam Press 2000), p 200).
5   See e g *Keppell v Bailey* (1834) 2 My & K 517 at 535, 39 ER 1042 at 1049; *Ackroyd v Smith* (1850) 10 CB 164 (1850) 10 CB 164 at 188, 138 ER 68 [**paras 2.95, 8.6**].

2.84 This preoccupation with definitional clarity is a consistent theme of English land law, and has served to draw particularly rigid limits around the species of right which may properly be asserted as tenancies,[1] easements,[2] and restrictive covenants.[3] Definitional rigour has traditionally been rationalised as delimiting those rights which may impinge upon later purchasers of land,[4] thereby preventing the proliferation of undesirable long-term burdens or 'clogs upon title' which sterilise land and render it unmarketable.[5] In the common law there has always been a powerful 'presumption ... for freedom in the occupation and use' of land,[6] a social value which would be severely threatened in the absence of constraints upon the kinds of entitlement which are recognised as proprietary burdens.[7] For exactly similar reasons judicial vigilance has tended to stigmatise loose, over-broad, vague or ill-defined claims over land as failing to exhibit a sufficient quantum of 'property' to qualify for potentially perpetual enforcement against strangers.

1 [**Para 7.88**].
2 [**Para 8.24**].
3 [**Para 9.154**].
4 Victims of this filter process include many forms of mere licence and contract [**paras 4.6, 12.223**].
5 Whether this rationale holds good today can be debated [**para 13.24**].
6 *Hunter v Canary Wharf Ltd* [1997] AC 655 at 726D per Lord Hope of Craighead (see similarly Lord Hoffmann at 709G–H, 710G).
7 See *Clos Farming Estates Pty Ltd v Easton* (2001) 10 BPR 18845 at [15], [50] per Bryson J; [2002] NSWCA 389 at [28].

'Property' as a discrete block of tradeable entitlement

2.85 A concentration on 'property' as an artificial or intangible jural construct has, if anything, intensified the conventional common law criterion of transferability as the test of proprietary character.[1] A preoccupation with 'property' as discrete blocks of conceptual entitlement conduces to the mistaken theory that 'property' is inherently commerciable. Common lawyers, having once conceived of 'property' as artificially pre-packaged commodities of carefully defined right, found it easy to embrace the seductive fallacy that only those rights which could be bought and sold could ever constitute 'property'. The crisp definitional quality which facilitates the commercial trading of identifiable assets began – in an illusory relationship of cause and effect – to make alienability or transmissibility appear as an essential qualifying characteristic or hallmark of 'property' itself. This commercialist perspective on 'property' also tended to suggest, in a closely associated *non sequitur*, that in order to enjoy 'proprietary' as distinct from merely 'personal' quality rights must be capable not only of conferring benefits on third parties, but also of imposing enforceable burdens on other strangers.[2]

1 [**Para 2.54**].
2 [**Para 2.57**].

'Property' as an intangible construct displaces any large theory of ownership

2.86 It remains one of the ironies of English law that the characterisation of 'property' as composite bundles of variously aggregated abstract entitlement has tended to preclude the formulation of any comprehensive or holistic theory of *dominium* in the continental sense.[1] The tabulation of discrete, but interlocking, estates and interests in land has quietly submerged any call to develop a fuller theory of title. Whether this shortcoming can ultimately survive the integration of English law within the emerging common law of Europe must now rank as a matter of heightening speculation.

1   Civilian systems of property law acknowledge ownership as an absolute jural relationship between a person and a thing [**para 1.119**].

PROPERTY AS STEWARDSHIP OF A COMMUNITY RESOURCE

2.87 An alternative (and increasingly important) model of 'property' in land emerges from the view that 'property' is neither fact nor right, but rather a form of community-oriented *responsibility*.[1] In terms of this perspective, 'property' in land comprises some form of social stewardship of a valuable, but finite, resource. 'Property' simply comprises those privileges of use and enjoyment which the state chooses to dispense to individuals and corporate actors in the implementation of public or communal strategies of social and environmental design.

1   See Gray and Gray, 'The idea of property in land', in S Bright and J K Dewar (ed), op cit, pp 39–51.

Conceptual severance

2.88 The utilities implicit in any land resource are variegated. Land may be turned to advantage in many overlapping ways; it may generate utilities of occupancy, enjoyment, consumption, investment, exploitation, exchange, endowment, aesthetic appreciation, and so on. When viewed in terms of a model of stewardship, 'property' in land does not consist in composite bundles of rights variously associated with the conventional estates or interests in land. 'Property' consists, instead, in each isolable *stick* of utility within the abstract bundle of advantages which comprises any particular estate or interest at any particular time. By virtue of some 'conceptual severance'[1] each individuated element of utility within the bundle can itself be characterised as a species of 'property'. The allocation of 'property' in land, ie the precise combination of sticks of utility contained within the bundle, is strictly regulated by the state; and the mix or balance of utilities associated with any landholding is subjected, through state intervention, to an overarching criterion of publicly defined responsibility. On this analysis, 'property' in land comprises not so much a 'bundle of rights', but rather a form of delegated responsibility for land as a valuable community resource. It is, in reality, this model of property which most closely corresponds to the state-directed control of land use which dominates the law of real property today.

1   The phrase originates in M J Radin, 'The Liberal Conception of Property: Cross Currents in the Jurisprudence of Takings' 88 Col L Rev 1667 (1988).

'Property' is allocated by the state

2.89   A plethora of regulatory and environmental constraints, over matters ranging from urban planning to the conservation of natural resources, testifies to the constant engagement of the modern state in the control of land use for purposes of public amenity and welfare.[1] The role of government in the regulation of land use is now so pervasive that all 'property' in land may be said to result from the distribution – on a vast scale – of diverse patterns of state-approved usufruct (or user right), each heavily conditioned and delimited by the public interest. Estate ownership is stripped back to a bare residuum of socially permitted power over land resources, the precise content of each estate or interest in land being determined by the state-controlled addition or subtraction of isolated elements of 'property'. Thus, for instance, when the state through the appropriate planning agency authorises the homeowner to build a garage or to extend his dwelling-house, the grant of planning permission marks the concession to that homeowner of an increased degree of socially permitted control over the land.[2] Effectively, in such cases, the homeowner's bundle of rights is augmented by the conferment of an extra component of 'property'.[3] Conversely, when the state designates a dwelling-house as a listed building or as falling within a conservation area, thereby curtailing its possible use or development, the state is effectively withdrawing from the homeowner certain important kinds of 'property' in respect of that land.

1   [**Para 13.10**].
2   See eg *McDougall v Council of the Shire of Warringah* (Unreported, Court of Appeal of New South Wales, 14 May 1993) per Cripps JA ('It must be steadily borne in mind that a development consent or a building approval is neither a right nor a privilege. In each case the consent or approval is no more than a relaxation of a prohibition imposed [by statute]').
3   'Property' was earlier defined in terms of socially permitted degrees of control over land resources [**para 2.11**].

2.90   'Property' in land is accordingly dispensed in various combinations by the state, subject only to occasional alterations, under strictly regulated circumstances, achieved through the exercise of a delegated bargaining power conferred on private citizens.[1] Thus it is open to landowners, by means of private agreement, to rearrange the balance of utility between adjacent parcels of land.[2] Such marginal shifts of utility occur, for example, on the grant of a restrictive covenant[3] or an easement (eg a right of way)[4] to a neighbour, both kinds of grant comprising the conferment of a limited, but not insignificant, quantum of 'property' upon the grantee.[5] In such cases both parties can truthfully assert that each holds some form of 'property' in the burdened (or 'servient') land, albeit graded by differing degrees of intensity,[6] and that each is

therefore, in some sense, a stakeholder in a common strategy for the constructive co-ordination of the parties' respective user-preferences.[7]

1   See R A Epstein, 'Covenants and Constitutions' 73 Cornell L Rev 906 at 926 (1987–88).
      Privately bargained restrictive covenants often operate as a localised form of private legisla-
      tion, preserving various kinds of residential and environmental amenity for future generations
      of successive owners. Indeed the modern rejuvenation of the 'building scheme' or 'scheme of
      development' is explicitly premised on the recognition of an intention 'to lay down what has
      been referred to as a local law for the estate for the common benefit of all the several
      purchasers of it' (see *Re Dolphin's Conveyance* [1970] Ch 654 at 662A per Stamp J
      [**para 13.101**]).
2   It follows that when there is any addition to, or subtraction from, the bundle of utilities
      enjoyed by any person, it can be suggested that a movement or transaction of 'property' has
      occurred – a proposition not only of venerable authority in English law (see e g the effect
      achieved by the decision in *Tulk v Moxhay* (1848) 2 Ph 774, 41 ER 1143 [**paras 9.147, 13.108**]),
      but also of huge contemporary relevance to the jurisprudence of environmental regulation
      and just compensation [**para 13.172**].
3   [**Paras 2.21, 9.138**].
4   [**Paras 2.22, 8.24**].
5   [**Paras 8.8, 9.151**]. See e g *Collins v Castle* (1887) 36 Ch D 243 at 254–255, where Kekewich J
      described a restrictive covenant as 'a species of property'. For some the proprietary status of
      the restrictive covenant is reinforced by the fact that the covenantee (or his successor) can
      commonly command a cash premium or equivalent value for release of the covenant; and the
      Lands Tribunal has statutory power to order the payment of compensation on discharge or
      modification of a restriction (LPA 1925, s 84(1)(c)).
6   The freehold or leasehold owner of land burdened by an easement or restrictive covenant
      clearly retains 'property' in this land, albeit limited by some qualified power of user or veto
      vested in the grantee of the rights concerned. Likewise the grantee, by virtue of the utility
      assigned to him, enjoys a form of 'property' (ie a significant degree of control) in respect of
      the same land.
7   In facilitating the simultaneous exercise of compatible modes of land use, both easements and
      restrictive covenants avoid costly buy-outs of neighbouring land merely for the purpose of
      securing the optimal utilisation of one's own land [**paras 8.3, 9.139**].

2.91   Privately contracted arrangements concerned with land use have nowadays been reinforced, but not entirely superseded,[1] by the public or socialised
obligations imposed through planning and environmental legislation.[2] This
development merely underscores the fact that the modern state retains an
eminent domain or overriding 'property' in all land – perhaps the most
significant present-day emanation of the Crown's radical title[3] – the state thus
holding a dominating stake in the determination of land use priorities. It is
equally arguable that the existence today of a substantial regime of public
planning control enables all citizens, in some significant sense, to claim a certain
quantum of 'property' in everyone else's land.[4]

1   See Gray and Gray, 'The Future of Real Burdens in Scots Law' (1999) 3 Edinburgh Law
      Rev 229 at 232–235 [**para 13.20**].
2   See also Town and Country Planning Act 1990, s 106, which adapts the restrictive covenant, in
      the guise of a 'planning obligation', as a significant instrument of planning control.
3   [**Para 1.122**]. Eminent domain – the public power to requisition land – has been aptly
      described as 'the proprietary aspect of sovereignty' (*Minister of State for the Army v Dalziel*
      (1944) 68 CLR 261 at 284 per Rich J).
4   [**Para 13.155**]. For reference to 'a growing attitude that there exists an inherent public right in

property that transcends the technicalities of title', see D W Large, 'This Land is Whose Land? Changing Concepts of Land as Property' (1973) Wisconsin L Rev 1039 at 1074.

'Property' is a socially derived privilege of use

2.92   'Property' in land can therefore be conceptualised as those publicly endorsed forms of user which the state allows individuals to enjoy.[1] In terms of this analysis the concept of 'property' denotes no more than a temporarily licensed form of utility or user-privilege which can be extended, varied or withdrawn at the sole discretion of the state and on terms dictated by it. 'Property' is no more than a defeasible privilege for the citizen; and even some privately bargained reallocations of 'property' are subject to defeasance where they cease to serve the public interest.[2] 'Property' thus incorporates a concept not of *right* but of *restraint*, reflecting a state-regulated responsibility to contribute towards the optimal exploitation of all land resources for communal benefit. 'Property' no longer articulates the arrogance of entitlement, but expresses instead the commonality of obligation, 'property' consisting simply of allocations of land-based utility co-ordinated towards a defined common good.[3]

1   Property in land, whether defined empirically or abstractly, is thus vulnerable to the all-invasive effect of socially derived land use regulation. The squatter's title may, for instance, be founded on brute fact, but he takes subject to all existing restrictive covenants affecting the land (see *Re Nisbet and Potts' Contract* [1906] 1 Ch 386 at 402–404 [**para 3.26**]) and his user of the land is just as clearly qualified by current planning controls.
2   See e g LPA 1925, s 84(1) [**para 13.127**].
3   See e g Art 14(2) of the German *Grundgesetz*, which provides that '[p]roperty imposes duties. Its use should also serve the welfare of the community.'

'Property' is enjoyed on terms of a civic trust

2.93   If, in this way, all 'property' in land is held subject to a wide range of publicly conditioned constraints, it follows that the deep structure of 'property' is not absolute or oppositional in nature.[1] It is, instead, delimited by a pervasive sense of community-directed obligation and is rooted in a contextual network of mutual restraint and social accommodation.[2] One American commentator has spoken of 'a new property jurisprudence of human interdependence', in which property law is based 'as much on responsibilities as on rights, on human connectedness rather than on personal autonomy.'[3] So distant is this perception from the classic liberal image of 'property' as a self-interested claim of unfettered power that some have now begun to predict a wholesale reconstruction or reinterpretation of 'property' in terms of socially derived privileges of use. 'Property' becomes not a summation of individualised power over scarce resources, but an allocative mechanism for promoting the efficient or ecologically prudent utilisation of such resources.[4] So analysed, this community-oriented approach to 'property' in land plays a pivotal role in the advancement of environmental welfare.[5] 'Property' becomes a form of *stewardship*[6] and resonates with the obligations of a civic or environmental trust.[7] This philosophy of stewardship has been widely espoused in the United States[8] and a similar perspective on property is now beginning to attract adherents in Britain.[9] It is not insignificant, moreover, that the newly approved Constitution of the European Union declares that enjoyment of the entitlements proclaimed in its Charter of Fundamental Rights (including, of course, the right to own and use property) 'entails responsibilities and duties with regard to other persons, to the human community and to future generations.'[10]

1   The European Court of Justice has emphasised that the right to property is not 'an absolute prerogative in Community law' (*O'Dwyer v Council of the European Union* (Joined Cases T-466/93, T-473/93 and T-477/93) [1995] ECR II-2071 at 2109 [93]), and that the fundamental rights recognised by the Court 'are not absolute ... but must be considered in relation to their social function' (*Wachauf v Federal Republic of Germany* (Case 5/88) [1989] ECR 2609 at 2639 [18]). See also *R v Chief Constable, ex p International Trader's Ferry Ltd* [1998] QB 477 at 495G–496B.

2   Thus, for instance, in spearheading the abandonment of an age-old (and controversial) restriction on the natural right of support for land [**para 1.63**], the Court of Appeal of Singapore announced that, consistently with the realities of the modern urban context, the law 'must ... take root in the terra firma of the principles of reciprocity and mutual respect for each other's property' (*Xpress Print Pte Ltd v Monocrafts Pte Ltd* [2000] 3 SLR 545 at 561H per Yong Pung How CJ).

3   Eric T Freyfogle, 'Context and Accommodation in Modern Property Law' 41 Stan L Rev 1529 at 1530–1531 (1988–89) ('Autonomous, secure property rights have largely given way to use entitlements that are interconnected and relative ... Property use entitlements will be phrased in terms of responsibilities and accommodations rather than rights and autonomy ... A property entitlement will acquire its bounds from the particular context of its use, and the entitlement holder will face the obligation to accommodate the interests of those affected by his ... use'). See also Prakash Pillai, 'The Primacy of the Principle of Reciprocity in the Singapore Land Regime' (2001) 13 SAcLJ 198 at 211–212.

4   See e g *State v Shack*, 277 A2d 369 at 372 (1971), where the Supreme Court of New Jersey observed that the viewpoint that 'he who owns may do as he pleases with what he owns' had given way to a perception which 'hesitatingly embodies an ingredient of stewardship.'

5   It also places a sharp focus on whether the regulatory control of land use is a compensable deprivation of a form of 'property' inherent in land or is merely a non-compensable affirmation that the use in question never comprised 'property' in that land in the first place [**para 13.173**]. See e g *Lucas v South Carolina Coastal Council* (1992) 505 US 1003, 120 L Ed 2d 798 (US Supreme Court); *Newcrest Mining (WA) Ltd v Commonwealth of Australia* (1997) 190 CLR 513 (High Court of Australia).

6   Modern environmental law is founded on a 'principle of stewardship, under which ownership or possession of land is viewed as a trust, with attendant obligations to future generations as well as to the present' (Lynton K Caldwell, 'Rights of Ownership or Rights of Use? – The Need for a New Conceptual Basis for Land Use Policy' 15 William and Mary Law Rev 759 at 766 (1973–74)).

7   See Gray, 'Equitable Property' (1994) 47(2) CLP 157 at 188–206. For the idea that the public has 'property rights in the non-commodity values of natural resources', see A Rieser, 'Ecological Preservation as a Public Property Right: An Emerging Doctrine in Search of a Theory' 15 Harv Envtl L Rev 393 at 432 (1991). See also C D Stone, 'Should Trees have Standing? – Towards Legal Rights for Natural Objects' 45 S Cal L Rev 450 (1972); 'Should Trees have Standing? Revisited: How far will law and morals reach? A pluralist perspective' 59 S Cal L Rev 1, 2 (1985); *Sierra Club v Morton*, 405 US 727 at 743–744, 31 L Ed 2d 636 at 648–649 (1972) per Justice Douglas.

8   See V J Yannacone, 'Property And Stewardship – Private Property Plus Public Interest Equals Social Property' 23 S Dak L Rev 71 (1978); L K Caldwell, 'Land and the Law: Problems in

Legal Philosophy' (1986) U Ill L Rev 319 at 325; J P Karp, 'A Private Property Duty of Stewardship: Changing Our Land Ethic' 23 Envtl L 735 at 748 (1992–93).

9   See e g W N R Lucy and C Mitchell, 'Replacing Private Property: The Case for Stewardship' [1996] CLJ 566; D W McKenzie Skene, J Rowan-Robinson, R Paisley and D J Cusine, 'Stewardship: From Rhetoric to Reality' (1999) 3 Edinburgh L Rev 151.

10   Constitution of the European Union, Part II (Charter of Fundamental Rights), Preamble (approved 18 June 2004).

THE MODERN TAXONOMY OF PROPRIETARY ENTITLEMENTS IN LAND

2.94   In common with many other regimes of property, English law has traditionally placed stringent limits on the kinds of entitlement which are considered 'proprietary' and therefore within the scope of the axiomatic rules of land law.[1] As Lord Brougham LC observed in *Keppell v Bailey*,[2] 'great detriment would arise and much confusion of rights if parties were allowed to invent new modes of holding and enjoying real property.'[3]

1   See *Charles v Barzey* [2003] 1 WLR 437 at [11] per Lord Hoffmann ('attempts to create interests unknown to the law are ineffectual').
2   (1834) 2 My & K 517 at 536, 39 ER 1042 at 1049.
3   'What cannot be done is to create new kinds of interests in land' (*Clos Farming Estates Pty Ltd v Easton* (2001) 10 BPR 18845 at [40] per Bryson J). The *Clos Farming* case involved an illicit attempt to impose 'seigneurial rights' on a freehold estate so as to 'change the nature of freehold ownership ... and to create a substantially different kind of land title' (10 BPR 18845 at [50]).

The numerus clausus principle

2.95   It has long been accepted that the catalogue of proprietary entitlements in land comprises a closed list – a *numerus clausus* – of recognised estates and interests. In fact, these permissible forms of conceptual entitlement probably total fewer than a dozen,[1] and, unlike the position in contract, land law allows the citizen no freedom to customise new species of right.[2] Alien forms may not intrude into the world of land law. The inhabitants of this world are required to construct their proprietary relationships using only the conventional building blocks constituted by the known 'estates' and 'interests'.[3] As Lord Brougham LC emphasised in *Keppell v Bailey*,[4] 'it must not ... be supposed that incidents of a novel kind can be devised and attached to property at the fancy or caprice of any owner.'[5]

1   See Bernard Rudden, 'Economic Theory v Property Law: The *Numerus Clausus* Problem', in J Eekelaar and J S Bell (ed), *Oxford Essays in Jurisprudence* (*Third Series*) (Clarendon 1987), pp 241–242.
2   'A new species of incorporeal hereditament cannot be created at the will and pleasure of an individual owner of an estate; he must be content to take the estate and the right to dispose of it subject to the law settled by decisions, or controlled by act of parliament' (*Hill v Tupper* (1863) 2 H & C 121 at 127–128, 159 ER 51 at 53 per Pollock CB). See likewise *Clos Farming Estates Pty Ltd v Easton* (2001) 10 BPR 18845 at [29] per Bryson J; [2002] NSWCA 389 at [68] per Santow JA (claim to a '*sui generis*' interest in land must ... fail').
3   See e g Law of Property Act 1925, s 4(1), proviso, which declares that, save for instances of

express enactment, an equitable interest in land 'shall only be capable of being validly created in any case in which an equivalent equitable interest in property real or personal could have been validly created' before 1 January 1926.
4   (1834) 2 My & K 517 at 535, 39 ER 1042 at 1049.
5   The owner 'is confined within certain limits by the view which the law takes of the nature of property' ((1834) 2 My & K 517 at 537, 39 ER 1042 at 1050 per Lord Brougham LC). See also *Ackroyd v Smith* (1850) 10 CB 164 at 188, 138 ER 68 at 77–78 per Cresswell J.

The rationale of the numerus clausus

2.96   At the root of *numerus clausus* principle undoubtedly lies a protective concern for the schematic order of land law. Historically the restriction on the proliferation of proprietary rights in land has served both to reinforce certainty in matters of ownership and obligation[1] and also to prevent the cluttering of land with long-term burdens of an idiosyncratic or anti-social nature.[2] Accordingly English courts have denied that proprietary status can ever be attained by such protean phenomena as the contractual licence[3] or the *ius spatiandi* (ie the right to wander at large over another's land).[4] The canon of proprietary rights does not embrace potentially expansive claims to protection from environmental degradation.[5] Nor, as some Victorian home owners were keen to establish, is there any such 'right of property' as an entitlement to exclusive use of a name attached to a house or other land.[6] Again, in much more modern times, it is significant that the long awaited form of stratified ownership known as 'commonhold' is to be given effect, not through the medium of some novel estate in the land known as a 'commonhold' (as distinct from a freehold or leasehold), but rather as a sub-species of fee simple ownership itself (ie as ownership of a 'freehold estate in commonhold land').[7]

1   '[I]t would hardly be possible to know what rights the acquisition of any parcel conferred, or what obligations it imposed' (*Keppell v Bailey* (1834) 2 My & K 517 at 536, 39 ER 1042 at 1049 per Lord Brougham LC).
2   Unrestricted freedom for estate owners to invent proprietary rights would 'impress upon their lands and tenements a peculiar character, which should follow them into all hands, however remote' (*Keppell v Bailey* (1834) 2 My & K 517 at 536, 39 ER 1042 at 1049 per Lord Brougham LC). See also *Ackroyd v Smith* (1850) 10 CB 164 at 188, 138 ER 68 at 77–78 per Cresswell J.
3   **[Para 12.223]**.
4   **[Para 5.30]**. See *Re Ellenborough Park* [1956] Ch 131 at 176 per Evershed MR (an 'indefinite and unregulated privilege').
5   *Phipps v Pears* [1965] 1 QB 76 at 84D–E per Lord Denning MR (no right to protection from the weather). See also *Hunter v Canary Wharf Ltd* [1997] AC 655 at 726F–H per Lord Hope of Craighead.
6   *Day v Brownrigg* (1878) 10 Ch D 294 at 302 per Jessel MR.
7   Commonhold and Leasehold Reform Act 2002, ss 1(1)(a), 2(1) **[para 7.359]**.

The decline of the numerus clausus

2.97   The *numerus clausus* has recently been described as a 'deep design principle of the law that is rarely articulated explicitly', the limited menu of estates and interests in land helping to ensure that property comes 'in standardized packages that the layperson can understand at low cost.'[1] Thus, it is claimed, the maintenance of the *numerus clausus* facilitates commerce in realty by reducing the transaction costs otherwise incurred in the process of trading with unfamiliar, non-uniform or unorthodox bundles of entitlement.[2] While this explanation of the *numerus clausus* certainly holds good in relation to the pre-digital era, it is already becoming apparent that the modern drive towards comprehensive recordation of land rights in a publicly accessible register has dramatically reduced the need to constrict the menu of rights deemed capable of proprietary status. It is also increasingly the case that changing social and commercial realities throw up new challenges to traditional proprietary classifications.[3] Accordingly, the categories of proprietary entitlement are now beginning to loosen up.[4] The contractual licence has long made periodic bids for inclusion amongst the canon of proprietary rights[5] and must surely one day succeed. The inchoate equity founded on estoppel – sometimes known as the 'equitable licence' – already seems set to claim its place amongst the field of acknowledged proprietary entitlements.[6] Current debate even extends to the possible proprietary status of the 'carbon sequestration rights' which will underpin future regimes of domestic and international trading in greenhouse gas emission credits.[7] The *numerus clausus* of realty suddenly looks rather more shaky than before.

1   Thomas W Merrill and Henry E Smith, 'What Happened to Property in Law and Economics?' 111 Yale LJ 357 at 359 (2001).
2   See Thomas W Merrill and Henry E Smith, 'Optimal Standardization in the Law of Property: The Numerus Clausus Principle' 110 Yale LJ 1 at 24–38 (2000).
3   See e g *Scurry-Rainbow Oil Ltd v Galloway Estate* [1993] 4 WWR 454 at [36], where Hunt J disavowed 'too heavy a reliance upon traditional legal concepts, crafted for another time and other circumstances.' See also *Bank of Montreal v Dynex Petroleum Ltd* (1999) 182 DLR (4th) 640 at [56] (referring to the notion of 'closed categories of interests in land' as 'an overly restrictive view of the law'); *Bank of Montreal v Dynex Petroleum Ltd* (2002) 208 DLR (4th) 155 at [20]–[21] (Supreme Court of Canada).
4   See Gray and Gray, 'The rhetoric of realty', in J Getzler (ed), *Rationalizing Property, Equity and Trusts: Essays in Honour of Edward Burn* (Butterworths 2003), pp 221–223.
5   [**Para 12.225**].
6   See LRA 2002, s 116 [**para 12.235**].
7   See also Carol M Rose, 'The Several Futures of Property: Of Cyberspace and Folk Tales, Emission Trades and Ecosystems' 83 Minn L Rev 129 at 164 (1998–99).

2.98   It is nevertheless safe to say that the principal species of proprietary right with which this book will be concerned include the following:
–   the fee simple absolute in possession[1]
–   terms of years absolute[2]
–   mortgages[3]
–   easements[4]
–   restrictive covenants[5]
–   profits *à prendre*[6]
–   beneficial interests existing under a trust of land[7]
–   estate contracts (including options)[8]
–   unpaid vendors' liens[9]
–   purchasers' liens to secure deposit[10]

- rights of entry[11] and
- rentcharges.[12]

1   [Para 7.2].
2   [Para 7.68].
3   [Para 8.232].
4   [Para 8.24].
5   [Para 9.138].
6   [Para 8.17].
7   [Para 9.172].
8   [Para 9.23].
9   [Para 9.130].
10 [Para 9.134].
11 [Para 8.263].
12 [Para 8.225].

A 'BIRD'S EYE VIEW' OF LAND LAW

2.99   Much of the difficulty in understanding English land law is connected with the problem of overall structure and perspective. It is not always easy to see the regime of land law as an integrated whole and it may help, at this relatively early stage, to provide a 'bird's eye view' of the entirety (see *Fig.* 6), leaving the detail to be elaborated later. The remaining pages of this chapter therefore seek to outline the way in which proprietary rights in land are incorporated within the framework of the legislation of 1925–2002. It is important, moreover, to emphasise that the scheme of English land law, as laid out in this legislation, extends only to those rights which, in the conventional understanding, are *proprietary* in nature. In other words, only those rights which comprise a sufficient or 'threshold' degree of property content are included within the statutory scheme. Only such rights can ever affect third parties; all other entitlements in respect of land remain unclassified in the grand design of our land law, usually having a mere personal or contractual significance between grantor and grantee.[1]

1   [Para 2.50].

DISTINCTION BETWEEN REGISTERED AND UNREGISTERED TITLE

2.100   The most fundamental structural classification in English land law is the distinction between estates whose title has been registered (i e centrally recorded) at Land Registry and estates whose title has not yet been so registered.[1] This major dichotomy between the regimes of *registered* and *unregistered* title exerts a deep impact upon the systematic organisation of land interests and upon the way in which these interests are protected on the disposition of any estate in land. For the time being there are, in effect, 'two systems of land ownership in this country which rest upon wholly different foundations.'[2] Registered titles derive their force from the fact of public registration – the official recordation of proprietary estates at Land Registry – whereas unregistered titles rest upon the pragmatic fact of

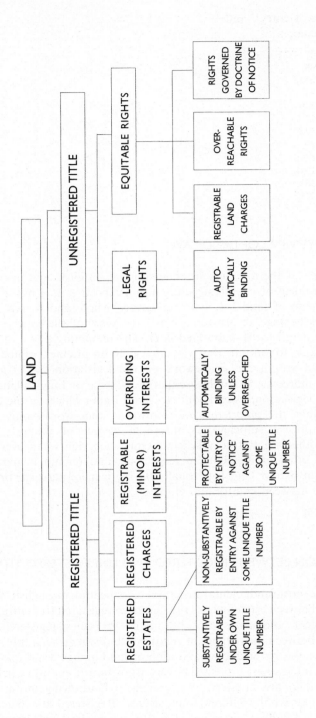

Fig. **6**

possession (as evidenced, usually, by the documentary history of recent transactions with the land concerned).[3] It is also possible that title to one form of estate in land (eg the fee simple estate) may be registered at Land Registry, whilst title to another estate in the same land (eg a short lease) remains unregistered. This merely makes the point that, although colloquial speech often distinguishes between registered and unregistered *land*, the strictly accurate contrast is between titles to estates which have been registered and those titles which have not.

1   A search of the Index Map at Land Registry (now in a vector polygon electronic format) indicates whether title to any estate in a particular parcel of land has been registered or whether there is currently any pending application for first registration (see LRR 2003, rr 10(1), 145).
2   Law Commission and Land Registry, *Land Registration for the Twenty-First Century* (Law Com No 254, September 1998), para 10.18.
3   [**Paras 2.112, 6.7**].

Origins of the two regimes

2.101   The present system of registration of title in England and Wales dates from the commencement of the Land Registration Act 2002[1] and is administered by Land Registry in conformity with the rules prescribed pursuant to this enactment.[2] This new and significantly rationalised legislative scheme replaces the Land Registration Acts 1925–1997[3] and marks an important advance towards the long-awaited goal of universal registration of electronically transactable titles in land. By contrast, the principles of unregistered land law have a somewhat older origin in the common law and currently lie scattered, in a less organised fashion, across the property legislation of 1925 and throughout its accompanying case law.

1   Most of this legislative scheme came into effect on 13 October 2003 (see Land Registration Act 2002 (Commencement No 4) Order 2003 (SI 2003/1725)).
2   See principally Land Registration Rules 2003 (SI 2003/1417).
3   The Land Registration Act 1925 always stood somewhat apart from the remainder of the 1925 legislation, both in style and (more obviously) in content. The registration statute of 1925 never enjoyed 'a good press' (*Central London Commercial Estates Ltd v Kato Kagaku Co Ltd* [1998] 4 All ER 948 at 953e per Sedley J), being commonly acknowledged to be 'legislation of extremely low quality' (see *Clark v Chief Land Registrar* [1994] Ch 370 at 385C–D per Nourse LJ). See similarly *Re White Rose Cottage* [1965] Ch 940 at 952B–E per Harman LJ; *Property Law: Fourth Report on Land Registration* (Law Com No 173, November 1988), para 2.1.

A future based on universal registration

2.102   During the latter years of the 20th century the heavily bureaucratised regime of registered title began rapidly to supersede unregistered title. It became clear that the future development of the law was likely to be based upon comprehensive registration of land titles and would eventually involve the introduction of a novel scheme of electronic conveyancing and 'paperless transactions'.[1] It was soon recognised that the system of unregistered title had

'had its day'[2] and would be phased out of existence within the foreseeable future. Today ever increasing numbers of unregistered estates have already been drawn on to the Land Register.[3] Registered title is incontestably the primary regime of modern land law and inevitably, therefore, we shall place it in the forefront of our analysis in this book.

1   See Land Registry, *Annual Report and Accounts 1999–2000* (HC661, July 2000), p 20 **[para 2.110]**.
2   Law Commission and Land Registry, *Land Registration for the Twenty-First Century: A Conveyancing Revolution* (Law Com No 271, July 2001), para 1.6.
3   **[Paras 7.38, 8.252]**.

THE BASIC STRUCTURE OF TITLE REGISTRATION

2.103   For well over a century the comprehensive registration of title to land has represented a fundamental aspiration of law reformers. In 1857 the Royal Commission on Land Transfer and Registration set itself the task of enabling owners 'to deal with land in as simple and easy a manner … as they can now deal with moveable chattels or stock.'[1] The achievement of this goal depended, in large measure, on the compilation of an accurate and definitive official record of the rights and obligations relating to all land in England and Wales. The law of conveyancing can serve the interests of the community only if it provides a secure, efficient and inexpensive mode of land transfer – an objective of extreme importance in a mobile and industrialised society.[2] Whilst the aims of the 1857 Royal Commission have never been fully realised, the Land Registration Act 2002 certainly provides a highly functional regime for the regulation of transactions with realty.

1   *Report of the Commissioners on the Registration of Title with reference to the Sale and Transfer of Land* (CP 2215, 1857 – Session 2), para XL.
2   It is one of the professed objectives of Land Registry to 'maintain and develop a stable and effective land registration system throughout England and Wales as the cornerstone for the creation and free movement of interests in land' (Land Registry, *Annual Report and Accounts 1999–2000* (2000), p 9).

Modern origins of title registration

2.104   The concept of formal registration of land titles was first adopted in the Torrens registration schemes introduced in Australia in the mid-19th century (and based on earlier Hanseatic systems of mercantile registration).[1] 'Torrens title' legislation has now spread across much of the common law world and is, in many ways, the inspirational force behind the registration scheme currently contained in the Land Registration Act 2002.[2]

1   The Torrens scheme was first adopted in the Real Property Act 1858 (South Australia). There is some controversy as to whether Sir Robert Torrens was the true author of the scheme that bears his name. Torrens was accused by even his contemporaries of some degree of plagiarism (see *Sackville and Neave's Property Law: Cases and Materials* (5th edn by M A Neave, C J Rossiter and M A Stone, Sydney 1994), paras 7.32–7.33). There is evidence to suggest that the

fundamental concept of the 'Torrens' scheme was formulated by Dr Ulrich Hübbe, a German lawyer living in South Australia in the 1850s, and was modelled largely on the Hanseatic system of title registration (see S Robinson, *Transfer of Land in Victoria* (Sydney, Melbourne, Brisbane, Perth 1979), pp 11–20).

2   In England a phase of experimentation over a period of two centuries with more limited schemes of deeds registration based in local registries in Middlesex and Yorkshire finally came to an end in 1974. Such schemes, albeit ultimately a failure, have been described as 'providing a vital intermediate step between a system of private conveyancing and a state system' (see Jean Howell, [1999] CLJ 366 at 397). Similar schemes have existed in other parts of the common law world (see e g Registration of Deeds Act 1897 (New South Wales), as amended by Conveyancing (Amendment) Act 1984 (New South Wales)).

The aim of title registration

2.105   The general aim of all registration schemes derived from the Torrens model is that the record of the Land Register should reflect, in a definitive form, the totality of estates, interests and charges affecting the land falling within its coverage.[1] The underlying philosophy is that, in relation to specified parcels of land, the administrative act of registration confers on each registered proprietor a legal title which, within the limits indicated by the register, is indefeasible.[2] This conclusive effect follows from the fact that all titles entered in the register are first examined, graded and guaranteed by the Chief Land Registrar and his staff. Any subsequent purchaser who, in good faith and for value, deals with the registered proprietor on the strength of his registered title likewise obtains 'an absolute and indefeasible title.'[3] In effect, registration dispenses with the need for any retrospective investigation of title behind or beyond the record of the register. As Lord Oliver of Aylmerton indicated in *Abbey National Building Society v Cann*,[4] the 'governing principle' of land registration is the idea that the title to land should 'be regulated by and ascertainable from the register alone.' The current aim of Land Registry is, accordingly, to 'provide ready access to up to date and guaranteed land information, so enabling confident dealings in property and security of title.'[5]

1   'Formal property records and titles ... represent our shared concept of what is economically meaningful about any asset. They capture and organise all the relevant information required to conceptualize the potential value of an asset and so allow us to control it' (Hernando de Soto, *The Mystery of Capital: Why Capitalism Triumphs in the West and Fails Everywhere Else* (Bantam Press 2000), p 39). The operation of the English Land Register is more fully described in Chapter 12 [**para 12.60**].

2   See *Racoon Ltd v Turnbull* [1997] AC 158 at 163C–D per Lord Jauncey of Tullichettle.

3   *British American Cattle Co v Caribe Farm Industries Ltd* [1998] 1 WLR 1529 at 1533E–F per Lord Browne-Wilkinson.

4   [1991] 1 AC 56 at 78C.

5   See Land Registry, *Annual Report and Accounts 2001–02* (HC1063, July 2002), p 9.

The organisation of registered entitlements

2.106   On first registration of a title at Land Registry most of the pertinent details of proprietary entitlement affecting the relevant parcel of land are recorded in an individual 'register of title' and the register so created is kept permanently updated thereafter. There is, moreover, a general requirement that subsequent dealings with any registered estate should be recorded in the register as a precondition of their effectiveness at law.[1]

1   [Paras 7.49, 7.244].

The key strategy of the Land Registration Act 2002

2.107   The linchpin of the Land Registration Act 2002 is the general idea that the most significant forms of 'estate' in any geographically defined parcel of land may, and often must, be recorded as an individual registered title in the Land Register under a uniquely assigned title number[1] – a process sometimes known as 'independent'[2] or 'substantive'[3] registration. Thus, for example, the fee simple estate in any particular plot of land and any leasehold estate carved out of it for a term of more than seven years can be recorded in the Land Register as an individual, numerically identified, registered title.[4] It is inherent in the statutory scheme that most other sorts of proprietary interest affecting either of these registered estates are then entered against the *burdened* title number (and often also entered against the title number of the estate *benefited*).[5] In this way each substantively registered title operates as a focal point for the recordation or protection of other rights and obligations. Each title number effectively identifies a *major* interest around which are clustered register entries relating to a range of *minor* interests.[6] The operative distinction is therefore between large forms of estate ownership (which are recorded substantively under unique title numbers) and all other kinds of interest in the land which enhance, diminish or qualify such ownership.

1   See LRR 2003, r 4(1).
2   See eg LRA 2002, Sch 2, para 6.
3   For use of the terminology of 'substantive registration', see *UCB Group Ltd v Hedworth* [2002] EWCA Civ 708 at [28] per Jonathan Parker LJ.
4   [Paras 7.38, 7.228].
5   [Para 2.151].
6   The terminology of 'major' and 'minor' interests does not appear in the Land Registration Act 2002, but this crude categorisation provided the means by which Viscount Dilhorne – not a trained exponent of land law principle – found it helpful to express the broad organisational strategy of registered land during argument before the House of Lords in *Williams & Glyn's Bank Ltd v Boland* [1981] AC 487. Contrast LRA 1925, ss 3(xv), 101–103 (referring explicitly to 'minor interests' in registered land).

The 'mirror' principle

2.108   Individual registers of title at Land Registry are publicly accessible sources of information relating to land, all such registers now existing in the form of digitally recorded data.[1] The information collated by the Chief Land Registrar at first registration[2] is held in one or other of the three subdivisions of each individually numbered register of title (ie the 'property register', the 'proprietorship register', and the 'charges register').[3] A register of title, once created, is updated not only on subsequent dealings with the title, but also in order to protect freshly arising minor interests relating to the land. Thus, in respect of any particular registered estate, the register of title is broadly intended to operate as a *mirror*, reflecting to potential purchasers (and to any other interested persons) the full range of the proprietary benefits and burdens which currently affect the land. The register provides, in effect, a fairly accurate snap-shot of title at any given moment. Any 'disponee'[4] of a registered estate is, of course, bound by the contents of the register[5] but the repetitive investigation of title which is characteristic of unregistered conveyancing[6] is rendered redundant. The definitive record of the register eliminates any need for retrospective documentary investigation outside that register.[7] The overall objective is that any prospective purchaser of registered land should always be able to verify, by simple examination of the register, the exact nature of all interests existing in or over the land which he or she proposes to buy.[8]

1   Contrary to popular supposition, the Land Register is not some vast Domesday Book, but exclusively takes the form of electronic databases maintained by Land Registry.
2   **[Para 12.266]**.
3   LRR 2003, rr 4–9 **[para 6.15]**.
4   The term 'disponee' covers not only the transferee and chargee of a registered estate, but also the grantee of any term of years or any easement or profit *à prendre* carved out of a registered title **[para 7.50]**. See the similarly extensive reference to 'registrable dispositions' in LRA 2002, s 27(1)–(3).
5   LRA 2002, s 29(1)–(2) **[para 12.76]**.
6   **[Para 2.113]**.
7   This has long been recognised as the primary merit of all Torrens legislation (see e g *Gibbs v Messer* [1891] AC 248 at 254 per Lord Watson; *Re Passburg Petroleums Ltd and Landstrom Developments Ltd* (1984) 8 DLR (4th) 363 at 368).
8   See *Registrar of Titles* (*Vic*) *v Paterson* (1876) 2 App Cas 110 at 116–117.

The 'crack in the mirror'

2.109   The perfection of the Torrens ideal has not been fully attained by the Land Registration Act 2002. The Act of 2002 – as indeed the earlier Land Registration Act 1925 – allows certain kinds of proprietary entitlement in land to exist 'off' (or outside) the register even in cases where the rights involved could, and should, have been protected by some entry in the register.[1] These unrecorded rights, which are generally detectable on a physical inspection of the land, are known as interests which 'override' registered titles. The most important comprise short legal leases granted for a period not exceeding seven years[2] and proprietary interests belonging to any 'person in actual occupation' of the land.[3] Such 'overriding interests' automatically bind any disponee of a registered estate and thereby detract, at least marginally, from the completeness of the mirror image which the Land Register is meant to reflect.

1   **[Paras 2.173, 12.132]**.
2   LRA 2002, ss 11(4)(b), 12(4)(c), Sch 1, para 1, s 29(1)–(2)(a)(ii), Sch 3, para 1 **[paras 7.247, 12.143]**.
3   LRA 2002, ss 11(4)(b), 12(4)(c), Sch 1, para 2, s 29(1)–(2)(a)(ii), Sch 3, para 2 **[paras 2.172, 12.146]**.

The eventual aim of dematerialised conveyancing

2.110   The ultimate goal of the Land Registration Act 2002 is the introduction of a new system of electronic or dematerialised conveyancing in which the process of transacting with land will become generally inseparable from simultaneous entry in, or amendment of, the Land Register.[1] The professed (and indeed the 'fundamental') objective of the Act of 2002 is to render the register a 'complete and accurate reflection of the state of the title to land at any given time, so that it is possible to investigate title on line, with the absolute minimum of additional enquiries and inspections.'[2] Towards this end the new legislation removes many of the deficiencies in the mirror image presented by the register, not least by severely reducing the categories of overriding interest permitted under the registered land scheme.[3]

1   **[Para 12.4]**.
2   Law Com No 271 (2001), para 1.5.
3   **[Para 12.134]**.

THE BASIC STRUCTURE OF UNREGISTERED TITLE

2.111   The regime of unregistered title contrasts markedly with the definitive public record of proprietary rights contained in the Land Register. In relation to estates whose title has not yet been registered, none of the details relevant to ownership (with the isolated exception of certain matters registrable under the Land Charges Act 1972[1]) appears on any central record or register.

1   Various categories of 'land charge' are publicly recorded in the Register of Land Charges against the name of the relevant estate owner **[para 12.278]**. It is necessary to distinguish clearly between the registration of various incumbrances affecting an unregistered estate (as land charges in the Register of Land Charges) and the substantive registration of title to an estate in land (under a distinct title number in the Land Register). The interests which are registrable in the Register of Land Charges are also protectable when they arise in relation to a substantively registered estate, in which case protection is provided as an integral part of a much more general process of registration at Land Registry.

Investigation of unregistered titles

2.112   Unregistered titles exist only in the form of chains of documentary records (or 'title deeds') which detail successive transactions with reference to a particular parcel of land. Title deeds – the historic documents of title – are generally held by the owner of the estate to which they relate. These title deeds (or 'deeds bundles') thus provide a privately controlled form of evidence as to title and must always be produced on a conveyance of land in order to enable the purchaser to verify his vendor's title.[1] By investigating title (ie by examining the relevant title deeds stretching back over a period of at least 15 years[2]), the purchaser of an unregistered estate is generally able to discover most of the proprietary estates, interests and charges impinging upon his vendor's land.[3] If this process of exploration enables him to find a 'good root of title' and an unbroken chain of subsequent dealings leading out of the past through to his vendor, the purchaser can safely complete the transaction by paying over the purchase money and taking a formal conveyance of the unregistered estate.[4]

1 Title deeds are, in effect, the 'essential indicia of title to unregistered land' (*Sen v Headley* [1991] Ch 425 at 437C per Nourse LJ).
2 LPA 1969, s 23 [**para 12.260**].
3 Unregistered conveyancing is based on the pragmatic assumption that the historic documents of title will generally throw up most of the pertinent details relating to the land which the purchaser wishes to buy. In the generality of cases this assumption proves to be correct.
4 The process of unregistered conveyancing is described in further detail in Chapter 12 [**para 12.259**].

Deficiencies of unregistered conveyancing

2.113 Unregistered conveyancing inevitably compares unfavourably with the more streamlined proof of title which constitutes the foundation of registered conveyancing. The underlying defect of unregistered conveyancing is precisely the fact that title must be investigated afresh on every occasion of purchase, irrespective of the length of time which has elapsed since the last conveyance and investigation of title. Each successive purchaser is obliged to form his or her own judgement as to the quality of the relevant title and to calculate the likelihood that any defects in that title may prejudice future value and market-ability. The process of unregistered land dealing is thereby rendered repetitive, protracted and costly.[1] Under the Land Registration Act 2002, by contrast, the title to an estate is investigated only once – definitively by the Chief Land Registrar prior to first registration – and is thereafter guaranteed by him in relation to the class of title awarded to the registered proprietor.[2] The individual register of title, which is constantly updated in order to reflect any changes of proprietary entitlement, thereafter provides an accurate record of all matters relevant to the ownership and enjoyment of that land (other than matters which are discoverable on physical inspection of the realty).[3] The regime of unregistered conveyancing affords the purchaser no similarly comprehensive record of the benefits and burdens attaching to the land. Indeed, in unregistered conveyancing, the purchaser's vulnerability to certain pre-existing entitlements is extended by an unsatisfactorily limited scheme of land charge registration[4] and by the operation of equitable rules relating to actual or constructive notice (ie real or deemed knowledge on the part of the purchaser).[5]

1 See *Williams & Glyn's Bank Ltd v Boland* [1981] AC 487 at 511D, where Lord Scarman referred to unregistered conveyancing as the 'wearisome and intricate task of examining title.' See likewise W Markby, *Elements of Law considered with reference to Principles of General Jurisprudence* (6th edn, Clarendon 1905), p 258 ('a very long, troublesome and expensive inquiry').
2 With the introduction of compulsory registration of title, property is 'no longer grounded in a practice of "social mnemonics" – the rich medium of practical social memory – but in administrative practice' (A Pottage, 'The Originality of Registration' (1995) 15 OJLS 371 at 386).
3 The record of the Land Register thus goes far beyond the one isolated category of interest –

the 'land charge' – which can be made the subject of registration in the context of unregistered land. Registration of title involves an entry in the register for almost every kind of interest (whether legal or equitable) relating to the land in question.

4   [Paras 2.185, 12.275].
5   [Paras 2.191, 12.337].

THE TRANSITION TO REGISTERED TITLE

2.114   For some time the jurisdiction of England and Wales has been moving inexorably towards the comprehensive registration of land titles. Compulsory registration of title in something like its present form was introduced only in 1926[1] and was superimposed upon an existing system of unregistered title. The registration regime was initially envisaged as extending fairly rapidly across England and Wales in a programme of incremental expansion,[2] but in reality the transition to registered title proceeded much more slowly than had been anticipated. Nevertheless by the 1980s most large urban centres had been designated as areas of compulsory registration,[3] with the consequent displacement of much of the regime of unregistered conveyancing.[4] As more estates were introduced to the Land Register, it became clear that the shift towards universal registration of title was both inevitable and irresistible. Significant catalysts in the process were provided by a gradual extension of the 'triggers' for compulsory first registration.[5]

1   Early title registration schemes appeared in the Land Registry Act 1862 (25 & 26 Vict, c 53), the Land Transfer Act 1875 (38 & 39 Vict, c 87) and the Land Transfer Act 1897 (60 & 61 Vict, c 65), but, as Lord Oliver of Aylmerton noted in *City of London Building Society v Flegg* [1988] AC 54 at 84D–E, these schemes did not prove 'wholly successful or popular.'
2   For further detail, see *Elements of Land Law* (3rd edn 2001), pp 197–198.
3   Designation of an area as one of compulsory registration of title did not achieve an immediate or automatic conversion of all unregistered land into land of registered title. The requirement of registration at Land Registry was initially 'triggered' only by the first conveyance 'on sale' following the relevant designation.
4   The transition has been described in terms of a movement from a 'devolutionary or genealogical model of property' to a system of 'tabular property' (A Pottage, (1995) 15 OJLS 371 at 383–386).
5   See Land Registration, England and Wales: The Registration of Title Order 1989 (SI 1989/1347) (effective 1 December 1990); LRA 1925, ss 123(1), 123A (effective 1 April 1998).

The modern requirement of first registration at Land Registry

2.115   Following the commencement of the Land Registration Act 2002, virtually all forms of disposition of an unregistered estate now trigger a compulsory first registration of title at Land Registry.[1] For example, such registration is mandatory in the case of most transfers of an unregistered legal freehold or of an unregistered legal leasehold with more than seven years left to run. Likewise all new grants of a leasehold term of more than seven years, together with most first legal mortgages relating to any unregistered freehold or leasehold estate, require to be completed by registration of title to the relevant estate and charge. The number of currently unregistered titles is therefore diminishing as newly transacted estates are brought on to the Land Register.[2]

1   See LRA 2002, ss 4(1)–(2), 6(1)–(3) [**paras 7.40, 7.237, 7.241**]. It is, of course, open to an estate owner to apply at any time for voluntary first registration of his title (LRA 2002, s 3(2)). After its arrival on the Land Register the new title must, of course, be transacted exclusively as a registered title in accordance with the terms of the Land Registration Act 2002.
2   The Land Registry estimates that some 82 per cent of all land titles in England and Wales are now registered under the Land Registration Act (Land Registry, *Annual Report and Accounts 2002–03* (HC891, July 2003), pp 41, 105).

A growing 'culture of registration'

2.116   A further implication of this steady conversion of title to the computerised format of the Land Register has been, quite clearly, the creation of the legal and technological framework for a system of paperless transactions and electronic dealings with interests in land,[1] a scheme which is expected to be piloted from 2006.[2] An important motivation underlying the enactment of the Land Registration Act 2002 was the vision, jointly entertained by the Law Commission and Land Registry, of a future founded upon a 'culture of registration.'[3] Against the background of what will soon become a world of electronic commerce and dematerialised conveyancing, both bodies accepted that it was right to 'lay to rest the notion ... that it is somehow unreasonable to expect those who have rights over registered land to register them.'[4] The aim of the modern registration regime is therefore a 're-engineering [of] the conveyancing process.'[5]

1   See Law Com No 271 (2001), paras 1.1, 1.4, 2.1, 2.41.
2   [**Para 12.4**].
3   Law Com No 254 (1998), para 1.14 [**para 6.52**].
4   Law Com No 271 (2001), para 8.58 (see likewise para 8.72).
5   Land Registry, *Annual Report and Accounts 2001–02* (HC1063, July 2002), p 20.

2.117   Accordingly the Land Registration Act 2002 not only makes the process of registration very much easier, but also envisages that, in relation to the express creation or transfer of most land rights, 'the execution of the transaction in electronic form and its simultaneous registration will be inextricably linked.'[1] Such synchronous registration of electronic dispositions is 'the single most important technical objective' of the Land Registration Act 2002,[2] the 'essential feature' of the new scheme of electronic conveyancing being the idea that registration will itself operate as the sole constitutive source of expressly created rights in registered land.[3]

1   Law Com No 271 (2001), para 1.9 [**paras 7.63, 12.4, 12.53**].
2   Law Com No 271 (2001), para 2.60.
3   Law Com No 271 (2001), para 5.3.

2.118   Following the arrival of electronic conveyancing it will not be possible to generate or dispose of most interests *except* by means of some contemporaneous entry in the register. Unregistered transactions will, quite simply, have no effect either at law or in equity. The fact that entitlement will be conferred by 'registration and registration alone' will serve dramatically to reinforce the 'fundamental principle of a conclusive register' which underpins the Act of 2002.[1] Indeed, one of the most striking effects of the Act of 2002 is to consolidate and protect the proprietorship of registered estates in land, making them far less vulnerable to unforeseen or adventitious claims which derogate from the plenary quality of the title achieved by registration.[2]

1   Law Com No 271 (2001), para 1.10.
2   See Gray and Gray, 'The rhetoric of realty', in J Getzler (ed), *Rationalizing Property, Equity and Trusts: Essays in Honour of Edward Burn* (Butterworths 2003), p 244.

Residue of unregistered estates

2.119   The steady extension of the regime of registered title has not yet obliterated the system of unregistered estates. A significant minority of land transactions still concern unregistered titles and the law relating to such titles is not quite ready to be discarded.[1] It is likely that a residue of estates in land will continue to exist off the Land Register (eg short leases and estates owned by corporations which have no need to sell or mortgage their land). Whilst these unregistered estates remain outstanding, the comprehensive conversion of unregistered land into registered titles may still be some distance away. Unregistered land principles are far from dead, not least because it is these principles which are brought into play, on any first registration, in determining the nature and priority of the estates, interests and charges which have accumulated around any unregistered title and which must therefore be reflected on the Land Register.

1   Although most modern transactions involve an already registered title, there remain large portions of the land area of England and Wales – estimated by the Land Registry to comprise some 35 per cent of the total – where the existing distribution of rights and obligations in land must still be ascertained with reference to the 'old system' rules (see Kevin Cahill, 'Who really owns Britain?' (2004) Walk (2) 41).

Divergent principles of registered and unregistered land law

2.120   For some purposes it is true to say that the system of registered title contained in the Land Registration Act utilises existing concepts of unregistered land conveyancing and simply provides more streamlined conveyancing machinery. It has become increasingly obvious, however, that registration of title achieves more than merely procedural changes in the law.

Inconsistent solutions

2.121   The regime of registered title incorporates rules and concepts which are substantively quite different from the principles which have regulated unregistered estates.[1] For instance, many of the classic concepts of unregistered land (such as the equitable doctrine of notice[2]) are rendered redundant in the scheme of registered title[3] and would, in any event, prove wholly incompatible with the successful operation of electronic conveyancing.[4] The registered and unregistered regimes often coincide in the solutions which they prescribe for similar problems, but from time to time a divergence of fundamental principle between registered and unregistered land law generates large discrepancies of substantive outcome.[5] The net effect is that, for the moment, two approximately parallel regimes of land law continue to operate in this country.[6] Although registered title clearly comprises the dominant regime, there remains an important sense in which – at least until relatively recently – the student of real property has been required to learn two slightly differing systems of land law.

1　See G Ferris, 'Structural Differences Between Registered and Unregistered Land Law', in P Jackson and D C Wilde (ed), *Contemporary Property Law* (Ashgate 1999), p 143.

2　**[Para 12.337]**. On the general elimination of the doctrine of notice in registered title, see *Williams & Glyn's Bank Ltd v Boland* [1981] AC 487 at 511E–F per Lord Scarman; *Kemmis v Kemmis* [1988] 1 WLR 1307 at 1332E per Nourse LJ; *Abbey National Building Society v Cann* [1991] 1 AC 56 at 93D per Lord Oliver of Aylmerton; *Barclays Bank plc v Boulter* [1998] 1 WLR 1 at 11B per Mummery LJ.

3　Even the fundamental dichotomy between legal and equitable rights tends to be submerged by a system where most minor interests (whether legal or equitable) are alike capable of recordation or protection by entry against substantively registered titles.

4　See Law Com No 271 (2001), paras 5.16, 5.21.

5　See e g *Lloyds Bank plc v Carrick* [1996] 4 All ER 630 at 642d–e, where the Court of Appeal reached a conclusion in terms of unregistered title which Morritt LJ openly conceded would have been resolved in a diametrically opposite direction if the title had been *registered*. Compare e g *Hollington Brothers Ltd v Rhodes* [1951] 2 TLR 691 **[para 12.287]** with *Grace Rymer Investments Ltd v Waite* [1958] Ch 831 **[para 12.160]**. In the former case an unprotected equitable lease carved out of an *unregistered* reversion was held void against a purchaser of that superior title, even though the purchaser had the clearest express notice of the tenant's rights. In the latter case, an equivalent (and, again, unprotected) equitable lease – carved this time out of a *registered* reversion – was held to be an overriding interest. See generally Law Com No 158 (1987), para 2.5.

6　See *City of London Building Society v Flegg* [1988] AC 54 at 84G per Lord Oliver of Aylmerton.

Demise of unregistered conveyancing

2.122　However unsatisfactory it is that the twin regimes of land law should give rise to divergent practical solutions, English courts and lawyers have long abandoned the task of striving for conformity between the principles governing registered and unregistered estates.[1] In 1987 the Law Commission acknowledged that 'there are substantive differences between registered and unregistered land' and that there was 'little justification in trying at all costs to keep the two systems in step.' Registered land, said the Commission, 'is after all to be the way forward, the new improving on the old.'[2] Much more recently the Commission observed that there 'seems little point in inhibiting the rational development of the principles of property law by reference to a system which is rapidly disappearing, and in relation to which there is diminishing expertise amongst the legal profession.'[3] This surrender to the inevitable has prepared the way for the hegemony of registered land principles and for the introduction of mechanisms of computerisation and electronic conveyancing which would have proved utterly impossible within the strictures of the unregistered land regime. It is now widely accepted that the continued existence of two separate systems of conveyancing – the registered and the unregistered – is 'absurd' and that the unregistered regime 'must be given its quietus.'[4] Immediately prior to the enactment of the Land Registration Act 2002, the Law Commission committed itself to the view that 'remaining unregistered land should be phased out as quickly as possible.'[5] It is now one of the 'strategic objectives' of Land Registry to achieve a Land Register with 'comprehensive content and national coverage' by 2012[6] and, accordingly, it seems likely that at some future point most surviving unregistered titles will be swept compulsorily on to the Land Register.

1   See e g *Spectrum Investment Co v Holmes* [1981] 1 WLR 221 at 230A–C per Browne-Wilkinson J; *Oceanic Village Ltd v United Attractions Ltd* [2000] Ch 234 at 252E per Neuberger J.
2   Law Com No 158 (1987), para 2.5.
3   Law Com No 254 (1998), para 1.6.
4   Law Com No 271 (2001), para 2.6.
5   Law Com No 271 (2001), para 2.9.
6   Land Registry, *Annual Report and Accounts 2002–03* (HC891, July 2003), p 10, Appendix 4 (p 99).

THE WATERSHED BETWEEN LEGAL AND EQUITABLE RIGHTS

2.123   Following the distinction between registered and unregistered titles, the next most significant structural classification in English land law is the differentiation of proprietary entitlements into categories of *legal* and *equitable* right (see *Fig.* 6[1]). Although historical factors underlie the distinction,[2] the borderline between legal and equitable rights in land is now drawn, definitively and arbitrarily, by the legislation of 1925 and 2002. The ultimate importance of the distinction has been eroded by the extension of title registration, but the statutory watershed between legal and equitable entitlements in land still provides a vital key to the resolution of many issues of disputed priority. Particularly in unregistered land the attribution of legal or equitable character may fundamentally determine the binding impact of rights upon third parties who purchase the land to which they relate. Any systematic review of English land law must therefore address, at its beginning, the way in which some proprietary rights in land are designated as 'legal' and others as merely 'equitable'.

1   **[Para 2.99]**.
2   **[Para 1.155]**.

THE STATUTORY STARTING-POINT

2.124   The potential significance of the distinction between legal and equitable rights may be inferred from the fact that a strenuous demarcation of these categories appears in the opening section of the primary enactment of 1925, the Law of Property Act 1925. In a schema which is explicitly adopted and developed by the Land Registration Act 2002,[1] section 1 of the Law of Property Act 1925 surveys the entire field of proprietary rights in land and indicates the basic criteria for identifying rights in land as having either 'legal' or 'equitable' quality.

1   See LRA 2002, s 132(1) (definition of 'legal estate').

Rights authorised to exist 'at law' (ie as legal rights)

2.125   In English law the range of proprietary entitlements in or over land comprises a relatively limited canon of rights (ie a *numerus clausus*[1]). From within this cluster of rights the Law of Property Act 1925 isolates a group of estates, interests and charges which are expressly declared to be 'capable of subsisting or of being conveyed or created at law' (ie as *legal* rights).[2] By reason of their exclusion from this category, all other proprietary rights in land are necessarily *equitable* only.[3] The entitlements which, in the words of section 1(4) of the Law of Property Act 1925, are 'authorised to subsist or to be conveyed or created at law' include:

–   the fee simple absolute in possession[4]
–   the term of years absolute[5]
–   easements[6]
–   profits *à prendre*[7]
–   rentcharges[8]
–   charges by way of legal mortgage[9] and
–   rights of entry.[10]

1   [Para **2.95**].
2   LPA 1925, s 1(1)–(2). For earlier legislation which was consolidated in the 1925 enactment, see Law of Property Act 1922, s 1(1).
3   LPA 1925, s 1(3).
4   [Para **7.2**].
5   [Para **7.68**].
6   [Para **8.24**].
7   [Para **8.17**].
8   [Para **8.225**].
9   [Para **8.232**].
10   [Para **8.263**].

2.126   The 1925 Act indicates merely that these kinds of proprietary entitlement are *capable* of existing at law. Whether, within any particular context, such rights *actually* attain legal quality usually depends on compliance with some requirement of formal creation or transfer or of due registration at Land Registry.[1]

1   [Paras **7.25**, **7.217**]. Requirements of form relate, essentially, to the use of a deed [para **7.29**].

Inherently equitable rights

2.127   The distinction between 'legal' and 'equitable' rights in land is both artificial and crude; but it is nonetheless clear. Whether an entitlement can *ever* be legal depends quite simply on whether reference to it can be found in the catalogue of rights contained in section 1(1)–(2) of the Law of Property Act 1925. It follows that, simply by virtue of their categorical exclusion from the statutory canon, certain proprietary entitlements *never* have the potential to rank as legal rights in or over land.[1] This residue of rights remains inherently and inevitably equitable.[2] These rights include:

- determinable fee simple estates[3]
- life interests[4]
- estate contracts (including options)[5]
- restrictive covenants[6] and
- beneficial interests existing under a trust of land.[7]

1   Such rights remain equitable irrespective of their mode of creation (eg even if created by deed).
2   See LPA 1925, s 1(3).
3   **[Para 7.6]**.
4   **[Para 9.205]**.
5   **[Para 9.23]**.
6   **[Paras 9.138, 13.63]**.
7   **[Para 9.172]**.

Rights made equitable by some deficiency of form or registration

2.128   There remains a further category of rights which, by reason of some deficiency of formal creation or transfer or of some failure of completion by registration at Land Registry, survive as merely equitable entitlements. These entitlements are, quite simply, the analogue of those rights which, to borrow the terminology of the old Land Registration Act 1925,[1] have the capacity to subsist validly at law if properly 'clothed with the legal estate', but which, for want of such clothing, are consigned to equitable status only. Most important amongst these rights are:

- the fee simple absolute in possession[2]
- the term of years absolute[3]
- easements[4]
- profits *à prendre*[5] and
- mortgage charges.[6]

1   See LRA 1925, s 3(xi).
2   **[Para 7.25]**.
3   **[Para 7.221]**.
4   **[Para 9.88]**.
5   **[Para 9.88]**.
6   **[Para 9.104]**.

Simplification of legal ownership

2.129   With its rigid redefinition of the boundary between law and equity, the 1925 legislation achieved at least three further simplifications of estate ownership at law.

Sweeping of limited interests into equity

2.130 Prior to 1 January 1926 many kinds of limited interest in land (eg life interests and fees tail[1]) could rank as legal estates in land. In order to obtain a comprehensively valid legal title, a purchaser was often required, in consequence, to take his conveyance not merely from the owner of the fee simple absolute but also, quite possibly, from an assortment of limited legal owners. The purchaser's task in investigating the component parts of a legal title could therefore be a complex and protracted affair. This difficulty was finally removed by the Law of Property Act 1925, which deliberately swept limited interests into equity behind the curtain of some form of trust.[2] Since 1 January 1926 all purchasers have known that the only person competent to transfer a freehold estate at law is the owner of an estate in fee simple absolute in possession. It is correspondingly clear that the only vendor now competent to transfer a legal leasehold estate is one who owns a term of years absolute in possession.

1 [Para **1.128**].
2 LPA 1925, s 1(1)–(3). The Trusts of Land and Appointment of Trustees Act 1996 goes one step further and altogether prohibits the creation of new entails after 1996 (TOLATA 1996, Sch 1, para 5(1) [**para 1.139**]).

Restriction of the number of owners of a legal estate

2.131 Before the enactment of the 1925 legislation, even an absolute legal estate (eg an estate in fee simple) could be held by, and fragmented between, an almost limitless number of persons, each holding a specific share or proportion of that legal estate. In order to take a good conveyance, a purchaser had to investigate each co-owner's individual title[1] and then ensure that the conveyance was executed by all concerned. The process could be cumbersome, costly and time-consuming. This potentially disadvantageous feature of co-ownership was greatly alleviated by the provision in the 1925 legislation that the maximum number of persons who may hold a legal estate is generally limited to four.[2] The number of persons from whom a disposition of a legal estate can now be taken is therefore at most four; and these four are regarded as owners of one and the same legal estate, with the result that the purchaser need investigate only *one* composite title.[3] In this way a much greater degree of simplicity and convenience was introduced into the process of title transfer, lease and charge.

1 See *City of London Building Society v Flegg* [1988] AC 54 at 76H–77A per Lord Oliver of Aylmerton.
2 TA 1925, s 34(2); LPA 1925, s 34(2) [**para 7.189**].
3 [Para **11.27**].

Prohibition of legal ownership by a minor

2.132 The 1925 legislation (and indeed subsequent enactments) confirmed that a legal estate in land may not be held by a minor (ie by a person who has not attained the age of 18 years)[1], although a minor may validly hold the *equitable* version of any estate[2] necessarily behind some trust of land.[3] Any attempt after 1996 to transfer a legal estate to a minor operates instead as a declaration that the land is held in trust for the minor.[4]

1   LPA 1925, ss 1(6), 20, 205(1)(v); TOLATA 1996, Sch 1, para 1(1)(a) **[para 7.1]**.
2   See e g *Kingston upon Thames BC v Prince* [1999] 1 FLR 593 at 603A–D.
3   **[Para 9.172]**.
4   TOLATA 1996, s 2(1), (6), Sch 1, para 1(1)(b).

Historical significance of the distinction between legal and equitable rights

2.133   The rigorous distinction drawn in the 1925 legislation between *legal* and *equitable* rights becomes more readily explicable when it is realised that the borderline between legal and equitable quality has provided, at least in historical terms, an important key to the resolution of the central question of land law. This central issue concerns whether subsidiary entitlements of various kinds survive a disposition of the land to which they relate, thereby remaining valid and enforceable against a purchaser.[1]

1   [Para 2.44].

The twin axioms of unregistered land law

2.134   In the context of unregistered estates in land it was (and still is) axiomatic that (i) *legal* rights automatically bind the world[1]; and (ii) *equitable* rights bind all persons other than a bona fide purchaser of a legal estate for value without notice of such equitable rights.[2] These foundational principles belong, of course, to an era prior to the advent of modern regimes of registration, but even under the Land Registration Act 2002 it remains broadly true that legal entitlements have an automatically binding quality and that equitable rights remain enforceable against those who (through the medium of register entry) are infected with a deemed knowledge of the rights concerned.

1   [Para 12.274].
2   [Para 12.337]. See *London and South Western Railway Co v Gomm* (1882) 20 Ch D 562 at 583; *Re Nisbet and Potts' Contract* [1906] 1 Ch 386 at 403, 405.

Deficiencies of the axiomatic rules of land law priority

2.135   By the early 20th century the deficiencies of the axiomatic rules of priority had become clearly apparent.[1] The purchaser of land was always bound, irrespective of knowledge or notice, by pre-existing legal rights in or over that land. Furthermore, the equitable doctrine of notice (or 'bona fide purchaser rule') often operated capriciously and unpredictably as a determinant of priority between the disponee and those who owned fragments of equitable entitlement. Equitable rights are commonly not referred to at all in the formal documents of title, and there was always a possibility that a disponee might be fixed by a deemed or 'constructive' notice of such rights – a consequence which could entirely stultify the purpose of the transaction.[2] It was inevitable by 1925 that such uncertainty – the antithesis of a rational law of property – could no longer be allowed to attach to equitable rights.

1   [**Para 12.339**].
2   The doctrine of notice was just as unsatisfactory from the viewpoint of the equitable incumbrancer, whose rights (often purchased for consideration) were exposed to uncompensated destruction with the advent of any purchaser who had no notice of their existence. No equitable owner could sleep easily at night for fear that he might be confronted at any time by a purchaser claiming to be 'Equity's Darling'. Even if this fear never materialised, the equitable owner was still disadvantaged when he came to sell the land which carried the benefit of his equitable rights. He was in no position to command the highest price in so far as he could not assure his successor in title that the appurtenant rights were indefeasible in the event of a later transfer of the burdened land.

Introduction of a general rule of register entry

2.136   The Land Registration Act 1925 radically modified the twin axioms of land law priority by establishing a regime of registration of title under which most kinds of entitlement in land could be reflected on the face of the Land Register.[1] With certain qualifications relating to 'overriding' interests[2] and 'overreachable' rights,[3] the impact of proprietary rights on disponees of a registered title was settled definitively by the record of the Land Register. In a pattern now incorporated within the Land Registration Act 2002, the facility of register entry not only ensures the indefinite protection of all relevant entitlements through subsequent changes in the ownership of title, but also provides a fail-safe means of alerting potential disponees of title to the existence of the rights in question.[4]

1   [**Para 2.108**] ('the mirror principle').
2   [**Paras 2.171, 12.129**].
3   [**Paras 2.165, 11.195**].
4   See e g *Kemmis v Kemmis* [1988] 1 WLR 1307 at 1332E, where Nourse LJ referred to the process of register entry as providing 'statutory notice' of rights affecting registered estates, thus affording a functional substitute for the old equitable doctrine of notice.

Taxonomy of rights under the Land Registration Act 2002

2.137   Although the rights governed by the Land Registration Act 2002 are still capable of identification as either *legal* or *equitable*, this dichotomous analysis is far less significant in the taxonomy of entitlements under the 2002 Act (see *Fig.* 6[1]). The Land Registration Act classifies proprietary interests in a manner quite unfamiliar to the common law. The statutory categories comprise the following forms of entitlement:

–   registered estates[2] and registered charges;[3]
–   minor interests[4] which may be noted against registered titles; and

–   interests which automatically 'override' first registrations of title and/or subsequent registered dispositions of registered estates and charges.[5]

1   **[Para 2.99]**.
2   **[Paras 2.148, 7.37]**
3   **[Paras 2.152, 8.242]**.
4   **[Paras 2.162, 12.84]**.
5   **[Paras 2.171, 12.129]**.

2.138   In the context of these autonomous classifications, the distinction between legal and equitable character generally assumes a secondary importance.[1] What matters much more is the extent to which various entitlements (whether legal or equitable) are protected by the process of registration of title or are specially exempted from that process. As it happens, registered estates and registered charges are always, by definition, legal in quality; and minor and overriding entitlements can, depending upon the circumstances, be either legal or equitable. We must return, however, to the underlying classifications of entitlement established by the 1925 legislation.

1   The distinction becomes virtually insignificant except, perhaps, for the purpose of defining the major estates against which all other register entries require to be made.

'LEGAL ESTATES' IN LAND

2.139   As indicated earlier,[1] the structural classification of rights in the 1925 legislation indicates merely whether a given proprietary right in land has the potential of legal status. For the purpose of attaining *actual* legal status, most potentially legal rights are subjected to certain basic requirements of formal creation or transfer (and sometimes also of registration). Once created or transferred in compliance with any appropriate requirement of formality or due registration, all potentially legal rights become known generically as 'legal estates' in land.[2]

1   [Para 2.126].
2   See LPA 1925, ss 1(4), 205(1)(x); LRA 2002, ss 7(1), 132(1). For reference to the inevitably 'proprietary' connotation of the word 'estate', see *R v Toohey; Ex parte Meneling Station Pty Ltd* (1982) 158 CLR 327 at 342 per Mason J.

Estates which 'subsist' at law

2.140   A limited class of estates can be said to subsist 'at law' without the necessity of compliance with *any* requirements of form or registration. The best examples are provided by certain kinds of lease granted for a term of not more than three years.[1] Such leases may be created either by informal writing or even orally and rank immediately as 'legal estates' quite irrespective of whether the land to which they relate has been the subject of any registration at Land Registry.[2]

1   LPA 1925, ss 52(2)(d), 54(2) **[para 7.221]**.

2   In other words a perfectly valid *unregistered* legal estate (e g a short lease) can be carved out of a *registered* parent estate.

Estates which must be created or conveyed by formal means

2.141   In most other cases the Law of Property Act 1925 stipulates a requirement of documentary formality before the creation or transfer of a potentially legal entitlement can generate a 'legal estate' in the hands of its recipient. With certain exceptions, all conveyances of land or of any interest in land are declared to be 'void for the purpose of conveying or creating a legal estate' *unless* made by 'deed' (ie formal writing).[1] Many 'legal estates' in unregistered land owe their origin precisely to compliance with this statutory requirement of a deed, although most new dealings with such estates now trigger an additional requirement of first registration at Land Registry as a condition of the continuance of the 'legal estate'.[2] It is clear, moreover, that the technical requirement of a deed will soon have to be modified to take account of the advent of electronic dealings (ie 'paperless' transactions) in respect of land.[3]

1   LPA 1925, s 52(1); LRR 2003, rr 58–60 **[paras 2.175, 7.26]**. For the constituent elements of a 'deed', see Chapter 7 **[para 7.29]**.
2   **[Paras 7.41, 7.238]**.
3   **[Paras 2.117, 12.4]**.

Estates which require registration at Land Registry

2.142   The generic category of 'legal estates' provides a vital bridge into the registration provisions of the Land Registration Act 2002. The Chief Land Registrar is empowered to register title to two broad sorts of entitlement.

Registration of previously unregistered estates

2.143   The Chief Land Registrar is statutorily authorised to register title to certain 'unregistered legal estates' in land,[1] ie to estates whose legal quality has already been established through compliance with the formality of creation or conveyance by deed, but which have never before been recorded in the Land Register. Registration of title to such estates may be 'voluntary' on the part of the estate owner[2] or 'compulsory' in the case of specified 'events' which trigger a mandatory requirement of first registration at Land Registry.[3]

1   LRA 2002, s 2(a).
2   LRA 2002, s 3 **[paras 7.39, 7.229]**.
3   LRA 2002, s 4 **[paras 7.40, 7.230–7.237]**.

Registration of interests created by a disposition of an already registered estate

2.144   The Chief Land Registrar is likewise authorised to register title to certain 'interests capable of subsisting at law' which are created by a 'disposition' of an estate whose title is *already registered* at Land Registry.[1] Here the term 'disposition' is broad enough to embrace not merely outright transfers of the registered estate itself, but also dealings under which lesser entitlements (e g certain leases, easements and profits *à prendre*) – are carved out of the registered estate.[2] In every case registration of the disponee's title to the interest in question is rendered a precondition of the vesting of any legal estate in that disponee.[3]

1   LRA 2002, s 2(b).
2   LRA 2002, s 27(2).
3   **[Paras 7.240, 8.117]**.

Effect of registration

2.145   It is a pervasive feature of the Land Registration Act 2002 that the *legal* status of any entitlement which is caught by a requirement of compulsory registration crystallises finally and permanently *only* when the disposition of that interest is duly registered at Land Registry. At this point the arrival of the 'legal estate' in the disponee is said, in the self-explanatory parlance of the Land Registration Act 2002, to equip the disponee in most cases with a 'registered estate', ie a 'legal estate the title to which is entered in the register.'[1] In this way the withholding of the legal quality of estate ownership until completion by registration provides an incentive for those dealing in land to apply for registration and also ensures that the Land Register is kept constantly updated.

1   LRA 2002, s 132(1).

Effect of non-registration

2.146   For want of appropriate registration, a transaction with a *previously unregistered* legal estate quickly becomes 'void as regards the transfer, grant or creation of a legal estate.'[1] An even more draconian outcome affects estates which are already recorded in the Land Register. The disposition of an *already registered* estate 'does not operate at law' – even briefly – unless and until it is appropriately 'completed by registration',[2] ie by entry of the disponee in the Land Register as proprietor of the relevant estate.

1   LRA 2002, s 7(1) **[paras 7.41, 7.237–7.243]**.
2   LRA 2002, s 27(1) **[paras 7.49, 7.245]**.

Equitable entitlement in default of due registration

2.147   Notwithstanding the failure of any attempted vesting of a 'legal estate', it remains quite possible that the *equitable* version of the same estate may already have vested in the intended disponee – usually by force of some pre-existing and specifically enforceable contract.[1]

1   **[Paras 2.128, 7.238, 9.48]**.

REGISTRATION OF ESTATES AT LAND REGISTRY

2.148   Under the inter-connecting provisions of the Law of Property Act 1925 and the Land Registration Act 2002, the generic category of 'legal estates' includes the fee simple and the term of years, together with easements,[1] profits *à prendre*, rentcharges, charges by way of legal mortgage[2] and rights of entry.[3] In the scheme of registered land, title to *any* of these 'estates' may be registered at Land Registry in the name of its proprietor, thus in most instances conferring on that proprietor a 'registered estate' in respect of the land concerned. However, only certain categories of 'estate' are 'independently registrable',[4] ie capable of 'substantive registration'[5] in the Land Register in a newly opened register of title identified by a unique title number. All other 'estates' are eligible for non-substantive registration, ie registration by some other form of entry in other registers of title.

1   See eg *Willies-Williams v National Trust* (1993) 65 P & CR 359 at 361 per Hoffmann LJ; *Singh v Sandhu* (Unreported, Court of Appeal, 4 May 1995) per Balcombe LJ.
2   See eg *City of London Building Society v Flegg* [1988] AC 54 at 90H–91A per Lord Oliver of Aylmerton; *First National Bank plc v Thompson* [1996] Ch 231 at 240C per Millett LJ. See also LRA 2002, s 7(1)–(2).
3   For a similarly broad understanding of 'estate' ownership as embracing freehold and leasehold estates together with incorporeal interests such as easements and profits *à prendre*, see *Stow v Mineral Holdings (Australia) Pty Ltd* (1979) 180 CLR 295 at 311 per Aickin J; *R v Toohey; Ex parte Meneling Station Pty Ltd* (1982) 158 CLR 327 at 351 per Wilson J.
4   See LRA 2002, Sch 2, para 6.
5   See *UCB Group Ltd v Hedworth* [2002] EWCA Civ 708 at [28] per Jonathan Parker LJ [**para 2.107**].

Substantively registrable estates

2.149   The principal estates capable of substantive registration in the Land Register under an independent title number are[1]

–   a fee simple absolute in possession[2]
–   a term of years absolute – subject to the proviso that substantive registration of leasehold estates extends, in general, only to legal terms of more than seven years[3]
–   a profit *à prendre* in gross[4]
–   a rentcharge[5] and
–   a franchise.[6]

1   See LRR 2003, r 2(2).
2   [**Para 7.38**].
3   [**Paras 7.237, 7.241**].
4   [**Para 8.116**].
5   [**Para 8.227**].
6   See LRA 2002, s 3(1)(c). A franchise is an unusual estate in land, acquired either by royal grant or by prescription, which entitles the holder to exercise some privilege (eg to hold a market or fair (see *Sevenoaks DC v Pattullo & Vinson Ltd* [1984] Ch 211) or to receive treasure [**para 1.102**]). A franchise may be registered with its own title if held in perpetuity or for a term of which more than seven years remain unexpired (LRA 2002, s 3(3)). A 'manor' (ie lordship of a manor) is now no longer registrable (see LRA 2002, s 119).

2.150   It is quite possible, of course, that one parcel of land may be the subject of substantive registrations of title to two or more estates under different title numbers, as, for instance, where the freehold title to Greenacre is subject to one or more long leaseholds.[1] As always, however, no subsequent transfer of a substantively registered estate can be effective to pass the legal estate unless the disposition is completed by registration of the transferee as the new proprietor.[2]

1   See *Ferrishurst Ltd v Wallcite Ltd* [1999] Ch 355 at 363F–G.
2   **[Paras 7.58, 7.244]**.

Other registrable estates

2.151   Other rights falling within the generic category of 'legal estates' are also eligible for registration under the Land Registration Act 2002. Thus, for instance, formally created easements, mortgage charges and rights of entry can be registered in the name of their respective proprietors. Such registrations are not accorded an independent title number, but are merely entered in the register of the substantively registered estate or estates which they affect.[1] In so far as no separately numbered title is generated, this form of registration can be described as *non-substantive* registration. Two examples may suffice.

1   In some cases an elaborate cross-referencing system links the correlative benefits and burdens associated with various kinds of entitlement **[paras 2.107, 8.119]**.

Charge by way of legal mortgage

2.152   The creation of a legal charge in favour of a bank, building society or other lender is completed by registration of details of the charge in the 'charges register' of the *borrower*'s substantively registered title, immediately followed by the entry of the *lender*'s name in that register as proprietor of the charge in question.[1] Such registration finally confers on the lender (or 'chargee') a legal estate in the mortgage charge. At this point the charge becomes known, in statutory terminology, not as a 'registered estate' but, more specifically, as a 'registered charge'.[2] In the absence of registration the chargee holds only an *equitable* charge.[3]

1   LRA 2002, ss 27(2)(f), 59(2), Sch 2, para 8; LRR 2003, r 9(c)–(e) **[para 8.244]**.
2   LRA 2002, s 132(1).
3   **[Para 9.107]**.

Legal easements

2.153   The express grant of an easement (eg a right of way[1]) is completed by registration of the benefit of the easement in the 'property register' of the substantively registered estate in the 'dominant' (or benefited) land.[2] The correlative burden imposed by this easement can and should be entered by 'notice'[3] in the 'charges register' of the substantively registered title of the 'servient' land.[4] The registered proprietor of the dominant land thus becomes the registered proprietor of the legal estate in any easement which benefits his land and he can be described as holding a 'registered estate' in that easement.[5]

1   [Paras 2.22, 8.89].
2   LRA 2002, ss 27(2)(d), 59(1), Sch 2, para 7(2)(b); LRR 2003, r 5(b)(ii).
3   [Paras 8.119, 12.84].
4   LRA 2002, ss 32, 38, Sch 2, para 7(2)(a); LRR 2003, r 9(a).
5   See LRA 2002, s 132(1).

Non-registrable estates

2.154   Some estates in land remain incapable of registration, even though the land to which they relate may be the subject of a title already registered at Land Registry. The number of non-registrable estates in land has, of course, been significantly diminished by the lowered threshold for leasehold registration introduced by the Land Registration Act 2002.[1] A lease granted for a term not exceeding three years now provides the prime example of an estate which remains ineligible for any form of registration of title, whether substantive or non-substantive. The tenant under such a term of years cannot appear any-where on the Land Register as proprietor of his estate[2]; nor can his lease be protected by the entry of a 'notice' in the register of his landlord's title.[3] Short terms of this nature may nevertheless qualify for an alternative form of protection under the Land Registration Act 2002, often constituting overriding interests which automatically bind all disponees of the lessor's registered estate.[4]

1   [Para 7.228].
2   Even in the absence of registration, this leasehold estate will generally constitute a legal estate in land. See LPA 1925, ss 52(2)(d), 54(2) [para 7.221].
3   LRA 2002, s 33(b).
4   LRA 2002, s 29(1), (2)(a)(ii), Sch 3, paras 1–2 [paras 7.247, 12.143, 12.146].

DEALINGS WITH REGISTERED ESTATES

2.155   Perhaps the most distinctive achievement of modern English land law consists in the way in which it has largely reconciled the commerciability of land titles with the long-term preservation of fragmented benefits carved out of land. This accommodation of divergent objectives is made possible by a series of statutory provisions, confirmed in 1925 and now reinforced by the Land Registration Act 2002, which guarantee for the disponee of a registered estate a substantial freedom from unpredictable incumbrances upon his or her title. By virtue of some legislative ingenuity, these provisions also ensure that fragments of benefit (which in the artificial schema of the Law of Property Act 1925 are often equitable interests) are simultaneously secured in such a way as to survive dispositions of the major legal estates. In this way the essential success of English property legislation has been the combination of a high degree of facility for the disponees of land with a large measure of protection for the owners of fragments of proprietary benefit in the same land.

Streamlined transactions with title

2.156　Much of this book is concerned with the way in which the Land Registration Act 2002 strives to ensure that the major estates whose title is registered at Land Registry are susceptible to convenient and efficient acts of transfer or other disposition.[1] The 2002 Act also sets the scene for the automated forms of electronic disposition which will arrive with the era of digital conveyancing. In the brave new world of electronic transacting, title to a legal estate will simply shift with the press of a key, thereby confirming that the land lawyer's attention will be left to concentrate on the question whether the disponee of the registered estate takes free of burdens which previously encumbered the land.

1　[Para 12.63].

Disponee's limited vulnerability to pre-existing burdens

2.157　Under the Land Registration Act 2002 – and pending the arrival of a scheme of purely electronic conveyancing[1] – the disponee of a registered estate in land receives a significant immunity from pre-existing burdens affecting the land, provided that the disposition is made 'for valuable consideration' and is itself completed by due registration (see *Fig.* 7). In this combination of circumstances, the disponee takes free of 'any interest affecting the estate immediately before the disposition' *unless* such interest enjoyed 'protected' priority at the time of registration.[2] In the terms of the 2002 Act, 'protected' priority is mostly confined to entitlements which comprise a registered charge (ie a mortgage),[3] a minor interest safeguarded by the entry of a 'notice' in the register[4] or an unregistered interest which is statutorily declared to 'override' registered dispositions.[5] The disponee of a registered estate is otherwise unburdened by pre-existing entitlements which might have qualified his proprietorship.

1　[Para 12.4].
2　LRA 2002, s 29(2) [para 12.73].
3　[Paras 8.242, 12.76].
4　[Paras 2.163, 12.84].
5　[Paras 2.171, 12.129–12.244].

2.158　The consequence of the statutory scheme is that, with the exception of overriding interests, the disponee of a registered estate takes subject only to those interests which have left some positive imprint on the face of the Land Register at the date of his or her own registration. The net result is the achievement of a previously unattainable transactional efficiency, the registration process effectively controlling the externalities (ie the economic costs and disincentives) which would otherwise flow from uncertainty in the outcome of land dealings.

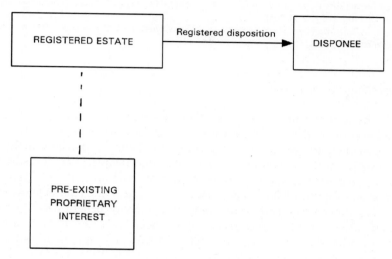

Fig. 7

Specific and non-specific burdens on land

2.159 For more than a century English legislation has drawn an implicit distinction between two categories of burden upon a freehold estate in land. Statutory strategies differ according to whether a relevant burden can be said to attach exclusively to one particular parcel of land or can instead be regarded as ultimately transferable to other parcels of realty.

Specific (or real) burdens on land

2.160 Some forms of entitlement carved out of land are highly specific to the land in respect of which they are created. Prime examples are provided by leases, easements, restrictive covenants and estate contracts (such as agreements or options to purchase land). Rights of these kinds are inherently tied to a precise block of land and indeed have meaning only with reference to that land. When, say, the owner of Redacre bargains with the owner of the adjoining Greenacre for a right of way over Greenacre which connects Redacre to a passing highway, the advantage conferred on Redacre makes sense only in relation to Greenacre itself. The benefit thereby accorded to Redacre constitutes a non-exchangeable burden imposed uniquely and irreplaceably upon the realty which is Greenacre.[1] For this reason, rights in the nature of leases, easements, restrictive covenants and estate contracts all generate, in the radical sense of the word, a *real* burden on the title of the estate owner affected.[2] Such burdens are generally intended to form long-term, if not indeed permanent, incumbrances on the land concerned, thus comprising 'rights which an adjoining owner enjoys over the land itself, regardless of its ownership from time to time.'[3]

1 The route of the way benefiting Redacre obviously cannot be transposed to Whiteacre, some 20 miles away, if and when the owner of Greenacre later sells up and moves there.

2   For further discussion of the implications of *general* (as distinct from *real*) burdens upon land,
     see Chapter 11 [**para 11.201**].
3   *Birmingham Midshires Mortgage Services Ltd v Sabherwal* (2000) 80 P & CR 256 at 262 per
     Robert Walker LJ.

Non-specific (or general) burdens

2.161   By way of contrast, certain other fragments of entitlement carved out
of land impose burdens which, at least in the money-oriented perspective of the
1925 legislation, are entirely non-specific to any particular parcel of realty. Such
cases involve entitlements whose enjoyment is, in principle, freely transferable to
another parcel of land (or even to some form of asset other than realty). Thus,
for example, a person who holds a fractional share of the equitable ownership
of a family home is regarded as retaining a fragment of benefit which could just
as easily attach to the capital proceeds generated by a sale of that home (or
indeed to other land or some other asset subsequently purchased out of that
fund of money).[1] In the unsympathetic view of the 1925 legislation, shared
rights of equitable ownership of land impose on the land a *general* burden
which is distinctly fungible or exchangeable in quality. The burden, being
non-specific and readily convertible into a cash value, is thoroughly translatable
to other forms of investment.

1   See *Birmingham Midshires Mortgage Services Ltd v Sabherwal* (2000) 80 P & CR 256 at 263.

Minor interests affecting a registered estate

2.162   Against the background of this distinction between specific and non-
specific burdens on registered estates, it now becomes possible to understand
the strategy adopted by the Land Registration Act 2002 for the protection of
subsidiary interests in land.

Protection by register entry

2.163   In keeping with the 'mirror principle' which underlies the entire statutory scheme,[1] the 2002 Act ensures that a range of entitlements which are
neither registered estates nor registered charges can be made the subject of a
'notice' entered in the register of title of the land which they affect.[2] If
safeguarded in this way, these rights become binding on subsequent disponees
of that registered freehold or leasehold estate.[3] The entitlements which are
protectable by 'notice' are sometimes termed *registrable* interests (in order to
distinguish them from 'registered estates' and 'registered charges'). It may
ultimately be easier – and it is certainly very tempting – to borrow the familiar
language of the Land Registration Act 1925 and describe this category of
protectable entitlements as 'minor' interests. Such terminology also has the
advantage that it highlights the essential strategy of the Land Registration

Act 2002, under which the substantively registered estates – Viscount Dilhorne's 'major' estates[4] – provide a vital point of reference for the entry of a range of 'minor' interests.

1   [**Para 2.108**].
2   LRA 2002, ss 32–33 [**para 12.84**].
3   LRA 2002, s 29(1), (2)(b)(i) [**para 12.76**]. It is likewise part of the overall statutory strategy that a 'minor' interest, if not protected in the relevant register of a 'major' title, is ineffective against a disponee for value under any subsequent registered disposition – unless, of course, the unprotected interest also happens to rank as an 'overriding' interest [**paras 2.171, 12.129**].
4   [**Para 2.107**].

Durable protection of real burdens

2.164   This heavily modified adaptation of the old axiomatic rules of priority is ideal for securing the long-term preservation of the kinds of entitlement which impose 'real burdens' on registered estates. Rights such as easements and restrictive covenants are not designed to be fungible or exchangeable. They do not command, in the abstract, any readily monetisable value and have never been viewed as mechanically convertible into the cash proceeds of overreaching dispositions.[1] Under the legislative scheme real burdens are not intended to be swept off land by transfers of title,[2] but are usually envisaged as permanent burdens on the specific land to which they are annexed. It is for precisely this reason that the Land Registration Act 2002 makes elaborate provision for such incumbrances to enjoy a continuing force over the affected land through the medium of 'notices' entered in the register.[3] The owners of relevant subsidiary interests in the land may therefore safeguard their rights by a simple protective entry in the Land Register, the fact of their entitlement being made perfectly visible to potential disponees of the title concerned.

1   Rights falling within this category 'cannot sensibly shift from the land affected ... to the proceeds of sale' (*Birmingham Midshires Mortgage Services Ltd v Sabherwal* (2000) 80 P & CR 256 at 263 per Robert Walker LJ).
2   'To overreach such interests is to destroy them' (*Birmingham Midshires Mortgage Services Ltd v Sabherwal* (2000) 80 P & CR 256 at 262 per Robert Walker LJ).
3   [**Paras 2.163, 12.84**]. 'Real burdens' (if subsisting in registered land) sometimes remain binding simply as 'overriding' interests even in the absence of protection on the register [**paras 2.173, 12.132**].

The principle of 'overreaching'

2.165   If the consequence of a 'notice' in the Land Register is to fix the disponee of a registered title with an inescapable awareness of certain kinds of subsidiary right affecting the land, the Law of Property Act 1925 confirms the operation of a rather different device which, in relation to *other* categories of interest, renders knowledge on the part of the disponee entirely irrelevant. This device – the principle of statutory 'overreaching' – provides an extremely neat means of resolving the tension between the requirement of facility for purchasers and the countervailing requirement of protection for certain kinds of lesser interest in land.[1] In the process, the disponee of a registered estate is accorded a substantial immunity from trust interests in the subject land,[2] whilst these same interests survive the transaction concerned and live on in permutated form in the capital proceeds of the disposition.[3]

1   The overreaching principle is just as readily applicable in the context of *unregistered* estates **[paras 2.190, 11.196]**.
2   This immunity goes beyond and supersedes the protection afforded the purchaser by the equitable doctrine of notice **[paras 1.184, 12.337]**.
3   See e g *City of London Building Society v Flegg* [1988] AC 54 at 73G per Lord Templeman ('One of the main objects of the legislation of 1925 was to effect a compromise between on the one hand the interests of the public in securing that land in trust is freely marketable and, on the other hand, the interests of beneficiaries in preserving their rights under the trusts').

Appropriateness to 'general burdens' on land

2.166   As observed earlier,[1] some kinds of entitlement in land have a general or non-specific character and are not therefore intrinsically diminished by their transmutation into some other form of holding. Prime examples are provided by the equitable rights of beneficiaries under a trust of land (whether in the guise of a fractional beneficial share or a life interest or, indeed, an absolute entitlement under a bare trust[2]). The ready convertibility of such 'general burdens' into cash renders them ideal candidates for a statutory mechanism which depends upon a convenient translation of economic value in and out of money forms. This mechanism – the 'overreaching' of rights – consists precisely in a clearing of the title taken by a disponee through the transmutation of pre-existing (and otherwise binding) equitable entitlements into their equivalent value in money.

1   **[Para 2.161]**.
2   **[Paras 9.27, 11.154]**.

Operation of overreaching

2.167   By means of the principle of statutory 'overreaching', the Law of Property Act 1925 oversees a compulsory surrender of the equitable interests of beneficial co-owners in exchange for money rights in the capital proceeds of the disposition of an estate held on trust. In the event of specified categories of conveyance or registered disposition, 'overreaching' has the effect of creating in the disponee a legal estate which, by force of statute,[1] takes 'an absolute priority' over beneficial trust interests already existing in the land.[2] An overreaching disposition of registered land mandatorily sweeps these interests off the land, thereby presenting the disponee with a title free of any beneficial rights behind the former trust of land. In short, the purchaser simply 'overreaches' the obstacles to achieving an unencumbered estate. At the same time, however, the beneficial rights swept off the land are *not* lost or extinguished. Instead they are deflected or 'shifted from the land'[3] so as to attach thereafter to the capital money arising on the disposition. Herein lies the genius of the overreaching device. The disponee is given an extended immunity from various forms of pre-existing equitable right – 'whether or not he has notice' of them[4] – whilst these rights are, in their turn, transmuted into equivalent entitlements in the money proceeds of the transaction. Long-term protection for equitable interests is thus coupled imaginatively with ultimate convenience for the disponee,[5] a combination of effects which remains untouched by the Land Registration Act 2002.[6]

1   See LPA 1925, s 2(1).
2   See *City of London Building Society v Flegg* [1988] AC 54 at 83G–H per Lord Oliver of Aylmerton. For a fuller account of the overreaching process, see Chapter 11 **[para 11.195]**.
3   *City of London Building Society v Flegg* [1988] AC 54 at 91A–B per Lord Oliver of Aylmerton.
4   LPA 1925, s 2(1).
5   Beneficial owners under a trust of registered land are generally entitled to apply for the entry of a 'restriction' on the relevant register of title, but such an entry merely ensures that Land Registry will process no subsequent disposition of the registered estate except in such manner as will inevitably overreach the relevant equitable interests, thereby translating them into the equivalent interests in the capital proceeds received by the trustees **[para 7.53]**.
6   See Law Com No 271 (2001), para 6.41.

Preconditions of overreaching

2.168   The device of overreaching radically extends the freedom from liability enjoyed by the purchaser of a legal estate. Provided that a potentially over-reaching conveyance is conducted in the manner prescribed by the Law of Property Act 1925,[1] the purchaser takes the legal title free of adverse equitable rights (irrespective of his awareness of the rights in question). However, the overreaching process operates only upon those equitable interests which are 'capable of being overreached'[2] – effectively, those interests which have a readily convertible or monetisable value.[3] Moreover, in order to safeguard the rights which are to be overreached, there is a general statutory requirement that the disponee must pay any capital money arising under the relevant disposition to trustees (of whom there must normally be at least two), who then hold the money on trust to give effect to the beneficial rights of those entitled. Any non-compliance with this 'two-trustee rule' has the serious consequence of disabling the disponee from automatically taking free of trust equities and these rights sometimes remain binding upon him as 'overriding' interests.[4]

1   **[Para 11.198]**.
2   LPA 1925, s 2(1).
3   The statutory device of overreaching therefore catches, principally, beneficial interests under a trust of land, but never affects such equitable rights as options, leases and other estate contracts, easements or restrictive covenants. The latter categories of right are protectable, in the registered land scheme of things, by the entry of a 'notice' in the relevant registered title or as interests which statutorily 'override' registered dispositions **[paras 12.89, 12.160]**.
4   See eg *Williams & Glyn's Bank Ltd v Boland* [1981] AC 487 **[paras 12.160, 12.203]**.

A practical example

2.169   The most significant category of overreaching transaction specified by the 1925 legislation comprises a conveyance of a legal estate by trustees of a trust of land.[1] Here, provided that the capital money arising under the disposition is paid to at least two persons as trustees, the beneficial interests under the former trust of land are translated forthwith into precisely equivalent interests in the money now held by those trustees as personalty. Thus, for example (see *Fig.* 8), if the registered title to a family home is held by T1 and T2 on trust for A and B as beneficiaries of 75 per cent and 25 per cent shares respectively,[2] an overreaching disposition of the legal estate by T1 and T2 in favour of X (eg by way of sale) has the effect of entitling A and B to 75 per cent and 25 per cent shares respectively in the capital money released by the disposition.[3]

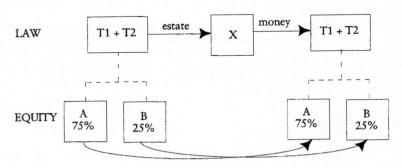

Fig. 8

1   LPA 1925, s 2(1)(ii), as amended by TOLATA 1996, s 25(1), Sch 3, para 4(1), (2)(a).
2   It will be seen later that it is quite possible that T1 and T2 may be the same people as A and B **[para 11.128]**.
3   The resulting capital money is often, of course, reinvested in the purchase of a new home for A and B, whereupon there arises for them both a new trust in the same proportions of equitable ownership.

2.170   At least from the limited perspective of the 1925 legislation,[1] this outcome is highly advantageous for all parties concerned. X, who would not have wished A and B to retain rights in the land following the acquisition of his own interest, takes a clean and unfettered title.[2] Meanwhile, the equitable rights of A and B are not destroyed, but are preserved by being diverted into the capital money raised by the transaction. In theory, at any rate, A and B can regard the disposition of the legal estate with indifference, since all that has happened is that the nature of their investment – the character of the trust asset – has undergone a transformation.

1   See Chapter 11 **[para 11.201]** for a different perspective on this issue.
2   The overreaching effect of a disposition by land trustees (in the plural) displaces any possibility that the equitable rights of trust beneficiaries may 'override' as the rights of persons 'in actual occupation of the land' (see *City of London Building Society v Flegg* [1988] AC 54 **[paras 11.212, 12.213]**). Contrast the outcome where legal title is held by a sole trustee and a disposition of that title is executed by that trustee alone (see eg *Williams & Glyn's Bank Ltd v Boland* [1981] AC 487 **[para 12.203]**). Here, for want of the payment of capital money to trustees (in the plural), the disposition can have no overreaching effect and the possibility remains that trust beneficiaries, if 'in actual occupation of the land', may claim that their interests 'override' as against a transferee or chargee of the registered estate.

'Overriding interests' affecting a registered estate

2.171 The Land Registration Act 2002 demarcates a number of *unregistered* interests in land as having the capacity to 'override' both the first registration of any title at Land Registry and also any subsequent registered disposition of the estate comprised within that title. These rights are commonly, if loosely, known as 'overriding interests'. Although by definition such entitlements never appear on the face of any register of title,[1] they remain automatically binding on the registered estate[2] and have hitherto played a significant role in the scheme of title registration. Registered estates are potentially burdened by a fairly extensive list of overriding interests, almost all proprietary in nature and detailed with some specificity.[3] The majority are uncontentious; many comprise entitlements such as very short leases which are non-registrable and otherwise unprotectable within the registered land scheme of things. Litigation has tended to cluster around the provisions which notoriously protect interests belonging to persons 'in actual occupation' of the land.[4] Although most 'overriding interests' relate to entitlements which are readily apparent from a physical inspection of the land concerned, the Land Registration Act 2002 has now imposed important restrictions on the range and scope of the interests which are allowed to 'override'.[5]

1   See LRA 2002, s 29(3).
2   LRA 2002, s 29(1), (2)(b)(ii) **[para 12.76]**.
3   LRA 2002, Sch 1, Sch 3.
4   **[Para 12.146]**.
5   **[Para 12.150]**. See Robert Walker LJ's reference, in *Ferrishurst Ltd v Wallcite Ltd* [1999] Ch 355 at 368G–369A, to the Law Commission's condemnation of the degree to which the existence of overriding interests 'may be a stumbling block in the law of registration of title, destroying the certainty which registration is intended to achieve' (Law Com No 158 (1987), paras 2.2–2.7).

Rights of occupiers

2.172 The unregistered interests of those 'in actual occupation' of land are statutorily declared to 'override' both first registration and subsequent registered dispositions of registered estates.[1] This category of overriding interest is rather open-ended, affording long-term shelter to *any* proprietary rights which are held by occupiers (other than the registered proprietor of the land). In practice, the overriding interest frequently offers a lifeline to vulnerable occupiers whose entitlement in land is the product of unwitting or casual undocumented creation (eg under some estoppel or informal trust). Such persons are protected from losing their rights amidst the confusion of any dealings with the land which they occupy. As Lord Denning MR pointed out in *Strand Securities Ltd v Caswell*,[2] the claimant whose interest overrides may simply 'stay there and do nothing', since nobody can 'buy the land over his head and thereby take away or diminish his rights.' Effectively, therefore, an onus is placed on all transferees or chargees of the land to carry out a physical inspection of the premises and to make inquiry of any person found to be present.

1   LRA 2002, ss 11(4)(b), 12(4)(c), Sch 1, para 2, s 29(1), (2)(a)(ii), Sch 3, para 2.
2   [1965] Ch 958 at 979G.

Possible overlaps of interest

2.173   Interests which 'override' registered dispositions under the Land Registration Act 2002 include certain entitlements which could (and ideally should) have been protected by some form of entry in the register of the burdened title. For example, options of purchase and certain leases for a term in excess of three years are protectable by the entry of a 'notice' in the Land Register,[1] but nevertheless qualify – in default of such protection – as overriding interests if held by persons who happen to be in 'actual occupation' of the land.[2] Some interests may therefore 'override' by force of statute even though they 'might have been protected by alternative means.'[3] This over-protection of certain kinds of proprietary entitlement has long been a controversial feature of the registration scheme, but it remains the case that the categories of entitlement in registered land are not mutually exclusive.[4] Indeed, rights in registered land may, at various stages in their existence, shift between the categories of registered estate/charge (ie 'major' interest), 'minor' interest and 'overriding' interest.

1   **[Paras 7.247, 9.82]**.
2   **[Para 12.146]**.
3   *Ferrishurst Ltd v Wallcite Ltd* [1999] Ch 355 at 370E–F per Robert Walker LJ. In recent years an additional threat to the title taken by a registered disponee – who may well be a chargee of a registered estate **[para 2.42]** – has been the possibility that some potentially 'overreachable' interests may 'override' the disposition (see e g *Williams & Glyn's Bank Ltd v Boland* [1981] AC 487 **[paras 11.199, 12.203]**).
4   See e g *Williams & Glyn's Bank Ltd v Boland* [1981] AC 487 at 508A per Lord Wilberforce.

LEGAL ESTATES IN UNREGISTERED LAND

2.174   In view of the modern expansion of registered title, the law governing unregistered estates in land is rapidly becoming little more than an obscure annexe to the law of registered estates under the Land Registration Act 2002. The law regulating unregistered estates nevertheless recognises the same initial demarcation of potentially legal and equitable rights as applies in respect of estates registered at Land Registry.[1] Thus the entitlements which are 'authorised to subsist or to be conveyed or created at law'[2] comprise the following:
–   the fee simple absolute in possession[3]
–   the term of years absolute[4]
–   easements[5]
–   profits *à prendre*[6]
–   rentcharges[7]
–   charges by way of legal mortgage[8] and
–   rights of entry.[9]

1   See LPA 1925, s 1(1)–(2) **[para 2.124]**.

2   LPA 1925, s 1(4).
3   **[Para 7.3]**.
4   **[Para 7.68]**.
5   **[Para 8.24]**.
6   **[Para 8.17]**.
7   **[Para 8.225]**.
8   **[Para 8.232]**.
9   **[Para 8.263]**.

STEADY ENCROACHMENT OF REGISTRATION OF TITLE

2.175   In those transactions with an unregistered estate which do not trigger a compulsory first registration at Land Registry,[1] the durable legal status of an entitlement rests solely on due compliance with any appropriate rules of formal creation and conveyance without any additional necessity of completion by registration. The only requirement is, effectively, that a 'legal estate' must normally be created or transferred by deed,[2] although an important exception to this rule of formality covers the grant of certain leasehold terms not exceeding three years.[3] Over the past 15 years, however, the steady extension of compulsory first registration of title at Land Registry has superimposed, in most cases, an extra requirement of completion by registration as the precondition of legally effective creation or transfer. Thus, for instance, the transfer of a previously unregistered estate generally now requires to be completed by the substantive registration of the transferee as proprietor of that estate in a newly created title on the Land Register.[4] Today, in unregistered land, the creation of legal rights outside the mandatory embrace of the Land Registration Act 2002 is confined primarily to the grant of a leasehold term for seven years or less[5] and the creation of a second mortgage charge.[6] Neither form of disposition at present triggers any requirement of registration at Land Registry, although power has been reserved to extend the circumstances which activate the requirement of registration.[7]

1   **[Paras 2.140, 7.40]**.
2   LPA 1925, s 52(1) **[paras 2.141, 7.26]**.
3   LPA 1925, ss 52(2)(d), 54(2).
4   LRA 2002, s 4(1)(a), Sch 2, para 2(1) **[paras 7.40, 7.242]**.
5   **[Paras 2.115, 7.247]**.
6   **[Para 8.257]**.
7   LRA 2002, ss 5(1), 118(1).

THE BINDING IMPACT OF LEGAL RIGHTS IN UNREGISTERED LAND

2.176   It is principally in relation to unregistered estates and interests that the two foundational axioms of English land law still retain some validity.[1] The primary rule of unregistered land holds that legal rights[2] are automatically effective against *all* persons irrespective of knowledge or 'notice'. When an unregistered estate is transferred to a third party, legal rights previously attached to the land remain attached and continue to bind the transferee. Legal rights thus bind the world; they require no artificial protection against third parties; their integrity is inviolable. With very few exceptions (relating to certain kinds of mortgage[3]), legal rights affecting unregistered estates effectively take care of themselves. This axiomatic rule of priority is part of the deep historic structure of unregistered land law, ensuring that one of the earliest sedimentary layers of English law still remains thoroughly exposed to view.

1   [Para 2.134].
2   As defined by reference to LPA 1925, ss 1, 52.
3   For special reasons one particular legal interest affecting an unregistered estate in land – the 'puisne mortgage' – is taken outside the scope of this general rule of binding effect. The enforceability of a puisne mortgage against third parties depends on the registration of a Class C(i) land charge under LCA 1972, s 2(4) [para 12.301].

No immunity from pre-existing legal rights

2.177   The primary axiom of unregistered land law ensures that a purchaser of an unregistered estate enjoys no immunity from pre-existing *legal* rights affecting that estate. If B owns a legal (rather than equitable) right in or over an estate held by A (see *Fig. 9*), and P later takes or acquires any kind of interest in A's land, B's right becomes automatically binding on P, regardless of whether P had any prior knowledge of the existence of B's entitlement.[1]

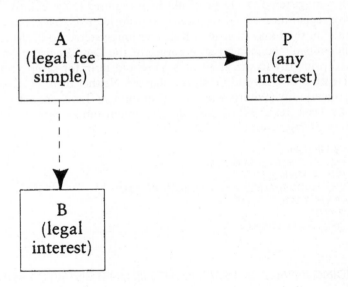

Fig. 9
1   See *Mercer v Liverpool, St Helen's and South Lancashire Railway Co* [1903] 1 KB 652 at 662 per Stirling LJ.

2.178   In this way the austere propositional logic of unregistered land law demands that purchasers[1] (and, indeed, all others[2]) take unregistered estates subject to such pre-existing rights as legal easements, legal terms of years,[3] legal mortgages and legal rights of entry. In the case of any transfer which triggers a requirement of first registration at Land Registry, the priority of such rights is, in most instances, reflected immediately in the entries made by the Chief Land Registrar in the newly opened title in the Land Register.[4]

1   The term 'purchaser' includes a mortgagee **[para 2.42]**.
2   The same inexorable logic applies to render legal rights binding even on one who is not a purchaser at all, but is instead an adverse possessor of the land (ie a 'squatter'). See *Re Nisbet and Potts' Contract* [1906] 1 Ch 386 at 401 **[para 3.26]**.
3   If the relevant term of years were not legal but equitable (eg if not created by deed in circumstances where a deed was required (see LPA 1925, ss 52(2)(d), 54(2))), its effect on a purchaser would depend on different principles **[paras 9.76, 12.308]**.
4   **[Para 12.266]**.

Discoverability of legal rights

2.179   The axiomatic rule that legal rights bind the world works, in a large degree, for efficiency and clarity in unregistered land transactions. The owner of legal rights knows that his position is secure notwithstanding any future transfer of the land; likewise purchasers are in general wholly aware that they take their disposition subject to any legal rights which belong to others. Such outcomes rarely cause injustice since the documentary formality normally required to constitute the legal quality of such rights also ensures their discoverability on a purchaser's investigation of the vendor's title. The existence of many legal interests is also fairly obvious on a physical inspection of the land, with the consequence that it is unlikely – although not altogether impossible – that a purchaser will be caught unawares by an existing legal entitlement affecting the land.

EQUITABLE RIGHTS IN UNREGISTERED LAND

2.180   In relation to land of unregistered title, the categories of equitable entitlement include, as in the case of registered land, not merely those rights which are inherently equitable, but also certain rights which would have been legal but for some want of formality or capacity.[1] Together, in the main, these categories comprise:

–   estate contracts[2] (including options[3] and equitable leases[4])
–   equitable easements[5]
–   equitable profits *à prendre*[6]
–   equitable charges[7]
–   restrictive covenants[8]
–   life interests and
–   beneficial interests under a trust of land.[9]

1   LPA 1925, s 1(3) **[para 2.127]**.
2   **[Para 9.23]**.
3   **[Para 9.77]**.
4   **[Para 9.42]**.

5   [Para 9.88].
6   [Para 9.88].
7   [Para 9.115].
8   [Para 9.138].
9   [Para 9.172].

THE BINDING IMPACT OF EQUITABLE RIGHTS IN UNREGISTERED LAND

2.181   The other major axiom of unregistered land law dictates, in its historic form, that equitable rights bind all persons *other than* a bona fide purchaser of a legal estate for value without notice.[1] According to this principle, a purchaser for value therefore takes the legal estate free of any equitable interests of which he had no notice at the date of purchase.[2]

1   [Para 1.184].
2   'The doctrine of notice lies at the heart of equity' (*Barclays Bank Plc v O'Brien* [1994] 1 AC 180 at 195G–H per Lord Browne-Wilkinson).

Modification of the notice doctrine in the 1925 legislation

2.182   As has already been observed,[1] the equitable doctrine of notice came in time to be regarded as uncertain and capricious in its operation.[2] Notwithstanding its defects, the doctrine continued to govern the binding effect of almost all equitable rights in land until the commencement of the property legislation of 1925. The impact of equitable rights on purchasers of unregistered estates was finally subjected to radical reorganisation by the legislation which took effect on 1 January 1926. The traditional doctrine of notice was overlaid by the two devices, one of which (ie a scheme of 'land charge' registration) rendered notice *inescapable*, whilst the other (ie the device of statutory overreaching) made notice altogether *irrelevant*.

1   [Paras 1.186, 2.135].
2   See W Markby, *Elements of Law considered with reference to Principles of General Jurisprudence* (6th edn, Clarendon 1905), pp 259–260.

Three-fold division of the field of equitable interests in unregistered land

2.183   The obvious intention of the 1925 legislation was to eliminate the role of the equitable doctrine of notice in the determination of unregistered land priorities. The legislation sought to achieve this objective by means of a statutory subdivision of the field of equitable interests into *two* distinct categories (see *Fig.* 6[1]). Some rights were rendered capable of surviving successive transfers of title by virtue of registration as 'land charges' under the Land Charges Act 1925. Other rights were earmarked as capable of being swept off the land by the process of statutory overreaching. It later became apparent that this subdivision had failed to exhaust the categories of equitable rights in unregistered land. There remains a third, residual, category of equitable entitlements to which the pre-1926 notice-based rules of priority continue to apply.[2]

1   [Para 2.99].
2   [Paras 2.191, 12.339].

2.184   As and when an unregistered title is brought on to the Land Register for the first time, it is this complex of priority rules (together with the axiomatic protection given to legal rights) which determines the range of entitlements which require to be reflected on the face of the newly registered estate at Land Registry.

REGISTRATION OF LAND CHARGES

2.185   The Land Charges Act 1972 (the modern successor of the Land Charges Act 1925) subjects certain categories of equitable rights in unregistered land to a limited regime of registration against the *name* of the estate owner whose land they affect.[1] Although, confusingly, a scheme of registration within the domain of 'unregistered' land,[2] this form of registration contrasts markedly with the comprehensive recordation of estates and interests (whether legal or equitable) under distinct title numbers in the wholly separate Land Register (maintained by Land Registry) which controls matters of 'registered title'.

1   [Para 12.275].
2   [Para 2.111].

Coverage of land charge registration

2.186   The land charges scheme applies to important kinds of right which, once created, merit either long- or short-term preservation against purchasers of a legal estate. Such rights include:
–   estate contracts (including options and equitable leases)[1]
–   equitable easements and profits *à prendre*[2]
–   certain equitable charges[3]
–   puisne mortgages and
–   restrictive covenants.[4]

1   [Para 9.23].
2   [Para 9.88].
3   [Para 9.115].
4   [Para 9.138].

Effect of land charge registration

2.187   The Land Charges Act is straightforward – almost brutal – in its operation. The Act modifies the traditional doctrine of notice by providing that the formal registration of certain kinds of equitable interest in the Register of Land Charges is 'deemed to constitute actual notice ... to all persons and for all purposes' of the existence of the rights in question.[1] Thus, in respect of relevant categories of entitlement, entry in the Register of Land Charges becomes in effect the only recognised form of notice for the purpose of binding third parties.[2] By registering his interest as a land charge against the name of the appropriate estate owner, the equitable owner utilises the element of publicity and certainty inherent in formal registration to fix the world with statutory notice of his own interest. He forecloses the possibility that any subsequent purchaser can ever claim to have bought an estate in the encumbered land *without* notice of his equitable interest. Once registered this equitable interest remains binding on the land into whosoever hands the legal estate may later pass.

1   LPA 1925, s 198(1) [**para 12.279**].
2   The Register of Land Charges is accessible by the public – usually by way of a computerised search conducted by officials of the Registry [**para 12.325**]. All prudent purchasers of unregistered land search the Register for entries which may have been effected against previous estate owners.

Effect of failure to register

2.188   The regime of land charge registration has a starkly crystalline quality. In a draconian corollary to the rule of registration, the Land Charges Act provides that *unregistered* rights are rendered statutorily void as against virtually all forms of purchaser.[1] Purchasers are declared unaffected by any registrable, but unregistered, right of which they have knowledge derived from a source outside the Register of Land Charges.[2] In this way the scheme of land charge registration removes many kinds of equitable interest in unregistered land from the scope of the conventional doctrine of notice, thereby diminishing yet further the role left to be played by this doctrine in modern land law.

1   LCA 1972, s 4 [**para 12.280**].
2   LPA 1925, s 199(1)(i). See *Midland Bank Trust Co Ltd v Green* [1981] AC 513 [**para 12.289**].

The net benefits of the Land Charges Act

2.189   The scheme for registration of land charges promotes the general strategy, incorporated in the 1925 property legislation, by which security for various kinds of equitable owner is reconciled with increased facility for third parties who deal with the legal estate. Although certain flaws will later be seen as attaching to this registration scheme,[1] its superficial advantages extend to both purchaser and equitable owner alike. By one simple act of registration, the incumbrancer immediately secures his rights for ever, whilst it remains open to any prospective purchaser to discover, by a simple search of the Register of Land Charges, a swathe of entitlements enforceable against the land which is the subject of his proposed dealing. Under this registration regime the purchaser is placed in the position of knowing exactly what he is buying; while the rights of the equitable owner are made absolutely binding on all later purchasers through the artificial but inexorable medium of notice as provided by the Register.

1   [**Para 12.329**].

STATUTORY OVERREACHING OF TRUST BENEFICIAL INTERESTS

2.190   The device of statutory overreaching[1] is just as applicable to *unregistered* as to *registered* land.[2] Thus the equitable interests of beneficiaries under a trust of land may be cleared off the title taken by a purchaser of an unregistered estate, provided as always that there is compliance with the statutory requirements respecting the payment of any capital money arising on the transaction.[3] The beneficial interests concerned are simultaneously deflected on to – and preserved in the form of – the capital money in the hands of the trustees.[4] In this way the 1925 legislation aims to guarantee the purchaser immunity from substantial categories of pre-existing equitable entitlement in the land, whilst safeguarding such rights in the alternative medium of money.

1   [**Para 2.165**].
2   See LPA 1925, s 2(1) [**para 11.196**].
3   [**Para 11.203**].
4   [**Para 11.210**].

THE RESIDUAL APPLICATION OF THE 'BONA FIDE PURCHASER RULE'

2.191   The enactment in the 1925 Acts of the devices of overreaching and land charge registration was initially thought to have rendered the orthodox doctrine of notice virtually irrelevant to equitable rights in unregistered land. It has become painfully obvious, however, that these devices did not exhaust the field of equitable interests and that 'there may well be rights, of an equitable character, outside the provisions as to registration and which are incapable of being overreached.'[1] Indeed, one of the more difficult problems left in modern unregistered conveyancing relates to the continued existence of a small, but consistently awkward, category of anomalous equitable rights which for one reason or another fall outside both major classifications of registrable and overreachable entitlement. In respect of these interests the classical doctrine of notice, for want of any other relevant rule, retains a residual application.[2] Such rights remain binding on all purchasers of an unregistered estate *other than* a bona fide purchaser of a legal estate for value without notice.[3]

1   *Shiloh Spinners Ltd v Harding* [1973] AC 693 at 721D per Lord Wilberforce.
2   [**Para 12.339**]. This doctrine of notice or 'bona fide purchaser rule' *never* applies in relation to titles which have already been registered under the Land Registration Act 2002.
3   [**Para 12.355**].

Remaining instances of notice-based entitlement

2.192   Of the category of surviving notice-based equitable rights in unregistered land perhaps the most prominent example comprises the equitable interest of a beneficiary under a trust of land where legal title has been conveyed by a sole land trustee.[1] In these circumstances the beneficiary's rights fall outside the major classifications of overreachable right (because capital money has not been paid over to at least two trustees) and registrable land charge (because the rights, being inherently overreachable, were excluded from the ambit of the Land Charges Act 1972).[2] The purchaser of the legal estate from the sole trustee takes free of the beneficiary's rights only if he is a bona fide purchaser for value without notice. Similarly notice-based equitable rights include certain restrictive covenants[3] and equitable easements created before 1926[4] and some forms of entitlement based on 'proprietary estoppel'.[5]

1   See e g *Kingsnorth Finance Ltd v Tizard* [1986] 1 WLR 783 [**para 12.361**].
2   [**Para 12.356**].
3   [**Para 12.372**].
4   [**Para 12.372**].
5   See e g *E R Ives Investment Ltd v High* [1967] 2 QB 379; *Birmingham Midshires Mortgage Services Ltd v Sabherwal* (2000) 80 P & CR 256 at 263.

Impulse towards curtailment of notice-based entitlements

2.193   With the advent of comprehensive registration of title now within view, it seems that there is an ever stronger judicial impulse to close down the scope available for the operation of the old notice-based priority rule. Residual applications of the bona fide purchaser principle keep alive all the uncertainty and unpredictability which the legislators of 1925 tried so hard to eradicate from both registered and unregistered land. It is not without significance that, in *Birmingham Midshires Mortgage Services Ltd v Sabherwal*,[1] Robert Walker LJ indicated, with ill-disguised impatience, that in the regime of unregistered title the category of unoverreached, unregistrable equities is nowadays 'limited ... to some unusual types of equitable interest arising in commercial situations.' Although the animus against this anomalous class of notice-based rights is manifest, it has to be said that the doctrine of notice still holds a key to the resolution of some quite important issues of unregistered land priority.

1   (2000) 80 P & CR 256 at 263.

CHAPTER 3

Possession

THE SIGNIFICANCE OF 'POSSESSION'

3.1 Throughout the history of English land law, the operative concept has been *possession* rather than ownership: the common lawyer's overwhelming concern has been with the phenomenon of possessory control over land.[1] The conceptualism of *ownership* is a relatively recent intrusion into the thought patterns of the common lawyer,[2] more relevant to the ordering of the personal property generated by the industrial revolution and the advent of the modern corporate state.[3] In relation to land the common lawyer's essential working tool has always been the earthily pragmatic notion of de facto possession[4] or, as earlier generations of lawyers would have expressed it, the concept of 'seisin'.[5] In some fairly primitive way the actuality of social or behavioural fact – in the form of sustained possession of land – has long functioned not only as the authentic origin of title[6] but also as the source of certain crucial guarantees of free enjoyment of land.[7] The imperative of peaceful possession finds timeless expression from Magna Carta[8] to the European Convention on Human Rights.[9] Yet, as will become apparent in following chapters, the philosophical base of title has, in recent times, shifted significantly from *possession* to *ownership*. The historic perception of property as rooted in empirically defined fact is being rapidly displaced by a more modern view of property as the exclusive product of a state-administered system of computerised entitlement.

1 'Exclusive possession de jure or de facto, now or in the future, is the bedrock of English land law' (*Hunter v Canary Wharf Ltd* [1997] AC 655 at 703F per Lord Hoffmann). See also *Bell v General Accident, Fire & Life Assurance Corpn Ltd* [1998] 1 EGLR 69 at 71D–E per Hutchison LJ ('The essence of the relationship of landlord and tenant is the granting of possession and not of title').

2 The earliest reference to 'ownership' seems to date back no further than 1583. Pollock and Maitland report that 'the term *absolute ownership* was very new when Coke thus applied it to the tenant in fee of English land' (*The History of English Law* (2nd edn, London 1968), Vol 2, p 153).

3 For reference to 'the nineteenth-century dogma that everything must be owned', see *Yanner v Eaton* (1999) 201 CLR 351 at [29] per Gleeson CJ, Gaudron, Kirby and Hayne JJ, citing Roscoe Pound, *An Introduction to the Philosophy of Law* (Yale University Press 1954), p 111.

4   'At common law, a premium is placed on the factual reality of occupation' (*Delgamuukw v British Columbia* (1997) 153 DLR (4th) 193 at [156] per Lamer CJC).
5   [**Para 3.5**].
6   For example, unregistered conveyancing ultimately comprises little more than the handing on from seller to buyer of a title evidenced by undisturbed possession (see LPA 1969, s 23 [**paras 6.2, 12.260**]).
7   Standing to sue in trespass and nuisance is, in strict terms, a derivative of possession [**paras 3.30, 7.143**].
8   'No free man shall be ... disseised ... except by the lawful judgment of his peers or by the law of the land' Magna Carta 1215, Art 39 (see J C Holt, *Magna Carta* (2nd edn, Cambridge UP 1992), pp 461, 465–466). See also *Mabo v Queensland (No 1)* (1988) 166 CLR 186 at 226 per Deane J.
9   ECHR Protocol No 1, Art 1 [**para 2.29**]. See Gray and Gray, 'The rhetoric of realty', in J Getzler (ed), *Rationalizing Property, Equity and Trusts: Essays in Honour of Edward Burn* (Butterworths 2003), pp 206–207.

THE NATURE OF 'POSSESSION'

3.2   'Possession' is no simple concept.[1] Although a central notion in English law, the term 'possession' has long lacked any concise judicial explication.[2] In relation to land, however, its key element is the idea of control over terrain. 'Possession' is perhaps best described as 'a conclusion of law defining the nature and status of a particular relationship of control by a person over land.'[3] In this sense, the concept of 'possession' is a free-standing notion which admits little qualification. In the view of the common law, possession is autonomous and indivisible.[4] Possession is simply a state of overall territorial control. Since exclusivity is 'of the essence of possession',[5] even the adjective 'exclusive' adds nothing to an understanding of the phenomenon.[6] Indeed, the misnomer of 'exclusive possession' can be said to have generated difficulties in several important respects.[7] Equally, the qualifier 'adverse' does little to illuminate the inherent nature of 'possession', since it indicates merely that the possessor's presence on land is contrary to the interests of others.[8]

1   See *Mabo v Queensland (No 2)* (1992) 175 CLR 1 at 207 per Toohey J. For Salmond there was, '[i]n the whole range of legal theory ... no conception more difficult than that of possession' (John W Salmond, *Jurisprudence (or The Theory of Law)* (London 1902), p 288). For classic explorations of possession, see O W Holmes, *The Common Law* (Boston 1881), p 206; F Pollock and R S Wright, *Possession in the Common Law* (Clarendon 1888).
2   See *United States of America and Republic of France v Dollfus Mieg et Cie SA and Bank of England* [1952] AC 582 at 605 per Earl Jowitt. Statute law has similarly fought shy of comprehensive definition (see eg LPA 1925, s 205(1)(xix); LRA 2002, s 131(1)–(2) [**para 12.253**]). Contrast the penetrating critique of 'possession' provided by McHugh J in *Western Australia v Ward* (2002) 191 ALR 1 at [477]–[478], [502]–[503].
3   *Mabo v Queensland (No 2)* (1992) 175 CLR 1 at 207 per Toohey J.
4   'The general rule ... is that only one person can be in possession at any one time' (*J A Pye (Oxford) Ltd v Graham* [2003] 1 AC 419 at [70] per Lord Hope of Craighead). See W Markby, *Elements of Law considered with reference to Principles of General Jurisprudence* (6th edn, Clarendon 1905), p 203. See also *Hills (Patents) Ltd v University College Hospital Board of Governors* [1956] 1 QB 90 at 99 per Denning LJ.
5   See *J A Pye (Oxford) Ltd v Graham* [2003] 1 AC 419 at [70] per Lord Hope of Craighead.
6   '[P]ossession that is not exclusive is a contradiction in terms, for the right of general control and exclusion is central to the concept of legal possession ... [I]t is a pity that the term

"exclusive possession" was ever used … ' (*Western Australia v Ward* (2002) 191 ALR 1 at [477], [502] per McHugh J). In any event, as Callinan J pointed out in *Wilson v Anderson* (2002) 190 ALR 313 at [194], it is simply a reality of the modern world that 'exclusive possession in absolute terms has long since ceased to exist.' See also *Ward*, supra at [624], [694] per Callinan J.

7 The phrase rather insinuates that those in 'possession' are automatically invested with a totalitarian privilege to exclude all comers [**para 4.20**]. The unnecessary qualifier 'exclusive' has also induced a blurring of the fundamental distinction between 'possession' and mere 'occupation' of land, with the result that the more intense forms of non-proprietary occupancy of land have come to be accorded legal consequences which properly attach only to 'possession' [**paras 3.51, 7.144**].

8 *J A Pye (Oxford) Ltd v Graham* [2003] 1 AC 419 at [36] per Lord Browne-Wilkinson, [69] per Lord Hope of Craighead ('a convenient label only'). See also *Wills v Wills* [2004] 1 P & CR 612 at [17] per Lord Walker of Gestingthorpe ('a convenient shorthand').

Possession is more than mere occupancy

3.3 At common law the term 'possession' connotes much more than the idea of a bare physical occupancy.[1] The relevant emphasis is on the deliberate, strategic control of land. Possession is the self-evident state of affairs which prevails where one person is in a position to 'control access to [land] by others and, in general, decide how the land will be used.'[2] Possession is thus an inherently behavioural phenomenon which incorporates a particular mindset. Far from denoting a mere physical presence upon land,[3] possession is constituted by a range of inner assumptions about the power relationships generated by such presence.[4] In other words, possession is necessarily reinforced by a demonstrable state of mind (or *animus*[5]) which encapsulates the possessor's own perception of the force and defensibility of his rights in relation to the land.[6] For this reason, whereas 'occupation' is a question of *fact*, 'possession' is a conclusion of *law*,[7] and its presence or absence can lead to important legal consequences.

1 See *J A Pye (Oxford) Ltd v Graham* [2003] 1 AC 419 at [70] per Lord Hope of Craighead; *Ocean Harvesters Ltd v Quinlan Brothers Ltd* [1975] 1 SCR 684 at 691–692 per Dickson J; *Western Australia v Ward* (2002) 191 ALR 1 at [518] per McHugh J ('Possession and occupation – even sole occupation – are different concepts').

2 *Western Australia v Ward* (2002) 191 ALR 1 at [52] per Gleeson CJ, Gaudron, Gummow and Hayne JJ. See similarly W Markby, op cit, p 180 ('a physical capacity to deal with a thing as we like, to the exclusion of everyone else'). Thus one may be in possession of land without ever having seen it or being aware of its full scope; one may be in possession of things concealed under the land surface without having any reason to suspect their presence or know their location (*Elwes v Brigg Gas Company* (1886) 33 Ch D 562 at 568–569 (prehistoric longboat)).

3 A person may be in possession of land without being in occupation of it (see *R v St Pancras Assessment Committee* (1877) 2 QBD 581 at 588 per Lush J; *Western Australia v Ward* (2002) 191 ALR 1 at [518] per McHugh J). See also *Nicholson v Samuel Property Management Ltd* (2002) 217 DLR (4th) 292 at [14]. 'Possession' includes 'receipt of rents and profits or the right to receive the same' (LPA 1925, s 205(1)(xix)).

4 See O W Holmes, *The Common Law* (Boston 1881), p 216 (possession is 'simply a relation of manifested power coextensive with the intent').

5 [**Para 6.133**]. See *J A Pye (Oxford) Ltd v Graham* [2003] 1 AC 419 at [40] per Lord Browne-Wilkinson.

6   Thus, for instance, no 'possession' can properly be attributed to a mere 'overnight trespasser' or to a friend who has expressly agreed to look after a house during its owner's absence on holiday (*J A Pye (Oxford) Ltd v Graham* [2003] 1 AC 419 at [40] per Lord Browne-Wilkinson). See likewise *Pemberton v Southwark LBC* [2000] 1 WLR 1672 at 1686B–C per Sir Christopher Slade (no possession for the 'casual intruder').

7   See *Mabo v Queensland (No 2)* (1992) 175 CLR 1 at 212 per Toohey J.

Differences between 'possession' and 'property'

3.4   In land law the 'property' denoted by the major estates in realty has tended, historically, to be a derivative of possessory control over defined terrain.[1] The concepts of 'property' and 'possession' are nevertheless distinct. A person can be described as being in 'possession' of land, but cannot (except in one very technical sense[2]) be said to be in 'possession' of a proprietary right. The *animus* which underlies 'possession' of land is subjective to the occupier,[3] whereas 'property' in land is ultimately validated by some social or collective judgement about the legitimacy of the claim involved.[4] 'Property' (in the sense of a power-relationship in respect of some valued resource) is a relative notion and is capable of many fine gradations.[5] 'Possession' (in the sense of overall territorial control) has a recognisable integrity and uniformity. Thus, for example, the grantee of an easement undoubtedly has a certain quantum of 'property' in the servient land,[6] but cannot be said to be in 'possession' of that land.[7]

1   See *Russell v Hill*, 34 SE 640 at 640 (NC 1899) ('property may be presumed from possession').
2   [Para 7.21].
3   [Para 6.142].
4   [Para 2.6].
5   [Para 2.13].
6   [Paras 2.14, 8.71].
7   See e g *Jackson v Mulvaney* [2003] 1 WLR 360 at [25] [para 8.71].

HISTORIC IMPORTANCE OF THE 'SEISIN-POSSESSION' CONCEPT

3.5   The 'seisin-possession' concept is deeply embedded in the historical development of English land law.[1] The notion of seisin reflects the empirical orientation of the early common law, which tended to analyse entitlement to land in terms of factual possession rather than in terms of some abstract or documentary title.

1   See F W Maitland, 'The Mystery of Seisin' (1886) 2 LQR 481; 'The Beatitude of Seisin' (1888) 4 LQR 24, 286.

Vindication of seisin

3.6   Seisin comprised the actual or de facto possession of land – quite irrespective of right.[1] As Pollock and Maitland expressed it, a man was 'in seisin' of land when he was 'enjoying it or in a position to enjoy it.'[2] Such possession, even if wrongful, was accorded a certain protection 'in the interests of peace.'[3] If a man with seisin was dispossessed (or 'disseised'), he could seek to recover the land through the action of novel disseisin. Significantly, this action protected *seisin* not *ownership*, but the process of recovery threw up the 'curiosity'[4] that the disseisee was able to rely on his earlier seisin as providing the basis of his title to the land. Although seisin was fact not right, right could flow from fact and find reinforcement in the passage of time.[5]

1   Since seisin was a matter of fact, even the thief could enjoy seisin. The wrongful possessor came to be regarded as having a tortious fee simple which he could alienate and devise [**para 3.31**].
2   *The History of English Law* (2nd edn, London 1968), Vol 2, p 34. 'Seisin' did not necessarily connote violence. To medieval lawyers it shared semantic roots with 'sitting' and 'setting' and 'suggested peace and quiet' (ibid, p 30).
3   See *Minister of State for the Army v Dalziel* (1944) 68 CLR 261 at 276 per Latham CJ.
4   See A W B Simpson, *A History of the Land Law* (2nd edn, Oxford 1986), p 38.
5   See A E-S Tay, 'Property and Law in the Society of Mass Production, Mass Consumption and Mass Allocation' (1977) 10 ARSP (New Series) 87 at 91–95.

Feoffments with 'livery of seisin'

3.7   Seisin thus expressed an organic element in the relationship between tenant, land and lord, and came to provide presumptive evidence of entitlement within the medieval framework of rights in land. Moreover, from the 15th century onwards, seisin was the technical term used to 'denote the completion of that investiture, by which the tenant was admitted into the tenure; and without which, no freehold could be constituted or pass.'[1] Indeed only the person seised could effect a 'feoffment' (or conveyance of freehold land) with 'livery of seisin' in the symbolic sense required by the common law. 'Livery of seisin' took the form of a solemn ceremony. The grantor and grantee entered upon the land to be conveyed and the feoffor, in the presence of witnesses, delivered seisin to the feoffee either by some symbolic act, such as handing him a twig or sod of earth, or by expressing appropriate words of alienation and leaving him in possession of the land.[2]

1   *Taylor d Atkyns v Horde* (1757) 1 Burr 60 at 107, 97 ER 190 at 216 per Lord Mansfield.
2   '"What's taking seizin?" said Dan, cautiously. "It's an old custom the people had when they bought and sold land. They used to cut out a clod and hand it over to the buyer, and you weren't lawfully seized of your land – it didn't really belong to you – till the other fellow had actually given you a piece of it – like this." He held out the turves' (Rudyard Kipling, *Puck of Pook's Hill* (London 1906), p 12). See also *Manton v Parabolic Pty Ltd* [1985] 2 NSWLR 361 at 367A–368C.

Respect for factual possession

3.8   The quaint ritual of feoffment with livery of seisin is no longer effective in English law to transfer an estate in land.[1] All interests in land now 'lie in grant' and may be conveyed 'without actual entry.'[2] The seisin-possession concept nevertheless left an indelible mark on the way in which the common lawyer thinks of all property and particularly of land. The protection accorded raw possession expresses a strong sense of respect for what one finds on the ground. The large social interest in preserving the peace and good order of the status quo comprises a subliminal theme which extends throughout the entire range of property law.[3] On this pragmatic view the avoidance of socially harmful disruption has been deemed to justify the compromise between fact and entitlement which is implicit in the historic law of adverse possession.[4] On a broader plane the seisin-possession concept has even played a significant constitutional role in protecting 'the citizen's actual behaviour and powers *against* the claims of privilege and authority.'[5] It can be maintained with some justification that the common law 'bias in favour of the factual situation' generated an early sense of the civil liberties of the subject,[6] of the inviolability of the Englishman's home as his castle,[7] and even of the general distaste for forcible eviction and violent seizure which pervades English law.[8]

1   LPA 1925, s 51(1).
2   The possibility of land transfer by livery of seisin seems to have survived longest in Ontario (see e g *Re Bouris and Button* (1976) 60 DLR (3d) 233 at 238).
3   See Gray, 'Property in Common Law Systems', in G E van Maanen and A J van der Walt (ed), *Property Law on the Threshold of the 21st Century* (MAKLU, Antwerp, 1996), pp 250–252.
4   **[Para 6.36]**.
5   Alice Tay, 'Law, the citizen and the state', in E Kamenka, R Brown and A E-S Tay (ed), *Law and Society: The Crisis in Legal Ideals* (London 1978), p 11.
6   See Tay, loc cit, pp 11–12 ('The role of the underlying seisin-possession concept in the common law is to recognise and protect those still important areas in which men live, work and plan as user-owners, to set out their rights and obligations, to give them an area of privacy in which they have a right to be free of state and community interference').
7   See *Semayne's Case* (1604) 5 Co Rep 91a at 91b, 77 ER 194 at 195 **[paras 3.20, 4.14]**.
8   The historic protection of seisin was the intellectual progenitor of the social housing legislation adopted during the 20th century throughout much of the common law world. Regardless of the merits of the case, eviction is not merely the compulsory vacation of property; it is the destruction of someone's way of life **[paras 14.109, 14.311]**.

Relevance of possession in the context of title registration

3.9   The significance accorded de facto possession even reaches into the modern statutory regulation of registered titles.

Protection at first registration

3.10   Possession-based notions of title retain a substantial relevance up to and including the point when unregistered estates in land are finally brought on to the register maintained by Land Registry.[1] First registration of title is, so to speak, the terminal event in the lifetime of an unregistered estate as it becomes translated into one of the registered titles governed by the Land Registration Act 2002. For this reason the priorities surrounding a previously unregistered estate require to be determined at first registration by reference to *unregistered* *land* principles which are still overshadowed by the significance traditionally assigned at common law to the fact of possession. Thus, for example, a squatter who is a mere trespasser on unregistered land may voluntarily apply to be entered in the register as a first registered proprietor with 'possessory title',[2] a status which may be granted if the registrar is 'of opinion that the person is in actual possession of the land' by virtue of his common law estate.[3]

1   **[Paras 2.143, 12.266]**.
2   **[Para 7.47]**.
3   LRA 2002, ss 9(5), 10(6).

Other protection for possessors

3.11   The idea of seisin also finds a contemporary echo in the force accorded to certain unregistered interests which are statutorily declared to 'override' first registrations of title and subsequent registered dispositions under the Land Registration Act 2002. Here, most controversially, unrecorded interests belonging to 'a person in actual occupation' of land[1] represent an exception to the general indefeasibility of registered titles,[2] although the 2002 Act makes a concerted effort to cut back the scope of such interests.[3] Likewise all first registered proprietors – irrespective of the quality of the title awarded to them by Land Registry – are bound by interests acquired by other persons under the Limitation Act of which they have notice.[4] A similar deference towards rights of possession is evident in the rule which, in other than exceptional circumstances, safeguards the title of a registered proprietor from unconsented and prejudicial alteration 'in relation to land in his possession.'[5]

1   LRA 2002, ss 11(2)–(4), 12(2)–(4), Sch 1, para 2 **[para 12.268]**, s 29(1), (2)(a)(ii), Sch 3, para 2 **[para 12.146]** (see formerly LRA 1925, s 70(1)(g)). See also *Hodgson v Marks* [1971] Ch 892 at 932C–D per Russell LJ ('a person in occupation is protected in his rights by that occupation').
2   In invoking this exception to protect the residential rights of family members in the family home, modern courts have used language strikingly reminiscent of the concept of seisin. See *Williams & Glyn's Bank Ltd v Boland* [1979] Ch 312 at 332E per Lord Denning MR ('actual occupation' is 'matter of fact, not matter of law ... It does not depend on title'). See also *Williams & Glyn's Bank Ltd v Boland* [1981] AC 487 at 505B per Lord Wilberforce ('what is required is physical presence, not some entitlement in law').
3   **[Para 12.134]**.
4   LRA 2002, ss 11(4)(c), 12(4)(d) **[paras 6.70, 12.268]**.
5   LRA 2002, ss 65, 131(1)–(2), Sch 4, paras 3(2), 6(2) **[para 12.252]**. See formerly LRA 1925, s 82(3).

POSSESSION, PROPERTY, TITLE AND ESTATE

3.12   At the base of any understanding of English realty is the network of relationships between 'possession', 'property', 'title' and 'estate'. The subtlety of these linkages reflects a deep historic ambivalence[1] as to whether 'property' in land is constituted by the empirical reality of behavioural fact or by the official regulation of abstract entitlements. Is 'property' in land determined socially or conceptually? Is the character of 'property' ultimately physical or cerebral?

Following chapters of this book will point to a clear distinction between the *common law* notion of title (as founded essentially on the raw fact of unchallenged possession) and the increasingly pervasive *statutory* perception of title (as based on the state-administered ordering of artificially defined legal entitlements).

1   See Gray and Gray, 'The Idea of Property in Land', in S Bright and J K Dewar (ed), *Land Law: Themes and Perspectives* (Oxford UP 1998), p 18.

'Property' in land

3.13   The law of real property has long exhibited a tension between empirical and conceptual models of entitlement. In terms of cerebral analysis, English law recognises only the ownership of abstract 'estates' rather than any ownership of land itself: 'property' in land is necessarily articulated through the medium of notional 'estates' or 'interests' in realty.[1] In terms of pragmatic analysis, the behavioural reality of 'possession' has tended to be regarded, in default of any better methodology, as the ultimate ground of claim to a 'title' to an 'estate' in land.[2] In less sophisticated times the derivation of title from visible physical possession performed a valuable function in limiting the information costs associated with the ascertainment of estate ownership.[3] As Kitto J once observed,[4] 'men generally own the property they possess' and the law simply 'recognises the probability which common experience suggests.' The common law theory of relativity of title therefore predicated that the best 'title' was that of the person whose claim to 'possession' was superior to that of anyone else. From these propositions emerged the ultimate integration of the material and the conceptual. Since the best possible 'title' flows from ownership of the largest common law 'estate', unchallenged de facto 'possession' of land is equated with, and legally generates, ownership of an 'estate' in fee simple.[5]

1   [**Para 1.121**]. See e g *Reilly v Booth* (1890) 44 Ch D 12 at 22–23 per Cotton LJ, 26 per Lopes LJ.
2   [**Para 2.78**].
3   See Thomas W Merrill and Henry E Smith, 'The Property/Contract Interface' 101 Col L Rev 773 at 803 (2001).
4   *Allen v Roughley* (1955) 94 CLR 98 at 138.
5   [**Para 3.24**].

'Title' and 'estate'

3.14   If 'possession' is concerned with a factual relationship of control over land, 'title' is certainly a more abstract concept. As will appear later,[1] the meaning of 'title' has undergone significant change over the years and its connotation varies between common law and statutory contexts.

1   [**Para 6.1**].

Meaning of 'title' at common law

3.15   At common law 'title' is the term used to denote the *right* or *entitlement* of an owner to assert his 'estate' (and its various incidents) against other persons. To have 'title' to an 'estate' means to be *entitled* – the etymological link is not accidental – to exercise the various rights associated with ownership of that estate. 'Title' in relation to a freehold or leasehold estate therefore comprises the legal authority to vindicate possessory rights as against strangers and to avail oneself of other rights to control the use, exploitation and disposition of the land.

Disjunctions of 'title' and 'estate'

3.16 On this analysis, 'title' and 'estate' are clearly not synonymous terms. The estate owner generally has 'title' to his 'estate'. It is possible, however, that one can own an 'estate' in land, but have no 'title' to assert it against a particular person (or even at all). In rare circumstances 'title' and 'estate' may become detached so that the estate owner loses his entitlement to enforce his estate quoad somebody else or even quoad the world at large. Under the Limitation Act 1980, for example, a twelve year period of adverse possession against an estate owner extinguishes that owner's 'title' to his 'estate',[1] but does not extinguish the 'estate' itself.[2] In such cases the relevant 'estate' remains vested in limbo in its disentitled owner, but it does not follow that the 'estate' is necessarily non-existent or dead. Adverse possession may, for instance, extinguish the 'title' of a leasehold estate owner quoad the squatter on his land, but leave the leasehold estate intact in the hands of the dispossessed tenant and therefore available to be surrendered to his landlord.[3] In effect, the tenant's title to assert his estate can be barred as against a squatter whilst remaining unbarred for the purpose of other dealings.[4]

1   Limitation Act 1980, s 17 [**para 6.46**].
2   See *St Marylebone Property Co Ltd v Fairweather* [1962] 1 QB 498 at 515 per Holroyd Pearce LJ, [1963] AC 510 at 538–540 per Lord Radcliffe. Compare *St Marylebone Property Co Ltd v Fairweather* [1963] AC 510 at 544–545 per Lord Denning; *Central London Commercial Estates Ltd v Kato Kagaku Co Ltd* [1998] 4 All ER 948 at 958h per Sedley J.
3   See e g *St Marylebone Property Co Ltd v Fairweather* [1963] AC 510 [**para 6.83**].
4   See *Spectrum Investment Co v Holmes* [1981] 1 WLR 221 at 226B–D per Browne-Wilkinson J.

'Property' as socially constituted fact

3.17 According to one of the major historic models of the common law, 'property' in land is simply a reflection of socially constituted fact.[1] De facto use and exploitation of land resources tend to generate legal entitlements of varying degrees of intensity. The most significant forms of 'property' in land – the possessory estates of freehold and leasehold – are associated with a powerful, perhaps deeply instinctive, sense of territorial belonging and control.[2] Correspondingly, an absence or deficit of overall possessory control generally points towards ownership of some lesser entitlement in the land.[3] On this empirical view, the critical determinant of the nature and extent of 'property' in land has therefore been the mode of behaviour consciously adopted by the claimant.[4] The claimant has been, in some elusive sense, the master of his own destiny. Estate ownership has been a self-defining phenomenon: each occupier or user of land is credited with the quantum of 'property' which corresponds most closely to the quality of his own behaviour.

1   On the constitutive effect of empirical fact, see Gray and Gray, 'The Idea of Property in Land', in S Bright and J K Dewar (ed), *Land Law: Themes and Perspectives* (Oxford UP 1998), pp 18–27.
2   **[Para 2.79]**.
3   See e g *R v Toohey; Ex parte Meneling Station Pty Ltd* (1982) 158 CLR 327 at 342–343, where the High Court of Australia declared a statutory grazing licence to constitute a mere personal right and no proprietary 'estate or interest' in land, emphasising the extraordinary fragility of the licence in question **[para 2.26]**. See also *Koowarta v Bjelke-Petersen* (1982) 153 CLR 168 at 184.
4   See *Western Australia v Ward* (2000) 170 ALR 159 at 188 per Beaumont and von Doussa JJ.

Possessory estates in land

3.18   The possessory estates of modern land law – the fee simple and the term of years absolute – connote distinctive concentrations of overall territorial control. Both estates resonate with a significant sovereignty over land: both carry extensive rights of quiet and exclusive enjoyment.[1] The fee simple absolute and the term of years absolute are acknowledged as the primary estates of land law[2] precisely because, in their different ways, they mark out the allocation of a predominating or strategic quantum of 'property' in the subject land.

1   'Exclusivity is a common law principle derived from the notion of fee simple ownership' (*Delgamuukw v British Columbia* (1997) 153 DLR (4th) 193 at [156] per Lamer CJC). Exclusive possession is also 'the proper touchstone' of a lease or tenancy (*Radaich v Smith* (1959) 101 CLR 209 at 223 per Windeyer J **[para 7.131]**). See similarly *Street v Mountford* [1985] AC 809 at 816C per Lord Templeman.
2   See LPA 1925, s 1(1).

Exclusive territorial control

3.19   Indeed, speaking from the pragmatic perspective which has dominated so much English land law, it can be said that the more obvious the possessory element, the more likely it is that the claimant of rights in land is the owner of a freehold or leasehold estate. The de facto assertion of dominion over land points unmistakably towards ownership of one or other of the possessory estates. As Lopes LJ observed in *Reilly v Booth*,[1] '[t]he exclusive or unrestricted use of a piece of land ... beyond all question passes the property or ownership in that land.' For example, a water company's insertion of a sewer in privately owned land necessarily invests the company as a freeholder with 'absolute property' in 'the whole of the space occupied by the sewer', thereby entitling the landowner to compensation for compulsory divestiture of a freehold estate.[2]

1   (1890) 44 Ch D 12 at 26. See similarly W Markby, *Elements of Law considered with reference to Principles of General Jurisprudence* (6th edn, Clarendon 1905), p 201.

2   See *Taylor v North West Water* (1995) 70 P & CR 94 at 107. Exclusive user of a defined
    quantum of air space likewise connotes a freehold estate rather than an easement (*Bursill
    Enterprises Pty Ltd v Berger Bros Trading Co Pty Ltd* (1971) 124 CLR 73 at 91; *Tileska v
    Bevelon* (1989) 4 BPR 9601 at 9606). See similarly *Telecom Auckland Ltd v Auckland CC* [1999]
    1 NZLR 426 at 440–441 (space exclusively occupied by underground cables held taxable as
    'land' owned by operator of communications network).

A 'stake' in the land

3.20   So potent is this behavioural dimension of property relationships that,
even today, common law courts frequently resort to curiously unlegalistic
language in seeking to identify the existence of the fee simple estate and the
term of years. Estate ownership is still articulated in language which is
strikingly crude and unsophisticated. Thus, for instance, the status enjoyed by
the leaseholder, and *a fortiori* by the freeholder, is often said to be characterised
by the freedom each has to 'call the place his own.'[1] In *Marchant v Charters*,[2] in
attempting to capture the essence of the leasehold estate, Lord Denning MR
could frame the issue only as a deeply intuitive empirical inquiry, ie whether the
relevant occupier had a 'stake' in the premises, as distinct from a mere
'permission for himself personally to occupy.' It is by virtue of such stakehold-
ing – by virtue of some gut sense of belonging or domain – that the leaseholder
or tenant can properly be described as 'able to exercise the rights of an owner of
land, which is in the real sense his land albeit temporarily and subject to certain
restrictions.'[3]

1   *Street v Mountford* [1985] AC 809 at 818A per Lord Templeman. As Coke CJ observed long
    ago, 'the house of every one is to him as his castle and fortress' (*Semayne's Case* (1604) 5 Co
    Rep 91a at 91b, 77 ER 194 at 195). By contrast, '[a] licensee lacking exclusive possession can in
    no sense call the land his own' (*Street v Mountford*, supra at 816C per Lord Templeman).
2   [1977] 1 WLR 1181 at 1185G **[para 7.163]**.
3   *Street v Mountford* [1985] AC 809 at 816B per Lord Templeman.

Absence of estate ownership

3.21   It follows that no freehold or leasehold estate can be claimed by one
whose mode of user of land exhibits no true possessory character. Thus, for
example, a lodger or licensee, by reason of his subordination to the supervisory
authority of another, lacks the essential element of territorial control which
would equip him with any credible claim to *possession*, as distinct from a mere
personal occupancy, of land.[1] The peculiar psycho-spatial dynamics of the
lodger relationship entail that the occupant lacks the self-validating inner
confidence of a stakeholder in the land. The lodger does not feel himself to be
quite 'at home'; his occupancy resonates with a certain permissive quality
rather than with the arrogance of right.[2] As Lord Templeman declared in *Street
v Mountford*,[3] no residential occupier can claim an estate in the land if he is
provided with attendance or services which require the owner or his servants to
'exercise unrestricted access to and use of the premises.'[4] In such circumstances
it is the owner who 'retains possession' precisely in order to supply the

attendance or services.[5] For example, the student lodger whose comings and goings are jealously overseen by his landlady cannot realistically claim to enjoy 'possession' of any part of his premises or to have any 'property' as such in his landlady's house. Similarly the hotel guest may enjoy a temporarily exclusive use of his room but does not have overall territorial control.[6]

1   On the lodger's subjection to the control exercised by the estate owner, see *Thompson v Ward* (1871) LR 6 CP 327 at 361 per Bovill CJ; *Bradley v Baylis* (1881) 8 QBD 195 at 219; *Ancketill v Baylis* (1882) 10 QBD 577 at 586 [**para 7.161**]). Significantly, in *Street v Mountford* [1985] AC 809 at 817H–818D, the House of Lords invoked the 'lodger' jurisprudence of the late 19th century to illuminate the essence of modern leasehold tenure.
2   [**Paras 2.80–2.81**].
3   [1985] AC 809 at 818A [**para 7.133**].
4   See e g *R v Tao* [1977] QB 141 at 146F–G [**para 2.80**].
5   *Antoniades v Villiers* [1990] 1 AC 417 at 459F–G per Lord Templeman; *Westminster CC v Clarke* [1992] 2 AC 288 at 301H–302A per Lord Templeman [**para 7.134**]. See also *Western Australia v Ward* (2002) 191 ALR 1 at [519] per McHugh J.
6   See *Bradley v Baylis* (1881) 8 QBD 195 at 216 per Jessel MR; *Customs and Excise Commrs v Sinclair Collis Ltd* [2001] STC 989 at [66] per Lord Slynn of Hadley.

Non-possessory estates in land

3.22   Not all estates in land are possessory in character. Thus, for instance, more limited assertions of power over land (as in the case of mere passage and re-passage along a road or path) are suggestive, at most, of ownership of some non-possessory estate (e g an estate of easement). Indeed, the distinction between the grant of a fee simple and an easement has been said to turn on whether a particular entitlement of user so derogates from the totality of the grantor's rights that the grantee is left 'free to act as if [he] were the owner of the freehold.'[1] On this basis the courts have generally rejected claims of easement[2] (or even *ius spatiandi*[3]) where the alleged entitlement is so over-broad or wide-ranging as to constitute, in effect, an assertion of a possessory estate in fee simple.

1   *Mercantile General Life Reassurance Co of Australia Ltd v Permanent Trustee Australia Ltd* (1989) NSW ConvR ¶55–441, at 58,211 per Powell J. See *Keefer v Arillotta* (1977) 72 DLR (3d) 182 at 189 (an easement can comprise user of a right of way merely as a means of non-exclusive passage and re-passage over another's land, but not a much more extensive claim to utilise the way as a parking lot). See also *Simpson v Fergus* (2000) 79 P & CR 398 at 402–403.
2   See *Reilly v Booth* (1890) 44 Ch D 12 at 26 per Lopes LJ ('there is no easement known to the law which gives exclusive and unrestricted use of a piece of land. It is not an easement in such a case; it is property that passes'). See similarly *Copeland v Greenhalf* [1952] Ch 488 at 498 [**para 8.75**]. See also *Ward v Kirkland* [1967] Ch 194 at 223E; *Grigsby v Melville* [1972] 1 WLR 1355 at 1364G, [1974] 1 WLR 80; *Harada v Registrar of Titles* [1981] VR 743 at 753; *Clos Farming Estates Pty Ltd v Easton* (2001) 10 BPR 18845 at [44].
3   [**Para 5.30**]. See *Attorney-General v Antrobus* [1905] 2 Ch 188 at 208 per Farwell J; and compare *Re Ellenborough Park* [1956] Ch 131 at 176 per Evershed MR [**para 8.45**].

POSSESSION AS THE ROOT OF TITLE

3.23 At the heart of the common law perception of property is the primacy accorded to possession in fact. For the common lawyer the origin of title has never truly been 'a set of words upon parchment',[1] but rather the raw datum of sustained possession of land.[2] The unchallenged arrogation of possessory control over land has tended to be viewed as the authentic root of title to an estate in the land. And it is an important consequence of the common law principle of relativity of title[3] that, even in advance of formal recognition of his possessory title, the person in possession of land acquires certain important rights which are good against all the world except those who are meanwhile able to claim a better title.[4]

1   *Bl Comm*, Vol II, p 2.
2   See *Calder v Attorney-General* (*British Columbia*) (1973) 34 DLR (3d) 145 at 185 per Hall J (Supreme Court of Canada); *Mabo v Queensland* (*No 2*) (1992) 175 CLR 1 at 208 per Toohey J (High Court of Australia). See also Richard A Epstein, 'Possession as the Root of Title' 13 Ga L Rev 1221 (1978–79); Carol M Rose, 'Possession as the Origin of Property' 52 U Chi L Rev 73 (1985–86). See also *Bl Comm*, Vol II, p 8.
3   **[Para 6.4]**.
4   *Asher v Whitlock* (1865) LR 1 QB 1 at 5 per Cockburn CJ; *Allen v Roughley* (1955) 94 CLR 98 at 145 per Taylor J. It may, of course, be that a better title can be claimed by a 'paper owner' whose documentary title to an estate in the land has not yet been barred.

Possession generates a common law freehold

3.24 Factual enjoyment of the more extensive forms of control over land has long been regarded as connoting ownership of either a freehold[1] or a leasehold[2] estate. Possession generates its own title, and English law came, in particular, to apply a pragmatic presumption that, unless and until the contrary were shown,[3] this title was a title to the full freehold estate.[4] The law 'gives credit to possession unless explained'[5] and possession is 'prima facie evidence of seisin in fee simple.'[6] Even today possession, whether or not tortiously acquired, still throws up for the possessor (or 'squatter') a 'common law freehold' which, in the absence of any superior title to a fee simple estate, is enforceable against the world.[7] It is even possible that the same parcel of land may yield up a multiplicity of common law freehold estates, as for instance where a number of different possessors enter upon the land *seriatim*.[8] In such a case it can become critically important to determine, as between these possessors, which one holds the *best* freehold 'title' (ie which of these possessors is now entitled to assert his own freehold estate against all others). This, in turn, depends on whether any of the rival freeholders has been able to perfect his own possessory title by establishing on his own behalf a period of adverse possession which statutorily bars all other claims to the land.[9]

1   See *Metropolitan Railway Co v Fowler* [1892] 1 QB 165 at 175; *Clos Farming Estates Pty Ltd v Easton* (2001) 10 BPR 18845 at [44] per Bryson J.
2   Courts commonly scrutinise the 'factual matrix and genesis' of written occupancy agreements **[para 7.184]** in order to determine whether, in reality, the occupier enjoys the exclusiveness of possession which identifies him as a leaseholder (*Crancour Ltd v Da Silvaesa* (1986)

52 P & CR 204 at 229 per Purchas LJ). See also *Wik Peoples v Queensland* (1996) 187 CLR 1 at 116 per Toohey J ('the conferring of exclusive possession is an indication that the arrangement in question is a lease').

3 For instance, the payment of rent by the possessor or the express restriction of his rights to a fixed term would demonstrate the existence of a leasehold (rather than freehold) estate (see *Street v Mountford* [1985] AC 809 at 818E–F per Lord Templeman).

4 See *Rosenberg v Cook* (1881) 8 QBD 162 at 165 per Jessel MR; *Central London Commercial Estates Ltd v Kato Kagaku Co Ltd* [1998] 4 All ER 948 at 951d per Sedley J. Even the squatter on leasehold land acquires, by virtue of his possession, a common law freehold estate (see Law Commission and Land Registry, *Land Registration for the Twenty-First Century* (Law Com No 254, September 1998), para 10.36). See also *St Marylebone Property Co Ltd v Fairweather* [1962] 1 QB 498 at 529 per Pearson LJ ('an independent possessory title').

5 *Asher v Whitlock* (1865) LR 1 QB 1 at 6 per Mellor J.

6 *Peaceable d Uncle v Watson* (1811) 4 Taunt 16 at 17, 128 ER 232 per Mansfield CJ. See also *Re Atkinson and Horsell's Contract* [1912] 2 Ch 1 at 9 per Cozens-Hardy MR; *Allen v Roughley* (1955) 94 CLR 98 at 136 per Kitto J.

7 'Every fee simple is not *legitimum*' (*Co Litt*, p 2a). As McHugh JA observed in *Newington v Windeyer* (1985) 3 NSWLR 555 at 563E, 'an estate gained by wrong is nevertheless an estate in fee simple'. See also *Leach v Jay* (1878) 9 Ch D 42 at 45 per James LJ; *Buckinghamshire CC v Moran* [1990] Ch 623 at 644D per Nourse LJ; *Mabo v Queensland (No 2)* (1992) 175 CLR 1 at 209–211 per Toohey J; *Yanner v Eaton* (1999) 201 CLR 351 at [85] per Gummow J.

8 [**Para 3.34**].

9 [**Para 6.40**].

Registration of the possessor's title

3.25 Possession confers a title at common law which is fully capable of registration at Land Registry. Even in the absence of any documentary grant or other evidence of title, the squatter may apply, in certain circumstances, to have his title to a fee simple estate registered.

Unregistered land

3.26 Where title in respect of the land occupied by the squatter has never previously been registered, the squatter may apply to Land Registry to be registered as the first proprietor of a 'possessory' freehold title. He may make this application even *before* the expiration of the twelve year limitation period which normally controls adverse possession against unregistered titles.[1] Such registration may be authorised if the registrar is of the opinion that the applicant is in 'actual possession' of the land (or in receipt of the rents and profits of the land) by virtue of his common law estate and that there is no other class of title with which he may be registered.[2] Registration neither improves nor disimproves the squatter's position: he takes his possessory title subject to 'any estate, right or interest adverse to, or in derogation of, the proprietor's title subsisting at the time of registration or then capable of arising.'[3] In other words, the squatter is bound at the point of first registration by all pre-existing legal and equitable entitlements affecting the land.[4] It is inevitable that this should be so. Legal rights in unregistered land always bind the world.[5] Not being a 'purchaser' under a 'conveyance' of land, the squatter can never claim to have defeated pre-existing equitable interests either on the basis of statutory overreaching[6] or as a 'bona fide purchaser' without notice[7] or even on the footing that he is immune from those equitable rights in unregistered land which normally require registration under the Land Charges Act.[8] For the same reasons the squatter also takes inescapably subject to any mortgage subsisting in respect of the land.[9]

1   LRA 2002, ss 3(1)(a), (2)(a), 9(1)(c). After a period of twelve years from the date of first registration with possessory freehold title, the title may, if the proprietor is still in possession, be upgraded into an 'absolute title' (LRA 2002, s 62(4) **[para 7.47]**).
2   LRA 2002, s 9(5). A squatter who dispossesses a tenant may apply for first registration with either 'possessory leasehold title' or 'qualified freehold title' (LRA 2002, ss 9(1)(b), 10(1)(d) **[paras 7.46, 7.235]**), the latter form of registration expressly reserving for the time being the rights of the landlord (see Law Com No 254 (1998), para 10.42).
3   LRA 2002, s 11(7).
4   The squatter takes his possessory interest subject to the rights and incidents of any notice to treat already served in respect of the land under a compulsory purchase order (see *Rhondda Cynon Taff County BC v Watkins* [2003] 1 WLR 1864 at [47] per Arden LJ).
5   **[Paras 2.176, 12.274]**.
6   LPA 1925, s 2(1) **[paras 2.165, 11.195]**.
7   **[Paras 2.191, 12.343]**. Thus he is clearly bound by equitable interests such as pre-1926 restrictive covenants, of which many examples survive to this day (*Re Nisbet and Potts' Contract* [1906] 1 Ch 386 at 402–404 per Collins MR, 406–408 per Romer LJ, 409 per Cozens-Hardy LJ). See F W Maitland, *Equity* (2nd edn revd by J Brunyate, London 1936), p 116.
8   Even if unregistered, such rights are void only as against a 'purchaser' (LCA 1972, s 4(3)–(8) **[paras 2.188, 12.343]**). The squatter is therefore bound, for example, by post-1925 restrictive covenants.
9   See *Carroll v Manek and Bank of India* (2000) 79 P & CR 173 at 188.

Registered land

3.27   Where title to the land is already registered, a squatter who has adversely possessed for an immediately preceding period of ten years may apply for registration at Land Registry as proprietor with 'absolute' title.[1] However, the making of such an application will almost inevitably alert the current registered proprietor to the adverse claim, thereby prompting an objection which quashes the claim.[2] The squatter's common law freehold nevertheless ranks, if he remains in actual occupation, as an overriding interest which will bind any disponee of the registered title[3] and may even ripen into registered estate ownership if the squatter is not removed from the land.[4]

1   LRA 2002, Sch 6, para 1(1).
2   **[Para 6.57]**.
3   LRA 2002, Sch 3, para 2 **[paras 2.172, 12.146]**.
4   LRA 2002, Sch 6, para 6 **[para 6.60]**.

PRIVILEGES OF POSSESSION

3.28   Possession confers valuable privileges against the world at large (including any paper owner of the land concerned).[1] From the inception of his possession the squatter's common law freehold carries an entitlement to vindicate his possession against, and to transfer his rights to, other persons.[2] Possession is presumed to confer a defensible and alienable form of fee simple ownership, notwithstanding the tortious nature of the squatter's entry into possession and irrespective of his vulnerability to eviction by legal process.[3] In the ancient words of Bracton, 'everyone who is in possession, though he has no right, has a greater right [than] one who is out of possession and has no right.'[4] Herein lies the essential relativity of real entitlement in English law. As Lord Millett emphasised in *Harrow LBC v Qazi*,[5] '[a] person who is in actual possession of land is entitled to remain in peaceful enjoyment of the property without disturbance by anyone except a person with a better right to possession. It does not matter that he has no title.'[6] Perhaps, more accurately, it might be said that the squatter's possession has generated its own form of title at common law.

1   Possessory rights may even be claimed by the paper owner himself where, following dispossession by another, he has re-entered into possession (see *Rhondda Cynon Taff County BC v Watkins* [2003] 1 WLR 1864 at [23] per Schiemann LJ).

2   The squatter is entitled to compensation if the land is compulsorily purchased before the perfection of his possessory title (*Perry v Clissold* [1907] AC 73 at 79–80). However, since his title does not derive from grant, the squatter cannot claim the benefit of any easement implied, for instance, on the basis of necessity (*Wilkes v Greenway* (1890) 6 TLR 449; *North Sydney Printing Pty Ltd v Sabemo Investment Corpn Pty Ltd* [1971] 2 NSWLR 150 at 159C–D **[para 8.130]**).

3   See *Wheeler v Baldwin* (1934) 52 CLR 609 at 632 per Dixon CJ; *Spark v Meers* [1971] 2 NSWLR 1 at 12A–C.

4   *Bracton on the Laws and Customs of England* (trans S E Thorne, Harvard UP, 1977), Vol III, p 134. See also A W B Simpson, *A History of the Land Law* (2nd edn, Oxford 1986), pp 38–39.

5   [2004] 1 AC 983 at [85].

6   It is this idea, declared Lord Millett, which is 'now enshrined, in suitably restrained and less colourful language, in article 8' of the European Convention on Human Rights **[para 2.60]**.

Limited protection even as against prior possessors

3.29   Even as against prior possessors (including the 'true owner') of the land concerned, the person currently in possession enjoys one valuable, though inevitably limited, form of protection. Until 'possession' of land has, in strict terms, been assumed by an intruder, a prior possessor is entitled to exercise the remedy of self-help against the intruder through eviction by reasonable force.[1] However, once possession has been taken over by the intruder, this summary remedy is no longer available and the intruder's position becomes correspondingly more secure. If he does not leave the land voluntarily, any rival claimant to possession will find himself obliged to bring proceedings for possession and, for this purpose, to prove his superior title.[2] Even then a prior possessor's right to recover possession may ultimately be barred by the effluxion of time[3] or by the statutory termination of his right to resist the intruder's application for registration as proprietor.[4]

1   **[Para 3.72]**.

2   See generally *Powell v McFarlane* (1977) 38 P & CR 452 at 476 per Slade J.

3   [Para 6.40].
4   [Para 6.60].

Locus standi in nuisance

3.30   It is, strictly speaking, possession which provides the authentic basis of the right to sue strangers in private nuisance.[1] Indeed, in *Hunter v Canary Wharf Ltd*[2] a majority in the House of Lords went to some pains to confirm that standing in nuisance is confined to those who are linked to the land by some form of possessory status or claim. The rigour of this ruling was mitigated by the controversial concession that some licensees may nowadays enjoy 'exclusive possession' of land and thus also have standing to sue in nuisance.[3]

1   *Foster v Warblington UDC* [1906] 1 KB 648 at 673–674; *Hunter v Canary Wharf Ltd* [1997] AC 655 at 688E–689D per Lord Goff of Chieveley; *Paxhaven Holdings Ltd v Attorney-General* [1974] 2 NZLR 185 at 189.
2   [1997] AC 655 at 692B–H per Lord Goff of Chieveley, 697G–698A, 698F–699A per Lord Lloyd of Berwick, 703B–F per Lord Hoffmann, 723D, 724D per Lord Hope of Craighead. See also *Sedleigh-Denfield v O'Callaghan* [1940] AC 880 at 903 per Lord Wright.
3   **[Para 3.51]**. See *Hunter v Canary Wharf Ltd* [1997] AC 655 at 688E per Lord Goff of Chieveley, 703E per Lord Hoffmann, 724C–F per Lord Hope of Craighead. See also *Pemberton v Southwark LBC* [2000] 1 WLR 1672 at 1682G–H, 1684H–1685A, 1686B–D (successful nuisance claim by 'tolerated trespasser').

Transmissibility of the possessor's rights

3.31   Having acquired a common law estate in fee simple on the inception of his possession, the squatter – even before the perfection or registration of his possessory title – is competent to assign his estate inter vivos or to dispose of it by will.[1] If the squatter dies intestate, his rights devolve upon his next of kin. Moreover, in registered land the successor in title to the squatter's common law freehold may count his predecessor's period of possession towards the period which must elapse before he can apply to be registered as proprietor at Land Registry.[2] Similarly, in unregistered land, one squatter's period of possession may be added to (or 'tacked' on to) the possession of the next successive squatter so as to build up a complete possessory title after a total of twelve years.[3]

1   *Asher v Whitlock* (1865) LR 1 QB 1 at 6–7; *Wheeler v Baldwin* (1934) 52 CLR 609 at 632–633; *Allen v Roughley* (1955) 94 CLR 98 at 108, 130–131, 145; *Mulcahy v Curramore Pty Ltd* [1974] 2 NSWLR 464 at 476C; *Public Trustee v Bellotti* (1986) 4 BPR 9196 at 9200; *Brown v Faulkner* [2003] NICA 5(2) at [41].
2   LRA 2002, Sch 6, para 11(2)(a), reinforcing an old common law principle (see *Asher v Whitlock* (1865) LR 1 QB 1 at 6–7; *Mulcahy v Curramore Pty Ltd* [1974] 2 NSWLR 464 at 476D). An assignment of rights (e g on gift or sale) – insecure though these rights may be – must 'on ordinary principles of law' preclude any subsequent ouster of the assignee by the assignor (see *Mount Carmel Investments Ltd v Peter Thurlow Ltd* [1988] 1 WLR 1078 at 1086E–F per Nicholls LJ). In effect, the assignment of the inchoate possessory title leaves the assignor with no entitlement to assert (see *Mulcahy*, supra at 476C–D, 479B–C; *Simpson v Council of North West County District* (1978) 4 BPR 9277 at 9298).
3   **[Para 6.43]**. See *Willis v Earl Howe* [1893] 2 Ch 545 at 553; *Salter v Clarke* (1904) 4 SR (NSW)

280 at 288; *Mulcahy v Curramore Pty Ltd* [1974] 2 NSWLR 464 at 471A–B. The process of 'tacking' requires no formal transmission of the predecessor's inchoate rights. See e g *Ellis v Lambeth LBC* (1999) 32 HLR 596 at 598, where, by being allowed to join an existing council house 'squat', the eventual claimant of an indefeasible fee simple title was held to have obtained an informal transmission of the possessory rights of earlier trespassers. Such transmission of rights marks an exception to the requirement (contained in LPA 1925, s 52(1)) of formal conveyance of estates by deed (see LPA 1925, s 55(c)).

PRIOR POSSESSION GENERATES A RIGHT TO RECOVER POSSESSION

3.32   One of the difficulties inherent in a possession-based rule of title is, of course, the aggressive free-for-all to which such a rule might conduce. Title could be contested by a mêlée of claimants, each struggling against the others to establish territorial control over the same piece of land.

The 'first-in-time' principle

3.33   In English law the major defence against this potential scramble for title has long been supplied by a 'first-in-time' principle. For want of any clearer conception of title, the primitive common law adapted the notion of title by first occupancy and held that possession, even if lost, gave rise to a right to recover possession,[1] since 'as between mere possessors prior possession is a better right.'[2] This visceral rule of priority still applies today (subject only to the barring of prior rights of recovery after the effluxion of the statutory limitation period[3]). In effect, the 'first-in-time' principle confirms that possession of land 'gives ownership good against everyone except a person who has a better, because older, title.'[4] The squatter cannot be evicted 'save at the suit of someone with a better right to possession, and even then that person must rely on the strength of his own title and not the weakness of the squatter's.'[5] The possessor of land has access, in effect, to a remedy of recovery in specie which goes far beyond the mere recovery of damages for another's trespass.[6]

1   See e g *Rhondda Cynon Taff County BC v Watkins* [2003] 1 WLR 1864 at [27] per Schiemann LJ, [47] per Arden LJ.
2   *Mabo v Queensland (No 2)* (1992) 175 CLR 1 at 210 per Toohey J. The roots of this principle are found in *Allen v Rivington* (1670) 2 Wm Saund 111 at 112, 85 ER 813 at 814; *Bristow v Cormican* (1878) 3 App Cas 641 at 657 per Lord Hatherley. See *Doe d Hughes v Dyeball* (1829) M & M 346 at 347, 173 ER 1184 (possession for only one year held good against stranger who had no title at all); *Doe d Smith and Payne v Webber* (1834) 1 Ad & E 119 at 121, 110 ER 1152 at 1153–1154 per Parke J.
3   [Para 6.40].
4   *Newington v Windeyer* (1985) 3 NSWLR 555 at 563E–F per McHugh JA. See also *Wheeler v Baldwin* (1934) 52 CLR 609 at 632 per Dixon CJ; *Spark v Meers* [1971] 2 NSWLR 1 at 12A–C.
5   *Harrow LBC v Qazi* [2004] 1 AC 983 at [87] per Lord Millett (reiterating, in effect, a dictum of Lord Ellenborough CJ in *Goodtitle d Parker v Baldwin* (1809) 11 East 488 at 495, 103 ER 1092 at 1095). See *Allen v Roughley* (1955) 94 CLR 98 at 125 per Fullagar J; *Chung Ping Kwan v Lam Island Co Ltd* [1997] AC 38 at 47F–G per Lord Nicholls of Birkenhead; *Rhondda Cynon Taff County BC v Watkins* [2003] 1 WLR 1864 at [27] per Schiemann LJ.
6   [Para 3.83].

Multiple freehold estates

3.34 Implicit in the notion of relativity of title is the recognition that one person's ownership of a common law freehold in no way forecloses the possibility that some other person (whether squatter or 'true owner') may have an older and better title to a fee simple estate in the land.[1] In a context of consecutive trespasses on the same land, each successive possessor is vulnerable to the assertion of the freehold estate held by any earlier possessor or, indeed, by the 'true owner'.[2] By virtue of his possession each individual squatter has acquired his own common law freehold; and at the inception of his possession each squatter's title to his own estate is necessarily an *unregistered* title. Thus, even where the true owner's title to *his* freehold estate has at all relevant times been registered at Land Registry, priority as between the various common law freeholds held by a series of squatters is still governed by the 'first-in-time' principle. Accordingly any earlier squatter may recover possession from any later squatter (subject only to the twelve year limitation period imposed by the Limitation Act 1980[3]). As between successive squatters, the *best* claim to a fee simple estate at any particular time therefore rests with the squatter who has statute-barred all earlier claims without, himself, having yet been excluded from possession of the land for the duration of the limitation period.[4]

1   See *Bell v General Accident, Fire & Life Assurance Corpn Ltd* [1998] 1 EGLR 69 at 71L–M per Hutchison LJ.
2   See e g *Heid v Connell Investments Pty Ltd and the Registrar-General* (1987) 9 NSWLR 628 at 637A–B. See also *Public Trustee v Bellotti* (1986) 4 BPR 9196 at 9201.
3   [**Para 6.41**]. The Land Registration Act 2002 regulates priority only as between a squatter and the registered proprietor [**para 6.53**].
4   Thus, where land is occupied by a series of trespassers, A, B, C, D and E, the best claim to possessory fee simple ownership is initially that of A, but later shifts down the line as time runs out against each squatter in favour of the next (see *Allen v Roughley* (1955) 94 CLR 98 at 131–132 per Fullagar J; *Mulcahy v Curramore Pty Ltd* [1974] 2 NSWLR 464 at 476D–477D; *Simpson v Council of North West County District* (1978) 4 BPR 9277 at 9298; *Public Trustee v Bellotti* (1986) 4 BPR 9196 at 9201).

Remedy by action for possession

3.35 Although the law provides a displaced possessor with the remedy of self-help in certain circumstances,[1] this is not usually a course to be encouraged.[2] As Lord Denning MR said in *McPhail v Persons (Names Unknown)*,[3] '[i]n a civilised society, the courts should themselves provide a remedy which is speedy and effective: and thus make self-help unnecessary.' For centuries therefore English law has provided a curial means by which a person dispossessed of land can dislodge trespassers, this legal process taking the form of the common law action for possession.[4] By the early 1970s, however, it had become obvious that the common law action for possession was subject to certain disadvantages. The action was particularly ineffective, for instance, where the occupiers of premises were unidentifiable and could not therefore be named as defendants in proceedings taken against them.[5] There were also great difficulties in making a possession order where one squatter followed another in quick succession.

1   [**Para 3.72**].
2   See, in a different context, the disapproval of self-help remedies expressed in *Billson v Residential Apartments Ltd* [1992] 1 AC 494 at 524C–525C per Nicholls LJ, 536F–H per Lord Templeman [**para 14.121**].
3   [1973] Ch 447 at 457B–C.
4   See *Norris and Norris v Walls* [1997] NI 45 at 53d–j per Girvan J.
5   See *Re Wykeham Terrace, Brighton, Sussex, ex p Territorial Auxiliary and Volunteer Reserve Association for the South East* [1971] Ch 204 at 209F.

The summary action for possession

3.36   Some relief from the technical defects of the common law action for possession came when the Supreme Court Rules and County Court Rules were reformulated in 1970 to provide a summary or 'short-cut' procedure for the recovery of possession against trespassers.[1] This procedure was intended to be used only in straightforward cases where there was no doubt that the occupiers of land were trespassers. The expedited procedure, as now provided by the Civil Procedure Rules 1998,[2] lends substantial assistance to those who are dispossessed by trespassers or squatters. The 'possession claim against trespassers' affords a speedy remedy, available in either the High Court or the county court,[3] against any person who occupies land without consent. This procedure has the advantage that it is available and enforceable whether or not trespassers are identifiable by name.[4] The summary action is, in effect, an action *in rem*.

1   RSC Ord 113 and CCR Ord 24.
2   SI 1998/3132, as amended (see Civil Procedure (Amendment) Rules 2001 (SI 2001/256)).
3   See CPR Rule 55.3. Only exceptional circumstances justify proceedings in the High Court (eg if there are complicated disputes of fact or points of law of general importance) (see *Practice Direction – Possession Claims*, para 1.1–1.3).
4   CPR Rule 55.3(4).

Availability of the summary action

3.37   In order to succeed in recovering land, the claimant in an action for possession must demonstrate that he has a title superior to that of the defendant. This title may be based on either estate ownership[1] or possession[2] (although the two grounds of claim ultimately coalesce[3]). The right to vindicate possession against strangers thus derives either from the proprietary estate held by the trespass victim or from his pre-existing (and unbarred) possession of the land.

1   See *Manchester Airport Plc v Dutton* [2000] QB 133 at 150B, where Laws LJ indicated that an estate owner may seek an order for possession 'whether he is in possession or not.' A leaseholder whose estate has been terminated by notice to quit may retain a continuing right to possession as against his subtenants where the leaseholder has covenanted to hand over the premises with vacant possession (see *Alamo Housing Co-operative v Meredith* [2003] HLR 947 at [41]–[43]).

2   See, analogously, *Sedleigh-Denfield v O'Callaghan* [1940] AC 880 at 903 per Lord Wright;
     Hunter v Canary Wharf Ltd [1997] AC 655 at 703C per Lord Hoffmann.
3   Possession of land is deemed to generate an estate in fee simple [**para 3.24**].

Extension to certain licensees

3.38   In recent years access to the summary action for possession has been
extended to claimants other than those qualified by virtue of estate ownership
or entitled, in the strict sense, to 'possession' of land. In *Manchester Airport Plc
v Dutton*[1] the Court of Appeal confirmed that even a contractual licensee who
is merely in 'effective control' or 'de facto occupation' of land may obtain a
summary possession order against trespassers who invade the land over which
he holds his licence. The Court also held by a majority that the same protection
is available to a licensee who holds an as yet unexercised and non-exclusive
contractual right to enter and occupy land, if a possessory remedy is necessary
in order to vindicate that licensee's contractual entitlement.[2] In *Dutton*'s case an
airport company, which had been granted a contractual licence by a landowner
to prepare a site for the construction of a second runway at Manchester
Airport, was held entitled – even in advance of its own entry upon the site – to
a summary possession order sweeping out trespassers who had invaded the land
and built a tree camp in order to impede the proposed development. In the view
of the Court of Appeal, a contractually created right to 'enter and occupy'
confers a relatively good title to possession of land as against a 'bare trespasser',[3] although not, of course, as against the licensor himself.[4]

1   [2000] QB 133 at 147C–G per Laws LJ [**paras 4.98, 7.145**].
2   [2000] QB 133 at 150A–E per Laws LJ, 151B–C per Kennedy LJ. See also *Monsanto plc v Tilly*
     [2000] Env LR 313 at 322 per Stuart-Smith LJ, 336 per Mummery LJ.
3   [2000] QB 133 at 150C per Laws LJ.
4   Contrast *Countryside Residential (North Thames) Ltd v (1) A Child; (2) Persons Unknown*
     (2001) 81 P & CR 10 at [12]–[13], where the Court of Appeal declined to extend *Dutton* to
     cover a licensee whose contract provided for only a temporary privilege of 'access' for limited
     purposes of survey and technical investigation prior to a planning application. The licensee
     had not entered the site prior to the setting up of protest camps by trespassing environmen-
     talists. Nor did the licensee's contractual right confer any entitlement to 'effective control over
     the land.'

Relative degrees of possession?

3.39   The generous extension of possessory remedies to those who, in conventional terms, have no 'possession' of land amounts, in effect, to the recognition
of a certain relativity in the concept of possession.[1] Certain kinds of licence,
which were not traditionally credited with proprietary significance, are now
beginning to be treated as if they carry some of the incidents of estate
ownership – yet further evidence of the modern breakdown of the *numerus
clausus* of recognised proprietary entitlements.[2] The trend is apparent even in
the House of Lords. In *Customs and Excise Commrs v Sinclair Collis Ltd*[3]
Lord Scott of Foscote referred to a 'licence to occupy' land as conferring a

permission 'to go into possession, not necessarily exclusive possession, or to go on to the land and take some degree of control of it.' Such an approach threatens to alter the delineation of 'property' in land, not least since a 'possessory' licence of this kind is regarded for many purposes in European law as the equivalent of a leasehold estate in land.[4]

1   See *Manchester Airport Plc v Dutton* [2000] QB 133 at 143G, where Chadwick LJ dissented precisely because he disfavoured the argument that there is 'now a concept of "relative possession".' The stance of the majority in *Dutton* clearly contravened the basic principle that possession is a uniform and ungradable phenomenon [**para 3.4**], but is nevertheless consistent with the drift towards fragmentation of the concept of possession [**para 3.51**].
2   [**Para 2.97**].
3   [2001] STC 989 at [73]–[74].
4   See e g EC Council Directive 77/388 (The Sixth VAT Directive), Title X, art 13B, implemented by Value Added Tax Act 1994, s 31, Sch 9 [**para 7.142**]. Compare, however, *Sinclair Collis Ltd v Customs and Excise Commrs* (*Case C-275/01*) [2003] STC 898 at [46] (installation of cigarette vending machine).

Service

3.40   For the purpose of pursuing a possession claim against trespassers, the claim form and supporting documents may be served on a named occupier either personally or by leaving a copy at, or sending a copy to, the premises occupied.[1] Service may be effected on unnamed occupiers by affixing the relevant documents to the main door or some other part of the land 'so that they are clearly visible', and, if practicable, by inserting a copy through the letter box at the premises.[2] Alternatively, the documentation may be addressed to 'the occupiers' and affixed in a sealed transparent envelope to stakes specially placed in the ground at locations where they are 'clearly visible.'[3] The court may hear the case for possession (in the case of residential premises) when five clear days have elapsed since the date of service and (in the case of other land) when two clear days have so elapsed.[4] The net effect is significantly to strengthen the interests of private property against the adverse claims of intruders.

1   See CPR Rule 55.8(5). Neither acknowledgement of service nor the filing of any defence is required (CPR Rule 55.7(1)–(2)).
2   CPR Rule 55.6(a).
3   CPR Rule 55.6(b). See e g *Drury v Secretary of State for the Environment, Food and Rural Affairs* [2004] EWCA Civ 200 at [8].
4   CPR Rule 55.5(2). Even these periods may be shortened by the court (e g in cases involving actual or threatened violence to the claimant or others) (see CPR Rule 3.1(2)(a); *Practice Direction – Possession Claims*, para 3.2).

Adjudication of the claim for possession

3.41   As a matter of domestic law the court, on hearing the claim, has no discretion to withhold an order for possession once the title to possession has been established.[1] The court has no power to examine, on the merits of the case, whether the granting of possession is reasonable or justified. The court has, equally, no discretion to have regard to humanitarian factors or even to government codes of good practice in relation to certain categories of eviction.[2]

1 See *McPhail v Persons (Names Unknown)* [1973] Ch 447 at 458E–G per Lord Denning MR ('The court cannot give any time ... It is ... for the owner to give such time as he thinks right to the squatters. They must make their appeal to his goodwill and consideration, and not to the courts'). See also *Northern Ireland Housing Executive v McAuley* [1974] NI 233 at 235–237; *Swordheath Properties Ltd v Floydd* [1978] 1 WLR 550 at 552B–G.

2 *R v Brighton and Hove Council, ex p Marmont* (1998) 30 HLR 1046 at 1050–1051; *R v Hillingdon LBC, ex p McDonagh* (1999) 31 HLR 531 at 543 (Department of Environment circular on gypsy sites merely evidence of good practice).

Possession as a vehicle of protest

3.42 The taking of adverse possession of land is sometimes used as a means of coercing political action, expressing protest or promoting social justice. During the 1970s and 1980s the organised sit-in emerged as a non-violent method of demonstration against mass redundancy at the work-place, oppressive actions of university authorities or the supposed obscenity of property lying idle during times of severe homelessness. In the late 1980s and early 1990s the collective invasion of privately owned agricultural land by groups of 'New Age' travellers provided another controversial focus for the law on recovery of possession. More recently mass trespass upon land has been prompted by concerns over animal rights, the pursuit of blood sports and the cultivation of genetically modified crops.[1]

1 See the well publicised acquittal in 2001 of 11 environmental activists on charges of criminal damage to GM crops (Decision of Stipendiary Magistrate Kevin Gray, Harwich Magistrates' Court, 27 June 2001: *The Independent*, 28 June 2001; *The Guardian*, 28 June 2001).

No defence of social utility

3.43 It is clear that the judicial reaction to these forms of trespass has generally taken the form of a stern reinforcement of the legal power of the paper owner of the land concerned.[1] The courts have not been prepared to endorse political, social or utilitarian justifications for even a temporary dispossession of a paper owner from 'his' land. The idea that existing distributions of land can, in themselves, express or conceal inequity is not a notion which the courts have been ready to explore.[2] In *McPhail v Persons (Names Unknown)*[3] a group of homeless persons secured entry to residential premises which had been left unoccupied and locked by the owner. Lord Denning MR held that the courts could not entertain, by way of defence to proceedings for the recovery of possession, any plea by a squatter[4] that 'he was homeless and that this house or land was standing empty, doing nothing.' No such excuse could avail at law, since, as Lord Denning himself had said in *Southwark LBC v Williams*,[5] if homelessness were once admitted as a defence to trespass, 'no one's house could be safe.'[6] The courts 'must, for the sake of law and order, take a firm stand. They must refuse to admit the plea of necessity to the hungry and the homeless: and trust that their distress will be relieved by the charitable and the good.'[7]

1   A further disincentive to trespass by a group in joint and exclusive occupation of premises is the possibility that any individual member of the group may be required to discharge the entirety of the group's liability in respect of local authority charges. See *Westminster CC v Tomlin* [1989] 1 WLR 1287 at 1296B–G (rates liability of over £27,000 for occupation of Cambodian Embassy).

2   The Supreme Court of Ireland has rejected the suggestion that the use of legal process against trespassers for the vindication of the landowner's possessory rights is an unconstitutional form of discrimination against the 'landless classes' (*Dooley v Attorney General* [1977] IR 205 at 210).

3   [1973] Ch 447. See A M Prichard, (1976) 40 Conv (NS) 255.

4   Lord Denning defined a 'squatter' as 'one who, without any colour of right, enters on an unoccupied house or land, intending to stay there as long as he can' ([1973] Ch 447 at 456B).

5   [1971] Ch 734 at 744B–C.

6   See *Perka v The Queen* (1985) 13 DLR (4th) 1 at 34, where, in the Supreme Court of Canada, Wilson J cited *Southwark LBC v Williams* in support of the proposition that '[t]he maximisation of social utility may well be a goal of legislative policy but it is not part of the judicial task of delineating right and wrong.'

7   [1971] Ch 734 at 744C–D. See also *Kensington and Chelsea LBC v Wells* (1974) 72 LGR 289 at 297–300 per Roskill LJ. The Court of Appeal has also ruled against the relevance in possession proceedings of matters which should properly be raised only in proceedings by way of judicial review (see *Avon CC v Buscott* [1988] QB 656 at 663F (challenge to reasonableness of local authority's failure to provide caravan site for gypsies)). Compare, however, *R v Brighton and Hove Council, ex p Marmont* (1998) 30 HLR 1046 at 1049–1051; *R v Hillingdon LBC, ex p McDonagh* (1999) 31 HLR 531 at 539–541; and see now *Connors v United Kingdom* (ECtHR, Application No 66746/01, 27 May 2004).

Relevance of the European Convention on Human Rights

3.44   In cases relating to residential land it is clear that a court order for possession necessarily interferes with the Convention right to respect for 'private and family life' and the integrity of the 'home'.[1] It has nevertheless been held that, in appropriate cases, the removal of trespassers from privately owned land can be justified in Convention terms[2] as 'necessary in a democratic society ... for the protection of the rights and freedoms of others.'[3] The very unlawfulness of the possession concerned has, of course, a significant bearing on the question whether 'a requirement that an individual leave his or her home is proportionate to the legitimate aim pursued.'[4] But proportionality is indeed the key factor. The very automaticity of court orders for possession under domestic law[5] may now fuel the argument that, in certain cases involving the eviction of long-standing residential occupiers, a summary procedure which affords the defendant no opportunity to ventilate the merits of his dispossession before an independent tribunal constitutes a denial of the procedural safeguards which would otherwise ensure that the interference with residential security is 'fair' and such as to accord 'due respect' to the defendant's Convention rights.[6]

1   ECHR Art 8(1). See *Connors v United Kingdom* (ECtHR, Application No 66746/01, 27 May 2004) at [68].

2   See ECHR Art 8(2).
3   *R (on application of Gangera) v Hounslow LBC* [2003] EWHC Admin 794 at [41] per Moses J;
    R (Fuller) v Chief Constable of Dorset Police [2003] QB 480 at [77] per Stanley Burnton J.
4   *Chapman v United Kingdom* (2001) 33 EHRR 399 at [102]. See similarly *Buckley v United
    Kingdom* (1997) 23 EHRR 101 at [63]; *R v Hillingdon LBC, ex p Ward* [2001] LGR 457
    at [31]–[32]; *R (Fuller) v Chief Constable of Dorset Police* [2003] QB 480 at [74].
5   This is a consideration which strikes with even greater force in relation to the jurisdiction to
    issue interim possession orders [**para 3.48**].
6   ECHR Art 8. See *Connors v United Kingdom* (ECtHR, Application No 66746/01, 27 May
    2004) at [94]–[95], [114] [**para 2.73**].

Enforcement of recovery

3.45   The court's power to postpone the giving up of possession pursuant to a
possession order is strictly limited. Possession cannot be postponed to a date
later than 14 days after the making of the order unless 'it appears to the court
that exceptional hardship would be caused by requiring possession to be given
up by that date'.[1] Even where 'exceptional hardship' is present, possession
cannot be postponed to a date later than six weeks after the making of the
court order.[2]

1   Housing Act 1980, s 89(1). This limit applies whether proceedings are brought in the county
    court or in the High Court (see *Hackney LBC v Side By Side (Kids) Ltd* [2004] 1 WLR 363
    at [32] per Stanley Burnton J, regarding as 'clearly wrong' the opposing view of Harman J in
    Bain & Co v Church Commissioners for England [1989] 1 WLR 24 at 28C–D). The limit also
    applies even in the case of possession orders made by consent (see *Hackney LBC v Side By
    Side (Kids) Ltd*, supra at [39]).
2   Housing Act 1980, s 89(1).

Effect of the possession order

3.46   The summary procedure has proved a useful means of recovering
possession of land from a wide variety of trespassers. It has been used
successfully against such persons as students participating in a campus 'sit-in',[1]
gypsies illegally camping on a roadside,[2] and residential licensees who refuse to
vacate premises following the expiry of their licence.[3] Once a possession order
has been granted, it can be enforced against any person who subsequently
returns to the site or premises covered by the original order, provided that there
is a 'plain and sufficient nexus between the original recovery of possession and
the need to effect further recovery of the same land.'[4]

1   *University of Essex v Djemal* [1980] 1 WLR 1301.
2   *Wiltshire CC v Frazer* (1984) 47 P & CR 69 at 75–77.
3   *GLC v Jenkins* [1975] 1 WLR 155 at 157A, 160B; *Turner v Burton* (Unreported, Court of
    Appeal, 12 March 1985).
4   *Wiltshire CC v Frazer (No 2)* [1986] 1 WLR 109 at 113D. See also *R v Wandsworth County
    Court, ex p Wandsworth LBC* [1975] 1 WLR 1314 at 1318H–1319A.

Territorial scope of the possession order

3.47   A possession order may relate to a larger area of the claimant's land than is adversely affected by the occupation in respect of which relief is initially sought.[1] In *University of Essex v Djemal,*[2] for instance, a group of university students occupied the university's administrative offices as a protest and threatened to extend their sit-in to other parts of the university's premises. The Court of Appeal took the view that the summary possession procedure confers 'a jurisdiction directed to protecting the right of the owner of property to the possession of the whole of his property, uninterfered with by unauthorised adverse possession.'[3] Accordingly the Court of Appeal expanded the terms of the original possession order to cover the university's premises in their entirety.[4] It is clear, however, that the judicial power to make wide-ranging pre-emptive orders *in rem* will be exercised cautiously.[5]

1   A possession order may therefore relate to other land of the claimant which is physically separate from the land trespassed upon (see *Ministry of Agriculture, Fisheries and Food v Heyman* (1990) 59 P & CR 48 at 50 per Saville J).
2   [1980] 1 WLR 1301. See [1981] Conv 317 (A A Preece).
3   [1980] 1 WLR 1301 at 1304E per Buckley LJ.
4   The extension of a possession order to neighbouring areas of land is justified only if there is convincing evidence (and not merely a belief) that there is 'a real danger of actual violation' of such other areas. There need, however, be no express threat by the trespassers to extend their occupation (see *Ministry of Agriculture, Fisheries and Food v Heyman* (1990) 59 P & CR 48 at 50). See also *Drury v Secretary of State for the Environment, Food and Rural Affairs* [2004] EWCA Civ 200 at [20] (anticipated trespass can, in rare circumstances, give rise to a cause of action).
5   In determining the range of the possession order, the court is likely to be guided by such factors as propinquity and the geographical and occupational unity of the claimant's land. For trespass on parcel A to justify an order in relation to parcel B, there must be a 'strong and unbroken link between the two parcels' (*Drury v Secretary of State for the Environment, Food and Rural Affairs* [2004] EWCA Civ 200 at [44]–[46] per Ward LJ).

Interim possession orders

3.48   Since 1995 the court has enjoyed an even more far-reaching jurisdiction to make an *interim* possession order (an 'IPO') against any alleged trespasser on residential premises.[1] The application must be made within 28 days of the date on which the claimant first knew, or ought reasonably to have known, that the land was occupied.[2] The interim order procedure is draconian.[3] The court must consider the application 'as soon as practicable' after the third day following the date of the claimant's application.[4] The defendant is entitled to file a witness statement in response to the application,[5] but the court must make an IPO if satisfied that the claimant has an immediate right to possession of the premises at the date of application and has been so entitled throughout the period of the alleged unlawful occupation.[6] Any IPO must be served within 48 hours after it is sealed by the court[7] and the defendant is obliged to vacate the premises within 24 hours of the service of that order.[8] The decision whether to make the possession order final is taken only at a date at least seven days later, when the defendant is already out of possession.[9] The interim order procedure is reinforced by the possibility of criminal sanction in the case of residential premises.[10] It is normally a criminal offence for *any* person to trespass on such premises during the currency of a duly served IPO[11] or for the original trespasser to return after the expiry of the order but within the year following the service of the order.[12]

1 CPR Rules 55.20–55.28 (introduced in their original form by SI 1995/1582). An IPO cannot be sought against any person who entered with consent (eg a tenant or licensee who now holds over after the expiration of the relevant term or period) (see CPR Rule 55.21(2)).
2 CPR Rule 55.21(1)(c).
3 It is a criminal offence to make false or misleading statements for the purpose of obtaining (or resisting) an IPO (Criminal Justice and Public Order Act 1994, s 75(1)–(2)). The claimant may have to undertake to reinstate and compensate the defendant if, after an IPO has been made, the court holds that the claimant was not entitled to the order (CPR Rule 55.25(1)(b)). The making of an IPO may also depend on whether the claimant is prepared to undertake, pending final determination, not to damage the premises or damage or dispose of any of the defendant's property (CPR Rule 55.25(1)(b)).
4 CPR Rule 55.22(6). The claimant must, within 24 hours of his application to the court, serve the relevant documentation on the defendant in almost exactly the same manner as prescribed by CPR Rule 55.6 [**para 3.40**] (see CPR Rule 55.23).
5 CPR Rule 55.24(1).
6 CPR Rules 55.21(1)(b), 55.25(2)(b)(i). The court must also be satisfied that there has been proper service of documentation and that any undertakings given by the claimant as a precondition of making the IPO are adequate (CPR Rule 55.25(2)(a)–(b)).
7 CPR Rule 55.26(1).
8 CPR Rule 55.25(3).
9 CPR Rules 55.25(4), 55.27(3). The defendant, if he has left the premises, may apply on grounds of urgency for the IPO to be set aside before the hearing of the claim (CPR Rule 55.28(1)).
10 See CJ&POA 1994, s 76(8).
11 CJ&POA 1994, s 76(2). The offender is arrestable without warrant on reasonable suspicion (CJ&POA 1994, s 76(7)). No offence is committed by a person who leaves the premises within 24 hours of the time of service of the order and does not return (CJ&POA 1994, s 76(3)(a)).
12 CJ&POA 1994, s 76(4).

ENTITLEMENT TO SUE IN TRESPASS

3.49 The wrongful assumption of possession of land inevitably constitutes a trespass to land; but not all infringements of land boundaries constitute an assumption of possession. Some sorts of invasion are merely intermittent or non-exclusive (eg that of the individual who takes a short cut across another's land or of the casual intruder whose presence is temporary). In the latter kinds of case the appropriate remedy lies, not in any action for the recovery of possession, but in the action for trespass to land. The person who currently enjoys possession of land may bring an action in trespass against anyone who enters the land without his consent, with the sole exception of a person who has a better title than himself.[1] In cases of *dispossession* from land, an action for trespass may, in conjunction with the recovery of possession, offer the additional prospect of recovering damages in respect of any loss inflicted by or during the period of dispossession, together with the further possibility of obtaining injunctive relief.

1   See *Hunter v Canary Wharf Ltd* [1997] AC 655 at 703E per Lord Hoffmann; *Lambeth LBC v Rumbelow* (Chancery Division, 25 January 2001) per Etherton J. See also *Anderson v Wilson* (2000) 171 ALR 705 at [45] per Black CJ and Sackville J.

A wrong against possession

3.50   Consistently with the empirical approach of much English law,[1] trespass to land is 'essentially a wrong against possession, not against ownership.'[2] It follows that, in strict terms, trespass to realty is actionable only at the instance of a person with a present right to possession of land.[3] Given the strong link between possession and title, the right to sue in trespass is also sometimes said, at the risk of slight inaccuracy, to rest upon estate ownership.[4] In some instances an action in trespass may also be available to the owner of a reversionary estate[5] and even to a beneficial owner of land.[6]

1   [Para 2.77].
2   *Simpson v Fergus* (2000) 79 P & CR 398 at 401 per Robert Walker LJ. See similarly *J A Pye (Oxford) Ltd v Graham* [2003] 1 AC 419 at [42] per Lord Browne-Wilkinson; *Powell v McFarlane* (1977) 38 P & CR 452 at 469 per Slade J; *Barker v The Queen* (1983) 153 CLR 338 at 372 per Dawson J; *TCN Channel Nine Pty Ltd v Anning* (2002) 54 NSWLR 333 at [23] per Spigelman CJ.
3   *Harper v Charlesworth* (1825) 4 B & C 574 at 585, 107 ER 1174 at 1178; *Attorney-General v Wilcox* [1938] Ch 934 at 938 per Farwell J; *Street v Mountford* [1985] AC 809 at 816B–C per Lord Templeman; *Hunter v Canary Wharf Ltd* [1997] AC 655 at 703C–F per Lord Hoffmann. The principle is broadly accepted (see *Simpson v Knowles* [1974] VR 190 at 195; *Sky Four Realty Co v State*, 512 NYS2d 987 at 989 (NY Ct Cl 1987); *Bradley v Wingnut Films Ltd* [1993] 1 NZLR 415 at 429; *Australian Broadcasting Corpn v Lenah Game Meats Pty Ltd* (2001) 208 CLR 199 at [43] per Gleeson CJ).
4   See *AG Securities v Vaughan* [1990] 1 AC 417 at 454A per Lord Bridge of Harwich.
5   See *Hunter v Canary Wharf Ltd* [1997] AC 655 at 688F, 692C per Lord Goff of Chieveley.
6   *Malory Enterprises Ltd v Cheshire Homes Ltd* [2002] Ch 216 at [65] per Arden LJ. Because he enjoys unity of possession with co-tenants [para 11.32], a tenant in common may maintain an action in trespass against either a stranger or another co-tenant (see *Incorporated Owners of Chungking Mansions v Shamdasani* [1991] 2 HKC 342).

Extension to certain licensees

3.51   In what seems an unprincipled erosion of the historic concept of possession,[1] English courts are nowadays beginning to accord some of the attributes of 'possession' to certain categories of licensee.[2] In the teeth of clear doctrine that a licence connotes a fragile, non-possessory presence on land,[3] the courts have in recent years conceded that 'exclusive possession' of land may be enjoyed by a licensee[4] and even by a 'tolerated trespasser'.[5] The result has been to extend the availability of trespass remedies to a number of persons otherwise unentitled to sue,[6] provided that in each case the claimant 'is enjoying or asserting exclusive possession of the land.'[7]

1   The temptation towards doctrinal deviation has been sternly resisted elsewhere (see *Western Australia v Ward* (2002) 191 ALR 1 at [504] per McHugh J; *Fatac Ltd v Commissioner of Inland Revenue* [2002] 3 NZLR 648 at [66] (NZ Court of Appeal)).

2   A similar indeterminacy as to the meaning of possession is beginning to colour the traditional requirement in English law that easements must be non-possessory in character [**para 8.74**].

3   [**Para 4.6**]. Other jurisdictions acknowledge, with greater insight, that 'a licence that gives exclusive possession is a contradiction in terms' (*Western Australia v Ward* (2002) 191 ALR 1 at [513] per McHugh J).

4   See eg *Hounslow LBC v Twickenham Garden Developments Ltd* [1971] Ch 233 at 257D–E per Megarry J; *Street v Mountford* [1985] AC 809 at 823D per Lord Templeman; *Hunter v Canary Wharf Ltd* [1997] AC 655 at 688E, 692C per Lord Goff of Chieveley, 702H–703E per Lord Hoffmann, 724C–F per Lord Hope of Craighead; *Leadenhall Residential 2 Ltd v Stirling* [2002] 1 WLR 499 at [19]–[23] per Lloyd J.

5   See eg *Pemberton v Southwark LBC* [2000] 1 WLR 1672 at 1682G–H, 1684H–1685A, 1686B–D.

6   See eg *Mehta v Royal Bank of Scotland* [1999] 3 EGLR 153 at 160E–F (successful trespass claim by licensee with exclusive possession).

7   *Hunter v Canary Wharf Ltd* [1997] AC 655 at 703E per Lord Hoffmann (see also 688E per Lord Goff of Chieveley, 724C–F per Lord Hope of Craighead). See similarly *Newcastle-under-Lyme Corpn v Wolstanton Ltd* [1947] Ch 92 at 106–108.

Occasional plurality of possession

3.52   Given the complex definition of 'land' in English law,[1] it is even possible that the same land co-ordinates may simultaneously support separate possessory claims by two or more persons – as, for instance, where one owns the soil and another owns growing crops – so that each may sue in trespass for damage to his respective interest.[2] In *Monsanto plc v Tilly*[3] the Court of Appeal was even prepared to hold that a company which contractually reserved title in a genetically engineered crop trial had a sufficient interest in the land, as against environmental campaigners, to maintain an action in trespass in respect of sites in which it held no estate or other interest.[4]

1   [**Para 1.13**].

2   *Crosby v Wadsworth* (1805) 6 East 602 at 609, 102 ER 1419 at 1423; *Back v Daniels* [1925] 1 KB 526 at 542 per Scrutton LJ; *Monsanto plc v Tilly* [2000] Env LR 313 at 322 per Stuart-Smith LJ.

3   [2000] Env LR 313 at 322 per Stuart-Smith LJ, 336 per Mummery LJ.

4   See also *Wellaway v Courtier* [1918] 1 KB 200 at 203–204; and compare *Manchester Airport Plc v Dutton* [2000] QB 133 at 150A–E, 151B–H [**paras 4.98, 7.145**].

TRESPASS

3.53   The idea of trespass and the correlative notion of licensed entry upon land[1] are ineradicable components of the deep structure of real property. Together these concepts provide the supportive sanction of the civil law for an ancient territorial imperative. Possession of land confers, at common law, an entitlement to dictate the terms on which access may be enjoyed (if at all) by others. 'Our law holds the property of every man so sacred, that no man can set his foot upon his neighbour's close without his leave.'[2] At the heart of this absolutist dogma is the notion of trespass. Trespass is the act of unauthorised and unjustifiable entry upon land in the possession of another.[3] In keeping with the supposedly sacrosanct nature of the territorial claim safeguarded by the law of trespass, the wrong of trespass is not only actionable regardless of the extent of the incursion,[4] but also actionable per se (ie without any necessary showing of injury or damage to the claimant).[5] In the case of a permanent structural encroachment across a boundary line, the invasion constitutes a continuing trespass in respect of which a fresh cause of action arises day by day.[6] In certain restricted circumstances, the commission of trespass to land is not merely a tort,[7] but also a crime.[8]

1   [**Para 4.3**].
2   *Entick v Carrington* (1765) 2 Wils KB 275 at 291, 95 ER 807 at 817 per Lord Camden CJ.
3   *Peck v United Kingdom* (2003) 36 EHRR 719 at [44] (European Court of Human Rights). See also *Coco v The Queen* (1994) 179 CLR 427 at 435 per Mason CJ, Brennan, Gaudron and McHugh JJ.
4   'If the defendant places a part of his foot on the plaintiff's land unlawfully, it is in law as much a trespass as if he had walked half a mile on it' (*Ellis v Loftus Iron Company* (1874) LR 10 CP 10 at 12 per Lord Coleridge CJ; *Drury v Secretary of State for the Environment, Food and Rural Affairs* [2004] EWCA Civ 200 at [39] per Ward LJ). See e g *Cudmore-Ray v Pajouheshnia* [1993] CLY 4040 (encroachment of granny flat into neighbour's airspace by 7/8th of an inch); *Daniells v Mendonca* (1999) 78 P & CR 401 at 408 (1½ inch annexation along 12 foot wall).
5   *Entick v Carrington* (1765) 19 Howell's State Trials 1029 at 1066, 2 Wils KB 275 at 291, 95 ER 807 at 817. See *League against Cruel Sports Ltd v Scott* [1986] QB 240 at 246G–H. Substantial damages can be awarded (even in the absence of loss) in sheer vindication of the right to exclude the trespasser (see *Plenty v Dillon* (1991) 171 CLR 635 at 645, 655 (High Court of Australia)).
6   *Earle v Martin* (1998) 172 Nfld & PEIR 105 at [15]. It is possible, however, that the trespass victim's right to recover possession of the airspace taken over by the encroachment may be barred by Limitation Act 1980 [**para 6.40**]. Airspace, in itself, comprises land [**para 1.40**].
7   It is increasingly recognised that trespass upon another's land may sometimes be actionable under other heads of claim, e g breach of confidence (see *Douglas v Hello! Ltd* [2001] QB 967 at [71], [96], [165]; *Douglas v Hello! Ltd* (*No 3*) [2003] 3 All ER 996 at [227]; *Australian Broadcasting Corpn v Lenah Game Meats Pty Ltd* (2001) 208 CLR 199 at [55] per Gleeson CJ).
8   [**Paras 3.94–3.102**].

Fundamental nature of trespass

3.54   The roots of trespass to realty lie in the medieval action of trespass *quare clausum fregit*.[1] The inviolability of land from the physical incursion of strangers is a principle deeply grounded in the common law,[2] as fundamental to the concept of property as it is to basic notions of individual freedom and personal privacy.[3] Laws relating to trespass have been described as 'important features of any government dedicated ... to a rule of law.'[4] At common law, therefore, it is virtually axiomatic that any entry upon land unsupported by consent or other authorisation or justification is a trespass.[5] The right to exclude unwanted strangers has been described as 'one of the essential sticks in the bundle of property rights'[6] and it is the 'fundamental right of the owner of land ... to object to trespass.'[7] It is in this area that property and privacy concerns most obviously coalesce and the common law tradition has long endorsed the 'right of a citizen ... to the control and enjoyment of his own property, including the right to determine who shall and who shall not be permitted to invade it.'[8]

1   Literally, trespass 'by which means he broke (or breached) the close'. See *Bl Comm*, Vol III, pp 209–210; J B Ames, 'Injuries to Realty', in *Lectures on Legal History* (Harvard UP, Cambridge Mass 1913), p 224.
2   The inviolability of privately held land from the invasion of outsiders is regarded as 'a fundamental principle going to the root of our social order' (*Reference re an Application for an Authorisation* (1984) 5 DLR (4th) 601 at 616 per Harradence JA).
3   See *TCN Channel Nine Pty Ltd v Anning* (2002) 54 NSWLR 333 at [52] per Spigelman CJ ('The protection of privacy interests has long been recognised as a social value protected by the tort of trespass').
4   *Bell v Maryland*, 378 US 226 at 346, 12 L Ed 2d 822 at 867 (1964) per Justice Black. See also *Harrison v Carswell* (1976) 62 DLR (3d) 68 at 83 per Dickson J.
5   *Kenyon v Hart* (1865) 6 B & S 249 at 255, 122 ER 1188 at 1190 per Blackburn J; *R v Fox* [1985] 1 WLR 1126 at 1129G–H per Lord Fraser of Tullybelton; *R v Somerset County Council, ex p Fewings* [1995] 1 WLR 1037 at 1050H–1051B per Simon Brown LJ; *DPP v Corrigan* [1986] IR 290 at 294; *DPP v McMahon* [1986] IR 393 at 398; *Coco v The Queen* (1994) 179 CLR 427 at 435; *Jacque v Steenberg Homes, Inc*, 563 NW2d 154 at 159–160 (Wis 1997).
6   *Prune Yard Shopping Center v Robins*, 447 US 74 at 82, 64 L Ed 2d 741 at 752 (US Supreme Court 1980) per Justice Rehnquist. See also Thomas W Merrill, 'Property and the Right to Exclude' 77 Neb L Rev 730 at 740–745 (1998); David L Callies and J David Breemer, 'The Right to Exclude Others From Private Property: A Fundamental Constitutional Right' 3 Wash J of Law and Policy 39 (2000).
7   *Newbury DC v Russell* (1997) 95 LGR 705 at 713 per Rattee J. The law of trespass is nowadays supplemented, in cases where there is no physical intrusion across a boundary, by the Protection from Harassment Act 1997 (see eg *R v DPP, ex p Moseley* (1999) Times, 23 June). See also *Daiichi Pharmaceuticals UK Ltd v Stop Huntingdon Animal Cruelty* [2004] 1 WLR 1503 at [36] (exclusion zones around homes of company employees).
8   *Colet v The Queen* (1981) 119 DLR (3d) 521 at 526 per Ritchie J. See likewise *Martin v City of Struthers*, 319 US 141, 87 L Ed 1313 at 1316 (1943) per Justice Black.

Aerial trespass

3.55   Land is a multi-dimensional resource. It therefore follows that some forms of trespass involve, not an unconsented footfall upon terrain, but rather a lateral invasion of lower stratum airspace. Such invasion is the endless stuff of neighbour disputes; and the stance of the law is strict. The law does not endorse the use of another's airspace for private convenience or profit. This is so even though the incursion causes no significant damage[1] and even though the airspace concerned had no commercial value prior to the artificial value conferred on it through the relevant invasive activity.[2] The point is simply that the intruder 'thereby takes into his possession air space to which his neighbour is entitled.'[3] It is well known, for instance, that where the branches of a neighbour's tree overhang the land of an adjoining owner, the latter is entitled, without giving prior notice,[4] to lop off the branches which intrude into his airspace.[5] In doing so, he must not enter upon his neighbour's land[6] save in cases of emergency for the purpose of protecting life or property.[7] (Because of the ever changing nature of the tree, neither the statute of limitations nor the law of prescription can validate the wrong.[8]) Likewise, either trespass or nuisance (or both[9]) can be committed through the projection of overhanging eaves,[10] protruding scaffolding,[11] advertising signs,[12] fire escapes,[13] and overhead cables and wires.[14] Illicit invasion of airspace is caused even by the poking of a horse's head across a dividing fence,[15] and certainly by the intrusion of low-flying aircraft.[16] Perhaps the most persistent of urban trespassers is the oversailing jib of the sky crane.[17]

1   *Woollerton and Wilson Ltd v Richard Costain Ltd* [1970] 1 WLR 411 at 413E. See also *Bernstein of Leigh (Baron) v Skyviews & General Ltd* [1978] QB 479 at 486F; *Didow v Alberta Power Ltd* [1988] 5 WWR 606 at 615–616.

2   *LJP Investments Pty Ltd v Howard Chia Investments Pty Ltd* (1989) 24 NSWLR 490 at 494D–495E.

3   *Anchor Brewhouse Developments Ltd v Berkley House (Docklands Developments) Ltd* (1987) 38 BLR 82 at 94 per Scott J.

4   *Lemmon v Webb* [1895] AC 1 at 6 per Lord Herschell LC, 8 per Lord Davey.

5   This right may be just as appropriately founded in nuisance as in trespass (see *Lemmon v Webb* [1894] 3 Ch 1 at 24; *Bernstein of Leigh (Baron) v Skyviews & General Ltd* [1978] QB 479 at 485E).

6   *Lemmon v Webb* [1894] 3 Ch 1 at 14–15, 17–18, 24.

7   *Jones v Williams* (1843) 11 M & W 176 at 182, 152 ER 764 at 767 per Lord Abinger CB; *Carr v Sourlos* (1994) 6 BPR 13626 at 13632.

8   *Lemmon v Webb* [1895] AC 1 at 6 per Lord Herschell LC. The adjoining owner is nevertheless liable for conversion if he appropriates either the overhanging branches or any fruit thereon (see *Mills v Brooker* [1919] 1 KB 555 at 558). Severance of fruit from the branch does not alter the ownership of the fruit. This remains after severance, as before, in the owner of the tree – even if the severance is caused by the action of the wind or the ripeness of the fruit (see *Mills v Brooker*, supra at 558 per Lush J).

9   The law of nuisance has been described as 'an extension of the idea of trespass into the field that fringes property' (see *Victoria Park Racing and Recreation Grounds Co Ltd v Taylor* (1937) 58 CLR 479 at 513 per Evatt J). The terminology of trespass has been considered particularly appropriate to encroachment by permanent structures (see *Didow v Alberta Power Ltd* [1988] 5 WWR 606 at 609, 615).

10   *Baten's Case* (1610) 9 Co Rep 53b at 54a/b, 77 ER 810 at 811–812; *Fay v Prentice* (1845) 1 CB 828 at 838, 840, 135 ER 769 at 773–774; *Ward v Gold* (1969) 211 EG 155 at 159. See also *Corbett v Hill* (1869–70) LR 9 Eq 671 at 673–674.

11   *LJP Investments Pty Ltd v Howard Chia Investments Pty Ltd* (1989) 24 NSWLR 490 at 495E–496D; *Meriton Apartments Pty Ltd v Baulderstone Hornibrook Pty Ltd* (1992) 9 BPR 17433 at 17435.

12   *Gifford v Dent* [1926] WN 336; *Kelsen v Imperial Tobacco Co (of Great Britain and Ireland) Ltd* [1957] 2 QB 334 at 345; *De Richaumont Investment Co Ltd v OTW Advertising Ltd* [2001] 2 NZLR 831 at [39].

13   *Straudley Investments Ltd v Barpress Ltd* [1987] 1 EGLR 69 at 70E.

14   *Barker v Corporation of the City of Adelaide* [1900] SALR 29 at 33–34; *Graves v Interstate Power Co*, 178 NW 376 at 377 (1920); *Didow v Alberta Power Ltd* [1988] 5 WWR 606 at 616. See also *Wandsworth Board of Works v United Telephone Co* (1884) 13 QBD 904 at 927 per Fry LJ.

15   *Ellis v Loftus Iron Company* (1874) LR 10 CP 10 at 12 per Lord Coleridge CJ ('That may be a very small trespass, but it is a trespass in law').

16   See *Smith v New England Aircraft Co*, 170 NE 385 at 393 (1930) (overflight at height of 100 feet); *Thrasher v City of Atlanta*, 173 SE 817 at 826 (1934). Similar problems are caused by low-level helicopter searches by police (see e g *People v Sneed*, 108 Cal Rptr 146 at 151 (1973); *R v Kelly* (1999) 169 DLR (4th) 720 at 735–738). See also Shawcross and Beaumont, *Air Law* (4th edn, London 2000), Vol I, V/127.

17   See *Photo Centre Ltd v Tersons Ltd* (1964) 192 EG 901 at 903; *Woollerton and Wilson Ltd v Richard Costain Ltd* [1970] 1 WLR 411 at 413D–E; *Graham v K D Morris & Sons Pty Ltd* [1974] Qd R 1 at 4D; *John Trenberth Ltd v National Westminster Bank Ltd* (1979) 39 P & CR 104 at 106–107; *Anchor Brewhouse Developments Ltd v Berkley House (Docklands Developments) Ltd* (1987) 38 BLR 82 at 94–95; *London & Manchester Assurance Co Ltd v O & H*

Construction Ltd [1989] 2 EGLR 185 at 186M–187A; *Franklin Mint Ltd v Baxtergate Investment Co* (Unreported, Court of Appeal, 12 March 1998).

Visual trespass

3.56 During most of the history of English law it has been generally true that no civil (as distinct from criminal[1]) wrong is committed by reason merely of visual penetration of one's premises from outside the boundaries of one's land.[2]

1 The peeping Tom may be guilty of a breach of the peace, criminal assault and/or an offence under the Vagrancy Act 1824, s 4 (*Smith v Chief Superintendent, Woking Police Station* (1983) 76 Cr App R 234 at 237–238). See also *Raffaelli v Heatly* 1949 JC 101 at 104–105; *Butcher v Jessop* 1989 SLT 593 at 600 per Lord Murray. It is now both a criminal offence and an actionable civil wrong for a person knowingly and unreasonably to pursue 'a course of conduct ... which amounts to harassment of another' (Protection from Harassment Act 1997, ss 1, 2(1), 3(1)). For this purpose 'harassing' includes 'alarming the person or causing the person distress' (s 7(2)).
2 In certain exceptional circumstances the act of overlooking may constitute the common law nuisance of 'watching and besetting' (see *J Lyons & Sons v Wilkins* [1899] 1 Ch 255 at 267, 271–272, 276; *Ward, Locke & Co (Ltd) v Operative Printers' Assistants' Society* (1906) 22 TLR 327 at 328–330).

Onus to resist visual intrusion

3.57 In the absence of any protectable easement of indefinite privacy[1] or any all-embracing tort of 'invasion of privacy',[2] there has existed no general common law right to resist having one's land and one's activities on that land overlooked by neighbours or indeed by others.[3] It is no trespass 'to watch your neighbour's pursuits in his garden as long as you do not enter his land, even if you employ binoculars to improve your view.'[4] Consistently with the idea that property inheres in 'excludability',[5] the onus has been firmly cast on the aggrieved landowner to 'shut out incursive eyes'[6] and to frustrate external visual access by raising his own boundary fence or other barrier.[7] More difficult issues are nowadays raised by thermal imaging which penetrates premises *ab extra*[8] and by CCTV street surveillance which also happens to record events inside a home.[9]

1 *Browne v Flower* [1911] 1 Ch 219 at 225 [**para 8.56**].
2 *Wainwright v Home Office* [2003] 3 WLR 1137 at [35] per Lord Hoffmann; *Campbell v MGN Ltd* [2004] 2 WLR 1232 at [11] per Lord Nicholls of Birkenhead, [43] per Lord Hoffmann [133] per Baroness Hale of Richmond. See also *Malone v Metropolitan Police Commissioner* [1979] Ch 344 at 357F per Megarry V-C; *Kaye v Robertson* [1991] FSR 62 at 66 per Glidewell LJ; *R v Khan* [1997] AC 558 at 577H per Lord Nolan; *Khan v United Kingdom* (2000) 8 BHRC 310 at [27]; *Douglas v Hello! Ltd* [2001] QB 967 at [71] per Brooke LJ, [113] per Sedley LJ; *Hosking and Hosking v Runting* [2004] NZCA 34 at [7] per Gault P and Blanchard J.
3 'Any person is entitled to look over the plaintiff's fences and to see what goes on in the plaintiff's land' (*Victoria Park Racing and Recreation Grounds Co Ltd v Taylor* (1937) 58 CLR 479 at 494 per Latham CJ). See also *California v Ciraolo*, 476 US 207 at 213, 90 L Ed 2d 210 at 216 (1986) (policemen do not have to 'shield their eyes when passing by a home on public

thoroughfares'). Freedom from view or inspection, although it may be a natural or acquired physical characteristic of a site, 'is not a legally protected interest' (*Victoria Park Racing*, supra at 508 per Dixon J). See Gray, 'Property in Thin Air' [1991] CLJ 252 at 259–273.

4   *Report of the (Younger) Committee on Privacy*, Cmnd 5012 (July 1972), Appendix I, para 12. See C S Kenny, *Cases on the English Law of Tort* (5th edn, Cambridge 1928), p 367, for an account of the unsuccessful complaint made in 1904 by the Balham dentist whose neighbours had carefully positioned large mirrors in such a way as to be able to observe operations in his surgery.

5   [**Paras 2.35, 2.78**].

6   *E I duPont deNemours & Co, Inc v Christopher*, 431 F2d 1012 at 1016–1017 (1970) per Judge Goldberg, cert denied 400 US 1024, 27 L Ed 2d 637 (1971), reh denied 401 US 976, 28 L Ed 2d 250 (1971).

7   *Chandler v Thompson* (1811) 3 Camp 80 at 81, 170 ER 1312 at 1313; *Cross v Lewis* (1824) 2 B & C 686 at 689, 107 ER 538 at 539; *Tapling v Jones* (1865) 11 HLCas 290 at 317, 11 ER 1344 at 1355; *Victoria Park Racing and Recreation Grounds Co Ltd v Taylor* (1937) 58 CLR 479 at 494 per Latham CJ, 507 per Dixon J (contrast Evatt J at 522).

8   The United States Supreme Court has held, by a bare majority, that such thermal imaging is a form of 'search' which requires a warrant (*Kyllo v United States*, 533 US 27, 150 L Ed 2d 94 (2001)). See also *Lyons v The Queen* (1985) 14 DLR (4th) 482 at 503 (trespass by laser); *Hosking and Hosking v Runting* [2004] NZCA 34 at [118] per Gault P and Blanchard J.

9   Such visual intrusion inevitably violates the right under ECHR Art 8(1) to respect for private and family life and for the home (compare e g *Peck v United Kingdom* (2003) 36 EHRR 719).

Ocular freedom

3.58   Provided that no physical entry is made upon the land, no trespass is committed by one who merely looks across a boundary into private premises[1] or who sketches,[2] photographs[3] or films[4] what he sees there. As Lord Camden CJ observed in *Entick v Carrington*,[5] 'the eye cannot by the laws of England be guilty of a trespass.'[6] By the mid-19th century it had become clear that concerns of personal privacy inevitably gave way to the competing merits of economic development and entrepreneurial activity. The householder could no more complain about being overlooked by the factory next door[7] than he could object to the noisome effects of the recently constructed road or railway which ran past his house.[8] The same approach has been generally adopted in relation to visual intrusion into commercial premises. In *Victoria Park Racing and Recreation Grounds Co Ltd v Taylor*,[9] the High Court of Australia held, by a majority, that no civil wrong was committed by a defendant who, from an elevated position outside the claimant's racecourse, broadcast for profit commentaries on the sporting events which he was able to view and hear over the low enclosure fence.[10]

1   *Cross v Lewis* (1824) 2 B & C 686 at 688–689, 107 ER 538 at 539–540; *Turner v Spooner* (1861) 30 LJ Ch 801 at 803; *Johnson v Wyatt* (1863) 2 De GJ & S 18 at 27, 46 ER 281 at 284; *Tapling v Jones* (1865) 11 HLCas 290 at 305, 317, 11 ER 1344 at 1350, 1355; *Bathurst City Council v Saban* (1985) 2 NSWLR 704 at 706B per Young J.

2   *Hickman v Maisey* [1900] 1 QB 752 at 756 per A L Smith LJ.

3   See *Sports and General Press Agency Ltd v 'Our Dogs' Publishing Co Ltd* [1916] 2 KB 880 at 884 per Horridge J, affd [1917] 2 KB 125.

4   *Bathurst City Council v Saban* (1985) 2 NSWLR 704 at 706B per Young J. See also *Aisenson v American Broadcasting Co, Inc*, 269 Cal Rptr 379 at 388 (1990); *Bradley v Wingnut Films Ltd* [1993] 1 NZLR 415 at 429; *TV3 Network Services Ltd v Broadcasting Standards Authority* [1995] 2 NZLR 720 at 732 per Eichelbaum CJ.

5   (1765) 19 Howell's State Trials 1029 at 1066. See also *Boyd v United States*, 116 US 616 at 628, 29 L Ed 746 at 750 (1886).
6   The use of floodlights and camera surveillance equipment positioned on one's own land in order to view activities in a neighbour's backyard may constitute an actionable nuisance (see *Raciti v Hughes* (1995) 7 BPR 14837 at 14840–14841 per Young J).
7   See *Tapling v Jones* (1865) 11 HLCas 290 at 305, 11 ER 1344 at 1350 per Lord Westbury LC.
8   *Duke of Buccleuch v Metropolitan Board of Works* (1870) LR 5 Ex 221 at 237; *Re Penny and the South Eastern Railway Co* (1857) 7 E & B 660 at 669–672, 119 ER 1390 at 1393–1394.
9   (1937) 58 CLR 479.
10   Latham CJ denied that a spectacle could be '"owned" in any ordinary sense of that word' ((1937) 58 CLR 479 at 496–497). See similarly *Detroit Base-ball Club v Deppert* (1886) 61 Mich 63 at 69, 1 Am St Rep 566 at 569, 27 NW 856 at 857–858; *N O C, Inc v Schaeffer*, 484 A2d 729 at 731–735 (1984). Compare *Australian Broadcasting Corpn v Lenah Game Meats Pty Ltd* (2001) 208 CLR 199 at [303], [316] per Callinan J.

Alternative approaches

3.59   The late 20th century saw a significant extension of the social interests and sensitivities deemed worthy of protection by the law.[1] A focus of concern has come to rest on those fundamental values of human dignity and autonomy[2] which underpin the personal privacy 'essential for the well-being and development of an individual.'[3] Accordingly, against the backdrop of heightened media encroachment upon the lives of individuals and corporate concerns, the courts of the common law world have begun to provide alternative remedies for the visual invasion of privately held land. The long recognised action for breach of confidence[4] is increasingly advocated as a means of protecting rights of privacy in the face of photographic intrusion.[5] The newly emerging law of harassment likewise goes some distance towards combatting derogations from individual privacy.[6] Above all, it is apparent that the gradual infiltration of a Convention-based 'right to respect' for one's private and family life and for one's home[7] has already done much to displace traditional common law perspectives. Although few judges have openly embraced a new generalised tort of 'invasion of privacy',[8] there are strong indications that the combined effect of European human rights jurisprudence and the resurgent law on breach of confidence has created the functional equivalent of such a tort in English law.[9] Here the civil wrong of breach of confidence has been reshaped[10] in such a way that, by absorbing the competing European Convention values of privacy and freedom of expression,[11] it now resembles a tort of 'misuse of private information'[12] or the infringement of a 'reasonable expectation' of privacy.[13]

1   'The law of civil liability may be said to be in transition' (*Hosking and Hosking v Runting* [2004] NZCA 34 at [2] per Gault P and Blanchard J).
2   See *Douglas v Hello! Ltd* [2001] QB 967 at [126] per Sedley LJ; *Campbell v MGN Ltd* [2004] 2 WLR 1232 at [50]–[51] per Lord Hoffmann; *Hosking and Hosking v Runting* [2004] NZCA 34 at [238]–[239] per Tipping J.
3   *Campbell v MGN Ltd* [2004] 2 WLR 1232 at [12] per Lord Nicholls of Birkenhead. There is, of course, a powerful counter-argument that an onus ultimately rests upon the landowner to shield from view those activities which he or she does not wish to be exposed to external scrutiny.

4   *Prince Albert v Strange* (1840) 1 Mac & G 25, 41 ER 1171, 2 De G & Sm 652, 64 ER 293; *Coco v A N Clark (Engineers) Ltd* [1969] RPC 41.

5   See *Hellewell v Chief Constable of Derbyshire* [1995] 1 WLR 804 at 807F–H per Laws J; *Earl Spencer v United Kingdom* (1998) 25 EHRR CD 105 at 117–118 (telephoto shot of patient in grounds of private clinic); *Douglas v Hello! Ltd* [2001] QB 967 at [86] per Brooke LJ, [117]–[118] per Sedley LJ, [165] per Keene LJ; *Campbell v MGN Ltd* [2004] 2 WLR 1232 at [75]–[76] per Lord Hoffmann; *Australian Broadcasting Corpn v Lenah Game Meats Pty Ltd* (2001) 208 CLR 199 at [34]–[35] per Gleeson CJ; *Peck v United Kingdom* (2003) 36 EHRR 719 at [110]–[111]; *Hosking and Hosking v Runting* [2003] 3 NZLR 385 at [47].

6   See Protection from Harassment Act 1997, s 1(1), (3)(c) **[para 3.56]**.

7   See ECHR Art 8(1). HRA 1998, s 12(1), (4)(b) effectively obliges the court, in touching upon any claim to freedom of expression, to have regard to the Press Complaints Commission's Code of Practice (ratified November 1997), para 3 of which states that the 'use of long lens photography to take pictures of people in private places without their consent is unacceptable.' See *Douglas v Hello! Ltd* [2001] QB 967 at [92]–[95] per Brooke LJ; *Douglas v Hello! Ltd (No 3)* [2003] 3 All ER 996 at [279] per Lindsay J. Contrast *Stewart-Brady v United Kingdom* (1998) 27 EHRR CD 284 at 286.

8   See, however, *Hosking and Hosking v Runting* [2004] NZCA 34 at [246] per Tipping J ('a self contained and stand-alone common law cause of action'). Compare the reluctance, in many jurisdictions, to recognise any high-level or overarching principle relating to 'invasion of privacy'. See *Douglas v Hello! Ltd (No 3)* [2003] 3 All ER 996 at [229] per Lindsay J; *Australian Broadcasting Corpn v Lenah Game Meats Pty Ltd* (2001) 208 CLR 199 at [41] per Gleeson CJ, [189] per Kirby J; *Hosking*, supra at [45] per Gault P and Blanchard J. There is, however, an increasing willingness to protect individuals against a particular invasion of privacy in the form of intrusive publicity (see *Hosking*, supra at [117] per Gault P and Blanchard J, [244] per Tipping J). There may also be an incremental movement towards more general rights of privacy (see *Bradley v Wingnut Films Ltd* [1993] 1 NZLR 415 at 423; *P v D* [2000] 2 NZLR 591 at [33]–[36]; *Lenah Game Meats*, supra at [125] per Gummow and Hayne JJ, [328]–[336] per Callinan J).

9   See *Douglas v Hello! Ltd (No 3)* [2003] 3 All ER 996 at [186(i)], [229] per Lindsay J; *Hosking and Hosking v Runting* [2004] NZCA 34 at [247] per Tipping J.

10   *Hosking and Hosking v Runting* [2004] NZCA 34 at [42], [109] per Gault P and Blanchard J, [245] per Tipping J. See likewise *Campbell v MGN Ltd* [2004] 2 WLR 1232 at [51] per Lord Hoffmann ('a shift in the centre of gravity of the action for breach of confidence').

11   See *A v B plc* [2003] QB 195 at [4] per Lord Woolf CJ; *Campbell v MGN Ltd* [2004] 2 WLR 1232 at [17] per Lord Nicholls of Birkenhead, [86], [105] per Lord Hope of Craighead, [132] per Baroness Hale of Richmond.

12   See *Campbell v MGN Ltd* [2004] 2 WLR 1232 at [14] per Lord Nicholls of Birkenhead. See G Phillipson, 'Transforming Breach of Confidence? Towards a Common Law Right of Privacy under the Human Rights Act' (2003) 66 MLR 726.

13   *Campbell v MGN Ltd* [2004] 2 WLR 1232 at [21] per Lord Nicholls of Birkenhead, [134]–[137] per Baroness Hale of Richmond. For a similar evolutionary development in New Zealand, see *Hosking and Hosking v Runting* [2004] NZCA 34 at [117] per Gault P and Blanchard J, [250] per Tipping J.

JUSTIFICATIONS FOR TRESPASS

3.60   In the absence of any licence authorising his access, an intruder upon land is left to show justification for his entry by reference to some paramount right of possession, some statutory or common law right of entry,[1] some 'involuntary and inevitable accident' arising in the absence of negligence,[2] some constitutional right or some freedom guaranteed by supra-national charter. In general, however, the common law has allowed very few forms of defence or justification to curtail the right to complain of trespass. For example, a mistaken belief by the trespasser (eg that he is on his own land) affords no recognisable excuse.[3] Nor, for the most part, do broadly stated guarantees of expressional or associational freedom confer any entitlement to trespass on privately held land for the purpose of exercising such freedoms.[4] Indeed, it has been argued (although not conclusively) that the European Convention on Human Rights explicitly subordinates freedoms of expression, assembly and association not only to the Convention-based protection of 'private and family life' and the integrity of the 'home', but also to the protection from intrusion which is inherent in the newly expanded law relating to the preservation of confidence.[5]

1   Extensive rights of entry are conferred by statute in connection with the enforcement of the criminal law and the regulation of public health and the environment. For a mundane, but important, example, see *Walkers Snack Foods Ltd v Coventry CC* (1998) Times, 9 April (right of authorised officer to 'enter any premises at any reasonable hour' (see now Food Standards Act 1999, s 11(4)(a))).

2   *Barker v The Queen* (1983) 153 CLR 338 at 356–357 per Brennan and Deane JJ. See *League against Cruel Sports Ltd v Scott* [1986] QB 240 at 249G.

3   See *Conway v George Wimpey & Co Ltd* [1951] 2 KB 266 at 273; *Barker v The Queen* (1983) 153 CLR 338 at 370–371 per Dawson J; *DPP v Wille* (1999) 47 NSWLR 255 at [20] per Kirby J. Likewise no defence is available to the purchaser who buys land in ignorance of an existing encroachment into a neighbour's airspace (see *Karuppannan v Balakrishnen* (1994) 3 MLJ 584 at 591D–F, 593F–G).

4   See eg *Brown v Louisiana*, 383 US 131 at 166, 15 L Ed 2d 637 at 659 (1966) per Black J; *Armes v City of Philadelphia*, 706 F Supp 1156 at 1164 (ED Pa 1989); *RMH Teleservices International Inc v British Columbia Government and Service Employees' Union* (2003) 223 DLR (4th) 750 at [55].

5   ECHR Arts 8(1), 10(2), 11(2), as construed in *Douglas v Hello! Ltd (No 3)* [2003] 3 All ER 996 at [186(ii)] per Lindsay J. See also *Douglas v Hello! Ltd* [2001] QB 967 at [137] per Sedley LJ.

Prevention or prosecution of serious crime

3.61   By long tradition the common law has upheld the right of the private citizen or police officer to enter another's premises (and, if necessary, to break down doors for the purpose[1]) in the case of compelling need to prevent serious imminent crime or to effect hot pursuit of a serious offender or to intercept one running away from an affray.[2] This power of entry is, nevertheless, of a most limited nature. Even a police officer has no common law power of entry merely because he suspects that something may be wrong.[3]

1   At common law it is a precondition of any lawful breaking of premises that there has been a demand for access and a refusal by the occupier to allow entry (*Swales v Cox* [1981] QB 849 at 855A–H per Donaldson LJ; *Plenty v Dillon* (1991) 171 CLR 635 at 647–648).

2   *Swales v Cox* [1981] QB 849 at 853F–G, 855A–C per Donaldson LJ. (In strict terms the power to enter in pursuit of an offender running from an affray was confined to police officers.) See similarly *Plenty v Dillon* (1991) 171 CLR 635 at 647 (High Court of Australia); *R v Landry* (1986) 26 DLR (4th) 368 at 392 per La Forest J (dissenting). See also *R v Macooh* (1993) 105 DLR (4th) 96 at 103–109; *R v Thomas* (1992) 67 CCC (3d) 81 at 93; *R v Anderson* (1996) 108 CCC (3d) 37 at 50.

3   *Great Central Railway Co v Bates* [1921] 3 KB 578 at 581–582 per Atkin LJ; *Plenty v Dillon* (1991) 171 CLR 635 at 648 per Gaudron and McHugh JJ. Common law may, however, provide

an implied authority for entry in special circumstances. See e g *Kay v Hibbert* [1977] CLR 226 at 227 (activation of burglar alarm wired into police station); *R v Godoy* (1997) 115 CCC (3d) 272 at 284–287 (disconnected '999' call).

Apprehended breach of the peace

3.62   In a development prudently avoided elsewhere,[1] English courts have confirmed the existence at common law[2] of an ill-framed and potentially over-broad police power to enter private premises without warrant, as a measure of preventative justice, where a police officer reasonably believes that a breach of the peace is imminent.[3] The European Court of Human Rights has upheld the validity of this power, but only in so far as it is based upon evidence that an individual has caused or 'appears likely' to cause harm to persons or property or 'acts in a manner the natural consequence of which would be to provoke violence in others.'[4]

1   Compare e g *Shattock v Devlin* [1990] 2 NZLR 88 at 110; *DPP v Delaney* [1996] 3 IR 556 at 564.
2   See Police and Criminal Evidence Act 1984, s 17(6); *Williamson v Chief Constable of West Midlands Police* [2004] 1 WLR 14 at [12].
3   *McLeod v Metropolitan Police Commissioner* [1994] 4 All ER 553 at 560e (domestic dispute); (1995) 111 LQR 562 (D Feldman); *Addison v Chief Constable of West Midlands Police* [2004] 1 WLR 29 (Note) at 32B. The idea that the public peace can be maintained in privately held premises gains support from *McConnell v Chief Constable of the Greater Manchester Police* [1990] 1 WLR 364 at 371B; *Addison*, supra at 32E–F; *R v Smith* (1983) 2 CCC (3d) 250 at 252–253. See also *Porter v Commissioner of Police of the Metropolis* [1999] All ER (D) 1129.
4   *McLeod v United Kingdom* (1999) 27 EHRR 493 at [42]. English courts are now well aware of the stringent limits thus imposed on the concept of breach of the peace (see *Foulkes v Chief Constable of the Merseyside Police* [1998] 3 All ER 705 at 711a–f per Beldam LJ; *Porter v Commissioner of Police of the Metropolis* [1999] All ER (D) 1129 per Sedley LJ).

De minimis principle

3.63   Some minor acts of trespass are excusable on a de minimis principle (or possibly as instances of inevitable accident[1]). Thus courts have been generally unprepared to acknowledge the commission of a trespass by such events as the mere protrusion of someone's head out of a window into someone else's airspace,[2] the passage of stray bullets across another's land,[3] an unintentional stepping on someone else's land to avoid an obstruction on the pavement[4] or the retrieval of a wind-blown hat or an errant child from some stranger's driveway.[5]

1   See *DPP v Wille* (1999) 47 NSWLR 255 at [19] per Kirby J.
2   *Gifford v Dent* [1926] WN 336 per Romer J.
3   *Pickering v Rudd* (1815) 4 Camp 219 at 220, 171 ER 70 at 70–71 per Lord Ellenborough CJ.
4   *Halliday v Nevill* (1984) 155 CLR 1 at 7 (High Court of Australia).
5   *Halliday v Nevill* (1984) 155 CLR 1 at 7. Compare *Bauman v Beaujean*, 53 Cal Rptr 55 at 58–59 (1966).

Necessity

3.64 Trespass to land can be justified at common law on the ground of necessity.[1] For this purpose necessity may be either public or private[2] and may extend beyond cases of sheer emergency to cover cases where intervention without the landowner's consent is necessary in order to preserve property.[3] The plea of necessity is, however, severely circumscribed.[4] The defence of necessity is available to an individual only where 'it is necessary for the private citizen to act in the face of immediate and serious danger to life or property and the citizen acts reasonably in all the circumstances.'[5] It has been said, moreover, that in all but 'very exceptional circumstances', trespass by an individual, even in cases of emergency, cannot be justified as necessary or reasonable 'if there exists a public authority responsible for the protection of the relevant interests of the public.'[6] Thus, for instance, in *Monsanto plc v Tilly*,[7] the genuine concern of a protest group over the harmful effects of genetically modified crops did not justify trespass upon land (or the destruction of plants thereon) where responsibility for the safety of such forms of cultivation fell squarely within the purview of the Department of the Environment. Likewise, in the light of the extensive public law obligations now fastened on local authority housing departments,[8] the plight of homelessness cannot comprise, in itself, a form of social necessity justifying unconsented entry upon another's land.[9] For similar reasons, any ancient doctrine of hot pursuit of vermin which may have existed before the advent of public environmental health controls can no longer be said to afford a present-day ground of immunity from trespass liability.[10]

1   *Re F (Mental Patient)* [1990] 2 AC 1 at 74A per Lord Goff of Chieveley. See *Rigby v Chief Constable of Northamptonshire* [1985] 1 WLR 1242 at 1253A; *Monsanto plc v Tilly* [2000] Env LR 313 at 325–327 per Stuart-Smith LJ, 338 per Mummery LJ; *Wilcox v Police* [1995] 2 NZLR 160 at 162–163; *R v Godoy* (1997) 115 CCC (3d) 272 at 285 (hypothetical example of forced entry in aid of heart attack victim). See also *State v Shack*, 277 A2d 369 at 373 (1971).

2   The classic common law examples arose where someone entered upon another's land in order to pull down a neighbour's burning house lest it cause a general catastrophe ('public necessity') or spread fire to his own house ('private necessity'). Such instances have now been said to be 'at least obsolescent' because of the availability of an organised and accessible public fire service (see *Burmah Oil Co Ltd v Lord Advocate* [1965] AC 75 at 164G–165B per Lord Upjohn; *Monsanto plc v Tilly* [2000] Env LR 313 at 326 per Stuart-Smith LJ).

3   *Re F (Mental Patient)* [1990] 2 AC 1 at 74H–75C per Lord Goff of Chieveley. The American Restatement of Torts holds that a landowner is not entitled to deny entry to a stranger where access 'is or reasonably appears to be necessary to prevent serious harm' to the stranger or to others. For instances of privileged entry in order to avert 'an imminent public disaster' or 'serious harm' to a person, land or chattels, see *Restatement of the Law, Second: Torts 2d*, (St Paul, Minn 1965), ¶¶ 196–197 (Vol 1, pp 353–361).

4   See *Southwark LBC v Williams* [1971] Ch 734 at 743H per Lord Denning MR. Necessity 'can very easily become simply a mask for anarchy' (Edmund Davies LJ at 746A). See also *Monsanto plc v Tilly* [2000] Env LR 313 at 337 per Mummery LJ. There is no common law right of non-consensual entry upon another's land or airspace merely for the purpose of effecting necessary repairs to one's own building (see *Meriton Apartments Pty Ltd v Baulderstone Hornibrook Pty Ltd* (1992) 9 BPR 17433 at 17435).

5   *Monsanto plc v Tilly* [2000] Env LR 313 at 338 per Mummery LJ. The danger must be 'immediate and readily perceivable' (Pill LJ at 335). Encroachment on private land is permitted only 'in case of great and imminent danger, in order to preserve life' (*Southwark LBC v Williams* [1971] Ch 734 at 743F per Lord Denning MR). See also *Rigby v Chief*

Constable of Northamptonshire [1985] 1 WLR 1242 at 1253A ('especially where human life is at stake'). Necessity nevertheless provides no excuse for trespass by anti-abortion protestors (see *Darcey v Pre-Term Foundation Clinic* [1983] 2 NSWLR 497 at 502B–D; *Sigma Reproductive Health Center v State*, 467 A2d 483 at 493–498 (Md 1983); *Jones v City of Tulsa*, 857 P2d 814 at 816–817 (1993); *Elizabeth Bagshaw Society v Breton* (1997) 75 ACWS 3d 183).

6   *Monsanto plc v Tilly* [2000] Env LR 313 at 338 per Mummery LJ.

7   [2000] Env LR 313 at 338 per Mummery LJ.

8   See Housing Act 1996, Part VII.

9   *McPhail v Persons* (*Names Unknown*) [1973] Ch 447 at 456B–D per Lord Denning MR; *Monsanto plc v Tilly* [2000] Env LR 313 at 327 per Stuart-Smith LJ. See *Southwark LBC v Williams* [1971] Ch 734 at 744B–C per Lord Denning MR ('If homelessness were once admitted as a defence to trespass, no one's house could be safe. Necessity would open a door which no man could shut ... the plea would be an excuse for all sorts of wrongdoing').

10   See *Paul v Summerhayes* (1878) 4 QBD 9 at 11; *League against Cruel Sports Ltd v Scott* [1986] QB 240 at 247C–F. A master of a hunt may, for instance, be liable in trespass where hounds are intentionally or negligently allowed to enter upon land, the relevant intention being inferable from a persistence in hunting over land which is relatively indefensible. The master's liability can extend to the intentional or negligent acts or omissions of any hunt servants, agents or followers (see *League against Cruel Sports Ltd*, supra at 252A–F).

Public interest

3.65   The closely related defence of public interest is construed even more tightly. In *Monsanto plc v Tilly*,[1] for example, Mummery LJ expressed no surprise at the absence of authority for the idea that 'the protection or promotion of the public interest (as distinct from necessity)' might justify a private citizen's entry upon another's land for the purpose of inflicting damage on that land or on personal possessions.[2] The Court of Appeal took the view that trespass in pursuit of narrowly conceived or subjective interpretations of the public interest threatens a subversion of the democratic process.[3]

1   [2000] Env LR 313 at 338–339.

2   It is also well established that the mere grant of a planning permission by a public authority confers no permission to trespass on another's land (see *Wheeler v J J Saunders Ltd* [1996] Ch 19 at 38B–C per Sir John May).

3   [2000] Env LR 313 at 329 per Stuart-Smith LJ, 339 per Mummery LJ. See *Morgentaler v The Queen* (1975) 53 DLR (3d) 161 at 209 per Dickson J ('No system of positive law can recognise any principle which would entitle a person to violate the law because on his view the law conflicted with some higher social value'). See also *Perka v The Queen* (1985) 13 DLR (4th) 1 at 34 per Wilson J.

Unavailing excuses

3.66   The traditional stance of the common law is reflected in the courts' refusal to accept a wide range of public interest concerns, however worthy, as justifying the tortious act of unconsented intrusion.[1] Unavailing excuses have included bona fide protest against the commissioning of a nuclear waste dump,[2] concern about the development of the nuclear industry,[3] sincere indignation about proven nuclear contamination,[4] a desire to stop a defence contractor's 'war crimes',[5] opposition to logging in ecologically sensitive forest areas,[6] support for environmental and planning legislation,[7] abhorrence of battery hen farming,[8] peaceful opposition to road-building proposals,[9] and a desire to preserve dignified buildings from demolition.[10]

1 Resort to the Protection from Harassment Act 1997 [**para 3.56**] is inappropriate for the purpose of stifling protest directed towards matters of public interest (*Huntingdon Life Sciences v Curtin* [1998] Env LR D9 at D10 per Eady J).
2 *United Kingdom Nirex Ltd v Barton* (1986) Times, 14 October.
3 *Commonwealth v Averill*, 423 NE2d 6 at 7–8 (Md App 1981); *Commonwealth v Hood*, 452 NE2d 188 at 196 (Mass 1983).
4 *British Nuclear Fuels Ltd v Greenpeace Ltd* (Unreported, Court of Appeal, 25 March 1986).
5 *State v Marley*, 509 P2d 1095 at 1109–1112 (1973).
6 *MacMillan Bloedel Ltd v Simpson* (1994) 113 DLR (4th) 368 at 384–385.
7 *Mayor and Burgesses of London Borough of Bromley v Susanna* (*a female*) [1999] Env LR D13.
8 *Mark v Henshaw* (1998) 155 ALR 118 at 125.
9 *Department of Transport v Williams* (Unreported, Queen's Bench Division, 2 July 1993).
10 *R v Bacon* [1977] 2 NSWLR 507 at 512–513.

Overriding social values

3.67 It is not entirely true to say that public interest concerns can *never* found a defence to trespass. There is a slowly emerging body of law which suggests that certain kinds of unconsented entry which cause no physical injury to land or person can be justified by reference to overriding concerns of general or social interest.[1] The values which claim primacy over the exclusory rights of the landowner tend to revolve around freedoms of association, communication and access to education, health care and legal aid. Thus, for instance, American courts have held that, in extreme circumstances, allegations of trespass can be countered by the need to ensure the effective provision of legal and social welfare services for indigents resident on privately owned land.[2] Again, in *Gerhardy v Brown*,[3] Deane J expressed the fear that an excessively tight regulation of access rights for non-tribal visitors to an aboriginal homeland could severely impair facilities for education and health.[4] The sorts of concern which thus take priority over the orthodox dictates of trespass law are not isolated or idiosyncratic readings of the public interest, but rather shared civic understandings about the fundamental value of human dignity.[5]

1 See e g *Dalury v S-K-I, Ltd*, 670 A2d 795 at 799–800 (Vt 1995); *Green Party of New Jersey v Hartz Mountain Industries, Inc*, 752 A2d 315 at 322 (2000) per O'Hern J.
2 See the American litigation relating to employer-owned camps for migrant farmworkers (*State v Shack* 277 A2d 369 at 374–375 (1971); *Franceschina v Morgan*, 346 F Supp 833 at 839 (1972); *Freedman v New Jersey State Police*, 343 A2d 148 at 150–151 (1975); *Baer v Sorbello*, 425 A2d 1089 at 1090 (NJ Super AD 1981)). In *Folgueras v Hassle* 331 F Supp 615 at 623–624 (1971), a Michigan court ruled that '[a]s a matter of property law, the ownership of a labor camp does not entail the right to cut off the fundamental rights of those who live in the camp.' See also *State v DeCoster*, 653 A2d 891 (Me 1995).
3 (1985) 159 CLR 70 at 152 (see also Brennan J at 133–134).
4 Deane J thought that the relevant landowner's strict exclusory control over the access of strangers was 'likely to create an over-isolated enclave within South Australia entrenched behind what amounts to a type of passport system.' He could only 'speculate about the danger that, particularly for the female and the weak, the difference between separate development

and segregation might become more theoretical than real.' See likewise *Toohey v Peach* (2003) 143 NTR 1 at [9] (echoing the fear that a permit system could stifle press freedom and 'keep the Australian people in the dark').

5   North American case law makes frequent appeal to the supreme importance of human 'dignity' as the reason why 'ownership does not vest the owner with dominion over the lives of those people living on his property' (*Folgueras v Hassle*, 331 F Supp 615 at 625 (1971)). See e g *State v Shack*, 277 A2d 369 at 374–375 (1971); *Vasquez v Glassboro Service Association, Inc*, 415 A2d 1156 at 1164 (NJ 1980); *Irwin Toy Ltd v Quebec* (*Attorney-General*) (1989) 54 DLR 577 at 612 per Dickson CJC; *The Queen in Right of Canada v Committee for the Commonwealth of Canada* (1991) 77 DLR (4th) 385 at 457d per McLachlin J ('conditions necessary for individual fulfilment and human flourishing'). Compare German *Grundgesetz*, Art 1(1) ('human dignity is inviolable').

Socially paramount forms of access

3.68   Recent developments of the public interest argument have brought into play more materialistic conceptions of the kinds of value which may be claimed to outweigh the territorial prerogative of those who own or possess land and the commercial plant installed thereon. Increasingly frequent demands for unconsented access are made on behalf of corporate entities which seek to take advantage of some exclusively owned infrastructure for the distribution of a socially valued utility. Thus, for example, in *Videotron Telecom Ltd v OPGI Management Limited Partnership*,[1] the owners of a large proportion of the commercial premises in the business core of Toronto refused to allow the city's primary provider of telecommunications services to have access (even for a fee) to the in-building wiring supplying that provider's customers in those premises. The Ontario Superior Court of Justice nevertheless held that, in view of the 'national importance of the telecommunications industry', it was seriously arguable that, even without legislative changes, the owners' private real property rights could be 'compromised ... to accommodate or advance a larger public interest.'[2] The service provider was therefore successful in obtaining an interlocutory injunction restraining the landowners from interfering with the provider's existing connections.[3] The social and commercial imperative of communicational efficiency trumped even the 'inviolate nature of property.'[4]

1   [2003] OJ No 2278.
2   [2003] OJ No 2278 at [14]–[20]. It appeared (at [2(e), (n)]) that the landowners controlled access to at least 50 per cent of the buildings serviced by the provider's network and that the owners' refusal to negotiate threatened not only irreparable harm to the provider's business, but also to the commercial activities of its customers.
3   Compare *NT Power Generation Pty Ltd v Power & Water Authority* [2002] FCAFC 302, where a majority of the Federal Court of Australia upheld the right of the owner of the only electricity supply infrastructure in the Northern Territory to deny access to its transmission and distribution services to a competitor which, it was feared, might otherwise 'cherry-pick' the larger consumers of electricity.
4   [2003] OJ No 2278 at [18].

LIMITS OF THE NOTION OF TRESPASS

3.69   Although its origins may lie in some absolutist notion of the inviolable nature of possession of land, the concept of trespass is not without its inherent limitations. There is nowadays increasing doubt whether an unqualified exclusory privilege is an inevitable incident of *all* property in land. Whilst strict adherence to traditional concepts of trespass may be entirely appropriate, for example, in relation to the domestic curtilage, in other locations the assertion of an absolute exclusory power may become both meaningless and unenforceable.

Indefensible tracts of land

3.70 Since the law of trespass protects possession of land, actionability in trespass can be affected, in extreme circumstances, by the relative defensibility of a particular tract of land.[1] There have been suggestions, particularly in Australia, that the sheer scale of a land holding may determine the degree to which that land can properly be subjected to an estate owner's comprehensive regulatory control.[2] In *Wik Peoples v Queensland*,[3] Kirby J thought it 'unlikely' that there could have been any parliamentary intention to invest an estate owner with absolute exclusory power under pastoral leases covering 'huge areas as extensive as many a county in England and bigger than some nations' in 'remote and generally unvisited' terrain.[4] Similarly, in *Gerhardy v Brown*,[5] Mason J envisaged that in 'exceptional circumstances' legislative guarantees of freedom of movement might allow unconsented access to the lands of private owners. Such derogation from the landowner's right of arbitrary exclusion would be justified if, for example, 'the purpose and effect of vesting extensive tracts of land in private ownership and denying a right of access to non-owners was to impede or defeat the individual's freedom of movement across a State or, more relevantly, to exclude persons of a particular race from exercising their freedom of movement across a State.'[6]

1   For reference to the significance of 'physically non-excludable' resources, see Gray, [1991] CLJ 252 at 269–273, 286–290.
2   See the suggestion that conventional notions of trespass may not be strictly applicable to isolated stations situated within the vast expanses of the outback (*Hackshaw v Shaw* (1984) 155 CLR 614 at 659 per Deane J). See also *McKee v Gratz*, 260 US 127 at 136, 67 L Ed 167 at 170 (1922) per Justice Holmes [**para 5.33**].
3   (1996) 187 CLR 1 at 244, 246.
4   In such areas 'talk of "exclusive possession" or "exclusive occupation" has an unreal quality' ((1996) 187 CLR 1 at 233 per Kirby J). See also Gaudron J (at 154).
5   (1985) 159 CLR 70 at 103–104.
6   In *Gerhardy v Brown* a land title covering 100,000 square kilometres – more than ten per cent of the total land area of South Australia – had been vested in a supposedly private non-government corporation controlled by a tribal council. Unconsented access to this huge tract was rendered a criminal offence (Pitjantjatjara Land Rights Act 1981, s 19(1)), but, in the view voiced in the High Court of Australia by Murphy J, the selective exclusion of strangers from an area of this scale could not be said to occur within 'a private zone' ((1985) 159 CLR 70 at 107).

Large scenic areas

3.71 The qualified 'right to roam' acknowledged by the Countryside and Rights of Way Act 2000[1] constitutes an important statutory recognition of the inapplicability of traditional trespassory concepts to large areas of scenic space which are vested in relatively small numbers of private estate owners. Persons entering 'access land' in pursuance of the entitlement created by this legislation are no longer regarded as trespassers.

1   [Para 5.46].

PHYSICAL RESISTANCE TO TRESPASS

3.72   Where a stranger enters upon land without consent, the owner or any other person with a right to possession is entitled at common law to use reasonable physical force in order to exclude or evict the trespasser.[1] The use of self-help as a response to trespass may take various forms.[2] Self-redress may also be relevant where the act of trespass comprises not a personal entry by the trespasser but some form of physical encroachment for which he is responsible.[3]

1   See *Revill v Newbery* [1996] QB 567 at 580C–D per Millett LJ; *R v Asante-Mensah* (2003) 227 DLR (4th) 75 at [58] (Supreme Court of Canada). It is a defence to a criminal charge of putting people in fear of violence to show that a particular course of conduct was 'reasonable' for the protection of someone's person or property (Protection from Harassment Act 1997, s 4(3)(c)).
2   See e g *Times*, 17 May 2000 (trespassing travellers sprayed with contents of septic tank when they demanded £500 payment to vacate farmer's land).
3   See e g *Burton v Winters* [1993] 1 WLR 1077 at 1081D, where Lloyd LJ pointed out that, in (say) the case of overhanging branches, a summary resort to self-redress is justified by the disproportionate expense of legal proceedings in response to such trivial encroachment [**para 3.80**]. See also *Chamberlain v Lindon* [1998] 1 WLR 1252 at 1262A–C; *Nelson v Nicholson* (Unreported, Court of Appeal, 1 December 2000) at [20] per Jonathan Parker LJ.

Preconditions of self-help

3.73   The right of physical resistance to an invasion of one's land applies only during the period before the intruder's presence matures into possession of the land.[1] The availability of the remedy of self-help is terminated by the inception of possession on the part of the trespasser,[2] and it is for precisely this reason that possession is defined fairly restrictively by the courts. A householder who returns home from a brief holiday to find his house occupied by squatters is entitled to throw the intruders out of his house without further ceremony. In these circumstances insufficient time has elapsed to allow the occupancy of the trespassers to harden into the elements of *factum* and *animus* which, for relevant purposes, comprise possession.[3] In such cases, as Lord Denning MR observed in *McPhail v Persons (Names Unknown)*,[4] the aggrieved party 'can go in himself and turn them out without the aid of the courts of law.' However, although Lord Denning considered the legality of this particular remedy 'beyond question', he cautioned that self-help 'is not a course to be recommended because of the disturbance which might follow'.[5] In most instances it is preferable to recover the premises by way of a 'possession claim against trespassers' brought in the county court (or, exceptionally, in the High Court).[6]

1   It may have been true in the time of Bracton that the interval between wrongful entry and the inception of 'possession' was as short as four days – supposedly the period of time required for the ejected owner to ride one day in each direction of the compass in order to gather arms and friends to help in the re-ejectment (see Pollock and Maitland, *The History of English Law* (2nd edn, London 1968), Vol 2, p 50). Nowadays the period may be somewhat longer and depends, in any event, on the circumstances of the case.

2   *Powell v McFarlane* (1977) 38 P & CR 452 at 476 per Slade J; *Lambeth LBC v Rumbelow* (Chancery Division, 25 January 2001) per Etherton J.

3   See Sir F Pollock, *Torts* (15th edn, London 1951), p 292.

4   [1973] Ch 447 at 456D–E.

5   [1973] Ch 447 at 456E. See similarly *Rhondda Cynon Taff County BC v Watkins* (Chancery Division, 11 December 2001) per Neuberger J.

6   CPR Rule 55 [**para 3.36**].

Restrictions on self-help

3.74   Recourse to self-help against a trespasser is inevitably limited by a number of factors.

Reasonably necessary force

3.75   If the owner or possessor of land uses force to secure the eviction of a trespasser, it is clear that he must use no more force than, in the circumstances, is reasonably necessary for the achievement of that purpose.[1] The mere fact of trespass does not justify extreme retaliation or disproportionate force[2] and the use of excessive violence against the trespasser may itself constitute an actionable wrong[3] or even a criminal offence.[4] It used to be said that a householder (or any servant, lodger or member of his household) might use lethal force in defence against thieves who invaded his home for purposes of robbery or murder,[5] but it will be rare nowadays that homicide can be excused on this basis.[6] As Millett LJ pointed out in *Revill v Newbery*,[7] '[c]hanges in society and in social perceptions have meant that what might have been considered reasonable at one time would no longer be so regarded.'

1   *Hemmings v Stoke Poges Golf Club Ltd* [1920] 1 KB 720 at 747; *Revill v Newbery* [1996] QB 567 at 580C per Millett LJ.

2   An occupier cannot 'treat a burglar as an outlaw' (*Revill v Newbery* [1996] QB 567 at 577D per Neill LJ).

3   See e g *Revill v Newbery* [1996] QB 567 at 578D, where the Court of Appeal held that '*some* duty' of care was owed to a trespassing burglar and that liability therefore attached to a trespass victim who lay in wait and recklessly shot blind at an intruder through a hole in a shed door. See also *Phillips v Wiles* (Unreported, Court of Appeal, 2 June 1998) (successful damages action following excessive brutality towards thief caught red-handed). Ancient remedies of self-help must 'be carefully scrutinised in the present day and certainly not extended' (*Stear v Scott* [1992] RTR 226 at 232D per Forbes J). See also *R v Bacon* [1977] 2 NSWLR 507 at 513.

4   See eg *Campbell v Lord Advocate* 1997 SCCR 269 at 272A–C (reckless shooting at eight-year old trespasser). See also *R v Freake* (1990) 85 Nfld & PEIR 25 at [19]; *R v Asante-Mensah* (2003) 227 DLR (4th) 75 at [72].

5   The proposition was put most emphatically by Coke CJ in *Semayne's Case* (1604) 5 Co Rep

91a at 91b, 77 ER 194 at 195 ('it is not felony, and he shall lose nothing'). See also *R v Hussey* (1924) 18 Cr App R 160 at 161 per Lord Hewart CJ.

6   See e g *R v Martin* (*Anthony*) [2003] QB 1 at [53]. The killing of the intruder must be both necessary (in that the mischief sought to be prevented could not have been be prevented by less violent means) and proportionate to that mischief (see *R v McKay* [1957] VR 560 at 573 per Smith J (dissenting)).

7   [1996] QB 567 at 580C–D.

Potential criminal liability

3.76 The exercise of self-help is also subject to an important qualification imposed by the Criminal Law Act 1977. Under section 6(1) of this Act it is a criminal offence for any person without lawful authority[1] to use or to threaten violence for the purpose of securing entry into any premises if, to his know-ledge, there is someone present on those premises who is opposed to his entry. This provision inevitably applies to some trespassers, but is not of course relevant to an intruder who enters premises by non-violent means.[2] Simply by virtue of his de facto possession of the land, such a trespasser is entitled to resist trespass by others, although his claims must naturally give way in the face of any superior claim (e g by the real owner) to regain possession.

1   Except in the case of a 'displaced residential occupier' or 'protected intending occupier', no lawful authority is provided by the mere fact that this person has some interest in or right to possession of the premises (Criminal Law Act 1977, s 6(2)).

2   Thus, for example, this provision would apply to a trespasser who breaks a door or window in order to secure entry, but not to one who merely manipulates a yale-type lock or window catch with a thin piece of metal (see Law Commission, *Report on Conspiracy and Criminal Law Reform* (Law Com No 76, 1976), para 2.61). See also (1985) LAG Bulletin (October), p 5.

3.77 The Criminal Law Act 1977 provides a defence to a charge of violent entry in the case of any person who can prove that he was a 'displaced residential occupier' seeking to secure access to residential premises from which he had been excluded by the trespasser.[1] Apart from the instance where the displaced occupier is himself a trespasser,[2] the status of 'displaced residential occupier' is defined as attaching to 'any person who was occupying any premises as a residence immediately before being excluded from occupation by anyone who entered those premises … as a trespasser.'[3] Such a person ranks as a 'displaced residential occupier' so long as he continues to be excluded from occupation of the premises by the original trespasser or by any subsequent trespasser.

1   Criminal Law Act 1977, s 6(1A). The defence is also available to a 'protected intending occupier' (see Criminal Law Act 1977, s 12A(1)).

2   Criminal Law Act 1977, s 12(4).

3   Criminal Law Act 1977, s 12(3).

Criminal eviction of former lawful occupier

3.78 The possession of a lawful occupier (e g a tenant or licensee) may not be terminated by recourse to the remedy of self-help, even where the interest granted to the occupier has expired or a court order for possession has been obtained.[1] Once possession has been enjoyed by a tenant or licensee the occupier cannot be evicted except by due process of law. In such cases a criminal offence is committed by any person who seeks to secure the eviction of the occupier by any means other than that of court order for possession.[2]

1   *Haniff v Robinson* [1993] QB 419 at 428D–E **[para 14.110]**.
2   Protection from Eviction Act 1977, s 3(1), (2B) **[paras 4.77, 14.109]**.

Self-help in cases of vehicular trespass

3.79   In modern urban conditions the motor car provides an important focus of trespass law. After some controversy[1] it seems settled that a person in possession of land may wheel-clamp a trespassing car and demand reasonable payment for its release,[2] but only if he can discharge a 'very high' onus of proof[3] that the offending driver consented to, or willingly assumed, the risk of the otherwise tortious clamping and detention of his car.[4]

1   Scottish courts have moved in a different direction. In Scotland private wheel clamping and the imposition of a release fee have been disallowed as a form of self-help remedy in respect of the wrongful parking of motor vehicles (see *Black v Carmichael* 1992 SLT 897 at 900H–901D).
2   The clamper is not entitled to exact any unreasonable or extortionate charge for release (*Arthur v Anker* [1997] QB 564 at 573B). Nor may the clamper delay in releasing the car after the owner offers to pay; and there must be means for the owner to communicate his offer ([1997] QB 564 at 573C). Forcible removal of a lawfully installed wheel-clamp may, however, constitute criminal damage (see *Stear v Scott* [1992] RTR 226 at 231H–K; *Lloyd v DPP* [1992] 1 All ER 982 at 992g; *Arthur v Anker*, supra at 576E–H).
3   See *Vine v Waltham Forest LBC* [2000] 4 All ER 169 at 179d per Waller LJ. In most cases this onus is discharged by establishing that the car owner must have seen and understood the significance of a notice warning that vehicles were liable to be clamped. In *Vine*'s case a car owner who was suffering from urgent medical distress and had failed to see any such warning notice was held entitled to recover the release fee together with £5 for loss of use of her vehicle.
4   *Arthur v Anker* [1997] QB 564 at 573A–B per Sir Thomas Bingham MR. It is now a criminal offence to engage in wheel-clamping without a licence issued by the Security Industry Authority (Private Security Industry Act 2001, s 6(1)).

REMEDIES FOR TRESPASS

3.80   In England and Wales trespass is actionable per se,[1] but the courts retain a significant discretion to determine the remedy appropriate in individual cases.[2] Potential remedies range from a declaration of rights to an award of money damages and/or various kinds of injunctive relief.[3] Something may depend on whether the trespass was an isolated occurrence or is of a continuing nature.

1   **[Para 3.53]**. Where a trespass has not yet occurred, but is objectively anticipated as an imminent probability, the court may issue a quia timet injunction. Such a remedy tends, however, to be ineffective in relation to fluctuating groups of unidentifiable persons (see *Drury v Secretary of State for the Environment, Food and Rural Affairs* [2004] EWCA Civ 200 at [19], [42]).

2   The self-help remedy of summary suppression of a trespass [**para 3.72**] is available in only the simplest of cases. For example, an entitlement to self-redress appropriate in the case of overhanging branches could not justify a trespass victim's demolition of a neighbour's garage which protruded very slightly into his land (*Chamberlain v Lindon* [1998] 1 WLR 1252 at 1262A).

3   Some forms of trespass also constitute a breach of the victim's right to respect for his private and family life and home (ECHR Art 8(1)). Nevertheless the European Court of Human Rights has generally declined to award compensation for the illicit installation of covert police surveillance devices which expose the criminality of the complainant of the trespass (see e g *Chalkley v United Kingdom* (2003) 37 EHRR 680 at [32], [36]; *Hewitson v United Kingdom* (2003) 37 EHRR 687 at [25]).

Past trespass

3.81   The primary response to a past act of trespass lies in the common law remedy of damages.[1] This remedy provides retrospective compensation in respect of causes of action which are complete at the date of the claim,[2] with the corollary that common law damages for future or repeated wrongs must therefore be made the subject of fresh proceedings.[3]

1   See *Jaggard v Sawyer* [1995] 1 WLR 269 at 276D per Sir Thomas Bingham MR; *Roberts v Rodney DC* [2001] 2 NZLR 402 at [21].

2   See *Attorney-General v Blake* [2001] 1 AC 268 at 281C per Lord Nicholls of Birkenhead.

3   *Jaggard v Sawyer* [1995] 1 WLR 269 at 284D per Millett LJ.

Declaration and nominal damages

3.82   Where no real injury is inflicted by a technical trespass upon land – particularly in circumstances of harmless recreational trespass upon scenic terrain[1] – the courts are generally unwilling to issue an injunction and may award nothing more than a declaration of rights and/or nominal damages.[2] In certain cases, where a disputed intrusion is extremely temporary or purely trivial, courts have even denied that any trespass has actually occurred.[3] An award of nominal damages does not preclude the granting of injunctive relief.[4] Indeed, in some circumstances, the absence of actual damage may provide the very reason why an injunction is needed, since otherwise the outcome would constitute a licence to continue the tort of trespass in return for some insubstantial payment.[5]

1   See e g *Behrens v Richards* [1905] 2 Ch 614 at 621–623 [**para 5.32**]. See also *Harrison v Duke of Rutland* [1893] 1 QB 142 at 156 per Kay LJ.

2   See *Llandudno UDC v Woods* [1899] 2 Ch 705 at 709–710; *Ward v Kirkland* [1967] Ch 194 at 243C–D; *Stonebridge v Bygrave* (Chancery Division, 25 October 2001). See also *Minor v Groves* (2000) 80 P & CR 136 at 143 per Millett LJ.

3   See e g *Pickering v Rudd* (1815) 4 Camp 219 at 220, 171 ER 70 at 71, where Lord Ellenborough CJ thought no trespass was occasioned by 'firing [a gun] across a field *in vacuo*, no part of the contents touching it.' See also *Evans v Finn* (1904) 4 SR (NSW) 297 at 308 (stray bullets only a nuisance), but compare *Clifton v Viscount Bury* (1887) 4 TLR 8 at 9 (bullet fragments fell on land); *Davies v Bennison* (1927) 22 Tas LR 52 at 55–57 (shooting of neighbour's cat on hot tin roof).

4   *Nelson v Nicholson* (Unreported, Court of Appeal, 1 December 2000) at [21] per Jonathan
      Parker LJ.
5   See *Woollerton and Wilson Ltd v Richard Costain Ltd* [1970] 1 WLR 411 at 413E–F; *John
      Trenberth Ltd v National Westminster Bank Ltd* (1979) 39 P & CR 104 at 107; *Jaggard v
      Sawyer* [1995] 1 WLR 269 at 280A–B per Sir Thomas Bingham MR.

Calculation of substantial damages

3.83 In the event that a court decides to award a substantial money remedy
(or 'mesne profits'), the trespass victim must elect before judgment[1] to have his
claim calculated on one or other of two bases, the preponderant emphases of
which are, respectively, compensatory and restitutionary in character.

1   See *Ministry of Defence v Ashman* (1993) 66 P & CR 195 at 200–201 per Hoffmann LJ;
      Roberts v Rodney DC [2001] 2 NZLR 402 at [16]; but compare *Lamru Pty Ltd v Kation
      Pty Ltd* (1998) 44 NSWLR 432 at 440B–D.

The compensatory approach

3.84 Where a past trespass has inflicted damage upon the land, the claimant
may ask for a money award which covers the cost of any works reasonably
required in order to restore his enjoyment of the land.[1] If reinstatement of the
land is impossible, the relevant measure of compensation is the diminution in
the value of the land.[2] On either footing this approach accords with the normal
compensatory aim of the law of tort (ie to place the tort victim in the position
which he would otherwise have enjoyed).[3] It seems unlikely that the trespass
victim can claim the mental trauma occasioned by the act of trespass as a
separate head of consequential loss,[4] although such distress may sometimes
generate a finding of aggravated damages.[5]

1   See *Heath v Keys* (1984) Times, 28 May; but compare *Mayfair Ltd v Pears* [1987] 1 NZLR 459
      (no liability to repair premises damaged when non-negligent trespasser's car caught fire).
      Where a group of trespassers join in a squat, all may be made liable in negligence on a 'joint
      venture' basis for damage which has been caused by one member only of the group (see
      Bushell v Hamilton (1981) 113 DLR (3d) 498 at 502). A similar form of collective liability is
      now proposed by Trespassers on Land (Liability for Damage and Eviction) Bill 2004, cl 1. See
      also *Lamb v Camden LBC* [1981] QB 625.
2   See *Burton v Winters* [1993] 1 WLR 1077 at 1082F; *Daniells v Mendonca* (1999) 78 P & CR 401
      at 408. Compare, however, *Severn Trent Water Ltd v Barnes* [2004] EWCA Civ 570 at [12], [19]
      (no loss of development value).
3   See *Attorney-General v Blake* [2001] 1 AC 268 at 278D–E per Lord Nicholls of Birkenhead;
      Roberts v Rodney DC [2001] 2 NZLR 402 at [25].
4   See *TCN Channel Nine Pty Ltd v Anning* (2002) 54 NSWLR 333 at [104]–[115].
5   See eg *Bruce v Rawlins* (1770) 3 Wils KB 61 at 63, 95 ER 934 at 934–935. There may also be
      a cause of action based on *Wilkinson v Downton* [1897] 2 QB 57 where a trespasser actually or
      presumptively intends to cause psychiatric harm. See *TCN Channel Nine Pty Ltd v Anning*
      (2002) 54 NSWLR 333 at [106], where Spigelman CJ offered the examples of the stalker or the
      trespasser who leaves a cobra snake in the bedroom. However, the constituent elements of the
      Wilkinson v Downton tort may be difficult to establish (see eg *Bradley v Wingnut Films Ltd*
      [1993] 1 NZLR 415 at 422).

The restitutionary approach

3.85 An alternative method of quantifying a money award involves not a computation of the loss inflicted on the claimant, but a calculation of the benefit deemed to have been received by the trespasser by reason of his unauthorised use of the land.[1] This basis of calculation is sometimes termed the 'user principle',[2] focusing as it does on the price which a reasonable person would have been prepared to pay for the user concerned had it been required to be purchased.[3] In some instances of trespass the award of mesne profits can therefore be based on the sum which the trespasser should reasonably have paid for his use and occupation (normally the ordinary letting value of the land on the open market).[4] Unlike the compensatory approach outlined above, this restitutionary approach requires no proof of loss on the victim's part.[5] The claimant need not demonstrate that he could have let the land for substantial commercial gain or that he would have occupied it himself.[6] Nor is it strictly relevant that the trespasser derived no actual or net benefit from his wrongful use of the land.[7]

1   *Attorney-General v Blake* [2001] 1 AC 268 at 278E–F, 281E–F per Lord Nicholls of Birkenhead. See likewise *Ministry of Defence v Ashman* (1993) 66 P & CR 195 at 200–201 per Hoffmann LJ; *Governing Body of Henrietta Barnett School v Hampstead Garden Suburb Institute* (1995) 93 LGR 470 at 512–513; *Lamru Pty Ltd v Kation Pty Ltd* (1998) 44 NSWLR 432 at 439A–441B; *Roberts v Rodney DC* [2001] 2 NZLR 402 at [12].

2   *Stoke-on Trent CC v W & J Wass Ltd* [1988] 1 WLR 1406 at 1413H–1414A per Nourse LJ, 1416A–E per Nicholls LJ. See *Severn Trent Water Ltd v Barnes* [2004] EWCA Civ 570 at [23]–[26] per Potter LJ.

3   *Attorney-General v Blake* [2001] 1 AC 268 at 278F per Lord Nicholls of Birkenhead (giving the examples of wrongful deposit of waste or illicit use of a path on another's land).

4   See *Swordheath Properties Ltd v Tabet* [1979] 1 WLR 285 at 287H–288D; *Dean and Chapter of Canterbury Cathedral v Whitbread Plc* (1995) 72 P & CR 9 at 16; *Lamru Pty Ltd v Kation Pty Ltd* (1998) 44 NSWLR 432 at 439B–D; *Yip Alice v Wong Shun* [2002] HKCU 1 at [93], [98]. This valuation is unaffected by the actual commercial value of the land to the particular occupier (see *Mayor and Burgesses of Lewisham v Masterson* (2000) 80 P & CR 117 at 123), but may be influenced by such factors as the claimant's real loss or the trespasser's real gain (see *Roberts v Rodney DC* [2001] 2 NZLR 402 at [32]) and the relative bargaining power of the parties (see *Bracewell v Appleby* [1975] Ch 408 at 420B–D).

5   See *Inverugie Investments Ltd v Hackett* [1995] 1 WLR 713 at 718A–B per Lord Lloyd of Berwick; *Roberts v Rodney DC* [2001] 2 NZLR 402 at [27]–[29].

6   *Inverugie Investments Ltd v Hackett* [1995] 1 WLR 713 at 717F per Lord Lloyd. See also *Swordheath Properties Ltd v Tabet* [1979] 1 WLR 285 at 288C–F per Megaw LJ.

7   *Inverugie Investments Ltd v Hackett* [1995] 1 WLR 713 at 718B per Lord Lloyd. See *Roberts v Rodney DC* [2001] 2 NZLR 402 at [28] per Barker J ('wrongful use damages are an anomalous measure of damages which rest upon an assumption that the plaintiff has incurred loss and the trespasser has incurred a profit as a result of the trespass').

3.86 The restitutionary approach has proved particularly appropriate in relation to incursions made by commercial developers and utility undertakers who trespass in the furtherance of their business interests.[1] Here it seems obvious that money awards for trespass should bear 'some relationship to the financial gain or saving' achieved through the developer's use of the victim's land or airspace.[2] Such awards have tended to evolve into participatory rights in entrepreneurial or development profits.[3] Although English courts have shied away from the idea that the trespass victim has some 'right to a share in, or account of, profits in any conventional sense', it is readily accepted that the defendant's profits are, in many cases, 'likely to be a helpful reference point' for the court's determination of a fair price for a notional licence.[4] Commercial trespassers are forced, in effect, to internalise the externalities of construction and other projects, often having to pay the substantial holdout prices demanded by victims of the relevant intrusion.[5] Restitutionary damages may also provide a means of stripping the profits wrongfully made by those who trespass on private premises and who seek to derive monetary gain from the sale of photographs of persons or events on those premises.[6]

1   A typical example concerns the aerial trespass committed by sky cranes operating on downtown construction sites **[para 3.55]**. See *Lewvest Ltd v Scotia Towers Ltd* (1982) 126 DLR (3d) 239 at 240–241, where it appeared that by trespassing the defendant building contractor was saving approximately \$500,000. Goodridge J ruled, however, that if 'a third party can gain economic advantage by using the property of another, then it must negotiate with that other to acquire user rights. The Court cannot give it to him'. See likewise *Franklin Mint Ltd v Baxtergate Investment Co* (Unreported, Court of Appeal, 12 March 1998).

2   *LJP Investments Pty Ltd v Howard Chia Investments Pty Ltd* (1989) 24 NSWLR 490 at 497C. See *Jaggard v Sawyer* [1995] 1 WLR 269 at 281H–282A.

3   See eg *LJP Investments Pty Ltd v Howard Chia Investments Pty Ltd* (1989) 24 NSWLR 490 at 497D–F, (1989) 24 NSWLR 499 at 507D–E, where Hodgson J assessed 'restitutory damages' for airspace trespass with reference not to the market value of the airspace used, but to the 'peculiar value' which that airspace had for the trespasser. Compare the similar approach to profit sharing adopted in *Bracewell v Appleby* [1975] Ch 408 at 419D–420D.

4   *Severn Trent Water Ltd v Barnes* [2004] EWCA Civ 570 at [41]–[42] per Potter LJ (although here there was 'no practical or sensible way' of assessing the profits accruing to a water undertaker which had wrongfully inserted a water main through 20 metres of the claimant's land).

5   See eg *LJP Investments Pty Ltd v Howard Chia Investments Pty Ltd* (1989) 24 NSWLR 499 at 509A–B per Hodgson J ('it should be made clear to developers that they cannot expect to do better by an unlawful trespass than by paying a price demanded by the adjoining owner, at least unless the price demanded is clearly unreasonable').

6   See *Hosking and Hosking v Runting* [2004] NZCA 34 at [269] per Anderson J (referring to cases such as *Kaye v Robertson* [1991] FSR 62 and *Douglas v Hello! Ltd* [2001] QB 967).

Future or continuing acts of trespass

3.87 In cases of continuing trespass the common law remedy of damages tends to be inadequate precisely because such damages operate retrospectively and cover only past, and not future, acts of trespass.[1] It has always seemed inappropriate, as a matter of principle, that a trespasser should be able to acquire an easement or licence over another's land on cynical payment of such damages as the court may award for each fresh act of trespass.[2] For this reason equity has long asserted a power to afford the trespass victim a prospective form of relief which goes far beyond the common law remedy of damages for a series of past wrongs. The court has discretion to issue a negative or prohibitory injunction restraining future trespass or even a mandatory injunction to reverse unlawful conduct by the removal of a trespass.[3] Furthermore the court has available a supplementary power, first conferred by the Chancery Amendment Act 1858 ('Lord Cairns's Act'), to award equitable damages in respect of future or continuing wrongs either in addition to or in substitution for injunctive relief.[4]

1   See *Jaggard v Sawyer* [1995] 1 WLR 269 at 284G–H per Millett LJ; *Attorney-General v Blake* [2001] 1 AC 268 at 281C per Lord Nicholls of Birkenhead.
2   See *Cowper v Laidler* [1903] 2 Ch 337 at 341 per Buckley J; *Anchor Brewhouse Developments Ltd v Berkley House (Docklands Developments) Ltd* (1987) 38 BLR 82 at 101.
3   *Jaggard v Sawyer* [1995] 1 WLR 269 at 276D–E per Sir Thomas Bingham MR.
4   See Chancery Amendment Act 1858, s 2.

Selection of trespass remedy

3.88   Injunctive relief is sometimes said to be a prima facie right of the trespass victim,[1] in that, in the generality of cases, the 'landowner whose title is not in issue is entitled to an injunction to restrain trespass on his land whether or not the trespass harms him.'[2] Nowadays, however, it is increasingly apparent that the remedy of injunction is no longer an automatic or necessary judicial response to trespass.[3] In cases of relatively minor infringement occurring in a context of close neighbourhood, there are gathering indications that proprietary and possessory rights may not always be capable of such ultimate or unlimited vindication.[4] Under the modern equivalent of Lord Cairns's Act,[5] injunctive relief is frequently withheld in favour of an award of equitable damages in respect of future or continuing acts of trespass.[6] Modern imperatives of social accommodation and of 'reasonableness between neighbours'[7] often point away from the absolutist remedy of the injunction, with the result that the courts increasingly exercise a power to license, on payment of compensation, a broadly acceptable compromise of conflicting interests.[8] As Millett LJ observed in *Jaggard v Sawyer*,[9] '[m]any proprietary rights cannot be protected at all by the common law', with the result that the aggrieved owner 'must submit to unlawful interference with his rights and be content with damages.' In the process it becomes steadily more apparent that the ability of proprietors and possessors to dictate what shall or shall not be done on their own land is rather more limited than may be generally thought.[10] But this merely reflects the wider reality that the law of trespass is slowly being modified, in certain contexts, by an overriding proviso of reasonableness.[11]

1   See *Shelfer v City of London Electric Lighting Co* [1895] 1 Ch 287 at 322; *Kelsen v Imperial Tobacco Co (of Great Britain and Ireland) Ltd* [1957] 2 QB 334 at 346–347; *Patel v W H Smith (Eziot) Ltd* [1987] 1 WLR 853 at 861D; *Jaggard v Sawyer* [1995] 1 WLR 269 at 277D.
2   *Anchor Brewhouse Developments Ltd v Berkley House (Docklands Developments) Ltd* (1987) 38 BLR 82 at 96 per Scott J; *Patel v W H Smith (Eziot) Ltd* [1987] 1 WLR 853 at 858E per Balcombe LJ; *Keating & Co Ltd v Jervis Shopping Centre Ltd and Pierce Contracting Ltd* [1997] 1 IR 512 at 518 per Keane J. See also *Pride of Derby and Derbyshire Angling Association Ltd v British Celanese Ltd* [1953] 1 All ER 179 at 197H per Evershed MR; *Jaggard v Sawyer* [1995] 1 WLR 269 at 280B–C per Sir Thomas Bingham MR, 287C per Millett LJ ('In many cases ... an injunction will be granted almost as of course').
3   Nowadays the cases in which injunctive relief is withheld are not nearly so rare as was indicated even some 15 or 20 years ago (compare *Patel v W H Smith (Eziot) Ltd* [1987] 1 WLR 853 at 863C–D per Neill LJ).

4   See Gray and Gray, 'The rhetoric of realty', in J Getzler (ed), *Rationalizing Property, Equity and Trusts: Essays in Honour of Edward Burn* (Butterworths 2003), pp 257–259.

5   Supreme Court Act 1981, s 50.

6   See *Jaggard v Sawyer* [1995] 1 WLR 269 at 284G, 290H per Millett LJ. It follows that equitable damages are available only if the court has jurisdiction to entertain an application for injunctive relief. The claimant must have established a prima facie entitlement to an injunction, so that the court could – though not necessarily would – grant an injunction (see *Jaggard v Sawyer*, supra at 285A–B, 287F, 289G–290B; *Daniells v Mendonca* (1999) 78 P & CR 401 at 406; *Roberts v Rodney DC* [2001] 2 NZLR 402 at [22]). The original claim need not have asked for a remedy in damages (*Severn Trent Water Ltd v Barnes* [2004] EWCA Civ 570 at [31]).

7   **[Para 13.122]**. See eg *Delaware Mansions Ltd v Westminster CC* [2002] 1 AC 321 at [29], [34] per Lord Cooke of Thorndon; *Abbahall Ltd v Smee* [2003] 1 WLR 1472 at [36]–[38] per Munby J.

8   '[P]roperty rules' are often commuted into 'liability rules' (see Guido Calabresi and A Douglas Melamed, 'Property Rules, Liability Rules, and Inalienability: One View of the Cathedral' 85 Harv L Rev 1089 (1971–72)). See in this context Scott Grattan's distinction between right- and goal-based modes of judicial reasoning ('Judicial Reasoning and the Adjudication of Airspace Trespass' (1996) 4 APLJ 128).

9   [1995] 1 WLR 269 at 287C.

10   See eg *Burton v Winters* (Unreported, Court of Appeal, 18 July 1991), where an owner, far from being able to insist on the removal of a neighbour's encroaching garage wall, found herself relegated to a claim for damages in respect of the trespass. She was later sentenced to two years' imprisonment for contempt when she continued to inflict physical damage on the offending wall and garage (*Burton v Winters* [1993] 1 WLR 1077 at 1080C). Lloyd LJ indicated (at 1082F) that she was still entitled to enforce a damages claim for any diminution in value of her property caused by the encroachment ([1993] 1 WLR 1077 at 1082F). See also *Chamberlain v Lindon* [1998] 1 WLR 1252 at 1260G–1261H; and compare the outraged response of the trespass victim in *Jaggard v Sawyer* [1995] 1 WLR 269 at 286F–G.

11   **[Para 4.38]**. Compare the way in which modern statutory developments have diminished the rigour of trespass law (see Access to Neighbouring Land Act 1992 **[para 8.135]**; Party Wall etc Act 1996 **[para 8.138]**; Countryside and Rights of Way Act 2000 **[para 5.46]**; Vehicular Access Across Common and Other Land (England) Regulations 2002 (SI 2002/1711) **[para 8.139]**).

A 'good working rule'

3.89   The choice between injunctive and monetary relief has long been constrained by the 'good working rule' propounded by A L Smith LJ in *Shelfer v City of London Electric Lighting Co.*[1] According to this guideline, damages for a continuing trespass may be awarded in lieu of an injunction[2] if the injury to the claimant's rights is small, if the damage can be estimated in money and would be adequately compensated by a small money payment, and if it would be 'oppressive' to the defendant to grant an injunction. In such cases the power to award damages in lieu of an injunction imports a power to 'give an equivalent for what was lost by the refusal of an injunction',[3] damages being calculable, if necessary, on a restitutionary basis by reference to the benefits likely to be obtained or enjoyed in the future by the trespasser.[4] Particularly where the court has declined the discretionary remedy of injunction, the 'use and occupation' mode of valuation may represent the only means of redress for the trespass victim in respect of a future wrongful presence on his land.[5]

1   [1895] 1 Ch 287 at 322–323.

2   In this context the courts have tended to exercise their remedial discretion on an explicit
     analogy with the curial response to breaches of restrictive covenant [**para 13.118**].
3   *Attorney-General v Blake* [2001] 1 AC 268 at 281D–E per Lord Nicholls of Birkenhead.
4   The award may therefore reflect the 'likely reasonable outcome' of hypothetical negotiations
     for settlement of the trespass issue between the parties (see *Severn Trent Water Ltd v Barnes*
     [2004] EWCA Civ 570 at [35] per Potter LJ).
5   See *Roberts v Rodney DC* [2001] 2 NZLR 402 at [19]–[23].

Indications in favour of a money award

3.90   Money awards are frequently preferred to the grant of injunctive relief,[1]
especially where the relevant intrusion has had only a slight impact on the
claimant's amenity and, not least for this reason, is easily compensable.[2] In
some instances (eg involving trespass on an access way), injunctive relief may
be a wholly disproportionate response, sterilising the beneficial enjoyment of a
landlocked plot and subjecting the trespasser to extortionate holdouts by the
claimant.[3] Additional indicators in favour of a money remedy may be present
where the claimant has delayed in seeking relief[4] or has demanded excessive
compensation or has indeed refused to consider some reasonable offer of
compensation.[5]

1   For evidence of the modern trend, see *Burton v Winters* [1993] 1 WLR 1077 at 1082B–F; *Snell
     & Prideaux Ltd v Dutton Mirrors Ltd* [1995] 1 EGLR 259 at 263L–264C; *Ketley v Gooden*
     (1996) 73 P & CR 305 at 312–313; *Greenwich Healthcare National Health Service Trust v
     London and Quadrant Housing Trust* (1999) 77 P & CR 133 at 139. See also *Das v Linden
     Mews Ltd* [2003] 2 P & CR 58 at [31].
2   See eg *Burton v Winters* (Unreported, Court of Appeal, 18 July 1991), where Balcombe LJ
     pointed to the 'minimal' nature of the encroachment (4½ inches) and its lack of impact on the
     claimant's enjoyment of her own land. See also *Ketley v Gooden* (1996) 73 P & CR 305 at 313;
     Ward v Dougall (Unreported, Court of Appeal, 16 January 1997) per Phillips LJ (protruding
     television aerial used as perch by birds); *Margiz Pty Ltd v The Proprietors – Strata Plan
     No 30234* (Supreme Court of New South Wales, 22 March 1993, BPR Casenote 95408).
3   See *Jaggard v Sawyer* [1995] 1 WLR 269 at 288C–D per Millett LJ.
4   *Jaggard v Sawyer* [1995] 1 WLR 269 at 283C, 289B–C (where an interlocutory injunction
     would almost certainly have been available had the claimant applied when the trespass
     commenced). See also *Ketley v Gooden* (1996) 73 P & CR 305 at 312–313; *LJP Investments
     Pty Ltd v Howard Chia Investments Pty Ltd* (1989) 24 NSWLR 490 at 496E–F.
5   *LJP Investments Pty Ltd v Howard Chia Investments Pty Ltd* (1989) 24 NSWLR 490 at
     497C–F.

The critical question

3.91   Ultimately the vital question relates, not to the balance of convenience,
but to whether, as of the date of the court hearing, the granting of injunctive
relief would be oppressive to the trespasser.[1] The extreme sanction of the
injunction tends to be reserved for acts of especially flagrant or repeated
trespass and for cases of permanent or continuing annexation of land. In less
significant instances of trespass, damages (usually inclusive of a 'once and for
all' award in respect of future wrongs[2]) are often thought to represent the more
appropriate remedy even though the withholding of injunctive relief causes the

court, in effect, to 'authorise the continuance of an unlawful state of affairs.'[3] Yet the controversial feature of a damages remedy is precisely the fact that the trespasser is enabled to buy his way out of a wrongful incursion and to purchase immunity from further enforcement of the trespass victim's possessory rights.[4] In effect, the restitutionary measure of damages for trespass represents 'the price payable for the compulsory acquisition of a right.'[5]

1   See e g *Jaggard v Sawyer* [1995] 1 WLR 269 at 283B–C, 288B, where the Court of Appeal declined to injunct a building development which involved both continuing trespass and a breach of restrictive covenant. Compare *Daniells v Mendonca* (1999) 78 P & CR 401 at 407–409.

2   *Jaggard v Sawyer* [1995] 1 WLR 269 at 281H–282A per Sir Thomas Bingham MR, 286A, 292C–D per Millett LJ. See e g *Valentine v Allen* [2003] EWCA Civ 915 at [66].

3   *Jaggard v Sawyer* [1995] 1 WLR 269 at 286B per Millett LJ. See also *Attorney-General v Blake* [2001] 1 AC 268 at 281G per Lord Nicholls of Birkenhead. Moreover, the refusal of injunctive relief exposes the trespass victim to liability for criminal damage if he thereafter resorts to self-redress in order to combat the trespass (see *Chamberlain v Lindon* [1998] 1 WLR 1252 at 1260G–1261H).

4   This approach does not command universal support: compare the objection in *Anchor Brewhouse Developments Ltd v Berkley House* (*Docklands Developments*) *Ltd* (1987) 38 BLR 82 at 101–105 per Scott J that 'once and for all' payments are tantamount to the compulsory purchase of some sort of easement or licence to do wrong. See similarly *Woollerton and Wilson Ltd v Richard Costain Ltd* [1970] 1 WLR 411 at 413E–F per Stamp J; *Patel v W H Smith* (*Eziot*) *Ltd* [1987] 1 WLR 853 at 861D–E per Balcombe LJ.

5   *Attorney-General v Blake* [2001] 1 AC 268 at 281G per Lord Nicholls of Birkenhead.

Circumstances appropriate for injunctive relief

3.92   The 'formidable weapon'[1] of the injunction is used with caution, not least because it carries the ultimate sanction of imprisonment for contemptuous breach.[2] Injunctive relief is, however, virtually inevitable where the trespasser has effected a flagrant or permanent expropriation of the victim's land[3] or where the claimant would otherwise be compelled to submit to an oppressive purchase of his rights by the trespasser.[4] The grant of an injunction is, again, particularly appropriate where the interference with the claimant's rights has been significant in nature and is not readily compensable in money,[5] or where the trespasser has made no attempt to proffer substantial compensation[6] or has simply acted throughout in high-handed or cavalier disregard of the victim's rights.[7] The mere fact that land is owned by an arm of local government provides no special reason for the grant of injunctive relief,[8] but a wholesale occupation of public land by protesters may more readily justify the intervention of the court.[9] There is also a strong indication in the case law that an injunction is more likely to issue where the trespasser asserts a claim of right in the context of a repeated trespass.[10]

1   See *Behrens v Richards* [1905] 2 Ch 614 at 621 per Buckley J.

2   See e g *CIN Properties Ltd v Rawlins* [1995] 2 EGLR 130 [**para 4.56**].

3   See e g *Harrow LBC v Donohue* [1995] 1 EGLR 257 at 259F–H (landowner 'totally dispossessed' by encroaching building); *Daniells v Mendonca* (1999) 78 P & CR 401 at 407–408 (claimant 'permanently … deprived of part of her land'). See also *Earle v Martin* (1998) 172 Nfld & PEIR 105 at [36]; *Vaz v Jong* (2000) 96 ACWS (3d) 1086 at [158]–[159].

4   See *Cowper v Laidler* [1903] 2 Ch 337 at 341 per Buckley J.
5   *Bromley LBC v Morritt* (1999) 78 P & CR D37 at D38 (obstruction of public highway). See also *LJP Investments Pty Ltd v Howard Chia Investments Pty Ltd* (1989) 24 NSWLR 490 at 496E; *Karuppannan v Balakrishnen* (1994) 3 MLJ 584 at 593F–H. It may be particularly relevant that a continuing encroachment is likely to impede or jeopardise a future sale of the victim's land (see e g *Earle v Martin* (1998) 172 Nfld & PEIR 105 at [30]).
6   See *Woollerton and Wilson Ltd v Richard Costain Ltd* [1970] 1 WLR 411 at 416C, where the operation of an injunction was suspended largely because the offending party had at all times offered a substantial sum as compensation for the trespass. Compare, however, *John Trenberth Ltd v National Westminster Bank Ltd* (1979) 39 P & CR 104 at 108; *Franklin Mint Ltd v Baxtergate Investment Co* (Unreported, Court of Appeal, 12 March 1998).
7   *Kelsen v Imperial Tobacco Co* (*of Great Britain and Ireland*) *Ltd* [1957] 2 QB 334 at 347; *Jaggard v Sawyer* [1995] 1 WLR 269 at 283C–D; *Gross v Wright* [1923] SCR 214 at 233; *Graham v K D Morris & Sons Pty Ltd* [1974] Qd R 1 at 6D–F; *LJP Investments Pty Ltd v Howard Chia Investments Pty Ltd* (1989) 24 NSWLR 490 at 496E; *Earle v Martin* (1998) 172 Nfld & PEIR 105 at [32].
8   *Llandudno UDC v Woods* [1899] 2 Ch 705 at 710; *Blacktown CC v Sharp* (2000) 10 BPR 18107 at [11].
9   See e g *University of Sydney v Greenland* [1970] 2 NSWR 350 at 351.
10 See e g *Harrison v Duke of Rutland* [1893] 1 QB 142 at 156, 159–160 per Kay LJ (trespass 'in assertion of a fancied right'). This tendency is mirrored in Scots law (see *Steuart v Stephen* (1877) 4 R 873 at 874–875; D M Walker, *Principles of Scottish Private Law* (4th edn, Clarendon 1989), Vol III, p 100; K G C Reid, *The Law of Property in Scotland* (Butterworths 1996), para 183).

Mandatory injunctions

3.93   Courts are generally reluctant to grant a mandatory injunction for the removal of a trespass to land, since in many cases the effect is to deliver the trespasser 'bound hand and foot' to the claimant, thereby exposing him to any 'extortionate demand' which the latter may care to make as the price of his release.[1] There are nevertheless circumstances in which a mandatory injunction is unavoidable.[2] In *Daniells v Mendonca*,[3] for example, the Court of Appeal ordered the removal of a bathroom extension which had been constructed using the support of a neighbour's wall in circumstances which threatened a fire danger and the risk of structural damage.

1   *Isenberg v East India House Estate Co Ltd* (1863) 3 De GJ & S 263 at 273, 46 ER 637 at 641 per Lord Westbury LC. See also *Jaggard v Sawyer* [1995] 1 WLR 269 at 287C–E per Millett LJ; *Blacktown CC v Sharp* (2000) 10 BPR 18107 at [18] per Young J.
2   See e g *Goodson v Richardson* (1874) LR 9 Ch App 221 (deliberate invasion of another's land for private gain); *Earle v Martin* (1998) 172 Nfld & PEIR 105 at [33]. See generally *Redland Bricks Ltd v Morris* [1970] AC 652 at 665F–666D per Lord Upjohn.
3   (1999) 78 P & CR 401 at 407–409.

CRIMINAL TRESPASS

3.94   In the generality of cases the act of trespass on another's land is merely a civil wrong.[1] In certain circumstances, however, trespass constitutes a criminal offence.[2] Indeed the criminalisation of trespass has been significantly extended in recent decades,[3] a process now furthered by amendments contained in the Anti-social Behaviour Act 2003.[4]

1   See, however, Criminal Law Act 1977, s 8 (crime of trespassing with a weapon of offence).
2   See Stephen Tromans and Colin Thomann, 'Environmental Protest and the Law' [2003] JPL
     1367. The statute book still contains the oddity of Vagrancy Act 1824, s 4, pursuant to which
     a person 'being found in or upon any dwelling house, warehouse, coach-house, stable, or
     outhouse, or in any inclosed yard, garden, or area, for any unlawful purpose ... shall be
     deemed a rogue and a vagabond.' See, however, *Talbot v Oxford City Justices* (2000) Times,
     15 February.
3   See eg the amendments of the Criminal Law Act 1977 and the Public Order Act 1986
     contained in CJ&POA 1994, ss 70–74.
4   See Anti-social Behaviour Act 2003 (Commencement No 1 and Transitional Provisions)
     Order 2003 (SI 2003/3300 (C 130)).

Failure to leave residential premises on request

3.95   Under the Criminal Law Act 1977 a criminal offence is committed[1] by
any person who, having entered residential premises as a trespasser, fails to
leave those premises on being required to do so by or on behalf of either a
'displaced residential occupier'[2] or a 'protected intending occupier'[3] of those
premises.

1   Criminal Law Act 1977, s 7(1). A uniformed police constable has power to arrest without
     warrant any person whom he 'reasonably suspects' of committing an offence under this
     provision (s 7(6)), and the offence is punishable summarily by six months' imprisonment
     and/or a fine (s 7(5)).
2   See Criminal Law Act 1977, s 12(3) [**para 3.77**].
3   A 'protected intending occupier' is defined in Criminal Law Act 1977, s 12A(1).

Aggravated trespass

3.96   The Criminal Justice and Public Order Act 1994 created a new criminal
offence of 'aggravated trespass' on 'land'.[1] This offence is committed by a
trespasser who does anything with the intention of intimidating any persons
engaged in 'lawful activity'[2] on land or with the intention of obstructing or
disrupting that activity.[3] The constituent elements of the offence require proof
not only of trespass, but also of some 'further act' accompanied by the
statutorily specified intention.[4] As originally drawn, the offence of aggravated
trespass related only to 'land in the open air',[5] being intended largely to
counteract the conduct of such persons as hunt saboteurs and environmental
protesters. The limitation to 'land in the open air' has now been removed,[6] with
the consequence that the offence can be committed either inside or outside a
building.[7] There is a strong likelihood that the charge of aggravated trespass
will seem particularly appropriate in respect of single-issue activists who invade
the buildings of a targeted company in order to protest against commercial or
other activities conducted on those premises.[8]

1   CJ&POA 1994, s 68.
2   Activity is not, for this purpose, 'lawful' if, in itself, it involves the commission of any trespass
     or criminal offence (CJ&POA 1994, s 68(2)). See eg *Nelder v DPP* (1998) Times, 11 June.
3   CJ&POA 1994, s 68(1). The trespasser is, once again, arrestable without warrant on reason-
     able suspicion (CJ&POA 1994, s 61(4)). A further criminal offence is committed on failure to

comply with a direction given by a senior police officer who 'reasonably believes', however erroneously, that an aggravated trespass has occurred (CJ&POA 1994, s 69(3)). See *Capon v DPP* (Queen's Bench Division, 4 March 1998) per Lord Bingham CJ.

4   *DPP v Bernard* [2000] Crim LR 371 per Laws LJ (prosecution dismissed because the claimed further act merely reiterated the allegation of trespass). However, the 'further act' required for the offence need not involve the successful disruption of the targeted activity (see *Winder v DPP* (1996) 160 JP 713 at 719B–G).

5   There was initially some fear that the offence of 'aggravated trespass' would be used to criminalise innocent, but trespassory, presence on open land or in wild country.

6   ASBA 2003, s 59 (effective 20 January 2004).

7   'Land' is defined by Interpretation Act 1978, s 5, Sch 1, to include buildings.

8   See Explanatory Notes to Anti-social Behaviour Act 2003 (HMSO, December 2003), para 129.

Trespassory assembly

3.97   Criminal liability may likewise attach to persons who knowingly take part in a prohibited trespassory assembly.[1] Such assemblies may be prohibited by a district council (or by the Commissioner of Police for the City of London) where the police reasonably believe that an assembly[2] is likely to be held on 'land in the open air'[3] without the permission of its occupier in such manner as to risk 'serious disruption to the life of the community' or 'significant damage' to certain kinds of building or monument.[4]

1   Public Order Act 1986, s 14B(2).

2   An 'assembly' must comprise 20 or more persons, but a peaceful, non-obstructive gathering on a highway is not necessarily 'trespassory' (*DPP v Jones* [1999] 2 AC 240 at 257D–258B per Lord Irvine of Lairg LC, 281D–H per Lord Clyde, 286H–287C per Lord Hutton).

3   Public Order Act 1986, s 14A(9).

4   Public Order Act 1986, s 14A(1)–(4).

Collective trespass

3.98   Public concern over various forms of mass trespass on agricultural land or heritage sites led in 1986[1] to the significant strengthening of the law now contained in the Criminal Justice and Public Order Act 1994.

1   See Public Order Act 1986, s 39.

Direction to leave land

3.99   The Criminal Justice and Public Order Act 1994 confers a power upon a senior police officer present at the scene to direct persons to leave land if the officer 'reasonably believes' that two or more such persons are trespassing on the land and 'are present there with the common purpose of residing there for any period'.[1] In order properly to exercise this power, the senior police officer must also have reason to believe that 'reasonable steps' have been taken by or on behalf of the occupier to ask such persons to leave[2] and that the trespassers have caused damage to property on the land or have used 'threatening, abusive or insulting words or behaviour' towards the occupier or associated persons or that the trespassers 'have between them six or more vehicles on the land'.

1   CJ&POA 1994, s 61(1). A proposed amendment would make this provision applicable to single trespassers (see Trespassers on Land (Liability for Damage and Eviction) Bill 2004, cl 2).

2   The person on whose behalf the request to leave the land is made need not, in fact, be the occupier, provided that the police officer reasonably believes that he is (see *Neizer v Rhodes* 1995 SCCR 799 at 807E–F).

Non-compliance

3.100   The direction to leave the land can properly be issued only if the trespassers have been given an opportunity to comply with some earlier request to depart.[1] Moreover, the direction, when it is given, must then be a direction to leave immediately.[2] A criminal offence is committed by any person who, knowing that a direction to leave the land has been given by a senior police officer, fails to leave the land 'as soon as reasonably practicable' or who, having left, returns as a trespasser within the following three months.[3] The offence is, however, limited in scope in that the 'land' to which it applies does not include buildings (other than agricultural buildings or scheduled ancient monuments) and does not, in most cases, include land forming part of a highway.[4] The criminalisation of collective trespass under the 1994 Act (together with forcible removal of trespassing vehicles) has been held to involve no violation of the fair trial and property guarantees of the European Convention.[5] Moreover, although eviction in pursuance of the 1994 Act engages the Convention right to respect for 'private and family life' and the integrity of the 'home',[6] interference with this right can be justified by reference to the national economic interest and to the illegality (and temporary nature) of the trespassory presence.[7]

1   *R (Fuller) v Chief Constable of Dorset Police* [2003] QB 480 at [46], [83].

2   *R (Fuller) v Chief Constable of Dorset Police* [2003] QB 480 at [47]–[48], [84].

3   CJ&POA 1994, s 61(4). The trespassers are, again, arrestable without warrant on reasonable suspicion (CJ&POA 1994, s 61(5)). The police have power to seize and remove any vehicle which a trespasser has failed to remove himself (CJ&POA 1994, s 62(1)), for which a reasonable financial charge may be levied as a civil debt (CJ&POA 1994, s 67) (see *R (Fuller) v Chief Constable of Dorset Police* [2003] QB 480 at [56]). Additional powers to direct the removal of trespassers are available where, after consultation with appropriate local authorities, it appears that there exist relevant caravan sites with suitable pitches for the trespassers to move to (CJ&POA 1994, s 62A, as introduced by ASBA 2003, s 60).

4   CJ&POA 1994, s 61(9).

5   *R (Fuller) v Chief Constable of Dorset Police* [2003] QB 480 at [57], [63] (see ECHR Art 6, Protocol No 1, Art 1).

6   ECHR Art 8(1).

7   *R (Fuller) v Chief Constable of Dorset Police* [2003] QB 480 at [76]–[78].

Criminalisation of anti-social behaviour

3.101   A far-reaching form of trespassory crime arises in the context of anti-social behaviour orders made by a magistrates' court pursuant to the

Crime and Disorder Act 1998.[1] The emergence of the anti-social behaviour order (or 'ASBO') reflects a modern *Zeitgeist* which has become increasingly intolerant of even 'relatively trivial' instances of destructive and offensive conduct.[2] An ASBO may prohibit (for an initial period of two years) the entry of any named person aged at least 10 years upon defined premises or parts of a locality. Breach of the order without reasonable excuse renders the subject of the order criminally liable.[3] Moreover, certain social landlords are eligible to apply to the High Court or the county court for an 'anti-social behaviour injunction' in respect of misconduct which relates to or affects the management of their housing stock.[4] In cases of actual or threatened violence or significant risk of harm to other residents or to agents of the landlord, the court may include in the injunction an exclusion order (coupled with a power of arrest) which, on pain of imprisonment for contempt, prohibits further entry into a specified area or building.[5]

1   Crime and Disorder Act 1998, s 1(4). 'Anti-social behaviour' comprises behaviour 'in a manner that caused or was likely to cause harassment, alarm or distress to one or more persons not of the same household as [the actor]' (Crime and Disorder Act 1998, s 1(1)(a)). See also Crime and Disorder Act 1998, s 14(1) (local child curfew schemes).
2   See *R (McCann) v Crown Court at Manchester* [2003] 1 AC 787 at [16] per Lord Steyn, [42] per Lord Hope of Craighead, [85]–[86] per Lord Hutton.
3   Crime and Disorder Act 1998, s 1(10).
4   Housing Act 1996, s 153A(1)–(2), as introduced by ASBA 2003, s 13(3) **[para 14.38]**.
5   Housing Act 1996, s 153C, as introduced by ASBA 2003, s 13(3). A similar power can be exercised in connection with the issue of an injunction against breach of a tenancy agreement (ASBA 2003, s 153D(3)–(4)). An exclusion order may also be made pursuant to Protection from Harassment Act 1997, s 5 (see e g *Silverton v Gravett* (Unreported, Queen's Bench Division, 19 October 2001)).

Other forms of criminal liability

3.102   Failure to depart from land may also generate criminal liability where a local authority has directed unauthorised campers to leave the area of a highway, vacant land or occupied land on which they are trespassing.[1] A similar result follows where a senior police officer has ordered the closure of a 'rave' (whether or not those who attend are trespassers).[2] A 'rave' involves a gathering on land in the open air of at least 20 persons at which 'amplified music is played during the night' in such manner as to be 'likely to cause serious distress to the inhabitants of the locality.'[3]

1   CJ&POA 1994, s 77(3). Failure to comply can lead to a magistrates' court order (CJ&POA 1994, s 78(1)), the magistrates having no discretion to review the reasonableness of the local authority's original direction (see *Shropshire CC v Wynne* (1997) Times, 22 July).
2   CJ&POA 1994, s 63(6).
3   CJ&POA 1994, s 63(1), as amended by ASBA 2003, s 58(1)–(2) (effective 20 January 2004). The same police powers apply to a 'rave' held in a building by 20 or more persons who are trespassers (CJ&POA 1994, s 63(1), as amended by ASBA 2003, s 58(3)).

3.103   The Anti-social Behaviour Act 2003 creates further forms of criminal liability in connection with presence on land. It becomes a criminal offence for any person to remain on or enter, in contravention of a closure order, any premises where drugs have been used unlawfully.¹ It is likewise a criminal offence for any person knowingly to contravene a direction given by a senior police officer for the dispersal of groups of persons reasonably suspected to have been associated with anti-social behaviour in a public place.²

1   ASBA 2003, s 4(1). See also ASBA 2003, s 4(4) (defence of reasonable excuse).
2   ASBA 2003, s 32(2) (see also ASBA 2003, s 30(4)).

CHAPTER 4

Licences

CATEGORIES OF LICENCE

4.1   Licences to enter upon land fall towards the lower end of the calibrated scale of 'property' value which distinguishes entitlements in respect of realty.[1] Licences may assume various forms and perform a multiplicity of purposes. The overlapping categories of licence recognised by the law include:

-   bare licences[2]
-   contractual licences[3]
-   equitable or irrevocable licences[4]
-   licences supported by proprietary estoppel[5] and
-   licences coupled with the grant of an interest.[6]

The precise proprietary content of each licence varies with the category concerned.

1   [Para 2.13].
2   [Para 4.2].
3   [Para 4.60].
4   [Para 4.88].
5   [Para 10.168].
6   [Para 4.91].

BARE LICENCES

4.2   The law of licence reflects the prerogative of the owner or possessor of land to dictate the terms on which access may be enjoyed by strangers. The phenomenon of the licence is, in this sense, the emanation of territorial sovereignty. 'By the laws of England', declared Lord Camden CJ in *Entick v Carrington*,[1] 'every invasion of land, be it ever so minute, is a trespass. No man can set his foot upon my ground without my licence.'[2] Accordingly, a bare licence is a personal permission or consent, granted otherwise than for consideration, to enter, traverse or be present upon the land of another. An indescribably broad range of everyday human activity is silently mediated by the availability of such permissions.[3] It is, indeed, the device of the licence which 'facilitate[s] the practical functioning of the community.'[4]

1   (1765) 19 Howell's State Trials 1029 at 1066.
2   See also *Morris v Beardmore* [1981] AC 446 at 464C–D per Lord Scarman; *Reference re an Application for an Authorisation* (1985) 14 DLR (4th) 546 at 554 per Dickson J (dissenting); *Cadman v The Queen* (1989) 51 DLR (4th) 52 at 56–57.
3   A classic example is the invitation to a dinner party [**para 2.51**].
4   *Edwards v Attorney-General* [1986] 2 NZLR 232 at 237 per Eichelbaum J.

A DEFENCE TO LIABILITY IN TRESPASS

4.3   The bare licence to enter or cross land performs the minimal function of affording a defence to what would otherwise be the tort of trespass.[1] The licensee's liability in trespass revives when his licence terminates.[2] A licence (if granted for a fixed term or until a specified event) normally comes to an end on the stipulated term date or the occurrence of the specified event, but may otherwise be terminable by the giving of notice to the licensee.[3]

1   [**Para 3.53**]. See *Goldsack v Shore* [1950] 1 KB 708 at 714 per Evershed MR; *R v Toohey; ex p Meneling Station Pty Ltd* (1982) 158 CLR 327 at 352 per Brennan J; *Beaton v McDivitt* (1985) 13 NSWLR 134 at 146E per Young J; *Church of Christ in Hollywood v Superior Court*, 121 Cal Rptr 2d 810 at 815–816 (2002).
2   *Thompson v Park* [1944] KB 408 at 410; *Goldsack v Shore* [1950] 1 KB 708 at 714; *Cowell v Rosehill Racecourse Co Ltd* (1937) 56 CLR 605 at 630–631 per Dixon J.
3   *Sandhu v Farooqui* [2004] 1 P & CR 19 at [20] per Chadwick LJ.

Straying outside the scope of the licence

4.4   A licence to enter land suspends trespass liability only so long as the licensee does not overstep the ambit of the licence as granted. If the licensee strays beyond the geographical or temporal scope of the permission given to him, his status becomes automatically that of a trespasser.[1] In the famous phrase of Scrutton LJ, '[w]hen you invite a person into your house to use the staircase, you do not invite him to slide down the bannisters'.[2]

1   *Hillen and Pettigrew v ICI (Alkali) Ltd* [1936] AC 65 at 69 per Lord Atkin; *Tomlinson v Congleton BC* [2004] 1 AC 46 at [7] per Lord Hoffmann, [52] per Lord Hutton; *O'Keeffe v Irish Motor Inns Ltd* [1978] IR 85 at 94, 100. See also *Wandsworth LBC v A* [2000] 1 WLR 1246 at 1251G per Buxton LJ.
2   *The Carlgarth* [1927] P 93 at 110.

Other excesses of authority

4.5   Trespass is likewise constituted by any other excess of the entrant's original authority to be present on the land.[1] Thus a person who has permission to enter land for one specific purpose (whether express or implied) commits a trespass if he enters for some other purpose[2] or if, whilst lawfully present on the land, he begins to pursue some alien and unauthorised purpose[3] or engages in some activity to which it is known or understood that the occupier would not have given consent.[4] The pursuit of an unauthorised purpose may even mark the inception of adverse possession by the entrant.[5] Trespass is not, however, committed by one who, under an entirely general or unlimited licence for access, enters with a number of purposes in mind (only some of which fall inside the anticipated purpose of the relevant permission).[6]

1   The character of an entry (as trespassory or not) may sometimes be quite significant, as, for instance, in demarcating theft from burglary. Compare Theft Act 1968, ss 1 (theft), 9(1)–(2) (burglary arising from entry 'as a trespasser').

2   *R v Pratt* (1855) 4 E & B 860 at 865, 119 ER 319 at 321 per Lord Campbell CJ; *Taylor v Jackson* (1898) 78 LT 555 at 556; *Gross v Wright* [1923] 2 DLR 171 at 185; *Farrington v Thomson & Bridgland* [1959] VR 286 at 297; *Barker v The Queen* (1983) 153 CLR 338 at 342, 346 per Mason J, 354 per Murphy J, 365 per Brennan and Deane JJ, 373 per Dawson J; *TCN Channel Nine Pty Ltd v Anning* (2002) 54 NSWLR 333 at [32], [78] per Spigelman CJ; *DPP v McMahon* [1986] IR 393 at 398. See also *Harrison v Duke of Rutland* [1893] 1 QB 142 at 147 per Lord Esher MR, 154 per Lopes LJ, 158 per Kay LJ.

3   *Hillen and Pettigrew v ICI (Alkali) Ltd* [1936] AC 65 at 69 per Lord Atkin; *Brunner v Williams* (1975) 73 LGR 266 at 273 per Lord Widgery CJ; *Tomlinson v Congleton BC* [2004] 1 AC 46 at [7] per Lord Hoffmann, [52] per Lord Hutton, [67] per Lord Hobhouse of Woodborough; *Barker v The Queen* (1983) 153 CLR 338 at 345 per Mason J, 357 per Brennan and Deane JJ. See also *R v Jones and Smith* [1976] 1 WLR 672 at 675A–C (as explained in *Barker*, supra at 360).

4   See *R v London CC, ex p Corrie* [1918] 1 KB 68 at 73 per Darling J (selling of books in public park); *TV3 Network Services Ltd v Broadcasting Standards Authority* [1995] 2 NZLR 720 at 732 per Eichelbaum CJ.

5   See *J A Pye (Oxford) Ltd v Graham* [2003] 1 AC 419 at [59] per Lord Browne-Wilkinson **[para 6.98]**.

6   *Barker v The Queen* (1983) 153 CLR 338 at 347–348 per Mason J, 357–365 per Brennan and Deane JJ. See likewise *Byrne v Kinematograph Renters Society Ltd* [1958] 1 WLR 762 at 776. Of course, an illicit supporting purpose, once put into effect, immediately converts the presence into a trespass.

ABSENCE OF POSSESSORY OR PROPRIETARY EFFECT

4.6   The licensee's immunity in trespass does not connote that a bare licensee has acquired possessory or proprietary rights in land.[1] In the time-honoured words of Vaughan CJ in *Thomas v Sorrell*,[2] a licence 'properly passeth no interest nor alters or transfers property in any thing, but only makes an action lawful, which without it had been unlawful.'[3] The licence has, in other words, a purely permissive quality. It confers no entitlement on the entrant,[4] but merely ensures that he 'cannot be treated as a trespasser.'[5]

1   See *Kerrison v Smith* [1897] 2 QB 445 at 449–450; *Allen v Allen* [2001] OTC 800 at [19]–[21].

2   (1673) Vaugh 330 at 351, 124 ER 1098 at 1109.

3   See similarly *Winter Garden Theatre (London) Ltd v Millennium Productions Ltd* [1948] AC 173 at 188 per Viscount Simon, 193 per Lord Porter; *Street v Mountford* [1985] AC 809 at 814F–G, 816C–D per Lord Templeman; *Ashburn Anstalt v Arnold* [1989] Ch 1 at 13E–F; *Reid v Moreland Timber Co Pty Ltd* (1946) 73 CLR 1 at 5; *Ocean Harvesters Ltd v Quinlan Brothers Ltd* [1975] 1 SCR 684 at 692; *Fatac Ltd v Commissioner of Inland Revenue* [2002] 3 NZLR 648 at [29].

4   *Bolch v Smith* (1862) 7 H & N 736 at 745–746, 158 ER 666 at 669–670 per Martin B **[para 5.31]**.

5   *Lowery v Walker* [1910] 1 KB 173 at 189 per Buckley LJ. See likewise *Winter Garden Theatre (London) Ltd v Millennium Productions Ltd* [1948] AC 173 at 188 per Viscount Simon; *Customs and Excise Commrs v Sinclair Collis Ltd* [2001] STC 989 at [67] per Lord Scott of Foscote.

4.7   The bare licensee has, accordingly, no rights which are directly assignable to a stranger.[1] Nor can he carve any proprietary estate out of the land for a third party (eg a term of years).[2] The licensee's fragile entitlement comprises, for the most part, a purely personal right as against his licensor. Thus the bare licensee probably cannot confer on a stranger any right of occupation by way of sub-licence,[3] although he may on occasion act as the licensor's agent for the purpose of conferring on others a permission to enter the land.[4] Furthermore, unlike the tenant at will,[5] the bare licensee does not enjoy 'possession' of the land and therefore has no intrinsic entitlement to take action against third parties for disturbance of his rights.[6] However, modern English law has made a pragmatic concession that the licensee may sue in trespass[7] or nuisance,[8] but only if, contrary to the basic principle of the matter, he can be said to have acquired 'possession' of the land.[9]

1   See eg *Bird v Province of New Brunswick* (1988) 43 DLR (4th) 153 at 155–156.

2   In some circumstances a licensee may be able to create a non-proprietary 'lease' or tenancy by estoppel **[paras 7.86, 7.265]**. See *LB of Camden v Shortlife Community Housing Ltd* (1992) 90 LGR 358 at 381 per Millett J; *Bruton v London & Quadrant Housing Trust* [2000] 1 AC 406. A licensee may also create a restrictive covenant which binds the freehold estate on his later acquisition of that estate (see *Ceda Drycleaners Ltd v Doonan* [1998] 1 NZLR 224 at 239–240).

3   See *Goldsack v Shore* [1950] 1 KB 708 at 714 per Evershed MR; but compare *Winter Garden Theatre (London) Ltd v Millennium Productions Ltd* [1948] AC 173 at 202 per Lord Uthwatt. A contractual licensee's competence in this regard may be somewhat greater (see *Bruton v London & Quadrant Housing Trust* [2000] 1 AC 406 at 414C–G per Lord Hoffmann, 417F–418D per Lord Hobhouse of Woodborough **[paras 7.86, 7.265]**).

4   **[Para 4.11]**.

5   **[Para 7.273]**.

6   See eg *Hill v Tupper* (1863) 2 H & C 121 at 127, 159 ER 51 at 53 **[para 8.36]**; *Western Australia v Ward* (2002) 191 ALR 1 at [504] per McHugh J. See also *Malone v Laskey* [1907] 2 KB 141 at 151; *Nunn v Parkes & Co* (1924) 158 LT Jo 431; *Hull v Parsons* [1962] NZLR 465 at 467–468; *Simpson v Knowles* [1974] VR 190 at 195; *Oldham v Lawson (No 1)* [1976] VR 654 at 657; *Moore v MacMillan* [1977] 2 NZLR 81 at 89; *Lyons v The Queen* (1985) 14 DLR (4th) 482 at 510 per Estey J.

7   See eg *Mehta v Royal Bank of Scotland* [1999] 3 EGLR 153 at 160E–F **[paras 3.51, 7.145]**.

8   Compare eg *Pemberton v Southwark LBC* [2000] 1 WLR 1672 at 1682H, 1684A–B, 1685H–1686A **[para 3.30]**.

9   **[Paras 3.51, 7.144]**. See *Hunter v Canary Wharf Ltd* [1997] AC 655 at 688E per Lord Goff of Chieveley, 702H–703E per Lord Hoffmann, 724C–F per Lord Hope of Craighead.

CREATION OF BARE LICENCES

4.8   A licence to enter and be present on land may be created either expressly or impliedly by any person 'in possession, using that word in its strict sense so as to include a person entitled to immediate and exclusive possession.'[1] No formality is required in the matter of creation. The licence need not be written or even oral. A permission to enter may flow from an 'expression of consent by non-verbal means.'[2] It may also arise by implication from circumstances or conduct.[3] A licence does not generally confer exclusive rights on the licensee unless exclusiveness is stipulated or necessary as a matter of implication.[4]

1   *Barker v The Queen* (1983) 153 CLR 338 at 341–342 per Mason J. See similarly *Robson v Hallett* [1967] 2 QB 939 at 954F per Diplock LJ; *Australian Broadcasting Corpn v Lenah Game Meats Pty Ltd* (2001) 208 CLR 199 at [43] per Gleeson CJ. On the meaning of possession, see Chapter 3 [**para 3.2**].
2   *R (Beresford) v Sunderland CC* [2004] 1 AC 889 at [75] per Lord Walker of Gestingthorpe (giving as examples the leaving open of a gate or front door, although such instances shade easily into the category of an implied licence generated by conduct).
3   *R (Beresford) v Sunderland CC* [2004] 1 AC 889 at [59] per Lord Rodger of Earlsferry, [75] per Lord Walker of Gestingthorpe. See also *Faulkner v Willetts* [1982] RTR 159 at 164H. Certain implied licences to enter land are inferably licences for daytime entry only (see *Coleshill v Manchester Corpn* [1928] 1 KB 776 at 789 per Scrutton LJ).
4   *Reid v Moreland Timber Co Pty Ltd* (1946) 73 CLR 1 at 5.

Express licences

4.9   Expressly created licences are the stuff of everyday social and commercial intercourse. Party invitations, business meetings and summonses to job interviews rest alike on an express permission to be present in or on defined premises. Where the land is in the possession of one person alone, the conferment of an express licence is usually a straightforward issue. More complicated questions arise where others are present on that land.

Licence granted by one co-owner unilaterally

4.10   It is probable, but not beyond all dispute, that a licence to enter land may be granted unilaterally by one of two persons (e g co-owners) who enjoy joint possession of the land concerned.[1] To disallow the possibility of unilateral grant could, for instance, inhibit the investigation of complaints of domestic violence.[2] On the other hand, unilateral grant enables one co-owner to inflict an intrusive personality upon a shared household in the teeth of objection from another co-owner[3] and it is arguable that one occupier's privacy should not be left 'completely at the mercy of another with whom he shares legal possession.'[4] The law in this area is not entirely satisfactory, although something may turn in practice on whether the intended licence is a long-term invitation to share a home or merely a casual permission for short-term entry.[5] It is sometimes said that the recipient of a unilateral licence enjoys a presence on the land which is lawful as against the actual licensor, but (in the absence of the latter's actual or ostensible authority to grant a licence on behalf of both) remains a trespasser vis à vis the other co-owner.[6] This proposition may not, however, alleviate all difficulties.

1   See e g *Robson-Paul v Farrugia* (1969) 20 P & CR 820 at 825; *Slade v Guscott* (Unreported, Court of Appeal, 28 July 1981).

2   See *Attorney-General v Hewitt* [2000] 2 NZLR 110 at 118. See also *R v Thornley* (1980) 72 Cr
App R 302 at 305–306, where the Court of Appeal indicated that, in the context of domestic
disputes, a police officer summoned by one occupier may not, at common law, be ordered off
the premises by the other at least until it has been possible to ascertain the safety of all parties
concerned and of any children present.

3   See *Sanders v McDonald and Pringle* [1981] CLY 1534, where a county court refused to allow
a joint tenant to import his lover into the house on the breakdown of his relationship with the
other joint tenant. Compare *Jolliffe v Willmett & Co* [1971] 1 All ER 478 at 483g–484–485;
and see also Family Law Act 1996, ss 33(3), 36(5).

4   *Tompkins v Superior Court of City and County of San Francisco*, 27 Cal Rptr 889 at 892 (1963)
per Traynor J. In *Tompkins* the Supreme Court of California held that a police officer could
not rely on a permission to enter co-owned premises which had been given by only one of the
co-owners, at least where there was no emergency and the officer did not explain to the
co-owner in residence that he had the consent of an absent co-owner.

5   See e g *Allen v Allen* [2001] OTC 800 at [40].

6   See *Ferguson v Walsh* [1987] 1 WLR 1553 at 1563A–D per Lord Goff of Chieveley;
Incorporated Owners of Chungking Mansions v Shamdasani [1991] 2 HKC 342; *Allen v Allen*
[2001] OTC 800 at [40]. For the suggestion that a co-owner may bring possession proceedings
only against third parties who do not hold under any other co-owner, see *Scott v McNutt*
(1870) 8 NSR (1st Ser) 118 at 120; *Tobin v McDougall* (1914) 16 DLR 359 at 360–361; *Grundel
v Registrar General* (1990) 5 BPR 11217 at 11223.

Licence granted by a non-owner

4.11   The capacity of persons other than those in possession of land to grant
a licence is ultimately governed by ordinary principles of agency.[1] Thus, for
example, a spouse (if not strictly in 'possession' of the land) has at the very least
a presumed authority, derived from the fact of marriage, to invite friends into
the home.[2] There seems, moreover, to be an implied and rebuttable authority
for someone inside a dwelling-house, in response to a knock at the door, to
admit a stranger to the house on behalf of the occupier.[3] A person who is
casually or temporarily present on land (e g at a party) has a limited presumed
authority to confer on a stranger a revocable permission to enter the premises.[4]
A building contractor in occupation of a construction site is empowered to give
access to the site, as is a parking attendant to confer upon a motorist a licence
to enter land of which the attendant has neither ownership nor possession.[5]
Similarly an employee has ostensible authority to admit a stranger to ancillary
parts of business premises.[6] The limits of ostensible authority are reached
where a licence to enter land is purportedly conferred by some person who
could not have been reasonably believed by the entrant to have 'common
authority' over admission to the premises.[7]

1   See *Ferguson v Walsh* [1987] 1 WLR 1553 at 1563D.

2   *Coles-Smith v Smith* [1965] Qd R 494 at 502–503 (although there is no implied authority to
invite strangers into the marital bedroom).

3   See *Robson v Hallett* [1967] 2 QB 939 at 954B–C; *DPP v Delaney* [1996] 3 IR 556 at 562. Any
licence granted by a casual guest can be countermanded by the true possessor and cannot
extend, in any event, to all parts of the premises (see *R v Thomas* (1992) 67 CCC (3d) 81 at
92g–93c (bedroom)).

4   See e g *Jones and Jones v Lloyd* [1981] Crim LR 340 at 341 (party guest had authority to invite
police into premises for purpose of demonstrating his own innocence).

5   *Meriton Apartments Pty Ltd v Baulderstone Hornibrook Pty Ltd* (1992) 9 BPR 17433 at 17436
     per Young J.
6   *Mountney v Smith* (1904) 1 CLR 146 at 157 (lavatory in hotel bar).
7   The terminology of 'common authority' has been used in the United States in determining the
     legality of consent to police entry (see *Illinois v Rodriguez*, 497 US 177 at 179, 111 L Ed 2d 148
     at 155 (1990); *People v Hopkins*, 870 P2d 478 at 480 (Colo 1994)). On this basis, for instance,
     babysitters and non-resident caretakers, although fortuitously present on land, have no
     competence to give lawful admission to strangers (see *Petersen v People*, 939 P2d 824 at
     828–830 (Colo 1997); *Kaspar v City of Hobbs*, 90 F Supp 2d 1313 at 1321 (DNM 2000); but
     compare *Butler v Commonwealth*, 536 SW2d 139 at 140 (Ky 1976)).

Implied licences

4.12   Bare licences frequently emerge by implication from circumstances or
conduct. The existence of such licences dramatically eases the conduct of
everyday life; and the ways in which they are upheld or revoked effectively
define the extent of the privacy available to be enjoyed by the individual
citizen.[1]

1   It is unlikely, for instance, that English courts would uphold the American doctrine that a
     licence is available by implied consent for media photographers to enter private premises
     where a disaster of great public interest has occurred (see *Florida Publishing Co v Fletcher*, 340
     So2d 914 at 918–919 (1976); but compare *Prahl v Bosamle*, 98 Wis 2d 130 at 149–150 (1980)).
     See also *Wilson v Layne*, 526 US 603, 143 L Ed 2d 818 at 829–830 (1999) (unconstitutionality
     of media ride-along during police arrest).

Domestic premises

4.13   In the absence of a locked gate or some warning notice, the occupier of a
dwelling-house is taken to have issued an implied licence to any member of the
public to come through the garden gate (if there is one) and to approach the
front door in order to inquire whether he may be admitted to the house or
perform some other act on the land.[1] An implied licence of this kind extends to
such persons as postmen or milkmen,[2] door-to-door salesmen,[3] media report-
ers,[4] Jehovah's witnesses,[5] election canvassers[6] and even police officers,[7] provided generally in each case that the person concerned has a genuine and
legitimate reason to be present[8] or proposes to conduct 'lawful business'.[9] The
implied licence is not even tethered necessarily to the purpose of going to the
entrance of the house.[10] As the High Court of Australia pointed out in *Halliday
v Nevill*,[11] a passer-by is not rendered a trespasser 'if, on passing an open
driveway with no indication that entry is forbidden or unauthorised, he or she
steps upon it either unintentionally or to avoid an obstruction such as a vehicle
parked across the footpath.'[12]

1   *Robson v Hallett* [1967] 2 QB 939 at 951F, 953G–954A. See also *Snook v Mannion* [1982] RTR
     321 at 326C–D; *Nevill v Halliday* [1983] 2 VR 553 at 556; *Halliday v Nevill* (1984) 155 CLR 1
     at 7. The implied licence of the general public has been held equally applicable to an occupier's
     back door (see *Pamplin v Fraser* [1981] RTR 494 at 500H; *Snook v Mannion* [1982] RTR 321 at
     327A–B; *Edwards v Attorney-General* [1986] 2 NZLR 232 at 237).
2   *Holden v White* [1982] QB 679 at 687D–E.

3 See, however, Property Repairs (Prohibition of Cold-calling) Bill (Bill 28 of 2004), cl 3, which would make it a criminal offence for a trader to make a 'cold-call' to a consumer's home or place of work with a view to offering to provide a 'property service' (ie works of repair, maintenance or improvement).
4 *TV3 Network Services Ltd v Broadcasting Standards Authority* [1995] 2 NZLR 720 at 732.
5 *Commonwealth v Richardson*, 48 NE2d 678 at 682–683 (1943).
6 *Evans v Forsyth* (1979) 90 DLR (3d) 155 at 156.
7 *Robson v Hallett* [1967] 2 QB 939 at 952A–B, 953F–954A. See also *Dobie v Pinker* [1983] WAR 48 at 51, 68; *R v Pou* [2002] 3 NZLR 637 at [15].
8 *Nevill v Halliday* [1983] 2 VR 553 at 556.
9 *Robson v Hallett* [1967] 2 QB 939 at 954A. In *Lambert v Roberts* [1981] 2 All ER 15 at 19d, Donaldson LJ was prepared to extend this implied licence to knock on the door to all citizens (including police officers) who 'reasonably think that they have' legitimate business on the premises. The 'business' need not be with the occupier of the house (see *Brunner v Williams* (1975) 73 LGR 266 at 272).
10 There is, however, no implied licence to visit an orchard (*R v Grayson and Taylor* [1997] 1 NZLR 399 at 409) and a 'for sale' sign constitutes no invitation to plunder around the grounds at random (*Wells v Polland*, 708 A2d 34 at 44 (Md App 1998)).
11 (1984) 155 CLR 1 at 7.
12 Nor is there any trespass if the passer-by goes upon the driveway or path 'to recover some item of his or her property which has fallen or blown upon it or to lead away an errant child.' The law is 'not such an ass' that the implied or tacit licence in such a case is restricted to stepping over the item of property or around the child for the purpose of going to the entrance and asking the householder whether the item of property can be reclaimed or the child led away ((1984) 155 CLR 1 at 7). (Indeed the landowner who prevents a chattel owner from recovering his chattel may be liable for conversion (see *Fitzgerald v Kellion Estate Pty Ltd* (1977) 2 BPR 9181 at 9187; *Elders Rural Finance Ltd v Westpac Banking Corporation* (1988) 4 BPR 9383 at 9388.)) See also *Grim v Robison*, 48 NW 388 at 389 (1891); *Lincoln Hunt Australia Pty Ltd v Willesee* [1986] 4 NSWLR 457 at 460C–E.

'An Englishman's home is his castle'

4.14 In its operation within the domestic curtilage, the law of implied licences trenches peculiarly upon the principle enunciated in *Semayne's Case*[1] that 'an Englishman's home is his castle.'[2] This brocard has 'immense importance in the history of this country, and it still has immense importance.'[3] The implied licence exercised by strangers (including any investigating police officer) extends only to the area outside the dwelling-house.[4] Further entry inside the premises may be made only with the express permission of the occupier (or of some person acting on his behalf[5]) or in pursuance of some common law[6] or statutory power.[7] It is ultimately a question of fact whether a police officer has been granted a licence to enter beyond the curtilage of premises, but the exigencies of law enforcement have sometimes led courts to assume (perhaps over-readily) that such a licence has been granted unless the owner or occupier of premises in some way manifested an intention to exclude.[8]

1 (1604) 5 Co Rep 91a at 91b, 77 ER 194 at 195 **[para 3.8]**. The maxim probably has an even older provenance (see *TCN Channel Nine Pty Ltd v Anning* (2002) 54 NSWLR 333 at [54] per Spigelman CJ; and see also *Deuteronomy* 24:10). For an extensive review of the idea that 'an Englishman's home is his castle', see *Nevill v Halliday* [1983] 2 VR 553 at 561–567 per

Brooking J. See also *Minnesota v Carter*, 525 US 83, 142 L Ed 2d 373 at 386–387 (1998) per Justice Kennedy; *R v Pou* [2002] 3 NZLR 637 at [15] (referring to 'the citizen's right to privacy in the sanctity of his or her home').

2   See similarly *Burdett v Abbot* (1811) 14 East 1 at 155, 104 ER 501 at 560 per Lord Ellenborough CJ. The broadly stated principle of *Semayne's Case* is of course subject to exceptions, but it is for the police to justify a forcible entry (*McLorie v Oxford* [1982] QB 1290 at 1296B per Donaldson LJ).

3   *Swales v Cox* [1981] QB 849 at 855A–B per Donaldson LJ. The inviolable nature of the private dwelling was described by Estey J in *Lyons v The Queen* (1985) 14 DLR (4th) 482 at 501 as 'a basic part of our free society ... a bulwark against tyranny of the State.'

4   *Robson v Hallett* [1967] 2 QB 939 at 951F; *Snook v Mannion* [1982] RTR 321 at 327E. The implied licence 'ends with the knock on the door' (*Edwards v Attorney-General* [1986] 2 NZLR 232 at 238) – at some reasonable hour of the day or night (*Howden v Ministry of Transport* [1987] 1 NZLR 747 at 754–755). See also *Great Central Railway Co v Bates* [1921] 3 KB 578 at 581 per Atkin LJ; *R v Pou* [2002] 3 NZLR 637 at [15].

5   *Robson v Hallett* [1967] 2 QB 939 at 954C. That a licence may be effectively granted by some person acting on the occupier's authority is clear from *Rossiter v Conway* (1893) 58 JP 350 at 351; *Jones and Jones v Lloyd* [1981] Crim LR 340 at 341; *Nevill v Halliday* [1983] 2 VR 553 at 557.

6   *Sandon v Jervis* (1858) EB & E 935 at 940–941, 120 ER 758 at 760. See eg *Hart v Chief Constable of Kent* [1983] RTR 484 at 491E–F (right of 'hot pursuit').

7   See eg Police and Criminal Evidence Act 1984, ss 8(1), 17(1), 18(1). 'The community interest in crime detection and suppression ... inevitably entails intrusion on the castle concept' (*Lyons v The Queen* (1985) 14 DLR (4th) 482 at 502 per Estey J). Furthermore, evidence obtained by trespassing police officers is not necessarily inadmissible in subsequent criminal proceedings (see *R v Fox* [1985] 1 WLR 1126 at 1131H, 1132D–E; *R v Grayson and Taylor* [1997] 1 NZLR 399 at 407).

8   *Nevill v Halliday* [1983] 2 VR 553 at 556. See eg *Faulkner v Willetts* [1982] RTR 159 at 164C–D, where the Divisional Court found an implied licence where a woman opened her front door to a police officer and walked back into the house, giving the officer the impression that he had an implied invitation to follow her into the house. Compare *R v Landry* (1982) 34 OR (2d) 697 at 704, (1986) 26 DLR (4th) 368 at 376–382; *TCN Channel Nine Pty Ltd v Anning* (2002) 54 NSWLR 333 at [46]–[49].

Licences in the family context

4.15   Certain categories of person clearly enjoy at least an implied licence to live in the family home. Such a licence extends, for example, to a de facto partner.[1] The status of parents or other relatives who are allowed to reside in the family home depends usually on some combination of express and implied licence.[2]

1   See *Public Trustee v Bellotti* (1986) 4 BPR 9196 at 9202–9203.
2   See also *Hoskins v Hoskins* (Unreported, 3 December 1981), where the Court of Appeal held that a deserted wife, who had been given temporary occupation of a flat belonging to her husband and his two brothers, was merely a bare licensee under 'an ad hoc short-term licence free of charge'.

4.16   A de iure spouse's entitlement to occupy the matrimonial home is, however, rather distinct. A spouse (if not legally or beneficially entitled to an estate in the land) has a common law right of residence in the matrimonial home which is often described as sui generis.[1] This right flows from the fact of marriage itself[2] and to describe a spouse as a mere licensee would be 'not only uncomplimentary but inaccurate.'³ A spouse's occupation of the marital home is not by bare permission of the other spouse, but is attributable to special rights incidental to the marital relationship.⁴

1   *National Provincial Bank Ltd v Ainsworth* [1965] AC 1175 at 1232F per Lord Upjohn. See also *Hall v King* (1988) 55 P & CR 307 at 309 per Lord Donaldson MR. A spouse's right to reside in the matrimonial home is now reinforced by the conferment of 'matrimonial home rights' pursuant to the Family Law Act 1996 **[para 12.93]**.
2   On the gender-neutrality of the modern common law right, see *Harman v Glencross* [1985] Fam 49 at 58B–C per Ewbank J.
3   *National Provincial Bank Ltd v Ainsworth* [1965] AC 1175 at 1223E–F per Lord Hodson (emphasising that a wife 'is not a person who needs any licence from her husband to be where she has a right to be as a wife'). See also Lord Upjohn (at 1239A).
4   *Blake v Stradford*, 725 NYS2d 189 at 192 (2001).

4.17   It used to be said that, except in cases of beneficial entitlement or court order, the residential status of a child in the family home, both before and after his attainment of the age of majority, rested on nothing more than a revocable bare licence.¹ Whilst this analysis doubtless remains true of an adult child, the presence of the minor child is increasingly recognised today, not as a matter of implied licence, but rather as an incident of a certain protected status.² The notion of enduring 'parental responsibility' confirmed by the Children Act 1989³ provides a statutory basis for a prima facie entitlement to shelter in the home of one or other parent.⁴ This right now gathers strength from the principle of respect for home and family life enshrined in the European Convention on Human Rights.⁵ The United Kingdom has also ratified the United Nations Convention on the Rights of the Child, which acknowledges that no child 'shall be subjected to arbitrary or unlawful interference with his or her … home'⁶ and, as Lord Cooke of Thorndon once observed, international standards of this kind 'may be taken into account in shaping the common law.'⁷

1   *Metropolitan Properties Co Ltd v Cronan* (1982) 44 P & CR 1 at 8 per May LJ. See also *Waterhouse v Waterhouse* (1905) 94 LT 133 at 134; *Stevens v Stevens* (1907) 24 TLR 20 at 21; *Egan v Egan* [1975] Ch 218 at 221D; *Hunter v Canary Wharf Ltd* [1997] AC 655 at 690G per Lord Goff of Chieveley.
2   See e g *Devon Lumber Co Ltd v MacNeill* (1987) 45 DLR (4th) 300 at 302–303 per Stratton CJNB (New Brunswick Court of Appeal), cited in *Hunter v Canary Wharf Ltd* [1997] AC 655 at 715B per Lord Cooke of Thorndon.
3   Children Act 1989, ss 2(1)–(2), 3(1).
4   See e g *Blake v Stradford*, 725 NYS2d 189 at 194–195 (2001). For confirmation that the performance of statutory obligations can impliedly generate a licence, see *Wandsworth LBC v A* [2000] 1 WLR 1246 at 1253C–D (school premises) **[para 4.54]**.
5   ECHR Art 8(1) envisages that family members have a right to live together in order that family relationships may 'develop normally' (see *Marckx v Belgium*, Series A No 31 at [31] (1979)) and that parent and child may have 'mutual enjoyment … of each other's company' (*Olsson v Sweden*, Series A No 130 (1988) at [59]). See similarly *Peck v United Kingdom* (2003) 36 EHRR 719 at [57]; *Anufrijeva v Southwark LBC* [2004] 2 WLR 603 at [11]–[12] per Lord Woolf CJ.
6   United Nations Convention on the Rights of the Child (1989), Art 16.
7   *Hunter v Canary Wharf Ltd* [1997] AC 655 at 714A.

Business and other premises

4.18   Business and other premises can be the subject of an implied licence permitting entry by members of the public, although such licences are sometimes less extensive than those which apply to domestic premises.[1] A commercial organisation may be taken, for instance, to offer an implied invitation to persons who in good faith seek to acquire information or to do business.[2] In relation to such premises as a shopping mall which are quite deliberately opened up for public use, the invitation may be rather broader, encompassing 'not just an invitation to shop, but to do whatever one would do downtown, including doing very little of anything.'[3] There is, however, no implied licence authorising entry by investigative television journalists who, accompanied by camera crews, intrude upon the business premises of unsavoury or controversial commercial operations.[4] There is no implied licence to enter a nuclear installation for the purpose of distributing protest literature[5] or to invade an abortion clinic in order to gather evidence of allegedly unlawful activities conducted there.[6] Members of the public (as distinct from parishioners[7]) have no implied right to enter a church even though the church may purport to be a place of public worship.[8] There is, however, implied authority facilitating 'unfettered access' to a police station by members of the public[9] and there may well be an implied licence permitting entry to the precincts of Parliament for purposes of political communication or protest.[10]

1   See *Great Central Railway Co v Bates* [1921] 3 KB 578 at 581–582 (no implied right to enter warehouse); *TCN Channel Nine Pty Ltd v Anning* (2002) 54 NSWLR 333 at [55]–[57] per Spigelman CJ. See also *Mackay v Abrahams* [1916] VLR 681 at 684–685; but compare *Davis v Lisle* [1936] 2 KB 434 at 438–439.

2   *Lincoln Hunt Australia Pty Ltd v Willesee* (1986) 4 NSWLR 457 at 460F per Young J, who added for the avoidance of doubt that there is, however, no implied licence for persons who wish 'to enter to hold up the premises and rob them.' See likewise *Barker v The Queen* (1983) 153 CLR 338 at 348 per Mason J, 373 per Dawson J. Nor is there any implied licence to enter a hospital room in order to photograph a famous patient (see *Hosking and Hosking v Runting* [2004] NZCA 34 at [269] per Anderson J).

3   *New Jersey Coalition Against War in the Middle East v JMB Realty Corporation*, 650 A2d 757 at 761, 772–773 (NJ 1994) per Wilentz CJ. See also *Barker v The Queen* (1983) 153 CLR 338 at 361–362 per Brennan and Deane JJ; *City of Jamestown v Beneda*, 477 NW2d 830 at 837–838 (ND 1991).

4   *Lincoln Hunt Australia Pty Ltd v Willesee* (1986) 4 NSWLR 457 at 460F; *TCN Channel Nine Pty Ltd v Anning* (2002) 54 NSWLR 333 at [62]. See also *Le Mistral, Inc v Columbia Broadcasting System*, 402 NYS2d 815 at 817–818 (1978); *Belluomo v Kake TV & Radio, Inc*, 596 P2d 832 at 844–845 (1979); *Emcorp Pty Ltd v Australian Broadcasting Corporation* [1988] 2 Qd R 169 at 172–176; compare *Silber v British Columbia Broadcasting System Ltd* (1986) 25 DLR (4th) 345 at 351.

5   *Semple v Mant* (1985) 39 SASR 282 at 287.

6   See *Darcey v Pre-Term Foundation Clinic* [1983] 2 NSWLR 497 at 500D–E, 502B–G.

7   *Cole v Police Constable 443A* [1937] 1 KB 316 at 330, 334–335.

8   *Canterbury MC v Moslem Alawy Society Ltd* (1985) 1 NSWLR 525 at 541B–C. See also *State v Steinmann*, 569 A2d 557 at 560 (Conn App 1990).

9   *Bethune v Heffernan* [1986] VR 417 at 423–424.

10 See *Police v Beggs* [1999] 3 NZLR 615 at 632.

Tolerated trespass and licence through acquiescence

4.19 It is possible that a tolerated trespass on land can shade into a presence which is validated by some form of implied licence. Such may occur, for example, where a landowner, with knowledge that strangers enjoy frequent access to his land, habitually makes no objection to their presence.[1] Mere inaction on the landowner's part allows the bare trespass to ripen into an implied licence, thereby affording the intruders a defence to trespass.[2] These instances are, in reality, cases of 'tacit permission'[3] in which the landowner is taken, by his acquiescence in the use of the land by trespassers, to have 'impliedly permitted such use, so as to raise the status of the persons concerned from that of trespassers to that of licensees.'[4] The implied licensees nevertheless have no irrevocable right,[5] but only a 'mere permission'[6] to be present on the land.

1   See *Deane v Clayton* (1817) 7 Taunt 489 at 532–533, 129 ER 196 at 213 per Gibbs CJ; *Slater v Clay Cross Co Ltd* [1956] 2 QB 264 at 268–269 per Denning LJ; *Ashdown v Samuel Williams & Sons Ltd* [1957] 1 QB 409 at 420 per Jenkins LJ.
2   See *R (Beresford) v Sunderland CC* [2004] 1 AC 889 at [76] per Lord Walker of Gestingthorpe.
3   *Lowery v Walker* [1910] 1 KB 173 at 195–196 per Kennedy LJ; *Latham v R Johnson & Nephew Ltd* [1913] 1 KB 398 at 410–411 per Hamilton LJ.
4   Law Reform Committee, *Third Report: Occupiers' Liability to Invitees, Licensees and Trespassers* (Cmd 9305, November 1954), para 29. A prime example of such acquiescence is found in *Canadian Pacific Railway Co v The King* [1931] AC 414 at 424, 428 per Lord Russell of Killowen ('original trespass, which, by dint of toleration over a period of time, became an occupation by leave and licence').
5   See e g *Countryside Legislation: De facto and de iure access to the countryside* (Department for Environment, Food and Rural Affairs Guidance Note published 21 December 2001, updated 27 September 2002), para 3.
6   *Hounsell v Smyth* (1860) 7 CB (NS) 731 at 743–744, 141 ER 1003 at 1008 per Williams J; *Binks v South Yorkshire Railway and River Dun Co* (1862) 3 B & S 244 at 252, 122 ER 92 at 96 per Wightman J; *Lowery v Walker* [1910] 1 KB 173 at 199 per Kennedy LJ.

TERMINATION OF BARE LICENCES

4.20 In the orthodox analysis of the matter, the prerogative of property in land confers a relatively unqualified right to determine who may enter or remain on that land.[1] The correlatives of licence and trespass belong to a simplified world in which stark concepts of permission and denial of permission are wholly in place.[2] In the generality of cases the common law has long invested those in possession of land with a power of arbitrary exclusion of unwanted strangers.[3] The law upholding this exclusory privilege conventionally makes no distinction between various categories of land (whether domestic dwellings, crowded urban spaces or open country) or between various kinds of landowner (whether private, corporate or governmental). The prerogative of property tends, in its way, to be both total and totalitarian.

1   *Forbes v New South Wales Trotting Club Ltd* (1979) 143 CLR 242 at 249, 259 per Barwick CJ, 281 per Aickin J; *Australian Broadcasting Corpn v Lenah Game Meats Pty Ltd* (2001) 208 CLR 199 at [43] per Gleeson CJ.
2   'The concept of licence stemmed from the feudal politico-economic system of land-holding ...

Under it the peasant and pedestrian could step on the land with the permission and sufferance of the squire who owned it but must step out when the licence was revoked' (*Tan Hin Leong v Lee Teck Im* [2000] 3 SLR 85 at 90E–F per G P Selvam J).
3   **[Para 4.2]**.

Revocability at will

4.21   Embedded in the common law of at least the last 150 years is the broad principle that, absent any limitation imposed by common law[1] or statute,[2] a bare or mere licence to enter land is always revocable at the will of the licensor[3] (even if the licence was granted by deed[4]). This doctrine is normally associated with the decision of the Court of Exchequer in *Wood v Leadbitter*[5] and, although its origins are somewhat debatable,[6] the doctrine has come to be widely accepted throughout the common law world.[7] In many instances a bare licence may lawfully be brought to an end even though its termination is sudden, unreasoned, arbitrary and unfair. A bare licence is subject to summary cancellation on the giving of reasonable notice,[8] even though the licensee had no prior warning that his permission to be present on the land was terminable in this way.[9] Moreover, in the absence of any contractual element in the licence, it cannot be argued that, on granting the licence, the licensor impliedly promised that, provided the licensee behaved properly, he would be left undisturbed to complete the purpose contemplated by the licence.[10]

1   Certain restrictions may be imposed by doctrines of contract **[para 4.79]** and estoppel **[para 10.168]**. See *Allen v Allen* [2001] OTC 800 at [22]–[23].
2   In most modern jurisdictions the power to control access is subject to legislation prohibiting discrimination on grounds of gender, race and disability (see e g Sex Discrimination Act 1975, s 29(1)–(2); Race Relations Act 1976, s 20(1)–(2); Disability Discrimination Act 1995, ss 19(1), (3), 22(3), 23).
3   See *Canadian Pacific Railway Co v The King* [1931] AC 414 at 430–431 per Lord Russell of Killowen; *Winter Garden Theatre (London) Ltd v Millennium Productions Ltd* [1948] AC 173 at 188–189 per Viscount Simon, 193–195 per Lord Porter, 198 per Lord Uthwatt. In *Wood v Leadbitter* (1845) 13 M & W 838 at 851–854, 153 ER 351 at 357–358, Alderson B referred to the inherent revocability of the 'mere' licence as one of 'the ancient landmarks of the common law.'
4   See *Wood v Leadbitter* (1845) 13 M & W 838 at 845, 153 ER 351 at 354–355; *Winter Garden Theatre (London) Ltd v Millennium Productions Ltd* [1948] AC 173 at 194 per Lord Porter; *Cowell v Rosehill Racecourse Co Ltd* (1937) 56 CLR 605 at 631, 636 per Dixon J.
5   (1845) 13 M & W 838 at 844–845, 153 ER 351 at 354 **[para 4.78]**. There remains a strong suspicion that, in *Wood v Leadbitter*, references to 'mere' or 'naked' licences became fatally disoriented in a slather of debate about the formalities attendant on the grant of interests in land ((1845) 13 M & W 838 at 852, 153 ER 351 at 357–358). In the course of litigation concerned with the termination of contractual licences, certain overbroad statements about the revocability of bare licences slipped out almost accidentally, thereby conducing to a confusion which has lasted well into modern times. The *Wood v Leadbitter* doctrine was later rejected in relation to licences supported by contract (see *Winter Garden Theatre (London) Ltd v Millennium Productions Ltd* [1948] AC 173 at 191 per Viscount Simon **[para 4.83]**).
6   Closer analysis of the history of the Anglo-American trespass rule indicates that the law relating to peremptorily terminable licences was not originally quite so absolutist as has been widely supposed (see Gray and Gray, 'Civil Rights, Civil Wrongs and Quasi-Public Space' (1999) 4 EHRLR 46 at 85–89). *Wood v Leadbitter* was initially regarded by American jurists as misrepresenting the common law (see *Macgoverning v Staples* (1873) 7 Lans 145 at 148–149;

Donnell v The State (1873) 48 Miss 661, 12 Am Rep 375 at 381) and its reasoning seems deeply at variance with the old English doctrine of the 'licence acted upon' **[para 4.89]** (compare *Tayler v Waters* (1816) 7 Taunt 374, 129 ER 150; and see *McBean v Howey* [1958] NZLR 25 at 28). In the United States the absolutist form of the *Wood v Leadbitter* rule emerged only later as a supposedly neutral rationale for racially motivated exclusion from public facilities (see *Uston v Resorts International Hotel Inc*, 445 A2d 370 at 374 (1982) per Pashman J).

7 See *Marrone v Washington Jockey Club*, 227 US 633 at 636, 57 L Ed 679 at 681 (1912) per Justice Holmes; *Cowell v Rosehill Racecourse Co Ltd* (1937) 56 CLR 605 at 627 per Starke J, 630 per Dixon J; *Mayfield Holdings Ltd v Moana Reef Ltd* [1973] 1 NZLR 309 at 315; *Graham v Northern Ireland Housing Executive* [1986] NI 72 at 74A; *Tan Hin Leong v Lee Teck Im* [2000] 3 SLR 85 at 91E.

8 See *Winter Garden Theatre (London) Ltd v Millennium Productions Ltd* [1948] AC 173 at 188 per Viscount Simon ('a purely gratuitous licence in return for which A gets nothing at all, eg, a licence to B to walk across A's field ... would plainly be revocable by notice given by A to B'). See also Lord Uthwatt (at 200–201).

9 *Lambert v Roberts* [1981] 2 All ER 15 at 19d. See *Meriton Apartments Pty Ltd v Baulderstone Hornibrook Pty Ltd* (1992) 9 BPR 17433 at 17437.

10 See *Winter Garden Theatre (London) Ltd v Millennium Productions Ltd* [1948] AC 173 at 189 per Viscount Simon; *White v Blackmore* [1972] 2 QB 651 at 675F–676A per Roskill LJ.

Arbitrariness of termination

4.22 In the conventional view bare licences are therefore terminable without any requirement of objectively reasonable cause[1] and without any obligation to proffer a rationally communicable explanation, either before or after, for any particular act of exclusion.[2] The licensor's control over selective access to his land is unfettered by any necessity to comply with rules of natural justice.[3] The licensor simply enjoys an unchallengeable discretion to withhold or withdraw permission to enter[4] and may enforce his paramount right by bringing possession proceedings, following revocation, against any former licensee who remains on the land.[5] Quite apart from the practicalities of the matter, there is no way in which a bare licensee, being a mere volunteer, can have his exclusion from the land restrained by the equitable remedy of injunction.[6]

1 See eg *CIN Properties Ltd v Rawlins* [1995] 2 EGLR 130 at 134G–J; *Russo v Ontario Jockey Club* (1988) 46 DLR (4th) 359 at 364; *Austin v Rescon Construction (1984) Ltd* (1989) 57 DLR (4th) 591 at 593; *Plenty v Dillon* (1991) 171 CLR 635 at 655 per Gaudron and McHugh JJ; *Jacque v Steenberg Homes, Inc*, 563 NW2d 154 at 159–160 (Wis 1997).

2 See *Russo v Ontario Jockey Club* (1988) 46 DLR (4th) 359 at 361–362; *Australian Broadcasting Corpn v Lenah Game Meats Pty Ltd* (2001) 208 CLR 199 at [43] per Gleeson CJ.

3 *Heatley v Tasmanian Racing and Gaming Commission* (1977) 137 CLR 487 at 511 per Aickin J; *Russo v Ontario Jockey Club* (1988) 46 DLR (4th) 359 at 362.

4 See *Madden v Queens County Jockey Club, Inc*, 72 NE2d 697 at 698 (1947) (race track operator); *Brooks v Chicago Downs Association, Inc*, 791 F2d 512 at 517 (1986) ('The proprietor wants to be able to keep someone off his private property even if they only look like a mobster').

5 There are strict limits on the court's power to postpone the giving up of possession pursuant to a possession order (see Housing Act 1980, s 89(1) **[para 3.45]**). See also *Roberts v Scarth* (2001) 81 P & CR D16 per Tuckey LJ (eviction 'very upsetting' for 74-year-old).

6 The mere granting of a licence to go on land 'raises no equity against its subsequent revocation' (*Milton v Proctor* (1988) 4 BPR 9654 at 9660 per McHugh JA).

Mode of revocation

4.23   A bare licence is effectively revoked by any words or actions which sufficiently indicate that a permission to be present on land has been withdrawn.[1] The crucial (and primarily factual) issue is whether the language or conduct used is such as to intimate a request to leave the land.[2] A bare licence may be revoked either by the landowner or by some person who enjoys possession or even immediate (albeit temporary) 'control'[3] of the land. A bare licence may also be revoked by some person acting on behalf of the true owner or possessor,[4] but it remains unclear whether a licence can be effectively revoked by one of two or more joint owners acting unilaterally. As a matter of principle, unilateral revocation should be possible,[5] but to allow unilateral revocation may jeopardise the victims of domestic violence.[6] A bare licence is revoked automatically by the death of the licensor or by any transfer of his land.[7]

1   See *Bethune v Heffernan* [1986] VR 417 at 423.
2   See *Gilham v Breidenbach* [1982] RTR 328 at 331E–F, where a Divisional Court declined to interfere with a ruling by magistrates who had decided, after hearing extracts from the *Oxford English Dictionary*, that the phrase 'fuck off' was properly interpreted as 'coarse abuse rather than a request to leave'. Donaldson LJ thought that the 'precise meaning of that observation was supremely a matter for the justices with their knowledge of the local vernacular'. See also *Snook v Mannion* [1982] RTR 321. These matters are obviously better understood in Australia (see *Halliday v Nevill* (1984) 155 CLR 1 at 19, where Brennan J declared himself 'unable to adopt the reasoning' in the English cases in relation to 'vulgar and vigorous injunctions to depart').
3   *Bethune v Heffernan* [1986] VR 417 at 423. See also the reference to revocation by the 'occupier' in *Edwards v Attorney-General* [1986] 2 NZLR 232 at 238–239.
4   In the absence of specific evidence, the authority of a casual visitor or guest to deal on the occupier's behalf with strangers coming on to the premises 'must be quite limited' (*Edwards v Attorney-General* [1986] 2 NZLR 232 at 238–239).
5   See *Robson-Paul v Farrugia* (1969) 20 P & CR 820 at 825; *Sanders v McDonald and Pringle* [1981] CLY 1534; *Annen v Rattee* (1985) 273 EG 503 at 507. To hold otherwise would enable an unwanted intruder to remain on premises against the wishes of the clear majority of those in possession, so long as one occupier can be found who does not object to his presence (see *People v Yutt*, 597 NE2d 208 at 215 (1ll App 3 Dist 1992)).
6   See *R v Thornley* (1980) 72 Cr App R 302 at 305–306 [**para 4.10**].
7   *Terunnanse v Terunnanse* [1968] AC 1086 at 1095G–1096A; *Public Trustee v Bellotti* (1986) 4 BPR 9196 at 9203; *Chicago and North Western Trans Co v City of Winthrop*, 257 NW2d 302 at 304 (1977). Revocation in these circumstances is the inevitable consequence of the highly personal nature of the bare licence.

REASONABLE NOTICE OF TERMINATION

4.24   Both common law and equity recognise that licensees must be protected against the utterly peremptory cancellation of their permission to be present on land.[1] This protection is reinforced, in the case of premises used for residential occupation, by the right to respect for the home which is guaranteed by the European Convention on Human Rights.[2] The generally accepted view is that all licences (whether bare or contractual) are terminable only by the giving of 'reasonable' advance notice.[3] In other words, 'a licensee whose licence is revocable is entitled to reasonable notice of revocation'[4] and the licence itself does not terminate until the expiration of a 'reasonable' period of time following the announcement of the revocation.⁵ This period of reasonable notice of termination is often followed by an extra period of grace which 'supervenes after the licence has terminated' and is intended to 'enable the former licensee to adjust himself to the new situation by vacating the premises.'⁶

1 In principle, the same rules in respect of revocation apply to both bare and contractual licences (see *Winter Garden Theatre (London) Ltd v Millennium Productions Ltd* [1948] AC 173 at 204 per Lord MacDermott), save for the fact that the revocation of a contractual licence is commonly restricted by the express or implied terms of the relevant contract [**para 4.82**]. See *Parker v Parker* [2003] EWHC 1846 (Ch) at [276] per Lewison J (no 'bright line difference' in modern law between a contractual licence and a consensual (i e bare) licence).

2 ECHR Art 8(1) [**para 2.60**]. See *Parker v Parker* [2003] EWHC 1846 (Ch) at [276] per Lewison J.

3 For an isolated voice to the contrary, see *Winter Garden Theatre (London) Ltd v Millennium Productions Ltd* [1948] AC 173 at 196 per Lord Porter (who was, nevertheless, prepared to allow a 'reasonable' time following the termination of the licence for the licensee to vacate the premises). See also J Hill, 'The Termination of Bare Licences' [2001] CLJ 89.

4 *Canadian Pacific Railway Co v The King* [1931] AC 414 at 432 per Lord Russell of Killowen. See similarly *Mellor v Watkins* (1874) LR 9 QB 400 at 405–406 per Blackburn J; *White v Blackmore* [1972] 2 QB 651 at 670A per Buckley LJ; *Parker v Parker* [2003] EWHC 1846 (Ch) at [271] per Lewison J.

5 See *Winter Garden Theatre (London) Ltd v Millennium Productions Ltd* [1948] AC 173 at 199–201 per Lord Uthwatt.

6 *Winter Garden Theatre (London) Ltd v Millennium Productions Ltd* [1948] AC 173 at 204 per Lord MacDermott. See likewise *Cowell v Rosehill Racecourse Co Ltd* (1937) 56 CLR 605 at 631 per Dixon J; *Parker v Parker* [2003] EWHC 1846 (Ch) at [282]. (Much of the confusion in the case law results from a judicial tendency to conflate the requisite period of reasonable notice and the immediately following period of 'packing up' time.)

Duration of 'reasonable' notice

4.25 The definition of 'reasonable' advance notice of termination clearly depends on all the circumstances of each case.¹

1 *Canadian Pacific Railway Co v The King* [1931] AC 414 at 432 per Lord Russell of Killowen.

The casual visitor

4.26 The licence of the average casual visitor – whether a party invitee or a travelling salesman – is terminable 'brevi manu at the will of the licensor' (i e with immediate effect).¹ In such an instance the period of notice regarded by the common law as 'reasonable' is minimal to the point of non-existence.² The licence can be withdrawn by summary communication on the spot and the unwanted visitor can be expected to leave the premises virtually instantly.

1 *Canadian Pacific Railway Co v The King* [1931] AC 414 at 432 per Lord Russell of Killowen. See also *Robson v Hallett* [1967] 2 QB 939 at 954C–D; *R v Doncaster MBC, ex p Braim* (1989) 57 P & CR 1 at 15.

2 *Robson v Hallett* [1967] 2 QB 939 at 952G–953A per Lord Parker CJ ('a very short time'). See

also *Winter Garden Theatre (London) Ltd v Millennium Productions Ltd* [1948] AC 173 at 205, where Lord MacDermott provided more than a hint that a 'bare and unqualified licence' can be 'withdrawn instanter'.

Family and other purposive arrangements

4.27 In other circumstances the duration of 'reasonable' notice may require to be inferred from the practicalities of the case. Thus the reasonableness of notice of termination of a bare licence enjoyed under a 'family arrangement'[1] is governed largely by the difficulty involved in finding alternative accommodation.[2] Here a 'reasonable' period may be measured in months or perhaps even in years.[3] In some contexts the definition of 'reasonable' time may even be influenced by the principle 'that he who sows should be allowed to reap',[4] with the result, for example, that notice to terminate a gratuitous sheep grazing licence should not expire until the end of a four week 'risk period' after lambing time.[5]

1   [**Para 4.15**].
2   Compare *Imperial Oil Ltd v Young* (1996) 65 ACWS 3d 269 (60 days to end parking privilege).
3   See eg *E & L Berg Homes Ltd v Grey* (1980) 253 EG 473 at 477 (one year); *Parker v Parker* [2003] EWHC 1846 (Ch) at [286]–[287] (two years). See also *Hannaford v Selby* (1976) 239 EG 811 at 813 (six months allowed).
4   This is a phrase borrowed, in the licence context, from *Winter Garden Theatre (London) Ltd v Millennium Productions Ltd* [1948] AC 173 at 199 per Lord Uthwatt.
5   *Elders Rural Finance Ltd v Westpac Banking Corporation* (1988) 4 BPR 9383 at 9388 per Young J.

Licences involving 'interests of public concern'

4.28 The common law draws a distinction between those forms of licensed user which are 'an entirely personal matter' and those whose revocation involves 'interests of public concern' or the 'disruption of [some] public service.'[1] Licences of the latter kind, particularly where they implicate the licensee in commercial obligations towards third parties, require to be terminated by the giving of much more substantial notice than is appropriate where the exercise of a licence 'involves nothing beyond'[2] and where, accordingly, the requirements of due notice are nugatory. In circumstances involving some element of 'public service' or 'public concern', reasonable notice may well extend to a period of several years.[3]

1   *Governing Body of Henrietta Barnett School v Hampstead Garden Suburb Institute* (1995) 93 LGR 470 at 509, 511 per Carnwath J (bare licence enjoyed by voluntary aided school). See, however, *Parker v Parker* [2003] EWHC 1846 (Ch) at [279] per Lewison J.
2   See *Canadian Pacific Railway Co v The King* [1931] AC 414 at 432 per Lord Russell of Killowen.
3   See eg *Governing Body of Henrietta Barnett School v Hampstead Garden Suburb Institute* (1995) 93 LGR 470 at 511–513 (2 years and 3 months for termination of licence to use school premises).

Effect of failure to give reasonable notice

4.29   A licensor's failure to give reasonable notice of termination of a licence does not automatically invalidate the act of termination itself.[1] The courts are more likely to hold that any deficiency in the matter of notice can be cured if, in fact, the licensee was allowed more time than was actually specified in the notice to vacate the land. In effect, a notice which falls short of that which would be 'reasonable' does not operate to determine the licence until a 'reasonable' time has elapsed.[2]

1   It has been suggested, however, that a failure to give reasonable notice is ineffective to terminate a licence which provides for 'an important public service' (see *Canadian Pacific Railway Co v The King* [1931] AC 414 at 432–433; *Governing Body of Henrietta Barnett School v Hampstead Garden Suburb Institute* (1995) 93 LGR 470 at 508–511). Compare also *Parker v Parker* [2003] EWHC 1846 (Ch) at [288], where Lewison J held that an insufficient notice of termination of a contractual licence (to occupy a castle) was simply ineffectual.

2   *Minister of Health v Bellotti* [1944] KB 298 at 308–309 (inadequate notice rendered sufficient by date of possession proceedings); *Ganandran v Cyma Petroleum* (Unreported, Court of Appeal, 15 October 1993) per Evans LJ.

An extra 'period of grace'

4.30   Although a bare licence is terminated on the expiration of a reasonable notice of revocation, the licensee is not immediately converted into a trespasser.[1] The former licensee is now obliged to get off the land 'by the most appropriate route for doing so ... [and] with reasonable expedition',[2] but, as a rule of law, he is afforded a 'reasonable period of grace'[3] for this purpose.[4]

1   *Vaughan v Vaughan* [1953] 1 QB 762 at 766 per Evershed MR.
2   *Robson v Hallett* [1967] 2 QB 939 at 954D per Diplock LJ.
3   *Elders Rural Finance Ltd v Westpac Banking Corporation* (1988) 4 BPR 9383 at 9388 per Young J.
4   *Winter Garden Theatre (London) Ltd v Millennium Productions Ltd* [1948] AC 173 at 204–208 per Lord MacDermott (Viscount Simon and Lord Simonds concurring at 191, 208).

Temporary suspension of trespasser status

4.31   Although any licence of future access has clearly been abrogated, the former licensee 'will not be considered a trespasser before he has had a reasonable time in which to vacate the premises.'[1] If, however, he fails to act 'with all reasonable speed',[2] he reverts to the status of a trespasser[3] and the withdrawal of the licence becomes enforceable against him.[4] The 'period of grace' is intended merely to give him a reasonable time to remove himself and not to enable him to complete the originally contemplated purpose of his licence.[5]

1   *Winter Garden Theatre (London) Ltd v Millennium Productions Ltd* [1948] AC 173 at 204 per Lord MacDermott (see similarly Viscount Simon at 188–189). See also *Minister of Health v Bellotti* [1944] KB 298 at 305–306; *Soames-Forsythe Properties Ltd v Tesco Stores Ltd* [1991]

EGCS 22; *Cowell v Rosehill Racecourse Co Ltd* (1937) 56 CLR 605 at 631 per Dixon J; *Sammons v American Automobile Association*, 912 P2d 1103 at 1106 (1996).

2   *Lambert v Roberts* [1981] 2 All ER 15 at 19c.

3   See *Warnes v Hedley* (Unreported, Court of Appeal, 31 January 1984).

4   Under a parol licence, the licensee 'has a right to a reasonable time to go off the land after it has been withdrawn before he can be forcibly thrust off it' (*Cornish v Stubbs* (1870) LR 5 CP 334 at 339 per Willes J).

5   The provision of reasonable time following the termination of the licence is not intended 'to prolong the user sanctioned by the licence merely for the benefit and convenience of the licensee' (*Winter Garden Theatre (London) Ltd v Millennium Productions Ltd* [1948] AC 173 at 205 per Lord MacDermott).

Reasonable 'packing up' time

4.32   In the case of a licence which authorises some purpose more complex than that of simple entry upon land, the period of grace allowed to the licensee following termination of his licence is generally known as 'packing up' time.[1] The objective of the law is, quite clearly, to allow the former licensee a 'breathing space',[2] usually in the light of any commercial commitments already undertaken by him,[3] to make 'substituted arrangements'[4] by way of adjustment to the changed circumstances generated by the withdrawal of the licence.[5] The provision of reasonable 'packing up' time is therefore particularly significant in relation to long-term licences whose cancellation raises matters of public, rather than purely private, concern.[6]

1   *Hounslow LBC v Twickenham Garden Developments Ltd* [1971] Ch 233 at 244E per Megarry J. See likewise *Winter Garden Theatre (London) Ltd v Millennium Productions Ltd* [1948] AC 173 at 206 per Lord MacDermott.

2   *Canadian Pacific Railway Co v The King* [1931] AC 414 at 432 per Lord Russell of Killowen.

3   See e g *Winter Garden Theatre (London) Ltd v Millennium Productions Ltd* [1948] AC 173 at 205, where Lord MacDermott referred to 'specialised user involving obligations to third parties or the public' and involving 'considerable expenditure and a host of contractual relationships.' See likewise *Canadian Pacific Railway Co v The King* [1931] AC 414 at 432 per Lord Russell of Killowen (licensee had incurred 'obligations in other directions, which the determination of the licence would disable him from fulfilling').

4   *Canadian Pacific Railway Co v The King* [1931] AC 414 at 432 per Lord Russell of Killowen.

5   See *Winter Garden Theatre (London) Ltd v Millennium Productions Ltd* [1948] AC 173 at 204 per Lord MacDermott. Alternatively, in rare cases, the period of grace may allow the licensee to reap the fruits of such investment as he has made in the licensor's land. See e g *Winter Garden Theatre (London) Ltd v Millennium Productions Ltd* [1948] AC 173 at 196–197 per Lord Porter, 199–200 per Lord Uthwatt (profits from the run of an expensively produced play).

6   See *Governing Body of Henrietta Barnett School v Hampstead Garden Suburb Institute* (1995) 93 LGR 470 at 508 per Carnwath J (voluntary aided school). See likewise *Canadian Pacific Railway Co v The King* [1931] AC 414 at 432, where the Privy Council stressed the importance of reasonable time for organising the relocation of hundreds of miles of telegraph poles and wires elsewhere than on the crown land on which they were no longer welcome.

RIGHTS OF REASONABLE ACCESS TO LAND

4.33   The conventional rules of licence and trespass appear to confirm, as a venerable dogma of the common law, that the legal right to possession of land carries with it a prerogative to determine – no matter how arbitrarily or capriciously – who may enter or remain there.[1] On this basis the possessor is entitled, however intransigently, to deny access even in spite of reasonable offers of payment[2] and, conversely, to permit access only on payment of an unreasonable premium.[3] According to the general principle, the landowner (whether freeholder[4] or leaseholder[5]) simply has an uncontrollable discretion to exclude any unwanted stranger from his land.[6] Some sense of defensible monopoly has always seemed to be an irreducible characteristic of ownership; and the common law, for the most part, has engaged in no subtle gradation of the exclusory powers inherent in ownership and possession.

1   See *Coco v The Queen* (1994) 179 CLR 427 at 435, 438 per Mason CJ, Brennan, Gaudron and McHugh JJ ('a fundamental common law right'). For a review of the common law jurisprudence on the subject, see Gray and Gray, 'Civil Rights, Civil Wrongs and Quasi-Public Space' (1999) 4 EHRLR 46 at 52–55.

2   See e g *Jacque v Steenberg Homes, Inc*, 563 NW2d 154 at 159–160 (Wis 1997).

3   *Anchor Brewhouse Developments Ltd v Berkley House* (*Docklands Developments*) *Ltd* (1987) 38 BLR 82 at 96 per Scott J. See e g *Newbury DC v Russell* (1997) 95 LGR 705 at 715–716, where the Court of Appeal upheld the common law right of a lord of the manor to charge any sum he chose for vehicular access rights across his common land on behalf of residents of homes built on the common (*Times*, 8 March 1997 reported that wayleave charges of up to £50,000 had been obtained from each of some 50 families). This particular form of holdout was eventually remedied by statute (see Countryside and Rights of Way Act 2000, s 68(1)–(3) [**para 8.139**]).

4   See *South Staffordshire Water Co v Sharman* [1896] 2 QB 44 at 46 per Lord Russell of Killowen CJ.

5   See *Street v Mountford* [1985] AC 809 at 816 per Lord Templeman [**para 7.133**].

6   'The right to exclude strangers is an ordinary incident of ownership of land' (*Gerhardy v Brown* (1985) 159 CLR 70 at 150 per Deane J).

4.34   Orthodoxy has thus tended to support a fairly universal facility of peremptory and arbitrary exclusion. But the live question today is whether, across widely differing kinds of location, the same starkly unfettered liberty to withhold or terminate licensed entry is ultimately compatible with fundamental principles of human freedom and dignity. For some the 'arbitrary exclusion' rule merely effectuates an outdated concept of untrammelled proprietary power. In relation to certain kinds of privately held land, it is becoming increasingly clear that a guarantee of public access is so integrally linked with personal autonomy and civic cohesion that the absoluteness of the owner's regulatory prerogative must finally give way.

Locations appropriately governed by an 'arbitrary exclusion' rule

4.35   It is, of course, undeniable that in many sorts of location the inherent revocability of the bare licence still makes perfect sense.

Special status of the home

4.36   In the context of the family home and its immediate environs, the 'arbitrary exclusion' rule has long served a noble purpose. It enabled Coke CJ to declare in *Semayne's Case*[1] that 'the house of every one is to him as his castle and fortress.' In a country without a written constitution, this recognition of territorial sovereignty provided a pillar of personal freedom, creating a vital defence for the citizen against the intrusion of the state.[2] Indeed, all common law-based systems have traditionally accorded the clearest protection to the 'sanctity of a man's home and the privacies of life',[3] a form of guarantee now enshrined in the European Convention on Human Rights.[4] In relation to the domestic residence an unchallengeable and unreviewable discretion to exclude strangers (whether for good reasons or bad) is entirely appropriate.[5] Here the 'arbitrary exclusion' rule plainly conduces towards the more effective protection of 'fundamental' values of privacy and civil liberty.[6]

1   (1604) 5 Co Rep 91a at 91b, 77 ER 194 at 195 [**para 3.20**]. See also *Bl Comm*, Vol IV, p 223.

2   See *Southam v Smout* [1964] 1 QB 308 at 320 for Lord Denning MR's quotation of the well known words of the Earl of Chatham ('The poorest man in his cottage may bid defiance to all the forces of the Crown … the King of England cannot enter'). See also *Robson v Hallett* [1967] 2 QB 939 at 951B–F; *Plenty v Dillon* (1991) 171 CLR 635 at 639 per Mason, Brennan and Toohey JJ.

3   *Boyd v United States*, 116 US 616 at 630, 29 L Ed 746 at 751 (1886) per Justice Bradley, citing *Entick v Carrington* (1765) 19 Howell's State Trials 1029, 2 Wils KB 275, 95 ER 807. In *Hester v United States*, 68 L Ed 898 at 900 (1923), Justice Holmes declared the distinction between the home and 'open fields' to be 'as old as the common law.' See also *Bell v Maryland*, 378 US 226 at 253, 12 L Ed 2d 822 at 873 (1964) per Justice Douglas ('The home … is the essence of privacy'); *Lyons v The Queen* (1985) 14 DLR (4th) 482 at 501 per Estey J ('The inviolable nature of the private dwelling is a basic part of our free society').

4   See ECHR Art 8 (right to respect for 'private and family life' and the 'home') [**para 2.60**].

5   '[D]omus sua cuique est tutissimum refugium' (*Semayne's Case* (1604) 5 Co Rep 91a at 91b, 77 ER 194 at 195). See likewise *People v Wolf*, 312 NYS2d 721 at 723 (1970); *Forbes v New South Wales Trotting Club Ltd* (1979) 143 CLR 242 at 274 per Murphy J; *Flack v National Crime Authority* (1997) 150 ALR 153 at 163.

6   See *Morris v Beardmore* [1981] AC 446 at 463F–464E per Lord Scarman; *TCN Channel Nine Pty Ltd v Anning* (2002) 54 NSWLR 333 at [52] per Spigelman CJ.

Other highly protected locations

4.37   A rule of arbitrary exclusion also seems appropriate, largely for reasons of public safety and operational convenience, in relation to many other locations. Case law across the common law world confirms, for instance, that bare licences for entry (whether granted expressly or impliedly) are normally revocable at will in relation to such premises as small business establishments and office workplaces, banks, churches, hospitals, clinics and nursing homes.[1] All of these locations comprise zones of 'private autonomy'[2] in which rights of self-determination preclude or outweigh general claims of unfettered access by strangers.[3] Persons in possession of such areas have a paramount claim to turn back unwelcome visitors by simple fiat or demand.[4]

1   See eg *Diamond v Bland*, 113 Cal Rptr 468 at 478 (1974) per Justice Mosk ('modest retail establishment'); *Love-Lee v Cameron of Lochiel* 1991 SCLR 61 at 68A–B (sub-post office); *Albertson's Inc v Young*, 131 Cal Rptr 2d 721 at 733–734 (2003) (single-use grocery store); *Bank of Stockton v Church of Soldiers of the Cross of Christ of the State of California*, 52 Cal Rptr 2d 429 (1996) (bank); *Canterbury MC v Moslem Alawy Society Ltd* (1985) 1 NSWLR 525 at 541B–C; *Church of Christ in Hollywood v Superior Court*, 121 Cal Rptr 2d 810 at 813,

819 (2002) (church); *Darcey v Pre-Term Foundation Clinic* [1983] 2 NSWLR 497 (abortion clinic); *Cape Cod Nursing Home Council v Rambling Rose Rest Home*, 667 F2d 238 at 241–242 (1981) (nursing home). For further detail, see Gray and Gray, (1999) 4 EHRLR 46 at 91–93.

2   *Johnson v Tait*, 774 P2d 185 at 190 (1989) (Supreme Court of Alaska).

3   This must be all the more so where the premises in question are secured and patrolled in such a way as to preclude general public access (see e g *Golden Gateway Center v Golden Gateway Tenants Assn*, 111 Cal Rptr 2d 336 at 352 (2001) (retail and residential apartment complex)).

4   This may not mean, however, that the courts will necessarily restrain publication of what has been seen or filmed on the premises during the trespasser's visit (see e g *Australian Broadcasting Corpn v Lenah Game Meats Pty Ltd* (2001) 208 CLR 199 at [44]–[55]). See analogously *Bradley v Wingnut Films Ltd* [1993] 1 NZLR 415 at 429–430.

The emergence of a rule of 'reasonable access'

4.38   It is nevertheless beginning to be acknowledged today that the uncontrolled exercise of potentially capricious powers of exclusion sometimes results in a denial of certain basic values intrinsic to the idea of a democratic community.[1] In a modern urban environment, where recreational, associational and expressional space is at a premium, monolithic privileges of arbitrary exclusion are no longer wholly tenable.[2] In respect of certain kinds of location it now seems increasingly unacceptable that licences for entry should be terminable without a showing of good cause. Several common law jurisdictions have come to regard it as extraordinary that a venerable doctrine of possessory control, once invoked to uphold the individual's immunity from state interference, should today be deployed in support of an unconstrained power of arbitrary exclusion from areas which, through general invitation, have been opened up to public use.[3] In relation to such land – often called 'quasi-public' land – the old common law rule of 'arbitrary exclusion' is being steadily displaced by a rule of 'reasonable access'.[4] However, this rule of reasonableness cuts both ways: it provides a guarantee of access to quasi-public premises during good (ie reasonable) behaviour, but also affords a clear ground for the exclusion of unreasonable users.[5]

1   See e g *CIN Properties Ltd v Rawlins* [1995] 2 EGLR 130 **[para 4.56]**. For recent emphasis of the importance of human dignity and human freedom, see *Ghaidan v Godin-Mendoza* [2004] 3 WLR 113 at [132] per Baroness Hale of Richmond.

2   See Gray and Gray, 'The idea of property in land', in Bright and Dewar (ed), *Law and Land: Themes and Perspectives* (Clarendon Press, Oxford, 1998), pp 38–39.

3   See *Harrison v Carswell* (1975) 62 DLR (3d) 68 at 73 per Laskin CJC.

4   An influential lead has been taken by the courts of New Jersey, which, without reliance upon any constitutional guarantee, have simply announced that the common law no longer entitles the owner of quasi-public premises arbitrarily 'to exclude anyone at all for any reason' (*Uston v Resorts International Hotel Inc*, 445 A2d 370 at 373 (NJ 1982)). See also *Green Party of New Jersey v Hartz Mountain Industries, Inc*, 752 A2d 315 at 330–331 (2000). A similar view is now beginning to emerge in New Zealand (see *Sky City Auckland Ltd v Wu* [2002] 3 NZLR 621 at [33] per Blanchard and Anderson JJ).

5   It has always been the case that privileged entry upon quasi-public premises is therefore terminated by any misbehaviour or unlawful activity on the part of the entrant (see e g *R v Ivens* (1835) 7 C & P 213 at 219, 173 ER 94 at 96–97; *Jencks v Coleman* (1835) 13 Fed Cas 442 at 443–444; *Markham v Brown* (1837) 8 NH 523, 31 Am Dec 209 at 210; *Hall v State of Delaware* (1844) 4 Harr 132 at 145). See also *Harrison v Carswell* (1975) 62 DLR (3d) 68 at 74 per Laskin CJC.

4.39   Several factors help to explain why the law of the arbitrarily terminable licence is being qualified by a rule of 'reasonable access'.

Modern distaste for irrationality

4.40   Nowadays the exercise of unchallengeable power runs entirely counter to the collective expectation of rationality engendered by modern processes of judicial review.[1] There exists no unbridgeable gulf between public and private law; and the extended legal surveillance of public decision-making renders it inevitable that comparable controls should gradually infiltrate the supposedly private domain of property.[2] It simply cannot be the case, for instance, that the private owner of a large shopping centre is today legally entitled to exclude someone merely 'for wearing a green hat or a paisley tie' or because he or she has 'blond hair, or ... is from Pennsylvania.'[3] As Laskin CJC indicated in his seminal dissent in *Harrison v Carswell*,[4] the common law cannot be 'so devoid of reason as to tolerate this kind of whimsy.'[5] For this reason the courts of the common law world are slowly beginning to impose some requirement of due process on the exercise of proprietary powers which affect community interests.

1   Gray and Gray, 'Private Property and Public Propriety', in J McLean (ed), *Property and the Constitution* (Hart Publishing 1999), pp 16–17. See *Ghaidan v Godin-Mendoza* [2004] 3 WLR 113 at [132] per Baroness Hale of Richmond ('[p]ower must not be exercised arbitrarily', for this is 'the reverse of the rational behaviour we now expect of government and the state').

2   Many argue today that reasoned communication provides a core element in the fair treatment of one's fellow citizens (see eg E L Pincoffs, 'Due Process, Fraternity, and a Kantian Injunction', in J R Pennock and J W Chapman (ed), *Due Process* (Nomos XVIII, New York 1977), p 172).

3   *Brooks v Chicago Downs Association, Inc*, 791 F2d 512 at 514, 518 (1986). See also *Harrison v Carswell* (1975) 62 DLR (3d) 68 at 70 per Laskin CJC ('an extravagant position'); *Kreimer v Bureau of Police for Town of Morristown*, 765 F Supp 181 at 183 (DNJ 1991) ('enforcement [of library exclusion policy] cannot be left to the whim or personal vagaries of the persons in charge').

4   (1975) 62 DLR (3d) 68 at 74.

5   Laskin CJC indicated that the shopping mall issue pointed to the need to 'search for an appropriate legal framework for new social facts which show up the inaptness of an old doctrine developed upon a completely different social foundation.'

Social choices

4.41   A central issue of modern quasi-public property jurisprudence concerns the tension between inclusive and exclusive strategies of civic design.[1] Over the next few decades large outcomes will turn on whether, in certain specialised contexts, the historic exclusory function of property is refashioned to endorse a more integrative vision of social relationships. The choice lies between a culture of exclusion (driven by motivations of fear and insecurity) and a culture of inclusion (driven by motivations of social justice and equal opportunity).[2] In an age overshadowed by terrorist threat and the need for situational crime prevention, the 'inclusion/exclusion' question comprises one of the most difficult problems of social philosophy.[3] For some the exercise of heightened control over access to all land simply represents the price to be paid for the greater security of the vast majority of the population. Yet in many contexts there is evidence that a subliminal ethic of social co-operation – an expanded concept of civic neighbourhood – is beginning to promote, in a quite contrary direction, various entitlements of reasonable access to certain kinds of land.[4]

1   See A Grear, 'A tale of the land, the insider, the outsider and human rights', (2003) 23 Legal Studies 33.
2   See eg L J Moran and B Skeggs, 'The property of safety', 23 JSWFL 379 (2001).
3   A critical issue, only just beginning to attract interest in this country, concerns the legal status of the gated community. For a preview of some of the problems thrown up by the phenomenon of exclusionary residential structures, see Gray and Gray, 'Private Property and Public Propriety', in J McLean (ed), *Property and the Constitution* (Hart Publishing 1999), pp 31–36.
4   See Gray and Gray, 'The rhetoric of realty', in J Getzler (ed), *Rationalizing Property, Equity and Trusts: Essays in Honour of Edward Burn* (Butterworths 2003), pp 259–265.

Privatisation of public space

4.42   Modifications of the principle of arbitrarily revocable licence have been rendered virtually inevitable by the changing nature of modern urban space.[1] The privatisation of much public space – usually in the form of corporate rejuvenation of town centres – has equipped a generation of property developers with unprecedented power to control the exercise of the citizen's essential freedoms of movement, assembly, association and speech. Large urban areas are now owned and policed by private enterprise.[2] The social and commercial life of the ordinary citizen is increasingly conducted on 'mass private property'[3] and in such locations the protection of property begins to coalesce with the preservation of public order.[4] Accordingly, protected rights of reasonable civic access assume a new significance precisely because the arbitrary exercise of uncontrolled exclusory power by the owners of quasi-public space impacts severely upon the enjoyment of essential civil liberties.[5] As Murphy J once remarked in the High Court of Australia, '[t]he distinction between public power and private power is not clear-cut and one may shade into the other.'[6]

1   '[T]he public common has largely ceased to exist' (*Green Party of New Jersey v Hartz Mountain Industries, Inc*, 752 A2d 315 at 328 (2000) (Supreme Court of New Jersey)).
2   See *Chicago Acorn, SEIU Local No 880 v Metropolitan Pier and Exposition Authority*, 150 F3d 695 at 704 (1998) per Chief Judge Posner. See also P Spearritt, 'The commercialisation of public space', in Patrick Troy (ed), *Equity, Environment, Efficiency* (Melbourne UP 2000), p 81.
3   See C D Shearing and P C Stenning, 'Private Security: Implications for Social Control', 30 Social Problems 493 at 496 (1982–83).
4   The privatisation of space has effectively 'relocate[d] the power to define and maintain order … from the state to property developers' (M Davis, 'Less Mickey Mouse, More Dirty Harry: Property, Policing and the Modern Metropolis', 5(2) Polemic 63 at 64 (1994)). See also Andrew von Hirsch and Clifford D Shearing, 'Exclusion from Public Space', in A von Hirsch, D Garland and A Wakefield (ed), *Ethical and Social Perspectives on Situational Crime Prevention* (Hart 2000), pp 77–96.
5   Shearing and Stenning (30 Social Problems 493 (1982–83)) see private policing of 'mass private property' as creative of a new sovereign force, distinct from the state, which dispenses a species of private justice accountable not to the citizen, but only to corporate capital. See also

M Davis, 'Fortress Los Angeles: The Militarization of Urban Space', in M Sorkin (ed), *Variations on a Theme Park: The New American City and the End of Public Space* (Hill and Wang, New York 1992), p 158.

6   *Gerhardy v Brown* (1985) 159 CLR 70 at 107.

QUASI-PUBLIC LAND

4.43   The conclusion which emerges from the foregoing analysis is that there are today certain categories of land whose use is sufficiently coloured by a public interest that access to and exclusion from such areas cannot ultimately be relegated to the unchallengeable discretion of the owner or possessor.[1] In relation to such land exclusory power has a public or civic dimension which requires that privileges of access be terminable only on grounds which are objectively reasonable and rationally defensible.[2]

1   This does not mean, however, that the owner or possessor of such premises is disabled, in protection of its own interests, from imposing reasonable and 'narowly tailored' limitations of time, place and manner on the exercise of quasi-public rights of access (see *Costco Companies, Inc v Gallant*, 117 Cal Rptr 2d 344 at 353–354 (2002)).

2   See *R v Asante-Mensah* (1996) 31 WCB 2d 84 at [150] ('Land, of a public function and character, presumptively clothes persons with the privilege and licence of attendance. The absolute right of exclusion, retained to the private citizen, ... is whittled away').

The civic commons

4.44   The sorts of location most closely affected by the 'reasonable access' rule comprise areas which, although privately owned, perform a vital function in shaping the political and social ecology of modern urban space. These locations facilitate humanising and civilising contacts between fellow citizens, a role which draws heightened significance from the contemporary emphasis on freedom of communication[1] and the importance of a 'free trade in ideas.'[2]

1   See *The Queen in Right of Canada v Committee for the Commonwealth of Canada* (1991) 77 DLR (4th) 385 at 449d–f per Justice McLachlin; *Appleby and Others v United Kingdom* (2003) 37 EHRR 783 at [39] **[para 4.58]**.

2   *Abrams v United States*, 250 US 616 at 630, 63 L Ed 1173 at 1180 (1919) per Justice Holmes. See similarly *Marsh v Alabama*, 326 US 501 at 510, 90 L Ed 265 at 270 (1946) per Justice Frankfurter. See Gray, 'Property in Thin Air', [1991] CLJ 252 at 286.

Pedestrian democracy

4.45   The social goods of citizenship increasingly include intangible 'quality of life' benefits derived from access to certain urban fora designed for recreational, educational, cultural and associational use. Examples include the communal leisure areas or parks (often situated beside water), sports venues, exhibition galleries, libraries, museums, art complexes, transport facilities and vast shopping precincts which are so much part of the modern inner city landscape.[1] Such premises are often described as a 'civic commons' in which the enjoyment of 'social capital', the attainment of 'civic sociability'[2] and the satisfaction of the sophisticated demands of the modern consumer are vitally dependent on a new form of 'pedestrian democracy'.[3] The freedom to go where one wills and to interact as one wishes provides the foundation of an integrative sense of community or neighbourhood as well as the essential basis of an egalitarian society.[4] But, while the civic commons may be all about the freedom to associate, communicate and participate, the core component of private property is a countervailing impulse to supervise, control and exclude.[5]

1   For reference to the way in which the 'cathedrals of private commerce' have evolved into civic and social fora of large public significance, see Gray and Gray, (1999) 4 EHRLR 46 at 56.

2   See F I Michelman, 'The Common Law Baseline and Restitution for the Lost Commons: A Reply to Professor Epstein', 64 U Chi L Rev 57 at 61 (1997).

3   See Gray and Gray, 'Private Property and Public Propriety', in J McLean (ed), *Property and the Constitution* (Hart Publishing 1999), pp 20–22.

4   See J Frug, 'The Geography of Community' 48 Stan L Rev 1047 at 1050, 1062–1064 (1996). The exercise of arbitrary power tends to accentuate the social exclusion of the marginalised and disadvantaged (P Williams, 'Spirit-Murdering the Messenger: The Discourse of Finger-pointing as the Law's Response to Racism', 42 U Miami L Rev 127 at 129 (1987)). See also R White and A Sutton, 'Crime prevention, urban space and social exclusion' 31(1) Australian and New Zealand Journal of Sociology 82 at 90 (1995); R White, 'No-Go in the Fortress City: Young People, Inequality and Space' 14(1) Urban Policy and Research 37 (1996).

5   There is an awkward tension between the civic tolerance of diversity – 'the experience of otherness' – and zero tolerance of adventitious criminal or anti-social behaviour in quasi-public places. Situational crime prevention relies heavily on potentially capricious strategies of exclusion which operate through intensive access controls, entry screening, proactive surveil-lance techniques and the pre-emptive profiling of perceived cases of risk (see e g R V Clarke, 'Situational Crime Prevention', in M Tonry and D Farrington (ed), *Building a Safer Society. Crime and Justice: A Review of Research* (University of Chicago Press 1995), p 91). Civil liberty and environmental criminology exist in uneasy relationship with each other: situational crime prevention is not designed to be socially integrative.

Public trust

4.46   A certain historical continuity is present, moreover, in the fact that many 'quasi-public' locations are simply 'the functional equivalent of the city streets, squares and parks of earlier days',[1] areas which have long been viewed, in the common law tradition, as affected by some public trust guaranteeing open access for all.[2] The public dimension of such space is intensified where the private landowner's functions comprise a degree of governance resembling state power[3] or where the financial interdependence between the landowner and the state is so marked as to indicate the 'symbiotic'[4] or 'hybrid'[5] nature of the enterprise conducted on the land.[6]

1   *City of Jamestown v Beneda* 477 NW2d 830 at 837–838 (ND 1991). See likewise *The Queen in Right of Canada v Committee for the Commonwealth of Canada* (1991) 77 DLR (4th) 385 at 396h per Lamer CJC, 430g per L'Heureux-Dubé J, 459g per McLachlin J (airport terminal concourse).

2   **[Para 5.3]**. See *Hague v Committee for Industrial Organization*, 307 US 496 at 515, 83 L Ed 1423 at 1436 (1939) per Justice Roberts; *The Queen in Right of Canada v Committee for the Commonwealth of Canada* (1991) 77 DLR (4th) 385 at 393d per Lamer CJC ('quasi-fiduciary' land); *First Unitarian Church of Salt Lake City v Salt Lake City Corp*, 308 F 3d 1114 at 1123

(2002). See also *Bathurst CC v PWC Properties Pty Ltd* (1998) 195 CLR 566 at 582–587, for the proposition that rights of public access to local government-owned land may sometimes be protected by a trust for public purposes (publicly accessible free car park).

3   See eg *Marsh v Alabama*, 326 US 501, 90 L Ed 265 (1946), where the private owner of 'company town' was deemed to stand 'in the shoes of the State' (*Lloyd Corp, Ltd v Tanner*, 407 US 551 at 569, 33 L Ed 2d 131 at 143 (1972) per Justice Powell). The spectre of the company town has returned to England (see eg *Appleby v United Kingdom* (2003) 37 EHRR 783; *R (Beresford) v Sunderland CC* [2004] 1 AC 889) [paras **4.58, 5.44**].

4   See *Citizens To End Animal Suffering And Exploitation, Inc v Faneuil Hall Marketplace, Inc*, 745 F Supp 65 at 74 (D Mass 1990). Compare, however, *State v Wicklund*, 589 NW2d 793 at 801–802 (Minn 1999).

5   See *Bock v Westminster Mall Co*, 819 P2d 55 at 60 (Colo 1991) (refutation of the 'simplistic division of the universe into public and private spheres').

6   Much urban development in England is now facilitated by public-private partnerships and involves the preferential leasing of local authority-owned land for the purpose of revitalising downtown areas for general community benefit (see eg *CIN Properties Ltd v Rawlins* [1995] 2 EGLR 130 (125 year lease of shopping mall premises)).

Private property affected by a public interest

4.47   The recognition that some kinds of land have a 'quasi-public' quality is, in fact, nothing new. The common law tradition has always accepted[1] that certain kinds of privately held land are not controlled by arbitrary principles of trespass law but by a more open-ended rule of reasonable public access.[2] It was a common theme in the Anglo-American jurisprudence of the 19th and early 20th centuries that private property became 'clothed with a public interest' when used in such manner as to make it 'of public consequence' and 'affect the community at large.'[3] Common law courts, particularly in the United States, developed an explicit jurisprudence of 'quasi-public' property precisely for the purpose of expressing the admixture of socially purposive function inherent in the exercise of certain species of proprietary power. The designation of 'quasi-public' status came, in particular, to identify those zones of commercial activity which were neither wholly public nor wholly private in character, but where regulatory control was needed to constrain aggregations of power over the supply of essential utilities under trading conditions of market dominance. In these areas private power, as it shades into public power,[4] must be exercised 'bona fide ... and with due regard to the persons affected by its exercise.'[5]

1   See Gray and Gray, 'Civil Rights, Civil Wrongs and Quasi-Public Space' (1999) 4 EHRLR 46 at 82–86.

2   It was Hale CJ who pointed out three centuries ago that private property, when 'affected with a public interest ... ceases to be *juris privati* only' (Hale, *De Portibus Maris*, 1 Harg L Tr 78).

3   *Munn v Illinois*, 94 US 113 at 126, 24 L Ed 77 at 84 (1877) per Chief Justice Waite. For earlier references to the same theme, see *Allnutt v Inglis* (1810) 12 East 527 at 542, 104 ER 206 at 212 per Le Blanc J; *Mobile v Yuille* (1841) 3 Ala (NS) 140, 36 Am Dec 441 at 444.

4   See *Gerhardy v Brown* (1985) 159 CLR 70 at 107 per Murphy J.

5   *Forbes v New South Wales Trotting Club Ltd* (1979) 143 CLR 242 at 275 per Murphy J.

The common callings doctrine

4.48   Perhaps the foremost historic demonstration of such control arose in the case of the common innkeeper who, in the absence of some reasonable ground of refusal,[1] has long been bound by the common law and custom of the realm to receive and provide lodging in his inn for all comers who are travellers. It is recognised in all common law jurisdictions that 'the business of an innkeeper is of a quasi public character, invested with many privileges, and burdened with correspondingly great responsibilities.'[2] Accordingly the premises of the inn-keeper (as indeed other premises used in pursuit of a public or common calling[3]) have been subjected from time immemorial to special rules which severely curtail the operator's freedom to turn away strangers arbitrarily and without good reason.[4]

1   *Hawthorn v Hammond* (1844) 1 Car & K 404 at 407, 174 ER 867 at 869. See *Bl Comm*, Vol III, pp 164, 212.
2   *De Wolf v Ford*, 86 NE 527 at 529 (1908) per Werner J. For further reference to the 'quasi-public' character of the innkeeper, see *Slaughter v Commonwealth* (1856) 54 Va 767 at 777; *Civil Rights Cases*, 109 US 3, 27 L Ed 835 at 849 (1883) per Justice Harlan.
3   Similar rules of reasonable access extended to other common callings such as those of the carrier, the ferryman and the farrier. Blackstone was also prepared to regard the requirement of reasonable access (and reasoned denial of access) as applying to places of public accommodation beyond the range of the traditionally common callings (see *Bl Comm*, Vol III, p 164; *Bell v Maryland*, 378 US 226 at 297 (n 17), 12 L Ed 2d 822 at 839 (1964) per Justice Goldberg). See also *Streeter v Brogan*, 274 A2d 312 at 315–317 (1971) per Furman J (common callings rule applied to operator of gasoline service station); *Sammons v American Automobile Association*, 912 P2d 1103 at 1105–1106 (Wyo 1996).
4   *R v Ivens* (1835) 7 C & P 213 at 219, 173 ER 94 at 96–97 per Coleridge J. See also *Lane v Cotton* (1701) 12 Mod 472 at 483–485, 88 ER 1458 at 1464–1465 per Holt CJ; *Markham v Brown* (1837) 8 NH 523, 31 Am Dec 209 at 210 and generally Gray and Gray, (1999) 4 EHRLR 46 at 83–84.

Private premises opened up by general invitation to the public

4.49   In developments originating in the United States[1] and Canada,[2] the term 'quasi-public' has been applied to describe areas of land which, although nominally subject to private ownership, have been so opened up to public use, through general or unrestricted invitation, that they can no longer be regarded as purely private zones.[3] The liberality of the implied dedication to public resort, particularly if coupled with the furtherance of the owner's economic interests, causes the land to lose its exclusively private quality[4] and become instead 'private property having an essential public character.'[5] In such circumstances the landowner 'should not defeat the reasonable expectation of an individual who wishes to accept the invitation by excluding him quite arbitrarily and capriciously.'[6] Many overseas jurisdictions have therefore applied a rule of reasonable public access to such areas as shopping plazas,[7] large retail outlets,[8] petrol service stations,[9] libraries[10] and educational establishments,[11] transport facilities,[12] airport concourses,[13] sports venues[14] and other fora for recreation.[15] Indeed in many of these locations the basis of the citizen's entitlement of access may even be explained in contractual terms. The operator of the facility in question receives the commercially valuable benefit of public visitation in return for an implied promise that the visitor will not be excluded unreasonably or arbitrarily.[16] Seen in this way, the entitlement of the general public verges upon a right, under contractual licence, to have access to commercial premises during good behaviour.

1   See *Central Hardware Co v National Labor Relations Board*, 407 US 539 at 547, 33 L Ed 2d 122 at 128 (1972) per Justice Powell.

2   See *Harrison v Carswell* (1976) 62 DLR (3d) 68 at 73 per Laskin CJC (dissenting).

3   Even the most sceptical observers have recognised the way in which recent thinking 'blurs the line between the public and nonpublic forum' (*Chicago Acorn, SEIU Local No 880 v Metropolitan Pier and Exposition Authority*, 150 F3d 695 at 703 (1998) per Chief Judge Posner). See likewise *Dalury v S-K-I, Ltd*, 670 A2d 795 at 799–800 (Vt 1995); *Australian Broadcasting Corpn v Lenah Game Meats Pty Ltd* (2001) 208 CLR 199 at [42] per Gleeson CJ.

4   In determining under what circumstances private property can be 'treated as though it were public', Justice Black of the United States Supreme Court famously declared that '[t]he more an owner, for his advantage, opens up his property for use by the public in general, the more do his rights become circumscribed by the statutory and constitutional rights of those who use it' (*Marsh v Alabama*, 326 US 501 at 506, 90 L Ed 265 at 268 (1946)). See also *Matthews v Bay Head Improvement Association*, 471 A2d 355 at 366 (NJ 1984).

5   *R v Layton* (1988) 38 CCC (3d) 550 at 568. For similar reference to private property which has assumed 'the functional attributes of public property devoted to public use', see *Central Hardware Co v National Labor Relations Board*, 407 US 539 at 547, 33 L Ed 2d 122 at 128 (1972) per Powell J.

6   *Forbes v New South Wales Trotting Club Ltd* (1979) 143 CLR 242 at 269 per Gibbs J (see also Murphy J at 275). See e g *Wu v Sky City Auckland Ltd* [2002] NZAR 441 at [16]–[20], where a casino, by reason of 'holding itself out to the public as being willing to serve all', was not entitled at common law to exclude a successful gambler.

7   *New Jersey Coalition Against War in the Middle East v JMB Realty Corporation*, 650 A2d 757 at 776–777 (NJ 1994); *Green Party of New Jersey v Hartz Mountain Industries, Inc*, 752 A2d 315 at 328–329 (2000).

8   *Stranahan v Fred Meyer, Inc*, 958 P2d 854 at 863–866 (1998); *National Labor Relations Board v Calkins*, 187 F3d 1080 at 1091–1092 (9th Cir 1999).

9   *Streeter v Brogan*, 274 A2d 312 at 315–317 (1971).

10   *Kreimer v Bureau of Police for Town of Morristown*, 958 F2d 1242 at 1255 (3rd Cir 1992).

11   *State v Schmid*, 423 A2d 615 at 631–633 (1980); *Commonwealth v Tate*, 432 A2d 1382 at 1390 (Pa 1981); *People v Leonard*, 477 NYS2d 111 at 115 (Ct App 1984).

12   *Re Hoffman*, 434 P2d 353 at 356 (1967); *Streetwatch v National Railroad Passenger Corporation*, 875 F Supp 1055 at 1061–1062 (SDNY 1995); *Rogers v New York City Transit Authority*, 680 NE2d 142 at 147–148 (NY 1997).

13   *Jamison v City of St Louis*, 828 F2d 1280 at 1283 (8th Cir 1987); *The Queen in Right of Canada v Committee for the Commonwealth of Canada* (1991) 77 DLR (4th) 385 at 393d–h per Lamer CJC (Sopinka and Cory JJ concurring), 402f per La Forest J, 421h–422b per L'Heureux-Dubé J, 449d–450c per McLachlin J.

14   *Dalury v S-K-I, Ltd*, 670 A2d 795 at 799–800 (Vt 1995); *Lewis v Colorado Rockies Baseball Club, Ltd*, 941 P2d 266 at 270, 274 (Colo 1997).

15   See eg *Uston v Resorts International Hotel, Inc*, 445 A2d 370 at 373–375 (NJ 1982).

16   It was on precisely this footing that, half a century ago, the Law Reform Committee indicated that higher duties were owed to an 'invitee' than to a mere 'licensee'. The 'invitee' was one of whom it could be said that 'the occupier has a material interest in the purpose of the other party's visit, whether the other party shares that interest, or has some separate interest of his own … If, so to speak, the visitor by coming obliges the occupier in some material respect, then in return for that service the occupier owes the visitor the higher standard of care' (Law Reform Committee, *Occupiers' Liability to Invitees, Licensees and Trespassers* (Third Report, Cmd 9305, November 1954), paras 7, 61). See likewise *Winter Garden Theatre (London) Ltd v Millennium Productions Ltd* [1948] AC 173 at 188 per Viscount Simon (referring to 'a purely gratuitous licence in return for which A gets nothing at all'); *Forbes v New South Wales Trotting Club Ltd* (1979) 143 CLR 242 at 269 per Gibbs J.

Virtual monopolies

4.50 By long tradition in the common law, the element of 'quasi-public' character is intensified where an owner's self-serving outreach to the general public arises in connection with his status as a monopoly supplier of some social, commercial or environmental utility. The old common law concept of private property infused with a public interest later came to be applied to cases of 'virtual monopoly',[1] where publicly valuable services were rendered in circumstances in which the supplier could dictate the terms of his dealings with the public. An early version of a rule of reasonable access was therefore invoked in order to ensure that public access to essential services and commodities was maintained on terms which were fair and reasonable.[2] In some jurisdictions this approach has generated a modern common law doctrine of 'prime necessity'[3] aimed at 'curbing the exploitation or abuse of monopoly power.'[4] Thus, for example, in *Sky City Auckland Ltd v Wu*,[5] a majority in the New Zealand Court of Appeal expressed its provisional preference for the view that at common law, in respect of a 'business affected by a public interest in circumstances where the operator enjoys a monopoly ... the operator's right to exclude members of the public may be qualified by an obligation to do so only for an articulated good reason.' The *Sky City* case concerned the exclusion of a highly successful gambler from Auckland's only casino, the gambler eventually losing his privileges of entry only because legislation relating specifically to casino premises was held to have ousted the common law rule.[6]

1   *Allnutt v Inglis* (1810) 12 East 527 at 540, 104 ER 206 at 211 per Lord Ellenborough CJ. See also *Bolt v Stennett* (1800) 8 TR 606 at 608, 101 ER 1572 at 1573; *Simpson v Attorney-General* [1904] AC 476 at 482 per Lord Macnaghten.
2   See *Attorney General of Canada v Toronto* (1893) 23 SCR 514 at 520 per Strong CJ (indispensable commodities held on trust 'for the benefit of the general public').
3   The phrase was coined by the Privy Council in a Canadian appeal (see *Minister of Justice for the Dominion of Canada v City of Lévis* [1919] AC 505 at 513 per Lord Parmoor). For further reference, see *Vector Ltd v Transpower New Zealand Ltd* [1999] 3 NZLR 646 at [35]–[51] per Richardson P, Gault, Blanchard and Tipping JJ; *Pacifica Shipping Ltd v Centreport Ltd* [2003] 1 NZLR 433 at [5]. The doctrine has been acknowledged as 'a strand of the broader principle which ... is adaptable to meet new legal and social situations' (*Sky City Auckland Ltd v Wu* [2002] 3 NZLR 621 at 630 [25]–[26] per Blanchard and Anderson JJ). See also Michael B Taggart, 'Public Utilities and Public Law', in P A Joseph (ed), *Essays on the Constitution* (Brooker's, Wellington 1995), p 214.
4   *Vector Ltd v Transpower New Zealand Ltd* [1999] 3 NZLR 646 at [77] per Thomas J.
5   [2002] 3 NZLR 621 at [34] per Blanchard and Anderson JJ.
6   The casino subsequently re-admitted the gambler on condition that he agreed not to appeal to the Judicial Committee of the Privy Council (personal communication from Professor Michael Taggart, 19 August 2002). See also *Jones v Sky City Auckland Ltd* [2004] 1 NZLR 192 at [25].

A 'reasonable access' rule in English law

4.51 In recent decades English courts have begun to accept that arbitrary powers of exclusion are no longer an inevitable or necessary incident of property in all kinds of land. The perceptible trend is, instead, towards the

6   [2000] 1 WLR 1246 at 1251G.
7   [2000] 1 WLR 1246 at 1253D.
8   [2000] 1 WLR 1246 at 1253C–F.

4.55 In certain contexts the standards to be expected of the public authority landowner have now been raised significantly by the principle of respect for home and family life incorporated in the European Convention on Human Rights.[1] There has always been a broad hope that, in exercising possessory control over its land (and particularly in seeking to recover possession of it), a public authority would act with 'common humanity'.[2] Since the enactment of the Human Rights Act 1998, this aspiration has been converted into a duty binding the authority, when deciding whether to enforce its right to possession of land, to 'consider the Convention rights of trespassers living on its land and their human needs generally.'[3] The recent decision of the European Court of Human Rights in *Connors v United Kingdom*[4] amply demonstrates how the assertion of arbitrary control over land may lead, in the residential sector, to a finding that there has been a denial of the procedural safeguards which surround the Convention entitlement.

1   ECHR Art 8 [**para 2.60**].
2   See *R v Hillingdon LBC, ex p McDonagh* (1999) 31 HLR 531 at 542 per Carnwath J.
3   *R (Fuller) v Chief Constable of Dorset Police* [2003] QB 480 at [67]. See also *Drury v Secretary of State for the Environment, Food and Rural Affairs* [2004] EWCA Civ 200 at [38] per Ward LJ ('due compassion').
4   Application No 66746/01, 27 May 2004 at [94]–[95], [114] [**para 2.73**].

Performance of non-statutory functions

4.56 It is now beginning to be suggested that similar constraints of reasonbleness affect the exclusory power of certain landowners whose functions are *not* underpinned by public law. In *CIN Properties Ltd v Rawlins*,[1] for example, a corporate leasehold owner of a down-town shopping centre purported to ban a group of unemployed youths indefinitely from further entry within the precincts of the shopping mall. The ban, which followed unsubstantiated allegations of misbehaviour, was reinforced by court injunction, thereby effectively excluding the youths for life from a large part of the centre of their own home town.[2] At first instance the county court ruled that the landowner's implied invitation to the defendant youths (as indeed to all members of the public) could not be arbitrarily withdrawn in this way. The county court held that members of the general public, subject only to a requirement of 'reasonable conduct', had an 'equitable' or 'irrevocable' right to enter and use the shopping mall during its normal opening hours 'even though they are passing through private property.'[3] The Court of Appeal overturned this ruling on appeal, declining to accept that a landowner's power to exclude must be exercised reasonably and only upon a showing of good cause.[4] The European Human Rights Commission was subsequently powerless to intervene,[5] largely because the United Kingdom has never ratified the Convention guarantee of liberty of movement.[6]

1　[1995] 2 EGLR 130. See [1995] Conv 332 (M Haley); Gray and Gray, 'Civil Rights, Civil Wrongs and Quasi-Public Space' (1999) 4 EHRLR 46 at 47–50.

2　The shopping centre covered some 12 acres of the down-town area, contained the town's main shopping facilities, a bank, various cafés and the town's gas and electricity payment offices, and provided employment for large numbers of local people.

3　Interim Judgment of Mr Recorder Philip Cox QC, 6 January 1994, Birmingham County Court, *Transcript*, pp 14–15.

4　[1995] 2 EGLR 130 at 134E–J per Balcombe LJ (leave to appeal to the House of Lords was refused).

5　See *Mark Anderson and Others v United Kingdom* (1998) 25 EHRR CD 172 at 174; (1998) 3 EHRLR 218.

6　ECHR Protocol No 4, Art 2 (see also Human Rights Act 1998, s 1(1)).

4.57　The decision in *CIN Properties Ltd v Rawlins* placed a fresh focus on the proper limits of estate ownership in English law. The outcome in *CIN Properties Ltd v Rawlins* effectively allowed a private landowner, on invoking a threat of indefinite incarceration for contempt of court, to exile a group of citizens permanently from a sizeable portion of their own town.[1] By converting this area into a perpetual no-go zone, the ruling immediately endangered these citizens' prospects of employment and their freedom to engage in the social and commercial relationships of their choice.[2] The feudal resonance of this exercise of proprietary power has subsequently caused more than a flicker of concern for the Court of Appeal. In *Porter v Commissioner of Police of the Metropolis*,[3] the Court, whilst noting that it was bound by the decision in *Rawlins*, spoke of the possibility of 'incremental development of the common law'[4] along the lines which succeeded at first instance in *Rawlins*.[5] The *Porter* case concerned a disgruntled customer of the London Electricity Board who staged a sit-down protest in the Board's showroom and, despite being ordered to do so, adamantly refused to leave the premises. The Court of Appeal took the view that she could not credibly maintain that she was entitled to remain in those premises indefinitely and that her right of access to the showroom had been lawfully terminated. Significantly, however, Sedley LJ was not prepared to accept that the customer's right of access was *arbitrarily* terminable by the landowner.[6] Sedley LJ indicated that '[b]oth because London Electricity is a statutory undertaker providing a service essential to most people's lives and because its shop premises, when open, constitute an invitation to the public to enter and remain there for proper purposes, it is arguable that it cannot arbitrarily or improperly exclude or expel members of the public.'[7]

1　See C Grant, 'Banning the Banning Notice' 25 Alternative LJ 32 (2000). Other jurisdictions have demonstrated a greater sensitivity to the need for proportionality between the scope of an exclusion from premises and the legitimate interests and purposes of the excluder (see e g *R v Layton* (1988) 38 CCC (3d) 550 at 566; *Kreimer v Bureau of Police for Town of Morristown*, 958 F2d 1242 at 1264 (3rd Cir 1992); *State v Morse*, 647 A2d 495 at 497 (NJ Super L 1994); *R v Heywood* [1994] 3 SCR 761 at 796; *O v Wedd* [2000] TASSC 74 at [10]–[11]).

2　The vesting of powers of arbitrary exclusion in private landowners has become less essential for purposes of ensuring public safety in that the new statutory authority to disperse groups from public places (see ASBA 2003, s 30 [**para 3.103**]) applies to 'any place to which ... the public ... has access, on payment or otherwise, as of right or by virtue of express or implied permission' (ASBA 2003, s 36).

3　[1999] All ER (D) 1129.

4   See *Pepsi-Cola Canada Beverages (West) Ltd v RWDSU, Local 558* (2002) 208 DLR (4th) 385 at [16] per McLachlin CJC and LeBel J ('any change to the common law should be incremental').

5   Per May and Sedley LJJ. Noting that 'the common law has historically limited certain private powers in the public interest', Sedley LJ observed that 'there may be more to be said in the future on the topic than was said by this court in *CIN Properties v Rawlins*.' See also *DPP v Jones* [1999] 2 AC 240 at 259A, where Lord Irvine of Lairg LC was prepared to concede that the common law of trespass may be 'uncertain and developing.'

6   'Were London Electricity entitled to rescind Mrs Porter's licence? ... I am prepared to accept that the answer may no longer be a cursory "Of course".'

7   Ultimately, however, on a test of reasonableness, the revocation of her right to be present was considered by Sedley LJ, quite correctly, to be not unreasonable.

Impact of the Human Rights Act 1998

4.58   It is foreseeable that the gradual assimilation of European jurisprudence under the Human Rights Act 1998 will eventually curtail the more capricious assertions of proprietary power over quasi-public areas of land. Although in *Mark Anderson and Others v United Kingdom*[1] the European Commission of Human Rights proved extremely cautious in its interpretation of the Convention freedoms of peaceful assembly and association,[2] there are indications that the European Court of Human Rights is prepared to hold that Convention guarantees may, in certain circumstances, qualify the plenitude of a property owner's rights to exclude from privately held land. In *Appleby and Others v United Kingdom*,[3] a majority in the Court, although finding no breach of the Convention in the particular circumstances,[4] expressed the view that a state may be obliged to 'protect the enjoyment of Convention rights by regulating property rights' where, for example, a bar on access to land has the consequence of 'preventing any effective exercise of freedom of expression or it can be said that the essence of the right has been destroyed.'[5] In a partial dissent, one of the judges went so far as to observe that

> 'It cannot be the case that through privatisation the public authorities can divest themselves of any responsibility to protect rights and freedoms other than property rights ... The old traditional rule that the private owner has an unfettered right to eject people from his land and premises without giving any justification and without any test of reasonableness being applied is no longer fully adapted to contemporary conditions and society.'[6]

1   (1998) 25 EHRR CD 172 at 174.

2   See ECHR Art 11. The Commission stressed, by a majority, that the Convention case law on Art 11 had not, to date, indicated that freedom of assembly 'is intended to guarantee a right to pass and re-pass in public places, or to assemble for purely social purposes anywhere one wishes.' Likewise, freedom of association was narrowly construed as a highly purposive right for individuals to associate 'in order to attain various ends.'

3   (2003) 37 EHRR 783. The circumstances of the *Appleby* case subsequently reached the House of Lords as *R (Beresford) v Sunderland CC* [2004] 1 AC 889 [**para 5.44**].

4   The Court held that the applicants had available other fora for the meaningful exercise of expressional freedom ((2003) 37 EHRR 783 at [48]).

5   37 EHRR 783 at [47]. The Court stressed the 'key importance of freedom of expression as one of the preconditions for a functioning democracy' and noted that this freedom 'may require

positive measures of protection, even in the sphere of relations between individuals' ((2003) 37 EHRR 783 at [39]). For further evidence that charter-based freedom of expression may provide a defence to trespass, see *Horse Lake First Nation v Horseman* (2003) 223 DLR (4th) 184 at [29].

6   (2003) 37 EHRR 783 at [O-16]–[O-17] per Judge Maruste.

4.59 It is likely therefore that in a limited range of circumstances this approach will require that landowners demonstrate that any exclusion from privately owned areas of quasi-public space is justified on reasonable grounds which do not contravene the guaranteed liberties of the citizen.

CONTRACTUAL LICENCES

4.60 A 'contractual licence' comprises a permission to use or occupy land which derives its force from some express or implied contract.[1] It differs from the bare licence in that it is not granted gratuitously but is founded upon valuable consideration moving from the licensee.[2] In recent years the precise legal status of the contractual licence has proved to be a matter of some controversy. Although plainly rooted in contract, this form of licence nowadays hovers ambivalently on the threshold of property, often performing much the same role and evincing some of the same characteristics as conventionally recognised proprietary rights.[3] There is little doubt that, in at least some of its manifestations, the contractual licence is undergoing the same evolutionary process which, in the 19th century, led to the recognition of the restrictive covenant as a proprietary interest of an equitable character.[4] Indeed some contractual licences already shade into the area of estoppel-based or equitable licences, phenomena which are increasingly accepted as having a proprietary dimension.[5] At present the contractual licence has not yet been accorded full proprietary status, although some kinds of contractual licence are certainly beginning to look like a species of 'quasi-proprietary right' in land.[6]

1   In the orthodox view most contractual licences may be created without any formality since they confer no interest in the land to which they relate [**paras 2.80, 4.96, 10.90, 12.226**].
2   *Horrocks v Forray* [1976] 1 WLR 230 at 236C–E per Megaw LJ.
3   [**Para 4.64**].
4   [**Paras 2.52, 9.146, 13.108**].
5   [**Paras 10.213, 12.233**].
6   See *Jones v Jones* [2001] NI 244 at 257c per Girvan J.

Disparate functions of the contractual licence

4.61 The precise classification of contractual licences turns, inevitably, on the quantum of property inherent in various claims of licence.[1] Much of the ambivalence surrounding the modern contractual licence flows from the fact that it is, above all, a chameleonic device which has been adapted at different times and in wildly divergent contexts in order to fill various sorts of legal hiatus.

1   [**Para 2.13**].

Short-term functions

4.62　At one end of the spectrum the contractual licence provides the legal medium for relationships of an extremely short-term or intensely purposive character.[1] The contractual licence frequently supplies a personal permission to be present on another's land for the purpose of business or entertainment. It is the contractual licence which underlies the right of the cinema fan to sit in the auditorium or that of the football spectator to cheer from the grandstand.[2] Temporary parking in a commercial car park usually takes effect behind a contractual licence.[3] It was the contractual licence which provided the legal basis of the classic 'coronation cases' of 1903 where would-be spectators had hired rooms in order to watch a coronation procession which was in fact postponed because of the illness of King Edward VII.[4]

1　See *Customs and Excise Commrs v Sinclair Collis Ltd* [2001] STC 989 at [71] per Lord Scott of Foscote (a 'contract under which a room were taken for half an hour so that a man might consort with a lady').
2　See *Winter Garden Theatre (London) Ltd v Millennium Productions Ltd* [1948] AC 173 at 189.
3　*Ashby v Tolhurst* [1937] 2 KB 242 at 249. Compare, however, the bailment analysis applied in *Davis v Pearce Parking Station Pty Ltd* (1954) 91 CLR 642 at 647; *Walton Stores Ltd v Sydney City Council* [1968] 2 NSWR 109 at 112–114. The bailment analysis may, of course, result in the imposition of a different standard of care.
4　*Krell v Henry* [1903] 2 KB 740 at 750.

Medium-term functions

4.63　The contractual licence is also quite capable of serving a number of medium-term objectives. The building contractor who works on a construction site enjoys a contractual licence to be present on that site for a number of months.[1] 'Front of the house' rights in a theatre are commonly enjoyed by way of contractual licence.[2] On payment of his annual subscription the member of a golf club acquires a contractual licence to play on the course and to enjoy a package of benefits, privileges and club facilities.[3]

1　*Hounslow LBC v Twickenham Garden Developments Ltd* [1971] Ch 233 at 246C, 247B–D; *Mayfield Holdings Ltd v Moana Reef Ltd* [1973] 1 NZLR 309 at 316.
2　*Clore v Theatrical Properties Ltd and Westby & Co Ltd* [1936] 3 All ER 483 at 490.
3　*The Banstead Downs Golf Club v The Commissioners* (1974) VATTR 219 at 227.

Long-term functions

4.64　At the other end of the spectrum the contractual licence has come, during the last 50 years, to play a rather different role from any mentioned so far. Although at times scarcely distinguishable from the parallel device of tenancy,[1] the contractual licence has emerged as peculiarly appropriate to certain modern social and commercial contexts.[2] Particularly in the residential sphere the contractual licence has acquired a wholly unaccustomed prominence as a 'possible mode of land-holding.'[3] The contractual licence provides the legal explanation for the social reality of occupancy enjoyed by lodgers[4] and, occasionally, for certain informal and loosely organised kinds of 'family arrangement'.[5] But it is often in connection with such long-term occupancy that the rights of the contractual licensee begin most closely to resemble those of a conventional estate owner.

1   [**Para 7.139**]. The similarity between the long-term functions of the contractual licence and the term of years was intensified by the statutory creation of 'a new animal' (see *Norris v Checksfield* [1991] 1 WLR 1241 at 1246G per Woolf LJ). Section 5(1A) of the Protection from Eviction Act 1977 introduced the concept of the 'periodic licence' on an analogy with weekly, monthly and quarterly tenancies (see *Norris*, supra at 1248A).
2   See eg *Hunts Refuse Disposals Ltd v Norfolk Environmental Waste Services Ltd* [1997] 1 EGLR 16 (21 year licence for non-exclusive use of waste disposal site).
3   *Heslop v Burns* [1974] 1 WLR 1241 at 1252C–D per Scarman LJ.
4   In the residential context there is a presumption in favour of contractual licence rather than bare licence. The onus is on the licensor to prove that only a bare licence was present and that no money was paid (see *Patel v Patel* [1983] Court of Appeal Unbound Transcript 930 per Slade LJ).
5   [**Para 4.74**].

Disjunctions of time and concept

4.65   The difficulties evident in the contemporary law of contractual licences are those which inevitably arise where one term, itself of ill-defined scope, is required to do service for a range of purposes which differ broadly in time-scale and context. The formative concepts relevant to the law of contractual licences were hammered out during the 19th and early 20th centuries some time before the residential dimension of the contractual licence began properly to emerge.[1] Rules which are quite appropriate for short- or medium-term dealings have now come to appear entirely inapposite to the expectations of parties caught up in long-term contractual arrangements. Conversely, ideas which would seem bizarre in the context of the 'cinema ticket' cases acquire a certain plausibility in the context of other kinds of arrangement which fall within the compass of the contractual licence.

1   Even in the 1930s the Rent Acts were as yet in their infancy and the possibility that this legislation might be circumvented through the grant of contractual occupation licences had not been fully realised. A brake on this process of circumvention came with the ruling of the House of Lords in *Street v Mountford* [1985] AC 809 [**para 7.177**].

Terms of the contractual licence

4.66   A contractual licence may be created either expressly or impliedly and its terms are left to be ascertained by normal contractual principles. Some terms may be stipulated explicitly by the parties, but other terms can be supplied by implication from their conduct and expectations. The courts are generally willing to imply such terms as are required to make the contract 'workable'[1] or to give it 'business efficacy'.[2]

1   *Cartwright v Merthyr Tydfil BC* (Unreported, Court of Appeal, 22 May 2000) per Hale J
    (implied term in street trading consent that local council would take reasonable steps to keep
    designated area free of parked cars).
2   *Cartwright v Merthyr Tydfil BC* (Unreported, Court of Appeal, 22 May 2000) per Roch LJ.

Implied term for quiet enjoyment

4.67   Some kinds of contractual licence contain an implied undertaking by
the licensor to afford quiet enjoyment to the licensee.[1] In *Smith v Nottinghamshire CC*,[2] for example, a number of students living in a hall of residence
complained that their preparation for an examination had been affected by
noisy repairs which their university had insisted on carrying out during term
time. The Court of Appeal held that there had indeed been a breach of a
contractual term that the university, as a contractual licensor, should do
nothing without just cause to disturb the students from getting on with their
studies with reasonable quietude in their own rooms.

1   On the covenant for quiet enjoyment implied in a lease, see Chapter 14 [**para 14.11**].
2   (1981) *Times*, 13 November.

Implied term relating to fitness for purpose

4.68   As demonstrated by *Smith v Nottinghamshire CC*, the judicial implication of terms can sometimes make the contractual licence seem the functional
equivalent of a tenancy. In some respects the courts have gone even further and
have been willing to imply in the contractual licence a term which has never
been implied in any lease. In *Wettern Electric Ltd v Welsh Development Agency*,[1]
for example, Deputy Judge John Newey QC was prepared to imply into a
contractual occupation licence a term that the premises hired should be fit for
the purposes envisaged by the licensee.[2] Here the claimants had been unable to
carry on their business in the licensed premises because, shortly after moving in,
they discovered foundations defects which made the property dangerous and
unusable. The defendants were found to be in breach of an implied term of
fitness and were therefore liable in damages.[3] The willingness of the courts to
imply such terms on the basis of 'business efficacy'[4] may well counteract the
perceived attraction – judged from the landowner's viewpoint – which the
contractual licence has seemed to enjoy over the lease. However, the ampler
protection conferred on the contractual licensee is not always easy to justify[5]
and, perhaps for this reason, more recent decisions have tended to qualify the
scope of the ruling in *Wettern Electric*[6] or to interpret restrictively the nature of
the licensor's obligations in respect of fitness of premises.[7]

1   [1983] QB 796. See (1983) 34 NILQ 349 (N Dawson); (1983) 80 Law Soc Gaz 2195 (H W
    Wilkinson); [1983] Conv 319 (J E M).
2   For a discussion of the courts' reluctance to imply an equivalent term in the context of a lease,
    see Chapter 14 [**para 14.20**].
3   [1983] QB 796 at 809A–E.
4   See *The Moorcock* (1889) 14 PD 64 at 68, cited in *Wettern Electric Ltd v Welsh Development
    Agency* [1983] QB 796 at 809A–B.

5 'Why ... should a person who agrees to purchase a licence ... be able to invoke an implied term as to fitness while the purchaser or lessee of business premises is fobbed off with the maxim caveat emptor?' (*Ware v Johnson* [1984] 2 NZLR 518 at 535 per Prichard J).

6 See e g *Morris-Thomas v Petticoat Lane Rentals* (1987) 53 P & CR 238 at 249–251, 255–256.

7 See e g *Cartwright v Merthyr Tydfil BC* (Unreported, Court of Appeal, 22 May 2000) per Mummery LJ.

Requirement of notice to quit

4.69 A fixed-term contractual licence comes to an end, without any requirement of notice, on the expiration of the fixed term.[1] Other kinds of contractual licence are normally terminable only upon the giving of some form of notice to quit.[2] Such notice may be the subject of express stipulation[3] but, in the absence of any expressly specified period of notice (and in the absence of any obligation not to revoke the licence), contractual licences of indefinite duration are impliedly terminable only by notice of a duration which is reasonable in all the circumstances.[4] This restriction on the right to revoke a contractual licence instanter usually arises (particularly in a contract involving specialised use of premises) where it is inferable that the parties never intended that the licence could be withdrawn without any period of notice at all.[5] In the case of a contractual licence of a room in a long-stay hotel, reasonable notice of termination may comprise a period of four months[6] whereas the termination of certain licences for commercial or educational use may reasonably require notice of a significantly lengthier period.[7]

1 See *Sandhu v Farooqui* [2004] 1 P & CR 19 at [20].

2 There is no requirement of notice to quit where a service occupancy is brought to an end by the summary dismissal of an employee for employment-related misconduct (see *Norris v Checksfield* [1991] 1 WLR 1241 at 1247H per Woolf LJ).

3 Where a contractual licence is a 'periodic licence', there is an overriding statutory provision that no notice of termination by either party is valid unless given in writing at least four weeks before the date on which the notice is to take effect (Protection from Eviction Act 1977, s 5(1A), as amended by HA 1988, s 32(2)). A valid notice to quit must also contain 'such information as may be prescribed.'

4 The period of notice required is not necessarily one full payment period. See the requirement of one month's notice (rather than seven or eight days) imposed by the Court of Appeal in *Smith v Northside Developments Ltd* (1988) 55 P & CR 164 at 168; [1989] Conv 55 (J E M).

5 See *Winter Garden Theatre (London) Ltd v Millennium Productions Ltd* [1948] AC 173 at 191 per Viscount Simon, 199–200 per Lord Uthwatt, 205 per Lord MacDermott (licence to use theatre for stage plays). See also *Canadian Pacific Railway Co v The King* [1931] AC 414 at 432 per Lord Russell of Killowen; *Australian Blue Metal Ltd v Hughes* [1963] AC 74 at 99 per Lord Devlin.

6 See *Mehta v Royal Bank of Scotland* [1999] 3 EGLR 153 at 158M. See also *Grundel v Registrar General* (1990) 5 BPR 11217 at 11222 (six months' notice reasonable in relation to 65 year-old who had lived in shared family home for 12 years).

7 Compare *Governing Body of Henrietta Barnett School v Hampstead Garden Suburb Institute* (1995) 93 LGR 470 at 511–513 **[para 4.28]**.

Governing contractual principles

4.70   Although the express and implied terms of a contractual licence may at times resemble those contained in a lease, the assimilation of the lease and the contractual licence is far from complete. Because of the dual function of the leasehold as both a contractual phenomenon and a proprietary estate,[1] certain rules derived from contract law are equally applicable to leases and licences. Thus, for instance, both the tenant[2] and the licensee[3] may invoke the contractual doctrine of frustration. However, neither the licensor nor the licensee can claim the benefit of many other rules and doctrines which presuppose the conferment of an estate in the land.[4] The contractual licensee enjoys no special rights in respect of the removal of fixtures from the realty.[5] The implied surrender of a contractual licence is governed by the rules on discharge of a contract by tacit abandonment[6] rather than by the principles which control the surrender of a leasehold estate.[7] It is generally thought in England, at any rate, that the contractual licensee cannot invoke the equitable doctrine of relief against forfeiture for breach of the terms of his licence.[8] In the conventional view such relief is available only in respect of proprietary interests in land,[9] although in reality much the same relief is often accorded to licensees through the invocation of the principle of proprietary estoppel.[10]

1   [**Para 7.75**].

2   [**Para 7.323**].

3   See *Krell v Henry* [1903] 2 KB 740 at 751–752; *National Carriers Ltd v Panalpina (Northern) Ltd* [1981] AC 675 at 690H–691A, 694A–B.

4   See e g *Burton v De Vere Hotels* [1997] ICR 1 at 10A, where a hotel which granted a contractual licence for a social function was held liable for racial discrimination under Race Relations Act 1976, s 4, when a comedian (Bernard Manning) hired to entertain the guests made racially offensive remarks.

5   *C & P Haulage v Middleton* [1983] 1 WLR 1461 at 1468B–C. Contrast the position of tenants [**para 1.84**].

6   *Bone v Bone* [1992] EGCS 81 per Nourse LJ. See *Paal Wilson & Co A/S v Partenreederei Hannah Blumenthal* [1983] 1 AC 854 at 924D–G per Lord Brightman.

7   [**Para 7.305**]. As Nourse LJ pointed out in *Bone v Bone* [1992] EGCS 81, the abandonment of a contractual licence requires no formalities and is not necessarily founded on estoppel. In particular, there is no need to show – as would be the case with surrender of a lease by operation of law – that the party who alleges implied abandonment has acted in detrimental reliance on some representation made by the other party.

8   *Scandinavian Trading Tanker Co AB v Flota Petrolera Ecuatoriana* [1983] 2 AC 694 at 702A–C per Lord Diplock; *Sport Internationaal Bussum BV v Inter-Footwear Ltd* [1984] 1 WLR 776 at 794C–G.

9   Compare, however, the increasing support in the Australian jurisdictions for the proposition that equity may relieve against the forfeiture of a mere contractual licence (*Chaka Holdings Pty Ltd v Sunsim Pty Ltd* (1987) 10 BPR 18171 at 18182 per Young J; *Milton v Proctor* (1988) 4 BPR 9654 at 9659–9660 per McHugh JA; *Federal Airports Corpn v Makucha Developments Pty Ltd* (1993) 115 ALR 679 at 700; *Liristis Holdings Pty Ltd v Wallville Pty Ltd* (2001) 10 BPR 18801 at [116]). See also *Stern v McArthur* (1988) 165 CLR 489; W M C Gummow, *Forfeiture and Certainty: The High Court and the House of Lords*, in P D Finn (ed), *Essays in Equity* (Sydney 1985), pp 43–44; Sir Anthony Mason, *Themes and Prospects*, ibid, p 248.

10   [**Para 10.168**]. See *Milton v Proctor* (1988) 4 BPR 9654 at 9655 per Mahoney JA, 9669–9671 per Clarke JA.

CONTRACTUAL LICENCES IN THE FAMILY CONTEXT

4.71 The device of the contractual licence has sometimes been adapted by the courts in order to rationalise and resolve the legal problems generated by informal or ill-defined arrangements for family living.[1] In the early 1970s the rulings of the House of Lords in *Pettitt v Pettitt*[2] and *Gissing v Gissing*[3] seemed to preclude the law of trusts from having much positive application to the phenomenon of the family arrangement[4] and the device of the contractual licence suddenly appeared to provide the flexibility of approach to family arrangements which the clumsy and doctrinaire concepts of trust law so conspicuously lacked.

1   The difficulties presented by multiple domestic occupation are likely to be accentuated by the housing needs of a rapidly ageing population. A further dimension of difficulty is introduced by the sharing of accommodation with vulnerable or incapacitated relatives who are consigned to 'care in the community'.
2   [1970] AC 777 [**para 10.123**].
3   [1971] AC 886 [**para 10.93**].
4   The element of conscious understanding of anticipated equitable entitlement in which the House of Lords rooted the origins of trust is inevitably alien to most kinds of family arrangement [**para 10.128**].

Non-commercial nature of family relations

4.72 Familial relations are in general non-commercial and do not often involve the prudential calculation of cash advantage which so heavily colours the relationships of strangers. Hard bargaining and the cold definition of legal rights are normally alien to the spirit in which family interaction is conducted.[1] There may, however, be a more subtle sense in which the reciprocity sought in the bargaining of strangers is no less effectively secured in the family context. Since family living implies at least some continuity of relationship, the expected reciprocity of family transactions often takes many years to be fully realised.[2] The net result is that members of family and kinship groups commonly participate in informally based living arrangements which are negotiated – if they are discussed at all – not in clearly defined terms of legal entitlement, but in vaguely expressed terms of anticipated mutuality.[3]

1   It is also generally true that younger members of family groups are subject to some measure of disability (both legal and economic), and are therefore more likely to be the beneficiaries of transactions motivated by generosity.
2   As William J Goode once said, the continuity of family relationships means that 'an individual can give more at one time to a family member, knowing that in the long run this will not be a loss, for the other person (or someone else) is likely to reciprocate at some point' (see 'The Resistance of Family Forces to Industrialisation', in J M Eekelaar and S N Katz (ed), *Marriage and Cohabitation in Contemporary Societies* (Toronto 1980), p xiv).
3   Family arrangements are thus commonly characterised by obscure intentions, unexpressed terms, mixed motives and a high degree of mutual misunderstanding. Croom-Johnson LJ was once moved to speak of such situations as 'family non-arrangements' (*Rogers v Eller* (Unreported, Court of Appeal, 20 May 1986)). See also *Gillies v Keogh* [1989] 2 NZLR 327 at 333 per Cooke P.

Decline of non-interventionism

4.73   Domestic living arrangements tend, by nature and form, to be so unlegalistic that for many years the courts declined, as a matter of principle, to attribute to family members any intention to create legally actionable relationships.[1] By the 1970s, however, English courts had become increasingly willing to accept and to enforce some degree of contractual ordering of family relationships by the parties themselves.[2] Even where a family arrangement involved an element of de facto or non-marital cohabitation, judges liberated themselves from the historic fear that the conferment of rights might be confused with a rewarding of supposed immorality.[3] Courts no longer regarded the withholding of property or other rights as an appropriate means of manifesting an official social displeasure with unorthodox living arrangements.[4]

1   See *Balfour v Balfour* [1919] 2 KB 571 at 579 per Atkin LJ **[para 10.52]**; *Pettitt v Pettitt* [1970] AC 777 at 796A; *Burns v Burns* [1984] Ch 317 at 335C. For many people discussion of the legal implications of their living arrangements is inconsistent with the mutual trust on which their relationship is based (see *Doohan v Nelson* [1973] 2 NSWLR 320 at 324G–325A).
2   See *Hardwick v Johnson* [1978] 1 WLR 683 at 688A–E.
3   See *Holman v Johnson* (1775) 1 Cowp 341 at 343, 98 ER 1120 at 1121. For a modern emanation of this moralistic approach in the Republic of Ireland, see *Ennis v Butterly* [1997] 1 ILRM 28 at 39–40.
4   This altered direction did not necessarily reflect a new judicial liberalism or even an incipient principle of moral neutrality in the courts. In many cases the modern approach was more clearly the product of a judicial desire to deprive unmarried male cohabitees of any possible haven of effective legal immunity. Alongside this motivation there was a strong impulse to ensure that unmarried partners were not left free to contract out of legal control by opting deliberately for some autonomous or supposedly free-thinking relationship above and beyond the law (see Gray, 'The Law of Trusts and the Quasi-Matrimonial Home' [1983] CLJ 30 at 34). It has been suggested that perceptions of a national moral decline may have induced a willingness to penalise relationships which, by reason of instability or supposed immorality, threatened the public weal or – more crudely – taxed the public purse (see eg P Sparkes, 'Morality, Amorality and Equity' [1990] Denning LJ 91 at 102–103).

Implication of contractual terms

4.74   During the 1970s the English Court of Appeal began to recognise an enforceable contractual element as inherent in at least some kinds of family arrangements, although the practice quickly exposed profound difficulties in the ascertainment of the express and implied terms regulating such relationships. The resort to some extended version of the contractual licence reached its high point in *Tanner v Tanner*.[1] Here a young mother of twins gave up a Rent Act protected tenancy in order to move into a house which the father of her children bought in his own name. When he later evicted her from that house, the Court of Appeal awarded the woman compensation of £2,000 for the loss of a 'contractual licence'.[2] According to Lord Denning MR, the house had obviously been 'provided for her as a house for herself and the twins for the foreseeable future.'[3] Having suffered the detriment of giving up her protected tenancy, she had acquired a contractual licence to 'have accommodation in the house for herself and the children so long as they were of school age and the accommodation was reasonably required for her and the children.'[4] The Court thus regarded the expectations of the parties as having given rise to a form of residential security which, although terminable in changed circumstances,[5] was none the less compensable by damages where the licence had already been wrongfully brought to an end.[6]

1   [1975] 1 WLR 1346.
2   On the rationale for calculation of this lump sum, see *Baker v Baker and Baker* (1993) 25 HLR 408 at 415.
3   [1975] 1 WLR 1346 at 1350B.
4   [1975] 1 WLR 1346 at 1350E.
5   [1975] 1 WLR 1346 at 1350F. For criticism of the 'concept of a wavering licence', see *McGill v S* [1979] IR 283 at 293 [**para 10.293**].
6   See also *Broughall v Hunt* (Unreported, Chancery Division, 1 February 1983); (1983) 80 Law Soc Gaz 2198 (G Gypps). The courts even attributed a notional cash value to a *Tanner v Tanner* licence in the reallocation of resources between husband and wife on divorce (see *W v W* (Financial Provision: Lump Sum) [1976] Fam 107 at 113A–B).

Shift towards other legal devices

4.75   As with many of Lord Denning's innovations, the liberal application of contractual licence theory proved controversial in the context of family arrangements. The implied contractual obligation found in *Tanner v Tanner* was an extremely artificial creation[1] and later courts proved much less ready to give contractual status to supposed undertakings whose scope and time-scale can scarcely have been present to the minds of both (or perhaps either of the) parties.[2] In consequence the contractual licence approach adumbrated in *Tanner v Tanner* faded into the background[3] and subsequent 'family arrange-ment' decisions have focused, not on strained and scarcely credible implications of contract, but rather on more appropriate variants of equitable or irrevocable licence,[4] proprietary estoppel[5] and constructive trust.[6] Indeed, with the modern convergence of estoppel and constructive trust theory as a means of giving effect to shared understandings about proprietary entitlement,[7] it seems increasingly unlikely that the implied contractual licence has much of a role left to play in the legal regulation of family cohabitation.

1   Lord Denning MR was forced to concede in *Tanner v Tanner* that there was 'no express contract ... but the circumstances are such that the court should imply a contract by the plaintiff – or, if need be, impose the equivalent of a contract by him' ([1975] 1 WLR 1346 at 1350E–F). Lord Denning also invoked a doctrine of remedial constructive trust [**para 10.96**], arguing that by his wrongful termination of the woman's licence the landowner had 'obtained an unjust benefit and should make restitution' ([1975] 1 WLR 1346 at 1351B).
2   Compare the reluctance of differently constituted Courts of Appeal to resort, in similar cases, to a finding of indefinite contractual licence (see e g *Horrocks v Forray* [1976] 1 WLR 230 at 238H–239E; *Chandler v Kerley* [1978] 1 WLR 693 at 698G). See also [1979] Conv 184 (J M Masson); A A S Zuckerman, (1980) 96 LQR 248 at 257.
3   See e g *Johnson v Johnson* (Unreported, Court of Appeal, 11 March 1986); *Rogers v Eller* (Unreported, Court of Appeal, 20 May 1986); *Perry v Dixon* (Unreported, Court of Appeal, 28 October 1992); *McGill v S* [1979] IR 283 at 292. As the contractual shortcomings of *Tanner* became increasingly evident, it was perhaps significant that Lord Denning himself began to address the same problems in terms, not of contractual licence, but of estoppel doctrine (see e g *Greasley v Cooke* [1980] 1 WLR 1306 [**para 10.295**]).

4   **[Paras 4.88, 10.38]**. See *Hardwick v Johnson* [1978] 1 WLR 683 at 688H, where Lord Denning MR invented the terminology of a 'personal licence ... in the nature of an equitable licence', in order to uphold an irrevocable right of occupation on behalf of a participant in a family arrangement. Lord Denning thought that the court could 'look at all the circumstances and spell out the legal relationship ... and will find the terms of that relationship according to what reason and justice require' ([1978] 1 WLR 683 at 688D), but this broad approach has subsequently been disapproved (see *Hoskins v Hoskins* (Unreported, Court of Appeal, 3 December 1981); *Rogers v Eller* (Unreported, Court of Appeal, 20 May 1986)). For further reference to the 'equitable licence', see *Re Sharpe* (*A Bankrupt*) [1980] 1 WLR 219 at 224A **[para 10.38]**; *Beaton v McDivitt* (1985) 13 NSWLR 134 at 157D–E.

5   **[Para 10.168]**. The factual situation present in *Tanner* would have been better analysed in terms of proprietary estoppel (see E Ellis, (1979) 95 LQR 11).

6   **[Para 10.58]**.

7   **[Para 10.68]**.

TERMINATION OF CONTRACTUAL LICENCES

4.76   The law relating to the revocation and termination of contractual licences has undergone an important transformation during the past half-century. The inevitable effect of this change has been to infuse at least some sort of quasi-proprietary character into the status of many kinds of contractual licence.[1]

1   See *Jones v Jones* [2001] NI 244 at 257c per Girvan J.

Statutory restraint on eviction of contractual licensees

4.77   An overriding restraint on the eviction of certain kinds of contractual licensee is imposed by the Protection from Eviction Act 1977. Where premises have been occupied 'as a dwelling' under a licence (other than an 'excluded licence'[1]), it is unlawful otherwise than by court proceedings to enforce any right to recover possession of these premises from a licensee who continues to reside after the termination of his licence.[2]

1   A licence is 'excluded' if it involves various forms of sharing with a resident owner or a member of his family (PEA 1977, s 3A(2)–(3)) or was granted as a 'temporary expedient' to a trespasser (PEA 1977, s 3A(6)) or if it confers a right of occupation for a holiday only (PEA 1977, s 3A(7)(a)) or was granted otherwise than for money or money's worth (PEA 1977, s 3A(7)(b)). Certain kinds of statutorily controlled hostel accommodation are also 'excluded' (PEA 1977, s 3A(8)).

2   PEA 1977, s 3(1), (2B). See *Harrow LBC v Qazi* [2004] 1 AC 983 at [36] per Lord Hope of Craighead.

The doctrine of termination at will

4.78   In the latter part of the 19th century it became settled law that a contractual licence could be terminated by the licensor at any time, even though he acted in clear breach of his contractual undertaking to give reasonable notice or to allow the contract to run its contemplated course.[1] Wrongful termination gave the licensee a right to recover contractual damages[2] and the measure of this liability was determined by ordinary contractual principles.[3] In *Wood v Leadbitter*,[4] however, the Court of Exchequer accepted that breach of a contractual licence gave rise to no further liability (whether in tort or otherwise) if, following the revocation, the licensee was forcibly ejected or barred from the land.[5] Indeed the decision in *Wood v Leadbitter* demonstrates in its most extreme historical form the owner's paramount right to exclude. Here the claimant had purchased a ticket of admission to the grandstand and enclosure during the four days of the Doncaster races. The owner of the racecourse knew the claimant to have been involved in alleged betting malpractices at another racecourse and therefore caused him to be unceremoniously flung out of the enclosure. The plaintiff's claim for damages for assault and false imprisonment was rejected: the landowner had, in short, an unchallengeable discretion to withhold or withdraw permission to enter.[6]

1   Even in cases of peremptory termination, the licensor was bound to permit the licensee a reasonable time to remove himself **[para 4.30]**.
2   See e g *Kerrison v Smith* [1897] 2 QB 445 at 448–451; *Milton v Proctor* (1988) 4 BPR 9654 at 9660 per McHugh JA.
3   The court should not, for example, place the aggrieved party in a better financial position than if the contract had been duly performed (*C & P Haulage v Middleton* [1983] 1 WLR 1461 at 1467H–1468A). It used to be thought that the contractual damages appropriate in the 'cinema ticket' cases amounted simply to the price of the ticket, but it may be that, following *Jackson v Horizon Holidays Ltd* [1975] 1 WLR 1468 at 1472B–C, the damages will now include an element of compensation for disappointment and lost enjoyment.
4   (1845) 13 M & W 838 at 855, 153 ER 351 at 359. For an interesting account of the background to the litigation in this case, see P Polden, *A Day at the Races: Wood v Leadbitter in Context*, (1993) 14 Journal of Legal History 28.
5   See also *Hounslow LBC v Twickenham Garden Developments Ltd* [1971] Ch 233 at 243D–E; *Heatley v Tasmanian Racing and Gaming Commission* (1977) 14 ALR 519 at 534.
6   See *Hounslow LBC v Twickenham Garden Developments Ltd* [1971] Ch 233 at 249B–C, where Megarry J referred to the 'old distinction' between the licensor's *power* to revoke the licence effectively and his *right* or *liberty* to do it lawfully ('[h]e had the power: he did it: if he did it wrongfully he may have to pay damages: but still he did it').

Submergence of the doctrine of revocation at will

4.79   More recent developments – stimulated by the fusion of law and equity[1] – have given a quietus to any doctrine that the contractual licensor may simply elect, on pain of liability in contractual damages, to bring about the arbitrary and wrongful termination of a contractual licence.

1   **[Para 1.154]**.

Extensive range of contractual remedies

4.80   A contractual licence is no longer effectively revocable 'at the whim and will' of the licensor.[1] It has been said that such an approach 'should have died with Queen Victoria.'[2] Whilst contractual damages still remain available as a remedy for breach of a contractual licence,[3] damages do not represent the only (or even the most important) remedy available to the contractual licensee.[4] Today the contractual licence is widely viewed as 'irrevocable except as contemplated by the terms of the contract.'[5] On wrongful revocation (or threatened revocation) of the licence, the court has a discretion to decide whether the licence should be enforced in specie by an injunction or order for specific performance or whether breach should be compensated by the mere award of damages.[6] Purported revocation of a contractual licence is no longer necessarily definitive and, more often than not, the licensee is nowadays held entitled to occupy the land in accordance with the parameters of his licence,[7] the courts vindicating his right through the award of specific performance.

1   *Tan Hin Leong v Lee Teck Im* [2000] 3 SLR 85 at 95B per G P Selvam J. The doctrine of arbitrary revocation has been replaced by one of 'implied irrevocability at will' ([2000] 3 SLR 85 at 95F).
2   *Verrall v Great Yarmouth BC* [1981] QB 202 at 207F–G per Watkins J.
3   See e g *Tanner v Tanner* [1975] 1 WLR 1346 at 1351C (award of £2,000); *Ivory v Palmer* (1976) 237 EG 411 at 413; *Broughall v Hunt* (Unreported, Chancery Division, 1 February 1983).
4   *Verrall v Great Yarmouth BC* [1981] QB 202 at 209E per Watkins J.
5   *Tan Hin Leong v Lee Teck Im* [2000] 3 SLR 85 at 92C. Failure to give a contractually specified period of notice actually renders the purported termination of the licence ineffective (see *Wallshire Ltd v Advertising Sites Ltd* [1988] 2 EGLR 167 at 168K–L; *McMahon v Rowston* (1958) 75 WN (NSW) 508 at 513; *Grundel v Registrar General* (1990) 5 BPR 11217 at 11223).
6   In some circumstances failure to provide specific performance of a contractual licence may constitute an interference with the right to peaceful enjoyment of possessions guaranteed by ECHR Protocol No 1, Art 1 (see *Iatridis v Greece* (1999) 30 EHRR 97 at [55], [62] (applicant evicted from cinema which he had 'a specific licence to operate')).
7   *Tan Hin Leong v Lee Teck Im* [2000] 3 SLR 85 at 90A.

Changing character of the contractual licence

4.81   As always the jural character of a right is heavily determined by the nature and extent of the remedies which the courts award for its violation.[1] Modern developments in this area have therefore had the indirect effect not only of altering the rules as to the termination of contractual licences but also of adjusting the status of the contractual licence within the broader field of property concepts. At the heart of these developments has been a new found judicial willingness to imply into many contractual licences a negative contractual term in restraint of arbitrary or premature revocation.

1   [**Para 4.97**].

The 'implied contract' theory

4.82   It has come to be accepted that, in a contractual licence, the element of licence is not a separate entity but is merely one of the manifestations of the contract within which it is contained.[1] Thus, where a contract contains a permission to occupy land for a specific purpose or period of time, it is frequently possible to spell out in the contract an implied negative obligation on the part of the licensor, ie an obligation not to revoke the licence wrongfully before the completion of that purpose or period. Such a term may be implied, for instance, in contractual licences which confer on the licensee a right to watch a theatre performance[2] or to carry out a building operation[3] or to hold a meeting in a public hall.[4] The recognition of this implied term facilitated an even more important step in the evolution of the law.

1   See *Millennium Productions Ltd v Winter Garden Theatre (London) Ltd* [1946] 1 All ER 678 at 680E–H; *Hounslow LBC v Twickenham Garden Developments Ltd* [1971] Ch 233 at 246C per Megarry J.
2   *Hurst v Picture Theatres Ltd* [1915] 1 KB 1 at 10 (regarded as 'rightly decided' in *Winter Garden Theatre (London) Ltd v Millennium Productions Ltd* [1948] AC 173 at 189 per Viscount Simon).
3   *Hounslow LBC v Twickenham Garden Developments Ltd* [1971] Ch 233 at 247B–C.
4   *Verrall v Great Yarmouth BC* [1981] QB 202 **[para 4.86]**.

The equitable approach to contractual licences

4.83   The implication of a negative term in restraint of premature or improper revocation revolutionised the power of the courts to regulate rights of contractual licence. It opened the way for the courts to exercise an equitable jurisdiction to restrain the licensor by injunction from wrongful eviction of the licensee before the due termination of the contract.[1] As the Court of Appeal explained in *Winter Garden Theatre (London) Ltd v Millennium Productions Ltd*,[2] the courts will not assist the licensor to act in breach of his contractual undertaking.[3] The settled practice of the courts of equity is 'to do what they can by an injunction to preserve the sanctity of a bargain.'[4]

1   Where no negative obligation arises either expressly or impliedly from the dealings of the parties, injunctive relief cannot be granted and the contractual licence is determinable on the giving of reasonable notice (see *Patel v Patel* [1983] Court of Appeal Unbound Transcript 930). If terminated in breach of contract, the licence gives rise to a mere action for damages (see *Ivory v Palmer* (1976) 237 EG 411 at 413–416). The *equitable* character of injunctive relief also explains why the new approach to contractual licences is unavailable in respect of bare or gratuitous licences: equity will not normally assist a volunteer **[para 9.6]**.
2   [1946] 1 All ER 678 at 685 per Lord Greene MR (reversed by the House of Lords on different grounds, [1948] AC 173). See also Sir R Evershed, (1954) 70 LQR 326 at 332–341.
3   See *Hounslow LBC v Twickenham Garden Developments Ltd* [1971] Ch 233 at 248C–E. The contrary view taken by the majority of the High Court of Australia in *Cowell v Rosehill Racecourse Co Ltd* (1937) 56 CLR 605 has since been explained as based on the separation then existing in New South Wales between the jurisdictions of law and equity (see *Munday v Australian Capital Territory* (Unreported, Supreme Court, ACT, 8 July 1998) per Higgins J).
4   *Winter Garden Theatre (London) Ltd v Millennium Productions Ltd* [1948] AC 173 at 202 per Lord Uthwatt. See also *Verrall v Great Yarmouth BC* [1981] QB 202 at 222D per Cumming-Bruce LJ; *Tan Hin Leong v Lee Teck Im* [2000] 3 SLR 85 at 96A per G P Selvam J.

The Errington decision

4.84   One of the first significant demonstrations of the new equitable approach occurred in *Errington v Errington and Woods*.[1] Here a father, wishing to provide a home for his son who had recently married, purchased a house in his own name with the aid of a mortgage loan. He promised that if his son and daughter-in-law continued in occupation of the house and paid all the instalments of the mortgage loan, he would then transfer the house to them absolutely. The son and his wife entered into occupation and began to make repayments of the loan to the building society. The father later died, leaving all his property (including the house) to his widow, the present claimant. Shortly after the father's death, the son left his wife and went to live with his widowed mother. The daughter-in-law, the defendant in the present proceedings, continued to occupy the house and to make the appropriate repayments to the building society. The claimant then brought an action for possession, alleging that the defendant had a mere revocable licence to occupy the house.

1   [1952] 1 KB 290. See generally H W R Wade, (1948) 64 LQR 57; R H Maudsley, (1956) 20 Conv (NS) 281.

4.85   The Court of Appeal unanimously rejected the claim for possession and declined to eject the daughter-in-law. Denning LJ found that the father's promise was 'a unilateral contract – a promise of the house in return for their act of paying the instalments. It could not be revoked by him once the couple entered on performance of the act.'[1] This being so, the couple were licensees who enjoyed 'a permissive occupation short of a tenancy', but who also had 'a contractual right, or at any rate, an equitable right to remain so long as they paid the instalments, which would grow into a good equitable title to the house as soon as the mortgage was paid.'[2] Denning LJ fully recognised that the couple had no right to remain at law, 'but only in equity, and equitable rights now prevail.'[3] The inevitable effect of the fusion of law and equity,[4] together with the ruling in the *Winter Garden Theatre* case, was to ensure that 'a licensor will not be permitted to eject a licensee in breach of a contract to allow him to remain.'[5]

1   [1952] 1 KB 290 at 295.
2   [1952] 1 KB 290 at 296. The case is 'a classic illustration of equity supplementing a contractual right so as to give effect to the intention of the parties to the arrangement' (*Chandler v Kerley* [1978] 1 WLR 693 at 697H–698A per Lord Scarman). See also *Hardwick v Johnson* [1978] 1 WLR 683 at 689H. The interest of the young couple in *Errington* has since been variously described as (i) an equitable interest in the form of an estate contract, (ii) an interest based on estoppel by representation, and (iii) an interest by way of constructive trust (see *Ashburn Anstalt v Arnold* [1989] Ch 1 at 17A–C).
3   [1952] 1 KB 290 at 298.
4   See also *Verrall v Great Yarmouth BC* [1981] QB 202 at 220B–C per Roskill LJ.
5   [1952] 1 KB 290 at 298–299 ('This infusion of equity means that contractual licences now have a force and validity of their own'). See also *Verrall v Great Yarmouth BC* [1981] QB 202 at 216D per Lord Denning MR.

Specific performance of contractual expectations

4.86   Although some of Denning LJ's observations in *Errington* were later disapproved by the Court of Appeal on other grounds,[1] the immediate (and lasting) effect of the *Errington* ruling was to confirm the demise of the *Wood v*

Leadbitter doctrine that contractual licences were *always* de facto revocable. Instead, the modern position appears to be that, practicalities of time and circumstance permitting, injunctive relief is available at the discretion of equity[2] to restrain threatened breaches of a contractual licence.[3] Where injunctive relief is available, the court is also frequently prepared to grant the further remedy of specific performance in order to ensure that the terms of a contractual licence are duly carried out. Where the parties have contracted for a licence, 'equity will today provide an equitable remedy to protect the legal right.'[4] The duration of the licence, no matter how limited, is no bar to equitable relief,[5] provided that application for such relief can be made in time to preserve the performance of the entitlement in question.[6] Nor does it matter whether the licensee seeks the assistance of equity prior to his entry upon the land or in defence of an existing occupancy.[7] Thus, in *Verrall v Great Yarmouth BC*,[8] the Court of Appeal granted specific performance of a two-day booking of a public hall for the annual conference of the National Front, notwithstanding the attempts of the landowner, the local council, to repudiate the relevant contractual licence and force a cancellation of the forthcoming conference.

1   In *Ashburn Anstalt v Arnold* [1989] Ch 1 at 22B–D, the Court of Appeal, whilst conceding the actual decision in *Errington* to have been correct, regarded as per incuriam Denning LJ's pronouncement as to the general impact of contractual licences upon third parties [paras 10.90, 12.226].

2   The court may be particularly inclined to intervene by way of injunction where (e g in the case of a large all-ticket meeting organised at an advertised venue) it is impossible to quantify in damages the inconvenience, disappointment and general disruption caused by a late cancellation (see *Alonso v Leichhardt Municipal Council* (1975) 1 BPR 9368 at 9373–9374). Defence of the principle of freedom of speech, albeit in expression of an odious cause, may also influence the exercise of judicial discretion in favour of specific performance of a contractual licence (see *Verrall v Great Yarmouth BC* [1981] QB 202 at 210A–C, 216H–217C per Lord Denning MR, 221C–F per Roskill LJ).

3   *Winter Garden Theatre (London) Ltd v Millennium Productions Ltd* [1946] 1 All ER 678 at 684; *Foster v Robinson* [1951] 1 KB 149 at 156 (as cited in *Binions v Evans* [1972] Ch 359 at 367D); *Hounslow LBC v Twickenham Garden Developments Ltd* [1971] Ch 233 at 247B–C, 248F; *Piquet v Tyler* [1978] CLY Unreported Court of Appeal Case No 119.

4   *Chandler v Kerley* [1978] 1 WLR 693 at 697C per Lord Scarman. See also *Mayfield Holdings Ltd v Moana Reef Ltd* [1973] 1 NZLR 309 at 316.

5   It matters not that the licence relates to a 'transient' use of premises for a comparatively short period of time (see *Verrall v Great Yarmouth BC* [1981] QB 202 at 207F–208A per Watkins J, 215D–F per Lord Denning MR, 220A–C per Roskill LJ).

6   The contractual licensee is otherwise relegated to an action in damages for breach of contract (*Tanner v Tanner* [1975] 1 WLR 1346 at 1351A–C). A licensee who has been wrongfully ejected from the land in breach of his contractual licence may also seek damages for assault and battery (see e g *Hurst v Picture Theatres Ltd* [1915] 1 KB 1 at 11, 15).

7   *Verrall v Great Yarmouth BC* [1981] QB 202 at 209G–H per Watkins J, 216D–F per Lord Denning MR, 220D–221B per Roskill LJ.

8   [1981] QB 202 at 216A–F, 218B, 220D–F.

Circumstances inappropriate for equitable relief

4.87   There may of course be some circumstances in which equity is either unwilling or unable to grant discretionary relief to a contractual licensee, notwithstanding that a threatened revocation is in clear breach of contract. In

Thompson v Park,[1] for example, the Court of Appeal held that a highly personal sharing arrangement was not enforceable by way of injunction.[2] Equity cannot enforce 'an agreement for two people to live peaceably under the same roof.'[3] The Court held that under these circumstances the revocation of a contractual licence, although wrongful, was nevertheless effective, with the consequence that when the ejected licensee forcibly re-entered the premises he was guilty of trespass.[4] Similarly, equity will not specifically enforce the continuation of a relationship which is based on mutuality of trust and obligation.[5]

1   [1944] KB 408.
2   Here the owners of two schools had agreed to share occupation of premises which were owned by one of them.
3   [1944] KB 408 at 409.
4   [1944] KB 408 at 411–412. In *Hounslow LBC v Twickenham Garden Developments Ltd* [1971] Ch 233 at 249F–G, Megarry J confessed to 'feeling great difficulty' about the grounds given for this decision. He suggested that the case was decided 'quasi in furore' by way of heated response to the licensee's 'high-handed and riotous behaviour'. Although the point remains somewhat unclear, it is possible that the observations of the House of Lords in *Winter Garden Theatre* (*London*) *Ltd v Millennium Productions Ltd* [1948] AC 173 have at least the effect of relieving the contractual licensee of liability for trespass in this kind of case (see *Verrall v Great Yarmouth BC* [1981] QB 202 at 216C–G, 219C–E).
5   See eg *Melbourne Anglican Trust Corpn v Greentree* (Unreported, 29 May 1997), where the Supreme Court of Victoria, on the Archbishop's revocation of an incumbent's licence to occupy a vicarage, granted a possession order against a priest who was embroiled in an 'irretrievable breakdown in pastoral relationships'.

LICENCES COUPLED WITH AN EQUITY

4.88　The modern equitable approach to contractual licences is merely one emanation of a more ancient doctrine relating to the irrevocability of certain kinds of licence. The doctrine of the 'licence coupled with an equity' or the 'licence acted upon' effectively foreshadowed the conscience-based theory which underlies the contemporary principle of proprietary estoppel.[1]

1   [**Para 10.168**].

Irrevocability of licences 'acted upon'

4.89　In the Court of Appeal in *National Provincial Bank Ltd v Hastings Car Mart Ltd*,[1] Lord Denning MR adverted to a long line of cases which establish the legal implications of the phenomenon known as the 'licence coupled with an equity.'[2] Lord Denning explained the 'licence coupled with an equity' as arising where the owner of land 'grants a licence to another to go upon land and occupy it for a specific period or a prescribed purpose, and on the faith of that authority the licensee enters into occupation and does work, or in some other way alters his position to his detriment'. In such circumstances, declared Lord Denning,

> the owner cannot revoke the licence at his will. He cannot revoke the licence so as to defeat the period or purpose for which it was granted. A

court of equity will restrain him from so doing. Not only will it restrain him, but it will restrain any successor in title who takes the land with knowledge of the arrangement that has been made.[3]

1   [1964] Ch 665 at 686.
2   Lord Denning drew an analogy with the 'licence coupled with the grant of an interest' [**para 4.91**], which has long been recognised as conferring on the licensee an irrevocable right binding on third parties.
3   [1964] Ch 665 at 686. For expositions of the doctrine that a licence, once acted upon, is irrevocable, see *Webb v Paternoster* (1619) 2 Rolle 143, 81 ER 713; Palm 71 at 72–73, 81 ER 983 at 984; Popham 151, 79 ER 1250; *Winter v Brockwell* (1807) 8 East 308 at 310, 103 ER 359 at 360; *Tayler v Waters* (1816) 7 Taunt 374 at 384, 129 ER 150 at 153; *Liggins v Inge* (1831) 7 Bing 682 at 691–692, 131 ER 263 at 267; *Feltham v Cartwright* (1839) 5 Bing (NC) 569 at 572–573, 132 ER 1219 at 1220; *Wood v Manley* (1839) 11 A & E 34 at 37–38, 113 ER 325 at 326; *Hounslow LBC v Twickenham Garden Developments Ltd* [1971] Ch 233 at 255A–F; *Woods v Donnelly* [1982] NI 257 at 266D–F; *Classic Communications Ltd v Lascar* (1986) 21 DLR (4th) 579 at 585–586.

Proprietary impact of the 'licence coupled with an equity'

4.90   The equity-laden connotations of the 'licence acted upon' have provided a powerful motivating force behind the modern development of closely allied notions of 'equitable' or 'irrevocable' licence and the licence founded on 'equitable' or 'proprietary' estoppel.[1] All such notions recognise some kind of informally created entitlement which is not arbitrarily terminable by the landowner. By making legal sense of certain ill-defined relationships in respect of land, the amalgam of these versions of licence has done much to counteract the deficiencies of the law of trusts. In common these concepts bear a strong proprietary resonance, not least as measured in terms of binding effect on third parties.[2] Indeed, the terminology of 'equitable licence' and 'equitable estoppel' goes some distance towards obscuring the precise borderline between personal and proprietary rights, since it is only in relation to proprietary interests that the distinction between *legal* and *equitable* quality is, in English law, strictly appropriate.

1   [**Paras 4.75, 10.168**]. In *National Provincial Bank Ltd v Hastings Car Mart Ltd* [1964] Ch 665 at 686–688, Lord Denning pointed to the close links existing between the doctrine of the 'licence coupled with an equity', the principle of proprietary estoppel and the modern equitable development of the contractual licence.
2   [**Paras 12.233, 12.368**].

LICENCES COUPLED WITH THE GRANT OF AN INTEREST

4.91   Another form of licence long recognised by the common law is the 'licence coupled with the grant of an interest'. If licences can be graded across a span of propertiness, with the bare licence most lacking in proprietary content, the form of licence which undoubtedly crosses the threshold of recognised proprietary rights in land is the licence coupled with the grant of an interest. Such a licence usually comprises a permission to enter upon another's land for the specific purpose of removing something from that land (eg timber, minerals, fish, crops, or game).[1] In effect this form of licence combines the grant of an interest (such as a profit *à prendre*[2]) with an ancillary permission to enter the land in order to realise or exploit that interest.[3]

1   *Muskett v Hill* (1839) 5 Bing (NC) 694 at 707–708, 132 ER 1267 at 1272–1273; *Wood v Leadbitter* (1845) 13 M & W 838 at 844–845, 153 ER 351 at 354–355; *Hounslow LBC v Twickenham Garden Developments Ltd* [1971] Ch 233 at 243D.

2   [**Para 8.17**]. The right to cut down and remove trees constitutes 'a licence as to the acts of cutting down timber but as to removing them it would be a grant' (*Reid v Moreland Timber Co Pty Ltd* (1946) 73 CLR 1 at 8 per Starke J, 13 per McTiernan J). See also *Thomas v Sorrell* (1673) Vaugh 330 at 351, 124 ER 1098 at 1109; *Muskett v Hill* (1839) 5 Bing (NC) 694 at 707–708, 132 ER 1267 at 1272–1273; *Sim v Nirvana Pty Ltd* (2000) SR (WA) 11 at 23–24 (mining licence).

3   See eg *Thomas v Sorrell* (1673) Vaugh 330 at 351, 124 ER 1098 at 1109; *Wood v Leadbitter* (1845) 13 M & W 838 at 844–845, 153 ER 351 at 354–355. A licence coupled with the grant of an interest need not always involve a profit *à prendre*: a profit *à prendre* presupposes severance from the realty. See eg *James Jones & Sons Ltd v Earl of Tankerville* [1909] 2 Ch 440 (licence to enter and take away timber which had already been felled); *Beaton v McDivitt* (1985) 13 NSWLR 134 at 146C–D.

Types of 'interest'

4.92   The courts have provided no authoritative definition of the categories of 'interest' to which a licence may be attached.[1] The the older English case law tended to include amongst the relevant types of 'interest' not merely interests in land and chattels but also the 'interest' which a licensee might have in attending a creditors' meeting[2] or in seeing a cinema performance.[3] The modern trend is, however, more restrictive. It is unlikely, for instance, that a relevant 'interest' can be asserted by a contractor who is engaged to work on a building site.[4] Nor can a spectator or competitor attending a motor sports event claim that his access to the competition area is supported by a 'licence coupled with an interest.'[5] The difficulty with many of the kinds of 'interest' claimed as coupled with a licence is that they involve 'no shred of proprietary interest in the … land or any chattels on it', yet, if correctly decided, make it difficult 'to see any fair stopping place in what amounts to an interest, short of any legitimate reason for being on the land.'[6] It is therefore best to regard the licence coupled with a grant as restricted to proprietary or possessory interests only.[7]

1   *Hounslow LBC v Twickenham Garden Developments Ltd* [1971] Ch 233 at 243G per Megarry J.

2   *Vaughan v Hampson* (1875) 33 LT 15 at 16. Compare, however, *Alonso v Leichhardt Municipal Council* (1975) 1 BPR 9368 at 9371.

3   *Hurst v Picture Theatres Ltd* [1915] 1 KB 1 at 7. (The *Hurst* case is better analysed in terms of a simple contractual licence [**para 4.60**]. For criticism of the reasoning in *Hurst*, see *Cowell v Rosehill Racecourse Co Ltd* (1937) 56 CLR 605 at 621–622 per Latham CJ, 631–632 per Dixon J, 652 per Evatt J; *Mayfield Holdings Ltd v Moana Reef Ltd* [1973] 1 NZLR 309 at 315. Compare, however, *Hounslow LBC v Twickenham Garden Developments Ltd* [1971] Ch 233 at 244G–245A, 248F.)

4   See *Hounslow LBC v Twickenham Garden Developments Ltd* [1971] Ch 233 at 244G, 248F; *Sports Australia Pty Ltd v Nillumbik SC* (Unreported, Supreme Court of Victoria, 29 January 1996).

5   See *White v Blackmore* [1972] 2 QB 651 at 669H per Buckley LJ, 675G per Roskill LJ
    [para 5.31].
6   *Hounslow LBC v Twickenham Garden Developments Ltd* [1971] Ch 233 at 244D–H per
    Megarry J. See also *Cowell v Rosehill Racecourse Co Ltd* (1937) 56 CLR 605 at 630–632 per
    Dixon J; *Sim v Nirvana Pty Ltd* (2000) SR (WA) 11 at 24–25 (purchase option insufficient).
7   See e g *Mayfield Holdings Ltd v Moana Reef Ltd* [1973] 1 NZLR 309 at 315 per Mahon J; *Sim
    v Nirvana Pty Ltd* (2000) SR (WA) 11 at 24; *Clos Farming Estates Pty Ltd v Easton* [2002]
    NSWCA 389 at [65].

Creation

4.93   In so far as the permission to enter on land is ancillary to the grant of
some recognised proprietary interest, it is necessary that this proprietary
interest should itself have been the subject of valid creation. In the case of a
profit *à prendre*, the interest concerned should normally have been granted by
deed[1] or duly acquired by prescription.[2] The same formality of grant is not
required where the licence is linked to some proprietary interest of a chattel
character, as for instance in the case of a licence to enter on land and remove a
crop of already harvested hay or cut timber.[3]

1   *Reid v Moreland Timber Co Pty Ltd* (1946) 73 CLR 1 at 8 per Starke J, 16 per Williams J. On
    the *Walsh v Lonsdale* principle **[para 9.66]**, equity is prepared to regard the non-gratuitous
    grant of a profit by informal writing as a specifically enforceable agreement to grant an
    interest and therefore as an equitable profit.
2   **[Para 8.168]**.
3   See e g *James Jones & Sons Ltd v Earl of Tankerville* [1909] 2 Ch 440 at 442; *Wood v Manley*
    (1839) 11 A & E 34 at 37, 113 ER 325 at 326.

Revocation

4.94   A licence coupled with the grant of a proprietary interest is irrevocable
during the subsistence of the interest to which it pertains.[1] So long as the
proprietary interest in question was validly created,[2] the licence is co-extensive
with it and enjoys the same durable character.[3] Thus a licence is irrevocable
even if coupled with an informal grant of a proprietary interest which is
effective only in equity.[4] A licence coupled with a grant is capable of assignment
to third parties.[5] Moreover, because this form of licence lives and dies with the
interest to which it is annexed, it binds not only the licensor, but also all his
successors in title against whom, on conventional principles,[6] the interest
granted (e g a profit *à prendre*) remains enforceable.[7]

1   *Doe d Hanley v Wood* (1819) 2 B & Ald 724 at 738–740, 106 ER 529 at 534–535; *Wood v
    Manley* (1839) 11 A & E 34 at 37, 113 ER 325 at 326; *Wood v Leadbitter* (1845) 13 M & W 838
    at 845, 153 ER 351 at 354; *Reid v Moreland Timber Co Pty Ltd* (1946) 73 CLR 1 at 8, 16;
    Hounslow LBC v Twickenham Garden Developments Ltd [1971] Ch 233 at 243D; *Mayfield
    Holdings Ltd v Moana Reef Ltd* [1973] 1 NZLR 309 at 314; *Woods v Donnelly* [1982] NI 257 at
    263A–C; *Sim v Nirvana Pty Ltd* (2000) SR (WA) 11 at 23–24.
2   *Wood v Leadbitter* (1845) 13 M & W 838 at 845, 153 ER 351 at 354–355.
3   See *Woods v Donnelly* [1982] NI 257 at 263C, where Hutton J held that a licence granted for
    life to draw sand and gravel could not be terminated without consent during the grantee's life.

A 'licence coupled with an interest' is irrevocable 'so long as the term of the grant of the ancillary interest continues' (*Patel v Patel* [1983] Court of Appeal Unbound Transcript 930 per Slade LJ).

4   *James Jones & Sons Ltd v Earl of Tankerville* [1909] 2 Ch 440 at 442–443; *Frogley v Earl of Lovelace* (1859) Johns 333 at 339–340, 70 ER 450 at 453; *Chandler v Kerley* [1978] 1 WLR 693 at 697D–E; *Reid v Moreland Timber Co Pty Ltd* (1946) 73 CLR 1 at 8, 16; *Woods v Donnelly* [1982] NI 257 at 263G [9.92].

5   *Muskett v Hill* (1839) 5 Bing (NC) 694 at 710, 132 ER 1267 at 1273; *Reid v Moreland Timber Co Pty Ltd* (1946) 73 CLR 1 at 15. The assignability of the licence may be restricted by an expression of contrary intention (see *Woods v Donnelly* [1982] NI 257 at 263C).

6   **[Paras 8.215, 9.99]**.

7   *Webb v Paternoster* (1619) Palm 71 at 72–73, 81 ER 983 at 984; 2 Rolle 143, 81 ER 713; Popham 151, 79 ER 1250. See also *Silovi Pty Ltd v Barbaro* (1988) 13 NSWLR 466 at 475C–D per Priestley JA.

JUST HOW PROPRIETARY IS THE MODERN LICENCE?

4.95   There is no entirely clear or complete answer to this controversial question – nor indeed any true consensus as to its meaning. Some forms of bare licence (eg the dinner party invitation[1]) have no sensible proprietary content and can never bind third parties. Other forms of licence, particularly those coupled with an 'equity'[2] or with the grant of an 'interest',[3] are widely regarded as having substantial proprietary significance.[4] It is, as usual, the *contractual licence* which poses the real dilemma in terms of proprietary character.[5]

1   **[Para 2.51]**.
2   **[Para 4.88]**.
3   **[Para 4.91]**.
4   **[Paras 4.90, 4.91]**.
5   See further Chapter 12 **[paras 12.223, 12.364]**.

Impact on purchasers

4.96   If the 'property' component in the contractual licence is measured by its capacity to bind a purchaser of the licensor's estate, the strong trend in the modern case law is to maintain that 'a contractual licence does not create a property interest.'[1] In the generality of cases contractual licences are not nowadays regarded as impacting on purchasers of land,[2] this approach being said to depend – although in a somewhat circular fashion[3] – on an historic view of 'an important and intelligible distinction between contractual obligations which gave rise to no estate or interest in the land and proprietary rights which, by definition, did.'[4] On this basis it is often asserted, somewhat blandly, that a contractual licence never confers on the licensee any interest in the land itself.[5]

1   *Ashburn Anstalt v Arnold* [1989] Ch 1 at 24D per Fox LJ. See likewise *Camden LBC v Shortlife Community Housing Ltd* (1992) 90 LGR 358 at 373 per Millett J; *Canadian Imperial Bank of Commerce v Bello* (1992) 64 P & CR 48 at 51 per Dillon LJ; *IDC Group Ltd v Clark* (1992) 65 P & CR 179 at 181 per Nourse LJ; *Nationwide Anglia Building Society v Ahmed* (1995) 70 P & CR 381 at 387, 389 per Aldous LJ; *Habermann v Koehler* (1996) 73 P & CR 515 at 520 per Evans LJ, 523 per Peter Gibson LJ; *Melbury Road Properties 1995 Ltd v Kreidi* [1999] 3 EGLR 108 at 110H–J; *Lloyd v Dugdale* [2002] 2 P & CR 13 at [52(4)] per Sir Christopher Slade.

2   Exceptional circumstances may arise in which the conscience of a purchaser is bound by a constructive trust to give effect to a contractual licence affecting the land purchased by him [**para 10.90**].
3   [**Para 2.55**].
4   *Ashburn Anstalt v Arnold* [1989] Ch 1 at 22B–C per Fox LJ.
5   See e g *Patel v Patel* [1983] Court of Appeal Unbound Transcript 930 per Slade LJ; *Melbury Road Properties 1995 Ltd v Kreidi* [1999] 3 EGLR 108 at 110H–J; *Teo Siew Peng v Neo Hock Pheng* [1999] 1 SLR 293 at 301h; *Tan Hin Leong v Lee Teck Im* [2000] 3 SLR 85 at 92C.

Proprietary effect of curial protection

4.97   If, on the other hand, the proprietary quality of a right is measured in terms of the protection afforded to it (particularly against all comers),[1] there is substantial ground for believing that most varieties of licence have now acquired some proprietary quality. Proprietary character is the effect, rather than the cause, of curial relief in support of a right.[2] Thus, for instance, in *Federal Airports Corpn v Makucha Developments Pty Ltd*,[3] the Federal Court of Australia held that equity's willingness to grant specific performance of a contractual licence[4] confers on the licensee a 'proprietary interest in the land, beyond a mere personal interest to use the land in common with others.'[5] It is not without significance, moreover, that many of the classic denials that a contractual licence can comprise an interest in land pre-date the fusion of legal and equitable jurisdictions.[6]

1   [**Para 2.55**]. For the doctrine that equitable property is 'commensurate with equitable relief', see *Hoysted v Federal Commissioner of Taxation* (1920) 27 CLR 400 at 423 per Isaacs J; *Hewitt v Court* (1982) 149 CLR 639 at 665 per Deane J [**para 9.33**].
2   See *Yanner v Eaton* (1999) 201 CLR 351 at [85] per Gummow J.
3   (1993) 115 ALR 679 at 700.
4   [**Para 4.86**].
5   See also *Sports Australia Pty Ltd v Nillumbik Shire Council* (Unreported, Supreme Court of Victoria, 29 January 1996).
6   See *Lowe v Adams* [1901] 2 Ch 598 at 600 per Cozens Hardy J; *Winter Garden Theatre (London) Ltd v Millennium Productions Ltd* [1948] AC 173 at 191 per Viscount Simon; *Cowell*, supra at 649 per Evatt J; *McBean v Howey* [1958] NZLR 25 at 28; *Adrian Messenger Services and Enterprises Ltd v Jockey Club Ltd* (1972) 25 DLR (3d) 529 at 544; *Munday v Australian Capital Territory* (Unreported, Supreme Court, ACT, 8 July 1998).

4.98   Nowadays, moreover, the enhanced defensibility of many kinds of licence against trespassers provides a basis for attributing at least some limited property content to the licensee's entitlement.[1] In *Manchester Airport Plc v Dutton*,[2] for example, the Court of Appeal held that a claimant armed with a contractual right to 'enter and occupy' land was entitled to possession of that land against trespassers, even though the licensee did not yet enjoy either possession or occupation. The fact that today this substantial degree of protection is available even to a contractual licensee is indicative of the evolutionary process which is operating upon licences generally.

1   '[T]he law has developed to a stage where it would no longer be accurate to say that a licence never creates an interest in land' (*Milton v Proctor* (1988) 4 BPR 9654 at 9672 per Clarke JA).
2   [2000] QB 133 at 150A–E, 151B–H [**paras 3.38, 7.145**].

4.99   It is far from impossible that the contractual licence will one day be recognised in the fullest sense as a species of proprietary interest in land. For years the *numerus clausus* principle[1] silently moved English courts to deny that proprietary status could ever be attained by such a protean phenomenon, but the force of this rationale may dissipate with the arrival of a regime of easy computerised registration of all land-related rights. There is already an increasing tendency for modern statute law to treat the contractual licence as the full equivalent of a proprietary estate in land.[2] It is also clear that certain contractual licences to occupy land[3] come within the concept of a 'leasing or letting of immovable property' for the purpose of exemption from value added taxation under the relevant EC Council Directive.[4] The lease and the licence also seem likely to become indistinguishably merged in the 'housing agreement' which forms the basic conceptual device underpinning current proposals for reform of the residential rented sector.[5]

1   [**Para 2.95**].
2   See Housing Act 1985, s 79(3) (secure tenancy) [**para 14.339**]; Agricultural Holdings Act 1986, s 2(2)(b) (agricultural holding) [**para 14.361**].
3   Examples of contractual licences to 'occupy' land might include a contract to take a room for a week or to park a car in a specified parking space (*Customs and Excise Commrs v Sinclair Collis Ltd* [2001] STC 989 at [71] per Lord Scott of Foscote). The 'leasing or letting' exemption does not, however, include a contractual licence for the mere 'use' of land, e g for the consumption of a cup of coffee (or more) in a cafe (see *Customs and Excise Commrs v Sinclair Collis Ltd*, supra at [26] per Lord Slynn of Hadley, [67] per Lord Scott of Foscote) or for the installation of cigarette vending machine in a public house or hotel bar (*Sinclair Collis Ltd v Customs and Excise Commrs* (*Case C-275/01*) [2003] STC 898 at Judgment [31]).
4   EC Council Directive 77/388 (The Sixth VAT Directive), Title X, art 13B [**para 7.142**].
5   See Law Commission, *Renting Homes 1: Status and Security* (Law Com Consultation Paper No 162, 28 March 2002), paras 9.21–9.42.

CHAPTER 5

Public rights in land

THE NATURE OF PUBLIC RIGHTS IN LAND

5.1 Earlier chapters have adverted to the nature of 'property' in land. It now becomes possible to examine some rights relating to land which fall towards the weaker end of the proprietary spectrum. At best, these rights generally confer only limited degrees of control over or access to land, although the intensity of the precise stake conferred in the land depends upon the right in question. For want of a better term, these entitlements may perhaps be termed 'quasi-proprietary',[1] in that they exhibit only tentatively or imperfectly the characteristics which are conventionally associated with 'property' in land. Many of the rights falling within this category nevertheless display at least one of the orthodox proprietary attributes: they comprise 'rights in reference to land which have the quality of being capable of enduring through different ownerships of the land.'[2]

1 It is sometimes said that access rights which are enjoyed in common with all the world as 'members of the public' cannot be classified as 'proprietary' (see *Kanak v Minister for Land and Water Conservation (NSW)* (2000) 180 ALR 489 at [31] (Bondi beach)). See also *Stow v Mineral Holdings (Australia) Pty Ltd* (1977) 180 CLR 295 at 311–312 per Aickin J.

2 See *National Provincial Bank Ltd v Hastings Car Mart Ltd* [1964] Ch 665 at 696 per Russell LJ **[para 2.54]**. The extended third party impact of public rights is often made statutorily explicit (see e g Highways Act 1980, s 35(4) **[para 5.25]**; CROWA 2000, s 16(7) **[para 5.46]**; LRA 2002, Sch 1, para 5, Sch 3, para 5 **[para 5.3]**).

5.2 Most of these 'quasi-proprietary' entitlements comprise rights of a *public* nature, ie rights which are exercisable by anyone, whether he owns land or not, merely by virtue of his being a member of the public.[1] Some public rights resemble profits *à prendre*[2] (e g the public right of fishing). Other public rights are akin to easements (e g the public right in respect of the highway). However, all public rights are distinct from easements,[3] since they do not presuppose the existence of any 'dominant tenement'[4] and are never the subject of a specific grant to any individual.[5]

1   See *Overseas Investment Ltd v Simcobuild Construction Ltd and Swansea CC* (1995) 70 P & CR 322 at 328.
2   **[Para 8.17]**.
3   The public right of passage along the highway is sometimes – albeit inaccurately – referred to as an 'easement' (see e g *Harrison v Duke of Rutland* [1893] 1 QB 142 at 154 per Lopes LJ; compare the more correct analysis in *Martin v Cameron* (1894) 12 NZLR 769 at 771; *Man O'War Station Ltd v Auckland CC* [2000] 2 NZLR 267 at [68]).
4   **[Para 8.26]**.
5   For an excellent account of public rights, see Tim Bonyhady, *The Law of the Countryside: the Rights of the Public* (Abingdon 1987).

PUBLIC RIGHT TO USE THE HIGHWAY

5.3   Every citizen has a right of reasonable use of any highway over which the public has acquired a right of way either by statute or by reason of dedication and acceptance at common law.[1] This public right has an obvious importance not only in facilitating transport by road, but also in promoting recreational access to the countryside and in underpinning vital liberties of movement, expression, association and assembly.[2] Public rights in respect of the highway have at least some proprietary dimension in that they constitute overriding interests pursuant to the Land Registration Act 2002[3] and probably cannot be defeated by adverse possession.[4] Such rights are also increasingly viewed as rights of generalised beneficial ownership pursuant to some public trust vested in the appropriate highway authority. The United States Supreme Court has long declared city streets and squares to be 'held in the public trust.'[5] This perception is now widely shared throughout the Commonwealth[6] and, although more muted in the English authorities,[7] is beginning to acquire juristic currency in this country too.[8]

1   Landowners adjoining the public highway likewise enjoy a right of access to that highway, but have no common law right to have an access *constructed* from their land to that highway (*Shellharbour Municipal Council v Rovili Pty Ltd* (1989) 16 NSWLR 104 at 109F–110A). See also *Frecklington v Wellington City Council* [1988] 1 NZLR 72 at 75–76.
2   See *DPP v Jones* [1999] 2 AC 240 at 259A–F per Lord Irvine of Lairg LC. See also H Kalven, 'The Concept of the Public Forum' 1965 Sup Ct Rev 1 at 13 (when an American citizen 'goes to the street … he is exercising an immemorial right of a free man, a kind of First-Amendment easement').
3   LRA 2002, Sch 1, para 5, Sch 3, para 5 **[para 12.244]**. See *Overseas Investment Ltd v Simcobuild Construction Ltd and Swansea CC* (1995) 70 P & CR 322 at 329–331. See similarly *Man O'War Station Ltd v Auckland CC* [2000] 2 NZLR 267 at [69].
4   See *Bromley LBC v Morritt* (1999) 78 P & CR D37 at D37–D38 per Mummery LJ **[para 6.41]**.
5   See *Hague v Committee for Industrial Organization*, 307 US 496 at 515, 83 L Ed 1423 at 1436 (1939) per Justice Roberts; *Frisby v Schultz*, 487 US 474 at 481, 101 L Ed 2d 420 at 429 (1988) per Justice O'Connor.
6   For the proposition that the relevant highway authority holds its fee simple estate in the soil of the highway upon trust for the public, see *Man O'War Station Ltd v Auckland CC* [2000] 2 NZLR 267 at [22]; *SW Properties Inc v Calgary (City)* (2003) 222 DLR (4th) 430 at [19]. See also *The Queen in Right of Canada v Committee for the Commonwealth of Canada* (1987) 36 DLR (4th) 501 at 509f per Hugessen J, (1991) 77 DLR (4th) 385 at 393d–f per Lamer CJC (Sopinka and Cory JJ concurring); *Bathurst CC v PWC Properties Pty Ltd* (1998) 195 CLR 566 at [48]–[49].
7   See *Ex parte Lewis* (1888) 21 QBD 191 at 198 per Wills J (Trafalgar Square).

8   See e g *Secretary of State for the Environment, Transport and the Regions v Baylis (Glouces-ter) Ltd* and *Bennett Construction (UK) Ltd* (2000) 80 P & CR 324 at 332. See also Gray 'Equitable Property' (1994) 47(2) CLP 157 at 176–181.

DEFINITION OF THE 'HIGHWAY'

5.4   A public highway does not necessarily lead to any public place.[1] Indeed, it has been said that the public highway is itself 'a public place which the public may enjoy for any reasonable purpose.'[2] There is, accordingly, no rule of law that a public highway must connect two other public highways[3] or that a right of way over a cul-de-sac can exist only in a town.[4] A public highway must follow a defined route,[5] but may lead merely to a dead end (eg a point of natural beauty[6]). The highway includes not only a 'carriageway' over which there is a right of way for vehicular traffic,[7] but also the adjoining pavement[8] or 'footway' on either side where there is merely a public right of way on foot.[9] The concept of the highway also includes public footpaths,[10] byways,[11] bridle-ways[12] and even certain areas of public traverse which do not conform to the physical shape of a path or way.[13] The inclusion of a right of way in a definitive map drawn up pursuant to the National Parks and Access to the Countryside Act 1949 or the Wildlife and Countryside Act 1981 provides presumptive support for the existence of the way[14] which can be displaced only by cogent contrary evidence.[15] Despite isolated statements that a navigable river is a 'public highway',[16] the analogy between rights on water and rights on land is generally regarded today as incomplete and misleading.[17]

1   See *Attorney-General v Antrobus* [1905] 2 Ch 188 at 206; *Williams-Ellis v Cobb* [1935] 1 KB 310 at 320. Compare *Marquis of Bute v M'Kirdy & M'Millan Ltd* 1937 SLT 241 at 250–251 per Lord Normand ('it need not be a very public place'); *Love-Lee v Cameron of Lochiel* 1991 SCLR 61 at 67E–68G.

2   *DPP v Jones* [1999] 2 AC 240 at 257D per Lord Irvine of Lairg LC.

3   *Moser v Ambleside UDC* (1925) 89 JP 118 at 120 per Atkin LJ; *Williams-Ellis v Cobb* [1935] 1 KB 310 at 320 per Lord Wright.

4   *Moser v Ambleside UDC* (1925) 89 JP 118 at 119 per Pollock MR; *Roberts v Webster* (1968) 66 LGR 298 at 305; *R v Secretary of State for the Environment, ex p Bagshaw and Norton* (1994) 68 P & CR 402 at 410–411. The existence of a cul-de-sac may, however, contra-indicate a public right of way (see *Isaac v Secretary of State for the Environment* (Unreported, Queen's Bench Division, 10 November 1995) per Sedley J).

5   *Skrenty v Harrogate BC* (Chancery Division, 26 October 1999). See e g *Robinson v Cowpen Local Board* (1893) 63 LJQB 235 at 236–237 per Lord Esher MR, 237 per Lopes and Kay LJJ; *Macpherson v Scottish Rights of Way and Recreation Society Ltd* (1888) 15 SC 68 at 70 per Lord Selborne.

6   *Roberts v Webster* (1968) 66 LGR 298 at 304. See *Williams-Ellis v Cobb* [1935] 1 KB 310 at 320 per Lord Wright (acknowledging that a public way may end at the sea).

7   The highway includes the road verges and lay-bys (*DPP v Jones* [1999] 2 AC 240 at 280B–C per Lord Clyde). However, a car park is not, in the 'ordinary use of language', a road or highway (*Clarke v Kato* [1998] 1 WLR 1647 at 1653C per Lord Clyde). See also *Buckle v Stevens* (1996) 137 DLR (4th) 594 at 606.

8   A door may not open outwards on to a street (Highways Act 1980, s 153) and, irrespective of the date of its installation, the relevant occupier can be required by the local authority to alter the door at his own expense (see e g *Wandsworth LBC v Lloyd* (1997) 96 LGR 607 at 616).

9   Highways Act 1980, ss 328(1), 329(1). See also *Attorney-General v Wilcox* [1938] Ch 934 at 939; *Hubbard v Pitt* [1976] QB 142 at 175D; *News Group Newspapers Ltd v SOGAT '82* [1986] IRLR 337 at 346.

10   There is no absolute duty to provide a footpath as part of the highway (see Highways Act 1980, s 66(1)). The financial resources of the relevant local authority may legitimately constrain the decision whether such a footpath is necessary or desirable (*R v Norfolk CC, ex p Thorpe* (1998) 96 LGR 597 at 605–606).

11   See Wildlife and Countryside Act 1981, s 66(1). Any way which is marked in a definitive map as a 'road used as a public path' is now treated as a 'restricted byway' (see CROWA 2000, s 47(2)).

12   It is a criminal offence to disturb the surface of a footpath, bridleway or highway (Highways Act 1980, s 131A), but not, except in the case of a field-edge path, to plough over a footpath or bridleway (Highways Act 1980, s 134(1)). See also *Ramblers Association v Kent CC* (1990) 60 P & CR 464 at 471.

13   See *Brady v Northern Ireland Housing Executive* [1990] NI 200 at 211C per Sir Brian Hutton LCJ (square leading off surrounding streets). See also *Brandon v Barnes* [1966] 3 All ER 296 at 304C–D.

14   The Countryside and Rights of Way Act 2000 imposes a 'cut-off date' (1 January 2026) for the recording of historic rights of way in the definitive map (CROWA 2000, ss 53–56).

15   *Trevelyan v Secretary of State for the Environment, Transport and the Regions* [2001] 1 WLR 1264 at [38] per Lord Phillips of Worth Matravers MR. See W&CA 1981, s 56(1). The evidence provided by the definitive map does not remain conclusive for ever (see *Suffolk CC v Mason* [1979] AC 705 at 714C per Lord Diplock). In cases of proven error the map may be amended by the surveying authority (W&CA 1981, s 52(2)–(3)) in order to present as accurate a picture as possible of the relevant rights of way. See e g *R v Secretary of State for the Environment, ex p Burrows* [1991] 2 QB 354 at 384A–385A (bridleway can be downgraded to footpath); *Trevelyan*, supra at [42] (bridleway deleted as non-existent).

16   See e g *York Bros (Trading) Pty Ltd v Commr of Main Roads* [1983] 1 NSWLR 391 at 393G.

17   See *Attorney-General ex rel Yorkshire Derwent Trust Ltd v Brotherton* [1992] 1 AC 425 at 435C per Lord Oliver of Aylmerton ('I cannot … think that any reader of Alfred Lord Tennyson would have regarded the Lady of Shalott, as she floated down to Camelot through the noises of the night, as exercising a right of way over the subjacent soil').

DEDICATION AND ACCEPTANCE OF A PUBLIC HIGHWAY

5.5   Apart from express statutory provision,[1] a public highway is created not by a process of grant,[2] but in accordance with the common law doctrine of dedication and acceptance.[3] Dedication and acceptance, once complete, are conclusive of the creation of a public right of way[4] and cannot later be repudiated by the relevant landowner.[5] Moreover, dedication and acceptance of a highway can be inferred at common law from uninterrupted long user by the public,[6] although neither the fact of continual trespass[7] nor statutory access pursuant to the Countryside and Rights of Way Act 2000[8] can generate a public right of way on the basis of implied dedication. The courts are generally cautious in declaring that, by some act of gift, a private road has become a public road.[9] Cogent evidence of both dedication and acceptance is required.[10]

1   There is considerable judicial reluctance to find that a statute has created a public right of way over private land (see *Hale v Norfolk CC* [2001] Ch 717 at [19] per Chadwick LJ).

2   For the distinction between private easements (which are created by a process of grant) and public rights of way (which emerge from a process of dedication and acceptance), see *R (Beresford) v Sunderland CC* [2004] 1 AC 889 at [39] per Lord Scott of Foscote; *Murphy v Wicklow CC* (Irish High Court, 19 March 1999) per Kearns J.

3 *DPP v Jones* [1999] 2 AC 240 at 256E–F per Lord Irvine of Lairg LC. For evidence of the
   wide reception of the common law doctrine, see *Hale v Norfolk CC* [2001] Ch 717 at [18] per
   Chadwick LJ; *Permanent Trustee Co of New South Wales Ltd v Campbelltown Municipal
   Council* (1960) 105 CLR 401 at 420 per Windeyer J; *Newington v Windeyer* (1985) 3 NSWLR
   555 at 558G; *Dunstan v Hell's Gate Enterprises Ltd* (1988) 45 DLR (4th) 677 at 689; *Smeltzer
   v Fingal CC* [1998] 1 IR 279 at 287.
4 The public's right of way cannot be lost or downgraded by subsequent disuse or abandonment
   (*Loder v Gaden* (1999) 78 P & CR 223 at 226 per Hale J).
5 See *R (Beresford) v Sunderland CC* [2004] 1 AC 889 at [46] per Lord Scott of Foscote. The
   oft-quoted principle is 'once a highway always a highway' (see *Permanent Trustee Co of New
   South Wales Ltd v Campbelltown Municipal Council* (1960) 105 CLR 401 at 422 per Windeyer
   J; *Suffolk CC v Mason* [1979] AC 705 at 710B per Lord Diplock, 727G per Lord Fraser of
   Tullybelton; *Man O'War Station Ltd v Auckland CC* (*Judgment No 2*) [2002] 3 NZLR 584
   at [39] per Lord Scott of Foscote).
6 Continual user over a very long period generates an almost irresistible presumption of
   dedication (see *R v Inhabitants of the Tithing of East Mark* (1848) 11 QB 877 at 884, 116 ER
   701 at 704 per Erle J (50 years)). See also *Cubitt v Lady Caroline Maxse* (1873) LR 8 CP 704
   at 715; *Turner v Walsh* (1881) 6 App Cas 636 at 639–640; *Spedding v Fitzpatrick* (1888)
   38 Ch D 410 at 414; *Coats v Herefordshire CC* [1909] 2 Ch 579 at 599–600; *Folkestone Corpn v
   Brockman* [1914] AC 338 at 352, 362; *Newington v Windeyer* (1985) 3 NSWLR 555 at 559B–C.
   User by a mere section of the public (e g by neighbouring occupiers and their visitors) may not
   be enough (see *Newington*, supra at 562E–F; *Cook's Road Maintenance Assn v Crowhill
   Estates* (2001) 196 DLR (4th) 35 at [33]–[35]).
7 *Newington v Windeyer* (1985) 3 NSWLR 555 at 559C per McHugh JA.
8 See CROWA 2000, s 12(3) **[para 5.46]**.
9 See *Cook's Road Maintenance Assn v Crowhill Estates* (2001) 196 DLR (4th) 35 at [45] per
   Borins JA ('It is a very serious step ... for a court to declare an individual's private property to
   be public property. Property rights are to be respected').
10 See also Highways Act 1980, s 32 (relevance of maps, plans and other documents).

Dedication

5.6 Dedication by the competent landowner[1] may, but need not, be effected
by deed. Nor is there any requirement that the dedication be contained in
writing; it can instead be manifested by conduct.[2] Any sufficient indication,
whether express or implied, that the right of the public to use a path or track is
intended to be permanent will usually constitute a dedication of a public right
of way[3] and, subject to acceptance by the public, creates a public right of way
immediately.[4] However, a longstanding permissive user which clearly rests only
on the landowner's revocable licence or consent cannot raise any inference of
dedication.[5] Furthermore, in the absence of an express dedication of the way,
the mere fact of long user by the public can never result in the creation of a
public highway if the object of transit involves the exercise of some species of
entitlement not recognised by law.[6] Thus, for example, an access route cannot
be claimed at common law to be a public highway if its purpose is not to
facilitate travel from point A to point B,[7] but rather to afford a means of
random circumambulation over an adjacent area of land.[8] A public highway
cannot support a *ius spatiandi* (i e a generalised right to roam at will).[9]

1 At common law the competent landowner is generally the person absolutely entitled in fee
   simple, subject (where relevant) to the consent of any mortgagee (see *Permanent Trustee Co of
   New South Wales Ltd v Campbelltown Municipal Council* (1960) 105 CLR 401 at 420 per

Windeyer J). Dedication is obviously impossible if, at the relevant time, there was no owner legally capable of dedicating a way, although this difficulty may sometimes be averted by a prolonged public user which raises a presumption of dedication in a period beyond living memory (see *Williams-Ellis v Cobb* [1935] 1 KB 310 at 318–319, 324–325).

2   *R (Beresford) v Sunderland CC* [2004] 1 AC 889 at [39] per Lord Scott of Foscote.

3   *R (Beresford) v Sunderland CC* [2004] 1 AC 889 at [45] per Lord Scott of Foscote.

4   *R (Beresford) v Sunderland CC* [2004] 1 AC 889 at [39] per Lord Scott of Foscote.

5   *Mann v Brodie* (1885) 10 App Cas 378 at 392 per Lord Watson; *Magistrates of Edinburgh v North British Railway Co* 1904 6 SC 620 at 633–634; *Attorney-General v Antrobus* [1905] 2 Ch 188 at 205–206; *Smeltzer v Fingal CC* [1998] 1 IR 279 at 287; *Murphy v Wicklow CC* (Irish High Court, 19 March 1999).

6   There 'cannot prima facie be a right for the public to go to a place where the public have no right to be' (*Attorney-General v Antrobus* [1905] 2 Ch 188 at 206 per Farwell J, citing *Giant's Causeway Co v Attorney-General* (Freeman's Journal, 15 January 1898) per Holmes LJ).

7   The outcome in *Attorney-General v Antrobus* [1905] 2 Ch 188 might have been different if the claim had involved an assertion of thoroughfares through the stone circle at Stonehenge (see [1905] 2 Ch 188 at 205, 208 per Farwell J). See *Alfred F Beckett Ltd v Lyons* [1967] Ch 449 at 482E–F per Winn LJ ('identifiable termini'); *Skrenty v Harrogate BC* (Chancery Division, 26 October 1999) (there must normally be a 'terminus ad quem').

8   See *Abercromby v Fermoy Town Commissioners* [1900] 1 IR 302 at 314 per Holmes LJ.

9   *Robinson v Cowpen Local Board* (1893) 63 LJQB 235 at 237 per Lord Esher MR (claim to meander over open space in all directions); *Attorney-General v Antrobus* [1905] 2 Ch 188 at 205 per Farwell J ('there can be no legal right of visiting, walking about, and inspecting the stones [Stonehenge] in the public') [**para 8.44**]. See also *DPP v Jones* [1999] 2 AC 240 at 280C per Lord Clyde. Compare *Brady v Northern Ireland Housing Executive* [1990] NI 200 at 211A–B per Sir Brian Hutton LCJ.

Animus dedicandi

5.7   The common law doctrine requires proof that the relevant fee simple owner[1] intended to dedicate the highway to public use,[2] which intention may be either express or implied from conduct.[3] However, a mere pattern of continuous uninterrupted public user cannot, in itself, conclusively establish the required dedicatory intent,[4] although it may raise a presumption of such intent.[5] In the absence of express words of dedication (and no matter how strong the evidence of user), the acts and circumstances from which a dedication is to be implied 'must justify the inference of an intention to bestow on the public a *continuing* right of user of the road.'[6] No dedication arises, for instance, from an intent to confer some right, whose continuance is 'subject to the occurrence, or non-occurrence, of some future event such as the payment of rent.'[7] A dedicatory intent may, however, be inferred from an owner's clear acquiescence in prolonged public use of a way on his land.[8] In such circumstances the law 'will assume a public right rather than an easy-going proprietor.'[9] In all cases the nature of the way dedicated is limited by the scope of the proven intention.[10]

1   Intention on the part of a mere lessee is not enough unless the fee simple owner clearly acquiesced in the dedication (see *Pryor v Pryor* (1872) 26 LT (NS) 758 at 760; *Newington v Windeyer* (1985) 3 NSWLR 555 at 561B) or must have been aware of the general belief that dedication had occurred (*Folkestone Corpn v Brockman* [1914] AC 338 at 362–363). See also *Behrens v Richards* [1905] 2 Ch 614 at 621.

2   See *Man O'War Station Ltd v Auckland CC* (*Judgment No 2*) [2002] 3 NZLR 584 at [36] per Lord Scott of Foscote. See also *Poole v Huskinson* (1843) 11 M & W 827 at 830, 152 ER 1039 at 1041 per Parke B; *Spedding v Fitzpatrick* (1888) 38 Ch D 410 at 414 per Cotton and Fry LJJ.

3   *R v Inhabitants of the Tithing of East Mark* (1848) 11 QB 877 at 883, 116 ER 701 at 704. See
     also *Man O'War Station Ltd v Auckland CC* [2000] 2 NZLR 267 at [23].
4   *Attorney-General v Antrobus* [1905] 2 Ch 188 at 206; *Behrens v Richards* [1905] 2 Ch 614 at
     619–620. See also *Stoney v Eastbourne RDC* [1927] 1 Ch 367 at 378–379 per Romer J ('it is
     dedication and not user that constitutes a highway'); *Poole v Huskinson* (1843) 11 M & W 827
     at 830, 152 ER 1039 at 1041 per Parke B ('user by the public is evidence, and no more', of
     animus dedicandi).
5   *Folkestone Corpn v Brockman* [1914] AC 338 at 368 per Lord Atkinson, 374 per Lord Dun-
     edin. See *Williams-Ellis v Cobb* [1935] 1 KB 310 at 331–336 per Talbot J.
6   *Man O'War Station Ltd v Auckland CC* (*Judgment No 2*) [2002] 3 NZLR 584 at [39] per
     Lord Scott of Foscote.
7   *Man O'War Station Ltd v Auckland CC* (*Judgment No 2*) [2002] 3 NZLR 584 at [39] per
     Lord Scott of Foscote. See e g *Barraclough v Johnson* (1838) 8 Ad & El 99 at 103–104, 112 ER
     773 at 775 (annual rental of 5 shillings). The payment of one-off compensation to the
     landowner is not, however, incompatible with an intention to dedicate (see *Man O'War
     Station Ltd v Auckland CC* (*Judgment No 2*) [2002] 3 NZLR 584 at [41] per Lord Scott of
     Foscote).
8   *Mann v Brodie* (1885) 10 App Cas 378 at 386 per Lord Blackburn; *Macpherson v Scottish
     Rights of Way and Recreation Society Ltd* (1888) 15 SC 68 at 69 per Lord Halsbury LC;
     Secretary of State for the Environment, Transport and the Regions v Baylis (*Gloucester*) *Ltd and
     Bennett Construction* (*UK*) *Ltd* (2000) 80 P & CR 324 at 329–330. A very extensive period of
     user raises a presumption that the landowner was aware of such user (see *Davies v Stephens*
     (1836) 7 C & P 570 at 571, 173 ER 251 at 252). The courts may nowadays be more receptive to
     dedication by acquiescence (see *Skrenty v Harrogate BC* (Chancery Division, 26 October
     1999); *Hale v Norfolk CC* [2001] Ch 717 at [36] per Chadwick LJ). See also *Marquis of Bute v
     M'Kirdy & M'Millan Ltd* 1937 SLT 241 at 251–252 per Lord Normand, cited in *R* (*Beresford*)
     v Sunderland CC [2004] 1 AC 889 at [66] per Lord Rodger of Earlsferry.
9   *Marquis of Bute v M'Kirdy & M'Millan Ltd* 1937 SLT 241 at 252 per Lord Normand.
10   Thus the ancient dedication of a way as a footway or bridleway cannot be the basis of a
     modern user by wheeled vehicles, although the dedication of a cartway, even if 'formed long
     before the invention of the internal combustion engine', would authorise modern vehicular
     traffic (see *Loder v Gaden* (1999) 78 P & CR 223 at 227 per Hale J).

Acceptance

5.8   The common law doctrine requires proof not merely of dedication but
also of the fact that the proffered dedication was accepted by or on behalf of
the public.[1] Acceptance is commonly demonstrated by evidence of actual
public use of the way,[2] but the local highway authority, as the representative of
the public, is competent to accept an express dedication by written agreement
with the landowner.[3] Acceptance imports a positive obligation to maintain the
highway[4] and the expenditure of public funds on the way generally connotes
acceptance by or on behalf of the public.[5] By the same token, a landowner
who, with the intention of dedicating a way, permits the expenditure of public
funds thereon cannot subsequently be heard to assert the private character of
the way.[6]

1   See *Secretary of State for the Environment, Transport and the Regions v Baylis* (*Gloucester*) *Ltd
     and Bennett Construction* (*UK*) *Ltd* (2000) 80 P & CR 324 at 330 per Deputy Judge Kim
     Lewison QC. It can equally be said that, absent an intention to dedicate, acceptance by the
     public is irrelevant (see *Hale v Norfolk CC* [2001] Ch 717 at [36]).
2   *Secretary of State for the Environment, Transport and the Regions v Baylis* (*Gloucester*) *Ltd and
     Bennett Construction* (*UK*) *Ltd* (2000) 80 P & CR 324 at 330–331. See also *Fisher v Prowse*

(1862) 2 B & S 770 at 780, 121 ER 1258 at 1262 per Blackburn J; *Hale v Norfolk CC* [2001] Ch 717 at [20] per Chadwick LJ; but compare *Forrester v Bataille* (2003) 175 FLR 411 at [27]–[32] (no evidence of use).

3   *Secretary of State for the Environment, Transport and the Regions v Baylis (Gloucester) Ltd and Bennett Construction (UK) Ltd* (2000) 80 P & CR 324 at 332 (express agreement effective even before actual use by the public).

4   See *Bellevue Crescent Pty Ltd v Marland Holdings Pty Ltd* (1998) 43 NSWLR 364 at 368C per Young J. On acceptance the public must take the way as it is (see *Gautret v Egerton* (1867) LR 2 CP 371 at 373 per Willes J; *McGeown v Northern Ireland Housing Executive* [1995] 1 AC 233 at 243E–F per Lord Keith of Kinkel). In the absence of misfeasance the dedicating owner bears no further liability in respect of its state or condition (*Brady v Northern Ireland Housing Executive* [1990] NI 200 at 220B–F).

5   See *Behrens v Richards* [1905] 2 Ch 614 at 620; *Permanent Trustee Co of New South Wales Ltd v Campbelltown Municipal Council* (1960) 105 CLR 401 at 422 per Windeyer J; *Village of Silverton v Hobbs* (1985) 17 DLR (4th) 518 at 522–524; *Man O'War Station Ltd v Auckland CC* [2000] 2 NZLR 267 at [24]; *Cook's Road Maintenance Assn v Crowhill Estates* (2001) 196 DLR (4th) 35 at [37].

6   See *Attorney-General v Antrobus* [1905] 2 Ch 188 at 207. The circumstances are analogous to those of proprietary estoppel (*Man O'War Station Ltd v Auckland CC (Judgment No 2)* [2002] 3 NZLR 584 at [47] per Lord Scott of Foscote).

Statutory presumption from long user

5.9 It has been said that in most modern cases the 'so-called intention of the landowner is no more than a legal fiction imputed to the landowner by the court.'[1] There is nowadays a general (although rebuttable) statutory presumption that a way is deemed to have been dedicated as a public highway where the way has been 'actually enjoyed by the public as of right and without interruption for a full period of 20 years.'[2]

1   *DPP v Jones* [1999] 2 AC 240 at 257A per Lord Irvine of Lairg LC.
2   Highways Act 1980, s 31(1). See generally *Gloucestershire CC v Farrow* [1985] 1 WLR 741 at 745H–746G. The statutory presumption has no application to the crown (*Tower Hamlets LBC v Sherwood* (Unreported, Chancery Division, 20 July 2001)).

Quality of relevant acts of user

5.10 The user by members of the public which triggers the statutory presumption must have been continuous rather than merely occasional or sporadic.[1] The user must also have been exercised *nec vi, nec clam, nec precario* (without force, secrecy or permission),[2] with the consequence that user pursuant to an overt communication of a revocable licence cannot found the statutory presumption.[3] The concept of enjoyment 'as of right' does not, however, imply any requirement of actual legal entitlement on the part of those members of the public who avail themselves of the route in question. The phrase 'as of right' means little more than 'as if of right',[4] with the corollary that a landowner's mere toleration of a continuing user by the public is not inconsistent with a claim of user 'as of right'.[5] Moreover, the subjective knowledge or understanding of those responsible for this user is quite irrelevant.[6] User 'as of right' merely entails enjoyment 'of a kind which would lead a reasonable landowner to believe that those using the land were asserting a public right.'[7]

1   *Rowley v Secretary of State for Transport, Local Government and the Regions* [2003] 2 P & CR 359 at [7] per Elias J. Enjoyment 'without interruption' may be established even though a route is temporarily barred for specific purposes or barred when unlikely to be utilised by members of the public (see *Lewis v Thomas* [1950] 1 KB 438 at 444–445; *Rowley*, supra at [38]).

2   See *Jones v Bates* [1938] 2 All ER 237 at 245E–F; *R v Secretary of State for the Environment, ex p Cowell* [1993] JPL 851 at 858; *R (Beresford) v Sunderland CC* [2004] 1 AC 889 at [33] per Lord Scott of Foscote.

3   *R (Beresford) v Sunderland CC* [2004] 1 AC 889 at [73]–[85] per Lord Walker of Gestingthorpe **[para 5.44]**. See also *R v Secretary of State for the Environment, ex p Billson* [1999] QB 374 at 393E–F. In the *Beresford* case Lord Scott of Foscote even regarded some forms of *express* permission as compatible with user 'as of right.' With the support of Lord Bingham of Cornhill ([2004] 1 AC 889 at [10]), Lord Scott thought, for instance, that an express notice to the effect that the public may use a route as a public highway evinces 'a sufficiently dedicatory character' that use by the public thereafter becomes use 'as of right' ([2004] 1 AC 889 at [47]).

4   See *Cumbernauld and Kilsyth DC v Dollar Land (Cumbernauld) Ltd* 1992 SLT 1035 at 1043K–L per Lord Cowie; *R (Beresford) v Sunderland CC* [2004] 1 AC 889 at [72] per Lord Walker of Gestingthorpe.

5   See *R v Oxfordshire CC, ex p Sunningwell PC* [2000] 1 AC 335 at 358F per Lord Hoffmann.

6   *Rowley v Secretary of State for Transport, Local Government and the Regions* [2003] 2 P & CR 359 at [19], [34].

7   *Rowley v Secretary of State for Transport, Local Government and the Regions* [2003] 2 P & CR 359 at [12].

Rebuttal of the statutory presumption

5.11   The presumption arising from 20 years' user 'as of right' is rebuttable by 'sufficient evidence' that, for some period during these 20 years, there was no relevant intention to dedicate.[1] Evidence of the landowner's intention to oust the statutory presumption must be 'overt and contemporaneous'[2] and often appears in the form of a visible sign or notice 'inconsistent with the dedication of the way as a highway.'[3] An intention left unexpressed by the landowner or 'locked in his own mind' is clearly insufficient for the purpose, although, in order to be effective, a landowner's intention need not be expressly publicised to users of the way.[4] Thus, for example, the intention to dedicate a way to the public is commonly negatived by a symbolic closure of the route for one day per year for the purpose of denying public access as of right.[5] More substantial impediments to freedom of passage during the statutory 20 year period merely reinforce the conclusion that an alleged way has not been enjoyed 'without interruption'.[6]

1   Highways Act 1980, s 31(1). See *Jaques v Secretary of State for the Environment* [1995] JPL 1031 at 1037–1038 per Laws J; *R v Secretary of State for the Environment, ex p Billson* [1999] QB 374 at 395G–396A.

2   *R v Secretary of State for the Environment, ex p Billson* [1999] QB 374 at 395A.

3   Highways Act 1980, s 31(3). See e g *Ward and Ward v Durham CC* (1994) 70 P & CR 585 at 590 (display of 'no right of way' sign). The notice, in order to be relevant under section 31(3), must be maintained in position for the full 20 year period (*R v Secretary of State for the*

Environment, ex p Blake [1984] JPL 101 at 103). Moreover, a notice which indicates merely that the land is private may not be sufficient to negative the relevant intention (*Secretary of State for the Environment v Beresford Trustees* [1996] NPC 128).

4   *R v Secretary of State for the Environment, ex p Billson* [1999] QB 374 at 395A. See also *Jaques v Secretary of State for the Environment* [1995] JPL 1031 at 1037–1038; *R v Secretary of State for Wales, ex p Emery* [1998] 4 All ER 367 at 380f–j; *Rowley v Secretary of State for Transport, Local Government and the Regions* [2003] 2 P & CR 359 at [34]–[35].

5   See *British Museum Trustees v Finnis* (1833) 5 C & P 460 at 465, 172 ER 1053 at 1056; *Fairey v Southampton CC* [1956] 2 QB 439 at 458 per Denning LJ; *R (Beresford) v Sunderland CC* [2004] 1 AC 889 at [83] per Lord Walker of Gestingthorpe. See also *Poole v Huskinson* (1843) 11 M & W 827 at 830, 152 ER 1039 at 1041 per Parke B (' ... a single act of interruption by the owner is of much more weight, upon a question of intention, than many acts of enjoyment').

6   See eg *R v Secretary of State for the Environment, ex p Blake* [1984] JPL 101 at 104 (the Green Drive over Burbage Moor).

DUTY OF MAINTENANCE

5.12   Every highway authority has a responsibility both at common law[1] and under statute[2] to assert and protect the rights of the public to the use and enjoyment of the highways within its area.[3] The highway authority has an absolute statutory duty[4] to keep the fabric of the highway surface in a good state of repair so as to render it reasonably passable for ordinary traffic at all seasons of the year,[5] but this duty does not comprise an absolute obligation to prevent the formation, or remove the accumulation, of snow and ice on that highway surface.[6]

1   *R v Welwyn Hatfield DC, ex p Brinkley* (1982) 80 LGR 727 at 735.
2   Highways Act 1980, s 130(1). Any person may, by a notice procedure, enforce the highway authority's duty to prevent obstruction of footpaths, bridleways and other byways (Highways Act 1980, s 130A (inserted by CROWA 2000, s 63(1))).
3   If a highway is maintainable by the relevant statutory highway authority at public expense, that authority holds a determinable fee simple interest in the surface of the highway and in so much of the subjacent land and superjacent airspace as is required for the discharge of its statutory duties [**para 1.30**]. See Highways Act 1980, s 263.
4   Highways Act 1980, s 41(1). See *Goodes v East Sussex CC* [2000] 1 WLR 1356 at 1366A per Lord Hoffmann, 1368E–F per Lord Clyde.
5   See *Burnside v Emerson* [1968] 1 WLR 1490 at 1496H–1497A per Diplock LJ.
6   *Goodes v East Sussex CC* [2000] 1 WLR 1356 at 1366A–D, 1367H–1368E per Lord Hoffmann, 1370C–D per Lord Clyde. See also *Cross v Kirklees MBC* [1998] 1 All ER 564 at 572d–j.

CONTENT OF THE CITIZEN'S RIGHTS OVER THE HIGHWAY

5.13   It used to be thought that the rights of members of the public over the public highway were confined to a 'right to pass and repass at their pleasure for the purpose of legitimate travel'[1] and also for 'purposes incidental to passage'.[2] Although 'very little activity could accurately be described as "ancillary" to passing along the highway',[3] user of the highway for other purposes, whether lawful or unlawful, was generally taken to constitute a trespass against the owner of the top-soil in the highway[4] and could well involve a criminal obstruction of that highway.[5] As Lord Irvine of Lairg LC observed in *DPP v Jones*,[6] this unnecessarily restrictive approach threatened to impose trespass liability in respect of a range of wholly innocent and reasonable activities on the public highway.[7]

1   *Harrison v Duke of Rutland* [1893] 1 QB 142 at 154 per Lopes LJ. See also *Hickman v Maisey* [1900] 1 QB 752 at 757; *Waite v Taylor* (1985) 149 JP 551 at 553; *Thomas v National Union of Mineworkers* (*South Wales Area*) [1986] Ch 20 at 64A.
2   *Hubbard v Pitt* [1976] QB 142 at 149G per Forbes J.
3   See *DPP v Jones* [1999] 2 AC 240 at 255G–H per Lord Irvine of Lairg LC, who proffered the examples of 'stopping to tie up one's shoe lace, consulting a street map, or pausing to catch one's breath.' In *Hubbard v Pitt* [1976] QB 142 at 149G–150A, Forbes J conceded that '[a] tired pedestrian may sit down and rest himself. A motorist may attempt to repair a minor breakdown ... [and] it is permissible to queue for tickets at a theatre or other public place of entertainment, or for a bus.' Even then such user was said to be limited in duration to 'a reasonable while', and required to be exercised 'reasonably and in such a way as not unduly to obstruct other users' ([1976] QB 142 at 150D). See also *Hadwell v Righton* [1907] 2 KB 345 at 348; *Iveagh* (*Earl*) *v Martin* [1961] 1 QB 232 at 273; *Waite v Taylor* (1985) 149 JP 551 at 553; *Cooper v Metropolitan Police Commissioner* (1985) 82 Cr App R 238 at 242.
4   *Harrison v Duke of Rutland* [1893] 1 QB 142 at 154 per Lopes LJ (disruption of grouse-shooting; *Hubbard v Pitt* [1976] QB 142 at 150C–F, 175C–D. See e g *R v Pratt* (1855) 4 E & B 860 at 865, 867–868, 119 ER 319 at 321–322 (hunting on highway); *Hickman v Maisey* [1900] 1 QB 752 at 756–760 (racing tout spying on horse trials). Compare *Reis v Miller*, 550 NW2d 78 at 82–83 (SD 1996) (hunting in South Dakota).
5   Highways Act 1980, s 137(1). For reference to potential liability for public and private nuisance, see *Hubbard v Pitt* [1976] QB 142 at 175A–E.
6   [1999] 2 AC 240 at 254F–G.
7   Lord Irvine thought that, on the restrictive view, trespass would be committed by 'two friends who meet in the street and stop to talk; so too a group of children playing on the pavement outside their homes; so too charity workers collecting donations; or political activists handing out leaflets; and so too a group of members of the Salvation Army singing hymns and addressing those who gather to listen.' Compare *Culkin v McFie and Sons Ltd* [1939] 3 All ER 613 at 620F–G (no trespass by child who chases ball into the roadway or runs across the roadway in play), but see also Highways Act 1980, s 161(3).

Relaxation of the law

5.14   In *DPP v Jones*,[1] the House of Lords declined to hold that the public right over the highway is confined to a minimal privilege of passage and activities strictly ancillary thereto. By a majority[2] the House significantly expanded the scope of the public right,[3] ruling that no trespass on the highway is committed by the conduct of activities which are 'reasonable, do not involve the commission of a public or private nuisance, and do not amount to an obstruction of the highway unreasonably impeding the primary right of the general public to pass and re-pass.'[4] In the view of Lord Irvine of Lairg LC, the public highway is 'a public place which the public may enjoy for any reasonable purpose' consistent with that 'primary right'.[5] Lord Irvine also indicated that the permitted public user may, in certain circumstances, extend to 'roaming about on the highway, or remaining on the highway', provided that such use is consistent with the public's primary right of passage.[6]

1   [1999] 2 AC 240 at 254H per Lord Irvine of Lairg LC, 280E per Lord Clyde. See (1999) 8(1) Nottingham LJ 49 (Tom Lewis).
2   See the strong dissents by Lord Slynn of Hadley (at 264B–G) and Lord Hope of Craighead (at 276E), who believed that the majority decision comprised 'a fundamental rearrangement of the respective rights of the public and those of public and private landowners.' Even Lord Clyde was anxious (at 281C) to stress 'the basic predominance of the essential use of a highway as a highway.'
3   [1999] 2 AC 240 at 256A per Lord Irvine of Lairg LC (a 'broader modern test'), although it is fair to point out that, in *Harrison v Duke of Rutland* [1893] 1 QB 142 at 146–147, Lord Esher MR endorsed any 'reasonable and usual' mode of using a highway as such.
4   [1999] 2 AC 240 at 254H per Lord Irvine of Lairg LC. To confine lawful use of the highway to that which is literally incidental or ancillary to the right of passage 'would be to place an unrealistic and unwarranted restriction on commonplace day-to-day activities' ([1999] 2 AC 240 at 255H–256A).
5   [1999] 2 AC 240 at 255E–G, 257D. See also Lord Clyde (at 280D–F), Lord Hutton (at 287A, 292H–293B).
6   [1999] 2 AC 240 at 256D–E. Lord Clyde (at 280C–D) was more restrictive, opining that the public right does not entitle one 'simply to wander about the road ... at will. Further, the public have no jus manendi on a highway, so that any stopping and standing must be reasonably limited in time. While the right may extend to a picnic on the verge, it would not extend to camping there.'

A 'test of reasonableness'

5.15   The introduction in this context of a 'reasonable user' test[1] is symptomatic of a more general infusion of a criterion of reasonableness in the regulation of access to land,[2] Lord Irvine making it clear in *DPP v Jones*[3] that this extension of the public's right over the highway makes no distinction between highways situated on publicly and privately owned land.[4] In *DPP v Jones* itself the 'test of reasonableness' was applied to uphold a public right of peaceful non-obstructive assembly on the public highway,[5] although the same test clearly does not 'afford carte blanche to squatters or uninvited visitors' and would not support any claim of right to gather on, and obstruct, a narrow footpath or bridleway.[6] The test obviously excludes any use of the highway which is unreasonable, obstructive or liable to constitute a nuisance.[7]

1   [1999] 2 AC 240 at 256B–C per Lord Irvine of Lairg LC.
2   [**Paras 3.88, 4.38**].
3   [1999] 2 AC 240 at 257H.
4   See the alarm which this prospect plainly caused to the dissentients in the House of Lords ([1999] 2 AC 240 at 264C–G per Lord Slynn of Hadley, 268D–E, 276B–E, 278B–F per Lord Hope of Craighead).
5   [1999] 2 AC 240 at 255A, 257D–258B per Lord Irvine of Lairg LC, 280G–281H per Lord Clyde, 286H–287C per Lord Hutton. In *DPP v Jones*, the defendants succeeded in overturning their conviction on a charge of trespassory assembly at the roadside beside Stonehenge (see Public Order Act 1986, ss 14A(1)–(4), 14B(2) [**para 3.97**]). See (2000) 63 MLR 252 (G Clayton).
6   [1999] 2 AC 240 at 256B–E per Lord Irvine of Lairg LC, 293C–D per Lord Hutton.
7   [1999] 2 AC 240 at 256B, 258A per Lord Irvine of Lairg LC. An injunction will issue, for instance, to restrain any individual who 'persistently follow[s] another on a public highway, making rude gestures or remarks in order to annoy or vex' (*Thomas v National Union of Mineworkers (South Wales Area)* [1986] Ch 20 at 64D).

Paramount nature of the public right of passage

5.16   According to ancient common law members of the public have a right to use the public highway 'for all purposes and at all times' at least so far as regards the pedestrian right to pass and re-pass.[1] Once a public right of passage is established and is being exercised reasonably, there is 'no warrant for making any distinction, or even for making any enquiry, as to the purpose for which it is exercised.'[2] The untrammelled nature of this right of passage is an integral feature of what is sometimes termed 'pedestrian democracy'.[3] Motorised use of the highway may be subject to more stringent control, but it is questionable whether this control legitimately extends as far as was indicated by the ruling in *Moss v McLachlan*.[4] Here a Divisional Court upheld a supposed right in the police to turn back convoys of 'flying pickets' from proceeding along the highway towards the scene of an organised labour demonstration. Skinner J held that police officers operating on a motorway were acting within the execution of their duty when they stopped cars carrying persons 'who appeared to be striking miners.'[5] The police had sought to justify their action on the basis that the continued progress of the vehicles gave rise to a reasonable expectation that a breach of the peace would ensue in the form of a mass demonstration at a colliery some miles distant.[6] In accepting this explanation, the Divisional Court endorsed the restriction of free movement along the highway on grounds of an apprehended (but as yet unproven) unlawfulness of the ultimate objective of the journey undertaken.[7] The decision in *Moss v McLachlan* set an extremely dangerous precedent for the censoring of the lawful activities of entirely innocent persons on grounds of visual similarity to those deemed inimical to an officially defined social interest.

1   *Rouse v Bardin* (1790) 1 H Bl 351 at 355, 126 ER 206 at 208 per Wilson J. See also *Wills' Trustees v Cairngorm Canoeing and Sailing School Ltd* 1976 SC (HL) 30 at 124 per Lord Wilberforce ('One cannot ... stop a pedestrian on a highway, and ask him what is the nature of his use').
2   *Wills' Trustees v Cairngorm Canoeing and Sailing School Ltd* 1976 SC (HL) 30 at 124 per Lord Wilberforce (dealing with the analogous right of passage on navigable waters). See also *DPP v Jones* [1999] 2 AC 240 at 276A per Lord Hope of Craighead.
3   **[Para 2.7]**.
4   (1985) 149 JP 167.
5   (1985) 149 JP 167 at 168.
6   (1985) 149 JP 167 at 170–172.
7   The Queen's Bench Division Administrative Court, although following the decision in *Moss v McLachlan*, has recently made it clear that any attempt to force a traveller back to his point of origin under police escort constitutes a form of detention which violates the citizen's right to liberty under ECHR Art 5 (see *R (Laporte) v Chief Constable of Gloucestershire Constabulary* [2004] 2 All ER 874 at [47]).

Criminal liability for user of the highway

5.17   Historically the public right over the highway has been delimited by various kinds of criminal liability imposed by statute. The House of Lords' redefinition in *DPP v Jones* of public rights over the highway has now produced a welcome 'symmetry in the law' between those unreasonable activities on the highway which constitute a trespass and those activities which comprise a violation of various heads of the criminal law.[1]

1   [1999] 2 AC 240 at 258H–259A per Lord Irvine of Lairg LC. See also Lord Hutton (at 287B, 290H–291B).

Trespass and obstruction

5.18   Of the relevant heads of criminal liability the most important are those concerned with trespassory assembly[1] and wilful obstruction of 'free passage along a highway' in the absence of any 'lawful authority or excuse'.[2] Whether the use made of the highway by a member of the public is 'so unreasonable as to amount to obstruction' is a question of fact and degree in every case.[3] The offence of obstruction used to catch many 'relatively minor activities which some of the public might consider to be beneficial',[4] but, with the advent of a more liberal view of public rights over the highway, it is likely that the ambit of wilful obstruction is now somewhat reduced.[5] The offence may nevertheless be relevant to activities which do not promote the public's primary right of passage, but are deemed to be unpleasant, socially undesirable or obtrusive in relation to passers by.[6]

1   Public Order Act 1986, ss 14A(1)–(4), 14B(2) [**para 3.97**].
2   Highways Act 1980, s 137(1). See *Nagy v Weston* [1965] 1 WLR 280 at 284C–D. It is no defence that the defendant's obstructive activity (eg operation of a street stall) has continued in the same position for several years and that he has duly paid rates (*Pugh v Pidgen* (1987) 151 JP 664 at 669D–E). A police constable has power to arrest without warrant any person whom he sees committing an offence of wilful obstruction (Highways Act 1980, s 137(2)); and an offender may be ordered to remove a continuing obstruction (Highways Act 1980, s 130ZA(1) (inserted by CROWA 2000, s 64(1))).
3   *Nagy v Weston* [1965] 1 WLR 280 at 284D–E. See also *Fitzgerald v Montoya* (1989) 16 NSWLR 164 at 171G–172A. In the aftermath of *DPP v Jones* [1999] 2 AC 240, it can no longer be asserted that unless it is de minimis 'any stopping on the highway ... is *prima facie* an obstruction' (see *Hirst and Agu v Chief Constable of West Yorkshire* (1987) 85 Cr App R 143 at 151).
4   *Waite v Taylor* (1985) 149 JP 551 at 553 per May LJ. Criminal liability has thus been imposed – with expressions of judicial regret – on hot dog vendors (*Nagy v Weston* [1965] 1 WLR 280 at 284F; *Pitcher v Lockett* (1966) 64 LGR 477 at 479), mobile snack bars (*Waltham Forest LBC v Mills* [1980] RTR 201 at 205G–H), and street buskers juggling with lit firesticks in a pedestrian precinct (*Waite v Taylor*, supra at 553–554). Compare, however, *Fitzgerald v Montoya* (1989) 16 NSWLR 164 at 166B–D (Court of Appeal of New South Wales).
5   Some sense of the modern law was foreshadowed in *Waite v Taylor* (1985) 149 JP 551 at 553, where May LJ pointed out that there is no obligation 'to keep moving all the time', so long as the 'stopping is part and parcel of passing and re-passing along the highway and is ancillary to it (such as a milkman stopping to leave a milk bottle on a doorstep).' Likewise, in *Cooper v Metropolitan Police Commissioner* (1985) 82 Cr App R 238 at 242, Tudor Evans J thought that there is clearly 'a right to look in a shop window or to talk to a passing friend without committing an offence.'
6   See eg *Cooper v Metropolitan Police Commissioner* (1985) 82 Cr App R 238 at 242–243 (club tout seeking to persuade passing pedestrians to enter Soho club). In *Kent CC v Holland* [1996] EGCS 135, a Divisional Court held that the protrusion of the heads of two Rottweiler dogs over a 4ft fence on private property constituted no obstruction of an adjoining public footpath which was 3ft or 4ft wide (although it was mooted that the facts might amount to nuisance).

Interruption of highway use

5.19   A further form of criminal liability arises where 'without lawful authority or excuse' any person deposits 'any thing whatsoever on a highway to the interruption of any user of the highway'.[1] It is a specially designated criminal offence to deposit a builder's skip on the highway without the permission of the relevant highway authority.[2] Moreover, a local authority has power to require the removal of any 'structure' erected or set up on the highway without lawful authority.[3]

1   Highways Act 1980, s 148(c). See *Putnam v Colvin* [1984] RTR 150 at 158B–E (placing of pots with shrubs in cul-de-sac to prevent unlawful parking held to be itself unlawful). An occupier is not, however, burdened by a duty of care to ensure that, on completion of building works, his building contractor leaves behind no remaining hazards on the highway which might injure a third party (*Rowe v Herman* [1997] 1 WLR 1390 at 1394H–1395D).
2   Highways Act 1980, s 139(1)–(3). The criminal offence also includes leaving a skip on the highway for longer than the permitted period (*Craddock v Green* (1983) 81 LGR 235 at 239–240).
3   *R v Welwyn Hatfield DC, ex p Brinkley* (1982) 80 LGR 727 at 734–735 (gypsy caravans). See also *Wiltshire CC v Frazer* (1984) 47 P & CR 69 at 74–77.

Protest and demonstration on the public highway

5.20   The decision of the majority in the House of Lords in *DPP v Jones*[1] confirms the existence, in many circumstances, of a public right of peaceful and non-obstructive assembly on the highway, provided that such assembly is reasonable, 'taking into account its size, duration and the nature of the highway on which it takes place.'[2] The origin of this right lies in a common law tradition which favours free speech and the right to peaceful protest on matters of public concern,[3] subject to the need for peace and good order.[4] The public right, which is one of the 'fundamental rights of a citizen in a democracy', is unduly restricted 'unless it can be exercised in some circumstances on the public highway.'[5] Not least in view of the Convention guarantee of the 'right to freedom of peaceful assembly',[6] contemporary English law inevitably starts from the premise that 'assembly on the highway will not necessarily be unlawful.'[7]

1   [1999] 2 AC 240 [**para 5.15**].
2   [1999] 2 AC 240 at 257F per Lord Irvine of Lairg LC. (It is irrelevant whether the assembly is 'premeditated or spontaneous'.) Neither Lord Clyde nor Lord Hutton was prepared, however, to hold that all reasonable, peaceful and non-obstructive assembly on the highway is necessarily a matter of public right ([1999] 2 AC 240 at 281C–F, 293A–D).
3   See *Hirst and Agu v Chief Constable of West Yorkshire* (1987) 85 Cr App R 143 at 151–152 per Otton J. (Here a number of 'animal rights' protesters exhibited banners and distributed leaflets in a pedestrian precinct outside a shop which sold fur coats. Their conviction on a charge of wilful obstruction of the highway was quashed.)
4   See also *Hubbard v Pitt* [1976] QB 142 at 174H–175A, where Lord Denning MR (dissenting) thought that a picket of an estate agent's premises carried out by half a dozen people for three hours on a Saturday morning was 'not an unreasonable use of the highway.' ('They did not interfere with the free passage of people to and fro'). In Lord Denning's view, 'so long as good order is maintained, the right to demonstrate must be preserved', although any violence 'should be firmly handled and severely punished' ([1976] QB 142 at 178H–179A).

5   *DPP v Jones* [1999] 2 AC 240 at 287A per Lord Hutton, citing (at 288E–H) *The Queen in Right
     of Canada v Committee for the Commonwealth of Canada* (1991) 77 DLR (4th) 385 at 394 per
     Lamer CJC ('No one could agree that the exercise of freedom of expression can be limited
     solely to places owned by the person wishing to communicate'). As L'Heureux-Dubé J
     confirmed in the same case, any other view entails that 'only those with enough wealth to own
     land, or mass media facilities (whose ownership is largely concentrated), would be able to
     engage in free expression' ((1991) 77 DLR (4th) 385 at 426). See *Halifax Antiques Ltd v
     Hildebrand* (1986) 22 DLR (4th) 289 at 298; *Ramsden v Peterborough (City)* (1994) 106 DLR
     (4th) 233 at 242; *Attorney-General of Ontario v Dieleman* (1995) 117 DLR (4th) 449 at
     708–709. See also Gray and Gray, 'Civil Rights, Civil Wrongs and Quasi-Public Space', (1999)
     4 EHRLR 46 at 70–71.
6   ECHR Art 11(1). The right to freedom of assembly 'is one of the foundations of a democratic
     society and should not be interpreted restrictively' (*Mark Anderson and Others v United
     Kingdom* (1998) 25 EHRR CD 172 at 174). See (1998) 3 EHRLR 218.
7   *DPP v Jones* [1999] 2 AC 240 at 259E–F per Lord Irvine of Lairg LC. See also Lord Clyde (at
     280G–281B).

Industrial or other protest

5.21   A difficult balance requires to be maintained between the right of the
citizen to use the highway as a forum for legitimate protest and the right of
other citizens to enjoy uninterrupted user of the same highway for their own
legitimate purposes. This issue has arisen with some force in connection with
the crossing of picket lines during strikes and the mobilisation of public protest
over rising fuel prices. In *Thomas v National Union of Mineworkers (South
Wales Area)*,[1] for instance, Scott J held that working miners were entitled under
the general law to exercise their right to go to work 'without unreasonable
harassment by others.' Since the working miners had a 'right to use the highway
for the purpose of going to work',[2] they were entitled to an injunction
protecting that right from 'unreasonable interference' by a group of 50 to 70
striking miners who on a daily basis hurled verbal abuse at them from the
picket line.[3] Scott J seemed to suggest that unreasonable collective interference
with public rights of user of the highway constitutes 'a species of private
nuisance'.[4]

1   [1986] Ch 20 at 64E–F. See [1985] CLJ 374 (K D Ewing).
2   [1986] Ch 20 at 64E.
3   [1986] Ch 20 at 65A–C. Regular picketing at the home of a working miner was held to be a
     common law nuisance, 'regardless of the number of people involved and regardless of the
     peaceful nature of their conduct' ([1986] Ch 20 at 65C–D). The decision in *Thomas v National
     Union of Mineworkers (South Wales Area)* indicates that the courts may be more prepared to
     allow the highway to be utilised as a means of protest by private or informal interest groups
     (such as 'animal rights' protesters) than by more highly organised representatives of unionised
     labour.
4   [1986] Ch 20 at 64E. In *News Group Newspapers Ltd v SOGAT '82* [1986] IRLR 337 at 346,
     Stuart-Smith J held that the owner of land adjoining the highway has a 'right of access to the
     highway from any part of his premises' (see also *Marshall v Ulleswater Steam Navigation Co*
     (1871) LR 7 QB 166 at 172; *Marshall v Blackpool Corpn* [1935] AC 16 at 22; *Shellharbour
     Municipal Council v Rovili Pty Ltd* (1989) 16 NSWLR 104 at 108F–109A; *Keating & Co Ltd v
     Jervis Shopping Centre Ltd and Pierce Contracting Ltd* [1997] 1 IR 512 at 519; *White v
     Chandler* [2001] 1 NZLR 28 at [64]). An actionable private nuisance arises in the event of
     interference with this right, so long as the obstruction of access amounts to 'an unreasonable

use of the highway'. In *News Group Newspapers Ltd v SOGAT '82* the daily presence of 50 to 200 dismissed print workers outside Rupert Murdoch's newspaper plant at Wapping was considered to be an 'unreasonable obstruction of the highway'.

Public nuisance

5.22 Public nuisance on the highway may constitute either a crime or a civil wrong.

Criminal liability

5.23 Some forms of user of the highway may involve the criminal offence of public nuisance,[1] although it is clear that not every obstruction of the highway constitutes such a nuisance. There must in addition be some 'unreasonable use of the highway by the defendant.'[2] Thus a march or procession which is conducted in an orderly manner is not a public nuisance, even though it may involve obstruction of the highway.[3] In determining the reasonableness of any particular user, the court must 'balance the rights of those who wish to demonstrate with those who wish to exercise their rights of passage.'[4] A meeting or demonstration on the highway is not necessarily unlawful,[5] although it is 'more likely to be than a procession.'[6]

1   A public nuisance may arise in connection with an 'unlawful act which endangers lives, safety, health, property or comfort of the public or by which the public are obstructed in the exercise or enjoyment of any right common to all Her Majesty's subjects' (*News Group Newspapers Ltd v SOGAT '82* [1986] IRLR 337 at 346).
2   *Lowdens v Keaveney* [1903] 2 IR 82 at 87–88; *R v Clark (No 2)* [1964] 2 QB 315 at 320–321. It may, for instance, be reasonable to place scaffolding on the highway for the purpose of erecting or repairing a building (see *Lord Advocate v Dumbarton DC* [1990] 2 AC 580 at 599H–600A per Lord Keith of Kinkel).
3   *News Group Newspapers Ltd v SOGAT '82* [1986] IRLR 337 at 346. See the stringent controls imposed on public processions by Public Order Act 1986, Part II.
4   *News Group Newspapers Ltd v SOGAT '82* [1986] IRLR 337 at 346.
5   See *Burden v Rigler* [1911] 1 KB 337 at 339–340.
6   *News Group Newspapers Ltd v SOGAT '82* [1986] IRLR 337 at 346.

Civil liability

5.24 Public nuisance is also actionable as a civil wrong if it 'materially affects the reasonable comfort and convenience of life of a class of Her Majesty's subjects' who come within the sphere or 'neighbourhood' of its operation.[1] The claimant must, moreover, show particular damage 'other than and beyond the general inconvenience suffered by the public.'[2] In *News Group Newspapers Ltd v SOGAT '82*,[3] Stuart-Smith J ruled that the holding of mass demonstrations outside Rupert Murdoch's print plant at Wapping constituted an actionable public nuisance. The demonstrations were directed by sacked print workers both against the claimants' continuing employees and against lorry drivers who distributed the claimants' newspapers. Stuart-Smith J held that the targets of these demonstrations comprised a sufficiently numerous 'class' for the purpose of rendering the mass show of force an actionable civil wrong.[4] The print firm had a right for its employees and visitors to pass on all roads (including pavements) approaching the plant, 'unobstructed by pickets or demonstrators acting in an abusive, insulting, threatening or violent manner.'[5] Injunctions were granted restricting the demonstrations at Wapping to a picket line consisting of no more than six workers whose function was confined to peaceful communication and persuasion.

1   *Attorney-General v P Y A Quarriers Ltd* [1957] 2 QB 169 at 184; *Wallace v Powell* (2000) 10 BPR 18481 at [32].
2   *News Group Newspapers Ltd v SOGAT '82* [1986] IRLR 337 at 346. The invasion of a particular city area by a group of prostitutes may constitute public nuisance (see *Attorney-General of British Columbia v Couillard* (1985) 11 DLR (4th) 567 at 572–576; but compare *Stein v Gonzales* (1985) 14 DLR (4th) 263 at 267–268).
3   [1986] IRLR 337.
4   *News Group Newspapers Ltd v SOGAT '82* [1986] IRLR 337 at 346. Stuart-Smith J thought that the 'class' requirement probably does not apply at all to obstruction of the highway, since obstruction in this context can generally be presumed to affect the public at large.
5   *News Group Newspapers Ltd v SOGAT '82* [1986] IRLR 337 at 357.

WALKWAY AGREEMENTS

5.25   Public rights of passage and re-passage may also be enjoyed under a 'walkway agreement' negotiated, pursuant to the Highways Act 1980, between a local authority and the owner of land on which a building is (or is to be) situated.[1] A 'walkway' is a footpath through or under a building, walkway agreements being frequently concluded in respect of shopping malls and other commercial urban developments. Particularly when constructed in an elevated or subterranean form, walkways provide a convenient means of easing pedestrian flow and segregating pedestrians from motorised transport.[2] The 'central feature' of the walkway agreement is its provision for 'the dedication by the building owner of the walkways as footpaths, ie as being subject to public rights of way.'[3] Walkways thus represent a kind of highway, albeit subject to special conditions and limitations set out in the relevant walkway agreement.[4] By statute the rights of the public over a walkway have been given a certain proprietary dimension, in that the covenants contained in a walkway agreement (whether positive or restrictive) are rendered binding on all persons deriving title to the land under the covenantor.[5] Even in the absence of any formal walkway agreement, similar pedestrian access routes through commercial developments may sometimes be converted into public rights of way by unhindered user over a period of 20 years.[6]

1   Highways Act 1980, s 35(1)–(2), re-enacting Highways Act 1971, s 18. A walkway agreement is registrable as a local land charge (Highways Act 1980, s 35(5)).
2   Although originally considered an extremely useful adjunct to the built environment, statutorily agreed walkways have attracted some concern on the ground that they provide a location for vandalism and petty crime (see [1998] Conv 160 (A Samuels)).
3   *CIN Properties Ltd v Rawlins* [1995] 2 EGLR 130 at 133L per Balcombe LJ. Walkway

agreements need take no special form, but a walkway agreement cannot be constituted by a mere leasehold covenant between a corporate tenant and a local authority landlord undertaking to allow 'full pedestrian access to the common parts of the demised premises' from 7.00 am to 11.00 pm daily (*CIN Properties Ltd v Rawlins*, supra at 133M).

4 A walkway may, for instance, be closed outside business hours, need not be of perpetual duration, and may be regulated by byelaws.

5 Highways Act 1980, s 35(4).

6 **[Para 5.9]**. See *Cumbernauld and Kilsyth DC v Dollar Land (Cumbernauld) Ltd* 1993 SLT 1318 at 1321B–E (House of Lords).

PUBLIC RIGHT OF PASSAGE IN NAVIGABLE WATERS

5.26 There is, as a 'foundational principle of the common law',[1] a public right of passage at will over all navigable tidal waters for the purposes of 'navigation, commerce, trade, and intercourse'.[2] The common law right includes a right of anchorage, mooring and grounding where necessary in the course of navigation.[3] There is also a public right of passage in respect of non-tidal rivers and lakes, although this right is subject to statutory regulation[4] and entitles the citizen to exercise only reasonable rights of user which are incidental to a right of passage and re-passage.[5] The reasonableness of any particular user is measured with reference to the 'capacity and quality' of the river or other waterway,[6] but the public right of passage does not confer any entitlement to indulge in wildfowling on a river.[7] Nor does the public have any right to use the bed or banks of the river other than for anchoring in an emergency or for landing at some place where they are entitled to do so.[8]

1 See *Commonwealth of Australia v Yarmirr* (2001) 208 CLR 1 at [278]–[282], where Kirby J spoke of the public right of navigation as based on a 'principle of freedom of movement across waters' analogous to the international right of innocent passage. See likewise *Wills' Trustees v Cairngorm Canoeing and Sailing School Ltd* 1976 SC (HL) 30 at 123–124 per Lord Wilberforce. The public navigational right prevails, in cases of conflict, over exclusive rights of fishing (see *Mayor of Colchester v Brooke* (1845) 7 QB 339 at 374, 115 ER 518 at 531; *Yarmirr*, supra at [278], [290]).

2 *Blundell v Catterall* (1821) 5 B & Ald 268 at 294, 106 ER 1190 at 1199–1200. See Tim Bonyhady, *The Law of the Countryside: the Rights of the Public* (Abingdon 1987), pp 130–131. The public right of navigation cannot be said to be exercised by a floating heliport (see *Thames Heliports Plc v LB of Tower Hamlets* (1997) 74 P & CR 164 at 177–178, 180).

3 *Gann v Free Fishers of Whitstable* (1865) 11 HLCas 192 at 208–210–211, 222, 11 ER 1305 at 1313, 1317; *Iveagh (Earl) v Martin* [1961] 1 QB 232 at 272–273.

4 See e g Water Resources Act 1991, Sch 25; Countryside Act 1968, s 22(6).

5 A public right of navigation cannot be lost by mere disuse (see *Wills' Trustees v Cairngorm Canoeing and Sailing School Ltd* 1976 SC (HL) 30 at 126 per Lord Wilberforce; *Rowland v Environment Agency* [2003] EWCA Civ 1885 at [49] per Peter Gibson LJ).

6 *Wills' Trustees v Cairngorm Canoeing and Sailing School Ltd* 1976 SC (HL) 30 at 123–124 at 191 per Lord Wilberforce.

7 *Lord Fitzhardinge v Purcell* [1908] 2 Ch 139 at 166.

8 *Attorney-General ex rel Yorkshire Derwent Trust Ltd v Brotherton* [1992] 1 AC 425 at 445G–H per Lord Jauncey of Tullichettle. Where the riparian owner's registered title extends to the edge of the bank, the mere existence of a towpath (and of a right of way along it) implies no easement to moor a houseboat to the river bank (*Sussex Investments Ltd v Jackson* (1993) *Times*, 29 July).

PUBLIC RIGHT OF FISHING

5.27   From ancient times there has been a common law right, vested in members of the public, to fish in the open sea[1] and in all tidal and salt waters.[2] (This venerable common law entitlement is regrettably unlimited by any reference to the deleterious environmental and ecological impact of unrestrained harvesting of the fruits of nature.[3]) The public right to fish includes the right to take shellfish from the exposed foreshore.[4] The common law also recognises, as ancillary to the public right to fish, a right of bait-digging on the foreshore provided that the taking of worms is directly related to an actual or intended exercise of the right to fish.[5] The public right of fishing is confined, however, to the open sea and tidal waters.[6] There is no similar public right in respect of a non-tidal river,[7] even if the river is subject to a public right of navigation.[8] It is also highly unlikely that any public right of fishing exists in relation to inland non-tidal lakes.[9]

1   '[E]very man may fish in the sea of common right' (1466) YB Mich 8 Edw IV, pl 30. See also *Blundell v Catterall* (1821) 5 B & Ald 268 at 294, 106 ER 1190 at 1199–1200. It has been suggested that the common law fishing right implies a public right of access to the foreshore at least for the purpose of launching a boat (see *Brinckman v Matley* [1904] 2 Ch 313 at 316; *Williams-Ellis v Cobb* [1935] 1 KB 310 at 320–322 per Lord Wright). In *Behrens v Richards* [1905] 2 Ch 614 at 620–621, Buckley J spoke similarly of foreshore access 'as the means of reaching the highway of the sea.'

2   *Case of the Royal Fishery of the Banne* (1610) Dav 55, 80 ER 540 at 541; *Stephens v Snell* [1939] 3 All ER 622H; *Harper v Minister for Sea Fisheries* (1989) 168 CLR 314 at 329–330. Private (ie exclusive or 'several') fisheries can exist in English waters only if created prior to Magna Carta 1215 (see *Malcomson v O'Dea* (1863) 10 HLCas 593 at 618, 11 ER 1155 at 1165–1166; *Stephens v Snell*, supra at 622G; *Adair v National Trust for Places of Historic Interest or Natural Beauty* [1998] NI 33 at 40j–41a). For an extant exclusive fishery, see *Loose v Castleton* (1978) 41 P & CR 19.

3   See *Adair v National Trust for Places of Historic Interest or Natural Beauty* [1998] NI 33 at 44b–d per Girvan J; *Commonwealth of Australia v Yarmirr* (2001) 208 CLR 1 at [282] per Kirby J.

4   *Adair v National Trust for Places of Historic Interest or Natural Beauty* [1998] NI 33 at 43d. See also *Bagott v Orr* (1801) 2 B & P 472 at 479, 126 ER 1391 at 1394–1395.

5   *Anderson v Alnwick DC* [1993] 1 WLR 1156 at 1169E–1170A; [1993] All ER Ann Rev 241 (P J Clarke). See similarly *Adair v National Trust for Places of Historic Interest or Natural Beauty* [1998] NI 33 at 43g–44a.

6   See *Blundell v Catterall* (1821) 5 B & Ald 268 at 294, 106 ER 1190 at 1199–1200; *Malcomson v O'Dea* (1863) 10 HLCas 593 at 618, 11 ER 1155 at 1165–1166.

7   **[Para 1.109]**.

8   *Pearce v Scotcher* (1882) 9 QBD 162 at 167; *Blount v Layard* [1891] 2 Ch 681 at 689–690.

9   See *Johnston v O'Neill* [1911] AC 552 at 568, 577–578, 592–593. Compare, however, *Toome Eel Fishery (Northern Ireland) Ltd v Cardwell* [1966] NI 1 at 12 per Lord MacDermott CJ.

LOCAL CUSTOMARY RIGHTS

5.28   Certain entitlements in respect of land may be enjoyed by way of local customary right,[1] although, on a strict view, rights of this nature are 'not necessarily considered to be rights of property.'[2] The entitlements which fall within this category normally have a quaint or archaic quality and their utility as a means of generalising rights of access is severely limited by the requirement that a distinct 'local dimension' should underpin the assertion of customary entitlement.[3] Customary rights are exercisable, not by the public at large,[4] but predominantly[5] by the inhabitants of a particular local community such as a town[6] or a parish[7] or 'district'.[8] 'Custom' is, in effect, a form of 'local common law' specific to a particular place,[9] and customary rights have been held to extend to such activities as the use of an access path to the local church,[10] the playing of sports and pastimes on a piece of land,[11] the drying of fishing nets in a certain location,[12] and the holding of an annual 'fair or wake'.[13] Local customary rights can arise at common law only if they are ancient, certain, reasonable and continuous.[14] In theory 'ancient' rights must pre-date 1189,[15] but in practice the requirement of ancient origin is satisfied by evidence of uninterrupted long user for 20 years (or perhaps within living memory), provided always that there is no proof that the user actually originated after 1189.[16]

1   Local customary rights differ from easements in that they are not appurtenant to any 'dominant tenement' [**para 8.33**].
2   *Mason v Tritton* (1993) 6 BPR 13639 at 13644 per Young J.
3   *Murphy v Wicklow CC* (Irish High Court, 19 March 1999) per Kearns J. See e g *Abercromby v Fermoy Town Commissioners* [1900] 1 IR 302 at 314–315 (recreational meeting place for inhabitants of town since time immemorial).
4   See e g *Fitch v Rawling* (1795) 2 H Bl 393 at 398, 126 ER 614 at 616–617; *R v Doncaster MBC, ex p Braim* (1989) 57 P & CR 1 at 8; *Mason v Tritton* (1993) 6 BPR 13639 at 13644 per Young J.
5   See *R v Oxfordshire CC, ex p Sunningwell PC* [2000] 1 AC 335 at 358B per Lord Hoffmann (pointing out that it is not fatal to the idea of a customary use that the use is not *exclusive* to the inhabitants of a particular locality).
6   *New Windsor Corporation v Mellor* [1975] Ch 380 at 391C–D.
7   *Brocklebank v Thompson* [1903] 2 Ch 344 at 354.
8   *Edwards v Jenkins* [1896] Ch 308 at 313.
9   *Hammerton v Honey* (1876) 24 WR 603 per Jessel MR. See also *Mercer v Denne* [1905] 2 Ch 538 at 582 per Stirling LJ. Customary rights arise only in the absence of a common law right (see *Adair v National Trust for Places of Historic Interest or Natural Beauty* [1998] NI 33 at 44f–g per Girvan J).
10 *Brocklebank v Thompson* [1903] 2 Ch 344 at 355.
11 *New Windsor Corporation v Mellor* [1975] Ch 380 at 392H. See *Fitch v Rawling* (1795) 2 H Bl 393 at 398, 126 ER 614 at 616 (cricket); *Hall v Nottingham* (1875) 1 Ex D 1 at 3–4 (dancing around maypole). See also *R v Oxfordshire CC, ex p Sunningwell PC* [2000] 1 AC 335 at 347F per Lord Hoffmann ('the traditional village green with its memories of maypole dancing, cricket and warm beer').
12 *Mercer v Denne* [1905] 2 Ch 538 at 581, 584.
13 *Wyld v Silver* [1963] Ch 243 at 256, 266.
14 *Lockwood v Wood* (1844) 6 QB 50 at 64, 115 ER 19 at 24; *Daly v Cullen* (1958) 92 ILTR 127 at 130.
15 See *R v Oxfordshire CC, ex p Sunningwell PC* [2000] 1 AC 335 at 347F.
16 See *Simpson v Wells* (1872) LR 7 QB 214 at 217; *Mercer v Denne* [1905] 2 Ch 538 at 577; *R v Oxfordshire CC, ex p Sunningwell PC* [2000] 1 AC 335 at 353F–H. See the reference to a 'regular usage of 20 years unexplained and uncontradicted' in *R v Suffolk CC, ex p Steed* (1998) 75 P & CR 102 at 106, citing *R v Joliffe* (1823) 2 B & C 54 at 59, 107 ER 303 at 305; *Brocklebank v Thompson* [1903] 2 Ch 344.

RIGHTS OF RECREATIONAL ACCESS

5.29   Historically English law has conferred on members of the public only extremely limited rights of recreational user in respect of land and water, although substantial de facto access has tended to be enjoyed in a rather ill-defined way.[1] Hitherto there has been no universal right of access to the hills or to ramble over open or uncultivated countryside.[2] For at least the last 250 years the common law has signally failed to recognise any general customary entitlement to enter another's land for recreational purposes.[3] Recreational access has represented, at best, a tolerated user in respect of which the landowner by long tradition – in the generality of cases – has sought no remedy in trespass.[4] Nor does the public have any general right to walk upon the foreshore[5] or to have access to the seashore for the purpose of swimming or other recreation.[6] Such rights are normally enjoyed only by way of licence.[7] The fact that members of the public have a right to swim or bathe in the sea implies no right to cross the foreshore in order to exercise that right.[8]

1   'It is not part of the normal function of a private landowner to provide facilities for the public on the land' (*R* (*Beresford*) *v Sunderland CC* [2001] 1 WLR 1327 at [45] per Smith J, cited with approval by Lord Scott of Foscote, [2004] 1 AC 889 at [21]). See also *Douglas v Hello! Ltd* [2001] QB 967 at [64] per Brooke LJ ('English law, as is well known, has been historically based on freedoms, not rights').

2   See *Earl of Coventry v Willes* (1863) 9 LT 384 at 385; *Hammerton v Honey* (1876) 24 WR 603 at 604. In *Spedding v Fitzpatrick* (1888) 38 Ch D 410 at 414, for example, it was significant that the Court of Appeal thought that a claim of public access to Latrigg Hill near Keswick was supportable only by reference to the common law doctrine of dedication and acceptance [**para 5.5**].

3   It may well be that, in medieval times, there was 'an early form of the right to roam' over open uncultivated land, but the dim recollection of such a practice has been said merely to reflect 'the gulf which existed between the medieval historian and the modern lawyer' (*Loder v Gaden* (1999) 78 P & CR 223 at 239 per Brooke LJ). See also *Robson v Hallett* [1967] 2 QB 939 at 953G per Diplock LJ. Even by 1673 there was no right 'to hunt in a man's park' without permission (see *Thomas v Sorrell* (1673) Vaugh 330 at 351, 124 ER 1098 at 1109 per Vaughan CJ, cited with clear approval in *Wood v Leadbitter* (1845) 13 M & W 838 at 844, 153 ER 351 at 354 per Alderson B).

4   [**Para 3.82**].

5   An exception is made for the case of 'peril or necessity' during the course of navigation (*Brinckman v Matley* [1904] 2 Ch 313 at 316 per Buckley J).

6   *Blundell v Catterall* (1821) 5 B & Ald 268 at 294, 299–300, 303–304, 106 ER 1190 at 1200–1203; *Brinckman v Matley* [1904] 2 Ch 313 at 324; *Williams-Ellis v Cobb* [1935] 1 KB 310 at 320–321; *Alfred F Beckett Ltd v Lyons* [1967] Ch 449 at 482E–F. The position is different in Scotland (see *Burnet v Barclay* 1955 SLT 282 at 284).

7   The common law doctrine of dedication and acceptance [**para 5.5**] cannot sanction the public use of private land otherwise than as a highway (e g for purposes of leisure and entertainment) (see *Skrenty v Harrogate BC* (Chancery Division, 26 October 1999)).

8   *Adair v National Trust for Places of Historic Interest or Natural Beauty* [1998] NI 33 at 41j per Girvan J. Nor is there any public right to hold meetings or deliver sermons on the foreshore (*Llandudno UDC v Woods* [1899] 2 Ch 705 at 708–710).

No general right to wander

5.30   The common law tradition refuses, in all but the most restrictive of contexts,[1] to accept that members of the public can ever acquire a *ius spatiandi* (or right to wander at large) over land in the proprietorship of another person.[2] Such an entitlement is simply not a species of right known to the common law[3] and cannot therefore be acquired either by grant or by prescription (ie long user).[4] The rationale for this position is the strong belief that such an unqualified and wide-ranging form of entitlement is exactly the sort of right which the landowner enjoys over his own land.[5] Indeed it is the unrestricted nature of the owner's right to go precisely where he pleases on his own land which symbolises the essence of a freehold or leasehold estate. In *Attorney-General v Antrobus*,[6] for instance, Farwell J denied the existence of a public right to visit and wander around the megalithic monument at Stonehenge, and underlined the legal impossibility that any member of the public may acquire a *ius spatiandi* over open countryside.[7]

1　See eg *Re Ellenborough Park* [1956] Ch 131 (communal suburban garden) **[para 8.45]**.
2　'[N]o right can be granted (otherwise than by Statute) to the public at large to wander at will over an undefined open space' (*Re Ellenborough Park* [1956] Ch 131 at 184 per Evershed MR). This unwillingness to recognise *iura spatiandi* over open land is echoed in many other jurisdictions (see eg *Randwick Corpn v Rutledge* (1959) 102 CLR 54 at 74 per Windeyer J; *Smeltzer v Fingal CC* [1998] 1 IR 279 at 286; *Murphy v Wicklow CC* (Irish High Court, 19 March 1999); *Kanak v Minister for Land and Water Conservation* (*NSW*) (2000) 180 ALR 489 at 497).
3　See *International Tea Stores Co v Hobbs* [1903] 2 Ch 165 at 172; *Skrenty v Harrogate BC* (Chancery Division, 26 October 1999).
4　See *Attorney-General v Antrobus* [1905] 2 Ch 188 at 198–200 per Farwell J; *Re Ellenborough Park* [1956] Ch 131 at 176, 184 per Evershed MR. Nor does even a prolonged user of open or scenic country for recreational purposes support any inference that the landowner has impliedly dedicated an access way as a public right of way (see *Antrobus*, supra at 205–208), a proposition widely accepted not merely in England (see *Behrens v Richards* [1905] 2 Ch 614 at 619–620), but also in Scotland (see *Duncan v Lees* (1870) 9 M 274 at 276) and in Ireland (see *Abercromby v Fermoy Town Commissioners* [1900] 1 IR 302 at 314).
5　See eg *Dyce v Lady James Hay* (1852) 1 Macq 305 at 309 per Lord St Leonards LC. See also *Re Ellenborough Park* [1956] Ch 131 at 176 per Evershed MR (an 'indefinite and unregulated privilege').
6　[1905] 2 Ch 188 at 208.
7　Farwell J castigated the claim of general public access as 'simply extravagant' and as an attempt 'to dispossess the [landowner] of his property' for which no 'serious argument' could be adduced ([1905] 2 Ch 188 at 208). The force of the *Antrobus* ruling has not been diminished by the passage of time (see *Skrenty v Harrogate BC* (Chancery Division, 26 October 1999)). See generally Tim Bonyhady, *The Law of the Countryside: the Rights of the Public* (Abingdon 1987), pp 123–131.

De facto access

5.31　At common law the generality of recreational access over open countryside has hitherto been enjoyed on the basis merely of fragile and arbitrarily revocable licence from the landowner.[1] The courts have not proved receptive to the idea that the recreational visitor (whether climber, rambler or motor sports enthusiast) may ground more secure entitlements of access on some less freely terminable 'equitable licence'[2] or 'licence coupled with an interest'[3] or even on the argument that scenic open space is held on some kind of implied charitable trust for the public benefit.[4] Instead, the legal basis of recreational access has been, almost uniformly, some licence for entry granted or withheld at the discretion of the landowner.[5]

1   [**Para 4.21**].
2   [**Para 4.90**]. Particularly in view of the unrecognised status of the *ius spatiandi* at common law [**para 5.30**], it is difficult to demonstrate that the recreational visitor has received any assurance of a proprietary entitlement in the land or has altered his position in detrimental reliance on some offer of open access. There are also 'the gravest doubts' whether the principle of equitable or estoppel-based licence 'could ever apply so as to create rights in favour of the public at large, since it is difficult to see how the acts or omissions of those individuals who rely on a representation could create rights in favour of the public' (*CIN Properties Ltd v Rawlins* [1995] 2 EGLR 130 at 134B).
3   [**Para 4.91**]. See e g *White v Blackmore* [1972] 2 QB 651 at 675G, 669H, where, in the case of a competitor killed whilst spectating at a jalopy car race, the Court of Appeal rejected the argument that the victim's recreational access to the competition area had been a 'licence coupled with an interest' and had therefore been irrevocable before the completion of its purpose (i e before the end of the day's racing). The Court took the view that his licence was 'revocable at will' ([1972] 2 QB 651 at 676G per Roskill LJ) and could always have been withdrawn 'summarily' at any time subject only to his right to collect and remove his jalopy after the termination of his licence ([1972] 2 QB 651 at 669G–670B per Buckley LJ, 676G per Roskill LJ).
4   See *Murphy v Wicklow CC* (Irish High Court, 19 March 1999) per Kearns J.
5   'Permission involves leave and licence, but it gives no right. If I avail myself of permission to cross a man's land, I do so by virtue of a licence, not of a right. It is an abuse of language to call it a right: it is an excuse or licence, so that the party cannot be treated as a trespasser' (*Bolch v Smith* (1862) 7 H & N 736 at 745–746, 158 ER 666 at 669–670 per Martin B). See similarly *Lowery v Walker* [1910] 1 KB 173 at 189 per Buckley LJ.

5.32   The liberality of the de facto access generally permitted by landowners has long been attributed to a clear understanding that the gratuitous provision of reasonable access to recreational visitors neither was rooted in, nor could ever mature into, any customary *right* of access.[1] The courts have been consistently anxious not to construct entitlements of access from 'acts of kindly courtesy' lest this should 'drive landowners to close their gates in order to preserve their property.'[2] Equally, however, judges have striven informally to hold a balance between the reasonable rights of landowners and the reasonable aspirations of the public to enjoy non-injurious access to open land.[3] Where no loss or harm to the private owner is caused by a trivial trespass upon his land, the courts have frequently been unwilling to employ 'the formidable weapon of an injunction' and have tended to award the churlish proprietor nothing more than a declaration or nominal damages.[4]

1   See eg *Ex parte Lewis* (1888) 21 QBD 191 at 197 per Wills J; *Attorney-General v Antrobus* [1905] 2 Ch 188 at 199–200, 205–206 per Farwell J; *Behrens v Richards* [1905] 2 Ch 614 at 619–620 per Buckley J; *Johnston v O'Neill* [1911] AC 552 at 592 per Lord Dunedin.
2   *Attorney-General v Antrobus* [1905] 2 Ch 188 at 199 per Farwell J. See also *Blount v Layard* [1891] 2 Ch 681n at 691 per Bowen LJ ('Nothing worse can happen in a free country than to force people to be churlish about their rights for fear that their indulgence may be abused').
3   The case law contains a strong undercurrent of required reasonableness on both sides. See e g *Behrens v Richards* [1905] 2 Ch 614 at 619–623, where Buckley J spoke of the need for the landowner to avoid the 'churlish and unreasonable' refusal of access to recreational visitors 'so long as they conduct themselves in an orderly and reasonable manner.'
4   [**Para 3.82**]. See *Behrens v Richards* [1905] 2 Ch 614 at 621–623 (innocent invasion of a

deserted beauty spot); *Llandudno UDC v Woods* [1899] 2 Ch 705 at 709–710 (harmless preaching on seashore). See likewise *Williams-Ellis v Cobb* [1935] 1 KB 310 at 322 per Lord Wright; *Ward v Kirkland* [1967] Ch 194 at 243C–D. In such circumstances English courts would probably incline towards the view taken in Canada that the landowner should be ordered to pay costs 'for seeking empty vindication' (see *Harrison v Carswell* (1976) 62 DLR (3d) 68 at 73 per Laskin CJC).

Comparison with other jurisdictions

5.33 In most aspects of the law of recreational access English common law contrasts unfavourably with the law of other jurisdictions. American courts, for example, are far more willing to infer the existence of an implied licence allowing public access to areas of privately owned open space. Many American courts have invoked broad doctrines of implied dedication,[1] customary right[2] and public trust[3] (or *ius publicum*[4]) in order to underpin public recreational access to wild country, national parks, navigable rivers and waters,[5] beaches and tidelands.[6] Extensive rights of entry for recreational purposes are also guaranteed by the laws of many European countries.[7] Even Scots common law demonstrates a deeper sensitivity than does English law to the claims of the recreational visitor.[8] Although Scots law traditionally recognises no right of unconsented recreational access to another's land,[9] the recreational visitor is left largely immune from legal sanction.[10] The Scots landowner is entitled to enclose his land in exclusion of all-comers[11] and to require any trespasser to leave his land immediately,[12] but, unlike the position in England, unconsented entry is not actionable in damages without a showing of injury.[13] Moreover, in the absence of proven harm or of actual or threatened violence by the intruder,[14] the landowner is not entitled to use force to eject the trespasser,[15] but is instead relegated to the discretionary (and little used) remedy of interdict (ie injunction) in respect of repeated incursions.[16] The Scottish landowner, aggrieved by an isolated act of harmless trespass, has in effect 'no remedy against the trespasser.'[17]

1   See eg *State ex rel Thornton v Hay*, 462 P2d 671 at 673–678 (1969); *Gion v City of Santa Cruz*, 465 P2d 50 at 55–59 (1970); *Department of Natural Resources v Ocean City*, 332 A2d 630 at 633–634 (1975); *County of Los Angeles v Berk*, 605 P2d 381 at 389–391 (1980).

2   See eg *McKee v Gratz*, 260 US 127 at 136, 67 L Ed 167 at 170 (1922) per Justice Holmes ('The strict rule of English common law as to entry upon a close must be taken to be mitigated by common understanding with regard to the large expanses of uninclosed and uncultivated land in many parts, at least, of this country. Over these it is customary to wander, shoot and fish at will until the owner sees fit to prohibit it. A licence may be implied from the habits of the country'). See likewise *Marsh v Colby*, 39 Mich 626 at 627 (1878) (Supreme Court of Michigan); *United States v Curtis-Nevada Mines, Inc and Curtis*, 611 F2d 1277 at 1283–1284 (1980).

3   See eg *Knight v United Land Association*, 142 US 161 at 181, 35 L Ed 974 at 981 (1891); *Texas v Bradford*, 50 SW2d 1065 at 1069 (1932); *Marks v Whitney*, 491 P2d 374 at 378–381 (1971); *Sierra Club v Department of the Interior*, 376 F Supp 90 at 93 (1974); *Matthews v Bay Head Improvement Association*, 471 A2d 355 at 366 (NJ 1984). See J L Sax, 'The Public Trust Doctrine in Natural Resource Law: Effective Judicial Intervention' 68 Mich L Rev 471 (1969–70).

4   See *Shively v Bowlby*, 152 US 1 at 11, 38 L Ed 331 at 336 (1894).

5   See eg *Diversion Lake Club v R W Heath*, 86 SW2d 441 at 444 (1935); *National Audubon*

Society v Superior Court of Alpine County, 658 P2d 709 at 718–721 (1983); *Adirondack League Club, Inc v Sierra Club*, 706 NE2d 1192 at 1195 (NY 1998).

6   See M L Bryan, 'Which Way to the Beach? Public Access to Beaches for Recreational Use', 29 So Car L Rev 627 (1977–79); J W Singer, 'The Reliance Interest in Property' 40 Stanford L Rev 611 at 674–675 (1987–88).

7   See eg the Swedish Allemansrätt (Everyman's Right), which confers a remarkably broad entitlement of public access to privately held land (see Marion Shoard, *A Right to Roam* (OUP 1999), pp 260–264).

8   The frequent assertion that there is no law of trespass in Scotland is, however, 'loose and inaccurate' (*Wood v North British Rly Co* (1899) 2 F 1 at 2 per Lord Trayner).

9   *Earl of Breadalbane v Livingston* (1790) M 4999 per Sir Ilay Campbell, as affd (1791) 3 Pat 221; *Dyce v Lady James Hay* (1852) 1 Macq 305 at 312–315. See similarly J Rankine, *The Law of Land-Ownership in Scotland* (4th edn, Edinburgh 1909), pp 134, 139.

10   The greater liberality of Scots law in this respect has prompted the suggestion that customary freedoms of access have acquired the status of legal entitlements, thereby displacing trespass as part of Scots law (see eg Alan Blackshaw, 'Implied Permission and the Traditions of Customary Access', (1999) 3 Edinburgh L Rev 368; 'The customary freedoms of Scottish access' (Winter 2003) 34 John Muir Trust Journal 13). Compare, however, J Rowan-Robinson and A Ross, 'The Freedom to Roam and Implied Permission' (1998) 2 Edinburgh L Rev 225; P Mackay, 'Customary freedoms of access in Scotland: a reply' (Summer 2003) 35 John Muir Trust Journal 34. Much of this debate has now been overtaken by the enactment of the Land Reform (Scotland) Act 2003 [**para 5.50**].

11   K G C Reid, *The Law of Property in Scotland* (Butterworths 1996), para 184. See *Earl of Breadalbane v Livingston* (1790) 10 Faculty Decisions 276 at 279.

12   J Rankine, op cit, p 140; D M Walker, *Principles of Scottish Private Law* (4th edn, Clarendon 1989), Vol III, p 99. See J Rowan-Robinson, 'Working Together for Access', in P Jackson and D C Wilde (ed), *Property Law: Current Issues and Debates* (Ashgate 1999), p 4.

13   *Lord Advocate v Glengarnock Iron and Steel Co Ltd* 1909 1 SLT 15 at 17.

14   See J Rankine, op cit, p 140; D M Walker, op cit, Vol III, p 99; K G C Reid, op cit, para 184.

15   Time has almost certainly diminished the rigour of the older case law (see eg *Bell v Shand* (1870) 7 SLR 267 at 268–269; *Wood v North British Rly Co* (1899) 2 F 1 at 2–3). The use of reasonable force is probably justified nowadays only where there is intrusion into a dwelling-house (see J Rankine, op cit, p 140; D M Walker, op cit, Vol III, p 100; K G C Reid, op cit, para 184).

16   See *Wills' Trustees v Cairngorm Canoeing and Sailing School Ltd* 1976 SC (HL) 30 at 70 per Lord President Emslie. An interdict will be refused if repeated intrusion is not anticipated (see *Hay's Trustees v Young* (1877) 4 R 398 at 401–402; *Inverurie Magistrates v Sorrie* 1956 SC 175 at 181–186) or if the impact of the trespass is negligible (see eg *Steuart v Stephen* (1877) 4 R 873 at 875; *Winans v Macrae* (1885) 12 R 1051 at 1062–1064). See also W M Gordon, *Scottish Land Law* (W Green & Son Ltd, Edinburgh, 1989), para 13–10.

17   K G C Reid, op cit, para 182. It is, however, a criminal offence to camp on private land (Trespass (Scotland) Act 1865, s 3) or to trespass in pursuit of game (Game (Scotland) Act 1832, s 1). See *Ferguson v MacPhail* 1987 SCCR 52.

GRADUAL EXTENSION OF RECREATIONAL ACCESS RIGHTS

5.34   In England and Wales it is now increasingly recognised that there is a large public interest in the promotion and protection of general access to open countryside. At least three sorts of inter-related factor have fed this concern. First, there is a growing acknowledgement of the humanising and socialising qualities of the encounter with nature and wild country.[1] High and open places lend a certain moral elevation.[2] Second, arguments of 'social equity' point towards ensuring that unique recreational sites and the non-commodity values which they represent should not be the reserve of the privileged few.[3] The social dividends of the outdoor experience are not merely spiritual, but also political, in quality. It was Justice William Douglas who wrote of the 'citizenship of the mountains' where '[p]overty, wealth, accidents of birth, social standing, race [are] immaterial.'[4] Third, the expansion of recreational access has now become a major driver of public health policy and planning.[5] A key strategy for the implementation of the current government's vision of a 'physically active Britain' is a programme aimed at ensuring by 2020 that 70 per cent of the population is reasonably physically active.[6]

1   An influential government consultation paper of 1998 stated that greater access to open countryside 'will benefit a wide range of people ... They will be able to improve their health; to experience the wonders of wildlife and the beauty of fine landscapes; to learn about countryside activities; and to refresh their spirits' (*Access to the Open Countryside in England and Wales* (DETR Consultation Paper, February 1998), Foreword).

2   There is some deep sense in which the mountain-top experience makes us more decent human beings. On the transcendental aspects of exposure to wilderness, see Gray 'Equitable Property' (1994) 47(2) CLP 157 at 199–202. On the emerging links between natural law theory and 'ecological morality', see further Jane Holder, 'New Age: Rediscovering Natural Law' (2000) 53 CLP 151.

3   *DETR Consultation Paper* (1998), para 3.67. See also Carol Rose, 'The Comedy of the Commons: Custom, Commerce, and Inherently Public Property' 53 U Chi L Rev 711 at 780 (1986).

4   *Of Men And Mountains* (London 1951), pp 211, 293.

5   'Walking can provide real benefits to people's physical and mental well-being ... The Government therefore proposes to extend access to open countryside' (*DETR Consultation Paper* (1998), para 1.8).

6   See *Game Plan: a strategy for delivering Government's sport and physical activity objectives* (Department for Culture, Media and Sport/Strategy Unit Report, December 2002). (The current activity level is rated at 32 per cent.)

5.35 A gathering array of legal provisions nowadays underpins the revitalised concern to diffuse the benefits of personal self-realisation and social hygiene which open-air access is perceived to confer. Each can be seen as part of the process described by Professor C B Macpherson in which the concept of proprietary entitlement evolves towards the achievement of access rights for all to the 'full and free life'.[1]

1   See C B Macpherson, 'Capitalism and the Changing Concept of Property', in E Kamenka and R S Neale (ed), *Feudalism, Capitalism and Beyond* (Canberra 1975), p 121.

The national footpaths network

5.36 The shortcomings of the English common law on recreational access to open country have always been compensated to some degree by the network of public rights of foot and horse way, often of medieval origin, which covers England and Wales.[1] The protection, expansion[2] and official recordation of this profusion of entitlement[3] reflects what has been described as the 'strong public interest in facilitating the preservation of footpaths for access to the countryside.'[4] As Scott LJ observed in *Jones v Bates*,[5] '[t]he rambler – sometimes called the "hiker" – needs the footpath more than ever.'[6] Local authorities now have compulsory powers to initiate a 'public path creation order', with possible rights to financial compensation for the landowner,[7] where it appears that there is need for a footpath or bridleway over land.[8] To date such powers have been little used, and a code of practice is currently in preparation for the purpose of promoting path creation by clarifying and standardising entitlements to compensation.[9] Once created, almost all public footpaths, bridleways and restricted byways are highways maintainable at public expense.[10]

1   See Marion Shoard, *A Right to Roam* (OUP 1999), pp 15–19.
2   All local highway authorities outside inner London are now obliged to prepare 'rights of way improvement plans' pursuant to CROWA 2000, ss 60–61.
3   A definitive mapping process was initiated by the National Parks and Access to the Countryside Act 1949.
4   *R v Oxfordshire CC, ex p Sunningwell PC* [2000] 1 AC 335 at 359D–E per Lord Hoffmann. See also *R v Secretary of State for Wales, ex p Emery* [1996] 4 All ER 1 at 19j per Deputy Judge Sir Louis Blom-Cooper QC (affd on appeal [1998] 4 All ER 387).
5   [1938] 2 All ER 237 at 249C–E.
6   For Scott LJ, '[t]he movement represented by the ramblers' societies is of national importance, and to the real lover of the country ... the footpath is everything. In short, it is of real public moment that no genuine footpath should be lost, without statutory action to close it'.
7   Highways Act 1980, s 28. See, however, the rejection (as out of time) of a claim for £1.12 million made by the third Baron Rotherwick in respect of a 2 kilometre footpath created in an Oxfordshire beauty spot (*Rotherwick's Executors v Oxfordshire CC* [2000] 2 EGLR 84).
8   Highways Act 1980, ss 26–27. See also CROWA 2000, s 58(1).
9   See 'Creation of New Public Rights of Way: A Draft Code of Practice for Local Highway Authorities Paying Compensation' (Countryside Agency and Countryside Council for Wales Consultation Paper, August 2003), para 2.2
10   CROWA 2000, s 49(1), (3).

Public rights of recreation implied from long user

5.37   In some circumstances it is possible that the grant of a public right of recreation can be presumed from the fact of long user, it being irrelevant, for this purpose, that the land which is subject to such a public right has not been registered under the Commons Registration Act 1965.[1] In *R v Doncaster MBC, ex p Braim*,[2] for example, McCullough J gave an unreserved judgment to the effect that a claimed right of general recreational access to Doncaster Common could be ascribed to a long lost deed of trust which inferably declared that the corporate body which owned the land held henceforth on trust for the public. The fictional nature of this derivation of rights is self-evident. The *Braim* decision almost certainly relates only to relatively confined areas of land[3] owned by public authorities[4] and its potential field of application is likely to be highly specialised or restricted. Anomalously, however, it seems that long user has succeeded in establishing public rights to navigate at will over the surface of certain non-tidal inland waters.[5]

1   [**Para 5.40**]. See *R v Doncaster MBC, ex p Braim* (1989) 57 P & CR 1 at 7.
2   (1989) 57 P & CR 1 at 11–15 (Doncaster Common); [1988] Conv 369 (J Hill).
3   (1989) 57 P & CR 1 at 12
4   McCullough J stressed that the borough corporation in *Braim* 'would have had an interest in affording the amenity' of Doncaster Common (and the delights of the St Leger) to its

residents and others ((1989) 57 P & CR 1 at 12). Compare *Goodman v Mayor of Saltash* (1882) 7 App Cas 633 at 647 per Lord Selborne LC (no implication of trust possible in relation to private landowner).

5   See e g *Marshall v Ulleswater Steam Navigation Co* (1871) LR 7 QB 166 at 172 (Ullswater); *Bloomfield v Johnston* (1868) IR 8 CL 68 at 87–89, 111–112 (Lough Erne); *Micklethwait v Vincent* (1892) 67 LT 225 at 230 (Norfolk Broads). See also *Attorney-General (ex rel Yorkshire Derwent Trust Ltd) v Brotherton* [1992] 1 AC 425 at 434D.

Rights over commons and waste lands

5.38   Members of the public have statutory 'rights of access for air and exercise'[1] to any land which comprises a metropolitan common or manorial waste or a local authority common or other land which is subject to rights of common.[2] Such areas include much park land in the cities and extensive commons in the Lake District and South Wales.[3]

1   LPA 1925, s 193(1). The 'rights' do not include any right to hunt (*R v Somerset CC, ex p Fewings* [1995] 1 WLR 1037 at 1050H–1051B per Simon Brown LJ).

2   In view of the existing statutory right of access, such land is not regarded as 'access land' for the purpose of the Countryside and Rights of Way Act 2000 (see CROWA 2000, s 15(1)(a)).

3   'Access to the Open Countryside in England and Wales' (DETR Consultation Paper, February 1998), para 1.4.

Municipal parks

5.39   Other areas of municipally owned park land are similarly subject to a species of public trust[1] which not only imposes duties of management and maintenance on the local authority owner, but also confers at least some form of access entitlement upon members of the public.[2] Ownership of such land takes on a fiduciary quality. The land is 'only the property of the Council for the public benefit'[3] and, as legal owner, the local authority has an obligation to afford reasonable rights of entry to the citizen,[4] coupled with a duty not to discriminate unfairly in excluding or ejecting any particular individual from the amenity concerned.[5] Where an area has been appropriated for the purpose of public recreation, local inhabitants are not simply potential or 'tolerated' trespassers upon the land,[6] but are more properly to be regarded as the equivalent of 'beneficiaries of a statutory trust of a public nature.'[7] On this analysis, and even though his access may be restricted by reference to opening times and good behaviour,[8] the citizen becomes the holder of a right of entry.[9]

1   It has been said that '"trust" is not a term of art in public law' (*Town Investments Ltd v Department of the Environment* [1978] AC 359 at 382C–D per Lord Diplock).

2   Again there is weighty American authority for the idea that parks are 'held in the public trust' (see *Hague v Committee for Industrial Organization*, 307 US 496 at 515, 83 L Ed 1423 at 1436 (1939); *Frisby v Schultz*, 487 US 474 at 481, 101 L Ed 2d 420 at 429 (1988)).

3   *R v London CC, ex p Corrie* [1918] 1 KB 68 at 73 per Darling J (emphasising that it was 'not true to say that these parks are the property of the County Council in the sense that a man's house is his property'). See also *Bathurst CC v PWC Properties Pty Ltd* (1998) 195 CLR 566 at [48]–[49].

4   The local authority is '(in a loose sense) in the position of a trustee with a duty to let [the

citizen] in' (*R* (*Beresford*) *v Sunderland CC* [2004] 1 AC 889 at [86] per Lord Walker of Gestingthorpe). See similarly *Hall v Beckenham Corpn* [1949] 1 KB 716 at 727–728 per Finnemore J.

5   See *R v London Borough of Brent, ex p Assegai* (1987) Times, 18 June, per Woolf LJ [**para 4.53**].

6   *R* (*Beresford*) *v Sunderland CC* [2004] 1 AC 889 at [86]–[87] per Lord Walker of Gestingthorpe (a local resident who takes a walk in a municipal park 'might indignantly reject any suggestion that he was a trespasser unless he obtained the local authority's consent to enter').

7   *R* (*Beresford*) *v Sunderland CC* [2004] 1 AC 889 at [87] per Lord Walker of Gestingthorpe. Certain recreational areas are the subject of a statutory trust imposed by Open Spaces Act 1906, s 10.

8   See *Randwick Corpn v Rutledge* (1959) 102 CLR 54 at 80 per Windeyer J.

9   *Kanak v Minister for Land and Water Conservation* (NSW) (2000) 180 ALR 489 at [28].

Registration of greens under the Commons Registration Act 1965

5.40   Certain rights of recreational access are indirectly preserved by registration under the Commons Registration Act 1965.[1] This statute was enacted in recognition of the public importance of open spaces and in order to protect such spaces from commercial development.[2] Land is eligible for registration if, for example, it comprises a 'town or village green'.[3] Although the 1965 Act is silent on the point,[4] it seems likely as a matter of statutory implication that, in addition to providing for the registration of relevant areas, the Act has created, in respect of such areas, certain positive rights of recreational user for members of the public.[5] It is evident, in any event, that registration under the Act serves to prevent adverse development of the land in question,[6] encroachment on or inclosure of or interference with a town or village green being deemed to constitute the crime of public nuisance.[7]

1   The commons registration scheme co-ordinated by the 1965 Act extends beyond town and village greens to include grazing land and now covers 3 per cent of the total area of England and 9 per cent of the total area of Wales (*DETR Consultation Paper* (1998), para 3.9).

2   See *Report of the Royal Commission on Common Land 1955–1958* (Cmnd 462, 1958); *R v Oxfordshire CC, ex p Sunningwell PC* [2000] 1 AC 335 at 347G–348A, 359D–E per Lord Hoffmann.

3   Commons Registration Act 1965, s 1(1). The idea underlying the 1965 Act was that no land capable of registration under the Act should be a 'town or village green' unless so registered within a prescribed period (s 1(2)). Registration was intended to afford a definitive record of the ownership of the land concerned, provision being made for a vesting of title in the local authority in default of any established claim of ownership (s 8).

4   It is clear that second-phase legislation (as yet non-existent) was expected to define in positive terms the rights of the public over commons and town or village greens (see *R* (*Laing Homes Ltd*) *v Buckingham CC* [2004] 1 P & CR 573 at [27]–[29]).

5   See *R v Suffolk CC, ex p Steed* (1998) 75 P & CR 102 at 114–115 per Pill LJ; *Oxfordshire County Council v Oxfordshire City Council* [2004] 2 WLR 1291 at [43] per Lightman J. Compare, however, the more restrictive view evident in *New Windsor Corporation v Mellor* [1975] Ch 380 at 391H–392G per Lord Denning MR, 395G per Browne LJ; *R* (*Laing Homes Ltd*) *v Buckingham CC* [2004] 1 P & CR 573 at [47]–[48] per Sullivan J. The point was left open by Lord Hoffmann in *R v Oxfordshire CC, ex p Sunningwell PC* [2000] 1 AC 335 at 347B–C.

6   Commons registration is now used with increasing frequency as a weapon of environmental warfare. Some doubt has been expressed as to the propriety of such registration as a means of bypassing 'normal development controls' (see *R* (*Beresford*) *v Sunderland CC* [2004] 1 AC 889

at [92] per Lord Walker of Gestingthorpe). There is also a further (unresolved) query whether registration of a green constitutes a de facto deprivation of property contrary to ECHR Protocol 1, Art 1 (see *R (Laing Homes Ltd) v Buckingham CC* [2004] 1 P & CR 573 at [156]–[163]).

7   See Inclosure Act 1857, ss 12, 29; Commons Act 1876, s 29; *R v Oxfordshire CC, ex p Sunningwell PC* [2000] 1 AC 335 at 347B–C per Lord Hoffmann.

Recreational user

5.41 Land constitutes a 'town or village green'[1] if it has been statutorily allotted 'for the exercise or recreation of the inhabitants of any locality' or is land on which such inhabitants have a 'customary right to indulge in lawful sports and pastimes.'[2] Land also qualifies as a 'town or village green' if it is land on which for not less than 20 years[3] a 'significant number of the inhabitants of any locality, or of any neighbourhood within a locality, have indulged in lawful sports and pastimes as of right.'[4] It is the last limb of the statutory coverage which has created most difficulty. The phrase 'sports and pastimes' is nowadays regarded as a composite term which covers a broad range of informal recreational activity and need not involve any communal element 'such as playing cricket, shooting at butts or dancing round the maypole.'[5] An evening stroll with a dog or playing with children or kicking a ball around probably qualifies.[6]

1   Dedication by the landowner is not available as a means of creating a 'town or village green' (see *R (Beresford) v Sunderland CC* [2004] 1 AC 889 at [40] per Lord Scott of Foscote).
2   See Commons Registration Act 1965, s 22(1).
3   The 20 year period need not precede immediately the application for registration, but in the case of any registrable green not registered on 31 July 1970, a fresh 20 year period of qualifying user is required to revive its registrability (*Oxfordshire County Council v Oxfordshire City Council* [2004] 2 WLR 1291 at [45], [64]).
4   Commons Registration Act 1965, s 22(1A), as introduced by CROWA 2000, s 98. The recreational user by these inhabitants must, furthermore, be a continuing or recent activity (see s 22(1A)(a)–(b)). Unlike other sub-categories of 'town or village green', greens which are the subject of a 20 year user may be registered even after the expiry of the normal statutory time limit prescribed for registration (*R v Oxfordshire CC, ex p Sunningwell PC* [2000] 1 AC 335 at 348D).
5   *R v Oxfordshire CC, ex p Sunningwell PC* [2000] 1 AC 335 at 356H–357E per Lord Hoffmann.
6   See also *R v Suffolk CC, ex p Steed* (1995) 70 P & CR 487 at 503 per Carnwath J; *R (Beresford) v Sunderland CC* [2004] 1 AC 889 at [53] per Lord Rodger of Earlsferry.

User 'as of right'

5.42 In *R v Oxfordshire CC, ex p Sunningwell PC*,[1] the House of Lords held that the concept of user 'as of right' requires no subjective personal belief in the reality of any underlying right.[2] Indeed, the requirement of user 'as of right' neither presupposes nor necessitates the existence of any positive legal entitlement at all,[3] as evidenced by the fact that the landowner remains free, prior to the expiration of the 20 year period, to terminate the relevant recreational user of his land.[4] The case law indicates that the focus of the statutory formula falls on the predictable reaction of the landowner to the particular user rather than on the state of mind of the members of the public whose activities generate the statutory presumption.[5] Thus, for the purpose of the Commons Registration Act 1965, user 'as of right' merely denotes a form of user 'which would suggest to a reasonable landowner that [the persons concerned] believed that they were exercising a public right.'[6] User which, on objective evaluation, *appears* to be user as of right cannot be discounted merely because many of the individuals exercising such user over a long period 'were subjectively indifferent as to whether a right existed, or even had private knowledge that it did not'[7] or believed in the existence of a right, but did not 'know its precise metes and bounds.'[8] A claim of recreational user 'as of right' under the 1965 Act may be precluded, however, if the land in question is normally subjected to agricultural operations inconsistent with recreational activity[9] or if the user occurs pursuant to some other statutorily derived entitlement.[10]

1   [2000] 1 AC 335 at 355G–356E per Lord Hoffmann.
2   See likewise *R (Beresford) v Sunderland CC* [2004] 1 AC 889 at [3] per Lord Bingham of Cornhill, [14], [44] per Lord Scott of Foscote.
3   *R (Beresford) v Sunderland CC* [2004] 1 AC 889 at [3] per Lord Bingham of Cornhill. User can be 'as of right' even though it is not adverse to the landowner's interests (ibid at [90]–[91] per Lord Walker of Gestingthorpe).
4   *R (Beresford) v Sunderland CC* [2004] 1 AC 889 at [46] per Lord Scott of Foscote.
5   See *R v Oxfordshire CC, ex p Sunningwell PC* [2000] 1 AC 335 at 352H–353A per Lord Hoffmann; *R (Laing Homes Ltd) v Buckingham CC* [2004] 1 P & CR 573 at [78], [82].
6   *R v Oxfordshire CC, ex p Sunningwell PC* [2000] 1 AC 335 at 354F per Lord Hoffmann. The public character of the land concerned – as in the case of land owned by a local authority – is highly relevant to any consideration of the conclusion which a reasonable person might draw from the circumstances of user (*R (Beresford) v Sunderland CC* [2001] 1 WLR 1327 at [45] per Smith J, as endorsed by Lord Scott of Foscote, [2004] 1 AC 889 at [21], [49]).
7   *R v Oxfordshire CC, ex p Sunningwell PC* [2000] 1 AC 335 at 356B–C per Lord Hoffmann. It is 'almost inevitable' that, over a 20 year period of user, user in the earlier years is exercised 'without any very confident belief in the existence of the legal right.' See likewise *R (Beresford) v Sunderland CC* [2004] 1 AC 889 at [3] per Lord Bingham of Cornhill, [44] per Lord Scott of Foscote.
8   *R v Oxfordshire CC, ex p Sunningwell PC* [2000] 1 AC 335 at 356D per Lord Hoffmann. See e g *R v Suffolk CC, ex p Steed* (1998) 75 P & CR 102.
9   *R (Laing Homes Ltd) v Buckingham CC* [2004] 1 P & CR 573 at [68], [86].
10   See *R (Beresford) v Sunderland CC* [2004] 1 AC 889 at [9] per Lord Bingham of Cornhill, [30] per Lord Scott of Foscote. Thus, for example, access to land in the exercise of the right conferred by the Countryside and Rights of Way Act 2000 **[para 5.46]** cannot convert land into a 'town or village green' (CROWA 2000, s 12(4)). Likewise the pre-existence of footpath rights around the perimeter of a field may render recreational user of the remainder of the field too insubstantial to qualify under the 1965 Act (*R (Laing Homes Ltd) v Buckingham CC* [2004] 1 P & CR 573 at [105]–[110]).

Relevance of permission, acquiescence and encouragement

5.43   The concept of user 'as of right' is clearly descended from the notion of user *nec vi, nec clam, nec precario* (without force, secrecy or permission).[1] Somewhere at the back of this idea is the proposition that consensual user cannot later be paraded as an exercise of independent and non-permissive entitlement. A permitted user is generally inconsistent with any claim of user 'as of right'.[2] It has proved difficult, however, to distinguish between those elements of permission which defeat the claim of user 'as of right' and those elements of acquiescence, toleration or encouragement which classically underlie prescriptive claims of rightful user.

1 [**Para 8.177**]. See *R (Beresford) v Sunderland CC* [2004] 1 AC 889 at [3] per Lord Bingham of Cornhill, [16], [33] per Lord Scott of Foscote, [55] per Lord Rodger of Earlsferry.
2 *R (Beresford) v Sunderland CC* [2004] 1 AC 889 at [5] per Lord Bingham of Cornhill, [51] per Lord Scott of Foscote. In *Beresford* (at [43]–[47]) Lord Scott went rather further than his brethren in suggesting that even express permissions given by a landowner can, in some circumstances, be wholly compatible with user 'as of right'.

5.44 The problem arose most recently in *R (Beresford) v Sunderland CC*,[1] where a local authority landowner sought to rebut a claim of 20 years' public recreational user 'as of right' of a playing field which it owned and now wished to develop as a college of further education. The local authority alleged that any claim 'as of right' was negatived by the fact that, by mowing the grassed area and installing some spectator seating, the authority had impliedly licensed public use of the playing field. The House of Lords unanimously rejected this argument,[2] holding that the permission which defeats a claim of user 'as of right' necessarily involves some positive act of grant of a revocable licence to use the land (as distinct from mere silent acquiescence in or passive toleration of its use).[3] The grant of such permission may be either express or implied from the relevant circumstances.[4] However, in the latter case there must be 'overt conduct' on the part of the landowner which contradicts any claim of 'right' through the communication of an unmistakably precarious permission to enter the land.[5] There must, in effect, be evidence of 'some overt act which is intended to be understood, and is understood, as permission to do something which would otherwise be an act of trespass.'[6]

1 [2004] 1 AC 889.
2 A licence to use land 'cannot be implied from mere inaction of a landowner with knowledge of the use to which his land is being put' ([2004] 1 AC 889 at [6]–[7] per Lord Bingham of Cornhill). The decision in *Beresford* marked a final victory for the applicants in *Appleby v United Kingdom* (2003) 37 EHRR 783 [**para 4.58**] (see [2004] 1 AC 889 at [92] per Lord Walker of Gestingthorpe).
3 [2004] 1 AC 889 at [57]–[60] per Lord Rodger of Earlsferry, [77]–[79] per Lord Walker of Gestingthorpe. In *Beresford* the conduct of the local authority was regarded as explicable not as connoting the grant of some revocable licence to the public, but as the natural action of any responsible public authority landowner ([2004] 1 AC 889 at [7] per Lord Bingham of Cornhill, [49] per Lord Scott of Foscote, [60] per Lord Rodger of Earlsferry, [83] per Lord Walker of Gestingthorpe).
4 [2004] 1 AC 889 at [59]–[60] per Lord Rodger of Earlsferry. See similarly Lord Walker's allusion (at [75]) to 'the expression of consent by non-verbal means.'
5 [2004] 1 AC 889 at [83], [85], [89(a)] per Lord Walker of Gestingthorpe (referring to such conduct as charging for admission and occasional or intermittent closure of the land to all-comers). See likewise [2004] 1 AC 889 at [5] per Lord Bingham of Cornhill, [45] per Lord Scott of Foscote.
6 [2004] 1 AC 889 at [75] per Lord Walker of Gestingthorpe.

5.45 A clear onus thus rests upon the landowner to indicate to members of the public that their licence to use his land is intended to be merely temporary, entirely permissive and inherently revocable.[1] This is particularly the case where the landowner (as in *Beresford*) is clothed with a public character and is obligated to discharge its functions and responsibilities for the benefit of the public at large.[2] To 'suffer in silence' in the face of general recreational resort to one's land is to engage in a form of acquiescence or 'passive inactivity' which is in no way inconsistent with a claim of user 'as of right'.[3] Indeed, such toleration is the antithesis of consent,[4] since it marks, in reality, the landowner's surrender to the eventual claim of right. Ultimately the critical issue revolves around whether the landowner has patently reserved for himself an overall control over access to his land so that visitors use his land only precariously (ie at his revocable will).[5]

1   [2004] 1 AC 889 at [68] per Lord Rodger of Earlsferry, [79] per Lord Walker of Gestingthorpe. The landowner 'must do something' to make the public aware 'that the route is being used by them only with his permission and not as of right' (*Cumbernauld and Kilsyth DC v Dollar Land (Cumbernauld) Ltd* 1992 SLT 1035 at 1041G per Lord President Hope). See also *Beresford* at [6] per Lord Bingham of Cornhill, [77] per Lord Walker of Gestingthorpe.
2   [2004] 1 AC 889 at [49]–[50] per Lord Scott of Foscote.
3   [2004] 1 AC 889 at [6] per Lord Bingham of Cornhill, [43] per Lord Scott of Foscote, [77]–[79] per Lord Walker of Gestingthorpe. Any positive encouragement of public use operates a fortiori in the same direction (see [2004] 1 AC 889 at [50] per Lord Scott, [67]–[68] per Lord Rodger).
4   See *R (Beresford) v Sunderland CC* [2004] 1 AC 889 at [81] per Lord Walker of Gestingthorpe.
5   See eg *R (Beresford) v Sunderland CC* [2004] 1 AC 889 at [58]–[59] per Lord Rodger of Earlsferry, [73], [83] per Lord Walker of Gestingthorpe.

A statutory 'right to roam'

5.46   To date the most ambitious extension of recreational access rights in England and Wales is that provided by the Countryside and Rights of Way Act 2000. In the absence of any 'prescriptive right to roam'[1] and in view of the relative ineffectiveness of voluntary arrangements for access,[2] it was clear by the 1990s that some statutory reinforcement of general access rights had become inevitable. The Act of 2000 effectuates a quite remarkable social and environmental initiative. It gives legislative force to an entitlement which the common law could never recognise, ie a generalised right of self-determining pedestrian access to open land – in effect, a statutory *ius spatiandi*. The enactment was deliberately directed towards 'improving public health and reducing social divisions'[3] and at securing a measure of 'social equity'.[4] Walking, declared the Government's consultation paper, 'is an antidote to the pressures of modern life.'[5] Significantly, the Act of 2000 was followed by even more far-reaching access legislation in Scotland,[6] the two enactments thus preparing the way for a new era of 'pedestrian democracy' in which individuals draw civic strength from the self-empowering, self-fulfilling freedom to ambulate wherever their feet take them.

1   *R v Suffolk CC, ex p Steed* (1995) 70 P & CR 487 at 503 per Carnwath J. See *Attorney-General v Antrobus* [1905] 2 Ch 188 at 198–199 per Farwell J.
2   The National Parks and Access to the Countryside Act 1949, Part V, brought into existence machinery for the creation of public rights of access to the countryside by means of access agreements and orders. However, these procedures secured public rights of access to only

50,000 of the estimated 1.2 to 1.8 million hectares of open country in England and Wales (see *DETR Consultation Paper* (1998), para 2.3). There are also weak and indirect requirements in Water Industry Act 1991, s 3(2)–(3) that water companies, which own large catchment areas in the hills, should promote freedom of public access to places of natural beauty and historic interest. EC Council Regulation 2078/92 (the Agri-Environment Regulation) now provides for member states to implement voluntary incentive schemes which include the management of land for public access and leisure activities.

3   *Access to the Open Countryside in England and Wales: A Consultation Paper* (DETR, February 1998), para 3.50. The paper emphasises 'the gains in physical and mental health from wandering in the countryside' (ibid, para 3.66). Likewise the access provisions of the Land Reform (Scotland) Act 2003 are explicitly intended 'to promote social inclusion by improving people's health and their quality of life' (see Scottish Executive, *Draft Land Reform (Scotland) Bill: Consultation Paper* (February 2001), para 1.5).

4   *DETR Consultation Paper* (1998), para 3.67 (access to fine countryside 'is something which should be enjoyed by the many, not the few').

5   *DETR Consultation Paper* (1998), para 3.67.

6   See Land Reform (Scotland) Act 2003 [**para 5.50**].

Rights of public access

5.47 The enactment of the Countryside and Rights of Way Act 2000 was intended to 'give greater freedom for people to explore open countryside.'[1] This aim is achieved through the conferment of an unprecedented public right 'to enter and remain ... for the purposes of open-air recreation' on any 'access land' as defined by the Act.[2] The category of 'access land' automatically includes land more than 600m above sea level,[3] together with other areas of 'open country',[4] registered common land,[5] and land which is irrevocably dedicated by the owner to purposes of public access.[6] There is statutory power to extend the right of public access to the foreshore and other coastal land,[7] and the effect of the 2000 Act is to provide a general access entitlement to something between 8 and 12 per cent of the total land area of England and Wales.[8]

1   Countryside and Rights of Way Bill (Session 1999–2000), *Explanatory Notes*, para 5. The Foreword to the *DETR Consultation Paper* (1998) stated that greater access to open countryside 'will benefit a wide range of people ... They will be able to improve their health; to experience the wonders of wildlife and the beauty of fine landscapes; to learn about countryside activities; and to refresh their spirits'.

2   CROWA 2000, s 2(1).

3   CROWA 2000, s 1(1)(d).

4   'Open country' is defined as land (other than registered common land) which appears to the appropriate countryside body to 'consist wholly or predominantly of mountain, moor, heath or down' (CROWA 2000, s 1(2)). 'Open country' does not necessarily mean unenclosed country (*DETR Consultation Paper* (1998), para 3.3). The CROWA 2000 provides for the definitive mapping of areas of open country (CROWA 2003, ss 4–11), a process which is expected to be completed in 2004.

5   CROWA 2000, s 1(1)(b)–(c).

6   CROWA 2000, ss 1(1)(e), 16. The dedication constitutes a registrable local land charge (s 16(8) [**para 12.7**]).

7   CROWA 2000, s 3.

8   *DETR Consultation Paper* (1998), para 3.10. See J Rowan Robinson, 'Reform of the Law Relating to Access to the Countryside: Realising Expectations?' [2003] JPL 1394.

Limits of the access entitlement

5.48　The statutory right of access is limited to access on foot[1] (although at all hours of day and night)[2] and is subject to extensive requirements of reasonable behaviour.[3] The statutory entitlement is conditional on not 'breaking or damaging any wall, fence, hedge, stile or gate.'[4] The entrant must also observe the general restrictions laid down in Schedule 2 and any other restrictions imposed in relation to the land under Chapter II of the Act.[5] Thus, for example, the statutory right does not extend to any criminal or commercial activity[6] or to camping, hang- or para-gliding, the playing of organised games,[7] swimming in any non-tidal water,[8] use of any metal detector,[9] hunting, shooting, fishing, snaring or otherwise harming wildlife.[10] Breach of any of these access conditions[11] renders the entrant a trespasser and causes a forfeiture of the statutory right of access for 72 hours in relation to any land within the ownership of the aggrieved landowner.[12] The 2000 Act attempts to reconcile reasonable public access with the legitimate requirements of those who live and work in the countryside.[13] In order to ensure the protection of privacy and of specified forms of commercial activity, certain areas are designated as 'excepted land' and remain outside the scope of the access provisions.[14] The Act therefore has no application to cultivated land,[15] land covered by buildings and their curtilages,[16] land used as a park or garden,[17] railways,[18] golf courses, racecourses, aerodromes,[19] and certain quarries[20] and areas used for military training and defence purposes.[21]

1　Access on foot embraces such activities as walking, running, climbing, picnicking, bird-watching and sightseeing.
2　CROWA 2000, Sch 2, para 1(a). The Act excludes access by bicycle or on horse, but dogs are allowed (if on a lead at certain prescribed times of the year) (Sch 2, paras 1(c), 4).
3　For the roots of this theme of licensed enjoyment of scenic spaces 'in an orderly and reasonable manner', see *Behrens v Richards* [1905] 2 Ch 614 at 622 per Buckley J. The Land Reform (Scotland) Act 2003, which creates even more extensive 'access rights' over land for recreational and other purposes, explicitly conditions such rights on a requirement that they be 'exercised responsibly' (LR(S)A 2003, s 2(1)). Under the Scottish legislation the concept of 'responsible' user is reciprocal. Affected landowners are equally obligated to 'conduct the ownership' of their land 'in a way which, as respects [access] rights, is responsible', ie causes no 'unreasonable interference' with such rights (LR(S)A 2003, s 3(1)–(2)). Moreover, the notion of 'responsible' behaviour is, in either case, defined in terms of user which is 'lawful and reasonable and takes proper account of the interests' of all relevant parties (LR(S)A 2003, ss 2(3), 3(3)). Rules of 'responsible conduct' are set out in a 'Scottish Outdoor Access Code' (LR(S)A 2003, s 10).
4　CROWA 2000, s 2(1)(a).
5　CROWA 2000, s 2(1)(b). See *DETR Consultation Paper* (1998), para 3.32. For what it is worth, de facto access is left untouched by the Countryside and Rights of Way Act 2000 (*Countryside Legislation: De facto and de iure access to the countryside* (Department for Environment, Food and Rural Affairs Guidance Note published 21 December 2001, updated 27 September 2002), paras 2, 10).
6　CROWA 2000, Sch 2, para 1(d), (t).
7　CROWA 2000, Sch 2, para 1(s).
8　CROWA 2000, Sch 2, para 1(i).
9　CROWA 2000, Sch 2, paras 1(k), 2(1).
10　CROWA 2000, Sch 2, para 1(f)–(g), (j).

11 These access conditions may be varied or abrogated with the consent of the landowner (CROWA 2000, Sch 2, para 7).

12 CROWA 2000, s 2(4). Significantly, this limited forfeiture of entitlement gives effect to a principle of proportionality which has not always been a strong feature of the law of exclusion from land [**para 4.56**].

13 *DETR Consultation Paper* (1998), para 3.15.

14 CROWA 2000, s 1(1)–(2), Sch 1.

15 The Act excludes land where the soil has been disturbed within the past year by ploughing or drilling undertaken for the purposes of planting or sowing crops or trees (CROWA 2000, Sch 1, Pt I, para 1). The Act is not intended to affect agricultural land other than that used for extensive grazing (*DETR Consultation Paper* (1998), para 3.17).

16 CROWA 2000, Sch 1, Pt I, para 2. On the meaning of 'curtilage', see *Skerritts of Nottingham Ltd v Secretary of State for the Environment, Transport and the Regions* [2001] QB 59 at 66G–67E.

17 CROWA 2000, Sch 1, Pt I, paras 3–4.

18 CROWA 2000, Sch 1, Pt I, para 6.

19 CROWA 2000, Sch 1, Pt I, para 7.

20 CROWA 2000, Sch 1, Pt I, para 5.

21 CROWA 2000, Sch 1, Pt I, para 13. See also CROWA 2000, s 28.

Impact of access rights on landowners

5.49 The general effect of the Countryside and Rights of Way Act 2000 is to deprive owners of 'access land' of the right to sue in trespass those who enter their land in the exercise of the public right conferred,[1] but such owners remain entitled to eject, or obtain other civil relief against, members of the public who exceed or violate their statutory entitlement.[2] The 2000 Act does not endorse any principle of compensation for affected landowners[3] or of payment of user charges by walkers,[4] but landowners are immunised against any liability to visitors not already imposed by existing law.[5] Entrants exercising their statutory right of access do not constitute 'visitors' for the purpose of the Occupiers' Liability Act 1984,[6] and no duty is owed to such persons 'in respect of a risk resulting from the existence of any natural feature of the landscape.'[7] In effect, occupiers of access land continue to be liable to entrants 'as if they were trespassers.'[8] Landowners also remain free to develop and use their land subject to the constraints of planning and other legislation.[9] The Act recognises, moreover, that a 'fair balance' must be maintained between public and private interests,[10] and for this reason the owner of access land (or other 'entitled person'[11]) has the right, on giving notice to the relevant countryside agency, to exclude or restrict public access on a maximum of 28 days per calendar year.[12] Additional exclusions or restrictions may be allowed by the relevant countryside agency for special purposes of land management,[13] for the avoidance of fire or other danger to the public,[14] for the protection of ecologically sensitive or archaeologically significant sites,[15] and in cases of emergency.[16]

1 *DETR Consultation Paper* (1998), paras 3.31, 3.37. It is also a criminal offence to place or maintain any false or misleading notice at or near any access land which is likely to deter the public from exercising the statutory right of access (CROWA 2000, s 14(1)–(2)).

2 *DETR Consultation Paper* (1998), para 3.31.

3 *DETR Consultation Paper* (1998), paras 3.51–3.52. Although there may be grants in aid of

certain measures undertaken by landowners to enable, improve or limit access to open country, the general absence of provision for compensation has been attacked as inconsistent with ECHR Protocol No 1, Art 1 [**para 2.29**]. See *Parliamentary Debates* (*Hansard*) *House of Lords: Official Report*, Vol 614 (26 June 2000), Col 645 (Lord Brittan of Spennithorne).

4   *DETR Consultation Paper* (1998), paras 3.60–3.61 ('The Government regard it as fundamental that such access should not depend on payment by members of the public').

5   CROWA 2000, s 12(1). In other jurisdictions such immunity is a common trade-off for the benefits of public recreational access (see eg *Bragg v Genesee County Agric Socy*, 644 NE2d 1013 at 1018 (NY 1994); *Albright v Metz*, 672 NE2d 584 at 589 (NY 1996)).

6   CROWA 2000, s 13(1).

7   CROWA 2000, s 13(2).

8   *DETR Consultation Paper* (1998), para 3.39. See F R Barker and N D M Parry, 'Private property, public access and occupiers' liability', (1995) 15 Legal Studies 335. See *Tomlinson v Congleton BC* [2004] 1 AC 46.

9   *DETR Consultation Paper* (1998), para 3.37.

10   *DETR Consultation Paper* (1998), para 3.58.

11   CROWA 2000, s 22(3). The 'entitled person', in relation to land held on a farm business tenancy, is the tenant (s 21(4)).

12   CROWA 2000, ss 2(1), 22(1)–(4). Access must not be excluded or restricted on Saturdays and Sundays in summer, bank holidays or Christmas Day or Good Friday (s 22(6)–(7)).

13   CROWA 2000, s 24.

14   CROWA 2000, s 25(1).

15   CROWA 2000, s 26(1)–(3). The provision of access and the preservation of ecological integrity are not necessarily or always compatible (see Gray (1994) 47(2) CLP 157 at 203–204). In extreme circumstances the sheer numbers of those who seek environmental access may sometimes jeopardise or sterilise a natural amenity and it may therefore be necessary to impose management strategies on environmental goods (see Carol Rose, 'Rethinking Environmental Controls: Management Strategies for Common Resources' (1991) Duke LJ 1).

16   CROWA 2000, s 31(1); Access to the Countryside (Exclusions and Restrictions) (England) Regulations 2003 (SI 2003/2713) (see also SI 2003/142). The period of exclusion or restriction may not exceed three months.

Future developments

5.50   The Countryside and Rights of Way Act 2000, although revolutionary in its way, still suffers from limitations which are exposed by comparison with the extensive access provision made by the Land Reform (Scotland) Act 2003. Under this enactment (likely to become effective in 2004) every citizen has a presumptive entitlement, not to defined 'access land', but to all land in Scotland subject only to express exclusions.[1] The statutory 'access rights' include the right to cross land and to use land for recreational, educational and certain commercial purposes.[2] The range of permissible forms of access is also much less restrictive than in England, including access by foot, horse or cycle, camping, canoeing, and air sports.[3] The Scottish legislation may well provide a model for adoption or adaptation in the next phase of English access legislation, not least in the light of its emphasis on the educational aspect of recreational access to the outdoors. The 2003 Act defines 'relevant educational activity' in terms of furtherance of the 'understanding of natural or cultural heritage',[4] an objective which aligns itself well with the newly emerging pressure for recognition of a fundamental human right of enjoyment of nature as a keystone of recreational access law.[5] It has likewise been suggested that the freedom of movement guaranteed by the European Convention on Human Rights should explicitly include a general right of 'access to hills, mountains, waterways and open countryside.'[6]

1   Land Reform (Scotland) Act 2003, ss 1(1)–(3), 6.
2   See Land Reform (Scotland) Act 2003, s 1(4)–(5).
3   The use of motorised transport is prohibited, as is hunting, shooting or fishing (Land Reform (Scotland) Act 2003, s 9).
4   Land Reform (Scotland) Act 2003, s 1(5).
5   See Alan Blackshaw, 'Human rights and access freedoms: Is nature a missing link?', in Scottish Wild Land Group, *Scotland's wild land – what future?* (October 2002), p 23.
6   See Neil MacCormick, 'An Idea for a Scottish Constitution', in W Finnie, C M G Himsworth and N Walker (ed), *Edinburgh Essays in Public Law* (Edinburgh UP 1991), pp 168, 180.

CHAPTER 6

Title

THE CHANGING NATURE OF TITLE

6.1 Whereas the term 'possession' expresses an essentially factual relationship of control over land,[1] the idea of 'title' is connected with a more conceptual understanding of estate ownership. Indeed the notion of title in English law is currently undergoing an important transformation. The changing nature of modern title marks the transition from a world in which title to an estate in land ultimately derives from physical possession towards a rather different world in which title is constituted by the bureaucratic registration of abstractly defined proprietary entitlements. The Land Registration Act 2002 has shifted the fundamental paradigm of English land law from the reality of *possession* towards the ideology of *ownership*. The quaintly medieval notion that unchallenged possession connotes a presumptive form of estate ownership is being rapidly displaced by the idea that ownership is established exclusively by the computerised record of a person's proprietorship of some artificial 'estate',[2] 'interest'[3] or 'charge'.[4]

1   [Para 3.3].
2   LRA 2002, ss 11 (freehold), 12 (leasehold), 58(1), 59(1), 97, Sch 6, para 9.
3   LRA 2002, s 27(4), Sch 2, paras 6–7.
4   LRA 2002, s 27(4), Sch 2, para 8.

THE COMMON LAW PERCEPTION OF TITLE

6.2 Reference has already been made to the difference between the *common law* notion of title and the increasingly pervasive *statutory* perception of title in English law.[1] At common law 'title' has always been the term used to denote the right or entitlement of an owner to assert his 'estate' in land (together with its various incidents) against strangers.[2] In this context 'title' to an estate proceeds from the raw fact of physical possession of land and is generally handed on through a succession of estate owners by documentary transfer, although, as

Blackstone astutely pointed out, '(accurately and strictly speaking) there is no foundation in nature or in natural law, why a set of words upon parchment should convey the dominion of land.'[3]

1   [Para 3.12].
2   [Para 3.15].
3   *Bl Comm*, Vol II, p 2.

Title, estate and possession

6.3   Although, in the common law analysis, possession of land generates for the possessor a 'title' to an 'estate', the notions of title, estate and possession are quite distinct.[1] A person can own an 'estate' in land, but sometimes have no 'title' to assert it against others.[2] Likewise 'title' and 'possession' may become detached in the sense that an estate owner may be dispossessed by a stranger, yet retain (for at least some period of time) his 'title' to assert his 'estate' for the purpose of recovering possession from the interloper. 'Title' can therefore survive a temporary loss of 'possession' – a proposition which, in the context of registered estates, has now been given a rather more general force by the Land Registration Act 2002.[3]

1   See *Mabo v Queensland* (*No 2*) (1992) 175 CLR 1 at 207 per Toohey J (referring to title as 'the abstract bundle of rights associated with that relationship of possession').
2   [Para 3.16].
3   [Para 6.53].

Relativity of title

6.4   One of the remarkable features of the common law of real property has always been the absence of any concept of 'absolute title'. It is in this context that the common law appears markedly to diverge from civilian systems of property law, which unambiguously acknowledge ownership as an absolute jural relationship between a person and a thing.[1] Following Roman law, the continental codes speak in highly generalised terms of *dominium*; and on this view *dominium* becomes the most comprehensive right which a person may have with regard to a resource. By contrast, a pre-eminent respect for de facto possession has always ensured that the common law recognises no absolute title to any estate in land. In relation to land – ultimately the most durable of assets – title remains both relative and essentially defeasible.[2]

1   [Para 2.86].
2   There exists, of course, a statutory concept of 'absolute title', this being one of the classes of title which the Chief Land Registrar may award to an applicant for first registration of a freehold or leasehold estate [**paras 7.45, 7.232**]. In this context, however, 'absolute title' merely denotes the view of the registrar that the applicant has a good holding title which is *unlikely* to be disturbed (see LRA 2002, ss 9(2)–(3), 10(2), (4)). Even 'absolute' titles can be defeated by later acts of adverse possession; and the constant possibility of 'rectification' of title to give effect to hitherto unrecorded rights underscores the point that a registered title is *never* wholly indefeasible [**para 12.245**].

All rights to possession are relative

6.5   In English law possession is not, in strict terms, a relative concept: possession (in the sense of overall territorial control of land) has its own recognisable integrity and uniformity.[1] But it does not follow that *rights* to possession cannot be relative. Deep at the heart of the common law perception of title is the proposition that some claims to possession of land are better than others. From this flow certain important implications. In typically pragmatic fashion the common law presumes that any person in possession of land has a fee simple estate *unless and until* the contrary is shown.[2] The current possessor's 'title' to a fee simple estate is therefore valid and effective except where a better claim is advanced on behalf of somebody else.[3] Titles are never absolute: they are always 'relatively good or relatively bad.'[4] They are inherently vulnerable to the showing of a superior claim to possession. In this strange world of relativity all claims to possession of land are gradable against each other and one claim, however fragile, may be adjudged marginally better than another. As the Court of Appeal indicated in *Manchester Airport Plc v Dutton*,[5] even a licensee, if armed with 'effective control' of land or with a contractual right to 'enter and occupy' it, has a better claim to possession than does a 'bare trespasser', a factor of increasing importance in confrontations today between property developers and environmental protesters.

1   **[Para 3.4]**.
2   See *Peaceable d Uncle v Watson* (1811) 4 Taunt 16 at 17, 128 ER 232.
3   As Cockburn CJ observed in *Asher v Whitlock* (1865) LR 1 QB 1 at 5, 'possession is good against all the world except the person who can shew a good title.' See similarly *Wibberley (Alan) Building Ltd v Insley* [1999] 1 WLR 894 at 898A–B per Lord Hoffmann.
4   *Shaw v Garbutt* (1996) 7 BPR 14816 at 14832 per Young J. See *St Marylebone Property Co Ltd v Fairweather* [1962] 1 QB 498 at 513 per Holroyd Pearce LJ ('Title to land is pragmatic. It is true if and so long as it works. It works if it only comes up against a weaker title. But if it is challenged by a stronger title, it ceases to be a true title, and must give way').
5   [2000] QB 133 at 150A–E per Laws LJ, 151B–C per Kennedy LJ **[paras 3.38, 4.98, 7.145]**.

Common law methodology

6.6   One curious consequence of this theory of relativity is that the common lawyer remains fundamentally unable to make definitive pronouncements as to the ownership of particular parcels of land. The entire methodology of the common law militates against any absolute identification of estate ownership. The crude proprietary technique of the common law is restricted to determinations as to which of two claimants of a possessory estate has the *better* claim to possession. In one sense the common lawyer can never say who owns, but only who does not, albeit that such a ruling tends in practice to leave the preferred claimant with a fee simple title which is at least *pro tempore* unchallengeable.[1]

1   See *Clough v Shefford* [1944] 4 DLR 67 at 69 (Supreme Court of Canada) ('Under our system of law, property can never be "res nullius" ').

Evidence of title

6.7 In the case of an estate title to which has never been registered at Land Registry,[1] there is no general or centralised public record of ownership.[2] Accordingly, the 'essential indicia of title' are provided by the title deeds, normally retained within the control of individual estate proprietors,[3] which relate to successive transactions with the land over time.[4] The documents contained in these 'deeds bundles', when coupled with the fact of undisturbed possession, generally identify the person who currently has the best 'title' to any relevant estate in the land. Title to an estate can also be claimed, however, by one who holds no supporting documentary evidence but relies instead on the sheer fact of his own possession. The possessor's undocumented claim usually exists concurrently with, and in direct competition against, some other person's paper title. In these circumstances extrinsic evidence of the possessor's title to a common law freehold may be provided by statutory declarations which attest to the sustained possession alleged by the claimant. Declarations of this kind, sworn under the Statutory Declarations Act 1835, generally provide a proof of estate ownership sufficient to satisfy a purchaser of the land.[5]

1   [Para 2.111].
2   Without access to the relevant title deeds and in the absence of any central record of estate ownership, it is notoriously difficult to ascertain the proprietorship of unregistered estates. An ancient, but still valuable, clue to the ownership of large tracts of dynastically owned unregistered land can be found in a little known publication sometimes called 'The New Domesday Book' (see Kevin Cahill, 'Who really owns Britain?' (2004) Walk (2) 41). This work is *England and Wales* (*Exclusive of the Metropolis*): *Return of Owners of Land, 1873* (London 1875), presented to both Houses of Parliament by the Local Government Board. The two volumes of *Return of Owners of Land, 1873* are extremely difficult to locate, but can be found in Cambridge University Library under class mark 'Acton.a.25.104' and contain the names, addresses and acreages of all landowners of more than one acre in the British Isles in 1873. This record is still remarkably informative as to the modern ownership of dynastic territory.
3   [Para 2.112].
4   *Sen v Headley* [1991] Ch 425 at 437C per Nourse LJ. See also Alain Pottage, 'Evidencing Ownership', in S Bright and J K Dewar (ed), *Land Law: Themes and Perspectives* (OUP 1998), p 129.
5   The purchaser may, in turn, present such proof in support of an application to Land Registry for registration as proprietor of the title to the estate (see LRA 2002, ss 9(5), 10(6); LRR 2003, r 27).

THE LAND REGISTER

6.8 In the common law analysis, 'title' to an 'estate' ultimately derives from the earthy reality of behavioural fact; and the potentially variable nature of behavioural fact ensures that all title is ultimately relative. Completely definitive identification of estate ownership is never possible. Yet this is precisely the major objective of the Land Register for England and Wales which is maintained pursuant to the Land Registration Act 2002. In relation to those estates whose title is registered (either voluntarily or compulsorily) under the 2002 Act,[1] the Land Register provides a decisive attribution of proprietorship. Estate owners are conclusively identified on the face of an authoritative public record;

and the statutory regulation of estate ownership has indirectly brought about a significant evolution in the nature of 'title' in English law.

1   For further detail of the circumstances which necessitate the registration at Land Registry of previously unregistered estates, see **[paras 2.115, 7.40, 7.230]**.

Function of the Chief Land Registrar

6.9   It is the statutory duty of the Chief Land Registrar to keep a register of title to land in England and Wales.[1] The current 'mission' of Land Registry is avowedly to provide 'the world's best service for guaranteeing ownership of land and facilitating property transactions.'[2] Accordingly, the linchpin of title registration under the Land Registration Act 2002 is the idea that the title to certain major estates in land – principally the fee simple estate and any leasehold term of more than seven years – is substantively registered under an individual title number in the Land Register.[3] Relevant information about the estate concerned is then entered against the title as appropriate and further transactions with the land are effected with reference to the proprietor's numerically identified estate.[4] The Land Register currently contains over 19 million separate registered titles[5] and is used each year to record some 4.5 million registered dealings with the land comprised in these titles.[6]

1   LRA 2002, ss 1(1), 99(2).
2   Land Registry, *Annual Report and Accounts 2002–03* (HC891, July 2003), p 10.
3   **[Paras 2.107, 7.40, 7.230]**.
4   Contrast, in unregistered land, the system of registration of land charges against the name of the estate owner responsible for their creation **[paras 2.185, 12.278]**.
5   Land Registry Press Release LRP05/04 (16 March 2004).
6   See Land Registry, *Annual Report and Accounts 2002–03* (HC891, July 2003), p 9, Appendix 2 (p 93).

Guiding principles of title registration

6.10   The purpose of the Land Registration Act is 'to achieve greater simplicity and certainty of title to land by a system of central registration of property, ownership and charges.'[1] Underlying the entire scheme is the philosophy that registration of title confers on the registered proprietor a generally indefeasible title to a specified parcel of land and 'dispenses with any need on the part of persons dealing with him to investigate further his right thereto.'[2] It has been said that the fundamental features of all schemes of Torrens title legislation are essentially three in number.[3]

1   *Freeguard v Royal Bank of Scotland Plc* (2000) 79 P & CR 81 at 86 per Robert Walker LJ.
2   *Racoon Ltd v Turnbull* [1997] AC 158 at 163C–D per Lord Jauncey of Tullichettle. See also *Williams & Glyn's Bank Ltd v Boland* [1981] AC 487 at 503F–G per Lord Wilberforce; *CN and NA Davies Ltd v Laughton* [1997] 3 NZLR 705 at 712–713 (NZ Court of Appeal); *British American Cattle Co v Caribe Farm Industries Ltd* [1998] 1 WLR 1529 at 1533E–F per Lord Browne-Wilkinson.
3   **[Para 2.104]**. See T B F Ruoff, *An Englishman Looks at the Torrens System* (Sydney, Melbourne and Brisbane 1957), p 8.

The 'mirror principle'

6.11 The register of title is intended to operate as a 'mirror', reflecting accurately and incontrovertibly the totality of estates and interests which at any time affect the registered land.[1] In this sense, the 'register is everything.'[2]

1   See Land Registry, *Annual Report and Accounts 2002–03* (HC891, July 2003), Appendix 3 (p 94).
2   See *Creelman v Hudson Bay Insurance Co* [1920] AC 194 at 197 per Lord Buckmaster; *Teh Bee v Maruthamuthu* [1977] 2 MLJ 7 at 12; *Re Cartlidge and Granville Savings & Mortgage Corp* (1987) 34 DLR (4th) 161 at 172; *Abbey National Building Society v Cann* [1991] 1 AC 56 at 78C per Lord Oliver of Aylmerton.

The 'curtain principle'

6.12 Trusts relating to the registered land are kept off the title,[1] with the result that third parties may transact with registered proprietors safe in the assurance that the interests behind any trust will be overreached.[2]

1   See LRA 2002, s 78.
2   See *Wolfson v Registrar General (NSW)* (1934) 51 CLR 300 at 308 per Rich and Evatt JJ. On overreaching see **[paras 2.165, 11.195–11.216]**.

The 'insurance principle'

6.13 The state itself guarantees the accuracy of the registered title, in that an indemnity is payable from public funds if a registered proprietor is deprived of his title or is otherwise prejudiced by the correction of any mistake in the register.[1]

1   **[Para 12.255].** The state-backed guarantee currently covers land assets worth in excess of £2.5 trillion (Land Registry Press Release LRP03/03 (4 February 2003)).

Administration of the Land Register

6.14 Land Registry matters are handled both centrally in London and at 24 regional offices (formerly known as district land registries).[1] The Land Register is entirely digital[2] and comprises a database which is maintained in Plymouth and is available on-line in a range of locations. The Chief Land Registrar presides over what is now the 'largest online transactional database in the world.'[3] In the interests of greater transparency and impartiality, the determination of various categories of dispute over the operation of the Land Register is entrusted to the Adjudicator to Land Registry,[4] the holder of a new office independent of the Registry, from whose decisions appeal lies to the High Court.[5]

1   Accepted practice in Land Registry effectively creates the law which governs much of the business of the Registry, but Lord Denning MR warned in *Strand Securities Ltd v Caswell* [1965] Ch 958 at 977E that the registrar is not allowed 'by his practice to make bad law' (see, however, [1981] Conv 395).

2   The register may be kept in either electronic or paper form (see LRR 2003, r 2(1)), but all
     registered titles are now computerised. The last 'blue card' register was symbolically torn up
     by Land Registry's Chief Executive in March 2004 (Land Registry Press Release LRP05/04
     (16 March 2004)).
3   Land Registry Press Release LRP05/04 (16 March 2004).
4   LRA 2002, ss 107–109. See Land Registration (Referral to the Adjudicator to HM Land
     Registry) Rules 2003 (SI 2003/2114) (effective 13 October 2003).
5   LRA 2002, s 111.

The individual register of title

6.15   On first registration of title to any estate, a register of title is opened
under a unique title number.[1] The individual register thus created is generally
subdivided into three sections or subregisters. These subdivisions are known
respectively as the property register, the proprietorship register and the charges
register.[2]

1   LRR 2003, r 4(1).
2   LRR 2003, r 4(2).

Property register

6.16   The property register under any particular title number contains a
geographical description of the registered estate (e g the freehold land known as
88 Mill Road, Sodcaster). The physical extent of the land contained within the
title is indicated in a title plan (based on the Ordnance Survey map) on which
the land concerned is edged in red.[1] The property register also records other
advantageous features of the land, noting (where possible) such matters as
easements, rights, privileges, conditions and covenants over other land which
benefit the land comprised within the title number.[2] The property register of a
leasehold estate also provides sufficient particulars of the registered lease to
enable that lease to be identified.[3]

1   LRR 2003, r 5(a).
2   LRR 2003, r 5(b)(ii).
3   LRR 2003, r 6(1).

Proprietorship register

6.17   The principal function of the proprietorship register is to identify, with
ultimate clarity, the name and address of the current registered proprietor of
the estate represented by any particular title number.[1] In sharp contrast to the
relative indeterminacy of common law title, the Land Register thus pinpoints,
as authoritatively as can be, the location of estate ownership. The proprietorship register also indicates the class of title awarded to the proprietor as either
'absolute', 'good leasehold', 'qualified' or 'possessory'.[2] The proprietorship
register likewise records the entry of any 'restriction'[3] which cuts back the
otherwise plenary powers of disposition enjoyed by the registered proprietor.[4]

1   LRR 2003, r 8(1)(b)–(c).
2   LRR 2003, r 8(1)(a) [**paras 7.44, 7.231**].
3   See LRA 2002, ss 40–43 [**para 7.52**].
4   LRA 2002, s 23(1).

Charges register

6.18   The charges register details the disadvantageous or negative features affecting the land comprised in the title.[1] The charges register therefore refers to burdens on the registered title which have been protected by the entry of a 'notice'[2] (eg leases,[3] easements,[4] freehold restrictive covenants,[5] liens,[6] estate contracts[7] and matrimonial home rights[8]). The charges register also contains the registration of any mortgage charge created by the registered proprietor of a freehold or leasehold estate.[9]

1   LRR 2003, r 9.
2   LRA 2002, ss 32–34 [**paras 2.163, 12.84**].
3   [**Paras 7.247, 9.75**].
4   [**Paras 8.215, 9.100**].
5   [**Para 13.114**].
6   [**Para 9.133**].
7   [**Para 9.23**].
8   [**Para 12.93**].
9   [**Para 8.244**].

Title documentation

6.19   The Land Registration Act 2002 makes outline provision for the issue by Land Registry to newly registered proprietors of some form of land certificate.[1] According to the historic pattern, this certificate should comprise a print-out of the register bound up in a cover, together with a photocopy of the title plan. However, such a certificate can never constitute conclusive evidence of title to a registered estate.[2] There is no guarantee, at any point following its issue, that the print-out contained in a land certificate will remain up to date and accurate – a difficulty likely to intensify with the introduction of electronic conveyancing.[3] The only truly reliable evidence of any registered proprietor's title is that contained in a contemporary official copy of the register of title supplied, on payment of a fee, by Land Registry.[4] This official copy bears a date and time of issue and reveals definitively the state of the register at that precise moment. Accordingly Land Registry has announced that, as a matter of practice, it will automatically issue a 'title information document' whenever a particular register of title is changed. Such documents, incorporating a contemporary official copy of the register and title plan as amended, will serve, in effect, to replace the traditional form of one-off and rapidly outdated land certificates.[5]

1   See LRA 2002, Sch 10, para 4.
2   *Freeguard v Royal Bank of Scotland Plc* (2000) 79 P & CR 81 at 86 per Robert Walker LJ.
3   See *Land Registration for the Twenty-First Century: A Conveyancing Revolution* (Law Com No 271, July 2001), paras 9.86–9.88.

4   LRA 2002, s 67; LRR 2003, r 134.
5   *Report on responses to Land Registration Rules 2003 – A Land Registry Consultation* (2003), p 11, paras 2.2, 2.18.

Public access to the Land Register

6.20   One of the more controversial features of the Land Register used to be the fact that it was not open to general public inspection – a point not without political significance since the preclusion of access to the register ultimately frustrated any attempt to compile an accurate record of the allocation of land ownership in this country. The denial of a public right of access to the Land Register was almost without parallel in other jurisdictions[1] and came eventually to be criticised as symptomatic of 'the obsession with unnecessary secrecy which pervades British society.'[2] In 1985 the Law Commission recommended that, consistently with the principle of 'freedom of information and publication' in an 'open society', the Register should be made available for general public scrutiny.[3] This proposal was realised with the enactment of the Land Registration Act 1988.[4]

1   See Law Commission, *Property Law: Second Report on Land Registration: Inspection of the Register* (Law Com No 148, July 1985), para 18(i).
2   Comment of the National Consumer Council (quoted in Law Com No 148 (1985), para 17(iii)).
3   Law Com No 148 (1985), paras 20–21.
4   See LRA 1925, s 112(1) (as substituted by LRA 1988, s 1(1)).

Limits of public access

6.21   The Land Register is now open to public access. On payment of a small fee any person may obtain a print-out of an individual register of title and a copy of any document referred to therein.[1] The Land Register is not, however, the subject of a general search facility. There is, for example, no unqualified public right to search Land Registry's Index of Proprietors' Names,[2] which cross-refers the names of current proprietors of registered estates and charges with subsisting title numbers, thereby revealing the extent of any named person's registered title portfolio. Special application must be made to search the Index of Proprietors' Names against a particular name, permission being granted only if the applicant can satisfy the registrar that he or she is interested generally (eg as a trustee in bankruptcy or a personal representative).[3]

1   LRA 2002, ss 66–67; LRR 2003, rr 134–135. First registrations and registrations of subsequent transfers of land now disclose the price paid or value declared by the applicant for registration (LRR 2003, r 8(2)).
2   See LRR 2003, r 11(1).
3   LRR 2003, r 11(3).

Exempt information

6.22   The open nature of the Land Register means that potentially sensitive information contained in leases and charges referred to in the Register can be exposed to public scrutiny unless the registrar has been called on to designate a particular document as an 'exempt information document' and this designation is subsequently upheld by the registrar on a stranger's application for an official copy of the document in question.[1] In this way 'prejudicial information' may be withdrawn from the public domain if, but only if, its disclosure would be likely to cause 'substantial unwarranted' damage or distress to the registered proprietor or would be likely to 'prejudice' his 'commercial interests'.[2] The registrar is ultimately obligated to disclose even sensitive documents if the balance of the 'public interest' so dictates.[3]

1   LRR 2003, rr 136–137.
2   LRR 2003, r 131.
3   LRR 2003, r 137(4).

Land information as public information

6.23   The access provisions of the Land Registration Act 2002 give effect to the view that the contents of the Land Register should no longer be regarded 'as a private matter relevant only to the parties to a conveyancing transaction.'[1] The Law Commission and Land Registry have observed that the general principle of an open register has 'fundamentally changed both the perception and the potential of land registration' as a means of affording on-line access and as a source of public information.[2] Land Registry's professed aim is nowadays to 'maintain and develop stable and effective land information systems for England and Wales.'[3] It is indeed this aspiration which underlies Land Registry's current provision of on-line viewing and searching services to account holders' office computers ('Land Registry Direct') and its commitment as a key supplier of data to the National Land Information Service (NLIS) as first envisaged in the 'Citizen's Charter' White Paper of 1992.[4]

1   Law Com No 271 (2001), para 9.37. Land Registry is now authorised to publish any information about land in England and Wales if it 'appears ... to be information in which there is legitimate public interest' (LRA 2002, s 104).
2   See Law Com No 271 (2001), para 9.37.
3   Land Registry, *Annual Report and Accounts 1999–2000* (HC661, July 2000), p 9.
4   Land Registry has also introduced an internet-based service ('LR On-line') designed to deliver information from Land Registry's database to the general public.

THE STATUTORY PERCEPTION OF TITLE

6.24   The enactment of the Land Registration Act 2002 and the rapidly expanding coverage of the Land Register have together conduced towards an important transformation of the concept of title in English law.[1] Title to an estate in land, once entered in the Land Register, is no longer primarily a function of undisturbed possession, but is constituted instead by the formal record of the register itself.[2] Titles to estates registered at Land Registry draw their legitimacy from the sheer fact of registration. The bureaucratic act of registration operates a certain 'statutory magic',[3] conferring an immediate title on the newly registered proprietor irrespective of the provenance of the estate concerned and subject only to the possibility that the register may subsequently be rectified in rare cases of mistake or irregularity.[4] It can therefore be said, with justification, that the Land Registration Act 2002 provides 'not a system of registration of title but a system of title by registration.'[5] The transition is from analogue to digital – from a common law perception of title as rooted in organic fact to a more crystalline statutory perception of title as inherent in a computerised record maintained by the state.[6] Registration has, in effect, become the exclusive source of title 'rather than a retrospective approbation of it as a derivative right.'[7] Indeed, under the Land Registration Act 2002 'title' is no more and no less than the register entry which records proprietorship of the relevant estate.[8]

1   The roots of this transformation can be traced back at least as far as the Land Registration Act 1925.
2   See Alain Pottage, 'The Originality of Registration' (1995) 15 OJLS 371 at 383–386 **[para 2.114]**.
3   The phrase was used by Slade LJ in *Argyle Building Society v Hammond* (1985) 49 P & CR 148 at 153, 155. See also *Hounslow LBC v Hare* (1990) 24 HLR 9 at 23 per Knox J.
4   **[Para 12.245]**.
5   *Breskvar v Wall* (1971) 126 CLR 376 at 385 per Barwick CJ. See similarly *Duncan v McDonald* [1997] 3 NZLR 669 at 681.
6   The Land Registration Act 2002 envisages that registration will soon operate as the *sole* constitutive source of almost all expressly created rights in registered land **[para 12.4]**.
7   *Breskvar v Wall* (1971) 126 CLR 376 at 400 per Windeyer J. See also Law Com No 271 (2001), para 5.3.
8   See LRR 2003, r 217(1) (defining 'registered title' as 'an individual register and any title plan referred to in that register').

Shift in the philosophical base of English land law

6.25   With its definitive record of estate ownership, the Land Registration Act 2002 confirms a large shift in the philosophical base of English land law away from the phenomenon of *possession* and towards the ideology of *ownership*. It was inevitable, in the context of this evolutionary process, that the impact of relativity of title, whilst not wholly eliminated from the law of registered land, should be greatly curtailed.[1] Indeed, the ultimate achievement of the Land Registration Act 2002 lies in its ruthless maximisation of rational legal order, an aim which is symbolised by the statutory vision of an electronic register of virtually indefeasible titles, transactable by automated dealings and guaranteed by the state. Under this tightly organised regime, estate ownership, as constituted by the register record, becomes a heavily protected phenomenon, leaving little room for the operation 'off the record' of some ancient and pragmatic principle of long possession.

1   **[Para 6.54]**.

Modern drift towards *dominium*

6.26 The regime of title registration inaugurated by the Land Registration Act 2002 offers a new degree of security for those estates which are brought on to the Land Register. An inevitable product of the modern statutory regime is the emergence of a much more robust and deeply stabilised form of state-endorsed title.[1] The major registered estates are elevated into something approaching absolute ownership of land. The concentrated quality of this new form of register-based title is encapsulated in the way in which the 2002 Act compresses the historic terminology of English land ownership into an amalgam of interchangeable concepts. The Act speaks indiscriminately of registration of an 'estate',[2] of registration of 'title' to an 'estate',[3] and of registration of a person as 'proprietor' of an 'estate'.[4] Correspondingly, a 'registered estate' is an 'estate the title to which is entered in the register'[5] and a 'registered estate' is declared, moreover, to be synonymous with 'registered land.'[6] The overall effect is to weld concepts of 'title', 'estate' and 'proprietor' into a form of statutory ownership of land which begins to resemble the civilian model of proprietorship. The 'registered proprietor' now holds a 'registered title' which is inseparable from – indeed has no meaning apart from – the 'registered estate' in the 'registered land' to which it relates.[7] With the enactment of the 2002 Act the brightlines of land ownership have been significantly intensified. A new *in rem* quality has been conferred on estate proprietorship (and particularly on ownership of the fee simple estate). The titles maintained by Land Registry are beginning to evince a more 'absolute' quality than they have ever previously enjoyed, thereby demonstrating, in effect, an inexorable drift towards the hitherto alien continental concept of *dominium*.[8]

1   **[Paras 2.48, 12.64]**.
2   LRA 2002, ss 9(1), 10(1), 74, Sch 10, para 1(1).
3   LRA 2002, ss 2(a), 15(1). See also LRA 2002, ss 7(2)(a), 96(1).
4   LRA 2002, ss 3(2), 6(1), 11(1), 12(1), 24, 44(1), 98(5), 131(1), Sch 6, paras 1(1)–(2), 9(1)–(2). See similarly LRA 2002, ss 35(1)(a), 36(1)(a), 42(3), 45(1)(a), (3), 58(1), 59(1), Sch 4, paras 3(4), 6(2), (4), Sch 8, para 1(2)(b). A 'proprietor' can also be said to 'hold' an 'estate' (LRA 2002, s 63(1)).
5   LRA 2002, s 132(1).
6   LRA 2002, s 132(1).
7   See Harold Potter, (1942) 58 LQR 356 at 367 **[para 7.48]**.
8   See Gray and Gray, 'The rhetoric of realty', in J Getzler (ed), *Rationalizing Property, Equity and Trusts: Essays in Honour of Edward Burn* (Butterworths 2003), p 244.

6.27 The Land Registration Act 2002 has thus overseen a remarkable transition from title as self-authenticating social fact to title as state-regulated administrative fact. Nothing better illustrates this change in the nature of title than the recent history of the law of adverse possession.

ADVERSE POSSESSION AND THE LIMITATION PRINCIPLE

6.28 The common law principle of relativity of title has always been open to one large difficulty: claims to land are secure only to the extent that no other person can assert a better claim. If, as the common law insisted, prior possession automatically generated a right to recover possession from a later possessor,[1] land titles could become the subject of potentially indefinite conflict. The current possessor of land would remain constantly vulnerable to a claim advanced by some earlier possessor. A further restrictive principle was therefore both necessary and inevitable.

1   [Para 3.33].

The principle of limitation

6.29   The answer was found in the introduction of a principle of limitation. From as early as the Limitation Act 1623 the prior possessor's right to recover possession was itself curtailed by the imposition of arbitrary time limits on the assertion of claims.[1] Unchallenged adverse possession by an intruder or 'squatter' was deemed conclusively to 'toll' or bar all prior rights of recovery following the expiration of a legally stipulated limitation period (usually a period of twelve years).[2] This principle still applies today to titles which have not been registered at Land Registry. If the assertion of *all* older titles becomes statute-barred by the effluxion of time, the current possessor's title – however wrongful in its inception – ripens into an unimpeachable fee simple title.[3] Nobody else can now claim a better title than the current possessor: all other challengers are, by force of statute, disabled from recovering the land concerned.[4] Title to land being relative, the current possessor acquires – as an indirect effect of the Limitation Act – an exclusive title which confirms the legitimacy of his continuing possession.[5]

1   The current statute, the Limitation Act 1980, came into force on 1 May 1981.
2   [**Para 6.41**]. '[A] person's title arising from prior possession can be defeated either by a defendant showing that he or she ... has a better, because older, claim to possession or by a defendant showing adverse possession against the person for the duration of a limitation period' (*Mabo v Queensland (No 2)* (1992) 175 CLR 1 at 211 per Toohey J).
3   '[T]he squatter's title becomes impregnable, giving him a title superior to all others' (*Buckinghamshire CC v Moran* [1990] Ch 623 at 644C per Nourse LJ). See also *St Marylebone Property Co Ltd v Fairweather* [1962] 1 QB 498 at 513 per Holroyd Pearce LJ. If the squatter vacates the land before the end of the limitation period, his adverse possession obviously lapses (see *Brown v Faulkner* [2003] NICA 5(2) at [40]).
4   See *Shaw v Garbutt* (1996) 7 BPR 14816 at 14832 per Young J. The title of the adverse possessor thus rests 'on the infirmity of the right of others to eject him' (*Cooke v Dunn* (1998) 9 BPR 16489 at 16501 per Santow J).
5   In *J A Pye (Oxford) Ltd v Graham* [2001] Ch 804 at [43(2)], Mummery LJ declined to see the extinction of title under the Limitation Act as a 'deprivation of possessions or a confiscatory measure for which the payment of compensation would be appropriate: it is simply a logical and pragmatic consequence of the barring of [the claimant's] right to bring an action after the expiration of the limitation period.'

The constitutive effect of empirical fact

6.30   The law of statutory limitation has survived to the present day, although its role in the context of registered land has now been very severely modified by the Land Registration Act 2002.[1] By pressing relativity of title to its ultimate, the limitation principle effectively confirms estate ownership in persons who can show no formal or documentary title. In unregistered land the inception of adverse possession generates a 'property' in land which, if unchallenged, eventually brings about one of the larger paradoxes of the law of realty – an uncompensated shift of economic value to the squatter or interloper. Adverse possession thus provides a remarkable illustration of the constitutive effect of empirical fact.[2] The owner of an unregistered estate who fails within the allotted statutory period to initiate the eviction of a squatter or trespasser finds that he is definitively barred from recovering the land and that his title to an estate in that land is peremptorily extinguished. Nowhere else is the self-defining quality of property in land so clearly demonstrated. Land claims, however unmeritorious, come in time to enjoy a certain self-righting quality. Estate ownership is fundamentally determined by behavioural fact rather than by documentary record.

1   [Para 6.54].
2   See Gray and Gray, 'The Idea of Property in Land', in S Bright and J K Dewar (ed), *Land Law: Themes and Perspectives* (OUP 1998), pp 24–25.

THE RATIONALE OF ADVERSE POSSESSION

6.31   The acquisition of rights by adverse possession has always differed significantly from any form of acquisition by conveyance or transfer. Acquisition through adverse possession often appears to be founded on some notion of title by successful taking[1] and reflects one of the oldest, and initially most perplexing, aspects of the concept of property. Title by adverse possession seems to resemble 'title by theft or robbery, a primitive method of acquiring land without paying for it.'[2] Wrongful taking eventually generates rightful title. Yet – historically – almost all systems of law have conceded that, irrespective of the formal or documentary record of ownership, uncontested long possession of land must ultimately confer a good title upon the actual possessor.[3] Certain powerful (and overlapping) policy arguments have lent support to the phenomenon of adverse possession.[4]

1   See Lord Hoffmann's reference, in *R v Oxfordshire CC, ex p Sunningwell PC* [2000] 1 AC 335 at 349D–E, to the Roman concept of *usucapio*, 'meaning literally a taking by use.' For the early American view that appropriation of land 'to steady individual purpose' established a 'quasi-private proprietorship, which entitles the holder to be protected in its quiet enjoyment', see *Tartar v Spring Creek Water & Mining Co* (1855) 5 Cal 395 at 399; *State v Moore* (1859) 12 Cal 56 at 70; *Boggs v Merced Mining Co* (1859) 14 Cal 279.
2   H W Ballantine, 'Title by Adverse Possession' 32 Harv L Rev 135 (1918–19) ('an anomalous instance of maturing a wrong into a right contrary to one of the most fundamental axioms of the law').
3   'Any legal system must have rules of prescription which prevent the disturbance of long-established de facto enjoyment' (*R v Oxfordshire CC, ex p Sunningwell PC* [2000] 1 AC 335 at 349D per Lord Hoffmann). See likewise *Bakewell Management Ltd v Brandwood* [2004] 2 WLR 955 at [9] per Lord Hope of Craighead, [27] per Lord Scott of Foscote.
4   See M Dockray, 'Why Do We Need Adverse Possession?' [1985] Conv 272; M J Radin, 'Time, Possession, and Alienation' 64 Wash ULQ 739 at 742–750 (1986); D K Irving, 'Should the

Law Recognise Acquisition of Title by Adverse Possession?' (1994) 2 APLJ 112. For a more sceptical view, see Jeffrey E Stake, 'The Uneasy Case for Adverse Possession' 89 Geo LJ 2419 (2001).

Psychological factors

6.32 The legal recognition of adverse possession finds its origins in the psycho-social nature of our perceptions of property. Long-term possession of land stimulates primal territorial bondings.[1] As Oliver Wendell Holmes once remarked, the connection between property and prolonged user is 'in the nature of man's mind.'[2] For Holmes, '[a] thing which you have enjoyed and used as your own for a long time ... takes root in your being and cannot be torn away without your resenting the act and trying to defend yourself, however you came by it.'[3] The doctrine of adverse possession thus rests upon a theory of loss aversion which causes the law to impose the loss inevitably occasioned by long possession upon the person 'who will suffer it least – the person whose roots are less vitally embedded in the land.'[4] If it is complained that retention by the long possessor causes disappointment to the former owner, Holmes's robust response was that the former owner's 'neglect' had allowed 'the gradual dissociation between himself and what he claims, and the gradual association of it with another.' As Dean Ames famously concluded, 'English lawyers regard not the merit of the possessor, but the demerit of the one out of possession.'[5]

1   See M J Radin, 'Property and Personhood' 34 Stan L Rev 957 (1981–82).
2   'The Path of the Law' 10 Harv L Rev 457 at 477 (1897). On the instinctual nature of personal attachments to valued resources, see Gray, 'Equitable Property' (1994) 47(2) CLP 157 at 158–160. Such attachments may also be intensified by the resonance of a 'frontier' mentality. For instance, the generally shorter limitation periods currently in force in many parts of the United States and particularly in the American West (often ranging from six to ten years) have been attributed to different cultural perceptions of the length of time required to generate the relevant attachment to land (see M J Radin, 64 Wash ULQ 739 at 749 (1986)).
3   See also *Marquis Cholmondeley v Lord Clinton* (1820) 2 Jac & W 1 at 139–140, 37 ER 527 at 577 per Sir Thomas Plumer MR.
4   See Jeffrey E Stake, 89 Geo LJ 2419 at 2420 (2001). According to the theory of loss aversion, losses have a greater subjective impact than objectively commensurate gains (ibid at 2459). Stake locates the ideology of adverse possession (and the imperative defence of assets in our possession) in an evolutionary biology which is triggered by a 'property-recognition gene' (ibid at 2424–2426).
5   J B Ames, 'The Nature of Ownership', in *Lectures on Legal History* (Cambridge Mass 1913), p 197. See *Re Nisbet and Potts' Contract* [1905] 1 Ch 391 at 402 per Farwell J. The historical reality is that English law did not originally treat long enjoyment as a method of acquiring title, but rather 'approached the question from the other end by treating the lapse of time as ... barring the remedy of the former owner' (*R v Oxfordshire CC, ex p Sunningwell PC* [2000] 1 AC 335 at 349G–H per Lord Hoffmann).

The quieting of possession

6.33 At the back of the common law's preoccupation with factual possession has always been some deep-seated instinct for the preservation of security in the enjoyment of utility. Seisin, even when based on wrongful possession, was accorded a certain protection by the common law 'in the interests of peace.'[1] From the earliest origins of the 'seisin-possession' concept in the common law, there has been a large social interest in 'the quieting of possession.'[2] As Lord St Leonards once observed,[3] all limitation statutes are intended to prevent the 'rearing up of claims at great distances of time when evidences are lost.' Underlying the Limitation Act is the potent policy consideration that 'there shall be an end of litigation.'[4] Limitation periods operate as an important check upon the crippling social and legal costs otherwise incurred in endless litigation over matters of title.

1   *Minister of State for the Army v Dalziel* (1944) 68 CLR 261 at 276 per Latham CJ.
2   See *A'Court v Cross* (1825) 3 Bing 329 at 332–333, 130 ER 540 at 541 per Best CJ ('Long dormant claims have often more of cruelty than of justice in them').
3   *Dundee Harbour Trustees v Dougall* (1852) 1 Macq 317 at 321.
4   Ibid. It is 'not in the interests of order or good government that property should lie ownerless or open to conflicting claims' (*Cunnius v Reading School District*, 56 A 16 at 17 (1903); *Nelson v Blinn*, 83 NE 889 at 890 (1908)).

Stabilisation of land titles

6.34 It is widely accepted that 'certainty of title to land is a social need and occupation of land which has long been unchallenged should not be disturbed.'[1] Indeed the pragmatic business of unregistered conveyancing has always rested to some degree on the assumption that proof of continued de facto enjoyment of land by the vendor and his predecessors provides a good source of title for the purchaser.[2] As Lord Bingham of Cornhill pointed out in *J A Pye (Oxford) Ltd v Graham*,[3] 'in the days before registration became the norm' the law of adverse possession 'could no doubt be justified as avoiding protracted uncertainty where the title to land lay.'[4]

1   See Law Reform Committee, *Report on Acquisition of Easements and Profits by Prescription* (14th Report, Cmnd 3100, 1966), para 36.
2   [**Para 3.1**]. See *Minister of State for the Army v Dalziel* (1944) 68 CLR 261 at 277.
3   [2003] 1 AC 419 at [2].
4   It has become increasingly obvious, however, that the certainty-based rationale of adverse possession has much less relevance to registered conveyancing, where the location of title is accurately pinpointed by the definitive record of the register (see *J A Pye (Oxford) Ltd v Graham* [2000] Ch 676 at 709G–710B per Neuberger J, [2003] 1 AC 419 at [2] per Lord Bingham of Cornhill).

6.35 The stabilisation of title procured by the Limitation Act has clearly conferred important benefits not only upon the adverse possessor himself but also upon those third parties (e g purchasers, tenants and mortgagees) who dealt with him in reliance on the expectations engendered by his long possession. It is undoubtedly true that third parties require certainty as to title.[1] The law of adverse possession has always been underpinned, therefore, by the belief that without at least some version of the limitation principle significant burdens would be imposed on the process of land transfer itself. In the absence of a long possession rule, every disposition of real property would be jeopardised by the encroachment of ancient or increasingly stale claims in derogation of the transferor's rights. Every grantor of land would be required to trace a documentary title back to the Garden of Eden; and every estate owner would live under the perpetual shadow of apprehended repossession at the behest of some earlier and more meritorious claimant of title. When, in *J A Pye (Oxford) Ltd v Graham*,[2] it was argued in the Court of Appeal that the principle of adverse possession violated the European Convention guarantee of 'peaceful enjoyment' of possessions,[3] Mummery LJ indicated that the divesting operation of the Limitation Act is justified 'in the public interest', in that it is required to 'avoid the real risk of injustice in the adjudication of stale claims, to ensure certainty of title and to promote social stability by the protection of the established and peaceable possession of property from the resurrection of old claims.'[4]

1   See J W Singer, 'The Reliance Interest in Property' 40 Stan L Rev 611 at 665–672 (1987–88). On the 'moral element' in securing stability in fundamental legal institutions, see Percy Winfield, 'Ethics in English Case Law' 45 Harv L Rev 112 at 119 (1931–32).
2   [2001] Ch 804 [**para 6.98**].
3   ECHR Protocol No 1, Art 1 [**para 2.29**].
4   [2001] Ch 804 at [43(3)], confirmed in *Harrow LBC v Qazi* [2004] 1 AC 983 at [124] per Lord Scott of Foscote.

Trade-off between moral right and social utility

6.36   Contrary to the apprehension that title by long possession connotes a species of legalised theft, there has often been thought to be a distinct merit in ensuring that land titles ultimately conform to lived boundaries (rather than the reverse).[1] The limitation principle certainly ensured that de facto possession never diverged too markedly from de iure title.[2] Although the consequence might be the occasional uncompensated shift of wealth, the end result was an avoidance of the excessive social and economic burden of continual investigation and legal attrition. Indeed, the ready association of title with visible possession was once defensible as cutting back the information costs involved in ascertaining estate ownership.[3] The law of adverse possession can therefore be said to have marked an important compromise between considerations of moral right and social utility[4] – a controlled trade-off between documentary title and pragmatic fact which served to limit expensively disruptive inquiry and controversy.[5]

1   The law of limitation thus provides the ultimate resolution of the 'mistaken improvement' problem exposed in cases like *Pull v Barnes*, 350 P 828 (1960) (mountain cabin built on another's land). See R J Sutton, 'What should be done for mistaken improvers?', in P D Finn (ed), *Essays on Restitution* (Sydney 1990), p 245.
2   See M Goodman, (1970) 33 MLR 281 at 282–283.
3   See Thomas W Merrill and Henry E Smith, 'The Property/Contract Interface' 101 Col L Rev 773 at 803 (2001). However, the strength of the information-cost rationale is obviously diminished in the age of the electronically accessible data base.
4   See e g *DeRocco v Young* (1981) 120 DLR (3d) 169 at 173, where a convicted murderer was held to be capable (after his release from prison) of acquiring a title by long possession of his victim's land, even though he was barred by public policy from claiming any interest in the victim's land by way of the beneficial interest which had been left to him in her will.
5   See *Giouroukos v Cadillac Fairview Corp Ltd* (1984) 3 DLR (4th) 595 at 604 (Ontario Court of Appeal).

Arguments of social and economic engineering

6.37 The law of adverse possession is sometimes described as giving effect to a pragmatic expectation, born of the more physical climate of earlier times, that an owner will rise with rugged fortitude to defend his title against unlawful intruders.[1] The Limitation Act accordingly reflects a policy that 'those who go to sleep upon their claims should not be assisted by the courts in recovering their property.'[2] On this basis the limitation principle can be described as rewarding, at the expense of the sluggard, the purposeful labourer who makes constructive use of available land resources.[3] One commentator has attributed to the law of adverse possession the important function of reinforcing politically constructed perceptions of 'the mythic character of the ideal English landowner' as a rational, self-interested, careful, hard-working and ultimately civic-minded individual, whose incursion upon another's land is 'justified by his reliability as a natural guardian of English earth.'[4]

1 See *Purbrick v Hackney LBC* [2004] 1 P & CR 553 at [25] per Neuberger J (emphasising the underlying assumption that the owner can be expected to be vigilant).

2 *RB Policies at Lloyd's v Butler* [1950] 1 KB 76 at 81 per Streatfield J. See also *Ellis v Lambeth LBC* (1999) 32 HLR 596 at 601, where the principal demerit of the paper owner's case was that, even with clear knowledge of widespread squatting in its council housing, 'over many years the local authority never troubled to take legal proceedings.'

3 See C M Rose, 'Possession as the Origin of Property' 52 U Chi L Rev 73 at 81 (1985–86). Nowadays, however, it is increasingly recognised that, by favouring more active or intensive forms of land use, the doctrine of adverse possession may run counter to modern environmental or conservationist objectives (see John G Sprankling, 'An Environmental Critique of Adverse Possession' 79 Cornell L Rev 816 (1994)).

4 K Green, 'Citizens and Squatters: Under the Surfaces of Land Law', in S Bright and J K Dewar (ed), *Land Law: Themes and Perspectives* (OUP 1998), pp 229–256. (This interesting analysis argues that the rules of adverse possession subtly delineate categories of deserving or socially approved adverse claimants, thus drawing invidious distinctions between 'adverse possessors' who simply extend the boundaries of their existing middle class terrain, 'squatters' who are 'have-nots who want to join the haves', and 'trespassers' who 'pose a direct threat to modern civilised society.') See *J A Pye (Oxford) Ltd v Graham* [2000] Ch 676 at 705G–H, where Neuberger J spoke of the successful adverse possessors as persons who did not 'merely benefit from the land on a short term ad hoc basis. They looked after it and kept it in good heart by rolling, harrowing and fertilising it and by maintaining the hedges, fences and ditches.'

Some realism about title

6.38 The principle of adverse possession underscores the fact that possession and title were never, in the past, discrete juristic phenomena. Across centuries of English law the paper titles brandished in land disputes have never been regarded as conclusive. When the arrogant nonsense of title terminology was finally stripped away, all that remained visible to the naked eye was the official enforcement of raw claims to physical possession.[1] It was wholly consistent with the pragmatic demeanour of the common law that estate ownership should have been thought crucially dependent on sustained possessory control. In some deep sense the successful exercise of exclusory power may be all there ever really was to the grand claim of proprietary ownership. Behind all the brave philosophical and political rhetoric of conventional property talk, there has lurked only the unattractive rumble of state-sanctioned *force majeure*.[2] On this analysis, claims of *meum* and *tuum* have never protected rights of a sacrosanct or *a priori* nature, but have merely purported, with varying degrees of sophistication, to add moral legitimacy to the naked assertion of self-interest in the advantageous control of socially valued resources.[3]

1   'A property right has value to the extent only that the court will enforce it or award damages for its infringement' (*Attorney-General v Blake* [2001] 1 AC 268 at 281G per Lord Nicholls of Birkenhead).
2   Gray, 'Property in Common Law Systems', in G E van Maanen and A J van der Walt (ed), *Property Law on the Threshold of the 21st Century* (MAKLU, Antwerp, 1996), pp 264–265.
3   Gray, 'Property in Thin Air' [1991] CLJ 252 at 306–307.

TERRITORIAL CONTEXT OF ADVERSE POSSESSION

6.39   In reality the function of the law of adverse possession turns out to have been more complex and diverse than is suggested by the popular paradigm of the aggressive intruder whose wrongful taking of land is eventually validated by long possession. Many of the subtle difficulties and uncertainties inherent in adverse possession flow directly from excessive concentration on the crudely limited model of the self-interested squatter who invades large or extremely valuable tracts of land.[1] The typology of adverse possession is richly varied and it is likely that consciously wrongful seizure of land nowadays constitutes its least common form.[2] Adverse possession rules are rather more frequently invoked to resolve ownership disputes which originate either in relatively innocent circumstances of entry under colour of title or in defective conveyancing practice. Statistically the most significant adverse possessor is one who claims that a minute sliver of land formally titled in his neighbour has been inaccurately fenced in his own favour[3] or has been the subject of a mistaken double conveyance to himself.[4] The areas of land involved in contemporary claims of long possession are rarely large tracts of uncharted wilderness.[5]

1   See, however, *Ellis v Lambeth LBC* (1999) 32 HLR 596 (successful squat in council house reportedly worth £200,000); *J A Pye (Oxford) Ltd v Graham* [2003] 1 AC 419 (25 hectares of development land allegedly worth 'untold millions with planning consent' (see *Times*, 5 February 2000)). There are possibly 'tens of thousands' of squatters in England today (C Harpum, quoted in *Times*, 13 April 2000).
2   Regardless of the context neither ignorance nor mistake will normally prevent the operation of adverse possession [**para 6.123**].
3   See e g *Nunn v Croft* (Unreported, Court of Appeal, 12 February 1997) (19 inch encroachment by replacement fence).
4   See e g *Bridges v Mees* [1957] Ch 475. As every conveyancer is fully aware, the principle of adverse possession promises an ultimate cure or longstop remedy for any defectively drawn ground plans which erroneously enclose a small portion of a neighbour's land (see *Belotti v Bickhardt*, 127 NE 239 at 243–244 (1920); *Kohua Pty Ltd v Tai Ping Trading Pty Ltd* (1985) 3 BPR 9705 at 9707).
5   Compare *Prudential Assurance Co Ltd v Waterloo Real Estate Inc* [1999] 2 EGLR 85, where the realty in dispute comprised one face of a seven metre stretch of wall in Knightsbridge.

ADVERSE POSSESSION OF UNREGISTERED LAND

6.40 Where title to an estate in land remains *unregistered* at Land Registry, the consequences of adverse possession are still governed by the Limitation Act 1980. Underlying this enactment is the broad principle that no action may be brought for the recovery of land after the expiration of a statutorily prescribed period of time running from the date when the right of action first accrued.[1] The period prescribed differs according to the nature of the particular action, but at the termination of the appropriate period the action for recovery becomes statute-barred.[2]

1   If proceedings are begun before the expiration of the limitation period, the right of action is unaffected by the expiration of the period whilst proceedings remain pending. Moreover, if a judgment for possession is obtained in an action begun in due time, the successful claimant has a further period of twelve years from the date of judgment in which to enforce the judgment (see *BP Properties Ltd v Buckler* (1988) 55 P & CR 337 at 344–345).
2   See *R v Oxfordshire CC, ex p Sunningwell PC* [2000] 1 AC 335 at 349F–G per Lord Hoffmann. For reference to a 'tenuous if picturesque' form of adverse possession, see A R Everton, 'Built in a Night ... ' (1971) 35 Conv (NS) 249. See also (1972) 36 Conv (NS) 241, (1975) 39 Conv (NS) 427.

The limitation period

6.41 The Limitation Act 1980 lays down as a general rule that '[n]o action shall be brought by any person to recover any land after the expiration of twelve years from the date on which the right of action accrued to him.'[1] In respect of actions for recovery brought by the crown or the Church of England the relevant limitation period is 30 years[2] and, in respect of actions brought by the crown to recover foreshore, 60 years.[3] However, no limitation period curtails the recovery of land over which a public right of way exists. Such land is, as a matter of law, immune from the principle of adverse possession.[4] It is also difficult, although perhaps not impossible, to establish an adverse possession of land over which there exists a private right of way.[5]

1   LA 1980, s 15(1). The limitation period may be prolonged by the disability (including infancy) of the person to whom a right of recovery has accrued (LA 1980, ss 28(1), 38(2)).
2   LA 1980, Sch 1, Pt II, para 10. The 30 year period covers land which vests in the crown as bona vacantia (e g land formerly owned by a company which has been dissolved under the Companies Acts (see Companies Act 1985, s 654)).
3   LA 1980, Sch 1, Pt II, para 11.
4   *Bromley LBC v Morritt* (1999) 78 P & CR D37 at D37–D38 per Mummery LJ. Compare, however, *Coverdale v Charlton* (1878) 4 QBD 104 at 122–123, where adverse possession was ruled out, not in principle, but only as a matter of deemed intention on the part of the owner.
5   See *Simpson v Fergus* (2000) 79 P & CR 398 at 401–402.

Accrual of the right of action

6.42 In order that a right of action should accrue, thereby triggering the commencement of the limitation period, the land concerned must be 'in the possession of some person in whose favour the period of limitation can run.'[1] Only then can the squatter's possession truly be described as 'adverse'.[2] The limitation period thus begins to run from the date of the owner's dispossession by an adverse possessor or from the date of the inception of adverse possession by a stranger following a discontinuance of possession by the original owner.[3] Mere non-use of land by an owner cannot, in itself, initiate the limitation period.[4]

1   LA 1980, Sch 1, para 8(1). Adverse possession cannot be claimed by any person who is not legally competent to hold title, e g an unincorporated association of persons (see *Afton Band of Indians v Attorney-General of Nova Scotia* (1978) 85 DLR (3d) 454 at 463–465). Compare, however, *Mabo v Queensland (No 2)* (1992) 175 CLR 1 at 214, where Toohey J thought it possible that a possessory title had been acquired by the Meriam people of the Murray Islands.
2   See *J A Pye (Oxford) Ltd v Graham* [2001] Ch 804 at [34(5)] per Mummery LJ.
3   LA 1980, Sch 1, para 1 [**para 6.96**].
4   [**Para 6.91**].

Aggregation of periods of adverse possession

6.43   For the purpose of establishing the expiration of the limitation period in unregistered land, immediately consecutive periods of adverse possession may be aggregated: the statutory period can be accumulated by possession on the part of a series of squatters. In other words, if X (the original 'paper owner') is dispossessed by A, who later transfers his 'estate, right and interest' to B, B is then entitled to add the period of A's adverse possession to his own in defence against any action for recovery brought by X,[1] provided that these two periods together total at least the statutory period (i e normally twelve years).[2] However, the adverse possession of successive squatters can operate cumulatively to extinguish a pre-existing title only if the periods of adverse possession are strictly continuous.[3] If A abandons his adverse possession within the limitation period and, after an interval, B begins adversely to possess, B cannot 'tack' to his own possession the period of adverse possession earlier established by A.[4] The break in adverse possession restores X's title to its pristine force. The statutory period therefore starts afresh from the inception of B's possession and B must establish the full period independently on his own behalf.[5]

1   LA 1980, s 15(1). See *Willis v Earl Howe* [1893] 2 Ch 545 at 553–554; *Mount Carmel Investments Ltd v Peter Thurlow Ltd* [1988] 1 WLR 1078 at 1087G–1088B; *Salter v Clarke* (1904) 4 SR (NSW) 280 at 288; *Mulcahy v Curramore Pty Ltd* [1974] 2 NSWLR 464 at 476D–E; *Brown v Faulkner* [2003] NICA 5(2) at [41] per Higgins J.
2   The same rule of aggregation applies, in principle, if (instead of transferring his rights to B) A is dispossessed by B, although B may find it difficult to enlist A's aid in attesting to the effluxion of the full statutory limitation period. B remains vulnerable, in any event, to any action for recovery by A himself before B's independent period of adverse possession has prevailed for at least twelve years (see *Mount Carmel Investments Ltd v Peter Thurlow Ltd* [1988] 1 WLR 1078 at 1086E per Nicholls LJ; *Rhondda Cynon Taff County BC v Watkins* [2003] 1 WLR 1864 at [31] per Schiemann LJ).
3   *Shaw v Garbutt* (1996) 7 BPR 14816 at 14824.
4   LA 1980, Sch 1, para 8(2).
5   *Willis v Earl Howe* [1893] 2 Ch 545 at 554; *Mulcahy v Curramore Pty Ltd* [1974] 2 NSWLR 464 at 476B–E, 477C. See also *Public Trustee v Bellotti* (1986) 4 BPR 9196 at 9200–9201.

Limitation periods isolated invisibly in the past

6.44   There is no requirement that the relevant statutory limitation period should immediately precede the bringing of the paper owner's action for recovery.[1] It follows that a paper owner's rights to an unregistered estate may have become barred at some point in the past – a clear hazard for strangers who later seek to rely on his apparent documentary title.[2]

1   See *J A Pye (Oxford) Ltd v Graham* [2003] 1 AC 419 at [26] per Lord Browne-Wilkinson. Provided that twelve years of adverse possession have elapsed, the adverse possessor may go out of possession and 'the clock as it were continues to tick' (*Hounslow LBC v Minchinton* (1997) 74 P & CR 221 at 226 per Millett LJ). The squatter's title has already been definitively established and can now be defeated (even by the former paper owner) only if a new adverse possession is set up for the requisite statutory period.
2   Where a completed period of adverse possession of unregistered land lies buried in the past and the paper owner has since resumed possession, the successful squatter is accorded a certain limited protection in the event that the land is later the subject of someone else's application for first registration of title at Land Registry [**para 6.70**].

Reduction of limitation periods

6.45   It is likely that future reform will reduce the limitation periods imposed by statute. The Draft Limitation Bill of 2001 aimed to provide a standard ten year limitation period in respect of actions for the recovery of unregistered land (whether by individuals, the crown or the Church of England).[1] Under the Bill claims in respect of foreshore would continue to be limited by the present period of 60 years.[2]

1   Draft Limitation Bill 2001, cl 16(1). See *Limitation of Actions: A Consultation Paper* (Law Com CP No 151, 1998), para 13.127; Law Commission and Land Registry, *Land Registration for the Twenty-First Century* (Law Com No 254, September 1998), para 10.2; Law Commission, *Limitation of Actions* (Law Com No 270, July 2001), paras 4.126–4.135.
2   Draft Limitation Bill 2001, cl 16(2).

Extinguishment of prior titles

6.46   The operation of the Limitation Act 1980 is essentially negative in nature. The effluxion of the limitation period does not *create* a title in the adverse possessor, but has the general effect of *terminating* the title of any former owner to whom the completed period of possession was adverse.

Effects of extinguishment

6.47   On the expiration of the statutory limitation period a dispossessed owner's title to his unregistered estate in land is extinguished immediately.[1] With his title also perishes any claim to recover rent or mesne profits in respect of the squatter's preceding occupation of the land.[2] The combined impact of the barring of all rights of recovery and the extinction of all prior titles leaves the successful adverse possessor with a relatively better title than anyone else.[3] The common law freehold which the squatter has held from the inception of his possession is now rendered unchallengeable.[4] In unregistered land the adverse possessor simply emerges with an unimpeachable legal title in fee simple, although he inevitably holds this title subject to all valid pre-existing legal and equitable rights over the land.[5] Adverse possession against a paper owner extinguishes only the paper owner's title and not the interest of any third party to which that title was already subordinated.[6] Thus, for example, a successful adverse possessor is bound by any mortgage charge affecting the land, the squatter effectively acquiring only the equity of redemption.[7]

1   LA 1980, s 17. This provision is 'concerned with tidying up a situation where, by virtue of section 15, someone has acquired squatter's rights' (*Rhondda Cynon Taff County BC v Watkins* [2003] 1 WLR 1864 at [31] per Schiemann LJ).

2   *Re Jolly* [1900] 2 Ch 616 at 617–618; *Mount Carmel Investments Ltd v Peter Thurlow Ltd* [1988] 1 WLR 1078 at 1089A–B. See *Cox Homes Ltd v Ideal Homes (Midlands) Ltd* (Unreported, Court of Appeal, 10 February 1998) (no damages for trespass even in respect of the immediately preceding period of six years).

3   **[Para 6.29]**. See *Cooke v Dunn* (1998) 9 BPR 16489 at 16501 per Santow J.

4   Since the squatter takes a legal (rather than equitable) title, the equitable doctrine of 'clean hands' has been said to have no relevance (*Shaw v Garbutt* (1996) 7 BPR 14816 at 14834). The possessory owner 'does not have to offer to do equity' (*Re North Sydney Council* (1997) 8 BPR 15677 at 15681).

5   **[Para 3.26]**.

6   *Chung Ping Kwan v Lam Island Co Ltd* [1997] AC 38 at 47D–E per Lord Nicholls of Birkenhead. See similarly *St Marylebone Property Co Ltd v Fairweather* [1963] AC 510 at 536 per Lord Radcliffe.

7   **[Para 3.26]**. See *Carroll v Manek and Bank of India* (2000) 79 P & CR 173 at 188.

No 'parliamentary conveyance'

6.48   The Limitation Act does not effect a 'parliamentary conveyance' to the adverse possessor (ie a transfer of the paper owner's estate by force of statute).[1] This possibility is ruled out precisely because the paper owner's title to deal with his estate has been extinguished by the operation of the Act.[2] When, however, the extinguishing effect of the Limitation Act is placed in conjunction with the positive effect of adverse possession, the indirect consequence is that the adverse possessor is enabled to assert, as against the world, a title which is truly his own.

1   *Tichborne v Weir* (1892) 67 LT 735 at 736–737. See also *St Marylebone Property Co Ltd v Fairweather* [1963] AC 510 at 535–536 per Lord Radcliffe, 544 per Lord Denning; *Central London Commercial Estates Ltd v Kato Kagaku Co Ltd* [1998] 4 All ER 948 at 951c–d per Sedley J; *Perry v Woodfarm Homes Ltd* [1975] IR 104 at 122–123.

2   There remains an intriguing question whether the statutory extinguishment of 'title' simultaneously destroys the paper owner's estate in the land (see *Central London Commercial Estates Ltd v Kato Kagaku Co Ltd* [1998] 4 All ER 948 at 958h per Sedley J) or leaves that estate 'like Peter Pan's shadow, unattached to anyone' (see *St Marylebone Property Co Ltd v Fairweather* [1962] 1 QB 498 at 515 per Holroyd Pearce LJ). See Gray and Gray, 'The rhetoric of realty', in J Getzler (ed), *Rationalizing Property, Equity and Trusts: Essays in Honour of Edward Burn* (Butterworths 2003), p 220. It seems, on the whole, preferable to maintain that the paper owner's estate remains with him, but that he no longer has any 'title' to assert it.

Comparison with prescription

6.49 Adverse possession often seems to resemble the way in which long user of land generates the prescriptive acquisition of easements and profits *à prendre*.[1] However, one marked difference between limitation and prescription is that prescription is based upon a fiction of grant in respect of long used rights, whereas adverse possession, far from being founded on some fictional grant, operates by extinguishing prior titles.[2] Moreover, prescriptive acquisition occurs only through a user 'as of right',[3] while it has been said, quite aptly, that adverse possession under the Limitation Act is based upon 'possession as of wrong'.[4] Again, with prescription the fictional intention of the putative grantor of rights is decisive, whereas in the context of limitation it is the intention of the adverse possessor which is significant.[5] In the law of adverse possession the intention of the paper owner is, in virtually every instance, 'irrelevant in practice.'[6]

1   [**Para 8.168**].
2   *Buckinghamshire CC v Moran* [1990] Ch 623 at 644B–C per Nourse LJ. See also *Shaw v Garbutt* (1996) 7 BPR 14816 at 14829 per Young J.
3   [**Para 8.177**].
4   *Buckinghamshire CC v Moran* [1990] Ch 623 at 644D per Nourse LJ; *Sze To Chun Keung v Kung Kwok Wai David* [1997] 1 WLR 1232 at 1235H per Lord Hoffmann. See also *Co Litt*, p 2a; *Bladder v Phillips* [1991] EGCS 109 per Mustill LJ; *Shaw v Garbutt* (1996) 7 BPR 14816 at 14832; *Alexander v Polk* (1861) 39 Miss 737 at 755 per Harris J (adverse possession 'commenced in wrong ... and is maintained against right').
5   *Buckinghamshire CC v Moran* [1990] Ch 623 at 644D per Nourse LJ.
6   *Buckinghamshire CC v Moran* [1990] Ch 623 at 645A per Nourse LJ. See similarly *J A Pye (Oxford) Ltd v Graham* [2003] 1 AC 419 at [45] per Lord Browne-Wilkinson.

DIMINISHING FORCE OF THE ADVERSE POSSESSION PRINCIPLE

6.50 In recent years it has come to seem increasingly strange that adverse possession should have any relevance in a regime where the formal registration of title is supposed to provide a definitive record of estate ownership.[1] The last decade of the 20th century saw a gathering of force behind the view that, while the limitation principle may play a valuable role in resolving uncertainties of title in unregistered land, these uncertainties are highly unlikely to arise under a regime of compulsory registration of land ownership.[2] Title to registered land is readily ascertainable by inspection of the relevant proprietorship register and, as Neuberger J observed at first instance in *J A Pye (Oxford) Ltd v Graham*,[3] it is 'hard to see what principle of justice entitles the trespasser to acquire the land for nothing from the owner simply because he has been permitted to remain there for 12 years.'[4]

1   See e g Land Transfer Act 1952 (New Zealand), s 64, which disallows adverse claims against a registered proprietor except in special circumstances of extremely long possession (in practice normally 30 years). See Law Commission, *Limitation of Actions* (CP No 151 (1998)), para 13.111. The law of adverse possession co-exists with Torrens title in other Australasian jurisdictions (see e g *Newington v Windeyer* (1985) 3 NSWLR 555 at 563G–564A; *Cooke v Dunn* (1998) 9 BPR 16489 at 16502 per Santow J). See also R A Woodman and P Butt, 'Possessory Title and the Torrens System in New South Wales' (1980) 54 ALJ 78.

2   *J A Pye (Oxford) Ltd v Graham* [2000] Ch 676 at 709G–710A per Neuberger J, [2003] 1 AC 419
     at [2] per Lord Bingham of Cornhill. It remains true, however, that the imprecision of the
     'general boundaries rule' in registered land [**para 1.18**] can still generate marginal cases of
     difficulty.
3   [2000] Ch 676 at 710B–C.
4   In upholding a claim of adverse possession, Neuberger J declared that he arrived 'with no
     enthusiasm' at a conclusion 'which does not accord with justice, and cannot be justified by
     practical considerations.' Neuberger J condemned the squatter's uncompensated acquisition of
     land as a result which was 'draconian to the owner, and a windfall for the squatter.' The
     outcome was 'illogical and disproportionate … particularly in a climate of increasing aware-
     ness of human rights, including the right to enjoy one's own property' ([2000] Ch 676 at
     709F–710E). Neuberger J's sentiments were echoed in the House of Lords by Lord Bingham
     of Cornhill ([2003] 1 AC 419 at [2]).

Perceptions of unfairness

6.51   The House of Lords' ruling in *J A Pye (Oxford) Ltd v Graham* resulted
in the success of an adverse possession claim in respect of 25 hectares of prime
development land reputedly worth £10 million,[1] an outcome which the senior
law lord, Lord Bingham of Cornhill, declared 'apparently unjust'.[2] This view
merely mirrored a growing public perception that it had become 'too easy for
squatters to acquire title',[3] a criticism which attracted added force where
difficulties in the effective policing of vacant premises by cash-strapped local
authorities could easily lead to substantial losses for the public purse.[4] With the
modern demise of much of the traditional rationale for adverse possession, the
operation of the Limitation Act 1980 suddenly seemed, in popular imagination,
to endorse a form of land theft.[5] If 'property' is indeed a relationship of
socially approved control over a valued resource,[6] it had become quite clear
that, in the Britain of the 21st century, adverse possession of land is a form of
control which is no longer socially approved.

1   See 'Britain's biggest ever land-grab' (*The Guardian*, 9 July 2002).
2   [2003] 1 AC 419 at [2]. For similar expressions of judicial distaste for the operation of the
     adverse possession principle, see eg *Trustees of Michael Batt Charitable Trust v Adams* (2001)
     82 P & CR 406 at [24] per Laddie J; *Lambeth LBC v Blackburn* (2001) 82 P & CR 494 at [36]
     per Clarke LJ; *Lambeth LBC v Rumbelow* (Chancery Division, 25 January 2001) per Etherton
     J; *Purbrick v Hackney LBC* [2004] 1 P & CR 553 at [7] per Neuberger J.
3   Law Com No 271 (2001), para 2.70. Much public attention was attracted by decisions such as
     that in *Ellis v Lambeth LBC* (1999) 32 HLR 596 [**para 6.39**] (see *Times*, 22 July 1999). See also
     the headlines 'Squatters sell home for £103,000 … and it is completely legal' (*Daily Express*,
     8 July 1996); 'Squatter lays claim to £400,000 house' (*Times*, 14 October 1999).
4   See Law Com No 271 (2001), paras 2.70–2.71, 14.4.
5   Carol Rose has spoken similarly, in the American context, of a 'widely shared intuition against
     purposeful market bypass' (see Rose, 'Property and Expropriation: Themes and Variations in
     American Law' (2000) Utah L Rev 1 at 9).
6   [**Para 2.11**].

The Law Commission's proposals

6.52   Increasing doubt as to the proper place of the limitation rule in a
modern registration-based law of land eventually led the Law Commission to

propose a severe diminution of the principle of adverse possession.[1] It was already obvious that the era of the silicon chip and the prospect of electronic conveyancing would inevitably shift the reality of title from its pragmatic base in social behaviour towards a much more artificial base in bureaucratic recordation.[2] The Law Commission accordingly declared that the doctrine of adverse possession 'runs counter to the fundamental concept of indefeasibility of title that is a feature of registered title.'[3] Simultaneously with the announcement of its vision of a future founded upon a 'culture of registration',[4] the Commission advocated changes in the law of adverse possession which significantly cut back the right of the squatter to derogate from the title of the registered proprietor of land. Acting in conjunction with Land Registry, the Commission recognised that 'unregistered title is possession-based whereas the basis of registered title is the fact of registration.'[5] Taking the view that registered proprietors should be able (absent compelling reasons) to rely on the protection afforded by easily discoverable registration,[6] the Commission proposed that mere adverse possession should no longer bar the title of the registered proprietor.[7] Although adverse possession still has 'an essential role to play in relation to unregistered land',[8] the Commission recommended that in registered land the operation of the limitation principle should be restricted to cases 'where it is essential to ensure the marketability of land or to prevent unfairness.'[9]

1   Law Com No 254 (1998), paras 10.65–10.69, 10.100–10.101.
2   Under the forthcoming regime of electronic conveyancing, most interests will actually have no existence except by reason of their presence on the register [**para 12.4**].
3   Law Com No 271 (2001), para 14.3.
4   Law Com No 254 (1998), para 1.14.
5   Law Com No 254 (1998), para 10.3. See Law Com No 271 (2001), paras 14.2–14.6.
6   Law Com No 254 (1998), paras 10.11, 10.44. The unqualified application of adverse possession rules to registered land 'cannot be justified' (Law Com No 254, para 10.18).
7   Law Com No 254 (1998), paras 10.44, 10.49 ('registration should in itself protect the proprietor from the claims of an adverse possessor'). See likewise Law Com No 271 (2001), para 14.10.
8   Law Com No 254 (1998), para 10.18.
9   Law Com No 254 (1998), para 10.19.

ADVERSE POSSESSION UNDER THE LAND REGISTRATION ACT 2002

6.53   The Law Commission's recommendations were given substantial effect by the Land Registration Act 2002. In the words of one commentator, the 'much watered-down version of adverse possession' contained in the 2002 Act is 'undoubtedly one of the most fundamental changes to property law in the past century.'[1]

1   Roger Smith, 'The role of registration in modern land law', in L Tee (ed), *Land Law: Issues, Debates, Policy* (2002), p 55.

Reinforcement of the title of the registered proprietor

6.54   The Land Registration Act 2002 has brought about a dramatic curtailment of the limitation principle within the registered context, with the result that the common law principle of relativity of title operates only marginally within the statutory regime of registered land.[1] As Lord Hope of Craighead noted in *J A Pye (Oxford) Ltd v Graham*,[2] the more rigorous regime contained in the 2002 Act will 'make it much harder for a squatter who is in possession of registered land to obtain a title to it against the wishes of the proprietor.' The Act has thus engineered a very substantial strengthening of the position of registered proprietors against the claims of squatters[3] – a feature which must have been intended, in part, as a powerful incentive towards voluntary first registration of titles.[4] The real force of adverse possession is now effectively confined to *unregistered* titles in land.

1   The Land Registration Act 2002 cannot apply to any title which had already been lost by reason of a period of adverse possession completed before the passing of the Act (*J A Pye (Oxford) Ltd v Graham* [2003] 1 AC 419 at [2] per Lord Bingham of Cornhill). Under the Land Registration Act 1925, adverse possession against a registered title had the awkward effect of imposing on the registered proprietor a statutory trust in favour of the successful squatter, entitling him as beneficiary to apply to be registered as proprietor in place of the paper owner (LRA 1925, s 75(1)–(2)). For a more detailed account, see *Elements of Land Law* (3rd edn 2001), pp 248–250.
2   [2003] 1 AC 419 at [73] (see also Lord Bingham of Cornhill at [2]).
3   See Law Com No 254 (1998), para 10.19.
4   See Law Com No 271 (2001), para 2.10. It is no accident that a number of local authorities and other institutional owners are currently engaged in highly active programmes of voluntary registration of their portfolios of property at fee rates specially negotiated with Land Registry.

Mere lapse of time no longer bars registered titles

6.55   The Land Registration Act 2002 makes a decisive break away from the historic tradition that estate ownership is rooted in behavioural fact. The Act puts in place a 'wholly new system of adverse possession ... applicable to registered land.'[1] The 2002 Act introduces, with prospective effect, an unprecedented premise in English law, ie that the mere lapse of time cannot, in itself, bar the rights of a registered proprietor.[2] The relevant terms of the Limitation Act 1980 are expressly disapplied by a provision that no period of limitation can 'run against any person, other than a chargee, in relation to an estate in land ... the title to which is registered.'[3] Time, in other words, no longer runs in favour of a squatter by reason of his possession of registered land. The squatter may remain in possession for decades, but this circumstance cannot in itself extinguish the registered proprietor's title at Land Registry.[4] It therefore becomes quite immaterial whether the registered proprietor has made any attempt to commence legal proceedings for the purpose of terminating the squatter's possession.[5]

1   Law Com No 271 (2001), para 14.2. See All ER Rev 2002, p 226 (P J Clarke).
2   Law Com No 271 (2001), paras 2.74, 14.5, 14.9.
3   LRA 2002, s 96(1) (disapplying LA 1980, s 15 [**para 6.41**]).

4   LRA 2002, s 96(3) (disapplying LA 1980, s 17 [**para 6.47**]).
5   See LRA 2002, Sch 6, para 11(3)(a).

Requirement of positive application by squatter

6.56   The Land Registration Act 2002 substitutes a very different order of things in place of the common law notion of title by possession and lapse of time. The Act promotes the 'fundamental concept of indefeasibility'[1] by placing on the squatter, if he wishes to take over an existing registered title, an onus to make a positive application to Land Registry to be registered as the proprietor of the estate to which his possession has been adverse.[2] A person may apply to be registered as proprietor of a registered estate if he has been in 'adverse possession'[3] for a period of *ten* years,[4] but this period must immediately precede the date of his application.[5] The estate in question need not itself have been registered at Land Registry throughout the entirety of this period,[6] but for all material purposes 'adverse possession' retains substantially the same meaning as in the law of unregistered land.[7]

1   Law Com No 271 (2001), para 14.3.
2   Land Registration Act 2002, s 97, Sch 6, para 1(1). No application may be made by a squatter during, or within twelve months following, any period when the registered proprietor is an enemy or detained in enemy territory or during any period when the registered proprietor is suffering from an impairment or disturbance of mental functioning (see LRA 2002, Sch 6, para 8(1)–(2)).
3   A squatter who has been in adverse possession for ten years may also apply within six months of being evicted otherwise than pursuant to a court judgment for possession (ie if he is evicted through the registered proprietor's resort to self-help) (see LRA 2002, Sch 6, para 1(2)).
4   The period of adverse possession applicable to foreshore is 60 years (LRA 2002, Sch 6, para 13(1)).
5   LRA 2002, s 97, Sch 6, para 1(1). The 2002 Act thus precludes the possibility that adverse possession may be claimed by reason of a period of possession completed at some point in the past long before the emergence of the squatter's claim to title [**para 6.44**].
6   LRA 2002, Sch 6, para 1(4).
7   LRA 2002, Sch 6, para 11(1)–(2) [**paras 6.40, 6.105**]. See Law Com No 271 (2001), para 14.23.

The squatter's application can normally be defeated by simple objection

6.57   In *J A Pye (Oxford) Ltd v Graham*,[1] Lord Bingham of Cornhill identified the major hazard of the traditional doctrine of adverse possession as 'the risk that a registered owner may lose his title through inadvertence.' The Land Registration Act 2002 now addresses this risk by initiating a process of notification and objection as the necessary precursor of any successful claim of adverse possession against a registered proprietor.

1   [2003] 1 AC 419 at [2] (see similarly Lord Hope of Craighead at [73]).

Notification by Land Registry

6.58   The squatter's application for registration is notified by Land Registry to the proprietor of the estate to which the application relates and also to other

interested persons such as the proprietor of any registered charge on that estate
and (in the case of a leasehold estate) the proprietor of any superior registered
estate.[1] In effect, such persons are given 'one chance, but only one chance', to
terminate the squatter's adverse possession[2] and, in normal circumstances, it
seems inconceivable that the opportunity to do so will not be eagerly grasped.

1   LRA 2002, Sch 6, para 2(1). Prudent registered proprietors keep their address for service up to
    date at Land Registry. Land Registry reserves the right to reject applications which show no
    arguable case of adverse possession (*Adverse possession of registered land under the new
    provisions of the Land Registration Act 2002* (Land Registry Practice Guide 4, March 2003),
    para 5.3).
2   See Law Com No 271 (2001), paras 2.74, 14.6.

The right to oppose the squatter's application for registration

6.59 Any party notified of the squatter's application for registration is
entitled, on stating his grounds for doing so, to object to the application.[1] If no
agreement can be negotiated between the relevant parties, the matter is referred
for resolution by the Adjudicator to Land Registry.[2] Alternatively (or in
addition[3]), any party notified of the application may serve a counter-notice on
the Registry requiring that the application be disposed of under the peremptory
terms of para 5 of Schedule 6 of the Land Registration Act 2002,[4] a procedure
which, in all but exceptional circumstances, will cause the application to be
summarily rejected.[5] The net effect is that in most cases the squatter's application for registration is liable to be defeated – and defeated conclusively – by
opposition from *any* of the persons notified by Land Registry.[6] Once again the
2002 Act confirms that the title derived from registration has a resilience which
equips its proprietor with carapace-like protection against strangers.[7] Any
assault on the registered proprietor's title can usually be rebutted, albeit after
many decades of adverse possession, by an arbitrary repudiation of the
squatter's claim.

1   LRA 2002, s 73(1).
2   LRA 2002, s 73(7) **[para 6.14]**. The Adjudicator may direct one of the parties to initiate court
    proceedings.
3   See Land Registry Practice Guide 4 (March 2003), para 5.3.
4   LRA 2002, Sch 6, para 3(1). This counter-notice must be served within 65 business days (LA
    2002, Sch 6, para 3(2); LRR 2003, r 189).
5   In the absence of a counter-notice (or other objection), however, the applicant squatter is
    statutorily entitled to be entered in the register as the new proprietor of the relevant estate
    (LRA 2002, Sch 6, para 4).
6   See Law Com No 254 (1998), para 10.46.
7   See Gray and Gray, 'The rhetoric of realty', in J Getzler (ed), *Rationalizing Property, Equity
    and Trusts: Essays in Honour of Edward Burn* (Butterworths 2003), pp 247–248.

Failure to serve counter-notice or to oust squatter

6.60 The counter-notice procedure under para 5 of Schedule 6 of the 2002
Act has stringent consequences. On service of the counter-notice the registrar

must reject the squatter's application for registration unless the squatter can demonstrate the existence of any one of three kinds of special circumstance stipulated by statute which entitle him to be registered as the new proprietor of the relevant estate.[1] However, even if the squatter cannot bring himself within one or other of these exceptional cases, he may still succeed if he remains in adverse possession throughout the period of two years immediately following the rejection of his application. On the expiration of this period the squatter may reapply for registration[2] and is now entitled, irrespective of objection from the registered proprietor, to be entered in the register as the new proprietor.[3] In effect, the current registered proprietor is afforded a longstop period of two additional years during which he may either evict the squatter or regularise his status by the grant of some licence or tenancy (which would, of course, negative automatically any further claim of adverse possession).[4]

1   [Paras 6.61–6.64].
2   LRA 2002, Sch 6, para 6(1). No application may be made at this stage by any squatter who is currently a defendant in possession proceedings or who has had a judgment for possession made or executed against him during the last two years (see LRA 2002, Sch 6, para 6(2)). If, however, a judgment for possession against the squatter has lain unenforced for more than two years, it ceases to be enforceable (LRA 2002, s 98(2)).
3   LRA 2002, Sch 6, para 7.
4   See Law Com No 271 (2001), paras 14.53–14.58.

Exceptions to the right to object to the squatter's application

6.61   Para 5 of Schedule 6 of the Land Registration Act 2002 provides three narrowly defined (and slightly overlapping) circumstances in which, notwithstanding the objection of the current registered proprietor, a squatter who can establish a ten-year period of possession is *entitled* to take over the relevant registered land.[1]

1   LRA 2002, Sch 6, para 5(1). Cases of unresolved dispute will be referred, once again, to the Adjudicator to Land Registry.

Equity by estoppel

6.62   The first exceptional case arises where it would be 'unconscionable because of an equity by estoppel' for the registered proprietor to seek to dispossess the applicant.[1] This special ground effectively imports into the registration arena the principles of proprietary estoppel.[2] The squatter's application for registration may therefore succeed if the registered proprietor expressly or impliedly encouraged the squatter to believe that the squatter owned the land which is now the subject of claim *and* the squatter acted, to the knowledge of the registered proprietor, in detrimental reliance on this belief. It must, moreover, be shown that it would now be 'unconscionable' for the registered proprietor to resile from the assurance of entitlement given to the squatter. In effect, the 'equity by estoppel' exception allows a ten-year period of possession to be presented as 'adverse' even though it originated in some permissive occupation conceded by the registered proprietor. However, the mere raising of an inchoate equity of estoppel does not necessarily guarantee that the squatter will be entitled to take over the registered estate. In accordance with the 'minimum equity' limitation which governs the framing of relief in estoppel cases,[3] the 2002 Act adds the rider that the circumstances must be such 'that the applicant ought to be registered as proprietor' of the estate in question.[4] An important discretion is therefore reserved – in practice for the Adjudicator to Land Registry – to satisfy the applicant's estoppel-based equity by means of an order falling short of his or her registration as proprietor of the land in dispute.[5] It thus remains possible that, even though it would be unconscionable for the registered proprietor to assert his strict legal rights against the squatter, the appropriate remedy for the latter may comprise merely the award of monetary compensation or the grant of some residential or other occupational privilege short of title.

1   LRA 2002, Sch 6, para 5(2)(a). See S Nield, 'Adverse Possession and Estoppel' [2004] Conv 123.
2   **[Paras 10.168–10.300]**.
3   **[Paras 10.221, 10.290]**. See Law Com No 271 (2001), para 14.40.
4   LRA 2002, Sch 6, para 5(2)(b). The Law Commission and Land Registry envisaged as typical circumstances the case in which a squatter mistakenly builds on the registered proprietor's land or in which an informal sale of land allows the buyer into possession, following his payment of the purchase price, but no steps are ever taken to perfect his title (see Law Com No 271 (2001), para 14.42).
5   See LRA 2002, s 110(4).

Some other entitlement to be registered

6.63   The second exceptional case arises, rather more straightforwardly, where the applicant for registration is entitled 'for some other reason' to be registered as proprietor of the registered estate.[1] Such circumstances occur, for example, where a person who has been in possession for ten years can show that he is entitled to the land, in any event, under the will or intestacy of the deceased proprietor. Similarly a purchaser of land who has paid the full price and has assumed possession (but without taking a formal transfer) is entitled as a beneficiary under a bare trust to present his possession as 'adverse' for the purpose of the Land Registration Act 2002.[2]

1   LRA 2002, Sch 6, para 5(3).
2   See *Bridges v Mees* [1957] Ch 475 at 484–486 [**para 6.88**]; Law Com No 271 (2001), para 14.43.

Reasonable mistake as to boundary

6.64   The third exceptional case involves some of the very few instances in which ignorance or mistake as to law is an essential component of a claim of adverse possession.[1] This special case emerges in the context of mistaken land boundaries which, for a prolonged period, are assumed by neighbouring owners to be good and correct.[2] Under certain conditions the Land Registration Act 2002 entitles a squatter to take over a registered title to land bordering upon land which clearly belongs to him already, the exact boundary line between the two areas never having been fixed.[3] For a period of at least ten years immediately preceding his application, the squatter (or his predecessor in title) must have been in adverse possession of the land now in dispute and must 'reasonably' have believed that that land belonged to himself.[4] The 'reasonable mistake as to boundary' exception is likely to apply, for instance, where physical features on the ground suggest that a boundary is in one location whereas the registered plan shows it to be elsewhere.[5] The requirement of reasonable belief on the part of the squatter has been said to be merely one specific form of the *animus possidendi* which is generally demanded of any claimant of adverse possession.[6]

1   [**Para 6.123**]. See *Purbrick v Hackney LBC* [2004] 1 P & CR 553 at [21] per Neuberger J.
2   LRA 2002, Sch 6, para 5(4)–(5) (effective 13 October 2004: see LRA 2002 (Commencement No 4) Order (SI 2003/1725)).
3   LRA 2002, Sch 6, para 5(4)(a)–(b). On 'general boundaries', see [**paras 1.16–1.17**]. If the conditions stipulated in para 5(4) are met, the squatter has a statutory defence to any action for possession even in advance of any application by him to be registered as proprietor (LRA 2002, s 98(1)).
4   LRA 2002, Sch 6, para 5(4)(c), (5). The estate to which the application relates must have been registered more than one year prior to the date of the squatter's application (LRA 2002, Sch 6, para 5(4)(d)).
5   See Law Com No 271 (2001), para 14.46. If the current registered proprietor has led the squatter to believe that the application land already belongs to the squatter, there may be an overlap with the 'equity by estoppel' exception [**para 6.62**].
6   [**Para 6.133**]. The Law Commission and Land Registry have suggested that long possession of land whose physical features suggest that the land belongs to the squatter should raise a rebuttable presumption of reasonable belief (or *animus*) (Law Com No 271 (2001), paras 14.51–14.52).

Registration of the successful adverse possessor as the new proprietor

6.65   The general effect of the Land Registration Act 2002 is to make it immensely difficult for a squatter to take over the registered estate of one whom he has dispossessed. However, in the unlikely event that a squatter's inchoate rights survive the process of legal attrition established by the 2002 Act, he is generally entitled to be registered as the new proprietor with absolute title.[1]

1   See Law Com No 254 (1998), paras 10.45–10.49.

A parliamentary transfer of the registered estate

6.66   Such registration serves to replace (and thereby extinguish) the common law freehold acquired by the squatter on his initial assumption of possession.[1] The overall outcome is therefore the conferment on the successful squatter of a statutory right to be substituted in the Land Register as the current estate proprietor – a process which is 'to all appearances a statutory conveyance' of the relevant registered estate.[2]

1   LRA 2002, Sch 6, para 9(1).

2   Compare *Central London Commercial Estates Ltd v Kato Kagaku Co Ltd* [1998] 4 All ER 948
     at 959d–e per Sedley J.

Rights binding on the successful squatter

6.67   It is fundamental that adverse possession 'defeats the rights, whatever
they may be, of the person against whom the possession is adverse. It does not
defeat the rights of others.'[1] It follows that the registered estate taken by a
squatter pursuant to the Land Registration Act 2002 remains subject to a range
of legal and equitable rights and interests already vested in third parties. The
squatter's registration as the new proprietor is declared by statute to have no
impact on 'the priority of any interest affecting the estate.'[2] The successful
adverse possessor is therefore bound by most third party rights (eg easements,
profits *à prendre* and restrictive covenants) which already encumber the land
and have not yet been extinguished. By way of exception the squatter generally
takes free of any registered charge affecting the registered estate immediately
before his own registration,[3] not least because the registered chargee will, by
definition, have failed to object to the squatter's application for registration.[4] A
registered charge continues to bind the erstwhile squatter only where his
registration as proprietor has been achieved by reliance on one or other of the
exceptional conditions laid down in para 5 of Schedule 6 of the 2002 Act.[5]

1   *Chung Ping Kwan v Lam Island Co Ltd* [1997] AC 38 at 47D–E per Lord Nicholls of
     Birkenhead. See also *St Marylebone Property Co Ltd v Fairweather* [1963] AC 510 at 536 per
     Lord Radcliffe; *Pollard v Jackson* (1994) 67 P & CR 327 at 330.
2   LRA 2002, Sch 6, para 9(2).
3   LRA 2002, Sch 6, para 9(3) (reversing *Carroll v Manek and Bank of India* (2000) 79 P & CR
     173).
4   See Law Com No 271 (2001), para 14.75 (referring to a 'clean break').
5   **[Paras 6.61–6.64]**. See LRA 2002, Sch 6, para 9(4). Charges other than registered charges
     (eg charging orders) may also bind the squatter if he cannot claim priority over them (see
     LRA 2002, ss 28–29). In all such cases the new registered proprietor may have his estate
     discharged from the charge on paying the full amount of the debt or (where the charge affects
     other land of the former registered proprietor) such part of that debt as may be statutorily
     apportioned to the squatter's new estate (see LRA 2002, Sch 6, para 10).

Protection of squatters' rights accrued prior to the Land Registration Act 2002

6.68   The Land Registration Act 2002 preserves, in some degree, the rights of
squatters in whose favour time had already successfully run *prior to* the
commencement of the 2002 Act.

Registered land

6.69   A squatter on registered land who had completed the requisite period of
adverse possession (ie normally twelve years) is automatically entitled to be

registered as proprietor of the relevant estate.[1] In the absence of such registration, his rights, if he is still in 'actual occupation', will 'override' any subsequent disposition of the registered estate.[2]

1   LRA 2002, s 134(2), Sch 12, para 18(1). The squatter has a statutory defence to any action for possession of the land and any court, on upholding this defence, must order his registration as proprietor of the relevant estate (LRA 2002, Sch 12, para 18(2)–(3)).
2   LRA 2002, s 29(1), (2)(a)(ii), Sch 3, para 2 [**para 12.146**].

Unregistered land

6.70   The rights accrued prior to the commencement of the Land Registration Act 2002 by a successful squatter on unregistered land are deemed to 'override' any first registration of that land if the squatter remains in 'actual occupation'.[1] Even if the successful squatter went out of 'actual occupation' following the completion of his adverse possession, his rights bind any first registered proprietor who has notice of them[2] and are otherwise specially protected until 13 October 2006,[3] during which period he can apply for first registration himself.

1   LRA 2002, ss 11(4)(b), (7), 12(4)(c), (8), Sch 1, para 2 [**para 12.268**]. A squatter who has been in adverse possesson for twelve years has the opportunity (until 13 October 2005) to lodge a caution against first registration at Land Registry (LRA 2002, Sch 12, para 14(1) [**para 12.270**]).
2   LRA 2002, ss 11(4)(c), 12(4)(d). See See Law Com No 271 (2001), para 5.18.
3   LRA 2002, Sch 1, para 15, as inserted by LRA 2002, s 134(2), Sch 12, para 7 (ie a period of three years from the effective date of Sch 1 of the Land Registration Act 2002).

Historic changes of emphasis

6.71   It can therefore be seen that the Land Registration Act 2002 has confirmed a number of significant changes of emphasis. Consistently with the demise of possession as the fundamental operative concept of English land law, the 2002 Act severely curtails the role of adverse possession in respect of registered titles. For the first time ever, estate ownership is no longer regulated by effective possession and the mere lapse of time. Registration has replaced possession as the source of title. With the inexorable movement towards comprehensive registration of title has come a new conceptualism of *ownership*. The philosophical base of English land law has finally shifted from empirically defined fact to state-defined entitlement, from property as a reflection of social actuality to property as a product of state-ordered or political fact. In short, instead of the citizen telling the state who owns land, the state will henceforth tell the citizen.

ADVERSE POSSESSION IN RELATION TO LEASEHOLD LAND

6.72   The rules of adverse possession require refinement in respect of land held by a tenant or lessee. Something turns on whether the adverse claim is made by the tenant against his landlord or against some stranger or is made against the tenant himself. In certain circumstances the squatter's adverse possession may entitle him to apply to be registered as proprietor of a registered estate. However, as already observed, the Land Registration Act 2002 promulgates a new general principle that time does not run against any person in respect of an estate whose title has already been registered at Land Registry.[1]

1   LRA 2002, s 96(1) [**para 6.55**].

ADVERSE POSSESSION BY A TENANT

6.73   Adverse possession by a tenant is strictly controlled by rules which operate heavily in the landlord's favour.

Land already subject to the tenancy

6.74   A tenant cannot, during the subsistence of his lease or tenancy, claim adverse possession against his landlord in respect of any land which is already the subject of that lease or tenancy.[1] During the currency of the landlord–tenant relationship time cannot run against the landlord (even where the landlord's title is unregistered). The tenant's possession is by consent and cannot therefore be considered adverse.[2] Every tenant is, moreover, estopped from denying his landlord's title.[3] Nor does mere non-payment of rent during a fixed term render the tenant's continuing possession adverse. The tenant can assert a possession adverse to his landlord only when the relationship has come (or been deemed to come) to an end. In the case of a periodic tenancy in writing, time starts to run against the landlord only when the tenancy has been determined. Other periodic tenancies, whether from year to year or for any other period, are treated as determined at the expiration of the first period,[4] except in so far as any rent is received subsequently, in which case the landlord's right of action for recovery against his tenant is treated as having accrued on the date of the last receipt of rent.[5] Thereafter a tenant's failure to pay rent may initiate a period of adverse possession leading potentially to the perfection of a freehold title in the tenant.[6]

1   However, a landlord may possess adversely to his own tenant (see *Sze To Chun Keung v Kung Kwok Wai David* [1997] 1 WLR 1232 at 1235F–H per Lord Hoffmann).
2   [**Para 6.114**]. See *Hayward v Chaloner* [1968] 1 QB 107 at 122C–D per Russell LJ.
3   [**Para 7.316**]. See also *Shillabeer v Diebel* (1980) 100 DLR (3d) 279 at 283.
4   LA 1980, Sch 1, para 5(1). See *Palfrey v Palfrey* (1974) 229 EG 1593 at 1595; *Williams v Jones* [2002] EWCA Civ 1097 at [18]. A 'lease in writing' for the purpose of para 5(1) does not include a tenancy document which merely evidences the terms of a future lease and does not, of itself, create a legal leasehold term (see *Long v Tower Hamlets LBC* [1998] Ch 197 at 210E–F, 219A; [1998] Conv 229 (S Bright)).
5   LA 1980, Sch 1, para 5(2). In consequence, non-payment of rent under an orally granted tenancy may generate an adverse possession effective to extinguish the landlord's freehold title (see *Moses v Lovegrove* [1952] 2 QB 533 at 538, 543; *Carroll v Manek and Bank of India* (2000) 79 P & CR 173 at 189).

6   See e g *Pollard v Jackson* (1994) 67 P & CR 327 at 330 [**para 6.129**] and compare *Smith v Lawson* (1998) 75 P & CR 466 at 471 [**para 6.113**].

Other land belonging to the landlord

6.75   If the tenant encroaches on any land belonging to his landlord which is not part of the subject matter of the lease, the encroachment is presumed[1] to be merely a unilateral extension by the tenant of the locus of his existing tenancy.[2] In the absence of some act by the tenant disclaiming the landlord's title,[3] the additional land becomes subject to the terms of the lease[4] and must be given up to the landlord on its termination.[5]

1   The presumption is rebuttable (see *Ali v Tower Hamlets LBC* [1996] EGCS 193) and probably applies only to land in the immediate vicinity of the tenant's original holding (see *Lord Hastings v Saddler* (1898) 79 LT 355, as construed in *Smirk v Lyndale Developments Ltd* [1975] Ch 317 at 328D–G per Pennycuick V-C).
2   *Lord Hastings v Saddler* (1898) 79 LT 355 at 356. See also *Kingsmill v Millard* (1855) 11 Exch 313 at 318, 156 ER 849 at 851 per Parke B; *Smirk v Lyndale Developments Ltd* [1975] Ch 317 at 324E–G, 332G–H, 337G. The principle has been described as akin to that of an estoppel binding the tenant (see *J F Perrott & Co Ltd v Cohen* [1951] 1 KB 705 at 710 per Denning LJ; *Trustees of Michael Batt Charitable Trust v Adams* (2001) 82 P & CR 406 at [36]).
3   Some doubt must attach to Parke B's statement in *Kingsmill v Millard* (1855) 11 Exch 313 at 318–319, 156 ER 849 at 851–852, that the tenant may defeat the presumption in favour of his landlord by conveying the disputed land to a third party before the end of his tenancy (but see *Trustees of Michael Batt Charitable Trust v Adams* (2001) 82 P & CR 406 at [48]).
4   No extra rent is payable unless the landlord has made clear his intention to make an additional demand (see *Ali v Tower Hamlets LBC* [1996] EGCS 193). The tenant is, however, liable on the leasehold covenants for repair (see *J F Perrott & Co Ltd v Cohen* [1951] 1 KB 705 at 709–711).
5   *Smirk v Lyndale Developments Ltd* [1975] Ch 317 at 333D. See also *Colchester BC v Smith* [1991] Ch 448 at 479E–G.

Land belonging to some third party

6.76   If the tenant encroaches on land belonging to a stranger, his adverse possession is traditionally presumed, again in the absence of demonstrable contrary intention,[1] to operate for the benefit of his landlord as reversioner.[2] Title is therefore gained on behalf of the landlord, this instance of possession by a tenant being sometimes termed 'quasi-adverse possession'.[3] The presumption in favour of the landlord has recently incurred some criticism as being 'feudal' in appearance and may generate further difficulty if the encroachment on adjacent land is made by one who holds a tenancy of two parcels of land owned by different landlords.[4] It is also highly arguable that the effect of this outmoded presumption is that, following successful encroachment, the estate in the third party's land passes to the landlord, but that only the tenant has title to assert this estate against the third party.[5]

1   See *Long v Tower Hamlets LBC* [1998] Ch 197 at 203C–H. Again the presumption is highly likely to be rebutted the more distant the stranger's land is from the tenant's holding (see *Smirk v Lyndale Developments Ltd* [1975] Ch 317 at 328D–G per Pennycuick V-C).

2   *Whitmore v Humphries* (1871) LR 7 CP 1 at 5 per Willes J; *Smirk v Lyndale Developments Ltd*
     [1975] Ch 317 at 324B–326B. See also *Kingsmill v Millard* (1855) 11 Exch 313 at 318 per Parke
     B, 320 per Alderson B, 156 ER 849 at 851–852; *Simpson v Council of North West County
     District* (1978) 4 BPR 9277 at 9302. Again, the underlying principle seems to be one of
     estoppel (see *Trustees of Michael Batt Charitable Trust v Adams* (2001) 82 P & CR 406 at [39],
     [41]).
3   See e g *Yankwood Ltd v Havering LBC* [1998] EGCS 75 per Neuberger J. Exactly the same
     principle applies where a stranger's land is adversely possessed by a licensee. The licensee's
     possession of land extraneous to his licence constitutes adverse possession on behalf of his
     licensor (see *Sze To Chun Keung v Kung Kwok Wai David* [1997] 1 WLR 1232 at 1235E–H per
     Lord Hoffmann).
4   See *Trustees of Michael Batt Charitable Trust v Adams* (2001) 82 P & CR 406 at [38], [48] per
     Laddie J.
5   *Trustees of Michael Batt Charitable Trust v Adams* (2001) 82 P & CR 406 at [40]–[42] per
     Laddie J.

ADVERSE POSSESSION AGAINST A TENANT

6.77   A trespasser on leasehold premises is much more vulnerable than a
trespasser on freehold land.[1] The stranger who seeks to establish a possessory
title to freehold land which is currently subject to a lease must prove adverse
possession for the requisite period not only against the *tenant* but also, in due
course, against the *landlord*. In the case of registered leasehold and freehold
titles, the squatter must also apply to be registered as proprietor of, first, the
registered leasehold title and, secondly, the registered freehold title.

1   *Chung Ping Kwan v Lam Island Co Ltd* [1997] AC 38 at 47D per Lord Nicholls of Birkenhead.

Unregistered titles

6.78   Where a squatter adversely possesses against a tenant in circumstances
where neither the tenant's title nor his landlord's title is yet registered at Land
Registry, the achievement of an unassailable fee simple title for the squatter
requires the separate extinguishment of *both* the leasehold title *and* the freehold
title.

Extinction of the tenant's unregistered leasehold title

6.79   The squatter's assumption of possession against a tenant during the
currency of his lease causes time to run as against the tenant (but not as against
his landlord).[1] The continuance of this adverse possession for the statutory
limitation period will certainly bar the right of the tenant (and all those
claiming through him as tenant) to recover the land from the squatter,[2]
although no corresponding bar affects the freehold title of the landlord.[3] The
statutory limitation period is not set running against the landlord until the
expiry of the lease[4]; adverse possession defeats only the rights of those to whom
it is truly adverse.[5] It would be 'utterly wrong if the title of the freeholder could
be eroded away during the lease without his knowledge.'[6]

1   *Chung Ping Kwan v Lam Island Co Ltd* [1997] AC 38 at 46C–D, 47C–D; *Perry v Woodfarm Homes Ltd* [1975] IR 104 at 130. The squatter is immediately deemed to hold a common law freehold estate [**para 3.24**].
2   The squatter's adverse possession against the tenant also bars any specifically enforceable option for renewal contained in the tenant's lease (see *Chung Ping Kwan v Lam Island Co Ltd* [1997] AC 38 at 48B–G). On options for renewal, see [**paras 9.80, 14.280**].
3   In rare circumstances it is possible that the squatter on the tenant's land may be not a true stranger, but rather the landlord himself (see *Rhondda Cynon Taff County BC v Watkins* [2003] 1 WLR 1864 at [23] per Schiemann LJ, [47] per Arden LJ).
4   *St Marylebone Property Co Ltd v Fairweather* [1963] AC 510 at 544 per Lord Denning. See LA 1980, Sch 1, para 4.
5   See *St Marylebone Property Co Ltd v Fairweather* [1963] AC 510 at 536 per Lord Radcliffe; *Central London Commercial Estates Ltd v Kato Kagaku Co Ltd* [1998] 4 All ER 948 at 951j.
6   *St Marylebone Property Co Ltd v Fairweather* [1963] AC 510 at 544 per Lord Denning.

Rights binding on the successful squatter

6.80   Even after he has defeated the tenant's leasehold title, the squatter's status is complicated by the fact that, although he is entitled to the residue of the ousted tenant's term of years, he is not an *assignee* of that term and has neither privity of contract nor 'privity of estate' with the landlord.[1] The landlord cannot therefore sue the squatter directly for rent or for damages for breach of the leasehold covenants.[2] Nevertheless, even though not strictly liable to observe the covenants of the lease, the adverse possessor is vulnerable to the landlord's paramount exercise of any right of re-entry contained in the lease in the event of non-performance of the covenants. In effect, the covenants bind the *land* – even if not strictly speaking the *squatter* – with the consequence that the squatter is liable to suffer forfeiture (and is, moreover, ineligible to claim relief against such forfeiture).[3]

1   [**Para 14.208**]. See *Tichborne v Weir* (1892) 67 LT 735 at 737–738; *St Marylebone Property Co Ltd v Fairweather* [1963] AC 510 at 535; *Perry v Woodfarm Homes Ltd* [1975] IR 104 at 120; *Giouroukos v Cadillac Fairview Corp Ltd* (1984) 3 DLR (4th) 595 at 605.
2   The ousted tenant continues to be contractually liable on his covenants (see *Perry v Woodfarm Homes Ltd* [1975] IR 104 at 130).
3   *St Marylebone Property Co Ltd v Fairweather* [1963] AC 510 at 547 per Lord Denning; *Tickner v Buzzacott* [1965] Ch 426 at 434E–G [**para 14.189**]. The threat of forfeiture may indirectly force the squatter to perform the leasehold covenants (see *Perry v Woodfarm Homes Ltd* [1975] IR 104 at 120). A squatter on registered leasehold land can, of course, discover the terms of the registered lease by applying to Land Registry for a copy of that lease [**para 6.21**]. The squatter on unregistered leasehold land may have more difficulty in ascertaining the covenants which bind the land.

Extinction of the landlord's unregistered freehold title

6.81   Dispossession of the tenant – even for a period vastly in excess of the limitation period – does not, in itself, prejudice the rights of the landlord. The squatter's intrusion is 'adverse' only to the tenant and not to the landlord. Thus far, the only title extinguished is the leasehold title held by the person dispossessed.[1] Regardless of the duration of the squatter's adverse possession, the landlord remains fully entitled to recover possession from the squatter on the determination of the lease.[2] There is, at this point, nothing to prevent the landlord from granting a new lease of the land – even to the former, and now ousted, tenant – with the consequence that the new tenant becomes entitled to eject the squatter at any time during the following twelve years.[3]

1   *Chung Ping Kwan v Lam Island Co Ltd* [1997] AC 38 at 46E per Lord Nicholls of Birkenhead.
2   *Taylor v Twinberrow* [1930] All ER Rep 342 at 344E per Scrutton LJ; *St Marylebone Property Co Ltd v Fairweather* [1963] AC 510 at 536 per Lord Radcliffe.
3   *Chung Ping Kwan v Lam Island Co Ltd* [1997] AC 38 at 47A–D. If, however, the new lease is granted to the tenant under an option contained in the original lease, the original term and the new term are treated as continuous so that the squatter's possession is uninterrupted by the expiry of the 'old' lease and the commencement of the 'new' lease ([1997] AC 38 at 49G–H).

Accrual of the landlord's right of action

6.82   In all these matters the landlord's freehold remains unaffected precisely because, while the lease is extant, he is disabled from asserting on his own behalf any right to physical possession of the land.[1] It is only on the determination of the lease that the landlord's right to recover possession revitalises.[2] Only then does his independent right of action accrue against the intruder[3]; and only then does time start running against him and in favour of the squatter.[4] Until then the landlord's freehold title remains wholly undisturbed by the fact of adverse possession, with the result that the freehold title cannot be extinguished until, at the earliest, twelve years *after* the end of the leasehold term. This may be a distant point in time if the leasehold term is of long unexpired duration (eg under a lease of 99 years or 999 years). For precisely this reason the optimist is able to point out that a freeholder can always ensure (through the device of an extremely long lease) that his own fee simple estate is never destroyed by the encroachments of adverse possessors.[5] However, the pessimist is all too conscious that, by the same token, the earliest date for the freeholder's recovery of possession from the squatter may be horribly distant.

1   *Chung Ping Kwan v Lam Island Co Ltd* [1997] AC 38 at 46G per Lord Nicholls of Birkenhead; *St Marylebone Property Co Ltd v Fairweather* [1962] 1 QB 498 at 530 per Pearson LJ.
2   The irreducible core of every lease is the concession to the tenant of a right of exclusive possession [**para 7.131**].
3   LA 1980, Sch 1, para 4. See *Tichborne v Weir* (1892) 67 LT 735 at 737; *St Marylebone Property Co Ltd v Fairweather* [1963] AC 510 at 537 per Lord Radcliffe, 544, 548 per Lord Denning, 553–554 per Lord Morris of Borth-y-Gest; *Chung Ping Kwan v Lam Island Co Ltd* [1997] AC 38 at 46E–F per Lord Nicholls of Birkenhead. See also *Gioukouros v Cadillac Fairview Corp Ltd* (1984) 3 DLR (4th) 595 at 605–609.
4   *Chung Ping Kwan v Lam Island Co Ltd* [1997] AC 38 at 46E. See also *Perry v Woodfarm Homes Ltd* [1975] IR 104 at 120; *Gioukouros v Cadillac Fairview Corp Ltd* (1984) 3 DLR (4th) 595 at 605.
5   In this sense the freeholder can achieve 'bulletproof' protection (see Richard A Epstein, 64 Wash ULQ 793 at 838–839 (1986)).

Surrender of the dispossessed tenant's term

6.83   Where a tenant's right to recover possession from a squatter becomes statute-barred, the landlord may seek to accelerate his own right to possession against the squatter by colluding with the tenant in a premature surrender of the tenant's leasehold estate to the landlord.[1] This strategy succeeded, controversially,[2] in *St Marylebone Property Co Ltd v Fairweather*[3] where a majority in the House of Lords held the landlord to be entitled to recover possession from the squatter, on the ground that the latter's possession had defeated only the tenant's 'title' to the leasehold estate and not the 'estate' itself, with which, as against his landlord, the tenant remained free to deal.[4]

1   **[Para 7.305]**.
2   See e g *Perry v Woodfarm Homes Ltd* [1975] IR 104 at 114, 119, 130–131. In *Chung Ping Kwan v Lam Island Co Ltd* [1997] AC 38 at 47E, the Judicial Committee of the Privy Council declined to comment on the correctness of the decision in *St Marylebone Property Co Ltd v Fairweather*.
3   [1963] AC 510 at 540–543, 548. See (1962) 78 LQR 541 (H W R Wade); and compare *Walter v Yalden* [1902] 2 KB 304 at 309–310.
4   See the explanation of the *Fairweather* case provided by Browne-Wilkinson J in *Spectrum Investment Co v Holmes* [1981] 1 WLR 221 at 226B–D.

Registered titles

6.84   In the case of leasehold or freehold titles which are already registered, no period of adverse possession can in itself extinguish any current estate proprietor's title.[1] Possession by the squatter does not cause time to run against the registered proprietor, but merely opens up the opportunity for the squatter to apply to take over the relevant registered leasehold and freehold titles.

1   LRA 2002, s 96(1), (3) **[para 6.55]**.

Registration as proprietor of the leasehold title

6.85   Where throughout an immediately preceding ten-year period a squatter has been in adverse possession of registered leasehold land, the squatter becomes entitled to apply to be registered as the new proprietor of the registered leasehold estate.[1] This application may – and almost certainly will – be defeated by objection from the current registered proprietor of that estate (or, indeed, from the proprietor of any superior registered estate or from any registered chargee).[2] If, however, the application succeeds (or if the applicant is not ejected from the land during the two years next following the rejection of his application), the squatter is entitled to be entered in the Land Register as the new proprietor of the registered leasehold estate.[3] He takes, in effect, as an assignee of the leasehold estate and is therefore bound by the covenants and obligations of the lease.[4]

1   LRA 2002, Sch 6, para 1(1) **[para 6.56]**.

2   LRA 2002, Sch 6, paras 2–5 [**para 6.59**].
3   LRA 2002, Sch 6, paras 6–7 [**para 6.60**].
4   See LRA 2002, Sch 6, para 9(2).

Registration as proprietor of the freehold title

6.86   Even if registered as proprietor of the leasehold title, the squatter is still some distance from being able to claim that his adverse possession is effective against the owner of the freehold estate (ie the landlord). It is only at the termination of the lease that the squatter may begin to mount an assault on the freehold title. A further ten years of adverse possession would entitle the squatter or his successor to apply for registration in place of the proprietor of a registered fee simple estate (although this application is, of course, again subject to arbitrary rebuttal by simple objection).[1] Alternatively, if the freehold estate has never yet been registered, the squatter would be required to show a further twelve years of adverse possession.

1   LRA 2002, Sch 6, paras 2–5 [**para 6.59**].

Surrender of the dispossessed tenant's term

6.87   Where a squatter has already taken over a registered leasehold estate (following a successful application for his own registration as proprietor), the dispossessed former proprietor of that estate cannot accelerate his landlord's right to possession against the squatter by a collusive surrender to the landlord. In such circumstances, which are quite different from those raised in *St Maryle-bone Property Co Ltd v Fairweather*,[1] the former tenant retains no estate which he can possibly surrender.[2] It is equally obvious that, unless and until the squatter successfully applies for registration as proprietor of the leasehold title at Land Registry, the current registered proprietor can (irrespective of the duration of the adverse possession) bring his own proceedings to recover possession from the intruder.[3] In this case the squatter will have failed to obtain title to any estate, whether leasehold or freehold.

1   [1963] AC 510 [**para 6.83**].
2   Compare, in effect, the reasoning of Browne-Wilkinson J in *Spectrum Investment Co v Holmes* [1981] 1 WLR 221 at 230E–231C.
3   [**Para 3.35**].

ADVERSE POSSESSION IN RELATION TO LAND HELD ON TRUST

6.88   Specially adapted rules of adverse possession regulate the position where land is held on trust.[1] The principle of statutory limitation of rights of recovery applies to equitable interests in land in much the same way as to legal estates,[2] but subject always to the proviso that a trustee's title to trust land is never extinguished by reason of a stranger's adverse possession until the rights of all the trust beneficiaries have been barred.[3] Adverse possession of trust land by a trustee himself can never bar the claims of beneficiaries,[4] except where the trustee is also a beneficiary and has acted 'honestly and reasonably' in making a distribution of trust property between himself and other beneficiaries.[5] Nor can adverse possession by a beneficiary (other than a beneficiary who is solely and absolutely entitled) bar the title of his trustee.[6]

1   On the trust of land, see **[para 9.172]**.
2   LA 1980, s 18(1). (The same right of action for recovery is treated as accruing to a beneficiary in possession as if he held a legal estate.)
3   LA 1980, s 18(2)–(4).
4   LA 1980, s 21(1). For this purpose a trustee includes a personal representative (LA 1980, s 38(1), TA 1925, s 68(17)) and an executor *de son tort* who, although not a personal representative, intermeddles with the administration of a deceased's property and thereby attracts the liability of a constructive trustee (see *James v Williams* [2000] Ch 1 at 10C–11A). Compare *Pollard v Jackson* (1994) 67 P & CR 327 at 329–332. The prohibition of adverse possession by a trustee also prevents time from running against a purchaser under an uncompleted, but specifically enforceable, contract of sale (see *Rhondda Cynon Taff County BC v Watkins* (Chancery Division, 11 December 2001) per Neuberger J).
5   LA 1980, s 21(2).
6   LA 1980, Sch 1, para 9. A purchaser in possession under an uncompleted contract of sale of land may, of course, plead the effluxion of time against a vendor who has been fully paid (see e g *Bridges v Mees* [1957] Ch 475 at 484–486). In such circumstances the vendor has become a bare trustee and no longer holds any beneficial entitlement in the land (*Lloyds Bank plc v Carrick* [1996] 4 All ER 630 at 637j per Morritt LJ **[para 9.33]**).

Co-ownership interests under a trust

6.89   It is a fundamental principle that co-beneficiaries under a trust of land can never assert adverse possession against each other. The Limitation Act 1980 clearly provides that no right of action accrues in favour of any trustee or beneficiary while trust land is 'in the possession of a person entitled to a beneficial interest in the land or in the proceeds of sale.'[1] Accordingly, in the absence of a right of action, time cannot begin to run against a co-beneficiary who enjoys possession of the trust land.[2]

1   LA 1980, Sch 1, para 9. The same principle applies as between successively entitled beneficiaries.
2   This 'doctrine of non-adverse possession amongst beneficial co-owners of land' has been extended to preclude a claim of adverse possession by the beneficiary of an unadministered estate (see *Earnshaw v Hartley* [2000] Ch 155 at 160G–161C per Nourse LJ). This result follows even though the claimant possessor is not strictly entitled to any beneficial interest in land or its proceeds, but merely to the proper administration of the estate concerned (see *Commissioner of Stamp Duties (Queensland) v Livingston* [1965] AC 694).

Successive interests under a trust or settlement

6.90   Where land is held in trust for successively entitled beneficiaries (e g a tenant for life (X) and a remainderman (Y)), the completion of twelve years of adverse possession by a stranger against X normally bars X's equitable interest under the trust or settlement concerned. However, this adverse possession can have no definitive effect upon Y's interest as remainderman while X is still alive. On X's death Y is allowed a further six years within which to bring proceedings for the recovery of the land from the squatting stranger.[1] If X's death intervened before the stranger's completion of the twelve year period, Y's own interest is not barred until the expiry of that twelve year period or until the end of six years following X's death, whichever occurs later.[2]

1   LA 1980, s 15(2).
2   LA 1980, s 15(2). Thus, if the adverse possession commenced four years before X's death, Y has eight years from X's death to oust the squatter. If, however, such possession commenced 10 years before X's death, Y still has six years from X's death within which to recover the land.

THE INCEPTION OF A NEW (AND ADVERSE) POSSESSION

6.91   Although possession is the historic root of title,[1] an unbarred title does not require to be supported by continuous possession or enjoyment of the land. There is 'no concept in English law of the abandonment of title to land',[2] a proposition richly reinforced by the new statutory principle that the lapse of time can never, in itself, extinguish a registered proprietor's title.[3] The paper owner is, accordingly, under no obligation to make use of his land. His title cannot be lost through mere neglect; his possession is not deemed to have been discontinued simply because the land is left empty, unoccupied or derelict.[4]

1   [Paras 3.23, 6.2].
2   *Ironmonger v Bernard International* (*Estate Division*) (Unreported, Court of Appeal, 9 February 1996) per Millett LJ.
3   [Para 6.55].
4   *Williams Brothers Direct Supply Ltd v Raftery* [1958] 1 QB 159 at 170–173; *Railtrack plc v Hutchinson* (Unreported, Chancery Division, 17 December 1998); *Riley v Penttila* [1974] VR 547 at 562.

Requirement of a new possession

6.92   There is, therefore, no necessity for a paper owner to assert any claim to his land unless and until someone else enters into adverse possession.[1] Without this element of a *new* possession asserted by an intruder there is no right of action in the paper owner which can possibly be defeated either through the effluxion of time or otherwise.[2]

1   *MacDonell v M & M Developments Ltd* (1998) 157 DLR (4th) 240 at 252.
2   See *Hughes v Cork* [1994] EGCS 25.

Unregistered land

6.93   The Limitation Act 1980 makes it clear that, in unregistered land, an estate owner's rights begin to be at risk only when the land comes into 'the possession of some person in whose favour the period of limitation can run.'[1]

Thus the limitation period is triggered only by a possession which is 'adverse' to the owner, ie only when a squatter has possession and the owner does not.[2] Even then title to an unregistered estate cannot be prejudiced by simple delay in complaining about the stranger's intrusion.[3] The paper owner's title is statutorily extinguished only on the expiration of the relevant limitation period.

1   LA 1980, Sch 1, para 8(1).
2   See *J A Pye (Oxford) Ltd v Graham* [2000] Ch 676 at 695A–B per Neuberger J.
3   *Jones v Stones* [1999] 1 WLR 1739 at 1745G–1746A per Aldous LJ.

Registered land

6.94   The same premise applies, albeit circuitously by way of statutory fiction, to the loss of title to a registered estate. Although the Land Registration Act 2002 provides that no period of limitation can run against the proprietor of a registered estate,[1] a squatter is deemed to be in 'adverse possession' of an estate in land if, but for this statutory prohibition, time would run in his favour under the Limitation Act.[2] But, even here, the adverse possessor's claim to take over the registered estate may be – and normally will be – defeated on objection by the registered proprietor or other interested persons.[3]

1   LRA 2002, s 96(1) **[para 6.55]**.
2   LRA 2002, Sch 6, para 11(1). See *J A Pye (Oxford) Ltd v Graham* [2003] 1 AC 347 at [68] per Lord Hope of Craighead.
3   **[Para 6.59]**.

Requirement of an adverse possession

6.95   Adverse possession thus involves two elements: a loss of possession by the paper owner and a taking of possession by the adverse possessor.[1] A claimant of title by possession must show[2] either a 'dispossession' (or 'ouster') of the paper owner or a 'discontinuance by the paper owner followed by possession.'[3] As Nourse LJ conceded in *Buckinghamshire CC v Moran*,[4] the distinction between these two kinds of event is 'a very fine one.'[5] The constitutive elements of adverse possession do not vary between dispossession and discontinuance.[6]

1   *J A Pye (Oxford) Ltd v Graham* [2003] 1 AC 419 at [69] per Lord Hope of Craighead.
2   The burden of proof rests on the claimant (see eg *Bolton MBC v Qasmi* (Unreported, Court of Appeal, 3 December 1998)).
3   *Treloar v Nute* [1976] 1 WLR 1295 at 1300E per Sir John Pennycuick. See similarly *Buckinghamshire CC v Moran* [1990] Ch 623 at 635H per Slade LJ, 644E per Nourse LJ; *Stacey v Gardner* [1994] CLY 568.
4   [1990] Ch 623 at 644F–G.
5   Nourse LJ referred also ([1990] Ch 623 at 645B) to the 'confusion' between the concepts of dispossession and discontinuance which is found in some of the decided cases. However, the distinction is usually immaterial (see eg *Hughes v Cork* [1994] EGCS 25 per Beldam LJ).
6   *Buckinghamshire CC v Moran* [1990] Ch 623 at 644H–645A per Nourse LJ; *Smith v Waterman* [2003] All ER (D) 72 (Jun) at [18] per Blackburne J.

DISPOSSESSION OF THE PAPER OWNER

6.96   'Dispossession' (or 'ouster') has been said to occur where a squatter 'comes in and drives out the true owner from possession.'[1] At least in relation to large tracts of land, true cases of dispossession are nowadays somewhat rare,[2] although the extrusion of a paper owner (and particularly a corporate or local authority owner) can sometimes occur even without its knowledge.[3] Dispossession typically arises on a smaller scale where, for instance, one neighbour, A, repositions a boundary fence so as to enclose part of the land belonging to his neighbour, B. Here the relevant period of adverse possession runs from the date of B's dispossession.[4]

1   *Buckinghamshire CC v Moran* [1990] Ch 623 at 644F per Nourse LJ, following *Rains v Buxton* (1880) 14 Ch D 537 at 539–540 per Fry J.
2   For modern instances of dispossession, see *Buckinghamshire CC v Moran* [1990] Ch 623; *J A Pye (Oxford) Ltd v Graham* [2003] 1 AC 419.
3   See e g *Buckinghamshire CC v Moran* [1990] Ch 623 [**para 6.103**]; *Lambeth LBC v Blackburn* (2001) 82 P & CR 494 [**para 6.138**].
4   LA 1980, Sch 1, para 1.

6.97   The terminology of 'ouster' and 'adverseness' of possession has nowadays fallen into some disfavour, largely because it seems to carry 'overtones of confrontational, knowing removal of the true owner from possession.'[1] In *J A Pye (Oxford) Ltd v Graham*,[2] Lord Browne-Wilkinson was content to adopt a more neutral or objective test of 'dispossession', opining that

'much confusion and complication would be avoided if reference to adverse possession were to be avoided so far as possible ... The question is simply whether the defendant squatter has dispossessed the paper owner by going into ordinary possession of the land for the requisite period without the consent of the owner.'

1   *J A Pye (Oxford) Ltd v Graham* [2003] 1 AC 419 at [38] per Lord Browne-Wilkinson. See also Lord Hope of Craighead (at [69]) (no implication of 'any element of aggression, hostility or subterfuge').
2   [2003] 1 AC 419 at [36].

6.98   Lord Browne-Wilkinson was accordingly prepared to apply the notion of 'dispossession' to all cases (other than those of 'discontinuance') where a squatter simply 'assumes possession in the ordinary sense of the word.'[1] On this analysis, 'dispossession' plainly catches the circumstances exemplified in *J A Pye (Oxford) Ltd v Graham* itself.[2] Here, following the expiration of G's written grazing licence over P's potentially valuable development land, P had repeatedly refused a request for renewal of the grazing agreement. G nevertheless continued, for over twelve years, to use the land for agricultural purposes in the self-confessed hope that a formal agreement authorising his use would be forthcoming. During this period the land was accessible only through a gate kept padlocked by G, who effectively farmed the disputed area as a unit with his own adjoining land. The House of Lords upheld G's claim to have taken title by adverse possession, not least because G and his family had '[f]or all practical purposes ... used the land as their own and in a way normal for an owner to use it.'³ By remaining on the land in the face of the clearest evidence that the original permission to be present had terminated without renewal, they had acted 'in a way which, to their knowledge, was directly contrary to the wishes of the proprietors.'⁴ G and his family had, in short, done 'everything which an owner of the land would have done' and indeed, said Lord Hutton, it was difficult to think of anything more that the 'occupying owner of the disputed land might have done' to demonstrate his possession.⁵

1   [2003] 1 AC 419 at [38].
2   [2003] 1 AC 419. See [2003] CLJ 36 (L Tee); [2002] Conv 480 (M P Thompson); All ER Rev 2002, pp 226–227 (P J Clarke).
3   [2003] 1 AC 419 at [61] per Lord Browne-Wilkinson.
4   [2003] 1 AC 419 at [59] per Lord Browne-Wilkinson.
5   [2003] 1 AC 419 at [75] per Lord Hutton.

DISCONTINUANCE OF POSSESSION BY THE PAPER OWNER

6.99   Except in cases of 'dispossession', a claim of adverse possession can succeed only if it can be shown that there was a 'discontinuance'¹ or 'abandonment'² of possession by the paper owner followed by the inception of a new 'possession' on the part of an adverse occupier.³ 'Discontinuance' of possession therefore occurs where the true owner 'goes out of possession and is followed in by the squatter.'⁴ A typical instance of discontinued possession occurs where B carelessly repositions a boundary fence so as to exclude part of his own land in favour of his neighbour, A, who then begins to use the land as his own.⁵ In cases of discontinuance, the relevant period of adverse possession runs from the date of the inception of the new possession.⁶

1   For the inevitable consequence of failure to show a 'discontinuance', see *Maguire v Browne* (1913) 17 CLR 365 at 368–369.
2   See *Milton v Proctor* (1988) 4 BPR 9654 at 9657 per McHugh JA, 9663–9664 per Clarke JA.
3   *Hounslow LBC v Minchinton* (1997) 74 P & CR 221 at 232–233.
4   *Buckinghamshire CC v Moran* [1990] Ch 623 at 644F per Nourse LJ.
5   See eg *Hounslow LBC v Minchinton* (1997) 74 P & CR 221.
6   LA 1980, Sch 1, paras 1, 8(1).

Presumption of continued possession

6.100   Any claim based on an alleged 'discontinuance' of possession requires, in its turn, the rebuttal of a fairly heavy presumption that possession is retained either by the paper owner or by some person who claims through him.¹ In the absence of persuasive evidence to the contrary, the owner of the paper title is deemed to remain in possession.² Intermittent acts of control by the paper owner merely serve to reinforce this presumption.³ The slightest acts done by or on behalf of the paper owner will generally negative any supposed 'discontinuance' of his own possession.⁴ Continuing possession may even be asserted on behalf of the paper owner through the proxy occupation of persons such as relatives.[5] Moreover, in the case of large areas of land the paper owner is regarded as maintaining constructive possession even if he is not in actual possession of the whole of the land.[6]

1   *Powell v McFarlane* (1977) 38 P & CR 452 at 470; *J A Pye (Oxford) Ltd v Graham* [2003] 1 AC 419 at [70] per Lord Hope of Craighead. See also *Re Lundrigans Ltd and Prosper* (1982) 132 DLR (3d) 727 at 731.
2   See eg *Morrice v Evans* (1989) Times, 27 February. See also *Rimmer v Pearson* (2000) 79 P & CR D21 at D22 per Robert Walker LJ ('Neighbours should not be encouraged to conduct themselves in such a way that it is necessary for adjoining owners to defend every last inch of territory or to lose it').
3   Thus, for instance, there is no 'abandonment' of possession where the paper owner has persisted in denying entry to a particular named person (see *Milton v Proctor* (1988) 4 BPR 9654 at 9657 per McHugh JA, 9663–9664 per Clarke JA). See also *Brackenbank Lodge Ltd v Peart* (1993) 67 P & CR 249 at 261–262.
4   *Williams Brothers Direct Supply Ltd v Raftery* [1958] 1 QB 159 at 171; *Powell v McFarlane* (1977) 38 P & CR 452 at 472 per Slade J; *Lambeth LBC v Blackburn* (2001) 82 P & CR 494 at [19] per Clarke LJ. See *Re St Clair Beach Estates Ltd v MacDonald* (1975) 50 DLR (3d) 650 at 656; *Masidon Investments Ltd v Ham* (1983) 39 OR (2d) 534 at 553–554.
5   *Milton v Proctor* (1988) 4 BPR 9654 at 9664.
6   See *Fletcher v Storoschuk* (1981) 128 DLR (3d) 59 at 62; *Masidon Investments Ltd v Ham* (1983) 39 OR (2d) 534 at 545d.

Dormant possession

6.101   It is not normally difficult to determine whether there has been either a 'dispossession' or a 'discontinuance' of the possession of the paper owner of land. More problematic, however, are those cases where a paper owner allows his land to lie dormant for the time being whilst intending to put the land to some specific use in the future.

The rule in Leigh v Jack

6.102   It used to be thought that such circumstances were, as a matter of law, governed by a special rule adumbrated by Bramwell LJ in *Leigh v Jack*.[1] Under this rule the 'possession' of the original paper owner was regarded as wholly undisturbed by the acts of a squatter, no matter how continuous and far-reaching these acts might be, so long as the squatter's conduct did not substantially interfere with any plans which the paper owner might have for the future use of the land.[2] On this basis even extensive and significant possessory acts by the intruder did not derogate from or destroy the continuing possession of the paper owner – provided only that they remained compatible with the specific future use intended by the latter.[3] In more recent times the significance accorded to the paper owner's internal reservations has fallen away with the increasing recognition that it is 'heretical and wrong' to suppose that the sufficiency of the relevant possession is governed by the intention of the paper owner rather than that of the squatter.[4]

1   (1879) 5 Ex D 264 at 273.

2   This approach was conveniently rationalised by reference to the theory that the intruder's
    presence could be attributed to some implied licence granted by the paper owner **[para 6.117]**.
3   See eg *Wallis's Cayton Bay Holiday Camp Ltd v Shell-Mex and BP Ltd* [1975] QB 94 at 103D
    per Lord Denning MR. It has since been said that many of the decisions and dicta in support
    of *Leigh v Jack* were referable to 'a time when many plots of waste land had been brought
    under the spade in digging for victory during the Second World War and afterwards' (see
    Buckinghamshire CC v Moran [1990] Ch 623 at 646E–F per Nourse LJ). It may be that by 1976
    Bramwell LJ's dictum had – albeit wrongly – 'assumed the dignity of a special rule'.
4   See *J A Pye (Oxford) Ltd v Graham* [2003] 1 AC 419 at [45] per Lord Browne-Wilkinson; *Wills
    v Wills* [2004] 1 P & CR 612 at [29] per Lord Walker of Gestingthorpe.

Disavowal of the rule

6.103   The *Leigh v Jack* presumption against the disturbance of the paper
owner's possession was finally 'exploded'[1] by the decision of the Court of
Appeal in *Buckinghamshire CC v Moran.*[2] Here a local authority had acquired a
plot of land, which it left undeveloped for the purpose of a future highway
improvement. Over the following 30 years a neighbouring landowner began to
maintain the plot as an annexe to his garden and his successor in title installed
a lock and chain which rendered the plot accessible only from his own land.[3]
Both were well aware that the local authority had plans for the future use of the
land. The Court of Appeal nevertheless ruled that the enclosure of the disputed
plot and its effective annexation to the squatter's house constituted an assertion
of 'complete and exclusive physical control' sufficient to found a successful plea
of adverse possession.[4] Slade LJ thought it much too broad a proposition 'to
suggest that an owner who retains a piece of land with a view to its utilisation
for a specific purpose in the future can never be treated as dispossessed,
however firm and obvious the intention to dispossess, and however drastic the
acts of dispossession of the person seeking to dispossess him may be.'[5]

1   See *Hounslow LBC v Minchinton* (1997) 74 P & CR 221 at 227 per Millett LJ.
2   [1990] Ch 623. Vestiges of the *Leigh v Jack* principle persist in other jurisdictions which rule
    out adverse possession if the particular manner or degree of the claimant's occupation has
    deprived the paper owner of only those uses of his own land which he never intended or
    desired to exploit (see eg *Keefer v Arillotta* (1977) 72 DLR (3d) 182 at 193; *Masidon
    Investments Ltd v Ham* (1983) 39 OR (2d) 534 at 550–553).
3   Christopher Moran, the defendant in the action for possession, is a former Lloyd's broker who
    regularly features in lists of Britain's most wealthy.
4   [1990] Ch 623 at 641B per Slade LJ.
5   [1990] Ch 623 at 639A.

6.104   The Court of Appeal agreed in *Moran*'s case that where a paper owner
harbours intentions for the future use of his land, a discontinuance of possession can indeed be prevented 'by the slightest acts of ownership on his part,
even by none at all'.[1] The paper owner can be dispossessed only if 'the squatter
performs sufficient acts and has a sufficient intention to constitute adverse
possession.'[2] Particularly is this the case where (as in *Moran*) the squatter is at
all times well aware of the paper owner's plans for future development.[3] In such
circumstances 'very clear evidence' of possessory acts and intentions is required
before a claim of adverse possession can succeed.[4] In *Moran*'s case, however, the

squatter had amply manifested such conduct and intentions, most relevantly and unequivocally by placing the new lock and chain on the gate to the disputed area.[5]

1   [1990] Ch 623 at 644G per Nourse LJ.
2   [1990] Ch 623 at 644H per Nourse LJ.
3   In rare circumstances a squatter's knowledge of the paper owner's intentions for future use may derogate from *animus* ([1990] Ch 623 at 640E per Slade LJ, 645A–B per Nourse LJ [**para 6.138**]). See likewise *J A Pye (Oxford) Ltd v Graham* [2003] 1 AC 419 at [45] per Lord Browne-Wilkinson.
4   [1990] Ch 623 at 639H–640A per Slade LJ. See also *Hounslow LBC v Minchinton* (1997) 74 P & CR 221 at 229.
5   See [1990] Ch 623 at 642D–F per Slade LJ. It may well be that, unless the claimant has actually enclosed and secured the disputed land, the courts will be slow to make a finding of adverse possession in cases where the paper owner has reserved some future intentions for use (see [1990] Ch 623 at 643G–H per Slade LJ, 645F–G, 646D per Nourse LJ).

THE MEANING OF ADVERSE POSSESSION

6.105   In the case of both dispossession and discontinuance of possession, the element of possessory control which activates the statute of limitation bears a heavily specialised meaning. The constituent features of adverse possession were recently the subject of a comprehensive review by the House of Lords in *JA Pye (Oxford) Ltd v Graham*,[1] a decision which now colours much of the law in this area.

1   [2003] 1 AC 419 [**para 6.98**].

6.106   As was confirmed in *J A Pye (Oxford) Ltd v Graham*,[1] the legal concept of 'possession' is an amalgam of externally verifiable physical and mental components: both elements are required.[2] The phenomenon of 'possession' involves much more than bare factual presence on land: it comprises a particular mindset in relation to the power conferred by such presence.[3] And 'possession' requires more than a mere declaration of intention, however plain that declaration may be.[4] 'Possession' is attributed to the squatter (and his possession is 'adverse') only if he has both factual possession (*factum possessionis*) and the requisite intention to possess (*animus possidendi*).[5] These elements of *factum* and *animus* interact heavily.[6] The squatter must have a 'subjective intention to possess the land but he must also show by his outward conduct that that was his intention.'[7] In practice, as Lord Hope of Craighead indicated in the *Pye* case,[8] 'the best evidence of intention is frequently found in the acts which have taken place.'

1   [2003] 1 AC 419 at [40] per Lord Browne-Wilkinson, [70] per Lord Hope of Craighead, [74] per Lord Hutton.
2   See *J A Pye (Oxford) Ltd v Graham* [2003] 1 AC 419 at [70] per Lord Hope of Craighead.
3   [**Para 3.3**]. It is this highly qualified (but historically accurate) sense of 'possession' which distinguishes the squatter from the mere persistent trespasser (see *Hunter v Canary Wharf Ltd* [1997] AC 655 at 703F per Lord Hoffmann) and the novel category of the 'tolerated trespasser' (see *Burrows v Brent LBC* [1996] 1 WLR 1448 at 1455C per Lord Browne-Wilkinson [**para 7.155**]). See also *Stacey v Gardner* [1994] CLY 568.

4   *Simpson v Fergus* (2000) 79 P & CR 398 at 402 per Robert Walker LJ.
5   *Powell v McFarlane* (1977) 38 P & CR 452 at 470 per Slade J; *J A Pye (Oxford) Ltd v Graham*
    [2003] 1 AC 419 at [40] per Lord Browne-Wilkinson, [70] per Lord Hope of Craighead, [74]
    per Lord Hutton.
6   See *J A Pye (Oxford) Ltd v Graham* [2003] 1 AC 419 at [70] per Lord Hope of Craighead.
7   *Prudential Assurance Co Ltd v Waterloo Real Estate Inc* [1999] 2 EGLR 85 at 87G per Peter
    Gibson LJ. See *Inglewood Investment Co Ltd v Baker* [2003] 2 P & CR 319 at [21], [33] per
    Aldous LJ (distinguishing between the 'objective' and 'subjective' elements of *animus possi-
    dendi*).
8   [2003] 1 AC 419 at [70].

FACTUAL POSSESSION

6.107 The factual possession required of the adverse possessor is of a
significantly qualified kind. His possession must be 'open, not secret; peaceful,
not by force; and adverse, not by consent of the true owner.'[1] In another
compendious statement it has been said that possession must be 'actual, open,
continuous and exclusive (and, of course, without the licence of the documentary owner).'[2]

1   *Mulcahy v Curramore Pty Ltd* [1974] 2 NSWLR 464 at 475D per Bowen CJ in Eq. There is a
    clear link with the formula *nec vi, nec clam, nec precario* which dominates the prescriptive
    acquisition of easements and profits *à prendre* **[para 8.177]** (see *Shaw v Garbutt* (1996) 7 BPR
    14816 at 14828 per Young J). See also *Cooke v Dunn* (1998) 9 BPR 16489 at 16502 per Santow
    J.
2   *Shaw v Garbutt* (1996) 7 BPR 14816 at 14827 per Young J. See also *Browne v Perry* [1991]
    1 WLR 1297 at 1302A per Lord Templeman (adverse possession 'must be peaceable and
    open').

Possession must be exclusive

6.108 Exclusive possession is of the essence of all claims to freehold or
leasehold estate ownership in English law.[1] In the context of adverse possession,
this criterion embodies, in part, the idea that the squatter must reserve the right
to exclude all others from the land occupied.[2] The claimant's possession must
be a 'single and exclusive possession',[3] although it is possible that a single
possession can be 'exercised by or on behalf of several persons jointly.'[4] The
concerted and collective actions of members of a council house 'squat' can
comprise a sufficient *factum possessionis*,[5] but a possession which is, for
instance, exercised at different times by several members of one family cannot
grow into a possessory title for one of those family members alone.[6] In the
absence of a prior agreement or arrangement that possession is being exercised
on behalf of others, it is difficult for isolated acts of user by members of an
amorphous group to be regarded as some form of joint possession.[7]

1   **[Paras 3.18, 7.3, 7.131]**.
2   See e g *Battersea Freehold & Leasehold Property Co Ltd v Wandsworth LBC* (2001) 82 P & CR
    137 at [12], [18]–[20] (squatter's distribution of keys to third parties negatived any claim of
    unequivocal intention to exclude the world at large from the disputed land).
3   *J A Pye (Oxford) Ltd v Graham* [2003] 1 AC 419 at [38], [41] per Lord Browne-Wilkinson. For

emphasis of the necessary exclusiveness of this possession, see *Clement v Jones* (1909) 8 CLR 133 at 139 per Griffith CJ; *Attorney-General of Canada v Acadia Forest Products Ltd* (1988) 41 DLR (4th) 338 at 343; *Simpson v Fergus* (2000) 79 P & CR 398 at 401.

4   *Powell v McFarlane* (1977) 38 P & CR 452 at 470 per Slade J. See likewise *J A Pye (Oxford) Ltd v Graham* [2003] 1 AC 419 at [38] per Lord Browne-Wilkinson. For an instance of joint possession, see *Newington v Windeyer* (1985) 3 NSWLR 555 at 564A–C (adverse possession by group of neighbours united by a common purpose). An extreme example was posited by Toohey J in *Mabo v Queensland (No 2)* (1992) 175 CLR 1 at 214 (adverse possession by the Meriam people).

5   *Ellis v Lambeth LBC* (1999) 32 HLR 596 at 598.

6   *Morris v Pinches* (1969) 212 EG 1141.

7   See e g *Brown v Faulkner* [2003] NICA 5(2) at [33]–[34] per Higgins J (no adverse possession by 'a wider family circle comprising two distinct families with no common focal point').

Possession must be continuous

6.109   The squatter's possession must demonstrate a continuity in respect of both *factum possessionis* and *animus possidendi*.[1] It is not fatal to a possessory claim that the acts of adverse user are intermittent in character,[2] but they must be marked by consistency and regularity.[3] The possession of the squatter may, for instance, be terminated, and possession regained by the documentary owner, if the latter places other persons in occupation of the land during the currency of the period claimed as adverse.[4]

1   *Railtrack plc v Hutchinson* (Unreported, Chancery Division, 17 December 1998). See LA 1980, Sch 1, para 8(2).

2   See *Bligh v Martin* [1968] 1 WLR 804 at 811F–G; *Smith v Waterman* [2003] All ER (D) 72 (Jun) at [61]; *Mulcahy v Curramore Pty Ltd* [1974] 2 NSWLR 464 at 475F.

3   See e g *Trustees of Michael Batt Charitable Trust v Adams* (2001) 82 P & CR 406 at [17] (seasonal crops of hay).

4   See *Cooke v Dunn* (1998) 9 BPR 16489 at 16510.

Possession must be open

6.110   The possession which founds a claim of adverse possession must be open, notorious and unconcealed.[1] It must be such that it would be noticed by a documentary owner 'reasonably careful of his own interests.'[2] This requirement of visibility or transparency[3] ensures that the paper owner is given every opportunity of challenging the possession before it can mature as a threat to his own title.[4] Indeed an element of openness provides critical reinforcement for claims of adverse possession,[5] while fraud or concealment simply precludes the inception of adverse possession until such time as the paper owner could, with reasonable diligence, have discovered the presence of either.[6]

1   *Lord Advocate v Lord Lovat* (1880) 5 App Cas 273 at 291, 296; *McConaghy v Denmark* (1880) 4 SCR 609 at 632–633; *Sherren v Pearson* (1887) 14 SCR 581 at 585; *Hamson v Jones* (1989) 52 DLR (4th) 143 at 153. The requirement of open user did not, however, prevent adverse possession of an underground cellar in *Rains v Buxton* (1880) 14 Ch D 537 at 539–540. Here Fry J noted that the door into the cellar had been 'quite visible to anybody', and that there had been no concealment of user even though such user 'from its very nature ... was not perhaps a thing at all times necessarily seen.' See also *Purbrick v Hackney LBC* [2004] 1 P & CR 553 at [25]–[26] per Neuberger J.

2　*Re Riley and the Real Property Act* [1965] NSWR 994 at 1001 per McLelland CJ in Eq. The unconcealed conduct of repair and maintenance work should alert the documentary owner (see *Cooke v Dunn* (1998) 9 BPR 16489 at 16505–16506).

3　See eg *Re Lundrigans Ltd and Prosper* (1982) 132 DLR (3d) 727 at 729–731, where the Newfoundland Court of Appeal rejected a claim of adverse possession based on the presence in a wilderness area of two log cabins which were not visible either from the ground or from the air. See also *Marengo Cave Co v Ross*, 10 NE2d 917 at 923 (1937) (no adverse possession of underground cavern).

4　The adverse possessor must 'unfurl his flag on the land, and keep it flying so that the owner may see, if he will, that an enemy has invaded his dominions and planted his standard of conquest' (*The Laird Properties New England Land Syndicate v Mad River Corp*, 305 A2d 562 at 567 per Shangraw CJ (1973)).

5　See eg *Ellis v Lambeth LBC* (1999) 32 HLR 596, where a squatter deliberately drew attention to his occupation of a council house by placing a notice on the front door saying that the property was not empty (*Times*, 22 July 1999). The squatter's failure to make a community charge (ie council tax) return was not regarded as giving rise to any estoppel or concealment (at least where the paper owner had other means of knowledge of his presence). Openness of possession 'has always been considered vis à vis the documentary owners, not authorities' (*Cooke v Dunn* (1998) 9 BPR 16489 at 16505 per Santow J).

6　LA 1980, s 32(1) [**para 6.137**].

Possession must be 'adverse' to the paper owner

6.111　The possession which is relevant under the Limitation Act comprises only that which is truly 'adverse' to the paper owner.

Shared possession is insufficient

6.112　No occupancy which is concurrent with that of the paper owner can found a claim of possessory title.[1] The paper owner and the intruder cannot both be in possession at the same time.[2] Shared user cannot be 'adverse'; nor is it, in the required sense, exclusive to the claimant.

1　*Treloar v Nute* [1976] 1 WLR 1295 at 1300E per Sir John Pennycuick.
2　*Powell v McFarlane* (1977) 38 P & CR 452 at 470. See also *Hamson v Jones* (1989) 52 DLR (4th) 143 at 156.

Possession must be adverse to an effective right of entry

6.113　Possession counts as 'adverse' only if, during the relevant period, the paper owner had available, but did not assert, an effective right of entry against the squatter. Thus, for instance, non-payment of rent by a tenant does not render her continued occupation of premises 'adverse' where her landlord has disabled himself, by conduct amounting to estoppel, from enforcing his right to recover possession for failure to pay that rent.[1]

1　*Smith v Lawson* (1998) 75 P & CR 466 at 470–471. See also *Warren v Murray* [1894] 2 QB 648 at 652–653, 658.

Adverse possession cannot be consensual

6.114   For similar reasons the adverse quality of the possession enjoyed by a claimant is more generally negatived by any consent by the paper owner to the claimant's presence on the land.

Grant of a lease or licence

6.115   Possession is never 'adverse' if enjoyed under a lawful title[1] or by the leave[2] or licence[3] of the paper owner.[4] For example, the presence of a landlord–tenant relationship between the paper owner and the occupier is plainly inconsistent with a claim of adverse possession.[5] Nor can adverse possession stem from other forms of mandate or permission given by the paper owner.[6] Thus no adverse possession arises on the basis of occupation which is exercised at the request or with the consent of the paper owner.[7] The courts have tended, in any event, to guard against the possibility that acts founded on mere 'amity and good neighbourliness' may ripen into some form of unassailable adverse possession.[8] The permission which negatives adverse possession may be present even where it is unaccompanied by any obvious process of offer and acceptance and unsupported by any consideration.[9] Successful squatting is, quite simply, pre-empted by *any* subsisting element of permission from the paper owner,[10] although it is also clear that a licensee whose licence has terminated[11] or expired[12] rapidly acquires the status of an adverse possessor in whose favour time can begin to run.[13]

1   *Buckinghamshire CC v Moran* [1990] Ch 623 at 636G per Slade LJ. See also *Smith v Lawson* (1998) 75 P & CR 466 at 472 per Morritt LJ; *Ramnarace v Lutchman* [2001] 1 WLR 1651 at [10] per Lord Millett. A squatter's possession is not prevented from being adverse merely because the squatter happens, for unconnected reasons, to have some lawful title. Possession ceases to be adverse only if it is possession *under* that lawful title (see eg *Rhondda Cynon Taff County BC v Watkins* [2003] 1 WLR 1864 at [25] per Schiemann LJ).

2   See *Canadian Pacific Ltd v Paul* (1989) 53 DLR (4th) 487 at 501 (Supreme Court of Canada). Rights granted originally as rights of way may, however, enlarge subsequently into a possessory title if the paper owner fails to challenge a different or more extensive user by the grantee which is no longer referable to any lawful right of easement but is wholly inconsistent with such a right (see *Thomas v Thomas* (1855) 2 K & J 79 at 84–86, 69 ER 701 at 703–704; *Keefer v Arillotta* (1977) 72 DLR (3d) 182 at 188–189). See also *Williams v Usherwood* (1983) 45 P & CR 235 at 251.

3   *J A Pye (Oxford) Ltd v Graham* [2003] 1 AC 419 at [37] per Lord Browne-Wilkinson. See, however, LRA 2002, Sch 6, para 5(2), which allows adverse possession to emerge from circumstances in which a permitted occupation of land has generated an 'equity by estoppel' **[para 6.62]**.

4   An exception to this principle occurs where possession which would otherwise be adverse is enjoyed pursuant to an agreement made under a mutual mistake of fact (eg as to the boundary between two properties **[para 6.64]**) (see *Bristow v Mathers* (1991) 74 DLR (4th) 445 at 448). It has also been said that time can run in favour of a tenant at will **[para 7.273]** (see *Nicholl's Estate v Nugent* (1975) 8 Nfld & PEIR 536 at [6], (1975) 12 Nfld & PEIR 377 at [12]; *Belfast CC v Donoghue* [1993] NICG 1117).

5   See *Hayward v Chaloner* [1968] 1 QB 107 at 122C–D; *Colchester BC v Smith* [1991] Ch 448 at 464F, 479E; *Shillabeer v Diebel* (1980) 100 DLR (3d) 279 at 283; *Sauerzweig v Feeney* [1986] IR 224 at 227.

6   If, however, a licensee significantly exceeds the scope of his licence (e g by using the land for purposes markedly different from those covered by the permission), the fact that his initial entry was consensual may not preclude the inception of adverse possession (see *J A Pye (Oxford) Ltd v Graham* [2003] 1 AC 419 at [59] per Lord Browne-Wilkinson **[para 6.98]**).

7   *Bladder v Phillips* [1991] EGCS 109 per Mustill LJ; *Ramnarace v Lutchman* [2001] 1 WLR 1651 at [10] per Lord Millett. Indeed any attempt by a contractual licensee to claim a possessory title may, by denying the licensor's title, constitute a fundamental breach of the contract entitling the licensor to repudiate the agreement (see *Milton v Proctor* (1988) 4 BPR 9654 at 9658 per McHugh JA).

8   See e g *N Allee & Co v David Hodson & Co* [2001] EWCA 951 at [33]–[34] per Clarke LJ (squatter's occupation confirmed as being merely permissive occupation).

9   *Lambeth LBC v Rumbelow* (Chancery Division, 25 January 2001) per Etherton J. See also *BP Properties Ltd v Buckler* (1988) 55 P & CR 337 at 346.

10   *E R Ives Investment Ltd v High* [1967] 2 QB 379 at 396D–E per Lord Denning MR; *Hughes v Griffin* [1969] 1 WLR 23 at 30A, 31G, 32F; *Palfrey v Palfrey* (1974) 229 EG 1593 at 1595; *Wallis's Cayton Bay Holiday Camp Ltd v Shell-Mex and BP Ltd* [1975] QB 94 at 103F–G; *Buckinghamshire CC v Moran* [1990] Ch 623 at 636G–H; *Murphy v Murphy* [1980] IR 183 at 195, 202; *Bellew v Bellew* [1982] IR 447 at 464.

11   See e g *Public Trustee v Bellotti* (1986) 4 BPR 9196 at 9203 (de facto wife's licence to occupy terminated automatically by her partner's death).

12   *Colchester BC v Smith* [1991] Ch 448 at 489E–F; *J A Pye (Oxford) Ltd v Graham* [2003] 1 AC 419 at [59] per Lord Browne-Wilkinson. See also *Sandhu v Farooqui* [2004] 1 P & CR 19 at [23]–[25] (occupation licence for purchaser pending completion not terminated without mutual communication); *Parker v Parker* [2003] EWHC 1846 (Ch) at [281]. It has been suggested that a former licensee may lack a sufficient *animus possidendi* during the immediate aftermath of the expiry of a licence, particularly if he is still negotiating with an apparently willing owner for a renewal of the licence (see *J A Pye (Oxford) Ltd v Graham* [2000] Ch 676 at 706B–D).

13   It has long been a moot point whether a paper owner's permission which subsequently founds a claim of proprietary estoppel can bar the running of a limitation period in respect of unregistered land. For discussion of whether an estoppel claimant can enlarge his rights through a plea of adverse possession, see M Welstead, [1991] Conv 280. The answer in relation to registered land now seems clear (see LRA 2002, Sch 6, para 5(2) **[para 6.62]**).

Willingness to take a lease or licence

6.116   There is nothing inherently inconsistent in a squatter *offering* to take a tenancy or a licence whilst he is still 'clocking up' the required period of adverse possession.[1] Although his offer may, in some circumstances, detract from his ability to demonstrate *animus possidendi*,[2] the offer in itself does not necessarily negative the required intention to possess or connote that the squatter is not in actual possession.[3] In particular, a mere preparedness to take a lease or pay rent[4] or even the adverse possessor's belief that he already has a lease or tenancy[5] is wholly compatible with the claim of possession which underlies the operation of the limitation principle. If anything, such behaviour often serves to confirm that the adverse claimant has the vital *animus* in respect of possession of the land.[6]

1   *J A Pye (Oxford) Ltd v Graham* [2000] Ch 676 at 695G–H, 696G–697B, 706E–G per Neuberger J.

2   *J A Pye (Oxford) Ltd v Graham* [2000] Ch 676 at 695H–696A, 697C–D.

3   See *J A Pye (Oxford) Ltd v Graham* [2000] Ch 676 at 693D ('The mere recognition of the
     owner's ability, if he chooses to exercise it, to reclaim possession is not an acknowledgement
     that the owner actually has possession').
4   See *Ocean Estates Ltd v Pinder* [1969] 2 AC 19 at 24E per Lord Diplock; *J A Pye (Oxford) Ltd
     v Graham* [2003] 1 AC 419 at [46], [60] per Lord Browne-Wilkinson (declaring per incuriam the
     Court of Appeal's contrary indication in *R v Secretary of State for the Environment,
     ex p Davies* (1990) 61 P & CR 487 at 496).
5   See *Lodge v Wakefield MCC* [1995] 2 EGLR 124 at 126L per Balcombe LJ.
6   After all, a lessee or tenant has, by definition, an exclusive possession opposable against the
     world, including even his landlord [**para 7.133**].

No doctrine of implied licence

6.117   For decades the law of adverse possession was stultified by a doctrine
which, as matter of law, attributed the presence of trespassers on unutilised or
vacant land to some implied 'licence or permission of the true owner'.[1] This
doctrine effectively precluded the inception of adverse possession by strangers
who occupied land which the paper owner, having no immediate use, had left
unoccupied.[2] This highly restrictive aspect of the law of limitation was finally
removed in 1980.[3] It is now clear that, in determining whether a person
occupying land is in adverse possession of the land, it is no longer to be
'assumed by implication of law that his occupation is by permission of the
person entitled to the land merely by virtue of the fact that his occupation is
not inconsistent with the latter's present or future enjoyment of the land.'[4]

1   See *Wallis's Cayton Bay Holiday Camp Ltd v Shell-Mex and BP Ltd* [1975] QB 94 at 103F,
     where Lord Denning MR thought that it did not lie in a trespasser's mouth 'to assert that he
     used the land of his own wrong as a trespasser.' Compare *Ramnarace v Lutchman* [2001]
     1 WLR 1651 at [13] per Lord Millett.
2   See likewise *Gray v Wykeham Martin* (Court of Appeal Transcript No 10A of 1977) (claimant
     must have realised that access had been permitted 'as of grace').
3   Limitation Amendment Act 1980, s 4. See also *Buckinghamshire CC v Moran* [1990] Ch 623 at
     646F–G per Nourse LJ for reference to Lord Denning's 'original heresy ... the implied licence
     theory'.
4   LA 1980, Sch 1, para 8(4). It is still open to the courts to apply the concept of the implied
     licence – just as before 1980 – but only where a finding of implied permission is 'justified on
     the actual facts of the case' (para 8(4)). See also Law Reform Committee 21st Report, *Final
     Report on Limitation of Actions* (Cmnd 6923, 1977), paras 3.47–3.52; *Buckinghamshire CC v
     Moran* [1990] Ch 623 at 637D–F, 646F–G.

Family relationships

6.118   There is a tendency to find that any possession exercised by one family
member against another within the context of a loosely organised family
arrangement is not in any real sense 'adverse', but is more realistically attributable to some form of licence, whether express or implied.[1]

1   *Murphy v Murphy* [1980] IR 183 at 195. See e g *Tunley v James* (Unreported, Court of Appeal,
     No 81 03701, 7 April 1982); *Fruin v Fruin* [1983] Court of Appeal Bound Transcript 448; *Re
     Lands situate within the Townlands of Eshywilligan and Bunlougher, County Fermanagh*
     (Unreported, Northern Ireland High Court, 10 April 1992) per Campbell J.

Acknowledgment of title

6.119   The adverse quality of possession is also nullified by certain conduct which confirms the superior title of the paper owner.

Written and signed acknowledgment of title

6.120   Any written acknowledgment of the owner's title signed by a squatter in whose favour time has already begun to run causes the required period of adverse possession to re-commence at the date of the acknowledgment.[1] For this purpose an acknowledgment of title may be constituted by a written offer to purchase the land in question[2] or to take a tenancy or licence.[3] No statutory acknowledgment of title arises merely from an *oral* offer to purchase the land[4] or from an oral request for a licence to use the land,[5] although such action may sometimes assist the paper owner's contention that the squatter did not have the requisite *animus possidendi*.[6] Nor, it seems, is any statutory acknowledgment of title generated by the squatter's application for some entry in the paper owner's register of title.[7]

1   LA 1980, ss 29(1)–(2), 30(1). See e g *Lambeth LBC v Archangel* [2002] 1 P & CR 230 at [14].
2   See *Edginton v Clark* [1964] 1 QB 367 at 376.
3   See *J A Pye (Oxford) Ltd v Graham* [2000] Ch 676 at 696D.
4   See *Shaw v Garbutt* (1996) 7 BPR 14816 at 14826.
5   See *J A Pye (Oxford) Ltd v Graham* [2000] Ch 676 at 696D, 697B–C.
6   See *J A Pye (Oxford) Ltd v Graham* [2000] Ch 676 at 697C–D.
7   See *Urban v Urban Estate* (1994) 155 AR 237 at 240; *Shaw v Garbutt* (1996) 7 BPR 14816 at 14826–14827.

Informal concessions of title

6.121   In some circumstances, other less formal concessions of title may defeat claims of adverse possession on the non-statutory ground that they detract from the *animus possidendi* required of the squatter.[1] Moreover, the courts will not permit a dispossessing trespasser, by proffering damages,[2] to force through what is effectively a purchase of an adverse title on the payment of money compensation.[3]

1   See eg *Basildon DC v Charge* [1996] CLY 4929 (enquiry as to possible purchase). Whether an informal offer of purchase impliedly concedes that the offeree has a better title than the offeror must ultimately depend on a consideration of the whole terms of the offer (*Cawthorne v Thomas* (1993) 6 BPR 13840 at 13845). See also *Shaw v Garbutt* (1996) 7 BPR 14816 at 14826 per Young J.
2   **[Para 3.87]**.
3   *Harrow LBC v Donohue* [1995] 1 EGLR 257 at 259G.

Adverse possession need not be hostile

6.122   Adverse possession operates as an essentially objective process of law. It follows that adverse possession is not necessarily *hostile* possession,[1] except in the sense that the squatter's presence must be 'hostile to the title of the true owner.'[2] Possession may be objectively adverse to the interests of the paper owner without the relevant parties becoming, in any subjective sense, adversaries in respect of the possessory acts which are subsequently a matter of dispute.

1   See *J A Pye (Oxford) Ltd v Graham* [2003] 1 AC 347 at [69] per Lord Hope of Craighead.
2   *Beever v Spaceline Engineering Pty Ltd* (1993) 6 BPR 13270 at 13283 per Bryson J.

Unwitting adverse possession

6.123   It follows that adverse possession may occur through ignorance or mistake, without any understanding of the legal position on the part of *either* the paper owner *or* the adverse possessor.[1] Thus a title may be acquired by adverse possession even though the claimant was unaware of the true ownership of the property or believed that it was already his.[2] Any other approach would reward the wilful trespasser whilst penalising the innocent occupier of land.[3] Indeed the *animus* required of the adverse possessor relates not to ownership of the land at all but rather to the assertion of a 'complete and exclusive physical control' over the land[4] – an assertion which is wholly consistent with an erroneous assumption of entitlement.[5] A plea of adverse possession can therefore succeed even though both parties[6] mistakenly but genuinely believed that the claimant was the true owner of the land and that his entry on that land was therefore 'as of right.'[7] Possession may likewise be asserted adversely to a paper owner who is unaware that title to the land was conveyed to him long ago and that, in reality, he has now been dispossessed.[8]

1   *Rains v Buxton* (1880) 14 Ch D 537 at 540–541; *Wilson v Martin's Executors* [1993] 1 EGLR 178 at 180L; *Prudential Assurance Co Ltd v Waterloo Real Estate Inc* (1998) Times, 13 May, per Park J; *Murphy v Murphy* [1980] IR 183 at 202.
2   *J A Pye (Oxford) Ltd v Graham* [2001] Ch 804 at [34(5)] per Mummery LJ; *Williams v Usherwood* (1983) 45 P & CR 235 at 251 per Cumming-Bruce LJ; *Taylor v Lawrence* [2001] EWCA Civ 119 at [12] per Peter Gibson LJ; *Purbrick v Hackney LBC* [2004] 1 P & CR 553 at [21] per Neuberger J. Compare, however, *Bladder v Phillips* [1991] EGCS 109 per Mustill LJ (question left open). See now LRA 2002, Sch 6, para 5(4) [**para 6.64**].
3   *Hughes v Cork* [1994] EGCS 25 per Saville LJ. See similarly *McGugan and McNeill v Turner* [1948] 2 DLR 338 at 344–346; *Beaudoin v Aubin* (1981) 125 DLR (3d) 277 at 292; *Guild v Mallory* (1983) 144 DLR (3d) 603 at 619. In the law of prescription [**para 8.181**], it has been said that to disallow user based on a mistaken belief effectively confines prescription to someone who 'is aware that he is a wrongdoer' (*Bridle v Ruby* [1989] QB 169 at 177D–E per Parker LJ).
4   *Buckinghamshire CC v Moran* [1990] Ch 623 at 641B per Slade LJ.
5   See *Hughes v Cork* [1994] EGCS 25 per Beldam LJ.
6   Some of the ultimate demonstrations of adverse possession follow from conveyancing muddles or surveying confusions. See e g *McGuinness v Registrar-General* (1998) 44 NSWLR 61 (where two neighbours in Broken Hill mistakenly occupied each other's house for some 50 years); *Howard v Kunto*, 477 P2d 210 (1970) (where each occupier's deeds of purchase actually referred to the immediately adjacent plot in a housing development).
7   *Pulleyn v Hall Aggregates (Thames Valley) Ltd* (1993) 65 P & CR 276 at 282; *Bristow v Mathers* (1991) 74 DLR (4th) 445 at 448. Entry 'as of right' is nothing to the point in the law of adverse possession, most cases of adverse possession comprising, at least objectively, possession 'as of wrong' (see *Buckinghamshire CC v Moran* [1990] Ch 623 at 644D per Nourse LJ [**para 6.45**]).

8   *Palfrey v Palfrey* (1974) 229 EG 1593 at 1595; *Powell v McFarlane* (1977) 38 P & CR 452 at 480; *Wilson v Martin's Executors* [1993] 1 EGLR 178 at 180L; *Burns v Anthony* (1997) 74 P & CR D41 at D42; *Prudential Assurance Co Ltd v Waterloo Real Estate Inc* (1998) Times, 13 May ('unwitting paper owner').

Use of force

6.124   There is some authority to the effect that relevant possession should be 'peaceful'[1] or 'peaceable'.[2] Certainly the adverse possessor must not resort to unreasonable violence in order to maintain himself in possession.[3] However, there is here a danger of excessive analogy with the law of prescription[4] and it should not be forgotten that, in some instances, the squatter's original entry upon the land may have been secured by some form of force.[5] The real relevance of force probably lies in the light which it may throw on the squatter's claim to possession as of right against the world. Acts of violence militate against a claim of right and thus detract from the requisite *animus*, but it would not be unnatural that, in the course of setting up a successful adverse possession, the squatter should encounter some resistance.[6] Indeed the essence of adverse possession lies in the squatter's persistence in making good a possessory presence which is effective against the world. Aggressive defence of his boundaries may therefore reinforce, rather than weaken, the adverse possessor's claim.[7]

1   See *Mulcahy v Curramore Pty Ltd* [1974] 2 NSWLR 464 at 475D.
2   See *Muthu Goundan v Anantha Goundan* AIR [1916] Madras 1001 at 1004 per Sadasiva Iyer J.
3   See *Muthu Goundan v Anantha Goundan* AIR [1916] Madras 1001 at 1004; *Shaw v Garbutt* (1996) 7 BPR 14816 at 14829–14830.
4   **[Para 8.182]**.
5   See *Shaw v Garbutt* (1996) 7 BPR 14816 at 14831–14832 per Young J.
6   Adverse possession is not terminated simply by written or oral protest (*Mount Carmel Investments Ltd v Peter Thurlow Ltd* [1988] 1 WLR 1078 at 1085H; *Cooke v Dunn* (1998) 9 BPR 16489 at 16499). See also *Muthu Goundan v Anantha Goundan* AIR [1916] Madras 1001 at 1004 (irrelevance of oral opposition or dissent).
7   See e g *Beever v Spaceline Engineering Pty Ltd* (1993) 6 BPR 13270 at 13281, where a squatter threatened an intruder with a shotgun ('very unsatisfactory behaviour' but nevertheless 'an act of possession, in that it asserted a right to control the presence of another person'). See also *Harnett v Green (No 2)* (1883) 4 LR (NSW) 292 at 301–304; *Shaw v Garbutt* (1996) 7 BPR 14816 at 14831.

NATURE OF THE PHYSICAL POSSESSION REQUIRED

6.125   The *factum* of possession depends ultimately on evidence that the claimant of adverse possession has asserted a 'complete and exclusive physical control' over the land.[1] Although the intensity of this control will vary with different kinds of terrain and with the circumstances of each case,[2] it must be shown that 'the alleged possessor has been dealing with the land in question as an occupying owner might have been expected to deal with it'[3] and that 'no-one else has done so.'[4] The acts relied upon as evidencing 'possession' need not have been uninterrupted,[5] but the duration of the squatter's occupation, its exclusivity and the acts of user relied upon must normally be verifiable by a physical survey of the land.[6]

1   *Buckinghamshire CC v Moran* [1990] Ch 623 at 641B per Slade LJ. See similarly *J A Pye (Oxford) Ltd v Graham* [2003] 1 AC 419 at [41] per Lord Browne-Wilkinson. The required 'custody and control' implies a 'hands on' user of the land (*Brown v Faulkner* [2003] NICA 5(2) at [30] per Higgins J).

2   *Lord Advocate v Lord Lovat* (1880) 5 App Cas 273 at 288; *Bligh v Martin* [1968] 1 WLR 804 at 811F; *Murphy v Murphy* [1980] IR 183 at 193; *Hamson v Jones* (1989) 52 DLR (4th) 143 at 155. The mere fact that it is difficult or even impossible to take physical possession of a particular area of land does not cause a lower test to apply to the existence of adverse possession (see *Simpson v Fergus* (2000) 79 P & CR 398 at 402–403 per Robert Walker LJ).

3   *Powell v McFarlane* (1977) 38 P & CR 452 at 471 per Slade J. See also *Mulcahy v Curramore Pty Ltd* [1974] 2 NSWLR 464 at 479E per Bowen CJ in Eq (the adverse possessor 'may be expected to act like a real owner would act'). See similarly *J A Pye (Oxford) Ltd v Graham* [2003] 1 AC 347 at [61] per Lord Browne-Wilkinson, [71]–[72] per Lord Hope of Craighead, [75]–[76] per Lord Hutton.

4   *Powell v McFarlane* (1977) 38 P & CR 452 at 471 per Slade J. The negative part of this formula may be extremely important in reinforcing a claim of adverse possession (see e g *Prudential Assurance Co Ltd v Waterloo Real Estate Inc* [1999] 2 EGLR 85 at 88H). See also *Brackenbank Lodge Ltd v Peart* (1993) 67 P & CR 249 at 261.

5   *Bligh v Martin* [1968] 1 WLR 804 at 811F–G; *Mulcahy v Curramore Pty Ltd* [1974] 2 NSWLR 464 at 475F. In *Re Taylor and Willigar* (1980) 99 DLR (3d) 118 at 125–126, it was held sufficient that the disputed property was used only in summer months and not at other times 'when the snow and ice of winter preclude their use in any practicable sense'. See similarly *Howard v Kunto*, 477 P2d 210 at 213–214 (1970); *Hamson v Jones* (1989) 52 DLR (4th) 143 at 156.

6   When a squatter applies to register a title based on adverse possession [**paras 7.47, 7.235**], it is Land Registry practice to instruct a surveyor to inspect the land in question. The surveyor records the exact position on site of physical boundary features such as fences and hedges; he estimates the age of these features; he reports on the way in which access to the land is obtained and controlled and on the person who appears to be in actual occupation; and he describes the use being made of the land by the squatter. Prior to inspection of the land the squatter is required to establish by statutory declaration the facts on which his claim is based and his intention in taking control of and making use of the land (see Land Registry Form FR1).

Territorial extent

6.126   Some care may be needed in delineating the extent of the land claimed by the squatter.

Possession of part

6.127   Adverse possession may be asserted in respect of only part of the land titled in the paper owner, the latter remaining in effective possession of the remainder of his land.[1] Provided that the squatter is in exclusive factual possession of an identifiable portion of the land, it is irrelevant that the owner of the paper title has not been wholly dispossessed. Thus, for example, there can be adverse possession of a different stratum of land from that occupied by the paper owner.[2] Alternatively, adverse possession may be claimed in respect of a portion of the paper owner's land which is marked off not horizontally but vertically.[3]

1   *Quach v Marrickville MC (Nos 1 & 2)* (1990) 22 NSWLR 55 at 67E–F, 69C.
2   See e g *Rains v Buxton* (1880) 14 Ch D 537 at 539–540 (adverse possession of underground cellar [**para 6.110**]).
3   *Quach v Marrickville MC (Nos 1 & 2)* (1990) 22 NSWLR 55 at 67E–F per Young J.

Constructive possession

6.128   Acts of possession done on parts of the land to which a possessory title is sought may sometimes constitute 'evidence of possession of the whole.'[1] However, the credibility of a claim to constructive possession of a larger whole depends vitally upon the nature of the land in question.[2] A degree of factual possession sufficient to justify a claim over a tract of wild country[3] may be entirely inadequate to found a similar claim over urban land.[4]

1   *Powell v McFarlane* (1977) 38 P & CR 452 at 471 per Slade J ('a matter of degree'). See *Coverdale v Charlton* (1878) 4 QBD 104 at 118 (horse turned on to one end of common is different from herd of cattle turned into enclosed and gated field).
2   See *Toome Eel Fishery (Northern Ireland) Ltd v Cardwell* [1966] NI 1 at 14 per Lord MacDermott LCJ.
3   See *Halifax County Pulp Co Ltd v Rutledge* (1982) 131 DLR (3d) 199 at 206–207; *Walker v Russell* (1966) 53 DLR (2d) 509 at 524–526. See *Weld v Scott* (1855) 12 UCQB 537 at 540 for the suggestion that the area which may be claimed by the adverse possessor is that covered by his 'pedal possession'. It may be that a consciously wrongful trespasser (as distinct from a trespasser who enters under colour of right) cannot plead a more extensive acquisition of title by reliance on constructive possession (see *Harris v Mudie* (1882) 7 OAR 414 at 427–428).
4   See *Pavledes v Ryesbridge Properties Ltd* (1989) 58 P & CR 459 at 480 (use of small part of adjoining area as car park insufficient to constitute possession of whole site). In *Williams v Usherwood* (1983) 45 P & CR 235 at 251, Cumming-Bruce LJ pointed out that, while the parking of cars on a strip of waste land might have no evidential value, such action within the enclosed curtilage of a private dwelling-house could well constitute adverse possession.

Exclusive physical control

6.129   Whether a claimant has exclusive physical control of the subject land must be determined with particular reference to 'the nature of the land and the manner in which land of that nature is commonly used or enjoyed.'[1] The nature of the required 'possession' may differ markedly according to whether the claim relates to a dwelling or to uncultivated land,[2] to a vast tract of land or to a small boundary strip.[3] In the simplest case 'possession' comprises a comprehensive appropriation of land with the manifest intention, as of right, of excluding the paper owner from any immediate user of his property.[4] Acts of alleged possession require to be viewed cumulatively in order that the court may determine whether, taken as a whole rather than in isolation, they establish a factual possession.[5]

1   *Powell v McFarlane* (1977) 38 P & CR 452 at 471 per Slade J. See also *Kirby v Cowderoy* [1912]

AC 599 at 603; *Wuta-Ofei v Danquah* [1961] 1 WLR 1238 at 1243 per Lord Guest; *West Bank Estates Ltd v Arthur* [1967] 1 AC 665 at 678A–B per Lord Wilberforce; *Bligh v Martin* [1968] 1 WLR 804 at 811F–H; *Williams v Usherwood* (1983) 45 P & CR 235 at 255; *McDonell v Giblin* (1904) 23 NZLR 660 at 662; *Riley v Penttila* [1974] VR 547 at 561; *Newington v Windeyer* (1985) 3 NSWLR 555 at 564A per McHugh JA.

2   *Mabo v Queensland (No 2)* (1992) 175 CLR 1 at 213 per Toohey J. See also *Lord Advocate v Lord Lovat* (1880) 5 App Cas 273 at 288; *Johnston v O'Neill* [1911] AC 552 at 583. 'Possession of a flat with a front door which can be locked is obviously different from possession of part of an unfenced moor or hillside' (*Simpson v Fergus* (2000) 79 P & CR 398 at 401).

3   In relation to a three-inch strip of boundary 'exceptionally strong' evidence of acts of adverse possession is required (see *Rimmer v Pearson* (2000) 79 P & CR D21 at D22 per Robert Walker LJ). See also *Rose v Curtis* (1995) 7 BPR 14430 at 14433.

4   See e g *Pollard v Jackson* (1994) 67 P & CR 327, where a tenant, on the death intestate of his reclusive resident landlord, cleared out the latter's premises on the upper floors of the house and, in the absence of any known relatives of the deceased, took over occupation of the whole.

5   See *Kingsalton Ltd v Thames Water Developments Ltd* (Chancery Division, 12 July 2000) at [38]; *Smith v Waterman* [2003] All ER (D) 72 (Jun) at [40] per Blackburne J.

Control over the access or activities of strangers

6.130   A critical feature of successful possessory claims is the consistent assertion of control over the access of strangers to, or the activities of strangers upon, the disputed land.[1] An occupier may establish possession, for instance, by controlling the front door of a council house 'squat' and deciding who should be allowed to join the 'squat'.[2] A similar effect is achieved by the erection of prominent 'no trespassing'[3] or 'no dumping'[4] signs on the land and even by the removal of graffiti from walls on the land.[5] The claim to exclusive possession is intensified by the aggressive warning off of strangers[6] and by the imposition of charges on strangers for intermittent use of the land.[7] Physical enclosure of the land (where feasible[8]) is especially relevant,[9] even though the enclosure may not be 'completely access proof.'[10] The construction of a wall or fencing is 'useful evidence of occupation to the exclusion of others'.[11] Extensive fencing almost always demonstrates the required degree of factual possession,[12] except where the fencing is primarily intended to serve some purpose other than the exclusion of strangers.[13] Of course, the absence of fencing does not in itself prove a lack of possession.[14] For example, a changing of locks may constitute 'an act of some significance' in support of a claim of adverse possession.[15]

1   See e g *J A Pye (Oxford) Ltd v Graham* [2003] 1 AC 419 at [41] per Lord Browne-Wilkinson.
2   *Ellis v Lambeth LBC* (1999) 32 HLR 596 at 598.
3   *Powell v McFarlane* (1977) 38 P & CR 452 at 478. See also *Newington v Windeyer* (1985) 3 NSWLR 555 at 564C per McHugh JA, but compare *Inglewood Investment Co Ltd v Baker* [2003] 2 P & CR 319 at [11]. It is not enough, however, to erect 'no parking' signs and monitor 'unauthorised' parking in defence of 'personal' parking spaces on a service road over which others have private rights of way (see *Simpson v Fergus* (2000) 79 P & CR 398 at 402–403).
4   *Hughes v Mulholland & McCann Ltd* [1982] 7 BNIL 72.
5   *Prudential Assurance Co Ltd v Waterloo Real Estate Inc* [1999] 2 EGLR 85 at 87M–88A, 88G per Peter Gibson LJ.
6   See e g *Beever v Spaceline Engineering Pty Ltd* (1993) 6 BPR 13270 at 13281; *Shaw v Garbutt* (1996) 7 BPR 14816 at 14831 **[para 6.124]**. Compare *Harnett v Green (No 2)* (1883) 4 LR (NSW) 292 at 300–302.

7   *Carroll v Manek and Bank of India* (2000) 79 P & CR 173 at 189–190.
8   Absolute physical control of extensive open land is normally impracticable 'if only because it is generally impossible to secure every part of a boundary so as to prevent intrusion' (*Powell v McFarlane* (1977) 38 P & CR 452 at 471 per Slade J).
9   *Buckinghamshire CC v Moran* [1990] Ch 623 at 641H–642A (chain and padlock); *Lambeth LBC v Blackburn* (2001) 82 P & CR 494 at [23]–[26] (replacement lock). See also *Strahan v Doxey* (Court of Appeal, 21 November 1994) per Millett LJ (squatter held only key to shed); *Purbrick v Hackney LBC* [2004] 1 P & CR 553 at [18] (installation of corrugated iron door with padlock). Contrast *Battersea Freehold & Leasehold Property Co Ltd v Wandsworth LBC* (2001) 82 P & CR 137 at [12], [18]–[20] (squatter distributed keys to third parties).
10   *Railtrack plc v Hutchinson* (Unreported, Chancery Division, 17 December 1998). See also *Marshall v Taylor* [1895] 1 Ch 639 at 645.
11   *Mulcahy v Curramore Pty Ltd* [1974] 2 NSWLR 464 at 475E; *Raab v Caranci* (1980) 97 DLR (3d) 154 at 157–160 (affd (1980) 104 DLR (3d) 160).
12   *George Wimpey & Co Ltd v Sohn* [1967] Ch 487 at 511A, 512A per Russell LJ; *Simpson v Fergus* (2000) 79 P & CR 398 at 402 per Robert Walker LJ. See e g *Seddon v Smith* (1877) 36 LT 168 at 169 per Cockburn CJ ('Enclosure is the strongest possible evidence of adverse possession'). Contrast, however, the effect of flimsy or temporary fencing: see *Boosey v Davis* (1988) 55 P & CR 83 at 87 (incomplete fence reinforcing existing fence erected by paper owner); *Marsden v Miller* (1992) 64 P & CR 239 at 241–244 (erection of fence for 24 hours); *Basildon DC v Charge* [1996] CLY 4929 (short-term fence).
13   Fencing, although cogent evidence of possession, is not conclusive (see *Brown v Faulkner* [2003] NICA 5(2) at [32]). The requisite *animus possidendi* may be absent where a fence was intended essentially as a containment device for livestock or geese (see eg *Basildon DC v Charge* [1996] CLY 4929; *Trustees of Michael Batt Charitable Trust v Adams* (2001) 82 P & CR 406 at [34]–[35]; *Inglewood Investment Co Ltd v Baker* [2003] 2 P & CR 319 at [30]–[32]; *Smith v Waterman* [2003] All ER (D) 72 (Jun) at [19]) or for the restraint of a senile family member who was 'apt to wander' (see *Fruin v Fruin* [1983] Court of Appeal Transcript 448). For a similar approach, see *Riley v Penttila* [1974] VR 547 at 564 (fence and netting primarily intended to facilitate the playing of tennis); *Brown v Faulkner*, supra at [37] (enclosure to prevent invasion of cattle). Compare, however, *Hounslow LBC v Minchinton* (1997) 74 P & CR 221 at 233.
14   *Mulcahy v Curramore Pty Ltd* [1974] 2 NSWLR 464 at 475E; *Beever v Spaceline Engineering Pty Ltd* (1993) 6 BPR 13270 at 13279.
15   *Cooke v Dunn* (1998) 9 BPR 16489 at 16504 per Santow J. See e g *Lambeth LBC v Blackburn* (2001) 82 P & CR 494 at [25]–[26], [45]–[46] per Clarke LJ.

Other sufficient acts of user

6.131   Possession may also be established by a wide variety of other acts of user in accordance with the nature of the terrain.[1] Acts which are insignificant in relation to large areas of open land may, for instance, take on a heightened relevance in a suburban garden.[2] In different contexts, sufficient possessory conduct can include the construction of buildings or extensions,[3] works of active maintenance and improvement,[4] use of the land for grazing[5] and storage purposes[6] and for shooting,[7] the clearing away of fallen trees,[8] the parking of cars,[9] and the installation of security cameras, security lighting and an entryphone system.[10] A squatter's voluntary payment of council tax or rates is a highly significant reinforcement of his claim to possession,[11] although non-payment is not, in itself, evidence of non-possession.[12]

1   It has been suggested that acts of user wholly in accordance with the paper owner's intended purposes in respect of the land cannot qualify as relevant 'possession' (see e g *Pulleyn v Hall*

Aggregates (Thames Valley) Ltd (1993) 65 P & CR 276 at 282). This approach seems both unnecessarily restrictive and of dubious authority (see Louise Tee, 'Adverse possession and the Intention to Possess' [2000] Conv 113).

2   See e g *Hounslow LBC v Minchinton* (1997) 74 P & CR 221 at 233 per Millett LJ (hedge trimming, weeding and creation of compost heap).

3   *Prudential Assurance Co Ltd v Waterloo Real Estate Inc* [1999] 2 EGLR 85 at 88B–D; *Beever v Spaceline Engineering Pty Ltd* (1993) 6 BPR 13270 at 13281. The execution of substantial work is unlikely to have been intended to benefit another. See *Shaw v Garbutt* (1996) 7 BPR 14816 at 14832–14833 per Young J ('people do not do work on another person's property without good reason'). However, a mere failure to improve premises does not connote insufficient possession (*Purbrick v Hackney LBC* [2004] 1 P & CR 553 at [21]–[22]).

4   See e g *Newington v Windeyer* (1985) 3 NSWLR 555 at 564B–C, where the Court of Appeal of New South Wales upheld a possessory claim to an area of open ground where, for nearly 50 years, a number of neighbouring owners had maintained the area as a garden; had employed a man to mow the lawn; had used the area for parties, receptions and the display of sculpture; and had been assessed for rates in respect of the land.

5   See *J A Pye (Oxford) Ltd v Graham* [2003] 1 AC 419 **[para 6.98]**.

6   *Treloar v Nute* [1976] 1 WLR 1295. See (1978) 41 MLR 204 (P F Smith).

7   *Red House Farms (Thorndon) Ltd v Catchpole* (1977) 244 EG 295 at 297–299.

8   *Smith v Waterman* [2003] All ER (D) 72 (Jun) at [37].

9   *Burns v Anthony* (1997) 74 P & CR D41 at D43; but compare *Central Midlands Estates Ltd v Leicester Dyers Ltd* [2003] 2 P & CR D2 at D3.

10   *Prudential Assurance Co Ltd v Waterloo Real Estate Inc* [1999] 2 EGLR 85 at 88A–B.

11   See *Bank of Victoria v Forbes* (1887) 13 VLR 760 at 765; *O'Neil v Hart* [1905] VLR 107 at 120; *Quach v Marrickville MC (Nos 1 & 2)* (1990) 22 NSWLR 55 at 66F–67B; *Shaw v Garbutt* (1996) 7 BPR 14816 at 14833–14834; *Cooke v Dunn* (1998) 9 BPR 16489 at 16505.

12   *Ellis v Lambeth LBC* (1999) 32 HLR 596 at 599–601. See also *Robinson v Attorney General* [1955] NZLR 1230 at 1235; *Smaglinski v Daly* (1971) 20 DLR (3d) 65; *Shaw v Garbutt* (1996) 7 BPR 14816 at 14833.

Trivial or equivocal acts of user

6.132   Trivial, intermittent or equivocal acts by the adverse occupier are generally inadequate as proof of 'possession'[1] and provide an exceedingly fragile foundation for claims of the requisite *animus possidendi*.[2] In *Tecbild Ltd v Chamberlain*,[3] for instance, the Court of Appeal declined to attach significance to the fact that the claimant's children had been accustomed to play on the disputed plots of land as and when they wished and that the family ponies had been tethered and exercised there.[4] As the Court of Appeal confirmed, 'trivial acts of trespass' do not constitute adverse possession,[5] although it is possible that a series of apparently insignificant forms of conduct may, in the round, establish factual possession.[6] It must in any event be demonstrated that the adverse occupier established a possession which was wholly inconsistent with and in denial of the rights of the paper owner as the legal owner of the land concerned.[7]

1   See *Kingsalton Ltd v Thames Water Development Ltd* (Chancery Division, 12 July 2000) at [38]–[39]; *Cobham v Frett* [2001] 1 WLR 1775 at 1785E–G per Lord Scott of Foscote (intermittent acts of cutting down trees, grazing cows, picking grapes and fishing). See similarly *Brown v Faulkner* [2003] NICA 5(2) at [37] (storage of boats); *Hamson v Jones* (1989) 52 DLR (4th) 143 at 153.

2   *Buckinghamshire CC v Moran* [1990] Ch 623 at 642E per Slade LJ. See e g *Taylor v Rugby BC* (Unreported, Court of Appeal, 4 February 1998).

3   (1969) 20 P & CR 633. See similarly *Inglewood Investment Co Ltd v Baker* [2003] 2 P & CR 319
     at [35] (intermittent clearance of rubbish, children playing, shooting of rabbits and foxes), but
     contrast *Smith v Waterman* [2003] All ER (D) 72 (Jun) at [38].
4   Compare *Powell v McFarlane* (1977) 38 P & CR 452 [**para 6.144**].
5   (1969) 20 P & CR 633 at 644, 646. In *Boosey v Davis* (1988) 55 P & CR 83 at 86–87, the Court
     of Appeal disallowed a claim of adverse possession which comprised a grazing use which was
     'minimal' in quantity and quality. See similarly *Smith v Waterman* [2003] All ER (D) 72 (Jun)
     at [40] (erection of washing line). See also *Attersley v Blakely* (1970) 13 DLR (3d) 39 at 47; *Re
     MacEachern and MacIsaac* (1978) 81 DLR (3d) 20 at 29.
6   See *Smith v Waterman* [2003] All ER (D) 72 (Jun) at [40], [55] per Blackburne J.
7   See *Moses v Lovegrove* [1952] 2 QB 533 at 538. In *Bladder v Phillips* [1991] EGCS 109,
     Mustill LJ disallowed a claim of adverse possession based on cleaning out parts of a ditch 'on
     a few brief occasions at long intervals.' Compare, however, *Lee v Parsons* (Unreported, Court
     of Appeal, 6 October 1998).

INTENTION TO POSSESS (*ANIMUS POSSIDENDI*)

6.133   In the law of adverse possession, the possessory claimant must establish not only a *factum possessionis* subsisting throughout the limitation period,
but also a continuous possessory intent or *animus possidendi*.[1] The squatter's
intention to possess must remain manifest throughout the relevant period of
possession[2] and, if present for only part of this period, cannot support a claim
of adverse possession.[3] Complete and exclusive physical control of the land
must be coupled with, and reinforced by, evidence of an 'intention, in one's own
name and on one's own behalf, to exclude the world at large, including the
owner with the paper title if he be not himself the possessor, so far as is
reasonably practicable and so far as the processes of the law will allow.'[4] The
required intent is, of course, heavily qualified by the reality that, until his
possessory title is perfected, the squatter's ability to exclude *all* persons from the
land is inevitably limited.[5] In truth the law of adverse possession currently
demands no more than that the squatter should intend to maximise for as long
as possible the benefits which he draws from his presence on the land.

1   *Lambeth LBC v Blackburn* (2001) 82 P & CR 494 at [29] per Clarke LJ; *Trustees of Michael
     Batt Charitable Trust v Adams* (2001) 82 P & CR 406 at [28] per Laddie J.
2   *Smith v Waterman* [2003] All ER (D) 72 (Jun) at [21] per Blackburne J.
3   *Smith v Waterman* [2003] All ER (D) 72 (Jun) at [83], [105].
4   *Powell v McFarlane* (1977) 38 P & CR 452 at 471–472 per Slade J (adopted as correct in *J A
     Pye (Oxford) Ltd v Graham* [2003] 1 AC 419 at [43] per Lord Browne-Wilkinson, [77] per
     Lord Hutton). It is not enough, for instance, that the interloper intends merely to assert a
     right of easement or profit *à prendre* (see *Convey v Regan* [1952] IR 56 at 59 per Black J
     (adopted in *Powell*, supra at 478)).
5   See *J A Pye (Oxford) Ltd v Graham* [2003] 1 AC 419 at [43] per Lord Browne-Wilkinson ('a
     squatter will normally know that until the full time has run, the paper owner can recover the
     land from him').

Changing content of the required *animus*

6.134   During recent years English courts (unlike their common law counter-
parts overseas) have engaged, somewhat unsatisfactorily, in a progressive

curtailment of the content of the possessory intent required of the adverse possessor.[1] Indeed, some judges have come perilously close to suggesting that a positive demonstration of *animus possidendi* is no longer a necessary element of the concept of possession.[2] Ironically, the modern relaxation of the requirements of adverse possession has emerged at just the point in time when, by virtue of the changes effected by the Land Registration Act 2002,[3] the acquisition of title by long possession appears likely to become a relatively unusual occurrence in English law.

1   Some index of this movement appears from the fact that Slade J's definition of *animus possidendi* in *Powell v McFarlane* (1977) 38 P & CR 452 was once regarded as 'yet another weapon in the armoury to be deployed against squatters', imposing such onerous restrictions on the notion that 'few squatters, if any, could satisfy it' (see P Jackson (1980) 96 LQR 333 at 334). In *J A Pye (Oxford) Ltd v Graham*, perhaps the most successful adverse possession claim of all time, Lord Browne-Wilkinson expressly adopted Slade J's exposition as a statement of principle which 'cannot be improved upon' ([2003] 1 AC 419 at [31]).

2   See e g *Lambeth LBC v Blackburn* (2001) 82 P & CR 494 at [18] per Clarke LJ; *J A Pye (Oxford) Ltd v Graham* [2003] 1 AC 419 at [79] per Lord Hutton (although compare Lord Browne-Wilkinson at [40]).

3   [**Para 6.55**].

There need be no intention to own

6.135   It was once thought that *animus possidendi* necessarily connoted an intention to *own* or acquire *ownership* of the land or to exercise 'acts of ownership' in relation to it.[1] While the assertion of rights of ownership may well provide strong support for a claim of *animus possidendi*, it is now widely accepted that the adverse possessor need not prove any intention at all with regard to ownership of the land,[2] but he must show that he manifestly intended to *treat* that land *as if* he did own it.[3]

1   See e g *Littledale v Liverpool College* [1900] 1 Ch 19 at 23 per Lindley MR; *George Wimpey & Co Ltd v Sohn* [1967] Ch 487 at 510G. An element of ambivalence inevitably flows from the fact that possession provides the root of title [**para 3.23**]. It is easy, in consequence, for adverse possession terminology to glide between references to possessory intent and descriptions of the adverse claimant as 'regarding itself as the owner', 'overtly treating the [land] as belonging to it' and maintaining an 'overt assertion of ownership' (see e g *Prudential Assurance Co Ltd v Waterloo Real Estate Inc* [1999] 2 EGLR 85 at 88D–G per Peter Gibson LJ). Compare, however, L Tee, [2000] Conv 113.

2   He may even believe that he owns the land already [**para 6.123**].

3   'What the law requires is factual possession, i e an exclusive dealing with the land as an occupying owner might be expected to deal with it, together with a manifested intention to treat the land as belonging to the possessor to the exclusion of everyone else' (*Hughes v Cork* [1994] EGCS 25 per Saville LJ). See also *J A Pye (Oxford) Ltd v Graham* [2000] Ch 676 at 703F (adverse possessors 'treated the disputed land as if they were the occupying owners'); *Brown v Faulkner* [2003] NICA 5(2) at [30] per Higgins J.

There must be an intention to possess

6.136   The historic operative concept underlying all land titles is possession rather than ownership. In English law the notion of behaving as an 'owner' translates itself more accurately into the physical and mental components of the technical idea of legal 'possession'. The critical factor in adverse possession is, therefore, 'not an intention to own ... but an intention to possess.'[1] The required *animus* relates to the empirical quality of the occupier's conduct rather than to its eventual legal effect. *Factum* and *animus* interact; and the occupier's behaviour (in both its physical and mental aspects) has a certain self-determining character. What is required, moreover, is an intention to possess, and not necessarily any intention to *dispossess*,[2] with the result, for instance, that the requisite *animus* can easily coexist with a belief on the part of a squatter that his entry was by right.

1   *Buckinghamshire CC v Moran* (1988) 56 P & CR 372 at 378–379 per Hoffmann J, cited with approval in the Court of Appeal ([1990] Ch 623 at 643E per Slade LJ) and regarded as 'manifestly correct' by Lord Browne-Wilkinson in *J A Pye (Oxford) Ltd v Graham* [2003] 1 AC 419 at [42]. See also *Lambeth LBC v Blackburn* (2001) 82 P & CR 494 at [53] per Clarke LJ; *Cooke v Dunn* (1998) 9 BPR 16489 at 16507 per Santow J.
2   *Hughes v Cork* [1994] EGCS 25 per Beldam LJ.

Irrelevance of bad faith

6.137   One of the initially surprising features of the English law of adverse possession is that the test of *animus* does not differentiate between cases of innocent and wilful trespass.[1] The doctrine of long possession operates even in favour of the opportunist or consciously wilful trespasser who is perfectly aware that the land he occupies is not his own[2] and that his possession is therefore 'possession as of wrong.'[3] Although the courts are clearly not anxious to strain the law in favour of unmeritorious claimants,[4] there is in English law no general requirement of good faith in the adverse possessor.[5] Bad faith becomes relevant only if the paper owner can establish that he was the victim of a fraud perpetrated by the adverse occupier or that any fact relevant to his right of action was deliberately concealed from him by the occupier.[6] In such circumstances the period of limitation does not begin to run until the claimant could with reasonable diligence have discovered the fraud or concealment.[7]

1   *Prudential Assurance Co Ltd v Waterloo Real Estate Inc* [1999] 2 EGLR 85 at 87E–H per Peter Gibson LJ.
2   Even a public body or local authority which asserts adverse possession owes the paper owner no fiduciary obligation not to deprive him of his land (*Re North Sydney Council* (1997) 8 BPR 15677 at 15681 per Young J). Equally the public status of the body dispossessed by the squatter does not avert the operation of adverse possession (*Rhondda Cynon Taff County BC v Watkins* [2003] 1 WLR 1864 at [28] per Schiemann LJ).
3   See *Buckinghamshire CC v Moran* [1990] Ch 623 at 644D per Nourse LJ.
4   See e g *Buckinghamshire CC v Moran* [1990] Ch 623 at 647A per Nourse LJ; *Trustees of Michael Batt Charitable Trust v Adams* (2001) 82 P & CR 406 at [24] per Laddie J; *Lambeth LBC v Blackburn* (2001) 82 P & CR 494 at [36] per Clarke LJ; *Lambeth LBC v Rumbelow* (Chancery Division, 25 January 2001) per Etherton J.
5   Compare, however, the good faith requirement imposed in Roman law and in most modern civilian systems (see R H Helmholz, 'Adverse Possession and Subjective Intent' 61 Wash ULQ 331 at 356 (1983–84)). Helmholz argues that North American courts have in practice operated a test of good faith in adjudicating claims of title by long possession. See also *Campeau v May* (1911) 19 OWR 751 at 752 per Middleton J (there is 'nothing in the policy of the law which

demands that it should be made easy to steal land or any hardship which requires an exception to the general rule that the way of the transgressor is hard'); *Giouroukos v Cadillac Fairview Corp Ltd* (1984) 3 DLR (4th) 595 at 616 per Robins JA. Compare, however, R A Cunningham, 'More on Adverse Possession: A Rejoinder to Professor Helmholz' 64 Wash ULQ 1167 (1986).

6   See, however, *Ellis v Lambeth LBC* (1999) 32 HLR 596 at 600, where a squatter's failure to make a community charge (ie council tax) return was not even considered as an instance of fraud or concealment in relation to the local authority paper owner.

7   See LA 1980, s 32(1). Protection is provided for innocent third parties who purchase property for valuable consideration (LA 1980, s 32(3)).

Possessory intent can be limited or qualified

6.138   The *animus* required of the squatter may be heavily qualified. In *Buckinghamshire CC v Moran*[1] the Court of Appeal confirmed that it is sufficient that the claimant by adverse possession should demonstrate merely 'an intention for the time being to possess the land to the exclusion of all other persons, including the owner with the paper title.'[2] It was not, therefore, fatal in *Moran's* case that the claimant had intended to continue in possession of the disputed plot of land only until such time as the paper owner activated its plans to build a proposed by-pass over it.[3] This consciously limited or tentative form of possessory intention in no way frustrates the normal operation of adverse possession. The required mental element need not involve any intention to 'exclude the owner of the paper title in all future circumstances.'[4] Likewise, in *Lambeth LBC v Blackburn*,[5] adverse possession of a council house was success-fully claimed by a squatter whose modest intention throughout his occupation had been merely to remain in temporary possession until such time as he was evicted. The limited nature of this possessory intent is wholly consistent with, and is indeed an inevitable consequence of, the squatter's vulnerability to the recovery of possession at any time before his possessory title is completed.[6]

1   [1990] Ch 623 at 643E per Slade LJ (see also Nourse LJ at 644E).
2   See also *Colchester BC v Smith* [1991] Ch 448 at 477F; *Carroll v Manek and Bank of India* (2000) 79 P & CR 173 at 190.
3   [1990] Ch 623 at 643E–G per Slade LJ.
4   [1990] Ch 623 at 642G–643E per Slade LJ. Sometimes, however, the court may impose a higher threshold of proof of possessory intention (see eg *Stacey v Gardner* [1994] CLY 568). For instance, a squatter's knowledge of some future use intended by the paper owner may 'affect the quality of his own intention, reducing it below that which is required to constitute adverse possession' (*Buckinghamshire CC v Moran* [1990] Ch 623 at 645A–B per Nourse LJ). See similarly *J A Pye (Oxford) Ltd v Graham* [2003] 1 AC 419 at [45] per Lord Browne-Wilkinson **[para 6.104]**; *Hounslow LBC v Minchinton* (1997) 74 P & CR 221 at 229–230 per Millett LJ.
5   (2001) 82 P & CR 494 at [50]. See similarly *J A Pye (Oxford) Ltd v Graham* [2003] 1 AC 419 at [78] per Lord Hutton.
6   See *Lambeth LBC v Blackburn* (2001) 82 P & CR 494 at [17], [53] per Clarke LJ; *Purbrick v Hackney LBC* [2004] 1 P & CR 553 at [24] per Neuberger J.

Shift from exclusory intent to conscious furtherance of self-interest

6.139   The older case law heavily emphasised exclusory intent as the essential element of *animus possidendi*.[1] Frequent reference was made to the need to manifest an intention 'to exclude the world at large, including the owner with the paper title.'[2] Whilst this requirement still represents the law in many other jurisdictions,[3] there are strong indications that English law has recently overseen a subtle, but important, diminution of the exclusory component of *animus*.

1   See e g *Littledale v Liverpool College* [1900] 1 Ch 19 at 23 per Lindley MR; *Powell v McFarlane* (1977) 38 P & CR 452 at 472, 476 per Slade J (intention to 'exclude the owner as best he can').

2   *Powell v McFarlane* (1977) 38 P & CR 452 at 471–472 per Slade J. This emphasis has even penetrated relatively recent case law (see e g *Trustees of Michael Batt Charitable Trust v Adams* (2001) 82 P & CR 406 at [24]–[28]; *Lambeth LBC v Blackburn* (2001) 82 P & CR 494 at [17]–[20] per Clarke LJ).

3   For reference to an 'intention to repel', see *Permanent Trustee Co Ltd v Pangas* (Unreported, Supreme Court of New South Wales, 5 June 1992, BPR Casenote 96783) per Young J. See also *Keefer v Arillotta* (1977) 72 DLR (3d) 182 at 193.

Self-interested control and exploitation

6.140   In *J A Pye (Oxford) Ltd v Graham*[1] Lord Browne-Wilkinson confirmed that possessory intent involves 'an intention to exclude the paper owner only so far as is reasonably possible.' Lord Hope of Craighead even went so far as to deny any necessity at all to 'show that there was a deliberate intention to exclude the paper owner or the registered proprietor.'[2] For Lord Hope, the relevant *animus* is simply 'an intent to exercise exclusive control over the [land] for oneself.'[3] The former emphasis on exclusory intent has been commuted, in large degree, into a concern with whether the squatter has engaged in a conscious furtherance of his own self-interest. 'The only intention which has to be demonstrated,' declared Lord Hope, is 'an intention to occupy and use the land as one's own.' The identifying characteristic of the successful squatter is the intention to 'stay as long as he can for his own benefit.'[4] Viewed in this way, *animus* becomes merely the 'intention to exercise ... custody and control on one's own behalf and for one's own benefit.'[5] Thus, in *J A Pye (Oxford) Ltd v Graham* the House of Lords thought it hugely significant that, notwithstanding the non-renewal of their licence in respect of the disputed land, the claimant possessor and his family had simply intended, throughout the adverse possession period, to 'use the land as they thought best.'[6]

1   [2003] 1 AC 419 at [46].

2   [2003] 1 AC 419 at [71].

3   Contrast *Trustees of Michael Batt Charitable Trust v Adams* (2001) 82 P & CR 406 at [27]–[28], where, in advance of the House of Lords' ruling in the *Pye* case, Laddie J regarded adverse possession as impossible in the absence of evidence of the occupier's intention 'to exclude the person whom he believed was the owner of the land.' An intention to *use* or even *possess* the land did not, for Laddie J, 'indicate a determination to exclude others to the extent permissible.'

4   [2003] 1 AC 419 at [40] per Lord Browne-Wilkinson.

5   Contrast the approach adopted elsewhere that adverse possession may be ruled out if the claimant's conduct indicates not so much a settled intention to exclude the true owner as an intention to confer a particular benefit upon the claimant (*Murnane v Findlay* [1926] VLR 80 at 88). See e g *Riley v Penttila* [1974] VR 547 at 562–564 (tennis court built on the disputed ground). See also *Masidon Investments Ltd v Ham* (1983) 39 OR (2d) 534 at 550–551.

6   [2003] 1 AC 419 at [64] per Lord Browne-Wilkinson (with the concurrence of the other law
      lords).

No inconsistency with informal recognition of a superior claim to the land

6.141   Particularly because of the limited nature of this requirement of
possessory intent, there is no inconsistency between a claim of *animus possidendi* and an evident historic preparedness on the part of an opportunistic
squatter, if challenged, to pay a money rent or otherwise negotiate the terms of
his occupancy.[1] Mere recognition of someone else's temporarily superior
entitlement does not, in itself, derogate from the fact that the squatter is
currently in 'possession'.

1   [2003] 1 AC 419 at [46], [60] per Lord Browne-Wilkinson, [78] per Lord Hutton.

Proof of animus possidendi

6.142   As Slade J emphasised in *Powell v McFarlane*,[1] the success of any claim
by a trespasser to have acquired 'possession' rests on affirmative evidence that
the trespasser 'not only had the requisite intention to possess, but made such
intention clear to the world.'[2] This *animus* is assessed subjectively,[3] although its
presence can often be established as a matter of inference from the conduct of
the claimant adverse possessor. In one way or another the squatter must
manifest an intention to possess the land to the exclusion of all others.
Although this intention is not necessarily incompatible with mistake or ignorance as to the true ownership of the land in question,[4] it must be shown that
the claimant consciously acted in a manner which was consistent with a claim
to exclusive possession on his own behalf. Thus, for example, a claim of adverse
possession is inconsistent with a request by the squatter that the paper owner
should discharge the responsibilities normally attached to possession of land.[5]

1   (1977) 38 P & CR 452 at 472. See generally M Dockray, [1982] Conv 256, 345.
2   For cases in which the courts have rejected claims to possessory titles by trespassers for want
      of sufficient evidence of the requisite intent, see e g *Littledale v Liverpool College* [1900]
      1 Ch 19 at 23–26; *George Wimpey & Co Ltd v Sohn* [1967] Ch 487 at 508F–G; *Techild Ltd v
      Chamberlain* (1969) 20 P & CR 633 at 643; *Wilson v Martin's Executors* [1993] 1 EGLR 178 at
      181C; *Stacey v Gardner* [1994] CLY 568.
3   *Prudential Assurance Co Ltd v Waterloo Real Estate Inc* [1999] 2 EGLR 85 at 87G per Peter
      Gibson LJ. It may be particularly difficult for a claimant adverse possessor who licensed
      others to join him in a squat of a council house to demonstrate that all members of the squat
      'jointly ... had the requisite intention' (see *Lambeth LBC v Rumbelow* (Chancery Division,
      25 January 2001) per Etherton J).
4   [**Para 6.123**].
5   *J A Pye (Oxford) Ltd v Graham* [2000] Ch 676 at 693D–E per Neuberger J. See e g *Pavledes v
      Ryesbridge Properties Ltd* (1989) 58 P & CR 459 at 480 (squatter requested the paper owner to
      exclude trespassers from the land on his behalf).

Manifestation of animus vis à vis the true owner

6.143 In the absence of fraud or concealment,[1] it is generally irrelevant in the law of adverse possession that the paper owner is unaware of the fact that he has been dispossessed.[2] However, in view of the potentially drastic consequences of a change of possession, the adverse claimant must 'at least make his intentions sufficiently clear so that the owner, if present at the land, would clearly appreciate that the claimant is not merely a persistent trespasser, but is actually seeking to dispossess him.'[3] Courts attach 'very little evidential value' to retrospective assertions of the required *animus*, because 'they are obviously easily capable of being merely self-serving, while at the same time they may be very difficult for the paper owner positively to refute.'[4] For the same reason even contemporary declarations by an adverse occupier to the effect that he is intending to assert a claim to the land provide but little support for a claim of 'possession' at the relevant time unless they are specifically brought to the attention of the true owner.[5]

1   **[Para 6.110]**.
2   See e g *Rains v Buxton* (1880) 14 Ch D 537 at 540–541.
3   *Powell v McFarlane* (1977) 38 P & CR 452 at 480. See also *Stacey v Gardner* [1994] CLY 568; *Lambeth LBC v Blackburn* (2001) 82 P & CR 494 at [18], [20] per Clarke LJ; *Inglewood Investment Co Ltd v Baker* [2003] 2 P & CR 319 at [21] per Aldous LJ; *Smith v Waterman* [2003] All ER (D) 72 (Jun) at [19] per Blackburne J.
4   *Powell v McFarlane* (1977) 38 P & CR 452 at 476. See also *Bolton MBC v Qasmi* (Unreported, Court of Appeal, 3 December 1998) per Peter Gibson LJ; *Lambeth LBC v Blackburn* (2001) 82 P & CR 494 at [21] per Clarke LJ; *J A Pye (Oxford) Ltd v Graham* [2003] 1 AC 419 at [60] per Lord Browne-Wilkinson.
5   *Powell v McFarlane* (1977) 38 P & CR 452 at 476 per Slade J.

Inference of intention from conduct

6.144 As Lord Browne-Wilkinson pointed out in *J A Pye (Oxford) Ltd v Graham*,[1] the intention to possess 'may be, and frequently is, deduced from the physical acts' of the squatter himself. It is perhaps inevitable that relevant evidence of *animus* is normally left to be inferred from conduct: 'actions speak louder than words.'[2] Such inferences can be made, however, only if the actions in question are 'unequivocal and manifested to the true owner.'[3] Where evidence of possessory conduct is *equivocal*, the intention underlying the squatter's acts becomes 'all-important'.[4] In *Powell v McFarlane*,[5] Slade J confirmed that 'compelling evidence' of *animus* is required where a trespasser's user of land does not by itself clearly betoken an intention on his part to possess the land to the exclusion of the true owner.[6] In *Powell's* case Slade J declined to find the necessary *animus* proved on behalf of a claimant who, at the age of 14, had begun to use land for the purpose of grazing his cow. In Slade J's view, the conduct of one so young was 'not necessarily referable' to any intention to dispossess the paper owner and to occupy the land 'wholly as his own property.'[7]

1   [2003] 1 AC 419 at [40].

2　*Burns v Anthony* (1997) 74 P & CR D41 at D43 per Simon Brown LJ. See also *Techild Ltd v Chamberlain* (1969) 20 P & CR 633 at 643 per Sachs LJ; *Taylor v Lawrence* [2001] EWCA Civ 119 at [12] per Peter Gibson LJ; *Lambeth LBC v Blackburn* (2001) 82 P & CR 494 at [46] per Clarke LJ ('intentions are to be judged entirely by reference to [the squatter's] acts').

3　*Lambeth LBC v Blackburn* (2001) 82 P & CR 494 at [20]–[21] per Clarke LJ. See also *Prudential Assurance Co Ltd v Waterloo Real Estate Inc* [1999] 2 EGLR 85 at 87F per Peter Gibson LJ (the occupier's conduct must be 'unequivocal in the sense that his intention to possess has been made plain to the world').

4　*Littledale v Liverpool College* [1900] 1 Ch 19 at 23 per Lindley MR. See also *Inglewood Investment Co Ltd v Baker* [2003] 2 P & CR 319 at [29]; *Clement v Jones* (1909) 8 CLR 133 at 140; *Riley v Penttila* [1974] VR 547 at 562.

5　(1977) 38 P & CR 452 at 476.

6　If the trespasser's acts are 'open to more than one interpretation and he has not made it perfectly plain to the world at large by his actions or words that he has intended to exclude the owner as best he can, the courts will treat him as not having had the requisite *animus possidendi* and consequently as not having dispossessed the owner' ((1977) 38 P & CR 452 at 472). See also *Buckinghamshire CC v Moran* [1990] Ch 623 at 642E–F; *Lambeth LBC v Blackburn* (2001) 82 P & CR 494 at [19]; *J A Pye (Oxford) Ltd v Graham* [2003] 1 AC 347 at [76]–[77] per Lord Hutton.

7　(1977) 38 P & CR 452 at 478. See also *Re MacEachern and MacIsaac* (1978) 81 DLR (3d) 20 at 28–29.

Intention as implicit in 'possession'

6.145　Further evidence of the modern downgrading of the requisite *animus possidendi* is to be found in the speeches of the House of Lords in *J A Pye (Oxford) Ltd v Graham*.[1] Here, for example, Lord Hutton seemed to suggest that a rebuttable presumption of *animus* arises where 'the actions of the occupier make it clear that he is using the land in the way in which a full owner would and in such a way that the owner is excluded.'[2] In such circumstances the squatter 'in the normal case ... will not have to adduce additional evidence to establish that he had the intention to possess.' Instead, an evidential onus shifts to the paper owner to 'adduce other evidence which points to a contrary conclusion.'[3]

1　[2003] 1 AC 419.

2　[2003] 1 AC 419 at [76]. Lord Hutton approved (at [79]) the statement of Clarke LJ in *Lambeth LBC v Blackburn* (2001) 82 P & CR 494 at [36] that it was 'not ... appropriate to strain to hold that a trespasser who had established factual possession ... did not have ... *animus possidendi*.' See also *Brown v Faulkner* [2003] NICA 5(2) at [30] per Higgins J.

3　Contrast the view expressed, prior to the House of Lords' ruling in the *Pye* case, by Etherton J in *Lambeth LBC v Rumbelow* (Chancery Division, 25 January 2001) ('it is not in the least surprising that over many years ... the courts have been reluctant to infer the necessary animus possidendi on the part of a squatter, even where the acts relied on could have sufficed to constitute actual occupation').

RECOVERY OF POSSESSION OF LAND

6.146　Any action for the recovery of *unregistered* land of which a paper owner has been dispossessed must be brought before his right of recovery becomes statute-barred (ie before the expiration of the relevant limitation period).[1] In the new order instituted by the Land Registration Act 2002, the mere effluxion of time affords no defence to the squatter. A dispossessed proprietor of *registered* land is therefore entitled, irrespective of the duration of the relevant adverse possession, to bring proceedings for the recovery of the land at any time before he loses his statutory right to resist the intruder's application to be registered as proprietor in his place.[2]

1   LA 1980, s 15(1) [**para 6.41**]. See *Mount Carmel Investments Ltd v Peter Thurlow Ltd* [1988] 1 WLR 1078 at 1086A per Nicholls LJ. In extremely rare circumstances it is possible that, even after the paper owner's rights have been extinguished by adverse possession, his title may be revived by a later acknowledgment by the squatter. See e g *Colchester BC v Smith* [1992] Ch 421 at 435B (adverse possessor estopped from relying on Limitation Act by reason of subsequent tenancy granted by paper owner in which it was agreed that adverse possession had never occurred); [1991] Conv 397 (A H R Brierley).

2   LRA 2002, Sch 6, paras 4–6 [**paras 6.58–6.60**]. See also LRA 2002, Sch 6, para 11(3)(a) [**para 6.55**].

6.147   In each circumstance the onus ultimately rests on the paper owner to take positive steps to recover possession (in the absence of the squatter's voluntary surrender of possession or written acknowledgment of title or acceptance of some lease or licence). These steps inevitably involve the institution of legal proceedings for recovery.[1] The 'possession' of the squatter is in no way terminated, nor does the paper owner recover a 'constructive possession', by reason of the squatter's mere receipt of an informal communication demanding that he should quit the land.[2] Nor is it sufficient for the paper owner to initiate court proceedings for a form of relief which does not necessarily involve the recovery of possession.[3]

1   The true owner cannot, merely by entering the land, resume possession so as to break the continuity of possession of a squatter who remains there (see *Smith v Waterman* [2003] All ER (D) 72 (Jun) at [60]–[64] per Blackburne J).

2   *Mount Carmel Investments Ltd v Peter Thurlow Ltd* [1988] 1 WLR 1078 at 1084H–1086A. See [1988] Conv 359 (J E M).

3   See *J A Pye (Oxford) Ltd v Graham* [2000] Ch 676 at 702B–C.

6.148   The process of recovering possession of land is examined in greater detail in Chapter 3.[1]

1   [**Paras 3.32–3.48**].

CHAPTER 7

Freehold and leasehold estates in land

THE SIGNIFICANCE OF ESTATES

7.1 Chapter 1 pointed to the way in which English law employs the abstract medium of the 'estate' as the closest approximation to ownership of land.[1] The present chapter focuses on estates in greater detail, for it is these estates which constitute the basis of the structural grammar of land law. At its very outset the Law of Property Act 1925 marks out, with particular emphasis, two potential *legal* estates in land – the freehold and leasehold estates.[2] Such is the significance of these estates that neither can be held at law by a minor (ie by a person who has not attained the age of 18 years)[3], although a minor may validly hold the *equitable* version of one or other estate,[4] necessarily behind some trust of land.[5]

1   [**Para 1.125**].
2   LPA 1925, s 1(1).
3   LPA 1925, ss 1(6), 20, 205(1)(v); TOLATA 1996, Sch 1, para 1(1)(a). Any attempt after 1996 to convey a legal estate to a minor operates instead as a declaration that the land is held in trust for the minor; and a purported transfer to two or more minors operates as a declaration of trust for both (TOLATA 1996, s 2(1), (6), Sch 1, para 1(1)(b)) [**para 2.132**]. If, however, the intention was that the minor or minors should hold on trust for some other person, the purported conveyance takes effect as a declaration of trust for that other person.
4   See e g *Kingston upon Thames BC v Prince* [1999] 1 FLR 593 at 603A–D (minor competent to succeed to secure tenancy as an equitable estate).
5   [**Para 9.172**].

THE FEE SIMPLE ABSOLUTE IN POSSESSION

7.2 At common law the primary estate in land is the *freehold* or *fee simple* estate, an estate of essentially unlimited duration. It is this estate which connotes the reality, if not the rigorous theory, of absolute ownership of land in England and Wales.[1]

1   For a description of the fee simple absolute, see Chapter 1 [**para 1.125**].

Dominance of freehold ownership

7.3 The fee simple estate comprises by far the most common kind of ownership of English realty today. Freehold owner-occupation accounts for the tenure of 70 per cent of all households in the country,[1] its pre-eminence being attributable to the relatively unqualified nature of the possessory control which it confers.[2] Leasehold ownership – ownership of a term of years absolute – is less prevalent, although it is still quite significant and, in many ways, more complex than the phenomenon of the fee simple.

1   *Social Trends No 34* (2004 edition, London), p 153. The Tory aim of 80 per cent home ownership by the end of the 1980s was never achieved (see speech by Mr Hugh Rossi, Conservative spokesman on housing and land, reported *Times*, 23 February 1976).
2   See *Delgamuukw v British Columbia* (1997) 153 DLR (4th) 193 at [156] per Lamer CJC.

Dominance of the absolute form of the fee simple estate

7.4 The fee simple can assume several forms, but it is only the fee simple *absolute in possession* which is statutorily declared to be 'capable of subsisting or of being conveyed or created' as a legal estate in land.[1] Other, more limited, forms of the fee simple estate can exist – usually in equity – but these qualified forms of estate are nowadays extremely rare and are almost always the ill-advised testamentary product of the wilfully eccentric. The dominance of the fee simple absolute – the 'local equivalent of full ownership'[2] – is virtually complete.

1   LPA 1925, s 1(1)(a). Whether this fee simple estate *actually* attains legal status usually depends on compliance with various formalities of transfer or registration [**paras 2.126, 7.25**].
2   See *Wik Peoples v Queensland* (1996) 187 CLR 1 at 250 per Kirby J.

DEFINITION OF THE FEE SIMPLE 'ABSOLUTE'

7.5 The term 'absolute' qualifies the character of a fee simple estate in such a way as to distinguish it from various forms of modified fee such as the 'determinable' and the 'conditional' fee simple. The fee simple absolute is nowadays infinitely more important than any of the modified fees. Whereas the absolute form of the fee simple is readily identifiable, the internal distinctions between the modified kinds of fee throw up a range of complication wholly disproportionate to their contemporary significance.

The determinable fee simple

7.6 A determinable fee simple is an estate of potentially perpetual duration which is liable to be cut short automatically by some specified change of circumstance or by the occurrence of some named but unpredictable event. An example occurs in a grant of 'Greenacre to X in fee simple until she joins the

Communist Party.' Here it is uncertain at the date of the grant whether the determining event will ever happen.[1] The grant confers on X a determinable fee simple which, because it is not 'absolute', can never subsist as a legal estate[2] and can only be equitable.[3] As such it must take effect under a strict settlement (if granted prior to 1997)[4] or otherwise behind a trust of land.[5] Throughout X's ownership of the determinable fee simple, the original grantor retains a 'possibility of reverter' in that X's estate will automatically terminate in favour of the revertee if the specified determining event occurs.[6] In this case the grantor's possibility of reverter matures into a resumption of the fee simple absolute.

1   It is of the essence of a determinable fee that there is a possibility that the determining event may *never* happen. No determinable fee simple can arise if the specified determining event is bound to occur sooner or later. For instance, a grant in fee simple to X 'until the death of Y' confers on X not a determinable fee simple, but an estate *pur autre vie* (*Challis*, p 252) **[para 1.129]**.
2   See LPA 1925, s 1(1)(a).
3   LPA 1925, s 1(3). See *Re Rowhook Mission Hall, Horsham* [1985] Ch 62 at 79B.
4   SLA 1925, s 1(1)(ii)(c) **[para 9.209]**.
5   **[Para 9.172]**.
6   The determinable fee comes to an end without any entry or claim requiring to be made by the revertee (*Challis*, p 252).

Examples ancient and modern

7.7   No special language need be used to create a determinable fee simple so long as it is made plain that the durability of the fee simple estate is dependent on the continuance of some specified state of affairs or the non-occurrence of some specified future event. The case law abounds with such curious examples as the grant of a fee simple 'during the time that such a tree shall grow',[1] or 'as long as the Church of St Paul shall stand',[2] or until A pay £100 to B.[3] Nowadays determinable fees simple are few in number and tend increasingly to be the product of statutory creation. In England and Wales, for instance, the relevant local highway authority is, in relation to the superficial and immediately subjacent soil of its public roads, statutorily invested with a fee simple estate determinable on these roads ceasing to be public highways.[4]

1   *Ayres v Falkland* (1697) 1 Ld Raym 325 at 326, 91 ER 1112 at 1113.
2   2 Plowd 557, 75 ER 820.
3   For other examples of a determinable fee simple, see *Challis*, pp 255–260. For a more recent instance, see *Re Rowhook Mission Hall, Horsham* [1985] Ch 62.
4   See Highways Act 1980, s 263 **[paras 1.30, 5.12]**. It has been suggested that a freehold estate in commonhold land **[para 7.356]** is necessarily a determinable (and therefore equitable) fee simple in that the estate is liable to be divested on a winding up of the commonhold association (see [2003] Conv 358 (J G Riddall); but compare [2004] Conv 164).

Subsequent impossibility

7.8   If the determining event indicated in the grant of a determinable fee simple later becomes impossible, the grantee's estate becomes a fee simple absolute and the grantor's possibility of reverter simply falls away.[1] If, in the example above of a grant to X in fee simple 'until she joins the Communist Party', X dies without ever expressing such a political affiliation, her determinable fee becomes absolute and passes to her successors as part of her estate.

1   *Challis*, p 254. See *Re Leach* [1912] 2 Ch 422 at 429.

Effect of invalidity

7.9 If the limiting element in a determinable fee simple is vitiated (eg by considerations of public policy or by reason of non-compliance with the Human Rights Act 1998), the determinable fee is rendered void in its entirety.[1] Since the limiting words are bound into the determinable fee simple as an integral component of the estate granted, any invalidity affecting these limiting words inevitably makes the entire grant defective.

1   *Bl Comm*, Vol II, p 157. See *Re Moore* (1888) 39 Ch D 116 at 130, 132; *Zapletal v Wright* [1957] Tas SR 211 at 218.

The conditional fee simple

7.10 A conditional fee simple is an estate of potentially perpetual duration which is defeasible on satisfaction of a specified 'condition subsequent'. An example occurs where Greenacre is granted to X in fee simple 'on condition that she shall not join the Communist Party.' The fee simple estate vested in X is liable to forfeiture if X fulfils the terms of the condition subsequent. As is the case with the determinable fee simple, the grant of a conditional fee provides, at least in theory, a means by which – however capriciously – a landowner may impose on the grantees of his largesse an idiosyncratic preference as to beliefs, morals or lifestyle.[1] Although, like the determinable fee simple, the conditional fee has spawned a rich case law, some of the common law elaboration of this form of estate ownership may have been rendered redundant by the advent of the Human Rights Act 1998. The capacity for invidious discrimination so freely available to the eccentric testator may in certain instances fall foul of Convention-based guarantees of individual freedom (if such guarantees are given horizontal effect).

1   See *Jenner v Turner* (1880–81) 16 Ch D 188 at 196–197 per Bacon V-C.

Ancillary rights of entry

7.11 The grant of a conditional fee simple is almost invariably accompanied by an express right of entry,[1] which entitles the grantor of the fee simple, should he so choose, to forfeit (or terminate) the estate on fulfilment of the specified condition.[2] Rights of entry have sometimes been attached to a grant in fee simple in order to enforce payment of a rentcharge undertaken by the grantee of the land.[3] In certain parts of England[4] and Northern Ireland[5] it used to be a common conveyancing practice for land to be sold not for a capital sum but in consideration of a continuing income in the form of a perpetual rentcharge known as a 'fee farm rent'. Although such conveyances are no longer possible in England and Wales,[6] those fee farm grants which still subsist invest the grantee with a conditional fee simple, the estate being defeasible on non-payment of the required periodic sum.

1   **[Para 8.263]**.
2   The grantor may in his conveyance specify that the right of entry is exercisable by and on behalf of some person other than himself (LPA 1925, s 4(3)).
3   Rentcharges are discussed elsewhere **[paras 8.225, 13.58]**.
4   Particularly in Manchester and East Lancashire, and around Bath and Bristol (see Law Commission, *Transfer of Land: Rentcharges* (Published Working Paper No 24, 1969), paras 10–14).
5   Much of the 17th and 18th Century plantation of Ulster was carried out effectively through the device of fee farm grants which still, even in recent times, appeared in chains of title **[para 1.148]**.
6   See Rentcharges Act 1977, s 2(1) **[para 8.228]**.

The legal quality of some conditional fee simple estates

7.12   The distinction between conditional and determinable fees would be almost entirely without significance but for one vital difference in their characterisation as property rights. By some legislative accident the conditional fee simple ranks, in most cases, as a legal estate in land, whereas the determinable fee is clearly equitable only. In strict logic, the absence of an 'absolute' quality should have the effect of relegating all conditional fees to merely equitable status.[1] However, it was considered inconvenient that fee farm grants, which were all but grants in fee simple absolute, should not enjoy legal quality.[2] Accordingly the Law of Property Act 1925 was amended to provide that those fee simple grants which are subject to a right of entry or re-entry should henceforth be treated, for the purpose of the Act, as grants of a fee simple absolute estate.[3] Whether or not intentionally, the amending provision appears to be sufficiently widely drafted to apply not merely to fee farm grants subject to a rentcharge, but to all forms of conditional fee simple which happen to be subject to a right of entry or re-entry.[4] Thus, somewhat confusingly, the conditional fee simple is rendered capable of existing in such cases as a *legal* estate in land.

1   See LPA 1925, s 1(1)(a).
2   There was a danger that such grants would come within the cumbersome provisions of the Settled Land Act 1925 **[para 9.206]**. See *Re Rowhook Mission Hall, Horsham* [1985] Ch 62 at 79C–D.
3   LPA 1925, s 7(1), as amended by Law of Property (Amendment) Act 1926, Schedule. See the further amendment of section 7(1) contained in Reverter of Sites Act 1987, s 1.
4   Any post-1996 grant of a conditional or determinable fee simple falling outside LPA 1925, s 7(1) brings the land within the scope of a 'trust of land' governed by the Trusts of Land and Appointment of Trustees Act 1996 **[para 9.172]**. See *Transfer of Land: Trusts of Land* (Law Com No 181, June 1989), paras 17.1, 20.4.

Distinction between conditional and determinable fees

7.13 The elusive distinction between the conditional and determinable forms of the fee simple has been described as 'little short of disgraceful to our jurisprudence.'[1] The difference rests on the fact that in a determinable fee the limiting circumstance is integral to the formulation of the duration of the estate,[2] whereas in the conditional fee the limiting proviso operates to cut short the estate before it reaches out to its normal span.[3] This narrow distinction is ultimately a matter of construction of the words used in the grant,[4] but from it flow certain technical differences of operation and effect. First, whereas a determinable fee terminates automatically in favour of the revertee when the limiting event occurs, the conditional fee does not so terminate. The conditional fee continues to exist unless and until the grantor elects to exercise his right of entry.[5] Second, the courts have tended to be more vigilant in applying rules of public policy to strike down undesirable conditions subsequent than has traditionally been the case with equivalent clauses contained in a determinable fee simple. Third, if a condition subsequent is vitiated as contrary to public policy, the offending condition is merely struck out, leaving the grant as a fee simple absolute,[6] whereas the grant of a determinable fee is destroyed in its entirety.

1   *Re King's Trusts* (1892) 29 LR Ir 401 at 410 per Porter MR.
2   *Preston on Estates*, Vol 1, p 49; *Bl Comm*, Vol II, p 155; *Challis*, pp 260–261; *Re Tilbury West Public School Board and Hastie* (1966) 55 DLR (2d) 407 at 410.
3   See *Preston on Estates*, Vol 1, p 49; *Bl Comm*, Vol II, p 155; *Challis*, p 261. In the words of Laskin JA in *Re North Gower Township Public School Board and Todd* (1968) 65 DLR (2d) 421 at 424, a conditional fee involves a 'superadded condition upon a grant of a fee simple rather than an integral part of the very limitation of the estate created ... ' See also *Re Essex County Roman Catholic Separate School Board and Antaya* (1978) 80 DLR (3d) 405 at 409.
4   Certain words and phrases have come to be indicia of a fee simple upon condition subsequent (eg 'on condition that', 'provided that') and of a fee simple determinable (eg 'while', 'until', 'as long as'), but these rules of thumb are not necessarily conclusive (see *Hopper v Liverpool Corporation* (1943) 88 Sol Jo 213 at 214; *Re North Gower Township Public School Board and Todd* (1968) 65 DLR (2d) 421 at 424).
5   *Litt*, s 347; *Bl Comm*, Vol II, p 155; *Challis*, p 219. See *Matthew Manning's Case* (1609) 8 Co Rep 94b at 95b, 77 ER 618 at 620.
6   *Bl Comm*, Vol II, pp 156–157. A void condition subsequent is simply 'treated as non scriptum' (*Gower v Public Trustee* [1924] NZLR 1233 at 1257 per Salmond J). See also *Morley v Rennoldson* (1843) 2 Hare 570 at 579–580, 67 ER 235 at 239; *Zapletal v Wright* [1957] Tas SR 211 at 218; *Charles v Barzey* [2003] 1 WLR 437 at [11] per Lord Hoffmann.

Judicial control over conditions and limitations

7.14 As indicated above, the courts have asserted an historic jurisdiction to strike down certain kinds of condition or limitation attached to a grant in fee simple where the constraints concerned have been regarded as either impossible[1] or illegal[2] or as inimical to public policy on moral, social or economic grounds. In practice the courts have guarded jealously against restraints of an absolute or virtually absolute nature imposed upon the grantee of a fee simple, but have been remarkably tolerant of restraints which are merely partial or particular.[3]

1   Blackstone held conditions to be void 'if they be impossible at the time of their creation, or afterwards become impossible by the act of God or the act of the feoffor himself' (*Bl Comm*, Vol II, p 156). See also *Sheppard's Touchstone of Common Assurances* (8th edn by E G Atherley, London 1826), p 129; *Gower v Public Trustee* [1924] NZLR 1233 at 1255 (grant to X 'on condition that he shall not become a Roman Catholic', where X is already a Roman Catholic at the date of the grant).

2   Blackstone gave the example of a grant to a man which is expressed to be defeasible 'unless he kills another' (*Bl Comm*, Vol II, p 157). The preclusion of illegality also implies that a condition subsequent cannot be allowed to frustrate the legally prescribed devolution of property. For instance, a condition subsequent cannot validly make a fee simple estate defeasible in the event of the grantee's intestacy (*Re Dixon* [1903] 2 Ch 458 at 460) or insolvency (*Re Machu* (1882) 21 Ch D 838 at 842; *Charles v Barzey* [2003] 1 WLR 437 at [11] per Lord Hoffmann). Strangely there seems to be no objection if a similar clause appears in the form of a determinable interest (see e g *Graves v Dolphin* (1826) 1 Sim 66 at 67, 57 ER 503 at 504).

3   Modern courts lean towards a construction of grants which will result in validity rather than voidness (see *Charles v Barzey* [2003] 1 WLR 437 at [12] per Lord Hoffmann).

7.15   The judicial power to override the expressed wishes of grantors has always represented a significant diminution of the owner's right under English law to dispose of his assets in any way he will. Yet common law principle (as supplemented by statute) merely exemplifies the proposition that claims of property are constantly curtailed by more fundamental human freedoms: property issues are ultimately questions about moral space.[1] There has always been a particular disinclination to allow a testator to direct the lives of his children from the grave.[2] The courts thus tend to construe strictly any clause which purports to operate a forfeiture of a proprietary estate[3] and also to exercise their equitable jurisdiction to relieve the defaulting party against the effect of such forfeiture.

1   [Para 2.9].

2   See *Clayton v Ramsden* [1943] AC 320 at 325 per Lord Atkin; *Re Sutcliffe* [1982] 2 NZLR 330 at 337. See also *Blathwayt v Baron Cawley* [1976] AC 397 at 427C–D; *Re Tepper's Will Trusts* [1987] Ch 358 at 370E.

3   See *Rawson v Inhabitants of School District No 5, in Uxbridge* (1863) 89 Mass 125 at 127, 83 Am Dec 670 at 672 per Bigelow CJ ('[c]onditions subsequent are not favored in law'); *Pearson v Adams* (1912) 7 DLR 139 at 144–145. The courts require a greater degree of certainty in advance as to the scope of a condition subsequent than is needed when the condition is precedent (*Blathwayt v Baron Cawley* [1976] AC 397 at 424H–425A). It may be, as suggested by Lord Wright in *Clayton v Ramsden* [1943] AC 320 at 329, that the 'modern idea, perhaps, is that the beneficiary should be in a position to know beyond a peradventure what he is to do or not to do if he is to avoid a forfeiture. That must be ascertainable by him.' See also *Clavering v Ellison* (1856) 3 Drew 451 at 470, 61 ER 975 at 982, (1859) 7 HLCas 707 at 715–716, 11 ER 282 at 285.

Restrictions on alienation

7.16   The common law has long held that the power of alienation is a standard incident of the right of private property.[1] Unrestricted alienability nevertheless contains an inherent contradiction. In its fullest form the freedom to alienate implies a power to suspend or destroy the *alienee's* freedom of future alienation.[2] Freedom of disposition is supremely evidenced in a grant which is limited in such a way that the grantee can never replicate the grantor's exercise of sovereign dispositive power.[3] The ultimate exercise of free alienation is, paradoxically, the negation of that power – an abuse of right which breaches the inner morality of alienation.[4] For this reason the freedom to alienate has always been qualified by a number of common law rules which curtail the alienor's otherwise comprehensive creative control over future holdings in his or her property.[5]

1   See e g *Re Ridley* (1879) 11 Ch D 645 at 648–649 per Jessel MR; *Scott v National City Bank*, 139 So 367 (1931); *Hall v Busst* (1960) 104 CLR 206 at 218 per Dixon CJ; *Re Permanent Trustee Nominees (Canberra) Ltd* [1989] 1 Qd R 314 at 316. The European Court of Human Rights has also emphasised that 'the right to dispose of one's property constitutes a traditional and fundamental aspect of the right of property' (*Marckx v Belgium*, Series A No 31 (1979) at [63]).

2   Some commentators nevertheless accept this outcome as an inevitable component of a libertarian view of property. See e g Richard A Epstein, 'Past and Future: The Temporal Dimension in the Law of Property' 64 Wash ULQ 667 at 705 (1986), where it is argued that the only justification for restraints on private alienation is 'to prevent the infliction of external harms, either through aggression or the depletion of common-pool resources.' See also Epstein, 'Why Restrain Alienation?' 85 Col L Rev 970 (1985).

3   'The exercise of the power to convey by any individual cannot begin to be full unless he can limit the power to convey of the individual to whom he conveys' (see C Donahue, 'The Future of the Concept of Property Predicted from its Past', in J R Pennock and J W Chapman (ed), *Property: Nomos XXII* (New York 1980), p 33).

4   See Gray, 'Property in Common Law Systems', in G E van Maanen and A J van der Walt (ed), *Property Law on the Threshold of the 21st Century* (MAKLU, Antwerp, 1996), pp 262–263.

5   Free alienability of land is even more significantly cut back where the alienor, in pursuit of dispositive freedom, effectively ties the land up for generations by the conferment of highly contingent future interests (i e interests subject to a 'condition precedent'). The common law rule against perpetuities, although now radically modified by statute, abridges the property owner's right to create precisely whatever interests he or she may choose (see *Elements of Land Law* (2nd edn 1993), pp 645–672). By prohibiting the creation of certain forms of remotely vesting future interest, the rule eliminates long-term and inevitably costly ownership restrictions, thereby striking a compromise between the desire of one generation to fetter the future allocation of property resources and the contrary desire of following generations to enjoy total freedom of disposition. See R C Ellickson, 'Adverse Possession and Perpetuities Law: Two Dents in the Libertarian Model of Property Rights' 64 Wash ULQ 723 at 736 (1986).

7.17   For centuries courts have invalidated any condition attached to an estate which wholly or substantially prohibits alienation of the estate by the grantee. Any absolute restriction on the alienation of land held in fee simple is therefore, in the words of Littleton, 'against reason',[1] being wholly repugnant to the essence of ownership in fee.[2] The courts have accordingly struck down conditions subsequent which prohibit any form of alienation of the estate by the grantee[3] or which allow alienation only to a named person.[4] By contrast, the courts have normally been prepared to uphold clauses which prohibit alienation to a specific named person[5] or which permit alienation only to a member or members of an identifiable class or group of persons.[6] Some sort of compromise has therefore been struck between the policy concern to promote the commerciability of land and the countervailing impulse to permit personal control over discretionary distributions of privately held assets.[7]

1   *Litt*, s 360.

2   *Co Litt*, p 223a; *Bl Comm*, Vol II, p 156. See *Re Rosher* (1884) 26 Ch D 801 at 812; *Re Elliot*
     [1896] 2 Ch 353 at 356; *Re Winnipeg Condominium Corp No 1 and Stechley* (1979) 90 DLR
     (3d) 703 at 706; *Charles v Barzey* [2003] 1 WLR 437 at [11] per Lord Hoffmann.
3   See *Hood v Oglander* (1865) 34 Beav 513 at 522, 55 ER 733 at 737; *Byrne v Byrne* (1953) 87
     ILTR 183 at 185–186; *Wollondilly Shire Council v Picton Power Lines Pty Ltd* (1991) 5 BPR
     11503 at 11508. 'Alienation' for this purpose includes a mortgage (*Ware v Cann* (1830) 10 B &
     C 433 at 438, 109 ER 511 at 513) and a testamentary disposition (*Re Jones* [1898] 1 Ch 438 at
     443). The general rule of public policy (see *Re Ridley* (1879) 11 Ch D 645 at 649) also strikes
     at the inclusion in a transfer of oppressive rights of option or pre-emption in favour of the
     transferor.
4   *Muschamp v Bluet* (1617) Bridgman J 132 at 137, 123 ER 1253 at 1256; *Re Cockerill* [1929]
     2 Ch 131 at 134–135.
5   *Litt*, s 361; *Co Litt*, p 223a/b. See, however, *Re Rosher* (1884) 26 Ch D 801 at 813–814.
6   *Doe d Gill v Pearson* (1805) 6 East 173 at 180, 102 ER 1253 at 1256; *Re Macleay* (1875) LR 20
     Eq 186 at 189 (alienation permitted within 'the family'). Compare, however, the invalidation of
     restrictive conditions in *Crofts v Beamish* [1905] 2 IR 349 at 356–357, 360; *Re Browne* [1954]
     Ch 39 at 50 (alienation limited to small and diminishing group of 'brothers'); *Kirby v Allen*
     (1997) 9 BPR 17445 at 17447 (alienation limited to 'members of my future family'). Where the
     class to which alienation is permitted is defined with reference to racial or sexual characteris-
     tics, the limiting clause is not prohibited by statute (see Race Relations Act 1976, s 21(1); Sex
     Discrimination Act 1975, s 30(1)), but would be invalidated by more general rules of public
     policy. See J F Garner, (1972) 35 MLR 478; J D A Brooke-Taylor, [1978] Conv 24.
7   The modern distaste for capricious restrictions is evident in *In the estate of Dunne* [1988] IR
     155 at 157. Here the Irish High Court struck down a prohibition of transfer to any member of
     the 'Meredith families of Mountmellick' as excessively vague and also, in that it sought to
     'perpetuate old family divisions', as contrary to public policy.

Restrictions on marriage

7.18 The state of marriage is similarly regarded as a socially approved
institution and the courts have been reluctant to uphold conditions subsequent
which militate against the institution in its entirety.[1] Conditions subsequent
have thus been invalidated which altogether preclude marriage[2] (as distinct
from remarriage[3]) on the part of the grantee, but the courts have approved
partial restraints on marriage which merely prohibit the grantee's marriage with
a named person[4] or with any of an ascertainable class of persons.[5] It is now
likely, however, that even these forms of restriction are incompatible with the
'right to marry' recognised by the European Convention on Human Rights.[6]

1   'Conditions in restraint of marriage are odious' (*Long v Dennis* (1767) 4 Burr 2052 at 2055, 98
     ER 69 at 72 per Lord Mansfield). The disfavour shown towards such conditions was justified
     in former times on grounds both of moral paternalism (i e the curtailment of 'licentiousness')
     and also of public policy (i e the avoidance of 'depopulation, the greatest of all political sins')
     (*Low v Peers* (1770) Wilm 364 at 372, 97 ER 138 at 141). See also *Maddox v Maddox's
     Administrator* (1854) 11 Grat (52 Va) 804 at 806; O L Browder, 'Conditions and Limitations in
     Restraint of Marriage' 39 Michigan L Rev 1288 (1940–41).
2   See e g *Morley v Rennoldson* (1843) 2 Hare 570 at 579–580, 583, 67 ER 235 at 239–240; *Jenner
     v Turner* (1880–81) 16 Ch D 188 at 197; *Duddy v Gresham* (1878) 2 LR Ir 442 at 464–465.
     Compare the greater willingness to tolerate the use of marriage as a limiting circumstance in a
     determinable fee simple (*Re King's Trusts* (1892) 29 LR Ir 401 at 410; *Oliver v Menton* [1945]
     IR 6 at 11–12; *Stewart v Murdoch* [1969] NI 78 at 82; *Re Dolan* [1970] IR 94 at 101).
3   Grants *durante viduitate* (for the duration of widowhood) were not formerly regarded as
     offensive to public policy (see e g *Jordan v Holkham* (1753) Amb 209, 27 ER 139). Compare,

however, the more enlightened approach evident in *Duddy v Gresham* (1878) 2 LR Ir 442, where a testator had left property to his widow on condition that she should not remarry, but should 'retire immediately after my death into a convent of her own choice.'

4   *Jarvis v Duke* (1681) 1 Vern 19 at 20, 23 ER 274 ('such an example of presumptuous disobedience highly meriting such a punishment; she being only prohibited to marry with one man by name, and nothing in the whole fair garden of Eden would serve her turn but this forbidden fruit'). See also *Jenner v Turner* (1880–81) 16 Ch D 188 at 196; *Re Bathe* [1925] Ch 377 at 382; *Re Hanlon* [1933] Ch 254 at 260.

5   *Duggan v Kelly* (1847) 10 Ir Eq R 295 at 301–302 ('a Papist'); *Perrin v Lyon* (1807) 9 East 170 at 183–184, 103 ER 538 at 543 ('a Scotchman'); *Jenner v Turner* (1880–81) 16 Ch D 188 at 197 ('a domestic servant').

6   ECHR Art 12.

Restrictions on religious belief

7.19   The courts have not been particularly astute to restrain attempts to perpetuate religious preference – bigoted or otherwise – in the grant of a fee simple, at least where there is no vitiating degree of uncertainty attaching to the faith prescribed or proscribed by the grantor.[1] In *Blathwayt v Baron Cawley*,[2] the House of Lords upheld a condition subsequent which had the effect of forfeiting the grantee's interest if he should 'be or become a Roman Catholic.'[3] It is questionable whether such an approach remains reconcilable with the protection afforded by the European Convention on Human Rights to the 'right to freedom of thought, conscience and religion.'[4]

1   See *Clayton v Ramsden* [1943] AC 320, where the House of Lords struck down as uncertain a prohibition of marriage with a person 'not of Jewish parentage and of the Jewish faith'. Compare, however, *Higgins v Bank of Ireland* [1947] IR 277 at 285–286; *McCausland v Young* [1948] NI 72 at 94, [1949] NI 49 at 60; *Blathwayt v Baron Cawley* [1976] AC 397 at 425D–G, 429E–F; *Re Tuck's ST* [1978] Ch 49 at 62F, 65F, 66C; *Re Tepper's Will Trusts* [1987] Ch 358 at 368C–F, 376F–377D.

2   [1976] AC 397. See generally J D A Brooke-Taylor, [1978] Conv 24.

3   The actual grant in this case involved an entailed interest, but the entail was duly barred by the tenant in tail [**para 1.128**], who thereupon claimed that his fee simple was absolute and not conditional.

4   ECHR Art 9.

Other forms of discrimination

7.20   At least prior to the commencement of the Human Rights Act 1998, there was no significant inclination on the part of English courts to give effect to supra-national guarantees against discrimination. The view was once expressed that discrimination 'is not the same thing as choice' and that 'neither by express provision nor by implication has private selection yet become a matter of public policy.'[1] The deference accorded the private prejudice of the propertied class has been substantial,[2] personal caprice becoming offensive to public policy only where it has imposed a comprehensive fetter upon the operation of the free market in either private property[3] or the supporting institution of bourgeois marriage.[4]

1   *Blathwayt v Baron Cawley* [1976] AC 397 at 426B–C per Lord Wilberforce (see also Lord Cross of Chelsea at 429G–430A, Lord Edmund-Davies at 441D–E).
2   See e g *Re Talbot-Ponsonby's Estate* [1937] 4 All ER 309 at 313A (upholding a condition that grantee should not allow a named person to 'set foot upon' the premises). The private prejudices endorsed by the courts may, of course, be anti-establishment in character. See *Blathwayt v Baron Cawley* [1976] AC 397 at 442G per Lord Fraser of Tullybelton (grant conditioned upon not sending children to fee-paying public school).
3   See *Blathwayt v Baron Cawley* [1976] AC 397 at 426G per Lord Wilberforce (endorsing the idea that 'in relation to landed estates … testators may … prefer one branch of the family to another upon religious grounds').
4   The courts regard as void a condition which militates against the continued cohabitation of spouses (see *Re Johnson's WT* [1967] Ch 387 at 395B–C, 396C, F–G).

DEFINITION OF THE FEE SIMPLE 'IN POSSESSION'

7.21   The only form of fee simple absolute capable of subsisting as a legal estate is the fee simple *in possession*.[1] The qualifying phrase 'in possession' connotes that the grantee is immediately entitled to occupation and enjoyment of the land from the effective date of the grant (ie the grantee is not subject to any interest prior in time to his own).[2] The term 'in possession'[3] distinguishes this form of fee simple sharply from those estates in fee simple which are merely 'in remainder' or 'in reversion'. Regardless of the manner of its creation, an estate in remainder or reversion can never be a legal estate.[4] According to the inexorable logic of the Law of Property Act 1925, such an estate ranks as an equitable fee simple absolute[5] and can therefore take effect only under an existing strict settlement[6] or behind a new trust of land.[7]

1   LPA 1925, s 1(1)(a).
2   See *Pearson v IRC* [1981] AC 753 at 772A–D, where Viscount Dilhorne accepted the time-honoured proposition that an 'estate in possession' is one which gives 'a present right of present enjoyment.'
3   'Possession' is statutorily defined as including 'receipt of rents and profits or the right to receive the same' (LPA 1925, s 205(1)(xix)). Thus a fee simple absolute does not cease to be an estate 'in possession' merely because the owner grants a lease to a tenant.
4   They may, of course, become legal estates when later they fall into possession [**para 7.22**].
5   LPA 1925, s 1(1)(a), (3).
6   [**Para 9.206**].
7   [**Para 9.172**].

Estates 'in remainder'

7.22   An interest 'in remainder' confers a present right to future enjoyment, in the sense that the 'remainderman' is excluded from immediate enjoyment only by reason of the presence of a prior interest or prior interests vested in somebody else.[1] An example occurs where H, by his will, leaves the family home to W for life, with remainder to their children in fee simple. As from the date of H's death, W holds a life interest *in possession*. However, it is important to realise that the children, although not immediately entitled 'in possession', receive a vested proprietary estate at the date of the grant. They hold a present right to future enjoyment – in the form of an equitable fee simple absolute *in remainder*.[2] This remainder must eventually 'fall into possession' on the termination of W's prior interest (ie when W dies). Even if the children should predecease W, their equitable fee simple estate will pass to their own successors, who will, in due course, take the estate 'in possession' when W eventually dies.

1   *Bl Comm*, Vol II, p 164; *Challis*, pp 78–79.
2   Compare e g *Charles v Barzey* [2003] 1 WLR 437 at [18] per Lord Hoffmann.

Estates 'in reversion'

7.23   An estate 'in reversion' is the sum total of the rights retained throughout by a grantor who fails to exhaust the entire interest in the land in the terms of his conveyance to another.[1] In other words, if a grantor fails to dispose of his fee simple estate, he necessarily retains a fee simple 'in reversion' from the moment of his non-exhaustive grant, this fee simple estate falling back into possession only on the expiration of the limited interest or interests which he has granted away. An example occurs where S, having purchased the fee simple estate in a house, grants his elderly mother, M, a life interest (but makes no other disposition). M clearly takes a life interest *in possession*, but S, since he has not granted away the entire interest in the land, retains the equitable fee simple absolute *in reversion*.[2]

1   See *Bl Comm*, Vol II, p 175; *Challis*, p 78.
2   The 'reversion' which arises here by operation of law must be distinguished from other forms of right which appear similar but which result from the conduct of the grantees themselves (e g the 'possibility of reverter' which rests with the grantor of a determinable fee simple and the 'right of entry' vested in the grantor of a fee simple which has been made the subject of a condition subsequent).

CREATION OF THE FEE SIMPLE ESTATE

7.24   The *creation* of a fee simple absolute in possession (as distinct from the subsequent transfer of such an estate) is today a relatively rare event.[1] It involves the formation of a new estate in land out of the allodium comprising the unalienated lands of the crown.[2] It used to be that the crown could not hold land of itself – an inevitable implication of the doctrine of tenures[3] – but this principle has now been reversed by the Land Registration Act 2002, which enables the crown to grant itself a freehold estate in 'demesne land' which is both registrable and disposable.[4] The crown is also competent to make an infeudatory grant of a fee simple estate in 'demesne land' to any other person, such a grant ranking as an 'event' which triggers a requirement that the grantee apply for first registration of title to the estate at Land Registry.[5] The grantee then holds, as indeed all owners of a fee simple today hold, by a direct 'socage tenure' from the crown.[6]

1   Except perhaps in the specialised sense that a common law freehold may be generated by adverse possession [**paras 3.24, 6.30**].

2　For many reasons the aboriginal or native title increasingly recognised throughout the common law world does not comprise any form of fee simple estate. Instead such title is *sui generis* (see *Mabo v Queensland (No 2)* (1992) 175 CLR 1 at 89 per Deane and Gaudron JJ; *Delgamuukw v British Columbia* (1997) 153 DLR (4th) 193 at [112] per Lamer CJC). It comprises a non-commerciable 'proprietary community title' which constitutes 'a burden on the Crown's radical title when the Crown acquires sovereignty' (*Mabo (No 2)*, supra at 51 per Brennan J). See also *Wik Peoples v Queensland* (1996) 187 CLR 1 at 206–207 per Kirby J; *Anderson v Wilson* (2000) 171 ALR 705 at 714. See Brendan Edgeworth, 'Tenure, Allodialism and Indigenous Rights at Common Law' (1994) 23 Anglo-American L Rev 397; Patricia Lane, 'Native Title – The End of Property As We Know It' (2000) 8 APLJ 1.

3　Tenure requires a *tenant* (in the sense of landholder) [**para 1.142**]. One consequence was that the ancient lands of the crown were incapable of registration at Land Registry (see *Scmlla Properties Ltd v Gesso Properties (BVI) Ltd* [1995] BCC 793 at 798).

4　LRA 2002, ss 79(1), 132(1) ('demesne land'). See Law Commission and Land Registry, *Land Registration for the Twenty-First Century: A Conveyancing Revolution* (Law Com No 271, July 2001), paras 2.7, 11.5–11.19.

5　LRA 2002, s 80(1).

6　[**Para 1.150**].

DEALINGS WITH THE FEE SIMPLE ESTATE

7.25　While a legal fee simple estate is in existence, its owner enjoys virtually plenary powers of disposition, for example by way of gift, sale or mortgage charge.[1] This policy in favour of marketability reflects the common law's longstanding concern with freedom of alienation as a standard incident of property.[2] Dealings with a fee simple estate must, however, be effected in due compliance with certain strict requirements of formal execution and registration at Land Registry. Failure to comply generally results in the disposition of, at most, a mere equitable interest to the grantee.[3]

1　See eg LRA 2002, ss 23(1), 24 (subject to any entry in the register of title restricting the proprietor's powers).

2　See eg *National Provincial Bank Ltd v Ainsworth* [1965] AC 1175 at 1233G–1234A per Lord Upjohn [**para 2.40**].

3　[**Para 7.41**]. This demonstrates, incidentally, that it is quite possible to hold an *equitable* fee simple absolute in possession (or, for that matter, an *equitable* term of years absolute). LPA 1925, s 1(1) merely provides that it is these estates alone which have the potentiality of *legal* existence (see *R v Tower Hamlets LBC, ex p Von Goetz* [1999] QB 1019 at 1024C–1025A per Mummery LJ, 1026F–G per Peter Gibson LJ; *Kingston upon Thames BC v Prince* [1999] 1 FLR 593 at 597A).

General requirement of deed

7.26　English law has a general distaste for the informal or undocumented creation or transfer of rights in land.[1] It has for centuries been the policy of the law that changes of ownership should be attended by various formalities 'so that possibilities of mistake are minimised and everyone knows where they stand.'[2] Accordingly section 52(1) of the Law of Property Act 1925 provides that '[a]ll conveyances of land or of any interest therein are void for the purpose of conveying or creating a legal estate unless made by deed.'

1   See e g *Sen v Headley* [1991] Ch 425 at 440G.
2   *Proudreed Ltd v Microgen Holdings Plc* (1996) 72 P & CR 388 at 389 per Schiemann LJ.

Exceptions to the requirement of a deed

7.27   There are a number of exceptions to the requirement of a deed, the most important of which relate to assents by personal representatives,[1] disclaimers of title made a company liquidator or trustee in bankruptcy in the context of insolvency,[2] vesting orders made by the court[3] and conveyances which take effect by operation of law.[4]

1   LPA 1925, s 52(2)(a).
2   LPA 1925, s 52(2)(b). See Insolvency Act 1986, ss 178(2), 315(1)–(2) **[para 7.67]**.
3   LPA 1925, s 52(2)(f).
4   LPA 1925, s 52(2)(g).

Oral or informal transfers of a fee simple estate

7.28   The statutory concept of a 'conveyance' excludes parol (or oral) transactions.[1] Thus a purported oral disposition of a fee simple estate generally confers no interest at all in the land other than a fragile 'interest at will'.[2] In exceptional circumstances a purported verbal conferment of a fee simple estate can give rise to a constructive trust of the legal title for the promisee[3] or to a court-ordered transfer of the fee simple following proof of a proprietary estoppel.[4] It is also possible that title to land may be transferred, under the doctrine of *donatio mortis causa*, by an informal oral gift made in contemplation of, and conditional upon, the death of the donor.[5]

1   *Rye v Rye* [1962] AC 496 at 504 per Viscount Simonds, 508 per Lord MacDermott, 511 per Lord Radcliffe.
2   LPA 1925, s 54(1) **[para 7.273]**. See *Palfrey v Palfrey* (1974) 229 EG 1593 at 1595; *Dubej v Dubej* (Supreme Court of New South Wales, 25 February 1991, BPR Casenote 95934).
3   **[Para 10.89]**.
4   See e g *Pascoe v Turner* [1979] 1 WLR 431 at 438H–439B (proprietary estoppel created by owner's assurance that 'the house is yours and everything in it' coupled with promisee's subsequent expenditure on maintenance and repair) **[para 10.193]**. Compare, however, *Wright v Johnson* (Unreported, Court of Appeal, 2 November 1999).
5   See *Sen v Headley* [1991] Ch 425 at 441B **[para 10.309]**.

The constitutive elements of a deed

7.29   The essence of a deed is that it should be 'intended by the party who does it to be the most solemn indication to the community that he really means to do what he is doing.'[1] For centuries the validity of a deed in English law rested on compliance with the requirement that the deed be *signed, sealed and delivered*. The force of these ancient conditions became less compelling under modern conditions and, with effect from 31 July 1990,[2] the Law of Property (Miscellaneous Provisions) Act 1989 significantly altered both the constitutive

elements of a deed and the formalities required for its due execution. The
validity of any deed executed on or after this date now depends on its being
signed, attested and delivered.[3]

1   *Manton v Parabolic Pty Ltd* [1985] 2 NSWLR 361 at 367F–G per Young J. See also *Monarch
    Petroleum NL v Citco Australia Petroleum Ltd* [1986] WAR 310 at 352 ('The Latin term for a
    deed is factum, a thing done').
2   See Law of Property (Miscellaneous Provisions) Act 1989 (Commencement) Order 1990
    (SI 1990/1175).
3   See *Bolton MBC v Torkington* [2004] Ch 66 at [33] per Peter Gibson LJ.

Material form

7.30   At common law a deed comprised a writing on paper, vellum or
parchment which was sealed and delivered.[1] The Law of Property (Miscellaneous Provisions) Act 1989 abolished, with effect from 31 July 1990, any rule of
law restricting the substances on which a deed may be written.[2] This amendment recognised that technological innovation has dramatically changed the
material form in which the writing of a deed may be contained. However, no
instrument executed on or after 31 July 1990 can constitute a deed unless 'it
makes it clear on its face that it is intended to be a deed by the person making
it or, as the case may be, by the parties to it.'[3] The deed must, moreover, be
'validly executed as a deed' by such person or parties.[4]

1   See R F Norton, *A Treatise on Deeds* (2nd edn by R J A Morrison and H J Goolden, London
    1928), p 3. To these raw elements statute law added a rudimentary requirement of signature in
    the case of the execution of a deed by an individual (see LPA 1925, s 73(1)).
2   LP(MP)A 1989, s 1(1)(a). See Law Commission, *Deeds and Escrows* (Law Com No 163, June
    1987), para 2.3 (recommending merely a requirement of writing on some durable substance).
3   LP(MP)A 1989, s 1(2)(a). The intention towards deed may be made evident by the instrument
    'describing itself as a deed or expressing itself to be executed or signed as a deed or otherwise'.
    The standard forms of transfer and charge of a registered estate introduced by the Land
    Registration Act 2002 are all drawn as deeds (LRR 2003, rr 58–59, 103, Sch 1 (see e g Forms
    TR1, TR2, CH1)).
4   LP(MP)A 1989, s 1(2)(b).

Signature

7.31   Signature is the single fundamental and irreducible feature of a deed[1]
and, accordingly, section 1(3)(a) of the Law of Property (Miscellaneous Provisions) Act 1989 imposes a requirement of signature as a condition of the valid
execution by an individual of an instrument as his deed.[2] The conclusive nature
of the signature is an important protection for those 'who habitually and rightly
rely on signatures when there is no obvious reason to doubt their validity.'[3]

1   See *Shah v Shah* [2002] QB 35 at [30] per Pill LJ.
2   LP(MP)A 1989, s 1(3)(a). For the purpose of signature it is sufficient if the individual makes
    his mark on the instrument (LP(MP)A 1989, s 1(4)).
3   *Hambros Bank Ltd v British Historic Buildings Trust* [1996] CLY 4987 per Stuart-Smith LJ
    (rejecting a plea of non est factum by an illiterate, non-English speaking immigrant who
    transferred his house for £1).

Attestation

7.32 Prior to 31 July 1990 attestation of the signature on a deed, although exceedingly common in practice, was not (except in registered conveyancing[1]) a formal requirement in the execution of the deed. A general requirement of witnessing has now been imposed, however, by the Law of Property (Miscellaneous Provisions) Act 1989. An instrument is validly executed as a deed by an individual only if it is signed by him 'in the presence of a witness who attests the signature.'[2] The absence of the alleged witness at the time of signature renders the instrument ineffective as a deed[3] and a false representation attesting to signature may constitute forgery.[4]

1　See LRR 1925, rr 74(3), 98, Sch 3.
2　LP(MP)A 1989, s 1(3)(a)(i). Alternatively the instrument may be signed at the direction of an individual and in his presence and the presence of two attesting witnesses (LP(MP)A 1989, s 1(3)(a)(ii)). See [1990] Conv 321.
3　*Ellison v Vukicevic* (1986) 7 NSWLR 104 at 112D–G; *Farnham v Orrell* (1989) NSW ConvR ¶55–443 at 58,219.
4　See *R v Brott* [1988] VR 1 at 6–8, 14–17.

Delivery

7.33 Although the idea of 'delivery' of a deed had its origin in some manual transfer of the relevant document, it has been clear since at least the 17th century that a deed may be 'delivered by words without any act of delivery.'[1] In the form in which the requirement of delivery is retained in the modern law,[2] delivery does not necessarily connote the physical transfer of any instrument, but merely that the transaction contained in the deed is *irreversible*. The essential feature of a deed is that it constitutes 'the most solemn act that a person can perform with respect to a particular piece of property or other right.'[3] Delivery of a deed thus comprises any unilateral act or statement by the person making the deed which signifies that he adopts the deed irrevocably as his own.[4] Delivery also operates as a representation that the deed has been duly signed and attested.[5] A deed, once delivered, is binding on its maker without any act of exchange.[6]

1　*Co Litt*, p 36a.
2　LP(MP)A 1989, s 1(3)(b). The Law Commission, although declaring the law of delivery to be 'not entirely satisfactory', thought that delivery serves at least the purpose of fixing the date at which a deed takes effect (Law Com No 163 (1987), paras 2.8–2.10).
3　*Manton v Parabolic Pty Ltd* [1985] 2 NSWLR 361 at 369B–C per Young J. See also *Hambros Bank Ltd v British Historic Buildings Trust* [1996] CLY 4987 per Stuart-Smith LJ ('[t]he courts do not lightly set aside solemn documents on which innocent third parties have relied').
4　*Xenos v Wickham* (1867) LR 2 HL 296 at 312 per Blackburn J; *Re Sammon* (1979) 94 DLR (3d) 594 at 597–600; *Monarch Petroleum NL v Citco Australia Petroleum Ltd* [1986] WAR 310 at 355. See also D E C Yale, [1970] CLJ 52; D N Clarke, [1990] Conv 85.
5　*Shah v Shah* [2002] QB 35 at [33] per Pill LJ.
6　*Vincent v Premo Enterprises (Voucher Sales) Ltd* [1969] 2 QB 609 at 619D–E. See also *Ansett Transport Industries (Operations) Pty Ltd v Comptroller of Stamps* [1985] VR 70 at 76. Purported delivery by a solicitor instructed in a transaction is, in favour of a purchaser, conclusive evidence of the solicitor's authority to deliver the instrument (LP(MP)A 1989, s 1(5)).

Sealing

7.34   It was always said at common law that 'no writing without a seal can be a deed.'[1] The importance attached to the seal was particularly appropriate in an age when the general illiteracy of the population meant that a personal seal provided the only reliable means of authenticating legal documents. The requirement of the seal also fulfilled a cautionary function. The procedure of sealing gave the parties a valuable pause for reflection before the conclusion of an irreversible transaction at law.[2] It can even be said that the seal exerted a significant psychological impact on the minds of the relevant actors. The presence of the seal caused the deed to be 'surrounded with a magic aura.'[3] Conveyancing, magic and mystery have never been wholly unconnected phenomena, as is made clear by the medieval ritual and symbolism which attended the feoffment with livery of seisin.[4] It is an interesting feature of the social anthropology of land law that the 'sacrosanct and talismanic effect'[5] of a little red wafer was thought sufficient to confer upon certain transactions a legal efficacy which they would not otherwise have possessed.[6]

1   *Sheppard's Touchstone of Common Assurances* (8th edn by E G Atherley, London 1826), p 56.
2   See Duncan Kennedy, 'Form and Substance in Private Law Adjudication' 89 Harv L Rev 1685 at 1691 (1975–76).
3   *Armor Coatings (Marketing) Pty Ltd v General Credits (Finance) Pty Ltd* (1978) 17 SASR 259 at 275 per Bray CJ. This perception probably underlies the ancient common law rule (see *Pigot's Case* (1614) 11 Co Rep 26b at 27a, 77 ER 1177 at 1178) that any alteration avoids a deed: '[a]nything which violated its integrity destroyed its mana' (*Armor Coatings*, supra at 275). See also *Warburton v National Westminster Finance Australia Ltd* (1988) 15 NSWLR 238 at 243B–C per Hope JA.
4   **[Para 3.7].** See *Manton v Parabolic Pty Ltd* [1985] 2 NSWLR 361 at 367A–368C per Young J.
5   *Armor Coatings (Marketing) Pty Ltd v General Credits (Finance) Pty Ltd* (1978) 17 SASR 259 at 275 per Bray CJ. See also F E Crane, 'The Magic of the Private Seal' 15 Col L Rev 24 (1915).
6   When used today the seal tends to be merely a mass-produced red adhesive paper disc which is attached to the bottom of the document concerned: the ceremony of sealing with the aid of sealing wax has almost entirely disappeared (see Law Com No 163 (1987), para 2.4).

7.35   In modern times it was inevitable that the archaic mystique of the seal should become the subject of critical scrutiny.[1] Personal signatures had clearly acquired a far greater practical significance than the seal in establishing documentary authenticity.[2] In 1989 long-standing denigration of the practice of sealing led to the statutory abolition of the redundant formality[3] or 'mumbo-jumbo'[4] of the seal. There is now no requirement of sealing in respect of deeds executed by an individual[5] on or after 31 July 1990,[6] although seals often continue to be used in practice in order to dignify documents of transfer.[7]

1   As long ago as 1937 Goddard J observed that 'a seal nowadays is very much in the nature of a legal fiction' (see Sixth Interim Report of the Law Revision Committee on *Statute of Frauds and the Doctrine of Consideration* (Cmd 5449, 1937), p 35).
2   *Stromdale and Ball Ltd v Burden* [1952] Ch 223 at 230 per Danckwerts J. The diminishing mystique of the seal was clearly evident in *First National Securities Ltd v Jones* [1978] Ch 109 at 118E–F, 119H, 121A–B (printed circle containing the letters 'LS' – *locus sigilli* (the place of a seal) – regarded as sufficient). See D C Hoath, 'The Sealing of Documents – Fact or Fiction?' (1980) 43 MLR 415.

3   See Law Com No 163 (1987), para 2.4.
4   The phrase is that of Lord Wilberforce in *Parliamentary Debates, House of Lords, Official Report* (1970–71), Vol 315, Col 1213 (25 February 1971).
5   A corporation is deemed to have executed a deed if its seal is affixed to the document in the presence of, and is attested by, its clerk or secretary and a member of the board of directors or other governing body (LPA 1925, s 74(1)). Delivery is, however, required and the mere act of signing and sealing an instrument amidst negotiations which are still 'subject to contract' discloses no intention to deliver the deed as an escrow (see *Bolton MBC v Torkington* [2004] Ch 66 at [53]–[54]; [2004] Conv 9 (J E A)). See also Companies Act 1985, s 36A(5)–(6).
6   LP(MP)A 1989, s 1(1)(b).
7   Sealing also appears to provide, for the purpose of LP(MP)A 1989, s 1(2)(a), clear evidence of an intention that an instrument should constitute a deed (see [1990] Conv 1 (H W W)).

The deed will soon become a statutory fiction

7.36   The regime of electronic conveyancing soon to be instituted under the Land Registration Act 2002 will necessitate profound changes in the modalities of dealings with estates in land.[1] In an age of paperless transactions the deed will become a mere fiction of statute. Although paper-based and electronic systems of transacting will coexist during a transitional period,[2] the 2002 Act provides that, on compliance with certain conditions, the electronic disposition of estates and interests in registered land will be deemed to satisfy the existing formality requirements for a written document or deed.[3] In order to be effective, an electronic disposition will be required[4] to make provision for the time and date at which it is to take effect and must contain the electronic signature of each person by whom it purports to be authenticated (ie the disponor and often, also, the disponee).[5] Electronic signatures will probably be effected with the aid of some form of dual key cryptography and must be certified by some certifying authority. An electronic disposition which satisfies these conditions will be statutorily deemed to constitute a 'deed'[6]; the concept of delivery will become irrelevant[7]; and the process of attestation will be unnecessary.[8]

1   See D Capps, 'Conveyancing in the 21st Century: An Outline of Electronic Conveyancing and Electronic Signatures' [2002] Conv 443.
2   See Law Com No 271 (2001), paras 1.12, 2.61.
3   LRA 2002, s 91(4). See Law Com No 271 (2001), paras 13.11, 13.18. The same facility of electronic disposition will apply to any conveyance which triggers a requirement of first registration at Land Registry (LRA 2002, s 91(2)(c)).
4   See LRA 2002, s 91(1)–(3).
5   See S Mason and N Bohm, 'The Signature in Electronic Conveyancing: An Unresolved Issue?' [2003] Conv 460.
6   LRA 2002, s 91(5).
7   See Law Com No 271 (2001), para 13.13.
8   LRA 2002, s 91(8). See Law Com No 271 (2001), para 13.31.

Requirement of registration

7.37   Nowadays almost all forms of dealing with a fee simple estate also require to be completed by registration at Land Registry. A distinction must be drawn between the registration provisions which relate to *first registration* and those provisions which govern *subsequent transfers* of an already registered estate.[1]

1   [**Para 7.49**].

FIRST REGISTRATION OF AN UNREGISTERED LEGAL FREEHOLD ESTATE

7.38   First registration of title to a freehold estate may be either voluntary or compulsory.

Voluntary first registration

7.39   Substantive registration of title to a previously unregistered legal freehold estate is always available under the Land Registration Act 2002 as a matter of voluntary election.[1] Application for registration as proprietor may be made by any person in whom the freehold estate is vested[2] or who is entitled to require that the estate be vested in him.[3] Voluntary registrations are increasingly sought by bodies (such as local authorities) which have substantial land holdings in respect of which it is desirable to procure the enhanced protection against adverse possession offered by the 2002 Act.[4]

1   LRA 2002, s 3(1)–(2). The facility of voluntary registration under a unique title number also extends to other unregistered legal estates such as certain leaseholds, rentcharges, franchises and profits *à prendre* in gross.
2   LRA 2002, s 3(2)(a). There is an inducement towards voluntary first registration in the form of a 25 per cent reduction in the registration fee (see Land Registration Fee Order 2004 (SI 2004/595), art 2(1)(b), (6)).
3   LRA 2002, s 3(2)(b). No application may be made by a person whose entitlement stems from a contract to purchase the estate (LRA 2002, s 3(6)).
4   [**Para 6.55**].

Compulsory first registration

7.40   First registration of an unregistered legal freehold estate at Land Registry is made mandatory on the occurrence of certain kinds of statutorily specified 'event' (or trigger).[1] The Land Registration Act 2002 provides[2] that first registration is obligatory on any transfer of a fee simple estate for valuable or other consideration, by way of gift,[3] in pursuance of an order of any court[4] or by means of an assent (ie perfection of a gift of land by will or on intestacy).[5] A requirement of first registration of an unregistered fee simple estate also arises on the grant of any 'protected first legal mortgage' of that estate.[6] For this purpose a 'protected' mortgage is a charge which is protected by the deposit of documents relating to the freehold estate and which, on its creation, ranks prior to any other mortgage affecting that estate.[7]

1   Power has been reserved to expand, by order, the triggers for compulsory first registration (LRA 2002, s 5(1)(a)).

2   LRA 2002, s 4(1)–(2). The requirement of first registration does not apply to transfers by operation of law (eg a vesting of an unregistered estate in a deceased owner's personal representatives (see LRA 2002, s 4(3))). Nor do dispositions of mines and minerals apart from the surface trigger any requirement of first registration (LRA 2002, s 4(1), (9)).

3   Gift includes a transfer of the estate to trustees holding otherwise than on a bare trust for the transferor (LRA 2002, s 4(7)(a)) and most cases of transfer to a trust beneficiary who is absolutely entitled to the land (LRA 2002, s 4(7)(b)).

4   An example is a property transfer order made on the dissolution of marriage.

5   The duty to apply for registration rests on the transferee of the freehold estate (LRA 2002, s 6(1)).

6   LRA 2002, ss 4(1)(g), 6(2)(a).

7   LRA 2002, s 4(8). The duty to apply for registration of the freehold estate charged by mortgage rests on the mortgagor (ie the owner of the mortgaged estate) (LRA 2002, s 6(1), (2)(b)). However, the mortgagee may also, in the mortgagor's name and irrespective of the mortgagor's consent, apply for such registration (LRA 2002, s 6(6); LRR 2003, r 21). The parties may, of course, agree that the mortgagee should, as a matter of convenience, apply for registration of the freehold simultaneously with its own application to be registered as legal chargee.

Consequence of failure to effect a first registration

7.41   The Land Registration Act 2002 requires that any application for first registration of title to an unregistered fee simple estate be made within two months of the date of any 'relevant event' which triggers the requirement of first registration.[1] Failure to apply for timely registration renders the triggering disposition 'void' for the purpose of transferring, granting or creating a legal estate.[2] As can be seen in the following examples, the rule is one of statutory defeasance: the disponee's title, having been initially legal, is relegated to equitable status.

1   LRA 2002, s 6(1), (4).

2   LRA 2002, s 7(1). The two-month period may be extended by order of the registrar (LRA 2002, s 6(5)), in which case the legal quality of the estate is revitalised until the end of the period of extension. It is therefore possible that the legal estate may shuttle backwards and forwards rather unsatisfactorily between vendor and purchaser. Ultimately the transferee may be forced to arrange (at his own cost) for a retransfer of the intended legal estate, followed this time by somewhat swifter registration (LRA 2002, s 8).

Transfer of an unregistered freehold estate

7.42   When V transfers an unregistered freehold estate to P, P immediately acquires the legal fee simple. If, however, P fails within the following two months to apply to Land Registry for first registration of his title, the legal estate reverts to V, who thereafter holds the estate on a bare trust for P.[1] In effect P's title, having been a *legal* title during the first two months, then becomes merely an *equitable* fee simple absolute.[2]

1   LRA 2002, s 7(2)(a). See *Buckley v SRL Investments Ltd and Cator and Robinson* (1971) 22 P & CR 756 at 767. On bare trusts, see Chapter 11 [**para 11.154**].

2   This may, in practice, seriously impair the unregistered transferee's capacity for a rapid re-sale of the land to another purchaser, if the latter's mortgagee refuses to advance loan money

except on the security of a legal estate (see e g *Pinekerry Ltd v Needs* (*Kenneth*) (*Contractors*) *Ltd* (1992) 64 P & CR 245; [1993] CLJ 22 (A J Oakley); (1994) 57 MLR 121 (J Howell)).

Mortgage of an unregistered freehold estate

7.43   When, for the purpose of securing a loan from his bank, M executes a deed of first legal charge over his unregistered freehold land and deposits his documents of title with the bank, the bank immediately acquires a legal mortgage charge. If, within the following two months, no application is lodged for first registration of M's fee simple title (and of the bank's charge over it), the disposition of mortgage becomes void as a legal charge.[1] M nevertheless continues to hold an unregistered legal fee simple estate, but the bank's deed of charge thereafter takes effect merely as a contract for valuable consideration to create a legal charge (ie as a mere equitable charge).[2]

1   LRA 2002, s 7(1).
2   LRA 2002, s 7(2)(b). The notional contract requires registration as an 'estate contract' pursuant to the Land Charges Act 1972, being otherwise void against a purchaser of the legal estate for money or money's worth **[para 12.282]**.

Classes of freehold title on first registration

7.44   On an application for first registration of title, the applicant's title deeds and other relevant claims are examined by the registrar, who determines which quality of title to award.[1] The class of title accorded to the first registered proprietor is then indicated at the head of the proprietorship register of the newly opened register of title.[2] In relation to freehold land there are three possible classes of title, each reflecting a different perception of the strength and reliability of the title offered for registration.

1   LRA 2002, s 9(1) **[paras 6.17, 12.52]**.
2   LRR 2003, r 8(1)(a).

Absolute freehold title

7.45   'Absolute freehold title', the most frequently awarded class,[1] is the most reliable and extensively guaranteed form of title. Absolute title is awarded if the registrar is of opinion that the applicant's title is 'such as a willing buyer could properly be advised by a competent professional adviser to accept.'[2] Absolute title connotes, in effect, a holding which is unlikely to be disturbed.[3] Although it cannot *enhance* the applicant's existing rights in relation to the land, first registration with absolute freehold title confers the most ample form of ownership known in English law. Such registration has the effect of vesting in the registered proprietor the legal fee simple absolute *together with* all interests subsisting for the benefit of that estate,[4] *subject* only to:

–   interests entered in the register (by the registrar) in order to reflect pre-existing rights which burden the land[5];

–   certain unregistered interests which are statutorily declared to 'override first registration', eg legal leases for a term of seven years or less and any proprietary interest belonging to a 'person in actual occupation'[6];

–   interests acquired by squatters under the Limitation Act 1980 of which the proprietor has notice[7] and

–   (where the proprietor takes land as a trustee) such beneficial interests of which he has notice (actual or constructive).[8]

1   Absolute title is granted in almost all freehold applications for first registration.
2   LRA 2002, s 9(2).
3   See LRA 2002, s 9(3).
4   LRA 2002, s 11(3) (eg the benefit of appurtenant easements).
5   LRA 2002, s 11(4)(a) **[para 12.267]**. Mere entry in the register cannot revitalise an interest which by the date of first registration has already ceased to be enforceable (eg on the ground of non-registration as a land charge). See *Kitney v MEPC Ltd* [1977] 1 WLR 981 at 992B–C, 994H–995B.
6   LRA 2002, s 11(4)(b), Sch 1 **[para 12.268]**.
7   LRA 2002, s 11(4)(c) **[para 6.70]**.
8   LRA 2002, s 11(5). The new proprietor's title is subject, in effect, to any beneficial interest under a trust of land which was not disclosed in his application for registration and of which he is deemed to have notice.

Qualified freehold title

7.46   Qualified title is awarded in rare cases to an applicant who can establish title only in respect of a limited period or only subject to certain reservations which cannot be disregarded by the registrar.[1] First registration with qualified freehold title produces a result similar to registration with absolute freehold title, but subject also to any estate, right or interest which was specifically excepted from the effect of the qualified registration.[2] A qualified title may later be converted into absolute title if the registrar is satisfied that the suspected flaw in title is no longer material.[3]

1   LRA 2002, s 9(1), (4).
2   LRA 2002, s 11(6). A qualified title is therefore precarious to the extent of the qualification which is set out in the Property Register.
3   LRA 2002, s 62(1). See LRR 2003, r 124.

Possessory freehold title

7.47   Possessory title to a freehold estate is awarded to an applicant who is in 'actual possession' (or in receipt of rents and profits drawn from the land) by virtue of his estate and where there is no other class of title with which he may be registered.[1] This class of title is commonly accorded to those who cannot produce sufficient documentary evidence of title. An applicant's title deeds may have been lost or destroyed or he may be relying on a period of adverse possession of the land concerned.[2] Registration with possessory title invests the applicant with a legal freehold estate (with the same benefits and burdens as in the case of an absolute title), but subject also to any adverse estates, rights and interests which existed at the date of first registration and were not revealed in the application.[3] Again, the registrar has power subsequently to upgrade the title to absolute freehold title 'if satisfied' as to its quality[4] and, in particular, may do so if a possessory title has been entered in the Land Register for at least twelve years and the registrar is satisfied that the proprietor is 'in possession of the land.'[5]

1   LRA 2002, s 9(5).
2   **[Para 6.7]**.
3   LRA 2002, s 11(7). Subsequent transferees of this possessory title also hold subject to these burdens. It follows that a possessory title may later be altered against the registered proprietor (without indemnity) in order to give effect to a superior title or if the possessory title was insufficiently grounded in a claim of adverse possession (see *Tester v Harris* (1964) 189 EG 337 at 339).
4   LRA 2002, ss 62(1), 63; LRR 2003, r 124.
5   LRA 2002, s 62(4).

A new statutory estate

7.48   Irrespective of the precise class of title awarded, the registered proprietor's title to land is so heavily regulated by statute that it is probably best to say that unregistered common law estates are replaced, at the point of first registration, by some new and artificial kind of *statutory* estate. Entry of a person in the register as the proprietor of a legal estate has the effect that, even if 'the legal estate would not otherwise be vested in him, it shall be deemed to be vested in him as a result of the registration.'[1] In the absence of any 'alteration' of the register,[2] registered proprietorship is pro tempore definitive and conclusive. The registered proprietor can indeed be regarded as 'a statutory person having a statutory title to a statutory "thing" with a statutory power to dispose of it.'[3] This perspective helps to make sense of much of the law of land registration and richly confirms that the principles of registered title have evolved into a law of land which is significantly different from the unregistered or 'old system' regime which preceded it.

1   LRA 2002, s 58(1).
2   **[Para 12.245]**.
3   See H Potter, (1942) 58 LQR 356 at 367 ('We have ceased to convey "land" within the meaning of the old law and now transfer or otherwise dispose of a statutory interest held by a statutory title'). See also *Chowood Ltd v Lyall (No 2)* [1930] 2 Ch 156 at 163 per Lord Hanworth MR.

SUBSEQUENT DISPOSITIONS OF A REGISTERED FREEHOLD ESTATE

7.49   The Land Registration Act 2002 confers plenary powers to dispose of any estate which has been registered at Land Registry.[1] 'Owner's powers' in relation to a registered estate are declared to consist of a power to make any kind of disposition permitted by the general law, together with a power to charge the estate at law with the payment of money.[2] 'Owner's powers', so defined, are available to the registered proprietor or any person entitled to be registered as proprietor.[3] In keeping with the overall philosophy of the 2002 Act, once title to an estate (whether freehold or leasehold[4]) has been registered at Land Registry, almost all subsequent dealings with the estate require to be 'completed by registration' as a precondition of their effectiveness at law.[5]

1   See, however, LRA 2002, s 26(1)–(2) **[para 11.220]**.
2   LRA 2002, s 23(1). The Act specifically rules out the possibility of a mortgage by subdemise **[para 8.242]**.
3   LRA 2002, s 24. 'Owner's powers' are therefore exercisable, in some circumstances, even before the registration of a person's proprietorship. See *Jerome v HM Inspector of Taxes* [2004] 1 WLR 1409 at [43] per Lord Walker of Gestingthorpe ('a person's disposal of an asset may sometimes precede his acquisition of it').
4   Much of what follows here is applicable to both the fee simple estate and any term of years title to which has been registered.
5   LRA 2002, s 27(1)–(2), Sch 2, paras 1–8. With the advent of electronic conveyancing, the processes of disposition and registration will become indistinguishable **[paras 2.118, 12.4]**.

Range of 'registrable dispositions'

7.50   The 'registration requirements' of the Land Registration Act 2002 are activated by certain specified kinds of 'disposition of a registered estate', a phrase which is broad enough to embrace not merely an outright transfer of the registered estate, but also a number of dealings under which lesser entitlements are carved out of that estate.[1] The range of 'disposition' which must be completed by registration therefore includes not only transfers of the registered freehold estate, but also the creation of various kinds of lease,[2] mortgage charge,[3] easement,[4] profit *à prendre*,[5] rentcharge[6] and right of entry[7] affecting the freehold estate.

1   See LRA 2002, s 27(2).
2   **[Paras 7.240, 7.244]**.
3   **[Para 8.244]**.
4   **[Para 8.117]**.
5   **[Para 8.117]**.
6   **[Para 8.227]**.
7   **[Para 8.266]**.

Requirements of form and content

7.51   The Land Registration Act 2002 also provides that several kinds of registrable disposition of a registered estate must comply with specified rules as to form and content.[1] Thus, for example, the transfer of a registered freehold estate normally requires to be made using one of the forms prescribed by the Land Registration Rules 2003.[2] A standard form of legal charge of the registered estate is now offered by the Land Registration Rules 2003[3]; and it seems likely that registrable leases granted out of a registered estate will soon also become the subject of some prescribed Land Registry form.[4] This general move towards standardised formats for land dealings is an obvious precursor to the scheme of electronic conveyancing envisaged by the Land Registration Act 2002.

1   LRA 2002, s 25(1).
2   LRR 2003, rr 58–59, 206, 209, Sch 1.
3   LRR 2003, r 103, Sch 1.
4   **[Para 7.240]**.

'Restrictions' upon disposition

7.52   It is possible that the dispositionary powers of a registered proprietor may be limited by the entry of certain kinds of 'restriction' in the proprietor-ship register pertaining to his title.[1] A 'restriction' comprises an entry in the register which regulates the circumstances in which a subsequent disposition of the registered estate (whether freehold or, for that matter, leasehold) may be recorded in the Land Register.[2] In cases governed by a 'restriction' entered in the register, Land Registry is disabled from processing any application for registration by a disponee of the registered estate *unless and until* there has been compliance with the terms of the relevant 'restriction'.[3] The entry of a restriction confers no priority for the interest thereby protected: the restriction merely compels compliance with its terms.[4]

1   See LRR 2003, r 8(1)(d).
2   LRA 2002, s 40(1).
3   LRA 2002, s 41(1). The restriction cannot, of course, affect dealings with a *minor* interest (e g a dealing by a trust beneficiary with his own equitable interest).
4   No restriction may ever be entered for the purpose of protecting the priority of an interest which is, or could be, the subject of a 'notice' in the register (LRA 2002, s 42(2)).

Entitlements appropriately protected by 'restriction'

7.53   The protection provided by the entry of a restriction is peculiarly appropriate in the case of beneficial interests which arise under a trust of land or strict settlement.[1] In the case of such interests the restriction stipulates that no disposition by the proprietor shall be registered unless the capital money arising is paid to trustees or to a trust corporation. This most common form of restriction deters dealings with the land (e g by a sole trustee) which would fail to attract the advantageous effects of statutory overreaching.[2] In this way the 'restriction' ensures not only that the disponee takes free of the beneficial interests under the trust, but also, indirectly, that these beneficial interests are translated into equivalent rights in the capital proceeds arising from the transaction.[3]

1   See *Re Gorman (A Bankrupt)* [1990] 1 WLR 616 at 621B.
2   LRA 2002, s 42(1)(b) **[paras 2.165, 11.195]**.
3   Of course, this result is not always welcomed by the beneficiaries whose interests are compulsorily overreached. The overreaching which is facilitated by the entry of the restriction may deprive the beneficiaries of their use value in the land, which for them may represent a matter of greater concern **[para 11.201]**. Although, in the absence of a restriction, it has always been open to any trust beneficiary to apply to the court for an injunction restraining disposition by a sole trustee (see *Waller v Waller* [1967] 1 WLR 451 at 453E–F, 454C; (1967) 31 Conv (NS) 140 (F R Crane)), this protection is of little avail to a beneficiary who is unaware of an impending disposition.

7.54 'Restrictions' may also take other forms and serve rather different purposes. A 'restriction' may be entered in the register where, for example, it is wished to make the consent of a named person or body a prerequisite to any disposition of land.[1] A 'restriction' may also be used in order to reflect the limited dispositionary powers of an incorporated body or to preclude the registered proprietor from disposing of his estate while it remains subject to a registered charge. Alternatively a restriction may be employed to compel the registered proprietor to require any transferee to enter into positive covenants directly with a named covenantee, effectively ensuring the transmission of the burden of positive freehold covenants already undertaken by the transferor himself.[2]

1   **[Para 11.193]**. The entry of a 'named person' restriction may be particularly useful in helping to ensure that a sole registered proprietor does not simply appoint a crony as co-trustee to join with him in an overreaching disposition of the registered estate (e g if the 'named person' is one of the beneficiaries). For another example of a 'named person' restriction, see HA 1985, Sch 9A, para 5(2)(b).
2   The burden of positive freehold covenants is not normally transferable in English law **[para 13.48]**.

Entry and removal of 'restrictions'

7.55 The registrar has certain powers of his own motion to enter a 'restriction' in the register.[1] Furthermore, applications for the entry of a 'restriction' may be made by the proprietor of any registered estate and, in certain cases, by other persons also.[2] Thus, for instance, a 'restriction' may be entered on the application of a person who claims some beneficial entitlement to the registered estate by way of resulting or constructive trust[3] or who is currently entitled to a charging order in respect of a beneficial interest under a trust of registered land.[4] The Land Registration Act 2002 imposes a duty not to apply for the entry of a restriction 'without reasonable cause.'[5] In appropriate cases, a restriction, once it has exhausted its protective function, may be cancelled or withdrawn from the register of title.[6]

1   LRA 2002, s 42(1). The court also has power, in certain instances, to order the entry of a 'restriction' (LRA 2002, s 46(1)).
2   LRA 2002, s 43(1); LRR 2003, rr 92–93.
3   **[Paras 10.8, 10.58]**.
4   **[Para 9.121]**.
5   LRA 2002, s 77(1).
6   LRA 2002, s 47; LRR 2003, rr 97–99.

Application for registration

7.56 All 'registrable dispositions' must be completed by the entry of the disponee in the Land Register as the proprietor of the relevant interest under the disposition.[1] Thus, in the case of a freehold transfer, the transferee must apply to be registered as proprietor of the fee simple estate in place of the transferor.[2] The transfer of the registered estate is made final and effective at law only when the registrar has entered the name of the transferee in the register as proprietor of the estate transferred.[3] But while an application for registration is the act of the transferee, the transfer of the legal title is ultimately an act of the *state* (or, more accurately, of the civil servant responsible for updating the Land Registry's computer record). In this way the scheme of land registration can be said to provide 'not a system of registration of title but a system of title by registration.'[4] In the process the accuracy of the register is maintained by requiring each successive transferee of a registered estate to perfect his legal title by applying to be registered as the new proprietor.

1   LRA 2002, s 27(1)–(2), Sch 2, paras 2(1), 3(2), 4(2)(a), 6(2)(a), 7(2)(b), 8.
2   The requirement of completion by registration does not apply to certain dispositions by operation of law, e g a transfer on the death or bankruptcy of an individual proprietor (LRA 2002, s 27(5)).
3   LRA 2002, Sch 2, para 2(1). For reasons of administrative convenience, the date of registration of the new proprietorship is deemed retrospectively to be the date on which the application for registration was lodged at Land Registry (LRA 2002, s 74).
4   *Breskvar v Wall* (1971) 126 CLR 376 at 385 per Barwick CJ.

Consequence of completion by registration

7.57   When a disposition of the freehold estate is duly completed by registration, entry of the disponee in the Land Register as proprietor has definitive effect. The title enjoyed by the transferee depends on the force of statute rather than on any intrinsic validity in the transfer itself. The legal estate in question is simply 'deemed to be vested in him as a result of the registration.'[1] Thereafter the register remains, for the time being, conclusive of title. The vesting of a full legal title in the transferee does not preclude the possibility that the register may subsequently be altered[2] but, pending such alteration, the transferee's registration is sufficient to constitute him the legal owner even though the transfer may be vitiated by some irregularity[3] or may even have been a complete forgery.[4] Moreover, the disponee of a registered estate for valuable consideration generally takes that estate free of all pre-existing interests other than registered charges, other interests already noted in the relevant register of title, and those unregistered interests which are statutorily declared to 'override' registered dispositions.[5] The disponee for value of an already registered estate therefore enjoys a fuller guarantee of his title than did the first registered proprietor.[6] The disponee is entitled to rely on the register as an accurate representation of title (apart from overriding interests) and is unaffected by other defects in the title which existed at the date of first registration and clearly bound his predecessor.[7]

1   LRA 2002, s 58(1).
2   LRA 2002, s 65, Sch 4 **[para 12.245]**.
3   See e g *Hounslow LBC v Hare* (1990) 24 HLR 9 at 23 (void disposition by charity); *Rockhampton Permanent Building Society v Peterson (No 2)* [1989] 1 Qd R 670 at 676.
4   See *Argyle Building Society v Hammond* (1985) 49 P & CR 148 at 153, 155 per Slade LJ; *Hayes v Nwajiaku* [1994] EGCS 106. See also *Registrar, Regina Land Registration District v Hermanson* (1987) 33 DLR (4th) 12; *Paramount Life Insurance Co v Hill* (1987) 34 DLR (4th) 150.

5   LRA 2002, s 29(1)–(2), Sch 3 [**paras 12.76, 12.80**].
6   See H Potter, (1942) 58 LQR 356 at 364.
7   The disponee of the registered estate takes free, for instance, of beneficial trust entitlements which neither are entered in the register nor are overriding interests even if he knows of their existence. The same is not true of the first registered proprietor [**para 7.45**].

Consequence of failure to complete by registration

7.58   It is a stern principle of the Land Registration Act 2002 that the registrable disposition of a registered estate does not 'operate at law' unless the 'relevant registration requirements' are met.[1] Thus, until the transferee of a registered freehold title has applied to be registered as the new proprietor, the transferor necessarily remains proprietor of the legal fee simple estate in the land.[2]

1   LRA 2002, s 27(1).
2   There is no provision, as with dispositions which necessitate first registration [**para 7.41**], for a reversible vesting of the legal estate during the two months immediately following the disposition.

Interest taken by the unregistered transferee

7.59   In the absence of an application to register the transfer, the transferor holds the legal estate as a bare trustee for the transferee.[1] The transferee acquires merely an equitable estate in fee simple,[2] this result following regardless of whether the transferee has purchased the estate[3] or is merely a donee. In the latter case the equitable interest in the land vests in the donee when the 'donor has done all that is necessary to place the vesting of the legal title within the control of the donee and beyond the recall or intervention of the donor.'[4] On this basis, the gift is effective in equity when the transferor places the transferee in possession of the duly executed transfer form, since the transferee now needs no further assistance from a court of equity in order to complete his title.[5] In such circumstances the donor is 'bound in conscience' to hold the property as trustee for the donee pending the vesting of the legal title.[6]

1   This is a standard feature of Torrens legislation the world over (see *IAC (Finance) Pty Ltd v Courtenay* (1963) 110 CLR 550 at 571; *Coffey and Moylan v Brunel Construction Co Ltd* [1983] IR 36 at 40).
2   In effect the disponee, for want of completion by registration, acquires only an equitable version of the estate which was intended to pass at law. See *E S Schwab & Co Ltd v McCarthy* (1976) 31 P & CR 196 at 201 per Oliver J; *Coffey v Brunel Construction Co Ltd* [1983] IR 36 at 40, 43; *Chan v Cresdon Pty Ltd* (1989) 168 CLR 242 at 248, 256–257, 261 (High Court of Australia).
3   Here the transferee's equitable interest follows from the fact that the specifically enforceable contract behind the (as yet unrecorded) instrument has created for the transferee an equitable right in the land [**para 9.48**]. The inefficacy of the transfer at law 'cannot cut down or merge the pre-existing right which led to its execution' (*Barry v Heider* (1914) 19 CLR 197 at 216 per Isaacs J).
4   *Corin v Patton* (1990) 169 CLR 540 at 582 per Deane J. According to Mason CJ and McHugh

J in the same case, '[s]o long as the donee has been equipped to achieve the transfer of legal ownership, the gift is complete in equity' ((1990) 169 CLR 540 at 559). See, by analogy, *Re Rose* [1952] Ch 499.

5   *Mascall v Mascall* (1984) 50 P & CR 119 at 125–126. Contrast *Anning v Anning* (1907) 4 CLR 1049 at 1069 per Isaacs J and *Corin v Patton* (1990) 169 CLR 540 at 563 per Brennan J, 588 per Toohey J, to the effect that, in the absence of a transaction for value, there is no fact or circumstance on which a court of equity may fasten as binding the conscience of the donor to hold the land on trust for the transferee.

6   See *Corin v Patton* (1990) 169 CLR 540 at 582 per Deane J.

Risk of adverse dealings

7.60   Statute imposes no time limit on the transferee's application for registration of his transfer,[1] but for so long as he remains unregistered as proprietor, the transferee is obviously exposed to the risk of adverse dealings by his transferor. In some cases – as for example where the transferee goes into 'actual occupation' of the land – his unregistered fee simple estate (ie his equitable interest) may 'override' dispositions made by the transferor in favour of strangers.[2] If, however, the protection of an overriding entitlement is not available, the transferee's equitable interest, arising as it does behind a bare trust, cannot be safeguarded by the entry of a 'notice' in the register.[3]

1   Pending registration the transferee is entitled to receive mesne profits accruing from the date of the transfer (*Choudhury v Meah* (Unreported, Court of Appeal, 21 September 1981) per Lawton LJ).

2   LRA 2002, s 29(2)(a)(ii), Sch 3, para 2 [**paras 2.172, 12.146**]. The advent of electronic conveyancing will eventually eliminate the possibility of 'off the register' transfers (see Law Commission and HM Land Registry, *Land Registration for the Twenty-First Century* (Law Com No 254, September 1998), para 2.47).

3   A bare trust is a 'trust of land' (see TOLATA 1996, s 2(1), (2)(a)). No 'notice' may be entered in the register in respect of any interest under a trust of land (LRA 2002, s 33(a)(i)).

Future dealings by the unregistered transferee

7.61   Even in the absence of due registration of his own title, the unregistered transferee has the statutory 'owner's powers' to deal with the land by way of sale, lease, mortgage and otherwise.[1] However, since he holds only an equitable estate, it follows that any further dealings by the unregistered transferee inevitably take effect merely in equity.[2] No party transacting with him can achieve registration of any disposition in their own favour so long as the legal estate remains outstanding in the earlier, and still registered, transferor.[3]

1   LRA 2002, s 24(b).

2   See eg *Halifax Building Society v Fanimi* [1997] EWCA Civ 1461, where a lease granted by an unregistered transferee, being merely equitable, was defeated by an earlier equitable mortgage charge.

3   See similarly *Brown & Root Technology Ltd v Sun Alliance and London Assurance Co Ltd* [2001] Ch 733 at 741G–H.

Electronic dispositions of registered land

7.62   The 'single most important function' of the Land Registration Act 2002 is to institute the necessary legal framework for a system of electronic conveyancing which will come into operation in some years' time and which will make land dealings quicker, safer and more efficient.[1]

1   See Law Com No 271 (2001), paras 2.41, 13.1.

The register as a 'real time' mirror image of interests in land

7.63   Under a regime of e-conveyancing most land interests will be incapable of creation or transfer without a simultaneous electronic manipulation of the register record. Disposition and registration will coincide exactly in point of time; and the register of title will accurately and definitively record the priority of such rights.

Dispositions wholly ineffective unless registered

7.64   The system of electronic transfer will simplify matters to the extent that, in accordance with the new principle of synchronous registration of dealings, dispositions of a registered estate will have *no* effect at all – either at law or in equity – until communicated electronically to the registrar and simultaneously recorded in the Land Register.[1]

1   LRA 2002, s 93(1)–(4), Sch 2.

TERMINATION OF THE FEE SIMPLE ESTATE

7.65   All estate owners in fee simple hold directly of the crown as 'tenants in chief' – the last relic of the medieval doctrine of tenures.[1] But if the tenurial relationship, even in its modern vestigial form, comes to an end, the freehold title 'goes back to the Crown on the principle that all freehold estate originally came from the Crown, and that where there is no one entitled to the freehold estate by law it reverts to the Crown.'[2]

1   [Para 1.149].
2   *Re Mercer and Moore* (1880) 14 Ch D 287 at 295 per Jessel MR. See also *Re David James & Co Ltd* [1991] 1 NZLR 219 at 223–224; *Rural Banking and Finance Corpn of New Zealand Ltd v Official Assignee* [1991] 2 NZLR 351 at 356; *Sandhurst Trustees Ltd v 72 Seventh Street Nominees Pty Ltd (In Liq)* (1998) 45 NSWLR 556 at 565G.

Escheat

7.66   'Escheat' is the term used to describe the process by which the fee simple estate falls in to the crown, the crown's seignory or radical title being thereafter 'no longer encumbered by the freehold interest.'[1] Thus, for example, a freeholder's estate passes by statute to the crown as bona vacantia – technically 'in lieu of any right to escheat' – in the event of death without any competent successor.[2] A similar result occurs where the freeholder was a company which has been dissolved under the Companies Acts.[3] The Land Registration Act 2002 contains provisions which, despite the destruction of the tenurial relationship, will prevent – at least temporarily – the closure of any registered title to escheated freehold land, thereby allowing register entries to remain on the Land Register until the land is disposed of by the crown or by order of the court (and a new register opened under a different title number).[4]

1   *Scmlla Properties Ltd v Gesso Properties (BVI) Ltd* [1995] BCC 793 at 804.
2   Administration of Estates Act 1925, s 46(1)(vi). See *Re Mitchell (decd)* [1954] Ch 525 at 529; *Sandhurst Trustees Ltd v 72 Seventh Street Nominees Pty Ltd (In Liq)* (1998) 45 NSWLR 556 at 563C.
3   Companies Act 1985, s 654. It is normal practice for the Treasury Solicitor then to disclaim such bona vacantia as onerous, whereupon the relevant estate determines and escheats to the crown anyway (see Law Com No 271 (2001), para 11.24).
4   LRA 2002, s 82; LRR 2003, rr 79(3), 173.

Escheat following disclaimer

7.67   The incidence of escheat is nowadays rare, arising in some 500 cases each year[1] and tending to cluster around instances of corporate and personal insolvency. It is open to company liquidators and trustees in bankruptcy to disclaim 'onerous property' held by an insolvent entity or person, usually, in the case of land, where the asset is subject to substantial financial burdens arising by covenant or mortgage.[2] The effect of such disclaimer is the termination of the freehold estate and the escheat of the relevant land to the crown.[3]

1   Law Com No 271 (2001), para 11.22.
2   See Insolvency Act 1986, ss 178(2), 315(1)–(2).
3   Escheat destroys only the estate disclaimed: the crown still takes subject to the burdensome obligations (eg of mortgage or covenant) which triggered the disclaimer (see *Scmlla Properties Ltd v Gesso Properties (BVI) Ltd* [1995] BCC 793 at 806–808; *Sandhurst Trustees Ltd v 72 Seventh Street Nominees Pty Ltd (In Liq)* (1998) 45 NSWLR 556 at 566F).

THE TERM OF YEARS ABSOLUTE

7.68   In the structural organisation of estates and interests confirmed in the Law of Property Act 1925, the *term of years absolute* is firmly marked out as a proprietary interest in land.[1] The 1925 Act identifies the 'term of years absolute' as one of the two major estates in land which are 'capable of subsisting or of being conveyed or created at law.'[2] The term of years absolute is the estate which a landlord confers upon his tenant.[3] Its distinctive feature is the grant to the tenant of exclusive possession of defined land for a period of pre-arranged maximum duration,[4] the grantee always holding some lesser term than that held by his grantor.[5] Any area of land, whether a large tract or a single room,[6] can constitute the locus of a tenancy if granted for a determinate period as the 'exclusive domain of a particular individual.'[7] It matters not whether the tenant's term is *fixed* and therefore self-determining or *periodic* and therefore capable of extension at the will of the parties. The term may be one week or thousands of years.[8] A term of years can exist in either case as an alienable and often highly commerciable estate in land. The estate commonly outlives its grantee[9] and may be the subject of a complex of transactions of 'assignment' (ie transfer) and sublease.[10]

1   See *Customs and Excise Commrs v Sinclair Collis Ltd* [2001] STC 989 at [58] per Lord Scott of Foscote ('an interest in rem in the land').

2   LPA 1925, s 1(1)(b) **[para 2.125]**.

3   In this context the qualifier 'absolute' appears to have no special significance. A 'term of years absolute' retains its absolute character notwithstanding that it is determinable by notice given by either the landlord or the tenant or is determinable by reason of the landlord's exercise of a right of re-entry for breach of covenant by the tenant (see LPA 1925, s 205(1)(xxvii); LRA 2002, s 132(1)). In commercial practice a term of years absolute is commonly made subject to automatic determination in the event of the tenant's bankruptcy or insolvency.

4   Consistently with the historic emphasis of English land law **[para 3.1]**, the essence of the relationship of landlord and tenant 'is the granting of possession and not of title' (*Bell v General Accident, Fire & Life Assurance Corpn Ltd* [1998] 1 EGLR 69 at 71D–E per Hutchison LJ). See also *Baynes & Co v Lloyd & Sons* [1895] 1 QB 820 at 824 per Lord Russell of Killowen CJ.

5   See generally S Bright and G Gilbert, *Landlord and Tenant Law: The Nature of Tenancies* (Clarendon 1995).

6   See *Antoniades v Villiers* [1990] 1 AC 417 at 459D–E per Lord Templeman.

7   See *AG Securities v Vaughan* [1990] 1 AC 417 at 471B–C per Lord Oliver of Aylmerton.

8   The longer the term the greater has been the tendency in the past to use the nomenclature of 'lease' rather than 'tenancy'.

9   A leaseholder's estate passes automatically to the crown as bona vacantia in the event of the leaseholder's death without any competent successor (Administration of Estates Act 1925, s 46(1)(vi)) or if a corporate tenant has been dissolved under the Companies Acts (Companies Act 1985, s 654; see eg *Toff v McDowell* (1995) 69 P & CR 535 at 536; *Cromwell Developments Ltd v Godfrey & Wright* (1998) 76 P & CR D14 at D15).

10   **[Para 7.210]**.

Nomenclature

7.69   A term of years is commonly known as a 'leasehold estate' and its owner as a *leaseholder* (as distinct from a *freeholder*). In a strict sense a 'lease' or 'demise' is the transaction in law which enables a landlord (or 'lessor') to vest a term of years in a tenant (or 'lessee').[1] Although 'lease', 'tenancy' and 'term of years' have tended, in practice, to be used as interchangeable descriptions of the leaseholder's proprietary estate,[2] the decision of the House of Lords in *Bruton v London & Quadrant Housing Trust*[3] has now added a dimension of hazard to the indiscriminate use of such terminology. The precise connotation of each of these phrases requires more detailed examination, the difficulties in this regard flowing largely from the ambivalent character of the leasehold device as a creature of both contract and property.

1   The term 'lease' is often used to refer to the document which grants possession to the lessee and spells out the covenants intended to bind lessor and lessee (see *Rye v Rye* [1962] AC 496 at 511 per Lord Radcliffe).

2   An orally granted tenancy cannot however, comprise a 'lease' within the definition of 'conveyance' contained in LPA 1925, s 205(1)(ii) (see *Rye v Rye* [1962] AC 496 at 508 per Lord MacDermott).
3   [2000] 1 AC 406 [**para 7.85**].

The political future of the leasehold estate

7.70   In modern Britain the term of years accounts for a large proportion of occupancy in the commercial or business sector and also for some 30 per cent of all household tenure.[1] There is, however, an increasing level of disenchantment with the fixed-term leasehold estate as a medium of residential ownership. The present Labour government views the existing residential leasehold system as 'fundamentally flawed.' The law of leasehold has, accordingly, been condemned as having 'its roots in the feudal system', as being 'heavily weighted in favour of one party (ie the landlord)', and as conferring on the tenant, in many cases, an asset of a wasting nature for which he has paid a full market price.[2]

1   *Social Trends No 34* (2004 edition, London), p 153.
2   See *Commonhold and Leasehold Reform: Draft Bill and Consultation Paper* (Lord Chancellor's Department, Cm 4843, August 2000), Pt I, para 2.3.1 (p 85), Pt II, para 1.1 (p 107), Annex A, para 7 (p 101).

Origins of the leasehold device

7.71   Largely in consequence of its ancient origins, the term of years is a curious hybrid which hovers between the worlds of property and contract.[1] The proprietary character of the term of years is nowadays so readily assumed that it can be easily overlooked that the leasehold relationship is founded essentially on contract.[2]

1   See e g *Linden Gardens Trust Ltd v Lenesta Sludge Disposals Ltd* [1994] 1 AC 85 at 108H per Lord Browne-Wilkinson; *Western Australia v Ward* (2002) 191 ALR 1 at [482] per McHugh J; *PW & Co v Milton Gate Investments Ltd* [2004] 2 WLR 443 at [73] per Neuberger J.
2   As Lord Browne-Wilkinson pointed out in *Hammersmith and Fulham LBC v Monk* [1992] 1 AC 478 at 491G–H, the lease provides a classic reminder of the fact that 'a contract between two persons can, by itself, give rise to a property interest in one of them.'

Gradual accretion of property in the term of years

7.72   The leasehold estate provides the pre-eminent historic demonstration of the transformation of contractual right into proprietary title.[1] The right to occupy another's land for a defined period of time was originally considered to confer no estate in the land, but merely to create rights *in personam*.[2] The lessee's remedies were restricted to a personal action in damages against the lessor on his covenant to give enjoyment of the land.[3] In time, however, it came to be accepted that the lessee for a term, although denied 'seisin' in the strict sense, had a right to possession which could be protected against third parties.

The enactment of the Statute of Gloucester 1278 and the steady development of the action of ejectment during the late Middle Ages[4] effectively converted the personal relationship of landlord and tenant into a new category of proprietary relationship based on the recognition of some form of estate ownership vested in the tenant.[5] The tenant's rights were now vindicated by a recovery not merely of damages but of possession of the land. Commensurately with this extension of protection, the leasehold relationship began to generate an entitlement which more closely resembled a right good against the world.

1   See *Transfield Properties (Kent Street) Pty Ltd v Amos Aked Swift Pty Ltd* (1994) 36 NSWLR 321 at 343B per Santow J.
2   See *Street v Mountford* [1985] AC 809 at 814E per Lord Templeman.
3   See generally A W B Simpson, *A History of The Land Law* (2nd edn, Oxford 1986), pp 71–77; F Pollock and F W Maitland, *The History of English Law* (London 1968), Vol II, pp 106–117.
4   See *Silkdale Pty Ltd v Long Leys Co Pty Ltd* (1995) 7 BPR 14414 at 14427 per Young J; T F T Plucknett, *A Concise History of the Common Law* (5th edn London 1956), p 373.
5   See T F T Plucknett, op cit, p 574.

Transmutation to proprietary status

7.73 It was by virtue of this metamorphosis that, almost unnoticed, the term of years began to cross the critical conventional borderline between contract and property. At this point the interest conferred by a lease could no longer be regarded as lying altogether outside the law of real property, although a lingering recollection of its contractual antecedents inhibited its full acceptance within the strict system of feudal tenements.[1] The hybrid character of the term of years, partaking as it did of the nature of both realty and personalty, caused the tenant's interest to be classified, with fitting ambiguity, as a 'chattel real'.[2] This hesitancy notwithstanding, the tenant's interest in the land came to be acknowledged 'as analogous to a form of feudal tenure.'[3]

1   *Progressive Mailing House Pty Ltd v Tabali Pty Ltd* (1985) 157 CLR 17 at 51 per Deane J.
2   See *National Carriers Ltd v Panalpina (Northern) Ltd* [1981] AC 675 at 708B–C per Lord Russell of Killowen. The terminology of 'chattel real' is now archaic (see *Crago v Julian* [1992] 1 WLR 372 at 377H per Nicholls V-C).
3   *Progressive Mailing House Pty Ltd v Tabali Pty Ltd* (1985) 157 CLR 17 at 51 per Deane J.

Versatility of the modern leasehold device

7.74 The proprietary quality of the term of years is firmly recognised today by statute. Yet it has been said, quite correctly, that a lease is 'chameleonic in both character and function.'[1] In the legal systems of the common law world the leasehold device has been adapted and manipulated for an extremely broad range of purposes. It currently provides a primary legal vehicle for the provision of premises for commercial enterprise, for the supply of residential housing, and for the regulation of agricultural use. The lease or tenancy has come to play a vital role in mediating a host of contractual, consumer, conveyancing and investment relationships. Essentially the same legal concept has had to do service for arrangements which, in their context and purpose, can differ as widely as the short-term letting for residential occupation and a leasehold term of 3,000 years used as a mortgage security.[2] The multiplicity of uses to which the uniform concept of tenancy has been put only barely conceals the difficulties which are inherent in the indifferent application of the same legal rules to the periodic tenant who pays £100 per week for her bed-sit, the home-owner who has just paid £100,000 for a 99 year lease of a new flat, and the large commercial concern which rents a warehouse for £10,000 per year.[3]

1   *219 Broadway Corp v Alexander's, Inc,* 387 NE2d 1205 at 1207 per Judge Jasen (1979).
2   **[Para 8.251]**.
3   See *Wood Factory Pty Ltd v Kiritos Pty Ltd* (1985) 2 NSWLR 105 at 120F per Priestley JA.

CONCEPTUAL AMBIVALENCE OF THE LEASE

7.75   In consequence of the nature of its origins and its various contemporary functions, the lease for a term of years possesses a duality of character which gives rise to conceptual difficulty. The lease is 'both an executory contract and an executed demise'[1] and there remains a significant latent tension between these divergent dimensions of the leasehold relationship.

1   *Progressive Mailing House Pty Ltd v Tabali Pty Ltd* (1985) 157 CLR 17 at 51 per Deane J (High Court of Australia). The dual character of the lease is widely recognised throughout the common law world (see *Rye v Rye* [1962] AC 496 at 505 per Vicount Simonds; *Harrow LBC v Qazi* [2004] 1 AC 983 at [145] per Lord Scott of Foscote; *Hoyt's Pty Ltd v Spencer* (1919) 27 CLR 133 at 142 per Isaacs J; *Brown v RepublicBank First National Midland,* 766 SW2d 203 at 204 (1988) per Kilgarlin J).

The proprietary perspective

7.76   Viewed from the perspective of property, a demise of land marks the grant of an exclusive possession sufficiently intense to be identified by the common law, in its more abstract mode, as a form of estate ownership. On this analysis the leasehold differs from the freehold only in respect of duration, both estates connoting, in principle, a plenitude of territorial control. Thus, indeed, the tenant is said today to be fully entitled 'to exercise the rights of an owner of land, which is in the real sense his land albeit temporarily and subject to certain restrictions.'[1]

1   *Street v Mountford* [1985] AC 809 at 816B per Lord Templeman. See likewise Law Commission, *Landlord and Tenant: Privity of Contract and Estate* (Law Com No 174, November 1988), para 3.26 ('temporary property ownership'); *Fatac Ltd v Commissioner of Inland Revenue* [2002] 3 NZLR 648 at [38] ('fundamental, if temporary, rights of ownership').

Leasehold ownership

7.77   The proprietary aspect of the leasehold device comes most obviously to the fore in the executed demise of a long term of years, granted for a premium with no rent (or only a nominal rent) reserved.[1] In many such instances the purchase of a leasehold estate begins to resemble the purchase of an estate in fee simple.[2] The estate ownership acquired by the young urban professional under a 125 year lease of a flat seems to differ little from freehold ownership of a house, particularly where both are acquired with the aid of substantial mortgage finance.[3] Yet essentially the same proprietary analysis remains applicable, at least in principle, to much shorter lettings of less extensive areas of land. A term of years can exist in a single room[4] and, indeed, it is often the strong resonance of proprietary status which most crucially underpins the protection of the short-term tenant in English law.

1   See *Progressive Mailing House Pty Ltd v Tabali Pty Ltd* (1985) 157 CLR 17 at 53 per Deane J.
2   The notion of the lease as a vehicle of estate ownership makes a certain conceptual sense in the context of 'broad acre' or 'green field' leases of land (see *Wood Factory Pty Ltd v Kiritos Pty Ltd* (1985) 2 NSWLR 105 at 120F per Priestley JA). It has been said that this conveyancing perspective is particularly apt to describe the effect of leasehold grants in the rural, agrarian society of a bygone era (*Javins v First National Realty Corporation*, 428 F2d 1071 at 1074 per Judge Skelly Wright (1970)). 'Leases acquired the character of conveyances of real property when their primary function was to govern the relationship between landowners and farmers' (*Trentacost v Brussel*, 412 A2d 436 at 442 per Pashman J (1980)).
3   The grantee under a long lease normally purchases his or her estate in the land on payment of an initial cash sum or premium not dissimilar from the purchase price of a freehold estate in equivalent realty. Like the freeholder, the leaseholder may use the subject matter of his purchase as security for a loan covering all or part of the purchase price. After acquisition the leaseholder's only remaining financial liabilities to the grantor relate to the continuing payment of what is usually a fairly nominal ground rent, together with payment of such periodic service or management charges as may be stipulated in the covenants of the lease.
4   *AG Securities v Vaughan* [1990] 1 AC 417 at 471B–C per Lord Oliver of Aylmerton [**para 7.68**].

Hierarchies of leasehold ownership

7.78   In the leasehold context, the structure of estate ownership conforms to the elementary proprietary principle: *nemo dat quod non habet*.[1] The creation of a term of years always presupposes the existence in the grantor of some larger estate in that land.[2] The largest leasehold estate is 'carved out of the freehold'[3] and this leasehold estate may, in its turn, sustain the creation of a hierarchy of derivative leasehold interests, provided that each is of lesser duration than its reversionary (or parent) estate.[4] It follows, in this conveyancing sense, that no lessee can take a proprietary interest in the land in the absence of a more ample estate vested in his lessor.[5]

1   'No one can give that which he does not have'. See *Bruton v London & Quadrant Housing Trust* [2000] 1 AC 406 at 415B per Lord Hoffmann.
2   The one exception to this principle is provided by the crown lease, which, being granted out of the allodium, cannot be a derivative of any superior estate in the land [**para 1.141**].
3   *Ingram v IRC* [2000] 1 AC 293 at 310C–D per Lord Hutton. See also *St Marylebone Property Co Ltd v Fairweather* [1962] 1 QB 498 at 512, 515 per Holroyd Pearce LJ.
4   See also *Lang v Webb* (1912) 13 CLR 503 at 515 per Isaacs J; *Wik Peoples v Queensland* (1996) 187 CLR 1 at 94 per Brennan CJ.
5   *Ingram v IRC* [2000] 1 AC 293 at 303G per Lord Hoffmann. See also *Southgate BC v Watson* [1944] KB 541 at 544; *Lewisham BC v Roberts* [1949] 2 KB 608 at 622; *Street v Mountford* [1985] AC 809 at 821B; *Dellneed Ltd v Chin* (1987) 53 P & CR 172 at 187.

Terms of years as commerciable property

7.79   Short-term lettings and periodic tenancies are seldom the subject of alienation, but leasehold grants comprise, in many cases, a substantial and highly commerciable proprietary estate in land.[1] The proprietor of a long leasehold (whether a head lease or a sublease) stands possessed of an asset which, although necessarily of a wasting nature, still commands for many years an inflating market value. The manipulability of leasehold estate ownership allows every leaseholder to grant under-leases out of his own reversionary estate or to transfer (or 'assign') his own estate in its entirety to a third party.[2] In particular, the potential for assignment enables the leaseholder, in principle, to transfer the unexpired portion of his term for such price as the current market will sustain, inflation ensuring that this price continues for some time to run ahead of the purchase price of his leasehold estate at the commencement of the term.

1   The standard purchase of a leasehold flat nowadays comprises, at its commencement date, a term of 99 or 125 years.
2   [**Para 7.210**]. Leases normally contain a covenant prohibiting the tenant from assigning or subletting without the prior written consent or licence of the landlord [**para 14.81**].

The contractual perspective

7.80   Viewed from the perspective of contract, the lease is manifestly different from a conveyance of a fee simple: the conveyance of a leasehold interest does not represent a fully executed contract. Even after grant the lease is 'partly executory: rights and obligations remain outstanding on both sides throughout its currency.'[1] The phenomenon of the completely unconditional long-term demise[2] is nowadays most unusual; the leasehold estate can seldom be divorced from its basis in the law of contract.

1   *National Carriers Ltd v Panalpina (Northern) Ltd* [1981] AC 675 at 705G per Lord Simon of Glaisdale. See also *Ingram v IRC* [2000] 1 AC 293 at 304B–C per Lord Hoffmann.
2   See e g *Knight's Case* (1588) 5 Co Rep 54b at 55a, 77 ER 137 at 138.

Lease as a specialised form of contract

7.81   Especially in the context of many modern forms of residential or business occupancy, the lease often emerges more obviously as a relatively short-term commercial relationship, framed in the language of executory promises of an all-inclusive character to which the terminology of conveyance or estate ownership seems peculiarly inappropriate. Some 70 years ago William Douglas and Jerome Frank argued that 'to assimilate leases of modern office buildings to feudal tenure in seventeenth century England is to disregard the essential elements of the bargain made, the present money economy, and the great development in contract law which has taken place since Coke wrote.'[1] In more recent times Laskin J of the Supreme Court of Canada accepted that it is 'no longer sensible to pretend that a commercial lease ... is simply a conveyance and not also a contract.'[2] It is increasingly recognised, moreover, that the modern residential letting represents a commercial transaction which results in the sale of a package of consumer utilities of shelter and convenience.[3] In reality the urban tenant is frequently a purchaser of goods and services under a specialised form of consumer contract,[4] a perspective which in England will shortly intensify with the overt adoption of a 'consumer approach' to the 'housing agreements' that are to serve as the basis of a major statutory rationalisation of the law of housing tenure.[5]

1   W O Douglas and J Frank, 'Landlords' Claims in Reorganizations' 42 Yale LJ 1003 at 1005 (1932–33).
2   *Highway Properties Ltd v Kelly, Douglas & Co Ltd* (1971) 17 DLR (3d) 710 at 721.
3   'When American city dwellers, both rich and poor, seek "shelter" today, they seek a well known package of goods and services – a package which includes not merely walls and ceilings, but also adequate heat, light and ventilation, serviceable plumbing facilities, secure windows and doors, proper sanitation, and proper maintenance' (*Javins v First National Realty Corporation* 428 F2d 1071 at 1074 per Judge Skelly Wright (1970)).
4   See *Green v Superior Court of City and County of San Francisco*, 517 P2d 1168 at 1175 (1974) per Tobriner J ('the modern urban tenant ... may reasonably expect that the product he is purchasing is fit for the purpose for which it is obtained, that is, a living unit'.
5   See Law Commission, *Renting Homes 1: Status and Security* (Consultation Paper No 162, April 2002), paras 6.1–6.2.

'Contractualisation' of the lease

7.82 Acknowledgement of the heavily contractual dimension of the landlord–tenant relationship inevitably counteracts the conventional common law analysis of the lease as a conveyance of a proprietary estate.[1] In many ways the modern social function of the tenancy relationship as a consumer contract marks a significant transformation from its former role as the medium of estate ownership. Recent years have accordingly seen a growing tendency to expose the law of leases to a comprehensive application of ordinary contract principles.[2] Such principles seemed largely irrelevant where the dominant analysis of the lease was that of an executed demise whose essential purpose was to invest the tenant with a proprietary estate in land. Nowadays it has become impossible to maintain the traditional assumption that leases lie generally beyond the reach of contractual doctrines such as those relating to frustration, repudiatory breach and mitigation of loss.[3] Indeed the gradual infiltration of such doctrines may perversely have brought the lease almost full circle to its medieval origin as a species of essentially contractual obligation.[4]

1   See *Hussein v Mehlman* [1992] 2 EGLR 87 at 88K–L per Sedley QC. See also *Brown v RepublicBank First National Midland* 766 SW2d 203 at 205 (1988) per Kilgarlin J (referring in the Supreme Court of Texas to the need to replace 'antiquated property law concepts with more equitable and contemporary solutions in contract').
2   See *Progressive Mailing House Pty Ltd v Tabali Pty Ltd* (1985) 157 CLR 17 at 29 per Mason J; *Bruton v London & Quadrant Housing Trust* [2000] 1 AC 406 at 417E–F per Lord Hobhouse of Woodborough. In particular, in the enforcement against landlords of implied warranties of habitability and fitness for use, American courts have increasingly stressed that the contractual

principles established in other areas of the law 'provide a more rational framework for the apportionment of landlord–tenant responsibilities' (see *Javins v First National Realty Corporation*, 428 F2d 1071 at 1080 (1970)).

3   [**Paras 7.323, 7.319, 14.203**]. It may be that the applicability of pure contractual doctrine decreases 'the further one moves away from the case where the rights of the parties are ... essentially defined by executory covenant or contractual promise to the case where the tenant's rights are, as a matter of substance, more properly to be viewed by reference to their character as an estate (albeit a chattel one) in land with a root of title in the executed demise' (see *Progressive Mailing House Pty Ltd v Tabali Pty Ltd* (1985) 157 CLR 17 at 53 per Deane J).

4   It has become a recurring judicial refrain that the courts see 'no reason' why a particular issue should 'receive any different answer in the context of the contractual relationship of landlord and tenant than that which it would receive in any other contractual context' (*Hammersmith and Fulham LBC v Monk* [1992] 1 AC 478 at 483B per Lord Bridge of Harwich). See also *Hadjiloucas v Crean* [1988] 1 WLR 1006 at 1022G, 1024G per Mustill LJ; *Prudential Assurance Co Ltd v London Residuary Body* (1992) 63 P & CR 386 at 399 per Scott LJ; *Hussein v Mehlman* [1992] 2 EGLR 87 at 89E per Sedley QC; *Muscat v Smith* [2003] 1 WLR 2853 at [11] per Sedley LJ.

Contractual regulation by statute

7.83   The many spheres of operation of the lease were originally left to the free play of market forces, but in recent decades the landlord–tenant relationship has been subjected to at least some minimal control exerted through regulatory legislation.[1] Perhaps the most conspicuous aspect of this legislation has tended to be that dealing with private residential tenancies, where landlords, operating from a superior bargaining position, were frequently able to impose oppressive rents and conditions. During the past 80 years the Rent Acts and other housing legislation did much to redress the balance of power in the residential context, by affording substantial security of tenure, by establishing effective rent controls, and by the implication of contractual terms for repair and reasonable standards of residential amenity. Some of this protectionism in the private residential sector has now receded, but less extensive forms of protection for the tenant survive in the statutory codes which govern other leasehold areas, ie in respect of public sector residential tenancies, business tenancies and agricultural tenancies.

1   [**Paras 14.311–14.363**].

Continuing tension between contract and property

7.84   Notwithstanding the modern 'contractualisation' of the lease,[1] the relationship between the property- and contract-based views of the leasehold nexus remains one of pervasive tension.[2] In certain significant respects English law persists in identifying the tenant in terms of proprietary ownership. The leasehold is no less a form of proprietary control than is the freehold.[3] Moreover, the role of the leasehold as a medium of proprietary ownership has been accentuated by recent reforms, such as the statutory extension of leasehold enfranchisement and the council tenant's 'right to buy',[4] which underscore the fact that tenant status in the residential sector frequently provides a gateway to enlarged rights of fee simple ownership. Even short-term or periodic tenancies, with their capacity for devolution upon members of the tenant's family,[5] have come, in some contexts, to evince a tantalising resemblance to a modern form of entailed estate. In these and many other ways the law of landlord and tenant remains pervaded by the ambivalence of the lease as a source of both proprietary and contractual entitlement.

1   See e g Hicks, 'The Contractual Nature of Real Property Leases' 24 Baylor L Rev 443 (1972); J Effron, 'The Contractualisation of the Law of Leasehold: Pitfalls and Opportunities' (1988) 14 Monash L Rev 83; K Mackie, (1988) 62 ALJ 53; [1993] Conv 71 (S Bright); M Pawlowski, [1995] Conv 379.

2   See e g *Hammersmith and Fulham LBC v Monk* [1992] 1 AC 478 at 491E per Lord Browne-Wilkinson **[para 7.299]**.

3   See e g *Street v Mountford* [1985] AC 809 at 816B per Lord Templeman **[para 7.133]**.

4   **[Paras 7.327, 7.347]**.

5   **[Paras 14.319, 14.340]**.

The contractual or non-proprietary lease

7.85   A new complexity in the nomenclature surrounding the leasehold estate has been generated by the ruling in *Bruton v London & Quadrant Housing Trust*.[1] Here the House of Lords refined the conceptualism of leasehold tenure in a way which starkly highlights the divergence between proprietary and contractual perceptions of the landlord–tenant relationship. In a highly controversial ruling the House drew an important distinction between the 'lease' (or 'tenancy') and the 'term of years'. Lord Hoffmann indicated that the terms 'lease' and 'tenancy' refer to the *contractual relationship* between two parties who are designated landlord and tenant and not necessarily to any *proprietary consequence* of that relationship. On this analysis a 'lease' is a sheer product of contract[2] and, in itself, implies no conferment of a proprietary estate in the form of a term of years.[3] In this most basic sense, a 'lease' is a mere agreement for exclusive possession for a term at a rent – a purely functional or relational description of the parties' contractual nexus. As Lord Hoffmann went on to say, a lease 'may, and usually does, create a proprietary interest called a leasehold estate or, technically, a "term of years absolute" ', but whether in fact it does so 'will depend upon whether the landlord had an interest out of which he could grant it. Nemo dat quod non habet.'[4]

1   [2000] 1 AC 406 **[para 7.86]**. See Mark Pawlowski and James Brown, '*Bruton*: a new species to tenancy?' (2000) 4 L & TR 119.

2   The contractual essence of the 'lease' is strongly signalled by the fact that, in 30 lines of judicial prose (see [2000] 1 AC 406 at 413A–H), Lord Hoffmann referred no fewer than 12 times to the 'agreement' between the parties. Likewise Lord Hobhouse of Woodborough emphasised (at 417E–F) that rules of contractual construction apply 'as much to contracts relating to property as to any other contract.'

3   'The term "lease" or "tenancy" ... is not concerned with the question of whether the agreement creates an estate or other proprietary interest which may be binding upon third parties' ([2000] 1 AC 406 at 415A–B per Lord Hoffmann). Lords Slynn of Hadley, Hope of Craighead and Hobhouse of Woodborough expressly associated themselves with the reasoning of Lord Hoffmann ([2000] 1 AC 406 at 410E, 416A, 416B).

4   [2000] 1 AC 406 at 415B. See also *Western Australia v Ward* (2000) 170 ALR 159 at 361 per
       North J.

The tenant without a title good against the world

7.86   The decision in *Bruton* confirmed the existence, in English law, of the
phenomenon of the contractual or non-proprietary lease.[1] A 'lease' is simply a
contractual agreement for possession, whereas a 'term of years' is the proprietary consequence of a 'lease' created by someone who holds a proprietary
estate in the land concerned.[2] It is therefore possible for someone to create a
'lease' over land – a so-called 'tenancy by estoppel'[3] – even though he has no
proprietary estate out of which he could grant a 'term of years'. The status of a
'tenant' may rest upon either contract or estate,[4] but the existence of a
landlord–tenant relationship does not, in itself, depend upon the tenant's ability
to establish a 'proprietary title good against all the world' or upon his showing
that his own rights derive from a legal estate previously conveyed to his
landlord.[5] On this basis the House of Lords was able to hold in *Bruton* that a
housing trust, which owned no proprietary estate in the relevant land, could
nevertheless, by agreeing to grant exclusive possession to a residential occupier,
create a 'lease' which attracted the repairing obligations imposed on a landlord
by the Landlord and Tenant Act 1985.[6]

1   Some have suggested that *Bruton* revitalises 'a beast long thought extinct: the lease as pure
       personalty' (see M Dixon, 'The Non-Proprietary Lease: The Rise of the Feudal Phoenix'
       [2000] CLJ 25 at 27).
2   [2000] 1 AC 406 at 415C per Lord Hoffmann.
3   **[Para 7.265]**. The estoppel can be 'fed', as it was in *Bruton*'s case (see [1998] QB 834 at 838B),
       by the landlord's subsequent acquisition of a proprietary estate in the land which would have
       supported the initial grant, in which case the tenant's lease then 'take[s] effect in interest' as a
       proprietary estate (*Cuthbertson v Irving* (1859) 4 H & N 742 at 754–755, 157 ER 1034 at 1039
       per Martin B).
4   'A "tenant", both by derivation and by usage, is someone who "holds" land of another, for
       which purpose it is immaterial whether he does so by contract or by estate' (*City of London
       Corpn v Fell* [1993] QB 589 at 604B per Nourse LJ).
5   [2000] 1 AC 406 at 418C–D per Lord Hobhouse of Woodborough. It has been mooted that a
       Bruton lease comprises 'a type of "quasi-estate" conferring a limited form of exclusive
       possession' enforceable only as against the immediate landlord (see Mark Pawlowski, 'Occu-
       pational Rights in Leasehold Law: Time for Rationalisation?' [2002] Conv 550).
6   [2000] 1 AC 406 at 416F–G per Lord Hoffmann, 417E per Lord Hobhouse of Woodborough.
       There is an overwhelming suspicion that the new terminological exactitude insisted upon by
       the House of Lords in *Bruton*'s case was driven by the social need to ensure, by means of a less
       restrictive identification of landlord–tenant relationships, that a wider range of residential
       occupiers qualified for the benefit of the repairing obligations fastened upon 'landlords' by
       L&TA 1985, s 11 **[para 14.43]**.

Implications of Bruton's case

7.87   The implications of the *Bruton* decision are substantial.[1] The ruling
illustrates the continuing steady drift towards a contractual characterisation of
leasehold relationships. In so doing, it further blurs the distinction between the

contractual lease and the contractual licence.[2] It is also likely that, viewed from a wider perspective, *Bruton* evidences the gradual eclipse of the leasehold relationship as involving the conferment of a proprietary estate, thus foreshadowing, at least in the short-term residential sector, the decline of this (nowadays) politically incorrect device into something much more closely resembling the civilian concept of a contract of hire of land.[3] Perhaps most significantly, the decision and the mixed reception accorded to it[4] reflect again the tension between a land law philosophy which focuses predominantly on the empirical reality of the parties' conduct and a rather different perspective which focuses primarily on the juristic manipulation of abstract entitlements.[5] On the former approach, a lease is simply the product of defined transactional behaviour; on the latter approach, a non-proprietary lease carved out of a non-existent estate in land is a self-evident absurdity.[6] The *Bruton* decision, with its exposition of 'tenancy by estoppel', is pervaded by the empiricism of relativity of title.[7]

1   For instance, the creation of a non-proprietary lease (ie a tenancy by estoppel) need not comply with the formality rules governing conveyances of land (LPA 1925, ss 52–54) (see *E H Lewis & Son Ltd v Morelli* [1948] 2 All ER 1021 at 1024F–G; *Universal Permanent Building Society v Cooke* [1952] Ch 95 at 103). On the other hand, only a term of years – and not a non-proprietary lease – can be protected by LRA 2002, s 29(1), (2)(a)(ii), Sch 3, paras 1–2 **[paras 12.143, 12.146]**.

2   The right to recover possession now applies equally to leases and licences, provided (in the latter case) that the licensee enjoys exclusive possession (*Hounslow LBC v Twickenham Garden Developments Ltd* [1971] Ch 233 at 257D–E) or 'effective control' or 'de facto occupation' (*Manchester Airport Plc v Dutton* [2000] QB 133 at 147C–G per Laws LJ) or even a mere contractual right to enter and occupy land (*Manchester Airport Plc v Dutton*, supra at 150A–C per Laws LJ) **[paras 3.38, 4.98]**.

3   See also *Customs and Excise Commrs v Sinclair Collis Ltd* [2001] STC 989 at [58] per Lord Scott of Foscote.

4   See (2000) 63 MLR 424 (P Routley); (2000) 116 LQR 7 (S Bright); [1999] Conv 517 (D Rook).

5   See Gray and Gray, 'The Idea of Property in Land', in S Bright and J K Dewar (ed), *Land Law: Themes and Perspectives* (OUP 1998), p 18.

6   For some commentators, a 'non-proprietary lease' is a 'contradiction in terms' (see [2000] CLJ 25 at 27 (M Dixon)).

7   **[Paras 3.23, 6.4]**.

ESSENTIAL ELEMENTS OF A LEASE OR TENANCY

7.88   In the absence of any particularly helpful statutory definition of the 'term of years',[1] it has been left to the courts to fashion the parameters of the lease or tenancy. The essential ambiguity of the leasehold device as both contract and property was vividly captured in the statement of Lord Templeman in *Prudential Assurance Co Ltd v London Residuary Body*[2] that '[a] demise for years is a contract for the exclusive possession and profit of land for some determinate period.' Some years earlier, in *Street v Mountford*,[3] Lord Templeman had indicated that '[t]o constitute a tenancy the occupier must be granted exclusive possession for a fixed or periodic term certain in consideration of a premium or periodical payments.' Neither formula entirely eliminates the definitional difficulty.

1   The statutory definition of a 'term of years absolute' (see LPA 1925, s 205(1)(xxvii)) is circular in nature and provides little assistance in isolating the main structural elements of the lease or tenancy.
2   [1992] 2 AC 386 at 390C (effectively following *Bl Comm*, Vol II, p 140).
3   [1985] AC 809 at 818E.

7.89   The case law of the late 1980s seemed to identify three large elements as inherent in any lease or tenancy. The lessee or tenant must be granted:
–   exclusive possession[1]
–   for a fixed or periodic term certain[2]
–   in consideration of a premium (ie lump sum) or periodical payments.[3]

1   **[Para 7.131]**.
2   **[Para 7.100]**.
3   **[Para 7.91]**.

7.90   The strict necessity for rent or other consideration has since been doubted, although such payment probably remains a sine qua non of at least the periodic tenancy. The other two elements lie, indubitably, at the core of the leasehold concept,[1] as was indicated in by Lord Hoffmann in *Bruton v London & Quadrant Housing Trust*[2]:

> A 'lease' or 'tenancy' is a contractually binding agreement, not referable to any other relationship between the parties, by which one person gives another the right to exclusive occupation of land for a fixed or renewable period or periods of time, usually in return for a periodic payment in money. An agreement having these characteristics creates a relationship of landlord and tenant to which the common law or statute may then attach various incidents.[3]

1   These elements are no less adaptable to a subtenancy (see *Monmouth BC v Marlog* (1994) 68 P & CR D4 at D5).
2   [2000] 1 AC 406 at 413E–F.
3   This definition is not perfect, in that Lord Hoffmann clearly regarded 'exclusive occupation' and 'exclusive possession' as interchangeable terms (see [2000] 1 AC 406 at 413E–414B), whereas a difference of significance may persist **[para 3.3]**.

RENT OR OTHER CONSIDERATION

7.91   An obligation on the part of the tenant to pay rent or, more properly, to perform 'rent-service', was once considered to be an integral aspect of the tenurial relationship of landlord and tenant.[1] Correspondingly, the landlord's right to receive rent or rent-service tended to be regarded as a normal incident annexed to his reversion in the land.[2] So long as the tenant was given exclusive possession by the conveyance of a leasehold estate, his obligation to pay rent was absolute and unqualified.[3] In recent years there has been a distinct movement away from this tenurial or property-based view towards a more contractual analysis of the concept of rent. The courts have come to characterise rent not as the incident of a medieval tenure, but rather as the likely outcome of the contractual bargain concluded between owner and occupier.[4]

On this basis rent represents the consideration which the tenant frequently agrees to pay in return for his continuing right of exclusive possession[5] and the repairing and other obligations which attach to the reversion.[6]

1   On the property-oriented view of the lease, rent simply 'issues out of the land' and carries unique rights of distraint and forfeiture. See W Holdsworth, *History of English Law* (2nd edn, London 1937), Vol VII, p 262; *Muscat v Smith* [2003] 1 WLR 2853 at [10] per Sedley LJ; *Shevill v Builders Licensing Board* (1980) 2 BPR 9662 at 9672 per Mahoney JA; *Todburn Pty Ltd v Taormina International Pty Ltd* (1990) 5 BPR 11173 at 11175. The common law has always been fairly ready, in the absence of an express covenant for rent, to imply a promise to pay reasonable compensation for the loss of land use caused to the landlord by reason of the occupation of the tenant (see *Dean and Chapter of Rochester v Pierce* (1808) 1 Camp 466 at 467, 170 ER 1023).
2   Thus there can in law be an assignment of the right to recover rent simpliciter (see *Knill v Prowse* (1884) 33 WR 163 at 164; *Rhodes v Allied Dunbar Pension Services Ltd* [1989] 1 WLR 800 at 806C per Nicholls LJ).
3   The tenant's rent obligation was held to survive a number of calamities. See *Paradine v Jane* (1647) Aleyn 26 at 27–28, 82 ER 897 at 898 (dispossession during civil war); *Monk v Cooper* (1727) 2 Stra 763, 93 ER 833 at 834; *Belfour v Weston* (1786) 1 Term Rep 310 at 312, 99 ER 1112 at 1113 (destruction of premises by fire). The tenant's obligation to pay rent could never, of course, survive wrongful eviction by the landlord (see *Wood Factory Pty Ltd v Kiritos Pty Ltd* (1985) 2 NSWLR 105 at 121B–C per Priestley JA).
4   See *Shevill v Builders Licensing Board* (1980) 2 BPR 9662 at 9672 per Mahoney JA.
5   See eg *C H Bailey Ltd v Memorial Enterprises Ltd* [1974] 1 WLR 728 at 732B–D, 735B–C; *United Scientific Holdings Ltd v Burnley BC* [1978] AC 904 at 935A per Lord Diplock; *Ingram v IRC* [1995] 4 All ER 334 at 340j–341a.
6   See *Muscat v Smith* [2003] 1 WLR 2853 at [30] per Sedley LJ.

Necessity for rent or other money payment

7.92   When seen from the viewpoint of the landlord, the lease or tenancy is nowadays primarily an instrument for the commercial exploitation of land. Most leases and tenancies are therefore granted expressly in consideration of money or money's worth. In recent years, however, some confusion has surrounded the question whether rent or other money payment is an essential indicium of leasehold relationships. In *Street v Mountford*[1] Lord Templeman went so far as to describe the payment of rent as one of the decisive 'hallmarks' of a tenancy of residential accommodation, thereby seeming to endorse the idea that rent payment remains a sine qua non of the conferment of a leasehold estate.[2] The courts later retreated from so broadly stated a proposition,[3] pointing out that while a lease or tenancy is granted 'usually in return for a periodic payment in money',[4] this is not inevitably so.[5]

1   [1985] AC 809 at 826E (see also at 818C, 821B–C).
2   'To constitute a tenancy the occupier must be granted exclusive possession for a fixed or periodic term certain in consideration of a premium or periodical payments' ([1985] AC 809 at 818E). See also *Scrimgeour v Waller* (1981) 257 EG 61 at 63 per Sir David Cairns; *Manchester Airport Plc v Dutton* [2000] QB 133 at 143A per Chadwick LJ.
3   The dogmatic insistence on rent or other consideration is not reflected in other authoritative expositions of the concept of tenancy (see eg *Radaich v Smith* (1959) 101 CLR 209 at 222 per Windeyer J). See also *Knight's Case* (1588) 5 Co Rep 54b at 55a, 77 ER 137 at 138; *Burns v Dennis* (1948) 48 SR (NSW) 266 at 267 per Jordan CJ; *Re British American Oil Co Ltd and*

DePass (1960) 21 DLR (2d) 110 at 115; *Hayes v Seymour-Johns* (1981) 2 BPR 9366 at 9369; *Fatac Ltd v Commissioner of Inland Revenue* [2002] 3 NZLR 648 at [41], [66].

4   *Bruton v London & Quadrant Housing Trust* [2000] 1 AC 406 at 413E per Lord Hoffmann. See similarly *Western Australia v Ward* (2002) 191 ALR 1 at [482] per McHugh J.

5   *AG Securities v Vaughan* [1990] 1 AC 417 at 430C–G per Fox LJ. See e g *Ashburn Anstalt v Arnold* [1989] Ch 1 at 9F–10C, 12G–13B, where the Court of Appeal expressly declined to treat *Street v Mountford* as having laid down a principle of 'no rent, no lease.' Lord Templeman's reference to the 'hallmark' quality of rent payment was read down as merely a positive pointer towards the existence of a tenancy and not as a negative and definitive proposition that 'you cannot have a tenancy without a rent.' *Ashburn Anstalt* was subsequently overruled on other grounds by the House of Lords in *Prudential Assurance Co Ltd v London Residuary Body* [1992] 2 AC 386 at 395G, but in the latter case (at 390C) Lord Templeman avoided any reference to rent payment as a necessary component of the definition of a lease (see, however, *Westminster CC v Clarke* [1992] 2 AC 288 at 299G–H per Lord Templeman).

7.93   It may be that the uncertainty over the requirement of a rent flows from a failure to differentiate sufficiently clearly between a 'lease' or 'tenancy' and a 'term of years'. The presence or absence of a rent is made expressly irrelevant in the statutory definitions of a 'term of years absolute'.[1] Indeed it must, on principle, be possible for a lessor, if he so wishes, to grant a proprietary estate by way of unconditional demise for a term of years at no rent.[2] By contrast, the lease or tenancy, being essentially a contractual rather than proprietary phenomenon,[3] requires to be supported by consideration (unless created by deed).[4] The distinct character of the term of years, emphasised afresh by the House of Lords in *Bruton v London & Quadrant Housing Trust*,[5] may finally make sense of the difficulties in this area. The *Bruton* ruling confirms the modern consensus – however ambiguously it is articulated – that the reservation of a rent is not strictly necessary for the creation of a term of years.[6] At the same time it is difficult in practice to conceive of a periodic tenancy without a rent[7] and it remains likely that the absence of rent payment often points persuasively towards the existence of a mere licence rather than a term of years.[8]

1   LPA 1925, s 205(1)(xxvii); LRA 2002, s 132(1).

2   See e g *Knight's Case* (1588) 5 Co Rep 54b at 55a, 77 ER 137 at 138; *Progressive Mailing House Pty Ltd v Tabali Pty Ltd* (1985) 157 CLR 17 at 53 per Deane J.

3   **[Para 7.85]**.

4   'Rent is an important indicator of an intention to be legally bound' (*Fatac Ltd v Commissioner of Inland Revenue* [2002] 3 NZLR 648 at [66]). The requirement of money consideration is reinforced in certain contexts: absence of a money rent precludes a tenancy from some special forms of statutory protection (see e g Rent Act 1977, s 5(1) **[para 14.315]**).

5   [2000] 1 AC 406 at 415A–C per Lord Hoffmann **[para 7.85]**.

6   See e g *Birrell v Carey* (1989) 58 P & CR 184 at 187 per Fox LJ; *Prudential Assurance Co Ltd v London Residuary Body* (1992) 63 P & CR 386 at 397 per Scott LJ; *Canadian Imperial Bank of Commerce v Bello* (1992) 64 P & CR 48 at 55 per Ralph Gibson LJ; *Skipton Building Society v Clayton* (1993) 66 P & CR 223 at 230 per Sir Christopher Slade; *Fatac Ltd v Commissioner of Inland Revenue* [2002] 3 NZLR 648 at [41], [66].

7   See *Prudential Assurance Co Ltd v London Residuary Body* (1992) 63 P & CR 386 at 397 per Scott LJ. It is fair to record that in *Street v Mountford* [1985] AC 809 at 826E, Lord Templeman's reference to rent payments as a decisive 'hallmark' was made in the immediate context of 'a periodical term'.

8   See e g *Colchester BC v Smith* [1991] Ch 448 at 485B–C (upheld [1992] Ch 421); *West Wiltshire CC v Snelgrove* (1998) 30 HLR 57 at 60–62; *Manchester Airport Plc v Dutton* [2000] QB 133 at 143A. See also [1988] Conv 201 at 203 (M P Thompson). It does not necessarily follow that a

tenancy always arises wherever the landowner demands compensation for use and occupation. See *Northern Ireland Housing Executive v McCann* [1979] NI 39 at 43E; *Westminster CC v Basson* (1991) 62 P & CR 57 at 59–60 (regular payments demanded from squatters in initially unlawful occupation).

Definition of 'rent'

7.94 In its ordinary or essential meaning, 'rent', where it is contractually due, comprises any periodical payment made for the possession of realty under a lease and for which distress[1] may be levied.[2] Thus rent usually takes the form of monetary compensation paid for the tenant's use of the demised premises,[3] although there is in principle no objection to a rent which is fixed in some other way,[4] eg in the form of services in kind,[5] bottles of wine,[6] or other chattels.[7] Where a rent is fixed in money terms, nothing turns on the adequacy of the consideration.[8]

1   **[Para 14.193]**.
2   See *Escalus Properties Ltd v Robinson* [1996] QB 231 at 243G–H per Nourse LJ; *Commr of Stamp Duties v J V (Crows Nest) Pty Ltd* (1987) 7 NSWLR 529 at 531F per Mahoney JA. See generally R G Lee, [1991] Conv 270.
3   See *United Scientific Holdings Ltd v Burnley BC* [1978] AC 904 at 935A per Lord Diplock, 947B per Lord Simon of Glaisdale, 963G per Lord Fraser of Tullybelton. A payment for the use of land may be 'rent' notwithstanding that there is no right of distraint **[para 14.195]** (see *T & E Homes Ltd v Robinson* [1979] 1 WLR 452 at 457E, 459E–F; *Commr of Stamp Duties v J V (Crows Nest) Pty Ltd* (1987) 7 NSWLR 529 at 532A per Mahoney JA).
4   *Co Litt*, p 142a. In certain restricted contexts 'rent' must nevertheless have a distinct quantifiable money value. For example, the rent restriction provisions of the Rent Act 1977 would be totally inoperable if the consideration for the tenant's occupation were not ultimately expressible in terms of money (*Barnes v Barratt* [1970] 2 QB 657 at 667E per Sachs LJ; *Bostock v Bryant* (1990) 61 P & CR 23 at 26–28 (performance of onerous services)).
5   *Co Litt*, p 96a; *Doe d Tucker v Morse* (1830) 1 B & Ad 365 at 369, 109 ER 822 at 824; *Duke of Marlborough v Osborn* (1864) 5 B & S 67 at 74, 122 ER 758 at 761; *Barnes v Barratt* [1970] 2 QB 657 at 666D, 670F–G. See also *Montague v Browning* [1954] 1 WLR 1039 at 1044–1045 (employee's wages subject to regular fixed deduction for occupation under service tenancy). Compare, however, *Scrimgeour v Waller* (1981) 257 EG 61 at 63; *Meier v Lucas* (Unreported, Court of Appeal, 4 March 1986).
6   *Pitcher v Tovey* (1692) 4 Mod 71 at 75–76, 87 ER 268 at 271.
7   *Co Litt*, p 142a. Rent may take the form of a notional rendering of one peppercorn per year.
8   *Royal Philanthropic Society v County* (1985) 276 EG 1068 at 1072.

Payments for use of the land

7.95 Not all money payments made by an occupier necessarily constitute rent. The coverage of the term 'rent' is restricted to only some of the payments which may arise as the result of a transaction of lease.[1] In its proper sense rent includes only those payments which a tenant is bound to make 'for the use of' the land in question,[2] thereby excluding those payments which are made 'merely in respect of' such use or are 'in reality only an accidental or incidental part of the transaction by which the right to use is granted.'[3] The parties' own description of a payment as 'rent' is persuasive but not conclusive.[4] In all cases

the test of rent is ultimately whether the relevant payment is made in consideration of the grant of the tenancy 'however it be described or allocated.'[5] It is
likely, therefore, that exorbitant payments made in respect of furniture hire
under otherwise rent-free tenancies will be treated as constituting rent.

1　See also *Holt v Wellington* (1996) 71 P & CR D40 (payments under adult care scheme,
　　although described as rent, held to be payments merely in respect of care).
2　*Bostock v Bryant* (1990) 61 P & CR 23 at 25 per Stuart-Smith LJ. See also *Ward v Warnke*
　　(1990) 22 HLR 496 at 498–500 per Fox LJ (payments deposited by landlord in trust account
　　as involuntary 'savings scheme').
3　*Commr of Stamp Duties v J V (Crows Nest) Pty Ltd* (1987) 7 NSWLR 529 at 532C–G per
　　Mahoney JA (periodical payments by health centre franchisee in respect of administration
　　and advertising by franchisor did not constitute 'rent').
4　See *Bostock v Bryant* (1990) 61 P & CR 23 at 25, where Stuart-Smith LJ held that the
　　occupiers' payment of gas and electricity bills for a house which they shared with the owner
　　represented not 'rent' but merely a reimbursement of expenses for shared consumables.
5　*Property Holding Co Ltd v Clark* [1948] 1 KB 630 at 649 per Evershed LJ. See also *Sidney
　　Trading Co Ltd v Finsbury BC* [1952] 1 All ER 460 at 462A, where Lord Goddard CJ indicated
　　that if 'there is a sum of money which the tenant agrees to pay as a consideration for the
　　tenancy, it is for this purpose a rent.'

Payments to third parties

7.96　'Rent' prima facie excludes money which the tenant may be obliged to
expend on repairs or improvements,[1] but may well include payments which the
tenant is directed to make for the purpose of indemnifying the landlord's
financial obligations to third parties (e g payment of part or all of the landlord's
monthly mortgage liability).[2] The definition of 'rent' may even extend to
obligatory payments made by way of donation to some third party nominated
by the landlord[3] or in discharge of certain unrelated liabilities of the landlord
(e g periodical instalments on store account or credit cards).

1　*Commr of Stamp Duties v J V (Crows Nest) Pty Ltd* (1987) 7 NSWLR 529 at 532C per
　　Mahoney JA.
2　A strong argument in favour of recognising obligatory payments to third parties as a form of
　　rent lies in the fact that such payments (if disclosed) are treated for tax purposes as the
　　equivalent of rent received by the property owner (see *Jeffries v Stevens* [1982] STC 639 at
　　651b per Walton J).
3　See, however, *Michel v Volpe* (1967) 202 EG 213, where the occupier was contractually obliged
　　to make 'donations' to a periodical supplied by the person who provided her accommodation.
　　The Court of Appeal held that this arrangement created a licence rather than a subtenancy,
　　even though the occupier's 'donations book' was eventually replaced by 'a kind of rent book'.

Certainty of rent obligation

7.97　It has long been established that the reservation of rent under a lease or
tenancy must be certain both as to the amount and as to the time when it is
payable.[1] The quantum of rent payable must therefore be certain at the
commencement of the term or at least capable of being calculated with
certainty at the due date for payment.[2] The historic rationale for the requirement of a 'rent certain' is that the landlord's remedy of distress for unpaid rent

(ie the right to remove goods to the value of the default[3]) can operate only where the rent obligation is clearly defined.[4]

1   *Parker v Harris* (1692) 1 Salk 262, 91 ER 230; *Booker Industries Pty Ltd v Wilson Parking (Qld) Pty Ltd* (1982) 149 CLR 600 at 610 per Brennan J.
2   *Greater London Council v Connolly* [1970] 2 QB 100 at 109A per Lord Denning MR; *Booker Industries Pty Ltd v Wilson Parking (Qld) Pty Ltd* (1982) 149 CLR 600 at 610 per Brennan J. If the rent, although quantifiable at the due date, has not yet been ascertained, it cannot be demanded retrospectively for periods preceding the date when it is finally quantified (*Re Essoldo (Bingo) Ltd's Underlease* (1971) 23 P & CR 1 at 4–5).
3   [Para 14.193].
4   See *Re Knight, ex p Voisey* (1882) 21 Ch D 442 at 457; *Greater London Council v Connolly* [1970] 2 QB 100 at 112D; *United Scientific Holdings Ltd v Burnley BC* [1978] AC 904 at 935B–C. For evidence of the diminishing impact in this area of the conceptual restrictions imposed by the largely archaic law of distress, see *T & E Homes Ltd v Robinson* [1979] 1 WLR 452 at 456H–457A.

Variable rent

7.98   Consistently with this qualified requirement of certainty, it is quite possible that the rent due from the tenant may fluctuate during the course of the term.[1] Rent may also be altered in accordance with an express rent review clause contained in the lease.[2] In such cases the variability of the rent obligation is perfectly valid so long as the rent payable can be ascertained with certainty at the due date for payment. It is less clear whether, in the absence of a rent review clause, the rent level may be validly adjusted by a wholly unilateral decision on the part of the landlord. In *Greater London Council v Connolly*[3] the Court of Appeal declined to hold void for uncertainty a provision that a council tenant's rent was 'liable to be increased or decreased on notice being given', even though such a clause admittedly rendered the rent level 'dependent ... on the whim of the landlords.' The Court of Appeal later held in *Dresden Estates Ltd v Collinson*[4] that such a clause was inconsistent with the existence of a tenancy and therefore pointed clearly to a relationship of licence. The divergence of approach is explicable, if at all, only on the basis that unilateral rent variation may be permissible as a matter of bureaucratic convenience for a social landlord running an extensive housing regime but is unacceptable in the context of a one-off commercial letting.

1   Coke gave the example of a rent-service comprising the shearing of 'all the sheep pasturing within the lord's manor' (*Co Litt*, p 96a). See also *Kendall v Baker* (1852) 11 CB 842 at 850, 138 ER 706 at 710 (rent riding on the price of wheat). A rent may be validly tied to some index of inflation (see e g *Blumenthal v Gallery Five Ltd* (1971) 220 EG 31 at 33; *Re Collins Cartage & Storage Co Ltd and McDonald* (1981) 116 DLR (3d) 570 at 571–572; *Trifid Pty Ltd v Ratto* [1985] WAR 19 at 29 (revd on different grounds [1987] WAR 237)).
2   Rent review clauses, although now a universal feature in commercial leases, are rarely found in residential long leases. It is common, however, for stepped increases of ground rent to occur at intervals throughout lengthy terms (e g every 25 years in a 125 year lease). The quantum of such increases may be specified in the lease itself or index-linked to inflation.
3   [1970] 2 QB 100 at 109D, 111H.
4   (1988) 55 P & CR 47 at 53.

Indeterminate rent

7.99   While the courts are disinclined to strike down purposeful transactions as void on the ground of uncertainty,[1] there are some circumstances in which a tenancy is liable to be invalidated by uncertainty as to the rent obligation. Although the courts' approach to such provisions may nowadays have become more liberal,[2] it has been held in the past that a tenancy 'at a rent to be agreed' is vitiated by uncertainty,[3] at least where no formula or mechanism was provided for quantifying the rent.[4] An option for renewal 'at a rental to be agreed' may, however, be valid if the option stipulated that the new rent should not exceed the existing rent and indicated a plain contractual intention in the relevant parties to be bound by the option.[5] Nor is a tenancy regarded as void for uncertainty merely because the rent is to be fixed 'having regard to the market value of the premises'[6] or is to be quantified as the current 'market rental'.[7] The concept of 'market rental' has a well known meaning in the context of landlord–tenant negotiations, and the courts will, if necessary, provide machinery for assessing the value of such a rental in any given case.[8]

1   *Greater London Council v Connolly* [1970] 2 QB 100 at 108F; *Brown v Gould* [1972] Ch 53 at 56F.
2   See eg *Corson v Rhuddlan BC* (1990) 59 P & CR 185 at 194 per Ralph Gibson LJ.
3   *King's Motors (Oxford) Ltd v Lax* [1970] 1 WLR 426 at 429A; *King v King* (1980) 41 P & CR 311 at 314; *Young v Van Beneen* [1953] 3 DLR 702 at 704–705; *Booker Industries Pty Ltd v Wilson Parking (Qld) Pty Ltd* (1982) 149 CLR 600 at 604 per Brennan J.
4   *Brown v Gould* [1972] Ch 53 at 58C. In *Beer v Bowden (Note)* [1981] 1 WLR 522, the Court of Appeal upheld a lease for 10 years which fixed an annual rent for the first five years, but provided that thereafter the rent should be such rent 'as shall ... be agreed'. Geoffrey Lane LJ indicated (at [1981] 1 WLR 522 at 527G–H) that the lease was saved from voidness only by reason of the tenant's 'subsisting estate in land' and the concession by the tenant that 'some rent must be paid in respect of these premises'. The Court implied an obligation to pay a 'fair rent'.
5   See *Corson v Rhuddlan BC* (1990) 59 P & CR 185 at 194–197; [1990] Conv 290 (J E Martin). See also *Trazray Pty Ltd v Russell Foundries Pty Ltd* (1988) 5 BPR 11232 at 11237.
6   *Brown v Gould* [1972] Ch 53 at 61F, 62C; *Sandhu v Ferizis* (1994) 6 BPR at 13320 at 13323.
7   *Andrews v Colonial Mutual Life Assurance Society Ltd* [1982] 2 NZLR 556 at 565.
8   *Andrews v Colonial Mutual Life Assurance Society Ltd* [1982] 2 NZLR 556 at 565. See also *Sudbrook Trading Estate Ltd v Eggleton* [1983] 1 AC 444 at 484A per Lord Fraser of Tullybelton.

A TERM OF YEARS MUST HAVE A FIXED MAXIMUM DURATION

7.100   As Blackstone explained,[1] the leasehold estate is commonly called a 'term' or *terminus* precisely 'because its duration or continuance is bounded, limited and determined: for every such estate must have a certain beginning, and certain end.'[2] In view of this strictly terminal aspect, the 'term of years' represents pre-eminently 'a time in the land' or 'land for a time'.[3] A lease or tenancy confers a right of exclusive possession of land for a prescribed quantum of time which is fixed in advance at the commencement date. This concern with discrete temporal definition embodies a *proprietary* (as distinct from *contractual*) perspective on the law of leases. The focus of English law on the artificial abstraction of the 'estate' has inevitably placed a premium on the maintenance of strict definitional boundaries around its central constructs.[4] In the context of leases, this emphasis on the hard-edged integrity of concepts has the following implications.

1   *Bl Comm*, Vol II, p 143.
2   See also *Prudential Assurance Co Ltd v London Residuary Body* [1992] 2 AC 386 at 390D–E per Lord Templeman.
3   **[Para 1.123]**.
4   **[Para 2.83]**. See Gray and Gray, 'The Idea of Property in Land', in S Bright and J K Dewar (ed), *Land Law: Themes and Perspectives* (OUP 1998), pp 31–32.

Lessor necessarily retains a reversionary interest

7.101   In English law the derivative structure of real rights is firmly founded upon a logic of magnitude.[1] A term of years always comprises a lesser estate granted out of a larger estate in land.[2] It is, accordingly, an inescapable feature of every term of years that the landlord retains throughout the term a reversionary interest in the land,[3] the reversion 'falling in' at the end of the quantum of time represented by the term. The presence of this reversionary interest in the landlord carries the further implication that, even during the currency of the tenancy, he holds an estate 'in possession' in the very specific statutory sense that 'possession' includes 'receipt of rents and profits or the right to receive the same.'[4] The landlord has, of course, no right to possession in the sense of immediate exclusive possession, for this has been surrendered to the tenant for the duration of the term.[5] The landlord's reversion is nevertheless recognised as a commerciable proprietary estate. It even connotes a sufficient estate in the land to constitute a 'dominant tenement' for the purpose of enforcing restrictive covenants against a subtenant.[6]

1   See Gray and Gray, 'The rhetoric of realty', in J Getzler (ed), *Rationalizing Property, Equity and Trusts: Essays in Honour of Edward Burn* (Butterworths 2003), p 215.
2   *Ingram v IRC* [2000] 1 AC 293 at 303G per Lord Hoffmann, 310C–D per Lord Hutton.
3   *Wik Peoples v Queensland* (1996) 187 CLR 1 at 94 per Brennan CJ. See also *Re British American Oil Co Ltd and DePass* (1960) 21 DLR (2d) 110 at 115.
4   LPA 1925, s 205(1)(xix) **[para 7.21]**. See also *St Marylebone Property Co Ltd v Fairweather* [1963] AC 510 at 536–537 per Lord Radcliffe. There are always at least two estates concurrently in possession in the landlord–tenant relationship, since both landlord and tenant enjoy 'possession' within the extended meaning of the statute.
5   See *St Marylebone Property Co Ltd v Fairweather* [1963] AC 510 at 550 per Lord Morris of Borth-y-Gest; *Reference Re Prince Edward Island Lands Protection Act* (1988) 40 DLR (4th) 1 at 10–11; *Northern Sandblasting Pty Ltd v Harris* (1997) 188 CLR 313 at 339. Nor, during the term, is the landlord in possession for the purpose of the law of adverse possession (see *Giouroukos v Cadillac Fairview Corp Ltd* (1984) 3 DLR (4th) 595 at 605–606).
6   **[Para 9.163]**. See *Hall v Ewin* (1888) 37 Ch D 74 at 79; *Teape v Douse* (1905) 92 LT 319 at 320; *Northern Ireland Carriers Ltd v Larne Harbour Ltd* [1981] 5 NIJB, Transcript, p 10; *Wik Peoples v Queensland* (1996) 187 CLR 1 at 94.

The term must commence at a 'time certain'

7.102   A term of years must have a definite *terminus a quo*.[1] The temporal structure of the leasehold concept means that a term of years must commence at a 'time certain' which is either expressly fixed by the parties or readily ascertainable before the start of the term.[2] Some difficulty may arise where the inception of a term is preceded by an agreement to grant a lease.[3]

1   Where a term is expressed to commence 'from' a specified day, the term does not, in the absence of clear contrary indication, include that day. Instead the term is normally presumed to begin at midnight following the day specified (see *Sunnyvale Services B O P Ltd v Bhana* [1986] 1 NZLR 314 at 316). A term expressed to commence 'on' a specified day is generally deemed to include that day (see *Clayton's Case* (1585) 5 Co Rep 1a, 77 ER 48). Compare, however, E Cooke, [1993] Conv 206.
2   *Bl Comm*, Vol II, p 143; *Say v Smith* (1563) 1 Plowd 269 at 272, 75 ER 410 at 415.
3   There is an exemption from any requirement of writing for a contract for the grant of a term not exceeding three years taking effect in possession at the best rent reasonably obtainable without taking a fine (ie premium) (LP(MP)A 1989, s 2(5)(a)).

Agreements for uncertain commencement

7.103   There can be no valid agreement in law for a lease to commence at some unspecified future date. If an agreement to create a future lease does not stipulate at least an ascertainable commencement date, there is no concluded contract.[1] If the commencement date is not specified, it may in some circumstances be inferred that the term begins immediately on the taking of possession, provided that there is no doubt as to the precise date on which this occurs.[2] There is, however, no want of certainty where a verbal agreement for a lease is followed by an immediate taking of possession pursuant to the agreement: the agreement coupled with entry ensures a certain commencement.[3]

1   *Harvey v Pratt* [1965] 1 WLR 1025 at 1026D–E, 1027C; *Dunlop Olympic Ltd v Ellis* [1986] WAR 8 at 11. The commencement date cannot simply be taken to be the date of the contract (*Marshall v Berridge* (1881) 19 Ch D 233 at 239). See also *Lace v Chantler* [1944] KB 368 at 370; *Brown v Gould* [1972] Ch 53 at 61B; *Secretary of State for Social Services v Beavington* (1982) 262 EG 551 at 554; *Kerns v Manning* [1935] IR 869 at 880; *McQuaid v Lynam* [1965] IR 564 at 574; *Omsac Developments Ltd v Colebourne* (1980) 110 DLR (3d) 766 at 768; *South Coast Oils (Qld and NSW) Pty Ltd v Look Enterprises Pty Ltd* [1988] 1 Qd R 680 at 696.
2   *James v Lock* (1977) 246 EG 395 at 397.
3   *Jopling v Jopling* (1909) 8 CLR 33 at 39 per Griffith CJ.

Reversionary leases

7.104   It is possible that the commencement date of a lease may be postponed to a date considerably later than that of the instrument which creates the leasehold term, in which case the lease is known as a 'reversionary' lease.[1] However, a statutory penalty of voidness attaches to any reversionary term granted at a rent or in consideration of a fine which is limited to take effect more than 21 years after the date of the instrument purporting to create it.[2]

1   In the case of an orally granted lease, the postponement of the commencement date ensures that the term does not take effect 'in possession'. The lease does not therefore benefit from the limited exemption from requirements of formality otherwise conferred by LPA 1925, s 54(2) **[para 7.220]**. See *Abjornson v Urban Newspapers Pty Ltd* [1989] WAR 191 at 206.

2   LPA 1925, s 149(3). This provision does not affect the validity of a *contract* to create a lease at
     some future time which, when created by instrument, will then take effect either immediately
     or within 21 years of the date of that instrument (Perpetuities and Accumulations Act 1964,
     s 9(2)). See *Re Strand and Savoy Properties Ltd* [1960] Ch 582 at 591; *Weg Motors Ltd v Hales*
     [1962] Ch 49 at 68, 78.

The term may be of any length

7.105   Subject to the requirement that its maximum duration be ascertainable,
a term of years may relate to any measurable length of time.

Short terms

7.106   A term of years may comprise merely a fraction of a year,[1] and could
in theory be extremely short.[2] In *National Carriers Ltd v Panalpina (Northern) Ltd,*[3] for instance, Lord Roskill agreed that a holiday-maker may well have
a legal estate in a cottage let to him for a short period as a holiday home,
although 'the estate in land which he acquires has little or no meaning for him.'
It is likely, however, that the shorter the supposed term, the greater the
probability that the grant will be construed as conferring not a leasehold
interest but a licence.[4]

1   A 'term of years' is statutorily defined as including 'a term for less than a year' and 'a fraction
     of a year' (LPA 1925, s 205(1)(xxvii)).
2   See e g *Boylan v Mayor of Dublin* [1949] IR 60 at 73, where Black J adverted to the possibility
     of a lease for three days or three hours.
3   [1981] AC 675 at 714D.
4   See e g the 'coronation cases' **[para 4.62]**. See also *Voli v Inglewood Shire Council* (1963) 110
     CLR 74 at 91 per Windeyer J.

Long terms

7.107   Equally a term of years may extend to vast expanses of time which
begin to resemble a grant in fee simple.[1] Leases of 3,000 years are not unknown
for the purpose of creating certain kinds of mortgage.[2] Outside the context of
mortgage, leases are sometimes created for a term of 999 years. A term of 99
years is commonly granted in respect of leasehold flats; and local authorities
are statutorily empowered to grant terms of 125 years in respect of dwelling-
houses covered by the 'right to buy' provisions of the Housing Act 1985.[3]

1   See *National Carriers Ltd v Panalpina (Northern) Ltd* [1981] AC 675 at 714B. The longest lease
     on record seems to be one of 10 million years, granted on 3 December 1868 in respect of a
     plot for a sewage tank adjoining Columb Barracks, Mullingar, County Meath, Ireland
     (*Guinness Book of Records 1993* (London 1992), p 186). Ireland tends to specialise in the
     granting of extremely long terms. Part of the Dublin cattle market was leased by John
     Jameson to the Dublin City Corporation on 21 January 1863 for a term of 100,000 years (see
     N McWhirter (ed), *Guinness Book of Records* (27th edn Enfield, Middx, 1980), p 190). See
     also *Re Sergie* [1954] NI 1 (mortgage demise for 10,000 years).

2　**[Para 8.251]**.
3　HA 1985, s 139(1), Sch 6, Pt III, para 12(1).

Discontinuous terms

7.108　It is not even essential that the quantum of time in respect of which possession is granted under a lease should comprise one single continuous period. The advent of the phenomenon of holiday timesharing has confirmed the idea that a lease may comprise an aggregate of discontinuous periods of time.[1] In *Cottage Holiday Associates Ltd v Customs and Excise Commissioners*,[2] Woolf J accepted as a lease a document which granted the lessee, in consideration of an initial premium, a right to occupy a holiday cottage for one week in each year for a term of 80 years.[3] The creation of timeshare arrangements is now regulated by statute.[4]

1　As early as *Smallwood v Sheppards* [1895] 2 QB 627 at 630, it was recognised that a lease granting a right of occupation for three successive bank holidays could constitute a single letting. See also *Bedford v A & C Properties Co Ltd* (Unreported, Chancery Division, 27 June 1997) (parking area for Sunday market).
2　[1983] QB 735 at 739D. However, Woolf J held (at 739H–740F) that the length of the 'term' granted by such a lease was 80 weeks rather than 80 years, expressly leaving open (at 738A) the effect of LPA 1925, s 149(3).
3　It is quite common nowadays that lessees of office buildings are not entitled to occupy the demised premises at certain times such as weekends (see *Cottage Holiday Associates Ltd v Customs and Excise Commissioners* [1983] QB 735 at 739G–H). See also [1983] Conv 319.
4　The Timeshare Act 1992 introduced various kinds of protection against oppressive dealing in relation to timeshare users. See [1992] Conv 301 (H W Wilkinson).

THE 'CERTAINTY OF TERM' PRINCIPLE

7.109　It is, at common law, an essential characteristic of every lease (whether long or short) that it should relate to a term of certain maximum duration.[1] From the outset of the term a finite point (or *terminus ad quem*) must be either expressed or implicit or must be capable of being rendered certain.[2] Any purported lease whose maximum duration is not ascertainable at the commencement date is void[3] in that it fails to show 'the certainty of the time for which the lessee shall have the land.'[4] This 'certainty of term' principle is a fundamental expression of the property-oriented view of leasehold relationships: it articulates a clear concern that property rights should be both defined and discrete.[5]

1　It does not follow that a lease must stipulate a *minimum* duration: it is only the outer limit of the term which must be fixed or capable of being rendered certain. Provided that the maximum duration is certain, it is irrelevant that the term is capable of an earlier determination (e g through surrender or the operation of some limiting condition or through the lessor's exercise of a right of entry). See *Co Litt*, p 45; *Bl Comm*, Vol II, p 143; *Prudential Assurance Co Ltd v London Residuary Body* [1992] 2 AC 386 at 395A per Lord Templeman.
2　For an excellent examination of the law of terminal certainty, see S Bright, (1993) 13 Legal Studies 38.
3　*Prudential Assurance Co Ltd v London Residuary Body* [1992] 2 AC 386 at 392B per

Lord Templeman. It is possible, however, that a tenant who enters under the void lease may acquire an implied periodic tenancy on the payment and acceptance of a periodic rent [**para 7.256**]. See eg *Lace v Chantler* [1944] KB 368 at 372; *Prudential Assurance*, supra at 392B.

4   *Say v Smith* (1563) 1 Plowd 269 at 272, 75 ER 410 at 415. See also *Eton College v Bard* [1983] Ch 321 at 332A; *Re Lehrer and the Real Property Act* (1961) 61 SR (NSW) 365 at 376–377.

5   [**Para 2.83**]. For the view that the 'certainty of term' rule is merely a variant of the *numerus clausus* principle [**para 2.95**], see Thomas W Merrill and Henry E Smith, 'Optimal Standardization in the Law of Property: The Numerus Clausus Principle' 110 Yale LJ 1 at 11 (2000); 'The Property/Contract Interface' 101 Col L Rev 773 at 832 (2001).

Applications of the 'certainty of term' principle

7.110   The 'ancient and technical rule of law'[1] relating to certainty of term has been applied with rigour in the law of landlord and tenant. The proprietary perspective dictates that it is simply not competent for landlord and tenant, as a sheer act of contractual volition, to bargain for open-ended or indefinite terms of years.[2] In *Lace v Chantler*,[3] for instance, the Court of Appeal held that no lease had been validly granted where a right of occupation was conferred 'for the duration of the war.'[4] The dogma of the common law rule has been similarly applied to strike down a letting of premises 'for so long as the lessee shall use them',[5] or 'so long as the company is trading.'[6] Likewise the courts have indicated that uncertainty of term vitiates a letting expressed to continue 'until Britain wins the Davis Cup'[7] or 'until the end of the peanut crop in 1968 or end of harvesting period or as otherwise agreed upon.'[8]

1   *Prudential Assurance Co Ltd v London Residuary Body* [1992] 2 AC 386 at 396G per Lord Browne-Wilkinson.
2   This 'certainty of term' rule does not prevent the use of a break clause which allows for determination of the lease by either party *before* the expiry of the full term granted [**para 7.283**].
3   [1944] KB 368 at 370–371.
4   See also *MW Investments Ltd v Kilburn Envoy Ltd* [1947] Ch 370 at 376. In view of the large number of supposed lettings affected, the ruling in *Lace v Chantler* had to be modified by retroactive legislation (see Validation of War-time Leases Act 1944, s 1(1), which converted such arrangements into determinable leases of 10 years). It has been suggested that the strict approach of *Lace v Chantler* may not properly have been applicable in cases where the terminal date of the lease, although unpredictable, was specified in much clearer words. See eg *Eker v Becker* (1946) 174 LT 410 at 411 (lease determinable on 'the cessation of ... hostilities ... meaning thereby the actual date of the cease fire order'); *Mrs Levin, Ltd v Wellington Co-operative Book Society* [1947] NZLR 83 at 86 (lease determinable automatically three months after the cessation of active hostilities in war). See also *Ashburn Anstalt v Arnold* [1989] Ch 1 at 11G per Fox LJ.
5   *Congregational Christian Church v Iosefa Tauga* (1982) 8 Comm Law Bull 129.
6   *Birrell v Carey* (1989) 58 P & CR 184 at 186 per Fox LJ. See [1990] Conv 288 (J E Martin).
7   *Prudential Assurance Co Ltd v London Residuary Body* (1992) 63 P & CR 386 at 397 per Scott LJ.
8   *Bishop v Taylor* (1968) 118 CLR 518 at 523.

Rationales for the common law rule

7.111   Although it is nowadays far from easy to provide any convincing rationale for the continued application of the 'certainty of term' principle,[1] there may have been several related historic motivations behind the common law rule. First, it is plain that the common law abhorred 'any such thing as a lease in perpetuity',[2] not least since such a lease, if granted imprudently, could endanger the productive exploitation of land over an indefinite period. Second, the perpetual lease was a conceptual nonsense in that it postulated a term without a *terminus.*[3] Such a lease struck at the heart of the doctrine of estates by threatening to confound the distinction between the term of years and the one perpetual estate recognised by the common law, the estate in fee simple.[4] The perpetual lease offended against the intrinsic orderliness of the common law arrangement of estates.[5] Third, the open-ended nature of an uncertain term militated against the clear concern of the common law that the parties to a bargain should 'know where they stand'[6] and that neither party should be left in 'a state of unknowing' as to his maximum enforceable commitment.[7] Absent the certain demarcation of borderlines, not even the court can identify true cases of breach.[8] Fourth, it may have been felt to be inherently unfair that parties who had contemplated a short, but uncertainly defined, term should find that they had mistakenly created an endless term.[9] Fifth, there was inevitably some fear that an obscurely defined terminal date might present insuperable problems of construction simply on grounds of linguistic, semantic or contextual uncertainty.[10]

1   See *Prudential Assurance Co Ltd v London Residuary Body* [1992] 2 AC 386 at 396G–H per Lord Browne-Wilkinson (no 'satisfactory rationale for the genesis of this rule').

2   *Sevenoaks, Maidstone, and Tunbridge Railway Co v London, Chatham, and Dover Railway Co* (1879) 11 Ch D 625 at 635 per Jessel MR. See also *Wotherspoon v Canadian Pacific Ltd* (1987) 39 DLR (4th) 169 at 205; *Wik Peoples v Queensland* (1996) 187 CLR 1 at 153 per Gaudron J, 201 per Gummow J; *Anderson v Wilson* (2000) 171 ALR 705 at 726 per Black CJ and Sackville J, 758 per Beaumont J.

3   That such a phenomenon was quite impossible appears in the rejection of a lease 'for ever' in *Doe d Roberton v Gardiner* (1852) 12 CB 319 at 333, 138 ER 927 at 933 per Jervis CJ.

4   See *Western Australia v Ward* (2002) 191 ALR 1 at [432] per Gleeson CJ, Gaudron, Gummow and Hayne JJ; and compare the reference to the fee simple as conferring 'a time in the land without end' (*Walsingham's Case* (1573) 2 Plowd 547 at 555, 75 ER 805 at 817 [**para 1.125**]).

5   This may account for the desperate means sometimes adopted by the common law in attempting to refashion leases of uncertain duration. A lease for an unspecified term of years was long ago held to be a good lease for two years certain, in that certainty was lacking in respect of any longer term and any shorter term would falsify the wording of the grant (see *Bishop of Bath's Case* (1605) 6 Co Rep 34b at 35b/36a, 77 ER 303 at 305–306). Alternatively, if all else failed, the indefinite term might be construed as a grant in fee simple subject to the payment of a rentcharge [**para 8.225**]. See *Doe d Roberton v Gardiner* (1852) 12 CB 319 at 333, 138 ER 927 at 933–934; *Wotherspoon v Canadian Pacific Ltd* (1987) 39 DLR (4th) 169 at 205.

6   See *Ashburn Anstalt v Arnold* [1989] Ch 1 at 12E per Fox LJ.

7   *Re Midland Railway Co's Agreement* [1971] Ch 725 at 732H–733A per Russell LJ.

8   'Put another way, the court does not know what to enforce' (*Ashburn Anstalt v Arnold* [1989] Ch 1 at 12E per Fox LJ).

9   Such, for instance, would have been the result if the determining, but uncertain, event subsequently proved to be impossible or unlikely to occur. See *Prudential Assurance Co Ltd v London Residuary Body* (1992) 63 P & CR 386 at 400–401 per Scott LJ.

10   As Anthony Brown J is reported to have said, uncertain words in a lease 'are but babble' (*Say v Smith* (1563) 1 Plowd 269 at 272, 75 ER 410 at 415). See also S Bright, (1993) 13 Legal Studies 38 at 40–41.

Disenchantment with the common law rule

7.112   Recent years have seen a growing disenchantment with the common law rule in respect of certainty of term. It is far from clear that the historic rationales for the rule retain today the force which they may once have enjoyed.

Frustration of sensible bargains

7.113   The common law rule is open to objection on the ground that it frequently denies efficacy to perfectly sensible arrangements derived from a process of conscious bargain between free-willing parties. After all, why should not a landlord and tenant, if they so wish, agree on an indefinite term which may be brought to an end at any time on, say, the giving of three months' notice by either party? Such agreements are scarcely likely, in all reality, to survive as perpetuities.[1] Why should the law frustrate clear contractual intentions for the sake of compliance with some archaic common law dogma? Quite often the availability of a flexible, open-ended letting makes enormous commercial sense in terms of the efficient short-term exploitation of land which lies temporarily redundant or unused.

1   See eg *Ashburn Anstalt v Arnold* [1989] Ch 1.

Circumvention of the common law rule

7.114   The operation of the common law rule is also arbitrary and artificial. The 'certainty of term' principle strikes arbitrarily at some attempts to create a leasehold relationship, whilst other attempts – in themselves no less flawed – have been rescued from voidness by modern statutory intervention.[1] A high degree of artificiality is inevitably present in any rule which solemnly strikes down a term whose voidness could have been averted by a minor (and purely cosmetic) redrafting of the words of grant. The 'vice of uncertainty' is easily evaded by the provision of a lengthy maximum term expressed to be subject to determination on some earlier and uncertain event.[2]

1   **[Para 7.120]**.
2   Whereas a lease 'until England wins the World Cup' is invalid, no objection can be raised against a lease for 99 years subject to determination on the earlier happening of this uncertain – indeed unlikely – event (see *Prudential Assurance Co Ltd v London Residuary Body* [1992] 2 AC 386 at 395A per Lord Templeman, (1992) 63 P & CR 386 at 397 per Scott LJ). The latter form of grant is entirely valid since it creates a determinable term certain of 99 years.

Temporary relaxation of the rule

7.115   In the light of such factors the Court of Appeal was clearly tempted during the late 1980s to relax the requirement that the maximum duration of a term of years be ascertainable in advance of the term.[1] In effect the Court diluted the force of the old common law rule by holding that certainty of term need not be predicated at the *commencement* of a supposed term of years, but could be sufficiently established with reference to the circumstances pertaining at its *termination*.[2] This short-lived – and somewhat unconvincing – departure from orthodoxy provided yet another vivid reflection of the continuing tension between contract- and property-oriented views of the landlord–tenant relationship.[3]

1   The relevant issues tended to arise in their most critical form in the context of rent-free occupancy. Here there is no possibility that the parties can fall back upon an implied periodic tenancy [**para 7.250**]: the choice lies starkly between valid long lease and mere licence.

2   See e g *Ashburn Anstalt v Arnold* [1989] Ch 1 at 12E–H, where the Court of Appeal upheld as a valid lease an agreement granting rent-free occupancy for an indefinite period which was expressly terminable on the giving of three months' notice by the owner. The 'vice of uncertainty' was supposedy averted by the fact that the arrangement could be brought to an end by either party 'in circumstances which are free from uncertainty in the sense that there would be no doubt whether the determining event had occurred.' The determination of the relationship – unlike the circumstances present in *Lace v Chantler* [1944] K B 368 – had lain within the full control of both parties, since the occupier was in no sense obliged to occupy the premises and 'could simply walk out' ([1989] Ch 1 at 11G–12D). See similarly *Canadian Imperial Bank of Commerce v Bello* (1992) 64 P & CR 48 at 54–56 per Staughton LJ; *Prudential Assurance Co Ltd v London Residuary Body* (1992) 63 P & CR 386 at 398 per Scott LJ.

3   [**Para 7.84**].

Reaffirmation of the common law rule

7.116   The approach adopted by the Court of Appeal plainly marked a none too subtle shift from a prospective requirement of *certainty of term* to a retrospective requirement of *certainty of termination*. In the process the Court accorded a new primacy to clearly expressed contractual intentions in preference to the narrow property-oriented concern that asset entitlements be defined with certainty *ab initio*. However, these developments came to a sharp halt in *Prudential Assurance Co Ltd v London Residuary Body*.[1] Here the old London County Council had in 1930 granted a 'lease' of a strip of land fronting a highway at an annual rent of £30, the tenancy being expressed to continue until the land was required by the council for the purpose of widening the highway. The council later abandoned any intention of widening the road and the freehold reversion eventually passed to the London Residuary Body (which was not a highway authority). Meanwhile shop premises had been erected by the occupier on the relevant strip of land and by the late 1980s it was clear that the likely current commercial rent was in excess of £10,000 per annum. Unsurprisingly the London Residuary Body claimed that the occupier held only a yearly tenancy arising from the original entry into possession and the payment of a periodic rent and that this tenancy was terminable on the giving of half a year's notice.[2] The occupier, equally unsurprisingly, asserted the existence of a valid indefinite term of years at a rent of £30 per annum and determinable only in the event of a road-widening proposal.

1   [1992] 2 AC 386; (1992) 63 P & CR 386. See [1992] Conv 118 (P F Smith); [1993] CLJ 26 (S
     Bridge); (1994) 57 MLR 117 (D Wilde). For the Court of Appeal's decision, see (1992)
     63 P & CR 386.
2   **[Para 7.291]**.

The Prudential Assurance ruling

7.117   When the *Prudential Assurance* case reached the House of Lords, the
orthodox understanding of the 'certainty of term' principle was rapidly
restored. The Lords, rejecting all casuistry founded upon relative degrees of
control over determining events, preferred to hold with brutal simplicity that an
agreement for indeterminate occupation can *never* constitute a legally recognisable term of years.[1] Lord Templeman took the straightforward view that
'principle and precedent dictate that it is beyond the power of the landlord and
the tenant to create a term which is uncertain.'[2] The House of Lords thus
applied the full force of the common law rule that the maximum duration of a
term of years must be ascertainable at the commencement of every lease. The
clear property-orientation of this approach was evident in Lord Templeman's
anxiety lest a more liberal view of the certainty rule should allow loosely
defined arrangements between parties to 'continue until the crack of doom' and
enable them to enjoy 'in perpetuity' rights which had originally been contemplated as purely temporary.[3]

1   The House of Lords overruled both *Re Midland Railway Co's Agreement* [1971] Ch 725 and
     Ashburn Anstalt v Arnold [1989] Ch 1 as having been wrongly decided ([1992] 2 AC 386 at
     395G per Lord Templeman). See *Ferrishurst Ltd v Wallcite Ltd* [1999] Ch 355 at 365G.
2   [1992] 2 AC 386 at 394E–H ('I consider that the principle of *Lace v Chantler* ... reaffirming
     500 years of judicial acceptance of the requirement that a term must be certain applies to all
     leases and tenancy agreements').
3   [1992] 2 AC 386 at 394G–H. Lord Templeman referred pointedly to the fact that the
     agreement, if upheld as an indefinitely long term, would have entitled the occupier 'to stay
     there for ever and a day at the 1930 rent of £30' ([1992] 2 AC 386 at 390B).

An 'unsatisfactory' outcome

7.118   In *Prudential Assurance* the consequence of Lord Templeman's uncom-
promising approach was to render the occupier, in the absence of a valid
indefinite term, a mere yearly tenant vulnerable to half a year's notice to quit.[1]
This conclusion was endorsed, albeit reluctantly, by other members of the
House of Lords. Lord Browne-Wilkinson noted, for instance, that this 'unsatisfactory' outcome, far from effectuating the initial contemplation and contractual intent of the parties, had brought about the 'bizarre' result that both
parties would be left with premises which were incapable of use.[2] Lord Browne-
Wilkinson, although accepting that a departure from a land law rule which had
been established for many centuries might upset long held titles, voiced a
concern that the archaic common law rule should be re-examined by the Law
Commission to 'see whether there is in fact any good reason now for maintaining a rule which operates to defeat contractually agreed arrangements between

the parties (of which all successors in title are aware) and which is capable of producing such an extraordinary result as that in the present case.'[3]

1   [1992] 2 AC 386 at 392B–C.
2   [1992] 2 AC 386 at 396E–G. The tenant's remaining premises, situated behind the street frontage, would be effectively cut off from frontage to a shopping street; the use of the landlord's premises, once severed from the tenant's, would almost certainly be sterilised.
3   [1992] 2 AC 386 at 397A. Lords Griffiths and Mustill (at 396B, 397B) expressly associated themselves with this concern.

Statutory conversion?

7.119 In the aftermath of the *Prudential Assurance* case there is a strong argument for enacting a statutory conversion of all uncertain terms (other than those already covered by legislation) into determinable terms of, say, 90 years.[1] Such a solution would preserve the integrity of the venerable common law principle of certainty of term, while enabling sensible effect to be given to the clearly intended bargains of contracting parties.

1   See LPA 1925, s 149(6) [**paras 7.121–7.122**].

SPECIAL PROBLEMS OF LEASEHOLD DURATION

7.120 The reinforcement of the common law requirement of a prefixed maximum duration leaves a number of grave difficulties in the leasehold area. Many of these difficulties would remain unresolved but for several statutory interventions which ensure that at least some of the problematic cases are forced artificially, but nevertheless effectively, within the procrustean dimensions of the 'certainty of term' rule.

Lease for life

7.121 Longevity having an unpredictable quality, a lease for life offends against the prescription that leases must be of fixed maximum duration.[1] As statutorily defined,[2] a 'term of years absolute' does not include a lease for life or a lease which is determinable on the death of some named person. However, legislation has intervened to reconcile the lease for life with the common law requirement.[3] If granted at a rent or in consideration of a fine,[4] a lease for life or lives or for any term of years determinable with life or lives[5] is automatically converted into a 90 year term.[6] The fixed term thus created is determinable after the death of the original lessee (or the dropping of any other specified life) by the giving of at least one month's written notice.[7]

1   *Co Litt*, p 45; *Bl Comm*, Vol II, p 143.
2   LPA 1925, s 205(1)(xxvii).
3   LPA 1925, s 149(6).
4   The device of statutory conversion therefore cannot save a tenancy for life under which no

rent or premium is payable (see e g *Binions v Evans* [1972] Ch 359 at 370D, 372E–G). Contrast *Skipton Building Society v Clayton* (1993) 66 P & CR 223 at 231–233 (discounted purchase price paid to sitting tenants in exchange for rent-free tenancy for life constituted a premium or fine for purpose of statutory conversion).

5   See *Bass Holdings Ltd v Lewis* [1986] 2 EGLR 40 at 40K per Nourse LJ (example of 'lease to A for a term of 20 years if he shall live so long').

6   It has been questioned whether an automatic conversion to a 90 year term should sensibly be the result of a short-term letting conditioned upon the survival of the lessee. See *Bass Holdings Ltd v Lewis* (Unreported, 17 February 1986 (appeal: [1986] 2 EGLR 40)) per Hoffmann J (who suggested that in this respect the 'great conveyancers' who drafted the 1925 Acts may have been guilty of 'simply a mistake').

7   The statutory conversion also operates in relation to a *contract* to create a lease determinable by death or marriage (LPA 1925, s 149(6)).

Lease until marriage

7.122   Likewise a lease terminable upon the marriage of the lessee is converted into a 90 year term, determinable after the marriage of the original lessee by the giving of at least one month's written notice.[1]

1   LPA 1925, s 149(6).

Perpetually renewable lease

7.123   A perpetually renewable lease again fails, for want of a clear finite point, to qualify as a valid leasehold term. In theory such a grant – now extraordinarily rare[1] – could endure for ever, but is now converted automatically by statute into a term of 2,000 years[2] determinable only by the lessee.[3]

1   The courts nowadays lean against construing a lease as perpetually renewable in the absence of an unequivocal covenant to this effect (see e g *Marjorie Burnett Ltd v Barclay* (1981) 258 EG 642 at 644).

2   LPA 1922, s 145, Sch 15, para 1. See *Parkus v Greenwood* [1950] Ch 644 at 648; *Caerphilly Concrete Products Ltd v Owen* [1972] 1 WLR 372 at 375F, 378C.

3   Law of Property Act 1922, Sch 15, para 10(1). This statutory conversion is the subject of some judicial distaste, largely because it frequently operates in a highly artificial way to subvert the likely expectations of the parties (see e g *Caerphilly Concrete Products Ltd v Owen* [1972] 1 WLR 372 at 376B per Sachs LJ).

Timeshare lease

7.124   It is clear that a 'timeshare lease' can readily be drafted in such manner as to satisfy the requirement of certain maximum duration. In *Cottage Holiday Associates Ltd v Customs and Excise Commissioners*,[1] Woolf J recognised that there is a distinction between the lease which created the timeshare interest and the interest itself. The lease might continue for 80 years, but the timeshare interest conferred by it comprised a term of only 80 holiday periods of one week each. On any construction, no difficulty could arise here in respect of fixed maximum duration, not least because the rule against perpetuities ensures the imposition of a strict outer limit on all interests granted by the timesharing arrangement.[2]

1   [1983] QB 735 at 740E–F.
2   See e g Perpetuities and Accumulations Act 1964, s 1(1).

Periodic tenancy

7.125   It has never been easy to reconcile the periodic tenancy (e g a weekly or monthly or yearly tenancy) with the common law requirement of certain prefixed maximum duration. A periodic tenancy does not come automatically to an end at some predetermined point,[1] but continues indefinitely until the expiry of a duly served notice to quit.[2] Some periodic tenancies may last for decades.

1   In this sense, only, a periodic tenancy has been said not to expire by reason of the effluxion of time (*Queen's Club Gardens Estates Ltd v Bignell* [1924] 1 KB 117 at 130; *Mitchell v Wieriks, ex p Wieriks* [1975] Qd R 100 at 102D).
2   **[Para 7.286]**.

An unbroken elongating term

7.126   The doctrinal embarrassment is heightened by the classical theory that, in the absence of a valid notice to quit, a periodic tenancy takes effect, not as an aggregation of distinct terms, but as a single, infinitely expandable, term. The units of time which constitute the periodic tenancy are seen as comprising (at least retrospectively[1]) one single unbroken term[2] which, unless and until duly determined, perpetually elongates itself by the superaddition of a fresh unit or period.[3] The term grows period by period 'as a single term springing from the original grant.'[4] There cannot be said to be a termination of one tenancy at the end of each period, followed by the commencement of a new letting on the tacit exercise of some option to renew the term.[5] The tenancy simply continues as one integral term until duly determined by notice[6] and no maximum term can be predicated at its outset.[7] The periodic tenancy has a certain *terminus a quo* but no certain or predictable *terminus ad quem*.

1   See *St Marylebone Property Co Ltd v Fairweather* [1962] 1 QB 498 at 512 per Holroyd Pearce LJ.
2   See *Hammersmith and Fulham LBC v Monk* [1992] 1 AC 478 at 490B per Lord Bridge of Harwich.
3   *Legg v Strudwick* (1709) 2 Salk 414, 91 ER 359; *Jones v Mills* (1861) 10 CB (NS) 788 at 798, 142 ER 664 at 667; *Gandy v Jubber* (1865) 9 B & S 15 at 18, 122 ER 914 at 916; *Bowen v Anderson* [1894] 1 QB 164 at 167; *Queen's Club Gardens Estates Ltd v Bignell* [1924] 1 KB 117 at 130. For this reason it is quite possible that a weekly tenancy may 'continue from week to week quite as long as a yearly tenancy from year to year' (*Jones v Chappell* (1875) LR 20 Eq 539 at 544).
4   *Re Midland Railway Co's Agreement* [1971] Ch 725 at 732F per Russell LJ. For further recognition of the integrity of the original letting, see *Oxley v James* (1844) 13 M & W 209 at

214, 153 ER 87 at 89; *Bowen v Anderson* [1894] 1 QB 164 at 167; *Amad v Grant, Grosglik v Grant* (1947) 74 CLR 327 at 336; *Re Belajev* (1979) 22 SASR 1 at 4.

5   See *Jones v Chappell* (1875) LR 20 Eq 539 at 544. For the distinction between a periodic yearly tenancy and a perpetually renewable one-year tenancy, see *Gray v Spyer* [1922] 2 Ch 22 at 38–39.

6   The periodic tenancy constitutes 'an open-ended term with a series of possible termination dates which will only become effective if a valid notice to quit is served' (Frank Webb, [1983] Conv 194 at 209). On this basis it has been suggested that the true analogy for a notice to quit is with a break notice, although this analysis now presents some problems in respect of unilateral exercise by one joint tenant [**para 7.283**].

7   See *Re Midland Railway Co's Agreement* [1971] Ch 725 at 732F, where Russell LJ pointed out that, in relation to a periodic tenancy, it 'cannot be predicated that in no circumstances will it exceed, for instance, 50 years.' Compare, however, *Centaploy Ltd v Matlodge Ltd* [1974] Ch 1 at 11C; (1973) 89 LQR 457.

Termination by effluxion of time

7.127   In spite of this difficulty there is no serious doubt as to the status of the periodic tenancy as a term of years.[1] The reconciliation of the periodic tenancy with the 'certainty of term' principle has been made easier by an increasing judicial emphasis upon the contractual dimension of leasehold relationships.[2] In *Hammersmith and Fulham LBC v Monk*,[3] the House of Lords emphasised that a periodic tenancy is 'founded on the continuing will of both landlord and tenant that the tenancy shall persist.' By declining to give notice of termination, 'each party signifies the necessary positive assent to the extension of the term for a further period.'[4] Each prolongation of the periodic tenancy is therefore an affirmative act of continued endorsement of the leasehold relationship on both sides, with the consequence that, at any given time, 'the tenancy ... has no greater life than the period up to the time when the next notice can be given and would terminate.'[5] The non-continuation of the periodic tenancy (by the giving of notice) simply terminates the tenancy by the effluxion of time 'in the same way as a tenancy for a term of years.'[6] As Lord Millett explained in *Barrett v Morgan*,[7] landlord and tenant, by entering into a periodic tenancy with an express or implied provision for a notice to quit, have 'agreed at the outset on the manner of its termination.'[8] On the expiry of any notice to quit, the tenancy merely reaches 'the end of its natural life' and comes to 'its predetermined end in accordance with the terms of the tenancy agreement.'[9]

1   For statutory recognition that a tenancy from year to year can constitute a 'term of years', see LPA 1925, s 205(1)(xxvii).

2   Even in *Re Midland Railway Co's Agreement* [1971] Ch 725 at 733C, the Court of Appeal preferred 'as a matter of justice to hold parties to their clearly expressed bargain' rather than extend to the periodic tenancy an ancient land law doctrine which would 'deny the efficacy of that bargain.'

3   [1992] 1 AC 478 at 492A per Lord Browne-Wilkinson.

4   [1992] 1 AC 478 at 490H–491A per Lord Bridge of Harwich.

5   *Crawley BC v Ure* [1996] QB 13 at 26G per Hobhouse LJ.

6   *Newlon Housing Trust v Alsulaimen* [1999] 1 AC 313 at 317F–G per Lord Hoffmann. For further reference to the proposition that periodic tenancies are terminated by the effluxion of time, see *Harrow LBC v Johnstone* [1997] 1 WLR 459 at 470F per Lord Mustill, 471G per Lord Hoffmann; *Barrett v Morgan* [2000] 2 AC 264 at 270D per Lord Millett.

7   [2000] 2 AC 264 at 270E, 272C.
8   This agreement binds the parties' successors in title, including all who derive title under them ([2000] 2 AC 264 at 270E per Lord Millett).
9   [2000] 2 AC 264 at 272E–H per Lord Millett.

Certainty through agreed terminability

7.128   The courts have thus endeavoured to impart an ascertainable or predetermined quality to the termination of periodic tenancies. On this basis it becomes vaguely arguable that the periodic tenancy conforms to the general requirement of prefixed maximum duration: the modalities of termination have been fixed long in advance by agreement at the commencement of the tenancy.[1] In *Prudential Assurance Co Ltd v London Residuary Body*,[2] Lord Templeman was able simultaneously to affirm that the certainty of term rule 'applies to all leases and tenancy agreements' and that a tenancy from year to year is 'saved from being uncertain because each party has power by notice to determine at the end of any year. The term continues until determined as if both parties made a new agreement at the end of each year for a new term for the ensuing year.'[3] Meanwhile, unless and until the power to determine the periodic tenancy is exercised, each occupational unit of time, as it is added to the preceding unit of time, is itself of strictly defined duration.[4]

1   Recent judicial efforts represent only a more subtle variant on the attempts made during the 1980s to rationalise the termination of the open-ended tenancy as a controllable event **[para 7.115]**. It is ironic that, in attempting to deflect an awkward implication of a property-based dogma about 'certainty of term', the courts have unashamedly resorted to a 'contractual approach' (see e g *Notting Hill Housing Trust v Brackley* [2002] HLR 212 at [26] per Peter Gibson LJ).
2   [1992] 2 AC 386 at 394E–F.
3   The same reasoning is, of course, applicable to preserve any other kind of periodic tenancy from falling foul of the ancient common law principle against uncertainty of term. Lord Templeman had already expressed the view that the 'term' which, in conjunction with the grant of exclusive possession, is constitutive of a tenancy can be either a 'fixed or periodic term certain' (*Street v Mountford* [1985] AC 809 at 818E). See also Lord Templeman's reference (at 826E) to a 'periodical term'. In *Bruton v London & Quadrant Housing Trust* [2000] 1 AC 406 at 413E, Lord Hoffmann spoke simply of 'a fixed or renewable period or periods of time.'
4   'Whether the tenancy be from year to year, quarter to quarter, month to month, or week to week, it is a tenancy for a definite term of a year, a quarter, a month, or a week, as the case may be, with a superadded provision that it is to continue for another definite term of the same period, unless, by proper notice to quit, it is terminated ... ' (*Commonwealth Life (Amalgamated) Assurance Ltd v Anderson* (1946) 46 SR (NSW) 47 at 50–51 per Jordan CJ).

7.129   It is ultimately questionable whether judicial sophistry has entirely succeeded in reconciling the 'certainty of term' principle with the amoebic growth potential of the periodic tenancy.[1] It may be that such a task is simply impossible and that Russell LJ was quite correct when, in a moment of great candour over three decades ago, he declared that the 'certainty of term' principle 'cannot ... have direct reference to periodic tenancies.'[2]

1   There is an irreducible difference between knowing in advance *how* a periodic tenancy will terminate and knowing in advance *when* it will so terminate.
2   *Re Midland Railway Co's Agreement* [1971] Ch 725 at 732F–G.

Service tenancy

7.130   In so far as a service occupancy is expressed to be co-terminous with the occupier's employment by the owner of property, there is some doubt as to whether the occupancy can constitute a tenancy.[1] If the employee's employment, and therefore his occupancy of service accommodation, are of uncertain maximum duration, it may be that the common law requirement necessary for a leasehold estate is not met.[2] It is much more likely, however, that where a periodic rent is paid for a service occupancy, there arises an irresistible inference that there exists a periodic tenancy terminable by the appropriate notice in the event that the employment comes to an end.

1   **[Para 7.100]**. There may be other reasons for doubting the leasehold character of a service occupancy enjoyed by an employee who is required to occupy his employer's premises for the better performance of his duties (see *Street v Mountford* [1985] AC 809 at 818F–G **[para 7.157]**).
2   See e g *Ball v Crawford* [1981] BCL 627 (NZ High Court). However, English courts seem not to have been particularly sensitive to the existence of this problem (see e g *Scrimgeour v Waller* (1981) 257 EG 61).

A LEASE OR TENANCY MUST CONFER A RIGHT OF EXCLUSIVE POSSESSION

7.131   The essence of the relationship of landlord and tenant 'is the granting of possession.'[1] Exclusory power is central to the notion of possession[2] and therefore of the major possessory estates in land; and it is entirely consistent with the proprietary character of the term of years that 'the proper touchstone' of a lease or tenancy should comprise the legal right to exclusive possession of the land.[3] It is intrinsic to any lease or tenancy that the grantee enjoys exclusive possession of the premises concerned.[4] A tenant without exclusive possession is a contradiction in terms.[5] No tenancy can exist unless such a right has been conferred on the occupier[6] and the recipient of anything less than exclusive possession is no tenant,[7] but at best a mere licensee of the land.[8] Indeed the sine qua non of exclusive possession has tended, in practice, to mark out the borderline between the leasehold estate and the mere personal permission to be present on land.[9]

1   *Bell v General Accident, Fire & Life Assurance Corpn Ltd* [1998] 1 EGLR 69 at 71D–E per Hutchison LJ. Here, again, the tension between the proprietary and contractual perspectives on leasehold tenure helps to explain the ambiguity as to whether the tenant has 'exclusive possession' or a 'right to exclusive possession'. In its proprietary dimension, a term of years grants 'possession'; in its contractual dimension, a lease or tenancy confers a 'right to exclusive possession'. The difference of emphasis reflects the difference between the juristic functions of conveyance and contract.
2   **[Paras 3.18, 7.90]**.
3   *Radaich v Smith* (1959) 101 CLR 209 at 223 per Windeyer J. The authoritative quality of *Radaich v Smith* has been enthusiastically endorsed by both the House of Lords (see *Street v Mountford* [1985] AC 809 at 827B–E) and the Privy Council (see *Ramnarace v Lutchman* [2001] 1 WLR 1651 at [15]). For the English adoption of Windeyer J's reference to the 'touchstone' of exclusive possession, see *Aslan v Murphy (Nos 1 and 2)* [1990] 1 WLR 766 at 770E–F per Lord Donaldson of Lymington MR. See also *Goldsworthy Mining Ltd v Federal*

Commissioner of Taxation (1973) 128 CLR 199 at 212 per Mason J; *Western Australia v Ward* (2002) 191 ALR 1 at [501] per McHugh J. Exclusive possession is 'the litmus' or 'fundamental test' of tenancy (see *Fatac Ltd v Commissioner of Inland Revenue* [2002] 3 NZLR 648 at [38], [40] (NZ Court of Appeal)).

4   *Radaich v Smith* (1959) 101 CLR 209 at 214 per McTiernan J; *AG Securities v Vaughan* [1990] 1 AC 417 at 454A–B per Lord Bridge of Harwich; *Antoniades v Villiers* [1990] 1 AC 417 at 459D–H per Lord Templeman. See also *Wright v Stavert* (1860) 2 E & E 721 at 727, 121 ER 270 at 273; *Hull v Parsons* [1962] NZLR 465 at 468; *Re Villa Otthon Management and Bamboulis* (1988) 40 DLR (4th) 574 at 576. In this context 'exclusive possession' includes the exclusive right to the receipt of rents and profits (*AG Securities v Vaughan*, supra at 455A per Lord Templeman).

5   See *Radaich v Smith* (1959) 101 CLR 209 at 222, where Windeyer J emphasised the 'self-contradictory and meaningless' quality of any assertion that a person legally entitled to exclusive possession for a term is a mere licensee. In his view, '[t]o say that a man who has, by agreement with a landlord, a right of exclusive possession for a term is not a tenant is simply to contradict the first proposition by the second.' See also *Goldsworthy Mining Ltd v Federal Commissioner of Taxation* (1973) 128 CLR 199 at 212; *Lapham v Orange City Council* [1968] 2 NSWR 667 at 670–671; *Lewis v Bell* [1985] 1 NSWLR 731 at 734E–F.

6   *Street v Mountford* [1985] AC 809 at 818E per Lord Templeman. The High Court of Australia has, exceptionally, held that a lease may exist without a conferment of exclusive possession, but only in the context of statutorily created pastoral leases covering vast and remote areas of empty country (see particularly *Wik Peoples v Queensland* (1996) 187 CLR 1 at 117–122 per Toohey J, 153–155 per Gaudron J, 201–203 per Gummow J, 244–247 per Kirby J). This ruling ensured that pastoral leases did not extinguish claims of native title over the same areas. See also *Anderson v Wilson* (2000) 171 ALR 705 at 726 per Black CJ and Sackville J.

7   *Street v Mountford* [1985] AC 809 at 816C per Lord Templeman. See also *Beaton v McDivitt* (1985) 13 NSWLR 134 at 146A–C per Young J.

8   **[Para 4.6]**. See e g *Wilson v Tavener* [1901] 1 Ch 578 at 581; *Peakin v Peakin* [1895] 2 IR 359 at 362; *Daalman v Oosterdijk* [1973] 1 NZLR 717 at 720. Thus, for example, the right to park a car in a large garage can take the form of a lease only if the right relates to an identified parking bay rather than to the entire parking area in general (see *Harley Queen v Forsyte Kerman* [1983] CLY 2077).

9   *Hunter v Canary Wharf Ltd* [1997] AC 655 at 703F per Lord Hoffmann. See also *Fatac Ltd v Commissioner of Inland Revenue* [2002] 3 NZLR 648 at [38]. For a salutary reminder that '[t]he adjective "exclusive" adds nothing to the concept of possession', see *Western Australia v Ward* (2002) 191 ALR 1 at [503] per McHugh J **[para 3.2]**.

Exclusive possession as territorial control

7.132   The centrality of exclusive possession in the conceptualism of the leasehold derives from the fact that such possession alone confers the degree of territorial control normally necessary to enable the tenant to carry out the purpose for which he took the letting.[1] As Windeyer J pointed out in *Radaich v Smith*,[2] the occupier of a lock-up shop would be 'astounded' to be informed that she had no right to control entry to the shop or that the freehold owner was simultaneously entitled to provide other persons with keys to the premises and to authorise them to carry on other sorts of business there.[3] The principal emanations of exclusive possession are two in number.[4]

1   See *Hayes v Seymour-Johns* (1981) 2 BPR 9366 at 9368–9369; *OH Ranch Ltd v Patton* (1996) 138 DLR (4th) 381 at 384b; *Fatac Ltd v Commissioner of Inland Revenue* [2002] 3 NZLR 648 at [38].
2   (1959) 101 CLR 209 at 224–225.

3   See also (1959) 101 CLR 209 at 215 per McTiernan J, 217 per Taylor J, 221 per Menzies J ('exclusive possession' clearly essential for reasonably convenient carrying on of milk bar business).
4   See the approach adopted in *Bruton v London & Quadrant Housing Trust* [2000] 1 AC 406 at 413G–414B per Lord Hoffmann.

Exclusory power

7.133   The right of exclusive possession justifies the exercise of exclusory power. The common law requirement of exclusive possession in the leasehold serves as a constant reminder of the fact that privacy and 'excludability' are intrinsic components of estate ownership.[1] As Lord Templeman pointed out in *Street v Mountford*,[2] the hallmark of exclusive possession is entirely consistent with the 'elevation of a tenancy into an estate in land.' Accordingly the tenant is entitled 'to exercise the rights of an owner of land, which is in the real sense his land albeit temporarily and subject to certain restrictions.'[3] Viewed from this perspective, estate ownership of a leasehold is not qualitatively different from estate ownership of a freehold (which may itself be subject to various kinds of restrictive covenant). The common feature of exclusive possession eliminates the false dichotomy which might otherwise suggest itself between these two forms of proprietary control. The tenant is simply owner pro tempore[4] and one of the more dramatic indicia of his ownership is his ability to 'keep out strangers and keep out the landlord unless the landlord is exercising limited rights reserved to him by the tenancy agreement to enter and view and repair.'[5] Indeed, the reservation of such rights merely emphasises the background assumption that the tenant intrinsically enjoys exclusiveness of possession.[6] Whether his term of years be long or short, whether the land area be large or small,[7] the tenant has, in respect of the demised premises, a right of territorial control which he may vindicate by action in trespass even as against his own landlord.[8] It is quite different, however, if an owner of premises has reserved a genuine contractual right to introduce other persons to share occupation of those premises: the existing occupier's assertion of tenancy status falls together with any semblance of a claim to exclusive possession.[9]

1   [**Para 2.35**]. See Gray, 'Property in Thin Air' [1991] CLJ 252 at 268–269; *Fatac Ltd v Commissioner of Inland Revenue* [2002] 3 NZLR 648 at [38].
2   [1985] AC 809 at 814E–F, 816B.
3   [1985] AC 809 at 816B. It has always been clearly recognised that the tenant's right to exclusive possession is not inconsistent with the imposition of restrictions on the uses to which he may put the land (see *Glenwood Lumber Co Ltd v Phillips* [1904] AC 405 at 408; *Re British American Oil Co Ltd and DePass* (1960) 21 DLR (2d) 110 at 116–117; *Fatac Ltd v Commissioner of Inland Revenue* [2002] 3 NZLR 648 at [42], [67]; *Western Australia v Ward* (2002) 191 ALR 1 at [507] per McHugh J).
4   By contrast a licensee, 'lacking exclusive possession can in no sense call the land his own' (*Street v Mountford* [1985] AC 809 at 816C per Lord Templeman [**para 3.20**]).
5   *Street v Mountford* [1985] AC 809 at 816B–C. See also *Lewis v Bell* [1985] 1 NSWLR 731 at 734F–G; *Fatac Ltd v Commissioner of Inland Revenue* [2002] 3 NZLR 648 at [38]; *Western Australia v Ward* (2002) 191 ALR 1 at [485] per McHugh J. It is widely accepted that a reservation to the landlord, either by contract or statute, of limited rights of entry is not

inconsistent with a tenant's right of exclusive possession (see e g *Radaich v Smith* (1959) 101 CLR 209 at 222 per Windeyer J). For a statutory right of entry, see L&TA 1985, ss 8(2), 11(6) **[para 14.94]**.

6   See *Goldsworthy Mining Ltd v Federal Commissioner of Taxation* (1973) 128 CLR 199 at 213 per Mason J; *Wik Peoples v Queensland* (1996) 187 CLR 1 at 117 per Toohey J; *Bruton v London & Quadrant Housing Trust* [2000] 1 AC 406 at 411B–C per Lord Jauncey of Tullichettle, 414A–B per Lord Hoffmann; *Fatac Ltd v Commissioner of Inland Revenue* [2002] 3 NZLR 648 at [46] (NZ Court of Appeal); *Western Australia v Ward* (2002) 191 ALR 1 at [509], [551] per McHugh J.

7   See *AG Securities v Vaughan* [1990] 1 AC 417 at 471B–C per Lord Oliver of Aylmerton; *Miller v Eyo* (1999) 31 HLR 306 (single room).

8   See *Wright v Stavert* (1860) 2 E & E 721 at 728–729, 121 ER 270 at 273; *Stocker v Planet Building Society* [1879] 27 WR 877 at 878; *Michael Santarsieri Inc v Unicity Mall Ltd* (2000) 181 DLR (4th) 136 at 143.

9   See *Parkins v City of Westminster* (1998) 30 HLR 894 at 901.

Immunity from supervisory control

7.134   The tenant's intrinsic territorial prerogative does not merely confer an entitlement to exclude the rest of the world; it implies a general immunity from any detailed supervision or regulation of his activities on the demised premises. No claim of tenancy can ultimately be sustained if a power of intensive supervisory control is reserved for the freehold owner.[1] Such an explanation underlay the denial, in *Westminster CC v Clarke*,[2] of the tenant status of an occupant of a room in a council-run hostel for homeless persons. In order to facilitate the 'efficient and harmonious' administration of the hostel on behalf of its vulnerable clientèle, the council had expressly limited the accommodation rights accorded to occupants.[3] Under the hostel's regulations no occupant was entitled to any particular room; each could be required to share with other persons; each was forbidden to entertain visitors without permission; and hostel staff were authorised to 'enter the accommodation at any time'. All occupants were obliged to comply with the directions of the hostel warden and with other stipulated conditions of occupation. In these circumstances the House of Lords concluded that an assertion of tenancy was incompatible with the 'totality, immediacy, and objectives of the powers exercisable by the council and the restrictions imposed on [the occupant].'[4] The curtailed nature of each occupant's rights confirmed that it was, in reality, the council which 'retained possession of all the rooms of the hostel in order to supervise and control the activities of occupiers.'[5] No individual occupier could on his own behalf assert a right of exclusive possession.

1   The power to admit people to the premises and to exclude people from them 'does not belong to the landlord once he has parted with possession' (*Northern Sandblasting Pty Ltd v Harris* (1997) 188 CLR 313 at 339 per Brennan CJ). 'The lessor who has given up possession of premises to a tenant has significantly relinquished capacity to control activities taking place within them' (*W D & H O Wills (Australia) Ltd v State Rail Authority of New South Wales* (1998) 43 NSWLR 338 at 357C per Mason P).

2   [1992] 2 AC 288. See [1992] JSWFL 334; [1992] Conv 113 (J Martin), 285 (D S Cowan).

3   [1992] 2 AC 288 at 301A–H.

4   [1992] 2 AC 288 at 302A. See also *Bruton v London & Quadrant Housing Trust* [2000] 1 AC 406 at 413H–414B per Lord Hoffmann.

5   [1992] 2 AC 288 at 301H–302A per Lord Templeman. See similarly *Noble v Centacare* (2003) 150 ACTR at [45] (detailed disciplinary regime in crisis support centre).

'Exclusive possession' distinguished from 'exclusive occupation'

7.135   It is this element of overall control that distinguishes the exclusive possession which characterises a true tenancy from the exclusiveness of occupation which is frequently the attribute of a mere licence. 'Exclusive occupation' is not synonymous with 'exclusive possession'.[1] As elsewhere in English land law,[2] the notion of possession extends far beyond a mere physical occupancy of land to incorporate some kind of conscious will to control that occupancy and to defend it against all comers. It is often the case that persons who are allowed to enjoy sole occupation in fact are not necessarily to be taken as having been given in law a right of 'possession' – let alone a right of 'exclusive possession'.[3] Many contractual licensees and lodgers (eg students in university halls of residence, residents in a hotel, and persons living in an old people's home) undoubtedly enjoy sole occupation in this sense, but equally clearly have no tenancy.[4] In such instances factual enjoyment of sole occupation falls significantly short of any conferment of 'exclusive possession'.[5]

1   See *Venus Investments Ltd v Stocktop Ltd* [1997] EWCA Civ 1696 per Schiemann LJ ('the mere fact that in practice someone is the only person on the site does not mean that he had, during that time, the right to exclude others'). See also *Esso Petroleum Co Ltd v Fumegrange Ltd* (1994) 68 P & CR D15 at D17 per Neill LJ, per Sir Christopher Slade.
2   **[Para 3.3]**.
3   *Radaich v Smith* (1959) 101 CLR 209 at 223 per Windeyer J. See eg *Smith v Northside Developments Ltd* (1988) 55 P & CR 164 at 167; [1989] Conv 55 (J E M). On the failure to distinguish between exclusive possession and exclusive occupation, see *Parkins v City of Westminster* (1998) 30 HLR 894 at 899–901 per Chadwick LJ; *Western Australia v Ward* (2002) 191 ALR 1 at [477]–[478], [518]–[519] per McHugh J.
4   **[Paras 7.158–7.163]**.
5   *Radaich v Smith* (1959) 101 CLR 209 at 223 per Windeyer J.

Circumstances negating a right of exclusive possession

7.136   Certain circumstances negate the existence of any exclusive possession in an occupier, thereby ruling out any claim by him or her to hold as a tenant.

Denial of quiet enjoyment

7.137   The existence of an unlimited right of access for the freeholder or of any intensive supervisory control over the occupier's activities clearly precludes any assertion of tenancy.[1] Still less is a claim of tenancy justified where the freehold owner has genuinely reserved a contractual right to exclude the occupier from the premises for a specific portion of each day[2] or to require the occupier to transfer his occupation to other premises belonging to the freeholder.[3] Furthermore any attempt to confer a right of exclusive possession on two or more persons simultaneously otherwise than as joint tenants or tenants in common[4] must inevitably be self-contradictory and meaningless.[5] It follows, *a fortiori*, that if premises are shared in joint occupation with the supposed landlord, so that exclusive possession cannot be claimed by either, there is no question of tenancy.[6]

1   In *Westminster CC v Clarke* [1992] 2 AC 288 at 301F–302A [**para 7.134**], the fact that hostel staff were entitled to 'enter the accommodation at any time' was destructive of any claim of tenancy. See also *Dresden Estates Ltd v Collinson* (1988) 55 P & CR 47 at 55 per Lloyd LJ; *Essex Plan Ltd v Broadminster* (1988) 56 P & CR 353 at 356–357; *Vandersteen v Agius* (1992) 65 P & CR 266 at 273; *Beaton v McDivitt* (1985) 13 NSWLR 134 at 146B–C; *Rental Bond Board v Bayman Development Pty Ltd* (1985) 3 BPR 9670 at 9676 per Street CJ.
2   For instances where an owner sought contractually to confine a resident's rights to discontinuous periods of occupation, see *Crancour Ltd v Da Silvaesa* (1986) 52 P & CR 204 and *Aslan v Murphy (No 1)* [1990] 1 WLR 766 (occupier supposedly excluded from premises every day between 10.30 am and 12.00 midday) [**para 7.186**].
3   See *Dresden Estates Ltd v Collinson* (1988) 55 P & CR 47 at 53 per Glidewell LJ ('The landlord can only do that by terminating the tenancy and creating a new one in other premises'). On the effect of a reserved power to move an occupier from room to room, see also *Crancour Ltd v Da Silvaesa* (1986) 52 P & CR 204 at 212–215; *Brennan v Lambeth LBC* (1998) 30 HLR 481 at 485; *Fatac Ltd v Commissioner of Inland Revenue* [2002] 3 NZLR 648 at [46].
4   [**Para 11.23**].
5   *Wetherby Apartments v Tootell* (Unreported, Court of Appeal, 27 October 1981); *Hindmarsh v Quinn* (1914) 17 CLR 622 at 630.
6   *Pearch v Gyucha* (1953) 73 WN (NSW) 122; *Walliker v Deveaux* (1959) 78 WN (NSW) 409 at 410; *Armstrong v Armstrong* [1970] 1 NSWR 133 at 135.

Possession of keys

7.138   The allocation of keys to the premises is an ambivalent guide to exclusiveness of possession. An occupier's mere possession of a key to the premises constitutes no proof of either exclusive possession or exclusive occupation.[1] Equally it is no requirement of a tenancy that the occupier should have exclusive possession of the keys.[2] As Lord Donaldson of Lymington MR indicated in *Aslan v Murphy (No 1)*,[3] the critical issue relates to the purpose underlying the provision or retention of keys. A landlord may genuinely need to retain a key in order to enter quickly in cases of emergency or to facilitate the reading of meters or the execution of repairs. The retention of a key for such purposes is not inconsistent with the existence of a tenancy.[4] The possibility of tenancy may, however, be negatived if an owner retains a key in order to enjoy occasional access to the premises for reasons of his own convenience,[5] or in order to monitor the observance of relevant conditions of occupation,[6] or to provide genuine services (e g frequent cleaning and daily bed-making) which are practicable only if access is facilitated by retention of a master key.[7] A prohibition on any interference with or changing of locks by the occupier does not in itself exclude the possibility that the occupier is a tenant, at least where there is no indication that the owner was obliged to supply services to the occupier or intended genuinely to share occupation of the premises.[8]

1   *Michel v Volpe* (1967) 202 EG 213.
2   *Aslan v Murphy (No 1)* [1990] 1 WLR 766 at 773E.

3   [1990] 1 WLR 766 at 773E. See likewise *Noble v Centacare* (2003) 150 ACTR at [43].
4   *Aslan v Murphy (No 1)* [1990] 1 WLR 766 at 773F.
5   *Garland v Johnson* (Unreported, Court of Appeal, 24 February 1982).
6   *Oxford Overseas Student Housing Association v Mukherjee* (Unreported, Court of Appeal, 21 November 1989) per Bingham LJ.
7   *Aslan v Murphy (No 1)* [1990] 1 WLR 766 at 773F–H; *Huwyler v Ruddy* (1996) 28 HLR 550 at 553–554; *Noble v Centacare* (2003) 150 ACTR at [43]–[44]. The fact that virtually no services are in fact provided may reverse the balance once more in favour of tenancy (see *Aslan* at 773G–H).
8   *Duke v Wynn* [1990] 1 WLR 766 at 776A per Lord Donaldson of Lymington MR.

THE DISTINCTION BETWEEN LEASE AND LICENCE

7.139   Except in cases of tenancy by estoppel,[1] a lease or tenancy confers upon the occupier of land a proprietary estate to which is annexed a right of exclusive possession enforceable against all persons including the landlord.[2] By contrast, a licence confers upon the occupier not an estate in the land but merely a personal permission to occupy.[3] When described in such abstract terms, the lease appears wholly different in nature from the licence. However, the distinction has proved in practice to be more problematical,[4] not least because the factual and physical evidence of a lease 'on the ground' often seems to differ in no substantial respect from that of a contractual licence. A landowner is, in theory, free to make premises available on either basis,[5] although both lease and licence commonly involve the payment of money in return for the right to some form of exclusive occupancy for a prefixed period of time. The demarcation of the lease from the licence used to represent a hugely significant boundary of the domain of property. Nowadays, however, the importance of the distinction between lease and licence is being displaced by the increasing recognition of the concept of possession (whether granted by way of lease *or* by way of licence) as the essential base of many vital kinds of entitlement.

1   **[Para 7.265]**.
2   **[Para 7.131]**.
3   See *Street v Mountford* [1985] AC 809 at 816C; *Fatac Ltd v Commissioner of Inland Revenue* [2002] 3 NZLR 648 at [29]. Licences are discussed in Chapter 4.
4   See e g *Brooker Settled Estates Ltd v Ayers* (1987) 54 P & CR 165 at 167 per O'Connor LJ ('this tortured question'); *KJRR Pty Ltd v Commr of State Revenue* [1999] 2 VR 174 at 179 per Tadgell JA ('tantalising problems').
5   *Aslan v Murphy* [1990] 1 WLR 766 at 770B–C per Lord Donaldson of Lymington MR. See also *Antoniades v Villiers* [1990] 1 AC 417 at 445C–E per Bingham LJ ('It is not a crime, nor is it contrary to public policy, for a property owner to license occupiers to occupy property on terms which do not give rise to a tenancy').

Significance of the distinction

7.140   The blurred nature of the distinction between the lease and the licence has been responsible for much confusion in the law of landlord and tenant.[1] Yet the distinction – however elusive – is a vital determinant of several legal issues.

1   See *National Carriers Ltd v Panalpina (Northern) Ltd* [1981] AC 675 at 714A per Lord Roskill.

Common law of landlord and tenant

7.141 In the common law of landlord and tenant the lease–licence distinction derives an immediate relevance from the fact that a proprietary estate in land is normally conferred by a lease but never by a licence. Only a tenant, for instance, has an estate in the land which is capable of assignment to a stranger.[1] Furthermore, it is orthodox teaching that leases – but not most kinds of licence – are capable of binding a transferee of land.[2] Only a tenant – and not a licensee – is properly subject to the remedy of distress for arrears of rent.[3] Only a tenant – and not a licensee – may ask for relief against forfeiture.[4]

1   **[Para 2.54]**. See *Richardson v Landecker* (1950) 50 SR (NSW) 250 at 255; *Lewis v Bell* [1985] 1 NSWLR 731 at 735G.
2   **[Paras 2.50, 12.222]**.
3   The assertion by the owner of a right to distrain upon the goods of the occupier may estop the owner from any future claim that the occupier had a mere licence (see e g *Carden v Choudhury* (Unreported, Court of Appeal, 29 February 1984)).
4   **[Paras 4.70, 14.149]**. See *Fatac Ltd v Commissioner of Inland Revenue* [2002] 3 NZLR 648 at [30].

Ambit of regulatory legislation

7.142 The distinction between lease and licence is also important in defining the coverage of various schemes of protective legislation. Historically the most controversial function of this conceptual divide was to delineate the scope of full protection under the Rent Act 1977. The ample benefits conferred by this Act apply only to the tenant and not to the licensee.[1] Similarly the distinction between lease and licence serves to fix the boundaries of the statutory codes governing assured tenancies[2] and business tenancies.[3] Tenants, but not licensees, are the beneficiaries of significant statutory obligations relating to the repair and maintenance of their premises.[4] The definitional knife-edge separating lease from licence may affect even wider categories of problems, ranging from the level of compensation payable to a householder on compulsory purchase[5] to the allocation of legal liability for defective premises.[6] However, there is also a countervailing tendency in modern statute law to treat the contractual licence as on a par with the leasehold estate. The distinction between tenancy and licence no longer controls the operation of the protective codes regulating secure tenancies[7] and agricultural holdings.[8] A 'secure tenancy' covers, for instance, not merely a tenancy in the strict sense but also a licence to occupy a dwelling-house provided that the licensee enjoys exclusive possession.[9] Even in the prosaic world of taxation, leases and licences to occupy land have alike been brought within the 'leasing or letting' exemption from value added tax required by the EC Sixth VAT Directive.[10] Again in the European context, the enforcement of procedural safeguards against unfair eviction by public authority landowners has caused certain kinds of residential licence to acquire a form of protection not essentially dissimilar from that accorded to a lease or tenancy.[11]

1   Rent Act 1977, s 1 **[para 14.315]**.

2   HA 1988, s 1(1) **[para 14.330]**.
3   L&TA 1954, s 23(1).
4   L&TA 1985, ss 11(1), 11(1A) **[para 14.354]**.
5   See *David v LB of Lewisham* (1977) 34 P & CR 112 at 115–116; *McHugh v LB of Islington* (1984) 270 EG 1095 at 1096.
6   Defective Premises Act 1972, s 4(1) **[para 14.48]**. See *Wheat v E Lacon & Co Ltd* [1966] AC 552 at 579A–B, 579F–580A; *McDonagh v Kent AHA* (Unreported, Court of Appeal, 7 October 1985).
7   See HA 1985, s 79(3) **[para 14.339]**.
8   See Agricultural Holdings Act 1986, s 2(2)(b) **[para 14.361]**.
9   See *Westminster CC v Clarke* [1992] 2 AC 288 at 300C per Lord Templeman; *Parkins v City of Westminster* (1998) 30 HLR 894 at 897–901.
10   EC Council Directive 77/388 (The Sixth VAT Directive), Title X, art 13B, implemented by Value Added Tax Act 1994, s 31, Sch 9. See *Lubbock Fine & Co v Commissioners of Customs and Excise* (*Case C-63/92*) [1993] ECR I-6665 at 6691; *Abbotsley Golf & Squash Club Ltd v Commissioners of Customs and Excise* [1997] V & DR 355 at 362C–I. Contrast the licence to *use* land, which in the present context is not treated as the equivalent of a lease (see *Customs and Excise Commrs v Sinclair Collis Ltd* [2001] STC 989 at [35] per Lord Nicholls of Birkenhead, [44], [50] per Lord Millett, [73]–[79] per Lord Scott of Foscote (installation of cigarette vending machine); *Sinclair Collis Ltd v Customs and Excise Commrs* (*Case C-275/01*) [2003] STC 898 at [46], [58] (Advocate General Alber), [31] (Judgment)).
11   ECHR Art 8. See *Connors v United Kingdom* (ECtHR decision, Application No 66746/01, 27 May 2004) **[para 2.74]**.

Disturbance of rights by strangers

7.143   It used to be said that a licensee, intrinsically lacking possession of the land, had no right to sue a third person in respect of any disturbance of his rights.[1] His remedy (if any) lay against his licensor alone. On this basis only a tenant[2] – and not a licensee[3] – could sue a third party for nuisance or trespass.

1   **[Paras 3.50, 4.7]**. See *Hill v Tupper* (1863) 2 H & C 121 at 127, 159 ER 51 at 53 **[para 8.36]**; *Lewisham BC v Roberts* [1949] 2 KB 608 at 622.
2   *Harper v Charlesworth* (1825) 4 B & C 574 at 585, 107 ER 1174 at 1178; *Street v Mountford* [1985] AC 809 at 816B–C.
3   See *AG Securities v Vaughan* [1990] 1 AC 417 at 454A–B per Lord Bridge of Harwich; *Simpson v Knowles* [1974] VR 190 at 195; *Western Australia v Ward* (2002) 191 ALR 1 at [504] per McHugh J.

Exclusive possession for some licensees

7.144   In more recent years it has become established that possession, although one of the 'badges' of a tenancy, is not necessarily denied to all kinds of licensee.[1] Exclusive possession of land may be claimed not only by one who owns an estate in the land, but also by certain categories of person who hold a mere licence.[2] Thus not only a tenant, but also a licensee, may nowadays sue in trespass[3] and nuisance,[4] provided in either case that the claimant 'is enjoying or asserting exclusive possession of the land.'[5]

1   See *Hounslow LBC v Twickenham Garden Developments Ltd* [1971] Ch 233 at 257D–E per

Megarry J [**para 3.51**]; but contrast strong contrary views expressed overseas (*Western Australia v Ward* (2002) 191 ALR 1 at [504] per McHugh J; *Fatac Ltd v Commissioner of Inland Revenue* [2002] 3 NZLR 648 at [66]).

2   *Street v Mountford* [1985] AC 809 at 823D per Lord Templeman. See also *Telecom Auckland Ltd v Auckland CC* [1999] 1 NZLR 426 at 441.

3   See e g *Mehta v Royal Bank of Scotland* [1999] 3 EGLR 153 at 160E–F (successful trespass claim by licensee with exclusive possession).

4   See e g *Pemberton v Southwark LBC* [2000] 1 WLR 1672 at 1682H, 1684H–1685A (successful nuisance claim by 'tolerated trespasser').

5   *Hunter v Canary Wharf Ltd* [1997] AC 655 at 703E per Lord Hoffmann (see also 688E per Lord Goff of Chieveley, 724C–F per Lord Hope of Craighead). The degree of possession required for this purpose is not necessarily the same as that which would found a claim of adverse possession under the Limitation Act (see *Pemberton v Southwark LBC* [2000] 1 WLR 1672 at 1681H–1682C per Roch LJ, 1686B–D per Sir Christopher Slade). See also *Newcastle-under-Lyme Corpn v Wolstanton Ltd* [1947] Ch 92 at 106–108.

Recovery of land from trespassers

7.145   Even more significant developments have occurred in relation to the recovery of land from trespassers,[1] a remedy which goes considerably further than the mere recovery of damages for wrong done. The tenant, relying on the title derived from his ownership of an estate in the land, has a clear right to recover possession from trespassers who invade his land.[2] The licensee – precisely because he lacks any estate in the land – has 'no legal title which will permit him to exclude other persons.'[3] In recent decades, however, the courts have begun to attach significance to the degree of possessory control exercised over the land by a licensee. Thus a contractual licensee who is in 'effective control'[4] or 'de facto occupation'[5] of a site is entitled to obtain an order for possession as against trespassers who have entered that site without consent. In *Manchester Airport Plc v Dutton*[6] the Court of Appeal upheld the right of a contractual licensee to claim summary possession against trespassing protesters on an environmentally sensitive development site. This form of eviction was made available to the contractual licensee even though that licensee had no right to exclusive possession of the area,[7] had at best merely limited rights of entry for specified purposes[8] and, most surprisingly, was not yet in occupation of the site at all.[9] Nevertheless a majority in the Court of Appeal could see no reason why such a contractual licensee should not obtain possession even before entry, in order to 'vindicate and give effect to such rights of occupation as by contract with [its] licensor [it] enjoys.'[10] The Court effectively regarded a contractually created right of occupation as conferring a relatively good title to possession of the land, certainly as against a 'bare trespasser',[11] although not, of course, as against the licensor itself.[12] This equiparation of contract-based and estate-based rights to vindicate possession[13] has dramatically closed the juristic gap between many forms of licence and the proprietary leasehold estate.[14]

1   [**Paras 3.32–3.48**].

2   *Manchester Airport Plc v Dutton* [2000] QB 133 at 150B per Laws LJ.

3   *AG Securities v Vaughan* [1990] 1 AC 417 at 471A per Lord Oliver of Aylmerton.

4   *Manchester Airport Plc v Dutton* [2000] QB 133 at 147C–D per Laws LJ. Contrast, however,
     Countryside Residential (North Thames) Ltd v (1) A Child; (2) Persons Unknown (2001)
     81 P & CR 10 at [12]–[13] **[para 3.38]**.
5   *Manchester Airport Plc v Dutton* [2000] QB 133 at 147F–G per Laws LJ.
6   [2000] QB 133 **[paras 3.38, 4.98]**. See [1999] Conv 535 (E Paton and G Seabourne).
7   [2000] QB 133 at 150C per Laws LJ, 151B–H per Kennedy LJ.
8   [2000] QB 133 at 151B per Kennedy LJ.
9   [2000] QB 133 at 147C.
10   [2000] QB 133 at 150A per Laws LJ.
11   [2000] QB 133 at 150C per Laws LJ.
12   Laws LJ conceded that no one 'can exclude any occupier who, by contract or estate, has a
     claim to possession equal to or superior to his own' ([2000] QB 133 at 150C).
13   'In this whole debate, as regards the law of remedies in the end I see no significance as a
     matter of principle in any distinction drawn between a plaintiff whose right to occupy the land
     in question arises from title and one whose right arises only from contract' ([2000] QB 133 at
     150C–D per Laws LJ).
14   See, however, (2000) 116 LQR 354 (W J Swadling).

Rare instances of superior protection for the licensee

7.146   Although it is generally true that a tenancy confers on the occupier a
greater degree of legal protection than does a licence in equivalent circumstances, this is not always the case. For example, a licensee (other than one with
exclusive possession) may sue his licensor in negligence for failure to exercise
reasonable care in safeguarding the licensee's belongings from burglary.[1] A
similar claim on behalf of a tenant founders on the fact that the tenant is the
owner of an estate in the land and is himself responsible for the defence of his
exclusive possession of that land.[2] It is also significant that various forms of
licence in land – notably the 'irrevocable licence' or licence based on proprietary
estoppel – are sometimes accorded a degree of security of tenure which exceeds
that conferred by a tenancy.[3]

1   *Appah v Parncliffe Investments Ltd* [1964] 1 WLR 1064 at 1067.
2   The landlord may still be liable for loss caused to a tenant through burglary or criminal
     damage if the landlord failed in his responsibility to repair an insecure front door to premises
     within which the tenant occupied a self-contained flat (see e g *Marshall v Rubypoint Ltd* [1997]
     1 EGLR 69 at 71J–M).
3   See e g *Hardwick v Johnson* [1978] 1 WLR 683 at 689H.

Exclusive possession is a necessary, but not sufficient, criterion of tenancy

7.147   Since medieval times the criterion of exclusive possession has tended to
mark off the boundary between the lease and the licence.[1] In the residential
context the conferment of a right of exclusive possession for a term has served,
in all but exceptional circumstances, to denote the grant of a leasehold estate in
the land. The right to exclusive possession symbolises the overall territorial
control characteristic of estate ownership in English law. Such entitlement gives
legal expression to the perception that, in some elemental sense, the tenant has
a 'stake' in the land[2] and not a mere fragile permission for temporary personal

occupation. It is indeed this 'stake' in the land which, in the words of Lord Templeman in *Street v Mountford*,[3] enables the tenant (unlike the licensee) to 'call the land his own.' It also sustains both the tenant's ability to resist intrusion by any trespasser and his capacity to transfer his rights to a stranger.[4] Precisely because exclusive possession provides 'the proper touchstone' of a lease or tenancy,[5] no tenancy can be present in circumstances which directly or indirectly negate the occupier's exclusive possession.

1   See [1985] CLJ 351 at 352 (S Tromans).
2   *Marchant v Charters* [1977] 1 WLR 1181 at 1185G per Lord Denning MR. See Gray and Gray, 'The Idea of Property in Land', in S Bright and J K Dewar (ed), *Land Law: Themes and Perspectives* (OUP 1998), pp 20–21. The terminology of a 'stake in the room' was explicitly adopted by Lord Templeman in *Street v Mountford* [1985] AC 809 at 825B–C. See also *Hadjiloucas v Crean* [1988] 1 WLR 1006 at 1021F–G; *Barclays Mercantile Industrial Finance Ltd v Melluish* [1990] STC 314 at 345; *Mehta v Royal Bank of Scotland* [1999] 3 EGLR 153 at 155E.
3   [1985] AC 809 at 816B–C.
4   See *Barnes v Barratt* [1970] 2 QB 657 at 669G–H; *Shell-Mex and BP Ltd v Manchester Garages Ltd* [1971] 1 WLR 612 at 617H–618A. The student who lives in a bed-sitting room provided in a hostel or hall of residence has, for instance, no estate which he can meaningfully transfer to a stranger.
5   *Radaich v Smith* (1959) 101 CLR 209 at 223 per Windeyer J [**para 7.131**].

7.148   While exclusive possession is the sine qua non of tenancy, it does not follow that a tenancy is necessarily present wherever someone is, or seems to be, in exclusive possession of land.[1] The existence of a landlord–tenant relationship may be excluded because

–   the occupier's exclusive possession is referable to some other category of legal relationship; or
–   the parties never intended to create a legally enforceable relationship of any kind; or
–   the occupation is explicable on the basis of someone else's exclusive possession; or
–   the occupier's exclusive possession is not for a fixed or periodic term; or
–   the occupation relates to interim accommodation granted in the context of homelessness.

1   *Street v Mountford* [1985] AC 809 at 823D per Lord Templeman.

7.149   These categories of circumstance can overlap or shade into each other.[1] Ultimately these contra-indications of tenancy are intricately interlinked explanations which meld together in the assertion that the occupier has failed to demonstrate that he or she had a stake in, or possessory control over, the land.[2]

1   See e g *Street v Mountford* [1985] AC 809 at 818E–H, 826G–827B per Lord Templeman.
2   Where, however, an occupier genuinely enjoys a right of exclusive possession, free of overriding external control of his premises, the relationship is almost inevitably one of tenancy, even if this classification imposes highly onerous operating conditions upon a social landlord such as a charitable housing trust (see *Bruton v London & Quadrant Housing Trust* [2000] 1 AC 406 at 410C–D per Lord Slynn of Hadley, 411C–412B per Lord Jauncey of Tullichettle, 414B–D per Lord Hoffmann).

Exclusive possession referable to some other category of legal relationship

7.150 In *Street v Mountford*[1] Lord Templeman pointed out that while, by definition, a tenant must have exclusive possession, an occupier who enjoys exclusive possession 'is not necessarily a tenant.' The enjoyment of exclusive possession is not inconsistent with other forms of legal status[2] and may easily arise outside the landlord–tenant relationship.[3] That exclusive possession of land may be 'referable to a legal relationship other than a tenancy'[4] is amply demonstrated by such persons as the owner in fee simple,[5] the adverse possessor,[6] the mortgagee in possession,[7] the beneficiary under a charitable trust,[8] the purchaser allowed into possession before completion,[9] and the occupier who retains land pending the exercise of an option.[10] All these categories of person enjoy an exclusiveness of possession which arises quite independently of any grant for a term at a rent,[11] possession being ancillary in each case to some other kind of interest in or status in relation to the land.[12] Such alternative forms of status or relationship, 'although exhibiting the ordinary badges of a tenancy',[13] do not create a term of years.

1   [1985] AC 809 at 818E.
2   See *Ramnarace v Lutchman* [2001] 1 WLR 1651 at [16] per Lord Millett.
3   This concern to distinguish exclusive possession as the substratum of tenancy from the exclusive possession inherent in other forms of legal status may perhaps account for Lord Templeman's unnecessary reference to the payment of some rent or premium as a 'hallmark' of tenancy.
4   *Street v Mountford* [1985] AC 809 at 826H–827A per Lord Templeman. See also *Bruton v London & Quadrant Housing Trust* [2000] 1 AC 406 at 413E, 414B per Lord Hoffmann, 417E per Lord Hobhouse of Woodborough.
5   **[Para 7.125]**. See *Delgamuukw v British Columbia* (1997) 153 DLR (4th) 193 at [156] per Lamer CJC.
6   **[Para 6.108]**. See *Hunter v Canary Wharf Ltd* [1997] AC 655 at 703F per Lord Hoffmann.
7   **[Para 15.109]**.
8   *Street v Mountford* [1985] AC 809 at 818E per Lord Templeman. There is no need to resort to a tenancy to explain the almsperson's right to exclusive possession of accommodation provided by a charitable trust (see *Gray v Taylor* [1998] 1 WLR 1093 at 1098H per Sir John Vinelott, 1099D per Nourse LJ).
9   See *Essex Plan Ltd v Broadminster* (1988) 56 P & CR 353 at 355–356. However, if an occupier enters into possession with the ultimate intention of negotiating a purchase of the property, and that purchase never materialises, the occupier will still rank as a lessee if the facts otherwise satisfy the *Street v Mountford* criteria of 'exclusive possession at a rent for a term' (see *Bretherton v Paton* [1986] 1 EGLR 172 at 174H). Compare *Ramnarace v Lutchman* [2001] 1 WLR 1651 at [18]–[20] (rent-free occupation pending negotiation of purchase created tenancy at will **[para 7.273]**).
10   *Essex Plan Ltd v Broadminster* (1988) 56 P & CR 353 at 355–357; [1989] Conv 55 (J E M).
11   See *Fatac Ltd v Commissioner of Inland Revenue* [2002] 3 NZLR 648 at [65] (referring to cases where 'the initial appearance of a right to exclusive possession is ... critically undermined by the potential for termination for reasons extraneous to the occupation of the exclusively occupied area'). See also *Leadenhall Residential 2 Ltd v Stirling* [2002] 1 WLR 499 at [23].
12   Thus, in *Essex Plan Ltd v Broadminster* (1988) 56 P & CR 353 at 356, Hoffmann J pointed out that the optionee's possession was 'ancillary and referable to' its right to call for a long lease, an entitlement which had given it 'in equity an immediate interest in the land' **[para 9.20]**. The same kind of analysis applies to each of the other cases of exclusive possession enjoyed otherwise than qua tenant. For instance, the fee simple purchaser and the trespasser can attribute their exclusive possession, respectively, to a rightful and wrongful estate in fee.
13   *Essex Plan Ltd v Broadminster* (1988) 56 P & CR 353 at 356 per Hoffmann J.

Absence of intention to create any enforceable legal relationship

7.151   The enjoyment of exclusive possession is sometimes consistent with a total absence of legal status or obligation.[1] In certain rare situations a tenancy classification is ruled out precisely because the relevant parties, whilst agreeing on a temporary occupation of the land, lacked any intention to enter into a binding legal or contractual relationship of any kind.[2] As Lord Browne-Wilkinson emphasised in *Burrows v Brent LBC*,[3] it cannot be right to impute to the parties an intention to create a tenancy 'unless the legal structures within which they made their agreement force that conclusion.'

1   See *Street v Mountford* [1985] AC 809 at 826H per Lord Templeman; *Hadjiloucas v Crean* [1988] 1 WLR 1006 at 1019D per Mustill LJ; *Colchester BC v Smith* [1991] Ch 448 at 484A–485D per Ferris J.
2   See *Street v Mountford* [1985] AC 809 at 819C, 820D per Lord Templeman; *Ramnarace v Lutchman* [2001] 1 WLR 1651 at [17] per Lord Millett; *Fatac Ltd v Commissioner of Inland Revenue* [2002] 3 NZLR 648 at [40], [67] (NZ Court of Appeal).
3   [1996] 1 WLR 1448 at 1454G.

SPECIAL CIRCUMSTANCES WHICH DISCLOSE NO LEASE OR TENANCY

7.152   The circumstances which disclose a hiatus of contractual intent to generate any leasehold relationship tend to revolve around instances of personal generosity and institutional indulgence. In *Facchini v Bryson*,[1] for example, Denning LJ indicated that the intention to create a tenancy might be negatived in the context of 'a family arrangement, an act of friendship or generosity, or such like.'[2] As Windeyer J later observed in *Radaich v Smith*,[3] most of these exceptional instances are probably better regarded as cases where a factual enjoyment of sole occupation falls significantly short of any conferment of a right to exclusive possession.[4]

1   [1952] 1 TLR 1386 at 1389.
2   In *Street v Mountford* [1985] AC 809 at 821H–822A, Lord Templeman referred with approval to the old *Facchini v Bryson* categories, which still seem to represent good law today (see eg *AG Securities v Vaughan* [1990] 1 AC 417 at 426H–427A, 431F per Fox LJ; *Ramnarace v Lutchman* [2001] 1 WLR 1651 at [17] per Lord Millett).
3   (1959) 101 CLR 209 at 223.
4   See also R Street, [1985] Conv 328 at 331; D N Clarke, [1986] Conv 39 at 43.

Accommodation based on friendship or generosity

7.153   In the law of landlord and tenant generosity has never been left to be its own dubious reward. In the classic case of *Marcroft Wagons Ltd v Smith*,[1] a landlord, acting in response to 'the ordinary decencies of human life',[2] had allowed the daughter of his now deceased tenants to remain in occupation in the immediate aftermath of her double bereavement, paying the same rent as had obtained under those tenancies. The Court of Appeal was unwilling to penalise the landlord's compassionate 'indulgence' by imposing on him the strictures of Rent Act control,[3] and the Court therefore rejected the daughter's contention that she had acquired a new tenancy.[4] This decision set the pattern for a number of cases in which occupancy motivated by altruism has been held, except in instances of explicitly granted tenancy,[5] to give rise to a mere licence.[6]

1   [1951] 2 KB 496.
2   [1951] 2 KB 496 at 502.
3   Evershed MR was particularly anxious that the courts should do nothing which might inhibit or stultify the human impulse towards altruism (see [1951] 2 KB 496 at 501). On closer analysis it is not always easy to understand why the fact that a particular transaction has been induced by friendship or generosity should necessarily bring the transaction within an exceptional category. Indeed, it has been trenchantly observed that until the effect of the transaction has been determined, it is impossible to appreciate the extent of the grantor's generosity or to know quite how far the ties of friendship have carried him (see *Radaich v Smith* (1959) 101 CLR 209 at 220 per Taylor J).
4   In *Street v Mountford* [1985] AC 809 at 820D, the House of Lords approved this decision as one in which the parties evidenced no intention to contract at all, but the ruling is equally explicable on the footing that the relevant occupation did not confer a 'stake' in the land or constitute 'exclusive possession' in any true legal sense. The disputed occupancy had an entirely personal character.
5   It should not be assumed that an occupancy coloured by circumstances of friendship or generosity always gives rise to a licence (see e g *Sopwith v Stutchbury* (1983) 17 HLR 50 at 55 (express grant of tenancy to friend in aftermath of broken marriage)).
6   In *Turner v Burton* (Unreported, Court of Appeal, 12 March 1985), a mere revocable licence was found where the occupier had initially asked for accommodation for 'one or two weeks at most' and was then allowed to stay on for a few more weeks because he had lost his job. See also *West Wiltshire CC v Snelgrove* (1998) 30 HLR 57 at 60–62.

Gentleman's agreement

7.154   In some cases of casually permitted occupation, the occupier's status, not being that of a trespasser, is simply that of a licensee.[1] In *Garland v Johnson*,[2] for example, a flat-owner who had recently been the victim of a burglary reached a 'gentleman's agreement' with a casual acquaintance under which the latter was allowed to occupy the former's flat during his absence abroad. The Court of Appeal upheld the existence of a mere licence, partly on the ground that the occupancy was a personal occupancy 'in the role of a caretaker or a friend looking after the place',[3] and partly because the agreed payments to be made by the occupier were so minimal as to fall far short of an economic rent.[4] Eveleigh LJ declared that the occupier had no 'stake in the land', but had merely been permitted, on part-payment of 'expenses', to occupy the flat 'as a precaution against burglars'.[5] The owner had not sought commercial gain but merely an occupier whom he could trust.[6]

1   See e g *Holt v Wellington* (1996) 71 P & CR D40 ('no intention to create any legal relationship' between a young handicapped person and the owner who provided temporary accommodation for her under a local authority Sympathetic Landladies Scheme for the adult care of vulnerable people).
2   Unreported, Court of Appeal, 24 February 1982.
3   'Caretaker's agreements' of this kind seem to have been long accepted in Ireland as giving rise only to a licence (see *Davies v Hilliard* (1967) 101 ILTR 50 at 56; *Gatien Motor Co Ltd v Continental Oil Co of Ireland Ltd* [1979] IR 406 at 421).

4   See e g *West Wiltshire CC v Snelgrove* (1998) 30 HLR 57 at 60–62 (mere licence created by
     payments in respect of food and utilities). See [1999] Conv 53 (Jill Morgan).
5   Once again, the element of overall control seems to have been a decisive factor. Eveleigh LJ
     noted that the parties had 'treated the place ... in their mutual contemplation, not as the
     [occupier's] flat but as the [owner's] home.'
6   'The grant of a legal right cannot be referable to an extra-legal relationship' (*LB of Camden v
     Shortlife Community Housing Ltd* (1992) 90 LGR 358 at 372 per Millett J).

The 'tolerated trespasser'

7.155   Another hiatus of contractual intent arises where a social landlord's
'humane and reasonable' exercise of its housing functions requires that indul-
gences of various kinds be granted to its tenants in order to reflect changes in
their circumstances.[1] The Housing Act 1985 permits the court to suspend or
postpone the execution of a possession order made against a secure tenant,
normally subject to the payment by the tenant of 'arrears of rent (if any) and
rent ... in respect of occupation after the termination of the tenancy (mesne
profits).'[2] In *Burrows v Brent LBC*[3] the House of Lords held that no tenancy or
licence arises where a local authority landlord, having obtained a possession
order against a defaulting tenant, allows that tenant to remain in occupation so
long as all instalments of rent arrears and future rent are paid. In such
circumstances of 'limbo',[4] the court imputes no intention to create any legal
relationship between the parties.[5] Whilst the threat of eviction hangs over his or
her head, the former tenant is simply characterised as 'a trespasser whom the
landlord has agreed not to evict – a "tolerated trespasser".'[6] The status is an
anomalous concomitant of severely pressured regimes of modern public housing.[7] The tolerated trespasser's possession, although 'precarious', is not wrongful and may well be exclusive.[8] The tolerated trespasser is, in fact, no 'mere
trespasser'.[9] He remains in occupation, not in pursuance of contract, but by
reason of a 'rule of law.'[10]

1   *Burrows v Brent LBC* [1996] 1 WLR 1448 at 1454A–E per Lord Browne-Wilkinson. See also
     Pemberton v Southwark LBC [2000] 1 WLR 1672 at 1681D–E per Roch LJ; *Leadenhall
     Residential 2 Ltd v Stirling* [2002] 1 WLR 499 at [12] per Lloyd J.
2   HA 1985, s 85(2)–(3)(a).
3   [1996] 1 WLR 1448 at 1455B–1456A. See A Cafferkey, [1998] Conv 39.
4   [1996] 1 WLR 1448 at 1455A–D per Lord Browne-Wilkinson. The period of suspension of the
     secure tenancy is now widely referred to as the 'limbo period' (see e g *Pemberton v South-
     wark LBC* [2000] 1 WLR 1672 at 1678G per Roch LJ). The court has discretion, pursuant to
     HA 1985, s 85(4), to discharge the possession order against the tenant and thereby revive the
     secure tenancy together with its covenants (see e g *Lambeth LBC v Rogers* [2000] 03 EG 127 at
     131–132).
5   The tolerated trespasser enjoys none of the rights of a tenant in respect of landlord's repairs
     or liability for defective premises; nor is the landlord entitled to evict the tolerated trespasser
     for any breach of the covenants contained in the secure tenancy agreement. The tolerated
     trespasser can be evicted only for breach of the conditions on which he or she was allowed to
     remain in the premises (see *Burrows v Brent LBC* [1996] 1 WLR 1448 at 1452F–G per
     Lord Browne-Wilkinson; *Pemberton v Southwark LBC* [2000] 1 WLR 1672 at 1678A–C).
6   [1996] 1 WLR 1448 at 1455C per Lord Browne-Wilkinson. See also *Colchester BC v Smith*
     [1991] Ch 448 at 485C–D; *Greenwich LBC v Regan* (1996) 72 P & CR 507 at 516–518, 520–521;
     Pemberton v Southwark LBC [2000] 1 WLR 1672 at 1677A–D; *Leadenhall Residential 2 Ltd v*

Stirling [2002] 1 WLR 499 at [36] per Latham LJ (occupation 'referable only to forbearance ... and not the grant of any new entitlement to exclusive possession').

7 See *Pemberton v Southwark LBC* [2000] 1 WLR 1672 at 1683A per Clarke LJ ('the tolerated trespasser is a recent, somewhat bizarre, addition to the *dramatis personae* of the law'). See Susan Bright, 'The Concept of the Tolerated Trespasser: An Analysis' (2003) 119 LQR 495.

8 *Pemberton v Southwark LBC* [2000] 1 WLR 1672 at 1682C per Roch LJ.

9 See *Pemberton v Southwark LBC* [2000] 1 WLR 1672 at 1683G per Clarke LJ, 1685G per Sir Christopher Slade.

10 *Burrows v Brent LBC* [1996] 1 WLR 1448 at 1455E per Lord Browne-Wilkinson. The tolerated trespasser therefore has a sufficient right of occupation to enable him to bring an action against the landlord council in trespass and/or nuisance (see *Pemberton v Southwark LBC* [2000] 1 WLR 1672 at 1682G–H per Roch LJ, 1684H–1685A per Clarke LJ, 1685H–1686A per Sir Christopher Slade [**para 3.51**]).

Exclusive occupation explicable as someone else's 'possession'

7.156 Exclusiveness of *occupation* does not indicate unambiguously the existence of a tenancy. The mere fact of exclusive occupation may be wholly consistent with a right of exclusive *possession* vested in someone else[1]; and it is only exclusive possession which constitutes an unequivocal indicium of tenancy.[2] In certain circumstances it becomes apparent that one person's sole occupation of land is explicable on the basis of, and by reference to, another's exclusive possession. Accordingly there remains, outside the landlord–tenant relationship, a range of cases where overall territorial control of the land is reserved, in reality, not for the actual occupier, but for the landowner himself.[3] In such instances the landowner retains possession in the strict legal sense, but his possession casts a shadow in the form of a factum of exclusive occupation enjoyed by the occupier. Appearances can nevertheless be hugely deceptive, since exclusive occupation at a rent often closely mimics tenancy. Amongst the forms of exclusive occupancy omitted from the ambit of the modern landlord–tenant relationship are the following inter-related categories of case. In each, a vital element of territorial dominion is retained by someone *other than* the occupier, albeit that the latter seems superficially to be in possession.

1 *Western Australia v Ward* (2002) 191 ALR 1 at [518] per McHugh J.

2 Clarity in this area is not assisted by the fact that the courts have often used the terms 'exclusive possession' and 'exclusive occupation' as if they were interchangeable (see e g *Street v Mountford* [1985] AC 809 at 826E per Lord Templeman; *Antoniades v Villiers* [1990] 1 AC 417 at 459A–B, F, 460F per Lord Templeman; *Bruton v London & Quadrant Housing Trust* [2000] 1 AC 406 at 413E–G per Lord Hoffmann). See also *Aslan v Murphy* [1990] 1 WLR 766 at 770E–G, where Lord Donaldson of Lymington MR spoke of a 'spectrum of exclusivity ranging from the occupier of a detached property under a full repairing lease, who is without doubt a tenant, to the overnight occupier of a hotel bedroom who, however up-market the hotel, is without doubt a lodger.' There is a strong argument for regarding the element of 'exclusive possession' as being truly present only in a lease or tenancy (see e g [1986] JSWL 46 at 49 (D Hoath)).

3 See *Street v Mountford* [1985] AC 809 at 818F per Lord Templeman.

Service occupancy

7.157 In *Street v Mountford*[1] the House of Lords expressly pointed to service occupancy as a form of occupancy entirely personal to the occupier and therefore incompatible with the relationship of landlord and tenant.[2] As Lord Templeman observed, 'the possession and occupation of the servant is treated as the possession and occupation of the master and the relationship of landlord and tenant is not created.'[3] Thus an employee who is required to occupy his employer's premises for the better performance of his duties ranks as a mere licensee.[4] The employee's occupancy – however exclusive its nature – is entirely personal to him and is ancillary to the specific relationship created by his employment.[5] The position may be different if the employee's occupancy of employer-owned accommodation is merely incidental to, rather than contingent upon, his employment (ie if the accommodation might just as readily have been allocated to a non-employee). Here the courts seem much more willing to identify the status of the accommodation in terms of tenancy.[6]

1   [1985] AC 809 at 818E–G, 827A.
2   Lord Templeman also referred, with similar effect, to 'occupancy referable to the holding of an office' ([1985] AC 809 at 827A).
3   [1985] AC 809 at 818F–G. See also *Wrotham Park Settled Estates v Naylor* (1991) 62 P & CR 233 at 237 per Hoffmann J.
4   [1985] AC 809 at 818F–G. See *Glasgow Corporation v Johnstone* [1965] AC 609 at 626E–G; *Scrimgeour v Waller* (1981) 257 EG 61 at 64; *Royal Philanthropic Society v County* (1985) 276 EG 1068 at 1072; *Norris v Checksfield* [1991] 1 WLR 1241 at 1246A per Woolf LJ; *H A Warner Pty Ltd v Williams* (1946) 73 CLR 421 at 429 per Dixon J; *Australian Convention & Exhibition Services Pty Ltd v Sydney City Council* (1998) 9 BPR 16753 at 16756–16757 per Handley JA.
5   See eg *Ramsbottom v Snelson* [1948] 1 KB 473 at 477 (chauffeur or gardener); *Carroll v Manek and Bank of India* (2000) 79 P & CR 173 at 184 (hotel manager); *Macann v Annett* [1948] NZLR 116 at 120; *Snell v Mitchell* [1951] NZLR 1 at 3 ('live-in' housekeepers).
6   A tenancy classification is not precluded by the fact that the employer-provided accommodation is part of the employee's recompense for his services or leads to a deduction from his wages (see *H A Warner Pty Ltd v Williams* (1946) 73 CLR 421 at 429 per Dixon J).

Accommodation based on charitable or therapeutic motivations

7.158   In *Street v Mountford*[1] Lord Templeman also indicated that the occupier who is 'an object of charity' will normally be excluded from the status of tenant.[2] However dubious the nomenclature, this reference to 'charity' has been construed as covering accommodation provided through various socialised forms of charity underpinned by therapeutic motivations.[3] In *Brent People's Housing Association Ltd v Winsmore*,[4] for example, mere licensee status was accorded to an occupier who lived in a house managed by a 'single homeless project group' sponsored by a registered (and necessarily charitable) housing association. The absence of any right of exclusive possession vested in the occupier was underscored by the fact that all the residents in the house lived under the close supervision of local authority social workers who were employed full-time at the house to provide support, advice and general assistance.[5] As Lord Templeman later emphasised in *Westminster CC v Clarke*,[6] a claim of independent possession on the part of a resident in a hostel is incompatible with the exercise of far-reaching supervisory control by the owner or its agents.[7]

1   [1985] AC 809 at 818E.

2   The undefined and open-ended category of 'charity' merges with cases of accommodation based on 'friendship or generosity' **[para 7.153]**.

3   See e g *Gray v Taylor* [1998] 1 WLR 1093 at 1097H–1098B (occupancy of almshouse).

4   Unreported, County Court, 20 November 1985. See (1986) 17 Jiro (Ed Supp) No 1, p ii.

5   The denial of tenant status probably extends to many other kinds of sheltered or 'special needs' accommodation. See e g *Holt v Wellington* (1996) 71 P & CR D40 (handicapped person housed under adult care scheme); *Noble v Centacare* (2003) 150 ACTR at [45] (resident in crisis support centre).

6   [1992] 2 AC 288 at 301H–302A **[para 7.134]**.

7   See also the denial of tenant status in *R v South Middlesex Rent Tribunal, ex p Beswick* (1976) 32 P & CR 67 (long-term resident in YWCA hostel); *Trustees of the Alcoholic Recovery Project v Farrell* (1976) LAG Bulletin 259 (resident in rehabilitative hostel); but compare *Bruton v London & Quadrant Housing Trust* [2000] 1 AC 406 at 413H–414F (where the occupier of charitable housing trust accommodation was not subject to supervision and clearly had exclusive possession).

Occupancy of a domestic or quasi-familial character

7.159   Informal arrangements for occupancy within a familial or quasi-familial context have always been liable to be analysed in terms of revocable licence rather than tenancy.[1] Such circumstances commonly disclose no grant of 'independent possession' to the occupier[2] and sometimes the parties may also lack any intention to form a legally enforceable relationship.[3] In *Barnes v Barratt*,[4] for instance, the Court of Appeal declined to attach the label of tenancy to an arrangement under which a couple were provided with exclusive occupation of three rooms in a house in return for their performance of cooking and other domestic services for the owner and their payment of certain household bills. There existed here merely a 'personal licence to occupy', not least, as Sachs LJ emphasised, because the situation 'was closely akin to those produced by family arrangements to share a house.'[5]

1   See e g *Booker v Palmer* [1942] 2 All ER 674 at 677C (evacuees); *Cobb v Lane* [1952] 1 All ER 1199 at 1201A (brother). See also *Errington v Errington and Woods* [1952] 1 KB 290 at 298.

2   See e g *Peakin v Peakin* [1895] 2 IR 359 at 361–362 (occupation by owner's sisters), although mere family relationship does not automatically preclude a finding of tenancy (see *Nunn v Dalrymple* (1990) 59 P & CR 231 at 239–240 per Stocker LJ).

3   *Street v Mountford* [1985] AC 809 at 824E–F. See also *Leadenhall Residential 2 Ltd v Stirling* [2002] 1 WLR 499 at [15].

4   [1970] 2 QB 657.

5   [1970] 2 QB 657 at 670A. Sharing between family members often creates a mere licence (see *David v LB of Lewisham* (1977) 34 P & CR 112 at 115–116; *Armstrong v Armstrong* [1970] 1 NSWR 133 at 135). See also *Heslop v Burns* [1974] 1 WLR 1241 at 1252G, where the relationship between the owner and the occupiers was not only 'very akin to a family arrangement' but also marked by an extreme degree of generosity on the part of the former towards the latter. There seems to have been some ground for believing that the owner had formed a romantic attraction for one of the occupiers (see [1974] 1 WLR 1241 at 1244C).

7.160   The critical issue in such cases is whether the occupancy has detracted from the landowner's exercise of overall control over the premises and the conduct which takes place there. Frequently the domestic or quasi-familial character of the arrangement positively reinforces the fact that, far from possessory control having been transferred to the occupier, the latter remains intimately subject to supervision and regulation by the owner.[1] In *Oxford Overseas Student Housing Association v Mukherjee*,[2] for example, Bingham LJ upheld the licensee status of a resident in a hostel set up with the 'laudable objective' of providing accommodation for overseas students 'arriving in a strange country and in a strange town with no friends and contacts'. The Court of Appeal attached great significance to the fact that the hostel warden retained a general power of surveillance to ensure the observance of relevant conditions of occupation.

1   See e g *Abbeyfield (Harpenden) Society Ltd v Woods* [1968] 1 WLR 374 at 376G–H per Lord Denning MR ('[t]he whole arrangement was ... personal in nature').
2   Unreported, Court of Appeal, 21 November 1989.

Occupancy of the 'lodger'

7.161   In *Street v Mountford* the House of Lords provided one further, and critically important, instance of residential occupation which coexists with exclusive possession vested in another. Even if a residential occupier enjoys rights of exclusive occupation for a term, he may still be precluded from the status of tenant if he falls into the category of a *lodger*.[1] Lord Templeman drew a crucial distinction between the 'tenant' and the 'lodger' based on the location of overall control in respect of the premises which he occupies.[2] The lodger lacks a vital territorial stake in the premises which he occupies: he is entitled to live in the premises 'but cannot call the place his own.'[3] In all his conduct on the premises the lodger is subject to the supervisory authority of the owner, who at all times 'retains his character of master of the house, and ... retains the general control and dominion over the whole house'.[4]

1   [1985] AC 809 at 817H–818D. See *Western Australia v Ward* (2002) 191 ALR 1 at [519], [522] per McHugh J.
2   Indeed Lord Templeman went so far as to say that 'save in exceptional circumstances' the only live question in the determination of the status of a residential occupancy is henceforth the inquiry 'whether ... the occupier is a lodger or a tenant' ([1985] AC 809 at 827E–F).
3   [1985] AC 809 at 818A. See *Allan v Liverpool Overseers* (1874) LR 9 QB 180 at 191–192.
4   *Thompson v Ward* (1871) LR 6 CP 327 at 361 per Bovill CJ. Other early legal definitions of the term 'lodger' similarly emphasised the idea that lodgers 'submit themselves to [the owner's] control' (*Ancketill v Baylis* (1882) 10 QBD 577 at 586). In *Bradley v Baylis* (1881) 8 QBD 195 at 219, Jessel MR saw the owner of lodgings as one who 'gives to the "inmates" ... merely a right of ingress and egress, and retains to himself the general control, with ... a right to interfere, a right to turn out trespassers, and so on.' For further use in this context of the terminology of 'inmate', see *Noblett & Mansfield v Manley* [1952] SASR 155 at 158.

7.162   An occupier is a 'lodger' if the 'landlord' provides attendance or services 'which require the landlord or his servants to exercise unrestricted access to and use of the premises.'[1] In such circumstances it is not the provision of services or attendance which negatives the possibility of tenancy.[2] The decisive factor is the absence of any right in the occupier to resist intrusion: it is the owner who 'retains possession' precisely in order to supply the services or attendance.[3] The essence of the lodger relationship lies in the freedom of the owner to enter the premises at will[4] even when the lodger is not present to let him in.[5] This facility of unrestricted entry, whether for the performance of cleaning duties or for other purposes, precludes any claim of exclusive possession by the occupier[6] unless the element of attendance or services is so minimal as to constitute a sham[7] or is provided by the owner qua independent contractor under a separate agreement rather than qua landlady under the contract of occupancy.[8]

1   *Street v Mountford* [1985] AC 809 at 818A. See also *Antoniades v Villiers* [1990] 1 AC 417 at 459F–G per Lord Templeman. This judicial emphasis on the relevance of attendance or services has led on occasion to the most fearful foisting of unwanted attendance or services upon occupiers (see e g *Crancour Ltd v Da Silvaesa* (1986) 52 P & CR 204 (promise to provide a housekeeper, cleaning and lighting of common parts, window cleaning, telephone, collection of rubbish and the laundering of bed linen)).

2   See e g Rent Act 1977, s 7 **[para 14.316]**. It appears that in exceptional cases a residential occupier may still be a licensee even though not in receipt of services or attendance (see *Brooker Settled Estates Ltd v Ayers* (1987) 54 P & CR 165 at 169–170; *Nicolaou v Pitt* (1989) 21 HLR 487 at 493 per Mustill LJ).

3   *Antoniades v Villiers* [1990] 1 AC 417 at 459F–G per Lord Templeman. Tenancy is precluded by the fact that the 'owner retains control and unrestricted access' ([1990] 1 AC 417 at 467A–B per Lord Oliver of Aylmerton). The mere fact that contractually stipulated attendance or services were declined by the occupier or were never actually provided by the owner does not necessarily convert a licence into a tenancy (*Crancour Ltd v Da Silvaesa* (1986) 52 P & CR 204 at 212, 230; *Huwyler v Ruddy* (1996) 28 HLR 550 at 556; *Uratemp Ventures Ltd v Collins & Carrell* (2000) 79 P & CR D18 at D19).

4   *Vandersteen v Agius* (1992) 65 P & CR 266 at 273.

5   See *Crancour Ltd v Da Silvaesa* (1986) 52 P & CR 204 at 211 per Ralph Gibson LJ; *Huwyler v Ruddy* (1996) 28 HLR 550 at 554 per Peter Gibson LJ.

6   In these circumstances the retention of a set of keys for entry at convenience points strongly towards mere licence (see *Huwyler v Ruddy* (1996) 28 HLR 550 at 554; *Uratemp Ventures Ltd v Collins & Carrell* (2000) 79 P & CR D18).

7   See *Huwyler v Ruddy* (1996) 28 HLR 550 at 554 (20 minutes of cleaning per week not a 'sham' obligation).

8   See eg *Vandersteen v Agius* (1992) 65 P & CR 266 at 273.

7.163 The 'lodger' classification endorsed in *Street v Mountford* simply confirms existing authority relating to the status of serviced accommodation. Such circumstances disclose a mere licence since the occupancy conferred is so clearly personal to the occupier and the supervision of his activities so intrusive as to exclude any possibility that he has an estate in the land.[1] Traditional examples within this category include the long-term hotel resident,[2] the casual hotel guest,[3] the lodger in a furnished room,[4] the flat-sharer in a serviced bedroom,[5] the student in the bed-sit or college hostel,[6] and the resident in an old people's home.[7] All of these persons enjoy at best a mere 'exclusive occupation' as distinct from any right of 'exclusive possession'.[8] The possibility of tenancy is kept alive, however, where there is no contractual undertaking to provide the occupier with intrusive attendance or services[9] or if in practice the contracted services or attendance can be provided without the necessity of actual entry into the occupier's premises.[10] In such circumstances an express reservation of limited rights for the landlord to enter and view the state of the premises or to repair and maintain 'only serves to emphasise the fact that the grantee is entitled to exclusive possession and is a tenant.'[11]

1   *Antoniades v Villiers* [1990] 1 AC 417 at 459B–D per Lord Templeman, 466E–G per Lord Oliver of Aylmerton.

2   *Appah v Parncliffe Investments Ltd* [1964] 1 WLR 1064 at 1071; *Luganda v Service Hotels Ltd* [1969] 2 Ch 209 at 217D; *Mehta v Royal Bank of Scotland* [1999] 3 EGLR 153 at 156A. See also *Re Canadian Pacific Hotels Ltd and Hodges* (1979) 96 DLR (3d) 313 at 318 (hotel retained 'a general, over-all control of the property').

3   *Brillouet v Landless* (1995) 28 HLR 836 at 840. The hotel guest may enjoy a temporarily exclusive use of his room but does not have overall territorial control (see *Bradley v Baylis* (1881) 8 QBD 195 at 216 per Jessel MR; *Aslan v Murphy* [1990] 1 WLR 766 at 770E–G per Lord Donaldson of Lymington MR).

4   *Marchant v Charters* [1977] 1 WLR 1181 at 1185G–H ('attractive bachelor service apartments', ie bed-sits each with its own gas-ring). This decision was approved in *Street v Mountford* [1985] AC 809 at 824G–825C. See also *Maxwell v Brown* (1982) 35 OR (2d) 770 at 772, where the rules and restrictions imposed by the owner of a rooming house as to cooking privileges and the number of occupants were held sufficient to deny the occupier a 'stake in the room'. Compare *Guppys (Bridport) Ltd v Brookling* (1984) 269 EG 846 at 850, where the character of the occupancy depended largely on whether the owner's 'janitor' had exercised effective control over the admission of visitors – particularly of the opposite sex.

5   *Huwyler v Ruddy* (1996) 28 HLR 550 at 556.

6   *R v Tao* [1977] QB 141 at 146F–G (exclusive occupation in King's College Cambridge hostel).

7   *Abbeyfield (Harpenden) Society Ltd v Woods* [1968] 1 WLR 374 at 376F–H, as approved in *Street v Mountford* [1985] AC 809 at 824B.

8   See *Luganda v Service Hotels Ltd* [1969] 2 Ch 209 at 219D–F.

9   *Street v Mountford* [1985] AC 809 at 818C (it was conceded at 818D, 826B–C that there had been no provision of attendance or services). The mere absence of any contracted provision of attendance or services does not guarantee the existence of a tenancy (see *Brooker Settled Estates Ltd v Ayers* (1987) 54 P & CR 165 at 168–169).

10   *Crancour Ltd v Da Silvaesa* (1986) 52 P & CR 204 at 211–212, 216–217 per Ralph Gibson LJ.

11   *Street v Mountford* [1985] AC 809 at 818C–D. See also *Dellneed Ltd v Chin* (1987) 53 P & CR 172 at 184; *Antoniades v Villiers* [1990] 1 AC 417 at 459G–H per Lord Templeman.

Exclusive possession otherwise than for a fixed or periodic term

7.164   The landlord–tenant relationship is established only where there is exclusive possession 'for a fixed or periodic term certain.'[1] It follows that certain categories of occupier, even if equipped with exclusive possession or 'de facto occupation'[2] of a site, can never claim any lease or tenancy precisely because their presence on the land has neither the finality of a fixed term nor the periodic quality which might have been imparted by the regular payment of rent. Examples of such occupancy are provided by the building contractor who is entrusted with the security of a construction site for the duration of building works[3] and the occupier under an indefinite agreement involving no payment of rent.[4] Here the occupancy can take effect only as a licence.

1   *Street v Mountford* [1985] AC 809 at 818E per Lord Templeman. See also *Prudential Assurance Co Ltd v London Residuary Body* [1992] 2 AC 386 at 390C per Lord Templeman ('exclusive possession and profit of land for some determinate period').

2   See *Manchester Airport Plc v Dutton* [2000] QB 133 at 147F–G per Laws LJ.

3   See e g *Hounslow LBC v Twickenham Garden Developments Ltd* [1971] Ch 233 at 268D–G.

4   See e g *Ashburn Anstalt v Arnold* [1989] Ch 1 at 9D–E.

Interim accommodation in the context of homelessness

7.165 Exclusive possession outside the landlord–tenant relationship may also be enjoyed by an occupier whose provision of interim or limited accommodation is referable to the fulfilment by a local housing authority of its statutory duty under the homeless persons legislation.[1] Although granted 'exclusive possession' of council accommodation pending the outcome of a 'homelessness inquiry'[2] or the securing of alternative accommodation after repossession,[3] such a person enjoys merely a licence unless the local authority has quite explicitly offered him a 'tenancy'.[4]

1 See Housing Act 1996, Pt VII (formerly Housing Act 1985, Pt III).
2 *South Holland DC v Keyte* (1985) 19 HLR 97 at 101–103. See also *Brennan v Lambeth LBC* (1998) 30 HLR 481 at 485–486.
3 *Ogwr BC v Dykes* [1989] 1 WLR 295 at 302H–303B per Purchas LJ. See [1989] Conv 194 (J E M).
4 See *Eastleigh BC v Walsh* [1985] 1 WLR 525 at 530F–H.

IDENTIFICATION OF THE 'NATURE AND QUALITY' OF AN OCCUPANCY

7.166 Even when the general parameters of the notion of tenancy are established, it sometimes remains difficult to know whether a particular agreement, on its true construction, confers a right of 'exclusive possession' which is strictly referable to the existence of a tenancy.[1] The court must therefore scrutinise the 'nature and quality'[2] of any disputed occupancy in order to determine whether the occupier has been granted the right to 'exclusive possession' in the relevant sense.[3] The task of the court is to ascertain the 'true bargain between the parties'[4] and this task may prove highly elusive.[5]

1 See *Street v Mountford* [1985] AC 809 at 826G–H per Lord Templeman. The difficulty is intensified where the relevant agreement is purely oral. Here the existence of a right of exclusive possession can be established by an examination of the 'circumstances and facts of the case' (*Smith v Northside Developments Ltd* (1988) 55 P & CR 164 at 167 per Arnold P).
2 *Marchant v Charters* [1977] 1 WLR 1181 at 1185G per Lord Denning MR; *Crancour Ltd v Da Silvaesa* (1986) 52 P & CR 204 at 229 per Purchas LJ.
3 *Street v Mountford* [1985] AC 809 at 825B–C.
4 *Aslan v Murphy* [1990] 1 WLR 766 at 770C per Lord Donaldson of Lymington MR.
5 The guidance of *Street v Mountford* notwithstanding, the distinction between tenancy and licence admits of 'no simple all-embracing test ... The search for such a test would be a search for a chimaera' (*Mehta v Royal Bank of Scotland* [1999] 3 EGLR 153 at 156B–C). See also *Hadjiloucas v Crean* [1988] 1 WLR 1006 at 1025B per Mustill LJ.

Irrelevant or ambivalent factors

7.167 The determination whether a given occupancy constitutes a lease or a licence is ultimately 'a question of law ... to be decided upon the basis of the primary facts.'[1] The difficulty facing the court is that many of the 'primary facts' remain neutral or ambivalent as between tenancy and licence. It is, for instance, irrelevant whether a disputed occupancy is permanent or merely temporary[2] or whether the premises are furnished or unfurnished.[3] It is of no significance that the parties refer to the money consideration for the occupancy as 'rent' or even make use of a 'rent book'.[4] The possible application of protective legislation is entirely irrelevant to the problem of determining the legal effect of the rights granted by an agreement for residential occupation.[5] Nor, in general, is any 'decisive importance' attached to the exercise or failure to exercise rights provided for in the parties' agreement.[6] Thus, even though there has in fact been no performance of a contractual obligation to provide the occupier with 'attendance', the mere fact that such services were stipulated for in the parties' agreement may be effective to classify their status in terms of licence rather than tenancy.[7]

1   *Carden v Choudhury* (Unreported, Court of Appeal, 29 February 1984) per Arnold P.
2   *Marchant v Charters* [1977] 1 WLR 1181 at 1185F. The mere effluxion of time cannot convert a licensee into a tenant (see *Crancour Ltd v Da Silvaesa* (1986) 52 P & CR 204 at 212 per Ralph Gibson LJ).
3   *Marchant v Charters* [1977] 1 WLR 1181 at 1185F.
4   See *Winter Garden Theatre (London) Ltd v Millennium Productions Ltd* [1948] AC 173 at 188 per Viscount Simon. Such terminology provides no more than a 'convenient means of verbal reference to the payments' (*Street v Mountford* (1984) 49 P & CR 324 at 328 per Slade LJ). See also *Lewis v Bell* [1985] 1 NSWLR 731 at 738G.
5   *Street v Mountford* [1985] AC 809 at 819G–H per Lord Templeman; *Crancour Ltd v Da Silvaesa* (1986) 52 P & CR 204 at 214–215, 230; *Antoniades v Villiers* [1990] 1 AC 417 at 445E–F per Bingham LJ.
6   *Crancour Ltd v Da Silvaesa* (1986) 52 P & CR 204 at 230 per Purchas LJ. See also *Hadjiloucas v Crean* [1988] 1 WLR 1006 at 1024F–1025A per Mustill LJ.
7   *Crancour Ltd v Da Silvaesa* (1986) 52 P & CR 204 at 222 per Nicholls LJ. Compare, however, *Aslan v Murphy (No 1)* [1990] 1 WLR 766 at 773G–H per Lord Donaldson of Lymington MR.

Consideration of documents and circumstances

7.168   In seeking to assess whether the 'nature and quality' of an occupancy disclose a grant of 'exclusive possession', the court looks to the substance of the disputed transaction and not merely to its external form.[1] In determining whether the grantee was entitled to 'exclusive possession' or merely to the use of land 'for limited purposes', the court must consider 'the purpose of the grant, the terms of the grant and the surrounding circumstances.'[2]

1   This principle finds universal acceptance (see eg *Antoniades v Villiers* [1990] 1 AC 417 at 466G–H per Lord Oliver of Aylmerton. See likewise *Shell-Mex & BP Ltd v Manchester Garages Ltd* [1971] 1 WLR 612 at 618D–E per Buckley LJ; *Gatien Motor Co Ltd v Continental Oil Co of Ireland Ltd* [1979] IR 406 at 414, 420; *KJRR Pty Ltd v Commr of State Revenue* [1999] 2 VR 174 at 181 per Tadgell JA).
2   *Street v Mountford* [1985] AC 809 at 817G–H per Lord Templeman. Powerful indications that an instrument is a lease rather a licence are found in the use of the word 'demise'; in any provision which defines the circumstances in which the grantor can enter the land or the premises; and in any term which confers a right of re-entry and forfeiture in the event of default (see *Western Australia v Ward* (2002) 191 ALR 1 at [485], [490], [511]–[513] per McHugh J).

Careful construction of the substance

7.169   The written terms of any agreement are always 'of prime importance' and frequently require 'a meticulous perusal'.[1] The court must apply the techniques of construction of the ordinary law of contract,[2] although judges are understandably reluctant to 'award marks for drafting' or to 'draw up a "shopping list" of clauses' in any given agreement as indicative of either tenancy or licence.[3] Nevertheless careful construction of any relevant written agreement usually indicates whether a right of exclusive possession has been genuinely conferred on or genuinely denied to the occupier concerned.[4] The issue is one of substance: if the agreement confers and imposes on the grantee in substance the rights and obligations of a tenant, and on the grantor in substance the rights and obligations of a landlord, then this finding is conclusive in favour of tenancy.[5] If this is not the case, the occupier must be a licensee.

1   *Hadjiloucas v Crean* [1988] 1 WLR 1006 at 1022E–F per Mustill LJ. See similarly *Crancour Ltd v Da Silvaesa* (1986) 52 P & CR 204 at 229 per Purchas LJ.
2   *Hadjiloucas v Crean* [1988] 1 WLR 1006 at 1022G per Mustill LJ.
3   *Crancour Ltd v Da Silvaesa* (1986) 52 P & CR 204 at 230 per Purchas LJ.
4   Imprecision in the definition of the area to be occupied militates against a finding of tenancy (see e g *Chaka Holdings Pty Ltd v Sunsim Pty Ltd* (1987) 10 BPR 18171 at 18176 per Young J).
5   *Addiscombe Garden Estates Ltd v Crabbe* [1958] 1 QB 513 at 522 per Jenkins LJ. Parker LJ thought, for example, that the inclusion of a covenant for quiet enjoyment was 'inconsistent with the document being a licence' ([1958] 1 QB 513 at 529). See also *Rental Bond Board v Bayman Development Pty Ltd* (1985) 3 BPR 9670 at 9676 per Street CJ.

Implicit affirmation of exclusive possession

7.170   The presence or absence of a right of exclusive possession may be inferable from some of the written terms of an occupancy agreement. In *Lewis v Bell*,[1] for instance, the Court of Appeal of New South Wales pointed out the special significance of any terms bearing upon the transferability of the occupier's rights. A leasehold estate is inherently assignable to third parties; and a term which affirms the occupier's right to transfer his entitlement to a stranger carries the clear implication that the occupier has an exclusive possession sufficient to sustain such a transfer. Almost paradoxically, an express prohibition of assignment of the occupier's rights may likewise reinforce the occupier's claim to exclusive possession,[2] since the specific restraint on transfer impliedly concedes that the occupier would otherwise have been competent to alienate his rights.[3] However, a term which stipulates merely that the occupier's rights are personal to him and are for that reason non-transferable has the effect of negativing any implication of exclusive possession.[4] Similarly a term which entitles the owner at his convenience to move the occupier from one room to another within the same house clearly precludes any claim of exclusive possession which the occupier might otherwise have in respect of the room originally allocated to him.[5]

1   [1985] 1 NSWLR 731 at 735G–736A per Mahoney JA.
2   See *J A Pye (Oxford) Ltd v Graham* [2003] 1 AC 419 at [56] per Lord Browne-Wilkinson. The

inference in favour of tenancy may be less strong if licences are also regarded as assignable (see *Western Australia v Ward* (2002) 191 ALR 1 at [517] per McHugh J). Compare, however, Chapter 4 [**para 4.7**].

3   See also *Dellneed Ltd v Chin* (1987) 53 P & CR 172 at 185. References to subletting may not connote quite so clearly the existence of a tenancy (see *Lewis v Bell* [1985] 1 NSWLR 731 at 738G). See, however, *Rental Bond Board v Bayman Development Pty Ltd* (1985) 3 BPR 9670 at 9676 per Street CJ (covenant not to part with possession 'more akin to a fetter on the right of possession than the absence of such a right'). Contrast *Tower Hamlets LBC v Miah* [1992] QB 622 at 627H–628B (undertaking by occupier to do nothing to create 'any secure or other tenancy').

4   *Dresden Estates Ltd v Collinson* (1988) 55 P & CR 47 at 53 per Glidewell LJ; *Lewis v Bell* [1985] 1 NSWLR 731 at 735G per Mahoney JA.

5   *Crancour Ltd v Da Silvaesa* (1986) 52 P & CR 204 at 222.

Non-residential lettings

7.171   The task of distinguishing between tenancy and licence sometimes arises outside the residential sector in relation to other forms of occupancy. Although classification in the non-residential sector cannot, of course, rest upon the borderline between 'tenant' and 'lodger',[1] the courts have been prepared in the context of commercial premises[2] and agricultural land[3] to refer to broadly the same indicia which identify a tenancy in the residential sphere.[4]

1   See e g *Dresden Estates Ltd v Collinson* (1988) 55 P & CR 47 at 52 per Glidewell LJ.

2   See e g *London & Associated Investment Trust PLC v Calow* [1986] 2 EGLR 80 at 84D per Judge Paul Baker QC; *Dellneed Ltd v Chin* (1987) 53 P & CR 172 at 187. Results are not always uniform or consistent. Compare *Kewal Investments Ltd v Arthur Maiden Ltd* [1990] 1 EGLR 193 at 194G–H (no tenancy in respect of advertising panels) and *Rochester Poster Services Ltd v Dartford BC* (1991) 63 P & CR 88 at 93 (tenancy).

3   See e g *Colchester BC v Smith* [1991] Ch 448 at 483G–484A; *Ashdale Land & Property Co Ltd v Manners* [1992] 2 EGLR 5 at 8C–J. See, however, *McCarthy v Bence* [1990] 1 EGLR 1; [1991] Conv 58 (C Rodgers), 207 (M Slater).

4   See *Dellneed Ltd v Chin* (1987) 53 P & CR 172 at 185–188; *Esso Petroleum Co Ltd v Fumegrange Ltd* (1994) 68 P & CR D15 at D17.

7.172   In the business context, for instance, the courts have consistently invoked the criterion of 'overall control' as the determining factor in the identification of a tenancy.[1] In *Shell-Mex and BP Ltd v Manchester Garages Ltd*,[2] the Court of Appeal construed an agreement relating to a petrol filling station as a mere personal licence. Lord Denning MR attached particular significance to a stipulation contained in the agreement that the owners should be allowed unimpeded access to the premises, observing that this clause seemed to connote that the owners 'remain in possession themselves.'[3] Everything turns, however, on 'the nature of the transaction itself' as disclosed by the written terms of the occupancy[4] and the surrounding circumstances.[5] In *Dresden Estates Ltd v Collinson*,[6] for example, the Court of Appeal found that a business occupancy was excluded from having tenancy character by reason of express terms which, without artifice, had entitled the owner to require the occupier to transfer his occupancy to other premises belonging to the owner.[7]

1   See e g *Esso Petroleum Co Ltd v Fumegrange Ltd* (1994) 68 P & CR D15 at D17; *Venus Investments Ltd v Stocktop Ltd* [1997] EWCA Civ 1696.

2   [1971] 1 WLR 612.
3   [1971] 1 WLR 612 at 616B–C, approved in *Street v Mountford* [1985] AC 809 at 824D–E.
     Contrast *University of Reading v Johnson-Houghton* (1985) 276 EG 1353 (grantee of rights to
     train and exercise racehorses found to be entitled to exclude even the owner).
4   The absence of any right of re-entry or reservation of rights of inspection by the owner may
     point towards a mere licence (see *Venus Investments Ltd v Stocktop Ltd* [1997] EWCA Civ
     1696).
5   See also *London & Associated Investment Trust PLC v Calow* [1986] 2 EGLR 80 at 84D.
6   (1988) 55 P & CR 47 at 53–54. See [1987] Conv 220 (P F Smith).
7   See also *Smith v Northside Developments Ltd* (1988) 55 P & CR 164 at 167–168; *Fatac Ltd v
     Commissioner of Inland Revenue* [2002] 3 NZLR 648 at [46].

THE PARTIES CANNOT CONTRACT AWAY THEIR TRUE LEGAL STATUS

7.173   The borderline between lease and licence has always depended upon
the relative freedom which the courts allow to the parties to contract away their
true legal status. In view of the temptation for landlords to circumvent
protective legislation, courts have, in recent years, reacted vigorously to occupancy agreements whose principal purpose is to exploit the vulnerability of
those desperately dependent on the market in rental housing. In consequence
there is no freedom to stipulate – even by express contractual provision – for a
status at law which does not correspond to the inner reality of the parties'
dealing.

Relevance of intention

7.174   The tenancy character of arrangements for occupation is not, except in
one marginal sense, controlled by the subjective intentions of the parties. Since
a tenancy comprises at its core a contractual nexus, it is clear that the parties to
a tenancy must at least intend to enter into a legally binding contractual
relationship. Their subjective intentions are otherwise irrelevant in determining
the quality or legal status of the rights created by their contract.[1] As Lord Templeman indicated in *Street v Mountford*,[2] 'the only intention which is relevant is
the intention demonstrated by the agreement to grant exclusive possession for a
term at a rent.' The presence of a tenancy is thus a coldly objective issue of
definition.[3] Everything depends on 'the intention of the parties, objectively
ascertained by reference to the language and relevant background.'[4] The
identification of a given occupancy as a lease or a licence is ultimately a legal
question which turns on the 'primary facts'.[5] Several related consequences
follow.

1   *Crancour Ltd v Da Silvaesa* (1986) 52 P & CR 204 at 230 per Purchas LJ; *Bruton v London &
     Quadrant Housing Trust* [2000] 1 AC 406 at 413F–G per Lord Hoffmann; *Fatac Ltd v
     Commissioner of Inland Revenue* [2002] 3 NZLR 648 at [39].
2   [1985] AC 809 at 826G. See also *Royal Philanthropic Society v County* (1985) 276 EG 1068 at
     1072; *Western Australia v Ward* (2002) 191 ALR 1 at [521] per McHugh J.
3   'The question ... is not "what did the parties intend?" The question is, "What is the effect in
     law of the rights which they actually created?" ' (*AG Securities v Vaughan* [1990] 1 AC 417 at
     431G per Fox LJ).

4　*Bruton v London & Quadrant Housing Trust* [2000] 1 AC 406 at 413F per Lord Hoffmann.

5　*Carden v Choudhury* (Unreported, Court of Appeal, 29 February 1984) per Arnold P. See also *Bruton v London & Quadrant Housing Trust* [2000] 1 AC 406 at 413H per Lord Hoffmann. The issue is decided on a balance of probabilities (see *University of Reading v Johnson-Houghton* (1985) 276 EG 1353 at 1356).

Definitional intent is not conclusive

7.175　It is ultimately for the court alone to characterise, as either tenancy or licence, the terms which the parties have agreed.[1] There is a long-standing doctrine that the superficial label attached by the parties to their transaction is not definitive of its legal status.[2] The descriptive labels (e g 'lease', 'tenancy' or 'licence') applied by the parties themselves have only a persuasive and not a conclusive quality,[3] and the court retains an undoubted jurisdiction to override any appellation or 'false label' which does not correspond to the inner reality of the transaction in hand.[4] It is open to the court in appropriate circumstances to regard a transaction, whether described as a 'licence',[5] 'management agreement',[6] 'option agreement',[7] 'memorandum of agreement',[8] or otherwise, as constituting in substance a lease. Conversely the court may take the view that a supposed 'lease' or 'tenancy' comprises in truth a mere licence.[9] The definitional intent of the parties is relevant only in so far as it correctly conveys the inner substance – the jural reality – of the transaction. As Bingham LJ graphically pointed out in *Antoniades v Villiers*,[10] '[a] cat does not become a dog because the parties have agreed to call it a dog.'[11]

1　*Bruton v London & Quadrant Housing Trust* [2000] 1 AC 406 at 413G–H per Lord Hoffmann. See likewise *Fatac Ltd v Commissioner of Inland Revenue* [2002] 3 NZLR 648 at [62] (NZ Court of Appeal). '[T]he parties' description of their transaction cannot affect the substance of it' (*Ashburn Anstalt v Arnold* [1989] Ch 1 at 13B per Fox LJ). See also *Nicolaou v Pitt* (1989) 21 HLR 487 at 492 per Mustill LJ.

2　*Antoniades v Villiers* [1990] 1 AC 417 at 466H–467A per Lord Oliver of Aylmerton; *Bruton v London & Quadrant Housing Trust* [2000] 1 AC 406 at 411B per Lord Jauncey of Tullichettle; *Wik Peoples v Queensland* (1996) 187 CLR 1 at 152 per Gaudron J; *Fatac Ltd v Commissioner of Inland Revenue* [2002] 3 NZLR 648 at [39] (NZ Court of Appeal).

3　See *Aslan v Murphy* [1990] 1 WLR 766 at 770D, where Lord Donaldson of Lymington MR stated that labels 'give no guidance at all' in circumstances in which there is 'enormous pressure on the homeless to agree to any label which will facilitate the obtaining of accommodation.' See also *Guppys (Bridport) Ltd v Brookling* (1984) 269 EG 846 at 850.

4　'The court is concerned to enquire into what is the real relationship between the parties' (*Hayes v Seymour-Johns* (1981) 2 BPR 9366 at 9370).

5　See e g *Bruton v London & Quadrant Housing Trust* [2000] 1 AC 406. See also *Addiscombe Garden Estates Ltd v Crabbe* [1958] 1 QB 513 at 525; *Demuren v Seal Estates Ltd* (1978) 249 EG 440 at 444; *O'Malley v Seymour* (1978) 250 EG 1083 at 1088; *University of Reading v Johnson-Houghton* (1985) 276 EG 1353 at 1356; *Ashburn Anstalt v Arnold* [1989] Ch 1 at 13B; *Irish Shell and BP Ltd v John Costello Ltd* [1981] ILRM 66 at 71.

6　*Dellneed Ltd v Chin* (1987) 53 P & CR 172 at 183–185. See also *Greenstreet v Moorchat Ltd* (Unreported, Court of Appeal, 12 November 1982), which concerned a 'management contract' under which the occupier agreed to pay £416,000 per annum ('payable weekly') in return for the privilege of being 'manager' of an all-night cinema in Soho. The Court of Appeal construed this as a lease.

7　*Rental Bond Board v Bayman Development Pty Ltd* (1985) 3 BPR 9670 at 9676–9677.

8　*Baron Hamilton v Edgar* (1953) 162 EG 568.

9   See e g *Taylor v Caldwell* (1863) 3 B & S 826 at 832, 122 ER 309 at 312; *Clore v Theatrical Properties Ltd and Westby & Co Ltd* [1936] 3 All ER 483 at 490, 491; *R A Sanson Investments Ltd v Sanson* (Unreported, Court of Appeal, 11 March 1982).
10   [1990] 1 AC 417 at 444B.
11   Bingham LJ added, however, that 'in deciding whether an animal is a cat or a dog the parties agreement that it is a dog may not be entirely irrelevant.' This may be particularly true when construing the legal effect of the terminology consciously adopted by well-advised commercial parties. See e g *National Car Parks Ltd v Trinity Development Co (Banbury) Ltd* [2002] 2 P & CR 18 at [28]–[29] per Arden LJ (reference to 'licence' was 'relevant as a pointer').

Evasion by false label

7.176   There has always been some incentive for property owners to mislabel the transaction of tenancy. During the 1970s and 1980s, for instance, the significant extension of statutory security in the area of residential[1] and business[2] tenancies made it increasingly attractive to circumvent such legislation by the grant of a licence as distinct from a tenancy.[3] In more recent times a similar temptation has been posed by the substantial repair and maintenance obligations implied by statute in favour of tenants (but not licensees).[4] In the mid-1980s the decision of the Court of Appeal in *Somma v Hazelhurst and Savelli*[5] gave some currency to the idea that the legal character of a transaction could be stipulated (or overridden) by express agreement between the parties. This meant in effect that the legal status of an occupancy could be dictated by the expressly imposed intention of the stronger bargaining party, who was almost invariably the landowner. It became a fairly common practice for intending occupiers to be required to sign a declaration that their rights were merely those of a licensee.

1   **[Para 14.312]**.
2   **[Para 14.354]**.
3   See *Antoniades v Villiers* [1990] 1 AC 417 at 459B–D per Lord Templeman, 466E–G per Lord Oliver of Aylmerton.
4   **[Para 14.43]**.
5   [1978] 1 WLR 1014 at 1024H–1025A per Cumming-Bruce LJ. See Gray, 'Lease or licence to evade the Rent Act?' [1979] CLJ 38. The approach in *Somma v Hazelhurst and Savelli* came to be applied not merely in the residential sector but also in relation to business tenancies (see *Rossvale Ltd v Green* (1979) 250 EG 1183; *Matchams Park (Holdings) Ltd v Dommett* (1984) 272 EG 549 at 555).

Judicial control of false labels

7.177   During the last two decades the House of Lords has consistently struck down all attempts to evade the reach of protective legislation by contractual manipulation of the parties' genuine legal status. In *Street v Mountford*[1] the occupier was given a right of exclusive occupancy of a self-contained flat on payment of a weekly 'licence fee'. The agreement signed by the occupier was expressly described as a 'licence agreement', and the occupier specifically and in writing disavowed any intention to take a tenancy.[2] Notwithstanding this unequivocal declaration, the House of Lords held that the facts disclosed the existence, not of a mere licence, but of a Rent Act protected tenancy.[3] Lord Templeman, who delivered the only substantial speech, declared that the parties 'cannot turn a tenancy into a licence merely by calling it one.'[4] In his view

> [i]f the agreement satisfied all the requirements of a tenancy, then the agreement produced a tenancy and the parties cannot alter the effect of the agreement by insisting that they only created a licence. The manufacture of a five-pronged implement for manual digging results in a fork even if the manufacturer, unfamiliar with the English language, insists that he intended to make and has made a spade.[5]

1   [1985] AC 809 (reversing (1984) 49 P & CR 324). See [1985] CLJ 351 (S Tromans); (1985) LAG Bulletin 77; [1986] JSWL 46 (D Hoath); P Vincent-Jones, (1987) 14 J Law and Society 445.
2   The owner of the flat – a local solicitor – later maintained that this form of agreement was explicitly framed with reference to the decisions emerging from the Court of Appeal during the period 1977–1979. He claimed to have 'decided to take the Court of Appeal at its word and drafted a document, using the simplest possible terms, expressed to be a personal non-assignable licence' (see R Street, 'Coach and Horses Trip Cancelled?' [1985] Conv 328 at 329).
3   The House of Lords overruled *Somma v Hazelhurst and Savelli* [1978] 1 WLR 1014 (see [1985] AC 809 at 825H–826A).
4   [1985] AC 809 at 821C.
5   [1985] AC 809 at 819E–F. In effect, the parties were declared unable, by misdescription, to contract out of the Rent Act. See also *Voli v Inglewood Shire Council* (1963) 110 CLR 74 at 91 per Windeyer J ('[m]isnomers are not ... to be used as a means for modifying law').

7.178   Lord Templeman was plainly moved by the consideration that if exclusive possession at a rent for a term does not constitute a tenancy, then 'the distinction between a contractual tenancy and a contractual licence of land becomes wholly unidentifiable.'[1] Unless these three hallmarks are 'decisive', the task of differentiation becomes 'impossible ... save by reference to the professed intention of the parties or by the judge awarding marks for drafting.'[2]

1   [1985] AC 809 at 825C, 827A–B.
2   [1985] AC 809 at 826E.

Concern for the integrity of legislative schemes

7.179   The ruling in *Street v Mountford* was dramatic and its outcome quite remarkable. The decision provides an extremely powerful confirmation that the 'professed intention of the parties' does not serve as the determinant of the precise legal status of the occupancy agreed by them.[1] Although the occupier had signed a written acknowledgement that she had no tenancy, this was precisely the interest which the House of Lords held had been conferred upon her by the disputed agreement. In placing significant limits on the parties' powers of self-determination, *Street v Mountford* effectively curtails private contractual autonomy in favour of a more stringent social regulation of property relationships.[2] In holding that landlord and tenant are not free to contract into other categories of legal relationship, the decision presents an unusually significant demonstration of the constant interplay between bargained outcomes and doctrinal constraints. It illustrates the pervasive tension between the paramount will and the need for systemic conformity, and touches ultimately upon the limits of coercive control over individual freedom to stipulate contractually for a particular status at law.

1   [1985] AC 809 at 819G–H. See likewise *Antoniades v Villiers* [1990] 1 AC 417 at 463H–464A per Lord Templeman; *LB of Camden v Shortlife Community Housing Ltd* (1992) 90 LGR 358 at 371–372 per Millett J. Other jurisdictions have followed suit in abandoning tests of tenancy status based on the intention or dominant purpose of the parties (see e g *Fatac Ltd v Commissioner of Inland Revenue* [2002] 3 NZLR 648 at [60]–[68]).

2   See Lord Browne-Wilkinson's reference in *Burrows v Brent LBC* [1996] 1 WLR 1448 at 1454G, to 'the legal structures within which [the parties] made their agreement'. Compare the very different approach to contractual autonomy adopted in Australia (*KJRR Pty Ltd v Commr of State Revenue* [1999] 2 VR 174 at 189 per Chernov JA (Court of Appeal of Victoria)).

7.180   Exactly the same fundamental issues arose more recently in *Bruton v London and Quadrant Housing Trust*.[1] Here a charitable housing trust allocated short-term accommodation in a block of flats to a homeless person on payment of a weekly 'licence' fee.[2] The occupier later claimed that he qualified for the benefit of various statutorily implied repairing obligations available only under a tenancy.[3] Notwithstanding the clear label of licence applied by the parties, the House of Lords ruled that the occupier, in so far as he enjoyed exclusive possession at a rent for a periodic term,[4] had been granted a tenancy[5] and came within the scope of the housing trust's repairing obligations. Lord Hoffmann declared that the fact 'that the parties use language more appropriate to a different kind of agreement, such as a licence, is irrelevant if upon its true construction it has the identifying characteristics of a lease.'[6] The housing trust might have 'agreed with [the occupier] to say that it was not a tenancy', but the parties could no more use such devices to contract out of landlord and tenant statutes than, in *Street v Mountford*, the parties could contract out of the Rent Acts.[7] A similar concern for the integrity of protective legislation has recently caused the courts, in even more general terms, to declare unenforceable any leasehold device which amounts to an 'improper attempt to evade the mandatory scheme for security of tenure' provided by housing statutes.[8] In *Bankway Properties Ltd v Pensfold-Dunsford*,[9] for example, the Court of Appeal struck down, as 'inconsistent with and repugnant to' the relevant statutory purpose a rent review clause which purported, wholly unrealistically, to raise the rent from £4,680 per annum to £25,000 per annum. This clause, which 'masqueraded as a provision for the increase of rent', was in truth a mere device designed to force the recovery of possession and therefore constituted a violation of 'the doctrine against unlawful contracting out … of an Act of Parliament.'[10]

1   [2000] 1 AC 406. See [2000] CLJ 25 (M Dixon); (2000) 116 LQR 7 (S Bright).

2   The trust itself was only a licensee of the block of flats and held as yet no proprietary estate out of which to grant any term of years. It had undertaken to the local authority freeholder that it would grant no occupant security of tenure.

3   See L&TA 1985, ss 11(1), 11(1A) **[para 14.43]**.

4   [2000] 1 AC 406 at 413H–414B per Lord Hoffmann, 417D–E per Lord Hobhouse of Woodborough.

5   His tenancy took effect by estoppel **[para 7.265]**.

6   [2000] 1 AC 406 at 413F.

7   [2000] 1 AC 406 at 416F–G.

8   *Bankway Properties Ltd v Pensfold-Dunsford* [2001] 1 WLR 1369 at [58] per Arden LJ.
9   [2001] 1 WLR 1369 at [68]–[70] per Pill LJ. See [2001] CLJ 474 (R Thornton).
10   [2001] 1 WLR 1369 at [55]–[57] per Arden LJ.

SHAMS AND PRETENCES

7.181   The strictures imposed by protective legislation provide an inevitable temptation for landlords to grant lettings which are not simply mislabelled, but are contractually structured so as to circumvent statutory control. The jurisprudence of landlord and tenant (in common with the law of taxation) has always attempted to maintain a strict distinction between the concepts of 'avoidance' and 'evasion'. Avoidance is the entirely legitimate objective of arranging legal relations so that they do not attract the operation of regulatory legislation.[1] Evasion involves the use of deceptive devices in order to avert the operation of regulatory legislation where it would otherwise clearly apply.[2] For the purpose of policing the blurred border between the two concepts, the courts for many years drew a distinction between 'genuine transactions' and 'shams'. As Lord Templeman urged in *Street v Mountford*,[3] the courts must 'be astute to detect and frustrate sham devices and artificial transactions whose only object is to disguise the grant of a tenancy and to evade the Rent Acts.'[4]

1   See *IRC v Duke of Westminster* [1936] AC 1 at 19 per Lord Tomlin; *Helvering v Gregory*, 69 F2d 809 (1934) at 810 per Judge Learned Hand. However, the contemporary trend is firmly against the upholding of purely artificial devices (see *Ramsay (W T) v Inland Revenue Commissioners* [1982] AC 300; *Furniss v Dawson* [1984] AC 474).
2   See generally A Nicol, 'Outflanking Protective Legislation – Shams and Beyond' (1981) 44 MLR 21; S Bright, 'Avoiding Tenancy Legislation: Sham and Contracting Out Revisited' [2002] CLJ 146.
3   [1985] AC 809 at 825H.
4   See also *Facchini v Bryson* [1952] 1 TLR 1386 at 1390, where Denning LJ pointed out that if the courts were not astute to denounce sham transactions, 'we should make a hole in the Rent Acts through which could be driven – I will not in these days say a coach and four – but an articulated vehicle.'

Ascertainment of the reality of transactions

7.182   In determining whether an agreement has sought cynically and improperly to conceal the grant of exclusive possession behind the guise of a licence, the primary duty of the court is to seek out 'the substance and reality of the transaction.'[1] In each case the court must establish the true nature of the contractual relationship and 'where the language of licence contradicts the reality of lease, the facts must prevail.'[2]

1   *Antoniades v Villiers* [1990] 1 AC 417 at 466C per Lord Ackner. The 'critical question' is 'the true nature of the arrangement' ([1990] 1 AC 417 at 466G–H per Lord Oliver of Aylmerton). See Mustill LJ's reference to 'camouflage' which may 'prevent the transaction from being seen for what it really is' (*Hadjiloucas v Crean* [1988] 1 WLR 1006 at 1022G). See also *Bankway Properties Ltd v Pensfold-Dunsford* [2001] 1 WLR 1369 at [43] per Arden LJ.
2   *Antoniades v Villiers* [1990] 1 AC 417 at 463C per Lord Templeman.

Recognition of human vulnerability

7.183 It has been stressed that the court should be particularly sensitive to the vulnerability of those who seek residential accommodation on the open rental market.[1] As Lord Templeman indicated in *Antoniades v Villiers*,[2] such persons 'may concur in any expression of intention ... may sign a document couched in any language ... [and] may sign any number of documents in order to obtain ... shelter.' Where the benefits of statutory protection cannot legally be contracted away, the language of a supposed licence must therefore be 'examined and construed ... in order to decide whether the rights and obligations enjoyed and imposed create a licence or a tenancy.'[3] In Lord Templeman's words, any document which 'expresses the intention, genuine or bogus, of both parties or of one party to create a licence will nevertheless create a tenancy if the rights and obligations enjoyed and imposed satisfy the legal requirements of a tenancy.'

1   Contrast the approach adopted widely during the 1970s and early 1980s and epitomised in such decisions as those of the Court of Appeal in *Somma v Hazelhurst and Savelli* [1978] 1 WLR 1014 **[para 7.188]**; *Buchmann v May* [1978] 2 All ER 993 **[para 14.316]**; *Aldrington Garages Ltd v Fielder* (1979) 39 P & CR 461 (see [1979] CLJ 38 (Gray)). During the late 1970s and early 1980s the courts may have allowed the boundary between legitimate avoidance and illicit evasion of the Rent Act to shift in response to a perceived need to stimulate the supply of rented accommodation in large urban centres. Certainly until the mid-1980s there were few bold decisions overturning the superficial labels attached to evasive devices. See, however, *Walsh v Griffiths-Jones and Durant* [1978] 2 All ER 1002 at 1010d–e (joint tenancy upheld on behalf of two young graduates of Trinity College, Cambridge); *Demuren v Seal Estates Ltd* (1978) 249 EG 440 at 442; *O'Malley v Seymour* (1978) 250 EG 1083 at 1087–1088; *R v Rent Officer for LB of Camden, ex p Plant* (1981) 257 EG 713 at 718 per Glidewell J.
2   [1990] 1 AC 417 at 458E–G.
3   For this purpose the court may read together, and treat as 'one single transaction', two or more separate licence agreements with different occupiers of the same premises, where it is clear that the agreements were interdependent and were executed contemporaneously ([1990] 1 AC 417 at 458G–459B, 460H per Lord Templeman, 468C per Lord Oliver of Aylmerton, 475D per Lord Jauncey of Tullichettle).

Reference to surrounding circumstances

7.184 In furtherance of this task of construction, the court may have regard not only to the express terms of documents, but also to the surrounding circumstances including any relationship between prospective occupiers, the course of negotiations and the nature and extent of the accommodation together with its intended and actual mode of user.[1] Although the conduct of the parties subsequent to the date of the relevant agreement is, as a matter of contractual principle, irrelevant as an aid to construction,[2] such conduct is both admissible and highly relevant as to 'whether the documents were or were not genuine documents giving effect to the parties' true intentions.'[3] Although the primary focus remains the written terms agreed by the parties, the court may, if necessary, give consideration to 'how the arrangement works in practice.'[4] The court is entitled, and indeed obliged, to take an agreement 'otherwise than at its face value'[5] where the agreement is a 'sham' or contains terms which constitute a 'pretence'.[6]

1   *Antoniades v Villiers* [1990] 1 AC 417 at 458G–H per Lord Templeman.
2   See *Hadjiloucas v Crean* [1988] 1 WLR 1006 at 1024F–1025A per Mustill LJ.
3   *Antoniades v Villiers* [1990] 1 AC 417 at 469C per Lord Oliver of Aylmerton, 475F per Lord Jauncey of Tullichettle. Thus 'de facto exclusive possession can be an important guide to contractual intentions' (*Fatac Ltd v Commissioner of Inland Revenue* [2002] 3 NZLR 648 at [45]). See also *Crancour Ltd v Da Silvaesa* (1986) 52 P & CR 204 at 229 per Purchas LJ (referring to the importance of the 'factual matrix and genesis' of the agreement).
4   *Esso Petroleum Co Ltd v Fumegrange Ltd* (1994) 68 P & CR D15 at D17 per Neill LJ.
5   *Hadjiloucas v Crean* [1988] 1 WLR 1006 at 1019D–F per Mustill LJ.
6   The modern trend is away from the terminology of 'sham devices' and 'artificial transactions' towards the terminology of 'pretence' (see *Antoniades v Villiers* [1990] 1 AC 417 at 462H per Lord Templeman). See also *Hadjiloucas v Crean* [1988] 1 WLR 1006 at 1019F per Mustill LJ; *Aslan v Murphy* [1990] 1 WLR 766 at 770G–H per Lord Donaldson of Lymington MR; *KJRR Pty Ltd v Commr of State Revenue* [1999] 2 VR 174 at 182; S Bright and G Gilbert, *Landlord and Tenant Law: The Nature of Tenancies* (Clarendon, Oxford 1995), pp 132–133.

Identification of misleading terms

7.185   In *Antoniades v Villiers*,[1] Lord Templeman indicated that, in seeking to identify elements of 'pretence' in an occupation agreement, the court must look beyond the parties' expression of intention and must 'pay attention to the facts and surrounding circumstances and to what people do as well as to what people say.' Any elements of 'pretence' detected in this process may then be eliminated or discarded from the agreement as 'obviously inconsistent with the realities of the situation', thereby isolating the genuine elements of the agreement as the basis for ascertaining the true nature of the transaction.[2]

1   [1990] 1 AC 417 at 463H–464A.
2   See *Hadjiloucas v Crean* [1988] 1 WLR 1006 at 1023H–1024A per Mustill LJ (see also Purchas LJ at 1013H–1014A); *Duke v Wynne* [1990] 1 WLR 766 at 775H–776A.

7.186   In practice the real clue to the existence of severable 'pretences' seems to be the inclusion of written terms which are so incomprehensible, blatantly improbable,[1] or cynically inconsistent with the reasonably practical circumstances of the envisaged occupancy,[2] that they cannot seriously have been intended to be operative or effective. In *Antoniades v Villiers*,[3] for instance, an unmarried couple entered into identical contemporaneous 'licence' agreements with the owner of a small attic flat. Both agreements recited, amidst multiple references to the terminology of 'licensor' and 'licensee', that the owner was unwilling to grant exclusive possession of any part of the premises and instead reserved on his own behalf a right 'at any time' to use the premises in common with the licensee 'and such other licensees or invitees as the licensor may permit from time to time to use the said rooms.' Each 'licensee' expressly agreed to 'use his best endeavours amicably and peaceably to share the use of the rooms' with others. An addendum to the document provided that the flat was 'for single people sharing' and accordingly each 'licensee', in signing this addendum, contracted to vacate the flat on marrying 'any occupier of the flat'. The owner nevertheless supplied a double bed on the express request of the two occupiers and throughout their occupancy of the flat the owner made no attempt to use any of the rooms himself or to authorise their use by third parties.[4]

1   See *Aslan v Murphy (No 1)* [1990] 1 WLR 766 at 772H–773A, where the Court of Appeal held that the 'true bargain between the parties' could not sensibly have included a 'wholly unrealistic' provision that the 'licensee' should vacate his rented room every day between 10.30 am and midday (see [1990] JSWL 128 (P T Evans)). See similarly *Crancour Ltd v Da Silvaesa* (1986) 52 P & CR 204 at 215 per Ralph Gibson LJ, 224 per Nicholls LJ.

2   See e g *Demuren v Seal Estates Ltd* (1979) 249 EG 440 at 443, where despite the payment of a year's rent by post-dated cheques the 'licensor' retained a right to terminate the 'licence' at any time on one week's notice. In upholding a tenancy, the Court of Appeal found these terms 'irreconcilable' and pointed out that there was 'something so badly wrong with this agreement that one is bound to look at it with the gravest suspicion.'

3   [1990] 1 AC 417. See [1989] CLJ 19 (C Harpum); [1989] Conv 128 (P F Smith); (1989) 52 MLR 408 (J Hill); (1989) 105 LQR 165 (P V Baker).

4   [1990] 1 AC 417 at 458B.

7.187   The agreements involved in *Antoniades v Villiers* conformed closely to the standard pattern of the 'non-exclusive occupation licence' which had become prevalent in England during the 1980s. When the status of these agreements was challenged in *Antoniades v Villiers*, the House of Lords unanimously declared them to contain not a licence but a disguised tenancy within the protection of the Rent Act 1977. In the view taken by the House of Lords, the agreements were riddled with 'pretence', but once the elements of 'pretence' were cut away the documents plainly revealed the existence of a term of years granted to the occupiers as joint tenants. In the light of the intended use of the flat as a quasi-matrimonial home, the House of Lords pointed out that there was 'an air of total unreality about these documents read as separate and individual licences.'[1] No 'realistic significance' could be attached to the owner's reservation of a supposed right to share, or authorise a stranger to share, accommodation which had been 'specifically adapted for the occupation by a couple living together.'[2] The physical circumstances of the small attic flat, with its sloping roof and limited facilities, were clearly so unsuitable for multiple occupation that nobody could seriously have imagined that the parties had genuinely contemplated a sharing arrangement with either the owner or limitless numbers of strangers.[3] It was equally implausible to suppose that the young couple had each genuinely undertaken, as appeared from the express terms of their agreements, to discharge all liabilities for gas and electricity by whomsoever consumed in the flat and to accept responsibility for the defaults of other nominee occupiers over whose behaviour they could have had no control.[4] The 'bizarre results'[5] produced by the literal operation of the agreements compelled the conclusion that such unrealistic clauses had not been 'seriously intended' to have any practical effect or to serve any other purpose than to avert 'the ordinary legal consequences attendant upon letting the appellants into possession at a monthly rent.'[6]

1   [1990] 1 AC 417 at 467H per Lord Oliver of Aylmerton. See *KJRR Pty Ltd v Commr of State Revenue* [1999] 2 VR 174 at 184 per Tadgell JA ('irreconcilable with commonsense').

2   [1990] 1 AC 417 at 468A per Lord Oliver of Aylmerton. Lord Jauncey of Tullichettle noted (at 476D–E) that, read literally, the 'common user' clause would have enabled the 'licensor' to 'pack the flat with as many people as could find some sleeping space therein.' An unlimited number of strangers could have been permitted to share the flat with the young couple 'even to the extent of sharing the joys of the double bed.' Compare *Somma v Hazelhurst and Savelli* [1978] 1 WLR 1014 at 1028E–G per Cumming-Bruce LJ.

3   In so far as the agreements reserved for the owner a right of joint occupation, Lord Temple-man considered such a power incapable of lawful exercise. Without a court possession order under Rent Act 1977, s 98 [**para 14.322**], such entry into possession by the landlord would have constituted a wholly improper ouster of the Rent Act scheme for the protection of tenants ([1990] 1 AC 417 at 461C–462C).

4   [1990] 1 AC 417 at 467H–468A per Lord Oliver of Aylmerton, 476B–D per Lord Jauncey of Tullichettle. See also *Venus Investments Ltd v Stocktop Ltd* [1997] EWCA Civ 1696.

5   [1990] 1 AC 417 at 476B per Lord Jauncey of Tullichettle.

6   [1990] 1 AC 417 at 468A–B per Lord Oliver of Aylmerton (see likewise Lord Templeman at 463B).

7.188   The unreality permeating the agreements in *Antoniades v Villiers* was only accentuated by the owner's reservation of a right of eviction without court order[1] and by the contracted forfeiture of the couple's occupation rights 'if their double-bedded romance blossomed into wedding bells.'[2] The 'pretence' character of all these provisions was underlined by the fact that the owner had never in practice sought to enforce any of his rights in their literal terms.[3] The superficial denial of the occupiers' overall territorial control was amply falsified by the actual behaviour of the parties. Once the crudely disingenuous elements within the agreements were stripped away as 'pro non scripto',[4] it became obvious that the residue of rights and obligations comprised a joint tenancy which had been only barely concealed behind the 'smokescreen' or 'window-dressing' of the supposed 'licences'.[5]

1   [1990] 1 AC 417 at 468B per Lord Oliver of Aylmerton (who considered that this right 'cannot seriously have been thought to be effective').

2   [1990] 1 AC 417 at 463F per Lord Templeman.

3   [1990] 1 AC 417 at 458B, 463F–G per Lord Templeman, 476G–H per Lord Jauncey of Tullichettle.

4   [1990] 1 AC 417 at 477A per Lord Jauncey of Tullichettle.

5   In *Street v Mountford* [1985] AC 809 at 825G, the House of Lords had already overruled the contrary conclusion reached on almost identical facts in *Somma v Hazelhurst and Savelli* [1978] 1 WLR 1014 (where in reality the joint occupiers had taken a room in order that they might 'live together in quasi-connubial bliss making weekly payments'). See also *Caplan v Marden* (1986) Legal Action 30, 136 NLJ 131 (joint tenancy upheld where three students had been granted three identical non-exclusive occupation licences). Contrast *Parkins v City of Westminster* (1998) 30 HLR 894 at 901 (genuine flat-sharing licence).

ARRANGEMENTS FOR MULTIPLE OCCUPATION

7.189   Difficulties of a different kind are raised in determining the character of informal arrangements for shared or multiple occupation. It is clear that the shared occupation of rented premises may give rise to alternative analyses that each occupier has exclusive possession (and therefore a tenancy) of a distinct part of the premises[1] *or* that all the occupiers are licensees[2] *or* that some of them (to a maximum of four[3]) hold as joint tenants *or* even that one or more, acting as tenant, may have granted an occupation licence to the other occupier or occupiers.[4] In such contexts the distinction between tenancy and licence may prove problematical.

1   This analysis would apply where, for instance, each occupier has been granted exclusive possession of at least *some* accommodation (e g a private bed-sitting room) in an otherwise shared house.

2   In extreme cases the licence conclusion is compelled simply because the sharing of premises has become so comprehensive as to preclude any claim by anybody to exclusive possession of any part of the premises (see e g *Choudhury v Meah* (Unreported, Court of Appeal, 21 September 1981), where the overcrowding of premises in Soho was so gross as to destroy any possible claims of exclusive possession).

3   TA 1925, s 34(2); LPA 1925, s 34(2) **[para 2.131]**.

4   See *Baker v Turner* [1950] AC 401 at 417; *Rogers v Hyde* [1951] 2 KB 923 at 932.

Doctrinal starting-points

7.190   The fixed points of reference are few, but they seem to follow from well established doctrine. It is elementary that no form of holding which fails to display the 'four unities' of joint ownership[1] can itself comprise a joint tenancy. Where the 'four unities' are evidenced by two or more persons who hold a term of years in the same premises, they must hold together as joint tenants. Collectively such persons are entitled 'to exclude everyone other than those who have concurrent estates.'[2] Such persons, as joint owners of the leasehold estate, bear a joint and several liability for the whole rent.[3] They are vulnerable to the operation of survivorship and are subject in their dealings to all the inhibitions placed by law on unilateral action by one joint tenant. Thus, for instance, no joint tenant, acting alone and without the concurrence of the others, may validly terminate the lease[4] (unless it is a periodic tenancy[5]) or surrender the term to the landlord.[6] These rules have no parallel application to mere licensees.[7]

1   **[Para 11.22]**.

2   *AG Securities v Vaughan* [1990] 1 AC 417 at 471G per Lord Oliver of Aylmerton. See also Lord Oliver at 469H.

3   *AG Securities v Vaughan* [1990] 1 AC 417 at 469G–H per Lord Oliver of Aylmerton, 473E per Lord Jauncey of Tullichettle. It seems that the absence of joint obligations of payment is evidence of a disunity of interest inconsistent with a claim of joint tenancy (*Mikeover Ltd v Brady* [1989] 3 All ER 618 at 625e–f, 627a–e; (1990) 106 LQR 215 (J L Barton); *Stribling v Wickham* (1989) 21 HLR 381 at 390).

4   *AG Securities v Vaughan* [1990] 1 AC 417 at 473E–F per Lord Jauncey of Tullichettle.

5   **[Para 7.295]**.

6   **[Para 7.306]**.

7   *AG Securities v Vaughan* [1990] 1 AC 417 at 471F–472A per Lord Oliver of Aylmerton.

A single occupation agreement

7.191   Where one document is used to confer concurrent rights of occupation on two or more persons, the true character of the transaction falls to be determined in the manner outlined by the House of Lords in *Street v Mountford*[1] and *Antoniades v Villiers*.[2] After the severance of any 'sham' term or 'pretence' which serves to disguise reality, the transaction must be identified as either a joint tenancy or a joint licence in accordance with ordinary principles of landlord–tenant law. A conclusion in favour of joint tenancy causes no great conceptual difficulty,[3] and may even be facilitated by the fact that only one document has been used to record the expression of joint rights and obligations. Since joint tenants comprise collectively one person in contemplation of law,[4] the unity of possession which crucially identifies joint ownership is not inconsistent with the exclusiveness of possession which is integral to the concept of tenancy.

1   [1985] AC 809 [**para 7.177**].
2   [1990] 1 AC 417 [**para 7.186**].
3   There was surprisingly belated statutory recognition of the possibility that a leasehold may be co-owned (HA 1980, s 27(3) [now HA 1985, s 81]). See *Howson v Buxton* (1929) 139 LT 504 at 506 per Scrutton LJ; J Martin, [1978] Conv 436.
4   [**Para 11.5**].

Interdependent occupation agreements

7.192   Greater difficulty arises where occupation rights are conferred on a number of persons by means of more than one document. In *Antoniades v Villiers*[1] Lord Templeman acknowledged the possibility of circumstances where two or more documents collectively disclose such an interdependent character that they must be read together as conferring a joint right of exclusive possession appropriate to tenancy.[2] Thus, for example, concurrent 'licences' granted to a husband and wife in respect of a one-bedroom flat would create a joint tenancy if each 'licence' envisaged joint occupation only with the other spouse.[3] The tenancy character of such interdependent agreements is not diminished by the fact that the landlord 'may choose to require' each of the joint tenants to agree expressly to pay his or her proportionate part of the total rent.[4] Nor does it detract from the occupiers' status as joint tenants that the documents contain terms, at variance with 'the substance and reality of the transaction',[5] which purport to deny them a collective right of exclusive possession.[6]

1   [1990] 1 AC 417 at 458G–459B.
2   It goes to the interdependent quality of such agreements that neither or none of the prospective occupiers would have been prepared to enter into the transaction alone. See e g *Antoniades v Villiers* [1990] 1 AC 417 at 460H per Lord Templeman ('Both would have signed or neither').
3   This in effect was the analysis accorded the two 'licence' agreements at the centre of *Antoniades v Villiers* [1990] 1 AC 417 at 460H–461B, 468C [**para 7.187**].
4   *Antoniades v Villiers* [1990] 1 AC 417 at 461B per Lord Templeman. See also *Walsh v Griffiths-Jones and Durant* [1978] 2 All ER 1002 at 1010a–b; *Demuren v Seal Estates Ltd* (1978) 249 EG 440 at 443.
5   *Antoniades v Villiers* [1990] 1 AC 417 at 466C per Lord Ackner.
6   See *Antoniades v Villiers* [1990] 1 AC 417 at 465D–F per Lord Templeman; *Nicolaou v Pitt* (1989) 21 HLR 487 at 491–493.

Multiple sharing by a shifting population of occupants

7.193   Problems of an insuperable nature tend to afflict any attempt to apply a tenancy classification to loose informal arrangements under which premises are shared by a constantly shifting population of occupants. Such multiple sharing – the classic flat-share prevalent amongst young urban professionals – frequently involves contemporaneous and overlapping occupation by a number of previously unassociated individuals. This context differs vitally from that envisaged by interdependent agreements, in that multiple sharers do not usually enter into occupation simultaneously in pursuance of any preconceived arrangement inter se. In *AG Securities v Vaughan*,[1] for instance, four individual occupiers shared a four-bedroom flat under four separate non-exclusive licence agreements with the owner, each of a different date at a different monthly rent and for different periods of six months. Each occupier had his own bedroom, sharing communal facilities in the flat with the other residents, and as one occupier moved out a replacement was found to take over his or her vacancy.

1   [1990] 1 AC 417. See [1989] Conv 128 (P F Smith).

7.194   In the absence of any assertion that each occupier held a separate tenancy in respect of his or her individual bedroom,[1] the House of Lords held that this factual matrix did not enable the four 'licensees' in residence at any given moment collectively to claim a tenancy of the entire flat.[2] As Lord Jauncey of Tullichettle pointed out, any joint tenancy asserted by them would be 'notably deficient in the four unities of interest, title, time and possession.'[3] Their rights and obligations having initially been several, they could not by some 'legal alchemy' ever become joint.[4] There was no artificiality in the terms of the licences themselves,[5] and indeed only the 'highest degree of artificiality' could force 'into the mould of a joint tenancy' contracts which had been made at different times and on different terms.[6] In particular the disunity of time could not be repaired by recourse to the 'strange and unnatural theory' that successive alterations in the membership of the flat-sharing group brought about some implied surrender of an existing tenancy followed immediately by an implied grant of a new joint tenancy to the group as most recently constituted.[7] Moreover even if some joint tenancy could be assembled from the facts it would necessarily involve the untenable assertion that a rule of survivorship would operate in the event of the death of any one occupier.[8] It would also entail the surprising consequence that any occupier could, unilaterally and without wider reference, terminate the occupation rights of all after the expiry of any six month period.

1   This assertion might have succeeded (see [1990] 1 AC 417 at 460E per Lord Templeman, 466B–C per Lord Ackner, 471B–C per Lord Oliver of Aylmerton, 473B per Lord Jauncey of Tullichettle).

2   See also *Stribling v Wickham* (1989) 21 HLR 381 at 389–390; [1989] Conv 192 (J E Martin); *Parkins v City of Westminster* (1998) 30 HLR 894 at 897, 901.

3   [1990] 1 AC 417 at 474F (see also Lord Oliver of Aylmerton at 472B). This fatal flaw had already been exposed in Sir George Waller's dissenting judgment in the Court of Appeal

([1990] 1 AC 417 at 436F). It is not sufficient that the occupiers have unity of possession, time and title if they do not also have unity of interest (see *Mikeover Ltd v Brady* [1989] 3 All ER 618 at 625d–f per Slade LJ).

4   [1990] 1 AC 417 at 454A per Lord Bridge of Harwich. See also *Stribling v Wickham* (1989) 21 HLR 381 at 389 per Parker LJ.

5   [1990] 1 AC 417 at 470C–D per Lord Oliver of Aylmerton.

6   [1990] 1 AC 417 at 454C. In the absence of interdependent agreements, each occupier's several liability in respect of disparate amounts of rent was regarded as inimical to any suggestion of joint tenancy ([1990] 1 AC 417 at 471H–472A per Lord Oliver of Aylmerton).

7   [1990] 1 AC 417 at 472A per Lord Oliver of Aylmerton, 474D–E per Lord Jauncey of Tullichettle.

8   [1990] 1 AC 417 at 460G per Lord Templeman.

CREATION AND DISPOSITION OF LEASEHOLD ESTATES

7.195   By contrast with the creation of fee simple estates in land,[1] the creation of *leasehold estates* is extremely common. Shop leases, business leases, residential long leases and periodic tenancies abound. Precisely because the term of years is an alienable proprietary estate in land, the creation and disposition of leasehold estates provide a highly flexible framework for the distribution of possessory rights in land. This flexibility is constrained by certain rules relating to the parties, the kinds of transaction in which they may engage, and the premises to which these leasehold transactions relate.

1   **[Para 7.12]**.

The parties to a lease must be legally competent

7.196   A lease requires a lessor and a lessee.[1] Under a properly constituted term of years some minimal requirements of legal competence must be satisfied by both parties.

1   *Ingram v IRC* [2000] 1 AC 293 at 300G per Lord Hoffmann.

Competent lessor

7.197   The lessor must have legal competence to create a leasehold estate in the intended lessee. Thus, for instance, a company cannot grant an effective term of years if title to the land in question is vested not in the company itself but in the name of the person who formed the company.[1] Nor has a corporate entity any capacity to grant leases over its land unless a leasing power has been duly included in its memorandum of association or (where applicable) within its statutory mandate.[2]

1   *Torbett v Faulkner* [1952] 2 TLR 659 at 660, 662.

2   See also *LB of Camden v Shortlife Community Housing Ltd* (1992) 90 LGR 358 at 377–378 (grant of tenancy by council void without consent of Secretary of State).

Competent lessee

7.198 The grantee of a lease must likewise be legally competent to hold a term of years. The lessee must be a legal person such as an individual or a corporate body and, in the latter case, must be duly empowered by the company constitution to be the recipient of leases. No tenancy can be granted to an unincorporated association since such a body has no legal personality or status.[1] Nor can the grant be construed as one to the members of the association from time to time: a legal estate cannot be vested in a fluctuating body of persons.[2]

1 *LB of Camden v Shortlife Community Housing Ltd* (1992) 90 LGR 358 at 374 per Millett J. See e g *Congregational Christian Church v Iosefa Tauga* (1982) 8 Comm Law Bull 129 (grant to church invalid because church was an unincorporated association).
2 *Jarrott v Ackerley* (1915) 113 LT 371 at 373 per Eve J.

7.199 Problems arise only rarely as to the legal competence of the lessee. However, two of the more common issues relate to grants (a) to a minor and (b) to the lessor himself.

Lease to a minor

7.200 No minor (ie a person under the age of 18 years) may hold a legal estate in land (whether freehold or leasehold).[1] This limitation on the competence of the *lessee* is seldom discussed but seems to be an inescapable conclusion of law.[2] There is, however, no prohibition on a minor holding an equitable estate; and any attempt after 1996 to grant a lease to a minor takes effect as a declaration that the land is held in trust for the minor,[3] the minor thus holding an equitable term of years in the land.[4] Terms of years are not often expressly conferred upon minors; and the local authority which grants a council tenancy to a 17-year-old may have little realisation that it is initiating a trust relationship. It also sometimes happens that, on the death of a secure tenant under the Housing Act 1985,[5] a minor takes an equitable tenancy by succession.[6]

1 LPA 1925, ss 1(6), 20, 205(1)(v); TOLATA 1996, Sch 1, para 1(1)(a) **[para 2.132]**.
2 See e g *Kingston upon Thames BC v Prince* [1999] 1 FLR 593 at 601C–D.
3 TOLATA 1996, s 2(1), (6), Sch 1, para 1(1)(b).
4 See 'Can an under-18-year old be a contractual tenant?' (1983) 147 Loc Gov Rev 259; and see Minors' Contracts Act 1987, s 1; *Portman Registrars v Mohammed Latif* [1987] 6 CL 217.
5 **[Para 14.340]**.
6 See e g *Kingston upon Thames BC v Prince* [1999] 1 FLR 593 at 603A–E.

Lease to the lessor himself

7.201 A person cannot grant a lease to himself (or to his corporate alter ego[1]) out of land of which he is the estate owner.[2] This proposition is at least consistent with the idea that it is meaningless to create for oneself a subsidiary right in one's own estate.[3] An additional obstacle has always been said to consist in the absurdity of covenanting with oneself and then enforcing leasehold covenants against oneself.[4] The latter objection fails, of course, to take account of the fact that it is entirely possible, albeit rare, for some leasehold grants to contain no express covenants and for all implied covenants to be expressly excluded. It is, in any event, widely accepted that A may validly grant a lease to A and B,[5] and that A and B may together grant a lease to A, B and C.[6] If A were subsequently to take the entire legal and beneficial interest in the lease by release[7] or survivorship,[8] there would, if the lease were registered, be no obligation on A to apply (and pay) for closure of the registered leasehold title on grounds of merger in his own reversionary estate.[9] In these circumstances, therefore, a lessor can achieve an outcome declared impossible at common law.

1   See *Hocking v Kerhardy* (Unreported, Court of Appeal, 26 August 1992), where the Court of Appeal frustrated an attempt by a registered proprietor to obtain priority over a legal chargee by alleging an earlier lease of the property to a company which merely provided a trading name for his own activities.

2   *Rye v Rye* [1962] AC 496 at 505 per Viscount Simonds, 514 per Lord Denning; *Ingram v IRC* [2000] 1 AC 293 at 300G per Lord Hoffmann; *Barrett v Morgan* [2000] 2 AC 264 at 271A per Lord Millett. LPA 1925, s 72(3) provides that 'a person may convey land to or vest land in himself', but this has been construed to mean merely that a sole executor may properly convey land to himself as devisee, or that a beneficial owner may convey land to himself as a trustee for charitable purposes (see *Rye*, supra at 514).

3   See, for instance, the equivalent rule in respect of easements [**para 8.47**]. Scots law emphasises the objection that the end of the 'lease' cannot be marked, since the tenant's right to possession continues unchanged (by virtue of his capacity as owner of the superior estate) even after the termination of the term (see *Clydesdale Bank plc v Davidson* 1998 SLT 522 at 526E per Lord Hope of Craighead).

4   See *Faulkner v Lowe* (1848) 2 Exch 595 at 597, 154 ER 628 at 629–630; *Ellis v Kerr* [1910] 1 Ch 529 at 536; *Napier v Williams* [1911] 1 Ch 361 at 368; *Coleman v Jones* (1986) 4 BPR 9228 at 9230. Contrast Property Law Act 1952 (New Zealand), ss 49, 66A; *Harding v Commissioner of Inland Revenue* [1977] 1 NZLR 337 at 341; *Samuel v District Land Registrar* [1984] 2 NZLR 697 at 701–702; *Robert Bryce & Co Ltd v Stowehill Investments Ltd* [2000] 3 NZLR 535 at [34]–[44].

5   See *Barrett v Morgan* [2000] 2 AC 264 (yearly tenancy granted by A to A, B and C).

6   *Joseph v Joseph* [1967] Ch 78 at 84E per Lord Denning MR. Although this possibility has been doubted in Australia (see *Coleman v Jones* (1986) 4 BPR 9228 at 9230), it is the established practice of Land Registry to register title to long leases of this kind. Compare, however, *Clydesdale Bank plc v Davidson* 1998 SLT 522 (HL (Scotland)).

7   [**Para 11.69**].

8   [**Para 11.8**].

9   See LRR 2003, r 79.

The subject matter of a term of years must be identified with certainty

7.202   All lands and all interests in land 'lie in grant'[1] and may be made the subject matter of a lease or tenancy.[2] A term of years may therefore be granted in either a corporeal or an incorporeal hereditament.[3] It is just as possible, for instance, to create a leasehold interest in a profit *à prendre* (such as shooting or fishing rights)[4] as to grant a term of years in a house. Irrespective of the precise nature of the letting, the subject matter of the term of years must be described and identified with certainty.[5]

1   LPA 1925, s 51(1).
2   For a definition of 'land', see Chapter 1 [**para 1.23**].
3   The complex questions arising in relation to pastoral leases in *Wik Peoples v Queensland* (1996) 187 CLR 1 could have been more satisfactorily addressed in terms of leases of profits *à prendre* [**para 8.17**] (see, however, *Wik Peoples*, supra at 247 per Kirby J).
4   A lease of an incorporeal hereditament cannot confer 'exclusive possession' of the land, ie in the sense of a right to exclude the fee simple owner (see *Duke of Sutherland v Heathcote* [1892] 1 Ch 475 at 484). The lessee has at most a right to 'possession of his property, namely the incorporeal hereditament and its products' (*Hindmarsh v Quinn* (1914) 17 CLR 622 at 636), although, as lessee of the profit, he may defend his 'exclusive possession' of the profit by action in trespass (see *Swayne v Howells* [1927] 1 KB 385 at 393; *Mason v Clarke* [1955] AC 778 at 794).
5   *Goldsworthy Mining Ltd v Federal Commissioner of Taxation* (1973) 128 CLR 199 at 211. On the difficulties caused by inadequate or imprecise plans, see *Wallington v Townsend* [1939] Ch 588 (leasehold boundary appeared to run through middle of tenant's bathroom); *Kohua Pty Ltd v Tai Ping Trading Pty Ltd* (1985) 3 BPR 9705 at 9707.

Conventions of leasehold conveyancing

7.203   The requirement of certain identification of demised premises is usually satisfied without excessive difficulty.[1] The boundaries of the leased property are often regarded as fixed, in the absence of contrary intention, by reference to certain conventions of leasehold conveyancing which have become rules of law. Thus, for instance, the external wall enclosing the demised premises is normally regarded as part of the demised premises.[2] A conveyance of a leasehold also passes void spaces above false ceilings in a flat.[3] In the case of a top-floor flat, the lease includes the immediately superjacent air space above the roof of the demised premises,[4] with the result that the tenant may properly seek to raise the roof and convert the loft into additional accommodation for himself.[5]

1   That two sets of premises can form the subject matter of a single tenancy is clear from *Walter v Rumbal* (1695) 1 Ld Raym 53 at 55, 91 ER 931 at 933.
2   *Sturge v Hackett* [1962] 1 WLR 1257 at 1265. A lease of a flat prima facie conveys an estate in the external walls of that flat, but not in the external walls of other flats in the same building (*Campden Hill Towers Ltd v Gardner* [1977] QB 823 at 834F–G). See, however, *Pumperninks of Piccadilly Ltd v Land Securities plc* [2002] Ch 332 at [3], where commercial parties expressly agreed on the grant of an 'eggshell tenancy' which excluded structural and load-bearing parts of the building.
3   *Graystone Property Investments Ltd v Margulies* (1983) 269 EG 538 at 541–542.
4   *Kelsen v Imperial Tobacco Co (of Great Britain and Ireland) Ltd* [1957] 2 QB 334 at 339–340 [**para 1.40**].
5   See *Haines v Florensa* (1990) 59 P & CR 200 at 205–206; *Davies v Yadegar* (1990) 22 HLR 232 at 235–237.

Fluctuating boundaries

7.204   It is sufficient that the description of the subject matter of a lease or tenancy is such as to enable the boundaries of the property to be ascertained or identified at any given time. Where, for example, the area of demised land fluctuates with changes in a littoral boundary caused by accretion,[1] the requirement of certainty is adequately met. The territorial limit of the lease is readily ascertainable, since it can simply be measured with reference to the surface as it exists from time to time.[2]

1   [**Para 1.20**].
2   *Goldsworthy Mining Ltd v Federal Commissioner of Taxation* (1973) 128 CLR 199 at 211–212.

FLEXIBILITY OF LEASEHOLD RELATIONSHIPS

7.205   The leasehold relationship provides a flexible base for a range of transactions in land. The potential versatility of the leasehold device may be demonstrated with reference to the following diagram:

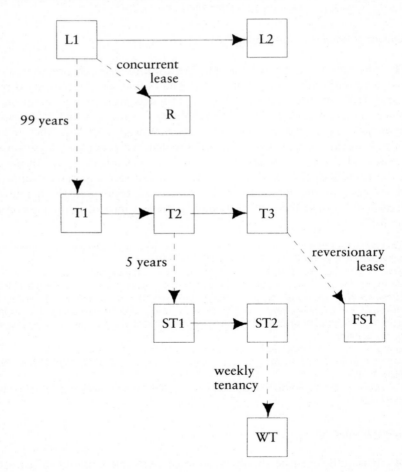

Fig. 10

Grant of a term of years

7.206   The events depicted in *Fig.* 10 find their origin in the grant by L1, the owner of an estate in fee simple absolute, of a 'head lease' for a term of 99 years to T1. This grant invests T1 with a proprietary estate in the land – a term of years absolute – thereby suspending L1's right to physical occupation of the land until the end of the leasehold term. The sum total of the rights meanwhile retained by L1 is known as the 'reversion' (or 'freehold reversion'), ie the residue of the rights reversionary upon the lease. It is of the essence of a legal lease that both L1 and T1 hold a legal estate in 'possession' (in L1's case, in the technical sense of his entitlement to rents and profits[1]). Each has an estate in the land with which – at least in theory – he may deal quite independently.

1   LPA 1925, s 205(1)(xix).

Subsequent dealings with L1's reversion

7.207   The freehold reversion on the lease granted by L1 to T1 remains a marketable asset and can be the subject of various kinds of dealing.

Assignment

7.208   It is open to L1 to assign the freehold reversion to an assignee, L2, by conveying to him the fee simple estate in the land which is subject to the lease. The essence of the device of assignment is that it comprises a disposition to the assignee of the assignor's entire interest in the land[1] and in effect L2 becomes landlord, initially to T1. L2 may, of course, execute a further assignment of the freehold reversion to someone else, the reversion normally increasing steadily in value as the lease approaches its expiration date.

1   **[Para 7.211]**. See *Burton v Camden LBC* [2000] 2 AC 399 at 408D per Lord Millett.

Concurrent lease

7.209   It is also possible – although much less common – for L1, during the currency of T1's lease, to grant a different lease to R of the same land as is comprised in T1's term of years. Thus, for instance, L1 may grant R a 'concurrent lease' for, say, 30 years. In such circumstances R cannot, of course, enter into physical occupation of the land, since this right has already been allocated to T1. However, R's concurrent lease confers upon him another form of 'possession', ie the right to receive rent for 30 years, the concurrent lease diverting to R an income stream which in a commercial context may be quite significant. Where the lease from L1 to T1 was granted before 1996, a concurrent lease to R is tantamount to a partial disposition of L1's reversionary estate to R.[1] In consequence L1 is substituted by R as T1's landlord[2] and the landlord–tenant relationship between L1 and T1 drops completely away. If, however, the lease from L1 to T1 was granted after 1995, R's concurrent lease operates, not to assign L1's reversionary interest to R, but rather to interpose a true lease to R of L1's reversionary estate. The concurrent lease thus engrafts a new and more complex range of landlord–tenant relationships upon the parties, the covenants of the lease now being enforceable between L1 and R, between R and T1, and even, at least in theory, between L1 and T1.[3]

1   See e g *Harmer v Bean* (1853) 3 C & K 307 at 308, 175 ER 566 at 567. As an assignment of L1's reversionary estate, the concurrent lease to R must be made by deed in order to be effective at law [**para 7.25**].

2   See *Wordsley Brewery Co v Halford* (1903) 90 LT 89 at 90. The rights and obligations of the lease now bind R and T1 respectively (see *Burton v Barclay and Perkins* (1831) 7 Bing 745 at 758–759, 131 ER 288 at 293–294; *Horn v Beard* [1912] 3 KB 181 at 188).

3   See Landlord and Tenant (Covenants) Act 1995, s 15(1)(a).

Subsequent dealings with T1's leasehold term

7.210   A term of years constitutes a proprietary estate in land which by its very nature is alienable and, in the absence of any limiting statutory[1] or contractual provision,[2] the tenant, T1, has an unqualified right to deal independently with the unexpired term of his lease either by assignment of the term or by the creation of a 'sublease' (or 'underlease').[3]

1   See the general prohibition on assignment of secure tenancies (HA 1985, s 91 [**para 14.340**]). See also *Burton v Camden LBC* [2000] 2 AC 399 at 406D per Lord Nicholls of Birkenhead.

2   [**Para 14.81**]. Any contractual restraint upon the tenant's right to assign or sublet is construed strictly against the landlord (see *Church v Brown* (1808) 15 Ves 258 at 265, 33 ER 752 at 755; *Wilson v Rosenthal* (1906) 22 TLR 233).

3   See *Williams v Earle* (1868) LR 3 QB 739 at 750; *Garry Denning Ltd v Vickers* [1985] 1 NZLR 567 at 569 per Woodhouse P and Richardson J.

Assignment

7.211   Here, again, assignment comprises a disposition to the assignee of the assignor's entire interest in the land,[1] thereby putting the assignee into the shoes of the assignor as henceforth the tenant under the lease.[2] When T1 assigns to T2 the unexpired portion of his term of 99 years,[3] T1 thereafter retains no interest, estate or reversion in the land,[4] although this does not mean that his obligations under the lease are necessarily terminated at this point.[5] In *Fig.* 10 T2 effects a further assignment of his steadily decreasing term in favour of T3, the premium (if any) commanded by this assignment being, in part, a reflection of the diminishing quantum of time available under the leasehold.

1   See *Milmo v Carreras* [1946] KB 306 at 310 per Lord Greene MR. Assignment involves 'a transfer of a lease, changing the identity of the tenants' (see *Burton v Camden LBC* [2000] 2 AC 399 at 405F per Lord Nicholls of Birkenhead).

2   See *City of London Corpn v Fell* [1993] QB 589 at 604B–C per Nourse LJ.

3   The transfer of a long lease (e g the residue of a 99 year lease of a flat) usually commands a cash premium (or lump sum) payable by T2 to T1. T2 may charge his newly acquired leasehold term in order to raise this sum by mortgage loan.

4   The assignor 'from that moment is a stranger to the land' (*Milmo v Carreras* [1946] KB 306 at
     310 per Lord Greene MR).
5   **[Para 14.217]**.

Sublease

7.212   By contrast the essence of a sublease consists in the fact that the
sublessor always retains a reversionary interest in the land, the sublease
bringing into existence a new tenurial relationship between sublessor and
sublessee.[1] A sublease effectively comprises the creation of a new (and subsidiary) leasehold estate out of the lessee's own leasehold term,[2] the sublessor
retaining a reversion on the sublease which will take effect (even if only
fleetingly) at the termination of the sublease. The logic of derivative interests
dictates that a sublease can be granted only for some shorter period of time
than the term enjoyed by the sublessor.[3] In *Fig.* 10 T2, the assignee from T1,
creates a five-year sublease for ST1, who in due course assigns the unexpired
portion of this sublease to ST2.[4] ST2 then creates a sub-underlease, by way of a
weekly tenancy, for WT.

1   *Garry Denning Ltd v Vickers* [1985] 1 NZLR 567 at 570.
2   In this way the relationship of landlord and tenant can be replicated many times over, each
     leasehold term being carved out of the immediately superior estate.
3   '[W]hen the grant is for the residue of the term of the grantor, there must be an exception of
     the last day or the last hour, or of some other period of the term' (*Jameson v London and
     Canadian Loan Agency Co* (1897) 27 SCR 435 at 442 per Strong CJ).
4   In the case of a short lease at an open market rent (eg the five year lease granted by T2 to
     ST1), the assignment of the lease to ST2 results in ST2 taking over the payment of the
     covenanted rent normally without any payment of a premium to ST1.

Test of substance not form

7.213   The distinction between assignment and sublease is subtle but important. Whether a particular dealing has produced a sublease or an assignment is
ultimately a matter of substance and not of form, and the court accordingly
has power to override any label erroneously attached to the transaction.[1] Any
purported sublease which attempts to carve out a term for the sublessee equal
to[2] or in excess of[3] the residue of the sublessor's own term is deemed to operate
not as a sublease but as an *assignment* of that term.[4]

1   *Milmo v Carreras* [1946] KB 306 at 310 per Lord Greene MR; *Gaumont v Luz* (1980) 111 DLR
     (3d) 609 at 614–615; *Garry Denning Ltd v Vickers* [1985] 1 NZLR 567 at 572.
2   *Parmenter v Webber* (1818) 8 Taunt 593 at 595–596, 129 ER 515 at 516; *Beardman v Wilson*
     (1868) LR 4 CP 57 at 58; *Hallen v Spaeth* [1923] AC 684 at 687.
3   *Hicks v Downing* (1696) 1 Ld Raym 99, 91 ER 962 (tenant cannot 'by this gain any tortious
     reversion'); *Wollaston v Hakewill* (1841) 3 Man & G 297 at 323, 133 ER 1157 at 1167–1168 per
     Tindal CJ; *Stretch v West Dorset CC* (1999) 77 P & CR 342 at 351–352; *Sunnyvale Services B
     O P Ltd v Bhana* [1986] 1 NZLR 314 at 319.
4   The sublessor has no 'property in his term ... left after he has made what is really a transfer'
     (*Hallen v Spaeth* [1923] AC 684 at 687–688 per Viscount Haldane). See similarly *PW & Co v
     Milton Gate Investments Ltd* [2004] 2 WLR 443 at [80] per Neuberger J; *Conoid Pty Ltd v*

International Theme Park Pty Ltd (2000) 10 BPR 18407 at [15] (New South Wales Court of Appeal). A sublease is not rendered excessive merely by the presence of an option for renewal (*Neva Holdings Ltd v Wilson* [1991] 3 NZLR 422 at 428). Nor is a sublease granted out of a periodic tenancy converted into an assignment by reason of the fact that the term of the sublease exceeds the relevant period (*Oxley v James* (1844) 13 M & W 209 at 215, 153 ER 87 at 89–90 (34 year lease granted out of yearly tenancy)), although termination of the periodic tenancy automatically ends the sublease (*Conoid Pty*, supra at [17]–[18]).

Preference for alienability

7.214   The tenant's general freedom to deal with his leasehold estate is merely a function of the traditional common law preference for unfettered alienability of land.[1] Moreover, even if a tenant assigns or sublets in clear breach of an express covenant in his lease,[2] the transaction vests a good title in the assignee or sublessee unless and until the wrongful dealing is invoked by the landlord as a ground for forfeiture of the lease.[3] In effect, the dealing operates to transfer or create the relevant estate subject only to the possible exercise of the landlord's right of re-entry.[4]

1   **[Paras 2.39, 7.16]**. However, a restriction on smoking by a tenant or any invitee of his is no more repugnant to freedom of alienation than is, say, a restriction on the permissible number of animals which may be kept. Neither restriction prohibits alienation, but merely limits the class of potential lessees (see *Salerno v Proprietors of Strata Plan 42724* (1997) 8 BPR 15457 at 15458).

2   It is different if the prohibition takes the form, not of a covenant against assignment or subletting, but of a proviso or condition that the head lease shall cease in the event of any unlawful dealing. In such circumstances any purported assignment or subletting is simply void (see *Paul v Nurse* (1828) 8 B & C 486 at 488, 108 ER 1123 at 1124; *Garry Denning Ltd v Vickers* [1985] 1 NZLR 567 at 570 per Woodhouse P and Richardson J).

3   *Williams v Earle* (1868) LR 3 QB 739 at 750; *Old Grovebury Manor Farm Ltd v W Seymour Plant Sales and Hire Ltd* (*No 2*) [1979] 1 WLR 1397 at 1398G; *Governors of the Peabody Donation Fund v Higgins* [1983] 1 WLR 1091 at 1095E–G, 1097C–D; *Massart v Blight* (1951) 82 CLR 423 at 440; *Garry Denning Ltd v Vickers* [1985] 1 NZLR 567 at 570, 572; *Ladies Sanctuary Pty Ltd v Parramatta Property Investment Ltd* (1997) 7 BPR 15156 at 1515; *Toronto Harbour Commissioners v T H C Parking Inc* (1999) 175 DLR (4th) 536 at 546.

4   The assignee of the term (not the assignor) becomes the proper applicant for relief against forfeiture, although any knowledge in the assignee of the assignor's wilful breach of covenant will almost certainly influence discretion against the granting of such relief (see e g *Ladies Sanctuary Pty Ltd v Parramatta Property Investment Ltd* (1997) 7 BPR 15156 at 15162).

Reversionary sublease

7.215   The lease held by T3 can also be the subject of further manipulation. For instance, T3 may wish immediately to secure a future letting to commence on the expiry of ST1's five-year sublease. This he can achieve by granting, say, a seven-year term to a future subtenant, FST. The consequence is instantly to confer on FST a 'reversionary lease'[1] which takes effect in possession when ST1's sublease ends.

1   **[Para 7.104]**.

Realignment of leasehold relationships

7.216 The relationship of landlord and tenant can be replicated many times over within the leasehold context, with a potentially infinite number of terms of years being carved out of the initial leasehold grant. At the end of the process described in *Fig.* 10,[1] L2 holds the legal fee simple absolute in possession, and T3, R, ST2 and WT all hold terms of years absolute in possession. At this stage five relationships of landlord and tenant currently exist: *first*, between L2 and T3; *second*, between T3 and ST2; *third*, between ST2 and WT; *fourth*, between L2 and R (the 'concurrent lease'); and *fifth*, between T3 and FST (the 'reversionary lease').

1   [**Para 7.205**].

STATUTORY FORMALITIES FOR THE CREATION (OR GRANT) OF A LEASE

7.217 The creation and assignment of most terms of years are subject to certain statutory requirements of formality. A leasehold interest in land comprises, at least in potentiality, a legal estate[1] and the creation and assignment of such an interest are therefore subject to stringent rules of form. In many cases the Land Registration Act 2002 has superimposed further requirements of completion or perfection by registration. A careful distinction must be drawn between the *creation* of a term of years (ie the grant of a head lease or of some sublease carved out of the head lease) and later *assignments* of any subsisting term of years.[2]

1   LPA 1925, s 1(1)(b) [**para 2.125**].
2   'A lease is not an assignment, because it does not transfer any pre-existing property from the lessor to the lessee, but creates a new interest and vests it for the first time in the lessee' (*Burton v Camden LBC* [2000] 2 AC 399 at 408D per Lord Millett).

Creation of a term of years

7.218 The statutory requirements of formality in respect of the initial grant or creation of leasehold interests are contained in an unco-ordinated series of provisions in the Law of Property Act 1925.[1]

1   These provisions stem from the Statute of Frauds 1677, ss 1, 2, and the Real Property Act 1845, s 3.

General rule

7.219 The starting point is the proposition that 'no interest in land can be created or disposed of except by writing signed by the person creating or conveying the same ... '[1] All interests created merely by parol have 'the force and effect of interests at will only.'[2] Furthermore, 'all conveyances of land or of any interest therein are void for the purpose of conveying or creating a legal estate unless made by deed.'[3]

1   LPA 1925, s 53(1)(a). This provision allows signature by an agent with written authority and also permits the creation and disposal of interests in land 'by will, or by operation of law.'
2   LPA 1925, s 54(1).
3   LPA 1925, s 52(1). The definition of a deed is considered elsewhere [**para 7.29**].

Exceptions

7.220   The general requirement of conveyance by deed is expressly subject to contrary statutory indication. No deed is required for assents by personal representatives,[1] disclaimers of leasehold title made by a company liquidator or trustee in bankruptcy in the context of insolvency,[2] surrenders of leases by operation of law[3] and vesting orders made by the court.[4] By far the most important exception to the requirement of creation by deed arises in relation to leases or tenancies 'not required by law to be made in writing.'[5] Further investigation of the statute[6] reveals that no writing of any kind is required for the creation of leases 'taking effect in possession'[7] for a term not exceeding three years 'at the best rent which can be reasonably obtained without taking a fine.'[8]

1   LPA 1925, s 52(2)(a).
2   LPA 1925, s 52(2)(b). See Insolvency Act 1986, ss 178(2), 315(1)–(2).
3   LPA 1925, s 52(2)(c) [**para 7.308**].
4   LPA 1925, s 52(2)(f).
5   LPA 1925, s 52(2)(d).
6   See LPA 1925, s 54(2).
7   'Possession' is defined in LPA 1925, s 205(1)(xix) [**para 7.21**]. Section 54(2) therefore has no saving impact on the grant of a 'reversionary lease' [**para 7.104**], ie a lease under which the commencement of possession is postponed to some future date (see *Long v Tower Hamlets LBC* [1998] Ch 197 at 218G–H; *Haselhurst v Elliot* [1945] VLR 153 at 155; *Abjornson v Urban Newspapers Pty Ltd* [1989] WAR 191 at 199). In consequence many short leases granted in advance of the taking of possession are denied exemption from the requirement of creation by deed (see [1998] Conv 229 (S Bright)), and the parties are thrown back upon the rights and obligations implied from entry into possession and payment of a periodic rent [**para 7.250**].
8   A 'fine' (or 'premium') is a lump sum payment demanded as part of the consideration for the grant of a term of years.

Net effect

7.221   The net effect of this 'hotchpotch of sections'[1] is that no deed is required for the creation of a legal lease or sublease which takes effect in possession at an open market rent without a premium for a period not exceeding three years. Such terms can be created at law by simple writing or even orally.[2] In all other cases no legal lease can be created otherwise than by *deed*.[3] Failure to use a deed may, however, result in the creation not of the fixed term *legal* lease originally intended, but of a broadly equivalent *equitable* lease[4] or – rather less likely – a legal periodic tenancy.[5] All of which demonstrates that the term of years absolute has merely the potentiality of *legal* existence.[6] It is entirely possible that, for want of appropriate formality, a term of years may comprise an *equitable* estate in land.[7]

1   See *Crago v Julian* [1992] 1 WLR 372 at 376C per Nicholls V-C.
2   *Kushner v Law Society* [1952] 1 KB 264 at 272; *Crago v Julian* [1992] 1 WLR 372 at 376D–E
    per Nicholls V-C. The creation of a term of exactly three years requires no formality (see
    Hayes v Seymour-Johns (1981) 2 BPR 9366 at 9371). See generally P Sparkes, [1992] Conv 252,
    337.
3   *R v Tower Hamlets LBC, ex p Von Goetz* [1999] QB 1019 at 1020G, 1024A. In certain cases the
    creation of a leasehold estate also requires that the leasehold proprietor's title be completed or
    perfected by registration **[para 7.236]**.
4   See e g *R v Tower Hamlets LBC, ex p Von Goetz* [1999] QB 1019 at 1020H, 1024B–C (10 year
    shorthold lease granted without deed). The equitable lease arises under the so-called doctrine
    in *Walsh v Lonsdale* **[para 9.66]**.
5   A lease which falls outside the statutory exemption from formality may, on entry into
    possession and the payment and acceptance of a periodic rent **[para 7.250]** give rise to a
    periodic tenancy by operation of law (see e g *Long v Tower Hamlets LBC* [1998] Ch 197 at
    218H–219A). This is the likely effect of an orally granted lease for a term in excess of three
    years, which otherwise has no validity at all either at law or in equity.
6   See LPA 1925, s 1(1)(b) **[para 2.125]**.
7   See *R v Tower Hamlets LBC, ex p Von Goetz* [1999] QB 1016 at 1024C–1025A per
    Mummery LJ, 1026F per Peter Gibson LJ.

Special cases

7.222   Special consideration must be given to four kinds of lease or tenancy.

PERIODIC TENANCIES

7.223   It follows from the provisions of the Law of Property Act 1925 that a
legal periodic tenancy can be created without any kind of formality,[1] even
though the tenancy may in fact continue for much longer than three years.[2]
Such a tenancy may be created simply by oral grant.[3] Moreover, a periodic
tenancy may be created either expressly or by implication from conduct. An
express periodic tenancy is one which is granted, for instance, 'from week to
week' or 'from month to month'. An implied periodic tenancy often arises
where a property owner accepts rent paid on a periodic basis by a 'tenant at
will'[4] (ie by one who occupies land with the consent of the owner) or by a
tenant under a formally invalid or incomplete lease.[5]

1   *Re Knight, ex p Voisey* (1882) 21 Ch D 442 at 456, 458; *Hammond v Farrow* [1904] 2 KB 332 at
    335.
2   The conclusive factor is that, at the commencement of the periodic tenancy, it is entirely
    uncertain that the tenancy will continue for more than three years and eminently possible that
    it may come to an end somewhat sooner (see *Re Knight, ex p Voisey* (1882) 21 Ch D 442 at
    456; *Duncan v Paki* [1976] 2 NZLR 563 at 565).
3   *Kushner v Law Society* [1952] 1 KB 264 at 274. However, no legal periodic term can be created
    by a tenancy document which merely evidences the terms of a proposed future lease and is
    not, in itself, dispositive (*Long v Tower Hamlets LBC* [1998] Ch 197 at 210E–F; [1998] Conv
    229 (S Bright)). See also *Battersea Churches Housing Trust v Hunte* [1996] CLY 3761.
4   **[Para 7.273]**.
5   **[Para 7.256]**.

RENEWABLE LEASES

7.224   The fact that a lease for a period not exceeding three years contains an option for renewal does not convert the lease into a term exceeding three years, even though the total period of possession enjoyed by the tenant ultimately extends beyond three years.[1] The option for renewal, if exercised by the tenant,[2] merely has the effect of creating a fresh lease for a new term.[3] No formality is required in respect of either the first term or the second term, provided that the second term does not itself exceed three years.

1   *Hand v Hall* (1877) 2 Ex D 355 at 358. See likewise *Markfaith Investment Ltd v Chiap Hua Flashlights Ltd* [1991] 2 AC 43 at 58E per Lord Templeman.
2   Where a lease is vested in more than one tenant, an option for renewal of the term cannot be exercised unilaterally by one joint tenant (see *Newman v Keedwell* (1977) 35 P & CR 393 at 398; *Hammersmith and Fulham LBC v Monk* [1992] 1 AC 478 at 490G per Lord Bridge of Harwich). See also *Churcher v Danis Hotels Pty Ltd* (1980) 8 BPR 15863 at 15877.
3   *Lewis v Stephenson* (1898) 67 LJQB 296 at 300; *Rider v Ford* [1923] 1 Ch 541 at 547; *Gerraty v McGavin* (1914) 18 CLR 152 at 163–164; *Minister v New South Wales Aerated Water and Confectionery Co Ltd* (1916) 22 CLR 56 at 78; *195 Crown Street Pty Ltd v Hoare* [1969] 1 NSWR 193 at 199; *Travinto Nominees Pty Ltd v Vlattas* (1973) 129 CLR 1 at 17 per Barwick CJ.

DETERMINABLE LEASES

7.225   The requirement of formal creation by deed applies to a lease which is granted for a definite term in excess of three years, notwithstanding that the lease is determinable by the tenant within the first three years.[1] The determinable 90 year term into which most leases for life are converted by statute[2] is, however, immune from the requirement of formal creation precisely because the 90 year term takes effect by operation of law.[3]

1   *Kushner v Law Society* [1952] 1 KB 264 at 274.
2   **[Para 7.121]**.
3   LPA 1925, s 52(2)(g) **[para 7.220]**.

CONTRACT FOR GRANT OF A LEASE

7.226   Parties who have in mind the creation of a lease of substantial duration frequently enter first into a *contract* to grant the lease envisaged. In negotiating the contract, the parties have effectively negotiated the terms of the lease and, on exchange of contracts, both parties sign a document which incorporates the lease in its final form. A copy of the proposed lease having been attached to their contract, it is not then unknown for the parties to leave their relationship on this purely contractual footing, thereby dispensing with the completion of their contract by formal grant.[1] In the result, the parties are bound by an 'estate contract'[2] which, if specifically enforceable, confers on the prospective tenant an *equitable* term of years[3] that is widely (if slightly inaccurately) supposed to be as good as a legal lease.[4]

1   There has obviously been compliance with the requirement of written contract imposed

by LP(MP)A 1989, s 2(1) **[para 9.15]**. Contracts for the grant of a term not exceeding three years are exempted from this requirement (LP(MP)A 1989, s 2(5)(a)).
2   **[Para 9.23]**.
3   Failure to execute the contracted lease activates the doctrine in *Walsh v Lonsdale* **[para 9.66]**.
4   **[Para 9.69]**.

Assignment of a term of years

7.227   The limited exemption from formality accorded by the Law of Property Act 1925 to certain kinds of lease or tenancy applies only to the *creation* of a term of years. It is clear that, in order to be effective at law, the *assignment* of any legal leasehold – irrespective of its duration – must be effected formally by deed.[1] (Depending on the duration of the term, the assignment may also require completion by registration of the new leasehold proprietor at Land Registry.[2]) Thus a yearly tenancy, although perfectly capable of oral creation, must be assigned by deed if it is to invest the assignee with a legal estate in the land.[3] An assignment by mere signed writing takes effect as an equitable assignment, investing the assignee with only an equitable term. An oral assignment is nowadays wholly ineffectual (except possibly in circumstances of proprietary estoppel).[4] In these respects the relevant statutory provisions doubtless compel a 'curious distinction' between the manner in which a short lease may be created and the manner in which it may be assigned, but this distinction is now too well established to be disturbed.[5]

1   *Crago v Julian* [1992] 1 WLR 372 at 376C–D, 377D–E per Nicholls V-C. See [1992] Fam Law 294 (S M Cretney); [1992] Conv 375 (P Sparkes). An assignment is a 'disposal' which requires signed writing (see LPA 1925, s 53(1)(a)); and, since it also ranks as a 'conveyance', must be made by deed (see LPA 1925, s 52(1)) if it is to take effect at law. The saving effect of LPA 1925, ss 52(2)(d), 54(2) is confined to the 'creation' of leases.
2   **[Paras 7.241, 7.244]**.
3   *Botting v Martin* (1808) 1 Camp 317 at 319, 170 ER 970 at 971; *Camden LBC v Alexandrou* (1998) 30 HLR 534 at 539. See also *Crago v Julian* [1992] 1 WLR 372 at 378B.
4   Prior to 27 September 1989 an oral assignment might arguably have been supported in equity on the basis of consideration and part performance (see *Crago v Julian* [1992] 1 WLR 372 at 378C–D; *Croydon LBC v Buston* (1991) 24 HLR 36 at 38). See now LP(MP)A 1989, s 2.
5   *Crago v Julian* [1992] 1 WLR 372 at 376F–377A per Nicholls V-C, who confessed (at 377B) that he saw 'common sense and practicality' in the argument that an orally created lease should be likewise capable of informal assignment. See [1992] Conv 268 (J Martin).

REGISTRATION OF TITLE TO LEASEHOLD ESTATES

7.228   Pursuant to the Land Registration Act 2002 it is possible, and sometimes compulsory, for the title to many kinds of leasehold estate to be registered at Land Registry.[1] Indeed the 2002 Act has considerably extended the dragnet of title registration, generally reducing the minimum registrable term to a term in excess of seven years.[2] The registration threshold formerly imposed by the Land Registration Act 1925 caught only terms in excess of 21 years,[3] but the 2002 Act effectively recognises the increasing commercial reality that business leases are now generally short-term leases.[4] The Land Registration Act 2002 therefore aims not only to bring a vast range of short-term leases on to the Land Register for the first time,[5] but also, in so doing, to render them eventually susceptible to processes of electronic grant (by way of sublease) and electronic disposition. It is also obvious that the leasehold relationship may easily produce two or more substantively registered titles in the same land, ie titles to (respectively) the estates of the freehold owner and of any owner of a subsidiary leasehold term of more than seven years.[6] Each independently registered estate will bear a unique title number and will have its own register of title.[7]

1   No registration can be effected in respect of a term of years created as security for a mortgage loan where there is a subsisting right of redemption (LRA 2002, ss 3(5), 4(5)).

2   Power has been reserved under the Land Registration Act 2002 to lower the threshold for substantive registration of title to cover leasehold terms in excess of *three* years (see LRA 2002, s 118(1)). Such a move is likely to occur when electronic conveyancing becomes fully operational, thereby ensuring that all leases which require formal grant by deed [**para 7.219**] also trigger compulsory registration at Land Registry (see Law Com No 271 (2001), para 3.17).

3   LRA 1925, ss 8(1)(a), 8(1A), 21.

4   The Law Commission had long been aware of the modern trend in favour of shorter, and therefore more flexible, commercial leases (see Law Com No 254 (1998), paras 3.7–3.10; Law Com No 271 (2001), para 3.16).

5   Substantive registration never applies, however, to periodic tenancies. Such tenancies are not transferred in practice and their registration would serve no useful purpose in facilitating dealings in registered land (see Law Commission, *Property Law: Land Registration* (Law Com No 125, October 1983), para 4.26(a)). See also *Newlon Housing Trust v Alsulaimen* [1999] 1 AC 313 at 318H–319A per Lord Hoffmann.

6   The bureaucratic act of registration cannot convert a licence into a lease (see e g *Re Lehrer and the Real Property Act* (1961) SR (NSW) 365 at 376–377) or otherwise validate any interest which is not viable under the general law (see *Re Ridgeway and Smith's Contract* [1930] VLR 111 at 117; *Karacominakis v Big Country Developments Pty Ltd* (2000) 10 BPR 18235 at [52]).

7   See *Ferrishurst Ltd v Wallcite Ltd* [1999] Ch 355 at 363F–G.

Voluntary first registration

7.229   Substantive registration of title to a previously unregistered legal leasehold estate is always available under the Land Registration Act 2002 as a matter of voluntary election,[1] but an application for such registration may be made only in respect of an estate granted for a term of which more than seven years remain unexpired.[2]

1   LRA 2002, s 3(1)–(2) [**para 7.39**]. Application for registration as proprietor may be made by any person in whom the leasehold estate is vested or who is entitled, otherwise than under a contract of purchase, to require that the estate be vested in him (LRA 2002, s 3(2), (6)).

2   LRA 2002, s 3(3). This limitation does not apply to leases under which the lessee's right to possession is discontinuous (LRA 2002, s 3(4)).

Compulsory registration of title

7.230   First registration of an unregistered legal leasehold estate at Land Registry is made mandatory on the occurrence of certain kinds of statutorily specified 'event' (or trigger). It is also the case that many forms of dealing with an already registered estate throw up a requirement of completion by registration of title to a leasehold estate. These various circumstances will shortly be examined in greater detail.[1]

1   [Paras 7.236–7.245].

Classes of leasehold title on first registration

7.231   As in the case of first registration of freeholds,[1] the registrar assigns an appropriate class of title to all leasehold estates presented, whether voluntarily or compulsorily, for first registration.[2] The class awarded depends on the extent to which the registrar has been able to investigate title to the estate out of which the leasehold has been granted.[3] There are four possible classes of title, as follows.

1   [Para 7.44].
2   LRA 2002, s 10(1).
3   The class of title awarded is indicated at the head of the relevant proprietorship register (LRR 2003, r 8(1)(a)).

Absolute leasehold title

7.232   'Absolute leasehold title' is the best and most frequently awarded class of title, the award operating effectively as a guarantee that the lease in question was validly granted. 'Absolute leasehold title' is accorded on the same conditions as pertain to absolute freehold titles,[1] with the additional requirement that the registrar must be able to approve the lessor's title to grant the lease.[2] First registration with absolute title vests the relevant leasehold estate in the lessee on much the same terms as apply to a successful freehold applicant, but subject also to 'all implied and express covenants, obligations, and liabilities incident to the estate.'[3] The new registered proprietor therefore takes subject to the covenants contained in the lease and any burdens affecting the lessor's reversion.

1   [Para 7.45].
2   LRA 2002, s 10(2).
3   LRA 2002, s 12(2)–(5).

Good leasehold title

7.233   If absolute title cannot be awarded, a leasehold application for first registration will almost certainly result in the award of a 'good leasehold title'. This class of title is conferred when the lessor's reversionary title cannot be examined, but the registrar is of opinion that the applicant's title is 'such as a willing buyer could properly be advised by a competent professional adviser to accept.'[1] First registration with good leasehold title is statutorily declared to have the same effect as registration with absolute title, save that it does not preclude 'the enforcement of any estate, right or interest affecting, or in derogation of, the title of the lessor to grant the lease.'[2] A good leasehold title may subsequently be upgraded to an absolute leasehold title if the registrar is satisfied as to the superior title.[3]

1　　LRA 2002, s 10(3).
2　　LRA 2002, s 12(6). In effect the registrar, in awarding a good leasehold title, certifies his approval of the lease, but cannot guarantee that it was validly granted by the lessor.
3　　LRA 2002, s 62(2).

Qualified leasehold title

7.234　A 'qualified leasehold title' is extremely rare and is awarded where there exists some fundamental uncertainty as to the subject matter of the registration.[1] A qualified title is precarious to the extent of the specified qualification (which may relate to a particular document or period of time which throws doubt on the title offered for registration). The qualified title is therefore subject to any adverse interests falling within the qualification which later emerge as having been in existence at the date of first registration.[2]

1　　LRA 2002, s 10(5).
2　　LRA 2002, s 12(7). A qualified leasehold registration may later be upgraded to good leasehold or even absolute leasehold title (LRA 2002, s 62(3)).

Possessory leasehold title

7.235　A 'possessory leasehold title' is awarded to any lessee who cannot produce sufficient documentary evidence of his title (eg in the case of loss or destruction of his title deeds) or who relies on a period of adverse possession of the land concerned.[1] First registration with a possessory leasehold title has the same effect as registration with absolute title, investing the applicant with a legal term of years, but subject to all adverse estates, rights and interests affecting the land which may later be shown to have existed at the date of first registration or to have been then capable of arising.[2]

1　　LRA 2002, s 10(6).
2　　LRA 2002, s 12(8). A possessory leasehold registration can be upgraded later to good leasehold or even absolute leasehold title (LRA 2002, s 62(3)). Where a leasehold title has been registered as possessory for at least twelve years and the proprietor is still in possession, the registrar may upgrade the title to good leasehold (LRA 2002, s 63(5)).

REGISTRATION OF NEWLY CREATED LEASEHOLD ESTATES

7.236　In the case of a lease granted for a term of more than *three* years but not more than *seven* years, the use of a deed is generally sufficient to confer legal quality on the leasehold estate thereby created – a proposition which is

an existing unregistered leasehold estate where, at the date of the dealing, the term of the lease still has more than seven years to run.[1]

1   LRA 2002, s 4(2)(b).

Events which trigger first registration

7.242 Compulsory first registration of title to a leasehold estate is triggered by any of a number of statutorily specified 'events'. The Land Registration Act 2002 requires[1] first registration following any transfer of the unregistered leasehold estate whether for valuable or other consideration, by way of gift, in pursuance of any court order or by means of an assent.[2] A requirement of first registration also arises on the grant of any 'protected first legal mortgage' of an unregistered leasehold estate.[3] On receipt of the application for first registration the registrar assigns an appropriate class of title to the newly registered estate.[4]

1   The requirement does not apply to transfers by operation of law (see LRA 2002, s 4(3)).
2   LRA 2002, s 4(1)(a). The duty to apply for registration of title rests on the transferee of the leasehold estate (LRA 2002, s 6(1), (3)(b)).
3   LRA 2002, ss 4(1)(g), 6(2)(a). On the meaning of 'protected first legal mortgage', see LRA 2002, s 4(8) **[para 7.40]**. Either the mortgagor or the mortgagee may apply for registration of the leasehold estate (LRA 2002, s 6(2)(b), (6); LRR 2003, r 21).
4   LRA 2002, s 10 **[para 6.9]**.

Consequence of failure to effect a first registration

7.243 Application for first registration of title to the leasehold estate must be made within two months of the date of the relevant 'event'[1] in the same way as described above on the grant of a new lease out of an unregistered reversion.[2] Failure to apply for timely registration of a transfer renders the disposition 'void' for the purpose of transferring a legal leasehold estate[3] and the transferee's term of years reverts to equitable status only. Where the trigger for first registration was a mortgage of an unregistered leasehold estate, failure to apply for such registration leaves the leasehold intact as an unregistered legal estate, but the mortgage takes effect only as a contract for value to create a legal charge (ie as a mere equitable mortgage).[4]

1   LRA 2002, s 6(1), (3)–(4).
2   **[Para 7.237]**.
3   LRA 2002, s 7(1).
4   LRA 2002, s 7(2)(b).

REGISTRATION OF DISPOSITIONS OF A REGISTERED LEASEHOLD ESTATE

7.244 A leasehold estate, once substantively registered at Land Registry, can be dealt with in much the same manner as a registered freehold title. In the absence of any 'restriction' entered in the register, the registered proprietor has, in principle, plenary powers of disposition over his leasehold estate.[1] However, certain 'dispositions' of a registered leasehold estate now require to be 'completed by registration' in order that they should 'operate at law.'[2] The category of registrable 'disposition' is wide enough to catch not merely the outright transfer of the registered leasehold estate, but also the creation of various kinds of sublease, mortgage charge, easement, profit *à prendre*, rentcharge and right of entry affecting the leasehold estate.[3]

1   LRA 2002, ss 23–24 ('owner's powers') **[para 7.49]**.
2   LRA 2002, s 27(1). This requirement does not apply to certain dispositions by operation of law, e g a transfer on the death or bankruptcy of an individual proprietor (LRA 2002, s 27(5)).
3   LRA 2002, s 27(2) **[para 2.144]**.

Transfer of a registered leasehold estate

7.245   As a matter of conveyancing practice, most dispositions of a registered leasehold are preceded by a specifically enforceable contract to engage in the dealing in question, with the result that the contract confers equitable rights on the disponee pending completion of the disposition.[1] In the case of an intended transfer of a registered leasehold estate, the contract is duly performed by the execution of an instrument of transfer in the form prescribed by the Land Registration Rules 2003.[2] The disposition of the registered estate must be completed by the entry of the transferee in the Land Register as the proprietor of the estate,[3] the transfer passing a legal estate only on due registration.[4] Pending registration of the transfer, the transferee holds merely an equitable leasehold term.[5] The legal title to the lease remains vested in the transferor.[6] In such cases the failure to vest the legal title in the transferee by registration has the effect of relegating all the latter's future transactions (e g by way of sale or mortgage) to equitable effect only, since none of these transactions is, for the moment, capable of registration.

1   **[Para 9.18]**.
2   LRA 2002, s 25(1); LRR 2003, rr 58, 206(1), Sch 1.
3   LRA 2002, s 27(1)–(2), Sch 2, para 2(1).
4   The date of registration of the new proprietorship is deemed retrospectively to be the date on which the application for registration was lodged at Land Registry (LRA 2002, s 74).
5   See e g *E S Schwab & Co Ltd v McCarthy* (1976) 31 P & CR 196 at 201, 213.
6   *Brown & Root Technology Ltd v Sun Alliance and London Assurance Co Ltd* [2001] Ch 733 at 741G–H.

Electronic disposition of registered leasehold estates

7.246   At present most unregistered dispositions generate at least an *equitable* entitlement in the disponee. However, under the stricter system of electronic conveyancing envisaged by the Land Registration Act 2002, dispositions of a registered leasehold estate will have no effect at all – either at law or in equity – until communicated electronically to the registrar and simultaneously recorded in the Land Register.[1]

1   LRA 2002, s 93(1)–(3), Sch 2 **[paras 2.118, 12.53]**.

RESIDUAL CATEGORIES OF UNREGISTRABLE LEASE

7.247 Irrespective of whether any superior estate has been substantively registered, leasehold terms of seven years or less are currently ineligible for substantive registration,[1] thus remaining off the register as mere 'deeds bundles'.[2] Certain categories of short lease may nevertheless qualify for other forms of protection under the Land Registration Act 2002. For instance, a lease granted for a term of more than three years can now be entered by 'notice' in the landlord's title, as and when that title is itself registered.[3] Furthermore, a lease granted for a term of seven years or less is statutorily declared to be an unregistered interest which 'overrides' any first registration of the superior estate out of which it has been carved.[4] Even after that superior estate becomes a registered title, such a lease continues to 'override' any subsequent disposition of the reversionary estate, thereby automatically binding all transferees or chargees of the landlord's title.[5]

1   It is likely that legal terms of more than *three* years will, at some future point, be drawn on to the register as substantively registrable estates (see LRA 2002, s 118(1)).
2   **[Para 2.112]**. An equitable lease (of any duration) likewise remains off the register, but, when issuing out of a registered reversion, may be protected as an overriding interest if the equitable lessee is in 'actual occupation' of the land (see LRA 2002, s 29(1), (2)(a)(ii), Sch 3, para 2; *Grace Rymer Investments Ltd v Waite* [1958] Ch 831 at 851).
3   LRA 2002, ss 32, 33(b).
4   LRA 2002, ss 11(4)(b), 12(4)(c), Sch 1, para 1 **[para 12.268]**.
5   LRA 2002, s 29(1), (2)(a)(ii), Sch 3, para 1 **[para 12.143]**.

PERIODIC TENANCY

7.248 A 'term of years' need not comprise a long or fixed term. It may instead take the form of a 'periodic tenancy' which runs from week to week, or from month to month, or from quarter to quarter, or from year to year,[1] continuing indefinitely until determined by the giving of the appropriate notice. Although it may actually endure for decades, no special formality of creation is required in respect of any periodic tenancy. Being at most a yearly tenancy, it need not be created by deed or other writing[2] and may be created at law by merely oral means.[3] Periodic tenancies are clearly ineligible for substantive registration of title or other entry in the Land Register but may 'override' both first registration and subsequent registered dispositions of registered estates.[4]

1   LPA 1925, s 205(1)(xxvii).
2   LPA 1925, ss 52(2)(d), 54(2) **[para 7.220]**.
3   Any transfer (or assignment) of a periodic tenancy must, however, be effected by deed if it is to vest a legal term of years in the assignee (*Crago v Julian* [1992] 1 WLR 372 at 377H–378A **[para 7.227]**).
4   LRA 2002, ss 11(4)(b), 12(4)(c), Sch 1, paras 1–2, s 29(1), (2)(a)(ii), Sch 3, paras 1–2.

Express periodic tenancy

7.249 A periodic tenancy may be created by express grant, such grants being most frequent in connection with the 'secure tenancies' allocated by local authority landlords[1] and the 'assured shorthold tenancies' created by private landlords.[2] Where a periodic tenancy is granted by express words, but the precise nature of the period is not explicitly declared, the periodicity of the tenancy is determined prima facie by the period with reference to which the rent payable is calculated, not by the frequency with which that rent is actually paid.[3]

1   **[Para 14.338]**. An expressly granted periodic tenancy is binding in its terms, even though the grantor was mistaken in believing the grantee to be eligible for the allocation of a tenancy (*Akinbolu v Hackney LBC* [1996] EGCS 73 (unwitting grant to immigrant 'overstayer')).

2   **[Para 14.329]**. Somewhat confusingly, a statutory minimum fixed term of six months has been imposed on most assured shorthold periodic tenancies granted on or after 28 February 1997. No order for possession may normally be made within this period (see HA 1988, s 21(5)(a) **[para 14.337]**).

3   Thus a tenant whose rent obligation amounts to '£5,200 per annum payable weekly' is presumed to hold a yearly tenancy, whereas a tenant whose rent obligation amounts to '£100 per week' is presumed to hold a weekly tenancy (see *Ladies' Hosiery & Underwear Ltd v Parker* [1930] 1 Ch 304 at 328–329). See similarly *E O N Motors Ltd v Secretary of State for the Environment* (1981) 258 EG 1300 (weekly tenancy arising from agreement to pay rent in quarterly instalments 'on the basis of £20 per week').

Implied periodic tenancy

7.250   By long tradition at common law, a periodic tenancy may also arise impliedly from circumstance. The historic motivation behind the implication of such periodic tenancies was the perceived need to protect the tenant from the landlord. Nowadays, however, the common law rules are increasingly directed towards the protection of the landlord from the tenant – and, even more so, the social landlord from the anti-social occupier. In consequence the presumption of implied periodic tenancy is neither so ready nor so frequent.[1]

1   This trend is mirrored in the innovation of the 'introductory tenancy' **[para 14.348]**, under which a local housing authority or housing action trust may now elect to grant rights of insecure possession for a probationary period of one year as a prelude to the creation of a 'secure tenancy' (HA 1996, ss 124(1), 125(1)). See *Manchester CC v Cochrane* [1999] 1 WLR 809 at 811C.

The old common law presumption

7.251   There used to be a strong common law presumption that, in the absence of express words, a periodic tenancy was impliedly created by entry into possession and the payment and acceptance of a periodic sum in the nature of rent.[1] Such circumstances were apt to generate a weekly, monthly, quarterly or yearly tenancy, depending on the period with reference to which the payment was calculated.[2] Indeed, until relatively recently it took little to raise a presumption that the implied periodic tenancy generated by the tenant's payments was a yearly tenancy.[3] The fact that rent was paid 'by reference to a year, or aliquot part of a year, affords evidence of a tenancy from year to year.'[4] Thus even the payment of a quarterly[5] or weekly[6] rent raised a rebuttable presumption of a periodic tenancy from year to year.[7] This tendency to presume, from the fact of regular payment, a *yearly* tenancy – or even *any* tenancy at all – is now outdated. In *Javad v Mohammed Aqil*,[8] the Court of Appeal, although emphasising the importance of inference from all the circumstances of the case, hinted that a greater realism may be applicable today. According to Nicholls LJ, where one party permits another to go into possession of his land on payment of a weekly or monthly rent, 'failing more the inference sensibly and reasonably to be drawn is that the parties intended that there should be a weekly or monthly tenancy.'[9]

1   *Doe d Lord v Crago* (1848) 6 CB 90 at 98–99, 136 ER 1185 at 1188–1189. This presumption 'dies very hard' (see *Longrigg, Burrough & Trounson v Smith* (1979) 251 EG 847 at 849 per Ormrod LJ), but see now *Javad v Mohammed Aqil* [1991] 1 WLR 1007 at 1011H–1012C per Nicholls LJ.

2   See *Cole v Kelly* [1920] 2 KB 106 at 132. It was sometimes suggested that a yearly tenancy came about only if the premises were 'ordinarily let from year to year' (*Doe d Lord v Crago* (1848) 6 CB 90 at 98, 136 ER 1185 at 1188) or if the tenant continued to pay a periodic rent for at least a whole year (*Moore v Dimond* (1929) 43 CLR 105 at 122–123 per Isaacs J. See also *Knight v Benett* (1826) 3 Bing 361 at 364, 130 ER 552 at 553; *Arden v Sullivan* (1850) 14 QB 832 at 839, 117 ER 320 at 323; *Hunt v Allgood* (1861) 10 CB (NS) 253 at 257, 142 ER 448 at 450).

3   There was, from the 18th century onwards, a strong presumption that a general occupation of land for which a periodic rent was paid should be construed as a tenancy from year to year (see *Doe d Martin and Jones v Watts* (1797) 7 Term Rep 83 at 85–86, 101 ER 866 at 868; *Low v Adams* [1901] 2 Ch 598 at 601; *Moore v Dimond* (1929) 43 CLR 105 at 116; *Progressive Mailing House Pty Ltd v Tabali Pty Ltd* (1985) 157 CLR 17 at 26 per Mason J). See *Bl Comm*, Vol II, p 147; W S Holdsworth, *History of English Law* (2nd edn, London 1937), Vol VII, pp 244–245.

4   *Moore v Dimond* (1929) 43 CLR 105 at 114 per Knox CJ, Rich and Dixon JJ. See *Braythwayte v Hitchcock* (1842) 10 M & W 494 at 497, 152 ER 565 at 567; *Landale v Menzies* (1909) 9 CLR 89 at 129–130; *Rochester Poster Services Ltd v Dartford BC* (1991) 63 P & CR 88 at 93; *Prudential Assurance Co Ltd v London Residuary Body* [1992] 2 AC 386 at 392B per Lord Templeman.

5   See eg *Doe d Thomson v Amey* (1840) 12 Ad & El 476 at 479–480, 113 ER 892 at 893; *Lee v Smith* (1854) 9 Exch 662 at 665, 156 ER 284 at 285; *Croft v William F Blay Ltd* [1919] 2 Ch 343 at 349, 357; *Moore v Dimond* (1929) 43 CLR 105 at 117.

6   The presumption of yearly tenancy was intensified where a tenant held under a formally invalid term of much greater duration [**para 7.256**]. See *Moore v Dimond* (1929) 43 CLR 105 at 116–117.

7   For further discussion of the implied periodic tenancy, see Chapter 9 [**para 9.62**].

8   [1991] 1 WLR 1007 at 1012E–G.

9   Where a landlord accepts rent paid on a periodic basis by a 'tenant at sufferance' [**para 7.272**], such payment may well be construed as giving rise to a weekly tenancy notwithstanding that the original tenancy comprised a fixed term of one year (see *Adler v Blackman* [1952] 2 All ER 41 at 44A–B, affd [1953] 1 QB 146 at 150–152). Compare, however, *Vaughan-Armatrading v Sarsah* (1995) 27 HLR 631 at 635–636.

The modern primacy of intention

7.252   The reservation of rent and its payment on some periodic basis were never wholly incompatible with the existence of something less than a term of years (eg a mere tenancy at will).[1] In cases of dispute it was ultimately the task of the court to examine the 'intentions of the parties in all the circumstances',[2] in order to determine whether it is 'right and proper to infer ... that the parties had reached an agreement' for a periodic tenancy.[3] The primacy of intention has been brought to the fore in the recent case law.[4] Particularly in view of the likelihood that tenancies may attract various kinds of long-term statutory protection, there is nowadays less inclination to presume the existence of a common law periodic tenancy from the mere fact of entry into possession and periodic payments of money.

1   *Doe d Bastow v Cox* (1847) 11 QB 122 at 123, 116 ER 421 at 422; *Hagee (London) Ltd v A B Erikson and Larson* [1976] QB 209 at 214F–G. The 'tenancy at will' is discussed shortly [**para 7.273**].
2   *Cardiothoracic Institute v Shrewdcrest Ltd* [1986] 1 WLR 368 at 378C. See also *Doe d Cheny v Batten* (1775) 1 Cowp 243 at 245, 98 ER 1066 at 1067 per Lord Mansfield CJ; *Irish Shell and BP Ltd v John Costello Ltd* [1984] IR 511 at 517–518 per Henchy J.
3   *Longrigg, Burrough & Trounson v Smith* (1979) 251 EG 847 at 849. See also *Uzun v Ramadan* [1986] 2 EGLR 255 at 257E–H; *Vaughan-Armatrading v Sarsah* (1995) 27 HLR 631 at 636 (no intention to create new tenancy for overstaying student taking resit examinations).
4   It remains uncertain whether, in this context, intention should be assessed subjectively or objectively (*Dreamgate Properties Ltd v Arnot* (1997) 76 P & CR 25 at 30). An objective assessment may be preferable in that it tends to overcome evidential difficulties and holds the parties more strictly accountable for their actions and inactions (compare the actual, and regrettable, outcome in *Dreamgate Properties* itself, where nobody thought fit to update a computer program for generating rent demands).

7.253   In *Javad v Mohammed Aqil*,[1] for instance, the Court of Appeal conceded that, in the total absence of any other 'material surrounding circumstances', the inference to be drawn from the periodic payment of rent is that the parties intended to create a periodic tenancy. Nicholls LJ indicated, however, that only relatively rarely will the fact of periodic payment stand isolated from other factors which may help to clarify the matter of intention.[2] Where other explanatory circumstances exist, the payment of rent on a periodic basis, although a 'very important' factor, is merely one of the indicators to which the court must have regard in ascertaining the nature of the parties' relationship.[3] The old common law presumption of yearly tenancy may still prevail in relation to the payment and acceptance of rent under an informal or defective fixed term lease. But nowadays, in many other instances, an intention towards tenancy is contra-indicated either by the statutory context within which the parties are operating or by the fact that the parties are still actively negotiating the future of their commercial relationship. Contrary to the old common law presumption, it is 'settled law' today that the payment and acceptance of rent 'raises an open question',[4] the onus resting on the occupier to demonstrate an agreement for a tenancy.[5]

1   [1991] 1 WLR 1007 at 1012E.
2   The typical case today 'invariably involves more than the simple facts of possession and an unexplained payment of rent' ([1991] 1 WLR 1007 at 1014H).
3   [1991] 1 WLR 1007 at 1012F–G. A landowner is, for instance, entitled to compensation for the use and occupation of his land by a trespasser. Thus mere periodic payments by one who enters as a trespasser are unlikely to connote any agreement to create a periodic tenancy (*Westminster CC v Basson* (1990) 62 P & CR 57 at 60; *Brent LBC v O'Bryan* (1992) 65 P & CR 258 at 262). See also *Colchester BC v Smith* [1991] Ch 448 at 485C–D.
4   *Dreamgate Properties Ltd v Arnot* (1997) 76 P & CR 25 at 27 per Hirst LJ.
5   *Leadenhall Residential 2 Ltd v Stirling* [2002] 1 WLR 499 at [48] per Judge LJ. See *Dreamgate*

Properties Ltd v Arnot (1997) 76 P & CR 25, where the fact that a tenant continued to pay (and the landlord to accept) rent in response to an automatic computer-generated demand was held, surprisingly, not to evidence any intention to create a periodic tenancy.

RELEVANCE OF POTENTIAL STATUTORY PROTECTION FOR THE TENANT

7.254 In determining whether the mere fact of payment and acceptance of rent generates an implied periodic tenancy, modern courts tend to draw inferences as to the parties' likely intentions against the background of prevailing protective legislation in respect of the landlord and tenant relationship.[1] In days of substantial statutory regulation of the landlord's right to recover possession, there is an increasing tendency to accept that the old common law presumption of periodic tenancy is 'unsound and no longer holds.'[2] In *Cardiothoracic Institute v Shrewdcrest Ltd*,[3] for instance, the potential impact of the protective scheme provided for business tenants by Pt II of the Landlord and Tenant Act 1954 made the court unwilling to believe that the parties had intended, by mere payment and acceptance of rent, to create a periodic tenancy.[4] Similarly, no term of years is created by the social landlord who, having obtained a possession order against a grievously defaulting council tenant, allows him to remain in occupation so long as all instalments of rent arrears and future payments (or mesne profits) are paid.[5]

1   See e g *Javad v Mohammed Aqil* [1991] 1 WLR 1007 at 1014H, where the Court of Appeal saw the 'widespread intervention of statute in the landlord–tenant area' as providing one highly potent reason why few cases arise to be dealt with nowadays purely on the footing of entry into possession coupled with the tendering of a periodic rent.
2   *Longrigg, Burrough & Trounson v Smith* (1979) 251 EG 847 at 849 per Ormrod LJ. See also *Javad v Mohammed Aqil* [1991] 1 WLR 1007 at 1017C–D per Nicholls LJ; *Leadenhall Residential 2 Ltd v Stirling* [2002] 1 WLR 499 at [48] per Judge LJ.
3   [1986] 1 WLR 368 at 379F–G. See [1987] Conv 55 (J E M); [1988] Conv 16 (J E A).
4   It is arguable that the common law presumption still retains its force where a tenancy unaffected by statutory prolongation has come to an end and the parties have not yet expressly agreed on the creation of a new tenancy. Under these circumstances the continuing payment and acceptance of a periodic rent may well generate a periodic tenancy 'on the footing that that is what the parties must have intended or be taken to have intended' (see *Cardiothoracic Institute v Shrewdcrest Ltd* [1986] 1 WLR 368 at 378B–C). See also *Cole v Kelly* [1920] 2 K B 106 at 127; *Bennett Properties v H & S Engineering* [1998] CLY 393.
5   *Burrows v Brent LBC* [1996] 1 WLR 1448 at 1455H–1456A **[para 3.51]**; *Leadenhall Residential 2 Ltd v Stirling* [2002] 1 WLR 499 at [47] per Judge LJ ('[m]esne profits are emphatically not rent'). The curious category of the 'tolerated trespasser' on local authority premises has, in recent years, gathered a certain momentum (see e g *Colchester BC v Smith* [1991] Ch 448 at 485C–D; *Greenwich LBC v Regan* (1996) 72 P & CR 507 at 516–518, 520–521; *Pemberton v Southwark LBC* [2000] 1 WLR 1672 at 1677A–D, 1683A; *Hounslow LBC v Adjei* [2004] 2 All ER 636 at [14]).

RELEVANCE OF PENDING NEGOTIATIONS

7.255 The implied creation of a tenancy is unlikely to have been intended where an occupier enters into (or stays in) possession paying a periodic rent whilst the owner remains locked in negotiations either with him or with some third party[1] about the commercial future of the premises. In *Javad v Mohammed Aqil*,[2] for example, an occupier had been allowed into possession of premises pending the conclusion of negotiations over a proposed ten year lease. The Court of Appeal declined to find that a periodic tenancy had been created by the occupier's payment during this period of quarterly amounts of rent. According to Nicholls LJ, entry into possession while negotiations proceed is 'one of the classic circumstances in which a tenancy at will may exist.'[3] There had been credible evidence here that the parties understood that the premises were to be vacated if negotiations broke down. The Court felt unable on this basis to accede to the occupier's argument that the periodic payments had generated a tenancy which would prematurely have qualified for extended protection under Pt II of the Landlord and Tenant Act 1954.[4] The lease contemplated by the parties had clearly been a long lease rather than any periodic tenancy. The Court was therefore reluctant, whilst the parties were 'in the throes of negotiating larger terms', to infer the creation of a different, and much more limited, interest on the mere basis of periodic payments of money.[5]

1   See e g *Dreamgate Properties Ltd v Arnot* (1997) 76 P & CR 25 at 27–28.
2   [1991] 1 WLR 1007.
3   [1991] 1 WLR 1007 at 1019E. Compare *Walji v Mount Cook Land Ltd* (2001) 81 P & CR D47 at D48 (quarterly tenancy).
4   **[Para 14.354]**.
5   [1991] 1 WLR 1007 at 1013B–C, 1017F–G. Likewise in *Uzun v Ramadan* [1986] 2 EGLR 255 at 257F, it was held that the parties' known intention to create a five-year term could not support an implication of periodic tenancy founded on periodic payments of rent. See [1988] Conv 17 (J E A). See also *Sopwith v Stutchbury* (1983) 17 HLR 50 at 74 per Stephenson LJ; *Brent LBC v O'Bryan* (1992) 65 P & CR 258 at 262–264.

Rent payment under an informal or defective fixed term

7.256   One context in which the old common law presumption of periodic tenancy survives is that in which an attempted grant of a substantial fixed term legal lease has failed by reason of some informality or technical imperfection.[1] The intended tenant clearly cannot take a legal estate in the fixed term. In many cases of abortive grant of a legal lease, equity regards the incomplete, informal or imperfect transaction as generating an *equitable* term of years which is the equivalent, in all but legal quality, of the term of years which was originally intended to pass.[2] This doctrine of equivalent equitable effect is, however, crucially dependent on the availability of specific performance and if, for some reason, the contractual dealings of the parties are *not* specifically enforceable, the analysis of their relationship reverts to the common law perception of their respective rights and obligations.

1   Such is the effect, for instance, where the creation of a legal term has been precluded by the informality of the grant (ie by the use of means other than a deed **[para 9.44]**) or simply by reason of the non-completion of a contract to create the leasehold term **[para 9.46]**.
2   **[Para 9.48]** (the so-called doctrine in *Walsh v Lonsdale*).

7.257   In the case of a long leasehold term, the intended tenant may well enter into possession of the land, often unaware that his fixed term leasehold estate is ineffective at law, and a periodic rent may begin to be paid and received. A tenant under an incomplete or imperfect lease, on being allowed into possession, immediately acquires the status of a tenant at will.[1] As soon as a periodic rent is offered by a tenant at will in virtue of his occupation of land and such payment is accepted by the landowner, the courts are apt to infer an intention in the parties to create a periodic tenancy. The tenancy at will is thus converted by implication of law into a periodic tenancy,[2] ie a term of years in the full common law sense.[3] This result follows whether the tenant entered by virtue of a formally defective lease[4] or under an agreement to create a future lease[5] or even under a purported lease which is altogether void on other grounds (eg uncertainty of term).[6]

1   [Para 7.273]. See *Braythwayte v Hitchcock* (1842) 10 M & W 494 at 497, 152 ER 565 at 567; *Moore v Dimond* (1929) 43 CLR 105 at 114–115; *Progressive Mailing House Pty Ltd v Tabali Pty Ltd* (1985) 157 CLR 17 at 25–26 per Mason J.
2   See *Javad v Mohammed Aqil* [1991] 1 WLR 1007 at 1012E–G per Nicholls LJ; *Brent LBC v O'Bryan* (1992) 65 P & CR 258 at 263 per Beldam LJ.
3   *Moore v Dimond* (1929) 43 CLR 105 at 112.
4   *Doe d Rigge v Bell* (1793) 5 Term Rep 471 at 472, 101 ER 265 at 266 per Lord Kenyon CJ; *Moore v Dimond* (1929) 43 CLR 105 at 113–114; *Chan v Cresdon Pty Ltd* (1989) 168 CLR 242 at 248; *Abjornson v Urban Newspapers Pty Ltd* [1989] WAR 191 at 199.
5   *Hamerton v Stead* (1824) 3 B & C 478 at 483, 107 ER 811 at 813; *Chapman v Towner* (1840) 6 M & W 100 at 104, 151 ER 338 at 340; *Doe d Thomson v Amey* (1840) 12 Ad & El 476 at 479–480, 113 ER 892 at 893; *Anderson v Midland Railway Co* (1861) 3 E & E 614 at 622, 121 ER 573 at 576; *Swain v Ayres* (1888) 21 QBD 289 at 293; *Moore v Dimond* (1929) 43 CLR 105 at 112–113; *Dockrill v Cavanagh* (1944) 45 SR (NSW) 78 at 80–81 per Jordan CJ; *Chan v Cresdon Pty Ltd* (1989) 168 CLR 242 at 248.
6   *Prudential Assurance Co Ltd v London Residuary Body* [1992] 2 AC 386 at 392B–C, 393G–H per Lord Templeman; *Southampton Community Health Services NHS Trust v Crown Estate Commissioners* [1997] EGCS 155. See also *Inntrepeneur Estates Ltd v Mason* (1993) 68 P & CR 53 at 72–73 (lease potentially struck down as anti-competitive by Art 85 of the Treaty of Rome).

Nature of the periodic term

7.258   The precise nature of this implied periodic tenancy is governed prima facie by the period with reference to which the rent is payable.[1] There is, however, a ready presumption that the parties intended to create a common law tenancy from year to year (terminable on half a year's notice),[2] there being a natural concern lest, for instance, the fact of weekly payments under an agreed term of substantial duration should relegate the tenant to a mere 'terminable holding of a week.'[3]

1   *Martin v Smith* (1874) LR 9 Ex 50 at 52; *Adams v Cairns* (1901) 85 LT 10 at 11.
2   See eg *Prudential Assurance Co Ltd v London Residuary Body* [1992] 2 AC 386 at 392B–C, 393G–H; *Inntrepeneur Estates Ltd v Mason* (1993) 68 P & CR 53 at 72.
3   *Moore v Dimond* (1929) 43 CLR 105 at 116–117 per Knox CJ, Rich and Dixon JJ.

Duration of the periodic tenancy

7.259   The common law tenancy implied from periodic payments continues only for the duration of the fixed term originally contemplated. Throughout this term the periodic tenancy is, of course, vulnerable to earlier determination by due notice to quit[1] and if not so determined will simply expire, without any further notice to quit, through the effluxion of time.[2]

1   *Doe d Davenish v Moffatt* (1850) 15 QB 257 at 265, 117 ER 455 at 458; *Progressive Mailing House Pty Ltd v Tabali Pty Ltd* (1985) 157 CLR 17 at 26 per Mason J; *Chan v Cresdon Pty Ltd* (1989) 168 CLR 242 at 248.
2   *Doe d Davenish v Moffatt* (1850) 15 QB 257 at 265, 117 ER 455 at 458; *Moore v Dimond* (1929) 43 CLR 105 at 113; *Progressive Mailing House Pty Ltd v Tabali Pty Ltd* (1985) 157 CLR 17 at 26 per Mason J.

Terms of the implied periodic tenancy

7.260   The implied periodic tenancy is deemed to incorporate all the originally agreed terms of the ineffective or incomplete fixed term lease[1] in so far as these terms are compatible with and transferable to the periodic tenancy.[2] Thus the tenancy includes prima facie any covenant in the invalid letting which related, for instance, to restrictions on the use of the premises or to a right of entry reserved for the landlord.[3] Some of the originally agreed terms may not, however, be so easily transferable. In *Martin v Smith*,[4] for example, a leasehold term requiring the tenant to redecorate the premises at the end of the seventh year was held to be inconsistent with a periodic tenancy, which by its nature could be no more than a tenancy from year to year.[5]

1   *Bennett v Ireland* (1858) El Bl & El 326 at 334–335, 120 ER 530 at 533; *Swain v Ayres* (1888) 21 QBD 289 at 293 per Lord Esher MR; *Moore v Dimond* (1929) 43 CLR 105 at 113; *Progressive Mailing House Pty Ltd v Tabali Pty Ltd* (1985) 157 CLR 17 at 26 per Mason J; *Chan v Cresdon Pty Ltd* (1989) 168 CLR 242 at 248.
2   *Prudential Assurance Co Ltd v London Residuary Body* [1992] 2 AC 386 at 392B–E per Lord Templeman. See *Doe d Rigge v Bell* (1793) 5 Term Rep 471 at 472, 101 ER 265 at 266 per Lord Kenyon CJ; *Arden v Sullivan* (1850) 14 QB 832 at 839, 117 ER 320 at 323; *Croft v William F Blay Ltd* [1919] 2 Ch 343 at 349.
3   See e g *Thomas v Packer* (1857) 1 H & N 669 at 672–673, 156 ER 1370 at 1371–1372.
4   (1874) LR 9 Exch 50 at 52.
5   Such a covenant would have been enforceable if the tenant had in fact continued to occupy, as a yearly tenant, for the originally anticipated term of seven years (*Martin v Smith* (1874) LR 9 Ex 50 at 52–53).

Inferior quality of the implied periodic tenancy

7.261   The common law tenancy generated by entry and payment of rent arises by sheer implication from conduct and takes effect automatically as a legal estate in the land. However, the broad equivalence which is generally maintained between the covenants contained in the implied periodic tenancy and the abortive fixed term legal lease which it replaces should not obscure the fact that these two leasehold interests are quite separate phenomena.[1] In the absence of specific enforcement of the longer fixed term lease, the intended tenant is relegated to a legal periodic tenancy which is vulnerable to termination – by the giving of appropriate notice to quit – long before the expiration of the originally intended fixed term.

1   See e g *Chan v Cresdon Pty Ltd* (1989) 168 CLR 242 at 249–250, where a majority in the High
     Court of Australia took the view that the implied common law tenancy was 'distinct from' the
     lease which had been rendered legally ineffective for want of registration. In consequence, a
     third party's guarantee of due performance under the abortive lease had no application to the
     performance of the tenant's obligations under the periodic tenancy. Compare, however, *Inglis
     v Clarence Holdings Ltd* [1997] 1 NZLR 268 at 272.

Legal quality of the periodic tenancy

7.262   Unless granted by someone who holds only an equitable interest in the
land, a periodic tenancy takes effect as a legal estate in both registered and
unregistered land.[1] Being at most a yearly letting, the periodic tenancy may be
created purely orally.[2]

1   Thus the tenant of a council house has a legal estate in his home (*Melluish v BMI (No 3) Ltd*
     [1995] Ch 90 at 103H per Vinelott J).
2   **[Para 7.220]**.

Matters binding on the periodic tenant

7.263   The grant of a periodic tenancy out of a registered reversion, whilst not
itself a registrable disposition, is statutorily deemed to be the equivalent of a
registered disposition. The tenant therefore holds subject to matters referred to in
the register and to any overriding interests.[1] Where a periodic tenancy has been
carved out of an unregistered estate, the tenant ranks as a purchaser for value of a
legal estate for the purpose of the 'bona fide purchaser rule',[2] but is clearly bound
by any interests which have been registered pursuant to the Land Charges Acts.[3]

1   LRA 2002, s 29(1)–(2), (4) **[para 12.76]**.
2   See *Melluish v BMI (No 3) Ltd* [1996] 1 AC 454 at 476C–D per Lord Browne-Wilkinson.
3   **[Paras 2.185, 12.275]**.

Binding impact of the periodic tenancy

7.264   A common law periodic tenancy granted out of a registered reversionary estate ranks as an overriding interest.[1] If granted out of an unregistered
estate, it is automatically binding on the world by virtue of its legal quality.[2]
Until duly determined, periodic tenancies therefore remain binding on the
landlord and upon any assignee of the landlord's reversion.

1   LRA 2002, s 29(1), (2)(a)(ii), Sch 3, paras 1–2 **[para 12.143]**.
2   **[Paras 2.176, 12.274]**.

TENANCY BY ESTOPPEL

7.265   A person who is not currently entitled to an estate in land cannot grant
a term of years, but remains competent to create a 'lease' or 'tenancy' which
takes effect by estoppel.[1]

1   **[Para 7.86]**.

Principle of estoppel between landlord and tenant

7.266   It is a 'fundamental principle'[1] of the common law that a grantor is not entitled to dispute the validity of his own grant[2] and may not therefore disaffirm the title of his grantee.[3] Thus a landlord is never permitted to deny that his grant of a lease has created an effective leasehold estate in his grantee. For his part, the grantee, so long as he continues in possession and enjoys the benefits of the lease, is debarred from questioning the validity of his landlord's title in any action brought against him by the latter.[4]

1   *First National Bank plc v Thompson* [1996] Ch 231 at 237A per Millett LJ; *Bruton v London & Quadrant Housing Trust* [1998] QB 834 at 844E per Millett LJ.
2   See *Goodtitle d Edwards v Bailey* (1777) 2 Cowp 597 at 600–601, 98 ER 1260 at 1262.
3   *First National Bank plc v Thompson* [1996] Ch 231 at 237F–G per Millett LJ.
4   *Cuthbertson v Irving* (1859) 4 H & N 742 at 754, 157 ER 1034 at 1039 per Martin B.

Attribution of relatively good titles

7.267   These propositions hold good even if, at the time of the leasehold grant, the landlord owned no proprietary estate in the land out of which he could carve a term of years. It follows from the basic relativity of title in English law[1] that, provided the tenant 'enjoys everything which his lease purports to grant', it cannot 'concern him what the title of the lessor … really is.'[2] The deficiency of the landlord's title is nothing to the point. If the landlord has no title, common law doctrine confers on him a title by estoppel which, at least vis à vis his tenant, supports the grant of a term of years.[3] On the execution of the lease – even if both parties knew of the landlord's defective title[4] – the doctrine of estoppel credits the landlord with a fee simple by estoppel[5] and regards the tenant as holding a tenancy by estoppel which binds all except those who can claim a superior title.[6]

1   **[Para 6.4]**. See also *First National Bank plc v Thompson* [1996] Ch 231 at 237B per Millett LJ; *Bell v General Accident, Fire & Life Assurance Corpn Ltd* [1998] 1 EGLR 69 at 72H per Mummery LJ.
2   *Cuthbertson v Irving* (1859) 4 H & N 742 at 758, 157 ER 1034 at 1041 per Martin B.
3   Tenancies by estoppel were developed at a time when title to land was often doubtful or difficult to establish (see *Bruton v London & Quadrant Housing Trust* [1998] QB 834 at 845B per Millett LJ).
4   *Morton v Woods* (1869) LR 4 QB 293 at 304.
5   *Cuthbertson v Irving* (1859) 4 H & N 742 at 754–755, 758, 157 ER 1034 at 1039, 1041 per Martin B. See eg *Bell v General Accident, Fire & Life Assurance Corpn Ltd* [1998] 1 EGLR 69 at 71H per Hutchison LJ, who pointed out that, in view of the principle of relative title, there is 'nothing surprising about the proposition that the title created in the lessor by estoppel is one in fee simple'.
6   *First National Bank plc v Thompson* [1996] Ch 231 at 239B. 'The law proceeds on a hypothesis that [the landlord] had a title which it did not in fact have. As between the tenants and [the landlord], that hypothesis is irrefutable by evidence … The effect of the common law doctrine is to bid you to treat an imaginary state of affairs as real' (*Bell v General Accident, Fire & Life*

Assurance Corpn Ltd [1998] 1 EGLR 69 at 72F per Mummery LJ). The doctrine of tenancy by estoppel applies regardless of whether the tenancy was created by deed, in writing or by parol (see *E H Lewis & Son Ltd v Morelli* [1948] 2 All ER 1021 at 1024F–G; *Universal Permanent Building Society v Cooke* [1952] Ch 95 at 103).

7.268   As Lord Hoffmann indicated in *Bruton v London & Quadrant Housing Trust*,[1] 'it is not the estoppel which creates the tenancy, but the tenancy which creates the estoppel ... it is the fact that the agreement between the parties constitutes a tenancy that gives rise to an estoppel.'[2] Thereafter each party may deal independently with his imaginary estate.[3] The estoppel runs with the land and binds it in the hands of successors in title.[4] The tenant's estate by estoppel also qualifies for the more general protection offered by statute to tenancies.[5] Both titles are, for the time being, better than any other extant claim.

1   [2000] 1 AC 406 at 416A **[para 7.85]**. See [1999] Conv 517 (D Rook); [2000] CLJ 25 (M Dixon); (2000) 116 LQR 7 (S Bright); (2000) 63 MLR 424 (P Routley).
2   'The estoppel arises when one or other of the parties wants to deny one of the ordinary incidents or obligations of the tenancy on the ground that the landlord had no legal estate. The basis of the estoppel is that having entered into an agreement which constitutes a lease or tenancy, he cannot repudiate that incident or obligation' ([2000] 1 AC 406 at 416A per Lord Hoffmann).
3   *Gouldsworth v Knights* (1843) 11 M & W 337 at 343–344, 152 ER 833 at 835–836; *Cuthbertson v Irving* (1859) 4 H & N 742 at 758, 157 ER 1034 at 1041.
4   See *First National Bank plc v Thompson* [1996] Ch 231 at 239B–H per Millett LJ. There is one exception to the principle of binding force. In the absence of some recital or unequivocal representation of the grantor's title, the estoppel cannot prevail against a bona fide purchaser from the grantor without notice of the earlier transaction (see *Right d Jefferys v Bucknell* (1831) 2 B & Ad 278 at 283, 109 ER 1146 at 1148; *General Finance, Mortgage, and Discount Co v Liberator Permanent Benefit Building Society* (1878) 10 Ch D 15 at 24; *First National Bank plc v Thompson*, supra at 239H per Millett LJ, 244A–B per Staughton LJ).
5   See e g *Stratford v Syrett* [1958] 1 QB 107 at 115–116 (Rent Act protection **[para 14.312]**); *Bell v General Accident, Fire & Life Assurance Corpn Ltd* [1998] 1 EGLR 69 at 72A, K (protection under Landlord and Tenant Act 1954, Pt II **[para 14.354]**).

Good leasehold equivalent

7.269   The common law phenomenon of tenancy by estoppel finds an echo in 'good leasehold title' under the Land Registration Act 2002.[1] Good leasehold title may be accorded by Land Registry even though the applicant for registration cannot prove his landlord's title. The lease presented by the applicant is simply taken at face value as a grant out of an unregistered reversion, of which, in the absence of deduction of the landlord's title, the Chief Land Registrar necessarily knows nothing. There is, in effect, a subset of persons for whom the chimaera of good leasehold title is very real: good leasehold title, once registered, is thereafter alienable by way of sale, mortgage and otherwise. But just as a good leasehold title has life breathed into it on registration, so too it will expire, should that title be closed on rectification, as if it had never existed. The 'good leasehold' remains always subject to the one matter never excluded by guarantee on registration, ie the possibility that it may ultimately be defeated by an owner whose title is better than that of the putative landlord.[2]

1   **[Para 7.233]**.

2   Where a good leasehold title is defeated by an interest derived from some superior title, no indemnity is payable on the closure of the registered title. Interests excepted from the effect of registration are always binding on the registered estate (LRA 2002, s 12(6)). Subsequent alteration of the registered title is not the effective cause of the loss suffered by the proprietor [**para 12.248**].

Feeding the estoppel

7.270   The application of estoppel theory brings into play one important 'companion'[1] or 'satellite'[2] doctrine, which relates to 'feeding' of the estoppel. If, after granting a lease out of a title which he did not currently own, a landlord by estoppel at some later date acquires a legal estate in the land which would have sustained his grant, the estoppel is said to be 'fed'. The tenant's lease, together with the landlord's reversion, 'then take[s] effect in interest and not by estoppel.'[3] The benefit of the grantor's subsequent acquisition thus 'goes automatically to the earlier grantee',[4] the tenant acquiring a legal term of years which is now good against the world.[5]

1   *First National Bank plc v Thompson* [1996] Ch 231 at 237B per Millett LJ.
2   *Bell v General Accident, Fire & Life Assurance Corpn Ltd* [1998] 1 EGLR 69 at 72J per Mummery LJ.
3   *Cuthbertson v Irving* (1859) 4 H & N 742 at 754–755, 157 ER 1034 at 1039 per Martin B. In effect, the estoppel is 'fed' by the later conveyance of the estate out of which the grantor purported to make the original grant (see *Church of England Building Society v Piskor* [1954] Ch 553 at 564–566). In *Bruton v London & Quadrant Housing Trust* [2000] 1 AC 406, for instance, the landlord by estoppel subsequently acquired a leasehold estate in the block of flats in which it had created a tenancy by estoppel (see [1998] QB 834 at 838B), at which point the estoppel was clearly fed.
4   *Rajapakse v Fernando* [1920] AC 892 at 897 per Lord Moulton.
5   See also *First National Bank plc v Thompson* [1996] Ch 231 at 239B–C.

7.271   The doctrine of 'feeding the estoppel' can have some unexpected consequences for the ordering of priorities between parties. In *Universal Permanent Building Society v Cooke*,[1] for example, a purchaser of land obtained possession in advance of the completion of her purchase. Before completion she orally granted a periodic tenancy to her sister, who went immediately into possession. One day after the completion of the transfer of the estate to her, the purchaser mortgaged the land, in a separate transaction, to a building society. The Court of Appeal held that, on the purchaser's acquisition of the legal estate, the sister's tenancy by estoppel became a tenancy in interest, which, since it preceded the grant of the mortgage (albeit by one day), took priority over it.[2]

1   [1952] Ch 95.
2   [1952] Ch 95 at 103. Where a landlord by estoppel mortgages the land simultaneously with, and for the purpose of financing, the purchase of the legal estate, the ruling of the House of Lords in *Abbey National Building Society v Cann* [1991] 1 AC 56 [**para 12.217**] has effectively terminated any possibility that the mortgagee may be defeated by the 'feeding' of any tenancy created in advance of the arrival of title. The rejection of the theory of the *scintilla temporis* prevents any metamorphosis of the tenant's rights between the purchaser/landlord's acquisition of his legal estate and the creation of the mortgage charge.

TENANCY AT SUFFERANCE

7.272 A tenancy at sufferance arises where a tenant who has enjoyed a perfectly valid term of years holds over at the end of his term without the consent or dissent of the landlord.[1] It is the absence of the landlord's consent which distinguishes a tenancy at sufferance from a tenancy at will.[2] Having no 'tenancy' in any true sense, the tenant at sufferance can neither create any form of tenancy out of his own interest[3] nor maintain any action in trespass.[4] The tenant at sufferance is not liable to pay rent as such, but is liable to a money claim for use and occupation of the land.[5]

1　See *Co Litt*, p 57b; *Remon v City of London Real Property Co Ltd* [1921] 1 KB 49 at 58. Active dissent by the owner would render the occupier a trespasser (see *Simms v Lee* (1945) 45 SR (NSW) 352 at 354). Active assent converts him into a tenant at will.
2　*Wheeler v Mercer* [1957] AC 416 at 426.
3　*Thunder d Weaver v Belcher* (1803) 3 East 449 at 451 per Lord Ellenborough CJ, 102 ER 669; *SEAA Enterprises Pty Ltd v Figgins Holdings Pty Ltd* [1998] 2 VR 90 at 95 per Brooking JA (reversed on other grounds, but see *Figgins Holdings Pty Ltd v SEAA Enterprises Pty Ltd* (1999) 196 CLR 245 at 287 per McHugh J).
4　*Schwartz v Zamrl* [1968] 2 NSWR 51 at 53; *Victa Sales Pty Ltd v Tucker* [1970] 1 NSWR 737 at 738–739. He may, however, be eligible for certain kinds of statutory protection. See e g *Remon v City of London Real Property Co Ltd* [1921] 1 KB 49 at 58 (Rent Act) **[para 14.312]**.
5　*Bayley v Bradley* (1848) 5 CB 396 at 406, 136 ER 932 at 936.

TENANCY AT WILL

7.273 The phenomenon of the 'tenancy at will' occupies an obscurely defined no-man's land between the periodic tenancy and the mere licence.[1] A tenancy at will is an extremely fragile form of entitlement[2] and cannot be generated by any transaction which is not intended to create legal relations.[3] It arises where, with the consent of the owner, a person enjoys occupation of land for an indefinite period in circumstances where either party may at any time terminate the arrangement at will, ie on demand.[4] Unlike the case of the periodic tenancy (which is terminable only by the giving of appropriate notice[5]), no notice to quit is required in order to determine a tenancy at will,[6] and the existence of any express stipulation relating to notice is itself inconsistent with such a tenancy.[7] It is of the essence of a tenancy at will that it continues indefinitely until terminated on demand. A tenancy at will is also brought to an end by the death of either party[8] or if either party (to the knowledge of the other) assigns his own interest in the land.[9]

1　For a definition of 'licence', see Chapter 4 **[para 4.2]**. See also *Ramnarace v Lutchman* [2001] 1 WLR 1651 at [14] per Lord Millett.
2　The tenant at will is effectively 'at the mercy of' the owner (*Colchester BC v Smith* [1991] Ch 448 at 483A–B).
3　*Ramnarace v Lutchman* [2001] 1 WLR 1651 at [17]–[19] per Lord Millett.
4　*Errington v Errington and Woods* [1952] 1 KB 290 at 296. See also *Doe d Groves v Groves* (1847) 10 QB 486 at 491–492, 116 ER 185 at 187–188; *Buck v Howarth* [1947] 1 All ER 342 at 343G; *Minister for Land and Water Conservation v NTL Australia Pty Ltd* [2002] NSWCA 149. With certain exceptions **[para 7.251]**, all interests in land created by parol have 'the force and effect of interests at will only' (LPA 1925, s 54(1)).

5   See *Javad v Mohammed Aqil* [1991] 1 WLR 1007 at 1009A–B per Nicholls LJ.
6   *Crane v Morris* [1965] 1 WLR 1104 at 1108B–C; *Cliffe v Cooper* (Unreported, Court of Appeal, 20 May 1985); *Parker v Parker* [2003] EWHC 1846 (Ch) at [269] per Lewison J. A tenancy at will may validly indicate a future date beyond which the tenancy shall not continue (*GLC v Minchin* (Unreported, Court of Appeal, 25 February 1981)).
7   See *Colchester BC v Smith* [1991] Ch 448 at 483C; *Re Crown Construction Ltd* [1979] ACWS 676. Compare, however, *Uzun v Ramadan* [1986] 2 EGLR 255 at 257H; [1988] Conv 16 (J E A).
8   *James v Dean* (1805) 11 Ves 383 at 391, 32 ER 1135 at 1138; *Wheeler v Mercer* [1957] AC 416 at 427. A tenancy at will is also terminated if the tenant commits acts of voluntary waste (see *Countess of Shrewsbury's Case* (1600) 5 Co Rep 13b, 77 ER 68 at 69; *Warren v Keen* [1954] 1 QB 15 at 21; *Nichols v R A Gill Ltd* (1975) 51 DLR (3d) 493 at 498). See also *Kater v Kater* (1960) 104 CLR 497 at 503.
9   *Doe d Davies v Thomas* (1851) 6 Exch 854 at 857, 155 ER 792 at 793; *Pinhorn v Souster* (1853) 8 Exch 763 at 772–773, 155 ER 1560 at 1564–1565. See also *Minister for Land and Water Conservation v NTL Australia Pty Ltd* [2002] NSWCA 149.

Transitional function

7.274   Tenancies at will tend nowadays to be fairly unusual and slightly anomalous. It is likely that such a tenancy 'can now serve only one legal purpose, and that is to protect the interests of an occupier during a period of transition'[1] pending the arrival of a more permanent interest in the land.[2] A tenancy at will normally confers some form of intermediate status and is readily (although not always) converted into an estate in the land – namely an implied periodic tenancy – as soon as the tenant offers and the owner accepts some payment of rent which is referable to a year or an aliquot part of a year.[3]

1   *Heslop v Burns* [1974] 1 WLR 1241 at 1253A per Scarman LJ. See also *Irish Shell and BP Ltd v John Costello Ltd* [1984] IR 511 at 515 per O'Higgins CJ.
2   See e g *Mayor and Burgesses of Lewisham v Masterson* (2000) 80 P & CR 117 (occupation for five years during abortive negotiations for lease); *Ramnarace v Lutchman* [2001] 1 WLR 1651 (occupation pending purchase of land by occupier).
3   [**Para 7.251**]. See *Roe d Bree v Lees* (1777) 2 W Bl 1171 at 1173, 96 ER 691 at 692; *Richardson v Langridge* (1811) 4 Taunt 128 at 132, 128 ER 277 at 278; *Doe d Hull v Wood* (1845) 14 M & W 682 at 687, 153 ER 649 at 651; *Landale v Menzies* (1909) 9 CLR 89 at 129–130.

Nature of a tenancy at will

7.275   A tenancy at will is something of a hybrid and its status in law is in many respects unclear. A tenancy at will comprises merely a 'personal relation between the landlord and his tenant.'[1] The tenant at will is a tenant only in the root sense that he holds land: he may thus have *tenure*, but he certainly has no *estate*.[2] The tenant at will holds no proprietary interest in the land capable of sublease or assignment to a stranger.[3] This being so, the tenant at will closely resembles the licensee, who similarly has no estate in the land and who avoids being classified as a trespasser only because the landowner consents to his occupancy. However, the status of the tenant at will differs vitally from that of most licensees in that, even if he has no estate as such, the tenant at will is accounted to be in possession of the land.[4] Unlike the licensee, who generally enjoys no positive (as distinct from defensive) rights,[5] the tenant at will has an 'exclusive right of occupation'.[6] It has been said to follow that, unlike the licensee, the tenant at will is entitled to maintain an action in trespass against a stranger[7] (although not against the owner himself[8]). The tenant at will is liable, however, to make payment in respect of his use and occupation, such payment normally corresponding to the open market value of that use and occupation.[9]

1   *Wheeler v Mercer* [1957] AC 416 at 427 per Viscount Simonds.
2   See *Irish Shell and BP Ltd v John Costello Ltd* [1984] IR 511 at 523 per McCarthy J ('In truth the tenant at will is a person with a licence and no more than a licence to occupy').
3   See *Murphy v Ford* (1855) 5 ICLR 19 at 23; *Anderson v Tooheys Ltd* (1937) 54 WN (NSW) 21 at 23; *Victa Sales Pty Ltd v Tucker* [1970] 1 NSWR 737 at 739; *Minister for Land and Water Conservation v NTL Australia Pty Ltd* [2002] NSWCA 149. Compare, however, *Ward v Ryan* (1875) IR 10 CL 17 at 19. The tenant at will has no estate which can vest in his trustee in bankruptcy (see *Re Keith G Collins Ltd and Director, Veterans' Land Act* (1987) 35 DLR (4th) 96 at 101).
4   *Lynes v Snaith* [1899] 1 QB 486 at 488–489. The concept of 'possession' is discussed further in Chapter 3.
5   See *Street v Mountford* [1985] AC 809 at 816C per Lord Templeman.
6   *Goldsack v Shore* [1950] 1 KB 708 at 714–715 per Evershed MR.
7   *Heslop v Burns* [1974] 1 WLR 1241 at 1253C; *Cuvet v Davis* (1883) 9 VLR 390 at 396; *Victa Sales Pty Ltd v Tucker* [1970] 1 NSWR 737 at 739.
8   Non-consensual entry by the owner amounts to a termination of the tenancy at will (see *Co Litt*, p 55b; *Doe d Bennett v Turner* (1840) 7 M & W 226 at 232–233, 151 ER 749 at 751; *Landale v Menzies* (1909) 9 CLR 89 at 133).
9   *Mayor and Burgesses of Lewisham v Masterson* (2000) 80 P & CR 117 at 122–124.

Eligibility for statutory protection

7.276   Although imprecisely drawn, the borderline between tenancy at will and periodic tenancy is sometimes disproportionately significant in defining the availability of various kinds of statutory protection. It is clear, for instance, that the tenant at will cannot invoke the code of protection applicable to business tenancies under Pt II of the Landlord and Tenant Act 1954,[1] although it seems that he does come within the protection of the Rent Act.[2]

1   *Wheeler v Mercer* [1957] AC 416 at 426–428, 435; *Hagee (London) Ltd v A B Erikson and Larson* [1976] QB 209 at 215C, 216F; *Cardiothoracic Institute v Shrewdcrest Ltd* [1986] 1 WLR 368 at 376E–F; *Javad v Mohammed Aqil* [1991] 1 WLR 1007 at 1009B–C.
2   *Francis Jackson Developments Ltd v Stemp* [1943] 2 All ER 601 at 603H–604A.

TERMINATION OF LEASES AND TENANCIES

7.277   A lease or tenancy may come to an end in many ways, of which the following are the most important:
—   effluxion of time[1]
—   activation of 'break clause'[2]
—   notice to quit[3]
—   forfeiture[4]
—   surrender[5]

– disclaimer[6]
– repudiatory breach[7]
– frustration[8]
– termination on statutory grounds[9]
– enlargement[10]
– merger[11] and
– enfranchisement.[12]

1   **[Para 7.282]**.
2   **[Para 7.283]**.
3   **[Para 7.284]**.
4   **[Para 7.304]**.
5   **[Para 7.305]**.
6   **[Para 7.315]**.
7   **[Para 7.319]**.
8   **[Para 7.323]**.
9   **[Para 7.324]**.
10   **[Para 7.325]**.
11   **[Para 7.326]**.
12   **[Para 7.327]**.

Effect of termination on derivative leasehold estates

7.278   The logic of derivative interests in land requires, as a matter of fundamental common law principle,[1] that when a superior lease determines and the estate created by it ceases to exist, any subsidiary estate carved out of it must likewise determine.[2] Every subordinate interest 'must perish with the superior interest on which it is dependent.'[3] Thus a subtenancy is almost always destroyed at common law when the relevant superior tenancy is itself terminated.[4]

1   Lessor and lessee have no competence, as a matter of law, to contract out of this principle (see *PW & Co v Milton Gate Investments Ltd* [2004] 2 WLR 443 at [71]–[85], [147], [279 (ii)] per Neuberger J).
2   *Barrett v Morgan* [2000] 2 AC 264 at 268F, 269B, 271D–272A, 272C–D per Lord Millett. See similarly *Gisborne v Burton* [1989] QB 390 at 395E per Dillon LJ.
3   *Bendall v McWhirter* [1952] 2 QB 466 at 487 per Romer LJ. In the absence of contrary provision in the sublease, the involuntary destruction of the inferior estate constitutes a derogation from grant which is actionable in damages by the sublessee (*Conoid Pty Ltd v International Theme Park Pty Ltd* (2000) 10 BPR 18407 at [19] (New South Wales Court of Appeal)).
4   See *Barrett v Morgan* [2000] 2 AC 264 at 268F, 269B per Lord Millett; *Walter v Yalden* [1902] 2 KB 304 at 310; *PW & Co v Milton Gate Investments Ltd* [2004] 2 WLR 443 at [73]–[74] per Neuberger J ('an example of the maxim nemo dat quod non habet'). The sole exception to the common law principle of automatic termination of derivative tenancies arises in the case of consensual surrender by the superior tenant **[para 7.305]**.

Closure of registered leasehold titles

7.279   Where title to a leasehold estate is registered, termination is completed by the lodging of an application to close the leasehold title and to cancel any 'notice' relating to the lease entered in the reversioner's registered title.[1] The application must be accompanied by evidence to satisfy the registrar that the estate has determined.[2]

1   LRR 2003, r 79(2).
2   LRR 2003, r 79(1).

Effect of the tenant's death

7.280   The death of the tenant does not in itself terminate a tenancy. If the tenant dies testate, the residue of his tenancy devolves in accordance with his will. If the tenant dies intestate, the residue of his tenancy vests in the Public Trustee until the grant of administration.[1]

1   Administration of Estates Act 1925, s 9(1), as substituted by LP(MP)A 1994, s 14(1).

Termination does not necessarily authorise recovery of possession

7.281   Where premises have been let 'as a dwelling', it is a 'basic rule'[1] of statute law that, even though the lease has determined, the landlord may not recover possession without due process of law. If some person is lawfully residing in those premises, no right of re-entry or forfeiture contained in the lease may be enforced otherwise than by proceedings in court.[2] Similarly, where a residential tenancy has come to an end but the occupier continues to reside in the premises, it is unlawful for the owner to enforce, otherwise than by proceedings in court, his right to recover possession.[3]

1   *Harrow LBC v Qazi* [2004] 1 AC 983 at [36] per Lord Hope of Craighead.
2   Protection from Eviction Act 1977, s 2.
3   Protection from Eviction Act 1977, s 3(1). This restriction does not apply to statutorily protected tenancies **[para 14.311]** and 'excluded tenancies'. The latter category relates principally to accommodation shared by the tenant with a resident owner-occupier (see Protection from Eviction Act 1977, s 3A).

EFFLUXION OF TIME

7.282   A lease or tenancy for a fixed term automatically terminates on the expiration of the term certain[1] without any requirement that the tenant should be given notice to quit.[2] At this point the landlord's reversion 'falls in' and the land is no longer encumbered by the term of years. Subject to any restriction imposed by statute,[3] the superior owner is once again free to resume physical possession and to deal with the property as he wishes. In some contexts, however, the effluxion of the contractually agreed fixed term does not terminate the tenant's rights. Under Pt II of the Landlord and Tenant Act 1954, for instance, the leasehold estate of the business tenant cannot 'come to an end' except in accordance with the Act and meanwhile persists in force indefinitely as a 'continuation tenancy'.[4] Under the Rent Act 1977 and the Housing Acts of

1985 and 1988 many fixed-term residential tenants are converted into periodic tenants or otherwise enjoy some form of security of tenure on the expiry of their term.[5]

1   *Barrett v Morgan* [2000] 2 AC 264 at 270D per Lord Millett.
2   A lease which is expressly limited to continue only so long as the tenant abstains from breaching any covenant takes effect as a lease which is determinable by a proviso for re-entry on such breach (LPA 1925, s 146(7)).
3   See e g Protection from Eviction Act 1977, s 3(1) **[para 7.281]**.
4   L&TA 1954, s 24(1) **[para 14.355]**. The business tenant is also given a statutory right to request the grant of a new lease.
5   **[Paras 14.317, 14.336, 14.342]**.

ACTIVATION OF 'BREAK CLAUSE'

7.283   In the commercial context a long lease often contains a 'break clause' which allows either the landlord or the tenant to determine the lease by notice at any one or more of a number of stipulated intervals in advance of the final expiry date of the term certain (e g at the end of every seventh year). Such a break clause cannot be exercised by a single joint tenant acting unilaterally.[1] In *Mannai Investment Co Ltd v Eagle Star Life Assurance Ltd*,[2] the House of Lords significantly relaxed the requirement that the valid exercise of the option of early termination of the lease must comply exactly with the terms of the break clause.[3] In the *Mannai Investment* case a tenant had mistakenly served a notice which expired one day before the date specified in the break clause, but the House of Lords, by a majority, held the error to be immaterial where a reasonable recipient of the notice, with a knowledge of the terms of the lease, would have been left in no doubt that the tenant wished to determine the lease.[4] The notice was effective to end the lease on the date with reference to which the tenant should, more correctly, have framed the notice.

1   See *Hammersmith and Fulham LBC v Monk* [1992] 1 AC 478 at 490G per Lord Bridge of Harwich; *Hounslow LBC v Pilling* [1993] 1 WLR 1242 at 1247A per Nourse LJ.
2   [1997] AC 749. See [1998] Conv 326 (P F Smith).
3   See *A & J Mucklow (Birmingham) v Metro-Cammell Weymann* [1994] EGCS 64.
4   [1997] AC 749 at 772C per Lord Steyn, 780C–G per Lord Hoffmann. The more liberal approach of the *Mannai Investment* case has since been widely applied (see e g *Garston v Scottish Widows' Fund and Life Assurance Society* [1998] 1 WLR 1583 at 1588E–G; *York v Casey* [1998] 2 EGLR 25 at 26M–27C).

NOTICE TO QUIT

7.284   A lease or tenancy may be determinable by notice to quit.[1] The availability of this method of termination depends to some extent on the quality of the tenancy concerned.[2]

1   Unless the contrary is proved, service of the notice to quit is deemed to have been effected if the notice is posted. An assertion that the notice was not received does not constitute proof to the contrary (see *Lex Service Plc v Johns* (1989) 59 P & CR 427 at 432–433). See also LPA 1925, s 196; L&TA 1927, s 23.

2   There are also certain rules, of archaic derivation, relating to a holding over by the tenant after the expiry of a notice to quit. A yearly tenant or tenant for years who holds over after the landlord's service of a written notice to quit becomes liable to pay the landlord double the annual value of the land in respect of the period of holding over (Landlord and Tenant Act 1730, s 1). Any holding over by any kind of tenant following due notice (written or verbal) by the *tenant* is penalised by the imposition of a liability to pay double rent which is enforceable by action or distress (Distress for Rent Act 1737, s 18). This double rent liability arises, however, only where the landlord treats the ex-tenant holding over as a trespasser and not where the landlord regards the tenancy as continuing (*Oliver Ashworth (Holdings) Ltd v Ballard (Kent) Ltd* [2000] Ch 12 at 38G–39A).

Fixed term tenancies

7.285   In the case of a fixed term of years a notice to quit is effective only if the parties have expressly agreed that this should be so, since otherwise such a lease simply continues until the expiry of the term. As noted above, such notice to quit a fixed term is effectively a 'break notice' permitting, according to its terms, either party to determine the lease in advance of the specified term date.[1]

1   [Para 7.283].

Periodic tenancies

7.286   It is intrinsic to the concept of a periodic tenancy that it is determinable by a notice to quit given by *either* the landlord *or* the tenant.[1] In terms of the currently fashionable contractual analysis of leasehold relationships,[2] periodic tenancies are 'founded on the continuing will of both landlord and tenant that the tenancy shall persist.'[3] Thus either landlord or tenant may terminate a periodic tenancy by serving on the other a notice to quit, thereby indicating that that will has lapsed.[4] Such a notice does not, on its expiry, bring about the assignment or surrender of any interest to the landlord.[5] The periodic tenancy simply 'comes to an end by effluxion of time, namely the expiry of the last period for which the tenant or tenants have been willing for it to continue.'[6] In effect, determination by notice to quit causes the periodic tenancy to 'come to the end of its natural life.'[7]

1   Where a tenant dies intestate in mid-term, the landlord's notice to quit should be served upon the Public Trustee (*Practice Direction (Probate: Notice to Quit)* [1995] 1 WLR 1120).
2   [Para 7.80].
3   *Hammersmith and Fulham LBC v Monk* [1992] 1 AC 478 at 492A–B per Lord Browne-Wilkinson.
4   The periodic tenancy ends at common law, not on the service of a valid notice to quit, but on its expiry (*Newlon Housing Trust v Alsulaimen* [1999] 1 AC 313 at 317E–F). Once given, the notice to quit cannot be withdrawn, although an agreement to do so may have the effect of substituting a new tenancy (see *Dagger v Shepherd* [1946] KB 215 at 221–222; *Kinch v Bullard* [1999] 1 WLR 423 at 428G–H).
5   *Harrow LBC v Johnstone* [1997] 1 WLR 459 at 471F per Lord Hoffmann. So much is evident from the rule that a subtenancy is determined on the expiry of a periodic tenant's notice to quit (see *Baron Sherwood v Moody* [1952] 1 All ER 389 at 394F–G) but is not determined by the surrender of a periodic tenancy (see *Barrett v Morgan* [2000] 2 AC 264 at 269A–B, 271D–H per Lord Millett; *Fleeton v Fitzgerald* (1998) 9 BPR 16715 at 16718).

6   *Newlon Housing Trust v Alsulaimen* [1999] 1 AC 313 at 317F per Lord Hoffman. According to
     Lord Hoffmann in *Harrow LBC v Johnstone* [1997] 1 WLR 459 at 471G, 'the interest comes to
     an end in accordance with the conditions by which it is defined, just as a life interest comes to
     an end upon the death of the tenant for life.' See also *Barrett v Morgan* [2000] 2 AC 264 at
     270D–E per Lord Millett.
7   *Barrett v Morgan* [2000] 2 AC 264 at 272E per Lord Millett. Until effective termination of the
     lease the tenant remains liable for any covenanted rent. Notwithstanding the tenant's service
     of a notice to quit, his liability persists if he fails to deliver up possession of the premises, e g if
     his spouse remains in occupation (see *Griffiths v Renfree* (1989) 21 HLR 338 at 344–345).

7.287 Although the continuance of a periodic tenancy thus rests upon
consent, its termination need not be consensual except in the minimal sense
that, by granting and accepting a periodic tenancy, the parties are taken to have
agreed at the outset of the term that their relationship should be terminable
unilaterally by notice to quit.[1] Thereafter the process of termination is in no
way dependent, at common law, upon the consent of the recipient of the
notice.[2] The notice to quit also destroys any other rights which were dependent
on the continuance of the tenancy. Thus, for example, the termination of the
tenancy cuts off the statutory occupation rights otherwise enjoyed by the
tenant's spouse pursuant to the Family Law Act 1996.[3] In such circumstances
the tenant's spouse has – as the domestic law currently stands – no right to
assert either that his entitlement to respect for his 'home' has been violated[4] or
that his right to a fair and impartial determination of his 'civil rights' has been
infringed.[5]

1   *Barrett v Morgan* [2000] 2 AC 264 at 270D–E, 272D per Lord Millett.
2   A tenant sometimes has a right, on receiving notice to quit, to apply to court for the grant of
     a new tenancy (see e g L&TA 1954, ss 25(5), 26(1)–(4) [**para 14.357**]).
3   [**Para 12.93**].
4   *Newham LBC v Kibata* [2003] 3 FCR 724 at [25] per Mummery LJ.
5   *Newham LBC v Kibata* [2003] 3 FCR 724 at [32]–[35] per Mummery LJ (local authority
     encouraged tenant to serve notice to quit on landlord following alleged domestic violence).

Contractual limitations on determination by notice

7.288 As the House of Lords made clear in *Prudential Assurance Co Ltd v
London Residuary Body*,[1] it is the constant and bilateral availability of the
power of determination by notice which alone prevents the periodic tenancy
from failing the general leasehold test of certainty of term. In accordance with
the certainty principle it is repugnant to the nature of periodic tenancy that the
entitlement to give a notice to quit should be contractually reserved for one
party alone in the leasehold relationship.[2] There can be no valid periodic
tenancy (whether weekly,[3] yearly,[4] or otherwise) which contains a provision that
the tenancy is determinable only by the tenant and not by the landlord. It is
likewise inconsistent with the concept of periodic tenancy that *both* parties
should be contractually denied the power to give the other notice to quit.[5]

1   [1992] 2 AC 386 at 394F–395C per Lord Templeman [**para 7.117**].
2   *Doe d Warner v Browne* (1807) 8 East 165 at 166–167, 103 ER 305 at 306; *Prudential
     Assurance Co Ltd v London Residuary Body* [1992] 2 AC 386 at 394F per Lord Templeman.
     See also *Roe d Prideaux Brune v Prideaux* (1808) 10 East 158 at 187, 103 ER 735 at 746.

3   *Centaploy Ltd v Matlodge Ltd* [1974] Ch 1 at 15A–B per Whitford J.
4   *Prudential Assurance Co Ltd v London Residuary Body* [1992] 2 AC 386 at 395G per Lord Templeman.
5   *Prudential Assurance Co Ltd v London Residuary Body* [1992] 2 AC 386 at 394F per Lord Templeman.

PARTIAL FETTERS ON NOTICE

7.289   Even a partial restraint or fetter on the landlord's power to determine by notice may be enough to invalidate the arrangement as a periodic tenancy.[1] As Lord Templeman emphasised in *Prudential Assurance Co Ltd v London Residuary Body*,[2] a term of years must 'either be certain or uncertain. It cannot be partly certain because the tenant can determine it at any time and partly uncertain because the landlord cannot determine it for an uncertain period.' A fetter on the landlord's power of determination may therefore be valid if limited to a defined period or portion of a lease,[3] but will otherwise cause the term to fail for uncertainty.[4]

1   See *Cheshire Lines Committee v Lewis & Co* (1880) 50 LJQB 121 at 124 per Lush J (periodic tenancy invalidated by proviso that landlord should not give notice until he is required to demolish demised premises). See similarly *Prudential Assurance Co Ltd v London Residuary Body* [1992] 2 AC 386 at 395G (overruling *Re Midland Railway Co's Agreement* [1971] Ch 725 at 733F–734A).
2   [1992] 2 AC 386 at 395B–C.
3   See *Prudential Assurance Co Ltd v London Residuary Body* [1992] 2 AC 386 at 395A, where Lord Templeman was prepared to uphold a yearly tenancy which disabled the landlord from determining 'before the expiry of five years unless the war ends.' Lord Templeman would have declared such a lease valid as a 'determinable certain term of five years.'
4   In *Prudential Assurance Co Ltd v London Residuary Body* [1992] 2 AC 386 at 395B, Lord Templeman indicated that the vice of uncertainty would taint a supposed yearly tenancy which suspended the landlord's right to give notice until the occurrence of some entirely unpredictable event (e g 'the end of the war').

NO IMPLIED FETTERS ON NOTICE

7.290   In the *Prudential Assurance* case itself, a local authority landlord's right to give notice of termination of a letting arrangement was made expressly dependent on the landlord's need to requisition the land for a road-widening scheme.[1] The indefinite nature of the term clearly invalidated the arrangement as a long lease, but in place of such a lease a yearly periodic tenancy later arose by reason of the tenant's entry into possession and payment of periodic rent. The tenant unsuccessfully argued that this yearly tenancy impliedly incorporated the originally agreed fetter suspending exercise of the landlord's power of determination in the absence of a road-widening scheme. The House of Lords ruled that a fetter of such uncertain duration was wholly repugnant to the notion of a periodic tenancy and could not therefore stand. According to Lord Templeman, such an inhibition on the landlord would have made 'a nonsense of the concept of a tenancy from year to year because it is of the essence of a tenancy from year to year that both the landlord and the tenant shall be entitled to give notice determining the tenancy.'² The yearly tenancy in this case was therefore terminable at any time by the giving of half a year's notice by either party.³

1   [1992] 2 AC 386.
2   [1992] 2 AC 386 at 392F–G. Compare the contrary view of the Court of Appeal ((1992) 63 P & CR 386 at 399–400 per Scott LJ).
3   [1992] 2 AC 386 at 393G–H.

Common law rules governing the length of notice

7.291   In the absence of express agreement between landlord and tenant,¹ the length of the notice required in order to terminate a periodic tenancy is governed in the first instance by the common law and depends on the nature of the tenancy concerned. A yearly tenancy may be determined by not less than half a year's notice expiring at the end of a year of the tenancy.² In the case of all other periodic tenancies, the notice required at common law comprises at least one full period³ (eg one month's notice in the case of a monthly tenancy,⁴ and one week's notice in the case of a weekly tenancy⁵). In each case there is a requirement at common law that, in the absence of contrary agreement,⁶ the notice should expire on the last day of a completed period of the tenancy (ie on a rent day).⁷ Thus a notice of termination in relation to a weekly tenancy cannot be made to expire during the currency of a week.⁸ The same approach is applicable mutatis mutandis to monthly and quarterly tenancies.⁹

1   *Re Threlfall* (1880) 16 Ch D 274 at 281–282 per Cotton LJ; *Ashburn Anstalt v Arnold* [1989] Ch 1 at 11F per Fox LJ; *Prudential Assurance Co Ltd v London Residuary Body* [1992] 2 AC 386 at 392C per Lord Templeman.
2   *Doe d Rigge v Bell* (1793) 5 Term Rep 471 at 472, 101 ER 265 at 266 per Lord Kenyon CJ; *Sidebotham v Holland* [1895] 1 QB 378 at 383; *Javad v Mohammed Aqil* [1991] 1 WLR 1007 at 1009B; *Prudential Assurance Co Ltd v London Residuary Body* [1992] 2 AC 386 at 392B–C per Lord Templeman. The notice need not be (but usually is) in writing (see *Doe d Lord Macartney v Crick* (1805) 5 Esp 196 at 197, 170 ER 784). For the purpose of computing the precise length of half a year's notice, the existence of a leap year is ignored (*Sunnyvale Services B O P Ltd v Bhana* [1986] 1 NZLR 314 at 317).
3   *Javad v Mohammed Aqil* [1991] 1 WLR 1007 at 1009B.
4   In a tenancy made by deed or in writing a month is, for present purposes, a calendar month (see LPA 1925, s 61(a)). Thus a month's notice should expire on the corresponding day of the next month (ie, a notice to quit given on 14 May should expire on 14 June). Where there is no 'corresponding day' (eg in relation to a month's notice given on 31 May), the notice should be made to expire on 30 June (see *Dodds v Walker* [1981] 1 WLR 1027 at 1030E–F). Under an orally granted monthly tenancy, a month's notice may still relate strictly to a lunar month (cf *P Phipps & Co (Northampton and Towcester Breweries) Ltd v Rogers* [1925] 1 KB 14 at 23), but this divergence of approach nowadays seems regrettably confusing.
5   *Queen's Club Gardens Estates Ltd v Bignell* [1924] 1 KB 117 at 124. For a suggestion that the common law rules relating to weekly and monthly tenancies are more flexible and may require the giving of *reasonable* notice, see E Cooke, [1992] Conv 263. See also *Simmons v Crossley* [1922] 2 KB 95 at 103–105 per Swift J.
6   *Soames v Nicholson* [1902] 1 KB 157 at 158. See, however, *Harler v Calder* (1988) 21 HLR 214 at 217.
7   See *Kemp v Derrett* (1814) 3 Camp 510 at 511, 170 ER 1463 at 1464; *Precious v Reedie* [1924] 2 KB 149 at 151–152. The courts in England and elsewhere have refused to split hairs over

whether a notice to quit on the anniversary date of a periodic tenancy is as effective as a notice to quit on the last day of the relevant period. In *Sidebotham v Holland* [1895] 1 QB 378 at 383, Lindley LJ observed that 'a notice to quit at the first moment of the anniversary ought to be just as good as a notice to quit on the last moment of the day before.' See also *Crate v Miller* [1947] KB 946 at 948–949; *Municipality of Metropolitan Toronto v Atkinson* (1977) 78 DLR (3d) 142 at 147–148 per Laskin CJC.

8   *Queen's Club Gardens Estates Ltd v Bignell* [1924] 1 KB 117 at 124, 131–132, 137; *Lynch v Dolan* [1973] IR 319 at 328.

9   *Ex parte Maddocks; Re Brown* [1968] 3 NSWR 651 at 652.

Statutory intervention

7.292   The common law rules relating to notice must be read subject to the overriding provision contained in the Protection from Eviction Act 1977.

Statutory minimum notice

7.293   In the case of 'premises let as a dwelling'[1] no notice to quit has any validity if it is given less than four weeks before the date on which it is to take effect.[2] This requirement applies irrespective of whether the notice is given by the landlord or by the tenant. In either case the notice must be in writing,[3] but a notice which is too short may be cured, for some purposes at least, by an agreement on the part of the recipient to waive his strict rights.[4]

1   This phrase excludes an agricultural holding, even with a dwelling on it (see *National Trust v Knipe* [1998] 1 WLR at 236H–237A, 243E). Highly purposive constructions of such statutory terminology are familiar in the law of landlord and tenant (see e g *Epsom Grand Stand Association Ltd v Clarke* [1919] WN 170 at 171; *Wolfe v Hogan* [1949] 2 KB 194 at 204–206; *Regalian Securities Ltd v Ramsden* [1981] 1 WLR 611 at 616C).

2   Protection from Eviction Act 1977, s 5(1)(b) (see e g *Ealing Family Housing Association Ltd v McKenzie* [2004] 1 P & CR D39). Section 5(1) of the 1977 Act does not apply to excluded tenancies under the Housing Act 1988 (see Protection from Eviction Act 1977, s 5(1B)(a)).

3   Protection from Eviction Act 1977, s 5(1)(a).

4   See *Elsden v Pick* [1980] 1 WLR 898 at 906A–B, 907H–908A, 909B. A unilateral waiver by one of a number of joint tenants cannot release the landlord from the obligation to comply with section 5 of the 1977 Act (*Hounslow LBC v Pilling* [1993] 1 WLR 1242 at 1248H–1249C).

Supply of prescribed information

7.294   Where the landlord gives the tenant notice to quit, the written notice must include certain statutorily prescribed information[1] which assures the tenant that even after the notice has expired the landlord must take proceedings in court before the tenant can be lawfully evicted. The tenant must also be informed that he may be able to obtain free legal advice relating to his rights. In effect every effort must be made to ensure that the notice to quit does not have an intimidating impact on the occupier or inhibit his exercise of such legal rights as he may have. A notice which fails to include the prescribed information is invalid and ineffective to determine the tenancy.[2]

1   Protection from Eviction Act 1977, s 5(1)(a). See The Notices to Quit (Prescribed Information) Regulations 1988 (SI 1988/2201). The landlord need not use the precise form of wording set out in these regulations, provided he transmits in substance the information required (see *Beckerman v Durling* (1981) 6 HLR 87 at 90; *Wilsher v Foster* [1981] CLY 1546).

2   A notice to quit is not invalidated by reason of the fact that it contains more information than is required by the Protection from Eviction Act 1977 (see *Meretune Investments v Martin* [1984] CLY 1917).

Notice to quit in relation to joint tenants

7.295   Special problems arise where a notice to quit is either served or received by only one of a number of co-owners of an estate in land.[1] Unilateral termination of a periodic tenancy can often be a highly controversial issue, not least because it makes a cohabiting joint tenant exceedingly vulnerable to vindictive action by a disaffected partner who has already secured an offer of alternative accommodation for herself.

1   Contrast a mere deed of release by one joint tenant to his fellow joint tenant, which does not normally affect the rent liability (or, more generally, the tenant status) of the releasing tenant in relation to the landlord (*Burton v Camden LBC* [2000] 2 AC 399 at 406D–E, 407E–F).

Internal logic of periodic tenancy

7.296   Some of the conceptual difficulties in this area were clarified by the decision of the House of Lords in *Hammersmith and Fulham LBC v Monk*.[1] Here Lord Bridge of Harwich adverted to the long established analysis of the periodic tenancy as creating between landlord and tenant an estate in land which 'continued only so long as it was the will of both parties that it should continue.'[2] Each prolongation of the periodic tenancy is thus a positive act of continued endorsement of the leasehold relationship on both sides, no less effective because it connotes what Lord Bridge termed a 'tacit relocation' of the obligations of the tenancy during the superadded unit of time.[3] The law implies consent to this tacit relocation 'if all the parties are silent on the matter.'[4] Thus, in the contemplation of law, each party 'signifies the necessary positive assent to the extension of the term for a further period' by his *omission* to give due notice of termination of the periodic tenancy.[5] Conversely, by the act of giving the appropriate notice to quit, either party may 'signify his unwillingness that the tenancy should continue' beyond the end of any period.[6] Were it not so, each joint tenant would be trapped by a 'potentially irrevocable obligation for the duration of their joint lives.'[7]

1   [1992] 1 AC 478. See [1992] Conv 279 (S Goulding); [1992] CLJ 218 (L Tee).

2   [1992] 1 AC 478 at 484F. See Blackstone's reference to tenancies from year to year as existing 'so long as both parties please' (*Bl Comm*, Vol II, p 147).

3   [1992] 1 AC 478 at 487H–488D.

4   See *Smith v Grayton Estates Ltd* 1960 SC 349 at 354 per Lord President Clyde.

5   [1992] 1 AC 478 at 490H–491A.

6   [1992] 1 AC 478 at 484F (see also Lord Browne-Wilkinson at 492B). Obvious reasons of convenience point in favour of a rule which compels a conscious opting *out* rather than a

regular opting *in* as the determinant of whether a periodic tenancy shall continue in force. See
also *Crawley BC v Ure* [1996] QB 13 at 26G–H per Hobhouse LJ.
7   *Hounslow LBC v Adjei* [2004] 2 All ER 636 at [8] per Pumfrey J.

Unilateral termination by a joint landlord

7.297   Where the interest of either the landlord or the tenant is held *jointly* by
two or more parties, it seems to follow from Lord Bridge's account of the logic
of periodic tenancy that 'the will of all the joint parties is necessary to the
continuance of the interest'[1] and that the withdrawal of any party's assent to
the continuance of a periodic tenancy has terminal effect. Accordingly the
House of Lords confirmed in *Hammersmith and Fulham LBC v Monk*[2] that an
effective notice to quit may be given unilaterally by any one of two or more
joint landlords.[3] The notice is, in other words, no less valid because it is given by
one freeholder without the concurrence of the other freeholder or freeholders.[4]

1   [1992] 1 AC 478 at 484F–G. See the statement of Lord Tenterden CJ in *Doe d Aslin v
Summersett* (1830) 1 B & Ad 135 at 140, 109 ER 738 at 739, that each joint tenant 'holds the
whole of all so long as he and all shall please'.
2   [1992] 1 AC 478.
3   [1992] 1 AC 478 at 485D per Lord Bridge of Harwich. In the words of Lord Browne-
Wilkinson (at 492G), where there are joint lessors of a periodic tenancy, the continuing 'will'
must be the 'will of all the lessors individually, not the conjoint will of all the lessors
collectively.'
4   See *Doe d Aslin v Summersett* (1830) 1 B & Ad 135 at 140–141, 109 ER 738 at 739–740; *Doe d
Kindersley v Hughes* (1840) 7 M & W 139 at 141–142, 151 ER 711 at 713; *Alford v Vickery*
(1842) Car & M 280 at 283, 174 ER 507 at 508; *Parsons v Parsons* [1983] 1 WLR 1390 at
1399A; [1984] Conv 166 (J T F). See generally F Webb, [1983] Conv 194.

Unilateral termination by a joint tenant

7.298   The issue which fell for decision in *Hammersmith and Fulham LBC v
Monk* concerned the related question whether a periodic tenancy may be
determined by a notice given unilaterally by one of the joint owners of the
leasehold interest. In *Monk*'s case, following a domestic dispute, one of two
cohabiting joint tenants of a council flat gave the landlord authority notice of
termination, thereby precipitating the homelessness of her erstwhile partner.[1]
The House of Lords upheld the effectiveness of this notice, albeit that it was
given without the knowledge or consent of the other cohabitee.[2] The House
declared itself clearly of the view that, in the absence of contrary provision in
the tenancy agreement, the power of determination by notice may validly[3] be
exercised independently and without the concurrence of the other joint lessee
or lessees.[4]

1   The female cohabitee had first ascertained the willingness of the council to rehouse her on
termination of the tenancy.
2   For trenchant criticism of this consequence of a supposedly 'secure tenancy', see [1998] Fam
Law 590 (S M Cretney). Even a well-intentioned attempt by one joint tenant to remove her
name from the joint tenancy, leaving the other joint tenant solely entitled, operates mandatorily to terminate the joint tenancy (see *Birmingham CC v Bradney* [2003] EWCA Civ 1783

at [9]–[11]). Nor is it relevant that the unilaterally acting joint tenant genuinely has no understanding of the inevitable impact of the notice to quit (see *Birmingham CC v NcCann* [2003] EWCA Civ 1783 at [28]).

3   However, no notice to quit given by a unilaterally acting joint tenant can be valid if (even with the landlord's agreement) it falls short of the period of notice required at common law or by statute (see *Hounslow LBC v Pilling* [1993] 1 WLR 1242 at 1246D, 1248H–1249C; *Osei-Bonsu v Wandsworth LBC* [1999] 1 WLR 1011 at 1020B–C; *Ealing Family Housing Association Ltd v McKenzie* [2004] 1 P & CR D39).

4   [1992] 1 AC 478 at 491A per Lord Bridge of Harwich, 492H–493A per Lord Browne-Wilkinson; (1992) 108 LQR 375 (J Dewar). The possibility of unilateral termination by a joint tenant has received the House of Lords' consistent endorsement as a matter of domestic law (see e g *Harrow LBC v Johnstone* [1997] 1 WLR 459 at 465G per Lord Mustill, 471C per Lord Hoffmann; *Burton v Camden LBC* [2000] 2 AC 399 at 402E–F per Lord Nicholls of Birkenhead, 407D–E per Lord Hobhouse of Woodborough; *Harrow LBC v Qazi* [2004] 1 AC 983 at [40]–[41], [74] per Lord Hope of Craighead, [90] per Lord Millett, [113] per Lord Scott of Foscote). See further *Doe d Lord Macartney v Crick* (1805) 5 Esp 196 at 197, 170 ER 784 per Lord Ellenborough; *Leek and Moorlands Building Society v Clark* [1952] 2 QB 788 at 793; *Greenwich LBC v McGrady* (1983) 46 P & CR 223 at 224.

Property or contract?

7.299   Once again, as Lord Browne-Wilkinson observed in *Monk*'s case, the relevant legal issues highlight the pervasive tension between property- and contract-based analyses of the landlord–tenant relationship.[1] An 'instinctive reaction' founded on a 'property based' perspective prompts a 'revulsion' against the idea that one joint tenant can unilaterally terminate her partner's proprietary rights: his 'property rights in the home cannot be destroyed without his consent.'[2] Juxtaposed to this response is a different 'contract based' reaction: the female cohabitee cannot be 'held to a tenancy contract which is dependent for its continuance on the will of the tenant.'[3] In the view supported by the House of Lords, English law for almost two centuries has resolved the instant question by adoption of the 'contractual, as opposed to the property, approach.'[4]

1   [**Para 7.84**].
2   [1992] 1 AC 478 at 491H–492A.
3   [1992] 1 AC 478 at 492A (see also Lord Bridge of Harwich at 483B–E).
4   [1992] 1 AC 478 at 492F–G per Lord Browne-Wilkinson. See *Doe d Aslin v Summersett* (1830) 1 B & Ad 135, 109 ER 738.

Attempts to reassert the property perspective

7.300   In consequence of the potentially devastating impact on the housing status of the parties involved,[1] the outcome in *Monk*'s case has since been the subject of various strenuous, and ultimately unsuccessful, attempts to avert its logic.[2]

1   The problem is exacerbated by the practice of most local housing authorities not to rehouse disaffected family members unless a notice to quit has been served in respect of existing council accommodation (see e g *Harrow LBC v Johnstone* [1997] 1 WLR 459 at 462C–D; *Osei-Bonsu v Wandsworth LBC* [1999] 1 WLR 1011 at 1018B; *Hounslow LBC v Adjei* [2004] 2 All ER 636 at [6]).

2   See eg *Hounslow LBC v Pilling* [1993] 1 WLR 1242 at 1247A, 1249B–C, where the Court of
Appeal strained hard to construe a tenant's unilateral notice as an invalid exercise of what
amounted to a break clause in the tenancy agreement **[para 7.283]**, thereby preventing a
collusive agreement between a joint tenant and her landlord authority from resulting in the
arbitrary eviction of her partner. See [1994] CLJ 227 (L Tee).

Breach of trust?

7.301   Any periodic tenancy held by joint tenants is, inevitably, held on a trust
of land.[1] The courts have nevertheless rejected the suggestion that a joint
tenant's unilateral notice to quit constitutes an improper exercise of a trustee's
'function' under the Trusts of Land and Appointment of Trustees Act 1996.[2]
Since the orthodoxy flowing from *Monk*'s case insists that the service of a
notice to quit is not a positive act, but rather a negative act of withdrawal of
consent to the continuation of the periodic tenancy, there is here no 'function'
which requires the consultation of trust beneficiaries.[3]

1   See *Crawley BC v Ure* [1996] QB 13 at 26D.
2   Under a trust of land a beneficiary normally has a right to be consulted about the exercise of
the trustees' functions and the trustees are obliged, within certain limits, to give effect to the
wishes of beneficiaries (see TOLATA 1996, s 11(1) **[para 11.159]**).
3   *Notting Hill Housing Trust v Brackley* [2002] HLR 212 at [23] per Peter Gibson LJ, [32] per
Jonathan Parker LJ. See likewise *Crawley BC v Ure* [1996] QB 13 at 25D–F, 27E–G
(insufficiently 'positive act' to constitute any breach of trust).

Relevance of injunction?

7.302   Unilateral notice to quit has been held effective, even though the
unilaterally acting joint tenant has defied an injunction restraining the exclusion of the other joint tenant from their shared home.[1] The existence of the
injunction does not vitiate the notice of termination, since the injunction is
concerned only with the exercise of rights under an existing joint tenancy and is
not intended to operate as a 'mandatory order requiring the wife to co-operate
in maintaining in force the rights created by the joint tenancy.'[2]

1   *Harrow LBC v Johnstone* [1997] 1 WLR 459 at 470F, 471B. See [1997] Conv 288 (M P
Thompson).
2   *Harrow LBC v Johnstone* [1997] 1 WLR 459 at 467G–468A per Lord Mustill.

Relevance of European Convention?

7.303   There have been suggestions that the arbitrary destruction of a joint
tenancy by a unilateral (and often self-serving) notice to quit amounts to a
violation of the dispossessed joint tenant's Convention guarantee of respect for
his 'home'.[1] In *Harrow LBC v Qazi*,[2] however, a majority of the House of
Lords confirmed – extremely controversially – that ECHR Art 8 provides no
escape from the inevitable effect under domestic law of a unilateral notice to
quit. The majority stressed that ECHR Art 8 is concerned with the protection
not of property, but of privacy,[3] with the consequence that the Convention

right is 'not ordinarily infringed by enforcing the terms on which the applicant occupies premises as his home.'[4] ECHR Art 8 is not, in other words, available as a defence to possession proceedings brought to enforce the 'ordinary property rights' of a local authority landlord.[5]

1   ECHR Art 8 [**para 2.60**].
2   [2004] 1 AC 983 [**para 2.70**].
3   [2004] 1 AC 983 at [50]–[53], [82] per Lord Hope of Craighead, [89] per Lord Millett, [125] per Lord Scott of Foscote.
4   [2004] 1 AC 983 at [100] per Lord Millett. See also *Newham LBC v Kibata* [2003] 3 FCR 724 at [32]–[35] (no infringement of ECHR Art 6) [**para 7.287**].
5   *Birmingham CC v Bradney*; *Birmingham CC v McCann* [2003] EWCA Civ 1783 at [15], [28] per Mummery LJ. See likewise *Hounslow LBC v Adjei* [2004] 2 All ER 636 at [49]. It has been suggested, however, that ECHR Art 8 may require a local authority landlord to inform and advise both joint tenants as to the consequences of a unilateral notice to quit (see (2004) 120 LQR 398 (S Bright)).

FORFEITURE

7.304   In the event of a breach of covenant by the tenant, a lease may become determinable according to the rules of forfeiture. The law in relation to forfeiture is discussed in detail in the general context of remedies available to the landlord.[1]

1   [**Para 14.99**].

SURRENDER

7.305   A lease or tenancy may be terminated prematurely by a surrender of the tenant's interest to his immediate landlord.[1] Surrender involves a yielding up of the tenant's estate to the landlord[2] and cannot be forced upon the latter. Being a premature mode of termination unsanctioned by any prior agreement between the parties,[3] surrender is ineffective without the landlord's consent.[4] If, however, the landlord accepts the surrender,[5] the tenant's term of years is 'absorbed by'[6] and merges forthwith in,[7] the landlord's reversion, being extinguished by operation of law.[8] Such surrender operates, however, only as between landlord and tenant[9] and cannot, for example, terminate the interest of any subtenant in the land,[10] even if the rights of the subtenant were unknown to the landlord and the grant of the subtenancy would have entitled the landlord to forfeit the lease.[11]

1   Surrender terminates the liability of any guarantor of the due performance of the tenant's covenants (*Proudreed Ltd v Microgen Holdings Plc* (1996) 72 P & CR 388 at 389; *BSE Trading Ltd v Hands* (1998) 75 P & CR 138 at 143).
2   See *St Marylebone Property Co Ltd v Fairweather* [1963] AC 510 at 546 per Lord Denning; *Tarjomani v Panther Securities Ltd* (1983) 46 P & CR 32 at 38 per Peter Gibson J.
3   In this respect surrender differs markedly from termination of a periodic tenancy by notice to quit, since the latter is a 'natural termination' of the tenancy relationship in strict accordance with its terms as agreed at the outset (see *Barrett v Morgan* [2000] 2 AC 264 at 272D per Lord Millett).

4   *Barrett v Morgan* [2000] 2 AC 264 at 270F–G, 272B per Lord Millett. 'Whether express or
    implied, surrender is essentially a consensual transaction' (*Barrett v Morgan* [1999] 1 WLR
    1109 at 1113H per Scott V-C).
5   A landlord's notice to quit served by agreement with his tenant does not operate as a
    surrender if the landlord has ascertained in advance merely that the tenant will not exercise his
    right to serve a counter-notice under relevant protective legislation (see *Barrett v Morgan*
    [2000] 2 AC 264 at 274H–275A).
6   *Barrett v Morgan* [2000] 2 AC 264 at 270F per Lord Millett. Coke spoke of the tenant's estate
    as 'absolutely drowned' in the reversion (*Co Litt*, s 338b). See also *St Marylebone Prop-
    erty Co Ltd v Fairweather* [1962] 1 QB 498 at 513 per Holroyd Pearce LJ, 532–533 per
    Pearson LJ.
7   As Lord Millett explained in *Barrett v Morgan* [2000] 2 AC 264 at 271A, no person can 'at the
    same time be both landlord and tenant of the same premises.' See *Rye v Rye* [1962] AC 496 at
    505, 514 [**para 7.201**], but compare *Robert Bryce & Co Ltd v Stowehill Investments Ltd* [2000] 3
    NZLR 535 at [34]–[44] (sale of landlord's reversion to tenant).
8   See *Allen v Rochdale BC* [2000] Ch 221 at 229H–230A per Morritt LJ. Surrender interposes a
    scintilla temporis which precludes any claim that the tenancy is immediately converted, on
    termination, into some other form of protected status (see e g *Foster v Robinson* [1951] 1 KB
    149 at 158, 160; *Dibbs v Campbell* (1988) 20 HLR 374 at 380–383).
9   See *Barrett v Morgan* [2000] 2 AC 264 at 271F–H per Lord Millett (citing *Doe d Beadon v Pyke*
    (1816) 5 M & S 146 at 154, 105 ER 1005 at 1008 per Lord Ellenborough CJ). As Lord Millett
    indicated ([2000] 2 AC 264 at 271D), it is 'a general and salutary principle of law that a person
    cannot be adversely affected by an agreement or arrangement to which he is not a party.'
10 *Barrett v Morgan* [2000] 2 AC 264 at 269A–B, 271D–H per Lord Millett [**para 7.278**]. See
    [2000] CLJ 251 (L Tee). See also *St Marylebone Property Co Ltd v Fairweather* [1962] 1 QB
    498 at 532 per Pearson LJ, [1963] AC 510 at 546–547 per Lord Denning. Surrender by the
    tenant leaves a 'sufficiency of the reversion' on the sublease to survive as a 'continuance' (see
    Co Litt, p 338b) in order to support the sublessee's title and to enable the enforcement of the
    sublessor's obligations (see *Robert Bryce & Co Ltd v Stowehill Investments Ltd* [2000] 3 NZLR
    535 at [33]). See also LPA 1925, ss 139, 150.
11 *Parker v Jones* [1910] 2 KB 32 at 38; *Fleeton v Fitzgerald* (1998) 9 BPR 16715 at 16718.

7.306   A surrender of the tenant's term may be made either expressly or
impliedly by operation of law.[1] Dispute as to whether surrender has occurred
may be generated by any of a number of causes.[2] The landlord may be anxious
to recover rent either from a tenant who has done a 'moonlight flit'[3] or, more
realistically, from that tenant's surety.[4] Alternatively, a tenant's resistance to the
suggestion that surrender has intervened may be attributable to his wish to avail
himself of rights which depend upon the subsistence of the lease.[5]

1   *Foster v Robinson* [1951] 1 KB 149 at 155.
2   It is clear that a surrender offered by only one of two or more joint tenants is ineffective (*Leek
    and Moorlands Building Society v Clark* [1952] 2 QB 788 at 795; *Greenwich LBC v McGrady*
    (1983) 46 P & CR 223 at 224; *Hammersmith and Fulham LBC v Monk* [1992] 1 AC 478 at
    490G per Lord Bridge of Harwich).
3   See e g *Relvok Properties Ltd v Dixon* (1972) 25 P & CR 1.
4   See e g *Proudreed Ltd v Microgen Holdings Plc* (1996) 72 P & CR 388.
5   See *Zionmor v Islington LBC* (1997) 30 HLR 822 (Housing Act 'right to buy').

Express surrender

7.307   Since the surrender of a tenant's term constitutes a disposition of an
estate in the land,[1] an express surrender must be contained in a deed in order to

be effective at law.[2] An express surrender made by mere writing can be effective only in equity as a specifically enforceable contract to surrender.[3] Even in equity an agreement to surrender is valid only if it complies fully with the statutory requirement of a written and signed contract incorporating all the terms relevant to the agreement.[4] Nor is surrender achieved by a document which merely contemplates the delivery up of possession at some future stage.[5] Surrender must be accompanied by some (even notional) yielding up of possession[6] and cannot operate in futuro.[7] Where there is an express surrender, the landlord has, of course, no claim for damages for the early termination,[8] although the surrender may, by virtue of its prematurity, command a money value payable by the tenant in the light of prevailing market factors.[9]

1   Surrender of a tenancy constitutes, for instance, a 'disposal' of assets in violation of a restraint order made in respect of the tenant pursuant to the Drug Trafficking Act 1994 (see *Re R (Restraint Order)* [1990] 2 QB 307 at 314D–E). However, a local authority landlord which accepts a surrender does not rank as an 'acquiring authority' within the Land Compensation Act 1973. Thus a tenant who surrenders a local authority tenancy on the assurance that alternative council accommodation will be provided has no entitlement to a 'disturbance payment' (see *R v Islington LBC, ex p Knight* [1984] 1 WLR 205 at 210E–G).

2   LPA 1925, s 52(1) **[para 7.219]**. See *Hoggett v Hoggett* (1980) 39 P & CR 121 at 126; *Ealing Family Housing Association Ltd v McKenzie* [2004] 1 P & CR D39 at D40. The requirement of a deed applies even to the surrender of an orally granted tenancy.

3   *Tarjomani v Panther Securities Ltd* (1983) 46 P & CR 32 at 39 per Peter Gibson J. See also *Hoggett v Hoggett* (1980) 39 P & CR 121 at 126. An oral agreement to surrender does not comply with LP(MP)A 1989, s 2, and therefore fails in the absence of some estoppel (see *Ealing Family Housing Association Ltd v McKenzie* [2004] 1 P & CR D39 at D40).

4   LP(MP)A 1989, s 2(1) **[para 9.15]**. See *Proudreed Ltd v Microgen Holdings Plc* (1996) 72 P & CR 388 at 393.

5   *Matthews v Pournasrollahzadeh* (1998) 76 P & CR D11 at D12. See also *Re Humphrey and Ontario Housing Corporation* (1979) 96 DLR (3d) 567 at 569.

6   See *Brown v Draper* [1944] KB 309 at 313. In *Foster v Robinson* [1951] 1 KB 149 at 154, Evershed MR thought that surrender might be sufficiently established by 'either an actual yielding up of possession, or its equivalent.' Subsequent cases have seized gratefully on this reference to an 'equivalent' of delivery up of possession (see eg *Collins v Claughton* [1959] 1 WLR 145 at 148), with the result that express surrender perhaps need not involve an actual abandonment of occupation 'providing that the intention of all parties is clear.' See *Dibbs v Campbell* (1988) 20 HLR 374 at 382 per Purchas LJ (tenants did not vacate because of 'inclement weather prevailing at the time').

7   *Whitehead v Clifford* (1814) 5 Taunt 518 at 519, 128 ER 791 at 792. An agreement between landlord and tenant to terminate the tenancy must be perfected, on the tenant's part, by relinquishment of possession and, on the landlord's part, by acceptance of possession (*Tasita Pty Ltd v Sovereign State of Papua New Guinea* (1991) 34 NSWLR 691 at 695G–696A). Until then the tenant's agreement is merely conditional (*Coupland v Maynard* (1810) 12 East 134 at 139–140, 104 ER 53 at 55–56) and the landlord has demonstrated no unequivocal intention to treat the lease as terminated.

8   *Wood Factory Pty Ltd v Kiritos Pty Ltd* (1985) 2 NSWLR 105 at 133B per Priestley JA.

9   A tenant has been held entitled to recover from a subtenant the cost demanded by the landlord for surrender, where the surrender was precipitated by the subtenant's breach (*Morrison Lamothe Inc v Bedok* (1986) 29 DLR (4th) 255 at 291–292).

Surrender by operation of law

7.308   Surrender occurs by operation of law where, with the landlord's concurrence or acquiescence, the tenant consciously does some act which is inconsistent with the continuance of the tenancy.[1] Surrender by operation of law is statutorily exempted from any requirement of formality.[2] This form of surrender operates independently of the subjective intentions of the parties[3] and is ultimately founded on the doctrine of estoppel.[4] Implied surrender effectively requires 'a change of possession, or something that is equivalent to a change of possession',[5] in circumstances where it would subsequently be unconscionable to plead the absence of a formal deed of surrender.[6] The conduct constituting surrender must be unequivocal on both sides,[7] rendering it inequitable thereafter for either landlord or tenant to dispute that the tenancy has ended.[8] In such circumstances, the parties are, in effect, estopped from asserting the continuance of the tenancy.[9]

1   *Fredco Estates Ltd v Bryant* [1961] 1 All ER 34 at 46G; *Tarjomani v Panther Securities Ltd* (1983) 46 P & CR 32 at 41; *Mattey Securities Ltd v Ervin* (1998) 77 P & CR 160 at 164; *Mavromatis v Mavromatis* [1968] 1 NSWR 647 at 649.
2   LPA 1925, s 52(2)(c) [**para 7.220**]. It is not sufficient that the parties enter into a mere parol agreement to surrender which is unsupported by any confirmatory act of delivery of possession (see *195 Crown Street Pty Ltd v Hoare* [1969] 1 NSWR 193 at 199).
3   *Zionmor v Islington LBC* (1997) 30 HLR 822 at 827.
4   *Foster v Robinson* [1951] 1 KB 149 at 155 per Evershed MR; *Tarjomani v Panther Securities Ltd* (1983) 46 P & CR 32 at 41 per Peter Gibson J; *Ealing Family Housing Association Ltd v McKenzie* [2004] 1 P & CR D39 at D40. See also *Wallis v Hands* [1893] 2 Ch 75 at 82; *RT & MI Abela Pty Ltd v Esso Australia Ltd* (1989) 89 ALR 485 at 501.
5   *Hoggett v Hoggett* (1980) 39 P & CR 121 at 126. See also *Oastler v Henderson* (1877) 2 QBD 575 at 578.
6   See *Proudreed Ltd v Microgen Holdings Plc* (1996) 72 P & CR 388 at 389–390 per Schiemann LJ; *Fleeton v Fitzgerald* (1998) 9 BPR 16715 at 16718.
7   *Brent LBC v Sharma & Vyas* (1992) 25 HLR 257 at 260 per Scott LJ.
8   *Tarjomani v Panther Securities Ltd* (1983) 46 P & CR 32 at 41.
9   *Tasita Pty Ltd v Sovereign State of Papua New Guinea* (1991) 34 NSWLR 691 at 695E per Young J. As in the area of disclaimer of the landlord's title [**para 7.316**], the estoppel may, in appropriate circumstances, relate to only part of the demised premises (see *Allen v Rochdale BC* [2000] Ch 221 at 233D–F).

Actual delivery up of possession

7.309   Surrender by operation of law is usually based on a relinquishment of possession and the acceptance or resumption of possession by the landlord.

Unequivocal yielding up of possession

7.310   Relinquishment of possession occurs where the tenant does all within his or her power to vacate the rented premises and deliver up possession to the landlord.[1] The return of the tenant's key, accompanied by the tenant's going out of occupation, represents a classic instance of surrender by operation of law,[2] although this implication may be less persuasive in the case of a commercial lease.[3] It must be clear that the tenant's actions mark the surrender of his term[4] and were accepted as such by his landlord.[5] The mere vacation of the rented property does not necessarily connote a surrender by the tenant,[6] even if he discontinues his payment of rent.[7] In such a case it is always open to the landlord to regard the tenancy as subsisting and to sue for the arrears of rent.[8] The courts may, however, be more ready to find a surrender by operation of law where a departing tenant has left behind him sizeable arrears of rent and remains absent for a substantial period of time.[9]

1   Thus the victim of domestic violence surrenders her tenancy when she abandons the property and rehouses herself, even though on her departure she leaves her spouse still in residence (*Sanctuary Housing Association v Campbell* [1999] 1 WLR 1279 at 1283B–C). She is not required to bring proceedings for the termination of his matrimonial home rights under the Family Law Act 1996 **[para 12.93]**. See also *Ealing Family Housing Association Ltd v McKenzie* [2004] 1 P & CR D39 at D40.

2   See *E S Schwab & Co Ltd v McCarthy* (1976) 31 P & CR 196 at 205, although Oliver J doubted (at 206–207) whether, in the case of registered land, such a surrender could in the absence of a registered disposition be effective to vest in the landlord anything more than a mere equitable interest in the tenant's lease. See also *Palfrey v Palfrey* (1974) 229 EG 1593 at 1595; *Filering Ltd v Taylor Commercial Ltd* [1996] EGCS 95.

3   See *Oastler v Henderson* (1877) 2 QBD 575 at 578–580; *Proudreed Ltd v Microgen Holdings Plc* (1996) 72 P & CR 388 at 393; *Matthews v Pournasrollahzadeh* (1998) 76 P & CR D11 at D12; *Buchanan v Byrnes* (1906) 3 CLR 704 at 722–723; *Wood Factory Pty Ltd v Kiritos Pty Ltd* (1985) 2 NSWLR 105 at 137B–C per Priestley JA, 146A–B per McHugh JA. Compare, however, *Borakat v Ealing LBC* [1996] EGCS 67 (return of keys accepted with intention of changing possession).

4   See *Heath Estates Ltd v Burchell* (1979) 251 EG 1173 at 1174.

5   *Charville Estates Ltd v Unipart Group Ltd* [1997] EGCS 36. See *Wood Factory Pty Ltd v Kiritos Pty Ltd* (1985) 2 NSWLR 105 at 146B per McHugh JA (continued assertion of rent liability inconsistent with acceptance of surrender).

6   See e g *Zionmor v Islington LBC* (1997) 30 HLR 822 at 828–829 (vacation after vandalism). See also *Todburn Pty Ltd v Taormina International Pty Ltd* (1990) 5 BPR 11173 at 11175.

7   *Addy v Donnelly* [1983] Court of Appeal Bound Transcript 506; *NRMA Insurance Ltd v B & B Shipping and Marine Salvage Co Pty Ltd* (1947) 47 SR (NSW) 273 at 282–283. The surrender of a statutorily protected tenancy 'is no easy matter' (*Hulme v Langford* (1985) 50 P & CR 199 at 202 per Stephenson LJ), not least because the courts are disinclined to allow the protection conferred by a special legislative regime to be contracted, or still less given, away. See also *Mavromatis v Mavromatis* [1968] 1 NSWR 647 at 651.

8   **[Para 14.202]**.

9   *Preston BC v Fairclough* (1982) 8 HLR 70 at 73.

Corpus and animus

7.311   In determining whether surrender has occurred, the courts have tended to have recourse to concepts of 'corpus possessionis' and 'animus revertendi'.[1] There is normally no surrender by operation of law while there remains any physical or symbolic evidence (or *corpus*) of the tenant's possession or so long as the tenant retains any intention (or *animus*) to return to the property. Thus the tenant's *corpus* of possession can be preserved intact where the tenant has departed but has deliberately left his spouse[2] or partner[3] or friend,[4] his furniture,[5] or his dog[6] installed on the premises in order to set up a protective presence on his behalf.[7]

1   Compare the concept of possession in the law of adverse possession **[para 6.106]**.

2   *Old Gate Estates Ltd v Alexander* [1950] 1 KB 311 at 318–320. A proxy occupation through a spouse may set up a continuing *corpus* of possession, notwithstanding that this person is

physically absent during the relevant period, provided that she intends to return to the property (see *Hoggett v Hoggett* (1980) 39 P & CR 121 at 127–128 (wife in hospital for operation)).

3   *Chamberlain v Scalley* (1994) 26 HLR 26 at 30.
4   *Zionmor v Islington LBC* (1997) 30 HLR 822 at 828.
5   *Old Gate Estates Ltd v Alexander* [1950] 1 KB 311 at 317; *Chamberlain v Scalley* (1994) 26 HLR 26 at 29–30.
6   *Hoggett v Hoggett* (1980) 39 P & CR 121 at 126–127.
7   It is different if a violent spouse is simply abandoned in situ (see eg *Sanctuary Housing Association v Campbell* [1999] 1 WLR 1279 at 1283B–C [**para 7.310**]).

Unequivocal acceptance of possession

7.312   It must be clear that, by resuming possession, the landlord has accepted that the tenancy no longer exists.[1] Changing of locks by the landlord can, in certain circumstances, amount to an unequivocal acceptance of surrender,[2] although the onus rests on the tenant to prove that such action was not simply motivated by the need to safeguard vacant premises.[3] Similarly, the landlord's institution of possession proceedings against trespassers may indicate, not that he has accepted a cesser of the tenancy, but only that he has acted sensibly in the protection of his own interests.[4] A mere attempt by the landlord to relet the premises does not necessarily connote an acceptance of surrender,[5] but the implication of perfected surrender inevitably strengthens with the continuing absence of a tenant who was also in substantial breach of other leasehold covenants.[6] At this point, where the landlord begins to use the vacated premises for his own purposes (eg by an actual reletting),[7] there is inevitably a powerful inference that the tenancy has been abandoned and that the landlord has finally accepted this fact.[8]

1   See eg *Brent LBC v Sharma & Vyas* (1992) 25 HLR 257 at 259–260; *Proudreed Ltd v Microgen Holdings Plc* (1996) 72 P & CR 388 at 393.
2   *McDougalls Catering Foods Ltd v BSE Trading Ltd* (1998) 76 P & CR 312 at 322.
3   *Relvok Properties Ltd v Dixon* (1972) 25 P & CR 1 at 5.
4   *McDougalls Catering Foods Ltd v BSE Trading Ltd* (1998) 76 P & CR 312 at 325–326. See also *Buchanan v Byrnes* (1906) 3 CLR 704 at 721–723 per O'Connor J; *Tasita Pty Ltd v Sovereign State of Papua New Guinea* (1991) 34 NSWLR 691 at 697C–D per Young J.
5   See *Oastler v Henderson* (1877) 2 QBD 575 at 578–579; *Boxsel v Bennett* (1981) ANZ ConvR 153 at 155.
6   *Andrews v Hogan* (1952) 86 CLR 223 at 252 per Fullagar J; *Wood Factory Pty Ltd v Kiritos Pty Ltd* (1985) 2 NSWLR 105 at 137D–F per Priestley JA.
7   *Oastler v Henderson* (1877) 2 QBD 575 at 579–580 per Brett LJ. See also *Hughes v NLS Pty Ltd* [1966] WAR 100 at 101–102; *Sandum v Holmes* (1985) 16 DLR (4th) 629 at 633; *Wood Factory Pty Ltd v Kiritos Pty Ltd* (1985) 2 NSWLR 105 at 133C–D per Priestley JA, 146A per McHugh JA.
8   *Wood Factory Pty Ltd v Kiritos Pty Ltd* (1985) 2 NSWLR 105 at 133C per Priestley JA. As the element of agreed termination becomes weaker, the concepts of surrender and repudiation tend to merge with a doctrine of abandonment. See *Stagg v Wyatt* (1838) 2 Jur 892, but compare *Sauerzweig v Feeney* [1986] IR 224 at 226–227.

Constructive delivery up of possession

7.313   There may be a delivery up of possession even where a tenant does not relinquish his possession but landlord and tenant engage in conduct which is consistent only with the cesser of the tenancy.[1] Thus possession may be yielded up constructively where the tenant accepts some new status inconsistent with that enjoyed under the former tenancy.[2] It seems, however, that where one kind of letting arrangement is supposedly replaced by another,[3] the court will not accept that there has been a valid surrender of the earlier tenancy unless there is clear evidence of the grant of a new tenancy or licence[4] as distinct from a mere variation of the terms of an existing lease.[5] Where the parties do not have in mind the 'substantial result' of bringing about a new arrangement on terms different from those of the earlier tenancy, the court will not infer that a new relationship has been formed between the parties and will therefore decline to accept that the earlier tenancy has been surrendered by operation of law.[6]

1   *Tarjomani v Panther Securities Ltd* (1983) 46 P & CR 32 at 41 per Peter Gibson J; *Ealing Family Housing Association Ltd v McKenzie* [2004] 1 P & CR D39 at D40–D41.
2   See *Foster v Robinson* [1951] 1 KB 149 at 159, where the tenant accepted a rent-free licence for life and Evershed MR thought it irrelevant for the purpose of this surrender that the key had not been 'handed over and then been handed back the next minute' to mark the superseding of the old relationship by a new and different one. See also *Palfrey v Palfrey* (1974) 229 EG 1593 at 1595; *Short Bros (Plant) Ltd v Edwards* (1979) 249 EG 539 at 542.
3   A landlord has no power to grant a new lease during the term of an existing tenancy except on the footing that the old lease has been surrendered. The tenant, by accepting the new lease, is estopped from denying such surrender (see *Jenkin R Lewis & Son Ltd v Kerman* [1971] Ch 477 at 496B–C per Russell LJ).
4   See *Bolnore Properties Ltd v Cobb* (1996) 75 P & CR 127 at 133–134; *Ealing Family Housing Association Ltd v McKenzie* [2004] 1 P & CR D39 at D40. See also *Hulme v Langford* (1985) 50 P & CR 199 at 203–205, where the tenant had requested that the landlord should transfer a tenancy out of his name into that of his wife. The Court of Appeal held that in order to be effective, such a surrender would necessarily have involved a 'tripartite agreement' between the tenant, the landlord and the wife. Compare, however, *Camden LBC v Alexandrou* (1998) 30 HLR 534 at 540.
5   *Smirk v Lyndale Developments Ltd* [1975] Ch 317 at 339H–340A. See e g *Joseph v Joseph* [1967] Ch 78 at 86B (new parties, new term and new rent).
6   *Take Harvest Ltd v Liu* [1993] AC 552 at 565F–H per Sir Christopher Slade (JCPC).

Wrongful termination by landlord

7.314   It has been suggested that a further instance of surrender by operation of law occurs where a landlord wrongfully terminates a tenancy and brings about the dispossession of the tenant. If in such circumstances the tenant takes no steps to recover possession, a time must come when as a matter of fact he will be treated as having elected to accept the landlord's wrongful act.[1] There is similarly a surrender by operation of law where the tenant gives up possession in response to an invalid notice to quit.[2]

1   See *Wood Factory Pty Ltd v Kiritos Pty Ltd* (1985) 2 NSWLR 105 at 121B–D per Priestley JA.
2   *Grimman v Legge* (1828) 8 B & C 324 at 326–327, 108 ER 1063 at 1064; *Dodd and Davies v Acklom* (1843) 6 Man & G 672 at 680–682, 134 ER 1063 at 1066–1067; *Sandum v Holmes* (1985) 16 DLR (4th) 629 at 632–633.

DISCLAIMER

7.315 A lease or tenancy may be terminated by various instances of disclaimer of the relationship of landlord and tenant.[1]

1   A unilateral disclaimer by one joint tenant alone is ineffective (see *Hammersmith and Fulham LBC v Monk* [1992] 1 AC 478 at 490G per Lord Bridge of Harwich).

Disclaimer by denial of title

7.316 One form of disclaimer is of medieval origin and occurs where the tenant denies or repudiates his landlord's title 'either by setting up the title of a rival claimant or by asserting a claim of ownership in himself.'[1] No tenant, whilst in possession and enjoying the benefits of the lease, is permitted to question the validity of his landlord's title.[2] Such conduct breaches the implied condition in every lease that the tenant shall do nothing which may prejudice the position of his landlord.[3] Repudiation of the superior title is incompatible with the tenant's fundamental obligations to his landlord[4] and indicates an intention to be no longer bound by the contract of tenancy.[5] The landlord is immediately entitled to re-enter the demised premises and forfeit the lease.[6]

1   *Warner v Sampson* [1959] 1 QB 297 at 318 per Hodson LJ, 324 per Ormerod LJ.
2   **[Para 7.266]**.
3   *W G Clark (Properties) Ltd v Dupre Properties Ltd* [1992] Ch 297 at 308D per Deputy Judge Thomas Morison QC.
4   *Doe d Ellerbrock v Flynn* (1834) 1 CM & R 137 at 141, 149 ER 1026 at 1028; *Vivian v Moat* (1881) 16 Ch D 730 at 734; *Wisbech St Mary Parish Council v Lilley* [1956] 1 WLR 121 at 125; *Warner v Sampson* [1959] 1 QB 297 at 312–313.
5   *W G Clark (Properties) Ltd v Dupre Properties Ltd* [1992] Ch 297 at 303C; *Milton v Proctor* (1988) 4 BPR 9654 at 9666–9667 per Clarke JA.
6   Precisely because the right to terminate the lease on the ground of denial of title operates as a forfeiture, the service of a notice under LPA 1925, s 146 **[para 14.128]** is a prerequisite to re-entry and the tenant may seek relief from forfeiture (see *W G Clark (Properties) Ltd v Dupre Properties Ltd* [1992] Ch 297 at 309E per Deputy Judge Thomas Morison QC; *Abidogun v Frolan Health Care Ltd* [2001] 45 EG 138 (CS); [2002] Conv 399 (M Pawlowski)).

7.317 Repudiation, in order to be effective, must be clear and unambiguous.[1] Thus a disclaimer of the landlord's title to a mere part of the demised premises does not necessarily constitute a disclaimer as to the whole of the premises.[2] Any repudiation of the leasehold relationship by the tenant may, of course, be ignored by the landlord, who is perfectly entitled to continue to enforce the terms of the demise.[3] Equally, however, the landlord may elect to re-enter and, by serving proceedings for possession, accept the tenant's repudiation and bring the relationship to an end.[4]

1   *Doe d Gray v Stanion* (1836) 1 M & W 695 at 703, 150 ER 614 at 617; *W G Clark (Properties) Ltd v Dupre Properties Ltd* [1992] Ch 297 at 303C per Deputy Judge Thomas Morison QC.
2   See *W G Clark (Properties) Ltd v Dupre Properties Ltd* [1992] Ch 297 at 304F–G, 305C–D (although a partial disclaimer may lead to a forfeiture of part of the premises).
3   *W G Clark (Properties) Ltd v Dupre Properties Ltd* [1992] Ch 297 at 303B.

4   *W G Clark* (*Properties*) *Ltd v Dupre Properties Ltd* [1992] Ch 297 at 306E–F, 307E.

Disclaimer by the tenant's trustee in bankruptcy

7.318   Another kind of disclaimer may arise on the bankruptcy of the tenant. It is open to a corporate tenant's liquidator (or a tenant's trustee in bankruptcy) to disclaim[1] any subsisting lease where that lease comprises property which is 'unsaleable or not readily saleable' or is likely to give rise to a 'liability to pay money or perform any onerous act.'[2] Such disclaimer automatically extinguishes the lease[3] and terminates the tenant's rights and obligations in their entirety,[4] although in some circumstances the landlord may be able to pursue a remedy against the tenant's guarantor or surety or other persons.[5] By ending the lease, disclaimer accelerates the landlord's right of reversion[6] and releases both the tenant and his estate from all further liability.[7] In the process, however, the landlord has lost the right to receive future rent and may prove for that loss in any subsequent winding-up or bankruptcy proceedings.[8] But, in so far as the landlord recovers this loss, he must submit to an appropriate discount for the accelerated receipt of the moneys which reflects the present value of the rents and other payments which would have accrued in the future but for the disclaimer.[9]

1   A disclaimer of interest in a licence to assign relating to a lease necessarily operates as a disclaimer of the lease itself (see *MEPC plc v Scottish Amicable Life Assurance Society* (1993) 67 P & CR 314 at 317).

2   Insolvency Act 1986, ss 178(2), 315(1)–(2) [**para 7.27**]. The disclaimer may require the approval of the court (Insolvency Act 1986, s 317).

3   *Christopher Moran Holdings Ltd v Bairstow, Re Park Air Services Plc* [2000] 2 AC 172 at 179F–180A per Lord Hobhouse of Woodborough, 183C–D per Lord Millett. Exercise of the statutory right to disclaim extinguishes the tenant's interest in the property immediately without any question of acceptance by the landlord (*W G Clark* (*Properties*) *Ltd v Dupre Properties Ltd* [1992] Ch 297 at 303B–C). A subtenant continues to hold his estate on the same terms as would be applicable if the tenant's interest had continued (*Hindcastle Ltd v Barbara Attenborough Associates Ltd* [1997] AC 70 at 89E–G) and may seek an order vesting the disclaimed property in himself (Insolvency Act 1986, ss 181(2), 320(3)), in which case the subtenant steps into the shoes of the tenant (*Hindcastle*, supra at 86G).

4   *Hindcastle Ltd v Barbara Attenborough Associates Ltd* [1997] AC 70 at 87D–F per Lord Nicholls of Birkenhead [**para 14.216**]. See Insolvency Act 1986, ss 178(4)(a), 315(3)(a).

5   Insolvency Act 1986, ss 178(4)(b), 315(3)(b). See *Hindcastle Ltd v Barbara Attenborough Associates Ltd* [1997] AC 70 at 87H–88A; *Beegas Nominees Ltd v BHP Petroleum Ltd* (1999) 77 P & CR 14 at 18.

6   *Hindcastle Ltd v Barbara Attenborough Associates Ltd* [1997] AC 70 at 87F per Lord Nicholls of Birkenhead; *Stubbs Investments Ltd v Thorp* [1997] 1 NZLR 310 at 315.

7   No vesting of the disclaimed property can be sought by the insolvent or bankrupt tenant under Insolvency Act 1986, ss 181(2), 320(3). See, in relation to analogous New Zealand provisions, *Auckland City Council v Glucina* [1997] 2 NZLR 1 at 4.

8   Insolvency Act 1986, ss 178(6), 315(5).

9   *Christopher Moran Holdings Ltd v Bairstow, Re Park Air Services Plc* [2000] 2 AC 172 at 180E–F per Lord Hobhouse of Woodborough, 183H–184C per Lord Millett. See (1999) 143 Sol Jo 193 (A Bruce).

REPUDIATORY BREACH

7.319 Relatively recent developments in the law of landlord and tenant have revived the possibility that the concept of disclaimer or repudiation may have a wider application to leases than was previously thought. Many common law jurisdictions have come to accept that the breach by either landlord or tenant of a 'fundamental term' of the lease constitutes a repudiation of the lease entitling the other party, at his election,[1] to regard the lease as terminated and to sue immediately for damages in respect of the loss of the lease.[2] On this basis a lease is terminable for breach if either landlord or tenant renounces his essential liabilities under the lease and thereby 'evinces an intention not to be bound by the contract or that he intends to fulfil the contract only in a manner substantially inconsistent with his obligations and not in any other way.'[3] The critical test becomes whether the default in question is such as to 'make further performance of the lease impossible' or effectively to deprive the innocent party of 'substantially the whole benefit of the lease.'[4] This view of repudiatory conduct is, of course, closely linked with the modern 'contractualisation' of the lease and the general drift away from the 'property-based' perspective on leasehold relationships.[5]

1   The repudiation of the lease need not be accepted by the injured party but, if accepted, releases both landlord and tenant from future performance under the lease (see eg *Lagouvardis v Brett and Janet Cottee Pty Ltd* (1994) 6 BPR 13467 at 13468–13469).

2   Landmark decisions were those of the Canadian Supreme Court in *Highway Properties Ltd v Kelly, Douglas & Co Ltd* (1971) 17 DLR (3d) 710 and the High Court of Australia in *Progressive Mailing House Pty Ltd v Tabali Pty Ltd* (1985) 157 CLR 17. See also *Wood Factory Pty Ltd v Kiritos Pty Ltd* (1985) 2 NSWLR 105 at 115E–F, 121A–B, 130A–133E, 143G–144C; *Nangus Pty Ltd v Charles Donovan Pty Ltd* [1989] VR 184 at 188–189; *Lehndorff Canadian Pension Properties Ltd v Davis Management Ltd* (1989) 59 DLR (4th) 1 at 16–17.

3   *Progressive Mailing House Pty Ltd v Tabali Pty Ltd* (1985) 157 CLR 17 at 33 per Mason J. See also *Lagouvardis v Brett and Janet Cottee Pty Ltd* (1994) 6 BPR 13467 at 13468 per Young J.

4   *Shun Cheong Holdings BC Ltd v Gold Ocean City Supermarket Ltd* (2002) 216 DLR (4th) 392 at [11] (British Columbia Court of Appeal).

5   [**Para 7.80**]. See *Hammersmith and Fulham LBC v Monk* [1992] 1 AC 478 at 491E–492A, 492G per Lord Browne-Wilkinson; *Liristis Holdings Pty Ltd v Wallville Pty Ltd* (2001) 10 BPR 18801 at [110]. Any proprietary prejudice brought about by a doctrine of repudiatory breach (e g in an executed demise for a long term where the tenant has already paid a premium) is likely to be overcome by a sensible application of a discretionary jurisdiction to afford relief from the rescission of the lease [**para 14.149**].

Contractualisation of the lease

7.320 For most of the last century English courts were unwilling to accept that ordinary contractual principles relating to wrongful repudiation could apply generally in the context of a term of years.[1] In retrospect, however, it is evident that the decision of the House of Lords in *National Carriers Ltd v Panalpina (Northern) Ltd*,[2] by exposing leases to the operation of the contractual doctrine of frustration, substantially opened the way for reconsideration of the issue.[3] A heavily persuasive force in this direction is already provided by the tempting analogy of disclaimer of title, which enables the landlord at his election to treat the lease as terminated.[4] There is, moreover, an increasing tendency to view forfeiture by a landlord as the effective equivalent of repudiation of the lease.[5] The steady intrusion of contractual principle has now placed in the hands of both landlord and tenant a potent means of terminating a tenancy. In this respect the controversial doctrine of repudiatory breach marks a dramatic reversal of the rule, well established in at least the modern English law of landlord and tenant, that performance of the parties' respective obligations is not interdependent.[6]

1   See e g *Total Oil of Great Britain Ltd v Thompson Garages (Biggin Hill) Ltd* [1972] 1 QB 318 at 324A–C per Lord Denning MR. Compare *Hussein v Mehlman* [1992] 2 EGLR 87 at 89K, where Assistant Recorder Sedley QC pointed out that the *Total Oil* case 'silently overruled an important line of cases ... in which, throughout the 19th century, the courts took it as axiomatic that a contract of letting could be terminated by the innocent party without notice if the other party failed to fulfil a fundamental term of the contract' (see e g *Smith v Marrable* (1843) 11 M & W 5, 152 ER 693 [**para 14.26**]).
2   [1981] AC 675.
3   See e g *Progressive Mailing House Pty Ltd v Tabali Pty Ltd* (1985) 157 CLR 17 at 28–29 per Mason J; *Wood Factory Pty Ltd v Kiritos Pty Ltd* (1985) 2 NSWLR 105 at 123G per Priestley JA.
4   [**Para 7.316**].
5   [**Para 14.99**]. See *Kingston upon Thames Royal LBC v Marlow* [1996] 17 EG 187 per Simon Brown LJ.
6   [**Para 14.8**].

The innovative doctrine

7.321   The doctrinal breakthrough is commonly attributed to the judgment of Assistant Recorder Sedley QC in *Hussein v Mehlman*.[1] Here the tenants under a three-year lease vacated their rented home after only 15 months on the ground of gross and persistent breaches by their landlord of his statutory obligations of repair and maintenance under the Landlord and Tenant Act 1985.[2] Declining to accept any 'major premise' that a lease of land is 'in its essence different from other contracts',[3] Sedley QC held that the tenants were entitled to throw up the tenancy (rather than seek other remedies for non-repair)[4] and claim immediately for damages for repudiatory breach of contract by their landlord.[5] This doctrine of repudiatory breach was later accepted by the Court of Appeal in *Chartered Trust Plc v Davies*,[6] where a tenant successfully claimed the right to rescind her lease of a unit in a shopping mall in circumstances of failure by the landlord to prevent acts of nuisance arising from other lettings in a supposedly 'high class retail' development.[7] The Court of Appeal agreed that there had been a repudiatory breach by the landlord and that the tenant had been correct in declining to keep her business open and in refusing to pay further rent.[8]

1   [1992] 2 EGLR 87; [1993] Conv 71 (S Bright). Although the terminology of repudiatory breach was expressly disclaimed, a similar – perhaps even more far-reaching – result was achieved in *Sampson v Floyd* [1989] 2 EGLR 49 at 50G–H, where the Court of Appeal, by way of damages for the grossest denial of quiet enjoyment, awarded a sum in excess of the purchase cost of the plaintiff's long lease.
2   See L&TA 1985, s 11 [**para 14.43**].
3   [1992] 2 EGLR 87 at 89E.

4   For a critical appraisal of *Hussein v Mehlman*, see W Barr, 'Repudiation of Leases: A Fool's Paradise', in P Jackson and D C Wilde (ed), *Contemporary Property Law* (Ashgate 1999), p 317.
5   Further evidence of the trend towards the application of general contractual doctrine in the English law of tenancies had already appeared in *Killick v Roberts* [1991] 1 WLR 1146 at 1149H–1150A, where the Court of Appeal held that a tenancy agreement which one party had been induced to enter into by reason of the fraud of the other could be rescinded at the innocent party's election. See [1992] CLJ 21 (L Tee); [1992] Conv 269 (J Martin).
6   (1997) 76 P & CR 396 at 409. See (1997) 141 Sol Jo 922 (A Bruce).
7   The tenant alleged that her business had been impeded, and driven towards bankruptcy, by the proximity of a pawnbroker's shop and a coffee shop whose tables littered the common parts of the mall premises. The landlord, despite imposing a service charge for its management and control of the mall, 'did nothing' to prevent the nuisance.
8   For further reference to the *Hussein v Mehlman* principle, see *Re Olympia & York Canary Wharf Ltd (No 2)* [1993] BCC 159 at 166 per Morritt J.

Implications of the doctrine

7.322   The application of repudiatory breach in a hitherto unfamiliar lease-hold context may have significant ramifications. The doctrine cuts both ways, in that the right to terminate the lease for breaches of essential terms is a remedy no less available to the landlord than to the tenant.[1] As Sedley QC acknowledged in *Hussein v Mehlman*,[2] the acceptance of a principle of elective termination by repudiatory breach appears equally applicable to certain kinds of default by a tenant in payment of rent in so far as 'the obligation to pay rent is as fundamental as the obligation to keep the house habitable.'[3] Nevertheless the courts have been generally slow to find that breaches of leasehold covenant, by depriving a party of substantially the whole contractual benefit, go to the root of the letting contract so as to justify disaffirmation of the entire tenancy.[4] In most cases of breach by landlord or tenant the appropriate remedy is damages not the termination of the lease.[5] In particular, the mere fact of nuisance or derogation from grant or breach of a covenant for quiet enjoyment will not, in itself, entitle the aggrieved party to collapse the leasehold estate.[6]

1   One of the criticisms directed at the doctrine of repudiatory breach is that a landlord's invocation of the principle may well convert the defaulting tenant into an 'involuntary guarantor' of the future rent due under the terminated lease (see J Effron, (1988) 14 Monash L Rev 83 at 90). See e g *Wood Factory Pty Ltd v Kiritos Pty Ltd* (1985) 2 NSWLR 105.
2   [1992] 2 EGLR 87 at 90H–J.
3   The better view is, however, that the mere failure to pay rent at specified times is not so fundamental a breach as to justify a summary termination of the lease. See *Shevill v Builders Licensing Board* (1982) 149 CLR 620 at 627 per Gibbs CJ, 634 per Wilson J (but compare *Ripka Pty Ltd v Maggiore Bakeries Pty Ltd* [1984] VR 629 at 634–635). It ought to be the case, as in the analogous area of disclaimer [**para 14.316**], that the service of some demand or statutory notice under LPA 1925, s 146 [**para 14.128**] is a necessary preliminary to termination for a tenant's repudiatory breach, thus opening up the possibility of relief from re-entry for the tenant. See *W G Clark (Properties) Ltd v Dupre Properties Ltd* [1992] Ch 297 at 308G–309E, but compare powerful authority to the contrary in *Marshall v Council of The Shire of Snowy River* (1994) 7 BPR 14447 at 14457 per Meagher JA.
4   See e g *Re Olympia & York Canary Wharf Ltd (No 2)* [1993] BCC 159 at 167–173; *Nynehead Developments Ltd v R H Fibreboard Containers Ltd* [1999] 1 EGLR 7 at 12H ('a judge must be careful not to allow an easy escape route from a disadvantageous contract'). See [1999] Conv

150 (M Pawlowski and J Brown). Compare *G S Fashions Ltd v B & Q Plc* [1995] 1 WLR 1088 at 1093G–H, where Lightman J thought that a tenant would be entitled to disaffirm a lease if his landlord wrongly treated him as a trespasser, either by exercising peaceable re-entry or by serving a writ for supposed breach.

5   See *Nynehead Developments Ltd v R H Fibreboard Containers Ltd* [1999] 1 EGLR 7 at 12L; *Firth v BD Management Ltd* (1990) 73 DLR (4th) 375 at 380.

6   [**Paras 14.15, 14.18**]. See *Nynehead Developments Ltd v R H Fibreboard Containers Ltd* [1999] 1 EGLR 7 at 12B–L; *Todburn Pty Ltd v Taormina International Pty Ltd* (1990) 5 BPR 11173 at 11176. Compare, however, *Shun Cheong Holdings BC Ltd v Gold Ocean City Supermarket Ltd* (2002) 216 DLR (4th) 392 at [11]–[14] (lease 'undermined' by leakages which prevented operation of grocery store).

FRUSTRATION

7.323   It has long been recognised that the individual covenants contained in a lease may be suspended or discharged in so far as supervening impossibility of performance affects continuing or future obligations.[1] Only relatively recently, however, has it been accepted that the contractual doctrine of frustration may sometimes apply to an executed lease as a *whole*.[2] In *National Carriers Ltd v Panalpina (Northern) Ltd*,[3] the House of Lords ruled by a majority that a lease can be affected by frustration, although the cases in which the doctrine will be applicable are likely to be 'exceedingly rare'.[4] It must be shown that a 'supervening event' has brought about such a 'fundamental change of circumstances as to enable the court to say – "this was not the bargain which these parties made and their bargain must be treated as at an end".'[5] In the *National Carriers* case itself the only access road leading to the demised premises had been closed by the local authority for a period of 18 months during a ten-year lease. The House of Lords declined to accept that this interruption of access had been of sufficient gravity to frustrate the entire lease.[6] It is unlikely that the doctrine of frustration can apply to a periodic tenancy – even, for instance, in circumstances of fire damage – where the subject matter of the tenancy can be restored by repair within a relatively short time.[7]

1   *Cricklewood Property and Investment Trust Ltd v Leighton's Investment Trust Ltd* [1945] AC 221 at 240. See *John Lewis Properties Plc v Viscount Chelsea* (1993) 67 P & CR 120 at 132–133 (covenant to demolish and rebuild frustrated by subsequent listed building status).

2   For the older law, see *Cricklewood Property and Investment Trust Ltd v Leighton's Investment Trust Ltd* [1945] AC 221 at 228–230, 233.

3   [1981] AC 675. See [1981] Conv 227 (K Hodkinson); (1981) 32 NILQ 162 (B Dickson); [1981] CLJ 217 (S Tromans); (1982) 60 Can Bar Rev 619 (J T Robertson).

4   [1981] AC 675 at 692B–D, 697A. See also *Prince v Robinson and Robinson* (1998) 76 P & CR D2 at D3 per Robert Walker LJ ('wholly exceptional circumstances').

5   [1981] AC 675 at 717D per Lord Roskill.

6   [1981] AC 675 at 697G–698A, 707B–F, 718A. It is likely that the answer would have been different in the case of a more lengthy interruption of access.

7   See *Prince v Robinson and Robinson* (1998) 76 P & CR D2 at D3.

TERMINATION ON STATUTORY GROUNDS

7.324   Leases and tenancies may also be terminated on a number of express statutory grounds which are examined more closely in Chapter 14.[1]

1   [**Paras 14.311–14.363**].

ENLARGEMENT

7.325   There exists a little used facility pursuant to section 153 of the Law of Property Act 1925 for the enlargement of certain long leases into a fee simple estate. It is open to the tenant to execute, by way of deed poll, an enlargement in respect of a lease which was granted for a term in excess of 300 years, of which at least 200 years remain unexpired.[1] Qualifying leases must not be liable to be determined by re-entry for condition broken,[2] nor must any rent of money value be payable.[3] The phenomenon of leasehold enlargement recognises that excessively lengthy terms tend, in effect, towards a form of freehold ownership. Accordingly, after enlargement, the tenant takes the fee simple subject to those few covenants and provisions which governed the now extinguished lease.[4]

1   LPA 1925, s 153(1). See e g *Bosomworth v Faber* (1993) 69 P & CR 288 at 292–293 (2,000 year lease granted in 1665). A sublease can be enlarged only if it was created out of a superior term which is itself capable of enlargement under the Law of Property Act 1925 (see LPA 1925, s 153(2)(ii)).
2   LPA 1925, s 153(2)(i).
3   LPA 1925, s 153(1)(b).
4   LPA 1925, s 153(8). The device of enlargement provides a rare means by which the burden of positive covenants may be made to run with freehold land [**para 13.56**].

MERGER

7.326   A lease may be determined by merger where the tenant acquires the landlord's reversion and holds both interests in the same name and in exercise of the same legal capacity.[1] Under these circumstances – at least so long as there is no contrary intention – the lease merges with the reversionary title and is extinguished.[2]

1   It is not sufficient, for instance, that the tenant has acquired the reversion merely qua personal representative (*Chambers v Kingham* (1878) 10 Ch D 743 at 746).
2   See LPA 1925, s 185. Closure of a registered leasehold title on grounds of merger is governed by LRR 2003, r 79.

LEASEHOLD ENFRANCHISEMENT AND EXTENSION

7.327   The role of the lease as a medium of proprietary ownership has been accentuated by recent decades of reform, which have introduced a number of statutory mechanisms enabling certain categories of tenant to purchase the freehold reversion on their leasehold estate or to acquire a greatly extended lease over their premises. The expansion of leasehold enfranchisement,[1] particularly in the form of the council tenant's 'right to buy',[2] has underscored the fact that leasehold status in the residential sector can frequently provide a gateway to enlarged rights of fee simple ownership. There has occurred, in Britain, a quite remarkable shift from leasehold to freehold tenure.[3] The expansion of the so-called 'property-owning democracy'[4] has been particularly promoted by several significant legislative schemes aimed at increasing domestic owner-occupation through leasehold enfranchisement and extension.

1   Leasehold enfranchisement – the compulsory acquisition of fee simple ownership – is, more correctly, a species of 'merger' [**para 7.326**], in that the tenant's acquisition of the fee simple brings about a merger of his lease in the freehold estate.
2   [**Para 7.347**].
3   The proportion of households subject to owner-occupation increased from 29 per cent in 1951 to 45 per cent in 1964 and, finally, to 70 per cent in 2002 (see *Social Trends* 34 (2004 edn London), pp 152–153.
4   See *Pettitt v Pettitt* [1970] AC 777 at 824C per Lord Diplock [**paras 2.43, 12.195**].

LEASEHOLD REFORM ACT 1967

7.328   A controversial means of leasehold enfranchisement is contained in the Leasehold Reform Act 1967. The principal object of this legislation is to confer on certain tenants holding long leases a right compulsorily to purchase either the freehold reversion or an extended term of years in the property which they occupy.

Origins of the legislation

7.329   On the expiry of a long lease the demised premises (inclusive of any construction, improvements or repairs effected by the tenant) revert to the landlord without any compensation for the tenant. In 1966 the Labour Government of the day recognised that residential long leases had 'worked very unfairly against the occupying leaseholder'[1] in that, although the freeholder had provided the land, it was the original leaseholder who, in the vast majority of cases, had either built the house at his own expense or had borne the cost of improvements and maintenance during the currency of the term.[2] The ensuing Leasehold Reform Act 1967 was therefore formulated on the broad premise that 'the land belongs in equity to the landowner and the house belongs in equity to the occupying leaseholder.'[3] The Act effectively confers on the tenant a right to acquire the freehold by compulsory purchase from the landlord.[4]

1   Leasehold Reform in England and Wales (Cmnd 2916, 1966), para 1.
2   It was acknowledged to be 'quite indefensible, if justice is to be done as between freeholder and occupying leaseholder', that property which had been cherished and improved as the home of the leaseholder should revert without compensation to the landlord at the expiry of the term (Cmnd 2916, para 1).
3   Cmnd 2916, para 4.
4   Any attempt by contractual means to exclude or modify the tenant's rights under the Leasehold Reform Act 1967 is in principle void (see LRA 1967, s 23(1)). See *Buckley v S R L Investments Ltd and Cator and Robinson* (1971) 22 P & CR 756 at 767; *Rennie v Proma Ltd & Byng* (1990) 22 HLR 129 at 140; *Woodruff v Hambro* (1991) 23 HLR 295 at 299–300. The operation of the 1967 Act may nevertheless be limited in certain circumstances where the

landlord requires the property concerned for redevelopment (LRA 1967, s 17) or as a residence for himself or for an adult member of his family (LRA 1967, s 18) or if the land is certified to be required for public purposes (LRA 1967, s 28).

Qualifying conditions

7.330   The qualifying conditions originally set out in the Leasehold Reform Act 1967 have been overlaid by a series of complex statutory amendments and additions.[1]

1   See principally Leasehold Reform, Housing and Urban Development Act 1993 and Commonhold and Leasehold Reform Act 2002 (the relevant provisions of the latter statute operating with prospective effect from 26 July 2002 (in England) and 1 January 2003 (in Wales)).

Qualifying property

7.331   The Leasehold Reform Act 1967 applies only to premises which consist of a 'house'.[1] For this purpose a 'house' can comprise a terraced or semi-detached house or an entire house divided up into flats or maisonettes,[2] but not an individual flat,[3] a tower block of flats[4] or a house which is 'not structurally detached and of which a material part lies above or below a part of the structure not comprised in the house.'[5] The 1967 Act originally imposed limits on the value of qualifying property (pegging these limits to the rateable value of the property at certain dates[6]), but, for the purpose of the right to acquire the freehold, these limits have now been abrogated in respect of most forms of otherwise qualifying tenancy.[7]

1   LRA 1967, s 2(1).
2   Vertical division of any part of the building renders the whole ineligible as a 'house' (*Malekshad v Howard de Walden Estates Ltd* [2003] 1 AC 1013 at [13], [24], [54]).
3   LRA 1967, s 2(1)(a). See [1982] Conv 241.
4   *Lake v Bennett* [1970] 1 QB 663 at 671A. See *Tandon v Trustees of Spurgeons Homes* [1982] AC 755 at 766F–H, where the House of Lords was prepared to accept that the Act could apply to leasehold premises which comprised a shop with living accommodation above. See also *Lake v Bennett* [1970] 1 QB 663 at 671C, 672D–E; *Sharpe v Duke Street Securities NV* (1988) 55 P & CR 331 at 334–336.
5   LRA 1967, s 2(2). See *Duke of Westminster v Birrane* [1995] QB 262 at 271A–D (mews basement extending beneath other property).
6   LRA 1967, s 1(1), (5)–(6).
7   LRA 1967, s 1A(1).

Qualifying tenancies

7.332   The tenant must hold a 'long tenancy', ie a term certain which when granted was in excess of 21 years,[1] and this tenancy must be 'at a low rent'.[2] The 1967 Act has been extended to cover certain tenancies granted before 18 April 1980 which are determinable by notice on the death or marriage of the tenant.[3]

an increasingly valuable capital asset, at a depressed and sometimes derisory price, just as the long leasehold term reaches towards its term date. It has been said with force that the Act 'greatly favours the tenant'[1] and is in effect 'an expropriatory Act'.[2]

1   *Tandon v Trustees of Spurgeons Homes* [1982] AC 755 at 761A per Lord Wilberforce (dissenting).
2   *Manson v Duke of Westminster* [1981] QB 323 at 332C per Stephenson LJ. It is often painfully clear that the benefits of the 1967 Act are not conferred on the deprived or disadvantaged. In spite of its socialist origins, the Act is primarily of benefit to those who are already possessed of sufficient capital resources or borrowing power to acquire a long lease in the first place.

7.337   In 1984 the Leasehold Reform Act 1967 was challenged as a violation of the property guarantee contained in the European Convention on Human Rights.[1] In *James v United Kingdom*,[2] trustees acting on behalf of the Duke of Westminster, the freehold owner of large areas of Belgravia, alleged that the operation of the 1967 Act had already caused losses to the Duke's estate in excess of £2.5 million.[3] The European Court of Human Rights rejected the claim, holding that the compulsory transfer of property from one individual to another 'may, depending upon the circumstances, constitute a legitimate means for promoting the public interest.'[4] Although the applicants' complaint was not 'groundless',[5] the United Kingdom Parliament's belief in the existence of social injustice in 1967 'was not such as could be characterised as manifestly unreasonable' in view of the relative capital investments of landlord and tenant.[6] In the Court's view, housing represents a 'prime social need, the regulation of which cannot entirely be left to the play of market forces.' There must be legislative competence to secure 'greater social justice in the sphere of people's homes, even where such legislation interferes with existing contractual relations between private parties and confers no direct benefit on the State or the community at large.'[7]

1   ECHR Protocol No 1, Art 1 [**para 2.29**].
2   Series A No 98 (1986).
3   Although the unencumbered freehold value of the properties so far enfranchised varied from £44,000 to £225,000, the prices paid by the tenants had ranged from £2,500 to £111,000. Many of the enfranchising tenants had since sold up their newly acquired freeholds, some at an instant profit (measured in 1980s values) in excess of £100,000.
4   Series A No 98 (1986) at [40]. The Court cited in support the US Supreme Court's endorsement of state legislation for the compulsory transfer of title from lessors to lessees in the interests of reducing the concentration of land ownership (*Hawaii Housing Authority v Midkiff*, 467 US 229 at 241–243, 81 L Ed 2d 186 at 198–199 (1984)). See also *Wilson v First County Trust Ltd (No 2)* [2004] 1 AC 816 at [68] per Lord Nicholls of Birkenhead.
5   Series A No 98 (1986) at [49].
6   Series A No 98 (1986) at [49]. The Court laid great emphasis on the fact that any 'windfall profits' gained through onward sales by the enfranchising tenants had been made, not at the expense of the applicants who had received the statutorily prescribed compensation, but at the expense of the predecessors in title of the enfranchising tenants.
7   Series A No 98 (1986) at [47].

LEASEHOLD REFORM, HOUSING AND URBAN DEVELOPMENT ACT 1993

7.338   One of the alleged shortcomings of the Leasehold Reform Act 1967 has always been that it has no application to a leasehold estate in a *flat* as distinct from a *house*.[1] This deficiency was remedied, at least in part, by the Leasehold Reform, Housing and Urban Development Act 1993, which confers significant rights on certain categories of 'qualifying tenant'.[2] The relevant provisions of the 1993 Act apply to 'flats' which form part of a building and are constructed or adapted for use as a dwelling.[3] A 'qualifying tenant' must hold a 'long lease' of a flat,[4] a 'long lease' being defined essentially as a term of years certain which when granted was in excess of 21 years.[5] Any agreement to exclude or modify the statutory entitlements of a qualifying tenant is generally void.[6]

1 [**Para 7.331**].
2 See M Davey, (1994) 57 MLR 773. The 1993 Act has been significantly amended by the Commonhold and Leasehold Reform Act, the relevant provisions of which took prospective effect from 26 July 2002 (in England) and 1 January 2003 (in Wales).
3 LRH&UDA 1993, s 101(1).
4 LRH&UDA 1993, s 5(1). The lease must not be a business lease (LRH&UDA 1993, ss 5(2)(a), 39(3)(a)) and the Act does not generally apply to leases held from a charitable housing trust (LRH&UDA 1993, ss 5(2)(b), 39(3)(a)).
5 LRH&UDA 1993, ss 7(1)(a), 39(3)(a). There is no longer any requirement that the lease should be 'at a low rent' (see LRH&UDA 1993, s 5(1), as amended by CALRA 2002, ss 117, 180, Sch 14).
6 LRH&UDA 1993, s 93(1). Even if coupled with actual occupation on the part of the tenant, the rights conferred by the Leasehold Reform, Housing and Urban Development Act 1993 are protectable only by the entry of a 'notice' in the register and never give rise an overriding interest pursuant to the Land Registration Act 2002 (LRH&UDA 1993, s 97(1) (as amended by LRA 2002, s 133, Sch 11, para 30(3)). See *Melbury Road Properties 1995 Ltd v Kreidi* [1999] 3 EGLR 108 at 109D.

Individual right to acquire a new lease

7.339 In relation to his individual flat, a 'qualifying tenant' is accorded a right, on payment of a premium, to have his existing lease replaced with a new lease at a peppercorn rent for a term expiring 90 years after the term date of the existing lease.[1] There is no longer any residence requirement. It is sufficient that the tenant has been a 'qualifying tenant' for the two years immediately preceding his notice of claim.[2] In this notice[3] the tenant must specify a bona fide, realistic and genuine proposal as to the premium which he is prepared to pay for the 'very valuable' asset which he seeks in the form of the new lease.[4] The tenant's right to acquire a new lease may be declared by court order to be incapable of exercise where the tenant's lease is due to terminate within five years and the landlord intends to demolish or redevelop the premises.[5]

1 LRH&UDA 1993, ss 39(1), 56(1), Sch 13. The right to a new lease may relate not merely to the tenant's flat, but also to a storeroom on a different floor (see *Cadogan v McGirk* [1996] 4 All ER 643 at 652e).
2 LRH&UDA 1993, s 39(2)(a), as amended by CALRA 2002, s 130.
3 LRH&UDA 1993, s 42(3)(c).
4 *Cadogan v Morris* (1999) 77 P & CR 336 at 340–341. In the absence of agreement, the premium payable is fixed in accordance with LRH&UDA 1993, Sch 13.
5 LRH&UDA 1993, s 47(1)–(2).

Right to collective enfranchisement

7.340   The Leasehold Reform, Housing and Urban Development Act 1993 also confers a 'right of collective enfranchisement' in relation to blocks of flats where 'qualifying tenants' hold at least two-thirds of the total number of flats in the building.[1] Subject to compliance with certain tightly drawn conditions, qualifying tenants may require that the freehold of the premises be 'acquired on their behalf' by a company specially created for the purpose (an 'RTE company'[2]) and at a price determined in accordance with the statute.[3]

1   LRH&UDA 1993, s 3(1)(c). The benefits of collective enfranchisement are therefore denied to those living in blocks of flats where more than one third of the flats are rented rather than held by long lease.
2   That is, a 'right to enfranchise' company (LRH&UDA 1993, ss 4A–4B, as added by CALRA 2002, s 122).
3   LRH&UDA 1993, s 1(1).

Statutory objective

7.341   The professed objective of the 1993 Act was to enable flat owners to gain effective ownership and managerial control of their blocks of flats, thereby overcoming the deleterious effects of oppressive or inefficient absentee landlordism. The legislation proved controversial partly because of the way in which it endorsed yet a further process of compulsory acquisition from existing freeholders and partly because its complexity withheld the benefits of statutory enfranchisement from a substantial minority of leaseholders. It has been said, however, that the 1993 Act should be construed purposively on behalf of tenants and not restrictively as a body of expropriatory legislation.[1]

1   See *Cadogan v McGirk* [1996] 4 All ER 643 at 648a–b per Millett LJ.

Eligible property

7.342   The 1993 Act applies to premises which consist of a building containing two or more flats held by 'qualifying tenants'.[1] The right to collective enfranchisement cannot be claimed where different persons own the freehold of different parts of the premises and any of those parts is a self-contained part of a building.[2] Certain other categories of property are excluded from the scope of the Act. The legislation does not apply to premises of which more than 25 per cent of the internal floor area is designated for non-residential use, e g as shops or other commercial premises.[3] Nor does the right to collective enfranchisement relate to premises where there is a resident landlord[4] and the premises do not contain more than four flats or units.[5]

1   LRH&UDA 1993, s 3(1)(a)–(b).
2   LRH&UDA 1993, s 4(3A), as added by HA 1996, s 107(2).
3   LRH&UDA 1993, s 4(1), as amended by CALRA 2002, s 115. Garage, parking space and storage areas, if ancillary to a particular dwelling in the premises, are taken to be occupied or designated for residential purposes (LRH&UDA 1993, s 4(2)). Common parts of the building are disregarded (LRH&UDA 1993, s 4(3)).

4   See LRH&UDA 1993, s 10.
5   LRH&UDA 1993, s 4(4).

Exercise of the right by qualifying tenants

7.343 The exercise of the statutory right to collective enfranchisement is initiated by the service of a notice of claim on the reversioner by the RTE company which has been formed by the tenants.[1] This notice can be served only if the 'qualifying tenants' own at least half of the flats contained in the building,[2] but there is no longer any precondition of residence.[3] No qualifying tenant may participate in giving a relevant notice of claim if at this date he is obliged to give up possession of his flat in pursuance of a court order.[4] Thereafter the conduct of all proceedings on behalf of the participating tenants is in the hands of the RTE company.[5] These proceedings, involving a statutory routine of notice and counter-notice, are designed to lead to a conveyance to the RTE company of the fee simple estate in the premises.[6] The price of this form of compulsory acquisition is fixed by reference to criteria laid down in the Act.[7] These criteria assume a sale on the open market by a willing seller[8] and incorporate elements of value designed to compensate the freeholder for his share of the 'marriage value' (ie the increased value generated by the merger of freehold and leasehold interests)[9] and for any other loss resulting to him from the enfranchisement.[10] The RTE company, on acquiring title, applies for registration at Land Registry and is now free to grant new long leases (usually terms of 999 years) to its participating members.

1   LRH&UDA 1993, s 13(1)–(2). The notice must include a plan of the property (s 13(3)(a)). See *Mutual Place Property Management Ltd v Blaquiere* [1996] 2 EGLR 78 at 80C–D.
2   LRH&UDA 1993, s 13(2)(b).
3   LRH&UDA 1993, s 6 was repealed by CALRA 2002, s 180, Sch 14.
4   LRH&UDA 1993, Sch 3, para 3(1). A qualifying tenant is likewise debarred (except with leave of the court) where any proceedings are pending to enforce a right of re-entry or forfeiture against him (Sch 3, para 3(2)), but no such proceedings may be instituted by the landlord (except with leave of the court) during the currency of any claim to exercise the right to collective enfranchisement (Sch 3, para 7(1)).
5   LRH&UDA 1993, s 15(1).
6   LRH&UDA 1993, s 34(1).
7   LRH&UDA 1993, s 32(1), Sch 6, as amended by HA 1996, s 109, and CALRA 2002, ss 127–128.
8   LRH&UDA 1993, Sch 6, para 3(1).
9   LRH&UDA 1993, Sch 6, para 4. The freeholder's share of the marriage value is normally deemed to be 50 per cent (see CALRA 2002, s 127), but no marriage value arises where the leasehold term of every participating member of an RTE company exceeds 80 years (see CALRA 2002, s 128).
10   LRH&UDA 1993, Sch 6, para 5.

LANDLORD AND TENANT ACT 1987

7.344 Purchase by a tenant of his landlord's superior interest was further promoted by the Landlord and Tenant Act 1987,[1] which introduced a limited

right of pre-emption for tenants of premises contained within a block of flats.[2]
Under the 1987 Act qualifying tenants[3] are entitled to a right of first refusal if
their landlord proposes to make a 'relevant disposal' of his interest in the
property.[4]

1   The enactment came in response to the concern expressed by the Nugee Committee in 1985 to
     provide increased safeguards for the interests of long leaseholders in mansion blocks (see
     Report of the Committee of Inquiry on the Management of Privately Owned Blocks of Flats
     (Chairman: E G Nugee QC, 1985), Vol 1, paras 7.9.13–7.9.23). The Landlord and Tenant
     Act 1987, an acknowledged victim of complicated and confused drafting (see eg *Belvedere
     Court Management Ltd v Frogmore Developments Ltd* [1997] QB 858 at 881C–F), was
     substantially modified by HA 1996, ss 92(1), 93(1), Sch 6.
2   The premises, which may be the whole or part of a building, must comprise at least two flats
     held by qualifying tenants and the number of flats held by qualifying tenants must exceed
     50 per cent of the total number of flats contained in the premises (L&TA 1987, s 1(2)).
3   A qualifying tenant need not satisfy any residence requirement (although see L&TA 1987,
     s 3(2)), but the 1987 Act excludes certain categories of tenant such as assured tenants, business
     tenants and protected shorthold tenants (L&TA 1987, s 3(1)).
4   See *Denetower Ltd v Toop* [1991] 1 WLR 945 at 948B–D per Browne-Wilkinson V-C.

Rights of pre-emption

7.345   The landlord may not dispose of his interest to a third party[1] without
first serving on the qualifying tenants a notice (an 'offer notice') indicating both
his intention to sell to a third party and the proposed sale price.[2] The notice
constitutes an offer by the landlord to dispose of the property to the tenants on
the same terms as agreed with the prospective purchaser.[3] The tenants must
then be allowed a period of not less than two months[4] within which they may
accept[5] or reject the offer. A binding acceptance of the landlord's offer may be
made by qualifying tenants with more than 50 per cent of the 'available votes',
ie by a bare majority of the qualifying tenants who own 'constituent flats' in
the relevant building on the expiry date of the landlord's notice.[6] If the
landlord's offer is rejected, the landlord is free during the next twelve months to
dispose of his interest provided that he does so for a consideration not less than
that specified in the original notice and on terms which correspond to the other
terms of that notice.[7]

1   The 'relevant disposal' occurs on completion of the transfer to the third party rather than on
     the mere exchange of contracts for such a transfer (*Mainwaring v Trustees of Henry Smith's
     Charity* [1998] QB 1 at 18B per Sir Thomas Bingham MR).
2   L&TA 1987, s 1(1). It is sufficient if the notice is served on at least 90 per cent of the
     qualifying tenants (L&TA 1987, s 5(5)). A criminal offence is committed by any landlord who,
     without reasonable cause, fails to serve the requisite notice (L&TA 1987, s 10A(1)).
3   L&TA 1987, s 5A(3), as substituted by HA 1996, s 92(1), Sch 6.
4   L&TA 1987, s 5A(4).
5   L&TA 1987, s 6.
6   L&TA 1987, ss 6(3), 18A(1). A tenant may withdraw his signature from the acceptance notice
     at any time before its service on the landlord, even though he has signed an irrevocable
     undertaking not to do so and even though his withdrawal destroys the majority for acceptance
     (see *Mainwaring v Trustees of Henry Smith's Charity (No 2)* (1996) Times, 9 October).
7   L&TA 1987, s 7(1)–(3).

Ancillary rights for qualifying tenants

7.346   The statutory scheme is buttressed by the entitlement of tenants to enforce their rights, in certain circumstances, against a purchaser to whom the landlord's interest is improperly disposed.[1] If the landlord makes a relevant disposal without first serving the requisite notice on the tenants or otherwise in contravention of key provisions of the statutory code, the tenants are entitled, on serving notice, to obtain information from the purchaser as to the terms of the actual disposal[2] and within six months to compel the purchaser to sell the property on the same terms to the nominee of the majority of the qualifying tenants.[3] Where, at the time of the tenants' notice, the purchaser no longer holds the subject matter of the original disposal, the rights of the tenants are enforceable against subsequent purchasers.[4]

1   The purchaser (ie the 'new landlord') is required to notify qualifying tenants not only of the assignment of the landlord's interest to him (L&TA 1987, s 3(1)) but also, on pain of criminal liability, of their right to obtain information as to the terms of the assignment and of their right to compel a sale of that interest to them (L&TA 1987, s 3A(1)–(3)).
2   L&TA 1987, ss 11(1)–(2), 11A(1). See *Staszewski v Maribella Ltd* (1997) Times, 28 March.
3   L&TA 1987, ss 11(1)–(2), 12B(1)–(2). The list of tenants specified as claiming this right must be accurate (see *Elnaschie v Pitt Place (Epsom) Ltd* (1999) 78 P & CR 44 at 48, where the relevant notice included the name of a deceased tenant and the names of several tenants who had not authorised the notice). Curiously the statute imposes no express obligation on the purchaser to comply with the tenants' notice, but the courts have supplied such an obligation by naked judicial legislation (see *Kay Green v Twinsectra Ltd* [1996] 1 WLR 1587 at 1597B–G, 1603A–G).
4   L&TA 1987, s 16. See *Belvedere Court Management Ltd v Frogmore Developments Ltd* [1997] QB 858.

HOUSING ACT 1985

7.347   A significant aspect of the charter of rights conferred on the public sector tenant takes the form of his statutory 'right to buy' the home in which he lives.[1] This right was introduced for council tenants by the Housing Act 1980 and is now contained in an expanded form in the Housing Act 1985.[2] One of the more notable political initiatives of the 1980s, the 'right to buy' scheme was commended to Parliament as fostering 'a deeply ingrained desire for home ownership' and as stimulating 'the attitudes of independence and self-reliance that are the bedrock of a free society.'[3] The scheme was intended to 'transform the personal prospects of millions of our citizens, offering to turn them at their wish from tenants to owners.'[4] It has been estimated that more than 10 per cent of all households in Britain today have participated in the purchase of public or quasi-public accommodation which they previously rented.[5]

1   See *R (O'Byrne) v Secretary of State for the Environment, Transport and the Regions* [2002] 1 WLR 3250 at [47] per Lord Scott of Foscote (referring to the 'right to buy' as an inaccurate, but 'attention catching' expression), [69] ('Parliament's equivalent of a soundbite').
2   In an attempt to tackle exploitation of the rules by property developers and tenants, the availability of the 'right to buy' is likely to be tightened by provisions currently contained in the Housing Bill 2004 (see *Housing Bill 2004 (HL Bill 71): Explanatory Notes*, para 30).

3　Michael Heseltine (Secretary of State for the Environment), *Parliamentary Debates, House of Commons, Official Report*, Vol 976 (Session 1979–1980), Col 1445 (15 January 1980).

4　Ibid, Col 1460 ('It will establish their rights as individuals above the bureaucracies of the State. It will come to be seen among the finest traditions and philosophies of the Conservative Party.') The implementation of the 'right to buy' scheme has not, however, lacked its critics. The scheme devastated an already impoverished public housing sector, withdrawing badly needed stock from circulation and leaving available for rental a disproportionate number of less desirable and less well maintained properties. The political drive for home ownership in the 1980s also caused substantial numbers of people to assume unaffordable financial liabilities, thereby contributing to the unprecedented phase of mortgage repossession experienced during the late 1980s and early 1990s (see *Social Trends 23* (1993), p 121 (Chart 8.19)).

5　*Social Trends 30* (2000 edn London), p 168.

Nature of the 'right to buy'

7.348　The Housing Act 1985 confers on certain qualifying categories of 'qualifying person'[1] the right, in statutorily defined circumstances, to purchase either the freehold or a long leasehold term in the property in which that person lives.[2] This right has been described as bearing a 'strong resemblance to an option to purchase.'[3] The qualifying public sector tenant is entitled to acquire the freehold if his dwelling-house is a 'house' and his landlord owns the freehold.[4] If his dwelling-house is not a 'house' but is a flat or if his landlord is not the owner of the freehold, the qualifying person has a right to be granted a long lease for a term of usually not less than 125 years at a rent which does not exceed £10 per annum.[5] The landlord is statutorily obliged, in advance of the purchase, to disclose defects affecting the premises[6] and to provide estimates of likely service charges and improvement contributions.[7]

1　HA 1985, s 118(1).

2　Where relevant property is occupied by two or more qualifying persons as joint tenants, the 'right to buy' may be exercised by such one or more of them as may be agreed between them (HA 1985, s 118(2)). In certain circumstances a qualifying person may nominate not more than three 'members of his family' to share the 'right to buy' with him, provided that such persons occupy the dwelling-house as their 'only or principal home' (HA 1985, s 123(1)). See e g *Savill v Goodall* [1993] 1 FLR 755 at 757A. If the public sector tenant dies before the completion of the purchase, the nominee or nominees may exercise the 'right to buy' by survivorship (*Harrow LBC v Tonge* (1992) 25 HLR 99 at 103). A child of a deceased tenant may also succeed to the 'right to buy' (see HA 1985, Sch 4, para 4(2)).

3　*Dance v Welwyn Hatfield DC* [1990] 1 WLR 1097 at 1100A per Nourse LJ. Compare *Bradford City MC v McMahon* [1994] 1 WLR 52 at 60H (right to buy is 'a creature of statute and is sui generis').

4　HA 1985, s 118(1)(a).

5　HA 1985, s 118(1)(b), Sch 6, Pt III, paras 11, 12(1).

6　HA 1985, s 125(4A).

7　HA 1985, ss 125A, 125B. See also HA 1985, ss 121A–121B, to be inserted by HB 2004, cl 166(1).

Conditions of eligibility

7.349　The 'right to buy' is conferred by the 1985 Act on any qualifying person who satisfies a complex series of statutory conditions.[1] Once the statutory conditions have been satisfied, the landlord has no discretion to resist the exercise of the right to buy.[2] As soon as all matters relating to the grant have been agreed or determined, the tenant has a statutory right to a conveyance[3] and the landlord's duty to convey becomes enforceable by injunction.[4]

1   The right to buy is not available to tenants of charitable housing trusts or housing associations or of co-operative housing associations (HA 1985, s 120, Sch 5, paras 1–2), but can be claimed (subject to certain conditions) by tenants of registered social landlords under a secure tenancy or an assured tenancy other than a shorthold or long tenancy (HA 1996, s 16(2)). The 'right to buy' also excludes an employee of the landlord who is required to occupy a rented dwelling-house for the better performance of his duties (HA 1985, Sch 1, para 2(1)), but such an obligation is not easily implied (see *Hughes v Greenwich LBC* [1994] 1 AC 170 at 179B per Lord Lowry).

2   HA 1985, s 138(1). See *Taylor v Newham LBC* [1993] 1 WLR 444 at 451C–D per Sir Thomas Bingham MR. For this reason the statutory right applies even in respect of 'green belt' land (see *R (O'Byrne) v Secretary of State for the Environment, Transport and the Regions* [2002] 1 WLR 3250 at [11], [58]–[59]).

3   See *Bristol CC v Lovell* [1998] 1 WLR 446 at 453H per Lord Hoffmann. It was once suggested that, at this point, the tenant becomes immediately the equitable owner of the property (see *Dance v Welwyn Hatfield DC* [1990] 1 WLR 1097 at 1104F–1105B per Nourse LJ), but this proposition has been denounced as 'positively misleading' (*Bristol CC v Lovell* at 455F per Lord Hoffmann; see also Lord Clyde at 459H). The qualifying tenant acquires no proprietary interest whatever until the grant of the freehold. See likewise *R (O'Byrne) v Secretary of State for the Environment, Transport and the Regions* [2002] 1 WLR 3250 at [70] per Lord Rodger of Earlsferry.

4   HA 1985, s 138(3). The county court has discretion to adjourn the tenant's application for an injunction pending the determination of any claim made against him by the council for possession of the property (see *Bristol CC v Lovell* [1998] 1 WLR 446 at 454F–455A per Lord Hoffmann, 460A per Lord Clyde).

7.350   The 'right to buy' relates only to a 'dwelling-house' which is a 'house' within the definition of the 1985 Act.[1] A tenant qualifies for the 'right to buy' if he has been a public sector tenant for a period of at least two years.[2] (The Housing Bill 2004 proposes to extend this qualifying period to five years.[3]) The tenant cannot, however, exercise the 'right to buy' if, at any stage before the completion of his purchase, a possession order is made against him on any of the grounds which permit the landlord to recover possession under the Housing Act 1985.[4] If the law were not so, as Slade LJ pointed out in *Enfield LBC v McKeon*,[5] a public sector tenant would always be able to frustrate the enforcement of any possession order against him – no matter how good the ground on which it was made – by the simple device of claiming the 'right to buy'. The tenant also loses the 'right to buy' if, at any point before completion of the purchase, he ceases to hold his qualifying tenancy.[6] Under the terms of the Housing Bill 2004 the 'right to buy' may also be suspended on grounds of anti-social behaviour.[7]

1   A dwelling-house is a 'house' if it is 'a structure reasonably so called' (s 183(2)) and a dwelling-house which is not a house is a 'flat' (s 183(3)). Where a building is divided horizontally, the resulting residential units are 'flats' rather than 'houses' (s 183(2)(a)). Certain kinds of property are excepted from the scope of the Act (HA 1985, s 120, Sch 5). See *Freeman v Wansbeck DC* (1983) 82 LGR 131 at 134–137.

2   HA 1985, s 119(1). This qualifying period need not be a continuous period (HA 1985, Sch 4, para 1), nor need it immediately precede the tenant's exercise of his 'right to buy' (see HA

1985, Sch 4, para 2). Moreover, even though a tenant has not himself resided for a period of two years, the requisite residence may include residence by a spouse with whom he was living at the date on which he claimed the 'right to buy' (HA 1985, Sch 4, para 2(b)).

3   HB 2004, cl 157(1), (5) (in respect of post-commencement tenancies only).

4   HA 1985, s 121(1). See *Enfield LBC v McKeon* [1986] 1 WLR 1007 at 1015G–H, where the Court of Appeal held that a tenant's attempt to exercise her 'right to buy' had been effectively pre-empted by the Council's recovery of possession on the ground that the accommodation afforded by the house was more extensive than she required. The 'right to buy' is also terminated by the tenant's bankruptcy (HA 1985, s 121(2)).

5   [1986] 1 WLR 1007 at 1015F–G. Compare, however, *Dance v Welwyn Hatfield DC* [1990] 1 WLR 1097 at 1105G.

6   See e g *Muir Group Housing Association Ltd v Thornley* (1992) 25 HLR 89 at 97 (tenant innocently sublet whole house shortly before completion date, thereby forfeiting his status as secure tenant pursuant to HA 1985, s 93(2) [**para 14.340**]).

7   HB 2004, cl 169.

Terms of purchase

7.351   A qualifying person exercises his 'right to buy' by serving a written notice on the landlord.[1] The eligible tenant has a right to purchase either the freehold or a long leasehold term at the price which such an interest would achieve on the open market,[2] minus a discount which is variable in accordance with the duration of the tenancy enjoyed by the qualifying person.[3] In the case of a house the appropriate discount currently ranges from 32 per cent to a maximum of 60 per cent after 30 years of qualifying residence and, in the case of a flat, from 44 per cent to a maximum of 70 per cent.[4] In order to prevent private profiteering at public expense, the 1985 Act imposes in cases of 'early disposal' an obligation to repay in part or whole any discount allowed to the tenant on the exercise of his 'right to buy'.[5] On purchase the tenant is required to covenant to repay a statutorily prescribed portion of the discount in the event of any onward sale of the fee simple or grant of a long lease during the three years immediately following his purchase.[6]

1   HA 1985, s 122(1).

2   HA 1985, ss 126(1)(a), 127(1)–(3).

3   HA 1985, s 126(1)(b). The maximum discount currently allowable varies generally from £38,000 in London to £22,000 in the North East. See HA 1985, s 131(2); The Housing (Right to Buy) (Limits on Discount) Order 1998 (SI 1998/2997, art 3(1), Sch 1), but the Secretary of State has power to restrict the maximum discount to £16,000 in designated areas (SI 1998/2997, art 3A(1), Sch 2, as added by SI 2003/498 (effective 27 March 2003)).

4   HA 1985, s 129(2)(a)–(b). The Housing Bill 2004 proposes, in respect of post-commencement tenancies, to start the discounts at 35 per cent and 50 per cent respectively (after a qualifying period of five years). See HB 2004, cl 157(2), (5).

5   Certain disposals are exempted from the liability to repay the discount (see HA 1985, s 160(1)), e g a disposal on divorce in pursuance of a court-ordered property transfer. See, however, *R v Rushmoor BC, ex p Barrett* [1989] QB 60 at 69A–B (immunity does not cover a court-ordered sale whose net proceeds are divided between the spouses).

6   HA 1985, ss 155(1)–(2), 159(1). The Housing Bill 2004 proposes, in respect of post-commencement exercises of the 'right to buy', to extend this period to five years (see HB 2004, cl 162(2)). Enforcement of the repayment covenant will, more generally, become a matter of discretion for the housing authority (e g in cases of illness, bereavement or violent relationship breakdown) (see HA 1985, s 155A(1), to be inserted by HB 2004, cl 162(4)). The housing

authority (or its nominee) will also have a right of first refusal in the event of any resale within ten years (see HA 1985, s 156A, to be inserted by HB 2004, cl 165(1)).

7.352   The completion of a purchase under the 'right to buy' terminates any tenancy previously enjoyed by the purchasing tenant.[1] Thereafter the position of the purchaser is governed largely by the terms and covenants which are attached by the Housing Act 1985 to the conveyance of his freehold or the grant of his lease.[2] The vendor is not entitled to impose any unreasonable terms on the purchaser,[3] although it is common to include a restrictive covenant which precludes the purchaser from further development of the land without the vendor's consent. In such cases it may not remain open to the vendor later to demand and receive payment for releasing the purchaser from this restriction.[4]

1   HA 1985, s 139(2).
2   HA 1985, s 139(1). See generally HA 1985, Sch 6. The conveyance or grant cannot normally exclude or restrict the general words implied under LPA 1925, s 62 [**para 8.153**]. See HA 1985, Sch 6, Pt I, para 1. See *Peckham v Ellison* (2000) 79 P & CR 276 at 296.
3   See *Guinan v Enfield LBC* [1996] EGCS 142.
4   *R v Braintree DC, ex p Halls* (2000) 80 P & CR 266 at 275–278.

The 'rent to mortgage' scheme

7.353   In aid of the public sector tenant's 'right to buy', the Leasehold Reform, Housing and Urban Development Act 1993 confers a right to acquire the freehold or a long lease 'on rent to mortgage terms'.[1] Under the 'rent to mortgage' scheme the periodic payments made by the tenant, if fixed at a specified level, enable him gradually to redeem the 'landlord's share' secured by mortgage to the landlord. The 'rent to mortgage' scheme effectively enables the qualifying tenant of a dwelling-house to make an immediate purchase of a fee simple estate or long leasehold interest,[2] the 'rent to mortgage' purchaser being entitled to a discount based on qualifying periods of residence.[3] Any pre-existing tenancy comes to an end on the occasion of a grant made in pursuance of the right to acquire on 'rent to mortgage' terms.[4] There is also provision for repayment of discount by the purchaser in the event of any disposal of the property within three years of purchase.[5] The 'rent to mortgage' scheme is due to be withdrawn, after an eight month period of grace following royal assent, by the terms of the Housing Bill 2004.[6]

1   HA 1985, s 143(1), as substituted by LRH&UDA 1993, s 108.
2   HA 1985, s 150(1).
3   HA 1985, s 148.
4   HA 1985, s 151(2).
5   HA 1985, s 155(3) (to be extended to five years by HB 2004, cl 162).
6   HB 2004, cl 167.

The 'preserved right to buy'

7.354   The Housing Act 1985 also provides measures designed to protect the tenant's 'right to buy' where the landlord's interest in his dwelling-house is 'privatised', ie transferred from public ownership into ownership within the private sector.[1] Where the secure tenant's dwelling-house is the subject of such a disposal to a private sector landlord, the tenant is given a 'preserved right to buy' which is effective against the new landlord in exactly the same terms as formerly against the original public sector landlord.[2] The bindingness of this 'preserved right to buy' on the new landlord depends, however, on the entry of a 'notice' in the appropriate register of title,[3] and if not duly protected in this way the 'preserved right to buy' becomes entirely ineffective.[4]

1   On the steady drive towards transfer of council housing stock to the private sector, see J Driscoll, (1994) 57 MLR 788.
2   HA 1985, s 171B(1).
3   HA 1985, Sch 9A, para 6(1).
4   It cannot be saved as an overriding interest pursuant to LRA 2002, s 29(1), (2)(a)(ii), Sch 3, para 2 (see HA 1985, Sch 9A, para 6(1)).

FREEHOLD OWNERSHIP OF COMMONHOLD LAND

7.356   The Commonhold and Leasehold Reform Act 2002 inaugurates a long-awaited form of estate ownership which is specially designed as a new form of landholding for blocks of flats and other multi-unit properties such as office blocks and similar commercial accommodation.[1]

1   See *Commonhold and Leasehold Reform: Draft Bill and Consultation Paper* (Lord Chancellor's Department, Cm 4843, August 2000) (foreshadowed by Law Commission, *Commonhold: Freehold Flats and freehold ownership of other interdependent buildings* (Cm 179, July 1987).

Commonhold ownership as a species of freehold ownership

7.357   'Commonhold ownership' is a species of *freehold* ownership of *registered* land which has been deliberately adapted to resolve many of the legal problems arising in respect of multiple occupation of premises.[1] Under the commonhold scheme each 'unit-holder' (eg each owner of a flat in a block) takes a registered freehold estate by way of exclusive ownership of his or her individual unit[2] and also becomes a member of a management or 'commonhold association' which owns the common parts of the grounds and building (including its structural walls and any garden or other communal facility). Commonholders thus enjoy 'the security of freehold ownership' coupled with a collective freedom to 'control and effectively manage their own common areas and to apply positive obligations to every successive owner of the individual units in the development.'[3]

1   **[Para 13.57]**. See D N Clarke, 'The Enactment of Commonhold – Problems, Principles and Perspectives' [2002] Conv 349.
2   A 'unit' could consist of two or more separate areas of land, eg a flat and separate garage, and units may be divided from each other either vertically or horizontally (CALRA 2002, s 11(3)(d); *Commonhold and Leasehold Reform* (2000), Pt I, para 1.3.4 (p 81)).
3   Land Registry, *Commonhold (Land Registration) Rules: A Land Registry Consultation Paper* (September 2002), p 11.

An alternative to long leasehold ownership

7.358   In many respects the device of commonhold ownership provides yet another way in which existing mechanisms of leasehold ownership (which have never proved entirely satisfactory as a means of regulating multi-occupied premises) can be converted into some form of freehold title.[1] Ownership of a lease, which is a wasting asset, 'will be replaced by ownership of a freehold, which is not', commonhold thus offering a distinctively different 'alternative to long leasehold ownership of flats and other interdependent properties.'[2] The introduction of the commonhold scheme, which is heavily derivative of 'condominium' and 'strata title' schemes practised in other parts of the common law world, represents a remarkable addition to, or variant of, the conceptual structure of estate ownership in English law.[3]

1   See, however, P F Smith, 'The Purity of Commonholds' [2004] Conv 194.
2   See *Commonhold Proposals for Commonhold Regulations: A Consultation Paper* (Lord Chancellor's Department, CP: 11/02 (October 2002)), p 10.
3   See N Roberts, 'Commonhold: A New Property Term – But No Property in a Term!' [2002] Conv 341.

Creation of a commonhold

7.359   A commonhold can only be created out of a freehold estate which is already registered at Land Registry; and the commonhold itself must be created expressly by a further act of registration at the Registry.[1] The Chief Land Registrar is authorised to register an estate as 'a freehold estate in commonhold land'[2] if the land concerned is not already commonhold land and if certain other conditions are fulfilled. Land can be 'commonhold land' only if there is in existence a 'commonhold association' (ie a private company limited by guarantee and registered at Companies House) whose memorandum of association specifies certain land as 'land in relation to which the association is to exercise functions'[3] and whose business it will be to own and manage the common parts of the development.[4] There must also be in existence a 'commonhold community statement' which makes provision for the rights and duties of the commonhold association and its unit-holders.[5] The commonhold community statement must specify not only the 'commonhold units' comprised within the scheme (these being at least two in number), but must also, by reference to a filed plan, define the extent of each relevant commonhold unit.[6]

1   CALRA 2002, ss 1(1)(a), 2(1).
2   CALRA 2002, s 2(1). Some categories of land (eg 'flying freeholds' and certain agricultural land) cannot comprise 'commonhold land' (CALRA 2002, s 4, Sch 2).
3   CALRA 2002, s 1(1)(b).
4   See CALRA 2002, Sch 3.
5   CALRA 2002, s 1(1)(c).
6   CALRA 2002, s 11.

Contents of application

7.360   An application for commonhold registration may be made by any person who is (or is entitled to be) registered as the proprietor of a freehold estate in the land with absolute title.[1] All applications must be accompanied[2] by the memorandum and articles of association of the commonhold association, by the commonhold community statement, and by evidence of a number of requisite consents to the application given by:

– the registered proprietor of the freehold estate in the whole or any part of the land;

– the registered proprietor of any leasehold estate in the whole or any part of the land granted for a term of more than 21 years[3];

– the registered proprietor of any charge over the whole or any part of the land;

and

– other prescribed classes of person (such as proprietors of a rentcharge and persons holding unregistered short leases).

1   CALRA 2002, s 2(3) [**para 7.45**].
2   CALRA 2002, s 2(2), Sch 1.
3   An existing leasehold development can therefore convert to commonhold tenure with the consent of 100 per cent of the leaseholders (*Commonhold and Leasehold Reform* (2000), Pt I, para 1.3.5 (p 81)). See, however, P F Smith, [2004] Conv 194 at 198 ('the prospect of one or two capricious or recalcitrant long lessees holding up a conversion from long leasehold to commonhold is unappealing').

New developments

7.361   The developer of a site which, as yet, has no unit-holders in occupation may apply for registration of the global commonhold title in respect of that site.[1] The developer then remains registered proprietor of the freehold estate in the entire commonhold land[2] until such time as at least one other person becomes entitled to be registered as freehold proprietor of one of the units. At this point, the Chief Land Registrar is obliged to register the commonhold association as proprietor of the freehold estate in the common parts,[3] and the rights and duties contained in the commonhold community statement come into effect.[4]

1   CALRA 2002, s 7(1).
2   CALRA 2002, s 7(2)(a).
3   CALRA 2002, s 7(3)(a)–(b).
4   CALRA 2002, s 7(3)(c).

Registration with existing unit-holders

7.362   Where an application for registration of commonhold land indicates that the relevant site has *existing* unit-holders, registration has the immediate effect of vesting the registered freehold estate in the common parts in the designated commonhold association.[1] Each person specified in the application as an initial unit-holder of a commonhold unit is then entitled to be registered as the proprietor of the freehold estate in that unit.[2] The commonhold community statement comes immediately into effect[3] and cross-referenced entries are made in the Land Register in order to reflect the emergence of these various freehold titles.[4] The corollary of this general mutation to freehold title is that any existing lease of the whole or any part of the commonhold land is extinguished,[5] although a partial system of compensation is provided for leaseholders who lose their interests and who were not persons whose consent was an essential precondition of the application for commonhold registration in the first place.[6]

1   CALRA 2002, s 9(3)(a).
2   CALRA 2002, s 9(3)(b).
3   CALRA 2002, s 9(3)(e).
4   CALRA 2002, s 9(3)(d).
5   CALRA 2002, s 9(3)(f).
6   CALRA 2002, s 10.

Effect of registration

7.363   When commonhold registration takes effect, the Land Register will thus carry cross-referenced entries relating to the freehold titles taken by the individual unit holders and by the commonhold association itself. The Chief Land Registrar is required, in respect of any commonhold land, to retain (and refer in the register to) certain prescribed details of the commonhold association, prescribed details of the registered freeholder of each commonhold unit, a copy of the commonhold community statement, and a copy of the memorandum and articles of association of the commonhold association.[1]

1   CALRA 2002, s 5(1).

Commonhold community statement

7.364   At the heart of the commonhold model is the idea that, in respect of his or her own commonhold unit, each unit-holder is governed by a charter of standardised rights and obligations defined by a 'commonhold community statement', which effectively operates as a binding constitutional document for the entire commonhold community.[1] The statement allocates the benefit and the burden of such matters as support, access, services, defects, repairs and common facilities and must also require the commonhold association to insure, repair and maintain the common parts.[2] The directors of the commonhold association have a statutory responsibility to establish and maintain a 'reserve' fund or funds for financing repair and maintenance. For this purpose all unit-holders within the commonhold scheme may be required to pay a proportionate levy or service charge.[3] The rights and obligations contained in the commonhold community statement attach automatically by force of statute to each unit, irrespective of subsequent changes in the ownership of the unit, thus forming a comprehensive framework for the long-term governance of relationships and mutual dealings within the commonhold community.

1   See CALRA 2002, ss 14, 31. These rights and obligations can be varied or extended (CALRA 2002, ss 32–33).
2   CALRA 2002, s 26.
3   CALRA 2002, s 39(1)–(2).

Management by the commonhold association

7.365   The commonhold association is a private company limited by guarantee,[1] which owns the common parts and is charged with a statutory duty to manage the development 'so as to permit or facilitate so far as possible' the exercise by each unit-holder (or his tenant) of his rights and the enjoyment by each unit-holder of the freehold estate in his unit.[2] Every unit-holder is entitled to be entered in the register of members of the relevant commonhold association[3] and to vote accordingly. The commonhold community will thus manage its own affairs without reference to a third party landlord, although some fears have been expressed that this may lead to tyranny by the majority in the matter of decisions affecting the whole community.[4] The directors of the community association also have certain powers to require or ensure due compliance by a unit-holder or his tenant with any duty imposed by the commonhold community statement or any relevant statutory provision.[5] There is, moreover, to be provision for the reference of disputes to some form of alternative dispute resolution (e g by reference to an approved Ombudsman of disputes arising between the commonhold association and individual unit-holders, but not of disputes between unit-holders themselves).[6]

1   See CALRA 2002, s 34(1).
2   CALRA 2002, s 35(1), (4).
3   CALRA 2002, Sch 3, Pt 2, para 7.
4   See e g P Kenny, [2003] Conv 3. Australian courts have been prepared to invoke the doctrine of fraud on the corporate minority (see *Young v Owners of Strata Plan No 3529* (2001) 10 BPR 19153 at [43]–[54] per Santow J).
5   CALRA 2002, ss 35(2), 37.
6   See CALRA 2002, s 42.

Dealings with a commonhold unit

7.366   The commonhold community statement must not prevent or restrict the transfer of a freehold estate in a commonhold unit,[1] although on any transfer the new unit-holder has a statutory obligation to notify the commonhold association of the fact of transfer.

1   CALRA 2002, s 15(2).

Automatic transmission of rights and obligations

7.367   One of the major advantages of commonhold ownership is undoubtedly the statutory provision that any right or duty conferred or imposed by the commonhold community statement will 'affect a new unit-holder in the same way as it affected the former unit-holder',[1] thus removing at a stroke the almost intractable difficulty which, for centuries, has impeded the transmission of the burden of freehold covenants on a transfer of land.[2]

1   CALRA 2002, s 16(1). The Law Commission has long advocated that the law of covenants should be amended to make the burden of positive covenants transmissible between freehold-ers. See Law Commission, *Commonhold: Freehold Flats and freehold ownership of other interdependent buildings* (Cm 179, July 1987), para 1.3.
2   **[Para 13.57]**.

Other dealings

7.368   The unit-holder is free to grant a mortgage charge over his or her unit,[1] although the creation, grant or transfer of other interests (e g an easement) in or over the whole or part of the unit may require the participation or written consent of the commonhold association.[2] Certain restrictions curtail the power of residential unit-holders to carve long leases out of the commonhold title in respect of their individual units,[3] thus reflecting yet again the current govern-ment distaste for leasehold estates in residential premises.[4]

1   CALRA 2002, s 20(1), (3), (6).
2   CALRA 2002, s 20(3)–(4).
3   CALRA 2002, s 17. There is a fear lest residential commonhold schemes degenerate into old-style leasehold developments.
4   **[Para 7.70]**.

Termination of a commonhold scheme

7.369   A commonhold scheme may be terminated either voluntarily by a winding-up resolution passed by the commonhold association (in some cases with the necessary addition of a court order) or compulsorily by court order.[1]

1   CALRA 2002, ss 43–55.

CHAPTER 8

Other legal estates in land

STATUTORY CATALOGUE OF POTENTIALLY LEGAL INTERESTS AND CHARGES

8.1 The last chapter provided an analysis of the fee simple absolute and the term of years absolute, two estates demarcated by the Law of Property Act 1925 as having the potential to exist at law.[1] The present chapter shifts the focus to other categories of entitlement in land which are also indicated[2] as 'capable of subsisting or of being conveyed or created at law.' The 1925 Act initially refers to these rights as 'interests' and 'charges',[3] perhaps in order to emphasise that they are essentially rights acquired in or over the land of another.[4] However, once created or transferred in compliance with relevant requirements of formality or registration, these lesser entitlements are also described generically as 'legal estates' in land.[5] The group includes certain:

— easements[6]
— profits *à prendre*[7]
— rentcharges[8]
— mortgage charges[9] and
— rights of entry.[10]

1 LPA 1925, s 1(1) [**paras 7.2, 7.68**].
2 See LPA 1925, s 1(2).
3 LPA 1925, s 1(2) [**para 2.125**].
4 The Law of Property Act 1925 also refers to an anomalous group of legal charges on land not created by the voluntary transactions of individuals but imposed by statute (see LPA 1925, s 1(2)(d)). These charges have been greatly diminished by repealing legislation and are now of virtually no consequence. (Tithe rentcharge was abolished by the Tithe Act 1936, s 1; and land tax by the Finance Act 1963, Part V, Sch 14.)
5 LPA 1925, s 1(4). See eg LRA 2002, s 13(a); LRR 2003, r 73(1) (easements and appurtenant profits *à prendre*); *First National Bank plc v Thompson* [1996] Ch 231 at 240C per Millett LJ (mortgages).
6 [**Para 8.24**].
7 [**Para 8.17**].
8 [**Para 8.225**].
9 [**Para 8.232**].

THE DISTRIBUTION OF PROPRIETARY ENTITLEMENT

8.2   Any rational scheme of real property is inevitably concerned to promote the most efficient utilisation of land resources. This objective is made less easily attainable by the fact that the physical asset of land can support a myriad of uses, whether social, commercial, recreational, industrial or agricultural.

8.3   The default allocation of rights and obligations in land is fixed by ownership of the fee simple estate and the term of years. It is the owner of the fee simple and, to the degree permitted by his lease, the tenant of a term of years, who have first call upon the functional and commercial advantages afforded by any particular block of land. There is no legal requirement that either of these estate owners should share such advantages with anyone else: historically the common law has not prescribed any duty of active co-operation between neighbours.[1] Nevertheless it is often true that the most efficient utilisation of land resources occurs only where the facilities implicit in estate ownership are parcelled out amongst a number of persons – frequently between neighbouring landowners – as part of a more general scheme of social or commercial interaction.[2] Thus the law of land permits estate owners to make permanent adjustments to their default allocations through the acquisition of legal rights over the land of others. For example, A may own a fee simple estate in his land, but it may make a great deal of practical sense that his neighbour, B, should simultaneously have a right to use part of A's land in a certain way or indeed a right to prevent a particular use of A's land.[3] Alternatively A may wish to harness the capital value of his land, short of outright sale, by mortgaging his estate to a commercial lender, C. The multiplicity of entitlements and user forms sustained by A's land need not, however, generate conflict. The law of property is complex precisely because it is possible for a number of people to acquire different, but compatible, rights in or over the same thing.

1   'No doctrinal rule of land law embodies the biblical command to "love thy neighbor as thyself"' (Stewart E Sterk, 'Neighbors in American Land Law' 87 Col L Rev 55 at 100 (1987)).
2   It can rarely be efficient to purchase an entire freehold or leasehold estate in land merely in order to secure permanent access to some valued user facility connected with that land, eg a right of way over it or a protected view (see, however, *Re Buchanan-Wollaston's Conveyance* [1939] Ch 738 [**para 11.244**]).
3   See *Commonwealth of Australia v Western Australia* (1999) 196 CLR 392 at [282] per Callinan J.

EASEMENTS, PROFITS À *PRENDRE* AND COVENANTS

8.4   Amongst the most important rights which may be acquired over the land of others are easements, profits à *prendre* and covenants.[1] The law relating to profits and positive covenants is of fairly ancient origin,[2] but the law of easements has developed rapidly in more recent times as a means of enabling private landowners to plan land use and to enhance the enjoyment or utility of their own land. Together the law relating to easements, profits *à prendre* and covenants can be said to comprise a general law of 'servitudes'.[3]

1   Covenants are the subject of extended treatment in Chapter 9 **[paras 9.138–9.171]** and Chapter 13 **[paras 13.16–13.154]**.
2   See A W B Simpson, *A History of The Land Law* (2nd edn, Oxford 1986), pp 106–115.
3   For a classification of both easements and profits *à prendre* under a general head of 'servitudes', see *Paine & Co Ltd v St Neots Gas & Coke Co* [1939] 3 All ER 812 at 823G–H per Luxmoore LJ. See also *Attorney-General (Ex rel Lumley) v T S Gill & Son Pty Ltd* [1927] VLR 22 at 35 per Dixon AJ. The terminology of 'servitude' is still more widely used in Scotland and in the United States.

8.5   Such servitudes, when created by A in favour of B, are normally binding between A and B as a matter of contract. For the land lawyer, however, the question inevitably arises whether the same rights will bind the successors of A and B. The distinctive feature of the category of servitudes is that almost all the rights contained within it are regarded as having *proprietary* (as distinct from merely *personal*) significance,[1] with the usual consequence in English law that they have the capacity to bind third parties.[2] But, for precisely this reason, the law draws stringent definitional boundaries around the species of incorporeal right which enjoy potential third party impact.[3] Received wisdom prescribes that the frontier between property and contract must be strictly patrolled.[4]

1   The one exception relates to positive covenants affecting freehold land, which bizarrely remain, for the most part, unenforceable against third parties (see *Rhone v Stephens* [1994] 2 AC 310 **[para 13.51]**).
2   **[Para 2.49]**.
3   **[Paras 2.83–2.84]**. For reference to 'public policy controls over the kinds of easements which may be created', see *Clos Farming Estates Pty Ltd v Easton* (2001) 10 BPR 18845 at [30] per Bryson J.
4   See Gray, 'Property in Thin Air' [1991] CLJ 252 at 302.

8.6   The imposition of severely limiting threshold criteria is traditionally rationalised as being necessary in order to prevent the proliferation of undesirable long-term burdens or 'clogs' upon title.[1] In the absence of restrictive rules governing the creation and distribution of proprietary entitlements, there is a longstanding fear that land may become encumbered by useless and anti-social rights of dubious enforceability, vested in a multitude of unspecified or unidentifiable third parties.[2] The resulting chaos, it is said, would be inimical to the large social interest which pervades the law of property – namely, that objects of property should be both readily alienable and capable of commercial exploitation.[3] Even more caution is evident when the law *implies* or *compels* the creation of incorporeal rights over land.

1   The philosophy underlying the *numerus clausus* principle **[para 2.95]** also suggests that bargaining for servitudes is aided by restricting the trading process to standardised species of entitlement which can be recognised and understood at low cost. See Gray and Gray, 'The rhetoric of realty', in J Getzler (ed), *Rationalizing Property, Equity and Trusts: Essays in Honour of Edward Burn* (Butterworths 2003), pp 210–213.
2   '[G]reat detriment would arise and much confusion of rights if parties were allowed to invent new modes of holding and enjoying real property, and to impress upon their lands and

tenements a peculiar character, which should follow them into all hands, however remote'
(*Keppell v Bailey* (1834) 2 My & K 517 at 535, 39 ER 1042 at 1049 per Lord Brougham LC
[**paras 2.95–2.96**]). See similarly *Voice v Bell* (1993) 68 P & CR 441 at 444; *London & Blenheim
Estates Ltd v Ladbroke Retail Parks Ltd* [1994] 1 WLR 31 at 37G–H; *Clos Farming Estates
Pty Ltd v Easton* (2001) 10 BPR 18845 at [29].
3   See *Clos Farming Estates Pty Ltd v Easton* (2001) 10 BPR 18845 at [15] per Bryson J.

EASEMENTS DISTINGUISHED FROM OTHER RIGHTS IN OR OVER LAND

8.7   An easement comprises either a positive or a negative right to derive some
limited advantage from the land of another. The easement must be annexed –
that is, its benefit must be attached – to one parcel of land (the 'dominant
tenement') and must be exercisable over another parcel of land (the 'servient
tenement'). The easement entitles the dominant owner to use the servient land
in a particular way or, indeed, to prevent the owner of the servient land from
using his own land in a particular way.[1] A typical easement is the restrained
form of user implicit in a right of way.[2]

1   Thus described, a negative easement differs little from a restrictive covenant [**para 9.138**]. A
restrictive covenant may prohibit a specified form of user on the entirety of the servient
tenement. A negative easement (e g an easement of support or an easement of access to light)
generally imposes no such blanket restriction on the servient owner, but merely requires him
so to use his tenement that a certain facility or advantage conferred by it on the dominant
tenement is not curtailed or destroyed.
2   [**Para 8.89**].

Easements as a species of land

8.8   In English law an easement has a 'dual character'.[1] In a characteristic
conflation of physical and cerebral perceptions of property,[2] the easement
comprises 'an estate or interest carved out of a larger estate or interest', but
also itself represents 'land' vested in the proprietor of the dominant tenement.[3]
The dominant owner (e g the grantee of a right of way) is regarded in English
law as holding a species of 'land' in the form of an incorporeal hereditament.
The dominant owner thus holds a certain limited quantum of property in the
land over which his right is exercisable[4]; and his proprietary interest in this
servient tenement is known as an easement.

1   *Willies-Williams v National Trust* (1993) 65 P & CR 359 at 361 per Hoffmann LJ.
2   [**Paras 1.117, 2.76**]. See Gray and Gray, 'The Idea of Property in Land', in S Bright and J K
Dewar (ed), *Land Law: Themes and Perspectives* (OUP 1998), pp 18, 31.
3   *Willies-Williams v National Trust* (1993) 65 P & CR 359 at 361 per Hoffmann LJ. Title to the
'estate' in an easement over registered land may be registered on behalf of the dominant
proprietor, i e in the register of the substantively registered estate which is benefited by the
easement [**paras 2.153, 8.119**].
4   [**Para 2.22**]. See *Macepark (Whittlebury) Ltd v Sargeant* [2003] 1 WLR 2284 at [12].

Easements as non-possessory rights in land

8.9   It is nevertheless clear that a right of easement, being carved out of some
larger estate in the servient tenement, cannot confer the intensity of possessory

control which is associated with either of the primary estates of freehold or leasehold.[1] No right can constitute an easement if it derogates from the servient owner's possession of his land. Indeed, any claim of right to a particularly intense form of land use (measured either geographically or temporally) almost always entails that the claimant is alleging an independent possession which is incompatible with the true character of an easement.[2]

1   [Paras 3.18, 8.71].
2   See eg *Copeland v Greenhalf* [1952] Ch 488 at 498 [para 8.75]; *Batchelor v Marlow* [2003] 1 WLR 764 at [18]. The principle is widely recognised (see *First Unitarian Church of Salt Lake City v Salt Lake City Corp*, 308 F 3d 1114 at 1122 (2002)).

Easements distinguished from profits à *prendre*

8.10   An easement cannot extend a right of user to the point where it becomes a right to take the natural produce of another's land or any part of his soil.[1] The latter kind of right is classified not as an easement but as a 'profit *à prendre*'.[2] An easement is ultimately a privilege *without* profit which the owner of one tenement has over another tenement and by which the servient owner permits (or refrains from) certain activities on his own land for the advantage of the dominant tenement. Furthermore a profit *à prendre* need not be appurtenant to any dominant land at all.

1   *Bevan v London Portland Cement Co Ltd* (1892) 67 LT 615 at 617; *Pennant Hills Golf Club v Roads and Traffic Authority of New South Wales* (1999) 9 BPR 17011 at 17015.
2   [Para 8.17].

Easements distinguished from licences

8.11   A licence grants a permission to do something on or affecting land which would otherwise constitute a trespass.[1] A licence is distinguishable from an easement not least because the categories of user which are capable of recognition as easements are both relatively limited and restrictively defined. By contrast a licence may be used to permit the conduct of almost any activity on the land of the licensor (ranging from the daily delivery of milk to the holding of an open-air pop festival). A licence may sometimes comprise an element of exclusive occupation of land, but any claim to wholly exclusive rights of user tends to be inconsistent with the concept of easement.[2]

1   For an examination of the law of licences, see Chapter 4.
2   [Paras 2.14, 8.71]. See eg *Sunset Properties Pty Ltd v Johnston* (1975) 3 BPR 9185 at 9193.

8.12   The creation of an easement often requires compliance with rules of formality and registration,[1] but a licence may be created without any formality at all. Furthermore, an easement cannot normally exist in gross,[2] whereas a licence need not be related to the ownership of any dominant tenement. An easement creates a proprietary interest which is capable of benefiting and binding third parties. At least in the conventional view, most licences do not generate any similar proprietary effect.[3]

1   [**Para 8.113**].
2   [**Para 8.26**].
3   [**Paras 4.95, 12.222**].

Easements distinguished from restrictive covenants

8.13   Restrictive covenants[1] are agreements restrictive of the user of land for the benefit of other land adjoining or in the vicinity.[2] Restrictive covenants are closely related to easements both in terminology and in substance, so much so that it has been said that restrictive covenants are in essence negative easements.[3] Certain differences nevertheless exist. Easements are enforceable both at law and in equity; restrictive covenants are the creation of equity and are enforceable *only* in equity. Moreover, easements may be acquired by prescription (ie long user),[4] whereas restrictive covenants may never be acquired in this way. Once again, whereas the permissible subject matter of an easement is relatively circumscribed, the possible content of a restrictive covenant is much less unlimited.

1   Positive covenants relating to freehold land and leasehold covenants throw up distinct problems which merit separate treatment [**paras 13.26, 14.208**].
2   [**Para 9.164**].
3   [**Para 9.153**]. Easements were recognised much earlier in the common law (see e g *Gateward's Case* (1606) 6 Co Rep 59b, 77 ER 344). Restrictive covenants have been accorded proprietary effect only since the mid-19th century [**para 13.108**].
4   [**Para 8.168**].

Easements distinguished from natural rights

8.14   Landowners have certain 'natural rights' which, unlike easements, come into being automatically and are not the subject of any grant. Examples include the natural right to support for land[1] and to the enjoyment of water flowing naturally in a defined channel.[2] The existence of a natural right precludes any claim of easement in the same regard: an easement can relate only to a benefit which is not already enjoyed as an essential incident of the claimant's ownership of his tenement.[3]

1   [**Para 1.56**].
2   [**Para 1.110**].
3   *Palmer v Bowman* [2000] 1 WLR 842 at 850A–B, 856A–B (natural right of drainage for percolating and undefined surface water could not also be claimed as easement).

Easements distinguished from public rights

8.15   Public rights are rights which are exercisable by anyone, whether he owns land or not, merely by virtue of his being a member of the public (e g the public right of fishing and the public right to use the highway).[1] Although often superficially similar to easements,[2] public rights are distinct in that they do not presuppose the existence of any dominant tenement and are never the subject of a specific grant to any individual.

1   **[Paras 5.3, 5.27]**.
2   See e g *Harrison v Duke of Rutland* [1893] 1 QB 142 at 154 per Lopes LJ **[para 5.2]**.

Easements distinguished from local customary rights

8.16   Local customary rights[1] differ from easements in that they are not necessarily appurtenant to any dominant tenement but are exercisable generally by the members of a particular local community such as a town or a parish.

1   **[Para 5.28]**.

DEFINING CHARACTERISTICS OF A PROFIT *À PRENDRE*

8.17   A profit *à prendre* is a 'very peculiar type of interest'[1] which entitles its holder 'to take something off another person's land.'[2] The owner of the profit may take or sever the subject matter of the profit from the land (e g some part of the soil, minerals or natural produce of the servient tenement[3]). A profit differs from an easement in that the latter right is essentially a privilege *without* profit,[4] but a profit resembles an easement in so far as both comprise non-possessory interests in the servient land.

1   *Ellison v Vukicevic* (1986) 7 NSWLR 104 at 113D per Young J.
2   *Duke of Sutherland v Heathcote* [1892] 1 Ch 475 at 484 per Lindley LJ.
3   *Alfred F Beckett Ltd v Lyons* [1967] Ch 449 at 482B. See also *Australian Softwood Forests Pty Ltd v Attorney-General for New South Wales; ex rel Corporate Affairs Commission* (1981) 148 CLR 121 at 130 per Mason J; *R v Toohey; ex p Meneling Station Pty Ltd* (1982) 158 CLR 327 at 344, 352; *The Queen v Tener* (1985) 17 DLR (4th) 1 at 16–17.
4   See *Hewlins v Shippam* (1826) 5 B & C 221 at 229–230, 108 ER 82 at 86 per Bayley J. The distinction between profits and easements was recognised at least as early as *Gateward's Case* (1606) 6 Co Rep 59b at 60b, 77 ER 344 at 345.

Subject matter of a profit

8.18   A profit *à prendre* is normally, but not necessarily, granted for the purpose of the grantee's commercial gain.[1] The subject matter of a profit *à prendre* must nevertheless be something which is capable of ownership.[2] Typical profits include the right to take either some part of the servient land itself (e g sand, soil,[3] gravel or turf[4]) or something which grows naturally on that land (e g grass, crops, fruit or timber[5]) or indeed wild animals,[6] fowl or fish[7] which are found on the servient owner's land or in his waters. The right to fell and remove standing timber is a particularly common profit *à prendre*, at least where it is intended that the trees should be remain in situ for some time while they grow to maturity.[8] Also common are profits of grazing or pasture.[9] A profit cannot be constituted by a mere right to enter the servient land in order to carry out a process of cultivation and harvesting.[10] The subject matter of profits *à prendre* is restricted to *fructus naturales* (the products of natural growth) and cannot extend to *fructus industriales* (the products of continuing human labour).[11] For example, a profit allows only the removal of a crop which requires no attention after initial planting[12] as distinct from a process of intensive ministration or care.[13]

1   See *Pennant Hills Golf Club v Roads and Traffic Authority of New South Wales* (1999) 9 BPR 17011 at 17015 per Stein JA.
2   For instance, a right to take water cannot comprise a profit, since water is incapable of being owned (*Alfred F Beckett Ltd v Lyons* [1967] Ch 449 at 481G–482A [**para 1.107**]). Such a right may, however, constitute an easement (see *Manning v Wasdale* (1836) 5 Ad & E 758 at 763–764, 111 ER 1353 at 1355; *Polden v Bastard* (1865) LR 1 QB 156 at 161).
3   A right to remove soil as an exercise merely ancillary to some other principal purpose (e g the insertion of rock anchors for a motorway) may not constitute a profit *à prendre* (see *Pennant Hills Golf Club v Roads and Traffic Authority of New South Wales* (1999) 9 BPR 17011 at 17015).
4   See *Convey v Regan* [1952] IR 56 at 61; *Re Bohan* [1957] IR 49 at 54–55. The right to dig peat and turf for fuel is sometimes called 'turbary'.
5   A profit involving the right to take wood for fuel and repairs is an 'estover' (see *Bettison v Langton* [2000] Ch 54 at 62F per Robert Walker LJ).
6   See *Finlay v Curteis* (1832) Hayes 496 at 499–500.
7   See *Kerry CC v O'Sullivan* [1927] IR 26 at 29–30; *Bolton v Forest Pest Management Institute* (1986) 21 DLR (4th) 242 at 248; *Gannon v Walsh* [1998] 1 IR 245 at 272.
8   See *Corporate Affairs Commission v ASC Timber Pty Ltd* (1989) 18 NSWLR 577 at 586–591. A mere contract for the sale of timber is more likely to have been intended where the trees were to be felled within a short period of time (*Australian Softwood Forests Pty Ltd v Attorney-General for New South Wales; ex rel Corporate Affairs Commission* (1981) 148 CLR 121 at 130–131 per Mason J). Profits have a certain continuing quality (*Lackie v The Queen* (2001) 78 DTC 6128 per Dubé J), with the result that a 'one-time sale of all the timber' may not be a profit (*Wright v Canada* (2002) 118 ACWS (3d) 921 at [28]). See also *James Jones & Sons Ltd v Earl of Tankerville* [1909] 2 Ch 440 at 442–443 (right to enter and remove already felled timber).
9   See e g *Bettison v Langton* [2002] 1 AC 27.
10   *Clos Farming Estates Pty Ltd v Easton* (2001) 10 BPR 18845 at [59] per Bryson J, [2002] NSWCA 389 at [55]–[56] per Santow JA.
11   On the distinction between fructus naturales and fructus industriales, see *Saunders (Inspector of Taxes) v Pilcher* [1949] 2 All ER 1097 at 1104B.
12   *Clos Farming Estates Pty Ltd v Easton* [2002] NSWCA 389 at [55] per Santow JA. In the case of timber it is the long cycle of production which excludes the subject of the taking from the category of *fructus industriales* (*Myola Enterprises Pty Ltd v Pearlman* (Supreme Court of NSW No 3920 of 1993) per Bryson J).
13   See e g *Clos Farming Estates Pty Ltd v Easton* [2002] NSWCA 389 at [62] (viticulture). Likewise a profit cannot relate to a crop which is sown and harvested annually (*Myola Enterprises Pty Ltd v Pearlman* (Supreme Court of NSW No 3920 of 1993); *Clos Farming Estates*, (2001) 10 BPR 18845 at [68] per Bryson J).

A profit is an incorporeal hereditament

8.19   A profit *à prendre* is an incorporeal hereditament[1] and therefore ranks as a proprietary interest in the servient land.[2] The holder of a profit *à prendre* does not own the subject matter of the profit while it remains in situ,[3] but has an option to sever or take it from the land. It is this act of severance which results in the holder acquiring title to the thing thereby severed or gathered. A profit is usually granted in conjunction with a licence to enter the servient land, in which case the licence is an incident of the grant of profit and is irrevocable during the term of the profit.[4]

1   *Bettison v Langton* [2000] Ch 54 at 61F; *Gannon v Walsh* [1998] 1 IR 245 at 273.
2   See *R v Toohey; ex p Meneling Station Pty Ltd* (1982) 158 CLR 327 at 352 per Wilson J. A profit *à prendre* can sustain an action in nuisance on behalf of its owner (see eg *Bolton v Forest Pest Management Institute* (1986) 21 DLR (4th) 242 at 249). A profit cannot be classified as a chattel (*Cream Silver Mines Ltd v The Queen in Right of British Columbia* (1986) 27 DLR (4th) 305 at 309).
3   *The Queen v Tener* (1985) 17 DLR (4th) 1 at 17. The holder of a profit has, for instance, no property in uncaptured game (*Bolton v Forest Pest Management Institute* (1986) 21 DLR (4th) 242 at 248).
4   **[Para 4.94]**. See *Cowell v Rosehill Racecourse Co Ltd* (1937) 56 CLR 605 at 615 per Latham CJ.

A profit may exist 'in gross'

8.20   A profit *à prendre* is distinguishable from an easement in that a profit may exist 'in gross',[1] ie the owner of the profit need not be the owner of any adjoining or neighbouring land or indeed of any land at all.[2] A profit may thus be 'freestanding'[3] and need not appertain to any 'dominant tenement'.[4] The rule relating to easements is quite different: it is an essential condition of an easement that it be appurtenant to 'dominant' land.[5]

1   *Bettison v Langton* [2002] 1 AC 27 at [49] per Lord Scott of Foscote.
2   *Bl Comm*, Vol II, p 34. See *Lovett v Fairclough* (1989) 61 P & CR 385 at 396; *The Queen v Tener* (1985) 17 DLR (4th) 1 at 17. Where a grant contains all the elements of a profit, the grant is presumed to create a profit rather than a mere licence unless there are 'strong indications that the grant was meant to be personal' (*Ellison v Vukicevic* (1986) 7 NSWLR 104 at 115A per Young J).
3   *Bettison v Langton* [2000] Ch 54 at 60E per Robert Walker LJ. In *Bettison's* case both the Court of Appeal ([2000] Ch 54 at 71G–72C) and the House of Lords ([2002] 1 AC 27 at [47], [63]) held that an appurtenant profit of grazing, if limited to a specific number of animals, was transferable separately from the dominant land to which it was annexed, thereby becoming a profit in gross in the hands of the transferee.
4   A profit in gross, once created, may be assigned and conveyed 'as a piece of real property' (see *Lovett v Fairclough* (1989) 61 P & CR 385 at 398).
5   **[Para 8.33]**.

Scope of the profit

8.21   A profit in gross is said to be 'unstinted' in the sense that it may be exhaustive of the fruit or produce of the servient land.[1] By contrast, a 'profit appurtenant' (ie a profit which is annexed to some dominant tenement) must not be exhaustive, but is instead limited by reference to the needs of that dominant tenement.[2] In either case, however, a profit *à prendre* (like so many other incorporeal rights in English law) is subject to an inherent restriction. Not being a possessory right in land, its exercise cannot be allowed to 'sterilise and neutralise' the servient owner's rights of ownership.[3]

1   See eg *Staffordshire and Worcestershire Canal Navigation v Bradley* [1912] 1 Ch 91 at 103.
2   *Bailey v Stephens* (1862) 12 CB NS 91 at 108, 110, 142 ER 1077 at 1084; *Lord Chesterfield v Harris* [1908] 2 Ch 397 at 410; *Anderson v Bostock* [1976] Ch 312 at 315F–G, 318B, 318H–319A.
3   *Clos Farming Estates Pty Ltd v Easton* [2002] NSWCA 389 at [57] per Santow JA.

A profit need not be exclusive

8.22 A profit *à prendre* may confer either an exclusive right or a right enjoyed in common with others (including the grantor).[1] An exclusive profit arises only where the terms of grant expressly so provide[2] or where an intention to this effect can be gathered from the language of the grant as a whole.[3] In the absence of such language the tendency to find a mere non-exclusive profit is accentuated where otherwise the grantor would be prejudiced by having contracted to take only a fixed royalty or where the grantor would suffer if the grantee were not active or diligent in severing the subject matter of the profit.[4] Conversely a profit may be confirmed as exclusive where there would be obvious physical difficulty in several persons exercising simultaneous rights of severance in relation to a confined area of realty.[5]

1   *R v Toohey; ex p Meneling Station Pty Ltd* (1982) 158 CLR 327 at 352 per Wilson J. The fact that in given circumstances a profit is not exclusive in nature does not derogate from its proprietary character (see *Unimin Pty Ltd v Commonwealth of Australia* (1974) 2 ACTR 71 at 78; *Ellison v Vukicevic* (1986) 7 NSWLR 104 at 118B).
2   See *Duke of Sutherland v Heathcote* [1892] 1 Ch 475 at 484–485.
3   *Reid v Moreland Timber Co Pty Ltd* (1946) 73 CLR 1 at 16.
4   *Ellison v Vukicevic* (1986) 7 NSWLR 104 at 118B–C.
5   *Reid v Moreland Timber Co Pty Ltd* (1946) 73 CLR 1 at 9 per Starke J.

Duration of profits à prendre

8.23 A profit *à prendre* may be granted either indefinitely[1] or for a fixed term[2] or indeed for any other temporal interest.[3] There is of course a danger that a perpetual and exclusive right (e g to cut timber) may permanently sterilise the servient land in the hands of its owner. Accordingly there is a general (although rebuttable) implication under a profit of indefinite duration that the grantee's exercise of his rights is restricted to a 'reasonable time' following the date of grant.[4] By contrast, a non-perpetual profit comes to an end on the expiration of the specified term, and profits may generally be terminated[5] by abandonment, release or surrender or by the giving of an agreed notice.[6]

1   A profit appurtenant is normally perpetual (see *Ex parte Florida Hills Townships Ltd* 1968 (3) SA 82 at 91H; *Ellison v Vukicevic* (1986) 7 NSWLR 104 at 113E).
2   See e g *Martyn v Williams* (1857) 1 H & N 817 at 829, 156 ER 1430 at 1436. A grant for a fixed term is effectively the lease of an incorporeal hereditament for a term of years (see e g *Mason v Clarke* [1955] AC 778 at 794 [**para 7.202**]).
3   See *Ex p Henry; Re Commissioner of Stamp Duties* (1963) SR (NSW) 298 at 303–305.
4   *Reid v Moreland Timber Co Pty Ltd* (1946) 73 CLR 1 at 13 per Dixon J.
5   See *Ellison v Vukicevic* (1986) 7 NSWLR 104 at 114A–B.
6   [**Para 8.216**]. See *Unimin Pty Ltd v Commonwealth of Australia* (1974) 2 ACTR 71 at 78. Breach of a contractual term governing a profit may afford a remedy in damages, but probable breach of a contractual condition is not enough to enable one party to terminate the profit (*Ellison v Vukicevic* (1986) 7 NSWLR 104 at 118C).

DEFINING CHARACTERISTICS OF AN EASEMENT

8.24   An easement is an incorporeal hereditament or proprietary estate in land, conferring on its owner (in the absence of contrary intention) such ancillary rights as are reasonably necessary[1] – as distinct from merely convenient[2] – for the effective exercise and enjoyment of the right granted.[3] An estate of easement may even be the subject of a trust and can therefore be held by way of legal or equitable title.[4] In view of the proprietary character of the easement, the courts have severely circumscribed the class of rights which may be asserted under this head.[5] In *Re Ellenborough Park*,[6] in a passage which has since become the locus classicus of the law of easements across the common law world,[7] Danckwerts J defined the essential qualities of an easement in these terms:

> (1) There must be a dominant and a servient tenement; (2) an easement must accommodate the dominant tenement, that is, be connected with its enjoyment and for its benefit; (3) the dominant and servient owners must be different persons; and (4) the right claimed must be capable of forming the subject-matter of a grant.

1   *Jones v Pritchard* [1908] 1 Ch 630 at 638 per Parker J; *Guth v Robinson* (1977) 1 BPR 9209 at 9215–9216; *Zenere v Leate* (1980) 1 BPR 9300 at 9305. See *Goodhart v Hyett* (1883) 25 Ch D 182 at 186 per North J.
2   *Fallowfield v Bourgault* (2003) 235 DLR (4th) 263 at [11]–[12].
3   Trespass is committed by the owner who exceeds the express or implied scope of the rights granted (*Mills v Silver* [1991] Ch 271 at 295A).
4   See e g *Guth v Robinson* (1977) 1 BPR 9209 at 9213 per Powell J.
5   See Anna Lawson, 'Easements', in L Tee (ed), *Land Law: Issues, Debates, Policy* (Willan Publishing 2002), p 64.
6   [1956] Ch 131 at 140.
7   See *Clos Farming Estates Pty Ltd v Easton* (2001) 10 BPR 18845 at [29] per Bryson J ('some of the foundational ideas of the modern law' of easements). The criteria confirmed by Danckwerts J have been widely adopted (see e g *Canadian Pacific Ltd v Paul* (1989) 53 DLR (4th) 487 at 499; *Shelf Holdings Ltd v Husky Oil Operations Ltd* (1989) 56 DLR (4th) 193 at 197–198 (Supreme Court of Canada); *White v Chandler* [2001] 1 NZLR 28 at [27]).

8.25   There is a strong tendency to accord the status of an easement to any right which satisfies these requirements, irrespective of the precise label which the right in question may have been given by the parties themselves.[1] Wrongful interference with an easement constitutes an actionable nuisance even in the absence of proof of actual damage, although damages are not awarded unless there has been a substantial interference with enjoyment.[2]

1   See e g *Riley v Penttila* [1974] VR 547 at 560 ('liberty' to use and enjoy an area of land construed as an easement).
2   *West v Sharp* (2000) 79 P & CR 327 at 333 per Mummery LJ.

THERE MUST BE A DOMINANT TENEMENT AND A SERVIENT TENEMENT

8.26   In English law, by contrast with the law of many other jurisdictions,[1] an easement cannot exist 'in gross' but only as appurtenant to a defined area of land.[2] Since an easement connotes a form of *real* as distinct from *personal* entitlement,[3] every easement is in principle linked with two parcels of land, its benefit being attached to a 'dominant tenement' and its burden being asserted against a 'servient tenement'.[4]

1   Compare e g the law of New Zealand, where statute has dispensed with the general requirement of a dominant tenement (see Property Law Act 1952, s 122; *Faloon and Piesse v District Land Registrar* [1997] 3 NZLR 498).

2   *Rangeley v Midland Railway Co* (1868) LR 3 Ch App 306 at 310–311; *Alfred F Beckett Ltd v Lyons* [1967] Ch 449 at 483E per Winn LJ; *Bettison v Langton* [2002] 1 AC 27 at [48] per Lord Scott of Foscote; *Commissioner of Main Roads v North Shore Gas Co Ltd* (1967) 120 CLR 118 at 134 per Windeyer J. See generally Michael F Sturley, (1980) 96 LQR 557.

3   An easement is 'no mere personal right' (*Gallagher v Rainbow* (1994) 179 CLR 624 at 633 per Brennan, Dawson and Toohey JJ).

4   *London & Blenheim Estates Ltd v Ladbroke Retail Parks Ltd* [1992] 1 WLR 1278 at 1283B per Deputy Judge Paul Baker QC.

8.27   It must, therefore, be possible to identify a particular piece of 'dominant' land as benefited or commoded by the right claimed as an easement.[1] There must also be 'servient' land over which the easement is exercised or exercisable.[2] At the date of grant of an easement, the grantor must own an interest[3] in the servient land and the grantee an interest in the dominant land.[4] As was confirmed in *London & Blenheim Estates Ltd v Ladbroke Retail Parks Ltd*,[5] there can be a valid grant of a future estate or interest in an easement,[6] but at the date of grant the essential requirements of an easement must be satisfied. Thus, for instance, there can be no valid grant of an easement by the owner of the potentially servient tenement in advance of the intended dominant owner's acquisition of the land supposed to be benefited.[7] Any other approach would effectively impose on the servient land a burden in gross capable of exposing later owners of that land to an unpredictable range of claimants of the right concerned.[8]

1   *London & Blenheim Estates Ltd v Ladbroke Retail Parks Ltd* [1992] 1 WLR 1278 at 1281F–G, [1994] 1 WLR 31 at 37G–H per Peter Gibson LJ. Thus, for instance, a member of a golf club cannot acquire any easement to play golf, since there exists no dominant tenement (*Banstead Downs Golf Club v The Commissioners* (1974) VATTR 219 at 226). Equally an annual horse race on common land cannot be the subject of an easement (*Mounsey v Ismay* (1865) 3 H & C 486 at 497, 159 ER 621 at 625 per Martin B).

2   *Re Gordon and Regan* (1985) 15 DLR (4th) 641 at 643. It is irrelevant that the servient tenement may serve more than one dominant tenement (see e g *Re Ellenborough Park* [1956] Ch 131 at 175 **[para 8.42]**; *Sunset Properties Pty Ltd v Johnston* (1975) 3 BPR 9185 at 9197; *Harada v Registrar of Titles* [1981] VR 743 at 751).

3   **[Para 8.50]**.

4   **[Para 8.54]**. It is sufficient – albeit rare – that the legal title to an easement should be vested in a bare trustee for the owner of the land to which the easement is intended to be appurtenant (see *Guth v Robinson* (1977) 1 BPR 9209 at 9213).

5   [1992] 1 WLR 1278 at 1284F per Deputy Judge Paul Baker QC (affd [1994] 1 WLR 31 at 37B).

6   Easements are subject to the rule against perpetuities (see *Dunn v Blackdown Properties Ltd* [1961] Ch 433 at 438 per Cross J; *Newham v Lawson* (1971) 22 P & CR 852 at 855–856).

7   *London & Blenheim Estates Ltd v Ladbroke Retail Parks Ltd* [1994] 1 WLR 31 at 37D–E. 'An estate or interest cannot subsist in a non-existent hereditament' (*London & Blenheim Estates Ltd v Ladbroke Retail Parks Ltd* [1992] 1 WLR 1278 at 1284F per Deputy Judge Paul Baker QC).

8   See *Voice v Bell* (1993) 68 P & CR 441 at 444 per Dillon LJ.

An easement runs with both tenements

8.32   The annexation of a defined burden to a servient tenement and of an equivalent benefit to an ascertained dominant tenement emphasises the proprietary character of the easement, with the consequence that burden and benefit can be made to run with their respective tenements in such manner as to affect the successors in title of the original grantor and grantee.[1]

1   [**Paras 8.204, 8.210**].

THE EASEMENT MUST 'ACCOMMODATE' THE DOMINANT TENEMENT

8.33   No right can qualify as an easement unless it can be shown that the right confers a significant benefit on dominant land as distinct from offering some merely personal advantage or convenience to the dominant owner.[1] As always, the impact of the easement must be *real* rather than *personal*.[2] The core idea is that an easement, properly so called, must make the use of the dominant land more beneficial or commodious in a way which applies indifferently to both the current dominant owner and all his successors in title.[3]

1   *Dukart v District of Surrey* (1978) 86 DLR (3d) 609 at 616 (Supreme Court of Canada); *Gallagher v Rainbow* (1994) 179 CLR 624 at 633 (High Court of Australia). There must be dominant land, but not necessarily a dominant building (see *Commonwealth v Registrar of Titles (Victoria)* (1918) 24 CLR 348 at 353, 355). For some of legal history's most unusual dominant tenements, see *R v Registrar of Titles; Ex parte Waddington* (1917) VLR 603 at 606–607 (a square link – ie 0.04 sq metre – used as conveyancing device to provide dominant land for each resident of private street).

2   See *City Developments Pty Ltd v Registrar General of the Northern Territory* (2000) 135 NTR 1 at [21]; *Depew v Wilkes* (2002) 216 DLR (4th) 487 at [20] (Ontario Court of Appeal).

3   This criterion of 'accommodation' must be determined at the date of grant (*Clos Farming Estates Pty Ltd v Easton* (2001) 10 BPR 18845 at [36]). It is generally irrelevant that the benefit conferred by the easement is diminished or altogether frustrated by subsequent events (see *Huckvale v Aegean Hotels Ltd* (1989) 58 P & CR 163 at 168).

Requirement of propinquity

8.34   In order to support the claim that a given right 'accommodates' the alleged dominant tenement, there is some requirement of propinquity in relation to the servient and dominant tenements. There is no rule that the dominant and servient land must be contiguous,[1] but the servient land must at least be sufficiently closely situated to confer a practical benefit on the dominant land.[2] Thus, in the famous dictum, there cannot be 'a right of way over land in Kent appurtenant to an estate in Northumberland.'[3]

1   *Re Salvin's Indenture* [1938] 2 All ER 498 at 506G; *Robinson Webster (Holdings) Ltd v Agombar* [2002] 1 P & CR 243 at [84]; *Guth v Robinson* (1977) 1 BPR 9209 at 9214; *Harada v Registrar of Titles* [1981] VR 743 at 751–752. See also *Re Ellenborough Park* [1956] Ch 131 at 175 [**para 8.42**], where the requirement of benefit was satisfied even in respect of those houses which did not front on to the park.

2   *Bailey v Stephens* (1862) 12 CB (NS) 91 at 115, 142 ER 1077 at 1086; *Todrick v Western*

National Omnibus Co Ltd [1934] Ch 561 at 572–574, 580–581, 589–591; (1934) 50 LQR 313; *Pugh v Savage* [1970] 2 QB 373 at 381C–D; *Dewhirst v Edwards* [1983] 1 NSWLR 34 at 51E–F.
3 See *Bailey v Stephens* (1862) 12 CB (NS) 91 at 115, 142 ER 1077 at 1086 per Byles J; *Todrick v Western National Omnibus Co Ltd* [1934] Ch 561 at 580.

Exclusiveness of benefit is not necessary

8.35 The benefit conferred by an easement need not relate exclusively to one dominant tenement. For instance, it is not fatal to the status of an easement that it confers a user privilege on a number of different dominant owners simultaneously.[1] Furthermore, in the case of an easement of way it is irrelevant that the route of the way is of incidental advantage to 'any passer-by, wholly unconnected with the dominant tenement, who chooses to use it as a short cut.'[2]

1 See e g *Re Ellenborough Park* [1956] Ch 131; *Simpson v Fergus* (2000) 79 P & CR 398 at 402.
2 *Re Ellenborough Park* [1956] Ch 131 at 172.

Exclusion of purely personal or commercial advantages

8.36 The test of 'accommodation' of the dominant tenement excludes from the status of an easement any privilege conferred on its recipient in a purely personal capacity rather than as an occupier of land.[1] The classic example of a purely personal advantage which could not be claimed as an easement is the right asserted by the plaintiff in *Hill v Tupper*.[2] Here the owner of a canal leased to the plaintiff some land on the canal bank (including a landing stage) and purported to grant him a 'sole and exclusive' right to put pleasure boats on that canal. When a third party, the landlord of a nearby inn, later interfered with the plaintiff's trade by putting rival boats on the canal, the plaintiff claimed to have an exclusive proprietary right over the waterway. This claim was rejected by the court, which took the view that the plaintiff had a mere licence (unenforceable except against his licensor[3]) as distinct from a generally enforceable easement over the canal.

1 In *Dewsbury v Davies* (Unreported, 21 May 1992), the Court of Appeal distinguished between rights enjoyed 'with' an alleged dominant tenement and rights enjoyed 'by' a person 'as an individual.' Thus a friendly parking permission given to a gardener who lived in a cottage next door to his employer was no easement (and could just as easily have been exercised if he had lived elsewhere). However, a way of access and egress across the employer's land to and from a bus stop was held to be an easement in that it was 'attached to or enjoyed with' the cottage. See L Tee, [1998] Conv 115.
2 (1863) 2 H & C 121, 159 ER 51.
3 See, however, *Manchester Airport Plc v Dutton* [2000] QB 133 [**paras 3.38, 4.98**].

8.37 The ground for the decision in *Hill v Tupper* is somewhat unclear.[1] Pollock CB observed that a 'new species of incorporeal hereditament cannot be created at the will and pleasure of the owner of property.'[2] Martin B held that to admit the right claimed by the plaintiff 'would lead to the creation of an infinite variety of interests in land, and an indefinite increase of possible estates.'[3] Such statements appear to express further variants of the policy against proliferating 'clogs' which might make a title uncommerciable. However, perhaps the most potent factor in the minds of the judges in this case was their clear apprehension that the right claimed by the plaintiff was not appurtenant to any dominant tenement. Pollock CB cited *Ackroyd v Smith*[4] in support of the proposition that it is impossible to create easements in respect of 'rights unconnected with the use and enjoyment of land.' In the present case it was scarcely realistic to argue that the plaintiff's contractual rights over the canal were such as to make his occupation of the land on the canal bank more convenient. Although the area in question included a landing stage, it was plainly the case that this landing stage facilitated the plaintiff's use of the canal rather than vice versa.[5]

1   See *Clos Farming Estates Pty Ltd v Easton* (2001) 10 BPR 18845 at [36] per Bryson J.
2   (1863) 2 H & C 121 at 127, 159 ER 51 at 53.
3   (1863) 2 H & C 121 at 128, 159 ER 51 at 53.
4   (1850) 10 CB 164, 138 ER 68 [**para 8.28**].
5   See *Re Ellenborough Park* [1956] Ch 131 at 175. It is possible that the right claimed would have been upheld as an easement if it had provided an effective means of access to and egress from the plaintiff's land and the defendant's boats had interfered with this means of traffic.

8.38   It may also be that in *Hill v Tupper*, in an early prohibition of anti-competitive practices and restraints on trade, the court was disinclined to allow the law of easements to be invoked in protection of blatantly commercial advantage. The plaintiff had effectively sought, under the banner of an easement, to set up a commercial monopoly in respect of the business of putting pleasure boats on the canal. There was no sense in which the plaintiff's occupation of the alleged dominant tenement was enhanced by the easement claimed. His use of that land was entirely incidental to his entrepreneurial exploitation of the waterway.[1] It is also possible that the judgments in *Hill v Tupper* concealed a distaste for rights which are over-broad. It is characteristic of the easement that it should not smack of exclusiveness of possession or control.[2]

1   See *Re Ellenborough Park* [1956] Ch 131 at 175, where Evershed MR said, with reference to *Hill v Tupper*, that 'it is clear that what the plaintiff was trying to do was to set up, under the guise of an easement, a monopoly which had no normal connexion with the ordinary use of his land, but which was merely an independent business enterprise. So far from the right claimed sub-serving or accommodating the land, the land was but a convenient incident to the exercise of the right.' Compare, however, [1956] CLJ 24 at 25 (R N Gooderson). See also *Clos Farming Estates Pty Ltd v Easton* (2001) 10 BPR 18845 at [36], [47], [2002] NSWCA 389 at [34], [43].
2   [**Para 8.71**].

Nature of the accommodation or benefit conferred

8.39   It is an elusive task to define in positive terms the nature of the benefit which must be shown to have been conferred on the alleged dominant tenement. There is, of course, a crude sense in which in the law of easements all benefits are ultimately enjoyable by people rather than by land.[1] In *Dukart v District of Surrey*,[2] the Supreme Court of Canada spoke of the need to show that 'the dominant tenement is accommodated, serviced or supported by the servient tenement.'[3] There must be between the dominant tenement and the servient tenement 'a connection of real benefit to the former ... which is of such a character as would ordinarily be classified as a right or condition running with the land and not merely a contractual right enuring to the benefit only of persons who are parties thereto at its inception.'[4] This test of 'accommodation' is often heavily coloured by value judgments as to the propriety of conferring long-term protection on various kinds of land use: easements do not exist to safeguard purely personal or idiosyncratic advantage.

1   **[Para 9.165]**.
2   (1978) 86 DLR (3d) 609 at 616.
3   The right claimed must be 'reasonably necessary for the better enjoyment' of the dominant tenement (*Re Ellenborough Park* [1956] Ch 131 at 170 per Evershed MR). See also *Depew v Wilkes* (2002) 216 DLR (4th) 487 at [19]–[26].
4   *Dukart v District of Surrey* (1978) 86 DLR (3d) 609 at 616. See *Clos Farming Estates Pty Ltd v Easton* (2001) 10 BPR 18845 at [22] per Bryson J ('The necessary nexus must exist in a real and intelligible sense').

Enhancement of land value

8.40   Whether a particular right increases the market value of the benefited land is a relevant but not conclusive index of 'accommodation'.[1] There are many kinds of right which may have this effect, but not all would qualify as easements. As the Court of Appeal indicated in *Re Ellenborough Park*,[2] there must be some 'sufficient nexus between the enjoyment of the right and the use of [the dominant property].' Thus a right granted to the purchaser of a particular house to use the Zoological Gardens free of charge or to attend Lord's Cricket Ground without payment, although possibly increasing the value of the property conveyed, could not at law run with the land as an easement. Such rights would be 'wholly extraneous to, and independent of, the use of a house as a house, namely as a place in which the householder and his family live and make their home.'

1   *Re Ellenborough Park* [1956] Ch 131 at 173.
2   [1956] Ch 131 at 174. See [1956] CLJ 24 (R N Gooderson); (1956) 72 LQR 16 (R E M).

Benefit to trade conducted on the dominant tenement

8.41   It seems to be a sufficient accommodation of the dominant tenement that the right claimed as an easement should facilitate or benefit some trade or business which is carried on in the dominant land.[1] In *Moody v Steggles*,[2] for instance, Fry J held that the owner of a public house could claim an easement to hang a signboard on the adjoining house.[3] An element of commercial benefit does not disqualify a right as an easement, provided that the conduct of the trade or business in question is a necessary incident of the normal enjoyment of the particular land concerned (eg the inn in *Moody v Steggles*) and not merely an independent or unconnected business enterprise.[4]

1   A commercial benefit extracted from business conducted on the *servient* tenement is not enough to validate the claim of easement (see *Hill v Tupper* (1863) 2 H & C 121, 159 ER 51 [**para 8.36**]; *Clos Farming Estates Pty Ltd v Easton* (2001) 10 BPR 18845, [2002] NSWCA 389).
2   (1879) 12 Ch D 261 at 266–268. See also *Ellis v Mayor of Bridgnorth* (1863) 15 CB (NS) 52 at 78, 143 ER 702 at 712; *Leon Asper Amusements Ltd v Northmain Carwash & Enterprises Ltd* (1966) 56 DLR (2d) 173 at 176.
3   See also *William Hill (Southern) Ltd v Cabras Ltd* (1987) 54 P & CR 42 at 46.
4   See *Clos Farming Estates Pty Ltd v Easton* [2002] NSWCA 389 at [34] per Santow JA.

Integral aspects of commodious domestic living

8.42   In the residential context the test of 'benefit' ultimately involves some qualitative or socio-spatial assessment[1] of the kinds of facility required for commodious domestic living.[2] In *Re Ellenborough Park*,[3] for example, a number of owners of residential properties had been given a right of common enjoyment of a park or pleasure ground which was enclosed by their houses and title to which was vested in trustees. Each adjoining owner paid a proportionate part of the cost of maintaining the pleasure ground as a well stocked and carefully ordered garden. The Court of Appeal held that the right granted each purchaser of 'full enjoyment ... of the pleasure ground' was capable of forming the subject matter of an easement. Underlying this decision was an almost unspoken perception that 'the use of a garden undoubtedly enhances, and is connected with, the normal enjoyment of the house to which it belongs.'[4] In the present circumstances the park had become a 'communal garden for the benefit and enjoyment of those whose houses adjoined it or were in its close proximity'[5] and as such amply satisfied the 'requirement of connexion with the dominant tenements to which it is appurtenant.'[6]

1   These judgments doubtless vary over time. See eg *Philipps v Halliday* [1891] AC 228 at 233 (upholding an easement to maintain and use a pew in a church as appurtenant to a mansion house).
2   '[W]hat is a land use-related promise changes somewhat according to contemporary views. The striving for amenities and security in densely populated areas has already caused some changes. Matters which were looked upon in the past as indicative of hypersensitivity or extreme fine taste, and accordingly merely personal, have become a market commodity today' (Uriel Reichman, 'Judicial Supervision of Servitudes' 7 J Legal Stud 139 at 155 (1978)).
3   [1956] Ch 131.
4   [1956] Ch 131 at 174 per Evershed MR. See *Riley v Penttila* [1974] VR 547 at 559–560 ('For gracious living it has been found for a very long time ... necessary to have space in areas around a house for the purposes of a garden and recreation, and even of a park. Undoubtedly, it adds to the enjoyment of the occupation of such house property'). See also *Evanel Pty Ltd v Nelson* (1995) 39 NSWLR 209 at 212B–C.
5   [1956] Ch 131 at 174.
6   [1956] Ch 131 at 175. See similarly *Jackson v Mulvaney* [2003] 1 WLR 360 at [23]. In *Wright v Macadam* [1949] 2 KB 744 at 752, Jenkins LJ accepted the easement character of a right to store 'such coal as might be required for the domestic purposes of the flat.'

8.43   As the *Ellenborough Park* case demonstrates, the definition of qualifying rights in the law of easements is heavily coloured by an element of value judgment.[1] Such evaluation relates not only to the sorts of activity claimed as amounting to an easement, but also to the relative degree of merit which is thought to attach to the party advancing the claim. In *Re Ellenborough Park* the Court of Appeal had little difficulty in applying the terminology of easements to the civilised user by civilised people of a communal garden situated in an excessively bourgeois location.

1   Thus, for instance, 'in a modern urban context' the right to park a motor car 'directly relates to the enjoyment of the benefited land' (*Owners Corp of Strata Plan 42472 v Menala Pty Ltd* (1998) 9 BPR 16337 at 16346 per Bryson J [**para 8.77**]).

A purely recreational user may not be an easement

8.44 There is some authority in English law for the view that a mere right of 'recreation and amusement' can never qualify as an easement since such a right is purely personal in its scope and cannot confer 'utility and benefit' on land.[1] There can, in short, be no easement merely to have fun. Consistent with this limitation is the once widely accepted notion that the concept of an easement cannot encompass a *ius spatiandi*, ie 'a privilege of wandering at will over all and every part of another's field or park.'[2]

1   *Solomon v Vintners' Company* (1859) 4 H & N 585 at 593, 157 ER 970 at 974; *Mounsey v Ismay* (1865) 3 H & C 486 at 498, 159 ER 621 at 625. See H S Theobald, *The Law of Land* (2nd edn, London 1929), p 263.
2   *Re Ellenborough Park* [1956] Ch 131 at 176 per Evershed MR. See *International Tea Stores Co v Hobbs* [1903] 2 Ch 165 at 172; *Attorney-General v Antrobus* [1905] 2 Ch 188 at 198–200 [**para 5.30**].

8.45 It is clear, however, that neither of these restrictions on the scope of easements is absolute. In *Re Ellenborough Park*[1] the Court of Appeal agreed that a *ius spatiandi*, being an 'indefinite and unregulated privilege', would indeed lack the essential qualities of an easement. The Court nevertheless considered a *ius spatiandi* to be 'substantially different' from the grant in the present case, which comprised 'the provision for a limited number of houses in a uniform crescent of one single large but private garden.'[2] Moreover, although 'a garden is a pleasure – on high authority, it is the purest of pleasures',[3] the right claimed here was 'appurtenant to the surrounding houses as such' and constituted 'a beneficial attribute of residence in a house as ordinarily understood.'[4] The Court of Appeal thus concluded that the use of the communal garden 'for the purposes, not only of exercise and rest but also for such domestic purposes as ... taking out small children in perambulators or otherwise ... is not fairly to be described as one of mere recreation or amusement, and is clearly beneficial to the premises to which it is attached.'[5]

1   [1956] Ch 131 at 176.
2   [1956] Ch 131 at 176. In *Dukart v District of Surrey* (1978) 86 DLR (3d) 609 at 616, the Supreme Court of Canada took the view that *Re Ellenborough Park* had established that some kinds of ius spatiandi are sufficiently determinate to deserve easement status. The Supreme Court pointed in particular to the fact that in *Re Ellenborough Park* Evershed MR had emphasised ([1956] Ch 131 at 179) that an easement may include a right of 'wandering at will

round each and every part of the garden except of course, such parts as comprise flower beds, or are laid out for some other purpose, which renders walking impossible or unsuitable.' In *Dukart* the Supreme Court held, on similar grounds, that there can be an easement to wander at large over a beach beside a resort development.

3   [1956] Ch 131 at 179 per Evershed MR (the reference is to Francis Bacon's *An Essay of Gardens* (1605)). The idea that a garden is a numinous place goes back as far as the first garden, where Adam communed with God in the cool of the evening (see J Delumeau, *History of Paradise: the Garden of Eden in myth and tradition* (trans M O'Connell, New York 1995), pp 3–15).

4   [1956] Ch 131 at 179.

5   [1956] Ch 131 at 179 (see also *R v Doncaster MBC, ex p Braim* (1989) 57 P & CR 1 at 9). For other instances of judicial indulgence towards perambulators, see *R v Mathias* (1861) 2 F & F 570 at 572–574, 175 ER 1191 at 1192; *Behrens v Richards* [1905] 2 Ch 614 at 622.

8.46   The judicial animus against recreational easements has undoubtedly receded in recent times. It may be an index of a more hedonistic (or even more health-conscious) age that it no longer seems inappropriate to acknowledge the easement character of certain recreational facilities annexed to dominant land.[1] This is particularly the case where the claim of easement refers to a defined area[2] over which a right of recreational enjoyment has been given not to the public but to a limited number of lot holders.[3]

1   See *City Developments Pty Ltd v Registrar General of the Northern Territory* (2000) 135 NTR 1 at [36] ('there is no reason in law why an easement cannot be granted for recreational purposes').

2   See *R v Doncaster MBC, ex p Braim* (1989) 57 P & CR 1 at 15 ('right to take recreation in a defined area' as distinct from a right to 'wander over an undefined area').

3   See e g *Riley v Penttila* [1974] VR 547 at 559; *City Developments Pty Ltd v Registrar General of the Northern Territory* (2000) 135 NTR 1 at [41] (recreational activities such as walking, swimming, boating, photography, and birdwatching).

DOMINANT AND SERVIENT TENEMENTS MUST BE OWNED OR OCCUPIED BY DIFFERENT PERSONS

8.47   An easement is by definition a right over somebody else's land. It is therefore impossible that the same person should both own *and occupy* the dominant and servient tenements.[1] A person cannot meaningfully have rights against himself,[2] but the required diversity of occupation is satisfied between landlord and tenant. It is therefore quite feasible for a tenant to be granted an easement over other land owned by his landlord since, although there is common freehold ownership of the dominant and servient tenements, there is no common occupation.[3] A landlord may likewise reserve an easement over land leased to his tenant.[4]

1   *Morris v Edgington* (1810) 3 Taunt 24 at 30, 128 ER 10 at 13; *Greathead v Morley* (1841) 3 Man & G 139 at 156, 133 ER 1090 at 1097; *Bolton v Bolton* (1879) 11 Ch D 968 at 970–971; *Roe v Siddons* (1888) 22 QBD 224 at 236; *Metropolitan Railway Co v Fowler* [1892] 1 QB 165 at 171; *Wright v Macadam* [1949] 2 KB 744 at 748; *Palmer v Bowman* [2000] 1 WLR 842 at 846B. See also *Attrill v Platt* (1884) 10 SCR 425 at 463; *Grizzard v Broom*, 71 SE 430 at 431 (1911); *Margil Pty Ltd v Stegul Pastoral Pty Ltd* [1984] 2 NSWLR 1 at 9D; *Re Lonegren and Rueben* (1987) 37 DLR (4th) 491 at 495–496.

2   See *Peckham v Ellison* (2000) 79 P & CR 276 at 295 per Cazalet J. It is likely that A and B, as

joint freehold owners of Greenacre, can grant a valid easement to A and C, as joint freehold owners of Redacre (see *Re Lonegren and Rueben* (1987) 37 DLR (4th) 491 at 495–496, affd (1988) 50 DLR (4th) 431 at 433) or even just to A, as sole freehold owner of Redacre (see *McDonald v McDougall* (1897) 30 NSR 298 at 300).

3   See *Borman v Griffith* [1930] 1 Ch 493 at 499.
4   *Beddington v Atlee* (1887) 35 Ch D 317 at 332.

THE RIGHT CLAIMED MUST BE CAPABLE OF FORMING THE SUBJECT MATTER OF A GRANT

8.48   It is commonly said that all easements 'lie in grant.' That is, all easements must be capable of forming the subject matter of a grant by deed (even if they are not actually so granted). This apparently innocuous require-ment contains a compendious subset of important and interlinking criteria for the constitution of a valid easement.[1] An easement cannot exist with respect to any advantage or facility whose parameters could not have been spelt out with particularity in the terms of an express grant. Once again, perceptions of the easement as an artificial jural abstraction have heightened the emphasis upon rigorous definitional clarity. Proprietary estates in easements must have a clear-cut, hard-edged quality. 'Property' ideally comes in neat, discrete, pre-packaged conceptual compartments.[2] Stringent limits are therefore drawn around the categories of entitlement which are capable of binding third parties. In the law of easements a number of implications follow.

–   There must be a capable grantor and a capable grantee[3]
–   The right must be sufficiently definite[4]
–   The right must be within the general nature of the rights traditionally recognised as easements[5]
–   The right must not impose any positive burden on the servient owner[6]
–   The right must not exclude reasonable alternative users of the servient tenement[7]

1   See *Clos Farming Estates Pty Ltd v Easton* (2001) 10 BPR 18845 at [23] per Bryson J.
2   See Gray and Gray, 'The Idea of Property in Land', in S Bright and J K Dewar (ed), *Land Law: Themes and Perspectives* (OUP 1998), pp 31–34.
3   [**Para 8.49**].
4   [**Para 8.55**].
5   [**Para 8.59**].
6   [**Para 8.66**].
7   [**Para 8.69**].

THERE MUST BE A CAPABLE GRANTOR AND A CAPABLE GRANTEE

8.49   It follows from the requirement of capacity for grant that the existence of any easement presupposes both a competent grantor and a competent grantee.

Capable grantor

8.50   The proprietary character of the easement brings into play the principle of *nemo dat quod non habet*.[1] Apart from cases of easement by estoppel,[2] no easement may be carved out of land except by a person who is himself entitled to a proprietary interest in the land.[3]

1   See *Rodwell v G R Evans & Co Pty Ltd* [1978] 1 NSWLR 448 at 452A ('The principle is that the quantum of the grantor's estate in the servient land determines the quantum of the easement').
2   **[Para 8.53]**.
3   A mere licensee (even under a licence coupled with an interest in land) is therefore incompetent to grant, either expressly or by implication, any easement as such over the land (see *Quicke v Chapman* [1903] 1 Ch 659 at 668, 671). A licensee is perfectly entitled, of course, to confer on a third party a purely personal right in respect of land which is effective only against himself (see *Hari v Trotter* (1958) 76 WN (NSW) 112 at 113; *Rodwell v G R Evans & Co Pty Ltd* (1977) 3 BPR 9114 at 9121, 9124).

Limits on grant

8.51   No person is competent to subject the land to an easement more extensive than his own proprietary interest.[1] It follows that only the owner of an estate in fee simple has power to grant an easement of a perpetual or permanent character.[2] A tenant for years or a tenant for life is competent to make an express grant of an easement so as to bind his own limited interest,[3] but in either case the easement so created cannot survive the termination of the limited interest.[4]

1   *Booth v Alcock* (1873) 8 Ch App 663 at 666; *Beddington v Atlee* (1887) 35 Ch D 317 at 327; *Rodwell v G R Evans & Co Pty Ltd* (1977) 3 BPR 9114 at 9123.
2   *Rodwell v G R Evans & Co Pty Ltd* [1978] 1 NSWLR 448 at 452A–B (Court of Appeal of New South Wales).
3   *Simmons v Dobson* [1991] 1 WLR 720 at 723C per Fox LJ. See also *Wheaton v Maple & Co* [1893] 3 Ch 48 at 64–65; *Kilgour v Gaddes* [1904] 1 KB 457 at 466.
4   *Lord Dynevor v Tennant* (1886) 32 Ch D 375 at 381.

Limits on competence

8.52   No easement can be claimed if at the date of its supposed creation the servient land was owned by someone who was legally incompetent to grant an easement (eg a statutory or other corporation which had no authority to grant incorporeal rights over its land[1]). A less obvious case of incompetent grant arises where an easement (eg a right of way) has already been validly created as appurtenant to a particular dominant tenement. In such circumstances and in the absence of contrary agreement,[2] the dominant owner has no right to assign any share of that same easement to the owner of another adjoining tenement.[3] It is possible (although not entirely clear) that an easement may be the subject of a valid unilateral grant by one of a number of joint owners of the servient tenement, provided that the encumbrance does not interfere with the rights of the other co-owners to possession and enjoyment of their land.[4]

1   *Mulliner v Midland Railway Co* (1879) 11 Ch D 611 at 619–623.
2   *Clapman v Edwards* [1938] 2 All ER 507 at 512D–H.
3   *Alvis v Harrison* (1990) 62 P & CR 10 at 15–16 per Lord Jauncey of Tullichettle [**para 8.85**]; *Bannister v Chiene* (1902) 22 NZLR 628 at 631. See also *Classic Communications Ltd v Lascar* (1986) 21 DLR (4th) 579 at 584. In effect, the benefit of the easement is normally transferable only in association with a transfer of the dominant estate (see *Il Giardino LLC v Belle Haven Land Co*, 757 A2d 1103 at 1113, 1116 (2000) (Supreme Court of Connecticut)).
4   *Hedley v Roberts* [1977] VR 282 at 288–289. Compare, however, *Paine & Co Ltd v St Neots Gas & Coke Co* [1939] 3 All ER 812 at 824A–D.

Easements by estoppel

8.53   Where a person expressly grants an easement over land to which he currently has no title, the grantor is estopped as against the grantee from denying the effectiveness of his grant.[1] Any subsequent acquisition of legal title by the grantor of the easement has the effect of 'feeding' the estoppel so that thereafter, and perhaps also retrospectively, the grant operates as if the grantor had held title at the date of grant.[2]

1   [**Para 7.266**]. See *Rowbotham v Wilson* (1857) 8 E & B 123 at 145, 120 ER 45 at 54, (1860) 8 HLCas 348 at 364, 11 ER 463 at 470. This estoppel doctrine cannot apply to any implied grant of easement (*Quicke v Chapman* [1903] 1 Ch 659 at 668, 670) or where, in the case of an express grant, the deficiency in the grantor's title was apparent on the face of the instrument of grant (*Bucknell v Mann* (1862) 2 NSWSCR 1 at 8; *Rodwell v G R Evans & Co Pty Ltd* (1977) 3 BPR 9114 at 9124).
2   *Rajapakse v Fernando* [1920] AC 892 at 897; *Hedley v Roberts* [1977] VR 282 at 285. See also *Universal Permanent Building Society v Cooke* [1952] Ch 95 at 101–103; *Bruton v London & Quadrant Housing Trust* [2000] 1 AC 406, [1998] QB 834 at 838B [**para 7.86**]. A variant of the principle of 'feeding the estoppel' was adverted to in *Voyce v Voyce* (1991) 62 P & CR 290 at 294, where the Court of Appeal expressed the obiter view that a prescriptive claim to an easement of light could be built up against an adjoining occupier who had an equity founded on proprietary estoppel which was later perfected by a conveyance to him in fee simple. See [1992] Conv 56 (J E Martin).

Capable grantee

8.54   No valid easement arises where, at the supposed date of grant, the alleged dominant owner was legally incompetent to receive such a grant (e g a company without power to acquire easements[1]) or comprised a fluctuating body of persons (e g 'the inhabitants for the time being' of a named village[2]). It is clear, however, that the dominant tenement relevant to an express grant may be held by the grantee either in fee simple or for a term of years.[3]

1   *National Guaranteed Manure Co Ltd v Donald* (1859) 4 H & N 8 at 17–18, 157 ER 737 at 741.
2   Such a body may enjoy a local customary right as distinct from an easement [**para 5.28**].
3   *London & Blenheim Estates Ltd v Ladbroke Retail Parks Ltd* [1992] 1 WLR 1278 at 1284H.

THE RIGHT MUST BE SUFFICIENTLY DEFINITE

8.55   In order to be capable of grant by deed, all easements must have a certain quality of definitional clarity. The category of easement thus excludes user rights which are amorphous, over-broad[1] or ill-defined.[2] Easement status can also be vitiated by a grant of vague or indeterminate duration.[3] Precision in these matters is required not least because it must always be possible to predicate whether a claimed right exists or has been breached.[4]

1   See *Copeland v Greenhalf* [1952] Ch 488 at 498 per Upjohn J **[para 8.75]**, where the rights asserted 'were both uncertain and too extravagant' (*Batchelor v Marlow* [2003] 1 WLR 764 at [13] per Tuckey LJ).

2   The right claimed must not be 'too vague and uncertain' (*Bryant v Lefever* (1879) 4 CPD 172 at 178) or 'too vague and too indefinite' (*Harris v De Pinna* (1886) 33 Ch D 238 at 249–250). See also *Dalton v Angus & Co* (1881) 6 App Cas 740 at 824; *Auerbach v Beck* (1985) 6 NSWLR 424 at 442C–D.

3   See *Duncan v Cliftonville Estates Pty Ltd* (2001) 10 BPR 19127 at [32].

4   See *Webb v Bird* (1861) 10 CB (NS) 268 at 282, 142 ER 455 at 460 per Erle CJ ('I am at a loss to conceive what would be an interruption of such a right as is claimed here'). See also *Duncan v Cliftonville Estates Pty Ltd* (2001) 10 BPR 19127 at [28] per Young CJ in Eq.

Exclusion of loosely defined rights

8.56   No easement can exist, for instance, in respect of a good view or prospect[1] (or, in modern jargon, a 'visibility splay'[2]). Such a right may be acquired only in the form of a restrictive covenant which precludes the owner of neighbouring land from building in such a way as to obstruct the view which it is desired to protect.[3] Likewise there is no such easement as an entitlement to the uninterrupted access of light or air except through defined apertures in a building.[4] There can be no easement in respect of an unimpeded and general flow of air across one's neighbour's land to a windmill sited on the supposed dominant tenement[5] or for the purpose of preventing chimneys from smoking.[6] Nor is there any easement of indefinite privacy.[7] Even a claim of harmless recreational user – such as the right to wander at will over another's land – is vulnerable as an easement, in part because it probably confers a merely personal benefit[8] and in part because it lacks the discreteness of definition required by the law of easements.[9]

1   *William Aldred's Case* (1610) 9 Co Rep 57b at 58b, 77 ER 816 at 821; *Harris v De Pinna* (1886) 33 Ch D 238 at 262 per Bowen LJ; *Campbell v Paddington Corpn* [1911] 1 KB 869 at 875–876. See also *Day v Brownrigg* (1878) 10 Ch D 294 at 304.

2   See *McKay Securities plc v Surrey CC* (Unreported, Chancery Division, 9 December 1998).

3   *Hunter v Canary Wharf Ltd* [1997] AC 655 at 699C–E per Lord Lloyd of Berwick, 709B per Lord Hoffmann, 727A–B per Lord Hope of Craighead. See e g *Buckleigh v Brown* [1968] NZLR 647 at 651–656. Construction on adjacent land which obliterates a good view is not actionable in nuisance (see *Venuto v Owens-Corning Fiberglas Corp*, 99 Cal Rptr 350 at 357 (1971)).

4   See *Harris v De Pinna* (1886) 33 Ch D 238 at 250–251, 262; *Levet v Gas Light & Coke Co* [1919] 1 Ch 24 at 27. The High Court of Australia has recognised the right to the uninterrupted access of light and air as an easement, even though not limited to access through defined apertures (see *Commonwealth v Registrar of Titles (Victoria)* (1918) 24 CLR 348 at 353–356). The English Court of Appeal has rationalised the easement of light enjoyed by the domestic greenhouse on the ground that a greenhouse is 'not to be regarded simply as a garden under glass, but as a building with apertures, namely, the glass roof and sides' (see *Allen v Greenwood* [1980] Ch 119 at 129C per Goff LJ). See also [1979] Conv 298 (F R Crane).

5   *Webb v Bird* (1861) 10 CB (NS) 268 at 283–286, 142 ER 455 at 460–462, (1863) 13 CB (NS)

841 at 843, 143 ER 332 at 333. See also *Harris v De Pinna* (1886) 33 Ch D 238 at 249–250. There can be no easement to drain off surface water from dominant land except through a defined channel or watercourse (see *McPhee v Township of Plympton* (1988) 43 DLR (4th) 233 at 245), although the natural drainage of percolating water on to lower land comprises a natural right or incident of ownership of the higher land (see *Gibbons v Lenfestey* (1915) 84 LJPC 158 at 160 per Lord Dunedin; *Palmer v Bowman* [2000] 1 WLR 842 at 855F per Rattee J [**para 1.113**]).

6   *Bryant v Lefever* (1879) 4 CPD 172 at 178, 180.
7   *Browne v Flower* [1911] 1 Ch 219 at 225 per Parker J. See Gray, 'Property in Thin Air' [1991] CLJ 252 at 260–263.
8   [**Para 8.36**].
9   *Re Ellenborough Park* [1956] Ch 131 at 176–178 [**para 8.42**]. See also *Attorney-General v Antrobus* [1905] 2 Ch 188 at 198–200 (Stonehenge).

Rationales for tightness of definition

8.57   According to conventional theory these definitional restrictions play a valuable role in delimiting the kinds of right which, unlike mere licences and contracts, have the capacity to affect later purchasers of land. The imposition of severely limiting criteria has been rationalised as necessary to prevent the proliferation of undesirable long-term burdens which inhibit the marketability of land. Nowadays, however, it is far from clear that the tight definitional regulation of servitudes has any particularly beneficial effect. A more relaxed categorisation of allowable servitudes may actually enhance the enjoyment of land in a crowded environment, promoting rather than inhibiting the character of a locality and its consequent attractiveness on the open market.

Limits of permissible development

8.58   The insistence on strict definitional parameters in the law of easements tends to conceal, just as effectively today as it did over a century ago, that the crucial issue at stake is often the boundary of permissible commercial initiative in the exploitation and development of land resources.[1] The recognition of easements of a vague or unlimited character threatens to impose significant limitations on the entrepreneurial exploitation of areas of servient land and, for this reason, may once have seemed contrary to the public interest. Nowadays it is arguable that the community interest in industrial or commercial development is counterbalanced by a wider concern for the enhancement of the environment and the preservation of residential amenity. In *Hunter v Canary Wharf Ltd*,[2] however, the House of Lords held unactionable the extensive interference with television reception brought about by the construction of the Canary Wharf Tower. Starting from the premise of a 'rule of common law which, absent easements, entitles an owner of land to build what he likes on his land',[3] the House of Lords indicated that, just as in the case of disputed access to a prospect or wind and air flow, English law knows no such right as a prescriptive easement to receive a television signal.[4] The House pointed in particular to the indeterminate nature of the amenity supposedly injured,[5] the inordinate range of potentially aggrieved viewers,[6] and the supposedly intolerable restriction otherwise imposed upon the freedom of the commercial developer.[7] The correctness of the outcome may be debated, but the *Canary Wharf* case clearly suggests that the discreteness of definition accorded to the conceptual abstractions of English land law has a critical interface with large issues of environmental protection and the quality of urban life in the 21st century.

1   Gray and Gray, 'The Idea of Property in Land', in S Bright and J K Dewar (ed), *Land Law: Themes and Perspectives* (OUP 1998), pp 33–34. See e g *Webb v Bird* (1861) 10 CB (NS) 268 at 284, 142 ER 455 at 461 where, in rejecting any easement of wind access for a windmill, Erle CJ observed that such a claim would 'operate as a prohibition to a most formidable extent to the owners of the adjoining lands – especially in the neghbourhood [sic] of a growing town.'
2   [1997] AC 655; [1997] Conv 145 (P R Ghandi); (1997) 113 LQR 515 (P Cane); [1997] CLJ 483 (J O'Sullivan).
3   [1997] AC 655 at 709G–H, 710G per Lord Hoffmann (see also Lord Goff of Chieveley at 685C–D, Lord Hope of Craighead at 726D–G). Compare Lord Cranworth's proposition in *Tapling v Jones* (1865) 11 HLCas 290 at 311, 11 ER 1344 at 1353, that each might 'use his own land by building on it as he thinks most to his interest.'
4   [1997] AC 655 at 709H per Lord Hoffmann, 719F–H per Lord Cooke of Thorndon, 727D per Lord Hope of Craighead.
5   'Radio and television signals ... may come from various directions over a wide area as they cross the developer's property. They may be of various frequencies ... Their passage from one point to another is invisible ... ' ([1997] AC 655 at 727C per Lord Hope of Craighead).
6   [1997] AC 655 at 710A per Lord Hoffmann.
7   [1997] AC 655 at 727C–D Lord Hope of Craighead ('If he were to be restricted by an easement from putting up a building which interfered with these signals, he might not be able to put up any substantial structures at all. The interference with his freedom would be substantial').

THE RIGHT MUST BE WITHIN THE GENERAL NATURE OF THE RIGHTS TRADITIONALLY RECOGNISED AS EASEMENTS

8.59   The law of easements is constrained by the innately conservative principle that the categories of admissible easement must not dramatically overstep the boundaries of the kinds of easement already recognised.

Novelty is not necessarily an objection

8.60   It is often said that the list of easements is not closed.[1] As Lord St Leonards observed in *Dyce v Lady James Hay*,[2] 'the category of servitudes and easements must alter and expand with the changes that take place in the circumstances of mankind.'[3] Nevertheless the courts are traditionally reluctant to admit new kinds of right to the status of easement,[4] and have not usually been prepared to recognise rights which lie markedly outside the range of entitlements hitherto acknowledged as easements. Occasionally a new right is admitted within the canon of allowable easements,[5] but in many cases alleged easements have been rejected either because they were in the nature of negative easements and therefore more appropriately created as restrictive covenants[6] or because the claimed entitlements were more properly characterised as rights of irrevocable licence.[7]

1   See e g *Re Ellenborough Park* [1956] Ch 131 at 140 per Danckwerts J; *Queanbeyan Leagues Club Ltd v Poldune Pty Ltd* (1996) 7 BPR 15078 at 15080 per McLelland J; *Clos Farming Estates Pty Ltd v Easton* [2002] NSWCA 389 at [41] per Santow JA.

2   (1852) 1 Macq 305 at 312.

3   Cited with approval in *Commonwealth v Registrar of Titles (Victoria)* (1918) 24 CLR 348 at 353 per Griffith CJ.

4   See e g *Hill v Tupper* (1863) 2 H & C 121, 159 ER 51 [**para 8.36**]; *Clos Farming Estates Pty Ltd v Easton* [2002] NSWCA 389 at [46] (no 'easement for vineyard').

5   See e g *Simpson v Godmanchester Corpn* [1897] AC 696 (right to enter another's land in order to open and shut sluice gates on a canal). See also *Attorney-General of Southern Nigeria v John Holt & Co (Liverpool) Ltd* [1915] AC 599 at 617.

6   [**Para 9.138**].

7   It has been held that an exclusive right to burial in a cemetery is neither an easement nor a proprietary right analogous to an easement (see *Beard v Baulkham Hills Shire Council* (1986) 7 NSWLR 273 at 278E–G). Such a right may, however, comprise an exclusive licence which becomes irrevocable on interment (see *Re West Norwood Cemetery* [1994] Fam 210 at 218A–B; *Smith v Tamworth CC* (1997) 41 NSWLR 680 at 694C per Young J). See P W Young, (1969) 39 ALJ 50; A Dowling, (1998) 18 Legal Studies 438. See also *Bradley v Wingnut Films Ltd* [1993] 1 NZLR 415 at 428–429.

Reluctance to accept new negative easements

8.61   By their nature negative easements require the servient owner to refrain from certain action on his own land.[1] Nowadays, however, the categories of negative easement are virtually closed.[2] In *Hunter v Canary Wharf Ltd*[3] Lord Hope of Craighead observed that, against the background of a general presumption 'for freedom in the occupation and use of property', negative easements 'represent an anomaly in the law because they restrict the owners' freedom.' The court therefore 'takes care not to extend them beyond the categories which are well known to the law.'[4] This caution is particularly marked where a negative easement is claimed by prescription (i e on the basis of long user[5]) and is therefore supported by no positive agreement on the part of the servient owner and evidenced by no change on his land which might reveal its existence.[6]

1   [**Para 8.7**]. See I Dawson and A Dunn, (1998) 18 Legal Studies 510.

2   In certain circumstances a claim of negative easement may connote an exclusive possession which is inconsistent with the nature of an easement [**para 8.69**]. See the debate in *Shelf Holdings Ltd v Husky Oil Operations Ltd* (1987) 38 DLR (4th) 441 at 448–455, (1989) 56 DLR (4th) 193 at 201–204; but compare *Pennant Hills Golf Club v Roads and Traffic Authority of New South Wales* (1999) 9 BPR 17011 at 17014–17015. See also M M Litman and B H Ziff, 57 Alta L Rev 326 (1988).

3   [1997] AC 655 at 726F–H [**para 8.58**].

4   See *Phipps v Pears* [1965] 1 QB 76 at 82G–83A per Lord Denning MR (the law 'has been very chary of creating any new negative easements').

5   [**Para 8.168**].

6   See *Hunter v Canary Wharf Ltd* [1997] AC 655 at 726G–H per Lord Hope of Craighead. See also I Dawson and A Dunn, 'Acquiring a Prescriptive Right to Commit a Nuisance', in P Jackson and D C Wilde (ed), *Contemporary Property Law* (Ashgate 1999), p 237.

8.62   In *Phipps v Pears*,[1] for instance, the claimant sought damages from the defendant on the ground that the latter had demolished his adjoining house thereby exposing the unpointed flank wall of the claimant's house to the rigours of the weather.² The Court of Appeal denied that the claimant could assert any prescriptive easement of protection from the weather.³ Such a right is entirely negative,⁴ effectively comprising 'a right to stop your neighbour pulling down his own house.'⁵ The Court accordingly viewed the proposed new negative easement as unduly restrictive of the rights of neighbouring owners to enjoyment of their own land⁶ and was disinclined to 'hamper legitimate development' in this way.⁷ Such inhibitions on the development of adjoining land can normally be enforced against a neighbouring landowner only after an explicit process of bargain resulting in the creation of a restrictive covenant.⁸

1   [1965] 1 QB 76.
2   See now Building Act 1984, ss 81(1), 82(1)(b), under which a local authority may require the weatherproofing of surfaces exposed by demolition.
3   See also *Giltrap v Busby* (1970) 21 NILQ 342; *Marchant v Capital & Counties Property Co Ltd* (1982) 263 EG 661.
4   *Phipps v Pears* did not concern any positive claim to support of the claimant's gable wall: the two houses were freestanding (see *Bradburn v Lindsay* [1983] 2 All ER 408 at 414j; *Rees v Skerrett* [2001] 1 WLR 1541 at [25]). The courts have tended to be much more responsive where a claimant alleges interference with an easement of support for his building (see e g *Tollemache & Cobbold Breweries Ltd v Reynolds* (1983) 268 EG 52 at 56; *Bradburn v Lindsay*, supra at 413e; *Brace v South East Regional Housing Association Ltd* (1984) 270 EG 1286 at 1288). See [1984] Conv 54 (P Jackson).
5   [1965] 1 QB 76 at 82G per Lord Denning MR.
6   For a critical view of this rationale, see (1964) 80 LQR 318 (R E M); M A Peel, (1964) 28 Conv (NS) 450 at 451–453. It has since been doubted whether Lord Denning's rejection of an easement of protection from the weather was intended to apply as between tenements which are separated horizontally rather than vertically (see *Sedgwick Forbes Bland Payne Group Ltd v Regional Properties Ltd* (1981) 257 EG 64 at 70 per Oliver J).
7   Provided that the appropriate planning permission is obtained, 'every man is entitled to pull down his house if he likes. If it exposes your house to the weather, that is your misfortune. It is no wrong on his part. Likewise every man is entitled to cut down his trees if he likes, even if it leaves you without shelter from the wind or shade from the sun' (*Phipps v Pears* [1965] 1 QB 76 at 83A per Lord Denning MR).
8   *Phipps v Pears* [1965] 1 QB 76 at 83E–F per Lord Denning MR.

8.63   The ruling in *Phipps v Pears* reflects a policy-based recognition that it is 'wrong to require too much of one of two adjoining owners as a consequence of or condition upon his entitlement to demolish his property.'¹ Nevertheless in more recent times the courts have striven to establish a principle of protection for neighbours not through the medium of negative easements, but in terms of a common law duty (based in either negligence or nuisance) to take reasonable steps to avoid foreseeable harm caused by the withdrawal of support from an adjoining structure. Thus failure to provide suitable weatherproofing for a neighbour's wall following demolition may give rise to a substantial damages liability which is not founded on the claimant's property rights, but is based instead on the law of torts.²

1   *Rees v Skerrett* [2001] 1 WLR 1541 at [21] per Lloyd J.
2   See e g *Rees v Skerrett* [2001] 1 WLR 1541 at [33]–[39]; [2002] Conv 7 (J E A).

Range of recognised easements

8.64 Notwithstanding the clear element of judicial caution in this context, the courts have, over the years, accepted many widely varying kinds of right as constitutive of an easement. The categories of easement (or, at any rate, of positive easement) are not yet closed.[1] An easement may therefore comprise an entitlement to do something on the servient tenement (e g to use a right of way,[2] to store goods,[3] to use a neighbour's kitchen,[4] to install electrical and telephone wires,[5] or to advertise a business[6]). An easement may also comprise a right to prevent the servient owner from doing certain acts on his land which he would otherwise be entitled to perform, although there is an increasing danger that such an entitlement may be considered to be both negative and novel and therefore not in the nature of an easement.[7]

1 See *Re Ellenborough Park* [1956] Ch 131 at 140 per Danckwerts J; *Ward v Kirkland* [1967] Ch 194 at 222; *Gypsum Carrier Inc v The Queen* (1977) 78 DLR (3d) 175 at 181; *Clos Farming Estates Pty Ltd v Easton* [2002] NSWCA 389 at [41].
2 *Borman v Griffith* [1930] 1 Ch 493 at 499.
3 *Attorney-General of Southern Nigeria v John Holt & Co (Liverpool) Ltd* [1915] AC 599 at 617.
4 *Heywood v Mallalieu* (1883) 25 Ch D 357.
5 *Prospect CC v Cross* (1990) 21 NSWLR 601; *Stasiuk v West Kootenay Power Ltd* (1996) 67 ACWS 3d 252.
6 *Moody v Steggles* (1879) 12 Ch D 261 at 266–268; *Henry Ltd v McGlade* [1926] NI 144 at 151–152.
7 Some negative rights have nevertheless been acknowledged as easements. In *Ough v King* [1967] 1 WLR 1547 at 1553A–C, for instance, the Court of Appeal upheld an easement of access to light flowing through a defined aperture. This right was effectively a right to prevent a neighbour from building on his land in such a way as to obstruct that right to light (damages awarded).

8.65 An easement may even sanction the conduct of an activity affecting the servient land which would otherwise constitute a nuisance.[1] In *Sturges v Bridgman*[2] the defendant claimed to have acquired a prescriptive easement to generate an excessive amount of noise and vibration in the course of his business as a confectioner. The Court of Appeal held that no easement had been acquired on the facts, but acknowledged that an easement to make noise could have been created by long user if during the period of user the noise had amounted to an actionable nuisance and the servient owner had failed to avail himself of the appropriate remedy in the law of tort.[3] This limited freedom to commit nuisance is nowadays reinforced by a potentially dangerous doctrine that immunity from nuisance liability can also arise by necessary implication from a statute which regulates an environmentally hazardous activity.[4] In other jurisdictions, however, the modern trend is to accord an implied immunity of this kind only if, in the carrying out of the relevant operation, it was 'practically impossible' to avoid the nuisance.[5] Significantly even in England the courts have declined to extend the analogy of statutory authority as a defence for nuisance committed in pursuit of a lawfully obtained planning permission.[6]

1 Courts have generally been disinclined, however, to allow the rights of neighbouring house-holders to be 'subordinated to the leisurely pursuits of sportsmen.' See *Kennaway v Thompson* [1981] QB 88 at 94E–95A (power boat racing) and *Banfai v Formula Fun Centre Inc* (1985) 19

DLR (4th) 683 at 692–693 (automobile racing). Even Lord Denning MR held that there is 'no such easement known to the law as a right to hit cricket balls into your neighbour's land' (*Miller v Jackson* [1977] QB 966 at 978G). In baseball, of course, the intrinsic object of the game may require a different outcome (see *Bank of New Zealand v Greenwood* [1984] 1 NZLR 525 at 535). See also the disobliging view taken of domestic bombardment by misdirected golf balls in *Lester-Travers v City of Frankston* [1970] VR 2 at 9–10; *Segal v Derrick Golf & Winter Club* (1977) 76 DLR (3d) 746 at 749–750.

2   (1879) 11 Ch D 852.

3   (1879) 11 Ch D 852 at 863–866. See also *Re The State Electricity Commission of Victoria & Joshua's Contract* [1940] VLR 121 at 125–126; D Wittman, (1980) 9 J Legal Stud 557; and compare Noise Act 1996, ss 2–8.

4   See *Allen v Gulf Oil Refining Ltd* [1981] AC 1001 at 1014A–C, 1016F, 1024A–B. See also *York Bros (Trading) Pty Ltd v Commr of Main Roads* [1983] 1 NSWLR 391 at 397D–398A; but compare *Lawrence v Kempsey Shire Council* (1995) 6 BPR 14111 at 14115–14116.

5   See *Tock v St John's Metropolitan Area Board* (1990) 64 DLR (4th) 620 at 651b per Sopinka J; *Ryan v Victoria (City)* (1999) 168 DLR 4th 513 at [54]–[55] (where nuisance is the 'inevitable result' of the exercise of statutory authority); *Rideau Falls Generating Partnership v Ottawa (City)* (1999) 174 DLR (4th) 160 at 163–164.

6   See *Wheeler v J J Saunders Ltd* [1996] Ch 19 at 31D–F, 38B (noxious smells caused by extension of pig farm). See similarly *Ports of Auckland Ltd v Auckland CC* [1999] 1 NZLR 601 at 610–611; *Hawkes Bay Protein Ltd v Davidson* [2003] 1 NZLR 536 at [19].

THE RIGHT MUST NOT IMPOSE ANY POSITIVE BURDEN ON THE SERVIENT OWNER

8.66   It is intrinsic to the concept of an easement that the role of the servient owner should be essentially passive. An easement requires of the servient owner nothing more than an act of sufferance, in that he must either allow the dominant owner to do something on the servient land or abstain from some action of his own on that land which would otherwise be entirely legitimate.[1]

1   See A J Waite, [1985] CLJ 458, for the argument that this limitation on the scope of the easement is a relatively recent development in English law and that some easements of positive obligation may have survived intact to the present day.

General absence of onerous obligation

8.67   In the absence of contrary agreement, an easement must not normally demand that the servient owner engage in any expenditure of money or undertake any positive or onerous action.[1] Thus, for example, the mere existence of a right of way imposes on the servient owner no duty to carry out necessary repair or maintenance of the way.[2] A tenant's easement to use drains running through his landlord's premises imposes no duty on the landlord to keep these drains in repair.[3] Likewise no easement can impose a positive obligation to maintain a supply of water or electricity,[4] although an easement may validly preclude the servient owner from taking any positive steps to interfere with an existing supply (e g by cutting it off[5] or otherwise preventing its transmission across the servient land[6]).

1   See *Liverpool City Council v Irwin* [1977] AC 239 at 256D–E per Lord Wilberforce, 259B per

Lord Cross of Chelsea; *Cardwell v Walker* [2004] 2 P & CR 122 at [19]. Nor does a dominant owner have any duty to repair or maintain a facility which is the subject matter of an easement (see *Soich v Sutherland SC* (1980) 2 BPR 9273 at 9275). See also Law Reform Committee, *Occupiers' Liability to Invitees, Licensees and Trespassers* (Third Report, Cmd 9305, November 1954), para 34.

2   *Transco plc v Stockport MBC* [2004] 2 AC 1 at [80] per Lord Scott of Foscote. See *Ingram v Morecraft* (1863) 33 Beav 49 at 51, 55 ER 284 at 285; *Jones v Pritchard* [1908] 1 Ch 630 at 637–638; *Gulliksen v Pembrokeshire CC* [2002] Ch 825 at [5]; *Lawrence v Griffiths* (1987) 47 SASR 455 at 488. See also *Holden v White* [1982] QB 679 at 684A–B, 685D, 687E–F, but compare *Bartlett v Robinson* (1980) 25 SASR 552 and see Occupiers' Liability Act 1984, s 1.

3   *Duke of Westminster v Guild* [1985] QB 688 at 702H–703C, 704A. See also *Ingram v Morecraft* (1863) 33 Beav 49 at 52, 55 ER 284 at 285. Where the maintenance of an easement requires positive action, the dominant owner has an implied right to enter the servient land, e g for the purpose of executing necessary repairs (see *Jones v Pritchard* [1908] 1 Ch 630 at 638; *Transco plc v Stockport MBC* [2004] 2 AC 1 at [80] per Lord Scott of Foscote).

4   *Regis Property Co Ltd v Redman* [1956] 2 QB 612 at 627–628 (positive obligation to secure and pay for a supply of hot water inconsistent with easement).

5   See *Duffy v Lamb* (1997) 75 P & CR 364 at 371 (electricity), although the Court of Appeal left open the question whether the servient owner might indirectly truncate the supply by inviting the Electricity Board to discontinue that supply.

6   See *Rance v Elvin* (1985) 50 P & CR 9 at 15–17 (right to uninterrupted passage of water from another's land imposes only a negative obligation).

Rare examples of positive imposition

8.68   Only in extremely special (and now possibly anomalous) circumstances can an easement properly impose any positive duty on the servient owner. In *Jones v Price*[1] the Court of Appeal held that a right to require a neighbour to maintain a boundary fence can be validly acquired as an easement. This fencing obligation has nevertheless been described as a 'spurious easement'[2] and it is doubtful whether it can arise otherwise than by prescription.[3] It is also possible that a landowner whose property fronts on to the sea may be burdened by an easement to repair the sea wall.[4]

1   [1965] 2 QB 618 at 633D–E, 639C.
2   *Lawrence v Jenkins* (1873) LR 8 QB 274 at 279.
3   Such an easement, if it exists, may be of some importance in determining the respective rights and obligations of holders of grazing rights on open moorland (see *Crow v Wood* [1971] 1 QB 77 at 84E–G; *Egerton v Harding* [1975] QB 62 at 68B–F). See [1975] CLJ 34 (C F Kolbert); A J Bradbrook, (1979) 53 ALJ 306.
4   *Keighley's Case* (1610) 10 Co Rep 139a at 139b, 77 ER 1136 at 1137.

THE RIGHT MUST NOT EXCLUDE REASONABLE ALTERNATIVE USERS OF THE SERVIENT TENEMENT

8.69   No claim of easement can be recognised if it involves an element of exclusive possession or joint occupation of the supposedly servient land. This proposition is open, however, to a number of ambivalent interpretations which revolve around the question whether user is 'exclusive to' the grantee or 'exclusive of' others (including the grantor).[1]

1   Much of the confusion in this area of the law of easements is usefully exposed in P Luther, 'Easements and exclusive possession' (1996) 16 Legal Studies 51 (pointing inter alia to the obscure origins of the supposed 'exclusive possession' principle).

An easement may or may not be exclusive to the grantee

8.70   The prohibition of easements involving exclusive possession has no bearing on whether rights claimed as easements are exclusive to the grantee. An easement may involve either sole or shared user of a privilege. Some forms of user are indeed exclusive to the grantee,[1] but others need not be. The same user privilege may often be the subject of simultaneous grant to a number of dominant owners.[2] Thus, unless otherwise specified, an easement of way gives the grantee merely a non-exclusive right of passage over the land,[3] the grantor remaining free to offer a similar right to others.

1   See eg *Moody v Steggles* (1879) 12 Ch D 261 (right to advertise a business).
2   See eg *Re Ellenborough Park* [1956] Ch 131 [**para 8.42**]; *Simpson v Fergus* (2000) 79 P & CR 398 at 402.
3   See *Sunset Properties Pty Ltd v Johnston* (1975) 3 BPR 9185 at 9193; *Rodwell v G R Evans & Co Pty Ltd* (1977) 3 BPR 9114 at 9118.

An easement must not exclude the grantor from possession

8.71   An easement may or may not be exclusive to the grantee, but it can never, ultimately, be exclusive of the *grantor*. Rights conferred as an easement, although they inevitably qualify the servient owner's enjoyment of his land, must not be such as to exclude the grantor from possession of that land.[1] English law traditionally inclines against possessory easements,[2] not least because territorial claims of such intensity connote, in reality, the assertion of either a fee simple estate or a term of years.[3] The archetypal easement merely permits some form of restrained, intermittent user of the servient land (as in the case of a right of way).[4] As Lord Hope of Craighead once observed,[5] easements are 'limited rights'.[6] The greater the intensity of user claimed, the less likely are the courts, in general, to admit the existence of an easement.[7] As confirmed by venerable authority, 'there is no easement known to the law which gives exclusive and unrestricted use of a piece of land.'[8] Thus, for example, an assertion that the alleged servient owner can visit his own land only by invitation of the supposed dominant owner is fatal to any claim of easement over that land.[9]

1   See eg *Clos Farming Estates Pty Ltd v Easton* [2002] NSWCA 389 at [46] ('the servient owner's rights are so attenuated as no longer to meet the description of exclusive possession'). See also the test of effective exclusion from land applied in *Jackson v Mulvaney* [2003] 1 WLR 360 at [25].
2   [**Para 8.74**].
3   [**Para 3.24**]. See *Dyce v Lady James Hay* (1852) 1 Macq 305 at 309; *Metropolitan Railway Co v Fowler* [1892] 1 QB 165 at 175; *Taylor v North West Water* (1995) 70 P & CR 94 at 107; *Bursill Enterprises Pty Ltd v Berger Bros Trading Co Pty Ltd* (1971) 124 CLR 73 at 91 per Windeyer J; *Tileska v Bevelon* (1989) 4 BPR 9601 at 9606; *Osoyoos Indian Band v Oliver (Town)* (2001) 206 DLR (4th) 385 at 413 per Iacobucci J.

4   See *Butler v Muddle* (1995) 6 BPR 13984 at 13986–13987 per Young J ('a right of way is not the equivalent of ownership … the prime thrust is that the land is still land belonging to the servient owner …'). See likewise *Finlayson v Campbell* (1997) 8 BPR 15703 at 15710–15711 per Young J.

5   *DPP v Jones* [1999] 2 AC 240 at 275D–E. See also *Transco plc v Stockport MBC* [2004] 2 AC 1 at [68] per Lord Hobhouse of Woodborough ('very limited rights and remedies').

6   The limited nature of a right of easement has the consequence that interference with an easement is actionable, not in trespass, but in nuisance (see *Paine & Co Ltd v St Neots Gas & Coke Co* [1939] 3 All ER 812 at 823G–H; *Transco plc v Stockport MBC* [2004] 2 AC 1 at [80] per Lord Scott of Foscote; *Simpson v Knowles* [1974] VR 190 at 195; *Finlayson v Campbell* (1997) 8 BPR 15703 at 15707).

7   See e g *Jackson v Mulvaney* [2003] 1 WLR 360 at [25], where an easement extended to use of another's land as a communal garden, but could not comprise any right to dictate the precise location of a particular flower bed [**para 2.14**].

8   *Reilly v Booth* (1890) 44 Ch D 12 at 26 per Lopes LJ.

9   *Hanina v Morland* (Unreported, Court of Appeal, 22 November 2000) at [34], [36] per Aldous LJ. See the rejection of the easement claim in *Clos Farming Estates Pty Ltd v Easton* [2002] NSWCA 389 at [38], where the New South Wales Court of Appeal pointed to the 'sterility and nominal character' of what remained to the servient owners.

Inconsistent applications of the general principle

8.72   Whilst it is plain that exclusive possessory rights over land are more appropriately conferred by freehold or leasehold grant, the time-honoured prohibition against exclusiveness in the law of easements often represents an intuitive rather than a reasoned response to the validity of certain claims. The non-possessory character of easements has not been enforced by the courts with consistency and rigour. Significant confusion flows from the almost universal failure to define with any three-dimensional precision the servient area in respect of which the exercise of an alleged easement may or may not be adjudged to constitute exclusive possession. The case law certainly discloses no uniform application of a criterion of non-exclusive possession.[1] There are many instances where the courts have upheld the easement character of rights which inevitably comprised some form of exclusive possession or user.[2] For example, the disputed use of the coal shed in *Wright v Macadam*[3] must surely have represented exclusive user.[4] To some extent the definitional problem remains 'one of degree.'[5] As Deputy Judge Paul Baker QC observed in *London & Blenheim Estates Ltd v Ladbroke Retail Parks Ltd*,[6] '[a] small coal shed in a large property is one thing. The exclusive use of a large part of the alleged servient tenement is another.' It may also be that the courts have used the supposed requirement of non-exclusive user as a smokescreen for judicial discretion, invoking the requirement in order to strike down claims felt to be unmeritorious, whilst suppressing the requirement in cases where it has been thought that a remedy should be given.[7]

1   It has been suggested that the case law is best understood as imposing a criterion of certainty (i e as requiring some clear limit to what the claimant can do on the servient land). See P Luther, (1996) 16 Legal Studies 51 at 55.

2   For confirmation of this point, see *Mercantile General Life Reassurance Co of Australia Ltd v Permanent Trustee Australia Ltd* (1989) NSW ConvR ¶55–441 at 58,208 per Powell J. See also

Berger Bros Trading Co Pty Ltd v Bursill Enterprises Pty Ltd [1970] 1 NSWR 137 at 140; *Miller v Emcer Products Ltd* [1956] Ch 304 at 316 (right to use lavatory on another's premises); *Hedley v Roberts* [1977] VR 282 at 289.

3   [1949] 2 KB 744 at 752–753. See (1959) 66 LQR 302 (R E M).
4   *Grigsby v Melville* [1972] 1 WLR 1355 at 1364F per Brightman J. See also *Hair v Gillman and Inskip* (2000) 80 P & CR 108 at 115 per Chadwick LJ; *Batchelor v Marlow* [2001] 1 EGLR 119 at 124E–F; *Jackson v Mulvaney* [2003] 1 WLR 360 at [17]; *Clos Farming Estates Pty Ltd v Easton* [2002] NSWCA 389 at [45].
5   *Grigsby v Melville* [1972] 1 WLR 1355 at 1364F; *London & Blenheim Estates Ltd v Ladbroke Retail Parks Ltd* [1992] 1 WLR 1278 at 1286C.
6   [1992] 1 WLR 1278 at 1286C–D.
7   See e g *Wright v Macadam* [1949] 2 KB 744, where the Court of Appeal had no hesitation in recognising the easement character of a hard-pressed tenant's claim to store coal in a coal shed provided by her landlord. (The landlord had asserted a right to make an extra charge for use of the coal shed and pulled down the coal shed before the date of the hearing.)

Boundary between ownership and mere user

8.73   Recent years have seen some judicial uncertainty about the scope of the rule against possessory easements.[1] There have long been suggestions[2] that exclusiveness of user is a vitiating circumstance only in cases of an alleged prescriptive user[3] or implied grant,[4] where in reality a claim of exclusive user is tantamount to an assertion that title to the land has been acquired by reason of long adverse possession.[5] It is nevertheless clear that, in the interests of systemic order, a distinction must be drawn between 'ownership of the land giving rights to the soil and to every inch of the soil' and the ownership of mere rights of enjoyment or user in respect of that land.[6] An easement cannot be allowed to become 'the equivalent of ownership' of the entire servient tenement.[7] The question to be determined in every instance is whether the subject matter of the claim is an estate in a *corporeal* hereditament (e g a fee simple estate in the land) or an estate in an *incorporeal* hereditament (i e an easement over the land).[8] All other matters aside, the difference may be hugely significant in determining, for instance, the length of time required to generate entitlement by long possession or user.[9]

1   See *Mercantile General Life Reassurance Co of Australia Ltd v Permanent Trustee Australia Ltd* (1989) NSW ConvR ¶55–441 at 58,208 per Powell J for a warning that the supposed rule against exclusiveness 'must be scrutinised with care.'
2   See e g *Dyce v Lady James Hay* (1852) 1 Macq 305 at 312, 315.
3   **[Paras 8.168–8.196]**.
4   **[Paras 8.128–8.166]**.
5   *Mercantile General Life Reassurance Co of Australia Ltd v Permanent Trustee Australia Ltd* (1989) NSW ConvR ¶55–441 at 58,208 per Powell J.
6   *Saggers v Brown* (1981) 2 BPR 9329 at 9331 per Rath J; *Butler v Muddle* (1995) 6 BPR 13984 at 13986; *Carlson v Carpenter* (1998) 8 BPR 15909 at 15914–15915. See also *Clifford v Hoare* (1874) LR 9 CP 362 at 370. A transfer of title or exclusive ownership of a building is inconsistent with the concept of easement (see *Bursill Enterprises Pty Ltd v Berger Bros Trading Co Pty Ltd* (1971) 124 CLR 73 at 91 per Windeyer J).
7   *Butler v Muddle* (1995) 6 BPR 13984 at 13986 per Young J.
8   One of the pivotal questions posed by Lord Evershed MR in *Re Ellenborough Park* [1956] Ch 131 at 175–176, was whether the grant was 'inconsistent with the proprietorship or possession of the alleged servient owners.'

9   Adverse possession may result in acquisition of a freehold title after ten (or sometimes twelve) years [**paras 6.41, 6.56**]; prescriptive acquisition of an easement generally involves 20 years of user [**para 8.190**].

A test of 'substantial interference'

8.74   In modern times the general disfavour of possessory easements has been commuted to a recognition that the class of easements cannot include any user which 'substantially interferes with the whole of the servient tract'[1] or exhausts its entire beneficial value. An easement, properly so called, may not assert a degree of possessory control which sterilises a significant proportion of the land claimed as servient.[2] Nowadays, therefore, it is likely that a claim of easement will be disallowed on the ground of intensity of user only if, 'in relation to the area over which it is to be exercisable', the right proposed as an easement is apt to 'leave the servient owner without any reasonable use of his land.'[3] The user asserted must not represent an unacceptable 'invasion of the servient land',[4] leaving the servient owner with 'no more than a shadow of ownership and possession.'[5] The issue is ultimately one of fact and degree,[6] the crucial question revolving around whether the disputed user so derogates from the totality of the grantor's rights that the grantee is left 'free to act as if [he] were the owner of the freehold.'[7] In this way the delimitation of the category of easements more effectively recognises that easements are designed not to sterilise land, but to facilitate the purposeful, profitable and collaborative exploitation of land resources.

1   See [1989] Conv 296 at 298 (Bruce Ziff and Moe Litman).
2   See *Clos Farming Estates Pty Ltd v Easton* (2001) 10 BPR 18845 at [41], [49] per Bryson J (affd [2002] NSWCA 389 at [40]).
3   *London & Blenheim Estates Ltd v Ladbroke Retail Parks Ltd* [1992] 1 WLR 1278 at 1288C per Deputy Judge Paul Baker QC (obiter). See likewise *Clos Farming Estates Pty Ltd v Easton* [2002] NSWCA 389 at [40] per Santow JA (servient owner left with 'little by way of residue', his rights being rights 'totally subordinated to the over-arching rights' of the dominant owner).
4   *London & Blenheim Estates Ltd v Ladbroke Retail Parks Ltd* [1992] 1 WLR 1278 at 1288C–D per Deputy Judge Paul Baker QC (affd [1994] 1 WLR 31).
5   *Clos Farming Estates Pty Ltd v Easton* (2001) 10 BPR 18845 at [41] per Bryson J (affd [2002] NSWCA 389 at [40]). A significant reduction in the monetary value of the allegedly servient land may point to a sterilisation of ownership (see *Batchelor v Marlow* [2003] 1 WLR 764 at [16] per Tuckey LJ; *Platt Ltd v Crouch* [2004] 1 P & CR 242 at [46] per Peter Gibson LJ).
6   See *Hair v Gillman and Inskip* (2000) 80 P & CR 108 at 112 per Chadwick LJ ('an ill-defined line'); *Batchelor v Marlow* [2003] 1 WLR 764 at [13]; *Platt Ltd v Crouch* [2004] 1 P & CR 242 at [45] per Peter Gibson LJ.
7   *Mercantile General Life Reassurance Co of Australia Ltd v Permanent Trustee Australia Ltd* (1989) NSW ConvR ¶55–441 at 58,211 per Powell J. See similarly *Carlson v Carpenter* (1998) 8 BPR 15909 at 15914–15915. As the Alberta Court of Appeal held in *Shelf Holdings Ltd v Husky Oil Operations Ltd* (1989) 56 DLR (4th) 193 at 202, the 'key to resolving the issue' is to balance the extent of the rights relinquished by the supposedly servient owner against the rights reserved by him. Thus in *Shelf Holdings* the grant of a right to construct an underground pipeline, coupled with a prohibition on any further building development by the grantor, did not impede the grantor's normal farming operations and thus constituted an easement.

Rationalisation of the case law

8.75   The adoption of a criterion of substantial interference does much to rationalise the rule against exclusiveness in the law of easements. It captures in a more articulate form the pragmatic response to circumstance which underlies much of the case law. In *Copeland v Greenhalf*,[1] for instance, the defendant in injunction proceedings was a wheelwright who for 50 years had used a narrow strip of land belonging to the claimant for the purpose of storing vehicles awaiting and undergoing repair. Upjohn J held that the prescriptive right asserted by the defendant was too extensive to constitute an easement in law. In his view, the right alleged went 'wholly outside any normal idea of an easement' since it amounted to a 'claim to a joint user of the land by the defendant.'[2] Indeed the defendant was arrogating to himself 'the whole beneficial user' of one strip of the land in question. Such a claim could not be established as an easement since it was 'virtually a claim to possession of the servient tenement, if necessary to the exclusion of the owner.'[3] There was, said Upjohn J, no authority in support of the idea that 'a right of this wide and undefined nature can be the proper subject-matter of an easement.'[4]

1   [1952] Ch 488.
2   [1952] Ch 488 at 498. Compare *V T Engineering Co Ltd v Richard Barland & Co Ltd* (1968) 19 P & CR 890 at 895–896.
3   [1952] Ch 488 at 498. Subsequent case law has declined to accept that *Copeland v Greenhalf* was wrongly decided (see eg *London & Blenheim Estates Ltd v Ladbroke Retail Parks Ltd* [1992] 1 WLR 1278 at 1286D per Deputy Judge Paul Baker QC).
4   [1952] Ch 488 at 498. See also *Harada v Registrar of Titles* [1981] VR 743 at 753, where the right of a public electricity authority to position pylons on private land and to prohibit the landowner from building thereon was considered to be a claim of joint user and thus inconsistent with a claim of easement.

8.76   The 'substantial interference' test likewise provides a useful explanation of other decisions often presented as applications of a supposed criterion of non-exclusive possession. In *Ward v Kirkland*[1] the plaintiff claimed to have a right to enter an adjoining farmyard in order to maintain the wall of his cottage abutting on to that farmyard. Ungoed-Thomas J held that the right claimed was capable of existence as an easement,[2] since the right involved no more than monthly visits to the servient land for the purposes of window-cleaning.[3] In *Grigsby v Melville*,[4] however, Brightman J doubted whether a right of storage in a cellar could constitute an easement in circumstances where the claim amounted to 'an exclusive right of user over the whole of the confined space representing the servient tenement.'[5] A valid claim of easement can, however, be asserted in the form of less obstructive users of more general areas of land.[6]

1   [1967] Ch 194.
2   See also *Auerbach v Beck* (1985) 6 NSWLR 424 at 442D (affd sub nom *Beck v Auerbach* (1986) 6 NSWLR 454).
3   Here the user did not 'in effect exclude the defendant from the use of part of the farmyard next to the cottage, or interfere substantially with such use', or otherwise resemble a claim of 'possession or joint possession of part of the defendant's property' ([1967] Ch 194 at 223C–E).
4   [1972] 1 WLR 1355 at 1364G.
5   Brightman J's decision was upheld by the Court of Appeal ([1974] 1 WLR 80), but without

further consideration of the question of exclusive user or possession. The disinclination to uphold claims of easement in respect of confined spaces may account for the ruling in *Dikstein v Kanevsky* [1947] VLR 216 at 219 (no easement to use an elevator).

6   See e g *Attorney-General of Southern Nigeria v John Holt & Co (Liverpool) Ltd* [1915] AC 599 at 617 (storage); *Capar v Wasylowski* (1983) 146 DLR (3d) 193 at 200–201.

Car parking

8.77   Further light is thrown by the 'substantial interference' test on the proper classification of that most valuable asset of the modern urban dweller – the right to park a car. There has been a drift towards acceptance of the idea that, in at least some circumstances, the right to park a car can constitute an easement[1] and that such a right may be acquired prescriptively.[2] However, even this limited proposition has not yet been endorsed unequivocally by the Court of Appeal (or any higher authority).[3] Although the required beneficial connection with the alleged dominant tenement is usually fairly obvious,[4] difficulties spring from the intensity of the user involved.

1   See *London & Blenheim Estates Ltd v Ladbroke Retail Parks Ltd* [1992] 1 WLR 1278 at 1287H per Deputy Judge Paul Baker QC, citing *Le Strange v Pettefar* (1939) 161 LT 300 at 301–302; *Bilkus v London Borough of Redbridge* (1968) 207 EG 803 at 805. See similarly *Handel v St Stephens Close Ltd* [1994] 1 EGLR 70 at 72B; *Patel v W H Smith (Eziot) Ltd* [1987] 1 WLR 853 at 859H.
2   *Bye v Mitchell* [1993] CLY 1627.
3   See e g *Saeed v Plustrade Ltd* [2002] 2 P & CR 266 at [22] where the Court of Appeal preferred to leave open the potential easement status of parking rights. Likewise in *London & Blenheim Estates Ltd v Ladbroke Retail Parks Ltd* [1994] 1 WLR 31 at 38G, the Court of Appeal neatly avoided any comment on the affirmative approach adopted at first instance by Deputy Judge Paul Baker QC. See also the doubts expressed by the Court of Appeal in *Batchelor v Marlow* [2003] 1 WLR 764 at [14].
4   See *Depew v Wilkes* (2002) 216 DLR (4th) 487 at [26] (Ontario Court of Appeal).

8.78   The preferable view today is that a parking easement can arise so long as the rights claimed do not amount to an arrogation of exclusive beneficial user of the entire servient tenement, thereby depriving the servient owner of 'any reasonable use of his land, whether for parking or anything else.'[1] Accordingly the courts have been ready to uphold as easements those parking rights which are limited in point of time or which relate only to a general area of land.[2] However, a claim to monopolise a limited area (e g by parking cars on it during all useful working hours of the day) constitutes such a usurpation of the rights of the alleged servient owner as to 'make his ownership of the land illusory.'[3] On the other hand – despite some doubts on the matter[4] – an easement may comprise a right to park in a numbered or individualised parking bay situated on the servient land.[5] There are indications that some courts are now beginning to take the view that the grantor has an implied obligation to make the grant of parking rights effective by designating a marked car park space.[6] The delimitation of such space merely underscores the fact that the user does not substantially interfere with the remainder of the servient owner's land.

1   *London & Blenheim Estates Ltd v Ladbroke Retail Parks Ltd* [1992] 1 WLR 1278 at 1288C per Deputy Judge Paul Baker QC.

2 *Sweet & Maxwell Ltd v Michael-Michaels Advertising* [1965] CLY 2192; *Newman v Jones* (Unreported, 22 March 1982, Megarry V-C); *Bye v Mitchell* [1993] CLY 1627. See e g *Hair v Gillman and Inskip* (2000) 80 P & CR 108 at 112 (non-exclusive parking on forecourt). Contrast *Central Midlands Estates Ltd v Leicester Dyers Ltd* [2003] 2 P & CR D2 at D3 (saturation parking of unlimited number of cars anywhere on strip of waste land rendered ownership of that land 'illusory').

3 *Batchelor v Marlow* [2003] 1 WLR 764 at [18] (parking rights during the period 8.30am–6.00pm Monday to Friday) (see All ER Rev 2003, pp 260–261 (P J Clarke)). Contrast *Leon Asper Amusements Ltd v Northmain Carwash & Enterprises Ltd* (1966) 56 DLR (2d) 173 at 176–179 (parking only after 6.00pm each day).

4 See (1973) 37 Conv (NS) 60 (D J Hayton). A claim to use a right of way as a parking lot is certainly too extensive to support a valid claim of easement (*Keefer v Arillotta* (1977) 72 DLR (3d) 182 at 189; *Butler v Muddle* (1995) 6 BPR 13984 at 13986–13987). See also *Simpson v Fergus* (2000) 79 P & CR 398 at 402.

5 The right to park in a strictly defined space may also connote the grant of a leasehold interest (*Harley Queen v Forsyte Kerman* [1983] CLY 2077). See also (1976) 40 Conv (NS) 317. Alternatively, car parking can be a form of bailment (see *Walton Stores Ltd v Sydney City Council* [1968] 2 NSWR 109 at 112–113), although this analysis may be applicable only where custody of the vehicle has actually been transferred, e g through a handing over of car keys (see *Fred Chappell Ltd v National Car Parks Ltd* (1987) Times, 22 May).

6 See e g *Owners Corp of Strata Plan 42472 v Menala Pty Ltd* (1998) 9 BPR 16337 at 16346 per Bryson J.

CHANGED USER OF AN EASEMENT

8.79 In view of the tight definitional characteristics of a valid easement in English law, difficult questions are raised by changes which, some time after the creation of an easement, affect the use or extent of the dominant tenement or the nature or intensity of the activity authorised by the easement. In this context a distinction has to be drawn between easements which are the product of express creation and those which arise by implication or prescription. Furthermore, the courts have traditionally attached greater significance to alterations in the purpose or quantum of a particular user than to any change in the mere form of that user. Underlying these propositions is a common principle that the servient tenement should never be exposed to the risk of any significant additional or different burden from that implicit at the point of creation of the easement in question.[1]

1 The claimed user 'must not diminish the servient tenement (or, to put it the other way, increase the grant to the dominant tenement)' (*White v Chandler* [2001] 1 NZLR 28 at [52] per Hammond J).

Expressly created easements

8.80 The scope of an expressly created easement is pre-eminently a matter of construction of the relevant grant or reservation[1] in the light of the circumstances existing at that time and known to the parties or within their reasonable contemplation.[2] There is, however, a principle of general application that, even in relation to the dominant tenement to which it is appurtenant, an expressly created easement may not be used subsequently for a purpose wholly different from that originally envisaged by the grantor and grantee.[3] It is unlikely, therefore, that an easement of way granted as appurtenant to an open space can be invoked if that open space is later built upon.[4] By contrast, a right of way granted for general purposes in respect of a house may survive the conversion of the house into a hotel,[5] subject always to the possibility that any excessive user of the easement may be an actionable tort.[6] In *Jelbert v Davis*,[7] for instance, a right of way had been expressly granted for access and egress 'at all times and for all purposes' in respect of a dominant tenement which was then used for agricultural purposes only. The dominant owner subsequently obtained planning permission to position up to 200 holiday caravans on the site. The Court of Appeal upheld an objection that the volume of the proposed user was likely to be 'so extensive as to be outside the reasonable contemplation of the parties at the time the grant was made.'[8] An injunction was granted.[9]

1   *McAdams Homes Ltd v Robinson* [2004] EWCA Civ 214 at [22] per Neuberger LJ. Absent evidence of contrary intention, the language of a grant is to be 'construed most strongly against the grantor' (*Williams v James* (1867) LR 2 CP 577 at 581 per Willes J). See also *Wood v Saunders* (1875) LR 10 Ch App 582 at 584 per Hall V-C; *Bulstrode v Lambert* [1953] 1 WLR 1064 at 1067; *Dunell v Phillips* (1982) 2 BPR 9517 at 9521.
2   *Todrick v Western National Omnibus Co Ltd* [1934] Ch 190 at 206 per Farwell J; *Laurie v Winch* [1952] 4 DLR 449 at 455 (Supreme Court of Canada). See e g *Wood v Saunders* (1875) LR 10 Ch App 582 at 585 per Hall V-C (easement restricted to reasonable user as determined at date of grant).
3   *Gallagher v Rainbow* (1994) 179 CLR 624 at 640 per McHugh J.
4   *Allen v Gomme* (1840) 11 A & E 759 at 772, 774, 113 ER 602 at 607–608. See, however, *Flavell v Lange* [1937] NZLR 444 at 449; *Grinskis v Lahood* [1971] NZLR 502 at 508–509.
5   *White v Grand Hotel, Eastbourne, Ltd* [1913] 1 Ch 113 at 116–117 (affd by Court of Appeal, (1915) 84 LJ Ch 938). See also *Robinson v Bailey* [1948] 2 All ER 791 at 796B–G; *Jelbert v Davis* [1968] 1 WLR 589 at 594H–595B; *Grinskis v Lahood* [1971] NZLR 502 at 509; *Finlayson v Campbell* (1997) 8 BPR 15703 at 15708. Compare *National Trust v White* [1987] 1 WLR 907 at 913G–914G.
6   *McAdams Homes Ltd v Robinson* [2004] EWCA Civ 214 at [27] per Neuberger LJ. See similarly *Wood v Saunders* (1875) LR 10 Ch App 582 at 585 per Hall V-C (easement of foul drainage inapplicable to house recently converted into lunatic asylum for 150 persons).
7   [1968] 1 WLR 589.
8   [1968] 1 WLR 589 at 596A, F per Lord Denning MR. See *Malden Farms Ltd v Nicholson* (1956) 3 DLR (2d) 236 at 239–241 (developer of holiday beach resort restrained from allowing general public, who came 'by the hundreds', to use lake shore pathway originally granted as private right of way). See also *Grinskis v Lahood* [1971] NZLR 502 at 509–510.
9   For discussion of the remedy appropriate in cases of unreasonable or excessive user, see *Rosling v Pinnegar* (1986) 54 P & CR 124 at 132–134 (application for variation of court order rejected: *Rosling v Pinnegar* (Unreported, Court of Appeal, 9 October 1998)).

Easements arising by implication or prescription

8.81   Easements which arise by implication or prescription have in common the fact that they derive from deemed grants whose nature and extent depend on the circumstances existing at the date of grant.[1] The effect of subsequent changes in the purpose, nature or quantum of the user concerned fall to be assessed by reference to principles which, for the most part, disclose little difference between cases of implied and prescriptive origin.[2] In *McAdams*

Homes Ltd v Robinson,[3] Neuberger LJ offered a significant rationalisation of a body of case law which is 'not entirely consistent and clear.' He indicated that the dominant owner is deprived of the right to enjoy an implied or prescriptive easement only if two conditions are satisfied. Where *both* of these conditions are met, the easement ceases to be enforceable or is at least suspended.

1   In the case of prescription, the relevant rules are coloured by the fact that prescriptive rights are founded on a deemed acquiescence in a user of a certain and uniform kind (see *Scott-Whitehead v National Coal Board* (1987) 53 P & CR 263 at 273).

2   See *McAdams Homes Ltd v Robinson* [2004] EWCA Civ 214 at [22] per Neuberger LJ, [79(i)] per Sir Martin Nourse.

3   [2004] EWCA Civ 214 at [50]–[55].

Radical alteration of purpose underlying the easement

8.82   First, there must have been an altered use of the dominant land which marks a 'radical change in the character' or a 'change in the identity' of the site, as distinct from a 'mere change or intensification in the use of the site.'[1] Thus, for example, an implied or prescriptive right of way may be terminated by the transformation of the dominant tenement from a small dwelling house into a large hotel,[2] but not by a substantial increase in the intensity of an existing user of the dominant land.[3] Similarly an implied easement of access to premises used for residential and warehousing purposes cannot survive the conversion of the dominant tenement into an underground railway station,[4] whereas a prescriptive right to abstract water for watering animals can, without prejudice, be extended to a right to extract significantly greater quantities of water for another agricultual purpose, ie crop spraying.[5]

1   *McAdams Homes Ltd v Robinson* [2004] EWCA Civ 214 at [50] per Neuberger LJ.

2   *British Railways Board v Glass* [1965] Ch 538 at 562F–G per Harman LJ. See also *Williams v James* (1867) LR 2 CP 577 at 582 per Willes J; *Wimbledon and Putney Commons Conservators v Dixon* (1875) 1 Ch D 362 at 368 (pasture turned into manufactory); *RPC Holdings Ltd v Rogers* [1953] 1 All ER 1029 at 1032B–C (field turned into caravan and camping site). The 'radical change' principle is less applicable to an implied or prescriptive easement of support, where even far-reaching alterations in the use of the dominant land do not necessarily increase the burden imposed on the servient land (see *Atwood v Bovis Homes Ltd* [2001] Ch 379 at 389A–B per Neuberger J).

3   See *British Railways Board v Glass* [1965] Ch 538 at 562E–563A, 567G–568D (increase from 6 to 30 caravans on site). See also *Woodhouse & Co Ltd v Kirkland (Derby) Ltd* [1970] 1 WLR 1185 at 1190H–1191A.

4   See *Milner's Safe Co Ltd v Great Northern and City Railway Co* [1907] 1 Ch 208 at 226–229.

5   See *Cargill v Gotts* [1981] 1 WLR 441 at 448H–449B.

Substantial increase in burden on servient land

8.83   The second condition which must be met relates to the intensity or quantum of the user claimed under an implied or prescriptive easement. The enforceability of such an easement is not jeopardised merely by a radical alteration of the use of the dominant tenement.[1] The changed user must also result in a 'substantial increase or alteration in the burden on the servient land.'[2] Even far-reaching changes result in no loss of the dominant owner's entitlement to the easement where no real prejudice has been caused to the servient owner.[3] Thus, for example, a prescriptive easement of natural surface water drainage is unaffected by the development of the dominant land from agricultural land into a large housing estate, provided that the change does not result in a user which is significantly greater in quantum or different in character.[4] But where the conversion of small industrial premises into a housing development causes a marked increase in the burden imposed by an implied easement of foul water drainage, this combination of circumstances renders the easement unenforceable.[5]

1   Such alteration may, of course, impact upon the nature or intensity of the burden on the servient land (*McAdams Homes Ltd v Robinson* [2004] EWCA Civ 214 at [33]).
2   *McAdams Homes Ltd v Robinson* [2004] EWCA Civ 214 at [50] per Neuberger LJ.
3   See *Luttrel's Case* (1601) 4 Co Rep 86a at 87a–87b, 76 ER 1065 at 1067.
4   See *Atwood v Bovis Homes Ltd* [2001] Ch 379 at 388C–D per Neuberger J (All ER Rev 2000, pp 238–239 (P J Clarke)). See similarly *Harvey v Walters* (1873) LR 8 CP 162 at 166 (burden of eavesdropping easement not increased by taller dominant building). The onus of proof is on the dominant owner (*Atwood*, supra at 388E).
5   See *McAdams Homes Ltd v Robinson* [2004] EWCA Civ 214 at [58], [71].

EXTENSION OF USER TO NON-DOMINANT LAND

8.84   In an era of increasingly intense land use and housing development, it is predictable that awkward questions should arise over the extent to which an easement created or acquired for the benefit of one tenement, Greenacre, may also be used for the benefit of an adjacent tenement, Redacre. While it may often seem 'bloody-minded'[1] to object to a sensible diffusion of the benefit of certain easements, there has always been enormous judicial resistance to the idea that a designated dominant tenement should be effectively capable of extension in a manner never bargained for by the parties.[2] It is frequently emphasised that in the law of easements it is 'property rights which are at issue' and that legal solutions should not foist upon servient owners 'a change to their ownership rights.'[3] To allow an unauthorised extension of the dominant tenement would be to 'exceed' (or, indeed, to reformulate) the terms of the original grant,[4] with the consequence that the additional user becomes an actionable trespass.[5] It is, moreover, almost always the case that to permit Redacre to enjoy a benefit conferred upon Greenacre is to impose a significantly increased burden of user upon the servient land.[6]

1   *White v Chandler* [2001] 1 NZLR 28 at [40] per Hammond J. In some jurisdictions there is now a tendency to allow rights of way to be utilised for access to ulterior land where the burden on the servient land is not increased (see e g *MacKenzie v Matthews* (2000) 180 DLR (4th) 674 at 680), particularly where the hardship which injunctive relief would impose on the dominant owner greatly exceeds the benefit to the servient owner (see e g *Brown v Voss*, 715 P2d 514 at 517–518 (Supreme Court of Washington 1986)).
2   In *Peacock v Custins* [2002] 1 WLR 1815 at [24], Schiemann LJ pointed to the 'self-evident commercial value' which had been left outside the scope of the parties' negotiations. See also *Macepark (Whittlebury) Ltd v Sargeant* [2003] 1 WLR 2284 at [52].

3   *White v Chandler* [2001] 1 NZLR 28 at [67] per Hammond J. See similarly *Brown v Voss*, 715
    P2d 514 at 517 (Supreme Court of Washington 1986); *Chevy Chase Land Co v United States*,
    733 A2d 1055 at 1077 (Md 1999).
4   See *Harris v Flower* (1904) 74 LJ Ch 127 at 132 per Vaughan Williams LJ; *White v Chandler*
    [2001] 1 NZLR 28 at [47] per Hammond J.
5   *Das v Linden Mews Ltd* [2003] 2 P & CR 58 at [32]. There still remains a large question as to
    whether the remedial response should take the form of an injunction or mere damages (see
    e g *Das*, supra at [29]–[33] **[para 3.88]**). There is inevitably some suspicion that modern courts,
    by declining injunctive relief, effectively permit dominant owners to purchase immunity from
    the classic rule against unauthorised extension of dominant land (see 62 Wash L Rev 295
    (1987)).
6   See *White v Chandler* [2001] 1 NZLR 28 at [47]. In *Peacock v Custins* [2002] 1 WLR 1815
    at [25], Schiemann LJ analysed the superadded burden, not in terms of any quantifiable
    increase in user, but in more stark terms of legal detriment to the servient land. See likewise
    Das v Linden Mews Ltd [2003] 2 P & CR 58 at [32].

Prohibition of ulterior purpose

8.85   There is longstanding authority, both in England[1] and throughout the
common law world,[2] that a right of way which is appurtenant to a particular
dominant tenement may not be used colourably for the purpose of enjoying a
further access to some other land outside the scope of the grant.[3] A servitude
right of access 'inures to the benefit of the dominant tenement and no other'
and cannot be 'communicated for the benefit of other tenements contiguous
thereto.'[4] Thus an easement of access to Greenacre may not be used for the
purpose of facilitating access to Redacre, quite regardless of whether Redacre is
owned by the proprietor of Greenacre[5] or is owned by some stranger.[6] Nor, for
the purpose of this general rule, does it matter whether the claimed additional
access to Redacre involves transit across Greenacre[7] or can actually be achieved
without any passage through Greenacre.[8] It is even irrelevant that the extension
of the benefit of Greenacre's easement to Redacre would not in fact enlarge,[9]
and in some unusual cases might even diminish,[10] the overall quantum of user
on the servient land.

1   *Allen v Gomme* (1840) 11 A & E 759 at 770, 113 ER 602 at 607; *Skull v Glenister* (1864) 16 CB
    (NS) 81 at 103, 143 ER 1055 at 1063; *Williams v James* (1867) LR 2 CP 577 at 580 per
    Bovill CJ, 582 per Willes J; *Harris v Flower* (1904) 74 LJ Ch 127 at 132; *Callard v Beeney* [1930]
    1 KB 353 at 359; *Bracewell v Appleby* [1975] Ch 408 at 417H–418A; *Jobson v Record and
    Record* (1998) 75 P & CR 375 at 378.
2   *Smith v Smith* (1895) 14 NZLR 4 at 6; *Grinskis v Lahood* [1971] NZLR 502 at 509; *Re Gordon
    and Regan* (1985) 15 DLR (4th) 641 at 647–648; *MacKenzie v Matthews* (2000) 180 DLR (4th)
    674 at 679; *White v Chandler* [2001] 1 NZLR 28 at [66]–[67]. See likewise the American
    Restatement (Third) of Property (Servitudes), para 4.8(3), comment (b) (p 620).
3   An exception to this principle occurs where, at the date of the grant, the dominant tenement
    was itself used as a means of access to the other property (see *Nickerson v Barraclough* [1980]
    Ch 325 at 336D–E).
4   *Alvis v Harrison* (1990) 62 P & CR 10 at 15 per Lord Jauncey of Tullichettle. See likewise
    Peacock v Custins [2002] 1 WLR 1815 at [24] per Schiemann LJ; *Macepark (Whittlebury) Ltd v
    Sargeant* [2003] 1 WLR 2284 at [12], [50].
5   *Macepark (Whittlebury) Ltd v Sargeant* [2003] 1 WLR 2284 at [12]. See eg *Harris v Flower*
    (1904) 74 LJ Ch 127; *Peacock v Custins* [2002] 1 WLR 1815; *Das v Linden Mews Ltd* [2003]
    2 P & CR 58.

6   *Irvine Knitters Ltd v North Ayrshire Co-operative Society Ltd* 1978 SC 109 at 117 per
    Lord President Emslie; *Macepark (Whittlebury) Ltd v Sargeant* [2003] 1 WLR 2284 at [13],
    [22], [28].
7   See e g *Harris v Flower* (1904) 74 LJ Ch 127 at 132; *Peacock v Custins* [2002] 1 WLR 1815. The
    true dominant tenement cannot be used 'merely as a bridge' to non-dominant land (*Irvine
    Knitters Ltd v North Ayrshire Co-operative Society Ltd* 1978 SC 109 at 117 per Lord President
    Emslie).
8   See eg *Das v Linden Mews Ltd* [2003] 2 P & CR 58 (disputed access directly over servient
    carriageway to non-dominant land at end of mews terrace).
9   *Peacock v Custins* [2002] 1 WLR 1815 at [24] per Schiemann LJ.
10 *White v Chandler* [2001] 1 NZLR 28 at [67]. Contrast the more relaxed approach adopted in
    the United States (see e g *Ogle v Trotter*, 495 SW2d 558 at 565–566 (1973)).

A doctrine of ancillary use

8.86   The foregoing principles are plainly directed at protecting the servient
owner from uncovenanted proprietary burdens, but the rigour of the common
law rule has long been qualified by a doctrine of 'ancillary use'.[1] Under this
doctrine an easement created for the benefit of Greenacre may properly serve
Redacre also if the user for purposes of Redacre is merely 'ancillary' to the
enjoyment of the easement for purposes of Greenacre.[2] The courts are,
however, extremely reluctant to expand the concept of 'ancillary use' and,
indeed, the definition of 'ancillary use' has proved somewhat elusive.

1   *Macepark (Whittlebury) Ltd v Sargeant* [2003] 1 WLR 2284 at [47]. See All ER Rev 2003, pp
    262–263 (P J Clarke).
2   *National Trust v White* [1987] 1 WLR 907 at 913C–D per Warner J. See *Massey v Boulden*
    [2003] 1 WLR 1792 at [44]–[45].

8.87   The core of the 'ancillary use' proviso is the idea that, whilst an
easement for Greenacre must not be used 'in substance'[1] for the benefit of
Redacre,[2] certain forms of user for purposes of Redacre are properly classified
as 'mere adjuncts to the honest user'[3] of the easement for Greenacre and do not
therefore constitute any unlawful extension of the original dominant tenement.[4]
Thus, for example, the dominant owner who accesses his land at Greenacre by
perfectly lawful exercise of his right of way over servient land need not 'retrace
his steps'[5] in order to engage in some purely incidental activity such as strolling
or picnicking on his own adjoining land at Redacre.[6] Such 'ancillary use' of the
subsisting easement for Greenacre does not connote any excess of grant.

1   *Harris v Flower* (1904) 74 LJ Ch 127 at 132 per Romer LJ.
2   Quite clearly, if a dominant owner's essential purpose is to use a legitimate access to
    Greenacre in order to obtain access to Redacre, the user is unlawful (*Macepark (Whittle-
    bury) Ltd v Sargeant* [2003] 1 WLR 2284 at [21]; *Miller v Tipling* (1918) 43 DLR 469 at 475).
3   *Harris v Flower* (1904) 74 LJ Ch 127 at 132 per Vaughan Williams LJ. See also *Peacock v
    Custins* [2002] 1 WLR 1815 at [25] per Schiemann LJ. In *Williams v James* (1867) LR 2 CP 577
    at 580–581, Bovill CJ spoke similarly of 'bona fide' use of a right of way consistent with the
    'ordinary and reasonable use of the land to which the right of way was claimed.'
4   The 'ancillary use' doctrine cannot operate where a grant has expressly confined the benefit of
    an easement to a tenement identified at the point of grant (see *McKay Securities plc v Surrey
    CC* (Unreported, Chancery Division, 9 December 1998)).

5   *Miller v Tipling* (1918) 43 DLR 469 at 475 per Mulock CJ Ex.
6   *Peacock v Custins* [2002] 1 WLR 1815 at [6], [22]; *Macepark (Whittlebury) Ltd v Sargeant* [2003] 1 WLR 2284 at [49]. See similarly *Lawton v Ward* (1696) 1 Ld Raym 75 at 75–76, 91 ER 946 at 947. It would be quite different if the dominant owner were to provide a picnic area for public use on Redacre (see *Das v Linden Mews Ltd* [2003] 2 P & CR 58 at [21]).

8.88   Recent case law[1] has clarified that use may be deemed merely 'ancillary' if the extent of the use for the benefit of the non-dominant land is 'insubstantial'[2] or if it involves no exploitation of the easement in such a way that a profit can be derived from use of the non-dominant land.[3] Conversely, no claim of merely 'ancillary' use can be made where it is sought to exercise Greenacre's right of way over servient land for the purpose of transporting building materials to Redacre[4] or recovering from Greenacre a store of timber felled on Redacre[5] or facilitating a commercially profitable access across Redacre to the grand prix circuit at Silverstone.[6] Nor can cultivation of Redacre be sensibly described as 'ancillary' to cultivation of the adjacent Greenacre, even if both are being farmed together as a unit.[7] Likewise a right of way affording access to a dwelling-house on Greenacre cannot be utilised as a lawful means of reaching vacant land at Redacre, since such use would improperly enlarge the dominant tenement by unlocking access to a wholly different (and highly valuable) facility at Redacre in the form of a car parking area.[8]

1   *Macepark (Whittlebury) Ltd v Sargeant* [2003] 1 WLR 2284 at [50] per Deputy Judge Gabriel Moss QC.
2   Although the examples in the case law fall very close to the margin, the category of 'insubstantial' use seems to cover circumstances where the original dominant tenement has later been amalgamated with relatively small premises. See e g *Graham v Philcox* [1984] QB 747 at 756D–757A, 764D–765A (conversion of flat to incorporate downstairs premises as single dwelling unit); *Massey v Boulden* [2003] 1 WLR 1792 at [45] (two rooms added as mere appendages of dominant land); *Macepark (Whittlebury) Ltd v Sargeant* [2003] 1 WLR 2284 at [48]–[49], [60]. See also *Collin Development (Pte) Ltd v Hong Leong Holdings Ltd* [1976] 2 MLJ 149 at 150; *Carbone v Vigliotti*, 610 A2d 565 at 569 (Conn 1992); *Il Giardino LLC v Belle Haven Land Co*, 757 A2d 1103 at 1111–1112 (2000); *White v Chandler* [2001] 1 NZLR 28 at [50].
3   The reference to 'profitable user' of the non-dominant land as indicating an excess of grant can be traced back to *Harris v Flower* (1904) 74 LJ Ch 127 at 132 per Vaughan Williams LJ.
4   *Harris v Flower* (1904) 74 LJ Ch 127 at 132–133.
5   *Jobson v Record and Record* (1998) 75 P & CR 375 at 379. See *Macepark (Whittlebury) Ltd v Sargeant* [2003] 1 WLR 2284 at [36].
6   *Macepark (Whittlebury) Ltd v Sargeant* [2003] 1 WLR 2284 at [57]–[59].
7   *Peacock v Custins* [2002] 1 WLR 1815 at [27]. See All ER Rev 2001, pp 262–263 (P J Clarke).
8   *Das v Linden Mews Ltd* [2003] 2 P & CR 58 at [24]–[27], [32]. See E Paton and G Seabourne, 'Can't get there from here?: permissible use of easements after *Das*' [2003] Conv 127.

RIGHTS OF WAY

8.89   Amongst the most common easements are those which confer a private right of way. A right of way is essentially a right to pass and re-pass along a way and also to do things which are ancillary to such passage[1] or are reasonably necessary for its use or enjoyment.[2] The grantee of the right of way thus has, for instance, certain ancillary rights to render the easement effective for the purposes originally contemplated.[3] In the case of an express grant the grantee is entitled not merely to repair but also to develop or improve the way in order to render it suitable for the reasonable accommodation or enjoyment of the dominant tenement.[4] Such action may involve excavating or sealing the route of the way,[5] constructing stairs where appropriate,[6] or otherwise carrying out alterations to meet changed conditions.[7]

1   *V T Engineering Ltd v Richard Barland & Co Ltd* (1968) 19 P & CR 890 at 896. Compare the public right to pass along the highway [**para 5.13**].
2   *Auerbach v Beck* (1985) 6 NSWLR 424 at 444D–E (affd sub nom *Beck v Auerbach* (1986) 6 NSWLR 454); *Owners of Strata Plan 48754 v Anderson* (1999) 9 BPR 17119 at 17123 per Young J; *MacKenzie v Matthews* (2000) 180 DLR (4th) 674 at 678–679. See also *White v Taylor (No 2)* [1969] 1 Ch 160 at 196E–G; *Duke of Westminster v Guild* [1985] QB 688 at 700D–E.
3   *Newcomen v Coulson* (1877) 5 Ch D 133 at 143 per Jessel MR; *Jones v Pritchard* [1908] 1 Ch 630 at 638; *Tomara Holdings Pty Ltd v Pongrass* (2002) 10 BPR 19531 at [16]. A right of way through a basement area implies, as a matter of reasonable necessity, a right to install and maintain artificial lighting to render the way trafficable (*Owners of Strata Plan 48754 v Anderson* (1999) 9 BPR 17119 at 17123–17124).
4   *Gerrard v Cooke* (1806) 2 Bos & P NR 109 at 115–116, 127 ER 565 at 567–568; *Newcomen v Coulson* (1877) 5 Ch D 133 at 143–144; *Mills v Silver* [1991] Ch 271 at 286H–287A per Dillon LJ; *Alvis v Harrison* (1990) 62 P & CR 10 at 15 per Lord Jauncey of Tullichettle; *Sunset Properties Pty Ltd v Johnston* (1975) 3 BPR 9185 at 9191; *Zenere v Leate* (1980) 1 BPR 9300 at 9305; *Butler v Muddle* (1995) 6 BPR 13984 at 13987.
5   See *Guth v Robinson* (1977) 1 BPR 9209 at 9215–9216; *Lawrence v Griffiths* (1987) 47 SASR 455 at 480–482.
6   See *Hemmes Hermitage Pty Ltd v Abdurahman* (1991) 22 NSWLR 343 at 347C–348G; *Hanny v Lewis* (1998) 9 BPR 16205 at 16208.
7   See *Finlinson v Porter* (1875) LR 10 QB 188 at 193–195.

Content of the right of way

8.90   A right of way across servient land extends to the entire width of the designated path or roadway,[1] but must have an ascertainable *terminus a quo* and *terminus ad quem*.[2] A right of way confers not merely a right to pass and re-pass along the way, but often also a right to halt on the way for a reasonable period of time for the purpose of loading and unloading a vehicle. In the absence of an express term of grant, the question whether a right of way includes ancillary rights of loading and unloading depends on whether such rights can be implied from the circumstances existing at the date of grant.[3] (The existence of ample room for loading and unloading on the dominant tenement argues strongly against the implication of similar rights on a servient way.[4]) Although a right of way does not normally confer any right to leave vehicles unattended[5] or to station gantries, cranes, hoists or other loading equipment on the way,[6] it does give the grantee certain rights over the superjacent airspace. The grantee can thus insist that the way remain unobstructed, not of course *usque ad coelum*, but to such height as is 'reasonable in all the circumstances.'[7]

1   *Simpson v Fergus* (2000) 79 P & CR 398 at 402–403.
2   *Zenere v Leate* (1980) 1 BPR 9300 at 9306–9307; *Butler v Muddle* (1995) 6 BPR 13984 at 13986.

3   *Zenere v Leate* (1980) 1 BPR 9300 at 9307; *SS & M Ceramics Pty Ltd v Kin* [1996] 2 Qd R 540 at 545–548; *Robmet Investments Pty Ltd v Don Chen Pty Ltd* (1997) 8 BPR 15461 at 15464–15465; *Tomara Holdings Pty Ltd v Pongrass* (2002) 10 BPR 19531 at [17]. See *Bulstrode v Lambert* [1953] 1 WLR 1064 at 1071; *McIlwraith v Grady* [1968] 1 QB 468 at 476E; *V T Engineering Ltd v Richard Barland & Co Ltd* (1968) 19 P & CR 890 at 894; *Grinskis v Lahood* [1971] NZLR 502 at 509; *Deanshaw and Deanshaw v Marshall* (1978) 20 SASR 146 at 150.

4   *London and Suburban Land and Building Co (Holdings) Ltd v Carey* (1991) 62 P & CR 480 at 483–484.

5   *Butler v Muddle* (1995) 6 BPR 13984 at 13986–13987 per Young J. A right to park a car may be regarded as 'ancillary' only if reasonably necessary for the effective enjoyment of the right of way (see *Zenere v Leate* (1980) 1 BPR 9300 at 9305; *Owners Corp of Strata Plan 42472 v Menala Pty Ltd* (1998) 9 BPR 16337 at 16346).

6   *V T Engineering Ltd v Richard Barland & Co Ltd* (1968) 19 P & CR 890 at 896. A right of way normally confers no right 'permanently or indefinitely to be in occupation of the road or to use it to the exclusion of the owner of the land' (*Rodwell v G R Evans & Co Pty Ltd* (1977) 3 BPR 9114 at 9118). See also *Keefer v Arillotta* (1977) 72 DLR (3d) 182 at 189; *Simpson v Fergus* (2000) 79 P & CR 398 at 402–403.

7   *Robmet Investments Pty Ltd v Don Chen Pty Ltd* (1997) 8 BPR 15461 at 15464. See *V T Engineering Ltd v Richard Barland & Co Ltd* (1968) 19 P & CR 890 at 895 per Megarry J (grantee entitled to reasonable amount of 'vertical swing space' for hoist, but not to 'lateral swing space' since this would 'in effect sterilise a strip of land of indefinite depth on each side of the way'). See, however, *Reilly v Booth* (1890) 44 Ch D 12 at 17 ('You cannot have a right of way described as so many feet high').

Relation to the dominant tenement

8.91   So long as a right of way is demonstrably beneficial to the dominant land to which it is appurtenant, it is irrelevant that other land intervenes between the dominant and servient tenements.[1] The grant of a right of way does not, however, confer any right on the dominant owner to enter upon the way from simply *any* part of the dominant tenement adjoining the route of that way.[2] The creation of a new point of access is permissible so long as it does not unreasonably interfere with the rights of other users,[3] but the servient owner is otherwise entitled to erect a fence, railing or wall along the route,[4] provided that the right of way offers such access from the dominant tenement as is reasonable (e g by means of intermediate gateways).[5]

1   *Todrick v Western National Omnibus Co Ltd* [1934] Ch 561 at 572–573.

2   *Pettey v Parsons* [1914] 2 Ch 653 at 663–664, 667, 669; *Saggers v Brown* (1981) 2 BPR 9329 at 9331.

3   *Fairview New Homes plc v Government Row Residents Association Ltd* [1998] EGCS 92.

4   *Pettey v Parsons* [1914] 2 Ch 653 at 663, 667, 669; *Saggers v Brown* (1981) 2 BPR 9329 at 9331–9332; *Dunell v Phillips* (1982) 2 BPR 9517 at 9522.

5   *Lewis v Wakeling* (1923) 54 OLR 647 at 650–654; *Owners Corp of Strata Plan 42472 v Menala Pty Ltd* (1998) 9 BPR 16337 at 16341.

Construction of an expressly created right of way

8.92   The precise scope of an expressly created right of way is construed by reference to the terms of the relevant grant[1] or reservation[2] considered in the light of the surrounding circumstances at the date of creation of the right.[3] Of these circumstances perhaps the most material is the 'nature of the locus in quo over which the right of way is granted.'[4] The sheer physical characteristics of the way may indicate that rights which are otherwise unlimited in their terms must by necessary implication be cut back to more restricted forms of user.[5] If the terms of the grant or reservation do not sufficiently describe the extent or location of a right of way, reference may be made not only to the plan attached to a transfer of the land but also to any planning permission which delimited the scope of the access in question.[6]

1   In the case of an implied grant, the actual user of the right is 'the only satisfactory guide' (*Milner's Safe Co Ltd v Great Northern and City Railway Co* [1907] 1 Ch 208 at 220). The same is inevitably true of prescriptive rights also (see *Williams v James* (1867) LR 2 CP 577 at 581).

2   **[Para 8.198]**. See *White v Richards* (1993) 68 P & CR 105 at 108.

3   *Wood v Saunders* (1875) LR 10 Ch App 582 at 585 per Hall V-C; *St Edmundsbury and Ipswich Diocesan Board of Finance v Clark* (*No 2*) [1975] 1 WLR 468 at 476G–477B; *Morgan Sindall plc v Sawston Farms* (*Cambs*) *Ltd* [1999] 1 EGLR 90 at 91K–L; *West v Sharp* (2000) 79 P & CR 327 at 332; *Saggers v Brown* (1981) 2 BPR 9329 at 9331; *Gallagher v Rainbow* (1994) 179 CLR 624 at 639–640 per McHugh J.

4   *Cannon v Villars* (1878) 8 Ch D 415 at 420 per Jessel MR. See *Minor v Groves* (2000) 80 P & CR 136 at 141 per Millett LJ; *Peacock v Custins* [2002] 1 WLR 1815 at [30] per Schiemann LJ.

5   A right granted in respect of a passageway which was only 2 ft 11 in wide is necessarily restricted to foot traffic (*Bridgwood v Keates* (Unreported, Court of Appeal, 1 November 1983)). See also *Milner's Safe Co Ltd v Great Northern and City Railway Co* [1907] 1 Ch 208 at 221. Similarly a right of way over a small country lane cannot support the passage of a large bus (*Todrick v Western National Omnibus Co Ltd* [1934] Ch 190 at 207 (reversed on other grounds, [1934] Ch 561)), nor can a right of way over a 2.7 metres wide roadway support the passage of 38-ton dumper trucks 14 times per day (*White v Richards* (1993) 68 P & CR 105 at 113).

6   *Scott v Martin* [1987] 1 WLR 841 at 849D–850A. A valid easement over an undefined route may also be granted where the parties agree that the route is to be fixed by some defined person (see *Talga Investments Pty Ltd v Tweed Canal Estates Pty Ltd* (1974) 1 BPR 9675 at 9681).

8.93   An express grant of a right of way must also be construed having regard to the purposes for which it was granted or which were within the reasonable contemplation of the parties at the date of grant.[1] Thus, for instance, the grant to a supermarket of a right of footway over surrounding pedestrian walkways includes, by implication, a right for the grantee's customers to wheel trolleys to an adjacent car park.[2] A right of passage 'on foot and with or without motor vehicles' has been held to include a right to walk dogs, ride horses and ride motorcycles, but not a right to drive cattle.[3]

1   *Hamble PC v Haggard* [1992] 1 WLR 122 at 136B per Millett J. See also *Finlayson v Campbell* (1997) 8 BPR 15703 at 15708–15709 per Young J.

2   *Soames-Forsythe Properties Ltd v Tesco Stores Ltd* [1991] EGCS 22 (drawing an analogy with the right to use a perambulator on a public footway (*R v Mathias* (1861) 2 F & F 570 at 572–574, 175 ER 1191 at 1192)). See [1992] Conv 199 (J Martin).

3   *White v Richards* (1993) 68 P & CR 105 at 114–115.

Changed user of a right of way

8.94   There has always been a reluctance to allow a dominant owner to extend the exercise of a right of way substantially beyond the contemplation of the original grant.[1] In this context, once again, it is necessary to draw a distinction between express and other rights of way and between changes of purpose, intensity and form of the user concerned.

1   See *Harris v Flower* (1904) 74 LJ Ch 127 at 132; *Re Gordon and Regan* (1985) 15 DLR (4th) 641 at 648.

Express rights of way

8.95   The courts tend to be more sensitive to changes in the purpose or volume of user of an expressly created right of way than to mere alterations in the form of that user. Thus, for example, objection may be raised if a changed user imposes an excessive burden on the servient tenement relative to that which existed at the date of creation of the right of way.[1] The courts are generally ready to restrain any 'abuse of the rights given to the grantee' where excessive traffic on the way causes the servient owner 'troubled days and sleepless nights.'[2] However, in the absence of any express restriction as to the form of user, the courts have been disinclined to hold that the permissible user is cut down by the past practice of the dominant owner[3] or is impliedly limited to certain kinds of person.[4] In particular an unlimited right of way may be exercised in any manner beneficial to the dominant tenement and consistent with the original purpose of the grant, even though this form of user may differ from the user at the date of the express grant.[5] Thus, for instance, a right of way which was originally used for transport by horse-drawn vehicles may quite properly extend to motorised transport for similar purposes.[6]

1   Excessive user constitutes trespass and may be restrained by injunction (see *Hamble PC v Haggard* [1992] 1 WLR 122 at 133E–134E; *Mercantile General Life Reassurance Co of Australia Ltd v Permanent Trustee Australia Ltd* (1989) NSW ConvR ¶55–441 at 58,210–58,212). The servient owner is entitled to obstruct an excessive user only where the excessive user cannot be severed from a perfectly lawful user (see *Hamble*, supra at 134E). Otherwise excessive user does not justify the termination or even the suspension of the easement in question (see *Graham v Philcox* [1984] QB 747 at 756E–F).

2   *Rodwell v G R Evans & Co Pty Ltd* (1977) 3 BPR 9114 at 9119 per Holland J. See e g *White v Richards* (1993) 68 P & CR 105 at 113; *Jobson v Record and Record* (1998) 75 P & CR 375 at 378–379.

3   *Newcomen v Coulson* (1877) 5 Ch D 133 at 138–139; *Bridgwood v Keates* (Unreported, Court of Appeal, 1 November 1983); *Lawrence v Griffiths* (1987) 47 SASR 455 at 479. Events subsequent to the date of grant are irrelevant to the scope of the grant, but may colour the court's willingness to grant injunctive relief (see *Andriopoulos v Marshall* (1981) 2 BPR 9391 at 9392).

4   See *Bridgwood v Keates* (Unreported, Court of Appeal, 1 November 1983) (access to back door not impliedly restricted to 'trade visitors').

5   See e g *Newcomen v Coulson* (1877) 5 Ch D 133 at 138–139; *Lawrence v Griffiths* (1987) 47 SASR 455 at 479.

6   *Sunset Properties Pty Ltd v Johnston* (1975) 3 BPR 9185 at 9191. See also *Lock v Abercester Ltd* [1939] Ch 861 at 863–864; *Kain v Norfolk* [1949] Ch 163 at 169–170; *Robmet Investments Pty Ltd v Don Chen Pty Ltd* (1997) 8 BPR 15461 at 15464.

Prescriptive rights of way

8.96   Prescriptive rights of way are governed by slightly more stringent rules. Such rights are for ever limited to the category and quantum of user which prevailed during the period which gave rise to the prescriptive claim.[1] Thus, for example, a prescriptive easement of way in respect of a field cannot survive the conversion of that land into a caravan and camping site.[2] It also follows that, although the grantees of a prescriptive way are entitled to repair the way,[3] there is no right to improve the way (eg by constructing a made road), since such action is liable to increase significantly the burden falling on the servient tenement.[4] Mere variants of the form of user which underlay the prescriptive claim are, however, immaterial. An easement which originated in user by horse-drawn vehicles remains available for modern user by way of motor car.[5]

1   *Ballard v Dyson* (1808) 1 Taunt 279 at 286, 127 ER 841 at 844; *Williams v James* (1867) LR 2 CP 577 at 582; *Bradburn v Morris* (1876) 3 Ch D 812 at 823; *RPC Holdings Ltd v Rogers* [1953] 1 All ER 1029 at 1032B–C; *Mills v Silver* [1991] Ch 271 at 287B–C. See also *Cargill v Gotts* [1981] 1 WLR 441 at 447H–448A.
2   *RPC Holdings Ltd v Rogers* [1953] 1 All ER 1029 at 1032B–C.
3   *Mills v Silver* [1991] Ch 271 at 286F–G.
4   *Mills v Silver* [1991] Ch 271 at 287B–C.
5   *Lock v Abercester Ltd* [1939] Ch 861 at 863–864. It is likewise irrelevant that an original user has dwindled away to less onerous traffic on foot (see *Davies v Stephens* (1836) 7 C & P 570 at 571, 173 ER 251 at 252).

Realignment or variation of route

8.97   In the absence of some express or implied entitlement, neither the servient owner[1] nor the dominant owner[2] has any right unilaterally to realign or vary the route of an easement of way. This inflexibility in the law has been criticised as detracting from the optimal efficiency of land use.[3] English law has, as yet, no statutory jurisdiction for the modification of easements in the interests of the beneficial development of servient land.[4] It is arguable, however, that unilateral relocation of a way should be regarded as constituting no 'substantial' (ie actionable[5]) interference with the dominant owner's rights if the relocation causes him no inconvenience or loss of utility and is 'necessary to achieve an object of substantial public and local importance and value.'[6]

1   *Greenwich Healthcare National Health Service Trust v London and Quadrant Housing Trust* (1999) 77 P & CR 133 at 138; *Gormley v Hoyt* (1982) 43 NBR (2d) 75 at 81. See also *Deacon v South-Eastern Railway Co* (1889) 61 LT 377 at 379.
2   *Slorach v Mount View Farm Pty Ltd* (Unreported, 20 July 1998, BPR Casenote 102110).
3   Significantly, the American *Restatement* (*Third*) *of Property* (*Servitudes*) allows the servient owner a right of unilateral variation 'when necessary to permit normal use or development of the servient estate', so long as the relocation of route does not lessen significantly the utility of the servitude, increase the burdens on the dominant estate, or frustrate the purpose of the easement (para 4.8(3)). See 109 Harv L Rev 1693 (1996).
4   Compare LPA 1925, s 84 **[para 13.127]**. A statutory facility for the modification of easements exists in other common law jurisdictions (see eg Conveyancing Act 1919 (New South Wales), s 88K; Property Law Act 1974 (Queensland), s 180).
5   **[Para 8.99]**.

6   See eg *Greenwich Healthcare National Health Service Trust v London and Quadrant Housing Trust* (1999) 77 P & CR 133 at 138–139 per Lightman J.

Interference with rights of way

8.98   Any wrongful interference with a private right of way is potentially an actionable nuisance.[1]

1   *Saint v Jenner* [1973] Ch 275 at 280A–E; *Jalnarne Ltd v Ridewood* (1989) 61 P & CR 143 at 150; *B & Q Plc v Liverpool and Lancashire Properties Ltd* (2000) 81 P & CR 246 at [75]–[76]; *McKellar v Guthrie* [1920] NZLR 729 at 731; *Finlayson v Campbell* (1997) 8 BPR 15703 at 15707. Even substantial interference with an easement may be quite lawful if authorised by the express terms of the grant (see eg *Overcom Properties v Stockleigh Hall Residents Management Ltd* (1989) 58 P & CR 1 at 10–11).

Test of 'substantial interference'

8.99   Unlike the case of the public highway (where any 'appreciable' obstruction is wrongful[1]), not every form of interference with a private right of way is actionable.[2] The courts are increasingly anxious to uphold an ethic of 'reasonableness between neighbours'[3] and frequently endorse the idea that in the law of nuisance there must be a large element of 'give and take'.[4] A right of way cannot, by definition, confer rights of exclusive user.[5] It necessarily follows that the threshold of actionable nuisance is reached only when there is 'substantial' interference with the way as granted[6] in a form which is plainly obstructive of its reasonable use.[7]

1   *Pettey v Parsons* [1914] 2 Ch 653 at 662 per Lord Cozens-Hardy MR. Compare, however, *DPP v Jones* [1999] 2 AC 240 at 257D **[para 5.14]**.
2   *Celsteel Ltd v Alton House Holdings Ltd* [1985] 1 WLR 204 at 216E. See eg *West v Sharp* (2000) 79 P & CR 327 at 333–336; *Finlayson v Campbell* (1997) 8 BPR 15703 at 15713. See also *York Bros* (*Trading*) *Pty Ltd v Commr of Main Roads* [1983] 1 NSWLR 391 at 394D.
3   *Delaware Mansions Ltd v Westminster CC* [2002] 1 AC 321 at [29], [34] per Lord Cooke of Thorndon; *Abbahall Ltd v Smee* [2003] 1 WLR 1472 at [36]–[38] per Munby J. See Gray and Gray, 'The rhetoric of realty', in J Getzler (ed), *Rationalizing Property, Equity and Trusts: Essays in Honour of Edward Burn* (Butterworths 2003), pp 256–257.
4   See eg *Cambridge Water Co v Eastern Counties Leather Plc* [1994] 2 AC 264 at 299D per Lord Goff of Chieveley, citing *Bamford v Turnley* (1862) 3 B & S 62 at 84, 122 ER 27 at 33 per Bramwell B ('live and let live'). See also *Costagliola v English* (1969) 210 EG 1425 at 1431 per Megarry J.
5   The grant of a right of way in respect of every part of a defined area 'does not involve the proposition that the grantee can in fact object to anything done on any part of the area which would obstruct passage over that part' (*West v Sharp* (2000) 79 P & CR 327 at 332 per Mummery LJ).
6   *Hutton v Hamboro* (1860) 2 F & F 218 at 219, 175 ER 1031 at 1032; *Pettey v Parsons* [1914] 2 Ch 653 at 662, 665; *Keefe v Amor* [1965] 1 QB 334 at 347D; *Overcom Properties v Stockleigh Hall Residents Management Ltd* (1989) 58 P & CR 1 at 8; *Zenere v Leate* (1980) 1 BPR 9300 at 9305; *Saggers v Brown* (1981) 2 BPR 9329 at 9331; *Carlson v Carpenter* (1998) 8 BPR 15909 at 15914–15915.
7   *Keefe v Amor* [1965] 1 QB 334 at 346G; *Celsteel Ltd v Alton House Holdings Ltd* [1985] 1 WLR 204 at 217B per Scott J; *West v Sharp* (2000) 79 P & CR 327 at 332 per Mummery LJ, 335 per Colman J.

8.100 Each case raises an issue of fact and degree,[1] to be determined with reference to the reasonable requirements of the dominant tenement from time to time.[2] The relevant test is one of obstruction rather than of dissuasion from use[3] and the pertinent question is not whether the residue of use left to the dominant owner is reasonable, but whether he is being reasonable in insisting on continued enjoyment of the facility for which he contracted.[4] In effect, the test turns on convenience rather than necessity: does the interference render the continuance of the dominant owner's reasonable user of the way 'materially less convenient than before'?[5] Thus, for example, no actionable interference occurs where an adjacent building encroaches into a roadway by merely two feet,[6] but there may well be a remedy where the width of the way is more than halved.[7] In some cases, where the dominant owner has specifically negotiated and paid for an ample or unimpeded form of access, it is not subsequently open to the servient owner to deprive him of any of that user unless the dominant owner's stance on the matter is 'unreasonable or perverse.'[8]

1 For a far-reaching review of the relevant case law, see *Finlayson v Campbell* (1997) 8 BPR 15703 at 15709–15711 per Young J.
2 *Saggers v Brown* (1981) 2 BPR 9329 at 9332; *Sinclair v Jut* (1996) 9 BPR 16219 at 16229–16231.
3 The installation of horror pictures along a right of way makes the way less attractive, but has been said not to constitute a substantial interference (see *Finlayson v Campbell* (1997) 8 BPR 15703 at 15711–15712 per Young J), although non-physical interference tends to shade into problems of physical obstruction.
4 *B & Q Plc v Liverpool and Lancashire Properties Ltd* (2000) 81 P & CR 246 at [45] per Blackburne J.
5 *B & Q Plc v Liverpool and Lancashire Properties Ltd* (2000) 81 P & CR 246 at [48]–[49], [71] per Blackburne J.
6 *Clifford v Hoare* (1874) LR 9 CP 362 at 370–372.
7 *Celsteel Ltd v Alton House Holdings Ltd* [1985] 1 WLR 204 at 218C–G; *Stonebridge v Bygrave* (Unreported, Neuberger J, 25 October 2001). See also *Powell v Linney* (1983) 80 Law Soc Gaz 1982.
8 *B & Q Plc v Liverpool and Lancashire Properties Ltd* (2000) 81 P & CR 246 at [45], [71] (injunction granted to prevent servient owner from developing so as cause a 26 per cent reduction of an access area for which dominant owner had specifically bargained). See also *CP Holdings Ltd v Dugdale* (Unreported, Park J, 30 March 1998).

Installation of gates and barriers

8.101 The erection of a gate across the way constitutes no nuisance[1] so long as the dominant owner is allowed free access at all times[2] or so long as the gate is kept open at least during the dominant owner's business hours.[3] The true test of interference here is whether the gate is 'locked against enjoyment',[4] and the locking of a gate across a right of way is not in itself inconsistent with a claim of right particularly where the dominant owner is provided with a key[5] or combination lock code.[6] An excessive number of awkward internal gates on a rural property may, however, constitute a substantial interference with the way.[7] Likewise the installation of a large cattle grid may be a source of actionable nuisance,[8] but the courts have looked more kindly on the construction of speed ramps on a driveway.[9]

1   *Carlson v Carpenter* (1998) 8 BPR 15909 at 15915 (unlocked boom gate).
2   See *Flynn v Harte* [1913] 2 IR 322 at 326–327; *Sunset Properties Pty Ltd v Johnston* (1975) 3 BPR 9185 at 9194–9195; *Owners Corp of Strata Plan 42472 v Menala Pty Ltd* (1998) 9 BPR 16337 at 16341; *MacKenzie v Matthews* (2000) 180 DLR (4th) 674 at 682. The existence of a right of way is not inconsistent with a duty in the dominant owner to close the gate after use (see *Lister v Rickard* (1969) 113 Sol Jo 981; *Gohl v Hender* [1930] SASR 158 at 163–164).
3   *Pettey v Parsons* [1914] 2 Ch 653 at 662–664; *Lister v Rickard* (1969) 113 Sol Jo 981. See also *Healy v Ellco Farm Supplies Pty Ltd* (1986) 3 BPR 9596 at 9599.
4   See *Sunset Properties Pty Ltd v Johnston* (1975) 3 BPR 9185 at 9195 per Holland J.
5   Such action may be intended to discourage unauthorised strangers or simply to preserve the relative privacy of the servient owner (see *Sunset Properties Pty Ltd v Johnston* (1975) 3 BPR 9185 at 9195).
6   *Cardwell v Walker* [2004] 2 P & CR 122 at [32].
7   *Sinclair v Jut* (1996) 9 BPR 16219 at 16231.
8   *Powell v Linney* (1983) 80 Law Soc Gaz 1982.
9   *Saint v Jenner* [1973] Ch 275 at 279D.

Remedies for substantial interference

8.102   An historic (but today little encouraged[1]) response to interference with an easement of way lies in the self-help remedy of abatement of the nuisance. Thus, for instance, a frustrated dominant owner may, under conditions of safety, use reasonable force to remove an obstruction to his right of way.[2] It is also permissible for the dominant owner, if unreasonably impeded in his use of a way, to divert (if he can) over another route on land belonging to the servient owner.[3] Nowadays, however, the more frequent form of response to substantial interference with a right of way lies in some court-ordered remedy. The court has discretion either to issue a declaration of the parties' rights[4] or to order the termination of the obstruction by mandatory or other injunction[5] or to make an award damages.[6] An injunction is generally inappropriate where the interference or threat of interference, although substantial, is merely temporary or is adequately remedied by damages.[7] All too often – particularly in a context of 'bad feeling between ... neighbours' – discord over an impeded right of way seems 'eminently a case for alternative dispute resolution.'[8]

1   See *Lagan Navigation Co v Lambeg Bleaching, Dyeing and Finishing Co Ltd* [1927] AC 226 at 244 per Lord Atkinson.
2   *Roberts v Rose* (1865) LR 1 Exch 82 at 89.
3   *Stonebridge v Bygrave* (Unreported, Neuberger J, 25 October 2001); *Slorach v Mount View Farm Pty Ltd* (Unreported, 20 July 1998, BPR Casenote 102110) (Supreme Court of Queensland).
4   See eg *Stonebridge v Bygrave* (Unreported, Neuberger J, 25 October 2001).
5   See eg *B & Q Plc v Liverpool and Lancashire Properties Ltd* (2000) 81 P & CR 246 at [83].
6   See *Snell & Prideaux Ltd v Dutton Mirrors Ltd* [1995] 1 EGLR 259 at 263L–264C, where, in circumstances of extended non-use of a right of way, the Court of Appeal quantified damages to reflect the difference in value of the dominant land with and without the disputed right of access.
7   *West v Sharp* (2000) 79 P & CR 327 at 333 per Mummery LJ.
8   *West v Sharp* (2000) 79 P & CR 327 at 334 per Mummery LJ. See also *Stonebridge v Bygrave* (Unreported, Neuberger J, 25 October 2001) (referring to the need 'to bang [the parties'] heads together so that they can sort matters out between them in the future').

RIGHTS OF LIGHT

8.103 In the absence of any natural right of access to light,[1] the preservation of access to sunlight must be sought by way of either a duly created easement of light or a restrictive covenant which precludes adverse building development. Rights of light are commonly acquired as prescriptive easements and are often termed 'ancient lights'.[2] In English law at any rate, an easement of light can arise only in respect of light which comes through a defined aperture (such as a window)[3] and easements of light are therefore restricted to buildings.[4] The obstruction of part of the light reaching a building on the dominant tenement may constitute an actionable nuisance.

1   **[Para 1.43]**.
2   **[Para 8.194]**.
3   **[Para 8.56]**. See *Levet v Gas Light & Coke Co* [1919] 1 Ch 24 at 27.
4   Other jurisdictions have shown a much greater interest in easements of solar access. See e g *Prah v Maretti*, 321 NW2d 182 (1982); D D Goble, 'Solar Rights: Guaranteeing a Place in the Sun' 57 Oregon L Rev 94 (1978); A J Bradbrook, (1982) 5 Univ of New South Wales LJ 229; (1983) 15 U of W Australia L Rev 148.

Quantum of light

8.104 The dominant owner is entitled to the uninterrupted access through his ancient windows of sufficient light to enable him to enjoy comfortable use of the building for the purposes of his occupancy,[1] whether that use is residential or business-related.[2] Judged against the criterion of 'ordinary user',[3] the relevant issue in any alleged interference with light is not 'How much light has been taken away?' but rather 'How much light is left?'[4]

1   *Colls v Home and Colonial Stores Ltd* [1904] AC 179 at 187, 198, 204; *Allen v Greenwood* [1980] Ch 119 at 130A–B, 135A–B. In *Carr-Saunders v Dick McNeil Associates Ltd* [1986] 1 WLR 922 at 928E–F, Millett J reiterated the 'well established' rule that no actionable wrong is committed if 'the amount of light remaining is sufficient for the comfortable enjoyment of his property by the dominant owner according to the ordinary notions of mankind.'
2   A photographic studio may be entitled to an unusually large quantity of light (see *Allen v Greenwood* [1980] Ch 119 at 133C–D, 136G–H), but a church, even if it has stained glass windows, cannot prescribe for more light than is needed in order to be 'comfortably used according to the ordinary requirements of people attending church' (see *Newham v Lawson* (1971) 22 P & CR 852 at 859–860).
3   The light required for 'ordinary user' depends also on the nature of the building concerned. A greenhouse may need much more light than a warehouse (see *Allen v Greenwood* [1980] Ch 119 at 131B, 135A–B). The standard of light enjoyed by way of easement may extend beyond that which would be justified by 'ordinary user' if, e g during a period sufficient for prescription, the servient owner has been aware of a specially enhanced or heightened requirement of light for the particular purposes of the dominant owner (see *Allen v Greenwood*, supra at 132D–F, 136A–B).
4   *Higgins v Betts* [1905] 2 Ch 210 at 215 per Farwell J. See also *Carr-Saunders v Dick McNeil Associates Ltd* [1986] 1 WLR 922 at 928F.

Fluctuations in user

8.105   The dominant owner is not entitled to impose an increased burden on the servient tenement merely by altering either the user of his building[1] or the position or size of his windows.[2] However, an easement of light acquired under the Prescription Act 1832[3] relates to the building as a whole and not to any particular room within it.[4] The extent of the dominant owner's right is neither increased nor diminished by the actual use to which the dominant tenement has been put in the past[5] or by any extraordinary use to which he now chooses to put the premises or any of the rooms in them.[6] The court must take account not only of present use, but also of 'other potential uses to which the dominant owner may reasonably be expected to put the premises in the future.'[7] In *Carr-Saunders v Dick McNeil Associates Ltd*,[8] for instance, it was not fatal to the dominant owner's allegation of obstruction that he had, during the prescription period, altered his premises by subdividing one large room into a number of smaller rooms. The windows had remained unchanged, even though the rooms behind them had not, and the dominant owner was therefore entitled to damages in respect of the elevation of an adjacent building which had recently obstructed the access of reasonable light to the reconstructed rooms.[9]

1   *Colls v Home and Colonial Stores Ltd* [1904] AC 179 at 203.
2   *Smith v Evangelization Society (Incorporated) Trust* [1933] Ch 515 at 533–541; *Scott v Goulding Properties Ltd* [1973] IR 200 at 219–221.
3   **[Para 8.194]**.
4   *Colls v Home and Colonial Stores Ltd* [1904] AC 179 at 204; *Price v Hilditch* [1930] 1 Ch 500 at 508; *Carr-Saunders v Dick McNeil Associates Ltd* [1986] 1 WLR 922 at 928D.
5   *Price v Hilditch* [1930] 1 Ch 500 at 506–508; *Carr-Saunders v Dick McNeil Associates Ltd* [1986] 1 WLR 922 at 928F–G.
6   *Carr-Saunders v Dick McNeil Associates Ltd* [1986] 1 WLR 922 at 928G.
7   *Carr-Saunders v Dick McNeil Associates Ltd* [1986] 1 WLR 922 at 928H. See also *Moore v Hall* (1878) 3 QBD 178 at 182.
8   [1986] 1 WLR 922 at 929F–930F.
9   It used to be said that where a building enjoying ancient lights was demolished and replaced by a new building, the ancient lights would be preserved only if the windows in the new building were in the same place and of the same number and dimensions as those in the old building (see *Cherrington v Abney Mil'* (1709) 2 Vern 646, 23 ER 1022). Compare, however, *Andrews v Waite* [1907] 2 Ch 500 at 510, where Neville J indicated that 'the real test ... is identity of light, and not identity of aperture, or entrance for the light'.

Actionable interference

8.106   The courts are nowadays disinclined to adopt inflexible methods of quantifying the degree of obstruction with light which gives rise to an actionable nuisance. There is no longer any '45 degrees rule',[1] and in *Carr-Saunders v Dick McNeil Associates Ltd*[2] Millett J resisted any rigid application of the '50–50 rule', under which an interference with light is actionable only where more than 50 per cent of the floor area of a room receives one lumen of light at table level. He took the view that the dominant owner is simply entitled to such access of light 'as will leave his premises adequately lit for all ordinary purposes for which they may reasonably be expected to be used.'[3]

1   *Colls v Home and Colonial Stores Ltd* [1904] AC 179 at 210; *Fishenden v Higgs & Hill Ltd* (1935) 153 LT 128 at 131–132, 136–137, 143–144. This rule operated against obstructions which rose above a line extended upwards from a room at a 45 degree angle out through the centre of a window.
2   [1986] 1 WLR 922 at 927B–C.
3   [1986] 1 WLR 922 at 928G–H. In appropriate cases of severe loss of light, the obstruction (even if constructed with planning permission) may be the subject of an injunction ordering its removal (see e g *Deakins v Hookings* [1994] 1 EGLR 190 at 195E–H).

CREATION OF EASEMENTS AND PROFITS À *PRENDRE*

8.107   Easements and profits *à prendre* are created in a variety of ways. Creation may be by way of either grant or reservation[1]; and the duration of the rights created can extend in perpetuity or for a fixed term or, indeed, for any other period of time.[2] Creation may be express,[3] implied[4] or – in some cases – presumed from long user.[5] The precise modalities of creation determine whether the rights created are legal or equitable in quality.

1   [Paras 8.108–8.109].
2   [Para 8.112].
3   [Paras 8.110, 8.198].
4   [Paras 8.128–8.166].
5   [Paras 8.168–8.196].

Grant

8.108   The difference between grant and reservation turns on the identity of the party in whose favour the easement or profit is created. Grant occurs where a landowner, A, creates in favour of B an easement or profit over land held by A.[1] Consistently with the prohibition of easements in gross,[2] B must, in the case of a grant of easement, hold some dominant land capable of deriving benefit. Although it is open to A, as landowner, to grant away easements or profits over his land at any time, the grant of easements usually occurs on a severance or subdivision of A's land, B (the transferee of a part of the land) taking the benefit of the rights granted. It is normally at this point that the minds of the parties are most clearly directed towards a consideration of their future needs in relation to their respective parcels of land.

1   [Paras 8.111, 8.120].
2   [Para 8.26].

Reservation

8.109   Reservation arises where a landowner, A, disposes of part of his land to B on terms that A shall nevertheless retain an easement or profit over the land transferred to B.[1] Here the easement or profit concerned is one created in favour of A, the transferor of the land.

1   [Para 8.197].

EXPRESS CREATION OF EASEMENTS AND PROFITS À *PRENDRE* AT LAW

8.110   An easement or a profit *à prendre* can be created at law only if certain cumulative conditions are fulfilled.

Creation out of a legal estate

8.111   Since easements and profits are 'carved out of a larger estate or interest',[1] a legal easement or profit must be created out of a legal estate in the servient land (ie a legal fee simple or a legal term of years). Any right granted out of a merely equitable estate can itself be *equitable* only.[2]

1   *Willies-Williams v National Trust* (1993) 65 P & CR 359 at 361 per Hoffmann LJ.
2   See D G Barnsley, (1999) 115 LQR 89 at 97, 102.

Duration of entitlement

8.112   It is a necessary, but not sufficient, condition of legal quality that an easement or profit *à prendre* must conform to certain statutorily defined requirements of duration. The legal easement or profit must be framed on the analogy of either a freehold or a leasehold estate and, accordingly, must be created 'for an interest equivalent to an estate in fee simple absolute in possession or a term of years absolute.'[1] Legal quality therefore attaches, at least potentially, to rights which are granted or reserved without limit of time or for a fixed period, but rights created for an indeterminate period other than in perpetuity (eg an easement for life or an easement pending the construction of an alternative access) can take effect only in equity.[2]

1   LPA 1925, s 1(2)(a); LRA 2002, s 27(4), Sch 2, paras 6(3), 7(1)(a). Reference may therefore be made, for instance, to a 'right of way in fee simple' (*Singh v Sandhu* (Unreported, Court of Appeal, 4 May 1995) per Balcombe LJ) and a 'tenancy of an easement' (*Cardwell v Walker* [2004] 2 P & CR 122 at [44] per Neuberger J).
2   LPA 1925, s 1(3).

Mode of creation

8.113   Unless arising by statute,[1] implication[2] or prescription,[3] all legal easements and legal profits *à prendre* must be created by deed.[4] There is no exception to this principle even in the case of an easement or profit which is granted for a period of three years or less,[5] there being no parallel with the rules concerning the informal creation of legal leases.[6]

1   [**Para 8.126**].
2   [**Paras 8.128–8.166**].
3   [**Paras 8.168–8.196**].
4   See LPA 1925, s 52(1) [**para 7.26**]. See *Carroll v Manek and Bank of India* (2000) 79 P & CR 173 at 190.

5 See e g *Mason v Clarke* [1954] 1 QB 460 at 468 per Denning LJ, 471 per Romer LJ, [1955] AC 778 at 794, 798 (oral one-year lease of rabbiting rights denied effect as legal profit). See also *Hewlins v Shippam* (1826) 5 B & C 221 at 229–230, 108 ER 82 at 86; *Wood v Leadbitter* (1845) 13 M & W 838 at 843, 153 ER 351 at 354; *Bayley v Marquis Conyngham* (1863) 15 ICLR 406 at 411–412 per Monahan CJ, 415, 418–419 per Christian J.

6 The curious consequence emerges that even though the oral grantee of a short lease takes a legal term of years, his access over his landlord's retained land may be unenforceable both at law and in equity **[para 9.91]**, unless supported by necessity **[para 8.130]** or by the rule in *Wheeldon v Burrows* **[para 8.142]**.

8.114 In the context of an easement or profit carved out of an unregistered estate, formal creation by deed is sufficient to establish the legal quality of the right, provided that the entitlement in question is inherently capable of subsisting at law. However, the mere use of a deed does not confer legal character on any right which was not created for one or other of the statutorily defined time scales. Thus, for instance, an easement for life,[1] even if granted by deed, can give rise to no more than an equitable easement.[2]

1 **[Para 9.90]**.
2 LPA 1925, s 1(3).

Registration

8.115 Consistently with the modern drive towards comprehensive registration of land rights, the Land Registration Act 2002 makes it possible – and in many cases compulsory – for the grantee of an easement or profit *à prendre* to register title to his estate in the incorporeal hereditament.

Voluntary registration of certain profits

8.116 The grantee of a profit *à prendre* in gross[1] over unregistered land is entitled to apply for voluntary first registration of title to his profit under a unique title number at Land Registry,[2] provided that the profit was granted in perpetuity or for a term which still has more than seven years left to run.[3] In this way the grantee can opt to appear on the Land Register as the substantively registered proprietor of a legal estate in the relevant profit.

1 **[Para 8.20]**.
2 LRR 2003, r 2(2)(b).
3 LRA 2002, s 3(1)(d), (2)–(3) **[para 2.149]**. See Law Com No 271 (2001), para 3.20.

Mandatory completion by registration

8.117 The express creation of an easement or a profit *à prendre* out of a registered estate ranks as a 'disposition' of that estate and, in order to 'operate at law', requires to be 'completed' by registration at Land Registry.[1] Non-compliance with the relevant 'registration requirements' relegates the easement or profit to merely equitable status and also ensures that it can never 'override' further registered dealings with the land.[2]

1   LRA 2002, s 27(1), (2)(d) **[para 7.50]**. For present purposes, an 'express' grant does not include any grant resulting from the operation of LPA 1925, s 62 **[para 8.153]** (see LRA 2002, s 27(7)). An exception is also made for rights registrable under the Commons Registration Act 1965.
2   See LRA 2002, s 29(1), (2)(a)(ii), Sch 3, para 3(1) **[para 12.238]**.

Profits à prendre in gross

8.118   The disponee of a profit *à prendre* in gross created out of registered land is required, as a precondition of taking a legal estate in the profit, to complete the disposition by applying to be entered under a unique title number in the Land Register as proprietor of the profit.[1] The holder of the profit thus acquires an independently registered title to his profit,[2] but only where the profit was created without limit of time or for a term of more than seven years. In order to take effect at law, the profit must also be entered by 'notice' in the register of title of the land over which it is exercisable.[3]

1   LRA 2002, Sch 2, para 6(1)–(2)(a) **[para 2.144]**.
2   See LRR 2003, r 2(2)(b).
3   LRA 2002, s 38, Sch 2, para 6(2)(b).

Easements and all other profits à prendre

8.119   The express creation of legal easements and other legal profits (ie appurtenant profits) out of registered land must be completed by the entry of a 'notice' in respect of the relevant burden in the registered title of the *servient* owner[1] and by the registration of the correlative benefit in the register of title (if any) of the *dominant* owner.[2] The dominant owner thus becomes, by non-substantive registration, the proprietor of a registered 'legal estate'[3] in the particular easement or profit.[4]

1   LRA 2002, s 38, Sch 2, para 7(2)(a); LRR 2003, r 9(a).
2   LRA 2002, ss 27(2)(d), 59(1), Sch 2, para 7(2)(b); LRR 2003, r 5(b)(ii) **[para 2.153]**. The benefit of a legal easement or non-appurtenant legal profit expressly created out of an unregistered estate in favour of already registered dominant tenement may, on a showing of satisfactory evidence, be registered as appurtenant to the dominant proprietor's registered estate (LRA 2002, s 13(a); LRR 2003, r 73(1)).
3   The quality of the dominant owner's title to the easement or profit (as absolute, possessory or qualified) generally follows the quality of the substantively registered dominant estate.
4   In leasehold land no separate entries are necessary in respect of easements granted by the lease itself, since the lease is incorporated by reference into the property register of the dominant land and is noted in the charges register of the servient land.

EXPRESS GRANT OF EASEMENTS AND PROFITS À PRENDRE

8.120   The express grant of a legal easement or profit *à prendre* may emerge in three categories of case – by means of express words of grant, by perfection of an equity of estoppel and by virtue of statute.

Express words of grant

8.121 Express words constitute the most common form of grant of easements and profits *à prendre*.

Easements

8.122 A grant of an easement by express words is normally incorporated in a transfer of a freehold estate or a grant of a leasehold estate where it is intended that the new estate owner and his successors in title should enjoy certain enduring rights over the land retained by the transferor or lessor. For example, the builder of a housing development almost invariably grants the purchaser of each individual plot certain rights of way, rights of drainage and other rights to the supply of mains services. The grant being contained in a deed of transfer or lease (subsequently registered where necessary), the easements so created are legal. There is no requirement at common law that the grant should make any explicit reference to the dominant tenement or in any other way identify the land benefited by the easement.[1] Where an easement is granted in favour of registered land, identification of the dominant tenement is implicit in the entry of the benefit of the easement as appurtenant to the registered estate.[2] It is a further statutory 'registration requirement' that the burden of any legal easement created out of registered land be entered in the register by a 'notice' which sufficiently identifies the servient estate or affected portion thereof.[3]

1 The court simply examines all the relevant circumstances in order to determine whether there was in fact a dominant tenement benefited by the supposed easement (see *Johnstone v Holdway* [1963] 1 QB 601 at 612; *The Shannon Ltd v Venner Ltd* [1965] Ch 682 at 693G–694A; *Gas & Fuel Corpn of Victoria v Barba* [1976] VR 755 at 764).
2 **[Para 8.119]**.
3 LRR 2003, r 84(2) **[para 8.119]**. Other jurisdictions apply even stricter identification rules. In New South Wales no easement is enforceable against a third party unless the instrument which created the interest clearly indicates both the land to which the benefit is appurtenant and the land which is subject to the burden of the easement (Conveyancing Act 1919, s 88(1)). See *Maurice Toltz Pty Ltd v Macy's Emporium Pty Ltd* (1969) 91 WN (NSW) 591 at 599D–F; *Papadopoulos v Goodwin* [1982] 1 NSWLR 413 at 417B–418E.

Profits à prendre

8.123 An expressly conferred profit *à prendre* is usually granted in conjunction with a licence to enter the servient land,[1] in which case the licence is an incident of the grant of profit and is irrevocable during the term of the profit.[2]

1 Thus, for instance, a grant of fishing rights in a river implies, at common law, a right of access to the river banks, such access to be exercised in a manner which is 'as little detrimental to the riparian owners as is consistent with the full beneficial use of the right of fishing' (*Gannon v Walsh* [1998] 1 IR 245 at 275 per Keane J). See also *Middletweed Ltd v Murray* 1989 SLT 11 at 14K–L.
2 **[Paras 4.94, 8.19]**.

Duration of grant

8.124   The grant of an easement or profit without words of limitation confers the most ample interest which the grantor is competent to confer, unless a contrary intention is apparent.[1] Thus an easement granted expressly in a transfer of the grantor's fee simple estate is effective to grant an easement for an interest equivalent to a fee simple. An easement which is expressly granted in a lease is an easement whose duration is the term of years created by the lease.[2]

1   **[Para 8.53]**. See *Reid v Moreland Timber Co Pty Ltd* (1946) 73 CLR 1 at 13 per Dixon J; *Gannon v Walsh* [1998] 1 IR 245 at 275–276.
2   **[Para 8.112]**.

Estoppel

8.125   The doctrine of proprietary estoppel[1] provides what is really a subset of the category of express grant of easements and profits. If relied upon to the grantee's detriment, an express grant of rights by informal means (ie otherwise than by deed) may sometimes generate an equity of estoppel which a court may perfect by declaring that the intended grantee takes an easement or profit.[2]

1   **[Para 10.168]**.
2   See e g *Crabb v Arun DC* [1976] Ch 179 at 190A, 192D, 199F **[paras 9.95, 10.198]**. For the effect on easements of 'feeding' the estoppel', see **[para 8.53]**.

Statutory easements

8.126   Easements and profits may be granted expressly by or pursuant to statute. Particularly in the case of easements, such grants are often made in favour of various public or privatised service utilities which provide and maintain supplies of gas, electricity and water.[1] These easements are usually an exception to the general principle which requires that an easement must accommodate a specific dominant tenement.[2]

1   See *Canadian Pacific Ltd v Paul* (1989) 53 DLR (4th) 487 at 498–501 (Supreme Court of Canada).
2   **[Para 8.33]**.

8.127   Various statutory undertakers are also indirectly empowered by statute to compel the creation of easements or wayleaves for the supply of vital commodities. For example, an electricity undertaker may apply to the Secretary of State for Trade and Industry for the compulsory grant, on payment of compensation to the landowner affected, of the right to install an electricity line in or over land.[1] In England, however, the courts have no general power – as do courts in Australia[2] and Canada[3] – to impose, on behalf of private parties, easements which are 'reasonably necessary for the effective use or development' of a proposed dominant tenement.[4]

1   Electricity Act 1989, Sch 4, para 6(1)–(3). See e g *R v Secretary of State for Trade and Industry*

and Northern Electric Plc, ex p Wolf (2000) 79 P & CR 299 at 302–304 (power lines over garden). See also *Wheeler v J J Saunders Ltd* [1996] Ch 19 at 38B–C.

2   Conveyancing Act 1919 (New South Wales), s 88K(1); Property Law Act 1974 (Queensland), s 180(1). See eg *Ex parte Edward Street Properties Pty Ltd* [1977] Qd R 86; *117 York Street Pty Ltd v Proprietors of Strata Plan No 16123* (1998) 43 NSWLR 504; *Marshall v City of Wollongong* (2000) 10 BPR 18163. See also H Tarlo, (1979) 53 ALJ 254.

3   Property Law Act (British Columbia) (RSBC 1979, c 340), s 32. See *Re Ferguson and Lepine* (1982) 128 DLR (3d) 188.

4   The court must be satisfied that use of the land in accordance with the easement 'will not be inconsistent with the public interest' (Conveyancing Act 1919 (New South Wales), s 88K(2)(a); Property Law Act 1974 (Queensland), s 180(3)(a)); and compensation must be paid to the involuntary servient owner (see eg *Wengarin Pty Ltd v Byron SC* (1999) 9 BPR 16985 at 16988–16989).

IMPLIED GRANT OF EASEMENTS AND PROFITS À *PRENDRE*

8.128   There are certain circumstances in which, in the absence of express conferment, the grant of an easement (or, much more rarely, a profit *à prendre*) can be *implied* or *inferred* in favour of the purchaser of land.[1] Since the grant in all such instances is deemed to derive from a deed of transfer,[2] the rights granted are inevitably legal in quality[3] and are therefore (in the case of unregistered land) automatically enforceable against successors in title of the servient land[4] and (in registered land) will 'override' subsequent dispositions of the servient estate.[5]

1   Implied grant cannot occur, however, except where an express grant would have been possible (see *MRA Engineering Ltd v Trimster Co Ltd* (1988) 56 P & CR 1 at 5, 7; *Re St Clement's, Leigh-on-Sea* [1988] 1 WLR 720 at 728E–H).
2   See *R (Beresford) v Sunderland CC* [2004] 1 AC 889 at [36] per Lord Scott of Foscote.
3   [Para 8.113].
4   [Para 12.274].
5   [Paras 2.171, 12.237].

8.129   The categories of implied grant often overlap, but generally give expression, in slightly differing ways, to the ancient principle that a grantor 'may not derogate from his grant' (ie he must not transfer land to another on terms which effectively negative the utility of the transfer).[1] The cases of implied grant relate principally to easements, but cannot convert into an easement any user which is intrinsically incapable of subsisting as an easement under the *Ellenborough Park* criteria.[2] Cases of implied grant fall into four categories.

1   *Aldridge v Wright* [1929] 2 KB 117 at 130 per Greer LJ. See *Birmingham, Dudley and District Banking Co v Ross* (1888) 38 Ch D 295 at 313 per Bowen LJ ('a grantor having given a thing with one hand is not to take away the means of enjoying it with the other').
2   [Para 8.24]. See *P & S Platt Ltd v Crouch* [2004] 1 P & CR 242 at [43] per Peter Gibson LJ.

EASEMENTS OF NECESSITY

8.130   It is open to the courts to imply the grant of an easement on grounds of necessity where a claimant can establish that, without the provision of the desired easement, it becomes impossible to make use of his own tenement.[1]

1   See P Jackson, (1981) 34 CLP 113; P G Glenn, 58 North Carolina L Rev 223 (1979–80).

Instances of necessity

8.131   The classic case of necessity is provided by the 'landlocked close'.[1] If V transfers land to P which has no legally enforceable means of access except across land retained by V, it is clear that the courts will imply in favour of P an easement of access even though the transfer to P made no express reference to such a right.[2] This implication of rights plainly emanates from the principle against derogation from grant.[3] It is for V to select the particular route of access,[4] but once nominated this route cannot later be varied without agreement.[5] Necessity may also generate an implied obligation of support between adjoining terraced or semi-detached houses.[6] It is likewise possible that an implied easement arises at common law where V transfers to P a house one of whose external walls is sited on the common boundary with V's retained land. Here it is arguable that P acquires by necessity a right to enter upon V's land in order to repair or maintain his own boundary wall,[7] although the implication of this right may now be less pressing in consequence of the Access to Neighbouring Land Act 1992.[8]

1   See D A Stroud, (1940) 56 LQR 93; A J Bradbrook, (1983) 10 Sydney L Rev 39.
2   *Clark v Cogge* (1607) 2 Roll Abr 60, pl 17, Cro Jac 170, 79 ER 149; *Pomfret v Ricroft* (1669) 1 Wms Saund 321 at 323, 85 ER 454 at 460 (n 6); *Pinnington v Galland* (1853) 9 Exch 1 at 12–13, 156 ER 1 at 6; *Pearson v Spencer* (1861) 1 B & S 571 at 584, 121 ER 827 at 831; *Gayford v Moffatt* (1868) 4 Ch App 133 at 135; *B & W Investments Ltd v Ulster Scottish Friendly Society* (1969) 20 NILQ 325.
3   See *Bolton v Bolton* (1879) 11 Ch D 968 at 971–972. As Cotton LJ observed in *Birmingham, Dudley and District Banking Co v Ross* (1888) 38 Ch D 295 at 306, 'when a man grants a house, he grants that which is necessary for the existence of that house.' See also *Parish v Kelly* (1980) 1 BPR 9394 at 9400.
4   *Clark v Cogge* (1607) 2 Roll Abr 60, pl 17, Cro Jac 170, 79 ER 149; *Bolton v Bolton* (1879) 11 Ch D 968 at 971; *Deacon v South-Eastern Railway Co* (1889) 61 LT 377 at 379; *Brown v Alabaster* (1887) 37 Ch D 490 at 500; *Barba v Gas & Fuel Corpn of Victoria* (1976) 136 CLR 120 at 132. The route selected must, however, be convenient (see *Pearson v Spencer* (1861) 1 B & S 571 at 585, 121 ER 827 at 832). If the servient owner fails to point out the way, the grantee must take the nearest way possible (see *Wimbledon and Putney Commons Conservators v Dixon* (1875) 1 Ch D 362 at 369–370). There is Australian authority that in default of a selection of way by the servient owner, the dominant owner has a right of selection (*Sunset Properties Pty Ltd v Johnston* (1975) 3 BPR 9185 at 9188).
5   *Pearson v Spencer* (1861) 1 B & S 571 at 584, 121 ER 827 at 832; *Deacon v South-Eastern Railway Co* (1889) 61 LT 377 at 379.
6   See *Williams v Usherwood* (1983) 45 P & CR 235 at 254. It is also likely that in these circumstances an implied obligation of support can be founded on the rule in *Wheeldon v Burrows*. See e g *Scouton & Co (Builders) Ltd v Gilyott & Scott Ltd* (1972) 221 EG 1499; *Kebewar Pty Ltd v Harkin* (1987) 9 NSWLR 738 at 741B–742A.
7   *Auerbach v Beck* (1985) 6 NSWLR 424 at 444D–E (affd sub nom *Beck v Auerbach* (1986) 6 NSWLR 454).
8   [**Para 8.135**].

Criterion of necessity

8.132 The criterion of 'necessity' has been extremely strictly construed in English law[1] and is, on this ground, vulnerable to criticism.[2] No necessity arises on a mere showing that a particular access or facility would be convenient or even 'reasonably necessary' for the proper enjoyment of the alleged dominant tenement,[3] although an easement based on such grounds is perhaps more easily implied under the head of 'common intention'.[4] The claimant must establish that, without the provision of the desired access or other easement, his tenement cannot be used at all.[5] It is not fatal to a claim to a way of necessity that some of the surrounding land belongs to third parties and not to the transferor[6] or that there exist alternative ways open to the landlocked owner by way of precarious user.[7] It is vital, however, that the necessity pleaded by the transferee (or by his successor) should have existed at the date of transfer of the land and not be merely a form of necessity which arose after that date.[8]

1 Compare the less exacting standard applied in Australia, where it is sufficient to show that, without an implied easement, there would be 'a substantial degree of practical difficulty of access' (*Tarrant v Zandstra* (1973) 1 BPR 9381 at 9386). See also *Torrisi v Magame Pty Ltd* [1984] 1 NSWLR 14 at 22E–G; *Lamos Pty Ltd v Hutchison* (1984) 3 BPR 9350 at 9354–9355. Even in Australia, however, a claim based on the mere reasonableness of the required access is not enough (*Parish v Kelly* (1980) 1 BPR 9394 at 9401).
2 The law relating to ways of necessity has been described as 'in some respects archaic' and as needing reformulation to meet 'modern circumstances' (see *MRA Engineering Ltd v Trimster Co Ltd* (1988) 56 P & CR 1 at 5 per Dillon LJ).
3 Compare New Zealand's Property Law Act 1952, s 129B, which vests a more general power in the courts to make an order on behalf of a landlocked owner granting access through the land of neighbours with compensation to the latter. Land is 'landlocked' if 'there is no reasonable access to it' as defined in Property Law Act 1952, s 129B(1)(c). See *Jacobsen Holdings Ltd v Drexel* [1987] 2 NZLR 52; *Cleveland v Roberts* [1993] 2 NZLR 17 at 23–24; *Brankin v MacLean* [2003] 2 NZLR 687. An area is not, for this purpose, 'landlocked' if it enjoys reasonable access by sea (see *Kingfish Lodge (1993) Ltd v Archer* [2000] 3 NZLR 364 at [36]).
4 **[Para 8.140]**. See e g *Stafford v Lee* (1992) 65 P & CR 172 at 176.
5 See *Union Lighterage Co v London Graving Dock Co* [1902] 2 Ch 557 at 573; *MRA Engineering Ltd v Trimster Co Ltd* (1988) 56 P & CR 1 at 6. Compare, however, *Morris v Edgington* (1810) 3 Taunt 24 at 31, 128 ER 10 at 13 per Mansfield CJ. For indications that a variable threshold of 'necessity' may apply in circumstances of emergency or special need, see *St Edmundsbury and Ipswich Diocesan Board of Finance v Clark* (No 2) [1975] 1 WLR 468 at 481D; [1989] Conv 355 (J E M).
6 *Serff v Acton Local Board* (1886) 31 Ch D 679 at 683–684; *Barkshire v Grubb* (1881) 18 Ch D 616 at 620.
7 See *Barry v Hasseldine* [1952] Ch 835 at 839. The availability of an alternative route enjoyable as of right is, of course, destructive of any claim of necessity, even though that alternative is inconvenient (see *Titchmarsh v Royston Water Co Ltd* (1899) 81 LT 673 at 675; *Manjang v Drammeh* (1990) 61 P & CR 194 at 197 per Lord Oliver of Aylmerton).
8 *Holmes v Goring* (1824) 2 Bing 76 at 84, 130 ER 233 at 237; *Corpn of London v Riggs* (1880) 13 Ch D 798 at 806–808. See also *BOJ Properties Ltd v Allen's Mobile Home Park Ltd* (1980) 108 DLR (3d) 305 at 312–314; *Parish v Kelly* (1980) 1 BPR 9394 at 9400; *Torrisi v Magame Pty Ltd* [1984] 1 NSWLR 14 at 22E–G.

Extent of the implied right

8.133   There is some authority that an easement of necessity confers only a right to pass and re-pass along the route of access to a landlocked dominant tenement.[1] This minimalist approach[2] derives force from a natural prejudice against the 'man who does not take the trouble to secure an actual grant of a right-of-way.'[3] Thus, for example, the dominant owner of a way of necessity cannot plead similar grounds of need in support of such ancillary easements as those relating to drainage, sewerage and the supply of electricity.[4] It is highly likely, however, that in modern conditions an implied grant of these auxiliary rights would be supportable on a principle of non-derogation from grant.[5]

1   There can be no easement of necessity in respect of access to light, since land is not rendered useless without such access (see *Ray v Hazeldine* [1904] 2 Ch 17 at 20–21; [1989] Conv 355 at 356 (J E M)).
2   See *Parish v Kelly* (1980) 1 BPR 9394 at 9400 per Rath J.
3   *London Corpn v Riggs* (1880) 13 Ch D 798 at 807 per Jessel MR.
4   See e g *Pryce v McGuinness* [1966] Qd R 591 at 607–608. See also *Union Lighterage Co v London Graving Dock Co* [1902] 2 Ch 557 at 573.
5   See *Auerbach v Beck* (1985) 6 NSWLR 424 at 444D–445B (affd sub nom *Beck v Auerbach* (1986) 6 NSWLR 454).

An overriding rule of public policy?

8.134   It has sometimes been suggested that implied easements of necessity rest ultimately on some freestanding rule of public policy which favours the efficient use of land resources.[1] At first instance in *Nickerson v Barraclough*[2] Megarry V-C thought that 'no transaction should, without good reason, be treated as being effectual to deprive any land of a suitable means of access.'[3] Megarry V-C thus saw no good reason to deprive the land in the present case of access to the highway, even though the terms of the relevant conveyance had seemed expressly to negative any right of way in favour of the transferee.[4] In the Court of Appeal, however, Brightman LJ ruled that 'the doctrine of way of necessity is not founded upon public policy at all but upon an implication from the circumstances.'[5] The Court of Appeal held that a way of necessity can exist only in association with a transfer of land[6] and rests on the implication, drawn from the circumstances of the case, that unless some way is implied a parcel of land will be inaccessible.[7] Considerations of public policy are relevant therefore only to the extent that the courts may *frustrate* a contract where the underlying intention is contrary to public policy.[8]

1   See E H Bodkin, (1973) 89 LQR 87; T A M Cooney, (1979) 14 Ir Jur (NS) 334. See also *Ex parte Edward Street Properties Pty Ltd* [1977] Qd R 86 at 89 per Andrews J.
2   [1980] Ch 325 at 334H–335A. See (1980) 96 LQR 187 (P Jackson).
3   Megarry V-C recognised exceptions to this principle, e g in the case of contaminated land or land designated as a bird sanctuary ([1980] Ch 325 at 334G).
4   In *Nickerson v Barraclough* the original vendor had sold the land as building land and Megarry V-C considered that to deny all means of access would constitute 'a plain instance' of derogation from grant ([1980] Ch 325 at 335B).
5   [1981] Ch 426; (1982) 98 LQR 11 (P Jackson); L Crabb, [1981] Conv 442. See e g *North Sydney*

Printing Pty Ltd v Sabemo Investment Corpn Pty Ltd [1971] 2 NSWLR 150 at 160D–E (cited in *Nickerson v Barraclough* [1981] Ch 426 at 440G).

6   It follows that no way of necessity can be implied on behalf of an owner who acquires title to the alleged dominant tenement by adverse possession (*Wilkes v Greenway* (1890) 6 TLR 449; *North Sydney Printing Pty Ltd v Sabemo Investment Corpn Pty Ltd* [1971] 2 NSWLR 150 at 159C–D). Normally, however, 20 years of uninterrupted user will eventually create a prescriptive right [**para 8.190**].

7   Thus no way of necessity will be implied unless there is evidence from which an intention to create an easement can be inferred at the date of the transfer of the land (see *Margil Pty Ltd v Stegul Pastoral Pty Ltd* [1984] 2 NSWLR 1 at 10B–C; *Auerbach v Beck* (1985) 6 NSWLR 424 at 441E–F).

8   [1981] Ch 426 at 441A.

Access to neighbouring land for the purpose of repair

8.135 In another, rather specific, case of necessity, statute now confers a judicial discretion to create temporary rights in the nature of an easement. English law has never recognised any general rule of access enabling a landowner lawfully to enter neighbouring land without his neighbour's permission in order to carry out necessary works on his own land.[1] In the past this legal hiatus has raised pressing problems where, for instance, a landowner needed to repair part of his property (eg a wall or roof gutter) which immediately abutted on to adjoining land. In the absence of some debatable easement of necessity,[2] there used to be no means of legal challenge to a refusal of access by a disobliging neighbour.[3] Nowadays, however, at least a partial remedy is provided by the Access to Neighbouring Land Act 1992.[4]

1   See eg *John Trenberth Ltd v National Westminster Bank Ltd* (1979) 39 P & CR 104 at 105–106. Such a right may arise as an easement where the two parcels of land were formerly in common ownership (see *Auerbach v Beck* (1985) 6 NSWLR 424 at 444D–E, affd sub nom *Beck v Auerbach* (1986) 6 NSWLR 454).

2   [**Para 8.132**].

3   See *Meriton Apartments Pty Ltd v Baulderstone Hornibrook Pty Ltd* (1992) 9 BPR 17433 at 17435 (no common law right of non-consensual entry).

4   Legislation was recommended in 1985 by the Law Commission (see *Rights of Access to Neighbouring Land* (Law Com No 151, Cmnd 9692, December 1985)).

Scope of the court's power

8.136 The Access to Neighbouring Land Act 1992 creates a novel jurisdiction in the High Court and county court to make an 'access order'[1] on the application of any person who desires to make an unconsented entry upon 'adjoining or adjacent land' for the purpose of 'carrying out works' on the entrant's own land.[2] The court *must* make an access order if satisfied that the works are 'reasonably necessary for the preservation' of the whole or any part of the 'dominant land' and would, absent a right of entry, be at least 'substantially more difficult to carry out.'[3] Equally the court *must not* make an order where to do so would be 'unreasonable',[4] having regard to the degree of interference with, or disturbance of, or hardship caused to, the servient owner.[5]

The statutory right of access is limited to the carrying out of 'basic preservation works', which include maintenance and repair, clearance of drains and sewers, and the care of trees, hedges and shrubs.[6] However, access for the purpose of effecting demolition or of making optional improvements and alterations to the dominant property can be ordered if such works are considered by the court to be 'fair and reasonable in all the circumstances of the case.'[7]

1   This order may be entered by 'notice' in the Land Register pursuant to LRA 2002, ss 32–34 **[para 12.90]** or entered in the register of writs and orders affecting land under LCA 1972, s 6(1) **[para 12.334]**. See ANLA 1992, s 5(1)–(2).
2   ANLA 1992, s 1(1)(a), (2). The definition of land is wide enough to cover a vertically divided party wall which requires repair (see *Dean v Walker* (1997) 73 P & CR 366 at 372).
3   ANLA 1992, s 1(2). An access order may require the payment of compensation for any loss, damage, injury, or 'substantial loss of privacy or other substantial inconvenience' (ANLA 1992, s 2(4)).
4   The legislative scheme is manifestly underpinned by a concept of 'reasonableness between neighbours' **[para 13.122]** (see Gray and Gray, 'The rhetoric of realty', in J Getzler (ed), *Rationalizing Property, Equity and Trusts: Essays in Honour of Edward Burn* (Butterworths 2003), p 260).
5   ANLA 1992, s 1(3).
6   ANLA 1992, s 1(4). Compare, in relation to similar New Zealand legislation, *De Richaumont Investment Co Ltd v OTW Advertising Ltd* [2001] 2 NZLR 831 at [59] (no entry for servicing of billboard).
7   ANLA 1992, s 1(5). Except in the case of residential land, compensation may be payable in respect of the 'likely financial advantage' conferred by the making of the access order (ANLA 1992, s 2(5)(a), (6)).

Limited compulsory acquisition of rights

8.137   The right of access granted by the court under the 1992 Act is not a permanent right, but is intended merely to provide a 'one-off' right appropriate to a particular need.[1] The short-term right of access authorised by the 1992 Act represents only a limited form of compulsory acquisition of user rights.[2] The Act thus effects a purposive and fairly successful compromise between the legitimate privacy interests of the servient owner and the wider public interest in preserving the utility of dominant land and particularly of any housing stock situated thereon.

1   See Law Com No 151 (1985), paras 4.62–4.63.
2   The compulsory acquisition of easements is already available on a more extensive scale in other jurisdictions **[para 8.127]**.

Party wall rights

8.138   Even more dramatically intrusive is the Party Wall etc Act 1996,[1] which confers certain important access rights without the interposition of any court order. The 1996 Act entitles a building owner, subject to the service of a notice and possible payment of compensation for damage, to insert such footings or foundations below the surface of his *neighbour*'s land as are necessary for the construction on his *own* land of a wall immediately inside the boundary line between them.[2] A building owner has similarly conditioned statutory rights to alter, repair or rebuild party structures and even to cut into the wall of an adjoining owner's building for purposes such as weather-proofing.[3] Perhaps most significant, the 1996 Act confirms – subject only to the giving of notice – an extraordinary entitlement for a building owner, his servants, agents, workmen and surveyors, 'during usual working hours [to] enter and remain on any land or premises' for the purpose of executing works in pursuance of the Act.[4]

1 The Party Wall etc Act 1996 extends the localised measures provided by the old London Buildings Acts (see e g London Building (Amendment) Act 1939).
2 PWA 1996, ss 1(4)–(7), 7(2).
3 PWA 1996, s 2(1)–(2).
4 PWA 1996, s 8(1), (5). Furniture and fittings may be removed (PWA 1996, s 8(1)) and, if premises are closed, fences and doors may be broken open for the purpose of entry (PWA 1996, s 8(2)). It is a criminal offence for an occupier to refuse to permit, or to obstruct, the exercise of these statutory rights (PWA 1996, s 16(1)–(2)). Disputes under the Act are remitted to a compulsory process of arbitration by a panel of surveyors, for the cost of which the unwilling adjacent owner may be rendered liable in whole or part (PWA 1996, s 10).

Statutory easement scheme on common land

8.139 The Countryside and Rights of Way Act 2000[1] makes provision for a statutory easement scheme under which certain owners may apply to a neighbouring landowner for the compulsory grant of rights of vehicular access over privately held common land in return for tiered rates of modest compensation proportioned to the age of the premises benefited by the grant. The scheme was aimed at reversing the exorbitant holdout strategies exposed in recent case law,[2] and is intended to 'strike a fair balance' between neighbours in consequence of which, in exchange for the creation of permanent rights over their land, the owners of common land may receive 'reasonable compensation'.[3] Ironically, more recent judicial development of the law of prescriptive acquisition has probably rendered the statutory easement scheme entirely unnecessary. In the light of the House of Lords' ruling in *Bakewell Management Ltd v Brandwood*,[4] it seems that rights of access over common land may be generated by long user without any payment of compensation under the 2000 Act.

1 See Countryside and Rights of Way Act 2000, s 68(1)–(3); Vehicular Access Across Common and Other Land (England) Regulations 2002 (SI 2002/1711), regs 3(1), 11(1)–(3); Vehicular Access Across Common and Other Land (Wales) Regulations 2004 (SI 2004/248).
2 See e g *Newbury DC v Russell* (1997) 95 LGR 705 at 715–716 [**para 4.33**]; *Bakewell Management Ltd v Brandwood* [2004] 2 WLR 955 at [5] per Lord Hope of Craighead (referring to opportunist companies buying up common land).
3 Department for Environment, Food and Rural Affairs, Countryside and Rights of Way Act 2000: A Regulatory Impact Assessment in respect of The Vehicular Access Across Common and Other Land (England) Regulations 2002 (11 May 2002), para 10.
4 [2004] 2 WLR 955.

EASEMENTS OF COMMON INTENTION

8.140   Easements may be implied in favour of the transferee of land in order to give effect to a common intention of transferor and transferee. Such easements may not be essentially different from those implied from necessity, in that a common intention to grant a particular easement will normally be found only in cases of necessity.[1] In *Pwllbach Colliery Co Ltd v Woodman*,[2] Lord Parker of Waddington stated that the law will readily imply the grant of 'such easements as may be necessary to give effect to the common intention of the parties to a grant of real property, with reference to the manner or purposes in and for which the land granted ... is to be used.'[3] Lord Parker added, however, that 'it is essential ... that the parties should intend that the subject of the grant ... should be used in some definite and particular manner.'[4]

1   See e g *Nickerson v Barraclough* [1980] Ch 325 at 336D, where Megarry V-C expressed the view that a 'way of necessity' should be 'more accurately referred to as a way implied from the common intention of the parties, based on a necessity apparent from the deeds'. For the affinity between necessity and common intention, see *Mobil Oil Co Ltd v Birmingham CC* [2002] 2 P & CR 186 at [42]; *BOJ Properties Ltd v Allen's Mobile Home Park Ltd* (1980) 108 DLR (3d) 305 at 315–316; *Auerbach v Beck* (1985) 6 NSWLR 424 at 444A–B.
2   [1915] AC 634 at 646–647.
3   See also *Squarey v Harris-Smith* (1981) 42 P & CR 118 at 127 per Oliver LJ.
4   [1915] AC 634 at 647. The relevant intention need not be express but may be established by implication from the surrounding circumstances. See e g *Stafford v Lee* (1992) 65 P & CR 172 at 176–177 (conveyancing plans provided evidence of shared intention to create easement).

8.141   The principle of implication from common intention was well illustrated in *Wong v Beaumont Property Trust Ltd*.[1] Here the defendant's predecessor in title had leased basement premises to the claimant's predecessor in title for the express purpose of use as a restaurant. The claimant later bought the residue of the lease, intending to use the premises as a Chinese restaurant. He covenanted to comply with public health regulations and to eliminate all noxious smells and odours. In fact, unknown to the parties at the date of the assignment of the lease, these obligations could be performed only by the installation of a new ventilation system leading through the upstairs premises retained by the defendant. The Court of Appeal held that the claimant was entitled to assert an easement for the construction of the ventilation duct which would enable him to comply both with the terms of the lease and with public health regulations.[2]

1   [1965] 1 QB 173. See (1964) 80 LQR 322 (R E M).
2   [1965] 1 QB 173 at 181E, 183E–F. See also *Re The State Electricity Commission of Victoria & Joshua's Contract* [1940] VLR 121 at 125–126 (implied grant of easement to transmit noise).

QUASI-EASEMENTS (THE RULE IN *WHEELDON V BURROWS*)

8.142   A third category of implied grant (relating only to easements[1]) is confirmed in the rule in *Wheeldon v Burrows*.[2] This class of implied easements is wider than that of easements of necessity,[3] and serves as another powerful illustration of the principle that a grantor may not derogate from his grant.[4]

(The presumption against derogation from grant may, however, be ousted by contrary agreement[5] or otherwise excluded by the terms of a grant.[6]) By virtue of its origin in the morality of grant, the rule in *Wheeldon v Burrows* applies only to grants, and not to reservations, of easements.[7]

1　It is generally thought that the rule in *Wheeldon v Burrows* has no application to profits *à prendre*.

2　(1879) 12 Ch D 31. The rule has been applied throughout the common law world (see e g *United States v Thompson*, 272 F Supp 774 at 784–785 (1967); J W Bruce and J W Ely, *The Law of Easements and Licences in Land* (Boston and New York, 1988), pp 4–33 – 4–54).

3　See *Wheeler v J J Saunders Ltd* [1996] Ch 19 at 25C per Staughton LJ.

4　**[Para 8.129]**. See e g *Bayley v Great Western Railway Co* (1884) 26 Ch D 434 at 453; *Aldridge v Wright* [1929] 2 KB 117 at 129–130, 134; *MRA Engineering Ltd v Trimster Co Ltd* (1988) 56 P & CR 1 at 7; *Re St Clement's, Leigh-on-Sea* [1988] 1 WLR 720 at 729A; *Wheeler v J J Saunders Ltd* [1996] Ch 19 at 31B; *Nelson v Walker* (1910) 10 CLR 560 at 582; *Tarrant v Zandstra* (1973) 1 BPR 9381 at 9385 per Mahoney J; *Wilcox v Richardson* (1997) 43 NSWLR 4 at 14B–C per Handley JA.

5　*Borman v Griffith* [1930] 1 Ch 493 at 499; *Squarey v Harris-Smith* (1981) 42 P & CR 118 at 123, 128–129. A contrary intention may, for this purpose, be inferred from the circumstances (*Selby DC v Samuel Smith Old Brewery (Tadcaster)* (2000) 80 P & CR 466 at 474, 478).

6　Rights cannot be implied under *Wheeldon v Burrows* if inconsistent with the words of an express grant or if contrary to the language of a conveyance (*Millman v Ellis* (1996) 71 P & CR 158 at 164–167). See *Wheeler v J J Saunders Ltd* [1996] Ch 19 at 31B–32C (where the implication of a right of access was held to be inconsistent with an express covenant to erect a stockproof boundary fence).

7　*Parish v Kelly* (1980) 1 BPR 9394 at 9399–9400 per Rath J.

Operation of the rule

8.143　The rule in *Wheeldon v Burrows* operates characteristically in the event of a subdivision of land (see *Fig. 11*).

Transfer of the quasi-dominant tenement

8.144　The rule confers on P, the purchaser of a part of V's land, the benefit of any acts of user over the land retained by V, which V (as owner of the whole) had found it reasonably necessary to exercise on his own behalf during the period prior to the subdivision. However, since such user could not strictly have been described as an easement before the transfer to P – for the simple reason that both tenements were then within the common ownership and possession of V[1] – the rights to be impliedly granted under *Wheeldon v Burrows* are usually referred to as 'quasi-easements'. The rule in *Wheeldon v Burrows* operates upon these quasi-easements and converts them, by implied grant, into legal easements in the hands of P.[2] In effect P receives such rights over V's retained land as had previously proved significant for the proper enjoyment and utilisation of the land now transferred to P.[3]

1　**[Para 8.47]**. See also *Roe v Siddons* (1888) 22 QBD 224 at 236 per Fry LJ; *Selby DC v Samuel Smith Old Brewery (Tadcaster)* (2000) 80 P & CR 466 at 471 per Peter Gibson LJ.

2　On severance of ownership the quasi-easement 'is capable of ripening by implication into an easement properly so called in favour ... of the land granted' (*Peckham v Ellison* (2000) 79 P & CR 276 at 295).

3   See *Australian Hi-Fi Publications Pty Ltd v Gehl* [1979] 2 NSWLR 618 at 621B; *Babine Investments Ltd v Prince George Shopping Centre Ltd* (2002) 212 DLR (4th) 537 at [52].

Transfer of both tenements

8.145   If, instead of retaining some land for himself, V on subdivision of his land simultaneously transfers the subdivided tenements to P and Q respectively, each transferee obtains by way of implied grant the same rights over the land of the other as he would have received if that other land had been retained by V.[1]

1   *Swansborough v Coventry* (1832) 9 Bing 305 at 309, 131 ER 629 at 631; *Selby DC v Samuel Smith Old Brewery (Tadcaster)* (2000) 80 P & CR 466 at 473–474, 477–478; *Holaw (470) Ltd v Stockton Estates Ltd* (2001) 81 P & CR 404 at [27]; *Sunset Properties Pty Ltd v Johnston* (1975) 3 BPR 9185 at 9188. This result follows at least if both P and Q were 'aware of the simultaneous conveyances' (see *Aldridge v Wright* [1929] 2 KB 117 at 130).

Practical examples

8.146   The doctrine in *Wheeldon v Burrows* provides a mode of implied grant applicable to rights of way, support, light and drainage,[1] together with many other users 'enjoyed *de facto* during unity of possession [which] would, had that unity not existed, have been easements.'[2] The doctrine frequently catches rights of way, although it is 'perhaps surprising' that so important a right is capable of being granted by mere implication in a modern conveyance.[3] Thus if V, while he occupied the quasi-dominant tenement prior to subdivision of his land, was accustomed to pass and re-pass along a path or driveway over land which he still retains after the subdivision (see *Fig.* 11), this user may now be claimed by P to be annexed, as of right, to what was the quasi-dominant tenement.[4] The rule in *Wheeldon v Burrows* extends far beyond rights of way.[5] Where, for instance, V was originally the common owner of two adjoining houses, the rule may be used to imply a right of support in favour of P on his purchase of one of these houses from V.[6]

1   See e g *Robins v Tupman* [1993] 15 EG 145 (drainage into soakaway).
2   *Nelson v Walker* (1910) 10 CLR 560 at 582 per Isaacs J. See also *Tarrant v Zandstra* (1973) 1 BPR 9381 at 9385.
3   *Wheeler v J J Saunders Ltd* [1996] Ch 19 at 31B per Peter Gibson LJ.
4   See *Bayley v Great Western Railway Co* (1884) 26 Ch D 434 at 452–453; *Borman v Griffith* [1930] 1 Ch 493 at 499; *Holaw (470) Ltd v Stockton Estates Ltd* (2001) 81 P & CR 404 at [26].
5   See *Goldberg v Edwards* [1950] Ch 247 at 254 per Evershed MR.
6   *Scouton & Co (Builders) Ltd v Gilyott & Scott Ltd* (1972) 221 EG 1499. See LPA 1925, s 38. The rule in *Wheeldon v Burrows* also enables a landlord to enforce a repairing obligation undertaken by a tenant even though the landlord has failed to reserve the appropriate right of entry for this purpose in the express terms of the lease (see *Sedgwick Forbes Bland Payne Group Ltd v Regional Properties Ltd* (1981) 257 EG 64 at 68).

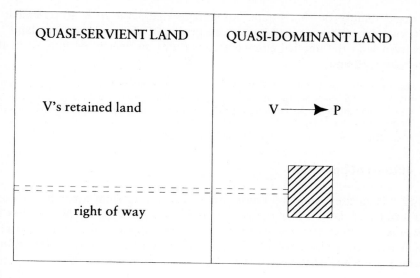

Fig. 11

Dealings which trigger the doctrine

8.147 The operation of the doctrine in *Wheeldon v Burrows* is triggered by a wide range of dealings by the common owner of quasi-dominant and quasi-servient tenements. The rule can apply whether the land is held by freehold or leasehold title.[1] It is therefore irrelevant whether the subdivision of the whole occurs by way of freehold transfer or lease or sublease.[2] The rule is applicable not merely following transfers on sale but also in the context of voluntary transfers and devises.[3] Moreover, the rule operates not only in relation to transactions which take effect at law (eg on the formal transfer of an estate in fee simple or a term of years), but also on dealings which take effect merely in equity (eg on a contract to transfer a fee simple estate[4] or to create or transfer a term of years[5]).[6]

1   See *Aldridge v Wright* [1929] 2 KB 117 at 124–132.
2   See *Wilcox v Richardson* (1997) 43 NSWLR 4 at 14A–B.
3   *Sunset Properties Pty Ltd v Johnston* (1975) 3 BPR 9185 at 9188.
4   **[Para 9.23]**.
5   **[Para 9.91]**.
6   *Borman v Griffith* [1930] 1 Ch 493 at 499. See (1930) 46 LQR 271 (H P); [1932] CLJ 219 (K K L). See also *Horn v Hiscock* (1972) 223 EG 1437 at 1441.

Legal quality of quasi-easements

8.148 An easement which, under the doctrine in *Wheeldon v Burrows*, arises as an implied incident of the formal transfer of a legal estate will itself share the legal quality of that estate.¹ In unregistered land such an easement is therefore enforceable against successors in title of the quasi-servient land. In registered land the implied easement constitutes an overriding interest in the quasi-servient land.²

1   *Tarrant v Zandstra* (1973) 1 BPR 9381 at 9385 per Mahoney J. Where, however, the rule in *Wheeldon v Burrows* is triggered by an uncompleted contract to take a legal estate in quasi-dominant land, the resulting easement can only be equitable (see *Borman v Griffith* [1930] 1 Ch 493 at 499).
2   LRA 2002, s 29(1), (2)(a)(ii), Sch 3, para 3 [**para 12.239**].

Conditions of operation

8.149   There are certain limitations upon the kinds of right which may pass to a transferee of land under the rule in *Wheeldon v Burrows*. The rule has no reference to 'mere personal conveniences',¹ but applies only to those rights which are intrinsically capable of being easements. Furthermore, in *Wheeldon v Burrows*² Thesiger LJ indicated that

> [O]n the grant by the owner of a tenement of part of that tenement as it is then used and enjoyed, there will pass to the grantee all those continuous and apparent easements (by which, of course, I mean *quasi* easements), or, in other words, all those easements which are necessary to the reasonable enjoyment of the property granted, and which have been and are at the time of the grant used by the owners of the entirety for the benefit of the part granted.³

1   *Nelson v Walker* (1910) 10 CLR 560 at 584 per Isaacs J.
2   (1879) 12 Ch D 31 at 49.
3   The *rule* in *Wheeldon v Burrows* is to be distinguished from the *decision* in that case, which concerned implied reservations [**para 8.199**]. A 'helpful translation' of the rule in *Wheeldon v Burrows* can be found in *Borman v Griffith* [1930] 1 Ch 493 at 499 (see *Horn v Hiscock* (1972) 223 EG 1437 at 1441 per Goulding J).

'Continuous and apparent' user

8.150   The requirement of 'continuous and apparent' user¹ does not appear to be applied by the courts with any great strictness.² The requirement has been held to be satisfied by any user which is enjoyed over substantial periods of time³ and which is discoverable or detectable on 'a careful inspection by a person ordinarily conversant with the subject.'⁴ Thus a worn track provides evidence of 'continuous and apparent' user,⁵ as does a 'plainly visible road' which is obviously intended to serve the alleged quasi-dominant tenement.⁶ Likewise 'continuous and apparent' user may be demonstrated by the presence of an underground drain into which water runs from the eaves of a house.⁷

1   It has been suggested that the criterion of 'continuous and apparent' user was borrowed in the 19th century from the analogous concepts of continuous and apparent servitudes in French law. See *Suffield v Brown* (1864) 4 De GJ & Sm 185 at 195, 46 ER 888 at 892; *Dalton v Angus & Co* (1881) 6 App Cas 740 at 821; A W B Simpson, 'The Rule in *Wheeldon v Burrows* and the Code Civile' (1967) 83 LQR 240.

2   The test of 'continuous and apparent' user merges with the requirement of user subsisting at the date of subdivision (see *Kebewar Pty Ltd v Harkin* (1987) 9 NSWLR 738 at 741E–G).

3   'Continuous user' is not necessarily incessant user, but refers to permanent rather than merely temporary user (see Gale, *Law of Easements* (1st edn, London 1839), p 53).

4   *Pyer v Carter* (1857) 1 H & N 916 at 922, 156 ER 1472 at 1475. See also *Scouton & Co (Builders) Ltd v Gilyott & Scott Ltd* (1972) 221 EG 1499.

5   *Hansford v Jago* [1921] 1 Ch 322 at 337–338. It is not necessary that the road be made up so long as it was 'established and visible' at the date of subdivision (*Sunset Properties Pty Ltd v Johnston* (1975) 3 BPR 9185 at 9189). See also *Re St Clement's, Leigh-on-Sea* [1988] 1 WLR 720 at 729B–C.

6   See *Horn v Hiscock* (1972) 223 EG 1437 at 1441 per Goulding J. See also *Millman v Ellis* (1996) 71 P & CR 158 at 162 ('unbroken and undivided area of Tarmac' inferably available for use by 'the occupant of the big house'). See [1995] Conv 346 (J West). Contrast *Robinson Webster (Holdings) Ltd v Agombar* [2002] 1 P & CR 243 at [81] (no evidence of visible track).

7   *Pyer v Carter* (1857) 1 H & N 916 at 922, 156 ER 1472 at 1475. See also *McAdams Homes Ltd v Robinson* [2004] EWCA Civ 214 at [8].

Reasonable necessity

8.151   It has never been entirely clear whether, for the purpose of the rule in *Wheeldon v Burrows*, the conditions of 'reasonable necessity' and 'continuous and apparent' user are alternative or cumulative.[1] The preponderant view in the authorities is that both conditions must be met,[2] but there are influential indications in the modern case law that the requirements are synonymous.[3] In any event the two requirements tend to interact heavily, so that if a particular user is 'reasonably necessary' it will almost always have been the subject of 'continuous and apparent' user.[4] It is also plain that the standard of necessity[5] demanded in the present context is rather less stringent than that applicable to 'easements of necessity',[6] although it would not be enough to assert merely that the claimed user is a convenient adjunct of dominant ownership.[7] The criterion of 'reasonable necessity' may be linked with the need to give 'business efficacy' to the transaction in hand.[8] In so far as there is any requirement to show 'reasonable necessity', it seems probable that this condition can be satisfied even in the presence of another available form of access or facility.[9]

1   The judgment of Thesiger LJ is itself ambiguous, but see (1879) 12 Ch D 31 at 58–59 where he seemed to regard the two requirements as 'discrete classes of case' (*Auerbach v Beck* (1985) 6 NSWLR 424 at 443B per Powell J). See also *Ward v Kirkland* [1967] Ch 194 at 224D–225A. The ambivalence on this issue is not diminished by the observations of Oliver LJ in *Squarey v Harris-Smith* (1981) 42 P & CR 118 at 124. In *Simmons v Dobson* [1991] 1 WLR 720 at 722F, Fox LJ made no reference at all to a requirement of necessity.

2   *Bayley v Great Western Railway Co* (1884) 26 Ch D 434 at 452–453; *Borman v Griffith* [1930] 1 Ch 493 at 499; *Horn v Hiscock* (1972) 223 EG 1437 at 1441; *Millman v Ellis* (1996) 71 P & CR 158 at 162–163; *Robinson Webster (Holdings) Ltd v Agombar* [2002] 1 P & CR 243 at [81]–[82]. See likewise *Israel v Leith* (1890) 20 OR 361 at 367; *Floyd v Heska* (1975) 50 DLR (3d) 161 at 167; *Sunset Properties Pty Ltd v Johnston* (1975) 3 BPR 9185 at 9188; *Margil Pty Ltd v Stegul Pastoral Pty Ltd* [1984] 2 NSWLR 1 at 11B; *Jones v Lockhart* (1989) 60 DLR (4th) 283 at 287–288.

3   *Wheeler v J J Saunders Ltd* [1996] Ch 19 at 31B–D per Peter Gibson LJ ('tolerably clear'). See similarly *Dewsbury v Davies* (Unreported, Court of Appeal, 21 May 1992) per Fox LJ. In

Costagliola v English (1969) 210 EG 1425 at 1431, Megarry J applied the requirement of 'reasonable necessity' in circumstances where there was some doubt as to the continuity of the disputed user.

4   See e g *Auerbach v Beck* (1985) 6 NSWLR 424 at 443A–B, where Powell J was happy to regard 'continuous and apparent' user as the essential and irreducible precondition for a quasi-easement. In *Tarrant v Zandstra* (1973) 1 BPR 9381 at 9384–9385, Mahoney J upheld a quasi-easement on the ground that the user was 'continuous' and would have been 'apparent as "necessary to the reasonable enjoyment"' of the dominant land.

5   The test of 'reasonable necessity' must be judged as of the date of the relevant subdivision (*Sunset Properties Pty Ltd v Johnston* (1975) 3 BPR 9185 at 9188).

6   **[Para 8.132]**. See *Wheeler v J J Saunders Ltd* [1996] Ch 19 at 31D–E per Peter Gibson LJ; *Re Standard and the Conveyancing Act 1919* (1970) 92 WN (NSW) 953 at 956A–B. The claimed user need not be 'essential' (see *Wilcox v Richardson* (1997) 43 NSWLR 4 at 8C–D per Meagher JA, 14F–15C per Handley JA). See similarly *Daar Pty Ltd v Feza Foundation Ltd* (2001) 10 BPR 19099 at [14].

7   *MCA Camilleri Building & Constructions Pty Ltd v H R Walters Pty Ltd* (1981) 2 BPR 9277 at 9281. See e g *Wheeler v J J Saunders Ltd* [1996] Ch 19 at 25E–G. Reasonable necessity may be measured by the demands of road safety (*Millman v Ellis* (1996) 71 P & CR 158 at 163).

8   *Wilcox v Richardson* (1997) 43 NSWLR 4 at 14B–15A per Handley JA (New South Wales Court of Appeal). See *The Moorcock* (1889) 14 PD 64 at 68.

9   See *Goldberg v Edwards* [1950] Ch 247 at 254–255; *Costagliola v English* (1969) 210 EG 1425 at 1431; *Horn v Hiscock* (1972) 223 EG 1437 at 1441; *Millman v Ellis* (1996) 71 P & CR 158 at 163–164; *Jones v Lockhart* (1989) 60 DLR (4th) 283 at 287–288. Compare, however, *Wheeler v J J Saunders Ltd* [1996] Ch 19 at 25F.

User at the date of transfer

8.152   The rule in *Wheeldon v Burrows* catches only those quasi-easements which had been used, and at the time of the relevant transfer were still used,[1] by the owner of the entirety for the benefit[2] of the part now conveyed away. *Wheeldon v Burrows* cannot, for instance, be invoked as the origin of an alleged easement of support for a building on a supposed quasi-dominant tenement if at the date of transfer no building stood on that tenement.[3] A claim will likewise fail unless it can be linked at the relevant date to 'some continuous and apparent feature upon the alleged servient tenement designed, or appropriate, for the exercise of the easement asserted'.[4] In *Costagliola v English*,[5] however, Megarry J did not consider that an 'established means of access' was deprived of status as a quasi-easement merely because it had not been 'actively enjoyed to any great extent' during the 10 or 11 months preceding the relevant conveyance.

1   See *Re St Clement's, Leigh-on-Sea* [1988] 1 WLR 720 at 729B–C; *Commission for New Towns v J J Gallagher Ltd* [2003] 2 P & CR 24 at [70].

2   The requirement that the claimed user should have existed 'for the benefit of' the supposed quasi-dominant tenement cannot be treated lightly. See e g *Dewsbury v Davies* (Unreported, 21 May 1992), where the Court of Appeal refused to apply *Wheeldon v Burrows* to a claim of parking rights.

3   *Kebewar Pty Ltd v Harkin* (1987) 9 NSWLR 738 at 741C–F per McHugh JA.

4   *Auerbach v Beck* (1985) 6 NSWLR 424 at 443B–D (affd sub nom *Beck v Auerbach* (1986) 6 NSWLR 454).

5   (1969) 210 EG 1425 at 1429.

EASEMENTS UNDER LAW OF PROPERTY ACT 1925, S 62

8.153   Another form of implied grant is made possible by the operation of the 'word-saving provision' contained in section 62 of the Law of Property Act 1925.[1] Section 62 contains 'general words' which, in the absence of any contrary intention expressed in the conveyance,[2] imply into any conveyance of a legal estate in land a number of rights thenceforth to be enjoyed by the transferee of that estate.[3] Section 62 passes to the transferee all 'liberties, privileges, easements, rights, and advantages whatsoever, appertaining or reputed to appertain to the land or any part thereof, or, at the time of conveyance, … enjoyed with … the land or any part thereof.'[4] This provision sometimes has the incidental – and perhaps surprising[5] – effect of creating entirely new easements and profits out of many kinds of quasi-easement, right or even merely revocable privilege subsisting at the date of the conveyance.[6] It is quite possible that rights which were not easements properly so called before the conveyance may be translated to the status of easement thereafter.[7]

1   See generally P Jackson, (1966) 30 Conv (NS) 340. Whether section 62 effects an *implied* form of grant is perhaps debatable. It may be more accurate to say that the use of general words, imported by statute, creates new easements and profits 'by way of express grant' (*Auerbach v Beck* (1985) 6 NSWLR 424 at 445F per Powell J). See also *Broomfield v Williams* [1897] 1 Ch 602 at 610; *Goldberg v Edwards* [1950] Ch 247 at 255.

2   LPA 1925, s 62(4). See *William Hill (Southern) Ltd v Cabras Ltd* (1987) 54 P & CR 42 at 46. It has been said more generally that section 62, since it operates by implication, yields to any contrary intention of the parties which is apparent from either their conveyance or their contract (see *Selby DC v Samuel Smith Old Brewery (Tadcaster)* (2000) 80 P & CR 466 at 474 per Peter Gibson LJ, 478–479 per Chadwick LJ).

3   Section 62 includes within a conveyance only intangible rights and privileges over land rather than any tangible or physical land which is not expressly the subject of the conveyance (see *Hanina v Morland* (Unreported, Court of Appeal, 22 November 2000) at [41], [44] per May LJ; *Commission for New Towns v J J Gallagher Ltd* [2003] 2 P & CR 24 at [63]–[65]).

4   LPA 1925, s 62(1) **[para 1.52]**. Section 62(2) provides, in very similar terms, that every conveyance of land which has 'houses or other buildings thereon' is deemed to include all 'cisterns, sewers, gutters, drains, ways, passages, lights, watercourses, liberties, privileges, easements, rights, and advantages' appertaining or reputed to appertain to the land or buildings.

5   *Commission for New Towns v J J Gallagher Ltd* [2003] 2 P & CR 24 at [61] per Neuberger J. See also *Dewsbury v Davies* (Unreported, Court of Appeal, 21 May 1992) per Fox LJ (it 'seems a rather odd result that a section whose purpose was to shorten conveyances should have the effect of turning … a permissive and precarious right into an irrevocable easement').

6   See *Peckham v Ellison* (2000) 79 P & CR 276 at 295 per Cazalet J; *Auerbach v Beck* (1985) 6 NSWLR 424 at 445F.

7   For incisive criticism of the logic underlying this transmutation of rights, see L Tee, 'Metamorphoses and Section 62 of the Law of Property Act 1925' [1998] Conv 115. See also *Hair v Gillman and Inskip* (2000) 80 P & CR 108 at 116, where Chadwick LJ expressed dismay that, under section 62, acts of benevolence may inadvertently create easements which bind land permanently, a consequence which 'may tend to discourage landlords from acts of kindness to their tenants' (see *Wright v Macadam* [1949] 2 KB 744 at 755 per Tucker LJ).

Operation of section 62

8.154   Section 62 operates only where there is common ownership by one person of two parcels of land.[1] The classic application of the provision arises in landlord–tenant relationships. In *International Tea Stores Co v Hobbs*[2] a landlord, L, owned two adjacent plots of land in fee simple, occupying one of them himself and leasing the other to a tenant, T. During the currency of the lease L permitted T, as a matter of grace and favour, to use a means of access to T's premises which ran across the plot occupied by L (see *Fig.* 12). T's user of this access was plainly precarious in the sense that, if he had so wished, L could at any time have revoked T's permission (or bare licence) to use this route. L later conveyed to T the freehold reversion in the previously rented premises. Farwell J held that this conveyance activated the statutory 'general words' provision[3] and vested in T not only a freehold estate in the land purchased but also a right by way of irrevocable easement to continue against L the user which had previously been merely precarious.[4] Moreover, since T's new easement was impliedly incorporated within a conveyance of a legal estate, it was likewise clothed with legal character and was enforceable against any successor in title to L.

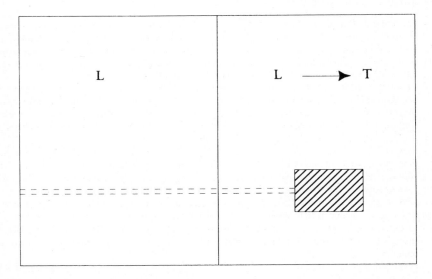

***Fig.* 12**

1   *MRA Engineering Ltd v Trimster Co Ltd* (1988) 56 P & CR 1 at 4–5 per Dillon LJ. Thus section 62 has no application where one fee simple owner, X, enjoys some privilege or licence over land owned by Y, and X then conveys his fee simple to Z (see [1997] Conv 453 at 455 (M P Thompson)).

2   [1903] 2 Ch 165.

3   The relevant provision was, of course, the statutory predecessor of section 62, ie Conveyancing Act 1881, s 6.

4   [1903] 2 Ch 165 at 170–173. See *MRA Engineering Ltd v Trimster Co Ltd* (1988) 56 P & CR 1 at 5. Exactly the same outcome would have followed upon a renewal of T's term of years (see eg *Wright v Macadam* [1949] 2 KB 744 at 747–751; *Goldberg v Edwards* [1950] Ch 247 at 257–259).

8.155   Section 62 thus affords a means by which the conveyance of a further legal estate to a sitting tenant may elevate to the status of a legal easement or profit even some purely precarious user (or 'factual advantage'[1]) enjoyed over the quasi-servient tenement. The provision confers on the transferee of the quasi-dominant land a new right of permanent enjoyment.[2] This result flows literally from the wording of section 62, which implies into a conveyance all such users as previously comprised 'privileges ... rights, and advantages ... appertaining ... to the land.'[3]

1   *Nickerson v Barraclough* [1981] Ch 426 at 446F per Eveleigh LJ. See also *Hair v Gillman and Inskip* (2000) 80 P & CR 108 at 112 per Chadwick LJ ('precarious permission').
2   See *Lewis v Meredith* [1913] 1 Ch 571 at 579; *Wright v Macadam* [1949] 2 KB 744 at 751; *Goldberg v Edwards* [1950] Ch 247 at 255–256; *Stafford v Pearson-Smith* (1962) 182 EG 539 at 541. The same effect would follow a conveyance of a legal estate (whether freehold or leasehold) made in favour of a *licensee* who was already in occupation of the quasi-dominant tenement (see *Commission for New Towns v J J Gallagher Ltd* [2003] 2 P & CR 24 at [63]).
3   See *Commission for New Towns v J J Gallagher Ltd* [2003] 2 P & CR 24 at [61] per Neuberger J.

Comparison with the rule in *Wheeldon v Burrows*

8.156   Although section 62 of the Law of Property Act 1925 is effective to pass many of the rights impliedly available under the rule in *Wheeldon v Burrows*, the statutory provision enjoys, in many respects, a rather wider significance than its common law counterpart. The creative impact of section 62 is, effectively, an overlay upon the rule in *Wheeldon v Burrows*[1] and it may be that the common law rule is now largely subsumed within the statute.[2] There is, for instance, no strict requirement that the rights to which section 62 has reference should be 'continuous and apparent'[3] or even 'necessary to the reasonable enjoyment of the land granted.'[4] Section 62 seems, furthermore, to provide a mode of implied grant relevant to profits *à prendre*,[5] which almost certainly are not covered by the rule in *Wheeldon v Burrows*.[6] However, although section 62 appears to have an extremely extensive application, its scope has been cut back by several important restrictions.

1   See *Auerbach v Beck* (1985) 6 NSWLR 424 at 445F per Powell J.
2   The operation of section 62 may, of course, be excluded by express words (LPA 1925, s 62(4) **[para 8.153]**).
3   See *White v Williams* [1922] 1 KB 727 at 740 per Younger LJ.
4   In *Goldberg v Edwards* [1950] Ch 247 at 256, for instance, the Court of Appeal held that section 62 could apply to a way of access through a landlord's house which was clearly not necessary for the tenant in view of the latter's separate means of access to the demised premises. See (1950) 66 LQR 302 (R E M). See also *Baron Hamilton v Edgar* (1953) 162 EG 568 at 569; *Ward v Kirkland* [1967] Ch 194 at 229G.
5   *White v Williams* [1922] 1 KB 727 at 737–741.
6   **[Para 8.142]**. See, however, *Auerbach v Beck* (1985) 6 NSWLR 424 at 445F per Powell J.

Section 62 operates only on a conveyance of a legal estate

8.157   The most obvious limitation on section 62 is that the 'general words' provision is activated only by a conveyance of a *legal* estate in land.[1] It is

privilege, advantage, easement or quasi-easement, by the owner or occupier of the dominant tenement over the servient tenement.'[1] The section envisages 'something which exists and is seen to be enjoyed either as a specific right in itself, or as an advantage in fact.'[2] Such rights or advantages need not be in the course of actual exercise at the precise moment of the conveyance which allegedly triggers section 62,[3] but there must be evidence of a 'pattern of regular user' during a 'reasonable period of time before the grant in question.'[4] In the elusive context of implied grant there have been two classic ways of demonstrating that rights and advantages appertain or are 'reputed to appertain' to the land or, at the time of conveyance, are 'enjoyed with … the land' so that section 62 can bite.

1   *Payne v Inwood* (1997) 74 P & CR 42 at 47 per Roch LJ. See [1997] Conv 453 (M P Thompson). The importance of actual user at the date of conveyance is heavily stressed in the older authorities (see eg *Broomfield v Williams* [1897] 1 Ch 602 at 615; *Lewis v Meredith* [1913] 1 Ch 571 at 579; *Goldberg v Edwards* [1950] Ch 247 at 256). See *Auerbach v Beck* (1985) 6 NSWLR 424 at 441G.

2   *Nickerson v Barraclough* [1981] Ch 426 at 446E per Eveleigh LJ.

3   The notion of enjoyment is not synonymous with actual user at the date of the conveyance (*Re Yateley Common* [1977] 1 WLR 840 at 850H–851A).

4   *Green v Ashco Horticulturist Ltd* [1966] 1 WLR 889 at 898G per Cross J. Compare *Pretoria Warehousing Ltd Co v Shelton* [1993] EGCS 120 (section 62 relevant to user terminating four months before conveyance) with *Re Broxhead Common, Whitehill, Hampshire* (1977) 33 P & CR 451 at 463–464 (section 62 inapplicable to grazing rights unexercised for previous 21 or 22 years). See also *Penn v Wilkins* (1974) 236 EG 203.

Continuous and apparent user

8.163   Section 62 operates to pass to the transferee of quasi-dominant land any right or factual advantage which was the subject of *continuous* and *apparent* exercise prior to the conveyance.[1] In such cases it is self-evident that the facility or user in question attaches to the quasi-dominant land and is enjoyed with it.[2] Under these circumstances it matters not that, prior to the conveyance, both tenements were within the common occupation of the transferor.[3] The common occupier was doubtless only too well aware that a particular factual user was intrinsic to his enjoyment of the quasi-dominant portion of the land.[4] To this extent section 62 can be said to replicate the function of the rule in *Wheeldon v Burrows*,[5] with the extra liberating factor that there is no statutory requirement that the quasi-easement impliedly granted be 'reasonably necessary' for the enjoyment of the relevant tenement. But, where there has been unity of occupation of both tenements prior to the relevent conveyance, it is fatal to any invocation of section 62 that the user claimed as a matter of implied grant was 'not obvious'.[6]

1   See eg *Broomfield v Williams* [1897] 1 Ch 602 at 610, 615–616, where the Court of Appeal upheld a clearly continuous and apparent quasi-easement of light under section 62 between tenements previously in common ownership and occupation. Easements of light are sometimes considered to be anomalous (see *Sovmots Investments Ltd v Secretary of State for the Environment* [1979] AC 144 at 176C per Lord Edmund-Davies), but this assumption is far from universal (see [1997] Conv 453 at 456–457 (M P Thompson)).

2   Section 62 can operate if there is evidence of user or a physical state of affairs which indicates the existence of a quasi-easement (*Payne v Inwood* (1997) 74 P & CR 42 at 47 per Roch LJ).

3   See eg *Dewsbury v Davies* (Unreported, Court of Appeal, 21 May 1992) per Fox LJ (access way to bus stop used 'a lot').

4   See eg *P & S Platt Ltd v Crouch* [2004] 1 P & CR 242 at [42], [59], where the Court of Appeal held that section 62 was effective, on a transfer of hotel premises on the Norfolk Broads, to pass to the new hotel proprietor certain mooring, fishing and other recreational rights over the transferor's adjacent retained land which had previously been available for hotel patrons. Even in the absence of 'prior diversity of occupation' of the various tenements, these rights were 'continuous and apparent' entitlements which 'appertain[ed] to and were reputed to appertain to and were enjoyed with the hotel.'

5   Section 62 is the statutory successor of Conveyancing Act 1881, s 6, enacted in the immediate aftermath of the enunciation of the rule in *Wheeldon v Burrows* (1879) 12 Ch D 31.

6   See eg *Payne v Inwood* (1997) 74 P & CR 42 at 48 per Roch LJ (albeit that here the unity of ownership and occupation subsisted for a mere seven days immediately preceding the conveyance which was later claimed to activate the 'general words' provision). See also *Robinson Webster (Holdings) Ltd v Agombar* [2002] 1 P & CR 243 at [80].

Prior diversity of occupation

8.164   In the absence of plainly visible factual user preceding the conveyance of the quasi-dominant tenement, section 62 has no application unless there was a diversity of occupation of the quasi-dominant and quasi-servient tenements prior to the conveyance in question.[1] A non-apparent right or privilege cannot pass by statutory implication to a transferee of a quasi-dominant tenement unless there has been 'de facto enjoyment of it by an occupier' who is, quite visibly, not the owner or occupier of the quasi-servient tenement.[2] Thus the element of prior diversity of occupation effectively provides, in itself, the basis for inferring the existence of some right or factual advantage exercisable over the quasi-servient tenement, in that the user now claimed as an easement would otherwise have comprised a sheer act of trespass in relation to that tenement and could never be upgraded by section 62 to the status of an easement by implication.

1   *Sovmots Investments Ltd v Secretary of State for the Environment* [1979] AC 144 at 176C per Lord Edmund-Davies, following *Long v Gowlett* [1923] 2 Ch 177 at 200 per Sargant J. Much controversy has been raised by the precise role of diversity of occupation in applications of section 62 (see C Harpum, (1977) 41 Conv (NS) 415; [1979] Conv 113, [1989] Conv 113; compare P Smith, [1978] Conv 449; [1979] Conv 311).

2   *Auerbach v Beck* (1985) 6 NSWLR 424 at 445D.

8.165   Such diversity of occupation is, of course, precisely what was present in the landlord–tenant situation dealt with in *International Tea Stores Co v Hobbs.*[1] Prior to the conveyance which activated the 'general words' provision in this case the two tenements were occupied by different persons, L and T. Without the element of prior diversity of occupation of two tenements it would have been difficult to point in any meaningful sense to 'rights' or 'liberties' or 'privileges' which might be caught by the operation of section 62.[2] But this requirement of prior diversity of occupation is relevant only where the claimed right or privilege is 'imperceptible or non-apparent, corresponding with inter-mittent and non-apparent user over one of two tenements held in common ownership.'[3]

1   [1903] 2 Ch 165.
2   *Squarey v Harris-Smith* (1981) 42 P & CR 118 at 129 per Oliver LJ. See *Long v Gowlett* [1923] 2 Ch 177 at 200 per Sargant J ('there must be something done on Blackacre ... of such a nature that it is attributable to a privilege, easement, right or advantage, however precarious, which arises out of the ownership or occupation of Whiteacre, altogether apart from the ownership or occupation of Blackacre').
3   *Auerbach v Beck* (1985) 6 NSWLR 424 at 445C–D per Powell J (affd sub nom *Beck v Auerbach* (1986) 6 NSWLR 454).

Avoidance of section 62

8.166   The far-reaching effect of section 62 can be averted only through the expression of contrary intention[1] or by the revocation of the relevant permission in advance of the conveyance which would otherwise activate section 62. The mere existence of an express (and more limited) grant of rights of easement in the terms of a transfer or conveyance does not necessarily exclude the acquisition by the purchaser of further and more extensive implied rights under section 62(1), if it is clear that the vendor effectively enjoyed the larger right prior to the transaction in question.[2]

1   LPA 1925, s 62(4). Section 62 is commonly excluded in consequence of standard form conditions of sale. For judicial disquiet that this provision can be ousted by a clause buried in the small print of a contract of sale which the parties may never have read, see *Squarey v Harris-Smith* (1981) 42 P & CR 118 at 128, 130.
2   *Gregg v Richards* [1926] Ch 521 at 527–530. See also *Stafford v Pearson-Smith* (1962) 182 EG 539 at 541; *Snell & Prideaux Ltd v Dutton Mirrors Ltd* [1995] 1 EGLR 259 at 263H–K per Stuart-Smith LJ, 264L–265A per Hoffmann LJ.

Jurisdiction to rectify

8.167   The court retains an equitable jurisdiction to rectify any conveyance which mistakenly transfers to a grantee more rights than were intended in the relevant contract for sale. Thus, in *Clarke v Barnes*,[1] the court rectified a conveyance which had failed to exclude as against the purchaser the user of a right of way over other land retained by the vendor. The equitable jurisdiction was available to rectify the vendor's omission to exclude the effect of section 62, even though the purchaser maintained that he had contracted to purchase the land on the assumption that the right of way in question was included in the conveyance. However, the remedy of rectification will not be extended in order to assist any vendor who has acted otherwise than in good faith.

1   [1929] 2 Ch 368 at 380–382.

PRESCRIPTION

8.168   A third method of acquisition of easements and profits *à prendre* is provided by the law of prescription or long user. This area of law has become extremely complex over the years. As long ago as 1966 the Law Reform Committee recommended, by a majority, the total abolition of the concept of prescriptive acquisition.[1] No reform has yet occurred, although the existing law is marked by 'much unnecessary complication and confusion.'[2] Prescriptive acquisition is something of a hybrid, since it combines elements of fictional express grant with implications from the fact of long-term user.

1   *14th Report of the Law Reform Committee* (Cmnd 3100, 1966), para 32. A minority of the Committee recommended the retention of a prescription period of 12 years' user in respect of easements (see (1967) 30 MLR 189 (H W Wilkinson)). Among the main considerations leading to the majority proposal that prescriptive acquisition be abolished entirely was the argument that 'there is little, if any, moral justification for the acquisition of easements by prescription, a process which either involves an intention to get something for nothing or, where there is no intention to acquire any right, is purely accidental.'

2   *Tehidy Minerals Ltd v Norman* [1971] 2 QB 528 at 543F per Buckley LJ. Contrast the almost total exclusion of the prescriptive principle from the operation of Torrens title legislation (see *Dewhirst v Edwards* [1983] 1 NSWLR 34 at 48A–D).

8.169   There is in English law a strong policy bias in favour of the legitimacy of a user which has been exercised de facto over extended periods of time.[1] This consideration underlies the law of adverse possession[2] and likewise affords the rationale for prescriptive acquisition.[3] Prescription provides the ground on which the courts may uphold as lawful the long user of any right in the nature of an easement or profit *à prendre*.[4] Although there is no evidence of any actual grant, the law of prescription spells a fictional grant out of the fact of prolonged enjoyment of rights over the land of another. As Fry J said in *Moody v Steggles*,[5] it is 'the habit, and ... the duty, of the court, so far as it lawfully can, to clothe the fact with right.'[6] The process of prescription is, however, quite distinct from that of adverse possession under the Limitation Act. The latter process extinguishes old titles by barring remedies, whereas prescription generates new rights through a presumption that 'enjoyment was pursuant to a right having a lawful origin.'[7] Limitation has a negative and extinctive effect, whereas prescription is positive and creative in its mode of operation.[8]

1   See also L Berger, 'An Analysis of the Doctrine That "First in Time is First in Right"', 64 Nebraska L Rev 349 at 361–363 (1985).

2   [**Para 6.31**].

3   See *Clippens Oil Co Ltd v Edinburgh and District Water Trustees* [1904] AC 64 at 69–70 per Earl of Halsbury LC; *R v Oxfordshire CC, ex p Sunningwell PC* [2000] 1 AC 335 at 349D per Lord Hoffmann; *Bakewell Management Ltd v Brandwood* [2004] 2 WLR 955 at [9] per Lord Hope of Craighead.

4   The right must be inherently capable of constituting an easement or profit (see *Palmer v Bowman* [2000] 1 WLR 842 at 850A). Thus a prescriptive claim, although not requiring any assertion of necessity, must still involve some user which accommodates the alleged dominant land (*Depew v Wilkes* (2002) 216 DLR (4th) 487 at [22]–[26]). It may also be difficult evidentially to establish a prescriptive right of a very detailed nature (eg 'a right to use a footpath between the hours of 8am and 12 noon') (*Batchelor v Marlow* [2001] 1 EGLR 119 at 124H–J).

5   (1879) 12 Ch D 261 at 265.

6   There has always been weighty support for the proposition that long user should if possible be

ascribed to a lawful origin (see *Davis v Whitby* [1974] Ch 186 at 192C–D per Lord Denning MR, 192E per Stamp LJ; *Bakewell Management Ltd v Brandwood* [2004] 2 WLR 955 at [27], [39] per Lord Scott of Foscote, [49] per Lord Walker of Gestingthorpe; *Dobbie v Davidson* (1991) 23 NSWLR 625 at 670F–671A per Handley JA).

7   *R v Oxfordshire CC, ex p Sunningwell PC* [2000] 1 AC 335 at 350A per Lord Hoffmann. See likewise *Massey v Boulden* [2003] 1 WLR 1792 at [30] per Simon Brown LJ.

8   *Lovett v Fairclough* (1989) 61 P & CR 385 at 399; *Shaw v Garbutt* (1996) 7 BPR 14816 at 14829. See M J Goodman, (1968) 32 Conv (NS) 270.

GENERAL PRINCIPLES OF PRESCRIPTIVE ACQUISITION

8.170   The basis of prescriptive acquisition is not merely long user per se. In order that a claim of prescription should succeed, it is necessary that there be a history of continuous user in fee simple, and that this user be a 'user as of right in which the servient owner has, with the requisite degree of knowledge, ... acquiesced.'[1] This element of acquiescence vitally underpins all claims of prescription.[2]

1   *Mills v Silver* [1991] Ch 271 at 281G per Dillon LJ. See also *Sunset Properties Pty Ltd v Johnston* (1975) 3 BPR 9185 at 9190.

2   *Dalton v Angus & Co* (1881) 6 App Cas 740 at 773 per Fry J ('the whole law of prescription ... rest[s] upon acquiescence'). See also *Sturges v Bridgman* (1879) 11 Ch D 852 at 863 per Thesiger LJ; *Piromalli v Di Masi* [1980] WAR 173 at 178.

User in fee simple

8.171   Since a prescriptively acquired right inevitably becomes a right in perpetuity,[1] it is always said that prescription is necessarily based on user in fee simple. The user alleged must be user by or on behalf of a fee simple owner against another fee simple owner.[2] Several consequences follow.

1   *Rodwell v G R Evans & Co Pty Ltd* (1977) 3 BPR 9114 at 9123.

2   *Bright v Walker* (1834) 1 CM & R 211 at 221–222, 149 ER 1057 at 1061–1062; *Davis v Whitby* [1973] 1 WLR 629 at 630E; *Simmons v Dobson* [1991] 1 WLR 720 at 723C. The fee simple owner of a supposed dominant tenement, if not himself in occupation, can claim the benefit of user enjoyed by the actual occupier (eg his tenant), although such a claim can equally be destroyed by a consent or licence negotiated by the latter with the alleged servient owner (*Hyman v Van den Bergh* [1907] 2 Ch 516 at 531).

Prescription against a tenant for years

8.172   Any claim to prescriptive acquisition at common law must fail if the user began against an occupier of the servient land who was not entitled in fee simple (eg a tenant for years).[1] In such circumstances it would almost certainly be unreasonable to hold the fee simple owner bound by a prescriptive user of which he may not have been aware and which, in any event, he may have been utterly powerless to prevent.[2] There can, in effect, be no common law prescription of an easement or profit for a term of years.[3]

1   *Barker v Richardson* (1821) 4 B & Ald 579 at 582, 106 ER 1048 at 1049; *Pugh v Savage* [1970] 2 QB 373 at 383G–H. (Some of the problems connected with tenure by limited owners are eased by Prescription Act 1832, ss 7, 8.) See also A K Kiralfy, (1948) 13 Conv (NS) 104.

2   See *Pugh v Savage* [1970] 2 QB 373 at 383G–H per Cross LJ. Here, however, the Court of Appeal took the view (at 383H–384A, 386F) that a user commenced against a fee simple owner is not prejudiced if the land in question is subsequently occupied by a tenant at some intermediate stage during the prescription period. See also *Rodwell v G R Evans & Co Pty Ltd* [1978] 1 NSWLR 448 at 451E; *Piromalli v Di Masi* [1980] WAR 173 at 176; *Connellan Nominees Pty Ltd v Camerer* [1988] 2 Qd R 248 at 256–257.

3   *Gayford v Moffatt* (1868) 4 Ch App 133 at 135; *Wheaton v Maple & Co* [1893] 3 Ch 48 at 63; *Kilgour v Gaddes* [1904] 1 KB 457 at 460.

Prescription by a tenant for years

8.173   A tenant cannot acquire rights by common law prescription against his own landlord,[1] not least because the tenant's user is, in the sight of the law, that of his landlord.[2] Nor, for the same reason, can a tenant acquire prescriptive rights against another tenant who holds under the same landlord.[3] Easements can arise, for instance, only where dominant and servient tenements belong to different persons.

1   See *Bosomworth v Faber* (1992) 69 P & CR 288 at 292. A tenant may, however, acquire an easement of light against his landlord under Prescription Act 1832, s 3 [**para 8.194**].

2   *Gayford v Moffatt* (1868) 4 Ch App 133 at 135 per Lord Cairns LC; *Kilgour v Gaddes* [1904] 1 KB 457 at 467 per Romer LJ.

3   *Kilgour v Gaddes* [1904] 1 KB 457 at 467; *Derry v Sanders* [1919] 1 KB 223 at 237; *Cory v Davies* [1923] 2 Ch 95 at 107–108. (The same result obtains under Prescription Act 1832, s 2 (*Simmons v Dobson* [1991] 1 WLR 720 at 724A–B)). The law is different in Ireland (see *Flynn v Harte* [1913] 2 IR 322 at 325–326) and even English courts have remarked on the anomalous nature of the rule which prevents a tenant under a 999 year term from prescribing against his neighbour who also holds a similar long lease from the same landlord (*Simmons v Dobson*, supra at 724A–H). See also V T H Delany, (1958) 74 LQR 82; P Sparkes, [1992] Conv 167.

Continuous user

8.174   The user which founds a prescriptive claim must be continuous user, although the degree of continuity required is dependent on the nature of the right claimed.[1]

1   In the case of prescriptive claims to an easement or profit appurtenant (but not a profit in gross), the continuous user pleaded in support need not be exercised by the same person throughout the entire prescription period (*Lovett v Fairclough* (1989) 61 P & CR 385 at 399).

Frequency of user

8.175   The mere fact that user is intermittent does not destroy a claim of continuous user,[1] but frequency of user does ultimately affect the validity of the claim. Thus, for instance, a prescriptive claim to a right of way may succeed where there has been user on six to ten occasions each year for 35 years,[2] but not where there have been merely three occasions of user, each separated by an interval of 12 years.[3]

1   *Axler v Chisholm* (1978) 79 DLR (3d) 97 at 101.

2   *Diment v N H Foot Ltd* [1974] 1 WLR 1427 at 1430G. Likewise the continuity of user of a roadway leading to a summer home is not vitiated by the fact that the access is closed off during winter (*Estey v Withers* (1975) 48 DLR (3d) 121 at 127–128). See also *Mills v Silver* [1991] Ch 271 at 286C–D. Nor is continuity of user interrupted by an agreement between the claimant and the landowner to alter the route of access (*Davis v Whitby* [1973] 1 WLR 629 at 631C–E, [1974] Ch 186 at 191D–H).

3   *Hollins v Verney* (1884) 13 QBD 304 at 315. See also *Ramsay v Cooke* [1984] 2 NZLR 680 at 687 ('merely isolated occasions' of permission by way of licence).

Uniformity of user

8.176   Embedded in the requirement of continuous user is also the idea that the user asserted as the subject matter of a prescriptive claim must have a reasonably certain or uniform quality.[1] Thus, where the branches of a tree intrude into the airspace over neighbouring land, the incursion cannot, in view of the ever changing nature of the tree, be justified on the ground of prescription.[2] Likewise no prescriptive right can be claimed to pollute a river where the amount of pollution introduced into the water has varied over time or at least has increased during the potentially prescriptive 20-year period preceding the claim.[3]

1   See *Hulley v Silver Springs Bleaching Co* [1922] 2 Ch 268 at 281 per Eve J; *Green v Lord Somerleyton* [2004] 1 P & CR 520 at [122] per Jonathan Parker LJ.

2   *Lemmon v Webb* [1895] AC 1 at 6 [**para 3.55**].

3   See *Millington v Griffiths* (1874) 30 LT 65 at 68; *Cargill v Gotts* [1981] 1 WLR 441 at 448D–E; *Scott-Whitehead v National Coal Board* (1987) 53 P & CR 263 at 273–274.

User as of right

8.177   It is only against a background of assumed entitlement that the courts can infer the existence of some earlier grant from which the lawful exercise of an easement or profit is deemed to have derived. Prescription is therefore based on a user 'as of right',[1] acquiesced in by the servient owner, which at the end of the prescription period finally becomes a user 'by right'.[2] The definition of user 'as of right' is elusive, for it must steer a skilful course between concepts of legality, illegality, mistake and specific permission. The nature of the required user is traditionally described in terms borrowed from Roman law. It is commonly said that prescriptive user must be exercised *nec vi, nec clam, nec precario* (without force, without secrecy and without permission).[3] User 'as of right' must be enjoyed 'openly and in the manner that a person rightfully entitled would have used it.'[4] The onus of proof lies on the claimant.[5]

1   See *Earl De La Warr v Miles* (1881) 17 Ch D 535 at 591 per Brett LJ; *Hanna v Pollock* [1900] 2 IR 664 at 671; *Hamilton v Joyce* [1984] 3 NSWLR 279 at 291D–G.

2   *Newnham v Willison* (1988) 56 P & CR 8 at 17 per Kerr LJ.

3   *Co Litt*, p 13b; *Eaton v Swansea Waterworks Co* (1851) 17 QB 267 at 275, 117 ER 1282 at 1285; *Solomon v Vintners' Co* (1859) 4 H & N 585 at 602, 157 ER 970 at 977; *Sturges v Bridgman* (1879) 11 Ch D 852 at 863; *Burrows v Lang* [1901] 2 Ch 502 at 510; *Newnham v Willison* (1988) 56 P & CR 8 at 12.

4   *Bright v Walker* (1834) 1 CM & R 211 at 219, 149 ER 1057 at 1060 per Parke B. See also
     Gardner v Hodgson's Kingston Brewery Co Ltd [1903] AC 229 at 239 per Lord Lindley; *R v
     Oxfordshire CC, ex p Sunningwell PC* [2000] 1 AC 335 at 351F–G per Lord Hoffmann.
5   *Earl De La Warr v Miles* (1881) 17 Ch D 535 at 591; *Gardner v Hodgson's Kingston
     Brewery Co Ltd* [1903] AC 229 at 233; *Patel v W H Smith (Eziot) Ltd* [1987] 1 WLR 853 at
     860A–B.

Acts already authorised by the general law

8.178   Long user cannot result in the acquisition of a right to do what one is
already entitled to do by the general law.[1] Thus there can be no prescription in
relation to matters already the subject of a public right (eg the public right of
every citizen to make reasonable use of the highway[2]) or which are a natural
incident of ownership of an alleged dominant tenement (eg a natural right of
drainage[3]).

1   See *London and Canadian Loan Co v Warin* (1885) 14 SCR 232 at 236, 240–241; *Monaghan v
     Moore* (1996) 140 DLR (4th) 188 at 190.
2   *Monaghan v Moore* (1996) 140 DLR (4th) 188 at 190.
3   *Palmer v Bowman* [2000] 1 WLR 842 at 850A–E, 856A **[para 1.113]**.

Illegal and unlawful acts

8.179   Some difficulty arises where a prescriptive claim is founded on the
illegal or unlawful activity of the claimant. At one level, of course, it is intrinsic
to the prescriptive process that prescription can be based on conduct which
begins as a tortious invasion of the servient owner's land and is eventually
cured by the effluxion of the prescriptive period.[1] At another level, however, it
would seem strange that prescription could be successfully alleged on the
footing of actions which violate the criminal law or are directly contrary to
some public statutory prohibition. This dilemma required resolution in
Bakewell Management Ltd v Brandwood.[2] Here, in relation to privately owned
common land,[3] the House of Lords was confronted by prescriptive claims of
access based on long user which technically involved the commission of a
criminal offence.[4] The House, in upholding this particular instance of prescriptive acquisition,[5] drew an important distinction between cases where it lies
within the servient owner's power to remove the criminality or unlawfulness of
the claimant's user and those cases in which it is simply not within the alleged
servient owner's competence so to do.

1   See *Bakewell Management Ltd v Brandwood* [2004] 2 WLR 955 at [7] per Lord Hope of
     Craighead, [46] per Lord Scott of Foscote.
2   [2004] 2 WLR 955.
3   **[Paras 5.40, 8.139]**.
4   See LPA 1925, s 193(4) (which makes it a criminal offence to drive 'without lawful authority'
     over common land which has been dedicated to public recreational user **[para 5.40]**).
5   In the *Bakewell Management* case ([2004] 2 WLR 955 at [38], [46]–[47], [59]), the House of
     Lords overruled, as excessively wide, earlier statements that the courts 'will not recognise an
     easement established by unlawful activity' (see eg *Cargill v Gotts* [1981] 1 WLR 441 at 446H;
     Hanning v Top Deck Travel Group Ltd (1994) 68 P & CR 14 at 20, 23).

8.180   Since all common law prescription presupposes a grant (albeit by way of fiction),[1] the circumstances of prescriptive acquisition are inevitably limited by the putative grantor's competence in matters of grant.[2] If a particular grant could not have had a lawful origin, its existence can never be presumed by virtue of long user.[3] Thus, for example, it is inconceivable that a putative grantor should have granted any right to do an act or acts which, if done, would constitute an irreversible breach of the law.[4] As a sheer issue of legal competence, a purported grant of this nature would be 'a legal impossibility'[5] and could never vest any entitlement in the grantee.[6] Most forms of user which involve criminal illegality or the breach of some public law prohibition cannot therefore generate any claim 'as of right'.[7] If, by contrast, the putative grantor inherently possessed the power to negative or condone the unlawfulness of the user, the fictional grant which underlies the prescriptive claim is presumed to have been an exercise of this power.[8] Thus in *Bakewell Management Ltd v Brandwood*[9] the House of Lords upheld the prescriptive claim of access precisely because the servient landowner had always enjoyed, in most cases, a 'dispensing power' to decriminalise the claimants' user of the common by a simple express grant of 'lawful authority' for that purpose.[10] Likewise more ordinary cases of prescriptive acquisition of a private right of way are entirely unaffected by the initially tortious nature of the claimant's user. The presumptive (albeit fictional) grant of entitlement raised by long user is itself effective to supply the landowner's prior authority for the user and thereby to counteract its essential unlawfulness.[11]

1   *Gardner v Hodgson's Kingston Brewery Co Ltd* [1903] AC 229 at 239 per Lord Lindley.
2   In effect, an apparent entitlement based on long and open user must be 'within grant' (or 'lie in grant') as a precondition of any inference of lawful origin (*Bakewell Management Ltd v Brandwood* [2004] 2 WLR 955 at [8] per Lord Hope of Craighead, [49]–[50] per Lord Walker of Gestingthorpe). See e g *Rochdale Canal Co v Radcliffe* (1852) 18 QB 287 at 314–315, 118 ER 108 at 118 (company lacking legal capacity to grant easements [para **8.50**]).
3   See *Neaverson v Peterborough RDC* [1902] 1 Ch 557 at 563–564 per Henn Collins MR (cited in *Bakewell Management Ltd v Brandwood* [2004] 2 WLR 955 at [32] per Lord Scott of Foscote).
4   Nor, in relation to common land belonging to a putative grantor, could a fictional grant have provided any lawful authority to conduct activities on that land (e g camping or other excesses of user) which would inevitably constitute a nuisance (e g to existing commoners with grazing rights) (*Bakewell Management Ltd v Brandwood* [2004] 2 WLR 955 at [24] per Lord Scott of Foscote). See similarly *Massey v Boulden* [2003] 1 WLR 1792 at [34] per Simon Brown LJ (but compare Sedley LJ at [68]).
5   See *George Legge & Son Ltd v Wenlock Corpn* [1938] AC 204 at 216 per Lord Macmillan.
6   *Bakewell Management Ltd v Brandwood* [2004] 2 WLR 955 at [39] per Lord Scott of Foscote. See e g *Cargill v Gotts* [1981] 1 WLR 441 at 446H (no prescriptive acquisition of easement to abstract water from mill pond in defiance of requirement of licence under Water Resources Act 1963).
7   *Bakewell Management Ltd v Brandwood* [2004] 2 WLR 955 at [60] per Lord Walker of Gestingthorpe. It has been suggested that the mere use of land without planning permission does not constitute sufficient illegality to preclude the operation of prescription, provided that no enforcement notice has yet been served or proceedings for injunctive relief commenced (see *Batchelor v Marlow* [2001] 1 EGLR 119 at 127C–D). See also *Glamorgan CC v Carter* [1963] 1 WLR 1 at 5, as construed in *Bakewell Management*, supra at [34] per Lord Scott of Foscote.
8   *Bakewell Management Ltd v Brandwood* [2004] 2 WLR 955 at [8] per Lord Hope of Craighead.
9   [2004] 2 WLR 955.

10 [2004] 2 WLR 955 at [56] per Lord Walker of Gestingthorpe (see likewise Lord Hope of Craighead at [9], Lord Scott of Foscote at [24], [46]).
11 *Bakewell Management Ltd v Brandwood* [2004] 2 WLR 955 at [59] per Lord Walker of Gestingthorpe.

Acts based on mistake

8.181   It is no bar to the acquisition of rights by long user that the prescriptive claimant suffered from a mistaken belief that he owned the disputed land anyway[1] or that he already enjoyed rights by express grant.[2] If anything, the claimant's misapprehension confirms rather than undermines the claim of rightful user.[3] A mere subjective mistake as to entitlement does not deprive the claimant's user of its quality as 'of right',[4] for the pre-eminent focus concentrates on the way 'in which that user is seen by the owner of the land over which the right is asserted.'[5]

1 *Capar v Wasylowski* (1983) 146 DLR (3d) 193 at 200–202.
2 *Bridle v Ruby* [1989] QB 169 at 177C–E, 178F–H. See G Kodilinye, [1989] Conv 261. To disallow user based on a mistaken belief would effectively confine prescription to someone who 'is aware that he is a wrongdoer' (*Bridle*, supra at 177D–E per Parker LJ).
3 A mistaken belief that the claimant owns the alleged servient tenement vitiates the claim of easement only if, in reliance on his assumption, the claimant has exercised acts of ownership involving exclusive possession of that tenement (see *Attorney-General of Southern Nigeria v John Holt & Co (Liverpool) Ltd* [1915] AC 599 at 617–618; *Warren v Yell* [1944] 1 DLR 118 at 129–130; *Capar v Wasylowski* (1983) 146 DLR (3d) 193 at 201; but compare *Lyell v Lord Hothfield* [1914] 3 KB 911 at 916).
4 However, a user based on a mistaken belief that it is justified on a right of limited duration, which belief is acquiesced in, cannot be made the foundation of a grant of unlimited duration (see *Chamber Colliery Co v Hopwood* (1886) 32 Ch D 549 at 556; *Bridle v Ruby* [1989] QB 169 at 177C–D).
5 *Bridle v Ruby* [1989] QB 169 at 178E per Ralph Gibson LJ.

User nec vi

8.182   It is clear that forcible user vitiates any claim to entitlement 'as of right'.[1] For this purpose the notion of forcible user includes not merely a violent exercise of the user (eg the removal of an obstruction[2]), but also any insistence upon a particular user in the face of continuing protest from the supposedly servient owner.[3] Here prescription differs significantly from adverse possession under the Limitation Act,[4] which involves a form of possession admittedly 'as of wrong'. In the law of prescription the claim of user 'as of right' is inevitably negated by the claimant's knowledge (actual or constructive[5]) that there is objection to his user.[6] Evidence of 'contentiousness'[7] or 'perpetual warfare'[8] between the parties destroys the element of acquiescence which is fundamental to prescription and palpably falsifies the shallow fiction that the claimant's user proceeded on the footing of some past grant.

1 *R v Oxfordshire CC, ex p Sunningwell PC* [2000] 1 AC 335 at 350H–351A per Lord Hoffmann.
2 See *Newnham v Willison* (1988) 56 P & CR 8 at 19.
3 The 'peaceable character' of the user is destroyed by 'continuous and unmistakable protests'

(*Dalton v Angus & Co* (1881) 6 App Cas 740 at 786 per Bowen J). In an analogous context in *R* (*Beresford*) *v Sunderland CC* [2004] 1 AC 889 at [56], Lord Rodger of Earlsferry spoke of force as involving an 'overcoming [of] any resistance on the owners' part.' See also *Newnham v Willison* (1988) 56 P & CR 8 at 18–19 per Kerr LJ. Prescription can be averted even by the erection of a notice declaring that user is by permission only (see *Rafique v Trustees of the Walton Estate* (1992) 65 P & CR 356 at 357). Compare, however, H Wallace, [1994] Conv 196 at 207–210.

4　**[Para 6.49]**.

5　*Smith v Brudenell-Bruce* [2002] 2 P & CR 51 at [12] per Pumfrey J.

6　*Newnham v Willison* (1988) 56 P & CR 8 at 19. See also *Shaw v Garbutt* (1996) 7 BPR 14816 at 14829–14830 per Young J.

7　*Newnham v Willison* (1988) 56 P & CR 8 at 19. See also *Dalton v Angus & Co* (1881) 6 App Cas 740 at 786; *Smith v Brudenell-Bruce* [2002] 2 P & CR 51 at [11], [21].

8　See *Eaton v Swansea Waterworks Co* (1851) 17 QB 267 at 273–274, 117 ER 1282 at 1285 per Lord Campbell CJ.

User nec clam

8.183　The user which founds a prescriptive claim must not be surreptitious or concealed in any way.[1] In *Union Lighterage Co v London Graving Dock Co*,[2] for instance, the Court of Appeal declined to accept that a prescriptive claim had been established by a defendant who fixed the side of a dock to the soil of a wharf by means of underground rods which remained undetected for more than 20 years.[3] Romer LJ held that a prescriptive right to an easement over another's land could be acquired only 'when the enjoyment has been open – that is to say, of such a character that an ordinary owner of the land, diligent in the protection of his interests, would have, or must be taken to have, a reasonable opportunity of becoming aware of that enjoyment.'[4] Where an access way has been used for many years, an onus may rest on the servient landowner to rebut the presumption that he had knowledge of the long user.[5] However, in cases involving other kinds of easement where the user is either less obvious[6] or extremely intermittent, the burden may be on the prescriptive claimant to prove that the alleged servient owner knew, or had reasonable means of knowledge, of the acts of user.[7]

1　*Bright v Walker* (1834) 1 CM & R 211 at 219, 149 ER 1057 at 1060 per Parke B (user must not be 'by stealth as a trespasser would have done'). See also *Gardner v Hodgson's Kingston Brewery Co Ltd* [1903] AC 229 at 238 per Lord Davey, 239 per Lord Lindley; *R v Oxfordshire CC, ex p Sunningwell PC* [2000] 1 AC 335 at 350H, 351F–G per Lord Hoffmann; *R* (*Beresford*) *v Sunderland CC* [2004] 1 AC 889 at [56] per Lord Rodger of Earlsferry.

2　[1902] 2 Ch 557.

3　See similarly *Liverpool Corpn v H Coghill and Son Ltd* [1918] 1 Ch 307 at 314 (secret discharge of factory effluent into sewer); *Barney v BP Truckshops* [1995] NPC 5 (unsuspected underground sewage pipe).

4　[1902] 2 Ch 557 at 571. See eg *Milne v James* (1910) 13 CLR 168 at 177–178, 186–187, 193–194; *Capar v Wasylowski* (1983) 146 DLR (3d) 193 at 199.

5　*Diment v N H Foot Ltd* [1974] 1 WLR 1427 at 1434F–G.

6　See eg *Scott-Whitehead v National Coal Board* (1987) 53 P & CR 263 at 275 per Stuart-Smith J (river pollution).

7　*Davies v Du Paver* [1953] 1 QB 184 at 205–206, 210–211; *Temma Realty Co Ltd v Ress Enterprises Ltd* (1968) 69 DLR (2d) 195 at 198. At the very least any onus of rebuttal which rests on the landowner in these circumstances is easily satisfied (see *Axler v Chisholm* (1978) 79

DLR (3d) 97 at 101–102). See also *Sunshine Retail Investments Pty Ltd v Wulff* (Unreported, Supreme Court of Victoria, 28 October 1999, BPR Casenote 102222) (constructive knowledge of the claimed user not sufficient).

User nec precario

8.184 No prescriptive claim can be based on a user which is positively permissive, ie precariously founded on an active licence or consent from the landowner.[1] Such permission, whether sought by a direct request or granted in a unilateral and unsolicited form,[2] is inconsistent with any claim of user 'as of right'.[3] Moreover, any practice of periodic payment to the landowner tends to indicate that a continuing user is acknowledged to be permissive only.[4] An actively permissive user leaves no scope for acquiescence on the part of the landowner.[5] It is nevertheless possible that a user which originated in a permission granted by the landowner may later lose its permissive character and arrogate to itself a kind of rightful quality if there is evidence that subsequent acts of user ceased to be reliant on the initial element of licence.[6]

1   *Gardner v Hodgson's Kingston Brewery Co Ltd* [1903] AC 229 at 239 per Lord Lindley. See similarly also *Hyman v Van den Bergh* [1907] 2 Ch 516 at 530; *R v Oxfordshire CC, ex p Sunningwell PC* [2000] 1 AC 335 at 350H, 351F–G per Lord Hoffmann; *R (Beresford) v Sunderland CC* [2004] 1 AC 889 at [35] per Lord Scott of Foscote; *Henderson v Volk* (1982) 35 OR (2d) 379 at 383; *Hamilton v Joyce* [1984] 3 NSWLR 279 at 291D–G.
2   *BP Properties Ltd v Buckler* (1988) 55 P & CR 337 at 345–347; *Rafique v Trustees of the Walton Estate* (1992) 65 P & CR 356 at 357; *O'Mara v Gascoigne* (1996) 9 BPR 16349 at 16355–16356.
3   Enjoyment at the will and pleasure of the owner is inconsistent with a claim of right (*Gardner v Hodgson's Kingston Brewery Co Ltd* [1903] AC 229 at 231 per Earl of Halsbury LC). See eg *Goldsmith v Burrow Construction Co Ltd* (1987) Times, 31 July (locking of gate on path for substantial periods rendered user merely precarious).
4   *Gardner v Hodgson's Kingston Brewery Co Ltd* [1903] AC 229 at 231–235; *Bridle v Ruby* [1989] QB 169 at 177G; *Mills v Silver* [1991] Ch 271 at 292G; *R (Beresford) v Sunderland CC* [2004] 1 AC 889 at [74] per Lord Walker of Gestingthorpe. It is fatal at common law to rest any prescriptive claim on an alleged contractual right to engage in the user concerned (see *Norton v Williams* [1939] NZLR 1051 at 1055).
5   *Monaghan v Moore* (1996) 140 DLR (4th) 188 at 190.
6   See *Gaved v Martyn* (1865) 19 CB NS 732 at 744–745, 144 ER 974 at 979–980.

Acquiescence by the servient owner

8.185 There is an important distinction between a positive permission or consent (which clearly precludes any prescriptive claim) and the passive assent or acquiescence which underlies the entire principle of prescriptive acquisition.[1] Prescription depends crucially on an acquiescence by the servient owner in the exercise of a user 'as of right'.[2] In *Dalton v Angus & Co*[3] Fry J expressed the view that acquiescence necessarily presupposes on the part of the servient owner (1) a knowledge of the acts done[4]; (2) a power in him to stop the acts or to sue in respect of them[5]; and (3) an abstinence on his part from the exercise of such a power.[6]

1   The phrase 'as of right' is governed by the same principles and bears the same meaning for the purposes of the law of prescription and the generation of entitlements under the Commons Registration Act 1965 **[para 5.41]** and Highways Act 1980, s 31 **[para 5.9]** (see *R v Oxfordshire CC, ex p Sunningwell PC* [2000] 1 AC 335 at 353E per Lord Hoffmann; *R (Beresford) v Sunderland CC* [2004] 1 AC 889 at [55] per Lord Rodger of Earlsferry).

2   *Hamilton v Joyce* [1984] 3 NSWLR 279 at 289B–290B. The user claimed must be 'inconsistent with any other reasonable inference than that it has been of right' (*Gardner v Hodgson's Kingston Brewery Co Ltd* [1903] AC 229 at 239 per Lord Lindley).

3   (1881) 6 App Cas 740 at 773–774.

4   Acquiescence is not, however, vitiated if the servient owner is unaware that he owns the land himself (*Capar v Wasylowski* (1983) 146 DLR (3d) 193 at 199).

5   In *Dalton v Angus & Co* the House of Lords held that the claimant had acquired a right of support for his building by reason of 20 years' enjoyment and could therefore sue the defendant in respect of the damage caused by the removal of the lateral support provided by the defendant's adjoining house. It is difficult to see how in practice this prescriptive claim could have been frustrated by the adjoining owner otherwise than by granting an express licence of support or by demolishing his building within the prescription period of 20 years. See also *Dynevor v Richardson* [1995] Ch 173 at 183C–E.

6   See also *Davies v Du Paver* [1953] 1 QB 184 at 210 per Morris LJ. This statement of the principle of acquiescence closely resembles the doctrine of proprietary estoppel, particularly where the prescriptive claimant undertakes expenditure in the belief that there has been acquiescence in his assumption of right (see e g *Annally Hotel Ltd v Bergin* (1970) 104 ILTR 65 at 66).

Informed acceptance of the user

8.186   A prescriptive right can be established where a particular user is 'such as to bring home to the mind of a reasonable person that a continuous right of enjoyment is being asserted.'[1] If, in these circumstances, the alleged servient owner does nothing, he will be 'taken to have recognised the right and not intended to resist it.' It will be no defence for him later to assert that he merely 'tolerated' the user in question.[2] The mere fact that the servient owner could have stopped the user within the prescription period 'is not inconsistent with the concept of user as of right.'[3] The critical point is precisely the fact that the servient owner took no steps to halt the adverse user.[4] But no claim 'as of right' can be asserted if the alleged servient owner has demonstrated a willingness to exclude from, or exert control over access to, the disputed facility on his own land. No acquiescence arises, for instance, where a supposed servient owner has allowed user under a purely temporary licence[5] or has retained control over the extent of the user (e g by means of a gate which is locked from time to time at his discretion).[6] 'Overt conduct' by the landowner which unmistakably under-scores the precarious nature of the user ultimately excludes the claim of prescription.[7] Positive acts of permissive control indicate conclusively that the landowner intended to retain the 'property' in his land and did not intend to concede any of that 'property' (in the form of an incorporeal hereditament) to any stranger.

1   *Mills v Silver* [1991] Ch 271 at 288D per Parker LJ. See *Loder v Gaden* (1999) 78 P & CR 223 at 232 per Hale J. Much assistance can be found in the analogous treatment of user 'as of

right' pursuant to the Commons Registration Act 1965 [**paras 5.42–5.45**]. See e g *R v Oxfordshire CC, ex p Sunningwell PC* [2000] 1 AC 335 at 352H–353A per Lord Hoffmann [**para 5.42**].

2   *Mills v Silver* [1991] Ch 271 at 288E per Parker LJ (see also Dillon LJ at 281G, 285E and Stocker LJ at 291B). For an identical approach, see *R* (*Beresford*) *v Sunderland CC* [2004] 1 AC 889 at [6] per Lord Bingham of Cornhill, [43] per Lord Scott of Foscote, [77]–[81] per Lord Walker of Gestingthorpe [**para 5.45**].

3   *Mills v Silver* [1991] Ch 271 at 282A per Dillon LJ; *Smith v Brudenell-Bruce* [2002] 2 P & CR 51 at [24] per Pumfrey J. At common law a servient owner could always frustrate the prescriptive acquisition of a right of access to light by erecting a 'spite fence' to obstruct the light. Nowadays the servient owner can achieve the same objective under the Rights of Light Act 1959 by registering a notional 'spite fence' in the local land charges register (Rights of Light Act 1959, s 2). See e g *Bowring Services Ltd v Scottish Widows' Fund & Life Assurance Society* [1995] 1 EGLR 158 at 161F.

4   See *Goldsmith v Burrow Construction Co Ltd* (1987) Times, 31 July, per May LJ, cited in *Mills v Silver* [1991] Ch 271 at 282C–D. The position may be very different if the relevant user is of such a nature that there were no possible or practicable means by which the servient owner could have brought it to an end. See e g *Webb v Bird* (1861) 10 CB (NS) 268 at 283–285, 142 ER 455 at 460–461, (1863) 13 CB (NS) 841 at 843, 143 ER 332 at 333 (no easement in respect of free flow of air over alleged servient tenement in direction of claimant's windmill). See also *Bryant v Lefever* (1879) 4 CPD 172 at 178.

5   *Sturges v Bridgman* (1879) 11 Ch D 852 at 863. In circumstances of temporary licence no entitlement arises merely because the servient owner has reserved the right not to renew the licence (see *Mills v Silver* [1991] Ch 271 at 282B).

6   *Lay v Wyncoll* (1966) 198 EG 887 at 889; *Goldsmith v Burrow Construction Co Ltd* (1987) Times, 31 July; *Mills v Silver* [1991] Ch 271 at 282B–D. See also *Bridle v Ruby* [1989] QB 169 at 177G ('permission from time to time').

7   See *R* (*Beresford*) *v Sunderland CC* [2004] 1 AC 889 at [75], [83], [85], [89(a)] per Lord Walker of Gestingthorpe [**para 5.44**].

Tolerated user

8.187   It may sometimes be difficult to distinguish acquiescence from active consent, particularly where an alleged servient owner has tolerated a user out of good neighbourliness or because the user was too insignificant to cause him concern or inconvenience. Sheer tolerance of a user without objection cannot bar the creation of prescriptive rights, for such a principle would be 'fundamentally inconsistent with the whole notion of acquisition of rights by prescription.'[1] Yet a landowner's 'mere tolerance of a trespass' which continues over many years should not necessarily clothe that trespass with the character of a user 'as of right'.[2] Courts are traditionally reluctant to allow tolerated trespasses to ripen into rights,[3] thereby stultifying the altruistic impulse,[4] and it is a constant refrain in the law of easements that 'between neighbours there must be give as well as take.'[5] Thus, in the past, many acts of neighbourly forbearance have given rise to no prescription, precisely because there was no reasonable apprehension that the permitted user was generated by *entitlement*.[6] The casual nature of a tolerated user between neighbours frequently indicates that 'the user was not a user asserting a right.'[7] For prescriptive purposes a neighbourly tolerance motivated by generosity of spirit tends therefore to be viewed more on the analogy of an implicit active permission than of sheer passive inactivity. In a proper case, however, the mere existence of neighbourly relations will not connote a consent or licence which frustrates prescriptive claims if there is evidence that the user was actually viewed as a matter of entitlement.[8]

1   *Mills v Silver* [1991] Ch 271 at 279H–280A per Dillon LJ, cited with approval in *R (Beresford) v Sunderland CC* [2004] 1 AC 889 at [80] per Lord Walker of Gestingthorpe.
2   *Ramsay v Cooke* [1984] 2 NZLR 680 at 685–686. See later *Cooke v Ramsay* [1984] 2 NZLR 689. As the Ontario Court of Appeal held in *Henderson v Volk* (1982) 35 OR (2d) 379 at 384, 'neighbourly acquiescence' in the occasional use of a path 'during inclement weather or in times of emergency such as a last minute attempt to catch a bus' should not too readily be accepted as evidence of submission to the use.
3   See *R v Oxfordshire CC, ex p Sunningwell PC* [2000] 1 AC 335 at 359B–C per Lord Hoffmann.
4   **[Para 5.32]**. As was pointed out by Cory JA in *Henderson v Volk* (1982) 35 OR (2d) 379 at 384, the essence of prescription is to 'subject a property owner to a burden without compensation.' The over-eager finding of successful prescriptive user 'may discourage acts of kindness and good neighbourliness; it may punish the kind and thoughtful and reward the aggressor.' See also *Blount v Layard* [1891] 2 Ch 681n at 691 per Bowen LJ; *Attorney-General v Antrobus* [1905] 2 Ch 188 at 206 per Farwell J **[para 5.30]**.
5   See *Costagliola v English* (1969) 210 EG 1425 at 1431 per Megarry J.
6   See e g *Henderson v Volk* (1982) 35 OR (2d) 379 at 384; *Bridle v Ruby* [1989] QB 169 at 177G.
7   *Mills v Silver* [1991] Ch 271 at 284D–E, citing *Ironside, Crabb and Crabb v Cook, Cook and Barefoot* (1978) 41 P & CR 326 at 339.
8   See *Sunset Properties Pty Ltd v Johnston* (1975) 3 BPR 9185 at 9191 per Holland J; *Rose v Krieser* (2002) 212 DLR (4th) 123 at [50]–[54] (Ontario Court of Appeal).

GROUNDS OF PRESCRIPTIVE ACQUISITION

8.188   At common law prescription depends on the idea that long user is evidence of past grant. In other words, the fact of long user is deemed to provide evidence that the easement or profit now claimed was once duly granted in proper form, with the consequence that any easement or profit established by prescription is necessarily legal.[1] The theory of prescriptive acquisition is, however, deeply marked by fiction.[2]

1   Once again prescriptive user cannot convert into an easement or profit any right which is inherently incapable of existing as such (see *Palmer v Bowman* [2000] 1 WLR 842 at 850A).
2   'I agree that the Court is endowed with a great power of imagination for the purpose of supporting ancient user' (*Neaverson v Peterborough RDC* [1902] 1 Ch 557 at 573 per Collins MR). See also *Bakewell Management Ltd v Brandwood* [2004] 2 WLR 955 at [52] per Lord Walker of Gestingthorpe.

Common law presumption from long user

8.189   At common law it was presumed that a long user stemmed from a valid grant if that user had continued 'from time whereof the memory of men runneth not to the contrary',[1] a date which was fixed somewhat arbitrarily as 1189 (the date of the accession of Richard I).[2] Any user which commenced before this date provided an unimpeachable basis for a claim of prescriptive acquisition. However, such proof of lawful origin came in time to be both impracticable and impossible and was, accordingly, replaced by another presumption. The courts of common law began to presume that if, at any point, a continuous user as of right during the period of living memory[3] or even for more than 20 years[4] could be shown, this user must have commenced before 1189.[5] This benevolent fiction was inevitably defeated by any demonstration that a particular user could not possibly have been exercised or enjoyed at all times since 1189[6] or if there had been unity of possession between the dominant and servient tenements at any stage since 1189.[7] It is therefore virtually impossible to satisfy the test of common law prescription[8] and it is generally assumed that the ancient common law principle nowadays adds nothing to the other grounds of prescriptive claim.[9]

1   *Co Litt*, p 114b.
2   Statute of Westminster I, 1275, c 39. See *Dalton v Angus & Co* (1881) 6 App Cas 740 at 811 per Lord Blackburn; *Simmons v Dobson* [1991] 1 WLR 720 at 722H; *R v Oxfordshire CC, ex p Sunningwell PC* [2000] 1 AC 335 at 349H–350B.
3   See *Hanna v Pollock* [1900] 2 IR 664 at 700.
4   *Angus & Co v Dalton* (1877) 3 QBD 85 at 105 per Cockburn CJ; *Clancy v Whelan and Considine* (1958) 92 ILTR 39 at 43–44.
5   See *R v Oxfordshire CC, ex p Sunningwell PC* [2000] 1 AC 335 at 350B.
6   Thus an easement of access to light cannot be claimed in respect of a building clearly constructed after 1189 (*Duke of Norfolk v Arbuthnot* (1880) 5 CPD 390 at 393, 402). See also *Hanna v Pollock* [1900] 2 IR 664 at 693, 700–701; *Simmons v Dobson* [1991] 1 WLR 720 at 722H–723A. For similar reasons there cannot, in Australia and New Zealand, be any presumption of user since before 1189 by a non-aboriginal (see *New Zealand Loan and Mercantile Agency Co Ltd v Wellington Corpn* (1890) 9 NZLR 10 at 18–19; *Richardson v Browning* (1936) 31 Tas LR 78 at 140–141; *Hamilton v Joyce* [1984] 3 NSWLR 279 at 287E).
7   [Para 8.47]. See *Dynevor v Richardson* [1995] Ch 173 at 182G.
8   *Simmons v Dobson* [1991] 1 WLR 720 at 722H per Fox LJ.
9   *Mills v Silver* [1991] Ch 271 at 278A–B.

Lost modern grant

8.190   In order to remedy the deficiencies of the common law presumption from user, the courts later developed a further resourceful fiction in the form of the doctrine of 'lost modern grant'.[1] This doctrine concedes that user dating back to 1189 cannot be proved. It therefore allows prescriptive claims to be made on the basis of a 'convenient and workable fiction'[2] that 20 years' user provides evidence of a 'modern grant' (ie a grant by deed at some date after 1189) which has since been misplaced and lost.[3] The doctrine of lost modern grant thus embodies another glaring juxtaposition of empirically founded and right-based notions of property in land. In the absence of evidence inconsistent with such a conclusion,[4] the sheer fact of long user supports an inference of formal grant of an incorporeal right.[5] The doctrine was definitively upheld by the House of Lords in *Dalton v Angus & Co*,[6] the only conditions for its application being proof of 20 years' enjoyment as of right,[7] coupled with an absence of any showing that the putative grantor was legally incompetent.[8] Proof of continuous user as of right for a period of 20 years is therefore normally sufficient nowadays to found a claim of prescriptive acquisition.[9] Emphasis has shifted from the 'brute fact' of immemorial (and almost always fictional) user to the inherent quality of the 20 year user which underlies the modern law of prescription.[10]

1   See *Pekel v Humich* (1999) 21 WAR 24 at 28 per Templeman J ('one of the last remaining legal fictions'). See also M A Clawson, 'Prescription Adrift in a Sea of Servitudes: Postmodernism and the Lost Grant' (1994) 43 Duke LJ 845.

2   *Simmons v Dobson* [1991] 1 WLR 720 at 723B per Fox LJ. Compare *Angus & Co v Dalton* (1877) 3 QBD 85 at 94, where Lush J made his classic reference to the 'revolting fiction of a lost grant.'

3   See *Bryant v Foot* (1867) LR 2 QB 161 at 181; *Dalton v Angus & Co* (1881) 6 App Cas 740 at 811–812; *Hanna v Pollock* [1900] 2 IR 664 at 694, 697–698; *Bakewell Management Ltd v Brandwood* [2004] 2 WLR 955 at [8] per Lord Hope of Craighead, [28] per Lord Scott of Foscote. The justification for the doctrine of 'lost modern grant' seems to be that the state of affairs which is shown to exist is otherwise unexplained (see *Attorney-General v Simpson* [1901] 2 Ch 671 at 698; *Bridle v Ruby* [1989] QB 169 at 177F; *Palmer v Bowman* [2000] 1 WLR 842 at 849H; *Hamilton v Joyce* [1984] 3 NSWLR 279 at 287G–288A).

4   *Bakewell Management Ltd v Brandwood* [2004] 2 WLR 955 at [8] per Lord Hope of Craighead.

5   It is rare, but not impossible, for a profit in gross to be acquired under the doctrine of lost modern grant (see *Bettison v Langton* [2000] Ch 54 at 61G).

6   (1881) 6 App Cas 740.

7   A claim of lost modern grant based on 20 years of actual enjoyment is not prejudiced by the fact that subsequent user may have been interrupted or discontinuous (see *Mills v Silver* [1991] Ch 271 at 278D).

8   The presumption of grant may be rebutted by evidence that the putative grantor suffered from mental incapacity or was a corporation which lacked the legal capacity to grant easements (see *Rochdale Canal Co v Radcliffe* (1852) 18 QB 287 at 314–315, 118 ER 108 at 118) or did not have a full fee simple estate in the supposed servient tenement (see *Rodwell v G R Evans & Co Pty Ltd* (1977) 3 BPR 9114 at 9121). See also *Oakley v Boston* [1976] QB 270 at 280F–281A, 285C–E; *Smith v Brudenell-Bruce* [2002] 2 P & CR 51 at [22].

9   See *Tehidy Minerals Ltd v Norman* [1971] 2 QB 528 at 546A, 552A–B; *Smith v Brudenell-Bruce* [2002] 2 P & CR 51 at [24]. The claimant need not state the dates of and parties to the lost deed of grant (*Palmer v Guadagni* [1906] 2 Ch 494 at 497); and it is likely that the presumption of grant is not rebuttable even by evidence that no grant was in fact ever made (see *Angus & Co v Dalton* (1878) 4 QBD 162 at 172–173, 187; *Tehidy Minerals*, supra at 552B).

10 See *R v Oxfordshire CC, ex p Sunningwell PC* [2000] 1 AC 335 at 350G. See also *Pekel v Humich* (1999) 21 WAR 24 at 29 per Templeman J.

Prescription Act 1832

8.191   Some of the difficulties of the common law are dealt with in the Prescription Act 1832, but this statute has been castigated as 'one of the worst drafted Acts on the Statute Book.'[1] The confused provisions of the 1832 Act are a self-evident eyesore and are long overdue for statutory reform. The Act is intended to supplement, rather than displace, the other grounds of prescription,[2] but its provisions are available only in the context of litigation which has already arisen in relation to an alleged incumbrance.

1   *14th Report of the Law Reform Committee* (Cmnd 3100, 1966), para 40. See also *Smith v Brudenell-Bruce* [2002] 2 P & CR 51 at [20] per Pumfrey J.

2   See *Hyman v Van den Bergh* [1907] 2 Ch 516 at 532.

Prescriptive periods

8.192   Any period of time pleaded in support of a claim under the Prescription Act 1832 must be the period 'next before some suit or action' in which the claim is challenged.[1] This requirement has the consequence that, however long the period of actual enjoyment, no absolute or indefeasible right can be acquired until the right is brought into question in court proceedings. Until it so crystallises, any right claimed is 'inchoate' only.[2] It follows, moreover, that irrespective of its duration, any discontinued period of long user isolated in the past cannot provide any basis of claim under the 1832 Act.[3] There is a further provision to the effect that no act of obstruction is deemed to be an interruption until it has been submitted to or acquiesced in for one year after the party interrupted had notice both of the interruption and of the person making it.[4]

1 Prescription Act 1832, s 4. See *Hyman v Van den Bergh* [1907] 2 Ch 516 at 528.
2 *Hyman v Van den Bergh* [1907] 2 Ch 516 at 524–525; *Newnham v Willison* (1988) 56 P & CR 8 at 17. See also *Pavledes v Ryesbridge Properties Ltd* (1989) 58 P & CR 459 at 481 (statutory period not yet elapsed).
3 See *Mills v Silver* [1991] Ch 271 at 278B–C. In such circumstances a claim based on lost modern grant [**para 8.190**] may still succeed (*Bakewell Management Ltd v Brandwood* [2004] 2 WLR 955 at [29] per Lord Scott of Foscote).
4 Prescription Act 1832, s 4. See *Dance v Triplow* (1992) 64 P & CR 1 at 3–7, 14–15; [1992] Conv 197 (J Martin). Again, an interruption lasting more than one year does not preclude a valid claim of lost modern grant (see *Ward (Helston) Ltd v Kerrier DC* (1984) 24 RVR 18 at 19).

Easements (other than easements of light)

8.193 In respect of easements other than easements of light, the 1832 Act provides that user as of right[1] and without interruption for 20 years cannot be defeated by evidence that such user commenced after 1189.[2] Such easements, if enjoyed for 40 years as of right and without interruption, are deemed to be 'absolute and indefeasible'[3] unless enjoyed by written consent or agreement.[4]

1 The user must have been *nec vi, nec clam, nec precario* (*Newnham v Willison* (1988) 56 P & CR 8 at 12, 17). See also *Jones v Price and Morgan* (1992) 64 P & CR 404 at 407; *R v Oxfordshire CC, ex p Sunningwell PC* [2000] 1 AC 335 at 351E–G per Lord Hoffmann.
2 Prescription Act 1832, s 2.
3 Prescription Act 1832, s 2.
4 Prescription Act 1832, s 2. In all cases under section 2 of the 1832 Act, a claim of user 'as of right' may be defeated by evidence of even verbal consent or agreement (whether given or made before or after the commencement of the statutory period), except that a consent or agreement before the commencement of the 40 year period must be by deed or writing. See *Hyman v Van den Bergh* [1907] 2 Ch 516 at 530; *Jones v Price and Morgan* (1992) 64 P & CR 404 at 407. An oral permission given before commencement of the 40 year period will bar a claim only if renewed during that period (see *Gardner v Hodgson's Kingston Brewery Co Ltd* [1903] AC 229 at 236).

Easements of light

8.194 Slightly different rules apply to the prescriptive acquisition of easements of light. Under the Prescription Act 1832, the actual enjoyment of access to light for a period of 20 years without interruption renders that access 'absolute and indefeasible'[1] unless it was enjoyed by reason of written consent or agreement.[2]

1   Prescription Act 1832, s 3. There is no requirement here that the user should have been as of right; it may be merely precarious (*Colls v Home and Colonial Stores Ltd* [1904] AC 179 at 205; *Hyman v Van den Bergh* [1907] 2 Ch 516 at 530).

2   A consent or agreement relevant under section 3 must be by deed or writing but may be given or made either before or after the commencement of the statutory period (*Hyman v Van den Bergh* [1907] 2 Ch 516 at 530–531). The 1832 Act does not specify the persons who must be parties to the agreement, but the consent or agreement referred to in section 3 must be such as would be effectual to negative prescription at common law or under presumed grant (*Hyman*, supra at 529–530). It is possible that the prescriptive effect of section 3 may be destroyed by an agreement or consent by the tenant of the supposed dominant owner (*Hyman*, supra at 531).

Profits à prendre

8.195   The 1832 Act provides that a profit *à prendre* which has been enjoyed as of right and without interruption for 30 years 'next before some suit or action' cannot be defeated by proof that the profit arose only after 1189.[1] Moreover, a period of 60 years' user on the same terms makes the prescriptive claim to the profit 'absolute and indefeasible'.[2]

1   Prescription Act 1832, s 1. Statutory prescription is impossible for a profit in gross (see *Bettison v Langton* [2000] Ch 54 at 61G–H).

2   Prescription Act 1832, s 1.

Possible statutory reform

8.196   The Law Commission, whilst acknowledging the deficiencies of the Prescription Act 1832, has made the provisional proposal that, for the future, no prescription of easements or profits *à prendre* should be permissible except under the terms of the 1832 Act.[1] The Commission is currently engaged in a comprehensive review of the law of easements.

1   Law Com No 254 (1998), paras 10.90–10.94, 10.111.

RESERVATION OF EASEMENTS AND PROFITS À PRENDRE

8.197   Reservation is the converse of grant and occurs where a transferor of land reserves for himself easements or profits over the land which he transfers to another. The technique of reservation is nowadays much simpler than it used to be before the enactment of the property legislation of 1925. Once again reservation may be either express or implied.

Express reservation

8.198   If a transferor wishes to retain an easement or profit *à prendre* in respect of land which he conveys to a transferee, it is open to him to do so by means of express words contained in the document of transfer.[1] The precise extent of a reservation is ultimately a matter of construction of the words used in the light of the general principle that the terms of a grant are, in cases of doubt or ambivalence, to be construed *against* the grantor. In the past the courts were accustomed to regard the reservation of an easement or profit as constituting in law a 'regrant' of that right by the purchaser of the servient tenement, with the consequence that the *contra proferentem* rule of construction operated not in favour of the servient owner but in favour of the party who had in effect reserved the right for himself (ie the dominant owner). After 1925 it was generally considered that the balance of advantage conferred by this rule of construction had been reversed by the provision in section 65(1) of the Law of Property Act 1925 that a reservation shall 'operate at law without ... any regrant'. However, the more recent case law seems, somewhat perversely, to favour the proposition that an express reservation of an easement or profit is still to be construed against the servient owner and in favour of the dominant owner.[2]

1 A reservation in favour of Z may be created by a transfer of a legal estate by X to Y which purports to be expressly subject to an easement (albeit not yet in existence at the date of the transfer) for the owner or occupier of a specified dominant tenement (LPA 1925, s 65(2)). Such a conveyance creates an enforceable easement for Z, even though Z is not referred to by name in the transfer (see *Wiles v Banks* (1985) 50 P & CR 80 at 87–90).

2 See *Johnstone v Holdway* [1963] 1 QB 601 at 612–613; (1963) 79 LQR 182 (R E M); *St Edmundsbury and Ipswich Diocesan Board of Finance v Clark (No 2)* [1975] 1 WLR 468 at 478F–G. Compare *Cordell v Second Clanfield Properties Ltd* [1969] 2 Ch 9 at 15B–16B.

Implied reservation

8.199 It is a rule of general application that if a transferor wishes to reserve any rights over land transferred by him, he must do so expressly in clear and unambiguous terms.[1] The law is much more inclined to imply easements in favour of the transferee of land than in favour of the transferor.[2] This stern resistance to the principle of implied reservation finds its locus classicus in the actual decision in (as distinct from the rule emanating from) *Wheeldon v Burrows*.[3] Here a vendor claimed a right of access to light as impliedly reserved in his conveyance to a purchaser. This claim was denied by the Court of Appeal on the ground that reservation can arise only by reason of express stipulation in the terms of the conveyance.[4] To this rule there appear to be only two exceptions.[5]

1 *Broomfield v Williams* [1897] 1 Ch 602 at 616; *Wiles v Banks* (1985) 50 P & CR 80 at 83–84.

2 *Peckham v Ellison* (2000) 79 P & CR 276 at 286 per Cazalet J; *Chaffe v Kingsley* (2000) 79 P & CR 404 at 417 per Parker J, 418 per Sedley LJ; *Holaw (470) Ltd v Stockton Estates Ltd* (2001) 81 P & CR 404 at [82] per Neuberger J.

3 (1879) 12 Ch D 31.

4 For reference to the extreme difficulty of making good a claim of implied reservation, see *Bayley v Great Western Railway Co* (1884) 26 Ch D 434 at 458 per Fry LJ; *Peckham v Ellison* (2000) 79 P & CR 276 at 291; *Parish v Kelly* (1980) 1 BPR 9394 at 9399. There is no room for the contention that a reservation can be implied wherever such would be equitable in all the circumstances (see *Re Webb's Lease* [1951] Ch 808 at 817 per Evershed MR).

5 The *rule* in *Wheeldon v Burrows* applies, of course, only as a ground of implied grant, not as a means of implied reservation (see *Barton v Raine* (1981) 114 DLR (3d) 702 at 706).

Easements of necessity

8.200   It is possible, although unusual, for an easement to be reserved by implication in cases of necessity.[1] Such necessity occurs where a transferor disposes of all the land adjacent to or surrounding the land which he retains, with the consequence that the only possible access to his landlocked close lies across the transferred land. In these circumstances an easement of way can be implied,[2] since without the reservation the transferor's land is rendered unusable.[3] Necessity is, however, strictly construed.[4] It is not sufficient that the easement claimed is merely convenient or reasonably necessary for the enjoyment of the land retained. It must be shown that, without the easement, the transferor's land is completely sterilised.[5] No implied reservation of a right of way may be claimed where the transferor has available to him a legal right (as distinct from a mere permission) to use some alternative access over a neighbour's land[6] or if the transferor retains an adjoining property which permits a means of access.[7]

1   See *Wheeldon v Burrows* (1879) 12 Ch D 31 at 49 per Thesiger LJ.
2   It is for the transferor to select the way (*Packer v Welsted* (1657) 2 Sid 39, 82 ER 1244, *Packer v Wellstead* (1658) 2 Sid 111 at 112, 82 ER 1284 at 1285; *Pearson v Spencer* (1861) 1 B & S 571 at 584–585, 121 ER 827 at 832; *Bolton v Bolton* (1879) 11 Ch D 968 at 972).
3   See *Titchmarsh v Royston Water Co Ltd* (1899) 81 LT 673 at 675; *Barry v Hasseldine* [1952] Ch 835 at 838–839; *Maude v Thornton* [1929] IR 454 at 457. See also *Mobil Oil Co Ltd v Birmingham CC* [2002] 2 P & CR 186 at [89] per Arden LJ.
4   The way of necessity is limited by the necessity existing at the date of grant (see *Parish v Kelly* (1980) 1 BPR 9394 at 9400).
5   *MRA Engineering Ltd v Trimster Co Ltd* (1988) 56 P & CR 1 at 6.
6   *Barry v Hasseldine* [1952] Ch 835 at 839. There is some authority to the effect that a reservation of necessity is extinguished if the claimant subsequently acquires an alternative means of access (see *Holmes v Goring* (1824) 2 Bing 76 at 83–85, 130 ER 233 at 236–237). Compare, however, *Maude v Thornton* [1929] IR 454 at 458, and see *Proctor v Hodgson* (1855) 10 Exch 824 at 828, 156 ER 674 at 675, where both Parke B and Alderson B expressed doubt as to the correctness of *Holmes v Goring*. Parke B opined that a way of necessity ought to be 'as much a grant for ever as if expressly inserted in a deed.'
7   *Ray v Hazeldine* [1904] 2 Ch 17 at 20–21 per Kekewich J.

Easements of common intention

8.201   In rare circumstances a reservation of an easement can be implied in order to give effect to a common intention left unexpressed on the subdivision of land.[1] A heavy onus of proof rests on the transferor who wishes to show that a reservation was mutually intended.[2] A common intention to reserve a right must be specific 'as to the precise nature and extent of that right'[3] and can be upheld only if the facts are 'not reasonably consistent with any explanation other than that of an implied reservation.'[4] It is not enough that the transferee of land knows that his transferor retains adjoining land and 'would probably wish to use [the facility] in the same way as before.'[5]

1   *Pwllbach Colliery Co v Woodman* [1915] AC 634 at 646–647.
2   See *Re Webb's Lease* [1951] Ch 808 at 820; *Chaffe v Kingsley* (2000) 79 P & CR 404 at 416–417; *Green v Lord Somerleyton* [2004] 1 P & CR 520 at [113]. Implied reservation has been

held to give a mutual right of support after the sale of one of two adjoining houses by their common owner (see *Richards v Rose* (1853) 9 Exch 218 at 221, 156 ER 93 at 94–95). See also *Barton v Raine* (1981) 114 DLR (3d) 702 at 706–710.
3   *Chaffe v Kingsley* (2000) 79 P & CR 404 at 417 per Parker J.
4   *Peckham v Ellison* (2000) 79 P & CR 276 at 291 per Cazalet J.
5   *Peckham v Ellison* (2000) 79 P & CR 276 at 291.

TRANSMISSION OF THE BENEFIT AND BURDEN OF LEGAL EASEMENTS

8.202   Easements are proprietary rights not least in the conventional sense that, once duly created or acquired, they annex a benefit to the dominant tenement (and a corresponding burden to the servient tenement) and therefore have the potential to affect the successors in title of either tenement. The precise effect of an easement on third parties depends to some extent on the legal or equitable quality of the easement[1] and on whether it relates to registered or unregistered land. The relevant problems arise where A has granted an easement to B (see *Fig. 13*). Are C and D affected by respectively the *burden* and *benefit* of that easement?

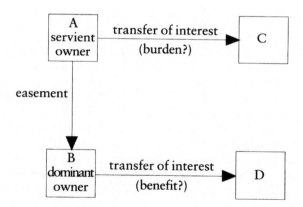

Fig. 13

1   [**Para 8.110**]. The transmission of the benefit and burden of equitable easements is discussed in Chapter 9 [**paras 9.97–9.101**].

8.203   The transmission of benefit and burden is complicated by the fact that English law treats these two aspects of an easement as severable from each other. Thus the mere fact that (in *Fig. 13*) the *benefit* of an easement may pass to B's successor, D, does not mean that the easement is necessarily enforceable against A's successor, C. Enforceability is achieved only if the *burden* of the easement was effectively transmitted to C under the rules which govern the binding effect of interests in land. There is here, of course, a difficulty for the lay person who imagines, in his or her innocence, that there can be no 'benefit' for anyone unless someone else is simultaneously subject to a correlative 'burden'.[1] However, English land law approaches the issue of enforceability in an artificial, and initially confusing, manner. Benefit and burden are treated as separate phenomena, the transmission of which is governed by independent principles. The apparent illogic of this approach is less bizarre when considered in a forensic context. Any action to enforce an easement will succeed only if the claimant can be shown to have the *benefit*, and the defendant the *burden*, of the easement in question. Thus, for the land lawyer, the real questions are whether (in *Fig.* 13) the benefit of the easement concerned has been got out of B into D, and the burden out of A into C.

1   See, however, *Rogers v Hosegood* [1900] 2 Ch 388 at 395 per Farwell J.

Benefit

8.204   Since no easement can exist in gross,[1] easements can never be transferred independently of the land which they benefit or be retained by a vendor who sells all of the benefited land.

1   [**Paras 2.24, 8.26**].

Registered land

8.205   The express grant of a legal easement out of a registered estate in favour of other registered land requires to be 'completed by registration.' The benefit of the easement must therefore be entered in the property register of the dominant title,[1] whereupon the owner of the dominant land becomes, effectively, the proprietor of two separate 'estates' – ie his own freehold or leasehold estate in the dominant land and also the estate of easement over the servient land.[2] His proprietorship of both estates is recorded within one and the same individual register of title,[3] with the result that, on any subsequent transfer of the dominant title, the benefit of the easement – now an intrinsic component of the property register[4] – automatically passes to the transferee. Thus, in *Fig.* 13, the benefit of the easement granted by A to B can be claimed by D.

1   [**Para 8.119**].
2   The benefit of implied and prescriptive easements, if established to the satisfaction of the registrar, can likewise be registered as appurtenant to the estate of the dominant land (LRR 2003, r 74).
3   See LRA 2002, s 59(1), Sch 2, para 7(2)(b); LRR 2003, r 3(1).
4   See LRR 2003, r 5(b)(ii).

8.206   The registration requirements of the Land Registration Act 2002 thus give indirect effect to the statutory prescription that the legal estate in an easement 'shall enure for the benefit of the land to which it is intended to be annexed.'[1] Legal easements become notionally affixed to the tenement to which they are appurtenant, in much the same way that fixtures become annexed to realty.[2]

1   LPA 1925, s 187(1).
2   [**Para 1.64**].

Unregistered land

8.207 The benefit of a legal easement in favour of unregistered land is automatically annexed to the dominant land and passes tacitly with any subsequent conveyance of that land.[1] The easement will normally be entered as appurtenant to the dominant estate on first registration of title at Land Registry.[2]

1   LPA 1925, s 62(1)–(2). See *Godwin v Schweppes Ltd* [1902] 1 Ch 926 at 932; *Wright v Macadam* [1949] 2 KB 744 at 754; *Sunset Properties Pty Ltd v Johnston* (1975) 3 BPR 9185 at 9189 (devise).
2   LRA 2002, s 14(b); LRR 2003, r 33.

Benefit available for tenants

8.208   In the case of either registered or unregistered land, the benefit of the easement is also available to any occupier for the time being of the land.[1]

1   *Leech v Schweder* (1874) 9 Ch App 463 at 474–475. See e g *Thorpe v Brumfitt* (1873) 8 Ch App 650 at 655–656 (lessee). Similarly, easements created in a lease can be enjoyed by a subtenant.

Subdivision of the dominant tenement

8.209   There is a prima facie inference that an easement becomes appurtenant to each and every part of the dominant land[1] and is not therefore destroyed by a later subdivision of that land.[2] The benefit of the easement may be claimed by the transferee of any part of the original dominant tenement,[3] so long as the claimant can show that the easement confers benefit on his portion of the whole and does not disproportionately burden the servient land.[4] This convenient inference of diffused benefit is rebuttable by contrary words of grant,[5] but where the benefit of the incorporeal right is distributable in this way the law of easements has been able to avoid the problems which once bedevilled the law of restrictive covenants following a fragmentation of the dominant tenement.[6]

1   *Callard v Beeney* [1930] 1 KB 353 at 360–361; *Gallagher v Rainbow* (1994) 179 CLR 624 at 633. See also *Laurie v Winch* [1952] 4 DLR 449 at 456–457; *Re Maiorana and the Conveyancing Act* [1970] 1 NSWR 627 at 634; *Re Gordon and Regan* (1985) 15 DLR (4th) 641 at 645; *Butler v Muddle* (1995) 6 BPR 13984 at 13985.
2   See e g *Newcomen v Coulson* (1877) 5 Ch D 133 at 141 per Jessel MR; *Gallagher v Rainbow* (1994) 179 CLR 624 at 632–634 per Brennan, Dawson and Toohey JJ; *Durack v De Winton* (1998) 9 BPR 16403 at 16437.
3   See *Guth v Robinson* (1977) 1 BPR 9209 at 9214; *Short v Patrial Holdings Pty Ltd* (1994) 6 BPR 13996 at 14002–14003; *Coles Myer NSW Ltd v Dymocks Book Arcade Ltd* (1996) 9 BPR 16939 at 16948.
4   See *Gallagher v Rainbow* (1994) 179 CLR 624 at 632–634.
5   See *Jennison v Traficante* (1980) 1 BPR 9657 at 9658–9659.
6   **[Para 13.75]**.

Burden

8.210   In certain instances the successful assertion of the benefit of the easement may depend on whether the *burden* has run with the servient land so as to affect successors in title of the original servient owner. Reception of the benefit of an easement is, of course, futile if it cannot be shown that its burden has come to rest upon the party against whom enforcement is sought.

Registered land

8.211   The burden of any legal easement expressly created out of a registered estate requires, by way of fulfilment of the relevant 'registration requirements', to have been entered by 'notice' in the charges register of the servient estate.[1] If protected in this way, the burden of the easement is clearly binding on all subsequent disponees of the servient estate (e g C in *Fig.* 13).[2] The burden of any easement over registered land which arises by way of implied grant or prescription generally 'overrides' any registered disposition of the servient estate. Such easements (which are necessarily legal easements) automatically bind transferees of the servient land, provided at least that the easements in question were 'obvious on a reasonably careful inspection of the land.'[3]

1   [**Para 8.119**]. For want of compliance with this 'registration requirement', the disposition of an expressly created easement cannot 'operate at law' and the easement takes effect only in equity (LRA 2002, s 27(1) [**paras 9.91, 12.87**]).
2   LRA 2002, s 29(1), (2)(a)(i) [**para 12.76**].
3   LRA 2002, s 29(1), (2)(a)(ii), Sch 3, para 3(1) [**para 12.239**].

Unregistered land

8.212   The rule governing the transmission of the burden of legal easements over unregistered land is straightforward. Simply by virtue of their legal quality, all such easements bind the world.[1] Thus, in *Fig.* 13, if the easement granted by A to B was legal, its burden automatically affects the servient tenement in the hands of C. When the servient land is finally brought on to the Land Register, the burden of the legal easement is noted in the newly opened register of title.[2]

1   [**Para 12.274**].
2   LRA 2002, s 14(b); LRR 2003, r 35(1) [**para 12.267**].

TRANSMISSION OF THE BENEFIT AND BURDEN OF LEGAL PROFITS À PRENDRE

8.213   Both the benefit and the burden of a legal profit *à prendre* may be transmitted to third parties.

Benefit

8.214   In the case of both registered and unregistered land, the benefit of a profit *à prendre* which is appurtenant to a particular dominant tenement normally passes on the transfer of the dominant land.[1] A profit in gross[2] is, by contrast, transferable only as an independent 'piece of real property.'[3] In the case of registered land, such a profit is substantively registrable under a unique title number as a 'registered estate' which is thereafter capable of independent disposition.[4]

1 LPA 1925, s 62(1); *Bettison v Langton* [2002] 1 AC 27 at [35] per Lord Scott of Foscote. See, in the case of registered land, LRA 2002, Sch 2, para 7(2)(b) [**para 8.119**].
2 [**Para 8.20**].
3 *Lovett v Fairclough* (1989) 61 P & CR 385 at 398.
4 [**Para 8.118**].

Burden

8.215 The burden of any legal profit *à prendre* expressly created out of a registered estate is necessarily noted in the charges register of the servient estate[1] and therefore binds all subsequent disponees of the land over which it is exercisable.[2] The burden of any profit over registered land which arises by way of implied grant or prescription generally 'overrides' a registered disposition of that land.[3] In unregistered land the burden of a legal profit automatically binds all (including purchasers of the servient tenement).[4]

1 [**Para 8.119**].
2 LRA 2002, s 29(1), (2)(a)(i) [**para 12.76**].
3 LRA 2002, s 29(1), (2)(a)(ii), Sch 3, para 3(1) [**para 12.239**].
4 [**Para 12.274**].

EXTINGUISHMENT OF EASEMENTS AND PROFITS À *PRENDRE*

8.216 Since an easement or profit *à prendre* represents for the dominant owner an important and valuable proprietary right, the courts have been slow to hold that such rights (if otherwise unlimited in their terms) are brought to an end by subsequent events. There are nevertheless several ways at common law in which easements and profits may be extinguished or suspended.[1]

1 In registered land the registrar is required to close the registered title to any estate which he is satisfied has been determined (LRR 2003, r 79(2)).

Unity of ownership and possession

8.217 Easements and appurtenant profits are automatically extinguished if at any time the dominant and servient tenements pass into the ownership and possession of the same person.[1] There is at least a surface logic in the proposition that 'a man cannot have an easement over his own land.'[2] The same proposition is nevertheless bounded by strong limiting factors. The extinctive merger must bring together two similar and equally perdurable estates.[3] Unity of possession without unity of ownership (or vice versa) has a merely suspensory effect on the existence of an easement.[4] There is, moreover, a highly

persuasive view that the doctrine of extinguishment by merger has no application to easements of necessity.[5] In respect of such easements the stringent
nature of the original necessity is not normally diminished by any intervening
union of title or possession.[6]

1   **[Para 8.47]**. See *Tyrringham's Case* (1584) 4 Co Rep 36b at 38a, 76 ER 973 at 980; *Payne v
    Inwood* (1997) 74 P & CR 42 at 51; *The Queen v Tener* (1985) 17 DLR (4th) 1 at 17; *Durack v
    De Winton* (1998) 9 BPR 16403 at 16437. See also J D A Brooke-Taylor, (1977) 41 Conv (NS)
    107. Contrast the effect of merger under other Torrens legislation (see e g Real Property
    Act 1900 (New South Wales), s 47(7)).
2   *Margil Pty Ltd v Stegul Pastoral Pty Ltd* [1984] 2 NSWLR 1 at 9D, citing *Roe v Siddons* (1888)
    22 QBD 224 at 236 per Fry LJ.
3   *R v Inhabitants of Hermitage* (1692) Carth 239, 90 ER 743; *Re Cockburn* (1896) 27 OR 450 at
    459–460; *Re Lonegren and Rueben* (1987) 37 DLR (4th) 491 at 496–497 (affd (1988) 50 DLR
    (4th) 431 at 433). There is authority that an easement extinguished by merger can be revived
    by subsequent reference to that easement in a later transfer document executed by the
    common owner in respect of the former dominant tenement (see *Cuvet v Davis* (1883) 9 VLR
    390 at 396; *Margil Pty Ltd v Stegul Pastoral Pty Ltd* [1984] 2 NSWLR 1 at 10G–11A).
4   *Hillman v Rogers* (Unreported, Court of Appeal, 19 December 1997). Thus, for instance, the
    fact that X owns the freehold of Greenacre and simultaneously holds a lease over the
    adjoining Redacre merely suspends any easement granted earlier in respect of these two
    premises. The easement revives when the unity of possession is severed (see *Thomas v Thomas*
    (1835) 2 Cr M & R 34 at 40, 150 ER 15 at 17). See also *Richardson v Graham* [1908] 1 KB 39
    at 43; *Post Investments Pty Ltd v Wilson* (1990) 5 BPR 11146 at 11147.
5   *Parish v Kelly* (1980) 1 BPR 9394 at 9400; *Margil Pty Ltd v Stegul Pastoral Pty Ltd* [1984]
    2 NSWLR 1 at 10A–C.
6   See *Pheysey v Vicary* (1847) 16 M & W 484 at 490, 153 ER 1280 at 1282 per Alderson B;
    Margil Pty Ltd v Stegul Pastoral Pty Ltd [1984] 2 NSWLR 1 at 9E–10C. This approach
    effectively treats implied rights of necessary access as being not so much easements as natural
    incidents of the right of ownership (see *Bowers v Kennedy* 2000 SC 555 at [16]–[18], [24]).

Express release

8.218   A legal easement or profit may be extinguished by an express release
executed in the form of a deed by its owner.[1] Express release is usually made for
valuable consideration and is complete without any supporting evidence of
non-user by the owner.[2] In the case of registered land, an application should be
made to cancel the relevant entries in the property register of the dominant title
and in the charges register of the servient title.

1   *Lovell v Smith* (1857) 3 CB (NS) 120 at 126–127, 140 ER 685 at 687. A release otherwise than
    by deed may be effective in equity, as for instance where the servient owner has incurred
    detriment in reliance on the informal release (see e g *Waterlow v Bacon* (1866) LR 2 Eq 514 at
    520).
2   See *Wolfe v Freijah's Holdings Pty Ltd* [1988] VR 1017 at 1024.

Implied release

8.219   Implied release of an easement or profit occurs where abandonment of
the exercise of the right is coupled with a clear intention to release the right in

question.[1] Abandonment, when it occurs, may extend to any or all of the multiple users permitted within the parcel of rights conferred by the original grant.[2]

1   *Ward v Ward* (1852) 7 Ex 838 at 839–840, 155 ER 1189 at 1190; *Swan v Sinclair* [1924] 1 Ch 254 at 266; *Tehidy Minerals Ltd v Norman* [1971] 2 QB 528 at 553D–F. In *Costagliola v English* (1969) 210 EG 1425 at 1431, Megarry J conceded the 'undoubted similarities' between the doctrines of abandonment and proprietary estoppel, but thought it wrong to 'equate' them.

2   Thus on sufficient evidence a dominant owner of a right of way may be found to have abandoned the user of the way as a carriageway but not as a footway (see eg *Snell & Prideaux Ltd v Dutton Mirrors Ltd* [1995] 1 EGLR 259 at 261J; *Guth v Robinson* (1977) 1 BPR 9209 at 9214; compare *Bulstrode v Lambert* [1953] 1 WLR 1064 at 1068).

Intention to abandon

8.220   In order to establish implied abandonment, it must be demonstrated that the dominant owner formed a 'fixed intention never at any time thereafter to assert the right himself or to attempt to transmit it to anyone else.'[1] Some circumstances are relatively clear-cut. For example, alterations to, or demolition of, a structure situated on the dominant tenement (eg a mill which enjoys an easement of water) may substantiate the intention to abandon user.[2] But it normally requires little evidence, particularly in the case of a right conferred by express grant, to counteract any supposed intention of abandonment. Since autonomous control is of the essence of proprietary rights, a grantee 'may always, if he chooses, not exercise his rights under the grant to the full without in any way prejudicing his full right if he finds it convenient to use it.'[3] It is therefore clear that no abandonment is established by a short-lived cessation of user[4] or by the temporary suspension of a user by agreement with the servient owner.[5] The courts are reluctant to allow a widely construed doctrine of abandonment to discourage or penalise neighbourly acts of co-operation or acquiescence.[6]

1   *Tehidy Minerals Ltd v Norman* [1971] 2 QB 528 at 553D per Buckley LJ. See also *Huckvale v Aegean Hotels Ltd* (1989) 58 P & CR 163 at 167 per Nourse LJ, 171 per Butler-Sloss LJ; *Guth v Robinson* (1977) 1 BPR 9209 at 9214; *Jennison v Traficante* (1980) 1 BPR 9657 at 9659; *Finlayson v Campbell* (1997) 8 BPR 15703 at 15717 per Young J.

2   *Liggins v Inge* (1831) 7 Bing 682 at 693, 131 ER 263 at 268. See similarly *McAdams Homes Ltd v Robinson* [2004] EWCA Civ 214 at [12]. A change of circumstances rendering the easement no longer of any benefit can be regarded, in clear cases, as demonstrating an intention to abandon (see *New England Structural Co v Everett Distilling Co*, 75 NE 85 at 87 (1905); *Dean v Colt*, 84 P2d 481 at 484–485 (1938)).

3   *Keewatin Power Co Ltd v Lake of the Woods Milling Co Ltd* [1930] AC 640 at 647 per Viscount Dunedin.

4   See *Bulstrode v Lambert* [1953] 1 WLR 1064 at 1068 (10 years); *Clark v Duckworth* [1984] 2 NZLR 58 at 64 (3 or 4 years).

5   *Payne v Sheddon* (1834) 1 Mood & R 382 at 383, 174 ER 131; *Sunset Properties Pty Ltd v Johnston* (1975) 3 BPR 9185 at 9195 (suspension of user on Sundays). Similarly, a variation of the route of an existing way by acquiescence or consent does not constitute abandonment (*Davis v Whitby* [1974] Ch 186 at 191E–192A; *Sunset Properties, supra* at 9192).

6   See *Snell & Prideaux Ltd v Dutton Mirrors Ltd* [1995] 1 EGLR 259 at 262C–E, 264H–J.

Non-use is not implied release

8.221   Mere failure to exercise a right is not, of itself, implied abandonment.[1] It is particularly difficult to show abandonment of a right of way.[2] Non-use of the right of way – even over a lengthy period – does not necessarily constitute implied release,[3] since 'it is one thing not to assert an intention to use a way, and another thing to assert an intention to abandon it.'[4] An extremely long suspension of user of an easement may, however, render it necessary for the dominant owner either to provide an explanation for the non-user[5] or to show that during the period of suspension some indication was given of an intention to preserve the relevant entitlement.[6]

1   See *Benn v Hardinge* (1992) 66 P & CR 246 at 255; *Bosomworth v Faber* (1992) 69 P & CR 288 at 294–295; *Snell & Prideaux Ltd v Dutton Mirrors Ltd* [1995] 1 EGLR 259 at 261M–262E; *Palmer v Bowman* [2000] 1 WLR 842 at 849A. It is equally the case that excessive use does not extinguish an easement (except perhaps in the case of continuous easements of support or light). See *Graham v Philcox* [1984] QB 747 at 756E–F; *Woodhouse v Consolidated Property Corpn Ltd* (1993) 66 P & CR 234 at 243.

2   *Finlayson v Campbell* (1997) 8 BPR 15703 at 15717 per Young J. See e g *Carder v Davies and Davies* (1998) 76 P & CR D33 at D34. Scots law goes even further, taking the view that non-use can never forfeit an implied right of necessary access. Such a right is an incident of ownership and it is inconsistent with the nature of ownership that the owner should be obliged to visit his land simply in order to maintain his entitlement to the access (see *Bowers v Kennedy* 2000 SC 555 at [16]).

3   *Crossley & Sons Ltd v Lightowler* (1867) 2 Ch App 478 at 482; *Swan v Sinclair* [1924] 1 Ch 254 at 266; *Treweeke v 36 Wolseley Road Pty Ltd* (1973) 128 CLR 274 at 282–285 per McTiernan J, 302–304 per Mason J; *Riley v Penttila* [1974] VR 547 at 570; *Guth v Robinson* (1977) 1 BPR 9209 at 9214; *Barton v Raine* (1981) 114 DLR (3d) 702 at 710; *Wolfe v Freijah's Holdings Pty Ltd* [1988] VR 1017 at 1024; *Finlayson v Campbell* (1997) 8 BPR 15703 at 15717; *Pekel v Humich* (1999) 21 WAR 24 at 37.

4   *James v Stevenson* [1893] AC 162 at 168 per Sir Edward Fry.

5   *Treweeke v 36 Wolseley Road Pty Ltd* (1973) 128 CLR 274 at 288 per Walsh J; *Riley v Penttila* [1974] VR 547 at 570–572; *McIntyre v Porter* [1983] 2 VR 439 at 444.

6   *Moore v Rawson* (1824) 3 B & C 332 at 337–338, 107 ER 756 at 759; *Crossley & Sons Ltd v Lightowler* (1867) 2 Ch App 478 at 482; *Riley v Penttila* [1974] VR 547 at 570.

No presumption of abandonment after 20 years

8.222   It used to be thought that, in the total absence of contrary evidence, an intention to abandon could be presumed after a discontinuation of user for 20 years.[1] Recent decisions have nevertheless shown the courts to be disinclined to uphold claims of abandonment even after relatively long periods of discontinued user.[2] In *Benn v Hardinge*,[3] for instance, the Court of Appeal was unwilling to presume an intention to abandon a right of way after a period of non-user of 175 years.[4] In the view of Hirst LJ, the abandonment of such a 'valuable latent piece of property' was not lightly to be inferred since the right might be of 'significant importance in the future.'[5] Here the fact of prolonged non-user was met by the explanation that throughout the period in question the dominant owner and his predecessors in title had enjoyed an alternative means of access to their tenement.[6]

1   *Moore v Rawson* (1824) 3 B & C 332 at 339, 107 ER 756 at 759. Compare, however, *Cook v Bath Corpn* (1868) LR 6 Eq 177 at 180.
2   To permit a servient owner too readily to claim an implied release would effectively allow him to expropriate the dominant owner without compensation (see U Reichman, 'Judicial Supervision of Servitudes' 7 J Legal Stud 139 at 157 (1978)).
3   (1992) 66 P & CR 246 at 260–262.
4   See also *Gotobed v Pridmore* (1970) 115 Sol Jo 78; *Williams v Usherwood* (1983) 45 P & CR 235 at 256; *Guth v Robinson* (1977) 1 BPR 9209 at 9214; *Grill v Hockey* (1991) 5 BPR 11421 at 11424.
5   (1992) 66 P & CR 246 at 262.
6   (1992) 66 P & CR 246 at 261–262.

Change of circumstance

8.223   It is inevitable that the problem of obsolescence should affect ease-ments and profits, since such rights usually arise in the context of legal arrangements which have an extended or undefined time horizon.[1] There is, however, no statutory provision in English law for the discharge or modification of easements or profits which have become redundant or obstructive with the effluxion of time.[2] In the absence of such interventionist legislation there is a strong argument for recognising in at least limited form a 'change of circum-stance' doctrine under which courts are empowered to modify or terminate obsolete forms of incumbrance.[3]

1   See S E Sterk, 'Foresight and the Law of Servitudes' 73 Cornell L Rev 956 (1987–88).
2   Compare (in relation to restrictive covenants) LPA 1925, s 84 **[para 13.127]**. New Zealand courts have a statutory power to modify or extinguish an easement on the ground that it is 'obsolete' or that its continued existence 'would impede the reasonable user of the land' (see Property Law Act 1952, s 127: *Masters v Snell* [1979] 1 NZLR 34 at 40–43; *Armishaw v Denby Horton (NZ) Ltd* [1984] 1 NZLR 44 at 45–47). Similar powers exist in Australia (see Conveyancing Act 1919 (NSW), s 89(1): *Manly Properties Pty Ltd v Castrisos* [1973] 2 NSWLR 420; *Pieper v Edwards* [1982] 1 NSWLR 336; *Durian (Holdings) Pty Ltd v Cavacourt Pty Ltd* (2000) 10 BPR 18099) and Canada (Property Law Act (RSBC 1996), s 35(2): *TDL Group Ltd v Harvey* (2002) 212 DLR (4th) 278).
3   The possibility of such intervention undoubtedly reopens the liberal dilemma prompted by the tension between private autonomy and sensible social regulation (see G S Alexander, 'Freedom, Coercion, and the Law of Servitudes' 73 Cornell L Rev 883 (1987–88)). The application of a 'change of circumstance' doctrine tends to inhibit undesirable holdout strategies on the part of dominant owners of now pointless servitudes, whilst reconciling foresightless private arrangements with vastly changed present realities.

8.224   Although a 'change of circumstance' doctrine appears a novel proposi-tion in English land law, it is neither wholly implausible nor wholly without precedent. A way of necessity is said, for instance, to be limited by the necessity which created it[1] and therefore to be extinguished by changed conditions which alleviate the necessity.[2] The obsolescence issue was raised in a more general form in *Huckvale v Aegean Hotels Ltd*.[3] Here the dominant owner's expressly granted right of way over the servient tenement became largely purposeless when that owner lost accompanying and complementary rights over other land belonging to the servient owner. The Court of Appeal felt that it could not altogether rule out the possibility that an easement may be extinguished by operation of law when it ceases to accommodate the dominant tenement.[4] In the *Huckvale* case, however, there could be no question of extinguishment since it was impossible to claim with certainty that the easement had ceased to confer a 'real and practical benefit' on the dominant land or could never be 'reasonably necessary for its better enjoyment in the future.'[5] Although agreeing that a court should be slow to hold that an easement has been 'extinguished by frustration', Slade LJ was prepared to contemplate precisely such an outcome if circumstances 'have changed so drastically since the date of the original grant of an easement (for example by supervening illegality) that it would offend common sense and reality for the court to hold that an easement still subsisted.'[6] In Slade LJ's view, however, the evidence must show clearly that, because of the later change of circumstance, there is 'no practical possibility' that the easement will ever again benefit the dominant tenement in the manner contemplated by the initial grant.

1   See *Holmes v Goring* (1824) 2 Bing 76 at 83–84, 130 ER 233 at 236–237.
2   Changed conditions arise, for instance, with the acquisition of a hitherto unavailable alternative means of access. Alteration of a servient tenement may likewise bring about the extinguishment of a profit *à prendre*, although the profit may automatically revive if the servient property is later restored to its former condition (see *Ellison v Vukicevic* (1986) 7 NSWLR 104 at 114B–C).
3   (1989) 58 P & CR 163; [1990] Conv 292 (G Kodilinye).
4   (1989) 58 P & CR 163 at 170 per Nourse LJ, 172 per Butler-Sloss LJ.
5   (1989) 58 P & CR 163 at 172 per Nourse LJ.
6   (1989) 58 P & CR 163 at 173.

RENTCHARGES

8.225   The rentcharge comprises a further form of potential entitlement in the land of another. A rentcharge is a right to a revenue – ie a right to a periodic payment of money charged on or issuing out of land other than under a lease or mortgage[1] – and is statutorily declared to be capable of creation at law.[2]

1   Rentcharges Act 1977, s 1.
2   LPA 1925, s 1(2)(b).

Creation

8.226   A rentcharge arises for instance where A has charged his own estate in land with a payment of £1000 per annum in favour of B. In such circumstances B is regarded as holding a proprietary estate in A's land. B's rentcharge can constitute a legal estate only if it was created by deed[1] and is 'either perpetual or for a term of years absolute',[2] being *equitable* in all other cases.[3]

1   LPA 1925, 52(1). Rentcharges may also, albeit rarely, be the product of statute and may also be created by will, although in the latter case the rentcharge becomes a legal interest only following a written assent by the personal representatives (Administration of Estates Act 1925, s 36(4)).
2   LPA 1925, s 1(2)(b).

3   LPA 1925, s 1(3).

Substantive registration of rentcharges

8.227 The creation of a legal rentcharge out of a registered estate in land ranks as a 'registrable disposition'[1] which must itself be 'completed', first, by the substantive registration of the grantee as proprietor of the 'registered estate' of the rentcharge under a unique title number and, second, by the entry of a corresponding 'notice' in the register of the estate charged.[2] Such registration is now compulsory, as the precondition of an effective grant 'at law', in respect of any rentcharge created without limit of time or for a term of more than seven years.[3] An existing rentcharge issuing out of an unregistered estate in land can be the subject of a voluntary first registration of title at Land Registry,[4] provided that the rentcharge in question was granted without limit of time or for a term which still has more than seven years left to run.[5]

1   LRA 2002, s 27(1), (2)(e).
2   LRA 2002, Sch 2, para 6(2).
3   LRA 2002, Sch 2, para 6(1).
4   LRR 2003, r 2(2)(b).
5   LRA 2002, s 3(1)(b), (2)–(3).

Phasing out of rentcharges

8.228 Rentcharges have become increasingly uncommon and are now being phased out of existence under the terms of the Rentcharges Act 1977.[1] This legislation recognises the anomalous nature of rentcharges in the modern context and provides, in principle, that no new rentcharge may be created after 21 August 1977 'whether at law or in equity.'[2] Rentcharges created prior to the 1977 Act are liable to be extinguished at the expiry of a period of 60 years beginning with the commencement of the 1977 Act (ie in 2037) or with the date on which the rentcharge in question first became payable (whichever is the later).[3] The enactment of this 60-year 'sunset rule' is subject to certain exceptions, of which the most significant are the following. (In effect the statutory embargo on new rentcharges covers only those created in a commercial context for money or money's worth.)

1   See Law Commission, *Report on Rentcharges* (Law Com No 68, August 1975).
2   Rentcharges Act 1977, s 2(1). Except in certain specific cases, any instrument which purports to create a new rentcharge is declared void (Rentcharges Act 1977, s 2(2)).
3   Rentcharges Act 1977, s 3(1).

Family charges

8.229 The Rentcharges Act 1977 does not prohibit the creation of a rentcharge which charges land voluntarily (or in consideration of marriage) or by way of family arrangement with the payment of capital or an annual or periodical sum for the benefit of a designated person.[1] Any instrument coming into operation after 1996, which in this way carves out of land a revenue entitlement for a family member, is statutorily deemed to be a declaration that the land is held in trust to give effect to the charge.[2]

1   Rentcharges Act 1977, s 2(3)(a).
2   TOLATA 1996, Sch 1, para 3. A similar instrument coming into operation prior to 1997 had the effect of imposing a strict settlement on the land charged (see SLA 1925, s 1(1)(v) **[para 9.210]**).

Estate rentcharges

8.230   Another exempted class is the 'estate rentcharge,'[1] which often plays a useful role in the enforcement of positive freehold covenants.[2] An estate rentcharge is one which couples an obligation of (usually nominal) money payment with some other much more onerous positive covenant (e g to repair or maintain premises), a right of entry[3] being annexed to the rentcharge in order to secure performance of the covenants. Because any legal right of entry annexed to the rentcharge is enforceable against the rentchargor's successors, the device of the estate rentcharge provides a circuitous means of ensuring – contrary to the usual common law rule[4] – that the burden of positive freehold covenants runs with the covenantor's land.

1   Rentcharges Act 1977, s 2(3)(c), (4)–(5).
2   **[Para 13.58]**.
3   **[Para 8.264]**.
4   See *Rhone v Stephens* [1994] 2 AC 310 **[para 13.50]**.

Termination

8.231   During the period before the final statutory extinguishment of all other than specifically exempted rentcharges,[1] a rentcharge may be terminated by express release. A rentcharge whose title has not been registered at Land Registry may also be extinguished under the Limitation Act if the charge is not paid for 12 years.[2] Save in exceptional cases (such as those relating to family charges and estate rentcharges), the rentchargor is also entitled to offer a capital sum in full settlement of the obligation of the rentcharge, the redemption price being calculated according to an algebraic formula prescribed by the Rentcharges Act 1977.[3] After payment of this premature settlement figure, the Secretary of State is empowered to issue a 'redemption certificate',[4] which records that the relevant land is no longer subject to the rentcharge.[5]

1   See Rentcharges Act 1977, s 3(1).
2   Limitation Act 1980, s 15(1). The limitation rule has been disapplied in relation to registered rentcharges (see LRA 2002, s 96(1) **[para 6.55]**).
3   Rentcharges Act 1977, ss 8–10.
4   Rentcharges Act 1977, s 9.
5   Rentcharges Act 1977, s 8.

MORTGAGES

8.232 A mortgage – or more accurately a 'charge by way of legal mortgage' – constitutes a further entitlement declared by the Law of Property Act 1925 to be capable of creation at law.[1] Where it is created in conformity with certain requirements of formality (and, if appropriate, registration), such a charge constitutes another species of legal estate in land.[2]

1   LPA 1925, s 1(2)(c).
2   The regulation of mortgages is examined in greater detail in Chapter 15.

Function

8.233 A mortgage is a security interest created by a borrower (or 'mortgagor') in favour of a lender (or 'mortgagee'). Most lenders of large amounts of money, being reluctant to rely merely upon the borrower's contractual promise to repay, require some form of security in respect of the debt owed to them. The device of the mortgage provides this security precisely because, in circumstances of contractual default, the capital debt (plus accumulated interest) is ultimately recoverable from the sale of the land which has been subjected to the mortgage charge.

8.234 Mortgages of realty provide a major means of financing commercial initiative and investment, money borrowed on the security of land being used to stimulate business and development.[1] Mortgage transactions have also become the primary means of financing home ownership in fee simple or on long lease,[2] the prospective home-owner often raising the bulk of the required purchase price by means of a loan from an institutional mortgagee such as a bank or building society.[3] In this way the purchaser acquires the fee simple estate or a long leasehold interest in the land purchased and contemporaneously grants the lender a charge by way of legal mortgage as security for the loan. The purchaser retains ownership of the estate throughout the loan term, although remaining under a contractual obligation to repay both the capital sum advanced and any interest which it bears. The home-owner – the mortgagor – is thereby enabled to acquire both a residential base and a major capital asset by way of instalment purchase over a lengthy period (usually 20 or 25 years). Meanwhile the creditor – the mortgagee – is protected since the charge taken as security can always be enforced by taking possession of the premises if the mortgagor becomes unable to discharge his obligations under the terms of the loan.

1   See *Royal Bank of Scotland plc v Etridge (No 2)* [2002] 2 AC 773 at [34] per Lord Nicholls of Birkenhead.
2   Within the residential sector almost 60 per cent of all properties are nowadays subject to some current mortgage liability (*Social Trends 32* (2002 edn London), p 167).
3   The unprecedented availability of mortgage funds has promoted a powerful ideology of home ownership in Britain (see Lord Diplock's reference in *Pettitt v Pettitt* [1970] AC 777 at 824C to 'the emergence of a property-owning, particularly a real-property-mortgaged-to-a-building-society-owning, democracy').

Definitions

8.235   In the law of mortgage there is a technical distinction between the concepts of 'mortgage' and 'charge'.

Mortgage

8.236   In strict terms a 'mortgage' is a disposition of some ownership interest in land or other property 'as a security for the payment of a debt or the discharge of some other obligation for which it is given.'[1] The mortgagee is thereby placed in the privileged position of being a secured creditor of the mortgagor, with the consequence that he enjoys priority over the mortgagor's unsecured creditors if he becomes insolvent. For the purpose of recovering the loan money, the mortgagee enjoys not merely a personal right based on the contract of loan with the borrower, but also a proprietary right, potentially enforceable against third parties, to realise the value of the mortgaged property by sale. Mortgage transactions thus represent one of the safest ways of lending money since, in the last resort, the asset offered as security can be appropriated by the mortgagee and the proceeds of sale applied in the repayment of the loan.[2]

1   *Santley v Wilde* [1899] 2 Ch 474 per Lindley LJ. See also *Swiss Bank Corpn v Lloyds Bank Ltd* [1982] AC 584 at 595C–D per Buckley LJ.
2   *Bevham Investments Pty Ltd v Belgot Pty Ltd* (1982) 149 CLR 494 at 499.

Charge

8.237   Whereas a mortgage actually invests the mortgagee with some form of estate ownership in relation to the secured property, a 'charge' strictly confers no ownership of any estate,[1] but merely gives the 'chargee' a bundle of rights and powers (eg of possession and sale) over the property which is charged as security for the loan.[2] Nevertheless the practical distinction between mortgages and charges is relatively unimportant and the terms are nowadays used virtually interchangeably.[3] Indeed the primary means of mortgaging a registered estate in land is now the 'registered charge'.

1   See *English Scottish and Australian Bank Ltd v Phillips* (1937) 57 CLR 302 at 321.
2   **[Paras 15.109, 15.171]**.
3   The distinction is finally blurred by the reference in the 1925 legislation to a 'charge by way of legal mortgage' (LPA 1925, ss 1(2)(c), 85(1)). See *Grand Junction Co Ltd v Bates* [1954] 2 QB 160 at 168–169; *Regent Oil Co Ltd v J A Gregory (Hatch End) Ltd* [1966] Ch 402 at 431B–E.

Modern rationalisation of the law of mortgage

8.238   Lord Macnaghten once remarked that 'no one ... by the light of nature ever understood an English mortgage of real estate',[1] an observation which certainly rang true in the days when security interests in land were created by highly artificial manipulations of the estate ownership inherent in the borrower's land.[2] The property legislation of 1925 and 2002 has now significantly rationalised the law of mortgage, injecting a much greater realism into the law and practice of real security.[3]

1   *Samuel v Jarrah Timber and Wood Paving Corpn Ltd* [1904] AC 323 at 326. Compare Maitland's famous description of the mortgage transaction as 'one long suppressio veri and suggestio falsi' (*Equity* (2nd edn revd by J Brunyate, London 1936), p 182).

2   Prior to 1926 the classic method of mortgage involved a transfer of the mortgagor's entire freehold or leasehold estate to the mortgagee, subject to a covenant for re-transfer on repayment of the loan money. Non-payment triggered the permanent forfeiture of the estate to the lender (see generally A W B Simpson, *A History of The Land Law* (2nd edn, Oxford 1986), pp 242–243). Legal mortgage by conditional transfer was made impossible by the 1925 legislation (LPA 1925, ss 85(1)–(2), 86(1)–(2)), but the further archaism of the mortgage by long demise [**para 8.251**] survived until relatively recently [**para 8.242**]. See also *Lavin v Johnson* [2002] EWCA Civ 1138; [2003] Conv 326 (C McNall).

3   In 1991 the Law Commission made recommendations for further sweeping changes in the law of mortgage (see *Transfer of Land – Land Mortgages* (Law Com No 204, November 1991)). The Commission advocated the introduction of two new standardised forms of mortgage – the 'formal land mortgage' and the 'informal land mortgage' – but its proposals were later abandoned as not commanding sufficiently wide support (see Law Com No 254 (1998), para 9.1).

Legal title remains in the borrower

8.239   The essence of the modern mortgage is that full legal title to the mortgaged estate remains in the mortgagor throughout the mortgage term.[1] This retention of formal title nowadays provides an important key to capital accumulation for the upwardly mobile private citizen. The mortgagor is automatically entitled to any increase in value of the mortgaged land even though initially he may have purchased the property entirely with borrowed funds. The mortgagee, in closer accord with the reality of the situation, takes merely a security interest (almost always a charge by way of legal mortgage) over the land and is generally entitled only to the return of his capital together with appropriate interest thereon.

1   That the 'owner' of the land is the mortgagor (rather than the mortgagee) is apparent from the fact that it is the former who is bound by statutory (e g tax or rating) obligations imposed on the 'owner' (see *Westminster City Council v Haymarket Publishing Ltd* [1981] 1 WLR 677 at 680C).

The 'equity of redemption'

8.240   Under the modern law of mortgage the borrower retains an 'equity of redemption', this being the term used to encapsulate the totality of his rights in equity. Historically the 'equity of redemption' marked the view that, irrespective of the strict legal and contractual position, the mortgagor remained in substance the owner of the mortgaged land – albeit subject to the mortgage created in favour of his creditor. Most importantly the mortgagor retained an equitable right to redeem the mortgage, by tender of the loan money, even after the contractual (or 'legal') date for repayment fixed by the mortgage terms had passed. The borrower's 'equity of redemption' is still jealously safeguarded by equity and can even be accorded a money value – effectively the difference at any given point in time between the market value of the land and the sum of the mortgage debt currently outstanding.[1] Such is the significance of the equity of redemption that the legal date for repayment of the mortgage loan is nowadays rendered almost entirely academic. For this reason most modern mortgage deeds incorporate a clause – which strikes terror into the heart of only the uninformed lay person – apparently requiring repayment of the entire capital sum within a very short period (eg three or six months) of the granting of the loan. This 'short date' for redemption is for most purposes meaningless,[2] neither mortgagor nor mortgagee having any intention that repayment should actually be made on this date.[3]

1 Thus, if land has a market value of £150,000 and is currently subject to a mortgage debt of £100,000, the value of the mortgagor's equity of redemption is £50,000. This surplus or uncharged value can fluctuate. If it plunges below zero (eg because of a slump in the market value of the mortgaged land), the borrower is exposed to the infamous phenomenon of 'negative equity'. Normally, however, the equity of redemption tends to increase in value both in consequence of the steady inflation of land prices and by reason of the gradual discharge of the mortgage debt.

2 Such a clause does, however, serve the important function of accelerating the point at which the mortgagee's power of sale becomes available [**para 15.172**] and also the date at which the mortgagor, for his part, becomes entitled to proffer repayment of the entire mortgage debt [**para 15.36**] – a course of action which may seem attractive if better mortgage terms are available elsewhere in the marketplace.

3 See *Stocks & Enterprises Pty Ltd v McBurney* (1977) 1 BPR 9521 at 9526 per Reynolds JA (Court of Appeal of New South Wales).

Acquisition mortgages and later mortgages

8.241   Borrowing on the security of land is not confined to *acquisition mortgages* (which facilitate the initial purchase of property), but often extends to *later mortgages* (which tap into the increased capital value derived from the steady inflation of land prices). The same land may be mortgaged many times over,[1] the limiting factor being the difference between its open market value and the total debt currently secured.

1 *Downsview Nominees Ltd v First City Corpn Ltd* [1993] AC 295 at 311F per Lord Templeman.

CREATION OF A LEGAL CHARGE OVER REGISTERED LAND

8.242   Pursuant to the Land Registration Act 2002 certain 'owner's powers' are conferred on the proprietor of a registered estate in land and upon any person entitled to be registered as proprietor.[1] These powers include a 'power to charge the estate at law with the payment of money.'[2] Under the 2002 Act an expressly created legal mortgage of registered land (whether freehold or leasehold) must be created by way of 'registered charge'.[3]

1   LRA 2002, s 24 [**para 7.49**].

2   LRA 2002, s 23(1)(b).

3   A 'registered charge' is defined as 'a charge the title to which is entered in the register' (LRA 2002, s 132(1)). The formerly available (and extremely cumbersome) method of mortgage by demise or subdemise of the registered estate [**para 8.251**] is no longer available (see LRA 2002, s 23(1)(a); Law Com No 254 (1998), para 9.5).

Registered charge

8.243   In the absence of any contrary entry in the register, the holder of the statutory 'owner's powers' may mortgage to a lender by declaring that the registered estate is charged by way of legal mortgage as security for the payment of the sums specified to be due under the charge. This charge can be executed, necessarily as a deed, in the standard form provided by the Land Registration Rules 2003.[1]

1   LRA 2002, s 25(1); LRR 2003, r 103, Sch 1 [**paras 7.50–7.51**].

Registration requirements

8.244   The grant of a charge over a registered estate ranks as a 'disposition' of the registered estate and therefore requires to be 'completed' by registration.[1] Under the current registration requirements of the Land Registration Act 2002, a charge becomes effective 'at law' only when the chargee is entered as the proprietor of the charge in the charges register of the chargor's title.[2] Such registration has definitive force. The charge takes effect, 'if it would not otherwise do so, as a charge by deed by way of legal mortgage.'[3] It is at this point that the chargee finally acquires a 'legal estate' in the mortgage.[4]

1   LRA 2002, s 27(2)(f).

2   LRA 2002, ss 27(1), 59(2), Sch 2, para 8 [**para 2.152**]. Failing such entry, the chargee holds only an equitable charge (see *E S Schwab & Co Ltd v McCarthy* (1976) 31 P & CR 196 at 201, 212; *Mortgage Corpn Ltd v Nationwide Credit Corpn Ltd* [1994] Ch 49 at 53F–54A [**para 9.107**]).

3   LRA 2002, s 51. Thus, for example, the registration of an otherwise void mortgage validates the mortgage as a security so that the innocent mortgagee may exercise a power of sale over the land, but does not render enforceable any other covenant-based right to recover a deficiency from the mortgagor (*Duncan v McDonald* [1997] 3 NZLR 669 at 682–683 (five-member NZ Court of Appeal); *Karacominakis v Big Country Developments Pty Ltd* (2000) 10 BPR 18235 at [57]–[58] (NSW Court of Appeal)).

4   See *First National Bank plc v Thompson* [1996] Ch 231 at 240C per Millett LJ. The drive towards 'dematerialisation' of the Land Register has brought about the disappearance of the charge certificate with which each mortgage lender used to be issued (see Land Registry, *Annual Report and Accounts 1999–2000* (2000), p 19).

Electronic mortgages

8.245   When electronic conveyancing becomes operational,[1] the 'relevant registration requirements' will comprise the transmission of an electronic mortgage document to Land Registry, with the result that unless and until such transmission occurs, the charge will have effect *neither* at law *nor* in equity.

1   [**Paras 2.117, 12.4**].

Rights of the registered chargee

8.246   All registered chargees are statutorily invested with a general power 'to make a disposition of any kind permitted by the general law' in relation to the registered charge.[1] The chargee also has available, most significantly, a power of sale in respect of the estate which has been charged.[2] Although, strictly speaking, the registered chargee holds no common law estate in the land charged,[3] he is deemed by statute to hold the equivalent of an estate in land.[4] A charge by way of legal mortgage over freehold land is deemed to confer on the chargee 'the same protection, powers and remedies (including the right to take proceedings to obtain possession …)' as if a leasehold term of 3,000 years had been created in his favour.[5] Mortgage by charge thus mimics the effects of mortgage by demise,[6] by equiparating the chargee's rights and powers with those which would have been incidents of any common law estate taken by him as mortgage security.

1   LRA 2002, s 23(2)(a) (e g a power of transfer [**para 8.259**]).
2   See LPA 1925, ss 87–108 [**paras 15.171–15.221**].
3   See *Weg Motors Ltd v Hales* [1962] Ch 49 at 74, 77.
4   See *Lai v Beem Construction Ltd* [1984] 2 NZLR 278 at 285 per Somers J (a 'statutory estate or interest as chargee or mortgagee simpliciter'). See also *English Scottish and Australian Bank Ltd v Phillips* (1937) 57 CLR 302 at 321; *Figgins Holdings Pty Ltd v SEAA Enterprises Pty Ltd* (1999) 196 CLR 245 at 262.
5   LPA 1925, s 87(1)(a). A charge by way of legal mortgage over leasehold land confers on the chargee equivalent protection to that which would have been provided by a subdemise of a term less by one day than the term vested in the mortgagor (LPA 1925, s 87(1)(b)).
6   [**Para 8.251**].

Rights of subsequent registered chargees

8.247   If the borrower subsequently wishes to create another legal charge in favour of a different lender, this later charge must likewise be completed by registration. Subject to any contrary indication in the register, registered charges over the same registered estate rank as between themselves according to the order in which they are entered in the register and not according to the order in which they are created.[1] A person dealing with the registered proprietor of an estate in land can readily discover how many registered charges exist over the land by obtaining an official copy of the title from Land Registry.[2] It is not uncommon that land should be burdened by two or three charges to different lenders, but thereafter a multiplicity of charges registered against the same title number usually indicates that the proprietor of the land is in deep financial difficulty.

1   LRA 2002, s 48(1); LRR 2003, r 101.
2   LRR 2003, r 134(1).

Mortgages by estoppel

8.248 The doctrine of estoppel by deed is applicable to the grant of a mortgage.[1] A mortgage may therefore be granted by one who, at the time of grant, holds no estate at all in the mortgaged land. The common law disables the mortgagor from denying the title of his mortgagee,[2] with the result that the mortgagee takes a mortgage by estoppel. In *First National Bank plc v Thompson*,[3] for example, the defendant had executed a charge in favour of a bank over freehold land which was transferred to him only some two months later, title in the land transferred not being registered in the defendant's name at Land Registry until a further three months thereafter. The Court of Appeal held that, in so far as the defendant's deed purported to create a charge by way of legal mortgage, this grant operated as a charge by estoppel.[4] This charge, although not initially eligible for registration, became registrable at Land Registry when the estoppel was 'fed' by the subsequent transfer of the freehold title.[5] In effect, nothing requires that the chargor of registered land must himself be registered as proprietor of the land *in advance of* his execution of the deed of charge.

1 See the parallel case of tenancy by estoppel [**para 7.265**].
2 *First National Bank plc v Thompson* [1996] Ch 231 at 237F per Millett LJ.
3 [1996] Ch 231.
4 [1996] Ch 231 at 240B–E per Millett LJ. Where, however, the purported charge contains (as in *First National Bank*) no recital or clear representation of the grantor's title, the estoppel cannot prevail against a bona fide purchaser from the grantor without notice of the earlier transaction (see *Right d Jefferys v Bucknell* (1831) 2 B & Ad 278 at 283–284, 109 ER 1146 at 1148–1149; *General Finance, Mortgage, and Discount Co v Liberator Permanent Benefit Building Society* (1878) 10 Ch D 15 at 24; *First National Bank plc v Thompson*, supra at 239H, 240E per Millett LJ, 244A per Staughton LJ).
5 [1996] Ch 231 at 241F–242B per Millett LJ, 244B per Staughton LJ.

CREATION OF A LEGAL MORTGAGE OVER UNREGISTERED LAND

8.249 A legal mortgage of an unregistered estate in land must be effected by deed[1] and may take either of two forms (one of which is now obsolete). In either case most first legal mortgages executed in England and Wales on or after 1 April 1998[2] have activated a requirement that title to the mortgagor's estate be registered at Land Registry and that details of the mortgage taken be entered in the charges register of the newly registered title.

1 LPA 1925, s 52(1). Any electronic creation of a mortgage charge in prescribed form which triggers a compulsory first registration at Land Registry is deemed to have complied with the statutory requirement of creation by deed (LRA 2002, s 91(2)(c), (5) [**para 7.36**]).
2 See LRA 1925, s 123(2), as substituted by LRA 1997, ss 1, 5(4) [**para 2.114**].

Charge by way of legal mortgage

8.250 Nowadays the almost invariable method of mortgaging unregistered land comprises the charge by deed which is expressed to be by way of legal mortgage. By statutory fiction this charge equips the chargee with the rights and powers incidental to the long leasehold estate which he might otherwise have taken as a mortgage security.[1]

1   LPA 1925, s 87(1) [**para 8.246**].

Mortgage by demise or subdemise

8.251   An alternative (and now archaic) method of legal mortgage of unregistered land lies in a special manipulation of the borrower's estate. In the case of unregistered freehold land the security granted to the lender takes the form of an express demise of a long lease in the borrower's land (usually again a term of 3,000 years).[1] The term is subject to a proviso for 'cesser on redemption' (ie automatic termination of the leasehold estate on full discharge of the borrower's loan liability).[2] The mortgagee by demise is thus invested with a legal estate – a term of years absolute – in the mortgagor's land and is nominally entitled to enjoy possession of the land. In the case of unregistered leasehold land the method of mortgage by subdemise requires that the borrower carve a sublease for the lender out of his own leasehold estate, the sublease being 'less by one day at least than the term vested in the mortgagor.'[3]

1   The leasehold estate taken as security is never eligible for substantive registration of title at Land Registry (LRA 2002, s 4(5)).
2   LPA 1925, s 85(1). The real value of the mortgagor's interest in the land is, of course, not so much the (fairly sterile) freehold reversion on a 3,000 year term, but rather the equity of redemption which he also still retains (ie the right to repay the loan and procure the termination of the mortgagee's technical leasehold interest).
3   LPA 1925, s 86(1). There is a statutory proviso that where the subdemise requires the licence of the lessor, this licence shall not be unreasonably refused.

Trigger for first registration of title

8.252   Any first legal mortgage of an unregistered freehold estate (or of a unregistered long leasehold estate[1]), if protected by the deposit of title deeds,[2] now triggers a requirement of first registration of title to that freehold (or leasehold) estate at Land Registry.[3]

1   The trigger for first registration operates only on the mortgage of an unregistered leasehold estate which, at the date of the mortgage, still has more than seven years to run.
2   Thus no registration requirement is triggered by a first legal mortgage which has been preceded by an equitable mortgage by deposit of the title deeds to an earlier lender [**para 7.40**].
3   LRA 2002, ss 4(1)(g), (8), 6(2)(a).

Requirement of entry in the charges register

8.253   In most circumstances a first legal mortgage of an unregistered estate quickly turns into a registered charge over the newly registered title.[1] An application for first registration of the mortgaged estate must be lodged at

Land Registry within two months of the date of disposition,[2] together with the consequent entry of the newly created mortgage in the charges register of the title affected.[3]

1   First registration of the borrower's estate is accompanied, in practice, by registration of the lender as proprietor of a mortgage charge [**paras 2.152, 7.43**].
2   LRA 2002, ss 6(2), (4), 7(1).
3   LRA 2002, Sch 2, para 8. The mortgage requires to be completed by registration of details of the mortgage in the charges register, coupled with the entry of the mortgagee's name as proprietor of the charge in question. Only then does the mortgagee acquire an enduring legal title to the charge [**para 7.43**].

Failure to complete by first registration

8.254   The relevant statutory provisions operate a rule of statutory lapse. On the execution of the deed of legal charge the mortgagee immediately acquires a legal mortgage, but a failure of timely registration relegates the mortgagee's security to that of a mere contract for valuable consideration to create a legal charge (ie a mere equitable charge).[1]

1   LRA 2002, s 7(2)(b). The chargee is inevitably disabled from full exercise of the statutory powers of a legal mortgagee. See eg *Lever Finance Ltd v L N & H M Needleman's Trustee* [1956] Ch 375 at 382 (power to appoint receiver [**para 15.137**]).

Deposit of title documents

8.255   By long tradition the first mortgagee of an unregistered estate enjoys the additional protection afforded by his legal right throughout the mortgage term to retain (at least the most significant of) the title deeds pertaining to the mortgaged property.[1]

1   See now LPA 1925, s 85(1). The mortgagor has a statutory right to inspect and make copies (at his own expense) of the title documents in the custody or power of the mortgagee (LPA 1925, s 96(1)). This right cannot be excluded by contract. On redemption of a mortgage, the mortgagee must hand the title deeds over either to the mortgagor or to the next mortgagee (see LPA 1925, s 96(2)).

Purpose of deposit

8.256   This requirement of deposit of the mortgagor's title documents used to provide a substantial safeguard against any subsequent attempt by the mortgagor to deal with his land.[1] The mortgagor is hampered by his inability to produce the original documents of title as evidence of his estate ownership; and any person dealing with the mortgagor is deemed to have notice of the existence of at least one mortgage. The protection of deposit is still important in relation to first legal mortgages executed before 1 April 1998, but in respect of first legal mortgages executed on or after that date serves merely to equip the mortgagee with the title documents required for production in support of the first registration application triggered by the transaction of mortgage.[2] Thereafter much more effective protection for the mortgagee is secured by the entry of the mortgage in the relevant charges register.

1   Apart from restraining prejudicial dealings by the mortgagor, the practice of depositing title documents with the mortgagee of unregistered land facilitates any later exercise of the mortgagee's power of sale. Should that power ever become exercisable [**para 15.173**], he is already equipped with the necessary documents of title for the purpose of dealing with third parties.

2   [**Para 8.252**].

Legal mortgages of unregistered land without deposit of title documents

8.257   The safeguard of deposit of title documents is not, of course, available to second and later mortgagees (a fact which may be particularly significant in respect of legal mortgages created before 1 April 1998). Even today unregistered land may still be subjected to a legal mortgage without activating any requirement of first substantive registration (eg where the mortgage is unaccompanied by deposit of the mortgagor's documents of title). In all such cases, legal mortgagees, if they are to preserve their priority over further dealings (whether by sale or mortgage), must protect their mortgage by the registration against their mortgagor's name of a Class C(i) land charge under the Land Charges Act 1972.[1] The legal mortgage not secured by the deposit of title deeds – the so-called 'puisne mortgage' – thus constitutes one of the anomalies of unregistered land. In that it requires protection by some form of registration, the puisne mortgage provides an exceedingly rare example of a *legal* interest in unregistered land which is not simply governed by the classic principle that legal rights bind the world.[2]

1   LCA 1972, s 2(4) [**para 12.301**]. An equitable mortgage may be protected as a Class C(iii) land charge [**para 12.303**].

2   [**Paras 2.176, 12.301**].

STATUTORILY CREATED CHARGES

8.258   A number of statutes nowadays provide for the creation of a charge over land for the recoupment of various kinds of liability incurred by the landowner. Such charges generally arise without the necessity of any deed and tend to constitute enforceable first legal charges in respect of the land, sometimes taking priority over securities already taken by banks and building societies.[1] For instance, local authorities have power to impose a charge for the recovery of costs incurred in connection with street works[2] or the abatement of a statutory nuisance on a landowner's premises.[3] Once registered as a local land charge, such levies take effect as if they had been created by deed by way of legal mortgage.[4] The statutory charges thus created have priority over any other registered charge affecting the property.[5] A further, particularly controversial, example is provided by the power enjoyed by local authorities to recover the costs of residential nursing home accommodation by imposing a charge on property retained by the elderly person concerned.[6] Likewise the Legal Services Commission takes a statutory charge in relation to any interest 'recovered or preserved' in legally aided litigation.[7]

1   Land Registry is now statutorily obliged to inform current registered chargees of the registration of any new statutory charge which displaces existing priorities (LRA 2002, s 50; LRR 2003, rr 105–106).

2   Highways Act 1980, ss 203(3), 212(1)–(3).

3   Environmental Protection Act 1990, s 81A. See also HA 1985, ss 193(3), 375(4), Sch 10, para 7; Housing Grants, Construction and Regeneration Act 1996, ss 87–88.

4   See Local Land Charges Act 1975, s 7. A charge over registered land which is a local land charge may be realised only if the title to the charge is registered at Land Registry (LRA 2002, s 55; LRR 2003, r 104).

5   See *Bristol Corpn v Virgin* [1928] 2 KB 622 at 627–628.

6   Health and Social Services and Social Security Adjudications Act 1983, s 22(7)–(8). See *R v Somerset CC, ex p Harcombe* (1997) 96 LGR 444 at 454–459.

7   Access to Justice Act 1999, s 10(7).

TRANSFER OF MORTGAGES

8.259   From the viewpoint of the lender a legal charge represents a valuable proprietary asset. During the lifetime of the mortgage the mortgagee normally receives interest on the capital sum outstanding and is entitled to repayment of the capital itself either by instalments during the mortgage term (under a repayment mortgage) or as a lump sum at its end (under an endowment mortgage). If the mortgagee wishes to accelerate his realisation of the value represented by a mortgage charge, he is perfectly entitled, without any requirement of consent from the mortgagor,[1] to sell the charge to a third party.[2] The disponee of the charge, having paid the market price for the security in question, thereafter collects all payments due under the mortgage.[3] The transfer of a charge over a registered estate is effected by registered disposition using the prescribed Land Registry form.[4] In order to take a legal security the transferee must then complete the disposition by registration,[5] ie must apply to be registered in the charges register of the borrower's title as the new proprietor of the charge concerned.[6] The transfer of a charge over an unregistered estate may be effected by a simple deed executed by the mortgagee.[7]

1   The only advantage of consent, from the mortgagee's viewpoint, is that the outstanding mortgage debt can be clarified as an agreed figure. If the mortgagee intends to transfer the mortgage at a discount, there is normally no fiduciary obligation to give a right of first refusal to the mortgagor or to a second mortgagee (see *Elders Rural Finance Ltd v Westpac Banking Corporation* (1988) 4 BPR 9383 at 9385 per Young J).

2   LRA 2002, s 25(2)(a). See also *Turner v Smith* [1901] 1 Ch 213 at 218–220.

3   The bona fide purchaser who takes a legal transfer of the mortgage at a discount or undervalue is entitled to be repaid the full face value of the mortgage debt (*Davis v Barrett* (1851) 14 Beav 542 at 553–555, 51 ER 394 at 398). See also *Silkdale Pty Ltd v Long Leys Co Pty Ltd* (1995) 7 BPR 14414 at 14415 per Young J.

4   LRA 2002, s 25(1); LRR 2003, r 116.

5   LRA 2002, s 27(3)(a).

6   LRA 2002, Sch 2, para 10.

7   LPA 1925, s 114(1).

DISCHARGE OF MORTGAGES

8.260   A mortgage may be discharged, and the mortgagor's equity of redemption extinguished, in a number of ways. Some forms of discharge are, from the borrower's perspective, less agreeable than others. A mortgage may be discharged, for instance, by sale of the mortgaged land under the mortgagee's power of sale,[1] by foreclosure[2] or by the operation of the Limitation Act 1980.[3] The more normal occasion for discharge arises where the borrower has met his contractual obligation to repay all sums due under the mortgage and becomes entitled to call for a discharge of the mortgage secured on his land. Discharge often occurs when the mortgagor sells his property and the mortgage debt is satisfied out of the proceeds of sale.[4] Alternatively, discharge may occur without any sale of the property, eg on a remortgage of the land to another lender, or if the mortgagor applies his lottery winnings or his late aunt's legacy in payment of his outstanding liability.

1   **[Para 15.178]**.
2   **[Para 15.222]**.
3   **[Para 6.28]**. Neither the mortgagor nor any person claiming through him may assert any right to redeem the mortgage where the mortgagee has been in possession in his capacity as mortgagee for a period of at least twelve years (Limitation Act 1980, s 16). See also *Park v Brady* [1976] 2 NSWLR 329 at 336B.
4   It is common conveyancing practice for completion to occur before the vendor's outstanding mortgage is actually discharged. The purchaser completes effectively on the basis of an undertaking by the vendor's solicitor that the mortgage debt will be discharged out of the proceeds of sale and the deed of discharge forwarded subsequently to the new owner's solicitor. Despite its prevalence, this practice carries enormous risks if anything goes wrong and may expose the purchaser's solicitor to liability in negligence (see *Edward Wong Finance Co Ltd v Johnson Stokes & Master* [1984] AC 296 at 308G (so-called 'Hong Kong style of completion')).

Mortgage charge over a registered estate

8.261   A registered charge of a registered estate is discharged when the registered chargee executes the statutory form of discharge.[1] The chargor is then able to apply to Land Registry for cancellation of the relevant entries in the charges register.[2] Alternatively a discharge may be delivered to the registrar in electronic form.[3]

1   LRR 2003, r 114(1).
2   LRR 2003, r 114(5).
3   LRR 2003, r 115(1).

Mortgage charge over an unregistered estate

8.262   A mortgage over an unregistered estate is usually discharged by the endorsement of a receipt on the mortgage deed (in the form required by statute) for all moneys due.[1]

1   LPA 1925, s 115(1). The discharge of building society mortgages is expressly governed by Building Societies Act 1986, s 6C, Sch 2A (inserted by Building Societies Act 1997, s 7, Sch 2).

RIGHTS OF ENTRY

8.263 One final form of estate in land which may take effect at law is the 'right of entry'.[1] A right of entry, although it sounds similar to a right of way or other easement, is a quite distinct kind of entitlement and performs a very different sort of function.[2]

1 LPA 1925, s 1(2)(e).
2 'To include a right of entry in the description of "equitable easement" offends a sense both of elegance and accuracy' (*Shiloh Spinners Ltd v Harding* [1973] AC 691 at 720B per Lord Wilberforce).

Function

8.264 A right of entry is not facultative but penal in nature,[1] in that it empowers its owner to enforce the forfeiture of land or to enter land compulsorily in order to remove some object from it.[2] Rights of entry are frequently attached to a lease[3] or rentcharge,[4] the right effectively comprising an entitlement to resume possession of land in the event of some non-compliance with the terms of the relevant lease or rentcharge (e g for non-payment of rent or for failure to perform any other covenanted obligation). Here the exercise of a right of entry (or, as it is sometimes known, a right of re-entry) results in a vesting or revesting of the delinquent's estate in the landlord or the rentchargee.[5] Far from comprising a 'right to use or draw profit from another man's land', the right of entry provides a means 'to take his land altogether away.'[6]

1 See *Shiloh Spinners Ltd v Harding* [1973] AC 691 at 719E per Lord Wilberforce.
2 [**Para 1.87**].
3 [**Para 14.99**]. See e g *Southampton Community Health Services NHS Trust v Crown Estate Commissioners* [1997] EGCS 155.
4 [**Para 8.230**].
5 The exercise of the right of entry is subject to the court's jurisdiction to afford the defaulting party relief against forfeiture [**para 14.149**].
6 *Shiloh Spinners Ltd v Harding* [1973] AC 691 at 720C per Lord Wilberforce.

Independent proprietary character

8.265 A right of entry constitutes a free-standing proprietary interest in the subject land which is distinct from the estate or rentcharge to which it is appended.[1] Thus L, the owner of an estate in fee simple, may have an additional proprietary entitlement against his tenant, T, in the form of a right of entry expressly conferred on L by the terms of the lease. A right of entry ranks as a *legal* entitlement in land if created by deed[2] and if exercisable in respect of a legal term of years absolute or annexed to a legal rentcharge.[3]

1 A right of entry affecting a legal estate is alienable and may become exercisable by some person other than the original grantee (LPA 1925, s 4(3)), provided, in the case of an estate in fee simple, that the right is exercised only within the perpetuity period.
2 LPA 1925, s 52(1) [**para 7.26**].

3   LPA 1925, s 1(2)(e). A right of entry created otherwise than by deed (or exercisable merely in
     respect of some equitable estate) can only be *equitable* (see LPA 1925, s 1(3)).

Creation

8.266   Where a right of entry is expressly created by deed in respect of a
registered term of years absolute or is expressly annexed to a rentcharge
affecting a registered estate, the grant or reservation of the right of entry ranks
as a 'disposition' which requires to be completed by registration.[1] A right of
entry annexed to a rentcharge can therefore 'operate at law' only if the
rentchargee is entered in the register of title to his rentcharge as the proprietor
of the right of entry and a corresponding 'notice' is entered in the charges
register of the registered estate affected.[2] In the case of a right of entry
exercisable over a leasehold estate, the burden of the right is incorporated by
reference in the particulars of the lease entered in the property register of the
lessee's title[3] and the benefit of the right is specifically exempted from any
requirement of entry in the registered title of the lessor's reversionary estate.[4]

1   LRA 2002, s 27(2)(e).
2   LRA 2002, s 27(1), Sch 2, para 7(1)–(2).
3   LRR 2003, r 6(1).
4   LRA 2002, Sch 2, para 7(3); LRR 2003, r 77.

Binding effect of rights of entry

8.267   The enforceability of a right of entry is not dependent on showing that
the burden of any particular obligation has passed to the party against whom it
is sought to assert the right. Enforcement does not, in strict terms, require that
the defendant be *bound* by the obligation for non-compliance with which the
right of entry is being exercised. In effect, a right of entry is a peremptory
self-help remedy often visited upon someone who is simply the wrong person in
the wrong place at the wrong time.[1] Thus, for instance, a landlord can enforce a
leasehold right of re-entry against a squatter who adversely possesses against
his tenant, not on any theory that the squatter is bound as an assignee of the
leasehold term but merely on the rather stark ground that the right of re-entry
is triggered by sheer non-performance of that which was promised in the lease.[2]

1   The Chief Land Registrar has power to record in any register of title the fact that a right to
     determine a registered estate in land appears to have become exercisable (LRA 2002, s 64(1)).
2   **[Paras 13.58, 14.105]**.

8.268   A right of entry in respect of a registered estate is binding on any disponee
of the affected estate if the subject of a 'notice' in the relevant register of title to the
burdened estate.[1] A legal right of entry affecting an unregistered estate automatically binds the world; and an equitable right of entry affecting an unregistered
estate is binding in accordance with the bona fide purchaser rule.[2]

1   LRA 2002, s 29(1), (2)(a)(i).
2   *Shiloh Spinners Ltd v Harding* [1973] AC 691 at 719B **[para 12.372]**.

CHAPTER 9

Equitable rights in or over land

THE CLASSIFICATIONS OF EQUITABLE ENTITLEMENT

9.1 Chapters 7 and 8 have described the principal forms of estate, interest and charge which are capable of existence *at law*. In the present chapter attention is turned to the range of proprietary entitlements which subsist – sometimes necessarily – *in equity*. Equitable rights have their origins deep in the doctrines and maxims of equity. This chapter explains how modern equitable entitlements in land have evolved from equity's historic thematic concerns with substance rather than form, with the inner reality of intent rather than the external manifestations of conduct, and above all with the priority of conscience-driven obligation over strict legal entitlement.[1] The equitable character of certain entitlements in or over land is ultimately confirmed by statute, but equitable rights fall into one or other of two broad groups.

1 'The fundamental principle according to which equity acts ... [is] that a party having a legal right shall not be permitted to exercise it in such a way that the exercise amounts to unconscionable conduct' (*Legione v Hately* (1983) 152 CLR 406 at 444 per Mason and Deane JJ). See also *Australian Broadcasting Corpn v Lenah Game Meats Pty Ltd* (2001) 208 CLR 199 at [98]–[99] per Gummow and Hayne JJ.

Inherently equitable rights

9.2 Some equitable rights enjoy their equitable status precisely because they are excluded from the categories of estate, interest and charge statutorily declared capable of 'subsisting or of being conveyed or created at law.'[1] Such rights have no potential to exist at law, and their inherently equitable status can usually be rationalised in terms of the maxims and historic jurisdiction of equity. Examples include:
– estate contracts[2]
– equitable liens[3]
– restrictive covenants[4] and
– beneficial interests existing under a trust of land.[5]

1   LPA 1925, s 1(1)–(3) **[para 2.127]**.
2   **[Para 9.23]**.
3   **[Para 9.130]**.
4   **[Para 9.138]**.
5   **[Para 9.172]**.

Equitable analogues of legal rights

9.3   Some equitable rights are, on the other hand, merely the analogue of rights which, on due compliance with some requirement of formal creation or transfer or of registration at Land Registry, would normally have ranked as *legal* rights. Examples include certain kinds of:

–   leases[1]
–   easements and profits *à prendre*[2] and
–   mortgage charges.[3]

1   **[Para 9.42]**.
2   **[Para 9.87]**.
3   **[Paras 9.104–9.108]**.

THE ROLE OF EQUITABLE PRINCIPLE

9.4   Much of land law cannot be understood without some sense of the way in which the conscience-based jurisdiction of equity has infused various sorts of *Leitmotiv* into the formulation and recognition of rights in land.

Preference for substance over form

9.5   Attention was drawn in Chapter 1 to the fact that legal rights frequently give expression to the external or formal elements of proprietary entitlement, whilst equitable rights tend to acknowledge the inner reality of transactions in respect of land.[1] If, for instance, the question arises who owns a particular piece of land, the common law instinct is to look either to the possessory position on the ground or to the name inscribed on the documentary title. Equity, by contrast, attempts rather more subtly to determine the inner motivations of the relevant parties and to allocate ownership accordingly. It is indeed a constant characteristic of equity to look beneath the superficial appearance of transactions in order to discover and, so far as conscience will allow, give effect to the substantive reality of the parties' actual or presumed intentions as responsible moral agents.[2]

1   **[Para 1.158]**. In relation to the equitable emphasis on 'the substance of the transaction rather than its form', see *Hewitt v Court* (1982) 149 CLR 639 at 668 per Deane J; *Corin v Patton* (1990) 169 CLR 540 at 579 per Deane J.
2   See e g *Corin v Patton* (1990) 169 CLR 540 at 558 per Mason CJ and McHugh J.

Subliminal effect of the maxims of equity

9.6 The law of property has long been overshadowed not only by conscience-laden equitable rules, but also by more ethereal or elastic 'maxims of equity'.[1] The maxims of equity are redolent with such notions as:

– equity has regard to intent rather than form[2]
– equity will not suffer a wrong to go without remedy[3]
– he who comes to equity must come with clean hands[4]
– equity will not assist a volunteer[5]
– equality is equity[6]
– equity follows the law[7]
– equity looks on that as done which ought to be done.[8]

1 These maxims function as the 'meta-principles' of equitable intervention (Gray and Gray, 'The rhetoric of realty', in J Getzler (ed), *Rationalizing Property, Equity and Trusts: Essays in Honour of Edward Burn* (Butterworths 2003), p 239). They reflect a 'professional consensus' based on the 'common learning of the ... legal community' (see *Harris v Digital Pulse Pty Ltd* (2003) 197 ALR 626 at [17] per Spigelman CJ).
2 **[Para 9.54]**.
3 **[Para 9.7]**.
4 **[Para 9.16]**.
5 **[Para 9.14]**.
6 **[Para 10.146]**.
7 **[Para 11.147]**.
8 **[Para 9.59]**.

9.7 These maxims of equity (and there are others) are far from being binding rules of inflexible application. In fact they are not rules at all, but operate merely as background formulae of powerful thematic content, exerting an almost subliminal influence on the reasoning processes of lawyers.[1] Sometimes these maxims come to the fore only as a last resort, where there exists no clearer signpost to the resolution of a difficulty. The idea that 'equity follows the law' falls clearly into this category of residual application,[2] but nevertheless reinforces the broad idea that equity, being merely a corrective system of justice, is needed only where the dogmatic assertion of a formal rule of law produces an unacceptably unfair or 'inequitable' outcome. Likewise the maxim that 'equality is equity' provides only an ultimate 'fall-back presumption' in the ascertainment of beneficial ownership under a trust.[3] Sometimes a maxim (eg 'equity will not suffer a wrong to go without remedy') expresses no more than a generalised moral imperative which, if actualised in other than extreme cases, would in fact spell the disintegration of any ordered or structured system of justice. Another of the maxims ('equity will not assist a volunteer', ie one who provides no consideration) is actually and richly falsified in the primary equitable phenomenon of the express trust, where most beneficiaries are indeed volunteers. Yet the maxims of equity continue to play an insidiously formative role in giving sense to many of the categories of entitlement discussed in this chapter. Indeed, it has been said that equity 'calls into existence and protects equitable rights and interests in property only where their recognition has been found to be required in order to give effect to its doctrines.'[4]

1   Each equitable maxim is 'not a specific rule or principle of law. It is a summary statement of a broad theme which underlies equitable concepts and principles. Its precise scope is necessarily ill-defined and somewhat uncertain' (*Corin v Patton* (1990) 169 CLR 540 at 557 per Mason CJ and McHugh J).

2   See e g *Forestview Nominees Pty Ltd v Perpetual Trustees WA Ltd* (1998) 193 CLR 154 at 162, where the High Court of Australia found this precept of 'little assistance'.

3   *Mortgage Corporation v Shaire* [2001] Ch 743 at 750H, 751E per Neuberger J. See *Gissing v Gissing* [1971] AC 886 at 908G per Lord Diplock [**para 10.146**].

4   *Commissioner of Stamp Duties (Queensland) v Livingston* [1965] AC 694 at 712E per Viscount Radcliffe. It can thus be said that 'equitable rights are commensurate with the protection which equity will afford them' (*Hewitt v Court* (1982) 149 CLR 639 at 665 per Deane J) and, by way of corollary in specific cases, that 'as equitable relief evaporated, so did any equitable estate' (*Marshall v Council of The Shire of Snowy River* (1994) 7 BPR 14447 at 14457 per Meagher JA). See also *Mills v Ruthol* (2002) 10 BPR 19381 at [122].

EQUITY ACTS IN PERSONAM

9.8   Of all the keynotes of equitable principle, perhaps the most influential is ultimately the idea that 'equity acts *in personam.*' Courts of equity have always intervened by ordering the defendant personally to do, or refrain from doing, a specific act.[1] In the exercise of this equitable jurisdiction courts thus fashion their orders and remedies so as to affect the litigant much more directly and coercively than any remedy devised in the traditional regime of the common law.[2] In civil matters the characteristic remedy of the common law is the award of damages.[3] In equity, however, the remedial range extends more widely, embracing forms of relief which act directly *in personam* (e g decrees of specific performance, injunctions and orders for rectification).[4]

1   See *Swiss Bank Corpn v Lloyds Bank Ltd* [1979] Ch 548 at 565C per Browne-Wilkinson J; *Mountney v Treharne* [2003] Ch 135 at [71] per Jonathan Parker LJ.

2   Courts of equity 'ordered the defendant to behave as a righteous man would have done' (*R Griggs Group Ltd v Evans (No 2)* [2004] EWHC 1088 (Ch) at [39]).

3   See *Harris v Digital Pulse Pty Ltd* (2003) 197 ALR 626 at [2] per Spigelman CJ.

4   The net effect is that, although originating in the ability of the court to make an order *in personam* against another party in respect of identified land, the claimant's rights frequently 'become an interest in the property itself, an equitable interest' (*Swiss Bank Corpn v Lloyds Bank Ltd* [1979] Ch 548 at 565G per Browne-Wilkinson J).

Remedial characteristics of equity

9.9   This procedural difference between law and equity acquires a vast significance in the context of land law. It means, for instance, that the usual remedy for breach of contract in relation to a land interest is not the mere award of money damages, but a much more far-reaching order of specific performance, which operates directly upon the party in breach by requiring him to do that which he contracted to do.[1] In most cases, therefore, a specifically enforceable contract relating to land must be completed by the delivery of the contracted performance. The defaulting party is not permitted to buy his way out of breach by the offer of money damages. Again, the remedy for non-compliance with a restrictive covenant is not only the award of compensation to the aggrieved party, but frequently also an injunction restraining further breach of the covenant on pain of liability for contempt. In these and many other ways equity, by virtue of the immediacy of its remedial impact, effectively converts contractual promises into a conferment of enforceable property in the promisor's land.

1   See *Swiss Bank Corpn v Lloyds Bank Ltd* [1979] Ch 548 at 565D–E per Browne-Wilkinson J; *R Griggs Group Ltd v Evans (No 2)* [2004] EWHC 1088 (Ch) at [40]–[43].

Discretionary nature of equitable remedies

9.10   Unlike the common law remedy of damages (which is available as of right once the claimant's case has been proved[1]), equitable remedies are always discretionary[2]; and equity has laid down guidelines for the exercise of this discretion.[3] For instance, equity will not, in general, lend its assistance to a volunteer. Again, even a claimant who has proved his case may be denied equitable relief on the ground that he has not come to court 'with clean hands'. That is, he may be precluded from relief simply because he has forfeited any claim to the assistance of equity by reason of his own inequitable or unconscionable conduct.[4] Equitable relief may also be withheld because the claimant is seeking such relief for improper purposes.[5]

1   The quantum of damages awarded remains a matter to be decided at the discretion of the court.
2   See *Bristol CC v Lovell* [1998] 1 WLR 446 at 453F–G per Lord Hoffmann.
3   See e g *Co-operative Insurance Society Ltd v Argyll Stores (Holdings) Ltd* [1998] AC 1 at 9E–G per Lord Hoffmann. Equitable remedies (such as an injunction) cannot be granted or withheld 'on a mere judicial whim' (see *Michael Santarsieri Inc v Unicity Mall Ltd* (2000) 181 DLR (4th) 136 at 141 per Twaddle JA).
4   [Para 9.16]. 'In a court of equity wrongful acts are no passport to favour' (*Winter Garden Theatre (London) Ltd v Millennium Productions Ltd* [1948] AC 173 at 203 per Lord Uthwatt). See similarly *Douglas v Hello! Ltd* [2001] QB 967 at [100] per Brooke LJ.
5   Thus, for instance, the award of an injunction may be refused on the ground that the claimant has sought this form of equitable relief in order to compel an extortionate buy-out of his rights (see *Isenberg v East India House Estate Co Ltd* (1863) 3 De GJ & S 263 at 273, 46 ER 637 at 641; *Baxter v Four Oaks Properties Ltd* [1965] Ch 816 at 829) or otherwise to strengthen his negotiating leverage (see *Michael Santarsieri Inc v Unicity Mall Ltd* (2000) 181 DLR (4th) 136 at 143–144).

PROPRIETARY EFFECT OF CONTRACTS RELATING TO LAND

9.11   Many forms of equitable right in land derive their existence from some contractual relationship affecting the land. Although it seems at first implausible, the doctrinal effect of equitable principle often elevates rights of mere *contractual* significance into rights of *proprietary* consequence. In this sense, the borderline between contract and property is much more fluid or ambivalent than initially appears.[1] Although the chain of propositional logic underlying this conclusion can be understood only against the background of historic equitable principle, the net effect is that those who enter into contracts to purchase various sorts of interest in land frequently find that the sheer fact of contract has already conferred on them some kind of proprietary entitlement in that land. Moreover, because this metamorphosis of the contractual into the proprietary occurs under the shadow of equitable doctrine, the proprietary rights created by contract are properly classifiable as *equitable* rights in land. The logic which produces this result turns on the significance of the remedy of specific performance.

1   Gray, 'Property in Thin Air' [1991] CLJ 252 at 302–303. See *Linden Gardens Trust Ltd v Lenesta Sludge Disposals Ltd* [1994] 1 AC 85 at 106D–E per Lord Browne-Wilkinson ('contractual rights are a species of property'); *Beneficial Finance Corpn Ltd v Multiplex Constructions Pty Ltd* (1995) 36 NSWLR 510 at 522E per Young J (contract and property as 'compartments of the law ... are no longer watertight').

SPECIFICALLY ENFORCEABLE CONTRACTS

9.12   Although the remedy is ultimately discretionary, it is now well settled that a contract relating to land is one in respect of which equity will generally grant specific performance. If a contracting party fails to grant or transfer the promised interest in land, the court will normally order him to perform the contract by completing the relevant disposition, whether the original undertaking was to transfer a freehold or grant a lease, or even to create an easement or mortgage over the land in question. Because of the availability of specific enforcement of the contractual promise, the disposition of the interest becomes almost *inevitable*. The contracting party will either perform his contract or be made to do so under the compulsion of a court-ordered decree of specific performance.[1] The end result is not in doubt. The rationale which underlies this equitable perspective on contracts relating to land is the recognition that the subject matter of such contracts is physically (and therefore commercially) unique and that contractual breach can rarely be compensated adequately by money.[2]

1   Even if the subject matter of the contract is a residence, an unwilling vendor cannot resist specific performance by reference to ECHR Art 8 (*Harrow LBC v Qazi* [2004] 1 AC 983 at [136] per Lord Scott of Foscote) [**para 2.60**].
2   See *Hall v Warren* (1804) 9 Ves 605 at 608, 32 ER 738 at 739 per Sir William Grant MR; *Hexter v Pearce* [1900] 1 Ch 341 at 346; *Rudd v Lascelles* [1900] 1 Ch 815 at 817; *Hewitt v Court* (1982) 149 CLR 639 at 665 per Deane J; *Norris and Norris v Walls* [1997] NI 45 at 53a per Girvan J; *Attorney-General v Blake* [2001] 1 AC 268 at 282C–E, 285B per Lord Nicholls of Birkenhead; *R Griggs Group Ltd v Evans* (*No 2*) [2004] EWHC 1088 (Ch) at [41].

PRECONDITIONS OF SPECIFIC PERFORMANCE

9.13   Although available in land transactions almost as a matter of course,[1] the award of specific performance is always dependent on the satisfaction of certain preconditions by the contractual party who invokes the aid of equity.

1   See *Patel v Ali* [1984] Ch 283 at 286G; *Graham v Pitkin* [1992] 1 WLR 403 at 406D per Lord Templeman; *AMEC Properties Ltd v Planning Research & Systems Plc* [1992] 1 EGLR 70 at 72L; *Kopec v Pyret* (1987) 36 DLR (4th) 1 at 8–9.

There must be a contract for value

9.14   Equity, being generally unwilling to assist a volunteer, grants specific performance only to contracting parties who provide valuable consideration.[1]

1   See *Brunker v Perpetual Trustee Co (Ltd)* (1937) 57 CLR 555 at 599 per Dixon J.

General requirement of written and signed contract

9.15   Specific performance cannot normally be ordered in respect of any oral contract in respect of land which is entered into on or after 27 September 1989. In relation to almost all contracts for the disposition of any interest in land, the Law of Property (Miscellaneous Provisions) Act 1989 imposes a requirement that the contract be 'made in writing' and signed by or on behalf of each contracting party.[1] The contract must incorporate all expressly agreed terms in one document or, where contracts are exchanged, in each document. The 1989 Act allows few exceptions from the scope of this requirement of signed writing.[2] Non-compliance renders a contract not merely *unenforceable*,[3] but entirely *ineffective*[4] in the absence of circumstances of estoppel or constructive trust.[5] Only contracts concluded prior to 27 September 1989 remain subject to the old rule on contractual formality which, apart from cases of part performance[6] and estoppel,[7] required that an enforceable contract relating to land be merely *evidenced in writing* signed by or on behalf of the party to be charged.[8]

1   LP(MP)A 1989, s 2(1), (3) **[para 12.28]**. See *Yaxley v Gotts* [2000] Ch 162 at 171B per Robert Walker LJ ('an entirely new provision which marks a radical change in the law').
2   One important exception relates to contracts to grant certain short leases not exceeding three years (LP(MP)A 1989, s 2(5)(a)).
3   The old doctrine of part performance, which used to save many oral contracts, has been abolished (LP(MP)A 1989, s 2(8)). See *Yaxley v Gotts* [2000] Ch 162 at 172F per Robert Walker LJ.
4   See, for example, the problem caused by the lack of one signature in *Chandler v Clark* [2003] 1 P & CR 239 at [13].
5   LP(MP)A 1989, s 2(5). See e g *Yaxley v Gotts* [2000] Ch 162 at 174F, 180C–E per Robert Walker LJ, 181E–F per Clarke LJ, 193C–D per Beldam LJ. See also *McCausland v Duncan Lawrie Ltd* [1997] 1 WLR 38 at 45H, 50B–C; *Target Holdings Ltd v Priestley* (2000) 79 P & CR 305 at 324–326.
6   **[Para 12.40]**.
7   **[Para 10.68]**.
8   LPA 1925, s 40(1) **[para 12.38]**.

The party seeking specific performance must come 'with clean hands'

9.16   The party who seeks to invoke specific performance must not have disqualified himself from equitable relief by unconscionable conduct: 'he who comes into equity must come with clean hands.'[1] The court retains a discretion to withhold specific performance from any party whose behaviour has been 'gross and wilful',[2] but the circumstances must be fairly extreme before the courts decline to award what has become the standard remedy for breach of contracts relating to land.[3] Equitable assistance is refused only where a party has forfeited such help by reason of some truly unconscionable act or default.[4]

1   See *Mason v Clarke* [1954] 1 QB 460 at 471–472 per Romer LJ (an exceptionally harsh application of the principle). See generally P H Pettit, [1990] Conv 416.

2   *Parker v Taswell* (1858) 2 De G & J 559 at 573, 44 ER 1106 at 1112. See also *Upper Hutt Arcade Ltd v Burrell and Burrell Properties Ltd* [1973] 2 NZLR 699 at 703; *Wilkie v Redsell* [2003] EWCA Civ 926 at [34] (inconsistency with earlier sworn testimony regarded as abuse of the facilities of the court).

3   It has been said, for instance, that 'general depravity' does not connote an absence of 'clean hands' (*Dering v Earl of Winchelsea* (1787) 1 Cox Eq Cas 318 at 319, 29 ER 1184 at 1185 per Eyre CB). See also *Attorney-General for the United Kingdom v Heinemann Publishers Australia Pty Ltd* (1987) 8 NSWLR 341 at 383B per Powell J.

4   See *Coatsworth v Johnson* (1886) 55 LJQB 220 at 222–223 [**para 9.57**]; *Harrigan v Brown* [1967] 1 NSWR 342 at 349–350. Mere 'general naughtiness' is not enough (*FAI Insurances Ltd v Pioneer Concrete Services Ltd* (1987) 15 NSWLR 552 at 554G–555B per Young J). See e g *Carlson v Sparkes* (1981) 2 BPR 9101 at 9102–9103 (specific performance awarded to purchaser who tortiously demolished house before completion).

Specific performance must not prejudice third parties or cause excessive hardship

9.17   Specific performance will not be granted if it would prejudice the rights of third parties[1] or would be 'oppressive'[2] or would cause a 'hardship amounting to injustice.'[3] For example, there can be no order for specific performance where the subject matter of the contract has already been transferred to a third party.[4]

1   *Warmington v Miller* [1973] QB 877 at 886F–G.

2   *Attorney-General v Blake* [2001] 1 AC 268 at 282H per Lord Nicholls of Birkenhead.

3   *Patel v Ali* [1984] Ch 283 at 288D–E per Goulding J. See also *Roberts v O'Neill* [1983] IR 47 at 55–56; *R D McKinnon Holdings Pty Ltd v Hind* [1984] 2 NSWLR 121 at 126D–E; *South Coast Oils (Qld and NSW) Pty Ltd v Look Enterprises Pty Ltd* [1988] 1 Qd R 680 at 692.

4   See e g *Babcock v Carr* (1982) 127 DLR (3d) 77 at 85–86. If, however, the third party transferee has been guilty of fraud (e g through unconscionable dealing in the face of a prior known incumbrance), he may himself be vulnerable to the remedy of specific performance. See *Potter v Sanders* (1846) 6 Hare 1 at 9–10, 67 ER 1057 at 1060–1061; *Canadian Long Island Petroleums Ltd v Irving Industries (Irving Wire Products Division) Ltd* (1975) 50 DLR (3d) 265 at 281 per Martland J; *Island Properties Ltd v Entertainment Enterprises Ltd* (1986) 26 DLR (4th) 347 at 351.

CONTRACT CONFERS SOME FORM OF EQUITABLE TITLE

9.18   The general inexorability of due transfer or grant under a specifically enforceable land contract activates the equitable maxim that 'equity looks on that as done which ought to be done.'[1] Equity, assuming that the contracted performance is unstoppable, simply accelerates, for its own purposes, the effect of such performance. Equity anticipates the completion of the contract and regards the contractual promisee as already entitled – in equity – to an interest in the subject matter of the contract.[2]

1   See *KLDE Pty Ltd v Commissioner of Stamp Duties (Queensland)* (1984) 155 CLR 288 at 296 (High Court of Australia).
2   See *Re Flint (A Bankrupt)* [1993] Ch 319 at 326; *Mountney v Treharne* [2003] Ch 135 at [76] per Jonathan Parker LJ.

Metamorphosis of contractual into proprietary rights

9.19   Since contracts relating to land must (by one means or another) eventuate in performance, equity views the contractual purchaser as having acquired, as of the date of the contract itself, certain substantial rights of a proprietary character.[1] Thus, from the moment of specifically enforceable contractual commitment, the purchaser of a land interest acquires not merely a *contractual* right against the vendor but also a *proprietary* right in the vendor's land, a right which is necessarily equitable.[2] Under a specifically enforceable contract for the sale of land the purchaser is 'treated in equity as the owner of the property whether or not an order for specific performance has been made.'[3] His interest under the contract is 'a proprietary interest of a sort, which arises ... in anticipation of the execution of the transfer for which the purchaser is entitled to call.'[4]

1   See *Sonenco (No 77) Pty Ltd v Silvia* (1989) 89 ALR 437 at 457 per Ryan and Gummow JJ.
2   See *Hewitt v Court* (1982) 149 CLR 639 at 666 per Deane J.
3   *Swiss Bank Corpn v Lloyds Bank Ltd* [1979] Ch 548 at 565F per Browne-Wilkinson J.
4   *Oughtred v IRC* [1960] AC 206 at 240 per Lord Jenkins. See also *Neville v Wilson* [1997] Ch 144 at 157G–H per Nourse LJ; *Mills v Ruthol* (2002) 10 BPR 19381 at [122] per Palmer J.

Transmission of equitable ownership

9.20   There may be some question as to the exact nature of the proprietary entitlement conferred by contract and perhaps even as to the precise moment at which it arises. There is, however, no doubt that the irresistible right to call for the disposition of a promised estate or interest effectively transmits to the intended disponee a significant quantum of equitable property in the land concerned.[1] In effect, contract generates some form of equitable title – a doctrine which accounts for many of the species of equitable proprietary entitlement discussed in this chapter.

1   See *Hoysted v Federal Commissioner of Taxation* (1920) 27 CLR 400 at 423 per Isaacs J ('equitable property is commensurate with equitable relief').

Contracts for the transfer of a fee simple estate or a term of years

9.21   The equitable consequences of specifically enforceable contractual commitment are most obvious in relation to contracts for the transfer of a fee simple estate or a term of years. Indeed it has sometimes been said that the existence of the contract has a 'remarkable effect' in that it 'converts the estate, so to say, in equity.'[1] That is, the contract 'actually changes the ownership of the estate in equity' and causes the land to become 'a part of the real estate of the vendee.'[2] With the exchange of contracts for the disposition of a freehold or leasehold estate, an equitable interest in the fee simple[3] or term of years absolute,[4] as the case may be, vests immediately in the disponee.[5] In many circumstances it can loosely be said that the disponee is already, with the contract, the 'equitable owner' of the estate concerned.[6] It is undoubtedly true that some form of beneficial ownership of the relevant estate passes silently at this point,[7] subject to the payment of the purchase money,[8] with the consequence that, pending the contracted disposition at law, the disponor holds his legal estate on some limited or specialised form of trust for the disponee.[9]

1   *Lysaght v Edwards* (1876) 2 Ch D 499 at 507 per Jessel MR.
2   *Lysaght v Edwards* (1876) 2 Ch D 499 at 507 per Jessel MR. See also *Raffety v Schofield* [1897] 1 Ch 937 at 943.
3   See e g *Lysaght v Edwards* (1876) 2 Ch D 499 at 506 per Jessel MR.
4   See e g *R v Tower Hamlets LBC, ex p Von Goetz* [1999] QB 1019 at 1024A–1025A **[para 9.61]**.
5   In *Rose v Watson* (1864) 10 HLCas 672 at 678, 11 ER 1187 at 1190, Lord Westbury LC took it to be 'very simple and very clear' that 'the ownership of the estate is, in equity, transferred by [the] contract.'
6   *R v Tower Hamlets LBC, ex p Von Goetz* [1999] QB 1019 at 1024B per Mummery LJ. See likewise *Shaw v Foster* (1872) LR 5 HL 321 at 338 per Lord Cairns ('the purchaser was the real beneficial owner, in the eye of a Court of Equity').
7   'Upon the exchange of contracts the purchaser acquires an equitable estate in the land' (*DKLR Holding Co (No 2) Pty Ltd v Commissioner of Stamp Duties* [1978] 1 NSWLR 268 at 279F per Sheppard J). See also *Appleton v Aspin* [1988] 1 WLR 410 at 417D per Nourse LJ; *Legione v Hately* (1983) 152 CLR 406 at 423; *KLDE Pty Ltd v Commissioner of Stamp Duties (Queensland)* (1984) 155 CLR 288 at 297, 301; *Lowther v Kim* [2003] 1 NZLR 327 at [23].
8   *Lloyds Bank plc v Carrick* [1996] 4 All ER 630 at 637g–638b.
9   See *Lysaght v Edwards* (1876) 2 Ch D 499 at 506 per Jessel MR.

Contracts for the disposition of other interests or charges in or over land

9.22   Similar equitable consequences attach to specifically enforceable contracts to grant other kinds of interest or charge in or over land. A contract to grant a legal easement or profit *à prendre* is effective to transfer an equitable estate in the incorporeal hereditament to the prospective grantee.[1] Likewise a specifically enforceable agreement to create a legal mortgage immediately confers on the lender an equitable mortgage over the borrower's legal estate.[2] Such outcomes are entirely consistent with equity's historic impact on dealings with land. The anticipatory doctrine of equity accelerates, at least in equity, the desired effect of the transaction in hand and accords to the promisee under the specifically enforceable contract some equitable version of the subject matter of that transaction.

1   **[Para 9.92]**. See *May v Belleville* [1905] 2 Ch 605 at 612–613; *McDonald v Peddle* [1923] NZLR 987 at 993; *Tarrant v Zandstra* (1973) 1 BPR 9381 at 9385.
2   **[Para 9.109]**. See e g *Re Beetham; Ex parte Broderick* (1887) 18 QBD 766 at 768; *National Provincial and Union Bank of England v Charnley* [1924] 1 KB 431 at 440; *Palmer v Carey* [1926] AC 703 at 706–707; *Swiss Bank Corpn v Lloyds Bank Ltd* [1982] AC 584 at 594H–595E; *Hoofstetter v Rooker* (1895) 22 OAR 175 at 179; *Hewitt v Court* (1982) 149 CLR 639 at 666; *Re Collens* (1983) 140 DLR (3d) 755 at 757–758.

ESTATE CONTRACTS

9.23 A contract to create or transfer a legal estate in land is termed an 'estate contract'. At the risk of some 'over-simplification',[1] a specifically enforceable estate contract has the effect of passing to the intended disponee some kind of equitable estate in land.[2] The potential range of the estate contract includes contracts to transfer a fee simple estate or a term of years, together with contracts to create a lease, mortgage or charge or to confer an estate in an incorporeal hereditament such as an easement, and also contractual options to take any of the foregoing interests in or over land. The proprietary dimension of the estate contract carries certain important implications.

1 See *Wollondilly Shire Council v Picton Power Lines Pty Ltd* (1991) 5 BPR 11503 at 11508 per Young J.
2 See *London and South Western Railway Co v Gomm* (1882) 20 Ch D 562 at 581 per Jessel MR ('The right to call for a conveyance of the land is an equitable interest or equitable estate').

Trusteeship of the vendor

9.24 The availability of the contractual remedy of specific performance engrafts, at least temporarily, some sort of trust upon the relationship between vendor and purchaser under an estate contract. Early equity jurisprudence tended to regard it as settled law 'that the moment you have a valid contract for sale the vendor becomes in equity a trustee for the purchaser of the estate sold.'[1] By contrast, recent case law has been more discriminating in its use of the terminology of trusteeship, imposing substantial qualifications on the adaptation of the trust model in the present context.[2] Nevertheless it is now 'obviously too late in the day' to doubt that in equity the contractual purchaser is 'entitled to many rights ... that closely resemble the rights of a beneficial owner.'[3] The interface between trust theory and the specifically enforceable vendor–purchaser relationship imparts much that is instructive about the inner nature of property.

1 *Lysaght v Edwards* (1876) 2 Ch D 499 at 506 per Jessel MR. See, to the same effect, *Daire v Beversham* (1661) Nels 76 at 77, 21 ER 793 at 794; *Green v Smith* (1738) 1 Atk 572 at 573, 26 ER 360; *Paine v Meller* (1801) 6 Ves 349 at 352–353, 31 ER 1088 at 1089–1090; *Broome v Monck* (1805) 10 Ves 597 at 606, 32 ER 976 at 979; *Shaw v Foster* (1872) LR 5 HL 321 at 333 per Lord Chelmsford, 338 per Lord Cairns. The applicability of trust concepts to vendor and purchaser was not, however, a matter of universal acceptance (see e g *Rayner v Preston* (1881) 18 Ch D 1 at 10–11 per Brett LJ ('With the greatest deference, it seems wrong to say that the one is a trustee for the other')).
2 The vendor under an uncompleted contract of sale becomes 'a trustee of some sort for the purchaser' (*Michaels v Harley House (Marylebone) Ltd* [2000] Ch 104 at 113G–H per Robert Walker LJ), but it would be wrong to treat the contract 'as equivalent to an immediate, irrevocable declaration of trust (or assignment of beneficial interest) in the land' (*Jerome v Kelly (Inspector of Taxes)* [2004] 1 WLR 1409 at [32] per Lord Walker of Gestingthorpe).
3 *Martin Commercial Fueling, Inc v Virtanen* (1997) 144 DLR (4th) 290 at 295 per Newbury JA.

Phased transfer of equitable property to the contractual purchaser

9.25   Far from being absolute or unitary in quality, property is a relative and highly gradable concept,[1] which can be calibrated across a wide range of proprietary intensity.[2] This is no less true of the equitable property which passes from vendor to purchaser under a specifically enforceable contract relating to land.

1   Gray, 'Property in Thin Air' [1991] CLJ 252 at 295–296 [**para 2.13**].
2   Gray and Gray, 'The Idea of Property in Land', in S Bright and J K Dewar (ed), *Land Law: Themes and Perspectives* (OUP 1998), pp 15–16.

9.26   An analysis of the nature of the vendor–purchaser relationship at different stages of a transaction of sale reveals a sophisticated, but constantly changing, trust relationship between the parties, corresponding to the gradual transmission of equitable property from one party to the other. The transactional history of the sale is all about the gradual accretion of equitable property in the purchaser.[1] The vendor–purchaser relationship, as it moves steadily through its various phases, involves the progressive transfer of beneficial property to the purchaser until the point when the purchaser finally becomes the full beneficial owner of the relevant estate in the land and the vendor ranks as no more than a bare trustee.[2] A specifically enforceable contract thus filters elements of beneficial ownership away from the vendor and towards the purchaser, these elements eventually merging with the legal estate at the point of transfer (or, where relevant, on registration of the transfer at Land Registry).

1   This analysis has now been accepted by the House of Lords. See *Jerome v Kelly* (*Inspector of Taxes*) [2004] 1 WLR 1409 at [32] per Lord Walker of Gestingthorpe ('If the contract proceeds to completion, the equitable interest can be viewed as passing to the buyer in stages, as title is made and accepted and as the purchase price is paid in full').
2   On bare trusteeship, see Chapter 11 [**para 11.154**]. Under a bare trust the beneficiary is the 'absolute beneficial owner', leaving the trustee 'without any beneficial interest' (*Lloyds Bank plc v Carrick* [1996] 4 All ER 630 at 637h–j). See, however, *Thorpe v Bristile Ltd* (1996) 16 WAR 500 at 505A–B.

Gradual intensification of the trust relationship

9.27   It follows that the trust relationship between vendor and purchaser under a specifically enforceable contract gathers in intensity as the relationship progresses. If there is any modern disinclination to use the terminology of trusteeship in the present context,[1] it stems from a distaste for the premature labelling of the vendor as a trustee at a stage when many of his rights and functions are still plainly non-fiduciary. The application of the trust model is necessarily a phased or incremental process.[2] On exchange of contracts the vendor first becomes a 'constructive trustee' of his legal estate,[3] holding on a trust which arises by *construction* of the court. But, as soon as the purchase money is received in full, he is converted (until the date of completion of the transfer) into a bare trustee for his purchaser[4] and the purchaser acquires an irresistible right to call for the transfer of the promised estate. This analysis can be demonstrated by reference to a hypothetical transaction in which a vendor (V) and a purchaser (P) contract for the transfer to P of a fee simple estate in Greenacre.

1   See *Chang v Registrar of Titles* (1976) 137 CLR 177 at 184 per Mason J; *Avondale Printers & Stationers Ltd v Haggie* [1979] 2 NZLR 124 at 141–142 per Mahon J.

2   See e g *Wall v Bright* (1820) 1 Jac & W 494 at 503, 37 ER 456 at 459 per Sir Thomas Plumer MR; *Rose v Watson* (1864) 10 HLCas 672 at 678, 11 ER 1187 at 1190 per Lord Westbury.

3   *Shaw v Foster* (1872) LR 5 HL 321 at 349 per Lord O'Hagan, 356 per Lord Hatherley LC; *Lysaght v Edwards* (1876) 2 Ch D 499 at 510 per Jessel MR.

4   See e g *Bridges v Mees* [1957] Ch 475 at 484 per Harman J; *Lloyds Bank plc v Carrick* [1996] 4 All ER 630 at 637h–j, 638b, 641c–d per Morritt LJ. See also *Morgan v Swansea Urban Sanitary Authority* (1878) 9 Ch D 582 at 586 per Jessel MR; *Weidman v McClary Man Co* (1917) 33 DLR 672 at 683; *McWilliam v McWilliams Wines Pty Ltd* (1964) 114 CLR 656 at 660; *Shanahan v Fitzgerald* [1982] 2 NSWLR 513 at 514G–515A; *Bell v Guaranty Trust Co of Canada* (1984) 4 DLR (4th) 624 at 633; *Stern v McArthur* (1988) 165 CLR 489 at 523 per Deane and Dawson JJ.

Pre-contractual stage

9.28   Before any exchange of contracts occurs it is clear that the entire interest in Greenacre is vested in V and there exists no trust of any kind.[1] Indeed, at this stage it is technically inaccurate to suppose that V's ownership comprises a summation of two distinct estates, legal and equitable.[2] Equitable doctrine resists the notion that absolute ownership requires, for all purposes and at every moment of time, the separate and concurrent existence of two different kinds of estate or interest, ie the legal and the equitable.[3] Where the 'whole right of property' is vested in one person, there is no need to isolate any beneficial component of ownership,[4] for equitable rights in property emerge only when required in order to give effect to the precepts of equity.[5] Prior to contract V simply holds the legal estate in Greenacre, together with all the rights and incidents which attach to that estate.[6]

1   See e g *Lloyds Bank plc v Carrick* [1996] 4 All ER 630 at 638b per Morritt LJ.

2   [**Para 1.161**]. A man 'cannot be a trustee for himself' (*Goodright v Wells* (1781) 2 Doug KB 771 at 778, 99 ER 491 at 495 per Lord Mansfield). See also *Selby v Alston* (1797) 3 Ves 339 at 341, 30 ER 1042 at 1043; *Harmood v Oglander* (1803) 8 Ves 106 at 127, 32 ER 293 at 301 per Lord Eldon; *Re Selous* [1901] 1 Ch 921 at 922; *Re Turkington* [1937] 4 All ER 501 at 504F; *Re Heberley (deceased)* [1971] NZLR 325 at 333, 346; *DKLR Holding Co (No 2) Pty Ltd v Commissioner of Stamp Duties (NSW)* (1982) 149 CLR 431 at 463; *Chief Commr of Stamp Duties v ISPT Pty Ltd* (1997) 45 NSWLR 639 at 647F–G per Mason P.

3   See *DKLR Holding Co (No 2) Pty Ltd v Commissioner of Stamp Duties* [1978] 1 NSWLR 268 at 278B–E per Sheppard J, (1982) 149 CLR 431 at 463 per Aickin J; *Re Transphere Pty Ltd* (1986) 5 NSWLR 309 at 311D–E per McLelland J; *Oughtred v IRC* [1960] AC 206 at 216 per Wilberforce QC (arguendo).

4   *Commissioner of Stamp Duties (Queensland) v Livingston* [1965] AC 694 at 712C–D per Viscount Radcliffe; *Westdeutsche Landesbank Girozentrale v Islington LBC* [1996] AC 669 at 706E per Lord Browne-Wilkinson; *Corin v Patton* (1990) 169 CLR 540 at 579 per Deane J. The absolute owner has no separate equitable estate since this is 'absorbed in the legal estate' (*DKLR Holding Co (No 2) Pty Ltd v Commissioner of Stamp Duties (NSW)* (1982) 149 CLR

431 at 442 per Gibbs CJ). See also *Grey v IRC* [1958] Ch 690 at 708 per Evershed MR; *Chief Commr of Stamp Duties v ISPT Pty Ltd* (1997) 45 NSWLR 639 at 648C per Mason P, 658B per Fitzgerald A-JA.

5   *Commissioner of Stamp Duties (Queensland) v Livingston* [1965] AC 694 at 712E per Viscount Radcliffe. See also *DKLR Holding Co (No 2) Pty Ltd v Commissioner of Stamp Duties* [1978] 1 NSWLR 268 at 278D–E.

6   *Re Transphere Pty Ltd* (1986) 5 NSWLR 309 at 311E per McLelland J.

Exchange of contracts

9.29   With the conclusion of an enforceable contract for the sale of Greenacre some form of beneficial entitlement in Greenacre clearly passes from V to P[1] and, correspondingly, V is subjected to a form of constructive trust in favour of P.[2] The emergence of a specifically enforceable contract produces a trusteeship 'of a peculiar kind',[3] since P receives only part of the beneficial interest in the property, V retaining some beneficial interest himself.[4] On this ground it is probably 'inaccurate to describe as ownership' the interest which is acquired by P in advance of transfer or conveyance[5] and it seems better to acknowledge, in more guarded terms, that the making of the contract transfers beneficial ownership to P merely 'to an extent'.[6] Until V is obliged on payment of the purchase moneys to convey title, P 'owns an interest in the property but he does not own the property.'[7] The most that can be said is that, to the extent that P pays any part of the purchase money to V (e g by way of deposit or otherwise), 'to that extent the vendor is a trustee for him', P taking an equitable lien over the land commensurate with his part payment.[8] The duties and functions of V at this stage remain, unquestionably, a strange blend of the fiduciary and non-fiduciary.

1   P has, with the contract, a sufficient interest in the land to support a subsale to a stranger (see *Gordon Hill Trust Ltd v Segall* [1941] 2 All ER 379 at 391G per Luxmoore LJ). Furthermore, the transmission of equitable entitlement to P is not precluded by the fact that the contract remains conditional, e g on the grant of planning permission (see *London and South Western Railway Co v Gomm* (1882) 20 Ch D 562 at 581; *Chattey v Farndale Holdings Inc* (1998) 75 P & CR 298 at 306).

2   *Lloyds Bank plc v Carrick* [1996] 4 All ER 630 at 639d–e per Morritt LJ; *Yaxley v Gotts* [2000] Ch 162 at 179E–F per Robert Walker LJ. See also *Central Trust and Safe Deposit Co v Snider* [1916] 1 AC 266 at 272 per Lord Parker of Waddington; *Hoysted v Federal Commissioner of Taxation* (1920) 27 CLR 400 at 423 per Isaacs J; *Shephard v Corindi Blueberry Growers Pty Ltd* (1994) 6 BPR 13672 at 13674 per Young J.

3   *Lloyds Bank plc v Carrick* [1996] 4 All ER 630 at 637g per Morritt LJ. See also *Rhondda Cynon Taff County BC v Watkins* (Chancery Division, 11 December 2001) per Neuberger J.

4   See *Chief Commr of Stamp Duties v ISPT Pty Ltd* (1997) 45 NSWLR 639 at 654E–F per Meagher JA. 'Beneficial ownership of the land is in a sense split between the seller and buyer' (*Jerome v Kelly (Inspector of Taxes)* [2004] 1 WLR 1409 at [32] per Lord Walker of Gestingthorpe).

5   *KLDE Pty Ltd v Commissioner of Stamp Duties (Queensland)* (1984) 155 CLR 288 at 300 per Brennan J. See also *Coffey v Brunel Construction Co Ltd* [1983] IR 36 at 43 per Griffin J.

6   *Haque v Haque (No 2)* (1965) 114 CLR 98 at 124 per Kitto J. See also *KLDE Pty Ltd v Commissioner of Stamp Duties (Queensland)* (1984) 155 CLR 288 at 301 per Brennan J.

7   *KLDE Pty Ltd v Commissioner of Stamp Duties (Queensland)* (1984) 155 CLR 288 at 300 per Brennan J. See also *Stern v McArthur* (1988) 165 CLR 489 at 522–523 per Deane and Dawson JJ.

8   *Rose v Watson* (1864) 10 HLCas 672 at 684, 11 ER 1187 at 1192 per Lord Cranworth (see also 10 HLCas 672 at 678, 11 ER 1187 at 1190 per Lord Westbury LC). See *Shirlaw v Taylor* (1991) 31 FCR 222 at 228; *Shephard v Corindi Blueberry Growers Pty Ltd* (1994) 6 BPR 13672 at 13674.

9.30   V is undoubtedly burdened by certain fiduciary responsibilities towards P in respect of the management and preservation of Greenacre during the interim between the contract and its completion by transfer.[1] For instance, V must repel trespassers and prevent decay or dilapidation to the property. V is liable to P if, by reason of his negligence, the subject matter of the estate contract is damaged by trespassers[2] or by the elements,[3] or if the property is damaged by V himself[4] or is prejudiced by unfavourable transactions entered into by V.[5] Moreover, if V in breach of his contract sells the land instead to a third party, V stands in relation to the proceeds of that sale as a trustee on behalf of P.[6]

1   See *Cumberland Consolidated Holdings Ltd v Ireland* [1946] KB 264 at 269–270; *Lukies v Ripley* (1994) 6 BPR 13471 at 13474. The Law Commission has recommended that the relationship between vendor and contractual purchaser should continue to be analysed in terms of trusteeship (Law Commission, *Transfer of Land: Risk of Damage after Contract for Sale* (Law Com No 191, April 1990), paras 2.7–2.8).

2   *Clarke v Ramuz* [1891] 2 QB 456 at 460–463. The vendor must take reasonable steps to exclude trespassers and prevent damage by them (see *Davron Estates Ltd v Turnshire Ltd* (1982) 133 NLJ 937).

3   *Lucie-Smith v Gorman* [1981] CLY 2866.

4   *Lysaght v Edwards* (1876) 2 Ch D 499 at 507; *Cumberland Consolidated Holdings Ltd v Ireland* [1946] KB 264 at 269 (deposit of rubbish). See *Phillips v Lamdin* [1949] 2 KB 33 at 41–45 (removal of door).

5   See *Abdulla v Shah* [1959] AC 124 at 132–133 (grant of unfavourable tenancies); *Sinclair-Hill v Sothcott* (1973) 226 EG 1399 at 1401 (withdrawal of application for planning permission). The vendor's powers to act as owner and change tenancies and holdings are generally suspended pending completion (*Riddington v Pye* (1989) 9 BPR 16643 at 16646).

6   *Lake v Bayliss* [1974] 1 WLR 1073 at 1076D–E.

9.31   There remain, however, distinct limitations on the proposition that V stands as trustee for P pending completion of their specifically enforceable contract.[1] V undeniably retains a substantial beneficial interest in the land[2] and enjoys a 'paramount right ... to protect his own interest as vendor of the property.'[3] He has a right to remain in possession of the land until completion of the contract and payment of the purchase moneys[4] and is beneficially entitled to the rents and profits which accrue before the date of completion[5] and to any statutory compensation payable before that date.[6] V may even mortgage the land provided that the mortgage is discharged on or before the date fixed for transfer.[7] If P enters upon the land without V's permission and without authority under the contract, V can maintain, for his own benefit, an action in trespass against P.[8] Moreover, any trusteeship fixed on V is inherently qualified by the fact that if P enters into possession prior to transfer of the legal estate, V retains an 'unpaid vendor's lien' over the land until the purchase moneys are paid in full.[9]

1   *Stern v McArthur* (1988) 165 CLR 489 at 521 per Deane and Dawson JJ ('the qualifications are such as to rob the proposition of much of its significance ... ').

this point the legal estate in Greenacre is effectively reunited with such beneficial interest as passed to P under the estate contract.[1] The equitable estate in the land now merges indistinguishably with the legal estate – is 'absorbed in the legal estate' – thereby confirming in P 'the whole right of property in the land.'[2] Thus is completed a process in which V, by entering into a specifically enforceable contract, allowed an obligation in favour of his purchaser to be 'impressed', by the force of equity, upon his own legal estate.[3] P's right to demand due performance of that contractual obligation became constitutive of an equitable proprietary right which was not so much 'carved out of', but rather 'engrafted on to', V's legal estate.[4] But when, on the transfer of the promised legal estate in Greenacre, P's equitable entitlement is no longer needed in reinforcement of V's conscientious obligation to deal with the land in conformity with the estate contract, P's equitable right simply falls away.[5]

1   If the estate contract is never completed by the appropriate transfer or assignment, P retains the estate in equitable form and, in almost all conceivable circumstances, can call irresistibly for specific performance of the contract by court order (see *R v Tower Hamlets LBC, ex p Von Goetz* [1999] QB 1019 at 1020H, 1024C–1025C per Mummery LJ).

2   *DKLR Holding Co (No 2) Pty Ltd v Commissioner of Stamp Duties (NSW)* (1982) 149 CLR 431 at 442 per Gibbs CJ. See also *Brydges v Brydges* (1796) 3 Ves 120 at 126, 30 ER 926 at 929.

3   *DKLR Holding Co (No 2) Pty Ltd v Commissioner of Stamp Duties (NSW)* (1982) 149 CLR 431 at 474 per Brennan J.

4   *Re Transphere Pty Ltd* (1986) 5 NSWLR 309 at 311E–F per McLelland J.

5   Equitable rights of property ultimately derive from some conscientious obligation to deal with a resource in accordance with equitable doctrine (see *Commissioner of Stamp Duties (Queensland) v Livingston* [1965] AC 694 at 712E per Viscount Radcliffe [**para 1.162**]).

Transmission of risk

9.35   The anticipatory effect of equitable doctrine attaches one further implication to a specifically enforceable estate contract. In the absence of contractual provision to the contrary, an estate contract passes to the purchaser all normal risks incidental to land ownership. Thus, for instance, the parties are not discharged from their agreement by the mere fact that a statutory power of compulsory purchase is unexpectedly exercised immediately following the date of their contract.[1]

1   *E Johnson & Co (Barbados) Ltd v NSR Ltd* [1997] AC 400 at 407B–F. See similarly *Amalgamated Investment & Property Co Ltd v John Walker & Sons Ltd* [1977] 1 WLR 164 at 173D–174A (listed building notice).

Insurable risk

9.36   It follows that (absent other contractual provision) the insurable risk in the land passes to the purchaser concurrently with the transmission of any part of the beneficial interest in the realty. It is therefore standard practice (and clearly advisable) for the purchaser to buy insurance cover effective from the date of his contract of purchase.[1] Such cover is essential since if a building on the land is destroyed (eg by fire) between contract and conveyance, the purchaser remains contractually bound to take the conveyance of the land and the charred remains at the full contracted purchase price.[2]

1   *Lysaght v Edwards* (1876) 2 Ch D 499 at 507 per Jessel MR.
2   See eg *Lysaght v Edwards* (1876) 2 Ch D 499 at 507; *Rayner v Preston* (1881) 18 Ch D 1 at 6; *Fletcher v Manton* (1940) 64 CLR 37 at 42, 48–49; *Budhia v Wellington City Corpn* [1976] 1 NZLR 766 at 768. For a strong counter-argument, see M P Thompson, 'Must a Purchaser buy a Charred Ruin?' [1984] Conv 43. See also LPA 1925, s 47; *Lonsdale & Thompson Ltd v Black Arrow Group Plc* [1993] Ch 361; *Kern Corporation Ltd v Walter Reid Trading Pty Ltd* (1987) 163 CLR 164; *Stephenson v State Bank of New South Wales Ltd* (1996) 39 NSWLR 101.

Contractual reallocation of risk

9.37 In 1990 the Law Commission condemned this allocation of risk between vendor and purchaser as 'fundamentally unsatisfactory and unfair', in that it imposes on the contractual purchaser a responsibility for the land at a time when he has no control over it.[1] The Commission was minded to propose that the risk of physical damage should pass to the purchaser only on completion of the contract of purchase rather than at the date of exchange of contracts.[2] In the event, legislation towards this end was considered unnecessary since the Standard Conditions of Sale, introduced in 1990 and now widely used in property transactions, effectively reallocate the risk of supervening physical damage.[3] Under these Conditions the seller undertakes to transfer the property 'in the same physical state as it was at the date of the contract (except for fair wear and tear), which means that the seller retains the risk until completion.'[4] Ironically, it is frequently the case in practice that the Standard Conditions are amended by the addition of a special condition which returns the risk to the purchaser.

1   Law Com No 191 (1990), para 2.9 (The purchaser 'cannot take steps physically to protect the property or to do running repairs').
2   Law Com No 191 (1990), para 2.25. The Commission did not, however, envisage a similar deferment of risk in relation to other kinds of changed circumstance which, without inflicting physical damage, may affect the value of a property between contract and completion (ibid, para 2.5). Such risks include fluctuations in market value or changes in value occurring outside the parties' control (eg flowing from listed building designation).
3   Law Com No 191 (1990), paras 3.8–3.10.
4   Standard Conditions of Sale (4th edition), Condition 5.1.1. See J E Adams, [1990] Conv 179 at 189–190.

Protection of the estate contract against strangers

9.38 The beneficial entitlement taken by a purchaser under a specifically enforceable estate contract, like other equitable interests in land, requires protection if it is to bind third parties. Until its completion by conveyance or transfer, the purchaser's estate contract comprises a contractual right to call for the legal estate and this right is always vulnerable to the possibility that the legal owner may transfer his estate, in breach of contract, to some other purchaser (usually in return for a higher price). Alternatively, the legal owner may charge the estate to a lender and abstract the value of the loan money advanced. The protection available to an estate contract differs in accordance with whether title to the estate is registered at Land Registry.

Contracts relating to a registered estate

9.39   An estate contract relating to a registered estate requires to be protected by the entry of a 'notice' in the register of the legal owner's title.[1] If safeguarded in this way, the estate contract becomes enforceable against any disponee of the registered estate (including a chargee) who takes in defiance of the contract.[2] The protected incumbrancer is then fully entitled to call upon the disponee for a transfer of the legal estate on the terms of the original contract. Conversely, a failure to protect the estate contract usually has the consequence, in the event of non-performance, of relegating the contractual purchaser to a mere money remedy against the other contracting party.[3] An unprotected estate contract is wholly ineffective against a disponee for value in all but those exceptional circumstances where the contractual purchaser has been allowed into possession of the land pending disposition of the legal estate and can claim an overriding interest as a person 'in actual occupation'.[4]

1   LRA 2002, ss 32(1)–(2), 33 [**para 12.84**]. In practice estate contracts are seldom protected by register entry except in cases of suspicion or delayed completion (see also H W R Wade, [1956] CLJ 216 at 223). The cost and effort involved in drawing up the application for entry is certainly a disincentive, whereas the intending purchaser's search with priority normally provides adequate protection against adverse dealings [**para 12.50**].

2   LRA 2002, ss 28(1), 29(1), (2)(a)(i).

3   An unprotected estate contract remains effective, however, against a disponee otherwise than for value or a disponee who takes merely equitable rights in or over the land, e g an equitable chargee (LRA 2002, s 29(1) [**para 12.80**]). See *Shephard v Corindi Blueberry Growers Pty Ltd* (1994) 6 BPR 13672 at 13675–13676; *Martin Commercial Fueling, Inc v Virtanen* (1997) 144 DLR (4th) 290 at 300.

4   LRA 2002, s 29(1), (2)(a)(ii). See e g *Grace Rymer Investments Ltd v Waite* [1958] Ch 831 at 849–851; *Webb v Pollmount Ltd* [1966] Ch 584 at 603C–D; *Ferrishurst Ltd v Wallcite Ltd* [1999] Ch 355 at 366G–367G.

Contracts relating to an unregistered estate

9.40   If the legal owner's title is not yet registered at Land Registry, an estate contract can be protected only by the registration of a Class C(iv) land charge against the estate owner's name.[1] Registration renders the estate contract binding against the world,[2] but a failure to ensure due registration makes the contract void against any subsequent purchaser of a legal estate in the land for money or money's worth.[3] In *Lloyds Bank plc v Carrick*,[4] for example, V contracted to sell a maisonette to his sister-in-law, P.[5] The legal estate was never transferred to P, although P paid the purchase price in full and moved into occupation of the maisonette. V later mortgaged his legal estate to Lloyds Bank. On V's subsequent default the Court of Appeal upheld the bank's right to recover possession from P. Morritt LJ indicated that, on full payment of the purchase money by P, V ranked as a bare trustee of the legal estate and P became 'the absolute beneficial owner of the maisonette.'[6] Her equitable interest, founded in the estate contract with V, was rendered statutorily void against the bank as mortgagee by reason of P's failure to register that estate contract against V as a land charge.[7] The Court of Appeal held, moreover, that in the presence of the trust relationship already created by the specifically enforceable contract (and here rendered statutorily unenforceable), there was no room for the superimposition on V of any further constructive trust which might arguably affect the rights of the bank.[8]

1   LCA 1972, ss 2(4)–3(1) [paras **2.186**, **12.306**].
2   LPA 1925, s 198(1) [paras **2.187**, **12.279**].
3   LCA 1972, s 4(6) [para **12.282**].
4   [1996] 4 All ER 630. See [1996] Conv 295 (M P Thompson); (1996) 112 LQR 549 (P Ferguson).
5   The contract was an oral contract entered into before the commencement of the Law of Property (Miscellaneous Provisions) Act 1989. Although initially unenforceable under LPA 1925, s 40 [para **12.38**], it later became specifically enforceable by reason of part performance when P paid the purchase price and went into possession ([1996] 4 All ER 630 at 637f–g).
6   [1996] 4 All ER 630 at 637j.
7   P could not establish the bare trust as against the bank 'for it has no existence except as the equitable consequence of the contract' ([1996] 4 All ER 630 at 638b–c per Morritt LJ). The Court of Appeal noted, however, that the result would have been different if title to the maisonette had been registered ([1996] 4 All ER 630 at 642d–e). P would, on the unusual facts of this case, have had an overriding interest binding the bank (LRA 2002, s 29(1), (2)(a)(ii), Sch 3, para 2) [para **2.121**].
8   See, however, N Hopkins, (1998) 61 MLR 486. The result in *Lloyds Bank plc v Carrick* means that, in unregistered land, a party may be positively disadvantaged by having entered into a specifically enforceable contract. Compare e g *Yaxley v Gotts* [2000] Ch 162 at 179E–F where, in the absence of a specifically enforceable contract, the Court of Appeal held that there was 'room for a constructive trust to operate so as to avoid injustice.'

Remedy in damages

9.41   In the case of failure to complete an estate contract by due performance, it is open to the aggrieved contracting party to rescind the contract and seek monetary compensation instead of specific performance of the contract. A failure to complete on the contractual date is remediable in damages for breach of contract or in damages in lieu of a decree for specific performance under the Supreme Court Act 1981.[1] However, no right to rescind arises until time becomes 'of the essence' by virtue of a notice to complete served by the party seeking completion or by virtue of unreasonable delay.[2] Where one contracting party has treated another's repudiation or breach of contract as discharging the contract, or where an order for specific performance is not complied with, damages may be recovered not only for restitution and indemnity in respect of sums paid and expenses incurred, but also for loss of bargain.[3]

1   Supreme Court Act 1981, s 50.
2   See *Raineri v Miles* [1981] AC 1050; [1980] CLJ 21 (D J Hayton). Where time has been made of the essence of contractual performance, there is an increasing tendency to deny relief to the

party in breach (see e g *Union Eagle Ltd v Golden Achievement Ltd* [1997] AC 514 (JCPC); *Tanwar Enterprises Pty Ltd v Cauchi* (2003) 201 ALR 359 (HCA)).

3   *Johnson v Agnew* [1980] AC 367. See also A J Oakley, [1980] CLJ 58.

EQUITABLE LEASES

9.42   It is entirely possible that a term of years may exist as an *equitable* estate in English law.[1] The circumstances in which this may occur are diverse; it is in the context of the equitable lease that equitable doctrine appears in its most curative guise. Equity is often efficacious in salvaging attempts at leasehold creation or transfer which have failed, for reasons of informality or technical imperfection, to invest the intended lessee with a legal term of years. There is, in equity, an understandable reluctance to treat as wholly ineffective a transaction which was deliberately, albeit misguidedly, entered into by independent, freewilling parties.[2] Ever mindful of human frailty, equity strains to accord at least some vitality to the terms which these parties have so patently agreed.

1   See *R v Tower Hamlets LBC, ex p Von Goetz* [1999] QB 1019 at 1024C–1025A per Mummery LJ, 1026F–G per Peter Gibson LJ.
2   See e g *Proudreed Ltd v Microgen Holdings Plc* (1996) 72 P & CR 388 at 389 per Schiemann LJ ('failure to adopt the appropriate formalities may be the result of laziness, ignorance, double dealing or a number of other causes. The law recognises that there comes a point when it will be seen as inequitable to maintain that, just because the due formalities have not been observed, no transfer has taken place').

Circumstances of defective, incomplete or informal grant or transfer

9.43   No legal term of years can be validly created otherwise than out of an existing legal estate and in appropriate compliance with strict statutory requirements of formality and registration.[1] The transfer or assignment of subsisting legal leases is likewise dependent on certain requirements of formality and, where appropriate, registration. Non-compliance with these elementary ground rules brings the consequence that the intended recipient of a leasehold estate is disabled from taking the contemplated leasehold as a *legal* term of years. Such an outcome inevitably arises in each of the following circumstances.

1   [Paras 7.217–7.247].

Formally defective grant or transfer of a legal lease

9.44   The informal grant of a term of years (ie a grant otherwise than by deed) prevents the creation of any legal leasehold estate for a term in excess of three years.[1] Furthermore, the informal transfer of a subsisting legal lease (irrespective of its duration) always precludes the assignment at law of any term of years.[2]

1   LPA 1925, ss 52(1), 54(2) [**para 7.221**].
2   [**Para 7.227**].

Failure to apply for substantive registration

9.45   A number of statutory provisions ensure that failure to secure substantive registration at Land Registry of certain kinds of leasehold disposition disables the intended recipient from taking a legal term of years. In cases of leasehold grant for a term in excess of seven years or of assignment of an unregistered term with more than seven years unexpired or of transfer of any registered leasehold estate, failure to complete the disposition by registration of the disponee as registered proprietor brings about the strict consequence that no legal term of years can pass or remain vested in the intended recipient.[1]

1   LRA 2002, ss 7(1)–(2), 27(1) [**paras 7.238, 7.243**].

Mere contract to create or transfer a leasehold term

9.46   A leasehold relationship may fail to create a legal term of years precisely because the parties never proceed beyond the stage of a contract to create a lease. Some parties to a leasehold relationship incorporate their mutual understanding in a written contract to create or transfer the lease envisaged,[1] but never actually move from contractual commitment to contractual performance, with the result that no formal legal lease is ever granted or assigned. In dispensing with the completion of their contract by formal grant or transfer, the parties effectively signify their willingness to leave their relationship on a purely contractual footing, often assuming it to be just as effective as a formal disposition of leasehold rights.

1   [**Para 7.226**].

Grant out of equitable title

9.47   A lessor or assignor who holds only an equitable entitlement (eg an equitable fee simple estate or an equitable term of years) is clearly unable to create or transfer a legal term of years of any kind.[1] Any term of years carved out of an equitable estate can itself have equitable quality only.

1   See eg *Marks v Attallah* (1966) 198 EG 685; (1966) 110 Sol Jo 709.

Intervention of equity

9.48   Certain transactions which have not resulted in any successful vesting of a *legal* leasehold estate may nevertheless be effective to confer an *equitable* term of years. In many cases of abortive grant or transfer of a fixed term lease at law, equity regards the incomplete, informal or imperfect transaction as generating an equitable term of years which is equivalent, in all but legal quality, to the term of years originally intended to pass. (Thus, for instance, an invalid grant of a ten-year lease *at law* is commuted, under this doctrine of broad equivalence, into a fully valid ten-year lease *in equity.*[1]) Such an outcome rests on a combination of factors, some statutory, some contractual, and some purely equitable in their application. All have in common the idea that the mere inefficacy of a transaction at law 'does not touch whatever rights are behind it' and 'cannot cut down or merge the pre-existing right which led to its execution.'[2] The vitiating informality or incompleteness strikes at the effectiveness of only the imperfect or unregistered instrument of disposition, leaving equitable doctrine free to operate upon other, closely associated, aspects of the transaction.

1   See *R v Tower Hamlets LBC, ex p Von Goetz* [1999] QB 1019 at 1020H, 1024A–D **[para 9.61]**.
2   *Barry v Heider* (1914) 19 CLR 197 at 216 per Isaacs J.

Statutory regulation

9.49   In each of the following four instances a failure to secure the substantive registration of the grantee or transferee of a term of years as proprietor of title to a leasehold estate has the statutory consequence that the grantee or transferee is left holding merely an equitable term of years.

Lease granted out of unregistered reversion

9.50   A long[1] lease granted out of an unregistered reversion (albeit with due formality) becomes, after a lapse of two months, a mere contract to grant a legal lease[2] and therefore takes effect, almost invariably, as an equitable lease.

1   In this context a long lease comprises a term of more than seven years measured from the date of grant **[para 7.237]**.
2   LRA 2002, s 7(2)(b) **[para 7.238]**.

Transfer of existing unregistered legal lease

9.51   The transfer of an existing unregistered long leasehold, if not substantively registered at Land Registry within two months, becomes void as a transfer of the legal estate.[1] At this point the transferor is left holding the legal leasehold estate on a statutory 'bare trust' for the intended transferee,[2] who thus holds an equitable leasehold estate.

1   LRA 2002, s 7(1) **[para 7.242]**.
2   LRA 2002, s 7(2)(a).

Lease granted out of existing registered reversion

9.52   Failure to register a long leasehold term granted out of an existing registered reversion ensures that the disposition cannot 'operate at law.'[1] The lease therefore subsists only in equity, the contractual intent underlying the unrecorded instrument effectively creating for the disponee an equitable right in the land.

1   LRA 2002, s 27(1) **[para 7.240]**.

Transfer of existing registered lease

9.53 Failure to register the transfer[1] of an already registered leasehold estate leaves the legal leasehold title outstanding in the transferor as registered proprietor,[2] the intended transferee being restricted to a merely equitable title to the leasehold term.[3]

1   Even a gratuitous, as distinct from a contracted, transfer of a term of years can give rise, in the absence of due registration of the donee as leasehold proprietor, to an equitable term of years vested in that donee (see *Mascall v Mascall* (1984) 50 P & CR 119 at 125–128; *Corin v Patton* (1990) 169 CLR 540 at 559–560, 582 [**para 7.59**]).
2   LRA 2002, s 27(1).
3   The principle is widely accepted. See *E S Schwab & Co Ltd v McCarthy* (1976) 31 P & CR 196 at 201; *Brown & Root Technology Ltd v Sun Alliance & London Assurance Co Ltd and London Assurance Co Ltd* [2001] Ch 733 at 741G–H; *National Trustees, Executors and Agency Co of Australasia Ltd v Boyd* (1926) 39 CLR 72 at 82; *Brunker v Perpetual Trustee Co (Ltd)* (1937) 57 CLR 555 at 581, 599; *Progressive Mailing House Pty Ltd v Tabali Pty Ltd* (1985) 157 CLR 17 at 27, 54; *Chan v Cresdon Pty Ltd* (1989) 168 CLR 242 at 248, 256–257, 261.

Reference to antecedent contractual intent

9.54 The statutory outcome of failure to complete certain leasehold dealings by substantive registration merely mirrors a more general approach adopted by equity, under which a grant or transfer which is defective at law may be rescued by reference to its underlying contractual intent. Equity looks always to intent rather than to form,[1] with the consequence that the mere fact that an informal or unregistered instrument of grant or assignment is ineffective at law (and cannot therefore be a source of *legal* rights) in no way prevents the court from basing equitable entitlements on the contractual substratum of the parties' antecedent dealings.[2] Since in most cases an incomplete or informal leasehold transaction is preceded by some sort of agreement – a fortiori if the parties never proceeded beyond the stage of contract anyway – equitable doctrine operates quite independently to give effect to the contractual rights which 'lie behind or beyond' any legal estate purportedly conferred.[3]

1   [**Para 9.6**]. See *Chan v Cresdon Pty Ltd* (1989) 168 CLR 242 at 252; *Gilbert v Cossey* (1912) 106 LT 607 at 608.
2   See *Telado Pty Ltd v Vincent* (1996) 7 BPR 14874 at 14880 per Powell JA ('the underlying agreement ... if capable of being made the subject of an order for specific performance, will ... be effective to bring into existence an equitable estate or interest in the land').
3   *Corin v Patton* (1990) 169 CLR 540 at 572 per Deane J.

Preconditions for the availability of specific performance

9.55 A contract for the disposition of an interest in land is a contract of which equity will usually grant specific performance.[1] Thus any breach of a contractual obligation to create or transfer a legal term of years normally generates a remedy not of mere money damages, but rather of a court order that the contracted performance be delivered, ie that a valid legal lease be granted or assigned to its intended recipient. In accordance with equitable principle, an antecedent agreement to vest a leasehold estate in an intended recipient causes this party to acquire an equitable interest in the land commensurate with his ability to obtain specific performance of his contract.[2] (For present purposes informal, incomplete and imperfect leasehold transactions are alike deemed to have an effect precisely equivalent to that of an unperformed contract to grant a future lease, in that they disclose an underlying contractual intent to create or assign a term of years.[3]) The equitable remedy of specific performance is not, of course, available as of right. Its award lies within the discretion of the court and is generally dependent on the following preconditions.[4]

1   **[Para 9.12]**.
2   *Corin v Patton* (1990) 169 CLR 540 at 588 per Toohey J. See also *Parker v Taswell* (1858) 2 De G & J 559 at 570–571, 44 ER 1106 at 1111; *Brunker v Perpetual Trustee Co (Ltd)* (1937) 57 CLR 555 at 581 per Latham CJ; *Marshall v Council of The Shire of Snowy River* (1994) 7 BPR 14447 at 14456 per Meagher JA.
3   See e g *R v Tower Hamlets LBC, ex p Von Goetz* [1999] QB 1019 at 1020H, 1024A–D, 1025B–C (ten-year tenancy granted by mere writing). See *Progressive Mailing House Pty Ltd v Tabali Pty Ltd* (1985) 157 CLR 17 at 26 per Mason J; *Starr v Barbaro* (1986) 4 BPR 9137 at 9138 per Powell J. See analogously *McDonald v Peddle* [1923] NZLR 987 at 1003 per Reed J (imperfect easement); *Katsaitis v Commonwealth Bank of Australia* (1987) 5 BPR 12049 at 12052 (imperfect mortgage).
4   **[Para 9.13]**.

There must be a transaction for valuable consideration

9.56   The claimant of specific performance must have given value: 'equity will not assist a volunteer.'

There must be a written and signed contract

9.56   In order that specific performance be available, the relevant contract for a lease must comply with the formality rules imposed by statute. In the absence of any estoppel or constructive trust, all contracts concluded on or after 27 September 1989[1] must be contained in writing signed by both parties.[2] For this purpose a formally defective instrument of legal grant or transfer (if signed by both parties) can be deemed to constitute the statutorily required written contract.[3]

1   An exception is made, by cross-reference to LPA 1925, s 54(2) **[para 7.220]**, for contracts to grant a lease or tenancy at a full market rent for a period not exceeding three years (see LP(MP)A 1989, s 2(5)(a)).
2   LP(MP)A 1989, s 2(1). In relation to contracts entered into prior to 27 September 1989, there must have been compliance with the more liberal requirement of written evidence (or of part performance) laid down by LPA 1925, s 40 **[para 12.37]**.
3   See e g *R v Tower Hamlets LBC, ex p Von Goetz* [1999] QB 1019 at 1020H per Mummery LJ. Although some doubt has been expressed on the matter (see J Howell, [1990] Conv 441), the prevailing view seems to be that expressed by Reed J in *McDonald v Peddle* [1923] NZLR 987 at 1003, i e that it is 'not essential that the document should contain a covenant to grant the legal right. The mere fact that it purports to grant a legal right is sufficient.' See *Telado Pty Ltd v Vincent* (1996) 7 BPR 14874 at 14880 per Powell JA.

The party seeking specific performance must come 'with clean hands'

9.57 The claimant of specific performance must not have forfeited his claim to equitable assistance through unconscientious conduct. In the context of an agreement for a lease, this last condition means that the court has a discretion to withhold specific performance from either party[1] on the ground of conduct which alienates the sympathy of equity. The scope of this 'clean hands' doctrine is, however, somewhat limited[2] and the court will not usually refuse specific performance unless the claimant's misconduct is 'gross and wilful'.[3] In extreme cases disqualifying conduct may include a failure to fulfil obligations fixed by the originally agreed lease[4] or dishonest concealment of a lease through non-registration in order to facilitate further mortgaging.[5] Nevertheless the courts tend not to refuse equitable assistance in those circumstances where relief against forfeiture would normally be granted under a legal lease.[6] Thus, for example, the court may grant specific performance to a tenant, notwith-standing past breaches of his covenant to pay rent, if the relevant arrears have since been paid to the landlord and accepted by him.[7]

1   Even the landlord may be precluded from obtaining specific performance if, by his conduct, he has forfeited the assistance of equity (*Warwick Grove Pty Ltd v Wright & Howson* [1979] 1 SR (WA) 69 at 73). In such a case the court will simply decline to compel the tenant to execute the legal lease.

2   **[Para 9.16]**.

3   *Parker v Taswell* (1858) 2 De G & J 559 at 573, 44 ER 1106 at 1112. See also *Upper Hutt Arcade Ltd v Burrell and Burrell Properties Ltd* [1973] 2 NZLR 699 at 703.

4   *Coatsworth v Johnson* (1886) 55 LJQB 220 at 222–223 (breach of covenant to cultivate land in 'a good and husbandlike manner'). See also *Williams v Frayne* (1937) 57 CLR 710 at 730; *Australian Hardwoods Pty Ltd v Commissioner for Railways* [1961] 1 WLR 425 at 432. The 'clean hands' rule can also apply to unfulfilled conditions precedent where there is no waiver by the landlord (see *Cornish v Brook Green Laundry Ltd* [1959] 1 QB 394 at 407; *Euston Centre Properties Ltd v H & J Wilson Ltd* (1982) 262 EG 1079 at 1082; *Shelley v United Artists Corpn Ltd* (1990) 60 P & CR 241 at 248).

5   See *Chan v Cresdon Pty Ltd* (1989) 168 CLR 242 at 256, 263.

6   **[Para 14.149]**. See *Parker v Taswell* (1858) 2 De G & J 559 at 573, 44 ER 1106 at 1112. Mere delay by the tenant in seeking specific performance of a contract for a lease does not fetter the equitable jurisdiction to award such relief (see *Tottenham Hotspur Football & Athletic Co Ltd v Princegrove Publishers Ltd* [1974] 1 WLR 113 at 122B–C; *Baxton v Kara* [1982] 1 NSWLR 604 at 611E).

7   *Baxton v Kara* [1982] 1 NSWLR 604 at 610D–E. See also *Kemp v Lumeah Investments Pty Ltd* (1983) 3 BPR 9203 at 9206 (specific performance conditional on payment of arrears).

Anticipatory effect of equity

9.58 Provided that the preconditions of equitable relief are satisfied,[1] the intended recipient of a lease has a right to compel specific performance of the agreed leasehold disposition by means of a court order directing the due execution of a formal lease or leasehold transfer in his favour.[2] His contractual rights, being specifically enforceable, have a certain quality of inevitability: they contain the potential of irresistible enlargement into a legal lease on the terms originally agreed.[3]

1   See, however, S Gardner, (1987) 7 OJLS 60; P Sparkes, (1988) 8 OJLS 350.
2   *Progressive Mailing House Pty Ltd v Tabali Pty Ltd* (1985) 157 CLR 17 at 26 per Mason J. In the early years after the Judicature Act there was a general expectation that specific performance would actually be obtained in such a case, the formal lease normally being decreed to extend back to the date agreed between the parties for the commencement of the term (see *McMahon v Ambrose* [1987] VR 817 at 829–830).
3   See e g *R v Tower Hamlets LBC, ex p Von Goetz* [1999] QB 1019 at 1025B per Mummery LJ.

Equity anticipates due performance

9.59   At this point equitable doctrine intervenes with decisive effect. Since 'equity looks on that as done which ought to be done', the technical availability of specific performance now enables the parties to be treated *as if* a legal lease had been granted or transferred and 'was actually in existence.'[1] Equity anticipates the due performance of the contractual obligation[2] and, in so doing, ensures that the agreement for a lease operates 'not merely to create contractual rights and duties, but to create an equitable term of years.'[3] Thus, although the absence of formal disposition or substantive registration is fatal to any claim that an intended recipient has taken a *legal* term of years,[4] his entitlement to specific performance enables him to assert that he holds an *equitable* term of years for the same fixed term and on essentially the same covenants and conditions as would have obtained if the transaction had been effective at law.[5] With its characteristic regard for substantive intent rather than mere form,[6] equity views the parties' respective rights and obligations on the fictional basis that the underlying agreement to create or transfer a legal lease has already been duly performed.[7]

1   *Swain v Ayres* (1888) 21 QBD 289 at 293 per Lord Esher MR. In *Lowther v Heaver* (1889) 41 Ch D 248 at 264, Cotton LJ made the point that the tenant 'being entitled in equity to have a lease granted, his rights ... do not depend on its actually having been granted.' See likewise *R v Tower Hamlets LBC, ex p Von Goetz* [1999] QB 1019 at 1025B–C.
2   The equitable doctrine 'applies without there being an actual order for specific perform-ance ... When issues as to the rights of the parties have come before the courts it has usually been enough that the court, by holding that it would grant specific performance, has established the existence of equitable rights and then enforced them' (*McMahon v Ambrose* [1987] VR 817 at 830).
3   *National Trustees, Executors and Agency Co of Australasia Ltd v Boyd* (1926) 39 CLR 72 at 82 per Knox CJ, Gavan Duffy and Rich JJ. See also *Progressive Mailing House Pty Ltd v Tabali Pty Ltd* (1985) 157 CLR 17 at 26 per Mason J.
4   *Lowther v Heaver* (1889) 41 Ch D 248 at 264 per Cotton LJ; *National Trustees, Executors and Agency Co of Australasia Ltd v Boyd* (1926) 39 CLR 72 at 82; *Chan v Cresdon Pty Ltd* (1989) 168 CLR 242 at 251–252.
5   See *Tinsley v Milligan* [1994] 1 AC 340 at 370F–G per Lord Browne-Wilkinson. This approach has a long and distinguished pedigree (see *Swain v Ayres* (1888) 21 QBD 289 at 293; *Goldstein v Sanders* [1915] 1 Ch 549 at 556; *Williams v Frayne* (1937) 58 CLR 710 at 730 per Dixon J; *Progressive Mailing House Pty Ltd v Tabali Pty Ltd* (1985) 157 CLR 17 at 27 per Mason J).
6   *Chan v Cresdon Pty Ltd* (1989) 168 CLR 242 at 252. See also *Gilbert v Cossey* (1912) 106 LT 607 at 608 per Darling J (justice demands 'that a person be held to have an interest in land, although the document under which he claimed it had only a signature upon a piece of paper ... instead of a piece of wax on parchment').
7   See *Warmington v Miller* [1973] QB 877 at 887C–E per Stamp LJ; *Rochester Poster Serv-ices Ltd v Dartford BC* (1991) 63 P & CR 88 at 93. The resulting equitable lease does not

necessarily incorporate a third party's guarantee of the tenant's due performance of the terms contained in the pre-existing agreement for a lease: the third party's guarantee may, depending on the precise wording used, be confined to performance under the legal term envisaged in the contract (see *Chan v Cresdon Pty Ltd* (1989) 168 CLR 242 at 256–258; but compare *Liley v Pipers-Furniture Makers of Tasmania Pty Ltd* [1997] ANZ Conv R 242, BPR Casenote 102501). See also *Shun Cheong Holdings BC Ltd v Gold Ocean City Supermarket Ltd* (2002) 216 DLR (4th) 392 at [20].

Emergence of equitable lease

9.60 In this way even though legal effect is withheld from the intended term of years, the disponee may claim *in equity* an alternative estate which finds its source, not in the abortive or incomplete legal transaction, but in some pre-existing contract for value.[1] The specifically enforceable rights generated behind a formally deficient or unregistered lease or an agreement for a future lease are treated as having given rise to the equitable equivalent of the intended legal term.[2]

1   *Corin v Patton* (1990) 169 CLR 540 at 563 per Brennan J. See also *Chan v Cresdon Pty Ltd* (1989) 168 CLR 242 at 257.
2   See *Swain v Ayres* (1888) 21 QBD 289 at 293 per Lord Esher MR; *York House Pty Ltd v Federal Commissioner of Taxation* (1930) 43 CLR 427 at 435–436; *Chan v Cresdon Pty Ltd* (1989) 168 CLR 242 at 252.

9.61 This outcome, although commonly attributed to the later decision of the Court of Appeal in *Walsh v Lonsdale*,[1] is more properly credited as the doctrine in *Parker v Taswell*,[2] Lord Chelmsford LC observing in the latter decision that 'the intention of the parties having been that there should be a lease ... the aid of equity [is] only invoked to carry that intention into effect.'[3] This equitable stance persists to the present day. In *R v Tower Hamlets LBC, ex p Von Goetz*,[4] for example, the Court of Appeal readily treated a ten-year shorthold tenancy granted by mere writing (ie not by deed) as a specifically enforceable contract for a term of years and gave effect to it as an *equitable* lease for ten years. Mummery LJ pointed out that the grantor could not have refused a request by the tenant for a deed to perfect her legal title and that the tenant's interest in the property was therefore 'as enduring and ascertained as if there had been a deed vesting the legal estate in her for a term of years.'[5]

1   (1882) 21 Ch D 9 [**para 9.64**]. See eg the reference to the tenant's entitlement to a '*Walsh v Lonsdale* equity' in *Cornish v Brook Green Laundry Ltd* [1959] 1 QB 394 at 406–407. See also *Progressive Mailing House Pty Ltd v Tabali Pty Ltd* (1985) 157 CLR 17 at 26.
2   (1858) 2 De G & J 559 at 570, 573, 44 ER 1106 at 1111–1112.
3   Lord Chelmsford LC therefore construed the obligations of the contracting landlord and tenant as if the stipulations of their original informal agreement had been 'converted into a covenant according to the intention of the parties.' See also *Warwick Grove Pty Ltd v Wright & Howson* [1979] 1 SR (WA) 69 at 73.
4   [1999] QB 1019 at 1020H, 1024A–D.
5   [1999] QB 1019 at 1025B–C.

Resolution of the conflict between law and equity

9.62   It was inevitable that equitable intervention in the landlord–tenant relationship should set up a tension between law and equity. The fixed term equitable lease produced by the so-called doctrine in *Walsh v Lonsdale* stands in marked contrast to the common law perspective on the consequences of an incomplete or informal lease. At common law a tenant's entry into possession under an imperfect lease, if followed by payment and acceptance of a periodic rent, is normally sufficient to found the implication of a yearly tenancy.[1] Unless terminated by notice, this implied common law tenancy continues for the duration of the fixed term originally contemplated and is deemed to incorporate all the terms of the incomplete or abortive legal lease in so far as they are compatible with and transferable to a periodic tenancy.

1   [Para 7.256].

Tension between legal and equitable perspectives

9.63   Notwithstanding their superficial resemblance, the legal periodic tenancy implied from conduct and the equitable *Walsh v Lonsdale* lease are significantly dissimilar in nature and effect. The covenants implied by common law in a periodic tenancy may be subtly different from the terms agreed under the original, but abortive, fixed term lease. Furthermore a common law periodic tenancy is extremely vulnerable to early termination by the giving of appropriate notice to quit[1] and, on this ground alone, is distinctly inferior to the fixed term yielded in equity by the application of *Walsh v Lonsdale*. Where the rights and obligations fixed by the periodic tenancy at common law are inconsistent with those incorporated within the equitable lease, a question arises as to which perspective on the leasehold relationship is to prevail. This problem posed itself, apparently for the first time, in *Walsh v Lonsdale*.

1   [Para 7.291].

The ruling in Walsh v Lonsdale

9.64   In *Walsh v Lonsdale*[1] L granted W a seven-year lease in writing under which W's rent was expressly indicated to be payable annually *in advance*. No lease by deed was executed, but W entered into possession and proceeded to pay rent *in arrear*, thereby appearing to become a yearly periodic tenant at common law. L then demanded a year's rent in advance and, on W's refusal to pay in advance, distrained for the rent (by seizing W's goods[2]). W brought an action seeking both damages for trespass and a decree of specific performance of the informal lease. A clear conflict arose between the common law analysis of the facts (under which W held a legal tenancy from year to year and, as is normal at common law, owed rent only in arrear[3]) and the equitable analysis (under which W held a seven-year equitable term which made the rent expressly payable in advance). L's liability in trespass obviously turned on the question whether the legal periodic tenancy or the equitable seven-year lease was determinative of the rights and duties of the parties.

1   (1882) 21 Ch D 9.
2   **[Para 14.193]**.
3   See *Coomber v Howard* (1845) 1 CB 440 at 443, 135 ER 611 at 612–613.

Priority accorded to the equitable analysis

9.65   In an historic judgment the Court of Appeal decided that, in consequence of the Judicature Acts 1873–1875, any conflict between the rules of law and equity should be resolved by an application of the rules of equity.[1] The parties' rights and obligations thus fell to be determined in accordance with the equitable analysis of their relationship. L's act in distraining upon the goods of W had therefore been perfectly lawful since L's rights were conclusively established by the terms of the *equitable* seven-year lease. With admirable clarity the Court disposed of the problem of apparently co-existing yet incompatible estates in the land. Jessel MR declared that

> there are not two estates as there were formerly, one estate at common law by reason of the payment of rent from year to year, and an estate in equity under the agreement. There is only one Court, and the equity rules prevail in it. The tenant holds under an agreement for a lease. He holds, therefore, under the same terms in equity as if a lease had been granted, it being a case in which both parties admit that relief is capable of being given by specific performance. That being so, he cannot complain of the exercise by the landlord of the same rights as the landlord would have had if a lease had been granted.[2]

1   Supreme Court of Judicature Act 1873, s 25(11). See now Supreme Court Act 1981, s 49(1) **[para 1.156]**.
2   (1882) 21 Ch D 9 at 14–15. However, as Jessel MR pointed out, the tenant could not, on this premise, be turned out on half a year's notice as would have been the case had he been merely a tenant from year to year. Under the equitable lease, the tenant had the right to insist that the landlord could re-enter only for breach of covenant.

The doctrine in *Walsh v Lonsdale*

9.66   This classic confirmation of the priority accorded to the equitable view of specifically enforceable land contracts has since become known as the doctrine in *Walsh v Lonsdale*. Operating far beyond the immediate leasehold context, this doctrine has established a principle of general application to such transactions as the granting of easements, profits and mortgages. Informal or incomplete dispositions of any such interests in land stand to be construed as contracts which, if capable of specific performance, confer an equitable interest of the relevant kind upon the intended disponee.[1]

1   **[Paras 9.92, 9.105]**.

Specific enforceability is the crucial criterion

9.67   Under the doctrine in *Walsh v Lonsdale* equitable protection is accorded to imperfect leasehold dealings only if and so long as the remedy of specific performance remains available to the claimant of this protection.[1] A tenant in possession under a specifically enforceable agreement for a fixed term is deemed to hold an equitable lease on the same terms as those contained in the abortive or incomplete leasehold disposition.[2] If, for any reason, the parties' antecedent dealings are not (or cease to be) specifically enforceable, the anticipatory doctrine of equity is inapplicable.[3] The parties are consequently relegated to the common law rights and obligations appropriate to the periodic tenancy implied from the tenant's entry into possession and payment of rent.[4]

1   *Walsh v Lonsdale* (1882) 21 Ch D 9 at 14–15 per Jessel MR. See likewise *Coatsworth v Johnson* (1886) 55 LJQB 220 at 222–223; *Swain v Ayres* (1888) 21 QBD 289 at 293 per Lord Esher MR; *Euston Centre Properties Ltd v H & J Wilson Ltd* (1982) 262 EG 1079 at 1082; *Chan v Cresdon Pty Ltd* (1989) 168 CLR 242 at 252.
2   The principle of *Walsh v Lonsdale* applies even where the agreement is embodied in a consent order of the court confirming a compromise between the parties (see *Tottenham Hotspur Football & Athletic Co Ltd v Princegrove Publishers Ltd* [1974] 1 WLR 113 at 122A).
3   The doctrine in *Walsh v Lonsdale* is applicable 'only in those cases where specific performance can be obtained between the same parties in the same court, and at the same time as the subsequent legal question falls to be determined' (*Manchester Brewery Co v Coombs* [1901] 2 Ch 608 at 617 per Farwell J). This may mean that the full effect of *Walsh v Lonsdale* cannot apply as between one of the original parties and an assignee from the other (see R J Smith, [1978] CLJ 98 at 102).
4   If, for instance, specific performance can be resisted on the ground of some gross breach by the claimant tenant, the tenant's term ceases to be regarded as an equitable fixed term lease and reverts instead to a legal and readily terminable periodic tenancy. See *Williams v Frayne* (1937) 57 CLR 710 at 730 per Dixon J; *Marshall v Council of The Shire of Snowy River* (1994) 7 BPR 14447 at 14456–14457 (right to specific performance lost on fundamental breach by tenant giving rise to landlord's repudiation of lease).

9.68   Paradoxical though it may at first appear, the periodic tenancy implied at law offers a form of protection far inferior to that ensured by an equitable lease for the originally agreed term. Although the common law tenancy is technically more potent in that it ranks as an overriding interest in registered land and is automatically binding in unregistered land, it suffers from the disadvantage that it is terminable at any time by service of the appropriate notice to quit. Unless supplemented by special protective legislation,[1] the security of tenure afforded even by a legal tenancy from year to year[2] falls short of that available under an equitable fixed term lease (which must be allowed to run its full course except where a right of re-entry arises for breach of covenant).

1   [**Paras 14.312–14.329**]. See [1988] Conv 16 (J E A).
2   Such a tenancy is determinable on half a year's notice [**para 7.291**].

Is a Walsh v Lonsdale lease as good as a legal lease?

9.69 The effect of the doctrine of *Walsh v Lonsdale* is, in most cases, to convert an informal, imperfect or merely contractual lease into a perfectly valid equitable lease on the terms of the parties' original agreement. In view of this result, it is commonly said that a specifically enforceable leasehold dealing is as good as the grant of an actual legal lease.[1] For this reason the parties to an formally defective or incomplete leasehold dealing often refrain from seeking specific performance[2] and remain content to allow their obligations to be governed by contract without any formal disposition to the tenant of a legal estate.[3] For most purposes the contractual relationship itself is as efficacious as any legal lease. Yet the substantial truth of this proposition conceals certain significant respects in which a contract for a lease falls vitally short of the disposition of a legal leasehold estate.[4]

1   See e g *Re Maughan, Ex parte Monkhouse* (1885) 14 QBD 956 at 958; *Lowther v Heaver* (1889) 41 Ch D 248 at 264 per Cotton LJ; *R v Tower Hamlets LBC, ex p Von Goetz* [1999] QB 1019 at 1024B–C per Mummery LJ. Indeed, there are even certain respects in which a contract for a lease offers more liberal remedies than does the equivalent legal lease. Under a contract for a lease, for instance, the landlord enjoys the benefit of an *implied* right of re-entry in the event of breach by the tenant [**para 14.107**].
2   'It is enough that a court can determine ex post that equitable relief could have been granted had it been sought at the earlier point of time' (*Chief Commr of Stamp Duties v ISPT Pty Ltd* (1997) 45 NSWLR 639 at 650C per Mason P).
3   See *McMahon v Ambrose* [1987] VR 817 at 830; *Re Eastdoro Pty Ltd* [1989] 2 Qd R 182 at 184.
4   See *Manchester Brewery Co v Coombs* [1901] 2 Ch 608 at 617 per Farwell J.

Parties are dependent on the availability of specific performance

9.70 The doctrine in *Walsh v Lonsdale* is entirely dependent on the theoretical availability of the discretionary remedy of specific performance.[1] If the parties' dealing is one in respect of which equity cannot or will not currently grant specific performance, the tenant's position is very different from that which would have obtained if a formal legal lease had been granted in the first place.[2]

1   'To that extent an equitable lease is vulnerable' (*Chan v Cresdon Pty Ltd* (1989) 168 CLR 242 at 261 per Toohey J).
2   The tenant's rights will simply be those (much less secure) rights which exist by virtue of an implied legal periodic tenancy.

There is no privity of estate under a Walsh v Lonsdale lease

9.71 In leases granted prior to 1996 most leasehold covenants are rendered binding on assignees from the original lessor and lessee by the doctrine of 'privity of estate'.[1] It is generally considered, however, that 'privity of estate' arises only where a leasehold term is validly granted as a legal estate in the land and all subsequent assignments by either lessor or lessee are effective at law. In the conventional view, no privity of estate obtains in respect of an equitable lease quite simply because there exists no 'estate' at law to which anyone can be 'privy'. The net result is that, under an equitable lease created prior to 1996,[2] the lessee's covenants are not directly enforceable against his assignees – an illustration of the general rule that the benefit but not the burden of a contract is assignable. This remains one significant respect in which, at least from the viewpoint of the lessor, a *Walsh v Lonsdale* lease is certainly not as good as a legal lease.

1   **[Para 14.242]**. Many of the essential features of 'privity of estate' are incorporated in the rules which govern all legal and equitable leases granted on or after 1 January 1996 (see Landlord and Tenant (Covenants) Act 1995, s 3(1), (6)(a)). Leases granted before 1996 are still governed, however, by the historic doctrine of 'privity of estate'.
2   Contrast, in relation to equitable leases created after 1995, the effect of Landlord and Tenant (Covenants) Act 1995, s 28(1) ('tenancy') **[para 14.249]**.

Equitable tenant cannot claim the benefit of Law of Property Act 1925, s 62

9.72   The 'general words' provision of section 62 of the Law of Property Act 1925 is activated only by a 'conveyance' of a legal estate.[1] The benefit of section 62 cannot therefore be claimed by a tenant under a contract for a lease,[2] with the result that no easements can be implied in favour of such a tenant on the basis of the 'general words'.

1   'Conveyance' is defined in LPA 1925, s 205(1)(ii).
2   *Borman v Griffith* [1930] 1 Ch 493 at 497–498 **[para 8.157]**.

Equitable tenant cannot plead purchase of a legal estate without notice

9.73   In the law governing unregistered estates in land, it is impossible for an equitable tenant to claim immunity from prior unregistrable, non-overreachable equitable interests. The binding effect of such interests is still dictated by the equitable doctrine of notice,[1] and in advance of acquiring a legal term of years the contractual tenant cannot claim to be a bona fide purchaser of a legal estate for value without notice.

1   **[Paras 2.191, 12.337]**.

Equitable tenant is insecure against third parties

9.74   Another drawback of the *Walsh v Lonsdale* lease consists in the fact that an equitable tenancy may, in some circumstances, be insecure against a disponee of the landlord's reversionary estate.

9.75   A tenant under a *Walsh v Lonsdale* lease granted out of a registered reversionary estate holds an interest in the land which requires to be protected by the entry of a 'notice' in his landlord's register of title.[1] If not duly protected, the tenant's equitable lease can 'override' subsequent dispositions of the landlord's registered estate only if the equitable tenant is 'in actual occupation' of the land.[2] If, conversely, a tenant's contract for a lease is not capable of specific performance, his position is that of a legal periodic tenant whose rights are automatically overriding,[3] but may nevertheless be terminated at any time by the appropriate notice to quit.

1   [Paras 2.163, 12.89].
2   LRA 2002, s 29(1), (2)(a)(ii), Sch 3, para 2. See e g *Grace Rymer Investments Ltd v Waite* [1958] Ch 831 at 849, 851.
3   LRA 2002, s 29(1), (2)(a)(ii), Sch 3, para 1 [para 12.143].

9.76   It is in relation to unregistered reversionary estates that the disadvantages of a *Walsh v Lonsdale* lease become more apparent. Here the equitable tenant holds an estate contract which is protectable by registration of a Class C(iv) land charge against the name of the landlord.[1] If not so registered, the equitable tenant's lease becomes void against a purchaser of a legal estate for money or money's worth (generally irrespective of any pre-existing knowledge in that purchaser of the existence of the lease).[2] If for some reason the leasehold dealing under which the tenant holds is incapable of specific performance, the tenant has at best a legal periodic tenancy which, although binding on the purchaser, may again be snuffed out prematurely by service of the appropriate notice to quit.

1   [Paras 2.186, 12.308].
2   LCA 1972, s 4(6). See e g *Hollington Bros Ltd v Rhodes* [1951] 2 TLR 691 at 696 [para 12.287]. See also *Midland Bank Trust Co Ltd v Green* [1981] AC 513 at 527H–528A [para 12.289].

OPTIONS

9.77   An option to purchase a legal estate comprises a form of estate contract.[1] It has been aptly said that the juridical nature of an option is an 'academic riddle'.[2] An option blends aspects of an irrevocable offer of sale[3] with features of a conditional contract in favour of the optionee.[4]

1   See generally *Barnsley's Land Options* (3rd edn by Richard Castle, London 1998); S Tromans, [1984] CLJ 55.
2   *Murray v Scott* [1976] 1 NZLR 643 at 655 per Cooke J; *Alexander v Tse* [1988] 1 NZLR 318 at 324 per Somers J. An option is 'nearly always a ticklish thing' (*Mackay v Wilson* (1947) 47 SR (NSW) 315 at 318 per Jordan CJ).
3   See *United Scientific Holdings Ltd v Burnley BC* [1978] AC 904 at 929A per Lord Diplock, 945F per Lord Simon of Glaisdale, 951A per Lord Salmon.
4   See *Helby v Matthews* [1895] AC 471 at 482; *Griffith v Pelton* [1958] Ch 205 at 225. For the view that an option ultimately constitutes a 'relationship sui generis', see *Spiro v Glencrown Properties Ltd* [1991] Ch 537 at 544G per Hoffmann J. See also *Armstrong & Holmes Ltd v Holmes* [1993] 1 WLR 1482 at 1488A–C; *Freeguard v Royal Bank of Scotland Plc* (2000) 79 P & CR 81 at 87 per Robert Walker LJ.

Nature of an option

9.78   An option is a contractual right which entitles the grantee of the option (the 'purchaser' or 'option holder' or 'optionee') to require that the grantor of the option (the 'vendor' or 'optionor') grant or transfer a legal estate to him in accordance with the agreed terms of the option (not least concerning price). The grant of an option imposes no obligation on the purchaser,[1] but merely confers on him a contractual right to call for the relevant disposition provided that he has satisfied any conditions to which the option was made subject.[2] Control over the exercise of the option lies wholly in the hands of the purchaser. The timing of its exercise (or whether it is exercised at all) is for the purchaser to determine.[3] The only act required of him is an act signifying his intention to exercise the option.[4]

1   *Spiro v Glencrown Properties Ltd* [1991] Ch 537 at 543C per Hoffmann J.
2   See *Laybutt v Amoco Australia Pty Ltd* (1974) 132 CLR 57 at 76 per Gibbs J.
3   See *Canadian Long Island Petroleums Ltd v Irving Industries* (*Irving Wire Products Division*) *Ltd* (1975) 50 DLR (3d) 265 at 277 per Martland J; *Stephens v Gulf Oil Canada Ltd* (1976) 65 DLR (3d) 193 at 218 per Howland JA.
4   *Kopec v Pyret* (1983) 146 DLR (3d) 242 at 248. On the requirements for exercise of an option, see *Ballas v Theophilos* (No 2) (1957) 98 CLR 193 at 204–205; *Traywinds Pty Ltd v Cooper* [1989] 1 Qd R 222 at 225.

Terms of an option

9.79   It is irrelevant that the purchase price of the contracted estate is not stipulated by the terms of the option, so long as the option provides machinery by which the price can later be objectively ascertained without the necessity of any further agreement between the parties.[1] Nor is an option rendered void for uncertainty by the absence of a time limit on its exercise (since the courts can supply a reasonable time by implication[2]), although it may be vitiated by perpetuity.[3] The sphere of options is, nevertheless, 'a cold hard world.'[4] An option must always be exercised in strict compliance with the requirements set out for its exercise.[5]

1   See e g *Sudbrook Trading Estate Ltd v Eggleton* [1983] 1 AC 444, where the House of Lords upheld the enforceability of an option where the price was to be settled by valuers nominated by the parties or, in default, by an umpire appointed by both parties. See also *Kopec v Pyret* (1983) 146 DLR (3d) 242 at 248. An option for renewal of a lease 'at a rental to be agreed' is prima facie void (*King's Motors* (*Oxford*) *Ltd v Lax* [1970] 1 WLR 426 at 429A), but may be saved by special circumstances (see *Corson v Rhuddlan BC* (1990) 59 P & CR 185 at 194–196; *Trazray Pty Ltd v Russell Foundries Pty Ltd* (1988) 5 BPR 11232 at 11237).
2   See *Reid v Moreland Timber Co Pty Ltd* (1946) 73 CLR 1 at 13 per Dixon J; *Malding Pty Ltd v Metcalfe* (1989) NSW ConvR ¶55–495 at 58,613.
3   A perpetuity period of 21 years applies to a disposition which confers an option to acquire for valuable consideration any interest in land (Perpetuities and Accumulations Act 1964, s 9(2)).
4   *Burrell v Cameron* (1997) 8 BPR 15443 at 15446.
5   See *Carradine Properties Ltd v Aslam* [1976] 1 WLR 442 at 446C; *Parras v FAI General Insurance Co Ltd* (2001) 10 BPR 19209 at [2]. See also *Spiro v Glencrown Properties Ltd* [1991] Ch 537, where an option was expressly exercisable only before 5 pm on the day of grant. Minor inaccuracies in the exercise of an option may not be fatal if a reasonable person would have understood the intent (see, by analogy, *Mannai Investment Co Ltd v Eagle Star Life Assurance Ltd* [1997] AC 749).

Types of option

9.80   Options can relate to a variety of transactions with a legal estate in land. An option may confer a right to call for a fee simple estate or a leasehold term[1] or an easement[2] or profit in the land. The range of possible options includes a tenant's contractual right to renew his leasehold term[3] or to purchase a superior reversionary interest[4] and even the right sometimes reserved by a landlord to require that his tenant should surrender the leasehold term to the landlord rather than assign it to a stranger.[5]

1   See *Phillips v Mobil Oil Co Ltd* [1989] 1 WLR 888 at 890H–891A per Nicholls LJ.
2   See *London & Blenheim Estates Ltd v Ladbroke Retail Parks Ltd* [1994] 1 WLR 31 at 37A; *Gas & Fuel Corpn of Victoria v Barba* [1976] VR 755 at 757–759.
3   *Beesly v Hallwood Estates Ltd* [1960] 1 WLR 549 at 558; *Phillips v Mobil Oil Co Ltd* [1989] 1 WLR 888 at 893F, 894E–G. See Jean Howell, [1990] Conv 169, 250.
4   *Phillips v Mobil Oil Co Ltd* [1989] 1 WLR 888 at 891C. See also Leasehold Reform Act 1967, s 5(5) [**para 7.334**].
5   *Greene v Church Commissioners for England* [1974] Ch 467 at 477B.

Proprietary character of options

9.81   In so far as an option connotes a specifically enforceable contractual right to call for a legal estate, the optionee holds, from the moment of grant of the option, a proprietary interest in the land.[1] This proprietary status is attributable to the anticipatory effect of equitable doctrine and marks a recognition that, with the granting of the option, a significant part of the property in the grantor's land has vested in the optionee.[2] It follows that – even before it is exercised[3] – the option confers upon the grantee an equitable interest in the land concerned.[4] The full interest in the land passes to the purchaser on the exercise of the option followed by completion, at which point the vendor's estate or interest 'is taken away from him without his consent.'[5]

1   *London and South Western Railway Co v Gomm* (1882) 20 Ch D 562 at 581 per Jessel MR. See also *Armstrong & Holmes Ltd v Holmes* [1993] 1 WLR 1482 at 1488G.
2   [**Para 2.23**]. The right of purchase 'crystallise[s] immediately upon the option being granted' (*Kopec v Pyret* (1983) 146 DLR (3d) 242 at 248) and can thereafter be revoked or varied only in accordance with the terms of the option itself.
3   The exercise of the option 'does not add to the burden on the land' (*Armstrong & Holmes Ltd v Holmes* [1993] 1 WLR 1482 at 1488G).
4   See *London and South Western Railway Co v Gomm* (1882) 20 Ch D 562 at 580–581; *Webb v Pollmount* [1966] Ch 584 at 596D; *Mountford v Scott* [1975] Ch 258 at 262; *London & Blenheim Estates Ltd v Ladbroke Retail Parks Ltd* [1992] 1 WLR 1278 at 1282A; *Frobisher Ltd v Canadian Pipelines & Petroleums Ltd* (1960) 21 DLR (2d) 497 at 532; *Laybutt v Amoco Australia Pty Ltd* (1974) 132 CLR 57 at 75; *Stephens v Gulf Oil Canada Ltd* (1976) 65 DLR (3d) 193 at 215; *Bahr v Nicolay (No 2)* (1988) 164 CLR 604 at 645–646 per Brennan J.
5   *London and South Western Railway Co v Gomm* (1882) 20 Ch D 562 at 581 per Jessel MR.

Protection of options against third parties

9.82   Like most other equitable rights in land, an option requires protection against the possibility that the grantor of the option may wrongfully transfer his legal estate to somebody other than the optionee. Accordingly, an option affecting a registered estate can be entered by 'notice' in the grantor's register of title,[1] although in some cases where the optionee is in 'actual occupation' of the land the option may automatically 'override' registered dispositions of the grantor's estate.[2] Where an option is exercisable over an unregistered estate, the rule is rather more strict. Here options must be protected by the registration of a land charge against the name of the grantor.[3]

1   LRA 2002, ss 32–34 [**para 12.89**].
2   LRA 2002, s 29(1), (2)(a)(ii), Sch 3, para 2. See e g *Webb v Pollmount* [1966] Ch 584 at 603C–D [**para 12.160**].
3   LCA 1972, ss 2(4), 4(6). See e g *Midland Bank Trust Co Ltd v Green* [1981] AC 513 at 527E–529B; *Phillips v Mobil Oil Co Ltd* [1989] 1 WLR 888 at 890H [**para 12.280**].

RIGHTS OF PRE-EMPTION

9.83   A 'right of pre-emption', although superficially similar to an option, differs in important respects. An option confers a right, solely within the purchaser's control, to compel a transfer of the vendor's land at some future date.[1] By contrast, a right of pre-emption confers upon its grantee merely a right of first refusal[2] in the event that the grantor should ever choose to sell the land concerned.[3] The grantee of a right of pre-emption is clearly not entitled, in the first instance, to compel any transfer of a legal estate.[4] The decision whether to sell at all lies always within the discretion of the grantor of the right.[5]

1   See *Stephens v Gulf Oil Canada Ltd* (1976) 65 DLR (3d) 193 at 218.
2   In so far as there is any distinction, a 'right of first refusal' describes a preferential right to refuse an offer of sale at the price at which the grantor is willing to sell, whereas a 'right of pre-emption' commonly denotes a preferential right to refuse to purchase at a fixed price (see *Bircham & Co Nominees (2) Ltd v Worrell Holdings Ltd* (2001) 82 P & CR 427 at [31] per Chadwick LJ).
3   On one view this phrase is 'a somewhat inept term, because what the potential offeree wants is an opportunity of *accepting* an offer rather than an opportunity of refusing an offer' (see *Woodroffe v Box* (1954) 92 CLR 245 at 257 per Fullagar and Kitto JJ). A right of pre-emption has been described as a 'conditional option' (*Pata Nominees Pty Ltd v Durnsford Pty Ltd* [1988] WAR 365 at 372 per Burt CJ).
4   In identifying whether a grant is one of option or of first refusal, the label applied by the parties is not conclusive. The court scrutinises the substance rather than the form of the transaction (see *Kopec v Pyret* (1983) 146 DLR (3d) 242 at 247, (1987) 36 DLR (4th) 1 at 4–5). The critical question is whether the grantor of the right has put it out of his control to prevent the grantee from acquiring the property (see *Bircham & Co Nominees (2) Ltd v Worrell Holdings Ltd* (2001) 82 P & CR 427 at [37] per Chadwick LJ; *Beneficial Finance Corpn Ltd v Multiplex Constructions Pty Ltd* (1995) 36 NSWLR 510 at 524A–B per Young J).
5   See *Brown v Gould* [1972] Ch 53 at 58F; *Dear v Reeves* [2002] Ch 1 at [43]; *Stephens v Gulf Oil Canada Ltd* (1976) 65 DLR (3d) 193 at 217–218. A right of first refusal operates in effect as a 'negative covenant on the part of the vendor not to part with his interest in the land until the first opportunity to purchase is accorded to the covenantee' (see *Canadian Long Island Petroleums Ltd v Irving Industries (Irving Wire Products Division) Ltd* (1975) 50 DLR (3d) 265 at 279–280; *Kopec v Pyret* (1983) 146 DLR (3d) 242 at 247).

Point of exercisability

9.84 The essential characteristic of a right of pre-emption is the intention on the part of the grantor to give to the grantee a preference over other potential buyers in the event that the grantor should decide to sell.[1] A right of pre-emption becomes 'exercisable' (or 'fructifies'[2]) only when the grantor signifies an intention to sell on certain defined terms[3] or receives a bona fide offer of purchase made by some third party.[4] In such cases the grantee's pre-emptive right is converted into a specialised form of option[5] at least to the extent that the pre-emptive terms oblige the grantor to leave the offer of sale outstanding and unrevoked for a specified period.[6] When the exercise of a right of pre-emption is triggered, the grantee may demand (subject to the precise terms of the pre-emptive right) to purchase on terms identical to any offer which the grantor was plainly willing to accept.[7]

1   See *Kopec v Pyret* (1983) 146 DLR (3d) 242 at 247 per Scheibel J. If the original grant of the pre-emptive right stipulated a fixed purchase price which has since been rendered 'grossly inadequate' by the subsequent inflation of land values, there is a possibility that the agreement to grant the right may be struck down as void on grounds of public policy: in extreme circumstances the fixed price may be regarded as an invalid restriction upon alienation [**para 7.16**]. See *Re Rosher* (1884) 26 Ch D 801 at 811; *Hall v Busst* (1960) 104 CLR 206 at 216–218; *Saliba v Saliba* [1976] Qd R 205 at 207D–E.
2   See *Transfield Properties (Kent Street) Pty Ltd v Amos Aked Swift Pty Ltd* (1994) 36 NSWLR 321 at 342D; *Jonns v Tan* (1999) 9 BPR 17113 at 17115 per Santow J.
3   A right of pre-emption becomes exercisable on various 'triggering' events. See e g *Kling v Keston Properties Ltd* (1983) 49 P & CR 212 at 217 per Vinelott J (contract to sell); *London & Blenheim Estates Ltd v Ladbroke Retail Parks Ltd* [1992] 1 WLR 1278 at 1282A per Deputy Judge Paul Baker QC (placing land on market); *Jonns v Tan* (1999) 9 BPR 17113 at 17115 (grant of an option to third party). See also *Kopec v Pyret* (1983) 146 DLR (3d) 242 at 252.
4   See *Turner v Mendenhall* 510 P2d 490 at 492 (1973); *Vancouver Key Business Machines Ltd v Teja* (1975) 57 DLR (3d) 464 at 472; *Associated Grocers Co-operative Ltd v Hubbard Properties Pty Ltd* (1986) 42 SASR 321 at 333. In advance of such an offer the right of pre-emption is not extinguished merely because the grantor offers to sell to the grantee at a price which the grantee is not prepared to pay (see *Kopec v Pyret* (1987) 36 DLR (4th) 1 at 6–7).
5   See *Kopec v Pyret* (1983) 146 DLR (3d) 242 at 252 per Scheibel J; *Motor Works Ltd v Westminster Auto Services Ltd* [1997] 1 NZLR 762 at 765 per Tipping J.
6   *Speciality Shops v Yorkshire and Metropolitan Estates Ltd* [2003] 2 P & CR 410 at [26] per Park J.
7   *Kopec v Pyret* (1987) 36 DLR (4th) 1 at 6. The grantee's equitable interest in the land is extinguished if he refuses to purchase the land in accordance with the terms of his pre-emptive right (see *Pata Nominees Pty Ltd v Durnsford Pty Ltd* [1988] WAR 365 at 375).

Proprietary status of rights of pre-emption

9.85 Over the years there has been an extended debate as to the proprietary status of rights of pre-emption. On one view a right of pre-emption remains a purely personal contractual right unless and until it becomes exercisable by reason of the estate owner's election to sell.[1] It is only at this point – and not before[2] – that the grantee's entitlement is transformed into an equitable interest in the land.[3] Until then, it was widely believed, a right of first refusal confers insufficient 'property' in the land to qualify its recipient as the owner of any equitable entitlement capable of protection by register entry.[4] This analysis, although probably a correct reflection of the highly contingent nature of the unfructified right of pre-emption,[5] attracted much criticism,[6] not least because there remains a strong argument that potential disponees of land deserve, in fairness, to be forewarned of all sale arrangements affecting the estate which they propose to buy.

1   *London & Blenheim Estates Ltd v Ladbroke Retail Parks Ltd* [1992] 1 WLR 1278 at 1282A per Deputy Judge Paul Baker QC. See also *McFarland v Hauser* (1978) 88 DLR (3d) 449 at 461 per Martland J; *Kopec v Pyret* (1987) 36 DLR (4th) 1 at 8; *Jonns v Tan* (1999) 9 BPR 17113 at 17115–17116.

2   See *Mackay v Wilson* (1947) 47 SR (NSW) 315 at 325; *Woodroffe v Box* (1954) 92 CLR 245 at 254; *Transfield Properties (Kent Street) Pty Ltd v Amos Aked Swift Pty Ltd* (1994) 36 NSWLR 321 at 341D–343C; *Motor Works Ltd v Westminster Auto Services Ltd* [1997] 1 NZLR 762 at 765.

3   See e g *Pritchard v Briggs* [1980] Ch 338 at 418C–D per Templeman LJ (the grantee under an unfructified right has 'a mere spes').

4   See the strong obiter view expressed in *Pritchard v Briggs* [1980] Ch 338 at 419F–G per Templeman LJ, 423A–B per Stephenson LJ. See likewise *Homsy v Murphy* (1997) 73 P & CR 26 at 38 per Beldam LJ. For a similar approach in other jurisdictions, see *Stephens v Gulf Oil Canada Ltd* (1976) 65 DLR (3d) 193 at 217–218; *Re Rutherford* [1977] 1 NZLR 504 at 510; *Kopec v Pyret* (1983) 146 DLR (3d) 242 at 247, (1987) 36 DLR (4th) 1 at 7–8; *Transfield Properties (Kent Street) Pty Ltd v Amos Aked Swift Pty Ltd* (1994) 36 NSWLR 321 at 341C–D, 343C; *Beneficial Finance Corpn Ltd v Multiplex Constructions Pty Ltd* (1995) 36 NSWLR 510 at 526D–E; *Motor Works Ltd v Westminster Auto Services Ltd* [1997] 1 NZLR 762 at 766; *Bruce v Edwards* [2003] 1 NZLR 515 at [54].

5   See *Bircham & Co Nominees (2) Ltd v Worrell Holdings Ltd* (2001) 82 P & CR 427 at [34] per Chadwick LJ; *Tiffany Investments Ltd v Bircham & Co Nominees (No 2) Ltd* [2003] 2 P & CR 381 at [36] per Lindsay J.

6   See [1980] CLJ 35 (C Harpum); [1980] Conv 433 (J Martin); (1980) 96 LQR 488 (H W R Wade); A R Everton, [1982] Conv 177 at 180; Law Com No 271 (2001), para 5.26; *Dear v Reeves* [2002] Ch 1 at [43] per Mummery LJ.

9.86   Much of the controversy surrounding the right of pre-emption has now been removed, with prospective force, by the Land Registration Act 2002. A right of pre-emption created in registered land after 13 October 2003 is declared to have effect 'from the time of creation as an interest capable of binding successors in title.'[1] Such a right is therefore protectable by the entry of a 'restriction' in the estate owner's register of title[2] and may even, in certain circumstances, 'override' registered dispositions of that title.[3] Although this confirmation of the proprietary status of the unexercised right of pre-emption obtains, strictly speaking, only in the context of registered land, its impact will inevitably strengthen the view that a similar entitlement arising in respect of an unregistered estate constitutes an 'estate contract' registrable against the estate owner as a Class C(iv) land charge.[4]

1   LRA 2002, s 115(1)–(2). See Law Commission and Land Registry, *Land Registration for the Twenty-First Century* (Law Com No 254, September 1998), para 3.32; Law Com No 271 (2001), para 5.28. A right of pre-emption is also sufficiently proprietary to vest in a trustee in bankruptcy (*Dear v Reeves* [2002] Ch 1 at [43]–[44]).

2   LRA 2002, ss 40–43 **[para 7.52]**.

3   LRA 2002, s 29(1), (2)(a)(ii), Sch 3, para 2 **[para 12.161]**.

4   The statutory definition of an 'estate contract' has always included an express reference to a

'right of pre-emption' (LCA 1972, s 2(4) [**para 12.306**]). Compare the extraordinary statement of Goff LJ in *Pritchard v Briggs* [1980] Ch 338 at 398A–399E that this legislation 'proceeded on a mistaken basis as to what the law was.'

EQUITABLE EASEMENTS AND PROFITS À *PRENDRE*

9.87   Unlike an estate contract (which can exist only in equity), an easement or profit *à prendre* can exist *either* at law *or* in equity, depending on a number of circumstances. The conditions necessary for the creation of a legal easement or profit have already been outlined,[1] but either interest can assume an equitable form where these conditions are not met.[2]

1   [**Para 8.110**].
2   See generally D G Barnsley, 'Equitable Easements – Sixty Years On' (1999) 115 LQR 89 (pointing inter alia to the paucity of explicit reference to equitable easements in the pre-1926 case law).

CREATION OF EQUITABLE EASEMENTS AND PROFITS

9.88   Equitable easements and profits *à prendre* arise in circumstances where *legal* creation founders on obstacles relating to the nature of the grantor's title, the duration of the grant or the mode of creation of the right (including the requirement of completion by registration).

Capacity of grantor

9.89   A grantor who is himself entitled merely in equity (eg to an equitable freehold or leasehold estate) is competent to create only *equitable* easements and profits.

Duration of entitlement

9.90   An easement or profit which is not framed on the analogy of either a freehold or a leasehold estate (ie is not perpetual or for a fixed period) can, again, be equitable only.[1] It follows that any easement or profit which is created for some other period (eg for the duration of a life) takes effect as an equitable right.[2]

1   LPA 1925, s 1(2)(a), (3) [**paras 2.125, 8.112**].
2   It has been argued that only a grantee with a current life interest in land can properly take an easement for life (see D G Barnsley, (1999) 115 LQR 89 at 100–101). On this view, a right of user for life granted to any other grantee (eg a fee simple owner) takes effect, at best, as a purely contractual right personal to the grantee.

Mode of creation

9.91   Equitable status also attaches, inevitably, to any easement or profit which is not created either by deed[1] or by implication,[2] prescription[3] or statute.[4]

Moreover, the legal quality of any easement or appurtenant profit *à prendre* granted expressly out of a registered estate is dependent on completion of the disposition by registration.[5] The net effect is that, in all cases of express non-statutory grant, any deficiency of formality or registration causes the grant to have force in equity only.[6] There is no exception even for easements and profits granted for a period of three years or less,[7] there being no analogy in this respect with the rules concerning the informal creation of legal leases.[8]

1   LPA 1925, s 52(1) [**para 8.113**]. See e g *E R Ives Investment Ltd v High* [1967] 2 QB 379 [**para 9.101**].

2   [**Paras 8.128, 8.199**]. It has been clear since *Borman v Griffith* [1930] 1 Ch 493 at 499 [**para 8.147**] that the rule in *Wheeldon v Burrows* can apply in favour of someone who merely contracts to take a lease of quasi-dominant land. If, however, the lease is never granted by deed, the dominant owner can take only an equitable easement (see D G Barnsley, (1999) 115 LQR 89 at 104).

3   [**Para 8.168**].

4   [**Para 8.126**].

5   LRA 2002, s 27(1), (2)(d) [**paras 7.50, 8.117**].

6   LPA 1925, s 1(3). See *Wood v Leadbitter* (1845) 13 M & W 838 at 843, 153 ER 351 at 354; *Mason v Clarke* [1954] 1 QB 460 at 468, 471. See also *Ellison v Vukicevic* (1986) 7 NSWLR 104 at 117E.

7   *Bayley v Marquis Conyngham* (1863) 15 ICLR 406 at 411–412 per Monahan CJ, 415, 418–419 per Christian J.

8   [**Para 7.220**]. This produces the odd result that, for instance, a one-year shorthold tenancy granted under hand (i e not by deed) which also confers on the tenant an easement of way does not create a legal burden on the landlord's retained land.

Written grant on or after 27 September 1989

9.92   An equitable easement or profit *à prendre* may emerge from a merely informal grant or written agreement for value.[1] A transaction of either kind (if entered into for value) can be accorded equitable effect as a specifically enforceable contract to grant an easement or profit,[2] provided that there is compliance with the requirements of contractual formality imposed with effect from 27 September 1989 by the Law of Property (Miscellaneous Provisions) Act 1989.[3] This outcome represents simply another application of the doctrine of *Walsh v Lonsdale*,[4] the specifically enforceable contract giving rise to rights of an equitable character[5] so long as the contract was intended to create immediate rights. It has been suggested, somewhat controversially, that an equitable easement arising from this kind of informal grant may, if enjoyed for a period of 20 years, graduate into a legal easement by reason of long user under the Prescription Act 1832.[6]

1   *Frogley v Earl of Lovelace* (1859) Johns 333 at 339–340, 70 ER 450 at 453; *May v Belleville* [1905] 2 Ch 605 at 613; *Carroll v Manek* (2000) 79 P & CR 173 at 190; *Reid v Moreland Timber Co Pty Ltd* (1946) 73 CLR 1 at 16. A formally deficient grant is simply treated as a *contract* to create the right in question (see *McDonald v Peddle* [1923] NZLR 987 at 1003).

2   *R (Beresford) v Sunderland CC* [2004] 1 AC 889 at [38] per Lord Scott of Foscote. See e g *E R Ives Investment Ltd v High* [1967] 2 QB 379 at 403E per Winn LJ (easement) [**para 9.101**]; *James Jones & Sons Ltd v Earl of Tankerville* [1909] 2 Ch 440 at 443; *Reid v Moreland Timber Co Pty Ltd* (1946) 73 CLR 1 at 16 per Williams J (profit).

3   LP(MP)A 1989, s 2(1) [**paras 9.15, 12.27**].

4   **[Para 9.66]**.
5   *Campbell, Wilson & Horne Ltd v Great West Saddlery Co* (1921) 59 DLR 322 at 327–328; *Tarrant v Zandstra* (1973) 1 BPR 9381 at 9385; *Salisbury (Village) v Collier* (1999) 169 DLR (4th) 560 at 563.
6   See *R (Beresford) v Sunderland CC* [2004] 1 AC 889 at [38], where Lord Scott of Foscote thought (sed quaere) that the long user, although deriving from an initial permission, would not subsequently be discounted as merely precarious but would instead constitute enjoyment by a person 'claiming right thereto' in the sense of the 1832 Act **[para 8.191]**.

Oral grant on or after 27 September 1989

9.93   Now that the doctrine of part performance no longer assists informal agreements concerning land,[1] the oral grant of an easement or profit can create equitable rights only in exceptional circumstances which justify a claim of proprietary estoppel on behalf of the intended grantee.[2]

1   LP(MP)A 1989, s 2(8) **[para 9.15]**. See Jean Howell, [1990] Conv 441.
2   See eg *Hair v Gillman and Inskip* (2000) 80 P & CR 108 at 112, 115, where Chadwick LJ ruled out an equitable easement on the ground that it purported to have been created orally and for no consideration.

Informal grant prior to 27 September 1989

9.94   Prior to 27 September 1989 an equitable easement or profit could be created even by mere oral agreement, where the agreement was supported by value or by acts of part performance.[1] Informal grant thus gave rise to an easement where, for instance, the grantee incurred expenditure or work in furtherance of the agreed easement.[2] Informal grant of this kind readily shades into the category of easements founded on estoppel.

1   *McManus v Cooke* (1887) 35 Ch D 681 at 697; *Thatcher v Douglas* (1995) 146 NLJ 282. See also *McDonald v Peddle* [1923] NZLR 987 at 993; *Clark v Duckworth* [1984] 2 NZLR 58 at 60; *Daigle v Clair (Village)* (1986) 70 NBR (2d) 129 at 136; *Salisbury (Village) v Collier* (1999) 169 DLR (4th) 560 at 563.
2   *Salisbury (Village) v Collier* (1999) 169 DLR (4th) 560 at 563.

Easements founded on estoppel

9.95   A further method of creation of easements and profits lies in the operation of the doctrine of proprietary estoppel. If relied upon to the grantee's detriment, a grant of rights by informal means (ie otherwise than by deed) may sometimes generate an equity of estoppel.[1] In these cases the court has discretion either to declare that the claimant has acquired an inchoate equitable right in the nature of an easement or profit[2] or even to require that such a right be granted forthwith to him at law.[3] Now that the doctrine of part performance can no longer operate upon informal agreements affecting land, the estoppel principle may acquire a new significance as a means of upholding the informal grant of an easement or profit which would otherwise be wholly ineffectual.[4] It has even been mooted that an estoppel-based easement may, if enjoyed for a period of 20 years, be converted into a legal easement by reason of long user under the Prescription Act 1832.[5]

1   See *R (Beresford) v Sunderland CC* [2004] 1 AC 889 at [37] per Lord Scott of Foscote **[para 10.239]**.
2   See e g *Ward v Kirkland* [1967] Ch 194 at 242–243; *E R Ives Investment Ltd v High* [1967] 2 QB 379 at 396E, 406B; *Classic Communications Ltd v Lascar* (1986) 21 DLR (4th) 579 at 587–588. It has been suggested that 20 years' enjoyment of an inchoate equity of estoppel would rank as enjoyment by a person 'claiming right thereto' for the purpose of the Prescription Act 1832, thereby enabling the beneficiary of the original permission to claim a prescriptive, and therefore legal, easement (see *R (Beresford) v Sunderland CC* [2004] 1 AC 889 at [37] per Lord Scott of Foscote).
3   See e g *Crabb v Arun DC* [1976] Ch 179 at 190A, 192D, 199F, where the estoppel claimant had allowed himself to become landlocked in reliance on an 'agreement in principle' that he should have a right of access and egress over land belonging to an adjacent owner. See also *Zelmer v Victor Projects Ltd* (1997) 147 DLR (4th) 216 at 228–229.
4   See P Pettit, [1989] Conv 431 at 442. See also *Transfer of Land: Formalities for Contracts for Sale etc of Land* (Law Com No 164, June 1987), paras 5.4–5.5.
5   See *R (Beresford) v Sunderland CC* [2004] 1 AC 889 at [37] per Lord Scott of Foscote.

TERMINATION OF EQUITABLE EASEMENTS AND PROFITS

9.96   As in the case of legal easements, an equitable easement is terminable by a merger of dominant and servient tenements in common ownership.[1] The dominant owner may also release equitable easements and profits either expressly or impliedly,[2] and express release may be made effective by means of an informal agreement which is supported by consideration given by the servient owner or which is attended by circumstances where it would be inequitable to revive the rights thereby abrogated.[3]

1   **[Para 8.217]**.
2   **[Para 8.218]**.
3   *Davies v Marshall* (1861) 10 CB (NS) 697 at 710–711, 142 ER 627 at 633. It is therefore possible that the extinguishment of an easement may be founded on the doctrine of proprietary estoppel **[para 10.168]**, although it may sometimes be difficult to establish the requisite elements of knowledge and reliance required in a claim of estoppel (see *Costagliola v English* (1969) 210 EG 1425 at 1431).

TRANSMISSION OF THE BENEFIT AND BURDEN OF EQUITABLE EASEMENTS AND PROFITS

9.97   As is the case with their equivalents at law,[1] the benefit and burden of equitable easements and profits must be treated separately.

1   **[Para 8.203]**.

Benefit

9.98   The benefit of equitable easements and appurtenant profits *à prendre* is transferable only in conjunction with the estate for whose advantage they exist.[1]

Any transfer of the dominant tenement is effective to pass the benefit of such rights to the transferee, either under the statutory 'general words' provision[2] or on the wider basis that equitable rights are annexed to the dominant realty no less effectively than legal rights.[3]

1   [**Para 8.204**]. An appurtenant profit can be severed from its dominant land, thereby becoming a profit in gross in the hands of a transferee (see *Bettison v Langton* [2000] Ch 54 at 72B–C, [2002] 1 AC 27 at [47], [63]).
2   See LPA 1925, s 62(1)–(2), under which a conveyance presumptively passes all 'liberties, privileges, easements, rights, and advantages' appertaining or reputed to appertain to land or buildings [**para 8.207**]. An easement is prima facie appurtenant to each and every part of the dominant tenement [**para 8.209**].
3   *Leech v Schweder* (1874) 9 Ch App 463 at 474–476. See similarly *McDonald v Peddle* [1923] NZLR 987 at 1003; D G Barnsley, (1999) 115 LQR 89 at 112.

Burden

9.99   The burden of equitable easements and profits *à prendre* is capable of passing to transferees of the servient land.

9.100   Where the servient estate is registered, equitable easements and profits are binding on a disponee who takes otherwise than for valuable consideration.[1] In all other cases the relevant burden is enforceable against a registered disponee of the servient land only if that burden was the subject of a 'notice' entered, prior to the registered disposition in question, in the charges register of the servient tenement.[2] Before the commencement of the Land Registration Act 2002 certain equitable easements were regarded as having an automatically binding status as overriding interests.[3] This much criticised extension of the field of overriding interests has now been reversed by the 2002 Act. Equitable easements and profits created *on* or *after* 13 October 2003 can no longer rank as interests which 'override' registered dispositions of the servient estate[4] and their protection depends upon register entry.[5]

1   LRA 2002, s 28(1) [**para 12.80**].
2   LRA 2002, s 29(1), (2)(a)(i) [**para 12.89**].
3   LRA 1925, s 70(1)(a); LRR 1925, r 258 (if 'openly exercised and enjoyed' as appurtenant to the dominant tenement). The Court of Appeal gave unexpected support to this controversial view (see *Celsteel Ltd v Alton House Holdings Ltd* [1985] 1 WLR 204 at 220H–221D (affd [1986] 1 WLR 512); *Thatcher v Douglas* (1995) 146 NLJ 282; *Valentine v Allen* [2003] EWCA Civ 915 at [72]–[73]). See M P Thompson, [1986] Conv 31 at 37.
4   An easement or profit which comprised an overriding interest *before* this commencement date will continue to 'override' pursuant to the LRA 2002 (see LRA 2002, s 134(2), Sch 12, para 9(1)–(2)).
5   [**Para 12.238**].

9.101   If created on or after 1 January 1926, all equitable easements and profits affecting an unregistered servient estate are rendered enforceable against subsequent purchasers of that estate by means of registration of a Class D(iii) land charge against the owner who granted the right in question.[1] If not so registered, qualifying easements and profits are rendered void against any purchaser of a legal estate in the servient land for money or money's worth.[2] It remains possible, however, that a statutorily unenforceable easement may arise in close association with rights based on proprietary estoppel. Rights founded on estoppel do not comprise a registrable category of land charge and thus have the potential to bind purchasers of the legal estate in the servient land who have actual or constructive notice of the circumstances of the estoppel. In *E R Ives Investment Ltd v High*,[3] for example, H had generously waived his right to complain of a neighbour's trespass in return for an informal written agreement giving him a right of way across his neighbour's land.[4] H failed to register a land charge in protection of his equitable easement, but built a garage on his own land which was accessible only across the informally agreed right of way. Although H's equitable easement was clearly void against I, who later purchased the servient land expressly subject to H's right of way, the Court of Appeal held that H's associated rights, as generated by his expenditure in reliance on the informally granted right of way, were not registrable at all under the Land Charges Act. Instead they constituted an 'equity', grounded on estoppel, which bound a purchaser who (as here) took the land with express actual notice of H's rights.[5]

1　LPA 1925, s 198(1); LCA 1972, s 2(5) **[para 12.318]**. Equitable easements and profits created prior to 1926 remain governed by the equitable doctrine of notice **[para 12.372]**.

2　LCA 1972, s 4(6) **[para 12.282]**. See eg *E R Ives Investment Ltd v High* [1967] 2 QB 379 at 399B–C per Danckwerts LJ, 403E–F per Winn LJ.

3　[1967] 2 QB 379 **[para 12.369]**. See (1967) 31 Conv (NS) 338 (F R Crane).

4　Compare *Sutton v O'Kane* [1973] 2 NZLR 304 at 333–334.

5　[1967] 2 QB 379 at 394F–395A per Lord Denning MR, 399C–400F per Danckwerts LJ, 404F–405C per Winn LJ. See also *Classic Communications Ltd v Lascar* (1986) 21 DLR (4th) 579 at 589–590. In *High*'s case the purchaser was an investment company which had bought with full knowledge of the agreement and was quite prepared to plead the statute in order to further its own unconscionable dealing. Unsurprisingly the Court of Appeal strained to uphold the county court judgment in favour of H. 'Could anything be more monstrous and inequitable afterwards to deprive [H] of the benefit of what he has done?' ([1967] 2 QB 379 at 399F per Danckwerts LJ).

EQUITABLE MORTGAGES AND CHARGES

9.102　Mortgage charges are normally created at law[1] – institutional lenders tend to accept nothing less on a first mortgage of realty – but it is entirely possible that various kinds of mortgage or charge may be created *in equity*. These can take various forms including:

– 　a mortgage of a borrower's equitable interest in land[2]
– 　an informal or incomplete mortgage of a legal estate in land[3]
– 　a mortgage by deposit of documents of title coupled with a written and signed contract of loan[4]
– 　an equitable charge[5]
– 　a charging order under the Charging Orders Act 1979[6]
– 　an unpaid vendor's lien[7] and
– 　a purchaser's lien to secure a deposit.[8]

1　**[Para 8.242]**.

2　**[Para 9.103]**.

3   **[Para 9.104]**.
4   **[Para 9.111]**.
5   **[Para 9.115]**.
6   **[Para 9.118]**.
7   **[Para 9.130]**.
8   **[Para 9.134]**.

MORTGAGE OF AN EQUITABLE INTEREST IN LAND

9.103   A mortgage may remain equitable precisely because it is created over a mere *equitable* interest in land (e g a beneficial interest under a trust of land[1] or a strict settlement[2]). Such a mortgage (or charge) is effected by the assignment of the whole equitable interest to the lender as security for money advanced,[3] the assignment being subject to a proviso for re-assignment on full repayment of the loan.[4] A mortgage or charge of an equitable interest is self-evidently equitable and is valid only if the assignment is made either by will or by other signed writing.[5] A mortgage of an equitable interest under a trust of land is normally overreached on a conveyance of the legal estate in the trust land[6] and is thereafter satisfied out of the capital proceeds received by the trustees.[7]

1   **[Para 9.172]**.
2   **[Para 9.206]**.
3   A prudent assignee immediately gives notice of the assignment to the relevant land trustees in order to obtain priority over other mortgagees under the rule in *Dearle v Hall* **[para 15.252]**.
4   See *Thames Guaranty Ltd v Campbell* [1985] QB 210 at 234F–G.
5   LPA 1925, s 53(1)(c). The mortgage of an equitable interest affecting a registered estate can never constitute a registered charge **[para 8.242]**.
6   **[Paras 2.165, 11.195]**.
7   LPA 1925, s 2(1)(ii).

INFORMAL OR INCOMPLETE MORTGAGE OF A LEGAL ESTATE IN LAND

9.104   An equitable mortgage also arises where the owner of a legal estate in land executes an informal or imperfect charge over that estate, or where the chargee fails to complete the disposition of charge by registration at Land Registry, or where a contract to mortgage the legal estate is never completed by the execution of a deed of charge.

Informal or imperfect mortgage of the legal estate

9.105   An informal or imperfect mortgage of a legal estate occurs where the mortgagor has failed to use one of the modes of legal mortgage indicated as appropriate by statute[1] or has mortgaged the legal estate otherwise than by deed.[2] In such circumstances equity 'looks on that as done which ought to be done' and, in accordance with the so-called doctrine in *Walsh v Lonsdale*,[3] treats the transaction as a valid equitable mortgage of the legal estate.[4]

1   **[Paras 8.242–8.244]**.
2   **[Para 8.243]**.
3   **[Para 9.66]**.
4   See *Parker v Housefield* (1834) 2 My & K 419 at 420, 39 ER 1004; *Swiss Bank Corpn v Lloyds Bank Ltd* [1982] AC 584 at 595D–F. The incomplete instrument is regarded in equity as evidence of an agreement to create a mortgage (see *Mestaer v Gillespie* [1803–13] All ER Rep 594 at 595F–G per Lord Eldon LC; *Katsaitis v Commonwealth Bank of Australia* (1987) 5 BPR 12049 at 12052). Alternatively the formally defective mortgage can be said to be 'equitable in so far as it touches the conscience of the mortgagor' (*Windella v Hughes* (1999) 9 BPR 17141 at 17143 per Santow J).

Failure to complete by registration

9.106   In registered land imperfection may result from a failure to complete a charge over a legal estate by entry of the chargee as registered proprietor of the charge in the charges register of the burdened title.[1]

1   **[Para 8.244]**.

Charge over a registered estate

9.107   Until completed by registration, a mortgage which is drawn as a legal charge over a registered estate does not operate at law and cannot constitute a 'registered charge' within the meaning of the Land Registration Act 2002.[1] Such a charge nevertheless 'operates in equity upon the conscience of the mortgagor'[2] and therefore takes effect as an equitable charge[3] – an outcome which merely reinforces a more general approach adopted by equity in cases of defective disposition. Provided that the preconditions of specific performance are met,[4] equity 'looks on that as done which ought to be done.'

1   LRA 2002, s 27(1).
2   *Windella v Hughes* (1999) 9 BPR 17141 at 17143 per Santow J.
3   See *E S Schwab & Co Ltd v McCarthy* (1976) 31 P & CR 196 at 201, 212; *Mortgage Corpn Ltd v Nationwide Credit Corpn Ltd* [1994] Ch 49 at 53F–54A.
4   **[Para 9.13]**.

First legal charge over an unregistered estate

9.108   Where a mortgage is drawn as a first legal charge over an unregistered estate (and is accompanied by the deposit of documents relating to the mortgaged estate), the charge requires to be completed, within two months of the date of the charge, by a first registration at Land Registry of the borrower's estate and of the lender's charge thereover.[1] Failure to register within this time limit causes the charge to lose its legal status, rendering it a mere contract for valuable consideration to create a legal charge (ie an equitable charge only).[2]

1   **[Para 8.253]**.
2   LRA 2002, s 7(1), (2)(b). In such circumstances the equitable chargee is protected by his retention of the title documents.

Contract to mortgage the legal estate

9.109 An equitable mortgage may also arise where the owner of a legal estate in land enters into a specifically enforceable agreement to create a legal mortgage.[1] Equity again 'looks on that as done which ought to have been done' and under the doctrine in *Walsh v Lonsdale*[2] regards the agreement as an informal equitable mortgage of the legal estate.[3] The operation of this equitable doctrine presupposes that the relevant preconditions of specific enforceability have been met.[4] Thus agreements entered into on or after 27 September 1989[5] must normally be contained in writing signed by both parties,[6] although in certain rare circumstances this requirement of writing may be outflanked by the doctrine of proprietary estoppel. For example, an oral agreement to mortgage a legal estate can generate a valid equitable charge if accompanied by additional detriment incurred by the lender in reliance on the verbal agreement.[7]

1 Specific performance (ie execution of a legal mortgage) may be ordered. See eg *Bridge Wholesale Acceptance Corp (Aust) Ltd v Burnard* (Court of Appeal of New South Wales, 17 July 1992, BPR Casenote 96220).
2 **[Para 9.66]**.
3 See eg *Re Beetham; Ex parte Broderick* (1887) 18 QBD 766 at 768; *Swiss Bank Corpn v Lloyds Bank Ltd* [1982] AC 584 at 594H–595A, D–E; *Hoofstetter v Rooker* (1895) 22 OAR 175 at 179; *Re Collens* (1983) 140 DLR (3d) 755 at 757–758.
4 If specific performance would not be granted (eg because the agreement is to create a mortgage in breach of trust), no equitable mortgage can be said to have arisen (see *Corozo Pty Ltd v Total Australia Ltd* [1987] 2 Qd R 11 at 21).
5 In respect of contracts entered into prior to this date, there must have been compliance with the requirement of written evidence or part performance contained in LPA 1925, s 40 **[para 12.37]**. See *Swiss Bank Corpn v Lloyds Bank Ltd* [1982] AC 584 at 595D–E.
6 LP(MP)A 1989, s 2(1) **[para 9.15]**. An agreement by only one of two owners of a legal estate to charge the jointly held legal estate to a lender may nevertheless effect a valid equitable charge over the chargor's equitable interest **[para 15.96]**. See eg *Bankers Trust Co v Namdar* [1997] EGCS 20.
7 See *Bankers Trust Co v Namdar* [1997] EGCS 20 per Peter Gibson LJ.

Protection of equitable mortgages of a legal estate

9.110 Where the mortgagor's estate is registered at Land Registry, the equitable charge which emerges from an informal or incomplete mortgage of that estate requires to be protected by the entry of a 'notice' in the mortgagor's register of title if it is to be enforceable against subsequent disponees of the registered estate.[1] An equitable mortgage over an unregistered estate is protectable by registration of a general equitable charge under Class C(iii) of the Land Charges Act 1972,[2] unless the equitable chargee holds the title deeds (in which case no registration is necessary).

1 LRA 2002, ss 32–34 **[para 12.89]**.
2 LCA 1972, s 2(4) **[para 12.303]**.

EQUITABLE MORTGAGE OR LIEN BY DEPOSIT OF DOCUMENTS OF TITLE

9.111   Under a venerable doctrine dating back more than two centuries to *Russel v Russel*,[1] it used to be possible to create an equitable mortgage of land, without the necessity of writing or any other formality, through the mere deposit by a landowner of his title deeds or, in the case of a registered estate, by deposit of the relevant land certificate.[2] Such deposit of documents with the lender readily gave rise to an equitable mortgage if coupled with an intention that the depositee should hold the document or documents as his security for a loan of money. The deposit of documentary title was generally construed as a sufficient act of part performance to evidence a contract to create a mortgage,[3] although this view was never entirely without difficulty.[4] Over the years mortgage by documentary deposit became an extremely convenient form of real security. For example a bank which rapidly required some form of security in respect of a customer's dangerously mounting overdraft had access to an easy means of protection, ie by way of a curt request that the customer lodge his documents of title with the bank.

1   (1783) 1 Bro CC 269 at 270, 28 ER 1121 at 1122. For an historical review of the doctrine, see *North West Trust Co v West* (1990) 62 DLR (4th) 749 at 755–756. See also J H G Sunnucks, (1970) 33 MLR 131.
2   For further detail, see *Elements of Land Law* (3rd edn 2001), pp 600–602.
3   See *Swiss Bank Corpn v Lloyds Bank Ltd* [1982] AC 584 at 594H–595A; *Thames Guaranty Ltd v Campbell* [1985] QB 210 at 218F; *United Bank of Kuwait Plc v Sahib* [1997] Ch 107 at 137A–B; *Bank of Ireland Finance Ltd v D J Daly Ltd* [1978] IR 79 at 82. The mere delivery of documents was normally effective without any express written or verbal agreement to mortgage, since the court readily inferred an intention to provide security as between debtor and creditor (see eg *Shaw v Foster* (1872) LR 5 HL 321 at 339–340; *Re Wallis & Simmonds (Builders) Ltd* [1974] 1 WLR 391 at 395A–E).
4   See e g *United Bank of Kuwait Plc v Sahib* [1997] Ch 107 at 132F; *North West Trust Co v West* (1990) 62 DLR (4th) 749 at 754; Law Com No 204 (1991), para 2.9 (n 26).

Informal mortgage by deposit prior to 27 September 1989

9.112   Mortgage by deposit remains today an entirely valid form of equitable mortgage in relation to title documents deposited before 27 September 1989. Although such mortgages by deposit controversially ignore the historic concern for writing expressed in the Statute of Frauds 1677,[1] no further formality is required to make the equitable mortgage effective.[2] It is sufficient that there has been a mere act of deposit,[3] coupled with the intention of thereby providing real security.[4]

1   It has always seemed extraordinary that an equitable mortgage could be made without any writing at all. See, for instance, the regret with which Maitland was forced to accept the existence and continuing force of the doctrine stemming from *Russel v Russel* (*Equity*, p 199). See also *Edge v Worthington* (1786) 1 Cox 211 at 212, 29 ER 1133; *Ex parte Mountfort* (1808) 14 Ves 606 at 606–607, 33 ER 653 at 653–654 per Lord Eldon LC; *United Bank of Kuwait Plc v Sahib* [1997] Ch 107 at 143E–H per Phillips LJ.
2   'The right created by the deposit is not limited to keeping the deeds until the money has been paid but gives an equitable estate in the lands' (*Allied Irish Banks Ltd v Glynn* [1973] IR 188 at 192). See eg *Freeguard v Royal Bank of Scotland Plc* (2000) 79 P & CR 81 at 86.

3   A joint owner of a freehold estate cannot validly create an equitable mortgage over that estate by means of a deposit of the documentary title without the consent of the other joint tenant or tenants (see *Thames Guaranty Ltd v Campbell* [1985] QB 210 at 233C–D).

4   There must be a genuine intention that the deposit of the documentary title should operate as security for the advance. It is not sufficient that, after an agreement has been made to provide security, the documentary title happens to come into the hands of the creditor for some other purpose (*Re Beetham; Ex parte Broderick* (1887) 18 QBD 380 at 383–384, 766 at 769–770; *Bank of Ireland Finance Ltd v D J Daly Ltd* [1978] IR 79 at 82).

Requirement of written contract on or after 27 September 1989

9.113   It is equally clear today that an equitable mortgage can no longer be created by the mere act of documentary deposit.[1] The Law of Property (Miscellaneous Provisions) Act 1989 invalidates all contracts relating to land (entered into on or after 27 September 1989) which are not contained in writing signed by all parties.[2] The rule in *Russel v Russel* undoubtedly rests upon an 'essential contractual foundation'[3] and the 1989 Act brings about the inescapable, if slightly unwelcome, conclusion that, contrary to two centuries of hallowed doctrine and commercial practice, the convenient facility of equitable mortgage by mere documentary deposit is no longer available.[4] Notwithstanding the deposit of all relevant documents, an agreement to mortgage land can no longer be made orally and any act of documentary deposit must be coupled with a written contract signed by both lender and borrower[5] in conformity with the requirements of the 1989 Act.

1   See J Howell, [1990] Conv 441 at 444; [1991] Conv 12 (J E Adams).
2   LP(MP)A 1989, s 2(1) [**paras 9.15, 12.28**].
3   *United Bank of Kuwait Plc v Sahib* [1997] Ch 107 at 137A per Peter Gibson LJ.
4   This was certainly the expectation of the Law Commission in proposing the introduction of the Law of Property (Miscellaneous Provisions) Bill 1989 (see Law Com No 204 (1991), para 2.9). See also *United Bank of Kuwait Plc v Sahib* [1997] Ch 107 at 138E–G per Peter Gibson LJ. It is significant that the Land Registration Act 2002 deliberately contains no replica of an earlier statutory provision (LRA 1925, s 66) authorising the creation of liens and charges over registered land by documentary deposit (Law Com No 271 (2001), para 7.10).
5   It is easily overlooked that both lender and borrower must sign the relevant agreement (see [1991] Conv 12 (J E Adams)). Moreover, if a deposit of documents is accompanied by an actual written charge agreement, it is the express terms of this charge which are definitive (see *Shaw v Foster* (1872) LR 5 HL 321 at 339–340; *Thames Guaranty Ltd v Campbell* [1985] QB 210 at 241D–E).

Protection of an equitable mortgage or charge by deposit

9.114   Where a registered estate has been mortgaged by means of documentary deposit and signed contractual writing, the resulting equitable charge may be protected against subsequent dealings by the entry of a 'notice' in the charges register of the title affected.[1] A similar mortgage over an unregistered estate is excluded from the category of registrable general equitable charges under Class C(iii) of the Land Charges Act 1972,[2] precisely because the lender's retention of the title deeds provides him with adequate protection against adverse dealings with the legal estate.

1   LRA 2002, ss 32–34 [**para 12.89**].
2   LCA 1972, s 2(4) [**para 12.303**].

EQUITABLE CHARGE

9.115   An equitable charge is created when land or any interest in it, whether legal or equitable, is 'expressly or constructively made liable, or specially appropriated, to the discharge of a debt or some other obligation.'[1] A charge of this kind differs from a mortgage,[2] in that, unlike a mortgage, it passes no property (either actually or notionally) to the creditor[3] nor any right of possession[4] or foreclosure,[5] but only a right of realisation by judicial process in case of non-payment of the debt (usually through the appointment of a receiver or an order for sale).[6]

1   *Swiss Bank Corpn v Lloyds Bank Ltd* [1982] AC 584 at 595A–B per Buckley LJ. See also *Re Cosslett (Contractors) Ltd* [1998] Ch 495 at 507H–508D per Millett LJ.
2   See *Shea v Moore* [1894] 1 IR 158 at 168; and compare LPA 1925, s 87(1) [**para 8.246**].
3   *Re Cosslett (Contractors) Ltd* [1998] Ch 495 at 508G per Millett LJ (equitable charge involves no 'transfer of legal or equitable ownership'). See also *Buhr v Barclays Bank plc* [2001] BPIR 25 at [47] per Arden LJ.
4   *Bland v Ingrams Estates Ltd* [2001] Ch 767 at [19] per Nourse LJ.
5   *Carreras Rothmans Ltd v Freeman Mathews Treasure Ltd* [1985] Ch 207 at 227C–D per Peter Gibson J.
6   *London County and Westminster Bank Ltd v Tompkins* [1918] 1 KB 515 at 528; *Weg Motors Ltd v Hales* [1962] Ch 49 at 77; *Bland v Ingrams Estates Ltd* [2001] Ch 767 at [17]–[19] per Nourse LJ.

Creation

9.116   The equitable charge provides a means by which, even without any deposit of title documents, an agreement under which land is identified as collateral for a debt is effective in equity to create a valid security.[1] The agreement must, however, identify specific property as being appropriated to the charge,[2] since the agreement is otherwise unenforceable 'on the ground of vagueness.'[3] The agreement must also disclose a clear common intention to make the land a form of present security.[4] A mere agreement that a creditor should share in future proceeds of sale in priority to the debtor is not, for instance, enough to create an equitable charge over the land.[5] In the absence of estoppel any agreement by which a debtor equitably charges his interest must be contained in a written contract signed by all relevant parties,[6] although it is arguable that a unilateral declaration of charge, setting aside specific land as security, may be effective if signed only by the chargor.[7]

1   In *Matthews v Goodday* (1861) 31 LJ Ch 282 at 283, for example, it was accepted that a written contract by B charging his real estate to A in the sum of £500 would not constitute an 'agreement to give a legal mortgage', but would amount to 'a security by which he equitably charged his land with the payment of a sum of money.' See also *Simmons v Montague* [1909] 1 IR 87 at 95–96; *Bank of Ireland Finance Ltd v D J Daly Ltd* [1978] IR 79 at 82; *Freeway Mutual Pty Ltd v Taylor* (1979) 22 ALR 281 at 285.

2   See *Bridge Wholesale Acceptance Corp (Aust) Ltd v Burnard* (Supreme Court of New South Wales, 31 May 1991, BPR Casenote 96206; Court of Appeal of New South Wales, 17 July 1992, BPR Casenote 96220).

3   *Re Clarke* (1887) 36 Ch D 348 at 352 per Cotton LJ.

4   See *National Provincial and Union Bank of England v Charnley* [1924] 1 KB 431 at 440 per Bankes LJ, 445–446 per Scrutton LJ, 449–450 per Atkin LJ; *Westfield Holdings Ltd v Australian Capital Television Pty Ltd* (1992) 5 BPR 11615 at 11620 per Young J.

5   *Re Sikorski and Sikorski* (1979) 89 DLR (3d) 411 at 415–416.

6   LP(MP)A 1989, s 2(1) **[paras 9.15, 12.28]**.

7   See LPA 1925, s 53(1)(a).

Protection

9.117   An agreement to create an equitable charge over a *legal* estate requires the protection appropriate for an estate contract in either registered or unregistered land[1] and an agreement to charge an equitable interest under a trust of land constitutes an overreachable interest in the case of both registered and unregistered land.[2]

1   **[Paras 12.89, 12.306]**.

2   **[Para 9.103]**.

CHARGING ORDER UNDER THE CHARGING ORDERS ACT 1979

9.118   The device of the charging order now provides an increasingly important mechanism for the recovery of debts. Under the Charging Orders Act 1979 it is open to a creditor, on obtaining a High Court or county court judgment in respect of a debt, to apply to the court for a 'charging order' for the purpose of enforcing the judgment in his favour.[1] The court has discretion whether or not to make a charging order,[2] but if an order is made, it converts what was at most a contractual debt into an enforceable security with proprietary attributes.[3]

1   COA 1979, s 1(1).

2   COA 1979, s 1(5). If the creditor's application is successful, the court first makes an order nisi and then an order absolute, the burden being on the judgment debtor to show cause why a charging order nisi should not be made absolute (see *Roberts Petroleum Ltd v Bernard Kenny Ltd* [1982] 1 WLR 301 at 307E). The mere fact that a court declines to make an order absolute does not, of course, discharge the debt owed to the creditor (see *Harman v Glencross* [1985] Fam 49 at 58D).

3   A charging order 'seems to be an assignment of some proprietary right, effected by the order of the court' (*Croydon (Unique) Ltd v Wright* [2001] Ch 318 at 328D).

Scope of the charging order

9.119   A charging order made by the court has the effect of imposing on specified property of the judgment debtor a 'charge for securing the payment of any money due ... under the judgment or order.'[1] The charge may be ordered in respect of any land or interest in land 'held by the debtor beneficially.'[2] A charging order may also be made with reference to any interest of the debtor under a trust of land[3] and may extend to land held on a bare trust for the debtor[4] or held by two or more joint debtors who are together entitled to the whole unencumbered beneficial interest under a trust.[5]

1   COA 1979, s 1(1).
2   COA 1979, s 2(1)(a)(i).
3   COA 1979, s 2(1)(a)(ii). See *National Westminster Bank Ltd v Stockman* [1981] 1 WLR 67 at 69C; *Perry v Phoenix Assurance Plc* [1988] 1 WLR 940 at 943E–F.
4   COA 1979, s 2(1)(b)(ii).
5   COA 1979, s 2(1)(b)(iii). See eg *National Westminster Bank Ltd v Allen* [1971] 2 QB 718 at 721B.

Effect of the charging order

9.120   The principal advantage of a charging order is that the court-imposed charge becomes enforceable 'in the same manner as an equitable charge created by the debtor by writing under his hand.'[1] Accordingly the judgment creditor is entitled to invoke legal process for the purpose of realising his security together with appropriate interest[2] and the costs of enforcing the charging order.[3] He can apply to the court either for an order for sale of the property charged or for the appointment of a receiver.[4] Whether the subject matter of the charging order is land in which the judgment debtor has a sole or only a shared beneficial interest,[5] the creditor may seek an order for the sale of the land itself, his own charge being satisfied out of the proceeds attributable to such beneficial entitlement as the debtor may have.[6]

1   COA 1979, s 3(4). See *Bland v Ingrams Estates Ltd* [2001] Ch 767 at [7] per Nourse LJ.
2   See *Ezekiel v Orakpo* [1997] 1 WLR 340 at 345H–346E.
3   *Holder v Supperstone* [2000] 1 All ER 473 at 479f–480b.
4   See *Midland Bank Plc v Pike* [1988] 2 All ER 434 at 435h; *Croydon (Unique) Ltd v Wright* [2001] Ch 318 at 333B.
5   The imposition of the charge effects a severance of any beneficial joint tenancy [**para 11.87**].
6   See *Midland Bank Plc v Pike* [1988] 2 All ER 434 at 438a.

Protection against third parties

9.121   A court-ordered charge over a *registered* estate held legally and beneficially by a debtor can be protected against third parties by the entry of a 'notice' in the charges register of the debtor's title.[1] A charging order in respect of a similarly held *unregistered* estate is protectable by registration under the Land Charges Act 1972.[2] Matters are more complex where a charging order operates upon a beneficial interest belonging to the debtor behind a trust of land. If the order relates to a beneficial entitlement under a trust of a registered estate, the appropriate protection comprises the entry of a 'restriction' in the proprietorship register of the registered title.[3] An equivalent order in respect of an equitable interest under a trust of an unregistered estate is, however, ineligible for protection by registration pursuant to the Land Charges Act 1972.[4]

1   LRA 2002, ss 32–34 **[para 12.84]**.
2   LCA 1972, s 6(1)(a) (register of writs and orders affecting land) **[para 12.334]**.
3   LRA 2002, s 42(1)(c), (4); LRR 2003, r 93(k) **[para 7.52]**. The assumption seems to be that the
     charging order, like the beneficial interest to which it relates, should, if necessary, take effect
     on overreaching against the proportion of the resulting sale proceeds of the trust land
     attributable to the debtor.
4   This legislation catches only orders 'affecting land' (LCA 1972, s 6(1)(a)) and for this purpose
     'land' is expressly defined, unless the context otherwise requires, as excluding 'an undivided
     share in land' (LCA 1972, s 17(1)). See also LCA 1972, s 6(1A); *Perry v Phoenix Assurance Plc*
     [1988] 1 WLR 940 at 945B–D per Browne-Wilkinson V-C.

Discretion to make a charging order

9.122   In view of its potentially drastic consequences, the making of a
charging order is not mandatory on proof of a judgment debt.[1] A judicial
discretion attaches both to the decision whether a charging order should be
made at all[2] and to subsequent decisions whether a charging order, once made,
should be discharged or varied.[3] The court has, moreover, a statutory discretion
to order an immediate sale of any co-owned land affected by a charging order.[4]

1   See Law Commission, *Report on Charging Orders* (Law Com No 74, Cmnd 6412, 1976),
     para 43.
2   COA 1979, s 1(5).
3   COA 1979, s 3(5). The jurisdiction to discharge or vary a charging order is open only to a
     'person interested in any property to which the order relates.' This person must have, in respect
     of the asset charged, 'a proprietary interest or an interest akin thereto, in the sense that they
     are a person who at least has some interest such that their legal rights and liabilities are
     directly affected by the charging order' (see *Banque Nationale de Paris plc v Montman Ltd*
     [2000] 1 BCLC 576 at 581a). This may include the debtor's spouse (*Harman v Glencross* [1985]
     Fam 49 at 56C–D, [1986] Fam 81 at 89H–90G) and the interest claimed may be the spouse's
     statutory matrimonial home rights (*Banque Nationale de Paris*, supra at 581b).
4   TOLATA 1996, s 14(1)–(2) **[para 11.229]**.

Factors generally relevant to discretion

9.123   In exercising the discretion to make a charging order,[1] the court must
consider 'all the circumstances of the case',[2] and in particular must have regard
to the 'personal circumstances of the debtor'[3] and to whether any other
creditor would be 'unduly prejudiced' by the making of the order.[4] Although
the creditor may normally expect a charging order to be made,[5] this expectation
is far from absolute[6] and in the context of the family home it has been said that
references to 'any presumption one way or the other' are unhelpful.[7]

1   The matters prescribed for consideration in section 1(5) are by necessary implication relevant
     also to decisions on discharge or variation (*Harman v Glencross* [1985] Fam 49 at 55C–D).
2   In the context of a jointly owned matrimonial home, the court has 'a duty at least to consider'
     whether the debtor's wife ought to be given notice of the hearing so that she can be heard and
     all the circumstances of the case can be considered (*Harman v Glencross* [1985] Fam 49 at
     54G–H, [1986] Fam 81 at 89D–E).
3   COA 1979, s 1(5)(a). See *Harman v Glencross* [1986] Fam 81 at 103D–E.
4   COA 1979, s 1(5)(b).

5   See *Roberts Petroleum Ltd v Bernard Kenny Ltd* [1982] 1 WLR 301 at 307A; *First National Securities Ltd v Hegerty* [1985] QB 850 at 866A–B.
6   The proposition is necessarily qualified where, for instance, the judgment creditor finds himself in competition with other creditors (see *Harman v Glencross* [1986] Fam 81 at 93A).
7   *Harman v Glencross* [1985] Fam 49 at 57B per Ewbank J.

Factors specially relevant to the family home

9.124   In dealing with the family home the court must seek to strike a balance between the normal expectation of the creditor and the hardship to the debtor's partner and children if an order is made.[1] The decision whether to make a charging order absolute often coincides, in point of time, with the decision whether to enforce the charge by ordering an immediate sale of the land concerned.[2] Where the land is co-owned by the debtor and his partner, the interests of the secured creditor (ie the chargee under the charging order) represent only one matter relevant to the exercise of discretion.[3] The court's attention is equally directed to other factors such as the welfare of any minor who occupies (or might reasonably be expected to occupy) the land as his home.[4]

1   *Harman v Glencross* [1986] Fam 81 at 104A per Fox LJ.
2   **[Para 11.248]**.
3   TOLATA 1996, s 15(1)(d). See e g *Mortgage Corpn v Shaire* [2001] Ch 743 at 758F–G, 760E–F per Neuberger J.
4   TOLATA 1996, s 15(1)(c) **[para 11.245]**.

Considerations in favour of the creditor

9.125   It can be argued that the debtor's partner may fairly be called on to share the debtor's adversity, just as he or she would doubtless have been willing in different circumstances to share in any prosperity which might have come their way.[1] In many instances the debtor's spouse may also have had the opportunity, by registration of her matrimonial home rights (ie statutory rights of occupation),[2] to acquire priority over any charging order later obtained against the debtor.[3] Moreover, as Balcombe LJ pointed out in *Harman v Glencross*,[4] not all judgment creditors are 'faceless corporations'. Some are private individuals for whom the denial or postponement of a charging order may entail just as much domestic hardship as for the debtor.

1   *Harman v Glencross* [1985] Fam 49 at 59A–B.
2   Family Law Act 1996, ss 30(2), 31(2); LCA 1972, s 2(1), (7) **[para 12.93]**.
3   *Harman v Glencross* [1986] Fam 81 at 94A–C.
4   [1986] Fam 81 at 93F–H.

Considerations in favour of the debtor and his family

9.126   From the viewpoint of the debtor's family it is often a significant consideration that the debtor's partner may not have been a party to his indebtedness.[1] It may also be relevant that the creditor could easily have insisted on taking some security prior to advancing money or credit to the debtor but clearly failed to do so.[2] In some circumstances it may be conclusive in favour of the debtor's family that the operation of a charging order on the debtor's beneficial share will precipitate a sale of the family home and leave insufficient funds to rehouse the debtor's partner and children. In *Harman v Glencross*,[3] for example, Ewbank J decided that the balance of these considerations pointed overwhelmingly against the making of a charging order, and the Court of Appeal declined to disturb his exercise of discretion.[4]

1   See e g *Harman v Glencross* [1986] Fam 81 at 98C.
2   [1986] Fam 81 at 98C.
3   [1985] Fam 49 at 59F. See [1985] Conv 129 (P F Smith).
4   [1986] Fam 81 at 98G, 105G. See [1986] Conv 218 (J Warburton).

Interaction with divorce proceedings

9.127   A complicating factor in the exercise of discretion under the Charging Orders Act 1979 is frequently the consideration that the making of a charging order in respect of the debtor's beneficial interest in his family home is liable to prejudice any claim which his spouse might otherwise have in the event of divorce.[1] In such circumstances the exercise of discretion under the Charging Orders Act 1979, although superficially an issue arising merely as between debtor and creditor, represents in reality a conflict between the commercial law jurisdiction conferred by the 1979 Act and the matrimonial jurisdiction which operates on divorce.[2] Even where divorce proceedings have been initiated between the debtor and his spouse,[3] a judgment creditor may still apply to have a charging order made absolute and unconditional, but may normally do so only if the balance of the proceeds of sale (after the judgment debt has been satisfied) are 'clearly sufficient to provide adequate alternative accommodation for the wife and children.'[4] If, as is more usual, the proceeds released by sale are unlikely to be sufficient for this purpose, the creditor's application for an order absolute is normally transferred to the court's family jurisdiction and considered in conjunction with the spouse's application for property adjustment. In this way one court (and one court only) is in a position to consider all the relevant circumstances of the case.[5]

1   Any subsequent property transfer order made in matrimonial proceedings clearly takes effect subject to the charging order (see *Harman v Glencross* [1986] Fam 81 at 102B, 103G).
2   See *Harman v Glencross* [1986] Fam 81 at 103F.
3   It would not normally constitute a proper exercise of the court's discretion under Matrimonial Causes Act 1973, s 24, to order an immediate property transfer to the wife for the express purpose of frustrating a pending application for a charging order (*Harman v Glencross* [1986] Fam 81 at 103G–H).
4   *Harman v Glencross* [1986] Fam 81 at 99C–D. See e g *Llewellin v Llewellin* (Unreported, Court of Appeal, Transcript No 640 of 1985, 30 October 1985). In this context, the provision of 'adequate alternative accommodation' is not inconsistent with the wife and children being 'housed at a lower standard than they might reasonably have expected' (*Harman v Glencross*, supra at 99F).
5   See *Harman v Glencross* [1986] Fam 81 at 99D–E, 105E–F.

9.128   In the ensuing proceedings[1] the creditor has a justifiable expectation of recovering his debt[2] and his legitimate interests should be relegated only if and to the extent that it is 'necessary to protect the wife's right to occupy (with the children where appropriate) the matrimonial home.'[3] With this end in view, the Court of Appeal suggested in *Harman v Glencross*[4] that a compromise solution may well lie in the equivalent of the *Mesher* order which at one time enjoyed currency under the Matrimonial Causes Act 1973.[5] A charging order based on the *Mesher* analogy imposes a charge on the debtor's share in the family home but effectively postpones its enforcement so long as the house is occupied by his spouse and a child of the family who is under the age of 17 and in full time education.[6] Such an order thus guarantees the creditor a deferred recovery of his debt, whilst alleviating at least temporarily the hardship inevitably suffered by the debtor's family.[7]

1   The transfer of the charging order application to the matrimonial jurisdiction does not detract from the essentially commercial character of these proceedings (see *Harman v Glencross* [1986] Fam 81 at 103F, 105F).
2   [1986] Fam 81 at 99E–F. Only in exceptional circumstances is the court ever justified in ordering an outright transfer of the debtor's share to his wife, thereby leaving nothing on which the judgment creditor's charging order can ever bite (*Harman v Glencross* [1986] Fam 81 at 100A).
3   *Harman v Glencross* [1986] Fam 81 at 99G per Balcombe LJ. See more generally Chapter 11 **[paras 11.266–11.270]**.
4   [1986] Fam 81 at 96C–97A, 104F–105E.
5   See *Mesher v Mesher* [1980] 1 All ER 126n.
6   Fox LJ pointed out ([1986] Fam 81 at 104F–G) that COA 1979, s 3(1) empowers the court to make a charging order subject to the condition that the creditor should not seek to enforce his charge by means of an order for sale during a specified period.
7   Fox LJ agreed ([1986] Fam 81 at 105A–B) that *Mesher* type orders were not in the long term particularly favourable from the wife's viewpoint, but thought that in a dispute between the wife and the husband's creditor 'the interests of the creditor cannot be disregarded.'

Interaction with bankruptcy proceedings

9.129   It is quite possible that a creditor may seek a charging order in respect of a debtor who is on the verge of bankruptcy. In view of the substantial preference given to the trustee in bankruptcy, even in the context of the family home, there may be little point in denying the creditor his charging order.[1] It is usually only a matter of time before the claims of the trustee in bankruptcy become paramount and a sale of the property is ordered.[2]

1   See *Harman v Glencross* [1986] Fam 81 at 100B per Balcombe LJ.
2   **[Para 11.252]**.

UNPAID VENDOR'S LIEN

9.130   From the moment of entering into a contract of sale the vendor of land retains a lien at common law until the purchase price is paid.[1] More pertinently the vendor retains an *equitable lien* on the land if he transfers the legal estate to the purchaser or gives him possession before the purchase money is paid in full.[2] This 'unpaid vendor's lien' arises automatically by operation of law,[3] quite independently of the parties' agreement or subjective intentions, except in rare cases[4] where the retention of a lien is manifestly inconsistent with the provisions of the contract or with the true nature of the transaction as disclosed by the documents.[5]

1   See *Re Birmingham, Decd* [1959] Ch 523 at 529 per Upjohn J.
2   *Winter v Lord Anson* (1827) 3 Russ 488 at 490–491, 38 ER 658 at 659–660; *Bridges v Mees* [1957] Ch 475 at 484; *Hewitt v Court* (1982) 149 CLR 639 at 645 per Gibbs CJ. The lien secures only the payment of purchase money, as distinct from the performance of other contractual obligations which are not expressed in money (see *Gracegrove Estates Ltd v Boateng* [1997] EGCS 103 per Aldous LJ).
3   *Re Beirnstein* [1925] Ch 12 at 17–18; *Hewitt v Court* (1982) 149 CLR 639 at 663 per Deane J. This lien, like all creatures of equity, is governed by the hard reality of the facts and is not excluded by the circumstance that the conveyance contains an express receipt for the money (*Barclays Bank Plc v Estates & Commercial Ltd* [1997] 1 WLR 415 at 420A–B).
4   See eg *Gracegrove Estates Ltd v Boateng* [1997] EGCS 103.
5   *Barclays Bank Plc v Estates & Commercial Ltd* [1997] 1 WLR 415 at 421E per Millett LJ. See also *McDowell v Kelic* (1998) 9 BPR 16669 at 16671.

Origin in equitable principle

9.131   The equitable lien gives expression to the elementary precept of justice that 'a person, having got the estate of another, shall not, as between them, keep it, and not pay the consideration.'[1] The lien arises where property has been specifically identified and appropriated to the performance of the contract between the parties and the purchaser would be acting 'unconscientiously and unfairly' if he were to dispose of the property without discharging the indebtedness which has arisen under the contract with the original vendor.[2] Although the point remains controversial, the preferable view is that the vendor's lien arises irrespective of whether the contract of sale is specifically enforceable.[3]

1   *Mackreth v Symmons* (1808) 15 Ves 329 at 340, 33 ER 778 at 782 per Lord Eldon LC.
2   *Hewitt v Court* (1982) 149 CLR 639 at 668 per Deane J.
3   *Hewitt v Court* (1982) 149 CLR 639 at 666–667 per Deane J. See likewise *Metcalfe v Archbishop of York* (1836) 1 My & Cr 547 at 557, 40 ER 485 at 489 per Lord Cottenham LC; *Western Wagon and Property Co v West* [1892] 1 Ch 271 at 275 per Chitty J; *Ecclesiatical Commissioners v Piney* [1899] 2 Ch 729 at 735, 738. For a contrary view, see *Capital Finance Co Ltd v Stokes* [1969] 1 Ch 261 at 278E–F per Harman LJ; *London and Cheshire Insurance Co Ltd v Laplagrene Property Co Ltd* [1971] Ch 499 at 514E–F per Brightman J; *Re Bond Worth Ltd* [1980] Ch 228 at 251D per Slade J.

Effect

9.132   The unpaid vendor's lien operates as the vendor's security for full payment of the agreed purchase price and is regarded, for the purpose of the Law of Property Act 1925,[1] as a species of mortgage. Unlike most mortgages, however, the equitable lien transfers no title[2] and confers on the unpaid vendor no right to possession of the land, but merely a right to enforce his lien through a declaration of charge and a court order for sale.[3] Such realisation by judicial process enables the vendor to recoup the unpaid money out of the sale proceeds, the equitable lien operating, in effect, as a 'form of equitable charge' implied by law.[4] The vendor is thus treated, in equity, as a secured creditor of the purchaser.[5] The lien is not a negative right to retain some legal or equitable interest, but essentially a positive right to obtain, in appropriate circumstances, an order for sale of property which, in equity, is bound by the contract concerned.[6]

1   LPA 1925, s 205(1)(xvi).
2   *Hewitt v Court* (1982) 149 CLR 639 at 663 per Deane J.
3   *Bowles v Rogers* (1800) 6 Ves 95n, 31 ER 957; *Re Stucley* [1906] 1 Ch 67 at 76–77, 80; *Hewitt v Court* (1982) 149 CLR 639 at 663 per Deane J.
4   *Hewitt v Court* (1982) 149 CLR 639 at 663 per Deane J. See similarly *Re Birmingham, Decd* [1959] Ch 523 at 529 per Upjohn J.
5   *Hewitt v Court* (1982) 149 CLR 639 at 645 per Gibbs CJ. One increasingly important consequence of this equitable charge is that a lender whose advance is intended to assist the purchase may claim, to the extent that this money reaches the vendor, to be subrogated to the unpaid vendor's security (see eg *Halifax plc v Omar* [2002] 2 P & CR 377 at [84] **[para 15.102]**).
6   *Hewitt v Court* (1982) 149 CLR 639 at 664–665 per Deane J.

Protection

9.133   The unpaid vendor's equitable lien arises simultaneously with the making of the contract of sale.[1] If a registered vendor's lien is to survive the contracted transfer of his title, the vendor must protect the lien by entering a 'notice' in *his own* register of title immediately following the contract which generates the lien.[2] In this way the vendor is enabled to claim protected priority for his lien as against the disponee who takes the registered estate on performance of the contract to transfer.[3] In rare cases, where an unpaid vendor remains 'in actual occupation' of the land following the transfer,[4] the equitable lien may 'override' the registered disposition notwithstanding a failure to protect it by 'notice'.[5] An equitable lien over an unregistered estate is protectable by the registration of a Class C(iii) general equitable charge under the Land Charges Act 1972.[6]

1   *Barclays Bank Plc v Estates & Commercial Ltd* [1997] 1 WLR 415 at 419H–420A per Millett LJ.
2   LRA 2002, ss 32–34 **[para 12.89]**.
3   LRA 2002, s 29(1), (2)(a)(i).
4   LRA 2002, s 29(1), (2)(a)(ii), Sch 3, para 2.
5   See *London and Cheshire Insurance Co Ltd v Laplagrene Property Co Ltd* [1971] Ch 499 at 504; *UCB Bank plc v Beasley and France* [1995] NPC 144; *Nationwide Anglia Building Society v Ahmed* (1995) 70 P & CR 381 at 386; *Gracegrove Estates Ltd v Boateng* [1997] EGCS 103.
6   **[Para 12.303]**. Once again this registration should be effected immediately following the contract of sale.

PURCHASER'S LIEN TO SECURE DEPOSIT

9.134   A converse principle applies in favour of a purchaser whose contract of purchase remains unperformed through no fault of his own. An equitable lien arises by operation of law as the purchaser's security for the recovery of any money (eg a contractual deposit[1]) which he has already paid under the unperformed contract.[2]

1   [Para 12.46].
2   *Rose v Watson* (1864) 10 HLCas 672 at 683–684, 11 ER 1187 at 1192 per Lord Cranworth; *Hewitt v Court* (1982) 149 CLR 639 at 664 per Deane J.

Origin in equitable principle

9.135   The purchaser's lien to secure his deposit gives effect to a principle of 'solid and substantial justice'[1] that the vendor should not be allowed to 'keep the price if he fails to make the conveyance.'[2] There is no necessity that the purchaser's lien be founded on a specifically enforceable contract to purchase a legal estate.[3] Indeed, an equitable lien may be most needed by a purchaser whose contract of sale is, for some reason, specifically *unenforceable*.[4]

1   *Rose v Watson* (1864) 10 HLCas 672 at 684, 11 ER 1187 at 1192 per Lord Cranworth. See similarly *Whitbread & Co Ltd v Watt* [1902] 1 Ch 835 at 838 per Vaughan Williams LJ.
2   *Hewitt v Court* (1982) 149 CLR 639 at 645 per Gibbs CJ.
3   *Middleton v Magnay* (1864) 2 H & M 233 at 236–237, 71 ER 452 at 453; *Barker v Cox* (1876) 4 Ch D 464 at 469; *Levy v Stogdon* [1898] 1 Ch 478 at 486–487; *Hewitt v Court* (1982) 149 CLR 639 at 650 per Gibbs CJ, 651 per Murphy J, 667 per Deane J; *Cox v Parker* (1987) 5 BPR 11208 at 11213.
4   See *Chattey v Farndale Holdings Inc* (1998) 75 P & CR 298 at 305–307 per Morritt LJ.

Effect

9.136   Like the vendor's equitable lien,[1] the purchaser's lien to secure his deposit operates as an equitable charge,[2] entitling the purchaser to apply for realisation by judicial process and payment out of the proceeds. Once again the holder of the lien is treated in effect as a secured creditor of the vendor,[3] a status which may be highly significant for the recovery of the purchaser's deposit from an insolvent vendor or for a claim of priority over a subsequent charge made by the vendor.[4] It is not uncommon, for example, that the commercial developer of a housing estate should market most of the plots 'off the plan' (ie in advance of the completion of construction), each purchaser contracting to buy a house and paying over the appropriate deposit to the developer.[5] If the developer goes into liquidation before finishing the construction, the lien may be vital in enabling the purchaser to recover his deposit money.[6]

1   [Para 9.130].
2   [Para 9.115].
3   *Hewitt v Court* (1982) 149 CLR 639 at 645 per Gibbs CJ.
4   See eg *Shephard v Corindi Blueberry Growers Pty Ltd* (1994) 6 BPR 13672 at 13675–13676.
5   See eg *Lyus v Prowsa Developments Ltd* [1982] 1 WLR 1044 at 1046G–1047B **[para 10.73]**.
6   See eg *Chattey v Farndale Holdings Inc* (1998) 75 P & CR 298 at 318.

Protection

9.137   The purchaser's equitable lien requires protection by the entry of a 'notice' in the vendor's register of title (in the case of registered land)[1] and by registration of a Class C(iii) land charge (in the case of unregistered land).[2]

1   [Para 12.89].
2   [Para 12.303].

RESTRICTIVE COVENANTS

9.138   A restrictive covenant is an agreement between two estate owners limiting the use of the land of one for the benefit of the other. Restrictive covenants rank in English law as equitable proprietary interests in land.[1] They have come to play a significant role in the preservation of environmental welfare and are almost invariably found in any residential context which involves multiple habitation in conditions of close proximity. Although far from confined to the residential sphere, restrictive covenants have as their primary function the safeguarding of various kinds of amenity considered important for enlightened urban planning and civilised coexistence.

1   [Paras **2.21**, **13.113**]. See also *Forestview Nominees Pty Ltd v Perpetual Trustees WA Ltd* (1996) 141 ALR 687 at 697.

Social and commercial functions of restrictive covenants

9.139   Restrictive covenants provide an important means of securing the segregation of land uses and are therefore entered into for a variety of purposes both commercial and aesthetic. Particularly in the era prior to planning legislation on a more general scale, restrictive covenants offered an appropriate method of protection for such intangible factors as the trading interests of a covenantee or the local atmosphere or 'tone' of a community.[1] Indeed restrictive covenants have played a vital role throughout the history of urban planning by shielding residential development from the undesired impact of industrial or commercial forms of land use. In this way restrictive covenants have been used widely for the purpose of preserving the residential character of particular districts or neighbourhoods.[2]

1   The enforcement of a restrictive covenant against business user may provide a solution for the vexed problem of the neighbour who keeps a huge lorry parked semi-permanently on the street outside his home (see *McDonagh v Cromie* [1982] 9 BNIL 72). See also *Balchin v Buckle* (1982) 126 Sol Jo 412 (injunction and damages).
2   So successful has been the device of the restrictive covenant in securing certain uniformities of urban development that some commentators have criticised the way in which 'strait jacket' restrictions impose an undesirable homogeneity on housing patterns, thereby invading 'aspects of home life previously left to personal choice' (see J L Winokur, 'The Mixed Blessings of Promissory Servitudes: Toward Optimizing Economic Utility, Individual Liberty, and Personal Identity' (1989) Wisc L Rev 1 at 4).

Typical restrictive covenants

9.140 A typical restrictive covenant comprises an undertaking that the covenantor's land shall not be used for any trade or business[1] or shall not be used for other than private residential purposes.[2] Restrictive covenants may likewise forbid any activity which causes nuisance, annoyance, danger or detriment to neighbours[3] or may seek to control the number or character of domestic animals which may be kept as pets. In their more extreme forms restrictive covenants can have the insidious effect of policing the lifestyles of those living within an area or development through reinforcement of the perceived character of the neighbourhood.[4] Other more prosaic restrictive covenants regulate the extent, type or density of the construction permissible in certain areas.[5] A restrictive covenant may require the covenantor to refrain, for example, from building within a certain distance from the frontage of his property or even to refrain from erecting certain kinds of construction on his land.[6]

1   A covenant against trade or business user is breached by the presence of lodgers who make fixed periodical payments, but not where a person merely agrees to share part of the expenses of a single household (*Heglibiston Establishment v Heyman* (1977) 36 P & CR 351 at 360).
2   See *C & G Homes Ltd v Secretary of State for Health* [1991] Ch 365 at 384F, 387C, 390B (breach by reason of district health authority's provision of supervised housing for former mental in-patients). In the *C & G Homes* case it was relevant, but not conclusive, that this 'care in the community' user fell within a permissible class of use under the relevant planning legislation ([1991] Ch 365 at 380D–G).
3   See *C & G Homes Ltd v Secretary of State for Health* [1991] Ch 365 at 386A–E, 387E (no breach where sheltered housing project allegedly inflicted financial detriment on neighbouring properties by reason of 'impaired marketability').
4   Some local authorities in England and Wales impose behaviour-related covenants on the disposition of council houses purchased under the 'right to buy' **[para 7.352]** as a means of combatting anti-social behaviour on mixed tenure estates (see Scottish Executive Central Research Unit, *The Use of Civil Legal Remedies for Neighbour Nuisance in Scotland* (2000), para 11.3).
5   A covenant not to 'cause or permit' a certain specified form of user is not breached merely because the covenantor later agrees to sell the land affected to a third party who, to his knowledge, intends to engage in one of the proscribed forms of user (*Tophams Ltd v Earl of Sefton* [1967] 1 AC 50 at 64D, 68G, 75A–76A).
6   See e g *Clothier v Snell* (1966) 198 EG 27 at 28 (restrictive covenant against any building other than bungalow). A covenant prohibiting any building other than a private dwelling-house is infringed by the construction of flats (*Carmichael v Ripley Finance Co Ltd* [1974] 1 NZLR 557 at 559), but not by the erection of a covered swimming pool in the grounds of a private house (*Harlow v Hartog* (1978) 245 EG 140). A covenant limiting construction on a site to one house is breached by a subsequent conversion of that one house into two dwelling units (*Lawton v SHEV Pty Ltd* [1969] 2 NSWR 238 at 241–242). See also *Windsor Hotel (Newquay) Ltd v Allan* (1980) 77 Law Soc Gaz 733 (large barbeque held to be a 'building').

Planning obligations

9.141 In recent times a particularly prolific source of restrictive covenants has been the statutory power vested in local planning authorities to enter into an agreement with 'any person interested'[1] in land in their area for the purpose of 'restricting or regulating the development or use of the land.'[2] Such agreements are frequently pressed on developers of land in order to limit the extent of the proposed development or to promote the preservation or improvement of local amenities.[3] A section 106 agreement creates a 'planning obligation' which, once undertaken, remains valid for five years or such other period as is prescribed by its terms[4] and is enforceable both against the person entering into the obligation and against any person deriving title from that person.[5] The agreement, although concluded in exercise of a statutory power, is 'intended in every way to operate as a true restrictive covenant as established by well-known equitable principles.'[6]

1   A 'person interested' in relevant land includes a lessee. In the absence of an expressly drawn prohibition in the covenants of his lease, a lessee can therefore conclude a 'section 106 agreement' which unilaterally restricts the utility of the demised premises – at least during the unexpired term of the lease – adversely to the interests of the lessor. (Such an agreement must in many situations prejudice the landlord's reversion, causing damage not least through the impact of the agreement upon the landlord's negotiating position in subsequent rent reviews.) There seems, surprisingly, to be no clear authority disentitling a tenant from derogating in this way from the rights of his landlord – unless such conduct is actionable as a form of 'waste' **[para 1.33]**.

2   Town and Country Planning Act 1990, s 106(1) (formerly Town and Country Planning Act 1971, s 52(1)).

3   See e g *Re Martin's Application* (1987) 53 P & CR 146 at 153–154, (1989) 57 P & CR 119 at 124.

4   Town and Country Planning Act 1990, s 106A(3)–(4). The modification and discharge jurisdiction of LPA 1925, s 84 **[para 13.127]** remains available (see e g *Re Martin's Application* (1989) 57 P & CR 119).

5   Town and Country Planning Act 1990, s 106(3).

6   *Re Martin's Application* (1987) 53 P & CR 146 at 153.

Interaction with planning control

9.142   In many respects the role of the privately bargained freehold restrictive covenant has been overtaken, since the late 1940s, by various regimes of public planning law.[1] There is, however, increasing evidence that restrictive covenants frequently function as the residual guarantor of a degree of environmental amenity which individual citizens can no longer count on receiving at the hands of their local planning authority.[2] Existing public planning controls, operating under conditions of increasing pressure, cannot be concerned with all the detailed matters for which private covenants make provision. The device of the restrictive covenant thus remains a valuable and efficient means of land use control, in that it enables land use preferences to be targeted accurately – at minimal transaction cost – by the very persons best positioned to assess the environmental utility required in given contexts.

1   **[Para 13.158]**.

2   See Gray and Gray, 'The Future of Real Burdens in Scots Law' (1999) 3 Edinburgh Law Rev 229 at 234.

THE LIMITATIONS OF CONTRACTUAL REGULATION

9.143 Restrictive covenants are usually entered into either as a condition of the sale of land to the covenantor or on the proffering by the covenantee of some money payment or other valuable consideration (such as a reciprocal covenant undertaken by the covenantee himself).[1] Restrictive covenants are often generated by a simple bilateral agreement between two estate owners. Even more frequently, as in the case of a large building development, a network of intersecting bilateral agreements between the developer and each individual purchaser brings about a complex structure of locally enforceable regulations regarding land use within the area concerned.

1   Most restrictive covenants, being contained in a deed, are contractually enforceable even in the absence of valuable consideration. See also *Commonwealth of Australia v Western Australia* (1999) 196 CLR 392 at [282] per Callinan J.

Consequences of contractual privity

9.144 In such contexts each covenantor's undertaking has clear contractual force, the covenantee acquiring an undoubted contractual interest in the due performance of the promise. But a profound difficulty arises – irrespective of whether the contractual model involves only two covenanting parties or many. Each restrictive covenant is contractually effective as between covenantor and covenantee but, in accordance with the traditional rules concerning privity of contract, can never confer rights or obligations on others who later purchase the estates of the original covenanting parties. At common law only the contracting parties may claim the benefit or be called upon to suffer the burden of contractual terms. Yet any purposive scheme of land use control is fundamentally flawed if bilateral constraints on use, designed to produce beneficial long-term effects, are liable to be frustrated by any change in ownership of the tenements involved. A purely contractual scheme of land regulation, precisely because it fails to impact on third parties, is doomed to failure.[1]

1   See *Forestview Nominees Pty Ltd v Perpetual Trustees WA Ltd* (1996) 141 ALR 687 at 696–697.

Intervention of equity

9.145 The ineffectiveness of land use covenants in relation to derivative owners came to be remedied by one of the most revolutionary contributions made by equity to the law of property. During the 19th century equity began to fashion special rules governing covenants between freeholders. These rules were founded, not on privity of contract or even privity of estate,[1] but rather on 'the equitable principle of privity of conscience.'[2] This equitable regime recognised that contractually bargained arrangements designed to protect the commercial and environmental value of land could 'go beyond the frame of contract' and find enforcement, at least in equity if not at law, against third parties.[3] In the process the contractual right of the covenantee arrogated to itself the character of a proprietary interest in the covenantor's land. As always, equitable property is 'commensurate with equitable relief'[4] and enforcement is constitutive of the proprietary nature of the right.[5] The propertiness of a right is not a predetermined or intrinsic quality, but simply follows from the fact of wide curial recognition of the claim involved.[6]

1   For over four centuries the common law concept of privity of estate underpinned the enforcement of leasehold covenants between the successors of the original landlord and tenant **[para 14.242]**.
2   *Forestview Nominees Pty Ltd v Perpetual Trustees WA Ltd* (1998) 193 CLR 154 at 167 (High Court of Australia). See E H Abbot, 31 Yale LJ 127 at 131 (1921).
3   *Forestview Nominees Pty Ltd v Perpetual Trustees WA Ltd* (1998) 193 CLR 154 at 160.
4   *Hoysted v Federal Commissioner of Taxation* (1920) 27 CLR 400 at 423 per Isaacs J. See also *Hewitt v Court* (1982) 149 CLR 639 at 665 per Deane J.
5   See e g *Wily v St George Partnership Banking Ltd* (1999) 161 ALR 1 at 3–4 per Sackville J, 9 per Finkelstein J.
6   Gray, 'Property in Thin Air' [1991] CLJ 252 at 295–301. See *Attorney-General v Blake* [2001] 1 AC 268 at 281G–H per Lord Nicholls of Birkenhead.

THE EVOLUTION OF A NEW PROPRIETARY INTEREST

9.146   The mid-19th century was a period of significant expansion, when the tension was greatest between the desire to keep land unfettered by private covenants (and therefore profitable for industrial development) and the conflicting desire to curb the deleterious effects of commercial and urban growth (by preserving residential amenity for the private householder). These conflicting policies were reflected in the case law of the period. In *Keppell v Bailey*[1] Lord Brougham refused to allow that 'incidents of a novel kind can be devised and attached to land at the fancy and caprice of any owner.' He thus declined to enforce the burden of a covenant against a successor in title of the original covenantor, taking the view that such a burden, if enforced, would fetter the use and development of the land in perpetuity.[2]

1   (1834) 2 My & K 517 at 535, 39 ER 1042 at 1049.
2   (1834) 2 My & K 517 at 536–537, 39 ER 1042 at 1049–1050.

The decision in *Tulk v Moxhay*

9.147   The emphasis had altered significantly by the time *Tulk v Moxhay*[1] came to be decided in 1847. Lord Cottenham LC's ruling in this case is usually taken as marking the inception of a major development in the equitable rules concerning freehold covenants,[2] thereby reversing the earlier disinclination to allow land to be sterilised by the imposition of permanently binding freehold covenants. In *Tulk v Moxhay*, the claimant had sold a vacant piece of land in Leicester Square to E, who covenanted on behalf of himself, his heirs and his assigns that he would keep and maintain that land 'in an open state, uncovered with any buildings, in neat and ornamental order.' The land subsequently passed by a further conveyance into the hands of the defendant. The defendant's conveyance did not contain any such covenant as that spelt out in the original conveyance from the claimant, but it was common ground that he had notice of the restrictive covenant imposed in respect of the open land. When the defendant attempted to build there in defiance of the covenant, the claimant sought an injunction to prevent him from doing so. Lord Cottenham LC upheld a decision at first instance granting the claimant the relief required.

1   (1848) 2 Ph 774, 41 ER 1143 [**para 13.108**].
2   The decision reached in *Tulk v Moxhay* was anticipated in two poorly reported cases decided by Sir Lancelot Shadwell, *Whatman v Gibson* (1838) 9 Sim 196 at 207, 59 ER 333 at 338, and *Mann v Stephens* (1846) 15 Sim 377 at 378, 60 ER 665 at 666. See A W B Simpson, *A History of The Land Law* (2nd edn Oxford 1986), pp 257–258.

9.148   Lord Cottenham took an entirely different view from that adopted earlier by Lord Brougham in *Keppell v Bailey*. In the present case, Lord Cottenham held that an injunction should be granted restraining the defendant from acting in violation of the restrictive covenant. This decision was grounded on the stern view taken by equity in matters of conscience. The Lord Chancellor accepted the argument that the real question was

> not whether the covenant runs with the land, but whether a party shall be permitted to use the land in a manner inconsistent with the contract entered into by his vendor, and with notice of which he purchased. Of course, the price would be affected by the covenant, and nothing could be more inequitable than that the original purchaser should be able to sell the property the next day for a greater price, in consideration of the assignee being allowed to escape from the liability which he had himself undertaken.[1]

In order to preclude such an unconscionable outcome, Lord Cottenham concluded that the court should enforce the relevant covenant against any party purchasing with notice of it, 'for if an equity is attached to the property by the owner, no one purchasing with notice of that equity can stand in a different situation from the party from whom he purchased.'[2]

1   (1848) 2 Ph 774 at 777–778, 41 ER 1143 at 1144.
2   (1848) 2 Ph 774 at 778, 41 ER 1143 at 1144.

The reception of *Tulk v Moxhay* in the case law

9.149   The decision in *Tulk v Moxhay* was broadly based. Equity was prepared to intervene in restraint of any unconscionable conduct in respect of a contractual undertaking in relation to land of which the wrongdoer – albeit not a contracting party – nevertheless had notice. The argument which had prevailed before Lord Cottenham LC was capable of wide application. Indeed, the view adopted in *Tulk v Moxhay*, far from leading to a sterilisation of land use, could even be seen as promoting the commerciability of land. As

Lord Cottenham clearly recognised, unless restrictive covenants could be enforced against a covenantor's successors, 'it would be impossible for an owner of land to sell part of it without incurring the risk of rendering what he retains worthless.'[1] The decision in *Tulk v Moxhay* was invoked with enthusiasm during the years which followed. The ruling was applied to both positive and negative covenants[2]; it was applied on behalf of litigants who held no estate in the land benefited by the covenant; it was even applied outside the realm of real property.[3]

1   (1848) 2 Ph 774 at 777, 41 ER 1143 at 1144.
2   *Forestview Nominees Pty Ltd v Perpetual Trustees WA Ltd* (1996) 141 ALR 687 at 697.
3   See A W B Simpson, *A History of The Land Law* (2nd edn Oxford 1986), p 259.

The mutation of contractual into proprietary interests

9.150   The doctrine in *Tulk v Moxhay* had a dramatic effect upon both the law of contract and the law of property. The covenantee was widely regarded as having not merely a contractual interest in the performance of the covenant made with him, but also a *proprietary* interest in the land of the covenantor.[1]

1   See *Re Nisbet and Potts' Contract* [1905] 1 Ch 391 at 398 per Farwell J; *Forestview Nominees Pty Ltd v Perpetual Trustees WA Ltd* (1996) 141 ALR 687 at 697 per French J.

Allocation of equitable property to the covenantee

9.151   As a consequence of the equitable innovation brought about by *Tulk v Moxhay*, both the affected freeholder and the restrictive covenantee could truthfully assert that each held some form of 'property' in the servient land, albeit graded by differing degrees of intensity.[1] The freeholder retained 'property' in his land although burdened by a qualified power of veto over user vested in the covenantee; and in so far as the covenantee enjoyed a significant control over user, he too could claim a significant quantum of 'property' in the same land.[2] In reality the proprietary interest created by restrictive land-related obligations gave both covenantor and covenantee a strategic stake in the constructive co-ordination of their respective user-preferences.[3] Consistently with its historic provenance, the covenantee's entitlement is nowadays formalised, within the canon of property rights enshrined in the 1925 legislation, as an *equitable* proprietary interest. Not being included within the category of proprietary interests capable of existence at law,[4] the restrictive covenant can subsist only in equity.[5]

1   See Gray and Gray, 'The Idea of Property in Land', in S Bright and J K Dewar (ed), *Land Law: Themes and Perspectives* (OUP 1998), pp 42–43.
2   'The benefit of a restrictive covenant ... can constitute a valuable asset. It is incorporeal but it is, nonetheless, property' (*Commonwealth of Australia v State of Tasmania* (1983) 158 CLR 1 at 286 per Deane J). See also *Collins v Castle* (1887) 36 Ch D 243 at 254–255 per Kekewich J; *Attorney-General v Blake* [2001] 1 AC 268 at 298E per Lord Hobhouse of Woodborough; *Commonwealth of Australia v Western Australia* (1999) 196 CLR 392 at [282] per Callinan J.

3   Restrictive covenants, rather like easements, have helped to coordinate the simultaneous exercise of compatible modes of land use, without necessitating costly buy-outs of neighbouring land in order merely to secure optimal benefits for one's own land **[para 8.3]**.
4   See LPA 1925, s 1(1)–(2) **[para 2.125]**.
5   See LPA 1925, s 1(3) **[para 2.127]**.

Effect on third parties

9.152   In a manner similar to the evolution of the estate contract,[1] the covenantee's contractual right to control activities on the land of the covenantor enlarged into a proprietary right in land.[2] As *Tulk v Moxhay* so palpably demonstrated, the covenantee's entitlement was capable of binding all third parties into whose hands that land came, until such time as the covenantor's land was conveyed to a bona fide purchaser of a legal estate for value without notice of the covenant.[3] However, the source of this binding effect was neither the old common law of privity of estate[4] nor even the fact that a successor in title to the covenantor had notice of the covenantee's entitlement.[5] The *Tulk v Moxhay* doctrine has been attributed to a recognition by the courts of equity of 'the importance attached to the preservation of the value of the benefited land against activities, not only of the covenantor, but also of third parties dealing in the burdened land.'[6] Accordingly (and in keeping with an equitable concept of 'privity of conscience') equity imposed on the covenantor's successor 'a "constructive duty", coextensive with the express duty of the covenantor to the covenantee', to observe the terms of the original covenant.[7] This was equitable intervention in its amplest form – the imposition of obligations of conscience on those who could fairly be regarded as 'privy' to the undertaking given by the covenantor. This expanded regime of enforcement made the privately bargained restrictive covenant effectively the forerunner of much modern state-controlled land use regulation. The new equitable regime relating to covenants not only supplemented the common law rules relating to the transmission of the benefit and burden of covenants,[8] but came to serve as an early and invaluable form of environmental protection in the developing urban context.[9]

1   **[Para 9.19]**.
2   See *Wily v St George Partnership Banking Ltd* (1999) 161 ALR 1 at 3–4 per Sackville J.
3   The equitable rules governing the enforcement of freehold restrictive covenants has now been heavily modified by statute. For further detail, see Chapter 13 **[paras 13.113–13.115]**.
4   If privity of estate were the basis of *Tulk v Moxhay*, absence of notice would be no defence to a claim for breach of a covenant (see *Forestview Nominees Pty Ltd v Perpetual Trustees WA Ltd* (1998) 193 CLR 154 at 163).
5   Under the *Tulk v Moxhay* doctrine, for example, a purchaser of an equitable estate from the covenantor was bound even without notice (see *London and South Western Railway Co v Gomm* (1882) 20 Ch D 562 at 583 per Jessel MR; *Rogers v Hosegood* [1900] 2 Ch 388 at 405; *Re Nisbet and Potts' Contract* [1906] 1 Ch 386 at 406; *Forestview Nominees Pty Ltd v Perpetual Trustees WA Ltd* (1998) 193 CLR 154 at 166).
6   *Forestview Nominees Pty Ltd v Perpetual Trustees WA Ltd* (1998) 193 CLR 154 at 164 (High Court of Australia).
7   *Forestview Nominees Pty Ltd v Perpetual Trustees WA Ltd* (1998) 193 CLR 154 at 167. See also *Doyle v Phillips (No 1)* (1997) 8 BPR 15523 at 15526 per Young J.
8   **[Para 13.63]**.

9   Restrictive covenants often operate as a localised form of private legislation, preserving various kinds of residential and environmental amenity for generations of successive owners. Indeed the modern rejuvenation of the 'building scheme' or 'scheme of development' is explicitly premised on the recognition of an intention 'to lay down what has been referred to as a local law for the estate for the common benefit of all the several purchasers of it' (see *Re Dolphin's Conveyance* [1970] Ch 654 at 662A per Stamp J [**para 13.101**]).

Gradual restriction of the scope of *Tulk v Moxhay*

9.153   It was inevitable that, with the passage of time, the broad doctrine of *Tulk v Moxhay* should be modified. Aware of the potential scope of the doctrine, the courts had begun even during the closing decades of the 19th century to limit its application by defining precise qualities which required to be possessed by covenants before they could rank as equitable interests in the land of the covenantor.[1] In *London and South Western Railway Co v Gomm*,[2] Jessel MR was already re-interpreting the doctrine in *Tulk v Moxhay* as 'either an extension in equity of the doctrine of *Spencer's Case* to another line of cases, or else an extension in equity of the doctrine of negative easements.'[3] Thus the new doctrine had its 'wings clipped'.[4] Covenants began to be enforced against third parties on the same conditions as attached to the enforcement of easements, with the result that equity imposed such extra requirements as that there be a servient and a dominant tenement.[5]

1   See H W R Wade, (1952) 68 LQR 337 at 348. It has been suggested that the laissez faire approach to land obligations following *Tulk v Moxhay* was ended when it was realised that the equitable theory had been widely manipulated for the purpose of enforcing commercial monopolistic interests. 'By defeating arrangements aimed at capturing part of the market in perpetuity, title was once again salvaged from becoming a permanent carrier of all sorts of obligations' (see U Reichman, 'Judicial Supervision of Servitudes' 7 J Legal Stud 139 at 147 (1978)).

2   (1882) 20 Ch D 562 at 583. See also *Re Nisbet and Potts' Contract* [1905] 1 Ch 391 at 397 per Farwell J.

3   This did not, and does not, mean that restrictive covenants in fact *are* easements (see *Norton v Kilduff* [1974] Qd R 47 at 53E–G per Hart J). See also *White v Lauder Developments Ltd* (1976) 60 DLR (3d) 419 at 427. Jessel MR's analogy has since been described as 'seriously imperfect' (*Forestview Nominees Pty Ltd v Perpetual Trustees WA Ltd* (1998) 193 CLR 154 at 163), but it is undeniable that in the early case law restrictive covenants were variously likened to a 'quasi-negative easement' (*Kelly v Barrett* [1924] 2 Ch 379 at 405 per Warrington LJ) and an 'equitable charge' (*Re Nisbet and Potts' Contract* [1905] 1 Ch 391 at 397 per Farwell J). For further analogy with the model of easement, see *Newton Abbot Co-Operative Society Ltd v Williamson & Treadgold Ltd* [1952] Ch 286 at 293 per Upjohn J; *Bell v Norman C Ashton Ltd* (1956) 7 P & CR 359 at 364 per Harman J.

4   *Challis*, p 185. See also *Forestview Nominees Pty Ltd v Perpetual Trustees WA Ltd* (1996) 141 ALR 687 at 697.

5   See e g *Newton Abbot Co-Operative Society Ltd v Williamson & Treadgold Ltd* [1952] Ch 286 at 293 per Upjohn J.

DEFINING CHARACTERISTICS OF ENFORCEABLE RESTRICTIVE COVENANTS

9.154 As the doctrine in *Tulk v Moxhay* was slowly refined, it became clear that certain strict conditions attached to any covenant which was claimed to be enforceable in equity otherwise than between the original parties. Precisely because of the potential impact on third parties, the courts were careful – even from a relatively early period – to lay down threshold criteria governing the recognition of enforceable covenants.[1] These limitations were initially aimed at preventing the proliferation of undesirable 'clogs upon the title' of land.[2] Tight controls came to be exerted not only over the range of social and economic interests accorded protection in the law of covenants, but also over the technical operation of the rules governing enforcement.[3]

1   **[Para 2.84]**.
2   **[Para 2.84]**.
3   For example, the courts construe strictly the specified duration of restrictive covenants (see e g *Dano Ltd v Earl Cadogan* [2004] 1 P & CR 169 at [14], [18]).

9.155 While something of this cautious concern still remains today at the core of the legal response, it is clear that in recent times the courts have adopted a more sympathetic view of restrictive covenants. This relaxation of approach may in part reflect a general change in community attitudes towards the importance of preserving the attractiveness of local environments.[1] It may also owe something to the increased availability of means for scrutinising the contemporary merit of restrictions and, where appropriate, for modifying or discharging unnecessary or outdated covenants.[2] Nevertheless certain requirements (over and above requirements of register entry[3]) must be met before a covenant can be enforced outside the original covenant relationship. The defining characteristics of the enforceable restrictive covenant include the following:
–   the covenant must be negative or restrictive of the user of land[4]
–   the covenant must relate to an identifiable dominant tenement[5]
–   the covenant must benefit or accommodate the dominant tenement[6]
–   the covenant must have been intended to run with the covenantor's land.[7]

1   See *Application of Fox* (1981) 2 BPR 9310 at 9321 per Wootten J.
2   **[Para 13.127]**.
3   **[Paras 13.113–13.115]**.
4   **[Para 9.156]**.
5   **[Para 9.159]**.
6   **[Para 9.164]**.
7   **[Para 9.170]**.

THE COVENANT MUST BE NEGATIVE OR RESTRICTIVE OF THE USER OF LAND

9.156 If the application of *Tulk v Moxhay* was to be limited by analogy to the doctrine of negative easements, the first limiting factor to emerge was the rule that equity would take cognisance of only those covenants which are, in their nature, truly negative or restrictive of the user of land.[1] In *Haywood v Brunswick Permanent Benefit Building Society*,[2] the Court of Appeal declared the equitable principle underlying *Tulk v Moxhay* to have no application to positive covenants and accordingly declined to enforce against an assignee from the covenantor a positive covenant to build and repair.[3] In the view of Brett LJ, equity would henceforth enforce only those covenants 'restricting the mode of using the land.'[4] Thus, from at least this point onwards, the burden of a positive covenant became unenforceable, both at law and in equity, against successors of the original covenantor. Furthermore, since the purview of equity was now confined to restrictive covenants, the remedy given by equity in respect of enforceable restrictive covenants became pre-eminently the remedy of injunction.[5]

1   See C D Bell, '*Tulk v Moxhay* Revisited' [1981] Conv 55. For the view that the doctrine in *Tulk v Moxhay*, as originally formulated, applied only to negative covenants, compare R Griffith, '*Tulk v Moxhay* Reclarified' [1983] Conv 29, but see also [1983] Conv 327 (C D Bell). The idea that the original doctrine related to both positive and negative covenants seems to be supported by *Morland v Cook* (1868) LR 6 Eq 252 at 265–266; *Cooke v Chilcott* (1876) 3 Ch D 694 at 701–702.
2   (1881) 8 QBD 403.
3   See *Shropshire CC v Edwards* (1983) 46 P & CR 270 at 274.
4   (1881) 8 QBD 403 at 408.
5   See *Forestview Nominees Pty Ltd v Perpetual Trustees WA Ltd* (1998) 193 CLR 154 at 164 (High Court of Australia).

Enforceable covenants must restrict the user of land

9.157   One corollary of the limiting approach of equity was that the emerging regime had no relevance to purely personal covenants which did not constrain the mode of user of a servient tenement.[1] In a strict sense a restrictive covenant must 'control the use of the land itself and not simply control a party to the agreement',[2] even if such control has the effect of 'indirectly restricting the use of the land.'[3] It has been said, although with some danger of beguiling circuity, that the test of a true restrictive covenant is that it must create on behalf of the covenantee 'an interest in the covenantor's land.'[4]

1   There is today some doubt, in this context, whether an anti-social behaviour covenant [**para 9.140**] is truly restrictive of the user of land (see Scottish Executive Central Research Unit, *The Use of Civil Legal Remedies for Neighbour Nuisance in Scotland* (2000), para 11.4).
2   A covenant restraining alienation of the covenantor's land has, nevertheless, been held to constitute a restrictive covenant in the required sense (*Hemingway Securities Ltd v Dunraven Ltd* (1995) 71 P & CR 30 at 33). Compare *Re Nylar Foods Ltd and Roman Catholic Episcopal Corp of Prince Rupert* (1988) 48 DLR (4th) 175 at 179. See also *Noble v Alley* [1951] 1 DLR 321 at 326.
3   See eg *Palm Beach Lands Pty Ltd v Marshall* (1988) NSW ConvR ¶55–411 at 57,773 per Needham J (covenant restricting building without covenantee's prior written approval held to be a mere personal covenant). Compare, however, *Cryer v Scott Brothers (Sunbury) Ltd* (1988) 55 P & CR 183.
4   *White v Lauder Developments Ltd* (1975) 60 DLR (3d) 419 at 427.

Criterion of negative or restrictive quality

9.158   The question whether a covenant is *restrictive* always involves a test of substance.[1] A covenant phrased in a positive manner may nevertheless constitute a restrictive covenant, as is the case, for instance, with a covenant 'to use the property for residential purposes only.'[2] Conversely, a covenant 'not to let the premises fall into disrepair' is, on closer examination, a positive repairing covenant. A rule of thumb commonly used to test the nature of a covenant of dubious status is the question whether the performance of the covenant requires the expenditure of money. If the covenantor is required 'to put his hand into his pocket', the covenant is usually positive in nature.[3] It is not fatal to enforceability that a covenant contains both positive and negative obligations. There is no 'doctrine of contagious proximity',[4] and a positive obligation may be binding if it is no more than a condition of an accompanying negative covenant.[5]

1   See *Shepherd Homes Ltd v Sandham (No 2)* [1971] 2 All ER 1267 at 1272b per Megarry J; *Ceda Drycleaners Ltd v Doonan* [1998] 1 NZLR 224 at 235.
2   *German v Chapman* (1877) 7 Ch D 271 at 277–278, 280. See also *Abbey Homesteads (Developments) Ltd v Northamptonshire CC* (1987) 53 P & CR 1 at 5, 7, where an agreement that land should be 'reserved for school purposes' was regarded as being a 'covenant ... just as restrictive as the seminal one in *Tulk v Moxhay*.' See also *Collins v Castle* (1887) 36 Ch D 243 at 253–255.
3   See *Haywood v Brunswick Permanent Benefit Building Society* (1881) 8 QBD 403 at 409 per Cotton LJ; *Ceda Drycleaners Ltd v Doonan* [1998] 1 NZLR 224 at 235. See, however, *Westhoughton UDC v Wigan Coal and Iron Co Ltd* [1919] 1 Ch 159 at 170 (covenant not to let down surface without payment of compensation held to be negative).
4   See *Shepherd Homes Ltd v Sandham (No 2)* [1971] 2 All ER 1267 at 1272d per Megarry J.
5   See eg *Ceda Drycleaners Ltd v Doonan* [1998] 1 NZLR 224 at 236–237 (covenant not to trade at premises unless a current fully paid-up member of local business association).

THE COVENANT MUST RELATE TO AN IDENTIFIABLE DOMINANT TENEMENT

9.159   On a clear analogy with the law of easements,[1] equity takes cognisance of only those covenants which create a relationship of benefit between two separate parcels of land. A restrictive covenant can be enforced against strangers only if it relates to a defined servient tenement and is appurtenant to an ascertainable dominant tenement.[2] The covenantee must own an estate in the dominant tenement at the date of the making of the covenant[3] and the covenantor must likewise own an estate in the servient tenement.[4] Thus there can generally be no restrictive covenant in gross: there must always be an 'anchor' parcel of land to which the benefit of the restrictive covenant is tied.[5] Any attempt to annex the benefit of a restrictive covenant to land not owned by the covenantee is ineffective.[6] The maximum period for which a covenantor can bind his land is limited, moreover, by the duration of his estate in that land.[7] Thus, for instance, a lessee covenanting with a party other than his lessor can impose a restrictive covenant on the leasehold premises in order to benefit other land during, but not beyond, the term of his lease.[8]

1   **[Para 8.26]**.
2   There is no strict requirement that the deed of covenant should positively and clearly identify the dominant and servient tenements. It is sufficient in English law that the dominant land is ascertainable with reasonable certainty (see *Renals v Cowlishaw* (1879) 11 Ch D 866 at 868–869; *Shropshire CC v Edwards* (1983) 46 P & CR 270 at 275). Contrast, on this point, the law of New South Wales (Conveyancing Act 1919, s 88(1); *Re Louis and the Conveyancing Act* [1971] 1 NSWLR 164 at 178A). Under the Land Registration Act 2002, however, the entry of a 'notice' in respect of a restrictive covenant must now sufficiently identify the servient estate or affected portion thereof (see LRR 2003, r 84(2)).
3   *Application of Fox* (1981) 2 BPR 9310 at 9312. This rule is particularly relevant where a vendor subdivides land and takes a restrictive covenant from each respective purchaser on sale. Only under a 'scheme of development' or 'building scheme' **[para 13.97]** can the vendor extract a covenanted benefit on behalf of a dominant tenement in which he no longer retains any interest (*Re Mack and the Conveyancing Act* [1975] 2 NSWLR 623 at 630E). In all other circumstances the courts are unwilling to sever away that part of a supposed dominant tenement which was not owned by the covenantee in order that the covenant should remain enforceable in respect of the portion in which he did have a relevant estate (see *Application of Magney* (1981) 2 BPR 9358 at 9359).
4   A restrictive covenant is normally extinguished by unity of possession of the dominant and servient tenements **[para 9.171]**.
5   For an argument that the prohibition on restrictive covenants in gross should be eliminated, see S F French, 73 Cornell L Rev 928 at 941–947 (1987–88).
6   See *Doyle v Phillips (No 1)* (1997) 8 BPR 15523 at 15525, where Young J refuted the claim that any assistance could be found in the equivalent of LPA 1925, s 56(1) **[para 13.39]**, since this provision relates to a 'covenant' in the sense of 'a promise by deed in a lease or conveyance rather than a restrictive covenant which is enforceable in equity under the doctrine of *Tulk v Moxhay*.'
7   Covenants may be imposed only to the extent that the land is not encumbered by prior interests. A prior right of way vested in a third party thus has controlling effect over any terms agreed between covenantor and covenantee (see *Doe v Registrar General* (1997) 8 BPR 15803 at 15810).
8   See *Wilkes v Spooner* [1911] 2 KB 473 at 480; *Doe v Registrar General* (1997) 8 BPR 15803 at 15810.

Purpose of requirement of dominant tenement

9.160   The prohibition on restrictive covenants in gross is sometimes rationalised on the basis that there must always be some identifiable landowner with whom it is possible to bargain for a discharge or modification of the covenant. Alternatively it can be said that the requirement of a dominant tenement operates effectively as a test of standing, ensuring that claimants have a legitimate interest in the enforcement of particular covenants.

Reasonable proximity of dominant and servient tenements

9.161   Dominant and servient tenements need not be immediately adjacent. However, the party who seeks to enforce a restrictive covenant must be able to demonstrate that his tenement – although not necessarily contiguous with – is at least reasonably proximate to the servient tenement, since otherwise the requirement of benefit is unlikely to be satisfied. As was indicated by Pollock MR in *Kelly v Barrett*,[1] 'land at Clapham would be too remote and unable to carry a right to enforce ... covenants in respect of ... land at Hampstead.'[2]

1   [1924] 2 Ch 379 at 404.
2   See also *McGuigan Investments Pty Ltd v Dalwood Vineyards Pty Ltd* [1970] 1 NSWR 686 at 690–691 (covenant held incapable of benefiting land 17 miles distant from supposed dominant tenement); *Clem Smith Nominees Pty Ltd v Farrelly* (1978) 20 SASR 227 at 236 (covenant not enforced where tenements separated by 35 km).

Reinforcement of the requirement of dominance

9.162   The classic requirement of dominant ownership was affirmed most clearly in *London County Council v Allen*.[1] Here the Court of Appeal held that the claimant was unable to enforce a restrictive covenant against the covenantor's successor, on the ground that the claimant was not in possession of, or interested in, any land for the benefit of which the covenant had been taken.[2] The requirement that there be a dominant tenement carries the additional implication that if the covenantee parts with all the land for the benefit of which the restrictive covenant was taken, he ceases to be able to enforce the covenant except against the original covenantor.[3] Even as against the latter, his remedy is limited to the recovery of nominal damages.

1   [1914] 3 KB 642. See D J Hayton, (1971) 87 LQR 539 at 542–543.
2   See also *Tophams Ltd v Earl of Sefton* [1967] 1 AC 50 at 81A per Lord Wilberforce; *Peabody Donation Fund v London Residuary Body* (1988) 55 P & CR 355 at 359–360.
3   *Chambers v Randall* [1923] 1 Ch 149 at 157–158 per Sargant J; *Formby v Barker* [1903] 2 Ch 539 at 550–551; *Miles v Easter* [1933] Ch 611 at 630–631; *Pirie v Registrar-General* (1963) 109 CLR 619 at 628. See e g *Thompson v Potter* [1980] BCL 764.

Exceptions to the requirement of dominant land

9.163   Only limited exceptions are made from the otherwise stringent requirement of dominant ownership. The requirement is abrogated, for instance, on the last sale under a scheme of development.[1] Moreover, following the decision in *Hall v Ewin*,[2] it is clear that a lessor's reversion provides a sufficient dominant tenement for the enforcement of restrictive covenants contained in a lease.[3] Nowadays many public and quasi-public bodies are exempted by statute from any requirement of dominant ownership. In consequence of the inconvenient ruling in *London County Council v Allen*,[4] numerous bodies have been given specific authority to enforce restrictive covenants in gross, ie even though they are not possessed of any dominant land which might serve as a base for enforcement in the conventional sense.[5] For example, local planning authorities may enter into restrictive planning agreements with land developers for the purpose of guaranteeing or enhancing the preservation of local amenities, even though such covenants are unattached to any definable dominant tenement.[6]

1   **[Para 13.97]**. Here, of course, the common vendor retains nothing which even remotely resembles a dominant tenement (see *Re Mack and the Conveyancing Act* [1975] 2 NSWLR 623 at 630E).

2   (1887) 37 Ch D 74 **[para 14.309]**. See also *Regent Oil Co Ltd v J A Gregory (Hatch End) Ltd* [1966] Ch 402 at 433A–B, F per Harman LJ.
3   Likewise a mortgagee's interest in mortgaged land is a sufficiently real interest to enable the mortgagee to enforce a restrictive covenant (see *Regent Oil Co Ltd v J A Gregory (Hatch End) Ltd* [1966] Ch 402 at 433D–F).
4   [1914] 3 KB 642 **[para 9.162]**.
5   The dispensation extends, for instance, to local authorities (see HA 1985, s 609), the National Trust (see National Trust Act 1937, s 8; *National Trust v Midlands Electricity Board* [1952] 1 All ER 298 at 302A), and the Nature Conservancy Council (Countryside Act 1968, s 15(4)).
6   Town and Country Planning Act 1990, s 106(1) **[para 9.141]**. A 'section 106 agreement' or 'planning obligation' is enforceable 'as if the local planning authority were possessed of adjacent land and as if the agreement had been expressed to be made for the benefit of such land' (T&CPA 1990, s 106(3)). See *Ransom & Luck Ltd v Surbiton BC* [1949] Ch 180 at 194; *Re Martin's Application* (1987) 53 P & CR 146 at 153, (1989) 57 P & CR 119 at 124.

THE COVENANT MUST BENEFIT OR ACCOMMODATE THE DOMINANT TENEMENT

9.164   No restrictive covenant can be enforced in equity unless the covenant in question was made for the *benefit* and *protection* of dominant land held by the covenantee.[1] For this purpose a 'benefit' must be 'something affecting either the value of the land or the method of its occupation or enjoyment.'[2] The restriction on the servient tenement must be directed, in some way, towards strengthening title to the dominant tenement or enhancing the dominant owner's enjoyment of his own land by encumbering the servient land with rights which 'enlarge, amplify, secure or improve' the dominant owner's use of his own tenement.[3] Thus, for example, a covenant which forbids a covenantor to compete with a business conducted on the covenantee's land can properly be held to 'touch and concern' or 'benefit' the land in the required sense.[4] A covenant may benefit a dominant tenement even though it is expressed to enure for the benefit only of the covenantee and his successors and not for the benefit of any tenant in occupation of the dominant land.[5] The categories of 'benefit' are not closed, and there is nowadays increasing recognition that these categories are not confined to demonstrable economic advantages accruing to the dominant owner but include benefits 'not readily translated into economic values such as preservation of amenity or environment' in the vicinity of the claimed dominant land.[6]

1   *Formby v Barker* [1903] 2 Ch 539 at 552 per Vaughan Williams LJ. It used to be said, in the hallowed terminology of the law of covenants, that the restrictive covenant must 'touch and concern' the land of the covenantee (see e g *Rogers v Hosegood* [1900] 2 Ch 388 at 395; *Re Ballard's Conveyance* [1937] Ch 473 at 480; *Marquess of Zetland v Driver* [1939] 1 Ch 1 at 8). However, in more recent times the courts have moved away from the concept of covenants which 'touch and concern' the covenantee's land, in favour of a requirement that the restrictive covenant should 'benefit' the covenantee's land. The tests of 'benefit' or 'accommodation' and 'touching and concerning' quality are nevertheless substantially the same test (see *Application of Fox* (1981) 2 BPR 9310 at 9312; *Ceda Drycleaners Ltd v Doonan* [1998] 1 NZLR 224 at 237; *Forestview Nominees Pty Ltd v Perpetual Trustees WA Ltd* (1998) 193 CLR 154 at 170 (High Court of Australia)).
2   *Re Gadd's Land Transfer* [1966] Ch 56 at 66B per Buckley J. Impact on land value is not, however, conclusive of the question of 'benefit' (see *Application of Fox* (1981) 2 BPR 9310 at 9314–9315).

3   *Attorney-General (Ex rel Lumley) and Lumley v T S Gill & Son Pty Ltd* [1927] VLR 22 at 35 per Dixon A-J; *Forestview Nominees Pty Ltd v Perpetual Trustees WA Ltd* (1996) 141 ALR 687 at 699.

4   *Newton Abbot Co-operative Society Ltd v Williamson and Treadgold Ltd* [1952] Ch 286 at 293–294; *Re Quaffers Ltd's Application* (1988) 56 P & CR 142 at 152.

5   *Forestview Nominees Pty Ltd v Perpetual Trustees WA Ltd* (1998) 193 CLR 154 at 162 (where the High Court of Australia pointed out that such a covenant is likely to have been so drafted in order to confine to the dominant freeholder the commercial advantage of any later bargain for discharge or variation of the covenant).

6   *Forestview Nominees Pty Ltd v Perpetual Trustees WA Ltd* (1996) 141 ALR 687 at 699 per French J (Federal Court of Australia).

The purpose of the 'benefit' requirement

9.165   There is a certain opaque quality in the requirement that enforceable restrictive covenants must be made for the 'benefit' or 'protection' of dominant land. As Ungoed-Thomas J once observed,[1] '[t]he protection of land, qua land, does not have any rational or, indeed, any human significance, apart from its enjoyment by human beings, and the protection of land is for its enjoyment by human beings.'[2]

1   *Stilwell v Blackman* [1968] Ch 508 at 524G–525A.
2   An environmentalist would certainly quibble with a proposition of so anthropocentric a nature.

Benefit must be real rather than personal

9.166   A restrictive covenant capable of enforcement against third parties must, in some way, enhance the dominant land rather than connote some purely personal advantage or benefit for the covenantee. It is nevertheless a fairly rare restrictive agreement which does not augment the utility of the claimed dominant land. There is nowadays a general presumption that covenants confer benefit in the required sense unless such a view is demonstrably untenable.[1] For instance, most covenants restricting premises to residential use or prohibiting various kinds of development are of clear 'benefit' to the dominant land.

1   **[Para 9.169]**.

The 'benefit' requirement filters out undesirable long-term burdens on land

9.167   Not least in the area of restrictive covenants, the law is wary of 'long-term inhibitions to the realisation of the full potential of the servient tenement.'[1] It is clearly undesirable that *every* promise concerning activities on or in respect of that tenement should run with the land so as to affect third parties. The truth is that the 'benefit' criterion, by excluding commitments of a substantially personal character, silently filters out those contractual undertakings which, in the public interest, ought not to be imposed as long-term burdens upon any parcel of land. Agreements which serve merely to gratify some personal interest or whim dear to the heart of the covenantee should not be allowed to become permament blots on the title of the covenantor.

1   *Forestview Nominees Pty Ltd v Perpetual Trustees WA Ltd* (1998) 193 CLR 154 at 163.

9.168   Quite apart from covenants which contravene protective legislation such as the Sex Discrimination Act 1975 or the Race Relations Act 1976,[1] it would be entirely wrong that a covenantee's personal, ideological or religious prejudices should be visited indefinitely on successive owners of a servient tenement. It may be that X can validly commit himself, by a contractual promise made to his neighbour Y, that X's land shall never be used for the purpose of watching a particular television programme or for the private consumption of alcohol. The enforcement of conformity with a covenantee's eccentric or capricious convictions may indeed ensure a certain emotional satisfaction for the covenantee, but cannot be said in any relevant sense to confer a 'benefit' upon his land. In so far as such obligations are inimical to social values of personal liberty and identity, it is generally thought preferable that the range of enforceable land interests should be insulated from personal commitments of this kind.[2] In practice, the 'benefit' requirement provides a residual legal control over the deleterious social consequences otherwise flowing from the foolishness or lack of foresight which caused the original covenantor to commit himself to such miscalculated obligations.[3]

1   **[Para 14.96]**. See J F Garner, 'Racial Restrictive Covenants in England and the United States' (1972) 35 MLR 478; J D A Brooke-Taylor, [1978] Conv 24.
2   See U Reichman, 7 J Legal Stud 139 at 147–150 (1978); J L Winokur, (1989) Wisc L Rev 1 at 87–88.
3   See e g Gregory S Alexander, 73 Cornell L Rev 883 at 895–900 (1987–88); J E Stake, (1988) Duke LJ 925 at 934–935.

Attachment of benefit to large areas of land

9.169   In the past certain difficulties afflicted the question whether a particular restrictive covenant could be said to confer true benefit upon an alleged dominant tenement which was excessively large. In *Re Ballard's Conveyance*,[1] for example, a restrictive covenant had been made in favour of a covenantee who retained approximately 1,700 acres of land. Clauson J held that the covenant was not enforceable by the covenantee's successor in title, since it could not reasonably be maintained that the covenant in question conferred benefit upon the entirety of such an extensive dominant tenement as that claimed by the successor.[2] This unnecessarily strict approach has been abandoned in the modern case law.[3] The courts nowadays presume that a covenant confers benefit upon the alleged dominant tenement unless it is evident that such a conclusion is untenable.[4] As Brightman J indicated in *Wrotham Park Estate Co Ltd v Parkside Homes Ltd*,[5] restrictive covenants tend to be upheld 'so long as an estate owner may reasonably take the view that the restriction remains of value to his estate.'[6] The restriction will not be discarded 'merely because others may reasonably argue that the restriction is spent.'

1   [1937] Ch 473. See G R Y Radcliffe (1941) 57 LQR 203 at 210–211.
2   [1937] Ch 473 at 480–481.
3   The existence of benefit to the whole of a claimed dominant tenement is nowadays rarely a
     matter of dispute (see *J Sainsbury Plc v Enfield LBC* [1989] 1 WLR 590 at 595F–G). See also
     Application of Fox (1981) 2 BPR 9310 at 9314.
4   See e g *Wrotham Park Estate Co Ltd v Parkside Homes Ltd* [1974] 1 WLR 798 at 808D, where
     Brightman J stated that there 'can be obvious cases where a restrictive covenant clearly is, or
     clearly is not, of benefit to an estate. Between these two extremes ... it is not for the court to
     pronounce which is the correct view ... the court can only decide whether a particular view is
     one which can reasonably be held.' See [1974] CLJ 214 (C T Emery); *Lord Northbourne v
     Johnston & Son* [1922] 2 Ch 309 at 318–320; *Forestview Nominees Pty Ltd v Perpetual Trustees
     WA Ltd* (1996) 141 ALR 687 at 699–700 per French J.
5   [1974] 1 WLR 798 at 808F. See G H Newsom, [1974] JPL 130 at 133.
6   The onus is on the covenantor's successor in title to show that breach of a restrictive covenant
     could not possibly hurt the whole of the area claimed as the dominant tenement (see *Cryer v
     Scott Brothers (Sunbury) Ltd* (1988) 55 P & CR 183 at 196–197, 202–203).

THE COVENANT MUST HAVE BEEN INTENDED TO BE MADE ON BEHALF OF THE COVENANTOR'S SUCCESSORS

9.170   Since equity looks always to matters of intention,[1] no restrictive
covenant is enforceable against third parties unless it was intended by those
who created it to have a wider than purely personal impact. Nowadays this
requirement is easily satisfied. Unless a covenant is phrased in such a way that it
patently binds only the original covenantor,[2] there is a statutory presumption
that a covenant relating to any land of a covenantor 'shall be deemed to be
made by the covenantor on behalf of himself his successors in title and the
persons deriving title under him or them, and ... shall have effect as if such
successors and other persons were expressed.'[3] This rebuttable presumption
that covenants are not intended to be merely personal operates as 'a necessary
condition, but not a sufficient condition, for making the burden of the
covenants run with the land.'[4]

1   See, in this context, the Australian High Court's reference to 'the preference of equity for
     intention over form' (*Forestview Nominees Pty Ltd v Perpetual Trustees WA Ltd* (1998) 193
     CLR 154 at 169).
2   See *Re Royal Victoria Pavilion, Ramsgate* [1961] Ch 581 at 589.
3   In this context, 'successors in title' are deemed to include the owners and occupiers for the
     time being of relevant land (LPA 1925, s 79(2)). Section 79 has reference only to restrictive
     covenants entered into on or after 1 January 1926 (LPA 1925, s 79(3)).
4   *Morrells of Oxford Ltd v Oxford United Football Club Ltd* [2001] Ch 459 at [40] per Robert
     Walker LJ. In order that the burden should run with the land so as to bind successors, other
     conditions (generally relating to register entry) also require to be fulfilled [**para 13.113**].

EXTINGUISHMENT, MODIFICATION AND DISCHARGE OF RESTRICTIVE COVENANTS

9.171   Freehold restrictive covenants are extinguished by any supervening
unity of possession of the dominant and servient tenements, unless revived by
their common owner in a subsequent transfer of one of those tenements.[1]

Restrictive covenants may also be terminated by voluntary release (usually in return for a cash premium or equivalent value). There exists, moreover, a statutory jurisdiction, vested in the Lands Tribunal, to discharge or modify – with or without compensation – restrictive covenants which have become 'obsolete' or have come to 'impede some reasonable user of the land for public or private purposes.'[2]

1   *Re Tiltwood* [1978] Ch 269 at 280F; *Kerridge v Foley* [1964–5] NSWR 1958 at 1961; *Application of Caroline Chisholm Village Pty Ltd* (1980) 1 BPR 9507 at 9515. See also *Gyarfas v Bray* (1989) 4 BPR 9736 at 9751–9752; *Post Investments Pty Ltd v Wilson* (1990) 5 BPR 11146 at 11147.
2   LPA 1925, s 84(1). This jurisdiction is described in greater detail in Chapter 13 [**para 13.127**].

BENEFICIAL INTERESTS UNDER A TRUST OF LAND

9.172   A further, and extremely important, category of equitable proprietary rights in land emerges in the range of beneficial entitlements generated by various forms of trust.[1] These rights comprise the subject of the remainder of this chapter and will also be dealt with in Chapters 10 and 11.

1   On the essential nature of a trust, see Chapter 1 [**para 1.164**].

THE CONSTITUTION OF A BENEFICIAL INTEREST IN LAND

9.173   Any claim to a beneficial interest in real property necessarily presupposes the existence of some kind of trust.[1] As Lord Diplock indicated in *Gissing v Gissing*,[2] it must be shown 'that the person in whom the legal estate is vested holds it as a trustee upon trust to give effect to the beneficial interest of the claimant as cestui que trust.' The origin of this beneficial ownership lies in the willingness of equity to direct the legal owner – the trustee – to carry out the trust which he has expressly or impliedly undertaken. And, because in the eyes of equity that which ought to have been done is regarded as having been done, the beneficiary is 'treated as immediately entitled to his interest in the trust property whether or not an order for the execution of the trust has been made against the trustee.'[3] In this way a moral obligation is converted into an equitable entitlement and the beneficiary's rights, although founded on the ability of the court to make an order *in personam*, become a proprietary interest in the trust asset.[4]

1   *Gissing v Gissing* [1971] AC 886 at 900B per Viscount Dilhorne; *Burns v Burns* [1984] Ch 317 at 326F, 330H–331A per Fox LJ; *Allen v Snyder* [1977] 2 NSWLR 685 at 689F; *Thwaites v Ryan* [1984] VR 65 at 69.
2   [1971] AC 886 at 904G–H.
3   *Swiss Bank Corpn v Lloyds Bank Ltd* [1979] Ch 548 at 565G per Browne-Wilkinson J. See also *Mountney v Treharne* [2003] Ch 135 at [71] per Jonathan Parker LJ.
4   [**Paras 1.162–1.189, 9.8**].

9.174   Fundamental to the ascertainment of the beneficial ownership of land is the proposition that a transfer of the legal title carries with it, prima facie, the absolute beneficial interest in the property conveyed.[1] Equity, in this respect, 'follows the law'[2] and, indeed, there is no strict need to distinguish between legal and equitable ownership whilst land is vested in one person absolutely.[3] Thus a conveyance to A of a legal estate in land vests in A the whole of the beneficial interest unless some other person, B, is able to 'establish a basis upon which equity would intervene on [his or] her behalf.'[4] Equity will intervene on behalf of B only if such action is necessary in order to give effect to one or other of its doctrines.[5]

1   *Pettitt v Pettitt* [1970] AC 777 at 813H–814A per Lord Upjohn. See also *Vandervell v IRC* [1966] Ch 261 at 287G; *Gissing v Gissing* [1971] AC 886 at 902A per Lord Pearson; *Bernard v Josephs* [1982] Ch 391 at 402D; *Burns v Burns* [1984] Ch 317 at 330H, 336D; *Currie v Hamilton* [1984] 1 NSWLR 687 at 690E; *Ali v Khan* [2002] EWCA Civ 974 at [19] per Morritt V-C.
2   **[Para 9.7]**.
3   **[Paras 1.161, 11.155]**.
4   *Allen v Snyder* [1977] 2 NSWLR 685 at 701E per Mahoney JA. The onus is on the claimant to demonstrate that the beneficial entitlement does not coincide with the legal title (*Crisp v Mullings* (1976) 239 EG 119 per Russell LJ). See also *Bernard v Josephs* [1982] Ch 391 at 404H–405B, 407D–E; [1983] CLJ 30 (Gray).
5   **[Para 1.162]**. See *Commissioner of Stamp Duties (Queensland) v Livingston* [1965] AC 694 at 712E per Viscount Radcliffe; *Muschinski v Dodds* (1985) 160 CLR 583 at 616 per Deane J.

Beneficial ownership is engrafted on to legal title

9.175   All trusts are founded on the willingness of equity, consistently with its historic concern with conscience, to call into existence some form of equitable interest or ownership in opposition to the legal title.[1] The legal owner has at law all the rights of an absolute owner, but the beneficiary is entitled to compel him to hold the legal title in conformity with obligations imposed by equity. In this way the owner of the legal estate is conventionally described as holding his legal title on trust (in whole or part) for the claimant or 'cestui que trust'; and the beneficiary's right constitutes an equitable estate engrafted on to the legal estate by the doctrinal force of equity.[2] Nowadays almost all claims to a beneficial interest in land involve the existence of a 'trust of land' governed by the Trusts of Land and Appointment of Trustees Act 1996.

1   **[Para 1.163]**.
2   See *Re Transphere Pty Ltd* (1986) 5 NSWLR 309 at 311E–F per McLelland J. It matters not, for present purposes, whether the legal ownership is concentrated in one trustee alone or in several trustees collectively. Nor is it relevant whether beneficial ownership is asserted by more than one claimant or even shared with some or all of the trustees in some independent capacity as cestui que trust.

The role of conscientious obligation

9.176   The point cannot be over-emphasised that the trust embodies the practical realisation of equity's historic *Leitmotiv* – the idea that conscientious obligation takes priority over strict legal right.[1] This does not mean, however, that a trust arises in *every* case where broad considerations of justice or fair play

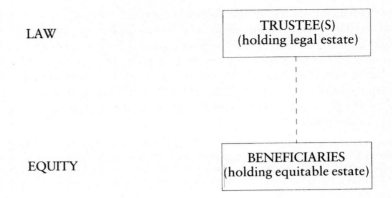

Fig. 14

seem to demand that a trust should come into existence. Such an outcome would ultimately cause every litigant's claim 'to be consigned to the formless void of individual moral opinion.'[2] The tradition of English equity (as distinct, perhaps, from that practised elsewhere in the common law world) is that the courts do not sit 'as under a palm tree, to exercise a general discretion to do what the man in the street, on a general overview of the case, might regard as fair.'[3] The ascertainment of a trust relationship is a measured task involving the structured application of equitable principle to pragmatic fact. It is nevertheless undeniable that some degree of controversy surrounds the definition of the precise circumstances which will permit equitable rights to be impressed on pre-existing legal titles under the mandate of conscience.

1   Gray, 'Equitable Property' (1994) 47(2) CLP 157 at 207, 214 [**para 1.162**].
2   See *Carly v Farrelly* [1975] 1 NZLR 356 at 367 per Mahon J.
3   *Springette v Defoe* [1992] 2 FLR 388 at 393D per Dillon LJ.

The role of intention

9.177   As befits a jurisdiction which is less impressed by form than by substance, equity's recognition of the trust focuses ultimately on matters of intention. Indeed, beneficial ownership depends fundamentally on intentions, proved or presumed, as to the equitable title in land.[1]

1   See *Hepworth v Hepworth* (1963) 110 CLR 309 at 317 per Windeyer J (an 'intention, proved or presumed, that a trust should exist is at the base of every trust'). See also *Pettitt v Pettitt* [1970] AC 777 at 813D per Lord Upjohn ('the beneficial ownership of the property in question must depend on the agreement of the parties determined at the time of its acquisition').

Express indications of beneficial ownership

9.178   Ownership of the legal estate in land is scarcely ever in doubt, since the identity of the current legal owner is usually firmly established by the relevant proprietorship register (in the case of a registered estate) or by the last deed of conveyance (in the case of an unregistered estate). In almost every case, therefore, the location of legal title is definitively ascertained by reference to a documentary source[1] and indeed the primary purpose of the transfer documents used in conveyancing is to indicate with precision the name of the next legal owner or owners.[2] These transfer documents may, of course, go on to clarify not merely matters of legal title but also details of beneficial ownership. Such declarations of beneficial entitlement, if included in the conveyance, are generally conclusive.[3]

1 Compare, however, the case of acquisition through adverse possession [**para 6.47**].
2 See *Tinsley v Milligan* [1992] Ch 310 at 337D per Ralph Gibson LJ.
3 [**Para 9.198**]. See *Pettitt v Pettitt* [1970] AC 777 at 813E per Lord Upjohn; *Bernard v Josephs* [1982] Ch 391 at 403C per Griffiths LJ; *Re Gorman (A Bankrupt)* [1990] 1 WLR 616 at 621C.

Unexpressed beneficial ownership

9.179 It is possible that the documentary title may remain silent as to beneficial ownership.[1] In such cases it is more difficult to ascertain the nature and quantum of the equitable interests in the land.[2] The details of beneficial ownership following transfer are sometimes not contained in any formal document or other writing and come into question only at some much later stage when a dispute arises.[3] When this happens it becomes necessary to render explicit that which was previously left unexpressed.[4]

1 See eg *McKenzie v McKenzie* [2003] EWHC 601 (Ch) at [63]–[67]. See now LRR 2003, rr 23(1), 58, 206(1), Sch 1 [**para 9.197**].
2 For evidence of the difficulties caused by undeclared beneficial ownership, see *Springette v Defoe* [1992] 2 FLR 388 at 390E, 396A–B; *Huntingford v Hobbs* [1993] 1 FCR 45 at 58C–D. Judges have long urged a general practice of declaring trust entitlements explicitly at the point of acquisition (see *Cowcher v Cowcher* [1972] 1 WLR 425 at 442C per Bagnall J; *Bernard v Josephs* [1982] Ch 391 at 403E–F per Griffiths LJ; *Goodman v Gallant* [1986] Fam 106 at 118F–G; but compare the despairing observations of Ward LJ in *Carlton v Goodman* [2002] 2 FLR 259 at [44]).
3 Disputes as to beneficial ownership may arise in many contexts. The issue of ownership may be precipitated by a bankruptcy or death, or in connection with tax liability, or even in unusual contexts such as arose in *Heron v Sandwell MBC* (1980) 255 EG 65 (payment of owner-occupier's supplement after compulsory purchase).
4 Occasionally a silence as to the precise nature of the intended beneficial ownership can be resolved by necessary implication from the terms of a conveyance. However, a standard declaration that the survivor of the transferees is entitled 'to give a valid receipt for capital money arising on a disposition of the land' does not constitute a declaration of trust indicating either beneficial joint tenancy or ultimate equality of entitlement (see *Harwood v Harwood* [1991] 2 FLR 274 at 288E–289C per Slade LJ; *Huntingford v Hobbs* [1993] 1 FCR 45 at 51F–52C per Sir Christopher Slade, 58E–59E per Steyn LJ; *Mortgage Corporation v Shaire* [2001] Ch 743 at 752E–753E per Neuberger J).

Family property

9.180 The ascertainment of undeclared beneficial ownership becomes particularly problematic in relation to land which is acquired for family use. The legal arrangements for joint family living are usually forged in a fairly ill-defined and inarticulate fashion, precise issues of beneficial entitlement emerging only years later on the termination of the relevant relationships by death or disaffection. Where parties have been married to each other, the courts are nowadays empowered by statute to overstep the technicalities of strict beneficial entitlement in resolving matters of dispute.[1] In dealing with the economic consequences of divorce, the law adopts 'a forward-looking perspective in which questions of ownership yield to the higher demands of relating the means of both to the needs of each, the first consideration given to the welfare of children.'[2] Where, however, the parties are not married, their economic rights must be worked out according to their strict entitlements in equity – a process which, as Waite J acknowledged in *Hammond v Mitchell*,[3] 'is anything but forward-looking and involves, on the contrary, a painfully detailed retrospect.' Nor is this process aided by the recognition in English law of any law of family or community property or any special regime of 'family assets'.[4] The mere fact that persons are members of the same family has no automatic effect on their respective property entitlements.[5] Their proprietary relations are still governed by the bleak and inflexible rules of the general law of property.

1   See Matrimonial Causes Act 1973, ss 23–25; Inheritance (Provision for Family and Dependants) Act 1975, ss 1–3. See also Matrimonial Proceedings and Property Act 1970, s 37 **[para 10.92]**.
2   *Hammond v Mitchell* [1991] 1 WLR 1127 at 1129D per Waite J. On the opposition between 'retrospective' and 'prospective' approaches to asset distribution on divorce, see Gray, *Reallocation of Property on Divorce* (Professional Books 1977), pp 278–325.
3   [1991] 1 WLR 1127 at 1129E.
4   See *Pettitt v Pettitt* [1970] AC 777 at 794G–795C per Lord Reid, 810F–G per Lord Hodson, 817A–G per Lord Upjohn; *Gissing v Gissing* [1971] AC 886 at 899G–900A per Viscount Dilhorne; *Burns v Burns* [1984] Ch 317 at 334F–G per May LJ.
5   *Grant v Edwards* [1986] Ch 638 at 651E–G per Mustill LJ.

Extrinsic aids to the discovery of intention

9.181   The method by which beneficial ownership is determined under such circumstances was explained in classic terms by the House of Lords in *Pettitt v Pettitt*.[1] Here Lord Upjohn pointed to the extrinsic aids which may be called into play when the documentary title performs only its minimal function of dealing with the legal ownership. Certain residual evidential devices exist to enable the court to discover the parties' intentions in respect of beneficial ownership and the court has recourse to these devices in the following order. *First*, the court may have regard to parol evidence as to the beneficial interests intended by the parties at the date of acquisition of the legal title.[2] *Second*, if such parol evidence is lacking or inadmissible or simply inconclusive, the court may draw inferences as to intention from the conduct of the parties both before and after the acquisition of the legal estate. *Third*, if even this fails to illuminate the relevant intentions of the parties, the court may apply the equitable presumptions as to intention. These presumptions represent merely the informed speculation of lawyers over the centuries as to the beneficial ownership most likely to have been intended by the parties in certain stylised situations.[3] These presumptions of equity are decisive of beneficial title only in the last resort[4] and they prevail only in the absence of other more compelling evidence of actual intention.[5]

1   [1970] AC 777 at 813F–G.
2   Parol evidence may be given not only by the parties to a transaction of purchase, but also by others (e g relatives or solicitors) who are in a position to testify to their intentions at that time (see *Hodgson v Marks* [1971] Ch 892 at 905C–E).
3   See *Pettitt v Pettitt* [1970] AC 777 at 823H per Lord Diplock [**para 10.22**]; *Muschinski v Dodds* (1985) 160 CLR 583 at 613.
4   See *McGrath v Wallis* [1995] 2 FLR 114 at 115A per Nourse LJ; *Stockholm Finance Ltd v Garden Holdings Inc* [1995] NPC 162 per Robert Walker J.
5   [**Para 10.22**].

CLASSIFICATION OF TRUSTS OF LAND

9.182   Classification is arid, but confusion is worse. 'Trusts of land' under the Trusts of Land and Appointment of Trustees Act 1996 can be classified as either *express* trusts or *implied* trusts, the latter category subdividing into further categories of *resulting* and *constructive* trusts (see *Fig.* 15).[1]

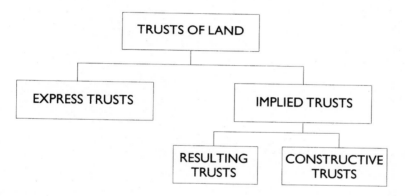

Fig. 15

1   This classification is widely accepted today (see *Cowcher v Cowcher* [1972] 1 WLR 425 at 430D, 431A per Bagnall J; *McKenzie v McKenzie* [2003] EWHC 601 (Ch) at [68]; *Barrios v Chiabrera* (1984) 3 BPR 9276 at 9278 per Powell J).

9.183   Consistently with the characteristic preoccupation of equity, the primacy of intention is highlighted in each of the three cases of trust with which following chapters of this book are concerned. The *express trust* is the very embodiment of an intention formulated by a legal owner regarding the beneficial ownership of his land.[1] The *resulting trust* gives effect to an intention presumed to have been formulated in the light of money contributions made in the context of a purchase of land.[2] The *constructive trust* arises in circumstances where it would be unconscionable not to give effect to a common intention or bargain which has provided the basis of the parties' mutual expectations and dealings.[3] The terminology used by courts and lawyers to refer to these different kinds of trust sometimes lacks uniformity and consistency,[4] but these confusions will be left aside for the moment in order to concentrate on the expressly created trust of land, thus reserving the difficulties of implied trusts for explanation in Chapter 10.

1   [Para 9.184].
2   [Para 10.8].
3   [Para 10.58].
4   [Para 10.6]. See *Birmingham Midshires Mortgage Services Ltd v Sabherwal* (2000) 80 P & CR 256 at 263 per Robert Walker LJ.

EXPRESS TRUSTS OF LAND

9.184   An express trust of land arises principally in two sorts of circumstance:
- *either* where A, the sole owner of an estate in Greenacre, expressly declares himself to be a trustee of that estate for B, whether absolutely or in respect of some limited or fractional beneficial interest[1] (*Fig.* 16)
- *or* where S, the sole owner of an estate in Redacre, transfers the legal estate to A, subject to a trust of that estate (accepted, and thus declared, by A) under which B is entitled to an absolute or limited or fractional beneficial interest (*Fig.* 17).

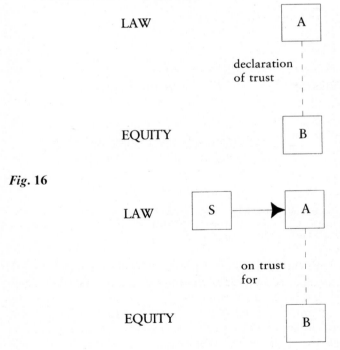

Fig. 16

Fig. 17

1   An estate owner cannot declare a valid trust in favour of himself absolutely: the declaration would give him no separate equitable rights [**paras 1.162, 9.174**]. See *DKLR Holding Co (No 2) Pty Ltd v Commissioner of Stamp Duties* [1980] 1 NSWLR 510 at 519B–C per Hope JA;

Wollondilly Shire Council v Picton Power Lines Pty Ltd (1991) 5 BPR 11503 at 11508 per
Young J; *Chief Commr of Stamp Duties v ISPT Pty Ltd* (1997) 45 NSWLR 639 at 647F–G per
Mason P. See also *Corin v Patton* (1990) 169 CLR 540 at 579 per Deane J.

Language creative of a trust

9.185   An express trust need not be couched in formal words or phrased in a
particular formula; any words which plainly evince an intention to create a trust
are sufficient.[1] It is even possible that 'by the use … of unguarded language, a
person may create a trust, as Monsieur Jourdain talked prose, without knowing
it',[2] but unless an intention to create a trust is clearly to be collected from the
language used and from the circumstances of the case, the courts will not be
astute to discover indications of such an intention.[3] An express trust can,
however, be generated by some loosely worded conferment of a fractional share
or life interest or even by the grant of some functional equivalent of a limited
interest, as where A undertakes to allow B rent-free occupation for life of some
of A's land.[4] Likewise the person who fondly indicates that he regards his
spouse or partner as having equal rights with him in his home may well find
that he has effectively created a trust of the legal estate in her favour.[5]

1   *Cowcher v Cowcher* [1972] 1 WLR 425 at 430E; *Bloch v Bloch* (1981) 37 ALR 55 at 59.
2   *Re Schebsman, decd* [1944] Ch 83 at 104 per Du Parcq LJ. See also *Tito v Waddell* (No 2)
    [1977] Ch 106 at 211F.
3   Trusts affecting certain kinds of person (i e the crown and its governmental agencies) tend not
    to be justiciable in the courts (see *Tito v Waddell* (No 2) [1977] Ch 106 at 222F–G). There are
    also certain kinds of premises in relation to the acquisition of which the courts seem anxious
    not to apply trust principles (e g barristers' chambers). See *Appleby v Cowley* (1982) Times,
    14 April.
4   See e g *Bannister v Bannister* [1948] 2 All ER 133, where an agreement for rent-free occupation
    for life was construed as a conferment of a life interest [**para 10.70**].
5   See *Rowe v Prance* [1999] 2 FLR 787 at 792–G, 795B–D, where persistent references to
    property as 'ours' were held to constitute an express declaration of trust in equal shares. (Here
    the trust property was a boat, but the same principle seems applicable to declarations in
    respect of realty which are supported by written evidence.)

Subject matter of the trust

9.186   An express declaration of trust may extend to the entire equitable
interest in the land (as where A constitutes himself a trustee for B absolutely) or
merely to some limited interest in the land (as where A holds henceforth on
trust to give effect to a life interest or a fractional share in B). However, no
express trust can be validly declared in respect of land in which the declarant
has as yet no proprietary interest.[1] Nor, obviously, can the declarant create a
trust of any larger estate than he himself owns.[2] Subject to these qualifications,
an express trust can be declared at any time and in respect of any land in which
the declarant is beneficially entitled.

1   *Dye v Dye* (1884) 13 QBD 147 at 157; *White v Cabanas Pty Ltd* (No 2) [1970] Qd R 395 at
    407E. By contrast, a *constructive* trust may attach to property which was not owned by the

declarant at the date of his declaration of trust (see *Stokes v Anderson* [1991] 1 FLR 391 at 398E–F per Nourse LJ; *Le Compte v Public Trustee* [1983] 2 NSWLR 109 at 111A).

2   *Dye v Dye* (1884) 13 QBD 147 at 157. A declaration of trust affecting the whole beneficial interest in co-owned land can be made only with the concurrence of all the co-owners (*Kronheim v Johnson* (1877) 7 Ch D 60 at 66).

STATUTORY REQUIREMENT OF FORMALITY

9.187   An express trust may take a wide variety of forms. It matters not whether an express trust is declared contemporaneously with the acquisition of the legal estate or at some later time. It is generally irrelevant whether an express trust nominates one beneficiary or many; the declaration may allocate various kinds or sizes of equitable entitlement. However, irrespective of the content of the express trust, one overriding rule prevails in English law. Although a declaration of trust relating to land need not itself be made in writing,[1] it is enforceable only if it is *evidenced* by signed writing.[2]

1   See *Randall v Morgan* (1805) 12 Ves 67 at 74, 33 ER 26 at 29 per Sir William Grant MR. There is, in other words, no superimposition of a requirement of writing by virtue of LPA 1925, s 53(1)(a). See, on equivalent Australian legislation, *Secretary, Department of Social Security v James* (1990) 95 ALR 615 at 622; *Hagan v Waterhouse* (1991) 34 NSWLR 308 at 385F–386A.

2   See D C Wilde, 'Formalities for Declaring Trusts of Land', in P Jackson and D C Wilde (ed), *Contemporary Property Law* (Ashgate 1999), p 204.

Written evidence of the trust

9.188   Section 53(1)(b) of the Law of Property Act 1925 provides that

a declaration of any trust respecting any land or any interest therein must be manifested and proved by some writing signed by some person who is able to declare such trust or by his will.

The declaration must comprise a present irrevocable declaration of trust and the writing must contain all the terms of the trust.[1] In the absence of the statutorily required evidence, an oral declaration of trust relating to land is valid[2] but simply unenforceable.[3] Where, however, written evidence is available in support of the declaration, the date of the writing is irrelevant[4] and the signed writing may provide purely retrospective evidence of the declarant's beneficial intendment.[5]

1   *Veale v Commissioners of Customs and Excise* (VAT and Duties Tribunal, 12 December 1996). See *Smith v Matthews* (1861) 3 De GF & J 139 at 150–153, 45 ER 831 at 835–837; *Re Cozens* [1913] 2 Ch 478 at 486–487.

2   *Gardner v Rowe* (1828) 5 Russ 258 at 262, 38 ER 1024 at 1025.

3   *Gissing v Gissing* [1969] 2 Ch 85 at 99A–B; [1971] AC 886 at 910E–F per Lord Diplock; *Cowcher v Cowcher* [1972] 1 WLR 425 at 430H–431A; *Midland Bank Plc v Dobson* [1986] 1 FLR 171 at 175C–D; *Wratten v Hunter* [1978] 2 NSWLR 367 at 371B.

4   *Forster v Hale* (1798) 3 Ves 696 at 711, 30 ER 1226 at 1233; *Rochefoucauld v Boustead* [1897] 1 Ch 196 at 206.

5   It would, for instance, be sufficient that the fondly generous domestic partner (supra)

subsequently recorded his generosity on the back of an envelope and signed it. Compare, however, *Veale v Commissioners of Customs and Excise* (VAT and Duties Tribunal, 12 December 1996), where the minutes of a board meeting could have evidenced a declaration of trust but for the fact that they were not signed by the appropriate parties.

Electronic declarations

9.189 As a concession to the digital age, the Land Registration Act 2002 provides for the possibility of an electronic declaration of trust in respect of an estate registered at Land Registry. Under the 2002 Act an electronically signed document[1] will be deemed to be a deed,[2] with the result that it necessarily satisfies the requirements for an enforceable declaration of trust under section 53(1)(b) of the Law of Property Act 1925.[3]

1   [**Para 7.36**].
2   LRA 2002, s 91(5).
3   See Law Com No 271 (2001), para 13.19.

Purpose of the requirement of written evidence

9.190 The venerable documentary requirement imposed by section 53(1)(b) dates back to the Statute of Frauds 1677[1] and performs at least two related functions. It curtails costly controversy arising from mistaken or fraudulent allegations of beneficial ownership (perhaps many years after the events in dispute); it also provides a classic illustration of the general disfavour shown in English land law towards informal mechanisms of rights creation. In particular, the requirement of written evidence severely restricts the possibility that informal language – especially in the domestic context – may lead to the creation of unsuspected trust relationships. In the absence of written evidence a trust 'does not come into being merely from a gratuitous intention to transfer or create a beneficial interest.'[2] The failure of documentary formality brings about, at least initially, a 'merely voluntary declaration of trust ... unenforceable for want of writing'[3] and traditionally equity will not assist a volunteer.[4]

1   Section 53(1)(b) is the modern emanation of section 7 of the Statute of Frauds 1677 (29 Car 2, c 3). For an account of the legislative motivations underlying this famous enactment, see Tim Youdan, [1984] CLJ 306 at 307–315.
2   *Austin v Keele* (1987) 10 NSWLR 283 at 291B per Lord Oliver of Aylmerton.
3   *Gissing v Gissing* [1971] AC 886 at 905E per Lord Diplock [**para 10.114**].
4   [**Para 9.6**]. See *Mascall v Mascall* (1984) 50 P & CR 119 at 126 per Browne-Wilkinson LJ.

EXEMPTIONS FROM THE REQUIREMENT OF FORMALITY

9.191 However compelling the policy motivation behind the statutory requirement of written evidence of an express trust of land, there are nevertheless certain instances where even this potent rationale is displaced by concerns ranking higher in the scale of values which animate equitable jurisdiction.

These concerns permit exceptions to be made to the statutory rule in cases where insistence on compliance with the rule would occasion an even greater offence against equitable principle. Such circumstances arise where failure to relax the statutory requirement would enable the declarant of an oral trust to profit from his own unconscionable conduct. The stern rule contained in section 53(1)(b) of the Law of Property Act 1925 is therefore subject to certain important exceptions, some of which go so far as to constitute 'a drastic judicial modification' of the statutory requirement of written evidence.[1]

1   T Youdan, [1984] CLJ 306 at 325.

Resulting, implied or constructive trusts

9.192   Certain kinds of trust are exempted by the Law of Property Act itself from any requirement of writing or written evidence. If the beneficial owner-ship protected by such forms of trust were to be shut out by a dogmatic exclusion of all supporting evidence of a merely parol nature, the inequity of outcome thereby caused would outweigh the policy motivation underpinning the statutory requirement of signed writing. In consequence section 53(2) of the Law of Property Act 1925 provides that the requirement of documentary formality does not affect the 'creation or operation of resulting, implied or constructive trusts.' It is therefore quite possible that an originally unenforce-able oral declaration of trust may sometimes become enforceable, not as an express trust, but rather as a *resulting* or *constructive* trust. The existence of an unenforceable express trust is not necessarily inconsistent with a claim alleging some other form of trust which is immune from the documentary requirements of section 53(1). In such cases the purely parol nature of the evidence in support of a trust relationship is irrelevant if the same facts which underlie an express declaration of trust also give rise to an enforceable trust of some other kind.[1]

1   For example, an informal declaration of beneficial entitlement for a spouse or partner may later acquire a new vitality as a constructive trust if the recipient of the declaration has since acted to her detriment in reliance on the substance of the initially unenforceable representa-tion [**para 10.114**]. See also *Hodgson v Marks* [1971] Ch 892 at 933C per Russell LJ; *Dalton v Christofis* [1978] WAR 42; *Stowe v Stowe* (1995) 15 WAR 363 at 367F.

Use of statute as an instrument of fraud

9.193   The fundamental purpose of requiring certain formalities to be observed in the creation and operation of express trusts is to prevent fraud being practised upon a trustee (and genuine beneficiaries) by those who fabricate allegations of trust. However, this insistence on formality is not pursued to the insensate degree that reliance upon an absence of writing is allowed to facilitate the commission of fraud by the trustee himself. It is clear doctrine that equity will never permit a statute to be used as an instrument of fraud.[1] In the present context equity's abhorrence of fraud finds expression in the rule in *Rochefoucauld v Boustead*.[2] Here the Court of Appeal confirmed that 'the Statute of Frauds does not prevent proof of a fraud', Lindley LJ holding that

> it is a fraud on the part of a person to whom land is conveyed as a trustee, and who knows it was so conveyed, to deny the trust and claim the land himself. Consequently, notwithstanding the statute, it is competent for a person claiming land conveyed to another to prove by parol evidence that it was so conveyed upon trust for the claimant, and that the grantee, knowing the facts, is denying the trust and relying upon the form of the conveyance and the statute, in order to keep the land himself.[3]

1   *Hutchins v Lee* (1737) 1 Atk 447 at 448, 26 ER 284 at 285; *Forster v Hale* (1798) 3 Ves 696 at 713, 30 ER 1226 at 1234; *Lincoln v Wright* (1859) 4 De G & J 16 at 22, 45 ER 6 at 9; *McCormick v Grogan* (1869) LR 4 HL 82 at 97; *Booth v Turle* (1873) LR 16 Eq 182 at 187; *Rochefoucauld v Boustead* [1897] 1 Ch 196 at 206; *Organ v Sandwell* [1921] VLR 622 at 630; *Last v Rosenfeld* [1972] 2 NSWLR 923 at 927E; *Barrios v Chiabrera* (1984) 3 BPR 9276 at 9278 per Powell J.
2   [1897] 1 Ch 196.
3   [1897] 1 Ch 196 at 206.

Limitations of the rule in Rochefoucauld v Boustead

9.194   The rule in *Rochefoucauld v Boustead* has a quite remarkable impact, but operates only within a fairly narrow range of circumstances. The rule cannot validate an express trust which is declared by A, with supposedly immediate effect, *before* the date of his acquisition of the legal title. Such a trust fails on the ground that the relevant trust property does not yet exist. Nor can the rule render enforceable an oral declaration of trust made *after* the date of acquisition by which A purports to constitute himself a trustee of property which he already owns. Such a declaration is unenforceable (in the absence of a constructive trust) since otherwise there would be no circumstances at all which came within the reach of section 53(1)(b).[1]

1   See *Wratten v Hunter* [1978] 2 NSWLR 367 at 371B.

Application of the rule in Rochefoucauld v Boustead

9.195   The rule in *Rochefoucauld v Boustead* therefore has a somewhat limited application, abrogating the statutory requirement of written evidence only where A acquires an estate in land on terms of his express oral undertaking that he will, from the moment of acquisition, hold on trust for B.[1] However, within this context it seems not to matter whether A acquires his legal title by conveyance from B himself[2] or by conveyance from a complete stranger, X.[3] More surprising is the fact that it seems to be irrelevant whether B has provided any consideration for A's undertaking.[4] From the date of acquisition onwards, A is affected by a fiduciary obligation towards B, and it would be fraud in equity if A were to rely on the absence of written evidence as a ground for disavowing the very trust on whose terms he was enabled to acquire title.

1   See *Lavette v Quin* (1980) 1 BPR 9609 at 9612; *Ash Street Properties Pty Ltd v Pollnow* (1985) 3 BPR 9646 at 9651.

2   *David v Szoke* (1974) 39 DLR (3d) 707 at 717.

3   See *Chattock v Muller* (1878) 8 Ch D 177 at 181; *Pallant v Morgan* [1953] Ch 43 at 48; *Devine v Fields* (1920) 54 ILTR 101 at 103–104; *Organ v Sandwell* [1921] VLR 622 at 630; *McGillicuddy v Joy* [1959] IR 189 at 212–214; *Gilmurray v Corr* [1978] NI 99 at 104E–G.

4   See T Youdan, [1984] CLJ 306 at 331–332.

Nature of the trust validated by the rule in *Rochefoucauld v Boustead*

9.196   There is some ambiguity as to whether the trust enforced under the rule in *Rochefoucauld v Boustead* is more accurately characterised as the original express trust or as an entirely new constructive trust which is statutorily exempt from the requirement of written evidence.[1] On the one hand, it could be said that, consistently with equity's utter detestation of fraud, the rule gives effect to the original express trust directly in the teeth of the statute.[2] Thus, without any attempt to circumvent section 53(1)(b) by a finding of resulting or constructive trust, 'equity simply enforce[s] the actual original trust upon which the person accepted the property in the first place.'[3] The alternative view – and the view more widely accepted today[4] – is that the trust enforced under *Rochefoucauld v Boustead* is a new constructive trust which arises as soon as A asserts his legal title in derogation of the rights to which he has agreed to take subject.[5]

1   See *Allen v Snyder* [1977] 2 NSWLR 685 at 699D–E per Samuels JA (who pointed out that the ambiguity is demonstrated most clearly in *Bannister v Bannister* [1948] 2 All ER 133 **[para 10.70]**). See also T Youdan, [1984] CLJ 306 at 330–334.

2   For instances where courts have leaned towards the 'express trust' analysis of the rule, see *Hodgson v Marks* [1971] Ch 892 at 909B per Ungoed-Thomas J; *Organ v Sandwell* [1921] VLR 622 at 630; *David v Szoke* (1974) 39 DLR (3d) 707 at 717; *Allen v Snyder* [1977] 2 NSWLR 685 at 689F–G, 693A–B; *Barrios v Chiabrera* (1984) 3 BPR 9276 at 9278 per Powell J; *Ash Street Properties Pty Ltd v Pollnow* (1985) 3 BPR 9646 at 9651, 9656 per McLelland J. As Fullagar J indicated in *Thwaites v Ryan* [1984] VR 65 at 93, it would be difficult to describe the trust enforced as 'implied or constructive' because it 'may often be actual and meticulously expressed.'

3   This approach has been colourfully described as 'no less than the exercise by equity of a suspending or dispensing power denied the executive branch of government since the Bill of Rights 1689' (R P Meagher, W M C Gummow and J R F Lehane, *Equity: Doctrines and Remedies* (3rd edn, Sydney 1992), para 1226). See, however, *Devine v Fields* (1920) 54 ILTR 101 at 103 per O'Connor MR: 'It is the duty of a court of equity to overcome all technicalities in order to defeat a fraud.'

4   In *Paragon Finance plc v D B Thakerar & Co* [1999] 1 All ER 400 at 409c, Millett LJ was content to treat *Rochefoucauld v Boustead* as simply a sub-species of constructive trust doctrine. See likewise *Neale v Willis* (1968) 19 P & CR 836 at 839. The 'constructive trust' analysis was favoured by the New South Wales Court of Appeal in *Ash Street Properties Pty Ltd v Pollnow* (1987) 9 NSWLR 80 at 84D, where Mahoney JA spoke of equity operating 'not by way of restraining reliance on the statute and so enforcing the transaction itself, but by creating equities independent of the transaction' (see also Priestley JA at 101A).

5   **[Para 10.5]**. This analysis does less violence to LPA 1925, s 53(1)(b), since constructive trusts are clearly a case of statutory exception under LPA 1925, s 53(2). However, it can be argued that where no consideration has been provided for the undertaking entered into by the legal owner, the trust to which the rule gives effect must be express rather than constructive (see *Ash Street Properties Pty Ltd v Pollnow* (1985) 3 BPR 9646 at 9651 per McLelland J).

CONCLUSIVE EFFECT OF A DECLARATION OF TRUST

9.197 If incorporated in an instument of transfer, an express declaration of trust plainly complies with the statutory requirement of written evidence.[1] The use of such declarations of trust will doubtless intensify in consequence of modern Land Registry requirements. In the event of any transfer of land to joint proprietors, the statutorily prescribed Land Registry forms (applicable to both first registration and subsequent transfer) now include a compulsory declaration of trust, to be executed by the transferees, which specifies the nature or quantum of the intended beneficial entitlements.[2] All new joint proprietors are therefore required, in effect, to execute a written declaration of trust which settles their equitable rights.

[1] LPA 1925, s 53(1)(b) [**para 9.188**].
[2] LRA 2002, s 25(1); LRR 2003, rr 23(1), 58, 206(1), Sch 1 (Forms FR1 and TR1). The transferees must indicate whether they hold on trust for themselves as joint tenants, as tenants in common in equal shares, or on some other trusts [**para 11.148**].

The general principle

9.198 The case law establishes that an express declaration of trust, when duly supported by signed writing, 'necessarily concludes the question of title ... for all time.'[1] The declaration provides virtually irrebuttable evidence as to the nature and extent of the beneficial rights subsisting under a trust of land. This definitive effect is certainly achieved where the declaration is executed by the transferees of the legal title as well as by the transferor.[2] Even if not so executed, a declaration inserted into a conveyance on the instruction of the purchasers may well be taken to provide conclusive evidence of their intentions as to beneficial ownership.[3] These rules sometimes have surprising implications.

[1] *Pettitt v Pettitt* [1970] AC 777 at 813E per Lord Upjohn. See similarly *Gissing v Gissing* [1971] AC 886 at 905A per Lord Diplock. An express declaration of the beneficial interests also excludes any discretionary jurisdiction of the court to value the parties' equitable shares as of the date on which they ceased to live together. The proper date for the valuation of shares in such cases is the date of realisation of the property (see *Turton v Turton* [1988] Ch 542 at 550F, 555F–H; *Passee v Passee* [1988] 1 FLR 263 at 268C–D, 272B–D).
[2] *Robinson v Robinson* (1977) 241 EG 153 at 155; *Re Gorman (A Bankrupt)* [1990] 1 WLR 616 at 621E. See, however, *City of London Building Society v Flegg* [1988] AC 54 at 70C–D, where Lord Templeman indicated that an express declaration of trust executed by joint transferees of a legal title could not exclude the beneficial entitlements of other contributors to the purchase price who had not executed the declaration [**para 11.212**].
[3] *Pink v Lawrence* (1978) 36 P & CR 98 at 101 per Buckley LJ; *Re Gorman (A Bankrupt)* [1990] 1 WLR 616 at 621F, 623H–624A per Vinelott J. See *Roy v Roy* [1996] 1 FLR 541 at 545G–546B, where Fox LJ held that a transfer, unexecuted by joint transferees, conveying land into their joint names to hold as joint tenants at law and in equity did not, in itself, constitute a declaration of trust within the ambit of LPA 1925, s 53(1). Instead, such a transfer simply took effect 'according to its language' in the absence of compelling grounds for rectification.

Declaration of beneficial joint tenancy

9.199   If a legal estate is transferred into the joint names of A and B, subject to an express trust for themselves as beneficial joint tenants,[1] the equitable rights of A and B are clarified definitively as those of joint tenants.[2] In other words, either A or B can later, and quite unilaterally, exercise the right of severance enjoyed by a beneficial joint tenant.[3] In such an event, both parties become beneficial tenants in common in equal shares, irrespective of their original proportions of contribution to the purchase price of the co-owned land and irrespective of the reasons which caused one party to desire a severance.[4] This result follows inexorably from the binding nature of what is effectively a settlement by the transferees designed to regulate the beneficial terms on which they agreed to hold the legal estate: the transferees committed themselves at the outset to an equitable joint tenancy.

1   On the significance of joint tenancy (as distinct from tenancy in common), see Chapter 11 **[para 11.4]**.
2   *Pettitt v Pettitt* [1970] AC 777 at 813E per Lord Upjohn. See also *Mayes v Mayes* (1969) 210 EG 935 at 937; *Re Johns' Assignment Trusts* [1970] 1 WLR 955 at 959C; *Pink v Lawrence* (1978) 36 P & CR 98 at 101; *Brykiert v Jones* (1981) 2 FLR 373 at 376A–B; *Goodman v Gallant* [1986] Fam 106 at 110H–111A; *Huntingford v Hobbs* [1993] 1 FCR 45 at 49F–G.
3   See the discussion of severance in Chapter 11 **[para 11.64]**.
4   *Bedson v Bedson* [1965] 2 QB 666 at 689C–D; *Pettitt v Pettitt* [1970] AC 777 at 813E per Lord Upjohn; *Re Johns' Assignment Trusts* [1970] 1 WLR 955 at 959C; *Bernard v Josephs* [1982] Ch 391 at 397F; *Goodman v Gallant* [1986] Fam 106 at 108D, 119D.

Declaration of other forms of beneficial ownership

9.200   An express declaration of trust is commonly used to stipulate for beneficial joint tenancy in the family home. However, a declaration of trust may take many forms[1] and is conclusive in its terms regardless of which precise form of beneficial ownership it provides.[2] Thus if a legal title is vested in A, B and C on trust for themselves as tenants in common in equal shares, it is entirely irrelevant that A, B and C have contributed the purchase money in unequal proportions.[3] It is clearly a matter of some importance that conveyancers should be able to rely on the face value of documents which purport to define in express terms both the legal and beneficial ownership of land.

1   See e g *Wright v Johnson* [2002] 2 P & CR 210 at [11]–[12], where a 'restriction' in the Land Register prohibiting disposition by the survivor of joint proprietors was regarded as the equivalent of an express declaration of beneficial tenancy in common.
2   It is also possible to provide, by way of express declaration, that joint tenancy should prevail in equity until and unless severance occurs, and that in the event of severance the parties' respective interests should be unequal (see *Goodman v Gallant* [1986] Fam 106 at 119C).
3   *Brown v Staniek* (1969) 211 EG 283. See also *Bedson v Bedson* [1965] 2 QB 666 at 689D–E. Where A and B take a transfer of legal title and execute a declaration of trust for themselves, it may nevertheless be relevant that part or all of the purchase money came from sources other than A and B. See e g *City of London Building Society v Flegg* [1988] AC 54 at 70C–D **[para 11.212]**, where the House of Lords envisaged that the express trusts set out in a conveyance could be displaced by the fact that persons other than the designated beneficiaries had contributed financially towards the purchase.

Exceptions to the general principle

9.201 Only extremely limited exceptions are permitted from the rule that an express declaration of trust has conclusive effect.

Rescission for fraud or mistake

9.202 It is always open to a party to go behind the express terms of a trust where there has been 'fraud or mistake at the time of the transaction' by which the legal title is vested.[1] This ground of exception, if proved, may lead to rescission of the declaration, but the ground is difficult to establish. Mistake, for instance, is not constituted merely by a failure on the part of a lay person to understand the precise technical significance of the declaration of trust.[2] Indeed, in *Pink v Lawrence*,[3] the parties were held bound by a declaration of equitable joint tenancy which they had neither read nor signed and which (it was conceded) they would probably not have understood anyway.

1   *Pettitt v Pettitt* [1970] AC 777 at 813E per Lord Upjohn. See also *Goodman v Gallant* [1986] Fam 106 at 116B.
2   *Mayes v Mayes* (1969) 210 EG 935 at 937; *Re Johns' Assignment Trusts* [1970] 1 WLR 955 at 958G–H; *Huntingford v Hobbs* [1993] 1 FCR 45 at 64D.
3   (1978) 36 P & CR 98 at 99.

Rectification

9.203 Apart from cases of fraud or mistake, it is possible that a court may grant rectification of a declaration of trust in order to give effect to intentions which the parties clearly had at the date of the transaction, but which were expressed only imperfectly or not at all in the declared trust. In rare cases the court may, for instance, reinstate an original common intention that the parties should be equitable tenants in common rather than joint tenants,[1] or that one party rather than two should be beneficially entitled,[2] or even that two parties instead of one should be grantees of the legal title under the deed of conveyance.[3]

1   See *Re Colebrook's Conveyances* [1972] 1 WLR 1397 at 1398H, but compare *Goodman v Gallant* [1986] Fam 106 at 116H–117C.
2   *Wilson v Wilson* [1969] 3 All ER 945 at 949A–B. Where the conveyance does not accurately represent the agreement of the parties, it may be possible for the court to give relief without actually employing the machinery of rectification (*Pink v Lawrence* (1978) 38 P & CR 98 at 101). See also *Gross v French* (1976) 238 EG 39.
3   *Armstrong v Armstrong* (1979) 93 DLR (3d) 128 at 135.

DISPOSITIONS OF LAND HELD ON TRUST

9.204 The legal estate in land held on trust should (in the case of registered land) be registered in the name of the trustee or trustees. The equitable interests

W B Simpson, 'Introduction' to W Blackstone, *Commentaries on the Laws of England* (Facsimile edn, Chicago and London 1979), Vol 2, p xi).

4   The tax consequences which flow from the creation of a strict settlement are onerous in the extreme, inheritance tax falling on the full capital value of the estate on the termination of each successive interest (see *Ingram v IRC* [2000] 1 AC 293 at 300E–F per Lord Hoffmann). Estate duty, the forerunner of this form of taxation, was introduced by the Finance Act 1894 and the wealth retrieved by the Revenue by means of this tax provided the basis of the great naval rearmament in this country immediately prior to the First World War. See F H Lawson, *Introduction to the Law of Property* (London 1958), pp 94–95.

5   During the 20th century the strict settlement was almost wholly displaced by the trust for sale of land [**para 9.221**]. In due course the Law Commission condemned the strict settlement as 'excessively complex and no longer necessary' (Law Commission, *Trusts of Land* (Law Com Working Paper No 94, September 1985), para 17.1) and modern successive interests in land are now assimilated within the trust of land regulated by the Trusts of Land and Appointment of Trustees Act 1996 [**para 9.205**]. See Law Com No 181 (1989), paras 4.3–4.12.

6   For a fuller acount of the operation of the Settled Land Act 1925, see *Elements Of Land Law* (2nd edn 1993), pp 608–644.

7   See e g *Bannister v Bannister* [1948] 2 All ER 133 [**para 10.70**]; *Ungurian v Lesnoff* [1990] Ch 206; *Costello v Costello* (1994) 70 P & CR 297 [**para 10.304**].

Constitution of a strict settlement

9.207   Although it has been impossible since 1996 to create any new strict settlement under the Settled Land Act 1925,[1] strict settlements of land created prior to 1997 continue to be governed by the 1925 Act. This legislation provides an ingenious and highly artificial mechanism for the regulation of successive and limited interests in land.

1   TOLATA 1996, s 2(1).

Coverage of the strict settlement

9.208   A 'settlement' within the meaning of the Settled Land Act 1925 was capable of arising in two generalised kinds of situation: (i) where limited successive equitable interests were carved out of ownership of a legal estate in land, and (ii) where an absolute (as distinct from a limited) interest in land was conferred on a grantee who was subject to some disability, liability or contingency which qualified his capacity or entitlement to hold such an interest.[1]

1   The Settled Land Act 1925 cannot apply to any bare trust or trust for sale of land (SLA 1925, s 1(7)).

Limited beneficial interests

9.209   A strict settlement arose where land 'stands ... limited in trust for any persons by way of succession.'[1] A primary instance occurred where land was granted to A for life, with remainder to B in fee simple.[2] Other examples involved the grant of an entailed interest[3] or an interest subject to some specified condition subsequent (ie an interest for A capable of divesting in favour of B if the specified condition was fulfilled).[4]

1   SLA 1925, s 1(1)(i).
2   See *Ungurian v Lesnoff* [1990] Ch 206 at 226B per Vinelott J.
3   SLA 1925, s 1(1)(ii)(a). An entailed interest could likewise take effect only as an equitable interest [**para 1.138**], but if the entail were barred [**para 1.128**], the land ceased to be subject to the Settled Land Act (*Re Alefounder's Will Trusts* [1927] 1 Ch 360 at 364; *Re Blake's Settled Estates* [1932] IR 637 at 640, 647–648).
4   SLA 1925, s 1(1)(ii)(b). A 'shifting interest' of this kind (eg 'Greenacre to X in fee simple until she joins the Communist Party, with remainder over to Y in fee simple' [**para 7.6**]) is inevitably equitable, the determinability of X's equitable interest providing the successive element so characteristic of strict settlement.

Cases of disability, liability or contingency

9.210   The Settled Land Act 1925 also governs the conferment prior to 1997 of absolute beneficial entitlements upon recipients who were, for some reason, subject to a disability, liability or contingency which precluded their holding an absolute legal interest. The Act thus catches any grant of a freehold or leasehold estate which was made contingent on the happening of some event (eg attainment of a stipulated age or qualification).[1] The Act likewise applies to the grant, prior to 1997, of an estate to a minor[2] or of a family rentcharge.[3]

1   SLA 1925, s 1(1)(iii). The imposition of the condition precedent to the grant gave rise, necessarily in equity, to a 'springing interest' which might or might not materialise at some future date. If the contingency was never satisfied, the estate reverted to the settlor or (if he was dead) to his successors.
2   SLA 1925, s 1(1)(ii)(d).
3   SLA 1925, s 1(1)(v).

Vesting of the legal estate in the tenant for life

9.211   Central to the scheme of the Settled Land Act 1925 is the concept that, wherever possible, the commerciable legal estate in the settled land – the fee simple or term of years – should be vested in the 'tenant for life' (usually the person currently entitled in possession to a beneficial life interest).[1] The legal title being a merely nominal or 'paper' title, it makes sense that legal ownership (with its attendant powers of management and disposition) should generally be allocated to the beneficial owner in possession at any given time.[2]

1   SLA 1925, s 19(1); LRA 2002, s 89(1), LRR 2003, r 186, Sch 7, paras 1, 4(3). Two or more persons, if granted land for their joint lives with remainder to the survivor for life, can occupy the position of tenant for life (SLA 1925, ss 19(2), 117(1)(xxviii)), holding the legal estate as joint tenants. They must, however, exercise their joint powers of management and disposition either unanimously or not at all (see *Re 90 Thornhill Road, Tolworth, Barker v Addiscott* [1970] Ch 261 at 265H, 267A).
2   In the absence of some person beneficially entitled in possession for life, the powers of the tenant for life are exercisable by any of a range of substitutes of full age (eg a tenant in tail) who hold limited or qualified interests in possession in the settled land (SLA 1925, s 20(1)). In default of any other person statutorily entitled to discharge the functions of the tenant for life, these functions devolve ultimately upon the trustees of the settlement (SLA 1925, s 23(1)).

Dual function of the tenant for life

9.212   In the standard case the holder of a life interest in possession governed by the Settled Land Act enjoys a dual entitlement. The quantum of his beneficial enjoyment is confined to his life interest (and measured in terms of either occupation of the land or receipt of rents and profits drawn from it). But he also holds (or is entitled to call for) the full legal estate in the settled land,[1] with which he then stands invested as a fiduciary on behalf of all those holding beneficial interests under the settlement (including himself).[2] In effect, the split role of the tenant for life marks the distinction between the managerial and administrative responsibilities in respect of the entire settled estate (which attach to his function as tenant for life) and his entitlement to personal beneficial enjoyment (as marked by his own equitable interest under the settlement).

1   SLA 1925, s 9(2); LRR 2003, r 186, Sch 7, para 9. See *Peach v Peach* (Unreported, Court of Appeal, 3 November 1981) per Templeman LJ; *Ungurian v Lesnoff* [1990] Ch 206 at 224D–E, 226D.
2   SLA 1925, ss 16(1)(i), 107(1). See also *Re Hunt's Settled Estates* [1905] 2 Ch 419 at 423 per Farwell J, [1906] 2 Ch 11 at 12.

Documentary formalities

9.213   It is integral to the proper constitution of a strict settlement that two documents should be executed. *First*, there must[1] be a vesting document or deed,[2] which vests the legal estate in the settled land in the appropriate recipient.[3] The vesting document may also nominate up to four persons[4] (who may include a settlement beneficiary) to act as 'trustees of the settlement'[5] and who play a residual role of oversight in relation to the affairs of the strict settlement.[6] *Second*, there must be a trust instrument, which details the beneficial entitlements intended to be held under the settlement trusts.[7] This use of separate documentation, relating respectively to matters of legal and equitable entitlement, lays the essential foundation for the 'curtain principle' which ensures that beneficial rights under the Settled Land Act are kept off the legal title, do not affect subsequent purchasers,[8] and are ultimately overreached on a disposition of the legal estate. Furthermore, where the proprietorship of a settled estate is registered at Land Registry, a 'restriction' should be entered in the register in order to ensure that the necessary preconditions of overreaching are met and the trusts of the settlement overreached.[9]

1   SLA 1925, ss 4(1) (settlement inter vivos), 6 (testamentary settlement). An informal instrument inter vivos which spells out the intended beneficial entitlements may be deemed to be an effective trust instrument (s 9(1)(iii)), the trustees of the settlement then being required to supply the necessary vesting deed (s 9(2)).
2   See SLA 1925, s 5(1).
3   If the legal estate in the settled land is never, by one or other means, properly vested in the tenant for life, most future dealings with the legal estate are paralysed and, except in favour of a bona fide purchaser, take effect only as a contract for valuable consideration to carry out the transaction after the requisite vesting instrument has been executed (SLA 1925, s 13). See, however, *Re Alefounder's Will Trusts* [1927] 1 Ch 360 at 364.

4   See TA 1925, s 34(1)–(2).
5   SLA 1925, s 30(1).
6   See *Re Boston's Will Trusts* [1956] Ch 395 at 405 per Vaisey J. If a settlement arises by way of
     will or intestacy, the functions of the settlement trustees default to the settlor's personal
     representatives (SLA 1925, s 30(3)). In the last resort any beneficiary or any person otherwise
     interested in the settlement may apply to the court for the appointment of a fit person as
     trustee (SLA 1925, s 34(1)).
7   In the case of a testamentary settlement, the will, laying out the trust interests of the various
     designated beneficiaries, is deemed to be the trust instrument, and a vesting assent is left to be
     supplied in favour of the appropriate tenant for life by the settlor's personal representatives
     (see SLA 1925, ss 6, 8(1)). See also *Re King's Will Trusts* [1964] Ch 542 at 548; *Re Edwards'
     Will Trusts* [1982] Ch 30 at 33C; [1982] Conv 4 (P W Smith).
8   See e g SLA 1925, s 110(2).
9   LRA 2002, s 42(1)(b); LRR 2003, r 186, Sch 7, paras 2, 3, 4(2), 7(1).

Powers of the tenant for life

9.214   The tenant for life, in addition to his competence to deal independently
with his own beneficial life interest,[1] is statutorily invested with a range of
important powers relating to the legal estate in the settled land.[2] He may sell the
settled land (or any part of it) or any easement, right or privilege over the land.[3]
He has power to lease the land (or any easement, right or privilege over it) for
any period not exceeding 50 years.[4] The tenant for life also has power to raise
money for certain limited purposes by mortgaging the settled estate,[5] but has,
for instance, no power to purchase land with the assistance of mortgage
finance. The tenant for life's powers in all foregoing respects can be expanded
by the express terms of the settlement,[6] but any provision which purports to
prohibit, restrict or inhibit the tenant for life's exercise of his statutory powers
is, by statute, declared 'void'.[7] Any improper exercise of the statutory powers
conferred upon the tenant for life constitutes a breach of trust, in respect of
which the settled land beneficiaries may seek an injunction[8] or damages.[9]

1   A tenant for life's dealings with his own equitable interest under the strict settlement normally
     have no effect upon the ownership of the legal estate in the settled land (SLA 1925, s 104(1);
     LPA 1925, s 137(2)(i), (4)). See *Re Earl of Pembroke and Thompson's Contract* [1932] IR 493 at
     501–503. The extinguishment of the tenant for life's beneficial interest in favour the next
     remainderman does, however, require that the legal estate in the settled land be conveyed to
     that person (SLA 1925, ss 7(4), 19(4), 105(1)).
2   The tenant for life must at all times consult the interests of the beneficiaries, although, in a
     delphic phrase (see [1956] CLJ 174 (H W R Wade)), he may 'legitimately exercise his powers
     with some, but not of course, an exclusive regard for his own personal interests' (*Re Boston's
     Will Trusts* [1956] Ch 395 at 405 per Vaisey J). An imminent and improvident transaction by
     the life tenant may be restrained by injunction (see *Wheelwright v Walker* (1883) 31 WR 912;
     Re Earl Somers (1895) 11 TLR 567; *Middlemas v Stevens* [1901] 1 Ch 574 at 577).
3   SLA 1925, s 38(i). The sale must normally be made for the 'best consideration in money that
     can reasonably be obtained' (SLA 1925, s 39(1)). The tenant for life may also make an
     exchange of settled land (SLA 1925, s 38(iii)).
4   SLA 1925, s 41(iv). It has been recommended that this power be extended to the grant of
     ordinary leases not exceeding 100 years (Law Reform Committee, *The powers and duties of
     trustees* (23rd Report, Cmnd 8733, October 1982), para 8.6). A tenant for life may also grant
     leases not exceeding 100 years for mining and not exceeding 999 years for building or forestry
     (see SLA 1925, s 41(i)–(iii)). In all cases the lease must normally be made by deed, must take

effect in possession within twelve months of its date, must reserve 'the best rent that can reasonably be obtained', and must contain a condition of re-entry on the covenanted rent not being paid within a specified time not exceeding 30 days (SLA 1925, s 42(1)).

5   SLA 1925, s 71(2).

6   SLA 1925, s 109(1). The powers may also be augmented by order of the court (SLA 1925, s 64(1)). The tenant for life cannot validly contract not to exercise his statutory powers (SLA 1925, s 104(2)).

7   SLA 1925, s 106(1). Any forfeiture of settled land beneficial rights which follows indirectly from the exercise of a tenant for life's statutory powers (eg when a tenant for life, on selling, ceases to fulfil a condition of residence) is thus rendered void (see *Re Acklom* [1929] 1 Ch 195 at 198–200; *Re Fitzgerald* [1902] 1 IR 162 at 165–166). If, however, the cesser of residence is not attributable to the exercise of any statutory power by the tenant for life, the beneficial interest is expressly terminated and the beneficiary is no longer eligible to receive the rents and profits drawn from the land (see *Re Haynes* (1887) 37 Ch D 306 at 309–310).

8   See eg *Hampden v Earl of Buckinghamshire* [1893] 2 Ch 531 at 544.

9   In the case of wilful refusal by the tenant for life to exercise his statutory powers, the court may authorise the trustees of the settlement to exercise those powers in his name and on his behalf (SLA 1925, s 24(1)).

Sale of the settled estate

9.215   The most significant of the tenant for life's powers is, ultimately, his power to sell the legal estate in the settled land.[1] Here the statutory device of overreaching ensures that the land can be disposed of entirely free of the beneficial interests of the settlement,[2] these interests surviving the disposition as beneficial entitlements in the capital money generated by the transaction (see *Fig.* 18). The simultaneous protection of both purchaser and settled land beneficiary is the culminating effect of the Settled Land Act 1925.

1   SLA 1925, s 38(i). A tenant for life may purchase the settled estate himself provided that the negotiations preceding sale are conducted by the trustees of the settlement (SLA 1925, s 68). See *Re Pennant's Will Trusts* [1970] Ch 75 at 81B.

2   **[Para 9.216]**.

Statutory overreaching of beneficial interests

9.216   The proprietorship register (in the case of registered land)[1] and vesting deed (in the case of unregistered land)[2] will make it obvious to any stranger that the land is subject to the trusts of a strict settlement and will, moreover, identify the trustees of that settlement. Provided that there is compliance with certain statutory preconditions, the disponee of settled land takes the legal estate entirely unencumbered by the beneficial interests existing under the settlement.[3] These interests are automatically swept off the land and exchanged for equivalent rights in the income and capital generated by the sale (see *Fig.* 18). Precisely because this is so, the trusts of the settlement are kept concealed behind the 'curtain' of the vesting instrument; and the purchaser normally has no right to call for or inspect the trust instrument relating to the settled land.[4]

The conditions of statutory overreaching are three in number.[5]

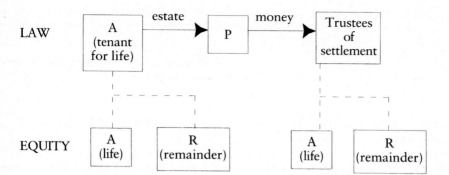

Fig. 18

1 LRR 2003, r 186, Sch 7, para 4(1).
2 SLA 1925, s 5(1).
3 SLA 1925, s 18(1)(c); LPA 1925, s 2(1)(i).
4 SLA 1925, s 110(2). The only occasions on which the purchaser may insist upon seeing the trust instrument relate to the exceptional cases in which an originally imperfect settlement has been rendered perfect under SLA 1925, s 9 [**para 9.213**]. See the proviso to SLA 1925, s 110(2).
5 See LPA 1925, s 2(1)(i).

The conveyance must be 'made under the powers conferred by the Settled Land Act 1925'

9.217 The powers of the Settled Land Act 1925 are unavailable, and statutory overreaching is accordingly denied, if for any reason settled land is withdrawn from the ambit of the Act (eg where a condition subsequent of the tenant for life's beneficial entitlement becomes satisfied and the absolute beneficial interest therefore vests in possession in some other beneficiary[1]).

1 Thus, where Greenacre was settled on X in fee simple 'until she joins the Communist Party, with remainder over to Y in fee simple' [**para 7.6**], Y becomes absolutely entitled in equity if the condition subsequent attached to X's interest is satisfied. X remains invested with the legal estate, but now holds on a bare trust for Y, the existence of a bare trust necessarily taking the land outside the reach of the Settled Land Act 1925 [**para 9.208**]. In these circumstances the preconditions of statutory overreaching under LPA 1925, s 2(1)(i) cannot be met by any transfer of the legal estate.

The equitable interests must be 'capable of being overreached'

9.218 Statutory overreaching applies only to those equitable interests which are 'capable of being overreached.'[1] Overreaching sweeps away the beneficial entitlements created under the trusts of the settlement, together with certain annuities, limited owner's charges and general equitable charges,[2] but not, of course, legal rights over the settled estate already granted to third parties (eg leases)[3] or equitable rights such as restrictive covenants, options or other estate contracts.[4]

1 LPA 1925, s 2(1)(i).

2   SLA 1925, s 72(3). Since such interests have a definite quantifiable money value, they may as
     well be satisfied out of the capital proceeds of the transaction and are therefore swept off the
     land at this convenient opportunity.
3   SLA 1925, s 72(2).
4   For an account of the way in which overreaching characteristically clears off 'general burdens'
     as distinct from 'real burdens', see Chapter 11 [**para 11.201**].

There must be compliance with the statutory requirements respecting the payment of capital money

9.219   Provided that the purchaser of the legal estate pays the capital money
arising on the disposition to the trustees of the settlement (of whom there must
be at least *two*[1]), the purchaser takes the legal title entirely unencumbered by
the beneficial interests of the settlement.[2] The trustees thereafter hold the
money on a trust of personalty.[3] From the moment when the purchaser obtains
his receipt from the settlement trustees, he is exonerated from any liability for
loss or misapplication of the funds now in the hands of those trustees[4] and is
conclusively deemed to have given 'the best price, consideration, or rent'
reasonably obtainable for the land and to have 'complied with all the requisitions of this Act.'[5]

1   SLA 1925, ss 94(1), 95(1). An exception is made in the case of payment to a trust corporation
     or to the personal representatives of the last surviving or continuing trustee.
2   SLA 1925, s 18(1)(c); LPA 1925, s 2(1)(i).
3   As trustees they are obliged to invest the capital prudently and to distribute income and
     capital in accordance with the terms of the original trust instrument.
4   SLA 1925, s 95.
5   SLA 1925, s 110(1).

Failure to comply with the preconditions of statutory overreaching

9.220   In the case of settled land the preconditions of statutory overreaching
are enforced with rigour. Any unauthorised disposition of the legal estate which
fails to ensure that the capital proceeds are safeguarded by payment to the
settlement trustees is declared void by statute.[1] It is arguable, but far from clear,
that this draconian penalty of voidness attaches only to transactions which, by
reason of fraud on the part of the tenant for life, are entirely ultra vires the
Settled Land Act.[2] If this is so, the purchaser who innocently fails to pay the
purchase money to at least two trustees is likely to be saved by the immunity
conferred on a purchaser who has dealt 'in good faith with a tenant for life or
statutory owner.'[3]

1   SLA 1925, s 18(1)(a). See e g *Weston v Henshaw* [1950] Ch 510 at 519 per Danckwerts J.
2   The problem will rarely arise in registered land, since the entry of a 'restriction' on the
     registered title will almost always prevent the registration of any unauthorised dealing with
     the legal title. For more detailed discussion of the position in unregistered land, see *Elements
     of Land Law* (2nd edn 1993), pp 631–634. See also R H Maudsley, (1973) 36 MLR 25; E H
     Scamell, [1957] CLP 152 at 163; D W Elliott, (1971) 87 LQR 338; J Hill, (1991) 107 LQR 596.
3   SLA 1925, s 110(1). See *Re Morgan's Lease* [1972] Ch 1 at 9A–C per Ungoed-Thomas J; but
     compare *Bevan v Johnston* [1990] 2 EGLR 33 at 34H–J. In *Re Morgan's Lease* it was noted that

the earlier authority of the Court of Appeal in *Mogridge v Clapp* [1892] 3 Ch 382 at 400–401 had not been cited before Danckwerts J in *Weston v Henshaw*.

BENEFICIAL INTERESTS UNDER A TRUST FOR SALE

9.221 Prior to 1997 virtually all concurrent interests in land – in effect all forms of co-ownership of a legal or equitable estate – were required to exist either under an express 'trust for sale' deliberately created for the purpose or under a 'trust for sale' arising by implication of statute.[1] It was possible that some successive interests (e g life interests) could also take effect expressly under a 'trust for sale' of land. The net effect of the important changes introduced by the Trusts of Land and Appointment of Trustees Act 1996 (effective 1 January 1997) is that the 'trust for sale' survives as a landholding device only where it has been explicitly created as such, whether before or after the commencement of the 1996 Act.

1   For a more detailed account of the origin and operation of the trust for sale of land, see *Elements of Land Law* (2nd edn 1993), Chapter 14.

Operation of the trust for sale

9.222 As with any trust,[1] the trust for sale separates the administrative functions of management and disposition from the beneficial enjoyment of the trust property. Under the scheme of the 1925 legislation it is open to a settlor to vest a legal estate in persons who are specifically directed to hold that estate 'on trust for sale' for certain nominated beneficiaries (see *Fig.* 19). These 'trustees for sale' are thenceforth bound by a fiduciary duty to deflect to their beneficiaries all advantages derived from the profitable exploitation of the land or from its physical enjoyment in specie (ie by way of actual occupation).[2] Powers of management and disposition in respect of the legal estate are conferred, in the first instance, on the trustees for sale.[3] The beneficiaries merely benefit: their interests are concerned with money and actual occupation.

1   **[Para 1.168]**.
2   It is not impossible that the trustees may be the same persons as the beneficiaries, albeit exercising quite distinct functions. Trustees for sale may hold a legal estate on trust for *themselves* as beneficiaries. In the capacity of trustee for sale, however, each is the owner of the legal estate; in the capacity of beneficiary, each owns an equitable interest.
3   Statutory powers of sale, lease and mortgage were originally conferred on trustees for sale by way of an express analogy with the powers enjoyed by the tenant for life and settlement trustees under the Settled Land Act 1925 (LPA 1925, s 28(1)). See *Re Conquest* [1929] 2 Ch 353 at 358. These powers have now been significantly widened by TOLATA 1996, s 6 **[para 11.158]**.

9.223 The trust for sale is more than simply a *trust* of property. It is, in precise terms, a trust *for sale*. The Law of Property Act 1925 superimposes certain features on the basic trust device which are designed to ensure that the land held on trust is ultimately converted (or sold) and its money value distributed in the manner specified either by the settlor or by law.[1] The trust for sale, as initially conceived by the 1925 legislation, placed its pre-eminent focus on the exchange value, as distinct from the use value, of land.[2] The overriding emphasis of the trust for sale was on land as capital rather than on land as a means of residential or commercial utility, the pervasive assumption being that the exact nature of the investment of trust funds was a matter of little consequence to the beneficiaries behind the trust for sale. With the passage of time, this money-oriented aspect was to make the trust for sale appear a somewhat inappropriate medium – not least in the residential context – for the legal formulation of co-ownership rights in land.

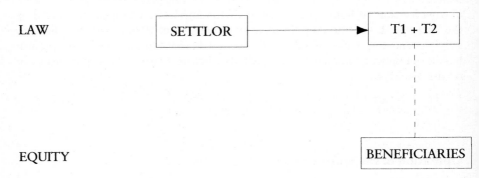

Fig. **19**

1   A 'trust for sale' was originally defined as 'an immediate binding trust for sale, whether or not exercisable at the request or with the consent of any person, and with or without a power at discretion to postpone the sale' (LPA 1925, s 205(1)(xxix)).

2   See *Mortgage Corporation v Shaire* [2001] Ch 743 at 758H per Neuberger J. For adoption of the terminology of 'use value', see *Transfer of Land: Overreaching: Beneficiaries in Occupation* (Law Com No 188, December 1989), para 3.3.

Functions of trustees for sale

9.224   The 'trust for sale' assumed an important role in the restructuring of property law which took effect on 1 January 1926. Although originally a form of landholding expressly created in favour of expressly designated beneficiaries,[1] the trust for sale was adapted by the Law of Property Act 1925[2] to provide a general medium of landholding suitable for most cases of co-ownership of land[3] and even for some cases of successive ownership.[4] Whether a trust for sale arose by express direction or by implication from statute, the trustees for sale were nevertheless fixed with an immediate duty to sell the land held on trust, albeit generally subject to a power vested in these trustees to postpone sale.[5]

1   The archetype was the 19th century 'trust for sale', which enabled a testator to direct his executors to sell his property after his death and distribute the money proceeds to a number of specified beneficiaries. The duty of these 'trustees' was unequivocal and immediate: they became subject to a duty to convert (ie to sell) the trust property, normally within a period of one year from the date of the testator's death (the so-called 'executor's year').

2   See LPA 1925, ss 23–36, 205(1)(xxix).

3 Thus it was possible for Lord Oliver of Aylmerton to declare, in *City of London Building Society v Flegg* [1988] AC 54 at 77H–78A, that the 1925 legislation 'established the trust for sale as the conveyancing machinery through which effect is given to the interests of owners in undivided shares.'

4 Prior to 1997 trusts for sale had become much more common than the extremely cumbersome form of settlement governed by the Settled Land Act 1925 (see G A Grove, (1961) 24 MLR 123 at 127). Strict settlements were rarely created deliberately and usually came into being only where a settlor unwisely attempted to confer a life interest by informal means **[para 10.302]**. Moreover, the flexible arrangement of the trust for sale fairly obviously avoided the probate difficulties and disastrous tax implications attaching to strict settlements of land.

5 LPA 1925, s 25(1). This power to postpone the sale of the trust land is now implied, in an unavoidable form, in every trust for sale (TOLATA 1996, s 4(1)–(2) **[para 9.243]**).

Duty to sell land held on trust for sale

9.225 The essence of the 'trust for sale' lies in the *duty* to sell which is imposed on all 'trustees for sale' by the very nature of their trust.[1] The prime object of the trust for sale involves, at least in theory, the conversion of the co-owned land into a monetary form in which all the beneficiaries may enjoy their respective rights. The trust for sale thus imposes a mandatory duty to sell the legal estate held on trust unless the trustees displace the primacy of this obligation by a unanimous exercise of their power to postpone sale.[2] Any disagreement between the trustees as to the desirability of sale should normally be resolved in favour of discharging the primary purpose of the trust for sale.[3] In the absence of proven mala fides in the trustee who presses for sale, the duty to sell thus overrides the power to postpone sale and, unless the court intervenes,[4] is determinative of the controversy.

1 The grant to trustees of a mere power of sale used to connote the existence of a strict settlement of land, in which case the power of sale belonged properly, not to the trustees in the first instance, but to the tenant for life **[para 9.212]**. The grant of a power of sale after 1996 connotes a trust of land **[para 9.243]**.

2 The requirement of unanimity does not apply to trustees holding land on charitable trusts. A proposal to introduce a general rule of decision by majority vote was rejected by the Law Reform Committee in 1982 (see Law Reform Committee, *The Powers and Duties of Trustees* (23rd Report, Cmnd 8733, October 1982), paras 3.60–3.65).

3 See *Re Mayo* [1943] Ch 302 at 304 per Simonds J. If, in the teeth of the primary duty to sell, one of the trustees for sale holds out against sale, application may be made for a court order directing the recalcitrant trustee to co-operate in a transfer of the land (TOLATA 1996, s 14(1)–(2)). See formerly LPA 1925, s 30.

4 TOLATA 1996, s 14(1)–(2) **[para 11.229]**.

Execution of the duty to sell

9.226 Central to the 1925 legislation is the idea that the due performance by trustees for sale of their paramount duty (ie sale) should attract the advantageous consequence of enabling the purchaser of the legal estate to overreach the equitable interests held by beneficiaries behind the trust.[1] Thus any conveyance of the legal estate in the land in conformity with certain statutory preconditions is designed to allow the purchaser to take an unencumbered legal title,[2] whilst ensuring that the equitable interests of the beneficial co-owners are translated into equivalent interests in the capital proceeds arising from the disposition.[3]

1   [**Paras 2.165, 11.195**].
2   LPA 1925, s 2(1)(ii).
3   See *City of London Building Society v Flegg* [1988] AC 54 at 73G–74A per Lord Templeman.

Concurrent and successive interests

9.227   In the scheme of the Law of Property Act 1925 the trust for sale was intended to provide a device capable of accommodating both concurrent and successive forms of expressly created beneficial entitlement.[1]

1   Where land is held on an express trust for sale, the details of ownership (both legal and equitable) are often – although not necessarily – contained in two separate documents. One of these documents is a vesting document (or transfer) which records the vesting of the legal title in the trustees for sale. The other document, if there is one, is a 'trust instrument' which records the equitable rights behind the trust. A subsequent purchaser of the land need normally concern himself only with the first of these documents (in unregistered conveyancing) or with the proprietorship register (in registered conveyancing), since he knows that any beneficial interests outlined in the trust instrument will be overreached on compliance with the relevant statutory requirements [**para 11.203**].

The 'co-ownership trust for sale'

9.228   By far the more common type of trust for sale provides expressly for *concurrent* beneficial entitlement on the part of nominated beneficiaries, as where Greenacre is transferred to trustees for sale on behalf of 'A, B and C in equal shares' (see *Fig.* 20). Under such a 'co-ownership trust for sale' the relevant legal estate in land (together with the ancillary powers of management and disposition) is vested in T1 and T2 as 'trustees for sale'. The equitable interests of the beneficiaries are held simultaneously in possession, the beneficiaries having proportional rights in any income drawn from the land before sale and enjoying specific aliquot shares of the capital proceeds of sale if and when sale takes place.

The 'successive interest trust for sale'

9.229   Under a 'successive interest trust for sale' it is possible to make express provision for a series of beneficial interests to be held *consecutively*, as for instance where Greenacre is conveyed to trustees for sale on behalf of 'A for life, remainder to B for life, remainder to C in fee simple' (see *Fig.* 21). Prior to 1997 it was the explicit nature of the direction that T1 and T2 should hold 'on trust for sale' which indeed brought about a trust for sale rather than a strict settlement under the Settled Land Act 1925.[1] After 1996, in default of some explicit reference to a trust 'for sale', a grant of successive beneficial entitlements necessarily takes effect under a 'trust of land' regulated by the Trusts of Land and Appointment of Trustees Act 1996.[2]

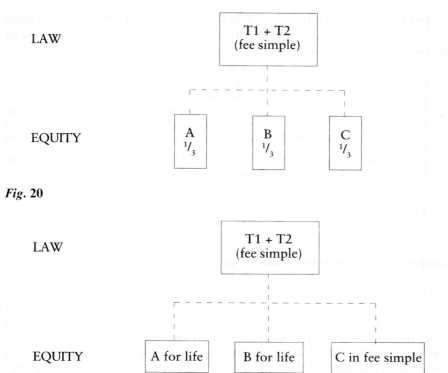

Fig. **20**

Fig. **21**

1   Merely to convey a legal estate to T1 and T2 'on trust for' successively entitled beneficiaries had the effect, prior to 1997, of generating a strict settlement (see *Peach v Peach* (Unreported, Court of Appeal, 3 November 1981)). In such circumstances the person entitled to hold the legal estate was the beneficiary currently in possession (rather than T1 and T2), with the consequence that any transfer to the latter 'on trust' was simply ineffective as a conveyance of the legal estate, the legal title remaining in the grantor pending its vesting in the appropriate tenant for life.

2   [**Para 9.205**].

9.230   Under a 'successive interest trust for sale' the legal estate in the land and the attendant decision-making powers are not vested, as under a pre-1997 strict settlement,[1] in the beneficiary currently entitled in possession (ie A). The essence of the trust for sale device is that the legal estate in the land is allocated to separate trustees (T1 and T2),[2] who thereafter exercise all the decision-making powers with regard to the administration of the land and its eventual disposition.[3] Pending sale of the land these trustees are required to deflect beneficial enjoyment of the land (whether in the form of rents and profits or rights of occupation) to A and B successively. If the trustees dispose of the legal estate while A is beneficially entitled in possession,[4] the beneficial interests of A, B and C are overreached and translated into the resulting proceeds.[5] If no sale occurs before C's beneficial interest falls into possession, C (if of full age) is

Suppression of implied trusts for sale

9.242   The statutorily implied trust for sale has now disappeared, all existing instances being automatically converted into 'trusts of land'.[1] Today there is, happily, no need to force cases of co-ownership within the ambit of some dubiously relevant statutory provision.

1   TOLATA 1996, ss 1(1)–(2), 5(1), Sch 2, paras 3–4.

Express trusts for sale are subsumed within the trust of land

9.243   Under the Trusts of Land and Appointment of Trustees Act 1996 express trusts for sale created prior to 1997 continue in existence. Such trusts are, however, subsumed within the general machinery of the new 'trust of land'. This transmutation of the old-style express trust for sale into a sub-species of 'trust of land' has certain important consequences. Irrespective of the date of creation of the trust for sale,[1] the supposed primacy of the duty of sale is now negatived by the overriding statutory mandate that, in every trust for sale of land created by a disposition, 'there is to be implied, despite any provision to the contrary made by the disposition, a power for the trustees to postpone sale of the land.'[2] The trustees now have not only (as before 1997) an implied power to postpone sale indefinitely but, more significantly, a power in this respect which is irreducible by any contrary indication.[3] The 1996 Act also completes the retreat from the equitable doctrine of conversion by providing that land held on trust for sale 'is not to be regarded as personal property'.[4]

1   See TOLATA 1996, s 4(2).
2   TOLATA 1996, s 4(1). Trustees for sale, acting in the exercise of their discretion, cannot now be made liable 'in any way' for postponing sale, although they must still act unanimously in deciding to do so [**para 9.225**].
3   Prior to 1997 the statutorily implied power to postpone the sale of land held on trust for sale could be excluded by an expression of 'contrary intention' (LPA 1925, s 25(1)). See eg *Re Atkins' Will Trusts* [1974] 1 WLR 761 at 767C–D.
4   TOLATA 1996, s 3(1). See Law Com No 181 (1989), paras 3.5, 20.2. This displacement of the doctrine of conversion does not apply to a trust created by the will of a testator who died before 1 January 1997 (s 3(2)), but is otherwise operative irrespective of the date of creation of the trust for sale (s 3(3)).

CHAPTER 10

Informal creation of rights in land

INFORMAL MECHANISMS OF RIGHTS CREATION

10.1   As is apparent from earlier chapters of this book, English law is heavily influenced by a distaste for informal mechanisms directed towards the creation of property rights in land.[1] Considerations of clarity and certainty argue strongly in favour of the use of formal means of rights creation such as those provided by a deed or other signed writing.[2] Yet the powerful policy motivation underlying the general requirement of formality sometimes comes into collision with even more significant concerns, particularly of equitable origin, which override the standard preference that rights in land should be created or evidenced by documentary means alone. Equity attaches ultimate priority to the underlying intent of transactions and to the demands of conscionable dealing. Although the conscience of equity is far from comprising a complete system of social or commercial morality, the longstop of equity is an abhorrence of fraud, especially where it subverts the basic intentions or shared understandings underpinning various sorts of transaction.

1   **[Paras 7.26, 9.190]**.
2   See LPA 1925, ss 52(1), 53(1) **[paras 7.26, 9.188]**.

10.2   In certain circumstances, therefore, English law permits the informal creation of rights in land if a dogmatic insistence on documentary formality would grossly controvert the relevant intentions of the parties or unconscionably frustrate their legitimate expectations.[1] Such cases are recognised principally, although not exclusively, by the law relating to

–   implied trusts[2]
–   proprietary estoppel[3]
–   informally conferred life interests[4] and
–   *donationes mortis causa.*[5]

1   See e g *Proudreed Ltd v Microgen Holdings Plc* (1996) 72 P & CR 388 at 389 per Schiemann LJ. For an excellent overview, see G Battersby, 'Informally Created Interests in Land', in S Bright and J K Dewar (ed), *Land Law: Themes and Perspectives* (OUP 1998), p 487.

2   **[Para 10.3]**.
3   **[Para 10.168]**.
4   **[Para 10.301]**.
5   **[Para 10.309]**.

CLASSIFICATION OF IMPLIED TRUSTS

10.3   Given that a transfer of a legal estate carries prima facie the entire beneficial interest,[1] substantial difficulties lie in the path of any person who alleges a beneficial entitlement not contained in the express terms of the transfer[2] or in an enforceable declaration of trust relating to the land in question.[3] The claimant is relegated to the contention that some variety of implied trust has been generated in his or her favour.[4] Implied trusts are of essentially two kinds, the *resulting trust* and the *constructive trust*.[5] Whereas express trusts are founded directly on declared intention, implied trusts arise by operation of law, albeit against a background of actual or presumed intention.[6] Moreover, the Law of Property Act 1925 makes it clear that the documentary requirements generally imposed in respect of trusts[7] have no application to the 'creation or operation of resulting, implied or constructive trusts.'[8] Resulting and constructive trusts, although alike in that they escape statutory requirements of writing, nevertheless have quite distinct spheres of operation.

1   **[Para 9.174]**.
2   See e g *Roy v Roy* [1996] 1 FLR 541 at 546A–F per Fox LJ.
3   **[Para 9.188]**.
4   See *Carlton v Goodman* [2002] 2 FLR 259 at [22(ii)] per Mummery LJ.
5   **[Para 9.192]**. See *Cowcher v Cowcher* [1972] 1 WLR 425 at 431A per Bagnall J; *McKenzie v McKenzie* [2003] EWHC 601 (Ch) at [68].
6   *Westdeutsche Landesbank Girozentrale v Islington LBC* [1996] AC 669 at 708C per Lord Browne-Wilkinson; *Avondale Printers & Stationers Ltd v Haggie* [1979] 2 NZLR 124 at 145 per Mahon J.
7   LPA 1925, s 53(1).
8   LPA 1925, s 53(2).

Resulting trusts

10.4   Resulting trusts are intrinsically concerned with the pattern of money contributions laid out in a purchase of land. A resulting trust gives effect to the intention which, in default of any other evidence, is presumed to underlie the way in which such moneys are put towards the acquisition of a legal title. In the absence of any countervailing intention, a money contribution towards the purchase of a legal estate in the name of another normally generates a resulting trust in favour of the contributor, the latter's equitable entitlement being proportionate to his or her cash contribution.

Constructive trusts

10.5   By contrast constructive trusts are intimately concerned, not so much with money, but rather with expressly or implicitly bargained commitments respecting equitable entitlement. A constructive trust arises where it would be fraudulent for the owner of a legal estate to maintain his sole beneficial ownership in derogation of rights which have already been bargained away informally to another. The existence of the prior agreement, once relied on to the detriment of the claimant party, renders it unconscionable for the legal owner to assert his beneficial title to the exclusion of the claimant. To prevent such inequitable outcomes, equity imposes or 'constructs'[1] a trust to give effect to the parties' earlier understanding as to their respective equitable rights.

1   See *Green v Green* [2003] UKPC 39 at [12] per Lord Hope of Craighead; *Grant v Edwards* [1986] Ch 638 at 646H–647A per Nourse LJ; *Melbury Road Properties 1995 Ltd v Kreidi* [1999] 3 EGLR 108 at 110L; *Thwaites v Ryan* [1984] VR 65 at 91 per Fullagar J.

Ambivalent relationship of resulting and constructive trusts

10.6   English case law abounds with indiscriminate references to resulting and constructive trusts as broadly interchangeable terminology for the same equitable phenomenon.[1] The nomenclature of trust law is 'unfortunately far from uniform'[2] and some doctrinal uncertainty has been generated by the temptation to merge the fields of resulting and constructive trust.[3] Lord Browne-Wilkinson has nevertheless pointed out that these forms of trust 'are two different animals' and that failure to distinguish them has caused 'great confusion'.[4] Further disorientation flows from the fact that the constructive trust coalesces with many applications of the principle of proprietary estoppel,[5] with the result that English law is in some danger of sliding into a generalised formula of equitable proprietary relief relevant to supposed instances of injustice.

1   Some of the confusion can be traced to a locus classicus of trust law, *Gissing v Gissing* [1971] AC 886 at 905B–C, where Lord Diplock spoke of a 'resulting, implied or constructive trust' and observed that 'it is unnecessary for present purposes to distinguish between these three classes of trust.'
2   *Birmingham Midshires Mortgage Services Ltd v Sabherwal* (2000) 80 P & CR 256 at 263 per Robert Walker LJ.
3   Compare the distaste of the New South Wales Court of Appeal for the 'apparent amalgamation of resulting and constructive trusts into one congruent class' (*Allen v Snyder* [1977] 2 NSWLR 685 at 698D per Samuels JA).
4   'Constructive Trusts and Unjust Enrichment' (1996) 10 Trust Law International 98 at 99. See similarly *Drake v Whipp* [1996] 1 FLR 826 at 827B–C per Peter Gibson LJ; *McKenzie v McKenzie* [2003] EWHC 601 (Ch) at [68], [89]; *Avondale Printers & Stationers Ltd v Haggie* [1979] 2 NZLR 124 at 145 per Mahon J; *Muschinski v Dodds* (1985) 160 CLR 583 at 596 per Gibbs CJ.
5   See e g *Chan Pui Chun v Leung Kam Ho* [2003] 1 FLR 23 at [91] per Jonathan Parker LJ; *Oxley v Hiscock* [2004] 3 WLR 715 at [66] per Chadwick LJ.

10.7   The ambivalent relationship between resulting and constructive trusts stems, in part, from the fact that both are exempted from any requirement of written form or written evidence. Both are premised, moreover, upon intended beneficial ownership – in one case as disclosed presumptively by the pattern of money purchase and in the other case as embodied in some antecedent bargain struck by the relevant parties. It is nevertheless important to separate out the

notions involved in the readily blurred classifications of resulting and constructive trust. The *resulting* trust finds its origins in the unilateral intention
attributed to a provider of purchase money. In the absence of any evidence of
actual intention, the doctrine of resulting trust articulates the presumption that
the money contributor to a purchase taken in the name of another intends no
gratuitous benefit for that other. By contrast the *constructive* trust is rooted in
the bilateral intentions of the relevant actors (whether expressed or inferred
from their conduct). The constructive trust 'arises out of, and is equity's way of
giving effect to, the common intentions of the parties' regarding the allocation
of beneficial ownership.[1] One further ground of distinction has emerged
between the two forms of implied trust. It is probably best nowadays to regard
the resulting trust as applicable only where contributions of cash have been
channelled directly towards the initial purchase of realty.[2] All other forms of
contributory activity (whether occurring before or after the acquisition of title)
are therefore relegated to the sphere of the constructive trust.[3]

1   *McKenzie v McKenzie* [2003] EWHC 601 (Ch) at [70].
2   There is a tendency to subsume under the heading of constructive trust even those direct
     forms of financial contribution to purchase (such as the payment of a cash deposit) which
     formerly would have been thought to raise a resulting trust (see eg *Halifax Building Society v
     Brown* [1996] 1 FLR 103 at 109D per Balcombe LJ).
3   See eg *Mollo v Mollo* [1999] EGCS 117 (Transcript at [22]–[23]), where a claim of resulting
     trust was rejected for want of financial contribution towards acquisition, but the doctrine of
     constructive trust was described as enjoying 'a wide flexibility in recognising other forms of
     input into the ultimate capital value of the house, for example, by way of subsequent
     expenditure of a capital nature such as an extension to the property or a new conservatory.'

RESULTING TRUSTS

10.8   A resulting trust is presumed, absent all other evidence of intention,
where information concerning the source of purchase money is recognised as
displacing the prima facie inference that equitable ownership follows legal title.
The legal title is, after all, a mere paper title; and equity's concern has long been
with the inner substance of transactions rather than with their outer form. A
resulting trust comes into existence in certain stereotyped situations where a
nominal purchaser of an estate (A) is deemed to hold on a trust which 'results'
back to the person (B) who financed the acquisition.[1] Under the resulting trust
A takes only the legal (or paper) title and the equitable interest is presumed to
belong to B, the 'real purchaser'.[2]

1   The word 'result' in this context is not used in any sense of causation and consequence, but
     rather in its root sense of 'leaping back' (Latin, *resultare*). A trust of the land springs back in
     favour of the real purchaser (see *Rathwell v Rathwell* (1978) 83 DLR (3d) 289 at 302 per
     Dickson J).
2   *Muschinski v Dodds* (1985) 160 CLR 583 at 589 per Gibbs CJ.

Presumption of resulting trust

10.9   Consistently with the character of equity, beneficial ownership depends
fundamentally on intention[1] and the origin of the resulting trust lies in a

presumption as to the intended beneficial ownership of the asset purchased.[2] This presumption is, however, an ultimate fall-back of judicial technique and operates only in the absence of all other evidence of intention.[3] The presumption readily gives way to any contrary intention manifested at the date of the purchase.[4] The presumption of resulting trust can also be displaced by a counter-presumption of equity[5] or even overtaken by some constructive trust which emerges at or subsequently to the date of acquisition.[6]

1   See *Hepworth v Hepworth* (1963) 110 CLR 309 at 317 per Windeyer J **[para 9.177]**.
2   *Gissing v Gissing* [1971] AC 886 at 902B per Lord Pearson; *Westdeutsche Landesbank Girozentrale v Islington LBC* [1996] AC 669 at 708C per Lord Browne-Wilkinson; *Rathwell v Rathwell* (1978) 83 DLR (3d) 289 at 303 per Dickson J.
3   *Stockholm Finance Ltd v Garden Holdings Inc* [1995] NPC 162 per Robert Walker J ('the equitable presumptions ... are presumptions of fact only, which will rarely be decisive today ... ').
4   *Dyer v Dyer* (1788) 2 Cox Eq Cas 92 at 93, 30 ER 42 at 43; *Pettitt v Pettitt* [1970] AC 777 at 814A–G per Lord Upjohn.
5   *Tinsley v Milligan* [1994] 1 AC 340 at 371G per Lord Browne-Wilkinson; *Westdeutsche Landesbank Girozentrale v Islington LBC* [1996] AC 669 at 708A–B per Lord Browne-Wilkinson; *Calverley v Green* (1984) 155 CLR 242 at 251 per Gibbs CJ, 258 per Mason and Brennan JJ; *Muschinski v Dodds* (1985) 160 CLR 583 at 589–590 per Gibbs CJ, 612 per Deane J.
6   **[Para 10.23]**.

Trust for the real purchaser

10.10   A resulting trust is presumed to come into existence when an interest in land[1] is purchased in the name of A, A having provided none or part only of the purchase price.[2] A resulting trust therefore arises in favour of B if (and to the extent that) B provided money for the purchase.[3] In the classic exposition of Eyre CB in *Dyer v Dyer*,[4] a 'trust of a legal estate ... results to the man who advances the purchase-money.'[5] Accordingly, if B provides all the purchase money for a vesting of a legal estate in A, A is presumed (absent evidence of contrary intention) to hold that legal estate on a resulting trust for B absolutely (*Fig. 22*).[6]

1   The interest subject to a resulting trust may sometimes have a limited lifespan. There is 'no reason in principle' why a resulting trust cannot attach to a one-year tenancy, at least where – although it must happen rarely – such an estate is purchased for a premium (*Savage v Dunningham* [1974] Ch 181 at 184G).
2   *Pettitt v Pettitt* [1970] AC 777 at 814A per Lord Upjohn; *Cowcher v Cowcher* [1972] 1 WLR 425 at 431B; *Wirth v Wirth* (1956) 98 CLR 228 at 235; *Goodfriend v Goodfriend* (1972) 22 DLR (3d) 699 at 702; *Allen v Snyder* [1977] 2 NSWLR 685 at 689G–690A; *Nelson v Nelson* (1995) 184 CLR 538 at 600 per McHugh J.
3   It is not fatal to a claim of resulting trust that B may have had improper motives for arranging to make money contributions towards the purchase of an estate vested strategically in A. See *Tinsley v Milligan* [1994] 1 AC 340, where a majority in the House of Lords upheld a claim of resulting trust notwithstanding that B's contributions were both motivated and facilitated by a conspiracy to defraud the Department of Social Security. Here the critical factor was that, in putting forward a claim of resulting trust, B was not required to rely on any fraud or illegality committed by her, but merely on the fact of money contributions creative of a trust ([1994] 1 AC 340 at 371F–372A, 376E–G per Lord Browne-Wilkinson). See also *Lowson v Coombes* [1999] Ch 373 at 381A–C per Nourse LJ.

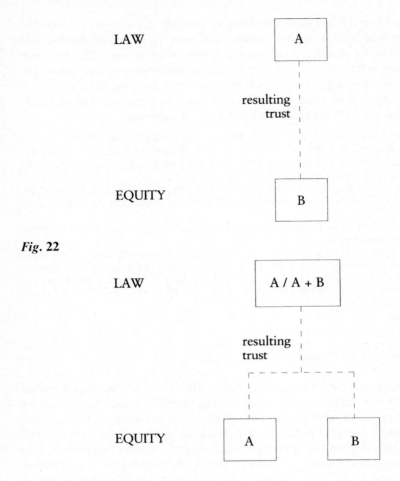

Fig. **22**

Fig. **23**

4   (1788) 2 Cox Eq Cas 92 at 93, 30 ER 42 at 43.
5   This dictum has become a commonplace in the jurisprudence of resulting trusts (see e g *Pettitt*
     v Pettitt [1970] AC 777 at 814B–E per Lord Upjohn; *Gissing v Gissing* [1971] AC 886 at 902D
     per Lord Pearson; *Carlton v Goodman* [2002] 2 FLR 259 at [36] per Ward LJ).
6   *Calverley v Green* (1984) 155 CLR 242 at 246 per Gibbs CJ, 266–267 per Deane J; *Stephenson*
     Nominees Pty Ltd v Official Receiver on behalf of Official Trustee in Bankruptcy; ex p Roberts
     (1987) 76 ALR 485 at 500 per Gummow J.

Effect of joint contributions of money

10.11   The principle of resulting trust is adaptable to any number of financial
contributors: each is presumed to intend to take beneficially in proportion to
his own contribution of money.[1] If A and B both contribute towards the
purchase of a legal estate in the name of A (or even of A and B), there is a
presumed resulting trust for A and B (see *Fig.* 23).[2] If A and B contribute
unequally, they are presumed, in the absence of contrary agreement,[3] to hold

beneficially as tenants in common[4] commensurately with their respective contributions.[5] If they contribute equally, their entitlement under the resulting trust has traditionally been deemed to take the form of beneficial joint tenancy.[6] Nowadays, however, there is increasing force in the argument that mere parity of contribution should not automatically render the contributors joint tenants (with the rights of survivorship so disfavoured by equity[7]), but should instead produce a presumptive tenancy in common in equal shares.[8] At all events it is clear that any beneficial joint tenancy can be easily converted by either party into a tenancy in common in equal shares.[9]

1 See *Harwood v Harwood* [1991] 2 FLR 274 at 292B–C, where *Dyer's* case was applied to raise a presumption of resulting trust of a legal estate purchased in the names of A and B, using the moneys of A, B and C. See also *Billinghurst v Reader* (1997) 151 DLR (4th) 753 at 756–757.

2 *Tinsley v Milligan* [1994] 1 AC 340 at 371D per Lord Browne-Wilkinson; *Westdeutsche Landesbank Girozentrale v Islington LBC* [1996] AC 669 at 708A per Lord Browne-Wilkinson; *Calverley v Green* (1984) 155 CLR 242 at 246 per Gibbs CJ. See also *Little v Little* (1988) 15 NSWLR 43 at 46A–C per Bryson J.

3 Any intention that A and B should take entitlements other than those dictated by their respective money contributions (eg as joint tenants or as tenants in common in different proportions) can be given effect only under a declaration of trust evidenced by writing (see LPA 1925, s 53(1)(b) [**para 9.188**]) or by way of constructive trust [**para 10.23**]. See *Cowcher v Cowcher* [1972] 1 WLR 425 at 431C–D per Bagnall J.

4 [**Para 11.29**].

5 The principle is almost as old as equity itself and has found global acceptance. See *Lake v Gibson* (1729) 1 Eq Ca Abr 290 at 291, 21 ER 1052 at 1053; *Aveling v Knipe* (1815) 19 Ves 441 at 444–445, 34 ER 580 at 582; *Bull v Bull* [1955] 1 QB 234 at 236 per Denning LJ; *Pettitt v Pettitt* [1970] AC 777 at 814B per Lord Upjohn; *Gissing v Gissing* [1971] AC 886 at 907C per Lord Diplock; *Williams & Glyn's Bank Ltd v Boland* [1981] AC 487 at 502F–G per Lord Wilberforce; *Scott v Scott* (1963) 109 CLR 649 at 663; *Calverley v Green* (1984) 155 CLR 242 at 246–247 per Gibbs CJ, 266–267 per Deane J.

6 [**Para 11.60**]. See *Lake v Gibson* (1729) 1 Eq Ca Abr 290, 21 ER 1052; *O'Connell v Harrison* [1927] IR 330 at 336; *Efstratiou, Glantschnig and Petrovic v Glantschnig* [1972] NZLR 594 at 598; *Taddeo v Taddeo* (1978) 19 SASR 347 at 365. See also *Vedejs v Public Trustee* [1985] VR 569 at 575.

7 [**Para 11.55**].

8 See eg *Knightly v Sun Life Assurance Society Ltd* (1981) Times, 23 July. In *Carmody v Delehunt* [1984] 1 NSWLR 667 at 669C Hutley JA found it 'wholly mysterious', in view of the equitable distaste for survivorship, that the resolution of equity should have 'faltered when it came to the rights of persons advancing equal sums of money.' See also *Tinsley v Milligan* [1992] Ch 310 at 321D, 326G per Nicholls LJ; *Allen v Rochdale BC* [2000] Ch 221 at 232D–E per Morritt LJ. It is likely, however, that a purchase paid for out of jointly held funds gives rise to a presumptive beneficial joint tenancy (see *Chandler v Clark* [2003] 1 P & CR 239 at [19] per Chadwick LJ).

9 The law relating to severance of beneficial joint tenancy is discussed in Chapter 11 [**para 11.64**].

RATIONALE OF THE RESULTING TRUST

10.12 In drawing a sharp distinction between the *nominal* and the *real* purchaser, equity emphasises the significance of the cash nexus in human dealings. Equity, with its superbly realistic grasp of human motivations, 'assumes bargains, and not gifts.'[1] In the normal run of things, people who lay out large sums in the context of a purchase of land do not harbour particularly altruistic intentions,[2] but really expect, regardless of the destination of the legal title purchased, to derive a beneficial return from their investment in the form of an aliquot share of the equity. Resulting trust doctrine ensures a default position which gives effect to this expectation. The resulting trust generated by the provision of purchase money is compelling evidence of what Woodhouse J once termed 'the solid tug of money'.[3] In a money-conscious world it is scarcely conceivable, absent clear evidence of donative intention, that B, the provider of money, intended to confer a gratuitous benefit on A, the nominal purchaser.

1   *Goodfriend v Goodfriend* (1972) 22 DLR (3d) 699 at 703 per Spence J (Supreme Court of Canada). See also *Gorog v Kiss* (1977) 78 DLR (3d) 690 at 694.

2   See *McKenzie v McKenzie* [2003] EWHC 601 (Ch) at [76]. The deep suspicion with which gifts of land were viewed in the 19th century may have been one of the underlying reasons for the presumption of resulting trust (see *Lohia and Lohia v Lohia* [2001] WTLR 101 at [22]).

3   *Hofman v Hofman* [1965] NZLR 795 at 800. See also *Reid v Reid* [1979] 1 NZLR 572 at 581 per Woodhouse J ('the hypnotic influence of money').

'Equities' fashioned by presumed intention

10.13   The critical intention in the creation of a resulting trust is that of the contributor of the purchase money.[1] Equity, with its obsessive focus on the animus underlying transactions, allows the consequence of money payment to be determined by the intention of the payer.

1   See *Cowcher v Cowcher* [1972] 1 WLR 425 at 431C per Bagnall J.

An 'equity' for the provider of money

10.14   In the absence of all other evidence, the resulting trust is founded on the presumed absence in the money contributor of any intention to surrender the benefit of his wealth to the recipient of the legal estate which has been purchased at his expense.[1] The doctrine of resulting trust thus recognises an 'equity' as inhering in B in direct proportion to his contribution to the purchase in the name of A. This 'equity' marks the concern of the jurisdiction of conscience lest the contributor be unjustly deprived of the value of his contribution, in much the same way that an 'equity' arises elsewhere to protect a vendor of land against the possibility that he might remain for ever unpaid.[2]

1   The resulting trust is 'equity's response to the failure of a gift or proof of lack of intention to make one' (*McKenzie v McKenzie* [2003] EWHC 601 (Ch) at [76]).

2   **[Para 9.130]**.

The 'equity' binds the nominal purchaser

10.15   The 'equity' raised in favour of the money contributor (B) binds the recipient of the legal estate (A) precisely because the latter has knowingly accepted (or now seeks to retain[1]) a title purchased through the use of another's funds.[2] It would clearly be unconscionable to allow A to assert absolute legal and beneficial ownership if B, intending to confer no largesse, has paid money in the character of a purchaser.[3] Equity, looking on as done that which ought to be done, assumes that A intends to honour the 'equity' which has accrued in favour of the unintending benefactor.[4] The resulting trust simply gives 'the force of law to moral obligations.'[5]

1   See *Westdeutsche Landesbank Girozentrale v Islington LBC* [1996] AC 669 at 705G–706A per Lord Browne-Wilkinson.
2   Compare *Allen v Rochdale BC* [2000] Ch 221 at 232D–F, where a resulting trust was rejected because the purchaser had no ground for believing itself to be buying otherwise than with its own money. See also *Westdeutsche Landesbank Girozentrale v Islington LBC* [1996] AC 669 at 705D per Lord Browne-Wilkinson.
3   See *Winkworth v Edward Baron Development Co Ltd* [1986] 1 WLR 1512 at 1516C–D per Lord Templeman.
4   See *Taddeo v Taddeo* (1978) 19 SASR 347 at 368, where Walters J attributed the operation of the resulting trust to equity's assumption that 'independently of any fraud … the purchaser … intended to act, and … was acting, in pursuance of his fiduciary duty.' See also *Gissing v Gissing* [1971] AC 886 at 902B per Lord Pearson; *Pettkus v Becker* (1981) 117 DLR (3d) 257 at 263 per Ritchie J.
5   *Sekhon v Alissa* [1989] 2 FLR 94 at 99C per Hoffmann J.

Resulting trust as an emanation of shared intention

10.16   The resulting trust arises, not from any intention in A to create a trust, but rather from a presumed lack of intention in B to enrich A. However, A's willingness to accept the legal title in the shadow of B's presumed intention now gives a semblance of commonality to their respective intentions. A, being unable conscionably to deny the absence of donative intent in B, is deemed to endorse B's expectation of beneficial ownership as a tangible return for B's material assistance in the purchase. By a circuitous route the resulting trust thus appears to reflect some kind of implied agreement,[1] arising from the circumstances of purchase, as to the way in which the equitable title should be held.[2]

1   The presumption of resulting trust is sometimes explained as 'the fact of contribution evidencing an agreement'. It has also been described as a form of 'constructive agreement' (see *Rathwell v Rathwell* (1978) 83 DLR (3d) 289 at 304 per Dickson J).
2   The foregoing analysis helps to resolve the doctrinal controversy as to whether the resulting trust is based on the unilateral negative intent of the money contributor (*Twinsectra Ltd v Yardley* [2003] 2 AC 164 at [92] per Lord Millett) or is rooted in the common intention of both parties (see *Westdeutsche Landesbank Girozentrale v Islington LBC* [1996] AC 669 at 708C per Lord Browne-Wilkinson). See e g *Carlton v Goodman* [2002] 2 FLR 259 at [23]–[26] per Mummery LJ, [33]–[34] per Ward LJ.

ORIGIN OF THE RESULTING TRUST

10.17   Resulting trusts arise by operation of law[1] rather than by reference to the actual intentions of the parties. There is, for instance, no requirement that a resulting trustee should necessarily know that a resulting trust exists.[2] Moreover, a resulting trust arises in favour of the provider of the purchase money even if the land actually purchased is not the land which he intended should be purchased (eg if A wrongfully uses B's money to purchase Redacre rather than Greenacre as agreed[3]).

1   *Blackburn v Y V Properties Pty Ltd* [1980] VR 290 at 293; *Re Levy* (1982) 131 DLR (3d) 15 at 23.
2   *Tattersfield v Tattersfield and the New Zealand Insurance Co Ltd* [1980] BCL 1110. See, however, *Allen v Rochdale BC* [2000] Ch 221 at 232D–F [**para 10.15**]).
3   *Scott v Scott* (1963) 109 CLR 649 at 663–664 (High Court of Australia).

Mode of acquisition of title

10.18 Since ownership at law concerns only a nominal or paper title, a resulting trust attaches to the legal estate irrespective of the identity of its owner. Exactly the same beneficial results follow whether the moneys of A and B are used to purchase a legal title taken in the name of A alone, or in the joint names of A and B[1] or of A and X,[2] or in the name of X alone[3] or in the joint names of X, Y and Z. Likewise, if a legal estate is purchased in the joint names of A and B, using only the money of B, a resulting trust is presumed exclusively for B.[4] Nor does it matter whether B purchases land with his own funds and directs that the legal title should be transferred by the vendor into the name of A,[5] or whether A, using funds provided by B, purchases a legal estate in his own name. In either case, if the money has been laid out by B in the character of a purchaser, there is a presumption of resulting trust.[6]

1   *Crisp v Mullings* (1976) 239 EG 119 at 121; *Walker v Hall* [1984] FLR 126 at 130C; *Calverley v Green* (1984) 155 CLR 242 at 246 per Gibbs CJ, 258 per Mason and Brennan JJ; *Muschinski v Dodds* (1985) 160 CLR 583 at 589 per Gibbs CJ.
2   *Hoare v Hoare* (1982) Times, 9 November.
3   *Hardy v Lane* (1994) 6 BPR 13968 at 13975.
4   *Benger v Drew* (1721) 1 P Wms 781, 24 ER 613; *Wilson v Wilson* [1969] 3 All ER 945 at 949E–F; *Young v Young* [1984] FLR 375 at 380E; *Noack v Noack* [1959] VR 137 at 139; *Allied Irish Banks Ltd v McWilliams* [1982] NI 156 at 161C–D. *Calverley v Green* (1984) 155 CLR 242 at 255 per Mason and Brennan JJ, 266 per Deane J.
5   *Pettitt v Pettitt* [1970] AC 777 at 814A; *Noack v Noack* [1959] VR 137 at 139; *Rathwell v Rathwell* (1978) 83 DLR (3d) 289 at 302.
6   See *Bateman Television Ltd v Bateman and Thomas* [1971] NZLR 453 at 462 per Turner J.

Voluntary transfer of legal estate

10.19 The resulting trust is sometimes known as a 'purchase money trust',[1] in that the doctrine of resulting trust presupposes a purchase for value in A's name of land previously owned by a stranger. However, no resulting trust is presumed from the mere fact that B, the owner of a legal estate, transfers this estate voluntarily (ie gratuitously) into the name of A. In this rather different context, statute has abolished the presumption of resulting trust[2] and, in the absence of any evidence of contrary intention,[3] A takes both legal and equitable title absolutely.[4]

1   See *Bhana v Bhana* (2002) 10 BPR 19545 at [12] per Hamilton J.
2   See the effect attributed to LPA 1925, s 60(3), in *Ali v Khan* [2002] EWCA Civ 974 at [24] per

Morritt V-C. The case law contains some expressions of caution as to the precise impact of this provision (see e g *Hodgson v Marks* [1971] Ch 892 at 933D per Russell LJ; *Lohia and Lohia v Lohia* [2001] WTLR 101 at [26] per Mummery LJ, [34] per Sir Christopher Slade), but the preferable view is that LPA 1925, s 60(3) simply means what it says. See also *DKLR Holding Co (No 2) Pty Ltd v Commissioner of Stamp Duties (NSW)* (1982) 149 CLR 431 at 442, 463–464, 473–474.

3   LPA 1925, s 60(3) in no way inhibits reliance on extrinsic evidence which shows that a trust was intended (*Ali v Khan* [2002] EWCA Civ 974 at [24]). See e g *Lohia and Lohia v Lohia* [2001] WTLR 101 at [21].

4   In jurisdictions where there is no statutory equivalent of LPA 1925, s 60(3), a gratuitous transfer of title from A to B produces a resulting trust in favour of B (see e g *Napier v Public Trustee (Western Australia)* (1980) 32 ALR 153 at 158). See also *Nelson v Nelson* (1995) 185 CLR 538 at 600–602 per McHugh J (obiter), but compare *Bhana v Bhana* (2002) 10 BPR 19545 at [27].

Time-frame of the relevant intentions

10.20   According to classical theory, a resulting trust is based on an intention presumed to exist at the date of acquisition of the land concerned,[1] at which point the precise distribution of beneficial entitlement definitively 'crystallises'.[2] In a very strict sense, the only intention relevant to a resulting trust – as distinct from a constructive trust[3] – is that which can be presumed to have been contemporaneous with the initial taking of legal title.[4] Resulting trusts cannot, in principle, be founded on intentions, events or circumstances which emerge only after the date of purchase.[5] Thus, for example, later contributions of money (whether towards improvement of land or otherwise) cannot, in the rigorous theory of resulting trust, generate any presumed intention as of the date of acquisition. The major difficulty with this concentration on the isolated moment of purchase is, of course, that it fails to take account of mortgage-assisted acquisitions of land, where the economic reality of purchase is elongated over many years. It is plainly inequitable to apply resulting trust theory in total disregard of mortgage instalments paid or shared over a prolonged period by some party other than the legal owner. Yet it is exceedingly difficult to accommodate the practice of instalment purchase within the dogmatic confines of resulting trust theory without extreme doctrinal contortion.

1   See *Sekhon v Alissa* [1989] 2 FLR 94 at 95G per Hoffmann J; *Currie v Hamilton* [1984] 1 NSWLR 687 at 691D per McLelland J.

2   *Bernard v Josephs* [1982] Ch 391 at 404F per Griffiths LJ.

3   **[Para 10.84]**.

4   *Pettitt v Pettitt* [1970] AC 777 at 800F–G per Lord Morris of Borth-y-Gest, 813D per Lord Upjohn; *Gissing v Gissing* [1971] AC 886 at 897C per Lord Reid, 900B–D per Viscount Dilhorne, 905D per Lord Diplock; *Bernard v Josephs* [1982] Ch 391 at 404C; *Burns v Burns* [1984] Ch 317 at 327A; *Hohol v Hohol* [1981] VR 221 at 225–226; *Baumgartner v Baumgartner* (1985) 2 NSWLR 406 at 417F.

5   See *Jeffries v Stevens* (1982) STC 639 at 651g.

Shift of emphasis to constructive trusts

10.21   In recent decades a new pragmatism has become apparent in the law of trusts. English courts have eventually conceded that the classical theory of resulting trusts, with its fixation on intentions presumed to have been formulated contemporaneously with the acquisition of title, has substantially broken down. For a period the courts seemed willing to accept that, contrary to the basic principles of resulting trust, conduct subsequent to the acquisition date might justify the retrospective inference of intentions assumed to exist at that date[1] and that the actual quantification of the ensuing beneficial interests might on occasion be deferred until a much later date.[2] But the inevitable artificiality of such inferences of intention has caused a gradual slippage away from resulting trust theory towards more liberating applications of the constructive trust, where the timing of relevant intentions has never been so critically defined. Simultaneously the balance of emphasis in the law of trusts has transferred from crude factors of money contribution (which are pre-eminent in the resulting trust) towards more subtle factors of intentional bargain (which are the foundational premise of the constructive trust). This process of intellectual migration has contributed in no small way to a blurring of the borderline between these two forms of trust. But the undoubted consequence is that the doctrine of resulting trust has conceded much of its field of application to the constructive trust, which is nowadays fast becoming the primary phenomenon in the area of implied trusts. The presumption of resulting trust may now be 'completely anachronistic'[3] and little more than a 'judicial instrument of last resort.'[4]

1   See eg *Gissing v Gissing* [1971] AC 886 at 906E per Lord Diplock; *Bernard v Josephs* [1982] Ch 391 at 404F–G.

2   See *Gissing v Gissing* [1971] AC 886 at 909C–D per Lord Diplock; *Bernard v Josephs* [1982] Ch 391 at 407G–H per Kerr LJ; *Winkworth v Edward Baron Development Co Ltd* [1986] 1 WLR 1512 at 1516C–D; *Burns v Burns* [1984] Ch 317 at 327A–B, 344E.

3   *Dullow v Dullow* (1985) 3 NSWLR 531 at 535A per Hope JA.

4   *Stockholm Finance Ltd v Garden Holdings Inc* [1995] NPC 162 per Robert Walker J; *Nightingale Mayfair Ltd v Mehta* (Unreported, Chancery Division, 21 December 1999) per Blackburne J. See now *Oxley v Hiscock* [2004] 3 WLR 715 **[para 10.140]**.

REBUTTAL OF THE PRESUMPTION OF RESULTING TRUST

10.22   The presumptions of equity are, of course, only that – they are *presumptions*, based on standardised expectations of human action and reaction.[1] As Lord Diplock observed in *Pettitt v Pettitt*,[2] the equitable presumptions of intention are 'no more than a consensus of judicial opinion disclosed by reported cases as to the most likely inference of fact to be drawn in the absence of any evidence to the contrary.' Presumptions shift the burden of adducing evidence, in that the onus of persuasion is thrown upon the party against whom the force of the presumption operates.[3] However, as an American judge once said,[4] 'presumptions may be looked on as the bats of the law, flitting in the twilight but disappearing in the sunshine of actual facts.' It follows that *presumed* intentions ultimately prevail only where there is no convincing evidence of *actual* intention.[5]

1 'Presumptions arise from common experience' (*Calverley v Green* (1984) 155 CLR 242 at 264 per Murphy J).
2 [1970] AC 777 at 823H.
3 *Russell v Scott* (1936) 55 CLR 440 at 451 per Dixon and Evatt JJ. See also *Calverley v Green* (1984) 155 CLR 242 at 266 per Deane J; *Muschinski v Dodds* (1985) 160 CLR 583 at 612 per Deane J. A presumption merely allocates the 'risk of non-persuasion' (*Carkeek v Tate-Jones* [1971] VR 691 at 695 per McInerney J).
4 *Mackowik v Kansas City*, 94 SW 256 at 264 (1906) per Lamm J. See also *Ebner v Official Trustee* (2003) 196 ALR 533 at [34].
5 The equitable presumptions of intention are 'readily rebutted by comparatively slight evidence' (*Pettitt v Pettitt* [1970] AC 777 at 814G per Lord Upjohn, who was admittedly 'the most loyal supporter of the presumptions' (see *Stockholm Finance Ltd v Garden Holdings Inc* [1995] NPC 162 per Robert Walker J)). See also *Westdeutsche Landesbank Girozentrale v Islington LBC* [1996] AC 669 at 708B per Lord Browne-Wilkinson; *Vajpeyi v Yusaf* [2004] 1 P & CR D2 at D3.

10.23 The presumption of resulting trust is therefore rebuttable, in whole or part,[1] by any evidence[2] (including parol evidence) which unambiguously demonstrates that B, although providing all or part of the finance for a purchase in the name of A, did not actually intend to take a commensurate (or even any) beneficial interest.[3] Evidence of a countervailing intention sufficient to oust the presumption of resulting trust can be provided in a number of ways. A presumed resulting trust may be displaced by evidence of contrary intention which founds an 'express bargain' constructive trust.[4] Alternatively, the proportions of beneficial ownership established under a presumed purchase money trust can be overturned (sometimes to the unexpected prejudice of the trust claimant[5]) by reference to a different pattern of intended beneficial entitlement as inferred, under an 'implied bargain' constructive trust, from the conduct and mutual dealings of the parties.[6]

1 *Rider v Kidder* (1805) 10 Ves 360 at 368, 32 ER 884 at 887. See also *Re Kerrigan; Ex parte Jones* (1947) 47 SR (NSW) 76 at 82; *Napier v Public Trustee* (*Western Australia*) (1980) 32 ALR 153 at 155, 158; *Dullow v Dullow* (1985) 3 NSWLR 531 at 540F–541D.
2 In determining whether the presumption of resulting trust has been rebutted, acts and declarations forming part of the transaction are admissible as evidence either for or against the party who did the act or made the declaration. However, subsequent declarations are admissible as evidence only against the party who made them (see *Shephard v Cartwright* [1955] AC 431 at 445; *Cowcher v Cowcher* [1972] 1 WLR 425 at 436D–E; *Hepworth v Hepworth* (1963) 110 CLR 309 at 319; *Calverley v Green* (1984) 155 CLR 242 at 262 per Mason and Brennan JJ; *Muschinski v Dodds* (1985) 160 CLR 583 at 590 per Gibbs CJ).
3 *Pettitt v Pettitt* [1970] AC 777 at 814F–G; *Allen v Snyder* [1977] 2 NSWLR 685 at 698F. Where one person has contributed all of the purchase money, it is his or her intention alone which is relevant; where two persons contributed, the intentions of both are material (*Calverley v Green* (1984) 155 CLR 242 at 251 per Gibbs CJ; *Muschinski v Dodds* (1985) 160 CLR 583 at 590 per Gibbs CJ).
4 **[Para 10.113]**. See eg *Winsper v Perrett* (Unreported, Chancery Division, 13 February 2001) at [36] per Deputy Judge Kim Lewison QC.
5 See eg *Drake v Whipp* [1996] 1 FLR 826 at 831E–G per Peter Gibson LJ (claimant's 40 per cent beneficial share under resulting trust dislodged by court's finding of 'implied bargain' constructive trust **[para 10.127]** under which her 'fair share' was only one third).
6 **[Para 10.5]**. See *Oxley v Hiscock* [2004] 3 WLR 715 at [64] per Chadwick LJ.

10.24 Whether a presumption of resulting trust is rebutted in any of these ways is ultimately a matter of probability and credibility, determined with reference to the facts of each individual case. It is unusual that there is not some living person who, by his or her evidence, can either confirm or refute the resulting trust presumed from the payment of money. However, if all the available evidence is neutral as to the purpose of the money payment by B to A, the 'prima facie inference' remains that it was intended that there should be a resulting trust commensurate with the funds contributed.[1]

1   *Gissing v Gissing* [1971] AC 886 at 907C per Lord Diplock.

Gift

10.25 The presumption of resulting trust is clearly excluded by any evidence that a money contributor to the purchase price intended to confer a gratuitous benefit upon the nominal purchaser.[1] Actual donative intent is inconsistent with any claim of resulting trust[2] and compelling evidence of a gift relationship, particularly in the family context, pre-empts any explanation that a provision of cash was intended to generate either loan-based contractual rights or equity shareholding behind a resulting (or any other) trust.[3]

1   *Cowcher v Cowcher* [1972] 1 WLR 425 at 431C. See also *Reber v Reber* (1988) 48 DLR (4th) 376 at 378; *Braaksma v Braaksma* (1996) 141 DLR (4th) 190 at 192. The onus of proving donative intent falls, not unnaturally, upon the recipient of the money (*Wirth v Wirth* (1956) 98 CLR 228 at 235 per Dixon CJ).
2   *Winkworth v Edward Baron Development Co Ltd* [1986] 1 WLR 1512 at 1516D; *Taddeo v Taddeo* (1978) 19 SASR 347 at 366–367; *Barrios v Chiabrera* (1984) 3 BPR 9276 at 9279.
3   No resulting trust can be claimed, for instance, by the father who announces at his son's wedding reception that he proposes to give the newly married couple money to set up a house (see *Walker v Walker* (Unreported, Court of Appeal, 12 April 1984)). See also *Julian v Furby* (Unreported, Court of Appeal, No 79 15962, 24 November 1981), where a father-in-law was held to have made a gift of his labour in effecting improvements; and compare *Mollo v Mollo* [1999] EGCS 117 (Transcript at [43]), where a trust claim was upheld precisely because there was no intended gift of labour.

10.26 The presumption of resulting trust may also be rebutted in a less obvious case of donative intent.[1] A and B may have contributed unequally to the purchase price of land in circumstances where A, having made the greater contribution, intended that B should have a beneficial quantum other than that strictly commensurate with B's financial contribution (eg a half-share or even the entire beneficial interest). On these facts the resulting trust presumed on the basis of actual contributions is rebutted in part by A's intention to advance B beyond the proportion fixed by B's own contribution.[2] In such cases, however, it is unlikely that B's enhanced beneficial entitlement, unsupported by resulting trust, can be validated except on the basis of some formally declared express trust or some constructive trust.

1   One specific case of donative intent is governed by statute (see LPA 1925, s 60(3) **[para 10.19]**).
2   See *Cowcher v Cowcher* [1972] 1 WLR 425 at 431C, 433H; *Springette v Defoe* [1992] 2 FLR 388 at 392E–F per Dillon LJ; *Allen v Snyder* [1977] 2 NSWLR 685 at 692C–D; *Currie v Hamilton* [1984] 1 NSWLR 687 at 690F.

Counter-presumption of advancement

10.27 The presumption of resulting trust is sometimes displaced by a countervailing equitable presumption, the 'presumption of advancement', which
relates to a specialised form of assumed gift. The presumption of advancement
operates, in certain restricted or stylised circumstances, to supply an all-
important inference of donative intent on the part of a money contributor. In
these cases the presumption of resulting trust which would normally arise on
the basis of B's provision of money for A's purchase of a legal estate is rebutted
by a contrary presumption that the contributor in fact wished to 'advance' (or
make a gift to) the nominal purchaser of the legal title. The presumption of
advancement effectively reverses the onus of proof of beneficial entitlement.
When the presumption of advancement applies, the subject of the purchase is
deemed to belong to A both at law and in equity, the onus now shifting to B to
rebut the inference that he intended to 'advance' A.[1] Although the presumption
of advancement has been criticised as inappropriate in the modern age[2] and as
inimical to the rational evaluation of the property consequences of personal
relationships,[3] it seems too well entrenched as a 'landmark' in the law of
property to be discarded in its entirety by pure judicial legislation.[4]

1   *Murless v Franklin* (1818) 1 Swan 13 at 18, 36 ER 278 at 280. See also *Sidmouth v Sidmouth*
     (1840) 2 Beav 447 at 454, 48 ER 1254 at 1257; *Pearson v Pearson* [1961] VR 693 at 698; *Martin
     v Martin* (1959) 110 CLR 297 at 303; *Pettitt v Pettitt* [1970] AC 777 at 814G per Lord Upjohn.
     The presumption of advancement is rebuttable by oral evidence, since the resulting trust which
     is reinstated by its rebuttal lies outside the scope of any statutory requirement of writing
     (*Nelson v Nelson* (1995) 184 CLR 538 at 547–548 per Deane and Gummow JJ).
2   See *Pettitt v Pettitt* [1970] AC 777 at 824C per Lord Diplock; *Lowson v Coombes* [1999] Ch 373
     at 385A–D.
3   See *Calverley v Green* (1984) 155 CLR 242 at 264 per Murphy J.
4   See *Calverley v Green* (1984) 155 CLR 242 at 266 per Deane J; *Nelson v Nelson* (1995) 184
     CLR 538 at 602 per McHugh J.

Rationale of advancement

10.28 The presumption of advancement tends to arise in familial contexts
where altruism, rather than cash calculation, may be expected to have been the
motivating force behind a transaction of purchase.[1] The presumption is applicable where a legal estate is purchased in the name of a person whose welfare
the provider of the purchase money would naturally have wished to promote or
'advance'.[2] Accordingly, a donative intent is presumed in favour of certain
persons who are deemed to come within the bonds of familial affection[3] and for
whom the real purchaser has some 'obligation in conscience to provide.'[4] The
primary example occurs where a father provides funds for the purchase of a
legal estate in the name of his adult son. The son is presumed to take the estate
both at law and in equity, the father being presumed, in the absence of all other
evidence, to have intended to make a gift of his money contribution. But
whether the presumption reflects a moral obligation to provide,[5] or the likelihood of accelerated inheritance,[6] or merely the actual probability that the real

purchaser would have wished to benefit the nominal purchaser,[7] the presumption of advancement simply reinforces 'the prima facie position ... that the equitable interest is presumed to follow the legal estate and to be at home with the legal title.'[8]

1   The categories of relationship giving rise to the presumption are probably 'not ... finally settled or closed' (*Calverley v Green* (1984) 155 CLR 242 at 268 per Deane J). The presumption has been said to arise 'where the relationship between the parties falls into a class where dependency, past, present or future, commonly exists or, at all events, commonly existed in the nineteenth and earlier centuries' (*Nelson v Nelson* (1995) 184 CLR 538 at 600 per McHugh J).
2   See also *Murless v Franklin* (1818) 1 Swans 13 at 17, 36 ER 278 at 280; *Dullow v Dullow* (1985) 3 NSWLR 531 at 535F–536A.
3   See *Wirth v Wirth* (1956) 98 CLR 228 at 237 per Dixon CJ ('relationships affording "good" consideration').
4   *Scott v Pauly* (1917) 24 CLR 274 at 281 per Isaacs J. See the reference, in *Calverley v Green* (1984) 155 CLR 242 at 259 per Mason and Brennan JJ, to certain categories of 'lifetime relationship'. See also *Nelson v Nelson* (1995) 184 CLR 538 at 585 per Toohey J.
5   See e g *Bennet v Bennet* (1879) 10 Ch D 474 at 477 per Jessel MR ('the presumption of gift arises from the moral obligation to give'). Compare, however, *Calverley v Green* (1984) 155 CLR 242 at 247–248 per Gibbs CJ.
6   See *Re Levy* (1982) 131 DLR (3d) 15 at 25.
7   See *Calverley v Green* (1984) 155 CLR 242 at 250 per Gibbs CJ; *Nelson v Nelson* (1995) 184 CLR 538 at 585–586 per Toohey J, 575–576 per Dawson J.
8   *Calverley v Green* (1984) 155 CLR 242 at 267 per Deane J. See also *Nelson v Nelson* (1995) 184 CLR 538 at 547 per Deane and Gummow JJ.

Relationships which raise a presumption of advancement

10.29   By circumscribing the field of recognised 'advancement', the presumption casts an incidental light on socially perceived boundaries of personal and familial responsibility. In the absence of clear evidence of contrary intention at the time of purchase,[1] the presumption of advancement infers a donative intent where a father provides the consideration for a transfer into the name of his child[2] or where a person (male or female) purchases land in the name of someone in relation to whom he or she currently stands *in loco parentis*.[3] The presumption of advancement also applies to a purchase in the name of an illegitimate child,[4] an adopted child,[5] a step-child,[6] and a grandchild whose father is dead.[7] The presumption does not, however, apply to a purchase in the name of a sibling,[8] a son-in-law[9] or a nephew.[10] Nor does it rebut the presumption of resulting trust where property is purchased in the name of a parent or parent-in-law.[11]

1   Subsequent acts and declarations of the child (but not of the parent) may operate to rebut the presumed advancement (*Sidmouth v Sidmouth* (1840) 2 Beav 447 at 455, 48 ER 1254 at 1257). See also *Cowcher v Cowcher* [1972] 1 WLR 425 at 436D; *Charles Marshall Pty Ltd v Grimsley* (1956) 95 CLR 353 at 366; *Blackburn v Y V Properties Pty Ltd* [1980] VR 290 at 293.
2   *Dyer v Dyer* (1788) 2 Cox Eq Cas 92 at 93–94, 30 ER 42 at 43; *Sidmouth v Sidmouth* (1840) 2 Beav 447 at 454, 48 ER 1254 at 1257; *Shephard v Cartwright* [1955] AC 431 at 445; *Re Vandervell's Trusts (No 2)* [1974] Ch 269 at 289A; *Charles Marshall Pty Ltd v Grimsley* (1956) 95 CLR 353 at 364; *Goodfriend v Goodfriend* (1972) 22 DLR (3d) 699 at 703; *Napier v Public*

Trustee (*Western Australia*) (1980) 32 ALR 153 at 158; *Calverley v Green* (1984) 155 CLR 242 at 247 per Gibbs CJ, 268 per Deane J; *Nelson v Nelson* (1995) 184 CLR 538 at 600–601 per McHugh J.

3   *Shephard v Cartwright* [1955] AC 431 at 445; *Re Vandervell's Trusts (No 2)* [1974] Ch 269 at 289A; *Tinsley v Milligan* [1994] 1 AC 340 at 372B per Lord Browne-Wilkinson; *Charles Marshall Pty Ltd v Grimsley* (1956) 95 CLR 353 at 364; *Young v Young* (1959) 15 DLR (2d) 138 at 139; *Napier v Public Trustee (Western Australia)* (1980) 32 ALR 153 at 158; *Calverley v Green* (1984) 155 CLR 242 at 247 per Gibbs CJ, 268 per Deane J.

4   *Beckford v Beckford* (1774) Lofft 490 at 492, 98 ER 763 at 764; *Soar v Foster* (1858) 4 K & J 152 at 160, 70 ER 64 at 67.

5   *Standing v Bowring* (1886) 31 Ch D 282 at 287.

6   *Re Paradise Motor Co Ltd* [1968] 1 WLR 1125 at 1140A; *Oliveri v Oliveri* (1993) 38 NSWLR 665 at 678G–679E per Powell J.

7   *Edbrand v Dancer* (1680) 2 Ch Cas 26, 22 ER 829; *Soar v Foster* (1858) 4 K & J 152 at 160, 70 ER 64 at 67.

8   *Noack v Noack* [1959] VR 137 at 140; *Gorog v Kiss* (1977) 78 DLR (3d) 690 at 694. It cannot be claimed that a brother stands *in loco parentis* to his sister (*O'Brien v Bean and Bean* (1957) 7 DLR (2d) 332 at 333).

9   *Knight v Biss* [1954] NZLR 55 at 57.

10   *Drury v Drury* (1675) 73 SS 205; *Russell v Scott* (1936) 55 CLR 440 at 451.

11   See *Binmatt v Ali* (Unreported, Court of Appeal, 6 October 1981) (money contribution to parent's acquisition of council house [**para 7.347**]); *Groves v Christiansen* (1978) 86 DLR (3d) 296 at 301.

Applicability to mothers

10.30   The presumption of advancement has not, historically, been applied to a provision of money or transfer of other benefits by a *mother* to her own son or daughter.[1] Even in recent times English courts have been prepared to impose a straightforward resulting trust on any legal estate purchased for an adult child with the aid of money contributed by a mother.[2] This distinction between father and mother used to be rationalised on the basis that the father was supposedly 'the head of the family' and therefore 'under the primary moral obligation to provide for the children of the marriage.'[3] However, this perspective has become hopelessly out of touch with the egalitarian nature of contemporary society[4] and fails, moreover, to reflect the fact that both parents, if married to each other, are nowadays statutorily burdened with 'parental responsibility' for their minor children.[5]

1   *Bennet v Bennet* (1879) 10 Ch D 474 at 478; *Re Vandervell's Trusts (No 2)* [1974] Ch 269 at 289A; *Preston v Greene* [1909] 1 IR 172 at 177–178; *Lattimer v Lattimer* (1978) 82 DLR (3d) 587 at 590. Compare *Bull v Bull* [1955] 1 QB 234 at 236, and *Rupar v Rupar* (1964) 49 WWR 226 at 234, where it seems to have been thought that the presumption of advancement could, in the absence of contrary intention, apply to a mother.

2   *Sekhon v Alissa* [1989] 2 FLR 94 at 100B per Hoffmann J. See likewise *Gross v French* (1975) 238 EG 39 per Scarman LJ ('even in these days of sex equality').

3   *Scott v Pauly* (1917) 24 CLR 274 at 282 per Isaacs J. An allied explanation may lie in the control exercised by a husband, until deep into the 19th century, over his wife's property (see *Nelson v Nelson* (1995) 184 CLR 538 at 601 per McHugh J).

4   See *Brown v Brown* (1993) 31 NSWLR 582 at 600C–D per Kirby P; *Nelson v Nelson* (1995) 184 CLR 538 at 585–586 per Toohey J.

5   Children Act 1989, s 2(1). See also *Nelson v Nelson* (1995) 184 CLR 538 at 586 per Toohey J, 601 per McHugh J. The discrepant approach to provision by fathers and mothers was always

particularly difficult to justify in relation to benefits conferred on her children by a mother who was widowed, divorced or single (see *Scott v Pauly* (1917) 24 CLR 274 at 282, where Isaacs J thought that the presumption of advancement might apply to a widow). It may not require very strong evidence to show that a mother is *in loco parentis* (*Re Orme* (1883) 50 LT (NS) 51 at 53).

10.31   Some of the modern embarrassment generated by the gender bias of the presumption of advancement has been cloaked beneath assertions that, in most instances, it is fairly easy for a child to prove an actual donative intent on the part of his mother.[1] Today it seems scarcely conceivable that the presumption can survive, in the parental context, in its offensively differential form. There is a powerful argument that English courts should follow the lead of the High Court of Australia in *Nelson v Nelson*[2] in declaring the presumption, if it retains any currency at all under modern conditions, to be equally applicable to fathers and mothers.[3] More pertinently perhaps, as McHugh J indicated in the High Court, the 'real question is whether the courts should continue to hold that the presumption applies to either parent.'[4] The stark truth is that the concept of presumed advancement has a distinctly patriarchal resonance which causes many to question today whether it properly has any substantial role in the ascertainment of beneficial intentions.[5]

1   This view dates back at least as far as *Bennet v Bennet* (1879) 10 Ch D 474 at 479–480 per Jessel MR. See also *Main v Main* [1939] 1 DLR 723 at 725; *Edwards v Bradley* (1957) 9 DLR (2d) 673 at 678 (Supreme Court of Canada); *Lattimer v Lattimer* (1978) 82 DLR (3d) 587 at 590; *Dullow v Dullow* (1985) 3 NSWLR 531 at 534G.
2   (1995) 184 CLR 538 at 548–549 per Deane and Gummow JJ, 576 per Dawson J, 585–586 per Toohey J, 601 per McHugh J. See also *Dullow v Dullow* (1985) 3 NSWLR 531 at 536C, 541D–E.
3   See similarly *Brown v Brown* (1993) 31 NSWLR 582 at 600C per Kirby P.
4   (1995) 184 CLR 538 at 601.
5   See e g *McGrath v Wallis* [1995] 2 FLR 114 at 115A per Nourse LJ; *Ali v Khan* [2002] EWCA Civ 974 at [30] per Morritt V-C.

Applicability to spouses

10.32   Perhaps the most controversial issue of all is whether the presumption of advancement has any relevance to husband and wife. It is clear that such a presumption once operated not only in favour of a married woman,[1] but also in favour of a woman to whom an estate was transferred in express contemplation of a marriage which subsequently took place with the transferor.[2] However, the presumption of advancement has not generally been thought to apply as between de facto spouses.[3] Nor has it ever applied in favour of a husband.[4]

1   *Christ's Hospital v Budgin et Ux* (1712) 2 Vern 683 at 684, 23 ER 1043 at 1044; *Martin v Martin* (1959) 110 CLR 297 at 303; *Hepworth v Hepworth* (1963) 110 CLR 309 at 317; *Heavey v Heavey* [1977] 111 ILTR 1 at 3; *M v M* [1980] 114 ILTR 46 at 49; *Napier v Public Trustee* (*Western Australia*) (1980) 32 ALR 153 at 158; *Nelson v Nelson* (1995) 184 CLR 538 at 600.
2   *Moate v Moate* [1948] 2 All ER 486 at 487G–H; *Wirth v Wirth* (1956) 98 CLR 228 at 237–238; *Nelson v Nelson* (1995) 184 CLR 538 at 600–601 per McHugh J. See also *Ibbotson v Kushner* (1978) 84 DLR (3d) 417 at 419. In *Eeles v Wilkins* (Unreported, Court of Appeal, 3 February 1998), Nourse LJ noted that in *Moate v Moate* the disposition preceded the marriage by only three weeks.

3   *Rider v Kidder* (1805) 10 Ves 360 at 367, 32 ER 884 at 887; *Soar v Foster* (1858) 4 K & J 152 at
     162, 70 ER 64 at 68; *Lowson v Coombes* [1999] Ch 373 at 381B; *Collins v Sanders* (1956) 3
     DLR (2d) 607 at 615; *David v Szoke* (1974) 39 DLR (3d) 707 at 716; *Allen v Snyder* [1977]
     2 NSWLR 685 at 690B; *Calverley v Green* (1984) 155 CLR 242 at 268–269 per Deane J. See,
     however, *Napier v Public Trustee* (*Western Australia*) (1980) 32 ALR 153 at 154 per Gibbs
     ACJ. It is always possible, of course, that there may be sufficient evidence of an actual
     donative intention to support the equitable entitlement of a cohabiting transferee (see
     Murdock v Aherne (1878) 4 VLR (E) 244 at 249; *Carkeek v Tate-Jones* [1971] VR 691 at
     698–701).
4   *Pettitt v Pettitt* [1970] AC 777 at 815E–F; *Northern Bank Ltd v Henry* [1981] IR 1 at 18; *Allied
     Irish Banks Ltd v McWilliams* [1982] NI 156 at 161D; *Doohan v Nelson* [1973] 2 NSWLR 320
     at 327D; *Brophy v Brophy* (1974) 3 ACTR 57 at 60; *Taddeo v Taddeo* (1978) 19 SASR 347 at
     365, 367; *Muschinski v Dodds* (1985) 160 CLR 583 at 590 per Gibbs CJ.

10.33   The relevance in modern conditions of the discriminatory concept of
'advancement' is highly questionable. In the marital context its application was
all too plainly an index of a former social climate in which wives enjoyed an
inferior status.[1] The archaic nature of the presumption was subjected to
devastating criticism by the House of Lords in *Pettitt v Pettitt*,[2] where
Lord Diplock considered it 'an abuse of legal technique ... to apply to
transactions between the post-war generation of married couples "presumptions" which are based upon inferences of fact which an earlier generation of
judges drew as to the most likely intentions of earlier generations of spouses
belonging to the propertied classes of a different social era.'[3]

1   See *Falconer v Falconer* [1970] 1 WLR 1333 at 1335H–1336A per Lord Denning MR.
2   [1970] AC 777 at 824C. See also Lord Reid (at 793E–F); *Lowson v Coombes* [1999] Ch 373 at
     385A–D per Robert Walker LJ.
3   Compare *Pettitt v Pettitt* [1970] AC 777 at 813G–H, where Lord Upjohn maintained that the
     equitable presumptions 'when properly understood and properly applied to the circumstances
     of today ... remain as useful as ever in solving questions of title.' This view still seems to be
     shared by lawyers steeped in a vibrant equity tradition (see e g *Tinsley v Milligan* [1994] 1 AC
     340 at 372B per Lord Browne-Wilkinson).

10.34   The contemporary disfavour for the social philosophy of advancement
has led to an almost irresistible movement away from the presumption, at least
in the context of spousal transactions concerning land. The presumption of
advancement can now play only an extremely marginal role in determining
questions of beneficial ownership between living spouses.[1] In few instances will
recourse to the presumption be necessary or conclusive, for it will be a rare case
in which evidence of actual intention is completely absent.[2] Where the presumption retains any application, its strength may have to be calibrated relative
to the date of the disputed purchase and to the age[3] and social or cultural
outlook[4] of the particular spouses. In the total absence of other evidence of
intention, it is just conceivable that the presumption has sufficient vitality to
support a wife's assertion of beneficial entitlement where a husband has
purchased a legal title either in her name[5] or in their joint names,[6] but it is much
more likely that modern courts will simply apply ordinary presumptions of
resulting trust to both spouses impartially.[7] If both spouses have contributed to
the purchase of a legal title, there is high authority for the view that they are to

be taken, in the absence of all other evidence, as having intended to be beneficial owners in the proportions contributed.[8]

1   *Pettitt v Pettitt* [1970] AC 777 at 811G per Lord Hodson; *Gissing v Gissing* [1971] AC 886 at 907C–D per Lord Diplock; *Re Berry (A Bankrupt)* [1978] 2 NZLR 373 at 378; *Napier v Public Trustee (Western Australia)* (1980) 32 ALR 153 at 154. See, however, *Harwood v Harwood* [1991] 2 FLR 274 at 294A–B, where Slade LJ found 'nothing sufficient to displace' the presumption of advancement, although noting that the presumption 'must be applied with caution in modern social conditions'.

2   What little force the presumption retains can be defeated by evidence of contrary intention (see *Organ v Sandwell* [1921] VLR 622 at 626, 629; *Allen v Snyder* [1977] 2 NSWLR 685 at 690A). See generally J Martin, [1992] Conv 153.

3   See *Re Hogg (Deceased)* (Unreported, Chancery Division, 11 July 1983), where the presumption was held more readily applicable to a husband and wife born at the end of the 19th century who married in 1930 with the benefit of a marriage settlement and who each possessed substantial capital assets. See also *Doohan v Nelson* [1973] 2 NSWLR 320 at 326A.

4   See *Taddeo v Taddeo* (1978) 19 SASR 347 at 366–367 per Bray CJ (advancement presumed in favour of a traditional Italian wife: sed quaere).

5   *Pettitt v Pettitt* [1970] AC 777 at 815E–G per Lord Upjohn (at least where the husband's financial contribution is 'very small'); *Pearson v Pearson* [1961] VR 693 at 698; *Calverley v Green* (1984) 155 CLR 242 at 259 per Mason and Brennan JJ. Compare, however, *Neo Tai Kim v Foo Stie Wah* (Unreported, Privy Council No 30 of 1982, 4 March 1985) per Lord Brightman; *McFarlane v McFarlane* [1972] NI 59 at 75 per Lowry J.

6   *Pettitt v Pettitt* [1970] AC 777 at 815E; *Calverley v Green* (1984) 155 CLR 242 at 256 per Mason and Brennan JJ.

7   See e g *Pearson v Pearson* [1961] VR 693 at 698 (Full Court of Supreme Court of Victoria). Thus, where a wife purchases a legal title in her husband's name, he holds on a resulting trust for her (see e g *Northern Bank Ltd v Henry* [1981] IR 1 at 8, 18), 'but in practice there will in almost every case be some explanation (however slight) of this (today) rather unusual course' (*Pettitt v Pettitt* [1970] AC 777 at 815E–F).

8   *Pettitt v Pettitt* [1970] AC 777 at 815F–G per Lord Upjohn; *McFarlane v McFarlane* [1972] NI 59 at 67 per Lord MacDermott LCJ. See also *Re Rogers' Question* [1948] 1 All ER 328 at 330A; *Hine v Hine* [1962] 1 WLR 1124 at 1132; *Bernard v Josephs* [1982] Ch 391 at 398A–C; *Pearson v Pearson* [1961] VR 693 at 698.

Relevance to colourable transactions

10.35 If and to the extent that the presumption of advancement has any marginal operation between spouses today, its main impact in English law may be to frustrate claims of resulting trust arising in the context of a transfer of title motivated by some illegal or fraudulent purpose. Thus it is arguable that an advancement may still be presumed in favour of a married woman if her husband's objective in placing or purchasing a legal title in her name was to evade the potential claims of his own creditors[1] or to defeat the financial claims of his divorced spouse[2] or to defraud the tax authorities.[3] In such circumstances, the husband cannot be heard to rebut the presumed advancement, since he can do so only by disclosing and relying on some unlawful purpose as representing the true explanation for the transaction.[4] No such impediment exists, of course, where the presumption of advancement is inapplicable (as in the case of unmarried partners[5]), since here the financial contributor can make good the claim of resulting trust without needing to rely on his own illegality.

1   A husband cannot be heard to maintain as against his creditors that his family home belongs to his wife, while maintaining as against his wife that the house still belongs in equity to himself (see eg *Tinker v Tinker* [1970] P 136 at 141G–H; *Cantor v Cox* (1976) 239 EG 121 at 123; *Phillips v Brewin Dolphin Bell Lawrie Ltd* [1998] 1 BCLC 700 at 725e–726a; *Maysels v Maysels* (1974) 45 DLR (3d) 337 at 345–346, affd (1976) 64 DLR (3d) 765 (Supreme Court of Canada)).

2   See *Lowson v Coombes* [1999] Ch 373 at 378G–H per Nourse LJ.

3   *Re Emery's Investment Trusts* [1959] Ch 410 at 422. See also *Webb v Webb* [1991] 1 WLR 1410 at 1419F–G (transfer designed to avoid exchange control), but compare *Sekhon v Alissa* [1989] 2 FLR 94 at 98A–C. It is not, however, improper to transfer a legal estate in order to enable the transferee to raise money on its security (*Ali v Khan* [2002] EWCA Civ 974 at [31], [35] per Morritt V-C).

4   See *Tinsley v Milligan* [1994] 1 AC 340 at 376C–G per Lord Browne-Wilkinson. Contrast the more liberated approach of the High Court of Australia in *Nelson v Nelson* (1995) 184 CLR 538; and see likewise *Duncan v McDonald* [1997] 3 NZLR 669 at 684, where the Court of Appeal of New Zealand adverted to 'the uncomfortable position reached by the House of Lords in *Tinsley v Milligan*.'

5   See eg *Lowson v Coombes* [1999] Ch 373 at 381A–C.

Loan

10.36   The presumption of resulting trust is likewise displaced by proof that purchase money was provided by way of loan.[1] A lender does not advance money in the character of a purchaser and therefore takes no beneficial interest under any presumed resulting trust.[2] Were it otherwise, a lender could recover his money twice over,[3] and banks and building societies would acquire a myriad of beneficial interests in the millions of properties bought on the strength of mortgage advances. In fact, one of the attractions of the mortgage device (from the borrower's viewpoint) is that, except in cases of express contrary agreement,[4] the lender is *not* an equity participant in the inflating value of the realty purchased with the help of the mortgage loan. The lender is almost invariably confined to contractually based rights to the repayment of capital plus interest, backed up by a right of possession and a power of sale should the borrower default.[5]

1   *Winkworth v Edward Baron Development Co Ltd* [1986] 1 WLR 1512 at 1516D per Lord Templeman. See *Hussey v Palmer* [1972] 1 WLR 1286 at 1292E; *Re Sharpe (A Bankrupt)* [1980] 1 WLR 219 at 222E–F, 223A–B; *Risch v McFee* [1991] 1 FLR 105 at 109B–C; *Avondale Printers & Stationers Ltd v Haggie* [1979] 2 NZLR 124 at 145; *Barrios v Chiabrera* (1984) 3 BPR 9276 at 9279.

2   *Re Cooke* (1857) 6 Ir Ch R 430 at 438; *Bateman Television Ltd v Bateman and Thomas* [1971] NZLR 453 at 459, 462. Loan money may later generate a trust for the lender if assimilated de facto into the provision of the purchase price (eg where the lender, acting in reliance on a promise of beneficial entitlement, never makes any attempt to recover either capital or interest). See *Risch v McFee* [1991] 1 FLR 105 at 110E–H.

3   *Re Sharpe (A Bankrupt)* [1980] 1 WLR 219 at 223B.

4   See the instance of the 'shared appreciation mortgage' **[para 15.17]**.

5   **[Paras 15.109, 15.171]**.

Occupation liens

10.37   Exceptionally a lender derives larger rights from a loan of money made as part of a family arrangement which contemplates, in an informal or inarticulate fashion, that pending repayment the lender should be afforded some kind of residential privilege in the premises purchased with the aid of the loan money. It is frequently the case in such arrangements that no term date is fixed in relation to the loan and there may be only the haziest of intentions as to how or when the money is to be repaid. Particularly where the lender is an elderly person, the provision of loan money returnable at some unspecified future date tends to merge obscurely with an anticipated devolution of property by way of succession. Even here, however, the existence of a loan excludes the possibility of an aliquot share under a resulting trust.[1] Nevertheless, whilst recognising the primarily contractual nature of loan relationships, the courts have often awarded the lender some form of occupation lien pending repayment of the money lent. This form of remedy is readily coupled, albeit imprecisely, with cognate notions of irrevocable equitable licence, constructive trust and proprietary estoppel.[2]

1   See e g *Mortgage Express Ltd v Raja* (Unreported, Court of Appeal, 2 July 1996).
2   **[Paras 4.88, 10.58, 10.168]**.

An example

10.38   In *Re Sharpe (A Bankrupt)*[1] A acquired a leasehold interest in a shop and maisonette, much of the purchase price being contributed by A's 77 year-old aunt, B. B had sold her existing home and had moved into the maisonette with A and his wife on the understanding that she would be able to stay there for as long as she wished. When A later became bankrupt, Browne-Wilkinson J held that B had no interest in the premises by way of resulting trust, taking the view that the money paid by B had been paid by way of loan.[2] However, he was inclined to agree that B had acquired 'something less than an aliquot share of the equity in the premises, namely, the right to stay on in the premises until the money she provided indirectly to acquire them has been repaid.'[3] The right generated on B's behalf, 'whether it be called a contractual licence or an equitable licence or an interest under a constructive trust',[4] was binding not only upon A but also upon A's trustee in bankruptcy, who simply stepped into the shoes of the debtor. B had a right to live in the premises until her loan was repaid, and it followed that the trustee in bankruptcy took the property subject to that right.[5]

1   [1980] 1 WLR 219. See [1980] Conv 207 (J Martin); (1980) 96 LQR 336 (G Woodman); A R Everton, [1982] Conv 118 at 125–129.
2   [1980] 1 WLR 219 at 222F (B had obtained a promissory note from A). See, however, *Stokes v Anderson* [1991] 1 FLR 391 at 396F–397A.
3   [1980] 1 WLR 219 at 223B–C. It was relevant that B had 'only loaned the money as part of a wider scheme, an essential feature of which was that she was to make her home in the property to be acquired with the money loaned' ([1980] 1 WLR 219 at 223H).
4   [1980] 1 WLR 219 at 224A.

5   [1980] 1 WLR 219 at 224F–225D. Although this was sufficient to dispose of the issue between
     B and A's trustee in bankruptcy, the trustee in bankruptcy had already contracted to sell the
     premises with vacant possession. Browne-Wilkinson J observed that the contractual pur-
     chaser, who was not a party to the proceedings, was not necessarily bound by such rights as B
     might have. In fact, Browne-Wilkinson J indicated that 'as a purchaser without express notice'
     he might well take priority over B in any action for specific performance of his contract
     ([1980] 1 WLR 219 at 226G).

CONTRIBUTIONS OF 'PURCHASE MONEY' RELEVANT TO THE RESULTING TRUST

10.39   The presumption of resulting trust depends on a finding that B has
acted in the character of a purchaser by providing funds for a purchase in the
name of A.[1] It is not always easy, however, to identify the kinds of financial
contribution which generate a resulting trust. Not every contribution of value
or assumption of liability constitutes 'purchase money' for the purpose of
raising the presumption, since the courts attach significance only to those
money contributions which can fairly be said to be 'referable to' the acquisition
of title.[2] In recent decades the definition of relevant 'purchase money' has
become strained to the point where it is probably best to reserve resulting trust
terminology for the relatively straightforward case where quantifiable contributions of money are laid down at the point of purchase,[3] leaving all other kinds
of contribution to be assessed in terms of constructive trust.

1   *Calverley v Green* (1984) 155 CLR 242 at 246 per Gibbs CJ. See also *Stephenson Nominees
     Pty Ltd v Official Receiver on behalf of Official Trustee in Bankruptcy; ex p Roberts* (1987)
     76 ALR 485 at 501 per Gummow J.
2   *Burns v Burns* [1984] Ch 317 at 328H–329B per Fox LJ. It is almost impossible to establish the
     'referable' character of a payment made some time *after* the acquisition of land and full
     payment of its purchase price (see e g *Winkworth v Edward Baron Development Co Ltd* [1986]
     1 WLR 1512 at 1515E–1516B).
3   See *Burns v Burns* [1984] Ch 317 at 326F–G per Fox LJ; *Ryan v Dries* (2002) 10 BPR 19497
     at [48] (New South Wales Court of Appeal).

Direct contribution to cash price at the point of purchase

10.40   The clearest instances of resulting trust emerge from direct cash
contributions made towards the purchase of land. Here, regardless of the name
or names in which the legal title is taken, a resulting trust arises for the
contributor in the absence of any contrary intention or countervailing presumption. The direct cash payment is regarded as sufficiently 'referable to' the
acquisition of title to generate a trust,[1] the contributor being presumed to have
intended to take a beneficial interest commensurate with his contribution.[2]
Thus, if a legal estate is transferred to A for £150,000, A providing £100,000 out
of his own available cash resources and B £50,000 out of hers, a resulting trust
is presumed under which A takes a two-thirds beneficial interest and B a
one-third beneficial interest.[3] A and B are taken, in effect, as having formulated
a 'money consensus' that their respective equitable interests should accord with

the relative proportions of their contributions.⁴ By virtue of its association with the resulting trust, this 'money consensus' requires no documentary formality under section 53(1) of the Law of Property Act 1925.⁵

1   *Burns v Burns* [1984] Ch 317 at 329B per Fox LJ.
2   *Pettitt v Pettitt* [1970] AC 777 at 794A–B per Lord Reid; *Gissing v Gissing* [1971] AC 886 at 897A–B per Lord Reid; *Cowcher v Cowcher* [1972] 1 WLR 425 at 431B–C; *Williams & Glyn's Bank Ltd v Boland* [1981] AC 487 at 502F–G per Lord Wilberforce.
3   *Cowcher v Cowcher* [1972] 1 WLR 425 at 431E–F per Bagnall J. See also *Gissing v Gissing* [1971] AC 886 at 907A–B per Lord Diplock.
4   *Cowcher v Cowcher* [1972] 1 WLR 425 at 431B–C, 436A–B per Bagnall J.
5   See *Cowcher v Cowcher* [1972] 1 WLR 425 at 432A–D, 436C–D.

Contribution to initial deposit or legal expenses

10.41   In the absence of evidence of contrary intention, a money contribution made by B towards the initial deposit or legal expenses payable in connection with the acquisition of a legal estate also raises a resulting trust in favour of B.¹ A contribution of this kind casts B in the character of a purchaser² and provides presumptive evidence of an intention from the very outset that B should take a commensurate beneficial share in the land acquired.³ Although it is sometimes suggested that the beneficial interest earned by B's contribution should be larger than that justified purely arithmetically,⁴ the allocation of a disproportionate share to B is strictly permissible only if some additional consensus between the parties has given rise to a *constructive* trust.⁵ It may be, however, that the payment of a deposit or expenses helps to establish a framework of shared intention in favour of beneficial co-ownership which makes it more feasible to regard subsequent payments by B as being 'referable to' the acquisition of the land.⁶

1   *Gissing v Gissing* [1971] AC 886 at 907E; *Davis v Vale* [1971] 1 WLR 1022 at 1026H; *Efstratiou, Glantschnig and Petrovic v Glantschnig* [1972] NZLR 594 at 598. Compare, however, *Little v Little* (1988) 15 NSWLR 43 at 44G–46F per Bryson J.
2   The basis of calculation under the resulting trust should be the 'aggregate cost' of purchase (ie inclusive of incidental costs, fees and disbursements) (*Currie v Hamilton* [1984] 1 NSWLR 687 at 691A per McLelland J). Likewise, in *Calverley v Green* (1984) 155 CLR 242 at 265, Murphy J spoke of 'contributions to the purchase', a phrase which may not mean the same thing as 'contributions to the purchase price' (*Little v Little* (1988) 15 NSWLR 43 at 45E per Bryson J). See also *Ryan v Dries* (2002) 10 BPR 19497 at [53] (New South Wales Court of Appeal).
3   *Burns v Burns* [1984] Ch 317 at 344G; *Carlton v Goodman* [2002] 2 FLR 259 at [22(iv)], [38].
4   See *Efstratiou, Glantschnig and Petrovic v Glantschnig* [1972] NZLR 594 at 598; *Pearson v Pearson* [1961] VR 693 at 699; *Re Whiteley and Whiteley* (1975) 48 DLR (3d) 161 at 170; *Suttor v Hutchinson* (Unreported, Supreme Court of New South Wales, 19 November 1987, BPR Casenote 95915).
5   [Para 10.78].
6   *Gissing v Gissing* [1971] AC 886 at 907F–H per Lord Diplock; *Burns v Burns* [1984] Ch 317 at 344G–H.

Contribution of public sector tenant's discount

10.42   A frequent form of input into the purchase of a legal estate nowadays takes the form of the statutory discount made available under the Housing Act 1985 to a qualifying public sector tenant who exercises his 'right to buy' the freehold reversion or to acquire a long leasehold in his rented home.[1] This discount from the purchase price, which varies in accordance with the duration of the pre-existing tenancy, may well amount to many thousands of pounds.[2] Family members often combine their efforts in the purchase, the benefit of the discount being contributed by the qualifying tenant, whilst mortgage money or other finance is provided by another family member.[3]

1   See HA 1985, s 118(1), Sch 6, Part III, paras 11–12 [**para 7.347**]. Essentially the same issues arise where a private landlord sells the freehold reversion at a discount to a sitting tenant (see e g *Carlton v Goodman* [2002] 2 FLR 259 at [22(iv)]).
2   See HA 1985, s 126(1)(b) [**para 7.351**].
3   See *Jiggins v Brisley* [2003] WTLR 1141 at [65]. Where a qualifying tenancy is a joint tenancy, the discount may be generated by relevant occupation on the part of one joint tenant alone and the court remains free to attribute the discount value solely to that tenant (see *Evans v Hayward* [1995] 2 FLR 511 at 516C per Dillon LJ).

Beneficial impact of the 'right to buy' discount

10.43   There has been some divergence of view as to whether the value of the public sector tenant's discount can be regarded as a direct cash contribution towards the purchase price of the premises acquired under the statutory 'right to buy'.[1] The case law throws up the occasional judicial grumble that the statutory discount is a handout from the state and is not, therefore, 'strictly speaking, purchase money provided by either party.'[2] Nevertheless it seems tolerably clear nowadays that if, pursuant to the 'right to buy', a legal estate is acquired by A, any reduction in price attributable to a qualifying period of occupation by B presumptively raises a resulting trust in favour of B.[3] The 'right to buy' discount simply generates for B a commensurate beneficial share. This presumed trust is rebuttable by any contrary agreement or countervailing presumption of equity. For example, A and B may reach an informal consensus that their respective beneficial shares should be other than those dictated by a purely mathematical calculation of their financial contributions to the purchase, in which case their reallocation of beneficial entitlement *inter se* takes effect – if at all – by way of constructive trust.[4]

1   See *Ashe v Mumford* (2000) 33 HLR 756 at [43] per Jonathan Parker LJ, for the suggestion that the fact of the discount might justify an inference that the parties had agreed that its value might be treated as a contribution towards the purchase. See also *Marsh v Von Sternberg* [1986] 1 FLR 526 at 531 per Bush J.
2   *Evans v Hayward* [1995] 2 FLR 511 at 516H per Staughton LJ.
3   *Springette v Defoe* [1992] 2 FLR 388 at 391D–F, 393H–394A per Dillon LJ, 395G per Steyn LJ; *McKenzie v McKenzie* [2003] EWHC 601 (Ch) at [87]; *Driver v Yorke* [2003] All ER (D) 103 (Apr) at [32], [35]. In effect the 'right to buy' discount is treated as a contribution towards the 'gross price' of purchase (see *Evans v Hayward* [1995] 2 FLR 511 at 515D–F per Dillon LJ).
4   *McKenzie v McKenzie* [2003] EWHC 601 (Ch) at [84], [87].

Shared 'right to buy'

10.44   Difficulties may arise if A and B, as joint occupiers under the relevant tenancy, can both point to qualifying periods of occupation, albeit of different duration. The Housing Act 1985 provides that the allowable discount shall be that generated by the longer of the two periods of occupation.[1] If, however, B has occupied for, say, ten years and A has jointly occupied for five of those ten years, it seems unfair that A's period of occupation should be entirely ignored in calculating the attributable value of the discount under a resulting trust.[2] In such circumstances the contributory effect of the discount figure should normally be allocated as to one-third to A and as to two-thirds to B.[3]

1   HA 1985, s 129(3).
2   See *Savill v Goodall* [1993] 1 FLR 755 at 759H–760C per Nourse LJ.
3   It was for precisely this reason that, in *Evans v Hayward* [1995] 2 FLR 511 at 517C, Staughton LJ preferred the more flexible view that the discount is not so much an imputed money contribution but rather a 'factor capable of giving rise to an inference that [the parties] may have reached an agreement as to how it should be allocated between them'. See also *Ashe v Mumford* (2000) 33 HLR 756 at [50].

Contributions of borrowed money

10.45   It is rare today for purchasers of land to finance their acquisition entirely from their own freely available cash reserves.[1] It is much more common that part (or all) of the purchase price should consist of money borrowed from a bank or building society. Where such money is used in the purchase of realty, there is a primary presumption that the loan money should be regarded as the exact equivalent of money contributed from the free available cash resources of the borrower.[2] Once money has been advanced by the lender, it is treated as being, legally and factually, the borrower's own money.[3] This being so, certain implications follow as a matter of resulting trust doctrine, although beneficial ownership is probably more accurately and easily ascertained nowadays by reference to the law of constructive trusts.

1   See *Bernard v Josephs* [1982] Ch 391 at 403G; *Burns v Burns* [1984] Ch 317 at 344D–E.
2   See *Cowcher v Cowcher* [1972] 1 WLR 425 at 431F, 433B; *Crisp v Mullings* (1976) 239 EG 119; *Young v Young* [1984] FLR 375 at 378D–H; *Carlton v Goodman* [2002] 2 FLR 259 at [18], [22(v)]; *Calverley v Green* (1984) 155 CLR 242 at 257–258 per Mason and Brennan JJ. Compare the contrary view taken in *Ulrich v Ulrich and Felton* [1968] 1 WLR 180 at 186E, 189F–G (in the days before mortgage-assisted purchase became a way of life).
3   See eg *Halifax Building Society v Brown* [1996] 1 FLR 103 at 109D per Balcombe LJ. Of course, where a legal estate is acquired in the name of A, using A's own money together with a mortgage advance for which A is solely responsible, the prima facie inference is that A was intended to be the sole beneficial owner (*Bernard v Josephs* [1982] Ch 391 at 403G–H).

Sole mortgage liability

10.46   Suppose, for example, that a legal estate is purchased in the name of A for £150,000, A providing £100,000 by way of mortgage advance from a bank (for which A undertakes sole liability) and B providing £50,000 out of her own available cash resources. In these circumstances and in the absence of any other evidence of intention, A takes a two-thirds interest and B a one-third interest under a presumed resulting trust.[1] The borrowed money is credited in full as a trust-generating contribution on the part of the person who has undertaken the covenant to repay.[2] The primary yardstick is effectively the idea that an assumption of personal liability to a lender has the same value in beneficial terms as a direct contribution of free cash.[3]

1   *Cowcher v Cowcher* [1972] 1 WLR 425 at 431E–F per Bagnall J.
2   See *Power v Brighton* (Unreported, Court of Appeal, 14 November 1984) per Cumming-Bruce LJ and Sir Denys Buckley; *Currie v Hamilton* [1984] 1 NSWLR 687 at 691C–D per McLelland J.
3   For an argument that, at least in the early years of a mortgage loan, this approach devalues the significance of cash down-payments, see P Sparkes, (1991) 11 OJLS 39 at 46–52.

Joint mortgage liability

10.47 Suppose, instead, that a legal estate is purchased in the joint names of A and B for £150,000, B providing £50,000 from her own available cash resources and the remaining £100,000 being funded by a mortgage advance in respect of which A and B have undertaken joint and several liability. In these circumstances A and B are each credited with having contributed half of the loan money towards the purchase.[1] In the absence of any contrary agreement or arrangement,[2] the legal estate is held on a presumed resulting trust[3] under which the proportions of beneficial entitlement are now reversed, A taking a one-third interest and B a two-thirds interest. B's enhanced share in this case reflects the fact that, in addition to undertaking joint and several liability to repay the loan, B has contributed the remainder of the purchase price either from personal cash reserves[4] or from some other source.[5] Equitable ownership behind the resulting trust is again fixed with reference to cash contributions and the extent to which the relevant parties have exposed themselves to a contractual liability vis à vis the lender of money.[6]

1   See *Springette v Defoe* [1992] 2 FLR 388 at 393H–394A; *Carlton v Goodman* [2002] 2 FLR 259 at [38].
2   An express declaration of trust in favour of A and B as beneficial joint tenants would, of course, be conclusive irrespective of the relative proportions of financial contribution (see *Mayes v Mayes* (1969) 210 EG 935 at 937).
3   See *Carlton v Goodman* [2002] 2 FLR 259 at [22(v)] per Mummery LJ; *McKenzie v McKenzie* [2003] EWHC 601 (Ch) at [80].
4   See e g *Ingram v Ingram* [1941] VLR 95 at 98–102 (direct cash contribution).
5   See e g *Springette v Defoe* [1992] 2 FLR 388 at 393H–394A, 395G–H ('right to buy' discount). See also *Currie v Hamilton* [1984] 1 NSWLR 687 at 691D–692C.
6   In the absence of any agreed reallocation of beneficial entitlement (see *Wright v Johnson* [2002] 2 P & CR 210 at [23]–[24] per Sir Martin Nourse), there may have to be an equitable accounting, on eventual sale, in respect of any mortgage payments by either party which exceed the respective proportions of contractual liability under the loan [**para 11.51**].

Mortgage payments

10.48   In *Gissing v Gissing*[1] Lord Diplock conceded that it would be 'unreasonably legalistic' to treat the transaction involved in a mortgage-assisted acquisition of property as restricted to the actual conveyance of title into the name of one or other party.[2] Speaking in relation to a family home, Lord Diplock pointed out that the intentions of the spouses are 'more likely to have been concerned with the economic realities of the transaction than with the unfamiliar technicalities of the English law of legal and equitable interests in land.' In his view, the 'economic reality' underlying a mortgage-assisted acquisition is 'that the freeholder is purchasing the family home upon credit and that the purchase price is represented by the instalments by which the mortgage is repaid in addition to the initial deposit in cash.'[3] In these circumstances the conduct of the parties in relation to the payment of the mortgage instalments may be no less relevant than their conduct in relation to the payment of a cash deposit.[4] Whilst the primary presumption is that the beneficial shares generated by contributions of borrowed money are governed by the parties' respective personal liabilities to the relevant lender, particular difficulties emerge if the parties, by private agreement, reorganise these liabilities *inter se* or subsequently make unanticipated or uncovenanted contributions to the discharge of the mortgage debt. Such reconfigurations of the parties' financial relationship are not easily accommodated within the strict theory of the resulting trust, under which beneficial shares crystallise in accordance with money contributions made contemporaneously with the acquisition of title.[5]

1   [1971] AC 886 at 906F–H.
2   See also *Little v Little* (1988) 15 NSWLR 43 at 45F per Bryson J.
3   See *Thwaites v Ryan* [1984] VR 65 at 93.
4   See also *Bloch v Bloch* (1981) 37 ALR 55 at 64. Compare *Calverley v Green* (1984) 155 CLR 242 at 263 per Mason and Brennan JJ.
5   **[Para 10.20]**.

Private reapportionment of loan liability

10.49   It is always quite possible that, irrespective of the formal responsibilities undertaken vis à vis a lender, the parties to a purchase of land may privately rearrange their liabilities *inter se*.[1] A and B may agree, for instance, that the legal estate should be vested in A and B (and a joint mortgage liability undertaken by A and B) merely for the limited purpose of attracting a mortgage advance (or perhaps a larger loan of money than might otherwise have been available).[2] In other words, A may simply lend his name to the transaction for some ulterior reason and subject to a mutual understanding between A and B that B will discharge the entirety of the joint mortgage liability.[3] In these circumstances A's nominal involvement in the transaction 'cannot fairly be described as a contribution to the purchase price.'[4] The presumption of resulting trust (which would normally attach beneficial value to A's exposure to contractual liability) is here rebutted by clear evidence of a contrary common intention.[5] The countervailing consensus reached between A and B has generated a constructive trust under which the jointly held legal estate is held for B alone in equity.[6] This constructive trust requires, of course, no statutory formality.[7]

1   The informal reorganisation of liability *inter se* has, of course, no legal impact upon the lender.

2   See e g *Allied Irish Banks Ltd v McWilliams* [1982] NI 156 at 160D, 161D. Alternatively, the lender may have required that A expressly join in the mortgage as a potential actual occupier of the mortgaged premises (see e g *Mellowes v Collymore* (Unreported, Court of Appeal, 27 November 1981) (mother-in-law in residence in family home)).

3   For many years the courts tried valiantly to accommodate such informal reallocations of the parties' loan obligations under some version of a resulting trust (see e g *Cowcher v Cowcher* [1972] 1 WLR 425 at 431G–432C; *Bernard v Josephs* [1982] Ch 391 at 403G–H; *Re Gorman* (*A Bankrupt*) [1990] 1 WLR 616 at 624D; *Huntingford v Hobbs* [1993] 1 FCR 45 at 55D–E). Nowadays it seems preferable to analyse these agreed reapportionments of responsibility under the head of constructive trust.

4   *Carlton v Goodman* [2002] 2 FLR 259 at [22(vii)]. A's potential liability is simply not regarded as a 'relevant' contribution (*McKenzie v McKenzie* [2003] EWHC 601 (Ch) at [81]). In *Carlton*, supra at [22(vii)], Mummery LJ pointed out that even subsequent enforcement of A's repayment covenant by the lender does not constitute a contribution to the purchase price, but merely a contribution to the discharge of the mortgage liabilities. A is entitled to be indemnified as a trustee and any loss suffered can be recouped by way of reimbursement from the trust estate (see *Allied Irish Banks Ltd v McWilliams* [1982] NI 156 at 161C–D; *Carlton v Goodman* [2002] 2 FLR 259 at [22(viii)]). See similarly *Robinson v Robinson* [2004] 1 P & CR D16 at D17.

5   A is regarded as 'making a "gift"' of his contribution to B (see *Carlton v Goodman* [2002] 2 FLR 259 at [41] per Ward LJ). See e g *McKenzie v McKenzie* [2003] EWHC 601 (Ch) at [80], [104], [113].

6   Alternatively, if A and B agree *inter se* that B will undertake a disproportionate part of their joint and several mortgage liability, this consensus clearly alters the ratio in which each is treated as putting money towards the purchase. The parties' private rearrangement of obligations under the mortgage rebuts the presumed resulting trust and raises a constructive trust to give effect to the proportions of beneficial ownership defined by their agreement.

7   LPA 1925, s 53(2). Conversely, where there is no convincing evidence of any explicit agreement between trust beneficiaries to share a mortgage liability formally undertaken in the sole name of one, the borrowed money is reckoned as the full equivalent of a cash contribution originating from this beneficiary alone (see *Power v Brighton* (Unreported, 14 November 1984); *Harwood v Harwood* [1991] 2 FLR 274 at 294D–H).

Unanticipated sharing of mortgage liability

10.50 Further difficulties arise where, during the lifetime of a mortgage, there is an unanticipated sharing of financial liability between A and B. Suppose, for instance, that a legal estate was purchased in the name of A and that B later begins to contribute from her own cash resources towards mortgage payments for which, technically, A is solely responsible. Such unplanned variations of the parties' finances may occur entirely informally in reaction to unforeseen family or business circumstances. A may be made redundant; B may have received an unexpected legacy or lottery win. Nevertheless B's payments in partial discharge of A's mortgage debt are unlikely to generate any (or any increased) beneficial interest for B under a trust of A's legal estate.[1] Occasional payments made towards mortgage instalments some time after the original acquisition do not have a sufficiently 'direct nexus with the purchase' to qualify as contributions to the purchase price and cannot therefore raise a resulting trust for B.[2] Even if B was already entitled under some resulting trust by reason of a cash contribution made at the point of purchase, subsequent payments by B build up an increased equitable share only in accordance with the strict conditions prescribed by the law of trusts.[3] Any successful claim of enhanced beneficial entitlement for B inevitably involves the assertion that an additional fragment of equitable ownership has been released by A to B.[4] To be valid and effective, such a disposition requires, as a matter of statutory formality,[5] to be contained 'in writing and signed by the person disposing of the same.'[6] In the absence of a written disposition, the claim to the increased beneficial share can be sustained only on the footing that the circumstances gave rise *either* to some new consensus about equitable entitlement which was validated by the doctrine of constructive trust *or* to some representation of entitlement which is protected by the law of proprietary estoppel.[7]

1   This does not alter the fact that B is normally entitled, on the winding up of the trust, to receive credit in respect of any mortgage payments made on behalf of A (see *Cowcher v Cowcher* [1972] 1 WLR 425 at 432G–433C [**para 11.51**]). McLelland J pointed out in *Currie v Hamilton* [1984] 1 NSWLR 687 at 692C that, in the absence of any evidence of gift, the provider of uncovenanted payments is entitled to an equitable contribution from the debtor and to an equitable charge over the land to secure this entitlement.
2   *McKenzie v McKenzie* [2003] EWHC 601 (Ch) at [82], [126]. Except in circumstances of constructive trust or estoppel, the conferment of a beneficial interest on a contributor who had no entitlement *at all* at the date of acquisition of the legal estate can be achieved only by means of an express declaration of trust in her favour, duly evidenced by signed writing, under LPA 1925, s 53(1)(b) [**para 9.188**] (see *Cowcher v Cowcher* [1972] 1 WLR 425 at 431C–D).
3   B's beneficial entitlement crystallised at the point of creation of the trust and cannot now be varied or supplemented by informal means (see *Sekhon v Alissa* [1989] 2 FLR 94 at 100C per Hoffmann J; *Currie v Hamilton* [1984] 1 NSWLR 687 at 691C–D per McLelland J).
4   As Bagnall J put it in *Cowcher v Cowcher* [1972] 1 WLR 425 at 436A–D, this amounts to a claim that the 'money consensus' underlying the original resulting trust (which was, of course, immune from any statutory requirement of formality) has been replaced by some different 'interest consensus' (which is not so immune). See LPA 1925, s 53(1)–(2).
5   LPA 1925, s 53(1)(c).
6   See e g *Cowcher v Cowcher* [1972] 1 WLR 425 at 432G–433B per Bagnall J (wife-beneficiary not entitled to increased beneficial share where she had used her own money in part discharge of her husband's sole mortgage liability). See (1972) 35 MLR 547 (J Levin).
7   Reliance to one's detriment in response to an offer of increased beneficial entitlement may subsequently make it 'unconscionable … to set up the statute and repudiate the agreement' (*Re Densham (A Bankrupt)* [1975] 1 WLR 1519 at 1525D–E).

Contributions to general household expenses

10.51   There are certain contexts, particularly of a domestic nature, where no resulting trust can be presumed from the mere fact of money payment.[1] These again involve circumstances in which it is extremely difficult to say that the contributor of funds has advanced money in the character of a purchaser.[2] Problems arise in two closely connected areas.

1   The payment may be an informal family loan (see e g *Mortgage Express Ltd v Raja* (Unreported, Court of Appeal, 2 July 1996)).

2   No resulting trust is raised by conduct on the part of a contributor which is 'explicable on a basis other than an expectation of a return by way of beneficial interest' (*McKenzie v McKenzie* [2003] EWHC 601 (Ch) at [77]).

Payments into a common pool

10.52   There is a longstanding reluctance to accept that recurrent payments of money made between family members are intended to create or reflect any legally binding relationship between the parties.[1] The son who gives his mother part of his jobseeker's allowance whilst living at home does not normally acquire thereby a beneficial trust interest in his parents' realty. Such payments are not usually attributable to any reasonable belief that a beneficial interest is being acquired, but are more readily analysed as merely a contribution towards current living expenses and the outgoings of a shared household.[2] Even a pattern of regular payments into a common pool may give rise to no more than minimal protection for the contributor.[3] In *Hannaford v Selby*,[4] for example, a young couple bought a house in their own names with the aid of a mortgage loan. The wife's elderly parents moved in with them, paying a weekly sum into the family purse over a substantial period of time. When friction later erupted between the generations, Goulding J rejected the parents' claim to a beneficial interest in the home,[5] holding that their payments into the common pool had resulted in no more than an occupation licence which was revocable on reasonable notice.[6]

1   *Balfour v Balfour* [1919] 2 KB 571 at 579 per Atkin LJ. See similarly *Pettitt v Pettitt* [1970] AC 777 at 796A; *Burns v Burns* [1984] Ch 317 at 335C; but compare *Sharp v Anderson* (1994) 6 BPR 13801 at 13808, where Santow J pointed to an increasing trend towards enforcement of informal family arrangements which involve substantial obligations or undertakings.
2   See e g *Gross v French* (1976) 238 EG 39 at 41; *Mehra v Shah* [2003] All ER (D) 15 (Aug) at [48] (affd [2004] EWCA Civ 632 at [64]); *Govorko v Vicelic* (1971) 2 BPR 9477 at 9485, 9487. See also *Springette v Defoe* [1992] 2 FLR 388 at 394A–F; *Baumgartner v Baumgartner* (1985) 2 NSWLR 406 at 419C.
3   This is so even if the common pool is used in part for the payment of mortgage instalments (*Buggs v Buggs* [2003] EWHC 1538 (Ch) at [48]–[50]; but see [2003] Conv 411 (M P Thompson)).
4   (1976) 239 EG 811.
5   See similarly *Mollo v Mollo* [1999] EGCS 117 (Transcript at [29]) ('payment of routine bills'). Compare, however, *Timms v Timms* (1973) 226 EG 1565, where the Court of Appeal preferred to find in favour of a tenancy rather than a family arrangement.
6   (1976) 239 EG 811 at 813 (six months' notice given).

Distributions of expenditure in a shared family home

10.53   For many years English courts tinkered at the edges of resulting trust theory in an attempt to clarify whether one person's financial contributions towards the general running expenses of a shared household could be said to generate any beneficial entitlement in her favour, particularly where such contributions freed another family member to discharge a mortgage commitment for which he was solely responsible. This problem arose with some acuteness in the context of a family home purchased with borrowed funds towards the repayment of which A had applied his own income, whilst B diverted her income towards the payment of household bills and in the purchase of domestic consumables such as food, clothing and heating.

10.54   It has long been recognised, as a matter of elementary fairness, that the beneficial ownership of family assets should not depend upon fortuitous patterns of family expenditure.[1] The courts have not been wholly insensitive to the argument that financial contributions to general household welfare should be accounted, under a resulting trust, as the equivalent of direct money contributions towards the purchase price of the family home.[2] Yet, in terms of resulting trust principle, there have always remained obvious difficulties in relating the discharge of general household expenses to any clear beneficial intention existing at the date of acquisition of the legal estate.[3] Moreover, any attempt to assimilate household expenditure under a resulting trust is apt to fall foul of the doctrinaire approach of the equity lawyer, whose view is both simple and logical: if B spends money in the purchase of item X, she generally acquires rights in item X, but not in item Y, which has been bought by A, even if the fact that B has purchased item X indirectly enables A to purchase item Y.[4] Thus, in the hardened perception of the equity lawyer, the woman who pays household food or electricity bills with her own funds does not magically acquire any beneficial entitlement in land which her partner has meanwhile managed to purchase with his own money.[5]

1   The line of authority begins with *Fribance v Fribance (No 2)* [1957] 1 WLR 384 at 387 per Denning LJ. See also *Gissing v Gissing* [1971] AC 886 at 909E–G per Lord Diplock; *Allen v Snyder* [1977] 2 NSWLR 685 at 707F–G; *Boccalatte v Bushelle* [1980] Qd R 180 at 184B.
2   See e g *McFarlane v McFarlane* [1972] NI 59 at 70, 72 per Lord MacDermott LCJ (at least if the parties had 'agreed to some quid pro quo in the nature of a proprietary benefit'). For emphasis of the need for some understanding between A and B that B's assumption of responsibility for more general aspects of household expenditure was part of a deliberate design to free A to discharge the acquisition cost of the home itself, see *Gissing v Gissing* [1971] AC 886 at 903B–C per Lord Pearson; *Burns v Burns* [1984] Ch 317 at 329A–B per Fox LJ.
3   [**Para 10.20**].
4   For an extreme example of this approach, see *Little v Little* (1988) 15 NSWLR 43 at 46F per Bryson J ('[w]hat one gets for paying stamp duty is a stamp, not a piece of land').
5   See *Burns v Burns* [1984] Ch 317 at 329C; *Allen v Snyder* [1977] 2 NSWLR 685 at 691C.

10.55   After an unsatisfactory period of experimentation with resulting trust theory, English courts eventually abandoned the suggestion that general household expenditure might sufficiently replicate the character of 'purchase money' as to raise a resulting trust of the legal estate in the family home.[1] It is widely recognised nowadays that the mere sharing of family living expenses is not intrinsically referable to the acquisition of family property.[2] Accordingly, economic contributions of this kind are best regarded, not as generating some strained form of resulting trust, but rather as evidence of a relevant detriment or 'change of position' for the purpose of founding a constructive trust. In this way the resulting trust is confined more narrowly to money payments which serve directly to finance the purchase of a legal estate.

1   *Gissing v Gissing* [1971] AC 886 at 901B–C per Viscount Dilhorne, 910G–H per Lord Diplock.
2   *Gissing v Gissing* [1971] AC 886 at 909G–H per Lord Diplock. See also *McGill v S* [1979] IR
     283 at 289; *Niederberger v Memnook* (1982) 130 DLR (3d) 353 at 360.

Contributions of domestic endeavour

10.56   It is also clearly established that contributions of domestic labour, even
though provided over many years, do not constitute the equivalent of 'purchase
money' for the purpose of creating a resulting trust.[1] The English law of real
property notoriously refuses to attach any money value to the homemaker's
intangible contribution to the general welfare of the family through services of
domestic management and child care. The courts take the view that 'the mere
fact that parties live together and do the ordinary domestic tasks is ... no
indication at all that they thereby intended to alter the existing property rights
of either of them.'[2] It is an enduring irony that reluctance to monetise the
unquantifiable economic impact of domestic endeavour has caused an invaluable form of activity to appear valueless.[3] However, if domestic effort were
accorded an imputed monetary significance in the law of resulting trusts, its
impact could hardly be confined to the acquisition of an isolated asset such as
the family home.[4] Domestic contributions can normally be related indiscriminately to all property acquired within the family context,[5] with the consequence
that vast ranges of household asset could be found to be trammelled by the
imposition of resulting trusts.[6] To this day English law recognises no distinct
regime of family property,[7] except, curiously, amidst the social pathologies of
divorce and death. The reward for generalised, and usually unquantifiable,
contributions of domestic performance is to be found – if at all – only in the
law of constructive trusts.

1   See e g *Burns v Burns* [1984] Ch 317 at 342G per May LJ.
2   *Burns v Burns* [1984] Ch 317 at 331A per Fox LJ. See also *Button v Button* [1968] 1 WLR 457
     at 462C.
3   'For those held spellbound by the fetishism of price theory, any operation not tagged with a
     price is *a priori* not economic' (Wally Seccombe, 'The Housewife and Her Labour under
     Capitalism' (1974) 83 New Left Review 3 at 4). See Gray, *Reallocation of Property on Divorce*
     (Professional Books 1977), pp 22–42, 68–71.
4   As Woodhouse J once pointed out, the 'physical association of domestic effort and domestic
     environment' provides only an illusory nexus of cause and effect (*Aitken v Aitken* (Auckland
     Registry, No M 105/70 and D 697/70, 22 November 1972), Transcript pp 10–11).
5   See *Gravina v Gravina* [1972] VR 678 at 682 per Menhennitt J.
6   Compare *E v E* [1971] NZLR 859 at 865 per Wild CJ (dissenting).
7   The mere fact of marriage or family relationship imports no special regime of community of
     property or family assets (see *Pettitt v Pettitt* [1970] AC 777 at 794G–795C per Lord Reid,
     810F–G per Lord Hodson, 817A–G per Lord Upjohn; *Gissing v Gissing* [1971] AC 886 at
     899G–900A per Viscount Dilhorne; *Burns v Burns* [1984] Ch 317 at 334F–G per May LJ;
     Grant v Edwards [1986] Ch 638 at 651E–G per Mustill LJ; *Stockholm Finance Ltd v Garden
     Holdings Inc* [1995] NPC 162 per Robert Walker J).

Payments of periodic rent

10.57   In order to be relevant under the doctrine of resulting trusts, money payments must be made in connection with the acquisition rather than the use of a capital asset.[1] This has a significance in relation to flat-sharing arrangements, where it is common for a tenancy to be taken in the name of one of the flat-sharers, the others holding technically as contractual licensees from him. No resulting trust is presumed on the basis of money payments made by flat-sharers who contribute proportionately to the rent charged to the nominal tenant.[2] The latter stands in no fiduciary relationship to the others, and it therefore follows that if he subsequently acquires a long lease in the flat on his own behalf, this valuable asset is not held on trust for the other erstwhile flat-sharers.[3] As Plowman J pointed out in *Savage v Dunningham*,[4] serious problems would result if flat-sharing were treated not as an entirely informal arrangement but as the potential source of a trust.[5]

1   See e g *Passee v Passee* [1988] 1 FLR 263 at 268D–E; *Annen v Rattee* (1985) 273 EG 503 at 504 (payments by lodger, although directed towards the legal owners' mortgage instalments, were never intended to generate a beneficial interest).
2   *Savage v Dunningham* [1974] Ch 181 at 184H–185A. See also *Annen v Rattee* (1985) 273 EG 503 at 504.
3   *Savage v Dunningham* [1974] Ch 181 at 185G. The position might be different if the flat-sharers had jointly contributed a cash premium towards the purchase of the tenancy in the name of one of their number. See also *Malayan Credit Ltd v Jack Chia-MPH Ltd* [1986] AC 549 at 561D–E.
4   [1974] Ch 181 at 185D–F.
5   Each flat-sharer would, for instance, hold a beneficial interest which would require written disposition when he or she moved out (LPA 1925, s 53(1)(c)).

CONSTRUCTIVE TRUSTS

10.58   The constructive trust is one of the more far-reaching devices used by equity in vindication of its own doctrines.[1] The constructive trust is the counter-agent of equitable fraud.[2] In the memorable words of Justice Benjamin Cardozo, the constructive trust is

> the formula through which the conscience of equity finds expression. When property has been acquired in such circumstances that the holder of the legal title may not in good conscience retain the beneficial interest, equity converts him into a trustee.[3]

1   See *Sen v Headley* [1991] Ch 425 at 440B per Nourse LJ ('a ready means of developing our property law in modern times').
2   The 'constructive trust' is, strictly speaking, distinguishable from the 'constructive trusteeship' (or personal liability as a trustee) which is imposed as a 'direct consequence of [some] unlawful transaction which is impeached by the plaintiff' (such as knowing assistance in some breach of trust). See *Paragon Finance plc v D B Thakerar & Co* [1999] 1 All ER 400 at 409a–g per Millett LJ; *Giumelli v Giumelli* (1999) 196 CLR 101 at [4] (High Court of Australia).
3   *Beatty v Guggenheim Exploration Co*, 225 NY 380 at 386 (1919), quoted in *Binions v Evans* [1972] Ch 359 at 368C per Lord Denning MR. 'A constructive trust is equity's way of enforcing conscience' (*McKenzie v McKenzie* [2003] EWHC 601 (Ch) at [76]). See similarly

Soulos v Korkontzilas (1997) 146 DLR (4th) 214 at 226f per McLachlin J ('good conscience is a theme underlying constructive trust from its earliest times').

10.59 The constructive trust derives from no direct intention on the part of the estate owner to hold as a fiduciary[1] – but rather because he has sought to *avoid* liability as a trustee. A constructive trust is generated by the circumstance that, through some prior agreement or bargain, the trustee has taken upon himself a fiduciary role which he cannot now be heard to disavow. As Dixon J said in *Cohen v Cohen*,[2] the constructive trust represents an instance where an equity 'is fastened upon the trustee not because he intended to become the fiduciary of property but because of the character of his dealings and in spite of his intention to take the property for himself.' The constructive trust is imposed precisely because the assertion of absolute beneficial ownership now appears unconscionable. Even when a constructive trust is declared by court order, the court's intervention merely reflects a pre-existing conclusion of equity that the relevant estate owner's conscience is bound.[3] The beneficial interest recognised under the constructive trust comes into being as soon as the estate owner unconsentiously denies the relevant bargain for entitlement on which the beneficial claimant has relied.[4]

1   See *Muschinski v Dodds* (1985) 160 CLR 583 at 613 per Deane J. The reality is usually quite the reverse: the imposition of the trust is normally the last result desired or contemplated by the constructive trustee (see *Rathwell v Rathwell* (1978) 83 DLR (3d) 289 at 305 per Dickson J).
2   (1929) 42 CLR 91 at 100.
3   See *Westdeutsche Landesbank Girozentrale v Islington LBC* [1996] AC 669 at 714G per Lord Browne-Wilkinson ('the function of the court is merely to declare that such a trust has arisen in the past').
4   *Grant v Edwards* [1986] Ch 638 at 652C–D per Mustill LJ; *Turton v Turton* [1988] Ch 542 at 555A per Kerr LJ.

The 'construction' of a trust

10.60 A constructive trust is always based on the perception that some relevant party deserves to be 'made liable in equity as trustee by the imposition or construction of the court of equity.'[1] A may own the legal estate in land, but still be required for reasons of equitable doctrine to hold that estate, in the character of a fiduciary, on an implied trust for B.[2] In its more dramatic manifestations, the imposition of a constructive trust on A resembles a decree of confiscation, awarding to B, in whole or part, a proprietary interest which A had previously thought belonged entirely to himself both at law and in equity.[3] Although not the direct product of intention, the constructive trust operates against the background of – and indeed is ultimately premised upon – some common intention formulated between A and B which now renders the assertion of an absolute beneficial title inequitable.[4]

1   *Selangor United Rubber Estates Ltd v Cradock (No 3)* [1968] 1 WLR 1555 at 1582A–B per Ungoed-Thomas J.
2   See *Muschinski v Dodds* (1985) 160 CLR 583 at 616–617 per Deane J. The court 'acts upon the conscience' of the title holder (*Nichols v Nichols* (1986) 4 BPR 9240 at 9246 per Needham J).

Constructive trust principles are equally applicable where title is held by a company controlled by A (see e g *Winkworth v Edward Baron Development Co Ltd* [1986] 1 WLR 1512; *Re Schuppan* (*a bankrupt*) (*No 2*) [1997] 1 BCLC 256 at 268h; *Chan Pui Chun v Leung Kam Ho* [2003] 1 FLR 23 at [97]–[99]).

3   Not every constructive trust confers an absolute equitable interest on B. In appropriate circumstances a constructive trust may be imposed on A, directing him to hold on trust for some lesser equitable entitlement (e g a life interest) on the part of B (see e g *Bannister v Bannister* [1948] 2 All ER 133 [**para 10.70**]).

4   See *Allen v Snyder* [1977] 2 NSWLR 685 at 693A–B; *Baumgartner v Baumgartner* (1985) 2 NSWLR 406 at 435A–B.

A means of informal rights creation

10.61   Whilst resulting trusts focus on *contributions* towards the purchase of realty, constructive trusts are more heavily concerned with *bargains* relating to beneficial ownership.[1] Consistently with its disfavour of informal mechanisms of rights creation, English law generally denies effect to mere oral gifts, agreements or transactions relating to land.[2] But once the repudiation of a promised beneficial entitlement crosses the threshold of unconscionable behaviour, equity is ultimately prepared to impose a special form of trust liability on the errant estate owner, thereby safeguarding the bargained interest notwithstanding the informality of its origin. Thus, where the owner of an estate in land has entered into an agreement, since acted upon, to allocate or share beneficial ownership in some particular way, equity will not allow him unconscionably to deny the beneficial interest conceded and will therefore 'construct a trust to give effect to it.'[3]

1   See *Grant v Edwards* [1986] Ch 638 at 651G–653A per Mustill LJ.
2   LPA 1925, s 53(1).
3   *Grant v Edwards* [1986] Ch 638 at 646H–647A per Nourse LJ.

THE OPERATION OF THE CONSTRUCTIVE TRUST

10.62   A constructive trust arises by operation of law whenever the circumstances are such that it would be 'unconscionable for the owner of property (usually but not necessarily the legal estate) to assert his own beneficial interest in the property and deny the beneficial interest of another.'[1] A prescription of this kind offers, at first sight, only an extremely vague formula of general equitable relief,[2] but the facts which attract the vigilant concern of equity are much more closely circumscribed. As Lord Diplock indicated in *Gissing v Gissing*,[3] the inequitable outcome which the constructive trust aims to prevent occurs primarily where an estate owner 'by his words or conduct ... has induced the cestui que trust [the claimant beneficiary] to act to [her] own detriment in the reasonable belief that by so acting [she] was acquiring a beneficial interest in the land.' This terminology has 'much in common' with the language of proprietary estoppel[4] and blends crucial elements of bargain and conscience in the articulation of the deep theory of the constructive trust.

1   *Paragon Finance plc v D B Thakerar & Co* [1999] 1 All ER 400 at 409a–b per Millett LJ. See
     also Millett, 'Restitution and Constructive Trusts' (1998) 114 LQR 399 at 400; *Banner Homes
     Group Plc v Luff Developments Ltd* [2000] Ch 372 at 383E–F per Chadwick LJ.
2   See eg *Gissing v Gissing* [1971] AC 886 at 905B–C, where Lord Diplock stated that a
     constructive trust is 'created by a transaction between the trustee and the cestui que trust in
     connection with the acquisition by the trustee of a legal estate in the land, whenever the
     trustee has so conducted himself that it would be inequitable to allow him to deny to the cestui
     que trust a beneficial interest in the land acquired.' Lord Denning MR was later accustomed,
     by way of selective quotation, to invoke the open-ended equity apparently adumbrated by
     Lord Diplock (see eg *Eves v Eves* [1975] 1 WLR 1338 at 1341F–G **[para 10.96]**; compare *Grant
     v Edwards* [1986] Ch 638 at 647G per Nourse LJ).
3   [1971] AC 886 at 905B–C.
4   *Banner Homes Group Plc v Luff Developments Ltd* [2000] Ch 372 at 384A–B per Chadwick LJ.
     See similarly *Lloyds Bank plc v Carrick* [1996] 4 All ER 630 at 640a per Morritt LJ; *Yaxley v
     Gotts* [2000] Ch 162 at 176B–177B, 180B–C per Robert Walker LJ, 191C per Beldam LJ
     [para 10.68]; *Chan Pui Chun v Leung Kam Ho* [2003] 1 FLR 23 at [91] per Jonathan Parker LJ;
     Oxley v Hiscock [2004] 3 WLR 715 at [66], [70]–[71] per Chadwick LJ.

The role of bargain

10.63   The role of bargain is central to the 'common intention' constructive
trust. In *Gissing v Gissing*[1] Lord Diplock observed that the preceding case law
on constructive trusts had largely passed over the first – and critical – stage in
the analysis of this form of trust, ie, 'the role of … agreement … in the creation
of an equitable estate in real property.'[2] The equitable entitlement protected by
the constructive trust derives almost invariably from an antecedent bargain or
agreement relating to the property, by which the owner of an estate or interest
in that property has undertaken to give effect to a beneficial entitlement in
someone else.[3] The trust-generating impact of contract is, of course, nothing
new in English law.[4] An express agreement by A that B should take a beneficial
interest in A's land is potentially creative of a trust in respect of that land, but
the difficulty is that express declarations of trust are enforceable only if
evidenced by signed writing in accordance with section 53(1)(b) of the Law of
Property Act 1925.[5]

1   [1971] AC 886 **[paras 10.93, 10.108]**.
2   [1971] AC 886 at 904G. For reference in this context to the terminology of 'bargain', see *Grant
     v Edwards* [1986] Ch 638 at 651G–653D per Mustill LJ. The pre-eminent significance of
     agreement as a factor in the formative phase of the constructive trust has since been heavily
     re-emphasised by the House of Lords (see *Lloyds Bank Plc v Rosset* [1991] 1 AC 107 at
     132E–F per Lord Bridge of Harwich **[para 10.91]**).
3   'Where a common intention can be proved or imputed … the technique of equity is to impose
     a constructive trust to fulfil it' (*McKenzie v McKenzie* [2003] EWHC 601 (Ch) at [70]).
4   For example, English law is prepared to construct a trust in recognition of the interest taken
     by a purchaser under a specifically enforceable contract for the transfer of an estate in land
     [para 9.27].
5   **[Para 9.188]**.

The role of conscience

10.64   The role of conscience now becomes vital in the genesis of a 'common intention' constructive trust. The constructive trust operates typically against a background in which A threatens unconscionably to resile from an informal understanding that B should receive some equitable entitlement in A's land.[1] Although unenforceable as an express declaration of trust, this agreement is not necessarily spent. In some circumstances, as Lord Diplock pointed out in *Gissing v Gissing*,[2] the court may still be able to give effect to the agreed beneficial ownership, notwithstanding the absence of statutory formality.

1　Had A granted B's entitlement under a written declaration of trust, B's equitable rights would, of course, have been conclusive and secure **[para 9.198]**.
2　[1971] AC 886 at 905D–E.

10.65   No court will impose a constructive trust 'unless it is satisfied that the conscience of the estate owner is affected.'[1] In the present context, the inequity which triggers the imposition of a constructive trust is established by the disclaimer of obligations of conscience originating in the prior agreement or understanding between the relevant parties. Such a disclaimer amounts to a 'breach of faith'[2] and equity immediately counteracts A's equitable fraud (or unconscionable behaviour) by 'constructing' a trust in B's favour.[3] Unlike the unenforceable declaration contained in the prior informal bargain, the constructive trust imposed by equity is fully enforceable by B, precisely because constructive trusts are exempted from any statutory requirement of written form or written evidence.[4] Depending upon the nature of the interest promised to B, the constructive trust may confirm B's entitlement to an absolute beneficial interest (e g an equitable fee simple estate) or to a limited beneficial interest (e g a life interest) or to some fractional beneficial interest. The constructive trust then takes effect as a 'trust of land' under the Trusts of Land and Appointment of Trustees Act 1996.[5]

1　*Ashburn Anstalt v Arnold* [1989] Ch 1 at 25H per Fox LJ; *Lloyd v Dugdale* [2002] 2 P & CR 167 at [52(2)] per Sir Christopher Slade; *Driver v Yorke* [2003] All ER (D) 103 (Apr) at [28].
2　*Gissing v Gissing* [1971] AC 886 at 900B–C per Viscount Dilhorne. See also *Ogilvie v Ryan* [1976] 2 NSWLR 504 at 518D–E per Holland J ('a species of fraud').
3　See *Grant v Edwards* [1986] Ch 638 at 646H–647A per Nourse LJ.
4　LPA 1925, s 53(2).
5　**[Para 9.172]**.

COMPONENT ELEMENTS OF THE CONSTRUCTIVE TRUST

10.66   Given this account of the general principle underlying the constructive trust, it can be said that the imposition of a constructive trust requires proof of three elements:[1]
–　'bargain' (or common intention)[2]
–　'change of position' (or detrimental reliance)[3] and
–　'equitable fraud' (or unconscionable denial of rights).[4]

1   See *Ogilvie v Ryan* [1976] 2 NSWLR 504 at 516G–517A; *Hohol v Hohol* [1981] VR 221 at 225;
     Butler v Craine [1986] VR 274 at 283; *Higgins v Wingfield* [1987] VR 689 at 690, 699.
2   **[Para 10.79].**
3   **[Para 10.100].**
4   **[Para 10.109].**

10.67   These three elements are inevitably interlinked. For the purpose of establishing a constructive trust, a common intention is recognised as relevant only if one party changes his position in detrimental reliance upon some form of bargain. A change of position occurs in the relevant sense only if it is truly referable to a common intention that some equitable entitlement should be conferred by one party upon the other. Equitable fraud is present only if an estate owner then tries to evade the bargain by asserting the absolute, exclusive or unqualified nature of his own rights.

10.68   Thus stated, the constituent elements of the constructive trust bear a remarkable similarity to the features of proprietary estoppel.[1] Indeed some even refer nowadays to 'the estoppel principle enunciated by Lord Diplock in *Gissing v Gissing*.'[2] The doctrines of constructive trust and proprietary estoppel are alike 'concerned with equity's intervention to provide relief against unconscionable conduct'[3] and, although the concepts do not always overlap, it is increasingly recognised that 'in the area of a joint enterprise for the acquisition of land (which may be, but is not necessarily, the matrimonial home) the two concepts coincide.'[4] It is not uncommon to find that in many cases arguments based on constructive trust and proprietary estoppel are pleaded in the alternative,[5] although the doctrinal congruence is now so marked that courts are beginning to complain of conceptual overkill.[6]

1   See *Grant v Edwards* [1986] Ch 638 at 656H per Browne-Wilkinson V-C **[para 10.62]**. The
     Canadian development of the constructive trust is likewise underpinned by the language of
     estoppel (see *Pettkus v Becker* (1981) 117 DLR (3d) 257 at 274; *Sorochan v Sorochan* (1986) 29
     DLR (4th) 1 at 7, 12–13) **[para 10.155]**. See also *Hayward v Giordani* [1983] NZLR 140 at 147
     (Court of Appeal of New Zealand); *Giumelli v Giumelli* (1999) 196 CLR 101 at [10], [34]–[48]
     (High Court of Australia).
2   *Mason v Brown* (Chancery Division, 10 November 1997) per Deputy Judge Lawrence
     Collins QC. See *Austin v Keele* (1987) 10 NSWLR 283 at 290F, where Lord Oliver of
     Aylmerton indicated that Lord Diplock's formulation of a doctrine of implied trusts in
     Gissing v Gissing [1971] AC 886 was '[i]n essence ... an application of proprietary estoppel.'
     See also *David v David* (Unreported, Supreme Court of New South Wales, 4 February 1998)
     per Young J ('no essential difference in the analysis').
3   *Yaxley v Gotts* [2000] Ch 162 at 176B–C per Robert Walker LJ (see also Beldam LJ at 191C).
4   *Yaxley v Gotts* [2000] Ch 162 at 176E per Robert Walker LJ. See also *Lloyds Bank Plc v Rosset*
     [1991] 1 AC 107 at 132F–G per Lord Bridge of Harwich; *Birmingham Midshires Mortgage
     Services Ltd v Sabherwal* (2000) 80 P & CR 256 at 263 per Robert Walker LJ; *Banner Homes
     Group Plc v Luff Developments Ltd* [2000] Ch 372 at 384A–385A per Chadwick LJ; *Beresford
     v Williamson* [2002] EWCA Civ 1632 at [10] per Chadwick LJ.
5   See e g *Chan Pui Chun v Leung Kam Ho* [2003] 1 FLR 23 at [91]–[93].
6   See e g *Birmingham Midshires Mortgage Services Ltd v Sabherwal* (2000) 80 P & CR 256 at
     263, where Robert Walker LJ stated that 'a trust, however labelled, does not then leave room
     for a separate interest by way of equitable estoppel. To do so would cause vast confusion in an
     area which is already quite difficult enough.'

CLASSIC DEMONSTRATIONS OF CONSTRUCTIVE TRUST

10.69   Constructive trust doctrine is classically demonstrated in the context of dealings with land where an estate owner has informally agreed that another shall acquire or retain some beneficial entitlement. In certain circumstances this agreement or bargain may have burdened the title of the estate owner with unavoidable obligations of conscience which give rise to the imposition of a constructive trust.[1] The spheres of operation of the constructive trust are various and are by no means confined to cases involving the family home.

1   See *Bahr v Nicolay* (*No 2*) (1988) 164 CLR 604 at 653 per Brennan J.

Agreement that B should retain an interest in land purchased from B by A

10.70   In *Bannister v Bannister*[1] B conveyed her freehold interest in two cottages to A, her brother-in-law, at much less than market value, upon A's oral undertaking that B would be allowed to live rent-free in one of the cottages for the remainder of her life. The conveyance made no reference to this oral promise. When, in the teeth of the agreement, A later sought to evict B from her home,[2] the Court of Appeal ruled that A held his legal title on constructive trust to give effect to the beneficial life interest promised to B.

1   [1948] 2 All ER 133.
2   A claimed that B was a mere tenant at will [**para 7.273**].

Constituent elements of constructive trust

10.71   The facts of *Bannister*'s case disclosed all the constituent elements of the 'common intention' constructive trust. There had been a bargain, in that B was induced to convey the cottages to A partly in consideration of money payment and partly on the strength of A's oral promise of rights of residence. B clearly changed her position in detrimental reliance on this bargain by transferring the property to A. Even though the initial conveyance was not in itself marked by fraud,[1] a fatal element of fraud was introduced as soon as A attempted, quite unconscionably, to set up an absolute entitlement for himself in derogation of the beneficial interest which he had already agreed should be taken by B.[2] Equitable fraud of this kind could not be covered up by the plea that 'no written evidence of the real bargain is available'.[3]

1   There was an express finding by the county court judge that no fraud was present in the conveyance ([1948] 2 All ER 133 at 135C).
2   [1948] 2 All ER 133 at 136C per Scott LJ.
3   [1948] 2 All ER 133 at 136D.

Extensions of the Bannister principle

10.72   The operative principles of *Bannister*'s case can be detected in other cases where there has been an unwritten agreement between A and B that B should retain either an absolute[1] or a limited[2] beneficial interest in land which B transfers to A. The precise nature or quantum of that interest is immaterial[3] and it is generally accepted that the statutory requirement of writing can never be employed to 'smother proof of an oral arrangement creating a trust.'[4] For this purpose, moreover, it is irrelevant whether the purchase price paid by A is reduced in the light of the oral arrangement[5] or is indeed non-existent.[6] The key question is 'whether the transferor would have parted with his property but for the oral undertaking of the transferee.'[7] If that question is answered in the negative, then A's repudiation of his promise or disavowal of the common intention formulated between A and B will 'operate in equity as a fraud' on B.[8]

1   *Hutchins v Lee* (1737) 1 Atk 447 at 448, 26 ER 284 at 285; *Childers v Childers* (1857) 1 De G & J 482 at 492, 44 ER 810 at 814; *Re Duke of Marlborough* [1894] 2 Ch 133 at 146.
2   *Booth v Turle* (1873) LR 16 Eq 182 at 183, 188; *Last v Rosenfeld* [1972] 2 NSWLR 923 at 936E.
3   *Bannister v Bannister* [1948] 2 All ER 133 at 136E–F; *Last v Rosenfeld* [1972] 2 NSWLR 923 at 936E; *Avondale Printers & Stationers Ltd v Haggie* [1979] 2 NZLR 124 at 163.
4   *Dalton v Christofis* [1978] WAR 42 at 46 per Smith J. See also *Organ v Sandwell* [1921] VLR 622 at 630.
5   *Booth v Turle* (1873) LR 16 Eq 182 at 183, 188; *Bannister v Bannister* [1948] 2 All ER 133 at 134F.
6   *Hutchins v Lee* (1737) 1 Atk 447 at 448, 26 ER 284 at 285; *Childers v Childers* (1857) 1 De G & J 482 at 492, 44 ER 810 at 814; *Re Duke of Marlborough* [1894] 2 Ch 133 at 146. In some cases the transfer to the alleged trustee is expressed to be for valuable consideration, but the consideration is never in fact paid (see e g *Davies v Otty (No 2)* (1865) 35 Beav 208 at 213, 55 ER 875 at 877; *Haigh v Kaye* (1872) 7 Ch App 469 at 473–474).
7   If the transferee pays the full market value, but on oral terms that he shall hold on trust for the transferor, the case is best seen as involving an oral declaration of an express trust which, but for the rule in *Rochefoucauld v Boustead*, would have been unenforceable **[para 9.193]**. There is no element of 'detriment' or 'sacrifice' sufficient to raise a constructive trust.
8   *Avondale Printers & Stationers Ltd v Haggie* [1979] 2 NZLR 124 at 163 per Mahon J.

Agreement that B should retain an interest in land purchased by A from X

10.73   The constructive trust principle is equally applicable where A's agreement that B should retain an interest in specified land takes the form of a bargain reached, not directly between between A and B, but between A and some other person, X, who, on the strength of the bargain, transfers the land to A.[1] In *Lyus v Prowsa Developments Ltd*,[2] for example, A, a development company, took a transfer from X of an uncompleted housing development which had earlier collapsed in insolvency.[3] In the contract of purchase A agreed to take the legal title expressly subject to any subsisting contractual rights of B, who, prior to the insolvency, had paid a substantial deposit on one of the houses yet to be built on the housing estate.[4] When A threatened to renege on its agreement to honour B's rights, Dillon J concluded that it had been 'a stipulation of the bargain' between A and X that A would give effect to such equitable rights as B held under his estate contract.[5] Applying *Bannister v Bannister*,[6] Dillon J held that A had taken the legal estate on a constructive trust for B[7] and accordingly ordered specific performance of the terms of B's estate contract.[8] The 'fraud' which underlay this finding of constructive trust consisted very largely in the repudiation of the 'positive stipulation' in favour of B contained in the 'bargain' under which the land was sold on.[9]

1   See e g *Bahr v Nicolay (No 2)* (1988) 164 CLR 604 at 654 per Brennan J ('The fraud which attracts the intervention of equity consists in the unconscionable attempt by the registered proprietor to deny the ... interest to which he has undertaken to subject his registered title').

2   [1982] 1 WLR 1044. See [1983] CLJ 54 (C Harpum); [1983] Conv 64 (P Jackson); (1983) 46 MLR 96 (P H Kenny); (1984) 47 MLR 476 (P Bennett).

3   The development had been financed by a loan of money from a bank, secured by a legal charge over the land.

4   B's estate contract had been protected by an entry in the relevant registered title, but was ineffective against the bank which, in exercise of its paramount power of sale as mortgagee, had initiated a chain of sales leading to A **[para 15.178]**.

5   [1982] 1 WLR 1044 at 1053E. On the equitable rights generated by an estate contract, see Chapter 9 **[para 9.18]**.

6   [1948] 2 All ER 133 **[para 10.70]**.

7   For confirmation of this constructive trust finding, see *Chattey v Farndale Holdings Inc* (1998) 75 P & CR 298 at 316 per Morritt LJ; *Lloyd v Dugdale* [2002] 2 P & CR 167 at [50]–[51] per Sir Christopher Slade.

8   [1982] 1 WLR 1044 at 1053F–G. For another application of the same principle, see e g *Binions v Evans* [1972] Ch 359 at 368B, 370D–G **[para 12.365]**. See also D J Hayton, (1983) 133 NLJ 188; C T Emery and B Smythe, (1983) 133 NLJ 798.

9   [1982] 1 WLR 1044 at 1054G–H. Mere knowledge of prior contracts or obligations is not, however, enough to justify the imposition of a constructive trust (see *Chattey v Farndale Holdings Inc* (1998) 75 P & CR 298 at 317; *Lloyd v Dugdale* [2002] 2 P & CR 167 at [50]).

Agreement that B should acquire an interest in land to be purchased by A from X

10.74   A constructive trust may also be imposed in order to give effect, not to a promised *retention* of entitlement, but to an otherwise unenforceable agreement between A and B that B should *acquire* an interest in land which is about to be purchased by A from X.[1] Against the background of such a 'pre-acquisition arrangement or understanding',[2] it is 'equitable fraud' for A to rely on the statutory requirement of writing in order to defeat the agreement reached between himself and B.[3] The pre-acquisition agreement 'colours the subsequent acquisition by [A] and leads to his being treated as a trustee if he seeks to act inconsistently with it.'[4] The obligation of conscience created by the anterior bargain casts A *ab initio* in the role of a fiduciary[5] and a person 'who accepts property in a fiduciary capacity cannot set up in himself the legal estate free of the trust.'[6] Accordingly any attempt by A to derogate from the rights informally conceded to B, particularly by reference to a statutory requirement of writing, would be 'to steal what was in equity never his.'[7]

1   See e g *Ogilvie v Ryan* [1976] 2 NSWLR 504 at 518D–E (oral agreement for rent-free occupation for life in return for care services for elderly legal owner). See also *Last v Rosenfeld* [1972] 2 NSWLR 923 at 928B–C; *Thwaites v Ryan* [1984] VR 65 at 94.

2   See *Banner Homes Group Plc v Luff Developments Ltd* [2000] Ch 372 at 383C per Chadwick LJ. It matters not that the pre-acquisition arrangement or understanding is, for reasons of uncertainty or otherwise, contractually unenforceable **[para 10.87]**.

3   *Allen v Snyder* [1977] 2 NSWLR 685 at 692E per Glass JA. See e g *Yaxley v Gotts* [2000]

Ch 162 at 177E–G ('oral bargain' preceding acquisition). This branch of constructive trust doctrine is closely analogous to the rule in *Rochefoucauld v Boustead* [1897] 1 Ch 196 **[para 9.193]**.

4   *Banner Homes Group Plc v Luff Developments Ltd* [2000] Ch 372 at 397G per Chadwick LJ. See *Thwaites v Ryan* [1984] VR 65 at 91 per Fullagar J ('equity is liable to say that A has received a benefit which binds his conscience and he cannot be allowed to assert against B the existence in A of something that A never had, namely the legal estate unencumbered by the trust'). See also *Vedejs v Public Trustee* [1985] VR 569 at 572–573.

5   *Paragon Finance plc v D B Thakerar & Co* [1999] 1 All ER 400 at 409b–c per Millett LJ.

6   *Thwaites v Ryan* [1984] VR 65 at 91 per Fullagar J.

7   *Thwaites v Ryan* [1984] VR 65 at 91–92 per Fullagar J.

Agreement that B should acquire an interest in land already owned by A

10.75   The operation of constructive trust doctrine is not dependent on a showing that A was a fiduciary at the date of his acquisition of the legal estate.[1] His assumption of fiduciary status may be deferred. It is now accepted that a constructive trust may be founded, long after the date of acquisition, on some agreement or bargain by which A informally constitutes himself a trustee for B.[2] Such circumstances arise typically from an oral understanding in which A concedes to B some beneficial interest in A's land. This declaration of B's entitlement is clearly unenforceable as an express trust,[3] but may be enforced as a constructive trust if A later attempts unconscionably to deny that he holds on trust for B.[4] Here the constructive trust is imposed, not on the basis of any fiduciary acquisition of title, but on the basis of some later 'change of position' by B which A cannot now conscientiously claim to ignore.[5]

1   *Gissing v Gissing* [1971] AC 886 at 905B–C; *Butler v Craine* [1986] VR 274 at 284–285.

2   See eg *Austin v Keele* (1987) 10 NSWLR 283 at 290E–F per Lord Oliver of Aylmerton.

3   LPA 1925, s 53(1)(b) **[para 9.190]**. An unenforceable post-acquisition declaration of trust cannot be salvaged either by reference to a resulting trust **[para 10.20]** or by the rule in *Rochefoucauld v Boustead* **[para 9.193]**. Both of these doctrines are activated by intentions (actual or presumed) which exist contemporaneously with A's acquisition of title.

4   See *Gissing v Gissing* [1971] AC 886 at 901D per Viscount Dilhorne, 906E–F, 908B–C per Lord Diplock; *Burns v Burns* [1984] Ch 317 at 327D per Fox LJ; *Grant v Edwards* [1986] Ch 638 at 651G–652A per Mustill LJ; *Gough v Fraser* [1977] 1 NZLR 279 at 283; *Allen v Snyder* [1977] 2 NSWLR 685 at 691C.

5   See *Nemeth v Nemeth* (1978) 17 ALR 500 at 506. The claimant's 'change of position' must be 'referable to' some bargain or common intention that a beneficial interest would be generated thereby. See eg *Winkworth v Edward Baron Development Co Ltd* [1986] 1 WLR 1512 at 1516A–B per Lord Templeman.

10.76   A controversial example of the way in which a constructive trust may be generated by post-acquisition agreements or arrangements is found in the ruling of the Court of Appeal in *Hussey v Palmer*.[1] Here H, an elderly widow, had been invited to live in a house already owned by her son-in-law, P. An extra bedroom was built for her as an extension to the existing house and the cost of this construction was met by H. Domestic discord brought the cohabitation to a premature end, it being typical of this kind of informal family arrangement that the parties had never clearly spelt out the legal implications of their relationship. Lord Denning MR stated the philosophy of the constructive trust in expansive terms,[2] holding it to be a trust imposed by law whenever justice and good conscience require it. It is a liberal process, founded upon large principles of equity, to be applied in cases where the legal owner cannot conscientiously keep the property for himself alone, but ought to allow another to have the property or the benefit of it or a share in it. The trust may arise at the outset when the property is acquired, or later on, as the circumstances require. It is an equitable remedy by which the court can enable an aggrieved party to obtain restitution.[3]

1   [1972] 1 WLR 1286. See (1973) 37 Conv (NS) 65 (D J Hayton); (1973) 89 LQR 2; (1973) 36 MLR 436 (T C Ridley). The majority ruling in *Hussey v Palmer* proved so controversial that for many years it arguably impeded, rather than promoted, the development of constructive trust theory in England.

2   Despite much deep-rooted scepticism about Lord Denning's judgment in *Hussey v Palmer*, it has been pointed out (see *Soulos v Korkontzilas* (1997) 146 DLR (4th) 214 at 225h–226a per McLachlin J) that he was not alone in his liberal perception of 'good conscience' as the basis of equitable intervention (see *Neste Oy v Lloyds Bank Plc* [1983] 2 Lloyd's Rep 658 at 665–666 per Bingham J).

3   [1972] 1 WLR 1286 at 1290A.

10.77   The Court of Appeal accordingly decided, by a majority,[1] to impose a constructive trust under which H received either a proportionate share of the beneficial ownership of the property or a lien for the money advanced by her.[2] The propriety of a constructive trust in these circumstances has been much debated.[3] Although there was clearly a recognisable change of position by H, it is not easy to identify any relevant bargain or common intention between the parties,[4] and even more difficult to pinpoint the precise interest which P, even by inference, supposedly agreed to confer upon H.[5] The majority decision may ultimately have been less influenced by the technicalities of constructive trust theory than by the fact that P had, on any view, behaved most oppressively towards H.[6]

1   Cairns LJ dissented, partly on the ground that H herself had testified in court to having merely 'lent' the money to P ([1972] 1 WLR 1286 at 1292C–D).

2   It was 'entirely against conscience that [P] should retain the whole house and not allow [H] any interest in it, or any charge upon it' ([1972] 1 WLR 1286 at 1291B per Lord Denning MR). See also *Murray v Murray* [1996] 3 IR 251 at 255.

3   For critical views of *Hussey v Palmer*, see *Re Sharpe* (*A Bankrupt*) [1980] 1 WLR 219 at 223A; *Avondale Printers & Stationers Ltd v Haggie* [1979] 2 NZLR 124 at 145; *Malsbury v Malsbury* [1982] 1 NSWLR 226 at 231B–C. As was suggested in *Holiday Inns Inc v Broadhead* (1974) 232 EG 951 at 1087 and *Savva v Costa and Harymode Investments Ltd* (1981) 131 NLJ 1114, the decision in *Hussey v Palmer* may be better analysed as an illustration of proprietary estoppel [**para 10.168**]. See e g *Clayton v Green* (1979) NZ Recent Law 139 at 140.

4   See *Avondale Printers & Stationers Ltd v Haggie* [1979] 2 NZLR 124 at 145; M Neave, (1978) 11 Melbourne ULR 343 at 361.

5   See *Re Sharpe* (*A Bankrupt*) [1980] 1 WLR 219 at 222H–223A. Compare *Broughall v Hunt* (Unreported, Chancery Division, 1 February 1983) (finding of contractual licence rather than constructive trust).

6   There was evidence, for example, that P had refused even to reply to H's plaintive request for an allowance of £1 per week to help her out after her departure from the home ([1972] 1 WLR 1286 at 1288D–E). The facts of *Hussey v Palmer* have been said to be 'very special' (*Re Sharpe* (*A Bankrupt*) [1980] 1 WLR 219 at 223A per Browne-Wilkinson J; *Firth v Mallender* (Unreported, Court of Appeal, 11 October 1999) per Parker J).

Agreement that B should acquire an enlarged interest in land owned by A

10.78 The quantum of beneficial entitlement under an express or resulting trust crystallises, in principle, at the commencement of the trust[1] and is not normally thereafter variable except by a signed disposition in writing.[2] In the absence of compliance with statutory formality, it is nevertheless possible that a claim to an enlarged beneficial share (ie over and above the beneficial entitlement already enjoyed) may sometimes be supported by a claim of constructive trust. In *Re Densham (A Bankrupt)*[3] Goff J took the view that if A, the owner of a legal title, expressly (but informally) agreed at any stage that B should receive a larger beneficial share under a trust of that title than was strictly justified by B's money contribution towards its purchase,[4] B could justifiably claim that larger share on the footing of a constructive trust. To hold the agreement in B's favour unenforceable for want of writing would be 'contrary to equitable principles', since it would be 'unconscionable for a party to set up the statute and repudiate the agreement.' A would become a 'constructive trustee of the property so far as necessary to give effect to the agreement.'[5] For her part, however, B would be required to prove the existence of some agreement for enhanced beneficial ownership[6] and also that, in reliance upon this bargain, she had undertaken some 'change of position' which was 'referable' to the promise of enhanced shareholding.[7]

1   *Bernard v Josephs* [1982] Ch 391 at 404F.
2   See *Cowcher v Cowcher* [1972] 1 WLR 425.
3   [1975] 1 WLR 1519. See (1976) 92 LQR 489 (F Webb).
4   To the extent that agreed beneficial shares deviate from the ratio of the parties' actual money contributions, there arises an 'express trust which lacks writing' (see *Allen v Snyder* [1977] 2 NSWLR 685 at 692C–D per Glass JA). See also *Cowcher v Cowcher* [1972] 1 WLR 425 at 431C, 433H; *Currie v Hamilton* [1984] 1 NSWLR 687 at 690F.
5   [1975] 1 WLR 1519 at 1525D–E. See, however, Insolvency Act 1986, s 339(3)(c).
6   See Lord Diplock's reference in *Gissing v Gissing* [1971] AC 886 at 906E to the necessity for 'some subsequent fresh agreement, acted upon by the parties, to vary the original beneficial interests created when the matrimonial home was acquired.'
7   See *Calverley v Green* (1984) 155 CLR 242 at 263 per Mason and Brennan JJ.

BARGAIN OR COMMON INTENTION

10.79 The role of bargain (express or implied) is both central and irreducible in the context of the classic constructive trust. For present purposes every constructive trust can be said to derive from some bargain which affects the conscience of the party who is eventually made liable as constructive trustee. Thus, if A, an estate owner, makes some informal agreement to recognise the existence of equitable rights in B,[1] it becomes unconscionable for A later to disown this common intention if, in the meantime, the agreement has induced a change of position to the potential detriment of B. No crucial importance is attached to the precise origin of the relevant bargain: it is sufficient merely that some anterior bargain for equitable entitlement so impinges on the conscience of A as to make him guilty of equitable fraud should he ever attempt to defeat the agreement.

1   See e g *Bannister v Bannister* [1948] 2 All ER 133 [**para 10.70**]. It is possible, for this purpose, that A may adopt an agreement entered into by an associate (see e g *Yaxley v Gotts* [2000] Ch 162 at 170C per Robert Walker LJ, but compare Clarke LJ at 180H–181C) or that A, knowing of the agreement, is estopped from repudiating its intended effect (see *Yaxley*, supra at 188B–D per Beldam LJ).

Objective reality of bargain

10.80   The English model of the constructive trust is sometimes known as the 'institutional' or 'substantive' constructive trust,[1] in that it seeks to fashion trust entitlements, on the analogy of the express trust, from the articulated intentions of the relevant parties.[2] It therefore follows that the element of bargain which underlies the constructive trust of land must have an objective and demonstrable reality.[3] The agreement or understanding may be *express* or *implied* – a difference which may have important consequences for the detailed operation of the trust[4] – but in either case there must be evidence of some actual agreement or common intention that B should be beneficially interested in A's land.[5] In the absence of some consensus relating to beneficial title, even substantial changes of position cannot generate rights by way of constructive trust.[6]

1   See *Westdeutsche Landesbank Girozentrale v Islington LBC* [1996] AC 669 at 714G per Lord Browne-Wilkinson; *Rawluk v Rawluk* (1990) 65 DLR (4th) 161 at 169e per Cory J.
2   See *Hepworth v Hepworth* (1963) 110 CLR 309 at 317 per Windeyer J [**para 9.177**].
3   It is 'not for the court to make a bargain for the parties' (*Stockholm Finance Ltd v Garden Holdings Inc* [1995] NPC 162 per Robert Walker J).
4   [**para 10.112**].
5   *Allen v Snyder* [1977] 2 NSWLR 685 at 694A; *Baumgartner v Baumgartner* (1985) 2 NSWLR 406 at 435B. No relevant bargain is present, however, if the parties' agreement is conditional on an event (e g marriage) which never occurs (see *Lightfoot v Lightfoot-Brown* [2004] All ER (D) 92 (Apr) at [10]).
6   See *Gissing v Gissing* [1971] AC 886 at 905C–F per Lord Diplock; *Springette v Defoe* [1992] 2 FLR 388 at 392C–D, 397E–F.

The threshold question

10.81   In *Oxley v Hiscock*[1] the Court of Appeal recently identified, as 'the primary, or threshold, question' in the area of co-ownership claims, the issue whether there was a common intention that each party 'should have a beneficial interest' in the land.[2] Provided that there has been an agreement for some form of shared beneficial entitlement, this bargain can generate a constructive trust even though it does not disclose any common intention as to the precise quantum of the parties' respective beneficial interests.[3] As the Court of Appeal indicated in *Oxley*, the exact extent of the parties' beneficial shares raises 'a secondary, or consequential question' which, in some circumstances, may require to be determined later by the court with reference to what is fair in the light of the parties' 'whole course of dealing' in relation to the land.[4] One important effect of this staged approach is to intensify the significance of the secondary phase where the court may have to quantify the beneficial entitlement brought about by the 'threshold' agreement that there should be at least some form of equitable sharing.

1   [2004] 3 WLR 715 at [47], [68], [71] per Chadwick LJ (Mance and Scott Baker LJJ concurring).
2   The origins in this approach are to be found in *Gissing v Gissing* [1971] AC 886 at 905B–C per Lord Diplock; *Lloyds Bank Plc v Rosset* [1991] 1 AC 107 at 132E–F per Lord Bridge of Harwich [**para 10.63**].
3   See *Drake v Whipp* [1996] 1 FLR 826 at 829H–830B per Peter Gibson LJ.
4   [2004] 3 WLR 715 at [47], [69], [73] per Chadwick LJ.

Inferred and imputed common intention

10.82   According to received doctrine, it is open to the court to *infer* the existence of a common intention for some kind of shared beneficial ownership if such an intention is plainly evidenced by the conduct of the parties. But the court may not – at least in the conventional view – *impute* to the parties an intention to share beneficial title if they never actually formulated, either by words or conduct, a consensus to this effect.[1] It is widely accepted[2] that there is no jurisdiction to attribute to A and B a fictitious common intention that B should be beneficially entitled, even though it is highly probable that such an agreement would have been reached by the parties had they only considered the issue[3] or would have been fair, just or reasonable in all the circumstances.[4] If, however, the parties clearly intended some sharing of beneficial ownership, the court remains free to *impute*, at some later stage, their intended quantification of the respective shareholdings.[5]

1   See *Grant v Edwards* [1986] Ch 638 at 651G–652A per Mustill LJ; *Butler v Craine* [1986] VR 274 at 285; *Cooke v Cooke* [1987] VR 625 at 638; *Stowe v Stowe* (1995) 15 WAR 363 at 368A–B. For recognition of 'the uncertain boundaries between inference and conjecture', see *Doohan v Nelson* [1973] 2 NSWLR 320 at 329E.
2   Isolated statements to the contrary can be found (see e g *Pettitt v Pettitt* [1970] AC 777 at 795C–F per Lord Reid; *Gissing v Gissing* [1971] AC 886 at 897F–G per Lord Reid; *Midland Bank plc v Cooke* [1995] 4 All ER 562 at 575a–j per Waite LJ), but these are not supported by traditional equity jurisprudence (see *Allen v Snyder* [1977] 2 NSWLR 685 at 694B; *Muschinski v Dodds* (1985) 160 CLR 583 at 595 per Gibbs CJ).
3   *Pettitt v Pettitt* [1970] AC 777 at 804H–805A per Lord Morris of Borth-y-Gest, 810E–F per Lord Hodson, 816D per Lord Upjohn; *Gissing v Gissing* [1971] AC 886 at 898C–D per Lord Morris of Borth-y-Gest, 900E–F per Viscount Dilhorne, 904E–F per Lord Diplock; *Grant v Edwards* [1986] Ch 638 at 652F; *Mollo v Mollo* [1999] EGCS 117 (Transcript at [25(d)]); *McFarlane v McFarlane* [1972] NI 59 at 71; *Allen v Snyder* [1977] 2 NSWLR 685 at 690F, 694A–B, 696F–G; *Avondale Printers & Stationers Ltd v Haggie* [1979] 2 NZLR 124 at 146; *McMahon v McMahon* [1979] VR 239 at 244.
4   *Pettitt v Pettitt* [1970] AC 777 at 805A per Lord Morris of Borth-y-Gest, 808B–C per Lord Hodson; *Gissing v Gissing* [1971] AC 886 at 900E–F per Viscount Dilhorne, 904E–F per Lord Diplock; *Cowcher v Cowcher* [1972] 1 WLR 425 at 429H; *McFarlane v McFarlane* [1972] NI 59 at 76–77; *Lloyds Bank Plc v Rosset* [1991] 1 AC 107 at 132G–H per Lord Bridge of Harwich; *Stockholm Finance Ltd v Garden Holdings Inc* [1995] NPC 162 per Robert Walker J;

Allen v Snyder [1977] 2 NSWLR 685 at 690D–F; *Avondale Printers & Stationers Ltd v Haggie* [1979] 2 NZLR 124 at 145–146; *Baumgartner v Baumgartner* (1985) 2 NSWLR 406 at 412F–G.

5   See *Oxley v Hiscock* [2004] 3 WLR 715 at [65]–[66] per Chadwick LJ **[para 10.139]**.

Identification of the bargain

10.83   The detailed substance (if any) of the bargain concluded between the parties falls to be determined objectively.[1] In *Gissing v Gissing*[2] Lord Diplock indicated that, in so far as the law of constructive trusts rests upon a common intention, 'the relevant intention of each party is the intention which was reasonably understood by the other party to be manifested by that party's words or conduct notwithstanding that he did not consciously formulate that intention in his own mind or even acted with some different intention which he did not communicate to the other party.'[3] Effect is given to 'the inferences as to the intentions of parties to a transaction which a reasonable man would draw from their words or conduct and not to any subjective intention or absence of intention which was not made manifest at the time of the transaction itself.'[4]

1   *Burns v Burns* [1984] Ch 317 at 336F per May LJ. See also *Pearson v Pearson* [1961] VR 693 at 698.

2   [1971] AC 886 at 906B–C.

3   See *Calverley v Green* (1984) 155 CLR 242 at 261 per Mason and Brennan JJ; *Baumgartner v Baumgartner* (1985) 2 NSWLR 406 at 412F–G.

4   [1971] AC 886 at 906C–D per Lord Diplock. See also *Eves v Eves* [1975] 1 WLR 1338 at 1342E; *Springette v Defoe* [1992] 2 FLR 388 at 397D per Sir Christopher Slade.

Timing of the bargain

10.84   Whereas a resulting trust can be generated only by intentions presumed to have been present at the date of acquisition of the trust property,[1] the precise timing of the agreement or bargain which underlies the constructive trust is less critical. The agreement guaranteeing equitable entitlement for B may precede[2] or emerge contemporaneously with[3] A's acquisition of title. On either basis A can be said to have taken his title subject to a fiduciary obligation towards B which, if breached by A, leads to the imposition of a constructive trust. A constructive trust can also be founded on a bargain or common intention between A and B which occurs only some time *after* A's acquisition of title.[4] As Lord Oliver of Aylmerton indicated in the Privy Council in *Austin v Keele*,[5] there is 'no reason in principle' why the doctrine should be 'limited to an intention formed at the time of the first acquisition of the property.'[6] In this respect the constructive trust is more flexible than the resulting trust. It is true that an express trust for B may be declared by A after the date on which he acquires his title to land, but the enforceability of this kind of post-acquisition trust is dependent upon compliance with the statutory requirement of written evidence.[7] A constructive trust arising in the same context is enforceable even though the agreement or common intention on which it is based was *never* statutorily evidenced.[8]

1   **[Para 10.20]**.
2   This is so at least if the property concerned is specific and identifiable and was, at the time of the agreement, within the contemplation of both A and B (see *Le Compte v Public Trustee* [1983] 2 NSWLR 109 at 111A). That a constructive trust can attach to an after-acquired estate or interest is confirmed in *Kowalczuk v Kowalczuk* [1973] 1 WLR 930 at 934G–935A per Buckley LJ; *Stokes v Anderson* [1991] 1 FLR 391 at 398E–F per Nourse LJ. See also *Chan Pui Chun v Leung Kam Ho* [2003] 1 FLR 23 at [96] per Jonathan Parker LJ.
3   *Pettitt v Pettitt* [1970] AC 777 at 813D per Lord Upjohn.
4   In *Lloyds Bank Plc v Rosset* [1991] 1 AC 107 at 132E–F, Lord Bridge of Harwich thought that only 'exceptionally' could a constructive trust be founded upon an express agreement reached at some date later than that of acquisition (see also *Bernard v Josephs* [1982] Ch 391 at 404D–F; *Hammond v Mitchell* [1991] 1 WLR 1127 at 1129F). However, this restrictive note is not generally echoed in the case law (see e g *Gissing v Gissing* [1971] AC 886 at 901D per Viscount Dilhorne; *Bernard v Josephs* [1982] Ch 391 at 404D–E; *Burns v Burns* [1984] Ch 317 at 327D per Fox LJ; *Grant v Edwards* [1986] Ch 638 at 651G–652A per Mustill LJ; *Oxley v Hiscock* [2004] 3 WLR 715 at [73] per Chadwick LJ). See also *Gough v Fraser* [1977] 1 NZLR 279 at 283; *Allen v Snyder* [1977] 2 NSWLR 685 at 691C; *McMahon v McMahon* [1979] VR 239 at 244; *Butler v Craine* [1986] VR 274 at 285–287.
5   (1987) 10 NSWLR 283 at 290E–F.
6   Lord Oliver conceded, however, that it may be 'more difficult to prove the requisite intention in relation to property already held beneficially by the trustee.'
7   LPA 1925, s 53(1)(b) **[para 9.188]**.
8   LPA 1925, s 53(2).

Form of the bargain

10.85   For the purpose of fixing a constructive trust on A in favour of B, it is not essential that the relevant bargain 'should include any express stipulation that [A] is in so many words to hold as trustee'[1] or that it should spell out the precise quantum of B's beneficial interest.[2] It is enough that 'the bargain ... included a stipulation under which some sufficiently defined beneficial interest in the property was to be taken by another.'[3]

1   *Bannister v Bannister* [1948] 2 All ER 133 at 136D per Scott LJ. See also *White v Cabanas Pty Ltd* (No 2) [1970] Qd R 395 at 397F; *Baumgartner v Baumgartner* (1985) 2 NSWLR 406 at 444C.
2   **[Para 10.139]**.
3   *Bannister v Bannister* [1948] 2 All ER 133 at 136D per Scott LJ.

Contractual uncertainty

10.86   It is not fatal that the language of the agreement (e g as to the timing or quantum of the promised entitlement) is insufficiently certain to constitute an enforceable contract.[1] Uncertainty such as would preclude the creation of a contract 'has never been regarded as necessarily preventing the beneficial intervention of equity.'[2]

1   See e g *Yaxley v Gotts* [2000] Ch 162 at 179G–180A, where the constructive trust beneficiary was promised that the ground floor of premises would be his 'for ever', but without any specification 'whether the objective was to be achieved by a conveyance which left the rest of the property as a "flying freehold", or by the grant of a long lease, or by a declaration of

trust.' This 'oral bargain' was 'definite enough to meet the test stated by Lord Bridge in *Lloyds Bank Plc v Rosset*' ([2000] Ch 162 at 177F–G per Robert Walker LJ).

2   *Flinn v Flinn* [1999] 3 VR 712 at [95] per Brooking JA. Compare the approach to uncertainty exhibited in the closely allied area of proprietary estoppel **[para 10.237]**.

Availability of contractual enforcement

10.87   If the agreement between the parties *is* contractually enforceable, there is likely to be no need at all for the imposition of a constructive trust.[1] Equity 'can act through the remedy of specific performance and will recognise the existence of a corresponding trust.'[2] Since in such cases the promisee of rights is already protected by the trust constituted by the enforceable contract,[3] there is no 'room for a constructive trust to operate so as to avoid injustice.'[4] In *Lloyds Bank plc v Carrick*,[5] for example, the Court of Appeal held that a vendor of a maisonette had become a trustee for his contractual purchaser, but that the latter's estate contract had been rendered void for non-registration as a land charge.[6] In response to the argument that the bargain for sale and purchase had conferred on the contractual purchaser certain non-registrable rights as a beneficiary behind some *additional* constructive trust, Morritt LJ indicated that the sole 'source and origin' of the contractual purchaser's rights as a trust beneficiary lay in her specifically enforceable contract. The trusteeship in her favour had no existence 'except as the equitable consequence' of that contract[7] and there was, accordingly, no room for the court to 'superimpose a further constructive trust on the vendor in favour of the purchaser over that which already exists in consequence of the contractual relationship.'[8] Ironically, the outcome in *Carrick* means that a purchaser of an unregistered estate is better placed if his or her rights derive from some 'oral or documentary consensus' which falls short of a valid, specifically enforceable contract.[9] The informal promise made to the intending purchaser in *Yaxley v Gotts*[10] was protected by a court-ordered constructive trust precisely because, in the absence of specifically enforceable contractual rights, further equitable assistance was indeed necessary in order to avoid the injustice which would have ensued from the unconscientious denial of the promised entitlement.[11]

1   See also LP(MP)A 1989, s 2(5), which explicitly preserves the operation of constructive trust doctrine in the context of contracts which fail to comply with the statutory requirement of writing. See *Yaxley v Gotts* [2000] Ch 162 at 180C–E per Robert Walker LJ.
2   *Banner Homes Group Plc v Luff Developments Ltd* [2000] Ch 372 at 398A–B per Chadwick LJ.
3   **[Para 9.18]**.
4   See *Yaxley v Gotts* [2000] Ch 162 at 179F per Robert Walker LJ.
5   [1996] 4 All ER 630 **[para 9.40]**.
6   **[Para 12.282]**.
7   [1996] 4 All ER 630 at 638b–c.
8   [1996] 4 All ER 630 at 639d–e. Any injustice which might have attracted the operation of a further constructive trust was averted by the fact that the contractual purchaser had failed to protect her rights by registration.
9   See *Yaxley v Gotts* [2000] Ch 162 at 172G per Robert Walker LJ.
10   [2000] Ch 162. See [2000] CLJ 23 (L Tee); (2000) 116 LQR 11 (R J Smith).
11   [2000] Ch 162 at 179F per Robert Walker LJ.

Subject matter of the bargain

10.88 Where a constructive trust is imposed on A in favour of B, the beneficial entitlement thereby confirmed in B normally – but not necessarily¹ – relates to some informal equitable right created de novo by A.

1 See e g *Binions v Evans* [1972] Ch 359 [**para 12.365**]; *Lyus v Prowsa Developments Ltd* [1982] 1 WLR 1044 at 1051E [**para 10.73**]; *White v Cabanas Pty Ltd* (No 2) [1970] Qd R 395 at 399B–C. Indeed, the imposition of a constructive trust on A in *Binions v Evans* has since been explained as having been necessary to save X from an unmerited, but otherwise unavoidable, liability in damages to B (*Lyus v Prowsa Developments Ltd*, supra at 1051F–G). See also *Ashburn Anstalt v Arnold* [1989] Ch 1 at 26A.

Recognisable equitable entitlements

10.89 The entitlement protected by constructive trust may comprise many different kinds of recognisable proprietary interest in land, provided that the interest conferred or conceded by A – whatever its nature or quantum – relates to a specific asset or to specific assets.¹ The subject matter of the bargain between A and B may therefore involve a promise to B of the entire equitable fee simple in A's land² or some lesser right such as a lease³ or a life interest,⁴ or some (possibly unquantified) share under a trust of land,⁵ or a contractual right of purchase⁶ or option⁷ or even a right to the conditional re-transfer of an interest already transferred by B to A.⁸ A testamentary promise that land shall belong to B on A's death likewise connotes a 'sufficiently defined beneficial interest' to attract the operation of a constructive trust in favour of the putative donee.⁹

1 *Layton v Martin* [1986] 2 FLR 227 at 237A–B, 238B; *Pasi v Kamana* [1986] 1 NZLR 603 at 607 per McMullin J. The asset must have positive value. A constructive trust cannot, for instance, be imposed on a 'negative equity' [**para 8.240**], precisely because, in such a case, there is 'no property … to which … a trust could attach' (see *Firth v Mallender* (Unreported, Court of Appeal, 11 October 1999)).

2 *White v Cabanas Pty Ltd* (No 2) [1970] Qd R 395 at 399B–C, 406B; *Doohan v Nelson* [1973] 2 NSWLR 320 at 329E.

3 *Yaxley v Gotts* [2000] Ch 162 at 169A.

4 *Bannister v Bannister* [1948] 2 All ER 133 at 137B. See also *Ungurian v Lesnoff* [1990] Ch 206 at 224A–D; *Citco (Suisse) SA v Glynne* (Unreported, Court of Appeal, 24 August 1999); *Malsbury v Malsbury* [1982] 1 NSWLR 226 at 230C–D; *Le Compte v Public Trustee* [1983] 2 NSWLR 109 at 111C–F. See TOLATA 1996, s 1(3) [**para 9.207**].

5 *Grant v Edwards* [1986] Ch 638 at 649A–E; *Malsbury v Malsbury* [1982] 1 NSWLR 226 at 231E; *Hayward v Giordani* [1983] NZLR 140 at 145.

6 See e g *Lyus v Prowsa Developments Ltd* [1982] 1 WLR 1044 [**para 10.73**].

7 *Avondale Printers & Stationers Ltd v Haggie* [1979] 2 NZLR 124 at 162, 164.

8 *Last v Rosenfeld* [1972] 2 NSWLR 923 at 937B; *Bahr v Nicolay (No 2)* (1988) 164 CLR 604 at 638 per Wilson and Toohey JJ, 654–656 per Brennan J. See also *Cadd v Cadd* (1909) 9 CLR 171 at 187.

9 See e g *Sharp v Anderson* (1994) 6 BPR 13801 at 13812–13813, where Santow J thought that the promise, once acted upon, precluded any power in A to dispose of the land during his lifetime. See also *Gillett v Holt* [2001] Ch 210 at 226A–227A [**para 10.243**]. An induced expectation of inheritance can also be given effect as an express bargain for beneficial joint tenancy (see e g *Beresford v Williamson* [2002] EWCA Civ 1632 at [14]).

Unconventional rights

10.90   More controversial is the suggestion that a constructive trust may enforce promised entitlements which fall outside the acknowledged categories of proprietary right. In *Binions v Evans*,[1] for instance, Lord Denning MR seemed to indicate that a constructive trust might give effect to A's undertaking that B should enjoy a contractual occupation licence for the remainder of her life, even though contractual licences are not generally recognised as coming within the conventional canon of proprietary rights in land.[2] Lord Denning's approach can perhaps be rationalised, as it was by Dillon J in *Lyus v Prowsa Developments Ltd*,[3] on the footing that 'even if the beneficial interest of the claimant in the property concerned has not yet been fully defined, the court may yet intervene to raise a constructive trust on appropriate terms if to leave the defendant retaining the property free from all interest of the claimant would be tantamount to sanctioning a fraud on the part of the defendant.'[4] Similar perceptions of the supremacy of good conscience[5] caused the Court of Appeal in *Ashburn Anstalt v Arnold*[6] to incline towards the proposition that, in certain rigidly controlled instances, a constructive trust may be raised in protection of a contractual licence.[7] Although the point was strictly obiter, the Court did not dismiss the possibility that a purchaser may acquire legal title in circumstances which fasten upon him a conscientious obligation towards the contractual licensee. It is highly arguable that, in the context of the constructive trust, the balance of emphasis rests nowadays on the conscientiousness of the legal owner rather than on the intrinsic nature of the rights which it is sought to enforce against him.[8]

1   [1972] Ch 359 at 367C, 369D [**para 12.365**].
2   [**Para 12.223**]. See *Ashburn Anstalt v Arnold* [1989] Ch 1 at 14D, 17E–F, 22B–D. See also J D Davies, (1979) 8 Sydney L Rev 578 at 579.
3   [1982] 1 WLR 1044 at 1053A.
4   See also *Eves v Eves* [1975] 1 WLR 1338 at 1342E–F, 1345B.
5   See *Soulos v Korkontzilas* (1997) 146 DLR (4th) 214 at 225–228 per McLachlin J (Supreme Court of Canada).
6   [1989] Ch 1 at 25H–26E per Fox LJ. See [1988] CLJ 353 (A J Oakley).
7   See also *Kewal Investments Ltd v Arthur Maiden Ltd* [1990] 1 EGLR 193 at 194D–J.
8   See e g *Melbury Road Properties 1995 Ltd v Kreidi* [1999] 3 EGLR 108 at 110J, where Judge Cowell observed that the existence of a constructive trust 'is not, at any rate obviously, going to depend upon whether the arrangement gives rise to an interest in property or is a personal obligation. It seems to me that unconscionable conduct is made of more virulent stuff, not on the conceptual difference between property rights and personal rights.'

Indefinite offers and joint ventures

10.91   The limits of constructive trust doctrine are quickly reached if the subject matter of the supposed bargain between the parties is so ill-defined as not even faintly to resemble a proprietary right. Thus, for instance, no constructive trust (or indeed proprietary estoppel) can be based on a vague offer of 'financial security'[1] or some general intimation or expectation of likely inheritance.[2] In the standard case the critical common intention or bargain must relate to the acquisition of some recognisable proprietary entitlement[3] – an approach which has done little to humanise the law of constructive trusts. In recent years English courts have gone to great lengths to confirm that a constructive trust cannot be founded merely on some mutual assumption that family life is to be shared as a form of joint venture. The restrictive trend was set by the House of Lords' ruling in *Lloyds Bank Plc v Rosset*.[4] Here Lord Bridge of Harwich indicated that the simple and normal expectation that parties will 'share the practical benefits of occupying the matrimonial home whoever owns it' is something 'quite distinct from sharing the beneficial interest in the property asset which the matrimonial home represents.'[5] In *Rosset*'s case the House of Lords thought it entirely irrelevant that the spouses had formed a common intention that a dilapidated house should be purchased and renovated as a 'joint venture' and then 'shared by parents and children as the family home'.[6] Lord Bridge did not believe that such evidence threw 'any light on their intentions with respect to the beneficial ownership of the property.'[7] On this basis the wife's constructive trust claim was, perhaps somewhat harshly, rejected.[8]

1   *Layton v Martin* [1986] 2 FLR 227 at 238B.
2   See *McKenzie v McKenzie* [2003] EWHC 601 (Ch) at [110].
3   See e g *Cooke v Cooke* [1987] VR 625 at 633, where Southwell J considered that expressions such as 'a house for her' might possibly be intended to import beneficial interest, whereas the expression 'a house for her to live in' imported no offer of beneficial entitlement.
4   [1991] 1 AC 107 [**para 10.115**].
5   [1991] 1 AC 107 at 128A. See also *Cooke v Cooke* [1987] VR 625 at 634 (claimant's belief that legal owner would not disturb her occupancy held to be consistent merely with 'safe' licence).
6   See similarly *Buggs v Buggs* [2003] EWHC 1538 (Ch) at [43], [48]–[50], where the fact that the purchase of a flat had been a 'joint exercise' on the part of a family did not 'amount to a general agreement that all property acquired involved an intention of shared ownership.' For a highly critical analysis of this decision, see [2003] Conv 411 (M P Thompson).
7   *Lloyds Bank Plc v Rosset* [1991] 1 AC 107 at 130C–D (compare the view adopted in the Court of Appeal ([1989] Ch 350 at 380F–H per Nicholls LJ)). Anticipated joint occupation of the family home was likewise regarded in *Mollo v Mollo* [1999] EGCS 117 (Transcript at [28]) as 'a long way from there being a common intention' of shared beneficial entitlement. See also *Stockholm Finance Ltd v Garden Holdings Inc* [1995] NPC 162 per Robert Walker J; *McKenzie v McKenzie* [2003] EWHC 601 (Ch) at [110]; *Stowe v Stowe* (1995) 15 WAR 363 at 370E.
8   A direct consequence of this ruling was to destroy any claim that the wife had an overriding interest taking priority over a chargee of her husband's legal title [**para 12.211**].

The practical unrealism of the bargain requirement

10.92 The fundamental historic problem inherent in the English law of constructive trusts consists in the dogmatic insistence that trust entitlement be premised on a common intention or conscious bargain endorsing at least some sharing of equitable ownership between the relevant parties.[1] Although the courts are now beginning to arrogate a greater freedom to make 'fair' determinations of the beneficial quantum of established trust claims,[2] access to this broader jurisdiction rests exclusively on a showing that the parties reached a preliminary consensus as to participation in, or sharing of, the now disputed beneficial interest.[3] Yet this requirement of demonstrable bargain, regularly confirmed by the House of Lords at twenty-year intervals,[4] has exerted a stranglehold over the development of any rational law of family property.[5] In modern times the stubborn adherence to the element of intention as the authentic root of beneficial ownership has come to seem inherently flawed: in many circumstances the search for such intention is unrealistic and highly artificial.[6] The inevitable result has been the frequent denial of beneficial entitlement in the context of family arrangements, purely and simply on the ground that the relevant participants failed to advert in any precise or legalistic way to the property consequences of their relationship.[7]

1   Contrast Matrimonial Proceedings and Property Act 1970, s 37, which, as between spouses, creates a rebuttable presumption that a substantial contribution in money or money's worth to the improvement of the property of either generates a beneficial entitlement for the 'improving' spouse which the court can ultimately quantify in terms of what 'may seem in all the circumstances just.' Section 37 is a little used and not entirely happy provision. See, however, *Re Nicholson (Decd)* [1974] 1 WLR 476 at 482G–483C (enhanced equitable share on the basis of installation of central heating in the family home).
2   **[Para 10.141]**.
3   See *Oxley v Hiscock* [2004] 3 WLR 715 at [71] per Chadwick LJ ('the hypothesis upon which it becomes necessary to answer the second question').
4   See *Gissing v Gissing* [1971] AC 886; *Lloyds Bank Plc v Rosset* [1991] 1 AC 107.
5   Compare the law of other jurisdictions which have abandoned the search for elusive or illusory common intentions in the application of the constructive trust **[para 10.151]**.
6   See Gray, 'The Law of Trusts and the Quasi-Matrimonial Home' [1983] CLJ 30 at 33. There has long been a weary recognition of the 'air of unreality about the whole exercise' (*Bernard v Josephs* [1982] Ch 391 at 404B per Griffiths LJ). Furthermore, litigation in pursuit of elusive intention can prove disastrously expensive (see e g the legal costs in excess of £100,000 incurred in *Tee v Tee* [1999] 2 FLR 613).
7   See e g *Buggs v Buggs* [2003] EWHC 1538 (Ch) at [49]–[50], where beneficial entitlement under a constructive trust was denied to a claimant who had been an 'impressive woman ... a determined, hard-working wife who made a strong contribution to the family's welfare in financial as well as personal terms.'

The Gissing decision

10.93   In *Gissing v Gissing*[1] the claimant wife alleged that, during the course of a 25 year marriage, she had made indirect contributions towards the purchase of the family home by devoting her own money to various forms of household and other family-related expenditure. The legal estate in the home had been purchased in the name of her husband and he was solely responsible for repayment of the mortgage loan secured on the realty. In the absence of any express agreement between the spouses as to how the beneficial interest in the house should be held,[2] the House of Lords declined to infer that the wife's expenditure had been referable to any bargain directed at beneficial co-ownership or could now be seen as reflecting any common intention that she should acquire an equitable share in the family home.[3] The mere fact of contribution to joint expenditure was not regarded as founding any constructive trust,[4] with the consequence that the claimant was left entirely without remedy in the law of trusts.

1   [1971] AC 886.

2   [1971] AC 886 at 910E.
3   [1971] AC 886 at 911B–C.
4   '[S]uch conduct is no less consistent with a common intention to share the day-to-day expenses of the household, while each spouse retains a separate interest in capital assets acquired with their own moneys or obtained by inheritance or gift' ([1971] AC 886 at 909H per Lord Diplock). See also *Grant v Edwards* [1986] Ch 638 at 657F per Browne-Wilkinson V-C; *Springette v Defoe* [1992] 2 FLR 388 at 392C–D, 397E–F.

10.94   The application of conventional trust doctrine in *Gissing*'s case, and later in *Lloyds Bank Plc v Rosset*,[1] proved regrettably unsympathetic to the realities of family living, the House of Lords effectively demanding that beneficial entitlement be established on the basis of intentions which are rarely articulated or contemplated in the daily round of domestic life.[2] The proprietary difficulties of married persons are now generally untangled pursuant to the discretionary jurisdiction which applies on divorce.[3] However, the inflexible principles of ordinary trust law still comprise, rather unsatisfactorily, the regime relevant to the ascertainment of beneficial entitlement not only within de facto relationships[4] and other forms of family arrangement but also in the event of death and insolvency affecting even married partners.

1   [1991] 1 AC 107.
2   It is, for instance, no great surprise that expressly bargained beneficial entitlement is rarely proved to the satisfaction of the court [**para 10.113**]. See also N Glover and P Todd, 'The myth of common intention' (1996) 16 Legal Studies 325.
3   Matrimonial Causes Act 1973, Part II. See *Tee v Tee* [1999] 2 FLR 613 at 619B–C.
4   See e g *Nova Scotia (Attorney General) v Walsh* (2002) 221 DLR (4th) 1, where a majority in the Supreme Court of Canada declined to include de facto partners within the definition of 'spouse' in Nova Scotia's Matrimonial Property Act (RSNS 1989, c 275).

An experimental abandonment of the requirement of bargain

10.95   In the orthodox English law of constructive trusts there exists no general jurisdiction to subject disputed property to a trust merely on the ground that such a result 'would be fair in all the circumstances.'[1] The court's role is conventionally restricted to declaring the doctrinal consequence in equity of such intentions as have already been expressed by the parties or can be inferred from their past conduct.[2] Nevertheless there was, at one stage, a suggestion that Lord Diplock's seminal formulation of trust principle in *Gissing v Gissing*[3] had endorsed the idea that, without any reference to bargains (either express or implied), the court might award a trust interest *ex aequo et bono* – whenever it would be 'inequitable' not to do so.

1   *Gissing v Gissing* [1971] AC 886 at 900F per Viscount Dilhorne.
2   *Westdeutsche Landesbank Girozentrale v Islington LBC* [1996] AC 669 at 714G per Lord Browne-Wilkinson ('the function of the court is merely to declare that such trust has arisen in the past').
3   [1971] AC 886 at 905B–D [**para 10.62**].

The 'new model' constructive trust

10.96   During the 1970s various versions of the 'remedial constructive trust'[1] emerged within the jurisdictions of the common law world, conferring on courts a new freedom to do justice in the resolution of property rights within family arrangements. The remedial constructive trust effectively substituted the broad restitutionary principle of unjust enrichment for a sterile and ritualistic preoccupation with illusory figments of common intention. For a brief period it seemed that some equally liberated version of constructive trust doctrine might take root and flourish in England. Lord Denning MR advanced a more relaxed theory of trust law of particular application to family relationships.[2] In his view, '[e]quity is not past the age of child bearing. One of her latest progeny is a constructive trust of a new model.'[3] Under the influence of this 'new model' constructive trust, Lord Denning championed a principle of virtually automatic beneficial co-ownership in the context of joint ventures in respect of the family home. Suppressing the severely limiting qualifications inherent in Lord Diplock's famous formulation of trust doctrine in *Gissing v Gissing*,[4] Lord Denning invoked the House of Lords' apparent support for the proposition that a trust arises 'whenever [a] trustee has so conducted himself that it would be inequitable to allow him to deny to the cestui que trust a beneficial interest.'[5] The consequence was the rapid development of a novel doctrine of constructive trust, at the high point of which the Court of Appeal seemed prepared to award spouses equal shares in the family home merely on the ground that there had been 'a general atmosphere of joint ownership to the income and capital of the parties.'[6]

1   **[Para 10.151]**.
2   See eg *Cooke v Head* [1972] 1 WLR 518 at 520F–G, where Lord Denning declared that the courts would 'impose or impute' a constructive trust 'whenever two parties by their joint efforts acquire property to be used for their joint benefit'. This trust was applicable to 'husband and wife, to engaged couples, and to man and mistress, and maybe to other relationships too.'
3   *Eves v Eves* [1975] 1 WLR 1338 at 1341F–G ('Lord Diplock brought it into the world and we have nourished it'). See (1976) 92 LQR 489 (Frank Webb).
4   [1971] AC 886 at 905B–D **[para 10.62]**.
5   For criticism of Lord Denning's overly selective technique, see *Avondale Printers & Stationers Ltd v Haggie* [1979] 2 NZLR 124 at 146–147 per Mahon J. Lord Denning consistently declined to adopt Lord Diplock's notion of 'referable' contributions. See *Hargrave v Newton* [1971] 1 WLR 1611 at 1613B–D ('very difficult to apply'). See also *Hazell v Hazell* [1972] 1 WLR 301 at 304C–E.
6   *Smith v Baker* [1970] 1 WLR 1160 at 1162D–E per Lord Denning MR. See also *Heseltine v Heseltine* [1971] 1 WLR 342 at 346D–F; *Hussey v Palmer* [1972] 1 WLR 1286 at 1289H–1290D; *Eves v Eves* [1975] 1 WLR 1338 at 1345B–F.

Palm-tree justice

10.97   The principal demerit of the 'new model' constructive trust was, almost inevitably, the arbitrary quality of the discretionary allocations of beneficial entitlement to which it gave rise. Unstructured applications of trust law are always vulnerable to the objection that they represent a form of 'palm-tree justice',[1] under which past decisions are worthless as precedent and future decisions are almost entirely unpredictable. The 'new model' constructive trust appeared to allow equitable intervention in property matters as a sheer instrument of redistributive justice. For many, the invocation of such a trust theory in one-off adjudications of proprietary entitlement was a self-evident argument of last resort – an act of intellectual bankruptcy – comprising a judicial confession that no convincing or respectable reason could be found in law for giving judgment in favour of a deserving claimant. As Deane J once observed,[2] proprietary rights ought to be governed by principles of law and not 'by some mix of judicial discretion ... subjective views about which party "ought to win" ... and "the formless void of individual moral opinion".'[3]

1   See *Springette v Defoe* [1992] 2 FLR 388 at 393D per Dillon LJ.
2   *Muschinski v Dodds* (1985) 160 CLR 583 at 616.
3   See *Carly v Farrelly* [1975] 1 NZLR 356 at 367 per Mahon J. Compare, however, *Pasi v Kamana* [1986] 1 NZLR 603 at 607 per McMullin J.

Prejudice to third parties

10.98   Proponents of orthodox trust theory advanced a further objection to the remedial or 'new model' constructive trust, namely that it served as an improper agent for the informal creation of proprietary rights. The unpredictability of outcome associated with the liberal creation of such trusts was said to be not only capricious in relation to the immediate parties but also severely prejudicial to purchasers and creditors who relied on the apparently unqualified title of someone who later was suddenly cast in the role of a trustee.[1] If, without the interposition of any judicial process, a constructive trust could attach itself silently and without warning to legal titles in land, there was a danger that constructive trust beneficial interests would gain an automatic priority over creditors of the constructive trustee in the event of the latter's insolvency. Furthermore, even if the constructive trustee remained perfectly solvent, there was always a risk that third parties who purchased the trust property from him might find themselves bound by the constructive beneficiary's equitable interest.[2]

1   See Browne-Wilkinson, 'Constructive Trusts and Unjust Enrichment' (1996) 10 Trust Law International 98 at 99. See also *Westdeutsche Landesbank Girozentrale v Islington LBC* [1996] AC 669 at 703G–704A, 716E–F per Lord Browne-Wilkinson. For far-reaching insights into this policy concern, see A J Oakley, 'Proprietary Claims and Their Priority in Insolvency' [1995] CLJ 377.
2   **[Para 12.201]**.

Demise of the 'new model'

10.99   The 'new model' constructive trust was ultimately to prove excessively controversial in the English context[1] and rather faded with Lord Denning's retirement from the bench.[2] As Nourse LJ pointed out in *Re Polly Peck International Plc (No 2)*,[3] the 'new model' constructive trust was subsequently rejected by the English Court of Appeal[4] as being 'at variance with the principles stated in *Gissing v Gissing*.'[5] Far from supporting a liberated view of the role of the trust, Lord Diplock's approach in *Gissing*'s case turned out to incorporate a severely restrictive application of trust doctrine. During the 1980s and 1990s many claims of beneficial entitlement were effectively stifled by the doctrinaire requirement that shared ownership be premised on some demonstrable intention formed by the relevant parties – a requirement which, notwithstanding Lord Denning's experimental 'new equity', still persists in the trust jurisprudence of the new century.

1   See A J Oakley, (1973) 26 CLP 17; P T Evans, [1989] Conv 418.
2   See also *Allen v Snyder* [1977] 2 NSWLR 685 at 700F–701A, where Samuels JA opined that 'the legitimacy of the new model is at least suspect; at best it is a mutant from which further breeding should be discouraged.'
3   [1998] 3 All ER 812 at 832b.
4   See *Burns v Burns* [1984] Ch 317 at 330G–331F per Fox LJ, 341C–342G per May LJ; *Grant v Edwards* [1986] Ch 638 at 647G per Nourse LJ; *Turton v Turton* [1988] Ch 542 at 555F–G per Kerr LJ.
5   Ironically, as Nourse LJ also observed, much of the early Canadian development of the remedial constructive trust drew strength from Lord Denning's application of the 'new model' trust ([1998] 3 All ER 812 at 832a). See also P B H Birks, 'The end of the remedial constructive trust?' (1998) 12 Trust Law International 202.

CHANGE OF POSITION OR DETRIMENTAL RELIANCE

10.100   In order that a constructive trust should arise in English law, it is not sufficient merely that a common intention should have been expressed or a bargain made that B should have some equitable entitlement in A's land.[1] If an assurance of beneficial entitlement is purely oral, further elements are required. One of these is that there must be a 'change of position' by the party who relies upon the bargain or agreement.[2] According to Lord Bridge of Harwich in *Lloyds Bank Plc v Rosset*,[3] 'even the clearest oral agreement' to hold property in trust is ineffective for want of writing unless the claimant has 'altered her position in reliance on the agreement', thereby acquiring 'an enforceable interest ... by way either of a constructive trust or of a proprietary estoppel.' In the absence of such a change of position the express verbal agreement constitutes a merely voluntary declaration of trust and remains unenforceable for lack of statutory formality.[4] Traditionally equity will not assist a volunteer.[5]

1   *Grant v Edwards* [1986] Ch 638 at 656A per Browne-Wilkinson V-C.
2   For reference to the terminology of 'change of position', see *Burns v Burns* [1984] Ch 317 at 327G–H per Fox LJ; *Austin v Keele* (1987) 10 NSWLR 283 at 291C–D per Lord Oliver of Aylmerton; *Chan Pui Chun v Leung Kam Ho* [2003] 1 FLR 23 at [93], [96] per Jonathan Parker LJ. It is indeed the change of position that constitutes the bargain by providing evidence of some 'quid pro quo moving from the claimant' (*Layton v Martin* [1986] 2 FLR 227 at 236H–237A per Scott J).
3   [1991] 1 AC 107 at 129C.
4   *Gissing v Gissing* [1971] AC 886 at 905E per Lord Diplock. See also *Eves v Eves* [1975] 1 WLR 1338 at 1345B–C per Brightman J; *Grant v Edwards* [1986] Ch 638 at 656A per Browne-Wilkinson V-C; *Midland Bank Plc v Dobson* [1986] 1 FLR 171 at 175C–D per Fox LJ.
5   See *Midland Bank Plc v Dobson* [1986] 1 FLR 171 at 175E; *McFarlane v McFarlane* [1972] NI 59 at 73; *Austin v Keele* (1987) 10 NSWLR 283 at 291B–C per Lord Oliver of Aylmerton.

A factual 'change of position'

10.101 In order that an unenforceable oral trust declared by A should become enforceable by B, there must have been an 'irrevocable change of position' by B.[1] Depending on the circumstances, this 'change of position' may take the form either of some detriment or sacrifice suffered by B or, more rarely, of some benefit conferred by B upon A.

1   *Austin v Keele* (1987) 10 NSWLR 283 at 291C–D per Lord Oliver of Aylmerton (JCPC).

The incurring of 'detriment' or 'sacrifice'

10.102 As Lord Diplock indicated in *Gissing v Gissing*,[1] a relevant 'change of position' is classically and most easily demonstrated where B can prove that, in response to some bargain for beneficial entitlement, she has suffered a 'detriment' or has made some 'material sacrifice' connected with the land vested in A.[2] Some form of 'contribution'[3] or 'consideration'[4] moving from B is universally regarded as a precondition of the imposition of a constructive trust.[5] The precise nature of the required change of position may vary greatly in accordance with whether the trust enforced is an 'express bargain' constructive trust or an 'implied bargain' constructive trust.[6] In general, however, the need to establish a change of position creates clear analogies between the constructive trust and the doctrines of part performance[7] and proprietary estoppel[8] and the historic willingness of equity to grant specific performance of agreements for consideration.[9]

1   [1971] AC 886 at 905C–F.
2   See *Christian v Christian* (1981) 131 NLJ 43 [**para 10.103**]. The legal owner's bad conscience and the claimant's disappointed expectation do not, without more, warrant equitable intervention: there must be acts of 'material detriment' (*Higgins v Wingfield* [1987] VR 689 at 695–696).
3   *Allen v Snyder* [1977] 2 NSWLR 685 at 691A per Glass JA. See also *Boccalatte v Bushelle* [1980] Qd R 180 at 185E.
4   *Taddeo v Taddeo* (1978) 19 SASR 347 at 365.
5   Compare *Neale v Willis* (1968) 19 P & CR 836 at 839 (consideration provided by B's mother). The decision is, in fact, a textbook illustration of the rule in *Rochefoucauld v Boustead* [**para 9.193**].
6   [**Para 10.112**].
7   See *Yaxley v Gotts* [2000] Ch 162 at 176B–C per Robert Walker LJ; *Taddeo v Taddeo* (1978) 19 SASR 347 at 365.
8   [**Para 10.168**]. See e g *Thwaites v Ryan* [1984] VR 65 at 90, 95 per Fullagar J.
9   See *Cowcher v Cowcher* [1972] 1 WLR 425 at 431A.

Limits of 'detriment' and 'sacrifice'

10.103 The forms of 'detriment' or 'sacrifice' which denote a relevant change of position are manifold. The most obvious kind of 'detriment' or 'sacrifice' asserted by constructive trust claimants comprises a contribution of money,[1] but a change of position may include other forms of conduct such as the devotion of onerous labour to a joint venture.[2] The notions of 'detriment' and 'sacrifice' are nevertheless circumscribed with some strictness and do not extend to matters of a merely emotional character. It is clear, for example, that the ascertainment of property interests 'cannot be dealt with on the basis of sentiment.'[3] Sheer emotional commitment to a joint venture does not represent a sufficient change of position.[4] In *Christian v Christian*,[5] for example, the claimant argued that she had suffered 'detriment' in the form of the social embarrassment caused by living with her de facto husband in a house situated in close proximity to the current home of his legal wife. Brightman LJ rejected this alleged 'detriment', observing that equity is 'concerned with the protection of property and proprietary interests, not with the protection of people's feelings.' In his view, 'the only contributions, detriments and sacrifices that move the court in this field are those of a monetary or proprietary nature.'

1   See e g *Strickson v Boyd* [2001] EWCA Civ 401 at [11] (assumption of mortgage liability).
2   See e g *Chan Pui Chun v Leung Kam Ho* [2003] 1 FLR 23 at [96]–[97] per Jonathan Parker LJ.
3   *Wood v Wood* (Unreported, 1979 W No 1393, 7 July 1982) per Lawton LJ. See also *Winkworth v Edward Baron Development Co Ltd* [1986] 1 WLR 1512 at 1516C, where Lord Templeman observed that 'Equity is not a computer. Equity operates on conscience but is not influenced by sentimentality.'
4   See e g *Lloyds Bank Plc v Rosset* [1991] 1 AC 107 at 130C–D per Lord Bridge of Harwich **[para 10.91]**.
5   (1981) 131 NLJ 43.

Net concept of 'detriment' or 'sacrifice'

10.104   The courts analyse even recognised forms of 'detriment' or 'sacrifice' in net terms. Thus a change of position ranks in terms of 'detriment' or 'sacrifice' only if it results in a net disadvantage to the individual concerned.[1] A claimed 'detriment' must hurt[2] and claims of constructive trust tend to fail to the extent that the claimant has already benefited from the contribution or effort alleged.[3] In *Hannaford v Selby*,[4] for instance, the claimant's work in cultivating vegetables in his son-in-law's garden was not accounted to be 'detriment' in any relevant sense, since he was regarded as merely indulging his 'one absorbing hobby.'[5] Likewise, in *Layton v Martin*[6] the claimant's house-keeping and other services had already been compensated at least in part by the award of a regular salary.[7] In *Thwaites v Ryan*[8] the Supreme Court of Victoria declined to accept that the claimant had acted to his detriment in 'leaving his moribund marriage and moribund tenancy and going to live rent free in the pleasant home of his old friend.'[9]

1   See e g *Cooke v Cooke* [1987] VR 625 at 634, 638–639 (no constructive trust for a woman who had been provided with rent-free accommodation by the father of her child: the total cost of any contributions made by her 'must have been small indeed when compared with the value of the benefits provided by [the father]'). Contrast the Canadian rejection of any suggestion that the benefits of past occupation preclude a claim of constructive trust (see *Palachik v Kiss* (1983) 146 DLR (3d) 385 at 397 per Wilson J; *MacDonald v Mackenzie Estate* (1990) 64 DLR (4th) 476 at 488).
2   See e g the reference by Marks J in *Higgins v Wingfield* [1987] VR 689 at 700 to the idea that the claimant must 'suffer materially (i e not just psychologically)'. See also *H v M* [2004] EWHC 625 (Fam) at [65].

3   See e g *Winstanley v Winstanley* (Unreported, Court of Appeal, 22 July 1999), where the claimant was himself the primary beneficiary of improvement works which he had effected as a nominal rent tenant. See likewise *Pasi v Kamana* [1986] 1 NZLR 603 at 604, 607 (financial contributions went towards support of claimant herself: no evidence that 'she gave or contributed without receiving, or that she suffered any deprivation').

4   (1976) 239 EG 811 at 813.

5   See also *Pettitt v Pettitt* [1970] AC 777 at 826A per Lord Diplock.

6   [1986] 2 FLR 227 at 231F–G.

7   See also *Heyland v Heyland* (1972) Times, 25 January; *McPhee v McPhee* (1980) NZ Recent Law 42.

8   [1984] VR 65 at 89.

9   Compare *Coombes v Smith* [1986] 1 WLR 808 at 820A–F (claim of proprietary estoppel rejected) [**para 10.266**].

The conferment of advantage

10.105   Whereas earlier case law seemed to emphasise 'detriment' or 'material sacrifice' for the claimant as an essential ingredient of constructive trust, in recent years there has been a gradual, almost imperceptible, widening of the concept of 'change of position'. It was noticeable that, in his seminal speech in *Lloyds Bank Plc v Rosset*,[1] Lord Bridge of Harwich viewed 'detriment' and 'change of position' as not entirely synonymous terms. For the purpose of establishing a constructive trust, declared Lord Bridge, the claimant must show that he or she has *either* 'acted to his or her detriment' *or* 'significantly altered his or her position in reliance on the agreement.'[2] In certain circumstances relevant conduct on the claimant's part can therefore go beyond the mere incurring of a detriment and may comprise the conferment of an advantage on the legal owner.[3]

1   [1991] 1 AC 107 at 132F–G.

2   See similarly *Hammond v Mitchell* [1991] 1 WLR 1127 at 1137A per Waite J; *Chan Pui Chun v Leung Kam Ho* [2003] 1 FLR 23 at [93] per Jonathan Parker LJ.

3   This extended understanding of 'change of position' may be especially relevant to 'express bargain' constructive trusts [**para 10.120**].

The 'Pallant v Morgan equity'

10.106   The courts have, accordingly, begun to impose constructive trusts in vindication of what is sometimes termed a '*Pallant v Morgan* equity'.[1] This 'equity' arises in circumstances of joint venture where an antecedent (and contractually unenforceable) bargain between two parties accords one party the *benefit* of acquiring land without competition from the other in return for the promise of shared rights in the land after purchase.[2] For example, in *Banner Homes Group Plc v Luff Developments Ltd*,[3] the Court of Appeal invoked a constructive trust where two corporate property developers, although initially rival purchasers of an area of land, reached an understanding that one would withdraw from the market in order to let the other secure the purchase on behalf of a jointly owned venture company.[4] When instead the land was purchased for the bidder's wholly-owned subsidiary company, the Court of

Appeal held that the circumstances made it 'inequitable for the acquiring party to retain the property for himself in a manner inconsistent with the arrangement or understanding on which the non-acquiring party has acted.'[5] Chadwick LJ considered that a *'Pallant v Morgan* equity' could be triggered by the presence *either* of advantage for the acquiring party (ie the absence of competition) *or* of detriment for the non-acquiring party (ie loss of the chance to acquire on equal terms).[6] The Court ordered that the shares of the acquiring company be held, as to one half, on constructive trust for the non-acquiring party.[7]

1   See S Nield, 'Constructive trusts and estoppel' (2003) 23 Legal Studies 311.
2   See *Pallant v Morgan* [1953] Ch 43 at 47–49 (agreement not to bid against potential rival at auction).
3   [2000] Ch 372.
4   Contrast the case where joint venture negotiations are clearly 'subject to contract', with the consequence that withdrawal from the joint venture cannot be said to be so unconscionable as to raise a constructive trust (see eg *London and Regional Investments Ltd v TBI plc* [2002] EWCA Civ 355 at [42]–[47] per Mummery LJ).
5   [2000] Ch 372 at 399B.
6   [2000] Ch 372 at 399A.
7   [2000] Ch 372 at 401D.

Need for a new 'equity'?

10.107   It is not entirely clear that the recent (and slightly surprising) resurgence of the *'Pallant v Morgan* equity' departs markedly from the traditionally understood constructive trust doctrine of bargain-based detrimental reliance.[1] Even Chadwick LJ thought, in the *Banner* case, that it could be said that the non-acquiring party had 'suffered detriment from the fact that it never regarded itself as free to consider the site as a potential acquisition of its own.'[2] Furthermore, in a world of finite opportunity, any advantage for another almost inevitably represents some form of detriment for oneself.

1   See N Hopkins, 'The *Pallant v Morgan* "Equity"' [2002] Conv 35. Courts in other jurisdictions have likewise been less convinced that the historic case law on the *Pallant v Morgan* 'equity' discloses 'a common thread of principle' (see *Seyffer v Adamson* (2001) 10 BPR 19349 at [21] (Supreme Court of New South Wales)).
2   [2000] Ch 372 at 401A.

The change of position must be 'referable to' the bargain

10.108   'Change of position' *per se* is insufficient to support a claim of constructive trust.[1] It must be shown that the claimant's change of position was broadly 'referable to' the earlier bargain on which beneficial entitlement is premised.[2] There must, in other words, be some causal nexus between the agreement and the claimant's active willingness to incur detriment or confer advantage upon the legal owner.[3] This requirement of a chain of causation is deeply entrenched in the law of constructive trusts. In his classic exposition in *Gissing v Gissing,*[4] Lord Diplock indicated that a constructive trust arises only if the estate owner has 'induced' the claimant to act to his or her own detriment 'in the reasonable belief that by so acting he [or she] was acquiring a beneficial interest in the land.'[5] This formulation seems to require a certain mental element or motivation on the part both of A, the estate owner, and of B, the claimant of an equitable interest. To raise a constructive trust, A's conduct must have been 'intended to induce [B] to act to his or her detriment upon the faith of the promise of a specified beneficial interest in the land',[6] and B must have 'so acted with the intention of acquiring that beneficial interest.'[7] Once again the precise content of the requirement of 'referability' seems to be graded according to whether the claim of constructive trust is founded on express or implied bargain.[8]

1   *Pettitt v Pettitt* [1970] AC 777 at 805E; *Gissing v Gissing* [1971] AC 886 at 900H, 901B–C, 909G–H, 910G–H; *Allen v Snyder* [1977] 2 NSWLR 685 at 691C; *McGill v S* [1979] IR 283 at 289. See eg *Springette v Defoe* [1992] 2 FLR 388 at 392C–D, 397E–F (requiring a communicated belief on the part of both parties 'that they would be sharing benefit as well as burden equally').

2   See *Chan Pui Chun v Leung Kam Ho* [2003] 1 FLR 23 at [96] per Jonathan Parker LJ. The claimant 'must expend some money or do some other act, or omission, on the faith of his belief' that the bargained entitlement is his (*Thwaites v Ryan* [1984] VR 65 at 90, 95 per Fullagar J).

3   See eg *Winkworth v Edward Baron Development Co Ltd* [1986] 1 WLR 1512 at 1515F per Lord Templeman; *Green v Green* [2003] UKPC 39 at [12] per Lord Hope of Craighead ('a sufficient link between the common intention and the conduct which is relied upon to show that the claimant has acted on the common intention to [her] detriment').

4   [1971] AC 886 at 905C.

5   There are some signs that, as constructive trust edges closer to proprietary estoppel (where reliance is readily presumed), there may be less need for 'positive evidence' of 'conscious reliance' on the common intention [**para 10.124**].

6   The requirement of intentional inducement may be less pressing in the context of the 'express bargain' constructive trust, where 'the agreement itself discloses the common intention' (see *Gissing v Gissing* [1971] AC 886 at 905H per Lord Diplock).

7   [1971] AC 886 at 905G–H. Thus, ironically, a claim of constructive trust will fail if the claimant is 'almost wholly unmercenary' (see *Layton v Martin* [1986] 2 FLR 227 at 235B, 239H–240A or if she merely continues to contribute the same onerous effort which she willingly gave before the alleged bargain was struck (see *Britannia Building Society v Johnston* (Northern Ireland Chancery Division, 13 May 1994)) or if there is a history of joint venture 'without an understanding of what the property rights would be between the parties' (see *Buggs v Buggs* [2003] EWHC 1538 (Ch) at [43]).

8   [**Para 10.112**].

EQUITABLE FRAUD

10.109 Before a constructive trust can be imposed, a third element must be established in addition to a 'change of position' premised on some 'bargain' between the relevant parties. This element is variously described in the case law, but in effect amounts to a requirement that 'equitable fraud'[1] be shown to exist. 'Equitable fraud' is present 'as soon as the absolute character of the conveyance is set up for the purpose of defeating the beneficial interest' guaranteed by the relevant bargain.[2] In this sense 'equitable fraud' provides the 'common denominator' or 'connecting link' which runs through the many categories of circumstance where constructive trusts have arisen.[3]

1   For an early reference to 'equitable fraud', see *Lincoln v Wright* (1859) 4 De G & J 16 at 23, 45 ER 6 at 9. See also *Nocton v Ashburton* [1914] AC 932 at 953–954 per Viscount Haldane LC (equitable fraud is 'not moral fraud in the ordinary sense, but breach of the sort of obligation which is enforced by … a Court of conscience'). See likewise *Le Compte v Public Trustee* [1983] 2 NSWLR 109 at 111B per Rath J.

2   *Bannister v Bannister* [1948] 2 All ER 133 at 136C–D. See also *Last v Rosenfeld* [1972] 2 NSWLR 923 at 934F; *Baumgartner v Baumgartner* (1985) 2 NSWLR 406 at 412A–B.

3   *Avondale Printers & Stationers Ltd v Haggie* [1979] 2 NZLR 124 at 159 per Mahon J. See also *South Yarra Project Pty Ltd v Gentsis* [1985] VR 29 at 37.

Unconscientious use of the legal title

10.110   The essence of 'equitable fraud' lies in the 'unconscientious use of the legal title.'[1] As Lord Diplock insisted in *Gissing v Gissing*,[2] a constructive trust arises only where an owner, A, 'has so conducted himself that it would be inequitable to allow him to deny to [B] a beneficial interest in the land.' However, the required inequity is plainly established by any 'disclaimer … of the obligations of conscience based upon an express agreement, or common intention of the parties.'[3] The disclaimer of the antecedent bargain amounts, in the words of Viscount Dilhorne in *Gissing v Gissing*,[4] to a 'breach of faith' and converts the estate owner's actions into a fraud on the claimant.[5] Were A's disclaimer to remain unchecked, the 'suffering which would otherwise occur' on the part of B 'makes it "a fraud on B" for A to assert his rights, that is to say, makes it unconscionable of A to assert his rights.'[6]

1   *Ogilvie v Ryan* [1976] 2 NSWLR 504 at 518E per Holland J. See also *Baumgartner v Baumgartner* (1985) 2 NSWLR 406 at 412A–B.

2   [1971] AC 886 at 905C.

3   *Allen v Snyder* [1977] 2 NSWLR 685 at 694E per Glass JA; *Baumgartner v Baumgartner* (1985) 2 NSWLR 406 at 435A–B.

4   [1971] AC 886 at 900B–C.

5   See also *Boccalatte v Bushelle* [1980] Qd R 180 at 186A per Matthews J.

6   *Thwaites v Ryan* [1984] VR 65 at 90 per Fullagar J.

Attempted derogation from agreed entitlements

10.111   Constructive trusts come into play primarily in order to frustrate fraudulent designs.[1] It is clear that the fraud required to activate a constructive trust need not have been present in the original agreement or bargain which purported to guarantee some kind of beneficial interest for B.[2] A constructive trust is imposed on A only if he later behaves inequitably by attempting to derogate from the beneficial rights conferred on B by the earlier bargain.[3] In particular, A must not seek to escape from that bargain by pleading its unenforceability through want of written evidence. It is a clear doctrine of equity that any 'reliance by the trustee on the statute requiring writing would be an equitable fraud.'[4] Equity will never allow a statute to be used as an instrument of fraud and the unconscientious use of title is therefore penalised by the imposition of a constructive trust.

1   *Avondale Printers & Stationers Ltd v Haggie* [1979] 2 NZLR 124 at 160 per Mahon J.

2   *Bannister v Bannister* [1948] 2 All ER 133 at 136C, F–G; *Last v Rosenfeld* [1972] 2 NSWLR 923 at 934F.

3   In *Yaxley v Gotts* [2000] Ch 162, for example, a builder was orally promised the ground floor of certain premises 'for ever' in exchange for supplying labour, materials and services in the conversion of the premises to a block of flats. Although the agreed conversion was carried out, the legal owner reneged on this 'gentleman's agreement' and refused to grant the builder any interest in the land. The Court of Appeal ruled that, in the clear absence of any specifically enforceable contract, the legal estate was held on a constructive trust to give effect to a 99 year lease of the ground floor for the builder. The constructive trust operated to avert 'injustice' in circumstances where it would have been 'unconscionable' to disregard the claimant's expectations ([2000] Ch 162 at 180C, 193E).

4   *Allen v Snyder* [1977] 2 NSWLR 685 at 692E per Glass JA. See also *Baumgartner v Baumgartner* (1985) 2 NSWLR 406 at 435A–B per Priestley JA.

TWO TYPES OF CONSTRUCTIVE TRUST

10.112   The law of constructive trusts has not remained static. It is possible, in retrospect, to discern distinct phases in the evolution of constructive trust doctrine and it may be that certain features of the older law have been overtaken by more recent developments.[1] In the case law of the late 1980s and early 1990s English courts, to the surprise of most land lawyers,[2] began to discriminate between two categories of constructive trust by reference to the nature of the agreement, bargain or common intention on which the trust is founded. The courts came to differentiate the 'express bargain' constructive trust[3] from the 'implied bargain' constructive trust[4] and this typology has now taken firm root in English constructive trust jurisprudence.[5] As Lord Bridge of Harwich indicated in *Lloyds Bank Plc v Rosset*,[6] the difference between express bargains and implied bargains is a 'critical distinction which [the] judge … should always have in the forefront of his mind'[7] since it directly controls the character of the evidence of detriment or 'change of position' which is required in support of a claim of constructive trust.

1   See e g *Oxley v Hiscock* [2004] 3 WLR 715 at [50], [60] per Chadwick LJ.

2   See *Stokes v Anderson* [1991] 1 FLR 391 at 398F–G per Nourse LJ; *Oxley v Hiscock* [2004] 3 WLR 715 at [29] per Chadwick LJ (referring to the decision of the Court of Appeal in *Grant v Edwards* [1986] Ch 638 as 'a turning point').

3   **[Para 10.113]**. The origin of the terminology of 'express bargain' seems to have been the judgment of Mustill LJ in *Grant v Edwards* [1986] Ch 638 at 651G–653D. See also the reference by Browne-Wilkinson V-C to the distinction between 'direct evidence' of common intention and 'inferred common intention' ([1986] Ch 638 at 654F–H).

4   **[Para 10.127]**.

5   The case law is now legion, but see e g *Savill v Goodall* [1993] 1 FLR 755 at 758E–H per Nourse LJ; *Lloyds Bank plc v Carrick* [1996] 4 All ER 630 at 638d–g per Morritt LJ; *Drake v Whipp* [1996] 1 FLR 826 at 828B–G per Peter Gibson LJ; *Yaxley v Gotts* [2000] Ch 162 at 176G–177B per Robert Walker LJ, 191D–F per Beldam LJ; *McKenzie v McKenzie* [2003] EWHC 601 (Ch) at [70]–[72]; *Hyett v Stanley* [2003] WTLR 1269 at [8]–[9] per Sir Martin Nourse; *Buggs v Buggs* [2003] EWHC 1538 (Ch) at [18].

6   [1991] 1 AC 107 at 132D–E, 133H–134A. Lord Bridge spoke with the concurrence of the other members of the House.

7   This is the 'first and fundamental question which must always be resolved' ([1991] 1 AC 107 at 132E per Lord Bridge of Harwich). See also *Mortgage Corporation v Shaire* [2001] Ch 743 at 750B–D per Neuberger J.

THE 'EXPRESS BARGAIN' CONSTRUCTIVE TRUST

10.113   Although it probably happens relatively rarely,[1] it is possible that A, the proprietor of a land title, may have reached an express bargain or understanding with B that B should take some share of the beneficial ownership of the land. Such express agreements must be sharply distinguished from implied bargains which rest merely upon inferences drawn from the conduct or dealings of the parties.

1   See *Grant v Edwards* [1986] Ch 638 at 647C per Nourse LJ; *Stokes v Anderson* [1991] 1 FLR 391 at 398A per Nourse LJ. As Lord Hodson observed in *Pettitt v Pettitt* [1970] AC 777 at 810E–F, the conception of 'a normal married couple spending the long winter evenings hammering out agreements about their possessions appears grotesque.' Compare, however, *Mollo v Mollo* [1999] EGCS 117 (Transcript at [25(b)]), for the assertion that 'express discussion' is unlikely not to have occurred where both parties contribute money towards a purchase (sed quaere).

Effect of express agreement

10.114   Where there is 'an express agreement … as to the way in which the beneficial interest shall be held,' said Lord Diplock in *Gissing v Gissing*,[1] the court 'will give effect to it – notwithstanding the absence of any written declaration of trust.'[2] Such an express agreement, if specific as to quantum, is generally conclusive of the measure of beneficial entitlement,[3] but in all cases the agreement must be supported by some change of position on the part of the constructive trust claimant.[4] As Lord Diplock pointed out,[5] an agreement by A which fails to 'provide for anything to be done' by B is 'a merely voluntary declaration of trust and unenforceable for want of writing.' In the absence of writing a trust 'does not come into being merely from a gratuitous intention to transfer or create a beneficial interest.'[6] There must be some form of *bargain* struck between the parties either before the acquisition of the legal title or possibly at some later date.[7]

1   [1971] AC 886 at 905D–E. See also *Clough v Killey* (1996) 72 P & CR D22 per Peter Gibson LJ.
2   In other words, what would have been wholly unenforceable as an express trust may become effective as a constructive trust.
3   **[Para 10.126]**.
4   See *Chan Pui Chun v Leung Kam Ho* [2003] 1 FLR 23 at [93] per Jonathan Parker LJ.
5   [1971] AC 886 at 905E.
6   *Austin v Keele* (1987) 10 NSWLR 283 at 291B–C per Lord Oliver of Aylmerton (JCPC). See *Re Vandervell's Trusts (No 2)* [1974] Ch 269 at 294C per Megarry J ('To yearn is not to transfer').
7   **[Para 10.84]**.

Communication of the express bargain

10.115   The requirement of common intention is stringent. In order to establish an express bargain for present purposes, a constructive trust claimant must adduce clear evidence that the relevant parties have 'orally declared themselves in such a way as to make plain their common intention that the claimant should have a beneficial interest in the property.'[1] As Lord Bridge of Harwich held in *Lloyds Bank Plc v Rosset*,[2] there must have been some 'agreement, arrangement or understanding reached between them that the property is to be shared beneficially.'[3] The court looks, in effect, for exchanges between the parties of 'a consensual character falling not far short of an enforceable contract.'[4] It is clear, however, that an expressly articulated common intention that B should participate beneficially in A's land can give rise to a constructive trust even though the precise nature or quantum of B's share has not been definitively settled by the parties' expressly concluded bargain. In *Oxley v Hiscock*[5] the Court of Appeal vigorously dispelled any suggestion that an agreement for some form of equitable sharing is incomplete for the purpose of establishing a constructive trust merely because it omits to specify the exact extent of the parties' intended shares.

1 *Stokes v Anderson* [1991] 1 FLR 391 at 398A per Nourse LJ.
2 [1991] 1 AC 107 at 132E–F. See (1990) 106 LQR 539 (J D Davies); [1991] CLJ 38 (M Dixon).
3 See also *Oxley v Hiscock* [2004] 3 WLR 715 at [37], [40] per Chadwick LJ.
4 *Chan Pui Chun v Leung Kam Ho* [2003] 1 FLR 23 at [91] per Jonathan Parker LJ.
5 [2004] 3 WLR 715 at [37], [40], [47]–[48] per Chadwick LJ.

Necessity for express discussions

10.116 Speaking in *Rosset*'s case in the context of a family home, Lord Bridge went on to indicate that the finding of a legally significant agreement or arrangement 'can only ... be based on evidence of express discussions between the partners, however imperfectly remembered and however imprecise their terms may have been.'[1] The express bargain must comprise 'a shared intention communicated between' the relevant parties.[2] The consensus ad idem must be a demonstrable reality.[3] The required common intention is not sufficiently established even if each of the parties independently 'happened to be thinking on the same lines in his or her uncommunicated thoughts.'[4] In this respect, as Steyn LJ remarked in *Springette v Defoe*,[5] the court does not recognise communication 'at a subconscious level ... Our trust law does not allow property rights to be affected by telepathy.'[6] In the absence of a bargain embodied in *express* negotiation and discussion,[7] claims of beneficial entitlement can be made good only under the somewhat more rigorous criteria which apply to constructive trusts founded on implied bargain.[8] Not for the first time English land law is shown to be fairly unsympathetic to the realities of family life, placing a premium upon intentions which are rarely articulated or even contemplated by domestic partners.

1 See also *Hammond v Mitchell* [1991] 1 WLR 1127 at 1129F; *Beresford v Williamson* [2002] EWCA Civ 1632 at [15].
2 *Springette v Defoe* [1992] 2 FLR 388 at 393D per Dillon LJ. See also *Hammond v Mitchell* [1991] 1 WLR 1127 at 1137A–B per Waite J; *Savill v Goodall* [1993] 1 FLR 755 at 760D per Nourse LJ; *Oxley v Hiscock* [2004] 3 WLR 715 at [52] per Chadwick LJ; *Lightfoot v Lightfoot-Brown* [2004] All ER (D) 92 (Apr) at [5].

3   The law must concentrate on the 'external signs of common intention' (*Mollo v Mollo* [1999] EGCS 117 (Transcript at [34])).
4   *Springette v Defoe* [1992] 2 FLR 388 at 393F–G per Dillon LJ.
5   [1992] 2 FLR 388 at 394H.
6   Thus, in *Mollo v Mollo* [1999] EGCS 117 (Transcript at [39]), a constructive trust claim was not impaired by the claimant's uncommunicated private intention or motivation that his contribution towards the shared family home should generate a beneficial share, not for himself, but for his sons.
7   See eg *Springette v Defoe* [1992] 2 FLR 388 at 393G, 397B.
8   [**Para 10.131**].

Timing of express discussions

10.117   Despite the fact that constructive trusts may, in principle, emerge at any time, some of the case law reveals a lingering (and unnecessarily restrictive) judicial expectation that express discussion as to the beneficial ownership of a family home will normally occur prior to the acquisition of the legal title and can occur only 'exceptionally' at some later date.[1] The more recent and more general trend in the case law is, however, to accept that express agreements creative of a constructive trust may arise at any time before, at, or after the acquisition of title.[2]

1   *Lloyds Bank Plc v Rosset* [1991] 1 AC 107 at 132E–F per Lord Bridge of Harwich. It has been suggested that the latter reference covers 'unusual cases' where there has been considerable subsequent expenditure on improvements financed by an increased mortgage commitment to which the claimant has contributed (see *First National Bank plc v Wadhwani* (Unreported, Court of Appeal, 22 April 1998) per Sir John Vinelott).
2   See eg *Clough v Killey* (1996) 72 P & CR D22 per Peter Gibson LJ; *Hyett v Stanley* [2003] WTLR 1269 at [26] per Sir Martin Nourse; *Oxley v Hiscock* [2004] 3 WLR 715 at [40], [73] per Chadwick LJ.

Instances of express bargain

10.118   The 'primary emphasis' now accorded to express discussions means that 'the tenderest exchanges of a common law courtship may assume an unforeseen significance many years later when they are brought under equity's microscope.'[1] Under this analysis 'many thousands of pounds of value may be liable to turn on fine questions as to whether the relevant words were spoken in earnest or in dalliance and with or without representational intent.'[2] In *Lloyds Bank Plc v Rosset*[3] Lord Bridge instanced, as outstanding examples of the 'express bargain' category of constructive trust, the circumstances of *Eves v Eves*[4] and *Grant v Edwards*.[5] In both cases the claimant (the female partner in a relationship) had been explicitly led by the male partner to believe, when they established a home together, that the property would belong to them jointly. In *Eves* the female partner had been told that the legal title in the home was vested in her partner's sole name only because she was then under 21 years of age. Similarly in *Grant v Edwards* the male partner had informed the claimant that the only reason for not acquiring their home in joint names was the fact that this might prejudice the divorce proceedings in which she was currently involved. In both cases the evidence pointed to a clear common intention, expressly adverted to in the parties' discussions, that, when these special circumstances were displaced, some form of shared ownership would be entirely appropriate.[6]

1   *Hammond v Mitchell* [1991] 1 WLR 1127 at 1139C–D per Waite J. See eg *Clough v Killey* (1996) 72 P & CR D22.
2   As Lord Bridge observed in *Lloyds Bank Plc v Rosset* [1991] 1 AC 107 at 127G, evidence of express discussions is now the 'vital issue' raised in pleadings in this area. It is 'of prime importance' for both parties that affidavit assertions of express agreement are made with a high degree of particularity, since the case may otherwise founder for vagueness or, alternatively, the legal owner may not know exactly what case he must meet (see *Hammond v Mitchell* [1991] 1 WLR 1127 at 1139E–F).
3   [1991] 1 AC 107 at 133C–F.
4   [1975] 1 WLR 1338 **[para 10.122]**.
5   [1986] Ch 638. See [1986] Conv 291 (J Warburton); [1986] CLJ 394 (D J Hayton); (1986) 130 Sol Jo 347 (P M Rank).
6   See *Eves v Eves* [1975] 1 WLR 1338 at 1345B per Brightman J; *Grant v Edwards* [1986] Ch 638 at 649A–B per Nourse LJ, 653D–F per Mustill LJ.

Change of position required in 'express bargain' constructive trusts

10.119   It used to be assumed that the same definition of recognisable 'change of position' applied indifferently throughout the law of constructive trusts. The case law of the last 15 years has emphatically confirmed, however, that the standard of proof relating to 'changes of position' varies markedly according to whether a constructive trust is based on an *express* or *implied* bargain. In an 'express bargain' constructive trust, a relevant 'change of position' may be established by a broader range of acts of reliance on the part of the claimant.

A wider category of 'change of position'

10.120   In delivering the only substantive speech in the House of Lords in *Lloyds Bank Plc v Rosset*,[1] Lord Bridge indicated that a less exacting probandum applies to the 'change of position' which underlies an 'express bargain' constructive trust. Once there is evidence of agreed beneficial entitlement based on direct negotiation or discussion, the claimant need show 'only ... that he or she has acted to his or her detriment or significantly altered his or her position in reliance on the agreement.'[2] Since express agreement has already been found as a fact, relevant changes of position extend well beyond that conduct which is explicable only on the basis of some bargain over beneficial title. The court is not therefore required to look for conduct from which a shared intention of beneficial ownership could be inferred.[3] The court looks only for 'conduct which amounts to an acting upon [the agreement] by the claimant.'[4] The court can thus take account of behaviour which falls 'far short of such conduct as would by itself have supported the claim in the absence of an express representation ... that [the claimant] should have ... an interest.'[5]

1   [1991] 1 AC 107 at 132F–G.

2   The alternative nature of this formula has an importance which was noted earlier [**para 10.105**].

3   *Grant v Edwards* [1986] Ch 638 at 655F–G per Browne-Wilkinson V-C.

4   *Grant v Edwards* [1986] Ch 638 at 647C per Nourse LJ. It may be that more recent analyses of 'change of position' as inclusive of the conferment of benefit on the legal owner are particularly appropriate to cases of expressly negotiated bargain (see e g *Banner Homes Group Plc v Luff Developments Ltd* [2000] Ch 372 [**para 10.106**]), leaving the traditional understanding of 'change of position' as connoting detriment or material sacrifice to be relevant primarily to situations of implied bargain [**para 10.131**].

5   *Lloyds Bank Plc v Rosset* [1991] 1 AC 107 at 133F–G per Lord Bridge of Harwich.

Relevant changes of position in relation to the family home

10.121   The change of position required in the context of the family home obviously includes the incurring of expenditure which is referable to the acquisition of that home,[1] but may also extend to more general contributions to the family economy, whether by way of domestic achievement, child rearing, indirect expenditure on the joint household or otherwise. Evidence that a direct agreement has been 'acted upon' may thus be established, for instance, by a claimant's contribution of physical labour towards the renovation of a joint home[2] or by her participation in commercial activities initiated or undertaken by her partner.[3] Although the precise parameters of relevant conduct are still somewhat unclear, relevant acts of reliance may include various forms of self-abnegation or self-imposed disadvantage.[4]

1   See *Grant v Edwards* [1986] Ch 638 at 649F–650C per Nourse LJ; *Stokes v Anderson* [1991] 1 FLR 391 at 398A–B.

2   *Eves v Eves* [1975] 1 WLR 1338 at 1340D–E, 1342F–G, 1344C–D, 1345C. See also *Cooke v Head* [1972] 1 WLR 518 at 519G–H, 520F–G; *Grant v Edwards* [1986] Ch 638 at 648D per Nourse LJ; *Hayward v Giordani* [1983] NZLR 140 at 142, 150, 152.

3   *Hammond v Mitchell* [1991] 1 WLR 1127 at 1137D–E ([1992] Conv 218 (A Lawson); (1993) 56 MLR 224 (P O'Hagan)); *Chan Pui Chun v Leung Kam Ho* [2003] 1 FLR 23 at [38], [87], [96]–[97].

4   *Chan Pui Chun v Leung Kam Ho* [2003] 1 FLR 23 at [38], [87] (foregoing of political career).

10.122   One of the broader formulations of relevant 'change of position' is to be found in *Grant v Edwards*.[1] Here, in dealing with a partner's claim to a beneficial share in a family home, Browne-Wilkinson V-C thought that 'useful guidance' could be obtained from the principles underlying the law of proprietary estoppel.[2] This instructive analogy tended to suggest that 'any act done by [the claimant] to her detriment relating to the joint lives of the parties is ... sufficient detriment to qualify. The acts do not have to be inherently referable to the house'. On this footing Browne-Wilkinson V-C was prepared in *Grant v Edwards* to have regard to such activities as '[s]etting up house together, having a baby, [and] making payments to general housekeeping expenses (not strictly necessary to enable the mortgage to be paid).'[3] Such conduct was relevant even though it might be 'referable to the mutual love and affection of the parties and not specifically referable to the claimant's belief that she has an interest in the house.'[4] In the same case, however, Nourse LJ expressed the more restrictive view that conduct is relevant only if it is 'conduct on which the woman could not reasonably have been expected to embark unless she was to have an interest in the house.'[5] Only by adopting the latter kind of conduct could the claimant be 'seen to act to her detriment on the faith of the common intention.'[6] Thus, in Nourse LJ's opinion, the mere fact that a woman moved into joint occupation of her lover's home would not normally constitute an incurring of recognisable detriment on her part, since the law is 'not so cynical as to infer that a woman will only go to live with a man to whom she is not married if she understands that she is to have an interest in their home.'[7] In *Eves v Eves*,[8] by contrast, a constructive trust had been quite correctly imposed because there, in the absence of some anticipated beneficial entitlement, the female claimant could not reasonably have been expected to undertake the arduous physical effort which in fact she devoted to the improvement of her lover's home.[9] It is likely that the recent liberalising trend in the law of constructive trusts has made Browne-Wilkinson V-C's approach seem more persuasive.

1   [1986] Ch 638 at 657A–B.
2   Browne-Wilkinson V-C considered the principles of proprietary estoppel to be 'closely akin to those laid down in *Gissing v Gissing*' ([1986] Ch 638 at 656F–H). See likewise *Oxley v Hiscock* [2004] 3 WLR 715 at [66] per Chadwick LJ.
3   See e g Waite J's willingness in *Hammond v Mitchell* [1991] 1 WLR 1127 at 1137A–G to hold that the claimant had 'acted to her detriment or significantly altered her position' by making a 'contribution as mother/helper/unpaid assistant and at times financial supporter to the family prosperity generated by [her partner's] dealing activities.'
4   [1986] Ch 638 at 657A.
5   [1986] Ch 638 at 648G–H.
6   [1986] Ch 638 at 648H. See also *Hohol v Hohol* [1981] VR 221 at 225.
7   [1986] Ch 638 at 648F–G. See likewise *Stowe v Stowe* (1995) 15 WAR 363 at 39F–G.
8   [1975] 1 WLR 1338.
9   Apart from redecorating the entire house and demolishing a garden shed single-handed, it was the formidable achievement of the claimant in *Eves v Eves* that she wielded a 14 lb sledgehammer to break up an area of concrete at the front of the house, dump the rubble in a skip, and prepare the garden for turfing ([1975] 1 WLR 1338 at 1340D–E). The success of her claim (albeit limited to a 25 per cent share) seems to have stimulated the emergence of a small army of women, all 'wielding a pickaxe' within the domestic curtilage (see *Ungurian v Lesnoff* [1990] Ch 206 at 223F–224A per Vinelott J). See also *Clough v Killey* (1996) 72 P & CR D22.

Matters of lifestyle

10.123   In the past there was some uncertainty over the extent to which highly personal circumstances and matters of lifestyle could support constructive trusts of the 'express bargain' variety. Here some of the law's least attractive characteristics tended to find expression in a general unconcern for the special needs and vulnerabilities of women claimants. The strictures imposed by orthodox trust theory were such that a relevant 'detriment' or 'change of position' was seldom established unless the claimant's conduct substantially overstepped boundaries of conventional expectation based on stereotyped perceptions of her appropriate gender role. As was once said of a wife's claim to a matrimonial home, 'before equity will intervene to protect the wife, her contribution must exceed that normally expected of a wife carrying out her normal matrimonial role.'[1] This institutional lack of empathy was mirrored in other statements that beneficial ownership is not altered by the performance of 'the ordinary domestic tasks'[2] or by the fact that the husband 'likes to occupy his leisure by laying a new lawn in the garden or building a fitted wardrobe in the bedroom while the wife does the shopping, cooks the family dinner or bathes the children.'[3] It is noticeable, however, that the tenor of such observations reflects a view of constructive trust law which flourished some 20 or 30 years ago. It is highly probable that these gender-based perspectives have ceased to have any prominence in the modern law.

1   *Lloyds Bank Plc v Rosset* [1989] Ch 350 at 402F per Purchas LJ. (Purchas LJ upheld the claim of beneficial entitlement). See *Cooke v Cooke* [1987] VR 625 at 639, where Southwell J rejected the idea that any 'detriment' could be claimed by a partner who, in response to the legal owner's request, had foregone an abortion, had remained 'chaste' and 'faithful' to him, had refrained from seeking outside employment and had brought up two young children in his house.
2   *Burns v Burns* [1984] Ch 317 at 331A per Fox LJ.
3   *Pettitt v Pettitt* [1970] AC 777 at 826A–B per Lord Diplock. See also *Burns v Burns* [1984] Ch 317 at 344E–F per May LJ ('that the husband may spend his weekends redecorating or laying a patio is neither here nor there'); *Mollo v Mollo* [1999] EGCS 117 (Transcript at [25(c)]) ('the normal sort of do-it-yourself activities').

Requirement of 'referability'

10.124   The requirement of 'referability' usually occasions little difficulty where A and B have reached an express agreement as to the beneficial ownership of land vested at law in the name of A. The explicit nature of the agreement obviates the need to demonstrate a positive causal connection between the verbal assurance of A and the detrimental reliance of B. Lord Diplock confirmed in *Gissing v Gissing*[1] that there need be no formal demonstration that A's conduct was intended to induce B to act to her detriment on the faith of the promise of some specified beneficial interest or that B acted with the intention of acquiring such an interest. As Browne-Wilkinson V-C suggested in *Grant v Edwards*,[2] the causal link is readily presumed, on an analogy with the law of proprietary estoppel, to be self-evident.

1   [1971] AC 886 at 905G–H. See e g *Le Compte v Public Trustee* [1983] 2 NSWLR 109 at 111C, E–F.
2   [1986] Ch 638 at 656B–D, 657C (in the absence of contrary evidence 'the right inference is that the claimant acted in reliance ... and the burden lies on the legal owner to show that she did not do so'). For a more restrictive view, compare [1986] Ch 638 at 648G–H per Nourse LJ.

10.125   In *Grant v Edwards* the claimant de facto wife had contributed financially towards household expenses, her partner having undertaken sole responsibility for the repayment of the mortgage on the family home. Browne-Wilkinson V-C noted that, without the woman's contributions, the man's means would have been 'insufficient to keep up the mortgage payments', and that her indirect contributions were therefore 'essentially linked to the payment of the mortgage instalments'.[1] The mere use of the claimant's money 'whether directly or indirectly' in the discharge of mortgage instalments provided, in Browne-Wilkinson V-C's view, 'a sufficient link between the detriment suffered by the claimant and the common intention.' The court could 'infer that she would not have made such payments were it not for her belief that she had an interest in the house.'[2] The claimant was accordingly recognised as having acquired a one-half interest in the beneficial ownership.

1   [1986] Ch 638 at 656D–E.
2   [1986] Ch 638 at 656E–F.

Quantification of entitlement

10.126   It is one thing to resolve the 'primary, or threshold, question' whether a constructive trust has come into existence at all.[1] It is an entirely different matter to address the 'secondary, or consequential question' posed by the need to quantify the beneficial entitlements which have emerged from a finding of trust. It is tolerably clear, however, that where parties have demonstrably formed some express agreement in respect of beneficial quantum, equitable ownership 'will be governed by the agreement, arrangement or understanding and no further inquiry will be necessary.'[2] In quantifying entitlement under the constructive trust, the court may depart from the agreement 'only if there is very good reason for doing so.'[3] The shares or interests agreed by the parties are therefore definitive[4] unless it can be shown that there has been some 'subsequent renegotiation'[5] or subsequent conduct 'so inconsistent with what was agreed' as to point unmistakably to a variation or cancellation of that agreement.[6] Where, however, the parties' express agreement did not define the extent of the shares to be taken, the court must do so in their place using the yardstick of what is 'fair having regard to the whole course of dealing between them in relation to the property.'[7]

1   **[Para 10.81]**.
2   See eg *Savill v Goodall* [1993] 1 FLR 755 at 758H–759A per Nourse LJ (express agreement for ownership in equal shares). See also *Clough v Killey* (1996) 72 P & CR D22 per Peter Gibson LJ; *Re Share (Lorraine)* [2002] 2 FLR 88 at [11]; *Hyett v Stanley* [2003] WTLR 1269 at [28].
3   *Mortgage Corporation v Shaire* [2001] Ch 743 at 750C–D per Neuberger J.
4   See *Gissing v Gissing* [1971] AC 886 at 905D–E per Lord Diplock. It matters not, for example, that the parties subsequently make money contributions which are disproportional to their agreed shareholdings (see *Wright v Johnson* [2002] 2 P & CR 210 at [17]).
5   *Mortgage Corporation v Shaire* [2001] Ch 743 at 750C–D per Neuberger J. See e g *Re Schuppan (a bankrupt) (No 2)* [1997] 1 BCLC 256 at 270c–d.
6   *Mortgage Corporation v Shaire* [2001] Ch 743 at 750C–D per Neuberger J.
7   See *Oxley v Hiscock* [2004] 3 WLR 715 at [69], [73] per Chadwick LJ. The beneficial shares awarded in such cases may thus be disproportional to the value of claimant's actual contribution to the acquisition or enhancement in value of the disputed land. See e g *Eves v Eves* [1975] 1 WLR 1338 (25 per cent) and *Grant v Edwards* [1986] Ch 638 (50 per cent), as analysed by Lord Bridge of Harwich in *Lloyds Bank Plc v Rosset* [1991] 1 AC 107 at 133G–H.

THE 'IMPLIED BARGAIN' CONSTRUCTIVE TRUST

10.127   In the absence of an express bargain based upon direct negotiations, a constructive trust may be founded upon an implied bargain[1] which demonstrates a common intention that the claimant should have at least some beneficial interest.[2] It has long been clear that the court, in eliciting the common intention relevant to claims of constructive trust, may rely on inferences drawn from the pattern of conduct and the mutual dealings of the parties.[3] Yet it is in precisely this context that, in recent years, the jurisprudence of the constructive trust has been most turmoiled and now, conversely, shows the most dramatic indications of positive evolution.

1   In *Grant v Edwards* [1986] Ch 638 at 655F–G, Browne-Wilkinson V-C emphasised that express verbal declarations of intended co-ownership – if present on the facts – make it unnecessary for the court to have recourse to inferences based on other forms of conduct.
2   See *Oxley v Hiscock* [2004] 3 WLR 715 at [40] per Chadwick LJ.
3   See *Gissing v Gissing* [1971] AC 886 at 900G per Viscount Dilhorne, 902G per Lord Pearson, 908E–G per Lord Diplock; *Lloyds Bank Plc v Rosset* [1991] 1 AC 107 at 132H–133A per Lord Bridge of Harwich; *Mortgage Corporation v Shaire* [2001] Ch 743 at 750D–E; *Allen v Snyder* [1977] 2 NSWLR 685 at 691D; *Hayward v Giordani* [1983] NZLR 140 at 151; *Butler v Craine* [1986] VR 274 at 285.

A turmoiled past

10.128   The bleak limitations of traditional trust theory have rarely been so amply illustrated as in the law of the last four decades relating to constructive trusts allegedly generated by the conduct of the parties. The stark outcome, as exemplified in landmark decisions of the House of Lords across this period,[1] has been the denial of women's rights to participate in family assets accumulated during relationships of even substantial duration.[2] The failure of these claims has not been based, at least overtly, on any perception that it was 'inequitable' to acknowledge a shared beneficial ownership of the family home. The decisions have rested on the fact that the conventional law of trusts is deeply unsympathetic to the dynamics of family living.[3] The structural principles of property law often sit badly beside the social phenomena which they attempt to regulate. The traditional law of trusts, which 'assumes bargains, and not gifts',[4] is ill suited to deal with those who contribute towards the success of a family partnership without any anticipation of material reward or tangible pay-off. The shared endeavours of family members are motivated less by the mercenary incentives of the exchange economy than by higher principles of affection and commitment. Yet underlying the operation of trust law is a considerable historic resistance to any suggestion that co-ownership of assets can be founded merely on the parties' mutual assumption that family life is to be shared as a form of joint venture or partnership.[5]

1   See *Gissing v Gissing* [1971] AC 886; *Lloyds Bank Plc v Rosset* [1991] 1 AC 107. See also *Allen v Snyder* [1977] 2 NSWLR 685 at 694B–695C.
2   In its darkest days the doctrinaire application of English trust law failed markedly to protect the more vulnerable members of domestic partnerships. See e g *Burns v Burns* [1984] Ch 317,

where the Court of Appeal sent away empty-handed a de facto wife who had lived with her partner for 17 years, had borne and reared two children by him, and had contributed both money and household services to the relationship.

3   For reference to 'a clash of cultures' between a failing, but classical, law of trusts dominated by a longstanding commercialist ethos and the rather different mutualist ethic which underlies the property relationships of families, see Simon Gardner, (1996) 112 LQR 378 at 382. For a further, highly insightful critique, see Anne Bottomley, 'Women and Trust(s): Portraying the Family in the Gallery of Law', in S Bright and J K Dewar (ed), *Land Law: Themes and Perspectives* (OUP 1998), p 206.
4   *Goodfriend v Goodfriend* (1972) 22 DLR (3d) 699 at 703 per Spence J.
5   See eg *Lloyds Bank Plc v Rosset* [1991] 1 AC 107 at 128A, 130C–D per Lord Bridge of Harwich. Contrast the approach adopted, with reference to the Canadian doctrine of remedial constructive trust [**para 10.155**], in *Peter v Beblow* (1993) 101 DLR (4th) 621 at 633g per Cory J ('[I]n today's society it is unreasonable to assume that the presence of love automatically implies a gift of one party's services to another').

10.129   At long last modern developments in the jurisprudence of the constructive trust afford some cautious promise that the law has begun to escape from the strictures of the past. Many of the difficulties of English constructive trust law have stemmed from the rigid application of the doctrinal components of the conventional trust theory.

Search for a phantom common intention

10.130   The classic 'implied bargain' constructive trust has always placed a premium on the detailed, time-consuming and laborious process of determining whether the parties' conduct discloses evidence of any implied bargain for shared ownership. Although the court is not confined to an examination of the parties' conduct at the date of acquisition, and can draw inferences from their subsequent actions,[1] the search for the requisite element of inferable intention has frequently proved both difficult and unrealistic.[2] In the absence of an implicit, but demonstrable, bargain for equitable sharing, the constructive trust claimant has all too often emerged from the court empty-handed.[3]

1   *Grant v Edwards* [1986] Ch 638 at 651H–652A per Mustill LJ; *Stokes v Anderson* [1991] 1 FLR 391 at 399G per Nourse LJ; *Mortgage Corporation v Shaire* [2001] Ch 743 at 750D–E per Neuberger J.
2   See eg *Hammond v Mitchell* [1991] 1 WLR 1127 at 1129H per Waite J.
3   See eg *Wood v Wood* (Unreported, Court of Appeal, 1979 W No 1393, 7 July 1982), where Lawton LJ observed that such an outcome merely provided a 'cautionary tale for women who cohabit with men without having clear understandings with them about their property dealings one with the other.'

A 'change of position'

10.131   Whatever the precise parameters of the 'change of position' required under an 'express bargain' constructive trust, it has become clear that 'more rigorous standards ... apply when intention has to be inferred from conduct alone.'[1] Under an 'implied bargain' constructive trust, much more exacting proof of 'change of position' is needed not least because, as Lord Bridge pointed out in *Lloyds Bank Plc v Rosset*,[2] the claimant is attempting to rely entirely on the conduct of the parties 'both as the basis from which to infer a common intention to share the property beneficially and as the conduct relied on to give rise to a constructive trust.'[3]

1   *Hammond v Mitchell* [1991] 1 WLR 1127 at 1137H per Waite J.
2   [1991] 1 AC 107 at 132H–133A.
3   There is here, as Mustill LJ pointed out in *Grant v Edwards* [1986] Ch 638 at 652G–653A, 'a risk of circularity'.

Change of position must normally involve direct money payment

10.132   A monetary bias dominates the identification of the 'change of position' relevant for the purpose of establishing an 'implied bargain' constructive trust. In *Rosset*'s case, Lord Bridge acknowledged that 'direct contributions to the purchase price by the partner who is not the legal owner, whether initially or by payment of mortgage instalments, will readily justify the inference necessary to the creation of a constructive trust',[1] but concluded significantly that 'it is at least extremely doubtful whether anything less will do.'[2] The ruling of the House of Lords in *Lloyds Bank Plc v Rosset* again underlined, in the context of the 'implied bargain' constructive trust, the intense preoccupation with money payments which colours so much of the law of trusts.

1   See also *Mollo v Mollo* [1999] EGCS 117 (Transcript at [23]).
2   [1991] 1 AC 107 at 133A. See, accordingly, *Halifax Building Society v Brown* [1996] 1 FLR 103 at 109D, where Balcombe LJ regarded the payment of a deposit as sufficient for the purpose.

Denigration of other forms of contribution

10.133   The conventional law of trusts has always been notorious for its disregard of the implications of any division of labour within the family home. English law has been slow to acknowledge that families live in a factual community of goods and that the economic activity of family members is characterised by constructive co-operation and partnership endeavour.[1] In the absence of express bargain, the strict effect of *Lloyds Bank Plc v Rosset* has been to exclude many forms of domestic contributory activity from the ambit of the constructive trust. Lord Bridge himself conceded that even the execution of substantial or arduous renovation works on property in such cases as *Eves v Eves*[2] fell 'far short' of the kind of conduct required.[3] Still less was any 'implied bargain' constructive trust triggered by many years of faithful domestic endeavour on the part of a wife, mother and homemaker[4] or by other effort devoted to a common venture or family business.[5]

1   For a recent exploration of marriage as an 'egalitarian liberal community', see Carolyn J Frantz and Hanoch Dagan, 'Properties of Marriage' 104 Col L Rev 75 (2004).
2   [1975] 1 WLR 1338.
3   [1991] 1 AC 107 at 133F–G. See likewise *Grant v Edwards* [1986] Ch 638 at 648D per Nourse LJ; *Clough v Killey* (1996) 72 P & CR D22 per Peter Gibson LJ.

4   *Button v Button* [1968] 1 WLR 457 at 462A–C; *Gissing v Gissing* [1969] 2 Ch 85 at 98E–F;
    Burns v Burns [1984] Ch 317 at 327H, 331A–B, 345B–C; *Layton v Martin* [1986] 2 FLR 227 at
    235H–236A, 238C–D; *C v C* [1976] IR 254 at 257.
5   See *Britannia Building Society v Johnston* (Northern Ireland Chancery Division, 13 May 1994)
    (wife's labour on farm); *Ivin v Blake* (1994) 67 P & CR 263 at 276 (daughter's unpaid work in
    family-owned public house).

The requirement of 'referability'

10.134   In 'implied bargain' constructive trusts the courts have tended to
apply a much more stringent requirement that the claimant's change of position
be shown to have been *induced* by the bargain in question. Where the relevant
common intention as to beneficial title is left to be inferred from the mutual
conduct of A and B, the acts or omissions alleged in reliance by B must be
demonstrated to have been 'referable to the acquisition' of a beneficial interest
in A's property.[1] Only if this test of 'referability' is satisfied can B rebut the
normal legal inference that the sole title taken by A invests him also with the
sole equitable interest.[2]

1   *Gissing v Gissing* [1971] AC 886 at 905B–C, 909G per Lord Diplock. See also *Burns v Burns*
    [1984] Ch 317 at 327G–H, 328H–329B; *Grant v Edwards* [1986] Ch 638 at 651G–H; *Winkworth
    v Edward Baron Development Co Ltd* [1986] 1 WLR 1512 at 1515F–G.
2   [1971] AC 886 at 909H–910A.

Diffuse motivations

10.135   The strict test of referability has caused the failure of innumerable
trust claims, throwing almost insuperable obstacles in the way of those who fail
to clarify at a sufficiently conscious mental level the motivations and implications of their day-to-day actions. As was said in *Mollo v Mollo*,[1] the difficulty
inherent in inferring beneficial intentions from indirect or non-financial contributions to the family home is that 'there may well be other reasons which
explain such actions which have everything to do with the love and affection
which exists between two people ... and nothing to do with the beneficial
ownership of the property.'[2] In *Philip Lowe* (*Chinese Restaurant*) *Ltd v Sau Man
Lee*,[3] for example, May LJ insisted in the Court of Appeal that a showing of
referability was 'at the very least a sine qua non' of equitable entitlement under
what would now be termed an 'implied bargain' constructive trust. In the *Philip
Lowe* case the claimant, a de facto wife, was denied all beneficial interest in the
family property on the ground that the detriment which she had incurred by
working in the family restaurant had been undertaken, not in any belief that
she was thereby acquiring an equitable interest, but simply 'because she was
part of the family.'[4] Likewise, in *Lloyds Bank Plc v Rosset*,[5] the House of Lords
declined to accept that the claimant wife had demonstrated any relevant change
of position where, in the absence of an express bargain, her efforts had
consisted merely of personal assistance in the renovation of the family home
whose legal title was vested in her husband.[6] In the view of Lord Bridge of
Harwich, her intensive efforts were explicable purely on the basis that she had

been 'extremely anxious' that the home should be available for occupation as soon as possible. Her labours did not comprise work 'upon which she could not reasonably have been expected to embark unless she was to have an interest in the house.'[7]

1   [1999] EGCS 117 (Transcript at [26]) per Deputy Judge Ian Hunter QC.
2   See *Mehra v Shah* [2003] All ER (D) 15 (Aug) at [29], [51], [63] (affd [2004] EWCA Civ 632 at [64]) (substantial transfers of capital and income within extended Kenyan Asian family connoted 'no direct contributions to the purchase price' of the family's various properties, but were merely made 'by way of loan or gift out of family feeling'). See A Lawson, 'The things we do for love: detrimental reliance in the family home' (1996) 16 Legal Studies 218.
3   Unreported, Court of Appeal, 9 July 1985.
4   See also *Coombes v Smith* [1986] 1 WLR 808 at 820F–G; *Layton v Martin* [1986] 2 FLR 227 at 235H–236A; *Midland Bank Plc v Dobson* [1986] 1 FLR 171 at 177E. Compare the broader and more humane approach adopted by Sir Robin Cooke in the Judicial Committee of the Privy Council in *Maharaj v Chand* [1986] AC 898 at 907G ('in the absence of evidence to the contrary, the right inference is that the claimant acted in the belief that she (or he) would have an interest in the house and not merely out of love and affection'). See likewise *Peter v Beblow* (1993) 101 DLR (4th) 621 at 633g per Cory J.
5   [1991] 1 AC 107 at 131C–G.
6   A potent reminder of the 'solid tug of money' appears in Lord Bridge's comment that 'the monetary value of [the claimant's] work expressed as a contribution to a property acquired at a cost exceeding £70,000 must have been so trifling as to be almost de minimis' ([1991] 1 AC 107 at 131G). Compare the reference to improvements of 'an ephemeral character' in *Pettitt v Pettitt* [1970] AC 777 at 796E per Lord Reid.
7   Lord Bridge's dismissive approach is apparent in his observation that 'it would seem the most natural thing in the world for any wife, in the absence of her husband abroad, to spend all the time she could spare and to employ any skills she might have, such as the ability to decorate a room, in doing all she could to accelerate progress of the work quite irrespective of any expectation she might have of enjoying a beneficial interest in the property' ([1991] 1 AC 107 at 131E). Compare, however, the approach adopted in the Court of Appeal ([1989] Ch 350 at 381G–382A per Nicholls LJ).

A premium on rational calculation

10.136   The *Rosset* ruling reinforced 20 years of case law which, in the absence of clear understandings about the property consequences of personal relationships, had denied beneficial entitlement to longserving mothers and homemakers.[1] Criticism has long been directed at the injustice generated by the criterion of 'referability'.[2] In particular, it is plain that the application of this criterion penalises those lay persons who, in the confused circumstances of domestic life and financial pressure, fail to advert to the implications of property and financial dealings.[3] Correspondingly, an unfair advantage in legal terms is conferred on those who are either more calculating in the advancement of their own self-interest or more sophisticated in their ability to provide (or fabricate) evidence which seems to substantiate the claim that the detriment incurred by them was 'referable to' some agreement with the legal owner.[4]

1   See eg *Gissing v Gissing* [1971] AC 886 [**para 10.93**]; *Burns v Burns* [1984] Ch 317 [**para 10.128**].
2   See eg *Hargrave v Newton* [1971] 1 WLR 1611 at 1613A–B; *Hazell v Hazell* [1972] 1 WLR 301 at 304C–D. However, Lord Denning MR's suggestion in *Falconer v Falconer* [1970] 1 WLR 1333 at 1336D–E that mere expenditure without the requisite intention can raise a trust was

later rejected as inconsistent with *Gissing v Gissing* (see *Savva v Costa and Harymode Investments Ltd* (1981) 131 NLJ 1114 per Ormrod LJ).
3   See e g *McKeown v McKeown* [1975] NI 139 at 142C–D.
4   The force of these criticisms was indeed recognised by Lord Reid in *Gissing v Gissing* [1971] AC 886 at 897C–E. See also *Grant v Edwards* [1986] Ch 638 at 656B–D.

A more optimistic future

10.137   The English law of constructive trusts has not stood still during the last few years. Some of the value judgments which inform the law have doubtless changed over time and there has been an incremental movement towards a more liberal resolution of disputes centred on the family home. Such developments have not been uniform or consistent: current judicial philosophy is still caught somewhere between mild reformist zeal[1] and conservative adherence to the strictures of conventional trust doctrine.[2] But there are strong indications that the courts are increasingly embarrassed by the historic injustices perpetrated by the classical law of constructive trusts and are beginning to propel the law in a more positive direction.

1   See e g *Grant v Edwards* [1986] Ch 638; *Midland Bank plc v Cooke* [1995] 4 All ER 562 **[para 10.147]**; *Mortgage Corporation v Shaire* [2001] Ch 743; *Le Foe v Le Foe and Woolwich Plc* [2001] 2 FLR 970 at [52]–[53]; *Re Share (Lorraine)* [2002] 2 FLR 88 at [11]; *Oxley v Hiscock* [2004] 3 WLR 715 at [66]–[73].
2   See e g *Mollo v Mollo* [1999] EGCS 117; *Mehra v Shah* [2003] [2003] All ER (D) 15 (Aug) (affd [2004] EWCA Civ 632 at [64]); *McKenzie v McKenzie* [2003] EWHC 601 (Ch); *Buggs v Buggs* [2003] EWHC 1538 (Ch).

Clarification of the required common intention

10.138   An important breakthrough has come with the decision of the Court of Appeal in *Oxley v Hiscock*.[1] This case concerned a woman claimant who had made some financial contribution towards the purchase of a home vested at law in her partner, the parties having never articulated any express understanding as to their beneficial rights.[2] The male partner argued that the claimant should be confined to a resulting trust interest commensurate with her actual financial contribution (ie a share possibly in the region of 20 per cent). The Court of Appeal awarded the claimant a share of 40 per cent and, in the process, reviewed and rationalised several decades of case law on the constructive trust.

1   [2004] 3 WLR 715 (Chadwick LJ, Mance and Scott Baker LJJ concurring). Chadwick LJ emphasised (at [68]) that the Court's observations were primarily relevant to family homes vested at law in one partner, where both parties had made some financial contribution towards purchase without expressly declaring any trust.
2   [2004] 3 WLR 715 at [73].

10.139   The Court confirmed that where a constructive trust is allegedly based on evidence of the parties' conduct and dealings, an affirmative answer to the 'threshold' question of intention to share beneficially will 'readily be inferred' from the fact that each party has made some kind of financial contribution to the purchase of the asset.[1] In this way even a minimal financial contribution can afford evidence of the implied bargain or common intention which is required in order to trigger the creation of a constructive trust; and the court is not precluded from holding in favour of constructive trust merely because the parties are 'honest enough to admit that they never gave ownership a thought or reached any agreement about it.'[2] Nor is it any bar to the creation of an 'implied bargain' constructive trust that the parties' inferable common intention never involved any precise quantification of their respective equitable entitlements.[3] Once the gateway has been opened to a finding of *some* constructive trust for the claimant, the quantum of the parties' shares can be left to be determined by the court against the background of the parties' 'whole course of dealing ... in relation to the property.'[4] This approach, when applied in *Oxley v Hiscock*, therefore ensured that the parties' ultimate shares were not necessarily defined, on a strict resulting trust basis, by their money contributions to the purchase,[5] but were fixed by reference to a much broader range of factors.

1   [2004] 3 WLR 715 at [68] per Chadwick LJ.
2   *Midland Bank plc v Cooke* [1995] 4 All ER 562 at 575d per Waite LJ [**para 10.147**]. In Waite LJ's view, to leave a range of home-buyers 'beyond the pale of equity's assistance' would involve an abandonment of the historic calling of equity as a jurisdiction of conscience.
3   *Gissing v Gissing* [1971] AC 886 at 908D–G per Lord Diplock; *Drake v Whipp* [1996] 1 FLR 826 at 829H–830B per Peter Gibson LJ.
4   [2004] 3 WLR 715 at [73] per Chadwick LJ [**para 10.141**].
5   [2004] 3 WLR 715 at [60].

Requisite 'change of position'

10.140   The Court of Appeal's ruling in *Oxley v Hiscock* has eased the law of constructive trusts in several further respects.[1] It will be a rare domestic partner who cannot point to at least some minimal qualifying contribution of money towards the purchase of a house, thereby opening up the court's jurisdiction to award a larger share of beneficial ownership than that strictly commensurate with her money contribution. The days of the resulting trust may now, indeed, be truly numbered.[2] In a new era of almost universal access to the labour market for both sexes, a trust rule which is triggered by money payment operates, for once, in favour of financially disadvantaged partners, offering beneficial rewards disproportional to their financial outlay. The money contributions which trigger a finding of implied bargain also embrace a wide range of circumstances. Although counter-examples can always be found in the case law,[3] there is longstanding House of Lords authority for the proposition that money contributions 'referable to' the acquisition of land can include not merely ongoing payments of mortgage money,[4] but also the discharge of the general expenses of a shared household.[5] And, although the homemaker's intangible non-financial contribution to the welfare of the family still seems to be irrelevant to the 'threshold' question of intended beneficial sharing, a history of domestic performance and achievement is precisely the kind of consideration which becomes highly relevant at the secondary stage when the court is called upon to quantify the parties' respective beneficial shares in the light of their 'whole course of dealing'.

1   In *Oxley v Hiscock* it is significant, for example, that Chadwick LJ's own understanding of the law of constructive trusts contained not one reference to the vexed notion of 'referability'.
2   **[Para 10.21]**.
3   See e g *Mollo v Mollo* [1999] EGCS 117 (Transcript at [26]); *Mehra v Shah* [2003] All ER (D) 15 (Aug) at [48] (affd [2004] EWCA Civ 632 at [64]).
4   See *Gissing v Gissing* [1971] AC 886 at 908B–C per Lord Diplock ('regular and substantial direct contribution to the mortgage instalments'); *Lloyds Bank Plc v Rosset* [1991] 1 AC 107 at 133A per Lord Bridge of Harwich. The inference of common intention is even more readily made if evidence of uncovenanted mortgage payments is reinforced by evidence of contribution to the initial cash deposit or legal expenses (see *Gissing*, supra at 907F–G per Lord Diplock; *Burns v Burns* [1984] Ch 317 at 344G; *C v C* [1976] IR 254 at 258).
5   See *Gissing v Gissing* [1971] AC 886 at 909F per Lord Diplock ('an adjustment to [the claimant's] contribution to other expenses of the household which it can be inferred was referable to the acquisition of the house'). See also *Burns v Burns* [1984] Ch 317 at 328G–329B; *Allen v Snyder* [1977] 2 NSWLR 685 at 691B.

Quantification of beneficial entitlement

10.141   Whilst proof of some kind of financial contribution is required in order to trigger the claim of an 'implied bargain' constructive trust,[1] thereafter the respective money contributions of the parties are far from determinative of the proper inference of intention to be drawn from the parties' conduct.[2] Once the existence of a constructive trust has been established, the mandate of the court is to 'do its best to discover from the conduct of the [parties] whether any inference can reasonably be drawn as to the probable common understanding about the amount of the share' to be taken by the claimant.[3] For this purpose the court must undertake a survey of the 'whole of the course of dealing between the parties relevant to their ownership and occupation of the property and their sharing of its burdens and advantages.'[4] In all cases the extent of the claimant's interest is 'prima facie ... that which the parties intended',[5] but the court is not precluded from inferring the parties' intention by clear evidence that the parties neither discussed nor intended any agreement as to the proportions of their equitable interests.[6]

1   **[Para 10.132]**.
2   See *Re Share (Lorraine)* [2002] 2 FLR 88 at [11] per Patten J.
3   *Gissing v Gissing* [1971] AC 886 at 908F per Lord Diplock.
4   *Midland Bank plc v Cooke* [1995] 4 All ER 562 at 574c–e per Waite LJ. It is recognised nowadays that 'all payments made and acts done by the claimant are to be treated as illuminating the common intention as to the extent of the beneficial interest' (*Stokes v Anderson* [1991] 1 FLR 391 at 400B per Nourse LJ).
5   *Grant v Edwards* [1986] Ch 638 at 657F–G per Browne-Wilkinson V-C. See similarly *Oxley v Hiscock* [2004] 3 WLR 715 at [73] per Chadwick LJ.
6   *Midland Bank plc v Cooke* [1995] 4 All ER 562 at 575j per Waite LJ; *Oxley v Hiscock* [2004] 3 WLR 715 at [65] per Chadwick LJ.

The judicial role

10.142   It is frequently said that, in relation to the quantification of beneficial entitlement, each case 'must depend upon its own facts.'[1] The judicial task is difficult. There has always been resistance to the idea that the court's role is to sit 'as under a palm tree, to exercise a general discretion to do what the man in the street, on a general overview of the case, might regard as fair.'[2] The judge does not have 'some sort of roving commission' to fix beneficial shares[3] and is certainly not invested with any power to reallocate these shares between disputants on the model of the discretionary exercise mandated by divorce legislation. Yet it has become painfully obvious in recent years that the inference of intended beneficial ownership almost inevitably collapses back into something approaching an assessment of fair outcome.

1   *Gissing v Gissing* [1971] AC 886 at 907A per Lord Diplock. See also *Mortgage Corporation v Shaire* [2001] Ch 743 at 754E per Neuberger J.
2   *Springette v Defoe* [1992] 2 FLR 388 at 393D per Dillon LJ. See likewise *Huntingford v Hobbs* [1993] 1 FCR 45 at 53F per Sir Christopher Slade.
3   *Mortgage Corporation v Shaire* [2001] Ch 743 at 755F–G per Neuberger J.

A 'fair presumed basis' for the sharing of beneficial title

10.143   The sheer unreality involved in the divination of a common intention supposedly implicit in half a lifetime of inarticulate dealings is evidenced in the way in which the courts often grudgingly concede that there is 'no practicable alternative to the determination of a fair share.'[1] As Nourse LJ expressed it in *Stokes v Anderson*,[2] the court must 'supply the common intention by reference to that which all the material circumstances have shown to be fair.'[3] Thus not only does the court 'construct' a trust in order to frustrate unconscionable dealing; the court may even 'construct' the intended entitlements to which the trust then gives effect.

1   *Stokes v Anderson* [1991] 1 FLR 391 at 400B–C per Nourse LJ. See also *Gissing v Gissing* [1971] AC 886 at 909D–E per Lord Diplock.
2   [1991] 1 FLR 391 at 400B–C per Nourse LJ.
3   See likewise *Mortgage Corporation v Shaire* [2001] Ch 743 at 750G per Neuberger J; *Allen v Rochdale BC* [2000] Ch 221 at 232D–E per Morritt LJ.

A new equity?

10.144   In *Midland Bank plc v Cooke*,[1] Waite LJ undisguisedly advocated a resort to 'general equitable principles' in formulating a 'fair presumed basis for the sharing of beneficial title.'[2] It thus seems to be open to the court to be 'reasonably broad-brush in the approach'[3] adopted in calculating the relevant proportions of beneficial entitlement behind the 'implied bargain' constructive trust.[4] In *Oxley v Hiscock*,[5] the Court of Appeal, whilst accepting that this solution was not easily reconciled with a 'traditional, property-based, approach', finally surrendered to the inevitable and acknowledged that each party 'is entitled to that share which the court thinks fair having regard to the whole course of dealing between them in relation to the property.'[6]

1   [1995] 4 All ER 562 at 575d–j.

2   See also *Grant v Edwards* [1986] Ch 638 at 657G–658A per Browne-Wilkinson V-C ('equity ... displayed at its most flexible').

3   *Mollo v Mollo* [1999] EGCS 117 (Transcript at [41]). For further reference to the 'broad-brush approach', see *Passee v Passee* [1988] 1 FLR 263 at 271H per Nicholls LJ; *Drake v Whipp* [1996] 1 FLR 826 at 830C–D per Peter Gibson LJ; *Oxley v Hiscock* [2004] 3 WLR 715 at [65] per Chadwick LJ.

4   In *McHardy & Sons v Warren* [1994] 2 FLR 338 at 340E, the Court of Appeal held that a parent's payment of a deposit on the purchase of a matrimonial home for a bride and groom leads irresistibly to an inference that it was intended by all three that the spouses should have equal shares in the entire beneficial interest (and not merely some proportion measured by the ratio of the deposit to the full purchase price).

5   [2004] 3 WLR 715 at [69]–[70], [73] per Chadwick LJ.

6   See also *Drake v Whipp* [1996] 1 FLR 826 at 831G per Peter Gibson LJ.

An arbitrary discretion?

10.145   The new emphasis in this area upon the dictates of conscience effectively means that, in cases involving disputed entitlements in the family home, 'the time has come to accept that there is no difference in outcome ... whether the true analysis lies in constructive trust or in proprietary estoppel.'[1] Yet there remains a real danger that the endorsement of a generalised culture of 'fair' adjudications of entitlement will not only spawn litigation, but will also introduce an excessive element of uncertainty or of arbitrary (and effectively unappealable) judgment into a field of law which is already unduly complex and unpredictable.

1   *Oxley v Hiscock* [2004] 3 WLR 715 at [71] per Chadwick LJ. See similarly *Chan Pui Chun v Leung Kam Ho* [2003] 1 FLR 23 at [91] per Jonathan Parker LJ.

Relevant factors

10.146   In quantifying the parties' beneficial entitlements in accordance with their inferred common intentions, the court must obviously have regard to the circumstances of each individual case. The 'fair result' may well not be *equal* beneficial ownership.[1] This is not a context in which the maxim 'equality is equity' can be applied 'unthinkingly'.[2] This maxim is a 'fall-back presumption' to be used merely 'at the last resort.'[3] Only if it is wholly impossible to ascertain the intended quantum of entitlement will the court rely on the equitable maxim for the conclusion that beneficial ownership belongs to the relevant parties in equal shares.[4] The recognition of disparate fractions of beneficial ownership may be just as common[5] and it is not impossible that beneficial entitlement may take the form of a life interest.[6]

1   *Oxley v Hiscock* [2004] 3 WLR 715 at [72] per Chadwick LJ. See, however, the equal shares awarded in *Grant v Edwards* [1986] Ch 638 at 651A, 654B, 658A; *Hammond v Mitchell* [1991] 1 WLR 1127 at 1137F–G.

2   *Hammond v Mitchell* [1991] 1 WLR 1127 at 1137F per Waite J. See also *Gissing v Gissing* [1971] AC 886 at 897B per Lord Reid, 903A–B per Lord Hodson; *McFarlane v McFarlane* [1972] NI 59 at 67.

3   *Mortgage Corporation v Shaire* [2001] Ch 743 at 750H, 751E per Neuberger J.

capital money arising on a disposition does not point unequivocally towards equality of entitlement, being no less consistent with a mere concern to facilitate sale of the property after the death of one ([2001] Ch 743 at 752G–753D).

Personal misconduct

10.150   The circumstances or conduct which brought about the breakdown of a personal relationship 'cannot be relevant in principle to the basis of calcula-tion.'[1] The only exceptions to the general irrelevance of misconduct arise in respect of marginal adjustments over mortgage payments[2] and where it is alleged that the claimant was coerced by domestic violence to agree to abandon her interest in the property.[3]

1   *Huntingford v Hobbs* [1993] 1 FCR 45 at 61E–F.
2   [**Para 11.46**].
3   See *Skelding v Hanson* [1992] NPC 148 per Dillon LJ.

THE FUTURE OF THE CONSTRUCTIVE TRUST

10.151   In view of the difficulties posed by traditional applications of trust doctrine, a powerful argument has emerged, across the common law world, that social justice is better served by the abandonment of any search for phantoms of common intention as the essential basis of trust entitlement.[1] During the past 35 years this doctrinal shift has led, in many jurisdictions, to the recogni-tion of a concept of 'remedial' constructive trust which breaks away decisively from the strictures of the constructive trust as an 'institutional' device.[2] In varying forms this free-ranging doctrine of trust entitlement has infiltrated a number of legal systems.[3]

1   See Gray, 'The Law of Trusts and the Quasi-Matrimonial Home' [1983] CLJ 30 at 33. See *Hayward v Giordani* [1983] NZLR 140 at 145 per Cooke J; *Stratulatos v Stratulatos* [1988] 2 NZLR 424 at 436 per McGechan J.
2   See *Avondale Printers & Stationers Ltd v Haggie* [1979] 2 NZLR 124 at 147 per Mahon J. In *Westdeutsche Landesbank Girozentrale v Islington LBC* [1996] AC 669 at 714H, Lord Browne-Wilkinson spoke of the remedial constructive trust as 'a judicial remedy giving rise to an enforceable equitable obligation.'
3   See Gray, 'Property in Common Law Systems', in G E van Maanen and A J van der Walt (ed), *Property Law on the Threshold of the 21st Century* (MAKLU, Antwerp, 1996), pp 243, 258–260.

Unjust enrichment

10.152   in North America the general inadequacy of the orthodox common law approach to family property catalysed a much more general revolution of property analysis and ideology. From the 1960s onwards an almost irresistible pressure for reform in the family context triggered a reformulation of trust law, the net effect of which was to realign the distribution of equitable property entitlements more closely with informed social perceptions of fair outcome.

This new approach found its roots in the elaboration by the courts of the United States, during earlier decades and in more commercial contexts, of leading concepts of good faith and unjust enrichment. These ideas were increasingly given effect through widespread resort to the constructive trust as an overtly remedial mechanism.[1]

1   See *Chase Manhattan Bank NA v Israel-British Bank (London) Ltd* [1981] Ch 105 at 126G–127D; *Simmonds v Simmonds*, 408 NYS2d 359 at 362–365 (1978). See also J L Dewar, 'The Development of the Remedial Constructive Trust' (1982) 60 CBR 265; Craig Rotherham, 'The Contribution Interest in Quasi-Matrimonial Property Disputes' (1991) 4 Canterbury L Rev 407.

A general discretionary power

10.153   Remedial constructive trusts do not depend on the parties' intentions, but provide the court with a general discretionary power to remedy or counter-act broadly defined instances of 'unjust enrichment'.[1] The concept of unjust enrichment operates, in effect, as a third source of civil obligation ranking alongside, but still rather distinct from, contract and tort. Under the remedial constructive trust the court subjects a person holding title to property to an equitable duty to convey it to, or to hold it on trust for, another on the ground that the current title holder would be 'unjustly enriched' if he were permitted to retain the property beneficially.[2]

1   See *Rawluk v Rawluk* (1990) 65 DLR (4th) 161 at 169h–170a per Cory J; *Soulos v Korkontzilas* (1997) 146 DLR (4th) 214 at 222f–g per McLachlin J.
2   The American *Restatement of Restitution* provides that 'a person who has been unjustly enriched at the expense of another is required to make restitution to that other' (¶1). Likewise, where 'a person holding title to property is subject to an equitable duty to convey it to another on the ground that he would be unjustly enriched if he were permitted to retain it, a constructive trust arises' (¶160). See also A W Scott, (1955) 71 LQR 39, *Scott on Trusts* (4th edn by W F Fratcher, Boston and Toronto 1989), Vol V, ¶462 (p 304), ¶462.1 (pp 310–311).

Reception in common law jurisdictions

10.154   The remedial perspective of the constructive trust based on 'unjust enrichment' is not without respectable antecedents,[1] but its importance lies nowadays in the fact that it has stimulated a remarkable loosening up of property concepts throughout the common law world.

1   See eg *Moses v Macferlan* (1760) 2 Burr 1005 at 1012, 97 ER 676 at 681 per Lord Mansfield (referring to obligations arising from 'the ties of natural justice and equity').

Canadian developments

10.155   By the late 1970s liberalised doctrines of constructive trust had begun to infiltrate the Canadian law of family property. In *Rathwell v Rathwell*[1] the Supreme Court of Canada invoked the concept of the remedial constructive trust in order to confer a half-share in the matrimonial property on a wife who had made substantial domestic contributions to the marriage partnership. In the words of Dickson J, such a trust

> comprehends the imposition of trust machinery by the Court in order to achieve a result consonant with good conscience. As a matter of principle, the Court will not allow any man to appropriate to himself the value earned by the labours of another. That principle is not defeated by the existence of a matrimonial relationship between the parties; but, for the principle to succeed, the facts must display an enrichment, a corresponding deprivation, and the absence of any juristic reason – such as a contract or disposition of law – for the enrichment.[2]

1   (1978) 83 DLR (3d) 289.
2   (1978) 83 DLR (3d) 289 at 306. For confirmation of these three constitutive elements of the 'unjust enrichment' constructive trust, see *Sorochan v Sorochan* (1986) 29 DLR (4th) 1 at 5 per Dickson CJC; *Peter v Beblow* (1993) 101 DLR (4th) 621 at 627a–b per Cory J, 643c per McLachlin J; *Soulos v Korkontzilas* (1997) 146 DLR (4th) 214 at 222g–h per McLachlin J; *Shannon v Gidden* (1999) 178 DLR (4th) 395 at 403; *Wilcox v Wilcox* (2000) 190 DLR (4th) 324 at [41]–[46].

10.156   The Supreme Court of Canada later extended the remedial constructive trust to provide similar beneficial entitlements for quasi-matrimonial partners who had contributed substantial effort towards a family business[1] or as a homemaker and mother.[2] As McLachlin J recognised in *Soulos v Korkontzilas*,[3] a constructive trust may be imposed on grounds of 'good conscience' wherever a defendant would be 'unjustly enriched to the plaintiff's detriment by being permitted to keep the property for himself.'

1   *Pettkus v Becker* (1980) 117 DLR (3d) 257. See M Welstead, (1987) 2 Denning LJ 151. In terms which closely resembled the language of proprietary estoppel, Dickson J noted that 'where one person in a relationship tantamount to spousal prejudices herself in the reasonable expectation of receiving an interest in property and the other person in the relationship freely accepts benefits conferred by the first person in circumstances where he knows or ought to have known of that reasonable expectation, it would be unjust to allow the recipient of the benefit to retain it' ((1980) 117 DLR (3d) 257 at 274).
2   *Sorochan v Sorochan* (1986) 29 DLR (4th) 1. Dickson CJC acknowledged that the claimant's unwaged domestic endeavour had clearly conferred a 'benefit' upon her partner, resulting in a corresponding 'deprivation' to herself ((1986) 29 DLR (4th) 1 at 6–7). There being no 'juristic reason' in the form of any obligation (contractual or otherwise) to perform such household services, the claimant was awarded a constructive trust of part of her de facto husband's land plus a money sum of $20,000. See also *Rawluk v Rawluk* (1990) 65 DLR (4th) 161 at 169–172 per Cory J; *Peter v Beblow* (1993) 101 DLR (4th) 621 at 633–635 per Cory J, 646–649 per McLachlin J.
3   (1997) 146 DLR (4th) 214 at 227h.

10.157   Such articulations of constructive trust theory mark a considerable extension of the potential liability of the owner of a legal estate.[1] If the operation of traditional trust law is triggered essentially by contributions of money, the constructive trust based on unjust enrichment is activated by an acknowledgement of the value conferred by more general dedications of effort or labour (particularly within the family context).[2] The orthodox theory of the constructive trust and the doctrine of proprietary estoppel are both largely dominated by the inquiry whether 'detriment' has been incurred by the contributor. By contrast, the remedial constructive trust, by giving palpable recognition to the property which men and women have in their own labour, places a more obvious and realistic emphasis on the element of 'benefit' conferred by that labour.[3] It is often the case that an emphasis on *benefit conferred* (rather than *detriment suffered*) more accurately reveals the true value of the respective contributions made in the context of family arrangements.[4]

1   There is, for instance, no need to relate specific contributions to particular assets (see *Nuti v Nuti* (1980) 108 DLR (3d) 587 at 603, (1982) 122 DLR (3d) 384), although the constructive trust may produce merely a money remedy for the claimant in the absence of some 'special link' between her efforts and the property in dispute (see *Peter v Beblow* (1993) 101 DLR (4th) 621 at 649f–650f per McLachlin J).

2   See e g *Peter v Beblow* (1993) 101 DLR (4th) 621 at 647g–h per McLachlin J.

3   See, however, *L (L) v B (M)* (2003) 231 DLR (4th) 665 at [31], [38]–[39] where the Quebec Court of Appeal held that, in the light of the Canadian Supreme Court's recent emphasis on the importance of couples' freedom of choice in deciding not to enter the statutory marital property regime, the unjust enrichment principle would not necessarily lead to equal sharing of gains by unmarried cohabitants (see *Nova Scotia (Attorney General) v Walsh* (2002) 221 DLR (4th) 1 [**para 10.94**]).

4   See e g *Wylie v Leclair* (2003) 226 DLR (4th) 439 at [13]–[14], [20], where the Ontario Court of Appeal stressed the importance of 'value received'.

Antipodean developments

10.158   The lead of the Canadian jurisdictions was soon followed elsewhere in the common law world.[1] Trust doctrine in Australia and New Zealand has nowadays shifted sharply away from its orthodox point of departure in English law. During the 1980s the Australian courts began to elaborate a versatile jurisprudence of 'unconscionability' in the resolution of claims of beneficial entitlement.[2] In the High Court of Australia in *Muschinski v Dodds*[3] Deane J took the view that

> in its modern context, the constructive trust can properly be described as a remedial institution which equity imposes regardless of actual or presumed agreement or intention (and subsequently protects) to preclude the retention or assertion of beneficial ownership of property to the extent that such retention or assertion would be contrary to equitable principle.[4]

1   See Marcia Neave, 'Three Approaches to Family Property Disputes – Intention/Belief, Unjust Enrichment and Unconscionability', in T G Youdan (ed), *Equity, Fiduciaries and Trusts* (Agincourt, Ontario 1989), p 247.

2   In *Baumgartner v Baumgartner* (1987) 164 CLR 137 at 152–153, Toohey J went so far as to suggest that 'unconscionable conduct' and 'unjust enrichment' approaches might well be but component – if not identical – aspects of a unifying legal concept of restitution. See also *Gillies v Keogh* [1989] 2 NZLR 327 at 343 per Richardson J; *Woodson (Sales) Pty Ltd v Woodson (Aust) Pty Ltd* (1996) 7 BPR 14685 at 14708–14709 per Santow J; Paul Finn, 'Commerce, The Common Law and Morality' (1989) 17 Melbourne ULR 87 at 89.

3   (1985) 160 CLR 583 at 614.

4   This recognition of the constructive trust as a remedial device did not, however, mean that it

'represents a medium for the indulgence of idiosyncratic notions of fairness and justice.' Deane J insisted that the remedy was available 'only when warranted by established equitable principles or by the legitimate processes of legal reasoning, by analogy, induction and deduction, from the starting point of a proper understanding of the conceptual foundation of such principles' ((1985) 160 CLR 583 at 615). See also *Stowe v Stowe* (1995) 15 WAR 363 at 372A–F.

10.159   For Deane J the relevant equitable principle was one which operates 'where the substratum of a joint relationship or endeavour is removed without attributable blame and where the benefit of money or other property contributed by one party on the basis and for the purposes of the relationship or endeavour would otherwise be enjoyed by the other party in circumstances in which it was not specifically intended or specially provided that that other party should so enjoy it.' In such cases, said Deane J, 'equity will not permit that other party to assert or retain the benefit of the relevant property to the extent that it would be unconscionable for him to do so.'[1] This judicial initiative has now been formalised by the introduction, in most Australian jurisdictions, of a statutory discretion vested in the court to do that which is 'just and equitable' in adjudicating the property rights of de facto couples, having reference, inter alia, to the parties' financial and domestic contributions.[2]

1   (1985) 160 CLR 583 at 620, citing *Atwood v Maude* (1868) 3 Ch App 369 at 374–375; *Lyon v Tweddell* (1881) 17 Ch D 529 at 531. This approach was soon applied in *Baumgartner v Baumgartner* (1987) 164 CLR 137 at 149, where the High Court of Australia held that the legal owner's assertion of exclusive beneficial title amounted to 'unconscionable conduct which attracts the intervention of equity and the imposition of a constructive trust'. (The claimant was awarded a 45 per cent share in the disputed property, this share reflecting the proportions in which the parties' respective earnings had been mixed in the common pool.)
2   See eg Property (Relationships) Act 1984 (New South Wales), s 20 (effective June 1999); Property Law Act 1958 (Victoria), s 285 (effective June 2001); Domestic Relationships Act 1994 (ACT), s 15(1).

10.160   New Zealand courts have likewise adapted the constructive trust, substantially relaxing the conditions of beneficial entitlement to accord with a more fundamental equity in property relationships. In *Gillies v Keogh*,[1] the New Zealand Court of Appeal rejected the notion that constructive trusts arise only on the basis of 'the actual subjective intention of the parties'.[2] Cooke P noted the practical nexus between constructive trust, unjust enrichment, imputed common intention and estoppel.[3] Accordingly, he was quite prepared to counteract the unjust enrichment reaped where one party claims to retain 'the entire fruits of contributions made by the other' if that other has 'suffered detriment or made a sacrifice and has reasonably expected ... that the contributions will carry rights.' In Cooke P's view such one-sided retention of benefit is so 'manifestly unfair' as to attract equity's historic jurisdiction 'to interfere where the assertion of strict legal rights is ... unconscionable.'[4] The New Zealand courts have since constructed a jurisprudence of trust entitlement based on the 'reasonable expectation' of both owner and claimant, reinforced by direct or indirect contributions of either a monetary or non-monetary kind, that the claimant should have an interest in the disputed property.[5] Denial of a claim under these circumstances is 'unconscionable' and the courts impose a constructive trust accordingly.[6] Using a wide concept of contribution,[7] the New Zealand courts have applied this approach, irrespective of the gender of the parties,[8] to all kinds of domestic relationship. The New Zealand initiative has now culminated in a new statutory rule of presumptive equal entitlement in the context of almost all forms of domestic partnership.[9]

1   [1989] 2 NZLR 327 at 332. See (1990) 106 LQR 213 (M Bryan).
2   See *Hayward v Giordani* [1983] NZLR 140 at 148, where Cooke J had found the approach of the Canadian Supreme Court 'very helpful … in working out the property rights of common law spouses' and indicated that it seemed 'only a small step to eliminate the need to strain for proof of common intention.' See also *Stratulatos v Stratulatos* [1988] 2 NZLR 424 at 436 per McGechan J.
3   [1989] 2 NZLR 327 at 330. See likewise *Depew v Wilkes* (2000) 193 DLR (4th) 529 at [54]–[58].
4   [1989] 2 NZLR 327 at 331.
5   See *Lankow v Rose* [1995] 1 NZLR 277 at 294 per Tipping J. 'Whatever legal label or rubric cases in this field are placed under, reasonable expectations in the light of the conduct of the parties are at the heart of the matter' (*Gillies v Keogh* [1989] 2 NZLR 327 at 331 per Cooke P). See also *Ball v Fawcett* [1997] 1 NZLR 743 at 745–746; *Kendon v Richards* [2000] NZFLR 353 at 360; *Farrelly v Gruar* [2000] NZFLR 694 at 697, 702–703. For further reference to the close link with Canadian jurisprudence, see *Lankow v Rose* [1995] 1 NZLR 277 at 282 per Hardie Boys J.
6   There is a ready presumption of 'expectation' of entitlement in the circumstances of a shared family life (see e g *Stubbs v Holmes* [1999] NZFLR 780 at 789), but a remedial constructive trust may be much more difficult to establish in the commercial sphere (see *Gillies v Keogh* [1989] 2 NZLR 327 at 333 per Cooke P, 348–349 per Casey J).
7   See *Lankow v Rose* [1995] 1 NZLR 277 at 294 per Tipping J; *King v Church* [2002] NZFLR 555 at [33] per Baragwanath J ('the different contributions are complementary and of equal worth').
8   See e g *Giltrap v Horsfield* [2000] NZFLR 1047 at [21] (22 year platonic relationship); *King v Church* [2002] NZFLR 555 at [18]–[21], [33] (same-sex couple).
9   Property (Relationships) Act 1976 (New Zealand), ss 11–15, as amended with effect from February 2002.

Possible directions for English law

10.161 Although broad principles of restitution for unjust enrichment are beginning to be accepted by English courts in other contexts,[1] there is still a considerable reluctance to introduce anything resembling the remedial constructive trust.[2] Such trusts appear, at least to the conservatively minded, to confer on the courts a novel discretion to vary property rights in a manner completely unsanctioned by parliamentary authority.[3] In *Re Polly Peck International Plc (No 2)*,[4] Nourse LJ emphasised that the courts have no 'inherent jurisdiction to vary … beneficial interests' in property.[5] Lord Browne-Wilkinson likewise indicated that, in his view, there are 'great dangers in seeking to turn equity into one comprehensive law of unjust enrichment based on some sweeping fundamental concept.'[6] Yet it has been painfully clear over the last two or three decades that the courts' resistance to more liberal variants of trust doctrine, coupled with the stern reassertion of orthodoxy expressed in *Lloyds Bank Plc v Rosset*,[7] has isolated English law from the leading edge of the developing common law of property. Recent trends in other Commonwealth jurisdictions have plainly given English lawyers much to ponder.[8] Speaking extra-judicially in 1991, Lord Browne-Wilkinson expressed the belief that 'the law took a wrong turning in *Gissing v Gissing*' and that 'the law of constructive and resulting trusts has been distorted'.[9] In his opinion, there is now a need for a 'rethink' of the common intention constructive trusts 'invented' in *Gissing's* case.[10] Amongst the possible directions of future reform are the following.

1   See e g *Westdeutsche Landesbank Girozentrale v Islington LBC* [1996] AC 669; *Kleinwort Benson Ltd v Lincoln CC* [1999] 2 AC 349.
2   See *Pettitt v Pettitt* [1970] AC 777 at 795G–H per Lord Reid; *Re Sharpe (A Bankrupt)* [1980] 1 WLR 219 at 225G per Browne-Wilkinson J ('a novel concept in English law').
3   In its most extreme form the remedial constructive trust concentrates the court's focus, not upon unconscionability of *conduct*, but upon unconscionability of *outcome*. Emphasis on an 'unconscionable outcome' approach involves the imposition of a constructive trust wherever the end result of parties' mutual dealings produces an imbalance in the parties' proprietary rights which is considered unacceptable to the conscience of equity. It is a large question whether such a far-reaching doctrine is ultimately sustainable as a principled approach to the resolution of property disputes in either the commercial or the familial context (see Gray, 'Property in Common Law Systems', in G E van Maanen and A J van der Walt (ed), *Property Law on the Threshold of the 21st Century* (MAKLU, Antwerp, 1996), pp 259–260).
4   [1998] 3 All ER 812 at 831a–b, 832d–f.
5   See also *Chapman v Chapman* [1954] AC 429 at 444–445 per Lord Simonds LC.
6   (1996) 10 Trust Law International 98 at 101.
7   [1991] 1 AC 107.
8   See e g M P Thompson, 'Reform of the Law Relating to Property Rights on the Breakdown of Cohabitation', in P Jackson and D C Wilde (ed), *Contemporary Property Law* (Ashgate 1999), p 120.
9   'Constructive Trusts and Unjust Enrichment' (1996) 10 Trust Law International 98 at 100. Browne-Wilkinson pointed out that the members of the House of Lords sitting on *Gissing v Gissing* did not include an equity or property lawyer. Lord Upjohn, who had sat on *Pettitt v Pettitt* [1970] AC 777, died on 27 January 1971, six weeks before the House of Lords' hearing in *Gissing*.
10   (1996) 10 Trust Law International 98 at 99. See also S Gardner, 'Rethinking Family Property' (1993) 109 LQR 263, 'Fin de Siècle chez *Gissing v Gissing*' (1996) 112 LQR 378.

Adaptation of estoppel principles

10.162   Although English courts have shown a profound reluctance to embrace any over-broad formula for change, it has been suggested that the law of unjust enrichment and restitution should be developed 'incrementally' and that the trust doctrine expounded in *Gissing v Gissing* could 'with advantage' be refashioned on the guiding analogy of the principles of proprietary estoppel.[1] Such a redirection of the law of trusts, it has been argued, could confer enormous benefit in terms of flexibility of judicial response and the need to accommodate emerging solutions to the legitimate claims of third parties. With the recent decision of the Court of Appeal in *Oxley v Hiscock*,[2] there are clear indications that a move in this direction has already occurred.

1   Browne-Wilkinson, (1996) 10 Trust Law International 98 at 100. See, similarly, *Gillies v Keogh* [1989] 2 NZLR 327 at 346 per Richardson J, but compare *Stokes v Anderson* [1991] 1 FLR 391 at 399C–D per Nourse LJ; *Hyett v Stanley* [2003] WTLR 1269 at [27] per Sir Martin Nourse.
2   [2004] 3 WLR 715 **[para 10.138]**.

Infiltration of guiding concepts of fairness

10.163 Recent case law has disclosed a spontaneous infiltration of factors of 'fairness' in the implementation of trusts of the family home. In allowing beneficial shares to be quantified in accordance with 'imputed' common intentions,[1] the English Court of Appeal has all but returned to the approach adumbrated by Lord Reid in *Pettitt v Pettitt*[2] and *Gissing v Gissing*.[3] Here Lord Reid, a lone voice in the House of Lords, urged that the courts be free to impute to family members a 'deemed intention' with respect to beneficial ownership based on the likely intentions of reasonable persons. Lord Reid made clear his sense of disquiet with any requirement of actual or inferred common intention as the necessary foundation of beneficial entitlement, noting that, if such a requirement were held to be good law, he himself 'could not contemplate the future results of such a decision with equanimity.'[4] It seems that Lord Reid's prognosis has been proved broadly correct.[5]

1   See e g *Stokes v Anderson* [1991] 1 FLR 391 at 400D per Nourse LJ; *Midland Bank plc v Cooke* [1995] 4 All ER 562 at 574f, 575d–j; *Allen v Rochdale BC* [2000] Ch 221 at 232D–E; *Oxley v Hiscock* [2004] 3 WLR 715 at [68]–[71].
2   [1970] AC 777 at 795C–G.
3   [1971] AC 886 at 897C–G.
4   *Gissing v Gissing* [1971] AC 886 at 897G. In *Pasi v Kamana* [1986] 1 NZLR 603 at 605, Cooke P doubted whether there was any 'significant difference' between Lord Reid's deemed common intention and the unjust enrichment concept used by the Supreme Court of Canada. 'Unconscionability, constructive or equitable fraud, Lord Denning's "justice and good conscience" and "in all fairness": at bottom in this context these are probably different formulae for the same idea ... One way of putting the test is to ask whether a reasonable person in the shoes of the claimant would have understood that his or her efforts would naturally result in an interest in the property.' See also *Stratulatos v Stratulatos* [1988] 2 NZLR 424 at 437 per McGechan J; *Gillies v Keogh* [1989] 2 NZLR 327 at 340 per Cooke P.
5   See now *Oxley v Hiscock* [2004] 3 WLR 715 at [65]–[66] per Chadwick LJ.

A statutory regime for home-sharers

10.164 It was at one stage hoped that the Law Commission would propose a special statutory regime for the resolution of the property problems of de facto partners and other home-sharers. Such a regime, loosely framed on the analogy of the reallocative jurisdiction applicable on divorce, would undoubtedly have liberated certain areas of trust law from the limitations imposed by current case law. On the other hand there is always some danger that a discretionary redistribution of property rights between home-sharers could disintegrate into an unprincipled wilderness of single instances, overladen with uncertainty and ever-present incentives towards oppressive out-of-court bargaining or ruinously expensive litigation. As it happens, the Law Commission announced in 2002 that, in view of the 'infinitely variable circumstances' affecting home-sharers, it had abandoned the task of constructing a special statutory regime for the property problems of de facto partners.[1] The outcome is disappointing, not least because this objective has proved eminently achievable in Australia and New Zealand, but it is clear that for the immediate future the initiative in England has been left to the courts.

1   Law Commission, *Sharing Homes: A Discussion Paper* (July 2002), paras 1.27–1.31, 3.100,
     Part VI.

Modified remedial mechanisms

10.165   Some indication of the possible direction of future change is also
evident in recent trends in the comparative law of trusts. Courts in other
common law jurisdictions have made it clear that remedial models based on
unjust enrichment or unconscionability can be developed with a flexibility
which displaces much conventional concern over their potentially oppressive
impact.

A new minimalist perspective

10.166   It is beginning to be recognised, in at least some jurisdictions, that the
function of remedial mechanisms is properly confined to the more modest
objective of neutralising or alleviating the conscience-based concerns of equity
rather than aiming at the achievement of a social justice which the parties have
signally failed to secure by more explicit means.[1] In *Hogan v Baseden*,[2] for
example, Stein JA emphasised in the New South Wales Court of Appeal that,
where it is 'unconscionable for a person to take the whole beneficial ownership
without recognising a contribution of some other party, equity orders the
minimal relief necessary to relieve the conscience of the legal owner.' Accordingly there is now an increasing acceptance that, in certain cases, the appropriate remedy may fall short of the award of some defined fraction of beneficial
entitlement in the disputed land (or even of any 'possessory property right' in
that land[3]), and may instead involve an order for payment to the successful
claimant of a liquidated sum of money.[4] The use of constructive trust principles to raise an obligation sounding only in money provides a flexibility which
crucially enables the court to prevent the imposition of any unjust impact on
innocent third parties.[5]

1   See eg *L (L) v B (M)* (2003) 231 DLR (4th) 665 at [31]–[39] (Quebec Court of Appeal).
2   (1997) 8 BPR 15723 at 15726.
3   *Rawluk v Rawluk* (1990) 65 DLR (4th) 161 at 185g–h per McLachlin J.
4   See eg *Peter v Beblow* (1993) 101 DLR (4th) 621 at 640b–g per Cory J, 649c–650f per
     McLachlin J (Supreme Court of Canada) and *Giumelli v Giumelli* (1999) 196 CLR 101 at [10],
     [50], [65] (High Court of Australia).
5   See *Soulos v Korkontzilas* (1997) 146 DLR (4th) 214 at 227c–d per McLachlin J.

Diminished impact on third parties

10.167   A further protection for third parties appears in a new judicial
willingness to frame the constructive trust remedy (of whatever kind) so that
'the consequences of its imposition are operative only from the date of
judgment or formal court order' rather than from any earlier date which might

result in prejudice to unsuspecting third parties.[1] Such curtailment of the impact of trust remedies was always implicit, in any event, in the 'unconscionability' doctrine developed by the Australian courts. A trust interest generated against one party on the footing of 'unconscionability' has no dogmatically predetermined or inexorable impact on any other party. Ironically the precise reverse may indeed be true. If the binding effect of jural claims is subjected to an overriding test of unconscionability, it may turn out in many circumstances to be unconscionable for a beneficiary under a remedial constructive trust to assert priority over the trustee's creditor or purchaser.[2]

1   *Muschinski v Dodds* (1985) 160 CLR 583 at 615 per Deane J. This restriction on the application of the constructive trust has been urged as one means of enabling English courts to adopt a more liberal view of the remedial function of trust doctrine (see (1996) 10 Trust Law International 98 at 100). Indeed, in *Westdeutsche Landesbank Girozentrale v Islington LBC* [1996] AC 669 at 714H–715A, Lord Browne-Wilkinson, in describing overseas exemplars of the remedial constructive trust, attached significance to the way in which the court retains a discretion to determine 'the extent to which it operates retrospectively to the prejudice of third parties.'
2   See e g *Re Osborn* (1989) 91 ALR 135 at 141–142 per Pincus J (Federal Court of Australia).

PROPRIETARY ESTOPPEL

10.168   The law relating to proprietary estoppel provides a further means, closely allied to the constructive trust, by which rights in land may be created informally.[1] Whereas the conventional law of the constructive trust places its primary emphasis on *bargains* in respect of beneficial ownership, the principle of proprietary estoppel focuses on *representations* which generate expectations of proprietary entitlement. First adumbrated by the courts over a century ago, the doctrine of proprietary estoppel has come to play an increasingly important role in the law of real property. The last 30 years have seen the emergence of a new 'equity' based on estoppel which, although its juristic basis remains ill-defined,[2] has helped to reshape the notion of proprietary rights in land and may, in some respects, comprise a form of restitution for unjust enrichment.[3]

1   See generally Mark Pawlowski, *The Doctrine of Proprietary Estoppel* (London 1996).
2   See *Re Sharpe (A Bankrupt)* [1980] 1 WLR 219 at 223D per Browne-Wilkinson J.
3   See *Sledmore v Dalby* (1996) 72 P & CR 196 at 208 per Hobhouse LJ.

The central concern of proprietary estoppel

10.169   The central concern of the doctrine of proprietary estoppel is the notion of conscientious dealing in relation to land.[1] The doctrine has been explained as having its root in 'the first principle upon which all courts of equity proceed', that is, 'to prevent a person from insisting on his strict legal rights – whether arising under a contract, or on his title deeds, or by statute – when it would be inequitable for him to do so having regard to the dealings which have taken place between the parties.'[2] Estoppel doctrine dictates that legal entitlements cannot be enforced in total isolation from the relational context in which relevant dealings have taken place. Accordingly the law of proprietary estoppel confers on the courts a residual power to scrutinise and to restrain (or estop) particular assertions of legal entitlement on grounds of conscience.[3] Although starting in this way as a principle of inhibition, the doctrine usually has the indirect (but more positive) effect of creating rights on behalf of the successful claimant of an 'equity' founded upon estoppel.

1   '[T]he fundamental principle that equity is concerned to prevent unconscionable conduct permeates all the elements of the [estoppel] doctrine' (*Gillett v Holt* [2001] Ch 210 at 225D per Robert Walker LJ). See also *Commonwealth of Australia v Verwayen* (1990) 170 CLR 394 at 440 per Deane J; *Driver v Yorke* [2003] All ER (D) 103 (Apr) at [28].

2   *Crabb v Arun DC* [1976] Ch 179 at 187H–188A per Lord Denning MR, citing *Hughes v Metropolitan Railway Co* (1877) 2 App Cas 439 at 448 per Lord Cairns LC.

3   See *R (Reprotech (Pebsham) Ltd v East Sussex CC* [2003] 1 WLR 348 at [35], where Lord Hoffmann referred to the 'moral values which underlie the private law concept of estoppel.'

Protection of fundamental assumptions

10.170   The concept of estoppel has evolved in both common law and equitable forms, the latter comprising doctrines grounded variously on estoppel by encouragement or acquiescence and upon promissory and proprietary estoppel.[1] The 'fundamental purpose' of estoppel is to 'afford protection against the detriment which would flow from a party's change of position if the assumption that led to it were deserted.'[2] In particular, the doctrine of proprietary estoppel gives expression to a general judicial distaste for any attempt by a legal owner unconscientiously to resile from assumptions which were previously understood, and acted upon, as the basis of relevant dealings in respect of his land.[3] In curtailing the unconscionable disclaimer of such underlying assumptions, the estoppel principle is ultimately directed against the abuse of power.[4]

1   See *Commonwealth of Australia v Verwayen* (1990) 170 CLR 394 at 409 per Mason CJ.

2   *Commonwealth of Australia v Verwayen* (1990) 170 CLR 394 at 410 per Mason CJ. See also *Waltons Stores (Interstate) Ltd v Maher* (1988) 164 CLR 387 at 419 per Brennan J.

3   See e g *Amalgamated Investment and Property Co Ltd v Texas Commerce International Bank Ltd* [1982] QB 84 at 122C per Lord Denning MR ('one general principle shorn of limitations'); *Gillies v Keogh* [1989] 2 NZLR 327 at 331 per Cooke P.

4   The rationale of estoppel is not to 'save persons from the consequences of their own mistake', but to counteract any exploitation of another's 'special vulnerability or misadventure ... in a way that is unreasonable and oppressive to an extent that affronts ordinary minimum standards of fair dealing' (*Commonwealth of Australia v Verwayen* (1990) 170 CLR 394 at 440–441 per Deane J).

Versatility of estoppel doctrine

10.171   Few other doctrines of modern property law demonstrate so clearly the courts' jurisdiction to arrive at broadly 'just' or 'equitable' solutions of the property difficulties of opposed parties. Frequently in the ill-defined and chaotic circumstances of everyday life – especially in the family context – problems of entitlement arise for which the relatively orderly framework of structural property principles provides no satisfactory answer.[1] It is here that proprietary estoppel has emerged as an important source of rights. The notion of proprietary estoppel is increasingly invoked in order to plug the awkward gaps which exist between well established heads of claim and between various accepted forms of entitlement. In these marginal or interstitial areas the estoppel principle now plays a significant role in enabling the courts to address difficult questions which would otherwise escape satisfactory analysis. The sheer flexibility of estoppel doctrine has proved uniquely suitable for translating into comprehensible legal form the more nebulous and confused aspects of lay persons' informal arrangements with regard to land. The doctrine thus provides an essential supplement to the law of licences[2] and trusts,[3] enabling the courts to fashion remedial justice on the basis of extremely loose and often ill-considered patterns of informal or formally defective dealing.

1　The reach of estoppel doctrine extends well beyond the context of family relationships to affect wide ranges of business dealings. It is likely, for example, that a new emphasis was placed on estoppel doctrine by the abolition of the doctrine of part performance [**paras 9.15, 12.35**]. Equity is 'flexible and strong enough to ensure that any estoppel results in a sensible commercial outcome, which is not thwarted by archaic and technical rules of property law, unless those rules are based on public policy or are so fundamental as to be incapable of being overridden' (*PW & Co v Milton Gate Investments Ltd* [2004] 2 WLR 443 at [207] per Neuberger J).

2　[**Para 4.88**].

3　[**Paras 9.172, 10.3**].

THE OPERATION OF PROPRIETARY ESTOPPEL

10.172　The doctrine of proprietary estoppel has rarely been defined in one clear analytical formula, but has instead been expounded at different times by different judges in slightly divergent terms. These varying formulae, although alike directed against unconscionable dealings with land, have not always made for certainty or consistency in the implementation of the fundamental premise of proprietary estoppel.

Essential elements of proprietary estoppel

10.173　The law of proprietary estoppel operates where the owner of an estate in land has expressly or impliedly given some informal assurance respecting present or future rights in that land. The doctrine of estoppel restrains that person from any unconscientious withdrawal of his representation if the person to whom it was made has meanwhile relied upon it to her own disadvantage.[1] The primary inquiry for the court is whether it is conscionable for the representor to deny that which he has allowed or encouraged the representee to assume to her detriment.[2] In this way estoppel doctrine finds its ultimate purpose in 'enabling the courts to do justice.'[3]

1   'At the heart of estoppel or acquiescence lies an encouragement or allowance of a party to believe something to his detriment' (*Jones v Stones* [1999] 1 WLR 1739 at 1745A per Aldous LJ). See also *Re Basham, decd* [1986] 1 WLR 1498 at 1503H; *Brinnand v Ewens* (1987) 19 HLR 415 at 416–417; *Gillies v Keogh* [1989] 2 NZLR 327 at 346–347 per Richardson J.

2   See *Taylors Fashions Ltd v Liverpool Victoria Trustees Co Ltd* [1982] QB 133 (Note) at 151H–152A per Oliver J.

3   *Sledmore v Dalby* (1996) 72 P & CR 196 at 205, 207, 209 per Hobhouse LJ ('the end result must be a just one'). See likewise *Jennings v Rice* [2003] 1 P & CR 100 at [36] per Aldous LJ.

10.174   A successful claim of proprietary estoppel thus depends, in some form or other, on the demonstration of *three* elements:

–   representation (or an 'assurance' of rights)[1]
–   reliance (or a 'change of position ')[2] and
–   unconscionable disadvantage (or 'detriment').[3]

1   **[Para 10.234]**.
2   **[Para 10.256]**.
3   **[Para 10.271]**.

10.175   An estoppel claim succeeds only if it is inequitable to allow the representor to overturn the assumptions reasonably created by his earlier informal dealings in relation to his land. For this purpose the elements of representation, reliance and disadvantage are inter-dependent and capable of definition only in terms of each other.[1] A representation is present only if the representor intended his assurance to be relied upon. Reliance occurs only if the representee is caused to change her position to her detriment. Disadvantage ultimately ensues only if the representation, once relied upon, is unconscionably withdrawn.

1   '[T]he doctrine of proprietary estoppel cannot be treated as subdivided into three or four watertight compartments' (*Gillett v Holt* [2001] Ch 210 at 225C per Robert Walker LJ). See also *Parker v Parker* [2003] EWHC 1846 (Ch) at [207].

Comparison with promissory estoppel

10.176   The doctrine of proprietary estoppel shares a common origin with its contractual analogue of promissory estoppel. In English law, however, the two doctrines differ in important respects. First, proprietary estoppel can arise even outside the scope of contractual relationships,[1] although in practice proprietary estoppel and contractual relations often overlap.[2] Second, proprietary estoppel does not merely provide a *shield* for the vulnerable but may also be relied on as a *sword*, conferring rights of action where none would otherwise exist.[3] Third, whereas the effect of promissory estoppel may be merely temporary, the effect of proprietary estoppel is often long-lasting or permanent.[4] Fourth, the equity arising in connection with proprietary estoppel may bind third parties and, in this sense, appears to constitute a substantive equitable proprietary right.[5]

1   *Holiday Inns Inc v Broadhead* (1974) 232 EG 951 at 1087; *Riches v Hogben* [1986] 1 Qd R 315 at 339; *Beaton v McDivitt* (1985) 13 NSWLR 134 at 150G–151B.

2   See e g *Tanner v Tanner* [1975] 1 WLR 1346 at 1350E, where Lord Denning MR described as a contractual licence something which might be more easily recognised in terms of proprietary

estoppel [**para 4.74**]. For conflicting views as to whether contractual licences and estoppels can logically overlap, see A Briggs, [1981] Conv 212, [1983] Conv 285; M P Thompson, [1983] Conv 50. See also John Dewar, 'Licences and Land Law: An Alternative View' (1986) 49 MLR 741.

3   [**Para 10.289**]. See *Crabb v Arun DC* [1976] Ch 179 at 187E; *Amalgamated Investment & Property Co Ltd v Texas Commerce International Bank Ltd* [1982] QB 84 at 105D–E; *J T Developments Ltd v Quinn* (1991) 62 P & CR 33 at 45; *Thomas v Thomas* [1956] NZLR 785 at 793; *Classic Communications Ltd v Lascar* (1986) 21 DLR (4th) 579 at 587; *Depew v Wilkes* (2000) 193 DLR (4th) 529 at [63].

4   See *Sledmore v Dalby* (1996) 72 P & CR 196 at 203.

5   [**Para 10.216**].

Comparison with constructive trust

10.177   An extremely close relationship exists between proprietary estoppel and the constructive trust[1] and the convergence of concept is today so marked that the two doctrines are, in many respects, indistinguishable.[2] The component elements of proprietary estoppel are overwhelmingly similar to those of constructive trust. The constructive trust originates in some 'equity' that one party in a joint relationship or endeavour should not 'assert or retain the benefit of the relevant property to the extent that it would be unconscionable for him to do so.'[3] In a very similar way estoppel doctrine gives substantial effect to the 'equity of expectation' generated by past dealings[4] and, for this reason, claims based on estoppel are almost invariably coupled with allegations of constructive trust.[5] Further conceptual assimilation follows from the fact that, in concretising the 'equity' of estoppel in the grant of some interest in land,[6] courts often award this interest behind a constructive trust.[7] Conversely, in fashioning constructive trust awards, courts frequently point quite explicitly to the parallel of the remedial flexibility offered by the law of proprietary estoppel.[8] Doctrinal developments in this area are clearly symbiotic.

1   [**Paras 10.62, 10.68**]. A sharper distinction can be drawn between the notions of proprietary estoppel and resulting trust (see *Walker v Walker* (Unreported, Court of Appeal, 12 April 1984) per Browne-Wilkinson LJ).

2   Proprietary estoppel involves 'the same general principle as that invoked in *Gissing v Gissing* ... namely, that courts applying equitable principles will prevent a person from insisting on his strict legal rights when it would be inequitable for him to do so having regard to the dealings which have taken place between the parties' (*Christian v Christian* (1981) 131 NLJ 43 per Brightman LJ). See also *Savva v Costa and Harymode Investments Ltd* (1981) 131 NLJ 1114 per Oliver LJ; *Yaxley v Gotts* [2000] Ch 162 at 176B–177B, 180B–C per Robert Walker LJ, 191C per Beldam LJ; *Oxley v Hiscock* [2004] 3 WLR 715 at [66] per Chadwick LJ.

3   *Muschinski v Dodds* (1985) 160 CLR 583 at 620 per Deane J.

4   *Riches v Hogben* [1986] 1 Qd R 315 at 327 per Macrossan J, 339 per Williams J.

5   The cases are innumerable in which constructive trust and estoppel are pleaded in the alternative. The two forms of claim may even operate cumulatively so that a claimant recovers a 50 per cent share of equitable ownership on each basis, thereby establishing entitlement to the beneficial whole (see *Preston and Henderson v St Helens MBC* (1989) 58 P & CR 500 at 505).

6   [**Para 10.219**].

7   See e g *Re Sharpe (A Bankrupt)* [1980] 1 WLR 219 at 225C–D [**para 10.38**]; *Re Basham, decd* [1986] 1 WLR 1498 at 1504A–F. See also *Sen v Headley* [1991] Ch 425 at 440A per Nourse LJ [**para 10.215**].

8   See e g *Grant v Edwards* [1986] Ch 638 at 656F–H, 657G–658A per Browne-Wilkinson V-C;
     Nichols v Nichols (1986) 4 BPR 9240 at 9244; *Gillies v Keogh* [1989] 2 NZLR 327 at 346 per
     Richardson J.

Balance of emphasis

10.178   In so far as any distinction exists between the doctrines of proprietary
estoppel and constructive trust,[1] it is sometimes said that the balance of
emphasis in the constructive trust falls on the notion of frustrated bargain,
whereas the 'equity' of estoppel is more obviously founded upon some concept
of frustrated expectation.[2] Proprietary estoppel may therefore extend beyond
the constructive trust to circumstances of passive representation of entitlement,[3] where the representor has in no sense 'bargained' with the representee
for a conferment of rights, but has simply stood back watching the representee
incur disadvantage in the expectation that she has rights.[4] The fields of bargain
and representation do not necessarily coincide, but in fact little today turns on
this.

1   See *Stokes v Anderson* [1991] 1 FLR 391 at 399C–D per Nourse LJ; *Hyett v Stanley* [2003]
     WTLR 1269 at [27] per Sir Martin Nourse.
2   '[E]stoppel puts weight on inducement, constructive trusts on undertakings' (J D Davies,
     (1980–81) 7 Adelaide L Rev 200 at 221). See the reference to a concept of 'legitimate
     expectation' in *Norris and Norris v Walls* [1997] NI 45 at 55a–b per Girvan J.
3   In this respect the estoppel doctrine may rest on 'wider equitable principles' (*Morris v Morris*
     [1982] 1 NSWLR 61 at 63F–G). See similarly *Shaida v Kindlane Ltd* (Unreported, Chancery
     Division, 22 June 1982) per Deputy Judge P V Baker QC.
4   **[Para 10.199]**. See *Yaxley v Gotts* [2000] Ch 162 at 176B–E per Robert Walker LJ, 192B–D per
     Beldam LJ. Compare *Te Rama Engineering Ltd v Shortlands Properties Ltd* [1982] BCL 692 for
     circumstances in which a claim based on constructive trust succeeded and an estoppel claim
     failed.

Range of relevant changes of position

10.179   It is unlikely that much real distinction exists today between the kinds
of contributory activity (or 'change of position') which underlie estoppel and
constructive trust. It may be that estoppel doctrine attaches significance to a
slightly broader range of contribution (inclusive of the more intangible elements of domestic commitment and endeavour),[1] which in the absence of
express agreement would not obviously generate a constructive trust.[2] Recent
case law has emphasised, however, that at least in the context of the family
home the 'concepts of trust and equitable estoppel are almost interchangeable.'[3] It is probable that any further relaxation of the rules concerning imputed
common intentions in the law of constructive trusts[4] will eradicate any remaining distinction based on the nature or content of recognised 'changes of
position'.[5]

1   See e g *Greasley v Cooke* [1980] 1 WLR 1306 at 1312A **[para 10.295]**. See also *Grant v Edwards*
     [1986] Ch 638 at 657A–C per Browne-Wilkinson V-C; *Preston and Henderson v St Hel-
     ens MBC* (1989) 58 P & CR 500 at 505. See P Ferguson, 'Constructive Trusts – A Note of

Caution' (1993) 109 LQR 114 at 119, for the suggestion that constructive trust doctrine may require a showing of a *specifically agreed* detrimental reliance on the part of the claimant beneficiary, whilst estoppel claims rest on changes of position which need not have been the subject of prior bargain.

2 **[Para 10.132]**.

3 *Birmingham Midshires Mortgage Services Ltd v Sabherwal* (2000) 80 P & CR 256 at 263 per Robert Walker LJ.

4 **[Para 10.260]**.

5 It is also probable that any presumption of reliance applied by the courts in cases of estoppel **[para 10.139]** is equally relevant nowadays to claims of constructive trust **[para 10.134]**.

Remedial differences

10.180 More important distinctions are perhaps apparent in the remedial mechanisms for giving effect to doctrines of proprietary estoppel and constructive trust. It has been pointed out, for instance, that the highly flexible nature of the estoppel remedy renders unnecessary the largely artificial attempt under constructive trust doctrine to quantify the interest awarded.[1] The most commonly awarded constructive trust remedy recognises the claimant's entitlement to an aliquot share of beneficial ownership, whereas proprietary estoppel may lead more easily to the allocation of less sharply defined entitlements such as 'the lesser property right of an irrevocable licence.'[2] But even this difference of approach is beginning to fade into unimportance as the remedial repertoire of the constructive trust assumes an expanded reach.[3] Of undoubted significance, however, is the fact that the court, in devising a remedy for proprietary estoppel (but not in cases of constructive trust), is free to fashion an order entirely unrelated to the property in dispute. Whilst a constructive trust must (at least in English law) take effect against the land itself, the court may satisfy the 'equity' of estoppel by a pure order for money payment.[4] This possibility opens up in estoppel cases a potential for compensatory relief, sounding only in money, which may be particularly valuable in circumstances where there is currently no property to which a constructive trust might attach.[5]

1 See Browne-Wilkinson, 'Constructive Trusts and Unjust Enrichment' (1996) 10 Trust Law International 98 at 100.

2 *Bristol & West Building Society v Henning* [1985] 1 WLR 778 at 782D per Browne-Wilkinson LJ.

3 **[Para 10.166]**.

4 Such an order, usually for reimbursement of money expended on improvements to land, is often, but not necessarily, reinforced by a lien or charge upon the land in question **[para 10.300]**.

5 See eg *Firth v Mallender* (Unreported, Court of Appeal, 11 October 1999), where a constructive trust was ruled out because the land concerned was affected by 'negative equity', but the Court of Appeal would have been prepared to order money reimbursement in respect of improvements had the facts supported the allegation of some induced expectation of the eventual return of funds spent on those improvements.

A TEXTBOOK ILLUSTRATION OF PROPRIETARY ESTOPPEL

10.181 The doctrine of proprietary estoppel tends to be controversial, not least because it frequently comes into conflict with a number of principles of broad application in English jurisprudence. The classic features of the estoppel concept were demonstrated in *Inwards v Baker*,[1] a case which typifies the way in which vaguely expressed entitlements are often left dormant for years until disaffection, death or insolvency necessitates a greater precision in the identification of land rights. In *Inwards v Baker* an elderly man, F, encouraged his adult son, S, to build a bungalow on F's land, telling S that the bungalow, once built, would be available indefinitely as long as S wished to use the property as his own home. Consistently with the messy way in which family dealings are usually conducted, no details of the arrangement were ever expressed formally or even in writing. Legal title remained in F, but S nevertheless proceeded, at his own expense, to construct the bungalow and to live there for some 30 years. When F then died leaving no will or binding contract in S's favour, S's half-brothers (acting as F's personal representatives) sought to revoke S's occupation licence and to recover possession from him.

1   [1965] 2 QB 29.

Countervailing principles of law

10.182 On the facts presented in *Inwards v Baker*, there seemed little likelihood that S could derive much assistance from conventional principles of property, tort or contract – for the following reasons.

The law disfavours the informal creation of rights in land

10.183 There is, in English law, a general requirement that rights in land should be created only in compliance with certain formalities.[1] Land law disfavours the informal creation of rights. In *Inwards v Baker*, F should have used a deed of grant or a formal declaration of trust or, at the very least, made some testamentary disposition in favour of S. He did none of these things.

1   **[Paras 7.26, 9.190]**. See *Sen v Headley* [1991] Ch 425 at 440G.

Gratuitous promises are unenforceable

10.184 Another fundamental principle of English law holds gratuitous promises to be essentially unenforceable.[1] There is no equitable jurisdiction to hold a person to a promise simply because a court thinks it unfair, unconscionable or morally objectionable for him to go back on it. If there were such a jurisdiction, one 'might as well forget the law of contract and issue every civil judge with a portable palm tree.'[2] In *Inwards v Baker* the relationship between F and S was not, for any number of reasons, contractual in nature.[3] Familial arrangements are seldom intended to have legal consequence[4] and if F, immediately after offering the land to S, had resiled from the offer, no contractual remedy would have been available. Nor could F have alleged any breach of contract if S had subsequently refused to construct the bungalow.

1 See e g *Watts and Ready v Storey* (1983) 134 NLJ 631 per Slade LJ.
2 *Taylor v Dickens* [1998] 1 FLR 806 at 820G per Deputy Judge Weeks QC.
3 [1965] 2 QB 29 at 36D–E, 37C per Lord Denning MR. See also *Gillett v Holt* [2001] Ch 210 at 230E per Robert Walker LJ.
4 See *Balfour v Balfour* [1919] 2 KB 571 at 579, where Atkin LJ, speaking in the more specific context of spousal relationships, observed that family arrangements 'are outside the realm of contracts altogether. The common law does not regulate the form of agreements between spouses. Their promises are not sealed with seals and sealing wax. The consideration that really obtains for them is that natural love and affection which counts for so little in these cold Courts ... The parties themselves are advocates, judges, Courts, sheriff's officer and reporter. In respect of these promises each house is a domain into which the King's writ does not seek to run, and to which his officers do not seek to be admitted.'

Voluntarily rendered services are not generally compensable

10.185 English law has not, historically, been ready to recognise any broad principle of compensation for gratuitously rendered service.[1] Pending the emergence of a more fully developed jurisprudence of restitution, there is in English law no equivalent of the Roman law concept of *negotiorum gestio*,[2] which gave the provider of a voluntary service the right to claim remuneration or reimbursement. Voluntarily rendered services are generally non-compensable.[3] To confer an uncontracted benefit and then expect reward is, in the blunt terms of Lord Cranworth LC, a 'folly'.[4] In *Inwards v Baker*, therefore, S's construction of a bungalow was apt to be considered, in principle, as bringing about merely an uncompensated accession to F's realty.[5]

1 Compensation for improvements cannot be claimed under any doctrine of unjust enrichment (see *Pettitt v Pettitt* [1970] AC 777 at 795G–H per Lord Reid).
2 See W W Buckland and A D McNair, *Roman Law and Common Law* (2nd edn, London 1952), p 344; W W Buckland, *A Text-book of Roman Law* (3rd edn by P Stein, Cambridge 1963), pp 537–539.
3 *Pettitt v Pettitt* [1970] AC 777 at 818B per Lord Upjohn. See also *Falcke v Scottish Imperial Insurance Co* (1886) 34 Ch D 234 at 248 per Bowen LJ ('work and labour done or money expended by one man to preserve or benefit the property of another do not according to English law create any lien upon the property saved or benefited, nor, if standing alone, create any obligation to repay the expenditure').
4 *Ramsden v Dyson* (1866) LR 1 HL 129 at 141. See also *Ruabon Steamship Co v London Assurance* [1900] AC 6 at 10, 15; *Re Vandervell's Trusts (No 2)* [1974] Ch 269 at 299F–H; *Avondale Printers & Stationers Ltd v Haggie* [1979] 2 NZLR 124 at 155.
5 **[Para 1.52]**.

Consensual presence cannot rank as adverse possession

10.186 Consensual presence on land is normally incompatible with any claim of adverse possession.[1] Any suggestion in *Inwards v Baker* that S might have acquired title by adverse possession was comprehensively negatived by the permissive character of his many years of occupancy.

1 **[Para 6.114]**.

The decision in *Inwards v Baker*

10.187 In *Inwards v Baker* the Court of Appeal nevertheless refused to order possession against S, holding that he had acquired 'a licence coupled with an equity' which bound not only F while alive, but also F's successors in title and indeed any purchaser with notice.[1] The Court took the view that F's executors were estopped from evicting S and that S's 'equity' could be satisfied only by a court order allowing him to 'remain there as long as he desires to [use the land] as his home.'[2] Three crucial elements had raised this 'equity' on behalf of S.

-   F had *represented* that S would have an indefinite right of occupation.
-   S had *relied* on this clear, albeit informal, conferment of entitlement by building his home on F's land in preference to any other location.
-   S had incurred *disadvantage* in that his money and labour had generated an improvement which was irretrievably and non-compensably annexed to F's land, a personal investment which stood to be snatched away by the assertion of a strict legal entitlement.

1   [1965] 2 QB 29 at 37F. For critical views of this decision, see F R Crane, (1967) 31 Conv (NS) 332 at 342; *Dodsworth v Dodsworth* (1973) 228 EG 1115.
2   [1965] 2 QB 29 at 37G. See also *Raffaele v F & G Raffaele* [1962] WAR 29 at 31.

10.188 Since it had been shown that S, 'at the request or with the encouragement' of F, had 'spent the money in the expectation of being allowed to stay there', the Court would not now allow that expectation to be defeated 'where it would be inequitable so to do.'[1]

1   [1965] 2 QB 29 at 37C–D per Lord Denning MR. Danckwerts LJ likewise spoke of 'an equity created by estoppel, or equitable estoppel' as arising where a person who undertakes expenditure has been 'induced by the expectation of obtaining protection'. This being so, 'equity protects him so that an injustice may not be perpetrated' ([1965] 2 QB 29 at 38F–G).

ESTOPPEL DOCTRINE APPLIES TO A WIDE VARIETY OF CIRCUMSTANCE

10.189 The concatenation of ideas underlying proprietary estoppel emerges from three broad, and not entirely distinct, categories of circumstance. These categories comprise (1) the 'imperfect gift' cases, (2) the 'common expectation' cases, and (3) the 'unilateral mistake' cases. These cases alike present the essential characteristics of proprietary estoppel, but each class of case in its turn gives a heightened emphasis to one or other of the constituent elements of representation, reliance and unconscionable disadvantage. The tendency in the modern case law is to synthesise the jurisprudence of proprietary estoppel in a more unified doctrine of 'detrimental reliance'. However, this threefold classification retains some significance because even today the criteria applied by the courts in response to estoppel claims differentiate, in certain respects, between these broad categories of circumstance.

The 'imperfect gift' cases

10.190 The 'imperfect gift' cases relate typically to circumstances in which the courts, in applying the basic estoppel notion, have attached overwhelming significance to the element of *representation* or 'assurance' of entitlement. A representation by X to Y that Y shall have rights in X's land is most clearly epitomised in a gift of that land by X to Y. However, a gift of an estate or interest in land must be effected in the appropriate form (eg by means of formal transfer).[1] In default of such formality, the gift remains incomplete and it is trite law that equity will not perfect an imperfect gift.[2] Equity will not normally enforce any claim by the putative donee based on the informal gift, no matter how sincere or convincing the assurance of the would-be donor that he wished to make a gift of the land.

1 **[Para 7.26]**. See, however, *Sen v Headley* [1991] Ch 425 **[para 10.311]**.
2 See *Milroy v Lord* (1862) 4 De G F & J 264 at 274, 45 ER 1185 at 1189 per Turner LJ. Exceptionally, the rule in *Strong v Bird* (1874) LR 18 Eq 315 may apply to perfect an informal gift of realty to one who later, as executor of the donor, receives a grant of probate in relation to the donor's will in circumstances where the testator at death retained his intention to give (see *Stewart v McLaughlin* [1908] 2 Ch 251 at 254–255 (personalty); *Re Comberbach* (1929) 73 Sol Jo 403; *Benjamin v Leicher* (1998) 45 NSWLR 389 at 402D).

Exceptional assistance in the perfection of a gift

10.191 There are, however, some circumstances in which equity is prepared to depart from the normal rule in order to assist the vesting of an informal gift of realty. These circumstances are classically illustrated in *Dillwyn v Llewelyn*.[1] Here a father placed his adult son in possession of land belonging to the father, both parties signing an informal memorandum which evidenced an intention that the land should be given to the son for the purpose of providing him with a dwelling-house. The son immediately proceeded at vast expense to build a residence for himself on that land. Lord Westbury LC recognised the imperfect (and therefore abortive) nature of the purported gift of realty, but held that 'the subsequent acts of the donor may give the donee that right or ground of claim which he did not acquire from the original gift.'[2] Since, with his father's knowledge, the son had incurred substantial expenditure 'on the strength of' the promised gift,[3] the son was held to have acquired 'a right from the subsequent transaction to call on the donor to perform that contract and complete the imperfect donation which was made.'[4] The Court thus decreed that the intention to give the fee simple interest must now be performed, even though title to the land had by this stage passed to the executors of the father's estate. The abortive gift must be honoured in the light of the subsequent reliance upon it.

1 (1862) 4 De G F & J 517, 45 ER 1285.
2 (1862) 4 De G F & J 517 at 521, 45 ER 1285 at 1286.
3 See *Giumelli v Giumelli* (1999) 196 CLR 101 at [6] (High Court of Australia).
4 Lord Westbury viewed the son's expenditure as ex post facto consideration for his father's promise (see also *Re Barker's Estate* (1875) 44 LJ Ch 487 at 490 per Jessel MR). He concluded

that, since 'the subsequent expenditure by the son, with the approbation of the father, supplied a valuable consideration originally wanting', the memorandum signed by both must be regarded as 'an agreement for the soil extending to the fee-simple of the land' ((1862) 4 De G F & J 517 at 522, 45 ER 1285 at 1287). See also *Beaton v McDivitt* (1985) 13 NSWLR 134 at 149B–C, 151A–B.

10.192 Although the issue in *Dillwyn v Llewelyn* was considered largely on the analogy of the doctrine of part performance,[1] Lord Westbury LC made an important reference to the idea that the donee had an 'equity' which entitled him to claim the estate purportedly given to him by the original and informal promise.[2] The attendant circumstances left no doubt but that the original intention had been to vest a fee simple in the donee.[3] The decision thus provides authority for the proposition that where a gratuitous representation is given that an estate or interest in land will be transferred, there arises an 'equity' in favour of the promisee based upon proprietary estoppel, provided that the promisee suffers unconscionable disadvantage in reliance on the assurance. Under these circumstances the doctrine of proprietary estoppel not only protects the informal promisee against adverse claims to possession; it also affords the promisee a ground on which he may claim the assistance of the courts towards the perfection of the intended gift.[4] In allowing an 'equity' to arise from an unequivocal, but abortive, gift of an interest in land, this branch of estoppel doctrine plainly overlaps with – and substantially replicates the function of – the 'express agreement' constructive trust.[5]

1 [**Para 12.40**].
2 (1862) 4 De G F & J 517 at 522, 45 ER 1285 at 1286–1287.
3 Lord Westbury declared that the 'estate was given as the site of a dwelling-house to be erected by the son … No one builds a house for his own life only, and it is absurd to suppose that it was intended by either party that the house, at the death of the son, should become the property of the father.'
4 This approach to imperfect gifts of realty has been followed in other cases, the courts regarding it as irrelevant whether the original representation of rights is contained in writing or is merely oral (see *Thomas v Thomas* [1956] NZLR 785 at 793–794; *Raffaele v F & G Raffaele* [1962] WAR 29 at 31; but compare *Jackson v Crosby* (No 2) (1979) 21 SASR 280 at 289).
5 [**Para 10.113**].

Far-reaching consequences

10.193 The recognition of an 'equity' raised by an informal donee's detrimental reliance may sometimes produce dramatic results. In *Pascoe v Turner*,[1] on the breakdown of their de facto relationship, P left T in occupation of his house in order to move in with another woman elsewhere. P informed T orally that she had nothing to worry about as the house and its contents were thenceforth entirely hers. T later effected repairs to the house costing about £230, a figure which amounted to approximately one quarter of her available capital. When P subsequently brought possession proceedings on the basis that T had a mere revocable licence to occupy, the Court of Appeal directed P to convey the fee simple in the house to his erstwhile partner. Cumming-Bruce LJ applied *Dillwyn v Llewelyn*, holding that the circumstances raised in favour of T an 'equity',[2] founded on proprietary estoppel, which could be satisfied only by ordering P to perfect his imperfect gift of the realty.[3]

1   [1979] 1 WLR 431. See (1979) 129 NLJ 1193 (R D Oughton); [1979] Conv 379.
2   Compare, however, *Wright v Johnson* (Unreported, Court of Appeal, 2 November 1999); *Dubej v Dubej* (Unreported, Supreme Court of New South Wales, 25 February 1991, BPR Casenote 95934).
3   The outcome in *Pascoe v Turner* is remarkable in that it effectively achieved a discretionary redistribution of assets on the breakdown of a de facto marriage relationship in a manner analogous to property adjustment on divorce. See B Sufrin, (1979) 42 MLR 574, and compare *McGill v S* [1979] IR 283 at 293 where Gannon J in the Irish High Court declined to follow *Pascoe v Turner*. See also *Gissing v Gissing* [1971] AC 886 at 910E–F.

The 'common expectation' cases

10.194   Whereas the central feature of the 'imperfect gift' cases is the representation of intended entitlement contained in an abortive gift of land, the element which comes to the fore in the 'common expectation' cases is the notion of *reliance*.[1] These cases concern not so much the situation where X has attempted to make a gift of land to Y, but rather the situation where X and Y have consistently dealt with each other in such a way as reasonably to cause Y to rely on a shared supposition that he would acquire rights of some kind in X's land. It often becomes unconscionable to permit X to frustrate the substance of the common expectation.

1   This is not to imply that the other key characteristics of proprietary estoppel are not present in such circumstances, but merely that the 'common expectation' cases particularly highlight the element of reliance.

Lord Kingsdown's speech in Ramsden v Dyson

10.195   The classic exposition of the 'common expectation' basis of proprietary estoppel occurs in the dissenting speech of Lord Kingsdown in *Ramsden v Dyson*.[1] Here Lord Kingsdown stated that

> If a man, under a verbal agreement with a landlord for a certain interest in land, or, what amounts to the same thing, under an expectation, created or encouraged by the landlord, that he shall have a certain interest, takes possession of such land, with the consent of the landlord, and upon the faith of such promise or expectation, with the knowledge of the landlord, and without objection by him, lays out money upon the land, a Court of equity will compel the landlord to give effect to such promise or expectation.[2]

1   (1866) LR 1 HL 129 at 170.
2   See also *Gregory v Mighell* (1811) 18 Ves 328 at 333, 34 ER 341 at 343.

10.196   Although, for the purpose of the instant decision, Lord Kingsdown couched his observations in terms of the landlord–tenant relationship, his remarks have been accepted as having a more general role in identifying the factors which can generate a proprietary estoppel.[1] In *Taylors Fashions Ltd v Liverpool Victoria Trustees Co Ltd*,[2] Oliver J pointed out that the circumstances postulated in Lord Kingsdown's example of proprietary estoppel 'presuppose ... the fostering of an expectation in the minds of *both* parties at the time but from which, once it has been acted upon, it would be unconscionable to permit the landlord to depart.' This formulation of estoppel is sometimes known as 'estoppel by encouragement'.[3] In so far as it attaches equitable consequences to the shared expectations of parties, this branch of estoppel doctrine substantially resembles – and is perhaps indistinguishable from – the 'implied agreement' constructive trust.[4]

1   See *Crabb v Arun DC* [1976] Ch 179 at 194D per Scarman LJ.
2   [1982] QB 133 (Note) at 147G.
3   The precise name given to the *Ramsden v Dyson* principle is 'really immaterial' (*Taylors Fashions Ltd v Liverpool Victoria Trustees Co Ltd* [1982] QB 133 (Note) at 151H per Oliver J).
4   **[Para 10.127]**. See *Mollo v Mollo* [1999] EGCS 117 (Transcript at [42]).

Classic illustrations of 'common expectation'

10.197   A good example of this form of proprietary estoppel is found in *Plimmer v Mayor etc of Wellington*.[1] Here a licensee of land had, at the request of the owner of that land, expended considerable sums of money on the extension of a jetty and the construction of a warehouse. The Judicial Committee of the Privy Council upheld a claim on behalf of appellants claiming through the licensee that the licence, although originally revocable, had been rendered irrevocable by reason of the expenditure. Sir Arthur Hobhouse declared that the parties could not 'go on dealing with one another in the way stated in this case for a series of years, except with a sense in the minds of both that the occupant has something more than a merely precarious tenure.'[2] The Privy Council decided that the circumstances fell 'within the principle stated by Lord Kingsdown as to expectations created or encouraged by the landlord', and that the appellants therefore had an 'equity arising from expenditure on land.'[3] Accordingly they had acquired 'an indefinite, that is practically a perpetual, right' to the jetty for the purposes of the original licence.

1   (1884) 9 App Cas 699.
2   (1884) 9 App Cas 699 at 712.
3   (1884) 9 App Cas 699 at 713.

10.198   It has been accepted in numerous cases since *Plimmer* that a common expectation engendered by encouragement from the owner of land can give rise to an 'equity' based on proprietary estoppel.[1] In *E R Ives Investment Ltd v High*,[2] for example, H incurred expenditure in reliance on an informal agreement reached with a neighbouring owner, X. Under this agreement H raised no objection to the encroachment of X's foundations upon his own land, provided that he could enjoy a right of way across X's adjacent back yard. H subsequently built a garage on his own land accessible only by means of the agreed right of way and even contributed part of the cost of resurfacing the yard over which this way was exercised. I later purchased X's land expressly subject to such rights as H might have and the Court of Appeal accordingly held I to be bound by the arrangement reached between H and X. By reason of his detrimental reliance, H had acquired an 'equity' founded on the fact that I's predecessor had 'created in [H's] mind a reasonable expectation that his access over the yard would not be disturbed.'[3]

1 See eg *Inwards v Baker* [1965] 2 QB 29 [**para 10.181**].
2 [1967] 2 QB 379 [**paras 9.101, 12.320**]. See F R Crane, (1967) 31 Conv (NS) 332.
3 [1967] 2 QB 379 at 394G. A similar approach was applied by the Court of Appeal in *Crabb v Arun DC* [1976] Ch 179 at 189E, 192A, 198G, where one party had allowed himself to become landlocked in reliance on an 'agreement in principle' that he should have a right of access and egress over land belonging to an adjacent owner. See (1976) 40 Conv (NS) 156 (F R Crane); (1976) 126 NLJ 772 (M Vitoria); (1976) 92 LQR 174 (P S Atiyah), 342 (P J Millett).

The 'unilateral mistake' cases

10.199 An equity of estoppel may also arise – albeit more rarely – in circumstances of unilateral mistake. Unlike the 'common expectation' cases, which give pre-eminence to the shared nature of the parties' assumptions as to their respective rights, the 'unilateral mistake' cases apply the doctrine of proprietary estoppel where only one party is in any error as to the precise nature or scope of his or her rights. Here primary importance is attached to the *unconscionable disadvantage* or 'detriment' which is liable to be suffered by the party who innocently, but mistakenly, supposes that he has some entitlement in the land of another.[1] This branch of estoppel – sometimes known as 'estoppel by acquiescence' – has no real counterpart in the orthodox law of the constructive trust.[2] Under this formulation of estoppel jurisprudence it is regarded as unacceptable that the owner of land should wilfully stand by and watch a stranger incur clear disadvantage in reliance on some uncorrected misapprehension of his genuine legal position.[3]

1 The 'detriment' often flows directly from the fact that any physical improvements effected on the land in reliance on a mistaken belief accede to the realty [**para 1.52**].
2 In other jurisdictions the case of 'unilateral mistake' is frequently addressed in terms of a remedial constructive trust based on the concept of unjust enrichment [**para 10.151**].
3 The availability of an estoppel remedy in these circumstances highlights a significant area in which the doctrines of constructive trust and proprietary estoppel are not exactly congruent (see *Yaxley v Gotts* [2000] Ch 162 at 176B–E per Robert Walker LJ, 192B–D per Beldam LJ).

Lord Cranworth LC's speech in Ramsden v Dyson

10.200 The foremost statement of the 'unilateral mistake' approach is found in the speech of Lord Cranworth LC in *Ramsden v Dyson*.[1] Here the Lord Chancellor gave the following instance:

If a stranger begins to build on my land supposing it to be his own, and I, perceiving his mistake, abstain from setting him right, and leave him to persevere in his error, a Court of equity will not allow me afterwards to assert my title to the land on which he had expended money on the supposition that the land was his own. It considers that, when I saw the mistake into which he had fallen, it was my duty to be active and to state my adverse title; and that it would be dishonest in me to remain wilfully passive on such an occasion, in order afterwards to profit by the mistake which I might have prevented.

1   (1866) LR 1 HL 129 at 140–141.

The volunteer improver

10.201 The 'unilateral mistake' cases are remarkable in that historically they exemplify some of the few instances in English law where the courts have recognised a right to payment or other compensation for services rendered gratuitously. True 'unilateral mistake' cases are fairly rare,[1] and the facts which require to be proved in support of this kind of estoppel claim are narrowly prescribed. As Lord Cranworth LC indicated in *Ramsden v Dyson*, the classic example is that of the volunteer improver who mistakenly ploughs uncompensated value into the realty of the true legal owner.

1   For an early example, see *Hamilton v Geraghty* (1901) 1 SR NSW (Eq) 81.

The *Willmott v Barber* probanda

10.202 It was over a century ago, in *Willmott v Barber*,[1] that Fry J, without making explicit reference to any existing case law,[2] laid down extremely strict probanda for the success of estoppel claims. In his view, the doctrine of estoppel could not deprive a man of his strict legal rights 'unless he has acted in such a way as would make it fraudulent for him to set up those rights.'[3] Fraud of this kind was based on dishonest encouragement and required that there be proof of five different elements. First, the claimant of an equity based on estoppel must have made a mistake as to his legal rights. Second, the claimant must have 'expended some money or must have done some act ... on the faith of his mistaken belief'. Third, the owner of the land must know of the existence of his own right which is inconsistent with the right claimed by the claimant. Fourth, the owner must know of the claimant's mistaken belief of his rights. Fifth, the owner must have encouraged the claimant in his expenditure of money or in the other acts which he has done, either directly or by abstaining from asserting his legal right.

1   (1880) 15 Ch D 96 at 105–106.
2   *Ramsden v Dyson* (1866) LR 1 HL 129 had been cited during argument before Fry J.
3   As Scarman LJ observed in *Crabb v Arun DC* [1976] Ch 179 at 195B–C, 'fraud' was a word 'often in the mouths of those robust judges who adorned the bench in the 19th century', but 'less often in the mouths of the more wary judicial spirits today who sit upon the bench.'

10.203 The five probanda laid down by Fry J related essentially to cases of 'unilateral mistake'. Here the element of 'fraud' which activates the estoppel lies in the wilful and self-interested silence of one who knows his rights and who realises that he may profit by reason of the detriment suffered by one who, not knowing his rights, acts under a mistake. Such facts were altogether absent from *Willmott v Barber*, where claimant and defendant were alike mistaken as to their true legal rights. The circumstances of the instant case could not properly be categorised as a genuine example of 'unilateral mistake' and the claim of estoppel was therefore rejected.

Long-term effects of Willmott v Barber

10.204 The observations of Fry J in *Willmott v Barber* were destined to have a much more enduring impact, for they imposed a strait-jacket on the development of proprietary estoppel during the following hundred years. The five probanda, because they were not explicitly limited to the category of 'unilateral mistake', came to be applied indiscriminately to all forms of estoppel claim (ie well beyond the category of unilateral mistake to which they obviously relate),[1] thereby dramatically curtailing the availability of estoppel-based remedies.[2] In particular the estoppel doctrine was rendered virtually inapplicable to cases of 'common expectation', in which mistaken assumptions of entitlement – if there are any – are usually bilateral and wholly innocent. The requirement that the estoppel claimant be positively mistaken as to his existing rights operated harshly where the claimant was in no doubt as to the absence of any strict entitlement on his own part, but had been led to expect that he would somehow or at some stage acquire rights by relying upon the representation made by the landowner. Dogmatic insistence on the five probanda caused special difficulty in the context of informal 'family arrangements', where full awareness of non-entitlement in strict law is often wholly compatible with an ill-defined expectation of future entitlement.[3]

1   The courts frequently attempted to force given fact-situations within Fry J's five probanda, even where the terminology of *Willmott v Barber* was ludicrously irrelevant or inapplicable to the circumstances in issue (see even *Crabb v Arun DC* [1976] Ch 179 at 195F–H).

2   This extensive view was not taken in the early development of estoppel doctrine. Only four years after *Willmott v Barber*, the Privy Council in *Plimmer v Mayor etc of Wellington* (1884) 9 App Cas 699 at 712, was careful to distinguish clearly between the categories of 'unilateral mistake' and 'common expectation', observing that in the instant case 'the equity is not claimed because the landowner has stood by in silence while his tenant has spent money on his land.'

3   For examples of 'hard cases' both in the family arrangement context and elsewhere, see *E & L Berg Homes Ltd v Grey* (1980) 253 EG 473; *Stilwell v Simpson* (1983) 133 NLJ 894; *Coombes v Smith* [1986] 1 WLR 808.

Diminishing force of Willmott v Barber

10.205 The rigid application of the *Willmott v Barber* criteria tended to attach an undue significance to Lord Cranworth LC's 'unilateral mistake' theory of estoppel and to divert attention away from Lord Kingsdown's alternative 'common expectation' rationale. Gradually, however, it came to be recognised that Fry J's five probanda did not provide a comprehensively applicable formula[1] and the way was therefore prepared for a more liberal restatement of the estoppel principle. This restatement has largely reversed the balance of emphasis so that the modern law of proprietary estoppel more closely approximates to the approach adumbrated by Lord Kingsdown.[2]

1   For staging posts along the way, see *Electrolux Ltd v Electrix Ltd* (1953) 71 RPC 23 at 33 per Evershed MR; *Shaw v Applegate* [1977] 1 WLR 970 at 978C–D, 980B–C.
2   See e g *Crabb v Arun DC* [1976] Ch 179 at 193H–194D per Scarman LJ; *Orgee v Orgee* [1997] EGCS 152 per Hirst LJ.

The modern synthesis: detrimental reliance

10.206   It fell to Oliver J in *Taylors Fashions Ltd v Liverpool Victoria Trustees Co Ltd*[1] to confirm a broader direction in the law of proprietary estoppel. The claimants here were the assignees of a leasehold term granted by the defendants' predecessors. Under the terms of the lease the lessee had been given an option to renew the lease at the expiration of the current term. At the commencement date of the lease such an option was generally considered, as a matter of law, to run with the land and to require no further protection by registration. A few months later the original lessor conveyed the freehold reversion to the defendants. In the firm belief that the option was still valid, the claimants then incurred substantial expenditure on renovations and improvements of the demised premises. Only some years later – and somewhat to the surprise of conveyancers – did the courts indicate that an option to renew a lease constitutes a registrable land charge.[2] The ineluctable result here was that the claimants' option was rendered void for non-registration.[3] When the defendants subsequently declined to renew the lease, the claimants argued that the defendants, by acquiescing in the expenditure, were estopped from pleading the voidness of the option. Oliver J rejected this claim of proprietary estoppel and held the defendants entitled to refuse to renew the lease.

1   [1982] QB 133 (Note). See (1981) 97 LQR 513; [1982] Conv 450 (P Jackson).
2   **[Para 14.280]**.
3   Oliver J did not pretend that the defendants' case was 'overburdened with merit', but took the view that 'it is no part of a judge's function to seek to impose upon a party to litigation his own idiosyncratic code of commercial morality' ([1982] QB 133 (Note) at 135E–F). The option was of course still binding upon the original lessor ([1982] QB 133 (Note) at 143G).

Retreat from the Willmott v Barber probanda

10.207   It was clear in *Taylors Fashions* that the claimants could not establish all of the *Willmott v Barber* criteria, not least because at all material times the defendants had been unaware of their own strict rights in the matter.[1] Oliver J nevertheless resisted a slavish application of the *Willmott v Barber* probanda and instead based his dismissal of the estoppel claim on much wider grounds.[2] He pointed out that Fry J's probanda, whilst arguably relevant to certain claims of estoppel, made no sense at all in relation to others. Oliver J accordingly drew a broad distinction between the 'common expectation' cases and the 'unilateral mistake' cases, observing that the *Willmott v Barber* probanda are more properly relevant (if at all) to the latter category of case, 'where all that has happened is that the party alleged to be estopped has stood by without protest while his rights have been infringed.'[3] Oliver J found it 'readily intelligible' in such cases of 'pure acquiescence' or 'mere passivity' that 'there must be shown a duty to speak, protest or interfere which cannot normally arise in the absence of knowledge or at least a suspicion of the true position.'[4] However, in the 'common expectation' cases exemplified in Lord Kingsdown's dictum in *Ramsden v Dyson*, 'there is no room for the literal application of the *probanda*, for the circumstances there postulated do not presuppose a "mistake" on anybody's part, but merely the fostering of an expectation in the minds of *both* parties at the time but from which, once it has been acted upon, it would be unconscionable to permit the landlord to depart.'[5]

1   They had not known that the claimants were mistaken in believing that their option was still enforceable.
2   [1982] QB 133 (Note) at 152A. See also *Andrews v Colonial Mutual Life Assurance Society Ltd* [1982] 2 NZLR 556 at 568.
3   [1982] QB 133 (Note) at 147B. Significantly, Oliver J thought that the strict relevance of the probanda even in 'unilateral mistake' cases 'must now be considered open to doubt.'
4   [1982] QB 133 (Note) at 146C, 147C.
5   [1982] QB 133 (Note) at 147G. See *Trethewey-Edge Dyking District v Coniagas Ranches Ltd* (2003) 224 DLR (4th) 611 at [67]–[74]. For confirmation that the *Willmott v Barber* probanda apply only to cases in which nothing more than 'a standing by' can be alleged, see *Starr v Barbaro* (1986) 4 BPR 9137 at 9140; *Jamino v Whitehall Investments Pty Ltd* (1986) 4 BPR 9210 at 9218.

A more general basis for proprietary estoppel

10.208   Having rejected the universal relevance of the *Willmott v Barber* probanda,[1] Oliver J proceeded in *Taylors Fashions Ltd v Liverpool Victoria Trustees Co Ltd* to derive support from the case law for 'a much wider equitable jurisdiction to interfere in cases where the assertion of strict legal rights is found by the courts to be unconscionable.'[2] On this 'very much broader approach' the application of all estoppel doctrine becomes fused or subsumed within a unitary test of conscience. The primary inquiry for the court is

> whether, in particular individual circumstances, it would be unconscionable for a party to be permitted to deny that which, knowingly or unknowingly, he has allowed or encouraged another to assume to his detriment.[3]

1   Oliver J conceded merely that the *Willmott v Barber* criteria might provide 'a valuable guide' in determining the applicability of proprietary estoppel ([1982] QB 133 (Note) at 153E, quoting *Crabb v Arun DC* [1976] Ch 179 at 194E per Scarman LJ. See also *Orgee v Orgee* [1997] EGCS 152 per Hirst LJ.
2   [1982] QB 133 (Note) at 147B.
3   [1982] QB 133 (Note) at 151H–152A. See also *Habib Bank Ltd v Habib Bank AG Zurich* [1981] 1 WLR 1265 at 1285C–F per Oliver LJ; *Amalgamated Investment & Property Co Ltd v Texas Commerce International Bank Ltd* [1982] QB 84 at 104D–E.

10.209   On this basis the state of mind of the party alleged to be estopped thus becomes 'merely one of the relevant factors ... in the overall inquiry.'[1] The unconscionability test centres, not on states of mind existing at the date of any relevant representation, but rather on the equity of allowing the representor to 'go back on the assumption which he permitted the representee to make.'[2]

1   [1982] QB 133 (Note) at 152A.
2   See also *Holee Holdings (M) Sdn Bhd v Chai Him* [1997] 4 MLJ 601 at 632G–H.

A watershed in the law of proprietary estoppel

10.210   Oliver J's judgment in *Taylors Fashions* represents a watershed in the law of proprietary estoppel.[1] Over the last 25 years the focus of estoppel doctrine has decisively turned away from applications of the *Willmott v Barber* probanda[2] and towards the 'essential test' as to whether the assertion of strict legal rights would be unconscionable.[3] Disapproval of unconscientious behaviour has been rightly identified as 'the driving force behind equitable estoppel.'[4] Accordingly the court must 'look at the matter in the round' as part of a 'broad inquiry as to whether the repudiation of an assurance is or is not unconscionable in all the circumstances.'[5] Demonstration of the *Willmott v Barber* probanda is no longer a precondition of all successful claims of estoppel[6] and in recent far-reaching reviews of estoppel doctrine the Court of Appeal has, rather significantly, made no reference at all to these probanda.[7] The old strictures on estoppel have rather faded into the background, a trend observed and reflected in many other common law jurisdictions.[8] The modern emphasis is on a generalised or overarching formula based on considerations of conscience, although as Robert Walker LJ was quick to observe in *Jennings v Rice*,[9] the court must always 'take a principled approach, and cannot exercise a completely unfettered discretion according to the individual judge's notion of what is fair in any particular case.'[10]

1   See *Gillett v Holt* [2001] Ch 210 at 225G per Robert Walker LJ; *Trethewey-Edge Dyking District v Coniagas Ranches Ltd* (2003) 224 DLR (4th) 611 at [65] per Newbury JA.
2   For lingering signs of fidelity to the *Willmott v Barber* criteria, see, however, *Matharu v Matharu* (1994) 68 P & CR 93 at 102 per Roch LJ. See also *Coombes v Smith* [1986] 1 WLR 808 at 817G–818B, where *Taylors Fashions Ltd v Liverpool Victoria Trustees Co Ltd* was not cited and the *Willmott v Barber* criteria were applied with full rigour.
3   *Gillett v Holt* [2001] Ch 210 at 232F per Robert Walker LJ. See similarly *Appleby v Cowley* (1982) Times, 14 April, per Megarry V-C; *Lim Teng Huan v Ang Swee Chuan* [1992] 1 WLR 113 at 117E–F per Lord Browne-Wilkinson; *Pridean Ltd v Forest Taverns Ltd* (1998) 75 P & CR 447 at 454–455 per Aldous LJ; *Trethewey-Edge Dyking District v Coniagas Ranches Ltd* (2003) 224 DLR (4th) 611 at [64].
4   *Commonwealth of Australia v Verwayen* (1990) 170 CLR 394 at 407 per Mason CJ; *Australian Broadcasting Corpn v Lenah Game Meats Pty Ltd* (2001) 208 CLR 199 at [98] per Gummow and Hayne JJ.
5   *Gillett v Holt* [2001] Ch 210 at 225D, 232D per Robert Walker LJ. See similarly *Parker v Parker* [2003] EWHC 1846 (Ch) at [241]–[246] per Lewison J.
6   See *Re Basham, decd* [1986] 1 WLR 1498 at 1508F–G; *Soames-Forsythe Properties Ltd v Tesco Stores Ltd* [1991] EGCS 22; *Lloyds Bank plc v Carrick* [1996] 4 All ER 630 at 640b–d per Morritt LJ; *Orgee v Orgee* [1997] EGCS 152 per Hirst LJ; *Jones v Stones* [1999] 1 WLR 1739 at 1743E–F per Aldous LJ.

7   See e g *Wayling v Jones* (1993) 69 P & CR 170; *Sledmore v Dalby* (1996) 72 P & CR 196; *Willis v Hoare* (1999) 77 P & CR D42; *Gillett v Holt* [2001] Ch 210; *Jennings v Rice* [2003] 1 P & CR 100.
8   For the distinct movement in Australia and New Zealand away from the *Willmott v Barber* probanda and towards the criterion of 'unconscionability', see *Wham-O MFG Co v Lincoln Industries* [1984] 1 NZLR 641 at 671; *Starr v Barbaro* (1986) 4 BPR 9137 at 9140; *Jamino v Whitehall Investments Pty Ltd* (1986) 4 BPR 9210 at 9218; *Stratulatos v Stratulatos* [1988] 2 NZLR 424 at 436; *Gillies v Keogh* [1989] 2 NZLR 327 at 345 per Richardson J; *Prudential Building and Investment Society of Canterbury v Hankins* [1997] 1 NZLR 114 at 121. See also *Holee Holdings (M) Sdn Bhd v Chai Him* [1997] 4 MLJ 601 at 630B–H (High Court of Malaysia). In Canada the equivalent movement has involved an increased resort to the concept of unjust enrichment (see *Carabin v Offman* (1989) 55 DLR (4th) 135 at 140–147; *Rawluk v Rawluk* (1990) 65 DLR (4th) 161 at 172c per Cory J; *Soulos v Korkontzilas* (1997) 146 DLR (4th) 214 at 222f–g per McLachlin J).
9   [2003] 1 P & CR 100 at [43].
10   Estoppel doctrine provides no 'charter for idiosyncratic concepts of justice and fairness' (*Legione v Hateley* (1983) 152 CLR 406 at 431 per Mason and Deane JJ). See likewise *Haslemere Estates Ltd v Baker* [1982] 1 WLR 1109 at 1119G per Megarry V-C; *Starr v Barbaro* (1986) 4 BPR 9137 at 9140 per Powell J; *Gillies v Keogh* [1989] 2 NZLR 327 at 331 per Cooke P.

OUTCOME OF ESTOPPEL DOCTRINE

10.211   The doctrine of estoppel begins as an inhibitory principle, conferring on the court a jurisdiction to control or restrain the immediate enforcement of the strict legal entitlements of the parties.[1] The doctrine is initially negative in operation: even the etymology suggests that estoppel is about *stopping* something.[2] Proprietary estoppel provides a holding mechanism which affords time for the court to interpose a considered judgment as to whether, in the light of the parties' dealings, the legal owner's assertion of power is ultimately conscionable. Estoppel doctrine thus works in two distinct stages.[3] First, the claimant who wishes to deflect the normal enforcement of the parties' legal rights must be able to point persuasively to the existence of an 'inchoate' equity of estoppel in his favour. Second, once the claimant has successfully invoked the court's jurisdiction to stay the hand of the legal owner, the court has a wide discretion to 'concretise' the claimant's equity by confirming his entitlement to some specific interest or remedy.

1   *Sledmore v Dalby* (1996) 72 P & CR 196 at 205 per Hobhouse LJ.
2   See e g *Re Basham, decd* [1986] 1 WLR 1498 at 1503H.
3   For a contrary view, see Ben McFarlane, 'Proprietary Estoppel and Third Parties after the Land Registration Act 2002' [2003] CLJ 661.

THE 'INCHOATE' EQUITY OF ESTOPPEL

10.212   The equity of estoppel arises in an inchoate form as soon as the conscience of the relevant landowner is affected by the transactions of the parties.[1] This inchoate equity is brought into being when the landowner unconscionably sets up his rights adversely to the legitimate demands of the estoppel claimant.[2] From this point onwards the claimant has 'an equity which would attract the discretion of the Court',[3] entitling him to bend the ear of the court of conscience to listen sympathetically to his plea for a restraint upon the landowner's exercise of his rights.[4] It then becomes the task of the court to decide whether, and if so in what form, to vindicate or perfect the 'equity' which has been claimed.

1   See *Silovi Pty Ltd v Barbaro* (1988) 13 NSWLR 466 at 473A–B per Priestley JA.
2   *Lim Teng Huan v Ang Swee Chuan* [1992] 1 WLR 113 at 117E–F per Lord Browne-Wilkinson.
3   See *Beaton v McDivitt* (1987) 13 NSWLR 162 at 172C–D per Kirby P.
4   See *Commonwealth of Australia v Verwayen* (1990) 170 CLR 394 at 435, where Deane J described 'an equity' as referring to 'any entitlement or obligation ... of which a court of equity will take cognisance', stating specifically that 'it is permissible to speak of the operation of estoppel ... as giving rise to "an equity".'

Proprietary character of the inchoate equity

10.213   It is now clear that, long before the inchoate equity of estoppel is formalised in any court-ordered remedy, this equity is proprietary in character. 'Property' in land is not a static or absolute jural phenomenon, but exists in varying grades of intensity.[1] The origin of the inchoate equity of estoppel and its subsequent mutation into some court-ordered proprietary interest merely exemplify the relativity – the constantly changing nature – of the notion of proprietary entitlement.[2]

1   [Para 2.13].
2   Even if the court holds the equity to be satisfied not by the recognition of any proprietary interest in the land but by a mere order for money compensation [**para 10.297**], this too demonstrates the infinitely gradable nature of the concept of property.

Gradual acceptance of proprietary nature

10.214   The inchoate (or unperfected) equity of estoppel has never, of course, been easily accommodated within the canon of proprietary rights and interests recognised by the Law of Property Act 1925. For many years the unorthodox or amorphous quality of the inchoate equity caused courts and commentators to relegate this entitlement to the status of a purely personal right.[1] Gradually, however, strength gathered behind the argument that equities of estoppel are endowed with proprietary quality simply because, in common with other more obvious categories of equitable proprietary right, they comprise entitlements which are engrafted[2] or impressed[3] upon the relevant legal estate 'in order to give effect to [equity's] doctrines.'[4] Estoppel-based equities emerged as the functional equivalent of beneficial entitlement behind a trust of land.[5] Consistently with the principle that 'equitable property is commensurate with equitable relief',[6] it became increasingly self-evident that the estoppel claimant acquires some kind of 'property' as soon as the preconditions of proprietary estoppel are met in any particular case.[7] English courts thus began, with growing confidence, to acknowledge the proprietary character of even the unperfected equity.[8]

1   See e g *Pennine Raceway Ltd v Kirklees MBC* [1983] QB 382 at 391A per Eveleigh LJ. For an argument that a licence coupled with an equity falls into some intermediate category of 'quasi-property' mid-way between rights *in rem* and rights *in personam*, see A R Everton, 'Towards A Concept Of "Quasi-Property"?' [1982] Conv 118 at 131–132.

2   *Re Transphere Pty Ltd* (1986) 5 NSWLR 309 at 311E–F per McLelland J.

3   *DKLR Holding Co (No 2) Pty Ltd v Commissioner of Stamp Duties (NSW)* (1982) 149 CLR 431 at 474 per Brennan J.

4   *Commissioner of Stamp Duties (Queensland) v Livingston* [1965] AC 694 at 712E per Viscount Radcliffe **[paras 1.162, 9.7]**.

5   See *Re Sharpe (A Bankrupt)* [1980] 1 WLR 219 at 223C–H, 225G–H per Browne-Wilkinson J.

6   **[Para 12.234]**.

7   For an early recognition of the proprietary quality of the inchoate equity of estoppel, see *Hoysted v Federal Commissioner of Taxation* (1920) 27 CLR 400 at 423 per Isaacs J. This perception came to be widely supported throughout Australia (see *Cameron v Murdoch* [1983] WAR 321 at 360 per Brinsden J; *Beaton v McDivitt* (1985) 13 NSWLR 134 at 158C per Young J; *Milton v Proctor* (1988) 4 BPR 9654 at 9661 per McHugh JA, 9672 per Clarke JA) and was eventually accepted in England (see *Voyce v Voyce* (1991) 62 P & CR 290 at 294 per Dillon LJ ('the equitable rights of the defendant had accrued long before' the instant litigation)).

8   See e g *E R Ives Investment Ltd v High* [1967] 2 QB 379 at 394G; *Sledmore v Dalby* (1996) 72 P & CR 196 at 201; *Lloyds Bank plc v Carrick* [1996] 4 All ER 630 at 642; *Habermann v Koehler (No 2)* (2000) Times, 20 November; *Birmingham Midshires Mortgage Services Ltd v Sabherwal* (2000) 80 P & CR 256 at 262–263 [24]–[31] per Robert Walker LJ; *Lloyd v Dugdale* [2002] 2 P & CR 167 at [39] per Sir Christopher Slade.

Prototype of court-ordered entitlement

10.215   This trend towards proprietary recognition was heavily reinforced by the view that, in most cases, the inchoate equity of estoppel already contains, in embryonic form, the proprietary interest later awarded by the court in perfection of the equity. English courts developed the theory that the estoppel claimant's interest in property 'predates any order of the court.'[1] The court order merely operates, by virtue of some doctrine of relation back (or even on the footing that 'equity looks on as done that which ought to be done') to vindicate some earlier, anticipatory prototype of the entitlement now ordered in favour of the claimant.[2] It thus became steadily more apparent that proprietary estoppel generates anticipatory beneficial rights behind a trust, constructed by the court,[3] which then provides the basis for the court's subsequent order of either specific performance or compensatory damages for breach.[4] All of which returns the argument full circle to the point that proprietary estoppel and constructive trust are intricately inter-related doctrines.[5]

1   *Re Sharpe (A Bankrupt)* [1980] 1 WLR 219 at 225H per Browne-Wilkinson J ('[I]t cannot be that the interest in property arises for the first time when the court declares it to exist. The right must have arisen at the time of the transaction in order for the plaintiff to have any right the breach of which can be remedied').

2   See e g *Voyce v Voyce* (1991) 62 P & CR 290 at 294 per Dillon LJ (claimant of inchoate equity recognised to be the 'equitable owner' of the land in advance of any court order). See similarly *Sen v Headley* [1991] Ch 425 at 440A per Nourse LJ.

3   In *Sen v Headley* [1991] Ch 425 at 440A, Nourse LJ expressed the view that an estoppel-based right to call for a conveyance of land 'is the consequence of an implied or constructive trust

which arises once all the requirements of the [estoppel] doctrine have been satisfied.' See likewise *Re Basham, decd* [1986] 1 WLR 1498 at 1503H–1504A ('a species of constructive trust').

4 See *Commonwealth of Australia v Verwayen* (1990) 170 CLR 394 at 437, where Deane J spoke of the estoppel claimant's cause of action as 'the ordinary one of a beneficiary against a trustee for actual or threatened breach of trust in which the estoppel was relied upon to establish the factual ingredient of [the claimant's] beneficial ownership of the alleged trust property.'

5 As Browne-Wilkinson J observed in *Re Sharpe* (*A Bankrupt*) [1980] 1 WLR 219 at 225H, '[t]he 'introduction of an interest under a constructive trust is an essential ingredient if the [estoppel claimant] has any right at all', since otherwise the right whose breach is remedied by court order would be vitiated by non-compliance with statutory requirements of form or writing (see LPA 1925, ss 52(1), 53(1)–(2)).

Statutory clarification

10.216 The culmination of the movement described above came with the enactment of the Land Registration Act 2002. For the 'avoidance of doubt' the 2002 Act declares that, in relation to registered land, an 'equity by estoppel' has effect 'from the time the equity arises as an interest capable of binding successors in title.'[1] The statute therefore places matters beyond all doubt by acknowledging that inchoate equities of estoppel already enjoy a proprietary character in advance of their perfection by court order.

1 LRA 2002, s 116(a) [paras **2.97, 12.235**].

Can the benefit of the inchoate 'equity' pass to a third party?

10.217 There has always been some doubt whether the inchoate equity raised in circumstances of proprietary estoppel can be asserted, not by the party who originally relied on the relevant assurance, but by his successor in title.[1] There have been isolated suggestions that the equity is merely a 'personal interest' vested in the original estoppel claimant himself[2] and is neither shareable with[3] nor transmissible to others.[4] In view of the modern acceptance of the proprietary quality of inchoate equities, the preferable view is that the benefit of the equity is transferable to third parties,[5] so that a successor in title is entitled to claim an inchoate 'equity' on the ground of an earlier assurance made to, and relied on by, his predecessor.[6] This approach is consistent with the status attached to other 'equities' (such as the right to seek rectification or specific performance) and finds further support in the ancient law of estoppel.[7]

1 See *E R Ives Investment Ltd v High* [1967] 2 QB 379 at 395A, where Lord Denning described an 'equity' based on proprietary estoppel as being available also to successors in title. Winn LJ declined to decide the 'subsidiary but important question whether Mr High's claim, if valid, is only a personal right' ([1967] 2 QB 379 at 403A).

2 See F R Crane, (1967) 31 Conv (NS) 332 at 341; (1990) 107 LQR 87 at 97 (D J Hayton).

3 In *Jones* (*A E*) *v Jones* (*F W*) [1977] 1 WLR 438 at 443D, Lord Denning MR held that the defendant had an 'equity ... of a possessory nature entitling [him] to remain in this house, but it would not ... extend to the defendant's wife.' See also *Matharu v Matharu* (1994) 68 P & CR 93 at 98 (equity not available to representee's widow).

4   See e g *Fryer v Brook* [1984] LS Gaz R 2856, where Oliver LJ tentatively opined that, like the
     personal right of occupation created by a statutory tenancy **[para 14.317]**, the inchoate equity
     was not transmissible to a trustee in bankruptcy.
5   Save in circumstances giving rise to a constructive trust, such a disposition seems to require
     signed writing (see (1995) 7 CFLQ 59 at 63 (G Battersby)).
6   For clear rulings to this effect, see *Hamilton v Geraghty* (1901) 1 SRNSW (Eq) 81 at 89;
     Cameron v Murdoch [1983] WAR 321 at 360 (affd (1986) 63 ALR 575 at 595); *Hill v A W J
     Moore & Co Pty Ltd* (1990) 5 BPR 11359 at 11365. See also M Neave and M Weinberg, 'The
     Nature and Function of Equities' (1978–80) 6 Tas U L Rev 24 at 30. The tortuous litigation in
     Neesom v Clarkson (1842) 2 Hare 163, 67 ER 68, (1845) 4 Hare 97, 67 ER 576 may provide
     support for the same idea.
7   See *Co Litt*, p 352a/b ('every estoppel ought to be reciprocal ... privies in estate, as the feoffee,
     lessee & c ... shall be bound and take the advantage of estoppels'). See also *Brikom
     Investments Ltd v Carr* [1979] QB 467 at 484G–485A per Lord Denning MR.

Can the burden of the inchoate 'equity' pass to a third party?

10.218   There is nowadays much clearer support for the proposition that the
burden of an inchoate equity of estoppel is transmissible to third parties who
purchase an interest in the land to which the equity relates. This matter is
examined in greater detail in Chapter 12 in the context of dealings with title
and their effect on disponees.

THE EQUITY OF ESTOPPEL SATISFIED

10.219   The mere fact that a claimant can demonstrate that an 'inchoate
equity' of estoppel has arisen in his favour does not mean that he has an
automatic right to some particular court-ordered remedy. His equity finally
crystallises only when it is concretised in the form of a specific interest, award
or order determined at the discretion of the court. The existence of the inchoate
equity merely opens up the court's jurisdiction to consider the effect of the
claimant's allegation against the good conscience of the landowner.

Wide judicial discretion

10.220   There is a consensus throughout the world's common law jurisdictions
that, once an equity of estoppel has been established, the court has an
extremely flexible discretion to mould relief in order to give effect to the equity.[1]
The court must 'look at the circumstances in each case to decide in what way
the equity can be satisfied.'[2] The range of possible relief extends widely.[3] In
some cases the court may simply dismiss claims adverse to the equity of
estoppel, effectively by interdicting the landowner's proposed exercise of his
own rights. In other instances more positive action may be required such as the
award to the claimant of some distinct proprietary interest or residential
privilege or financial compensation (possibly secured by lien on the disputed
land).[4]

1   See *Beaton v McDivitt* (1985) 13 NSWLR 134 at 158D per Young J; *Stratulatos v Stratulatos* [1988] 2 NZLR 424 at 438 per McGechan J; *Commonwealth of Australia v Verwayen* (1990) 170 CLR 394 at 412 per Mason CJ; *Stiles v Tod Mountain Development Ltd* (1992) 88 DLR (4th) 735 at 742 (Supreme Court of British Columbia).

2   *Plimmer v Mayor etc of Wellington* (1884) 9 App Cas 699 at 714 per Sir Arthur Hobhouse **[para 10.197]**.

3   See e g *Yaxley v Gotts* [2000] Ch 162 at 175E–G per Robert Walker LJ.

4   **[Para 10.286]**.

A minimalist approach

10.221   It is a recurrent theme in estoppel cases that the court is confined to formulating relief in terms of the 'minimum equity' required to do justice to the claimant.[1] It is the court's duty 'to do equity and no more than equity.'[2] In fashioning its order, 'the court, as a court of conscience, goes no further than is necessary to prevent unconscionable conduct.'[3] The court thus seeks, amongst other aims, to preserve some kind of proportionality between the detriment which has been incurred by the estoppel claimant and the remedy eventually awarded.[4] As Robert Walker LJ indicated in *Gillett v Holt*,[5] it is the function of the court in each case to identify the 'maximum extent of the equity' claimed on grounds of estoppel and then 'to form a view as to what is the minimum required to satisfy it and do justice between the parties.' The court may never award estoppel claimants 'a greater interest in law than was within their induced expectation',[6] but may in some circumstances award rather less.[7] In *Jennings v Rice*,[8] for example, R, a childless widow had told J, her gardener and odd-job man, that 'he would be alright' and that her house (worth over £400,000) would all be his 'one day'. In what emerged later as the mistaken belief that J would benefit under R's will, J and his wife provided substantial nursing care services for R during her declining years. Whilst agreeing that a proprietary estoppel had arisen in favour of J, the Court of Appeal upheld an award of only £200,000 from R's estate on the ground that any larger award would have been out of all proportion to what J might reasonably have charged for his services.[9]

1   **[Para 10.290]**. See *Crabb v Arun DC* [1976] Ch 179 at 198G per Scarman LJ; *Baker v Baker and Baker* (1993) 25 HLR 408 at 412, 415; *Campbell v Griffin* [2001] WTLR 981 at [30] per Robert Walker LJ. The reference to 'minimum equity' does not 'require the court to be judicially parsimonious, but it does recognise that the court must also do justice to the defendant' (*Jennings v Rice* [2003] 1 P & CR 100 at [48] per Robert Walker LJ).

2   *Cameron v Murdoch* [1983] WAR 321 at 360 per Brinsden J.

3   *Waltons Stores (Interstate) Ltd v Maher* (1988) 164 CLR 387 at 419 per Brennan J. See similarly *Commonwealth of Australia v Verwayen* (1990) 170 CLR 394 at 411 per Mason CJ, 429 per Brennan J, 501 per McHugh J; *Stratulatos v Stratulatos* [1988] 2 NZLR 424 at 438 per McGechan J.

4   *Jennings v Rice* [2003] 1 P & CR 100 at [36] per Aldous LJ, [56] per Robert Walker LJ; *Campbell v Griffin* [2001] WTLR 981 at [34] per Robert Walker LJ; *Parker v Parker* [2003] EWHC 1846 (Ch) at [210] per Lewison J; *Lissimore v Downing* [2003] 2 FLR 308 at [9]. See e g *Sledmore v Dalby* (1996) 72 P & CR 196 at 207–209 per Hobhouse LJ **[para 10.280]**.

5   [2001] Ch 210 at 237A.

6   *Dodsworth v Dodsworth* (1973) 228 EG 1115 at 1117 per Russell LJ. See likewise *Baker v Baker*

and Baker (1993) 25 HLR 408 at 415 per Dillon LJ; *Lloyds Bank plc v Carrick* [1996] 4 All ER 630 at 641g–h per Morritt LJ; *Parker v Parker* [2003] EWHC 1846 (Ch) at [210], [244] per Lewison J.

7   See *Sledmore v Dalby* (1996) 72 P & CR 196 at 204 per Roch LJ; *Norris and Norris v Walls* [1997] NI 45 at 55b per Girvan J.

8   [2003] 1 P & CR 100 See [2003] Conv 225 (M P Thompson).

9   'The essence of the doctrine of proprietary estoppel is to do what is necessary to avoid an unconscionable result, and a disproportionate remedy cannot be the right way of going about that' ([2003] 1 P & CR 100 at [56] per Robert Walker LJ). See similarly *Campbell v Griffin* [2001] WTLR 981 at [34]–[36] (promise of home for life satisfied by award of charge in sum of £35,000).

OVERALL AIM OF ESTOPPEL REMEDIES

10.222   Since the principle of proprietary estoppel is an equitable doctrine, it falls to the court to determine 'the equitable way in which to give effect to it.'[1] This discretionary process has always concealed fundamental uncertainties which impinge upon the overall aim of the law of proprietary estoppel.

1   *Sledmore v Dalby* (1996) 72 P & CR 196 at 207 per Hobhouse LJ.

Enforcement of expectations or mere reversal of unacceptable prejudice?

10.223   The history of proprietary estoppel is marked by an ambivalence as to whether the proper role of estoppel doctrine is to give effect to the expectations of entitlement engendered by the parties' dealings or merely to protect against the detrimental consequences caused when these expectations are undermined by an unconscientious insistence upon legal rights. In other words, does estoppel doctrine provide for the specific performance of expectations or only the reversal of unacceptable prejudice? Is estoppel aimed at the validation of the claimant's assumptions or only the recovery of his reliance loss? Much may depend on the precise perspective adopted. The *expectation-based* approach leads to the mandatory delivery of an otherwise unenforceable promise of entitlement. The *compensation-based* approach seeks more modestly to require the landowner to compensate, and thereby eliminate, any unduly burdensome detriment or loss caused by his frustration of the other party's assumptions.

The $100 shed on the $1 million block of land

10.224   The distinction between these remedial perspectives was dramatically illustrated in the hypothetical instance considered by the High Court of Australia in *Commonwealth of Australia v Verwayen.*[1] Here Deane J postulated a case in which A, the owner of a block of land valued at $1,000,000, induces B to incur expenditure on the faith of a wholly gratuitous verbal representation that B is henceforth the fee simple owner of the land. B erects on the land a shed worth $100. It is a matter of critical importance whether the estoppel remedy awarded to B is aimed at the specific vindication of his expectation of entitlement or directed instead towards compulsory restitution of B's outlay as a precondition of A's exercise of his legal right to possession.[2] Under an *expectation-based* approach the court orders A to transfer the fee simple estate to B in order to make good the expectation induced in B. Under a *compensation-based* approach the court merely orders A to indemnify B in respect of the $100 loss flowing from the non-realisation of his initial expectation. The distinction between these two approaches effectively involves the difference between guaranteeing the claimant what he was originally promised and awarding him what he has actually lost.

1   (1990) 170 CLR 394 at 441.
2   On established principle, the shed has, of course, become a part of A's land [**para 1.52**].

Specific performance of expectations

10.225   Many of the early formulations of proprietary estoppel doctrine emphasised the court's jurisdiction to ensure specific performance of the entitlement on which the estoppel claimant had placed reliance.[1] On this basis the estoppel doctrine operates effectively as a procedural mechanism for sanctioning or legitimising the informal creation of property rights in land.[2] The court seeks, in general terms, to frame the remedy in accordance with the representation on which the claimant has relied, so that the outcome guarantees the claimant no more and no less than was actually promised in the original assurance of entitlement.

1   See e g *Ramsden v Dyson* (1866) LR 1 HL 129 at 170 per Lord Kingsdown [**para 10.195**].
2   See generally S Moriarty, (1984) 100 LQR 376.

10.226   The expectation-oriented measure of relief has always been vulnerable to the objection that it subverts both the formality rule which inhibits the informal grant of rights in land and the contractual rule which renders gratuitous promises unenforceable. It also has the incongruous effect, as demonstrated by Deane J's example above, of sometimes awarding fairly substantial rights in return for rather insubstantial investments of money or effort. There is considerable force in the argument that expectation-based estoppel threatens an improper outflanking of the requirement for contractual consideration.[1] The mere fact that a person does not keep his promise is not, in legal terms, an unconscionable form of behaviour.[2] The breach of a voluntary promise ought not of itself to give rise to an estoppel.[3]

1   See e g *Giumelli v Giumelli* (1999) 196 CLR 101 at [34] (High Court of Australia). As McHugh J observed in *Commonwealth of Australia v Verwayen* (1990) 170 CLR 394 at 501, 'the enforcement of promises is not the object of the doctrine of equitable estoppel. The enforcement of promises is the province of contract.'
2   See *Commonwealth of Australia v Verwayen* (1990) 170 CLR 394 at 416 per Mason CJ ('morally reprehensible, but not unconscionable').
3   It is indeed the superadded requirement of unconscionable conduct which is generally seen as

the protection against undue intrusion by estoppel upon the law of contract (see *Commonwealth of Australia v Verwayen* (1990) 170 CLR 394 at 454 per Dawson J).

Recovery of reliance loss

10.227 In response to these objections many jurisdictions in the common law world have seen a gradual, but not wholly uniform,[1] drift away from the expectation-oriented basis of relief towards a more limited rationale founded upon the recovery of the estoppel claimant's reliance loss. In terms of this rather different perspective the court discards any concern to make good the claimant's expectation of entitlement[2] and instead aims merely to compensate the loss directly incurred by reason of the falsification of the claimant's basal assumptions.[3] As Mason CJ observed in *Commonwealth of Australia v Verwayen*,[4] this less expansive rationale permits the court to 'do what is required, but no more, to prevent a person who has relied upon an assumption ... from suffering detriment ... as a result of the denial of its correctness.' Yet this *compensation-based* approach runs the danger, in its turn, that it may often reduce the estoppel remedy to the analogue of a money recovery in the law of tort or restitution. There is, as Deane J pointed out in *Verwayen*'s case,[5] a strongly competing view that estoppel operates '[p]rima facie ... to preclude departure from the assumed state of affairs' and that some lesser form of relief should be awarded only where an expectation-based measure of relief would be 'inequitably harsh'.

1 See, for instance, the division of opinion evident in the High Court of Australia in *Commonwealth of Australia v Verwayen* (1990) 170 CLR 394.
2 See eg *Waltons Stores (Interstate) Ltd v Maher* (1988) 164 CLR 387 at 423 per Brennan J; *Commonwealth of Australia v Verwayen* (1990) 170 CLR 394 at 413 per Mason CJ.
3 On this footing the appropriate estoppel remedy may well be a simple return of the claimant's outlay rather than any large conferment of proprietary title. It 'does not follow that a single act of expenditure would require a transfer of the fee simple' (*Grimison v Union Fidelity Trustee Co of Australia Ltd* (1984) 3 BPR 9469 at 9475). See also *Veitch v Caldicott* (1945) 173 LT 30 at 34 per Atkinson J.
4 (1990) 170 CLR 394 at 413 (High Court of Australia). See similarly P D Finn, 'Equitable Estoppel', in P D Finn (ed), *Essays in Equity* (Sydney 1985), p 61.
5 (1990) 170 CLR 394 at 443.

A flexible compromise

10.228 The proper scope of estoppel doctrine is far from settled. In the English Court of Appeal in *Sledmore v Dalby*,[1] Hobhouse LJ professed to find Mason CJ's compensation-based analysis in *Verwayen*'s case 'of particular value', whilst declaring certain passages in Deane J's judgment 'similarly illuminating'.[2] It is also undoubtedly true that the expectation- and compensation-based approaches sometimes coincide. In certain situations the 'minimum equity' required to satisfy the estoppel claim cannot be attained by anything short of an order compelling the landowner to fulfil the expectation which he created.[3] On occasion 'the only way to prevent the promisee suffering detriment will be to enforce the promise.'⁴ In many instances, however, the two rationales for relief do not coalesce and, in relation to such cases, some firmer guidance has begun to emerge from the case law. In a series of recent decisions the Court of Appeal has confirmed what appears to be a graded response to the remedial conundrum. The estoppel claimant's expectations are said to 'set the maximum limit to the relief' available from the court⁵ and within this outer limit the court then attempts to ascertain the minimum relief required to satisfy the claimant's 'equity'.⁶ On this basis, as Robert Walker LJ stated in *Jennings v Rice*,⁷ compensation for reliance loss may sometimes be the appropriate aim of relief, but 'only where, on the facts, a higher measure would amount to overcompensation.'

1   (1996) 72 P & CR 196 at 208.
2   The High Court of Australia has since ruled that nothing in *Verwayen*'s case confines the court, in granting relief in estoppel cases, to ordering a mere reversal of detriment (*Giumelli v Giumelli* (1999) 196 CLR 101 at [33], [48] per Gleeson CJ, McHugh, Gummow and Callinan JJ, [63] per Kirby J).
3   *Commonwealth of Australia v Verwayen* (1990) 170 CLR 394 at 454 per Dawson J. See e g *Barrios v Chiabrera* (1984) 3 BPR 9276 at 9281 per Powell J; *Singh v Sandhu* (Unreported, Court of Appeal, 4 May 1995) per Balcombe LJ ('the only realistic way of fulfilling the equity').
4   *Commonwealth of Australia v Verwayen* (1990) 170 CLR 394 at 501 per McHugh J. The avoidance of reliance loss may thus 'require that the party estopped make good the assumption' on which the claimant relied, even though in other cases the relief required 'may be considerably less' (*Commonwealth of Australia v Verwayen*, supra at 454 per Dawson J). See also Brennan J at 429, Toohey J at 475–476.
5   *Bawden v Bawden* [1997] EWCA Civ 2664 per Robert Walker LJ.
6   See *Gillett v Holt* [2001] Ch 210 at 237A per Robert Walker LJ.
7   [2003] 1 P & CR 100 at [54].

Specific enforcement of expectations

10.229   Specific vindication tends to correlate with specific expectation. As Robert Walker LJ indicated in *Jennings v Rice*,¹ the expectation-based measure of relief seems most relevant where the representor's assurances and the claimant's reliance on them have 'a consensual character falling not far short of an enforceable contract.'² In such cases the expectation and the element of detriment 'will have been defined with reasonable clarity',³ as for example where a live-in carer is promised that he or she will eventually inherit the home or enjoy lifelong occupancy. Here the parties have reached 'a mutual understanding ... in reasonably clear terms' in circumstances where the 'consensual element' suggests that both parties probably regarded the expected benefit and the accepted detriment as 'being (in a general, imprecise way) equivalent, or at any rate not obviously disproportionate.'⁴ The specific enforcement of identifiable expectations is most clearly appropriate in those cases where the representation of promised entitlement persists over many years and the avoidance of the reliance loss otherwise incurred by reason of the claimant's prolonged onerous efforts is impossible except through the validation of his underlying assumption of right.[5] In such cases the making good of expectations and the reversal of compensable detriment are so closely intertwined as to be indistinguishable.[6]

1   [2003] 1 P & CR 100 at [45].
2   The argument in favour of specific enforcement of reasonably clearly defined expectations is merely reinforced by the doctrinal proximity of proprietary estoppel and constructive trust, the essential emphasis of the latter falling upon the specific vindication of commonly intended entitlements (see *Lloyds Bank plc v Rosset* [1991] 1 AC 107 at 132F–G per Lord Bridge of Harwich; *Yaxley v Gotts* [2000] Ch 162 at 176B–177B, 180B–C per Robert Walker LJ, 191C–F per Beldam LJ).
3   *Jennings v Rice* [2003] 1 P & CR 100 at [45].
4   Thus if the claimant can point to some expectation of a 'readily identifiable equitable interest', this entitlement tends to provide the prima facie measure of relief. As Auld LJ pointed out in *Willis v Hoare* (1999) 77 P & CR D42 at D43, the cases 'show that the courts, as a matter of practicality, look for some ready marker of the parties' intent and of what will do justice in the case.' See *Wayling v Jones* (1993) 69 P & CR 170; *Singh v Sandhu* (Unreported, Court of Appeal, 4 May 1995); *Price v Hartwell* [1996] EGCS 98; *Gillett v Holt* [2001] Ch 210.
5   The foremost recent example of such circumstances is provided by *Gillett v Holt* [2001] Ch 210 (lifetime of labour on farm in return for promise of testamentary gift) **[para 10.243]**.
6   As Robert Walker LJ emphasised in *Jennings v Rice* [2003] 1 P & CR 100 at [51], detriment in some cases 'may be even more difficult to quantify, in financial terms, than the claimant's expectations' (eg the detriment of 'an ever-increasing burden of care for an elderly person').

A lesser measure of relief

10.230   In other cases a more limited judicial response may well be appropriate.[1] A compensation-based approach is likely to be relevant where the dealings between the parties are relatively shortlived and the change of position undertaken by the estoppel claimant is both fairly insubstantial and readily calculable in money terms.[2] A lesser measure of relief is likewise appropriate where, as in *Jennings v Rice*[3] itself, the estoppel claimant's expectations are 'uncertain, or extravagant, or out of all proportion to the detriment which the claimant has suffered.'[4] The overarching task facing the court is to satisfy the *equity* raised by 'the combination of expectations, detrimental reliance, and the unconscionableness of allowing the [representor or his/her estate] to go back on the assurances.' The task is not simply, necessarily or even in principle to satisfy the claimant's *expectations* as such.[5]

1   Mere proof of the factual basis for some proprietary estoppel does not mean that 'a right of enjoyment for life is more or less automatically established' (*Bawden v Bawden* [1997] EWCA Civ 2664 per Robert Walker LJ; *Jennings v Rice* [2003] 1 P & CR 100 at [31]).
2   See eg *Dodsworth v Dodsworth* (1973) 228 EG 1115 (minor expenditure on improvement of realty).
3   [2003] 1 P & CR 100 at [50] **[para 10.221]**.
4   See also *Grundy v Ottey* [2003] WTLR 1253 at [58] per Arden LJ ([2004] Conv 137 (M P Thompson)).
5   *Jennings v Rice* [2003] 1 P & CR 100 at [49]–[51] per Robert Walker LJ.

Fair dealings or fair outcomes?

10.231   An associated uncertainty in the contemporary law of proprietary estoppel relates to whether the central test of 'unconscionability' is measured in terms of *conduct* or in terms of *outcome*. Does the relevant test relate to the conscientiousness of the parties' mutual dealings or to the overall fairness of their outcome? The explicit application of a criterion of 'unconscionability' inevitably places a focus upon personal, subjective and ultimately moral concerns surrounding a relevant insistence upon strict legal entitlements.[1] An outcome-oriented test of estoppel introduces factors which often relate rather more objectively to the social welfare implications of the parties' respective positions before and after the application of court-ordered relief.[2]

1   See e g *Inwards v Baker* [1965] 2 QB 29 at 37D–G [**para 10.181**], where estoppel relief was granted on the ground that it would have been 'inequitable' to allow investment-backed expectations of residential security to be defeated by the claims of rapacious siblings. '[E]quity protects [the claimant] so that an injustice may not be perpetrated' ([1965] 2 QB 29 at 38F–G per Danckwerts LJ). See also *E R Ives Investment Ltd v High* [1967] 2 QB 379 at 399F per Danckwerts LJ [**para 9.101**] ('Could anything be more monstrous and inequitable afterwards to deprive [the estoppel claimant] of the benefit of what he has done?').

2   See e g *Sledmore v Dalby* (1996) 72 P & CR 196 at 198, 204, 209 [**para 10.280**].

10.232   This ambivalence of perspective raises issues which are just as pertinent to the operation of constructive trusts. A preoccupation with fairness of *outcomes* (as distinct from fairness of *dealings*) causes estoppel doctrine to operate as a silent agent of distributive justice. Outcome-oriented applications of estoppel are concerned with the correction of unexplained disparities of entitlement between the parties even where such maldistributions are not attributable to unconscionable dealing by either. At this point there is, of course, a danger that property rules will lose their characteristically clear-cut, crystalline form and dissolve into the 'mud' of discretion-laden formulae aimed simply at producing an 'equitable' outcome in each isolated instance.[1] Some have expressed the fear that estoppel doctrine, like the constructive trust, may degenerate into a blunt instrument of social justice premised on ill-defined notions of fairness and a perceived need to prevent unjust enrichment.[2] The conversion of estoppel doctrine into some virtually unregulated precept of general equitable relief contrasts markedly with the common lawyer's historic belief that relatively hard-edged rules of property are ultimately more efficient in minimising confusion, limiting costly controversies and facilitating the productive processes of commerce.[3]

1   See Carol Rose, 'Crystals and Mud in Property Law' 40 Stanford L Rev 577 at 590 (1987–88).
2   See Browne-Wilkinson, 'Constructive Trusts and Unjust Enrichment' (1996) 10 Trust Law International 98 at 100–101.
3   By settling the ground rules ex ante, crystalline legal principles have a certain social and commercial utility. As Carol Rose says in her racy way, 'sticking it to those who fail to protect themselves in advance ... will encourage people to plan and to act carefully, knowing that no judicial cavalry will ride to their rescue later' (40 Stanford L Rev 577 at 592 (1987–88)).

10.233   Against the background of this discussion of the proper objectives of the law of estoppel, it is now possible to examine more closely the constituent elements of a successful estoppel claim.

REPRESENTATION (OR 'ASSURANCE' OF ENTITLEMENT)

10.234 In order to found a claim of proprietary estoppel, some representation or allowance of entitlement or other assurance or encouragement must have been given by or on behalf of the relevant landowner.[1] Reliance *without* representation generates no 'equity'. Clearly no estoppel can arise where the landowner has always explicitly denied that the claimant has any rights in the land.[2] Nor is there any 'category of proprietary estoppel outside the *Ramsden v Dyson* principle, resting simply on expenditure with consent.'[3] Thus one who voluntarily improves another's land without encouragement or promise of reward does so, in English law, 'entirely at his own risk.'[4] It remains to be seen how the developing law of restitution will affect this position, but existing exceptions to the rule tend to be of statutory origin[5] and few in number.

1   *Jones v Stones* [1999] 1 WLR 1739 at 1745A per Aldous LJ; *Parker v Parker* [2003] EWHC 1846 (Ch) at [235]–[237] per Lewison J; *Easterbrook v The King* [1931] 1 DLR 628 at 636; *Rodgers v Moonta Town Corporation* (1981) 37 ALR 49 at 53 per Gibbs CJ (High Court of Australia).
2   See e g *Haughan v Rutledge* [1988] IR 295 at 301 (expectation of lease rebutted by prior refusal to agree to grant lease); *Gillies v Keogh* [1989] 2 NZLR 327 at 347 per Richardson J (no encouragement of any expectation of rights where cohabitee consistently emphasised her own sole ownership of assets).
3   *Savva v Costa and Harymode Investments Ltd* (1981) 131 NLJ 1114 per Oliver LJ. See likewise *Milton v Proctor* (1988) 4 BPR 9654 at 9660 per McHugh JA; *Haughan v Rutledge* [1988] IR 295 at 301–302.
4   *Stilwell v Simpson* (1983) 133 NLJ 894. See also *Harry Neal Ltd v Clarke* (1997) 75 P & CR D47 at D48 (repair works entirely consistent with what might be expected of rent-free tenant).
5   See e g Matrimonial Proceedings and Property Act 1970, s 37 [**para 10.92**]. Other jurisdictions provide more general statutory relief in respect of improvements effected under mistake of title. See e g Queensland's Property Law Act 1974, ss 196–197 (*Newman v Powter* [1978] Qd R 383; *Ex parte Goodlet & Smith* [1983] 2 Qd R 792).

Source of the representation or assurance

10.235 Where an alleged proprietary estoppel relates to the exercise of rights normally incident to a fee simple estate, the representation or assurance on which the estoppel is based must have been given by someone speaking as fee simple owner[1] or by some other person entitled to act on his behalf.[2] A relevant assurance can be given by a corporate body acting through its employees or agents.[3] There is no strict requirement that the representor should already own the land in relation to which the assurance is made.[4] The assurance may come, for instance, from a licensee who subsequently acquires a fee simple estate, in which case the estoppel is 'fed' at the point of later acquisition.[5]

1   *Ward v Kirkland* [1967] Ch 194 at 241D per Ungoed-Thomas J. The assurance must come from some party qua owner of the land concerned (*Western Fish Products Ltd v Penwith DC* [1981] 2 All ER 204 at 218a–b). The relevant assurance may even come from the crown (see *Attorney-General to the Prince of Wales v Collom* [1916] 2 KB 193 at 204; *The Queen v Smith* (1981) 113 DLR (3d) 522 at 582).
2   The relevant assurance may be communicated by the landowner's spouse (*Matharu v Matharu* (1994) 68 P & CR 93 at 103) or by other relatives (*Greasley v Cooke* [1980] 1 WLR 1306 at

1310A–E) or by his agents or employees (see *Ivory v Palmer* (1976) 237 EG 411), but not by a tenant of the freehold owner (see *Ward v Kirkland* [1967] Ch 194 at 241D; *Swallow Securities Ltd v Isenberg* (1985) 274 EG 1028 at 1030).

3   See e g *Swallow Securities Ltd v Isenberg* (1985) 274 EG 1028 at 1030, where the Court of Appeal would have held a landlord company estopped had the relevant assurance been mediated through its resident porter in a block of flats. No meaningful representation can, however, be made by one company to a related company which is controlled by identical shareholders and management (see *Te Rama Engineering Ltd v Shortlands Properties Ltd* [1982] BCL 692 (High Court of New Zealand)).

4   See e g *Riches v Hogben* [1986] 1 Qd R 315 at 321, 327, 342, where an estoppel claim was successfully based on a mother's promise that she would purchase a house and put it in her son's name if he was prepared to emigrate to Australia to live near her.

5   *Watson v Goldsbrough* [1986] 1 EGLR 265 at 267F per Browne-Wilkinson V-C. On the 'feeding' of estoppels, see Chapter 7 [**para 7.270**].

Subject matter of the representation or assurance

10.236   In order to raise an equity of estoppel, a representation or assurance must confirm in its recipient *either* an understanding that he is already the owner *or* an expectation that he will become the owner of some interest or entitlement which would not otherwise be his.[1] The representation or assurance need not relate to any specific asset,[2] provided that the scope of the intended expectation can later be identified with reasonable certainty.[3] Thus, for example, a valid estoppel claim may arise from an expectation that the claimant would inherit the owner's residuary estate.[4] Even loose language (e g 'this will all be yours one day') can be found in context to relate to an objectively ascertainable asset.[5] It is always said that the assurance of entitlement must be 'clear and unequivocal',[6] although this proposition conceals a number of further difficulties.[7] In practice the courts draw an important distinction between two different sorts of certainty. In the law of estoppel relevant assurances must always be certain as to the *existence* or *inevitability* of the representee's entitlement, but need not be absolutely precise in relation to the *nature* or *quantum* of that entitlement.[8]

1   See e g *Parker v Parker* [2003] EWHC 1846 (Ch) at [218], where the ninth Earl of Macclesfield was held unable to claim a right of life occupancy in the ancestral castle merely on the basis of a 'tradition' that the Earl would live there ([2003] Conv 516 (M P Thompson)).

2   *Jennings v Rice* [2003] 1 P & CR 100 at [46] per Robert Walker LJ; *Parker v Parker* [2003] EWHC 1846 (Ch) at [223]–[224] per Lewison J.

3   It must be possible to make an 'objective assessment … of what is being promised' (*Lissimore v Downing* [2003] 2 FLR 308 at [18]).

4   See *Re Basham, decd* [1986] 1 WLR 1498 at 1510C–E.

5   *Jennings v Rice* [2003] 1 P & CR 100 at [17]. A claim may fail, however, if framed merely in generalised terms of guaranteed welfare or otherwise unidentified benefit (see e g *Lissimore v Downing* [2003] 2 FLR 308 at [15]).

6   See eg *J T Developments Ltd v Quinn* (1991) 62 P & CR 33 at 46, 51 per Ralph Gibson LJ.

7   As Robert Walker LJ indicated in *Gillett v Holt* [2001] Ch 210 at 225C–D, 'the quality of the relevant assurances may influence the issue of reliance'.

8   A promise may be 'definite in the sense that there is a clear promise to do something even though the something promised is not precisely defined' (*Flinn v Flinn* [1999] 3 VR 712 at [80] per Brooking JA).

Certainty as to the nature or quantum of the entitlement

10.237 The rights assured to the estoppel representee must be rights in or over land and must be such as fall within the capacity of the representor to grant.[1] Beyond this the law is relatively relaxed as to the nature or quantum of the rights assured.

1 *Ezekiel v Orakpo and Scott* (Unreported, Court of Appeal, 1976 E No 1773, 20 February 1980) per Brightman LJ. For example, no estoppel can be founded on any assurance made by a person who has no power to alienate, or create any interest in, land or whose dispositive power is fettered by an unfulfilled condition precedent (see *Starr v Barbaro* (1986) 4 BPR 9137 at 9139).

Ex post facto identification of rights

10.238 It is not essential, for instance, that the precise nature of the representee's entitlement should have been explicitly identified by the representor in terms of some specific proprietary right. There is high authority for the view that the equity of estoppel 'need not fail merely on the ground that the interest to be secured has not been expressly indicated.'[1] The expectation engendered by the assurance may involve a fairly inarticulate understanding that the representee will acquire rights of some kind.[2] It is sufficient that, if the other elements of the alleged estoppel are upheld, the court is eventually able to clothe the claimed entitlement in some recognisable form as a 'readily identifiable equitable interest.'[3] In consequence it is entirely possible that an arrangement so equivocal in its terms as to be incapable of giving rise to a binding contract may sometimes be held to confer upon the representee a 'right in equity to a transfer of the whole property.'[4]

1 *Plimmer v Mayor etc of Wellington* (1884) 9 App Cas 699 at 713 per Sir Arthur Hobhouse. See also *Inwards v Baker* [1965] 2 QB 29 at 37B; *Denny v Jensen* [1977] 1 NZLR 635 at 638; *Vinden v Vinden* [1982] 1 NSWLR 618 at 624E; *Cameron v Murdoch* [1983] WAR 321 at 351 (affd (1986) 63 ALR 575 at 595).
2 See e g *Pascoe v Turner* [1979] 1 WLR 431 at 438H–439B ('the house is yours and everything in it' [**paras 7.28, 10.193**]); *Wayling v Jones* (1993) 69 P & CR 170 at 172 ('It'll all be yours one day'); *Yaxley v Gotts* [2000] Ch 162 at 179H, 186B–C, 188B (ground floor 'for ever').
3 *Willis v Hoare* (1999) 77 P & CR D42 per Auld LJ.
4 *Jones v Watkins* [1987] CA Transcript 1200 per Slade LJ.

Categories of recognisable right

10.239 In many cases the subject matter of the representation takes the form of some objectively recognisable right in or over land.[1] In appropriate circumstances the courts have shown themselves willing to identify and give effect to assurances of entitlement ranging from a fee simple interest in land[2] to the beneficial ownership of a share in land,[3] a right of pre-emption,[4] a lease,[5] a licence,[6] and even an easement.[7]

1 Even the inclusion of chattels within an estate agent's printed particulars of sale may constitute a representation that these items will pass with the conveyance of the realty, with

the result that the vendor is estopped from denying that they are within the scope of the sale (see *Hamp v Bygrave* (1983) 266 EG 720 at 726).

2   *Pascoe v Turner* [1979] 1 WLR 431 **[paras 7.28, 10.193]**; *Singh v Sandhu* (Unreported, Court of Appeal, 4 May 1995); *Norris and Norris v Walls* [1997] NI 45 at 55f.

3   *Lim Teng Huan v Ang Swee Chuan* [1992] 1 WLR 113 at 119F–G.

4   *Stilwell v Simpson* (1983) 133 NLJ 894.

5   *Watson v Goldsbrough* [1986] 1 EGLR 265 at 266F–H; *J T Developments Ltd v Quinn* (1991) 62 P & CR 33 at 50–51; *Yaxley v Gotts* [2000] Ch 162 at 177F–G; *Lloyd v Dugdale* [2002] 2 P & CR 167 at [38].

6   *Inwards v Baker* [1965] 2 QB 29 **[para 10.181]**; *Greasley v Cooke* [1980] 1 WLR 1306.

7   *Ward v Kirkland* [1967] Ch 194; *Crabb v Arun DC* [1976] Ch 179; *Singh v Sandhu* (Unreported, Court of Appeal, 4 May 1995); *Dewhirst v Edwards* [1983] 1 NSWLR 34; *Classic Communications Ltd v Lascar* (1986) 21 DLR (4th) 579 at 587–588; *Hill v A W J Moore & Co Pty Ltd* (1990) 5 BPR 11359 at 11365.

Excessively uncertain representations

10.240   Although the entitlements upheld under estoppel doctrine may be indicated in only imprecise or approximate terms, there comes a point at which the court's capacity to intervene is precluded by the excessively vague or uncertain quality of the entitlement allegedly secured by the representor's assurance.[1] As Auld LJ remarked in *Willis v Hoare*,[2] '[t]here are parts that sometimes even equity cannot reach.'[3] Recent case law has stressed that estoppel cannot be claimed in defence of an expectation which falls short of a 'sufficiently concrete character to enable the court to give effect to it.'[4] In rare cases the translation of ill-defined assurances into recognisable proprietary terms may simply prove to be too difficult.[5] A promise of a tenancy may, for example, be wholly inefficacious if unaccompanied by any adequate identification of the terms and conditions of the proposed leasehold grant.[6] It is similarly arguable that no estoppel is generated by a legal owner's general assurance of 'financial security' both before and after his death.[7] Still less is an estoppel raised by an undertaking that a live-in lover 'did not need to worry her pretty little head about money.'[8] Conversely, the more specific the promised entitlement, the more likely the court is to award an expectation-based measure of estoppel relief.[9]

1   See e g *Lissimore v Downing* [2003] 2 FLR 308 at [17]–[18], [54] per HH Judge Norris QC; *Parker v Parker* [2003] EWHC 1846 (Ch) at [232] per Lewison J. The excessively equivocal nature of an assurance undoubtedly influences the issue whether it is unconscionable to allow the landowner, in all the circumstances, to rely on his strict legal title (see *Jones v Watkins* [1987] CA Transcript 1200 per Slade LJ).

2   (1999) 77 P & CR D42 at D43.

3   Some transactions, although involving unconscionable behaviour, may produce a detriment so uncertain in nature and extent 'that even equity may not be able to devise an appropriate remedy for it' (*Willis v Hoare* (1999) 77 P & CR D42 at D43 per Auld LJ).

4   *Orgee v Orgee* [1997] EGCS 152 per Hirst LJ. See e g *Parker v Parker* [2003] EWHC 1846 (Ch) at [222] (insufficient specification of area covered by supposed lease).

5   'I am unable to recognise an equitable estoppel based on a representation which is so uncertain' (*Willis v Hoare* (1999) 77 P & CR D42 at D43 per Chadwick LJ).

6   See e g *Orgee v Orgee* [1997] EGCS 152; *Parker v Parker* [2003] EWHC 1846 (Ch) at [222] per Lewison J (rights of access, obligations of repair and renovation). It is difficult to do justice if, in these circumstances, the representee 'cannot even point in the vaguest way to what form his

ultimately arguable equity might take' (*Willis v Hoare* (1999) 77 P & CR D42 at D43 per Auld LJ). In such cases arbitration is scarcely a feasible solution (see *Parker v Parker*, supra at [232]) and the difficulties left for the court may well be 'insuperable' (*Flinn v Flinn* [1999] 3 VR 712 at [93] per Brooking JA).

7 *Layton v Martin* [1986] 2 FLR 227 at 238G–239D (offer made without reference to any specific asset or assets). Nowadays, however, such representations could be construed as raising at least an 'expectation of an indefinite right of residence' (see *eg Baumgartner v Baumgartner* (1985) 2 NSWLR 406 at 414D, 419D–E per Kirby P).

8 *Lissimore v Downing* [2003] 2 FLR 308 at [17]–[18].

9 **[Para 10.229]**. The restrictive tendency of recent case law also contrasts with the liberality with which 19th century courts were prepared to uphold unspecific agreements for the running of canals and watercourses, referring rent and other terms for settlement by a Master of the court (see *eg Duke of Devonshire v Eglin* (1851) 14 Beav 530 at 534, 51 ER 389 at 391). Compare also *Crabb v Arun DC* [1976] Ch 179 **[para 10.253]**, where again a lack of specific terms of grant did not prevent the Court of Appeal from upholding an estoppel (see *Flinn v Flinn* [1999] 3 VR 712 at [89] per Brooking JA).

Certainty as to the existence or inevitability of entitlement

10.241 It is clear that estoppels may be raised by representations of either *existing* or *future* entitlement,[1] but promises of future rights must leave no room for doubt as to the inevitability of the entitlement concerned.[2] Thus, for example, a mere expression of opinion as to likely future entitlement cannot rank as a relevant assurance for the purpose of estoppel.[3] Nor can a speculative possibility of future entitlement found a good claim.[4] Special difficulties have been caused in two areas.

1 See *eg Re Basham, decd* [1986] 1 WLR 1498 at 1510B–C, where an estoppel claim was successfully founded on acts undertaken on the faith of a promise that the representee would be granted rights in the future. The claimant and her husband had for many years looked after the claimant's elderly step-father, having been encouraged by him to believe that his entire residuary estate would become theirs on his death. It was held to be irrelevant that the claimant's expectations were not related to any existing entitlement, and that she had never enjoyed any (even lesser) form of right in the property promised. See also *Davies v Messner* (1975) 12 SASR 333 at 341; *Barrios v Chiabrera* (1984) 3 BPR 9276 at 9279 per Powell J.

2 It need not have been clear in the mind of the estoppel claimant precisely how the entitlement would arise, but he must have believed that he would become entitled 'in due course of time … in some way' (*Cameron v Murdoch* [1983] WAR 321 at 354, 360). See also *Hardwick v Johnson* [1978] 1 WLR 683 at 687G.

3 *E & L Berg Homes Ltd v Grey* (1980) 253 EG 473 at 477 per Sir David Cairns.

4 The promise of entitlement must be unconditional (*eg* not dependent on the parties staying together). See *Grundy v Ottey* [2003] WTLR 1253 at [49] ([2004] Conv 137 (M P Thompson)).

Pre-contractual negotiations for sale

10.242 Doctrines of proprietary estoppel and constructive trust may sometimes render enforceable a 'gentleman's agreement' for the sale of land which fails to reach the stage of a valid written contract.[1] Such circumstances are, however, highly unusual and arise only where the informal bargain between the parties is both definite and intended as irrevocable. In *Attorney-General of Hong Kong v Humphrey's Estate (Queen's Gardens) Ltd*[2] the Judicial Committee of the Privy Council declined to regard a vendor as estopped from withdrawing from a transaction which had been agreed 'in principle'.[3] Here the intending purchaser of land, acting in the 'confident and not unreasonable hope' that the agreement would subsequently be formalised, had meanwhile paid for improvements to the land, but could not prove that the vendor had ever created or encouraged any expectation that he would not withdraw from the transaction. The Privy Council advised that, in so far as the purchaser had known at all times that the vendor retained the right to resile from the informal agreement, there was no representation of entitlement on which estoppel could be based.[4] Furthermore, an awareness of the possibility of withdrawal from the transaction generally negatives any suggestion that there was true reliance or that the withdrawal is unconscionable.[5] It is therefore extremely unlikely that the conduct of negotiations 'subject to contract'[6] can ever found a later allegation of proprietary estoppel.[7]

1   See e g *Yaxley v Gotts* [2000] Ch 162 [**para 10.111**]. See [2000] CLJ 23 (L Tee); (2000) 116 LQR 11 (R J Smith).
2   [1987] AC 114 at 124F–125A.
3   See also *J T Developments Ltd v Quinn* (1991) 62 P & CR 33 at 47; *Pridean Ltd v Forest Taverns Ltd* (1998) 75 P & CR 447 at 453–455; *Gillies v Keogh* [1989] 2 NZLR 327 at 331 per Cooke P.
4   In *Gillett v Holt* [2001] Ch 210 at 228A, Robert Walker LJ analysed the *Humphrey's Estate* case as 'essentially an example of a purchaser taking the risk, with his eyes open, of going into possession and spending money while his purchase remains expressly subject to contract.' See likewise *London and Regional Investments Ltd v TBI plc* [2002] EWCA Civ 355 at [43].
5   See *Edwin Shirley Productions Ltd v Workspace Management Ltd* [2001] 2 EGLR 16 at [50] per Lawrence Collins J.
6   [**Para 12.20**]. The attachment of the 'subject to contract' qualification to correspondence presumptively colours all negotiations thereafter (see *Cohen v Nessdale Ltd* [1982] 2 All ER 97 at 103f–104b).
7   See e g *James v Evans* [2000] 3 EGLR 1 at 4D; *Edwin Shirley Productions Ltd v Workspace Management Ltd* [2001] 2 EGLR 16 at [49]; *Adegbulu v Mayor and Burgesses of London Borough of Southwark* [2003] 2 P & CR D 58 at D59.

Testamentary promises

10.243   Similar difficulties arise in relation to oral assurances by a legal owner that, in consideration of either past or future services, he will dispose of his land by a will made out in favour of the provider of these services.[1] Testamentary dispositions being inherently revocable,[2] there is always substantial doubt as to whether a representation of testamentary intent can be construed as an assurance that there should be a 'present acquisition of [a] future right by the representee.'[3] The representee would be exceedingly unwise to 'count his chickens before they were hatched',[4] since the courts are fully aware of the notorious tendency of the elderly to exploit their testamentary power by dropping hints as to their intentions.[5] Accordingly the case law of the recent past reflects a deep ambivalence as to whether representations of testamentary impulse can ever be more than mere unenforceable expressions of intention.[6] In *Gillett v Holt*,[7] however, the Court of Appeal indicated that the intrinsic revocability of a will is nothing to the point where consistent and unambiguous intimations of testamentary intent, coupled with substantial acts of reliance, 'make clear that the assurance is more than a mere statement of present (revocable) intention, and is tantamount to a promise.'[8] In *Gillett v Holt* a wealthy gentleman farmer's promises to a favoured farm worker that 'all this will be yours' were considered to impose an 'exceptionally strong claim' on the representor's conscience which could not be disclaimed after 40 years of underpaid labour on the part of that farm worker.[9]

1   Such a promise is, of course, contractually ineffective (see LP(MP)A 1989, s 2(1) **[para 9.15]**).
2   The courts are mindful that 'the right to decide, and change one's mind as to, the devolution of one's estate is a basic and well understood feature of English law' (*Gillett v Holt* [1998] 3 All ER 917 at 929j per Carnwath J).
3   *Philip Lowe (Chinese Restaurant) Ltd v Sau Man Lee* (Unreported, Court of Appeal, 9 July 1985) per May LJ. See also *Layton v Martin* [1986] 2 FLR 227 at 238G–239D. It may be easier to infer a fixed intent in relation to a specific asset rather than the testator's residuary estate, especially if the representee was allowed to enjoy that asset in return for services rendered (see *Gillett v Holt* [1998] 3 All ER 917 at 930f per Carnwath J).
4   *Gillett v Holt* [1998] 3 All ER 917 at 929j per Carnwath J.
5   *Gillett v Holt* [2001] Ch 210 at 228C per Robert Walker LJ. Even more is this the case where an estoppel claimant has actual knowledge that the representor has already made a will leaving the relevant property to somebody else (*Stilwell v Simpson* (1983) 133 NLJ 894).
6   Compare *Re Basham, decd* [1986] 1 WLR 1498 ([1987] CLJ 215 (D J Hayton)) and *Wayling v Jones* (1993) 69 P & CR 170 ((1996) 16 Legal Studies 218 (A Lawson)) with *Taylor v Dickens* [1998] 1 FLR 806 ([1998] Conv 210 (M P T)) and *Gillett v Holt* [1998] 3 All ER 917 ([1999] CLJ 25 (P Milne); [1999] Conv 46 (M Dixon)).
7   [2001] Ch 210 at 227H–228A **[para 10.221]**.
8   See also *Flinn v Flinn* [1999] 3 VR 712 at [76] per Brooking JA; *Rogers v Rogers* [2001] VSC 141 at [98]. Contrast *Lissimore v Downing* [2003] 2 FLR 308 at [40] (where inclusion in a will was regarded not as the performance of a promise, but as a 'pure gift').
9   In *Gillett v Holt* the legal owner had, over the years, made a series of wills leaving the bulk of his estate to the representee. After a sudden breakdown in their personal and working relationship, he made a new will which completely excluded the representee from benefit. See also *Durant v Heritage* [1994] EGCS 134; *Sharp v Anderson* (1994) 6 BPR 13801 at 13814.

The manner of the representation or assurance

10.244   The representation which generates an equity of estoppel may be express or implied; it may be 'active or passive'.[1] A proprietary estoppel can arise in either case if the representee was led to believe that he either had or would acquire rights over the land in question.[2] The determining factor in this context is the impact which the assurance or encouragement had upon the mind of the claimant as a reasonable person.[3] It is irrelevant that the representor did not himself realise the legal implications of his informal concession of rights.[4] The precise manner and context of the representation may, of course, interact significantly with other elements of reliance and change of position.[5] The sheer informality or excessively casual nature of the alleged assurance of entitlement may sometimes,[6] but not always,[7] militate against a claim of estoppel.

1   *Warnes v Hedley* (Unreported, Court of Appeal, 31 January 1984) per May LJ. See also *Singh v Sandhu* (Unreported, Court of Appeal, 4 May 1995) per Balcombe LJ.
2   It is doubtful whether a representation can validly create estoppel rights in favour of the public at large (see *CIN Properties Ltd v Rawlins* [1995] 2 EGLR 130 at 134B–C per

Balcombe LJ), although a similar effect may be achieved by reference to the emerging public law doctrine of 'legitimate expectation' (see *Rowland v Environment Agency* [2004] 3 WLR 249 at [102] per May LJ **[para 10.284]**).

3   *Commonwealth of Australia v Verwayen* (1990) 170 CLR 394 at 445 per Deane J. See *J T Developments Ltd v Quinn* (1991) 62 P & CR 33 at 50, where Ralph Gibson LJ thought that the claimant's subjective belief that he has been promised rights 'cannot be decisive: he must show that the assurance given was in the circumstances such that he could reasonably so regard it.'

4   *Preston and Henderson v St Helens MBC* (1989) 58 P & CR 500 at 503. See also *Wellington CC v New Zealand Law Society* [1988] 2 NZLR 614 at 627.

5   See *Jones v Stones* [1999] 1 WLR 1739 at 1745G–1746C per Aldous LJ; *Gillett v Holt* [2001] Ch 210 at 225C–D per Robert Walker LJ.

6   See *Dubej v Dubej* (Unreported, Supreme Court of New South Wales, 25 February 1991, BPR Casenote 95934), where McLelland J held that a mother's casual comments to the effect 'Well it's your house' could not be construed as representations of an intention to confer a proprietary interest. See also *Wright v Johnson* (Unreported, Court of Appeal, 2 November 1999).

7   See *Pascoe v Turner* [1979] 1 WLR 431 **[paras 7.28, 10.193]**.

Relevant forms of representation

10.245   Relevant assurances may fall anywhere within a broad spectrum which extends from a direct and positive request to incur expenditure, through incitement or encouragement, to mere silent abstention from the assertion of one's rights.[1] In determining the applicability of proprietary estoppel, the courts look for evidence of 'anything done or left undone' which may have induced the change of position alleged by the claimant.[2] The representation of entitlement need not be made, and commonly is not made, in any manner which gives rise to contractual liability.[3] The assurance of rights may even derive from the terms of an agreement which is void for uncertainty[4] or for non-compliance with some statutory requirement of writing.[5]

1   *Ward v Kirkland* [1967] Ch 194 at 239B–C. See also *Taylors Fashions Ltd v Liverpool Victoria Trustees Co Ltd* [1982] QB 133 (Note) at 148E–F.

2   *E & L Berg Homes Ltd v Grey* (1980) 253 EG 473 at 477 per Sir David Cairns.

3   See e g *Inwards v Baker* [1965] 2 QB 29 **[para 10.181]**. See also *Holiday Inns Inc v Broadhead* (1974) 232 EG 951 at 1087; *Gillett v Holt* [2001] Ch 210 at 226C–D, 230B–E per Robert Walker LJ; *Flinn v Flinn* [1999] 3 VR 712 at [95] per Brooking JA.

4   *Lim Teng Huan v Ang Swee Chuan* [1992] 1 WLR 113 at 116F, 118B–C.

5   See e g *Yaxley v Gotts* [2000] Ch 162 at 180B–E.

Representation by silence

10.246   It is in relation to the role of silence or tacit acquiescence that the most controversial questions arise. It is clear that an estoppel can be founded on conscious silence.[1] As Lord Wensleydale said in *Ramsden v Dyson*,[2] if a stranger 'builds on my land, supposing it to be his own, and I, knowing it to be mine, do not interfere, but leave him to go on, equity considers it to be dishonest in me to remain passive and afterwards to interfere and take the profit.'[3]

1   See *The Queen v Smith* (1981) 113 DLR (3d) 522 at 583 (Federal Court of Appeal of Canada).
2   (1866) LR 1 HL 129 at 168.
3   In *Warnes v Hedley* (Unreported, Court of Appeal, 31 January 1984), Slade LJ readily
     accepted that 'in some circumstances passive conduct, even if unaccompanied by any words,
     may suffice to constitute the relevant encouragement, if the facts are such that it is reasonable
     for the other party so to construe it.' See also *Denny v Jensen* [1977] 1 NZLR 635 at 638.

10.247   The courts are nevertheless reluctant to attach significance to mere
silence on the part of a landowner unless it is quite clear that he deliberately
intended that his silence should be construed as endorsing the supposed
entitlement of the estoppel claimant.[1] In the absence of other encouragement,
mere delay in complaining of a neighbour's trespass constitutes no acquiescence in that neighbour's assumption of right,[2] although failure to repel the
trespass may eventually lead to a successful claim of adverse possession.[3]
Silence in the face of adverse occupation can be explicable on the ground that
the landowner 'wanted to avoid trouble' and therefore 'made no fuss'.[4] Likewise
sheer inaction by a landlord in respect of past breaches of covenant by a tenant
does not amount to an assurance that the lease will not be forfeited by reason
of future breaches.[5] But if the owner of an interest in or over land remains
wilfully silent about his interest in the knowledge that a mortgagee would
otherwise be inhibited from accepting the land as security for a loan, this degree
of non-disclosure may estop a future assertion of priority over the rights taken
by the mortgagee.[6]

1   See *Salvation Army Trustee Co Ltd v West Yorkshire MCC* (1981) 41 P & CR 179 at 196 per
     Woolf J.
2   *Jones v Stones* [1999] 1 WLR 1739 at 1745G–1746A per Aldous LJ. See also *Soames-Forsythe
     Properties Ltd v Tesco Stores Ltd* [1991] EGCS 22 ('acquiescence in the sense of laches may
     not raise an equity').
3   [**Para 6.41**].
4   See *Williams v Coleman* (Unreported, Court of Appeal, 27 June 1984) per Fox LJ (no estoppel
     upheld against physically disabled lady confined to wheelchair).
5   *Boxbusher Properties Ltd v Graham* (1976) 240 EG 463 at 465. Prolonged inaction by a
     liquidator while a bankrupt improves his property cannot be taken to connote the degree of
     encouragement or acquiescence required to generate a proprietary estoppel (*Pennell v Nunn*
     (Unreported, Chancery Division, 2 April 1982)).
6   [**Para 12.164**]. See *Midland Bank Ltd v Farmpride Hatcheries Ltd* (1981) 260 EG 493 at
     497–500; *Ulster Bank Ltd v Shanks* [1982] NI 143 at 150A; *Bristol and West Building Society v
     Henning* [1985] 1 WLR 778 at 782G, 783C. An often quoted dictum is that of Lord Tomlin in
     Greenwood v Martins Bank Ltd [1933] AC 51 at 57: 'Mere silence cannot amount to a
     representation, but when there is a duty to disclose deliberate silence may become significant
     and amount to a representation' (see *Canadian Superior Oil Ltd v Paddon-Hughes Develop-
     ment Co Ltd* (1969) 3 DLR (3d) 10 at 16, (1970) 12 DLR (3d) 247 at 253; *Maurice Demers
     Transport Ltd v Fountain Tire Distributors (Edmonton) Ltd* (1974) 42 DLR (3d) 412 at 421).

Reliance without representation or encouragement

10.248   There is, in practice, an indistinct borderline between representation
by silence and the situation where a party acts in detrimental reliance upon
some assumed entitlement which has never been the subject of any representation or encouragement at all (either express or implied). This troubled frontier

represents one of the potential growth-points of the modern law of estoppel, as indeed also of the emerging law of restitution. In English law proprietary estoppel cannot be founded on a mere anticipation or expectation of entitlement, however reasonable, if the relevant landowner has failed to 'encourage or allow a belief or expectation' that the claimant would acquire rights.[1] Detrimental reliance upon a self-generated expectation gives rise to no valid claim of estoppel[2] and the mere existence of a long-standing practice or course of dealings between the parties cannot suffice.[3]

1   *Attorney-General of Hong Kong v Humphrey's Estate (Queen's Gardens) Ltd* [1987] AC 114 at 124F–125A [**para 12.20**]. See likewise *Watkins v Emslie* (1982) 261 EG 1192 at 1194; *Barclays Bank plc v Zaroovabli* [1997] Ch 321 at 330H–331C per Scott V-C; *Harry Neal Ltd v Clarke* (1997) 75 P & CR D47 at D48 per Millett LJ; *Parker v Parker* [2003] EWHC 1846 (Ch) at [235] per Lewison J.

2   See *Gillett v Holt* [2001] Ch 210 at 227H–228B per Robert Walker LJ. See also *Rogers v Eller* (Unreported, 20 May 1986), where the Court of Appeal rejected a claim of estoppel made by long-term permissive occupants who for 40 years had never received any express indication that they would eventually be turned out. Something more was needed in the form of an assurance of entitlement to continue to reside.

3   *Keelwalk Properties Ltd v Waller* [2002] 3 EGLR 79 at [62] per Jonathan Parker LJ (practice of renewing leases at a ground rent rather than a premium). See similarly *Parker v Parker* [2003] EWHC 1846 (Ch) at [213].

10.249   It is at precisely this point that developments in other jurisdictions threaten to outstrip the English doctrine of estoppel. Even in the absence of any assurance or representation made by the landowner, Australian courts have indicated a willingness to order that the owner compensate spontaneously incurred detriment where a failure to do so would be 'unconscionable' or would lead to unjust enrichment of the owner.[1] Such a sweeping doctrine of estoppel relief seems, at least for the time being, unlikely to find a ready acceptance in English courts.[2]

1   See eg *Knox v Knox* (Unreported, Supreme Court of New South Wales, 16 December 1994, BPR Casenote 96808) ('quasi-constructive trust' in respect of 'incontrovertible benefit' conferred by unauthorised improvements). See similarly *Beaton v McDivitt* (1987) 13 NSWLR 162 at 171F–G per Kirby P; *Nepean District Tennis Association Inc v Council of City of Penrith* (1988) 4 BPR 9645 at 9651–9653 (New South Wales Court of Appeal).

2   See eg Browne-Wilkinson, 'Constructive Trusts and Unjust Enrichment' (1996) 10 Trust Law International 98 at 101.

The state of mind of the owner of the land

10.250   Certain difficulties in the application of the doctrine of proprietary estoppel relate to the state of mind which must be shown on the part of the owner of the land which is the subject of an estoppel claim.

Must the owner have acted unconscionably in making the assurance?

10.251   It is widely accepted that, for the purpose of establishing a proprietary estoppel, there is no need to show that the representor acted unconscionably at the point of making the assurance of entitlement in favour of the eventual estoppel claimant. The relevant element of unconscionability relates, not to the initial representation made, but to the later denial of the assumptions thereby engendered in the mind of the estoppel claimant.[1]

1   See *Crabb v Arun DC* [1976] Ch 179 at 195C–D per Scarman LJ; *Taylors Fashions Ltd v Liverpool Victoria Trustees Co Ltd* [1982] QB 133 (Note) at 147H per Oliver J; *Lim Teng Huan v Ang Swee Chuan* [1992] 1 WLR 113 at 117E–F per Lord Browne-Wilkinson; *Olsson v Dyson* (1969) 120 CLR 365 at 379.

Must the owner have known of the reliance by the claimant?

10.252   In order that a proprietary estoppel be raised, it must be shown that the representor gave the relevant assurance of entitlement, whether actively or passively, with the intention that it should be relied on to another's detriment.[1] It must be proved, moreover, that the representor knew[2] or ought to have known[3] that the representee was likely to undertake detrimental action in the belief that he was acquiring some entitlement on the strength of the assurance.[4] If there is no actual or constructive knowledge of the representee's intention to rely on the assurance given, the claim of proprietary estoppel must fail.[5]

1   *J T Developments Ltd v Quinn* (1991) 62 P & CR 33 at 46 per Ralph Gibson LJ.
2   *Ward v Gold* (1969) 211 EG 155 at 161; *Gross v French* (1976) 238 EG 39 at 41; *Savva v Costa and Harymode Investments Ltd* (1981) 131 NLJ 1114; *Appleby v Cowley* (1982) Times, 14 April; *J T Developments Ltd v Quinn* (1991) 62 P & CR 33 at 51–52. See also *Denny v Jensen* [1977] 1 NZLR 635 at 639.
3   *Salvation Army Trustee Co Ltd v West Yorkshire MCC* (1981) 41 P & CR 179 at 194, 196; *Swallow Securities Ltd v Isenberg* (1985) 274 EG 1028 at 1030 per Cumming-Bruce LJ; *Watson v Goldsbrough* [1986] 1 EGLR 265 at 266M, 267E; *Bibby v Stirling* (1998) 76 P & CR D36 at D37–D38.
4   There is no absolute obligation on the representee to point out to the representor that he is just about to act in reliance by incurring expenditure (see *Crabb v Arun DC* [1976] Ch 179 at 198A–D per Scarman LJ; *J T Developments Ltd v Quinn* (1991) 62 P & CR 33 at 52–53).
5   See *Costagliola v English* (1969) 210 EG 1425 at 1431; *Franklin Mint Ltd v Baxtergate Investment Co* (Unreported, Court of Appeal, 12 March 1998) per Chadwick LJ. A fortiori, if there is a requirement (eg as a condition of grant aid) that the landowner be informed in advance of the intention to begin making improvements on the land (*Devlin v Northern Ireland Housing Executive* [1983] NI 377 at 391E per Lord Lowry LCJ).

10.253   Where reliance supervenes during a prolonged period of repeated representation or encouragement, no estoppel can emerge in the absence of knowledge that the assurance was being relied upon by the eventual claimant of the equity.[1] Usually there will be knowledge of such facts as that the representee is engaging in expenditure on the improvement of land,[2] but the representor's knowledge need not extend to the precise nature of the estoppel claimant's change of position.[3] In *Crabb v Arun DC*,[4] for instance, the Court of Appeal upheld an estoppel claim even though the representor was unaware at the material time that, in direct reliance on the representation, the representee was selling part of his land without reserving an appropriate right of access.[5] It was sufficient that the representor had knowingly undertaken the risk that the representee might, in some way, act in reliance on the common expectation engendered by their mutual dealings.

1   *Griffiths v Williams* (1978) 248 EG 947 at 949 per Goff LJ.
2   Such knowledge may be actual or a matter of irresistible inference (see *E & L Berg Homes Ltd v Grey* (1980) 253 EG 473 at 476, 479).
3   There is some suggestion that, in estoppel claims founded on silent acquiescence, the party sought to be estopped must know of the acts constituting the detriment to the other party (*Barclays Bank plc v Zaroovabli* [1997] Ch 321 at 330H–331C per Scott V-C).
4   [1976] Ch 179 at 189D, 197H **[para 10.288]**.
5   Scarman LJ admitted that the Court was applying the estoppel doctrine where the representor knew merely of the representee's 'intention' to rely on the assurance given, as distinct from having knowledge of 'the realisation of that intention' ([1976] Ch 179 at 197H–198A).

Must the owner have been aware of his own strict rights?

10.254   It used to be a precondition of all claims of proprietary estoppel that, at the date of his representation, the representor must have been consciously aware of his own strict proprietary rights.[1] This requirement of knowledge is nowadays confined to cases of 'pure acquiescence', where the only assurance given by the landowner takes the form of sheer silence or, at most, passive encouragement.[2] Accordingly the landowner's ignorance or misapprehension of his strict legal rights does not preclude a claim of proprietary estoppel where the relevant assurance takes a more forceful or active form.[3] Estoppel may apply if one party, although unaware of his precise rights, has by his words or conduct positively induced another party to rely on the strength of a common expectation generated by their dealings or negotiations.[4]

1   See e g *Ward v Kirkland* [1967] Ch 194 at 240B. This requirement stemmed from *Willmott v Barber* (1880) 15 Ch D 96 at 105 per Fry J **[para 10.202]**.
2   *Taylors Fashions Ltd v Liverpool Victoria Trustee Co Ltd* [1982] QB 133 (Note) at 152A, 157B–C **[para 10.207]**.
3   It is irrelevant in such cases that the rights which the owner now seeks to enforce were not strictly pre-existing rights, but were instead rights which came into existence only upon the change of position induced by his assurance (see *Bank Negara Indonesia v Hoalim* [1973] 2 MLJ 3 at 5A–B per Lord Wilberforce).
4   See *Canadian Superior Oil Ltd v Paddon-Hughes Development Co Ltd* (1969) 3 DLR (3d) 10 at 16–17, (1970) 12 DLR (3d) 247 at 253. See also *Sarat Chunder Dey v Gopal Chunder Laha* (1892) 19 LR Ind App 203 at 215–217 per Lord Shand (Privy Council); *Cameron v Murdoch* [1983] WAR 321 at 351.

Must the owner realise that the claimant is acting under a mistake?

10.255   Again it used to be thought that, in order to establish a proprietary estoppel, a claimant must show that the owner knew that the claimant's belief in his own supposed rights was erroneous or mistaken.[1] However, after *Taylors Fashions Ltd v Liverpool Victoria Trustees Co Ltd*[2] this requirement seems to have been displaced at least in relation to cases of the 'common expectation' variety,[3] although it may have a greater relevance to cases of 'unilateral mistake'. As Oliver J pointed out, 'knowledge of the true position by the party alleged to be estopped becomes merely one of the relevant factors – it may even be a determining factor in certain cases – in the overall inquiry.'[4]

1　See *Willmott v Barber* (1880) 15 Ch D 96 at 105 **[para 10.202]**.
2　[1982] QB 133 (Note) **[para 10.206]**.
3　[1982] QB 133 (Note) at 147B.
4　[1982] QB 133 (Note) at 152A.

RELIANCE (OR 'CHANGE OF POSITION')

10.256　In order to raise an equity based on proprietary estoppel, the claimant must show that he has changed his position in reliance on the representation made by the owner of the land.[1] In the absence of such a change of position, what remains is, at best, an informal and unenforceable declaration of entitlement by the legal owner[2] and the claim of estoppel simply cannot succeed.[3] It is the element of prejudice to the representee which confers a legal significance upon the parties' dealings and renders it unconscionable that the relevant assurance, once given, should be subsequently withdrawn or denied.[4]

1　*Re Basham, decd* [1986] 1 WLR 1498 at 1504D per Deputy Judge Edward Nugee QC ('alteration of ... position on the faith of [an] understanding'). It may be difficult, however, to show that a representation to the public at large has been sufficiently relied upon by individuals to found an estoppel in favour of members of the general public (see *CIN Properties Ltd v Rawlins* [1995] 2 EGLR 130 at 134B–C per Balcombe LJ).
2　See LPA 1925, ss 53(1)(b) **[paras 9.188, 10.63]**.
3　See *Jones v Stones* [1999] 1 WLR 1739 at 1745H–1746C per Aldous LJ. See also *Beaton v McDivitt* (1985) 13 NSWLR 134 at 157C–D per Young J (affd on appeal, (1987) 13 NSWLR 162 at 167E, 172D–E).
4　See *Lissimore v Downing* [2003] 2 FLR 308 at [20]–[21]. In *Greasley v Cooke* [1980] 1 WLR 1306 at 1311H–1312A, Lord Denning MR seemed to suggest that there is 'no need for [the estoppel claimant] to prove that she acted to her detriment or to her prejudice.' This view was expressly disavowed in *Watts and Ready v Storey* (1983) 134 NLJ 631 by Dunn LJ (who was a party to the decision in *Greasley v Cooke*) and has found no support in the later case law (see e g *Coombes v Smith* [1986] 1 WLR 808 at 821B–E; *Gillett v Holt* [2001] Ch 210 at 232A–F per Robert Walker LJ).

Ambiguity of 'detriment'

10.257　The notion of detrimental reliance thus lies at the very core of proprietary estoppel, so much so that this central ingredient of estoppel doctrine is often predicated, slightly ambiguously, in terms of a requirement that the claimant should demonstrate that he or she has suffered some form of 'detriment'.[1] As Dixon J astutely observed in *Grundt v Great Boulder Pty Gold Mines Ltd,*[2] no 'detriment' in the relevant sense ever truly arises unless and until the assurance which induced the claimant's reliance is revoked or withdrawn.[3] So long as the relevant representation of entitlement is honoured, the representee who alters his situation upon the faith of it cannot complain.[4] It is only if the representor successfully disclaims his representation by asserting some adverse right that the representee's 'own original change of position will operate as a detriment.'[5] Only then, as Dixon J indicated, does the claimant's act of reliance constitute for him a 'source of prejudice'.[6]

1　See e g *Greasley v Cooke* [1980] 1 WLR 1306 at 1313H–1314A per Dunn LJ; *Wayling v Jones* (1993) 69 P & CR 170 at 173 per Balcombe LJ; *Sledmore v Dalby* (1996) 72 P & CR 196 at 207 per Hobhouse LJ; *Riches v Hogben* [1986] 1 Qd R 315 at 341–342; *Commonwealth of Australia v Verwayen* (1990) 170 CLR 394 at 416 per Mason CJ.

2   (1937) 59 CLR 641 at 674 (High Court of Australia).

3   See *Olsson v Dyson* (1969) 120 CLR 365 at 379 per Kitto J; *Grimison v Union Fidelity Trustee Co of Australia Ltd* (1984) 3 BPR 9469 at 9475.

4   See e g *Sledmore v Dalby* (1996) 72 P & CR 196 at 209 per Hobhouse LJ (defendant's assumption 'was never falsified').

5   *Grundt v Great Boulder Pty Gold Mines Ltd* (1937) 59 CLR 641 at 674.

6   *Grundt v Great Boulder Pty Gold Mines Ltd* (1937) 59 CLR 641 at 675. See also *Wayling v Jones* (1993) 69 P & CR 170 at 173 per Balcombe LJ.

10.258   There are, in truth, 'two distinct types of detriment.'[1] In a strict sense, 'detriment' comprises the *legal* disadvantage which flows from the ultimate falsification of the estoppel claimant's assumptions. In a less accurate sense, the terminology of 'detriment' is often applied rather indiscriminately to refer to the *factual* disadvantage suffered by the estoppel claimant in reliance on those initial assumptions.[2] In many ways it seems preferable to reserve the language of 'detriment' for the prejudice which is inflicted on the estoppel claimant if an assurance initially given is later unconscionably withdrawn. There is, correspondingly, a movement in the modern case law to refer to the estoppel claimant's onerous acts of reliance in terms, not of 'detriment', but of a 'change of position'.[3] This shift in language not only highlights the close parallel between proprietary estoppel and constructive trust, but also confirms the contemporary tendency to envelop the several elements of estoppel doctrine within a composite formula of unconscionability.[4]

1   *Commonwealth of Australia v Verwayen* (1990) 170 CLR 394 at 415 per Mason CJ.

2   See, however, *Gillett v Holt* [2001] Ch 210 at 232F–233E per Robert Walker LJ.

3   For an early reference to 'change of position' as an element of proprietary estoppel, see *E R Ives Investment Ltd v High* [1967] 2 QB 379 at 405F per Winn LJ. See also *Re Basham, decd* [1986] 1 WLR 1498 at 1504D. The terminology of 'change' or 'alteration' of position is commonly used in other jurisdictions (see e g *Maurice Demers Transport Ltd v Fountain Tire Distributors (Edmonton) Ltd* (1974) 42 DLR (3d) 412 at 423; *Mahony v Danis*, 469 A2d 31 at 36 (1983) (Supreme Court of New Jersey); *Wellington CC v New Zealand Law Society* [1988] 2 NZLR 614 at 627).

4   **[Para 10.208]**. See e g *Watts and Ready v Storey* (1983) 134 NLJ 631, where Slade LJ thought it neither possible nor desirable to define 'detriment' except in terms of such 'prejudice … that it would be inequitable to allow the party who made the relevant representation to go back on it.'

Causal link between representation and change of position

10.259   In the law of proprietary estoppel there must be a 'sufficient causal link' between the representation and the change of position which constitutes the detriment to the representee.[1] The representee's reliance on the owner's representation must be clearly established[2] or at least be demonstrated to have been a matter of 'inevitable inference.'[3] Thus the courts have stressed that the representation claimed as the basis of an estoppel must be an *effective* cause of the detriment alleged to flow from its repudiation.[4] As Robert Walker LJ observed in *Gillett v Holt*,[5] 'reliance and detriment are often intertwined.' It must be proved that the assurance has 'induced'[6] or at least 'influenced'[7] the representee's conduct.[8] In all cases other than rare instances of 'unilateral mistake', the estoppel claimant's change of position must be 'referable' to a belief that he would acquire some interest in or over the land,[9] and in the absence of such a belief the claim of estoppel is likely to fail.[10]

1 *Gillett v Holt* [2001] Ch 210 at 232E Robert Walker LJ. See also *Wayling v Jones* (1993) 69 P & CR 170 at 173 per Balcombe LJ; *Ellis v Lambeth LBC* (1999) 32 HLR 596 at 600. The relevant question is not whether, in the absence of any representation, the representee would voluntarily have altered his position, but rather whether, given the representation made to him, the representee would have discontinued his change of position if subsequently informed that the representor was no longer prepared to implement his promises (see *Wayling v Jones*, supra at 175).

2 See *Attorney-General of Hong Kong v Humphrey's Estate (Queen's Gardens) Ltd* [1987] AC 114 at 124D per Lord Templeman.

3 *Lim Teng Huan v Ang Swee Chuan* [1992] 1 WLR 113 at 118D per Lord Browne-Wilkinson.

4 The promise relied upon need not be the *sole* inducement to the claimant's change of position: it may be merely one of several factors which 'influenced' the claimant's conduct (see *Amalgamated Investment & Property Co Ltd v Texas Commerce International Bank Ltd* [1982] QB 84 at 104G–105C per Robert Goff J; *Wayling v Jones* (1993) 69 P & CR 170 at 173; *Gillett v Holt* [2001] Ch 210 at 226G–H; *Campbell v Griffin* [2001] WTLR 981 at [29] per Robert Walker LJ; *Flinn v Flinn* [1999] 3 VR 712 at [117] per Brooking JA).

5 [2001] Ch 210 at 225D per Robert Walker LJ. See similarly *Greasley v Cooke* [1980] 1 WLR 1306 at 1311G per Lord Denning MR.

6 See *Dodsworth v Dodsworth* (1973) 228 EG 1115 at 1117. In *Swallow Securities Ltd v Isenberg* (1985) 274 EG 1028 at 1030, Cumming-Bruce LJ found it 'helpful to use the term "inducing an expectation" rather than the nearly synonymous "encouraging".'

7 *Amalgamated Investment & Property Co Ltd v Texas Commerce International Bank Ltd* [1982] QB 84 at 105A per Goff J. See also *Coombes v Smith* [1986] 1 WLR 808 at 820A; *Layton v Martin* [1986] 2 FLR 227 at 235G.

8 It is notoriously difficult, however, to pinpoint motivations in some estoppel cases. Is the person who pays for improvements in her mother's home 'thinking predominantly of her own inheritance rather than the care and comfort of her mother' (see *Griffiths v Williams* (1977) 248 EG 947 at 949)?

9 The terminology of 'referability', reminiscent of *Gissing v Gissing* [1971] AC 886 at 909F–G, seems to have been introduced in this context by May LJ (see *Warnes v Hedley* (Unreported, Court of Appeal, 31 January 1984); *Philip Lowe (Chinese Restaurant) Ltd v Sau Man Lee* (Unreported, Court of Appeal, 9 July 1985)).

10 See e g *Warnes v Hedley* (Unreported, Court of Appeal, 31 January 1984) per Slade LJ (no credible evidence of 'belief or expectation that [the claimant] was being offered an interest in the house'). See likewise *Clayton v Singh* (Unreported, Court of Appeal, 12 April 1984).

Burden of proof

10.260 The element of reliance is often easily demonstrable as a matter of evidence, but in order to assist proof of reliance the courts apply a 'common-sense and rebuttable presumption of fact' which has been said to 'arise from the natural tendency of a promise.'[1] In respect of any representation claimed as the basis of an estoppel, reliance by the representee is presumed as soon as it is shown that that representation was 'calculated to influence the judgment of a reasonable man.'[2] Once the estoppel claimant establishes the relevant representation and a change of position which is capable of causal relation to it, the burden shifts to the representor to establish that the representee did *not* rely on the promise of entitlement which was given.[3]

1   *Flinn v Flinn* [1999] 3 VR 712 at [117] per Brooking JA.
2   *Greasley v Cooke* [1980] 1 WLR 1306 at 1311C–E per Lord Denning MR. See also *Brikom Investments Ltd v Carr* [1979] QB 467 at 483A; *Hamp v Bygrave* (1983) 266 EG 720 at 726; *Gillett v Holt* [2001] Ch 210 at 228F; *Grimison v Union Fidelity Trustee Co of Australia Ltd* (1984) 3 BPR 9469 at 9474.
3   *Wayling v Jones* (1993) 69 P & CR 170 at 173 per Balcombe LJ. See also *Grant v Edwards* [1986] Ch 638 at 657C; *Re Basham, decd* [1986] 1 WLR 1498 at 1507F–G; *Gillett v Holt* [2001] Ch 210 at 226H–227A; *Grundy v Ottey* [2003] WTLR 1253 at [56]; *Campbell v Griffin* [2001] WTLR 981 at [27]–[29].

Failures of causality

10.261   The importance of causality in this area is such that estoppel claims have often been rejected by the courts on the ground that the representor's assurance cannot be shown to have been an operative factor in bringing about the representee's change of position.[1] Thus, for instance, no estoppel can be raised where a claimant's change of position precedes, and is unconnected with, the representation alleged by her.[2] In the past the requirement of causality has sometimes led to surprising – and even harsh – decisions. The courts have on occasion disallowed estoppel claims in respect of improvements made to living conditions in the family home which, in the courts' view, the claimant would have effected in any case simply for reasons of domestic comfort or convenience.[3] Likewise the courts have refused to apply the doctrine of proprietary estoppel where it is felt that the claimant contributed money and labour, not in the belief that she was acquiring either an interest in the family home or a right to live there, but merely because 'she was part of the family.'[4] In this respect the judicial approach echoes some of the more unpleasantly restrictive features of the related doctrines of resulting and constructive trusts.[5]

1   See eg *Taylors Fashions Ltd v Liverpool Victoria Trustees Co Ltd* [1982] QB 133 (Note) at 156C, where Oliver J distinguished between action undertaken 'on the faith of' a belief that the claimants had a valid right of option and action undertaken merely 'in' that belief. See also *Brinnand v Ewens* (1987) 19 HLR 415 at 417; *Avondale Printers & Stationers Ltd v Haggie* [1979] 2 NZLR 124 at 144; *Concept Projects Ltd v McKay* [1984] 1 NZLR 560 at 565.
2   See eg *Southwark LBC v Logan* (1995) 29 HLR 40 at 46 (estoppel claimant had severed her connection with previous accommodation before offer of new premises).
3   See *E & L Berg Homes Ltd v Grey* (1980) 253 EG 473 at 479 per Sir David Cairns; *Rogers v Eller* (Unreported, Court of Appeal, 20 May 1986). In *Stilwell v Simpson* (1983) 133 NLJ 894, it was considered that the claimant had effected the disputed improvements, not in response to the assurance given to him, but because it was 'natural to him to make the best of his home.' For an extension of this principle to commercial premises, see *Gan v Wood* [1998] EGCS 77.
4   *Philip Lowe (Chinese Restaurant) Ltd v Sau Man Lee* (Unreported, Court of Appeal, 9 July 1985) per May LJ. See also *Coombes v Smith* [1986] 1 WLR 808 at 820F–G; *Layton v Martin* [1986] 2 FLR 227 at 235H–236A; *Lissimore v Downing* [2003] 2 FLR 308 at [53] (cohabitation 'represented an exciting opportunity' and an escape from 'a humdrum life' rather than a 'change ... underwritten by a commitment' from the legal owner).
5   **[Paras 10.54, 10.128]**.

Relevant changes of position

10.262 The change of position required in support of a claim of proprietary estoppel is 'not a narrow or technical concept': the definition of relevant conduct must be approached as part of a broad inquiry as to 'whether the repudiation of an assurance is or is not unconscionable in all the circumstances.'[1] The acts undertaken by the claimant in reliance on the relevant representation must be 'distinct and substantial',[2] but can extend well beyond the expenditure of money or the incurring of other quantifiable financial detriment.[3] The test of substantiality is, again, intimately bound up with the 'essential test of unconscionability', in that the relevance of an alleged change of position turns ultimately on 'whether it would be unjust or inequitable to allow the assurance to be disregarded.'[4]

1   *Gillett v Holt* [2001] Ch 210 at 232D per Robert Walker LJ.
2   *Sledmore v Dalby* (1996) 72 P & CR 196 at 207 per Hobhouse LJ.
3   *Gillett v Holt* [2001] Ch 210 at 232D per Robert Walker LJ.
4   *Gillett v Holt* [2001] Ch 210 at 232E–F per Robert Walker LJ. See also *Greasley v Cooke* [1980] 1 WLR 1306 at 1311G per Lord Denning MR.

Improvement of realty

10.263 It has sometimes been said that the improvement of land constitutes the 'classic way'[1] in which an estoppel claimant can establish that he has undergone a factual detriment or change of position in reliance on an assurance. It is certainly true that reliance is most clearly and tangibly expressed in the form of expenditure on the enhancement of realty, provided at least that these alterations are relatively 'permanent'[2] or 'substantial'.[3] Thus proprietary estoppels have been recognised where the claimant has built a dwelling-house on another's land,[4] or has financed an improvement to or extension of some existing construction.[5]

1   *Shaida v Kindlane Ltd* (Unreported, Chancery Division, 22 June 1982) per Deputy Judge Paul Baker QC.
2   *Griffiths v Williams* (1977) 248 EG 947; *Taylor v Taylor* [1956] NZLR 99 at 103. Compare *Appleby v Cowley* (1982) Times, 14 April per Megarry V-C ('little weight' attached to electrical re-wiring, redecoration and damp-repair of premises), but see also *Beaton v McDivitt* (1985) 13 NSWLR 134 at 157C (maintenance of a road regarded as sufficient).
3   *Pascoe v Turner* [1979] 1 WLR 431 at 436B; *Gillett v Holt* [2001] Ch 210 at 233F–G. See also *Stratulatos v Stratulatos* [1988] 2 NZLR 424 at 436; *Milton v Proctor* (1988) 4 BPR 9654 at 9659. Compare *Gan v Wood* [1998] EGCS 77, where the Court of Appeal rejected an estoppel claim founded on extremely minor alterations and improvements to the premises (£300 spent on blinds). See also *Harry Neal Ltd v Clarke* (1997) 75 P & CR D47 at D48.
4   *Dillwyn v Llewelyn* (1862) 4 De G F & J 517, 45 ER 1285 [**para 10.191**]; *Inwards v Baker* [1965] 2 QB 29 [**para 10.181**].
5   *Hussey v Palmer* [1972] 1 WLR 1286 [**para 10.76**]; *Dodsworth v Dodsworth* (1973) 228 EG 1115 [**para 10.298**]; *Soames-Forsythe Properties Ltd v Tesco Stores Ltd* [1991] EGCS 22 (supermarket refit); *Sledmore v Dalby* (1996) 72 P & CR 196 at 199 (estoppel claim rejected on other grounds [**para 10.280**]).

Disadvantage unrelated to land

10.264   The categories of relevant 'change of position' are not closed.[1] The disadvantage incurred by the relier may be land-related,[2] but there is no requirement that the claimant's change of position should necessarily involve any qualitative improvement of land[3] or comprise expenditure on the representor's land[4] or, for that matter, comprise any form of expenditure related to land at all.[5]

1   See *Watts and Ready v Storey* (1983) 134 NLJ 631 per Dunn LJ.
2   See e g *Watkins v Emslie* (1982) 261 EG 1192 at 1194 (deliberate omission to serve statutory notice of application for new lease); *Crabb v Arun DC* [1976] Ch 179 at 197G (failure to reserve appropriate rights of way on the sale of land). See also *Vinden v Vinden* [1982] 1 NSWLR 618 at 624F.
3   See e g *Pennine Raceway Ltd v Kirklees MBC* [1983] QB 382 at 386B (preparation of motor racing track).
4   *Willmott v Barber* (1880) 15 Ch D 96 at 105; *Dewhirst v Edwards* [1983] 1 NSWLR 34 at 49F. See *Cook v Minion* (1979) 37 P & CR 58 at 65 (installation of water closets on estoppel claimant's own land in reliance on neighbour's permission for ancillary rights of drainage).
5   *Holiday Inns Inc v Broadhead* (1974) 232 EG 951 at 1087; *Re Basham, decd* [1986] 1 WLR 1498 at 1509D; *Gillett v Holt* [2001] Ch 210 at 232D; *Riches v Hogben* [1986] 1 Qd R 315 at 342.

Personal effort and personal disadvantage

10.265   The estoppel claimant's change of position may be measurable in money terms,[1] but there is ample authority that the change of position required need not involve the payment of money.[2] It may instead take the form of a contribution of labour and services in the family home,[3] the devoted performance of 'all the functions of a live-in carer',[4] the working of a farm property,[5] the abandonment of an existing job and home in order to live with or near the representor,[6] or indeed the undergoing of any sacrifice which is not of exclusively emotional significance.[7] The disadvantage incurred may comprise a forgoing of opportunities for alternative employment[8] or for a career outside the home,[9] a failure to purchase[10] or retain[11] other land for use as a home or for business purposes, stepping off the 'property owning ladder',[12] or any conduct which indicates that the claimants 'deprived themselves of the opportunity of trying to better themselves in other ways.'[13]

1   See e g *Timber Top Realty Pty Ltd v Mullens* [1974] VR 312 at 318 (sale of land to representor at heavy discount). See also *Baumgartner v Baumgartner* (1985) 2 NSWLR 406 at 419C.
2   *Re Sharpe (A Bankrupt)* [1980] 1 WLR 219 at 223E; *Greasley v Cooke* [1980] 1 WLR 1306 at 1311G, 1314A; *Watts and Ready v Storey* (1983) 134 NLJ 631; *Gillett v Holt* [2001] Ch 210 at 232D. Money payment in itself is no guarantee that an estoppel will be raised. Payments towards shared household expenses (such as food) or running costs (such as household bills) may more readily be seen as a mere contribution to the current living expenses of the family (see *Hannaford v Selby* (1976) 239 EG 811 at 813 [**para 10.52**]; *Griffiths v Williams* (1977) 248 EG 947).
3   *Greasley v Cooke* [1980] 1 WLR 1306 [**para 10.295**].
4   *Campbell v Griffin* [2001] WTLR 981 at [15] per Robert Walker LJ ([2003] Conv 157 (M P Thompson)).
5   *Gillett v Holt* [2001] Ch 210 at 233E–F; *Beech v Beech* [1982] BCL 231 (High Court of New Zealand).

6   *Jones (A E) v Jones (F W)* [1977] 1 WLR 438 at 442D. See also *Riches v Hogben* [1986]
     1 Qd R 315 at 321 (where a son sold up at a loss and emigrated to Australia in order to live
     near his aged mother). Contrast *Lissimore v Downing* [2003] 2 FLR 308 at [36] (no true
     abandonment of 'career').
7   See *Christian v Christian* (1981) 131 NLJ 43 **[para 10.103]**. See also *Re Basham, decd* [1986]
     1 WLR 1498 at 1505G–H (claimant and her husband 'subordinated their own interests to the
     wishes of the deceased'); *Gillett v Holt* [2001] Ch 210 at 235B–C (claimants 'devoted the best
     years of their lives to working for [the representor], showing loyalty and devotion to his
     business interests, his social life and his personal wishes').
8   *Gillett v Holt* [2001] Ch 210 at 233F.
9   *Greasley v Cooke* [1980] 1 WLR 1306 at 1312A. Compare, however, *Coombes v Smith* [1986]
     1 WLR 808 at 820H–821A.
10   *Cameron v Murdoch* [1983] WAR 321 at 360 (affd without comment by JCPC, (1986) 63 ALR
     575 at 595); *Lloyd v Dugdale* [2002] 2 P & CR 167 at [38] per Sir Christopher Slade. See also *Re
     Basham, decd* [1986] 1 WLR 1498 at 1505F, where the claimant and her husband had refrained
     from moving home in order that they could continue living near the claimant's step-father.
11   *Parker v Parker* [2003] EWHC 1846 (Ch) at [238]–[239] per Lewison J (estoppel claim rejected
     on other grounds).
12   *Gillett v Holt* [2001] Ch 210 at 234H.
13   *Gillett v Holt* [2001] Ch 210 at 235A.

Matters of lifestyle

10.266   It remains uncertain quite how far the liberal understanding of a
relevant 'change of position' can go. Courts intermittently emphasise that, in
response to a representation of entitlement, an estoppel claimant must demonstrate something more than the undergoing of mere emotional trauma[1] or the
inconvenience of an altered personal lifestyle.[2] In *Coombes v Smith*,[3] for
example, a court rejected an estoppel claim brought by a woman who had left
her husband to move in with the defendant, had become pregnant by him, and
had generally looked after the child, the defendant and their shared home.
Deputy Judge Jonathan Parker QC held that none of these actions was
sufficient to found a claim of proprietary estoppel, but simply represented the
kind of conduct to be expected of the claimant 'as occupier of the property, as
the defendant's mistress, and as [the child's] mother, in the context of a
continuing relationship with the defendant.'[4]

1   See e g *Christian v Christian* (1981) 131 NLJ 43 **[para 10.103]**.
2   See e g *Watts and Ready v Storey* (1983) 134 NLJ 631, where the Court of Appeal rejected a
     claim of estoppel in spite of substantial evidence of disadvantage suffered by the claimant,
     who, in response to a promise of testamentary benefits, had given up a Rent Act protected flat
     and had moved from a settled life in his home town in order to live with and look after his
     elderly grandmother. See also *Rogers v Eller* (Unreported, Court of Appeal, 20 May 1986).
3   [1986] 1 WLR 808. See [1986] CLJ 394 (D J Hayton); [1988] Conv 59.
4   [1986] 1 WLR 808 at 820F–G. See also *Lissimore v Downing* [2003] 2 FLR 308 at [20].

10.267   It is likely that courts today are more willing to recognise intangible
personal sacrifice as relevant to the foundation of an estoppel claim. It is clear,
in retrospect, that an important landmark was established by the ruling of the
Court of Appeal in *Grant v Edwards*.[1] Here Browne-Wilkinson V-C drew an
explicit analogy between the doctrines of proprietary estoppel and constructive

trust. He indicated that, under either head, a wide range of ordinary acts of domestic endeavour would constitute a sufficient change of position even though such acts might be referable more to 'the mutual love and affection of the parties' than to any specific belief by the claimant that she had an interest in the house.'[2] It is probable that this broader approach marks the path of future developments in the law of estoppel.[3]

1   [1986] Ch 638. See [1986] Conv 291 (J Warburton).
2   [1986] Ch 638 at 657A–B. Against the background of a mutual understanding that the claimant should have an interest in the disputed property, Browne-Wilkinson V-C thought that 'any act done by her to her detriment relating to the joint lives of the parties is ... sufficient detriment to qualify' ([1986] Ch 638 at 657B).
3   The more positive approach adumbrated in *Grant v Edwards* is symptomatic of the increasing embarrassment of the English courts at the apparent inability of the law to provide satisfactory remedies for those who have devoted labours of love in the context of ultimately abortive family arrangements. There nevertheless continue to be suggestions that the estoppel claimant must be able to point to conduct 'which goes beyond what might normally be expected of the relationship between the parties' (see *Lissimore v Downing* [2003] 2 FLR 308 at [21]).

State of mind of the relier

10.268   The operation of proprietary estoppel is inevitably founded on some misconception generated by an active or passive representation as to the claimant's rights. However, many of the inconsistencies evident in the history of estoppel doctrine are attributable to a failure to distinguish between the differing kinds of misapprehension required in cases of 'common expectation' and 'unilateral mistake'.[1] Following the ruling of Oliver J in *Taylors Fashions Ltd v Liverpool Victoria Trustees Co Ltd*,[2] it is now clear that the claimant need demonstrate a positive misconception as to his existing rights only in instances of 'unilateral mistake' estoppel and not in cases of 'common expectation' estoppel.

1   **[Para 10.204]**. The requirement of misapprehension was, of course, classically expressed in the first probandum in *Willmott v Barber* (1880) 15 Ch D 96 at 105 per Fry J **[para 10.202]**.
2   [1982] QB 133 (Note) **[para 10.207]**.

'Common expectation' cases

10.269   In cases of 'common expectation' the essence of estoppel lies in the fact, not that a unilateral mistake about current entitlement has been made by someone, but that both parties have dealt with each other on the footing of shared assumptions as to their future rights. In all likelihood both representor and representee were fully aware that the representee had no existing rights, but intended that the relevant change of position should generate new rights for him. In such circumstances the offence against conscience which attracts the operation of the estoppel is the representor's subsequent withdrawal from this mutual understanding. However, no misapprehension was ever present except in the sense that the estoppel claimant was induced to believe that he would[1] receive some entitlement in the land which he would not otherwise have[2] and, on the basis of this assurance, exposed himself to recognisable factual and legal prejudice.[3]

1 It is not sufficient that the estoppel claimant believed merely that he 'might' acquire some entitlement (see *Parker v Parker* [2003] EWHC 1846 (Ch) at [218]).
2 See *Holiday Inns Inc v Broadhead* (1974) 232 EG 951 at 1089.
3 See e g *Griffiths v Williams* (1977) 248 EG 947 at 949 per Goff LJ.

'Unilateral mistake' cases

10.270 In the 'unilateral mistake' cases, by contrast, the state of mind required in the estoppel claimant comprises a total misunderstanding of his existing entitlements.[1] An estoppel can arise in these cases only if the claimant undertook his acts of reliance under some complete misconception as to the nature or quantum of his current rights.[2] It is indeed in this context that the requirement of 'mistake' makes perfect sense, for no equity can possibly avail a claimant who, without active encouragement, voluntarily pours his money or effort into land which he is fully aware is not his own.[3] The equity generated for the 'unilateral mistake' category of claimant flows directly from the dishonesty implicit in the landowner's wilful inaction in standing by and omitting to correct the claimant's misapprehension as he altered his position to his potential detriment.

1 See e g *Ramsden v Dyson* (1866) LR 1 HL 129 at 141 per Lord Cranworth LC [**para 10.200**]. See also *Hastings Minor Hockey Association v Pacific National Exhibition* (1982) 129 DLR (3d) 721 at 728 (British Columbia Court of Appeal).
2 'Unilateral mistake' can generate an estoppel even where the claimant had constructive notice of the fact that the land on which he built was not his own. The relevant question is 'simply whether a mistake has been made, not whether the plaintiff ought to have made it' (see *Willmott v Barber* (1880) 15 Ch D 96 at 101 per Fry J). The knowledge required to bar a claim of estoppel based on 'unilateral mistake' is 'real knowledge which would involve a wilful act on the part of the party who has done the building' (*McMahon v Kerry County Council* [1981] ILRM 419 at 421).
3 *Ramsden v Dyson* (1866) LR 1 HL 129 at 141 per Lord Cranworth LC. See also *Ezekiel v Orakpo and Scott* (Unreported, Court of Appeal, 20 February 1980) per Brightman LJ (estoppel claimant had 'spent his money ... with his eyes open').

UNCONSCIONABLE DISADVANTAGE (OR 'DETRIMENT')

10.271 The preconditions for the application of proprietary estoppel are met only if and to the extent that the representee is left *unconscionably disadvantaged* by his reliance on the relevant assurance of entitlement. Only then does his change of position truly operate to his detriment. The minimal objective of estoppel doctrine is to neutralise any unacceptable prejudice which would otherwise flow from the representor's departure from the assumptions engendered by his assurance of rights.[1] Accordingly the element of 'detriment' which underlies all successful estoppel claims is ultimately measurable only in terms of whether it would be 'unfair or unjust' if the party who induced the expectation or assumed state of affairs 'were left free to ignore it.'[2] It must be shown that, by surrendering the representee to a subsisting and unremedied prejudice, the representor is 'taking advantage of him in a way which is unconscionable, inequitable or unjust.'[3]

1   See *Gillett v Holt* [2001] Ch 210 at 233A per Robert Walker LJ (quoting *Grundt v Great Boulder Pty Gold Mines Ltd* (1937) 59 CLR 641 at 674 per Dixon J [**para 10.257**]). See also *Amalgamated Investment and Property Co Ltd v Texas Commerce International Bank Ltd* [1982] QB 84 at 122C per Lord Denning MR.
2   *Grundt v Great Boulder Pty Gold Mines Ltd* (1937) 59 CLR 641 at 675 per Dixon J. See also *Nationwide Anglia Building Society v Ahmed* (1995) 70 P & CR 381 at 390 per Aldous LJ.
3   *Crabb v Arun DC* [1976] Ch 179 at 195B–C per Scarman LJ. See also *Swallow Securities Ltd v Isenberg* (1985) 274 EG 1028 at 1030 per Cumming-Bruce LJ.

Criterion of unconscionability

10.272   Whether the recipient of an assurance is left exposed to unconscionable disadvantage in consequence of his reliance demands a sophisticated evaluation of all the circumstances of the case.[1] The presence of 'detriment' can be assessed only at the moment when the representor resiles from his assurance of rights and seeks to enforce his own strict legal entitlement.[2] The task of the court is to determine whether the prejudice currently suffered by the representee is so substantial 'that it would be inequitable to allow the party who made the relevant representation to go back on it.'[3]

1   'The notion of unconscionability is better described than defined' (*Commonwealth of Australia v Verwayen* (1990) 170 CLR 394 at 440 per Deane J).
2   *Gillett v Holt* [2001] Ch 210 at 232E per Robert Walker LJ. See likewise *Jones v Watkins* [1987] CA Transcript 1200; *Territory Insurance Office v Adlington* (1992) 84 NTR 7 at 18.
3   *Watts and Ready v Storey* (1983) 134 NLJ 631 per Slade LJ.

Cautious approach of the courts

10.273   In spite of the modern acceptance of a broadly based test of unconscionable dealing, the approach of the courts when faced with estoppel claims tends to be restrictive. The courts treat such claims 'with a degree of caution', mindful of the fact that the doctrine of proprietary estoppel 'may have the drastic effect of conferring on one person a permanent, irrevocable interest in the land of another, even though he has given no consideration for such acquisition, by way of contractual arrangement, and no legally effective gift of it has been made in his favour.'[1] There is an obvious reluctance to allow estoppel claims to generate rights disproportionate to the assumed entitlements in which they originate.[2] There is, moreover, a natural anxiety lest the courts should curtail the human impulse of generosity, by creating 'the impression that people are liable to be penalised for not enforcing their strict legal rights.'[3]

1   *Watts and Ready v Storey* (1983) 134 NLJ 631 per Slade LJ. See also *Gillett v Holt* [2001] Ch 210 at 235E–F per Robert Walker LJ.

2   See eg *Commonwealth of Australia v Verwayen* (1990) 170 CLR 394 at 413 per Mason CJ.
3   *E & L Berg Homes Ltd v Grey* (1980) 253 EG 473 at 479 per Ormrod LJ. See also *Marcroft Wagons Ltd v Smith* [1951] 2 KB 496 at 501 per Evershed MR **[para 7.153]**.

Relevant factors

10.274   Numerous factors affect the question whether the strict enforcement of rights is unconscionable. Each case is a matter of 'fact or degree'.[1]

1   *Watts and Ready v Storey* (1983) 134 NLJ 631 per Dunn LJ.

Alternative protection negativing detriment

10.275   In determining whether it would be inequitable to leave unremedied the disadvantage which the representee has incurred, it is relevant that the representee may have had access to other means of safeguarding his own position.[1] To the extent that such other means of protection existed, the argument of unconscionable detriment is plainly blunted (irrespective of whether the estoppel claimant availed himself fully of that protection). Thus, for example, the fact that the claimant was already covered by some relationship of trust in his favour tends substantially to deflect any contention that the subsequent behaviour of the representor abandoned him to some unconscionable fate. As Robert Walker LJ observed in *Birmingham Midshires Mortgage Services Ltd v Sabherwal*,[2] 'a trust, however labelled, does not then leave room for a separate interest by way of equitable estoppel.' The point was well illustrated in *Lloyds Bank plc v Carrick*,[3] where the Court of Appeal ruled that any suggestion of unconscionable disadvantage was negatived by the fact that the estoppel claimant had failed to utilise the protection available to her under an existing bare trust created by her contract of purchase.[4] The existence of this alternative protection displaced any allegation that the detriment suffered by her was unconscionable.[5] Indeed, it could properly be said that the defeat of her expectations was due not to any action of the representor in resiling from his assurance of rights, but rather to the claimant's failure to preserve her estate contract by registration of a land charge.[6]

1   Likewise where the parties have already agreed a contractually binding formula for compensating extra expenditure incurred by one, 'no intervention of equity is needed' in order to bring about a fair result (*Appleby v Cowley* (1982) Times, 14 April, per Megarry V-C).
2   (2000) 80 P & CR 256 at 263.
3   [1996] 4 All ER 630 **[para 9.40]**.
4   Morritt LJ could not 'see how there is any room for the application of the principles of proprietary estoppel when at the time of the relevant expenditure there was already a bare trust arising in consequence of an enforceable contract to the same effect as the interest sought pursuant to the proprietary estoppel' ([1996] 4 All ER 630 at 641c–d).
5   The availability of public sector accommodation for a claimant is irrelevant in determining the unconscionability of the position in which he is left by reason of the representor's withdrawal of an assurance given. Provision out of scarce public resources should not reduce a private liability for the unconscionable denial of an interest promised to the representee (see *Baker v Baker and Baker* (1993) 25 HLR 408 at 416–417 per Beldam LJ, 419 per Roch LJ).
6   [1996] 4 All ER 630 at 641e–g.

Counter-balancing advantages

10.276   In evaluating the totality of the circumstances the courts have been particularly sensitive to the presence of counter-balancing advantages enjoyed by the relier which partially or completely offset the disadvantage which he has suffered[1] and which thereby counteract any unconscionability of outcome. It may be especially important in this context that the claimant of an equity through improvements has meanwhile enjoyed rent-free occupation,[2] or that the representor has in the past shown some forbearance towards the claimant[3] or made generous gifts of money towards the claimant's other commitments,[4] or that the claimant has received more by way of profits drawn from a business than she ever invested in that business in the first place.[5] The courts may therefore deny an estoppel claim if of the opinion that no net disadvantage would be suffered by the claimant if the assurance originally given were allowed to be withdrawn.[6] Correspondingly, estoppels may be upheld if the representor would otherwise be unjustly enriched by the retention of improvements of an excessive or opulent nature.[7]

1   See eg *Watts and Ready v Storey* (1983) 134 NLJ 631 per Slade LJ (detriment involved in relocation offset by benefits of rent-free occupation). For a more recent instance, see *Lissimore v Downing* [2003] 2 FLR 308 at [55] (benefits derived from cohabitation with member of heavy metal band 'Judas Priest').

2   *Sledmore v Dalby* (1996) 72 P & CR 196 at 204 per Roch LJ, 209 per Hobhouse LJ (15 years of rent-free accommodation). See also *E & L Berg Homes Ltd v Grey* (1980) 253 EG 473 at 477 per Brandon LJ, 479 per Sir David Cairns and Ormrod LJJ; *Watts and Ready v Storey* (1983) 134 NLJ 631; *Beaton v McDivitt* (1985) 13 NSWLR 134 at 158G, (1987) 13 NSWLR 162 at 172E–F. Compare *Campbell v Griffin* [2001] WTLR 981 at [31]–[33] (equity of estoppel not extinguished by nine years of rent-free occupation).

3   *Appleby v Cowley* (1982) Times, 14 April, per Megarry V-C (prolonged rent forbearance was 'sufficient satisfaction' for claimants' expenditure).

4   *Jackson v Crosby (No 2)* (1979) 21 SASR 280 at 298, 302 per Zelling J (estoppel claim abated to the extent that defendant had helped to discharge previous mortgage created by claimant). See also *Re Basham, decd* [1986] 1 WLR 1498 at 1505E, where it was indicated that the claim of estoppel would not have succeeded if the claimant's labour on behalf of her step-father had received any 'commensurate reward … during his lifetime'.

5   *Cullen v Cullen* [1962] IR 268 at 282.

6   See *Winstanley v Winstanley* (Unreported, Court of Appeal, 22 July 1999), where the principal beneficiary of the expenditure on improvements had been the estoppel claimant himself.

7   See eg *Clayton v Green* (1979) NZ Recent Law 139 at 140 (installation of swimming pool and carpeted bar).

The equity of estoppel may fluctuate over time

10.277   In assessing whether the representee is left the victim of unconscionable disadvantage, the approach of the courts remains extremely flexible. The equity generated by an estoppel may fluctuate over time. In *Williams v Staite*,[1] Cumming-Bruce LJ expressed a view, now generally accepted, that the claimant's 'rights in equity' do not necessarily 'crystallise forever at the time when the equitable rights come into existence.' Instead, when the owner of land seeks to enforce his strict legal rights against the claimant, all relevant maxims of equity must be brought into play 'so that the court is entitled then on the facts to look at all the circumstances and decide what order should be made, if any, to satisfy the equity.' This approach highlights two sorts of factor.

1   [1979] Ch 291 at 300G–H. See H Bowie, (1981) 11 VUWLR 63.

Misconduct of representee

10.278   An inchoate equity of estoppel may be offset by misconduct on the part of the claimant occurring after the date of the reliance from which the claimant's equity originates.[1] Subsequent misbehaviour derogates from the argument of unconscionability, with the result that the claimant who is guilty of misconduct in relation to the owner of the land may be considered to have come to the court without 'clean hands'.[2] In an extreme case the claimant is 'left with no right at all' and it simply ceases to be unconscionable for the representor to exercise his strict legal rights.[3] In *Brynowen Estates Ltd v Bourne*,[4] for example, there was clear evidence that the estoppel claimant had behaved in a 'quite extraordinarily disturbing and objectionable way', not least by swearing and making obscene gestures at visitors to the caravan park in respect of part of which she claimed an equity.[5] The Court of Appeal had no hesitation in holding that any inchoate equity of estoppel which might have been generated by the circumstances of the case had been amply negatived or dissipated by the claimant's misconduct.

1   Relevant misconduct may sometimes take the form of non-compliance with an agreement which underlay the estoppel in the first place. A party cannot enforce his equity of estoppel whilst in default under such an agreement (see *E R Ives Investment Ltd v High* [1967] 2 QB 379 at 400A–B; *Vinden v Vinden* [1982] 1 NSWLR 618 at 625B; *Beaton v McDivitt* (1985) 13 NSWLR 134 at 157C–D, (1987) 13 NSWLR 162 at 172D).
2   A finding of unclean hands requires evidence of substantial misconduct (see *Parker v Parker* [2003] EWHC 1846 (Ch) at [240]).
3   *Williams v Staite* [1979] Ch 291 at 299D per Goff LJ. See likewise *Milton v Proctor* (1988) 4 BPR 9654 at 9671 per Clarke JA.
4   (1981) 131 NLJ 1212.
5   The claimant had also driven round the caravan park at speed late at night, continuously sounding her horn.

Exhaustion of the claimant's equity

10.279   The claimant's inchoate equity of estoppel may be exhausted in other ways. Estoppel doctrine restrains the representor's denial of an assumed state of affairs only 'until the detriment is removed or the innocent party otherwise compensated.'[1] Equity requires parties to act on the basis of the assumed relationship only so long as the 'equity' raised by estoppel persists. Once the detriment has 'ceased or been paid for', there is 'nothing unconscionable in a party insisting on reverting to his or her former relationship with the other party and enforcing his or her strict legal rights.'[2]

1   *Commonwealth of Australia v Verwayen* (1990) 170 CLR 394 at 500 per McHugh J.
2   *Commonwealth of Australia v Verwayen* (1990) 170 CLR 394 at 501 per McHugh J.

10.280   The gradual exhaustion of an estoppel-based equity is well illustrated in *Sledmore v Dalby*.[1] Here the Court of Appeal agreed that the defendant had initially acquired an equity by reason of his substantial improvements to a house purchased by his parents-in-law for occupation by their daughter and himself. The defendant had undoubtedly acted in reliance on his expectation, encouraged by his father-in-law, that he would be allowed rent-free occupation for the remainder of his life. Following the death of the daughter the defendant indeed enjoyed rent-free residence for a further 15 years. The defendant's mother-in-law, now a widow, eventually sued for possession on the grounds that she required the house for her own occupation and the defendant lived elsewhere with his new partner. The Court of Appeal held that the force of the defendant's initial equity had become spent over the intervening years.[2] In view both of his prolonged period of rent-free residence and of the balance of the parties' respective accommodation needs, it was 'no longer inequitable' to allow the defendant's expectation of rights to be defeated by the assertion of the legal rights of the owner.[3] Taking account, moreover, of the need for 'proportionality between the remedy and the detriment which is its purpose to avoid', it could not be 'properly said that there was anything unconscionable' in the owner now seeking to recover possession of her house.[4]

1   (1996) 72 P & CR 196.
2   'The effect of any equity that may at any earlier time have existed has long since been exhausted' ((1996) 72 P & CR 196 at 209 per Hobhouse LJ). As Roch LJ observed, the defendant would now have 'to be content with something less than his expectations' ((1996) 72 P & CR 196 at 204). See also *Southwark LBC v Logan* (1995) 29 HLR 40 at 47 (any arguable equity now exhausted by fact that children had reached adulthood).
3   (1996) 72 P & CR 196 at 204 per Roch LJ. See similarly *Allen v Allen* [2001] OTC 800 at [39].
4   (1996) 72 P & CR 196 at 209 per Hobhouse LJ ('it is unreal to say that the Defendant has suffered any injustice'). In *Sledmore v Dalby* estoppel doctrine was effectively used as an instrument of housing policy, private law obligations being manipulated in order to secure public law objectives. (The legal owner was living on state benefit and the mortgage interest on her existing home was being paid out of public funds.)

Bars to a claim of unconscionable behaviour

10.281   Several other factors may operate as a bar in any given case to the claim that considerations of conscience require a holding of proprietary estoppel.

Infringement of statute

10.282   Difficult questions arise if the expenditure on which the claim to an equity is based was undertaken in positive breach of some statutory provision or regulation – a problem which is particularly live if the supposed equity was grounded on some improvement to realty which required, but did not receive, a relevant planning permission. In *Chalmers v Pardoe*,[1] the Privy Council advised that the aid of equity could not be lent in support of an estoppel claim based on a land transaction which contravened regulatory legislation.[2] In this respect, an estoppel claim may be barred for want of 'clean hands'.[3] However, the courts, although recognising the force of the argument of illegality,[4] have sought almost any refuge to avoid having to sanction the unmerited retention of an unjustly received benefit by way of improvement.[5]

1   [1963] 1 WLR 677 at 685.
2   See also *Holee Holdings (M) Sdn Bhd v Chai Him* [1997] 4 MLJ 601 at 624C–D (lease purportedly granted in contravention of statute).
3   See *Dewhirst v Edwards* [1983] 1 NSWLR 34 at 51B; *Jackson v Crosby (No 2)* (1979) 21 SASR 280 at 291 per Bright J. Estoppel claims are not precluded, however, where the facts on which they rest represent, not a positive violation of some legislative provision (e g building without appropriate planning permission), but merely a failure to comply with a statutory requirement of formality, writing or registration which would have rendered the claimant's conduct legally effective (see e g *E R Ives Investment Ltd v High* [1967] 2 QB 379 at 399B–C, 403E–F; *Yaxley v Gotts* [2000] Ch 162 at 180B–E). The latter forms of statutory regulation are not infused with so obvious a 'social aim' as the former and the upholding of an estoppel does not therefore collide with irresistible arguments of public policy (see *Yaxley v Gotts*, supra at 175B–C, 191A–C).
4   See e g *Dewhirst v Edwards* [1983] 1 NSWLR 34 at 51B–C; *Wood v Browne* [1984] 2 Qd R 593 at 597–598; *Beaton v McDivitt* (1985) 13 NSWLR 134 at 157F–158C, 159B–C; *Starr v Barbaro* (1986) 4 BPR 9137 at 9139 per Powell J.
5   See e g *Jackson v Crosby (No 2)* (1979) 21 SASR 280 at 301 (strict construction of builder's licensing requirement). See also *Singh v Sandhu* (Unreported, Court of Appeal, 4 May 1995) (retrospective planning permission); *Lepel v Huthnance* (1979) NZ Recent Law 269; *Beaton v McDivitt* (1985) 13 NSWLR 134 at 156A; *Starr v Barbaro* (1986) 4 BPR 9137 at 9139; *Silovi Pty Ltd v Barbaro* (1988) 13 NSWLR 466 at 473D–474B.

Lack of 'clean hands'

10.283   In rare cases the claim to an equity of estoppel can be defeated by other kinds of circumstance which disclose a lack of 'clean hands'. If, for example, the original assurance pleaded in aid by the estoppel claimant was procured by reason of his own false representations, 'it does not ... lie in the mouth of the claimant to set up any form of estoppel.'[1]

1   *Ildebrando de Franco v Stengold Ltd* (Unreported, Court of Appeal, 14 May 1985) per Parker LJ.

Integrity of statutory duties and discretions

10.284   It has long been clear that no public body or agency can be estopped, by reason of representations made by it, from performing a duty imposed by statute or from exercising a discretion conferred by legislation.[1] Indeed, the House of Lords recently emphasised in *R (Reprotech (Pebsham) Ltd v East Sussex CC,*[2] that the private law concept of estoppel has no proper role to play in the public arena, although there is a public law analogue in the form of a concept of a 'legitimate expectation created by a public authority, the denial of which may amount to an abuse of power.'[3] A 'legitimate expectation' of this kind may be raised by a representation or regular practice or course of dealing by a public body which gives rise to circumstances in which that body may not properly resile from the expectation.⁴ No 'legitimate expectation' can be generated under domestic law by any representation which was ultra vires the public authority.⁵ It has been held, nevertheless, that certain 'legitimate expectations' relating to realty may constitute 'possessions' within the meaning of the property guarantee of the European Convention on Human Rights.⁶ Thus, for instance, the European Court of Human Rights has upheld a claim to protection in respect of a tenant's option to renew his lease – an option long assumed by the parties to be valid – in circumstances where the grant of the option eventually turned out to be null and void as ultra vires the supposed grantor.⁷

1   *Western Fish Products Ltd v Penwith DC* [1981] 2 All ER 204 at 218h–219c (no estoppel based on representation that planning permission would be available). See also *Southwark LBC v Logan* (1995) 29 HLR 40 at 46–47 (no estoppel raised by local authority's stated housing policy or by authority's written promise of residential security in council premises in which representee was squatting).
2   [2003] 1 WLR 348 at [33]–[35] per Lord Hoffmann. See [2002] CLJ 3 (S Atrill).
3   *R v North and East Devon Health Authority, ex p Coughlan* [2001] QB 213. See similarly *Challis v Destination Marlborough Trust Board Inc* [2003] 2 NZLR 107 at [105] per Wild J.
4   See *Rowland v Environment Agency* [2003] Ch 581 at [68] per Lightman J.
5   See e g *Rowland v Environment Agency* [2004] 3 WLR 249 at [81] per Peter Gibson LJ, [102] per May LJ.
6   ECHR Protocol No 1, Art 1 **[para 2.29]**. See e g *Rowland v Environment Agency* [2004] 3 WLR 249 at [85], [92] per Peter Gibson LJ, [104] per May LJ. Compare, however, [2003] Conv 184 (P Kenny).
7   *Stretch v United Kingdom* (2004) 38 EHRR 196 at [35]–[41].

Delay

10.285   It is possible¹ that a claim based on proprietary estoppel may be barred by excessive delay on the part of the claimant in seeking relief. The court will not, however, be over-ready to penalise delay by a claimant who has enjoyed unchallenged possession for a lengthy period and whose only default is that he has not taken steps to perfect an informal gift of title.²

1   See *Beaton v McDivitt* (1987) 13 NSWLR 162 at 172G–173A per Kirby P.
2   *Voyce v Voyce* (1991) 62 P & CR 290 at 293 per Dillon LJ.

THE SPECTRUM OF ESTOPPEL REMEDIES

10.286   At root all estoppel remedies involve the judicial curtailment of a strict legal entitlement, often operating as the functional equivalent of relief against forfeiture.¹ In many cases the owner of land is effectively restrained from obtaining the arbitrary eviction of the estoppel claimant or from otherwise causing him prejudice.² But in deciding how to reinforce or concretise the estoppel claimant's inchoate equity, the court can go much further. The upholding of a claim of proprietary estoppel opens up the court's jurisdiction to fashion new rights for relevant parties; and the court may select, in the light of individual circumstances, from a fairly well established spectrum of remedial possibilities.[3]

1   [**Para 14.149**]. See *Milton v Proctor* (1988) 4 BPR 9654 at 9655 per Mahoney JA, 9668–9670 per Clarke JA.
2   Estoppel may interact with adverse possession (see e g *Cullen v Cullen* [1962] IR 268 at 292, where Kenny J deliberately intended that the upholding of an estoppel claim, whilst not conferring any immediate right upon the estoppel claimant, would enable him to be registered as the proprietor of the land at the end of the relevant limitation period).
3   See *Stratulatos v Stratulatos* [1988] 2 NZLR 424 at 438 per McGechan J. See also S Gardner, 'The Remedial Discretion in Proprietary Estoppel' (1999) 115 LQR 438.

The general principle

10.287   The general principle of relief relevant to proprietary estoppel was stated over a century ago in *Plimmer v Mayor etc of Wellington*.[1] Here the Judicial Committee of the Privy Council held that when an equity has been raised, 'the Court must look at the circumstances in each case to decide in what way the equity can be satisfied.'[2] The court has an extremely wide discretion to formulate the remedy required to do justice to the claimant.[3] Sometimes the remedial outcome is tantamount to specific enforcement of the original promise of rights[4]; at the other end of the remedial spectrum the circumstances may call for nothing more than an order for money compensation[5] or a simple injunction restraining the landowner's exercise of his adverse rights.

1   (1884) 9 App Cas 699 at 714 [**para 10.197**].
2   See also *Chalmers v Pardoe* [1963] 1 WLR 677 at 682; *Inwards v Baker* [1965] 2 QB 29 at 37B; *E R Ives Investment Ltd v High* [1967] 2 QB 379 at 395A; *Amalgamated Investment & Property Co Ltd v Texas Commerce International Bank Ltd* [1982] QB 84 at 122D; *Voyce v Voyce* (1991) 62 P & CR 290 at 293.
3   For an extreme example, see *Stiles v Tod Mountain Development Ltd* (1992) 88 DLR (4th) 735 at 753–755, where the Supreme Court of British Columbia directed the representor's successor in title to offer an alternative plot of land to the representee and ordered the representee to move the house which he had constructed to that plot.
4   Such relief 'represents the outer limits within which the relief appropriate to do justice between the parties should be framed' (*Commonwealth of Australia v Verwayen* (1990) 170 CLR 394 at 446 per Deane J).
5   *Commonwealth of Australia v Verwayen* (1990) 170 CLR 394 at 442 per Deane J.

Guidelines for the exercise of discretion

10.288   The court's discretion to fashion the appropriate remedy is substantial. As Lord Denning MR observed in *Crabb v Arun DC*,[1] here 'equity is displayed at its most flexible.' The remedy required to satisfy the claim of proprietary estoppel may fluctuate over time.[2] The court may take into account all supervening circumstances occurring before the date of the hearing.[3] Developments subsequent to the date on which the equity was initially raised may move the court either to withhold relief from the claimant or to grant relief in terms other than those which it would have been inclined to order at an earlier stage.[4] In *Crabb v Arun DC*,[5] for example, the Court of Appeal satisfied the equity claimed by ordering the grant of a right of access without compensation, even though had the same equity been asserted earlier, the Court would have ordered the claimant to make some payment in respect of the access sought. During the intervening period the party denying the equity had acted with 'high-handedness' and had sterilised the user of an industrial estate by the denial of access, and for this the Court was prepared to impose a penalty.

1   [1976] Ch 179 at 189F.
2   [**Para 10.279**].
3   *Williams v Staite* [1979] Ch 291 at 298F per Goff LJ; *Voyce v Voyce* (1991) 62 P & CR 290 at 296 per Nicholls LJ.
4   See e g *Dodsworth v Dodsworth* (1973) 228 EG 1115, where the Court of Appeal took into account the changed circumstances caused by the death of the legal owner following the original assurance of accommodation rights.
5   [1976] Ch 179 at 189G–190A, 192E, 199C–F [**para 10.198**].

Use of estoppel as either a 'sword' or a 'shield'

10.289   It is now a commonplace that the doctrine of proprietary estoppel can be used as a sword and not merely as a shield.[1] 'In its enlarged and elevated nature as proprietary estoppel, equity stands ready to strike or defend as and when conscience demands.'[2] There is nevertheless some evidence that proprietary estoppel is more readily applied as a shield rather than as a sword. The courts tend to demonstrate a greater tolerance of defensive claims (e g where the representee seeks to resist some immediate threat to his residential security) than of positive claims where, in the absence of any threat to the claimant's security of tenure, estoppel doctrine is used as a platform for demanding new rights.[3]

1   See *Crabb v Arun DC* [1976] Ch 179 at 187D–E per Lord Denning MR; *Thomas v Thomas* [1956] NZLR 785 at 793; *Dewhirst v Edwards* [1983] 1 NSWLR 34 at 49E; *Zelmer v Victor Projects Ltd* (1997) 147 DLR (4th) 216 at 228; *Depew v Wilkes* (2000) 193 DLR (4th) 529 at [63]; *Trethewey-Edge Dyking District v Coniagas Ranches Ltd* (2003) 224 DLR (4th) 611 at [66]. 'Purists may regret the use of the word "estoppel" as the name of a sword but it seems now too late to challenge the usage' (*Jackson v Crosby (No 2)* (1979) 21 SASR 280 at 287 per Bright J).
2   *Classic Communications Ltd v Lascar* (1986) 21 DLR (4th) 579 at 587 per Pennell J.
3   See e g *Savva v Costa and Harymode Investments Ltd* (1981) 131 NLJ 1114, where, in rejecting a positive claim for a property transfer or a reimbursement for improvements, the Court of Appeal indicated that it would have regarded the plea of proprietary estoppel much more favourably if the litigation had been precipitated by a threat to dispossess the claimant and her children from the defendant's property. See also *Stilwell v Simpson* (1983) 133 NLJ 894.

Proportionality of relief

10.290   As Mason CJ stated in *Commonwealth of Australia v Verwayen*,[1] a 'central element' of estoppel doctrine is that there must be 'a proportionality between the remedy and the detriment which is its purpose to avoid.'[2] In responding to the claim on conscience implicit in the plea of proprietary estoppel, the court is therefore restricted to framing relief in terms of the 'minimum equity' required to satisfy the equity raised by the claimant.[3]

1   (1990) 170 CLR 394 at 413.
2   Mason CJ emphasised that it would be 'wholly inequitable and unjust to insist upon a disproportionate making good of the relevant assumption.' For Deane J it was clear that 'a doctrine based on good conscience' should not be converted by excessively zealous application into 'an instrument of injustice or oppression' ((1990) 170 CLR 394 at 442).
3   *Crabb v Arun DC* [1976] Ch 179 at 198G per Scarman LJ. The reference to 'minimum equity' **[para 10.221]** is a consistent feature of estoppel case law across the world (see *Pascoe v Turner* [1979] 1 WLR 431 at 438A per Cumming-Bruce LJ; *Sledmore v Dalby* (1996) 72 P & CR 196 at 204–205 per Roch LJ; *Yaxley v Gotts* [2000] Ch 162 at 175E–F per Robert Walker LJ; *Gillett v Holt* [2001] Ch 210 at 235E–F, 237A per Robert Walker LJ; *Waltons Stores (Interstate) Ltd v Maher* (1988) 164 CLR 387 at 404 per Mason CJ and Wilson J; *Commonwealth of Australia v Verwayen* (1990) 170 CLR 394 at 429 per Brennan J; *Trethewey-Edge Dyking District v Coniagas Ranches Ltd* (2003) 224 DLR (4th) 611 at [77], [84]).

Range of possible remedies

10.291   In the determination of appropriate relief each case 'is one of degree'.[1] Certain factors may point towards the larger and more radical forms of relief.[2] The circumstance that an assumption has been relied upon for an extended period may justify a court in requiring that the assumption be made good.[3] The same result may follow where the detriment incurred by the claimant is 'substantial and irreversible' or 'cannot satisfactorily be compensated or remedied'.[4] In different circumstances the 'equity' raised by estoppel may be wholly satisfied by a binding offer of money compensation[5] (possibly charged on the land concerned[6]). Alternatively – particularly in cases involving an assumption about a future state of affairs – significant detriment to the claimant may be avoided altogether if he is given 'reasonable notice of the intended departure' from the relevant assumption.[7] The range of possible estoppel-based remedies includes the following.

1   *Commonwealth of Australia v Verwayen* (1990) 170 CLR 394 at 416 per Mason CJ.
2   See generally P D Finn, 'Equitable Estoppel', in P D Finn (ed), *Essays in Equity* (Sydney 1985), pp 92–93.
3   *Commonwealth of Australia v Verwayen* (1990) 170 CLR 394 at 416 per Mason CJ. See *Voyce v Voyce* (1991) 62 P & CR 290 at 293.
4   *Commonwealth of Australia v Verwayen* (1990) 170 CLR 394 at 416 per Mason CJ.
5   *Commonwealth of Australia v Verwayen* (1990) 170 CLR 394 at 441–442 per Deane J, who thought such relief to be the appropriate solution of the 'million dollar block' problem **[para 10.224]**.
6   See e g *Campbell v Griffin* [2001] WTLR 981 at [36].
7   *Commonwealth of Australia v Verwayen* (1990) 170 CLR 394 at 442 per Deane J.

Grant of an unqualified estate or interest in land

10.292   In some cases the detriment flowing from dislocation of a promised entitlement is such that the equity of estoppel can be satisfied only by a court order that the full assumed entitlement be transferred or granted to the estoppel claimant. In such circumstances the court translates the claimant's expectation of rights into some identifiable proprietary entitlement which the representor is then directed to transfer to or otherwise recognise on behalf of the claimant. In relatively rare cases a court may even direct the conveyance of a fee simple estate,[1] particularly where a 'clean break' is advisable in order to avoid or minimise future friction.[2] In *Pascoe v Turner*,[3] for example, the Court of Appeal recognised that only the freehold title could protect the claimant from the 'ruthless' behaviour of her former lover and provide her with an interest which she might charge in order to raise finance for future repairs and improvements to the property.[4] In these circumstances the Court preferred to enforce the claimant's expectation of title, rather than to award a mere restitution of her outlay on repairs and improvements, and accordingly ordered the representor to perfect his imperfect gift of realty.[5] In other cases the courts have seen fit to satisfy the equity by granting or confirming such entitlements as a leasehold estate in land[6] or a fractional beneficial share.[7] In appropriate circumstances the courts have also granted rights akin to an easement,[8] or have allowed the claimant to purchase the disputed land at a discount.[9]

1   See e g *Norris and Norris v Walls* [1997] NI 45 at 55f. Such orders are far from inevitable (see *Barrios v Chiabrera* (1984) 3 BPR 9276 at 9279 per Powell J). The transfer of an interest in the land is often wholly 'disproportionate to the identified detriments to which the [claimant] can point' (*Beaton v McDivitt* (1987) 13 NSWLR 162 at 172F per Kirby P).

2   See *Gillett v Holt* [2001] Ch 210 at 237A–B per Robert Walker LJ; *Jennings v Rice* [2003] 1 P & CR 100 at [52] per Robert Walker LJ. The 'clean break' argument may, of course, incline the court to make only a money award to the estoppel claimant (see eg *Campbell v Griffin* [2001] WTLR 981 at [34]) or even to order no relief at all (see e g *Parker v Parker* [2003] EWHC 1846 (Ch) at [243]–[244]).

3   [1979] 1 WLR 431 at 439B [**paras 7.28, 10.193**].

4   See *Jennings v Rice* [2003] 1 P & CR 100 at [26] per Aldous LJ, [52] per Robert Walker LJ.

5   See also *Dillwyn v Llewelyn* (1862) 4 De G F & J 517 at 523, 45 ER 1285 at 1287; *Cameron v Cameron* (1892) 11 NZLR 642 at 659; *Eagleson v Public Trustee* [1922] NZLR 1054 at 1057. Contrast *Stratulatos v Stratulatos* [1988] 2 NZLR 424 at 439, where McGechan J thought that it would 'offend conscience' to order a conveyance of the family home to a 'former wife now remarried and effectively a stranger to the family'.

6   *Siew Soon Wah v Yong Tong Hong* [1973] AC 836 at 846B (JCPC); *Watson v Goldsbrough* [1986] 1 EGLR 265 at 266F–H; *J T Developments Ltd v Quinn* (1991) 62 P & CR 33 at 50–51; *Andrews v Colonial Mutual Life Assurance Society Ltd* [1982] 2 NZLR 556 at 570. Compensation may be awarded if it is no longer possible or practicable to enforce a lease (see *Brownlee v Duggan* (1976) 27 NILQ 291).

7   *Preston and Henderson v St Helens MBC* (1989) 58 P & CR 500 at 505; *Barrios v Chiabrera* (1984) 3 BPR 9276 at 9280f–9281; *Lim Teng Huan v Ang Swee Chuan* [1992] 1 WLR 113 at 119G–H.

8   *E R Ives Investment Ltd v High* [1967] 2 QB 379 at 396E, 406B [**para 10.198**]; *Crabb v Arun DC* [1976] Ch 179 at 190A, 192D, 199F [**para 10.288**]; *Hill v A W J Moore & Co Pty Ltd* (1990) 5 BPR 11359 at 11365; *Trethewey-Edge Dyking District v Coniagas Ranches Ltd* (2003) 224 DLR (4th) 611 at [56].

9   *Cameron v Murdoch* [1983] WAR 321 at 360 (affd by JCPC, (1986) 63 ALR 575 at 595).

10.293   Restrictions or conditions may be attached to any proprietary interest granted by the court.[1] In *Williams v Staite*,[2] for instance, Goff LJ accepted that any right awarded to an estoppel claimant could be limited in point of time or made determinable on express conditions,[3] in which case a court might later have to rule on whether the interest had expired or the determining event had occurred.[4] However, once the claimant's equity of estoppel has crystallised in some proprietary interest awarded by the court, this right (unlike the inchoate equity which preceded it[5]) cannot be curtailed or forfeited by 'subsequent excessive user or bad behaviour towards the legal owner.'[6]

1   *Bank Negara Indonesia v Hoalim* [1973] 2 MLJ 3 at 5C. See e g *Riches v Hogben* [1986] 1 Qd R 315 at 321–322, 327, 343, where the Full Court of the Queensland Supreme Court ordered a transfer of the legal title to the estoppel claimant, subject to an equitable life interest for the maker of the relevant assurance, thereby enabling the latter to reside in a 'granny flat' associated with the property.
2   [1979] Ch 291 at 300B–C.
3   See e g *E R Ives Investment Ltd v High* [1967] 2 QB 379 at 395A (right of way so long as neighbour's foundations encroached); *Classic Communications Ltd v Lascar* (1986) 21 DLR (4th) 579 at 588 (easement to install cable on hydro poles so long as hydro poles remained on land).
4   See also *Riches v Hogben* [1986] 1 Qd R 315 at 321.
5   See *J Willis & Son v Willis* (1986) 277 EG 1133 per Parker LJ.
6   *Williams v Staite* [1979] Ch 291 at 300B per Goff LJ. (Such misconduct may, of course, give rise to injunctive or damages remedies in both trespass and nuisance.) Lord Denning MR thought ([1979] Ch 291 at 298B) that there might be extreme circumstances under which even a court-ordered interest might be revoked on the ground of subsequent misconduct by the successful estoppel claimant, but this reservation has not been adopted in the case law (see e g *J Willis & Son v Willis* (1986) 277 EG 1133). See also the criticism in *McGill v S* [1979] IR 283 at 293 of the 'concept of a wavering licence terminable ... upon the possibility of changeable circumstances affecting the licensee.'

Grant of a right to occupy

10.294   A more commonly granted remedy is a recognition by the court that the estoppel claimant has an irrevocable or 'equitable' licence to occupy land rent-free either for life[1] or for some shorter period (whether fixed or not).[2] This form of order was made in *Inwards v Baker*[3] and often seems to mirror the ill-defined but nevertheless very real expectations of parties under informal family arrangements.[4] The courts have indicated, however, that it would be wrong to suppose that, once the factual basis for some proprietary estoppel has been put in place, a 'right of enjoyment for life is more or less automatically established.'[5]

1   See *Pearce v Pearce* [1977] 1 NSWLR 170 at 177F. Compare *Binions v Evans* [1972] Ch 359 **[para 12.365]**. If it is no longer practicable to enforce such an occupation licence, money compensation may awarded in lieu (*Broughall v Hunt* (Unreported, Chancery Division, 1 February 1983); *Baker v Baker and Baker* (1993) 25 HLR 408 at 412–413).
2   See *Silovi Pty Ltd v Barbaro* (1988) 13 NSWLR 466 at 474B–D.
3   [1965] 2 QB 29 at 37G **[para 10.181]**.
4   See e g *Matharu v Matharu* (1994) 68 P & CR 93 at 103; (1995) 58 MLR 412 (P Milne); [1995] Conv 61 (M Welstead); (1995) 7 CFLQ 59 (G Battersby); *Price v Hartwell* [1996] EGCS 98. It is not impossible that the estoppel doctrine may even protect a right of occupation granted *pur autre vie* (see *Habermann v Koehler* (1996) 73 P & CR 515 at 519–520).
5   *Bawden v Bawden* [1997] EWCA Civ 2664 per Robert Walker LJ.

10.295   A good example of a grant of long-term occupation rights occurred in *Greasley v Cooke*.[1] Here C, a 16 year old girl, started employment as a live-in maid in a house owned by A, a widower with four children. Although initially paid a weekly wage, she began some eight years later to cohabit in the house with one of the owner's sons, K. For almost the next 30 years C looked after members of the family, including a daughter who suffered from severe mental illness, but received during this period no financial reward for her services. C later alleged that she had been encouraged by members of the family (including G, one of the present plaintiffs) to believe that she could regard the house as her home for the rest of her life. Following the deaths of A and K, the remaining members of the family brought an action for possession against her.[2] The Court of Appeal upheld C's claim of proprietary estoppel, declaring that she was entitled to occupy the house rent-free for the remainder of her life. Lord Denning MR emphasised that neither the expenditure of money nor strict proof of reliance was required in estoppel claims.[3] Here it was sufficient that C had 'stayed on in the house', looking after its needy occupants, 'when otherwise she might have left and got a job elsewhere.'[4] An equity had been raised in favour of C in that she had acted on the faith of an assurance given to her 'in such circumstances that it would be unjust and inequitable for the party making the assurance to go back on it.'[5]

1   [1980] 1 WLR 1306. See [1981] Conv 154 (R E Annand); (1981) 44 MLR 461 (G Woodman).
2   The county court judge declined to recognise that any proprietary estoppel had arisen in favour of C, holding that such a claim must fail because C had spent no money on the property.
3   [1980] 1 WLR 1306 at 1311G–1312A.
4   [1980] 1 WLR 1306 at 1312A.
5   [1980] 1 WLR 1306 at 1311G–H.

10.296   The award of a lifelong right of occupation used to be fraught with complication. It was arguable that such a right constituted a 'life interest' which, however improbably, activated the cumbersome machinery of the Settled Land Act 1925.[1] In order to avoid the awkward implications of a strict settlement,[2] the courts tended to resolve estoppel claims by making alternative kinds of order either for the award of monetary compensation for a claimant's improvements[3] or for the compulsory grant of a long lease for life at a nominal rent and subject to an absolute covenant against assignment.[4] Nowadays the difficulties are substantially relieved since a court-ordered grant of lifelong occupation takes effect, if indeed it constitutes anything more than a mere licence, under a statutorily regulated 'trust of land',[5] although it remains the case that the administrative inconvenience and expense of the trust form tends to make this remedial solution seem rather less attractive.[6]

1   [Para 9.206].
2   In many cases it seemed undesirable that the estoppel claimant should be entitled to call for the legal estate and be invested with the statutory powers of a 'tenant for life' to sell, lease or mortgage that estate (see SLA 1925, s 19(1); *Dodsworth v Dodsworth* (1973) 228 EG 1115; *Griffiths v Williams* (1977) 248 EG 947 at 949).
3   See e g *Dodsworth v Dodsworth* (1973) 228 EG 1115.

4   See *Griffiths v Williams* (1977) 248 EG 947 at 950 per Goff LJ (thereby avoiding the complications of both the Settled Land Act 1925 and the Rent Act 1977). See F R Crane, (1967) 31 Conv (NS) 332 at 342).

5   **[Para 9.205]**.

6   See *Campbell v Griffin* [2001] WTLR 981 at [34] per Robert Walker LJ.

Grant of monetary compensation

10.297   In certain circumstances it may not be appropriate to grant a remedy which involves any form of long-term occupation right, the equity of estoppel calling for only an award of money compensation.[1] This less extensive remedy appears particularly relevant where the equity is founded on expenditure on improvements which are not in themselves substantial[2] or where it is impossible for practical reasons to enforce a sharing arrangement between parties whose personal relationship has broken down.[3] Although courts are naturally reluctant to allow a landowner to use a tender of compensation as a means of buying his way out of an estoppel claim or of forcing an inequity upon the claimant,[4] there may well be circumstances in which a simple offer of compensation negates any question of unconscionability.[5] However, the award of a remedy which sounds only in money may assist in avoiding any potential prejudice to third parties who have meanwhile relied, as purchasers or creditors, on the apparently unencumbered title of the legal owner.[6]

1   See eg *Campbell v Griffin* [2001] WTLR 981 at [36] (disputed land charged with fixed sum award of £35,000). The estoppel claimant may not have sought an occupation right in the first place (see *Hamilton v Geraghty* (1901) 1 SRNSW (Eq) 81 at 88 per Darley CJ) or may already have given up possession voluntarily (*Cushley v Seale* (Unreported, Court of Appeal, 28 October 1986)).

2   See *Jennings v Rice* [2003] 1 P & CR 100 at [51] per Robert Walker LJ; *Commonwealth of Australia v Verwayen* (1990) 170 CLR 394 at 441–442 per Deane J.

3   *Shaida v Kindlane Ltd* (Unreported, Chancery Division, 22 June 1982) per Deputy Judge Paul Baker QC, giving the example of *Dodsworth v Dodsworth* (1973) 228 EG 1115.

4   See *Milton v Proctor* (1988) 4 BPR 9654 at 9656 per Mahoney JA.

5   *Milton v Proctor* (1988) 4 BPR 9654 at 9671 per Clarke JA. See *Commonwealth of Australia v Verwayen* (1990) 170 CLR 394 at 442 per Deane J, 500–501 per McHugh J; *Campbell v Griffin* [2001] WTLR 981 at [36] per Robert Walker LJ; *Grundy v Ottey* [2003] WTLR 1253. Compare, however, *Singh v Sandhu* (Unreported, Court of Appeal, 4 May 1995).

6   See *Giumelli v Giumelli* (1999) 196 CLR 101 at [10], [49], where the High Court of Australia emphasised that in estoppel cases the court should first decide whether there is an appropriate equitable remedy which falls short of the imposition of a trust or other order for the acquisition of title to land.

10.298   In *Dodsworth v Dodsworth*[1] the owner of a bungalow had allowed the present defendants (who were her younger brother and his wife) to live with her in that property. The defendants proceeded to spend some £700 on improvements to the bungalow in the expectation that they could live in the property during the indefinite future. It was not contested that an equity of estoppel had arisen on these facts, but the Court of Appeal considered that the appropriate remedy in the circumstances comprised merely the return of the defendants' capital outlay together with some compensation for the labour invested in making the improvements.[2] The defendants' complaint had been essentially that it would be unfair to evict them in the light of their detrimental reliance on the assurances given to them, but in the Court's view this objection was easily deflected by a simple reimbursement of the money expended by them.[3]

1   (1973) 228 EG 1115.
2   (1973) 228 EG 1115 at 1117. The defendants' occupation was secured pending their reimbursement. See also *Mayes v Mayes* (1969) 210 EG 935 at 938.
3   Other complicating factors were the death of the owner during the hearing and the fear expressed by the Court of Appeal lest the remedy granted to the defendants should bring them within the scope of the Settled Land Act 1925.

10.299   The court's broad discretion in this area extends even to the basis adopted for assessment of compensatory payments. In some cases compensation has been fixed with reference to the enhanced value of the realty.[1] Sometimes compensation has been based on the actual cost of the improvements themselves, either with[2] or without[3] payment of interest, or with some adjustment designed to counter-balance the falling value of money over time.[4] In other cases the court has ordered compensation on the basis of an intermediate figure representing a compromise between the 'enhanced value' basis and the 'actual cost' basis.[5]

1   *Montreuil v Ontario Asphalt Co* (1922) 69 DLR 313 at 334–335; *Jackson v Crosby (No 2)* (1979) 21 SASR 280 at 294–295, 310; *Van den Berg v Giles* [1979] 2 NZLR 111 at 123; *The Queen v Smith* (1981) 113 DLR (3d) 522 at 583. In *Lepel v Huthnance* (1979) NZ Recent Law 269 at 270, Speight J assessed compensation in terms of the added value of the property, rather than on the basis of the cost of the improvements, not least because the claimant's labour had been misdirected and the end result was not up to workmanlike standards.
2   *Morris v Morris* [1982] 1 NSWLR 61 at 64F; *Grimison v Union Fidelity Trustee Co of Australia Ltd* (1984) 3 BPR 9469 at 9475.
3   *Re Whitehead* [1948] NZLR 1066 at 1071; *J N Elliot & Co (Farms) Ltd v Murgatroyd* (Unreported, Court of Appeal of New Zealand, CA 52/82, 12 September 1984).
4   *Cameron v Murdoch* [1983] WAR 321 at 351 (affd by JCPC, (1986) 63 ALR 575 at 595); *Stratulatos v Stratulatos* [1988] 2 NZLR 424 at 439–440.
5   *Clayton v Green* (1979) NZ Recent Law 139 at 140. For a comparable issue arising between beneficiaries under a trust of land, see Chapter 11 [**para 11.52**].

Grant of an occupation lien

10.300   A further, and rather hybrid, form of remedy lies in an award which combines an element of occupation with the grant of monetary compensation. This remedial variant involves a recognition that the estoppel claimant has a lien or charge over the disputed property to the appropriate value of the improvements effected[1] or of any money which has been contributed, given or loaned.[2] The lien or charge effectively creates a 'security interest to satisfy an obligation sounding in money', thus conferring on the estoppel claimant a right to occupy the property until such time as the money is paid or repaid.[3]

1   *Unity Joint Stock Mutual Banking Association v King* (1858) 25 Beav 72 at 78, 53 ER 563 at 565 (although foreclosure was decreed against both owner and holders of lien); *Hamilton v Geraghty* (1901) 1 SRNSW (Eq) 81 at 91; *Taylor v Taylor* [1956] NZLR 99 at 103–104.

2   *Hussey v Palmer* [1972] 1 WLR 1286 at 1291A–C [**para 10.76**], as explained in *Re Sharpe (A Bankrupt)* [1980] 1 WLR 219 at 222H–223A and *Savva v Costa and Harymode Investments Ltd* (1981) 131 NLJ 1114.
3   *Dodsworth v Dodsworth* (1973) 228 EG 1115 at 1117; *Re Sharpe (A Bankrupt)* [1980] 1 WLR 219 at 224B; *Stratulatos v Stratulatos* [1988] 2 NZLR 424 at 439–440 per McGechan J.

INFORMALLY CONFERRED LIFE INTERESTS

10.301   This chapter has been concerned throughout with the informal crea-tion of rights in land. A further context in which such interests may arise informally occurs in connection with the casual conferment of life interests. It is not impossible that such proprietary entitlements may be generated where loosely worded kinds of grant, particularly in dealings between family mem-bers, envisage the enjoyment of informal rights of rent-free occupation for life. The accommodation of such grants within the framework of the 1925 legisla-tion has always caused disproportionate difficulty.

Pre-1997 grants

10.302   Prior to 1997 the informal grant of a life interest[1] in land had the potential to enmesh the grantor and grantee unwittingly within the cumber-some machinery of a strict settlement governed by the Settled Land Act 1925, thereby provoking a chain of consequence usually unforeseen by the parties.[2] The relatively broad ambit of the notion of 'settlement'[3] ensures that the Settled Land Act is sometimes applicable in circumstances where its operation is least anticipated. No great formality of language is required in order to constitute a tenant for life for the purpose of the Act. Prior to 1997 it was quite possible that, in the absence of express reference to the existence of a 'trust for sale',[4] an equitable life interest under the Act could be denoted by the grant of a right to reside for life[5] or to receive rents and profits for life.[6]

1   A right of occupation for so long as the grantee wishes is classified as a life interest (see *Charles v Barzey* [2003] 1 WLR 437 at [7] per Lord Hoffmann).
2   [**Para 9.206**].
3   [**Para 9.208**].
4   [**Para 9.221**].
5   *Re Carne's Settled Estates* [1899] 1 Ch 324 at 329–330 per North J; *Re Boyer's Settled Estates* [1916] 2 Ch 404 at 409 per Sargant J. A grantee may be sufficiently marked out as a tenant for life by the conferment of a non-exclusive right to reside until death (see *Re Potter, decd* [1970] VR 352 at 354–358) or of a right to reside for a period determinable on some earlier event (see *Ungurian v Lesnoff* [1990] Ch 206 at 226A–B). See also *Re Gibbons* [1920] 1 Ch 372 at 377–379 (option to occupy and enjoy use of a house); *Bogdanovic v Koteff* (1988) 12 NSWLR 472 at 475A–C.
6   See *Peach v Peach* (Unreported, Court of Appeal, 3 November 1981) per Cumming-Bruce LJ.

The Bannister ruling

10.303   Much of the difficulty in this area flows from the ruling of the Court of Appeal in *Bannister v Bannister*.[1] Here B conveyed her freehold interest in two cottages to her brother-in-law, A, on his oral undertaking that she could live thereafter in one of the cottages rent-free for the remainder of her life. The Court of Appeal held that A was bound by a constructive trust to give effect to the interest thereby promised to B. This interest, said Scott LJ, was an equitable life interest determinable on her ceasing to live in the cottage,[2] and the imposition of the constructive trust had 'the effect of making the beneficiary a tenant for life within the meaning of the Settled Land Act'.[3]

1   [1948] 2 All ER 133 [**para 10.181**].
2   [1948] 2 All ER 133 at 136B.
3   [1948] 2 All ER 133 at 137B–C. See SLA 1925, s 19(1) [**para 9.211**].

Doubts left by the Bannister ruling

10.304   The Court of Appeal was not required in *Bannister*'s case to pursue the implications of holding that the defendant occupier came within the Settled Land Act, but there has long been doubt as to the correctness of this aspect of the Court's ruling.[1] The inter vivos creation of a strict settlement requires the execution of at least two deeds (a trust instrument and a vesting document),[2] and it seems wholly impossible that the occupier in *Bannister* could have been constituted a tenant for life by way of merely oral grant.[3] The decision of the Court of Appeal in *Bannister* nevertheless provides an uncomfortable precedent in support of the proposition that an informal grant – and, a fortiori, the creation of a life interest by deed[4] – may attract the operation of the Settled Land Act.[5] Most recently, in *Costello v Costello*,[6] Dillon LJ declared it impossible to say that *Bannister* was wrongly decided.

1   See A J Hawkins, (1966) 30 Conv (NS) 256; J A Hornby, (1977) 93 LQR 561.
2   SLA 1925, s 4(1) [**para 9.213**].
3   It has been suggested that in such cases the court order itself may be the instrument which constitutes the settlement within SLA 1925, s 1(1) (*Griffiths v Williams* (1977) 248 EG 947 at 950 per Goff LJ). See also [1978] Conv 250 at 251, but compare J Hill, (1991) 107 LQR 596 at 598.
4   *Ingram v IRC* [2000] 1 AC 293 at 300E–F per Lord Hoffmann. See e g *Costello v Costello* (1994) 70 P & CR 297 at 304–305, where the Court of Appeal held that a trust deed which conferred a right of rent-free occupation for life confirmed the grantee as a tenant for life under the Settled Land Act 1925. Although it was never contemplated at the date of the trust deed, this status entitled the grantee to sell the house and require the trustees of the settlement to purchase another property in which she would have a similar right of occupation for life.
5   See e g *Binions v Evans* [1972] Ch 359 at 370D–G per Megaw LJ (although admitting that the application of the Settled Land Act 'may produce some odd consequences'), 372E–G per Stephenson LJ. Likewise, in *Ungurian v Lesnoff* [1990] Ch 206 at 224A–D, Vinelott J perhaps surprisingly inferred an intention to create a right of residence for life on the basis of the conduct and oral dealings of the relevant parties.
6   (1994) 70 P & CR 297 at 305.

Implausible conveyancing consequences

10.305   Unlikely conveyancing consequences follow if an informal lifetime right of occupation is brought within the scope of the Settled Land Act 1925:

so long as he is of full age, the grantee appears to be entitled to call for a vesting of the full legal estate in his own name.[1] In *Bannister's* case this would have involved the improbable result that the defendant occupier, having conveyed the legal estate to her brother-in-law, would immediately have been entitled to insist that the legal estate be reconveyed to herself as tenant for life.[2] It seems strange that the informal grantee, consistently with the scheme of the Settled Land Act, should be empowered to sell, lease or mortgage the entire settled estate – a consequence which must almost inevitably have been outside the contemplation of the grantor.[3] It was indeed the incongruous nature of these Settled Land Act implications which, in *Binions v Evans*,[4] caused Lord Denning MR to diverge from the majority of the Court of Appeal by classifying a right of lifelong rent-free residence as a mere contractual licence.[5] Lord Denning declined to follow *Bannister* precisely on the ground that he thought it 'entirely contrary to the true intent of the parties' that the informal occupier in *Binions v Evans* should have acquired, by reason of the grant, a statutory power of sale or lease of the land.[6]

1   [**Para 9.211**].
2   However unattractive in the present context, this outcome merely reflects the fundamental design which lies at the root of the Settled Land Act – that the tenant for life should hold two distinct interests in the land [**para 9.212**].
3   See, however, *Ungurian v Lesnoff* [1990] Ch 206 at 226D, where Vinelott J held the informal grantee, on receiving a vesting of legal title in her favour, to be entitled to sell the land and 'reinvest the proceeds in the sale of another house or ... enjoy the income from them.' See [1990] Conv 223 (P Sparkes).
4   [1972] Ch 359 [**para 12.365**].
5   [1972] Ch 359 at 367C. The majority, although ultimately arriving at a decision in favour of the grantee, felt constrained by grudging deference to *Bannister v Bannister* to hold the grant to be caught by the Settled Land Act 1925. See *Ungurian v Lesnoff* [1990] Ch 206 at 225C per Vinelott J.
6   [1972] Ch 359 at 366D. Lord Denning construed SLA 1925, s 1(1)(i) restrictively as covering only cases where land is 'expressly limited' in trust and where there is a genuine 'succession of one beneficiary after another.' In an informal arrangement of the kind present in *Binions v Evans*, Lord Denning took the view that there was no true 'limitation' of land and therefore no 'settlement' ([1972] Ch 359 at 366E–F).

10.306   The approach adopted by Lord Denning in *Binions v Evans*, although heavily reinforced by common sense, is not easily reconciled with the ruling in *Bannister*.[1] On one hand it is the deliberate policy of the 1925 legislation that land should be rendered easily marketable[2] and there is therefore a strong argument in favour of maximising the coverage of the Settled Land Act, thereby extending as widely as possible the benefits of its conveyancing and overreaching machinery.[3] On the other hand, such extended coverage frequently exposes parties to the unwelcome operation of a statutory mechanism which was never intended by them to be relevant.

1   See e g *Griffiths v Williams* (1977) 248 EG 947 at 950, where Goff LJ suggested that *Dodsworth v Dodsworth* (1973) 228 EG 1115 was decided per incuriam in that the Court of Appeal in the latter case failed to advert to SLA 1925, s 1.
2   [**Para 2.39**]. See *Ungurian v Lesnoff* [1990] Ch 206 at 226C per Vinelott J.
3   [**Para 9.215**].

Avoidance of the Settled Land Act 1925

10.307   There is a general consensus that the machinery of the Settled Land Act 1925 should not, in principle, be activated by loosely phrased grants of some limited interest or residential privilege.[1] The implausibility of such a statutory application is reinforced where the relevant parties had no conscious understanding that their dealings would attract such specific legal effects.[2] In view of the difficulties implicit in the operation of the Settled Land Act 1925, the courts have often resisted the over-ready application of the Act to the informal conferment of amorphous rights of lifelong occupation.[3] The most obvious means of averting the complexities of the statute seems to lie in the reinterpretation of informally granted life interests as merely a species of personal residential licence or tenancy at will.[4] Although it is not entirely clear that the licence construction necessarily or properly excludes the heavy-handed operation of the statutory provisions, there is now a divergent line of authority to the effect that there can be such a phenomenon as a licence for life which exists outside the clutches of the Settled Land Act 1925.[5]

1   See eg Law Commission, *Transfer of Land: Trusts of Land* (Law Com No 181, June 1989), paras 4.1–4.2.
2   See *Ivory v Palmer* (1976) 237 EG 411 at 413, where Cairns LJ thought that the majority view in *Binions v Evans* had 'stretched to the very limit the application of the Settled Land Act'. For further reference to the over-large effect of the Settled Land Act powers, see *Dodsworth v Dodsworth* (1973) 228 EG 1115; *Griffiths v Williams* (1977) 248 EG 947 at 949.
3   See eg *Griffiths v Williams* (1977) 248 EG 947 at 950 (alternative solution in terms of grant of long tenancy at nominal rent [**para 10.296**]). Such is the embarrassment caused by *Bannister* that in *Ivory v Palmer* (1976) 237 EG 411 at 416 Browne LJ was at pains to stress that 'the court did not in fact ... base its decision on the Settled Land Act 1925, but on more general principles of the law of trusts.'
4   See eg *Buck v Howarth* [1947] 1 All ER 342 at 343F; *Foster v Robinson* [1951] 1 KB 149 at 158–160. For a discussion of the law of licences, see Chapter 4.
5   See eg *Ivory v Palmer* (1976) 237 EG 411 at 413; *Dent v Dent* [1996] 1 WLR 683 at 693C–F; *Re Walker's Application for Judicial Review* [1999] NI 84 at 91c–e.

Post-1996 grants

10.308   Much of the difficulty in this area is now relieved by the fact that no new strict settlements of land may be created after 1996.[1] Any life interest created in relation to land on or after 1 January 1997 takes effect, not under the Settled Land Act 1925, but under a 'trust of land' governed by the Trusts of Land and Appointment of Trustees Act 1996.[2] Thus any grant of a life interest on or after 1 January 1997 requires a declaration of trust in compliance with the Law of Property Act 1925,[3] unless the informality of grant can be cured by reliance on some claim of constructive trust or estoppel.[4] A purely oral grant of a life interest can now take effect only as an interest at will.[5]

1   [**Para 9.207**].
2   TOLATA 1996, s 2(1) [**para 9.205**]. Under a 'trust of land' there is no question of vesting the legal estate (or the attendant powers of management and disposition) in the beneficiary of any life interest: the legal estate is held by the appropriate trustee or trustees.

3   See LPA 1925, s 53(1)(b) **[para 9.188]**.
4   LPA 1925, s 53(2).
5   LPA 1925, s 54(1).

DONATIONES MORTIS CAUSA

10.309   Recent developments have disclosed one final, and rather unusual, context in which land may be subjected to effective informal disposition. The normal rule relating to dispositions of property on death requires, of course, that the disponor, as testator or testatrix, should incorporate his or her wishes in written form in a will which is duly signed and attested.[1] In the law of personal property there has always existed a startling exception to this requirement of formality. The documentary formality of a will may be circumvented by a *donatio mortis causa*, ie a parol (or oral) gift made in contemplation of death.

1   Wills Act 1837, s 9.

Preconditions for validity

10.310   A valid *donatio mortis causa* requires that three preconditions be met.[1] *First*, the gift must be made in contemplation (although not necessarily in expectation) of impending death. *Second*, the gift must be made on the condition that it is to be absolute and perfected only on the death of the donor, being revocable until then and entirely ineffective if death does not occur. *Third*, the subject matter of the gift, or the essential indicia of title to it, must be delivered to the donee, thereby signifying a 'parting with dominion and not mere physical possession' over that subject matter.[2]

1   See *Sen v Headley* [1991] Ch 425 at 431G–432A per Nourse LJ.
2   See A J Bradbrook, 'A Reassessment of the Scope of the Gift Mortis Causa' 17 McGill LJ 567 (1971).

Extension to realty

10.311   Prior to 1991 it was generally accepted that land could never form the subject matter of a *donatio mortis causa*,[1] partly because oral gifts of land seem to be precluded generally by statute[2] and partly because a handing over of title documents relating to land could not prevent an owner from dealing with his estate (eg through the grant of a short tenancy, the tenant having no right to call for evidence of his landlord's title). In *Sen v Headley*,[3] however, the Court of Appeal – to the surprise of most – upheld a *donatio mortis causa* in respect of land, apparently suggesting that the exemption of such a gift from the normal rules of formality is sanctioned by the last century of developments in the law of constructive trusts and proprietary estoppel.[4] In *Sen v Headley*, three days before his death from inoperable cancer, H told his long-time partner, M: 'The house is yours, Margaret. You have the keys. They are in your bag. The deeds are in the steel box.' After H's death intestate, M discovered that H had put her in possession of the only key to the deeds box. The Court of Appeal held that H's words and conduct sufficiently connoted a parting with dominion over H's house and that, all the other conditions of a *donatio mortis causa* being satisfied, H had effectively transferred the house to M.[5]

1   See *Bayliss v Public Trustee* (1988) 12 NSWLR 540 at 544G; C E F Rickett, [1989] Conv 184.
2   LPA 1925, ss 52–54.
3   [1991] Ch 425 at 441B. See [1990] Conv 132 (H B Parry); [1991] Conv 307 (M Halliwell).
4   [1991] Ch 425 at 439H–440B.
5   [1991] Ch 425 at 438G–439A.

10.312   The applicability of the *donatio mortis causa* to land is still less than clear. The best that can be said is that the dealing which comprises a *donatio mortis causa* operates upon the conscience of the deceased's personal representatives and thus either generates some kind of constructive trust or constitutes some strained version of the rule in *Rochefoucauld v Boustead*.[1]

1   [Para 9.193].

CHAPTER 11

Regulation of trusts and co-ownership

THE MODERN TREND TOWARDS CO-OWNERSHIP

11.1 Co-ownership is the term used to describe the form of ownership in which two or more persons are simultaneously entitled in possession to an interest or interests in the same asset. Co-ownership thus connotes some form of concurrent (as distinct from successive) holding. Virtually all forms of co-ownership of land nowadays operate in conjunction with a trust of land regulated by the Trusts of Land and Appointment of Trustees Act 1996.[1]

1   [**Paras 9.172, 11.124**].

11.2 Co-ownership of land has been given a contemporary prominence largely, although not exclusively, by the shared rights of ownership found in the family home. Concurrent ownership long ago displaced successive ownership as the dominant model of landholding in England and Wales, the demise of the strict settlement coinciding with fundamental alterations in the norms governing family relationships. The family patterns of today are far removed from those of a former age when the grant of patriarchal largesse was epitomised in the marriage settlement.[1] Concurrent ownership of an absolute interest in land – rather than successive entitlement to limited interests – became the expression of this more liberated social order. The general movement from status-dependent family relationships to non-hierarchical relationships based on equality inevitably placed a new emphasis on shared entitlements.[2] From the mid-20th century onwards an important catalyst in this process of normative change was provided by a post-war affluence which generated unprecedented levels of residential owner-occupation[3] and which, in its turn, came to depend heavily on harnessing the labour-power of more than one family member.[4] Nowadays the resort to co-operative purchase of realty is accentuated by additional factors which include the rising cost of housing, increased longevity and the extended family relationships so prevalent in a multicultural society. It is unsurprising that such transformations of social and economic fact should reflect themselves pervasively in the law of co-ownership of land.

1   **[Para 9.206]**.
2   See Oliver Ross McGregor, 'Equality, sexual values and permissive legislation: the English experience' (1972) 1 Jnl Soc Pol 44; Gray, *Reallocation of Property on Divorce* (Professional Books 1977), pp 11–21. See also *European Asian of Australia Ltd v Kurland* (1985) 8 NSWLR 192 at 200B–C per Rogers J.
3   See *Midland Bank plc v Cooke* [1995] 4 All ER 562 at 575a per Waite LJ ('The mass diffusion of home ownership has been one of the most striking social changes of our own time').
4   See e g *Williams & Glyn's Bank Ltd v Boland* [1981] AC 487 at 508G, where Lord Wilberforce spoke of 'the extension, beyond the paterfamilias, of rights of ownership, itself following from the diffusion of property and earning capacity.' See also *Brown v Brown* (1993) 31 NSWLR 582 at 600C–D per Kirby P (referring to the impact of increased female employment during the Second World War).

11.3   English law has known four types of co-ownership, of which only the first two now have any real significance: (1) joint tenancy,[1] (2) tenancy in common,[2] (3) tenancy by entireties,[3] and (4) coparcenary.[4]

1   **[Para 11.4]**.
2   **[Para 11.29]**.
3   **[Para 11.122]**.
4   **[Para 11.123]**.

JOINT TENANCY

11.4   The essence of joint tenancy consists in the theory that each joint tenant is wholly entitled to the whole of the interest which is the subject of co-ownership.[1] Joint tenancy can subsist in either a legal estate or an equitable estate in land (or in both at the same time). The key to understanding joint tenancy is the realisation that no joint tenant holds any specific or distinct *share* himself, but each is (together with the other joint tenant or tenants) invested with the totality of the co-owned interest.[2] The whole is not so much the sum of the parts, for each and every part is itself co-extensive with the whole.[3] Of each joint tenant it can be said, in Bracton's expressive language: *totum tenet et nihil tenet*.[4] Each holds everything and yet holds nothing.[5]

1   See *Burton v Camden LBC* [2000] 2 AC 399 at 408E per Lord Millett. In the present context, the term 'tenant' has nothing necessarily to do with the landlord–tenant relationship: it merely signifies 'owner'. There arises a possible ambiguity in that the total interest which is subject to 'joint tenancy' may be either an estate in fee simple, or a life interest, or even a term of years (i e a 'tenancy' in the landlord–tenant sense).
2   See *Wright v Gibbons* (1949) 78 CLR 313 at 329 per Dixon J; *Re Rushton* (*A Bankrupt*) [1972] Ch 197 at 203A per Goff J.
3   'Joint tenancy is based on the theory that together the joint tenants have but one estate, not a number of estates equal to the number of joint tenants' (*Re Estate of King*, 572 SW2d 200 at 211 (1978)).
4   'Quilibet totum tenet, et nihil tenet; scilicet, totum in communi, et nihil separatim per se' (Bracton, fo 430 (Woodbine's edn), Vol 4, 336). See also Co Litt, p 186a; *Dawson v IRC* [1988] 1 WLR 930 at 934D, 938C; *HKSAR v Lee Hang Wing* [1999] HKCFI 851 at [6]. According to Pollock and Maitland, joint tenancy was already in existence by the 13th century and is 'decidedly older' than tenancy in common (*The History of English Law* (2nd edn, London 1968), Vol 2, p 20). See also *Carmody v Delehunt* [1984] 1 NSWLR 667 at 675E–G per Priestley JA; R H Helmholz, 'Realism and Formalism in the Severance of Joint Tenancies' 77 Neb L Rev 1 at 4 (1998).

5   See *Challis*, p 367.

An undifferentiated form of co-ownership

11.5   Joint tenancy is thus an undifferentiated kind of co-ownership in which an entire estate or interest in land – rather than any defined proportion or aliquot share – is vested simultaneously in all the co-owners. Joint owners are bound up in a 'thorough and intimate union of interest and possession.'[1] So comprehensive is this co-ownership that joint tenants comprise, in the eyes of the law, a collective entity – one composite person – together holding one and the same estate in the subject land, whether that estate be freehold or lease-hold.[2] Accordingly, any transfer of land to two or more persons as joint tenants 'operates so as to make them, vis à vis the outside world, one single owner.'[3]

1   *Bl Comm*, Vol II, p 182. See also *Corin v Patton* (1990) 169 CLR 540 at 579 per Deane J.
2   It has been said that the concept of pervasive co-ownership of the whole is an 'esoteric notion ... remote from the realities of life. It should be handled with care, and applied with caution' (*Burton v Camden LBC* [2000] 2 AC 399 at 404H–405A per Lord Nicholls of Birkenhead). In *Burton* the strict theory of joint tenancy was not permitted to obscure the fact that a 'release' by one joint tenant to another [**para 11.69**] constituted, in reality, an assignment of a secure tenancy invalidated by Housing Act 1985, s 91(1) [**para 14.340**]. Compare, however, *Big Rivers Timber Pty Ltd v Stewart* (Supreme Court of New South Wales, 22 May 1998, BPR Casenote 101909) per Young J (transfer by one joint tenant to another held to be no conveyance, but merely an abandonment of right of survivorship).
3   *Hammersmith and Fulham LBC v Monk* [1992] 1 AC 478 at 492B per Lord Browne-Wilkinson. See also Joshua Williams, *Principles of the Law of Real Property* (23rd edn by T C Williams, London 1920), p 143; *Duncan v Suhy*, 37 NE2d 826 at 828 (1941); *Re Lorch's Estate*, 33 NYS2d 157 at 166 (1941); *Osterloh's Estate v Carpenter*, 337 SW2d 942 at 946 (1960); *Diemasters Pty Ltd v Meadowcorp Pty Ltd* (2001) 10 BPR 18769 at [17].

11.6   Any reference to ownership in specific shares (e g A owns a one-quarter interest and B a three-quarters interest) is normally sufficient to establish that A and B co-own not as joint tenants, but rather as tenants in common.[1] Even to say that A and B hold in equal shares is, in strict terms and in the absence of any other evidence, to indicate that A and B are, again, tenants in common.[2] Such ambivalence as may seem to attach to the nature of co-ownership in equal shares or half-shares is almost certainly attributable to the fact that a joint tenancy is fairly easily convertible by 'severance'[3] into a tenancy in common in equal shares. In consequence, every joint tenancy is also potentially a tenancy in common,[4] and every joint tenant is proleptically a co-owner in equal shares and thus entitled to dispose of his aliquot share or to grant a lease, mortgage or life interest out of that share.[5] There is sometimes an irresistible temptation to refer to joint tenants as being already entitled to equal shares,[6] but this merely reflects the extremely marginal nature of the legal distinction between the actual and the inchoate rights of the joint tenant.

1   *Cowcher v Cowcher* [1972] 1 WLR 425 at 430H; *Paluszek v Wohlrab*, 115 NE2d 764 at 766 (1953).
2   See *Martin v Martin* (1987) 54 P & CR 238 at 240 per Millett J; *Public Trustee v Pfeiffle* [1991] 1 VR 19 at 37–40 per Ormiston J. Blackstone almost certainly misled generations of lawyers

when, in expounding Littleton's law-French (*Litt*, s 288), he taught that joint tenants are 'seised *per my et per tout*, by the half or moiety, and by all' (*Bl Comm*, Vol II, p 182). See, for instance, *Doe d Aslin v Summersett* (1830) 1 B & Ad 135 at 140, 109 ER 738 at 739 per Lord Tenterden CJ. In effect, Littleton's phrase '*per my et per tout*' is merely a reiteration of Bracton's '*totum tenet et nihil tenet*'. On the 'singular infelicity' of Blackstone's translation, see Serjeant Manning's notes to *Daniel v Camplin* (1845) 7 Man & G 167 at 172, 135 ER 73 at 75 (note (c)). See also *Murray v Hall* (1849) 7 CB 441 at 455, 137 ER 175 at 180 (note (a)).

3   [**Para 11.64**].

4   It was with this possibility in mind that Coke, whilst conceding that joint tenants are wholly seised of the whole, was nevertheless careful to point out that 'yet to divers purposes each of them hath but a right to a moiety, as to enfeoff, give, or demise' (*Co Litt*, p 186a).

5   See *Challis*, p 367. Such forms of alienation automatically bring about either a total or partial severance of the joint tenancy [**para 11.84**]. See also *U-Needa Laundry Ltd v Hill* [2000] 2 NZLR 308 at [24]–[26].

6   See e g *Bl Comm*, Vol II, p 182.

Distinguishing characteristics

11.7   The distinguishing characteristics of joint tenancy are two in number. First, joint tenants enjoy as between themselves a 'right of survivorship'. Second, the existence of joint tenancy always presupposes the presence of the 'four unities'. These ideas must now be explored.

RIGHT OF SURVIVORSHIP (*IUS ACCRESCENDI*)

11.8   It has been said that the right of survivorship (or *ius accrescendi*) is the 'grand and distinguishing' incident of joint tenancy.[1] On the death of any one joint tenant,[2] the entire co-owned estate 'survives to' the remaining joint tenant or tenants.[3] Ultimately, in the manner of the medieval tontine, the last surviving joint tenant becomes the sole owner – the winner takes all. This concentration of ownership by right of survivorship was elegantly described by Blackstone:

> [W]hen two or more persons are seised of a joint estate ... the entire tenancy upon the decease of any of them remains to the survivors, and at length to the last survivor ... The interest of two joint-tenants is not only equal or similar, but also is one and the same. One has not originally a distinct moiety from the other ... but ... each ... has a concurrent interest in the whole; and therefore, on the death of his companion, the sole interest in the whole remains to the survivor.[4]

1   *De Witt v San Francisco*, 2 Cal 289 at 297 (1852). See also *Re Robertson* (1944) 44 SR (NSW) 103 at 105; *Matter of Estate of Oney*, 641 P2d 725 at 727 (1982).

2   The right of survivorship operates even where the death of a joint tenant is presumed (see *Chard v Chard* [1956] P 259 at 272) on the basis of seven years' continuous absence (*Grieve v Registrar General of New South Wales* (1997) 8 BPR 15729 at 15731).

3   Joint tenancy can exist even though one of the co-owners has the potential of perpetual existence. A corporate body, being an artificial person in the eyes of the law, enjoys in theory a kind of immortality. A corporate body may nevertheless become a joint tenant (see Bodies Corporate (Joint Tenancy) Act 1899, s 1(1)), and survivorship operates in the sense that the jointly owned property devolves on the other joint tenant or tenants if the company is ever dissolved (see Bodies Corporate (Joint Tenancy) Act 1899, s 1(2)).

4   *Bl Comm*, Vol II, p 183–184. See likewise *Wharton's Law Lexicon* (11th edn 1711), p 471 ('a general concentration of property from more to fewer … till it passes to a single hand, and the joint tenancy ceases').

Operation of the survivorship principle

11.9 The right of survivorship ensures that the entitlement of each joint tenant is eliminated on his death. The operation of survivorship can be illustrated in the following way.

Progressive concentration of ownership

11.10 Suppose that a fee simple estate in Greenacre is registered in the names of three joint tenants, A, B and C, holding for themselves as beneficial joint tenants.[1] If C dies, the legal and equitable estates remain vested in A and B as survivors,[2] and C's entitlement simply evaporates.[3] A and B are already fully entitled as joint tenants to the entire fee simple estate in Greenacre and no further vesting in them as survivors is required.[4] Nor is it true to say that any 'interest' in Greenacre passes to either of them on C's death. The entire interest in the land simply 'survives' to them as the remaining joint tenants. C drops out of the picture, the register of title being rectified (where appropriate) in order to reflect the fact that the legal estate has ceased to be vested in him.[5] Furthermore, regardless of whether C died testate or intestate, no 'share' in Greenacre can devolve upon his successors[6] precisely because as a joint tenant C had no 'share' in any estate in the land.[7] He had no fraction of ownership which was capable of transmission on his death, since together with A and B he was wholly entitled to the whole.[8]

1   **[Para 11.146]**.
2   *Litt*, s 280; *Co Litt*, p 181a.
3   *Wright v Gibbons* (1949) 78 CLR 313 at 323 per Latham CJ; *Corin v Patton* (1990) 169 CLR 540 at 575 per Deane J. See also *Green v Skinner*, 197 P 60 at 62 (1921); *Fleming v Fleming*, 174 NW 946 at 953 (1921).
4   'Technically, joint tenants are originally entitled to all which they ever have' (*Fadden v Deputy Federal Commissioner of Taxation* (1943) 68 CLR 76 at 84 per Williams J).
5   See LRR 2003, r 164.
6   The operation of survivorship is frustrated only rarely. An example occurs under the Inheritance (Provision for Family and Dependants) Act 1975 where an application is made for provision out of the estate of a decedent. The 'severable share' of a deceased beneficial joint tenant may be treated as part of his net estate 'to such extent as appears to the court to be just in all the circumstances of the case' (Inheritance (Provision for Family and Dependants) Act 1975, s 9(1)).
7   Administration of Estates Act 1925, s 3(4); *Challis*, p 366 (citing *Litt*, s 280); *Dando v Dando*, 99 P2d 561 at 562 (1940); *Eastgate v Equity Trustees Executors And Agency Co Ltd* (1964) 110 CLR 275 at 289–290.
8   Even if C attempted by will to leave his own 'share' to X, survivorship operates immediately on C's death – before his will can take effect – with the result that there is nothing on which his testamentary disposition can bite (see *Carr-Glyn v Frearsons* [1999] 1 FLR 8 at 9D; *Campbell v Griffin* [2001] W&TLR 981 at [13]). A joint tenancy cannot normally be severed by will **[paras 11.16, 11.68]**.

11.11   Similarly, if B now predeceases A, the right of survivorship operates once more. B disappears from the co-ownership and the entire fee simple estate in Greenacre 'survives to' A as sole legal and equitable owner.[1] Under the strict theory of survivorship, A's ownership never enlarges throughout this course of events (except to the extent that A is no longer subject to the hazard of survivorship).[2] In reality, however, the *ius accrescendi* brings about a 'distinct shifting of economic interest, a decided change for the survivor's benefit'[3] – regardless, incidentally, of whether the ultimate survivor made much (or any) contribution towards the initial purchase of the land.[4]

1   *Corin v Patton* (1990) 169 CLR 540 at 575 per Deane J.
2   See *Re Peterson's Estate*, 45 P2d 45 at 48–49 (1935); *Craig v Federal Commissioner of Taxation* (1945) 70 CLR 441 at 452; *Re Foster's Estate*, 320 P2d 855 at 859 (1958); *Eastgate v Equity Trustees Executors And Agency Co Ltd* (1964) 110 CLR 275 at 283.
3   *United States v Jacobs*, 306 US 363 at 371, 83 L ed 763 at 769 (1939) per Justice Black.
4   *Wright v Bloom*, 359 P2d 1080 at 1083 (1961). See also *Paluszek v Wohlrab*, 115 NE2d 764 at 766 (1953); *Brockway's Estate v CIR*, 219 F2d 400 at 403 (1954).

Commorientes rule

11.12   Any doubt as to the identity of the surviving joint tenant is resolved in England by the rule governing *commorientes*. Under this rule where two or more persons have died in circumstances rendering it uncertain which survived the other or others, the deaths are presumed to have occurred in order of seniority, and the younger is deemed to have survived the elder.[1] The *commorientes* rule is not entirely satisfactory: the solution provided in the United States by the Uniform Simultaneous Death Act is much to be preferred.[2] Under this Act, which has been adopted for instance in California, the death of two or more joint tenants simultaneously is treated as a severance and an equal share of the property devolves with the estate of each decedent.[3]

1   LPA 1925, s 184. See, in relation to the equivalent New South Wales provision, *Edwards v Mansfield* (1988) 5 BPR 11626 at 11627 (murder-suicide within family). The *commorientes* rule is subject to any order made by the court (see *Re Lindop* [1942] Ch 377 at 382; *Hickman v Peacey* [1945] AC 304 at 316). See also Administration of Estates Act 1925, s 46(3), as added by Intestates' Estates Act 1952, s 1(4).
2   See *Hickman v Peacey* [1945] AC 304 at 314, 317, where Viscount Simon LC, whilst acknowledging that time is infinitely divisible, opined that LPA 1925, s 184 has no application if the relevant deaths are 'absolutely simultaneous.'
3   See Cal Prob Code, s 296.2; *Re Estate of Meade*, 39 Cal Rptr 278 at 282 (1964).

Advantages of the survivorship principle

11.13   The capricious outcome of the joint tenants' gamble on longevity[1] might provoke concern were it not for several significant factors which combine to make joint tenancy a sensible and convenient medium of co-ownership. Indeed the undifferentiated nature of this co-ownership model has proved so appropriate for certain important purposes that, ever since 1925, co-ownership of a legal estate in land in England and Wales has been *required* to take the form of joint tenancy.[2] Co-owners of any legal estate (whether freehold or leasehold) are therefore, automatically, joint tenants and they hold that estate as trustees.[3] The joint nature of their co-ownership at law confers distinct advantages both on the internal administration of their trust and on the conduct of their transactions with strangers.

1   The Supreme Court of California has pointed out that 'a joint tenant's right of survivorship is an expectancy that is not irrevocably fixed upon the creation of the estate; it arises only upon success in the ultimate gamble – survival – and then only if the unity of the estate has not theretofore been destroyed' (*Tenhet v Boswell*, 133 Cal Rptr 10 at 14 (1976) per Mosk J). See also *Green v Skinner*, 197 P 60 at 62 (1921).
2   **[Para 11.21]**.
3   The interface between co-ownership and trust relationships is discussed elsewhere in this chapter **[para 11.124]**.

Avoidance of probate difficulties

11.14   The rule of survivorship avoids the inconvenience of fresh vestings of the trust estate on every occasion of death within the trusteeship. It is of the essence of joint tenancy that, on the death of a trustee, the surviving trustees are already invested with the entire interest in the estate and require no further vesting in their names.[1]

1   New trustees of a legal estate can be appointed quite easily (TA 1925, ss 36(1), 40, 41(1); TOLATA 1996, s 19(2)). See, however, *Adam & Co International Trustees Ltd v Theodore Goddard (a firm)* [2000] WTLR 349 at 354G–355E (existing trustees cannot simply be replaced by a single trustee other than a trust corporation).

Facility of dealings with title

11.15   Joint tenancy serves admirably the needs which arise in connection with the administration and disposition of the legal estate in co-owned land. A purchaser from joint tenants need be concerned with only one title[1] – the title held concurrently by each and all of the joint tenants – with the result that co-ownership by way of joint tenancy not only facilitates the internal management of the trust, but also promotes the free alienation of land.[2]

1   Prior to 1926 it was possible for a legal estate to be held in undivided shares **[para 11.55]**, with consequent conveyancing inconvenience for purchasers, who were effectively obliged to investigate title to a fragmented legal estate held by potentially numerous tenants in common (each of whom might have dealt independently, by sale, lease or mortgage, with his or her individual share of that legal estate). See *City of London Building Society v Flegg* [1988] AC 54 at 77D–E per Lord Oliver of Aylmerton.
2   'A principal objective of the 1925 property legislation was to simplify conveyancing and the proof of title to land' (*State Bank of India v Sood* [1997] Ch 276 at 281F per Peter Gibson LJ).

Indestructibility of survivorship

11.16   A unique and intimate union exists between joint tenants.[1] This identity of interest is so complete that the principal feature of their relationship

– the right of survivorship – takes precedence over any testamentary disposition made by a joint tenant. A disposition contained in the will of a joint tenant is ineffective in respect of any land to which his joint tenancy relates, simply because a joint tenant has no specific share or interest which he can pass on his death.[2] Moreover, by the time the will takes effect survivorship has already operated.[3] The same point is expressed in the proposition that severance of a joint tenancy cannot normally be effected by will.[4] Unless a severance of the joint tenancy has occurred inter vivos, the right of survivorship is unavoidable and indestructible.[5]

1   It has been postulated that there is a 'deep-rooted need for survivorship – the people want it' (N Sterling, 'Joint Tenancy and Community Property in California' 14 Pacific LJ 927 at 929 (1982–83)). It has been surmised that the sharp rise in the incidence of joint tenancies from the 1940s onwards may have been stimulated both by increasing social recognition of the emancipation of married women and by the ever-present reality of death under war-time conditions (see N W Hines, 'Real Property Joint Tenancies: Law, Fact, and Fancy' 51 Iowa L Rev 582 at 590, 623 (1965–66)).

2   The event which triggers survivorship 'cannot at the same time be the event which would destroy it' (*Re Levy* (1982) 131 DLR (3d) 15 at 25). See also *Swift d Neale v Roberts* (1764) 3 Burr 1488 at 1496–1497, 97 ER 941 at 946; *Carr-Glyn v Frearsons* [1999] 1 FLR 8 at 9D; *Re Fritz' Estate*, 20 P2d 361 at 363 (1933); *Re Estate of Moy*, 31 Cal Rptr 374 at 377 (1963).

3   *Co Litt*, p 185b; *Bl Comm*, Vol II, p 186.

4   The law of severance is dealt with elsewhere [**para 11.64**], but contrast the effect of mutual wills [**para 11.99**].

5   See *Carr-Glyn v Frearsons* [1999] 1 FLR 8 at 16F–17E, 20B–C (firm of solicitors held negligent in not advising testatrix to sever before death).

Utility as an estate planning device

11.17   Not only does the right of survivorship override testamentary dispositions; it often has the effect of rendering testamentary gifts quite unnecessary. As between husband and wife or other domestic partners, the operation of survivorship assumes its clearest modern function as a simple and cost-effective estate planning device. In a country where the majority of the population still make no will,[1] the *ius accrescendi* permits a co-owned estate to vest automatically in the surviving member of a domestic partnership – an outcome desired, it seems, by most married couples.[2] The rule of survivorship thus provides a speedy and inexpensive testamentary substitute designed to benefit a surviving partner whilst necessitating only minor administrative adjustments to the formerly joint title.[3]

1   Survivorship may even be coupled with taxation advantages for the survivor, as for instance under New Zealand's Joint Family Homes Act 1964, s 22(1) [**para 11.264**]. For the motivation behind this conferment of tax exemption, see Vol 292, *New Zealand Parliamentary Debates*, 3692; Vol 340, *New Zealand Parliamentary Debates*, 2995.

2   In Britain joint tenancy has long been the predominant form of freehold ownership for young married couples (see J E Todd and L M Jones, *Matrimonial Property* (London 1972), p 80; A J Manners and I Rauta, *Family Property in Scotland* (1981), p 5).

3   Survivorship is 'the poor man's will' (Y B Griffith, 'Community Property in Joint Tenancy Form' 14 Stan L Rev 87 at 108 (1961–62)).

Safety from unsecured creditors

11.18 A further, and rather more dubious, benefit of survivorship is that its operation leaves the surviving joint tenant or tenants immune from unsecured debts incurred independently by the deceased joint tenant during his lifetime.[1] On the death of the debtor the entire co-owned interest vests by operation of law in the survivor or survivors free of any claims which may be advanced by the deceased joint tenant's creditors.[2] Consistently with the theory of joint tenancy, the decedent's estate has no interest in the co-owned property from which outstanding unsecured claims can be satisfied.[3] Unsecured creditors are therefore unable to reach into the joint tenancy after the debtor's death. This rule has attracted criticism in that it renders unsecured creditors extremely vulnerable when dealing with a debtor who contrives to tie up his assets in joint tenancy form.[4] It is at precisely this point that 'the ineluctable logic of received property law strains in one direction while common humanity and sound public policy strain in the other.'[5]

1   The unilateral creation of a secured charge over jointly owned property normally has the effect of severance **[para 11.84]**, with the result that the chargee can look for satisfaction to the severed share of the debtor.

2   *Re Palmer, decd (A Debtor)* [1994] Ch 316 at 342B–D, 350A; [1995] CLJ 52 (L Tee). See also *Power v Grace* [1932] 2 DLR 793 at 798; *Re Maroukis and Maroukis* (1985) 12 DLR (4th) 321 at 325 per McIntyre J; *King v King*, 236 P2d 912 at 913 (1951); *Schlichenmayer v Luithle*, 221 NW2d 77 at 83 (1974). The corollary is, of course, that if the *debtor* is the survivor, the creditors have access to the entire estate formerly held under joint tenancy (see e g *Rupp v Kahn*, 55 Cal Rptr 108 at 112–113 (1966)).

3   Unless a creditor can prove that the decedent deliberately put his property in joint tenancy form in order to defraud his creditors.

4   This aspect of joint tenancy law has been criticised as 'anachronistic' and as conferring 'an unjustified windfall' on the surviving joint tenant or tenants (California Law Reform Commission, *Recommendation Relating To Non-Probate Transfers*, 15 Cal Law Revision Commission Reports (1980), 1620–1621).

5   See *Harris v Crowder*, 322 SE2d 854 at 855 (1984) per Neely J. See also J W Fisher, 91 W Va L Rev 267 (1988–89).

Joint tenancy is ideal for co-ownership of legal estates

11.19 In the context of co-ownership, title to a legal estate in land comprises a merely formal ownership. Here legal title, although enforceable against all the world, is otherwise relatively unimportant.

Practical significance of survivorship in equity

11.20 In relation to a legal estate held in co-ownership, the arbitrary nature of survivorship is normally quite harmless. The legal title is a nominal or 'paper' ownership, carrying only fiduciary powers of management and disposition in respect of the co-owned realty. The substance of ownership resides in equity. It is beneficial ownership which determines such matters as rights of occupation of the land,[1] the allocation of the rents and profits derived from it[2] and, ultimately, entitlement to the capital proceeds of any disposition.[3] When applied to these kinds of beneficial entitlement, joint tenancy can indeed operate capriciously although, even here, it does so only because the equitable co-owners have actively chosen joint tenancy as the vehicle of their concurrent entitlement.

1   [**Para 11.173**].
2   [**Para 11.39**].
3   [**Para 11.187**].

Mandatory nature of joint tenancy at law

11.21   Joint tenancy, albeit accompanied by the unpredictability of survivorship, is uniquely adapted to the efficient management of the formal legal title. For this reason the Law of Property Act 1925 made joint tenancy the mandatory medium of co-owned titles at law: since 1 January 1926 all co-ownership of a legal estate in land has necessarily taken the form of joint tenancy. Deep at the heart of the 1925 legislation is the declaration that a legal estate is 'not capable of subsisting or of being created in an undivided share in land',[1] with the obvious corollary that '[n]o severance of a joint tenancy of a legal estate, so as to create a tenancy in common in land, shall be permissible.'[2] These provisions merely extend the common law presumption in favour of joint tenancy[3] to its logical conclusion by providing that co-ownership at law may never take the form of tenancy in common and by ensuring that all co-ownership in distinct shares is inevitably swept into equity.[4] The cumulative effect of the 1925 Act has therefore been to facilitate the purchaser of the legal estate, who no longer faces the risk of investigating a fragmented title.[5] His task is further eased by the fact that the maximum number of persons who may be joint tenants of one and the same legal estate in land is now generally restricted to four.[6]

1   LPA 1925, s 1(6).
2   LPA 1925, s 36(2).
3   [**Para 11.55**].
4   See also *Rothera v Nottingham City Council* (1980) 39 P & CR 613 at 617.
5   [**Para 11.15**].
6   See TA 1925, s 34(2); LPA 1925, s 34(2) [**paras 2.131, 7.189**].

THE 'FOUR UNITIES'

11.22   It is axiomatic that the 'four unities' must be present before a joint tenancy can be said to exist[1]; and that where all 'four unities' are present in a multiple holding of land there is joint tenancy.[2] These unities – the 'hallmark inhabitants of the institution of joint tenancy'[3] – are the unities of possession, interest, title and time.[4] By contrast, only unity of possession is required as a precondition of tenancy in common.[5]

1   See *Bl Comm*, Vol II, pp 180–182; *AG Securities v Vaughan* [1990] 1 AC 417 at 431H per Fox LJ.
2   *Corin v Patton* (1990) 169 CLR 540 at 572 per Deane J.
3   *Corin v Patton* (1990) 169 CLR 540 at 572 per Deane J.
4   'This analysis has perhaps attracted attention rather by reason of its captivating appearance of symmetry and exactness, than by reason of its practical utility' (*Challis*, p 367). See also *Corin v Patton* (1990) 169 CLR 540 at 572–573 per Deane J. The requirement of the 'four unities' has not been literally adhered to in other jurisdictions: see e g *Estate of Grigsby*, 184 Cal Rptr 886 at 889 (1982); R H Helmholz, 'Realism and Formalism in the Severance of Joint Tenancies' 77 Neb L Rev 1 (1998).
5   **[Para 11.32]**.

Unity of possession

11.23   Unity of possession means that each joint tenant is as much entitled to possession of every part of the co-owned land as the other joint tenant or tenants: their possession is indivisible.[1] Thus no joint tenant may ever physically delineate any part of the land as being his to the exclusion of the other co-owner or co-owners[2] or prevent another co-owner from taking his appropriate allocation of the rents and profits derived from the land.[3] Between joint tenants the concept of internal physical boundaries and the consequent idea of trespass have no meaning, except in the sense that any ouster or interference with another's rights over the co-owned whole constitutes an actionable trespass. Absent any infringement of his or her rights, a joint tenant who finds the presence of another joint tenant irritating or even intolerable has no remedy at common law and can do nothing but leave the co-owned premises.[4] The joint tenants' unity of possession is only rarely displaced by statutory intervention (e g by a court order based on circumstances of domestic violence).[5]

1   The implications of unity of possession for joint tenants are, in general, the same as those for tenants in common and are therefore considered in greater detail in the context of the latter form of co-tenancy **[paras 11.32–11.54]**.
2   *Meyer v Riddick* (1990) 60 P & CR 50 at 54 per Fox LJ. See also *Swartzbaugh v Sampson*, 54 P2d 73 at 75 (1936).
3   **[Para 11.39]**. As between joint tenants, rents and profits must be divided equally.
4   *Wiseman v Simpson* [1988] 1 WLR 35 at 42E–G per Ralph Gibson LJ.
5   See e g *Davis v Johnson* [1979] AC 264 (CA), 317 (HL); *Wilde v Wilde* [1988] 2 FLR 83.

Unity of interest

11.24   Unity of interest follows from the proposition that each joint tenant is 'wholly entitled to the whole.' Unity of interest requires that the interest held by each joint tenant should be the same in extent, nature and duration.[1] Unity of interest also brings about the consequence that dealings with the whole legal estate in favour of third parties cannot be valid and effectual at common law without the active participation of all the joint tenants, each of whom must assent to the transaction and (where there is a document of disposition) add his or her signature to it.[2]

1   Joint tenancy cannot therefore exist between a freeholder and a leaseholder, between an owner

in possession and an owner in remainder, or between an owner of a fee simple interest and an owner of a life interest (*Bl Comm*, Vol II, p 181). A minor may nevertheless, in relation to the same interest, hold as an equitable joint tenant with an adult (see *Re Gardner* [1924] 2 Ch 243 at 251).

2   See *U-Needa Laundry Ltd v Hill* [2000] 2 NZLR 308 at [24].

Dealings with the whole legal estate

11.25   Whether the transaction is by way of transfer, lease or mortgage, a disponee of a legal estate owned by joint proprietors takes an unimpaired title to the whole estate only if he receives a disposition from all of the joint tenants. Thus no title to the whole legal estate in land can normally pass under a written disposition which does not bear the genuine signature of all the legal co-owners (although the 'statutory magic'[1] brought about by registration of an irregular disposition confers a legal title until such time as the register is rectified against the disponee[2]). The requirement of joint participation applies just as much to a leasehold as a freehold estate. Thus all positive dealings with a jointly held term of years, in order to be effective at law, require the concurrence of all the joint leaseholders.[3] It is indeed the mandatory participation of all the joint tenants in disposing of jointly held land which has led to a number of (ultimately unsuccessful) proposals that the legal title in the matrimonial home should automatically be held by husband and wife as joint tenants.[4] Such proposals, if accepted, would have gone far to minimise the social mischief which flows from unilateral dealings undertaken by one or other partner.

1   [**Para 6.24**]. See *Argyle Building Society v Hammond* (1985) 49 P & CR 148 at 155 per Slade LJ.
2   LRA 2002, s 65, Sch 4 [**para 12.249**]. See eg *Hayes v Nwajiaku* [1994] EGCS 106 (forgery of other joint tenant's signature on transfer document presented for registration). See also *Ahmed v Kendrick* (1988) 56 P & CR 120 at 123–124.
3   See *AG Securities v Vaughan* [1990] 1 AC 417 at 432E per Fox LJ; *Hammersmith and Fulham LBC v Monk* [1992] 1 AC 478 at 490G–H per Lord Bridge of Harwich. The co-operation of all the joint tenants is required for the purpose of surrendering the lease [**para 7.306**], claiming a right to relief against forfeiture [**para 14.150**], and exercising a break clause [**para 7.283**] or an option to renew the lease [**para 7.224**]. Only in the matter of giving notice to quit is unilateral action – by either landlord or tenant – fully effective [**para 7.295**], a principle which has been extended to allow unilateral termination of a licence granted by another joint tenant (see *Sanders v McDonald and Pringle* [1981] CLY 1534 [**para 4.23**]). See also *Lehmann v Herman* [1993] 1 EGLR 172 at 174D (party wall notice under London Building Acts (Amendment) Act 1939 invalid unless served by all joint tenants).
4   See Law Commission, *Family Law: Third Report on Family Property* (Law Com No 86, June 1978); *Property Law: The Implications of Williams & Glyn's Bank Ltd v Boland* (Law Com No 115, Cmnd 8636, August 1982). Parliamentary initiatives to give effect to these proposals have consistently failed (see *Parliamentary Debates, House of Lords, Official Report*, Vol 437 (Session 1982–1983), Col 642; *Parliamentary Debates, House of Lords, Official Report (Fifth Series)*, Vol 460 (Session 1984–85), Col 1262).

Effect of unilateral dealings by one legal co-owner

11.26   It is possible – although unusual – for one of a number of joint owners of a legal estate to attempt to deal with that estate unilaterally. Such dealings cannot operate effectively upon the whole legal estate in the land,[1] but have the consequence of severing, either completely or sometimes partially, any joint tenancy which exists in equity. Thus a purported transfer or charge of the whole estate which is executed by only one joint tenant takes effect in equity in relation to the severed beneficial share of that joint tenant.[2] Similarly a joint legal owner may grant a lease of jointly held land without the concurrence of the other co-owner or co-owners.[3] This unilateral letting cannot carve a term of years out of the whole co-owned legal estate,[4] but operates in equity to sever or suspend joint ownership of the parent estate during the term of the lease.[5] Such a lease, although it confers on the lessee a right to possession exclusive of the lessor and the rest of the world,[6] does not entitle the lessee to exclude the non-participating co-owners.[7] These non-participating co-owners retain the right to share possession of the leased premises, or to recover possession from the unilateral lessee,[8] or even to lease the premises to another, quite different, tenant.[9] In all such cases rights of occupation and the allocation of any rents and profits drawn from the land are ultimately governed by the Trusts of Land and Appointment of Trustees Act 1996.[10]

1   Any attempt to register a dealing patently executed by only one of two or more living joint tenants would simply be rejected by Land Registry.
2   [**Paras 11.80, 15.96**]. See LPA 1925, s 63(1).
3   See *Tilling v Whiteman* [1980] AC 1 at 24B per Lord Fraser of Tullybelton; [1980] CLJ 27 at 29–30 (Gray).
4   This outcome exemplifies the distinction between a 'lease' (which merely connotes the contractual conferment of a right to possession for a term) and a 'term of years' (which connotes the grant of a proprietary estate in the land). See *Bruton v London & Quadrant Housing Trust* [2000] 1 AC 406 at 415A–C per Lord Hoffmann [**para 7.85**].
5   [**Para 11.85**].
6   A truly joint letting, by carving a proprietary interest out of the whole jointly owned estate, confers on the lessee a right to exclusive possession vis à vis all persons without exception.
7   This result follows a fortiori where a lease is granted unilaterally by one who is already a tenant in common (see *U-Needa Laundry Ltd v Hill* [2000] 2 NZLR 308 at [22]–[26]).
8   See *Incorporated Owners of Chungking Mansions v Shamdasani* [1991] 2 HKC 342. In view of the impracticality of the arrangement, the court may be reluctant to grant specific performance of a unilaterally granted lease (see *U-Needa Laundry Ltd v Hill* [2000] 2 NZLR 308 at [22], [29]).
9   See *Frieze v Unger* [1960] VR 230 at 245; *Beaton v McDivitt* (1985) 13 NSWLR 134 at 145F.
10   [**Para 11.169**].

Unity of title

11.27   Unity of title entails that each joint tenant must derive his title to the land from the same act (e g of adverse possession) or the same document (e g of transfer or grant).[1] Unity of title confers the obvious advantage that a purchaser from joint tenants need investigate only one title.

1   *Bl Comm*, Vol II, p 181. Joint tenants, it was always said, 'are in under the same feudal contract or investiture' (R Preston, *Essay on Abstracts of Title* (1824), Vol 2, p 62). See e g *Brown v Faulkner* [2003] NICA 5(2) at [39] per Higgins J.

Unity of time

11.28   Unity of time expresses the idea that the interest of each joint tenant must normally vest at the same time.[1]

1   *Bl Comm*, Vol II, p 181. See *Elements of Land Law* (2nd edn 1993), pp 653–655.

TENANCY IN COMMON

11.29   In contrast to joint tenancy, tenancy in common is a form of co-ownership in which the co-owners hold distinct shares or notional proportions of entitlement. It is frequently said that, unlike joint tenants, tenants in common hold land in 'undivided shares'. This phrase is initially confusing to the extent that it appears to conjure up a picture of the amorphous undifferentiated co-ownership which characterises joint tenancy. However, the key to the distinction between joint tenancy and tenancy in common lies in the reference to the word 'shares'.[1] It is only in the tenancy in common that the co-owners hold distinct shares at all. It is only of tenants in common that it can be meaningful to say, for instance, that A has a three-quarters interest and B a one-quarter interest, or even that A and B are each entitled to a one-half share. The allocation of shares or proportions is simply not possible as between joint tenants, who are of course wholly entitled to the whole.[2] Tenants in common are owners of distinct shares, albeit in land which has not yet been divided up physically. It is impossible to point to one parcel or area of the co-owned land rather than any other as belonging to a particular tenant in common.[3] In this sense it can be said that tenants in common own specific, but undivided, shares in the land.

1   See *Re Davies (Deceased)* [1950] 1 All ER 120 at 123.
2   **[Para 11.4]**. 'A joint interest in equal shares is a contradiction in terms; the words of severance create a tenancy in common' (*Cowcher v Cowcher* [1972] 1 WLR 425 at 430H per Bagnall J). See also *Malayan Credit Ltd v Jack Chia-MPH Ltd* [1986] AC 549 at 559E–G; *Bl Comm*, Vol II, p 193 ('joint tenants do not take by distinct halves or moieties').
3   See *Co Litt*, p 189a; *Bl Comm*, Vol II, p 191 ('because none knoweth his own severalty … they all occupy promiscuously').

11.30   The principal characteristics of tenancy in common are two in number. First, there is no right of survivorship as between tenants in common; and second, only unity of possession is required.

THERE IS NO RIGHT OF SURVIVORSHIP

11.31   No right of survivorship obtains between tenants in common. The size of a tenant in common's share is a fixed quantum which does not alter merely by reason of the death of any other tenant in common. In the absence of a right of survivorship, the share of each passes on his death either in accordance with the terms of his will or according to the rules of intestate succession.

ONLY UNITY OF POSSESSION IS REQUIRED

11.32   Of the four unities required in joint tenancy only unity of possession is an essential constitutive element of tenancy in common.[1] Unity of interest is not required between tenants in common. It is indeed the potential *disunity* of interest which enables one tenant in common to own, say, a one-third share and another tenant in common to own a two-thirds share in the co-owned land. Nor is unity of title or unity of time essential; as has just been seen, it is possible for the share of a tenant in common to be passed to some third party by will or on an intestacy. Unity of possession is the irreducible component of tenancy in common: without it there would exist no co-ownership at all,[2] merely separate ownership of physically distinct areas of land.

1   *Bl Comm*, Vol II, pp 191–192.
2   *Bl Comm*, Vol II, p 192.

Indivisibility of possession

11.33   As is true of joint tenants,[1] the unity of possession enjoyed by tenants in common entails that each tenant is as much entitled to possession of the co-owned land as is any other.[2] No co-tenant[3] may physically demarcate any part of the land as his to the exclusion of his brethren.[4] Instead, each co-tenant has 'a right to exercise acts of ownership over the whole property',[5] subject to the qualification that in so doing he must not interfere with the like right of any other co-tenant.[6] It follows that no co-tenant has any right to demand compensation in respect of the simultaneous enjoyment of the land by a fellow co-owner except where the latter has received 'more than comes to his just share or proportion'.[7] However, this notion of a 'just share or proportion' has been construed so widely that in practice there is now relatively little left of the original rule that unity of possession precludes compensation claims between co-tenants. The implications of unity of possession must now be explored in greater detail.

1   [**Para 11.23**].
2   *Wight v IRC* (1982) 264 EG 935 at 936–937; *Swartzbaugh v Sampson*, 54 P2d 73 at 75 (1936); *Dimmick v Dimmick*, 24 Cal Rptr 856 at 858 (1962); *Govorko v Vicelic* (1971) 2 BPR 9477 at 9490; *Barrios v Chiabrera* (1984) 3 BPR 9276 at 9279–9280; *Dunkel v Izsak* (1984) 3 BPR 9668. Contrast *Chhokar v Chhokar* [1984] FLR 313 at 332D–F [**para 12.187**], where Cumming-Bruce LJ refused to allow one tenant in common to occupy a house which was already occupied by a married woman and her family.
3   Since the possessory rights of joint tenants and tenants in common are in general the same, the following description of shared possession uses the term 'co-tenant' as a generic reference to both forms of co-owner.
4   Perhaps the most bizarre circumstance in which this principle has been applied arose in *Galasso v Del Guercio*, 276 A2d 186 at 189–190 (1971). Here the Superior Court of New Jersey was called upon to resolve a dispute between co-owners as to which family member should be laid to rest in precisely which location in the family mausoleum. See also *Silvia v Helger*, 67 A2d 27 at 28 (1949).
5   *Griffies v Griffies* (1863) 8 LT (NS) 758 per Kindersley V-C. See likewise *Goodwyn v Spray* (1786) Dick 667, 21 ER 431; *Job v Potton* (1875) LR 20 Eq 84 at 97 per Bacon V-C; *Flynn v United States*, 205 F2d 756 at 760 (1953); *Dunkel v Izsak* (1984) 3 BPR 9668 per Powell J.

6   *Saulsberry v Saulsberry*, 121 F2d 318 at 321 (1941); *Sayers v Pyland*, 161 SW2d 769 at 773 (1942); *Tompkins v Superior Court of City and County of San Francisco*, 27 Cal Rptr 889 at 892 (1963); *Jemzura v Jemzura*, 330 NE2d 414 at 419 (1975).

7   This formula was first used in a statute of 1705 (4 Anne, c 16, s 27) which gave both the joint tenant and the tenant in common an action of account in respect of profits derived from undue exploitation of the co-owned land by another co-tenant. This statute has now been repealed (see Law of Property (Amendment) Act 1924, Sch 10), but the idea persists that co-owners are accountable to each other if one of them should take 'more than his proper share' (*Bull v Bull* [1955] 1 QB 234 at 237 per Denning LJ). See also *Job v Potton* (1875) LR 20 Eq 84 at 93. Even before the repeal in the 1924 Act, the notion of a 'just share or proportion' was construed as referring not merely to the 'receipt of issues and profits' but more widely to any 'receiving' in excess of one's 'just share' (see *Henderson v Eason* (1851) 17 QB 701 at 719, 117 ER 1451 at 1457).

Occupation and use

11.34   It has long been clear that at common law each co-owner (whether joint tenant or tenant in common) has 'a perfect right'[1] to possession of the entire co-owned land and to the 'use and enjoyment of it in a proper manner.'[2] This right exists regardless of the precise quantum of the co-tenant's interest and has been influential in fixing the degree of mutual tolerance which the law still requires of co-tenants in their dealings *inter se*.[3] The relations of co-owners in England and Wales are now subject to adjudication under the Trusts of Land and Appointment of Trustees Act 1996. This legislation reinforces the occupation entitlement of co-tenants[4] and confers on the courts an armoury of powers to regulate the exercise of rights of occupation and use.[5] Although the 1996 Act equips the courts with wide-ranging discretion, judicial determinations in this area are inevitably influenced by a substantial body of case law which has emerged over the last two centuries concerning the privileges of co-ownership.[6]

1   *Henderson v Eason* (1851) 17 QB 701 at 720, 117 ER 1451 at 1458 per Parke B. See also *Hole v Thomas* (1802) 7 Ves 589 at 590, 32 ER 237 per Eldon LC.

2   *Bull v Bull* [1955] 1 QB 234 at 237 per Denning LJ. The insistence upon use 'in a proper manner' is an echo of Lord Hatherley LC's statement in *Jacobs v Seward* (1872) LR 5 HL 464 at 474, that no action will lie against a co-owner if he uses the co-owned property 'in an ordinary and legitimate way' or for 'a perfectly legitimate purpose'.

3   There is a recurring assertion that a co-tenant is immune from liability if he was adopting the only (or only reasonable) means of enjoying or exploiting his right of ownership (see e g *Job v Potton* (1875) LR 20 Eq 84 at 93, 97 per Bacon V-C).

4   TOLATA 1996, s 12(1) [**para 11.175**].

5   TOLATA 1996, s 14(2) [**para 11.235**]; Family Law Act 1996, ss 33(3), 36(5) [**para 12.93**].

6   This case law is not merely indigenous to England and Wales. The courts of the United States have undertaken more than their fair share of the exploration of co-ownership law.

Trespass and ouster

11.35   Save in cases of physical ouster of another co-tenant or gross interference with mutual rights of enjoyment, the notion of trespass has no meaning between co-owners. In this context an important distinction is drawn between exclusive use and exclusory behaviour.

Exclusive use

11.36   No action lies in trespass against a co-tenant merely on the ground that he exclusively occupies and exploits the whole or any one part rather than another of the co-owned land.[1] He is not thereby taking 'more than comes to his just share or proportion.' In *Jacobs v Seward*,[2] for instance, the House of Lords rejected a claim in trespass based partly upon the allegation that one tenant in common had cut a crop of grass on the co-owned land. Lord Hatherley LC declared that it was 'idle to talk of trespass as a consequence of a man making hay upon his own field – for it is his own – or a moiety of it at least, and no definite portion of it is mapped out as his moiety.'[3]

1   *Co Litt*, p 199b; *Bl Comm*, Vol II, pp 183, 194.
2   (1872) LR 5 HL 464 at 473.
3   As counsel argued in *Job v Potton* (1875) LR 20 Eq 84 at 90, '[o]wners are not trespassers.' However, in *Jacobs v Seward* (1872) LR 5 HL 464 at 474, 478, both Lord Hatherley and Lord Westbury conceded that there might have been a legitimate case for an accounting in respect of the profit made from the harvesting of the hay [**para 11.43**]. See also *Harper v O'Neal*, 363 So2d 930 at 932 (1978). It is clear beyond doubt that the harvesting co-owner cannot be guilty of theft (see *State v McCoy* (1883) NC 466; Annot, 17 ALR3d 1394 at 1396).

Exclusory behaviour

11.37   A remedy for trespass is available against a co-tenant only in cases of 'ouster',[1] it being settled law that no co-tenant may go so far as to turn another co-tenant off the land.[2] Ouster comprises any unequivocal and express 'denial of the title and right to possession' of a co-tenant[3] and is wide enough to cover not merely instances in which one co-owner evicts or excludes another from the land,[4] but also circumstances where he otherwise interferes with the common enjoyment of that land.[5] The old cases suggest that, in order to establish trespass, this interference must be such as to tend towards the destruction of the co-owned property in its original form.[6] The modern understanding of ouster is undoubtedly somewhat broader, extending beyond 'actual' ouster to include 'constructive' ouster (eg where an innocent co-tenant is indirectly caused to leave the co-owned property).[7] Although conduct which merely makes life 'nasty' for a co-tenant may not constitute ouster,[8] ouster may occur with the unconsented introduction of a new partner to share co-owned premises[9] or with a persistent denial of the title of the other co-tenant.[10]

1   *Co Litt*, p 199b; *Bl Comm*, Vol II, p 194; *Jacobs v Seward* (1872) LR 5 HL 464 at 472, 478. See also *Stedman v Smith* (1857) 8 El & Bl 1 at 6, 120 ER 1 at 3.
2   *Bull v Bull* [1955] 1 QB 234 at 237 per Denning LJ. See also *Smith v United States*, 153 F2d 655 at 661 (1946); *Zaslow v Kroenert*, 176 P2d 1 at 5 (1946). The obtaining of a court order excluding a co-owner on the ground of apprehended domestic violence is no true ouster (*Biviano v Natoli* (1998) 43 NSWLR 695 at 697A, 702G–703A (Court of Appeal of New South Wales)).
3   *Biviano v Natoli* (1998) 43 NSWLR 695 at 701A per Beazley JA. See *Doe d Fishar v Prosser* (1774) 1 Cowp 217 at 218, 98 ER 1052 at 1053; *Doe d Hellings v Bird* (1809) 11 East 49 at 51, 103 ER 922 at 922–923; *Howell v Bradford*, 570 So2d 643 at 646 (1990); *Re Kostiuk* (2002) 215 DLR (4th) 78 at [43]–[44].
4   See *Bull v Bull* [1955] 1 QB 234 at 237. In *Jacobs v Seward* (1872) LR 5 HL 464 at 473,

477–478, the House of Lords held that the mere putting of a lock upon a gate by one co-tenant could not constitute 'ouster', unless there was direct evidence that by this means another co-tenant had been intentionally denied entry. See likewise *Spiller v Mackereth*, 334 So2d 859 at 862 (1976), but contrast *Zaslow v Kroenert*, 176 P2d 1 at 5–6 (1946), where there was manifest evidence of an intention to exclude the other co-tenant, not least in the form of a change of locks and the prominent display of 'no trespassing' notices. For the suggestion that 'ouster' can occur where one co-tenant unilaterally leases the co-owned land to a stranger, see *Oates v Oates* [1949] SASR 37 at 40.

5   See e g *Stedman v Smith* (1857) 8 El & Bl 1 at 7, 120 ER 1 at 3. Here D rested part of the roof of his wash-house on the top of a dividing wall which he co-owned with P. P was held to have been 'excluded from the top of the wall: he might have wished to train fruit trees there, or to amuse himself [sic] by running along the top of the wall'. Ouster from a party wall may, of course, lead in the fullness of time to a successful claim of title to the whole by adverse possession (see e g *Prudential Assurance Co Ltd v Waterloo Real Estate Inc* [1999] 2 EGLR 85 [**para 6.96**]). See also *De La Cuesta v Bazzi*, 118 P2d 909 at 915 (1941).

6   As Lord Hatherley LC pointed out in *Jacobs v Seward* (1872) LR 5 HL 464 at 475, 'where the act done by the tenant in common is right in itself, and nothing is done which destroys the benefit of the other tenant in common in the property, there no action will lie, because he can follow that property as long as it is in existence and not destroyed.' See e g *Cubitt v Porter* (1828) 8 B & C 257 at 268, 108 ER 1039 at 1043 (no ouster by destruction of old wall and building of new and better wall); *Ferguson v Miller* [1978] 1 NZLR 819 at 825 (no ouster by temporary disturbance of access way). For an example of 'ouster' by destruction of the common property, see *Wilkinson v Haygarth* (1847) 12 QB 837 at 845, 116 ER 1085 at 1088 (removal of turf).

7   See *Dennis v McDonald* [1982] Fam 63 at 70C, 71D per Purchas J (spouse no longer 'a free agent').

8   *Chieco v Evans* (1990) 5 BPR 11297 at 11299. A statement by one tenant to the effect that the other tenant could leave if she did not like his behaviour does not constitute constructive ouster (*Diotallevi v Diotallevi* (1982) 134 DLR (3d) 477 at 479). See also *Spiller v Mackereth*, 334 So2d 859 at 862 (1976).

9   See *Biviano v Natoli* (1998) 43 NSWLR 695 at 702C–F per Beazley JA. Contrast *Thrift v Thrift* (1975) 10 ALR 332 at 338 per Hutley JA (introduction of mother); *Chieco v Evans* (1990) 5 BPR 11297 at 11299.

10   *Biviano v Natoli* (1998) 43 NSWLR 695 at 703C–D. Ouster is not present in the mere action of ignoring another co-tenant's request for a sale of the property (see *Biviano v Natoli*, supra at 703A–C).

Other forms of liability

11.38   It is possible that two other forms of claim may arise from an illegitimate user exercised by a co-tenant on the land. There appears to be no reason why the tort of nuisance cannot be alleged by one co-tenant against another, although it may be difficult to prove that the alleged interference with the claimant's beneficial use of the land is sufficiently severe to meet the criterion of 'unreasonableness' which is constitutive of the tort.[1] It is also possible that one co-tenant may be guilty of voluntary waste by reason of his activity on the co-owned land,[2] but again it is both necessary and difficult to demonstrate that the activity in question has tended to the destruction of the property.[3] However, where waste is proved, the remedy for the other co-tenant may take the form of either an action of account[4] or an injunction[5] or both.

1   See e g *Ferguson v Miller* [1978] 1 NZLR 819 at 828, where McMullin J declined to apply the term 'nuisance' to a property developer's proposal to widen a carriageway on a co-owned access strip and resurface the accessway in permanent materials.

2   *Co Litt*, p 200b. The definition of waste marks out, as always, the boundaries of permissible advancement of self-interest and the proper limits of entrepreneurial zeal **[para 1.133]**. Thus the mere cutting of timber is not destructive waste (*Arthur v Lamb* (1865) 2 Dr & Sm 428 at 430, 62 ER 683 at 684), but the cutting of saplings or felling of timber 'at unseasonable times' would be (*Hole v Thomas* (1802) 7 Ves 589 at 590, 32 ER 237).

3   In *Ferguson v Miller* [1978] 1 NZLR 819 at 826, McMullin J considered the proposed development to be 'an act of repair rather than an act of waste.' See also *Jacobs v Seward* (1872) LR 5 HL 464 (where the allegation of waste seems not even to have been raised).

4   *Sayers v Pyland*, 161 SW2d 769 at 771–772 (1942).

5   See *The Durham and Sunderland Railway Co v Wawn* (1841) 3 Beav 119 at 123, 49 ER 47 at 48; *Foshee v Foshee*, 143 So2d 301 at 303–304 (1962), 177 So2d 99 at 101 (1965). No injunction will issue unless there is evidence of 'malicious destruction' (*Hole v Thomas* (1802) 7 Ves 589 at 590, 32 ER 237) as distinct from acts done in 'the proper course of husbandry' and 'good management' (*Arthur v Lamb* (1865) 2 Dr & Sm 428 at 430, 62 ER 683 at 684). See also *Twort v Twort* (1809) 16 Ves 128 at 131, 33 ER 932 at 934, 2 Ves Supp 431, 34 ER 1165; *Bailey v Hobson* (1869) 5 Ch App 180 at 182.

Rents, profits and other compensation received from a stranger

11.39   A co-tenant is entitled to share in any monetary advantage derived from an external source by reason of ownership of the co-owned land (e g by way of a lucrative letting to a stranger).[1] Within a joint tenancy each co-owner shares equally in the pecuniary gain.[2] The rights of a tenant in common are measured in strict proportion to the quantum of his individual share as a co-owner,[3] so that, for example, a tenant in common with a one-third interest is entitled to receive one third of the net rents and profits derived from the land.[4] Exactly the same principles apply to other forms of money payment received by one co-tenant from a third party in virtue of co-ownership of the land.[5]

1   Not all the co-tenants need join in the letting, and a non-participant co-tenant, precisely because he is not bound by any agreement, is entitled to an account direct from the stranger in respect of a proportionate share of the net profits drawn from the land by the latter (see *Job v Potton* (1875) LR 20 Eq 84 at 97–98, where the non-participant co-tenant was not limited to a share of a mining royalty agreed by the other co-tenants). Alternatively a co-tenant may claim mesne profits on a restitutionary basis from the third party as trespasser (*Lamru Pty Ltd v Kation Pty Ltd* (1998) 9 BPR 16571 at 16577–16578).

2   **[Para 11.23]**.

3   *Henderson v Eason* (1851) 17 QB 701 at 719, 117 ER 1451 at 1458. See also *Wright v Johnson* [2002] 2 P & CR 210 at [34]; *Hitchins v Hitchins* (1998) 9 BPR 16659 at 16665–16666.

4   See *Job v Potton* (1875) LR 20 Eq 84 at 93–94, 97. However, the rents and profits shared in this way must be carefully confined to 'those receipts which can properly be regarded as rents and revenue of the common property itself as distinct from profits which the defendant [who ran a caravan park] may have made by his use and occupation of the common property (e g fees for services and for use of items of equipment)' (*Squire v Rogers* (1980) 27 ALR 330 at 345).

5   See e g *Roberts v Rodney DC* [2001] 2 NZLR 402 at [54] (duty to share money damages recovered in respect of a third party's trespass on the land).

11.40   Co-owners are liable to account *inter se* in respect of any income received by one co-tenant from a stranger in excess of his own 'just share or proportion'.[1] However, this liability to account applies only to actual (rather than constructive) receipts of income drawn from the land. Co-owners are not fiduciaries one for another[2]; nor is their relationship one of partnership or agency. Even if one co-tenant is left to manage the land, he is under no duty to extract the maximum (or indeed any) rental value.[3] There is therefore no liability to account for such rents or profits as might have been (but were not in fact) derived from prudent letting of the land to an outsider.[4]

1   *Henderson v Eason* (1851) 17 QB 701 at 719, 117 ER 1451 at 1457–1458; *Kennedy v De Trafford* [1897] AC 180 at 187; *Bernard v Josephs* [1982] Ch 391 at 401C, 410B; *Chhokar v Chhokar* [1984] FLR 313 at 332G. See similarly *Zanzonico v Zanzonico*, 2 A2d 597 at 598 (1938); *Rehfuss v McAndrew*, 33 So2d 16 at 17 (1947); *Jeffress v Piatt*, 370 SW2d 383 at 386 (1963); *Squire v Rogers* (1980) 27 ALR 330 at 345; *Ryan v Dries* (2002) 10 BPR 19497 at [65].
2   *Kennedy v De Trafford* [1897] AC 180 at 189. See also *Pure Oil Co v Byrnes*, 57 NE2d 356 at 361 (1944); *Taylor v Brindley*, 164 F2d 235 at 240 (1947); *Britton v Green*, 325 F2d 377 at 383 (1963). See 86 CJS 377.
3   Nor, in the absence of agreement, may a co-tenant demand any fee for his personal services in managing the property (see *Kahnovsky v Kahnovsky*, 21 A2d 569 at 573 (1941); *Curl v Neilson*, 167 P2d 320 at 322–323 (1946); *Re Estate and Guardianship of Purton*, 441 P2d 561 at 570 (1968); *Neal v Neal*, 470 SW2d 383 at 386–387 (1971)).
4   *Wheeler v Horne* (1740) Willes 208 at 210, 125 ER 1135 at 1136; *Henderson v Eason* (1851) 17 QB 701 at 718–719, 117 ER 1451 at 1457. In *Chhokar v Chhokar* [1984] FLR 313 at 332F, a co-tenant was not required to account for any notional rent attributable to occupation by her husband, whom she allowed to live with her in the co-owned property. See also *Boulter v Boulter* (1898) 19 LR (NSW) Eq 135 at 138–139; *Re Tolman's Estate* (1928) 23 Tas LR 29 at 31; *Thompson v Flynn*, 58 P2d 769 at 771 (1936); *Mastbaum v Mastbaum*, 9 A2d 51 at 54 (1939); *Riechmann v Riechmann*, 283 NE2d 734 at 736 (1972); *Thrift v Thrift* (1976) 10 ALR 332 at 339.

Profit derived from industry of one co-tenant

11.41   A different problem arises where one co-tenant enjoys sole occupation of the co-owned land and derives a profit or income from that land by reason of his own exertions.

Legitimate profit

11.42   In *Henderson v Eason*[1] Parke B thought that in many such instances it would be 'impossible' to say that the occupying co-tenant 'has received more than comes to his just share.' He held that there is no liability to account for profits where a co-owner 'employs his capital and industry in cultivating the whole of a piece of land … in a mode in which the money and labour expended greatly exceed the value of the rent or compensation for the mere occupation of the land.'[2] In a 'hazardous venture' undertaken under such circumstances,[3] the risk of which is entirely his own,[4] the co-tenant is entitled to retain all the produce of the venture.[5] In a spirited endorsement of free enterprise, Parke B concluded that the co-tenant, in taking all the 'fructus industriales', receives in truth merely 'the return for his own capital and labour, to which his co-tenant has no right.'[6] This statement almost certainly still represents good law, at least so long as the co-tenant's activities have caused no long-term destruction of the revenue potential or capital value of the land.

1   (1851) 17 QB 701 at 720, 117 ER 1451 at 1458.

2   (1851) 17 QB 701 at 720–721, 117 ER 1451 at 1458.

3   Parke B gave the example of cultivating hops. Contrast *Jacobs v Seward* (1872) LR 5 HL 464 at 474, 478, where the cultivation of hay was considered not to be sufficiently hazardous, nor the investment of personal energy so excessive, as to exclude a liability to account. Lord Hatherley LC conceded (at 476) that any expense incurred in making the hay would have to be allowed for in the accounting.

4   Parke B pointed out that 'if the speculation had been a losing one altogether, he could not have called for a moiety of the losses, as he would have been enabled to do had [the land] been cultivated by the mutual agreement of the cotenants' ((1851) 17 QB 701 at 721, 117 ER 1451 at 1458). For further reference to the profit-sharing implications of a risk-sharing agreement between co-owners, see *Anon* (1684) Skinner 230, 90 ER 106.

5   This approach, correlating profit with risk, has been applied fairly widely to farming operations conducted by one co-owner (see e.g. *Swartzbaugh v Sampson*, 54 P2d 73 at 75 (1936); *Black v Black*, 204 P2d 950 at 953 (1949); *Reid v Reid* (1978) 87 DLR (3d) 370 at 372). See similarly *Spelman v Spelman* [1944] 2 DLR 74 at 77–79 (risk inherent in running a rooming-house counteracted any duty to account for rents).

6   See also *Pico v Columbet*, 12 Cal 414 at 421, 73 Am Dec 550 at 553–554 per Field J (1859). For a modern (and very similar) defence of the same approach, see L Berger, 'An Analysis of the Economic Relations between Cotenants' 21 Arizona L Rev 1015 (1979).

Liability to account

11.43 In *Henderson v Eason* there is a clear implication that there may be some cases in which a co-tenant will indeed have received more than his 'just share or proportion', even though his profit derives from engaging his own personal efforts in productive use of the co-owned land.[1] For instance, a co-tenant may, by his industrious exploitation of the common land, have exhausted or diminished the capital value of the property through activities such as mining, quarrying or oil drilling.[2] Here, even though the co-tenant has invested his own energy and risk-capital, he cannot retain the entire profit himself but must submit to a fair accounting with his co-tenants.[3] His liability to account is not affected by the fact that he did not in any way exclude his co-tenants from similar exploitation of the resource or even that he did not extract any more than his proportionate share of that resource.[4]

1   See e.g. *Jacobs v Seward* (1872) LR 5 HL 464.

2   Such activities may technically constitute waste (see 86 CJS 420). In Britain the ownership of petroleum reserves is vested by statute in the Crown [**para 1.35**].

3   *Payne v Callahan*, 99 P2d 1050 at 1057 (1940). Such accounting relates only to the *net* profit derived from the operation. It allows the entrepreneur co-tenant reimbursement of reasonable and necessary expenses incurred in extraction and marketing (see *Job v Potton* (1875) LR 20 Eq 84 at 97; *Cox v Davison*, 397 SW2d 200 at 203 (1965); *P & N Investment Corp v Florida Ranchettes Inc*, 220 So2d 451 at 454 (1968)) and recognises his right to 'reasonable compensation' for his personal services (see *White v Smyth*, 214 SW2d 967 at 975 (1948)).

4   *White v Smyth*, 214 SW2d 967 at 975 (1948) (Supreme Court of Texas).

Rent obligations as between co-tenants

11.44 It is often said that in the absence of agreement[1] no obligation in respect of rent or mesne profits can normally arise at common law as between co-tenants by reason merely of the fact that one of their number may happen to enjoy sole occupation of the entire co-owned property.[2]

1   *M'Mahon v Burchell* (1846) 2 Ph 127 at 135–136, 41 ER 889 at 893; 1 Coop T Cott 457 at 475, 47 ER 944 at 951; *Henderson v Eason* (1851) 17 QB 701 at 720, 117 ER 1451 at 1458; *Roberts v Roberts*, 150 SW2d 236 at 237 (1941).
2   *M'Mahon v Burchell* (1846) 2 Ph 127 at 135, 41 ER 889 at 893; 1 Coop T Cott 457 at 475, 47 ER 944 at 951; *Kennedy v De Trafford* [1897] AC 180 at 190–191; *Jones (A E) v Jones (F W)* [1977] 1 WLR 438 at 443B. See also *Re Randall's Estate*, 132 P2d 763 at 766 (1942); *Rehfuss v McAndrew*, 33 So2d 16 at 17 (1947); *Baird v Moore*, 141 A2d 324 at 329 (1958); *Seesholts v Beers*, 270 So2d 434 at 436 (1972); *Barrios v Chiabrera* (1984) 3 BPR 9276 at 9280; *Dunkel v Izsak* (1984) 3 BPR 9668; *Biviano v Natoli* (1998) 43 NSWLR 695 at 700A–B.

The general common law principle

11.45   Since co-tenants, whether joint tenants or tenants in common, enjoy unity of possession, each is equally entitled with his fellow co-owners to physical possession of the co-owned land.[1] The traditional common law view used to be that no co-tenant should be charged a rent for the sole enjoyment of that which is his 'perfect right' and which the other co-tenant or co-tenants are likewise free to enjoy.[2] Any concession of sole occupancy to one co-tenant was regarded as a matter of voluntary choice and one co-owner's unilateral decision to vacate the land should not 'change his status into that of a landlord over the remaining cotenant in possession.'[3]

1   *Jacobs v Seward* (1872) LR 5 HL 464 at 473; *Bull v Bull* [1955] 1 QB 234 at 237.
2   *Henderson v Eason* (1851) 17 QB 701 at 720, 117 ER 1451 at 1458 per Parke B. See similarly *Griffies v Griffies* (1863) 8 LT (NS) 758; *McCormick v McCormick* [1921] NZLR 384 at 385; *Thompson v Flynn*, 58 P2d 769 at 771 (1936); *Henderson v Henderson* (2000) 184 DLR (4th) 128 at [23]; *Re Kostiuk* (2002) 215 DLR (4th) 78 at [41].
3   *Seesholts v Beers*, 270 So2d 434 at 437 (1972) per Walden J.

The proliferation of exceptions

11.46   To this basic common law principle of rent-immunity between co-tenants there emerged, over the years, a number of overlapping exceptions, most of which involved some trauma in the personal or family relationship of the co-owners. It came to be accepted that an occupation rent is payable, for instance, by a co-tenant whose sole occupation was achieved by the intentional ouster or violent exclusion of another co-tenant[1] or where termination of a personal relationship made it 'unreasonable' to expect continued joint occupation.[2] Likewise a co-tenant who claims credit for improvements, repairs or mortgage outgoings paid on the co-owned land must normally give credit for a notional rent to be assessed in respect of any sole occupation which he has enjoyed.[3]

1   *Jones (A E) v Jones (F W)* [1977] 1 WLR 438 at 442B; *Dennis v McDonald* [1982] Fam 63 at 71D, 80A; *Bernard v Josephs* [1982] Ch 391 at 401B, 409B. See also *Mastron v Cotton* [1926] 1 DLR 767 at 768; *Luke v Luke* (1936) 36 SR (NSW) 310 at 314; *Szuba v Szuba* [1951] OWN 61 at 63; *Spiller v Mackereth*, 334 So2d 859 at 862 (1976); *Roberts v Roberts*, 584 P2d 378 at 380

(1978); *Biviano v Natoli* (1998) 43 NSWLR 695 at 700B; *Re Kostiuk* (2002) 215 DLR (4th) 78 at [40]–[48]; *Ryan v Dries* (2002) 10 BPR 19497 at [12], [61].

2   *Cousins v Dzosens* (1981) Times, 12 December. See also *Bernard v Josephs* [1982] Ch 391 at 405F. The court can also impose a rent obligation on a sole occupier on or pending the granting of a divorce (see e g *Bedson v Bedson* [1965] 2 QB 666 at 682F; *Harvey v Harvey* [1982] Fam 83 at 89B; *Brown v Brown* (1981) Times, 11 December) or as the condition of postponing a sale to which another co-owner would otherwise be entitled (*Bedson v Bedson*, supra at 682F, 683C; *Eves v Eves* [1975] 1 WLR 1338 at 1343A; *Dennis v McDonald* [1982] Fam 63 at 74A; *Bernard v Josephs*, supra at 411C).

3   **[Para 11.53]**.

A rule of fairness

11.47   These exceptions have proliferated to the point where the courts, in determining the applicability of an occupation rent, nowadays have regard simply to what is 'fair'[1] or 'just'[2] or 'necessary in order to do equity between the parties.'[3] The mere fact that there has been no ouster or forcible exclusion is 'far from conclusive.'[4] Today the proper presumption is that an occupation rent should always be payable in respect of sole occupancy except where the non-resident co-owner was 'in a position to enjoy [his or her] right to occupy but chose not to do so voluntarily and [was] not excluded by any relevant factor.'[5] In cases of family breakdown the co-tenant who leaves the shared home will normally be 'regarded as excluded from the family home', with the result that an occupation rent is payable by the co-tenant who remains.[6] This change in the balance of the prima facie position at common law is reinforced by the fact that trustees of land now have a statutory power to exclude one or more (but not all) of the beneficial co-owners from occupation under a trust.[7] In such cases it is open to the trustees to require the payment of 'compensation' to any beneficiary whose enjoyment of the land has been precluded or restricted.[8]

1   *Chhokar v Chhokar* [1984] FLR 313 at 332E per Cumming-Bruce LJ. The criterion of 'simple fairness' as the determinant of rent obligations between co-owners had already been propounded in New Zealand (see *Mayo v Mayo* [1966] NZLR 849 at 851). In *Chhokar* the Court considered it unfair to burden a wife with a rent obligation in favour of another tenant in common who had acted with 'moral turpitude' in conspiring with her husband to evict her from the matrimonial home **[para 12.187]**.

2   *Re Pavlou (A Bankrupt)* [1993] 1 WLR 1046 at 1050C–F per Millett J. See also *Chan Pui Chun v Leung Kam Ho* [2003] 1 FLR 23 at [106] per Jonathan Parker LJ.

3   *Re Pavlou (A Bankrupt)* [1993] 1 WLR 1046 at 1050C–D per Millett J. See likewise *Re Byford (Decd)* [2004] 1 P & CR 159 at [40] per Collins J. In *Henderson v Henderson* (2000) 184 DLR (4th) 128 at [24], the British Columbia Court of Appeal described the principle of the co-tenants' rent immunity as a 'principle of law, and not … a principle of modern equity.' The Court preferred to leave rent liability to be determined on principles of unjust enrichment.

4   *Re Pavlou (A Bankrupt)* [1993] 1 WLR 1046 at 1050D per Millett J; *Re Byford (Decd)* [2004] 1 P & CR 159 at [40] per Collins J.

5   *Dennis v McDonald* [1982] Fam 63 at 71A–B per Purchas J. See likewise *Re Pavlou (A Bankrupt)* [1993] 1 WLR 1046 at 1050E per Millett J; *Ryan v Dries* (2002) 10 BPR 19497 at [13] per Giles JA.

6   *Re Pavlou (A Bankrupt)* [1993] 1 WLR 1046 at 1050D per Millett J.

7   TOLATA 1996, s 13(1) **[para 11.178]**.

8   TOLATA 1996, s 13(6)(a). Pursuant to the Family Law Act 1996 the court may direct that the recipient of an occupation order should make periodical payments in respect of accommodation from which a beneficial owner is excluded (see Family Law Act 1996, s 40(1)).

Quantification of rent liability

11.48   The courts have always been anxious to deny that the introduction of a periodic money liability between co-tenants compulsorily creates between them any relationship of landlord and tenant.[1] Any money liability imposed is, in any event, more accurately attributed to mesne profits rather than rent.[2] The courts have accordingly resisted the suggestion that the occupation fee for sole occupancy by a co-tenant should be premised on a rack rent or open market letting value.[3] There is a tendency in many cases to calculate the rent payable on the footing that the sole occupier's liability is offset by payments of mortgage interest (and possibly of such other outgoings as council tax) made by him in respect of his own share in the land.[4] In this way the computation of any money liability imposed on the sole occupier combines an element of compensation for lost enjoyment of the land with a component of restitution for contributions made by the sole occupier which have preserved or enhanced the value of the co-owned estate.[5]

1   See eg *Dennis v McDonald* [1982] Fam 63 at 81C per Sir John Arnold P.
2   *Dennis v McDonald* [1982] Fam 63 at 81A; *Harvey v Harvey* [1982] Fam 83 at 89B; *Biviano v Natoli* (1998) 43 NSWLR 695 at 704A.
3   See eg *Dennis v McDonald* [1982] Fam 63 at 75C per Purchas J (rack rent 'was not the concept behind an occupation rent'); *Biviano v Natoli* (1998) 43 NSWLR 695 at 704B–E.
4   *Re Pavlou (A Bankrupt)* [1993] 1 WLR 1046 at 1050H–1051A per Millett J. See also *Leake v Bruzzi* [1974] 1 WLR 1528 at 1533B, H; *Suttill v Graham* [1977] 1 WLR 819 at 822C, 823H; *Bernard v Josephs* [1982] Ch 391 at 401B, 405G; *Kangas v Tsangaras* (1990) 5 BPR 11254 at 11256–11257. The crude set-off between rent and mortgage interest is only a 'rule of convenience' more readily applicable as between co-owners than in relation to the trustee in bankrupty of one of them. A trustee in bankruptcy may be inclined to ask for a stricter accounting in respect of rent and interest (see *Re Gorman (A Bankrupt)* [1990] 1 WLR 616 at 625G, 626E–G; *Re Pavlou (A Bankrupt)*, supra at 1051A–D).
5   See *Inverugie Investments Ltd v Hackett* [1995] 1 WLR 713 at 718B per Lord Lloyd of Berwick; *Ministry of Defence v Ashman* (1993) 66 P & CR 195 at 201–202 per Hoffmann LJ; but compare *Swordheath Properties Ltd v Tabet* [1979] 1 WLR 285 at 288C–F. See also *Dennis v McDonald* [1982] Fam 63 at 75D–F per Purchas J, 80G–81A, 82A–B per Sir John Arnold P.

Preservation or enhancement of the value of co-owned land

11.49   Difficult questions arise where voluntary expenditure by one co-tenant preserves or enhances the value of the co-owned land. Such expenditure occurs typically in connection with the repair or permanent improvement of the co-owned premises. The general principles applicable in this context were classically stated in *Leigh v Dickeson*[1] in terms which, more recently, have been extended to cover payments made by one co-tenant in respect of the capital component[2] (and, in some cases, the interest element[3]) of a mortgage debt affecting the land.

1   (1884) 15 QBD 60. This decision was in its turn confirmed and applied by the Australian High Court in *Brickwood v Young* (1905) 2 CLR 387 at 394–395, 400. See also *Miller v Prater*, 100 SW2d 842 at 844 (1937); *Lewis v Latham*, 79 So2d 811 at 814 (1955); *Cox v Davison*, 397 SW2d 200 at 201 (1965); *Cummings v Anderson*, 614 P2d 1283 at 1287 (1980).

2   See *Cowcher v Cowcher* [1972] 1 WLR 425 at 432G–433C per Bagnall J; *Re Pavlou (A Bankrupt)* [1993] 1 WLR 1046 at 1049B–C per Millett J; *Ryan v Dries* (2002) 10 BPR 19497 at [71] per Hodgson JA.

3   See *Re Gorman (A Bankrupt)* [1990] 1 WLR 616 at 626F–627A per Vinelott J; *Re Byford (Decd)* [2004] 1 P & CR 159 at [23] per Collins J ([2003] Conv 533 (H Conway)).

The general rule

11.50 In *Leigh v Dickeson* the Court of Appeal held that no co-tenant is entitled to demand an immediate contribution from his co-tenants towards expenses which he has voluntarily and unilaterally incurred in respect of the co-owned land.[1] This immunity from arbitrary calls for contribution does not avail the other co-tenants if, for instance, repairs or improvements were effected by agreement with them[2] or at their express or implied request.[3] Nor does any immunity apply if work was done pursuant to an existing obligation to a third party binding all the co-tenants to maintain or repair their property.[4] In such cases there is, of course, an immediate contractual liability to contribute towards the costs incurred. More particularly, in the case of mortgage payments made by one co-owner, any express or implied agreement between the co-owners relating to the effect of such payments may have an immediate impact on the configuration of their respective equitable entitlements in accordance with principles of constructive trust[5] or proprietary estoppel.[6]

1   'If the law were otherwise, a part-owner might be compelled to incur expense against his will: a house might be situate in a decaying borough, and it might be thought by one co-owner that it would be better not to repair it' ((1884) 15 QBD 60 at 65 per Brett MR). Compare the law in many jurisdictions in the United States, where there is power to demand contributions from co-tenants in respect of repairs which are absolutely necessary, although there is no similar liability in respect of permanent improvements (see 48A CJS 364, 86 CJS 445, 449–450).

2   *Anon* (1684) Skin 230, 90 ER 106; *Leigh v Dickeson* (1884) 15 QBD 60 at 64; *Harwood v Harwood* [1991] 2 FLR 274 at 294E–G. See also *Re Holyman* (1935) 30 Tas LR 15 at 26, 29–30; *Collier v Collier*, 242 P2d 537 at 542 (1952); *Ruptash and Lumsden v Zawick* [1956] 2 DLR (2d) 145 at 158; *Young v Young*, 376 A2d 1151 at 1157 (1977). However, a covenant by one co-owner to share the cost of repairs or improvements, being a positive covenant, does not run with the land to affect the covenantor's successors in title **[para 13.48]**. See *Ruptash and Lumsden v Zawick* [1956] 2 DLR (2d) 145 at 160 (Supreme Court of Canada).

3   *Leigh v Dickeson* (1884) 15 QBD 60 at 64, 66. It seems that a request or agreement will not be implied merely from the making of improvements or from their necessity or utility (*Young v McKittrick*, 267 Ill App 267 (1932); *Currie v Hamilton* [1984] 1 NSWLR 687 at 693A–C per McLelland J).

4   *Leigh v Dickeson* (1884) 15 QBD 60 at 66 per Cotton LJ. There is an indirect liability to contribute if the work was done by a co-owner who was also a trustee acting in the proper discharge of his duties (see *Gross v French* (1975) 238 EG 39 at 41).

5   **[Para 10.58]**.

6   **[Para 10.168]**.

A passive equity of reimbursement

11.51 Although a co-owner may not assert against his co-tenants any active entitlement to immediate reimbursement in respect of expenditure on repairs and improvements,[1] there arises in his favour an 'equity' which may be vindicated defensively[2] when the value of the property is eventually realised or distributed between the co-tenants.[3] This passive or dormant equity enables money laid out by one co-owner on substantial repair[4] or permanent improvement to be recovered on the subsequent sale of the land.[5] Likewise, in the absence of contrary agreement,[6] there must normally be an accounting out of the sale proceeds in respect of mortgage payments which increase the value of the equity of redemption enuring to the benefit of the co-owners.[7] In this way effect is given to a 'guiding principle of the Court of Equity' that the distribution of sale proceeds between co-owners 'must have regard to any increase in ... value which has been brought about by means of expenditure by one of them.'[8] The equity of reimbursement is available not only to a tenant in common but also to a joint tenant,[9] and effectively shares between all the co-owners the cost of any repair, improvement or other enhancement of value which has resulted in an increased sale price.[10] The rationale underlying the rule is the prevention of unjust enrichment of other co-owners,[11] but this principle obviously has no application if there was a clear intention to make a gift to the other co-owners of the relevant expenditure.[12]

1   *Leigh v Dickeson* (1884) 15 QBD 60 at 65–66; *Brickwood v Young* (1905) 2 CLR 387 at 395; *Squire v Rogers* (1980) 27 ALR 330 at 346; *Houghton v Immer (No 155) Pty Ltd* (1997) 44 NSWLR 46 at 56E; *Ryan v Dries* (2002) 10 BPR 19497 at [66]–[68].

2   For the original reference to a 'defensive' equity, see *Brickwood v Young* (1905) 2 CLR 387 at 395, 397 per Griffith CJ.

3   *Leigh v Dickeson* (1884) 15 QBD 60 at 65, 67, 69; *Re Jones* [1893] 2 Ch 461 at 476; *Re Cook's Mortgage* [1896] 1 Ch 923 at 925; *Mayes v Mayes* (1969) 210 EG 935 at 938; *Gross v French* (1975) 238 EG 39 at 41. See also *Brickwood v Young* (1905) 2 CLR 387 at 395–396 per Griffith CJ, 399 per O'Connor J; *Ruptash and Lumsden v Zawick* [1956] 2 DLR (2d) 145 at 159 (Supreme Court of Canada); *Noack v Noack* [1959] VR 137 at 142–143, 146; *Houghton v Immer (No 155) Pty Ltd* (1997) 44 NSWLR 46 at 56E–F.

4   See *Re Jones* [1893] 2 Ch 461 at 477–478; *Cardinaels-Hooper v Tierney* (1995) 7 BPR 14435 at 14444.

5   For present purposes no distinction is generally made between improvements (which usually add value) and repairs (which possibly only preserve value) (see e g *Ryan v Dries* (2002) 10 BPR 19497 at [67]). However, minor refurbishments are sometimes disregarded on the ground that they are merely 'in the nature of ordinary maintenance' and constitute no permanent improvement of the realty (see *McMahon v The Public Curator of Queensland* [1952] St R Qd 197 at 204 (painting of house)). See also *Currie v Hamilton* [1984] 1 NSWLR 687 at 693C; *Forgeard v Shanahan* (1994) 35 NSWLR 206 at 224B–C.

6   See *Wright v Johnson* [2002] 2 P & CR 210 at [23]–[24] per Sir Martin Nourse.

7   *Re Pavlou (A Bankrupt)* [1993] 1 WLR 1046 at 1049B–C per Millett J (spouse entitled to credit in respect of half of her contributions towards capital repayment of mortgage). See also *Cowcher v Cowcher* [1972] 1 WLR 425 at 432G–433C; *Leake v Bruzzi* [1974] 1 WLR 1528 at 1533B, H; *Suttill v Graham* [1977] 1 WLR 819 at 822C, 823H; *Re Gorman (A Bankrupt)* [1990] 1 WLR 616 at 626F–628A; *Ryan v Dries* (2002) 10 BPR 19497 at [5]–[6]. The accounting may extend to payments of mortgage interest, although this may be set off against a notional occupation rent [**para 11.53**].

8   *Re Pavlou (A Bankrupt)* [1993] 1 WLR 1046 at 1048H per Millett J. See also *Re Byford (Decd)* [2004] 1 P & CR 159 at [22] per Collins J.

9   *Re Pavlou (A Bankrupt)* [1993] 1 WLR 1046 at 1048F–G per Millett J. See also *Re Byrne* (1906) 6 SR (NSW) 532 at 536; *Noack v Noack* [1959] VR 137 at 143, 146. Some difficulty attaches to any attempt to claim this equity on behalf of a deceased joint tenant, since it involves 'a claim against an estate in which the joint tenant's interest had entirely ceased' (*Re*

Byrne (1906) 6 SR (NSW) 532 at 536–537). See D Mendes da Costa, (1961–62) 3 Melbourne ULR 137 at 146, but compare *Isaryk v Isaryk* [1955] OWN 487 at 489, where the extinction of a joint tenant's interest on death was not thought to preclude his estate from recovering from a co-tenant an excess over the latter's just share of rents and profits arising from the land.

10 See *Leigh v Dickeson* (1884) 15 QBD 60 at 67 ('the execution of the repairs and improvements is adopted and sanctioned by accepting the increased value').

11 See *Swan v Swan* (1820) 8 Price 518 at 519, 146 ER 1281; *Boulter v Boulter* (1898) 19 LR (NSW) Eq 135 at 137; *Re Byrne* (1906) 6 SR (NSW) 532 at 536; *Cummings v Anderson*, 614 P2d 1283 at 1287–1288 (1980). In *Knox v Knox* (Unreported, Supreme Court of New South Wales, 16 December 1994, BPR Casenote 96808), Young J was prepared to impose a 'quasi-constructive trust' in order to deprive one co-owner of the 'unconscionable windfall' otherwise comprised in the 'incontrovertible benefit' conferred through unauthorised improvements effected by other co-owners.

12 'No principle of equity can be invoked to recall a gift once made' (*Noack v Noack* [1959] VR 137 at 146).

Measure of reimbursement

11.52 The precise measure of reimbursement in respect of a co-owner's expenditure remains controversial. The sum expended by the co-owner is not always or necessarily reflected in a corresponding increment in the value of the land.[1] Some cases therefore take the view that the measure of compensation should not be related to the actual expenditure, but should be fixed by, and limited to, the actual increment in land value thereby achieved.[2] On this basis it matters not whether the 'sum expended' exceeds the 'value added': in either case the co-owner's recovery is assessed with reference to the increase in value.[3] The generally preferred, although more restrictive view, is that compensation should be limited to the amount of the actual expenditure or the extent of the increment in value generated by that expenditure, whichever is the lesser figure.[4] Thus where the 'value added' exceeds the 'sum expended', the equity of the claimant is to recover his due proportion of the actual expenditure and then share rateably with his co-tenants in any enhanced value over and above his outlay costs.[5] In this way '[a]n increase in value above cost accrues to all the co-owners, and any loss because the cost exceeded the increase in value falls on the improver.'[6] In any event all calculations are complicated by the fact that account may have to be taken of the 'present day equivalent in value' of historic expenditure.[7]

1 See *Re Pavlou (A Bankrupt)* [1993] 1 WLR 1046 at 1049A per Millett J.

2 *Parker v Trigg* (1874) WN 27 at 28; *Watson v Gass* (1881–82) 45 LT (NS) 582 at 585; *Williams v Williams* (1899–1900) 81 LT (NS) 163; *Gross v French* (1975) 238 EG 39 at 41; *Brickwood v Young* (1905) 2 CLR 387 at 397–398; *Mastin v Mastin's Administrator*, 50 SW2d 77 at 79 (1932); *Noack v Noack* [1959] VR 137 at 146; *Re Kostiuk* (2002) 215 DLR (4th) 78 at [51].

3 See e g *Currie v Hamilton* [1984] 1 NSWLR 687 at 693B–C, where McLelland J could find no 'evidence of any quantifiable enhancement of the realizable value of the property.'

4 *Re Jones* [1893] 2 Ch 461 at 479; *Re Cook's Mortgage* [1896] 1 Ch 923 at 925; *Re Pavlou (A Bankrupt)* [1993] 1 WLR 1046 at 1049B. See also *Boulter v Boulter* (1898) 19 LR (NSW) Eq 135 at 137; *Forgeard v Shanahan* (1994) 35 NSWLR 206 at 223G; *Cardinaels-Hooper v Tierney* (1995) 7 BPR 14435 at 14444; *Ryan v Dries* (2002) 10 BPR 19497 at [14].

5 It has been said that the equity of reimbursement can take no account of the outlay of time or effort (*Cardinaels-Hooper v Tierney* (1995) 7 BPR 14435 at 14444) and cannot make any allowance for risk or for borrowing charges necessitated by the relevant improvement (*Houghton v Immer (No 155) Pty Ltd* (1997) 44 NSWLR 46 at 57A).

6   *Houghton v Immer (No 155) Pty Ltd* (1997) 44 NSWLR 46 at 56G–57A per Handley JA. On
     this basis a successful improvement does not enure as a sheer windfall gain to an unenterpris-
     ing fellow co-owner; and the improver does not retain the entire increase in value generated by
     his unconsented use of co-owned land.

7   See e g *McMahon v The Public Curator of Queensland* [1952] St R Qd 197 at 202–203.

Equitable counterclaims

11.53   There is an important limitation on the right of a co-owner to assert an
'equity' based on expenditure incurred by him in respect of the co-owned land.
Such a claim is normally allowable only if he submits to payment of an
occupation rent in respect of any occupation enjoyed solely[1] or primarily[2] by
him.[3] The claimant of the 'equity' must similarly account for any rents and
profits which he may have derived from lettings of the land.[4] The relevant
principle here seems to be that he who comes to equity must himself do equity.[5]
Thus, when the value of the co-owned land is finally distributed amongst the
co-owners, there must be a counter-balancing of various types of income and
expenditure connected with that land. Only in this way can it be ensured that
each co-owner receives no more and no less than his proportionate share of the
net rental value derived from the land during the period of co-ownership,
together with his proper share of the net increase in the capital value of the
land accruing over that period. This may require relatively refined calculation
particularly where, for example, rents and profits drawn from the land have
been ploughed back into the land in the form of permanent improvements.[6]

1   **[Para 11.46].** See *Pascoe v Swan* (1859) 27 Beav 508 at 509, 54 ER 201 at 202; *Teasdale v
     Sanderson* (1864) 33 Beav 534, 55 ER 476; *Re Jones* [1893] 2 Ch 461 at 477–478; *Williams v
     Williams* (1899–1900) 81 LT (NS) 163; *Brickwood v Young* (1905) 2 CLR 387 at 398;
     McCormick v McCormick [1921] NZLR 384 at 387–388 per Salmond J; *Luke v Luke* (1936)
     36 SR (NSW) 310 at 313–314, 318; *Roberts v Roberts*, 150 SW2d 236 at 238 (1941); *Carkeek v
     Tate-Jones* [1971] VR 691 at 702–703; *Reid v Reid* (1978) 87 DLR (3d) 370 at 372; *Forgeard v
     Shanahan* (1994) 35 NSWLR 206 at 223C; *Cardinaels-Hooper v Tierney* (1995) 7 BPR 14435 at
     14444–14445; *Re Kostiuk* (2002) 215 DLR (4th) 78 at [50]–[51].

2   See *Ryan v Dries* (2002) 10 BPR 19497 at [7], [75].

3   It is also now open to the trustees of land, in allocating a right of occupation of the co-owned
     land to one or more of the beneficial co-owners, to impose conditions relating to 'expenses in
     respect of the land' (see TOLATA 1996, s 13(5)), a power which seems wide enough to cover
     the cost of repairs and improvements.

4   *Attorney-General v Magdalen College, Oxford* (1854) 18 Beav 223 at 255, 52 ER 88 at 100;
     Pascoe v Swan (1859) 27 Beav 508 at 509, 54 ER 201 at 202; *Re Jones* [1893] 2 Ch 461 at 478;
     Williams v Williams (1899–1900) 81 LT (NS) 163; *Brickwood v Young* (1905) 2 CLR 387 at
     398, 401; *Mastin v Mastin's Administrator*, 50 SW2d 77 at 79 (1932); *Vasili v Cross* (Unre-
     ported, Supreme Court of New South Wales, 14 February 1996, BPR Casenote 101901).

5   See *Luke v Luke* (1936) 36 SR (NSW) 310 at 317 per Long Innes CJ in Eq; *Roberts v Roberts*,
     150 SW2d 236 at 238 (1941) (Supreme Court of Texas); *Forgeard v Shanahan* (1994)
     35 NSWLR 206 at 223C per Meagher JA; *Ryan v Dries* (2002) 10 BPR 19497 at [2] per
     Sheller JA, [14] per Giles JA, [71], [75] per Hodgson JA. See also *Leigh v Dickeson* (1884) 15
     QBD 60 at 64–65 per Brett MR; *Squire v Rogers* (1980) 27 ALR 330 at 348. Because the taking
     of reciprocal accounts falls so clearly within the jurisdiction of equity, the approach of the
     courts is flexible and is heavily determined by notions of simple fairness (see e g *Baird v
     Moore*, 141 A2d 324 at 330–333 (1958); *Weh v Weh*, 164 A2d 508 at 513 (1960)).

6   See e g *Squire v Rogers* (1980) 27 ALR 330 at 347.

Impact of the equity on third parties

11.54 The 'defensive' equity of a co-owner to claim an account from his co-tenants in respect of expenditure on the co-owned land is not a merely personal right. The claimant's expenditure raises an equity which attaches to the land,[1] analogous to an equitable charge created by the owners for the time being, although enforceable only in the event of a later partition or distribution of the value of the land amongst the co-owners.[2] This equity is fully capable of running with the land. Thus it may enure to the benefit of the successor in title of the original owner of the equity[3] and may also bind the successor in title to the share of any other co-owner.[4]

1   See eg *Houghton v Immer (No 155) Pty Ltd* (1997) 44 NSWLR 46 at 57A per Handley JA (equity of reimbursement 'is normally an interest in the land').
2   *Brickwood v Young* (1905) 2 CLR 387 at 396; *Noack v Noack* [1959] VR 137 at 146.
3   *Brickwood v Young* (1905) 2 CLR 387 at 396. See also *Williams v Williams* (1899–1900) 81 LT (NS) 163, 68 LJ Ch 528 at 529; *Re Jones* [1893] 2 Ch 461 at 476–477.
4   See *Dietsch v Long*, 43 NE2d 906 at 916–917 (1942); *Ruptash and Lumsden v Zawick* [1956] 2 DLR (2d) 145 at 159; *Squire v Rogers* (1980) 27 ALR 330 at 346. Compare, however, *Canada Life Assurance Co v Kennedy* (1978) 89 DLR (3d) 397 (Ontario Court of Appeal).

THE EQUITABLE PREFERENCE FOR TENANCY IN COMMON

11.55 Historically the common law always preferred joint tenancy to tenancy in common as the medium of co-ownership, largely because the operation of survivorship tended to restrict the numbers of persons from whom feudal obligations might be due.[1] Later joint tenancy came to be preferred simply because conveyancers could more easily investigate the single title held by joint tenants than if the legal title were fragmented between tenants in common, each of whom could in turn dispose separately of his share. In short, the common law favoured the sweeping together of interests by means of survivorship and leaned away from tenancy in common. The law, said Holt CJ in 1700, 'loves not fractions of estates, nor to divide and multiply tenures.'[2]

1   *Bl Comm*, Vol II, p 193.
2   *Fisher v Wigg* (1700) 1 Salk 391 at 392, 91 ER 339 at 340.

11.56 Equity, in contrast to the common law, traditionally preferred tenancy in common to joint tenancy as the medium of co-ownership. Tenancy in common represents certainty and fairness in the property relations of co-owners. Each tenant in common holds a fixed beneficial interest immune from the caprice of survivorship.[1] Equity thus 'avoids the gamble of the tontine',[2] and in a tenancy in common each share constitutes a distinct and indefeasible quantum of wealth which can serve as the subject of either commercial exploitation or family endowment. Thus, whereas the law leaned in favour of joint tenancy largely for reasons of convenience, equity has always inclined towards tenancy in common for reasons of fairness.[3]

1   Survivorship 'is looked upon as odious in equity' (*R v Williams* (1735) Bunb 342 at 343, 145 ER 694). See also *Re Woolley* [1903] 2 Ch 206 at 211; *Carmody v Delehunt* [1984] 1 NSWLR 667 at 669B–C per Hutley JA; *Public Trustee v Pfeiffle* [1991] 1 VR 19 at 33 per Ormiston J.

2   *Corin v Patton* (1990) 169 CLR 540 at 573 per Deane J.
3   See *Gould v Kemp* (1834) 2 My & K 304 at 309, 39 ER 959 at 961 per Lord Brougham LC;
    Cowcher v Cowcher [1972] 1 WLR 425 at 430F–H per Bagnall J; *Martin v Martin* (1987)
    54 P & CR 238 at 240 per Millett J; *Kinch v Bullard* [1999] 1 WLR 423 at 430D per Neuberger
    J; *Public Trustee v Pfeiffle* [1991] 1 VR 19 at 29–30 per McGarvie J, 33 per Ormiston J.

Equity follows the law

11.57   The common law presumption in favour of joint tenancy finally crystallised in an irrebuttable form in the property legislation of 1925: co-ownership of a legal estate in land must now take the form of joint tenancy.[1] It is, moreover, undoubtedly true in some extremely general sense that 'equity follows the law.'[2] Equity's starting assumption is therefore that joint tenants of the legal estate likewise hold the equitable estate as joint tenants.[3] But this assumption as to the nature of equitable co-ownership is readily displaced by any of a number of contra-indications that, regardless of the mandatory joint tenancy at law, equitable ownership was intended to take the form of *tenancy in common*.[4] Indeed, these contra-indications have now become so prevalent that it is relatively rare that the nature of equitable co-ownership falls to be ascertained by a despairing resort to the residual proposition that 'equity follows the law.'

1   LPA 1925, ss 1(6), 36(2) **[paras 11.21, 11.80]**.
2   **[Para 9.6]**.
3   See *Pettitt v Pettitt* [1970] AC 777 at 814A per Lord Upjohn; *Cowcher v Cowcher* [1972]
    1 WLR 425 at 430E; *Bernard v Josephs* [1982] Ch 391 at 402B–C; *Marshall v Marshall*
    (Unreported, Court of Appeal, 2 October 1998) per Mummery LJ.
4   See *McKenzie v McKenzie* [2003] EWHC 601 (Ch) at [65].

Cases where equity does not follow the law

11.58   Irrespective of the position at law, some circumstances necessarily indicate that co-ownership in equity comprises a tenancy in common. Thus, for instance, equitable co-ownership can never take the form of joint tenancy if the 'four unities' are absent or if 'words of severance' have been employed in the terms of the grant to the co-owners. Words of severance can be either express or implied, and are constituted by any language denoting that the transferees are intended to take distinct and identifiable shares in the land granted,[1] thereby negativing the existence of joint tenancy in equity[2] and its concomitant of survivorship.[3] In such cases, even though the legal estate may be held by way of joint tenancy, the equitable estate is held by the transferees as tenants in common.

1   See *Robertson v Fraser* (1871) 6 Ch App 696 at 699 per Lord Hatherley LC ('anything which in
    the slightest degree indicates an intention to divide the property must be held to abrogate the
    idea of a joint tenancy, and to create tenancy in common').
2   Examples of express words of severance include the terms 'equally' (see *Lewen v Dodd* (1595)
    Cro Eliz 443 at 444–445, 78 ER 684 at 685; *Lewen v Cox* (1595) Cro Eliz 695 at 696, 78 ER 931
    at 932; *Right d Compton v Compton* (1808) 9 East 267 at 276, 103 ER 575 at 579), to 'be

divided between two' (see *Peat v Chapman* (1750) 1 Ves Sen 542, 27 ER 1193; *Re Crow* (1985) 12 DLR (4th) 415 at 422), and 'among' (*Richardson v Richardson* (1845) 14 Sim 526 at 528, 60 ER 462). Words of severance are implicit in, for instance, a direction that the co-owners should pay an annuity to a third party 'in equal shares'.

3   Difficulty has been occasioned by the self-contradictory quality of a grant to 'A and B as beneficial joint tenants in common in equal shares.' Following *Slingsby's Case* (1587) 5 Co Rep 18b at 19a, 77 ER 77 at 78, such a grant was generally taken to confer a joint tenancy if contained in a deed inter vivos, but to create a tenancy in common if contained in a will (see e g *Joyce v Barker Bros (Builders) Ltd* (1980) 40 P & CR 512 at 513–514; [1980] Conv 171 (J E Adams)). In *Martin v Martin* (1987) 54 P & CR 238 at 243–244, Millett J considered the rule of construction in *Slingsby's Case* to be a rule of last resort. In *Martin* (unlike in *Joyce*) the purchasers had themselves executed the ambiguous declaration of trust and it was therefore held that the 'meaningless jumble of words' in question pointed towards a beneficial tenancy in common. Millett J preferred to view the instant case as one in which the purchasers, having declared a trust for themselves as joint tenants, immediately severed that tenancy with the further reference to ownership 'in common in equal shares'. In *Joyce*, however, the grantor, having already conveyed away an estate to purchasers as beneficial joint tenants, had put it out of his power thereafter to sever the tenancy. See [1988] Conv 57 (J E M).

11.59 Quite apart from these instances of doctrinal necessity, reasons of fairness have always predisposed equitable co-ownership towards tenancy in common in a further range of specialised situations. In these cases the superficial presumption that legal joint tenancy entails equitable joint tenancy is overridden by the concern of equity to avoid the caprice of survivorship. In such circumstances, and in the absence of contrary agreement (as expressed for example in a declaration of trust[1]), equity presumes – quite irrespective of the position at law – that the co-owners hold as equitable tenants in common (see *Fig. 24*).[2] These instances of presumed beneficial tenancy in common are not rigidly circumscribed by the courts. Equity leans in favour of tenancy in common in the following cases – and the list is not exhaustive.[3]

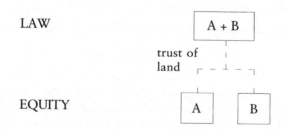

LAW

A + B

trust of land

EQUITY

A   B

Fig. 24

1   **[Para 9.184]**.
2   There is ultimately no inconsistency between joint tenancy at law coupled with tenancy in common in equity **[para 11.148]**.
3   *Malayan Credit Ltd v Jack Chia-MPH Ltd* [1986] AC 549 at 560E–F per Lord Brightman.

Contributors of purchase money in unequal proportions

11.60 By far the most important case in which equity prefers tenancy in common to joint tenancy arises where two or more persons contribute money in *unequal* proportions towards the purchase of land (or some other asset). Equity has consistently presumed that, as between persons who contribute differing amounts of money 'in the character of a purchaser', the resulting equitable ownership is intended to reflect the disparity of contribution, each contributor taking a proportionate beneficial share.[1] In this way, in the absence of express contrary agreement, the equitable entitlements of the contributors do not fall to be regulated by the crude rule of survivorship.[2]

1   Where the contributions are equal in amount, there may be a joint tenancy between the contributors, although even here the modern instinct is towards tenancy in common [**para 10.11**].
2   For an account of the presumption of resulting trust, see Chapter 10 [**para 10.8**].

Commercial partners

11.61   Where commercial partners acquire title to land for the purpose of their joint business enterprise, equity has always presumed that they hold the equitable interest in the land as tenants in common. The rationale for this equitable preference lies in the belief that the incidents of joint tenancy are inimical to commerce.[1] In particular the hazards of survivorship are alien to the essence of commercial partnership.

1   See *Jeffereys v Small* (1683) 1 Vern 217, 23 ER 424; *Lake v Craddock* (1732) 3 P Wms 158 at 159, 24 ER 1011 at 1012.

Business tenants

11.62   Business tenants who take a joint tenancy of a legal leasehold estate 'for their several individual business purposes' are similarly presumed to have intended to hold as tenants in common in equity.[1]

1   *Malayan Credit Ltd v Jack Chia-MPH Ltd* [1986] AC 549 at 560F.

Joint mortgagees

11.63   Where two or more persons lend money on the security of property, equity presumes that the lenders hold the equitable estate in their mortgage security as tenants in common as between themselves, even though as against the mortgagor they took the legal title to their mortgage as joint tenants. The basis of this presumption is the belief that each mortgagee, irrespective of his posture towards the outside world, intended as against his co-mortgagee to 'lend his own and take back his own.'[1]

1   *Morley v Bird* (1798) 3 Ves 628 at 631, 30 ER 1192 at 1193. See also *Re Jackson* (1887) 34 Ch D 732 at 737, and compare LPA 1925, s 111.

SEVERANCE

11.64   Certain acts or events cause the undifferentiated equitable co-ownership of joint tenancy to crystallise into co-ownership in distinct and undivided shares.[1] The process by which joint tenancy may thus be converted into tenancy in common is known as severance,[2] and it is ultimately a 'mere matter of evidence' whether severance has occurred.[3]

1   See A J McClean, (1979) 57 Can Bar Rev 1; P Butt, (1979–82) 9 Sydney L Rev 568.
2   'Severance is ... the process of separating off the share of a joint tenant, so that the concurrent ownership will continue but the right of survivorship will no longer apply. The parties will hold separate shares as tenants in common' (*Harris v Goddard* [1983] 1 WLR 1203 at 1210E per Dillon LJ).
3   *Crooke v De Vandes* (1805) 11 Ves 330 at 333, 32 ER 1115 at 1116. The onus of proof that severance has occurred rests upon the party seeking to establish severance (see *Re Denny* (1947) 116 LJR 1029 at 1031; *Greenfield v Greenfield* (1979) 38 P & CR 570 at 578; *Barton v Morris* [1985] 1 WLR 1257 at 1260G; *Flynn v Flynn* [1930] IR 337 at 343; *Re Sorensen and Sorensen* (1979) 90 DLR (3d) 26 at 33).

Facility of severance

11.65   Historically the common law has been willing to mitigate the hazards of survivorship by allowing severance to occur relatively easily.[1] Any act or event which is incompatible with the characteristic features of joint tenancy is apt to precipitate a severance. Thus, for instance, any dealing by a joint tenant which excludes the future operation of survivorship results in severance. Joint tenancy depends, moreover, upon the continued existence of the three unities of possession, interest and title,[2] and the destruction of either unity of interest or unity of title also automatically brings about a severance.[3] For the purpose of severance under the common law rules the consent of the other joint tenant or joint tenants is not necessarily required,[4] and severance may in this sense be quite unilateral.[5] It is inherent in the nature of beneficial joint tenancy that any joint tenant may sever at any time.[6]

1   See *Cray v Willis* (1729) 2 P Wms 529, 24 ER 847 ('the duration of all lives being uncertain, if either party has an ill opinion of his own life, he may sever the jointenancy ... so that survivorship can be no hardship, where either side may at pleasure prevent it').
2   Unity of time of vesting applies only to the original creation of the joint tenancy and cannot be affected by subsequent acts (*Re Murdoch and Barry* (1976) 64 DLR (3d) 222 at 225). See also *Nielson-Jones v Fedden* [1975] Ch 222 at 228F; *Bank of Montreal v Bray* (1997) 153 DLR (4th) 490 at 500.
3   *Bl Comm*, Vol II, p 192. See *Corin v Patton* (1990) 169 CLR 540 at 548 per Mason CJ and McHugh J, 573 per Deane J. See also *Power v Grace* [1932] 2 DLR 793 at 795; *Tenhet v Boswell*, 133 Cal Rptr 10 at 14 (1976); *Samuel v District Land Registrar* [1984] 2 NZLR 697 at 702. Destruction of unity of possession terminates co-ownership altogether by means of a physical 'partition' of the land [**para 11.273**].
4   *Burke v Stevens*, 70 Cal Rptr 87 at 91 (1968). A form of unseverable joint tenancy (the 'tenancy by entireties') was available to husband and wife in England before 1926 [**para 11.122**]. In some jurisdictions joint tenancy has been made unseverable without the consent of all the joint tenants, with the express purpose of guaranteeing to each joint tenant the indestructibility of his right of survivorship (see e g Land Titles Act (Saskatchewan) (RSS 1978, c.L-5), s 240; *Re The Queen And Peters* (1983) 141 DLR (3d) 508 at 516).
5   See *Staples v Maurice* (1774) 4 Bro Parl Cas 580 at 585, 2 ER 395 at 399. The joint tenants may of course bind themselves by agreement *inter se* not to do any act which will result in the severance of the joint tenancy (see *Re Debney* (1960) 60 SR (NSW) 471 at 473; *Anderson v O'Donnell* (2000) 10 BPR 18501 at [15]). However, if such a contractual undertaking is broken (e g if an erstwhile joint tenant sells a severed share to a stranger), it can sound only in

damages against the errant co-owner: the illicit severance cannot prejudice the rights of the stranger (see *Fitts v Stone*, 166 SW2d 897 at 899 (1942)). An injunction may be available to restrain an impending dealing which threatens wrongfully to sever the joint tenancy. See D Mendes da Costa, (1961–62) 3 Melbourne ULR 137, 306, 433 at 440.

6   *Bedson v Bedson* [1965] 2 QB 666 at 690E per Russell LJ. See similarly *Re Draper's Conveyance* [1969] 1 Ch 486 at 494A; *Cowcher v Cowcher* [1972] 1 WLR 425 at 430F–H; *Harris v Goddard* [1983] 1 WLR 1203 at 1208G; *Fleming v Hargreaves* [1976] 1 NZLR 123 at 127.

Consequence of severance

11.66   When it occurs, severance separates off a distinct beneficial share for the severing joint tenant.[1] In the absence of any contrary agreement between the co-owners,[2] this share is quantified on the basis of equality between the joint tenants, irrespective of the relative proportions of their original contributions to the purchase of the co-owned land.[3] If title is *registered*, an application (together with evidence of severance) should be made to Land Registry for entry of the appropriate restriction in the proprietorship register of the trustees' title.[4] If title is *unregistered*, the fact of severance should be noted in a memorandum of severance signed by at least one of the joint tenants and endorsed on or annexed to the conveyance which created the joint tenancy.[5]

1   Except where there are merely two joint tenants, severance affects the interest of only the severing tenant or tenants. Thus, in a joint tenancy comprising A, B and C, if A severs, he separates off for himself a one-third share as a tenant in common, leaving B and C as joint tenants of the whole of the remaining two-thirds share [**para 11.80**].

2   An agreement deviating from equality of shares after severance may be present in rare cases of a partnership arrangement involving joint tenants (see e g *Barton v Morris* [1985] 1 WLR 1257 at 1262D–H) or may be incorporated in a declaration of trust (see *Goodman v Gallant* [1986] Fam 106 at 119C).

3   '[U]pon a severance the person severing will take 1/nth of the property beneficially', where 'n' is the number of the joint tenants (see *Nielson-Jones v Fedden* [1975] Ch 222 at 228E per Walton J). See also *Bedson v Bedson* [1965] 2 QB 666 at 689C; *Goodman v Gallant* [1986] Fam 106 at 119D; *Corin v Patton* (1990) 169 CLR 540 at 573, 575 per Deane J.

4   [**Para 11.190**].

5   [**Para 11.278**].

GENERAL LIMITATIONS ON SEVERANCE

11.67   Few constraints limit the availability of severance, but two are of some importance.

Severance cannot be effected by will

11.68   Although severance can often be quite unilateral, it is an inveterate rule that severance can be effected only inter vivos. There can be no unilateral severance by will,[1] although the execution of mutual wills by joint tenants may sometimes bring about a severance.[2]

1　[Paras **11.10**, **11.16**].
2　[Para **11.99**].

Severance cannot be effected in relation to a legal estate

11.69　Following the commencement of the Law of Property Act 1925, joint tenancy has been capable of severance only in respect of an equitable estate in land. There can be no severance of a joint tenancy in a legal estate[1] and severance in equity has, in itself, no immediate impact on co-ownership at law. Severance by a co-owner who is, for example, a joint tenant of the fee simple estate both at law and in equity does not affect his trusteeship of the legal estate or his fiduciary status as a trustee of land. Although after severance he becomes a tenant in common of the equitable estate, he remains a joint tenant of the legal estate until such time as he (i) 'releases' his legal estate to the other joint tenant or tenants,[2] (ii) retires or is otherwise removed from the trust[3] or (iii) dies.

1　LPA 1925, s 36(2) [paras **11.21**, **11.80**].
2　LPA 1925, s 36(2) [para **11.5**].
3　See TOLATA 1996, s 19 [para **11.182**].

11.70　The net effect of these rules is that co-ownership of any legal estate automatically and unavoidably takes the form of joint tenancy; co-ownership in equity may take the form of *either* joint tenancy *or* tenancy in common (with the possibility that equitable joint tenancy may be converted, by severance, into an equitable tenancy in common).

METHODS OF SEVERANCE OF AN EQUITABLE JOINT TENANCY

11.71　Severance is a process now confined to *equitable* joint tenancy and is governed in English law by rules of unnecessary complexity.[1] The Law of Property Act 1925 provides two major categories of severing event.[2] The 1925 Act introduced a convenient form of severance by written notice, but also took care to preserve the classic law of severance laid down in *Williams v Hensman*[3] by Page Wood V-C (later Lord Hatherley LC). Although its usefulness has been doubted,[4] the pre-1926 case law on severance throws up three sub-categories of circumstance which result in severance.[5] Equity jurisprudence, considerations of public policy and the intrinsic doctrinal requirements of joint tenancy add three further classes of severing event, with the consequence that, when all recognised means of severance are taken into account, they number seven in total. Severance in equity may take the form of:

- severance by statutory notice in writing[6]
- severance under *Williams v Hensman*, ie by
  - an act operating on a joint tenant's share[7]
  - mutual agreement[8] or
  - mutual conduct[9]
- severance by court order[10]

- severance by homicide[11] and
- severance by merger of interests.[12]

1   See Louise Tee, 'Severance Revisited' [1995] Conv 104. There is a strong argument that modern severance should be confined to the statutory method of written notice; and there is evidence that a wilful failure to take advantage of this method may fatally weaken a claim of severance based on other grounds (see *Marshall v Marshall* (Unreported, Court of Appeal, 2 October 1998)). There is also, however, a contrary argument that the classical non-statutory modes of severance provide a flexible recognition of the informality often present in the dealings of co-owners.

2   See LPA 1925, s 36(2).

3   (1861) 1 John & H 546 at 557, 70 ER 862 at 867, approved by the Privy Council in *Tan Chew Hoe Neo v Chee Swee Cheng* (1929) LR 56 Ind App 112 at 115. LPA 1925, s 36(2) makes it clear that severance can be effected in equity if a joint tenant does 'such other acts or things as would, in the case of personal estate, have been effectual to sever the tenancy in equity' before 1926. This provision merely 'put into statutory language the other ways of effecting severance to which Page Wood V-C referred in *Williams v Hensman*' (*Harris v Goddard* [1983] 1 WLR 1203 at 1208H per Lawton LJ). See also P Luther, (1995) 15 Legal Studies 219.

4   In 1985 the Law Commission expressed the view that 'as time goes by, it is increasingly undesirable to have to refer to pre-1926 law' (see Law Commission, *Trusts of Land* (Law Com Working Paper No 94, September 1985), para 3.24). However, the Commission reserved further consideration of the law of severance for a future project (see *Transfer of Land: Trusts of Land* (Law Com No 181, June 1989), para 1.3).

5   *Williams v Hensman* related to personalty, but the principles enunciated there have been applied indifferently to property real and personal. See *Burgess v Rawnsley* [1975] Ch 429; *Re Murdoch and Barry* (1976) 64 DLR (3d) 222 at 224; *McNab v Earle* [1981] 2 NSWLR 673 at 675G; *Abela v Public Trustee* [1983] 1 NSWLR 308 at 316E.

6   **[Para 11.73]**.
7   **[Para 11.76]**.
8   **[Para 11.90]**.
9   **[Para 11.95]**.
10   **[Para 11.107]**.
11   **[Para 11.108]**.
12   **[Para 11.120]**.

11.72   Some of these modes of severance are unilateral, some definitely not; some sanctioned by statute, some by case law, and one method fairly clearly lacking encouragement from either source. In general terms, in the context of a dealing between a joint tenant and a stranger the issue of severance tends to focus on whether the transaction in question has destroyed one of the essential unities of joint tenancy. Where, however, the context is that of a dealing of the joint tenants *inter se*, the more useful question seems to be whether any of the co-owners has evinced an intention which is clearly inconsistent with the future operation of the *ius accrescendi*.[1]

1   See *Bradley v Mann*, 525 P2d 492 at 493 (1974), affd 535 P2d 213 at 214 (1975); *Mangus v Miller*, 532 P2d 368 at 369 (1975).

SEVERANCE BY WRITTEN NOTICE

11.73   The Law of Property Act 1925 radically altered the law of severance by introducing an entirely new method of severance as regards land.[1] Section 36(2) of the 1925 Act enables a joint tenant to effect a severance by giving to the other joint tenants a 'notice in writing' of his 'desire' to sever the joint tenancy.[2]

1   See *Burgess v Rawnsley* [1975] Ch 429 at 444G per Browne LJ, 447E per Sir John Pennycuick; *Harris v Goddard* [1983] 1 WLR 1203 at 1208H per Lawton LJ.
2   In *Burgess v Rawnsley* [1975] Ch 429 at 440B, Lord Denning MR thought section 36(2) merely declaratory of the pre-1926 law as to severance. See also *Hawkesley v May* [1956] 1 QB 304 at 313, as commented upon in *Davies v Davies* [1983] WAR 305 at 308 per Burt CJ.

Advantages

11.74   The statutory method of severance by written notice is undoubtedly convenient.[1] There is no prescribed form of notice.[2] The notice may be quite unilateral[3]: no consent is required from other joint tenants.[4] The 'notice in writing' need not be signed[5] and may even comprise various sorts of application for a judicial determination of the rights of the joint tenants *inter se*, at least where such an application clearly indicates a desire to sever.[6] The severance is effective if there is evidence that the notice was duly posted to the other joint tenants[7]; it is not necessary that the notice should actually have been read (or even received) by them.[8] In *Kinch v Bullard*,[9] for instance, a wife, who was terminally ill, posted a notice of severance to her disaffected husband at their shared home address, the parties being beneficial joint tenants of the matrimonial home. Shortly before the arrival of the notice, her husband suffered a serious heart attack and was hospitalised. The wife, reckoning that her chances of survivorship had dramatically improved, intercepted the letter on its delivery and destroyed it. Her husband died a week later. Neuberger J held that, once the process of delivery to the addressee's last-known abode or place of business had been set in train and the notice served, it was no longer open to the sender to change her mind as to severance and withdraw the notice.[10] Severance had already occurred and the husband's estate was thus entitled to a one-half share in what had been the matrimonial home.[11]

1   The written notice method of severance has the great advantage of speed and simplicity in circumstances where much can turn on the precise sequence of rapidly occurring events (see e g *First National Securities Ltd v Hegerty* [1985] QB 850 at 865B–E). For an appropriate form of words, see *Goodman v Gallant* [1986] Fam 106 at 109B.
2   See *Marshall v Marshall* (Unreported, Court of Appeal, 2 October 1998) per Mummery LJ.
3   The availability of statutory severance by written notice relieves joint tenants of any necessity to undertake the charade of executing a mortgage charge or an assignment to a trustee or even a self-directed assignment, these being the only other means by which a joint tenant can unilaterally sever whilst retaining a proprietary right in the common property. See *Corin v Patton* (1990) 169 CLR 540 at 584 per Deane J.
4   *Harris v Goddard* [1983] 1 WLR 1203 at 1209B per Lawton LJ. Even if the conveyance of an unregistered estate to joint tenants stipulates that no severance is valid unless annexed to the conveyance, this limitation has no application as between the joint tenants, but serves merely to protect a purchaser of the legal estate in good faith (see *Grindal v Hooper* (2000) Times, 8 February).
5   *Re Draper's Conveyance* [1969] 1 Ch 486 at 492A.
6   See e g *Re Draper's Conveyance* [1969] 1 Ch 486 at 492B–C, where Plowman J regarded a wife's application for an order directing a sale of the jointly owned matrimonial home and equal distribution of the proceeds of sale as not only a written notice of severance but also an act

'operating upon' her own share [**para 11.76**]. Following her husband's death shortly after a court order made in these terms, the wife held the legal estate (as sole surviving trustee) on trust for herself and her husband's estate in equal shares. See (1968) 84 LQR 462 (P V Baker). See also *Burgess v Rawnsley* [1975] Ch 429 at 447F per Sir John Pennycuick; *Harris v Goddard* [1983] 1 WLR 1203 at 1209H–1210A; *Marshall v Marshall* (Unreported, Court of Appeal, 2 October 1998).

7   See LPA 1925, s 196(3).
8   *Re 88 Berkeley Road, NW9* [1971] Ch 648 at 655C.
9   [1999] 1 WLR 423; [1999] Conv 60 (M Percival).
10   [1999] 1 WLR 423 at 428G–H ('[o]nce the sender has served the requisite notice, the deed is done and cannot be undone').
11   Neuberger J thought that the notice of severance could probably have been withdrawn at any point preceding its postal delivery if the sender had informed the addressee that she wished to revoke it ([1999] 1 WLR 423 at 429B–D).

Limitations

11.75   Despite its obvious utility, severance by written notice is subject to certain limitations. Notice must be served on all the existing joint tenants. The notice must express a desire to sever with immediate effect rather than at some time in the future.[1] It was on this ground that the Court of Appeal in *Harris v Goddard*[2] refused to find that severance had occurred where a spouse had merely included in her divorce petition a prayer that the divorce court should make such order respecting the matrimonial property 'as may be just.'[3] It is likewise insufficient that joint tenants should refer to severance in a draft separation agreement which, although sent by one party to the other, was never accepted by the recipient.[4] The convenience of severance by written notice may also be unavailable where the names on the legal title are not identical to the beneficiaries behind the trust (eg where A, B and C hold the legal estate on trust for sale for A, B, C and D, or where T1 and T2 hold the legal estate on trust for sale for X, Y and Z).[5] Likewise it seems that the written notice method of severance is inapplicable if the co-owned land has already been sold: the land is no longer 'vested in joint tenants beneficially' as required by section 36(2).[6] Here a severance of entitlements in the funds produced by the sale can be achieved only by other means.

1   *Harris v Goddard* [1983] 1 WLR 1203 at 1209B per Lawton LJ. See also *Lyons v Lyons* [1967] VR 169 at 172. For confirmation of the paramount importance of intention under LPA 1925, s 36(2), see *Gore and Snell v Carpenter* (1990) 60 P & CR 456 at 462.
2   [1983] 1 WLR 1203. See (1984) 100 LQR 161; [1984] Conv 148 (S Coneys); (1984) 134 NLJ 63 (H W Wilkinson).
3   Both Lawton LJ (at 1209D) and Dillon LJ (at 1210H) also pointed out that the general prayer in the wife's petition could have been satisfied by relief which did not involve 'severance' at all (eg by an order extinguishing the interest of one spouse or settling the land on the spouses successively). Contrast *Re Draper's Conveyance* [1969] 1 Ch 486 [**para 11.74**], where the claim plainly involved a severance of the beneficial joint tenancy.
4   *Gore and Snell v Carpenter* (1990) 60 P & CR 456 at 462–463 (severance clause merely a 'part of the package of proposals').
5   It is possible that such a construction is compelled by the strict wording of section 36(2), ' ... where a legal estate ... is vested in joint tenants beneficially ... ' However, there is much to commend a more liberal construction which would enable all beneficial joint tenants to take advantage of the facility of severance by written notice. See, in favour of this wider view,

Burgess v Rawnsley [1975] Ch 429 at 439G per Lord Denning MR, 444F per Browne LJ, 447G per Sir John Pennycuick. See, contra, [1976] CLJ 20 at 24 (D J Hayton).
6   *Nielson-Jones v Fedden* [1975] Ch 222 at 229E. See, contra, *Burgess v Rawnsley* [1975] Ch 429 at 440A per Lord Denning MR.

SEVERANCE BY AN ACT OF A JOINT TENANT 'OPERATING UPON HIS OWN SHARE'

11.76   The first of the classic pre-1926 forms of severance laid down by Page Wood V-C in *Williams v Hensman*[1] comprises 'an act of any one of the persons interested operating upon his own share.' This mode of severance can also be unilateral[2] and the act of severance may be concealed – even dishonestly – from the other joint tenant or tenants.[3] However, in order to amount to severance the 'act' of the joint tenant must be 'such as to preclude him from claiming by survivorship any interest in the subject-matter of the joint tenancy.'[4] In other words, the 'act' which operates upon the joint tenant's share must have a final or irrevocable character which estops any future claim that longevity has conferred the benefits of survivorship on that co-owner.[5]

1   (1861) 1 John & H 546 at 557, 70 ER 862 at 867.
2   *Harris v Goddard* [1983] 1 WLR 1203 at 1209B; *Clark v Carter*, 70 Cal Rptr 923 at 925 (1968); *Gonzales v Gonzales*, 73 Cal Rptr 83 at 87 (1968).
3   See e g *First National Securities Ltd v Hegerty* [1985] QB 850 [**para 15.95**]; *Ahmed v Kendrick* (1988) 56 P & CR 120 at 126; *First National Bank plc v Achampong* [2004] 1 FCR 18 at [54]; *Burke v Stevens*, 70 Cal Rptr 87 at 91 (1968); *Corin v Patton* (1990) 169 CLR 540 at 585–586 per Deane J. See also *Re Estate of Casella*, 64 Cal Rptr 259 at 265 (1967).
4   *Re Wilks* [1891] 3 Ch 59 at 61 per Stirling J.
5   For express reference to the terminology of estoppel in this context, see *Re Murdoch and Barry* (1976) 64 DLR (3d) 222 at 229. Compare, however, A J McClean, (1979) 57 Can Bar Rev 1 at 29–30.

Disposition inter vivos

11.77   A sufficient 'act' for the purpose of the rule in *Williams v Hensman* typically involves the disposition of a joint tenant's equitable share to a third party by way of sale or security.[1] That this should be so is, in one sense, entirely consistent with the theory of joint tenancy. A joint tenancy is severed if one of the 'four unities' ceases to be present, as for instance where one joint tenant disposes of his proprietary interest in the joint tenancy to a stranger.[2] In such circumstances the stranger, as disponee, cannot enjoy unity of title with the remaining joint tenants.[3]

1   A disposition of the entire estate by all of the joint tenants, whether to a stranger or to one of their own number, cannot, of course, bring about any severance (see *Re Hayes' Estate* [1920] 1 IR 207 at 211; *Re Allingham* [1932] VLR 469 at 472; *Oboohoff v Melnicke* (Unreported, Supreme Court of New South Wales, 23 August 1990); *Penny Nominees Pty Ltd v Fountain* (*No 3*) (1990) 5 BPR 11284 at 11289 [**para 11.93**]).
2   *Litt*, s 292; *Co Litt*, p 189a. See also *Partriche v Powlet* (1740) 2 Atk 54 at 55, 26 ER 430 at 431 per Lord Hardwicke LC: '*Alienatio rei praefertur iuri accrescendi*'. This proposition is yet

another expression of one of the historic premises of English property law, ie that the highest consummation of a thing lies in its alienation [**para 7.16**].

3   *Bl Comm*, Vol II, p 185. See also *Re Murdoch and Barry* (1976) 64 DLR (3d) 222 at 225–226. Conversely, no severance is brought about where one joint tenant grants to a stranger some incorporeal or non-possessory right (eg an easement or profit *à prendre*) which does not disrupt unity of title (see *Lyons v Lyons* [1967] VR 169 at 174, 176; *Hedley v Roberts* [1977] VR 282 at 288–289). Nor does severance occur if A merely releases his legal ownership in favour of B and C (*Penny Nominees Pty Ltd v Fountain (No 3)* (1990) 5 BPR 11284 at 11290).

11.78   There is, however, a logical difficulty at this point. As a matter of definition, it cannot be said that a joint tenant owns any interest or 'share' which is sufficiently distinct to provide the subject matter of a disposition. The only way in which the alienor can validly dispose of an 'interest' is on the assumption that severance has already occurred. The act of alienation is thus, paradoxically, both the source and the vehicle of the interest conveyed. In some curious dislocation of time and causation, the completed act of transfer brings into being the very 'interest' which purported to be the subject matter of the transfer in the first place. It is small wonder that Dixon J observed in *Wright v Gibbons*[1] that joint tenancy is 'a form of ownership bearing many traces of the scholasticism of the times in which its principles were developed.'

1   (1949) 78 CLR 313 at 330.

Dealings with strangers

11.79   The effect of this form of severance may be seen in the following examples. Suppose that A, B and C are joint tenants of the legal and equitable estate in Greenacre (see *Fig. 25*).

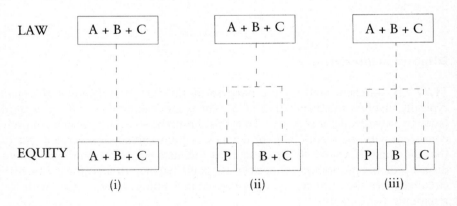

Fig. 25

11.80   If A transfers to P his 'share' or 'interest' in the joint tenancy,[1] A thereby destroys the pre-existing unity of equitable title and thus severs the joint tenancy.[2] This severance affects only the equitable ownership, since there can be no tenancy in common of a legal estate.[3] The result (as reflected in situation (ii) above) is that A, B and C remain as trustees of land, holding the legal estate as joint tenants on trust for P (as a tenant in common owning a one-third share in equity) and B and C (as joint tenants *inter se* of the remaining two-thirds).[4]

1   The transfer must be made by written disposition or otherwise under the aegis of a constructive trust (LPA 1925, ss 53(1)(c), (2)).
2   *Corin v Patton* (1990) 169 CLR 540 at 588 per Toohey J. No severance occurs merely because A grants P an irrevocable but as yet unexercised option to purchase A's 'interest' (*Re McKee and National Trust Co Ltd* (1975) 56 DLR (3d) 190 at 196).
3   LPA 1925, ss 1(6), 36(2) [**para 11.21**]. Even an ineffective attempt by a joint tenant to deal unilaterally with the entire jointly held estate normally operates in equity to sever his own aliquot share and to confer upon the disponee rights in relation to that share (see LPA 1925, s 63(1) [**para 15.96**]; *First National Securities Ltd v Hegerty* [1985] QB 850 at 854B, 862G–H; *Ahmed v Kendrick* (1988) 56 P & CR 120 at 126; *Re Ng (A Bankrupt)* [1998] 2 FLR 386 at 387A–B; *Bank of Ireland Home Mortgages Ltd v Bell* [2001] 2 All ER (Comm) 920 at [22]; *First National Bank plc v Achampong* [2004] 1 FCR 18 at [54]; *Westpac Banking Corporation v Sansom* (1994) 6 BPR 13790 at 13797–13798). There is no severance, however, if the disponee was privy to a dishonest attempt to deal with the entire legal estate (see *Penn v Bristol & West Building Society* [1995] 2 FLR 938 at 946G–947E, [1997] 1 WLR 1356; but compare (1996) Fam Law 28 at 29 (S M Cretney)).
4   *Litt*, s 294; *Co Litt*, p 189a; *Wright v Gibbons* (1949) 78 CLR 313 at 323 per Latham CJ; *Bedson v Bedson* [1965] 2 QB 666 at 689D per Russell LJ; *Corin v Patton* (1990) 169 CLR 540 at 575 per Deane J.

11.81   From one objective viewpoint, this situation can be described as disclosing a form of tenancy in common as between P, B and C. In strict analytical terms P is a tenant in common of a one-third share and the collective entity of (B + C) becomes a tenant in common of a two-thirds share. As between themselves, however, B and C are 'wholly entitled to the whole' of their two-thirds interest as joint tenants.[1] The right of survivorship continues to operate between them with respect to this two-thirds interest unless and until either severs. In the event of such further severance A, B and C will still hold the legal estate as joint tenants, but will now hold it on trust for P, B and C as tenants in common, each owning a one-third share in equity (ie situation (iii) above).[2] Any contradictions which appear in this context are more apparent than real, and merely mark the distinction between the external and the internal view of the property relations of A, B, C and P.

1   See *Denne d Bowyer v Judge* (1809) 11 East 288 at 289, 103 ER 1014 at 1015; *Shelton v Vance*, 234 P2d 1012 at 1014 (1951); *First National Bank of Denver v Groussman*, 483 P2d 398 at 401, affd 491 P2d 1382 (1971); *First National Bank of Southglenn v Energy Fuels Corp*, 618 P2d 1115 at 1118 (1980); *Corin v Patton* (1990) 169 CLR 540 at 575 per Deane J.
2   It is entirely irrelevant to this outcome that P later transfers his share back to A (see *Palmer v Palmer*, 121 P2d 822 at 825 (1942); *Alden v Alden*, 393 P2d 5 at 6 (1964)).

Dealings by joint tenants inter se

11.82   Exactly the same kind of result will apply where A, instead of transferring his interest to P, transfers it to B.[1] In such an event B acquires a dual status in equity. He becomes a tenant in common of a one-third interest in his own right and a joint tenant with C of the remaining two-thirds interest.[2] More difficult questions arise, however, if A and B as joint tenants *exchange* their 'interests' under the joint tenancy. Clearly, if A transfers his 'interest' to B one day before B transfers his 'interest' to A, two distinct severances will occur in close succession and A, B and C will all become tenants in common each as to a one-third share.[3] In *Wright v Gibbons*[4] precisely such transfers were made, but they were contained in one and the same instrument of transfer executed simultaneously by A and B. The High Court of Australia ruled that this mutual assurance or transposition of interests likewise had the effect of rendering A, B and C tenants in common each as to a one-third interest.[5]

1   *Hammond v McArthur*, 183 P2d 1 at 3 (1947); *Bank of Montreal v Bray* (1997) 153 DLR (4th) 490 at 500. It has even been held in some jurisdictions that A may sever by transferring his 'share' to himself, at least where such a transfer is made irrevocable e g through registration or delivery of the deed of transfer (see *Re Murdoch and Barry* (1976) 64 DLR (3d) 222 at 228; *Re Sammon* (1979) 94 DLR (3d) 594 at 597; *McNab v Earle* [1981] 2 NSWLR 673 at 677A). It is unlikely that English courts will accept a self-dealing transfer as sufficient for severance (see *Rye v Rye* [1962] AC 496 at 514) in the absence of amending legislation such as that found in New Zealand's Property Law Act 1952, s 66A (see *Samuel v District Land Registrar* [1984] 2 NZLR 697 at 702).

2   See *Wright v Gibbons* (1949) 78 CLR 313 at 324, 332; *Re Galletto's Estate*, 171 P2d 152 at 156 (1946). B's two separate holdings are distinguished by their different incidents: his joint tenancy of the two-thirds interest is still subject to the right of survivorship.

3   *Wright v Gibbons* (1949) 78 CLR 313 at 324–325 per Latham CJ.

4   (1949) 78 CLR 313.

5   Dixon J thought that an exactly similar result would follow if A and B as joint tenants were to grant their two aliquot shares to X effectively as a trustee for A and B as tenants in common in equal shares ((1949) 78 CLR 313 at 332).

Alienation in equity

11.83   It makes no difference to the steps outlined above in *Fig.* 25 if, instead of transferring his 'interest' to P outright, A merely enters into a specifically enforceable *contract* to transfer it to P.[1] Equity looks on that as done which ought to be done, and the contract operates in equity to transfer A's equitable interest to P under the so-called doctrine in *Walsh v Lonsdale*.[2] The effect of the unperformed, but specifically enforceable, contract is identical for purposes of severance to that of an actual transfer.[3] Severance similarly occurs if A declares himself a trustee of his own 'interest' on behalf of X[4] or if A transfers his 'interest' to T in order that T should hold on trust for A.[5]

1   *Brown v Raindle* (1796) 3 Ves 256 at 257, 30 ER 998 at 999; *Gould v Kemp* (1834) 2 My & K 304 at 309, 39 ER 959 at 961; *Wilson v Bell* (1843) 5 Ir Eq R 501 at 507; *Kingsford v Ball* (1852) 2 Giff (App) i at iii, 66 ER 294 at 295; *Caldwell v Fellowes* (1870) LR 9 Eq 410 at 418; *Re Hewett* [1894] 1 Ch 362 at 367. The elements of a specifically enforceable contract are discussed elsewhere [**para 9.13**].

2   (1882) 21 Ch D 9 [**para 9.66**]. Severance is not defeated by the death of the contracting joint tenant before he can perform his contract to transfer (see *Thomas v Johnson*, 297 NE2d 712 at 714–715 (1973)).

3   See *Burgess v Rawnsley* [1975] Ch 429 at 443G; *Freed v Taffel* [1984] 2 NSWLR 322 at 325C.

4   *Re Mee* (1971) 23 DLR (3d) 491 at 497; *Re Sorensen and Sorensen* (1979) 90 DLR (3d) 26 at 37; *Earl v Earl* [1979] 6 WWR 600 at 611. No severance is effected merely because A and B release their legal ownership in favour of C in order that C should hold on trust for A, B and C (*Groves v Christiansen* (1978) 86 DLR (3d) 296 at 306).

5   *Cray v Willis* (1729) 2 P Wms 529, 24 ER 847; *Staples v Maurice* (1774) 4 Bro Parl Cas 580 at
     585, 2 ER 395 at 399; *Clark v Carter*, 70 Cal Rptr 923 at 925–926 (1968); *Re Murdoch and
     Barry* (1976) 64 DLR (3d) 222 at 226; *In the Marriage of Badcock and Badcock* (1979) FLC
     ¶90–723 at p 78,896; *Corin v Patton* (1988) 13 NSWLR 15 at 25D–F.

Alienation by mortgage or lease

11.84   It is clear that a severing 'act' of alienation may include a mortgage or
charge.[1] Thus if one joint tenant purports to mortgage a jointly held entitlement either at law or in equity, severance follows in precisely the same way as if
there had been an outright transfer of that joint tenant's 'share'.[2] Such a
mortgage may, of course, be effected unilaterally without disclosure to the other
co-tenant or co-tenants.[3] The device of mortgage therefore offers the only
means (other than the cumbersome and legally dubious possibility of assignment to oneself or to a trustee[4]) of achieving a secret severance of a joint
tenancy without thereby alienating the severing tenant's proprietary rights in
their entirety.

1   See e g *First National Securities Ltd v Hegerty* [1985] QB 850 at 862G–H.
2   See LPA 1925, s 63(1); *First National Securities Ltd v Hegerty* [1985] QB 850 at 854B
     [para 15.95]. A specifically enforceable agreement to mortgage land will also, on the *Walsh v
     Lonsdale* principle, effect a severance. Not least because of the requirement of written contract
     signed by both parties (LP(MP)A 1989, s 2(1)), it is unlikely that one joint tenant's mere
     application for a secured loan can constitute a sufficient act of alienation for the purpose of
     severance (see *Lyons v Lyons* [1967] VR 169 at 176–181; *Wildschut v Borg Warner Acceptance
     Corporation (Aust) Ltd* (1987) 4 BPR 9453 at 9454). Compare *First National Securities Ltd*,
     supra at 862G–H per Sir Denys Buckley (pre-1989 Act case).
3   There is, of course, no severance if all the joint tenants together grant a mortgage over the
     joint property (see *Wollam v Barclays Bank Plc* (Unreported, 22 February 1988) per Knox J).
     Nor is it in any way inconsistent with the nature of joint tenancy that joint tenants should
     mortgage in order to provide security for the indebtedness of only one of their number (see
     Hall v Westpac Banking Corpn (1987) 4 BPR 9578 at 9581).
4   **[Para 11.83]**.

11.85   The severing effect of a lease granted unilaterally by one joint tenant is
a matter of some doubt.[1] There is good modern authority that the creation of
such a lease leads not to the complete severance of a joint tenancy but merely to
a partial severance or suspension of the joint tenancy during the leasehold
term.[2]

1   The possibility of such a unilateral grant seems clear **[para 11.26]**.
2   See *Wright v Gibbons* (1949) 78 CLR 313 at 327 per Rich J, 330 per Dixon J; *Corin v Patton*
     (1990) 169 CLR 540 at 573 per Deane J.

Alienation by will

11.86   The alienation of a joint tenant's 'share' by will does not normally
constitute an 'act ... operating upon his own share' for the purpose of severance. Neither death nor the execution of a testamentary document before
death[1] is a severing event. The *ius accrescendi* prevails over the testamentary

always be abandoned or discontinued.[2] However, English courts have tended to regard the possibility of a discontinuance of the proceedings either as negligible[3] or as entirely irrelevant.[4]

1   See *Re Draper's Conveyance* [1969] 1 Ch 486 at 492C. See also *Harris v Goddard* [1983] 1 WLR 1203 at 1209H, where Lawton LJ thought that the service of the summons and the filing of the affidavit in *Re Draper's Conveyance* could have been 'acts effectual to sever' within *Williams v Hensman*.

2   See e g Re Wilks [1891] 3 Ch 59 at 61; *Nielson-Jones v Fedden* [1975] Ch 222 at 236C; *Munroe v Carlson* (1976) 59 DLR (3d) 763 at 765; *In the Marriage of Badcock and Badcock* (1979) FLC ¶90–723 at p 78,897; *In the Marriage of Pertsoulis and Pertsoulis* (1980) FLC ¶90–832 at p 75,272; *Berdal v Burns* [1990] WAR 140 at 144.

3   *Re Draper's Conveyance* [1969] 1 Ch 486, as interpreted in *Harris v Goddard* [1983] 1 WLR 1203 at 1210B. See in any event (1968) 84 LQR 463 (P V B).

4   *Burgess v Rawnsley* [1975] Ch 429 at 440C, 447G. If, despite widespread doubts, *Burgess v Rawnsley* is correct in upholding the severing effect of an agreement which is later cancelled, it is difficult to see why severance is not irreversibly achieved by the mere commencement of litigation irrespective of the subsequent conduct of the parties.

SEVERANCE BY MUTUAL AGREEMENT

11.90   In *Williams v Hensman*[1] Page Wood V-C recognised that severance may also be brought about by 'mutual agreement' on the part of all the co-owners who currently enjoy the status of joint tenants.[2] Although it may sometimes be difficult to distinguish this form of severance from the third method outlined by Page Wood V-C ('mutual conduct'),[3] it is clear that joint tenants by acting together may effectively agree *inter se* to sever their joint tenancy.[4] Their agreement to do so may be either *express* or *implied* (ie such as can be inferred from conduct which necessarily involves severance[5]). In the absence of any contrary intention or arrangement, severance by mutual agreement results in a tenancy in common in equal shares.[6]

1   (1861) 1 John & H 546 at 557, 70 ER 862 at 867 [**para 11.76**].

2   There is no authority for severance where only some of the current joint tenants are party to the agreement (see *Wright v Gibbons* (1949) 78 CLR 313 at 322; *Tyson v Tyson* [1960] NSWR 177 at 180; *Corin v Patton* (1990) 169 CLR 540 at 547). Compare, however, A J McClean, (1979) 57 Can Bar Rev 1 at 2.

3   [**Para 11.95**]. The possibility of confusion between 'mutual agreement' and 'mutual conduct' is intensified by judicial statements that the court will 'infer an agreement' to sever 'if the acts and dealings of the parties in respect to the joint property *indicate an intention* to treat it as property held in common and not jointly' (*Wilson v Bell* (1843) 5 Ir Eq R 501 at 507). See also *Mann v Bradley*, 535 P2d 213 at 214 (1975); *Corin v Patton* (1990) 169 CLR 540 at 574 per Deane J, 587 per Toohey J. For an argument which fundamentally questions the validity of any distinction between 'mutual agreement' and 'mutual conduct', see A J McClean, (1979) 57 Can Bar Rev 1 at 16. See also *Lyons v Lyons* [1967] VR 169 at 171.

4   *Staples v Maurice* (1774) 4 Bro Parl Cas 580 at 585–586, 2 ER 395 at 399; *Wardlow v Pozzi*, 338 P2d 564 at 565 (1959); *Re Knowlton and Bartlett* (1985) 16 DLR (4th) 209 at 211.

5   See *Burgess v Rawnsley* [1975] Ch 429 at 446B per Sir John Pennycuick.

6   *Paterson v Paterson* (1980) 108 DLR (3d) 234 at 236.

Form of the agreement

11.91 Mutual agreement provides a flexible and informal mode of severance. The agreement need not take the form of a specifically enforceable contract.[1] Although valuable consideration will have passed between the severing joint tenants,[2] the agreement need not be in written form.[3] There is some authority for the proposition that severance is accomplished even though the agreement is revocable and is never, in fact, carried through to performance.[4] It is likewise irrelevant that the agreement depends, for its effectiveness, upon the approval of the court.[5] In all these respects the significance of the agreement is not that it binds the parties,[6] but rather that it 'serves as an indication of a common intention to sever.'[7] If such a mutual intention can be shown to have existed, the severance which it effects is not reversed merely because of some subsequent repudiation or failure of the parties' agreement. Caution is required, however, in relation to the severing quality of a mere 'agreement in principle' if there is evidence that the parties reserved the right to alter their respective bargaining positions in the light of later developments.[8] The conduct of contractual negotiations between parties can amount to 'mutual agreement' only if the parties have unequivocally indicated a common intention to sever and, irrespective of the outcome of the negotiations, their 'mutual attitude' in respect of this matter is 'unchanging'.[9] The presence of 'mutual agreement' is ultimately a question of fact dependent on the circumstances of each case.[10]

1   *Burgess v Rawnsley* [1975] Ch 429 at 444B–C, 446B–F; *Abela v Public Trustee* [1983] 1 NSWLR 308 at 315F. Contrast the case of severance under the first rule in *Williams v Hensman* (see *Burgess v Rawnsley*, supra at 444B–C per Browne LJ, 446C per Sir John Pennycuick [**para 11.83**]).

2   As Deane J indicated in *Corin v Patton* (1990) 169 CLR 540 at 574, 'mutual agreement' is inevitably supported by valuable consideration: 'each party agrees to relinquish the beneficial interest of a joint tenant of the common property, including the right of accretion by survivorship, in return for the share of a tenant in common.'

3   *Wilson v Bell* (1843) 5 Ir Eq R 501 at 507; *Lagar v Erickson*, 56 P2d 1287 at 1288 (1936). Severance follows *a fortiori* where the agreement is in written form (see *Smith v Morton*, 106 Cal Rptr 52 at 55 (1972)). For a strong contention that, for the purpose of severance by 'mutual agreement', writing is indeed required under the old Statute of Frauds (now LP(MP)A 1989, s 2(1)), see A J McClean, (1979) 57 Can Bar Rev 1 at 16–17; *Lyons v Lyons* [1967] VR 169 at 171.

4   *Burgess v Rawnsley* [1975] Ch 429 at 444D per Browne LJ; *Abela v Public Trustee* [1983] 1 NSWLR 308 at 314C, 315F.

5   See e g *Hunter v Babbage* [1994] 2 FLR 806 at 817B–E (agreement to draft consent order).

6   See e g *Hunter v Babbage* [1994] 2 FLR 806 at 817G–H, 818F–G (severance triggered by mutual agreement may result in shares quite different from those contemplated by the agreement) [**para 11.93**].

7   *Burgess v Rawnsley* [1975] Ch 429 at 446C per Sir John Pennycuick. See also *Frewen v Relfe* (1787) 2 Bro CC 220 at 224, 29 ER 123 at 125; *Hunter v Babbage* [1994] 2 FLR 806 at 817D; *Marshall v Marshall* (Unreported, Court of Appeal, 2 October 1998) per Mummery LJ; *Gebhardt v Dempster* [1914] SALR 287 at 309; *Abela v Public Trustee* [1983] 1 NSWLR 308 at 315F; *Magill v Magill* (1996) 7 BPR 14996 at 15005–15006.

8   *Gore and Snell v Carpenter* (1990) 60 P & CR 456 at 461–462.

9   *Slater v Slater* (1987) 4 BPR 9431 at 9435 per Cohen J.

10   *Slater v Slater* (1987) 4 BPR 9431 at 9434; *Magill v Magill* (1996) 7 BPR 14996 at 15004.

Content of the agreement

11.92   An effective 'mutual agreement' may contemplate severance either *expressly* or *impliedly*.[1]

1   *Burgess v Rawnsley* [1975] Ch 429 at 444A per Browne LJ, 446C per Sir John Pennycuick. See also *Wilson v Bell* (1843) 5 Ir Eq R 501 at 507; *Re Pozzi* [1982] Qd R 499 at 501C.

Illustrations

11.93   Severance can be implied from conduct which inevitably presupposes a common intention to sever a joint tenancy and renounce the operation of survivorship. Thus, for example, severing effect has been attributed to an agreement between two joint tenants that on the death of either co-owner the interest of the decedent should be passed to their daughter.[1] Conversely, in the normal case, no severance results from a simple agreement by co-owners to join in a sale[2] or lease[3] of the jointly owned property to a third party[4] or even to one of the joint tenants themselves.[5] Such action does not, in itself, eliminate the possibility of future survivorship in respect of the capital proceeds of the transaction.[6] However, an agreement that the proceeds of sale should be divided (whether equally or unequally) between the co-owners *does* effect a severance, for the precise reason that further survivorship is now excluded.[7] Thus, where the joint tenants are spouses, severance may be brought about by an agreement for separation or divorce which envisages a sale and distribution of sale proceeds in specific proportions.[8] Such agreements nevertheless throw up the potential irony that, regardless of the precise distribution agreed by the parties, the shares which follow from severance by 'mutual agreement' are necessarily *equal* shares rather than the shares as agreed between the parties.[9] No severance occurs at all, however, in the absence of agreed proportions of division.[10]

1   *McDonald v Morley*, 101 P2d 690 at 692 (1940).
2   *Marshall v Marshall* (Unreported, Court of Appeal, 2 October 1998) (mere agreement to put house on market). See similarly *Re Hayes' Estate* [1920] 1 IR 207 at 211; *Re Allingham* [1932] VLR 469 at 472; *County of Fresno v Kahn*, 24 Cal Rptr 394 at 397 (1962); *Lyons v Lyons* [1967] VR 169 at 172; *Public Trustee v Grivas* [1974] 2 NSWLR 316 at 320C; *Abela v Public Trustee* [1983] 1 NSWLR 308 at 314B. No severance is brought about by the compulsory acquisition of jointly owned land (see *Ex Parte Railway Commissioners for NSW* (1941) 41 SR (NSW) 92 at 95).
3   *Palmer v Rich* [1897] 1 Ch 134 at 143; *Lyons v Lyons* [1967] VR 169 at 170.
4   Nor is severance brought about by a mere agreement between the joint tenants for a splitting of the rental income derived from a joint letting (see *Flannigan v Wotherspoon* [1953] 1 DLR 768 at 775–776). Such an agreement does not extinguish the possibility of survivorship in respect of the freehold. For the same reason an agreement allowing one joint tenant sole residence does not connote a severance by 'mutual agreement' (see *Gillette v Nicolls*, 262 P2d 856 at 859 (1953); *Cole v Cole*, 294 P2d 494 at 496 (1956); *Lyons v Lyons* [1967] VR 169 at 170; *Compton v Compton*, 624 P2d 345 at 346 (1981)).
5   *Magill v Magill* (1996) 7 BPR 14996 at 15004–15006.
6   Incidental references in correspondence to 'half-shares' or 'half interests' do not necessarily connote a mutual agreement to sever (see e g *Magill v Magill* (1996) 7 BPR 14996 at 15004).
7   Severance may even be implied from the fact that joint tenants have agreed to divide between

themselves the deposit paid over by the purchaser at the point of contract (see *Crooke v De Vandes* (1805) 11 Ves 330 at 333, 32 ER 1115 at 1116; *Flannigan v Wotherspoon* [1953] 1 DLR 768 at 776). See also *Penny Nominees Pty Ltd v Fountain (No 3)* (1990) 5 BPR 11284 at 11287–11289; *Public Trustee v Pfeiffle* [1991] 1 VR 19 at 35. Some doubt must attach to the refusal to recognise that severance had occurred by 'mutual agreement' in *Nielson-Jones v Fedden* [1975] Ch 222 at 229G (see e g *Burgess v Rawnsley* [1975] Ch 429 at 440B, 448B; *Bank of British Columbia v Nelson* (1979) 17 BCLR 223).

8   *Hunter v Babbage* [1994] 2 FLR 806 at 817A. See likewise *Re McKee and National Trust Co Ltd* (1975) 56 DLR (3d) 190 at 196; *Re Pozzi* [1982] Qd R 499 at 502E; *Public Trustee v Pfeiffle* [1991] 1 VR 19 at 24–25, 31.

9   *Hunter v Babbage* [1994] 2 FLR 806 at 817G–H, 818F–G (spouse died before draft consent order for unequal shares could be finalised by the court).

10   *Marshall v Marshall* (Unreported, Court of Appeal, 2 October 1998).

An extreme example

11.94   An extremely controversial illustration of severance by 'mutual agreement' was provided by the decision of the Court of Appeal in *Burgess v Rawnsley*.[1] Here H and R, elderly lovers, purchased a dwelling-house as legal and beneficial joint tenants, each providing half of the purchase price.[2] On the subsequent breakdown of the relationship, H and R orally agreed (according to a dubious finding of fact by the trial judge) that R would sell her share in the house to H for a specified price. R subsequently revoked this agreement and demanded a higher price, but H died before negotiations could proceed further. The Court of Appeal held that the beneficial joint tenancy had indeed been severed before H's death and that his estate was therefore entitled to a half-share in any proceeds of sale of the property. Both Browne LJ and Sir John Pennycuick reluctantly based this conclusion on the ground that severance had been effected by the agreement which the county court judge had found on the somewhat unsatisfactory evidence before him.[3] The decision represents an unacceptably broad construction of 'mutual agreement' and has not been followed in other jurisdictions.[4]

1   [1975] Ch 429. See [1976] CLJ 20 (D J Hayton); (1975) 39 Conv (NS) 433 (F R Crane); (1976) 50 ALJ 246 (P B); (1976) 40 Conv (NS) 77 (J F Garner); (1977) 41 Conv (NS) 243 (S M Bandali).

2   The judgment of Lord Denning MR ([1975] Ch 429 at 435F–H) contains an account of a love story – as poignant as any to be found in the bleak pages of the law reports – which began at a scripture rally in Trafalgar Square.

3   'The evidence upon which that finding was based appears to be rather weak' ([1975] Ch 429 at 445H per Sir John Pennycuick). See also [1975] Ch 429 at 442G, 443G per Browne LJ. It has been suggested that a doctrine of temporary severance may be appropriate in cases of short-lived agreement, with a reversion to joint tenancy when the agreement is terminated or revoked (see Peter Butt, (1979–82) 9 Sydney L Rev 568 at 576–577).

4   See e g *Corin v Patton* (1990) 169 CLR 540 at 547–548, 565–566, 584 (High Court of Australia); *Magill v Magill* (1996) 7 BPR 14996 at 14998 (Court of Appeal of New South Wales).

SEVERANCE BY MUTUAL CONDUCT

11.95   The third method of severance adverted to by Page Wood V-C in *Williams v Hensman* has been termed severance by the 'mutual conduct' of the existing joint tenants. In the words of Page Wood V-C, severance may be effected 'by any course of dealing sufficient to intimate that the interests of all were mutually treated as constituting a tenancy in common.'[1] In spite of the close conceptual similarity,[2] the balance of judicial opinion is now to the effect that this third category of severing circumstance is not 'a mere sub-heading of rule 2' of Page Wood V-C's categories.[3] This third category may be particularly relevant to cases where, in ignorance of the fact that they were joint tenants, parties could not formulate any common intention to sever but nevertheless dealt with each other on the footing that their interests were those of tenants in common.[4]

1   (1861) 1 John & H 546 at 557, 70 ER 862 at 867 [**para 11.76**].
2   The temptation to merge Page Wood V-C's second and third categories intensifies if they are simply regarded as, respectively, examples of express and implied agreement (see e g *Corin v Patton* (1990) 169 CLR 540 at 574 per Deane J, 587 per Toohey J).
3   *Burgess v Rawnsley* [1975] Ch 429 at 447D per Sir John Pennycuick (see also Lord Denning MR at 439B, Browne LJ at 444F); *Greenfield v Greenfield* (1979) 38 P & CR 570 at 577; *Gore and Snell v Carpenter* (1990) 60 P & CR 456 at 462; *Abela v Public Trustee* [1983] 1 NSWLR 308 at 315A; *Re Knowlton and Bartlett* (1985) 16 DLR (4th) 209 at 211; *Berdal v Burns* [1990] WAR 140 at 144; *Corin v Patton* (1990) 169 CLR 540 at 547–548, 574. Contra, *Re Wilks* [1891] 3 Ch 59 at 61–62; *Flynn v Flynn* [1930] IR 337 at 343; *Lyons v Lyons* [1967] VR 169 at 170–171; *Nielson-Jones v Fedden* [1975] Ch 222 at 231B.
4   See *Hunter v Babbage* [1994] 2 FLR 806 at 812E.

General nature of 'mutual conduct'

11.96   'Mutual conduct' has been taken to comprise any conduct of the joint tenants which falls short of evidencing an express or implied *agreement* to sever but which nevertheless indicates an unambiguous common intention that the joint tenancy should be severed.[1] Severance by 'mutual conduct' requires neither an express act of severance, nor a contract, nor a declaration of trust. It requires merely a consensus between the joint tenants, disclosed by a pattern of dealings with the co-owned property, which effectively excludes the future operation of the right of survivorship.[2]

1   See *Abela v Public Trustee* [1983] 1 NSWLR 308 at 315G (but compare the greater hesitancy of Deane J in *Corin v Patton* (1990) 169 CLR 540 at 574). A common intention to sever may be more readily inferred from a course of conduct where the joint tenants are married to each other (see *Harris v Goddard* [1983] 1 WLR 1203 at 1208F; *Estate of Gebert*, 157 Cal Rptr 46 at 51 (1979)) or where the personal relationship of the joint tenants has broken down (see *In the Marriage of Badcock and Badcock* (1979) FLC ¶90–723 at p 78,898; *Abela v Public Trustee* [1983] 1 NSWLR 308 at 315E). See also *Re Walters and Walters* (1978) 79 DLR (3d) 122 at 127.
2   See *Szabo v Boros* (1967) 64 DLR (2d) 48 at 49 per Davey CJBC.

Examples of 'mutual conduct'

11.97   Examples of the 'course of dealing' required to establish severance are manifold and depend on the individual facts of each case. The following issues are close to the centre of judicial concern.

Long-term assumptions about ownership

11.98 It is clear that severance by 'mutual conduct' occurs where co-owners, although originally joint tenants, have acted over a long period of time on the assumption that each owns a severed share as a tenant in common.[1] However, the mere fact that joint property is for tax reasons included among the assets of a partnership with separate capital accounts for the co-owners does not necessarily constitute a severing 'course of dealing'.[2]

1 See e g *Wilson v Bell* (1843) 5 Ir Eq R 501 at 507–508; *Re Denny* (1947) 116 LJR 1029 at 1037. See also *Gore and Snell v Carpenter* (1990) 60 P & CR 456 at 462, where long-term assumptions were regarded as the pre-eminent manifestation of 'mutual conduct'.

2 *Barton v Morris* [1985] 1 WLR 1257 at 1262D–H. See also *Brown v Oakshot* (1857) 24 Beav 254 at 258, 53 ER 355 at 357, but compare *Bedson v Bedson* [1965] 2 QB 666 at 690F per Russell LJ.

Mutual wills

11.99 The consensus required for 'mutual conduct' can be provided by the simultaneous execution of mutual wills by two joint tenants, at least where the co-owners have formulated a precise agreement which contemplates severance.[1] Severance has thus been upheld in the case of mutual wills which direct the future disposition of the 'share' of each joint tenant.[2]

1 Compare *Re Goodchild , decd* [1996] 1 WLR 694 at 699A–C.

2 *Re Wilford's Estate* (1879) 11 Ch D 267 at 269; *In the Estate of Heys* [1914] P 192 at 195; *Szabo v Boros* (1967) 64 DLR (2d) 48 at 52. In *Re Bryan and Heath* (1980) 108 DLR (3d) 245 at 250, mutual wills distributing the respective shares of the co-owners among the surviving co-owner and the children of the family were held to constitute severance both by 'mutual agreement' and by 'mutual conduct'. See also *Re Sorensen and Sorensen* (1979) 90 DLR (3d) 26 at 38; *University of Manitoba v Sanderson Estate* (1998) 155 DLR (4th) 40 at 45.

Physical conversion of co-owned property

11.100 'Mutual conduct' is not necessarily constituted by a mere physical division of the co-owned property without partition or sale, where for reasons of convenience the joint tenants are left in sole and separate occupation of self-contained portions of the converted property.[1] A territorial realignment of this kind is not incompatible with continuing joint tenancy.[2]

1 *Greenfield v Greenfield* (1979) 38 P & CR 570 at 578; *Sanders v McDonald and Pringle* [1981] CLY 1534; *Haughabaugh v Honald*, 5 Am Dec 548 at 550 (1812); *Stiff v Stiff*, 168 NW2d 273 at 274 (1969). Compare *Gore and Snell v Carpenter* (1990) 60 P & CR 456 at 462, where severance might have followed from the co-owners' tentative plans for a severance of their joint tenancies of two houses and for the transfer of one property to each party. Their negotiations never crystallised sufficiently to effect a true severance.

2 Cp *Roche v Sheridan* (1857) 9 Ir Jur 409.

Commencement of litigation

11.101 'Mutual conduct' is not brought about simply by reason of the fact that the joint tenants have initiated court proceedings for partition[1] of the co-owned property or for a sale and distribution of proceeds.[2] However, the formal commencement of such litigation between joint tenants may well effect a severance on other grounds.[3]

1   [Para **11.273**].
2   *Dando v Dando*, 99 P2d 561 at 562 (1940); *Teutenberg v Schiller*, 291 P2d 53 at 56 (1955); *Munroe v Carlson* (1976) 59 DLR (3d) 763; *Rodrigue v Dufton* (1977) 72 DLR (3d) 16.
3   [Para **11.74**].

Negotiations between joint tenants

11.102   Perhaps the most difficult issue in this area is whether a process of inconclusive negotiation between joint tenants in relation to their respective 'shares' can amount to 'mutual conduct'. Severance by 'mutual conduct' provided the ground on which Lord Denning MR preferred to rest his judgment in *Burgess v Rawnsley*.[1] In his view, this head of severance includes any 'course of dealing in which one party makes clear to the other that he desires that their shares should no longer be held jointly but be held in common.'[2]

1   [1975] Ch 429 [**para 11.94**].
2   [1975] Ch 429 at 439C. This description of severance seems dubious in so far as it gives effect to unilateral declarations of intention [**para 11.88**]. It is significant that the High Court of Australia has declined to follow *Burgess v Rawnsley* (see *Corin v Patton* (1990) 169 CLR 540 at 547–548 per Mason CJ and McHugh J, 565–566 per Brennan J, 584 per Deane J). See also *Hall v Public Trustee (ACT)* (2003) 150 ACTR 8 at [11]. If Lord Denning's view is defensible at all, it must be on the basis that it was the communication of the desire to sever, rather than its mere formulation, which was 'the effective act' (see *Corin*, supra at 584–585 per Deane J).

11.103   It is likely that this approach to negotiations would today be considered over-broad.[1] Even in *Burgess v Rawnsley* Lord Denning's finding of 'mutual conduct' in the context of abortive negotiations for purchase did not receive support from the other members of the Court of Appeal. Both Browne LJ[2] and Sir John Pennycuick doubted whether a 'course of dealing' was sufficiently clearly established to bring into play Page Wood V-C's third category of severing circumstance. Sir John Pennycuick admitted that 'where one tenant negotiates with another for some rearrangement of interest, it may be possible to infer from the particular facts a common intention to sever even though the negotiations break down.'[3] However, he thought such an inference to be entirely dependent on the individual facts of any given case.[4] In his view, the negotiations in *Burgess v Rawnsley*, 'if they can be properly described as negotiations at all', fell far short of warranting an inference of severance: '[o]ne could not ascribe to joint tenants an intention to sever merely because one offers to buy out the other for X and the other makes a counter-offer of Y.'[5]

1   See e g *Gore and Snell v Carpenter* (1990) 60 P & CR 456 at 462 ('negotiations are not the same thing as a course of dealing'). See also *McDowell v Hirschfield Lipson & Rumney and Smith* [1992] 2 FLR 126 at 130C–E; *Slater v Slater* (1987) 4 BPR 9431 at 9434.
2   [1975] Ch 429 at 444E.
3   [1975] Ch 429 at 447A–B.
4   In *Gore and Snell v Carpenter* (1990) 60 P & CR 456 at 462, the court refused to infer the

common intention necessary for a finding of 'mutual conduct' where 'there were simply negotiations between the husband and the wife and ... there was no finality and there was no mutuality.' See also *Robichaud v Watson* (1983) 147 DLR (3d) 626 at 633.

5   [1975] Ch 429 at 447B. For a significant adoption of the observations of Sir John Pennycuick in preference to those of Lord Denning MR, see *Harris v Goddard* [1983] 1 WLR 1203 at 1211B per Dillon LJ. Elsewhere the test of severance by negotiations has been said to involve a 'clear indication by each party that the severance is regarded by them as having occurred' (see *Slater v Slater* (1987) 4 BPR 9431 at 9434–9435 per Cohen J (no severance effected by agreement in solicitors' correspondence to seek severance by court order)).

11.104   Courts in other jurisdictions have occasionally been more prepared to uphold severance as resulting from abortive or inconclusive negotiations between the joint tenants with respect to their individual 'shares'. This is particularly so where the negotiations have been incorporated in correspondence between the parties[1] or have been mediated through their respective legal advisers,[2] and where the parties have plainly begun to conceptualise their entitlements in terms of individualised shareholding.[3]

1   *Ginn v Armstrong* (1969) 3 DLR (3d) 285 at 288.
2   *Re Walters and Walters* (1978) 79 DLR (3d) 122 at 127, affd (1978) 84 DLR (3d) 416n; *Robichaud v Watson* (1983) 147 DLR (3d) 626 at 636. See, however, A J McClean, (1979) 57 Can Bar Rev 1 at 23.
3   See *Slater v Slater* (1987) 4 BPR 9431 at 9435.

Limitations on 'mutual conduct'

11.105   Most of the limitations imposed on the concept of 'mutual conduct' stem from the judicial disinclination to accept that severance may be achieved by a merely unilateral and unwritten declaration of intention expressed by one of the joint tenants. In this context the largely unspoken fear is that the facility of informal declaration, once admitted as a head of severance, would enable an unscrupulous joint tenant to hedge his bets in the gamble surrounding longevity by engaging in 'strategic behaviour'.[1] If the declarant subsequently failed to outlive his fellow co-owners, he would have ensured that a severed share devolved upon his own estate; if, however, he did survive them, he would be able simply to deny that he had ever made a severing declaration.[2] It was for this reason that in *Williams v Hensman*[3] Page Wood V-C emphasised explicitly that, in the absence of an express act of severance, 'it will not suffice to rely on an intention, with respect to the particular share, declared only behind the backs of the other persons interested.' Instead, ruled Page Wood V-C, it is imperative to 'find in this class of cases a course of dealing by which the shares of all the parties to the contest have been affected.'[4]

1   See R H Helmholz, 'Realism and Formalism in the Severance of Joint Tenancies' 77 Neb L Rev 1 at 26 (1998).
2   The formality of an irrevocable delivery or registration may be an all-important indication of a joint tenant's intention to exclude himself from the possibility of future survivorship **[para 11.72]**. See *Re Sammon* (1979) 94 DLR (3d) 594 at 600–601.
3   (1861) 1 John & H 546 at 558, 70 ER 862 at 867.
4   See (1861) 30 LJ 878 at 880 (more accurate report).

11.106   Thus, while Sir John Pennycuick was quite ready to concede in *Burgess v Rawnsley* that the 'policy of the law as it stands today ... is to facilitate severance at the instance of either party',[1] neither he nor any other member of the Court of Appeal was prepared to hold that severance could be effected either by an uncommunicated declaration by one joint tenant[2] or indeed by a mere verbal notice by one joint tenant to the other joint tenant or tenants.[3] It follows, *a fortiori*, that a declaration made by a joint tenant to a third party outside the joint tenancy is likewise incapable of bringing about a severance.[4]

1   [1975] Ch 429 at 448A [**para 11.56**].
2   [1975] Ch 429 at 439C per Lord Denning MR, 444G per Browne LJ, 448A per Sir John Pennycuick.
3   [1975] Ch 429 at 439E per Lord Denning MR, 448A per Sir John Pennycuick.
4   *Greenfield v Greenfield* (1979) 38 P & CR 570 at 578 (communication to wife of other joint tenant held ineffective).

SEVERANCE BY COURT ORDER

11.107   It is increasingly clear that severance of an equitable joint tenancy is brought about by certain kinds of court order (even before the order is duly carried through to performance).[1] Such cases arise where, following litigation, a court order settles the interests of joint tenants in co-owned land 'in a manner inconsistent with continuation of the joint tenancy.'[2] If, for example, a court resolves a dispute between joint tenants by directing that the land be sold and the proceeds distributed between them in defined proportions, it seems wrong in principle that this otherwise binding order should be rendered abortive by the continued operation of the *ius accrescendi*.[3] Equity jurisprudence steps in to ensure that the untimely death of one of the parties before the court order is perfected cannot have the capricious consequence of triggering survivorship.[4] From the date on which it takes effect, the court order is specifically enforceable.[5] Equity characteristically regards as done that which ought to be done, with the result that severance is viewed as having already occurred.[6] The correctness of this outcome is even clearer where a court order in respect of jointly owned land takes full effect only over an elongated period.[7] It would be quite wrong, for instance, that the death of one co-owner in advance of the postponed sale and distribution envisaged by the order should allow the other co-owner to take the whole estate as survivor.[8]

1   It has long been suggested that *Re Draper's Conveyance* [1969] 1 Ch 486 [**para 11.74**] is explicable on the footing that the court order in that case effected a severance (see *Davies v Davies* [1983] WAR 305 at 306–307 per Burt CJ).
2   See *Berdal v Burns* [1990] WAR 140 at 144 per Burt CJ. There can be no severance by court order where the court's jurisdiction is confined to a mere declaration of the existing rights of the parties (e g pursuant to Married Women's Property Act 1882, s 17) and where, accordingly, the court cannot authorise a conversion of these rights into a tenancy in common (see *Re Draper's Conveyance* [1969] 1 Ch 486 at 494D per Plowman J).
3   For this reason it has been suggested that the courts may have a more general equitable jurisdiction to impose a constructive trust on a surviving joint tenant, with severing effect, in cases where it would be unconscionable that this co-owner should take the entire benefit of the

joint property by survivorship (see *Public Trustee v Grivas* [1974] 2 NSWLR 316 at 322D per Bowen CJ in Eq). See also *Gray v Gray*, 412 A2d 1208 at 1211 (1980); *Berdal v Burns* [1990] WAR 140 at 144.

4 See *Re Johnstone* [1973] Qd R 347 at 351E; *Public Trustee v Grivas* [1974] 2 NSWLR 316 at 321E; *Gillette v Cotton* [1979] 4 WWR 515 at 525–526; *In the Marriage of Pertsoulis and Pertsoulis* (1980) FLC ¶90–832 at p 75,272; *McKee v McKee* (1986) 10 Fam LR 754 at 757.

5 See *Mountney v Treharne* [2003] Ch 135 at [76] ('All that remains is … to enforce it'). The same applies to a consent order (see *Public Trustee v Grivas* [1974] 2 NSWLR 316 at 322C; *Re Estate of Estelle*, 593 P2d 663 at 666 (1979); *Slater v Slater* (1987) 4 BPR 9431 at 9434–9435).

6 See *Penny Nominees Pty Ltd v Fountain (No 3)* (1990) 5 BPR 11284 at 11290 per Young J. The argument in favour of severance is even stronger here than that which would normally flow from a joint tenant's specifically enforceable agreement to transfer his share to another [para 11.83]. In the present context 'the court has in effect already made a decree of specific performance' (*Mountney v Treharne* [2003] Ch 135 at [76]).

7 See e g the *Mesher* order which, in the event of divorce, enables the court to impose a trust on the former family home, occupation pending sale being reserved for one or other ex-spouse as custodial parent. Sale (and the consequent division of capital proceeds in the proportions ordered by the court) are normally postponed until the youngest child of the parties reaches the age of 17 or 18 (see *Mesher v Mesher* [1980] 1 All ER 126n). A variant of this order, the *Harvey* order, postpones sale and distribution of capital proceeds until the death, remarriage, cohabitation or voluntary removal of the custodial parent (see *Harvey v Harvey* [1982] Fam 83; [1982] CLJ 228 (Gray)). Here, even more clearly, the reference to death as one of the contingencies conditioning sale makes it clear that no rule of survivorship can have been intended to operate.

8 See e g *Berdal v Burns* [1990] WAR 140 at 150 (Western Australian equivalent of a *Harvey* order held to have immediate severing effect).

SEVERANCE IN CONSEQUENCE OF UNLAWFUL KILLING

11.108 Severance of a joint tenancy may occur on a footing quite different from any so far considered. It is possible that severance may result, not from any lawful act of a joint tenant, but rather in consequence of the unlawful killing of one joint tenant by another.[1]

1 See generally J B Ames, 'Can a Murderer Acquire Title by his Crime and Keep it?', in *Lectures on Legal History* (Cambridge Mass 1913), p 310; J Chadwick, (1914) 30 LQR 211; J W Wade, 49 Harvard L Rev 715 (1935–36); J L Toohey, 'Killing the Goose that lays the Golden Eggs' (1958) 32 ALJ 14; Tim Youdan, 'Acquisition of Property by Killing' (1973) 89 LQR 235.

The general rationale

11.109 In *Cleaver v Mutual Reserve Fund Life Association*,[1] Fry LJ gave classic expression to the view that 'no system of jurisprudence can with reason include amongst the rights which it enforces rights directly resulting to the person asserting them from the crime of that person.'[2] A forfeiture rule[3] is therefore applied by the courts as a rule of public policy in order to ensure that no wrongdoer shall profit from his crime[4] and, in particular, to ensure that 'a man shall not slay his benefactor and thereby take his bounty.'[5] This principle has a special application to joint tenants who, in fact if not in strict legal theory, derive benefit from the earlier decease of one of their number.[6]

1   [1892] 1 QB 147 at 156.

2   See also *Beresford v Royal Insurance Co Ltd* [1938] AC 586 at 596 per Lord Atkin; *Davitt v Titcumb* [1990] Ch 110 at 114D–115C; *Helton v Allen* (1940) 63 CLR 691 at 709 (High Court of Australia); *Rosenfeldt v Olson* (1985) 16 DLR (4th) 103 at 125–127, (1986) 25 DLR (4th) 472 at 475.

3   The term 'forfeiture rule' now has legislative status, being defined for the purpose of the Forfeiture Act 1982 as comprising 'the rule of public policy which in certain circumstances precludes a person who has unlawfully killed another from acquiring a benefit in consequence of the killing' (Forfeiture Act 1982, s 1(1)). Not only the wrongdoer but also his own issue are disqualified from claiming any benefit (see *Re D W S, decd* [2001] Ch 568 at [31], [47]).

4   This rule is a narrower formulation (see e g *Helton v Allen* (1940) 63 CLR 691 at 710) than the idea that 'no man shall profit from his own wrong', since otherwise the slightest negligence by a beneficiary resulting in the death of the benefactor would bar recovery (see *Public Trustee v Evans* [1985] 2 NSWLR 188 at 191F–G). In the present context this may be an important qualification, given the proclivity of joint tenants to inflict death on each other in car accidents caused through the negligent driving of one.

5   *In the Estate of Hall* [1914] P 1 at 7 per Hamilton LJ. See also *Re Sigsworth* [1935] Ch 89 at 92; *Re Giles, decd* [1972] Ch 544 at 552B; *Re Nordstrom* (1962) 31 DLR (2d) 255 at 263. Courts in other jurisdictions have questioned whether the forfeiture rule is, in every circumstance, an inflexible rule of public policy. See e g the refusal to apply the rule in *Public Trustee v Evans* [1985] 2 NSWLR 188 at 193B–F (joint tenant killed husband whilst attempting to avert lethal violence directed against herself and her children).

6   [**Para 11.11**].

The operation of the forfeiture rule

11.110   The operation of the forfeiture rule differs according to the number of joint tenants involved.

Two joint tenants

11.111   The forfeiture rule operates easily in the case where the joint tenancy is limited to two persons who are joint tenants both of the legal estate and the equitable interest in co-owned land. If, for instance, A and B are joint tenants, and A unlawfully kills B, A remains invested with the legal interest by survivorship, but henceforth holds it on trust for himself and B's successors as tenants in common in equal shares,[1] subject only to the proviso that A may not take (directly or indirectly) as a beneficiary under B's estate.[2] In other words, the right of survivorship does not operate in an unqualified form: the killer cannot claim the benefit of the *ius accrescendi* in relation to the equitable interest. As Cardozo said,[3] 'the social interest served by refusing to permit the criminal to profit by his crime is greater than that served by the preservation and enforcement of legal rights of ownership.'

1   *Re Thorp and the Real Property Act* (1963) 80 WN (NSW) 61 at 65; *Schobelt v Barber* (1967) 60 DLR (2d) 519 at 524; *Re Pechar (Deceased)* [1969] NZLR 574 at 587; *Rasmanis v Jurewitsch* (1970) 70 SR (NSW) 407 at 411; *Re Gore* (1972) 23 DLR (3d) 534 at 536. Where, as sometimes happens, the murder of B is followed by the suicide of A, A's personal representatives hold the joint property on trust for A's estate and B's estate as tenants in common in equal shares (see *Re Dreger* (1976) 69 DLR (3d) 47 at 49, 60). The beneficiary under both estates may well be the same person (see e g *Whitfield v Flaherty*, 39 Cal Rptr 857 (1964)).

There is much to be said in favour of treating the murder-suicide phenomenon, not in terms of rules which aim to frustrate cupidinous slaying, but rather in terms analogous to the Californian rule relating to simultaneous death [**para 11.12**]. See *Johansen v Pelton*, 87 Cal Rptr 784 at 789 (1970).

2   *Re K, decd* [1985] Ch 85 at 100G; *Johansen v Pelton*, 87 Cal Rptr 784 at 786, 788 (1970). This proviso is explicitly incorporated, for instance, in California's Probate Code, s 258. See also *Re Pechar (Deceased)* [1969] NZLR 574 at 587. The same proviso must also preclude A from taking as a beneficiary under the estate of Z if Z was himself the beneficiary of B's estate. See *Public Trustee v Evans* [1985] 2 NSWLR 188 at 193D; Tim Youdan, (1973) 89 LQR 235 at 236–237. It seems preferable simply to regard the wrong-doing joint tenant as 'notionally not being in existence, so that the other next of kin took the estate' (*Public Trustee v Fraser* (1987) 9 NSWLR 433 at 444E). See also *Re Jane Tucker, Decd* (1920) 21 SR (NSW) 175 at 177H. There appears to be no justification for Vaisey J's improbable suggestion in *Re Callaway* [1956] Ch 559 at 565, that the disentitled beneficiary's portion should pass to the crown as bona vacantia. See (1956) 72 LQR 475; [1956] CLJ 167 (F J Odgers).

3   See B N Cardozo, *The Nature of the Judicial Process* (New Haven and London 1969), p 43.

Homicide as a severing event

11.112   Although this conclusion has been accepted as correct in most jurisdictions, it is much less easy to articulate the precise legal reasoning which underlies the outcome. Differing explanations have been put forward. It has sometimes been suggested that the act of killing constitutes so clear a violation of the intimate union of joint tenancy that the inherent feature of this co-ownership form – the right of survivorship – can no longer operate.[1] The rule of survivorship has, in effect, been displaced by the unlawful attempt by one joint tenant to predetermine in his own favour the gamble on longevity.[2] A more widely accepted explanation is quite simply that homicide is itself a severing event.[3] However, this explanation has been criticised by some courts on the ground that it controverts the long-established principle that severance can be effected only before death.[4] Moreover, the proposition has been considered undesirable in so far as it appears to countenance the addition of homicide as an approved method of terminating joint tenancy.[5]

1   See *Re Barrowcliff* [1927] SASR 147 at 151 per Napier J ('a repudiation of the terms on which [joint tenants] hold'). See also *Kemp v The Public Curator of Queensland* [1969] Qd R 145 at 149; *Bradley v Fox*, 129 NE2d 699 at 705–706 (1955).

2   See *Re Pupkowski* (1957) 6 DLR (2d) 427 at 430. In *Re K, decd* [1985] Ch 85 at 100H, Vinelott J seemed prepared to accept that the operation of the forfeiture rule simply severs the joint tenancy.

3   *Re Barrowcliff* [1927] SASR 147 at 151; *Bradley v Fox*, 129 NE2d 699 at 706 (1955); *Kemp v The Public Curator of Queensland* [1969] Qd R 145 at 149; *Johansen v Pelton*, 87 Cal Rptr 784 at 786, 788 (1970).

4   See *Re Thorp and the Real Property Act* (1963) 80 WN (NSW) 61 at 63; *Rasmanis v Jurewitsch* (1970) 70 SR (NSW) 407 at 411C; *Public Trustee v Evans* [1985] 2 NSWLR 188 at 193A–B.

5   See *Re King's Estate*, 52 NW2d 885 at 889 (1952); *Abbey v Lord*, 336 P2d 226 at 233 (1955); *Rasmanis v Jurewitsch* (1970) 70 SR (NSW) 407 at 412A.

Application of constructive trust principles

11.113   Increasingly the view is taken that the forfeiture imposed on the killer is best justified in terms of the application of an equitable doctrine of constructive trust based on unjust enrichment.[1] In other words, the killer is recognised as taking the entirety by survivorship but is, by reason of his misconduct, subjected to the full rigour of equitable control. He is made to hold the legal estate on a constructive trust for himself and the victim's estate in equal shares.[2]

1   See B N Cardozo, *The Nature of the Judicial Process*, p 42; *Abbey v Lord*, 336 P2d 226 at 230–231; *Re Pechar (Deceased)* [1969] NZLR 574 at 587–588; *Re Stone* [1989] 1 Qd R 351 at 352; Tim Youdan, (1973) 89 LQR 235 at 253–254. See also the exposition of constructive trust doctrine in the context of unjust enrichment in *Rosenfeldt v Olson* (1985) 16 DLR (4th) 103 at 121–125, but compare (1986) 25 DLR (4th) 472 at 476–477.
2   *Bradley v Fox*, 129 NE2d 699 at 706 (1955); *Re Stone* [1989] 1 Qd R 351 at 352. In *Re K, decd* [1985] Ch 85 at 100F–H, Vinelott J noted this approach, but thought that English law already provided an easier solution.

Unjust enrichment

11.114   The constructive trust approach has major merits. The legal devolution of title is left untouched, whilst the principle of public policy is enforced through the medium of trust.[1] The imposition of a constructive trust efficiently prevents unjust enrichment.[2] The killer is stripped of any profit arising from his crime, but is not otherwise subjected to penalty or forfeiture in respect of his own inchoate interest under the joint tenancy.[3] Moreover, the application of constructive trust principles enables a focus to be placed on the wider question whether the taking of a benefit by the wrongdoer would be so 'unconscionable' as to attract the operation of the public policy rule.[4] Thus, although the devolution of title is allowed to take its normal course, the relative culpability of the killer's conduct becomes relevant at this secondary stage in determining whether, and if so to what extent, a constructive trust should be imposed on the title-holder.[5] In effect, the constructive trust approach allows a flexible grading of judicial response to the relative wrongfulness of the co-owners.[6] Furthermore, where a constructive trust is actually imposed, this trust is capable of binding a third party to whom the killer has transferred the property.[7]

1   See *Re Thorp and the Real Property Act* (1963) 80 WN (NSW) 61 at 65. In *Re Stone* [1989] 1 Qd R 351 at 352 McPherson J spoke of the constructive trust approach as conferring the advantage of certainty.
2   *Scott on Trusts* (4th edn by W F Fratcher, Boston and Toronto 1989), Vol V, ¶492 (pp 436–437), ¶493.2 (pp 475–485); *Johansen v Pelton*, 87 Cal Rptr 784 at 787 (1970).
3   *Schobelt v Barber* (1967) 60 DLR (2d) 519 at 523–524; *Re Gore* (1972) 23 DLR (3d) 534 at 536, 538; *Re Dreger* (1976) 69 DLR (3d) 47 at 60. There is a marked disinclination in the civil law area against the imposition of a double penalty where the killer has already been subjected to the censure of the criminal law. See *Schobelt v Barber*, supra at 523–524; 41 Minnesota L Rev 639 at 654 (1956–57).
4   See *Public Trustee v Fraser* (1987) 9 NSWLR 433 at 443E–F, 444B per Kearney J.
5   See *Abbey v Lord*, 336 P2d 226 at 230 (1959); *Re Thorp and the Real Property Act* (1963) 80 WN (NSW) 61 at 63; *Re Stone* [1989] 1 Qd R 351 at 353. Compare *Re K, decd* [1985] Ch 85 at 98E–F, where Vinelott J declined to evaluate the degree of moral culpability once it had been established that death was 'the consequence, albeit unintended, of [a] deliberate threat'. This approach has been described as 'blinkered' (see *Public Trustee v Fraser* (1987) 9 NSWLR 433 at 444C, although Kearney J went on to say that consideration of relative culpability would displace the operation of forfeiture only in the 'most exceptional circumstances').

6   See *Re Public Trustee of Manitoba and LeClerc* (1982) 123 DLR (3d) 650 at 651, where the right of survivorship was allowed to operate freely in favour of a killer who had been found not guilty of manslaughter by reason of insanity. In strict terms the case involved no unlawful or wrongful act which could attract the imposition of a constructive trust by way of forfeiture. See also *Re Giles, decd* [1972] Ch 544 at 552A; *Re H (deceased)* [1990] 1 FLR 441 at 446G–447E. Compare, however, *Re Stone* [1989] 1 Qd R 351 at 354 (surviving joint tenant guilty of manslaughter on ground of diminished responsibility). See also *Public Trustee v Fraser* (1987) 9 NSWLR 433 at 444C–E (paranoid schizophrenia leading to finding of diminished responsibility but no lack of moral culpability sufficient to displace forfeiture rule).

7   *Bradley v Fox*, 129 NE2d 699 at 706 (1955) (killer transferred property to defence attorney as security for legal fees). However, the bona fide purchaser without notice should be protected (see Tim Youdan, (1973) 89 LQR 235 at 255–256, commenting on *Re Cash (Deceased)* (1911) 30 NZLR 577 at 580–581).

Form of the constructive trust remedy

11.115   The precise form of the constructive trust required by public policy is open to question. Since the principal concern is that the killer should not be allowed to retain any benefit flowing to him from the slaying of his co-tenant,[1] any benefit coming to him must be held on trust for someone other than himself.[2] In the two-person joint tenancy, this leads fairly clearly to the designation of the victim's estate as the appropriate recipient of that which the killer may not properly retain. Few courts have gone so far as to maintain that there should be a constructive trust for the victim's estate of the entire interest in the co-owned property.[3] The balance of authority favours a solution under which the killer holds the legal title in the co-owned property on constructive trust for himself and the victim's estate in equal shares.

1   In strict theory the killer has not acquired by his wrongful act any larger interest in the property than he had formerly, since joint tenants are each invested with the entire estate from the very inception of the joint tenancy **[para 11.11]**. However, the courts have had little hesitation in ruling that this 'common law fiction' should not be allowed to blind the eyes of equity to the fact that a wrongdoer has in reality benefited by his own wrongful conduct (see *Bradley v Fox*, 129 NE2d 699 at 705 (1955); *National City Bank of Evansville v Bledsoe*, 144 NE2d 710 at 714 (1957)).

2   'Where two persons have an interest in property and the interest of one of them is enlarged by his murder of the other, to the extent to which it is enlarged he holds it upon a constructive trust for the estate of the other' (*Restatement of the Law of Restitution* (St Paul 1937), ¶188 (p 773).

3   See *Colton v Wade*, 80 A2d 923 at 926 (1951); *Neiman v Hurff*, 93 A2d 345 at 347 (1952).

11.116   Even this solution has been challenged on the ground that it indirectly confers upon the killer the benefit of retaining behind the constructive trust a severed one-half share which is henceforth free from the uncertainty of survivorship.[1] Had events taken their normal course, the survivor might well have lost the gamble of longevity anyway.[2] For this reason some courts and commentators have inclined towards a more sophisticated form of constructive trust which allows the killer only a life interest in one half of the co-owned property, the entirety being otherwise held on constructive trust for the victim's estate.[3] However, even this variant of the constructive trust approach is vulnerable to criticism[4] and the preferable view seems to be the simpler conclusion that the co-owned property is held on constructive trust for the killer and his victim's estate equally.

1   *Scott on Trusts* (4th edn by W F Fratcher, Boston and Toronto 1989), Vol V, ¶493.2 (p 476).
2   It ought for this purpose to be immaterial that, because of their respective ages or states of health, it is likely that the killer would have been the survivor in any event (see *Restatement of the Law of Restitution*, ¶188, comment a (p 773)).
3   This is the view favoured in the *Restatement of the Law of Restitution*, ¶188 (pp 773–774). See also *Colton v Wade*, 80 A2d 923 at 925 (1951).
4   The restriction of the killer to a mere life interest in half of the joint property has been criticised as concentrating undue attention on what the victim has lost in derogation of what the killer has always had at least in inchoate form (see *Johansen v Pelton*, 87 Cal Rptr 784 at 791 (1970)). The 'life interest' approach may even comprise an unconstitutional deprivation of the killer's property interest (see *Re Estate of Hart*, 135 Cal Rptr 544 at 547 (1982)). The 'life interest' approach has no application to the phenomenon of double killing (ie murder followed by suicide) where, in any event, the public policy concern to prevent unjust enrichment of the killer is abundantly falsified by the killer's patent lack of interest in the fruits of his crime (see *Johansen v Pelton*, 87 Cal Rptr 784 at 789 (1970); *Re Gore* (1972) 23 DLR (3d) 534 at 537).

Forfeiture Act 1982

11.117   Although the conclusion stated above almost certainly represents the current law in England, the courts in this jurisdiction have a limited statutory discretion to override the draconian effect of this forfeiture rule in cases other than those involving murder.[1] Section 2 of the Forfeiture Act 1982 empowers the court to modify the operation of the rule if, having regard to the conduct of the offender and of the deceased and other material circumstances, 'the justice of the case requires the effect of the rule to be so modified.'[2] The evidence so far available suggests that this discretion is humanely, if not liberally, exercised.[3]

1   Forfeiture Act 1982, s 5.
2   Forfeiture Act 1982, s 2(2).
3   See *Dunbar v Plant* [1998] Ch 412. Compare, however, *Re K, decd* [1986] Ch 180 at 193A–C, 196D–E, affirming [1985] Ch 85 at 100H–102A.

More than two joint tenants

11.118   Where unlawful killing occurs between two joint tenants, the legal conclusion examined above is the same irrespective of whether the reasoning employed is that based on a supposed severance by reason of homicide or on an imposition of constructive trust.[1] However, the mode of legal reasoning adopted may well make a difference where the original joint tenancy comprises more than two co-owners.

1   See *Rasmanis v Jurewitsch* (1970) 70 SR (NSW) 407 at 411F.

11.119   Where A, B and C are joint tenants and A kills B unlawfully (C being entirely blameless), the resulting legal title is clearly vested in A and C as survivors. On the assumption that homicide effects a severance, a tenancy in common of the equitable interest should now arise between A as to one third, B's estate as to one-third, and C as to one third. However, in *Rasmanis v Jurewitsch*,[1] the Court of Appeal of New South Wales preferred the constructive trust approach in ruling that any benefit flowing to the killer from his crime must be held on trust for some person other than himself. That person, decided the Court, was C. In other words, the equitable interests behind the constructive trust belong to C as a tenant in common of one-third, and to A and C as joint tenants of the remaining two-thirds. In this way any profit arising from A's wrong passes to C rather than A, and A retains merely a chance of survivorship in relation to a two-thirds interest. The justice achieved by this result is highly questionable. It would be more consistent with the consensus attained in the case of two joint tenants that B's estate should take a one-third share, A and C remaining joint tenants of a two-thirds interest. Whilst A must not be allowed to derive benefit from his crime, there is no convincing reason why C should benefit either.

1   (1970) 70 SR (NSW) 407 at 412B–G.

SEVERANCE BY MERGER OF INTERESTS

11.120   Severance is also brought about in certain rare situations where the four unities characteristic of joint tenancy are destroyed by a 'merger' of interests. Such a merger occurs, for instance, where A, B and C are joint tenants for life, with remainder to D in fee simple, and A later acquires D's remainder. The effect of this transaction is to destroy unity of interest between A, B and C. A's life interest is seen as merging with the fee simple interest, A's entitlement thereby becoming distinguishable from that of B and C. Under these circumstances severance affects the life interest, A becoming a tenant in common while B and C remain joint tenants for life. A different result occurs, however, if A, B and C begin as joint tenants for life with remainder to A in fee simple. Oddly enough, the dual nature of A's initial entitlements seems not to connote any merger of interests which would precipitate a severance.[1] However, if C subsequently acquires A's fee simple in remainder, C's joint life interest is immediately severed.[2]

1   *Bl Comm*, Vol II, pp 181, 186. It has been doubted whether a modern court would adhere to the logic (or illogic) of this ancient rule: see D Mendes da Costa, (1961–62) 3 Melbourne ULR 137, 306, 433 at 444.
2   *Morgan's Case* (t Eliz 1) 2 And 202, 123 ER 620; *Wiscot's Case* (1599) 2 Co Rep 60b, 76 ER 555 at 556–557.

ARCHAIC FORMS OF CO-OWNERSHIP

11.121   Apart from joint tenancy and tenancy in common, English law has known two other forms of co-ownership, both now archaic.

Tenancy by entireties

11.122 Before 1 January 1926 there existed in England a type of co-ownership known as 'tenancy by entireties'. This form of co-ownership comprised an unseverable joint tenancy between husband and wife,[1] supposedly symbolising the medieval theory of indivisible unity between marital partners.[2] The creation of new tenancies by entireties had been prohibited in 1882[3] and in 1926 all remaining tenancies by entireties were transmuted automatically into joint tenancies.[4]

1   See *Challis*, p 377. See also *Re Estate of King*, 572 SW2d 200 at 211 (1978).
2   For condemnation of this adaptation of the fiction of conjugal unity, see *Registrar-General of New South Wales v Wood* (1926) 39 CLR 46 at 53 per Isaacs J; *United States v Jacobs*, 306 US 363 at 369, 83 L ed 763 at 768 (1939).
3   Married Women's Property Act 1882, ss 1, 5.
4   LPA 1925, Sch 1, Part VI. For a famous, but abortive, attempt to resurrect an unseverable form of co-ownership between spouses, see *Bedson v Bedson* [1965] 2 QB 666 at 678B. Here Lord Denning MR expressed the view that if either spouse could sell his or her severable share, 'it would mean that the purchaser could insist on going into possession himself – with the other spouse there – which is absurd'. It was left to Russell LJ (at 690E) to reiterate the modern consensus that such a prohibition on unilateral severance by spouses is 'without the slightest foundation in law or in equity'. A more direct attempt to revive the tenancy by entireties is to be found in New Zealand's Joint Family Homes Act 1964, s 9(2)(c)(proviso), which states that neither spouse may sever the statutory joint tenancy under which a registered joint family home is held [**para 11.264**].

Coparcenary

11.123 Coparcenary is a form of co-ownership which is now virtually extinct.[1] It arose before 1926 where a person died intestate leaving two or more persons as his 'heir': the latter, if female, inherited together as 'coparceners'. Coparcenary was a hybrid form of co-ownership, bearing attributes of both joint tenancy and tenancy in common: coparceners held in undivided shares without any right of survivorship, even though in most cases the 'four unities' were present.[2]

1   See *Bl Comm*, Vol II, pp 187–191; *Challis*, pp 373–375.
2   For further details, see *Elements of Land Law* (2nd edn 1993), pp 484–485.

THE CO-ORDINATION OF LEGAL AND EQUITABLE CO-OWNERSHIP UNDER A TRUST OF LAND

11.124 Integral to any understanding of concurrent interests in modern land law is the maintenance of a rigid distinction between ownership *at law* and ownership *in equity*.[1] Co-ownership of land is now co-ordinated by the device of the 'trust of land' pursuant to the Trusts of Land and Appointment of Trustees Act 1996.[2] The 1996 Act offers a unified model of landholding suitable for the regulation of various forms of concurrent and also (more rarely) successive entitlement.

1   If this distinction is preserved, it becomes possible to view with equanimity the apparent contradiction that, for instance, the same persons may be simultaneously joint tenants at law and tenants in common in equity [**para 11.148**].
2   See L M Clements, (1998) 61 MLR 56; N Hopkins, [1996] Conv 411; G Ferris and G Battersby, [1998] Conv 168.

Legal and equitable ownership

11.125   The co-ordination of legal and equitable co-ownership under a trust of land becomes much easier to understand once it is realised that, in general terms, legal and equitable title are really concerned with rather different matters. Ownership *at law* comprises merely a nominal or 'paper' title and identifies the persons who are entrusted with fiduciary powers of management and disposition in respect of the land. In other words, the legal title is concerned with the allocation of duties relating to the internal administration and eventual disposition of the land. By contrast, ownership *in equity* determines the distribution of actual beneficial enjoyment – enjoyment of the utility conferred by occupation of the land or of the rents and profits derived from letting the land or, ultimately, of the capital proceeds generated by any transfer of the land.

Mandatory joint tenancy of the legal estate

11.126   Co-ownership of the legal estate under a trust of land mandatorily takes the form of joint tenancy.[1] Unity of title and interest ensures that legal co-owners hold one and the same estate[2] and, under the scheme of the Trusts of Land and Appointment of Trustees Act 1996, hold that legal estate as 'trustees of land'. Thus, if A and B hold as joint tenants at law (ie are joint tenants of a legal estate), all that is meant is that A and B are jointly invested with the paper title and are jointly charged with the managerial and dispositive functions connected with it. Since they are joint tenants, the right of survivorship operates between them in relation to the exercise of these functions.

1   LPA 1925, ss 1(6), 36(2) [**paras 11.21, 11.57**].
2   [**Para 11.24**].

Co-ownership in equity

11.127   Co-ownership of the equitable estate under a trust of land may – depending on the circumstances – take the form of *either* joint tenancy *or* tenancy in common.[1] The difference revolves essentially around the question whether survivorship operates between the co-owners in respect of beneficial entitlement or whether the co-owners have crystallised matters of entitlement in the form of individually distinct and indefeasible shareholdings. If the co-owners are *joint tenants* in equity, this means merely that each equitable joint tenant is exposed to the risk that his premature death will concentrate beneficial enjoyment in the surviving joint tenant or joint tenants to the exclusion of the deceased's successors. If, however, an equitable co-owner is a *tenant in common* (whether from the outset or by subsequent severance), this co-owner is immune from the caprice of survivorship and his quantum of beneficial ownership remains irreducibly within his own control.

1   [Para 11.56].

Trustees of land may also be beneficiaries

11.128 A firm distinction between legal and equitable ownership lies at the heart of every trust of land, but there is nothing, in principle, to prevent some or all of the trustees and beneficiaries from being the same persons, ie A and B may hold a legal estate on trust for themselves as beneficiaries. Where, however, the identity of the trustees and beneficiaries coalesces in this way, their respective functions remain crucially different. In their capacity as trustees of the legal estate, A and B are concerned with fiduciary powers of management and disposition; in their capacity as co-owners of the equitable estate, A and B are concerned with beneficial enjoyment in the form of money and actual occupation. In the performance of their different roles they wear quite separate hats; their various headgear must never be confused.

Differing status at law and in equity

11.129 It is therefore entirely possible that, in certain cases, two co-owners, A and B, may be joint tenants of both the legal and equitable estates (see *Fig. 26*). There is, however, no inherent contradiction in the idea that, in other circumstances, A and B may be simultaneously *joint tenants* at law and *tenants in common* in equity (see *Fig. 27*). In the latter kinds of case, all that is really being said is that A and B are jointly charged with the administrative functions connected with the paper title and that these functions will eventually be concentrated in the survivor. In relation, however, to the fruits of beneficial enjoyment, A and B, as tenants in common, each enjoy a distinct and irreducible share free from the fateful gamble on longevity. Each has a quantifiable share in the money value of the co-owned property and, should A and B (as legal joint tenants) ultimately transfer their legal estate to a purchaser, it is in their respective capacities as beneficial tenants in common that each will claim a share in the capital proceeds of sale.

COVERAGE OF THE TRUST OF LAND AFTER 1996

11.130 The 'trust of land' introduced by the Trusts of Land and Appointment of Trustees Act 1996 provides a unitary structure for the governance of a wide variety of beneficial entitlements in land which, before the commencement of the 1996 Act, were incompletely regulated by an untidy collection of

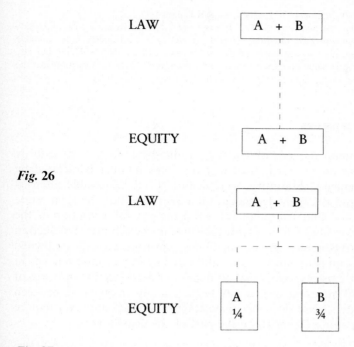

Fig. 26

Fig. 27

legislative measures.[1] Principal amongst the forms of beneficial entitlement covered by the 1996 Act are cases of concurrent interests,[2] successive interests[3] and bare trusts.[4] The regime of the 'trust of land' has undoubtedly brought about a significant rationalisation of the less attractive and more artificial features of the law governing trusts for sale and strict settlements.

1   [**Para 9.231**].
2   [**Para 11.145**].
3   [**Para 11.153**].
4   [**Para 11.154**].

OVERRIDING CONSTRAINTS ON THE TRUST OF LAND

11.131   Few restraints curtail the potential shape of the trust of land, but the following are important.

No trusteeship for minors

11.132   The legal estate subject to a trust of land may be held only by persons who have attained the age of 18 years,[1] although there is no prohibition on a minor holding some beneficial entitlement behind the trust. Any attempt to convey a legal estate to a minor is clearly ineffective and operates instead as a declaration that the land is held in trust for the minor.[2]

1   LPA 1925, ss 1(6), 20, 205(1)(v); TOLATA 1996, Sch 1, para 1(1)(a).
2   TOLATA 1996, s 2(1), (6), Sch 1, para 1(1)(b) [**paras 2.132, 7.1**]. A conveyance of a legal estate
     to a minor before 1997 operated under the Settled Land Act 1925 as an agreement for valuable
     consideration to execute a settlement in favour of the minor (SLA 1925, s 27(1)), but any
     agreement of this nature subsisting on 1 January 1997 is converted into a declaration that the
     land is held on trust for the minor (TOLATA 1996, s 2(6), Sch 1, para 1(3)).

Maximum of four trustees

11.133   The maximum number of trustees of the legal estate – necessarily
joint tenants of that estate – is limited to *four*.[1] This number is dictated by
conveyancing convenience. Statutory overreaching[2] of the equitable interests
behind a trust of land is largely dependent on a disposition of the legal estate
effected by 'trustees of land' (in the plural).[3] But the general restriction of the
trusteeship to a maximum of four – with the constant possibility of reduction
by mortality and survivorship – greatly facilitates conveyances of the co-owned
legal estate.[4] The compulsory unity of the title vested by way of joint tenancy in
a limited number of trustees means that no purchaser need face the prospect of
investigating title to an estate which has been horribly fragmented between
numerous shareholders.[5] Nor does any disposition of a legal estate ever require
more than four signatures (at most) on the part of the disponors.

1   TA 1925, s 34(2); LPA 1925, s 34(2). The limitation to four trustees does not apply to land
     vested in trustees for charitable, ecclesiastical or public purposes (TA 1925, s 34(3)).
2   [**Paras 2.165, 11.195**].
3   See LPA 1925, s 2(1)(ii) [**para 11.199**].
4   See *State Bank of India v Sood* [1997] Ch 276 at 281F per Peter Gibson LJ.
5   [**Para 11.27**].

No limit on the number of beneficial owners

11.134   Although the number of legal owners is strictly limited, there is no
corresponding restriction on the number of potential co-owners of the equitable estate under a trust of land (except in the ultimate sense that the number of
beneficiaries must not be so impossibly large as to render the trust unworkable).

Aberrant transfers of the legal estate

11.135   Any attempt to transfer a legal estate into the names of more than
four persons results, by force of statute, in a vesting of this estate by way of
joint tenancy in the first four persons named in the transfer who are willing and
able to act as trustees.[1] A difficulty likewise ensues in respect of any misguided
attempt to transfer a legal estate to persons otherwise than as joint tenants.
Clearly no legal estate can be held in undivided shares and aberrant transfers of
this kind are now given effect in equity behind a trust of land implied by
statute. If, for instance, a legal estate is purportedly transferred to A, B and C as

tenants in common in equal shares, then, provided that all are of full age, the transfer is construed as a grant of the legal estate to A, B and C as joint tenants, to hold on an implied trust for themselves as equitable tenants in common (see *Fig. 28*).[2] A similar result follows if a legal estate is transferred to more than four persons as tenants in common (eg to A, B, C, D, E and F in equal shares). The first four persons named in the grant become necessarily joint tenants of the legal estate, thereafter holding on a statutorily implied trust of land for all six grantees as tenants in common of the equitable interest (see *Fig. 29*).[3] In other words, the tenancy in common envisaged by the transfer is given effect only in the beneficial ownership of the land.[4]

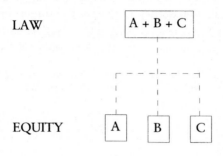

Fig. 28

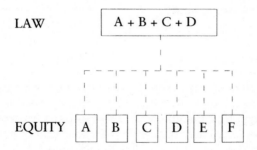

Fig. 29

1   TA 1925, s 34(2); LPA 1925, s 34(2).
2   LPA 1925, s 34(2).
3   LPA 1925, s 34(2). See eg *Persey and Another v Bazley* (1984) 47 P & CR 37 at 39; [1985] Conv 292 (J Martin). Designated grantees other than the first four named are thus relegated, rather arbitrarily, to beneficial ownership only (see (1944) 9 Conv (NS) 37 at 38). The significance of exclusion from the trusteeship is diminished by the presence of a duty under TOLATA 1996, s 11(1) to consult all beneficiaries prior to the exercise of trustees' functions **[para 11.183]**.
4   If, in either of the cases considered here, the grant is made not by a deed inter vivos but by testamentary disposition, the legal estate is likewise held on a statutorily implied trust of land, the only difference being that the legal estate vests in the testator's personal representatives (LPA 1925, s 34(3)).

LEGAL OWNERSHIP VESTED IN ONLY ONE TRUSTEE

11.136 Statute does not directly specify the *minimum* number of trustees required to hold the legal estate under a trust of land. It is, however, the clear policy of the 1925 property legislation (as reinforced by the Trusts of Land and Appointment of Trustees Act 1996 and the Land Registration Act 2002) that the legal estate associated with a trust of land should, at least for the purpose of dealings, be held by not fewer than two trustees.[1] No overreaching conveyance can normally be made by fewer than two trustees of land.[2] Nor can a sole trustee (other than a trust corporation) give a valid receipt for the proceeds of sale or other capital money arising under a trust of land.[3] In consequence a sole trustee of land who deals unilaterally is generally acting in breach of trust.

1   See *Taylor v Taylor (1968)* [1968] 1 WLR 378 at 382G per Danckwerts LJ; *Family Law: Third Report on Family Property* (Law Com No 86, June 1978), para 1.250. See now TOLATA 1996, s 19(3)(c) **[para 11.182]**.
2   LPA 1925, ss 2(1)(i)–(ii), 27(2). See *City of London Building Society v Flegg* [1988] AC 54 at 74C per Lord Templeman, 89A–G per Lord Oliver of Aylmerton.
3   TA 1925, s 14(2)(a).

Express trusts of land

11.137 For present purposes a distinction must be drawn between registered and unregistered estates in land.

Unregistered estates

11.138 Where there is an express trust of an unregistered legal estate, practical motivations require that this estate (unless owned by a trust corporation) should be held by a minimum of two persons as trustees. If the trust has been created by an instrument of transfer to a sole legal owner, the existence of the trust appears on the face of the documentary title and no prudent purchaser will thereafter accept a disposition of the legal estate except where payment of capital money can be made to trustees of land (in the plural).[1]

1   Where a sole legal owner declares a trust *subsequently* to his own acquisition of the legal title, documentary evidence of the trust may become separated from the deeds bundle. In such circumstances the existence of the trust will not be evident from the title offered to any later purchaser, who then takes free of the trust interests only if he can show that he is a bona fide purchaser of a legal estate for value without notice **[para 12.356]**.

Registered estates

11.139 A similar conveyancing objective is achieved in registered land by rules which require the entry of a 'restriction' in the relevant registered title prohibiting the registration of future dispositions by any sole proprietor who holds on trust.[1] On the acquisition of an unregistered estate which requires first registration of title or on the acquisition of an already registered estate, the primary onus is on the sole trustee (other than a trust corporation) to apply for the appropriate 'restriction' to be entered in the proprietorship register of his title.[2] If the trustee fails to comply with his obligation in this regard, application for entry of the 'restriction' may be made by any beneficiary of the trust.[3] The net effect of these rules is, in practice, to necessitate the appointment of at least one additional trustee for the purpose of any disposition of the registered estate.

1   **[Para 7.53]**.
2   LRR 2003, r 94(2). If a sole registered proprietor becomes subject to a trust subsequently to his registration as legal owner, he again must apply for the necessary 'restriction' to be entered in the register of his title (LRR 2003, r 94(1)(a)).
3   LRA 2002, s 43(1)(c); LRR 2003, r 93(a).

Implied trusts of land

11.140   Sole trusteeship under an *implied* trust of land raises more problematic issues. As has already been observed, there must be numerous trusts of land which arise by implication from circumstance and which involve some kind of resulting or constructive trust silently engrafted upon an existing sole ownership of a legal estate. In such cases the equitable co-ownership created by the trust – usually in the form of beneficial tenancy in common – leaves no documentary trace precisely because the trust in question is implied.[1] In most instances the legal owner himself is blissfully unaware that he is a 'trustee of land' under the Trusts of Land and Appointment of Trustees Act 1996 and, for this reason, is unlikely, in cases of registered title, to comply with the obligation to apply for the entry of a 'restriction' on dispositions of the registered estate by a sole proprietor.[2] Under the 'two trustee rule', however, a purchaser who innocently deals with such a trustee, on the basis of his apparently sole legal title, is clearly unable to claim that he has statutorily overreached the beneficial interests behind the trust and may find, to his cost, that these interests remain binding on him.[3]

1   See, however, LRA 2002, s 42(1)(b) **[para 11.191]**.
2   See LRR 2003, r 94(1)(a), (2).
3   **[Para 12.201]**. Precisely the same hazard affects the purchaser of an unregistered legal estate which is held on an implied trust **[para 12.361]**.

ASSIMILATION OF EXISTING TRUST FORMS WITHIN THE 'TRUST OF LAND'

11.141   Concurrent ownership arises under a trust of land in a variety of cases. The concurrent ownership may be the result of an express trust[1] or may emerge from some resulting[2] or constructive[3] trust. Prior to 1997 the courts endeavoured, sometimes by way of strained statutory construction, to bring virtually all co-ownership of land within the legislative device of the 'trust for sale',[4] largely in order that co-ownership trusts should attract the advantageous consequence of overreaching which statute provided in the case of 'trusts for sale'. Nowadays such judicial ingenuity is unnecessary. The 'trust of land' introduced by the Trusts of Land and Appointment of Trustees Act 1996 resolves many of the difficulties which beset the operation of the old trust for sale. As Neuberger J observed in *Mortgage Corporation v Shaire*,[5] the 1996 Act 'has the effect of rendering trusts for sale obsolete, including those in existence on 1 January 1997, and replacing them with the less arcane and simpler trusts of land.'

1   **[Para 9.184]**.
2   **[Para 10.8]**.
3   **[Para 10.58]**.
4   **[Para 9.232]**.
5   [2001] Ch 743 at 757E–F.

Broad definition of the 'trust of land'

11.142   The device of the 'trust of land' is liberally defined by the 1996 Act. A 'trust of land' comprises 'any trust of property which consists of or includes land',[1] irrespective of the date of creation or origin of that trust.[2] The 'trust of land' is explicitly defined as inclusive of 'any description of trust', with the consequence that it embraces all relevant trusts, 'whether express, implied, resulting or constructive', together with trusts for sale and bare trusts.[3] A 'trust of land' cannot, however, include land governed by the Settled Land Act 1925: trusts of land and strict settlements are mutually exclusive.[4]

1   TOLATA 1996, s 1(1)(a). A 'trust of land' cannot, however, include land governed by the Universities and College Estates Act 1925, s 1(3).
2   TOLATA 1996, s 1(2)(b).
3   TOLATA 1996, s 1(2)(a).
4   TOLATA 1996, s 1(3). See also SLA 1925, s 1(7).

Suppression of implied 'trusts for sale'

11.143   The old cases of implied (or 'statutory') trusts for sale,[1] which were forced – sometimes in procrustean manner – within the reach of the Law of Property Act 1925,[2] are now automatically converted into 'trusts of land'.[3] This conversion operates irrespective of the date of origin of such trusts,[4] although it is perhaps surprising that no explicit attempt is made in the 1996 Act to regularise the haphazard coverage of the former implied 'trusts for sale'. It is at least debatable whether a statutory trust for sale truly arose, for instance, in the circumstances of *Bull v Bull*.[5] However, the legislative omission to address such cases by more direct provision in the 1996 Act is doubtless attributable to the draftsman's assumption that all cases of legal and/or equitable co-ownership of land are now safely gathered within the expansive definition of the 'trust of land' as inclusive of trusts of 'any description ... whether express, implied, resulting or constructive.'[6] The lacunae which were left exposed by the incomplete coverage of the old statutory 'trusts for sale' related, in the main, to beneficial entitlements arising under some form of express or (more usually) implied trust.[7]

1   See LPA 1925, ss 34(2)–(3), 36(1) (original version).
2   **[Para 9.232]**.
3   TOLATA 1996, s 5(1), Sch 2, paras 3–4.
4   TOLATA 1996, Sch 2, paras 3(6), 4(4).
5   [1955] 1 QB 234 **[para 9.233]**.
6   TOLATA 1996, s 1(2)(a).
7   For example, the circumstances of *Bull v Bull* [1955] 1 QB 234 comprised a perfectly standard case of resulting trust arising from the unequal provision of purchase money. Under the inclusive definitional terms of TOLATA 1996, s 1(2)(a), these circumstances would today generate a trust of land pursuant to which the relevant legal estate is held on trust for the financial contributors as beneficial tenants in common.

Express trusts for sale are subsumed

11.144   Old and new express trusts for sale can exist under the Trusts of Land and Appointment of Trustees Act 1996 if the author of the trust has explicitly directed that land should be held on trust 'for sale', thereby demonstrating an intention that the subject land be sold and the proceeds divided between the designated beneficiaries. But such trusts for sale are now subsumed within the general machinery of the 'trust of land' and are, indeed, made relatively pointless by the overriding statutory mandate that the trustees have, in all cases, an irreducible implied power to postpone sale indefinitely.[1] Moreover, the Trusts of Land and Appointment of Trustees Act 1996 explicitly abandons the old overworked doctrine of conversion,[2] under which the equitable interests of trust for sale beneficiaries were treated as mere interests in the prospective sale proceeds of the land. Land held subject to a trust for sale is no longer, therefore, to be regarded as personalty.

1   TOLATA 1996, s 4(1) **[para 9.243]**. The Law Commission recommended that a power to retain land should be statutorily implied irrespective of contrary intention (Law Com No 181 (1989), para 3.7).
2   See TOLATA 1996, s 3(1) **[para 9.234]**.

CONCURRENT INTERESTS UNDER A TRUST OF LAND

11.145   The range of concurrent entitlement brought within the ambit of the trust of land includes the following permutations of concurrent entitlement by way of joint tenancy and tenancy in common. In all these cases the co-ownership in question (and its rights and obligations) are governed by the statutory regime contained in the Law of Property Act 1925 as adapted by the Trusts of Land and Appointment of Trustees Act 1996 and the Land Registration Act 2002.

Joint tenancy both at law and in equity

11.146   A legal estate subject to a trust of land may be held by two or more (but not normally more than four) joint tenants, holding on trust for themselves or any number of others as joint tenants of the equitable estate.[1] Indeed joint ownership both at law and in equity is today the landholding of choice for most matrimonial homes (see *Fig.* 30), largely because of the convenience conferred by the right of survivorship.[2] Such an arrangement is usually brought about as an express trust of land contained in the document of transfer of the legal estate (thus complying with section 53(1)(b) of the Law of Property Act 1925[3]).

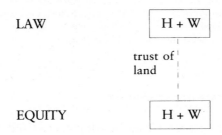

Fig. 30

1   In this case and in the following examples, it matters not whether the legal estate held on trust is a fee simple or a term of years absolute. Unfamiliar though the terminology may be, a trust of land is interposed even in the case of co-ownership of the legal estate comprised in a periodic tenancy. The co-owners hold that legal estate as joint tenants on trust for themselves as joint tenants in equity (see *Hammersmith and Fulham LBC v Monk* [1992] 1 AC 478 at 490C–F per Lord Bridge of Harwich, 493B–F per Lord Browne-Wilkinson). See also *Savage v Dunningham* [1974] Ch 181 at 184G–H.
2   [**Para 11.13**].
3   [**Para 9.188**].

11.147   More rarely beneficial joint tenancy arises by implication from the sheer circumstance that a legal estate has been vested in joint names without any specification of the equitable ownership. In such cases the transfer document has performed its minimal purpose of identifying the new owners at law but does not contain any express stipulation as to beneficial ownership.[1] In the total absence of any evidence of the transferees' intentions as to beneficial entitlement or as to the way in which the purchase money was contributed,[2] 'equity follows the law' and the transferees take as joint tenants both at law and in equity.[3] In default of any expressly created trust of land, these transferees hold their legal estate on a trust of land implied by statute.[4]

1   See, however, LRA 2002, s 25(1); LRR 2003, rr 23(1), 58, 206(1), Sch 1 (Forms FR1 and TR1) [**paras 9.179, 9.197**].
2   The relevance of such matters in determining beneficial ownership is discussed in Chapter 10 [**paras 10.9, 10.14**].
3   See *Pettitt v Pettitt* [1970] AC 777 at 814A; *Cowcher v Cowcher* [1972] 1 WLR 425 at 430E; *Bernard v Josephs* [1982] Ch 391 at 402B–C; *Marshall v Marshall* (Unreported, Court of Appeal, 2 October 1998) per Mummery LJ; *McKenzie v McKenzie* [2003] EWHC 601 (Ch)

at [65]. The onus of proving otherwise rests on any person who disputes that the beneficial entitlement coincides with the legal entitlement (*Crisp v Mullings* (1975) 239 EG 119 per Russell LJ).

4   LPA 1925, s 36(1); TOLATA 1996, s 1(1)–(2).

Joint tenancy at law coupled with tenancy in common in equity

11.148   It is possible that the legal estate subject to a trust of land may be held by two or more trustees as joint tenants on trust for two or more persons as beneficial tenants in common (see *Fig. 31*).[1] Such an outcome may, of course, emerge under a trust of land which expressly declares the existence of an equitable tenancy in common in specified proportions.[2] It more commonly arises, in the absence of an express declaration of trust, where there is evidence that the purchase of a legal estate was funded by unequal contributions of money provided by persons who, in consequence of a presumed resulting trust,[3] take proportionate shares of the equitable ownership.[4] Here the transferees of the legal estate hold for themselves as beneficial tenants in common under a trust of land which arises impliedly from an expansive judicial gloss upon the Law of Property Act 1925[5] or (more appropriately) from the clear indication in the 1996 Act that any resulting or constructive trust necessarily comes within the statutory definition of a 'trust of land'.[6]

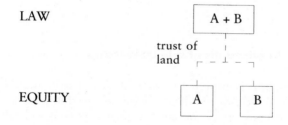

Fig. **31**

1   The beneficial tenants in common may well be the same persons as the joint tenants of the legal estate **[para 11.128]**.

2   See LPA 1925, s 53(1)(b) **[para 9.188]**. Joint transferees of a registered estate may now indicate a preference for beneficial tenancy in common in equal or other shares (see LRA 2002, s 25(1); LRR 2003, rr 58, 206(1), Sch 1 **[para 9.197]**).

3   **[Para 10.11]**. See *Winsper v Perrett* (Unreported, Chancery Division, 13 February 2001) at [28] per Judge Kim Lewison QC (although here the presumed resulting trust was displaced by an express agreement for beneficial joint tenancy creative of a constructive trust).

4   This is one of those cases in which, regardless of the position at law, equity leans in favour of undivided shares **[para 11.60]**.

5   See LPA 1925, ss 34(1), 36(1); *Re Buchanan-Wollaston's Conveyance* [1939] Ch 738 at 744; *Goodman v Gallant* [1986] Fam 106 at 110C–D.

6   See TOLATA 1996, s 1(1)–(2) **[para 11.130]**.

Sole trusteeship coupled with co-ownership in equity

11.149 Some instances of implied trust (whether resulting or constructive) can cause a legal title held by one person alone to be impressed by a trust of land for two or more beneficial owners (almost always as equitable tenants in common). Such is often the case where two or more persons join together in funding a purchase of a legal estate which is transferred into the name of only one (see *Fig.* 32). In default of any expressly declared trust and in the absence of any intention of gift or loan, there arises, in favour of the financial contributors, an implied trust of the legal estate under which each holds beneficially as a tenant in common in proportion to his or her own contribution. This implied trust constitutes a 'trust of land' within the meaning of the Trusts of Land and Appointment of Trustees Act 1996.

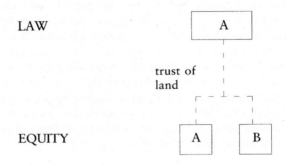

Fig. 32

Conveyancing implications of sole trusteeship

11.150 Although it is entirely proper that such a trust should be accommodated within the 1996 Act, the beneficial co-ownership generated by informal circumstances of co-operative purchase is highly unlikely to be disclosed by the documentary title of the sole trustee. Precisely because the trust arises by implication, the legal owner appears to the outside world to be solely entitled both at law and in equity. Indeed, the operation of the equitable doctrines of resulting and constructive trust brings about the consequence that vast numbers of landowners are elevated to the status of a trustee of land – a status which may not only surprise the unwitting owner but can also introduce unsuspected complications for third parties with whom he later deals. On any subsequent disposition relating to the legal estate, the sole trustee almost inevitably – and usually quite innocently – seems to be offering a good title by declaring that he transfers the land or makes a mortgage with 'full title guarantee' (ie free of any trust interests affecting the land). Such circumstances raise difficult questions of priority between third parties who deal with the trustee in good faith and those beneficiaries (other than the trustee) whose beneficial entitlement may have subsisted undisclosed behind the implied trust. In particular, the scene is set for an awkward confrontation between the residential interests of beneficial co-owners behind a trust of the family home and the commercial interests of strangers who purchase the legal estate to which that latent trust relates.[1]

1   See Chapter 12 [**paras 12.201, 12.356**].

Duty to appoint a second trustee

11.151   Largely in view of these potential difficulties, the scheme of the 1925 legislation has always implicitly required that sole trusteeship of a legal estate in land be regularised, at least for the purpose of dealings,[1] by the appointment of a second trustee as co-owner of that estate. Dispositions of the legal estate executed by two trustees are liable to have overreaching effect,[2] thus facilitating the disponee (who takes a title free of beneficial interests) whilst safeguarding those same beneficial interests as equivalent entitlements in the capital proceeds of the transaction. There is no direct statutory provision which makes it mandatory for a sole trustee of land to appoint an additional trustee as co-owner of the legal estate. However, the same effect is procured indirectly by the imposition of a duty on a sole trustee of a registered estate (other than a trust corporation) to apply for the entry of a 'restriction' against his own title which prohibits any future disposition by a sole proprietor.[3] Precisely how many sole trustees are likely to comply with (or even know about) this obligation is unclear, but the purpose of entering such a 'restriction' is, quite plainly, to prevent any future dealings by a sole trustee which would fail to attract the advantageous effects of statutory overreaching.

1   See LPA 1925, s 27(2).
2   [**Paras 2.168, 11.199**].
3   LRR 2003, r 94(1)(a), (2) [**paras 7.53, 11.139**].

Transfer to co-owners one of whom is a minor

11.152   Further problems are raised by a transfer of a legal estate to persons who include amongst their number one who is a minor. Land may be conveyed, for instance, to A, B and C, under circumstances where C is not yet aged 18. C, being a minor, clearly cannot hold a legal estate in land,[1] but the Trusts of Land and Appointment of Trustees Act 1996 directs that the conveyance (if made on or after 1 January 1997) operates instead to vest the relevant estate in A and B on a trust of land for A, B and C.[2]

1   [**Para 11.132**].
2   TOLATA 1996, ss 1(1)–(2), 2(6), Sch 1, para 1(2).

SUCCESSIVE INTERESTS UNDER A TRUST OF LAND

11.153   Since the Trusts of Land and Appointment of Trustees Act 1996 prohibits any further creation of strict settlements under the Settled Land

Act 1925,[1] new successive interests can be created only under a trust of land. The declaration of trust containing the successive equitable interests must be evidenced by signed writing.[2] Of the many possible forms of successive entitlement, the most obvious is the equitable life interest followed by an equitable remainder in fee simple.[3] In order to bring about such successive ownership in equity, the settlor must *either* constitute himself a trustee of land, holding the legal estate on the terms of the trust which he has declared (see *Fig.* 33) *or* vest the legal estate in nominated trustees of land for the same purpose (see *Fig.* 34). Once again, if the legal title under such a trust is or becomes vested in only one person as trustee (other than in the case of a trust corporation), the sole proprietor is obliged, in the case of registered land, to apply for the entry of a 'restriction' against his own title which prohibits future dispositions of the registered estate without the appointment of an additional trustee.[4]

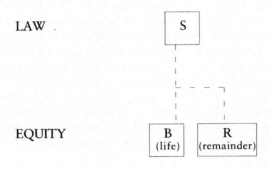

Fig. 33

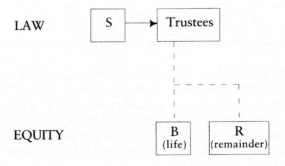

Fig. 34

1   TOLATA 1996, s 2(1) **[para 9.207]**.
2   LPA 1925, s 53(1)(b) **[para 9.188]**.
3   **[Para 1.140]**.
4   LRR 2003, r 94(1)(a), (2) **[para 11.139]**.

BARE TRUSTS

11.154 A bare trust arises where a title is vested in a trustee who has no active duties of management to perform.[1] The trustee is merely the repository of the naked or bare title. A bare trust is a species of trust in which the trustee's control over the trust property is minimal and the beneficiary's control is paramount.[2] The most common example is found where, in relation to the same estate in land, A is absolutely entitled at law and the entire beneficial interest is, for some reason or other, isolated in B (see *Fig. 35*).[3]

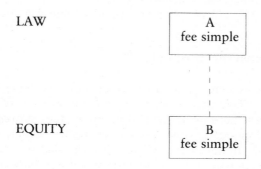

LAW — A fee simple

EQUITY — B fee simple

Fig. 35

1   *Re Cunningham and Frayling* [1891] 2 Ch 567 at 572 per Stirling J. See *Thorpe v Bristile Ltd* (1996) 16 WAR 500 at 505D–G; *Chief Commr of Stamp Duties v ISPT Pty Ltd* (1997) 45 NSWLR 639 at 651C–D per Mason P. A bare trust is not incompatible with the existence of some active duties in the trustee – but not of management. See *Corumo Holdings Pty Ltd v C Itoh Ltd* (1991) 24 NSWLR 370 at 398E per Meagher JA ('as a matter of strict logic, almost no situation can be postulated where a trustee cannot in some circumstances have active duties to perform').
2   The beneficiary of the bare trust 'has the entire economic interest in the assets' (*Jerome v HM Inspector of Taxes* [2004] 1 WLR 1409 at [2] per Lord Hoffmann).
3   A 'bare trustee' or 'naked trustee' means 'a trustee without any beneficial interest' (*Morgan v Swansea Urban Sanitary Authority* (1878) 9 Ch D 582 at 585 per Jessel MR). See also *Lloyds Bank plc v Carrick* [1996] 4 All ER 630 at 637h–j per Morritt LJ, but compare *Thorpe v Bristile Ltd* (1996) 16 WAR 500 at 505A–B.

The balance of power within a bare trust

11.155 Although he has power to dispose of the legal title in the trust property, the bare trustee must at all times comply with the directions as to disposition given by his beneficiary.[1] The beneficiary, as owner of the absolute beneficial interest is the only person with any right to enjoy the land and derive value from it. In this sense, the bare trust provides the ultimate demonstration of the idea that legal ownership is merely formal or titular, the substance of ownership residing in equitable title.[2] By an application of the rule in *Saunders v Vautier*,[3] the bare beneficiary, if *sui iuris* (ie of full age and sound mind), may terminate the trust and direct a transfer of the legal estate to himself[4] or to some nominated third person.[5]

1   See *Christie v Ovington* (1875) 1 Ch D 279 at 281 per Hall V-C.
2   **[Paras 1.189, 11.20]**.
3   (1841) 4 Beav 115 at 116, 49 ER 282, Cr & Ph 240 at 249, 41 ER 482 at 485.
4   Such a transfer destroys the bare trust by constituting B the sole owner at law and in equity
     (see *Commissioner of Stamp Duties (Queensland) v Livingston* [1965] AC 694 at 712C–D per
     Viscount Radcliffe **[para 1.161]**). Unification of title in the beneficiary is the natural end of a
     bare trust. Bare trusts are intrinsically anomalous arrangements which connote some state of
     disequilibrium: the 'paper' title is for the time being vested in one who has no beneficial stake
     in the property. Equity accordingly favours a return to a state of equilibrium, this being most
     easily achieved by means of a transfer of title to the equitable owner. This outcome is now
     reinforced by the bare trustee's statutory right to insist that the beneficiary, if *sui iuris*, must
     take the legal title from him (TOLATA 1996, s 6(2)).
5   It was uncertain prior to 1997 whether such a transfer destroyed the bare trust (infra).

Assimilation within the 'trust of land'

11.156   Bare trusts were always a source of difficulty under the 1925 legislation. Particularly where they took the form (as in *Fig.* 35) of absolute estates
isolated in different persons at law and in equity, they proved extraordinarily
awkward to accommodate within the conveyancing machinery of the Law of
Property Act 1925. In the absence of any co-ownership subsisting either at law
or in equity, the configuration of interests within the bare trust provided no
ground for the implication of a statutory trust for sale.[1] Accordingly it seemed
problematic to attribute to a bare trustee any competence to make an overreaching conveyance of the legal estate,[2] and the Law Commission finally
suggested that, in order to secure greater protection for purchasers, the bare
trust should be brought within the scope of its proposed new 'trust of land'.[3]
This result has now been achieved under the Trusts of Land and Appointment
of Trustees Act 1996[4] although, for the sake of conformity with the legislative
scheme, the legal title associated with a bare trust should – at least for the
purpose of dealings – be vested in not fewer than two trustees.

1   See eg Law Commission, *Trusts of Land: Overreaching* (Law Com Working Paper No 106,
     January 1988), para 3.3; *Transfer of Land: Overreaching: Beneficiaries in Occupation* (Law
     Com No 188, December 1989), paras 1.4, 2.17.
2   The Law Commission expressed the view in 1988 that a beneficial interest under a bare trust
     was overreachable only through the creation of an *ad hoc* trust pursuant to LPA 1925, s 2(2)
     [para 11.202]. See Law Commission, Working Paper No 106 (1988), para 3.3, but compare C
     Harpum, [1990] CLJ 277 at 303–304, 310. For want of overreaching, the impact on a
     purchaser of the beneficial interest under a bare trust probably depended in unregistered land
     on the equitable doctrine of notice (see *Thorpe v Bristile Ltd* (1996) 16 WAR 500 at 505) or, if
     the bare trust arose from an estate contract, on registration of a land charge (see *Lloyds
     Bank plc v Carrick* [1996] 4 All ER 630 **[paras 9.40, 10.87]**). In registered land the effect of a
     bare trust turned on whether that interest was a protected minor interest or an overriding
     interest (see *Hodgson v Marks* [1971] Ch 892 **[para 12.178]**).
3   Law Com No 181 (1989), paras 7.1, 20.2.
4   See TOLATA 1996, s 1(2)(a).

POWERS OF THE TRUSTEES OF LAND

11.157 Irrespective of the precise nature of the beneficial entitlement involved (whether concurrent or successive), the Trusts of Land and Appointment of Trustees Act 1996 attempts to confer a uniform range of powers upon those who hold the legal estate under the new unitary trust of land.[1] In keeping with the broad concept of a trust, the functions of the trustees are essentially concerned with management and disposition, beneficial enjoyment being reserved for those who hold the equitable interests under the trust.[2]

1   The conferment of powers is, however, cloaked in language of some obscurity. On some of the difficulties of construction exposed in the 1996 Act, see G Ferris and G Battersby, 'The General Principles of Overreaching and the Modern Legislative Reforms, 1996–2002' (2003) 119 LQR 94.
2   **[Paras 1.164, 11.125]**.

Trustees generally have the powers of an absolute owner

11.158   In marked contrast to the more limited powers statutorily conferred on legal owners under the historic strict settlement or trust for sale, the 1996 Act declares that, in relation to the land subject to the trust, the trustees of land have 'all the powers of an absolute owner.'[1] These extensive powers may be excluded by express provision in any 'disposition'[2] creating a trust of land[3] and are, in any event, available to trustees of land only for the purpose of 'exercising their functions as trustees.'[4] The powers of the trustees (except in relation to charitable trusts) must be exercised unanimously or not at all.[5]

1   TOLATA 1996, s 6(1). In the case of a registered estate, see also LRA 2002, ss 23(1), 24 **[para 7.49]**.
2   A 'disposition' is defined, by reference to LPA 1925, s 205(1)(ii), as including a 'conveyance', a term which is itself broad enough to embrace a declaration of trust by a settlor (see TOLATA 1996, s 23(2)).
3   TOLATA 1996, s 8(1). The statutorily defined powers of trustees may not be cut back in the case of charitable, ecclesiastical or public trusts (TOLATA 1996, s 8(3)) or in contravention of any enactment which inhibits such a limitation of the trustees' powers (TOLATA 1996, s 8(4)). Compare the much more comprehensive prohibition in Settled Land Act 1925, s 106(1), of any curtailment of powers under a strict settlement **[para 9.214]**.
4   TOLATA 1996, s 6(1). The trustees' powers must not be 'exercised in contravention of … any other enactment or any rule of law or equity' (TOLATA 1996, s 6(6)). Nor may the powers be exercised in breach of any order of the court or of the Charity Commissioners (TOLATA 1996, s 6(7)).
5   Application may always be made to the court for an order resolving any disagreement between the trustees (TOLATA 1996, s 14(1)–(2)).

The powers of trustees are fiduciary

11.159   Trustees of land clearly stand as fiduciaries in respect of their powers. In the exercise of the 'powers of an absolute owner', they are obliged, somewhat tautologically, to 'have regard to the rights of the beneficiaries.'[1]

Thus for instance, in making any disposition of the trust land, they must obtain the best price reasonably obtainable.[2] Moreover, in the exercise of any function relating to trust land, the trustees – in the absence of contrary provision – have a duty, so far as practicable, to 'consult the beneficiaries of full age' and, so far as consistent with the 'general interest of the trust', to give effect to 'the wishes of those beneficiaries, or (in case of dispute) of the majority (according to the value of their combined interests).'[3] In addition to these responsibilities, the Trustee Act 2000 now imposes a 'duty of care' on trustees, ie a duty to exercise 'such care and skill as is reasonable in the circumstances', having particular regard to any special knowledge or experience possessed or professed by any relevant trustee or which it would be 'reasonable to expect' of that trustee if acting as trustee in the course of a particular business or profession.[4] This 'duty of care' applies generally to the exercise by land trustees of any of the 'powers of an absolute owner'.[5]

1   TOLATA 1996, s 6(5).
2   See eg *George v McDonald* (1992) 5 BPR 11659 at 11670 (sale by trustees at undervalue).
3   TOLATA 1996, s 11(1) [**para 11.183**]. See, however, *Notting Hill Housing Trust v Brackley* [2002] HLR 212 [**para 7.301**].
4   TA 2000, s 1(1).
5   TOLATA 1996, s 6(9), as inserted by TA 2000, s 40(1), Sch 2, para 45(3).

CONTENT OF THE TRUSTEES' POWERS

11.160   Pursuant to the Trusts of Land and Appointment of Trustees Act 1996, trustees of land enjoy substantial powers in respect of the following matters.

Sale, lease and mortgage

11.161   Trustees of land have a general power to sell, lease or charge the legal estate in the trust land.[1] These powers are significantly wider than those previously available under a trust for sale or strict settlement.[2]

1   The duty to sell (with power to postpone) imported by the old trust for sale is effectively replaced by the conferment of a power either to sell or to retain the land (see Law Com No 181 (1989), paras 10.4–10.6) [**para 11.237**].
2   The powers available to trustees for sale were defined by reference to the limited powers enjoyed by the tenant for life and settlement trustees under the Settled Land Act (see LPA 1925, s 28(1); SLA 1925, ss 38–72). These powers were normally enlarged by express provision in the relevant trust instrument (see SLA 1925, s 109(1); *City of London Building Society v Flegg* [1986] Ch 605 at 612H–613A), but there was otherwise no general power, for instance, to grant a lease for a term exceeding 50 years (see SLA 1925, s 41). For the recommendation that the maximum term permissible could usefully have been increased to 100 years, see Law Reform Committee, *The powers and duties of trustees* (23rd Report, Cmnd 8733, October 1982), para 8.6.

Acquisition of freehold or leasehold land

11.162   In the absence of any restriction or exclusion imposed by their trust instrument or by statute, trustees of land are empowered to acquire freehold or leasehold land anywhere in the United Kingdom.[1] This power is exercisable regardless of whether the acquisition is by way of investment,[2] for occupation by any beneficiary[3] or for any other reason. The trustees may therefore sell trust land and reinvest the proceeds in the purchase of other land.[4] The trustees have a further (and highly significant) power, unavailable prior to the Trusts of Land and Appointment of Trustees Act 1996, to purchase land with the assistance of mortgage finance.[5] Unless disapplied by the relevant trust instrument, the 'duty of care' introduced by the Trustee Act 2000 applies to a trustee when exercising any power to acquire land or when exercising any power in relation to land so acquired.[6]

1   TOLATA 1996, s 6(3); TA 2000, s 8(1).
2   Effect has at last been given to recommendations that the investment powers of trustees should be extended to cover the purchase of freeholds and leaseholds (Law Reform Committee, 23rd Report (1982), paras 3.2–3.5; Law Com No 181 (1989), paras 10.8, 20.3).
3   Prior to 1997, trustees of mere personalty, even if expressly authorised by their trust instrument to invest in land, had no power to purchase land for occupation by a beneficiary (see *Re Power* [1947] Ch 572 at 575).
4   See TOLATA 1996, s 17(1). Under the old trust for sale, this power to re-invest in land was probably lost if the trustees sold *all* the land originally held on trust for sale, thereby forfeiting their status as 'trustees for sale' within the statutory definition (LPA 1925, s 205(1)(xxix)). See *Re Wakeman* [1945] Ch 177 at 181–182, but compare *Re Wellsted's Will Trusts* [1949] Ch 296 at 319.
5   This power was not included within the limited mortgaging powers conferred by SLA 1925, s 71(1).
6   TA 2000, s 2, Sch 1, paras 2, 7.

Partition

11.163 Trustees of land have power to partition the trust land (or any part of it) between absolutely entitled beneficiaries of full age by conveying to each his separate portion of the realty.[1] Partition – the physical division of the trust land – destroys co-ownership of any kind by reducing the land to separate ownership of individual parcels.[2] The power to partition is rarely exercised, and the conveying of the partitioned land in severalty, in accordance with the rights of the beneficiaries, requires that the trustees obtain the prior consent of each of those beneficiaries.[3]

1   TOLATA 1996, s 7(1). The trustees may additionally provide, by way of mortgage or otherwise, for the payment of any equality money.
2   [Para 11.32].
3   TOLATA 1996, s 7(2)–(3).

Compulsory conveyance to sui iuris beneficiaries who are absolutely entitled

11.164 Trustees of land have a statutory right to terminate their trust by demanding that their beneficiaries, all being of full age and capacity and absolutely entitled to the land, should take a conveyance of the legal estate in the trust land from them.[1]

1   TOLATA 1996, s 6(2).

Delegation of functions

11.165 Trustees of land have certain authority to delegate the exercise of their functions to other persons.

Individual delegation

11.166 A trustee of land, if also a beneficial owner, may individually, by power of attorney, delegate any of his functions as a trustee provided that such delegation is not prohibited by any relevant trust instrument.[1]

1 Trustee Delegation Act 1999, s 1(1), (5). The delegate may be a co-trustee, notwithstanding that the donor and donee of the power of attorney are the only trustees (*Trustees' Powers and Duties* (Law Com No 260, July 1999), para 4.1). However, no delegate can count as a second trustee for the purpose of giving a valid receipt for capital money or ensuring that beneficial interests are overreached (Trustee Delegation Act 1999, s 7(1)).

Collective delegation

11.167 Trustees of land also have power[1] collectively to delegate 'any of their functions as trustees which relate to the land' to any one or more of the beneficiaries of full age who are entitled to an interest in possession in the trust land.[2] The delegable powers comprise the full range of 'the powers of an absolute owner.'[3] The delegation, made by power of attorney, must be given by all the trustees jointly and, unless expressed to be irrevocable and given by way of security, may be revoked by any one or more of the trustees.[4] The delegation may be for any definite or indefinite period.[5] The recipient of delegated functions stands generally in 'the same position as trustees' and is subject to the same duties and liabilities, but is not to be regarded as a trustee for the purpose (inter alia) of any statutory requirements relating to the payment of capital money.[6]

1 A refusal by the trustees may be the subject of a court application under section 14(1) of the 1996 Act [**para 11.229**].
2 TOLATA 1996, s 9(1). A mere annuitant (ie a beneficiary with a mere interest in income drawn from the trust land) is not eligible to receive a delegation of functions (see TOLATA 1996, s 22(3)). The power of delegation conferred by the 1996 Act is, however, significantly wider than that previously conferred on trustees for sale by LPA 1925, s 29(1) (see Law Com No 181 (1989), paras 11.1, 20.3) and cannot be excluded by contrary intention on the part of a settlor. Delegations already made under section 29 are unaffected by the 1996 Act (see TOLATA 1996, s 9(7)).
3 See TOLATA 1996, s 6(1) [**para 11.158**]. Although the wording of the provision for delegation is entirely unqualified in scope, the Law Commission has expressed the view that the trustees' power to delegate is still restricted to 'ministerial functions' (eg purely administrative acts) and cannot, in the absence of express authority in a trust instrument or will, extend to 'fiduciary discretions' (eg the decision whether to sell or lease trust property). See Law Com No 260 (1999), paras 4.4–4.5, Appendix C, paras 2–4. The statutory use of the expansive term 'functions' may indicate, however, that Parliament intended to overstep the limitations of this technical (and nowadays scarcely tenable) distinction.
4 TOLATA 1996, s 9(3). The collective delegation of functions is automatically revoked by the appointment of a new trustee, but not by the death or resignation of an existing trustee.

5   TOLATA 1996, s 9(5).
6   TOLATA 1996, s 9(7). The delegated beneficiary cannot therefore constitute one of the trustees to whom payment of capital money ensures an overreaching of trust interests (see LPA 1925, ss 2(1)(ii), 27(2) **[para 11.203]**).

Duty of care in respect of the delegation

11.168   The 'duty of care' imposed by the Trustee Act 2000[1] attaches both to the trustees' decision whether to delegate at all and (unless the relevant delegation was expressed to be irrevocable) to the trustees' statutory responsibility to keep the delegation under review.[2] In monitoring the delegation, the trustees owe a statutory 'duty of care' in determining whether, at any stage, to exercise a 'power of intervention' by giving directions to the beneficiary or even by revoking the delegation itself.[3] Absent some breach of the 'duty of care', however, no trustee is liable for the delegate's acts or defaults in the exercise of the delegated functions.[4] Third parties dealing in good faith with a beneficiary to whom the functions of a trustee have been purportedly delegated are entitled to assume, in the absence of contrary knowledge at the time of the transaction, that the beneficiary was a proper recipient of the relevant delegation.[5]

1   TA 2000, s 1.
2   TOLATA 1996, s 9A(1)–(3) (as inserted by TA 2000, s 40(1), Sch 2, para 47).
3   TOLATA 1996, s 9A(4)–(5).
4   TOLATA 1996, s 9A(6).
5   TOLATA 1996, s 9(2). This presumption becomes conclusive in favour of a purchaser whose interest depends on the validity of the transaction, where the purchaser makes a statutory declaration, either before or within three months after the completion of his purchase, that he dealt in good faith and had no knowledge of any improper delegation.

Regulation of the beneficiary's right to occupy

11.169   The Trusts of Land and Appointment of Trustees Act 1996 confirms that most trust beneficiaries enjoy a general 'right to occupy' the land held on trust.[1] Trustees of land have certain discretionary powers to regulate, as between beneficiaries, the exercise of this entitlement.[2]

1   TOLATA 1996, s 12(1) **[para 11.175]**. In a total reversal of the classical law of trusts **[para 11.173]**, this entitlement represents a default position which now obtains in the absence of intervention by the trustees of land.
2   **[Para 11.178]**.

Application to court

11.170   Trustees of land may apply for court orders resolving various kinds of dispute relating to the trust land.[1]

1   TOLATA 1996, s 14(1) **[para 11.229]**. The court has no power under this provision to make any order as to the appointment or removal of trustees (s 14(3)).

RIGHTS OF BENEFICIARIES UNDER A TRUST OF LAND

11.171   Beneficiaries under a trust of land have a number of rights in respect of the trust land, its management and disposition, and ultimately the application of any proceeds of a sale or charge of the estate held on trust. Some of these rights are inherent in the idea of any trust; some emerged from the now archaic jurisprudence of the trust for sale; and some are more recently conferred by the Trusts of Land and Appointment of Trustees Act 1996.

The democratisation of the trust

11.172   The Trusts of Land and Appointment of Trustees Act 1996 saw the culmination of decades of slow movement towards a significant alteration in the balance of power between trustees and their beneficiaries. When, under the regime of the old trust for sale, the rights of trust beneficiaries were characterised as mere notional rights in prospective proceeds of sale, it seemed quite consistent that decisions as to the proper management or disposition of trust property should remain essentially within the control of the trustees. But with increasing judicial awareness of the 'use' value of property as distinct from its 'exchange' or capital value, it became inevitable that courts should begin to recognise certain kinds of entitlement in trust beneficiaries to intercept the decision-making processes of their trustees and to gain some control over dealings relevant to their own enjoyment of the trust land.[1] The 1996 Act accordingly confirmed the continuing emancipation of the trust beneficiary within the framework of a trust relationship in which the terminology of trustees' powers has tended to be replaced by reference to the responsible exercise of trustees' 'functions' with due regard to the 'rights' of beneficiaries.[2]

1   The movement towards change coincided, in the context of the matrimonial home, with the conferment upon many trust beneficiaries of statutory 'rights of occupation' pursuant to the Matrimonial Homes Acts 1967 and 1983 and now under the Family Law Act 1996 **[para 12.93]**.
2   TOLATA 1996, s 6(1), (5).

Right to occupy the trust land

11.173   The changing status of trust beneficiaries has emerged, perhaps most dramatically, in respect of rights to occupy trust land. In the case of the *trust for sale*, the courts came only gradually to recognise a right of beneficial occupation as an incident of equitable ownership under the trust. The doctrine of conversion, as extended and distorted by generations of property lawyers, insisted that the beneficiary's rights were classified as mere personalty: the beneficiary had no interest in land and certainly no *right* as such to physical occupation of the land vested at law in the trustees for sale. The beneficiary had an undoubted entitlement to receive his due share of any rents and profits derived from the land, but could not insist on going into possession himself.[1]

Occupation was a privilege to be accorded or withheld by the trustees in the fiduciary exercise of their powers of management of the land.[2]

1   See eg *Hoysted v Federal Commissioner of Taxation* (1920) 27 CLR 400 at 410 per Knox CJ and Starke J (High Court of Australia).

2   This was the position before 1926 (see *Re Bagot's Settlement* [1894] 1 Ch 177 at 180–181; *Re Earl of Stamford and Warrington* [1925] Ch 162 at 171) and seems to have been confirmed in the restructuring of property law in the enactments of 1925 (see *Re Landi (Deceased)* [1939] Ch 828 at 835; (1955) 19 Conv (NS) 146 at 147 (F R Crane)). On this view the beneficiary in possession by permission of the trustees ranked as a mere tenant at will (see *Cuvet v Davis* (1883) 9 VLR 390 at 396; *DKLR Holding Co (No 2) Pty Ltd v Commr of Stamp Duties* [1980] 1 NSWLR 510 at 519A–520A) and his tenancy was determinable at any time on the trustees' demand for possession (see *Garrard v Tuck* (1849) 8 CB 231 at 250, 137 ER 498 at 506; *Melling v Leak* (1855) 16 CB 652 at 668–669, 139 ER 915 at 921).

Modified perceptions of the trust for sale

11.174   This approach to beneficial occupation appeared increasingly unsustainable as it became clear in more recent decades that entitlement to unhindered residential utility is usually more significant than any rights to the exchange value of land on eventual sale. Although the rationale was never entirely straightforward,[1] the courts gradually acknowledged that an entitlement to occupy the land was necessarily an integral component of the rights enjoyed by the trust for sale beneficiary.[2] This uneasy evolution was complete by the time when, in *City of London Building Society v Flegg*,[3] Lord Oliver of Aylmerton spoke of the beneficiary's possession or occupation as 'no more than a method of enjoying in specie the rents and profits pending sale in which he is entitled to share.'[4] The changing social consensus on the importance of residential utility and residential security had finally forced a recognition that, despite its confused historical antecedents, the beneficiary had a right of occupation of land held on trust for sale.[5]

1   See eg *Williams & Glyn's Bank Ltd v Boland* [1981] AC 487 at 507B–D, where Lord Wilberforce observed that the trust for sale beneficiary's rights in respect of occupation were 'obscure'.

2   Lord Denning MR led the way by upholding a beneficiary's right of residence in cases where it could be inferred that occupation rather than sale had been the 'prime object of the trust' (see *Bull v Bull* [1955] 1 QB 234 at 238–239 per Denning LJ, as construed in *Barclay v Barclay* [1970] 2 QB 677 at 684A–B per Lord Denning MR). See also *Williams & Glyn's Bank Ltd v Boland* [1981] AC 487 at 510G, 511H per Lord Scarman. (In *Boland* it was a trust beneficiary's 'critically important' right of occupation which became overriding against the chargee of the legal estate in the family home.

3   [1988] AC 54 at 70D–E per Lord Templeman. See also [1986] Ch 605 at 614E, 617F–G per Dillon LJ.

4   [1988] AC 54 at 83F. In the view adopted by Lord Oliver, the right to occupy 'derives from and is … fathered by the interests under the trust for sale.'

5   See similarly *Kemmis v Kemmis* [1988] 1 WLR 1307 at 1325D per Purchas LJ, 1335H–1336A per Nourse LJ; *Meyer v Riddick* (1990) 60 P & CR 50 at 54 per Fox LJ; *Re Citro (A Bankrupt)* [1991] Ch 142 at 158H per Nourse LJ; *State Bank of India v Sood* [1997] Ch 276 at 281B per Peter Gibson LJ.

Rights of occupation under the 1996 Act

11.175   The Trusts of Land and Appointment of Trustees Act 1996 signifi-cantly clarified the entitlement of beneficiaries to occupy land held on trust.[1] The Act confers a general 'right to occupy' on any beneficiary who is 'benefi-cially entitled to an interest in possession' under a trust of land.[2] This 'right to occupy' under a trust of land may sometimes assume a crucial importance. In certain circumstances it becomes enforceable against third parties who receive a disposition of the legal estate in the trust land.[3] The beneficial right of occupation recognised by the 1996 Act is nevertheless hedged around by certain limitations.

1   See D G Barnsley, [1998] CLJ 123; but compare J G Ross Martyn, [1997] Conv 254.
2   TOLATA 1996, s 12(1). The statutory right thus applies only to a beneficiary with a present vested interest under the trust (see Law Com No 181 (1989), paras 13.3–13.4, 20.3).
3   **[Paras 12.205, 12.362]**.

11.176   A trust beneficiary may claim the statutory 'right to occupy' only where the 'purposes' of the trust include 'making the land available' for occupation by him or by beneficiaries of a class of which he is a member or by all the beneficiaries generally.[1] The essence of a trust 'purpose' is left perilously undefined. It is inferable, however, that the draftsman was attempting to incorporate a distinction (which gained some currency under the old trust for sale) between those trusts whose 'prime object' lay in the long-term provision of residential utility for one or more beneficiaries and trusts whose 'prime object' was expressly concerned with an immediate disposition of the trust land and division of the sale proceeds.[2]

1   TOLATA 1996, s 12(1)(a). There is also an obscure rider to the effect that the land must be 'held by the trustees so as to be' available for occupation (TOLATA 1996, s 12(1)(b)), which almost certainly serves merely to underline that the trust land is not available for occupation by a beneficiary if, for example, it is already occupied by a tenant under a lease granted by the trustees.
2   See e g *Barclay v Barclay* [1970] 2 QB 677 at 684A–B per Lord Denning MR, 684G per Edmund Davies LJ, 685G–H per Megaw LJ. Thus beneficiaries have a right to occupy trust land which was specifically acquired for their occupation, but not land governed (as in *Barclay v Barclay* **[para 11.240]**) by a testamentary trust under which a testator directed a sale and distribution of proceeds between family members.

11.177   A trust beneficiary has no 'right to occupy' land which is either 'unavailable' or 'unsuitable' for occupation by him.[1] Thus, for instance, a beneficiary may be unable to claim the statutory occupation right in respect of a house which is vastly disproportionate to his or her needs.[2] Likewise a beneficiary of a trust of an office block has no right to residential occupation of it.

1   TOLATA 1996, s 12(2). The notion of suitability relates not merely to the 'general nature and physical characteristics' of the premises, but also to the 'personal characteristics, circum-stances and requirements' of the particular beneficiary (*Chan Pui Chun v Leung Kam Ho* [2003] 1 FLR 23 at [101] per Jonathan Parker LJ).
2   Compare, however, *Chan Pui Chun v Leung Kam Ho* [2003] 1 FLR 23 at [102].

Regulation of the 'right to occupy'

11.178 Pursuant to the Trusts of Land and Appointment of Trustees Act 1996, the trustees of land have a discretion to exclude or restrict the statutory 'right to occupy'.[1] In other words, the trustees hold a power of selection between the beneficiaries, but, under the terms of the 1996 Act, may not exclude *all* of them from occupation of the land (or otherwise limit the rights of *all*).[2] In the exercise of this power the trustees may not 'unreasonably exclude' any beneficiary's entitlement to occupy land or restrict that entitlement to an 'unreasonable extent.'[3] It is, furthermore, an overriding condition[4] of the trustees' exercise of discretion in all these matters that no person already in occupation of the land[5] should be prevented from continuing to occupy it[6] except by that person's consent or with the approval of the court.[7]

1   TOLATA 1996, s 13(1). This discretion is, fairly obviously, available only where two or more beneficiaries are initially entitled, under TOLATA 1996, s 12, to occupy the trust land.
2   The trustees' discretion is necessarily limited in this way since a blanket exclusion of all beneficiaries collectively 'would make no sense' (*Rodway v Landy* [2001] Ch 703 at [33] per Peter Gibson LJ).
3   TOLATA 1996, s 13(2).
4   TOLATA 1996, s 13(7).
5   It matters not whether this occupancy is by reason of an entitlement under section 12 of the 1996 Act or arises on some other basis (e g in virtue of matrimonial home rights conferred by the Family Law Act 1996 **[para 12.93]**).
6   Nor may the trustees' powers be exercised in a manner likely to result in any such person ceasing to occupy the land.
7   In deciding whether to give approval, the court must have regard to the factors spelt out in TOLATA 1996, s 13(4) (see TOLATA 1996, s 15(2) **[para 11.179]**).

Factors relevant to the trustees' exercise of discretion

11.179 In excluding or restricting occupation, the trustees must have regard to a range of factors[1] including
−   the intentions of the person or persons (if any) who created the trust
−   the purposes for which the land is held[2]
−   the circumstances and wishes of each of the beneficiaries who would normally be entitled to occupy the land.

1   TOLATA 1996, s 13(4).
2   In relation to a building which lends itself to physical partition, the trustees' discretion is sufficiently wide to permit the allocation of different parts of the building for exclusive occupation by different beneficiaries (see e g *Rodway v Landy* [2001] Ch 703 at [33], [41] per Peter Gibson LJ (squabbling partners in a medical practice)).

Imposition of conditions

11.180 The trustees of land may from time to time impose 'reasonable conditions' on any beneficiary in relation to his enjoyment of the statutory 'right to occupy'.[1] Moreover, where one beneficiary's 'right to occupy' has been excluded or restricted by the trustees, financial or other conditions may be imposed by the trustees as the price of the occupation retained by any other beneficiary or beneficiaries.[2] A beneficiary who remains in occupation may be required to 'make payments by way of compensation' to the ousted beneficiary or to forgo, in favour of the ousted beneficiary, any payment or other benefit otherwise accruing under the trust.[3]

1   TOLATA 1996, s 13(3). The conditions which can be prescribed by the trustees may require the payment of 'outgoings or expenses' in respect of the land or the assumption of other obligations in relation to the land or to any activity which may be conducted there (TOLATA 1996, s 13(5)). This discretion appears sufficiently wide to cover a requirement of immediate compensation, in appropriate cases, for improvements effected by one beneficiary on the co-owned land, thereby supplementing the old case law on the equity of deferred reimbursement [**para 11.51**].

2   A beneficiary may properly be required, for instance, to contribute to the cost of adapting premises to make separate parts of these premises suitable for independent occupation by each beneficiary (see *Rodway v Landy* [2001] Ch 703 at [41]).

3   TOLATA 1996, s 13(6).

Application to court

11.181   It seems likely that most disputes concerning the 'right to occupy' trust land will arise, not under the provisions relating to the trustees' discretion to exclude or restrict the entitlement, but under the more general powers of judicial resolution conferred by the 1996 Act[1] and usually in the context of disagreement over a proposed sale of the trust land.[2]

1   [**Para 11.229**].
2   [**Para 11.236**].

Right to appoint and remove trustees

11.182   In general, trust beneficiaries have neither any right to be appointed as a trustee nor any entitlement to select, or veto the appointment of, any particular trustee. Nevertheless, in a significant innovation, the Trusts of Land and Appointment of Trustees Act 1996 confers such rights on certain kinds of beneficiary under a trust of land.[1] Absolutely entitled beneficiaries now have an important degree of control over the composition of the trusteeship where the relevant trust instrument (if there is one) fails to nominate some person as responsible for the appointment of trustees and does not otherwise exclude the beneficiaries' statutory rights.[2] Acting unanimously, the beneficiaries (if of full age and capacity) may give written directions[3] that one or more of their trustees should retire from the trust[4] or that the existing trustee or trustees should by writing appoint a designated person as an additional or replacement trustee.[5]

1   The Law Commission proposed in 1978 that a beneficial owner of the matrimonial home should have statutory 'trusteeship rights'. These rights would have included a right to prevent other persons from becoming trustees of the home without the consent of the spouse-beneficiary, and a right for the latter himself or herself to apply to the court for appointment

as a trustee (see Law Com No 86 (1978), paras 1.295–1.309). These proposals later evolved into a more general recommendation that trust beneficiaries be entitled to exercise, by direction to the existing trusteeship, a 'priority right of appointment' (Law Com No 181 (1989), paras 9.1, 20.3).

2   TOLATA 1996, ss 19(1), 21(5). The powers conferred by the 1996 Act in the matter of appointment and removal of trustees do not apply to trusts of land created by a disposition before 1997 if the settlor, being alive and of full capacity, by irrevocable deed exempts his trust from the operation of these powers (s 21(6)–(7)).

3   A single direction may be given jointly by all relevant beneficiaries or given individually and in identical terms by each of these beneficiaries, provided in the latter case that no beneficiary by writing withdraws his direction before it has been complied with (TOLATA 1996, s 21(1)–(2)).

4   The direction to retire should be served only on the trustee or trustees whose retirement is required (TOLATA 1996, s 19(2)(a)). Such trustee or trustees must then make a deed declaring their retirement, provided, inter alia, that there remain at least two other persons as trustees (or a trust corporation) to perform the trust and either a substitute trustee is to be appointed or the continuing trustees consent by deed to the retirement (TOLATA 1996, s 19(3)). There is separate provision for the appointment of a substitute for a trustee who is incapable by reason of mental disorder of exercising the functions of a trustee (TOLATA 1996, s 20).

5   TOLATA 1996, ss 19(2), 21(1)–(2). The direction for a new appointment must be given to all the trustees for the time being or, if there are none, to the personal representative of the last surviving trustee (TOLATA 1996, s 19(2)(b)). There is, curiously, no explicit statutory duty to comply with a direction for appointment (as distinct from retirement), but such an obligation is implicit. It would be a breach of trust to fail to give effect to the beneficiary's statutory rights.

Right to be consulted

11.183   The 1996 Act confers on certain trust beneficiaries a limited right of consultation in relation to the exercise of their trustees' functions. The Act provides that, in the exercise of any function relating to trust land, the trustees must, 'so far as practicable', consult the beneficiaries[1] of full age who are beneficially entitled to an interest in possession in the land,[2] and, 'so far as consistent with the general interest of the trust', give effect to the wishes of those beneficiaries or (in case of dispute) of 'the majority (according to the value of their combined interests).'[3] This duty of consultation initially applies only to trusts of land created or arising after 1996 and, in relation to such trusts, may be excluded or limited by express provision contained in the disposition by which a trust is created.[4] The duty of consultation may also be suspended by order of the court[5]; and there seems to be no duty to consult a beneficiary who is also a trustee.[6]

1   If a trust beneficiary is bankrupt, the consultation must not be with him, but with his trustee in bankruptcy (see *Fryer v Brooks* [1984] LS Gaz R 2856).

2   The wording of the 1996 Act may, in rare instances, exclude beneficiaries under a trust for sale on the ground that their interests are not in land, but rather in money [**para 9.243**]. See TOLATA 1996, s 3(2).

3   TOLATA 1996, s 11(1) (formerly LPA 1925, s 26(3)).

4   TOLATA 1996, s 11(2)(a). The statutory duty of consultation does not apply to trusts created or arising under a will made before 1997 (TOLATA 1996, s 11(2)(b)) and applies to other pre-1997 trusts only if the settlor expressly incorporates the statutory duty of consultation into the relevant trust by irrevocable deed (TOLATA 1996, s 11(3)–(4)). See, however, *X v A* [2000] 1 All ER 490 at 495h–496g.

5   TOLATA 1996, s 14(1)–(2)(a).

6   See *Notting Hill Housing Trust v Brackley* [2002] HLR at [25] per Peter Gibson LJ.

11.184   The duty of trustees to accede to the wishes of beneficiaries is somewhat restricted.[1] The duty of consultation ultimately comprises only a duty to listen coupled with a privilege to say 'no'. There is no duty in the trustees to comply with the wishes of the beneficiaries, except where the wishes are those of the majority shareholder(s) in equity and are also 'consistent with the general interest of the trust.'[2] Weak though this right of consultation may be, it does, however, entitle a trust beneficiary to apply for an injunction restraining the trustees from completing a sale of the land without having first discharged their minimal duty to consult the beneficiaries' wishes.[3]

1   See e g *Notting Hill Housing Trust v Brackley* [2002] HLR 212 at [23] [**para 7.301**].
2   See e g *Bull v Bull* [1955] 1 QB 234 at 238 [**para 9.233**], where Denning LJ accepted (in relation to LPA 1925, s 26(3)) that the trustee of the legal estate could have forced a sale of the property against the wishes of his mother as beneficial tenant in common. All he needed to do was to appoint a second trustee for sale to act with him. In Denning LJ's view, the two trustees would 'no doubt have to consider the mother's wishes, but as the son appears to have made the greater contribution, he could in theory override her wishes about a sale.'
3   See *Waller v Waller* [1967] 1 WLR 451 at 453D.

Right to insist that requisite consents be obtained

11.185   It is open to the author of an express trust of land to impose, by provision in the trust instrument, a requirement that specified acts by the trustees (e g sale or other disposition) should be subject to a right of consent vested in a named person or persons (usually one or more of the trust beneficiaries).[1] The imposition of an express named consent may be used, for example, to ensure that a particular trust beneficiary is guaranteed rent-free use or occupation of the trust property for so long as he or she wishes.[2] Indeed, if a settlor of land wishes to render the land effectively unsaleable in the hands of the trustees, all he need do is to transfer the land to those trustees subject to an express consent to sale vested in some person who is extremely unlikely ever to agree to any disposition.[3]

1   In *Bull v Bull* [1955] 1 QB 234 at 238, Denning LJ rather dubiously invoked, on behalf of trust for sale beneficiaries, an implied requirement of consent to any disposition by a trustee where a beneficiary in possession was de facto in a position to frustrate the delivery up of vacant possession. See H W R Wade, [1955] CLJ 157; (1955) 18 MLR 303 (V Latham); and compare *Barclay v Barclay* [1970] 2 QB 677 at 684A–B, 684G, 685G–H [**para 11.240**]. The ulterior purpose of the Denning strategy, i e the indirect conferment on trust beneficiaries of a right of occupation, is now rendered unnecessary by TOLATA 1996, ss 12–14 [**para 11.175**].
2   For the employment of such a technique under a trust for sale, see *Re Herklots' Will Trusts* [1964] 2 All ER 66 at 69I, 71C–D; *Ayer v Benton* (1967) 204 EG 359 at 360; *Abbey National Plc v Moss* [1994] 1 FLR 307 at 311G–H.
3   See e g *Re Inns* [1947] Ch 576 at 582. The consent requirement should be protected, in registered land, by the entry of a 'restriction' in the relevant registered title (see LRA 2002, s 40(2), (3)(b); LRR 2003, r 93(c) [**para 11.193**]). It is possible to seek a court order dispensing the trustees from securing a requisite, but unobtainable, consent where the unavailability of the consent threatens unreasonably to stultify a proposed transaction (TOLATA 1996, s 14(1)–(2)(a) [**para 11.230**]). See also *Abbey National Plc v Moss* [1994] 1 FLR 307 at 312E–F.

Right to apply for a court order

11.186   All beneficiaries have the right to apply to the court under the Trusts of Land and Appointment of Trustees Act 1996 for an order resolving various kinds of dispute in relation to the trust land.[1]

1   TOLATA 1996, s 14(1).

Right to an appropriate interest in capital proceeds

11.187   The ultimate entitlement of trust beneficiaries relates to the capital money arising on a disposition of the legal estate in the trust land. When overreaching occurs,[1] the beneficiaries' rights are deflected on to that capital money and each beneficiary may assert a claim to

 —   an aliquot share (if a joint tenant or tenant in common);
 —   a life interest in the income drawn from the invested capital fund (if a tenant for life); or
 —   the entire capital fund (if an absolutely entitled beneficiary under a bare trust).

1   **[Para 11.210]**.

THE REGISTERED LAND DIMENSION OF THE TRUST OF LAND

11.188   Where a registered estate is transferred to persons holding on a trust of land, the trustees are registered as proprietors of the legal estate but, so far as possible, references to the trust are excluded from the register.[1] This so-called 'curtain principle'[2] tends to keep beneficial interests off the title, consistently with the general policy that trust interests are unobtrusively overreached on subsequent dealings by the trustees. Once registered as proprietors, trustees of land have unfettered powers of registered disposition subject only to any 'restriction' which is entered in their proprietorship register for the purpose of curtailing their dispositive powers.[3] Such 'restrictions' are required usually, but not exclusively, where the registered estate is held in such a way that, in the event of a disposition of that estate, no valid receipt for capital money can be given to the disponee.

1   See LRA 2002, s 78.
2   **[Para 6.12]**.
3   LRA 2002, ss 40–44 **[para 7.52]**.

Joint tenancy at law and in equity

11.189   No 'restriction' of the proprietors' powers is, in fact, necessary where trustees of land hold on trust for themselves (and for no others) as joint tenants in equity. In the event of any disposition of the registered estate, the joint proprietors remain competent to give a valid receipt for any capital money arising,[1] in which case their beneficial entitlement is automatically deflected on to the money which they themselves hold as trustees. In these circumstances, the overreaching of the trust interests can never be in doubt. The disponee inevitably takes free of all beneficial interests, precisely because *all* the beneficiaries have joined in executing the disposition. None can possibly claim to retain any priority over the disponee. Quite clearly, in this context, no 'restriction' is needed 'for the purpose of securing that interests which are capable of being overreached ... are overreached.'[2] If, however, no disposition ever occurs and the legal and beneficial estates later come to vest in a sole owner by reason of survivorship, the surviving registered proprietor simply ranks as the absolute owner at law and in equity free of any trust.

1   **[Para 11.218]**.
2   See LRA 2002, s 44(1).

All other cases of co-ownership at law and in equity

11.190   The entry of a 'restriction' in the proprietorship register is obligatory where joint registered proprietors hold otherwise than solely on trust for themselves as equitable joint tenants.[1] Here, for the protection of any disponee of the registered estate (and, also indirectly, of the beneficial owners under the trust), the relevant 'restriction'[2] has the effect, in the absence of authorisation by court order, of inhibiting further registered dealings with the legal estate unless any capital money arising is paid to at least two trustees.[3] The net consequence of the 'restriction' is that the beneficial trust interests are inevitably overreached.[4] No registered disposition can occur if the trusteeship of the legal estate falls below two in number and, in practice, any intending disponee is mandatorily caused to pay the capital money to not fewer than two trustees. The entry of the 'restriction' merely ensures, in other words, that the overreaching provisions of the Law of Property Act 1925 are implemented for the mutual safeguard of disponee and beneficiaries.

1   LRA 2002, s 44(1); LRR 2003, r 95(2)(a).
2   See LRR 2003, r 91(1), Sch 4 ('restriction in Form A').
3   An exception is made in the case of payment to a trust corporation.
4   LPA 1925, ss 2(1)(ii), 27(2). Even the rights of beneficiaries in actual occupation of the land are overreached by the payment of capital money to two trustees (see *City of London Building Society v Flegg* [1988] AC 54 **[para 11.212]**).

Restrictions on disposition by a sole proprietor

11.191   The entry of a 'restriction' in the proprietorship register is also required where a registered estate in sole proprietorship is subject to a trust of land. Here, again, the relevant restriction (a 'restriction in Form A'[1]) directs that no disposition by the sole proprietor/trustee under which capital money arises is to be registered by Land Registry unless authorised by an order of the court.[2]

Application for the entry of this 'restriction' should be made by a sole proprietor/trustee himself.[3] Alternatively any other person interested in the registered estate (eg a trust beneficiary) may seek the appropriate entry.[4] The relevant 'restriction' will, in practice, be entered by the registrar if he ever becomes aware of the existence of a trust of land.[5] The 'restriction' on dispositions by a sole proprietor effectively forces the appointment of a second trustee for the purpose of any disposition involving the payment of capital money. The entry of the 'restriction' indirectly guarantees that overreaching of the beneficial trust interests *must* occur, but, having been overreached, these beneficial interests are themselves safeguarded – in the vast generality of cases – by their transmutation into equivalent entitlements in the money received by the trustees.[6]

1   LRR 2003, r 91(1), Sch 4.
2   Again, an exception is made in the case of a disposition by a trust corporation.
3   LRR 2003, r 94(1)(a), (2) [**para 11.139**].
4   LRA 2002, s 43(1)(c); LRR 2003, r 93(a).
5   LRA 2002, s 42(1)(b) [**para 11.140**].
6   In combination with the beneficiaries' enhanced rights to control the composition of the trusteeship [**para 11.182**], the entry of a 'restriction' affords substantially greater protection than was previously available under the trust for sale (compare *Waller v Waller* [1967] 1 WLR 451 at 453E–F, 454C; (1967) 31 Conv (NS) 140 (F R Crane)).

Additional forms of restriction on the register

11.192   Additional forms of restriction may be used to indicate that some other specific limitation has been imposed on the trustees' powers as registered proprietors.

Enforcement of requisite consents

11.193   The entry of a 'restriction' in the register is also appropriate where there exists an express requirement of some consent – usually on the part of a beneficiary – which needs to be obtained by the trustees as a precondition of any disposition of the registered estate.[1] Again it is the duty of the trustees to apply for the appropriate 'restriction' (usually a 'restriction in Form B'[2]) to be entered in the register[3] but, in default, application may also be made by any person with an interest in the registered estate (eg a trust beneficiary).[4] The protection achieved by entry of the 'restriction' is important, not merely for the trust beneficiaries, but also for prospective disponees, who inevitably want to ensure that any relevant limitations have been complied with in advance of completion of the transaction with the trustees. A disponee's insistence on compliance with the terms of 'restrictions' thus reinforces, of course, not only his own position but also the rights of trust beneficiaries.

1   [**Para 11.185**].
2   LRR 2003, r 94(4)(a), Sch 4.
3   LRR 2003, r 94(4) (a).
4   LRA 2002, s 43(1)(c); LRR 2003, r 93(c).

Dispute as to the existence of a trust of land

11.194   In the case of dispute as to the existence of a resulting or a constructive trust affecting a sole proprietor's registered title, it is open to the claimant beneficiary to apply for entry of a 'restriction' in the register.[1] However, in the absence of an entry in the register, any beneficial interest belonging to the claimant potentially 'overrides' a disposition of the registered estate by the sole trustee.[2]

1   LRA 2002, s 43(1)(c); LRR 2003, r 93(a).
2   LRA 2002, s 29(1), (2)(a)(ii), Sch 3, para 2 **[para 12.160]**.

OVERREACHING OF BENEFICIAL INTERESTS UNDER A TRUST OF LAND

11.195   One of the major achievements of the property legislation of 1925 was to make land generally marketable without simultaneously destroying its utility as a medium of beneficial endowment.[1] These twin objectives were largely realised through the technical device of 'overreaching'.

1   **[Para 2.48]**.

Significance of overreaching

11.196   'Overreaching' is a pivotal concept in English land law.[1] The term is used to describe the way in which the disponee of a legal estate in land (whether registered or unregistered) acquires an important immunity from various kinds of beneficial entitlement otherwise affecting the land. Provided that a potentially overreaching conveyance is conducted in the required manner, the Law of Property Act 1925 allows the disponee to *overreach* (ie to deflect or take free of) many kinds of pre-existing equitable interest. The title taken by the disponee is effectively cleared or unburdened by the translation of these rights into an equivalent money form.

1   See C Harpum, [1990] CLJ 277.

11.197   Overreaching thus confers, by force of statute, a substantial degree of protection on the disponee of trust land.[1] Overreaching creates in the disponee a legal estate and incidental powers which 'have an absolute priority over the beneficial interests' already existing in the land.[2] As Lord Oliver of Aylmerton explained in *City of London Building Society v Flegg*,[3] the transaction overreaches the adverse equities 'by subordinating them to the estate' taken by the disponee. The antecedent equitable rights and powers are not thereby extinguished, but are instead diverted or 'shifted from the land'[4] so that thereafter they attach not to the land but to the capital money generated by the disposition. Important categories of concurrent, successive and absolute entitlements are accordingly swept off the land and on to the capital proceeds. In the result the disponee of trust land enjoys an absolute statutory defence against future claims founded on the equitable rights of trust beneficiaries (regardless of whether he knew of them). He acquires a good title unencumbered by these trust interests. In effect, overreaching brings about the surrender of beneficial rights in land in compulsory exchange for equivalent rights in money. The disponee of trust land is fully protected, whilst pre-existing beneficial ownership is safeguarded by its transmutation into money form. In this way conveyancing convenience is coupled with security for the owners of equitable interests.

1   The overreaching provisions governing the trust for sale and strict settlement were adapted by the Trusts of Land and Appointment of Trustees Act 1996 to meet the needs of the new unitary 'trust of land' (see Law Com No 181 (1989), paras 1.7, 3.6, 6.1–6.2, 20.2).
2   *City of London Building Society v Flegg* [1988] AC 54 at 83G–H per Lord Oliver of Aylmerton. Pursuant to LPA 1925, s 2(1)(i)–(iv), the categories of potentially overreaching transaction also include a conveyance made under the powers conferred by the Settled Land Act 1925 [**para 9.216**], a conveyance made by a mortgagee or personal representative [**para 15.178**] and a conveyance made under court order.
3   [1988] AC 54 at 91B–C.
4   [1988] AC 54 at 91A–B per Lord Oliver of Aylmerton.

STATUTORY PRECONDITIONS OF OVERREACHING

11.198   Before the disponee of a legal estate held on trust can properly claim to have overreached, or taken title free of, the interests of beneficiaries under that trust, he must show that the statutory preconditions for overreaching have been satisfied. Section 2(1)(ii) of the Law of Property Act 1925 provides that

> A conveyance to a purchaser of a legal estate in land shall overreach any equitable interest or power affecting that estate, whether or not he has notice thereof, if ... the conveyance is made by trustees of land and the equitable interest or power is at the date of the conveyance capable of being overreached by such trustees ... and the requirements of section 27 of this Act respecting the payment of capital money arising on such a conveyance are complied with ...

The conveyance must be made by trustees of land

11.199   No overreaching can occur in respect of a trust of land except in the context of a 'conveyance' made by 'trustees of land' (in the plural),[1] a 'conveyance' including, for this purpose, a mortgage, charge[2] and lease.[3] The conveyance must be executed by *all* the trustees (being at least two in number) and, in default of such a disposition, overreaching cannot operate in favour of the purchaser.[4]

1   'Trustees of land' are defined as 'trustees of a trust of land' (TOLATA 1996, s 1(1)(b)).
2   See eg *City of London Building Society v Flegg* [1988] AC 54 at 70H–71A, 73F per Lord Templeman, 78A–D per Lord Oliver of Aylmerton; *State Bank of India v Sood* [1997] Ch 276 at 282C–D.
3   LPA 1925, s 205(1)(ii) [**para 2.42**].

4   Thus a disposition by a sole trustee (other than a trust corporation) has no statutory overreaching effect in either registered land (see e g *Williams & Glyn's Bank Ltd v Boland* [1981] AC 487 at 503D–E per Lord Wilberforce [**para 12.204**]; *City of London Building Society v Flegg* [1988] AC 54 at 74C per Lord Templeman; *State Bank of India v Sood* [1997] Ch 276 at 285D–F) or unregistered land (see e g *Kingsnorth Finance Co Ltd v Tizard* [1986] 1 WLR 783 at 792H–793A [**para 12.361**]).

The equitable interests must be capable of being overreached

11.200   Not all kinds of equitable interest in land are 'capable of being overreached' by a purchaser.[1] Statutory overreaching operates only upon those equitable rights which comprise *general* (as distinct from *real*) burdens on the land which has been conveyed.[2]

1   Trustees of land have, of course, no power to make a conveyance which overreaches *legal* estates in the land.
2   This distinction is sometimes expressed as a dichotomy between overreachable 'family interests' and non-overreachable 'commercial interests', perhaps on the ground that overreachable equities are frequently found within a family context (see e g *Birmingham Midshires Mortgage Services Ltd v Sabherwal* (2000) 80 P & CR 256 at 262–263 per Robert Walker LJ). Nowadays this typology is imperfect not least because overreachable rights do not arise exclusively in relation to the family home. Furthermore, a significant modern category of non-overreachable rights – the 'matrimonial home rights' conferred by the Family Law Act 1996 [**para 12.93**] – clearly originates within a family context but, like the so-called 'commercial' interests, still require protection by various kinds of register entry. For present purposes, therefore, it seems preferable to adapt a mixture of English and Scots terminology and to speak instead of 'general' and 'real' burdens on land.

General (or non-specific) burdens

11.201   The category of statutorily overreachable rights is composed of those interests which are readily convertible into quantifiable equivalents in the capital proceeds of the relevant disposition.[1] Although they may also incorporate strong elements of use value (as measured in terms of beneficial occupation of land),[2] overreachable rights must have an exchange value. They must have a *general* or *fungible* character in the sense that they are not intrinsically diminished by transmutation from one mode of investment into another. Overreaching is therefore peculiarly appropriate in relation to the beneficial interests which subsist behind a trust of land (e g the beneficial rights of co-owners, tenants for life and bare beneficiaries).[3] Such equitable entitlements can easily attach to many different kinds of asset (whether land, funds of money or other forms of valuable resource).[4] Under the theory of the 1925 legislation, these non-specific rights possess a profoundly exchangeable quality which makes them ideal candidates for the statutory mechanism of overreaching.[5]

1   [**Paras 2.166, 12.339**].
2   The framers of the 1925 legislation failed to appreciate the significance which, particularly in the family setting, would later be accorded to the utility-based aspects of proprietary entitlement. In the money-oriented perspective of the Law of Property Act 1925 it seemed fair

to assume that owners of overreachable rights within the scheme of the Act would react with relative indifference to the compulsory transformation of their rights into cash. This assumption was falsified with the advent of widespread owner-occupation of the family home. Measured in terms of use (rather than exchange) value, an overreached right to some portion of capital nowadays seems distinctly less preferable to the retention of occupation rights and residential security in bricks and mortar [**para 2.161**].

3   The judicial impulse to allow overreaching to sweep equities off the land is sufficiently strong to have prompted the suggestion that where, as in the context of the family home, 'concepts of trust and equitable estoppel are almost interchangeable ... both are affected in the same way by the statutory mechanism of overreaching' (see *Birmingham Midshires Mortgage Services Ltd v Sabherwal* (2000) 80 P & CR 256 at 263 per Robert Walker LJ [**para 10.179**]). See also (2000) 116 LQR 341 (C Harpum), but compare *Lloyd v Dugdale* [2002] 2 P & CR 167 at [55] per Sir Christopher Slade.

4   See e g *Birmingham Midshires Mortgage Services Ltd v Sabherwal* (2000) 80 P & CR 256 at 263, where Robert Walker LJ pointed out that the equitable interest of a tenant in common was convertible into a quantifiable money value which could be used to acquire another home.

5   When converted into the cash proceeds of an overreaching disposition, a beneficial tenant in common fairly obviously takes a proportionate or fractional share of those capital proceeds absolutely; the owner of a life interest, again obviously, takes the annual income drawn from the investment of the capital; and the beneficiary under a bare trust is entitled to the entirety of the cash product of the disposition.

Real (or specific) burdens

11.202   By contrast non-overreachable equitable rights comprise entitlements which are not fungible or exchangeable, but have meaning only in respect of the specific land to which they relate.[1] Examples include options and other estate contracts,[2] easements,[3] restrictive covenants[4] and rights of entry.[5] Rights falling within this category are not readily monetisable and were never viewed, in the scheme of the 1925 legislation, as mechanically convertible into cash.[6] Instead it was envisaged that for the large part these rights imposed, in respect of specific land, permanent 'real burdens' which were not designed to be swept away by later dispositions of title. Being deliberately intended to remain binding on land, these entitlements lay (and still lie) outside the scope of the statutory overreaching process.[7] Indeed, the 1925 legislation makes elaborate provision for these 'real burdens' to enjoy a continuing force over the affected land through the medium of various schemes of register entry.[8]

1   [**Para 2.164**].
2   [**Para 9.23**].
3   [**Para 9.87**].
4   [**Para 9.138**].
5   [**Para 8.265**].
6   A right falling within this category 'cannot sensibly shift from the land affected by it to the proceeds of sale' (*Birmingham Midshires Mortgage Services Ltd v Sabherwal* (2000) 80 P & CR 256 at 263 per Robert Walker LJ).
7   Apart from these 'real burdens', the only types of equitable interest which cannot be overreached on an ordinary conveyance by trustees of land are equities created *prior* to the trust of land itself. Such equitable interests are nowadays extremely rare, and can be overreached by the purchaser only if recourse is had to the special machinery of an *ad hoc* trust of land, ie only if the trust of land is converted into a trust under which the trustees are either a trust corporation or persons appointed or approved by the court (see LPA 1925,

s 2(2)). There is, in the context of the trust of land, no equivalent of SLA 1925, s 72(3) **[para 9.218]**. See *Re Ryder and Steadman's Contract* [1927] 2 Ch 62 at 82–83.

8   **[Paras 12.84, 12.275]**. 'Real burdens' (if subsisting in registered land) sometimes remain binding simply as overriding interests even in the absence of protection in the register. See LRA 2002, s 29(1), (2)(a)(ii), Sch 3, para 2 **[paras 2.172, 12.146]**.

Capital money must be paid over in the prescribed manner

11.203   It is a vital precondition of overreaching under section 2(1)(ii) of the Law of Property Act 1925 that the disponee must comply with 'the require-ments of section 27 of this Act respecting the payment of capital money.' Under this provision 'the proceeds of sale or other capital money shall not be paid to or applied by the direction of fewer than two persons as trustees.'[1] This 'two trustee rule' is a principle of stern application. The requirement of payment to the trustees (being at least two in number) is mandatory, overriding any contrary provision in the instrument, if any, which created the trust of land. Payment to fewer than two persons as trustees precludes the disponee from claiming that he has statutorily overreached the beneficial interests under the trust of land.[2] This insistence on strict observance of the 'two trustee rule' marks a pragmatic recognition that a payment made to two trustees of land is much less likely to be misappropriated or misapplied than a payment made to a single individual,[3] although in some instances the protection for beneficiaries admittedly turns out to be 'no safeguard at all.'[4] Only limited exceptions are allowed from the scope of the rule.[5]

1   LPA 1925, s 27(2).
2   These beneficial interests remain binding on a purchaser of an unregistered estate unless he can show that he purchased without notice of them **[para 12.356]**. Beneficial entitlements in respect of a registered estate may sometimes constitute overriding interests **[para 12.146]**.
3   See Law Com No 86 (1978), para 1.250.
4   *State Bank of India v Sood* [1997] Ch 276 at 290B per Peter Gibson LJ. See also *City of London Building Society v Flegg* [1988] AC 54 **[para 11.214]**.
5   There is no provision for the payment of purchase money into court.

Payment to a trust corporation

11.204   Statute allows overreaching to occur where payment has been made to a trust corporation (eg a bank trust corporation).[1]

1   LPA 1925, s 27(2).

Payment to a sole personal representative

11.205   The 'two trustee rule' does not affect the right of a sole personal representative to give a valid receipt for, or direct the application of, proceeds of sale or other capital money.[1]

1   LPA 1925, s 27(2).

Absence of capital money arising on disposition

11.206 A mere failure to pay capital money to two trustees of land cannot, in itself, prevent the overreaching of trust interests if no capital money *actually* arises on the disposition of the legal estate by the trustees (eg in the case of an exchange of land or a lease granted otherwise than for a premium).[1] This third category of exception to the otherwise stringent 'two trustee rule' is beginning to gather a previously unsuspected importance. In *State Bank of India v Sood*,[2] the Court of Appeal confirmed that the requirement that capital money be paid to at least two persons as trustees has no application to money which has *already* been paid in advance of the relevant disposition or is left to be drawn down *subsequently* to that disposition. Since, in either case, no capital money arises contemporaneously with the disposition, compliance with the 'two trustee rule' is not a statutory precondition of overreaching.[3]

1   See *State Bank of India v Sood* [1997] Ch 276 at 287C–D.
2   [1997] Ch 276; [1997] Conv 134 (M P Thompson).
3   [1997] Ch 276 at 288B per Peter Gibson LJ. 'If capital money does not arise, compliance does not arise' ([1997] Ch 276 at 291D–E per Pill LJ).

11.207 *Sood*'s case concerned a fairly common form of overdraft mortgage, under which the registered proprietors of a freehold estate charged their estate to a bank in order to secure their existing and future overdraft liabilities for business and other purposes. The bank advanced no mortgage money contemporaneously with the charge, but provided a drawdown facility for the future. When over £1 million later became outstanding on this facility, the bank called in the debt and sought possession of the land, only to be opposed by other members of the registered proprietors' family who claimed to have been in actual occupation of the land as beneficial co-owners at the date of the charge. The Court of Appeal nevertheless held that the equitable interests of all the beneficiaries had been overreached by the charge and did not therefore affect the bank as chargee.[1] According to the Court, the requirement of actual payment to two trustees (or to a trust corporation) applies only when capital money arises *at the date of* disposition of the legal estate.[2]

1   [1997] Ch 276 at 289F–G per Peter Gibson LJ. Even if the bank had subsequently made payments under the mortgage facility otherwise than to two or more trustees (or at their direction), 'that would not affect the overreaching which would have occurred on the mortgage' ([1997] Ch 276 at 289D).
2   [1997] Ch 276 at 288B per Peter Gibson LJ, 291H–292A per Pill LJ. The *Realpolitik* of *Sood* was, of course, that the courts could not afford to jeopardise the protection which banks assume they have under overdraft mortgages.

EFFECTS OF OVERREACHING

11.208 If the three statutory preconditions for overreaching are met, the disponee of trust land overreaches the beneficial interests behind the trust irrespective of whether he has notice of such entitlements.[1]

1   Thus even a purchaser with *express* notice of adverse beneficial rights takes title free of them

provided that there is compliance with the statutory preconditions of overreaching (*City of London Building Society v Flegg* [1988] AC 54 at 83E–F per Lord Oliver of Aylmerton).

Disponee can henceforth ignore all trusts

11.209   Section 27(1) of the Law of Property Act 1925 provides clearly that the disponee who complies with the preconditions of overreaching 'shall not be concerned with the trusts affecting the land, the net income of the land or the proceeds of sale of the land whether or not those trusts are declared by the same instrument by which the trust of land is created.'[1] In other words, the beneficial interests behind the trust now take effect conclusively in the capital money arising from the disposition. The disponee takes a good legal title free from all beneficial claims, and even does so irrespective of actual occupation by the claimant beneficiaries which would otherwise have founded an overriding interest (in registered land) or provided constructive notice (in unregistered land).[2]

1   According to Lord Oliver of Aylmerton, 'the scheme of the Act is to enable a purchaser or mortgagee, so long as he pays the proceeds of sale or other capital moneys to not less than two trustees or to a trust corporation, to accept a conveyance or mortgage without reference at all to the beneficial interests of co-owners ... which are kept behind the curtain and do not require to be investigated' (*City of London Building Society v Flegg* [1988] AC 54 at 78H–79A). See also *State Bank of India v Sood* [1997] Ch 276 at 281F per Peter Gibson LJ; LPA 1925, s 10(1).
2   See *Williams & Glyn's Bank Ltd v Boland* [1981] AC 487 at 503D–E per Lord Wilberforce; *City of London Building Society v Flegg* [1988] AC 54 at 89F–G per Lord Oliver of Aylmerton [**para 11.212**]. See also J Martin, [1980] Conv 361 at 362, [1981] Conv 219.

Impact on beneficial rights

11.210   The disposition of a legal estate held on trust, when coupled with compliance with the preconditions for overreaching, sweeps the interests of trust beneficiaries off the land. The beneficiaries' rights, although no longer capable of assertion against the disponee, nevertheless remain binding on and enforceable against the trustees, who now stand not as trustees of land but as trustees of the capital proceeds of the transaction.

Application of overreaching to transactions of mortgage

11.211   Overreaching of beneficial interests applies just as readily on a mortgage or charge of the trust estate as on a transfer by way of sale.[1] Provided that the relevant statutory preconditions are met, the equitable interests of trust beneficiaries are, 'eo instante with the creation of the charge, overreached.'[2] Such interests, in so far as they can properly be considered interests in land, thereafter subsist only in relation to the equity of redemption,[3] although there is a more general sense in which they also attach to the mortgage money paid over by the chargee.[4] In other words, these beneficial interests are deflected on to the legal estate as subject to the mortgage charge.[5] But since the value of this equity of redemption (ie the value of the encumbered legal estate) is inevitably diminished by the extraction of the loan money, the beneficiaries are compensated, at least in theory, by the fact that their rights are also regarded as having 'shifted from the land to the capital moneys in the hands of the trustees.'[6] It may, however, be of little comfort to trust beneficiaries that their rights now attach to the equity of redemption and to proportionate shares in the loan money advanced to their trustees. The equity of redemption may well have been rendered valueless by the aggregation of loan liability[7] and the loan money may have been dissipated.[8]

1   See e g *State Bank of India v Sood* [1997] Ch 276 [**para 11.206**].
2   *City of London Building Society v Flegg* [1988] AC 54 at 90F per Lord Oliver of Aylmerton.
3   *City of London Building Society v Flegg* [1988] AC 54 at 84B–C, 90F, 91C–D per Lord Oliver of Aylmerton (see also Lord Templeman at 73F). In effect, the beneficial interests are 'overreached on to the proceeds of sale of the equity of redemption' (*National Westminster Bank Plc v Malhan* [2004] EWHC 847 (Ch) at [44], [52] per Morritt V-C). For further discussion of the equity of redemption, see Chapter 15 [**para 15.12**].
4   See *City of London Building Society v Flegg* [1988] AC 54 at 71D, 71H–72A per Lord Templeman, 91A–B per Lord Oliver of Aylmerton.
5   See *State Bank of India v Sood* [1997] Ch 276 at 289F–G per Peter Gibson LJ; *Birmingham Midshires Mortgage Services Ltd v Sabherwal* (2000) 80 P & CR 256 at 261 per Robert Walker LJ.
6   *City of London Building Society v Flegg* [1988] AC 54 at 91A–B per Lord Oliver of Aylmerton.
7   See e g *State Bank of India v Sood* [1997] Ch 276 at 289G–H per Peter Gibson LJ.
8   See *State Bank of India v Sood* [1997] Ch 276 at 290A–B, where Peter Gibson LJ confessed that he could not pretend that the outcome in that case was 'entirely satisfactory'. The supposed 'safeguard' of overreaching had been rendered 'no safeguard at all' for the beneficial co-owners in *Sood*.

Irrelevance of potentially overriding interests

11.212   The comprehensively overreaching character of a conveyance which complies with the preconditions set down in the Law of Property Act 1925 has seldom been in question. Nevertheless the litigation in *City of London Building Society v Flegg*[1] posed a serious challenge to the conventional understanding of overreaching and the machinery of conveyancing. In *Flegg*, H and W purchased in their joint names a registered title in premises ominously called 'Bleak House', the greater part of the purchase money having been provided by W's elderly parents, F1 and F2, who therefore became beneficiaries behind a trust (see *Fig. 36*).[2] F1 and F2 moved into occupation of the house with H and W and remained there at all material times.[3] Without the knowledge or consent of either F1 or F2, H and W later charged their legal estate to a building society, dissipated the ensuing mortgage advance and were adjudicated bankrupt. The building society sought possession of 'Bleak House', plainly assuming that a charge executed by two trustees had an unchallengeably overreaching effect in relation to such equitable interests as might exist. F1 and F2 claimed, however, that by reason of their actual occupation at the date of the charge their own beneficial rights under the trust (or at least the occupation rights incidental thereto) overrode the charge.[4] Somewhat surprisingly this claim succeeded in the Court of Appeal, which decided that, pursuant to the Land Registration Act, the simple association of beneficial entitlement and actual occupation always overrode a registered disposition irrespective of the number of registered proprietors.[5]

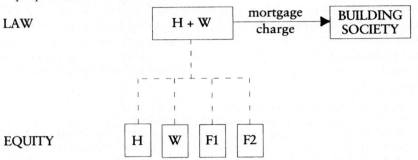

Fig. 36

1   [1988] AC 54; [1986] Ch 605.
2   Although the transfer contained an express declaration of trust for H and W as beneficial joint tenants, the House of Lords regarded H, W, F1 and F2 as together beneficial tenants in common (see [1988] AC 54 at 70A–E per Lord Templeman, 77G per Lord Oliver of Aylmerton). The declaration of trust, precisely because not executed by F1 and F2 [**para 9.198**], could not preclude the assertion of a competing beneficial entitlement by F1 and F2 as contributors of value. See M P Thompson, [1988] Conv 108 at 109.
3   [1986] Ch 605 at 614E–F.
4   The claim was made pursuant to LRA 1925, s 70(1)(g) [**para 12.147**].
5   Dillon LJ thought that the reasoning of Lord Wilberforce in *Williams & Glyn's Bank Ltd v Boland* [1981] AC 487 [**para 12.205**] did 'not depend at all … on the fact that [in *Boland*] there was only one registered proprietor of the land and therefore only one trustee' ([1986] Ch 605 at 616H–617D). The Court of Appeal's ruling was reinforced by reference to LPA 1925, s 14 ([1986] Ch 605 at 618D–620E).

Descent into heresy

11.213   The ruling of the Court of Appeal in *Flegg* immediately threatened a number of extraordinary consequences.[1] First, a disposition of title and receipt of capital money by two trustees for sale would no longer automatically overreach otherwise overriding interests in registered land and probably would not overreach the equivalent equitable interests in unregistered land either.[2] Second, the Court of Appeal's decision had the effect of ripping apart the 'curtain' which supposedly conceals trust equities from the purchaser who deals with two trustees. Third, a new onus was placed on the purchaser to identify all beneficiaries in possession (in either registered or unregistered land) and ensure that each gave consent to the transaction in hand. In effect, as Lord Oliver of Aylmerton later observed in the House of Lords, the Court of Appeal's ruling was of 'very considerable importance not only to conveyancers but to anyone proposing to lend upon the security of property'.[3]

1   For a good summary of these consequences, recounted with an appropriate frisson of horror, see [1988] AC 54 at 76E–77A per Lord Oliver of Aylmerton. For further critical views, see [1986] CLJ 202 (C Harpum); [1986] Conv 131 (D J Hayton); (1986) 136 NLJ 208 (D J Hayton); (1986) 49 MLR 519 (R J Smith); (1986) 102 LQR 349.
2   [1988] AC 54 at 77A.
3   [1988] AC 54 at 76G. '[F]inancial institutions advancing money on the security of land will face hitherto unsuspected hazards' ([1988] AC 54 at 77A).

Reinstatement of orthodoxy

11.214   Much to the relief of conveyancers,[1] the House of Lords unanimously overturned the ruling of the Court of Appeal as contrary to several structural tenets of the property legislation of 1925.[2] The House of Lords held that overriding status could attach only to such occupiers' rights as affected the registered estate on the completion of the mortgage charge. In *Flegg*, however, the trustees' receipt of the mortgage money (as acknowledged in the charge executed by them) had already overreached the beneficial interests of F1 and F2,[3] with the consequence that F1 and F2 no longer retained any rights affecting the land which could rank as overriding interests.[4] The mere fact of payment to the trustees had instantly ensured that the beneficiaries' rights were 'shifted from the land to the capital moneys in the hands of the trustees',[5] with the result that the immunity conferred on the lender by the 'two trustee rule' was already in place.[6]

1   The reversal of the Court of Appeal came too late to avert the trauma suffered by a generation of examination candidates. With sadistic timing, the House of Lords' ruling in *Flegg* first saw the light of day in (1987) Times, 18 May, only a few days before most summer law examinations.
2   [1988] AC 54. See [1987] CLJ 392 (C Harpum); (1987) 103 LQR 520 (R J Smith); (1988) 51 MLR 365 (S Gardner); M P Thompson, [1988] Conv 108.
3   Lord Oliver of Aylmerton thought it not 'merely part of the narrative but … an essential part of the reasoning' in *Williams & Glyn's Bank Ltd v Boland* [1981] AC 487 that in that case there had been a receipt of capital money by only one trustee. In *Boland* 'it was a critical feature of the [wives'] argument that their interests were not overreached but were kept alive as against the purchaser' ([1988] AC 54 at 89C–D).
4   [1988] AC 54 at 91F–G per Lord Oliver of Aylmerton.
5   [1988] AC 54 at 91A–B per Lord Oliver of Aylmerton. 'If, then, one asks what were the subsisting rights of the respondents referable to their occupation, the answer must … be that they were rights which, vis à vis the appellants, were, *eo instante* with the creation of the charge, overreached and therefore subsisted only in relation to the equity of redemption' ([1988] AC 54 at 90F per Lord Oliver of Aylmerton). See also Lord Templeman at 73F.
6   The beneficiaries' critical right, that of occupation of the land, was dependent on and 'co-terminous with' its parent interest, with the result that once the 'parent interest', by which alone occupation could be justified, had been overreached, 'nothing remains to which a right of occupation can attach' ([1988] AC 54 at 84A, 90H–91C per Lord Oliver of Aylmerton).

The modern scope of overreaching

11.215   The ruling of the House of Lords in *Flegg*'s case conclusively reinstated an important part of the orthodoxy of English land law and has since been declared to be undisturbed by the enactment of the Trusts of Land and

Appointment of Trustees Act 1996.[1] In holding that a mortgage charge can overreach the beneficial rights of persons in 'actual occupation', the House of Lords significantly reinforced the principle that, in registered land, compliance with the 'two trustee rule' confers a statutory immunity even in respect of potentially overriding interests.[2] The purchaser of registered land can indeed, in one sense, overreach overriding interests.[3] The outcome may be different, however, if the registered estate is held in the name of a sole trustee of land and a disposition of that estate is executed by that trustee alone.[4] Here, for want of the payment of capital money to land trustees (in the plural), such a disposition attracts no statutory overreaching effect. The possibility therefore remains – although the courts have recently striven mightily to counteract this effect[5] – that a beneficiary under a trust of this kind, if 'in actual occupation' of the land, may claim that his or her equitable interest 'overrides' the disposition.

1   *Birmingham Midshires Mortgage Services Ltd v Sabherwal* (2000) 80 P & CR 256 at 261–262 per Robert Walker LJ.
2   See *City of London Building Society v Flegg* [1988] AC 54 at 76E–F per Lord Oliver of Aylmerton.
3   A more accurate (and more modern) way of expressing the impact of *Flegg* is that the case demonstrates that Schedule 3, para 2 of the Land Registration Act 2002 requires not merely that the claimant of an overriding interest be in 'actual occupation' but also that he or she must still hold, at the relevant date, an 'interest affecting the estate' of the disponor (see LRA 2002, s 29(1) **[para 12.141]**).
4   See e g *Williams & Glyn's Bank Ltd v Boland* [1981] AC 487 **[para 12.205]**.
5   **[Paras 12.210–12.221]**.

Justice of the overreaching principle

11.216   The principle of overreaching undoubtedly serves the simplification of conveyancing, but the case law demonstrates some of the shortcomings of the mechanism. As Peter Gibson LJ observed in *State Bank of India v Sood*,[1] the safeguards for beneficiaries supposedly inherent in the 'two trustee rule' fall away when capital money does not arise contemporaneously with the disposition of the legal estate held on trust or is paid over to two dishonest trustees who act jointly in fraud of their beneficiaries. In *City of London Building Society v Flegg*,[2] for example, two elderly and entirely innocent beneficial co-owners lost their home and their life savings, their dilemma sadly illustrating that the 'two trustee rule' may still leave beneficiaries in occupation 'insufficiently protected.'[3] A further source of inequity flows from the fact that the entire process of overreaching turns, rather capriciously, on the precise composition of the trusteeship in a trust of land. The combined effect of the decisions in *Williams & Glyn's Bank Ltd v Boland*[4] and *City of London Building Society v Flegg*[5] is, in certain limited circumstances, to make the priority enjoyed by a beneficial co-owner depend on whether there is *one* trustee of land or *two*.[6] Yet, consistently with the modern drive towards the rationalisation of land dealings, the courts have progressively reinforced the statutory overreaching of beneficial trust interests in order to strip away, so far as possible, the obstacles to the reception of a clear title by transferees and chargees.[7] In particular, the courts have been concerned to counter any suggestion that the arbitrary effects which flow from the composition of the trusteeship amount to a discriminatory violation of the protection afforded by the European Convention on Human Rights in respect of the 'home' and 'family life' and the 'peaceful enjoyment' of possessions.[8]

1   [1997] Ch 276 at 290A–C.
2   [1988] AC 54 **[para 11.212]**.
3   *State Bank of India v Sood* [1997] Ch 276 at 290B per Peter Gibson LJ. During the 1980s the Law Commission acknowledged that almost all other occupiers of residential property have some form of protection against arbitrary eviction (see Law Commission, Working Paper No 106 (1988), para 6.1; *Transfer of Land: Overreaching: Beneficiaries in Occupation* (Law Com No 188, December 1989), para 3.4). In an initiative now long forgotten (and indeed quite foreign to more recent thinking), the Commission proposed that overreaching of the beneficial rights of any actual occupier should, in all cases, require the positive or 'real' consent of that occupier if a person 'of full age and capacity' (Law Com No 188 (1989), paras 4.3, 5.3(i)).
4   [1981] AC 487 **[para 12.205]**.
5   [1988] AC 54 **[para 11.212]**.
6   For recognition of the arbitrariness of this distinction, see Law Com No 188 (1989), paras 1.4, 2.28–2.32, 3.5.
7   See Gray and Gray, 'The rhetoric of realty', in J Getzler (ed), *Rationalizing Property, Equity and Trusts: Essays in Honour of Edward Burn* (Butterworths 2003), pp 248–253.
8   ECHR Art 8 **[para 2.60]**; Protocol No 1, Art 1 **[para 2.29]**. See e g *National Westminster Bank Plc v Malhan* [2004] EWHC 847 (Ch) at [48]–[53] per Morritt V-C.

OTHER PROTECTION FOR THE DISPONEE OF TRUST LAND

11.217   Under the property legislation of 1925 (as supplemented by more recent statutes) the process of overreaching is buttressed by the conferment of further protection on the disponee or purchaser from trustees of land. Some of these safeguards operate irrespective of whether the land is registered or unregistered; others are specific to one or other regime. The most significant forms of protection are those ancillary provisions which enable the purchaser of trust land to maintain that the disposition has not been vitiated by some transactional irregularity and therefore still ranks as a valid 'conveyance' of the legal estate with potentially overreaching effect.

Exoneration in respect of capital money

11.218   On compliance with the statutory prescription for overreaching, the disponee of the legal estate in trust land (whether registered or unregistered) is not answerable for the application of any capital money paid over. A receipt in writing operates as a 'sufficient discharge' for the disponee and exonerates him from seeing to the application of the money by the trustees or from being 'answerable for any loss or misapplication thereof.'[1] The combined effect of statute[2] is therefore that the purchaser who fulfils the three preconditions for overreaching[3] takes a legal title free of the beneficial interests, of the terms of the trust, and of any further responsibility for the capital money arising on the transaction.

1   TA 1925, s 14(1). A valid receipt cannot, of course, be given by a sole trustee other than a trust corporation (TA 1925, s 14(2)(a)).
2   See also LPA 1925, ss 2(1)(ii), 27(1).
3   [Para 11.198].

Protection in respect of multiple requisite consents

11.219   In most instances the purchaser of trust land (whether registered or unregistered) enjoys additional protection in the matter of multiple requisite consents.[1] Where, in a disposition creating a trust of land, the exercise of any of the functions of the trustees was expressly made subject to the consent of more than two persons, the consent of any two of such persons is deemed sufficient in favour of the purchaser.[2] The title taken by the purchaser cannot thereafter be challenged on the ground that some further consent was not obtained. Furthermore, if a *minor* was specified as having a requisite consent, this consent is deemed, in favour of the purchaser, not to be required, although the trustees are statutorily obliged instead to obtain the relevant consent either from the parent who has parental responsibility or from the minor's guardian.[3]

1   [Para 11.185].
2   TOLATA 1996, s 10(1). This dispensation does not apply to consents to the exercise of any function by trustees of land held on charitable, ecclesiastical or public trusts (s 10(2)).
3   TOLATA 1996, s 10(3). Power to give consent on behalf of a mental patient is vested in a receiver appointed by the Court of Protection (Mental Health Act 1983, ss 95–96, 99) or in an attorney who holds an enduring power of attorney for that patient.

Freedom from limitations on a registered proprietor's powers

11.220   It has long been a working principle in the regime of registered land that, save in respect of overriding interests, a disponee is affected only by matters which are the subject of some entry in the register of title.[1] This principle is perpetuated in section 26(1)–(2) of the Land Registration Act 2002, pursuant to which the title of the disponee of a registered estate or charge is declared to be undisturbed by any limitation on the disponor's powers which was *not* reflected by some entry in the latter's register of title[2] or imposed by or under the 2002 Act itself.[3] The registered proprietor's right to exercise 'owner's powers' is taken otherwise to be 'free from any limitation affecting the validity of a disposition.'[4] Subject to the stated exceptions, the disponee is, in effect, entitled to assume that the disponor had plenary powers of disposition.[5]

1   See *Securities Ltd v Caswell* [1965] Ch 373 at 390A–B per Cross J.
2   A limitation of this kind should be entered as a 'restriction' in the relevant proprietorship register (see Law Com No 271 (2001), para 4.8).
3   See also *State Bank of India v Sood* [1997] Ch 276 at 284C per Peter Gibson LJ.
4   LRA 2002, s 26(1).
5   See Law Com No 271 (2001), para 4.4.

11.221   It follows that, in the event of certain irregularities in the exercise of 'owner's powers' by trustees of land, the disponee's 'title' cannot be 'questioned',[1] although the unlawfulness of the disposition may still be a matter of

complaint against the trustees (or even against the disponee if he was implicated in the impropriety). Thus, for example, a disponee's title cannot be
'challenged'[2] – in the absence of some appropriate 'restriction' entered in the
register – on the ground that some requisite written consent to the disposition
was not obtained by the trustees. Without the relevant consent the disposition is
clearly unlawful, but the legal title taken by the disponee is statutorily protected. The disponee is therefore in a position to assert that he has received a
'conveyance' of a 'legal estate' in land from 'trustees' (within the terms of
section 2(i)(ii) of the Law of Property Act 1925[3]) which enables him to
overreach all beneficial interests behind the trust.[4] However, the protection
afforded by section 26 of the 2002 Act extends only 'for the purpose of
preventing the title of the disponee being questioned.'[5] The errant trustees are,
of course, personally liable to the person whose requisite consent has been
ignored; and the disponee, if privy to the wrongfulness of the transaction, may
also be personally accountable in equity for knowing receipt of trust property.[6]
But in none of these circumstances can the validity of the proprietary title
taken by the disponee be brought into question.[7]

1   LRA 2002, s 26(3).
2   See Law Com No 271 (2001), para 4.9.
3   **[Para 11.199]**.
4   This conclusion is unaltered by the possibility that the person whose consent was required
    may have been a trust beneficiary in 'actual occupation' of the land. No overriding interest
    can be claimed by such a beneficiary because the 'conveyance' from two trustees is perfectly
    valid (at least vis à vis the disponee) and therefore automatically overreaches the trust equities
    (see *City of London Building Society v Flegg* [1988] AC 54 **[para 11.214]**; Law Com No 271
    (2001), para 4.10).
5   LRA 2002, s 26(3).
6   See e g *Cowan de Groot Properties Ltd v Eagle Trust Plc* [1992] 4 All ER 700 at 759g–760e;
    Eagle Trust Plc v SBC Securities Ltd [1993] 1 WLR 484 at 503F–504A per Vinelott J.
7   Law Com No 271 (2001), para 4.11.

Registered disposition by a sole trustee in breach of trust

11.222 A broader question can be raised as to whether the protection
conferred on the disponee by section 26 of the Land Registration Act 2002
applies to all breaches of trust by the disponor. A critical example concerns the
disposition of trust land by a sole trustee in circumstances which preclude the
statutory overreaching of the beneficial interests behind the trust.[1] This sce-
nario becomes problematical if, having received the capital proceeds of the
transaction, the sole trustee applies the money dishonestly or becomes insolvent. Although non-compliance with the 'two trustee rule' is deeply contrary to
the statutory scheme underpinning the trust of land,[2] it is equally clear that the
disponee from the sole trustee takes a good title at law.

1   **[Para 11.199]**. Here the breach of trust is made possible by the absence of any 'restriction'
    entered in the disponor's register of title. The breach of trust is itself evidenced by the trustee's
    inability to give a valid receipt for the capital money arising on the disposition (see TA 1925,
    s 14(2)(a) **[paras 11.136, 11.218]**).
2   See LPA 1925, s 27(2) ('this subsection does not ... except where capital money arises on the

transaction, render it necessary to have more than one trustee'). There have even been isolated suggestions in the past that a disposition of land by a sole trustee is invalid as a conveyance of a legal estate (see e g *Bull v Bull* [1955] 1 QB 234 at 238 per Denning LJ; *Waller v Waller* [1967] 1 WLR 451 at 453C; *Northern Bank Ltd v Henry* [1981] IR 1 at 19 per Kenny J). See also S M Clayton, [1981] Conv 19 (referring, by analogy, to SLA 1925, s 18(1)(a) **[para 9.220]**); but compare B Rudden, (1963) 27 Conv (NS) 51 at 56.

11.223   This conclusion can be supported in two ways. First, it could be said, in reliance on section 26, that the disponee's title is immune from being 'questioned', precisely because any relevant 'limitation' on the exercise of the owner's powers, not being reflected by an entry in the register, stems from a source outside the Land Registration Act 2002, viz from the 'two-trustee rule' imposed by the Law of Property Act 1925. Alternatively, and at a more radical level, it could be argued that the disponee's protection does not flow from section 26 at all (which relates only to limitations 'affecting the validity of a disposition'). The breach of trust inherent in non-compliance with the 'two trustee rule' does not, in itself, threaten the *validity* of the disposition of the registered estate, although it may expose the disponee to other consequences of the undoubted breach of trust. As Lord Browne-Wilkinson once observed, the mere fact 'that a trustee acts in breach of trust does not mean that he has no capacity to do the act he wrongly did.'[1] As a matter of general registered land principle, the registration of the disposition of the sole trustee's legal estate therefore operates a 'statutory magic'[2] in favour of the transferee or chargee. This outcome reflects not only the plenary competence of the unrestricted registered proprietor under the scheme of the Land Registration Act, but also a cogent public policy in favour of the protection of the innocent disponee.[3]

1   *Hammersmith and Fulham LBC v Monk* [1992] 1 AC 478 at 493E.
2   **[Para 6.24]**.
3   See e g *National Westminster Bank Plc v Malhan* [2004] EWHC 847 (Ch) at [43] per Morritt V-C. The disponee would otherwise be required to satisfy himself of the non-existence of any implied trust (or to assume the risk that such a trust may have been generated by the disponor's past dealings) or to insist on the appointment of a second legal owner. There is a general argument of public policy that the burdens fastened on bona fide purchasers should not be increased save for good cause. The multiplication of risk may act as a disincentive for banks and other institutional lenders to advance money on the security of realty (see e g *Multiservice Bookbinding Ltd v Marden* [1979] Ch 84 at 104H per Browne-Wilkinson J; *Barclays Bank Plc v O'Brien* [1994] 1 AC 180 at 188G–H per Lord Browne-Wilkinson; *Royal Bank of Scotland plc v Etridge* (*No 2*) [2002] 2 AC 773 at [35] per Lord Nicholls of Birkenhead).

11.224   On either of these footings the wrongful transfer or charge executed by the sole trustee is left intact as a valid registered disposition of the legal estate,[1] in which case it takes its due effect according to the Law of Property Act 1925 and the Land Registration Act 2002.[2] Pursuant to the former statute[3] the disposition cannot, in default of payment of capital money to at least two trustees, be said automatically to have overreached the equitable interests of trust beneficiaries. But under the latter statute the disponee of the registered estate still takes the legal title free of these beneficial interests unless their 'priority' is 'protected' by virtue of their status as 'overriding' interests belonging to persons in 'actual occupation' of the land.[4] Thus, in some circumstances, the disponee, whilst taking a good legal title from a sole trustee of land, may take this title subject to beneficial interests existing behind the trust.[5]

1   No question was raised as to the validity at law of the charge executed by a sole trustee in *Williams & Glyn's Bank Ltd v Boland* [1981] AC 487 **[para 12.204]**. See similarly *Knightly v Sun Life Assurance Society Ltd* (1981) Times, 23 July; *Chhokar v Chhokar* [1984] FLR 313 **[para 12.187]**. Likewise, a disposition of the registered estate by a bare trustee has always been considered effective at law, even though the trustee is acting in gross breach of trust (see *Hodgson v Marks* [1971] Ch 892 at 899C).

2   For a similar analysis, see G Ferris and G Battersby, 'The General Principles of Overreaching and the Modern Legislative Reforms, 1996–2002' (2003) 119 LQR 94 at 121–122.

3   LPA 1925, ss 2(1)(ii), 27(2) **[para 11.203]**.

4   LRA 2002, s 29(1), (2)(a)(ii), Sch 3, para 2 **[para 12.146]**.

5   This replicates, in effect, the outcome reached by the House of Lords in *Williams & Glyn's Bank Ltd v Boland* [1981] AC 487. The Law Commission and Land Registry seem to have had no expectation that the enactment of the Land Registration Act 2002 would effect any dramatic reversal of this decision (see Law Com No 271 (2001), paras 4.8–4.10).

Various immunities for the purchaser of unregistered land

11.225   The Trusts of Land and Appointment of Trustees Act 1996 confers various forms of immunity on a purchaser of an unregistered estate in land held on trust.[1] Thus, for example, the purchaser is 'not concerned to see'[2] that trustees of land have properly discharged their statutory duty to consult their beneficiaries and give effect to their wishes[3] or to 'have regard' to their 'rights'[4] or to ensure their consent to any partition of the co-owned land.[5] Several other forms of protection are important.

1   See TOLATA 1996, s 16(7).

2   TOLATA 1996, s 16(1).

3   TOLATA 1996, s 11(1) **[para 11.183]**.

4   TOLATA 1996, s 6(5) **[para 11.159]**.

5   TOLATA 1996, s 7(3) **[para 11.163]**.

Failure to secure a requisite consent

11.226   A conveyance of the legal estate by trustees of land[1] is not invalidated by the fact that the trustees have failed to obtain a consent to the conveyance which was expressly required by the disposition which created the trust.[2] This immunity for the purchaser prevails except where the purchaser had 'actual notice' of the limitation on the trustees' dispositionary powers.[3] In all other cases, notwithstanding that the trustees are obviously guilty of a wrongful omission,[4] the transaction still ranks as a 'conveyance' of the legal estate for the purpose of enabling the purchaser to overreach outstanding trust equities, provided of course that the preconditions of statutory overreaching are fulfilled.[5]

1   Except in the case of land held on charitable, ecclesiastical or public trusts (TOLATA 1996, s 16(6)).

2   TOLATA 1996, s 16(3)(b).

3   The trustees have a statutory obligation to 'take all reasonable steps to bring the limitation to the notice of any purchaser of the land from them' (TOLATA 2001, s 16(3)(a)).
4   See TOLATA 1996, s 8(2).
5   There remains, of course, the possibility that the purchaser may, if implicated in the impropriety, render himself personally liable to the trust beneficiaries.

Contraventions of statute or any rule of law or equity

11.227   In similar terms a conveyance by trustees of land is not invalidated by reason of the mere fact that the trustees have contravened some statute (other than the Trusts of Land and Appointment of Trustees Act 1996) or have contravened some 'rule of law or equity.'[1] Notwithstanding the impropriety, the purchaser takes a good legal title unless he had 'actual notice of the contravention.'[2] Thus, for example, a conveyance of an unregistered estate by a sole trustee of land – technically acting in breach of his trust – remains effective at law.[3] The mere fact that the trustee's disposition violated a rule of equity does not invalidate the transaction as a 'conveyance'; and the effect of this 'conveyance' is simply left to be governed by the Law of Property Act 1925 and the ordinary rules of equity.[4] According to the Law of Property Act 1925, however, the purchaser from a sole trustee cannot – for want of payment to two trustees – assert that he has statutorily overreached the equitable interests of the trust beneficiaries.[5] Instead, the purchaser, although taking an unimpeachable title at law, may find that in some circumstances he is bound in equity by actual or constructive notice of these unoverreached beneficial rights.[6]

1   TOLATA 1996, s 16(2)(a) (referring to TOLATA 1996, s 6(6), (8)). The plural 'trustees' presumptively includes a singular 'trustee' (see Interpretation Act 1978, s 6(c)).
2   TOLATA 1996, s 16(2)(b).
3   See *Caunce v Caunce* [1969] 1 WLR 286 at 289F–G; *Kingsnorth Finance Co Ltd v Tizard* [1986] 1 WLR 783 at 785C; *Ulster Bank Ltd v Shanks* [1982] NI 143 at 144E.
4   This analysis seems to be broadly in accordance with the conclusion preferred by G Ferris and G Battersby, 'The General Principles of Overreaching and the Modern Legislative Reforms, 1996–2002' (2003) 119 LQR 94 at 113–115.
5   LPA 1925, ss 2(1)(ii), 27(2) [**para 11.203**].
6   This outcome replicates, in effect, the result reached prior to the 1996 Act in cases like *Kingsnorth Finance Co Ltd v Tizard* [1986] 1 WLR 783 [**para 12.361**], with the one qualification that 'actual notice' of the trustee's breach of trust now seems, for the first time, to invalidate the transmission of the legal estate itself.

Deed of discharge

11.228   A purchaser of land which was formerly subject to a trust is entitled, in the absence of actual notice of any irregularity, to rely on a deed of discharge executed by the trustees on their conveyance of the trust land to 'persons believed by them to be absolutely entitled beneficiaries of full age and capacity.'[1] The purchaser is safe, in other words, if he takes his conveyance from erstwhile trust beneficiaries whose trust has visibly terminated in a deed of discharge.

1   TOLATA 1996, s 16(4)–(5). The trustees are statutorily obliged to execute a deed declaring their discharge.

JUDICIAL RESOLUTION OF DISPUTES OVER TRUST LAND

11.229   The Trusts of Land and Appointment of Trustees Act 1996 provides machinery for the resolution of a number of disputes which may emerge in relation to trusts of land.[1] Application for a court order resolving any of these disputes may be made by any trustee of land or any person who 'has an interest in property subject to a trust of land',[2] a phrase which is broad enough to include not merely trust beneficiaries,[3] but also a personal representative, a trustee in bankruptcy, a chargee or mortgagee, a receiver, and a judgment creditor who has obtained a charging order against a trust beneficiary. The court may, in general, make any order which it 'thinks fit' in relation to the exercise by the trustees of any of their functions or in order to declare the 'nature or extent' of any person's interest in the trust land or its proceeds.[4]

1   This jurisdiction under the 1996 Act is somewhat wider than the resolution power conferred on the courts by the now repealed LPA 1925, s 30, which comprised principally a 'one-dimensional' power to order or refuse a sale. See *Abbey National Mortgages Plc v Powell* (1999) 78 P & CR D16 at D17 per Brooke LJ; Law Com No 181 (1989), paras 12.4–12.8, 20.3.
2   TOLATA 1996, s 14(1).
3   Including the beneficiary of a discretionary trust.
4   TOLATA 1996, ss 14(2), 17(2). The declaratory power conferred on the court creates no jurisdiction to vary the beneficial entitlements of the parties (see *Mortgage Corporation v Shaire* [2001] Ch 743 at 755F–G).

Range of potential dispute

11.230   The issues which call for resolution under Trusts of Land and Appointment of Trustees Act 1996 include the following kinds of dispute:

–   disputes as to the trustees' allocation of the 'right to occupy'[1]
–   questions whether trustees should be relieved from any obligation to consult beneficiaries[2] or obtain otherwise requisite consents to the performance of any of their functions[3]
–   disagreement between the trustees whether to sell the trust land[4]
–   attempts by one or more beneficiaries to prevent (or force) a sale by the trustees[5] and
–   applications by creditors for sale of the trust land.[6]

1   [Para 11.178].
2   [Para 11.183].
3   [Para 11.185].
4   [Para 11.236].
5   [Para 11.236].
6   [Para 11.248].

Relevant criteria

11.231   In determining these questions the court is generally directed, by section 15(1) of the 1996 Act, to have regard to a range of considerations, including

–   the intentions of the person or persons (if any) who created the trust
–   the purposes for which the property subject to the trust is held

—   the welfare of any minor who occupies or might reasonably be expected to occupy the trust land as his home, and
—   the interests of any secured creditor of any beneficiary.

11.232   These criteria are neither exhaustive nor weighted or ranked in any way,[1] but they are matters to which the court must have regard in the exercise of its general discretion to make such order as it 'thinks fit'. The statutory criteria are supplemented by provisions which detail several factors of special application to particular kinds of case.[2]

1   See *A v B* (Unreported, Family Division, 23 May 1997) per Cazalet J.
2   The criteria set out in TOLATA 1996, s 15, are expressly declared to be inapplicable on an application for sale brought by a beneficiary's trustee in bankruptcy [**para 11.249**].

Applications relating to the trustees' allocation of the 'right to occupy'

11.233   In any application challenging the manner of the trustees' exercise of their power to regulate the statutory 'right to occupy' enjoyed by trust beneficiaries,[1] the court must also have regard to 'the circumstances and wishes of each of the beneficiaries' who would normally be entitled to occupy the land.[2]

1   TOLATA 1996, s 13 [**para 11.178**].
2   TOLATA 1996, s 15(2).

All other applications

11.234   In the context of applications other than those relating to the trustees' allocation of occupation or to a compulsory conveyance of the trust land to absolutely entitled *sui iuris* beneficiaries,[1] the statutory direction given to the court is somewhat broader.[2] In such other applications the court must have regard to 'the circumstances and wishes' of *all* beneficiaries of full age who are entitled to an interest in possession in the trust land.[3]

1   TOLATA 1996, s 6(2) [**para 11.164**].
2   See *Mortgage Corporation v Shaire* [2001] Ch 743 at 761G–H per Neuberger J.
3   TOLATA 1996, s 15(3). A qualified majority rule applies: in cases of disagreement between the beneficiaries, the court must have regard to the circumstances and wishes of the majority 'according to the value of their interests.'

APPLICATIONS RELATING TO OCCUPATION OF TRUST LAND

11.235   Unresolved disagreement may occur – between trustee and trustee or between trustees and beneficiaries or even between beneficiaries themselves – as to the occupation of trust land. Such disputes tend to be submerged in larger questions whether the co-owned land should be sold or otherwise disposed of. Such questions frequently highlight an underlying tension between the exchange value of land and its use value.[1] Sooner or later the objectives of use and exchange become incompatible and the court may be asked to decide whether trust land should be retained (for purposes of occupation or investment) or sold (thereby releasing the proceeds for immediate distribution between the beneficial owners under the trust). In determining issues of this kind, the court is guided by statutory criteria which incorporate the effect of much pre-1997 case law. The court's discretion is influenced, not only by the general criteria specified by section 15(1) of the 1996 Act, but also by the statutory injunction to have regard to 'the circumstances and wishes' of the beneficiaries. The outcome of the discretionary process may be problematic, particularly where disputes over occupation take on a sharper edge in the context of a proposed sale of the trust land.

1   Some forms of dealing with land reflect this tension in only an attenuated form. By means of a mortgage, owners of land may not be forced into an immediate or irrevocable choice between the realisation of the exchange value and the use value of their land. The mortgage transaction is commonly a device for allowing the mortgagor to enjoy both kinds of value simultaneously.

DISPUTES OVER SALE ARISING BETWEEN TRUSTEES AND BENEFICIARIES

11.236   The court is given jurisdiction under section 14(1)–(2) of the Trusts of Land and Appointment of Trustees Act 1996 to make such order as it 'thinks fit' in resolution of any dispute as to whether trust land should be sold or the land retained for occupation or other use by one or more of the trust beneficiaries.[1] This jurisdiction is never invoked in the context of marriage dissolution, since the property difficulties of divorcing parties are nowadays dealt with as part of a specialised matrimonial regime of ancillary relief. The court's discretion is characteristically directed, however, to disputes arising between trustees and/or beneficiaries who are unmarried partners or members of a wider family group or, indeed, entirely unrelated persons caught up in commercial or other partnerships. Dilemmas of a peculiarly acute nature are thrown up where, in the quasi-marital or familial context, one party wishes the property to be sold and the proceeds of sale distributed in the appropriate beneficial shares, while another party simply wishes to remain living in the home with or without children of the family.

1   See also Civil Partnership Bill (Bill 132–1 of 2004), cl 66(2), which would empower the court, at its discretion, to order a sale of property on the application of one partner in a civil partnership.

Relevance of pre-1997 case law

11.237   Prior to 1997 the jurisdiction to order sale was exercised pursuant to section 30 of the Law of Property Act 1925, which likewise conferred a broad discretion on the court to make such order as it thought fit. The extensive case law generated by this provision was overshadowed, however, by a predisposition towards sale which was thought to be intrinsic to the device of the trust for sale.[1] The judicial discretion conferred by the 1996 Act deliberately reflects the removal of any bias towards sale in the new 'trust of land'.[2] Trusts of land are now premised on the vesting in trustees of twin (and equally balanced) powers either to sell or to retain the trust land. The Law Commission hoped that this restructuring of the trust powers would 'clear the way for a genuinely broad and flexible approach', in consequence of which the courts would 'not be required to give a preference to sale.'[3] The Commission expressed the view that, with the displacement of any presumption in favour of sale, the reformulated judicial discretion would 'consolidate and rationalise the present approach' to disputes between co-owners.[4] This prediction has proved broadly correct: the pre-existing case law has not been rendered redundant.[5]

1   *Mortgage Corporation v Shaire* [2001] Ch 743 at 758H per Neuberger J. See e g *Re Mayo* [1943] Ch 302 at 304 [**para 9.225**]. The jurisprudence of section 30 was dominated by the question whether the primacy of sale had been displaced by other considerations which made it inequitable to press for realisation of the 'prime object' of the trust for sale (ie sale). For further details, see *Elements of Land Law* (2nd edn 1993), pp 583–597.
2   Under the 1996 Act 'there is no duty to sell the property but only a power to do so' (*White v White* [2003] EWCA Civ 924 at [20] per Arden LJ).
3   Law Com No 181, para 12.5.
4   The Commission thought that the new statutory guidelines would put the criteria developed under section 30 on a statutory footing and that there would be 'much of value in the existing body of case law, even though these cases assume that there is a duty to sell' (Law Com No 181 (1989), para 12.9).
5   See *A v B* (Unreported, Family Division, 23 May 1997) per Cazalet J; *Wright v Johnson* (Unreported, Court of Appeal, 2 November 1999) per Robert Walker LJ.

Relationship with factors of reasonableness

11.238   The test to be applied between trustees and/or beneficiaries under section 15 of the 1996 Act cannot simply be converted into some ultimate or universal test of 'reasonableness'.[1] It is inherent in most circumstances of disputed sale that all parties are probably reacting entirely reasonably in expressing a vigorous preference either for sale or for retention of the trust land. It is usually quite reasonable, for instance, that one party (if beneficially entitled) should wish to realise his or her equitable share in cash while another who is likewise entitled should wish to continue to enjoy the use value of the property.[2] Recourse must therefore be had to the criteria specified by section 15 of the 1996 Act, which enable the court to address the specific needs and vulnerabilities present in the often complex world of trust relationships.

1   A similar view was taken of LPA 1925, s 30 (see e g *Jones v Challenger* [1961] 1 QB 176 at 180, 184; *Rivett v Rivett* (1966) 200 EG 858; *Mayes v Mayes* (1969) 210 EG 935 at 937; *Re Turner (A Bankrupt)* [1974] 1 WLR 1556 at 1558B–C).
2   See *Jones v Challenger* [1961] 1 QB 176 at 184 per Devlin LJ.

Relevant criteria

11.239   The statutory criteria relevant to the resolution of disputed issues of sale are overlapping and interactive. There is 'no order of precedence' between them.[1] Just as under the old jurisdiction conferred by section 30 of the Law of Property Act 1925, the court 'must look into all the circumstances of the case and consider whether or not, at the particular moment and in the particular circumstances when the application is made to it, it is right and proper' that an order for sale should be made.[2] It falls to the court to decide whose voice should be allowed in equity to prevail.[3]

1   See *A v B* (Unreported, Family Division, 23 May 1997) per Cazalet J.
2   *Re Buchanan-Wollaston's Conveyance* [1939] Ch 738 at 747 per Sir Wilfred Greene MR.
3   See e g *Chhokar v Chhokar* [1984] FLR 313 at 329–330.

Intentions of the person (if any) who created the trust

11.240   The 1996 Act instructs the court to have regard to the 'intentions of the person or persons (if any) who created the trust.'[1] This consideration, which tends to merge with the statutory reference to the 'purposes' of a trust of land, is primarily relevant to trusts created by express disposition or by will, particularly where the trust takes the form of a 'trust for sale'.[2] In *Barclay v Barclay*,[3] for example, a testator had left his bungalow on trust, the property to be sold after his death and the proceeds divided between five members of his family. In ordering sale the Court of Appeal declined to accede to the wishes of one of the beneficiaries, who during the testator's lifetime had been allowed to occupy the property and who selfishly wished to remain in occupation permanently. The Court attached decisive significance to the fact that the patent intention of the creator of the testamentary trust had been that the bungalow should be sold and his largesse distributed immediately to all the nominated beneficiaries.[4]

1   TOLATA 1996, s 15(1)(a). These 'intentions' must have been formulated prior to the creation of the trust and, if more than one person created the trust, the relevant 'intentions' are the intentions which the authors of the trust had in common (*White v White* [2003] EWCA Civ 924 at [22]–[23] per Arden LJ).
2   **[Para 9.221]**.
3   [1970] 2 QB 677. See (1970) 86 LQR 443 (P V Baker).
4   [1970] 2 QB 677 at 684A–B, 684G, 685G–H. For a similar decision under the 1996 Act, see *Swain v Foster* (Unreported, Court of Appeal, 14 October 1998).

Purposes for which the land is held on trust

11.241   The purposes for which land is held on trust represent a significant, although not decisive, consideration in determining whether that land should be sold.[1] The element of purpose, if initially shared by all parties concerned, often operates almost by way of estoppel[2] in pointing either towards sale or towards retention of the trust land.[3] The 1996 Act does not define the term 'purposes' or indicate whether the statutorily relevant 'purposes' are necessarily fixed ab initio.[4] The courts have indicated, however, that the 'purposes' of a trust can be formulated informally and are subsequently open to variation by agreement between the parties who created the trust.[5] Alternatively, the initial purpose of a trust can be destroyed by a fundamental change of circumstance.[6]

1   TOLATA 1996, s 15(1)(b). Under LPA 1925, s 30, the courts developed a doctrine of 'collateral purpose', holding it to be generally wrong to order sale of the trust property if the original or collateral purpose (written or unwritten) which underlay the trust was still capable of substantial fulfilment (see *Jones v Challenger* [1961] 1 QB 176 at 181 per Devlin LJ; *Rivett v Rivett* (1966) 200 EG 858; *Cousins v Dzosens* (1981) Times, 9 December). Conversely, if the collateral purpose of a trust was no longer capable of fulfilment, the courts tended to sanction the proposed sale unless it was clearly inequitable to do so (see generally *Abbey National Plc v Moss* [1994] 1 FLR 307 at 314E per Peter Gibson LJ).
2   See Chapter 10 [**para 10.168**].
3   For an explicit use of estoppel terminology, see e g *Jones (A E) v Jones (F W)* [1977] 1 WLR 438 at 442D–G, 443D–E. Here a father had induced his son to give up his employment and to contribute money towards the purchase of the father's house on the basis of a reasonable expectation, encouraged by the father, that the son could live in that house for the rest of his life. The Court of Appeal held that the father's widow (who later succeeded to the father's interests under the relevant trust) was estopped from obtaining an order for sale. The Court considered it inequitable to defeat the purpose originally contemplated by the father and son, which was to provide long-term housing for the latter.
4   See, however, *Luciv v Filinov* (Unreported, Court of Appeal, 15 May 1980), where Megaw LJ stressed that the fundamentally discretionary nature of the court's jurisdiction is inconsistent with any dogmatic assertion that the initial purpose of the trust is determinative for all time.
5   See *White v White* [2003] EWCA Civ 924 at [24] per Arden LJ.
6   See e g *Bankers Trust Co v Namdar* [1997] EGCS 20, where at first instance Evans-Lombe J regarded the initial purpose of a matrimonial home trust as having been brought to an end by the husband's unilateral mortgage of the property and his abandonment of his wife 'in circumstances in which it is plain that their marriage was at an end.' See also *Barclays Bank plc v Hendricks* [1996] 1 FLR 258 at 263D; *Mortgage Corporation v Shaire* [2001] Ch 743 at 762A–F per Neuberger J.

11.242   The motivation underlying a co-operative living arrangement can be hugely important. In *Stott v Ratcliffe*,[1] for example, the original purpose of a trust had been to provide a home for two elderly people during their joint lifetimes and thereafter for the surviving co-owner. On the death of one of the co-owners, the Court of Appeal declined to order sale at the behest of the personal representatives of the deceased tenant in common, the explicit object of the acquisition of the co-owned property having been to secure a home for the survivor.[2]

1   (1982) 126 Sol Jo 310.
2   See also *Wight v IRC* (1982) 264 EG 935 at 936–937; *Ngatoa v Ford* (1990) 19 NSWLR 72 at 77D; and contrast *Grindal v Hooper* (2000) Times, 8 February (where there was no proven intention to house the survivor). In *Power v Brighton* (Unreported, 14 November 1984), the Court of Appeal likewise declined to order a sale of property purchased for the purpose of providing a home for the new legal owner with the aid of money contributions from friends. When these contributors demanded to withdraw their respective cash investments, the Court of Appeal held that the 'underlying purpose of the trust' was still in existence and therefore precluded sale.

11.243   A trust of the family home is almost always founded upon the purpose of providing a base for joint residential occupation by family members.[1] Accordingly, the courts have tended to refuse any order for sale while that purpose remains substantially capable of fulfilment, sale being sanctioned only where the underlying residential purpose has clearly been exhausted or frustrated.[2] Except in cases of insolvency,[3] the court will rarely compel a sale of the family home so long as the relevant family members continue to live there in amity.[4]

1   See, however, the unattractively strict view taken in *White v White* [2003] EWCA Civ 924 at [24], where Arden LJ considered that, in the absence of agreement between the parties, the original purpose of a trust of a house could not be expanded to cover the provision of a home for children who were born subsequently.

2   The court thus leans in favour of ordering sale of a family home if the property was initially purchased in order to house a relationship which has since broken down irretrievably, leaving no minor children who still require the home as a base (see *Jones v Challenger* [1961] 1 QB 176 at 183–184 per Devlin LJ). See also *Rivett v Rivett* (1966) 200 EG 858; *Re Holliday (A Bankrupt)* [1981] Ch 405 at 415F per Goff LJ. See also *Grindal v Hooper* (2000) Times, 8 February (survivor had moved to Wales 'many many years ago').

3   See *Re Citro (A Bankrupt)* [1991] Ch 142 at 147B, 158G–159A per Nourse LJ [**para 11.257**].

4   *Jones v Challenger* [1961] 1 QB 176 at 182 per Devlin LJ; *Re Citro (A Bankrupt)* [1991] Ch 142 at 147B–C, 158G per Nourse LJ. See also *Chhokar v Chhokar* [1984] FLR 313 at 327E–G, 328C–G, where the Court of Appeal refused to countenance an application for sale made by a third party who had purchased the family home in fraud of the beneficial entitlement of the vendor's wife [**para 12.187**]. The wife continued to live in the home and later became reconciled with her husband. The Court held that the 'underlying objects' of the original trust were still in subsistence at the date of the application for sale, and there appeared now to be no special reason for frustrating the initial intention of the spouses to use the property as their matrimonial home.

11.244   The notion that an underlying purpose may render the sale of trust land inequitable is just as clearly demonstrated in circumstances where the participants in the trust have covenanted not to dispose of the land without the agreement of all parties. In *Re Buchanan-Wollaston's Conveyance*[1] four individuals, who each owned separate but neighbouring properties overlooking the sea, jointly purchased a piece of land which they desired to keep as an open space in order to preserve their common sea view.[2] The parties covenanted *inter se* not to part with the co-owned land except by unanimous consent or majority vote.[3] When one, on later selling his own house, sought a court order directing his fellow trustees to join with him in a sale of the co-owned open land,[4] the Court of Appeal refused the order on the ground that the plaintiff 'could not ... ask the Court to act in a way inconsistent with his own contractual obligations.'[5] Sale would not be ordered while the parties' underlying contractual purpose subsisted.[6]

1   [1939] Ch 217, 738.

2   They held the legal estate on trust for themselves as tenants in common in the proportions of their respective financial contributions towards the purchase [**para 10.11**].

3   An agreement between co-owners postponing or displacing otherwise available powers of sale is not void as a restraint on alienation [**para 7.16**], at least where the restriction facilitates a collateral benefit which is itself both lawful and reasonable. See eg *Re Permanent Trustee Nominees (Canberra) Ltd* [1989] 1 Qd R 314 at 316–318 (powers could be reactivated on the giving of 12 months' notice); *Elton v Cavill (No 2)* (1994) 34 NSWLR 289 at 301F–G.

4   The co-owner seeking sale argued that the trustees had indeed determined the question of sale by vote, in that this vote had consisted of 'a vote at a meeting which he and he alone had attended, although the [other trustees] were invited to come' ([1939] Ch 738 at 748).

5   [1939] Ch 738 at 745 per Sir Wilfred Greene MR. See also *Abbey National Plc v Moss* [1994]

1 FLR 307 at 313B–C; *L M Rosen Realty Ltd v D'Amore* (1982) 132 DLR (3d) 648 at 661, (1984) 7 DLR (4th) 285 at 296. Compare, however, *Miller v Lakefield Estates Ltd* (1989) 57 P & CR 104 at 107–109.

6 The Court of Appeal approved the stance taken at first instance by Farwell J, who thought that 'he who seeks equity must do equity' ([1939] Ch 217 at 223–224). The Court of Appeal did indicate, however, that sale might be ordered if circumstances were to change, in that if 'all the parties died, and all their houses were sold, ... the Court ... would not be disposed to listen to arguments against such a sale adduced by people who had no real interest in keeping this land unsold' ([1939] Ch 738 at 747–748).

Welfare of any minor who occupies the trust property as his home

11.245 The element of trust purpose interacts heavily with another factor rendered relevant by the Trusts of Land and Appointment of Trustees Act 1996. It is far from true that the underlying purpose of a trust of the family home is necessarily spent or exhausted when a family relationship breaks down. The existence of minor children of the family may well serve to prolong the trust purpose beyond the termination of the mutual relationship of the trustees or beneficiaries if the home is still required as accommodation for these children.[1] This family-oriented perspective is reflected in the requirement, contained in the 1996 Act, that the court must have regard to 'the welfare of any minor who occupies or might reasonably be expected to occupy any land subject to the trust as his home.'[2] In many cases such a consideration argues forcefully against any immediate sale of trust property.[3]

1 For an early realisation of this aspect, see *Rawlings v Rawlings* [1964] P 398 at 419 per Salmon LJ. Compare, however, *Burke v Burke* [1974] 1 WLR 1063 at 1067D–E, where Buckley LJ thought that the interests of children were 'only incidentally to be taken into consideration ... so far as they affect the equities in the matter as between the two persons entitled to the beneficial interests in the property.' To treat the children's father as being 'obliged to make provision for his children by agreeing to retain the property unsold' was, in Buckley LJ's view, to 'confuse with a problem relating to property considerations which are relevant to maintenance.' In *Williams (J W) v Williams (M A)* [1976] Ch 278 at 285E–G, Lord Denning MR was later to refer to Buckley LJ's perspective as exemplifying 'the old approach' which was 'now out-dated'.

2 TOLATA 1996, s 15(1)(c).

3 The court now has jurisdiction, in appropriate cases, to require that compensation be paid for the exclusive use of the trust property (TOLATA 1996, s 14(1)–(2) **[para 11.236]**).

11.246 The controlling relevance of this more utilitarian approach was classically foreshadowed in *Re Evers' Trust*.[1] Here a cohabiting couple had purchased a home in joint names largely with the aid of a joint mortgage loan. When the parties later separated, the woman and three children (including two from an earlier union) remained in the house. The Court of Appeal refused, at least for the time being, to endorse a sale which would have allowed the male partner to evict the woman and the children from their home merely in order to extract his capital investment and apply it for other purposes.[2] Ormrod LJ pointed out that the underlying purpose of the trust had been to provide a home for the couple and their three children 'for the indefinite future' and that this purpose was still capable of substantial fulfilment.[3] The decision in *Re Evers' Trust* has proved to be an important landmark in the development of a greater judicial and legislative sensitivity to the balance which requires to be maintained in this area between property and family considerations.

1   [1980] 1 WLR 1327. See [1981] Conv 79 (A Sydenham).
2   The Court of Appeal took into account that the man now had a secure home with his own mother and had no present need to realise his investment, while the woman was prepared to accept full responsibility for the outstanding mortgage liability and would have found it extremely difficult to rehouse herself if the property had been sold. The Court indicated, however, that sale might become appropriate at some future stage if circumstances changed, as for instance if the woman remarried or if it became financially possible for her to buy the man out.
3   [1980] 1 WLR 1327 at 1333E–1334D. Ormrod LJ cited with approval the 'modern view' articulated by Lord Denning MR in *Williams (J W) v Williams (M A)* [1976] Ch 278 at 285E–F, according to which the courts 'nowadays have great regard to the fact that the house is bought as a home in which the family is to be brought up. It is not treated as property to be sold, nor as an investment to be realised for cash.' See also *Browne v Pritchard* [1975] 1 WLR 1366 at 1371H per Ormrod LJ ('[I]nvestment in a home is the least liquid investment that one can possibly make. It cannot be converted into cash while the children are at home and often not until one spouse dies unless it is possible to move into much smaller and cheaper accommodation').

Other relevant factors

11.247   The specification of relevant criteria in section 15(1) is not exhaustive.[1] In any particular case it is open to the court to have regard to other factors which legitimately bear upon the sale of the trust property. The court is required to respond humanely to a wide variety of competing needs presented by the beneficial owners under a trust of land. It is clear, for instance, that the court may, in its discretion, withhold a sale of the family home where a co-owner who wishes to retain the home is out of work.[2] It may, on the other hand, be just and equitable to release the cash shares of the equitable co-owners where the trust property comprises an excessively large house which is plainly unsuitable for sole occupation by the beneficial co-owner resisting sale.[3] Likewise, it may be highly relevant that a refusal to order sale will severely prejudice the value of a beneficiary's equitable share[4] or otherwise keep this share locked up in the land for an unduly lengthy or indefinite period. Sometimes the balance of the parties' respective accommodation requirements may, almost as a matter of responsible housing policy, point towards the solution of the problem. In *Bernard v Josephs*[5] Kerr LJ observed that 'above all, in these times of housing shortage, a sale has the disadvantage that the property ceases to be available as a home for either of the parties.' The fact that a court-ordered sale throws an increased strain upon already hard-pressed social housing stock may be a ground which influences the court to decline to order the sale of co-owned homes.[6]

1   See *Swain v Foster* (Unreported, Court of Appeal, 14 October 1998), per Holman J; *White v White* [2003] EWCA Civ 924 at [26] per Arden LJ.
2   See *Mayes v Mayes* (1969) 210 EG 935 at 937.
3   See *Jackson v Jackson* [1971] 1 WLR 1539 at 1543G–H.
4   See e g *Jones v Challenger* [1961] 1 QB 176 at 187 (lease with only six years to run). Compare

Mayes v Mayes (1969) 210 EG 935 at 937, where in the case of a relatively long leasehold term the urgency of sale was considerably abated, the co-owned asset not being a wasting asset but one which was liable to inflate in value.

5   [1982] Ch 391 at 410D. See [1983] CLJ 30 at 33–34 (Gray).

6   This consideration has become a relevant concern in the resolution of property matters on divorce (see e g *Harvey v Harvey* [1982] Fam 83 at 88E–F; [1982] CLJ 228 at 230–231 (Gray)), and certainly influenced the court in *Bernard v Josephs* to hold that an order for sale should not be enforced if the defendant were willing and able to buy out the claimant's share for cash.

APPLICATIONS FOR SALE OF TRUST LAND BROUGHT BY OR ON BEHALF OF CREDITORS

11.248   The tension between the use value and the exchange value of trust land takes on an even more poignant character when the pressure towards a court-ordered sale of the land comes, not from any of the participants in the trust of land, but from some external creditor who requires that the land be sold in order to release funds for the discharge of debts incurred by one or more of the trust beneficiaries.[1] The introduction of a third party element profoundly affects the balance of the relevant issues.[2] In this respect the Trusts of Land and Appointment of Trustees Act 1996 draws an important distinction between the claims represented by a beneficiary's trustee in bankruptcy and claims in circumstances which fall short of bankruptcy.

1   As Hoffmann J observed in *Re Citro (A Bankrupt)* [1991] Ch 142 at 150A–B, the resolution of this tension is 'by no means an easy thing … The two interests are not in any sense commensurable. On the one hand, one has the financial interests of the Crown, some banking institutions and a few traders. On the other, one has personal and human interests of these two families.'

2   See *Re Bailey (A Bankrupt)* [1977] 1 WLR 278 at 281F–G per Megarry V-C (distinguishing the Court of Appeal's family-oriented approach in *Williams (J W) v Williams (M A)* [1976] Ch 278 **[para 11.245]** as irrelevant to disputes 'in which matters of commercial obligation [arise], as in the case of bankruptcy').

APPLICATIONS MADE BY A TRUSTEE IN BANKRUPTCY

11.249   Bankruptcy is personal financial crisis in its most extreme form, leading as it does to a severe diminution of legal capacity for the individual who is the subject of a bankruptcy order.[1] Bankruptcy tends to occur in close association with such events as redundancy, business failure or marriage breakdown and in each case the advent of bankruptcy has a potentially devastating impact on family life.[2] This impact is intensified by the fact that frequently the only substantial capital asset available to meet the claims of creditors is the family home in which the bankrupt's partner and children (and often the bankrupt himself) are still living. Where bankruptcy affects a beneficial owner of land, it is inevitable that his or her trustee in bankruptcy will seek a sale of the trust land – almost certainly contrary to the clear wishes of trustees and beneficiaries alike – where such sale is likely to raise money for distribution amongst the creditors.

1   See e g Insolvency Act 1986, s 284(1).
2   'Eviction from the family home ... may be a disaster not only to the debtor himself ... but also to those who are living there as his dependants' (*Insolvency Law and Practice* (Report of the Review Committee chaired by Sir Kenneth Cork, Cmnd 8558, June 1982), para 1116).

11.250   The balance to be struck between family and commercial interests in the context of insolvency was considered over 20 years ago by a review committee chaired by Sir Kenneth Cork. This committee concluded that it would be 'consonant with present social attitudes to alleviate the personal hardships of those who are dependent on the debtor but not responsible for his insolvency, if this can be achieved by delaying for an acceptable time the sale of the family home.'[1] The present law of bankruptcy gives partial effect to the Cork Committee's recommendations and also incorporates certain liberalising features introduced by the Enterprise Act 2002.

1   *Insolvency Law and Practice* (Cmnd 8558, June 1982), para 1118.

Locus standi of the trustee in bankruptcy

11.251   Bankruptcy has, of course, no direct impact on any legal title held by the bankrupt as a trustee,[1] but all property owned by the bankrupt beneficially (ie the bankrupt's 'estate') vests by operation of law in his or her trustee in bankruptcy.[2] The trustee in bankruptcy is then statutorily bound to 'get in, realise and distribute' that estate in satisfaction of the claims of creditors.[3] Where the bankrupt is beneficially entitled to trust land, the trustee in bankruptcy ranks as a person with 'an interest in property subject to a trust of land' for the purpose of applying for a court order for sale of that land.[4] The application is heard by the bankruptcy court[5] and, if an order for sale is made, the net proceeds thus released become available to meet the bankrupt's debts to a maximum value represented by the bankrupt's beneficial share under the trust.[6]

1   See *Worrall v Harford* (1802) 8 Ves 4 at 8, 32 ER 250 at 252; *Re Morgan* (1881) 18 Ch D 93 at 104.
2   Insolvency Act 1986, ss 283(1)(a), (3)(a), 306. The involuntary alienation to the trustee in bankruptcy operates an automatic severance of any beneficial joint tenancy held by the bankrupt.
3   Insolvency Act 1986, s 305(2). On application by a trustee in bankruptcy, the court may also review any transaction 'at an undervalue' entered into by the bankrupt within the five years immediately preceding the presentation of the bankruptcy petition (Insolvency Act 1986, ss 339(1), 341(1)(a)). The court may order that property transferred by the bankrupt (or its money proceeds) be vested in the trustee and treated as part of the bankrupt's distributable estate (Insolvency Act 1986, s 342(1)). See e g *Re Densham* (*A Bankrupt*) [1975] 1 WLR 1519 at 1529C per Goff J; *Elements of Land Law* (1st edn), pp 884–887. Transactions are, however, immune from review if they were entered into more than *two* years before the presentation of the bankruptcy petition and if the bankrupt can prove that he was not insolvent at the date of the transaction and did not become insolvent in consequence of it (Insolvency Act 1986, s 341(2)).
4   TOLATA 1996, s 14(1). See *Re Solomon* (*A Bankrupt*) [1967] Ch 573 at 586 (trustee in bankruptcy a 'person interested' in land for the purpose of LPA 1925, s 30). A trustee in bankruptcy must not incur costs deliberately in order to benefit a secured creditor who has

not surrendered his security, but is generally left to be 'the best judge of what is commercially prudent or expedient in the interests of the creditors' (see *Judd v Brown* [1999] 1 FLR 1191 at 1197H–1198C).

5   Insolvency Act 1986, s 335A(1) (as added by TOLATA 1996, s 25(1), Sch 3, para 23).

6   It is generally no abuse of process for a mortgagee, being unable to rely on his own paramount power of sale, to instigate bankruptcy proceedings for the purpose of obtaining a sale of trust land by other means (see *Alliance and Leicester plc v Slayford* [2001] 1 All ER (Comm) 1 at [20], [28] per Peter Gibson LJ [**para 15.129**]). But the court may view with suspicion a mortgagee's attempt to achieve, through a trustee in bankruptcy, a sale which, for reasons of the adverse publicity connected with evicting a family, it is unwilling to bring about through the exercise of its power of sale (see *Re Ng (A Bankrupt)* [1998] 2 FLR 386 at 387F–H, 388H–389A).

Exercise of the court's discretion

11.252 On an application for sale brought by a beneficiary's trustee in bankruptcy, the liberal criteria laid out in section 15(1) of the Trusts of Land and Appointment of Trustees Act 1996[1] are expressly declared to be inapplicable.[2] The bankruptcy court is instead directed by the Insolvency Act 1986 to make 'such order as it thinks just and reasonable', having regard to 'the interests of the bankrupt's creditors'[3] and 'all the circumstances of the case other than the needs of the bankrupt.'[4] This judicial discretion is ultimately curtailed by an overriding statutory direction that, in any application made more than one year after the bankrupt's estate vests in his trustee in bankruptcy, the court must assume, unless the circumstances of the case are 'exceptional', that 'the interests of the bankrupt's creditors outweigh all other considerations.'[5] In other words, after the bankrupt has been allowed a breathing space of (at most) one year to retrieve his situation or make alternative financial or residential arrangements, the needs of the bankrupt's creditors are normally regarded as paramount.[6]

1   [**Para 11.231**].
2   TOLATA 1996, s 15(4).
3   The statutory reference to 'creditors' includes not only secured, but also unsecured, creditors, although a trustee in bankruptcy will generally 'pay special attention' to the interests of unsecured creditors (*Judd v Brown* [1999] 1 FLR 1191 at 1197G–1198B per Robert Walker LJ).
4   Insolvency Act 1986, s 335A(2).
5   Insolvency Act 1986, s 335A(3). A trustee in bankruptcy has three years from the date of the bankruptcy within which to apply for an order for the sale of any dwelling-house in which the bankrupt has an interest and which served as the sole or principal residence of the bankrupt or his spouse (Insolvency Act 1986, s 283A(1)–(3), inserted with effect from 1 April 2004 by Enterprise Act 2002, s 261(1) (see SI 2003/2093, art 2(2), Sch 2)). Thereafter, for want of any sale or application to court, the relevant interest reverts to the bankrupt (Insolvency Act 1986, s 283A(2)).
6   The balance thereby maintained between bankrupt and creditor seems sufficient to avert any suggestion that the Insolvency Act 1986 inevitably violates the principle of respect for 'private and family life' and for the 'home' expressed in ECHR Art 8 [**para 2.60**]. This principle is qualified by reference to the 'protection of the rights and freedoms of others' (see ECHR Art 8(2)), a phrase which must 'plainly encompass the rights of the creditors of the bankrupt' (*Jackson v Bell* [2001] Fam Law 879 at [24] per Morritt V-C).

Matrimonial homes

11.253   The Insolvency Act 1986 specifies certain additional considerations as relevant in applications for sale which involve a dwelling house which is (or has been) the home of the bankrupt or his spouse or former spouse. Here the court must also take account of

–   the conduct of the bankrupt's spouse or former spouse, so far as contributing to the bankruptcy
–   the needs and financial resources of the spouse or former spouse,[1] and
–   the needs of any children.

1   The Cork Committee endorsed, more broadly, the idea that consideration be given to the needs of a de facto partner and any 'dependant parent of the debtor or of his wife who has been living there as part of the family on the basis of a long term arrangement' (Cmnd 8558 (1982), paras 1124–1125).

11.254   These statutory criteria are unranked and somewhat general in their tenor.[1] Their relevance is restricted to the determination whether the bankrupt and his family should be allowed a moratorium of up to one year before an order for sale, in the absence of 'exceptional' circumstances, becomes inevitable. The Enterprise Act 2002 has now added one further (and highly marginal) control on any application for sale made by a trustee in bankruptcy. The court must dismiss the application if the net value of the bankrupt's interest in the home is below an amount prescribed by secondary legislation.[2] This limitation at least serves to minimise the possibility of pointless realisations of assets which ultimately produce nothing for the bankrupt's creditors.[3]

1   The criteria contrast strongly with the express recommendation of the Cork Committee that, in balancing familial and commercial interests, the court should 'give primary consideration to the welfare of dependant children, to the circumstances of the wife, and to the situation of dependant parents who are resident in the family dwelling' (Cmnd 8558 (1982), para 1129).
2   Insolvency Act 1986, s 313A(2), inserted with effect from 1 April 2004 by Enterprise Act 2002, s 261(3)–(4) (see SI 2003/2093, art 2(2), Sch 2). The amount currently prescribed is £1,000 (SI 2004/547, Art 2, Sch).
3   See *Judd v Brown* [1999] 1 FLR 1191 at 1197G; *Trustee of the Estate of Bowe (A Bankrupt) v Bowe* [1997] BPIR 747.

Matrimonial home rights

11.255   The limited security of tenure which a bankrupt may thus be allowed in respect of his home is reinforced by the fact that any 'matrimonial home rights' under the Family Law Act 1996 which his spouse may have acquired prior to the bankruptcy[1] are expressly declared to subsist notwithstanding the bankruptcy.[2] These rights are terminable only by court order and, in deciding such an issue, the court must make 'such order … as it thinks just and reasonable', having regard to the interests of the creditors, the spouse's conduct, her needs and financial resources, the needs of any children, and 'all the circumstances of the case other than the needs of the bankrupt.'[3] Again the court's discretion is peremptorily limited by the statutory direction that, in cases arising more than one year after the vesting of the bankrupt's estate in his trustee, the court must assume, 'unless the circumstances of the case are exceptional, that the interests of the bankrupt's creditors outweigh all other considerations.'[4] This provision clearly signals that the bankrupt's home will rarely be immune from sale for more than a limited adjustment period of one year following his bankruptcy.[5]

1   The bankrupt's spouse is expressly precluded from acquiring any such rights (e g by reason of marriage) during the period which intervenes between the presentation of the petition for a bankruptcy order and the vesting of the bankrupt's estate in his trustee (Insolvency Act 1986, s 336(1)).
2   Insolvency Act 1986, s 336(2)(a).
3   Insolvency Act 1986, s 336(4).
4   Insolvency Act 1986, s 336(5).
5   See, however, *Re Bremner* [1999] 1 FLR 912 at 915A **[para 11.258]**.

'Exceptional' circumstances

11.256   The statutory direction given to the bankruptcy court closely mirrors the historic pattern of the case law which, even before the introduction of the Insolvency Act 1986 (as amended),[1] almost invariably accorded priority to the claims of trustees in bankruptcy for the sale of trust property.[2] Notwithstanding frequent protestations of neutrality in the exercise of judicial discretion,[3] the solid tug of money consistently prevailed over family interests,[4] the record revealing virtually no instances[5] in which the residential needs of spouses or children were adjudged superior to the claims of creditors as represented by a trustee in bankruptcy.[6] As Bingham LJ observed in *Re Citro (A Bankrupt)*,[7] sale must be ordered 'unless there are, at least, compelling reasons, not found in the ordinary run of cases, for refusing it.'

1   Insolvency Act 1986, s 335A came into effect on 1 January 1997, most applications for sale prior to that date being determined pursuant to LPA 1925, s 30 **[para 11.237]**. See generally *Abbey National Plc v Moss* [1994] 1 FLR 307 at 314F per Peter Gibson LJ.
2   See e g *Re Densham (A Bankrupt)* [1975] 1 WLR 1519 at 1532B; *Bird v Syme-Thomson* [1979] 1 WLR 440 at 445E–F; *Re Lowrie (A Bankrupt)* [1981] 3 All ER 353 at 358h, 359h; *Re Holliday (A Bankrupt)* [1981] Ch 405 at 425G; *Re Citro (A Bankrupt)* [1991] Ch 142 at 153F, 157A–B per Nourse LJ, 160C per Bingham LJ.
3   See e g *Re Turner (A Bankrupt)* [1974] 1 WLR 1556 at 1558A–C; *Re Densham (A Bankrupt)* [1975] 1 WLR 1519 at 1531E; *Re Holliday (A Bankrupt)* [1981] Ch 405 at 420C; *Thames Guaranty Ltd v Campbell* [1985] QB 210 at 239A–B.
4   See the statement of Cumming-Bruce LJ in *Chhokar v Chhokar* [1984] FLR 313 at 327G that, because he represents 'innocent creditors', the court 'will usually pay great regard to the voice of a trustee in bankruptcy'.
5   The case law had a self-fulfilling quality. See e g *Re Bailey (A Bankrupt)* [1977] 1 WLR 278 at 283C, where Walton J attributed great significance to the fact that 'no case of the many referred to yet has thrown up the case where [the trustee in bankruptcy's] voice was not allowed to prevail.'
6   See, for example, the admission in *Harman v Glencross* [1985] Fam 49 at 58A–B that the 'only real question' is 'how long is the wife to continue to have possession and not whether there should be a sale at all.' See also *Re Citro (A Bankrupt)* [1991] Ch 142 at 147D–E, 157A–B per Nourse LJ.
7   [1991] Ch 142 at 160C–E, 161E.

11.257 The reference to 'exceptional' circumstances in the Insolvency Act 1986 has been construed with the same restrictiveness of approach as was evident in the preceding case law.[1] A powerful influence in this direction is inevitably the fact that trustees in bankruptcy are bound by a statutory duty to realise the assets of the bankrupt.[2] The balance of emphasis clearly rests upon 'the purely property aspect of the matter,'[3] it being endemic in the circumstances of bankruptcy cases that the vulnerabilities of the bankrupt's spouse and children are submerged by the need to satisfy the claims of creditors.[4] In *Re Citro (A Bankrupt)*,[5] Nourse LJ declined to accept as 'exceptional circumstances' the fact that a court-ordered sale 'would cause difficulties with children's schooling and result in the eviction of a wife with young children … in circumstances where the realisation of her beneficial interest will not produce enough to buy a comparable home in the same neighbourhood, or indeed elsewhere.'[6] These effects, said Nourse LJ, 'while engendering a natural sympathy in all who hear of them … are the melancholy consequences of debt and improvidence with which every civilised society has been familiar.'[7]

1   Insolvency Act 1986, s 335A(3) echoes the Court of Appeal's analysis in *Re Citro (A Bankrupt)* [1991] Ch 142 at 157B that the voice of a bankrupt's spouse will only 'in exceptional circumstances' prevail against that of the trustee in bankruptcy. See also *Judd v Brown* [1999] 1 FLR 1191 at 1195E–F per Robert Walker LJ. The terminology of 'exceptional' circumstances had already been adopted in Insolvency Act 1986, ss 336(5), 337(6). In *Citro*, supra at 160E–F, Bingham LJ had been 'inclined to think that a test of exceptional circumstances was, in the absence of statutory guidance, more stringent than was warranted', but obviously deferred to the force of the statute.

2   For heavy emphasis of this point, see e g *Re Turner (A Bankrupt)* [1974] 1 WLR 1556 at 1558E; *Re Densham (A Bankrupt)* [1975] 1 WLR 1519 at 1531G; *Re Citro (A Bankrupt)* [1991] Ch 142 at 160B–C.

3   *Re Bailey (A Bankrupt)* [1977] 1 WLR 278 at 283E per Walton J.

4   See e g *Re Bailey (A Bankrupt)* [1977] 1 WLR 278 at 283A–B, where Walton J observed that the maxim *pacta sunt servanda*, 'although somewhat out of fashion, must be borne in mind. A person must discharge his liabilities before there is any room for being generous. One's debts must be paid, and paid promptly.' Walton J went on to say that the outcome 'may be yet another case where the sins of the father have to be visited on the children, but that is the way in which the world is constructed, and one must be just before one is generous' ([1977] 1 WLR 278 at 284E). See likewise *Pickering v Wells* [2002] 2 P & CR DG23 at [2].

5   [1991] Ch 142 at 157B–D. See S M Cretney, (1991) 107 LQR 177; [1991] CLJ 45 (J C Hall); (1992) 55 MLR 284 (D Brown).

6   Sir George Waller, in a dissenting judgment, was prepared to accept as 'exceptional circumstances' the housing difficulty and educational disruption which emerged from the evidence at trial ([1991] Ch 142 at 163D).

7   At first instance Hoffmann J had granted a postponement of sale until the youngest child reached the age of 16. This outcome was rejected by Nourse LJ as based on an erroneous analogy with orders 'which might have been made in the Family Division in a case where bankruptcy had not supervened' ([1991] Ch 142 at 159B). In overruling the first instance decision with 'regret', Bingham LJ felt that Hoffmann J's approach, although foreclosed by authority, had been 'conducive to justice in the broadest sense', as reflecting 'the preference which the law increasingly gives to personal over property interests' ([1991] Ch 142 at 161D–F).

11.258 Thus, even though a family home may still be required for the bankrupt's partner and children, applications for sale are highly unlikely to be declined under the Insolvency Act 1986 on the sheer ground of collateral damage to the family casualties of financial misfortune.[1] It does not, for instance, constitute an 'exceptional' circumstance that sale of the family home will interrupt a child's studies at a local school for his 'A' level examinations.[2] It is conceivable, however, that an 'exceptional' case for the court's discretion may arise where a house has been specially adapted to suit the needs of a handicapped child[3] or where postponement of sale will enable the bankrupt's debt to be paid in full out of the proceeds of forthcoming litigation.[4] In *Claughton v Charalambous*[5] it was thought that the severe ill-health and immobility of the bankrupt's wife, coupled with her special housing needs and reduced life expectancy, amounted to 'exceptional circumstances' justifying the indefinite suspension of an order for sale of her home.[6] 'Exceptional' circumstances were also, perhaps generously, found to be present in *Re Holliday (A Bankrupt)*,[7] where the Court of Appeal declined to order an immediate sale of a former matrimonial home in which the bankrupt's ex-wife was still living with three young children. Her ex-husband had been adjudicated bankrupt on his own petition[8] and the outstanding equity of redemption in the home was considerably larger than his liabilities.[9] The Court found that postponed payment was highly unlikely to cause great hardship to any of the creditors[10] and thus deferred sale for five years (by which time the two eldest children would be over 17 years of age).[11] Subsequent reaction to the decision in *Holliday* has been, significantly, to regard it as a 'high water-mark for the protection of the wife and children'[12] and it is unlikely that the temporary concession to family hardship demonstrated in this case has much precedential value under the Insolvency Act 1986.

1   It sometimes requires to be emphasised that many commercial creditors also have mortgages, spouses and children.
2   See *Re Bailey (A Bankrupt)* [1977] 1 WLR 278 at 284A (postponement of sale for two years denied).
3   See the example postulated in *Re Bailey (A Bankrupt)* [1977] 1 WLR 278 at 284B–C per Walton J.
4   See *Re Gorman (A Bankrupt)* [1990] 1 WLR 616 at 629H–630B, where Vinelott J proposed to postpone sale for long enough to enable the bankrupt's wife to pursue a negligence action the proceeds of which could be used to buy out the trustee in bankruptcy. (The trustee was meanwhile entitled to a market rate of interest.)
5   [1999] 1 FLR 740 at 745A–B, where Jonathan Parker J pointed out that the criterion of 'exceptional' circumstance necessitated a 'value judgment' by the court of first instance which was almost inherently unreviewable by an appellate court.
6   See also *Re Raval (A Bankrupt)* [1998] 2 FLR 718 at 725C–E (paranoid schizophrenia regarded as sufficiently 'exceptional' to justify year-long suspension of order for sale). Similarly, in *Re Bremner* [1999] 1 FLR 912 at 915A, sale was postponed until three months after the death of the bankrupt, who was terminally ill.
7   [1981] Ch 405 at 424D, 425D–E. See (1981) 97 LQR 200 (C Hand).
8   The courts are aware that self-induced bankruptcy is used, in rare cases, in an attempt to defeat a first wife's claims for property adjustment on divorce (see eg *Re Holliday* [1981] Ch 405 at 412G, 414C–D; *Re Lowrie (A Bankrupt)* [1981] 3 All ER 353 at 355j–356a). On the general irrelevance of the motive underlying a self-induced bankruptcy, see *Ex parte Painter* [1895] 1 QB 85 at 91; *Re Harry Dunn* [1949] Ch 640 at 647; *Re A Debtor* [1967] Ch 590 at 596C; *Re Mottee* (1977) 29 FLR 406 at 415.
9   Immediate sale was thought 'unfair' to the ex-wife, particularly having regard to the

bankrupt's desertion and the fact that the ex-wife was now 'saddled with the burden of providing a proper home for her children' without the resources necessary for this purpose ([1981] Ch 405 at 424A–B).

10 In *Re Citro (A Bankrupt)* [1991] Ch 142 at 157D–158A, Nourse LJ thought this factor to have been the 'one special feature' decisive of *Holliday's* case.

11 The Court meanwhile reserved power to order a sale on the application of any interested party should circumstances change ([1981] Ch 405 at 424E).

12 *Harman v Glencross* [1986] Fam 81 at 95F–H per Balcombe LJ ('very much against the run of the recent authorities'). See also *Re Lowrie (A Bankrupt)* [1981] 3 All ER 353 at 356a ('One can scarcely … imagine a more exceptional set of facts'); *Abbey National Plc v Moss* [1994] 1 FLR 307 at 314G ('somewhat unusual').

Equity of exoneration

11.259 If and when a trustee in bankruptcy finally succeeds in obtaining a court order for the sale of jointly owned property, the division of the resulting proceeds of sale may be affected by the operation of the 'equity of exoneration'. This little known equity is founded on the general proposition that if two joint owners of property charge that property in order to secure the debts of only one of the joint owners, the other joint owner stands merely in the position of a surety and is entitled, as between the two joint owners, to have the secured indebtedness discharged so far as is possible out of the equitable interest of the debtor.[1] The equity of exoneration in effect allocates more fairly as between joint mortgagors the ultimate burden of an indebtedness which was incurred for the benefit of only one co-owner.

1 See *Re Pittortou (A Bankrupt)* [1985] 1 WLR 58 at 61B; *Judd v Brown* [1998] 2 FLR 360 at 362H–363C.

Operation of the equitable principle of exoneration

11.260 The operation of this equitable doctrine can be demonstrated in a practical context where two co-owners of a family home have jointly charged that property as security for the debts of one co-owner who is subsequently adjudicated bankrupt. Such a charge may arise, for instance, where a bank insists on the provision of some security in respect of the husband's bank overdraft. Were it not for the equity of exoneration, the burden of this indebtedness could quite properly be thrown in exactly equal proportions upon the funds which represent the beneficial half-shares of the co-owners in the net proceeds of an enforced bankruptcy sale. However, the equity of exoneration entitles the bankrupt's co-owner to insist that the burden of the creditors' claims should be diverted primarily on to the bankrupt's share in those proceeds. The result of this process is *pro tanto* to preserve the proprietary interest of the bankrupt's co-owner and to augment her eventual money recovery.[1]

1 *Re Pittortou (A Bankrupt)* [1985] 1 WLR 58 at 61F. See also *Re A Debtor (No 24 of 1971)* [1976] 1 WLR 952 at 955.

Relevance of intention

11.261   The equity of exoneration depends upon the presumed intention of the parties.[1] The equity comes into play only if it can be inferred from the circumstances of the case that the joint mortgagors together intended that the burden of the secured indebtedness should fall primarily on the share of the actual debtor. The equity cannot operate if the indebtedness in question was incurred for the purpose of financing a higher standard of living for both co-owners and their family.[2] In other words, the equity cannot be invoked if in reality both joint mortgagors received and enjoyed the benefits of the indebtedness.[3] Thus, in *Re Pittortou (A Bankrupt)*,[4] Scott J held that the equity of exoneration should be confined to payments other than those made for the 'joint benefit of the household.' On this basis the bankrupt's wife was not entitled to any exoneration in respect of debts arising in connection with the running of the joint family household. She was, however, entitled to require that debts incurred by her husband for purely business purposes and in supporting another woman should be treated as charged primarily on his own half-share in the mortgaged property.[5]

1   *Re Pittortou (A Bankrupt)* [1985] 1 WLR 58 at 62A.
2   See *Paget v Paget* [1898] 1 Ch 470 at 475–477; *Re Pittortou (A Bankrupt)* [1985] 1 WLR 58 at 62G.
3   *Re Woodstock (A Bankrupt)* (Unreported, Walton J, 19 November 1979). See also *Re Kostiuk* (2002) 215 DLR (4th) 78 at [57]–[59] (British Columbia Court of Appeal).
4   [1985] 1 WLR 58 at 62H.
5   [1985] 1 WLR 58 at 62H–63A. See also *Re Berry* [1976] 2 NZLR 449 at 451–452; *Farrugia v Official Receiver in Bankruptcy* (1982) 43 ALR 700 at 703.

Comparison with homestead legislation

11.262   It was one of the original purposes of the Insolvency Act 1986 to bring about a better and more compassionate balance in the consideration of competing interests in the family home on bankruptcy. In particular the statutory compromise was aimed at establishing a legal mechanism which would delay rather than cancel the rights of creditors.[1] The heightened emphasis thus accorded the residential expectations of family members was intended to mark a significant advance on the pattern of decision-making evident in the earlier case law under section 30 of the Law of Property Act 1925. In practice it appears that the limiting statutory formulae, coupled with strict construction by the courts, have produced a substantial continuity with the bankruptcy case law rather than a quantum step into a new jurisprudence of insolvency.

1   See *Insolvency Law and Practice* (Cmnd 8558, June 1982), para 1118.

11.263   Even at face value the innovative measures of the Insolvency Act 1986 fall short of the objectives of the 'homestead legislation' which is currently in force in New Zealand and in many of the common law jurisdictions of Canada and the United States. At the heart of each of these homestead schemes is a large presumption in favour of long-term security of tenure in the family home.

By contrast, the balance of emphasis expressed in the Insolvency Act 1986 still heavily favours the recovery of creditors' claims, at most subject to a limited delay in the enforcement of these claims against family assets.

11.264   One of the oldest and most typical schemes of homestead rights is contained in New Zealand's Joint Family Homes Act 1964. Under this statute it is possible for spouses to register their home as a 'joint family home'.[1] Upon registration the spouses become legal and beneficial joint tenants,[2] and so long as the joint family home settlement remains registered the interests of the husband and wife are unaffected by bankruptcy or assignment for the benefit of creditors.[3] Creditors of either spouse may oppose the initial registration,[4] but may subsequently attack the joint family home settlement only on the restricted grounds laid down in the Act.[5] Under the Act the court retains a discretion to cancel any existing joint family home registration,[6] but this discretion is not exercised in favour of sale on the mere ground that one of the spouses has been declared bankrupt.[7] Cancellation followed by sale and distribution is ordered only in exceptional circumstances. Such circumstances may arise, however, where there has been unconscientious dealing by the debtor with his creditors,[8] or where *both* spouses have been adjudicated bankrupt and there remains a very substantial equity from which the creditors could be satisfied without undue hardship to the family.[9] Even if the court decides in a particular case that the joint family home must be sold to meet the claims of unsecured creditors, the proceeds of that sale remain to a level specified by statute immune from third party claims,[10] with the result that the family salvages something from the calamity of insolvency.[11]

1   Joint Family Homes Act 1964, s 5. Registration is voluntary.
2   Joint Family Homes Act 1964, s 9(1)(b).
3   Joint Family Homes Act 1964, s 9(2)(d). See *Official Assignee v Lawford* [1984] 2 NZLR 257 at 263.
4   Joint Family Homes Act 1964, s 6(1).
5   Joint Family Homes Act 1964, ss 16–20.
6   Joint Family Homes Act 1964, s 16(1).
7   See e g *Official Assignee of Pannell v Pannell* [1966] NZLR 324 at 325, where Wilson J did not think the very considerable total of the bankrupt's debts or the large number of his creditors to be 'sufficient, without more, to warrant ... an order for sale.'
8   See *Official Assignee of Pannell v Pannell* [1966] NZLR 324 at 326.
9   See e g *Official Assignee v Lawford* [1984] 2 NZLR 257 at 264–266, where even after satisfaction of the creditors' claims the equity amounted to over $70,000. The Court of Appeal considered that this surplus was sufficient to enable the bankrupts to purchase a quite adequate home and that 'on an objective view the present appellants and their family cannot possibly be said to be in a situation of hardship ... True, their standard of living has fallen; the home will be more modest and they no longer own a yacht' ([1984] 2 NZLR 257 at 265). Compare *Rukat v Rukat* [1975] Fam 63 at 73F ('The rich gourmet who because of financial stringency has to drink vin ordinaire with his grouse may well think that he is suffering a hardship; but sensible people would say he was not').
10   In the event of cancellation of a joint family home registration on the ground of bankruptcy, $82,000 must be set aside for the beneficiaries of the joint family home settlement, notwithstanding that this pro tanto defeats the claims of unsecured creditors (see Joint Family Homes Act 1964, s 16(1)(a), as amended by Joint Family Homes (Specified Sum) Order 2002 (SR 2002/364)). See, however, *Official Assignee v Noonan* [1988] 2 NZLR 252 at 255–256.

11   Similar schemes of limited immunity from the effects of bankruptcy are contained in
     Canadian provincial legislation (see Bruce Ziff, *Principles of Property Law* (3rd edn 2000), pp
     173–174).

11.265   The priorities expressed in New Zealand's Joint Family Homes Act
are quite different from those which prevail in English insolvency law. The New
Zealand legislation was enacted with the express object of promoting the
stability and permanence of family life as a higher social end than that
represented by commercial security for the creditor.[1] The 1964 Act indeed
embodies an imaginative attempt to strike a humane social balance between
competing interests and it is arguable that English law would be enriched by the
enactment of similar legislation.[2]

1   See Vol 292, *New Zealand Parliamentary Debates*, 3493 (Hon T C Webb, Attorney-General);
    Vol 340, *New Zealand Parliamentary Debates*, 2294 (Hon J R Hanan, Minister of Justice). In
    Fairmaid v Otago District Land Registrar [1952] NZLR 782 at 786, North J described the
    legislation as ensuring that 'husband and wife can live contentedly in their home in the
    knowledge that it is secured to them as a family home so long as they need it whatever the
    vicissitudes of life may bring.' See also *Sutherland v Sutherland* [1955] NZLR 689 at 691;
    Official Assignee v Lawford [1984] 2 NZLR 257 at 261; *Official Assignee v Noonan* [1988] 2
    NZLR 252 at 255 per Richardson J, 255–256 per Somers J; *King v Church* [2002] NZFLR 555
    at [33] per Baragwanath J.
2   Ironically the future of the 1964 Act is currently in some doubt, partly because of a fall in the
    marriage rate in New Zealand and partly because the benefits of the Act are felt to
    discriminate against sole owners (New Zealand Law Commission, *The Future of the Joint
    Family Homes Act 1964* (Report 77, December 2001), paras 15, 22).

APPLICATIONS MADE BY OTHER CREDITORS

11.266   Not all cases of financial exigency affecting a trust beneficiary result
in bankruptcy. Instead of pressing for bankruptcy (where their claims would
merely rank alongside those of other creditors), some creditors simply attempt
to enforce their existing security. Thus the sale of trust property is often sought
by legal or equitable chargees or by creditors who invoke legal process in the
enforcement of charging orders made in their favour.[1] Where creditors' claims
are not represented by a trustee in bankruptcy, contested applications for sale
of trust land fall to be dealt with in accordance with the general criteria
enunciated in section 15(1) of the Trusts of Land and Appointment of Trustees
Act 1996.[2]

1   [**Para 11.248**].
2   [**Para 11.231**].

The dawn of a more liberal era

11.267   There was an early suggestion that, under the Trusts of Land and
Appointment of Trustees Act 1996, the courts would adopt a significantly
different approach to applications for sale brought outside the context of
bankruptcy.[1] In *Mortgage Corporation v Shaire*,[2] Neuberger J pointed out that,

in such cases, section 15(1) of the 1996 Act expressly specifies the interests of secured creditors as ranking alongside, and having no automatic priority over, such factors as 'the welfare of any minor'.[3] Neuberger J also noted that, even under the bankruptcy jurisdiction, there had been 'indications of judicial dissatisfaction' with the predisposition towards sale[4] and that nothing in the 'new code' of the 1996 Act replicated the bias towards sale implicit in the now 'obsolete' trust for sale.[5] Against this background Neuberger J thought it 'not ... unlikely that the legislature intended to relax the fetters' on the court's exercise of discretion in cases other than bankruptcy 'so as to tip the balance somewhat more in favour of families and against banks and other chargees.'[6] In the light of this perceived change in the law, Neuberger J declined to order an immediate sale of a family home on the application of a chargee where it remained possible that a trust beneficiary, whose signature on the charge had been forged, might be able to service the interest payments on the outstanding debt.

1   It had always been said that in sale applications brought not by a trustee in bankruptcy, but by a mortgagee or chargee, different considerations are applicable, partly because such creditors, unlike a trustee in bankruptcy, have no statutory duty to realise the debtor's assets (see R J Smith, (1979) 95 LQR 501 at 506; J Martin, [1980] Conv 361 at 376–377). See *Mortgage Corporation v Shaire* [2001] Ch 743 at 759A per Neuberger J.
2   [2001] Ch 743 at 758F–G. See S Pascoe, [2000] Conv 315; [2000] Conv 329 (M P Thompson).
3   TOLATA 1996, s 15(1)(c)–(d) **[para 11.245]**.
4   [2001] Ch 743 at 760D. See e g *Re Citro* (*A Bankrupt*) [1991] Ch 142 at 161F per Bingham LJ, 163D per Sir George Waller; *Abbey National Plc v Moss* [1994] 1 FLR 307 at 321D.
5   [2001] Ch 743 at 758H.
6   [2001] Ch 743 at 760C. In relation to the 'wealth of learning and thought' found in the old case law on creditors' applications for sale, Neuberger J opined that, although it would be 'wrong to throw over all the earlier cases without paying them any regard', they were to be 'treated with caution ... and in many cases are unlikely to be of great, let alone decisive, assistance' ([2001] Ch 743 at 761A–C).

A false dawn

11.268   Subsequent experience has demonstrated that the new approach to court-ordered sale evident in *Mortgage Corporation v Shaire* has not been widely adopted by the courts. It has been said that, although the Trusts of Land and Appointment of Trustees Act 1996 'may have given the court somewhat greater flexibility' in non-bankruptcy cases, section 15(1) 'has hardly revolutionised things.'[1] There has even been a lingering sense that, in applying for a sale of trust land, a chargee creditor may be better placed than a trustee in bankruptcy, in that, if sale is postponed, the chargee suffers a postponement of the full amount of a potentially large and increasing debt, whereas on a bankruptcy 'each creditor may suffer very little.'[2] Recent case law has indicated that the courts remain strongly influenced by the argument that, unless an order for sale is made, 'the bank will be kept waiting indefinitely for any payment out of what is, for all practical purposes, its own share of the property.'[3] Nor have the courts allowed this concern for the lender's commercial interests to be deflected by reference to the principle of respect for 'private and family life' and for the 'home' enshrined in Article 8 of the European Convention on Human Rights.[4] Indeed, the major thrust of the House of Lords' majority ruling in *Harrow London Borough Council v Qazi*[5] is the insistence that Article 8 is not violated by the simple enforcement of entitlements which have been determined to belong to parties as a matter of private domestic law.

1   *Re A; A v A* [2002] 2 FLR 274 at [115] per Munby J.
2   See *Lloyds Bank plc v Byrne* [1993] 1 FLR 369 at 372D–F per Parker LJ.
3   *First National Bank plc v Achampong* [2004] 1 FCR 18 at [65] per Blackburne J. See [2003] Conv 314 (M P Thompson).
4   **[Para 2.60]**.
5   [2004] 1 AC 983 **[para 2.70]**.

The Bell case

11.269   The decision of the Court of Appeal in *Bank of Ireland Home Mortgages Ltd v Bell*[1] is now commonly regarded as epitomising the tone of the jurisprudence emerging from the courts' application of the 1996 Act.[2] In *Bell's* case W held a 10 per cent beneficial share in a family home which was owned at law by H and W. H forged W's signature on a mortgage of the legal estate to the claimant bank, with the result that the bank ranked as only an equitable chargee of H's beneficial interest in the home. H then abandoned W to live and work abroad, but for most of a decade after H ceased making mortgage payments W, together with the son of the family, continued to live in the home. When the question of sale finally reached the Court of Appeal, H's debt to the bank was well over £300,000 'and increasing daily'. The Court thought it 'plainly wrong' not to order a sale of the house, emphasising that 'a powerful consideration is and ought to be whether the creditor is receiving proper recompense for being kept out of his money.'[3] Here, regardless of the needs of the son and W's ill-health, it was 'very unfair to the bank' that it should be 'condemned ... to go on waiting for its money ... and with the debt increasing all the time, that debt already exceeding what could be realised on a sale.'[4] The bank after all, said Sir Christopher Staughton 'is a beneficiary of the trust referred to in section 15 as much as Mrs Bell.'[5]

1   [2001] 2 All ER (Comm) 920. See [2002] Conv 61 (R Probert).
2   See *Re A; A v A* [2002] 2 FLR 274 at [127]–[130], [171] per Munby J; *First National Bank plc v Achampong* [2004] 1 FCR 18 at [61]; [2003] Conv 314 (M P Thompson).
3   [2001] 2 All ER (Comm) 920 at [31] per Peter Gibson LJ.
4   [2001] 2 All ER (Comm) 920 at [31] per Peter Gibson LJ.
5   [2001] 2 All ER (Comm) 920 at [38].

Other restrictive factors

11.270   The exercise of judicial discretion under section 15(1) of the Trusts of Land and Appointment of Trustees Act 1996 now seems to replicate many of the unsympathetic features which characterise the bankruptcy jurisdiction.[1] Sale of trust land is ordered on behalf of creditors in all save exceptional circumstances.[2] As against such creditors, the 'purposes'[3] of a family home trust are widely regarded as spent and therefore no longer operative where, as is so often the case, the family relationship has also broken down.[4] Likewise, compassionate factors weighing against sale – such as ill-health or disability[5] within the family – are frequently taken as pointing towards a mere postponement (rather than refusal) of the sale order sought by the lender.[6] Moreover, the hardship caused by forced sale is regularly treated as offset by the fact that the evicted family has already effectively enjoyed a prolonged period of rent- and mortgage-free accommodation.[7] In a further devastating inroad into family security, the Court of Appeal has also indicated in *Bank of Baroda v Dhillon*[8] that a mortgagee may neutralise the effect of a trust beneficiary's overriding interest by the simple tactic of obtaining a court-ordered sale of the trust land (rather than by relying on the mortgagee's independent power of sale). The existence of the overriding interest, whilst it might have defeated any claim to possession by the bank, is utterly irrelevant to the exercise of a statutory discretion to order sale.[9]

1 **[Para 11.239].**
2 Indeed the courts' approach has largely returned to the pattern of the pre-1997 case law where the courts uniformly sanctioned the sale of trust land on behalf of creditors who held an equitable charge over a beneficiary's interest (see *TSB Bank plc v Marshall* [1998] 3 EGLR 100 at 102M–103A; *Bankers Trust Co v Namdar* [1997] EGCS 20; *Bank of Baroda v Dhillon* [1998] 1 FLR 524 at 530B–E) or who had obtained a charging order under the Charging Orders Act 1979 (see e g *Midland Bank Plc v Pike* [1988] 2 All ER 434 at 438a; *Lloyds Bank plc v Byrne* [1993] 1 FLR 369 at 375B–D; *Barclays Bank plc v Hendricks* [1996] 1 FLR 258 at 262A–D).
3 See TOLATA 1996, s 15(1)(b).
4 See e g *Bank of Ireland Home Mortgages Ltd v Bell* [2001] 2 All ER (Comm) 920 at [28] per Peter Gibson LJ; *First National Bank plc v Achampong* [2004] 1 FCR 18 at [61], [65] per Blackburne J.
5 See e g *First National Bank plc v Achampong* [2004] 1 FCR 18 at [65] (handicapped child).
6 See e g *Bank of Ireland Home Mortgages Ltd v Bell* [2001] 2 All ER (Comm) 920 at [29].
7 See *Bank of Ireland Home Mortgages Ltd v Bell* [2001] 2 All ER (Comm) 920 at [32]; *First National Bank plc v Achampong* [2004] 1 FCR 18 at [62].
8 [1998] 1 FLR 524 at 530B–E (where the creditor's application was made under LPA 1925, s 30, but the same principle applies pursuant to TOLATA 1996, ss 14–15).
9 The trust beneficiary was entitled, however, to first payment out of the ensuing proceeds of sale **[para 12.220]**. See also *Halifax Mortgage Services Ltd v Muirhead* (1997) 76 P & CR 418 at 428–429.

TERMINATION OF CO-OWNERSHIP

11.271 Co-ownership of land may be terminated in a variety of ways, of which the most obvious are the following.

Transfer to a purchaser who takes free of the trust of land

11.272 Co-ownership of land, together with any trust of land, plainly terminates if the legal estate held on trust is transferred to a third party who takes free of the trust.[1] Compliance with the conditions of statutory overreaching[2] ensures precisely this result, the transferee thereafter enjoying immunity from the trust beneficial interests.[3]

1   Of course, a transfer to a single purchaser in circumstances where two or more persons have contributed to the purchase money creates a new co-ownership in the land (and a new trust of the land), as does a transfer of the legal estate to more than one person [**paras 10.11, 11.145**].
2   [**Para 11.208**].
3   Likewise the ultimate performance of duty by a bare trustee – conveyance on the direction of his beneficiary to the beneficiary himself – terminates any trust of land, since the former beneficiary is now entitled absolutely both at law and in equity [**para 11.155**].

Partition

11.273   The unity of possession which is essential to both joint tenancy and tenancy in common is destroyed if, with the consent of the beneficiaries, the trustees physically divide up or partition co-owned land amongst the individual co-owners.[1] Partition effectively involves the transfer to each co-owner of an appropriate portion of the trust land, thereby reducing the former co-ownership to separate ownership of individual parcels. If the trustees or any of the beneficiaries refuse to consent to a partition, it is open to a trustee or any person with an interest in the trust land to apply to the court for such order in resolution of the matter as the court thinks fit.[2]

1   TOLATA 1996, s 7(1) [**para 11.163**].
2   TOLATA 1996, s 14(1)–(2) [**para 11.229**]. Partition is rare in England, but is more common in other jurisdictions. See, on the court's discretion, *Schnytzer v Wielunski* [1978] VR 418 at 423–427 (Property Law Act 1958 (Victoria), s 223); *Hayward v Skinner* [1981] 1 NSWLR 590 at 593F–595A (Conveyancing Act 1919 (New South Wales), s 66G(1), (4)). Partition may not be sanctioned by the court if it conflicts with planning controls or zoning regulations which prohibit subdivision of the land (see e g *Cochrane v Cochrane* (1980) 108 DLR (3d) 395 at 397–398; *Crawford v Durrant* (1998) 156 DLR (4th) 292 at 300).

Union of the property in one joint tenant

11.274   Co-ownership clearly ends if a co-owned estate comes into the sole ownership of one joint tenant. In the context of a joint tenancy originally affecting both the legal and equitable interest in land, this may happen in two different ways.

Release inter vivos

11.275   In strict terms a joint tenant has no interest with which he can deal unilaterally at law.[1] However, the Law of Property Act 1925 permits a joint tenant to 'release' his interest inter vivos to the other joint tenant or tenants[2] and even makes provision for him to 'convey' his interest to another joint tenant.[3] It is clearly possible that the process of release may cause the entire co-owned interest to be held by only one of the original joint tenants, in which case all forms of co-ownership have been extinguished by the union in the single tenant.

1   [**Para 11.25**].
2   LPA 1925, s 36(2). See *Harris v Goddard* [1983] 1 WLR 1203 at 1210F; *Burton v Camden LBC* [2000] 2 AC 399 at 404E–F per Lord Nicholls of Birkenhead [**para 7.211**]. Although it is open to a joint tenant to release his joint tenancy at any time subsequent to the creation of this form of co-ownership, it seems that he may disclaim his interest ab initio only if the other joint tenants are parties to his disclaimer (see *Re Schär, Decd* [1951] Ch 280 at 285).
3   LPA 1925, s 72(4).

Operation of survivorship

11.276   The same effect may be brought about by the operation of survivorship.[1] On the death of one of two remaining joint tenants of the legal and equitable estate, the entire interest both at law and in equity survives to the remaining joint tenant. Any trust of land which previously gave effect to the co-ownership terminates with the demise of the joint tenancy.[2]

1   [**Para 11.8**].
2   See *Re Cook* [1948] Ch 212 at 215–216.

The problem with subsequent dealings

11.277   The Law of Property Act 1925 provides that nothing affects 'the right of a survivor of joint tenants, who is solely and beneficially interested, to deal with his legal estate as if it were not held in trust.'[1] It is plain that the sole surviving proprietor of a registered estate is perfectly competent to deal with the land as the absolute owner.[2] In relation to an *unregistered* estate there is, however, a practical problem. The survivor is faced with the difficulty that, if he ever tries to sell the land, his purchaser will require proof that none of the now deceased joint tenants severed in equity prior to his death. The original joint tenancy will, of course, be obvious from the face of the vendor's title deeds and the vendor is consequently put on proof of a negative. If severance had occurred prior to the death of a deceased joint tenant, the purchaser would stand in danger of receiving only part of the beneficial interest in the land since the deceased's share would have devolved with his own estate.

1   LPA 1925, s 36(2). A restriction will not have been entered on the proprietorship register of the trustees' title [**para 11.190**] and the survivor therefore retains plenary powers of disposition.
2   See LRR 2003, r 164.

A statutory solution for unregistered land

11.278   The last surviving joint tenant of an unregistered estate can always circumvent the present difficulty by appointing another trustee to act with him in giving an overreaching conveyance to a purchaser. However, legislation has intervened in order to spare the surviving joint tenant both the inconvenience of such a manoeuvre and the impossibility of proving that no severance has ever taken place. Under the Law of Property (Joint Tenants) Act 1964, the surviving joint tenant is deemed to be solely and beneficially entitled if the conveyance to his purchaser contains a statement that he is so interested.[1] The 1964 Act has no application to registered land[2] and is ineffective in relation to unregistered land if a memorandum of severance has been endorsed on or annexed to the original conveyance to the joint tenants[3] or if a bankruptcy order made against any of the joint tenants (or a petition for one) has been registered under the Land Charges Act before the date of the survivor's conveyance.[4] In all other cases, however, it is safe for a bona fide purchaser for value to rely on the statutory presumption against severance of the equitable joint tenancy.[5] He may assume that his vendor is competent to convey the absolute estate and, even if this turns out not to have been so, the purchaser takes priority over any owner of a severed share.

1   Law of Property (Joint Tenants) Act 1964, s 1(1). On the 1964 Act, see (1964) 28 Conv (NS) 329; (1966) 30 Conv (NS) 27 (P Jackson).
2   Law of Property (Joint Tenants) Act 1964, s 3. See G Ferris and G Battersby, [1998] Conv 168 at 184. It has been suggested that parallel protection for purchasers of registered land could be achieved by amendment of the Land Registration Act 2002 to provide that, in the absence of any 'restriction' in the register, a survivor of joint tenants is deemed to be solely entitled beneficially if his disposition so states and the disponee obtains a clear bankruptcy search (see E J Cooke, [2004] Conv 41).
3   Law of Property (Joint Tenants) Act 1964, s 1(1)(a). The memorandum of severance must be signed by at least one of the joint tenants and must record that the joint tenancy was severed in equity on a specified day. See e g *Grindal v Hooper* (2000) Times, 8 February, where a purchaser of the survivor's legal title was fully aware of the fact of severance (a memorandum of which was endorsed on the deeds) and therefore took subject to the severed beneficial share of a deceased equitable co-owner.
4   Law of Property (Joint Tenants) Act 1964, s 1(1)(b).
5   The 'purchaser' entitled to the benefit of the statutory presumption must be a purchaser in good faith for valuable (i e not nominal) consideration (LPA 1925, s 205(1)(xxi)). See *Grindal v Hooper* (2000) Times, 8 February. Even in the absence of a memorandum of severance or land charge registration, it is doubtful whether a purchaser with actual express notice of a severance can rely on the 1964 Act (see (1984) 100 LQR 149 (P Jackson)).

CHAPTER 12

Dealings with title

AN INTEGRATED ACCOUNT OF DEALINGS WITH TITLE

12.1 This book has now reached the point where it becomes possible to integrate the information contained in previous chapters to form a composite account of the central problem of conveyancing – the way in which dealings with title impact on the various categories of legal and equitable right already outlined. Chapter 2 provided a preliminary glimpse of the overall effect of land dealings[1] and this analysis is expanded in the present chapter. As always, the primary distinction lies between estates whose titles have been registered at Land Registry and estates whose titles have not yet been brought on to the Land Register. In keeping with the theme of this book, registered title is treated as the self-evidently dominant regime of modern land law, but this chapter also provides a parallel account of the process and outcome of dealings with unregistered titles.[2]

1   See the 'bird's eye view' of the terrain of land law contained in Chapter 2 [**paras 2.99–2.193**].
2   [**Paras 12.259–12.372**].

THE TRANSACTION OF SALE OF LAND

12.2 In England and Wales the sale of land is essentially a two-stage process: first contract, then transfer of title (ie 'completion' of the contract by registered disposition). It is irrelevant for this purpose whether the subject matter of the transfer is a freehold or long leasehold estate. In either case the relationship between vendor and purchaser (ie between 'seller' and 'buyer', as modern conveyancing terminology increasingly expresses it) normally develops through three sharply defined phases:
–   pre-contractual negotiations and enquiries[1]
–   exchange of contracts[2] and
–   disposition of the legal estate followed by registration of the disposition at Land Registry.[3]

1   **[Paras 12.5–12.25]**.
2   **[Paras 12.26–12.48]**.
3   **[Paras 12.49–12.53]**.

The process of contract and registered transfer

12.3   When preliminary negotiations and enquiries have been concluded, the prospective vendor and purchaser enter into a formal contract to execute in favour of the purchaser a transfer of the legal estate in the land, this transfer usually following on the contractually specified completion date. Nowadays almost all forms of dealing with a legal estate require a further act of completion by registration at Land Registry.[1] The present chapter therefore traces the legal implications of the conveyancing process from the initiation of negotiations between vendor and purchaser to the conclusion of this process in a perfected transfer of title.

1   **[Paras 2.145, 7.40, 7.56]**.

The move to paperless transactions

12.4   The process of transacting with land has been placed under intense scrutiny during the past two decades, not least because of the need to accommodate the modern revolution in information technology.[1] The Land Registration Act 2002 and the advent of electronic conveyancing within the foreseeable future[2] will undoubtedly transform the business of conveyancing.[3] In an era of 'paperless' transactions it is clear that entry in the digital record of the Land Register will relatively soon become the essential constitutive source of entitlement to realty.[4] In other words, entry in the register will be integral to the very process of dealing with most kinds of interest in registered land. Transfer of land and the creation of rights over land will become inseparably linked with a simultaneous act of registration.[5] And with the realisation of these objectives, the historic 'mirror principle'[6] will take on a new and different significance: the register will reflect a 'real time' mirror image of land interests, since most interests will actually have no existence outside the register.

1   See the Law Commission's prolonged engagement with the subject (*Property Law: Third Report on Land Registration* (Law Com No 158, March 1987); Law Commission and Land Registry, *Land Registration for the Twenty-First Century* (Law Com No 254, September 1998); *Land Registration for the Twenty-First Century: A Conveyancing Revolution* (Law Com No 271, July 2001)).

2   The current government has indicated that '[w]hen it comes to the delivery of public services, e-conveyancing is one of [its] highest priorities' (David Lammy, Under-Secretary of State, Department of Constitutional Affairs). Spurred on by this encouragement, Land Registry aims to pilot the e-conveyancing service during the spring of 2006 and begin an 'incremental process of national rollout during 2007' (see Land Registry Press Release LRP08/04 (22 July 2004)).

3   'The transition to a system of paperless transfer of land is a very major one' (Law Com No 254 (1998), para 11.8).

4   **[Paras 2.117, 6.24, 12.53]**. See Law Com No 254 (1998), paras 11.10, 11.56; Law Com No 271 (2001), para 5.3.

5   Law Com No 254 (1998), paras 2.47, 11.9; Law Com No 271 (2001), paras 8.2, 8.53, 8.74.
6   **[Paras 2.108, 6.11]**.

NEGOTIATIONS AND ENQUIRIES PRIOR TO CONTRACT

12.5   During the period preceding exchange of contracts, the parties inch towards agreement on such matters as price and the timing of the sale. The purchaser arranges any necessary mortgage finance and he or his prospective mortgagee obtains a professional survey or valuation of the land concerned.[1] The purchaser likewise directs a number of searches and enquiries to the local authority responsible for the area.[2] It is also essential at this stage that the purchaser should carry out a full inspection of the land, noting in particular the identity of the current occupiers, not least because the rights of such persons could become binding following the transfer of title.[3] In domestic conveyancing, where the transaction is conducted under the Law Society's National Conveyancing Protocol, the period prior to exchange of contracts is also used for the investigation of the vendor's title.[4] Significantly, however, all of these potentially onerous activities are undertaken at a time when there is no subsisting contractual commitment on either side and when, indeed, there is no assurance that such contractual commitment will ever materialise. Perhaps even more difficult is the fact that, in certain circumstances – most notably in cases of sale by auction or sealed bid – many of the expensive preliminary steps outlined above are taken by a number of prospective purchasers, each acting independently, with enormous duplication of effort and cost.

1   **[Para 12.6]**.
2   **[Para 12.7]**.
3   **[Paras 12.146, 12.358]**.
4   **[Para 12.11]**. In the case of a registered land transaction, it is therefore open to the purchaser to examine an official copy of the register entries, a copy of the title plan, and copies of any documents which are referred to in the registered title. In the case of an unregistered land transaction, the purchaser is enabled to satisfy himself that there is an unbroken chain of ownership leading from a good root of title through to his vendor and that all incumbrances affecting the land are reflected in the draft contract **[para 12.260]**.

Surveys

12.6   In advance of any exchange of formal contracts, the purchaser often wishes to commission a survey of the land to be acquired. Moreover, any lending institution which helps to finance his purchase will certainly insist that some kind of valuation is made on its own behalf (but at the purchaser's expense) in order that the security offered be shown to be reasonably sound and the amount of the mortgage advance not disproportionate to the current market value of the land. Such assessments, if conducted negligently, provide a fertile source of legal liability. A surveyor or valuer who is careless in carrying out a survey commissioned privately by a potential purchaser before exchange of contracts is liable in negligence for the difference between the contracted purchase price and the true market value at the date of purchase.[1] The damages awarded to the purchaser may also include interest on this difference in property values, together with damages for vexation and inconvenience.[2] A surveyor who values property for a lender owes a duty of care not only to the lender[3] but also to the mortgage applicant who proposes to purchase the property.[4] Furthermore, the lender may itself be liable to the mortgage applicant in respect of any loss caused by the negligence of the surveyor commissioned by the lender to report on the property in relation to which the mortgage loan is sought.[5]

1   *Perry v Sidney Phillips & Son* [1982] 1 WLR 1297 at 1302D–E, 1303F–H, 1304G, 1306C–D; [1984] Conv 60 (K Hodkinson). See *Oswald v Countryside Surveyors Ltd* [1996] EGCS 100 (death watch beetle in timber-framed farmhouse). The surveyor's duty of care is limited to the person who commissioned his survey. The surveyor's negligence affords no cause of action to potential purchasers of adjacent properties, even though their properties, when purchased, are discovered to contain the same defect (eg dry rot) which he failed to reveal in the commissioned survey (see *Shankie-Williams v Heavey* [1986] 2 EGLR 139 at 141A–C). See also *Merivale Moore plc v Strutt & Parker* (1999) Times, 5 May.

2   *Perry v Sidney Phillips & Son* [1982] 1 WLR 1297 at 1302G–1303D, 1305F, 1307A–E.

3   *London and South of England Building Society v Stone* [1983] 1 WLR 1242 at 1249H–1250A. On the quantum of damages recoverable, see *Swingcastle Ltd v Gibson* [1991] 2 AC 223 at 238F–G. A negligent valuer may not be liable for the full extent of the loss incurred by the lender, eg where a depreciation in value is caused by a fall in the property market (see *Banque Bruxelles Lambert SA v Eagle Star Insurance Co Ltd* [1997] AC 191 at 222F; (1997) 113 LQR 1 (J Stapleton); (1998) 61 MLR 68 (J Wightman)). The valuer's liability is restricted to the extent of the overvaluation (*Nykredit Mortgage Bank Plc v Edward Erdman Group Ltd* (*No 2*) [1997] 1 WLR 1627 at 1631H–1632A) and principles of contributory negligence are applicable (see *Platform Home Loans Ltd v Oyston Shipways Ltd* [2000] 2 AC 190).

4   *Yianni v Edwin Evans & Sons* [1982] QB 438 at 456B–C; *Roberts v J Hampson & Co* [1990] 1 WLR 94 at 104D–E; *Merrett v Babb* [2001] QB 1174 at [10], [44]. See also *Smith v Eric S Bush* [1990] 1 AC 831 at 854E–F, 859F, 874A, where the House of Lords held that it was not fair and reasonable, for the purposes of the Unfair Contract Terms Act 1977, that a surveyor or valuer should rely on general disclaimers of negligence liability contained in the survey report and mortgage application. See [1989] Conv 359 (C Francis); (1989) 52 MLR 841 (T Kaye). Such disclaimers may, however, be effective in relation to a third party who, unknown to the valuer, lends money in reliance on a favourable report (see *Omega Trust Co Ltd v Wright Son and Pepper* (*A Firm*) *and Baker & Co* (*A Firm*) (1996) 75 P & CR 57 at 62–63).

5   See *Stevenson v Nationwide Building Society* (1984) 272 EG 663 at 670. See also, in the case of a local authority lender, *Harris v Wyre Forest DC* [1990] 1 AC 831 at 848A–G; *Ward v McMaster* [1988] IR 338 at 351.

Local authority searches and other searches and enquiries

12.7   The period prior to exchange of contracts is also used by the purchaser for the purpose of requisitioning a variety of searches for information controlled by local or central government bodies or by statutory undertakers (such as water utilities) and the Environment Agency.[1] In relation to the subject matter of a proposed purchase, a 'local authority search' elicits information which is held in the local authority's register of local land charges,[2] together with more general information relating to local development and conservation, local structure plans, the maintenance of adjacent roads, tree preservation orders, smoke control orders and many other matters of local amenity.[3] Local land charges cover such issues as local authority financial charges on the land, planning and listed building matters, light obstruction notices and drainage scheme charges. The local authority may be liable to the purchaser in negligence in respect of any misleading replies which cause him loss.[4] In certain areas of the country it may be appropriate to carry out searches relating to commons registration[5] and the registration of mining rights.[6]

1   Many of the matters concerned under these heads, because they have the potential to constitute overriding interests pursuant to the Land Registration Act 2002 [**para 12.242**], merit careful investigation.
2   A register of local land charges is maintained by the City of London, by each of the London Boroughs, and by every district council (see Local Land Charges Act 1975, s 3).
3   The National Protocol indicates that the vendor should, at his own cost, supply the purchaser with the result of a recent local land charges search relating to the land. Such searches are, however, relatively expensive and have a necessarily limited shelf-life. If a sale falls through and another purchaser does not appear speedily, the investment in a local authority search is wasted.
4   See *L Shaddock & Associates Pty Ltd v Parramatta City Council* (1981) 150 CLR 225 at 234–236 (High Court of Australia).
5   See Commons Registration Act 1965, s 3(2) [**para 5.40**].
6   See Coal Industry Act 1994, s 56(1) (register of notices relating to withdrawal of support and assumption of compulsory rights).

Enquiries in relation to unregistered land

12.8   Where the land is held under a title which has not yet been brought on to the Land Register, the period preceding exchange of contracts also provides an opportunity to accelerate the making of searches for land charges registered against estate owners pursuant to the Land Charges Acts.[1] The prudent purchaser of what appears to be unregistered land also requisitions a search of the Index Map at Land Registry[2] for confirmation that title to the estate which he is proposing to purchase is not already registered or subject to an application for first registration or a caution against first registration.[3]

1   [**Paras 12.323–12.329**].
2   [**Para 2.100**].
3   [**Para 12.270**].

THE *CAVEAT EMPTOR* PRINCIPLE

12.9   The historic rule underlying land transfer is the principle of *caveat emptor*: let the buyer beware. It was (and still is) essentially the responsibility of the purchaser to inform himself in all relevant respects concerning the property which he seeks to purchase. The vendor must, of course, disclose latent defects in his title[1] and, if asked by the intending purchaser for specific information, must give it accurately to the best of his ability.[2] But only relatively rarely has there been any onus on the vendor to disclose pertinent information on his own initiative. For example, the Court of Appeal has expressed the view that there is no duty of care which obliges a vendor to disclose to a prospective purchaser the fact that the subject matter of the sale was once the scene of a horrific murder.[3]

1 Latent defects comprise incumbrances and other adverse matters of title which a prospective purchaser could not discover for himself by inspecting the property with reasonable care (see *Yandle v Sutton* [1922] 2 Ch 199 at 207–210 per Sargant J).

2 See *Terrene v Nelson* [1937] 3 All ER 739 at 744E per Farwell J. It is a criminal offence (but not necessarily a ground of civil liability) to make a 'false or misleading statement' about certain prescribed matters in the course of an estate agency business or a property development business (see Property Misdescriptions Act 1991, s 1(1)). An estate agent's disclaimer of responsibility for the accuracy of sale particulars may (notwithstanding the Unfair Contract Terms Act 1977) relieve the agent from liability to a purchaser for negligent misstatement (see *McCullagh v Lane Fox and Partners Ltd* (1995) Times, 22 December, where Sir Christopher Slade and Nourse LJ thought that, even in the absence of an express disclaimer, there was probably no breach of a duty of care).

3 *Sykes v Taylor-Rose* [2004] EWCA Civ 299 at [37] (even though this fact may significantly affect the resale value of the house). Contrast the view adopted in California (*Reed v King*, 193 Cal Rptr 130 at 133 (1983)). See also R B Brown and T H Thurlow, 'Buyers beware: statutes shield real estate brokers and sellers who do not disclose that properties are psychologically tainted' 49 Okla L Rev 625 (1996).

Gradual erosion of *caveat emptor*

12.10 In recent years it has been increasingly recognised not only that the essential basis of the transaction of sale is an element of trust between the parties, but also that the vendor has much more ready access than the purchaser to information about the land being sold. The result has been a steady movement away from the *caveat emptor* principle towards a regime of more liberal communication of relevant information to prospective purchasers.[1] In 1988 the Law Commission's Conveyancing Standing Committee issued a Consultation Paper which provisionally proposed that the caveat emptor rule should be reversed and that vendors should be required to make disclosure of 'all material facts' about properties offered for sale. This recommendation emerged in 1990, in a more muted form, as the Law Society's 'National Protocol' governing the standard steps to be taken in all domestic conveyancing transactions.[2] This Protocol greatly expedites the process of land transfer by rationalising the way in which information is transmitted or distributed between seller and buyer.

1 It was already quite clear that the *caveat emptor* principle has no application where a purchaser is induced to enter into a contract of purchase by means of fraud or deceit (see e g *Gordon v Selico Co Ltd* [1986] 1 EGLR 71 at 77J (deliberate concealment of dry rot)). Other exceptions to *caveat emptor* include instances of uberrimae fidei or fiduciary relationship and circumstances where a positive representation is distorted by silence on the part of a vendor (see Law Commission's Conveyancing Standing Committee, *Caveat Emptor in Sales of Land* (November 1988)).

2 See *Let the buyer be well informed* (Recommendations of Conveyancing Standing Committee of the Law Commission, December 1989).

The Law Society's National Conveyancing Protocol

12.11 Most domestic conveyancing is nowadays conducted in voluntary compliance with the National Protocol, the general aim of which is to provide purchasers with convenient and speedy access to all relevant information in respect of the property to be purchased.[1] Thus the vendor's solicitor commonly supplies, along with the draft contract for sale, an official copy of the vendor's register of title (if the vendor's title is registered)[2] or a full certified epitome of title (if the vendor's title is unregistered).[3]

1   See [1990] Conv 137 (H W Wilkinson).
2   **[Para 12.5]**.
3   This epitome of title takes the form of a chronological summary of all dealings and events concerning the land from the 'good root of title' **[para 12.260]** forward to the current date. Included with this epitome is a certified photocopy of every document to which reference is made. It is also usual to include copies of the results of earlier official searches made under the Land Charges Acts **[para 12.329]**.

The Property Information Form

12.12 Under the National Protocol the purchaser is also furnished with a duly completed 'Property Information Form', which fulfils much the same function as was once performed by solicitors' standard form preliminary enquiries. The 'Property Information Form' covers such issues as the identity of current occupiers, existing disputes concerning the property, the ownership of boundary features, guarantees in respect of work carried out on the building, the existence of mains services to the property, rights of way, planning matters and compulsory purchase orders. The vendor bears a duty of care in relation to the accuracy of his replies and liability cannot be excluded by a term in the written contract between vendor and purchaser.[1] Incorrect information may found a liability in negligence[2] or deceit.[3]

1   *Walker v Boyle* [1982] 1 WLR 495 at 507A–E; *South Western General Property Co Ltd v Marton* (1982) 263 EG 1090 at 1092; [1983] Conv 8.
2   See e g *Wilson v Bloomfield* (1979) 123 Sol Jo 860; [1980] Conv 401.
3   See *Alevizos v Nirula* (2003) 234 DLR (4th) 352 at [38] (Manitoba Court of Appeal).

Other disclosable information

12.13 The Law Society's National Protocol also recommends that the prospective purchaser be supplied with a 'Fixtures, Fittings and Contents Form'[1] and with the result of a recent local land charges search relating to the land.[2] The objective of this process of communication is to enable the purchaser, at an early stage in the transaction, to know exactly what he is buying.

1   **[Para 1.68]**. See *Taylor v Hamer* [2003] 1 P & CR D9 (Transcript at [76], [82], [93]).
2   **[Para 12.7]**.

Additional enquiries prior to contract

12.14   Additional enquiries may be necessitated by the information disclosed by the 'Property Information Form', by the documentary title or by the physical inspection conducted by the purchaser or his surveyor. Answers to such enquiries must be made honestly and carefully. The Court of Appeal has recently emphasised the importance of '[c]ommon sense and common decency' in the transaction of house sales[1] and it follows that misleading or dishonest responses to additional enquiries cannot be cured by a subsequent contractual term that the buyer is deemed to purchase with full notice of the actual state and condition of the property.[2]

1   *Taylor v Hamer* [2003] 1 P & CR D9 (Transcript at [82]) per Sedley LJ. See [2003] Conv 108 (J E A), 432 (C McNall).
2   *Taylor v Hamer* [2003] 1 P & CR D9 (Transcript at [69–[71] per Wall J, [85] per Sedley LJ).

The 'home information pack'

12.15   The Law Society's National Protocol remains voluntary rather than mandatory, but Part 5 of the Housing Bill 2003/2004 contains controversial provisions which would impose a general statutory duty to provide prospective purchasers with a 'home information pack'.[1] This innovation, already tried and tested in other jurisdictions,[2] effectively shifts to the vendor the burden of eliciting certain basic information about the subject matter of the sale. The home information pack is defined as a 'collection of documents'[3] which discloses 'relevant information'[4] in respect of the property and its title, the contents of any register entry relating to the property and details of any warranties, guarantees, taxes, service charges or other charges relating to it.[5] In particular, the home information pack will include a 'home condition report', prepared by a member of an approved certification scheme, which contains a description of the physical condition of the property and an analysis of its energy efficiency.[6] The seller or his estate agent will be required to make the home information pack available, on payment of a reasonable charge,[7] in any case where 'residential property' is 'put on the market' for sale with vacant possession.[8] For the most part, the Housing Bill merely converts good professional practice into a binding statutory obligation, but will nevertheless help to avoid the duplication of effort and cost which has previously marked many conveyancing transactions.

1   See [2003] Conv 1, 263 (P Kenny).
2   See e g Conveyancing Act 1919 (New South Wales), s 52A(2); Conveyancing (Sale of Land) Regulation 1995. See also *Timanu Pty Ltd v Clurstock Pty Ltd* (1988) 15 NSWLR 338 at 339G–340A.
3   Housing Bill 2003/2004, cl 130(2).
4   'Relevant information' means 'information about any matter ... that would be of interest to potential buyers' (Housing Bill 2003/2004, cl 144(4)). The information must relate to the property 'as it stands' (Housing Bill 2003/2004, cl 138(2)), i e must be up to date.
5   Housing Bill 2003/2004, cl 144(5). The pack will also contain replies to standard preliminary enquiries made on behalf of buyers (Housing Bill 2003/2004, cl 144(6)).

6   Housing Bill 2003/2004, cl 145.
7   The reasonable charge covers only the cost of making and sending the paper copy of the home information pack (Housing Bill 2003/2004, cl 138(7)). The seller is otherwise burdened with the cost of drawing up the required information (i e the cost of obtaining surveys, searches and copies of register entries).
8   Housing Bill 2003/2004, cls 130–138, 142. The requirement of a home information pack will be enforceable by local weights and measures authorities who will have power to impose penalty charge notices for non-compliance (Housing Bill 2003/2004, cls 147–148).

ABSENCE OF CONTRACTUAL COMMITMENT

12.16   It is likely that, while pre-contractual negotiations and enquiries are being pursued, the prospective vendor and purchaser will express some tentative consensus ad idem in the matter of sale. It used to be invariable practice at this stage for vendor and purchaser to mark all correspondence as being 'subject to contract' so that no binding contractual commitment could emerge in the absence of a formal contract for sale signed and exchanged by the parties. In view of the comprehensive modern requirement of written contract,[1] the necessity for such caution has now largely disappeared.[2]

1   See LP(MP)A 1989, s 2(1) [para **12.27**].
2   See particularly *Commission for the New Towns v Cooper (Great Britain) Ltd* [1995] Ch 259 at 287F–H, 294C–E.

Agreements for sale 'subject to contract'

12.17   It is universally accepted that an agreement for sale 'subject to contract',[1] even if contained in written form, is not contractually binding unless and until its terms are incorporated in a formal contract of sale signed and exchanged by the parties.[2] In advance of a formal contract, the parties have merely a 'gentleman's agreement',[3] which in reality incorporates little more than a mutual hope that 'the other will act like a gentleman' in circumstances where neither 'intends so to act if it is against his material interests.'[4] This lack of legal consequence enables either party with impunity to disregard agreements in principle for the sale and purchase of land.[5] In order to curb abuses of the 'subject to contract' rule,[6] various attempts were made by the courts during the 1970s to dislodge its suspensive effects,[7] but the orthodox understanding of the proviso was soon reinstated[8] and eventually put beyond all doubt by the Law of Property (Miscellaneous Provisions) Act 1989.[9]

1   Compare the phrase 'without prejudice', which does not preclude the formation of a valid contract (see *Hooper v Sherman* [1995] CLY 840).
2   *Winn v Bull* (1877) 7 Ch D 29 at 32 per Jessel MR; *Coope v Ridout* [1921] 1 Ch 291 at 297–298; *Chillingworth v Esche* [1924] 1 Ch 97 at 104–105; *Lockett v Norman-Wright* [1925] Ch 56 at 62; *Keppel v Wheeler* [1927] 1 KB 577 at 592–593; *Eccles v Bryant and Pollock* [1948] Ch 93 at 100–101; *D'Silva v Lister House Development Ltd* [1971] Ch 17 at 28F; *London and Regional Investments Ltd v TBI plc* [2002] EWCA Civ 355 at [38].
3   Only in 'a very strong and exceptional context' will the words 'subject to contract' not be given their clear prima facie meaning (*Alpenstow Ltd v Regalian Properties PLC* [1985] 1 WLR 721

at 730A–B per Nourse J). See also *Mulhall v Haren* [1981] IR 364 at 386, but compare *Farah v Moody* [1998] EGCS 1 where, as a matter of 'commercial sense', the Court of Appeal refused to hold that an explicit undertaking by one party to reimburse the cost of improvements specifically requested of the other party pending the conclusion of a formal contract was deprived of legal effect merely because included within 'subject to contract' correspondence.

4   *Goding v Frazer* [1967] 1 WLR 286 at 293B per Sachs J. See also *Edward Wong Finance Co Ltd v Johnson Stokes & Master* [1984] AC 296 at 307E, where Lord Brightman observed that 'the conception of courtesy as between vendor and purchaser would be a nonsense.'

5   See *Pitt v PHH Asset Management Ltd* [1994] 1 WLR 327 at 333D–H per Sir Thomas Bingham MR ('For very many people their first and closest contact with the law is when they come to buy or sell a house. They frequently find it a profoundly depressing and frustrating experience ... No explanation is given, no apology made'). The Law Commission long ago accepted that the 'subject to contract' proviso 'has drawbacks and is capable of being abused in certain circumstances' (*Report on 'Subject to Contract' Agreements* (Law Com No 65, January 1975), para 4). Compare the practice in Scots law under which even informal agreements for the sale of land are contractually binding (see *House Selling the Scottish Way for England and Wales* (Conveyancing Standing Committee of the Law Commission, September 1987)).

6   See *Mulhall v Haren* [1981] IR 364 at 378.

7   See e g *Law v Jones* [1974] Ch 112 at 125H–126A ('subject to contract' correspondence held capable of constituting written memorandum necessary for the purpose of LPA 1925, s 40(1) [paras 12.38–12.39]); *Griffiths v Young* [1970] Ch 675 at 685H–686D, 687A–E (agreement 'subject to contract' held to have been superseded by subsequent unconditional offer and acceptance made by the same parties and communicated by telephone).

8   See *Tiverton Estates Ltd v Wearwell Ltd* [1975] Ch 146 at 160F–G, 161D, 171E; *Munton v GLC* [1976] 1 WLR 649 at 655D; *Daulia Ltd v Four Millbank Nominees Ltd* [1978] Ch 231 at 249B–250D; *Cohen v Nessdale Ltd* [1982] 2 All ER 97 at 105a–j. See generally R W Clark, [1984] Conv 173, 251.

9   [Para 12.27]. The 1989 Act reflects the Law Commission's earlier endorsement of the 'sound concept ... that the buyer should be free from binding commitment until he has had the opportunity of obtaining legal and other advice, arranging his finance and making the necessary inspection, searches and enquiries' (Law Com No 65 (1975), para 4).

'Gazumping'

12.18   The delay in contractual commitment opens up the possibility of 'gazumping'[1] at times when the property market becomes unstable and volatile. By resort to this unpleasant practice a potential vendor may withdraw from an existing 'gentleman's agreement' for sale if it transpires that a more favourable price can be extracted from a different potential purchaser.[2] The gazumped purchaser has no remedy in the absence of a 'lock-out' or 'exclusivity' agreement, ie a prior collateral contract for valuable consideration that during a stipulated period the vendor will not negotiate with other prospective purchasers.[3] Such an agreement confers on the purchaser no right to require that the land be sold to him, but merely entitles the purchaser to recover damages in respect of transaction costs thrown away when the vendor elects to deal with somebody else during the period of exclusivity.[4]

1   See *Mulhall v Haren* [1981] IR 364 at 378 per Keane J ('a practice as unattractive as its name').

2   It has been pointed out that the duty of trustees to sell only at the best price reasonably obtainable [para 11.159] imposes a duty to 'gazump' (see *Buttle v Saunders* [1950] 2 All ER 193 at 195C–E; [1979] Conv 451; *Cowan v Scargill* [1985] Ch 270 at 288A–C). An agent may be liable in damages to a vendor for breach of duty in failing to 'gazump' if offered a higher price (see *Keppel v Wheeler* [1927] 1 KB 577 at 585–586).

3   *Pitt v PHH Asset Management Ltd* [1994] 1 WLR 327 at 332H–333B. See also *Walford v Miles*
      [1992] 2 AC 128 at 139C–G per Lord Ackner.
4   *Tye v House and Jennings* (1997) 76 P & CR 188 at 190. In the absence of a 'lock-out' or
      'exclusivity' agreement, the purchaser has no right to restitution of wasted expenditure (see
      Regalian Properties Plc v London Docklands Development Corpn [1995] 1 WLR 212 at
      230E–231C; [1995] RLR 100 (E McKendrick)).

12.19   There are intermittent suggestions that 'anti-gazumping' legislation
should be introduced in England and Wales which would require that a
prospective vendor and purchaser should both put down a 'pre-contract
deposit' as soon as an offer of purchase has been made and accepted 'subject to
contract'.[1] This deposit – perhaps 0.5 per cent of the purchase price – would be
forfeited by any party who, otherwise than for good cause, withdrew or refused
to exchange contracts within an agreed period.[2] The implementation of such a
scheme would afford at least some redress for the victim of gazumping in
respect of his wasted expenditure on professional fees connected with the
abortive transaction.

1   See e g Law Commission, *Pre-Contract Deposits: A Practice Recommendation by the Convey-*
      ancing Standing Committee (1987), paras 5–7.
2   A similar scheme operates in New South Wales in relation to the sale of residential property
      (Conveyancing Act 1919, ss 66Q, 66R, 66W; Conveyancing (Sale of Land) Regulation 1995).

Applicability of estoppel and constructive trust

12.20   In relatively rare instances the more inequitable effects of the 'subject
to contract' rule may be challengeable by reference to the doctrines of proprietary estoppel and constructive trust. An intending purchaser who, in advance
of a formal contract, incurs expenditure or other detriment may have a valid
claim founded on trust or estoppel if he has acted in reliance on some supposed
contractual commitment between the vendor and himself.[1] Claims of this kind
are, however, unlikely to succeed in ordinary transactions of purchase.[2] It must
be shown that the vendor created or encouraged an expectation in the purchaser that the vendor would not withdraw from a transaction which had been
agreed in principle between the parties.[3] There must also be evidence that the
purchaser relied, at least implicitly, on this expectation.[4] A claim of estoppel
failed in *Attorney-General of Hong Kong v Humphreys Estate (Queen's Gar-*
dens) Ltd[5] precisely because it was clear that the purchaser had at all times
known[6] that the vendor retained the right to resile from the agreement which
had been informally reached between them.[7] As Lord Templeman pointed out,
no estoppel could be founded on the mere fact that the purchaser had acted 'in
the confident and not unreasonable hope that the agreement in principle would
come into effect.'[8]

1   *Attorney-General of Hong Kong v Humphreys Estate (Queen's Gardens) Ltd* [1987] AC 114 at
      127H–128A per Lord Templeman. See also *Salvation Army Trustee Co Ltd v West Yorkshire*
      MCC (1981) 41 P & CR 179; *Gonthier v Orange Contract Scaffolding Ltd* [2003] EWCA Civ
      873; [2003] Conv 360 (J E A).
2   See *Clark v Follett* (1973) STC 240 at 263–264; *Thwaites v Ryan* [1984] VR 65 at 96. In
      Salvation Army Trustee Co Ltd v West Yorkshire MCC (1981) 41 P & CR 179 at 199, Woolf J

was careful to emphasise that his upholding of a claim of estoppel on unusual facts was not intended to 'interfere with the normal conduct of negotiations "subject to contract"'.

3   See e g *Nepean District Tennis Association Inc v Council of City of Penrith* (1989) NSW ConvR 55–438 at 58,180.

4   [**Para 10.242**]. See e g *Milchas Investments Pty Ltd v Larkin* (1989) NSW ConvR 55–487 at 58,536–58,537, where Young J lamented the tendency for estoppel claims to be advanced 'as a back-up submission in every case where parties have failed to obtain an exchange of contracts'. In deprecating the unprincipled enforcement of *nuda pacta* by reference to estoppel, Young J pointed out that 'generally speaking, the mere fact that a person does not keep his promise is not unconscionable. There must be something more and that something more will usually be found in looking to see what the opposing party did to his detriment ... in reliance on the promise.'

5   [1987] AC 114 at 124G–125B, 127G–128A.

6   See *Gillett v Holt* [2001] Ch 210 at 228A per Robert Walker LJ.

7   See *Waltons Stores (Interstate) Ltd v Maher* (1988) 164 CLR 387 at 423, where Brennan J pointed out that 'so long as both parties recognise that either party is at liberty to withdraw from the negotiations at any time before the contract is made, it cannot be unconscionable for one party to do so.'

8   [1987] AC 114 at 124F–G. Even if a plea of estoppel does not succeed in fixing the parties with a binding contract of sale, the principle of unjust enrichment has been held in some jurisdictions to justify a return of the intending purchaser's expenditure on the land (see *Nepean District Tennis Association Inc v Council of City of Penrith* (1989) NSW ConvR 55–438 at 58,180–58,181).

Chain transactions

12.21   Especially in the context of domestic conveyancing, a transaction of sale and purchase rarely occurs in isolation. As homeowners move up (or down) the property ladder, transactions tend to involve highly complex chains of transfer. Each individual transaction is reliant upon the successful and simultaneous completion of a number of interlinked dealings. It is this interdependence of dealings which makes the pre-contractual phase of land transactions a particularly fraught affair, since an entire chain of sales and purchases may be frustrated if all parties concerned are not ready (and equipped, where necessary, with offers of mortgage finance) to exchange contracts on the same day.

Implications of electronic conveyancing

12.22   The 'single most important function' of the Land Registration Act 2002 is to set in place the necessary legal framework for the introduction of electronic conveyancing.[1] The move from paper-based transactions to electronic dealing is already underway and, in the joint view of the Law Commission and Land Registry, e-conveyancing 'seems certain to become the only form of dealing with registered land within a comparatively short time.'[2] It is envisaged that the system of e-conveyancing will be operated through a secure electronic communications network (or 'intranet') accessible on a contractual basis by professionals (e g solicitors, licensed conveyancers,[3] estate agents and mortgage lenders) who are authorised for this purpose by Land Registry.[4] The network will be employed to conduct all stages of a transaction in electronic form and will have three particular functions during the pre-contractual phase.

1   Law Com No 271 (2001), paras 2.41, 13.1 **[para 7.62]**.
2   Law Com No 271 (2001), para 13.45.
3   The Administration of Justice Act 1985 allows 'licensed conveyancing' to be carried out by persons who are not qualified solicitors (see AJA 1985, ss 11–39), but the bulk of conveyancing work is still carried out by solicitors.
4   See LRA 2002, s 92, Sch 5.

Dissemination of information

12.23   The electronic communications network will be used for the dissemination of information about properties being sold, thereby dispensing with many of the routine enquiries and surveys which make the conveyancing process repetitive and costly. This communicative function is likely to dovetail with the proposed statutory requirement that vendors of residential premises should be obliged, at their own expense, to provide prospective purchasers with a 'home information pack' relating to the land.[1]

1   [Para 12.15].

The 'chain manager'

12.24   It is probable that a 'chain manager' – almost certainly an official of Land Registry – will oversee and coordinate the linked transactions within a chain of sales and purchases (at least within the area of domestic conveyancing).[1] The expedited flow of information through the secure intranet to all chain members about the achievement of successive stages in the pre-contractual phase will relieve much of the uncertainty and tension currently experienced in conveyancing transactions and will enable the chain manager to monitor the progress of a chain and identify any party in that chain who is delaying the process of eventual transfer.[2]

1   Law Com No 271 (2001), paras 2.52, 13.63.
2   See LRA 2002, s 92, Sch 5, para 9.

Early involvement of Land Registry

12.25   Land Registry's involvement in the conveyancing process will begin much earlier than is currently the case.[1] For instance, the draft terms of any proposed contract will require to be transmitted to the Registry in electronic form for checking by electronic means in order to eradicate, even at this stage, discrepancies or other difficulties which might impede the transaction later.

1   Law Com No 271 (2001), paras 2.49–2.53.

CONTRACT

12.26   When vendor and purchaser finally reach a state of preparedness for contractual commitment, they enter into a formal contract for the disposition of the vendor's legal estate in the land (whether freehold or leasehold).[1] The contract may be 'open', ie may provide expressly for nothing beyond the identification of the parties, the definition of the subject property and the price to be paid.[2] Infinitely more common than 'open' contracts for the sale of land are 'closed' contracts which incorporate a number of standardised conditions relevant to the generality of land transactions. Solicitors operating under the Law Society's National Protocol use the current edition of the Standard Conditions of Sale, coupled with any special conditions relevant to the transaction in hand.[3]

1   The contract can be – but in normal domestic conveyancing rarely is – protected as an 'estate contract' [**para 12.89**]. The purchaser is usually better protected by the process of priority search [**para 12.50**] (see Law Com No 271 (2001), para 2.43).
2   The rights and duties of vendor and purchaser under an 'open' contract are then determined with reference to the general law of property.
3   It is a salutary fact that the small print in such standard form contracts has binding effect even in relation to 'conditions which it is probable that nobody ever read' (see *Squarey v Harris-Smith* (1981) 42 P & CR 118 at 130 per Lawton LJ).

STATUTORY REQUIREMENTS OF CONTRACTUAL FORMALITY

12.27   In spite of the frequent use of standard written terms of contract, there used to be few legal requirements of form in respect of the exchange of contracts. The relative informality of the contract stage was dramatically altered by the Law of Property (Miscellaneous Provisions) Act 1989 in relation to all contracts concluded on or after 27 September 1989.[1]

1   LP(MP)A 1989, s 2(7).

Contracts entered into on or after 27 September 1989

12.28   The Law of Property (Miscellaneous Provisions) Act 1989 was intended to bring about a 'markedly different regime' in the area of contract.[1] For modern land contracts, the message is unmistakable: in order to be valid, contracts must be in writing and signed by all contracting parties.[2] Parliament has concluded, in the public interest, 'that the need for certainty as to ... formation ... must in general outweigh the disappointment of those who make informal bargains in ignorance of the statutory requirement.'[3]

1   *Firstpost Homes Ltd v Johnson* [1995] 1 WLR 1567 at 1571E per Peter Gibson LJ. See likewise *Yaxley v Gotts* [2000] Ch 162 at 171B per Robert Walker LJ [**para 9.15**]. On the impact of the 1989 Act, see G Griffiths, 'Continuing Problems of Formality in Contracts for the Sale of Land? The Issue of Substantive Interpretation', in P Jackson and D C Wilde (ed), *Contemporary Property Law* (Ashgate 1999), p 183.
2   In relation to contracts entered into on or after 27 September 1989, the less demanding

formality rules contained in LPA 1925, s 40 cease to have effect (LP(MP)A 1989, s 2(8)). See P H Pettit, [1989] Conv 431; (1989) 105 LQR 553 (R E Annand).

3   *Yaxley v Gotts* [2000] Ch 162 at 175B–C per Robert Walker LJ. See also *Proudreed Ltd v Microgen Holdings Plc* (1996) 72 P & CR 388 at 389 per Schiemann LJ.

Requirement of written contract

12.29 Following upon recommendations made by the Law Commission in 1987,[1] the Law of Property (Miscellaneous Provisions) Act 1989 imposes a requirement of written form in relation to almost all kinds of contract relating to the disposition of an interest in land.[2] Section 2(1) of the Act provides that

> A contract for the sale or other disposition of an interest in land can only be made in writing and only by incorporating all the terms which the parties have expressly agreed in one document or, where contracts are exchanged, in each.

1   See Law Commission, Transfer of Land: Formalities for Contracts for Sale etc of Land (Law Com No 164, June 1987), Part IV.
2   The term 'disposition' bears the same meaning as in the Law of Property Act 1925 (see LP(MP)A 1989, s 2(6); LPA 1925, s 205(1)(ii)), thus including leases, mortgages, and charges (see *United Bank of Kuwait Plc v Sahib* [1997] Ch 107 at 136A–B).

12.30 This statutory innovation removes what the Law Commission considered to be the 'indefensibly confusing' feature of the pre-existing law, namely that it allowed oral contracts to be binding but unenforceable. The old law has been replaced by a 'simple, straightforward rule' that contracts concerning land cannot be made orally.[1] An unwritten contract is now not merely unenforceable but utterly void and ineffective.[2] The requirements of the 1989 Act have the substantial merit of requiring a much greater degree of clarity in respect of both the existence of a binding contract and the nature of its terms. Towards this end the courts have striven to assure the 1989 Act wide coverage. For example, the Act applies even where, at the date of contract, neither party has a proprietary interest in the subject matter of the contract.[3]

1   Law Com No 164 (1987), para 4.2. For a bizarre instance, arising in Australia, of an oral 'contract' made at a dinner party, see *Lezabar Pty Ltd v Hogan* (1989) 4 BPR 9498.
2   *Firstpost Homes Ltd v Johnson* [1995] 1 WLR 1567 at 1571E–F per Peter Gibson LJ. See e g *Singh v Beggs* (1995) 71 P & CR 120 at 122.
3   *Singh v Beggs* (1995) 71 P & CR 120 at 122.

Requirement of signatures

12.31 The 1989 Act also extends the requirement of signature. The document incorporating the terms of the contract agreed by the parties must be signed not simply 'by the party to be charged'[1] but by or on behalf of all parties to the contract.[2] Signature by one party alone is ineffective.[3] Moreover, signature must be a real signature by hand and is not constituted by the printing or typing of a party's name as the addressee of a supposedly contractual undertaking.[4]

1   Compare LPA 1925, s 40(1).
2   LP(MP)A 1989, s 2(3). In the case of an option to purchase land, it is sufficient for the purpose of section 2(1) of the 1989 Act that the agreement conferring the option complies with the requirement of writing signed by all parties (but see *Jelson Ltd v Derby CC* [2000] JPL 203 at 214–215 (agreement invalidated for want of all required signatures)). It is irrelevant that the notice under which the option is later exercised does not so comply (eg because signed only by the option holder (see *Spiro v Glencrown Properties Ltd* [1991] Ch 537 at 546E–F; [1991] CLJ 236 (A J Oakley); [1990] Conv 9 (J E Adams); [1991] Conv 140 (P F Smith))).
3   *Chandler v Clark* [2003] 1 P & CR 239 at [13] per Chadwick LJ.
4   *Firstpost Homes Ltd v Johnson* [1995] 1 WLR 1567 at 1575F–1576E per Peter Gibson LJ, 1577C–F per Balcombe LJ.

Documentation and terms

12.32   The 1989 Act aims to 'simplify the law and to avoid disputes'[1] and therefore requires that, except where contracts are exchanged,[2] the contract must be contained in one document and this single document must itself contain all the terms of the contract.[3] The 1989 Act preserves the pre-existing rules on the joinder of documents, with the result that some contractual terms may be incorporated by reference to another document.[4] Thus, for example, an Ordnance Survey plan may be incorporated by reference in the contractual document, in which case it is essential that all parties concerned should sign the contractual document (although not necessarily the plan).[5] Subsequent variations of a material term in any contract must also be signed by all parties.[6]

1   *Firstpost Homes Ltd v Johnson* [1995] 1 WLR 1567 at 1571H per Peter Gibson LJ.
2   Where contracts are exchanged, it is sufficient that one of the relevant contractual documents (but not necessarily the same one) is signed by or on behalf of each party.
3   *Firstpost Homes Ltd v Johnson* [1995] 1 WLR 1567 at 1571H per Peter Gibson LJ ('Thereby it has been sought to avoid the need to have extrinsic evidence as to that contract').
4   LP(MP)A 1989, s 2(2). A number of separate and intrinsically incomplete documents may therefore be linked in order to form a complete contract in writing (see *Long v Millar* (1879) 4 CPD 450 at 454–455). However, if two or more documents are to be joined in this way, the primary contractual document must be signed and must contain 'some reference, express or implied, to some other document or transaction' (*Timmins v Moreland Street Property Co Ltd* [1958] Ch 110 at 130 per Jenkins LJ; *Elias v George Sahely & Co (Barbados) Ltd* [1983] 1 AC 646 at 655A–656A). Thus, although this outcome was not intended by the Law Commission (see Law Com No 164 (1987), para 4.15), a valid contract cannot normally be created by a mere exchange of correspondence unless the correspondence acknowledges the existence of an already concluded agreement (see *Commission for the New Towns v Cooper (Great Britain) Ltd* [1995] Ch 259 at 287F–H, 294C–E; [1995] Conv 319 (M P Thompson); [1995] CLJ 502 (A J Oakley)).
5   *Firstpost Homes Ltd v Johnson* [1995] 1 WLR 1567 at 1573C–E per Peter Gibson LJ. See [1996] CLJ 192 (A J Oakley).
6   *McCausland v Duncan Lawrie Ltd* [1997] 1 WLR 38 at 44H–45A, 49G.

Exceptions

12.33   Few exceptions are permitted from the requirements laid down in section 2 of the 1989 Act. However, the Act expressly excludes from its ambit any contract to grant a lease for not more than three years at a full market rent.[1] The courts have also elaborated a number of implied exceptions from the scope of section 2. The 1989 Act has been held to have no application to a genuinely collateral contract[2] or to an executed agreement supplemental to a contract.[3] Nor does the 1989 Act catch a mortgagee's agreement to allow a mortgagor to return into possession on payment of loan arrears.[4] Moreover, the requirement of signed writing relates only to an executory contract for the future disposition of an interest in land as distinct from a contract of disposition (ie a contract which itself effects the disposition of such an interest).[5] Most recently the Court of Appeal has indicated that the Act does not apply to agreements between neighbours which, in the interests of 'quieting strife and averting litigation', demarcate a boundary line (even though such agreements may involve some trivial transfer of land).[6]

1   LP(MP)A 1989, s 2(5)(a) (by cross-reference to LPA 1925, s 54(2)). Other exceptions comprise a contract made in the course of a public auction and a contract made on a recognised investment exchange regulated by the Financial Services Act 1986 (LP(MP)A 1989, s 2(5)(b)–(c)).
2   *Record v Bell* [1991] 1 WLR 853 at 860D, 862A–B (purchaser's acceptance of an oral warranty as to the state of the vendor's title not invalidated by absence of signed writing); *Pitt v PHH Asset Management Ltd* [1994] 1 WLR 327 at 333C, 334B ('lock-out' agreement).
3   *Tootal Clothing Ltd v Guinea Properties Management Ltd* (1992) 64 P & CR 452 at 455–456 (agreement to grant lease); [1993] Conv 89 (P Luther).
4   *Kumah v Osbornes* [1997] EGCS 01.
5   See e g *Target Holdings Ltd v Priestley* (2000) 79 P & CR 305 at 318–320 (no application to contractual repayment scheme under an already executed mortgage charge).
6   *Joyce v Rigolli* [2004] 1 P & CR D55 (Transcript at [32] per Arden LJ, [43] per Sir Martin Nourse).

Abolition of the doctrine of part performance

12.34   A further – and at least superficially far-reaching – effect of the Law of Property (Miscellaneous Provisions) Act 1989 is the disapplication[1] of the historic doctrine of part performance to contracts concluded on or after 27 September 1989.[2] This equitable doctrine was expressly preserved by section 40(2) of the Law of Property Act 1925[3] and used in practice to ensure the enforceability of many oral contracts relating to land.[4] The law of part peformance eventually came to be criticised as uncertain and unsatisfactory in its operation[5] and in 1987 the Law Commission advocated that it should cease to play any role in contracts concerning land.[6] This objective has been achieved by the comprehensive statutory requirement of written contract. Where an agreement relating to land fails to comply with section 2 of the 1989 Act, there is simply no contract in support of which acts of part performance can ever be pleaded.[7] The statutory avoidance of unwritten contracts has caused a fatal detachment of the entire doctrine.

1   See LP(MP)A 1989, s 2(8); *Yaxley v Gotts* [2000] Ch 162 at 172F per Robert Walker LJ.
2   **[Para 12.40]**. The doctrine of part performance remains relevant to agreements entered into prior to this date (see e g *Lloyds Bank plc v Carrick* [1996] 4 All ER 630 at 637f–j **[paras 9.40, 10.87]**).
3   See *Yaxley v Gotts* [2000] Ch 162 at 171C per Robert Walker LJ.
4   *Firstpost Homes Ltd v Johnson* [1995] 1 WLR 1567 at 1571G per Peter Gibson LJ.

5   See eg Law Commission, *Transfer of Land: Formalities for Contracts for Sale etc of Land* (Law Com Working Paper No 92, July 1985), para 5.14; Law Com No 164 (1987), para 5.4.
6   Law Com No 164 (1987), para 4.13.
7   See P H Pettit, [1989] Conv 431 at 441.

Role of constructive trust and estoppel

12.35   The demise of the doctrine of part performance has not brought about such wide-ranging effects as might at first have been supposed. In the context of non-compliance with prescribed formalities, the abolition of part performance has simply thrown a heightened emphasis upon the application of alternative equitable doctrines.[1] The 1989 Act in no way exhausts the capacity of equity to avert unconscionable outcomes where the need demands.[2] Even in the absence of a written contract, the court can declare in appropriate cases that a vendor holds land subject to an 'equity' which requires him to transfer it to the purchaser as on a performance of the agreement.[3]

1   The Law Commission predicted that the function of part performance in counteracting the unconscionable repudiation of oral undertakings would be taken up by other remedies founded in estoppel, negligence, deceit, restitution and rectification (Law Com Working Paper No 92 (1985), para 5.8; Law Com No 164 (1987), paras 5.1–5.6). See P H Pettit, [1989] Conv 431 at 442.
2   See *Yaxley v Gotts* [2000] Ch 162 at 190H per Beldam LJ.
3   See *Ash Street Properties Pty Ltd v Pollnow* (1987) 9 NSWLR 80 at 101A–D per Priestley JA (referring to 'an equity which has arisen extra the contract and as a result of what the parties have done'). In giving effect not to the agreement, which is statutorily void, but to an external 'equity' generated by the circumstances, the court simply ensures that the statute is not used as an instrument of fraud.

12.36   Thus, in certain circumstances, doctrines of proprietary estoppel and constructive trust may render enforceable an oral bargain or 'gentleman's agreement' for the sale of land.[1] In particular, section 2(5) of the 1989 Act explicitly preserves the operation of constructive trust doctrine in relation to contracts which fail to comply with the statutory requirement of writing. In *Yaxley v Gotts*[2] the Court of Appeal confirmed that this provision allows a 'limited exception ... for those cases in which a supposed bargain has been so fully performed by one side, and the general circumstances of the matter are such, that it would be inequitable to disregard the claimant's expectations, and insufficient to grant him no more than a restitutionary remedy.'[3] The Court took the view that, although this deviation from the general statutory objective had the effect of enforcing contracts which would otherwise be void,[4] the outcome was not so offensive to the 'public policy principle' as to subvert or frustrate the basic parliamentary purpose.[5] On the contrary, Beldam LJ declined to believe that it is 'inherent in a social policy of simplifying conveyancing by requiring the certainty of a written document that unconscionable conduct or equitable fraud should be allowed to prevail.'[6]

1   The doctrine of estoppel may 'operate to modify (and sometimes even counteract) the effect of section 2' of the 1989 Act (*Yaxley v Gotts* [2000] Ch 162 at 174F per Robert Walker LJ).

2   [2000] Ch 162 [**paras 10.86, 10.111**]. See [2000] CLJ 23 (L Tee); (2000) 116 LQR 11 (R J Smith); [2000] Conv 245 (M P Thompson).

3   [2000] Ch 162 at 180D–E per Robert Walker LJ. For present purposes the Court of Appeal viewed the doctrine of constructive trust as 'indistinguishable' from the principle of proprietary estoppel [**para 10.68**]. For earlier intimations that estoppel might provide an escape route from the statutory requirement of written contract, see e g *McCausland v Duncan Lawrie Ltd* [1997] 1 WLR 38 at 45H, 50B–C; *Bankers Trust Co v Namdar* [1997] EGCS 20; *Target Holdings Ltd v Priestley* (2000) 79 P & CR 305 at 324–325.

4   In *Yaxley v Gotts* the Court of Appeal enforced, by way of constructive trust, an oral agreement by an estate owner to grant a builder the ground floor of premises in exchange for labour, materials and services supplied.

5   [2000] Ch 162 at 172F–175C.

6   [2000] Ch 162 at 193C.

Contracts entered into prior to 27 September 1989

12.37   Only contracts concluded prior to 27 September 1989 remain subject to the old rule of contractual formality which, apart from cases of part performance and estoppel,[1] required that an enforceable contract relating to land be merely evidenced in writing and signed only by or on behalf of the party to be charged.[2] A binding contract could thus be concluded quite validly in either oral or written form, although the *enforceability* of the contract depended on compliance with a minimal evidential requirement imposed by statute.[3]

1   See *Photo Art & Sound (Cremorne) Pty Ltd v Cremorne Centre Pty Ltd (In Liquidation)* (1987) 4 BPR 9436 at 9441–9442 (Court of Appeal of New South Wales).

2   LPA 1925, s 40(1). Only the party who signed the evidential note or memorandum could be sued. For reference to this 'lack of mutuality', see *Commission for the New Towns v Cooper (Great Britain) Ltd* [1995] Ch 259 at 287D per Stuart-Smith LJ.

3   In so far as a binding contract for the sale of land is generally thought to vest some equitable interest in the purchaser at the date of contract [**para 9.18**], it was sometimes argued that an oral agreement, even if supported by a memorandum or note pursuant to section 40, still fell foul of LPA 1925, s 53(1)(a). This contention was finally rebutted in *Target Holdings Ltd v Priestley* (2000) 79 P & CR 305 at 318–319. See also Nicholas Seddon, 'Contracts for the Sale of Land: Is a Note or Memorandum Sufficient?' (1987) 61 ALJ 406; D Everett, (1987) 17 U W Australia L Rev 301.

Requirement of written memorandum

12.38   Pursuant to section 40(1) of the Law of Property Act 1925, no action could be brought upon any contract for the sale or other disposition of land or any interest in land unless the agreement upon which such action was brought, or 'some memorandum or note thereof', was 'in writing, and signed by the party to be charged or by some other person thereunto by him lawfully authorised.'[1] This provision derived from section 4 of the Statute of Frauds 1677 and was plainly designed to prevent dispute over oral dealings in land.[2] Section 40(1) did not render void a purely oral contract for the sale of land: it merely provided that such a contract should be unenforceable unless evidenced in some written memorandum.[3]

1   Although for reasons of clarity this account of section 40 is couched in the past tense, section 40 still governs the enforceability of contracts entered into prior to 27 September 1989.

2   The requirement of a written memorandum had no application to any contract between A and B that A should purchase land from C (*Lees v Fleming* [1980] Qd R 162 at 167E–F).

3   See *Lloyds Bank plc v Carrick* [1996] 4 All ER 630 at 637f per Morritt LJ. In practice there was little confusion as to whether section 40(1) had been satisfied by the provision of a written memorandum or note, since most contracts for the sale of land were not only evidenced in writing but were actually contained in written form.

Contents of written memorandum

12.39   There were few limitations on the form or contents of the memorandum required by section 40(1).[1] It was enough that some note of all the material terms of the contract was recorded in documentary form.[2] It was necessary that the material terms should identify the parties beyond any possibility of later dispute.[3] These terms also had to render ascertainable both the physical subject matter of the contract[4] and the price to be paid,[5] specify a date for the handing over of possession to the purchaser[6] and afford evidence of other expressly agreed terms.[7] According to the more generally accepted view, the memorandum or note was also required to incorporate some acknowledgement or recognition by the signatory that a contract had actually been entered into.[8]

1   A memorandum could comprise, for example, a minute of a meeting of directors (see *Jones v Victoria Dock Graving Co* (1877) 2 QBD 314 at 322).

2   *Hawkins v Price* [1947] Ch 645 at 659–660; *Tiverton Estates Ltd v Wearwell Ltd* [1975] Ch 146 at 161G; *Mulhall v Haren* [1981] IR 364 at 394.

3   *Potter v Duffield* (1874) LR 18 Eq 4 at 7–8; *Davies v Sweet* [1962] 2 QB 300 at 307–308.

4   *Davies v Sweet* [1962] 2 QB 300 at 306.

5   See *Sudbrook Trading Estate Ltd v Eggleton* [1983] 1 AC 444.

6   *Mulhall v Haren* [1981] IR 364 at 394. See also *Walker v Bower* [1975] NZ Recent Law 138 at 139.

7   *Hawkins v Price* [1947] Ch 645 at 654.

8   *Tiverton Estates Ltd v Wearwell Ltd* [1975] Ch 146 at 160F–G, 171C–D. See also *Kelly v Park Hall School Ltd* [1979] IR 340 at 352; *Mulhall v Haren* [1981] IR 364 at 391; but compare *Law v Jones* [1974] Ch 112 at 124H per Buckley LJ. A pre-contractual document cannot satisfy the requirement of written memorandum (see *Haydon v McLeod* (1901) 27 VLR 395; *John Wakim & Sons Pty Ltd v BBA Industries Pty Ltd* (2000) 10 BPR 18475 at [14]). Nor, of course, may a party seek to rely on a written memorandum or note brought into existence only after the commencement of enforcement proceedings (see *Lucas v Dixon* (1889) 22 QBD 357 at 359–362; *Farr, Smith & Co Ltd v Messers Ltd* [1928] 1 KB 397 at 405; *South Coast Oils (Qld and NSW) Pty Ltd v Look Enterprises Pty Ltd* [1988] 1 Qd R 680 at 690).

Doctrine of part performance

12.40   Irrespective of non-compliance with the provisions of section 40(1) of the Law of Property Act 1925, a contract for the sale of land remained actionable pursuant to section 40(2) if it could be shown that there had been acts of 'part performance'.[1] For this purpose part performance generally required that the party seeking to enforce the contract had, in reliance upon that contract,[2] undertaken some action to his own detriment or prejudice. The doctrine of part performance is thus closely related both to the doctrine of proprietary estoppel[3] and to the long-standing disinclination of the courts to allow a statute to be used as an instrument of fraud.[4] The law of part performance is thematically linked with the historic pattern of 'equity's intervention to provide relief against unconscionable conduct.'[5]

1 See Gerwyn Griffiths, 'Part performance – Still Trying to replace the Irreplaceable?' [2002] Conv 216.

2 The doctrine of part performance could never render enforceable an agreement which was itself void for uncertainty (see eg *Cook v Norlands Ltd* [2001] UKPC 52 at [11] per Sir Andrew Leggatt (Appeal from the High Court of Justice of the Isle of Man)).

3 **[Paras 10.168–10.300]**.

4 **[Para 9.193]**. See *Maddison v Alderson* (1883) 8 App Cas 467 at 474 per Earl of Selborne LC; *Last v Rosenfeld* [1972] 2 NSWLR 923 at 927E–F; *Thwaites v Ryan* [1984] VR 65 at 91.

5 *Yaxley v Gotts* [2000] Ch 162 at 176B–C per Robert Walker LJ. The courts are nevertheless 'cautious' in allowing equitable doctrines to circumvent the requirements of LPA 1925, s 40 (*Inglorest Investments Ltd v Campbell* [2004] EWCA Civ 408 at [32] per Mummery LJ).

Acts sufficient to constitute part performance

12.41 The doctrine of part performance rendered a contract enforceable, even in the absence of a written memorandum, where the claimant had done acts which, on a balance of probability, were referable to and explicable only in terms of the existence of a contract in relation to land.[1] Although these acts did not need to be such as would demonstrate the precise terms of the contract,[2] part performance was premised on the current existence of an actual contract. Acts of reliance were irrelevant if performed on the footing of mere negotiations which might or might not ripen later into contract.[3] The doctrine of part performance was substantially relaxed during the 1970s and 1980s.[4] A claim of part performance came to be supportable on the basis of any acts which could be shown to have been undertaken in reliance on a contract, where it would in effect have constituted a fraud for the defendant to take advantage of the fact that the contract was not evidenced in writing. Relevant acts included the payment of money either to the other contracting party[5] or to some third party,[6] the entry into possession of land with the vendor's consent,[7] or the making of substantial improvements or alterations to the land.[8] In *Steadman v Steadman*[9] it even appeared to be the majority view in the House of Lords that a sufficient act of part performance could arise where a purchaser instructed solicitors to prepare and submit a draft conveyance or transfer.[10]

1 The acts relied upon must point to a contract in respect of *land* (*Re Gonin, Decd* [1979] Ch 16 at 31B–D), although compare the doubts expressed in *Steadman v Steadman* [1976] AC 536 at 541C–D per Lord Reid, 554C–D per Viscount Dilhorne.

2 *Steadman v Steadman* [1976] AC 536 at 546F per Lord Morris of Borth-y-Gest.

3 *Thynne v Earl of Glengall* (1848) 2 HLCas 131 at 158, 9 ER 1042 at 1052; *Ex parte Foster* (1883) 22 Ch D 797 at 811; *Biss v Hygate* [1918] 2 KB 314 at 317; *J C Williamson Ltd v Lukey and Mulholland* (1931) 45 CLR 282 at 300; *O'Rourke v Hoeven* [1974] 1 NSWLR 622 at 625E–F. See eg *Gely v Scobell* (1989) NSW ConvR ¶55–439 at 58,186–58,187 (arrangement of purchase finance constituted merely 'preparatory acts' and no part performance).

4 In *Steadman v Steadman* [1976] AC 536 the House of Lords departed significantly from the

classic requirements of part performance as laid down in *Maddison v Alderson* (1883) 8 App Cas 467. See (1974) 90 LQR 433 (H W R Wade); (1974) 38 Conv (NS) 354 (F R Crane); [1974] CLJ 205 (C T Emery). This new liberality was eventually to doom the doctrine of part performance (see Law Com No 164 (1987), para 5.4, condemning the doctrine as 'very confused').

5   *Steadman v Steadman* [1976] AC 536 at 541B per Lord Reid, 565B per Lord Simon of Glaisdale, 570F–G per Lord Salmon; *Lloyds Bank plc v Carrick* [1996] 4 All ER 630 at 637f–g per Morritt LJ. See also *Re Gonin, Decd* [1979] Ch 16 at 30G–H.

6   See *Shillabeer v Diebel* (1980) 100 DLR (3d) 279 at 282.

7   *Smallwood v Sheppards* [1895] 2 QB 627 at 630; *Sharman v Sharman* (1893) 67 LT 834 at 836–837; *Kingswood Estate Co Ltd v Anderson* [1963] 2 QB 169 at 181, 189, 193. See also *Wakeham v Mackenzie* [1968] 1 WLR 1175 at 1181D; *Re Gonin, Decd* [1979] Ch 16 at 31D–E; *Regent v Millett* (1976) 133 CLR 679 at 682–683, affirming *Millett v Regent* [1975] 1 NSWLR 62.

8   *Reddin v Jarman* (1867) 16 LT 449 at 450; *Broughton v Snook* [1938] Ch 505 at 514–516; *Starlite Variety Stores Ltd v Cloverlawn Investments Ltd* (1979) 92 DLR (3d) 270 at 276.

9   [1976] AC 536 at 540C per Lord Reid, 553H–554B per Viscount Dilhorne, 563A–B per Lord Simon of Glaisdale, 573D per Lord Salmon.

10 See also *Sutton v Sutton* [1984] Ch 184 at 193A–D, where part performance of an oral agreement for transfer of a former matrimonial home was found in the giving of consent to divorce on agreed financial terms.

CONDITIONAL CONTRACTS

12.42   A contract for the sale of land may be made in conditional terms, the courts tending towards a generous view of the kinds of condition which are compatible with the existence of a binding contract for the sale and purchase of land.[1] Effect can thus be given, for instance, to a contract which is expressed to be subject to satisfactory survey,[2] since this condition can be construed as imposing on the purchaser an obligation to act reasonably in obtaining a surveyor's report on the property and then in deciding whether to adopt its recommendations.[3] Similarly, a binding contract may quite validly be conditioned upon the purchaser's sale of his own property[4] or upon the obtaining of a planning permission[5] or satisfactory mortgage finance.[6] Some conditions are, however, so vague or so general as to deprive an agreement of any genuine contractual force. Thus no binding contract can be created by acceptance 'subject to the approval of' a named third party, although such an acceptance may itself constitute a counter-offer.[7]

1   No equitable interest passes to the purchaser unless and until the condition is met (see *McWilliam v McWilliams Wines Pty Ltd* (1964) 114 CLR 656 at 660; *Brown v Heffer* (1967) 116 CLR 344 at 350; *Re Androma Pty Ltd* [1987] 2 Qd R 134 at 150).

2   *Ee v Kakar* (1980) 255 EG 879 at 881–883. See [1980] Conv 446 (J E A); [1981] CLJ 23 (A J Oakley).

3   It may even be possible to exchange contracts 'subject to satisfactory searches' (see *Ganton House Investments Ltd v Corbin* [1988] 43 EG 76; but compare [1988] Conv 397 at 398 (J E A)).

4   *Perri v Coolangatta Investments Pty Ltd* (1982) 149 CLR 537 at 543; *Wiebe v Bobsien* (1985) 20 DLR (4th) 475 at 476–477.

5   *Heron Garage Properties Ltd v Moss* [1974] 1 WLR 148; *McKillop v McMullan* [1979] NI 85.

6   See *Graham v Pitkin* [1992] 1 WLR 403 at 405F–406A per Lord Templeman; *Meehan v Jones* (1982) 149 CLR 571 at 582 per Gibbs CJ, 588–592 per Mason J. Compare, however, *Lee-Parker v Izzet (No 2)* [1972] 1 WLR 775 at 779F–G, 780A–B; (1976) 40 Conv (NS) 37; *Grime v Bartholomew* [1972] 2 NSWLR 827 at 837G.

7   See *Framton v McCully* [1976] 1 NZLR 270 at 276. See also H W Wilkinson, [1985] Conv 90.

MANNER OF EXCHANGE OF CONTRACTS

12.43 The Law of Property (Miscellaneous Provisions) Act 1989 makes explicit reference to the time-honoured practice of 'exchange of contracts' as a likely component of the greater formality now demanded in respect of contracts relating to land.[1] Although 'not a term of art',[2] the exchange of contracts between vendor and purchaser is no mere matter of machinery. Exchange constitutes the 'mutual acknowledgement that the bargain has been struck'[3] and is 'the crucial and vital fact which brings the contract into existence.'[4] The process of exchange requires that each party should sign his 'part' of the contract in the expectation that the other has also executed or will execute a corresponding part incorporating the same terms.[5] At the time of execution neither party is contractually bound, since it is mutually intended that neither will be bound until the duplicate executed parts are exchanged.[6] The act of exchange then comprises the formal delivery by each party of its part into the actual or constructive possession of the other 'with the intention that the parties will become actually bound when exchange occurs, but not before.'[7] Although the traditional method of exchange was once 'mutual exchange across the table',[8] the precise modalities of exchange are nowadays left to be determined by the parties.

1 LP(MP)A 1989, s 2(3). See *Commission for the New Towns v Cooper (Great Britain) Ltd* [1995] Ch 259 at 289F per Stuart-Smith LJ.
2 *Commission for the New Towns v Cooper (Great Britain) Ltd* [1995] Ch 259 at 285B per Stuart-Smith LJ.
3 *Sindel v Georgiou* (1984) 154 CLR 661 at 666 (High Court of Australia).
4 *Eccles v Bryant and Pollock* [1948] Ch 93 at 99 per Lord Greene MR.
5 If the two parts of the contract are not identical, there can be no contract (see *Harrison v Battye* [1975] 1 WLR 58 at 60E–F).
6 See *Commission for the New Towns v Cooper (Great Britain) Ltd* [1995] Ch 259 at 285D per Stuart-Smith LJ.
7 *Commission for the New Towns v Cooper (Great Britain) Ltd* [1995] Ch 259 at 285D–E per Stuart-Smith LJ.
8 *Commission for the New Towns v Cooper (Great Britain) Ltd* [1995] Ch 259 at 285E per Stuart-Smith LJ.

Postal exchange

12.44 Until late in the 20th century the most common method of exchanging contracts for the sale of land consisted of a postal exchange of the two parts signed by vendor and purchaser respectively. The general rule in the law of contract is that a postal acceptance of a contractual offer is complete when the offeree actually posts his acceptance to the offeror.[1] There has always been some doubt whether this postal rule applies to the exchange of contracts for the sale of land,[2] since the security sought by both parties in a land transaction seems to require that acceptance be complete only at the point of actual delivery of the acceptance to the offeror.[3] The legal difficulty is usually obviated now by the fact that the Standard Conditions of Sale provide that, in cases of exchange by post or through a document exchange (eg the DX system), the contract is made when the last copy is actually posted or deposited at the document exchange.[4]

1   *Household Fire Insurance Co (Ltd) v Grant* (1879) 4 Ex D 216 at 219–220.
2   See the ambivalent reference in *Commission for the New Towns v Cooper (Great Britain) Ltd* [1995] Ch 259 at 285E–F to the completion of exchange when 'the second document to be dispatched has been received or posted.'
3   *Eccles v Bryant and Pollock* [1948] Ch 93 at 99f per Lord Greene MR.
4   Condition 2.1.1.

Telephonic exchange

12.45   Just as postal exchange of contracts superseded any form of manual or ceremonial exchange of contracts, the postal mode of exchange has now been overtaken by the device of simultaneous telephonic exchange.[1] The practical realities of synchronised chain transactions require that solicitors should be able to use the instantaneous medium of the telephone. Accordingly, in *Domb v Isoz*,[2] the Court of Appeal ruled that telephonic exchange may be used, under strictly regulated conditions,[3] wherever it appears both effectual and appropriate.[4] The Court took the view that an exchange of a written contract for sale is complete as soon as each part of the contract, duly signed by the appropriate party, is in the actual or *constructive* possession of the other party or of his solicitor. Telephonic exchange can thus take place where a contract signed by a client is 'in the physical possession of his own solicitor or in the possession of the solicitor on the other side who has agreed to hold that part to the order of the despatching solicitor.'[5] Used carefully under one or other of the standard formulae published by the Law Society, telephonic exchange greatly simplifies the process of exchange and reduces the danger that any client may lose his bargain.

1   *Commission for the New Towns v Cooper (Great Britain) Ltd* [1995] Ch 259 at 285F.
2   [1980] Ch 548. See [1980] Conv 227 (H W Wilkinson); (1980) 96 LQR 323.
3   '[A]s a matter of professional practice, exchange by telephone should only be carried out by a partner or proprietor of a firm of solicitors … [I]f two solicitors exchange by telephone, they should then and there agree and record identical attendance notes' ([1980] Ch 548 at 564E per Templeman LJ).
4   [1980] Ch 548 at 557G per Buckley LJ. The practice of telephonic exchange is widely accepted in other jurisdictions (see eg *Sindel v Georgiou* (1984) 154 CLR 661 at 666).
5   [1980] Ch 548 at 564D per Templeman LJ. No exchange is effected if one party's signed copy is not in the possession of his solicitor or held to the latter's order (see *Henderson v Hopkins* (1988) 4 BPR 9257 at 9258).

Deposits

12.46   It is customary for a deposit of 10 per cent of the purchase price to become payable by the purchaser on the exchange of contracts.[1] The requirement that such a deposit be paid is not a condition precedent to the existence of a binding contract, but is a fundamental contractual term which, if breached, entitles the injured party to sue for damages including the unpaid deposit.[2] The deposit operates effectively both as a part-payment of the contractually agreed purchase price and as a guarantee that the purchaser will complete the transaction. If the purchaser breaches the contract in such a way as to relieve the vendor from any further obligation under the terms of that contract, the vendor may retain any deposit already paid by the purchaser.[3] If, however, the contract goes off by reason of the vendor's default, the purchaser is of course entitled to recover his deposit money.

1   See Standard Conditions of Sale, Condition 2.2.1. Even in advance of the completion date, the vendor may use part or all of this deposit as his own deposit in connection with the purchase of another property in England and Wales for his residence (Standard Conditions of Sale, Condition 2.2.5). For an attempted payment of a deposit by a transfer of gemstones, see *D & J Constructions Pty Ltd v Machello Pty Ltd* [1987] 2 Qd R 350 at 352–353.
2   *Millichamp v Jones* [1982] 1 WLR 1422 at 1430G–H. See also *Alarm Facilities Pty Ltd v Jackson Constructions Pty Ltd* [1975] 2 NSWLR 22 at 28F–29A.
3   The courts have an equitable jurisdiction to grant relief against forfeiture of a contractual deposit of disproportionate size (see e g *Workers Trust & Merchant Bank Ltd v Dojap Investments Ltd* [1993] AC 573 at 582C–F (25 per cent deposit)). See also *Linggi Plantations Ltd v Jagatheesan* [1972] 1 MLJ 89 at 94 (JCPC); *Legione v Hateley* (1983) 152 CLR 406 at 444–445; *Tanwar Enterprises Pty Ltd v Cauchi* (2003) 201 ALR 359 at [69], [123], [147].

Electronic contracts

12.47   The Land Registration Act 2002 envisages that, under the regime of electronic conveyancing soon to be inaugurated, contracts for the sale of registered land will be made in electronic form and signed electronically by the parties or their agents.[1] Pursuant to the 2002 Act estate contracts will require, as a condition of their validity, to be protected by the entry of a pre-agreed form of 'notice' in the charges register of the vendor's title.[2] There will be no 'exchange' of contracts in the traditional sense, but rather a consensual transmission of the agreement to Land Registry. The making of the contract (ie the moment of contractual commitment) will be synchronous with the entry of the parties' pre-agreed 'notice' in the register[3] and in this way the contractual purchaser will acquire clear (and immediate) priority protection for his contract.[4]

1   See LRA 2002, s 93(1)–(2). The Electronic Communications Act 2000 prepared the ground for a more general introduction of electronic contracting with interests in land (see ECA 2000, s 8; LP(MP)A 1989, s 2A, as proposed by Draft Law of Property (Electronic Communications) Order 2001, art 4). This innovation, not yet brought into effect, would significantly supplement the requirements of contractual formality affecting both registered and unregistered land, but is likely – in the former context – to be superseded by the advent of electronic contracting under the Land Registration Act 2002.
2   LRA 2002, ss 32–34 [**paras 12.84–12.89**].
3   Law Com No 271 (2001), para 2.54.
4   See LRA 2002, s 72(1)–(2).

UNCONSCIONABLE BARGAINS

12.48   A person who signs a legal document is in general bound by the act of signature, even if he did not read or understand the document concerned. Any other approach 'would make chaos of everyday business transactions.'[1] Nevertheless the court, in the exercise of its equitable jurisdiction, retains a discretion to set aside a contract of sale of land on the ground that it constitutes an unconscionable bargain. As the Privy Council indicated in *Hart v O'Connor*,[2] cases which attract equitable intervention of this kind arise where a 'bargain of an improvident character' has been made by a 'poor and ignorant person acting without independent advice.'[3] Such circumstances typically involve an agreement to transfer land at a considerable undervalue[4] and the court will intervene to set aside the contract unless the contractual purchaser can prove that the transaction in question was fair, just and reasonable.[5] However, the discretion to set aside unconscionable bargains is exercised only in exceptional circumstances.[6] In *Hart v O'Connor*[7] Lord Brightman drew a vital distinction between transactions which are marked by 'procedural unfairness' (as, for instance, where there is an element of undue influence) and those which are merely affected by 'contractual imbalance'. Equity cannot set aside a transaction as an unconscionable bargain where there is no victimisation, no taking advantage of another's weakness, and the sole allegation [is] contractual imbalance with no undertones of constructive fraud.[8]

1   *Wilton v Farnworth* (1948) 76 CLR 646 at 649 per Latham CJ.
2   [1985] AC 1000 at 1024B–C.
3   According to Megarry J in *Cresswell v Potter* (1968) [1978] 1 WLR 255 (Note) at 257F–H, the persons who nowadays fall within the scope of this classical equitable formula are those who, in more contemporary idiom, comprise members of 'the lower income group' and who may be said to be 'less highly educated.' See also *Watkin v Watson-Smith* (1986) Times, 3 July.
4   See *How v Weldon* (1754) 2 Ves Sen 516 at 518–520, 28 ER 330 at 331–332; *Fry v Lane* (1888) 40 Ch D 312 at 322. See also *Chrispen v Topham* (1986) 28 DLR (4th) 754 at 758–759.
5   *Wood v Abrey* (1818) 3 Madd 417 at 423–424, 56 ER 558 at 560–561; *Fry v Lane* (1888) 40 Ch D 312 at 322; *Hart v O'Connor* [1985] AC 1000 at 1024B–C; *Langton v Langton* [1995] 2 FLR 890 at 907F.
6   See *Mountford v Scott* [1975] Ch 258 at 264E.
7   [1985] AC 1000 at 1017H–1018C.
8   [1985] AC 1000 at 1024D. Compare the broader and arguably more humane jurisdiction exercised in Australia (see *Commercial Bank of Australia Ltd v Amadio* (1983) 151 CLR 447 at 474) and New Zealand (see *Nichols v Jessup* [1986] 1 NZLR 226 at 234–235), where a primary emphasis is placed upon the objectively unconscionable character of 'the conduct of the stronger party in attempting to enforce, or retain the benefit of, a dealing with a person under a special disability in circumstances where it is not consistent with equity or good conscience that he should do so.' See also *Louth v Diprose* (1992) 175 CLR 621; *Bridgewater v Leahy* (1998) 194 CLR 457.

TRANSFER OF THE LEGAL ESTATE

12.49   Exchange of contracts marks the point at which vendor and purchaser are legally committed to complete their transaction of sale and purchase. Transfer of the legal estate normally follows on the completion date specified in the contract for sale.[1] Whereas the burden of drawing up the contract of sale falls upon the vendor (who alone is cognisant of the full extent of the title which he has to sell), the onus of preparing the draft transfer of the legal estate shifts to the purchaser (who has, of course, a sharpened interest in acquiring the full extent of the subject matter of the contract). The purchaser sends for the vendor's approval a draft transfer in prescribed Land Registry format[2] or, in the case of unregistered land, a draft conveyance of the legal estate. The practical arrangements for completion (relating, for instance, to the destination of purchase money and the handing over of keys) are finalised. A fair copy of the approved transfer document is sent to the vendor for execution 'in escrow'[3] in compliance with the statutory rules relating to formality.[4]

1   In the context of domestic conveyancing, this date is generally 20 working days after the date of exchange of contracts (see Standard Conditions of Sale, Condition 6.1.1).
2   LRR 2003, rr 58, 206, Sch 1 [**para 7.51**].
3   An 'escrow' is a deed which has been duly executed, but has not yet been delivered [**para 7.33**]. A transfer or conveyance executed on a date *later* than that borne on its face takes effect from the date of the actual signature (*Grindal v Hooper* (2000) Times, 8 February).
4   In the case of a registered estate, the appropriate transfer form is necessarily drawn as a deed [**para 7.30**] in order to ensure compliance with the general requirement of formality in the conveyance of a legal estate in land (see LPA 1925, s 52(1); LP(MP)A 1989, s 1 [**paras 7.26, 7.227**]).

Searches with priority in registered land

12.50   Shortly before the completion date, the purchaser applies for an official search 'with priority' of his vendor's registered title in order to verify that the land remains vested in the vendor and free of undisclosed adverse interests.[1] The result of this search details any entries made in the register since the issue of the official copy of the register supplied earlier by the vendor.[2] If any adverse entries are revealed, the purchaser is entitled to withdraw from the transaction. The search 'with priority' provides the purchaser with a 'priority period' of 30 business days within which to lodge his dealing for registration at Land Registry.[3] Any entry made in the register during this period is normally postponed to the title taken by the purchaser pursuant to his 'priority protection'.[4]

1   LRR 2003, r 147(1).
2   [**Para 12.11**].
3   The Supreme Court of Canada has held that, absent special knowledge of the significance of their contents, a courier is not liable in negligence for the late delivery of registration documents to the registry (see *BDC Ltd v Hofstrand Farms Ltd* (1986) 26 DLR (4th) 1 at 5, 14–15).
4   LRA 2002, s 72(2); LRR 2003, r 131.

Searches with priority in unregistered land

12.51   In the case of unregistered land, a prudent purchaser, again shortly prior to the completion date, requisitions an official search against the name of his vendor in the Register of Land Charges.[1] The result contained in the certificate of official search is deemed to be conclusive in favour of the purchaser.[2] An official search carries the further advantage that the purchaser is not bound by any entry made in the Register of Land Charges after the issue of the certificate provided that he takes a conveyance of the legal estate within 15 working days of the issue of the certificate.[3]

1   **[Para 12.325]**.
2   **[Para 12.326]**.
3   LCA 1972, s 11(5)–(6). An exception is made for entries made under a 'priority notice' pursuant to LCA 1972, s 11(1)–(3), although the existence of any priority notice is revealed by the search.

Completion by registration

12.52   On the date fixed for completion of the contract of sale, the purchaser pays over the balance of the purchase money[1] and the vendor hands over the duly executed and attested transfer document[2] (together with all appropriate title documents or deeds).[3] The contract has thus been completed by the transfer (or 'disposition') of the vendor's estate, but the disposition itself is completed only when the transfer document, duly stamped with ad valorem duty, is lodged at Land Registry for amendment of the proprietorship register. No legal estate in registered land can pass until the disponee is entered as the new owner of the estate,[4] with the consequence that a 'registration gap' – possibly a matter of several weeks – opens up between the dates of disposition and registration.[5] By contrast, the formal conveyance of an unregistered estate is immediately effective to vest that legal estate in the purchaser, but the purchaser's ownership of the legal estate lapses if the conveyance is not presented within two months for first registration of title at Land Registry.[6]

1   On the electronic transfer of funds under the CHAPS system (Clearing Houses Automatic Payment Scheme), see [1990] Conv 145 (H W Wilkinson). Electronic banking enables solicitors' firms to direct the transfer of funds from a computer terminal situated in their own accounts department.
2   **[Paras 7.26, 7.51, 7.246]**. Where solicitors act for both parties, completion normally takes place in accordance with the Law Society's Code for Completion by Post.
3   The vendor's obligation to deliver a good title and the purchaser's obligation to pay the purchase money are concurrent and mutually dependent obligations in the sense that they are 'simultaneous acts to be performed interchangeably' (*Palmer v Lark* [1945] Ch 182 at 184–185). See also *Foran v Wight* (1989) 168 CLR 385 at 396 per Mason CJ.
4   LRA 2002, s 27(1), (2)(a), Sch 2, para 2(1) **[paras 7.49, 7.245]**.
5   **[Para 12.81]**.
6   LRA 2002, ss 6(4), 7(1)–(2) **[paras 7.41, 7.243]**.

Electronic dispositions

12.53   The Land Registration Act 2002 envisages the eventual elimination of the 'registration gap' which currently intervenes between the dates of disposition and registration at Land Registry.[1] The essence of electronic conveyancing is the idea that the disposition of any estate or interest in registered land should be synchronous with the registration of the disponee as the new proprietor.[2] Accordingly the final stage in an electronic conveyance will involve the execution of a pre-agreed form of electronic transfer (together with any related mortgage charge) and its electronic transmission to Land Registry. This release to the Registry will result, with instantaneous effect, in a *simultaneous* registration of these various dispositions and the electronic movement of purchase and mortgage moneys, stamp duty land tax and Land Registry fees.[3] All will happen in less than the twinkling of an eye; the moment of disposition and registration will exactly coincide; and the register of title will then accurately and definitively record the resulting priority of all relevant rights.

1   Law Com No 271 (2001), para 2.56.
2   **[Paras 2.117, 7.64]**.
3   See LRA 2002, ss 91–94, Sch 5.

TRANSFERS VITIATED BY UNDUE INFLUENCE

12.54   The law of real property is not conventionally regarded as a branch of moral philosophy. The law is concerned with procedural efficiency in the transfer of land and not with the achievement of justice in the distribution of goods.[1] Few concessions are made to the concept of fairness as a criterion of lawful transfer, but at some point the law has set limits to the means which may properly be employed for the purpose of procuring a transfer of land. The court has always retained an important power to set aside the gift of an estate in land on the ground that the transfer was induced by undue influence.[2] Whether a transaction has been so influenced is always a question of fact[3] and undue influence may take several forms. In all its manifestations, however, the law relating to undue influence represents a 'fetter' on the donee's conscience which 'arises out of public policy and fair play.'[4]

1   See, however, the jurisdiction to set aside unconscionable bargains **[para 12.48]**.
2   In *Niersmans v Pesticcio* [2004] EWCA Civ 372 at [4], Mummery LJ pointed out that, in days of rising property values and increased longevity, a new focus is being cast on the validity of lifetime dispositions of houses made by the elderly and infirm in response to suggestions by family members that the wealth tied up in such assets will otherwise be seriously diminished by the high cost of long-term care or the impact of inheritance tax on death.
3   *Royal Bank of Scotland plc v Etridge (No 2)* [2002] 2 AC 773 at [13] per Lord Nicholls of Birkenhead.
4   *Allcard v Skinner* (1887) 36 Ch D 145 at 190 per Bowen LJ.

Actual undue influence

12.55   In cases of alleged actual undue influence, the complainant is required to prove affirmatively that the wrongdoer exerted undue influence on the complainant to enter into the particular transaction which is now impugned.[1] Where such proof is forthcoming, there is no need to demonstrate that the transaction was disadvantageous (whether financially or otherwise) to the influenced person, although in the nature of things some disadvantage will normally have been suffered.[2] The court will then intervene, on behalf of the dependent and the vulnerable, to reverse the effects of the proven abuse of influence.[3]

1   *Barclays Bank plc v O'Brien* [1994] 1 AC 180 at 189D per Lord Browne-Wilkinson.
2   *CIBC Mortgages Plc v Pitt* [1994] 1 AC 200 at 209A–B; *Royal Bank of Scotland plc v Etridge (No 2)* [2002] 2 AC 773 at [12].
3   See e g *Ransome v Leeder* [1994] CLY 2246; *Langton v Langton* [1995] 2 FLR 890.

Presumed undue influence

12.56 In certain standardised categories of relationship the presence of undue influence is, as a matter of law, irrebuttably presumed to have affected transactions between the parties.[1] The relationships in question include those between parent and child, trustee and beneficiary, solicitor and client, and medical advisor and patient.[2] Within the context of these relationships the dependent party is automatically entitled to have the court set aside any gift which he has made to the dominant party.

1   *Niersmans v Pesticcio* [2004] EWCA Civ 372 at [3] per Mummery LJ.
2   *Royal Bank of Scotland plc v Etridge (No 2)* [2002] 2 AC 773 at [18] per Lord Nicholls of Birkenhead. No such presumption arises between husband and wife (*Bank of Montreal v Stuart* [1911] AC 120 at 137; *Barclays Bank plc v O'Brien* [1994] 1 AC 180 at 190A–B per Lord Browne-Wilkinson; *Etridge (No 2)*, supra at [19]).

12.57 In other cases a presumption of undue influence arises, not because of any generic categorisation, but simply because the relationship between particular parties discloses elements of 'trust and confidence, reliance, dependence or vulnerability on the one hand and ascendancy, domination or control on the other.'[1] The fact that one party 'reposed trust and confidence' in the other,[2] when 'coupled with a transaction which calls for explanation', is prima facie evidence that the dominant party abused the influence which he enjoyed over the other.[3] The dependent party need not produce any evidence that undue influence was actually exerted or that the dominant party indeed abused his position of trust and confidence.[4] Instead the burden shifts to the dominant party to resist the inference that undue influence was used to procure the transaction which is now being challenged.[5] If this onus cannot be discharged, the court interferes, not because any wrongful act has been committed by the transferee,[6] but 'on the ground of public policy, and to prevent the relations which existed between the parties and the influence arising therefrom being abused.'[7] In the absence of evidence disproving undue influence, the court will set aside the challenged transaction. There has not, objectively, been 'fair play' between the parties.[8]

1   *Royal Bank of Scotland plc v Etridge (No 2)* [2002] 2 AC 773 at [11] per Lord Nicholls of Birkenhead. See *Niersmans v Pesticcio* [2004] EWCA Civ 372 at [3] per Mummery LJ.
2   *Barclays Bank plc v O'Brien* [1994] 1 AC 180 at 189H–190A per Lord Browne-Wilkinson.
3   *Royal Bank of Scotland plc v Etridge (No 2)* [2002] 2 AC 773 at [14] per Lord Nicholls of Birkenhead.
4   *Allcard v Skinner* (1887) 36 Ch D 145 at 183 per Lindley LJ; *Niersmans v Pesticcio* [2004] EWCA Civ 372 at [20] per Mummery LJ.
5   *Barclays Bank plc v O'Brien* [1994] 1 AC 180 at 189D–F per Lord Browne-Wilkinson; *Royal Bank of Scotland plc v Etridge (No 2)* [2002] 2 AC 773 at [14] per Lord Nicholls of Birkenhead. See *Nel v Kean* [2003] 2 P & CR D19 per Simon J.

6   There is no need to show that the dominant party has behaved in any 'sinister' way (*Hammond v Osborn* [2002] EWCA Civ 885 at [32]). There need be no 'specific reprehensible conduct' (*Niersmans v Pesticcio* [2004] EWCA Civ 372 at [4] per Mummery LJ).

7   *Allcard v Skinner* (1887) 36 Ch D 145 at 171 per Cotton LJ. See *Huguenin v Baseley* (1807) 14 Ves 273 at 299–300, 33 ER 526 at 536 per Lord Eldon LC; *Hammond v Osborn* [2002] EWCA Civ 885 at [1], [32] per Sir Martin Nourse; *Niersmans v Pesticcio* [2004] EWCA Civ 372 at [20] per Mummery LJ.

8   *Hammond v Osborn* [2002] EWCA Civ 885 at [61] per Ward LJ.

Gifts which call for further explanation

12.58   This presumption of undue influence is triggered by certain kinds of transaction which are 'not readily explicable by the relationship between the parties' and cannot be 'accounted for by the ordinary motives of ordinary persons in that relationship.'[1] Such transactions have an unusual or irrational quality which serves only to heighten the anxiety that improper pressure has been brought to bear. Thus, for example, an act of generosity entirely out of proportion to any kindness or service which may have been rendered by the donee affords an immediate gound for suspicion.[2] This is particularly the case where the donor is a person of impaired intelligence and understanding[3] or has failed to advert to the fiscal and personal financial consequences of his act of gift. It may be extremely significant that the transaction deprives the donor of the resources required to support his future needs in retirement and old age.[4] In all such instances the act of gratuitous transfer is not, objectively, a 'good' decision[5] and therefore raises an inference which requires to be repelled by the donee.

1   *Royal Bank of Scotland plc v Etridge (No 2)* [2002] 2 AC 773 at [13], [21] per Lord Nicholls of Birkenhead. See likewise *Niersmans v Pesticcio* [2004] EWCA Civ 372 at [20] per Mummery LJ.

2   See *Hammond v Osborn* [2002] EWCA Civ 885 at [58] per Ward LJ. Contrast *Jennings v Cairns* [2003] 2 P & CR D39 at D40.

3   See e g *Niersmans v Pesticcio* [2004] EWCA Civ 372 at [10].

4   *Hammond v Osborn* [2002] EWCA Civ 885 at [29] per Sir Martin Nourse, [54] per Ward LJ.

5   *Hammond v Osborn* [2002] EWCA Civ 885 at [58] per Ward LJ.

Disproving undue influence

12.59   Where undue influence is presumed to have induced a transfer of land by gift, an onus rests on the donee to establish affirmatively that 'the donor's trust and confidence in the donee has not been betrayed or abused.'[1] The donee must show that 'the disposition was made in the independent exercise of free will after full and informed consideration.'[2] The most obvious way in which to counter the presumption of undue influence is to demonstrate that the transaction was entered into only after its nature and effect had been 'fully explained ... by some independent and qualified person.'[3] The availability of independent advice is therefore usually 'the crucial evidence' going to the rebuttal of the presumption.[4] However, the participation of a solicitor is effective towards this end only if the 'outside advice had an emancipating effect',[5] liberating the donor from any impairment of his free will and giving him the 'necessary independence of judgment and freedom to make choices with a full appreciation of what he was doing.'[6] The donor must have been made aware that the gift was not mandatory, but that, once made, it was irreversible. If the donor was deprived of the opportunity to consider these implications of the transaction, the gift is liable to be set aside.[7]

1 *Hammond v Osborn* [2002] EWCA Civ 885 at [32] per Sir Martin Nourse; *Niersmans v Pesticcio* [2004] EWCA Civ 372 at [20] per Mummery LJ.

2 *Niersmans v Pesticcio* [2004] EWCA Civ 372 at [4] per Mummery LJ. There must have been a 'spontaneous act of the donor acting under circumstances which enabled him to exercise an independent will' (*Allcard v Skinner* (1887) 36 Ch D 145 at 171 per Cotton LJ). See likewise *Inche Noriah v Shaik Allie Bin Omar* [1929] AC 127 at 135 per Lord Hailsham LC; *Zamet v Hyman* [1961] 1 WLR 1442 at 1444, 1446 per Lord Evershed MR; *Hammond v Osborn* [2002] EWCA Civ 885 at [26] per Sir Martin Nourse.

3 *Inche Noriah v Shaik Allie Bin Omar* [1929] AC 127 at 135 per Lord Hailsham LC; *Niersmans v Pesticcio* [2004] EWCA Civ 372 at [23] per Mummery LJ. See also *In re Coomber* [1911] 1 Ch 723 at 730 per Fletcher Moulton LJ. In *Hammond v Osborn* [2002] EWCA Civ 885 at [50], a gift was set aside because it was a 'stark feature of the case ... that [the donor] was given no advice whatsoever.'

4 *Hammond v Osborn* [2002] EWCA Civ 885 at [49] per Ward LJ.

5 *Royal Bank of Scotland plc v Etridge (No 2)* [2002] 2 AC 773 at [20] per Lord Nicholls of Birkenhead. See similarly *Hammond v Osborn* [2002] EWCA Civ 885 at [50] per Ward LJ.

6 *Niersmans v Pesticcio* [2004] EWCA Civ 372 at [23] per Mummery LJ. Proof of outside advice 'does not, of itself, necessarily show that the subsequent completion of the transaction was free from the exercise of undue influence' (*Royal Bank of Scotland plc v Etridge (No 2)* [2002] 2 AC 773 at [20] per Lord Nicholls of Birkenhead). It sometimes works to this effect (see eg *Longmuir v Holland* (2000) 192 DLR (4th) 62 at [123], [150]) and sometimes not (see eg *Niersmans*, supra at [23]).

7 *Allcard v Skinner* (1887) 36 Ch D 145 at 185 per Lindley LJ; *Hammond v Osborn* [2002] EWCA Civ 885 at [44] per Ward LJ.

CLASSIFICATION OF INTERESTS IN REGISTERED LAND

12.60 In its regulation of dealings with registered titles, the Land Registration Act 2002 confirms the existence of certain classifications of proprietary interest unknown to the common law. These classifications, which correspond in all but terminology to the familiar entitlements met in unregistered conveyancing, comprise the following:

– registered estates[1]
– registered charges[2]
– registrable interests (sometimes known as 'minor' interests) which can be protected by the entry of a 'notice' in the register[3]

and
– unregistered interests which 'override' registered dispositions of a registered estate or registered charge (sometimes known as 'overriding' interests).[4]

1 **[Paras 2.107, 7.49, 7.228]**.
2 **[Paras 2.152, 8.243]**.
3 **[Paras 2.162, 12.84]**.
4 **[Paras 2.171, 12.129]**.

Terminology

12.61   It is appropriate to add a further explanatory note about terminology. Although the Land Registration Act 2002 (unlike its predecessor[1]) does not refer expressly to 'minor interests' within the registered land scheme, it is still useful to harness this compact phrase to indicate certain categories of subsidiary right which can be 'entered in the register.'[2] Likewise the Land Registration Act 2002 does not explicitly retain the primary reference in the Land Registration Act 1925[3] to various groups of 'overriding interest'. Instead, the 2002 Act refers rather more formally to 'unregistered interests' which 'override' first registrations of title and subsequent registered dispositions of a registered estate.[4] The 2002 Act nevertheless speaks also of the 'overriding status' of such entitlements[5] and the Land Registration Rules 2003 even advert to 'disclosable overriding interests' affecting an already registered estate.[6] For clarity of exposition it therefore seems both convenient and justifiable to revert occasionally to the familiar shorthand of the 'overriding interest'.

1   See LRA 1925, ss 3(xv), 101–103.
2   See LRA 2002, s 132(1).
3   See LRA 1925, ss 3(xvi), 70(1).
4   LRA 2002, Sch 1, Sch 3.
5   See LRA 2002, s 133, Sch 11, para 26(4) (amending Access to Neighbouring Land Act 1992, s 5(5)).
6   LRR 2003, r 57(3)–(5) [para 12.142].

Focus on minor and overriding interests

12.62   Registered estates and registered charges – principally the fee simple absolute, the term of years absolute and various kinds of legal mortgage – have already provided the focus of much discussion in this book.[1] The present chapter now turns to the way in which other categories of interest affecting registered land are dealt with on the disposition of a registered estate.

1   [Paras 7.2–7.24, 7.68–7.194, 8.242–8.257].

EFFECT OF DISPOSITIONS OF A REGISTERED ESTATE

12.63   One of the main objectives of the Land Registration Act 2002 is to define, with maximum certainty and accuracy, the consequences of dealings with estates which are registered at Land Registry.[1]

1   [Paras 2.155, 12.64].

Minimising potential threats to title

12.64   Rational, clear-sighted transacting with land requires a heightened degree of transparency in relation to the benefits and burdens associated with title. The overall drive of the Land Registration Act 2002 is therefore towards cleaning up the titles taken by registered transferees and chargees. It is a primary aim of the statute to minimise the range of matters which potentially trammel the estate taken by a newly registered proprietor, thereby safeguarding the disponee from adventitious, unforeseen or effectively undiscoverable derogations from his title. The general effect is undoubtedly to sharpen up the outcome of land dealings between strangers, to strip away many of the obstacles to the reception of an unencumbered title, and ultimately to equip the registered proprietor with a robust and highly protected form of state-guaranteed ownership.[1]

1   [**Para 6.26**]. See Gray and Gray, 'The rhetoric of realty', in J Getzler (ed), *Rationalizing Property, Equity and Trusts: Essays in Honour of Edward Burn* (Butterworths 2003), pp 243–253.

The statutory language of 'priority' and 'postponement'

12.65   The central provisions of the Land Registration Act 2002 are therefore concerned with the dynamic of land dealings and with the impact that dispositions of registered land have on various sorts of interest pre-existing in or over that land.[1] For this purpose it becomes imperative to ascertain whether, following the disposition of a registered estate in a parcel of land (say, 'Greenacre'), some pre-existing interest affecting Greenacre (ie *entitlement A*) remains binding on and effective against the interest (ie *entitlement B*) which is taken by the disponee of that registered estate (see *Fig.* 37). The technical terminology used by the Land Registration Act 2002 to express this problem of continuing enforceability revolves around the question whether *entitlement A* enjoys 'priority' over *entitlement B*. In this context the word 'priority' has nothing necessarily to do with temporal order or sequence, but merely expresses the idea of dominance or superiority (ie which of the two entitlements, *A* or *B* ranks above the other in terms of jural potency). Using the correlative statutory language of 'postponement',[2] a conclusion that *entitlement A* enjoys 'priority' over *entitlement B* can just as easily be expressed in terms that *entitlement B* is 'postponed' to *entitlement A*. Here, again, the concept of 'postponement' has nothing necessarily to do with temporal order or sequence, but merely articulates a notion of subjugation or relegation.

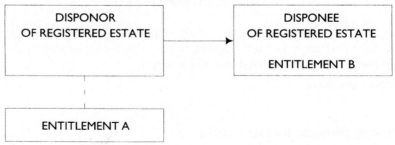

Fig. 37

1   Special provisions govern the effect of a disposition of a registered estate after the proprietor

has become bankrupt (LRA 2002, s 86(5)) or in respect of which an Inland Revenue charge has arisen (Inheritance Tax Act 1984, ss 237(6), 238; LRA 2002, s 31). In both cases – contrary to the general tenor of the Land Regstration Act 2002 – good faith affords an explicit ground of immunity for the disponee in the absence of any registration of the liability.

2   **[Para 12.74]**.

Extra dimensions of 'priority'

12.66   The issue of 'priority' is often given an extra complexity in land law precisely because, as already observed,[1] the range of 'registered dispositions' (ie the range of dealings which can throw up a question of disputed 'priority') includes not merely the transfer of a registered freehold or leasehold estate, but also the grant out of a registered estate of certain other kinds of interest. In terms of our hypothetical disposition, *entitlement B* may therefore comprise a term of years or mortgage charge taken by a disponee of the registered estate in Greenacre.

1   **[Paras 2.42, 7.50]**.

THE 'BASIC RULE': PRIORITY IS NOT AFFECTED BY A DISPOSITION

12.67   In order to resolve problems of priority, section 28(1) of the Land Registration Act 2002 announces a new, surprisingly stark (and somewhat inelegantly expressed) 'basic rule':

> 'Except as provided by sections 29 and 30, the priority of an interest affecting a registered estate ... is not affected by a disposition of the estate ...'

A simple ordering of 'priority'

12.68   In the context of our hypothetical disposition of Greenacre,[1] the 'basic rule' seems, in effect, to arrange priority as between *entitlement A* and *entitlement B* simply as a matter of temporal order of creation.[2] *Entitlement A*, if already effective against a registered estate in Greenacre, cannot be disturbed by any later disposition of that estate which gives rise to *entitlement B*. In other words, *entitlement A* enjoys, on a 'first in time' basis, an automatic and unassailable priority over *entitlement B* and, in a strictly accurate explication of this rule, it is declared to make 'no difference' whether the pre-existing interest or the disposition is registered.[3]

1   **[Para 12.65]**.
2   See Law Com No 271 (2001), paras 2.17, 5.5. The 'basic rule' effectively restates, in a more absolute form, the historic principle that the priority *inter se* of competing minor interests is governed, not by the order of their entry in the register, but by their respective dates of creation (see *Freeguard v Royal Bank of Scotland Plc* (2000) 79 P & CR 81 at 86 per Robert Walker LJ).
3   LRA 2002, s 28(2).

The key to the 'basic rule'

12.69   An important key to understanding the 'basic rule' of priority under the Land Registration Act 2002 is the realisation that its ulterior purpose is the governance of registered land interests *after* the introduction of the forthcoming regime of electronic conveyancing.[1] It is at this point that the 'basic rule' will actually come into its own.[2] With the advent of electronic dealings, the intention is that most interests in registered land will have no existence at all (either at law or in equity) *unless and until* they actually appear in the Land Register.[3] Order of creation will coincide exactly with order of registration. Since all disponees of a registered estate will plainly be bound by existing entries in the register of title, it will then become self-evident, in the words of section 28(1), that 'the priority of an interest affecting a registered estate ... is not affected by a disposition of the estate.' The validity of most interests will depend, by definition, on register entry; and register entries will be automatically enforceable against all subsequent disponees of the registered estate.

1   [**Paras 2.117, 12.4**]. See Law Com No 271 (2001), paras 5.3, 7.17.
2   See LRA 2002, ss 27(1), 93(2)–(4).
3   [**Paras 2.118, 12.53**].

Exceptions to the 'basic rule'

12.70   Meanwhile – largely for want of any presently available scheme of electronic dealings with registered land – the 'basic rule' of priority is rendered expressly subject to certain exceptions contained in a *special priority rule* set out in sections 29–30 of the Land Registration Act 2002. Although the 'basic rule' still plays, even now, a residual role in determining some issues of priority,[1] the statutory exceptions from its scope exert, for the moment, a quite devastating impact on the apparent import of the rule. Indeed, it is likely that, during the immediately foreseeable future, many more transactions in registered land will be governed by these exceptions than by the 'basic rule' itself.

1   [**Para 12.79**].

Extended coverage of the statutory priority rules

12.71   The priority rules of the Land Registration Act 2002 are declared, for the avoidance of doubt, to extend to certain cases where *entitlement A* consists of one or other of several rights whose proprietary status was previously a matter of some controversy. These rights comprise a right of pre-emption,[1] an 'equity by estoppel'[2] and a 'mere equity' (eg a right to have a document rectified on the ground of mistake[3] or to have a deed set aside on the ground of fraud or undue influence[4]). Rights of pre-emption created on or after 13 October 2003 are declared to have effect 'from the time of creation as an interest capable of binding successors in title.'[5] All equities by estoppel and mere equities are accorded a similar effect 'from the time the equity arises.'[6]

1   **[Para 9.83]**.
2   **[Para 10.168]**.
3   **[Para 9.203]**.
4   **[Para 12.54]**.
5   LRA 2002, s 115 **[para 9.86]**.
6   LRA 2002, s 116 **[para 12.235]**.

A SPECIAL PRIORITY RULE FOR REGISTERED DISPOSITIONS

12.72   Pending the arrival of a fully electronic regime of land dealings, the 'basic rule' of priority propounded by the Land Registration Act 2002 is subjected to the gravest of qualifications in the event of any 'registrable disposition of a registered estate ... for valuable consideration.'[1] When a disposition of this kind is completed by registration at Land Registry, registration has the statutory effect of reversing the thrust of the 'basic rule'. This has radical consequences for the ascertainment of priority in Greenacre[2] as between a hypothetical pre-existing *entitlement A* and the *entitlement B* taken by a disponee of the registered estate. In effect, the occurrence of a registered disposition for value dramatically limits the circumstances in which the recipient of *entitlement B* is required to take subject to some *entitlement A* that was previously enforceable over Greenacre. The trigger of the transaction for value has activated a rather stricter rule system for the ordering of priority.

1   LRA 2002, s 29(1). 'Valuable consideration' does not include marriage consideration or any nominal consideration in money (LRA 2002, s 132(1)).
2   **[Paras 12.65–12.68]**.

Reversal of priority for unprotected interests

12.73   In the context of a registered disposition for value, the priority which the 'basic rule' normally accords to a pre-existing interest (ie *entitlement A*) over the estate taken by the disponee (ie *entitlement B*) is now overturned by force of statute unless it can be shown that *entitlement A* enjoyed a 'protected' priority at the time of registration of *entitlement B*. For this purpose, the priority of an interest is taken to be 'protected' only in certain tightly regulated circumstances,[1] which must soon be examined.[2]

1   See LRA 2002, s 29(2).
2   An equivalent effect follows a registrable disposition of a registered charge (LRA 2002, s 30(1)–(2) **[para 8.259]**).

Consequence of unprotected priority

12.74   In the absence of 'protected' priority for *entitlement A*, the completed disposition of *entitlement B* is said, in the convoluted terms of section 29(1) of the Land Registration Act 2002, to have

' ... the effect of postponing to the interest under the disposition [ie *entitlement B*] any interest affecting the estate immediately before the disposition [ie *entitlement A*].'

12.75   In plainer language – and by way of exception to the 'basic rule' enunciated in the 2002 Act – it is *entitlement B* which now enjoys priority over *entitlement A*. The registered disponee of the registered estate in Greenacre takes free of the pre-existing interest. *Entitlement A*, although it may still generate a personal remedy as against its original grantor, is no longer enforceable against the registered estate in Greenacre.

Instances of 'protected' status

12.76   When translated out of the needlessly opaque language of the statute, the net effect of the special priority rule is as follows. Under the Land Registration Act 2002, the disponee of a registered estate receives an immunity from pre-existing interests affecting the land, provided that the disposition is made 'for valuable consideration' and is itself completed by due registration. In this combination of circumstances, the disponee takes free of 'any interest affecting the estate immediately before the disposition' *unless* such interest enjoyed 'protected' priority at the time of registration.[1] For this purpose, the priority of *entitlement A* is 'protected' if the interest is:
–   a registered charge[2]
–   an interest safeguarded by the entry of a 'notice' in the register[3]
–   an unregistered interest which is statutorily declared to 'override' registered dispositions[4] or
–   an interest which appears from the register to be excepted from the effect of registration (eg in the case of first registration with less than absolute title).[5]

or
–   if (in the case of a disposition of a leasehold estate) the burden of the interest is incident to the leasehold estate (eg where covenants and obligations arise under a registered lease).[6]

1   See LRA 2002, s 29(2).
2   **[Para 8.242]**. See LRA 2002, s 29(2)(a)(i).
3   **[Paras 12.84–12.104]**. See LRA 2002, s 29(2)(a)(i).
4   **[Paras 12.129–12.244]**. See LRA 2002, s 29(2)(a)(ii), Sch 3.
5   **[Paras 7.44, 7.231]**. See LRA 2002, s 29(2)(a)(iii). Thus all interests excluded from the scope of the guarantee given to the first registered proprietor continue to be binding on subsequent disponees of the registered estate.
6   **[Para 12.96]**.

12.77   This book has already dealt with the binding impact of registered charges[1] and will, in due course, examine leasehold burdens.[2] The primary concern of the present chapter revolves around those interests which attain 'protected' priority either by reason of the entry of a 'notice' or by reason of their overriding status.

1   [**Para 8.232**].
2   [**Paras 14.208–14.310**].

Effect of non-registrable leasehold grant

12.78   The special priority rule for registered dispositions is obviously inapplicable, in its terms, to dispositions out of registered land which do not require completion by registration (eg leases granted for a period not exceeding seven years[1]). However, the special priority rule is extended, by statutory fiction, to unregistrable dispositions of precisely this kind.[2] Thus the disponee of a registered estate who takes a term granted for no more than seven years holds his leasehold estate free of any interest affecting the parent registered estate immediately before the disposition which did not enjoy 'protected' priority at the time of the grant.

1   [**Para 7.247**].
2   LRA 2002, s 29(4).

CASES NOT COVERED BY THE SPECIAL PRIORITY RULE

12.79   Certain dispositions of a registered estate are *not* covered by the special priority rule promulgated by section 29(1) of the Land Registration Act 2002. In these cases the disponee is obviously disabled from claiming that he automatically takes free of pre-existing interests whose priority was unprotected at the date of registration of the disposition. Under such circumstances the 'basic rule' laid down in section 28(1) of the 2002 Act comes back into play to resolve the issue of priority.

Dispositions other than for value

12.80   The special priority rule has no application to registered dispositions made otherwise than for valuable consideration.[1] It follows that the disponee who provides no value enjoys no priority over pre-existing interests affecting the land.[2] Instead, we fall back on the 'basic rule' for the proposition that the priority of any interest affecting a registered estate is unchanged by the disposition of that estate.[3] Indeed, the Act goes so far as to declare it irrelevant, for the purpose of the 'basic rule', whether the interest or disposition in question is registered.[4] In consequence, the donee of a registered estate takes inevitably subject to all interests which pre-date the disposition to him. This outcome accords with the commonsense view that, in this instance, the record of the register is irrelevant precisely because the volunteer has placed no reliance upon it.[5]

1   LRA 2002, ss 29(1), 132(1) [**para 12.72**].
2   See Law Com No 271 (2001), para 5.9.
3   See LRA 2002, s 28(1) [**para 12.67**].

4   LRA 2002, s 28(2) [**para 12.68**].
5   The volunteer 'does not look to the register to decide whether or not he will accept a gift ...
     He is happy to receive whatever interest the registered owner has to give' (*Re Passburg
     Petroleums Ltd and Landstrom Developments Ltd* (1984) 8 DLR (4th) 363 at 368 per Moir JA).

Priority in relation to interests created during the 'registration gap'

12.81   Under the scheme of the Land Registration Act 2002, registrable
dispositions are still imperfect at the date of disposition (ie the date of
execution of the relevant dispositionary instrument) and require to be completed by registration at Land Registry.[1] Pending registration, such dispositions
take effect only in equity.[2] It also follows that a period of time – the so-called
'registration gap' – elapses between the date of *disposition* and the deemed date
of *registration*.[3] Pending registration of the disponee as the proprietor of an
estate or charge, the disponor obviously remains registered proprietor of the
registered estate. As such, he is technically competent to create interests in the
land adverse to the disponee (although to do so is usually a clear breach of
both contract and trust[4]). It is therefore possible that, during the 'registration
gap', the disponor may create interests (eg a lease or easement) which could not
have been detected or predicted on any inspection of the land by the intending
disponee prior to the date of disposition.[5] The question is whether the disponee
of the registered estate can claim priority over such a lease or easement.

1   [**Para 2.145**].
2   [**Paras 7.58, 7.245, 8.244**].
3   See LRA 2002, s 74 [**paras 7.56, 12.139**].
4   [**Para 9.30**].
5   See eg *Barclays Bank plc v Zaroovabli* [1997] Ch 321.

Reversion to the 'basic rule' of priority

12.82   In these circumstances the disponee can derive no comfort from the
special priority rule applicable to registered dispositions, for this rule allows
him to take free only of certain interests which affected the estate 'immediately
before the disposition.'[1] Instead, the case is governed by the 'basic rule' of
priority.[2] Any interest created by the disponor during the 'registration gap' is
postponed to the interest already taken by the (as yet) unregistered disponee,
precisely because the 'basic rule' sets in place a principle of 'first in time'. The
supervening interest (eg the lease or easement) is postponed to the equitable
entitlement which has already passed to the disponee by virtue of the disposition of the registered estate (it being, again, entirely irrelevant whether either
the interest or the disposition is registered[3]).

1   LRA 2002, s 29(1) [**para 12.74**]. Precisely the same reason precludes the disponee from taking
     free of an interest which he *himself* has created in favour of some third party during the
     'registration gap' (see Law Com No 271 (2001), para 5.10).
2   See LRA 2002, s 28(1) [**para 12.67**].
3   LRA 2002, s 28(2) [**para 12.68**].

Eventual elimination of the 'registration gap'

12.83 The introduction of electronic conveyancing pursuant to the Land Registration Act 2002 will finally remove the possibility that interests may supervene during a 'registration gap'. Electronic dealing with land interests is premised on the *synchronous* nature of the creation and registration of expressly conferred rights,[1] with the consequence that the 'registration gap' will completely disappear and the resulting record of the register will become, on its very face, conclusive as to the priority of expressly created interests.[2]

1   **[Paras 2.117, 12.53]**.
2   Law Com No 271 (2001), paras 2.1(2), 2.56.

PROTECTION OF PRIORITY BY ENTRY OF A 'NOTICE' IN THE REGISTER

12.84 For the purposes of the Land Registration Act 2002 a 'notice' is defined as an 'entry in the register in respect of the burden of an interest affecting a registered estate or charge.'[1] The 2002 Act recognises the existence of a range of entitlements in registered land whose priority, in the context of a registered disposition of a registered estate, can be 'protected' by such an entry.[2] These entitlements are sometimes called *registrable interests* (in order to distinguish them from 'registered estates' and 'registered charges').[3] Alternatively, in a loose evocation of the terminology employed under the Land Registration Act 1925, this diverse class of protectable entitlements may also be described as a category of *minor interests* in registered land. Whatever the terminology, the unifying feature of this group of interests is that each casts a burden on some registered estate or charge and constitutes therefore a subsidiary interest carved therefrom.[4]

1   LRA 2002, s 32(1). The interest protected by 'notice' may, in some cases, be another substantively registered estate (e g a long lease).
2   LRA 2002, s 29(1), (2)(a)(i) **[para 12.76]**. The entry of a 'notice' in the register operates, in effect, as a statutory substitute for the old equitable doctrine of notice **[para 12.338]** (see *Eng Mee Yong & Ors v Letchumanan* [1979] 2 MLJ 212 at 214 per Lord Diplock; *Kemmis v Kemmis* [1988] 1 WLR 1307 at 1332E per Nourse LJ **[para 2.136]**).
3   **[Para 2.163]**.
4   The interests involved here comprise principally those matters which, if affecting an unregistered estate, would be registrable under the Land Charges Act 1972 **[paras 12.275–12.329]**. However, a second legal mortgage (which in unregistered land would rank as a registrable 'puisne mortgage' **[para 12.301]**) requires registration, in its own right, as a registered charge affecting a registered estate **[para 8.242]**.

Rationalisation of the process of register entry

12.85 The Land Registration Act 2002 significantly simplified the ways in which minor interests affecting registered land can be safeguarded by register entry.[1] With prospective effect[2] the 2002 Act abolished some of the forms of protection previously available under the Land Registration Act 1925. It is no longer possible to record a 'caution against dealings',[3] a unilateral form of entry which gave the cautioner the opportunity to contend that a particular proposed operation of the register would infringe his rights.[4] Likewise the 2002 Act prohibits further use of the 'inhibition',[5] a form of entry which had the effect of freezing the registered title in circumstances of emergency or fraud.[6] Instead the 2002 Act preserves entry by 'notice' as the only means by which a minor interest can be made enforceable against a disponee following his registration as proprietor.[7] Many 'notices' (e g those relating to easements and restrictive covenants) stay on the register indefinitely and bind all subsequent disponees.[8] Other 'notices' which serve a short-term purpose (e g those relating to estate contracts) may, when that purpose is spent, be cancelled on application to Land Registry. 'Notices' can arrive on the Land Register in a variety of ways.

1   The Law Commission condemned the former means of protection as 'unnecessarily complex' (Law Com No 254 (1998), para 6.44).
2   See Law Com No 271 (2001), para 2.19.
3   See LRA 1925, s 54(1); LRR 1925, r 6.
4   See *Barclays Bank Ltd v Taylor* [1974] Ch 137 at 147A–D per Russell LJ. The caution against dealings, although conferring no priority over existing interests, provided a limited or temporary protection in hostile situations. Unless and until warned off, the caution effectively suspended dealings with the registered title until some superior or more permanent protection – usually in the form of the entry of a 'notice' – became available for the cautioner (see *Elements of Land Law* (3rd edn 2001), pp 1039–1041). Under the Land Registration Act 2002 the role of the caution against dealings has been taken over by the 'notice' and 'restriction', although existing cautions against dealings continue to be governed by LRA 1925, ss 55–56 (see LRA 2002, s 134, Sch 12, para 2(3)).
5   See LRA 1925, s 57(1).
6   Entry of an inhibition precluded the registration of further dealings either until the occurrence of some specified event or until some order of the court or registrar. The Law Commission eventually concluded that inhibitions constituted a specialised form of 'restriction' **[para 7.52]** and should therefore be assimilated within a new streamlined version of that device (Law Com No 254 (1998), paras 6.55–6.57, 6.73; Law Com No 271 (2001), paras 2.19, 6.32).
7   See Law Com No 254 (1998), paras 6.52, 6.72; Law Com No 271 (2001), para 6.6. The 2002 Act applies equally to 'notices' entered under the Land Registration Act 1925 (LRA 2002, s 134, Sch 12, para 2(1)).
8   **[Para 12.76]**.

Burdens entered on the initiative of the registrar

12.86   At the point of first registration of title to an estate, it is the task of the Chief Land Registrar to enter in the newly opened register a 'notice' in respect of the burden of any interest which appears from his examination of title to affect the registered estate.[1] The registrar also has a general power to enter 'notices' in respect of potentially overriding interests[2] and interests which have been omitted from the register by mistake.[3]

1   LRR 2003, r 35 **[paras 2.105, 12.267]**. The duty to enter a 'notice' is subject to certain statutory constraints (see e g LRA 2002, ss 33, 90(4)), ie the interest must be capable of protection by 'notice'.
2   LRA 2002, s 37(1); LRR 2003, r 89 **[para 12.136]**.
3   LRA 2002, Sch 4, para 5 **[para 12.248]**. See Law Com No 271 (2001), para 6.21.

Entry in compliance with statutory 'registration requirements'

12.87 It is essential to the strategy of the Land Registration Act 2002 that most dispositions out of a registered estate require, as a precondition of their effectiveness at law, to be 'completed by registration.'[1] This mandate applies to the creation of various kinds of lease, easement, profit *à prendre*, rentcharge and right of entry affecting a registered freehold or leasehold estate. The 'relevant registration requirements' necessitate not only that the benefits conferred by such dispositions be appropriately recorded in the Land Register, but also that the burdens thereby created should be noted in the register of title to the encumbered estate.[2] This cross-referencing process ensures not only that the recipient takes a good legal title to the interest concerned (whether it be a lease, easement or so forth), but also that subsequent disponees of the registered estate out of which these rights have been carved inevitably take subject to the burden of the protected interest.[3]

1   LRA 2002, s 27(1)–(4).
2   A 'notice' in respect of certain categories of lease granted out of registered land must be entered in the register of the landlord's title (LRA 2002, s 27(2)(b), Sch 2, para 3(2)(b) [**para 7.240**]). Likewise a 'notice' in respect of certain categories of easement, profit *à prendre*, rentcharge and right of entry granted or reserved out of registered land must be entered in the register of title to the 'servient' estate (LRA 2002, s 27(2)(d)–(e), Sch 2, paras 6(2)(b), 7(2)(a) [**paras 8.118, 8.119, 8.266**]). See Law Com No 271 (2001), para 6.20.
3   LRA 2002, s 29(1), (2)(a)(i) [**para 12.76**].

Entry for the purpose of updating the Land Register

12.88 The entry of a 'notice' may sometimes be required in order to record in the Land Register the burden of some interest which a court (or the Adjudicator to Land Registry) has determined to exist with reference to a registered estate.[1]

1   See Law Com No 271 (2001), para 6.21.

Voluntary entry of other minor interests

12.89 Entry by 'notice' in the register also provides an appropriate form of voluntary protection for a number of entitlements created out of a registered estate which have not been (and often cannot be) recorded in the Land Register in any other way. The entry of a 'notice' in the register of the burdened title guarantees that the minor interests in question bind subsequent disponees of the registered title. Such interests include:

–   leases granted for a term of more than *three* years[1]
–   leases created out of a registered estate which remain equitable for want of due formality or due registration at Land Registry[2]
–   contracts to grant a lease[3]
–   other estate contracts[4]

–   equitable easements and equitable profits *à prendre*[5]
–   equitable mortgages and equitable charges created out of a registered estate[6]
–   unpaid vendors' liens[7]
–   purchasers' liens to secure deposits[8] and
–   freehold restrictive covenants.[9]

1   LRA 2002, ss 32, 33(b) [paras **2.173, 7.247**].
2   [Paras **7.240–7.244, 9.52**].
3   [Paras **7.226, 9.75**].
4   [Paras **9.39, 9.82**].
5   [Paras **9.99, 9.100**].
6   [Paras **9.110–9.114**].
7   [Para **9.133**].
8   [Para **9.137**].
9   [Paras **9.138, 13.114**].

Statutory rights protectable by 'notice'

12.90   Some special categories of statutory entitlement are protectable by the entry of a 'notice' in the charges register of the burdened title. Common examples include rights conferred by an access order pursuant to the Access to Neighbouring Land Act 1992,[1] rights relating to leasehold enfranchisement,[2] rights to call for an 'overriding lease'[3] and 'preserved rights to buy' under the Housing Act 1985.[4]

1   Access to Neighbouring Land Act 1992, s 5(1)–(2) [paras **8.136, 12.169**].
2   Leasehold Reform Act 1967, s 5(5) [paras **7.334, 12.170**]; Leasehold Reform, Housing and Urban Development Act 1993, s 97(1) [paras **7.339, 12.170**].
3   Landlord and Tenant (Covenants) Act 1995, s 20(6) [paras **12.172, 14.236**].
4   Housing Act 1985, Sch 9A, para 5(2) [paras **7.354, 12.171**].

Matrimonial home rights

12.91   Perhaps the most important statutory rights protectable by 'notice' in the Land Register comprise the 'matrimonial home rights' conferred by the Family Law Act 1996. These rights enjoy a history and significance which require more detailed explanation.

Common law rights to occupy the family home

12.92   The common law has long acknowledged that a de iure wife has a right to occupy the matrimonial home,[1] this right being quite distinct from any right of occupation which she may happen to enjoy as a beneficiary behind a trust of land.[2] The spousal right to be housed arises from the fact of marriage itself and, in an age of sex equality, is almost certainly available nowadays on a basis of mutuality between husband and wife.[3] During the 1950s Denning LJ led the

Court of Appeal in developing the doctrine of the 'deserted wife's equity'.[4] According to this doctrine a wife, if abandoned in occupation of the family home, acquired at the date of her desertion an 'equity' to remain in the home which became enforceable against any third party to whom her husband subsequently sold or mortgaged the premises. This controversial doctrine, although an innovative response to a post-war era of increasing family break-down, eventually proved to be unacceptable in terms of conventional concepts of proprietary entitlement.[5] The doctrine was finally destroyed in *National Provincial Bank Ltd v Ainsworth*,[6] where the House of Lords conclusively rejected the idea that a spouse's common law right of occupation of the matrimonial home could be anything more than a purely personal right enforceable against the other spouse.[7]

1   *National Provincial Bank Ltd v Ainsworth* [1965] AC 1175 at 1220B–C per Lord Hodson, 1232F per Lord Upjohn [**para 4.16**]. For further detail, see *Elements of Land Law* (3rd edn 2001), pp 1044–1045.
2   [**Para 11.175**].
3   See *Harman v Glencross* [1985] Fam 49 at 58B–C per Ewbank J.
4   See *Bendall v McWhirter* [1952] 2 QB 466 at 475–477; *Ferris v Weaven* [1952] 2 All ER 233 at 236F–H; *Lee v Lee* [1952] 2 QB 489 at 492; *Jess B Woodcock & Sons Ltd v Hobbs* [1955] 1 WLR 152 at 154–156; *Westminster Bank Ltd v Lee* [1956] Ch 7 at 17–18.
5   See e g *Rock Permanent Building Society v Kettlewell* (1956) 168 EG 397 where Harman J described the 'equity' as 'a new terror in the surveyor's professional life' and as 'a sore subject between lawyers ... a thorn in the flesh of the equitable branch of the law.' See also F R Crane, (1955) 19 Conv (NS) 343.
6   [1965] AC 1175. See F R Crane, (1965) 29 Conv (NS) 254 at 464.
7   The principal demerit of the 'deserted wife's equity' was that it represented an unregistrable, non-overreachable incumbrance which threatened to destabilise any title taken under a disposition executed by a man whose household included a resident adult female. See the trenchant criticisms expressed in *Ainsworth* [1965] AC 1175 at 1234C–E per Lord Upjohn, 1249A–B per Lord Wilberforce.

Statutory rights of occupation

12.93   The immediate consequence of the House of Lords' ruling in *National Provincial Bank Ltd v Ainsworth* was the enactment of the Matrimonial Homes Act 1967 (now consolidated in the Family Law Act 1996), which was designed to fulfil some of the purposes previously served by the judge-made doctrine of the 'deserted wife's equity'. The Family Law Act 1996 confers 'matrimonial home rights' on certain categories of spouse[1] and, although these rights are intrinsically personal,[2] they may be made enforceable against third parties[3] by entry of a 'notice' in the charges register of the title to the family home.[4] The legislation thereby 'uses the machinery of publicity in order to transform the internal right of enjoyment into a modification of title.'[5] The statutory rights confer on a qualifying spouse, if in occupation of the home, an entitlement not to be evicted or excluded except in pursuance of a court order and, if not in occupation of the home, a right with the leave of the court to enter and occupy.[6]

1   The statutory rights are sex-neutral and may be claimed by any spouse other than one who holds a legal estate in the home (or has some contractual or statutory right to occupy) and

whose residential status is therefore adequately protected (see the extension of the original legislation now confirmed in FLA 1996, s 30(9)). The other spouse must, of course, have some proprietary, contractual or statutory right to occupy the premises (FLA 1996, s 30(1)).

2   See *Wroth v Tyler* [1974] Ch 30 at 46F–G per Megarry J. A court order regulating occupation of the home may be applied for by a spouse (FLA 1996, s 33(1)), a former spouse (FLA 1996, s 35(1)–(2)) or by a cohabitant or former cohabitant (FLA 1996, ss 36(1)–(2), 62(1)) and may even be made where the relevant dwelling-house is or has been the home of the entitled person and of 'another person with whom he is associated' (FLA 1996, ss 33(1)(b), 62(3)).

3   Even if protected by register entry, matrimonial home rights have only a limited impact on a trustee in bankruptcy of the proprietor of the estate on which they are charged [**para 11.255**]. Contrast the effect of the former 'deserted wife's equity' (*Bendall v McWhirter* [1952] 2 QB 466 at 478).

4   Matrimonial home rights constitute a charge on the beneficial estate or interest held by the other spouse (FLA 1996, s 31(2)). Matrimonial home rights burdening an unregistered estate are registrable as a Class F land charge [**para 12.322**].

5   O Kahn-Freund, (1970) 33 MLR 601 at 610. See *Harman v Glencross* [1986] Fam 81 at 94A–B per Balcombe LJ ('Parliament has looked with particular favour upon a spouse's right to occupy the matrimonial home and has given it the status of an equitable interest').

6   FLA 1996, s 30(2).

12.94   Despite its ambitious social motivations, the matrimonial homes rights scheme has never proved entirely satisfactory. For want of extensive public awareness of its existence,[1] the statutory regime has operated 'in the main ... on a basis of the mass invalidation of the statutory charges for want of registration, with registration being effected only in cases of actual or impending disputes.'[2] Moreover, the ease with which a register entry can be effected, when combined with the potentially hostile impact of this entry,[3] has often provoked the criticism that the statutory scheme facilitates registrations for malicious or ulterior purposes.[4] Particularly if the protective entry occurs at an inconvenient moment in the process of contract and transfer, the incumbrancer is presented with a relatively simple, speedy and secret means of frustrating any proposed transaction with the family home with which he or she does not agree.[5] The stubborn or ruthless spouse is thus enabled to force on the other a purely private and unshared desire for domestic inertia or, even worse, is enabled to require the other spouse to buy off the charge.[6]

1   See *Williams & Glyn's Bank Ltd v Boland* [1979] Ch 312 at 328E–F per Lord Denning MR, who pointed out that the statutory scheme 'was of precious little use to [the wife], at any rate when she was living at home in peace with her husband. She would never have heard of [it]: and she would not have understood it if she had.'

2   *Wroth v Tyler* [1974] Ch 30 at 46A–B per Megarry J. All too often the assistance offered by the register entry of matrimonial homes rights is 'too little and too late' (*Williams & Glyn's Bank Ltd v Boland* [1979] Ch 312 at 339G per Ormrod LJ). Unprotected rights enjoy no overriding status even if claimed by a spouse who remains in 'actual occupation' of the home (see FLA 1996, s 31(10)(b) [**para 12.167**]).

3   See *Williams & Glyn's Bank Ltd v Boland* [1979] Ch 312 at 339F per Ormrod LJ.

4   *Wroth v Tyler* [1974] Ch 30 at 46B per Megarry J. See eg *Barnett v Hassett* [1981] 1 WLR 1385 at 1388H, 1389C (ulterior motive to freeze proceeds of sale).

5   See e g *Wroth v Tyler* [1974] Ch 30, where W's entry of a 'notice' on the day following exchange of contracts by H (and her subsequent refusal to remove the entry) had the effect of bankrupting H (who was unable to pay the contractual damages awarded to the frustrated purchaser), with the ironic result that W's rights were defeated in any event by H's trustee in bankruptcy. As Megarry J observed ([1974] Ch 30 at 64F), 'there should be displayed in every

conveyancer's office the minatory legend *Cave uxorem.*' See also D J Hayton, 'The Femme Fatale in Conveyancing Practice' (1974) 38 Conv (NS) 110, but compare the Law Commission's defence of W's exercise of her right to register (*Family Law: Third Report on Family Property* (Law Com No 86, June 1978), para 2.83).

6   Considerations such as these led Megarry J to condemn the matrimonial home rights charge as 'a companion in obloquy for what in *Keeves v Dean* ... Scrutton LJ stigmatised as monstrum horrendum informe ingens' (*Wroth v Tyler* [1974] Ch 30 at 64A–B [**para 14.317**]).

12.95   The fundamental difficulty associated with the regime of matrimonial homes rights is the fact that an inherently worthwhile measure of social reform has been weakened by the attempt to engraft family-based rights on to an existing system of registration of incumbrances governed by the general law of property. The residential security of spouses will ultimately be assured only when the existing matrimonial home rights scheme gives way to a rule of automatic co-ownership of the legal estate in the matrimonial home during marriage – a regime not brought about by the application of commercialist principles of property law but resulting instead from the status of marriage. The adoption of this solution would mean that no disposition of the legal estate could ever occur without the active participation of both spouses.[1] Automatic co-ownership of the family home would cut clean through the difficulties which have been exposed in the operation of the Family Law Act 1996 (and its statutory predecessors), but as yet no legislation incorporating this principle has been enacted in England.[2]

1   Both spouses would have to sign any document of transfer, lease or mortgage [**para 11.25**].
2   In 1988 the Law Commission thought that a scheme of statutory legal ownership would be 'impossibly complex' (*Family Law: Matrimonial Property* (Law Com No 175, December 1988), para 4.15) and proposed instead a regime of joint equitable ownership of the matrimonial home (ibid, paras 4.1, 5.1).

Interests ineligible for protection by 'notice'

12.96   Certain kinds of entitlement are statutorily excluded from the facility of protection by 'notice'. These include principally:

–   beneficial interests under a trust of land and any charging order affecting such interests[1]
–   beneficial interests under a Settled Land Act settlement[2] and any charging order affecting such interests[3]
–   leasehold terms of three years or less (which are not otherwise required to be registered)[4]
–   restrictive covenants made between lessor and lessee (so far as relating to the demised premises)[5] and
–   rights of common which are registrable under the Commons Registration Act 1965.[6]

1   [**Paras 9.172, 9.121**]. These interests are generally protectable by the entry of a 'restriction' in the proprietorship register [**paras 7.53, 11.190**] (Law Com No 271 (2001), para 6.9).
2   [**Para 9.206**]. These interests are, again, protectable by the entry of a 'restriction'.
3   [**Para 9.121**].
4   [**Para 7.247**]. See Law Com No 271 (2001), paras 6.10–6.12. A 'notice' cannot therefore be entered in protection of a lease which is an overriding interest [**para 12.143**].

5   [**Para 14.309**]. Such covenants are normally apparent from the lease itself and their burden is automatically binding (LRA 2002, s 29(2)(b) [**para 12.76**]).
6   LRA 2002, s 33(e). See Law Com No 271 (2001), para 6.14.

MODE OF ENTRY OF A 'NOTICE' IN THE REGISTER

12.97   Any person who claims to be entitled to a protectable minor interest may apply to Land Registry for the entry of a 'notice' in respect of his interest in the charges register of the title affected.[1]

1   LRA 2002, ss 32(2), 34(1); LRR 2003, r 84(1).

Reasonable cause for application for entry

12.98   The Land Registration Act 2002 imposes an obligation not to apply for the entry of a notice 'without reasonable cause',[1] this duty being owed to any person who may suffer damage in consequence of its breach.[2] Moreover, the 2002 Act goes to some pains to indicate that the mere fact that an interest is the subject of a 'notice' in the register does not necessarily mean that the interest itself is 'valid', but only 'that the priority of the interest, if valid, is protected' in the event of subsequent registered dispositions of the relevant registered estate or charge.[3] The entry of a 'notice' does not in any way augment the rights which are the subject of entry: these rights are enforceable only to the extent that they remain independently valid under the general law.[4] The entry of a 'notice' does not even confer priority over existing unprotected minor interests.[5] The benefit gained through entry of a 'notice' is limited to securing priority over interests which are granted *subsequently* and which might otherwise achieve priority by registration.[6]

1   LRA 2002, s 77(1). This duty is particularly relevant in the case of an application for a 'unilateral notice' [**para 12.101**].
2   LRA 2002, s 77(2).
3   LRA 2002, s 32(3). See Law Com No 271 (2001), para 6.6.
4   For example, a restrictive covenant against building is unenforceable, even though protected by 'notice', if the covenantee has acquiesced in a disregard of the covenant [**para 13.128**].
5   See e g *Mortgage Corpn Ltd v Nationwide Credit Corpn Ltd* [1994] Ch 49 at 56B–C (charge protected by 'notice' had no priority over earlier and unprotected charge in respect of same land). Equitable charges rank in order of creation, not in order of protection on the register [**para 12.68**].
6   See *Mortgage Corpn Ltd v Nationwide Credit Corpn Ltd* [1994] Ch 49 at 54C–E per Dillon LJ; *Clark v Chief Land Registrar* [1994] Ch 370 at 382E–F per Nourse LJ.

Alternative forms of application

12.99   An application for entry of a 'notice' may, in general, take either of two forms.[1] It may comprise an application for an 'agreed notice' (or consensual entry) in the register which is, accordingly, immune from challenge at the point of entry by the consenting registered proprietor. Alternatively the application may seek the entry of a 'unilateral notice' which is capable of being 'warned off' on objection made by the registered proprietor.

1   LRA 2002, s 34(2).

Agreed notices

12.100   The entry of an 'agreed notice', which in the nature of things relates to non-contentious matters, requires the consent of the registered proprietor[1] or proof of the validity of the applicant's claim.[2] Alternatively, the registered proprietor himself may apply for the entry of an 'agreed notice'.[3] An 'agreed notice' is the only[4] appropriate form of entry in respect of certain kinds of entitlement (e g matrimonial home rights[5] and orders made under the Access to Neighbouring Land Act 1992[6]). 'Agreed notices' are not subject to the statutory cancellation procedure which applies to 'unilateral notices', with the consequence that this form of entry offers greater security to the beneficiary of the notice. An 'agreed notice' can, of course, be cancelled where the interest protected by it has come to an end.[7]

1   LRA 2002, s 34(3)(b).
2   LRA 2002, s 34(3)(c).
3   LRA 2002, s 34(3)(a).
4   LRR 2003, rr 80, 82.
5   **[Paras 12.93–12.95]**.
6   **[Paras 8.136, 12.90]**.
7   LRR 2003, r 87.

Unilateral notices

12.101   By contrast, an application for entry of a 'unilateral notice' relates essentially to hostile or contested claims of entitlement (and replicates in part the function of the old 'caution against dealings'[1]). The application initiates a process of notification of, and possible objection by, the registered proprietor.[2] A 'unilateral notice' can be entered without any proof of the validity of the applicant's claim,[3] but the 'notice' must indicate that it is 'unilateral' and must identify the beneficiary of the notice.[4] The entry of a 'unilateral notice' does not require the co-operation of the registered proprietor, but the proprietor is entitled to apply at any time for the cancellation of the notice (in which case the beneficiary of the notice has certain rights of objection to the proposed cancellation).[5] Equally, the beneficiary of the notice may apply to the registrar for removal of a notice which has become spent or redundant.[6]

1   **[Para 12.85]**.
2   LRA 2002, s 35(1); LRR 2003, r 83.
3   Law Com No 271 (2001), para 6.26.
4   LRA 2002, s 35(2).
5   LRA 2002, s 36; LRR 2003, r 86. Disputes are ultimately resolved by reference to the Adjudicator to Land Registry (LRA 2002, s 73(7)).
6   LRA 2002, s 35(3); LRR 2003, r 85.

CONSEQUENCE OF ENTRY BY 'NOTICE'

12.102   One of the fundamental objectives of any system of registered title is to ensure that the register remains an accurate record – or 'mirror'[1] – of the interests affecting the registered estate. It is a 'cardinal principle' that 'the register is everything'[2] and it is important that there should be a strong incentive towards the protection of minor interests by appropriate entry.

1   **[Paras 2.108, 6.11]**.
2   See *Fels v Knowles* (1906) 26 NZLR 604 at 620; *Bunt v Hallinan* [1985] 1 NZLR 450 at 458. See also *Abbey National Building Society v Cann* [1991] 1 AC 56 at 78C per Lord Oliver of Aylmerton **[para 2.105]**; *Re Cartlidge and Granville Savings & Mortgage Corp* (1987) 34 DLR (4th) 161 at 172.

The registration rule

12.103   Ultimately, in common with most schemes of Torrens-style registration, the protection of minor interests under the Land Registration Act 2002 operates on the basis of a 'registration rule' which can be expressed in two simple inter-related propositions:

–   A minor interest, if the subject of a 'notice' entered in the register, acquires 'protected' priority and therefore becomes automatically binding on any registered disponee for value of the registered estate, regardless of whether he inspected the register.[1]

–   A protectable minor interest, if *not* the subject of a 'notice' entered in the register, is postponed to the interest which passes under any registered disposition of the registered estate made for valuable consideration, even if the disponee had contemporaneous actual knowledge of the unprotected interest from another source.[2]

1   LRA 2002, s 29(1), (2)(a)(i) **[para 12.76]**. A prudent disponee obtains an official copy of the register before committing himself to the disposition and, shortly before taking the disposition, procures a priority search of the register, thereby acquiring a 30 day priority period during which to lodge his application for registration of that disposition **[para 12.50]**.
2   LRA 2002, s 29(1). Ultimately, of course, with the introduction of routine electronic conveyancing **[para 12.4]**, the making of an entry in the register will become an essential component of the creation of interests in registered land. When this happens, the concept of an unprotected minor interest will become, in most instances, a sheer contradiction in terms.

Rationale for the registration rule

12.104   The Land Registration Act 2002 thus causes unregistered minor interests to become unenforceable against most disponees[1] of the registered estate.[2] The motivation behind this principle is readily understandable: the registration rule is clear-cut and easily applicable. The medium of the publicly accessible register ensures a straightforward and effective notification of entitlement to the entire world.[3] The statutory sanction for non-protection goes a long way towards guaranteeing that the register remains an accurate, current and comprehensive record of the interests affecting the land concerned. More-over, the displacement of the traditional equitable doctrine of notice achieves a certain kind of efficiency, albeit at the expense of some moral exactitude.[4] Unlike the 'bona fide purchaser' principle,[5] the registration rule obviates any general inquiry into the state of mind or moral standing of the individual disponee in each transaction.[6] Above all, the rule preserves the integrity of the register as a safe basis for dealings with registered estates[7] and promotes a major objective of the 2002 Act by ensuring 'that all conveyancing inquiries should, so far as is possible, be capable of being conducted on line.'[8]

1　An unprotected minor interest remains enforceable, of course, against a disponee otherwise than for value (eg a donee) **[para 12.80]**. All disponees – whether or not for value – also take title subject to other burdens imposed directly by statute or common law (eg the consequences of planning legislation). See Law Com No 158 (1987), para 2.1.

2　There remains a possibility that, in certain circumstances, an entitlement left unprotected by 'notice' may still qualify for protected priority as an unregistered interest which statutorily 'overrides' registered dispositions of the estate (LRA 2002, s 29(1), (2)(a)(ii) **[paras 2.171, 12.146–12.236]**).

3　See *Williams & Glyn's Bank Ltd v Boland* [1981] AC 487 at 504A per Lord Wilberforce ('The only kind of notice recognised is by entry on the register'). See similarly *Freeguard v Royal Bank of Scotland Plc* (2000) 79 P & CR 81 at 86 per Robert Walker LJ.

4　See *Frazer v Walker* [1967] 1 AC 569 at 582A per Lord Wilberforce. For reference to 'the necessity of this business consideration predominating over the moral aspect', see *Holt, Renfrew & Co Ltd v Henry Singer Ltd* (1982) 135 DLR (3d) 391 at 399.

5　**[Paras 2.191, 12.337–12.372]**.

6　'[T]he system is designed to free the purchaser from the hazards of notice – real or constructive – which, in the case of unregistered land, involved him in enquiries, often quite elaborate, failing which he might be bound by equities' (*Williams & Glyn's Bank Ltd v Boland* [1981] AC 487 at 503G–H per Lord Wilberforce). See likewise *Miles v Bull (No 2)* [1969] 3 All ER 1585 at 1590D–H; *Parkash v Irani Finance Ltd* [1970] Ch 101 at 108A.

7　See *Wicks v Bennett* (1921) 30 CLR 80 at 95 per Higgins J ('a man may purchase land safely from the registered proprietor, closing his mind to the mere fact of any unregistered interest').

8　Law Com No 271 (2001), para 5.16.

RELEVANCE OF FRAUD

12.105 It is a standard feature of land registration the world over that a disponee's mere knowledge of a protectable, but unprotected, interest does not normally affect the title derived from registration.[1] This reluctance to allow the traditional doctrine of notice to intrude upon registers of title lies deeply embedded in the origins of the Land Register[2] and has persisted to the present day.[3] As Cross J observed in *Strand Securities Ltd v Caswell*,[4] it is 'vital to the working of the land registration system that notice of something which is not on the register should not affect a transferee unless it is an overriding interest.'[5] Title registration is intended to mark a 'complete break'[6] from the equitable rules which formerly governed land law priorities.[7] In consequence there has been a general rejection, no less so in England[8] than elsewhere,[9] of any temptation to qualify the system of title registration by the importation of an equitable doctrine alien to its central purpose.[10]

1　See eg *Union Bank of Canada v Boulter-Waugh Ltd* (1919) 46 DLR 41 at 48; *Waimiha*

Sawmilling Co Ltd v Waione Timber Co Ltd [1926] AC 101 at 106–108; *Ruptash and Lumsden v Zawick* (1956) 2 DLR (2d) 145 at 159–160; *Bahr v Nicolay (No 2)* (1988) 164 CLR 604 at 613 per Mason CJ and Dawson J, 630–631 per Wilson and Toohey JJ, 652–653, 655 per Brennan J.

2   See *Report of the Real Property Royal Commissioners* (1830), p 37 ('greatly for the public good, that civil rights should be capable of being ascertained without difficulty'). See similarly *Report of the Commissioners on the Registration of Title with reference to the Sale and Transfer of Land* (CP 2215, 1857 – Session 2), para LXXIII.

3   There is 'no general principle which renders it unconscionable for a purchaser of land to rely on a want of registration of a claim against registered land, even though he took with express notice of it. A decision to the contrary would defeat the purpose of the legislature in introducing the system of registration' (*Lloyd v Dugdale* [2002] 2 P & CR 167 at [50] per Sir Christopher Slade). See likewise *Mills v Stockman* (1967) 116 CLR 61 at 78 per Kitto J.

4   [1965] Ch 373 at 390A–B per Cross J.

5   See also LRA 1925, s 59(6) – a provision not replicated in the Land Registration Act 2002 – which provided that a purchaser acquiring title under a registered disposition was unaffected by notice 'express, implied, or constructive.'

6   See *United Trust Co v Dominion Stores Ltd* (1977) 71 DLR (3d) 72 at 75 per Laskin CJC (dissenting). See also *Nilson v Zagrodney* (2000) 183 DLR (4th) 564 at 574–576.

7   See *Chan Yiu Tong v Wellmake Investments Ltd* (1996) 1 HKC 528 at 534C per Godfrey JA ('the statutory requirements as to the necessity of registration for the protection of [minor] interests were intended to, and do, supplant ... general equitable principles').

8   See eg *De Lusignan v Johnson* (1973) 230 EG 499; *Melbury Road Properties 1995 Ltd v Kreidi* [1999] 3 EGLR 108 at 109M.

9   See *Wicks v Bennett* (1921) 30 CLR 80 at 91; *Bank of South Australia Ltd v Ferguson* (1998) 192 CLR 248 at [10]; *Nilson v Zagrodney* (2000) 183 DLR (4th) 564 at 574–576.

10   For isolated exceptions to the general pattern, see *Marsden v Campbell* (1897) 18 NSWR Eq 33 at 38; *Peffer v Rigg* [1977] 1 WLR 285 at 294C–E (where Graham J held that a transferee 'cannot ... be in good faith if he has in fact notice of something which affects his title'). For strong disapproval of the decision in *Peffer v Rigg*, see (1977) 41 Conv (NS) 207 (F R Crane); (1977) 93 LQR 341 (R J Smith); [1977] CLJ 227 (D J Hayton); [1978] Conv 52 (J Martin); Law Com No 158 (1987), para 4.15; Law Com No 254 (1998), para 3.44. See also *Dougbar Properties Ltd v Keeper of the Registers of Scotland* 1999 SCLR 458 at 469C.

The longstop of fraud

12.106 Notwithstanding the general irrelevance of equitable concepts of notice under the Land Registration Act, it has always been clear that cases of *unconscionable* dealing by a disponee constitute an exception to the principle of indefeasibility of title.[1] Registration of title does not wholly 'abrogate the principles of equity.'[2] The ultimate jurisdiction of conscience is not so easily ousted.[3] Alongside the historic emphasis upon the importance of certainty in the ascertainment of land rights there exists an overwhelming abhorrence of fraud.[4] Concern for the integrity of the register can never be allowed to eclipse all concern for the integrity of the disponee of a registered estate.[5] It is an enduring principle that 'fraud unravels everything' and no court in the land 'will allow a person to keep an advantage which he has obtained by fraud.'[6] In effect, all legal rules come with an implicit 'anti-fraud' proviso. In the present context a disponee for value of a registered estate who is guilty of fraud may well find that the long arm of equity intervenes to prevent him from disclaiming or disregarding minor interests simply on the ground that they were unprotected by register entry.

1   *De Lusignan v Johnson* (1973) 230 EG 499 per Brightman J. See generally M P Thompson, 'Registration, Fraud and Notice' [1985] CLJ 280.
2   *Wilkins v Kannammal* [1951] MLJ 99 at 100 per Taylor J; *CN and NA Davies Ltd v Laughton* [1997] 3 NZLR 705 at 712 per Thomas J.
3   Certain progressions of land law logic are simply deemed to be so offensive to good conscience that the conceptual process must be – and is – stopped in its tracks. At some barely definable point, axiomatic rules reach the moral, if not logical, limits of their application (see Gray and Gray, 'The rhetoric of realty', in J Getzler (ed), *Rationalizing Property, Equity and Trusts: Essays in Honour of Edward Burn* (Butterworths 2003), pp 224–227).
4   **[Para 10.1]**. The distaste for fraud goes back to the earliest days of land registration (see e g *Report of the Real Property Royal Commissioners* (1830), p 39). See also C F Brickdale and W R Sheldon, *The Land Transfer Acts, 1875 and 1897* (2nd edn by C F Brickdale, London 1905), p 14.
5   Although the system of registration of title is 'designed to provide simplicity and certitude in transfers of land', these qualities are 'amply achieved without depriving equity of the ability to exercise its jurisdiction *in personam* on grounds of conscience' (*Oh Hiam v Tham Kong* (1980) 2 BPR 9451 at 9453 per Lord Russell of Killowen). See similarly *Boyd v Mayor of Wellington* [1924] NZLR 1174 at 1223; *Frazer v Walker* [1967] 1 AC 569 at 585B–C per Lord Wilberforce; *Bank of South Australia Ltd v Ferguson* (1998) 192 CLR 248 at [9] (High Court of Australia).
6   *Lazarus Estates Ltd v Beasley* [1956] 1 QB 702 at 712 per Denning LJ. In the pungent phrase of one Scots judge, 'offside goals are disallowed' (*Rodger (Builders) Ltd v Fawdry* 1950 SC 483 at 501 per Lord Justice Clerk Thomson). See likewise *Burnett's Trustee v Grainger* [2004] UKHL 8 at [141] per Lord Rodger of Earlsferry.

The consequences of fraud under the Land Registration Act 2002

12.107   The intersecting policy motivations discussed above are reflected in the Land Registration Act 2002 and in the series of law reform proposals which preceded its enactment. The 2002 Act is certainly underpinned by the idea that registration displaces the historic doctrine of notice.[1] The Law Commission and Land Registry finally endorsed the view that the question whether a disponee has knowledge or notice of a pre-existing interest, or even whether a disponee has acted in good faith, should be irrelevant to the disponee's title.[2] Contrary to their recommendation, however, the Land Registration Act 2002 does not explicitly redefine the term 'purchaser' so as to exclude a requirement of 'good faith'.[3] The 2002 Act seems to preserve several respects in which, against a background of failure to register rights, bad faith or unconscionable behaviour on the part of a disponee of a registered estate may disable him from taking title entirely free of adverse claims.

1   Law Com No 254 (1998), para 3.46.
2   Law Com No 254 (1998), para 3.55; Law Com No 271 (2001), para 5.16. Law Commission's stance varied over the years (contrast the requirement of 'good faith' advocated in Law Com No 158 (1987), para 4.15; Law Com No 173 (1988), para 3.7).
3   The Land Registration Act 2002 altogether omits any definition of 'purchaser', 'transferee' or 'disponee'.

Assertion of in personam equities

12.108   Lord Russell of Killowen once pointed out in the Privy Council that indefeasibility of title does not interfere with 'the ability of the court, exercising its jurisdiction *in personam*, to insist upon proper conduct in accordance with the conscience which all men should obey.'[1] The enforcement of an *in personam* equity against a disponee of the registered title involves a principle which is 'essentially non-proprietary in nature' and has as its basis 'the enforcement of personal claims arising out of the registered proprietor's conduct.'[2] Thus, for example, the court clearly retains a power to subject a fraudulent disponee to personal liability for any loss suffered by the owners of interests which have been left unprotected by register entry. In such cases the disponee takes his title free of the unprotected interests, but is exposed to a personal financial liability. Alternatively the court has jurisdiction, in appropriate circumstances, to set aside a disposition to a fraudulent disponee, with the consequence that unprotected minor interests survive the abortive transaction and can then be duly protected by entry in the register.[3]

1   *Oh Hiam v Tham Kong* (1980) 2 BPR 9451 at 9454. See also *Frazer v Walker* [1967] 1 AC 569 at 585. Thus, for example, the supposed 'indefeasibility' of a registered title affords its proprietor no defence against a claim of specific performance brought by a purchaser under a contract of sale or against a beneficiary who seeks to enforce a trust affecting the registered estate (*CN and NA Davies Ltd v Laughton* [1997] 3 NZLR 705 at 711–712).
2   *CN and NA Davies Ltd v Laughton* [1997] 3 NZLR 705 at 712 per Thomas J; *Smith v Hugh Watt Society Inc* [2004] 1 NZLR 537 at [85]. A statutory scheme of registration 'does not protect moral fraud' (see *Cottee Dairy Products Pty Ltd v Minad Pty Ltd* (Unreported, Supreme Court of New South Wales, 25 August 1997) per McLelland CJ in Eq).
3   In their earlier deliberations the Law Commission and Land Registry expressly contemplated the possibility of *in personam* relief in the form of financial recovery or the award of rescission (see Law Com No 254 (1998), paras 3.48–3.49).

Postponing conduct

12.109   Under the Land Registration Act 2002 there also remains a strong possibility that the court will take the view that priority over an unprotected minor interest is simply unavailable to a disponee who seeks *unconscionably* to take advantage of the want of register entry. On this analysis the unconscientious disclaimer of unprotected interests constitutes a form of 'postponing conduct' which displaces or reverses the special priority rule adumbrated in section 29 of the Land Registration Act 2002.[1] The dishonest disponee therefore takes his title subject – by way of constructive trust[2] – to the unprotected interests in question.[3]

1   See, in relation to the old doctrine which reversed the normal priority of competing minor interests on the ground of 'postponing conduct', *Abigail v Lapin* [1934] AC 491 at 507; *Barclays Bank Ltd v Taylor* [1974] Ch 137 at 147E; *Strand Securities Ltd v Caswell* [1965] Ch 958 at 991B; *Freeguard v Royal Bank of Scotland Plc* (2000) 79 P & CR 81 at 89.
2   See Law Com No 254 (1998), para 3.48.
3   For the vitality of this approach in the thinking of the Court of Appeal, see *Lloyd v Dugdale* [2002] 2 P & CR 167 at [50]–[52] [**para 12.228**].

Definition of fraud

12.110 The difficulty remains that, as an exception to the principle of indefeasibility, the concept of 'fraud' has no clear statutory or other definition. In fact courts have usually gone to enormous lengths to avoid the limiting consequences of any strict definitional formula.[1] The threshold of 'fraud' remains elusive, the precise content of the term being left to be identified in the particular circumstances of each case.[2] For present purposes, however, 'fraud' seems to require more than a mere showing of 'equitable' or 'constructive' fraud.[3] The core meaning of 'fraud' involves concepts of 'dishonesty' and 'deprivation'.[4] There must be a 'taking from someone else, literally or metaphorically, [of] that which is his due or is due to him.'[5] If the 'designed object' of a transfer is to 'cheat a man of a known existing right, that is fraudulent.'[6] The purchaser must, in effect, be guilty of 'something in the nature of personal dishonesty or moral turpitude.'[7]

1 'No definition of fraud can be attempted, so various are its forms and methods' (*Stuart v Kingston* (1923) 32 CLR 309 at 359 per Starke J). See also *Moore v Moore* (1971) 16 DLR (3d) 174 at 185; *R v Olan, Hudson and Hartnett* (1978) 86 DLR (3d) 212 at 218 per Dickson J.
2 *Bunt v Hallinan* [1985] 1 NZLR 450 at 461. There is, for example, no 'fraud' if a disponee merely acts on professional legal advice that he is free to ignore the unprotected rights of some other person (*Bunt v Hallinan* [1985] 1 NZLR 450 at 462–463). See also *Babcock v Carr* (1982) 127 DLR (3d) 77 at 84–85. 'Fraud' is relevant only if it has been 'brought home to the person whose registered title is impeached or to his agents' (*Assets Co Ltd v Mere Roihi* [1905] AC 176 at 210 per Lord Lindley). On 'fraud' committed by an agent, see *National Commercial Banking Corpn of Australia Ltd v Hedley* (1984) 3 BPR 9477 at 9482.
3 There must be 'actual fraud' (see *Assets Co Ltd v Mere Roihi* [1905] AC 176 at 210; *Bunt v Hallinan* [1985] 1 NZLR 450 at 458; *Ong Ban Chai v Seah Siang Mong* [1998] 3 MLJ 346 at 366I). 'Not all species of fraud which attract equitable remedies will amount to fraud' in the present context (*Bank of South Australia Ltd v Ferguson* (1998) 192 CLR 248 at [10]).
4 *R v Olan, Hudson and Hartnett* (1978) 86 DLR (3d) 212 at 217–218 per Dickson J.
5 *Sutton v O'Kane* [1973] 2 NZLR 304 at 322 per Turner P. See also *Midland Bank Trust Co Ltd v Green* [1980] Ch 590 at 625B per Lord Denning MR [**para 12.120**].
6 *Waimiha Sawmilling Co Ltd v Waione Timber Co Ltd* [1926] AC 101 at 106 per Lord Buckmaster. Lord Buckmaster's dictum has been described as a 'convenient starting point' for the definition of fraud in this context (*Bahr v Nicolay (No 2)* (1988) 164 CLR 604 at 630 per Wilson and Toohey JJ).
7 *Butler v Fairclough* (1917) 23 CLR 78 at 90; *Wicks v Bennett* (1921) 30 CLR 80 at 91; *Stuart v Kingston* (1923) 32 CLR 309 at 329 per Knox CJ. See also *Frazer v Walker* [1967] 1 AC 569 at 584C; *Whittingham v Whittingham* [1979] Fam 9 at 12F; *Bunt v Hallinan* [1985] 1 NZLR 450 at 458, 463.

Variant interpretations of 'fraud'

12.111 Whilst all would agree that 'fraud' should never be allowed to succeed, the identification of 'fraud' is not a universally shared perception. Individual judges differ in the liberality with which they discern fraud in given situations.[1] The threshold of 'fraud' may even shift or oscillate over long historical cycles. The critical issue is ultimately the demarcation of the borderline between 'fair game' and 'foul play'. In marginal cases views will inevitably diverge on whether the disponee of a registered estate has played, albeit robustly, within the four corners of a game whose rules were presumed to be known to all or has strayed so far outside its rules that his dealings must be held vitiated by 'fraud'.[2] Significant differences of philosophy separate two approaches to this question, illustrating yet again the endemic tension between certainty and justice as determinants of land law priorities.

1   See *Tanwar Enterprises Pty Ltd v Cauchi* (2003) 201 ALR 359 at [83] per Kirby J ('What is "unconscionable" or "exceptional" in the opinion of one decision-maker may not be so regarded by another. Inescapably, such language invites differing evaluations by different people'). See e g the unregistered land parallel of *Midland Bank Trust Co Ltd v Green* [1981] AC 513, [1980] Ch 590 [**para 12.289**], where a majority in the Court of Appeal found 'fraud' to be present in circumstances which caused the House of Lords to be adamant that 'fraud' was not in issue.
2   The playing field analogy may usefully be pursued. By selling an enormous dummy to an opponent, an attacking player may deceive him thoroughly and bring about a score. However, no referee would penalise this behaviour as a 'foul'. The outcome is in no sense vitiated by 'fraud': all parties concerned are playing fairly within the four corners of the game.

A restrictive interpretation of fraud

12.112   The common lawyer is characteristically inclined to favour certainty over fairness in the ascertainment of proprietary rights.[1] In the law of property, justice is never quite as important as order.[2] In this respect English law reflects the widely held theory that, by minimising confusion over property entitlements, hard-edged rules promote socially useful commerce and avert costly controversy.[3] On this view it seems preferable that property rules should maintain a clear-cut, crystalline form and should not dissolve into the 'mud' which results from discretion-laden formulations supposedly designed to secure 'fair' outcomes in isolated cases.[4] The simple integrity of the rule system should not be compromised by well-intentioned, but open-ended, exceptions based on potentially subjective assessments of fraud, moral desert or the like.[5] As Mahon J once observed, '[n]o stable system of jurisprudence could permit a litigant's claim to justice to be consigned to the formless void of individual moral opinion.'[6]

1   Blackstone categorised property rules as relating to 'things in themselves indifferent' (*Bl Comm*, Vol I, p 55). See likewise *Vallejo v Wheeler* (1774) 1 Cowp 143 at 153, 98 ER 1012 at 1017 per Lord Mansfield ('it is of more consequence that a rule should be certain, than whether the rule is established one way or the other').
2   See *Burnet v Coronado Oil & Gas Co*, 285 US 393 at 406, 76 L Ed 815 at 823 (1932) per Justice Brandeis ('in most matters it is more important that the applicable rule of law be settled than that it be settled right'). See also *Western Australia v Ward* (2002) 191 ALR 1 at [479] per McHugh J.
3   For the argument that certainty and justice are not truly independent and oppositional, but are instead deeply interactive, see *Cowcher v Cowcher* [1972] 1 WLR 425 at 430A–C per Bagnall J ('[I]n determining rights, particularly property rights, the only justice that can be attained by mortals, who are fallible and not omniscient, is justice according to the law; the justice which flows from the application of sure and settled principles to proved or admitted facts. So in the field of equity the length of the Chancellor's foot has been measured or is capable of measurement. This does not mean that equity is past childbearing; simply that its progeny must be legitimate – by precedent out of principle. It is well that this should be so; otherwise no lawyer could safely advise on his client's title and every quarrel would lead to a law suit'). See also *Harris v Digital Pulse Pty Ltd* (2003) 197 ALR 626 at [8] per Spigelman CJ.

4   See Carol Rose, 'Crystals and Mud in Property Law' 40 Stan L Rev 577 at 591 (1987–88) ('In the absence of clear definitions around property rights, individuals dissipate resources in conflicts and bullying, or in taking precautions against being bullied. Crystalline rules, it seems, can halt this frittering away, be it public or private. Hard-edged rules define assets and their ownership in such a way that what is bought stays bought and can be safely traded to others, instead of repeatedly being put up for grabs'). See also D Baird and T Jackson, 'Information, Uncertainty and the Transfer of Property' 13 J Legal Stud 299 (1984); C G Holderness, 'A Legal Foundation for Exchange' 14 J Legal Stud 321 at 344 (1985).

5   '[T]he law inclines to prefer the certainty of rules over the uncertainty of exceptions. This is especially so where the exceptions are expressed in discretionary language or in open-textured criteria such as "unconscionable or unconscientious behaviour of an exceptional kind"' (*Tanwar Enterprises Pty Ltd v Cauchi* (2003) 201 ALR 359 at [83] per Kirby J).

6   *Carly v Farrelly* [1975] 1 NZLR 356 at 367.

12.113   This restrictive approach, when applied in the context of the Land Registration Act 2002, suggests that the normal consequence of the registration rule should not be deflected by an over-ready ascription of 'fraud' to a disponee of title. Thus, it can be argued, no 'fraud' inheres in the mere exploitation by a transferee of legal consequences which flow from the incautious or negligent failure of others to protect their own rights by register entry.[1] '[I]t is not fraud to take advantage of legal rights, the existence of which may be taken to be known to both parties.'[2] As Lord Rodger of Earlsferry announced with brutal candour in an analogous Scots case, '[n]ice guys finish last',[3] a result which at least secures a certain clarity and systemic efficiency in the operation of the Land Register. The clear-cut quality of the registration requirement enables parties to make reliable *ex ante* assessments of their respective rights and liabilities; and all parties to land transactions are given an important incentive to 'plan and to act carefully, knowing that no judicial cavalry will ride to their rescue later.'[4]

1   See e g *Burnett's Trustee v Grainger* [2004] UKHL 8 at [145] per Lord Rodger of Earlsferry (holding the respondent 'fully entitled to take advantage of the [appellants'] mistake' in failing to register).

2   *Re Monolithic Building Co* [1915] 1 Ch 643 at 663 per Lord Cozens-Hardy MR. See also *Markfaith Investment Ltd v Chiap Hua Flashlights Ltd* [1991] 2 AC 43 at 60D; *Chan Yiu Tong v Wellmake Investments Ltd* (1996) 1 HKC 528 at 533I–534B per Godfrey JA.

3   *Burnett's Trustee v Grainger* [2004] UKHL 8 at [141] (Those taking part in the race towards registration of rights 'are no Corinthians and swear no Olympic oath of sportsmanship. If your opponent is slow off the mark, mistakes the way or stumbles, you do not chivalrously wait for him to catch up: you take full advantage of his mistakes').

4   Carol Rose, 'Crystals and Mud in Property Law' 40 Stan L Rev 577 at 592 (1987–88).

An expansive interpretation of 'fraud'

12.114   Notwithstanding this powerful rationale for a restrictive interpretation of 'fraud', there are also cogent arguments in favour of a more flexible balance between hard-edged rules and the ethical realities of individual circumstances. More inclusive interpretations of the notion of 'fraud' tend towards fairness of outcome in the unique context of each case. A more expansive concept of 'fraud' not only enables the courts to determine priorities *ex post* (ie in the light of proven actualities rather than with reference to categorical abstractions), but also re-introduces a much needed 'ethical element' into the system of registered land.[1] There is nowadays increasing support in the common law world for the view that judicial assessments of moral neighbourhood and the margin of tolerance for exploitative behaviour must adjust to compensate for the demise of traditional cultural and religious constraints on aggressive individualism and unfair dealing.[2]

1   See e g G Battersby, 'Informal Transactions in Land, Estoppel and Registration' (1995) 58 MLR 637 at 655.
2   See Paul Finn, 'Commerce, The Common Law and Morality' (1989) 17 Melbourne UL Rev 87 at 96–99; Gray and Gray, 'The rhetoric of realty', in J Getzler (ed), *Rationalizing Property, Equity and Trusts: Essays in Honour of Edward Burn* (Butterworths 2003), p 255.

12.115   Arguments of this kind pinpoint the need for a greater responsiveness to moral criteria in the determination of land law priorities. A more extensive definition of 'fraud' would have the salutary effect of imposing visible sanctions on sharp practice. The disponee of a registered estate would know that he took title subject to any adverse (but unprotected) minor interests which could be said to impinge on his conscience. At a higher level of abstraction this approach reflects the more general contention that hard-edged rules of property law must ultimately give way to more open-textured 'standards' or 'principles' which express certain basic moral relativities.[1] It is even arguable that a more judgmental or ethically based system of property rules is itself an instrument of economic efficiency. The prospect of *ex post* redistributions of entitlement in accordance with moral equities may go far to dissuade the wrongdoer from even attempting bad faith manipulations of the rules and may therefore have a generally reassuring and stabilising effect on the expectations of the transacting community.

1   See Duncan Kennedy, 'Form and Substance in Private Law Adjudication' 89 Harv L Rev 1685 at 1710 (1975–76); Ronald Dworkin, *Taking Rights Seriously* (Duckworth, London 1977), pp 22–31. See also Geoffrey Samuel, 'Epistemology and Legal Institutions' 4 Intl J for the Semiotics of Law 311 at 315 (1991).

Differing views of the function of property law

12.116   Underlying these differing approaches to the identification of 'fraud' are divergent perspectives on the true function of the law of property. The dominant ideology of modern property law places a clear emphasis upon the simple mechanics of contract and transfer, leaving the morality of exchange largely unquestioned. On this view, the principal purpose of the law of property is to provide clarity and procedural efficiency in the combined operation of bargain and disposition. In many ways the law of property implicitly assumes a world of assertive individualism in which all are presumed to be equal, self-determining and competent to protect their own self-interest. Land transactions therefore have no particularly significant moral dimension. There is, however, another perspective according to which the ultimate business of the law of property is, quite inescapably, the administration of distributive justice. In this context there is no such thing as moral neutrality. The priorities which we allow to govern the law of property simply reflect the moral sensitivity of an entire legal culture; and the precise threshold of 'unconscionable' behaviour can be seen as providing a significant index of the value system which underlies modern social and commercial relationships.

RECOGNISED CASES OF 'FRAUD'

12.117 Regardless of differences of judicial philosophy in the identification of 'fraud', there is a broad consensus that mere knowledge of the existence of unprotected rights does not connote 'fraud' on the part of the disponee of a registered title.[1] Indeed, the dissociation of fraud and notice is intrinsic to the operation of most schemes of title registration in the common law world.[2] It is equally plain that a disponee cannot be allowed to disclaim unprotected minor interests following a transfer which is marked by manifest dishonesty on his own part. The court's jurisdiction to intervene on grounds of conscience[3] has been held to be wholly compatible with the concept of indefeasibility of title.[4] As Brennan J observed in the Australian High Court in *Bahr v Nicolay (No 2)*,[5] an indefeasible title is 'designed to protect a transferee from defects in the title of the transferor, not to free him from interests with which he has burdened his own title.'[6]

1   See e g *De Lusignan v Johnson* (1973) 230 EG 499; *Melbury Road Properties 1995 Ltd v Kreidi* [1999] 3 EGLR 108 at 109M; *Wicks v Bennett* (1921) 30 CLR 80 at 91; *Bank of South Australia Ltd v Ferguson* (1998) 192 CLR 248 at [10].
2   In some jurisdictions there is specific statutory confirmation that mere knowledge on the part of a purchaser that a trust or unregistered interest is in existence 'shall not of itself be imputed as fraud' (Real Property Act 1900 (New South Wales), s 43(1)). See also New Zealand's Land Transfer Act 1952, s 182; Alberta's Land Titles Act (RSA 1980, c L-5), s 195. See generally P Butt, 'Notice and Fraud in the Torrens System: A Comparative Analysis' (1977–78) 13 Univ of Western Australia L Rev 354.
3   [Para 12.108].
4   *Bahr v Nicolay (No 2)* (1988) 164 CLR 604 at 637 per Wilson and Toohey JJ; *CN and NA Davies Ltd v Laughton* [1997] 3 NZLR 705 at 712 per Thomas J.
5   (1988) 164 CLR 604 at 653. See J G Tooher, 'Muddying the Torrens Waters with the Chancellor's Foot?; *Bahr v Nicolay*' (1993) 1 APLJ 1.
6   See similarly *Penrith RSL Club Ltd v Cameron* (2001) 10 BPR 18621 at [25]; *CN and NA Davies Ltd v Laughton* [1997] 3 NZLR 705 at 711.

12.118   The following circumstances, which are not mutually exclusive, illustrate the conduct which has been classified as 'fraud' for present purposes. Most – but not all – of these instances arise where a disponee of a registered estate has expressly or impliedly undertaken to give effect to the unprotected rights of an incumbrancer and it would be plainly unconscionable for him later to repudiate the undertaking.

Deliberate ploy to defeat unprotected rights

12.119   The term 'fraud' is properly applied in relation to the transfer of a registered title which was quite blatantly intended to defeat an incumbrancer's rights whilst they remained unprotected.[1] The element which confirms the unconscionable nature of such a device is the deliberate or calculating character of the attempt to cheat the incumbrancer of his entitlement.[2]

1   The mere fact that the transferor warned the incumbrancer that his rights were unprotected may not be enough to avert a subsequent finding of fraud (see *Alberta* (*Minister of Forestry, Lands and Wildlife*) *v McCulloch* [1991] 3 WWR 662 at 669, [1992] 1 WWR 747).
2   See *Waimiha Sawmilling Co Ltd v Waione Timber Co Ltd* [1926] AC 101 at 106 per Lord Buckmaster. Such a transaction carries overtones of the *machinatio ad circumveniendum* which was condemned by Lord Hardwicke LC in *Le Neve v Le Neve* (1747) Amb 436 at 447, 27 ER 291 at 295.

Irregular transfers of title

12.120   A label of 'fraud' is likely to be attached to transfers of title marked by some irregularity which heightens the suspicion that the transaction was aimed principally at the defeat of unprotected rights. The taint of bad faith tends to infect dealings which are conducted with undue haste or secrecy[1] and which result in the payment of an obvious undervalue.[2] In *Efstratiou, Glantschnig and Petrovic v Glantschnig*,[3] for example, the New Zealand Court of Appeal found fraud to be present where, with inordinate speed,[4] a disaffected husband transferred his registered title in the matrimonial home to a friend for cash. The deliberate purpose of the transaction had been to defeat the unprotected equitable rights of the transferor's wife.[5]

1   See e g *Buttigeig v Micallef* (Unreported, Supreme Court of New South Wales, 4 October 1988, BPR Casenote 95922).
2   Compare Lord Denning MR's explication of 'fraud' as covering 'any dishonest dealing done so as to deprive unwary innocents of their rightful dues', the hallmarks of such fraud including 'transactions done stealthily and speedily in secret for no sufficient consideration' (*Midland Bank Trust Co Ltd v Green* [1980] Ch 590 at 625B **[para 12.294]**). See also *R v Olan, Hudson and Hartnett* (1978) 86 DLR (3d) 212 at 217–218 per Dickson J; *Funes v Brahimi* (Unreported, Supreme Court of Victoria, 17 May 1996) ('something very strange going on' in relation to unadvertised sale at two-thirds of market value).
3   [1972] NZLR 594 at 598–599.
4   The transfer was executed one day after the exchange of contracts and the transferee's title was registered one day after that. ('We are not persuaded that conveyancing transactions are so expeditiously conducted as a matter of course' ([1972] NZLR 594 at 600 per Turner J).)
5   The sale occurred following the husband's discovery of his wife *in flagrante delicto* ('[t]here was a scene'). The sale price was only 60 per cent of the true market value and the purchaser made no inspection of the house or its contents. The transferor immediately dissipated the proceeds of sale.

Use of a corporate alter ego

12.121   A similarly motivated transfer to a company which is in reality the alter ego of the transferor is likewise apt to be stigmatised as 'fraud'.[1] In *Jones v Lipman*[2] Russell J held that an unprotected estate contract remained binding upon, and specifically enforceable against, the transferee of a registered title. Here the transferee was a limited company which, on closer inspection, turned out to be merely the alter ego of the transferor who had earlier granted the estate contract to the present claimant.[3] In Russell J's view, the defendant company was 'the creature of the [transferor], a device and a sham, a mask which he holds before his face in an attempt to avoid recognition by the eye of equity.'[4]

1 See e g *Moore v Moore* (1971) 16 DLR (3d) 174 at 183 ('a device intended to defeat the rightful claims of the [transferor's] wife').
2 [1962] 1 WLR 832.
3 The company was a private £100 company, whose directors were the transferor himself and a clerk employed by his solicitors.
4 [1962] 1 WLR 832 at 836.

Transfer expressly subject to unprotected rights

12.122 If a transfer of title is expressly made subject to an unprotected minor interest, the court may, in certain circumstances, impose a constructive trust upon a transferee who later claims an unencumbered legal estate.[1] Here the element of 'fraud' comprises the transferee's deliberate disregard of the express terms on which the bargain between transferor and transferee was allowed to take effect.[2] There is, however, a limiting factor. A constructive trust can be imposed only if the court is satisfied that the conscience of the transferee is affected.[3] As Sir Christopher Slade indicated in *Lloyd v Dugdale*,[4] in determining 'whether or not the conscience of the new estate owner is affected ... the crucially important question is whether he has undertaken a new obligation, not otherwise existing, to give effect to the relevant encumbrance or prior interest.' The existence of this new level or dimension of self-imposed obligation is not demonstrated by the mere fact that the transferee is aware of unprotected rights[5] or that the transferor stipulated that the transfer should be 'subject to' specified incumbrances or pre-existing interests.[6] The incantation of a 'subject to' formula neither converts unenforceable rights into binding interests in land[7] nor connotes that it is 'fraudulent' for the transferee to repudiate the rights in question.[8] Something more is required before the court can impose a constructive trust to give effect to the unprotected minor interest.[9] This additional component, which fastens definitively upon the conscience of the transferee, usually arises in one or other of two overlapping kinds of circumstance.

1 *Lyus v Prowsa Developments Ltd* [1982] 1 WLR 1044 at 1053F–G **[paras 10.73, 12.123]**. It has even been suggested that such a stipulation may be enforceable as an *express* trust (see *Bahr v Nicolay* (*No 2*) (1988) 164 CLR 604 at 618–619 per Mason CJ and Dawson J).
2 See *Bahr v Nicolay* (*No 2*) (1988) 164 CLR 604 at 654 per Brennan J.
3 **[Para 10.65]**.
4 [2002] 2 P & CR 167 at [52(3)]. See [2002] Conv 584 (M Dixon).
5 See *Chattey v Farndale Holdings Inc* (1998) 75 P & CR 298 at 317; *Oertel v Hordern* (1902) 2 SR (Eq) 37 at 47 per Simpson CJ in Eq; *Munro v Stuart* (1924) 41 SR 203(n) at 205–206; *Goff v The Albury Soldier, Sailors & Airmen's Club Ltd* (1995) 6 BPR 14029 at 14037.
6 As Fox LJ pointed out in *Ashburn Anstalt v Arnold* [1989] Ch 1 at 26A, the use of a 'subject to' formula in a transfer may even 'be at least as consistent with an intention to protect the grantor against claims by the grantee as an intention to impose an obligation on the grantee.'

See similarly *Melbury Road Properties 1995 Ltd v Kreidi* [1999] 3 EGLR 108 at 110F; *Lloyd v Dugdale* [2002] 2 P & CR 167 at [52(1)] per Sir Christopher Slade; *Jamino v Whitehall Investments Pty Ltd* (1986) 4 BPR 9210 at 9216 per Powell J; *Chan Yiu Tong v Wellmake Investments Ltd* (1996) 1 HKC 528 at 533C per Godfrey JA.

7   It is possible that, in relation to contractual commitments entered into on or after 11 May 2000, a transferee's promise to take title 'subject to' otherwise unprotected rights may be enforceable by the incumbrancer by way of injunction, specific performance or otherwise (see Contracts (Rights of Third Parties) Act 1999, s 1(1)–(2)). Much depends on whether such an undertaking can be construed as 'purporting to confer a benefit' on the incumbrancer (s 1(1)(b)). The historic impulse of English law is, however, to treat this kind of contractual commitment as explicable merely as providing contractual immunity for the transferor rather than as an adjustment of the rights or liabilities of others (see e g *Lyus v Prowsa Developments Ltd* [1982] 1 WLR 1044 at 1051F–G; *Ashburn Anstalt v Arnold* [1989] Ch 1 at 26A).

8   See *Ashburn Anstalt v Arnold* [1989] Ch 1 at 25H–26B per Fox LJ ('The words "subject to" will, of course, impose notice. But notice is not enough to impose on somebody an obligation to give effect to a contract into which he did not enter'). See likewise *Melbury Road Properties 1995 Ltd v Kreidi* [1999] 3 EGLR 108 at 109K.

9   'The principles of equity cannot be used to defeat the statutory provisions; they can be used only to prevent those provisions from being misused as an instrument of fraud' (*Chan Yiu Tong v Wellmake Investments Ltd* (1996) 1 HKC 528 at 533C, 534E per Godfrey JA (Court of Appeal of Hong Kong)).

Positive stipulation by the transferee

12.123   An undertaking by a transferee to take title 'subject to' unprotected minor interests may generate a constructive trust if the undertaking can be construed as a 'positive stipulation'[1] or 'special promise'[2] by the transferee to give effect to such interests. The added significance of such a stipulation is precisely to highlight the fact that the parties had 'the express object of conferring new rights on the [incumbrancers] which they would not otherwise have enjoyed.'[3] Thus, for instance, in *Lyus v Prowsa Developments Ltd*[4] Dillon J imposed a constructive trust on the transferee of an uncompleted housing development who reneged on a 'positive stipulation' under which he had agreed to honour the contractual rights of a purchaser who had already paid his deposit.[5]

1   For reference to the terminology of 'positive stipulation', see e g *Lyus v Prowsa Developments Ltd* [1982] 1 WLR 1044 at 1054G–H; *Chan Yiu Tong v Wellmake Investments Ltd* (1996) 1 HKC 528 at 533C.

2   *Melbury Road Properties 1995 Ltd v Kreidi* [1999] 3 EGLR 108 at 110G.

3   *Chan Yiu Tong v Wellmake Investments Ltd* (1996) 1 HKC 528 at 533C per Godfrey JA ('It is quite clearly not fraud for a purchaser to rely on his statutory rights except in the special case where ... he has engaged himself to give effect to the rights which, but for that engagement, he would have been entitled to assert were rights not binding on him'). For cases in which claims of fraud failed precisely for want of any positive agreement to give effect to unprotected rights, see *Melbury Road Properties 1995 Ltd v Kreidi* [1999] 3 EGLR 108 at 110G; *Carvita Holdings Pty Ltd v Mitsubishi Bank of Australia Ltd* (1993) 6 BPR 13327 at 13329 per McLelland CJ in Eq; *Uechtritz v Watson* (1993) 6 BPR 13582 at 13586.

4   [1982] 1 WLR 1044 at 1054G–H [**para 10.73**].

5   The imposition of a constructive trust in these circumstances has since been approved by the Court of Appeal (see *Ashburn Anstalt v Arnold* [1989] Ch 1 at 24G–25A per Fox LJ; *Chattey v Farndale Holdings Inc* (1998) 75 P & CR 298 at 316 per Morritt LJ).

Ancillary circumstances binding on conscience

12.124 An undertaking to take title 'subject to' unprotected minor interests may also give rise to a constructive trust in the transferee where the undertaking is coupled with ancillary circumstances which clearly impinge on his conscience. Thus, for example, as the Court of Appeal indicated in *Ashburn Anstalt v Arnold*,[1] an unprotected interest may be regarded as binding a transferee of title where the relevant transfer was induced, at lower than market value, by the transferee's agreement to take title expressly subject to the entitlement in question. In effect, such circumstances justify the inference of a positive undertaking by the transferee that he would honour the unprotected rights,[2] not least since his failure to do so would expose the transferor to a liability in damages to the unprotected incumbrancer.[3] Here, again, a constructive trust arises in the exercise of the court's *in personam* jurisdiction to counteract unconscionable conduct.

1   [1989] Ch 1 at 23D–H. See [1988] Conv 201 (M P Thompson); (1988) 51 MLR 226 (J Hill); (1988) 104 LQR 175 (P Sparkes). The Court of Appeal's observations were strictly obiter **[para 7.115]**.
2   *Lloyd v Dugdale* [2002] 2 P & CR 167 at [52(5)] per Sir Christopher Slade.
3   *Ashburn Anstalt v Arnold* [1989] Ch 1 at 23G–H per Fox LJ.

Collateral representation

12.125 'Fraud' is likewise present where the transfer of a registered title has been induced by the transferee's express collateral representation that he would respect the unprotected rights of a third party. 'Fraud' may thus be found where, prior to the transfer, the transferee indicated to the transferor either verbally or in writing that he would not disturb the rights of the unprotected incumbrancer.[1] In *Loke Yew v Port Swettenham Rubber Co Ltd*,[2] for instance, the Privy Council had no doubt that a vitiating element of fraud would be present if the transferee later repudiated the undertaking.[3] If the purchaser's representation in fact induces in the vendor 'a false sense of security as to the purchaser's intention',[4] it would be fraudulent for the purchaser later to act inconsistently with its terms.[5] In such cases the purchaser is liable to be fixed with a constructive trust in favour of the incumbrancer.[6]

1   See *Stiles v Tod Mountain Development Ltd* (1992) 88 DLR (4th) 735 at 750.
2   [1913] AC 491 at 502–504.
3   One of the lesser ironies of legal history is the fact that Loke Yew, the unprotected incumbrancer, was not the vulnerable private citizen one might perhaps have supposed. Owning hugely valuable brothel businesses and opium import duty franchises, he controlled virtually every immoral enterprise in Selangor. It was said of him in 1896 that '[i]f he were crippled financially the revenues of the state would suffer serious loss' (see J G Butcher, 'The Demise of the Revenue Farm System in the Federated Malay States' (1983) 17 Modern Asian Studies 387 at 399). He petitioned in 1893 against the Women and Girls Protection Enactment on the ground that state regulation of his brothels would diminish the rents payable 'to no slight injury to Your Petitioner'. Thus it was that the man who later came to be known as the 'Carnegie of Malaya' helped to set the legal bench-mark of 'fraud'. See J G Butcher, *Revenue, Morality, and the Gambling Farms in the Federated Malay States* (1988).

4   *Holt, Renfrew & Co Ltd v Henry Singer Ltd* (1982) 135 DLR (3d) 391 at 408.

5   Here a finding of 'fraud' is closely allied to the doctrine of estoppel by representation [**para 10.168**], and rests on clear proof of a causal link between the representation and the transfer (see e g *Holt, Renfrew & Co Ltd v Henry Singer Ltd* (1982) 135 DLR (3d) 391 at 410, 421–422).

6   *Bahr v Nicolay (No 2)* (1988) 164 CLR 604 at 638 per Wilson and Toohey JJ.

Acquiescence in the exercise of unprotected rights

12.126   If a transferee not merely knows of the existence of unprotected rights in the land transferred, but positively acquiesces in their continued exercise after the date of transfer, it may constitute a species of 'fraud' if the transferee subsequently claims to have taken title free of these rights.[1]

1   See e g *Maurice Demers Transport Ltd v Fountain Tire Distributors (Edmonton) Ltd* (1974) 42 DLR (3d) 412 at 420–422; *Gough v Kiddeys Korner Ltd* [1976] BCL 62.

Post-registration acknowledgement of unprotected rights

12.127   In the present context the boundaries of 'fraud' are probably wide enough to attach equitable consequence to certain kinds of acknowledgement, made by the registered transferee *after* the date of his registration, that he is bound by unprotected rights created by his transferor in favour of a third party prior to the transfer.[1] In *Bahr v Nicolay (No 2)*[2] an owner of land, A, transferred title to B, the latter having contracted to reconvey the land later to A. B subsequently transferred the title to C pursuant to a contractual undertaking between B and C in which C acknowledged the existence of the repurchase agreement between A and B. Some time after the registration of C's title, C confirmed the repurchase clause in a written communication to A and recognised that C would honour its terms when A sought to exercise his rights. C later repudiated the repurchase clause as not having been protected by entry in the register. The High Court of Australia held that C was bound, by either an express[3] or a constructive[4] trust, to give effect to A's unprotected interest. Whilst C's agreement to take title subject to A's rights might have been enough to fix C with liability on more conventional grounds,[5] at least some members of the High Court considered it crucial that, almost immediately after taking the registered title, C had sent A written confirmation of his entitlement.[6] In this way C had 'burdened his own title' with rights which could not now in conscience be disavowed.[7]

1   See *CN and NA Davies Ltd v Laughton* [1997] 3 NZLR 705 at 711 (NZ Court of Appeal); *Bank of South Australia Ltd v Ferguson* (1998) 192 CLR 248 at [9] (High Court of Australia). Compare *Old & Campbell Ltd v Liverpool Victoria Friendly Society* [1982] QB 133 (Note) at 159A [**para 12.282**]. If there were evidence of detrimental reliance by the unprotected incumbrancer on this undertaking, there would, of course, be an even plainer argument based on estoppel.

2   (1988) 164 CLR 604.

3   (1988) 164 CLR 604 at 618–619 per Mason CJ and Dawson J.

4   (1988) 164 CLR 604 at 638–639 per Wilson and Toohey JJ, 654–655 per Brennan J.

5　The trial judge found that C had 'bought with the knowledge that they were bound by the terms of the Agreement' ((1988) 164 CLR 604 at 632).

6　(1988) 164 CLR 604 at 633–634 per Wilson and Toohey JJ.

7　(1988) 164 CLR 604 at 653 per Brennan J [**para 12.228**]. See also *Stiles v Tod Mountain Development Ltd* (1992) 88 DLR (4th) 735 at 746–747.

Purchase by a fiduciary agent

12.128　A further case of 'fraud' is present where a fiduciary agent purchases land on behalf of his principal, but procures the registration of title in the name of an associate who knows of the agent's fiduciary status. Here the associate cannot properly claim, pursuant to the provisions of the Land Registration Act 2002, to take the registered title free of the principal's unprotected equitable interest in the land.[1]

1　*Du Boulay v Raggett* (1989) 58 P & CR 138 at 153–154. See also *Loke Yew v Port Swettenham Rubber Co Ltd* [1913] AC 491 at 504; *Bahr v Nicolay* (*No 2*) (1988) 164 CLR 604 at 614, 654.

INTERESTS WHOSE PRIORITY IS 'PROTECTED' BY VIRTUE OF 'OVERRIDING STATUS'

12.129　Under the special priority rule of the Land Registration Act 2002, a registered disposition of a registered estate takes effect subject to certain unregistered interests which are specified to 'override' the disposition.[1] The disponee is automatically bound by these interests even though, by definition, they never appear in any register of title[2] and even though the disponee may have no actual knowledge of their existence.[3] Almost all the sub-categories of interest which enjoy this overriding status are currently detailed in Schedule 3 of the Land Registration Act 2002.[4]

1　LRA 2002, s 29(1), (2)(a)(ii) [**para 12.76**].

2　See LRA 2002, ss 29(3), 30(3); Law Com No 271 (2001), paras 5.12, 8.95.

3　See *Williams & Glyn's Bank Ltd v Boland* [1981] AC 487 at 506B per Lord Wilberforce.

4　An exceptional sub-category of overriding interest, the 'public-private partnership lease' (arising out of arrangements for the running of the London underground railway) is referred to in LRA 2002, s 90(5).

Function of the overriding interest

12.130　In English law disponees of registered estates have long taken their titles subject to the potential burden of an extensive range of unregistered rights.[1] These overriding interests comprise a number of entitlements which have been singled out either as having sufficient social importance or as involving such conveyancing difficulty as to merit a protection which derives not from the force of the register but from the force of statute. Substantial guidance on the operation of overriding interests pursuant to the Land Registration Act 2002 can be derived from the case law generated by its immediate predecessor, the Land Registration Act 1925.

1　See Land Transfer Act 1875, s 18; Land Transfer Act 1897, Sch 1; LRA 1925, s 70(1).

Conveyancing background of overriding interests

12.131   The rights which are rendered automatically binding as overriding interests relate principally to matters which, in unregistered conveyancing, are not normally included in title deeds or revealed by abstracts of title.[1] Since such matters are not generally disclosed by investigation of the documentary title, they are matters in respect of which it becomes impossible to compile a trustworthy record in any register of title.[2] As to these interests, the onus rests on persons dealing with a registered estate to seek information outside the register in the same manner as would persons dealing with an unregistered title. The disponee of a registered title must therefore discover the presence of overriding interests through a physical inspection of the land itself and by resort to other customary sources of information (eg the register of local land charges maintained by every local authority[3]).

1   See C F Brickdale and W R Sheldon, *The Land Transfer Acts, 1875 and 1897* (2nd edn by C F Brickdale, London 1905), pp 17–18.
2   *Lloyds Bank Plc v Rosset* [1989] Ch 350 at 370H per Nicholls LJ.
3   [**Para 12.7**].

Binding effect of overriding interests

12.132   For the most part the sub-categories of overriding interest comprise rights (eg short legal leases) which have no other means of protection within the registered land scheme of things and whose automatically binding status merely replicates the unregistered land rule that legal rights bind the world.[1] It is also true that many overriding interests are such as would be immediately apparent to any purchaser on a physical inspection of the land.[2] But certainly, in the case of at least some sub-categories of overriding interest,[3] overriding status is accorded to rights which could have been – but have not been – protected by the entry of a 'notice' in the register.[4]

1   [**Paras 2.109, 12.143**]. See *Abbey National Building Society v Cann* [1991] 1 AC 56 at 87F–G per Lord Oliver of Aylmerton.
2   See *Lloyds Bank Plc v Rosset* [1989] Ch 350 at 394G per Mustill LJ, 402B per Purchas LJ.
3   See eg LRA 2002, Sch 3, paras 1–2.
4   [**Para 12.84**]. See *Ferrishurst Ltd v Wallcite Ltd* [1999] Ch 355 at 370E per Robert Walker LJ.

Problematic nature of overriding interests

12.133   The principal difficulty posed by overriding interests is that their existence fundamentally distorts the mirror image of the register: the register can no longer be relied upon as a comprehensive record of the totality of interests affecting registered estates.[1] During the closing years of the 20th century overriding interests came to be seen not only as a 'major obstacle' to the achievement of the 'ultimate goal of total registration' of land rights,[2] but also as incompatible with the on-line investigation of title which was envisaged as the principal benefit of any future regime of electronic conveyancing.[3] Although the Law Commission appeared at one stage to favour the virtual abolition of overriding interests,[4] this category of rights has survived the enactment of the Land Registration Act 2002[5] and continues to play an important role in the law of registered estates. It was nevertheless a conscious objective of the 2002 Act to cut back the scope of overriding interests 'so far as possible.'[6]

1   See *Overseas Investment Ltd v Simcobuild Construction Ltd and Swansea CC* (1995) 70 P & CR 322 at 327 per Peter Gibson LJ.
2   Law Com No 271 (2001), paras 3.58, 8.1 (see also paras 2.24, 3.16). It also became increasingly apparent that, in spite of the original (and vaguely comforting) theory that overriding interests were normally apparent upon physical inspection of the land, several kinds of overriding interest could remain undiscovered even by a purchaser who carefully inspected both land and title (see *Kling v Keston Properties Ltd* (1983) 49 P & CR 212 at 222 per Vinelott J). The case law of the 1970s and 1980s tended, moreover, to increase rather than diminish the number of rights which claimed overriding status (see eg *Williams & Glyn's Bank Ltd v Boland* [1981] AC 487 **[para 12.205]**).
3   **[Paras 2.110, 12.104]**. The ultimate irony was (and still is) that the disponee who is ensnared by a virtually undiscoverable overriding interest is not entitled to any statutory compensation if the register is altered to give effect to this interest **[para 12.258]**.
4   See Law Commission, *Property Law: Second Report on Land Registration (Provisional)* (November 1984), para 9 ('our approach in this Report is robust: it is to close the cavernous crack in the mirror principle').
5   There has always been some apprehension that the wholesale abolition of overriding interests without compensation could violate ECHR Protocol No 1, Art 1 **[para 2.29]** (see Law Com No 254 (1998), paras 4.27–4.30; Law Com No 271 (2001), para 8.82).
6   Law Com No 271, para 2.25. This aim was also reflected in the increasingly restrictive view of overriding interests adopted in the contemporary case law. See eg *Overseas Investment Ltd v Simcobuild Construction Ltd and Swansea CC* (1995) 70 P & CR 322 at 327 per Peter Gibson LJ (the courts 'should … not be astute to give a wide meaning to any item constituting an overriding interest'); *Secretary of State for the Environment, Transport and the Regions v Baylis (Gloucester) Ltd* (2000) 80 P & CR 324 at 338 per Deputy Judge Kim Lewison QC ('it is necessary to keep to a minimum the number of matters which may defeat the title of a registered proprietor').

Modern curtailment of the scope of overriding interests

12.134   In 2001 the Law Commission indicated that, in its view, the 'guiding principle' underlying the overriding interest provisions of the new Land Registration Act was the proposition that interests should have overriding status only 'where protection against buyers is needed, but where it is neither reasonable to expect nor sensible to require any entry on the register.'[1] Consistently with this principle the role of overriding interests under the Land Registration Act 2002 has been restricted in a number of ways.

1   Law Com No 271 (2001), para 8.87 (see likewise paras 2.25, 8.6). See also Law Com No 158 (1987), para 2.64; Law Com No 254 (1998), para 5.61.

Abolition or phasing out of certain overriding interests

12.135   With prospective effect the 2002 Act withdraws overriding status from certain sub-categories of overriding entitlement previously permitted by the

Land Registration Act 1925. Prime examples include equitable easements and equitable profits *à prendre*,[1] the rights of persons in adverse possession[2] and the proprietary rights of non-resident landlords.[3] The Act also provides that some existing, but unusual, overriding interests will lose their overriding status after 13 October 2013,[4] although prior to this cut-off point they are capable of permanent protection, without payment of any fee, by entry in the Land Register.[5]

1   Formerly protected by LRA 1925, s 70(1)(a) [**para 12.237**].
2   Rights 'acquired or in course of being acquired under the Limitation Acts' were formerly protected by LRA 1925, s 70(1)(f) (see e g *Bridges v Mees* [1957] Ch 475 at 486–487 per Harman J; *Elements of Land Law* (3rd edn 2001), p 980). The Law Commission concluded that the 'unqualified overriding status of squatters' rights over-protects such rights.' The Commission thought that 'people would be astonished to discover that there was any possibility that a squatter who had long ago abandoned a piece of land could reappear and successfully claim it from an innocent purchaser' (Law Com No 254 (1998), para 5.48). See also Law Com No 271 (2001), paras 8.76–8.78.
3   Formerly protected by LRA 1925, s 70(1)(g) [**para 12.147**].
4   See, for instance, the ten-year 'sunset clause' thereby imposed on franchises, manorial rights, certain crown rents, non-statutory rights relating to embankments or sea or river walls, and rights to payment in lieu of tithe (LRA 2002, s 117(1), Sch 3, paras 10–14). See Law Com No 254 (1998), paras 4.33, 4.39; Law Com No 271 (2001), paras 8.2, 8.35–8.46.
5   LRA 2002, s 117(2). When coupled with this facility of register entry, the ten-year phase-out was thought unlikely to violate ECHR Protocol No 1, Art 1 (Law Com No 271 (2001), paras 8.81–8.89). A franchise is also capable of substantive registration under its own title number [**para 7.39**].

Incorporation of unregistered interests in the register

12.136   The Land Registration Act 2002 also provides various mechanisms for ensuring that, wherever possible, existing overriding interests are brought positively on to the register. At this point, of course, they cease to have overriding status[1] and become binding simply by virtue of their entry in the register. For this purpose the registrar has power, of his own motion, to enter potentially overriding interests in the register by 'notice'.[2] A further impetus towards incorporation in the register is provided by the statutory requirement that all applicants for registration of a registrable disposition must disclose to the registrar information relating to any unregistered interests within their 'actual knowledge' which affect the registered estate and fall within Schedule 3 of the 2002 Act.[3] The registrar then has discretion to enter a 'notice' in the register in respect of these 'disclosable overriding interests'.[4]

1   See LRA 2002, ss 29(3), 30(3); Law Com No 271 (2001), para 8.95.
2   LRA 2002, s 37(1). The registrar must normally give prior notice to the registered proprietor and any other appropriate person (LRR 2003, r 89).
3   LRA 2002, s 71(b); LRR 2003, r 57(1), (4). The duty of disclosure has no application to public rights, local land charges, leases with one year or less to run and interests which cannot be protected by 'notice' (LRR 2003, r 57(2)).
4   LRR 2003, r 57(5).

Impact of electronic conveyancing

12.137 Ultimately the shift towards electronic conveyancing will have the consequence of diminishing (if not eliminating) the function of the overriding interest. The scheme of the Land Registration Act 2002 already makes it increasingly difficult to grant or dispose of land interests 'off the register'.[1] Under the forthcoming regime of electronic conveyancing,[2] entry in the register will become integral to the very process of creating interests in registered land. Few interests will be capable of creation except as part of a simultaneous process of register entry: most interests will actually have no existence off the register. In these circumstances the concept of an unregistered, and therefore overriding, entitlement in land may soon seem a contradiction in terms.

1   **[Paras 2.118, 12.4]**. See Law Com No 254 (1998), paras 4.35, 5.62; Law Com No 271 (2001), paras 8.2, 8.53, 8.74.
2   **[Paras 2.117, 12.69]**.

PRINCIPAL SUB-CATEGORIES OF OVERRIDING INTEREST

12.138 As indicated by Schedule 3 of the Land Registration Act 2002, the principal sub-categories of unregistered interest which 'override' registered dispositions of a registered estate are the following:
−   legal leases granted for a term of not more than seven years[1]
−   proprietary interests of persons in actual occupation of the land[2]
−   certain legal easements and profits *à prendre*[3] and
−   local land charges.[4]

1   **[Paras 12.143–12.145]**.
2   **[Paras 12.146–12.236]**.
3   **[Paras 12.237–12.241]**.
4   **[Para 12.242]**.

Effective date of overriding interests

12.139 Under the 2002 Act most dispositions of a registered estate require to be completed by registration.[1] For reasons of administrative convenience, the date of registration is deemed to be the date of lodgment of the application for registration,[2] but this still means that a period of time – the so-called 'registration gap' – elapses between the date of *disposition* and the deemed date of *registration*. In advance of this registration the disponor, as the current registered proprietor, remains technically competent – however wrongful his actions may be – to create interests in the land adverse to his disponee.[3]

1   **[Paras 2.146, 7.58, 7.245, 12.81]**.
2   LRR 2003, s 74(b).
3   **[Paras 9.30, 12.81]**.

Danger of supervening overriding interests

12.140   Although interests which supervene during the registration gap cannot normally become enforceable against the disponee by means of the entry of a 'notice' in the disponor's register of title,[1] there was, under the old Land Registration Act of 1925, a real possibility that such interests could steal priority as 'overriding' interests. In *Abbey National Building Society v Cann*,[2] the House of Lords conceded, in an unhappy compromise, that the general date for determining the existence of overriding interests under the 1925 Act was the date of *registration* of the relevant disposition.[3] This construction clearly exposed the disponee to the risk[4] that overriding interests might arise some time following the date of disposition,[5] long after the disponee's inspection of land and title, in respect of which rights he had no realistic opportunity of discovery.[6] The Land Registration Act 2002 has, however, taken good care to ensure that such hazards can no longer affect the disponee of a registered title.

1   In most cases the disponee's priority search of the register gives him a 30 day period during which to apply for registration free from such entries [**para 12.50**].

2   [1991] 1 AC 56. See [1990] CLJ 397 (A J Oakley); [1991] Conv 116 (S Baughen), 155 (P F Smith).

3   [1991] 1 AC 56 at 87C per Lord Oliver of Aylmerton, 106C per Lord Jauncey of Tullichettle. In order to avoid 'conveyancing absurdity', the House of Lords held that the definitive date for ascertaining 'actual occupation' of land as the basis of an overriding claim was the date of *disposition* ([1991] 1 AC 56 at 83G, 88B–H per Lord Oliver of Aylmerton, 104H–105B, 106C–D per Lord Jauncey of Tullichettle). See likewise *Lloyds Bank Plc v Rosset* [1991] 1 AC 107 at 126D per Lord Bridge of Harwich.

4   That this risk was far from theoretical was demonstrated in *Barclays Bank Plc v Zaroovabli* [1997] Ch 321 at 329D–F (Rent Act regulated tenancy created during 'registration gap' overrode unregistered charge to bank pursuant to LRA 1925, s 70(1)(k)). See [1997] CLJ 496 (D G Barnsley).

5   Indeed, as Lord Oliver of Aylmerton observed in *Abbey National Building Society v Cann* [1991] 1 AC 56 at 85C, overriding interests can come into being at any time and some may arise without any volition on the part of the registered proprietor (eg a prescriptive easement or profit *à prendre* or rights derived from adverse possession).

6   See *Abbey National Building Society v Cann* [1991] 1 AC 56 at 75F–G per Lord Bridge of Harwich, 83G–84A, 88B per Lord Oliver of Aylmerton, 105A–B per Lord Jauncey of Tullichettle; *Lloyds Bank Plc v Rosset* [1989] Ch 350 at 372G–373B per Nicholls LJ.

Preconditions of priority for modern 'overriding' entitlements

12.141   Under the Land Registration Act 2002, two preconditions must be met before any entitlement falling within Schedule 3 can 'override' a registered disposition.[1] *First*, the 2002 Act expressly provides that no interest can claim overriding status unless it subsisted 'immediately before the disposition' and affected the estate which is the subject of that disposition.[2] On this basis no interest created during the 'registration gap' between the dates of disposition and registration can possibly be said to 'override'. *Second*, no interest can 'override' a registered disposition unless its priority is 'protected at the time of registration' as an unregistered interest falling within one or more of the paragraphs of Schedule 3. This requirement entails, quite logically, that no unregistered entitlement can 'override' a registered disposition unless it remains subsisting at the date of registration.

1   LRA 2002, s 29(1).
2   In the case of an overriding interest based on 'actual occupation' of land, it has been made clear that the claimant's occupation of the land must have been 'obvious ... at the time of the disposition' (LRA 2002, Sch 3, para 2(c)(i) **[para 12.177]**).

Duties to disclose overriding interests

12.142   Some overriding interests are readily ascertainable from documentary sources. The remaining entitlements, if not voluntarily disclosed by a disponor, can usually be discovered by a physical inspection of the land concerned, coupled with an inquiry directed to those persons who are in actual occupation. In addition to his statutory obligation to inform the registrar of 'disclosable overriding interests',[1] the disponor has a general duty to disclose the existence of such interests to any disponee and, in default of such disclosure, the latter may subsequently have valuable contractual rights of recovery against the disponor.[2]

1   **[Para 12.136]**.
2   See *Ferrishurst Ltd v Wallcite Ltd* [1999] Ch 355 at 371D per Robert Walker LJ.

LEGAL LEASES FOR A TERM NOT EXCEEDING SEVEN YEARS

12.143   Schedule 3, para 1 of the Land Registration Act 2002 confers overriding protection on most leasehold estates granted for a term not exceeding seven years from the date of grant.[1] This special protection for short-term leases is generally justified as safeguarding the interests of vulnerable tenants[2] and is, in some form or other, a standard feature of most Torrens statutes.[3] Moreover, it seems correct in principle that, at least until the arrival of electronic conveyancing, registers of title should not be cluttered by the recordation of leasehold arrangements of relatively short duration.[4]

1   LRA 2002, s 29(1), (2)(a)(ii) (see formerly LRA 1925, s 70(1)(k)). See also Law Com No 254 (1998), paras 5.94, 5.118. The protection of the overriding interest extends to certain protected and statutory tenancies under the Rent Act (see *Woolwich Building Society v Dickman* [1996] 3 All ER 204 at 214; *Barclays Bank Plc v Zaroovabli* [1997] Ch 321 at 329A–F; *Prince v Robinson and Robinson* (1998) 76 P & CR D2 at D3–D4).
2   'Many short tenancies are informal and where they relate to dwelling-houses and flats are often granted without the tenant being legally represented. We cannot think that it would be desirable that a monthly tenant or even a tenant of a flat for, say, three years, who has not yet moved in, would have to register notice of this tenancy against the reversionary title at the Land Registry to protect himself against a purchaser of the reversion ... Where there is a conflict we think that the law should incline in favour of the tenant' (Law Commission, *Property Law: Land Registration* (*Second Paper*) (Published Working Paper No 37, July 1971), para 89).
3   The duration of the qualifying term under Torrens legislation varies from jurisdiction to jurisdiction. Typical provisions give overriding effect, usually subject to a requirement of

actual possession, to a term not exceeding three years (see eg Real Property Act 1877 (Queensland), s 11; Real Property Act 1900 (New South Wales), s 42(1)(d); Land Titles Act 1980 (Tasmania), s 40(3)(d); Land Titles Act (Alberta), RSA 1980, c L-5, s 65(1)(d)). For other examples, see Real Property Act 1886 (South Australia), ss 69, 119 (term not exceeding one year); Transfer of Land Act 1893 (Western Australia), s 68 (term not exceeding five years). See also Transfer of Land Act 1958 (Victoria), s 42(2)(e) (exception for leases generally).

4   Where a short lease has overriding status, the binding effect of the covenants contained in the lease is still governed by the ordinary rules **[para 14.241]** relating to the running of leasehold benefits and burdens (see Law Com No 158 (1987), para 2.49).

The seven-year threshold

12.144   The overriding status accorded to most leasehold terms of not more than seven years is a corollary of the legislative requirement that leasehold estates with an unexpired term of more than *seven* years should be substantively registered at Land Registry.[1] It also reflects the fact that short leases are otherwise unprotectable under the regime of the Land Registration Act 2002[2] (save that leases granted for a term of more than *three* years can now be entered by 'notice' in a superior registered title[3]). There are, however, certain exceptional cases where even terms which are not in excess of seven years are excluded from overriding status. Thus no overriding quality can attach to any lease which (irrespective of its duration) is actually *required* to be the subject of first registration under the 2002 Act.[4] Likewise excluded from overriding status are certain kinds of lease granted out of a registered estate where the grant constituted a registrable disposition and was therefore required to be completed by registration.[5]

1   **[Paras 2.149, 7.228]**. Leases which, on 13 October 2003, were overriding interests pursuant to LRA 1925, s 70(1)(k) continue to override (LRA 2002, s 134, Sch 12, para 12).
2   **[Paras 2.175, 7.247]**.
3   LRA 2002, ss 32, 33(b).
4   LRA 2002, Sch 3, para 1(a). This exception catches a reversionary lease granted out of unregistered land to take effect in possession more than three months after the date of grant, together with any lease granted out of an unregistered legal estate under the 'right to buy' or 'preserved right to buy' provisions of the Housing Act 1985 (see HA 1985, ss 154(7), 171G, Sch 9A, para 3 **[para 7.237]**).
5   LRA 2002, Sch 3, para 1(b). The excluded categories embrace reversionary leases granted to take effect in possession more than three months after the date of grant; discontinuous leases; leases granted under the 'right to buy' or 'preserved right to buy' provisions of the Housing Act 1985; and leases of a franchise or manor (see LRA 2002, s 27(2)(b)(ii)–(v), (c) **[para 7.240]**).

Protection for legal leases only

12.145   Protection under Schedule 3, para 1 does not require any showing that the tenant is in actual occupation of the land,[1] but one important limitation on this head of overriding entitlement is said to follow from the technical connotation of the term 'grant' as used in para 1. Overriding status attaches to *legal* leases only.[2] An equitable lease is not protected under para 1, although it may still be protected (pursuant to Schedule 3, para 2) against disponees of the reversionary estate provided that the tenant was in 'actual occupation' of the land at the date of the disposition.[3]

1   See Law Com No 158 (1987), paras 2.50–2.51.
2   *City Permanent Building Society v Miller* [1952] Ch 840 at 853. Compare, however, *Halifax Building Society v Fanimi* [1997] EWCA Civ 1461, where Peter Gibson LJ rejected a lease as an overriding interest within LRA 1925, s 70(1)(k), but not, curiously, on the ground that it was merely equitable.
3   **[Paras 12.146–12.160]**.

UNREGISTERED INTERESTS OF PERSONS IN ACTUAL OCCUPATION

12.146   Without doubt the most difficult and controversial of the unregistered interests which 'override' registered dispositions are those which comprise the rights of occupiers of land. Subject to certain provisos,[1] Schedule 3, para 2 of the Land Registration Act 2002 confirms the overriding status of any 'interest belonging at the time of the disposition to a person in actual occupation, so far as relating to land of which he is in actual occupation …'[2]

1   **[Paras 12.173–12.179]**.
2   This provision has, significantly, no exact equivalent in the Torrens legislation of Australia, Canada and New Zealand, although most jurisdictions give overriding status to various kinds of unregistered short lease.

Rationale of Schedule 3, para 2

12.147   This important exception to the indefeasibility of registered titles provides yet another illustration of the primacy traditionally accorded to factual possession in English law.[1] The class of overriding interests confirmed in Schedule 3, para 2 replicates, in large part, the protection previously given, by the 'notorious' section 70(1)(g) of the Land Registration Act 1925,[2] to 'the rights of every person in actual occupation of the land … save where enquiry is made of such person and the rights are not disclosed.'[3] This venerable statutory formula was intended to benefit persons who held unprotected interests (generally of limited scope and duration or created under informal trusts or estoppels), where the sheer fact of actual occupation would normally have signalled to prudent purchasers both the possible existence of unrecorded interests affecting the land and the necessity of further inquiry.[4]

1   **[Para 3.11]**. See *Taylor v Stibbert* (1794) 2 Ves 437 at 440, 30 ER 713 at 714 per Lord Loughborough LC; *Hodgson v Marks* [1971] Ch 892 at 932C–D per Russell LJ ('a person in occupation is protected in his rights by that occupation'). For the earliest use of the phrase 'actual occupation', see *Barnhart v Greenshields* (1853) 9 Moo PCC 18 at 34, 14 ER 204 at 210. The phrase first appeared in statutory form in the list of overriding interests contained in Law of Property Act 1922, Sch 16, Part I, para 5(3)(i), amending Land Transfer Act 1875, s 18.
2   See Law Com No 254 (1998), para 5.56.
3   See Louise Tee, 'The Rights of Every Person in Actual Occupation: An Enquiry into Section 70(1)(g) of the Land Registration Act 1925' [1998] CLJ 328.
4   Law Com No 158 (1987), para 2.6; Law Com No 254 (1998), paras 4.4, 5.61. See also

Ferrishurst Ltd v Wallcite Ltd [1999] Ch 355 at 372C per Robert Walker LJ. The provision of statutory protection for occupiers probably caused fewer problems when, consonantly with earlier conveyancing practice, completion usually took place at the premises which were the subject of the instant transaction.

Protection amidst the welter of registration

12.148   The purpose of the modern formula in Schedule 3, para 2 is likewise to preserve the entitlements of any person who happens to have a physical presence on the ground at the date of disposition of a registered estate and for whom it may not be feasible, or even possible, to safeguard his rights by register entry.[1] The paragraph aims to strike a social balance between the integrity of the register and the legitimate claims of actual occupiers of registered land.[2] A person in 'actual occupation' of the land is protected from 'having his rights lost in the welter of registration' and may simply 'stay there and do nothing.'[3] No one 'can buy the land over his head and thereby take away or diminish his rights.'[4] An onus of inquiry is placed firmly upon the disponee and is ignored by the latter at his peril.[5] In determining whether the occupier's entitlement 'overrides', it is irrelevant whether the disponee had actual notice of the rights concerned.[6] The strong underlying principle is that the simple fact of visible occupation should have alerted the disponee to the possibility of adverse entitlement.

1   The Law Commission came to accept that the law 'pragmatically recognises that some rights can be created informally' and that to require their positive protection by entry on the register 'would defeat the sound policy that underlies that recognition' (Law Com No 254 (1998), para 5.61).
2   **[Para 2.109]**.
3   *Strand Securities Ltd v Caswell* [1965] Ch 958 at 979G per Lord Denning MR. See also *Lloyds Bank Plc v Rosset* [1989] Ch 350 at 402B per Purchas LJ.
4   *Strand Securities Ltd v Caswell* [1965] Ch 958 at 979G.
5   See *Ferrishurst Ltd v Wallcite Ltd* [1999] Ch 355 at 372C per Robert Walker LJ. There is an added dimension of hazard for the disponee. A successful claim of overriding entitlement on the part of even one of a number of multiple occupiers disables the disponee from asserting his rights against any of the occupiers (see eg *Kemmis v Kemmis* [1988] 1 WLR 1307 at 1325D–F, 1336A). Nor can any rent be recovered from occupiers who shelter behind an overriding interest claimed by one of their number (see *Kemmis*, supra at 1325E–F, 1336A–B).
6   *Singh v Sandhu* (Unreported, Court of Appeal, 4 May 1995) per Balcombe LJ.

Reaction against overriding protection for actual occupiers

12.149   In recent decades it has become clear that the overriding rights of actual occupiers comprise an 'intermediate, or hybrid, class' of interest in registered land.[1] The scheme of the Land Registration Act 1925 plainly allowed for an area of overlap between various categories of entitlement,[2] with the consequence that certain kinds of right which could and should have been entered in the register were paradoxically, in default of such protection, preserved as overriding interests.[3] During the latter part of the 20th century this duplication of protection increasingly came to be viewed as 'disquieting'.[4] The overriding status accorded to the rights of actual occupiers appeared to confer an unmerited reward upon the negligent and to inflict an uncompensable hazard upon disponees of title. This concern was intensified partly because overriding interests detracted from the reliability of the 'mirror image' of the register and partly because overriding interests generated no right to any statutory indemnity for a disponee trapped by their existence.[5] Pressure accordingly developed for a drastic curtailment of such over-solicitous and one-sided protection.

1　*Williams & Glyn's Bank Ltd v Boland* [1981] AC 487 at 503B per Lord Wilberforce.
2　See *Williams & Glyn's Bank Ltd v Boland* [1981] AC 487 at 508A per Lord Wilberforce; *City of London Building Society v Flegg* [1988] AC 54 at 89G–90B, 90G–H per Lord Oliver of Aylmerton.
3　It is 'by now uncontroversial ... that an interest may be protected as an overriding interest even though it might have been protected by other means' (*Ferrishurst Ltd v Wallcite Ltd* [1999] Ch 355 at 370E per Robert Walker LJ). See likewise *Williams & Glyn's Bank Ltd v Boland* [1981] AC 487 at 512A per Lord Scarman.
4　See *Kling v Keston Properties Ltd* (1983) 49 P & CR 212 at 222 per Vinelott J ('It is disquieting that the system of land registration ... should be so framed that a person acquiring an interest in registered land may find his interest subject to [a right] which has not been registered and notwithstanding that there is no person other than the vendor in apparent occupation of the property and that careful inspection and enquiry has failed to reveal anything which might give the purchaser any reason to suspect that someone other than the vendor had any interests in or rights over the property').
5　**[Para 12.258]**.

The compromise of the Land Registration Act 2002

12.150　A certain fluidity or potential overlap between the classes of registered land interest remains a feature of the Land Registration Act 2002. The Act retains the overriding status accorded to the rights of persons in actual occupation, but nevertheless strives, in important respects, to cut back the parameters within which the unregistered rights of occupiers can now impinge on disponees of registered estates. There is an underlying expectation that, in time, potentially overriding entitlements will be increasingly drawn on to the Land Register by positive entry.[1] There is, furthermore, a certain confidence that the synchronicity of disposition and registration promised by electronic conveyancing will finally eliminate the possibility that unregistered rights can exist at all in registered land. Within the comparatively near future, registration will become an 'essential part of the process by which rights over registered land are expressly created.'[2] When this occurs, actual occupation will then protect only those rights which are capable of creation without the need for registration and the ambit of overriding interests, existing by definition 'off the register', will be greatly limited.[3]

1　**[Para 12.136]**.
2　Law Com No 254 (1998), para 5.62.
3　Law Com No 254 (1998), para 4.35.

THE FORMULA OF SCHEDULE 3, PARA 2 OF THE LAND REGISTRATION ACT 2002

12.151 The operation of Schedule 3, para 2 of the Land Registration Act 2002 collapses into a virtually mathematical formula:

'Interest'	+	'actual occupation'	—	'inquiry'	=	Interest which 'overrides'

12.152 In other words, an interest in land, if coupled with actual occupation on the part of its owner, becomes an interest which, minus inquiry, 'overrides' dispositions of the registered estate.

Constituent elements of the formula

12.153 On closer examination Schedule 3, para 2 reveals itself to be a complex verbal structure, which consists of a lead proposition (ie overriding status attaches to 'an interest belonging ... to a person in actual occupation'), qualified by a number of exceptional circumstances in which this overriding protection becomes lost or unavailable. Thus the interest of an actual occupier is declared to 'override' a registered disposition of a registered estate *except* in cases where:
—   the actual occupier has unreasonably failed, on inquiry, to disclose his own entitlement[1] or
—   the relevant occupation was neither reasonably discoverable by nor actually known to the disponee.[2]

1   LRA 2002, Sch 3, para 2(b) **[para 12.173]**.
2   LRA 2002, Sch 3, para 2(c) **[para 12.177]**.

Occupation is merely a trigger

12.154 It is intrinsic to the scheme of Schedule 3, para 2 that the 'interest' claimed by an occupier as the basis of an overriding interest is quite distinct from the fact of his occupation.[1] What becomes binding under Schedule 3, para 2 is not necessarily any occupancy on the part of the claimant[2] but rather the specific proprietary entitlement which he happens to own.[3] Occupation is merely the trigger which activates the statutory protection of the occupier's rights – whatever these rights may be.[4] A successful claim under Schedule 3, para 2 does not imply that the claimant is necessarily entitled to enforce some right of *occupation* against the disponee of the registered title. In certain cases the claimant may indeed have such a right, but in other instances the 'interest' which 'overrides' is entirely unrelated to occupancy of the land. The 'interest' rendered overriding by Schedule 3, para 2 may comprise, for example, an unpaid vendor's lien[5] or an option to purchase a freehold or leasehold estate[6] or a right of pre-emption.[7]

1   See *Ferrishurst Ltd v Wallcite Ltd* [1999] Ch 355 at 372C–D per Robert Walker LJ.
2   'Actual occupation is not an interest in itself' (*City of London Building Society v Flegg* [1988] AC 54 at 74D per Lord Templeman).
3   The capacity in which a person occupies (eg as a tenant) is not necessarily indicative of the right which he claims. Thus in *Webb v Pollmount* [1966] Ch 584 a tenant's occupation of a dwelling-house sent out no 'obvious message' that he also had an option to purchase the reversion' (see *Ferrishurst Ltd v Wallcite Ltd* [1999] Ch 355 at 367F–G).
4   See the view adopted, in relation to LRA 1925, s 70(1)(g), by Lord Oliver of Aylmerton in *Abbey National Building Society v Cann* [1991] 1 AC 56 at 87E.
5   See *London and Cheshire Insurance Co Ltd v Laplagrene Property Co Ltd* [1971] Ch 499 at 502H; *Ferrishurst Ltd v Wallcite Ltd* [1999] Ch 355 at 372C–D.
6   *Webb v Pollmount* [1966] Ch 584 at 603C–D.
7   [**Para 12.161**]. See *Kling v Keston Properties Ltd* (1983) 49 P & CR 212 at 215–219.

Continuing enforceability of the overriding interest

12.155   Once overriding interest protection has been triggered by the fact of 'actual occupation', the 'interest' protected under Schedule 3, para 2 remains enforceable against the registered disponee even if the owner of the overriding interest ceases to occupy the land following the registration of the relevant disposition.[1] The subsequent effectiveness of the overriding interest against that disponee is not, in other words, dependent on continued long-term actual occupation.[2]

1   *London and Cheshire Insurance Co Ltd v Laplagrene Property Co Ltd* [1971] Ch 499 at 505A–B, 509E–F.
2   The conditions of Schedule 3, para 2 must, of course, be satisfied de novo in the event of any further registered disposition.

Overriding protection is confined to the area actually occupied

12.156   The Land Registration Act 2002 clarifies beyond doubt that overriding protection is accorded to an occupier's interest only in so far as it relates to 'land of which he is in actual occupation.'[1] Thus an occupier of one flat in a block who holds an option to purchase the entire block cannot claim that, by reason of his actual occupation of part of the land, this option 'overrides' a subsequent registered disposition to someone else of the whole block of flats.[2] The option, in so far as it affects the entire block, must be protected by the entry of a 'notice' in the register of title to the whole block.

1   LRA 2002, Sch 3, para 2. See Law Com No 254 (1998), paras 5.70, 5.121; Law Com No 271 (2001), paras 8.55–8.58.
2   This effectively reverses the rule applied under the Land Registration Act 1925 in *Ferrishurst Ltd v Wallcite Ltd* [1999] Ch 355 at 372D–F per Robert Walker LJ (who declined to follow on this point *Ashburn Anstalt v Arnold* [1989] Ch 1 at 28F–G per Fox LJ). See [1999] CLJ 483 (L Tee); (2000) 63 MLR 113 (J Hill); [1999] Conv 144 (S Pascoe).

12.157   We must now analyse more carefully the three elements which are vital to the formula in Sch 3, para 2: the nature of the 'interests' protected; the role of 'inquiry'; and the meaning of 'actual occupation'.

RANGE OF 'INTERESTS' PROTECTED BY SCHEDULE 3, PARA 2

12.158   Extensive though the sweep of Schedule 3, para 2 may appear to be, there are certain implicit limitations on the range of interests which come within its scope.

Overriding interests must be recognisably proprietary in character

12.159   Although Schedule 3, para 2 seems to attach an overriding quality to any 'interest belonging ... to a person in actual occupation', this statutory protection applies only to entitlements of a recognisably proprietary character.[1] This restriction flows from the statutory requirement that the 'interest' which overrides a registered disposition must be one 'affecting the estate' of the disponor.[2] Exactly similar wording in the Land Registration Act 1925[3] caused the courts to confine the overriding rights of occupiers under that legislation to proprietary rights as already defined under the general law.[4] It is inevitable that courts today will likewise resist any suggestion that the Land Registration Act 2002 accords overriding status to 'any right, of howsoever a personal character, which a person in occupation may have.'[5] Thus, for example, actual occupation cannot protect the rights of a bare licensee since, by common agreement, his entitlement falls far short of the required proprietary threshold.[6] As Lord Wilberforce emphasised in *National Provincial Bank Ltd v Ainsworth*,[7] any contrary approach would effect 'a substantive change in real property law' since, in the conventional view, purely personal rights in respect of land never have the potential to bind third parties.[8]

1   See *Guckian v Brennan* [1981] IR 478 at 486, where Gannon J pointed out that the Irish equivalent 'does not create burdens: it merely classifies burdens which are created aliunde.' See also *City of London Building Society v Flegg* [1988] AC 54 at 88A–E per Lord Oliver of Aylmerton.
2   LRA 2002, s 29(1).
3   See LRA 1925, ss 20(1), 23(1).
4   See e g *National Provincial Bank Ltd v Hastings Car Mart Ltd* [1964] Ch 665 at 696, where Russell LJ thought that LRA 1925, s 70(1)(g) dealt throughout only with 'rights in reference to land which have the quality of being capable of enduring through different ownerships of the land, according to normal conceptions of title to real property.' In the House of Lords in the same case, Lord Wilberforce likewise emphasised that the 'whole frame of section 70 ... shows that it is made against a background of interests or rights whose nature and whose transmissible character is known, or ascertainable, aliunde, ie, under other statutes or under the common law' (*National Provincial Bank Ltd v Ainsworth* [1965] AC 1175 at 1261F). Such statements involve, of course, a certain circularity in so far as they define proprietary status in terms of transmissibility of burden to third parties [**para 2.55**].
5   See, in relation to LRA 1925, s 70(1)(g), *Ashburn Anstalt v Arnold* [1989] Ch 1 at 8F–G per Fox LJ; *Canadian Imperial Bank of Commerce v Bello* (1992) 64 P & CR 48 at 51 per Dillon LJ; *Nationwide Anglia Building Society v Ahmed* (1995) 70 P & CR 381 at 387–388 per Aldous LJ; *Habermann v Koehler* (1996) 73 P & CR 515 at 519–520 per Evans LJ.
6   See e g *Strand Securities Ltd v Caswell* [1965] Ch 958 at 980C–D (rent-free licence of flat enjoyed by step-daughter of non-resident leaseholder). See also Law Com No 158 (1987), para 2.56; *Kemmis v Kemmis* [1988] 1 WLR 1307 at 1335B–D.
7   [1965] AC 1175 at 1261C–D.
8   Likewise, although more controversially, a tenant's contractual right to recover a security

deposit at the end of his tenancy has been held to generate no overriding interest against the landlord's successor, even though the tenant remained at all times in 'actual occupation' (*Eden Estates Ltd v Longman* (Unreported, 19 May 1980); [1982] Conv 239 (P H Kenny)). See also *Hua Chiao Commercial Bank Ltd v Chiaphua Industries Ltd* [1987] AC 99 at 112D–113C [**para 14.262**]; *NLS Pty Ltd v Hughes* (1966) 120 CLR 583 at 588–590.

Proprietary interests

12.160   The following rights are generally considered to be sufficiently propri-etary in nature to constitute 'interests' which, if coupled with actual occupa-tion, can override registered dispositions:

- a legal lease or tenancy,[1]
- an equitable lease or tenancy[2]
- a beneficial interest under a bare trust[3]
- a beneficial interest under some other trust of land[4]
- an estate contract (including an option to purchase a legal estate)[5]
- an unpaid vendor's lien[6]
- a Rent Act entitlement as a protected or statutory tenant[7]
- a tenant's right to recoup repair costs from future rent owed to his landlord[8] and
- a right to rectification of a disposition.[9]

1   *Ashburn Anstalt v Arnold* [1989] Ch 1 at 27D; *Canadian Imperial Bank of Commerce v Bello* (1992) 64 P & CR 48 at 51–54.

2   *Grace Rymer Investments Ltd v Waite* [1958] Ch 831 at 849–851; *Greaves Organisation Ltd v Stanhope Gate Property Co Ltd* (1973) 228 EG 725 at 729.

3   *Hodgson v Marks* [1971] Ch 892 at 934F–G [**para 12.178**]; *Collings v Lee* [2001] 2 All ER 332 at 336c–d (All ER Rev 2001, p 253 (P J Clarke)).

4   *Williams & Glyn's Bank Ltd v Boland* [1981] AC 487 at 508A–B. See also *Winkworth v Edward Baron Development Co Ltd* (1986) 52 P & CR 67 at 78; *Kemmis v Kemmis* [1988] 1 WLR 1307 at 1325D, 1330F, 1335G.

5   *Webb v Pollmount Ltd* [1966] Ch 584 at 603C–D; *Habermann v Koehler* (1996) 73 P & CR 515 at 520, 523; *Ferrishurst Ltd v Wallcite Ltd* [1999] Ch 355 at 367F–G. There may be some question whether Schedule 3, para 2 can catch an oral option which is unenforceable save by proprietary estoppel (*Habermann v Koehler*, supra at 523 per Peter Gibson LJ). Compare, however, *Lloyds Bank plc v Carrick* [1996] 4 All ER 630 at 637f–j, 642d–e, where the Court of Appeal was prepared to concede the proprietary status of an oral agreement enforceable only on the basis of part performance [**paras 9.40, 10.87, 12.210**].

6   *London and Cheshire Insurance Co Ltd v Laplagrene Property Co Ltd* [1971] Ch 499 at 502H; *Ferrishurst Ltd v Wallcite Ltd* [1999] Ch 355 at 367G–H.

7   *National Provincial Bank Ltd v Hastings Car Mart Ltd* [1964] Ch 665 at 689 per Lord Den-ning MR. In *Barclays Bank plc v Zaroovabli* [1997] Ch 321 at 328G–329F, Scott V-C regarded a statutory tenancy as 'overriding' only if it grew out of a protected (ie contractual) tenancy which, when granted, was itself potentially 'overriding'. An additional difficulty is caused by the fact that the degree of residential occupation sufficient to sustain a statutory tenancy under the Rent Act [**para 14.318**] may not always amount to the 'actual occupation' required for the purpose of the Land Registration Act (see Law Com No 158 (1987), para 2.15 (n 71)). On the nature of a statutory tenancy, see [**para 14.317**].

8   *Lee-Parker v Izzett* [1971] 1 WLR 1688 at 1693F–G [**para 14.60**].

9   *Blacklocks v J B Developments (Godalming) Ltd* [1982] Ch 183 at 196D–E; *Nurdin & Peacock plc v D B Ramsden & Co Ltd* [1999] 1 EGLR 119 at 126E; *Holaw (470) Ltd v Stockton*

Estates Ltd (2001) 81 P & CR 404 at [69]; *Malory Enterprises Ltd v Cheshire Homes Ltd* [2002] Ch 216 at [81] per Arden LJ ((2003) 119 LQR 31 (D Sheehan)).

Statutory clarification

12.161   Albeit by use of somewhat indirect language, the Land Registration Act 2002 has clarified that, in relation to registered estates, three other kinds of entitlement are sufficiently proprietary to rank as potential overriding interests. A right of pre-emption created on or after 13 October 2003 is now declared to have effect 'from the time of creation as an interest capable of binding successors in title.'[1] Furthermore, all equities by estoppel and mere equities are accorded a similar effect 'from the time the equity arises.'[2]

1   LRA 2002, s 115 [**para 9.86**]. The overriding status of rights of pre-emption had already been recognised even prior to 2003 (see *Kling v Keston Properties Ltd* (1983) 49 P & CR 212 at 215–219; *Homsy v Murphy* (1997) 73 P & CR 26 at 35).
2   LRA 2002, s 116 [**para 10.216**]. This provision merely reflected a growing recognition of the overriding character of equities by estoppel (see e g *Birmingham Midshires Mortgage Services Ltd v Sabherwal* (2000) 80 P & CR 256 at 262–263 per Robert Walker LJ [**para 12.234**]).

Overriding interests must be intrinsically enforceable

12.162   It is an implicit precondition of overriding status pursuant to the Land Registration Act 2002 that, at the date of the relevant registrable disposition, the interest which is alleged to 'override' should be fully enforceable and undiminished by any estoppel, postponement or waiver (express or implied).[1] The operation of Schedule 3, para 2 cannot enhance or alter the intrinsic quality of the rights which comprise the overriding interest.[2] The effect of the provision is to render the pre-existing claims of occupiers no less – but also no more – enforceable after the disposition than they were before.

1   See e g *Woolwich Building Society v Plane* (Unreported, Court of Appeal, 25 September 1997) per Mummery LJ; *UCB Bank plc v Beasley and France* [1995] NPC 144 per Morritt LJ.
2   See *Abbey National Building Society v Cann* [1991] 1 AC 56 at 87E–H per Lord Oliver of Aylmerton, 95F per Lord Jauncey of Tullichettle.

Express postponement

12.163   The enforceability of an occupier's rights is obviously curtailed by any express agreement on his part, immediately before a registrable disposition, to concede priority to the competing rights of some other person.[1] It is, for instance, an almost invariable condition of any mortgage advance that all persons who enjoy joint occupation with the borrower must sign a document which postpones their rights (if any) to the title taken by the lender as chargee of the registered estate.[2] This express waiver of rights or consent to the transaction operates as an estoppel[3] and precludes any future claim of priority for the occupier over the chargee.[4]

1   See *Nationwide Anglia Building Society v Ahmed* (1995) 70 P & CR 381 at 390; *Le Foe v Le Foe and Woolwich Plc* [2001] 2 FLR 970 at [55].
2   See *Woolwich Building Society v Dickman* [1996] 3 All ER 204 at 206j.
3   In some relatively rare cases the rights of occupiers are irreducibly conferred by statute and cannot therefore be diminished or destroyed by private agreement. One instance is provided by the Rent Act protected tenancy [**para 14.314**], where no estoppel can abrogate the benefits of the statute (see *Welch v Nagy* [1950] 1 KB 455 at 460, 464; *Keen v Holland* [1984] 1 WLR 251 at 261D–F). The protected tenant is 'under the shelter of the Act, whether or not he so desires' (*Brown v Draper* [1944] KB 309 at 313), with the result that even an express consent to the postponement of the tenant's rights cannot take him outside the Rent Act or subordinate his tenancy to the interest taken by a later chargee of the registered title (see *Woolwich Building Society v Dickman* [1996] 3 All ER 204 at 214; [1997] CLJ 37 (L Tee); [1997] Conv 402 (J Morgan)).
4   See e g *Woolwich Building Society v Plane* (Unreported, Court of Appeal, 25 September 1997).

Implied postponement (or estoppel)

12.164   Schedule 3, para 2 cannot protect an occupier's interest against a disponee of the registered estate if the priority otherwise accorded the occupier's interest has been impliedly waived in advance of the relevant dealing.[1] In *Paddington Building Society v Mendelsohn*,[2] for instance, S purchased a registered title in his own name, the purchase money being provided partly by S's mother, M, and partly through a mortgage loan advanced by PBS to S alone. M was clearly a beneficial tenant in common behind an implied trust and she moved into joint occupation of the property with S and his girlfriend during the interim between the transfer of title and the registration of PBS's charge over the premises.

1   That this rule applies as much to a transfer as to a charge was confirmed in *Nightingale Mayfair Ltd v Mehta* (Unreported, Chancery Division, 21 December 1999).
2   (1985) 50 P & CR 244.

12.165   M later claimed that her beneficial interest, coupled with her actual occupation of the property, gave her an interest which overrode the charge executed by S in favour of PBS.[1] The Court of Appeal held, however, that since M had both known and intended at the date of purchase that there was to be a charge in favour of PBS, the 'only possible intention to impute to the parties' was an intention that M's rights were to be subject to those of PBS.[2] It followed that M, having impliedly conceded priority to PBS, no longer retained any interest adverse to PBS which was capable of overriding the latter's legal charge.[3] By virtue of her silent representation M was effectively estopped[4] from later advancing any claim to priority over PBS's security.[5] As Browne-Wilkinson LJ observed, '[i]f the rights of the person in actual occupation are not under the general law such as to give any priority over the holder of the registered estate, there is nothing in [the statute] which changes such rights into different and bigger rights.'[6]

1   *Mendelsohn* was decided several years before the House of Lords' ruling in *Abbey National Building Society v Cann* [1991] 1 AC 56, in the light of which M's assertion of an overriding interest would now be disallowed on the additional grounds that PBS's charge was an

'acquisition mortgage' [**para 12.217**] and M's 'actual occupation' did not pre-date the disposition of charge [**para 12.180**]. However, the principle demonstrated in *Mendelsohn*'s case remains applicable in respect of any rights claimed by a person who (for whatever reason) happens to be in occupation in advance of the relevant disposition date (e g in the context of a post-acquisition mortgage).

2   (1985) 50 P & CR 244 at 247. *Mendelsohn*'s case seems to convert the traditional responsibility of the purchaser to investigate potential equitable claims into an onus upon equitable owners to disclose their rights. For a similar approach in unregistered land, see *Bristol and West Building Society v Henning* [1985] 1 WLR 778 at 781G–782G. Compare the more restrictive application of estoppel doctrine in Canada (*Re Quesnel & District Credit Union and Smith* (1988) 45 DLR (4th) 386 at 399–400).

3   The approach adopted in *Mendelsohn*'s case received the implicit approval of the House of Lords in *Abbey National Building Society v Cann* [1991] 1 AC 56 at 82F–G, 89B, 94B–G per Lord Oliver of Aylmerton. See also *Nightingale Mayfair Ltd v Mehta* (Unreported, Chancery Division, 21 December 1999), where Blackburne J indicated that a claim of overriding beneficial entitlement would have been precluded by the conduct of a beneficial owner 'in requesting (or at the very least in not objecting to)' the relevant transfer of the registered title.

4   [**Para 10.168**].

5   No estoppel or implied concession of rights can arise where the beneficial co-owner has *no* prior knowledge of the relevant disposition (see *Lloyds Bank Plc v Rosset* [1991] 1 AC 107 at 127C per Lord Bridge of Harwich, [1989] Ch 350 at 387C–E per Nicholls LJ, 406B–C per Purchas LJ). See e g *Williams & Glyn's Bank Ltd v Boland* [1981] AC 487 [**para 12.204**].

6   (1985) 50 P & CR 244 at 248. See also *E S Schwab & Co Ltd v McCarthy* (1976) 31 P & CR 196 at 205; *City of London Building Society v Flegg* [1988] AC 54 at 88A–B per Lord Oliver of Aylmerton.

STATUTORY EXCLUSION FROM THE CATEGORY OF INTERESTS WHICH 'OVERRIDE'

12.166   It is entirely consistent with conventional principle that Schedule 3, para 2 of the Land Registration Act 2002 should afford no overriding protection to rights which, although related to land in some broad sense, are classified either by statute or by the general law of property as merely personal or contractual in character. Amongst the interests specifically excluded by statute from overriding status are the following.

Matrimonial home rights under the Family Law Act 1996

12.167   The demarcation of overriding interests pursuant to the Land Registration Act first became controversial some 40 years ago when the courts were required to rule on the registered land impact of the so-called 'deserted wife's equity'.[1] In *National Provincial Bank Ltd v Ainsworth*,[2] the House of Lords finally rejected the idea that this 'equity' was anything more than a purely personal right effective against the other spouse.[3] In view of its nature and origin, the wife's 'equity' did not rank as having proprietary character under the general law and could not therefore 'override' her husband's disposition of charge to the bank. This analysis of occupation rights in the matrimonial arena was promptly carried over into the legislation which replaced the ill-fated doctrine of the deserted wife's equity.[4] This legislation, now consolidated in the

Family Law Act 1996, confers statutory occupation rights on specified categories of spouse,[5] but provides quite explicitly that these 'matrimonial home rights' can never 'override' a registered disposition even though the person entitled to them is in 'actual occupation' of the family home.[6]

1   [**Para 12.92**].
2   [1965] AC 1175.
3   See the contrary view expressed by Lord Denning MR in the Court of Appeal (sub nom *National Provincial Bank Ltd v Hastings Car Mart Ltd* [1964] Ch 665 at 689).
4   See Matrimonial Homes Act 1967, s 2(7); Matrimonial Homes Act 1983, s 2(8)(b).
5   [**Para 12.93**].
6   Family Law Act 1996, s 31(10)(b) (as amended by LRA 2002, s 133, Sch 11, para 34(1)–(2)). Matrimonial home rights thus require protection by the entry of a 'notice' in the appropriate register of title [**para 12.93**]. Nor can overriding status be claimed in respect of a spouse's right to set aside a prejudicial transaction aimed at defeating financial relief on divorce (see *Kemmis v Kemmis* [1988] 1 WLR 1307 at 1329F–G, 1332C).

Equitable rights of settled land beneficiaries

12.168   The equitable rights of beneficiaries arising under the Settled Land Act 1925[1] are expressly excluded from the field of overriding interests in land.[2] There is therefore no possibility that such entitlement, even if coupled with actual occupation on the part of a beneficiary of a settlement, can ever claim overriding status pursuant to Schedule 3, para 2 of the Land Registration Act 2002.

1   [**Para 9.206**].
2   LRA 2002, Sch 3, para 2(a).

Rights conferred by an access order under the Access to Neighbouring Land Act 1992

12.169   The Access to Neighbouring Land Act 1992 confers on the court certain powers to make an 'access order' permitting unconsented entry upon adjoining or adjacent land for the purpose of carrying out basic preservation works on the entrant's own land.[1] This order may be protected by the entry of a 'notice' on the register of title of the burdened land,[2] but the rights conferred by the access order are specifically precluded from constituting an overriding interest pursuant to Schedule 3, para 2 of the Land Registration Act 2002.[3]

1   ANLA 1992, s 1(1)(a), (2) [**para 8.136**].
2   LRA 2002, s 32. See ANLA 1992, s 5(1)–(2).
3   ANLA 1992, s 5(5) (as amended by LRA 2002, s 133, Sch 11, para 26(4)).

Rights arising under notices relating to leasehold enfranchisement

12.170   No overriding interest may ever be claimed to have arisen from a notice served by a qualifying tenant in support of his right to acquire a freehold or extended leasehold estate under the Leasehold Reform Act 1967.[1] A similar statutory exclusion relates to rights to collective enfranchisement or the acquisition of a new lease which become the subject of a notice under the Leasehold Reform, Housing and Urban Development Act 1993.[2] In all such cases the relevant entitlement is instead protectable by the entry of a 'notice' in the Land Register 'as if it were an estate contract.'[3]

1   Leasehold Reform Act 1967, s 5(5) (as amended by LRA 2002, s 133, Sch 11, para 8(2)(a)). On the operation of the 1967 Act, see Chapter 7 [**paras 7.328–7.337**].
2   LRH&UDA 1993, s 97(1) (as amended by LRA 2002, s 133, Sch 11, para 30(3)(a)). See *Melbury Road Properties 1995 Ltd v Kreidi* [1999] 3 EGLR 108 at 109D. On the operation of the 1993 Act, see [**para 7.338**].
3   Leasehold Reform Act 1967, s 5(5) (as amended by LRA 2002, s 133, Sch 11, para 8(2)(b)); LRH&UDA 1993, s 97(1) (as amended by LRA 2002, s 133, Sch 11, para 30(3)(b)).

Preserved right to buy

12.171   On the fulfilment of certain conditions a qualifying tenant in the public rented sector is entitled, under the Housing Act 1985, to acquire the freehold of, or a long leasehold estate in, the home occupied by him.[1] In the event of any disposal of this property to a private sector landlord, the tenant's original 'right to buy' continues to exist as a 'preserved right to buy' only if it has been protected by the entry of a 'notice' in the charges register of the new landlord's title.[2] If the 'preserved right to buy' is not duly protected in this way, it becomes ineffective against the new private sector landlord and is statutorily excluded from the category of overriding interests 'notwithstanding that the qualifying person is in actual occupation of the land.'[3]

1   [**Para 7.348**].
2   The registrar must enter a 'notice' in respect of the rights of qualifying tenants (see HA 1985, Sch 9A, para 4(2)(a)).
3   HA 1985, Sch 9A, para 6(1).

Right to call for an 'overriding lease'

12.172   In certain circumstances a former tenant has a statutory right to apply to the landlord for the grant of what, in the present context, is misleadingly entitled an 'overriding lease'.[1] The right to call for such a lease cannot constitute an overriding interest within the meaning of Schedule 3, para 2 of the Land Registration Act 2002, although it may be protected 'as if it were an estate contract' by the entry of a 'notice' in the relevant register of title.[2]

1   [**Para 14.236**].
2   Landlord and Tenant (Covenants) Act 1995, s 20(6).

NO PROTECTION FOR UNDISCLOSED RIGHTS

12.173   Schedule 3, para 2(b) of the Land Registration Act 2002 withholds overriding status from the interest of any actual occupier 'of whom inquiry was made before the disposition and who failed to disclose the right when he could reasonably have been expected to do so.'[1] In this respect, the statute aims for a balance between the respective responsibilities of an intending disponee of a registered estate and any actual occupier of the land concerned.

1   Compare LRA 1925, s 70(1)(g) (conferring overriding status on the actual occupier 'save where enquiry is made of such person and the rights are not disclosed').

Onus on disponee

12.174   An onus is effectively placed on the disponee or his agent[1] to ensure that each occupier (other than the disponor himself) is asked 'what rights he or she has in the land.'[2] This inquiry must be made 'before the disposition'[3] and is not satisfactorily achieved by mere interrogation of the disponor himself.[4] In order to take the land free of overriding interests, the disponee must address his inquiry to all persons who happen to be in actual occupation and whose rights might otherwise 'override'.[5] For this purpose inquiry can properly be directed, in most cases, to a solicitor acting on behalf of an actual occupier,[6] but it would be insufficient, for instance, to make inquiry of a hall porter in a block of flats as to the potential rights of occupiers of those flats.[7] The burden of inquiry resting on the intending disponee is often therefore quite substantial,[8] but where an actual occupier does disclose some existing entitlement, the disponee is well placed to demand a waiver of that entitlement as a precondition of going ahead with the transaction.[9] If, however, the disponee completes the disposition without obtaining such a waiver – or if the disponee makes no inquiry at all of those in actual occupation – the entitlement of any occupier simply 'overrides' in terms of the Act.[10]

1   See [1980] Conv 161. Inquiry made by a purchaser's solicitor can be taken to have been made on behalf also of the purchaser's mortgagee where the responses, as is normal practice, are communicated to that mortgagee (see *UCB Bank plc v Beasley and France* [1995] NPC 144 per Morritt LJ).
2   See *Winkworth v Edward Baron Development Co Ltd* (1986) 52 P & CR 67 at 77 per Nourse LJ, who added that it was not sufficient merely to ask all occupiers to confirm in writing that they hold 'as bare licensees and not by virtue of any tenancy or lease'. The Court of Appeal's ruling in *Winkworth* was later reversed by the House of Lords on different grounds ([1986] 1 WLR 1512).
3   LRA 2002, Sch 3, para 2(b). A disponee of a registered estate is well advised to have written proof of inquiry (see [1980] Conv 361 (J Martin)).
4   '[R]eliance on the untrue ipse dixit of the vendor will not suffice' (*Hodgson v Marks* [1971] Ch 892 at 932D per Russell LJ). In *Hodgson v Marks* the transferee (M) of the registered estate was bound by the overriding interest of the occupier (H) precisely because he had directed his inquiries not to H, but to the transferor (E) [**para 12.178**].
5   See *Habermann v Koehler* (1996) 73 P & CR 515 at 522 per Peter Gibson LJ.
6   See *Winkworth v Edward Baron Development Co Ltd* (1986) 52 P & CR 67 at 77 per Nourse LJ.
7   The porter is the agent of the landlord rather than any of the tenants and has no authority to make (or withhold) any relevant reply (see *Kling v Keston Properties Ltd* (1983) 49 P & CR 212 at 220).
8   The onus can be particularly significant in cases of multiple occupation of a family home [**para 12.200**]. See also *Ferrishurst Ltd v Wallcite Ltd* [1999] Ch 355 at 371D, where Robert

Walker LJ acknowledged that a purchaser of, say, the entire Barbican estate would undoubtedly be advised by his solicitors to 'make inquiries of every person who appeared to be in actual occupation of any part of the estate.'

9   [**Para 12.163**].
10   See *Lloyds Bank Plc v Rosset* [1989] Ch 350 at 396G–H per Mustill LJ.

Onus on actual occupier

12.175   Appropriate inquiry having been made, an onus rests on the actual occupier to disclose any proprietary right belonging to him if he 'could reasonably have been expected to do so.' An omission to make reasonable disclosure operates, in effect, as a form of estoppel.[1] The priority accorded to an overriding interest is obviously unavailable to any person who, upon inquiry, fails to reveal (or even conceals) the existence of his rights.[2] Moreover, the statutory reference to circumstances in which the occupier 'could reasonably have been expected' to disclose his interest is probably broad enough to catch circumstances such as those of *Paddington Building Society v Mendelsohn*,[3] where an actual occupier looked on in silence whilst a chargee took a mortgage security over a registered estate in which the chargee was unaware the occupier was beneficially entitled.

1   Law Com No 271 (2001), para 8.60. An estoppel of this kind is probably raised nowadays if an actual occupier fails to respond to a communication from an intending disponee to the effect that it will be assumed, in the absence of reply, that the occupier claims no adverse interest (see J Russell, (1981) 32 NILQ 3 at 21).
2   *Holaw (470) Ltd v Stockton Estates Ltd* (2001) 81 P & CR 404 at [73]. See e g *UCB Bank plc v Beasley and France* [1995] NPC 144, where overriding status was denied to an unpaid vendor's lien on the ground of its non-disclosure in pre-contract enquiries made of the vendor.
3   (1985) 50 P & CR 244 [**para 12.164**].

MEANING OF 'ACTUAL OCCUPATION' WITHIN SCHEDULE 3, PARA 2

12.176   Schedule 3, para 2 of the Land Registration Act 2002 confers protection on the interest of any person in 'actual occupation' of land which is the subject of a registered disposition.[1] The term 'actual occupation' has a long history in the context of land registration legislation.[2] Although this critical expression has never been statutorily defined, some guidance as to its meaning emerges from the case law under the Land Registration Act 1925.[3] It is clear, for instance, that the acts which constitute 'actual occupation' vary in accordance with the nature of the premises concerned.[4] More than one person may be in 'actual occupation' at the same time.[5] The presence pleaded as 'actual occupation' need not be, in any sense, adverse to that of the registered owner.[6] Perhaps most significant, certain constraints upon the nature of 'actual occupation' are imposed by the internal logic of the Land Registration Act itself.

1   In a rare case (e g involving an unpaid vendor's lien) this person may be the transferor herself (see *UCB Bank plc v Beasley and France* [1995] NPC 144).
2   See LPA 1922, Sch 16, Part I, para 5(3)(i).

3   In *Lloyds Bank Plc v Rosset* [1989] Ch 350 at 393H, Mustill LJ pointed out that no conclusive guidance could be obtained from the interpretation accorded in other branches of the law to the term 'occupation'.

4   See *Lloyds Bank Plc v Rosset* [1989] Ch 350 at 394F per Mustill LJ ('the acts which constitute actual occupation of a dwelling house, a garage or woodland cannot all be the same'). In *Rosset's* case there was general agreement in the Court of Appeal that differing standards of 'actual occupation' might be relevant to an ordinary dwelling house fit for habitation and a semi-derelict property ([1989] Ch 350 at 376H–377A, 398G–H).

5   *Lloyds Bank Plc v Rosset* [1989] Ch 350 at 394D per Mustill LJ; *Lloyd v Dugdale* [2002] 2 P & CR 167 at [43] per Sir Christopher Slade.

6   *Williams & Glyn's Bank Ltd v Boland* [1981] AC 487 at 505B per Lord Wilberforce, echoing the view of Ormrod LJ in the Court of Appeal ([1979] Ch 312 at 339A).

'Actual occupation' must be reasonably discoverable

12.177   It was once thought that, for the purposes of the Land Registration Act, the phrase 'actual occupation' stood to be construed as a matter of sheer physical fact.[1] As Lord Denning MR remarked in *Williams & Glyn's Bank Ltd v Boland*,[2] actual occupation is 'matter of fact, not matter of law'.[3] This approach was upheld by the House of Lords in the same case, Lord Wilberforce observing that the phrase comprised 'ordinary words of plain English'.[4] Lord Scarman noted, moreover, that the Land Registration Act had 'substituted a plain factual situation for the uncertainties of notice, actual or constructive.'[5] In later years, however, it became increasingly evident that this simplistic approach was unsustainable.[6] The internal logic of overriding interests requires that relevant occupation be not merely factual, but also reasonably discoverable, since otherwise the process of inquiry and disclosure envisaged by the statute becomes futile. The disponee must be placed in a position where he can identify potential holders of overriding entitlements and make meaningful inquiry of them. In consequence, the courts moved steadily towards the view under the 1925 Act that 'actual occupation' must be not only 'actual' but also 'apparent' or 'patent', ie such as to 'put a person inspecting the land on notice that there was some person in occupation.'[7] This more purposive understanding of the role played by 'actual occupation' in the ordering of registered land priorities is now formalised in the Land Registration Act 2002.[8] The 2002 Act provides that an actual occupier cannot claim that his interest 'overrides' in any circumstances where his occupation 'would not have been obvious on a reasonably careful inspection of the land at the time of the disposition.'[9] The only exception to this requirement of reasonable discoverability arises where the disponee of the land had 'actual knowledge' of the occupier's interest at the time of the disposition.[10] The legislative intention is quite plainly to protect disponees for value where the fact of occupation is neither subjectively known to them nor readily ascertainable.[11]

1   See *Hodgson v Marks* [1971] Ch 892 at 932C–D, where the Court of Appeal overturned the view of Ungoed-Thomas J (at 916C–H) that 'actual occupation' connoted 'actual and apparent occupation ... occupation by act recognisable as such.'

2   [1979] Ch 312 at 332E.

3   See also *Lloyds Bank Plc v Rosset* [1989] Ch 350 at 397C, 398H per Mustill LJ (posing the simple question whether the claimant of an overriding interest was '"there" on the property').

4   [1981] AC 487 at 504F.

5   [1981] AC 487 at 511E–F.

6   As Lord Oliver of Aylmerton pointed out in *Abbey National Building Society v Cann* [1991] 1 AC 56 at 93D, 'even plain English may contain a variety of shades of meaning'.

7   *Malory Enterprises Ltd v Cheshire Homes Ltd* [2002] Ch 216 at [81] per Arden LJ. The courts increasingly referred to the parallel function of overriding interest protection and the doctrine of constructive notice in unregistered conveyancing (see e g *National Provincial Bank Ltd v Ainsworth* [1965] AC 1175 at 1260G–1261A per Lord Wilberforce; *Hodgson v Marks* [1971] Ch 892 at 915C per Ungoed-Thomas J; *Lloyds Bank Plc v Rosset* [1989] Ch 350 at 397A–C per Mustill LJ, 403B per Purchas LJ; *Ferrishurst Ltd v Wallcite Ltd* [1999] Ch 355 at 372C per Robert Walker LJ).

8   See Law Com No 254 (1998), paras 5.75, 5.121; Law Com No 271 (2001), paras 8.61–8.62. See also L Tee, [1998] CLJ 328 at 347–348.

9   LRA 2002, Sch 3, para 2(c)(i).

10   LRA 2002, Sch 3, para 2(c)(ii).

11   See, however, N Jackson, 'Title by Registration and Concealed Overriding Interests: The Cause and Effect of Antipathy to Documentary Proof' (2003) 119 LQR 660.

12.178   It is a moot point whether this restrictive approach to 'actual occupation' would today ensure the same outcome as was reached in the classic litigation in *Hodgson v Marks*.[1] Here an elderly registered proprietor, H, was persuaded by her lodger, E, to effect a voluntary transfer of her title into his name on the verbal understanding that H would remain the real owner.[2] H and E continued to live together in the house at all material times – both before and after the transfer. E later dishonestly transferred the legal estate to M, without the knowledge or concurrence of H, and then promptly died.

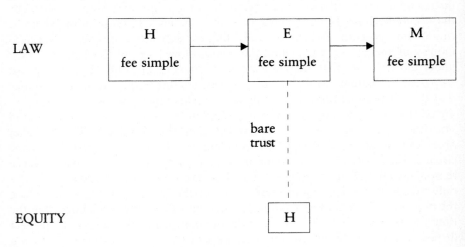

Fig. 38

1   [1971] Ch 892. See (1971) 35 Conv (NS) 225 (I Leeming); (1972) 88 LQR 14 (J L Barton); (1973) 36 MLR 25 (R H Maudsley).

2   There was evidence that H had come to regard E as a man of substance and therefore entrusted him with the management of her affairs.

12.179   The Court of Appeal held that, before his transfer to M, E had held the registered estate on an implied (or bare) trust for H (see *Fig.* 38).[1] The beneficial interest of H, as a person in 'actual occupation', therefore overrode the disposition to M (and also M's disposition of a legal charge to a building society). Although it was not at all clear how apparent H's presence on the land had been from the viewpoint of either M or his chargee,[2] the Court placed the onus of inquiry firmly on the disponees. Russell LJ declared that 'a wise purchaser or lender will take no risks' and that 'however wise he may be, [the disponee] may have no ready opportunity of finding out; but nevertheless the law will protect the occupier.'[3] Such sweeping propositions now require to be revised in the light of the Land Registration Act 2002.

1   It was found that H had not intended to part with the beneficial interest in the property and that the transfer to E brought about a trust of the legal estate in her favour ([1971] Ch 892 at 906D, 933C–G). H was not precluded from asserting the existence of this trust, since implied trusts are exempted from the requirements of writing or other formality normally imposed by LPA 1925, s 53(1) [**para 9.192**]. Compare, however, *Thwaites v Ryan* [1984] VR 65 at 93.
2   There was some evidence that M had seen H coming up the garden path on one occasion when he visited the property prior to the transfer and even that E had dishonestly attempted to implant in M's mind the impression that H was E's wife and had no beneficial interest in the land.
3   [1971] Ch 892 at 932D.

Date of relevant 'actual occupation'

12.180   The Land Registration Act 2002 also confirms a point which was a matter of some dispute in the earlier case law. In *Abbey National Building Society v Cann*,[1] the House of Lords held that a claim of overriding entitlement based on 'actual occupation' could succeed only where the claimant was already in 'actual occupation' of the land at the date of disposition of the registered estate.[2] The clear consequence of this ruling was to deny overriding effect to the interest of any person[3] who entered into occupation only during the 'registration gap' between the date of disposition (or completion of the transaction) and the deemed date of registration.[4] The *Cann* decision nevertheless made enormous 'conveyancing sense',[5] particularly in the context of dispositions of mortgage, in that it precluded the possibility that a chargee might be vulnerable to the claims of occupiers whose existence was wholly undetectable at the time of the advance of the loan money.[6] Relevant occupation must take a form and must subsist at a time which enables a disponee to make purposeful and 'fruitful' inquiry *before* he completes the transaction under which he takes his estate or interest.[7] Routine inquiries as to occupation at the disposition date would be rendered entirely futile if adverse rights could still emerge by reason of actual occupation supervening at any time prior to registration.[8] The conclusion reached in *Cann*'s case is now richly reinforced by the provision in the Land Registration Act 2002 that relevant occupation, for the purpose of any claim to overriding status, must have been 'obvious ... at the time of the disposition.'[9]

1   [1991] 1 AC 56 at 88C–H per Lord Oliver of Aylmerton, 104H–105B, 106C–D per

Lord Jauncey of Tullichettle. See likewise *Lloyds Bank Plc v Rosset* [1989] Ch 350 at 374A–C per Nicholls LJ, 397A–B, 398E per Mustill LJ, [1991] 1 AC 107 at 126D per Lord Bridge of Harwich.

2   Earlier case law had suggested the registration date as definitive (see eg *Re Boyle's Claim* [1961] 1 WLR 339 at 344–345 per Wilberforce J; *E S Schwab & Co Ltd v McCarthy* (1976) 31 P & CR 196 at 204; *Kling v Keston Properties Ltd* (1983) 49 P & CR 212 at 218). Compare, however, *Paddington Building Society v Mendelsohn* (1985) 50 P & CR 244 at 247; and see Law Com No 158 (1987), para 2.76.

3   See eg *Barclays Bank Plc v Zaroovabli* [1997] Ch 321 at 328H–329B (tenant assumed 'actual occupation' after date of disposition of mortgage charge).

4   See *Abbey National Building Society v Cann* [1991] 1 AC 56 at 76D per Lord Bridge of Harwich. See also *Lloyds Bank Plc v Rosset* [1989] Ch 350 at 374D–E per Nicholls LJ.

5   *Lloyds Bank Plc v Rosset* [1989] Ch 350 at 374A per Nicholls LJ.

6   See *Abbey National Building Society v Cann* [1991] 1 AC 56 at 88A–B per Lord Oliver of Aylmerton. If overriding rights could be set up during the 'registration gap', the chargee would already have become irretrievably committed to the mortgage transaction and the die would be cast (*Lloyds Bank Plc v Rosset* [1989] Ch 350 at 372G–373B per Nicholls LJ; *Abbey National Building Society v Cann* [1991] 1 AC 56 at 105B per Lord Jauncey of Tullichettle).

7   *Abbey National Building Society v Cann* [1991] 1 AC 56 at 88C–E per Lord Oliver of Aylmerton. See also *Lloyds Bank Plc v Rosset* [1989] Ch 350 at 374A–C per Nicholls LJ, 397A–B, 398E per Mustill LJ.

8   The date of disposition thus represents 'the only date at which ... inquiry ... could, in practice, be made and be relevant' (*Abbey National Building Society v Cann* [1991] 1 AC 56 at 88E per Lord Oliver of Aylmerton).

9   LRA 2002, Sch 3, para 2(c)(i).

Leases taking effect in possession more than three months after grant

12.181   The logic of reasonably detectable occupation as the trigger of overriding interest protection is further underscored by the provision in the 2002 Act that a reversionary lease granted to take effect in possession more than three months after the date of grant cannot 'override' if it has not yet taken effect in possession by the time of the registrable disposition to which it is adverse.[1]

1   LRA 2002, Sch 3, para 2(d). See Law Com No 271 (2001), para 8.63.

Rights of commercial landlords

12.182   Under the Land Registration Act 1925 overriding status was also accorded to the rights of any person who, although not in actual occupation, was 'in receipt of the rents and profits' derived from the land.[1] Such receipt by a non-resident landlord was effectively viewed as the symbolic equivalent of actual occupation,[2] with the consequence that the landlord's proprietary rights, albeit unregistered, could survive the registered disposition of any superior estate in the land.[3] This over-generous protection of commercial landlords has now been abandoned, with prospective effect,[4] by the Land Registration Act 2002,[5] thereby emphasising yet again the bias displayed by the 2002 Act against the conferment of overriding status on entitlements of persons who are not readily visible or detectable.

1   LRA 1925, s 70(1)(g).

2   For this purpose the landlord was required to show that he was in actual receipt of the rents and profits drawn from the land and not merely that he had an unenforced right to receive the same (see *E S Schwab & Co Ltd v McCarthy* (1976) 31 P & CR 196 at 205, 213).

3   Just to prove that no good deed goes unpunished, the Court of Appeal held in *Strand Securities Ltd v Caswell* [1965] Ch 958 at 981A–B, 983D–E [**para 12.159**], that no overriding interest could be claimed by a leaseholder who, as an act of generosity, had moved out of his flat and allowed his homeless step-daughter rent-free occupation of the premises. The Court acknowledged that the result would have been quite different if the step-daughter had made a 'token' payment of rent – even 'a penny a week for the privilege of remaining there.'

4   An interest which, immediately before 13 October 2003 and in accordance with LRA 1925, s 70(1)(g), was an overriding interest by reason of a person's receipt of rents and profits continues to 'override' thereafter, but only so long as that person remains in receipt of rents and profits under the same lease (LRA 2002, s 134(2), Sch 3, para 2A as inserted by Sch 12, para 8).

5   [**Para 12.135**]. See Law Com No 158 (1987), para 2.70; Law Com No 254 (1998), paras 5.67, 5.122; Law Com No 271 (2001), paras 8.18, 8.64.

Vicarious or symbolic 'actual occupation'

12.183   The Land Registration Act 2002 does nothing to address certain other ambiguities in the concept of 'actual occupation' which make it difficult to ascertain the presence of an overriding entitlement. The definition of 'actual occupation' cannot depend entirely on crude factual criteria: Schedule 3, para 2 inevitably necessitates some more sophisticated qualitative assessment of the nature of 'occupation'. It is clear, for instance, that in appropriate circumstances the requirements of Schedule 3, para 2 can be satisfied by certain kinds of vicarious or symbolic occupation on behalf of one who later asserts an overriding entitlement.[1] 'Actual occupation' may be preserved by the presence on the land of a close relative,[2] a resident caretaker,[3] a company employee[4] and a servant[5] or other 'agent'.[6] However, the occupation of such persons must be in some representative capacity[7] and must be required for and related to the proper discharge of the function of the proxy occupier.[8] 'Actual occupation' cannot be asserted vicariously through the presence of casual licensees[9] or labourers[10] or on the basis of occasional visits by an employee.[11] Nor, for the purpose of alleging an overriding entitlement on his own behalf, can a company's managing director claim to have been in 'actual occupation' of premises which were used by his company.[12]

1   See *Abbey National Building Society v Cann* [1991] 1 AC 56 at 93G, where Lord Oliver of Aylmerton adverted to the fact that actual occupation 'does not necessarily ... involve the personal presence of the person claiming to occupy.' See likewise *Williams & Glyn's Bank Ltd v Boland* [1979] Ch 312 at 338D per Ormrod LJ. The Land Registration Bill originally provided that 'a person is only to be regarded as in actual occupation of land if he, his agent or employee, is physically present there', (Land Registration Bill 2001/2002 (HL Bill 11), Sch 3, cl 2(2)), but this subclause was omitted from the eventual enactment.

2   See *Strand Securities Ltd v Caswell* [1965] Ch 958 at 984G–985A, where Russell LJ thought that the claimant of an overriding interest could establish 'actual occupation' through the presence of his spouse, although on the facts of the case he was unwilling to extend this notion of vicarious occupation to a step-daughter. Some helpful general guidance may be found in the analogy of vicarious occupation for the purpose of preserving a statutory

tenancy under the Rent Act [**para 14.318**]. See *Skinner v Geary* [1931] 2 KB 546 at 562 per Scrutton LJ (wife and family); *Brown v Brash and Ambrose* [1948] 2 KB 247 at 255 (de facto wife); *Roland House Gardens Ltd v Cravitz* (1975) 29 P & CR 432 at 438–439 (children); *Atyeo v Fardoe* (1979) 37 P & CR 494 at 498 (son).

3   *Abbey National Building Society v Cann* [1991] 1 AC 56 at 93G per Lord Oliver.

4   *Abbey National Building Society v Cann* [1991] 1 AC 56 at 93G per Lord Oliver. See also *Strand Securities Ltd v Caswell* [1965] Ch 958 at 981B per Lord Denning MR; *Stockholm Finance Ltd v Garden Holdings Inc* [1995] NPC 162 per Robert Walker J. Compare, however, *Strand Securities Ltd v Caswell*, supra at 984D–985A per Russell LJ, and see Law Com No 158 (1987), para 2.57.

5   *Strand Securities Ltd v Caswell* [1965] Ch 958 at 981B per Lord Denning MR.

6   *Lloyds Bank Plc v Rosset* [1989] Ch 350 at 377F–G per Nicholls LJ.

7   *Lloyd v Dugdale* [2002] 2 P & CR 167 at [45] per Sir Christopher Slade.

8   See *Strand Securities Ltd v Caswell* [1965] Ch 958 at 984E–G per Russell LJ; *Lloyds Bank Plc v Rosset* [1989] Ch 350 at 377G–378A per Nicholls LJ, 397H, 398B–C per Mustill LJ, 405D per Purchas LJ.

9   *Strand Securities Ltd v Caswell* [1965] Ch 958 at 981A–C, 984D–985A. Referring to *Strand Securities*, Purchas LJ accepted in *Lloyds Bank Plc v Rosset* [1989] Ch 350 at 405E that 'occupation by a friend for her own purposes with the leave and licence of the tenant is no "actual occupation".' See similarly *Lloyd v Dugdale* [2002] 2 P & CR 167 at [45] per Sir Christopher Slade.

10   See *Lloyds Bank Plc v Rosset* [1989] Ch 350 at 398E–G where, in a strong dissenting judgment, Mustill LJ took the view that no intending purchaser with inquiries to make as to adverse interests 'would imagine that masons and plasterers working on the fabric ... could be in occupation of the site, in any relevant sense, rather than coming and going to work upon it' (see [1988] Conv 453 at 457 (M P Thompson); (1988) 104 LQR 507 (R J Smith); [1989] CLJ 180 (P G McHugh)). The House of Lords reversed the Court of Appeal's decision on other grounds ([1991] 1 AC 107 at 134A–B), but the tenor of the principal speech, delivered by Lord Bridge of Harwich, indicated a clear preference for the dissent in the Court of Appeal.

11   See e g *Stockholm Finance Ltd v Garden Holdings Inc* [1995] NPC 162, where Robert Walker J rejected as 'actual occupation' the ministrations of a domestic cleaner and the intermittent visits of a chauffeur-caretaker whose function it was to give a house a 'lived-in look'.

12   *Lloyd v Dugdale* [2002] 2 P & CR 167 at [48]–[49] (managing director's presence on company premises held to be as agent of the company and 'not on his own account').

12.184   Schedule 3, para 2 is unlikely to be satisfied by the presence on the premises of persons who cannot possibly offer any helpful insight in response to inquiries made by intending disponees of title. It has been held, however, that 'actual occupation' may sometimes comprise the symbolic presence established by inanimate objects such as furniture[1] or may be evidenced by the claimant's recent works of construction on the land.[2] In *Kling v Keston Properties Ltd*[3] P claimed a contractual right to purchase a garage which was disputed by D. D maliciously parked her car across the entrance to the garage, thereby trapping inside a car belonging to P's wife, which D plainly regarded as being wrongfully there. When the garage was later let on a long lease to D, Vinelott J held that the enforced presence of the car in the garage constituted a form of 'actual occupation' of that garage on behalf of P, thus rendering his right of pre-emption an overriding interest binding on D.[4]

1   See e g *Chhokar v Chhokar* [1984] FLR 313 at 317E–F [**para 12.187**].

2   See e g *Goodger v Willis* [1999] EGCS 32 (installation of concrete base).

3   (1983) 49 P & CR 212. See [1985] Conv 406 (J E M).

4   (1983) 49 P & CR 212 at 218–219. Vinelott J thought that the result would have been the same even if the car had not been trapped inside the garage. An intermittent user of the garage 'in

the ordinary way' would have been sufficient to establish 'actual occupation'. Compare, however, *Epps v Esso Petroleum Co Ltd* [1973] 1 WLR 1071 at 1080A (regular parking of car on strip of land held not to be 'actual occupation').

Continuity of 'actual occupation'

12.185 Actual occupation must involve 'some notion of continuity', since it cannot have been the statutory intention that a claimant's interest should 'override the legal estate intermittently, according to momentary changes in the proprietor's degree of actual physical connection with the land'.[1] However, the concept of 'actual occupation' within Schedule 3, para 2 does not require an uninterrupted personal presence on the land by the claimant of an overriding interest.[2]

1   *Lloyds Bank Plc v Rosset* [1989] Ch 350 at 394E per Mustill LJ.
2   See *Stockholm Finance Ltd v Garden Holdings Inc* [1995] NPC 162 per Robert Walker J, adopting for registered land purposes the view expressed in *Kingsnorth Finance Ltd v Tizard* [1986] 1 WLR 783 at 788D–E [**para 12.361**]. Compare the statutory tenant under the Rent Act, whose continuing protection does not require that he should 'spend twenty-four hours in all weathers under his own roof for three hundred and sixty-five days in the year' (*Brown v Brash and Ambrose* [1948] 2 KB 247 at 254 per Asquith LJ).

Temporary absence

12.186 Some kinds of temporary absence do not detract from the 'actual occupation' of a person who is normally in residence. In this context the courts have applied something akin to the notions of *corpus possessionis* and *animus revertendi* which are familiar in the law of landlord and tenant,[1] with the result that 'actual occupation' is regarded as subsisting so long as the temporarily absent occupier can point to some physical evidence or symbol of continued residence coupled with an intention to return to the property.[2]

1   [**Para 14.318**].
2   See e g *Kling v Keston Properties Ltd* (1983) 49 P & CR 212 at 218–219 (parked car). See also *Hoggett v Hoggett* (1980) 39 P & CR 121 at 130, where, in a different context, 'occupation' was not regarded as necessarily interrupted by the fact that the occupier might have gone into hospital for a few days, or gone on a weekend visit to a friend, or gone out shopping for a few hours.

12.187 In determining whether there has been relevant 'actual occupation', the court may have regard not only to the length of an absence, but also to the reason for it.[1] In *Chhokar v Chhokar*,[2] for example, H held the registered legal title in the matrimonial home on an implied trust for himself and W in equal shares. H secretly agreed to transfer the registered estate at an undervalue to an acquaintance, P, H intending to rid himself of W whilst extracting for himself much of the outstanding equity in the matrimonial home.[3] H and P deliberately arranged that completion of the transfer should occur while W was in hospital having a baby. Immediately after the transfer of title, H disappeared with the balance of the proceeds of the sale and P advertised the property for sale at its full market value. When W emerged from hospital clutching her new-born child, she found that the locks had been changed and that she was denied access to her home.[4] Both Ewbank J and the Court of Appeal confirmed that W held an overriding interest which was binding on P.[5] Notwithstanding W's personal absence from the premises at the relevant time, the continuing presence of W's furniture and belongings in the house, coupled with her consistent intention to resume residence, comprised a notional or token occupation sufficient for the purpose of the Land Registration Act.[6] Ironically, before the litigation in *Chhokar* commenced, W managed to break back into her home and become reconciled with her prodigal husband. The family thereafter lived happily together in their original home, much to the discomfiture of P,[7] who ended up as registered proprietor of a house which he could neither occupy[8] nor sell[9] and from which he could derive no rental income.[10]

1   *Stockholm Finance Ltd v Garden Holdings Inc* [1995] NPC 162 per Robert Walker J ('a holiday or a business trip may be easier to reconcile with continuing and unbroken occupation than a move to a second home').
2   [1984] FLR 313.
3   In the words of Ewbank J, the transaction between H and P was similar to that which might have taken place 'in relation to property ... asserted to have fallen off the back of a lorry' ([1984] FLR 313 at 318A–B). P was fully aware of H's fraudulent intent.
4   Shortly after leaving the hospital W briefly secured a re-entry into the premises but was violently evicted by 'heavies' employed by P. Cumming-Bruce LJ declared it difficult 'to find language which, with becoming moderation, describes the moral turpitude of every step taken by [P] throughout this transaction' ([1984] FLR 313 at 330G).
5   [1984] FLR 313 at 317F.
6   The approach taken here is broadly regarded as superseding the view of Russell LJ in *Strand Securities Ltd v Caswell* [1965] Ch 958 at 985A–B, that a valid claim of 'actual occupation' could not be founded on either the presence of furniture or the retention of a key by an absent occupier.
7   Cumming-Bruce LJ observed ([1984] FLR 313 at 331H) that there was no room here for the shedding of 'crocodile tears' on behalf of P merely because his unlawful enterprise had not succeeded. ('I can see no reason for giving him anything more than the court in an unreported case gave to the money-lender who had rights over a debtor. The proceedings are recorded in a play of Shakespeare'.)
8   **[Para 11.33]**.
9   **[Para 11.243]**.
10   **[Para 11.47]**.

Fleeting presence

12.188   Whilst temporary absence is not fatal to a claim under Schedule 3, para 2, the concept of 'actual occupation' does connote 'some degree of permanence and continuity which would rule out mere fleeting presence.'[1] There must come a point at which a person's absence is 'so prolonged that the notion of his continuing to be in actual occupation ... becomes insupportable.'[2] In *Stockholm Finance Ltd v Garden Holdings Inc*,[3] for instance, a Saudi princess who had not 'set foot' in her London home for over a year was regarded as being no longer in 'actual occupation' of that property.[4] Nor can 'actual occupation' be established by a brief and marginal presence immediately prior to the completion of the transfer which is claimed to have been overridden by adverse rights. In *Abbey National Building Society v Cann*[5] it was alleged that a trust beneficiary had acquired an overriding interest in a house purchased by her son. It appeared that (with the consent of the transferor) the mother's furniture had started to be unloaded into the house from a removal van some 35 minutes prior to the completion of the transaction and the accompanying mortgage charge to the Abbey National Building Society. Lord Oliver of Aylmerton was, quite rightly, unprepared to accept that 'acts of this preparatory character carried out by courtesy of the vendor prior to completion' could ever constitute 'actual occupation' for the purpose of the Land Registration Act.[6]

1   *Abbey National Building Society v Cann* [1991] 1 AC 56 at 93D per Lord Oliver of Aylmerton.
2   *Stockholm Finance Ltd v Garden Holdings Inc* [1995] NPC 162 per Robert Walker J.
3   [1995] NPC 162.
4   See also *Nightingale Mayfair Ltd v Mehta* (Unreported, Chancery Division, 21 December 1999) (alleged actual occupier had been a tax exile for several years).
5   [1991] 1 AC 56 [**para 12.180**].
6   [1991] 1 AC 56 at 94A. See also Lord Oliver at 93H ('A prospective tenant or purchaser who is allowed, as a matter of indulgence, to go into property in order to plan decorations or measure for furnishings would not, in ordinary parlance, be said to be occupying it, even though he might be there for hours at a time'). For a similar view of acts preparatory to (but not constitutive of) 'actual occupation', see *Lloyds Bank Plc v Rosset* [1989] Ch 350 at 399A–B per Mustill LJ.

No actual occupation of an easement

12.189   Mere user of a right of way cannot constitute 'actual occupation' of the land over which that right of way is exercised.[1] A claim of easement necessarily implies some limited form of user[2] and the intermittent exercise of a right of way simply lacks the intensity of user required for the purpose of claiming an overriding interest by reason of 'occupation'.[3]

1   *Celsteel Ltd v Alton House Holdings Ltd* [1985] 1 WLR 204 at 219E. See also Law Com No 158 (1987), para 2.57.
2   'Actual occupation' would appear to be incompatible with the essentially non-exclusive character of an easement [**para 8.71**]. See M P Thompson, [1986] Conv 31 at 36.
3   See *Holaw (470) Ltd v Stockton Estates Ltd* (2001) 81 P & CR 404 at 424 per Neuberger J.

Some persons cannot be said to be in 'actual occupation'

12.190   Not every individual human being who is physically present on relevant premises at a relevant time can automatically be described as a 'person in actual occupation' for purposes of Schedule 3, para 2 of the Land Registration Act 2002. This initially strange conclusion is forced by the fact that not every occupier is necessarily competent to reply to the inquiry which Schedule 3, para 2 clearly envisages that an intending disponee may wish to carry out. The definition of 'actual occupation' is inevitably qualified by some purposive assessment of the capacity to make intelligent and intelligible response to inquirers.

The 'shadow' theory of personal occupation

12.191   This approach to the construction of Schedule 3, para 2 finds an uncomfortable precedent in the now discredited view that a wife's residence in the family home is somehow subordinated to, and submerged within, the occupation enjoyed by her husband. In *Bird v Syme-Thomson*[1] Templeman J rejected a wife-beneficiary's claim that she had an overriding interest enforceable against a chargee of her husband's registered title. In Templeman J's view, 'when a mortgagor is in actual occupation of the matrimonial home, it cannot be said that his wife also is in actual occupation.'[2] 'Actual occupation' thus belonged exclusively to the owner of the registered title, the wife being present 'only ... as a shadow of occupation of the owner.'[3] This 'shadow' theory, which barely concealed a number of outdated assumptions about the significance of a woman's presence and function in the family home, was finally and convincingly refuted in *Williams & Glyn's Bank Ltd v Boland*.[4] Here Lord Wilberforce noted that, in its application to wives, the 'shadow' theory was 'heavily obsolete'[5] and that the statutory phrase 'actual occupation' is neutral between male and female, involving 'no question of matrimonial law, or of the rights of married women or of women as such.'[6] It was 'unacceptable' to suggest that the apparent occupation of the wife of a vendor/mortgagor could be 'satisfactorily accounted for by his'[7] and Lord Wilberforce had no difficulty in concluding that 'a spouse, living in a house, has an actual occupation capable of conferring protection, as an overriding interest, upon rights of that spouse.'[8]

1   [1979] 1 WLR 440.
2   [1979] 1 WLR 440 at 444A.
3   [1979] 1 WLR 440 at 444E. See also *Williams & Glyn's Bank Ltd v Boland* (1978) 36 P & CR 448 at 454, where Templeman J pointed to the 'wide and almost catastrophic' nature of the extensive burden of enquiry which would be forced on prospective purchasers by any other holding.
4   [1981] AC 487.
5   [1981] AC 487 at 505G. The Court of Appeal had already condemned Templeman J's approach as 'unrealistic and anachronistic' ([1979] Ch 312 at 343B per Browne LJ) and as representing the law 'a hundred years ago when the law regarded husband and wife as one: and the husband as that one' ([1979] Ch 312 at 332C per Lord Denning MR). Ormrod LJ voiced the objection that the notion of vicarious occupation through a wife 'resurrects the outmoded concept of the head of the family' ([1979] Ch 312 at 338H).
6   [1981] AC 487 at 502E. See also [1979] Ch 312 at 333D–E per Ormrod LJ.
7   [1981] AC 487 at 505G–H. According to Ormrod LJ ([1979] Ch 312 at 338F), it would be difficult to 'imagine clearer examples of "actual occupation" in the ordinary sense' than the case of a wife living with her husband in the matrimonial home. See also [1979] Ch 312 at 332D–E per Lord Denning MR.
8   [1981] AC 487 at 506C. The pre-*Boland* view of the position of a wife in the family home has now been turned on its head. In *Bird v Syme-Thomson* [1979] 1 WLR 440 at 444E Templeman J held that a wife who was physically resident in her home was not in 'actual occupation'. In *Chhokar v Chhokar* [1984] FLR 313 at 317F **[para 12.187]**, a wife was unhesitatingly declared to be in 'actual occupation' notwithstanding that she was clearly absent from the property at the relevant time.

No overriding status for minors

12.192   Although most adult occupiers of relevant land are plainly persons in 'actual occupation',[1] the same is not, however, true of minors (albeit that minors may easily hold rights of a kind normally eligible for protection under Schedule 3, para 2[2]). A child of tender years – even though a trust beneficiary in residence in the family home – cannot claim to be a 'person in actual occupation', if only because a minor is almost certainly incapable of responding adequately to a purchaser's inquiries or of giving any valid consent to the transaction in hand.[3] In *Hypo-Mortgage Services Ltd v Robinson*[4] Nourse LJ regarded it as 'axiomatic that minor children of the legal owner are not in actual occupation … they are only there as shadows of occupation of their parent'.[5] Any other view would leave lenders potentially defenceless, for their security 'could always be frustrated by simple devices' if a parent were left free to use the beneficial interests of children 'as a shield against an order for possession against him.'[6]

1   It is likely that Schedule 3, para 2 also excludes certain persons suffering from severe senility or extreme cases of Alzheimer's disease, simply on the ground that such persons may be unable to respond adequately to inquiries as to their rights. For reference to the mentally infirm as lacking capacity to give a valid consent to any release of their rights, see Law Commission, *Property Law: The Implications of Williams & Glyn's Bank Ltd v Boland* (Law Com No 115, Cmnd 8636, August 1982), para 42(i)(b).
2   A child may be a beneficiary under a trust of the family home, as for instance where part of the purchase money for that home originated in a fund held on trust for that child.
3   See Law Com No 115 (1982), para 42(i)(b).
4   [1997] 2 FLR 71 at 72F–G.
5   'The minor children are there because their parent is there. They have no right of occupation of their own' ([1997] 2 FLR 71 at 72G per Nourse LJ). See likewise *Bird v Syme-Thomson* [1979] 1 WLR 440 at 444D per Templeman J; and compare J Martin, [1980] Conv 361 at 372.
6   [1997] 2 FLR 71 at 72H–73A.

The corporate alter ego

12.193   The registered title to land may sometimes be held by a company (often an off-shore company) which operates as the alter ego of the occupier of the land concerned. In *Stockholm Finance Ltd v Garden Holdings Inc*[1] title to an 'opulent second home' in London was purchased in the name of a Panamanian company using the cash contributed by a Saudi princess who was also the sole legal and beneficial owner of that company's shares. Robert Walker J rejected the claim that the princess had an overriding interest enforceable against a subsequent chargee of the title, on the ground inter alia that there was, in these circumstances, 'very little room for the application of traditional presumptions' of trust. The princess had no rights enforceable against the company (and, therefore, no rights which could become 'overriding'), since the corporate veil only thinly concealed the fact that the claimant beneficiary and the proprietor of the registered title were in reality, if not in legal form, one and the same person.[2]

1   [1995] NPC 162.

2   In these circumstances 'there is no basic economic difference between the company being sole beneficial owner of the house and being a nominee for the occupying shareholder' (per Robert Walker J). Similar reasoning applies even where the contributor of money towards a corporate purchase, although not a director or shareholder, has effective control of the company (see *Nightingale Mayfair Ltd v Mehta* (Unreported, Chancery Division, 21 December 1999) per Blackburne J). The courts' approach is tantamount to the application of a presumption of advancement in relation to companies wholly owned or controlled by the contributor of purchase money.

TRUST INTERESTS AS OVERRIDING INTERESTS

12.194   Following the rationalisation of trust law brought about by the Trusts of Land and Appointment of Trustees Act 1996, it is clear that the equitable interests (whether absolute, concurrent or successive) held by beneficiaries under a trust of land come within the field of interests which, if coupled with 'actual occupation', override dispositions of the registered estate. The major qualification on this proposition arises where a registered title is dealt with by two or more trustees in circumstances where the preconditions of statutory overreaching are met.[1] Here, as the House of Lords confirmed in *City of London Building Society v Flegg*,[2] the interests of trust beneficiaries are unquestionably overreached by the disposition, notwithstanding that the beneficiaries were, at the time of the disposition, persons 'in actual occupation of the land'. Equally plainly, any failure to comply with the 'two trustee rule' precludes the disponee from claiming that he has statutorily overreached the interests of trust beneficiaries (including such rights of occupation as may be comprised within their beneficial entitlements).[3] The remaining question is whether, in such circumstances, the equitable interests of the trust beneficiaries necessarily survive as overriding interests enforceable against the disponee.

1   LPA 1925, ss 2(1)(ii), 27(2) [paras 2.170, 11.212].
2   [1988] AC 54 [para 11.212].
3   A disposition by a sole trustee of land (other than a trust corporation) enjoys no statutorily overreaching effect (see *City of London Building Society v Flegg* [1988] AC 54 at 74C per Lord Templeman, 89A–G per Lord Oliver of Aylmerton).

Modern diffusion of home ownership

12.195   Over the last 25 years the inclusion of trust interests as potentially overriding entitlements has taken on a highly controversial aspect largely because such interests provide the focal point for a longstanding tension between claims to residential security in the family home and conflicting claims to commercial security for purchasers.[1] In *Midland Bank plc v Cooke*[2] Waite LJ remarked that '[t]he mass diffusion of home ownership has been one of the most striking social changes of our own time.'[3] The ideology of home ownership in Britain has been promoted both by a new form of prosperity and also by the unprecedented availability of mortgage finance.[4] The provision of loan money for home purchase has, in its turn, made it almost inevitable that the purchase of realty should be a co-operative endeavour between family members. Changing social mores and the increasing access of women to the labour market have made it possible, and frequently essential, to harness the income capacity of two or more family members for the purpose of meeting the level of mortgage commitment encouraged by the modern generation of institutional lenders.

1   In its extended statutory sense, the term 'purchaser' includes both a lessee and a mortgagee (see LPA 1925, s 205(1)(xxi)). A chargee of a legal estate stands in the same position as if he had taken a notional estate in the land charged (ie a long leasehold) (see LPA 1925, s 87(1) **[para 8.246]**).
2   [1995] 4 All ER 562 at 575a.
3   In *Williams & Glyn's Bank Ltd v Boland* [1981] AC 487 at 508G, Lord Wilberforce spoke of 'the extension, beyond the paterfamilias, of rights of ownership, itself following from the diffusion of property and earning capacity.' Owner-occupation forms the tenure of 70 per cent of all households in Britain today **[para 7.3]**, as compared with an incidence not greatly in excess of 10 per cent at the time of enactment of the 1925 property legislation (see John Stanley MP, Minister for Housing and Construction, Department of the Environment, 'Government Policies on Home Ownership in the 1980s', in SHAC, *Home Ownership in the 1980s* (Policy Paper No 3, July 1980), p 6). The number of owner-occupied dwellings in Britain more than doubled over the 30 year period from 1961 to 1991 (*Social Trends 23* (1993), pp 113–114 (Chart 8.1)).
4   See Lord Diplock's reference in *Pettitt v Pettitt* [1970] AC 777 at 824C to 'the emergence of a property-owning, particularly a real-property-mortgaged-to-a-building-society-owning, democracy.'

Proliferation of informal co-ownership

12.196   One inescapable consequence of this social and economic transformation has been the proliferation of informal co-ownership of the family home.

Prevalence of latent entitlements

12.197   Trust law has adapted, albeit slowly and rather awkwardly, to the fact that co-operative purchase – even in the context of vague, informal and ill-defined family arrangements – may give rise to various kinds of shared proprietary entitlement. There is nowadays a distinct probability that the average family home is held on some implied trust for two or more family members.[1] Relevant contributory activity extends beyond mere money provision to include household-related labour and other forms of effort or detriment.[2] The distribution of property rights on an unprecedented scale, whether by way of trust or estoppel,[3] has become an endemic feature of the law of family property.

1   The range of trust beneficiary may well include the registered proprietor's parents or children, a de facto partner, or 'his Uncle Harry or his Aunt Matilda' (see *Caunce v Caunce* [1969] 1 WLR 286 at 293H per Stamp J).
2   **[Paras 10.100, 10.120]**.
3   It is increasingly difficult, in the present context, to disentangle trust and estoppel (see eg *Birmingham Midshires Mortgage Services Ltd v Sabherwal* (2000) 80 P & CR 256 at 263 per Robert Walker LJ **[paras 10.62, 10.68]**).

Existence off the register

12.198   In so far as equitable rights emerge under an implied trust or through proprietary estoppel, such entitlements arise *dehors* the formal legal title and normally subsist off the register. They leave little or no documentary trace. Owners of a legal title may indeed be entirely unaware either that they are trustees or that their title is encumbered by rights founded on estoppel. Likewise those whose rights are recognised in equity may be unaware of their precise entitlements and even less conscious of their need for formal protection against third parties. In consequence, the existence of equities based on trust or estoppel may often remain concealed from disponees of the registered title in the family home.

Trend towards joint ownership of the legal title

12.199   The problems raised by latent equities in the family home are alleviated, to some extent, by the widespread vesting of legal title in joint names. It has been estimated that over 75 per cent of matrimonial homes are nowadays held in the joint names of husband and wife.[1] From the viewpoint of disponees of the registered title, joint ownership at law unmistakably indicates the existence of a trust either as the result of an express declaration or as a matter of obvious inference,[2] although it does not necessarily identify the full range of beneficial co-owners behind the trust.[3] The co-ownership revealed by the documentary title immediately signals to disponees the necessity of paying capital money to the trustees (being at least two in number) or to a trust corporation in order to ensure that all beneficial interests behind the trust, irrespective of their precise ownership, are statutorily overreached and, in the process, safeguarded as equivalent entitlements in the capital proceeds.[4]

1   Law Com No 115 (1982), paras 29, 60.
2   **[Paras 9.184, 11.146]**.
3   See e g *City of London Building Society v Flegg* [1988] AC 54 **[para 11.212]**.
4   There remains the problem that some dispositions by way of mortgage charge may be vitiated by undue influence (see *Barclays Bank plc v O'Brien* [1994] 1 AC 180; *Royal Bank of Scotland plc v Etridge* (*No 2*) [2002] 2 AC 773 **[para 15.68]**).

Residue of concealed beneficial co-ownership

12.200   Despite the drift towards joint proprietorship, there nevertheless remains a considerable residue of titles registered in the name of a sole owner. Implied trusts of land (or estoppels affecting that land) continue to lie concealed behind sole registered proprietorship.[1] Contemporary evidence suggests, moreover, that trusts and estoppels are disproportionately hidden behind sole ownership in ethnic minority communities, where cultural traditions cause deference to, and therefore a vesting of title in, a male head of household. More generally, sole legal titles are often unwittingly held on trust in the context of volatile or experimental de facto liaisons which develop over time into longerterm relationships. In either instance latent equities frequently arise on behalf of persons – usually female or elderly – who are unlikely to articulate their rights or to have access to specialised legal advice and services in their defence.

1   Not many sole trustees of a registered estate are aware of their obligation to apply for the entry in the register of a 'restriction' on dealings with their own title (LRR 2003, r 94(1) [**para 11.140**]).

Tension between family and commercial claims

12.201   The informality of beneficial co-ownership behind implied trusts of land usually presents no problem except in the event of dealings by a sole registered proprietor.[1] Difficulties begin to occur if the title held on trust is transferred or charged to someone who is unaware that he is dealing with a sole trustee of land[2] and that there are beneficial rights concealed behind the trust which can be statutorily overreached only on payment of capital money to two trustees (or to a trust corporation).[3] In such cases the trust beneficiaries may be equally unaware of the potential threat to their rights, particularly where the disposition takes the form, not of an outright transfer,[4] but of a post-acquisition mortgage charge.[5] This kind of transaction can often be completed without any knowledge or consent on the part of the beneficiaries,[6] with grave consequences if a subsequent default precipitates the enforcement of the security. At this point there arises a clear tension between the need to protect vulnerable occupiers of the family home and the equally pressing need to uphold the legitimate interests of a disponee suddenly faced with previously undisclosed beneficial claims. The stakes are high: the contest generally involves two innocent parties, one of whom must suffer the negative impact of a transaction entered into by a sole registered proprietor acting in breach of trust.[7] The disponee faces a temporary or permanent loss of his money investment.[8] Trust beneficiaries face the loss of their home.

1   Even then few problems arise in practice if the relevant disposition is effected with the knowledge or consent of all concerned. There must be thousands of home sales completed each year by transferors who are sole trustees of land although neither they nor their transferees realise this fact. In most cases a failure to comply with the preconditions of statutory overreaching makes no difference to anyone, since the proceeds of the sale are re-invested in the purchase of another family home and the beneficial co-owners can, if necessary, trace their equitable rights into the new property. In 1978 the Law Commission urged (unsuccessfully) that each spouse should have a statutory right to require that the other's share of the sale proceeds of the matrimonial home be used in the acquisition of a new home (see Law Com No 86 (1978), paras 1.365–1.369).

2   See e g *Equity & Law Home Loans Ltd v Prestidge* [1992] 1 WLR 137 at 141E.

3   A registered disposition by a sole trustee (albeit acting wrongfully and in breach of trust) is effective at law (see LRA 2002, s 26 [**para 11.224**]). See *Hodgson v Marks* [1971] Ch 892 at 899C [**para 12.178**]; *Williams & Glyn's Bank Ltd v Boland* [1981] AC 487 [**para 12.204**]; *Chhokar v Chhokar* [1984] FLR 313 [**para 12.187**]; *Bank of Baroda v Dhillon* [1998] 1 FLR 524 [**para 12.220**].

4   See, however, *Chhokar v Chhokar* [1984] FLR 313 [**para 12.187**].

5   In the case of a post-acquisition mortgage, beneficial co-ownership interests may already have been generated quite silently by a range of contributory activity on the part of family members during the period since the initial acquisition of the property. A mortgage of land is

usually a much less visible transaction than a sale or lease of land (where the trust beneficiaries are more likely to be aware of an impending transaction and therefore better positioned to assert their equitable rights).

6   This possibility is given a new twist where the registered title is vested in a company (see e g *Winkworth v Edward Baron Development Co Ltd* [1986] 1 WLR 1512).

7   As Murray J once observed in the High Court of Northern Ireland in *Northern Bank Ltd v Beattie* [1982] 18 NIJB, p 1, the phrase 'the eternal triangle' has taken on a new meaning for the judge in the Chancery Division. A strangely recurring feature of the case law involves the sole trustee of the family home who dishonestly charges the legal estate in order to extract a cash sum with which to disappear and make a new life elsewhere (see *Caunce v Caunce* [1969] 1 WLR 286 at 289F; *Kingsnorth Finance Co Ltd v Tizard* [1986] 1 WLR 783 at 787A; *Equity & Law Home Loans Ltd v Prestidge* [1992] 1 WLR 137 at 140G, 141C–E, 145D–E). See also *Chhokar v Chhokar* [1984] FLR 313 [**para 12.187**]; *Le Foe v Le Foe and Woolwich plc* [2001] 2 FLR 970 at [25] (a 'low, deceitful and ruthless subterfuge to strip the majority of the equity out of the former matrimonial home').

8   If a transferee is bound by the adverse rights of trust beneficiaries, he takes beneficially only such interest as was held by his transferor and thus holds the legal estate as a sole trustee on behalf of himself and any beneficiary whose interest has not been overreached. See e g *Chhokar v Chhokar* [1984] FLR 313 ([**paras 12.187, 12.201**]).

A confrontation of ideologies

12.202   During the last 30 years an ideological battle has been fought out at the heart of English land law doctrine. The confrontation has focused principally, but not exclusively, on transactions of mortgage which involve the family home. Social concern to preserve the integrity of the family home does not always accord easily with the lender's concern to recover loan money advanced on the security of this home.[1] The friendly bank manager who magically provided large sums for the purchase of a family residence – or for the business purposes of one of the family members – may adopt a very different stance at the onset of financial adversity. An obvious conflict of interest arises between the need to promote efficient banking and conveyancing practice and the need to ensure residential security and social justice for members of the borrower's family. It becomes critically important to determine whether latent beneficial rights behind an implied trust of registered land take priority over those who unwittingly lend money to a sole trustee of a family home. Given that the sole trustee stands defenceless, as chargor, against the lender's claim to repossess his home, everything turns on whether other trust beneficiaries can claim to 'override' the claim to possession and the exercise of the chargee's power of sale (or at least salvage some of the family's assets from the hands of the secured creditor). The law must grant priority to one or other competing interest. It is here that, in recent decades, English courts have witnessed a stark confrontation of philosophical and conceptual starting points.

1   Yet, in all fairness, it is 'essential that a law designed to protect the vulnerable does not render the matrimonial home unacceptable as security to financial institutions' (*Barclays Bank plc v O'Brien* [1994] 1 AC 180 at 188G–H per Lord Browne-Wilkinson).

The Boland ruling

12.203   Before the 1980s the courts simply used to deny that beneficial co-ownership rights behind an implied trust could *ever* constitute an overriding interest in land.[1] It was commonly believed that members of a registered proprietor's household could never assert an 'actual occupation' independent of his.[2] The effect was to collapse any claim that a beneficial interest (and particularly a right of beneficial occupation of the land) might take priority over a disponee of the registered title in a family home. An historic change of course was eventually signalled by the Court of Appeal and the House of Lords in *Williams & Glyn's Bank Ltd v Boland*,[3] although, paradoxically, the courts have spent much of the recent past attempting to counteract the liberal effects of the *Boland* ruling.[4]

1   This restrictive approach was sometimes rationalised on the basis that trust interests were precluded, by virtue of the equitable doctrine of conversion from constituting interests in *land* [paras 9.234, 11.173].
2   See eg *Bird v Syme-Thomson* [1979] 1 WLR 440 at 444A–E.
3   [1981] AC 487 (HL); [1979] Ch 312 (CA); (1978) 36 P & CR 448 (Templeman J).
4   [Paras 12.210–12.221].

The facts of Boland

12.204   *Williams & Glyn's Bank Ltd v Boland* was a conjoined appeal[1] from two decisions which held that a wife-beneficiary under an implied trust of the family home was not entitled to priority over a bank to which her husband, as sole registered proprietor, had charged his title as security for money lent for his business purposes (see *Fig. 39*). The bank had sought to enforce its security when the husband's business failed.[2] It was alleged (and generally accepted) that the wife had acquired a beneficial interest by reason of past financial contributions towards purchase. It was likewise common ground that the bank made no inquiry of the wife before advancing the mortgage money; and the wife claimed that she had had no contemporaneous knowledge of the creation of the mortgage charge. It was also painfully clear that the wife had not protected any entitlement by entry in her husband's registered title.[3] It followed that the issue of priority against the bank depended wholly on whether the wife's beneficial interest under the implied trust 'overrode' the disposition of charge by reason of her 'actual occupation' of the home. At the heart of *Boland*, therefore, lay fundamental questions relating to the scope of the inquiry incumbent on disponees of land and the extent to which lenders of money should be required to assume the risk of defects in their borrowers' titles.

1   An identical fact situation had arisen in *Williams & Glyn's Bank Ltd v Brown*. (In the present account the two cases are named collectively as *Boland*, although the nature of the appeals explains the courts' references to the claims of the 'wives'.)
2   The propensity of Williams & Glyn's Bank to call in business loans at short notice became the subject of considerable concern in 1979 (see *Economist*, 5–11 May 1979). In *Williams & Glyn's*

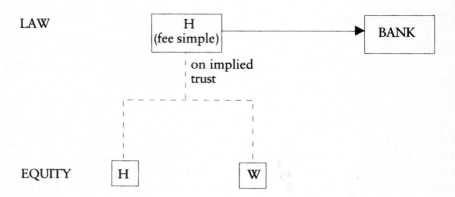

Fig. 39

Bank Ltd v Barnes [1981] Com LR 205, Gibson J upheld the bank's claim that money lent on overdraft is prima facie repayable on demand (see *Elements of Land Law* (3rd edn 2001), p 1004).

3   In *Boland* the wife could, by timely intervention, have entered *two* kinds of entitlement in her husband's register of title. She could have protected her equitable proprietary interest under the trust by the entry of a 'restriction' **[para 7.53]**; she could also have protected her statutory 'rights of occupation' (or 'matrimonial home rights' **[paras 12.93–12.95]**). The latter rights can never rank as an overriding interest (see now Family Law Act 1996, s 31(10)(b) **[para 12.167]**), with the consequence that in *Boland* all attention was focused on the potentially overriding quality of the wife's *trust* entitlement.

The decision in Boland

12.205   In *Boland* the House of Lords unanimously upheld the wife's claim to an overriding interest,[1] ruling that, in the absence of inquiry, a beneficial owner in 'actual occupation'[2] behind an implied trust of land[3] has an interest binding those who deal with the sole registered proprietor of that land.[4] Since in *Boland* the vital component of the interest thus rendered 'overriding' was the right of occupation implicit in beneficial entitlement,[5] the bank was unable to exercise its normal right, as registered chargee, to recover possession for the purpose of selling up and recouping the outstanding loan.

1   The claimant bank had succeeded in its action for possession before Templeman J, only to lose in both the Court of Appeal and the House of Lords. On the Court of Appeal's ruling, see [1979] Conv 377 (F R Crane); (1979) 42 MLR 567 (W T Murphy); (1979) 95 LQR 501 (R J Smith); (1979) 129 NLJ 700 (H W Wilkinson). On the House of Lords' decision, see (1980) 43 MLR 692 (S Freeman); [1980] Conv 361 (J Martin); (1981) 97 LQR 12 (R J Smith); (1980) 130 NLJ 896 (R L Deech).

2   Both the Court of Appeal and the House of Lords rejected the idea that joint occupation of land by a spouse could be discounted as only a 'shadow of occupation of the owner.' As Lord Denning MR observed of the matrimonial home in *Boland* [1979] Ch 312 at 332D–E, 'Visit the home and you will find that [the wife] is in personal occupation of it just as much as [the husband] is.'

3   *Boland* concerned a 'trust for sale' of the family home **[para 9.221]**.

4   The relevant principles do not in general depend on whether the parties involved are married or related by family connection (see *Williams & Glyn's Bank Ltd v Boland* [1979] Ch 312 at 333D–E per Ormrod LJ, [1981] AC 487 at 502F per Lord Wilberforce).

5   [Para 11.174]. One of the major obstacles in the way of an affirmative outcome was removed
     fairly early in the *Boland* litigation. It was accepted by all concerned that, despite the doctrine
     of conversion, an equitable interest behind a trust for sale was a right sufficiently referable to
     land for the purposes of the Land Registration Act (see now TOLATA 1996, s 3(1)
     [para 9.238]).

The rhetoric of social justice

12.206 The *Boland* decision was remarkable in that it reversed an entire
ideology of family property and finance. Until *Boland* the courts had fairly
consistently endorsed the view that those who lent money expected to be repaid
in full even if that meant that wives and families must be evicted from their
homes – a view somewhat crudely expressed in the adage that 'an Englishman's
home is his bank manager's castle!' In *Boland*, by contrast, the courts reached a
policy decision to uphold the integrity of the family home in preference to the
convenience of conveyancers and bankers.[1] By reallocating the risk of defects in
the titles offered by borrowers, *Boland* effectively traded off protection for
banks and other lenders against what was then perceived to be a higher social
interest. The ruling promised a significant shift in the balance between owners
and lenders, leaving it to the latter to adopt means of self-protection.

1   There was unattractive evidence in *Boland* that Williams & Glyn's Bank, in a cavalier exercise
     of its power of sale as mortgagee, had already sold up Boland's business premises (valued at
     £22,500) for merely £1,500 and now wanted to attack his home as well ((1978) 36 P & CR 448
     at 450–451). In the Court of Appeal Lord Denning MR caught the mood of the moment in
     fastening an obligation of social morality upon institutional lenders: 'If a bank is to do its
     duty, in the society in which we live, it should recognise the integrity of the matrimonial home.
     It should not destroy it by disregarding the wife's interest in it – simply to ensure that it is paid
     the husband's debt in full – with the high interest rate now prevailing' ([1979] Ch 312 at
     332H–333A).

12.207 This adjustment of judicial stance was forcefully underpinned by the
rhetoric of social justice.[1] The decision in *Boland* was, at its roots, a statement
of social ethics about the importance of providing security for the family – and
in particular the married woman – in occupation of the family home.[2] In the
Court of Appeal in *Boland* Lord Denning MR declared that the courts 'should
not give monied might priority over social justice.'[3] He did not see that this new
approach would cause any difficulty to conveyancers[4] or impair the proper
conduct of businesses since

> [a]nyone who lends money on the security of a matrimonial home
> nowadays ought to realise that the wife may have a share in it. He ought
> to make sure that the wife agrees to it, or to go to the house and make
> inquiries of her. It seems to me utterly wrong that a lender should turn a
> blind eye to the wife's interest or the possibility of it – and afterwards seek
> to turn her and the family out – on the plea that he did not know she was
> in actual occupation.[5]

1   In Lord Scarman's view, the 'achievement of social justice' now required that the courts
     should give a meaning to the Land Registration Act which militated in favour of, and not

against, the preservation of those rights of co-ownership in the family home which the courts had come to recognise over the past three decades as having been earned by various kinds of family member ([1981] AC 487 at 510B–C).

2   See, for example, the extra-judicial statement by Lord Simon of Glaisdale that running through the judgments in *Boland* was 'a strong sense of the social issues that were involved' (*Parliamentary Debates, House of Lords, Official Report*, Vol 437 (Session 1982–1983), Col 641 (15 December 1982)).

3   [1979] Ch 312 at 333A. In Lord Denning's view the bank was 'not entitled to throw these families out into the street – simply to get the last penny of the husband's debt' ([1979] Ch 312 at 333C).

4   See *Brikom Investments Ltd v Carr* [1979] QB 467 at 484F per Lord Denning MR ('I prefer to see that justice is done: and let the conveyancers look after themselves').

5   [1979] Ch 312 at 332G (see also Ormrod LJ at 339B–C). For a modern echo of the same approach, see *Le Foe v Le Foe and Woolwich Plc* [2001] 2 FLR 970 at [74].

12.208   The House of Lords in *Boland* unanimously confirmed this relegation of the commercial interest of the bank-mortgagee behind the claims of residential security. Lord Wilberforce acknowledged that this 'extension of the risk area' for purchasers might 'add to the burdens of purchasers, and involve them in enquiries which in some cases may be troublesome.'[1] He was not, however, unhappy to see a 'departure from an easy-going practice of dispensing with enquiries as to occupation beyond that of the vendor.'[2] The intensification of the duty of enquiry was simply the inevitable concomitant of 'the widespread development of shared interests of ownership.'[3]

1   [1981] AC 487 at 508G.
2   [1981] AC 487 at 508H.
3   An even more robust unconcern for the protests of conveyancers emerged in the speech of Lord Scarman, who thought that the alleged difficulties in conveyancing and banking practice had been 'exaggerated'. In his view, 'bankers and solicitors exist to provide the service which the public needs. They can – as they have successfully done in the past – adjust their practice, if it be socially required' ([1981] AC 487 at 510B–C).

Criticism of the Boland ruling

12.209   Although the *Boland* ruling was initially greeted both as a resounding victory for women's rights and as a timely blow in the eye for overweening institutional lenders, the correctness of the decision soon came under critical scrutiny.[1] Quite apart from the danger of collusive and fabricated claims of shared beneficial ownership,[2] it was at least debatable, as a matter of principle, whether wives should be able to participate in their husbands' business prosperity whilst claiming the right to remain immune from the effects of their commercial failure. It was also seriously questionable whether a trust beneficiary deserved the protection of an overriding interest if she had failed to safeguard any of her rights by appropriate entry in the register of title.[3] The *Boland* ruling demonstrated in a most salutary fashion that reliance could no longer be placed on an apparently unencumbered registered title.[4] According to *Boland* the disponee of registered land must, at his own risk, take steps to prove a negative, ie that no overriding interest affected the title which he took.[5] An onerous duty of this kind ran clearly counter to the traditionally vigorous preference of English land law for the protection of purchasers.[6] It was therefore scarcely surprising that, in *Boland*, counsel for the bank expressed the view that the banking world needed 'a workable system'[7] and that this goal would be made quite unattainable if lenders (and other purchasers) were required to make comprehensive and intrusive enquiries in every case.[8] Yet, as Lord Hailsham LC later pointed out, the world did 'not come to an end as a result of the decision in *Boland*.'[9] If a reason be sought, it lies in the way in which silently but surely the original *Boland* principle was, in following years, eroded almost to the point of extinction.[10]

1 Even Lord Wilberforce confessed, in an extra-judicial statement in 1985, that he had subsequently 'had some misgivings about whether or not we were right' in *Boland* (see *Parliamentary Debates, House of Lords, Official Report*, Vol 460 (Session 1984–85), Col 1271 (5 March 1985)). See also the reproach delivered by Lord Templeman in *Winkworth v Edward Baron Development Co Ltd* [1986] 1 WLR 1512 at 1515C.

2 The wife in *Boland* was not locked in mortal combat with her husband. Instead her husband was seeking to retain the family home by setting up against the bank an alleged beneficial entitlement in his wife. It was noticeable that, at first instance in *Boland*, Templeman J was careful to say merely that the wife 'claimed' to have made the cash contributions which supposedly generated an implied trust of her husband's legal title. Templeman J also emphasised that the protection of matrimonial home rights would be rendered otiose if the spouse of a legal owner 'could say or allege at any time that he or she had contributed to the purchase price' ((1978) 36 P & CR 448 at 454). The Law Commission likewise pointed to the danger that the rights of occupiers 'may be invoked primarily to frustrate proceedings brought by a mortgagee against the legal owner, as in fact they were in *Boland* itself' (Law Com No 115 (1982), para 30).

3 One of the bank's counsel, Robert Reid QC, was later to condemn the decision in *Boland* as 'one of the furthest extensions of what is sometimes called "The Nanny State"; that is the state in which people are presumed incapable of taking any coherent decision for themselves about any important matter' (see *Williams & Glyn's Bank Ltd v Boland: Report of a Conference on Problems of Conflict of Interest in the Matrimonial Home* (Gower 1981), p 26).

4 The bank in *Boland* was surely entitled to wonder why, having dutifully scrutinised the register of title, it lost priority to a wife who had failed to protect herself by entry in that register.

5 As Lord Wilberforce indicated in *Williams & Glyn's Bank Ltd v Boland* [1981] AC 487 at 508F, the class of protected co-ownership interests extends beyond that of the spouse to include the rights of 'other members of the family or even outside it' (see also [1979] Ch 312 at 333F per Ormrod LJ). Lord Wilberforce envisaged that overriding interests could easily arise in 'the case of a man living with a mistress, or of a man and a woman – or for that matter two persons of the same sex – living in a house in separate or partially shared rooms' ([1981] AC 487 at 506B). Inquiry may have to be made of many kinds of domestic *ménage* (each of possibly intermittent or discontinuous quality) such as those involving homosexual partners, 'old cronies', platonic friends, and polygamous spouses.

6 Even the Law Commission, for decades the firmest advocate of family property rights, was moved to remark that *Boland*, while consistent with the 'current social policy which favours the protection of the wife in the matrimonial home', is inconsistent with 'the policy of property law which upholds the security of titles, the marketability of land and the simplification of conveyancing' (Law Com No 115 (1982), para 70).

7 [1981] AC 487 at 502C (Donald Nicholls QC, now Lord Nicholls of Birkenhead). Indeed, so anxious was the bank to obtain a declaratory ruling from the House of Lords in support of a 'workable system' that the bank undertook, in the event of a favourable judgment, not to pursue any order for possession against the respondent wives. See also Mustill LJ's reference to the 'workmanlike solution' reached in decisions favouring banks in the area of unregistered land (*Lloyds Bank Plc v Rosset* [1989] Ch 350 at 397B).

8 The reaction to *Boland* from the banking and conveyancing world was predictably fierce. See e g *Times*, 24 June 1980 (letter from Derek Wheatley, Legal Adviser, Lloyds Bank Head

Office). Speaking extra-judicially in 1982, Lord Templeman observed that 'no one has great sympathy for lenders or banks but the point is that at the end of the day it is the borrower who pays, unless there is some speedy and efficient method of conveyancing' (see *Parliamentary Debates, House of Lords, Official Report*, Vol 437 (Session 1982–1983), Col 650 (15 December 1982)).

9   *Parliamentary Debates, House of Lords, Official Report*, Vol 437 (Session 1982–1983), Col 662 (15 December 1982). See also the reference in *Barclays Bank Plc v Zaroovabli* [1997] Ch 321 at 330B to 'Cassandra-like prophecies of disaster' emanating from mortgagees.

10   This reaction against *Boland* merely realigns English law with that of other jurisdictions, where the courts have not afforded spouses protection against third parties who take a mortgage charge from the legal owner of the family home (see eg *Royal Bank of Canada v Nicholson* (1981) 112 DLR (3d) 364 at 367; *Containercare (Ireland) Ltd v Wycherley* [1982] IR 143 at 153). A leading Australian commentator has observed that 'it would be striking at the most basic tenets of the Torrens system' to apply in the *Boland* situation any of the statutory exceptions to the Torrens principle of indefeasibility of title (see Peter Butt, 'Conveyancing and the Rights of Persons in Occupation' (1981) 55 ALJ 119 at 123).

Subsequent erosion of the Boland principle

12.210   The *Boland* ruling reflected an ideology whose day had come,[1] only to flourish briefly and recede with the passage of time. Recent years have seen the submergence of *Boland*'s more humane perspective on property priorities under the overwhelmingly commercialist ethos engendered during the late 1980s and 1990s.[2] The balance which shifted so dramatically with the *Boland* ruling has been readjusted by a relentless retreat from the high point of judicial activism evident in that decision. The *Boland* approach has been emasculated by a series of developments and strategems in which courts and lawyers have sought to minimise the hazards for conveyancers and lenders posed by beneficial entitlements which are concealed behind a trust of land.[3]

1   In the relatively liberated days of 1980 few judges were prepared to hold that a married woman resident in the family home was not 'in actual occupation' of it or was a mere 'shadow' of her husband as legal owner. No court willingly orders the eviction of spouses and children in order to satisfy the claims of an aggressive banking corporation if there is any feasible ground for an alternative legal outcome. Long before the phrase became fashionable, the *Boland* ruling was 'politically correct'.

2   See Gray and Gray, 'The rhetoric of realty', in J Getzler (ed), *Rationalizing Property, Equity and Trusts: Essays in Honour of Edward Burn* (Butterworths 2003), pp 250–253.

3   Little use has so far been made of the device of title insurance as a means of neutralising the hazard of overriding interests (but see G Morgan, 'Title Insurance: Its Relevance to Lenders', in P Jackson and D C Wilde (ed), *Contemporary Property Law* (Ashgate 1999), p 168).

Strict proof of beneficial entitlement

12.211   It has become increasingly common for disponees of a registered title, when confronted by an allegedly overriding interest, to demand strict proof of the origin of the claimed beneficial entitlement on which overriding status depends.[1] Often the only evidence for such entitlement lies in vague, self-serving and possibly collusive claims of financial contribution towards some long distant purchase. There is, in many cases, a fear that fabrications of past contributory effort by a spouse may enable an insolvent proprietor of the family home to shield himself from his own creditors.[2] It is therefore entirely predictable that the disponee's first line of attack should nowadays take the form of a full-frontal assault on the existence of the claimed beneficial entitlement.[3] It was precisely the rebuttal of such entitlement which devastated the claim made by the defendant wife in *Lloyds Bank Plc v Rosset*[4] that she had an overriding interest binding upon the chargee of her husband's title.

1 *Williams & Glyn's Bank Ltd v Boland* itself concerned a preliminary point of law and it was assumed for this purpose that the wife was entitled as an equitable co-owner behind an implied trust.

2 See the judicial caution evident in cases such as *Knightly v Sun Life Assurance Society Ltd* (1981) Times, 23 July; *Midland Bank PLC v Dobson* [1986] 1 FLR 171 at 174D per Fox LJ; *Buggs v Buggs* [2003] EWHC 1538 (Ch) at [19].

3 This line of attack is equally applicable in the case of unregistered land (see *Midland Bank PLC v Dobson* [1986] 1 FLR 171 at 177G).

4 [1991] 1 AC 107 at 134A–B per Lord Bridge of Harwich **[para 10.91]**.

Requirement of express consent from putative beneficiaries

12.212 Whilst inquiry made directly of the disponor cannot in itself neutralise the adverse rights of others,[1] such an inquiry may help to resolve the difficulties exposed in *Boland*[2] by identifying the persons who are in 'actual occupation' of the land which is the subject of a proposed disposition.[3] The disponee may require, as a *sine qua non* of the transaction, that such persons sign an express waiver of rights or otherwise consent to the dealing. This waiver or consent, unless vitiated by misrepresentation or undue influence,[4] precludes any future claim that an occupier has an overriding beneficial interest.

1 See *Hodgson v Marks* [1971] Ch 892 at 932D per Russell LJ **[para 12.174]**. The Law Commission long ago dismissed the suggestion that a declaration by the disponor should be deemed conclusive as to the existence or non-existence of co-ownership rights (Law Com No 115 (1982), Appendix 2, paras 21–23).

2 See Law Com No 115 (1982), Appendix 2, para 15. Transferors are asked in the Law Society's 'Property Information Form' **[para 12.12]** to identify all other persons in actual occupation of the land.

3 Physical inspection of the premises prior to completion of the transaction, whilst advisable, is not necessarily conclusive in favour of the purchaser and may not be realistic in the context of 'chain' transactions of sale and purchase (see Law Com No 115 (1982), paras 39–40). Such inspections may not detect all existing occupiers and, in any event, new occupiers may arrive during the period between the inspection and the date of the disposition.

4 **[Paras 12.54, 15.67]**.

Exclusion of jointly held titles

12.213 The limits of the *Boland* ruling were strenuously reaffirmed by the decision of the House of Lords in *City of London Building Society v Flegg*.[1] In *Flegg* the Court of Appeal held that the ratio of *Boland* also applied to a disposition of a registered title jointly held by two or more trustees of land, with the result that trust beneficiaries in 'actual occupation' were entitled, as against a chargee, to the protection of an overriding interest.[2] This heresy was terminated when, on appeal, the House of Lords immediately reinstated the orthodox view that a disposition of a registered estate held by two or more trustees of land inevitably overreaches the equitable co-ownership interests of even those beneficiaries who are in 'actual occupation'.[3] Accordingly it is clear that a disponee of land held on an implied trust can always obtain an unimpeachable title simply by insisting on a disposition effected by two trustees.[4] In such circumstances the disponee is automatically assured that the transaction (whether of sale or mortgage) overreaches all beneficial interests which lurk behind the trust.[5]

1   [1988] AC 54 [**para 11.212**].
2   [1986] Ch 605 at 616H–617D.
3   [1988] AC 54 at 76E–F per Lord Oliver of Aylmerton.
4   See e g *Owen v Williams* (Unreported, Court of Appeal, 21 November 1985) per Nourse LJ ('the obvious way out').
5   A sole trustee of registered land is now obliged to place a 'restriction' on his own title prohibiting unilateral dealings (LRR 2003, r 94(1) [**para 11.151**]). See, however, Law Com No 115 (1982), para 42(ii) (in relation to the inconvenience of finding a second legal owner).

Applications of estoppel doctrine

12.214   A further curtailment of the *Boland* ruling has been brought about by estoppels founded on the implied waiver of rights.[1] Courts will not allow a trust beneficiary to remain deliberately silent about his or her equitable rights at the date of a transaction of sale or charge,[2] only to assert these rights later as having priority over a third party who has dealt in good faith with the sole registered proprietor. In such circumstances the owner of the undisclosed rights cannot conscionably raise his or her rights in derogation of the interest or security taken by the disponee.[3]

1   The effect of the estoppel approach was to suspend the 'general philosophy of the decision of the House of Lords in *Williams & Glyn's Bank Ltd v Boland*' (see *Kemmis v Kemmis* [1988] 1 WLR 1307 at 1335A–B per Nourse LJ).
2   On the role of representation by silence in the law of estoppel, see [**para 10.246**].
3   See e g *Midland Bank Ltd v Farmpride Hatcheries Ltd* (1981) 260 EG 493 at 497 per Shaw LJ, 498–499 per Oliver LJ; *Ulster Bank Ltd v Shanks* [1982] NI 143 at 150A (highly relevant that wife-beneficiary had been present during negotiations between husband and bank manager). It has been suggested that a beneficial owner may be estopped from asserting her rights against a transferee if she appeared to acquiesce in a sale, for example by showing the intending purchaser around the house and encouraging him in expenditure (see [1980] Conv 361 at 368 (J Martin); *Spiro v Lintern* [1973] 1 WLR 1002 at 1013B–D).

12.215   The applicability of estoppel doctrine in this context depends vitally on the trust beneficiary's awareness of the relevant disposition of the registered title.[1] Where a trust beneficiary had no contemporaneous knowledge that the registered proprietor was dealing with his title (e g by charging it to a lender), the courts have allowed the beneficiary to retain the protection of her overriding interest.[2] But where such knowledge was present, the courts have ruled that trust beneficiaries – usually members of the registered proprietor's family – are estopped from overriding the priority of the disponee.[3] Wilful non-disclosure of an interest capable of undermining the security offered is 'conduct which would leave the owner of the equitable interest open to the charge of coming to the court with hands that were not clean.'[4] Any other approach is 'unarguable' and 'would go near to saying that our system of conveyancing permits a mortgagor to obtain money under a false pretence.'[5] Thus for instance, in *Paddington Building Society v Mendelsohn*,[6] a beneficial co-owner was deemed, by non-disclosure of her rights to a mortgagee, to have conceded priority to the latter.[7]

1   See *Paddington Building Society v Mendelsohn* (1985) 50 P & CR 244 at 248–249 per Browne-Wilkinson LJ.

2   See e g *Williams & Glyn's Bank Ltd v Boland* [1981] AC 487 [**para 12.204**], where a wife alleged that her husband had negotiated a mortgage without her knowledge or consent. See also *Winkworth v Edward Baron Development Co Ltd* (1986) 52 P & CR 67 at 77 (reversed on other grounds [1986] 1 WLR 1512); *Lloyds Bank Plc v Rosset* [1991] 1 AC 107 at 127C per Lord Bridge of Harwich; *Equity & Law Home Loans Ltd v Prestidge* [1992] 1 WLR 137 at 144A; *Bank of Baroda v Dhillon* [1998] 1 FLR 524 at 527E–F.

3   The principle is equally applicable to unregistered land (see e g *Bristol and West Building Society v Henning* [1985] 1 WLR 778 at 782G, 783C).

4   *Ulster Bank Ltd v Shanks* [1982] NI 143 at 150D per Murray J. Likewise Browne-Wilkinson LJ declared in *Bristol and West Building Society v Henning* [1985] 1 WLR 778 at 782G that he 'would not impute to the parties an intention to mislead the society by purporting to offer the unencumbered fee simple of the property as security when in fact there was to be an equitable interest which would take priority to the society.'

5   *Knightly v Sun Life Assurance Society Ltd* (1981) Times, 23 July per Nourse J. See also *Bristol and West Building Society v Henning* [1985] 1 WLR 778 at 781G–782A, where Browne-Wilkinson LJ observed that there was a 'risk that the common sense answer in this case may get lost in the many different technicalities which can arise. The basic fact is that the mortgage was granted to the society with the full knowledge and approval of Mrs Henning.'

6   (1985) 50 P & CR 244 [**para 12.164**].

7   Overriding status attaches only to those rights which, by their 'inherent quality', are enforceable at the date of the relevant disposition ((1985) 50 P & CR 244 at 248–249 per Browne-Wilkinson LJ).

12.216   In *Equity & Law Home Loans Ltd v Prestidge*[1] the same approach was extended to defeat the beneficial claim of a mortgagor's wife who had certainly known of the existence of an acquisition mortgage, but who was wholly unaware that this mortgage had later been replaced by a new mortgage covering an even larger loan advanced to her husband.[2] In this context, said Mustill LJ, the wife's beneficial interest was one 'which from the outset had carved out of it by anticipation a recognition of the rights of the mortgagees whose finance was intended to bring the purchase into being.'[3] The wife was therefore deemed to have consented to the replacement mortgage to the extent of the amount (plus accrued interest) secured by the first mortgage.[4]

1   [1992] 1 WLR 137 at 143H–145B.

2   The wife's imputed consent to the first mortgage 'must, in common sense, apply to the creation of a new encumbrance in replacement of the old, whether [the wife] knew about it or not, provided that it did not change [her] position for the worse' ([1992] 1 WLR 137 at 144B per Mustill LJ).

3   [1992] 1 WLR 137 at 145D.

4   Mustill LJ conceded ([1992] 1 WLR 137 at 144G) that the mortgagee should not be able to

enforce its security against the wife in any sum larger than that of the original mortgage advance. See also *Locabail (UK) Ltd v Waldorf Investment Corpn* (1999) Times, 31 March, per Deputy Judge Lawrence Collins QC.

Exclusion of acquisition mortgages

12.217   An even more significant limitation on the effect of the *Boland* ruling emerged from the decision of the House of Lords in *Abbey National Building Society v Cann*.[1] Where a taking of title is funded by a mortgage loan from a third party, it used to be thought that a *scintilla temporis* (or fraction of time) was interposed between the arrival of the legal title in the new registered proprietor and the creation by him of the mortgage charge which secured the money advance necessary for his acquisition.[2] Accordingly it was believed that, where a collaborative purchase was funded by disparate contributors in conjunction with an acquisition mortgage loan, the all-important interval of a micro-second allowed an implied trust of land to engraft itself upon the newly acquired title in advance of the disposition of charge.[3] The beneficial interests of the contributing co-owners would therefore take priority – albeit by the narrowest of margins – over the charge taken by the lender.

1   [1991] 1 AC 56 [**para 12.188**].
2   See *Church of England Building Society v Piskor* [1954] Ch 553 at 564–565 [**para 15.105**].
3   See Law Com No 115 (1982), paras 33–34.

12.218   In *Cann*'s case the House of Lords denied the operation of any *scintilla temporis* in the creation of acquisition mortgages.[1] The House ruled that, in the vast majority of cases of acquisition mortgage, the acquisition of the legal title and the creation of the charge are 'not only precisely simultaneous but indissolubly bound together.'[2] In consequence the legal owner who can fund his acquisition of title only 'by borrowing money for the security of which he is contractually bound to grant a mortgage to the lender eo instante with the execution of the conveyance in his favour cannot in reality ever be said to have acquired even for a *scintilla temporis* the unencumbered fee simple or leasehold estate in land whereby he could grant interests having priority over the mortgage.'[3] In such cases the estate taken by the legal owner is an already encumbered interest or 'equity of redemption'.[4] Thus any trust which comes into being is necessarily carved out of the attenuated rights of the legal owner, with the consequence that the mortgagee's security under the charge enjoys an inevitable priority over any equitable rights asserted by beneficial owners behind the trust.[5] By eliminating the operation of any *scintilla temporis*, *Cann*'s case effectively excluded acquisition mortgage transactions from the scope of the *Boland* ruling, indirectly destroying any possibility that financial contributors towards a purchase may ever claim priority over the mortgagee in respect of their beneficial interests.

1   See also *Nationwide Anglia Building Society v Ahmed* (1995) 70 P & CR 381 at 389.
2   [1991] 1 AC 56 at 92F per Lord Oliver of Aylmerton.
3   [1991] 1 AC 56 at 102A–B per Lord Jauncey of Tullichettle. See also *Ingram v IRC* [2000] 1 AC 293 at 303F–G per Lord Hoffmann ('I do not think that a theory based upon the notion of a scintilla temporis can have a very powerful grasp on reality').

4   **[Para 15.17]**.
5   This consequence of the *Cann* ruling obtains irrespective of any knowledge on the part of the beneficiaries that the acquisition depended vitally on mortgage finance. The logic of *Cann's* case is, moreover, equally applicable to unregistered titles.

Exclusion of trusts involving a minor

12.219   The courts have also confirmed that the *Boland* principle has no application to trusts of land under which one of the beneficiaries is a minor. In *Hypo-Mortgage Services Ltd v Robinson*[1] the Court of Appeal ruled that minor children of the legal owner are incapable, in their own right, of asserting an 'actual occupation' sufficient for any claim that their beneficial entitlement 'overrides' a disposition of the registered estate.

1   [1997] 2 FLR 71 at 72F.

Application for a court-ordered sale

12.220   The recourse for a chargee who is trapped by beneficial interests hidden behind an implied trust of land may ultimately lie in the pursuit of remedies other than those which are incidents of his charge over the trustee's legal estate. A successful claim of overriding entitlement (or even some defence based on misrepresentation or undue influence[1]) may disable the chargee from taking possession of the land and exercising the mortgagee's paramount power of sale.[2] But if frustrated in the independent exercise of his rights at law, the chargee still holds a charge which is valid and enforceable, with the aid of the court, over the chargor's *equitable* interest in the land. As a secured creditor holding 'an interest in property subject to a trust of land', the chargee has locus standi to apply for a court order directing sale pursuant to the Trusts of Land and Appointment of Trustees Act 1996.[3] Alternatively it remains open to the chargee to sue on the borrower's personal covenant to repay the mortgage debt.[4] On obtaining a money judgment against the sole registered proprietor in respect of this personal liability, the lender is then free, as a judgment creditor, to apply for a charging order under which he can seek a court order for sale of the property charged.[5] In an even more draconian response, the lender may elect to abandon his security altogether in order to bring bankruptcy proceedings against the registered proprietor.[6] In such a case, it is extremely unlikely under the Insolvency Act 1986 that the court will postpone sale for more than a limited period of perhaps one year.[7] Whichever of these three courses of action is adopted, a means is opened up for the lender, albeit ultimately at the discretion of the court,[8] to have access to the cash value of the chargor's beneficial share under the trust in at least partial satisfaction of the mortgage debt. The mere fact that some other trust beneficiary has an overriding interest affecting the registered estate does not, in itself, preclude a court-ordered sale.[9] The 'overriding' nature of such an interest ensures, at this stage, only that the owner of the overriding interest is entitled on sale to be paid the value of his or her interest unaffected by the chargee's claims.[10]

1   See e g *Zandfarid v Bank of Credit and Commerce International SA* [1996] 1 WLR 1420 at
     1424A–E; *Alliance and Leicester plc v Slayford* [2001] 1 All ER (Comm) 1 at [3] (wife-
     beneficiary misled over consent to charge and deprived of adequate legal advice).
2   See *Zandfarid v Bank of Credit and Commerce International SA* (Court of Appeal, 12 July
     1996) per Millett LJ. The chargee's remedies are cumulative and it is no abuse of process to
     seek by one means redress which cannot be obtained by another (see *Alliance and Leicester plc
     v Slayford* [2001] 1 All ER (Comm) 1 at [20], [28] per Peter Gibson LJ).
3   TOLATA 1996, s 14(1) **[para 11.266]**. See *Bank of Baroda v Dhillon* [1998] 1 FLR 524 at
     531C–D; [1998] Conv 415 (S Pascoe).
4   **[Para 15.133]**.
5   **[Para 9.118]**.
6   See e g *Zandfarid v Bank of Credit and Commerce International SA* [1996] 1 WLR 1420 at
     1425E–F. In *Williams & Glyn's Bank Ltd v Boland* [1981] AC 487 the bank could still have
     issued a bankruptcy notice and forced a sale of the land notwithstanding the wife's overriding
     interest (see Lord Hailsham LC in *Parliamentary Debates, House of Lords, Official Report*,
     Vol 437 (Session 1982–1983), Col 663 (15 December 1982)). However, the bank, having
     undertaken not to press for possession if it won the case **[para 12.209]**, was precluded from
     taking this course when it lost.
7   Insolvency Act 1986, s 335A(3) **[para 11.252]**.
8   For discussion of the likely outcome of this discretion, see **[paras 11.252–11.270]**.
9   See *Halifax Mortgage Services Ltd v Muirhead* (1997) 76 P & CR 418 at 428–429 per Evans LJ.
10   See e g *Northern Bank Ltd v Beattie* [1982] 18 NIJB, Transcript, p 25, per Murray J; *Bank of
     Baroda v Dhillon* [1998] 1 FLR 524 at 530E, 531C–D.

Net effect

12.221   The overall effect of many derogations from the *Boland* principle over
the last two decades is that, in the context of dispositions by way of mortgage
charge, this principle now catches only post-acquisition mortgages of a registered estate held by a sole trustee of land, and then only where latent equities
belong to adult persons who had no contemporary knowledge of the charge
and are not otherwise estopped from asserting their rights against the chargee.
Even if, notwithstanding all these qualifications, a beneficial trust interest is
found to have overriding status under the Land Registration Act 2002, this may
mean no more than that, on a court-ordered sale of the land, the value of that
interest is paid out to the relevant beneficiary ahead of any payment to the
secured lender.

LICENCES AND ESTOPPELS AS OVERRIDING INTERESTS

12.222   Although bare licences[1] are clearly excluded from the scope of
Schedule 3, para 2 of the Land Registration Act 2002,[2] predictable difficulty
has been generated by the question whether contractual licences, equitable (or
irrevocable) licences and estoppel-based rights can ever constitute overriding
interests. Partly because these sorts of entitlement hover uncertainly around the
threshold of proprietary character,[3] the law in this area has gone through a
period of evolution.[4] Some of the difficulties are now relieved by the Land
Registration Act 2002.

1   **[Para 4.2]**.

2   See, in relation to LRA 1925, s 70(1)(g), *Strand Securities Ltd v Caswell* [1965] Ch 958 at
      980C–D; Law Com No 158 (1987), para 2.56. See also *Kemmis v Kemmis* [1988] 1 WLR 1307
      at 1335B–D.
3   **[Para 4.95].**
4   The following account of the status of licences and estoppels in registered land must be read
      in conjunction with the parallel narrative concerning unregistered land **[paras 12.363–12.371].**
      Many of the important indications of the proprietary significance of such rights have arisen in
      the latter context and have exerted a persuasive impact on the field of registered land.

Contractual licences

12.223   Received doctrine holds that a contractual licence confers on the
licensee no proprietary interest in the land.[1] Thus, even if coupled with actual
occupation of land, the contractual licence can never 'override' dispositions of
a registered estate. This deeply orthodox view is founded on a firm belief that
the rights of contractual licensees are at all times merely personal rights and
bind only the immediate contracting parties.[2] In English law this non-
proprietary analysis of the contractual licence derives from the longstanding
House of Lords' authority of *King v David Allen and Sons, Billposting, Ltd*[3] and
is heavily reinforced by the influential decision of the Court of Appeal in *Clore
v Theatrical Properties Ltd and Westby & Co Ltd*.[4] The history of the contractual licence is nonetheless one of controversy, with the result that even
venerable authority has never entirely suppressed the recurring suggestion that
certain kinds of contractual licence may, in some circumstances, bind third
parties.

1   **[Para 4.96].** See e g *Patel v Patel* [1983] Court of Appeal Unbound Transcript 930 per Slade LJ
      [para 12.367].
2   The benefit of a contractual licence may be expressly assigned to a third party (see
      e g *Picton-Warlow v Allendale Holdings Pty Ltd* [1988] WAR 107 at 114 (parking bay)).
3   [1916] 2 AC 54 at 59–62 per Lord Buckmaster LC. See likewise firm rulings in the High Court
      of Australia in *Minister of State for the Army v Dalziel* (1944) 68 CLR 261 at 300 per Williams
      J; *Howie v New South Wales Lawn Tennis Ground Ltd* (1956) 95 CLR 132 at 156–157 per
      Dixon CJ, McTiernan and Fullagar JJ.
4   [1936] 3 All ER 483 at 490–491 per Lord Wright MR and Romer LJ. See also *Walton
      Harvey Ltd v Walker and Homfrays Ltd* [1931] 1 Ch 274 at 277.

The conceptual dilemma

12.224   The orthodox view of the contractual licence represents sound commonsense in relation to those licences which have only a short lifespan and are
directed towards intensely purposive activity. It would be absurd, for instance,
to suggest that the holder of a cinema ticket has a proprietary interest in the
cinema. 'Fifty thousand people who pay to see a football match do not obtain
fifty thousand interests in the football ground.'[1] Yet the field of contractual
licences also includes rights which take effect over a much longer time-scale and
operate virtually indistinguishably from some forms of estate ownership.[2] In
relation to such licences the attribution of proprietary character is not nearly so
bizarre. During the past half-century, moreover, the emergence of an equitable

jurisdiction to restrain the premature revocation of contractual licences has reinforced the idea that at least certain species of contractual licence – particularly those which may be viewed as licences 'coupled with an equity'[3] – could have an extended impact upon third parties. It became no longer outrageous to contend that the protective vigour of the courts in satisfying the 'equity' of the licence had effectively converted contractual licences into something closely resembling rights of property.[4]

1   *Cowell v Rosehill Racecourse Co Ltd* (1937) 56 CLR 605 at 616 per Latham CJ.
2   **[Para 4.64]**.
3   **[Para 4.88]**.
4   The chasm between contract and property has been spanned before in English law – for example in the case of the restrictive covenant – but the courts have strictly defined the qualities which must be possessed by restrictive covenants before they cross the threshold of the law of property **[paras 9.154–9.170]**. See H W R Wade, (1952) 68 LQR 337 at 348.

The Denning doctrine

12.225   It was, perhaps predictably, Lord Denning who became the foremost protagonist of the theory that the contractual licence had been elevated to the status of a virtual equitable interest in land.[1] Notwithstanding the suggestion that such a development could properly be achieved only by statutory intervention,[2] Lord Denning consistently maintained that, at least where equity was prepared to protect the licensee from wrongful revocation, the contractual licence had acquired the capacity, if coupled with actual occupation, to override registered transactions.[3] Lord Denning sought to deflect the contrary authority of *King* and *Clore* by arguing that these decisions had involved contractual licensees who were not 'in actual occupation of the land.'[4] However, such significant landmarks in the law of contractual licences were less easily moved than may have been supposed. Even at its height the Denning doctrine encountered opposition from property lawyers of a more orthodox cast. In *National Provincial Bank Ltd v Hastings Car Mart Ltd*,[5] for example, Russell LJ indicated his own view that the inescapable basis for the decisions in *King* and *Clore* was the courts' refusal to accept that a contractual licence could be anything other than a private agreement binding only the immediate parties.[6]

1   See, however, LPA 1925, s 4(1) (proviso) **[para 2.95]**.
2   See e g *National Provincial Bank Ltd v Hastings Car Mart Ltd* [1964] Ch 665 at 699 per Russell LJ. On appeal the House of Lords, although cautious as to the current status of the contractual licence, was less definite about the need for legislation and was not wholly unsympathetic to the idea of further judicial development (see *National Provincial Bank Ltd v Ainsworth* [1965] AC 1175 at 1239E per Lord Upjohn, 1251E per Lord Wilberforce).
3   See e g *National Provincial Bank Ltd v Hastings Car Mart Ltd* [1964] Ch 665 at 686–689. Lord Denning's stance drew substantial strength from his own view, expressed earlier in *Errington v Errington and Woods* [1952] 1 KB 290 at 298–299 that, by reason of equitable intervention, contractual licences now had a 'force and validity of their own' which could bind third parties. See also *Binions v Evans* [1972] Ch 359 at 368D–369C **[paras 10.90, 12.365]**.
4   *National Provincial Bank Ltd v Hastings Car Mart Ltd* [1964] Ch 665 at 688; *Binions v Evans* [1972] Ch 359 at 369A–B. Compare, however, *Hastings Car Mart Ltd*, supra at 697 per Russell LJ; R H Maudsley, (1956) 20 Conv (NS) 281 at 295.
5   [1964] Ch 665 at 697–698.

6   Russell LJ was unmoved by the impact of equitable intervention following *Winter Garden Theatre (London) Ltd v Millennium Productions Ltd* [1948] AC 173. He confessed that he found it 'not easy to see, on authority, how that which has a purely contractual basis between A and B is, though on all hands it is agreed that it is not to be regarded as conferring any estate or interest in property on B, nevertheless to be treated as producing the equivalent result against a purchaser C, simply because an injunction would be granted to restrain A from breaking his contract while he is still in a position to carry it out' ([1964] Ch 665 at 698).

Return to orthodoxy

12.226   Recent years have seen a significant return to the conventional analysis of the contractual licence as articulated in the cases of *King* and *Clore*. In *Ashburn Anstalt v Arnold*[1] the Court of Appeal gave a stern indication that contractual licences have no general binding impact on third parties. In *Ashburn Anstalt* it was argued that the transferee of a registered title, having agreed to take 'subject to' the rights of a contractual licensee, was bound by an overriding interest. The Court of Appeal was forthright in rejecting this contention.[2] According to Fox LJ (who delivered the Court's judgment[3]), the *King/Clore* line of authority rested on an 'important and intelligible distinction between contractual obligations which gave rise to no estate or interest in the land and proprietary rights which, by definition, did.'[4] The Court firmly endorsed the view that 'a contractual licence does not create a property interest'.[5] As Millett J noted later in *Camden LBC v Shortlife Community Housing Ltd*,[6] *Ashburn Anstalt* 'finally repudiated the heretical view that a contractual licence creates an interest in land capable of binding third parties.'[7] It would, accordingly, be difficult today to suggest that the rights of a contractual licensee (even in actual occupation of land) can properly be described as an interest 'affecting the estate' within the terms of the Land Registration Act 2002[8] so as to 'override' registered dispositions of that land.[9]

1   [1989] Ch 1. See [1988] CLJ 353 (A J Oakley); [1988] Conv 201 (M P Thompson); (1988) 51 MLR 226 (J Hill); (1988) 104 LQR 175 (P Sparkes); [1988] All ER Rev 176 (P J Clarke).

2   The point was obiter since the Court of Appeal decided that the rights in issue in *Ashburn Anstalt* were in fact rights of lease not licence [**para 7.115**]. See also the Court of Appeal's dismissal, albeit obiter, of a similar argument in *Canadian Imperial Bank of Commerce v Bello* (1992) 64 P & CR 48 at 51.

3   The other judges were Neill and Bingham LJJ.

4   [1989] Ch 1 at 22B–C. Although agreeing that the decision in *Errington v Errington and Woods* [1952] 1 KB 290 was correct on its facts, the Court of Appeal in *Anstalt Arnold* thought that Denning LJ's 'far-reaching statement of principle' in *Errington* had been unnecessary and, indeed, per incuriam ([1989] Ch 1 at 22C).

5   [1989] Ch 1 at 24D.

6   (1992) 90 LGR 358 at 373.

7   The observations of the Court of Appeal in *Ashburn Anstalt v Arnold* have had a profound declaratory significance in settling the status of the contractual licence. See e g *Canadian Imperial Bank of Commerce v Bello* (1992) 64 P & CR 48 at 51 per Dillon LJ; *IDC Group Ltd v Clark* (1992) 65 P & CR 179 at 181 per Nourse LJ; *Nationwide Anglia Building Society v Ahmed* (1995) 70 P & CR 381 at 387, 389 per Aldous LJ; *Habermann v Koehler* (1996) 73 P & CR 515 at 520 per Evans LJ, 523 per Peter Gibson LJ; *Melbury Road Properties 1995 Ltd v Kreidi* [1999] 3 EGLR 108 at 110H–J; *Lloyd v Dugdale* [2002] 2 P & CR 167 at [52(4)] per Sir Christopher Slade.

8   LRA 2002, s 29(1).
9   It remains awkward, however, to explain why a promise of rights based on consideration cannot 'override', whilst precisely this effect has been conferred on similar promises which induce detrimental reliance by the promisee **[para 10.168]**. See G Battersby [1991] Conv 36 at 37.

A conscience-based resolution

12.227   Although the tide of judicial opinion has now turned decisively against overriding status for the contractual licence, the Court of Appeal in *Ashburn Anstalt* left open the possibility that such a licence may still affect disponees of a registered title on other, rather different, grounds.

Imposition of constructive trust

12.228   In *Ashburn Anstalt* Fox LJ indicated that, in certain special circumstances, a disponee of title may be held bound by a *constructive trust* to give effect to a pre-existing contractual licence.[1] This analysis places a critical emphasis on the conscientiousness of the third party rather than on the intrinsic nature of the rights which it is sought to enforce against him.[2] The constructive trust does not operate against the disponee on the basis that the title which he takes is inherently encumbered by some binding proprietary right. Instead the trust arises precisely because – and only if – the disponee has 'burdened his own title' with an independent conscientious obligation towards the contractual licensee.[3] No court will impose a constructive trust 'unless it is satisfied that the conscience of the estate owner is affected.'[4] Accordingly it is always a question of fact whether there are any circumstances which a court of equity might regard as binding the conscience of the disponee so that he must hold on trust for the licensee.[5]

1   On constructive trusts, see Chapter 10 **[paras 10.58–10.167]**.
2   See *Melbury Road Properties 1995 Ltd v Kreidi* [1999] 3 EGLR 108 at 110J.
3   See *Bahr v Nicolay (No 2)* (1988) 164 CLR 604 at 653 per Brennan J **[para 12.127]**; *Lloyd v Dugdale* [2002] 2 P & CR 167 at [52(3)] per Sir Christopher Slade **[para 12.109]**.
4   *Ashburn Anstalt v Arnold* [1989] Ch 1 at 25H per Fox LJ. See also *Canadian Imperial Bank of Commerce v Bello* (1992) 64 P & CR 48 at 51 per Dillon LJ.
5   In *Lloyd v Dugdale* [2002] 2 P & CR 167 at [56], for example, the Court of Appeal was unwilling to impose a constructive trust on the basis of what, perhaps harshly, it viewed as 'very slender materials.' See similarly *Ashburn Anstalt v Arnold* [1989] Ch 1 at 26D–E per Fox LJ.

Triggers for the imposition of a constructive trust

12.229   In *Ashburn Anstalt* the Court of Appeal felt unable to accept 'as a general proposition' that a constructive trust could be upheld merely because a disponee takes title under a sale which is stipulated to be 'subject to' the rights of some other party.[1] However, Fox LJ indicated at least three instances, each involving some 'new' level or dimension of self-imposed obligation, where the court may properly exercise an *in personam* jurisdiction to counteract unconscientious conduct. First, a constructive trust may be applied in order to compel a disponee to give effect to a contractual licence subject to which he took title and in consequence of which he paid a lower than market price.[2] Second, a constructive trust may be appropriate where the contractual licence in question was not in fact enforceable against the disponor. In such a case the disponee's agreement to take subject to the rights concerned appears, not as an attempt to immunise his predecessor against contractual liability,[3] but rather as an entirely willing assumption of a new conscientious obligation towards the licensee.[4] Third, it may be relevant that an obligation of conscience has already been acknowledged (e g in writing) in respect of the relevant contractual entitlement.[5]

1 [1989] Ch 1 at 25D–26A. See likewise *Lloyd v Dugdale* [2002] 2 P & CR 167 at [52(1)] per Sir Christopher Slade, but compare *Kewal Investments Ltd v Arthur Maiden Ltd* [1990] 1 EGLR 193 at 194D, H–J per Deputy Judge Thomas Morison QC.
2 See similarly *Lloyd v Dugdale* [2002] 2 P & CR 167 at [52(5)] per Sir Christopher Slade. This view probably accounts for the outcome in *Binions v Evans* [1972] Ch 359 [**para 12.365**], which the Court of Appeal in *Ashburn Anstalt* [1989] Ch 1 at 23F considered to be 'a legitimate application of the doctrine of constructive trusts.'
3 See [1989] Ch 1 at 26B–C.
4 It was on this basis that the Court in *Ashburn Anstalt* [1989] Ch 1 at 24G–25A approved of *Lyus v Prowsa Developments Ltd* [1982] 1 WLR 1044 [**paras 10.73, 12.123**] as 'a case where a constructive trust could justifiably be imposed'. (*Lyus*, however, involved an estate contract and not a contractual licence.)
5 [1989] Ch 1 at 26D. See also *Bahr v Nicolay (No 2)* (1988) 164 CLR 604 at 633 per Wilson and Toohey JJ [**para 12.127**].

The future

12.230 The observations of the Court of Appeal in *Ashburn Anstalt v Arnold* have given a new and more subtle dimension to the question whether a contractual licence can exert a proprietary impact on disponees of a registered title. The law of contractual licences awaits an authoritative modern clarification by the House of Lords. Such clarification will necessarily touch upon the boundaries of the concept of property and, as already indicated in this book,[1] these boundaries are not definitive but are instead graded in relation to the context and function of the rights in question. Thus, for example, in *Sports Australia Pty Ltd v Nillumbik Shire Council*[2] the Supreme Court of Victoria overtly recognised the 'proprietary' status of a contractual licence to manage a golf course. This analysis was based on the ground that the contract did not simply entitle the licensee to 'enter upon the land for the purpose of viewing or taking part in some activity on the land', but authorised the licensee for a specified period to conduct a business on the land 'from which it makes its livelihood' and required it to spend money on capital improvements to the land.[3]

1 [**Para 2.13**].
2 Unreported, 29 January 1996.

3   See *Milton v Proctor* (1988) 4 BPR 9654 at 9672 per Clarke JA ('the law has developed to a
     stage where it would no longer be accurate to say that a licence never creates an interest in
     land').

12.231   The disavowal of proprietary character for the contractual licence in
Ashburn Anstalt v Arnold must be assessed in conjunction with other recent
developments which rather strengthen the perception that at least certain kinds
of contractual licence enjoy some proprietary or quasi-proprietary status in
relation to land. The increasing willingness of equity to protect contractual
licences by specific performance or injunction[1] has inevitably enhanced the
property content of the contractual licensee's entitlement in so far as the curial
guarantee of his rights confirms that he has some defensible 'stake' (as distinct
from a merely revocable privilege) in the land.[2] Precisely this effect is reinforced
by the Court of Appeal's ruling in *Manchester Airport Plc v Dutton*[3] that a
contractual licence to 'enter and occupy' land entitles the licensee to summary
possession of that land against trespassers. In certain contexts, moreover,
modern statute law has also abandoned, as a false dichotomy, any idea that the
contractual licence is essentially different from conventional proprietary estates
such as the lease.[4] Moreover, the facility now offered of universal recordation of
rights in a publicly accessible Land Register renders it far less necessary than
previously to constrict the menu of entitlements deemed capable of proprietary
status.[5] The law of the contractual licence has long been in flux. It is currently,
and self-evidently, caught up in yet another of those historic transformations of
perspective which cause rights of an initially personal quality to evolve into
entitlements of a generally accepted proprietary character.[6]

1   This willingness has been apparent even in cases of short-term user (see *Verrall v Great
     Yarmouth BC* [1981] QB 202 at 216A–F, 218B, 220D–F **[para 4.86]**).
2   See *Federal Airports Corpn v Makucha Developments Pty Ltd* (1993) 115 ALR 679 at 700
     [para 4.97].
3   [2000] 1 QB 133 at 150A–E, 151B–H **[paras 3.38, 4.98, 6.5, 7.145]**.
4   **[Para 4.99]**. See e g Housing Act 1985, s 79(3) (secure tenancy); Agricultural Holdings
     Act 1986, s 2(2)(b) (agricultural holding).
5   **[Para 2.97]**.
6   If, accordingly, the contractual licence becomes more widely acknowledged as an interest in
     land, one implication follows immediately. Except in so far as a contractual licence is
     protected by some constructive trust (see LPA 1925, s 53(2)), contractual licences will
     normally require to be created in writing signed by the licensor (LPA 1925, s 53(1)(a)).

Irrevocable licences and inchoate equities of estoppel

12.232   Similar issues are raised by the question whether, if coupled with
actual occupation, an irrevocable (or 'equitable') licence[1] or the inchoate rights
asserted by a claimant of proprietary estoppel[2] can 'override' registered dispositions under the Land Registration Act 2002.[3] The problem is dramatically
illustrated by a hypothetical extension of the facts present in *Pascoe v Turner*.[4]
If in this case, following the claimant's acts of detrimental reliance (but before
the dispute over occupation arose), the fee simple owner had sold or charged his
legal estate, would the disponee have taken subject to the inchoate equity of the

still resident estoppel claimant? Would the disponee have become liable to have his title qualified – or even extinguished – by the grant of some court-ordered property interest to that claimant? It seems inconceivable that an inchoate entitlement which, as between the immediate parties, provided the gateway to so large a remedy as an outright freehold transfer should be snuffed out by a simple disposition of the land to a stranger.[5]

1   [Paras 4.90, 10.38].
2   [Para 10.212]. There is, of course, a substantial conceptual and contextual overlap between the categories of irrevocable licence and estoppel-based equity, not least since both are derived from the idea of a 'licence coupled with an equity' [para 4.88].
3   Once the court has perfected or formalised an 'inchoate equity' of estoppel by awarding some conventional property right (eg a fee simple or term of years or easement or life interest), the subsequent binding impact of the court-ordered interest turns on wholly orthodox principles of land law. The courts have sometimes regarded third parties as bound even where claims are satisfied by the recognition of lesser entitlements in the form of an irrevocable licence (*Re Sharpe* (*A Bankrupt*) [1980] 1 WLR 219 at 224G). See also *Williams v Staite* [1979] Ch 291, where the point seems to have been assumed without explicit argument. Compare, however, G Battersby, 'Contractual and Estoppel Licences as Proprietary Interests in Land' [1991] Conv 36 at 39, for a strong argument that the court-ordered remedy will bind third parties only if the right awarded by the court constitutes a conventionally recognised species of proprietary interest.
4   [1979] 1 WLR 431 [paras 7.28, 10.193].
5   The 'equity' of the estoppel claimant is not qualitatively different from the right of the trust beneficiary to have the trust property dealt with as his trust requires. The latter right 'is regarded for the purposes of equity as equivalent to a right in the property itself' (*Glenn v Federal Commissioner of Land Tax* (1915) 20 CLR 490 at 503 per Isaacs J), equitable ownership being 'always commensurate with the right to relief in a Court of Equity' (*Trustees, Executors and Agency Co Ltd v Acting Federal Commissioner of Taxation* (1917) 23 CLR 576 at 583 [para 9.33]).

Gradual recognition of proprietary significance

12.233   In the older case law it was taken largely for granted that, although an inchoate 'equity' based on estoppel could comprise an 'interest in land' for isolated statutory purposes,[1] this form of entitlement never constituted a 'property interest' or 'interest in land' in the strict conveyancing sense.[2] The claimant of an 'equity' held no property right[3] and thus qualified for no overriding interest unless and until a court finally awarded him some form of conventional property right in satisfaction of his 'equity'.[4] In more recent years this analysis became increasingly hard to sustain as equities based on estoppel or irrevocable licence emerged as the functional equivalent of beneficial entitlement behind a trust of land.[5] Indeed, in some areas of its operation, the estoppel principle is nowadays acknowledged to 'coincide' with the field of constructive trust[6] and there is a distinct difficulty in maintaining that informal trust entitlements can be overriding interests[7] but that equities based on irrevocable licence or estoppel cannot.

1   *Pennine Raceway Ltd v Kirklees MBC* [1983] QB 382 at 389F, 391D–E (eligibility for compensation pursuant to Town and Country Planning legislation). See [1983] Conv 317 (J E M). See also *Plimmer v Mayor etc of Wellington* (1884) 9 App Cas 699 at 714 [para 10.197].

2   See e g *Pennine Raceway Ltd v Kirklees MBC* [1983] QB 382 at 391A. The same analysis extended to the relatively inarticulate entitlement comprised in the irrevocable or equitable licence.

3   The reluctance to recognise any significant proprietary content in these forms of entitlement flowed, in part, from the perceived difficulty of placing such interests within the canon of rights recognised by the Law of Property Act 1925. This issue relates, in its turn, to the question whether there exists any *numerus clausus* in respect of recognisable proprietary interests in land [**para 2.95**].

4   See *Canadian Imperial Bank of Commerce v Bello* (1992) 64 P & CR 48 at 52 per Dillon LJ.

5   See *Re Sharpe* (*A Bankrupt*) [1980] 1 WLR 219 at 223C–H, 225G–H per Browne-Wilkinson J. See also [**paras 10.213–10.215**] for an account of the way in which courts have come to recognise that estoppel doctrine generates anticipatory beneficial rights on the basis of which the judge then fashions an order for specific performance or compensatory damages (see e g *Sen v Headley* [1991] Ch 425 at 440A per Nourse LJ; *Voyce v Voyce* (1991) 62 P & CR 290 at 294 per Dillon LJ; *Commonwealth of Australia v Verwayen* (1990) 170 CLR 394 at 437 per Deane J).

6   *Yaxley v Gotts* [2000] Ch 162 at 176E per Robert Walker LJ [**para 10.111**]. See also *Lloyds Bank Plc v Rosset* [1991] 1 AC 107 at 132F–G per Lord Bridge of Harwich; *Banner Homes Group Plc v Luff Developments Ltd* [2000] Ch 372 at 384A–D per Chadwick LJ; *Birmingham Midshires Mortgage Services Ltd v Sabherwal* (2000) 80 P & CR 256 at 263 per Robert Walker LJ.

7   [**Para 12.226**].

12.234   The case law generated by the Land Registration Act 1925 inevitably began to demonstrate a steady drift towards an acceptance of the proprietary character of all conscience-based equities in land.[1] In *Birmingham Midshires Mortgage Services Ltd v Sabherwal*[2] the Court of Appeal was prepared to assume that a claimant, on proof of detrimental reliance on another's promises, would obtain 'through the medium of estoppel ... equitable rights of a proprietary nature' and that her actual occupation of relevant land 'would then have promoted those rights into an overriding interest.'[3] The trend evidenced in *Sabherwal*'s case was reinforced by the even more obvious tendency, in the parallel context of unregistered title, to treat equities founded on irrevocable licence or estoppel as binding purchasers other than those who take for value and without notice.[4] In either context a similar outcome could have been supported, in any event, by recourse to the *in personam* jurisdiction to restrain unconscionable conduct by third parties. It was always open to the courts to hold that an inchoate equity of estoppel affected a third party who had 'burdened his own title' with an independent conscientious obligation towards the estoppel claimant whose terms he could not now disavow.[5]

1   [**Para 12.227**]. It became increasingly clear that Land Registry was prepared to accept the entry in the Land Register of unperfected equities founded on proprietary estoppel and irrevocable licence (see Law Com No 254 (1998), para 3.36; Law Com No 271 (2001), para 5.30; *Bhullar v McArdle* (2001) 82 P & CR 481 at [50]). This approach was already reflected in the practice of other Torrens title jurisdictions (see e g *Holee Holdings (M) Sdn Bhd v Chai Him* [1997] 4 MLJ 601 at 645–653).

2   (2000) 80 P & CR 256 at 262–263 per Robert Walker LJ. See also G Battersby, 'Informal Transactions in Land, Estoppel and Registration' (1995) 58 MLR 637 at 642.

3   See similarly *Habermann v Koehler* (1996) 73 P & CR 515 at 520 per Evans LJ, 522–523 per Peter Gibson LJ; *Lloyd v Dugdale* [2002] 2 P & CR 167 at [39] per Sir Christopher Slade. This trend simply followed the lead given many years earlier by Lord Denning MR in *National*

Provincial Bank Ltd v Hastings Car Mart Ltd [1964] Ch 665 at 689 and by Goulding J in *Lee-Parker v Izzet (No 2)* [1972] 1 WLR 775 at 780G.

4   **[Paras 12.363–12.371]**.
5   See *Bahr v Nicolay (No 2)* (1988) 164 CLR 604 at 653 per Brennan J **[para 12.228]**. See also Wilson and Toohey JJ (at 638–639). In the context of this jurisdiction, it would not matter whether the claimant was in 'actual occupation' of the land or even whether his 'equity' was proprietary in character. The 'policing' function of the *in personam* jurisdiction operates regardless of the intrinsic character of the rights violated by the disponee: the critical question relates, once again, to the conscientiousness of the relevant actor **[para 12.228]**.

Statutory clarification

12.235   The Land Registration Act 2002 has finally placed the proprietary character of estoppel-based rights beyond all dispute. For the 'avoidance of doubt' the 2002 Act declares that, in relation to registered land, an 'equity by estoppel' has effect 'from the time the equity arises as an interest capable of binding successors in title.'[1] This innovative provision seems to have been crafted deliberately to ensure that an unperfected or inchoate equity of estoppel, if coupled with actual occupation on the part of the claimant, can now 'override' registered dispositions by virtue of Schedule 3, para 2 of the Act.[2]

1   LRA 2002, s 116(a) **[para 12.161]**.
2   See Law Com No 271 (2001), paras 5.30–5.31. The Law Commission acknowledged, with regret, the impossibility of securing a similar clarification for unregistered land (see para 5.28), but comforted itself with the thought that 'unregistered land is unlikely to have an extended future.'

12.236   The fact that an inchoate equity of estoppel 'overrides' a registered disposition is not, in itself, determinative of its actual impact on the disponee of the registered title. The newly recognised overriding status of the inchoate equity certainly marks an important acknowledgement that third parties are not immune from the requirements of conscionable dealing: the mandate of conscience is no respecter of persons. But the binding effect of the inchoate equity simply means that third parties must discharge the burden of showing that *their* proposed assertion of strict legal entitlement is not, in its own turn, unconscionable.[1] The call of conscience requires to be measured de novo in the light of the circumstances in which each disponee takes title. The ultimate effect of the inchoate equity is tailored specifically, in the discretion of the court, to the particular disponee whom it is sought to affect. The mere fact that an 'equity' of estoppel might command a particular remedial outcome as against one estate owner in no way precludes the possibility that another estate owner remains free, without injury to conscience, to enforce his strict legal rights or to proffer only some limited money compensation as the precondition for doing so.[2] The question of overriding conscientious obligation arises afresh on each occasion and may well admit of divergent responses on different occasions.

1   See Browne-Wilkinson, 'Constructive Trusts and Unjust Enrichment' (1996) 10 Trust Law International 98 at 100 ('[o]nly if the third party's conduct is such as to raise an estoppel against the third party individually will the third party be affected').
2   There is thus no inherent contradiction in the idea that the inchoate equity may bind third

parties even though the entitlement in which it is perfected has only personal effect. The inchoate equity is, in reality, merely a claim to be heard by a court of conscience **[para 10.212]**.

LEGAL EASEMENTS AND PROFITS *À PRENDRE*

12.237   Schedule 3, para 3 of the Land Registration Act 2002 confers overriding status on certain kinds of easement and profit *à prendre*, but it is important to observe the limitations of this provision. In the years preceding the enactment of the 2002 Act it came to be widely believed that disponees of registered estates were unacceptably disadvantaged by the extensive range of easements and profits deemed capable of overriding a registered disposition. The relevant provision in the Land Registration Act 1925[1] clearly gave overriding status to legal easements[2] and to profits *à prendre* (whether legal or equitable). Rather late in the history of the 1925 legislation the same provision was also held to include a category of *equitable* easements which were 'openly exercised and enjoyed' over registered land.[3] Such rights, although they could have been the subject of an entry in the register of the servient land, remained overriding, for want of such protection, as against unwitting disponees of that land. It therefore became a major purpose of the Land Registration Act 2002 to cut back the kinds of easement or profit which could 'override' registered dispositions under the Act.[4]

1   LRA 1925, s 70(1)(a). See *Elements of Land Law* (3rd edn 2001), p 978.
2   See *Britel Developments (Thatcham) Ltd v Nightfreight (Great Britain) Ltd* [1998] 4 All ER 432 at 433g.
3   See *Celsteel Ltd v Alton House Holdings Ltd* [1985] 1 WLR 204 at 220H–221D per Scott J (relying on LRR 1925, r 258). Scott J's ruling was affirmed without comment on appeal ([1986] 1 WLR 512). For a similar conclusion, see *Payne v Adnams* [1971] CLY 6486; *Thatcher v Douglas* (1995) 146 NLJ 282, 140 SJ LB 36; *Valentine v Allen* [2003] EWCA Civ 915 at [72]–[73] per Hale LJ. On this basis, only concealed equitable easements (e g undetectable easements of underground drainage) fell outside the class of overriding easements.
4   See Law Com No 158 (1987), paras 2.26–2.33; Law Com No 254 (1998), paras 5.24, 5.119; Law Com No 271 (2001), para 8.66.

No overriding status for equitable easements and profits

12.238   Overriding interest protection for newly created easements and profits is strictly confined by the Land Registration Act 2002 to *legal* rights alone.[1] Irrespective of its mode of creation, no equitable easement or profit brought into being following the commencement of the 2002 Act can ever override a registered disposition. Instead, the objective of the 2002 Act is to ensure that the express disposition of any new easement or profit out of registered land must, if the disposition is to 'operate at law', be completed by registration.[2] If duly completed by registration, the relevant disposition creates rights which appear quite visibly on the register and cannot therefore be overriding. If not so completed, the disposition creates merely *equitable* rights for the disponee which, under the altered regime of the Land Registration Act 2002, are explicitly excluded from the category of easements and profits which can 'override' later dispositions of the servient land.

1   LRA 2002, Sch 3, para 3(1). See Law Com No 271 (2001), para 8.67.
2   LRA 2002, s 27(1), (2)(d) **[para 8.119]**.

Overriding status for legal easements and profits created by implication or prescription

12.239   The net effect of the Land Registration Act 2002 is, at least prospectively, to confine the overriding interest category to rights which arise by prescription[1] or by implied grant[2] or reservation.[3] Even in relation to these kinds of entitlement, a disponee of a registered estate for value is bound *only if*, at the time of the disposition, the right in question:

−   was 'within the actual knowledge' of the disponee[4] or
−   was 'obvious on a reasonably careful inspection of the land over which the easement or profit is exercisable'[5] or
−   had been exercised within the period of one year immediately preceding the date of the disposition[6] or
−   was registered under the Commons Registration Act 1965[7] (in which case, the right was easily discoverable by the disponee).

1   **[Para 8.168]**.
2   **[Para 8.128]**.
3   **[Para 8.199]**.
4   LRA 2002, Sch 3, para 3(1)(a).
5   LRA 2002, Sch 3, para 3(1)(b). The overriding right must, in effect, be 'patent … so that no seller of land would be obliged to disclose it' (Law Com No 271 (2001), para 8.69).
6   LRA 2002, Sch 3, para 3(2). The burden of so proving rests on the person entitled to the relevant easement or profit. The category of right envisaged here includes 'invisible' easements such as rights of drainage or the right to run a water supply pipe over a neighbour's land (see Law Com No 271 (2001), para 8.70).
7   LRA 2002, Sch 3, para 3(1).

12.240   Again the legislative concern is plainly to protect disponees for value against any burden which was neither subjectively known to them nor readily detectable by inspection or otherwise. The change effected by the 2002 Act removes the safety net previously provided for equitable easements which were 'openly exercised and enjoyed' and accords with the general strategy of ensuring that all easements expressly granted out of registered land must be completed by registration if they are to bind subsequent disponees of the servient land.

Pre-existing easements and profits

12.241   Any easement or profit which was an overriding interest immediately before the commencement of Schedule 3 of the Land Registration Act 2002 automatically retains its overriding status under the new Act.[1] Furthermore, for

a transitional period of three years following commencement, *all* legal easements and profits will 'override' registered dispositions irrespective of whether
they were reasonable discoverable or actually known to the relevant disponee.[2]
Thereafter all such rights will require protection by register entry.[3]

1   LRA 2002, s 134(2), Sch 12, para 9(1)–(2). There is, however, a general hope that such rights
    will be voluntarily registered (see Law Com No 271 (2001), para 8.73(1)).
2   LRA 2002, s 134(2), Sch 12, para 10.
3   See Law Com No 271 (2001), para 8.73(2).

LOCAL LAND CHARGES

12.242   Under the Land Registration Act 2002 local land charges 'override'
registered dispositions of title.[1] Such charges relate to a range of local government impositions and restrictions in respect of highway repair, drainage and
sewerage, the abatement of statutory nuisances, preservation of listed buildings,
planning and environmental controls, and tree preservation orders.[2]

1   LRA 2002, Sch 3, para 6 (see formerly LRA 1925, s 70(1)(i)). See also now LRA 2002,
    s 134(2), Sch 12, para 13.
2   **[Para 12.7]**.

RIGHTS IN RESPECT OF REPAIR OF A CHANCEL

12.243   The Land Registration Act 1925 provided that a liability to repair the
chancel of a church comprised a further head of overriding interest.[1] This
controversial liability (of ancient common law origin) imposes a financial
responsibility for chancel repairs – effectively a duty to contribute towards the
preservation of the national architectural heritage – on certain landowners in
their capacity as the current proprietors of former rectorial glebe land adjacent
to the church in question.[2] The obligation is quaint, but can often expose
proprietors to an onerous and wholly unexpected form of financial liability.[3]
Chancel repair liability was originally omitted from the list of potentially
overriding interests contained in the Land Registration Act 2002, largely on the
surmise that this arbitrary form of local taxation had become unenforceable
under the Human Rights Act 1998.[4] This assumption was later falsified by the
House of Lords in *Aston Cantlow and Wilmcote with Billesley PCC v Wallbank*,[5] with the consequence that the right to repair of a chancel has had to be
reinstated amongst the head of interests which 'override' a registered disposition of the burdened land,[6] albeit subject to the proviso that all chancel repair
liabilities will cease to be overriding on 13 October 2013.[7]

1   LRA 1925, s 70(1)(c).
2   Chancel repair liability applies in the case of probably one third of all parish churches in
    England and Wales, the land affected by this liability being estimated to cover nearly four
    million acres (*Property Law: Liability for Chancel Repairs* (Law Com No 152, November
    1985), para 1.2).
3   In *Aston Cantlow and Wilmcote with Billesley PCC v Wallbank* [2004] 1 AC 546, a liability in

excess of £95,000 was imposed on an elderly couple who had inherited their land some 30 years earlier. See also *Chivers & Sons Ltd v Air Ministry* [1955] Ch 585 at 594–595 (land sold by Queens' College Cambridge).

4   See *Aston Cantlow and Wilmcote with Billesley PCC v Wallbank* [2002] Ch 51. The Law Commission had, at one stage, proposed that all chancel repair liabilities should be phased out without compensation over a period of ten years (Law Com No 152 (1985), para 4.18). See also Law Com No 271 (2001), para 8.75; Gray, 'Land Law and Human Rights', in Louise Tee (ed), *Land Law: Issues, Debates, Policy* (Willan Publishing 2002), p 234.

5   [2004] 1 AC 546 [**para 2.69**]. See [2003] Conv 351 (P Kenny); [2004] CLJ 7 (L Turano).

6   LRA 2002, Sch 3, para 16, as inserted by Land Registration Act 2002 (Transitional Provisions) (No 2) Order 2003 (SI 2003/2431), Art 2 (effective 13 October 2003).

7   [**Para 12.135**]. Until that date rights to chancel repair will be permanently protectable, without payment of any fee, by entry in the Land Register (LRA 2002, s 117(2)).

OTHER OVERRIDING ENTITLEMENTS

12.244   The Land Registration Act 2002 accords a general overriding status to customary rights[1] (ie rights enjoyed by inhabitants of a particular locality[2]) and public rights,[3] together with certain entitlements to coal and coal mines[4] and certain rights to minerals in land whose title was registered prior to 1926.[5]

1   LRA 2002, s 29(2)(a)(ii), Sch 3, para 4.

2   [**Para 5.28**]. See Law Com No 271 (2001), para 8.27.

3   LRA 2002, s 29(2)(a)(ii), Sch 3, para 5. Public rights include the right of any member of the public under the general law to use the public highway (see *Secretary of State for the Environment, Transport and the Regions v Baylis (Gloucester) Ltd* (2000) 80 P & CR 324 at 339 [**para 5.3**]) or to discharge effluent into a public sewer, but cannot extend to rights acquired by a public authority which, although existing for public benefit, are not intrinsically exercisable by members of the public as individuals. See eg *Overseas Investment Ltd v Simcobuild Construction Ltd and Swansea CC* (1995) 70 P & CR 322 at 329–331 (local authority's right to bring about future construction of highway on private owner's land).

4   LRA 2002, s 29(2)(a)(ii), Sch 3, para 7. See Law Com No 271 (2001), para 8.32.

5   LRA 2002, s 29(2)(a)(ii), Sch 3, paras 8–9. See Law Com No 271 (2001), paras 8.33–8.34.

ALTERATIONS OF THE REGISTER

12.245   An 'absolute title' to land is the most secure form of title recognised under the Land Registration Act 2002. It is nevertheless an inherent feature of the 2002 Act that no registered title is ultimately unalterable or indefeasible.[1] Although it is 'critical to keep to a minimum the number of matters which may defeat the title of the registered proprietor',[2] it remains the case that, regardless of the class of title awarded to an applicant for first registration, no register of title is ever bullet-proof. Even 'absolute' titles are liable to be altered in certain kinds of circumstance. The Land Registration Act 1925 specified a number of grounds of 'rectification' of the register,[3] but the 2002 Act has recast these provisions in a simplified and 'much more transparent form.'[4] The Law Commission, in proposing this rationalisation, was firmly of the view that alteration of the register should be encompassed within one general principle that there is a discretionary power to amend the register 'whenever there has been an error or omission in it.'[5]

1   **[Para 6.4]**.
2   *British American Cattle Co v Caribe Farm Industries Ltd* [1998] 1 WLR 1529 at 1533H per Lord Browne-Wilkinson.
3   LRA 1925, s 82(1).
4   Law Com No 271 (2001), para 10.4.
5   Law Com No 254 (1998), paras 8.41–8.43, 8.58.

The potential for inaccuracy in the register

12.246   When lodged for first registration, unregistered titles are examined and classified on behalf of the Chief Land Registrar,[1] one merit of the procedure being that technical defects can be cleared off at this stage. Applicants with a good holding title are normally awarded an 'absolute title' but, irrespective of the precise class of title awarded, all registered titles are backed by a state guarantee that indemnity will be paid in any case of error resulting in loss. In view of the sheer volume of titles being handled, errors are bound to occur, whether at first registration or at some later date, notwithstanding the care exercised by officials of the Land Registry.[2] Title plans may be ever so slightly awry; pre-registration deeds and subsequent dispositionary documents may themselves contain inaccuracies; undisclosed interests may suddenly emerge as affecting the land; initial assessments of the reliability of the title offered for first registration may turn out, in the event, to have been misjudged. Further inaccuracy in the register inevitably occurs when interests which were duly entered in the register terminate or are forfeited or become otherwise unenforceable. Spent or redundant entries require to be removed. In all these respects there is an obvious need for some mechanism which will enable the Land Register to be kept accurate and up to date. This mechanism is now found in the 'alteration' powers conferred by Schedule 4 of the Land Registration Act 2002.[3]

1   **[Paras 2.113, 12.266]**.
2   Mistakes made by Land Registry are 'a rare occurrence' (*Clark v Chief Land Registrar* [1993] Ch 294 at 299G per Ferris J). Land Registry currently prides itself on processing 98.74 per cent of all registrations free of any error (see Land Registry, *Annual Report and Accounts 2002–03* (HC891, July 2003), pp 8, 91).
3   LRA 2002, s 65.

'Alteration' and 'rectification'

12.247   The Land Registration Act 2002 draws a careful distinction between 'alteration' and 'rectification' of the Land Register.

Alteration

12.248   The 2002 Act uses the generic term 'alteration' to describe *any* change which is made to a register of title. Both the court[1] and the registrar[2] are given wide statutory powers to bring about the 'alteration' of any register of title for the purpose of 'correcting a mistake',[3] bringing the register 'up to date'[4] or giving effect to any estate, right or interest excepted from the effect of registration.[5] The registrar has an additional power to remove superfluous entries from the register.[6] 'Alteration' therefore covers a broad range of changes in the register, many of which may be entirely harmless or purely administrative in their scope.[7]

1   LRA 2002, Sch 4, para 2(1). A court order for alteration of the register, when served on the registrar, imposes on him a duty to give effect to the order (LRA 2002, Sch 4, para 2(2)).
2   LRA 2002, Sch 4, para 5. Where an application to the registrar for rectification is contested by the registered proprietor and the issue cannot be resolved by agreement, the registrar must refer the matter to the Adjudicator to Land Registry (LRA 2002, s 73(7)).
3   See e g *Calgary and Edmonton Land Co Ltd v Discount Bank (Overseas) Ltd* [1971] 1 WLR 81 at 85A–C (interest wrongly omitted by registrar on first registration).
4   An example would arise where the court determines that a claimant has established a prescriptive easement in his favour, in which case the court could order the entry of the benefit and burden of the easement in the relevant registers of title [**para 8.168**]. Alternatively an interest protected by register entry may have ceased to exist (see e g *Lester v Burgess* (1973) 26 P & CR 536 at 542–543).
5   Registered dispositions always take effect subject to any rights which were specifically excepted from the effect of first registration [**paras 7.46, 7.234**], with the consequence that if the register is subsequently altered in recognition of such rights, no genuine 'rectification' has occurred and no indemnity is payable (see Law Com No 271 (2001), para 10.10).
6   LRA 2002, Sch 4, para 5(d). This power is exercisable where, for instance, an interest protected in the register by one entry is adequately protected by another or where a 'restriction' on the registered proprietor's powers has ceased to apply (see Law Com No 271 (2001), para 10.19).
7   Some alterations benefit the registered proprietor by cleaning up his title whilst causing no loss to the person whose entry is cancelled. For example, a 'notice' entered for the purpose of protecting an estate contract may be cancelled once it has been established that the estate contract has been rescinded. In certain circumstances the registrar has power to pay costs and expenses reasonably incurred in connection with an 'alteration' which is not a 'rectification' (LRA 2002, Sch 8, para 3).

Rectification

12.249   By contrast, the 2002 Act uses the term 'rectification' to indicate a sub-species of 'alteration'. 'Rectification' is reserved for that narrower category of 'alterations' of a register which involve 'the correction of a mistake'[1] and which 'prejudicially affect' the title of a registered proprietor.[2] This refinement of the concept of 'rectification' provides an essential link with the circumstances in which an indemnity becomes payable from Land Registry funds to persons who suffer loss.[3] The availability of an indemnity represents the practical realisation of the 'insurance principle' which classically underlies all schemes of state-regulated registration of title.[4] An integral part of the strategy of the 2002 Act is the idea that entitlement to the award of an indemnity will coincide exactly with cases of 'rectification'.[5] Indemnity is payable only in circumstances of loss; and 'rectification' connotes, by definition, the correction of a mistake which has a prejudicial impact[6] on the title of a registered proprietor.[7] In other words, 'alterations' of the register which cause no loss do not rank as 'rectifications' of the register and give rise to no indemnity. For example, an 'alteration' which gives visible effect in the register to an overriding interest merely confirms a subsisting, albeit previously unrecorded, entitlement. Such 'alteration' inflicts no true derogation from the rights of the registered proprietor and does not qualify him for any indemnity.[8]

1   Thus, for example, no 'rectification' is involved in a mere alteration of the register made for the purpose of giving effect to an interest acquired over the land since the date of registration (Law Com No 271 (2001), para 10.7).

2   LRA 2002, Sch 4, para 1. Rectification shares one feature in common with the phenomenon of the overriding interest. Rectification and overriding interests alike provide for derogations from the title of the registered proprietor: they both represent ways in which reliance on the register may ultimately prove to be misplaced (see Law Com No 158 (1987), paras 1.4, 2.10).

3   [**Paras 12.255–12.258**].

4   [**Para 6.13**].

5   Law Com No 271 (2001), para 10.7.

6   It follows that not every correction of a mistake constitutes a 'rectification' (Law Com No 271 (2001), para 10.7).

7   Rectification may, for example, divest a registered proprietor of some or all of the land comprised within his title or subject his estate to burdens which were not previously entered on the register. Rectification can extend to all parts of the register and the title plan (see *Argyle Building Society v Hammond* (1985) 49 P & CR 148 at 157, 162 per Slade LJ).

8   [**Para 12.258**]. Similarly no true 'rectification' occurs where the register is altered simply in order to give effect to a court order declaring that some person is entitled to an estate, right or interest in any registered land or charge (Law Com No 254 (1998), paras 8.37–8.41; Law Com No 271 (2001), para 10.16).

Impact of rectification on derivative interests

12.250   The Land Registration Act 2002 makes it clear that rectification of the register can affect even innocent third parties.[1] The power to rectify is expressly stated to 'extend to changing ... the priority of any interest affecting the registered estate or charge concerned.'[2] Rectification may therefore impact (whether adversely or not) on derivative interests such as leases, easements and covenants which have already been created out of a registered estate. Rectification can, however, change the priority of such interests only 'for the future', ie prospectively from the date of the rectification.[3]

1   See similarly, in relation to the Land Registration Act 1925, *Argyle Building Society v Hammond* (1985) 49 P & CR 148 at 162 per Slade LJ; *Norwich and Peterborough Building Society v Steed* [1993] Ch 116 at 137A–C.

2   LRA 2002, Sch 4, para 8.

3   LRA 2002, Sch 4, para 8.

Remote electronic alteration of the register

12.251   The regime of electronic dealing envisaged by the Land Registration Act 2002 involves not merely the conduct of electronic dispositions by solicitors or licensed conveyancers operating under the terms of a 'network access agreement'.[1] It will also enable authorised practitioners to initiate alterations to the register of title (or to the cautions register) from a remote location. These persons will be empowered to set in train the removal from the register of such matters as discharged mortgages and other spent entries.[2]

1 [**Para 12.22**].
2 See LRA 2002, Sch 5, para 1(2)(b); Law Com No 271 (2001), para 10.23.

RESTRICTIONS ON RECTIFICATION

12.252 Certain restrictions are imposed on the right to obtain rectification, largely because the unlimited availability of such a remedy would be 'productive of future uncertainty and contrary to the raison d'être of registration of title.'[1] The Land Registration Act 2002 gives effect to a 'principle of qualified indefeasibility'[2] by providing that, except in cases of consent, no rectification may normally be made 'affecting the title of the proprietor of a registered estate in land … in relation to land in his possession.'[3] This protection for proprietors in possession constitutes an important acknowledgement of the reasonable expectations of transferees who have paid the full price, taken possession and become proprietors in reliance on the register.[4] It also recognises that a third party's loss of a land interest through the withholding of rectification is likely to be much less grievous for that party (particularly if compensated by payment of an indemnity) than the loss suffered by a registered proprietor who, having enjoyed possession of a unique piece of land, then has his title rectified against him.[5] In land law, once again, significant effect is accorded to an underlying theory of loss aversion.[6]

1 Law Com No 158 (1987), para 3.5. As Lord Elwyn-Jones LC declared in Parliament, it is 'important that the entry of a person on the Land Register as the registered proprietor of a piece of land should, so far as possible, be conclusive as to his title' (*Parliamentary Debates, Official Report, House of Lords*, Vol 386 (Session 1976–77), Col 871 (26 July 1977)).
2 See Law Com No 254 (1998), para 8.47; Law Com No 271 (2001), para 10.13.
3 LRA 2002, Sch 4, paras 3(2), 6(2).
4 The objective is to 'strengthen the position of registered proprietors in possession and to put them in general in a better position than that of persons with unregistered interests in registered land' (*Kingsalton Ltd v Thames Water Developments Ltd* [2002] 1 P & CR 15 at [40] per Arden LJ). Registered titles 'thereby come to reflect the reality of the situation' (Law Com No 271 (2001), para 10.13).
5 See *Kingsalton Ltd v Thames Water Developments Ltd* [2002] 1 P & CR 15 at [53] per Sir Christopher Slade. On the historic importance attached to factual possession of land, see [**paras 2.77, 3.5**].
6 See Jeffrey E Stake, 'The Uneasy Case for Adverse Possession' 89 Geo LJ 2419 at 2420 (2001) [**para 6.32**].

Proprietor 'in possession'

12.253 The Land Registration Act 2002 has taken the opportunity to clarify that, in the present context, land is 'in the possession of the proprietor' if it is 'physically in his possession' or in the possession of his tenant, mortgagee or licensee or of a beneficiary of a trust of which he is trustee.[1] The criterion of 'possession' is also met where land is physically in the possession of some person who is entitled to be registered as the proprietor of the registered estate[2] (except where that entitlement arises in consequence of adverse possession[3]).

1   LRA 2002, s 131(1)–(2). See Law Com No 271 (2001), para 10.17.
2   LRA 2002, s 131(1).
3   LRA 2002, s 131(3).

Exceptional cases of rectification against a proprietor 'in possession'

12.254   The Land Registration Act 2002 effectively supplies two strong presumptions in respect of rectification of the register. Where a registered proprietor is not 'in possession' of the land within his title, the existence of grounds for rectification *must* lead to rectification unless there are 'exceptional circumstances' which justify a refusal to rectify.[1] Conversely, where a registered proprietor *is* 'in possession', there arises a countervailing presumption against rectification of the register.[2] It is consistent with the principle of 'qualified indefeasibility' that this protection against the prejudicial correction of mistakes in the register shoud give way in only two instances, ie where the proprietor in possession has 'by fraud or lack of proper care caused or substantially contributed to the mistake' in question[3] or where it 'would for any other reason be unjust for the alteration not to be made.'[4]

1   LRA 2002, Sch 4, paras 3(3), 6(3). See Law Com No 271 (2001), paras 10.18, 10.22.
2   See Law Com No 271 (2001), para 10.13.
3   LRA 2002, Sch 4, paras 3(2)(a), 6(2)(a). See, in relation to LRA 1925, s 82(3)(a), *Re 139 High Street Deptford, ex p British Transport Commission* [1951] Ch 884 at 890–892; *Claridge v Tingey, Re Sea View Gardens* [1967] 1 WLR 134 at 140H–141A.
4   LRA 2002, Sch 4, paras 3(2)(b), 6(2)(b). See, in relation to LRA 1925, s 82(3)(c), *Horrill v Cooper* (1999) 78 P & CR 336 at 345–347 (where rectification was ordered against a proprietor who had deliberately discounted the price paid for land in the knowledge of defects which did not appear on the register). See also *Epps v Esso Petroleum Co Ltd* [1973] 1 WLR 1071 at 1080F–1083B; [1974] CLJ 60 (S N Palk).

INDEMNITY

12.255   It is integral to the insurance principle underlying title registration that any person who innocently suffers loss by reason of the operation of the Land Register should receive compensation. Accordingly Schedule 8 to the Land Registration Act 2002 makes provision for the payment of indemnity in certain specified circumstances.[1] Land Registry acts, in effect, as a statutory insurer of titles in England and Wales and is currently estimated to guarantee land assets worth in excess of £2.5 trillion.[2]

1   LRA 2002, s 103. During 2002–2003 a total of 799 indemnity claims were settled, involving substantive losses of £1,559,424 and costs of £1,102,573. The largest payment was in excess of £194,000 in respect of loss arising from a forged transfer (Land Registry, *Annual Report and Accounts 2002–03* (HC891, July 2003), pp 24–25). Indemnity moneys actually represented only a small fraction of Land Registry's total fee income for 2002–2003 (£415.3 million). On the valuation of estates, interests and charges for the purpose of indemnity, see LRA 2002, Sch 8, para 6.
2   Land Registry Press Notice LRP03/03 (issued 4 February 2003).

Entitlement to indemnity

12.256 An entitlement to indemnity arises where any person suffers loss by reason of a 'rectification' of the register (as narrowly defined by the 2002 Act[1]). 'Rectification' necessarily connotes a prejudicial alteration of the register, with the result that any person who suffers loss in consequence of the rectification has a statutory right to be indemnified.[2] An indemnity is also payable where any person suffers loss by reason of various kinds of 'mistake'[3] or 'failure'[4] by Land Registry (including a mistake whose correction would involve rectification of the register[5]).

1   LRA 2002, Sch 4, para 1, Sch 8, para 11(2) **[para 12.249]**.
2   LRA 2002, Sch 8, para 1(1)(a).
3   The term 'mistake' includes mistakes in official searches and official copies (LRA 2002, Sch 8, para 1(1)(c)–(d)). Indemnity is also payable in cases of loss or destruction of a document lodged at Land Registry for inspection or safe custody (LRA 2002, Sch 8, para 1(1)(f)).
4   See LRA 2002, Sch 8, para 1(1)(h) (failure to issue notification of the creation of an overriding statutory charge pursuant to LRA 2002, s 50 **[para 8.258]**).
5   LRA 2002, Sch 8, para 1(1)(b). This means, in effect, that an indemnity can be paid *either* where, notwithstanding the mistake, the register is not rectified *or* where, notwithstanding rectification, the person in whose favour it is granted has still suffered loss in consequence of the mistake (see Law Com No 271 (2001), para 10.32).

Definition of loss

12.257 For present purposes, the notion of 'loss' is accorded an extended definition so as to include the prejudice caused by the statutory upgrading of any class of title.[1] The 2002 Act also provides that the proprietor of a registered estate or charge who, in good faith, claims under a disposition which was in fact forged is to be regarded, when the register is rectified against him, as having suffered a relevant loss and as therefore deserving of indemnity.[2] This is so even though, in strict terms, a rectification which merely confirms the outcome of a null disposition inflicts no technical loss on the disponee.

1   LRA 2002, Sch 8, para 1(2)(a) (see LRA 2002, s 62 **[para 7.47]**).
2   LRA 2002, Sch 8, para 1(2)(b). See Law Com No 271 (2001), para 10.31. Indemnity payments are not therefore confined to cases of mistake made by Land Registry itself, but can cover losses flowing from wrongs perpetrated by third parties.

Restrictions on indemnity

12.258 The right to receive an indemnity in cases of prejudice is not as unqualified as might at first appear.[1] Where a registered title is rectified to give effect to a subsisting overriding interest, the proprietor is ineligible for compensation. The cold rationale for this denial of indemnity lies in the fact that, in such cases, rectification merely confirms an existing, though latent, entitlement and therefore inflicts no genuine loss on the registered proprietor.[2] The title taken by him was at all material times subject to the overriding interest in question: there can be no compensation where there has been no loss. The right to indemnity is also withheld in the case of any loss suffered by a claimant 'wholly or partly as a result of his own fraud' or 'wholly as a result of his own lack of proper care.'[3] Where a claimant suffers loss *partly* as a result of his own lack of proper care, the 2002 Act recognises a principle of contributory negligence. Any indemnity may be reduced 'to such extent as is fair having regard to [the claimant's] share in the responsibility for the loss.'[4] The registrar also has powers to recover amounts paid by way of indemnity from any person who turns out to have caused or substantially contributed to the loss by his fraud.[5]

1   Any claim for indemnity is statute-barred six years after the claimant knows or, but for his own default, might have known of the existence of his claim (LRA 2002, Sch 8, para 8(2); Limitation Act 1980, s 5).
2   See eg *Re Chowood's Registered Land* [1933] Ch 574 at 581–582. The Law Commission did, at one stage, propose that an indemnity be available in such cases (Law Com No 158 (1987), paras 2.12–2.14, 3.29), but this recommendation was later abandoned (Law Com No 254 (1998), para 8.57(1)). See Law Com No 271 (2001), para 10.16.
3   LRA 2002, Sch 8, para 5(1). See also *Dean v Dean* (2000) 80 P & CR 457 at 462.
4   LRA 2002, Sch 8, para 5(2).
5   LRA 2002, Sch 8, para 10. See Law Com No 271 (2001), para 10.51.

DEALINGS WITH UNREGISTERED ESTATES

12.259   Even when (as is today increasingly the case) a dealing with an unregistered estate triggers a requirement of substantive registration of title to that estate at Land Registry,[1] the pre-registration rights and liabilities attaching to the land fall to be determined largely by reference to the principles which regulate unregistered estates. These principles settle the priority of the estates, interests and charges which have accumulated around the unregistered estate and which require to be recorded on a first registration of title in the Land Register.

1   [**Paras 7.40, 7.230**].

Investigation of unregistered titles

12.260   Investigation of an unregistered title nowadays occurs mainly during the period between the receipt of the draft contract of sale and exchange of contracts. Such investigation is necessary because, as Lord Erskine LC observed in *Hiern v Mill*,[1] 'no man in his senses would take an offer of a purchase from a man, merely because he stood upon the ground.' The purchaser must form his own judgement as to whether the title offered by his vendor is good.[2] This the purchaser does by examining the deeds or documents of title[3] relating to dispositions of the land during at least the preceding 15 years.[4] Ultimately the vendor must satisfy the purchaser that he has title to the estate and that it is subject only to the adverse interests specified in the contract.[5] The purchaser takes a conveyance of the legal estate (and pays the balance of the purchase money) only if he has verified that there is an unbroken chain of ownership leading from a good root of title straight through to his vendor.

1   (1806) 13 Ves 114 at 122, 33 ER 237 at 240.

2   This investigation must uncover a 'good root of title' which is at least 15 years old. Such a root of title is constituted by any instrument which unambiguously deals with or shows title to the whole legal and equitable interest in the correctly identified property. It is generally considered that such instruments as leases and wills are insufficient for this purpose.

3   The title deeds are, in effect, the 'essential indicia of title to unregistered land' (see *Sen v Headley* [1991] Ch 425 at 437C per Nourse LJ).

4   LPA 1925, s 44(1), as amended by LPA 1969, s 23 [**para 2.112**]. Thus, if the first conveyance which is at least 15 years old was executed in 1970, then the relevant title commences in 1970. In the absence of contrary contractual stipulation, the period of investigation of title was originally fixed by the common law as 60 years (see *Barnwell v Harris* (1809) 1 Taunt 430 at 432, 127 ER 901). This period was progressively reduced to 40 years (Vendor and Purchaser Act 1874, s 1), 30 years (LPA 1925, s 44(1)), and now 15 years.

5   If the title offered by the vendor discloses any apparent defects, the purchaser may raise 'requisitions' in order to clarify matters of doubt.

Transition to registered title

12.261   Although nowadays the overall importance of the rules governing unregistered titles is greatly diminished by the steady translation of these titles on to the Land Register, the law of unregistered estates retains a significance which merits fuller exploration.[1]

1   A bird's eye view of the law of unregistered estates was provided in Chapter 2 [**paras 2.174–2.193**].

HISTORIC PRIORITY RULES GOVERNING UNREGISTERED TITLES

12.262   The law regulating unregistered estates has much earlier origins than the regime of registered title and operates on the basis of axioms which lie deeply embedded in the sedimentary layers of English law.[1] These axioms remain exposed to view at a few vantage-points across the terrain of modern property law, thus continuing to provide a solution for certain contemporary problems of land law priority. In other places the historic axioms of unregistered land have been overlaid by different strata deposited by the later action of legislative change, although even here the erosive activity of judge-made law has occasionally stripped back the more recent strata to reveal the bed-rock of original principle.

1   [**Para 2.134**].

Fundamental axioms of land law priority

12.263   The fundamental axioms which underlie the law of unregistered estates turn on the all-important distinction between *legal* and *equitable* rights.

As observed in earlier chapters, this distinction is fixed by statute,[1] subject to the rider that the *legal* quality of many kinds of entitlement depends also upon creation or conveyance by the formal means of a deed.[2] The historic axioms at the base of unregistered land law prescribe that:

– legal rights automatically bind all persons in the world (irrespective of notice)

– equitable rights bind all persons except a bona fide purchaser of a legal estate for value who takes without notice of such rights.

1 **[Para 2.124]**.
2 **[Paras 2.126, 7.26]**.

Modern displacement of the fundamental axioms

12.264 Whilst the first of these axioms – that relating to the impact of legal rights – still determines the outcome of many priority problems in the unregistered sector, the second axiom has been largely superseded by various schemes of registration[1] and by a device of statutory overreaching which transmutes certain equitable rights in land into an equivalent money form.[2] In consequence the equitable doctrine of notice or 'bona fide purchaser rule' now plays only a residual role in circumstances where other determinants of priority have failed or are inapplicable.

1 **[Paras 2.185, 12.275]**.
2 **[Paras 2.165, 11.195]**.

EFFECT OF DISPOSITIONS OF AN UNREGISTERED ESTATE

12.265 The principles which regulate unregistered land priorities ensure that a purchaser (including a mortgagee) of an unregistered legal estate takes title subject to:

– any other pre-existing legal estates[1]

– any registered land charges[2] or local land charges[3]

– any unoverreached equitable interests[4] of which he has notice (actual, constructive or imputed)[5] and

– (in the case of leasehold land) certain covenants and obligations arising under the lease.[6]

1 **[Para 12.274]**.
2 **[Para 12.279]**.
3 **[Para 12.7]**. Local land charges are enforceable whether or not they are registered (Local Land Charges Act 1975, s 10(1)).
4 Statutory overreaching operates in relation to dispositions of unregistered estates just as in relation to registered estates **[para 11.196]**.
5 **[Paras 12.345–12.353]**.
6 **[Para 14.241]**.

First registration at Land Registry

12.266   Most forms of dealing with an unregistered estate (whether freehold or leasehold) nowadays trigger a requirement of first registration of title to that estate at Land Registry.[1] At this point the Chief Land Registrar collates, in the newly opened register of title, as complete a list as possible of those interests which appear, from his examination of the unregistered title, to benefit or burden the estate in question.[2]

1   **[Paras 7.40, 7.230]**.
2   See LRR 2003, rr 29–30.

Entry of benefits and burdens

12.267   The registrar enters in the property register the benefit of any appurtenant rights – such as easements and covenants – enjoyed over other land[1] (including other land which is as yet unregistered[2]). Likewise the registrar enters in the charges register any charges which burden the newly registered estate,[3] together with a 'notice' in respect of any registrable lease, easement, profit *à prendre* or other burden which appears to affect the registered estate.[4] First registration then vests the freehold or leasehold estate (as the case may be) in the first registered proprietor together with the benefits, and subject to the burdens, thus entered in the register.[5]

1   LRA 2002, s 14(b); LRR 2003, rr 5(b)(ii), 33(1).
2   LRA 2002, s 13(a).
3   LRR 2003, rr 9(a), 22(2), 34.
4   LRR 2003, rr 9(a), 35(1).
5   LRA 2002, ss 11–12 **[paras 7.45–7.47, 7.232–7.235]**.

Unregistered interests which 'override' first registration

12.268   The first registered proprietor also takes the newly registered estate subject to certain interests which are specified by statute to 'override' first registration and which, for one reason or another, have escaped the dragnet of entry in the register.[1] These interests, listed in Schedule 1 of the Land Registration Act 2002, resemble fairly closely the interests which, as detailed in Schedule 3,[2] 'override' subsequent registered dispositions of the registered estate. The interests which override first registration thus include various categories of short lease,[3] the rights of persons in actual occupation[4] and legal easements and profits *à prendre*.[5] However, the list of overriding interests contained in Schedule 1 is more broadly defined than that in Schedule 3, in that the first registered proprietor takes subject to Schedule 1 overriding interests *without* reference to any question of prior inquiry made by him as to such rights. The first registered proprietor is, at the date of his registration, already bound by the interests which 'override' and cannot be saved therefrom by *any* amount of inquiry.[6] The number of interests which override first registration is, of course, minimised by the fact that the registrar has power, of his own motion, to enter a 'notice' in the register in respect of those unregistered interests which appear to him to fall within Schedule 1.[7] For this purpose, moreover, an applicant for first registration has a statutory obligation to disclose potentially overriding interests which are 'within his actual knowledge' and are capable of entry by 'notice'.[8] In these ways, it is hoped, most interests which pre-exist at first registration will be revealed to the registrar and thus find their way on to the first registered proprietor's register of title.[9]

1   See LRA 2002, ss 11(4)(b), 12(4)(c).
2   **[Para 12.138]**.
3   LRA 2002, Sch 1, para 1.
4   LRA 2002, Sch 1, para 2. There is no requirement that the occupation must have been 'obvious on a reasonably careful inspection of the land' (compare LRA 2002, Sch 3, para 2(c)(i) **[para 12.177]**).
5   LRA 2002, Sch 1, para 3. Similarly the user need not have been 'obvious on a reasonably careful inspection of the land' (compare LRA 2002, Sch 3, para 3(1)(b) **[para 12.239]**).
6   See Law Com No 271 (2001), paras 8.3–8.4.
7   LRA 2002, s 37(1); LRR 2003, r 89.
8   LRA 2002, s 71(a); LRR 2003, r 28(1). 'Disclosable overriding interests' do not include public rights, local land charges, leases which at the time of the application have one year or less to run, or interests which are apparent from the deeds and documents of title accompanying the application for first registration (LRR 2003, r 28(2)).
9   LRR 2003, r 28(4). See Law Com No 271 (2001), para 8.25.

Equitable easements and profits à prendre

12.269   The first registered proprietor takes his estate free of any equitable easements and equitable profits *à prendre* granted by his predecessors which were not, before the disposition to him, protected by registration of a Class D(iii) land charge.[1] If such rights have been duly protected, the registrar will, as a matter of course, enter them in the first registered proprietor's newly opened register of title.[2] Equitable rights of this nature never rank as overriding interests on first registration.[3]

1   **[Para 12.318]**.
2   LRR 2003, rr 9(a), 35(1).
3   See LRA 2002, Sch 1, para 3.

Cautions against first registration

12.270   The Land Registration Act 2002 provides a means by which certain persons interested in unregistered land may be informed of any application for first registration of title to an estate in that land. A 'caution against first registration' may be lodged at Land Registry by a person who claims, in relation to the land, to be the owner of (or to have an interest affecting) a fee simple absolute in possession, a term of years absolute, a rentcharge, franchise or profit *à prendre*.[1] A leaseholder can therefore lodge a caution against first registration of the reversionary freehold estate; cautions can likewise be lodged by those who claim to be entitled to an option or a beneficial interest affecting an unregistered estate.[2]

1   LRA 2002, s 15(1)–(2), (4); LRR 2003, r 42. A squatter who has been in adverse possesson for twelve years has the opportunity (until 13 October 2005) to lodge a caution against first registration (LRA 2002, Sch 12, para 14(1) **[para 6.70]**). A person may not lodge a caution 'without reasonable cause' (LRA 2002, s 77(1)(a)).

2   The caution against first registration affords particularly useful protection for trust beneficiaries in unregistered land (who are unable to safeguard their rights by any form of land charge registration **[para 12.356]**). The caution ensures that their rights will be protected by the entry of a 'restriction' in any newly opened register of title (see Law Com No 271 (2001), para 3.62).

12.271   The mechanism of the caution is not intended, however, to be a substitute for first registration of any unregistered estate which is itself capable of registration. Thus, for example, no caution can be lodged in respect of his own estate by the owner of a fee simple estate or a leasehold term of which more than seven years remain unexpired.[1]

1   LRA 2002, s 15(3) (effective from 13 October 2005) (LRA 2002, s 134, Sch 12, para 14(1)).

Effect of a caution against first registration

12.272   Following lodgment of a caution against first registration,[1] the registrar is statutorily obliged to notify the cautioner of any application for first registration and of the cautioner's right to object to the application.[2] Objection must be made (if at all) within a period of 15 business days from the date of the notification,[3] during which time the registrar cannot normally determine the application for first registration.[4] Unless satisfied that the objection is groundless, the registrar must refer the matter to the Adjudicator to Land Registry.[5] The lodgment of a caution has, in itself, no effect on the validity or priority of the cautioner's interest in the land.[6] The caution merely provides a procedure for ensuring that the cautioner has an opportunity to oppose first registration or to secure appropriate protection for his interest when a new register of title is created.[7]

1   Cautions against first registration are recorded in Land Registry's Index Map (LRA 2002, s 68(1)(c)) and are also detailed in a 'cautions register' in which a 'caution register' bearing a unique 'caution title number' is opened for each separate area of land affected by a caution (LRR 2003, rr 40–41).

2   LRA 2002, s 16(1). The notification may come directly from an agent (e g solicitor) of the applicant for first registration (LRA 2002, s 16(4)).

3   LRA 2002, s 16(2); LRR 2003, r 53(1). This period may be extended on request by up to a further 15 business days (LRR 2003, r 53(1)–(2)).

4   LRA 2002, s 16(2).

5   LRA 2002, s 73(7).

6   LRA 2002, s 16(3).

7   Law Com No 271 (2001), para 3.62.

Cancellation of the caution

12.273   The 2002 Act also creates a procedure under which the owner of a legal estate to which the caution relates (and certain other persons) may apply to the registrar for cancellation of the caution.[1] The caution may also be withdrawn by the cautioner on application to the registrar.[2]

1   LRA 2002, s 18; LRR 2003, rr 44–45. An estate owner who has consented to the lodgment of the caution may apply for cancellation only if the interest protected by the caution has come to an end or if his consent was procured by fraud, misrepresentation, mistake, undue influence or duress (LRA 2002, s 18(2); LRR 2003, r 46).
2   LRA 2002, s 17; LRR 2003, r 43.

LEGAL RIGHTS BIND THE WORLD

12.274   The force of the rule which governs legal rights in unregistered land is entirely straightforward. It is a fundamental principle that, if B owns a legal right in or over land belonging to A, B's right binds all persons irrespective of their knowledge or notice of the interest in question.[1] B's legal entitlement is therefore enforceable against any subsequent purchaser of an estate in A's land, against any squatter on that land[2] and indeed against the whole world. It matters not whether B's entitlement is one of lease, easement, mortgage or rentcharge. With the exception of certain tightly limited cases of mortgage (or charge),[3] his right automatically binds all comers. The axiomatic nature of this result conduces to efficiency and clarity in the ascertainment of land rights. The owner of legal rights knows that his position is secure notwithstanding future transfers of the land; likewise the purchaser is made generally aware that he takes his disposition subject to any legal rights which belong to others.

1   See *Mercer v Liverpool, St Helen's and South Lancashire Railway Co* [1903] 1 KB 652 at 662 per Stirling LJ.
2   *Re Nisbet and Potts' Contract* [1906] 1 Ch 386 at 401 [**para 3.26**].
3   See, for instance, the case of the 'puisne mortgage' [**paras 12.301, 15.246**].

REGISTRATION OF LAND CHARGES

12.275   Prior to 1926 the enforceability of equitable rights turned largely on the hazardous operation of the equitable doctrine of notice.[1] The 'bona fide purchaser rule', whilst motivated by a basic principle of fairness or equity, was productive of uncertainty for both the equitable owner and any subsequent purchaser of the land.[2] In particular, neither party could confidently predict the scope of constructive notice, which, depending on its presence or absence, would determine whether a purchaser was bound by, or took free of, subsisting equitable interests. In order to address this mutual insecurity, the 1925 legislation introduced a limited regime of registration of rights whose objective is to harness the publicity of registration as an inescapable means of notifying the world about certain entitlements in unregistered land.

1   [**Para 12.182**].
2   The rule also cast an onerous burden of enquiry on intending purchasers (see *R Griggs Group Ltd v Evans (No 2)* [2004] EWHC 1088 (Ch) at [33]).

Scope of the Land Charges Act 1972

12.276   The Land Charges Act 1972 – the modern consolidated version of the Land Charges Act 1925 – provides a scheme of public registration not merely for certain categories of interest (as 'land charges'), but also for a number of other matters, actions and documents relating to land.[1] The interests eligible for registration as land charges comprise, in the main, those real or specific burdens on unregistered land which are appropriate for long-term enforcement irrespective of the identity of the current estate owner.[2] Registration of land charges thus affords a means of enabling such interests to endure through changes of ownership of the land.[3] With the steady movement towards universal registration of title under the Land Registration Act 2002, this particular function will gradually become redundant. However, it may take some time for title to all estates in England and Wales to be registered[4] and some familiarity with the operation of the land charges legislation is therefore essential.[5]

1   [**Para 12.330**].
2   [**Paras 2.160, 11.202**]. See *Birmingham Midshires Mortgage Services Ltd v Sabherwal* (2000) 80 P & CR 256 at 262–263 per Robert Walker LJ.
3   Registration of isolated categories of interest under the Land Charges Act must be firmly distinguished from the much more comprehensive scheme of registration of title which is governed by the Land Registration Act 2002 [**paras 2.103, 6.8**]. Land charges affecting unregistered estates are recorded in the Register of Land Charges; registrations of title are recorded in the Land Register. The interests which comprise 'land charges', if arising in respect of registered estates, are normally protectable by the entry of a 'notice' in the Land Register [**paras 2.163, 12.84**].
4   [**Para 2.122**].
5   For a more detailed account of the Land Charges Act 1972, see *Elements of Land Law* (3rd edn 2001), pp 1086–1114.

Basic concept of registration

12.277   At the heart of the Land Charges Act 1972 is the idea that owners of certain statutorily designated categories of interest (almost always equitable in quality) should be given the opportunity to register their rights in the Register of Land Charges against the estate owner whose estate is intended to be affected.[1] But, whereas registration of title under the Land Registration Act 2002 involves the substantive registration of estates identified by title number, it is the *names* of estate owners which provide the vital 'fixed point of reference' in the scheme of land charge registration.[2] Under the Land Charges Act registrations are effected against names and searches of the register are likewise conducted against names.[3] Thereafter the registration scheme proceeds on the basis of two general (and rather blunt) rules. First, any interest or matter, once registered, is deemed to infect all persons with notice and therefore becomes enforceable against the entire world. Second, a registrable interest or matter, if not duly registered, is normally rendered void and ineffective against third parties.

1   LCA 1972, s 3(1). The Register of Land Charges is maintained by the Land Charges Department of the Land Registry, whose operations are governed by the Land Charges Rules 1974 (SI 1974/1286), as amended by SI 1990/485 and SI 1995/1355.
2   See *Standard Property Investment plc v British Plastics Federation* (1985) 53 P & CR 25 at 28–30 per Walton J. The function of the registrar in registering land charges is purely ministerial (see S M Cretney, (1969) 32 MLR 477 at 486–487). No inquiry is made into the validity of the charge registered and there is no requirement that the estate owner be informed of the application for registration (see e g *Taylor v Taylor* (1968) [1968] 1 WLR 378 at 383A–B). It is therefore possible that land charge registration may be used for tactical reasons to impose an apparent (but fictitious) blot on an owner's title.
3   LCA 1972, ss 3(1), 10(1). There is no legal duty to register a land charge (although see LPA 1925, s 200(4)). It therefore follows that damages for breach of an unregistered estate contract are not reduced by reason of the failure to register the contract and thus render it binding on a purchaser (see *Wright v Dean* [1948] Ch 686 at 696).

Mode of entry in the register

12.278   Any interest entered in the Register of Land Charges must be 'registered in the name of the estate owner whose estate is intended to be affected.'[1] The registration must also specify the correct address or location of the land in respect of which the charge is registered.[2] For present purposes the definitive version of the estate owner's name is deemed to be that disclosed on the face of the conveyance to him (ie his full name as recorded on his deeds of title).[3] Registration in any other name – even in an informal or incomplete variant of the correct name[4] – is ineffective against a purchaser who subsequently obtains a certificate of official search against the complete and correct version of the estate owner's name.[5] However, a registration in 'what may be fairly described as a version of the full names of the vendor' is not rendered a nullity as against a purchaser who 'does not search at all, or who … searches in the wrong name.'[6]

1   LCA 1972, s 3(1). In rare circumstances the owner of a land charge may be required to register the charge against his own name. Such a case arises where a purchaser of land agrees to lease back the premises to the vendor on completion of the purchase. Here the vendor holds an estate contract pending completion which is registrable against himself as the current estate owner (see [1980] Conv 170).
2   See *Buhr v Barclays Bank plc* [2001] BPIR 25 at [4] per Arden LJ (registration referring to incorrect postal address held ineffective).
3   Where A, the owner of an unregistered legal estate in fee simple, contracts to sell his estate to B, who immediately contracts to sub-sell to C, both estate contracts require registration against the name of A, who remains at all relevant times the 'estate owner' (see *Barrett v Hilton Developments Ltd* [1975] Ch 237 at 244A, F).
4   See e g *Diligent Finance Co Ltd v Alleyne* (1971) 23 P & CR 346 at 349–350 (ineffective registration of Class F charge against 'Erskine Alleyne' rather than 'Erskine Owen Alleyne').
5   See likewise *Oak Co-operative Building Society v Blackburn* [1968] Ch 730 at 743E–F per Russell LJ; *Standard Property Investment plc v British Plastics Federation* (1985) 53 P & CR 25 at 33. Registration rules tend to be strictly construed in other jurisdictions. See *Re Wilson* (1984) 8 DLR (4th) 271 at 273–274 (registration against 'Tom' instead of 'Thomas' held

defective); *Re Gibbons* (1984) 8 DLR (4th) 316 at 317 (registration against name by which debtor commonly known in the community held inadequate). See also *Federal Business Development Bank v Registrar of Personal Property Security* (1984) 7 DLR (4th) 479 at 489–490.

6   *Oak Co-operative Building Society v Blackburn* [1968] Ch 730 at 743E–F per Russell LJ (registration of Class C(iv) charge against 'Frank David Blackburn' – rather than the correct 'Francis David Blackburn' – held good against a mortgagee which obtained a clear certificate of official search against 'Francis Davis Blackburn').

Effect of registration

12.279   As indicated by section 198(1) of the Law of Property Act 1925, registration of a land charge in the name of the appropriate estate owner is 'deemed to constitute actual notice ... of the fact of such registration, to all persons and for all purposes connected with the land affected.' In respect of relevant categories of interest, due registration under the Land Charges Act 1972 therefore has the hugely significant effect of rendering notice of the registered rights utterly inescapable.[1] As Richard Epstein has observed, a registration system is 'routine and ministerial – a notable social triumph of the humdrum ... the problem of notice disappears in all but the most unusual case.'[2]

1   The effect of LPA 1925, s 198(1) even overrode the protection seemingly afforded by LPA 1925, s 44(5) to a lessee who was not entitled to investigate his lessor's title and was therefore vulnerable to undiscoverable registrations effected against previous owners of the superior title (see *White v Bijou Mansions Ltd* [1937] Ch 610 at 619 per Simonds J). This dilemma has now been relieved by the recent extension of the lessee's right to call for the superior title (see LPA 1925, s 44(4A), as inserted by LRA 2002, s 133, Sch 11, para 2).
2   'Covenants and Constitutions' 73 Cornell L Rev 906 at 909 (1987–88).

Effect of non-registration

12.280   Just as the effect of registration is phrased in absolute terms in section 198(1) of the Law of Property Act 1925, so the consequence of failure to register a registrable interest is specified in similarly draconian language. The precise effect of non-registration depends on the category of land charge concerned,[1] but the general result of failure to register is the voidness of the registrable interest against most kinds of purchaser.[2]

1   Land charges are divided by the Land Charges Act 1972 into six major categories (ie Classes A–F). These classifications are examined shortly [**paras 12.297–12.322**].
2   Non-registration does not affect the validity of the charge as between the original parties to its creation (see *Buhr v Barclays Bank plc* [2001] BPIR 25 at [36] per Arden LJ).

Classes A, B, C(i), (ii) and (iii), and F

12.281   For want of registration a land charge of Class A, Class B, Class C(i), (ii) and (iii), or Class F is rendered void 'as against a purchaser of the land charged with it, or of any interest in such land.'[1] A 'purchaser' is defined as any person (including a mortgagee or lessee) who gives 'valuable consideration'.[2]

1   LCA 1972, s 4(2), (5), (8). In some circumstances an unregistered interest may be void against a purchaser for non-registration, but nevertheless survive (by way of substitution) as a security interest in the sale proceeds arising from the disposition (see e g *Buhr v Barclays Bank plc* [2001] BPIR 25 at [45], where Arden LJ held that, although an unregistered puisne mortgage was destroyed by an unauthorised disposition of the fee simple estate, the mortgagee, as a matter of law, acquired a security interest in the sale proceeds of the land).
2   LCA 1972, s 17(1).

Classes C(iv) and D

12.282   The most significant categories of land charge (i e land charges of Class C(iv) and Class D) are rendered void for non-registration against a somewhat narrower category of purchaser. Unregistered charges falling within these Classes are void only as against 'a purchaser for money or money's worth of a legal estate in the land charged.'[1] An important statutory immunity is thus conferred on the purchaser, although in rare circumstances this immunity may be lost if the purchaser either fails to plead his statutory defence[2] or is precluded from doing so by some argument based upon constructive trust[3] or estoppel.[4]

1   LCA 1972, s 4(6). See e g *E R Ives Investment Ltd v High* [1967] 2 QB 379 at 399B–C per Danckwerts LJ, 403E–F per Winn LJ **[paras 9.101, 12.320]**; *Lloyds Bank plc v Carrick* [1996] 4 All ER 630 at 638b, 639e–f **[paras 9.40, 10.87]**.
2   See e g *Balchin v Buckle* (1982) Times, 1 June, 126 Sol Jo 412.
3   **[Para 10.58]**.
4   See e g *Old & Campbell Ltd v Liverpool Victoria Friendly Society* [1982] QB 133 (Note) at 159A per Oliver J (defendants estopped from pleading non-registration following represention to tenant that his unregistered estate contract was still valid and subsisting). See also *E R Ives Investment Ltd v High* [1967] 2 QB 379 at 405D–F per Winn LJ.

Differential outcomes

12.283   The different consequences attached to non-registration may have important practical results. Thus, for example, non-registration by an incumbrancer causes a 'general equitable charge' (which belongs to Class C(iii)[1]) to become void as against a purchaser of *any* estate or interest in the land (whether legal or equitable). However, a similar failure to register an 'estate contract' (which belongs to Class C(iv)[2]) makes the relevant charge void only as against a purchaser of a legal estate for money or money's worth.

1   **[Para 12.303]**.
2   **[Para 12.306]**.

Charges which remain valid notwithstanding non-registration

12.284   Unprotected land charges are not universally void for reasons of non-registration. An unregistered land charge remains binding upon a subsequent *donee* of the estate concerned (e g the recipient of land under a will or on intestacy). Likewise an unregistered estate contract remains valid against a purchaser of an *equitable* interest in the land.[1]

1   See LCA 1972, s 4(6); *McCarthy and Stone Ltd v Hodge* [1971] 1 WLR 1547 at 1555D–E.

Irrelevance of the traditional doctrine of notice

12.285   As indicated above, the statutory consequences of non-registration are spelt out with precision in the Land Charges Act 1972. Furthermore, where an unregistered charge is statutorily declared void as against a purchaser, it is entirely irrelevant that at the date of the conveyance the purchaser had actual express knowledge – from some other source – of the existence of the registrable but unregistered interest.[1] Once 'void' by virtue of statute, the charge cannot be revitalised by any residual application of the traditional doctrine of notice.[2] Nor can a want of registration be cured by the fact that the incumbrancer was in actual occupation of the land at the date of the relevant conveyance and could reasonably have expected that his presence would signal the possibility of some subsisting entitlement.[3] The courts have rigorously maintained the integrity of the rules surrounding land charge registration,[4] although the process has required that some fundamental issues about the nature or texture of legal rules be squarely addressed. As with the problem of unprotected minor interests in registered land,[5] disputed questions of priority in this context expose an underlying tension between the desiderata of certainty of entitlement and fairness of outcome.[6]

1   LPA 1925, s 199(1)(i). See *E R Ives Investment Ltd v High* [1967] 2 QB 379 at 399B–C per Danckwerts LJ, 403E–F per Winn LJ.
2   See *Markfaith Investment Ltd v Chiap Hua Flashlights Ltd* [1991] 2 AC 43 at 60D per Lord Templeman ('null and void' must be construed 'as meaning null and void').
3   LPA 1925, s 14, which protects persons 'in possession or in actual occupation of land' applies only within Part I of the Law of Property Act 1925 and has no impact on the consequences of non-registration under the Land Charges Act (see *Coventry Permanent Economic Building Society v Jones* [1951] 1 All ER 901 at 904A–B). Contrast LPA 1922, ss 3(5), 33, whose beneficial effects, in an accident of legislative history, were lost with the formal restructuring of the 1922 legislation in the various enactments of 1925 (see *Lloyds Bank Plc v Carrick* [1996] 4 All ER 630 at 642f–g per Morritt LJ; M Friend and J Newton, [1982] Conv 213 at 215–217).
4   See e g *Coventry Permanent Economic Building Society v Jones* [1951] 1 All ER 901 at 904B–C per Harman J; *Beesly v Hallwood Estates Ltd* [1960] 1 WLR 549 at 558; *Buckley v SRL Investments Ltd and Cator and Robinson* (1971) 22 P & CR 756 at 764, 768.
5   **[Para 12.105]**.
6   This tension highlights what Carol Rose has described as the temptation to transmute 'crystalline' rules into 'muddy' rules. 'A strong element of moral judgment runs through the cases in which mud supersedes crystal. These cases are often rife with human failings – sloth and forgetfulness on the one hand, greed and self-dealing on the other' (see C M Rose, 40 Stan L Rev 577 at 597 (1987–88)).

Drastic adaptation of the doctrine of notice

12.286   The property legislation of 1925 was heavily influenced by a policy preference for certainty[1] – not least in the approach adopted in respect of land charge registration. The major objective of the 1925 enactments was the simplification of conveyancing. In the context of land charges this objective is more effectively ensured if the consequences of registration and non-registration are absolutely clear-cut and conclusive. For this purpose the traditional doctrine of notice was displaced or, more accurately, adapted by the land charges scheme. With effect from 1 January 1926 land charge registration became the *only* recognised form of notice to third parties in respect of certain categories of entitlement affecting unregistered estates. An interest which falls within the registrable heads under the Land Charges Act is *either* duly registered as a land charge and therefore rendered binding *or* is not so registered and rendered void against most purchasers. The Act obviates any general enquiry into the state of the mind or conscience of each individual purchaser.

1　[**Paras 2.47, 12.112**].

Statutory incorporation of an amoral rule

12.287　The 1925 legislation aimed to reinforce the overall efficiency of the system of land charge registration through a rigorous extrusion of the equitable doctrine of notice. In unregistered land the doctrine was superseded by a 'mechanical principle of registration' which was said to have marked a 'shift from a moral to an a-moral basis' in the protection of equitable interests in land.[1] In its quest for long-term certainty rather than short-term justice, the law relating to land charges is largely indifferent to the relative moral claims of litigants. Thus, for example, in *Hollington Bros Ltd v Rhodes*[2] an unregistered contract to grant a lease was held ineffective even as against a purchaser of the leasehold reversion who had expressly agreed to take title 'subject to and with the benefit of such tenancies as may affect the premises.'[3] Notwithstanding this undertaking and even though the purchase price had been calculated in the light of the subsisting equitable tenancy, the purchaser was held entitled to repudiate the incumbrance and coerce a renegotiation of the tenancy at a new and higher rent level. The result was controversial in so far as the purchaser was allowed, in 'defiance of ethics',[4] to trample flagrantly over unregistered rights.[5]

1　H W R Wade, [1956] CLJ 216 at 227. See *R Griggs Group Ltd v Evans (No 2)* [2004] EWHC 1088 (Ch) at [33] ('under a pure registration system the drawback is that the first man to register always wins, irrespective of business ethics').

2　[1951] 2 TLR 691 at 696 per Harman J.

3　On the status of the contract for a lease as a species of estate contract registrable under Class C(iv) of the Land Charges Act, see Chapter 9 [**para 9.76**].

4　See H W R Wade, [1956] CLJ 216 at 217 (remarking that the outcome in *Hollington v Rhodes* attached a disproportionate penalty to the 'venial fault of non-registration'). See also G Battersby, 'Informal Transactions in Land, Estoppel and Registration' (1995) 58 MLR 637 at 653.

5　There would nowadays be a strong argument that the taking of title expressly 'subject to' the rights of another may raise a constructive trust to give effect to those rights [**paras 10.73, 12.122**]. In some circumstances the unregistered rights may even be enforceable against the dishonest purchaser pursuant to Contracts (Rights of Third Parties) Act 1999, s 1(1)–(2) [**para 12.122**].

Unconscionable repudiation of rights

12.288 In the present context the only available control over unethical outcomes stems from the overarching prohibition of fraud.[1] The aims of efficiency and convenience secured by the land charges scheme must not be attained at the price of fraud on the part of the main actors, for ultimately fraud unravels all.[2] The difficulty is that any reference to an exceptional category of 'fraud' merely re-opens a fierce controversy over the precise boundaries of permissible behaviour.[3] It has long been suggested, for instance, that one means of reintroducing an element of 'fairness' into the operation of the land charges system lies in the proposal that purchasers should be prejudicially affected by actual notice (as distinct from merely constructive notice) of unregistered incumbrances.[4] In cases of actual notice – it is argued – the purchaser is acting inconsistently with the requirements of conscience and thus becomes a fair target for a limited application of the traditional doctrine of notice. In spite of its attractions this approach was firmly rejected by the House of Lords in *Midland Bank Trust Co Ltd v Green*.[5]

1 Compare *London, Chatham & Dover Railway Co v South Eastern Railway Co* [1892] 1 Ch 120 at 143 per Lindley LJ (affd [1893] AC 429).
2 **[Para 12.106]**.
3 See the analogous discussion in the context of registered title **[paras 12.107–12.128]**.
4 There are parallels in other registration areas (see e g LCA 1972, s 5(7) **[para 12.333]**; Patents Act 1977, s 33(1)). See *R Griggs Group Ltd v Evans (No 2)* [2004] EWHC 1088 (Ch) at [33].
5 [1981] AC 513, on appeal from [1980] Ch 590. See [1981] CLJ 213 (C Harpum); [1981] Conv 361 (H E Johnson); (1981) 97 LQR 518 (B Green); (1980) 96 LQR 8 (R J Smith).

Midland Bank Trust Co Ltd v Green: the facts

12.289 In *Midland Bank Trust Co Ltd v Green*, W, the owner of a fee simple in unregistered land, granted his son, G, an option to purchase the land for £22,500.[1] G failed to register this option as an estate contract under Class C(iv) of the Land Charges Act.[2] Six years later, in consequence of some family discord, W sought to revoke the option. Upon discovering that the option had never been registered, W speedily conveyed the land (which was by now worth £40,000) to his own wife, E, for a consideration of £500, with the clear intention of defeating G's unprotected rights (see *Fig. 40*). When G, who had at all material times been a tenant in occupation of the land, later purported to exercise his option, his mother claimed that the option was void for non-registration. G began proceedings against his father and the executors of his mother's estate – his mother meanwhile having died – claiming both a declaration that the option was binding on his mother's estate and an order of specific performance of the option. G himself then died and his executors, the claimant bank, continued the action with, of course, the benefit of a large sympathy factor weighing on behalf of G's bereaved widow and children.

1 G purchased the option from his father for the sum of £1.
2 **[Para 12.309]**.

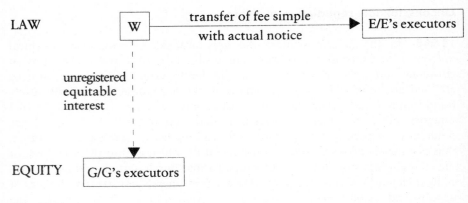

LAW

W

transfer of fee simple
with actual notice

E/E's executors

unregistered
equitable
interest

EQUITY   G/G's executors

Fig. **40**

12.290   By the time the action reached the courts, the value of the disputed land had inflated to over £400,000. It was plain that a decision against E's executors would effectively enable G's widow and children to buy the land for £22,500 in accordance with the option. A decision in favour of E's executors would result in a sale of the land and the division of the proceeds of sale between the five children of W and E, G's widow and children receiving in effect only 20 per cent of the value of the land.

Midland Bank Trust Co Ltd v Green: the ruling

12.291   The problem raised in *Midland Bank Trust Co Ltd v Green* was essentially one of statutory construction. E's executors claimed that, in accordance with the provision which is now section 4(6) of the Land Charges Act 1972,[1] E had taken free of the option as a 'purchaser for money or money's worth of a legal estate', notwithstanding her actual knowledge of the subsisting, but unregistered, incumbrance. At first instance Oliver J upheld this defence and ruled that the unregistered option was not binding on E's estate.[2] This ruling was reversed by a majority decision in the Court of Appeal, only to be reinstated by the unanimous decision of the House of Lords.[3]

1   The crucial provision in the *Green* litigation was LCA 1925, s 13(2) (the similarly worded predecessor of LCA 1972, s 4(6)). In the following discussion the courts' references in *Green* to section 13(2) are rendered as references to section 4(6).

2   Oliver J confessed that he reached this conclusion 'with regret', since it seemed that G's clear rights had been 'deliberately frustrated by his parents in breach of the contract created by the option.' However, Oliver J took the view that, 'with the best will in the world', he could not allow his 'subjective moral judgment to stand in the way of ... the clear meaning of the statutory provisions' ([1980] Ch 590 at 614D).

3   The result would have been different in registered land since G, being 'in actual occupation' of the land, would have had an overriding interest binding upon his mother's estate (see *Lloyds Bank plc v Carrick* [1996] 4 All ER 630 at 639d–e per Morritt LJ [**para 2.121**]).

Was there a purchase 'for money or money's worth'?

12.292 In *Midland Bank Trust Co Ltd v Green* E's immunity from the unregistered option depended upon a showing that E was a 'purchaser ... for money or money's worth'. In giving judgment in the Court of Appeal in favour of G's executors, Lord Denning MR ruled that the statutory immunity from unregistered options presupposed the payment of 'a fair and reasonable value in money or money's worth: not an undervalue.'[1] Accordingly he regarded E's 'grotesquely small' payment of £500 as 'a gross undervalue' for this purpose and, furthermore, as providing evidence of a degree of collusion which 'would open the door to fraud of the worst description.'[2]

1   [1980] Ch 590 at 624E.
2   [1980] Ch 590 at 624D. Eveleigh LJ ([1980] Ch 590 at 628B–C) likewise thought that the transaction between W and E was 'a gift coupled with a token of £500 ... to meet the requirements of [section 4] of the Land Charges Act.' Accordingly Eveleigh LJ held that the disputed conveyance had not been made 'for' money or money's worth within the meaning of section 4(6). Compare the dissenting judgment of Sir Stanley Rees ([1980] Ch 590 at 632A).

12.293 Lord Denning's requirement that consideration be 'adequate' for the purpose of section 4(6) was conclusively rejected by the House of Lords.[1] In delivering the only substantial speech in the House, Lord Wilberforce ruled that the purchaser need only show that she had paid 'money or money's worth' and that she had thereby provided 'valuable consideration'.[2] In this case E had certainly paid money and, in Lord Wilberforce's view, the notion of 'valuable consideration' is quite capable of including a 'nominal consideration'.[3] The House of Lords thus disposed of one of the principal bases for the decision of the majority in the Court of Appeal.

1   Lord Wilberforce referred to the criterion of adequacy as 'an expression of transparent difficulty' ([1981] AC 513 at 531D).
2   LCA 1972, s 17(1) defines a 'purchaser' as one who gives 'valuable consideration', a 'term of art which precludes any enquiry as to adequacy' ([1981] AC 513 at 531E per Lord Wilberforce).
3   Lord Wilberforce added that, in any event, he would have had 'great difficulty' in holding that £500 was merely a 'nominal sum of money' ([1981] AC 513 at 532B).

Is there any requirement of good faith in section 4(6)?

12.294 The definition of 'purchaser' in the Land Charges Act does not explicitly impose any requirement of good faith on the purchaser who claims the statutory immunity from unregistered land charges.[1] In the Court of Appeal, however, both Lord Denning MR and Eveleigh LJ denied E's estate the protection of section 4(6) on the ground that E had not purchased in good faith. In Lord Denning's view, the statutory immunity could never avail a purchaser 'when the sale to him is done in fraud of the holder of the estate contract.'[2] Here the facts disclosed all the characteristics of 'fraud' thus defined, in that W and E had 'hatched a plot ... [of which] the predominant purpose was to damage [G].'[3] An absurdly low price (one eightieth of the then current market value) had been paid in connection with a covert transaction whose plain object had been to deprive G of his unregistered option. It would, said Lord Denning, be 'most unfair to [G], his widow and children', if the fraud perpetrated by W and E were allowed to succeed.[4]

1   See LCA 1972, s 17(1) (formerly LCA 1925, s 20(8)).
2   [1980] Ch 590 at 624F. In support of this conclusion Lord Denning invoked the general principle that 'fraud unravels everything' (*Lazarus Estates Ltd v Beasley* [1956] 1 QB 702 at 712 [**para 12.106**]).
3   [1980] Ch 590 at 622G, 625D (contrast Sir Stanley Rees, dissenting, at 632F–633B).
4   [1980] Ch 590 at 622D. (It did not escape the notice of Lord Denning MR that W had treated other members of the family more generously than G.)

12.295   On further appeal the majority view in the Court of Appeal was roundly rejected by the House of Lords. Lord Wilberforce expressed the firm conviction that the omission of any explicit requirement of 'good faith' in the land charges legislation was entirely deliberate. To read into section 4(6) a requirement of good faith purchase would, he believed, introduce 'the necessity of enquiring into the purchaser's motives and state of mind'[1] – a re-emergence of the very doctrine of notice which the 1925 legislation had sought to avoid.[2] In support of this conclusion Lord Wilberforce invoked the well known principle that 'it is not fraud to take advantage of legal rights, the existence of which may be taken to be known to both parties.'[3] He pointed out that it had been perfectly open to G to protect his option by a simple act of registration, which he had failed to carry out.[4] The House of Lords thus re-asserted the crude but efficient rule that the only form of notice relevant in the land charges context is the notice constituted by due entry in the register, declining (in the absence of 'fraud') to import any general moral criterion of good faith into the operation of the Land Charges Act 1972.[5]

1   [1981] AC 513 at 530A.
2   [**Para 12.339**].
3   [1981] AC 513 at 531A ('it is not "fraud" to rely on legal rights conferred by Act of Parliament'). Lord Wilberforce cited the dictum of Lord Cozens-Hardy MR in *Re Monolithic Building Co* [1915] 1 Ch 643 at 663 [**para 12.113**]. See also *Markfaith Investment Ltd v Chiap Hua Flashlights Ltd* [1991] 2 AC 43 at 60D.
4   [1981] AC 513 at 528A–B ('The case is plain: the Act is clear and definite … [T]he Act itself provides a simple and effective protection for persons in [G's] position – viz – by registration'). See similarly *Lloyds Bank plc v Carrick* [1996] 4 All ER 630 at 639e–f per Morritt LJ.
5   In *Midland Bank Trust Co Ltd v Green* the House of Lords effectively relegated G's estate to such non-proprietary remedies as might be available. The 'unfairness' of the result achieved by the House of Lords was mitigated by the fact that, in different proceedings before Oliver J, G's estate succeeded in recovering damages in respect of the negligence of G's solicitor in failing to register G's Class C(iv) land charge (see *Midland Bank Trust Co Ltd v Hett, Stubbs and Kemp (A Firm)* [1979] Ch 384 at 433B–D). G's estate also recovered damages against W's estate for the tort of conspiracy (see *Midland Bank Trust Co Ltd v Green (No 3)* [1982] Ch 529 at 539H–540B, 541H–542A).

12.296   The decision of the House of Lords in *Midland Bank Trust Co Ltd v Green* is entirely consistent with the amoral approach to economic relations which infuses the market concept of property.[1] The ruling confirmed the traditional inclination of the property lawyer to trade off justice in return for enhanced security and stability in commercial transactions. The result was controversial[2] and it remains unclear whether the House of Lords' approach could have been sustained if the facts had presented a more blatant form of deception than simple manipulation of the Register of Land Charges.[3] It is difficult to maintain that fraudulent or unconscionable conduct can never deflect the operation of a statutory scheme. More recent case law in the analogous area of title registration suggests that, even in the absence of any explicit statutory requirement of good faith, modern courts are more ready to impose a constructive trust on a purchaser who takes title in circumstances which connote a breach of conscientious obligation.[4] Detestation of fraud or bad faith eventually colours the outworking of even the most rigorously structured statutory rules. It may not be fraud to take advantage of the folly of others, but it remains an uncomfortable fact of life that most fraud consists in doing precisely that.

1   **[Para 12.116]**.
2   The Law Commission later indicated that the outcome was not an 'acceptable' resolution of the problem in hand (*Property Law: Third Report on Land Registration* (Law Com No 158, March 1987), para 4.15).
3   Lord Wilberforce thought that the purchaser in *Green* could not necessarily be stigmatised as having acted in bad faith ([1981] AC 513 at 530A–D). He regarded the case as no more heinous than one in which, albeit with the addition of a profit motive, a purchaser who had notice of an existing option 'decided nevertheless to buy the land, relying on the absence of notification.'
4   **[Paras 12.117–12.128]**.

CATEGORIES OF REGISTRABLE LAND CHARGE

12.297   Six general classes of registrable land charge are defined in section 2 of the Land Charges Act 1972, of which the most important are Classes C, D, and F. All matters eligible for registration within the six general classes must, as a threshold qualification, involve some form of 'charge on or obligation affecting land'.[1]

1   LCA 1972, s 2(1).

CLASS A

12.298   Class A charges comprise various kinds of land charge which derive ultimately from statute and which arise only on the making of some statutory application.[1]

1   An example is the landlord's right to compensation under Agricultural Holdings Act 1986, s 86.

CLASS B

12.299   Class B charges likewise arise by virtue of statute. Such charges include the Legal Services Commission's charge (in respect of unpaid contributions towards legal aid) which attaches to land recovered or preserved for a legally assisted client under the Access to Justice Act 1999.[1] Class B charges differ from Class A charges in that they originate directly in the statute concerned and do not arise merely on the chargee's application.

1   Access to Justice Act 1999, s 10(7).

CLASS C

12.300   Class C charges fall under four heads:

Class C(i)

12.301   This class comprises the 'puisne mortgage', ie a legal mortgage which is not protected by a deposit of documents relating to the legal estate affected. A puisne mortgage is therefore a second (or subsequent) mortgage granted by a mortgagor who has already deposited his title deeds with the first mortgagee.[1] The second (or subsequent) mortgagee, being unable to enjoy the security provided by retention of the title deeds, is offered the alternative security of being able to register his mortgage as a land charge notwithstanding that it is *legal*. Class C(i) thus provides an unusual example of a legal interest which is registrable under the Land Charges Act.

1   **[Para 8.257]**.

Class C(ii)

12.302   Class C(ii) comprises the 'limited owner's charge'. Such a charge arises where, for instance, a tenant for life of settled land[1] discharges out of his own pocket a liability to taxation attracted by the settled estate as a whole. The limited owner's charge is an equitable charge which, if registered, secures the right of the limited owner (ie the tenant for life) to reimbursement of the money paid by him to the Revenue.

1   **[Para 9.211]**.

Class C(iii)

12.303   This class comprises the 'general equitable charge' and includes many kinds of equitable charge or mortgage which are not otherwise registrable.

Registrable equitable charges

12.304   Amongst the incumbrances registrable under Class C(iii) are a rentcharge granted for life (or 'equitable annuity'),[1] an equitable mortgage of a legal estate,[2] and an unpaid vendor's equitable lien on land which has been sold.[3]

1   **[Para 8.226]**. 'Equitable annuities outside trusts for sale and settlements must be extremely rare, even if only because most kinds of annuity charged upon land make it settled land' (H W R Wade, [1956] CLJ 216 at 224).
2   **[Para 9.104]**.
3   **[Para 9.130]**.

Non-registrable charges

12.305   Class C(iii) does not include any charge which is secured by a deposit of documents relating to the legal title affected.[1] Informal mortgages created by a contractually supported deposit of title deeds are therefore excluded from the registrable category.[2] Nor does Class C(iii) cover any equitable charge which arises, or affects an interest arising, under a trust or settlement of land.[3] Class C(iii) likewise excludes an agreement to share the proceeds of sale of land[4] and an estate agent's charge on these proceeds for the purpose of securing his commission.[5] The chargee's interest in such cases is, effectively, an interest in money rather than an interest in land and Class C(iii) is appropriate only in respect of interests in land.

1   LCA 1972, s 2(4).
2   **[Para 9.111]**.
3   LCA 1972, s 2(4). Mortgages of an equitable interest under a trust or settlement of land are swept away as an inherent consequence of the normal process of overreaching of the beneficiary's interest on sale. Since such charges are normally satisfied out of the proceeds of that sale, it follows that there is no basis for their enforcement against a later purchaser (see LPA 1925, s 2(1)(i)–(ii); SLA 1925, s 72(2)).
4   *Thomas v Rose* [1968] 1 WLR 1797 at 1808G–H.
5   *Georgiades v Edward Wolfe & Co Ltd* [1965] Ch 487 at 501F, 504G, 508C.

Class C(iv)

12.306   Class C(iv) comprises the 'estate contract', which is statutorily defined as

> a contract by an estate owner or by a person entitled at the date of the contract to have a legal estate conveyed to him to convey or create a legal estate, including a contract conferring either expressly or by statutory implication a valid option to purchase, a right of pre-emption or any other like right.[1]

1   LCA 1972, s 2(4).

Conveyancing function of the estate contract

12.307   It is an integral feature of the conveyancing process that, from the formation of a specifically enforceable contract of sale, the purchaser of a legal estate in land acquires not merely a contractual right but also a proprietary right of an equitable character.[1] This indirectly explains why one of the most significant categories of registrable land charge – the 'estate contract' – is designed precisely to protect the purchaser's right to require the conveyance of an unregistered legal estate in accordance with his contract.[2] There is always a possibility that between contract and conveyance the vendor may, in breach of contract, convey the legal estate to a third party who has no notice of the equitable rights generated by the contract. Moreover, a contract for the sale and purchase of land, by its very nature, creates merely a short-term interest and is therefore peculiarly appropriate for protection under a system of name-registration such as the land charges scheme.[3] Ironically it appears that, in practice, estate contracts are seldom registered by solicitors, being entered in the Register of Land Charges only in cases of suspicion or delayed completion.[4]

1   For an account of the anticipatory effect of equitable doctrine, see Chapter 9 [**paras 9.18–9.22**].
2   It matters not that the legal estate to be conveyed under the contract is greater than the estate currently vested in the estate owner (*Sharp v Coates* [1949] 1 KB 285 at 293). Class C(iv) even includes unwritten contracts which are enforceable only by reference to estoppel or part performance (see *Lloyds Bank plc v Carrick* [1996] 4 All ER 630 at 638b, 639e–f).
3   H W R Wade, [1956] CLJ 216 at 222.
4   See also Law Com No 271 (2001), para 9.69.

Accepted forms of registrable estate contract

12.308   Estate contracts include not merely contracts for the sale of an estate in fee simple, but also contracts for a lease,[1] contracts to create a mortgage of a legal estate[2] and certain kinds of option.[3]

1   See *Phillips v Mobil Oil Co Ltd* [1989] 1 WLR 888 at 890H per Nicholls LJ.
2   [**Para 9.109**].
3   [**Para 9.77**]. See e g *Midland Bank Trust Co Ltd v Green* [1981] AC 513 [**para 12.289**]; *Phillips v Mobil Oil Co Ltd* [1989] 1 WLR 888 at 890H per Nicholls LJ. Once an option is registered, there is no need for additional registration of any contract which results from its exercise (*Armstrong & Holmes Ltd v Holmes* [1993] 1 WLR 1482 at 1488H). On options, see generally *Barnsley's Land Options* (3rd edn by Richard Castle, London 1998).

Options and rights of pre-emption

12.309   An option to purchase a legal estate may take various forms apart from the obvious case of an option to purchase an estate in fee simple. The options registrable under Class C(iv) include an option to purchase a legal lease,[1] together with a tenant's option to renew his term[2] or to purchase the immediately superior reversionary interest.[3] A tenant may also, under Class C(iv), register his right to call for an 'overriding lease'.[4] He may likewise register any notice served by him in respect of his rights under various kinds of leasehold enfranchisement legislation.[5] A Class C(iv) charge is registrable by a landlord in protection of any right which he may have to require his tenant to surrender (rather than assign) his leasehold term.[6] The statutory definition of the Class C(iv) charge plainly includes a reference to a 'right of pre-emption' and, by analogy with the new status of such rights in registered land,[7] it seems preferable to regard equivalent rights in unregistered land as capable, from the moment of their creation, of registration under Class C(iv).

1   *Phillips v Mobil Oil Co Ltd* [1989] 1 WLR 888 at 890H–891A per Nicholls LJ.
2   *Beesly v Hallwood Estates Ltd* [1960] 1 WLR 549 at 558; *Phillips v Mobil Oil Co Ltd* [1989] 1 WLR 888 at 893F, 894E–G. See Jean Howell, [1990] Conv 169, 250. The Roxburgh Committee suggested that such options should cease to be registrable (*Report of the Committee on Land Charges* (Cmd 9825, 1956), para 15).
3   *Phillips v Mobil Oil Co Ltd* [1989] 1 WLR 888 at 891C.
4   Landlord and Tenant (Covenants) Act 1995, s 20(6) **[para 14.236]**.
5   Leasehold Reform Act 1967, s 5(5) **[para 7.334]**; Leasehold Reform, Housing and Urban Development Act 1993, s 97(1) **[para 7.338]**. The mere service of a statutory notice by the tenant confers no priority over a transferee from the landlord: for the latter purpose the notice must be registered (see e g *Buckley v SRL Investments Ltd and Cator and Robinson* (1971) 22 P & CR 756 at 764).
6   *Greene v Church Commissioners for England* [1974] Ch 467 at 477B.
7   See LRA 2002, s 115(1), finally countering the effect of obiter dicta in *Pritchard v Briggs* [1980] Ch 338 at 419F–G, 423A–B **[paras 9.85–9.86]**.

Conditional contracts other than options

12.310   Outside the context of options and rights of pre-emption some uncertainty still attaches to the registrable status of contracts which remain subject to an unfulfilled condition (e g the grant of a planning permission or receipt of a satisfactory survey). In practice many such conditional contracts have been registered within Class C(iv) without any objection whatsoever.[1] Registration is self-evidently appropriate where the condition in question is one which was included for the benefit of the purchaser and may be waived by him[2] or where the relevant condition requires to be satisfied not by either of the transacting parties but by some extraneous person or event.[3] In such cases the conditional contract imposes an 'obligation affecting land' within the required statutory sense,[4] precisely because the vendor has placed entirely outside his control the fulfilment or frustration of the relevant condition.

1   See e g *Re Longlands Farm* [1968] 3 All ER 552 at 553I.
2   See *Wood Preservation Ltd v Prior* [1969] 1 WLR 1077 at 1094E–G (contract conditional upon purchaser obtaining planning permission 'to its entire satisfaction').
3   *Haslemere Estates Ltd v Baker* [1982] 1 WLR 1109 at 1118H–1119A (contract conditional upon the grant of planning permission and the consent of the Charity Commissioners).
4   LCA 1972, s 2(1).

Contracts of agency

12.311   There has always been some doubt as to the place of contracts of agency within Class C(iv) and as to whether the class of registrable estate contracts can include a contract to *create* a contract in relation to land. In *Turley v Mackay*[1] Uthwatt J thought that Class C(iv) covered a contract by A to sell to any nominee put forward by B.[2] In *Thomas v Rose*,[3] however, Megarry J regarded Class C(iv) as properly applicable only where the estate owner undertakes a clear legal obligation to convey his estate to *somebody*.[4] No registration may be validly effected in respect of a contract 'at one remove' which merely provides 'machinery whereby such an obligation may be created by some other transaction.'[5]

1   [1944] Ch 37 at 40.
2   For confirmation that a contract to convey to an as yet unidentified nominee may be an estate contract, see *London & Blenheim Estates Ltd v Ladbroke Retail Parks Ltd* [1994] 1 WLR 31 at 37C–D per Peter Gibson LJ. It is irrelevant that no nomination is in fact ever made (*Thomas v Rose* [1968] 1 WLR 1797 at 1804B).
3   [1968] 1 WLR 1797 at 1804G.
4   [1968] 1 WLR 1797 at 1805C.
5   A contract between A and B conferring on B the power to accept 'any offer for the sale' of A's land is at most an authority to do some further act which might (or might not) bring an estate contract into being (*Thomas v Rose* [1968] 1 WLR 1797 at 1805F–G).

CLASS D

12.312   Class D falls under three heads:

Class D(i)

12.313   This class comprises an Inland Revenue charge for tax payable on death under the Inheritance Tax Act 1984.[1]

1   LCA 1972, s 2(5).

Class D(ii)

12.314   This class comprises the restrictive covenant,[1] which for present purposes is defined as 'a covenant or agreement (other than a covenant or agreement between a lessor and a lessee) restrictive of the user of land and entered into on or after 1 January 1926.'[2]

1   On restrictive covenants, see Chapter 9 [**paras 9.138–9.171**] and Chapter 13 [**paras 13.63–13.154**].
2   LCA 1972, s 2(5).

Proprietary status of the restrictive covenant

12.315   Ever since the decision in *Tulk v Moxhay*[1] the covenantee under a restrictive covenant has been viewed in English law as holding, by virtue of his contractual right of control, some kind of equitable proprietary entitlement in the covenantor's land. Accordingly in the years preceding 1926 the binding effect of restrictive covenants over freehold land was governed by the equitable doctrine of notice. The burden of the restrictive covenant fell on all purchasers of the covenantor's land other than a bona fide purchaser for value of a legal estate in that land who had no notice of the restrictive covenant.[2]

1   (1848) 2 Ph 774, 41 ER 1143 **[paras 9.147, 13.108]**.
2   The successors of such a person would also take free of the covenant **[para 12.195]**.

Introduction of a rule of registration

12.316   Consistently with the aim of much of the 1925 legislation,[1] the equitable doctrine of notice, in its application to freehold restrictive covenants over unregistered land, was displaced by a statutory mechanism of registration under Class D(ii). The transmission of the burden of such covenants to the covenantor's successors now depends on the registration against the covenantor of a land charge under Class D(ii). The traditional doctrine of notice has thus been modified to the extent that the only recognised form of notice of the covenantee's equitable interest is today the notice which is ensured by land charge registration. Registration disables any successor of the covenantor from claiming that he had no 'actual notice' of the covenant in question,[2] whilst failure to register the land charge renders the restrictive covenant void against most third parties.[3]

1   **[Para 12.339]**.
2   LPA 1925, s 198(1) **[para 12.279]**.
3   LCA 1972, s 4(6) **[para 12.282]**.

Exclusions from Class D(ii)

12.317   Class D(ii) excludes from its ambit two significant categories of restrictive covenant. *First*, the binding quality of restrictive covenants entered into before 1926 continues to be governed by the equitable doctrine of notice.[1] *Second*, the enforcement against third parties of restrictive covenants entered into between lessor and lessee, in so far as they relate to the user of the land leased, has always been governed by a special framework of rules stemming from *Spencer's Case*.[2] In rare instances, however, a restrictive covenant between lessor and lessee relates, not to the user of the land demised, but to the user of other land held by the lessor. Such a covenant cannot be registered as a Class D(ii) charge and its enforcement against third parties in unregistered land therefore depends on the continuing operation of the equitable doctrine of notice.[3]

1   **[Para 12.372]**.
2   (1583) 5 Co Rep 16a, 77 ER 72 **[para 14.243]**.
3   *Dartstone v Cleveland Petroleum Co Ltd* [1969] 1 WLR 1807 at 1812A **[para 12.372]**.

Class D(iii)

12.318   This class comprises the 'equitable easement',[1] which is statutorily defined as 'an easement, right or privilege over or affecting land created or arising on or after 1 January 1926, and being merely an equitable interest.'[2] An equitable easement generally arises where a right in the nature of an easement has been created otherwise than by deed (eg by mere contract, unsealed writing or verbal grant) or has been created otherwise than for an interest equivalent to an estate in fee simple absolute in possession or a term of years absolute.[3] In unregistered land such a right depends, for enforcement against the grantor's successors, upon registration of a Class D(iii) charge against the name of the grantor.

1　Easements are discussed more fully in Chapter 8 [**paras 8.24–8.224**] and Chapter 9 [**paras 9.87–9.101**].
2　LCA 1972, s 2(5).
3　[**Para 9.88**].

Uncertain coverage of Class D(iii)

12.319　The Class D(iii) land charge has proved to be problematic in both scope and operation. The very persons in whose favour such a charge commonly arises are precisely those persons who tend to be unaware of the need to secure protection by registration. The category of Class D(iii) charges is obscure and ill-defined.[1] Despite the width of the statutory description of Class D(iii), this category of charge has been held to have no application to a tenant's right to remove fixtures at the end of a lease[2] or to an equitable right of entry for breach of a leasehold covenant.[3] In *E R Ives Investment Ltd v High*[4] Lord Denning MR even suggested that Class D(iii) embraces only those equitable easements which, prior to 1926, would have ranked as legal interests in land but were cut back to equitable status by the effect of the 1925 legislation.[5]

1　See *Poster v Slough Estates Ltd* [1968] 1 WLR 1515 at 1520C–D, 1521F per Cross J.
2　*Poster v Slough Estates Ltd* [1968] 1 WLR 1515 at 1521B–C.
3　*Shiloh Spinners Ltd v Harding* [1973] AC 691 at 721G. See [1973] CLJ 218 (Paul Fairest). Enforcement against a later purchaser depends, in unregistered land, on the equitable doctrine of notice [**para 12.372**].
4　[1967] 2 QB 379 at 395F–396B. See (1967) 31 Conv (NS) 338 (F R Crane).
5　See C V Davidge, (1937) 53 LQR 259 at 260.

Estoppel-related easements

12.320　The Court of Appeal's decision in *E R Ives Investment Ltd v High* concerned an agreed right of way which was never completed by a deed of grant and never registered as a Class D(iii) land charge.[1] Since this equitable easement was supported, on the facts, by strong elements of acquiescence and mutuality of benefit and burden, Lord Denning indicated that the right, being inherently equitable, was immune from any requirement of land charge registration.[2] Its impact on third parties was therefore governed simply by the doctrine of notice.[3] Although concurring in the result, the other members of the Court of Appeal did not go quite so far. Danckwerts and Winn LJJ regarded the informally granted right of way as void for non-registration,[4] but held that the purchaser was estopped from pleading such non-registration in view of a history of acquiescence in the grantee's expenditure in reliance on his supposed entitlement.[5] The element of acquiescence, together with the doctrine of mutual benefit and burden,[6] created an 'equity' in favour of the grantee which bound all subsequent purchasers who took the land with actual notice.[7] Unlike the original equitable right of way, this 'equity' was not registrable under the Land Charges Act and was therefore unaffected by failure to enter a Class D(iii) charge.[8] The multi-stranded ruling in *E R Ives Investment Ltd v High* underscores the imprecision of Class D(iii) and indicates that, in one way or another, at least some post-1925 equitable easements effectively escape from the registrable category if associated with non-registrable rights founded on estoppel.

1   **[Paras 9.101, 10.198]**.
2   [1967] 2 QB 379 at 395E–396B.
3   It therefore followed that the purchaser of the land, having agreed to take expressly subject to the right of way, was bound by it. See also P V Baker, (1972) 88 LQR 336; D Yates, (1974) 37 MLR 87. For reasoning similar to that of Lord Denning MR, see *Montague v Long* (1972) 24 P & CR 240 at 247–248.
4   [1967] 2 QB 379 at 399B–C, 403E–F.
5   On estoppel doctrine, see Chapter 10 **[paras 10.168–10.300]**. Compare *Sutton v O'Kane* [1973] 2 NZLR 304 at 334.
6   On the doctrine of 'mutual benefit and burden' (and its strict limitations), see Chapter 13 **[para 13.59]**.
7   **[Para 12.369]**.
8   See also *Classic Communications Ltd v Lascar* (1986) 21 DLR (4th) 579 at 589–590.

CLASS E

12.321   Class E land charges comprise annuities arising before 1926 but not registered until after the Land Charges Act 1925 came into force.

CLASS F

12.322   Class F land charges comprise charges which are registrable in protection of the 'matrimonial home rights' conferred by the Family Law Act 1996.[1] Where title to the estate affected by matrimonial home rights has not yet been brought on to the Land Register, a matrimonial home rights charge may be registered as a Class F land charge against the name of the relevant estate owner.[2] Once so registered, a spouse's rights are rendered durable and enforceable against almost all third parties,[3] but failure to register the charge has the consequence that the rights become ineffective against a purchaser for value of any interest in the land.[4]

1   **[Para 12.93]**.
2   LCA 1972, s 2(1), (7).
3   LPA 1925, s 198(1) **[para 12.279]**. Spousal rights of occupation, even though duly registered, are at best effective for only a limited period against the estate owner's trustee in bankruptcy (see Insolvency Act 1986, s 335A(3) **[para 11.255]**).
4   LCA 1972, s 4(8) **[para 12.281]**.

SEARCH OF THE REGISTER OF LAND CHARGES

12.323   Search of the Register of Land Charges is governed by rules drawn from both statute and judge-made law.

Timing of search

12.324   It may seem strange that in unregistered conveyancing a prospective purchaser's investigation of title is sometimes not completed until after he has entered into a contractual commitment to purchase. The purchaser requires a 'good root of title' which is at least 15 years old[1] and the deed which constitutes the good root is specified in the contract itself. Where, however, the transaction is not conducted under the Law Society's 'National Protocol',[2] the vendor has no obligation to deduce his title from this good root until after exchange of contracts has occurred.[3] In such cases it is only following the exchange of contracts that the purchaser enjoys any contractual right of access to the documentary title which discloses the names of previous estate owners against whom land charges may have been registered.

1   LPA 1925, s 44(1), as amended by LPA 1969, s 23 [**para 12.260**].
2   [**Para 12.11**].
3   It is possible for the vendor to speed up or otherwise facilitate a transaction by affording access to the relevant documents before exchange of contracts, but this practice is not invariable (see *Rignall Developments Ltd v Halil* [1988] Ch 190 at 201A–C).

Process of search

12.325   At some point prior to the projected date of completion the purchaser searches the Register of Land Charges against the names of estate owners comprised within the relevant title. Search of the Register may be conducted personally,[1] but virtually all purchasers take advantage of an official search which is available upon application and payment of a small fee. An official search takes the form of a computer-aided check of the Register for subsisting entries against the names of the estate owners included in the purchaser's requisition for search.[2]

1   LCA 1972, s 9(1). '[A]nyone who nowadays is foolish enough to search personally deserves what he gets' (*Oak Co-operative Building Society v Blackburn* [1968] Ch 730 at 744A–B per Russell LJ).
2   LCA 1972, s 10(1)–(2).

Conclusive effect of an official search certificate

12.326   The principal advantage of an official search of the Register of Land Charges consists in the fact that the search result is set out in a certificate issued to the intending purchaser.[1] This certificate is irrebuttably deemed, in favour of a purchaser or an intending purchaser, to be 'conclusive, affirmatively or negatively, as the case may be.'[2] Thus, even if the Registry mistakenly issues a clear or 'nil' certificate of official search in respect of a particular estate owner named in the relevant title, the certificate is conclusive according to its tenor. In these circumstances the unrevealed land charge, albeit duly registered against the relevant estate owner, is rendered void and the purchaser takes the land free of the charge. The owner of the now destroyed charge is thrown back upon a remedy in damages against the Land Registry for the tort of negligence.[3]

1   A further advantage conferred by official search is that the purchaser is not bound by any entry made in the Register after the issue of the certificate (other than an entry made under a 'priority notice' pursuant to LCA 1972, s 11(1)–(3)), provided that completion of the purchaser's conveyance takes place within 15 working days of the date of issue of the certificate (LCA 1972, s 11(5)–(6)).
2   LCA 1972, s 10(4) (formerly LCA 1925, s 17(3)).
3   Compare *Ministry of Housing and Local Government v Sharp* [1970] 2 QB 223 (dealing with the equivalent problem in the analogous context of local land charges). See also LCA 1972, s 10(6) (immunity of Registry officers and employees from personal liability except in cases of fraud).

Consequence of discovering a registered charge

12.327   Where a search of the Register of Land Charges reveals the existence of a registered charge unknown to the purchaser at the date of the contract, the purchaser may nowadays plead his prior ignorance of the charge as a ground for rescission of the contract. The contractual liability of the purchaser is no longer governed by the fictitious 'actual notice' attributed by section 198(1) of the Law of Property Act 1925.[1] Instead the question whether, at the time of entering into the estate contract, the purchaser had knowledge of a registered land charge is determined 'by reference to his actual knowledge and without regard to the provisions of section 198.'[2]

1   Contrast the 'indefensible' rule previously enforced under the decision in *Re Forsey and Hollebone's Contract* [1927] 2 Ch 379 at 392–393 (see H W R Wade, [1956] CLJ 216 at 228–230).
2   LPA 1969, s 24(1) (effective in respect of all contracts entered into on or after 1 January 1970).

Defective search

12.328   To err is human. Mistakes (usually as to name) can be made in the process of search of the Register of Land Charges. A purchaser who requisitions an official search against an incorrect name must inevitably lose priority to an incumbrancer who has registered a land charge against the correct name of the estate owner as it appears on the title deeds.[1] Other forms of error in the process of search are nowadays rare.[2] With the advent of a computerised Register of Land Charges, the certificate of search reveals a result which, on its face, is inextricably linked to the name keyed in by the staff of the Land Charges Department. In consequence an erroneous search result can flow only from intrinsic defects in the database itself, since in all other instances the purchaser who requisitions a search simply receives, at worst, the outcome of a search which he did not actually request. The purchaser must, in effect, verify that the estate owner named in the certificate issued to him is the estate owner as named in his original search application.

1   The purchaser is inescapably affected by a deemed 'actual notice' of the correct entry (LPA 1925, s 198(1)). The same conclusion follows even if the search is requisitioned not against the name of the estate owner as disclosed by his title deeds, but against some more complete version of his name, e g the full names contained in his birth certificate (see e g *Standard Property Investment plc v British Plastics Federation* (1985) 53 P & CR 25 at 30–35; [1987] Conv 135 (J E A)).
2   For an ambiguity arising in relation to the precise plot of land concerned in an application for official search against a specific name, see *Du Sautoy v Symes* [1967] Ch 1146.

Registrations concealed behind a root of title

12.329   It is possible, although rare, that land charges may have been duly registered against the names of persons whose identity now lies hidden behind the 15-year root of title obtained by a contemporary purchaser.[1] The purchaser normally has no contractual right of access to the pre-root deeds of conveyance but, according to the draconian terms of section 198(1) of the Law of Property Act 1925, is still fixed with 'actual notice' of any registered interests concealed behind the short modern root of title.[2] Although it was once feared that the draftsmen of the 1925 legislation might have created 'the conveyancing equivalent of a Frankenstein's monster, which with the passing years would become not only more dangerous but also more difficult to kill',[3] the hazard of the undiscoverable registration has, in fact, remained more apparent than real.[4] In any event, the Law of Property Act 1969 now confers a right to compensation in the unlikely case that, following a transaction completed on or after 1 January 1970, a purchaser of an estate or interest in land suffers loss by reason of a registered land charge hidden behind a good root of title.[5] In order to qualify for this compensation (which is payable by the Chief Land Registrar[6]), the purchaser must have had no 'actual knowledge' of the charge at the date of completion of his purchase.[7]

1   See LPA 1969, s 23. If, for example, a restrictive covenant was registered in 1950 against N, then the estate owner of Greenacre, a purchaser of Greenacre today may well be unaware of this registration if his root of title is constituted by a much more modern conveyance of Greenacre (e g a conveyance from X to Y in 1983). The purchaser's investigation of title will, of course, elicit the names of X and Y as former estate owners (against whom a search can be requisitioned under the Land Charges Act), but not necessarily the name of N.
2   The fact that the purchaser has obtained a clear certificate of official search against the names of intervening estate owners is quite irrelevant. Through no fault of his own, he has failed to obtain a certificate of search against the name of N – which is all that matters here.
3   See H W R Wade, [1956] CLJ 216 at 220.
4   In practice the difficulty of concealed registrations has been largely avoided because most registered land charges tend to be referred to in later title deeds so long as there remains any possibility that these charges remain relevant. It is also common practice for the official search certificates obtained by successive purchasers to be tied into deeds bundles, although this may not, in itself, be enough to compile an accurate or comprehensive record of all the charges

affecting the land. There is, for instance, no guarantee that in each case the official search was requisitioned against the correct full names of former estate owners.

5 LPA 1969, s 25(1). The charge in question must have been registered 'against the name of an owner of an estate in the land who was not as owner of any such estate a party to any transaction, or concerned in any event, comprised in the relevant title' (LPA 1969, s 25(1)(c)). In other words, the registration in respect of which compensation is sought must be truly concealed behind the root of title.

6 LPA 1969, s 25(4).

7 LPA 1969, s 25(1)(b). For this purpose, 'actual knowledge' is to be determined without regard to LPA 1925, s 198(1) (see LPA 1969, s 25(2)).

OTHER REGISTERS MAINTAINED UNDER THE LAND CHARGES ACT 1972

12.330 The Land Charges Act 1972 provides a number of additional registers, which include the following.

Pending actions

12.331 The existence of certain kinds of litigation or disputed claim affecting a title to land may be entered in the Register of Pending Actions which is maintained under the Land Charges Act 1972.

Matters registrable as a pending action

12.332 The Register of Pending Actions may be used for the registration of bankruptcy petitions filed on or after 1 January 1926 and for the entry of 'pending land actions'.[1] A pending land action (or *lis pendens*) must comprise an action or proceeding pending in court 'relating to land or any interest in or charge on land.'[2] The matters registrable under this head thus cover most claims affecting the title to land or asserting some (even inchoate) proprietary interest in land. A pending land action may include such disparate matters as a spouse's claim to a property adjustment order on divorce[3] and a claim of entitlement to an easement.[4] A pending land action cannot, however, be registered in respect of a merely *monetary* claim in respect of land,[5] but may possibly provide a means of protecting rights of occupation based on proprietary estoppel.[6]

1 LCA 1972, s 5(1). See (1986) 136 NLJ 157 (H W Wilkinson).
2 LCA 1972, s 17(1). Pending land actions are deemed to include applications for an acquisition order pursuant to the Landlord and Tenant Act 1987 (L&TA 1987, s 28(5)) or for an access order under the Access to Neighbouring Land Act 1992 (ANLA 1992, s 5(6)), together with applications to the court for a restraint order under Criminal Justice Act 1988, s 77(12)(b) or Drug Trafficking Act 1994, s 26(12)(b).
3 See *Whittingham v Whittingham* [1979] Fam 9 at 13E, but compare *Sowerby v Sowerby* (1982) 44 P & CR 192 at 195. In *Perez-Adamson v Perez-Rivas* [1987] Fam 89 at 96D–E, 97D, the Court of Appeal held that even a general claim for property adjustment in respect of unidentified land, if registered as a lis pendens against specific property, could take priority over a mortgage charge subsequently executed by the other spouse (see [1988] Conv 58 (J E M)).

4　See *Greenhi Builders Ltd v Allen* [1979] 1 WLR 156 at 159G.
5　See *Taylor v Taylor* (*1968*) [1968] 1 WLR 378 at 384C, 385B–C.
6　See *Haslemere Estates Ltd v Baker* [1982] 1 WLR 1109 at 1119H–1120A; [1983] Conv 69 at 70.

Effects of registration and non-registration

12.333　An entry in the Register of Pending Actions has effect for an initial period of five years but is thereafter renewable for further periods of five years.[1] The inevitable consequence of an entry is that any prospective purchaser of the land concerned is affected by a deemed 'actual notice' of potentially contentious issues relating to the title which he proposes to purchase.[2] However, a failure to register renders a pending land action ineffective against any purchaser 'without express notice of it.'[3] Likewise an unregistered petition in bankruptcy has no binding effect on 'a purchaser of a legal estate in good faith, for money or money's worth.'[4]

1　LCA 1972, s 8.
2　LPA 1925, s 198(1) [**para 12.279**].
3　LCA 1972, s 5(7).
4　LCA 1972, s 5(8).

Writs and orders affecting land

12.334　Certain kinds of writ or order issued in the enforcement of a court order or judgment may be registered in the Register of Writs and Orders affecting land.[1] Included within this category are charging orders,[2] orders appointing a receiver or sequestrator of land,[3] bankruptcy orders[4] and access orders made pursuant to the Access to Neighbouring Land Act 1992.[5] If duly registered, the writ or order is binding on all persons,[6] but if not so registered is generally ineffective against a 'purchaser of the land.'[7]

1　As with pending actions, registration is for a renewable period of five years (LCA 1972, s 8).
2　LCA 1972, s 6(1)(a) [**para 9.121**]. A freezing order is not registrable under section 6(1)(a) (see *Stockler v Fourways Estates Ltd* [1984] 1 WLR 25 at 27B). However, following the Canadian example (see e g *Re Kumar and Kumar* (1988) 48 DLR (4th) 559), it is now open to the county court to direct that amounts unpaid under a liability order made pursuant to the Child Support Act 1991 be recoverable as a charging order (see Child Support Act 1991, s 36(1)).
3　LCA 1972, s 6(1)(b). Registration is available in respect of a receivership order made against a landlord following non-performance of repairing covenants (see *Clayhope Properties Ltd v Evans* [1986] 1 WLR 1223 at 1227E).
4　LCA 1972, s 6(1)(c).
5　LCA 1972, s 6(1)(d) [**para 8.136**].
6　LPA 1925, s 198(1) [**para 12.279**].
7　LCA 1972, s 6(4).

Annuities

12.335　Certain annuities created between 1855 and 1926 were capable of entry in a Register of Annuities which was closed in 1925.[1] This register contains only anomalous annuities which by now must be almost extinct. Most modern annuities are registrable as Class C(iii) or Class E land charges under the Land Charges Act 1972.[2]

1   LCA 1925, s 4.
2   **[Paras 12.303, 12.321].**

Deeds of arrangement

12.336   Certain deeds of arrangement entered into by a bankrupt debtor for the benefit of his creditors may be recorded in the Register of Deeds of Arrangement affecting land.[1] If so registered, they remain valid and effective against third parties for a renewable period of five years,[2] but if unregistered are void against any purchaser of the land concerned.[3]

1   LCA 1972, s 7(1).
2   LCA 1972, s 8.
3   LCA 1972, s 7(2).

THE 'BONA FIDE PURCHASER RULE' (OR EQUITABLE DOCTRINE OF NOTICE)

12.337   According to the second major historic axiom of English land law, equitable rights in or over land are binding on all persons *other than* a bona fide purchaser of a legal estate for value without notice of those rights.[1] This basic proposition incorporates what is known as the 'bona fide purchaser rule' (or equitable doctrine of notice).[2]

1   *London and South Western Railway Co v Gomm* (1882) 20 Ch D 562 at 583; *Re Nisbet and Potts' Contract* [1906] 1 Ch 386 at 403, 405. A purchaser who demonstrates that he is possessed of all these attributes is sometimes known simply as 'Equity's Darling' – one to whom the favour of equity has been extended **[para 1.185]**.
2   See Jean Howell, 'Notice: A Broad View and a Narrow View' [1996] Conv 34.

Modern displacement of the equitable doctrine

12.338   Although forming a fundamental stratum of English land law, the equitable doctrine of notice has, in modern times, been heavily overlaid by various regimes for the registration of land interests and by the statutory mechanism for 'overreaching' prior equitable rights. The operation of the doctrine is nowadays marginal: it applies only to unregistered land and, even here, its role is severely limited.[1] There are nevertheless certain circumstances in which the enforceability of equitable interests against a purchaser of an unregistered estate in land can be determined only by a residual application of the 'bona fide purchaser rule'.

1   See *Birmingham Midshires Mortgage Services Ltd v Sabherwal* (2000) 80 P & CR 256 at 263,

where Robert Walker LJ observed that the field of unoverreached and unregistrable equitable interests in unregistered land was now 'limited … to some unusual types of equitable interest arising in commercial situations.'

Disruption of the 1925 strategy

12.339   The survival of the equitable doctrine of notice severely disrupts the simple two-fold classification of equitable rights envisaged by the 1925 legislation.[1] It was a large part of the strategy of this legislation to eliminate the equitable doctrine of notice and, with it, the uncertain transactional outcomes generated by its application.[2] In relation to unregistered land, the legislation effectively divided the field of equitable rights into a category of 'specific' burdens on land (which constitute registrable land charges) and a category of 'general' burdens (which are, in principle, overreachable). It slowly became plain, however, that there still exists, in a twilight zone beyond these major categories of interest, a third (and inevitably awkward) category of equitable rights which are neither registrable as land charges nor statutorily overreached and whose effect on a purchaser of unregistered land falls to be determined by the equitable doctrine of notice in its traditional formulation.

1   **[Para 2.183]**.
2   **[Paras 2.193, 12.355]**. See *Holaw (470) Ltd v Stockton Estates Ltd* (2001) 81 P & CR 404 at [79] per Neuberger J.

CONTENT OF THE BONA FIDE PURCHASER RULE

12.340   In *Midland Bank Trust Co Ltd v Green*[1] Lord Wilberforce explained the equitable doctrine of notice as an instance of equity's tendency to fasten upon conscience, observing that the 'composite expression' of the doctrine was 'used to epitomise the circumstances in which equity would or rather would not do so.'[2] Before the equitable doctrine of notice can release a purchaser from pre-existing equitable rights, the purchaser must discharge a heavy onus.[3] In order to establish his immunity from unoverreached and non-registrable equitable interests, the purchaser must demonstrate the following.

1   [1981] AC 513 at 528D.
2   **[Para 1.184]**.
3   The onus of proof rests clearly on the purchaser (see *Attorney-General v Biphosphated Guano Co* (1879) 11 Ch D 327 at 337; *Re Nisbet and Potts' Contract* [1906] 1 Ch 386 at 403–404; *Northern Bank Ltd v Henry* [1981] IR 1 at 19).

Bona fides

12.341   It is generally assumed that the requirement of bona fides or good faith on the part of the purchaser relates primarily to the element of notice. In order that the purchaser may claim immunity from equitable interests, he must show not only that he had no notice of those interests but also that his absence of notice was 'genuine and honest.'[1] Part of this idea is now incorporated in the concept of constructive notice,[2] but it may be that the requirement of good faith imports something more than a mere want of notice.[3] There are indications that even if the purchaser establishes an absence of notice, the courts may still enquire into his honesty.[4] In other words, the requirement of good faith is neither obsolete nor descriptive merely of an absence of actual or constructive notice.[5] However, it seems in reality that nowadays this requirement is readily deemed to be satisfied and little ever turns upon it.[6]

1   *Midland Bank Trust Co Ltd v Green* [1981] AC 513 at 528E per Lord Wilberforce.
2   **[Para 12.346]**.
3   See *Grindal v Hooper* (2000) Times, 8 February ('notice is an essential but not an exclusive aspect of good faith').
4   See *Pilcher v Rawlins* (1872) 7 Ch App 259 at 269; *Oliver v Hinton* [1899] 2 Ch 264 at 273; *Taylor v London and County Banking Co* [1901] 2 Ch 231 at 256; *Midland Bank Trust Co Ltd v Green* [1981] AC 513 at 528F–G.
5   It is significant that the term 'purchaser', which appears in the statutory formulation of the notice doctrine contained in LPA 1925, s 199(1)(ii) **[para 12.346]**, is itself defined as incorporating an element of good faith (see LPA 1925, s 205(1)(xxi)).
6   See, however, *Grindal v Hooper* (2000) Times, 8 February **[para 11.278]**.

Purchase of a legal estate

12.342   In order to defeat pre-existing equitable rights, the purchaser must take a *legal* estate in the land concerned.[1] He must purchase either a legal fee simple absolute in possession or a legal term of years absolute.[2] Moreover, by a special statutory fiction a lender who takes a charge by way of legal mortgage is also regarded for some purposes as having purchased a legal estate. He is deemed to have the same protection as if a term of years had been created in his favour by the mortgagor.[3] By contrast, a purchaser who takes only an equitable interest in the land is, in principle, subject to all prior equitable interests irrespective of notice.[4] The latter case is governed by the general rule that where the equities are equal, the first in time prevails.[5]

1   The effective date of the conveyance is the date of its duly witnessed execution, rather than any other date borne by the deed (see e g *Grindal v Hooper* (2000) Times, 8 February). Even a purchaser who has paid the purchase money in full is not safe if notice of the adverse equitable interest reaches him before he takes a formal conveyance of the legal estate (*Wigg v Wigg* (1739) 1 Atk 382 at 384, 26 ER 244 at 245). However, this is true only in respect of those adverse equitable rights which existed prior to the contract to purchase. Any adverse equitable interest arising between contract and conveyance inevitably yields priority to the equitable interest taken by purchaser himself at the date of contract **[para 9.18]**.
2   LPA 1925, s 1(1)(a)–(b). Even a lessee at a rack rent constitutes a purchaser of a legal estate (*Goodright d Humphreys v Moses* (1775) 2 Wm Bl 1019 at 1022, 96 ER 599 at 600), with the result that a council tenant can rank as a bona fide purchaser for value (see *Melluish v BMI (No 3) Ltd* [1996] 1 AC 454 at 476C–D per Lord Browne-Wilkinson **[para 7.262]**).
3   LPA 1925, s 87(1) **[para 8.246]**.
4   *London and South Western Railway Co v Gomm* (1882) 20 Ch D 562 at 583. See e g *Cave v Cave* (1880) 15 Ch D 639 at 648–649 (one of the purchasers was an equitable mortgagee).
5   **[Para 12.68]**.

Purchase for value

12.343   The equitable doctrine of notice operates in favour only of a purchaser for value. The concept of a purchaser 'for value' may appear pleonastic but, in the strictest common law sense,[1] a 'purchaser' is one who takes property by reason of the *act* of another (as distinct from one whose title arises by operation of law).[2] On this basis, even a donee (or 'volunteer') ranks technically as a 'purchaser', since his interest derives from an act of gift; whereas an adverse possessor can never rank as a 'purchaser', since his title derives from the legal effect of the effluxion of time.[3] The person who seeks immunity from prior equitable interests must therefore demonstrate not merely that he is a 'purchaser' in the technical sense, but also that he gave valuable consideration.[4] The status of 'Equity's Darling' can never be achieved by a donee[5] or a squatter.[6] However, if the purchaser gave value, it is irrelevant for the purposes of the bona fide purchaser rule whether the consideration given was adequate.[7]

1   See *Powell v Cleland* [1948] 1 KB 262 at 272 for a recognition that, in its old common law significance, 'purchase' covers all means of acquisition otherwise than by descent or escheat. See also Inheritance Act 1833, s 1.
2   See *IRC v Gribble* [1913] 3 KB 212 at 218 per Buckley LJ; *Frederick Lawrence Ltd v Freeman, Hardy & Willis Ltd* [1959] Ch 731 at 744–745; *Snape v Kiernan* (1988) 13 NSWLR 88 at 97A.
3   [Para **3.26**].
4   'Value' includes money, money's worth, marriage consideration, and even the satisfaction of an existing debt (*Thorndike v Hunt* (1859) 3 De G & J 563 at 569, 44 ER 1386 at 1388). If the transfer to the purchaser is for a money consideration, the purchaser does not rank as a 'purchaser for value' until he has paid the money over. He cannot plead the doctrine of notice in his own favour merely because a legal estate has been conveyed to him in advance of payment (*Story v Windsor* (1743) 2 Atk 630 at 631, 26 ER 776).
5   *Burgess v Wheate* (1759) 1 Eden 177 at 195, 28 ER 652 at 659. See also *Wu Koon Tai v Wu Yau Loi* [1997] AC 179 at 190B–C per Lord Browne-Wilkinson.
6   *Re Nisbet and Potts' Contract* [1906] 1 Ch 386 at 406, 408, 410. (It is inconceivable that by his trespass a squatter should place himself in a more favourable position than if he had entered upon the land by right.)
7   *Basset v Nosworthy* (1673) Cas temp Finch 102 at 104, 23 ER 55 at 56.

Absence of notice

12.344   The crux of the equitable doctrine of notice is the idea that immunity from prior equitable interests is conferred only on the purchaser who, at the date of his purchase, had no knowledge or notice of the existence of such interests.[1] Only in the absence of notice can it truly be said that the conscience of the purchaser is unaffected by adverse pre-existing rights.[2] For this purpose the concept of 'notice' has an extended meaning and embraces not only 'actual' notice, but also 'constructive' and 'imputed' notice.[3]

1   'The doctrine of notice lies at the heart of equity. Given that there are two innocent parties, each enjoying rights, the earlier right prevails against the later right if the acquirer of the later right knows of the earlier right (actual notice) or would have discovered it had he taken proper steps (constructive notice)' (*Barclays Bank Plc v O'Brien* [1994] 1 AC 180 at 195G–H per Lord Browne-Wilkinson).

2   If only one of two joint purchasers is affected by notice of some equitable right, that
     purchaser alone is bound by the right and his knowledge does not sever the joint tenancy (see
     Myers v Smith (1992) 5 BPR 11494 at 11500).
3   *Kemmis v Kemmis* [1988] 1 WLR 1307 at 1333B per Nourse LJ.

Actual notice

12.345   Actual notice refers to matters of which the purchaser was consciously aware at the date of his purchase or which, in the statutory formulation
of the doctrine of notice,[1] were 'within his own knowledge.'[2] Clearly no
purchaser can be allowed to take priority over equitable interests whose
existence was fully known to him, since otherwise the purchaser would be guilty
of a form of equitable fraud. The source of the purchaser's knowledge is in
most cases entirely irrelevant. If the purchaser has actual knowledge of an
adverse equitable interest, it matters not that this knowledge is derived from
some person other than the vendor or that the purchaser came by the
information fortuitously. It is probable, however, that knowledge derived from
casual conversations does not constitute actual notice except where the mind of
the purchaser 'has in some way been brought to an intelligent apprehension of
the nature of the incumbrance ... so that a reasonable man, or an ordinary man
of business, would act upon the information and would regulate his conduct by
it.'[3]

1   LPA 1925, s 199(1)(ii)(a).
2   Formal registration of certain kinds of equitable interest is sometimes deemed, by a statutory
     fiction, to constitute *actual* notice to the purchaser of the subject matter of the registration
     (see e g LPA 1925, s 198(1) **[para 12.279]**).
3   *Lloyd v Banks* (1868) 3 Ch App 488 at 490–491 per Lord Cairns LC. See also *Barnhart v
     Greenshields* (1853) 9 Moo PCC 18 at 36, 14 ER 204 at 211 ('A purchaser is not bound to
     attend to vague rumours').

Constructive notice

12.346   Constructive notice relates to matters of which the purchaser would
have been consciously aware if he had taken reasonable care to inspect both
land and title. It used to be thought that constructive notice arose only in
circumstances of 'gross negligence' on the part of the purchaser,[1] but it seems at
least since the Conveyancing Act 1882 that the standard of care required of the
purchaser is somewhat higher.[2] Although phrased in a negative or restrictive
form, section 199(1)(ii)(a) of the Law of Property Act 1925 indicates that the
purchaser is prejudicially affected by notice of those matters which 'would have
come to his knowledge if such inquiries and inspections had been made as
ought reasonably to have been made by him.'[3] Constructive notice therefore
arises in the following categories of circumstance.[4]

1   See e g *Ware v Lord Egmont* (1854) 4 De GM & G 460 at 473, 43 ER 586 at 592 per
     Lord Cranworth. See similarly *Jones v Smith* (1841) 1 Hare 43 at 56, 66 ER 943 at 949 per
     Wigram V-C.
2   See Conveyancing Act 1882, s 3(1)(i) (now LPA 1925, s 199(1)(ii)(a)). It is a source of some

perplexity (see *Northern Bank Ltd v Henry* [1981] IR 1 at 16) that section 3(3) of the 1882 Act (now section 199(3) of the 1925 Act) appears to provide that the purchaser is not to be affected by notice in any case in which he would not have been regarded as having constructive notice before the enactment of the statutory formula. The reality is, however, that 19th century judges were prone to stigmatise all actionable negligence as 'gross' or 'culpable' (see e g the statement of Rolfe B in *Wilson v Brett* (1843) 11 M & W 113 at 115, 152 ER 737 at 739, that negligence and gross negligence were 'the same thing, with the addition of a vituperative epithet'). See also *Bailey v Barnes* [1894] 1 Ch 25 at 35 per Lindley LJ.

3   A purchaser who negligently fails to make any inquiry is unaffected if such inquiries as he *might* have made would not in any event have revealed the matters with constructive notice of which he is alleged to be fixed (see *Kemmis v Kemmis* [1988] 1 WLR 1307 at 1324B–C per Purchas LJ, 1328E–F per Lloyd LJ, 1333H–1334A per Nourse LJ).

4   'The basic concepts are "knowing something" which ought to have stimulated inquiry or "wilfully abstaining from inquiry to avoid notice"' (*Kemmis v Kemmis* [1988] 1 WLR 1307 at 1317H per Purchas LJ).

Knowledge which should have stimulated inquiry

12.347   Where the purchaser has actual notice of some defect or incumbrance in relation to the land, enquiry into which would have disclosed others, he is fixed with constructive notice of such matters as this further enquiry would have revealed.[1]

1   *Jones v Smith* (1841) 1 Hare 43 at 55, 66 ER 943 at 948 per Wigram V-C. See e g *Birch v Ellames* (1794) 2 Anst 427 at 431–432, 145 ER 924 at 926, where a mortgagee who lent money in the full knowledge that the borrower's title deeds were deposited with a third party was held to take subject to a prior mortgage secured by that deposit.

Wilful abstention from inquiry

12.348   The purchaser is likewise affected by constructive notice where he has 'designedly abstained from inquiry for the very purpose of avoiding notice.'[1]

1   *Jones v Smith* (1841) 1 Hare 43 at 55, 66 ER 943 at 948 per Wigram V-C. See also *Hunt v Luck* [1901] 1 Ch 45 at 52 per Farwell J.

Matters of reasonable enquiry

12.349   The purchaser is fixed, perhaps most significantly, with constructive notice of all those matters which a reasonable or prudent purchaser, acting with skilled legal advice,[1] would have investigated.[2] He is judged objectively by reference to that which any ordinary purchaser, advised by a competent lawyer, would reasonably have enquired about or inspected for the purpose of obtaining a good title. A reasonable purchaser is one who 'not only consults his own needs or preferences but also has regard to whether the purchase may affect, prejudicially and unfairly, the rights of third parties in the property.'[3] As Henchy J explained in *Northern Bank Ltd v Henry*,[4] 'the reasonable man, in the eyes of the law, will be expected to look beyond the impact of his decisions on his own affairs, and to consider whether they may unfairly and prejudicially affect his "neighbour", in the sense in which that word has been given juristic currency by Lord Atkin in *Donoghue v Stevenson*.'[5]

1 See *Northern Bank Ltd v Henry* [1981] IR 1 at 18 for the assertion by Kenny J that no prudent purchaser 'who was without legal qualifications would undertake the investigation of title to land.'
2 *Barclays Bank Plc v O'Brien* [1994] 1 AC 180 at 195H–196A per Lord Browne-Wilkinson.
3 *Northern Bank Ltd v Henry* [1981] IR 1 at 9 per Henchy J. It is for this reason that the doctrine of notice is not tied to the standards observed by the prudent man of business. The latter is, almost by definition, no altruist and consequently sees no further than his own interests. As Henchy J said ([1981] IR 1 at 12), the 'test for constructive notice is legal reasonableness, not business prudence.'
4 *Northern Bank Ltd v Henry* [1981] IR 1 at 12.
5 Thus a reasonable purchaser can legally be expected to 'make such inquiries and inspections as would normally disclose whether the purchase will trench, fraudulently or unconscionably, on the rights of such third parties in the property' (*Northern Bank Ltd v Henry* [1981] IR 1 at 11).

Reluctance to extend constructive notice

12.350 The imposition of the standard of care outlined above represents a significant restraint on the ability of the purchaser of an unregistered title to take free of adverse equitable interests. Accordingly the courts have been reluctant to expand the ambit of constructive notice to any large degree, a persuasive element of policy favouring protection for the purchaser of land.[1] The classic observation in this context is still that of Farwell J, who stated in *Hunt v Luck*[2] that the doctrine of constructive notice, 'imputing as it does knowledge which the person affected does not actually possess, is one which the Courts of late years have been unwilling to extend.'[3] In consequence the duty of care expected of a purchaser covers only two major areas, concerning respectively an inspection of *land* and an inspection of *title*.

1 [**Para 12.357**].
2 [1901] 1 Ch 45 at 48, affd [1902] 1 Ch 428 at 434–435.
3 See e g *Caunce v Caunce* [1969] 1 WLR 286 at 291H–292F [**para 12.359**]; *Kemmis v Kemmis* [1988] 1 WLR 1307 at 1334G–H per Nourse LJ.

Inspection of land

12.351 An inspection of *land* may reveal facts which are inconsistent with the title offered by the vendor.[1] This inspection may disclose the presence of persons other than the vendor, in which case the purchaser is likely to be fixed with constructive notice of such rights as these persons may have in the land.[2] For instance, the presence of a tenant provides constructive notice of his leasehold interest[3] and of the terms of his lease[4] (although not necessarily of the rights of any person to whom the tenant may be paying rent[5]). It is also often the case that the purchaser is bound by the trust entitlements of members of the vendor's family (and perhaps even of others) who are in joint occupation of the land with the vendor.[6]

1   See *Hervey v Smith* (1856) 22 Beav 299 at 302, 52 ER 1123 at 1124, where a purchaser of a
    house with fourteen chimney pots but only twelve flues was held to have received constructive
    notice of his neighbour's equitable easement to use the other two flues. See, however, *Allen v
    Seckham* (1879) 11 Ch D 790 at 794; R A Pearce, 'Joint Occupation and the Doctrine of
    Notice' (1980) 15 Ir Jur (NS) 211 at 213.
2   This possibility was reinforced by the parallel registered land decision of the House of Lords
    in *Williams & Glyn's Bank Ltd v Boland* [1981] AC 487 **[para 12.203]**. In *City of London
    Building Society v Flegg* [1988] AC 54 at 80F–G, Lord Oliver of Aylmerton observed that the
    constructive notice doctrine is also reflected in the protection accorded by LPA 1925, s 14, to
    the interests of persons 'in possession or in actual occupation of land' **[para 12.285]**. See also
    Clyne v Lowe (1968) 69 SR (NSW) 433 at 436.
3   *Hunt v Luck* [1902] 1 Ch 428 at 432. See also *Hayes v Seymour-Johns* (1981) 2 BPR 9366 at
    9372.
4   *Taylor v Stibbert* (1794) 2 Ves 437 at 440–441, 30 ER 713 at 714–715.
5   *Hunt v Luck* [1901] 1 Ch 45 at 49–51, affd [1902] 1 Ch 428 at 434–435. The question of
    constructive notice becomes controversial here only if the vendor is not the person to whom
    the tenant is paying his rent.
6   **[Para 12.358]**.

Inspection of title

12.352   An inspection of *title* comes within the scope of constructive notice in
that the purchaser is fixed with constructive notice of all rights or interests
affecting the land which would have been disclosed if he had investigated the
vendor's title for the period allowed by statute.[1] The purchaser takes the land
subject to any adverse equitable rights arising within this period, even where he
has contracted for a shorter period of investigation than he is entitled by statute
to require.[2] However, unless he positively chooses to investigate title for a longer
period, the purchaser is not bound by equitable interests created prior to the
statutory period of title investigation.[3]

1   The period of investigation of title fixed by statute now covers at least the 15 years preceding
    the current transaction (see LPA 1969, s 23 **[paras 2.112, 12.260]**).
2   *Re Cox and Neve's Contract* [1891] 2 Ch 109 at 118; *Re Nisbet and Potts' Contract* [1906]
    1 Ch 386 at 408.
3   LPA 1925, s 44(8).

Imputed notice

12.353   Imputed notice is notice which is attributed to a purchaser in virtue of
knowledge possessed actually or constructively by the purchaser's 'counsel …
solicitor or other agent.'[1] Thus a purchaser is deemed to have notice of those
matters of which his own solicitor was actually aware or should reasonably have
been aware. The scope of imputed notice is, however, subject to certain
restrictions. The knowledge of a solicitor or other agent is imputed to the
purchaser only if it arises within the current transaction of purchase and only if
the solicitor or other agent acquired his knowledge whilst acting in his capacity
'as such'.[2] Notice derived from any other transaction or circumstance is
irrelevant and cannot be fastened upon the purchaser.[3]

1 LPA 1925, s 199(1)(ii)(b).
2 LPA 1925, s 199(1)(ii)(b). See *Abbey National Plc v Tufts* [1999] 2 FLR 399 at 404H.
3 See e g *Rock Permanent Benefit Building Society v Kettlewell* (1956) 168 EG 397 (no imputed notice where mortgagee's solicitor was mortgagor's brother and was therefore aware of mortgagor's matrimonial difficulties).

DESTRUCTIVE EFFECT OF PURCHASE FOR VALUE WITHOUT NOTICE

12.354 If the purchaser succeeds in establishing all the foregoing elements of the 'composite expression' which epitomises the doctrine of notice, he has an 'absolute, unqualified, unanswerable defence'[1] against adverse equitable claims. This defence is so complete that the mere fact of purchase for value without notice has the effect of *destroying* the equitable rights involved. The advent of a good faith purchaser of a legal estate is sufficient to defeat these rights for ever so that they cannot thereafter revive even against a subsequent purchaser who *does* have notice of the fact that equitable rights once existed. In *Wilkes v Spooner*,[2] for example, C acquired a legal estate free of B's equitable interest on the ground that C was a bona fide purchaser of A's legal estate for value without notice (see *Fig.* 41). It was held that C's successor, D, likewise took the legal estate free of B's equitable interest, albeit that D had actual notice of the entitlement in question. By this stage B's interest had already been destroyed by the transfer to a good faith purchaser who had no notice of its existence,[3] leaving B with merely personal rights against A arising from the transaction by which B's rights were originally created.

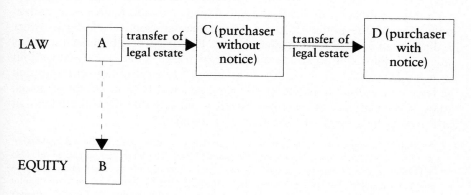

Fig. **41**

1 *Pilcher v Rawlins* (1872) 7 Ch App 259 at 269 per James LJ.
2 [1911] 2 KB 473 at 487–488. See also *Lowther v Carlton* (1741) 2 Atk 242, 26 ER 549 at 550 per Lord Hardwicke ('It is certainly the rule of this court, that a man who is a purchaser with notice himself from a person who bought without notice, may shelter himself under the first purchaser, or otherwise it would very much clog the sale of estates'). See likewise *Nottingham Patent Brick and Tile Co v Butler* (1886) 16 QBD 778 at 788.
3 This result does not apply, however, if A and D are the same person. A cannot destroy the equitable interest to which he is subject by selling the land to C and then purchasing that land back from C (see e g *Barrow's Case* (1880) 14 Ch D 432 at 445).

SURVIVING APPLICATIONS OF THE BONA FIDE PURCHASER RULE

12.355   Only relatively few examples remain of equitable rights in unregistered land which are neither overreached nor capable of registration as land charges.[1] In relation to these entitlements the problem of priority against a purchaser can be resolved only by reference to the traditional doctrine of notice. The rights affected by this residual doctrine tend to be both anomalous and awkward, presenting conveyancing difficulties wholly disproportionate to their number. Amongst the range of equitable rights in unregistered land governed by the bona fide purchaser rule are the following.

1   In *Shiloh Spinners Ltd v Harding* [1973] AC 693 at 721D, Lord Wilberforce was nevertheless quite ready to confirm the persistence of the category of the unoverreached and non-registrable equitable interest in unregistered land. See similarly *Birmingham Midshires Mortgage Services Ltd v Sabherwal* (2000) 80 P & CR 256 at 262–263 per Robert Walker LJ.

EQUITABLE INTERESTS OF BENEFICIARIES UNDER CERTAIN TRUSTS OF LAND

12.356   Perhaps the most significant entitlements still regulated by the bona fide purchaser rule are beneficial interests which, in the context of a dealing by a sole owner of an unregistered legal estate, remain hidden behind an implied trust of land.[1] In the absence of payment of capital money to trustees (or to a trust corporation) these beneficial interests are not statutorily overreached by the purchaser[2] and do not constitute any species of registrable charge under the Land Charges Act 1972.[3] For the purpose of determining their priority in relation to a purchaser of the legal estate,[4] there is no alternative to a residual application of the notice doctrine. The purchaser from a sole legal owner holding on an implied trust[5] therefore takes free of adverse beneficial interests only if he ranks as a bona fide purchaser of a legal estate for value without notice (either actual, constructive or imputed).[6] Most disputes centre around the issue of *constructive* notice. If the purchaser had been in receipt of actual notice of the existence of trust interests, it is unlikely that the transaction – at least in its current form – would have been completed.

1   This situation represents the unregistered land analogue of the problem addressed in *Williams & Glyn's Bank Ltd v Boland* [1981] AC 487 [**para 12.203**]. The bona fide purchaser rule also applies to equitable interests created behind a joint tenancy of the legal estate, where a purchaser acquires that legal estate with full knowledge that his vendor is a survivor of joint tenants and that the joint tenancy has already been severed in equity (see *Grindal v Hooper* (2000) Times, 8 February [**para 11.278**]).

2   [**Para 11.203**].

3   A beneficial interest under an implied trust cannot be registered under the Land Charges Act either as a land charge (see *Kingsnorth Finance Co Ltd v Tizard* [1986] 1 WLR 783 at 792H) or as a *lis pendens* (see *Taylor v Taylor* (1968) [1968] 1 WLR 378 at 384C). Some trust beneficiaries may, of course, have registrable 'matrimonial home rights' pursuant to the Family Law Act 1996 [**para 12.93**], but these rights are quite distinct from beneficial entitlement under a trust. Matrimonial home rights are not proprietary in nature [**para 12.167**] and are almost invariably rendered void for lack of registration [**para 12.281**].

4   It is generally accepted that the purchaser dealing innocently with a vendor who acts in breach of trust nevertheless takes a good title at law [**para 11.227**].

5   The position is quite different under an *express* trust. If the legal title reveals the existence of a trust, the purchaser cannot disclaim notice of the beneficial interests, but must pay the capital money to trustees (being at least two in number) or to a trust corporation. He may even need, for this purpose, to demand the appointment of a second trustee **[para 11.151]**.

6   *Caunce v Caunce* [1969] 1 WLR 286 at 289G per Stamp J; *Kingsnorth Finance Co Ltd v Tizard* [1986] 1 WLR 783 at 792H–793A per Deputy Judge Finlay QC. See also *Williams & Glyn's Bank Ltd v Boland* [1979] Ch 312 at 330D, 334C; *Ulster Bank Ltd v Shanks* [1982] NI 143 at 150H; *Allied Irish Banks Ltd v McWilliams* [1982] NI 156 at 161F; *Northern Bank Ltd v Beattie* [1982] 18 NIJB, p 20.

Nature of constructive notice

12.357   The purchaser of unregistered land is bound by adverse equities in the present context only if he has failed to make reasonable enquiries as to the possible existence of undisclosed equitable ownership. English law traditionally disfavours any unnecessary extension of the concept of constructive notice.[1] Purchasers are not lightly held to have a duty of enquiry into otherwise undisclosed rights in the land which they seek to purchase.[2] The issue depends not upon the nature of the right but upon the individual circumstances of the case. A purchaser is not to be fixed with constructive notice merely because he had special access to information which might have prompted the realisation that someone other than the sole trustee contributed financially towards the purchase of land. In *Caunce v Caunce*,[3] for instance, Stamp J rejected an argument that a bank-mortgagee should have realised that the premises offered as security had five years earlier been purchased in part with money withdrawn by the mortgagor's wife from an account at the very same branch of the very same bank. Stamp J considered that the onus of enquiry urged on behalf of the wife 'would … have been more appropriate to a police inquiry or that of a detective agency than to a bank manager who often no doubt arranges finances daily in the ordinary course of business.'[4]

1   See *Hunt v Luck* [1901] 1 Ch 45 at 48 **[para 12.350]**.
2   Thus, for example, a mortgagee has been held not to be bound by constructive notice of a wife's beneficial interest merely because the mortgagor requested the mortgagee to direct all correspondence to him at his business address rather than at the family home (*Northern Bank Ltd v Henry* [1981] IR 1 at 6 per McWilliam J).
3   [1969] 1 WLR 286 at 291C–H.
4   [1969] 1 WLR 286 at 292F. Moreover, as Stamp J pointed out, such a duty of enquiry, if once accepted, could not logically be confined to the financial relations of the vendor/mortgagor and his spouse. The bank would be obliged to conduct similar research into the bank accounts of the borrower's father and perhaps other relatives ([1969] 1 WLR 286 at 292G).

Relevance of joint occupation of land

12.358   Often the crucial question is whether constructive notice of beneficial co-ownership arises merely by reason of the fact that, at the date of the disputed transaction,[1] the vendor/mortgagor shared joint occupation of the land with other persons.

1   The clearest case of constructive notice must arise if, at the date of the transaction, the

vendor/mortgagor is not himself in occupation but has left other persons in possession of the premises. Here the purchaser is confronted with 'another party whose presence demands an explanation and whose presence one ignores at one's peril' (*Caunce v Caunce* [1969] 1 WLR 286 at 294A per Stamp J). In such cases the presence of strangers is obviously inconsistent with the sole title ostensibly offered by the legal owner.

The traditional approach

12.359   For many years the courts adopted a severely restrictive approach to this question. In *Caunce v Caunce*[1] Stamp J declined to accept that a wife's shared occupation of the matrimonial home had been other than 'wholly consistent with the sole title offered by the husband' to a bank as mortgagee. In Stamp J's view the wife had not been 'in apparent occupation or possession' since her presence in the family home was 'ostensibly because she was the husband's wife.'[2] The fact of joint residence was not in itself so remarkable as to cause the bank reasonably to suspect that the wife was in residence in the capacity of a beneficial co-owner as distinct from that merely of a dutiful wife.[3] It followed therefore that the husband's mortgagee was not fixed with constructive notice of her rights merely by reason of a failure to make further enquiries on the premises.[4]

1   [1969] 1 WLR 286 at 293G.
2   At the date of *Caunce v Caunce*, the protection afforded by registrable matrimonial home rights had not yet been extended to beneficial co-owners (see Matrimonial Proceedings and Property Act 1970, s 38).
3   Stamp J was moved by the possible existence of many other persons whose presence in a family home would be similarly compatible with the sole legal title vested in the vendor. Such persons would include, for instance, 'the vendor's father, his Uncle Harry or his Aunt Matilda, any of whom, be it observed, might have contributed money towards the purchase of the property' ([1969] 1 WLR 286 at 293H).
4   Any contrary holding, added Stamp J, would be adverse to the public interest in that bank-mortgagees would be rendered 'snoopers and busybodies in relation to wholly normal transactions of mortgages' ([1969] 1 WLR 286 at 294D). See also *Ulster Bank Ltd v Shanks* [1982] NI 143 at 150F.

The conveyancing perspective

12.360   The limitation of the notice doctrine evident in *Caunce v Caunce* was entirely consistent with a hard-nosed view of land law priorities. English law is pervaded by an inherent bias in favour of the lender's commercial interests.[1] The conveyancing perspective places a premium on the free commerciability of land, thereby elevating the exchange value of realty in preference to its use value.[2] Transactions in land are naturally facilitated by reducing the burden of enquiry imposed on purchasers and by protecting the latter from the claims of undetected beneficial co-owners.[3] The commercialist concern for smooth conveyancing practice is therefore promoted by subordinating the social interest which favours residential protection for family members.[4]

1   The 'solid tug of money' (see *Hofman v Hofman* [1965] NZLR 795 at 800 per Woodhouse J) tended to exert an hypnotic influence over the determination of priorities in this area.

2　See H W R Wade, [1956] CLJ 216 at 219.

3　In *Caunce v Caunce* [1969] 1 WLR 286 at 292H, Stamp J relied heavily on the famous dictum of Lord Upjohn in *National Provincial Bank Ltd v Ainsworth* [1965] AC 1175 at 1233G–1234A, that it 'has been the policy of the law for over a hundred years to simplify and facilitate transactions in real property. It is of great importance that persons should be able freely and easily to raise money on the security of their property' [**para 2.40**].

4　The decision in *Caunce v Caunce* [1969] 1 WLR 286 epitomised the standard view that it is virtually conclusive of any issue of land law priority to declare the matter to be a matter of conveyancing or banking practice (see *National Provincial Bank v Ainsworth* [1965] AC 1175 at 1233G per Lord Upjohn; *Caunce v Caunce* (Martin Nourse QC arguendo: see [1969] 1 WLR 286 at 294A–B per Stamp J); *Williams & Glyn's Bank Ltd v Boland* [1981] AC 487 at 500D–G (Donald Nicholls QC arguendo)).

Modern applications of constructive notice

12.361　Recent years have seen a more expansive approach to issues of constructive notice in the context of the family home.[1] The scope of the *Caunce* ruling began to be cut back by the parallel registered land decision in *Williams & Glyn's Bank Ltd v Boland*[2] and the change in emphasis was dramatically confirmed in *Kingsnorth Finance Co Ltd v Tizard*.[3] Here H held a legal title on an implied trust for himself and his estranged wife, W. H and two children of the family lived in the house and W visited the home twice a day in order to cook meals for the children. H secretly charged the legal title to K, a finance company, and then disappeared to America with one of the children. (K's agent had made a pre-arranged visit to the premises on a Sunday afternoon for the purpose of the usual mortgagee's inspection and valuation and it was clear in retrospect that the timing of the visit had been organised by H to coincide with W's absence from the home and that all signs of her occupation had been 'temporarily eliminated'.[4])

1　The movement towards change appeared first in the Irish jurisdictions (see eg *Northern Bank Ltd v Henry* [1981] IR 1 at 19–21; *Somers v W* [1979] IR 94 at 111, 114–115; *Allied Irish Banks Ltd v McWilliams* [1982] NI 156 at 161H–162A; *Northern Bank Ltd v Beattie* [1982] 18 NIJB, p 20).

2　[1981] AC 487 [**para 12.203**]. Although the House of Lords expressly declined to overrule *Caunce*, Lord Scarman indicated ([1981] AC 487 at 511G) that he himself was 'by no means certain' that the case had been correctly decided (see similarly Lord Wilberforce at 505E).

3　[1986] 1 WLR 783; (1986) 136 NLJ 771 (P Luxton); [1986] Conv 283 (M P Thompson). See also *Bristol and West Building Society v Henning* [1985] 1 WLR 778 at 781G per Browne-Wilkinson LJ.

4　[1986] 1 WLR 783 at 793C. The agent of course discovered evidence of occupation by two teenage children, but was told by H that their mother had left the home some time before and lived elsewhere.

12.362　In *Tizard* the High Court rejected the mortgagee's action for possession of the home following default by the mortgagor. H had originally described himself in his loan application as being 'single' and Deputy Judge Finlay QC held that the agent's reference in his report to the presence of the children should have alerted K to the need to make further enquiry as to the possible rights of a wife.[1] Here W had indeed been in 'occupation' of the property in that she had been present 'virtually every day for some part of the day.'[2] The failure to make further enquiry as to her possible entitlements, coupled with a form of inspection which the judge condemned as unsatisfactory,[3] led the Court to the conclusion that K was fixed with constructive notice of W's beneficial interest under the implied trust.[4] Following the *Tizard* ruling it became widely recognised that the purchaser of unregistered land must carefully examine the possibility of concealed beneficial entitlement on the part of those who share occupation of the land with the vendor.[5] Failure to make enquiry of occupiers almost inevitably precludes the purchaser from disclaiming notice of those co-ownership interests which lie hidden behind an implied trust,[6] although such beneficial entitlements may, just as in registered land, be defeated none the less by circumstances of estoppel.[7]

1   [1986] 1 WLR 783 at 792D.
2   Deputy Judge Finlay QC considered that 'occupation' for this purpose did not require 'continuous and uninterrupted presence; such a notion would be absurd.' In this case the relevant 'presence' of the wife was not 'negatived by regular and repeated absence' ([1986] 1 WLR 783 at 788D–E).
3   Deputy Judge Finlay QC was not satisfied that in the present circumstances a 'pre-arranged inspection on a Sunday afternoon fell within the category of "such inspections which ought reasonably to have been made," the words in section 199 of the Law of Property Act 1925 ...' ([1986] 1 WLR 783 at 795B). Compare, however, *Le Foe v Le Foe and Woolwich Plc* [2001] 2 FLR 970 at [68]–[70].
4   [1986] 1 WLR 783 at 794E.
5   The purchaser's duty of care does not, however, extend to any obligation to inform a beneficial co-owner of prejudicial dealings with the legal title in sufficiently good time to enable her to enlist the aid of state benefit in keeping up instalments payments under a mortgage (see *Equity & Law Home Loans Ltd v Prestidge* [1992] 1 WLR 137 at 144H–145B per Mustill LJ).
6   In *City of London Building Society v Flegg* [1988] AC 54 at 81D, Lord Oliver of Aylmerton readily conceded that enjoyment of land 'in specie' readily serves 'to give notice to third parties of the occupier's interest under the trust'. See similarly *Lloyds Bank Plc v Semmakie* [1993] 1 FLR 34 at 42C–D per Scott LJ; *Le Foe v Le Foe and Woolwich Plc* [2001] 2 FLR 970 at [68].
7   See eg *Bristol and West Building Society v Henning* [1985] 1 WLR 778 at 781G–782G [para 12.165].

LICENCES AND ESTOPPELS

12.363   Controversy has consistently dogged the question whether the equitable doctrine of notice applies to various kinds of licence or estoppel affecting land so as to render such entitlements binding on purchasers other than those who take a legal estate for value and without notice of the rights concerned. As always, the fundamental issue turns on the level of proprietary content perceived to be inherent in the rights themselves. For present purposes a conventional distinction must be drawn between contractual licences and other forms of interest founded on irrevocable licence or proprietary estoppel.

Contractual licences

12.364   The impact of contractual licences on purchasers of unregistered land has proved, over recent decades, to be a source of considerable confusion. Such licences are neither statutorily overreachable nor registrable as land charges under the Land Charges Acts. The only remaining means by which a contractual licence may conceivably bind a purchaser thus rests upon the potential application of the equitable doctrine of notice. This doctrine, in its turn, relates only to those entitlements which have a sufficient 'property' content to rank as equitable interests in land. Accordingly there arises, in the context of the contractual licence, the difficult delineation of the borderline between property and contract.[1] The issue is one of some practical importance, for the ever-present fear of the conveyancer is that the purchaser of land may be trapped, and his title rendered less valuable, by unregistrable, non-overreachable equitable interests. For reasons rehearsed earlier in the parallel area of registered title,[2] the orthodox rule in English law holds that purchasers are never affected by a contractual licence even though they purchase with express notice of the licensee's rights.[3]

1   See e g A Briggs, [1981] Conv 212, [1983] Conv 285; M P Thompson, [1983] Conv 50. For an incisive examination of the implications of the licence debate, see John Dewar, (1986) 49 MLR 741.
2   **[Para 12.223]**.
3   See e g *Clore v Theatrical Properties Ltd and Westby & Co Ltd* [1936] 3 All ER 483 at 490–493.

The challenge of the Denning doctrine

12.365   As already noted,[1] Lord Denning MR made diligent efforts over many years to elevate the status of contractual licences so that they should receive the same protection under the general law as that accorded to equitable proprietary rights. Lord Denning therefore maintained that in unregistered land the contractual licence was governed by the equitable doctrine of notice.[2] The high-point of the Denning doctrine came in *Binions v Evans*.[3] Here E had been allowed by T, the trustees of the estate for which her late husband had worked, to reside rent-free for the remainder of her life in a cottage on the estate (in which she had already lived for some 50 years).[4] This permission was granted in a written agreement which imposed on E an obligation to maintain the interior of the cottage and to keep the garden in good condition. T later conveyed the property to a married couple, B, expressly 'subject to' E's rights[5] and at a reduced price in view of E's occupation. B promptly brought possession proceedings against E (who was by this stage 79 years of age).

1   **[Para 12.225]**.
2   The root of the Denning doctrine lay in *Errington v Errington and Woods* [1952] 1 KB 290 at 299, where Denning LJ propounded that '[n]either the licensor nor anyone who claims through him can disregard the contract except a purchaser for value without notice.' See also *Bendall v McWhirter* [1952] 2 QB 466 at 478–483.
3   [1972] Ch 359. See R J Smith, [1973] CLJ 123; (1972) 36 Conv (NS) 266 (J E Martin), 277 (D J Hayton); (1972) 88 LQR 336 (P V Baker); (1972) 35 MLR 551 (A J Oakley).
4   It was provided that E could terminate the arrangement on giving four weeks' notice.
5   B were in fact supplied with a copy of the earlier agreement which conferred those rights on E.

12.366   The success of B's possession action plainly depended on the status of the rights held by E. In the Court of Appeal Lord Denning MR took the view that the original written agreement could not have conferred on E either a determinable 90 year lease[1] or indeed any other kind of lease.[2] Nor could it be said that E was a tenant at will[3] or a tenant for life under a strict settlement.[4] Instead, Lord Denning rather tenuously construed E's rights as constituting a contractual licence to reside in the cottage for the remainder of her life.[5] In accordance with authority he then held that the courts of equity would not allow the occupier under such a contract to be evicted in disregard of its terms.[6] Since B had bought the land expressly 'subject to' the contractual rights of E, B were bound by a 'constructive trust to permit the defendant to reside there during her life, or so long as she might desire.'[7] The constructive trust arose here 'for the simple reason that it would be utterly inequitable for [B] to turn [E] out contrary to the stipulation subject to which they took the premises.'[8]

1   [1972] Ch 359 at 366C. E's occupation was rent-free (compare LPA 1925, s 149(6) **[para 7.121]**).
2   [1972] Ch 359 at 366G–H. See *Lace v Chantler* [1944] KB 368 at 371 **[para 7.110]**.
3   [1972] Ch 359 at 366A. The right to determine the agreement was neither mutual nor at will **[para 7.273]**.
4   [1972] Ch 359 at 366E–G **[para 9.209]**.
5   [1972] Ch 359 at 367C, 369D. The other two judges in the Court of Appeal (Megaw and Stephenson LJJ) preferred, although with no great conviction, to analyse E's rights in terms of the Settled Land Act 1925.
6   '[T]he defendant, by virtue of the agreement, had an equitable interest in the cottage which the court would protect by granting an injunction against the landlords restraining them from turning her out' ([1972] Ch 359 at 369C–D).
7   [1972] Ch 359 at 369D. On the operation of the constructive trust, see Chapter 10 **[paras 10.58–10.167]**. Lord Denning distinguished the present case from *King v David Allen and Sons, Billposting, Ltd* [1916] 2 AC 54 and *Clore v Theatrical Properties Ltd and Westby & Co Ltd* [1936] 3 All ER 483 **[para 12.223]**, pointing out that in neither of these cases had there been any 'trace of a stipulation, express or implied, that the purchaser should take the property subject to the right of the contractual licensee' ([1972] Ch 359 at 368G). There is even some room for the argument that a stipulation of this kind is enforceable as an *express* trust (see *Bahr v Nicolay (No 2)* (1988) 164 CLR 604 at 618–619 per Mason CJ and Dawson J **[para 10.90]**).
8   [1972] Ch 359 at 368B. Some further support for the binding effect of a contractual licence may be found in *DHN Food Distributors Ltd v LB of Tower Hamlets* [1976] 1 WLR 852 at 859H, although there is an objection that the imposition of a constructive trust gives effect to a right which is not conventionally acknowledged as an equitable proprietary interest (see, however, *Lyus v Prowsa Developments Ltd* [1982] 1 WLR 1044 at 1053A per Dillon J **[para 10.90]**; *Eves v Eves* [1975] 1 WLR 1338 at 1342E–F, 1345B **[para 10.118]**).

The present position

12.367 The Denning doctrine seemed strongly to suggest that (contrary to venerable precedent) the contractual licence had become, for the purpose of the bona fide purchaser rule, the functional equivalent of an unregistrable, non-overreachable equitable interest in land. Indeed, in *Midland Bank Ltd v Farmpride Hatcheries Ltd*,[1] a Court of Appeal no longer dominated by Lord Denning accepted without question that a contractual licence was fully capable of binding any purchaser who was fixed with actual or constructive notice of the licensee's rights.[2] Orthodoxy soon began, however, to reassert its presence. In *Patel v Patel*[3] a differently constituted Court of Appeal affirmed 'the general rule ... that a mere licence to occupy land, albeit of a contractual nature, as opposed to a lease, does not confer any interest on the licensee in the land.' Indeed Slade LJ went so far as to declare it a 'heresy' to suggest that 'the mere fact that a licence to occupy land has been given for consideration ... confers any interest in the land on the licensee.' The reaction against the Denning doctrine culminated in the Court of Appeal's stern rejection in *Ashburn Anstalt v Arnold*[4] of the idea that contractual licences comprise a species of proprietary interest inherently capable of binding third parties. Against this background and pending definitive clarification by the House of Lords, it seems nowadays improbable that the equitable doctrine of notice is ever effective to render contractual licences binding on third parties. It is probable that third parties are affected by such licences only in circumstances which generate liability to a constructive trust.[5]

1   (1981) 260 EG 493 (Buckley, Shaw and Oliver LJJ).
2   It was found, on the facts, that the purchaser was not fixed with such notice.
3   [1983] Court of Appeal Unbound Transcript 930 (Dunn and Slade LJJ).
4   [1989] Ch 1 [**para 12.226**].
5   See e g *Ashburn Anstalt* [1989] Ch 1 at 23F, where the Court of Appeal approved the outcome in *Binions v Evans* [1972] Ch 359 as 'a legitimate application of the doctrine of constructive trusts.'

Irrevocable licences and inchoate equities of estoppel

12.368   It seems fairly clear that the 'equity' inherent in a claim of irrevocable licence or proprietary estoppel cannot rank as a registrable land charge.[1] It is, moreover, unlikely any other form of registration can make such rights binding upon a purchaser of unregistered land.[2] Equally plainly irrevocable licences and inchoate estoppel-based equities do not constitute equitable interests which are capable of being overreached[3] (except, perhaps, where they are so closely linked with overreachable claims of trust as to leave no 'room for a separate interest by way of equitable estoppel'[4]). It is also readily accepted in the case law that inchoate rights of estoppel can run with land so as to affect certain kinds of successor in title to the estate owner whose conduct has generated the estoppel.[5] Thus an estoppel-based equity, albeit not yet concretised in any court-ordered remedy, has been held to bind not merely the owner of the land, but also his trustee in bankruptcy,[6] his personal representatives,[7] an associated company,[8] and a successor local authority.[9]

1   *E R Ives Investment Ltd v High* [1967] 2 QB 379 at 395G per Lord Denning MR, 400B per Danckwerts LJ, 405G per Winn LJ; *Pascoe v Turner* [1979] 1 WLR 431 at 439A; *Bristol & West Building Society v Henning* [1985] 1 WLR 778 at 781F.
2   See [1982] Conv 80 (J E M). It has been suggested, on the basis of dicta in *Haslemere Estates Ltd v Baker* [1982] 1 WLR 1109 at 1119H–1120A per Megarry V-C, that an estoppel claim may be registrable under the Land Charges Act 1972 as a *lis pendens* (see [1983] Conv 69 at 70 (J E M)). This may be true, but would in any event require (i) that litigation should already have commenced and (ii) that the estoppel claimant should assert an interest in land (see LCA 1972, s 17(1) [**para 12.332**]).
3   *Shiloh Spinners Ltd v Harding* [1973] AC 693 at 721C per Lord Wilberforce. See, however, M P Thompson, [1988] Conv 108 at 120; and compare P T Evans, [1989] Conv 418 at 427.

4   See *Birmingham Midshires Mortgage Services Ltd v Sabherwal* (2000) 80 P & CR 256 at 263
    [**para 11.201**]. See also *Lepel v Huthnance* (1979) NZ Recent Law 269 at 270 (an 'equity' can be
    traced into the proceeds of sale of the land and into further investments bought out of those
    proceeds).
5   See *Voyce v Voyce* (1991) 62 P & CR 290 at 293–294 per Dillon LJ; *Torrisi v Magame Pty Ltd*
    [1984] 1 NSWLR 14 at 23A–C.
6   *Re Sharpe (A Bankrupt)* [1980] 1 WLR 219 at 224F.
7   *Inwards v Baker* [1965] 2 QB 29 at 37F; *Jones (A E) v Jones (F W)* [1977] 1 WLR 438 at 442F.
8   *E & L Berg Homes Ltd v Grey* (1980) 253 EG 473 at 475.
9   *Salvation Army Trustee Co Ltd v West Yorkshire MCC* (1981) 41 P & CR 179 at 193.

Purchasers with actual notice

12.369   It was inevitable, in unregistered land, that this case law should tend
towards the more general proposition that irrevocable licences and estoppels
have a sufficiently proprietary quality to bind all purchasers other than a bona
fide purchaser of a legal estate for value without notice of the rights concerned.
Thus an 'equity' raised by a representation of entitlement given by a landowner
is enforceable against the purchaser of a legal estate in the land who has actual
notice of the circumstances which gave rise to the 'equity'.[1] In *E R Ives
Investment Ltd v High*,[2] for example, an 'equity' generated both by detrimental
reliance and by elements of mutual benefit and burden was held to be binding
upon a purchaser who took title with express actual notice of the circumstances
of entitlement.[3] When, more recently, it was suggested to the Court of Appeal
in *Lloyds Bank plc v Carrick*[4] that proprietary estoppels could not give rise to
an 'interest in land capable of binding successors in title', Morritt LJ observed
that it was hard to see how such an argument could 'surmount the hurdle
constituted by the decision of this court in *E R Ives Investment Ltd v High*.'

1   See e g *Stiles v Tod Mountain Development Ltd* (1992) 88 DLR (4th) 735 at 750. The impact of
    the 'equity' on the purchaser follows *a fortiori* if the purchaser takes only an equitable interest
    in the land or if the purchaser gives no value and is a mere volunteer or donee (see *Voyce v
    Voyce* (1991) 62 P & CR 290 at 293 per Dillon LJ, 296 per Nicholls LJ).
2   [1967] 2 QB 379 [**paras 9.101, 12.320**]. See (1967) 31 Conv (NS) 338 (F R Crane).
3   All the members of the Court of Appeal in *E R Ives Investment Ltd v High* stressed the fact
    that the purchaser had received explicit notice of the circumstances of the claimant's 'equity'
    (see [1967] 2 QB 379 at 393G per Lord Denning MR, 400A–E per Danckwerts LJ, 405B per
    Winn LJ). See to similar effect *Sledmore v Dalby* (1996) 72 P & CR 196 at 201 per Roch LJ
    [**para 10.280**]; *Salisbury (Village) v Collier* (1999) 169 DLR (4th) 560 at 564 (New Brunswick
    Court of Appeal).
4   [1996] 4 All ER 630 at 642b–c.

Purchasers with constructive notice

12.370   It is less clear whether irrevocable licences and inchoate estoppels bind
purchasers of a legal estate who have merely constructive notice. If such rights
are treated as more or less the equivalents of conventional equitable interests in
land, there seems to be no reason in principle why a purchaser should not be
bound if he has constructive notice. In *Re Sharpe (A Bankrupt)*,[1] however,
Browne-Wilkinson J remarked somewhat pointedly that the 'equity' raised in

the case before him might be defeated by a purchaser from a trustee in bankruptcy, provided that such purchaser did not have 'express notice'.[2] The balance of authority nonetheless supports the proposition that even a purchaser with constructive notice is bound by irrevocable or estoppel-based interests.[3]

1   [1980] 1 WLR 219 at 226G **[para 10.38]**.
2   For an argument in favour of limiting the category of purchasers affected by an 'equity' to those with actual or express notice, see M P Thompson, [1983] Conv 50 at 56. See also R H Maudsley, (1956) 20 Conv (NS) 281 at 295–301.
3   *Duke of Beaufort v Patrick* (1853) 17 Beav 60 at 78, 51 ER 954 at 961; *Bristol & West Building Society v Henning* [1985] 1 WLR 778 at 781G. See F R Crane, (1967) 31 Conv (NS) 332 at 339.

Range of remedy against successors in title

12.371   In the present context resistance to the application of the doctrine of notice – and particularly the idea of constructive notice – is largely founded upon an abhorrence of unregistrable, unoverreachable (and virtually undiscoverable) equities which threaten to trap innocent purchasers of unregistered land.[1] It may therefore be relevant that, in estoppel cases, the precise nature of the remedy granted by the court against a successor in title may not be quite the same or quite as far-reaching as the remedy which the court might have granted had the 'equity' been asserted against the party who gave the initial assurance or representation.[2]

1   See, for instance, the criticism that estoppel interests fall outside the 'necessarily tidy world of the conveyancer', in that they tend to 'diminish both certainty of title and the availability of land on the market' (F R Crane, (1967) 31 Conv (NS) 332 at 341–342).
2   **[Para 10.167]**.

OTHER NOTICE-BASED EQUITABLE RIGHTS

12.372   Certain other forms of entitlement in unregistered land fall, rather anomalously, outside the categories of registrable land charge and statutorily overreachable right. In consequence their impact on purchasers falls to be determined – *faute de mieux* – by an application of the equitable doctrine of notice. Although of diminishing importance as unregistered estates are steadily brought on to the Land Register, this residual class includes restrictive covenants entered into between freeholders prior to 1926,[1] equitable easements likewise created prior to 1926,[2] equitable rights of entry[3] (eg under an equitable lease[4]) and restrictive covenants entered into between lessor and lessee which relate, not to the user of the land demised, but to the user of other land of the lessor.[5]

1   **[Para 13.116]**.
2   **[Para 9.101]**.
3   *Melluish v BMI (No 3) Ltd* [1996] 1 AC 454 at 476C–F per Lord Browne-Wilkinson.
4   *Shiloh Spinners Ltd v Harding* [1973] AC 691 at 719B **[paras 8.268, 12.319]**.
5   *Dartstone v Cleveland Petroleum Co Ltd* [1969] 1 WLR 1807 at 1812A **[para 12.317]**.

CHAPTER 13

Freehold covenants and environmental regulation

AN OBLIGATIONAL VIEW OF LANDHOLDING

13.1   Much of this book has analysed 'property' in land from the perspective of either socially constituted fact or abstractly defined entitlement. Yet, in terms of the future, perhaps the most significant and durable image of 'property' will emerge as the perception that all 'property' in land comprises a form of delegated responsibility for land as a community resource.[1] Land may, of course, be turned to advantage in many overlapping ways; it can be occupied or exploited commercially; it can be a vehicle of investment, consumption, endowment or exchange; it can simply be an object of aesthetic or recreational appreciation. These elements all require to be held in balance. An obligational analysis of 'property' in land focuses on the way in which the enjoyment of land is ultimately governed by socially conditioned restraints which seek to maximise the efficient utilisation, in the general public interest, of even privately owned land resources.[2]

1   [**Para 2.87**].
2   One of the controversial, yet vital, challenges for the future is the question whether, in some radical sense, all land resources are held on trust for the public good (see Gray, 'Equitable Property' (1994) 47(2) Current Legal Problems 157).

THE HISTORIC VIEW

13.2   The view that modern estate ownership is permeated by community- or even neighbour-oriented expectations of responsible land use stands in stark contrast to the historic analysis of 'property' in land. With their ringing assertions of property absolutism, the great judges of the Victorian era acknowledged no overriding duty on the part of the private owner to safeguard wider interests in the exploitation of land.[1] The estate owner remained free to utilise 'his' land selfishly with little or no regard for community concerns or environmental sensitivities.[2] 'Every man', declared Lord Cranworth amidst an age of unrestrained industrial expansion, '[has] a right to use his own land by building on it as he thinks most to his interest.'[3]

1   See *Anchor Brewhouse Developments Ltd v Berkley House (Docklands Developments) Ltd* (1987) 38 BLR 82 at 96 per Scott J (referring to the 'robust Victorian approach').

2   The untrammelled nature of the common law perception of ownership still surfaces in relatively recent judicial utterances. See e g *Phipps v Pears* [1965] 1 QB 76 at 83E–F per Lord Denning MR [**para 8.62**]. Likewise, in *R v Denton* [1981] 1 WLR 1446 at 1148G, 1149C, Lord Lane CJ held it to be no offence under the Criminal Damage Act 1971 'for a man to damage or injure or destroy or set fire to his own premises ... [He] was lawfully entitled to burn the premises down.'

3   *Tapling v Jones* (1865) 11 HLCas 290 at 311, 11 ER 1344 at 1353. See also *Webb v Bird* (1861) 10 CB (NS) 268 at 284, 142 ER 455 at 461 per Erle CJ (no easement of wind access for a windmill lest it 'operate as a prohibition to a most formidable extent to the owners of the adjoining lands' [**para 8.60**]). Even in 1997 Lord Hoffmann adopted the premise that the common law, in the absence of any contrary easement, 'entitles an owner of land to build what he likes on his land' (*Hunter v Canary Wharf Ltd* [1997] AC 655 at 709G–H, 710G). See also *Rhone v Stephens* [1994] 2 AC 310 at 317D–E per Lord Templeman; *Re Hydeshire Ltd's Application* (1994) 67 P & CR 93 at 99.

13.3   In the past the common law has not, in general, mandated any duty of co-operation or neighbourly concern between adjoining owners. The common law recognised, for instance, no such right as a prescriptive (or any other) easement to preserve a good view over an adjacent landscape.[1] Beauty of prospect could be secured only by means of some bargained restriction under which the owner of neighbouring land covenanted not to develop his land so as to obstruct the vista.[2] Equally clearly, when measured against the imperatives of economic development, the claim to extreme (and what may have seemed self-indulgent) forms of personal privacy came off very much second best.[3] The householder whose neighbour constructed a factory next door could not avert the oafish gaze of the new urban proletariat from intruding upon the privacy of his garden[4] any more than he could object to the loss of amenity inflicted by the recently constructed road or railway which ran past his house.[5] In the competition of life each estate owner took no prisoners; his autonomy was almost unqualified; the 'bundle of rights' inherent in ownership remained virtually intact.

1   [**Para 8.56**]. See *William Aldred's Case* (1610) 9 Co Rep 57b at 58b, 77 ER 816 at 821; *Harris v De Pinna* (1886) 33 Ch D 238 at 262 per Bowen LJ; *Campbell v Paddington Corpn* [1911] 1 KB 869 at 875–876.

2   [**Para 9.138**]. See *Hunter v Canary Wharf Ltd* [1997] AC 655 at 699C–E per Lord Lloyd of Berwick, 709B per Lord Hoffmann, 727A–B per Lord Hope of Craighead.

3   [**Para 3.58**]. See Gray, 'Property in Thin Air' [1991] CLJ 252 at 261–263.

4   See *Tapling v Jones* (1865) 11 HLCas 290 at 305, 11 ER 1344 at 1350 per Lord Westbury LC.

5   *Re Penny and the South Eastern Railway Co* (1857) 7 E & B 660 at 669–672, 119 ER 1390 at 1393–1394; *Duke of Buccleuch v Metropolitan Board of Works* (1870) LR 5 Ex 221 at 237 per Blackburn J.

13.4   The Victorian approach to the responsibilities of land ownership is for ever crystallised in the response of the courts to the facts of *Bradford Corpn v Pickles*.[1] Here P owned land whose underground strata formed a 'natural

reservoir' of subjacent water supplies.[2] This water would normally have perco-
lated, in undefined channels, into rock strata in neighbouring land owned by
Bradford Corporation and from which the Corporation drew the water needed
to support the rapidly developing domestic and industrial requirements of the
city of Bradford. When P began to sink a shaft on his own land with the object
of abstracting and diverting a large portion of the underground water, Bradford Corporation sought an injunction, contending that P was motivated, not
by any intention to benefit the commercial stone-working operations carried
out on his own land, but by a malicious desire to inflict injury upon the city and
its inhabitants. The House of Lords declined to issue any injunction against P.
Lord Macnaghten, expressing with admirable clarity the viewpoint of the
property absolutist, held P entitled 'to force the corporation to buy him out at a
price satisfactory to himself' and questioned why P should 'without fee or
reward keep his land as a store-room for a commodity which the corporation
dispense, probably not gratuitously, to the inhabitants of Bradford.'[3] Noting
that P preferred 'his own interests to the public good', Lord Macnaghten
readily conceded that P might be 'churlish, selfish, and grasping', but, although
his conduct might seem 'shocking to a moral philosopher',[4] the House of Lords
refused to inhibit what it viewed as a landowner's sovereign power to exploit his
land as he saw fit without regard to any social or environmental constraint.[5]

1   [1895] AC 587. See Michael Taggart, *Private Property and Abuse of Rights in Victorian
     England: The Story of Edward Pickles and the Bradford Water Supply* (Oxford UP 2003).
2   In English law water is incapable of being owned and is considered simply as part of the land
     in or on which it is contained [**para 1.107**].
3   [1895] AC 587 at 600–601.
4   [1895] AC 587 at 601.
5   'If the act, apart from motive, gives rise merely to damage without legal injury, the motive,
     however reprehensible it may be, will not supply that element' ([1895] AC 587 at 601 per
     Lord Macnaghten). See also *Bakewell Management Ltd v Brandwood* [2004] 2 All ER 305
     at [20] per Lord Scott of Foscote.

THE MODERN PERSPECTIVE

13.5   It is significant that virtually every single exercise of the landowner's
prerogative described in the last three paragraphs would today be rendered
impossible by the pervasive impact of public and private regimes directed
towards the socially beneficial regulation of land resources.[1] Planning control
(and also, in many instances, privately bargained covenants) would prohibit the
construction of factories in residential areas,[2] control the location of roads and
railways[3] and secure the preservation of scenic landscape views.[4] The right to
abstract water is nowadays regulated by a strict statutory licensing scheme.[5] The
property absolutism of a bygone era has been largely replaced by a property
relativism which holds that the estate owner's 'bundle of rights' contains no
entitlement ruthlessly to exploit land resources regardless of the communal
good. Indeed, at the heart of contemporary environmental law lies the proposition that the estate owner's 'bundle of rights' is intrinsically delimited by
social or community-oriented obligations of a positive nature. According to

this line of argument, the owner's 'bundle of rights' is inherently restricted by various sorts of communitarian concern for environmental integrity.[6]

1 See *South Bucks DC v Porter* [2003] 2 AC 558 at [10] per Lord Bingham of Cornhill.
2 See Town and Country Planning Act 1990, Part III **[para 13.158]**. See also *Hunter v Canary Wharf Ltd* [1997] AC 655 at 710A–B per Lord Hoffmann ('The common law freedom of an owner to build upon his land has been drastically curtailed by the Town and Country Planning Act 1947 and its successors').
3 See Town and Country Planning (General Development Procedure) Order 1995 (SI 1995/419), art 15.
4 See e g *Gilbert v Spoor* [1983] Ch 27.
5 Water Resources Act 1991, ss 24(1), 24A (as supplemented by Water Act 2003, s 1(1)); Environment Act 1995, s 2(1)(a)(i).
6 **[Paras 2.17, 2.87]**. See Eric T Freyfogle, 'Ownership and Ecology' 43 Case W Res L Rev 1269 at 1285 (1993) ('the right to degrade cannot be a stick in the owner's bundle of entitlements').

THE REALLOCATION OF 'STICKS' IN THE 'PROPERTY' BUNDLE

13.6 This relativist view of 'property' is entirely consistent with the major theme of modern property theory. 'Property' in land correlates with varying degrees of socially approved power exercisable over the resource of realty; and distinct quantums of 'property' in the same land can be distributed simultaneously amongst a number of persons and entities (including the state).[1] The amount of 'property' which a person may assert either in relation to his own land or in relation to somebody else's is determined by a range of factors, some of which stem from the law of torts (and particularly the law of nuisance and negligence) and some from within land law itself. This book has already discussed the way in which, for instance, the law of easements brings about marginal shifts in the 'property' implicit in a landholding (as where one estate owner grants to his neighbour a right of way or drainage or support).[2] The present chapter analyses the means by which the quantum of 'property' enjoyed in land may be varied either through privately negotiated covenant or by direct state intervention. Indeed, most modern environmental regulation involves the voluntary reallocation of various 'sticks' within the 'property' bundle (as in the case of private covenants relating to land use) or the more profound recognition that the state has always held a 'retained stick in the bundle of rights.'[3]

1 **[Para 2.18]**.
2 **[Paras 2.22, 8.3]**.
3 John E Cribbet, 'Concepts in Transition: The Search for a New Definition of Property' (1986) U Ill L Rev 1 at 26.

THE BALANCE BETWEEN PRIVATE AND PUBLIC REGULATION OF LAND USE

13.7 It is clear that regimes of private ordering may substantially alter the balance of advantage associated with landholding – one theory being that private contracting enables land use preferences to be determined by the persons best positioned to assess the environmental utility required in specific contexts. Thus one neighbour may covenant with another to safeguard a quiet residential enclave from intrusive or disruptive development; groups of neighbours may covenant with each other to preserve the civilised ambience or aesthetic character of their surrounding area. Increasingly, however, the *private* regulation of land use has been supplemented or superseded by *public* regulation imposed by agencies of the state. These agencies exercise a vast range of controls relating to urban planning, the built environment, the conservation of natural resources and the preservation of the local and national heritage. The local authority planning officer can make or break a homeowner's aspirations for an extension or 'granny annexe' in his back garden.[1] The same planning department will instruct the owner exactly how he can and cannot renovate his listed building.[2] A local authority official can demand that the owner maintains his land to a certain standard and ultimately force its sale or effect a compulsory purchase if he does not.[3] In the most dramatic manifestation of state power, land can be compulsorily acquired by the state in order to further some supervening community purpose such as the construction of a new highway or the regeneration of an urban area or, perhaps more controversially, the profitable operation of a privatised utility company.[4] The landowner's proud claim of 'property' begins, in reality, to appear immensely fragile.

1   Town and Country Planning Act 1990, Part III.
2   Planning (Listed Buildings and Conservation Areas) Act 1990, Part I, Ch III.
3   HA 1985, ss 193(3), 300(3), Sch 10, para 7(3); Environmental Protection Act 1990, ss 81(4), 81A(4); T&CPA 1990, ss 215–219. See e g *Miles v Secretary of State for the Environment and the Royal Borough of Kingston upon Thames* [2000] JPL 192 at 199–202 **[para 13.166]**.
4   **[Para 13.170]**.

THE RESIDUAL QUALITY OF MODERN ESTATE OWNERSHIP

13.8   So pervasive is the intervention of the state that, in many ways, the 'property' of estate ownership has nowadays been stripped back to a bare residue of socially permissible power. 'Property' in land can be seen, quite realistically, as resulting from the distribution of state-approved usufructs (or mere rights of user), each exercisable subject to an overarching criterion of publicly defined responsibility.[1] 'Property' is constituted simply by those publicly endorsed user-forms which the state, at its discretion, allows individuals to enjoy; and 'property' in land means no more and no less than what the state actually permits an individual to do with 'his' land. Although European Union law purports in no way to 'prejudice the rules in Member States governing the system of property ownership',[2] it is inevitable that the common lawyer's understanding of property will be increasingly coloured by the emphatic insistence of the European Court of Justice that the right to property is not 'an absolute prerogative in Community law.'[3] In common with all fundamental rights recognised by the Court, rights of property, far from being 'absolute', must be 'considered in relation to their social function.'[4] Moreover, although the European Convention on Human Rights guarantees the 'peaceful enjoyment' of possessions, this protection is expressly made subject to the 'public interest' and to the right of the state 'to enforce such laws as it deems necessary to control the use of property in accordance with the general interest.'[5]

1   As we move slowly in the direction of European harmonisation, it is interesting to compare the prescription in Article 14(2) of the German *Grundgesetz* that 'property imposes duties. Its use should also serve the welfare of the community' **[para 2.92]**.
2   Treaty of Rome, art 222.
3   See *O'Dwyer v Council of the European Union* (Joined Cases T-466/93, T-473/93 and T-477/93) [1995] ECR II-2071 at [93].
4   *Wachauf v Federal Republic of Germany* (Case 5/88) [1989] ECR 2609 at [18]. See also *R v Chief Constable, ex p International Trader's Ferry Ltd* [1998] QB 477 at 495G–496B.
5   ECHR Protocol No 1, Art 1 **[paras 2.29, 13.166]**.

13.9 'Property' in land has become, in effect, a form of stewardship in which land resources are held on some kind of civic or environmental trust.[1] This analysis is far removed from the classic liberal perception of 'property' as a self-interested claim of absolute or arbitrary power. 'Property' in land has become little more than a highly qualified, ultimately defeasible privilege for the citizen. The modern state retains an eminent domain or overriding 'property' in all land – perhaps the most significant present-day emanation of the crown's radical title[2] – holding a dominating stake in the determination of all land use priorities. Eminent domain has been aptly described as 'the proprietary aspect of sovereignty'[3] and even the regulation of land use by privately bargained covenant is, in truth, merely a delegated form of a more general social control exercisable by, and adjudicated through, courts and tribunals acting as guardians of the public interest.[4]

1   **[Paras 2.87, 13.156]**. See Gray, 'Equitable Property' (1994) 47(2) CLP 157 at 188–214. See the promotion of voluntary stewardship agreements pursuant to The Countryside Stewardship Regulations 1998 (SI 1998/1327), reg 4; The Countryside Stewardship Regulations 2000 (SI 2000/3048), reg 3 (as amended by SI 2003/3991, SI 2004/114).
2   **[Para 1.120]**.
3   *Minister of State for the Army v Dalziel* (1944) 68 CLR 261 at 284 per Rich J.
4   Even privately bargained covenants remain subject to a power of review vested in the Lands Tribunal pursuant to LPA 1925, s 84 **[para 13.127]**.

THE CONTEXTUAL NATURE OF 'PROPERTY'

13.10 In terms of the modern relativist view, the deep structure of 'property' is not absolute, autonomous and oppositional. It is instead delimited by the pervasive influence of community-directed obligation[1] and is rooted in a contextual network of mutual constraint and social accommodation mediated by the agencies of the state.[2] 'Property' in land is constantly shaped and redefined, even at one remove, by a concern to protect and enhance the integrity of the local and regional environment. Supervening community need operates ab initio as a tacit qualification upon title.

1   '[L]and ownership entails community membership; it means belonging to the various communities whose values and goals are reflected in the ownership norms and processes that apply to a given parcel' (Eric T Freyfogle, 'Land Ownership and the Level of Regulation: The Particulars of Owning' 25 Ecology LQ 574 at 579 (1999)).

2   For reference to 'a new property jurisprudence of human interdependence', see Eric T
Freyfogle, 'Context and Accommodation in Modern Property Law' 41 Stan L Rev 1529 at
1530–1531 (1988–89) **[para 2.93]**. See also *Xpress Print Pte Ltd v Monocrafts Pte Ltd* [2000]
3 SLR 545 at 561H per Yong Pung How CJ **[para 1.63]**.

Interpenetration of the public and the private

13.11   A community-oriented approach to 'property' in land nowadays plays
a pivotal role in the advancement of our overall environmental welfare,
although in the process it raises peculiar tensions of its own. The preservation
and enhancement of environmental quality are heavily dependent on the
assertion of regulatory control over the exercise of proprietary power. The scale
and intensity of this control seem certain to increase in years to come, casting
an unprecedented emphasis on the extent to which the owners of 'private'
property should be called upon to bear the economic costs of the environmental utility which the community demands.[1] The environmental perspective
falsifies any clean dichotomy between the public and the private: in the
environmental context private autonomy and public need have an interpenetrating quality.

1   **[Paras 13.171–13.184]**.

Allocation of the costs of commercial development

13.12   Some sense of the interconnected nature of property relationships is
revealed by the recent history of the law relating to 'planning gains'.

Planning gains

13.13   Following the property boom of the 1970s many local planning
authorities in England and Wales began to demand 'planning gains' (in the
form of off-site benefits of general community significance) in exchange for the
grant of planning consent for proposed commercial developments.[1] In this way
improvements to the infrastructure of the local environment (comprising, in
large part, the provision of roads, parking facilities and recreational amenities)
could be financed as the price of a relevant planning permission. Although the
'bargain and sale' aspect of this practice was later curtailed by Department of
the Environment circulars,[2] it remains open to a planning authority to seek
benefits which are 'related to the development and necessary to the grant of
permission.'[3] By such means, as the House of Lords recognised in *Tesco
Stores Ltd v Secretary of State for the Environment*,[4] planning authorities are
encouraged to cause developers to pay for infrastructure and other facilities
which would otherwise require to be provided at public expense. These policies,
as Lord Hoffmann pointed out, 'reflect a shift in Government attitudes to the
respective responsibilities of the public and private sectors.'[5]

1 Such authorities 'appeared to regard themselves as entitled to share in the profits of commercial development, thereby imposing an informal land tax without the authority of Parliament' (*Tesco Stores Ltd v Secretary of State for the Environment* [1995] 1 WLR 759 at 774C–D per Lord Hoffmann).

2 *Planning Gain* (Circular 22/83), replaced by *Planning Obligations* (Circular16/91). The planning process 'began to look more like bargain and sale than democratic decision-making' (*Tesco Stores Ltd v Secretary of State for the Environment* [1995] 1 WLR 759 at 774F per Lord Hoffmann).

3 Circular 16/91, para B5. T&CPA 1990, s 106 explicitly envisages that a developer who enters into a 'planning obligation' [**paras 9.141, 13.15**] may be required to pay sums of money. See likewise Highways Act 1980, s 278(1); *R v Cardiff CC, ex p Sears Group Properties Ltd* [1998] 3 PLR 55 at 62–63; *Wards Construction (Medway) Ltd v Kent CC* [1999] LGR 675 at 685c–686b.

4 [1995] 1 WLR 759 at 776H–777A.

5 'While rejecting the politics of using planning control to extract benefits for the community at large, the Government has accepted the view that market forces are distorted if commercial developments are not required to bear their own external costs' ([1995] 1 WLR 759 at 777A). See also *R v South Northamptonshire DC, ex p Crest Homes Plc* (1994) 93 LGR 205 at 216 per Henry LJ. Compare the very different view adopted in the United States, where the exaction of advantages as a condition of planning permission is regarded as a compensable 'taking' by the state (see *Nollan v California Coastal Commission*, 483 US 825 at 841–842, 97 L Ed 2d 677 at 692 (1987) (exaction of beachfront easement); *Dolan v City of Tigard*, 512 US 374 at 394–396, 129 L Ed 2d 304 at 322–323 (requirement to dedicate land for flood control and pedestrian/cycle way) [**para 13.171**]).

Material considerations

13.14 The materiality in the planning process of proffered planning gains fell to be considered by the House of Lords in *Tesco Stores Ltd v Secretary of State for the Environment*.[1] Here Tesco applied for planning permission to construct a food superstore outside Oxford. The House of Lords, although upholding the refusal of permission in the instant case,[2] indicated that the considerations properly regarded as material to the outcome of Tesco's application nevertheless included the fact that Tesco had offered £6.6 million to fund communal off-site benefits (such as a new link road and river crossing which would help to relieve the local traffic congestion likely to be exacerbated by the development). Thus a willingness on the part of a developer to defray the external costs imposed on the community by a proposed development of land can legitimately provide one of the bases on which a planning authority may grant permission for the development.[3] The House of Lords was, however, keenly alert to the fact that the offer of an *unrelated* planning gain is tantamount to 'an attempt to buy planning permission'[4] and that the coupling of such offers with planning applications may lead to the 'auction' of planning permissions to the highest bidder.[5] For these reasons the House confirmed that planning obligations may properly impose burdens on developers only if such burdens are necessary, proportionate and directed bona fide towards meeting or contributing to the external costs of the development.[6] Even within these constraints, the *Tesco* case amply demonstrates the heavily contingent quality of 'property' in land. The 'property' implicit in estate ownership is nowadays permeated by a wide

range of socially driven obligation: 'property' in land is both defined and
delimited by overriding responsibilities to the wider community.

1   [1995] 1 WLR 759.
2   The planning application of another developer was preferred on the ground that its site was
     marginally more suitable ([1995] 1 WLR 759 at 783D).
3   [1995] 1 WLR 759 at 770A–D per Lord Keith of Kinkel, 783C–D per Lord Hoffmann.
4   [1995] 1 WLR 759 at 770A per Lord Keith of Kinkel. See *Bradford City Metropolitan Council
     v Secretary of State for the Environment* (1986) 53 P & CR 55 at 64 per Lloyd LJ ('It has
     usually been regarded as axiomatic that planning consent cannot be bought or sold. As a
     broad general proposition, that must be true').
5   [1995] 1 WLR 759 at 782B–C per Lord Hoffmann.
6   [1995] 1 WLR 759 at 776A–C.

Planning contributions

13.15   The role of planning gains in the public planning process is shortly to
be intensified with the introduction of the concept of 'planning contributions'
pursuant to the Planning and Compulsory Purchase Act 2004. When the 2004
Act (together with its accompanying regulations) comes into force, the 'planning obligations' authorised by the Town and Country Planning Act 1990[1] will
be replaced by a new scheme under which local planning authorities will be
required to indicate the 'developments' or 'uses' in relation to which they will
(or will not) consider accepting a 'planning contribution' from applicants for
planning permission.[2] The 'planning contribution' which, in certain cases, can
be expected of such applicants may take the form of 'compliance with the
relevant requirements' (eg by way of entry into appropriate restrictive or other
covenants).[3] Alternatively (or in combination), a 'planning contribution' may
be made by 'the prescribed means'[4] (ie the payment of a sum of money[5] or the
provision of a 'benefit in kind' or both[6]). The exaction of a socially beneficial
'quid pro quo' in the planning process will be heightened by the requirement
that local planning authorities publish the criteria by reference to which the
value of a contribution made by 'prescribed means' is to be determined and
also the 'purposes' to which such contributions in money form are, in whole or
part, to be put.[7] The element of 'price tagging' in development control is
further underlined by the fact that regulations to be drawn up under the 2004
Act may prescribe maximum and minimum amounts for any payment required
to be made.[8]

1   T&CPA 1990, s 106 [**para 9.141**] (repealed by P&CPA 2004, s 118, Sch 6, para 5).
2   P&CPA 2004, s 46(1), (3)(a)–(b).
3   P&CPA 2004, s 46(2)(b).
4   P&CPA 2004, s 46(2)(a).
5   This payment has been euphemistically termed an 'optional planning charge' (see *Explanatory
     Notes to Planning and Compulsory Purchase Act 2004* (HMSO 2004), para 73).
6   P&CPA 2004, s 46(5).
7   P&CPA 2004, s 46(3)(c)–(d).
8   P&CPA 2004, s 47(2).

FUNCTION OF PRIVATE COVENANTS RELATING TO LAND

13.16 Alongside the laws relating to easements, nuisance and planning, the law of private freehold covenants provides an important means of asserting external control over the use of land.[1]

1   Covenants relating to leasehold land are governed by different principles discussed in Chapter 14 [**para 14.208**].

Efficient use of land resources

13.17 A 'covenant' is an undertaking contained in a deed by which one party (the 'covenantor') promises another party (the 'covenantee') that he will or will not engage in some specified activity in relation to a defined area of land. As between covenantor and covenantee the covenant is then fully enforceable as a form of contract. In a manner similar to the law relating to easements,[1] the law of covenants promotes the efficient utilisation of land resources. Covenants provide a highly convenient means of adjusting neighbourhood relationships for mutual benefit. The freehold owners of Greenacre and Redacre may wish to prevent each other from engaging in certain kinds of activity or construction on their adjoining plots of land. Alternatively the owner of Greenacre may desire that the owner of Redacre should supply some sort of commodity or service to Greenacre (eg a supply of water or electricity). It rarely makes sense for the owner of Greenacre to buy out the entire freehold (or even a leasehold estate) in the adjoining Redacre simply in order to secure, on behalf of Greenacre, some on-going advantage over that land.[2] Such acquisitions are almost always wasteful (in so far as the investment in realty is disproportionate to the benefits derived) and may not resolve the problem anyway (in so far as the rights purchased are often incomplete without the acquisition of similar rights from other adjacent landowners).[3] Without the need for resort to such inefficient manoeuvres, the law of covenants provides a means of binding adjacent landowners to common strategies for the user of their respective lands, often co-ordinating their mutual interests over a period of many generations.[4] Schemes of enforceable covenants tend, moreover, to enhance the value of land on the open market, increasing the commercial attraction of particular sites or areas through the promise that certain advantages or local amenities or desirable neighbourhood characteristics will be preserved indefinitely.

1   [**Para 8.3**].
2   See, however, *Re Buchanan-Wollaston's Conveyance* [1939] Ch 738 [**para 11.244**].
3   See U Reichman, 'Judicial Supervision of Servitudes' 7 J Legal Stud 139 at 144 (1978).
4   Covenants have sometimes been likened to a form of political or public constitutional document (see Richard A Epstein, 'Covenants and Constitutions' 73 Cornell L Rev 906 at 926 (1987–88)).

Positive and negative covenants

13.18 Freehold covenants may be either *positive* or *negative* in quality. A positive covenant is one which imposes on the covenantor an obligation to perform some specified act or provide some service in relation to a defined parcel of land (eg to maintain in good repair a boundary fence shared with the covenantee). By contrast, a negative covenant seeks, on behalf of the covenantee, to restrict some disadvantageous activity on adjacent land of the covenantor. A negative (or 'restrictive') covenant may, for example, preclude the covenantor from using his own land for the conduct of trade or business or from engaging in certain kinds of development. Such covenants clearly promote the amenity enjoyed on the covenantee's land by curtailing disruptive or inconvenient activities which might otherwise be undertaken on the covenantor's land.

Development of private control of land use

13.19   The basic principles governing the creation and enforcement of private freehold covenants were formulated during a period when government agencies played little part in planning the use and development of the community's land resources. It was accordingly both natural and inevitable that the law should seek to give long-term effect to the agreements by which landowners attempted to control land use through private treaty. The law of covenants came in this way to provide an important facility for the private planning of land use. In particular, the device of the restrictive covenant came to function as an early form of environmental regulation in a developing urban context.[1]

1   For reference to private restrictive covenants as constitutive of 'a local law', see *Re Dolphin's Conveyance* [1970] Ch 654 at 662A per Stamp J **[para 9.152]**.

13.20   Although public planning processes have now taken over much of the function of privately contracted arrangements, there still remains an important role for private and quasi-private governance of land use. It is often the case that private covenants deal more satisfactorily with the detailed organisation of land use than can existing public planning controls. Private covenants can be particularly significant in regulating the immediately local environment of neighbours as, for instance, where parties contract for the maintenance and repair of boundary features or agree to adhere to a vernacular style of construction or a specific pattern of density in any future development. More generally, however, it is painfully apparent nowadays that privately bargained covenants operate frequently as the longstop guardian of wider, community-oriented, conservationist concerns, protecting a range of environmental amenities which are no longer necessarily assured by the local planning process.[1] It is even observable that other private law devices – such as the trust – are beginning to be invoked for the purpose of guaranteeing the conservation of areas of special character.[2] The modern protection of environmental quality often involves a combination of private and public law controls which it is the purpose of this chapter to explore.

1   **[Para 9.142]**.
2   See, for instance, the creation of the Covent Garden Area Trust described in R Cooper and T O'Donovan, 'Covent Garden: A Model for Protection of Special Character?' [1998] JPL 1110.

THE BOUNDARY BETWEEN CONTRACT AND PROPERTY

13.21 The essential historic limitation on the utility of the freehold covenant has always been the fact that, by virtue of the rule of privity, contracts confer enforceable benefits and burdens upon only the initially contracting parties, the covenantor and the covenantee. In this respect the law of covenants simply reflects a profound common law principle governing the impact of contractual commitments.

Disadvantages of the purely contractual dimension

13.22 The function of covenants as devices for the long-term regulation of land use would be severely impeded if covenants could *never* affect successors in title of the original covenantor and covenantee. Although the traditional rule of contractual privity doubtless serves to 'curtail the social losses of destructive bargaining',[1] it is enormously important that the purposeful benefits and burdens created by private covenants respecting land should be transmissible to third parties. Unless these benefits and burdens can be made to 'run with the land' to which they relate (no matter into whose hands that land may subsequently pass), covenanted obligations are liable to be destroyed or rendered worthless by any later transfer of the land.

1   See R A Epstein, 73 Cornell L Rev 906 at 914 (1987–88).

Transmission of covenanted rights and obligations to third parties

13.23 One of the large achievements of English law over the centuries has been the fashioning of various means by which private freehold covenants can impose long-term consequences upon the ordering of land use. Both the benefit and (less consistently) the burden of covenanted obligations can now run with the land so as to affect third parties such as the successors in title of the covenantee and covenantor. An inevitable by-product of this evolution of principle has been to blur the boundary between contract and property, by conceding the conventional attributes of *proprietary* character to obligations of purely *contractual* derivation.[1]

1   [Paras 2.52, 9.146]. See generally S Gardner, (1982) 98 LQR 279.

Guarding the frontier

13.24 There is a significant public interest that the law of covenants should delimit with some clarity the circumstances in which covenanted obligations may not only have contractual force but also impose benefits and burdens on third parties. If covenants of *any* kind, however loosely or capriciously defined, were allowed to affect successors in title, there would be a danger that the encumbered land could be rendered effectively unmarketable. The law has always been wary of 'long-term inhibitions to the realisation of the full potential of the servient tenement'[1] and has been correspondingly cautious lest durable burdens sterilise land titles.[2] No purchaser wishes to buy land whose future use is fettered by trivial or obscure covenants limiting the activities permissible on that land.[3] It is for good reason therefore that the law of covenants has always demarcated a firm boundary between contract and property.[4] It is also clear, however, that a creative tension exists between the need to render land alienable and the need to allow private ordering by consensual arrangement. The stability and convenience of land use secured by durably binding covenants often ensures, in practice, that enforceable covenants, far from 'clogging' or sterilising title, operate to enhance the market value of both the benefited and the burdened land.

1   *Forestview Nominees Pty Ltd v Perpetual Trustees WA Ltd* (1998) 193 CLR 154 at 163.
2   [Paras 2.96, 9.146].
3   For a discussion of the difficulty in reconciling the running of covenants with individual freedom and the liberal concept of property, see Gregory S Alexander, 'Freedom, Coercion, and the Law of Servitudes' 73 Cornell L Rev 883 at 889 (1987–88).
4   See H W R Wade, (1952) 68 LQR 337 at 347–348 ('rights which can bind third parties ought to be of a limited and familiar kind').

13.25   The transmission of covenanted benefits and burdens is simultaneously governed in English law by rules of *common law* and *equitable* origin. These must be examined in turn.

COVENANTS AT LAW

13.26   The common law rules relating to covenants are of extremely ancient origin.[1] It has been clear from early times that a covenant relating to land may be enforced at law even though the covenantor owns no estate of any kind in land.[2] This proposition was first established by *The Prior's Case*[3] in 1368, when it was decided that a positive covenant to sing divine service in the covenantee's chapel was enforceable at law by the covenantee's successor even though the covenantor held no estate in land which could be burdened by the obligation. The approach adopted in *The Prior's Case* has been applied in more recent times, as in *Smith and Snipes Hall Farm Ltd v River Douglas Catchment Board*,[4] where the Court of Appeal enforced against the defendant river authority a positive covenant to repair and maintain the floodbanks of a river. In practice, however, most covenantors *do* own an estate in the vicinity of the 'dominant' (or benefited) land and the common law requires, in any event, that the covenantee *must* hold an estate in land to which the benefit of an enforceable covenant can accrue. The more significant problem inevitably attaches to the question whether the benefit and burden of the covenant can be transmitted to third parties.

1   See A W B Simpson, *A History of The Land Law* (2nd edn Oxford 1986), pp 116–118.
2   It is this principle which underpins the liability of the modern surety who, without owning any

estate in land, guarantees the due performance of the leasehold obligations of a tenant (see eg *P & A Swift Investments v Combined English Stores Group Plc* [1989] AC 632 **[paras 13.33, 14.268]**).

3   (1368) YB 42 Edw III, pl 14, fol 3A (sometimes referred to as *Laurence Pakenham's Case*: see *Keppell v Bailey* (1834) 2 My & K 517 at 539, 39 ER 1042 at 1050 per Lord Brougham LC).
4   [1949] 2 KB 500 at 506–507, 514–515. See (1949) 12 MLR 498 (A K R Kiralfy).

TRANSMISSION OF THE BENEFIT OF A FREEHOLD COVENANT AT LAW

13.27   A freehold covenant relating to land is normally enforceable in contract by the original covenantee,[1] but it is a different order of question whether at law the benefit of this covenant can be transmitted to, or claimed by, the covenantee's successors in title.[2] The common law has traditionally imposed strict preconditions on the passing of covenanted benefits, although more modern statutory provisions have tended to relax the rigour of the common law rules. In their statutorily modified form the common law rules now operate effectively as the analogue of the equitable principles which enable the benefit of a restrictive covenant to be annexed as an incident of the covenantee's estate in the land.[3]

1   See *P & A Swift Investments v Combined English Stores Group Plc* [1989] AC 632 at 639G. The covenantee who parts with the dominant land may sue a covenantor who subsequently breaches the terms of the covenant (*Stokes v Russell* (1790) 3 TR 678 at 681, 100 ER 799 at 801; *London County Council v Allen* [1914] 3 KB 642 at 664), but can recover only nominal damages since the real loss is likely to have fallen upon the person to whom the dominant land has been transferred.
2   Benefit can travel quite independently of burden **[para 8.203]**, with the result that it is entirely possible that the 'benefit' of a covenant runs with the covenantee's land while the 'burden' of the same covenant does *not* run with the covenantor's land (*Rogers v Hosegood* [1900] 2 Ch 388 at 395 per Farwell J).
3   **[Para 13.69]**.

13.28   The common law sets out conditions under which the benefit of a covenant (whether positive or negative) may pass at law to a third party who takes an estate in the dominant land.[1] The common law rules governing the transmission of benefit have existed since the earliest days, although equity was later to formulate its own rules for the passing of the benefit of covenants (and did so on the assumption that it was largely following the rules laid down by the common law).[2] The common law rules were authoritatively elucidated by the House of Lords in *P & A Swift Investments v Combined English Stores Group Plc*,[3] where Lord Oliver of Aylmerton confirmed that the benefit of a covenant runs at law with the covenantee's estate in the following circumstances.[4]

1   Where the common law rules apply, the benefit attaches presumptively to each and every part of the dominant land with the consequence that, notwithstanding subsequent fragmentation of that land, any successor in title may claim the benefit (see LPA 1925, s 78(1), as construed in *Federated Homes Ltd v Mill Lodge Properties Ltd* [1980] 1 WLR 594 at 606F–H **[para 13.81]**).
2   The common law rules continue to apply in cases not covered by the equitable rules, as for instance where the covenantor has no land upon which the burden of the covenant can be imposed.

3   [1989] AC 632 at 639H–640A. For earlier statements of the common law rules, see *Rogers v Hosegood* [1900] 2 Ch 388 at 395 per Farwell J; *Smith and Snipes Hall Farm Ltd v River Douglas Catchment Board* [1949] 2 KB 500 at 506 per Tucker LJ.
4   Although the common law speaks loosely of covenants as running with the land, it is more accurate to say, under the common law rules, that the benefit runs 'not with the land but with the covenantee's estate in the land' (see S J Bailey, 'The Benefit of a Restrictive Covenant' [1938] CLJ 339 at 350; *Forestview Nominees Pty Ltd v Perpetual Trustees WA Ltd* (1998) 193 CLR 154 at 167).

The covenant must 'touch and concern' the land

13.29   It must be shown that the covenant 'touches and concerns' the land owned by the covenantee, ie that it was entered into for the benefit of the covenantee's *land* and not merely for his own personal benefit.

Effect of the 'touch and concern' requirement

13.30   It is notoriously difficult to provide any definitive explanation of the terminology of 'touching and concerning' covenants. Nowadays, however, the clear effect of the 'touching and concerning' requirement is to confine the durable creation of land burdens to genuine and objective purposes of land use planning.[1] It has been said that the 'touch and concern' condition, by filtering out purely personal, idiosyncratic or oppressive covenants, 'eliminates the possibility of creating modern variations of feudal serfdom.'[2] The requirement certainly confers upon the courts an important power to determine the parameters within which the private planning of land use may occur.

1   For a vigorous argument that the 'touch and concern' requirement should be abolished, see S F French, 73 Cornell L Rev 928 at 939 (1987–88). For a counter-argument that the requirement promotes an efficient allocation of the responsibilities of land management, see J E Stake, 'Toward an Economic Understanding of Touch and Concern' (1988) Duke LJ 925.
2   U Reichman, 'Judicial Supervision of Servitudes' 55 S Cal L Rev 1177 at 1233 (1982).

The criterion of 'touching and concerning'

13.31   The test of whether a covenant 'touches and concerns' the land[1] is essentially the same as that which is applied in the context of leasehold covenants,[2] with the obvious qualification that the land in question here is of course the land of the *covenantee* rather than any land of the covenantor.[3] It must, in effect, be shown that, between the substance of the covenant and the covenantee's land, there exists some connection of benefit or protection similar to that required by the equitable rules of annexation.[4]

1   For this purpose the covenantee's land is usually a corporeal hereditament, but may also include an incorporeal hereditament such as an easement (see *Gaw v Córas Iompair Éireann* [1953] IR 232 at 257–258) or indeed may, as in the case of a surety covenant under a lease, include the covenantee's reversion on the lease (see *P & A Swift Investments v Combined English Stores Group Plc* [1989] AC 632 at 640E per Lord Oliver of Aylmerton).

2   **[Para 14.253]**. See *P & A Swift Investments v Combined English Stores Group Plc* [1989] AC 632
     at 640E–F per Lord Oliver of Aylmerton. In its turn, the 'touch and concern' test is in
     substance the same test as that which stipulates that restrictive covenants and easements must
     'accommodate' (or confer benefit upon) the land owned by their respective grantees
     [paras 8.33, 9.164]. See *Application of Fox* (1981) 2 BPR 9310 at 9312, 9314 per Wootten J,
     who pointed out that the transfer of the phrase 'touching and concerning' to freehold
     covenants 'has created some confusion.'
3   It is in fact irrelevant, in the case of a positive covenant, whether the covenantor has any land
     to be burdened (see *The Prior's Case* (1368) YB 42 Edw III, pl 14, fol 3A **[para 13.26]**). The
     rule against perpetuities has no application to covenants which touch and concern the land
     (*Coronation Street Industrial Properties Ltd v Ingall Industries Ltd* [1989] 1 WLR 304 at 307H
     per Lord Templeman).
4   **[Para 13.71]**.

Exclusion of collateral advantages

13.32   The classic test of a 'touching and concerning' covenant is derived from
Mayor of Congleton v Pattison.[1] As elaborated in more recent case law,[2] this test
requires that a covenant which 'touches and concerns' the covenantee's land
'must either affect the land as regards mode of occupation, or it must be such
as per se, and not merely from collateral circumstances, affects the value of the
land.'[3] It is arguable, of course, that these conditions are flawed by an element
of circularity, but the requirement of some intrinsic nexus with *land* means, for
instance, that a pure covenant in gross to pay an annuity of £x per annum to the
owner for the time being of Greenacre cannot constitute a 'touching and
concerning' covenant.[4]

1   (1808) 10 East 130 at 135, 103 ER 725 at 727 **[para 14.253]**.
2   *P & A Swift Investments v Combined English Stores Group Plc* [1989] AC 632 at 640F per
     Lord Oliver of Aylmerton. See also *Rogers v Hosegood* [1900] 2 Ch 388 at 395 per Farwell J;
     Smith and Snipes Hall Farm Ltd v River Douglas Catchment Board [1949] 2 KB 500 at 506 per
     Tucker LJ.
3   In *Smith and Snipes Hall Farm Ltd v River Douglas Catchment Board* [1949] 2 KB 500 at 508,
     Tucker LJ ruled that the required connection between the covenant and the land concerned
     need not appear expressly in the terms of the covenant but may be proved by extrinsic
     evidence: 'Id certum est quod certum reddi potest.'
4   See *P & A Swift Investments v Combined English Stores Group Plc* [1989] AC 632 at 639D–E
     per Lord Oliver of Aylmerton. However, a surety's guarantee of the due performance of a
     'touching and concerning' covenant undertaken by a tenant (eg a covenant to pay rent) *does*
     constitute a 'touching and concerning' covenant, even though it comprises a money obligation
     to the covenantee ([1989] AC 632 at 637H per Lord Templeman).

A 'satisfactory working test'

13.33   In dealing in *P & A Swift Investments v Combined English Stores Group
Plc*[1] with a surety covenant given to a landlord, Lord Oliver of Aylmerton
propounded what he termed a 'satisfactory working test' for determining
whether, in any given case, a covenant 'touches and concerns' the land. *First*, a
'touching and concerning' covenant must benefit only the dominant owner for
the time being, so that, if separated from his land, it ceases to be advantageous

to him.[2] *Second*, the covenant must affect the nature, quality, mode of user or value of the land of the dominant owner. *Third*, the covenant must not be expressed to be personal (ie must not have been given only to one specific dominant owner or in respect of obligations undertaken by only one specific servient owner). According to Lord Oliver, the sheer fact that a covenant involves the payment of a sum of money 'will not prevent it from touching and concerning the land so long as the three foregoing conditions are satisfied and the covenant is connected with something to be done on, to or in relation to the land.'[3] On this basis the House of Lords was able, in the *Swift* case, to hold that a guarantor's surety covenant sufficiently 'touched and concerned' land to run with the covenantee landlord's reversion and become enforceable in the hands of the transferee of that reversion.

1   [1989] AC 632 at 642E–F.
2   Thus the benefit of a freehold covenant can run with the land only if the covenant is 'beneficial to the owner for the time being of the covenantee's land and to no one else' (see *Forestview Nominees Pty Ltd v Perpetual Trustees WA Ltd* (1996) 141 ALR 687 at 699 per French J).
3   [1989] AC 632 at 642F.

There must have been an intention that the benefit should run with the estate owned by the covenantee at the date of the covenant

13.34   In *Smith and Snipes Hall Farm Ltd v River Douglas Catchment Board*,[1] Tucker LJ indicated that it must be shown that 'it was the intention of the parties that the benefit [of the covenant] should run with the land.' This element of intention comprises the central and most important precondition for the running of a covenanted benefit at law.[2] There must be 'an intention that the benefit of the obligation ... shall attach [to the land] into whosesoever hands the lands shall come.'[3] This element of intention was not specifically emphasised in *P & A Swift Investments v Combined English Stores Group Plc*[4] except in so far as Lord Oliver indicated that the covenant must not be expressed to be 'personal' to the covenantee. In any event it is clear that, in relation to covenants undertaken after 1925, the requirement of intention is closely intertwined with the provision in section 78(1) of the Law of Property Act 1925 that covenants 'relating to' the land of the covenantee are deemed to have been made with not merely the covenantee but also his successors in title.[5]

1   [1949] 2 KB 500 at 506. See, however, D W Elliott (1956) 20 Conv (NS) 43 at 53. *Smith and Snipes Hall Farm Ltd v River Douglas Catchment Board* was followed in *Williams v Unit Construction Co Ltd* (1955) 19 Conv (NS) 262.
2   In *Smith and Snipes Hall Farm Ltd v River Douglas Catchment Board* [1949] 2 KB 500, the deed in question showed that the object of the covenant was 'to improve the drainage of land liable to flooding and prevent future flooding.' Herein lay the required evidence of an intention permanently to benefit the covenantee's land.
3   [1949] 2 KB 500 at 506 per Tucker LJ.
4   [1989] AC 632.
5   **[Para 13.79]**.

The covenantee must have a legal estate in the dominant land

13.35 It is a basic feature of the common law rules that a covenant can run with the dominant land only if made with a covenantee who has a *legal* estate in that land.[1] No benefit can pass at law where the original covenantee has merely an *equitable* interest in the land.

1   *Webb v Russell* (1789) 3 TR 393 at 402, 100 ER 639 at 644.

The transferee of the dominant land must also take a legal estate in that land

13.36 The common law probably also required that any third party who sought to claim the benefit of a covenant relating to land must show that he held the *same* legal estate in that land as the original covenantee. In other words, if the original covenantee was an owner in fee simple, the benefit of the covenant could pass only to a transferee of the fee simple,[1] precisely because the benefit constituted an incident of this estate. In *Smith and Snipes Hall Farm Ltd v River Douglas Catchment Board*,[2] however, the Court of Appeal took the view that this common law requirement had finally been abrogated by section 78(1) of the Law of Property Act 1925.[3] This statutory modification of the common law effectively enabled covenanted benefits to run at law with the dominant land itself (as distinct from merely with the covenantee's *estate* in that land). In *Smith*'s case D had covenanted with X to repair and maintain the floodbanks of a river. X later sold the dominant land to P1, who in turn leased the land to P2. The Court of Appeal allowed an action for damages for breach of covenant on the suit of both P1 (the owner in fee simple) and P2 (who held a term of years). The Court held that section 78(1) rendered the covenant enforceable on behalf of not only the original covenantee but all successors in title and all persons deriving title from such successors. Here, for the purpose of enforcement, it was sufficient merely that subsequent claimants of the covenanted benefit held *some* legal estate in the relevant land, it being clear that the covenant touched and concerned X's land and had been intended to run with that land.[4]

1   Thus the benefit could not pass to a lessee (see e g *Westhoughton UDC v Wigan Coal and Iron Co Ltd* [1919] 1 Ch 159 at 171).
2   [1949] 2 K B 500.
3   **[Para 13.79]**.
4   See also *P & A Swift Investments v Combined English Stores Group Plc* [1989] AC 632 at 639H per Lord Oliver of Aylmerton.

STATUTORY METHODS OF TRANSMITTING COVENANTED BENEFITS

13.37 The common law rules for the transmission of covenanted benefits are supplemented by several statutory provisions which ensure, not so much that these benefits run with the covenantee's land, but rather that parties other than the immediate or primary covenantee become entitled to claim the benefits in question.

Assignment of a chose in action

13.38   The benefit of a covenant which is not exclusively personal may always be assigned in writing as a chose in action pursuant to section 136 of the Law of Property Act 1925. In order to be effective at law, this form of assignment requires to be in writing and express written notice of the assignment must be served upon the covenantor.

Law of Property Act 1925, s 56

13.39   It is clear that, on purely contractual principles, a deed of covenant may confer an enforceable benefit upon any one or more of the covenantees. Thus if A covenants directly with B *and* C to confer a benefit upon C, C is automatically entitled to sue in the event of breach. At common law, however, there was for many years a strict rule that no person could sue on a deed made *inter partes*[1] unless he was expressly *named* in that deed as a party.[2] This rule was modified in the mid-19th century[3] and section 56(1) of the Law of Property Act 1925 now provides that

> A person may take an immediate or other interest in land or other property, or the benefit of any condition, right of entry, covenant or agreement over or respecting land or other property, although he may not be named as a party to the conveyance or other instrument.

1   A deed made *inter partes* must be distinguished from a *deed poll*, ie a deed executed unilaterally by one party.
2   See *Lord Southampton v Brown* (1827) 6 B & C 718 at 719–720, 108 ER 615 at 616.
3   Real Property Act 1845, s 5.

The doctrine of contractual privity

13.40   Few statutory provisions have generated so much confusion as section 56(1). It was once thought that this section had abrogated the entire doctrine of privity of contract,[1] but the ambivalent utterances of the House of Lords in *Beswick v Beswick*[2] indicate on balance that this is not so.[3] Thus, if A covenants merely with B to confer a benefit upon C, C is still disabled from enforcing the covenant under section 56(1), since he is excluded from doing so by the rules of privity.[4] It is, of course, open to B (in the absence of other impediments) to seek an order for specific performance against A, requiring A to fulfil the covenant in favour of C,[5] but there is rarely any incentive for B to press for this form of remedy.

1   See eg *Smith and Snipes Hall Farm Ltd v River Douglas Catchment Board* [1949] 2 KB 500 at 517 per Denning LJ; *Drive Yourself Hire Co (London) Ltd v Strutt* [1954] 1 QB 250 at 274 per Denning LJ; *Beswick v Beswick* [1966] Ch 538 at 556G–557C per Lord Denning MR, 563A–B per Danckwerts LJ.
2   [1968] AC 58. See (1967) 30 MLR 687 (G H Treitel). For a review of the disparate approaches adopted in the House of Lords in *Beswick*, see *Amsprop Trading Ltd v Harris Distribution Ltd* [1997] 1 WLR 1025 at 1029H–1030C.

3   In *Beswick v Beswick* [1968] AC 58 the House of Lords thought that section 56(1) could not facilitate the recovery of a contractual benefit by a non-party, but only two of the law lords explicitly rejected Lord Denning's expansive view of this statutory provision (see [1968] AC 58 at 94C–D per Lord Pearce, 106A–G per Lord Upjohn). See also *Jones v Bartlett* (2000) 205 CLR 166 at [68]–[74] per Gaudron J, [141]–[142] per Gummow and Hayne JJ.

4   See *White v Bijou Mansions Ltd* [1937] Ch 610 at 624–625 per Simonds J, [1938] Ch 351 at 365; *Amsprop Trading Ltd v Harris Distribution Ltd* [1997] 1 WLR 1025 at 1031D, 1032D–E per Neuberger J.

5   *Beswick v Beswick* [1968] AC 58 at 88F–92C per Lord Pearce; *Woodar Investment Development Ltd v Wimpey Construction UK Ltd* [1980] 1 WLR 277 at 293D–E per Lord Russell of Killowen, 300C per Lord Scarman; *Rattrays Wholesale Ltd v Meredyth-Young & A'Court Ltd* [1997] 2 NZLR 363 at 380 per Tipping J. In *Woodar Investment*, supra at 293D, Lord Russell thought that, following the making of an order for specific performance against A at the suit of B, that order could be enforced by C.

Generic descriptions

13.41   The generally accepted view is that section 56(1) merely removes the old rule which restricted the enforceable benefit of a covenant to those parties who were referred to expressly *by name* in the original deed of covenant. After 1925 it is sufficient that the claimant-beneficiary is designated as a covenantee under some *generic* description. Thus, for instance, a covenantor may covenant with a named party (e g the vendor of land) and also with the 'owners for the time being' of identified adjoining or adjacent plots of land. In such cases the benefit of the covenant is enforceable not only by the *named* covenanting party but also by those other owners who are included in the category of covenantees, albeit that their inclusion is merely by generic reference.[1] It is not enough that the covenant purports to confer a benefit: the covenant must actually draw the intended beneficiary or beneficiaries 'within the ambit of the expressly identified covenantee.'[2] But even where this is so, the scope of section 56(1) remains significantly limited. Persons who are generically described as covenantees may claim the covenanted benefit only if they are existing and identifiable individuals at the date of the covenant.[3] Section 56(1) does not enable a covenant to confer benefit directly upon *future* purchasers of plots of land. Thus a covenant which purports to be made with a named owner of land 'and with his successors in title' does not bring these successors within the scope of section 56(1).

1   See e g *Wiles v Banks* (1985) 50 P & CR 80 at 87; *Re Shaw's Application* (1995) 68 P & CR 591 at 597–599.

2   *Amsprop Trading Ltd v Harris Distribution Ltd* [1997] 1 WLR 1025 at 1031D–E per Neuberger J.

3   *Kelsey v Dodd* (1881) 52 LJ Ch 34 at 39; *Forster v Elvet Colliery Co Ltd* [1908] 1 KB 629 at 636–637; *Grant v Edmondson* [1931] 1 Ch 1 at 27; *Re Ecclesiastical Comrs for England's Conveyance* [1936] Ch 430 at 441–442; *Pinemain Ltd v Welbeck International Ltd* (1984) 272 EG 1166 at 1171; *Bohn v Miller Bros Pty Ltd* [1953] VLR 354 at 358; *Re Wilsons' Settlements* [1972] NZLR 13 at 32.

Law of Property Act 1925, s 78(1)

13.42 Although section 56(1) may not be effective for the purpose, section 78(1) of the Law of Property Act 1925 appears, in its broad terms, to authorise the enforcement of covenants by third parties. Section 78(1) provides that a covenant 'relating to' any land of the covenantee is presumptively 'made with the covenantee and his successors in title and the persons deriving title under him or them, and shall have effect as if such successors and other persons were expressed.' The impact of section 78(1) is limited to covenants which relate to (or 'touch and concern') the covenantee's land and is further confined to covenants entered into after 1925.[1] Notwithstanding these constraints, it remains one of the enigmas of 20th century statutory interpretation that the ample terms of this provision were not invoked more overtly to confirm the distribution of covenanted benefits to the covenantee's successors and, indeed, to other 'occupiers for the time being of the land' (such as adverse possessors or licensees).[2] For decades courts have seemed reluctant to credit the plain message conveyed by the statutory language – doubtless because of its devastating incursion into the hallowed principle of privity of contract – but this conspiracy of silence has finally been abandoned in the related context of the enforcement of restrictive covenants by third parties.[3] Ironically, just as the full potential of section 78(1) began to impinge on the judicial consciousness, a further statutory innovation emerged whose scope travels even further than that of section 78(1).

1   *J Sainsbury Plc v Enfield LBC* [1989] 1 WLR 590 at 601D–E **[para 13.83]**.
2   'Why the decided cases make no reference to this legislation is a mystery ... why ... should counsel never argue the point, judges never mention it, and textbooks not discuss it?' (H W R Wade, [1972B] CLJ 157 at 171–173). See also G R Y Radcliffe, (1941) 57 LQR 203 at 205.
3   See the benevolent construction accorded to section 78(1) in the decision of the Court of Appeal in *Federated Homes Ltd v Mill Lodge Properties Ltd* [1980] 1 WLR 594 **[para 13.81]**.

Contracts (Rights of Third Parties) Act 1999

13.43 A dramatically extended third party impact for certain kinds of covenant is achieved by the Contracts (Rights of Third Parties) Act 1999,[1] although the operation of this statute is limited to contracts (including, by implication, covenants) entered into on or after 11 May 2000.[2] The Contracts (Rights of Third Parties) Act 1999 provides that a person who is not a party to a contract may 'in his own right' enforce a term of that contract if *either* the contract expressly provides that he may *or* the term in question 'purports to confer a benefit upon him' (unless, on a proper construction of the contract, it 'appears that the parties did not intend the term to be enforceable by the third party').[3] In order to enforce a contractual term, the third party must be expressly identified in the contract by name or as a 'member of a class or as answering a particular description.'[4] The latter provision for inclusion by generic description achieves an effect similar to that of section 56(1) of the Law of Property Act 1925, with the important rider that, for the purpose of the 1999 Act, persons described generically 'need not be in existence when the contract is entered into.'[5] The 1999 Act thus appears to allow the benefit of a covenant to be claimed by wide categories of non-party to the covenant provided that they are included in the covenant by way of generic description as 'successors in title' of the covenantee. Likewise the 1999 Act oversteps the ambit of section 78(1) of the Law of Property Act 1925, in that there is no requirement under the 1999 Act that enforceable covenants should relate to or 'touch and concern' the covenantee's land or even that the non-party enforcing the covenant should be entitled to any sort of estate in land at all.

1　See (1999) 143 Sol Jo 1082 (S Bright and P J G Williams).
2　It was open to contracting parties to opt into the provisions of the Act during a period of six months preceding 11 May 2000 (C(RTP)A 1999, s 8(2)–(3)).
3　C(ROTP)A 1999, s 1(1)–(2).
4　C(ROTP)A 1999, s 1(3).
5　C(ROTP)A 1999, s 1(3). Compare LPA 1925, s 56(1) **[para 13.41]**.

Commonhold and Leasehold Reform Act 2002

13.44　One of the essential features of the new regime of freehold ownership of 'commonhold land' is the idea that rights which are attached to the freehold proprietorship of a commonhold unit (by a 'commonhold community statement') are automatically transmitted to the new unit-holder on any transfer of the registered freehold estate in that commonhold unit.[1] To this extent, the device of commonhold ownership has introduced a novel and important means by which the benefit of certain obligations undertaken by freeholders can run with the fee simple estate into the hands of successors in title.

1　CALRA 2002, s 16(1) **[para 7.367]**. Upon transfer of the estate, the former unit-holder cannot take any new benefit under or by virtue of the commonhold community statement (CALRA 2002, s 16(2)), but remains entitled to any right which accrued before the transfer (CALRA 2002, s 16(3)(b)).

Statutory covenants for title

13.45　Special statutory provisions govern the transmission of the benefit of the most important covenants relating to land, ie covenants in respect of title.

Conveyances prior to 1 July 1995

13.46　Various covenants for title are implied by section 76 of the Law of Property Act 1925 in respect of conveyances made prior to 1 July 1995. The benefit of these covenants is 'annexed and incident to, and shall go with, the estate or interest of the implied covenantee, and shall be capable of being enforced by every person in whom that estate or interest is, for the whole or any part thereof, from time to time vested.'[1]

1　LPA 1925, s 76(6).

Dispositions on or after 1 July 1995

13.47   In respect of dispositions of property made on or after 1 July 1995, the Law of Property (Miscellaneous Provisions) Act 1994 implies certain covenants for title, depending on whether the relevant disposition is expressed to be made with 'full title guarantee' or 'limited title guarantee'.[1] The benefit of any covenant so implied is 'annexed and incident to, and shall go with, the estate or interest of' the disponee and shall be 'capable of being enforced by every person in whom that estate or interest is (in whole or in part) for the time being vested.'[2]

1   LP(MP)A 1994, ss 1(1)–(2), 2–5.
2   LP(MP)A 1994, s 7.

TRANSMISSION OF THE BURDEN OF A COVENANT AT LAW

13.48   One of the scarcely credible features of the modern law of freehold covenants is that there exists no relatively straightforward means by which the burden of a positive covenant can be transmitted to third parties.[1] English common law dogmatically insists that only the benefit, and not the burden, of a freehold covenant may run with the land.[2] As Lord Templeman observed in *Rhone v Stephens*,[3] it is a truth 'imparted at an elementary stage to every student of the law of real property that positive covenants affecting freehold land are not directly enforceable except against the original covenantor.' This orthodox principle was recognised classically in *Austerberry v Oldham Corpn*,[4] where the Court of Appeal confirmed as a clear rule of law that the burden of a covenant between freeholders cannot run with the land.[5] This common law rule is, of course, consonant with the general principle that the benefit, but never the burden, of a contract can be assigned to a third party.[6] It was indeed this unwillingness to hold covenants enforceable at law against the covenantor's successors which ultimately made it necessary, in the mid-19th century, for the jurisdiction of equity to devise a means by which at least the burden of *restrictive* covenants could be made to run with the land and affect third parties.[7]

1   It is, of course, futile to establish that a particular claimant is fully entitled to the *benefit* of a freehold covenant if the intended target of his enforcement action is someone who is not subject to the *burden* of the covenant concerned [**para 13.67**].
2   See *Rhone v Stephens* [1994] 2 AC 310 at 317B–C per Lord Templeman; *Thamesmead Town Ltd v Allotey* (2000) 79 P & CR 557 at 558 per Peter Gibson LJ; *Durham Condominium Corp No 123 v Amberwood Investments Ltd* (2002) 211 DLR (4th) 1 at [17].
3   [1994] 2 AC 310 at 321E–F.
4   (1885) 29 Ch D 750 at 781. See also *Jones v Price* [1965] 2 QB 618 at 633E–F, 639G, 646D; *Regent Oil Co Ltd v J A Gregory (Hatch End) Ltd* [1966] Ch 402 at 433B–D; *Application of Fox* (1981) 2 BPR 9310 at 9311–9312; *Government Insurance Office (NSW) v K A Reed Services Pty Ltd* [1988] VR 829 at 837.
5   Lindley LJ thought that the burden of a positive covenant could run with the land only if the covenant amounted, upon the true construction, 'to either a grant of an easement, or a rent-charge, or some estate or interest in the land' ((1885) 29 Ch D 750 at 781).
6   The refusal to allow the burden of a positive covenant to run with the land conflicts with

efficiency-based arguments which dictate that it is clearly preferable to allocate the relevant burden to the current owner of the servient land rather than to the original promisor (see J E Stake, (1988) Duke LJ 925 at 954–955).

7   See *Tulk v Moxhay* (1848) 2 Ph 774, 41 ER 1143 [**paras 9.147**, **13.108**].

Modern disadvantages of non-transmissible burdens

13.49   The principle of *Austerberry v Oldham Corpn* was motivated by a policy that land should remain substantially unfettered for future generations. Nevertheless the general incapacity of positive covenants to affect the covenantor's successors in title has proved remarkably inconvenient in a crowded urban world where many features of orderly co-existence depend upon the ready enforceability of positive burdens of maintenance, repair and support undertaken by one's neighbours.[1] The anxiety of 19th century judges to limit the kinds of incumbrance which might be imposed upon the freehold estate is not particularly apposite to the vastly changed conditions of modern life where most people live in large cities. The property law of the 19th century was highly individualistic and made little provision for 'freeholders living like battery hens in urban developments' where much of the land area may consist of amenities which belong to none personally but which are socially necessary for all.[2] The non-transmissible character of positive burdens has until recently made it difficult to envisage the possibility of freehold conveyancing of flats.[3] It remains none the less a bizarre fact that, outside the original contractual nexus and apart from express instances of statutory intervention,[4] most positive freehold covenants are today unenforceable – a conclusion 'whose discovery has shocked more than one eminent judge unversed in the subtleties of English real property law.'[5]

1   See eg *Xpress Print Pte Ltd v Monocrafts Pte Ltd* [2000] 3 SLR 545 at 558A, 562D–E [**para 1.63**]. The orthodox common law rule 'impedes transactions in land which have become socially desirable' (H W R Wade, [1972B] CLJ 157). See also *Durham Condominium Corp No 123 v Amberwood Investments Ltd* (2002) 211 DLR (4th) 1 at [17], [95].
2   H W R Wade, [1972B] CLJ 157 at 158. See also C D Bell, (1984) 128 Sol Jo 323; (1995) 58 MLR 486 at 490–492 (D N Clarke).
3   See now CALRA 2002, s 16(1) [**paras 7.367**, **13.44**].
4   See eg T&CPA 1990, s 106(3)–(4) (planning obligation enforceable against 'any person deriving title' from the person entering into the obligation [**para 9.141**]); Highways Act 1980, s 35(4) (covenants in 'walkway agreement' binding on all persons deriving title under the covenantor [**para 5.25**]).
5   *Rhone v Stephens* (1993) 67 P & CR 9 at 14 per Nourse LJ.

Reaffirmation of the common law dogma

13.50   The rule in *Austerberry v Oldham Corpn* now retains few committed supporters. Commentators and law reformers have frequently urged that the law be amended to allow positive burdens to run with the land,[1] but the challenge has certainly not been taken up by the highest levels of the judiciary. A prime opportunity for modification of the common law rule arose in *Rhone v*

Stephens,[2] where, in the Court of Appeal, Nourse LJ thought it 'hard to justify' the retention of the rule and also 'hard to see why the rule applicable to negative or restrictive covenants by virtue of the doctrine of *Tulk v Moxhay* should not apply to positive covenants as well.'[3]

1   **[Para 13.150]**.
2   [1994] 2 AC 310, (1993) 67 P & CR 9. See [1994] CLJ 446 (L Tee); (1994) 110 LQR 346 (N P Gravells); [1994] Conv 477 (J Snape). See also S Gardner, [1995] CLJ 60 at 63–68.
3   Nourse LJ pointed out ((1993) 67 P & CR 9 at 14) that the Court of Appeal was itself bound by the century-old precedent of *Austerberry v Oldham Corpn*, but hinted that the House of Lords might feel able to abolish or modify it, not least because, by virtue of the standard indemnity covenant **[para 13.53]**, each successor in title of the covenantor invariably has 'the clearest possible notice of the covenant and effectively agrees to perform it, albeit not with the owner of the benefited land.'

13.51   In *Rhone v Stephens* S's predecessor covenanted with R's predecessor to keep in repair a roof which projected from S's house over the adjoining cottage now owned by R. Although invited to overrule the decision in *Austerberry v Oldham Corpn*, the House of Lords held this covenant to be unenforceable by R against S when a lack of repair later caused water leakage into R's cottage. Lord Templeman regarded the enforcement of a positive covenant as a matter which 'lies in contract.'[1] He accordingly held that to enforce a positive covenant in the circumstances of *Rhone v Stephens* against a successor in title 'would be to enforce a personal obligation against a person who has not covenanted', a conclusion contrary to more than a century of 'clear and accepted law.'[2] Lord Templeman also indicated that no assistance could be gained from section 79(1) of the Law of Property Act 1925. This provision declares that a covenant relating to the covenantor's land 'is deemed to be made by the covenantor on behalf of himself his successors in title and the persons deriving title under him or them, and ... shall have effect as if such successors or other persons were expressed.' With the concurrence of the other law lords, Lord Templeman viewed section 79(1) as having merely 'word-saving' significance and denied that it could cause the burden of positive covenants to run with the land from one freeholder to another.[3] The net effect of the ruling in *Rhone v Stephens* was thus to breathe 'new life and vigour' into the orthodox rule of *Austerberry v Oldham Corpn*,[4] the House of Lords expressly declining to indulge in any judicial legislation aimed at overturning a much criticised precedent.[5]

1   [1994] 2 AC 310 at 318B.
2   [1994] 2 AC 310 at 321A.
3   *Rhone v Stephens* [1994] 2 AC 310 at 322A–D. See also *Morrells of Oxford Ltd v Oxford United Football Club Ltd* [2001] Ch 459 at [40]. Compare a New Zealand variant of this provision which renders all covenants (whether positive or negative) binding in equity on all persons who acquire a fee simple estate in the burdened land or are occupiers for the time being of that land (Property Law Act 1952, s 64A(2) (effective 1 January 1987)).
4   See *Duke of Westminster v Birrane* [1995] QB 262 at 269F–G per Nourse LJ.
5   [1994] 2 AC 310 at 321D–G. See also *Marlton v Turner* [1998] 3 EGLR 185 at 186M; *Thamesmead Town Ltd v Allotey* (2000) 79 P & CR 557 at 558 per Peter Gibson LJ. A similar conclusion has been reached in Ontario (see *Durham Condominium Corp No 123 v Amberwood Investments Ltd* (2002) 211 DLR (4th) 1 at [50], [90]).

INDIRECT MECHANISMS OF ENFORCEMENT OF POSITIVE BURDENS

13.52   In default of any judicial relaxation of the common law rule of contractual privity, there exist several indirect (and not wholly successful) means by which it may be sought to render the burdens of positive freehold covenants binding on successors of the covenantor.[1] These devices include the following.

1   See A Prichard, (1973) 37 Conv (NS) 194.

Chains of indemnity covenants

13.53   Although the burden of a freehold covenant cannot be made to run with the covenantor's land, something faintly resembling this result can be circuitously achieved if the covenantee requires a chain of indemnity covenants to be undertaken by successive purchasers of the covenantor's land. On this basis the original covenantor remains liable on his initial covenant but, if sued for his successor's breach, may claim on the indemnity covenant to recover any damages which he himself has been required to pay.[1] The chain of indemnity covenants can extend indefinitely, each successive purchaser of the covenantor's land entering into a covenant with his predecessor to indemnify in respect of future breaches.[2] This method of transmitting the financial consequences of covenanted burdens is, however, unwieldy and hazardous. From the covenantee's viewpoint the chain of covenants is largely irrelevant since the only remedy available to him is an action in damages, whereas the remedy which he really wants is usually an injunction or order of specific performance. From the covenantor's viewpoint the chain has limited utility because it is only as strong as its weakest link. The chain is liable to be ruptured by the disappearance or insolvency of any successor of the original covenantor.

1   See e g *Radford v De Froberville* [1977] 1 WLR 1262 at 1266G; *TRW Steering Systems Ltd v North Cape Properties Ltd and Cornerstone Estates Ltd* (1995) 69 P & CR 265 at 272–274.
2   See *Rhone v Stephens* (1993) 67 P & CR 9 at 14 per Nourse LJ.

Compulsorily renewed covenants

13.54   A more successful variant of the chain of indemnity covenants lies in the practice by which the covenantor is required to promise to compel his own successor, first, to enter into a direct covenant with the covenantee (or *his* successors) in the same terms as the initial positive covenant and, second, to promise to impose the same obligation of direct covenant in turn on his successor.[1] On this basis the covenantee (and his successors) retain a direct contractual nexus with the each successive owner of the covenantor's land.

1   This device for ensuring the transmission of covenanted burdens operates more effectively in relation to registered land, where the entry of an appropriately worded 'restriction' in the covenantor's title can indirectly compel the registered proprietor to require any transferee to enter into the relevant positive covenants with a named covenantee or with his successor (see S Bright, [1988] Conv 99 at 100).

Use of long leaseholds

13.55   It has long been true that the burden of covenants (whether positive or negative) can run with *leasehold* land.[1] In consequence the disadvantages implicit in the ruling in *Austerberry v Oldham Corpn* may always be averted if a vendor, instead of transferring the freehold title in his land to a covenantor, grants him a long leasehold estate (eg for a term of 125 years or 999 years). The long leasehold term is in practice indistinguishable from an estate in fee simple, although, in almost all circumstances, the burden of the covenants binds the covenantor's successors either by virtue of 'privity of estate'[2] or by virtue of statute.[3]

1   **[Para 14.243]**.
2   **[Para 14.212]**.
3   **[Para 14.247]**.

Enlargement of leaseholds into freeholds

13.56   Positive covenants in certain long leases may be rendered enforceable against the covenantor's successors if the leasehold is enlarged into a freehold. Such conversion into a freehold estate may be achieved by several statutory means. Pursuant to section 153 of the Law of Property Act 1925, a long lease may be enlarged into a freehold if the lease was originally created for a term of at least 300 years of which no fewer than 200 years remain unexpired.[1] The enlarged estate becomes subject 'to all the same covenants ... as the term would have been subject to if it had not been so enlarged.'[2] This device may be significant in the present context since the freehold is then governed by the principle which applies to leasehold covenants, ie the principle that the burden of covenants may run with the estate. Similar results are brought about by the enfranchisement of a long lease under the Leasehold Reform Act 1967[3] and by the purchase of a freehold estate by a public sector tenant in exercise of his 'right to buy'.[4]

1   The lease must not involve the payment of any rent or money value and must not be liable to be determined by re-entry for condition broken (see LPA 1925, s 153(1)–(2)).
2   LPA 1925, s 153(8).
3   LRA 1967, s 8(3) **[para 7.334]**.
4   HA 1985, s 139(1). See generally HA 1985, Sch 6 **[para 7.352]**.

Commonhold schemes

13.57   A further circumvention of the common law rule relating to covenanted burdens is now to be found in the Commonhold and Leasehold Reform Act 2002.[1] The rules governing any registered commonhold scheme and its various participants are contained in a 'commonhold community statement'.[2] Each unit-holder takes a registered freehold estate in his or her unit and the 2002 Act explicitly provides that, on the transfer of that estate by the unit-holder, any duty imposed by the commonhold community statement 'shall affect a new unit-holder in the same way as it affected the former unit-holder.'[3] Not only do the obligations comprised within the commonhold community statement shift immediately to the transferee of the commonhold unit. The former unit-holder, having transferred his or her estate, is freed from any new liability under or by virtue of the commonhold community statement.[4] This clean cut is reinforced by the stern prohibition of any attempted disapplication or variation of the statutory principle by contrary agreement,[5] although a former unit-holder always remains subject to any liability incurred before the transfer took effect.[6] The device of commonhold ownership thus offers a 'framework in which freehold ownership of a part of a multi-occupied development will be combined with the ability to enforce positive covenants against other owners.'[7] This far-reaching effect marks an important step forward in the rationalisation of the law of covenants.

1   For a description of commonhold, see Chapter 7 [**paras 7.356–7.369**].
2   CALRA 2002, ss 14, 31.
3   CALRA 2002, s 16(1).
4   CALRA 2002, s 16(2).
5   CALRA 2002, s 16(3)(a).
6   CALRA 2002, s 16(3)(b).
7   Commonhold Proposals for Commonhold Regulations: A Consultation Paper (Lord Chancellor's Department, CP: 11/02 (October 2002)), p 12.

Reservation of a right of entry

13.58   It remains possible to reserve a right of entry in respect of freehold land (usually annexed to an 'estate rentcharge'[1]) on terms that the right of entry becomes exercisable, not merely in the event of non-payment of money, but also on non-performance of other positive covenants.[2] The right of entry, if duly created, becomes a legal interest in the land.[3] The burden of the right of entry can therefore run with the covenantor's land so as to affect his successors in title,[4] compelling them to perform the covenants or risk forfeiting their freehold estate.[5]

1   An estate rentcharge [**para 8.230**] is a rentcharge created specifically for the purpose of ensuring the enforceability of covenants affecting the land to which the rentcharge relates or of ensuring payments towards the provision of services or carrying out of maintenance or repairs or any other financial liability relating to the land charged (Rentcharges Act 1977, s 2(4)). See S Bright, [1988] Conv 99.
2   It is not necessary for the enforcement of the right of entry that the person against whom it is raised should technically be bound by the positive covenants in question: it is sufficient merely that there is, de facto, a non-performance of these covenants (see *Shiloh Spinners Ltd v Harding* [1973] AC 691 at 717C–H [**paras 8.267, 14.105**]). See also *Peabody Donation Fund v London Residuary Body* (1988) 55 P & CR 355 at 362 (referring to 'that rather rare animal, the determinable fee').
3   [**Para 8.266**]. For reference to the artificial use of rentcharges as a means of enforcing positive covenants between freeholders, see *Clem Smith Nominees Pty Ltd v Farrelly* (1980) 20 SASR 227 at 253; *Davison Properties Ltd v Manukau City Council* (1980) NZ Recent Law 225; B Hunter, (1963–66) 2 Adelaide L Rev 208.
4   The right, if annexed to a rentcharge, is not subject to the rule against perpetuities (Perpetuities and Accumulations Act 1964, s 11(1); LPA 1925, s 121).

5   See [2002] Conv 507 (Susan Bright). It is always possible, of course, that relief may be granted against forfeiture.

Doctrine of 'mutual benefit and burden'

13.59   In some circumstances the burden of a freehold covenant may pass to the covenantor's successors in title by virtue of the doctrine of 'mutual benefit and burden'. This doctrine gives expression to a 'broad principle of justice'[1] to the effect that 'he who takes the benefit must bear the burden.'[2] Thus, for example, in *Halsall v Brizell*[3] D's predecessor in title, the purchaser of a house on a building estate, had been granted a right to use the roads and sewers on that estate and had covenanted to pay a proportionate share of the cost of the maintenance of these facilities. Upjohn J held that D could not now exercise these rights without contributing appropriately to the costs of ensuring that they could be exercised.[4]

1   *Tito v Waddell (No 2)* [1977] Ch 106 at 305H per Megarry V-C.
2   See *Tito v Waddell (No 2)* [1977] Ch 106 at 292C–D per Megarry V-C, who pointed (at 289F–G) to 'the simple principle of ordinary fairness and consistency that from the earliest days most of us heard in the form "You can't have it both ways," or "You can't eat your cake and have it too," or "You can't blow hot and cold."'
3   [1957] Ch 169 at 182–183. See (1957) 73 LQR 154 (R E M); (1957) 21 Conv (NS) 160 (F R Crane); [1957] CLJ 35 (H W R Wade).
4   For other cases upholding correlative burdens of maintenance and repair, see *Hopgood v Brown* [1955] 1 WLR 213 at 226 (discharge of water into a common drainage system); *Montague v Long* (1972) 24 P & CR 240 at 247–248 (use of bridge). See also *E R Ives Investment Ltd v High* [1967] 2 QB 379 at 394B–E [**paras 9.101, 12.320, 12.369**]; *Bhullar v McArdle* (2001) 82 P & CR 481 at [51].

The expanding universe of the doctrine

13.60   The 'benefit and burden' principle seems to prescribe that any successor in title who claims the benefit of a freehold grant must also take subject to burdens associated with that grant.[1] Although the principle began as a technical rule relating to deeds,[2] its ambit today is not necessarily restricted to the benefit of rights granted by a deed.[3] The doctrine of 'benefit and burden' has the potential, however, to become dangerously expansive in scope and the courts have recognised that, if applied broadly to everyday land transactions involving covenants, would 'very likely lead to wholesale circumventions of the rule in *Austerberry v Oldham Corpn*.'[4] The view has been forcefully put that a wide application of the doctrine 'confounds the law relating to covenants affecting land', by indiscriminately making almost any covenant an indefinitely binding incumbrance on land. Despite its initial attractions, the doctrine may be 'in truth a mere maxim masquerading as a rule of law, false and misleading ... when read literally.'[5]

1   Indeed, in *Tito v Waddell (No 2)* [1977] Ch 106 at 303E, Megarry V-C held that the doctrine covers not merely successors in title but also anybody 'whose connection with the transaction

creating the benefit and burden is sufficient to show that he has some claim to the benefit whether or not he has a valid title to it.' See also (1977) 41 Conv (NS) 432 (F R Crane); E P Aughterson, [1985] Conv 12.

2   The rule maintained that if a person is named as a party to a deed, but does not personally execute this deed, he is nevertheless bound by the deed if he takes the benefit conferred by it (see *Tito v Waddell (No 2)* [1977] Ch 106 at 289D).

3   *Thamesmead Town Ltd v Allotey* (2000) 79 P & CR 557 at 564 per Peter Gibson LJ (citing in support *E R Ives Investment Ltd v High* [1967] 2 QB 379 [**paras 9.101, 12.320**]).

4   *Rhone v Stephens* (1993) 67 P & CR 9 at 15 per Nourse LJ. See, however, *Green v Lord Somerleyton* [2004] 1 P & CR 520 at [103].

5   *Government Insurance Office (NSW) v K A Reed Services Pty Ltd* [1988] VR 829 at 840–841 per Brooking J.

Constrictions of the doctrine

13.61   Largely in view of the difficulty generated by over-liberal applications of the 'benefit and burden' principle, the trend of recent case law has been towards a steady retrenchment of the doctrine.[1] The doctrine operates, if at all, on the basis of what is 'real and substantial'[2] and cannot be invoked to uphold the transmission of the burden of a positive covenant where the reciprocal benefit is 'technical or minimal'.[3] In *Rhone v Stephens*[4] it was argued that S, albeit a successor in title, was bound by the burden of a positive repairing covenant because she had enjoyed the benefit of having her roof supported by R's adjoining cottage together with the benefit of roof water drainage. The Court of Appeal considered the easement of eavesdrop to be 'if not technical … certainly minimal', and the House of Lords was even more emphatic in holding that the 'benefit and burden' doctrine does not imply that simply 'any condition can be rendered enforceable by attaching it to a right.'[5] Nor, in Lord Templeman's view, is every covenanted burden ultimately enforceable in the name of mutuality 'by depriving the covenantor's successor in title of every benefit which he enjoyed thereunder.'[6]

1   See *Durham Condominium Corp No 123 v Amberwood Investments Ltd* (2002) 211 DLR (4th) 1 at [72]. Compare, however, C J Davis, [1998] CLJ 522 for an argument that the 'benefit and burden' principle has much in common with doctrines of constructive trust and proprietary estoppel and should be more widely invoked in the interests of 'fairness' between parties. This argument, if taken to extremes, could be thought to reduce the 'benefit and burden' principle to an uncontrollable formula of 'palm tree justice'.

2   *Tito v Waddell (No 2)* [1977] Ch 106 at 305H per Megarry V-C.

3   *Rhone v Stephens* (1993) 67 P & CR 9 at 15 per Nourse LJ. See likewise *Tito v Waddell (No 2)* [1977] Ch 106 at 305G–H per Megarry V-C.

4   [1994] 2 AC 310 at 314D–E. Lord Templeman (at 322F) nevertheless expressed approval of the decision in *Halsall v Brizell* [1957] Ch 169.

5   See also *Thamesmead Town Ltd v Allotey* (2000) 79 P & CR 557 at 565 per Peter Gibson LJ.

6   [1994] 2 AC 310 at 322F–G per Lord Templeman.

Two preconditions of the 'benefit and burden' doctrine

13.62   In *Thamesmead Town Ltd v Allotey*[1] the Court of Appeal summarised Lord Templeman's reasoning as pointing to two preconditions for the enforceability of a positive covenant against the covenantor's successors in title. *First,* the condition of discharging the covenanted burden must be 'relevant to the exercise of the rights which enable the benefit to be obtained.'[2] There must be a 'correlation between the burden and the benefit which the successor has chosen to take.' The mere taking of an incidental benefit – particularly if that benefit is not conferred as of right – cannot 'enable the enforcement of a burden against a person who has not himself covenanted to undertake the particular burden.'[3] *Second*, the covenantor's successors in title must have the opportunity to elect[4] whether to take the benefit or having taken it to renounce it, even if only in theory, and thereby to escape the burden.[5] Where these preconditions are met, the 'benefit and burden' principle may fasten the burden of positive covenants upon a successor, but it simply cannot be the case that any benefit obtained by a successor, following a transfer of title to him, is sufficient to justify the enforcement against him of covenanted burdens set out in an earlier transfer.[6] It is clear that the courts have now begun to construe the rule of reciprocity extremely narrowly. The law relating to the transmission of covenanted burdens between freeholders is left in a deeply unsatisfactory state and in *Thamesmead Town Ltd v Allotey*[7] the Court of Appeal could only express a sense of urgency that the deficiencies of the law be addressed by Parliament.

1   (2000) 79 P & CR 557 at 563–564 per Peter Gibson LJ.
2   In *Rhone v Stephens* the mutual obligations of support were 'unrelated to, and independent of, the covenant to maintain the roof' ((2000) 79 P & CR 557 at 564). See also *Rhone v Stephens* [1994] 2 AC 310 at 322G–H per Lord Templeman.
3   (2000) 79 P & CR 557 at 565 (owners supposedly charged with the burden of maintenance of communal or landscaped areas on estate enjoyed no strict entitlement of access).
4   This element of choice has been consistently emphasised in the case law since *Halsall v Brizell* [1957] Ch 169 at 182 per Upjohn J. See *Tito v Waddell (No 2)* [1977] Ch 106 at 291A–D per Megarry V-C; *Thamesmead Town Ltd v Allotey* (2000) 79 P & CR 557 at 562.
5   The latter precondition makes sense, of course, only if 'the successors in title can be deprived of the benefit if they fail to assume the burden' ((2000) 79 P & CR 557 at 564). Thus, whereas in *Halsall v Brizell* [1957] Ch 169 **[para 13.59]** D could 'at least in theory' choose between enjoying the rights in respect of roads and sewerage (and paying the proportionate cost) and abandoning his rights (and saving his money), S in *Rhone v Stephens* **[para 13.50]** 'could not in theory or in practice be deprived of the benefit of the mutual rights of support if they failed to repair the roof' (see *Rhone v Stephens* [1994] 2 AC 310 at 322H–323A per Lord Templeman).
6   (2000) 79 P & CR 557 at 565.
7   (2000) 79 P & CR 557 at 566.

COVENANTS IN EQUITY

13.63   It was largely the inability of the common law to ensure straightforward enforcement of covenants against successors in title which stimulated a series of revolutionary equitable developments in the 19th century aimed at facilitating the transmission of both the benefit and the burden of at least negative covenants.[1] These developments coincided with – indeed were necessitated by – an age of unprecedented urban and industrial expansion which gave a critical significance to the rudimentary environmental protection afforded by negative covenants. The major innovations achieved by the courts of equity – mainly during the period prior to the fusion of the administration of law and equity – have since been modified and refined by legislation. But it can generally be said that whereas enforcement of a positive covenant 'lies in contract' – whence the common law's fundamental difficulty with the transmission of burdens – the enforcement of a negative covenant 'lies in property.'[2]

1   [Paras 2.52, 9.146].
2   *Rhone v Stephens* [1994] 2 AC 310 at 318A–B per Lord Templeman.

Reallocations of 'property' in land

13.64   The changes initiated by mid-19th century equitable doctrine had a remarkable impact on proprietary relations between covenantor and covenantee. In the analysis articulated by Lord Templeman in *Rhone v Stephens*,[1] the restrictive covenant deprives the covenantor (and his successors) of 'some of the rights inherent in the ownership of [otherwise] unrestricted land.'[2] The covenantor plainly retains a substantial quantum of 'property' in his own land, but the covenantee's qualified power of veto over the user of this land confirms that the covenantee has also been allocated a form of 'property' in the servient land.[3] The subtraction of a limited quantum of 'property' from the totality of the covenantor's rights[4] corresponds exactly with the accretion of a quantum of 'property' to the covenantee's rights – which is, of course, why the restrictive covenant came to be classified, in the latter's hands, as an equitable proprietary interest.[5]

1   [1994] 2 AC 310 at 317E.
2   A negative covenant 'deprives the owner of a right over property' ([1994] 2 AC 310 at 318B).
3   [Para 9.151].
4   In the view expressed in the early cases, the making of a restrictive covenant calls into existence, in relation to the covenantor's land, 'an equity attached to the property ... [which] stands on the same footing with and is completely analogous to an equitable charge on real estate created by some predecessor in title of the present owner of the land charged' (*Re Nisbet and Potts' Contract* [1905] 1 Ch 391 at 398 per Farwell J).
5   [Para 9.151]. See *Re Nisbet and Potts' Contract* [1905] 1 Ch 391 at 398 per Farwell J ('the person entitled to the benefit of the restrictive negative covenant over Blackacre has an equitable interest in Blackacre').

Definitional precision

13.65   Precisely because equitable intervention in the area of covenants was attended by such extensive proprietary significance, it was inevitable that the 'property' of the restrictive covenant should require to be demarcated with care. In order that a restrictive covenant should affect parties other than the original covenantor and covenantee, it is necessary to show that the covenant in question conforms to the special characteristics which equity came to demand of any restrictive covenant falling within its purview. The defining characteristics of the enforceable negative covenant were discussed earlier in this book when the restrictive covenant was introduced as a species of equitable proprietary interest.[1]

1   [Paras 9.154–9.170].

The character of equitable intervention

13.66　The range of equitable intervention in the law of covenants is firmly limited to covenants of a negative or restrictive variety, but, as might perhaps be expected, the keynote of equitable involvement in this area has tended, with some historic exceptions, to be characterised by a concentration on matters of *knowledge* or *intention* rather than on matters of formality or technicality.[1] If anything, recent decades have seen the courts adopt an even more sympathetic stance in relation to the definition and enforcement of restrictive covenants. This relaxation of approach may in part reflect a general change in community attitudes towards the importance of preserving the integrity and attractiveness of local environments, but may also owe something to the residual availability of a statutory jurisdiction to modify or discharge unnecessary or outdated covenants.[2]

1　**[Para 13.81]**. See *Forestview Nominees Pty Ltd v Perpetual Trustees WA Ltd* (1998) 193 CLR 154 at 169.
2　**[Para 13.127]**.

Necessary correlation of benefit and burden

13.67　The proprietary analysis of negative covenants also explains why an even sharper edge has been given to the need for the party seeking to enforce a restrictive covenant to establish both that he is entitled to the *benefit* of the covenant and that the person against whom he seeks enforcement is subject to the *burden* of the covenant.[1] If he can prove only one of these requirements, his action must fail.[2] Successful enforcement depends upon an appropriate transmission of both the benefit and the burden originally taken, respectively, by covenantee and covenantor. If he is not himself the original covenantee, the enforcer bears the onus of demonstrating that the 'property' inherent in the restrictive covenant has been engrafted on to his own estate in land (or that the benefit of the restrictive covenant has been otherwise transmitted to him). He must also prove that the burden of the restrictive covenant has been duly transmitted to his proposed defendant (ie that the subtraction of 'property' from the estate of the original covenantor still applies to the servient land in the hands of its current owner).

1　If the covenantee parts with all the dominant land, he ceases to be able to enforce the covenant except against the original covenantor (see *Chambers v Randall* [1923] 1 Ch 149 at 157–158 per Sargant J; *Formby v Barker* [1903] 2 Ch 539 at 550–551; *Miles v Easter* [1933] Ch 611 at 630–631; *Pirie v Registrar-General* (1963) 109 CLR 619 at 628).
2　See eg *J Sainsbury Plc v Enfield LBC* [1989] 1 WLR 590 at 601E–F where, although the burden of a restrictive covenant had duly passed to the covenantor's successors, there now remained no persons entitled to claim the benefit **[para 13.83]**.

TRANSMISSION OF THE BENEFIT OF A RESTRICTIVE COVENANT

13.68　In order that the benefit of a restrictive covenant should be transmitted in equity to a successor in title of the covenantee,[1] it is necessary not only that the covenant should 'touch and concern' or 'benefit' some dominant land, but also that the benefit be transmitted in one or more of the modes prescribed by equity.[2] In keeping with the historic primacy of matters of intention,[3] the means recognised by equity for the carriage of the benefit to third parties are alike concerned with the manifestation of a clear intention that the covenanted benefit should be available to non-parties to the original undertaking. The equitable modes of transmission have traditionally been defined in fairly narrow terms. Nowadays, however, there is a strong contrary tendency on the part of the courts to relax the strict requirements of equity by allowing third party access to covenanted benefits to be determined with ever closer reference to the intentions of the covenanting parties rather than in accordance with stipulated requirements of form.[4] This gradual movement away from heavy technicality has done much to simplify the law of restrictive covenants.[5]

1   See S J Bailey, [1938] CLJ 339.
2   In relation to covenants undertaken on or after 11 May 2000, the benefit may, in certain circumstances, be enforceable by a third party 'in his own right' irrespective of whether such covenants 'touch and concern' the covenantee's land (see Contracts (Rights of Third Parties) Act 1999, s 1(1)–(2) **[para 13.43]**).
3   The High Court of Australia has referred, in this context, to the characteristic 'preference of equity for intention over form' (*Forestview Nominees Pty Ltd v Perpetual Trustees WA Ltd* (1998) 193 CLR 154 at 169).
4   The modern tendency is 'to assimilate the law of covenants to the law of easements, where no formalities are required for establishing the right as appurtenant to the dominant tenement' (see H W R Wade, [1972B] CLJ 157 at 163). The focus on intention is now intensified by the potential impact of the Contracts (Rights of Third Parties) Act 1999 on the carriage of covenanted benefits (whether positive or negative) **[para 13.43]**.
5   See, however, D J Hayton, (1971) 87 LQR 539.

Modes of transmission

13.69   If the benefit of a restrictive covenant is to be transmitted in equity to a successor in title of the covenantee, it must be shown that the benefit was effectively *annexed* to the covenantee's land,[1] or was expressly *assigned* to the successor,[2] or has become enforceable by reason of the presence of a *building scheme* or *scheme of development*.[3] It is sometimes said that these equitable modes of transmission of benefit – and particularly the rules relating to annexation – are merely an elucidation of the common law rules governing the passing of the benefit of covenants.[4] It is not impossible that the benefit of a restrictive covenant may sometimes pass both at law and in equity. There are nevertheless certain circumstances where the benefit of a restrictive covenant can be claimed only under the *equitable* rules concerning transmission: these cases are essentially situations in which the common law rules are not satisfied. Thus there can be no passing of the benefit at law if, for instance, either the covenantee or his successor has merely an equitable interest in land,[5] or (possibly) if an assignee from the covenantee takes title to part only of the original dominant tenement.[6] In such circumstances, the transmission of the benefit of a restrictive covenant is thrown back upon the operation of the equitable rules.

1　**[Para 13.71]**.
2　**[Para 13.84]**.
3　**[Para 13.94]**.
4　*Rogers v Hosegood* [1900] 2 Ch 388 at 397 per Farwell J. See also *Keates v Lyon* (1869) 4 Ch App 218 at 223. Compare, however, *Forestview Nominees Pty Ltd v Perpetual Trustees WA Ltd* (1998) 193 CLR 154 at 168.
5　See *Fairclough v Marshall* (1878) 4 Ex D 37 at 44–47.
6　See *Miles v Easter* [1933] Ch 611 at 630 per Romer LJ ('at law the benefit could not be assigned in pieces. It would have to be assigned as a whole or not at all').

Combined operations of law and equity

13.70　The benefit of a restrictive covenant can pass *at law* (if the common law conditions for transmission are fulfilled), even though successful enforcement of the covenant depends ultimately on the transmission of the burden in accordance with *equitable* principles (as now supplemented by legislation).[1] In general, however, the enforcement of restrictive covenants is widely viewed as a matter allocated to the realm of equity, whereas the enforcement of positive covenants – if enforcement is feasible at all – is a matter for the common law.

1　See *Rogers v Hosegood* [1900] 2 Ch 388 at 394 per Farwell J, 404 per Collins LJ.

ANNEXATION

13.71　Annexation is the process by which the benefit of a restrictive covenant is metaphorically 'nailed' to a clearly defined area of land belonging to the covenantee, in such a way that the benefit passes with any subsequent transfer of the covenantee's interest in that land.[1] Annexation mirrors the importance attached to the element of intention by the common law rules for the passing of covenanted benefits,[2] for annexation traditionally comprises a formal recognition that both covenantor and covenantee intend that the benefit should run with the dominant land so as to avail future owners. Once that intention has been manifested in the express terms of the covenant, the benefit is notionally fastened upon, or annexed to, the covenantee's land and passes automatically to all later estate owners and occupiers of the land, without any specific assignment and entirely irrespective of their knowledge or notice.[3] In recent decades the linguistic formalism required in annexation has tended to be relaxed by the courts, with the result that it is now possible to distinguish three different types of annexation.

1　Once annexed to the servient land the benefit of the restrictive covenant clearly passes to the covenantee's successors as an incident of the dominant estate (LPA 1925, s 62(1)). The Land Registration Rules 2003 envisage that the benefit of a restrictive covenant can be entered in the property register of the dominant land (see LRR 2003, r 5(b)(ii)), but the registrar appears to have been empowered to enter only those appurtenant rights which constitute a *legal* estate (see LRR 2003, rr 33(1), 73(1), 74(1)). See *Ruoff & Roper*, para 4.003.
2　**[Para 13.34]**.
3　In the words of Collins LJ in *Rogers v Hosegood* [1900] 2 Ch 388 at 407, annexation is effective to make the benefit of a covenant run, 'not because the conscience of either party is affected,

but because the purchaser has bought something which inhered in or was annexed to the land bought.' It is for this reason, of course, that the purchaser's ignorance of the existence of the covenant does not defeat the presumption that the benefit passes on a sale of the land ([1900] 2 Ch 388 at 408). See also *Pirie v Registrar-General* (1963) 109 CLR 619 at 628.

Express annexation

13.72 Express annexation is the oldest and least controversial form of annexation. Express annexation occurs where the wording of a restrictive covenant crystallises the intention of the parties that a covenanted benefit should run with the land of the covenantee. In other words, some clear verbal formula of annexation is embedded in the very document which brings the restrictive covenant into being.

Formulae of express annexation

13.73 It is always a question of construction whether the benefit of any restrictive covenant is intended to run with a defined parcel of land. Annexation is essentially a conferment of benefit upon *land*, not upon *persons*, and it is therefore imperative that the formula of annexation should incorporate some reference to the covenantee's land. Thus the covenanted benefit is effectively annexed to a particular parcel of land if that land is sufficiently identified in the instrument containing the covenant and the covenant is expressed to be made 'for the benefit of the land' or 'for the benefit of the [owner] in his capacity of owner of a particular property.'[1] Such formulae plainly indicate an intention that the benefit of the relevant covenant should not be personal to the covenantee, but should enure to the advantage of future owners of the covenantee's land. In *Rogers v Hosegood*,[2] for instance, the Court of Appeal was able to find an effective annexation in the parties' clearly expressed 'intent that the covenant may enure to the benefit of the vendors [ie the covenantees] their successors and assigns and others claiming under them to all or any of their lands adjoining.'[3] In *Renals v Cowlishaw*,[4] however, a claim of annexation was rejected where a covenant had been made merely with the vendors, 'their heirs, executors, administrators, and assigns.'[5] It was fatal in this case that no reference had been made to the *land* which was intended to receive the benefit.[6]

1   *Osborne v Bradley* [1903] 2 Ch 446 at 450 per Farwell J. See likewise *Drake v Gray* [1936] Ch 451 at 466 per Greene LJ.

2   [1900] 2 Ch 388 at 408.

3   It was of no great importance that this formula of annexation defined the benefited tenement in only general terms **[para 9.159]**.

4   (1878) 9 Ch D 125 at 130–131 (affd (1879) 11 Ch D 866). See *Rogers v Hosegood* [1900] 2 Ch 388 at 396, 408.

5   See also *Re MCA East Ltd* [2003] 1 P & CR 118 at [24]. No annexation is achieved by the similar statutory wording contained in Conveyancing Act 1881, s 58 (see *J Sainsbury Plc v Enfield LBC* [1989] 1 WLR 590 at 601D–E **[para 13.83]**).

6   See also *Reid v Bickerstaff* [1909] 2 Ch 305 at 321; *Ives v Brown* [1919] 2 Ch 314 at 323–324; *J Sainsbury Plc v Enfield LBC* [1989] 1 WLR 590 at 598A–C; *Jamaica Mutual Life Assurance Society v Hillsborough Ltd* [1989] 1 WLR 1101 at 1105B–1106B per Lord Jauncey of Tullichettle.

Express annexation to a large dominant tenement

13.74   In the past there has been some difficulty as to whether there could be an effective annexation where a restrictive covenant purported to confer benefit upon the *whole* of an excessively large dominant tenement.[1] The court in *Re Ballard's Conveyance*[2] was plainly unwilling to sever a covenanted benefit and treat it as specific only to a portion of the alleged dominant tenement. However, it has long been clear that none of the problems raised by *Re Ballard's Conveyance* has any substance if the benefit of the relevant restrictive covenant has been annexed, not to the undifferentiated whole of a large dominant tenement, but to 'each and every part' of that tenement.[3] In the case of annexation to 'each and every part', the covenantee's successors are entitled to claim the benefit of the covenant in respect of *any* part of a large dominant tenement which is particularly adversely affected by any breach of the covenant, provided always that the successor has a proprietary interest in the portion of land in respect of which he claims the benefit.

1   These difficulties are now substantially reduced in the light of the decision of Brightman J in *Wrotham Park Estate Co Ltd v Parkside Homes Ltd* [1974] 1 WLR 798 [**paras 9.169, 13.76**].
2   [1937] Ch 473.
3   See *Marquess of Zetland v Driver* [1939] Ch 1 at 3, 10 (where the Marquess of Zetland succeeded in depriving the citizens of Redcar in Yorkshire of the facility of 'an eating-house for the consumption of fried fish and other food').

Fragmentation of the dominant tenement

13.75   Most instances of express annexation effected since *Marquess of Zetland v Driver*[1] have made clear reference to 'each and every part' of the covenantee's land or have used words of similar import. In such cases the subsequent fragmentation of the dominant tenement between a number of successors in title does not therefore prevent each of these owners from claiming the benefit in relation to his or her own parcel of land. There was always, however, a real danger that, in the absence of an express annexation to 'each and every part' of the covenantee's land, the benefit of the covenant might be lost by any successor who acquired only part of the dominant tenement[2] or who, having acquired the whole dominant tenement, subsequently sold away a portion of that land.[3] In either case it could be objected that the successor no longer retained the precise tenement to which the benefit had been annexed. For a period technical complexity seemed to threaten good sense and to elevate arid formalism as the keynote of the law.[4]

1   [1939] Ch 1.
2   *Russell v Archdale* [1964] Ch 38 at 47 per Buckley J; (1962) 78 LQR 334, 482 (R E M). See also *Re Arcade Hotel Pty Ltd* [1962] VR 274 at 277–279.
3   See *Stilwell v Blackman* [1968] Ch 508 at 519D–F (where, as in *Russell v Archdale*, the point was obiter because there was on the facts a valid assignment of the benefit of the restrictive covenant in question). See P V Baker (1968) 84 LQR 22, and compare *Re Selwyn's Conveyance* [1967] Ch 674 at 689A–B.
4   See *Griffiths v Band* (1974) 29 P & CR 243 at 246 per Goulding J (a 'somewhat muddy corner of legal history'). It is noteworthy that the technical principles adumbrated in *Russell v*

Archdale and *Stilwell v Blackman* have no counterpart in the law relating to assignment [**para 13.89**] or, for that matter, in the law of easements [**para 8.209**].

13.76   In the 1980s the Court of Appeal finally liberated the law of restrictive covenants from these strictures. In *Federated Homes Ltd v Mill Lodge Properties Ltd*[1] Brightman LJ declared that 'if the benefit of a covenant is, on a proper construction of a document, annexed to the land, prima facie it is annexed to every part thereof, unless the contrary clearly appear.'[2] This observation, although technically obiter dictum,[3] clearly reflected a more general relaxation of the rules relating to restrictive covenants,[4] although falling somewhat short of the simplification which has been achieved in other jurisdictions by the more direct means of statutory intervention.[5]

1   [1980] 1 WLR 594 at 606G. Brightman LJ had already resolved some of the present problems in *Wrotham Park Estate Co Ltd v Parkside Homes Ltd* [1974] 1 WLR 798 at 806E, holding that a successor in title – albeit that he had sold a part of the dominant tenement – might nevertheless claim the benefit if he could show that he retained 'in substance' the tenement for the benefit of which the covenant was unqualifiedly taken.

2   Brightman LJ confessed to finding the 'idea of the annexation of a covenant to the whole of the land but not to a part of it a difficult conception fully to grasp' ([1980] 1 WLR 594 at 606F). See likewise *Re Arcade Hotel Pty Ltd* [1962] VR 274 at 291 per Sholl J ('[W]hy should the benefit of the covenant not be understood to be distributed over the benefited land, in the same way as the burden over the burdened land?').

3   The observations of the Court of Appeal were criticised as inconsistent with earlier authorities (see G H Newsom (1981) 97 LQR 32 at 48–49). Compare e g *Miles v Easter* [1933] Ch 611 at 628 per Romer LJ.

4   Such is the impact of the Court of Appeal's approach in *Federated Homes* that it is rarely argued today that an express annexation has other than a fully distributive effect (see e g *J Sainsbury Plc v Enfield LBC* [1989] 1 WLR 590 at 595C–D; *Hale v Bellway Homes Ltd* [1998] EGCS 83).

5   See, for instance, Victoria's Property Law Act 1958, s 79A (effectively vindicating the dissenting judgment of Sholl J in *Re Arcade Hotel Pty Ltd* [1962] VR 274 at 287–293). Section 79A provides that, in the absence of contrary provision, annexation is presumptively 'to the whole and to each and every part' of the land capable of benefiting from the restriction. See also *Re Miscamble's Application* [1966] VR 596 at 598–601; *Gyarfas v Bray* (1989) 4 BPR 9736 at 9744–9747.

Implied annexation

13.77   Although the matter was for many years the subject of some doubt,[1] annexation of a covenanted benefit can also occur by implication of the covenant in question. Annexation, although not expressed in the deed containing the restrictive covenant, may nevertheless have been so obviously intended by the covenanting parties that to ignore it would be 'not only an injustice but a departure from common sense.'[2] On this basis annexation of the benefit of a restrictive covenant can be implied from the circumstances surrounding a deed of covenant,[3] where it is clear that the covenant had reference to a defined piece of land and that the parties themselves intended that the benefit should attach to the land rather than to the covenantee personally.[4]

1   In favour of implied annexation, see H W R Wade, [1972B] CLJ 157 at 169–170. Compare, however, D J Hayton, (1971) 87 LQR 539; P V Baker (1968) 84 LQR 22 at 30. See also E C Ryder, (1972) 36 Conv (NS) 20.

2   *Marten v Flight Refuelling Ltd* [1962] Ch 115 at 133 per Wilberforce J; (1962) 26 Conv (NS) 298 (J F Garner).

3   See *Rogers v Hosegood* [1900] 2 Ch 388 at 408 per Collins LJ; *Owen v Blathwayt* [2003] 1 P & CR 444 at [52] per Neuberger J.

4   *Shropshire CC v Edwards* (1983) 46 P & CR 270 at 277–278. See also *Robins v Berkeley Homes (Kent) Ltd* [1996] EGCS 75 per HH Judge Colyer QC. It is likely that schemes of development are ultimately instances of annexation by implication from surrounding circumstances [**para 13.94**].

13.78   The scope of implied annexation is somewhat limited. If a court is to find an intention to annex, notwithstanding the absence of express words of annexation in the relevant transfer, the required element of intention must be manifested in the transfer, as construed in the light of the surrounding circumstances 'including any necessary implication in the conveyance from those surrounding circumstances.'[1] The primary focus is, in other words, to be placed on the language of the transfer and the implications to be drawn therefrom, rather than on the surrounding circumstances together with such inferences as can be derived from the latter.[2]

1   *J Sainsbury Plc v Enfield LBC* [1989] 1 WLR 590 at 595H–596F per Morritt J. See also *Jamaica Mutual Life Assurance Society v Hillsborough Ltd* [1989] 1 WLR 1101 at 1106A–B, 1108A–C per Lord Jauncey of Tullichettle; [1991] Conv 52 (S Goulding).

2   See *Re MCA East Ltd* [2003] 1 P & CR 118 at [24]–[28] (no evidence of implied annexation).

Statutory annexation

13.79   In recent decades one of the more dramatic developments in the law of covenants is the way in which the courts have at last begun to have recourse to long dormant provisions of the Law of Property Act 1925.[1] Section 78(1) of this Act provides that

> A covenant relating to any land of the covenantee shall be deemed to be made with the covenantee and his successors in title and the persons deriving title under him or them, and shall have effect as if such successors and other persons were expressed. For the purposes of this subsection in connexion with covenants restrictive of the user of land 'successors in title' shall be deemed to include the owners and occupiers for the time being of the land of the covenantee intended to be benefited.

1   For the suggestion that LPA 1925, s 62 may also enable the benefit of a restrictive covenant to pass on a conveyance of the dominant land, see H W R Wade, [1972B] CLJ 157 at 175; D J Hayton, (1971) 87 LQR 539 at 567, 570. This view was endorsed by Deputy Judge John Mills QC at first instance in *Federated Homes Ltd v Mill Lodge Properties Ltd* (see [1980] 1 WLR 594 at 601C–D), but traditionalists have shied away from so expansive a construction (compare e g *Rogers v Hosegood* [1900] 2 Ch 388 at 398; *Shropshire CC v Edwards* (1983) 46 P & CR 270 at 278–279; *Roake v Chadha* [1984] 1 WLR 40 at 47F–G; *Kumar v Dunning* [1989] QB 193 at 198; *Briggs v McCusker* [1996] 2 EGLR 197 at 200I–J).

13.80 At first sight, section 78(1) appears to provide, in statutory language, a formula of annexation no less efficacious than the classic formula which was upheld in *Rogers v Hosegood*.[1] Yet to the obvious puzzlement of many commentators, section 78(1) was never regarded as supplying a general statutory implication of the necessary words of annexation.[2]

1 [Para 13.73].
2 For many years section 78(1) was regarded as a mere 'word-saving' provision, operating only when a valid annexation had *already* been established without reliance on the subsection, but nevertheless making it unnecessary to name the covenantee's successors in title (see D J Hayton (1971) 87 LQR 539 at 554).

The Federated Homes ruling

13.81 The spell was finally broken by the landmark decision of the Court of Appeal in *Federated Homes Ltd v Mill Lodge Properties Ltd*.[1] The restrictive covenant involved here contained a reference to 'any adjoining or adjacent property retained by' the covenantee. One parcel of the covenantee's adjoining lands was subsequently transferred to the present claimant and the question arose whether this claimant could assert the benefit of the restrictive covenant on the footing of a valid annexation.[2] The Court was of the opinion that in the present case 'the benefit of [the] covenant was annexed to the retained land, and ... this is a consequence of section 78.'[3] Brightman LJ liberated the law of restrictive covenants from generations of needless technicality by recognising that 'if the condition precedent of section 78 is satisfied – that is to say, there exists a covenant which touches and concerns the land of the covenantee – that covenant runs with the land for the benefit of his successors in title, persons deriving title under him or them and other owners and occupiers.'[4] In other words, section 78(1) supplies a statutory formula which effectively annexes covenanted benefits to the land of the covenantee provided that these covenants can genuinely be described as *relating to* that land.[5] In *Federated Homes* itself the wording of the relevant restrictive covenant was sufficient to intimate that the covenant was one 'relating to ... land of the covenantee' and in consequence, pursuant to section 78(1), the benefit was caused 'to run with the ... land and therefore to be annexed to it.'[6]

1 [1980] 1 WLR 594. See (1980) 43 MLR 445 (D J Hayton); [1980] JPL 371 (G H Newsom); (1980) 130 NLJ 531 (T Bailey).
2 There was here a valid chain of express assignments, but the Court nevertheless dealt also with the possibility of an effective annexation.
3 [1980] 1 WLR 594 at 603H. Brightman LJ rejected any narrow interpretation of section 78(1) as 'merely a statutory shorthand for reducing the length of legal documents' ([1980] 1 WLR 594 at 604D). Although this effect has often been ascribed to its companion section, section 79 (see e g *Tophams Ltd v Earl of Sefton* [1967] 1 AC 50 at 73A–C per Lord Upjohn), Brightman LJ considered section 79 to involve 'quite different considerations' and to provide no 'helpful analogy' ([1980] 1 WLR 594 at 606B).
4 [1980] 1 WLR 594 at 605B–C. Brightman LJ found support for his view of section 78 in *Smith and Snipes Hall Farm Ltd v River Douglas Catchment Board* [1949] 2 KB 500, and *Williams v Unit Construction Co Ltd* (1955) 19 Conv (NS) 262. See, however, G H Newsom (1981) 97 LQR 32 at 44–47.
5 The land which is intended to be benefited must, however, be so defined as to be easily

ascertainable (*Marquess of Zetland v Driver* [1939] Ch 1 at 7–8). This requires, in effect, that the dominant land be capable of identification by reference to the express words of the instrument containing the covenant (or by necessary implication therefrom) (see *Crest Nicholson Residential (South) Ltd v McAllister* [2004] 2 All ER 991n at [31]–[34]).

6   [1980] 1 WLR 594 at 607C. The effect of the *Federated Homes* decision was to prevent the construction of 300 homes on the servient land by successors in title of the covenantor. See also *Bridges v Harrow LBC* (1981) 260 EG 284 at 290; [1982] Conv 313 (F Webb).

Subsequent case law

13.82   Although *Federated Homes Ltd v Mill Lodge Properties Ltd* greatly simplified the law, the approach adopted by the Court of Appeal proved highly controversial.[1] It was pointed out that if section 78 of the Law of Property Act 1925 achieves an automatic annexation effect, this renders largely otiose the device of express assignment as an alternative means of transmitting the benefit of restrictive covenants.[2] The Court of Appeal was also criticised on the ground that, in determining a question of annexation, which 'is not a question of words but of intention', it seemed to attach paramount significance to statutory words which are 'neutral as to intention.'[3] The Court of Appeal has subsequently indicated, however, that section 78 is not in fact 'neutral as to intention', in that the statutory reference to 'the land of the covenantee intended to be benefited' leaves it open to the covenanting parties to avert the effects of the section by express contrary provision.[4] Thus, for instance, in *Roake v Chadha*[5] the original covenanting parties had expressly stipulated that their covenant should 'not enure for the benefit of any owner or subsequent purchaser of any part of the ... estate unless the benefit ... shall be expressly assigned.' Deputy Judge Paul Baker QC held that section 78 did not operate here so as to pass the benefit of a covenant which so clearly excluded the consequence of annexation.[6]

1   For the view that *Federated Homes* may be confined to much narrower limits than is generally supposed, see P N Todd, 'Annexation After Federated Homes' [1985] Conv 177.
2   (1980) 43 MLR 445 at 447 (D J Hayton).
3   G H Newsom (1981) 97 LQR 32 at 34. Unlike section 79(1) [**para 13.51**], section 78(1) does not expressly advert to any 'contrary intention' articulated by the covenanting parties. See also G H Newsom, (1982) 98 LQR 202.
4   *Crest Nicholson Residential (South) Ltd v McAllister* [2004] 2 All ER 991n at [43]–[44] per Chadwick LJ.
5   [1984] 1 WLR 40 at 46B–H. See [1984] Conv 68 (P N Todd).
6   When construed as a whole against the background of its explicit terms, the covenant in *Roake v Chadha* was considered not to relate to, and therefore not to be annexed to, the land of the covenantee. See, similarly, *Robins v Berkeley Homes (Kent) Ltd* [1996] EGCS 75 per HH Judge Colyer QC; *Crest Nicholson Residential (South) Ltd v McAllister* [2004] 2 All ER 991n at [41]–[42] per Chadwick LJ.

Exclusion of pre-1926 restrictive covenants

13.83   Notwithstanding the criticisms cited above, the *Federated Homes* decision has received the inferential approval of the House of Lords.[1] The ruling is now widely accepted as establishing the automatic annexation of all 'touching and concerning' covenants except where the original covenanting parties have unqualifiedly indicated that the benefit of their covenant attaches only to the whole of a now fragmented dominant tenement or was intended to be personal to the covenantee or transmissible only by express assignment.[2] The only major limitation of the liberalising influence of *Federated Homes* concerns restrictive covenants undertaken prior to 1 January 1926. Such covenants are governed, not by the wording of section 78 of the 1925 Act,[3] but by the more narrowly expressed language of the Conveyancing Act 1881.[4] In *J Sainsbury Plc v Enfield LBC*[5] Morritt J held that the latter formula contained significantly different terms which do not automatically annex the benefit of pre-1926 covenants to the covenantee's land.[6] The *Sainsbury* decision thus places an important curb on the otherwise impressive span of the *Federated Homes* approach, not least since the uninhibited view of annexation adopted in *Federated Homes* is effectively withheld from restrictive covenants affecting most buildings in England and Wales constructed before 1926.

1 See *Rhone v Stephens* [1994] 2 AC 310 at 322A–D per Lord Templeman.
2 See *Robins v Berkeley Homes (Kent) Ltd* [1996] EGCS 75 per HH Judge Colyer QC.
3 See LPA 1925, s 78(2).
4 See Conveyancing Act 1881, s 58 [**para 13.73**], pursuant to which annexation occurs only if an intention to benefit identifiable land of the covenantee can be found in (or implied from) the express words of the instrument creating the relevant restriction (see *Re MCA East Ltd* [2003] 1 P & CR 118 at [20]–[21]).
5 [1989] 1 WLR 590 at 601D–E. See [1989] Conv 358 (J E M).
6 This much had already been acknowledged in *Federated Homes Ltd v Mill Lodge Properties Ltd* [1980] 1 WLR 594 at 604H–605A per Brightman LJ.

ASSIGNMENT

13.84 A second method of transmitting the benefit of a restrictive covenant in equity is provided by express assignment of that benefit. Thus, even though a successor in title of the covenantee cannot claim to enforce the covenant on the basis of an effective annexation, he may be able to show that the benefit of the covenant was the subject of an express assignment to him.

Relation between assignment and annexation

13.85 The broad view of annexation adopted by the Court of Appeal in *Federated Homes Ltd v Mill Lodge Properties Ltd*[1] has removed much of the scope left for assignment of covenanted benefits. The device of assignment nevertheless differs from annexation in the following respects.

1 [1980] 1 WLR 594 [**para 13.81**].

Difference of focus

13.86 Annexation and assignment are directed at quite different targets. Annexation involves the attachment of benefit to *land*; assignment involves the conferment of benefit upon a *person*.

Difference of timing

13.87   Annexation and assignment occur (if at all) at different times. Annexation is effected at the date of the making of the restrictive covenant. Assignment is effected, perhaps many years later, on subsequent transfers of the dominant land.[1]

1   It is possible that a successor of the covenantee may claim the benefit of a covenant on the basis of both assignment and annexation [**para 13.75**]. Assignment and annexation are not mutually exclusive.

Difference of effect

13.88   Annexation and assignment have quite different consequences. Annexation has the effect of fastening the benefit of a restrictive covenant upon the dominant land for ever, with the result that the benefit passes automatically with that land on any subsequent transfer of title. Assignment is almost certainly efficacious only in relation to the immediate assignee, with the result that the benefit of the restrictive covenant requires to be assigned afresh with every subsequent transfer of the dominant land.[1]

1   See *Re Pinewood Estate, Farnborough* [1958] Ch 280 at 287; *Stilwell v Blackman* [1968] Ch 508 at 526C–E. For the alternative view that assignment effects a 'delayed annexation', see *Renals v Cowlishaw* (1878) 9 Ch D 125 at 130–131; *Rogers v Hosegood* [1900] 2 Ch 388 at 408; *Reid v Bickerstaff* [1909] 2 Ch 305 at 320. See also S J Bailey, [1938] CLJ 339 at 360–361; [1957] CLJ 146 (H W R Wade); P V Baker, (1968) 84 LQR 22 at 31–32; H W R Wade, [1972B] CLJ 157 at 166.

13.89   There used to be one further contrast between assignment and annexation. Before the *Federated Homes* decision it was thought that a benefit annexed to the whole of a dominant tenement could not be claimed by a successor in title of merely a portion of that land.[1] There has never been any corresponding limitation in respect of the *assignment* of covenanted benefits in equity, notwithstanding that these benefits originally related to the entirety of the dominant tenement.[2] Fragmentation of the dominant land has no prejudicial impact upon equitable assignment since such assignment is an essentially personal transaction which involves the transmission of a benefit from one person or body to another.

1   [**Para 13.75**].
2   See e g *Russell v Archdale* [1964] Ch 38 at 47–48; *Stilwell v Blackman* [1968] Ch 508 at 528G–529A (assignment, but not annexation, held effective) [**para 13.75**].

Preconditions of assignment

13.90   Assignment is usually brought about by the inclusion of an appropriately worded clause in the document of transfer executed by the covenantee in favour of his successor or executed by that successor in favour of a later owner.

Certain specific conditions must be fulfilled in order that assignment be effective, but in general terms the essential requirement is that assignor and assignee should express some agreement that the benefit shall pass to the latter.

The covenant must have been taken for the protection or benefit of land owned by the covenantee at the date of the covenant

13.91 The assignee of the benefit of a restrictive covenant must be able to show that the covenant was originally taken for the benefit or protection of land owned by the covenantee at the date of the covenant.[1] (If this were not so, the covenant would be a 'covenant in gross' and would be unenforceable except as between covenantor and covenantee.) This requirement may be satisfied by showing that the circumstances surrounding the making of the covenant clearly point to an intention to benefit the covenantee's land. In *Newton Abbott Co-operative Society Ltd v Williamson and Treadgold Ltd*,[2] for instance, Upjohn J was prepared to accept that the requirement of intended benefit was met by a covenant which precluded the covenantor from conducting trade in competition with the business carried on by the covenantee in his nearby premises. Here it was quite clear that the covenant had been taken for the protection of the covenantee's land.

1   *Miles v Easter* [1933] Ch 611 at 625 per Bennett J. See (1933) 49 LQR 483 (H A Hollond). (This case is sometimes known as *Re Union of London and Smith's Bank Ltd's Conveyance*.)
2   [1952] Ch 286 at 293–294.

The assignment must be contemporaneous with the transfer of the dominant land

13.92 If the assignee of the benefit of a restrictive covenant seeks to enforce the covenant against a successor in title to the servient land, he must show that the benefit was assigned to him contemporaneously with the transfer of the title in the dominant land[1] (ie that the assignment was part of the transaction of transfer[2]). If the benefit of a restrictive covenant becomes separated from the dominant land, it ceases to be operative.[3]

1   A transferor who disposes of the entirety of the dominant tenement renders himself unable thereafter to assign the covenanted benefit in equity (see *Chambers v Randall* [1923] 1 Ch 149 at 157–158; *Miles v Easter* [1933] Ch 611 at 632–633, 638).
2   See *Miles v Easter* [1933] Ch 611 at 632; *Newton Abbot Co-operative Society Ltd v Williamson & Treadgold Ltd* [1952] Ch 286 at 294. See also L Elphinstone, (1952) 68 LQR 353.
3   See *Miles v Easter* [1933] Ch 611 at 632, where Romer LJ explained the assignability of a covenant as being necessary to enable the covenantee to 'dispose of his property to advantage.' This protection is unnecessary if he has already managed to sell the dominant land without simultaneously assigning the benefit.

The dominant tenement must be ascertainable

13.93 In *Miles v Easter*[1] the Court of Appeal held that the land benefited by the restrictive covenant which the assignee seeks to enforce must be 'ascertainable' or 'certain'. As Romer LJ observed, the existence and location of the dominant land cannot be ascertained unless these have been 'indicated in the conveyance or have been otherwise shown with reasonable certainty.' It is clear, however, that the dominant land will be regarded as sufficiently identified if it is ascertainable with reference to extrinsic evidence.[2]

1   [1933] Ch 611 at 631.
2   See e g *Newton Abbot Co-operative Society Ltd v Williamson & Treadgold Ltd* [1952] Ch 286 at 297, where Upjohn J considered that he was entitled to 'look at the attendant circumstances to see if the land to be benefited is shown "otherwise" with reasonable certainty.' See likewise *Re Memvale Securities Ltd's Application* (1975) 233 EG 689 at 691, but compare D J Hayton, (1971) 87 LQR 539 at 568–570.

SCHEME OF DEVELOPMENT

13.94   A third method of transmitting the benefit of restrictive covenants in equity is provided by the 'scheme of development' or 'building scheme'.[1] It is not unusual for a property developer to subdivide a large area of land into plots with the intention of selling these plots seriatim to individual purchasers. In order to preserve the value of each plot and the residential amenity of the whole area, the vendor commonly extracts certain restrictive covenants from each purchaser in turn. The object of the exercise is plainly to institute a scheme of mutually enforceable restrictive covenants which will be valid not only for the initial purchasers vis à vis each other but also as between all successors in title of the original covenantors. This aim, if duly realised, has the effect of creating a 'local law' for maintaining the character of the neighbourhood for the indefinite future,[2] but this strategy can be threatened by technical difficulties rooted in the law of restrictive covenants and, in particular, in the chronology of the sales effected by the developer.

1   For the view that '"scheme of development" … is the genus; "building scheme" a species', see *Brunner v Greenslade* [1971] Ch 993 at 999F per Megarry J. Although the terms are, in practice, used fairly interchangeably, it seems preferable to subsume both concepts within the single generic term 'scheme' (see C H S Preston and G H Newsom, *Preston & Newsom's Restrictive Covenants Affecting Freehold Land* (9th edn by G L Newsom, London 1998), para 2–59 (p 46)).
2   See *Application of Fox* (1981) 2 BPR 9310 at 9317 per Wootten J.

Problems of timing

13.95   The transmission of the burden of the restrictive covenants undertaken by the original purchasers of the individual plots depends, of course, on the due protection by register entry of the incumbrances created in favour of the developer of the site.[1] The transmission of the benefit received by the developer as covenantee is, however, a matter of greater difficulty. As the developer extracts restrictive covenants from each initial purchaser, the dominant tenement to which each covenant appertains comprises the area constituted by the currently unsold plots; and this area inevitably shrinks with each successive sale. The dominant tenement in respect of any one covenant plainly cannot include the plots which have already been sold away[2] and neither annexation nor assignment can enable the developer/covenantee to distribute the benefits of later covenants to earlier purchasers.[3] Given the irreversible chronology of the transfers on sale, the enforcement of the original restrictive covenants must fairly quickly break down in the absence of some other more general mechanism for transmitting the covenanted benefits to all purchasers and their successors.

1   [**Paras 12.89, 12.314, 13.113–13.115**]. See e g *Sawyer v Starr* [1985] 2 NZLR 540 at 551. See also (1928) 78 LJ 39 (J M L).
2   See e g *Application of Magney* (1981) 2 BPR 9358 at 9359.
3   See *Re Louis and the Conveyancing Act* [1971] 1 NSWLR 164 at 178F.

The solution

13.96   The solution for the problem outlined above lies in the distinctly equitable rules which have evolved for the governance of 'schemes of development' or 'building schemes'. If such a 'scheme' is present in any given circumstances, equity takes the view that the restrictive covenants appurtenant to each and every plot of land comprised within the scheme can be enforced by all who currently own any land covered by the scheme (provided, where appropriate, that these covenants have been protected by entry in the Land Register or Register of Land Charges).[1] If a scheme of reciprocal covenants is shown to exist, it matters not whether the party seeking to enforce a relevant covenant is the original covenantee or a successor in title.[2] Within a proven building scheme or scheme of development, restrictive covenants are enforceable on a general basis, quite irrespective of the relative timing of the original covenants or of the date of purchase by either of the parties in any enforcement action. Thus earlier purchasers can claim the benefit of covenants entered into by later purchasers.[3] The chronology of covenant and purchase becomes utterly irrelevant, both conceding to the overwhelming force of an equitable principle of conscience founded upon reciprocity of obligation.[4]

1   Schemes of development can relate to both vertical and horizontal subdivisions of land (see *Hudson v Cripps* [1896] 1 Ch 265 at 269 (flats)). For 'letting schemes' where tenants from a common landlord enter into interlocking restrictive covenants governing the user of their respective premises, see further *Kelly v Battershell* [1949] 2 All ER 830; *Williams v Kiley t/a CK Supermarkets Ltd* [2003] 1 P & CR D38 at [2] ([2003] Conv 105 (P Kenny); *Re Spike and Rocca Group Ltd* (1980) 107 DLR (3d) 62 at 64–65 (tenanted units in shopping plaza).
2   The scheme of development 'crystallises' on the disposition of the first plot sold within the scheme; and all land comprised within the scheme is automatically bound by the terms of the scheme (*Brunner v Greenslade* [1971] Ch 993 at 1003F–G).
3   See *Re Louis and the Conveyancing Act* [1971] 1 NSWLR 164 at 183D–E; *Application of Magney* (1981) 2 BPR 9358 at 9359.
4   'To endeavour to pick [a building scheme] to pieces and examine the relationship between a lot in one corner and a lot in another corner is to miss the point of a building scheme' (*Application of Fox* (1981) 2 BPR 9310 at 9317 per Wootten J).

Equitable origins of the scheme of development

13.97   The scheme of development has a special equitable character which makes it quite immune from many of the normal rules governing the enforceability of restrictive covenants.[1] The authentic basis for the enforcement of schemes of development lies in a 19th century notion of community of interest.[2] As Lord Macnaghten said in *Spicer v Martin*,[3] 'community of interest necessarily ... requires and imports reciprocity of obligation.'[4] The intended mutuality of the covenants created within a scheme of development is seen as generating a 'local law' for the area covered by the scheme.[5] This mutuality attracts the protection of a jurisdiction founded upon notions of conscience, for it gives rise to 'an equity which is created by circumstances and is independent of contractual obligation.'[6] It is precisely this recognition of the 'equities arising from the reciprocity of obligations undertaken by purchasers'[7] which underlies the modern scheme of development.

1   It is, for instance, irrelevant that, on the final sale under a scheme of development, the covenantee (logically) retains no dominant tenement to which the last purchaser's covenant could be said to appertain. In this case the requirement of benefit to dominant land is simply dispensed with (see *Re Mack and the Conveyancing Act* [1975] 2 NSWLR 623 at 630D–F).

2   See *Child v Douglas* (1854) Kay 560 at 572, 69 ER 237 at 242; *Renals v Cowlishaw* (1878) 9 Ch D 125 at 129 (affd (1879) 11 Ch D 866); *Nottingham Patent Brick and Tile Co v Butler* (1885) 15 QBD 261 at 268–269 (affd (1886) 16 QBD 778); *Collins v Castle* (1887) 36 Ch D 243 at 247.

3   (1888) 14 App Cas 12 at 25.

4   See also *Re Seifeddine and Governors & Co of Hudson Bay* (1980) 108 DLR (3d) 671 at 679; *Berry v Indian Park Assn* (1999) 174 DLR (4th) 511 at 518.

5   See *Reid v Bickerstaff* [1909] 2 Ch 305 at 319 per Cozens-Hardy MR. For possibly the earliest building scheme (dating from 1853, sited in Halifax, West Yorkshire, and still 'virtually intact'), see *Re John Horsfall & Sons (Greetland) Ltd* (Unreported, Lands Tribunal, 24 July 1990).

6   *Lawrence v South County Freeholds Ltd* [1939] Ch 656 at 682 per Simonds J. See also *Re Mack and the Conveyancing Act* [1975] 2 NSWLR 623 at 629F–630C.

7   *Application of Fox* (1981) 2 BPR 9310 at 9316.

Preconditions for an enforceable scheme of development

13.98   The equitable consequence of a finding that there exists a scheme of development is, of course, a vast simplification of the difficulties which would otherwise bedevil the enforcement of the mutual covenants. In view of the potent effects of a scheme of reciprocal covenants, the courts used to impose extremely restrictive preconditions on the establishment of such schemes.

The original preconditions

13.99   The severely technical nature of the preconditions originally applied to schemes of reciprocal covenants was illustrated, in classic terms, in *Elliston v Reacher*.[1] Here Parker J described the constituent elements of the building scheme or scheme of development as requiring strict proof (1) that both the claimant and defendant derived title from one common vendor; (2) that the common vendor had laid out the estate in defined plots in advance of the sales of the plots now owned by claimant and defendant respectively; (3) that the restrictions imposed by the common vendor were intended to benefit all of the plots within the scheme; and (4) that the claimant and defendant (or their predecessors in title) purchased their respective plots on the footing that the restrictions imposed were mutually enforceable by the owners of all the plots within the scheme. It was further stipulated by the Court of Appeal in *Reid v Bickerstaff*[2] that the area to which the scheme extends must be clearly defined.

1   [1908] 2 Ch 374 at 384.
2   [1909] 2 Ch 305 at 319.

Subsequent relaxation of the requirements

13.100   So ferocious were these preconditions for a binding 'scheme of development' that between 1908 and 1965 it seems that such schemes were upheld in only two reported English cases.[1] In more recent years, however, the courts have substantially relaxed the requirements demanded of enforceable schemes by having recourse to the equitable principles which animated the recognition of schemes of development during the era before *Elliston v Reacher*.[2] As Megarry J observed in *Brunner v Greenslade*,[3] when the broader perspective of equity is adopted '[t]he major theoretical difficulties based on the law of covenant seem ... to disappear.' The courts have accordingly returned to the authentic root of equitable obligation which underlies the scheme of development.[4]

1   See *Newman v Real Estate Debenture Corpn Ltd and Flower Decorations Ltd* [1940] 1 All ER 131.
2   'I am fabricating no new equity, but merely emphasising an established equity' (see *Brunner v Greenslade* [1971] Ch 993 at 1005H per Megarry J).
3   [1971] Ch 993 at 1005G.
4   See *Application of Fox* (1981) 2 BPR 9310 at 9316.

13.101   In *Re Dolphin's Conveyance*[1] the court was presented with a scheme which was defective in terms of the traditional requirements as laid down in *Elliston v Reacher*. The scheme lacked a single common vendor, and the vendors had not, prior to the relevant sales, laid out the estate or any defined portion of it in predetermined lots. Stamp J nevertheless held that there was a valid scheme of development in existence.[2] He noted that in the present case it had been intended 'as well by the vendors as the several purchasers ... to lay down what has been referred to as a local law for the estate for the common benefit of all the several purchasers of it.'[3] There had been a clear intention that each purchaser should 'have, as against the other purchasers, in one way or another, the benefit of the restrictions to which he had made himself subject.'[4] Accordingly Stamp J upheld a scheme of development, not on the ground of any implication derived from the existence of the four points specified by Parker J in *Elliston v Reacher*, but rather on the basis of 'a wider principle.'[5] In

Stamp J's view, there arose on the present facts an 'equity' which was ultimately founded on the 'common interest and the common intention actually expressed in the conveyances themselves.'[6]

1   [1970] Ch 654. See (1970) 86 LQR 445 (P V Baker); (1970) 117 Sol Jo 798 (G H Newsom).
2   See also *Baxter v Four Oaks Properties Ltd* [1965] Ch 816 at 828B–E; *Re Mack and the Conveyancing Act* [1975] 2 NSWLR 623 at 629C–630D. Compare, however, the stubborn adherence to *Elliston v Reacher* in Canada (*Re Lakhani and Weinstein* (1981) 118 DLR (3d) 61 at 67–68; *Berry v Indian Park Assn* (1999) 174 DLR (4th) 511 at 519–521) and in New Zealand (*Sawyer v Starr* [1985] 2 NZLR 540 at 544–545).
3   For other references to the implications of a 'local law' or 'common law' designed to govern a defined area, see *Baxter v Four Oaks Properties Ltd* [1965] Ch 816 at 826B per Cross J; *Texaco Antilles Ltd v Kernochan* [1973] AC 609 at 624E per Lord Cross of Chelsea; *Re Lee's Application* (1996) 72 P & CR 439 at 444.
4   [1970] Ch 654 at 662A.
5   See also *Re Mack and the Conveyancing Act* [1975] 2 NSWLR 623 at 634E–F.
6   [1970] Ch 654 at 664C–D, citing *Nottingham Patent Brick and Tile Co v Butler* (1885) 15 QBD 261 at 268 per Wills J.

The modern requirements

13.102   By returning to its broad origins in obligations of reciprocity and conscience, the courts have been able to refashion the scheme of development so that it once more becomes a useful and workable device in the enforcement of restrictive covenants.[1] The constitutive element in a scheme of development is not 'the "one to one" relationship between lots, but the definition of an area within which the scheme operates to create a local environment by the application of a local law.'[2] Accordingly it is now generally accepted that a scheme of development arises where there is an intention that a well defined area of land should be sold off in units or plots and that, for the benefit of the common purchasers *inter se*, restrictive obligations should be imposed on the user of each portion sold.[3] Equity thus steps over the trip-wires of technicality in order to give effect to a generally shared intention to institute a regime of reciprocal liability.[4]

1   For reference to the possibility that the vigilant enforcement of a scheme of development may protect the character and amenity of a housing estate 'to a standard which planning control would lamentably have failed to achieve', see *Re Hornsby's Application* (1968) 20 P & CR 495 at 502. See also *Re Mack and the Conveyancing Act* [1975] 2 NSWLR 623 at 635A–B.
2   *Application of Fox* (1981) 2 BPR 9310 at 9318 per Wootten J.
3   There must be a sale and consequent acquisition of a number of lots. No scheme of development can arise by reason of the mere fact that, unrelated to the acquisition of land, two persons have entered into restrictive covenants. The existence of the scheme depends upon the purchase of land by persons with the knowledge that, and in reliance upon the fact that, each will obtain the protection of covenants of a like nature entered into by others (see *Application of Caroline Chisholm Village Pty Ltd* (1980) 1 BPR 9507 at 9514).
4   The fundamental test relates to the presence of a 'mutuality of covenants' (*Briggs v McCusker* [1996] 2 EGLR 197 at 199J). See also *Re Bromor Properties Ltd's Application* (1995) 70 P & CR 569 at 579–582.

13.103 Ultimately there are but two requirements which are universally insisted upon,[1] and if these two requirements are fulfilled, it may not matter greatly that the other requirements elucidated by Parker J in *Elliston v Reacher* are not satisfied.[2]

1 These two requirements were confirmed by the Privy Council in *Jamaica Mutual Life Assurance Society v Hillsborough Ltd* [1989] 1 WLR 1101 at 1106F–G per Lord Jauncey of Tullichettle. See also *Williams v Kiley t/a CK Supermarkets Ltd* [2003] 1 P & CR D38 at [2] per Carnwath LJ.
2 Thereafter the onus of proof rests on the party who wishes to rebut the existence of a scheme of development (*Application of Fox* (1981) 2 BPR 9310 at 9316).

There must be an identifiable 'scheme'

13.104 It is essential to a scheme of development that there should be a *scheme* and this in turn necessarily presupposes that it is at least possible to identify the perimeters of the land to which the scheme relates.[1] It is not, however, sufficient that the vendor/developer has defined the area. The basal notion of reciprocal benefits and burdens implies that each purchaser must also know the extent of the area covered by the scheme.[2] Moreover, if the evidence presented in favour of a scheme rests upon the terms of a series of transfers, it may be fatal to the existence of a supposed scheme that none of these transfers shows any defined area over which reciprocal obligations are to be enforceable.[3] If, however, the original outline or boundaries of the intended scheme can be demonstrated from filed plans or documents of transfer, there is no need to show that the area covered by the scheme was already subdivided into plots of uniform or predetermined size.[4]

1 *Reid v Bickerstaff* [1909] 2 Ch 305 at 319 per Cozens-Hardy MR; *Jamaica Mutual Life Assurance Society v Hillsborough Ltd* [1989] 1 WLR 1101 at 1106F per Lord Jauncey of Tullichettle. An identifiable scheme of development may even be constituted by a network of integrated and overlapping sub-schemes within the area of the scheme (*Application of Fox* (1981) 2 BPR 9310 at 9316).
2 *Emile Elias & Co Ltd v Pine Groves Ltd* [1993] 1 WLR 305 at 310H per Lord Browne-Wilkinson.
3 *Lund v Taylor* (1975) 31 P & CR 167 at 175. The absence of any 'scheme' accounted for the failure of the claims put forward in *Harlow v Hartog* (1978) 245 EG 140; *Re Crest Homes Plc's Application* (Unreported, Lands Tribunal, 12 January 1984); *Thompson v Potter* [1980] BCL 764; *Emile Elias & Co Ltd v Pine Groves Ltd* [1993] 1 WLR 305 at 311B–D.
4 *Baxter v Four Oaks Properties Ltd* [1965] Ch 816 at 828C–E; *Briggs v McCusker* [1996] 2 EGLR 197 at 199D–K; *Application of Caroline Chisholm Village Pty Ltd* (1980) 1 BPR 9507 at 9514. The absence of lotting may nevertheless make it much more difficult to prove that there was any coherent intention to create an effective 'local law' (see *Baxter v Four Oaks Properties Ltd*, supra at 828C; *Re Crest Homes Plc's Application* (Unreported, Lands Tribunal, 12 January 1984); *Re Worth's Application* (Unreported, Lands Tribunal, 12 July 1984)).

There must be a mutually perceived common intention

13.105 The essence of a scheme of development resides in a 'reciprocity of obligations.'[1] As the Privy Council indicated in *Jamaica Mutual Life Assurance*

Society v Hillsborough Ltd,[2] each purchaser from the original vendor must have accepted 'that the benefit of the covenants into which he has entered will enure to the vendor and to others deriving title from him and that he correspondingly will enjoy the benefit of covenants entered into by other purchasers of part of the land.'[3] It must, in effect, be shown that the participants in the scheme purchased on the common footing that all would be mutually bound by, and mutually entitled to enforce, a defined set of restrictions.

1   *Jamaica Mutual Life Assurance Society v Hillsborough Ltd* [1989] 1 WLR 1101 at 1106G per Lord Jauncey of Tullichettle.
2   [1989] 1 WLR 1101 at 1106G.
3   'It is one of the badges of an enforceable building scheme, creating a local law to which all owners are subject and of which all owners take the benefit, that they accept a common code of covenants' (*Emile Elias & Co Ltd v Pine Groves Ltd* [1993] 1 WLR 305 at 311D–E per Lord Browne-Wilkinson).

13.106 Evidence of the required commonality of intention underpinning a scheme of development may be found in the terms of the individual transfers to the several purchasers.[1] In the absence of such proof the court may seek out extrinsic evidence as to the circumstances of the original purchases.[2] The existence of a scheme of development may be negatived if, for instance, it cannot be shown that the estate plan was brought to the attention of any of the individual purchasers.[3] Similarly, a 'scheme' cannot be established if there is no indication that the prospective purchasers were told that the vendor was proposing to exact similar covenants, or indeed any covenants, from the purchasers of other plots[4] or if there is any substantial disparity between the covenants which govern various lots within the alleged 'scheme'.[5] The existence of a scheme of development is unlikely to be inferred from the mere entry of restrictive covenants in a charges register.[6]

1   In determining the intentions of the original and subsequent purchasers, the court will have regard to as many of the relevant instruments of conveyance as possible (see C H S Preston and G H Newsom, *Preston & Newsom's Restrictive Covenants Affecting Freehold Land* (9th edn by G L Newsom, London 1998), para 2–71 (pp 53–54)). See, however, *Re Worth's Application* (Unreported, Lands Tribunal, 12 July 1984), where the relevant conveyances failed to disclose evidence of any scheme.
2   A court would be concerned, for instance, to examine the terms of advertisements relating to the relevant sales, the nature of any representations made by the vendors to the original purchasers, and whether the latter were aware of other parallel transactions within an alleged 'scheme' (see *Jamaica Mutual Life Assurance Society v Hillsborough Ltd* [1989] 1 WLR 1101 at 1108C).
3   *Lund v Taylor* (1975) 31 P & CR 167 at 174; *Harlow v Hartog* (1978) 245 EG 140. In the case of an estate sold by auction, it may be sufficient that the covenants to be entered into by each purchaser were set out in the auction particulars. See *Lund v Taylor*, supra at 174; *Re Crest Homes Plc's Application* (Unreported, Lands Tribunal, 12 January 1984). Compare, however, *Carmichael v Ripley Finance Co Ltd* [1974] 1 NZLR 557 at 560.
4   *Lund v Taylor* (1975) 31 P & CR 167 at 174; *Jamaica Mutual Life Assurance Society v Hillsborough Ltd* [1989] 1 WLR 1101 at 1108C–D. See also *Nottingham Patent Brick and Tile Co v Butler* (1885) 15 QBD 261 at 269. The existence of a coherent common intention may also be put in doubt by any subsequent waiver of breaches or inconsistent or irregular imposition of the restrictions on other purchasers (see *Re Lakhani and Weinstein* (1981) 118 DLR (3d) 61 at 67–68).
5   It is not essential that all lots within a 'scheme' must be subject to identical covenants, since a

scheme may comprise a mixture of residential and commercial development. But in relation to lots of a similar nature (eg intended for high class development of a single dwelling on each plot), a disparity in the covenants imposed is 'a powerful indication that there was no intention to create reciprocally enforceable rights' (*Emile Elias & Co Ltd v Pine Groves Ltd* [1993] 1 WLR 305 at 311E–G per Lord Browne-Wilkinson).

6   *Re Crest Homes Plc's Application* (Unreported, Lands Tribunal, 12 January 1984).

13.107   Where a scheme of development is successfully asserted, it is, however, relatively free of many of the more technical rules relating to restrictive covenants.[1] There is, for example, no need to apply to schemes of development any 'detailed "touch and concern" requirement'.[2] An irregular distribution of benefit amongst the lots within an alleged scheme may not be fatal to the existence of a valid 'scheme'. It is unnecessary to insist that every lot under the scheme is beneficially affected by every covenant or that the precise effect of each covenant was related to nominated lots when the covenants were being drafted.[3]

1   A scheme of development cannot be enforced, however, if unity of seisin intervenes during the course of the scheme, although the scheme can revive if and when that unity once again disappears (see *Texaco Antilles Ltd v Kernochan* [1973] AC 609 at 625E–626D).
2   *Application of Fox* (1981) 2 BPR 9310 at 9317.
3   *Application of Fox* (1981) 2 BPR 9310 at 9318.

TRANSMISSION OF THE BURDEN OF A RESTRICTIVE COVENANT

13.108   The idea that the burden of a restrictive covenant may be imposed upon a non-party is a concept alien to the common law. Yet earlier chapters of this book have pointed to the way in which, in *Tulk v Moxhay*,[1] the courts of equity began to enforce freehold restrictive covenants on a par with other equitable interests in land.[2]

1   (1848) 2 Ph 774, 41 ER 1143 [**paras 2.21, 9.147**]. See S I George, '*Tulk v Moxhay* Restored – To Its Historical Context' (1990) 12 Liverpool L Rev 173. On the role of Lord Cottenham in this important decision, see also Fiona Burns, 'Lord Cottenham and the Court of Chancery', 24 Jnl of Legal History 187 at 201–203 (2003).
2   See *Re Nisbet and Potts' Contract* [1905] 1 Ch 391 at 397–398 per Farwell J.

Carriage of the burden prior to the 1925 legislation

13.109   Following *Tulk v Moxhay* and until the commencement of the 1925 property legislation, the transmission of the burden of freehold restrictive covenants was governed uniformly by the equitable doctrine of notice. Such covenants bound all third parties *except* a purchaser for value of a legal estate in the covenantor's land who took without notice of the covenant[1] and any successor of such a person (even if this successor *had* notice of the covenant[2]). The precise rationale underlying the doctrine of *Tulk v Moxhay* is susceptible of a number of interacting, but slightly variant, interpretations.[3]

1   **[Para 1.185]**. See *Luker v Dennis* (1877) 7 Ch D 227 at 235–236 per Fry J; *Haywood v Brunswick Permanent Benefit Building Society* (1881) 8 QBD 403 at 407–408 per Brett LJ; *London and South Western Railway Co v Gomm* (1882) 20 Ch D 562 at 583 per Jessel MR; *Rogers v Hosegood* [1900] 2 Ch 388 at 405 per Collins LJ; *Re Nisbet and Potts' Contract* [1906] 1 Ch 386 at 403–404 per Collins MR, 410 per Cozens-Hardy LJ; *Oceanic Village Ltd v United Attractions Ltd* [2000] Ch 234 at 249D per Neuberger J. Restrictive covenants did, however, bind an adverse occupier of the servient land, precisely because he was not a *purchaser* (see *Re Nisbet and Potts' Contract*, supra at 402–404 per Collins MR, 409–410 per Cozens-Hardy LJ **[para 3.26]**). Mere licensees of the land were likewise bound (see *Mander v Falcke* [1891] 2 Ch 554 at 557–558).

2   *Wilkes v Spooner* [1911] 2 KB 473 at 487–488 **[para 12.354]**. See also *Nottingham Patent Brick and Tile Co v Butler* (1886) 16 QBD 778 at 788.

3   See *Forestview Nominees Pty Ltd v Perpetual Trustees WA Ltd* (1998) 193 CLR 154 at 164.

The conscience-based analysis

13.110   At one level the covenantor's entry into a restrictive covenant can be seen as generating an equity in favour of the covenantee[1] which binds the conscience of any successor of the covenantor who, with notice of the outstanding covenant, 'sets up the legal estate.'[2] Equity thus intervenes, on the basis of some concept of 'privity of conscience', in order to enforce obligations of conscience against those who can fairly be regarded as 'privy' to the undertaking given by the covenantor.[3] As Lord Cottenham LC emphasised in *Tulk v Moxhay*,[4] 'no one purchasing with notice of that equity can stand in a different situation from the party from whom he purchased.' The operation of this conscience-based approach produces a result similar to that brought about by the role of conscience in matters of trust.[5] In the context of negative covenants equity imposes on the covenantor's successor, not a constructive trust, but rather a 'constructive duty', replicating the express duty of the covenantor to the covenantee, which binds the successor to perform the terms of the original covenant.[6]

1   See *Haywood v Brunswick Permanent Benefit Building Society* (1881) 8 QBD 403 at 409 per Cotton LJ ('an equity attaches to the owner of the land').

2   *Re Nisbet and Potts' Contract* [1905] 1 Ch 391 at 398 per Farwell J. See also *Doyle v Phillips (No 1)* (1997) 8 BPR 15523 at 15526 per Young J.

3   See the Australian High Court's reference to 'the equitable principle of privity of conscience' (*Forestview Nominees Pty Ltd v Perpetual Trustees WA Ltd* (1998) 193 CLR 154 at 167 **[para 9.145]**).

4   (1848) 2 Ph 774 at 778, 41 ER 1143 at 1144.

5   **[Para 10.64]**.

6   *Forestview Nominees Pty Ltd v Perpetual Trustees WA Ltd* (1998) 193 CLR 154 at 167. See E H Abbot, 'Covenants in a Lease which Run With the Land' 31 Yale LJ 127 at 131 (1921); R R Reno, 'The Enforcement of Equitable Servitudes in Land' 28 Va L Rev 951 at 973 (1942).

The unjust enrichment analysis

13.111   Although Lord Cottenham did not express it in such overt terms, the doctrine of *Tulk v Moxhay* aims at the preservation of the value of the benefited land against activities undertaken by third parties who later acquire the burdened land.[1] The doctrine seeks to avert the unjust enrichment which would otherwise be reaped by a covenantor who knew that he could always sell the servient land, even to a purchaser with actual notice of the covenant, at a higher price than he himself had paid to the covenantee.[2]

1   *Forestview Nominees Pty Ltd v Perpetual Trustees WA Ltd* (1998) 193 CLR 154 at 164 (High Court of Australia) **[para 9.152]**.
2   *Tulk v Moxhay* (1848) 2 Ph 774 at 777–778, 41 ER 1143 at 1144 **[para 9.148]**.

The proprietary analysis

13.112   A further perspective on *Tulk v Moxhay* was provided in *Rhone v Stephens*[1] by Lord Templeman. In his view equity enforces covenanted restrictions against third parties, not by any manipulation of contractual doctrine,[2] but by a conscience-driven application of a deeply proprietary analysis of the role of negative covenants. The enforcement of a negative covenant, declared Lord Templeman, 'lies in property.'[3] When, in *Tulk v Moxhay*, the covenantor's successor was restrained from developing his land in contravention of a restriction of which he was aware on purchase, equity simply prevented him 'from exercising a right which he never acquired.'[4] In terms of the original covenant, the right to build on that land without the covenantee's consent had *never* been vested in the original covenantor and could not therefore pass to any of his successors who knew of this limitation on their rights. Instead the right to control development on the servient land had at all times been reserved for the covenantee (and his successors), who consequently could claim, with justification, that they held 'property' in the servient land to the extent of the right of veto conferred by their restrictive covenant. To enforce negative covenants, said Lord Templeman in *Rhone v Stephens*,[5] 'is only to treat the land as subject to a restriction.'

1   [1994] 2 AC 310 **[para 13.50]**.
2   See *Rhone v Stephens* [1994] 2 AC 310 at 317F, where Lord Templeman made it clear that equity 'does not contradict the common law by enforcing a restrictive covenant against a successor in title of the covenantor', but merely restrains the successor from exercising rights which were never his.
3   [1994] 2 AC 310 at 318A–B per Lord Templeman.
4   See *Rhone v Stephens* [1994] 2 AC 310 at 317F–G per Lord Templeman ('the owner of Leicester Square ... never acquired the right to build without the consent of the persons ... entitled to the benefit of the covenant against building'). An equity 'completely analogous to an equitable charge on real estate' had attached to the land (see *Re Nisbet and Potts' Contract* [1905] 1 Ch 391 at 397 **[para 9.153]**).
5   [1994] 2 AC 310 at 321A.

Statutory modifications of the notice doctrine

13.113   The entitlement of the restrictive covenantee is today formalised as an equitable proprietary interest within the canon of estates and interests recognised by the Law of Property Act 1925 and the Land Registration Act 2002.[1]

The 1925 legislation (as supplemented by later statutes) also transformed the way in which the burden of a freehold restrictive covenant created after 1925 is transmitted to later owners of the servient land. In effect, the notice principle incorporated in the traditional bona fide purchaser rule has been replaced by the indirect statutory notification of rights achieved through the entry of covenanted burdens in various sorts of register.[2]

1   Not being included amongst the statutory list of entitlements which can exist at law (LPA 1925, s 1(1)–(2)), the restrictive covenant can subsist only in equity (see LPA 1925, s 1(3) [**para 2.127**]) – a result entirely consistent with its historic provenance.
2   It remains true, however, that the transmission of burden is irrelevant for the purpose of enforcement against the covenantor's successor if the benefit of the restrictive covenant has not passed to the covenantee's successor (see *J Sainsbury Plc v Enfield LBC* [1989] 1 WLR 590 at 601E–F [**para 13.67**]).

Restrictive covenants affecting a registered estate

13.114   The burden of a freehold restrictive covenant created after 1925 passes to the disponee of the covenantor's registered estate only if the covenantee entered a 'notice' in the charges register of the servient title.[1] A restrictive covenant cannot rank as any category of overriding interest.

1   LRA 2002, ss 29(1), (2)(a)(i), 32–34. The protection of the entry of a 'notice' is now available in respect of any restrictive covenant between lessor and lessee which relates to land other than the demised premises (see LRA 2002, s 33(c)) (compare, pursuant to the Land Registration Act 1925, *Oceanic Village Ltd v United Attractions Ltd* [2000] Ch 234).

Restrictive covenants affecting an unregistered estate

13.115   A restrictive covenant made between freeholders after 1925 and affecting an unregistered estate constitutes a land charge of Class D(ii) under the Land Charges Acts of 1925 and 1972.[1] The transmission of the burden of this covenant depends upon the due registration of the land charge in the Register of Land Charges against the name of the covenantor.[2] In effect, the equitable doctrine of notice generally applicable prior to 1926 has been modified in so far as the *only* recognised form of notice is now the notice brought about by registration of the land charge.

1   LCA 1925, s 10(1); LCA 1972, s 2(5) [**paras 2.186, 12.314**]. A restrictive covenant made between a lessor and a lessee in respect of the demised premises can never constitute a protectable Class D(ii) land charge (LCA 1972, s 2(5)) and is governed instead by the rules which regulate the enforcement of leasehold covenants [**para 14.309**].
2   LCA 1972, s 4(6) [**para 12.316**]. See *Wrotham Park Estate Co Ltd v Parkside Homes Ltd* [1974] 1 WLR 798 at 809A.

13.116   The equitable doctrine of notice still governs the transmission of the burden of freehold restrictive covenants created before 1926 (ie affecting most buildings which are more than 80 or so years old). The traditional equitable doctrine also applies to any post-1925 restrictive covenant – albeit contained in a lease – which relates to unregistered land not comprised within the lease.[1]

1   *Dartstone Ltd v Cleveland Petroleum Co Ltd* [1969] 1 WLR 1807 at 1812A [**para 12.372**].

REMEDIES FOR BREACH OF A RESTRICTIVE COVENANT

13.117   A range of remedies may be available to a claimant who successfully asserts both that he is entitled to the benefit of a restrictive covenant and that the defendant is subject to its burden and in breach of its terms.[1] The remedy available as of right is the award of money damages, but the real issue is usually whether the court should vindicate the right of the covenantee (or his successor) by exercising its discretion to grant more far-reaching remedies such as a negative injunction to restrain further breach or even a mandatory injunction requiring, for instance, that a construction in breach of the covenant be demolished. What is at stake is whether the court should require specific compliance with the terms of the covenant or should effectively sanction the relevant wrong by allowing the party in breach to buy his way out of further liability.[2]

1   See J Martin, 'Remedies for Breach of Restrictive Covenants' [1996] Conv 329.
2   The law relating to this vexed question mirrors very closely the exercise of remedial discretion in the analogous context of trespass **[paras 3.87–3.93]**.

Selection of remedy

13.118   The basic common law remedy for breach of covenant is, of course, an award of damages affording retrospective compensation for past wrongs.[1] In equity the range of available remedy extends to injunctive relief and, since the mid-19th century, has included the award of damages by way of compensation for prospective loss.[2] In addressing the question of remedy, modern courts have generally adopted the approach that equitable damages in respect of future or continuing breaches may be awarded in lieu of an injunction[3] if the injury to the claimant's legal rights is small, if the damage can be estimated in money and can be adequately compensated by a small money payment[4] and if it would be 'oppressive' to the defendant to grant an injunction.[5]

1   *Jaggard v Sawyer* [1995] 1 WLR 269 at 276D per Sir Thomas Bingham MR.
2   See Chancery Amendment Act 1858, s 2 ('Lord Cairns's Act') **[para 3.87]**.
3   Supreme Court Act 1981, s 50. See J A Jolowicz, [1975] CLJ 224.
4   These days the value of money awards made in lieu of injunctive relief may not seem quite so small (see eg the award of £375,000 in *Amec Developments Ltd v Jury's Hotel Management (UK) Ltd* (2001) 82 P & CR 286 at [36] in respect of a hotel built four metres over a building line in breach of covenant).
5   This classic statement of the appropriate conditions for the award of damages derives from the judgment of A L Smith LJ in *Shelfer v City of London Electric Lighting Co* [1895] 1 Ch 287 at 322–323 and has been described as a 'good working rule' (*Jaggard v Sawyer* [1995] 1 WLR 269 at 278B per Sir Thomas Bingham MR, 287G–H per Millett LJ). See also *Kelly v Barrett* [1924] 2 Ch 379 at 396–397; *Federated Homes Ltd v Mill Lodge Properties Ltd* [1980] 1 WLR 594 at 607E–F; *Arbutus Park Estates Ltd v Fuller* (1977) 74 DLR (3d) 257 at 263–265.

The realities of the situation

13.119   In the present context it has been emphasised that the relevant test is one of 'oppression' (judged at the date of an application for injunctive relief) and not one which turns on a 'general balance of convenience.'[1] The court must respond to 'the reality with which it is confronted'[2] and this may mean that certain sorts of fait accompli are effectively irreversible. In *Wrotham Park Estate Co Ltd v Parkside Homes Ltd*,[3] for example, Brightman J declined to grant a mandatory injunction for the demolition of houses which had been built in breach of a restrictive covenant and which were 'now the homes of people.'[4] Brightman J warned, however, that developers who act in breach of restrictions 'may be in for a rude awakening' and he awarded money compensation in the sum of what 'might reasonably have been demanded ... as a quid pro quo for relaxing the covenant.'[5]

1   *Jaggard v Sawyer* [1995] 1 WLR 269 at 283B per Sir Thomas Bingham MR. The criterion of 'oppression' to the defendant has been described as the 'essential prerequisite' of an award of damages (*Gafford v Graham* (1998) 77 P & CR 73 at 86 per Nourse LJ).
2   *Jaggard v Sawyer* [1995] 1 WLR 269 at 283C per Sir Thomas Bingham MR.
3   [1974] 1 WLR 798 at 811A.
4   [1974] 1 WLR 798 at 811B–C ('an unpardonable waste of much needed houses to direct that they now be pulled down'). See *Attorney-General v Blake* [2001] 1 AC 268 at 282H–283A per Lord Nicholls of Birkenhead (attributing the refusal of mandatory relief in *Wrotham Park* to 'social and economic reasons').
5   On this basis damages were assessed as 5 per cent of the developer's anticipated profit.

No absolute protection for proprietary rights

13.120   In recent years the courts have reinforced the point that injunctive relief is not an automatic response to breaches of restrictive covenants.[1] Damages (inclusive of a 'once and for all' award in respect of future wrongs[2]) may often represent the more appropriate remedy even though the withholding of injunctive relief causes the court, in effect, to 'license future wrongs.'[3] In *Jaggard v Sawyer*,[4] for example, the Court of Appeal declined to issue an injunction to enforce a restrictive covenant against building development. Millett LJ pointed out that '[m]any proprietary rights cannot be protected at all by the common law', with the result that the aggrieved owner 'must submit to unlawful interference with his rights and be content with damages.'[5] The award of injunctive relief is ultimately discretionary and, if such relief is refused, the defendant, even though he 'may have no right to act in the manner complained of ... cannot be prevented from doing so.'[6] In *Jaggard v Sawyer* the Court of Appeal awarded damages measured on the basis of the amount which the covenantee might reasonably have expected to receive for the release of the covenant in question.[7] The Court rejected the suggestion that such a solution was effectively an 'expropriation' of the covenantee,[8] taking the view that a 'once and for all' award of damages for future wrongs and continuing breaches of covenant could fairly reflect the value of the rights which had been lost.[9]

1   See eg *Gafford v Graham* (1998) 77 P & CR 73 at 85–86. See generally Craig Rotherham, *Proprietary Remedies in Context* (Hart Publishing 2002), p 343.
2   *Jaggard v Sawyer* [1995] 1 WLR 269 at 281H–282A per Sir Thomas Bingham MR, 286A, 292C–D per Millett LJ.
3   *Jaggard v Sawyer* [1995] 1 WLR 269 at 285H per Millett LJ.
4   [1995] 1 WLR 269. See [1995] Conv 141 (T Ingman).

5   [1995] 1 WLR 269 at 287C.

6   [1995] 1 WLR 269 at 286A.

7   [1995] 1 WLR 269 at 282E per Sir Thomas Bingham MR, 292C–D per Millett LJ. See *Gafford
     v Graham* (1998) 77 P & CR 73 at 86 per Nourse LJ ('A welcome consequence of *Jaggard v
     Sawyer* is that it has firmly established the *Wrotham Park* basis of assessing damages as the
     basis appropriate to cases such as this'). See also *Oceanic Village Ltd v United Attractions Ltd*
     [2000] Ch 234 at 257F–G per Neuberger J.

8   '[R]eferences to the "expropriation" of the plaintiff's property are somewhat overdone' ([1995]
     1 WLR 269 at 287B per Millett LJ).

9   [1995] 1 WLR 269 at 286A per Millett LJ. It may tip the balance in favour of a monetary
     award that the claimant has already indicated a willingness to accept a cash sum in settlement
     (see *Gafford v Graham* (1998) 77 P & CR 73 at 84 per Nourse LJ).

13.121   Although this approach remains controversial (in that it allows legal
wrongs to go unabated[1]), it appears increasingly that damages for breach of
restrictive covenants are being awarded on the '*Wrotham Park* basis'[2] as an
approximation of likely release settlements.[3] Although the courts have not
overtly allowed money awards to serve the restitutionary purpose of stripping
the wrongdoer of any gains made by means of wrongful conduct,[4] there is clear
evidence of a new willingness to allow damages for breach of covenant to be
measured, in suitable cases, by the benefit reaped by the wrongdoer in consequence of his breach.[5]

1   See e g *Anchor Brewhouse Developments Ltd v Berkley House (Docklands Developments) Ltd*
     (1987) 38 BLR 82 at 101 per Scott J [**para 3.91**].

2   See *Jaggard v Sawyer* [1995] 1 WLR 269 at 282E per Sir Thomas Bingham MR.

3   See e g *Amec Developments Ltd v Jury's Hotel Management (UK) Ltd* (2001) 82 P & CR 286
     at [11].

4   In *Jaggard v Sawyer* [1995] 1 WLR 269 at 281G–282E Sir Thomas Bingham MR explicitly
     denied that the *Wrotham Park* measure of damages is, strictly speaking, restitutionary.

5   See e g *Attorney-General v Blake* [2001] 1 AC 268 at 283G–H, where Lord Nicholls of
     Birkenhead preferred the approach adopted in *Wrotham Park Estate Co Ltd v Parkside
     Homes Ltd* [1974] 1 WLR 798 [**para 13.76**] to that of the Court of Appeal in *Surrey CC v
     Bredero Homes Ltd* [1993] 1 WLR 1361 at 1364F–G, 1368G per Dillon LJ, 1370A–H per
     Steyn LJ. Compare also (1993) 109 LQR 518 (P B H Birks). In *Bredero Homes* the covenantee
     was confined to a nominal damages award of £2 against a developer which had erected 77
     houses in breach of covenant.

A new social ethic of 'reasonableness between neighbours'

13.122   The contemporary prevalence of monetary pre-estimates of the damage caused by breach of restrictive covenants is associated with a highly
relativist view of relationships between neighbours.[1] There is, in modern
English law, a growing sense that the dealings of neighbours require to be
regulated by a large measure of 'give and take.'[2] Some have even pointed to the
emergence of a 'law of neighbourhood' which is 'closely linked with the law of
property.'[3] The outcome has been the fresh articulation of an ethos of 'good
neighbourliness'[4] or 'reasonableness between neighbours.'[5]

1   See Gray and Gray, 'The rhetoric of realty', in J Getzler (ed), *Rationalizing Property, Equity
     and Trusts: Essays in Honour of Edward Burn* (Butterworths 2003), pp 257–259.

2   See e g *Hunter v Canary Wharf Ltd* [1997] AC 655 at 711F per Lord Cooke of Thorndon;

Earle and Earle v East Riding of Yorkshire Council [1999] RVR 200 at 218; *Southwark LBC v Mills* [2001] 1 AC 1 at 15G–H per Lord Hoffmann, 20G per Lord Millett. See also *Wildtree Hotels Ltd v Harrow LBC* [2001] 2 AC 1 at 10A–B per Lord Hoffmann.

3   *Hunter v Canary Wharf Ltd* [1997] AC 655 at 723D per Lord Hope of Craighead.

4   *Southwark LBC v Mills* [2001] 1 AC 1 at 20D–E per Lord Millett.

5   *Delaware Mansions Ltd v Westminster CC* [2002] 1 AC 321 at [29], [34] per Lord Cooke of Thorndon; *Abbahall Ltd v Smee* [2003] 1 WLR 1472 at [36]–[38] per Munby J.

13.123   Almost as a matter of definition,[1] restrictive covenants involve the relationships of adjacent owners, with the consequence that the new emphasis on social co-operation between neighbours points away from the absolutist remedy of the injunction in cases of breach of covenant.[2] Consistently with the burgeoning theme of social accommodation, the courts have begun to make it clear that, as between neighbouring owners, proprietary and possessory rights are not always capable of vindication in an absolute form. Instead – quite outside the normal market process – the courts have started to engineer the socially optimal redistribution of various kinds of utility in land between parties who must somehow be enabled to continue to live in co-operative proximity.[3] It seems that this judicial objective is not to be impeded by the fact that the provision of a mere money remedy for breach effectively allows a wrongdoing neighbour to purchase immunity from further enforcement of proprietary rights. Today there are, in truth, relatively severe curbs on the ability of an owner, when troubled by his interactions with neighbours, to assert the sanctity of contracted obligations. In the interdependency of neighbourhood, property rules are apt to be commuted into liability rules.[4] But this merely reflects the wider reality that the law of neighbourhood is gradually being infiltrated by an overriding proviso of reasonableness.

1   [Para 9.161].

2   As Carol Rose has pointed out, 'damage remedies have received excellent press in law-and-economic circles, in part because they suppress unneighbourly behavior ... [where] an owner hold outs for no reason except to make claims on another' (see Rose, 'Property and Expropriation: Themes and Variations in American Law' (2000) Utah L Rev 1 at 10).

3   The subtlety of remedial choice 'permits the courts to vindicate rights but at the same time control their socially harmful exploitation' (Robert J Sharpe, *Injunctions and Specific Performance* (Canada Law Book Co, Toronto 1983), p 216 [433]).

4   See Guido Calabresi and A Douglas Melamed, 'Property Rules, Liability Rules, and Inalienability: One View of the Cathedral' 85 Harv L Rev 1089 (1971–72).

Injunctions

13.124   Although courts are today much more inclined than formerly to award monetary remedies for breaches of restrictive covenant, it is clear that some cases of breach call imperatively for the award of an injunction.[1] Thus, where a defendant has acted in 'blatant and calculated disregard' of the claimant's rights,[2] the court will not enable him to neutralise these rights on payment of a cash sum, but will grant a mandatory order requiring the reversal of the breach. In *Wakeham v Wood*,[3] for example, the defendant had acted in 'flagrant disregard of the plaintiff's rights' by constructing, in breach of covenant, a building which obstructed the plaintiff's view of the sea. The Court of Appeal was not inclined to allow the defendant to 'buy his way out of his wrong' and granted a mandatory order requiring the demolition of the obstruction.[4]

1   See e g *Walker v Arkay Caterers Ltd* [1997] EGCS 107 (injunction to restrain use as restaurant).
2   *Jaggard v Sawyer* [1995] 1 WLR 269 at 283C–D per Sir Thomas Bingham MR.
3   (1982) 43 P & CR 40.
4   (1982) 43 P & CR 40 at 45–47. See also *Lund v Taylor* (1974) 230 EG 363 at 367. A mandatory injunction may be refused if the claimant stood by while the work in breach progressed (see *Clothier v Snell* (1966) 198 EG 27 at 28).

Statutory compensation

13.125   In limited categories of circumstance the courts cannot use the award of either damages or an injunction in order to enforce private covenant-based rights against certain statutory bodies. This consequence occurs where the legislature has entrusted a statutory body with functions to be discharged in the public interest (e g in connection with the running of the health service). In such cases private restrictions affecting land held by the statutory body (and which would otherwise impede its functions) are rendered unenforceable where the legislature has empowered the body in question to acquire and to hold land and has provided an exclusive remedy of statutory compensation for the loss of the covenantee's rights.[1] Privately bargained restrictive covenants are not therefore allowed to stand in the way of the statutory purpose for which the land is held.

1   *Brown v Heathlands Mental Health NHS Trust* [1996] 1 All ER 133 at 136J–137a; *Cadogan v Royal Brompton Hospital National Health Trust* [1996] 2 EGLR 115 at 116D; *Greenwich Healthcare National Health Service Trust v London and Quadrant Housing Trust* (1999) 77 P & CR 133 at 137–138. See *Kirby v School Board for Harrogate* [1896] 1 Ch 437 at 449, 455.

Discharge or modification

13.126   It is always open to the defendant in proceedings brought for the enforcement of a restrictive covenant to request leave to apply to the Lands Tribunal for discharge or modification of the covenant.[1]

1   LPA 1925, s 84(9) [**para 13.127**]. See e g *Robins v Berkeley Homes (Kent) Ltd* [1996] EGCS 75; *Luckies v Simons* [2003] 2 P & CR 397 at [41].

DISCHARGE OR MODIFICATION OF RESTRICTIVE COVENANTS

13.127   Like all 'property' in land,[1] the benefit of a restrictive covenant cannot be regarded as 'absolute and inviolable for all time.'[2] Restrictive covenants place a long-term fetter upon the affected land,[3] but in some cases it is clearly undesirable that the inhibition upon land use should continue indefinitely.[4] There may arise changes of circumstance where it becomes preferable, in the interests of general social utility, that the constraints imposed by a particular covenant should be abrogated or otherwise modified. Narrowly conceived private interests cannot be allowed to frustrate proposed developments which promise a distinct benefit to the entire community or to some significant section of it.

1   [**Para 2.12**].
2   *Jaggard v Sawyer* [1995] 1 WLR 269 at 283F per Sir Thomas Bingham MR. See also G O Robinson, 'Explaining Contingent Rights: The Puzzle of "Obsolete" Covenants' 91 Col L Rev 546 (1991).
3   In committing themselves to restrictive covenants, parties tend to undertake obligations over an extended time-frame without any proviso for cesser in the event of later changes of circumstance.
4   Restrictive covenants are free from the strictures of any rule against perpetuity (*Mackenzie v Childers* (1889) 43 Ch D 265 at 279) and the court has no inherent jurisdiction to declare restrictive covenants redundant (see *Westminster CC v Duke of Westminster* [1991] 4 All ER 138 at 142j per Harman J).

13.128 In rare instances a restrictive covenant may cease to be enforceable (on grounds of estoppel or implied waiver) where the covenantee or his successors can be shown to have acted over a prolonged period in disregard of patent breaches of the covenant[1] or if a covenant, by reason of supervening changes in the neighbourhood, has become self-evidently nugatory or valueless.[2] The problem of obsolescence is, however, addressed more generally by section 84 of the Law of Property Act 1925,[3] which vests in the Lands Tribunal a discretionary power to discharge or modify restrictive covenants (with or without compensation[4]) on any of a number of narrowly specified grounds.[5] It is inferable that the modern relaxation of many of the threshold requirements affecting the recognition of enforceable covenants[6] owes much to the increasingly wide scope of the Lands Tribunal's statutory power to deal with outdated or inappropriate land obligations. Section 84 has accordingly become an arena where those who apply for the removal or variation of restrictions (usually for reasons of private financial gain[7]) engage in mortal combat with objectors who allege, characteristically, that threatened developments will degrade their neighbourhood.[8]

1   *Hepworth v Pickles* [1900] 1 Ch 108 at 110 per Farwell J; *Chatsworth Estates Co v Fewell* [1931] 1 Ch 224 at 230–231 per Farwell J. See also *Gaskin v Balls* (1879) 13 Ch D 324 at 328–329; *Shaw v Applegate* [1977] 1 WLR 970 at 979B, 981B (refusal of injunction). It may, in particular, be inequitable to single out one covenantor for strict enforcement when comparable covenants given by others have long lain in abeyance (see *Robins v Berkeley Homes (Kent) Ltd* [1996] EGCS 75 per HH Judge Colyer QC).
2   *Chatsworth Estates Co v Fewell* [1931] 1 Ch 224 at 230. A heavy burden attaches to showing that there has been a relevant change in the character of the neighbourhood (*Robins v Berkeley Homes (Kent) Ltd* [1996] EGCS 75).
3   Section 84 was significantly amended and extended by LPA 1969, s 28. On section 84, see generally E H Bodkin, (1943) 7 Conv (NS) 17; N Dawson, (1978) 29 NILQ 223; P Polden, (1986) 49 MLR 195.
4   Uncompensated interference with existing covenant-based rights may be challengeable as a violation of the European Convention guarantee of 'peaceful enjoyment' of possessions (ECHR Protocol No 1, Art 1 [**para 2.29**]).

5   LPA 1925, s 84(1). See Lands Tribunal Rules 1996 (SI 1996/1022), as amended by SI 1998/22, SI 2003/2945. There is appeal to the Court of Appeal on points of law (Lands Tribunal Act 1949, s 3).
6   **[Paras 13.81, 13.100]**.
7   See *Re Kennet Properties' Application* (1996) 72 P & CR 353 at 363.
8   It is not unknown for objectors to have breached the covenants which they purport to defend – a factor which is unlikely to escape the attention of the Lands Tribunal (see e g *Re Kennet Properties' Application* (1996) 72 P & CR 353 at 362).

Scope of section 84 of the Law of Property Act 1925

13.129   The discharge and modification jurisdiction conferred by section 84 relates only to restrictive (ie negative) covenants[1] and is of principal application to freehold rather than leasehold obligations.[2] In general, section 84 applies to restrictive covenants irrespective of their date of creation, but never covers restrictions imposed on the occasion of a disposition made gratuitously (or for a nominal consideration) for public purposes.[3] The powers available under section 84 may be invoked regardless of whether the dominant and servient lands are still held by the parties to the covenant or have passed to their respective successors.[4] Section 84 applies to both bilateral covenants between neighbours and the multilateral covenants characteristic of a typical 'scheme of development',[5] although in the latter context there is 'a greater presumption that restrictions imposed ... will be upheld and therefore a greater burden of proof on the applicant to show that the requirements of [the statute] are met.'[6] Jurisdiction is reserved for the *court* to declare, in any case of doubt, whether given land is affected by a restrictive covenant and, if so, by whom it is enforceable and on what terms.[7]

1   *Bedwell Park Quarry Co Ltd v Hertfordshire CC* [1993] JPL 349 at 352 per Purchas LJ and Sir Christopher Slade.
2   Leasehold restrictive covenants come within section 84 only in the case of a lease created for a term of more than 40 years and where at least 25 years of that term have already expired by the date of application for discharge or modification (LPA 1925, s 84(12)). Mining leases are excluded from section 84 and the jurisdiction is, in general, less freely exercised in respect of leasehold (as distinct from freehold) covenants (see e g *Ridley v Taylor* [1965] 1 WLR 611 at 617H–618A per Harman LJ).
3   LPA 1925, s 84(7).
4   *Ridley v Taylor* [1965] 1 WLR 611 at 618A–B. The Lands Tribunal cannot order a discharge or modification which is merely personal to the applicant and does not affect successors (see *Re Ghey and Galton's Application* [1957] 2 QB 650 at 660–661 per Lord Evershed MR; *Re Willis' Application* (1998) 76 P & CR 97 at 115).
5   **[Para 13.94]**.
6   *Re Lee's Application* (1996) 72 P & CR 439 at 444. See also *Re Bromor Properties Ltd's Application* (1995) 70 P & CR 569 at 583.
7   LPA 1925, s 84(2).

GROUNDS OF DISCHARGE OR MODIFICATION

13.130   The Lands Tribunal's discretion under section 84 is exercised with extreme caution,[1] not least because, in many instances, a decision to discharge or modify privately bargained restrictive covenants comes close to enabling a person 'to expropriate the private rights of another purely for his own profit.'[2] In so far as the Lands Tribunal has a significant power to 'interfere with property rights', it is clear that 'the public interest is material to the exercise of the Tribunal's discretion.'[3] The Tribunal is therefore directed to take into account the local authority's development plan and any declared or ascertainable pattern in the grant or refusal of planning permissions in the relevant areas,[4] together with any other material circumstances.[5] Discharge or modification of a restrictive covenant may be ordered on any of the following grounds.[6]

1   In 1991 the Law Commission reported that, in its survey of a decade of case law (1981 to 1990), 14 out of 32 applications to the Lands Tribunal (ie 44 per cent) had met with an outright rejection of any discharge or modification of the challenged covenants (*Transfer of Land: Obsolete Restrictive Covenants* (Law Com No 201, July 1991), para 3.19). A later survey covering 42 cases during the period 1991 to 1998 suggested that the resistance of the Lands Tribunal had (if anything) hardened, with only six orders for discharge (ie 14 per cent of the field) and a complete rejection of discharge or modification in 20 cases (ie 48 per cent) (see Gray and Gray, 'The Future of Real Burdens in Scots Law' (1999) 3 Edinburgh Law Rev 229 at 233).
2   *Re Henderson* [1940] Ch 835 at 846 per Farwell J ('I do not think the section was designed with a view to benefiting one private individual at the expense of another private individual'). See also *Re Truman, Hanbury, Buxton & Co Ltd's Application* [1956] 1 QB 261 at 270–271 per Romer LJ; *Durack v De Winton* (1998) 9 BPR 16403 at 16443.
3   *Re Kennet Properties' Application* (1996) 72 P & CR 353 at 363. In view of the dangers of mercenary holdout by dominant owners, it has been emphasised that the object of restrictive covenants is 'to preserve the value and/or amenity of the land to be benefited and ... not to provide a source of income from fees from licences' (*Robins v Berkeley Homes (Kent) Ltd* [1996] EGCS 75 per HH Judge Colyer QC). The European Human Rights Commission has likewise insisted that landowners should not be facilitated in 'securing large sums in return for a waiver of obsolete restrictions' (*S v United Kingdom* (1984) 41 DR 226 at 233).
4   See eg *Re Page's Application* (1996) 71 P & CR 440 at 450.
5   LPA 1925, s 84(1B).
6   The Lands Tribunal has drawn attention to the disadvantages (in terms of imprecise or 'grapeshot' argument) which flow from the current practice of pleading a multiplicity of grounds under section 84 (*Re Kennet Properties' Application* (1996) 72 P & CR 353 at 357). See also *McMorris v Brown* [1999] 1 AC 142 at 146G–147B per Lord Cooke of Thorndon ('omnibus application').

Obsoleteness (section 84(1)(a))

13.131   The Lands Tribunal has power to discharge or modify a restrictive covenant where, 'by reason of changes in the character of the property concerned or the neighbourhood' or otherwise, the restriction 'ought to be deemed obsolete.'[1] The test of obsoleteness is whether the original object of the restriction can still be achieved[2] and there is inevitably some difficulty in attempting to demonstrate that a restrictive covenant entered into only recently has already become 'obsolete'.[3] Moreover, a restriction which tends to preserve the quality of a particular environment is not to be deemed obsolete merely because it 'frustrates proposals which, were it not for the covenant, would seem entirely reasonable.'[4] Accordingly the Lands Tribunal has not shown itself to be particularly inclined to discharge restrictions which continue to serve a valid environmental purpose in protecting local amenity,[5] but has been prepared to strike down restrictions whose utility has been utterly submerged by supervening events. In *Re Quaffers Ltd's Application*,[6] for instance, the Lands Tribunal discharged a restrictive covenant (prohibiting the sale of alcohol and other trade or business user) on the ground that, since the creation of the covenant, the immediate environment – once an area of open land – had been devastated through being enveloped by dual carriageway roads including the M62.[7]

1   A restriction cannot normally be rendered obsolete by a *voluntary* change in the applicant's circumstances (see *Re Bewick's Application* (1997) 73 P & CR 240 at 248–249).
2   See *Re Truman, Hanbury, Buxton & Co Ltd's Application* [1956] 1 QB 261 at 272; *Driscoll v Church Commissioners* [1957] 1 QB 330 at 341–342, 349; *Abbey Homesteads (Developments) Ltd v Northamptonshire CC* (1987) 53 P & CR 1 at 12, (1992) 64 P & CR 377 at 381; *Re Martins' Application* (1988) 57 P & CR 119 at 125.
3   See *Balchin v Buckle* (1982) 126 Sol Jo 412.
4   *McMorris v Brown* [1999] 1 AC 142 at 147A per Lord Cooke of Thorndon.
5   See e g *Re John Horsfall & Sons (Greetland) Ltd* (Unreported, Lands Tribunal, 24 July 1990) (covenant protecting residential character had ensured 'good state of preservation' of estate for 140 years); *Re Hoyle* (Unreported, Lands Tribunal, 9 December 1992) (restrictive covenants dated 1870 underpinning conservation area in Bristol); *Re Hopcraft's Application* (1993) 66 P & CR 475 at 483 (planning agreement dated 1980 still protected visual amenity of pleasant tract of open countryside in Hampshire); *Re North's Application* (1998) 75 P & CR 117 at 121 (covenants preserving 'attractive semi-rural character'); *Re Azfar's Application* [2002] 1 P & CR 215 at [41] (covenant of 1864 still provided 'real protection'). Compare *Re Wards Construction (Medway) Ltd's Application* (1994) 67 P & CR 379 at 389–390 (area not one of 'rural character', but 'an eyesore').
6   (1988) 56 P & CR 142 at 152.
7   See also *Re Cox's Application* (1985) 51 P & CR 335 at 344 (restriction to occupation by 'domestic staff' obsolete); *Re Kennet Properties' Application* (1996) 72 P & CR 353 at 361 (covenant to protect unimpeded view rendered obsolete by neighbouring housing development); *Re Nichols' Application* [1997] 1 EGLR 144 at 147G–J, 148B (house on dominant land now demolished and replaced by nursing home).

Obstruction of reasonable user of the land (section 84(1)(aa), (1A))

13.132   The Lands Tribunal may likewise intervene where the continued existence of a restriction 'would impede some reasonable user of the land for public or private purposes'[1] and the restrictive covenant no longer secures 'any practical benefits of substantial value or advantage'[2] to the relevant dominant owners or has become 'contrary to the public interest.'[3] In order to establish this ground it must also be shown that money would be 'an adequate compensation for the loss or disadvantage (if any)' which the dominant owner would suffer from the discharge or modification. The introduction of this composite ground in 1970 was clearly intended to open up the Tribunal's discretion to suppress those restrictions on land use whose utility is largely spent and whose removal is conveniently compensable by money.[4]

1   LPA 1925, s 84(1)(aa).
2   The phrase 'substantial value or advantage' has a significance which goes far beyond a purely pecuniary criterion (see *Re Bass Ltd's Application* (1973) 26 P & CR 156 at 162).
3   LPA 1925, s 84(1A). See *Stannard v Issa* [1987] AC 175 at 187A–B.

4   See Law Commission, *Report on Restrictive Covenants* (Law Com No 11, 1967), p 23; *Re Kennet Properties' Application* (1996) 72 P & CR 353 at 357; *McMorris v Brown* [1999] 1 AC 142 at 146D–E per Lord Cooke of Thorndon.

Surviving practical benefit

13.133   Whereas the 'touchstone' of the obsolescence ground in section 84(1)(a) relates to the original purpose of the relevant restriction and whether it is now out of date, the focus of section 84(1)(aa) falls on the nature of the contemporary benefits conferred by the restriction.[1] The Lands Tribunal is understandably cautious in determining that an existing restriction no longer secures a 'practical benefit' for the dominant owner.[2] Given that the Tribunal is authorised to 'take away from a person a vested right either in law or in equity', it is not surprising that the Tribunal is required to 'consider the adverse effects upon a broad basis.'[3]

1   *Re Kennet Properties' Application* (1996) 72 P & CR 353 at 358. (Thus a restriction, without being 'obsolete', may confer contemporary benefits which are merely insubstantial and can be compensated by money.) The Lands Tribunal is not concerned with the benefits which the *applicant* would gain from discharge or modification of the relevant covenant (*Re Page's Application* (1996) 71 P & CR 440 at 452).
2   It is commonly said that the right to maintain the status quo is, in itself, a relevant benefit (see *Re Chandler's Application* (1958) 9 P & CR 512 at 517; *Re Bromor Properties Ltd's Application* (1995) 70 P & CR 569 at 583; *Re Page's Application* (1996) 71 P & CR 440 at 453). For reference to the 'thin end of the wedge argument', see *Re Solarfilms (Sales) Ltd's Application* (1994) 67 P & CR 110 at 116; *Re Page's Application*, supra at 454; *Re Hunt's Application* (1997) 73 P & CR 126 at 135.
3   *Gilbert v Spoor* [1983] Ch 27 at 32F per Eveleigh LJ. It is, however, a moot question whether a restrictive covenant in respect of land can be said to confer a 'practical benefit' in respect of a house built on that land only 40 years later (see *Re North's Application* (1998) 75 P & CR 117 at 124).

13.134   A good view over surrounding landscape may, for instance, constitute a 'practical benefit'[1] (even if this benefit is not palpably enjoyed by the objector from a location on his own land[2]). Relevant benefit may also consist in the preservation of a house value which would demonstrably depreciate were a pertinent restriction to be discharged.[3] The category of 'practical benefits' also includes the prevention of an increase in traffic movement[4] and the preservation of 'environmental pleasure'[5] and of 'privacy and seclusion and peace and quiet.'[6] Likewise the maintenance of a predetermined housing density may comprise a relevant 'benefit'[7] and the fact that nearby housing already exhibits a density in excess of that allowed by the challenged covenant may well render it 'rather more than less important' that the status quo on the application land be preserved.[8] A relevant 'benefit' can also be asserted by a local authority covenantee acting in its capacity as 'custodian of the public interest.'[9] Thus a local authority has standing to resist a proposed relaxation of restrictions in order to defend the environmental benefits secured for ramblers by a planning agreement which protects scenic countryside.[10] In recent years, moreover, the local authority's role as guardian of the 'public interest' has assumed a new and significant dimension in the context of restrictions imposed under the 'right to buy' provisions of the Housing Act 1985.[11]

1 *Re Lee's Application* (1996) 72 P & CR 439 at 446; *Re Nichols' Application* [1997] 1 EGLR 144 at 148G.
2 See e g *Gilbert v Spoor* [1983] Ch 27 at 33A–C, 35G–36B (no discharge of covenant aimed at preservation of landscape view, not from the dominant land itself, but from land in its vicinity). See [1982] Conv 452 (P H Kenny); P Polden, [1984] Conv 429. See also *Re Manson & Gill Construction Ltd* (Unreported, Lands Tribunal, 9 April 1991).
3 See *Re Azfar's Application* [2002] 1 P & CR 215 at [58]–[60] (threatened reduction in value of £40,000 if residential home for elderly were built nearby).
4 *Re Lee's Application* (1996) 72 P & CR 439 at 446; *Re Azfar's Application* [2002] 1 P & CR 215 at [51]–[55].
5 *Re Manson & Gill Construction Ltd* (Unreported, Lands Tribunal, 9 April 1991).
6 *Re Page's Application* (1996) 71 P & CR 440 at 453 (one-bedroom residential development rejected in green belt close to North Downs Area of Special Character). Compare *Re Willis' Application* (1998) 76 P & CR 97 at 111 (conversion of former council house for bed and breakfast use did not threaten any benefits secured by restriction); *Re Love and Love's Application* (1994) 67 P & CR 101 at 106–108 (construction of garage permissible on estate 'of no special architectural merit').
7 *Re Hydeshire Ltd's Application* (1994) 67 P & CR 93 at 99.
8 *Re Snaith and Dolding's Application* (1995) 71 P & CR 104 at 118. Even marginal increases in density may deprive objectors of a substantial and valued practical benefit by jeopardising the 'assurance of continued integrity of a building scheme' (*Re Hunt's Application* (1997) 73 P & CR 126 at 135). See also *Re Lee's Application* (1996) 72 P & CR 439 at 445–446.
9 [**Para 13.143**]. The mere fact that an objector under section 84 holds the benefit as 'custodian of the public interest' is not in itself, however, conclusive against discharge or modification (see e g *Re Willis' Application* (1998) 76 P & CR 97 at 113–114). See also *Re Wards Construction (Medway) Ltd's Application* (1994) 67 P & CR 379 at 390–391 (council no longer retained land remotely capable of benefiting from restriction). Compare, however, *Re Wallace and Co's Application* (1993) 66 P & CR 124 at 128.
10 *Re Hopcraft's Application* (1993) 66 P & CR 475 at 483.
11 See *Re Beech's Application* (1990) 59 P & CR 502 at 509–510 (council entitled, in the interests of preserving housing stock, to resist conversion to office use); *Re Milius's Application* (1995) 70 P & CR 427 at 433–434 (council entitled, in the interests of providing affordable housing, to defend restriction of future sales to locally qualified purchasers); *Re Willis' Application* (1998) 76 P & CR 97 at 111–113 (council was custodian of 'public interest' represented in amenity of estate, parts of which had been sold, subject to restrictions, under the 'right to buy').

Public interest

13.135 In the determination of the 'public interest' criterion, the relevant test is not whether the applicant's proposed user is in the public interest, but whether the continued enforcement of the restrictive covenant is *contrary to* the public interest.[1] The Lands Tribunal tends to be slow to accept that an alleged 'public interest' is sufficiently weighty to justify a 'serious interference with private rights and the sanctity of contract.'[2] Thus, for instance, a severe under-supply of local land available for housing or construction does not automatically cause an existing restriction on development to conflict with the 'public interest'.[3] Moreover, a restriction imposed pursuant to, and in support of, the planning policies evident in a local authority development plan is generally presumed to be a restriction in the public interest.[4] It is clear, however, that the 'public interest' criterion enables the Lands Tribunal to balance the competing social merits of environmental protection and reasonable development of local infrastructure. In *Re Lloyd's and Lloyd's Application*,[5] for example, the Lands Tribunal, in pursuance of a government policy of 'care in the community', modified a restrictive covenant in order to address a 'desperate' need within the locality for a psychiatric community care home.[6] In other cases, however, no contravention of the 'public interest' has been found in the fact that existing restrictive covenants prohibit developments which, although inherently reasonable, would merely provide another local children's day care nursery[7] or old people's home[8] or would make only a negligible contribution to local housing stock.[9]

1   *Re Bass Ltd's Application* (1973) 26 P & CR 156 at 159; *Re Styles' Application* (Unreported, Lands Tribunal, 8 April 1993); *Re Azfar's Application* [2002] 1 P & CR 215 at [46]–[47].
2   *Re Collins' Application* (1974) 30 P & CR 527 at 531.
3   See *Re Beardsley's Application* (1972) 25 P & CR 233 at 238; *Re New Ideal Homes Ltd's Application* (1978) 36 P & CR 476 at 480–481.
4   *Re Bewick's Application* (1997) 73 P & CR 240 at 250–251.
5   (1993) 66 P & CR 112 at 122–123.
6   See also *SJC Construction Ltd v Sutton LBC* (1974) 28 P & CR 200 at 205 (sheltered housing for old people already under construction) (not challenged before Court of Appeal: (1975) 29 P & CR 322 at 324); *Re Hounslow and Ealing LBC's Application* (1996) 71 P & CR 100 at 103 (use of part of public park as commercial plant nursery and horticultural training and educational centre). See also *Re Shah and Shah's Application* (1991) 62 P & CR 450 at 456–457.
7   *Re Solarfilms (Sales) Ltd's Application* (1994) 67 P & CR 110 at 115 ('not of the same degree of urgency' as was demonstrated in *Re Lloyd's and Lloyd's Application*, '[n]or ... the same social importance').
8   *Re Azfar's Application* [2002] 1 P & CR 215 at [46]–[47].
9   *Re Lee's Application* (1996) 72 P & CR 439 at 446.

Consent (section 84(1)(b))

13.136   The Lands Tribunal's power is also exercisable where the persons entitled to the benefit of a restriction have agreed expressly or by implication to its discharge or modification.[1]

1   In order to effect a voluntary release, the dominant owners must be persons of full age and capacity (LPA 1925, s 84(1)(b)). Consent cannot be implied from a mere failure to respond to an application for discharge or modification (*Re University of Westminster* [1998] 3 All ER 1014 at 1020e–j).

Non-injurious discharge or modification (section 84(1)(c))

13.137   The Lands Tribunal may also allow a proposed discharge or modification which 'will not injure' the persons entitled to the benefit of the restriction.[1] This ground sets up the 'most stringent test' within section 84,[2] but provides a 'long-stop against vexatious objections' from dominant owners.[3] If made out, this ground justifies no award of compensation precisely because, ex hypothesi, no loss has been suffered. The Lands Tribunal tends to apply section 84(1)(c) rather sparingly,[4] partly because, even though the applicant's particular proposal may not in itself cause any harm, the relaxation of a restrictive covenant can 'materially alter the context' in which possible future applications are considered.[5] The Tribunal is sensitive to the 'familiar and at times legitimate argument ... known as the thin end of the wedge argument'[6] and it is entirely possible that one application, by opening a breach in a carefully maintained scheme of restrictions, may ultimately threaten the viability of the scheme as a whole.

1   See *Re Bewick's Application* (1997) 73 P & CR 240 at 251. In *Re Bushell's Application* (1987) 54 P & CR 386 at 390, a proposed modification in Wimbledon was rejected where the resulting construction would have obstructed an unusually fine view from a neighbouring property (resulting in a diminution of its value by some £30,000) and would have destroyed the 'air of spaciousness' in the local environment.
2   *Re Kennet Properties' Application* (1996) 72 P & CR 353 at 357. The consents of other dominant owners cannot affect the right of an objector to contest this ground of application (*McMorris v Brown* [1999] 1 AC 142 at 151A per Lord Cooke of Thorndon).
3   *Ridley v Taylor* [1965] 1 WLR 611 at 622F per Russell LJ. See also *McMorris v Brown* [1999] 1 AC 142 at 149E–F per Lord Cooke of Thorndon.
4   See, however, *Re Nichols' Application* [1997] 1 EGLR 144 at 149D–F (no injury because of screening of application land).
5   *Re Snaith and Dolding's Application* (1995) 71 P & CR 104 at 118.
6   See *McMorris v Brown* [1999] 1 AC 142 at 151B per Lord Cooke of Thorndon.

THE BALANCE BETWEEN PRIVATE AND PUBLIC PLANNING UNDER SECTION 84

13.138   One of the ironies of modern environmental protection is that the relationship between public and private planning regimes has in some degree been transmuted, with private covenant-based regimes now taking over some of the social or community-directed function of public planning schemes. The beneficial conservationist potential of conventional public planning processes, although hugely important, can sometimes be overstated. Public planning control, operating under conditions of increasing pressure, cannot concern itself with all the detailed matters for which private covenants commonly make provision.[1] Many significant changes of land use do not even require planning permission,[2] with the result that only local regulation by covenant[3] (or even by mechanisms of trust[4]) can avert disadvantageous development.[5] In reality it is often the case that a vigilant insistence on private covenants preserves the character and amenity of an area much more effectively than either the law of nuisance[6] or the application of public planning controls.[7] Even local authorities themselves have come to recognise the utility of privately covenanted restrictions on land use in that, as a condition of granting planning permission, they have frequently imposed 'planning obligations'[8] for the specific purpose of retaining a control over relevant developments which is 'untrammelled by interference by the Secretary of State' when he hears appeals from a carefully limited planning permission.[9]

1   See *Transfer of Land: The Law of Positive and Restrictive Covenants* (Law Com No 127,

January 1984), para 2.6. Likewise, 'covenants can be drawn so as to apply rigorous standards of control which the listed building control system would struggle to replicate' (R Cooper and T O'Donovan, [1998] JPL 1110 at 1111).

2   **[Para 13.158]**. See *Lothian Regional Council v George Wimpey & Co Ltd* 1985 SLT (Lands Tr) 2 at 3.

3   For reference to the way in which covenants can operate as instruments of conservation, see I Hodge, R Castle and J Dwyer, *Covenants as a Conservation Mechanism* (Granta Editions 1993); R Castle and I Hodge, 'Covenants for the Countryside' [1994] Conv 122.

4   See, for instance, the creation in London of the Covent Garden Area Trust in a context 'where the general planning law is likely to prove an inadequate protector' (R Cooper and T O'Donovan, [1998] JPL 1110 at 1111).

5   Such is the breadth of jurisdiction of the modern local planning authority that '[w]hat is good policy for the area as a whole may be damaging to a particular part. This is particularly the case now that development control is more plan-based' (R Cooper and T O'Donovan, [1998] JPL 1110 at 1111).

6   See *Wilson and Another's Application* (Unreported, Lands Tribunal, 14 May 1992).

7   *Re Hornsby's Application* (1968) 20 P & CR 495 at 503. As long ago as 1975 G H Newsom QC spoke of the way in which planning standards 'are still too often below the standards imposed by restrictive covenants' (*Preston & Newsom's Restrictive Covenants Affecting Freehold Land* (6th edn by G H Newsom, London, 1976), p vii).

8   See T&CPA 1990, s 106 **[paras 9.141, 13.15]**. Planning obligations will be replaced by 'planning contributions' following the commencement of the Planning and Compulsory Purchase Act 2004 **[para 13.15]**.

9   *Re Jones' and White's Application* (1989) 58 P & CR 512 at 516. See also *Re Bewick's Application* (1997) 73 P & CR 240 at 247.

Relevance of planning permission

13.139   The mere fact that planning permission has already been granted in respect of a proposed development does not necessarily indicate that the Lands Tribunal *must*, under section 84, discharge or modify a particular restrictive covenant.[1] Almost all applications under section 84 are supported by planning consent for the development proposed. The availability of such consent is merely one of the considerations relevant to the Lands Tribunal's exercise of discretion[2] although in some cases it may prove strongly persuasive.[3]

1   See *Re Martins' Application* (1988) 57 P & CR 119 at 125; *Re Azfar's Application* [2002] 1 P & CR 215 at [55]. For the adoption of a similar stance in Australia, see *Kort Pty Ltd v Shaw* [1983] WAR 113 at 115, although in New South Wales restrictive covenants are routinely struck down, under Environmental Planning and Assessment Act 1979, s 28, for inconsistency with a development approval (see *Coshott v Ludwig* (1997) 8 BPR 15519 at 15521; *Doyle v Phillips (No 2)* (1997) 8 BPR 15523 at 15527–15528; *Owens v Longhurst* (1998) 9 BPR 16731 at 16733). See also J Tooher, 'Restrictive Covenants and Public Planning Legislation– Should the Landowner Feel "Touched and Concerned"?' (1992) 9 Environmental and Planning LJ 63.

2   See *Re Beech's Application* (1990) 59 P & CR 502 at 509; *Re Bromor Properties Ltd's Application* (1995) 70 P & CR 569 at 579; *Re Willis' Application* (1998) 76 P & CR 97 at 110.

3   See *Re Hextall's Application* (2000) 79 P & CR 382 at 388.

Protective function of the Lands Tribunal

13.140   It used to be that the Lands Tribunal's discharge and modification jurisdiction provided longstop protection against narrowly conceived private interests which might frustrate proposed developments of benefit to the entire community. Nowadays it is much more likely that the private interests which merit careful scrutiny are those of property development corporations which, armed with sometimes easily obtainable planning permissions,[1] seek to over-turn covenanted arrangements which were originally designed to secure the environmental quality of urban or rural neighbourhoods. Section 84 applica-tions are frequently resisted by covenantees (or their successors) who fear, often quite rightly, that a proposed development will degrade their neighbourhood, usually by devastating quiet residential enclaves.[2] It is far from unknown for a council planning department (or for the Secretary of State on appeal) to grant permission for a local development which nonchalantly cuts through a conser-vation area[3] or an area of green belt or special character,[4] only for the Lands Tribunal ultimately to come to the rescue by refusing to relax private covenants originally created in order to safeguard the threatened amenity.[5]

1   See the wry observation that a local planning authority, although 'sympathetic to the protection of a special area', has to be 'careful' in dealing with applications 'because of the risk of appeal against a refusal (and the associated risk of having to pay the applicant's costs)' (R Cooper and T O'Donovan, 'Covent Garden: A Model for Protection of Special Charac-ter?' [1998] JPL 1110 at 1111).
2   See e g *Re Peck* (Unreported, Lands Tribunal, 31 December 1992).
3   See e g *Re Manson & Gill Construction Ltd* (Unreported, Lands Tribunal, 9 April 1991).
4   See e g *Re Page's Application* (1996) 71 P & CR 440.
5   Half of the cases during the 1990s in which the Lands Tribunal declined to modify or discharge a restrictive covenant involved developments already sanctioned, for planning purposes, by the Secretary of State (see Gray and Gray, (1999) 3 Edinburgh Law Rev 229 at 233–234). See also G Chesman, [1994] JPL 783.

Parallel, but different, regimes of statutory control

13.141 The divergent outcomes sometimes reached by the Lands Tribunal and the public planning process are generally said to illustrate the contrasting criteria applied in the context of these two rather different statutory regimes for the control of land use.[1] The case law contains many assertions of the proposition that two regimes exist in parallel.[2] However, despite classic declara-tions that it is no proper role of the Lands Tribunal to 'act as a substitute for the planning authority',[3] the Tribunal's increasing vigilance may simply under-score the point that it has begun to function as the residual guarantor of an environmental amenity which the individual citizen can no longer count on receiving at the hands of his or her planning authority.[4]

1   *Re Hunt's Application* (1997) 73 P & CR 126 at 135. See similarly *Re Wallace & Co's Application* (1993) 66 P & CR 124 at 127; *Re Williamson's Application* (1994) 68 P & CR 384 at 388; *Re Page's Application* (1996) 71 P & CR 440 at 449; *Re Willis' Application* (1998) 76 P & CR 97 at 109–110.
2   See e g *Re Martins' Application* (1988) 57 P & CR 119 at 124–125; *Re Bewick's Application* (1997) 73 P & CR 240 at 248; *Re Wiggins's Application* [1998] JPL 599 at 599–600.
3   *Re Sheehy's Application* (1992) 63 P & CR 95 at 107, following *Re Ghey and Galton's Application* [1957] 2 QB 650 at 662 per Lord Evershed MR. See also *Gilbert v Spoor* [1983] Ch 27 at 34F–G; *Re Willis's Application* (1998) 76 P & CR 97 at 109–110. For a characteristic

description of the role of the Lands Tribunal, see *Re Bromor Properties Ltd's Application* (1995) 70 P & CR 569 at 579 ('my function is not to act as a tribunal of appeal as to the correctness of these [planning] permissions').

4   Gray and Gray, (1999) 3 Edinburgh Law Rev 229 at 232–235. See e g *Re Azfar's Application* [2002] 1 P & CR 215 at [55]–[57].

DISCHARGE AND MODIFICATION OF PLANNING OBLIGATIONS AND AGREEMENTS

13.142   Planning obligations entered into on or after 25 October 1991 are not subject to the jurisdiction of the Lands Tribunal under section 84 of the Law of Property Act 1925.[1] Instead, such obligations (whether positive or negative in nature) may be discharged or modified only by consent or following a process of application to the local planning authority by which the relevant obligations are enforceable.[2] That authority may determine that the planning obligation should continue to have effect without modification or, if the obligation 'no longer serves a useful purpose', may decide upon its discharge.[3] When, following the commencement of the Planning and Compulsory Purchase Act 2004, planning obligations are replaced by covenanted 'planning contributions',[4] the Secretary of State will draw up regulations making provision for the modification or discharge of such commitments.[5]

1   T&CPA 1990, s 106A(10).
2   T&CPA 1990, s 106A(1). See Town and Country Planning (Modification and Discharge of Planning Obligations) Regulations 1992 (SI 1992/2832).
3   T&CPA 1990, s 106A(6)(a)–(b). The local planning authority may, alternatively, modify an obligation in such a manner that it still serves a useful purpose (T&CPA 1990, s 106A(6)(c)). See G Soloman, [2000] JPL 351.
4   **[Para 13.15]**.
5   P&CPA 2004, s 47(7)(c).

13.143   Planning agreements and obligations entered into prior to 25 October 1991 remain subject to the discharge and modification jurisdiction of section 84 in so far as they relate to covenants of a negative nature.[1] In respect of such covenants it has been said that the local authority acts as the 'custodian of the public interest.'[2] Cases are curiously frequent in which local authorities, despite having sanctioned a proposed development by way of a planning permission granted by its planning arm, have nevertheless attempted to reassert control over the development by refusing to agree to any later discharge or modification of covenants of which they stand as the public or nominal beneficiary.[3]

1   See *Bedwell Park Quarry Co Ltd v Hertfordshire CC* [1993] JPL 349 at 352.
2   *Re Jones' and White's Application* (1989) 58 P & CR 512 at 517; *Re Hopcraft's Application* (1993) 66 P & CR 475 at 483. See also *Re Wallace & Co's Application* (1993) 66 P & CR 124 at 127.
3   The objector may be the planning arm of the local authority, where the covenant in question is contained in a planning agreement, or the housing committee in respect of restrictive covenants imposed under the 'right to buy' legislation. See H C Abraham, 'The Local Authority as Objector to Applications for Modification or Discharge of Restrictive Covenants' [1994] JPL 792.

13.144 In *Re Jones' and White's Application*,[1] for example, the Lands Tribunal pointed out that the effect of a planning agreement is to 'give to the council a means of control of development additional to that provided by the ... Town and Country Planning Act', adding trenchantly that it affords 'a means of control untrammelled by interference by the Secretary of State.' The Tribunal observed that, by entering into a planning agreement, the local authority was 'enabled to consider matters from a subjective point of view whereas in exercising its functions in relation to applications for planning permission it must be objective.' Thus, in justifying opposition to a discharge or modification of a planning agreement – even against the background of a planning permission granted by itself – the council is 'entitled to look at matters from its own point of view and from that of members of the public whom it represents.'[2] Many are the cases in which a local authority's low view of the conservationist potential of planning processes appears to have been justified. In *Hopcraft's Application*,[3] for example, the Lands Tribunal accepted that the local planners had in 1991 given permission for the extension of a caravan site which would have damaged severely the visual amenity of an area of open countryside in Hampshire. The Tribunal nevertheless held that the District Council, the only objector to a section 84 application to remove a planning agreement of 1980 affecting the same land, had been entirely correct, 'as custodian of the public interest', to oppose the application.[4] Equally significantly, in *Re Bewick's Application*,[5] the evidence quite plainly revealed that the local council, after granting planning permission for limited occupancy only, had imposed a planning agreement to the like effect precisely because they had been 'apprehensive that they might subsequently lose an appeal against the occupancy condition and wished to retain control by a separate agreement.'[6]

1   (1989) 58 P & CR 512 at 516.
2   (1989) 58 P & CR 512 at 517.
3   (1993) 66 P & CR 475.
4   (1993) 66 P & CR 475 at 484 ('the public interest requires that the application land be kept free from development').
5   (1997) 73 P & CR 240.
6   (1997) 73 P & CR 240 at 247.

CONVERSION OF DWELLING-HOUSE INTO TWO OR MORE TENEMENTS

13.145 The county court has power under the Housing Act 1985 to vary any provision in a lease or restrictive covenant which, by prohibiting the conversion of a dwelling-house into two or more tenements, has the effect of impeding a letting of the house for residential use.[1]

1   HA 1985, s 610(1)–(2). The converted units must still be contained within one house (see *Josephine Trust Ltd v Champagne* [1963] 2 QB 160 at 168).

REFORM OF THE LAW OF COVENANTS

13.146 It has long been recognised that the law of covenants is in need of radical reform. Debate over possible reform has centred on three major issues.

Utility of privately covenanted arrangements

13.147 Over 20 years ago the Royal Commission on Legal Services expressed the view that the time 'may have come to make past and present restrictive covenants unenforceable except as between the parties to the original agreement.'[1] The Royal Commission accordingly suggested that the use of restrictive covenants should be 'curtailed by statute and reliance placed in the main on planning uses as controlled by planning legislation.'[2] Subsequent experience has, however, modified the view that privately bargained restrictions represent an unworthy or inconvenient object of aspiration. Describing the Royal Commission's view as 'radical',[3] the Law Commission later endorsed the facility which the law offers for imposing private restrictions on land use. Noting that such covenants 'are still felt by the public to meet a real need', the Law Commission observed that any limitation of this power would 'curtail a freedom which people do in fact exercise to a very considerable degree.'[4]

1   *Final Report* (Cmnd 7648, October 1979), Vol 1, para 21.1, Annex 21.1, para 3 ('Many thousands of words of restrictive covenants clutter the titles of house property and bedevil modern conveyancing').
2   Ibid, Annexe 21.1, para 12.
3   See *Transfer of Land: Obsolete Restrictive Covenants* (Law Com No 201, July 1991), para 2.6 (n 2).
4   Law Com No 127 (1984), paras 2.8, 2.10, 6.19. See also P Polden, (1986) 49 MLR 195 at 212.

13.148 The assault on the appropriateness of privately covenanted arrangements relating to land has meanwhile continued north of the border. The Scottish Law Commission was, at one stage, minded to impose severe constraints on the availability of private bilateral covenants between landowners, on the ground that such covenants allegedly involve one-off, unidirectional impositions of an owner's user preferences upon his neighbour[1] and evince 'the potential to be oppressive.'[2] Taking the view that the relationship of dominance and servience obtaining in respect of restrictive covenants between neighbours was, in effect, 'to continue the feudal system by other means',[3] the Scottish Commission adopted the preliminary stance that, for the future, it 'should not be possible to create a neighbour burden with perpetual duration.'[4] Although this animus against restrictive covenants has since been considerably muted,[5] the underlying sense of the Scottish Commission is that restrictions conceived in the private interest may 'require to be justified more carefully than restrictions in the public interest.'[6]

1   *Real Burdens* (Scot Law Com Disc Paper No 106, October 1998), paras 2.9, 5.79, 7.12.
2   Draft Discussion Paper on Real Burdens (1998), para 2.40.
3   Draft Discussion Paper on Real Burdens (1998), para 2.11.
4   Draft Discussion Paper on Real Burdens (1998), paras 2.40, 2.44.
5   *Report on Real Burdens* (Scot Law Com No 181, October 2000), para 1.21. See Gray and Gray, 'The Future of Real Burdens in Scots Law' (1999) 3 Edinburgh Law Rev 229.
6   *Real Burdens* (October 1998), para 2.1; Scot Law Com No 181, 2000, para 1.17.

13.149 The factor which has contributed most substantially, in both England and Scotland, to continuing support for private mechanisms of land use control has been the realisation that the privately bargained covenant nowadays serves as a crucial instrument of much needed environmental regulation.[1] It has become increasingly apparent that the regime of covenants, far from symbolising the imposition of selfish or isolated or eccentric protectionist impulses, operates as a vital supplement to public regimes of land use planning. Privately covenanted arrangements (whether bilateral or multilateral in nature) frequently secure the protection of environmental quality much more effectively than any other scheme of planning regulation.[2] Covenants are not, for the most part, anti-social devices aimed at the satisfaction of selfish user-preferences, but tend to embody rather more attractive preoccupations with local environmental management and conservation. The privately bargained covenant is beginning to come into its own as the residual guardian of a more general, community-directed concern with environmental welfare.

1   See D Grinlinton, 'Property Rights and the Environment' (1996) 4 APLJ 41 at 62.
2   [**Para 13.138**]. See the standard wide-ranging restrictive covenant of the Victorian era, which prohibited 'any nuisance or act which may injure the amenity of the place and neighbourhood' and which provided more comprehensive protection than contemporary planning control is able to afford. Such covenants often remain in place today (see eg *Re Hoyle* (Unreported, Lands Tribunal, 9 December 1992) (restrictive covenants dated 1870)).

The enforcement of obligations

13.150   The principal defect in the current English law of covenants centres around the disastrously limited enforceability of positive burdens. As long ago as 1965 the Wilberforce Committee acknowledged that, in practice, many positive covenants in respect of property in this country are wholly unenforceable.[1] The Committee agreed that the time had come for statutory intervention 'to introduce legal order and consistency into the present (inevitably) haphazard techniques of multi-unit property development.'[2]

1   See *Report of the Committee on Positive Covenants Affecting Land* (Cmnd 2719, 1965).
2   Ibid, para 9.

The land obligation

13.151   No legislation was ever introduced to implement the proposals of the Wilberforce Committee. In 1984, however, the Law Commission issued a renewed proposal for the comprehensive reformulation of the law of freehold covenants, both positive and negative, which rested heavily on the analogy of the law of easements.[1] The Commission envisaged the creation of a new interest in land (the 'land obligation'), by means of which it would be possible to impose both positive and negative obligations on one piece of land (the 'servient land') for the benefit of another piece of land (the 'dominant land').[2] 'Land obligations' were to comprise two types of obligation. It was proposed that they should include 'neighbour obligations' (ie the equivalents of existing positive and negative covenants)[3] and 'development obligations' (ie the kinds of reciprocal obligation much needed for the regulation of multi-occupied areas such as blocks of flats).[4]

1   *Transfer of Land: The Law of Positive and Restrictive Covenants* (Law Com No 127, January 1984). See (1984) 134 NLJ 459, 481 (H W Wilkinson); (1984) 47 MLR 566 (P Polden).
2   Law Com No 127 (1984), paras 4.21, 5.2.
3   Law Com No 127 (1984), paras 6.3–6.6.
4   Law Com No 127 (1984), paras 6.7–6.14.

13.152   The Law Commission's proposed scheme, had it been implemented,[1] would have had the highly beneficial consequence of eliminating the extremely technical rules relating to the transmission of the benefits and burdens of covenants.[2] It was envisaged that all land obligations (including legal obligations) should be protected by entry in the register of the titles of both dominant and servient tenements (in the case of registered land) and by the registration of a new category of Class C land charge (in the case of unregistered land).[3] In this way the benefits and burdens created by the 'land obligation' were designed to attach to the relevant tenements, being enforceable only as between the current owners of the respective tenements.[4]

1   The Lord Chancellor announced in 1998 that there was no intention to introduce legislation based on Law Com No 127. The Law Commission is currently engaged in a review of the law of easements which may result in a more co-ordinated regime of land obligations that accommodates both covenants and commonholds.
2   Law Com No 127 (1984), para 4.22.
3   Law Com No 127 (1984), paras 9.4–9.25.
4   Law Com No 127 (1984), para 4.22, Parts X and XI. It was proposed that the person burdened by a land obligation would cease to be liable when he ceased to be owner of the relevant servient land (ibid, para 11.32).

Link with commonhold

13.153   The commonhold scheme introduced by the Commonhold and Leasehold Reform Act 2002[1] does not obviate the need for a fundamental reconsideration of the law of covenants. There are still many situations in which it would be inappropriate to adopt the communal management machinery which is integral to commonhold schemes[2] and in such cases something akin to the 'land obligation' may well provide all that is required for the orderly transmission of the benefit and burden of covenanted obligations between freeholders and their successors in title.[3] The commonhold scheme is principally aimed at facilitating the co-operative multi-ownership of buildings such as residential blocks of flats. Outside this context there remains a need to enable owners to create 'land obligations' inter se of a fully and permanently enforceable character.[4]

1   [**Paras 13.44, 13.57**].
2   The Law Commission instanced the case of suburban property owners who covenant inter se to make periodic contributions towards the upkeep of a private road [**para 13.59**]. Here it would be excessively burdensome to require the creation of a complex commonhold simply in order to provide a legal mechanism for the transmission of the positive burden from one individual property owner to his or her successor (see *Commonhold: Freehold Flats and freehold ownership of other interdependent buildings* (Cm 179, July 1987), para 17.2).
3   Law Commission, *Commonhold* (1987), paras 1.9, 17.2.
4   Law Commission, *Commonhold* (1987), para 17.2.

A possible 'sunset' rule

13.154 A further area of possible reform relates to the introduction of a 'sunset' rule which would cause covenanted obligations to be automatically extinguished on the expiry of a statutorily fixed period following their creation. The Law Commission recommended some time ago that most restrictive covenants between freeholders should cease to have effect 80 years after their creation,[1] any person aggrieved by the lapse being entitled to apply to the Lands Tribunal for the conversion of the relevant covenant into a 'land obligation'.[2] This proposal for the systematic removal of redundant land burdens reflects a disinclination to allow the dead hand of the past to order the affairs of the present, but the Law Commission's recommendation has been taken no further. There is nowadays a strong possibility that, if unaccompanied by compensation, the arbitrary destruction of existing covenanted arrangements may fall foul of the European Convention guarantee of 'peaceful enjoyment' of possessions.[3]

1   *Transfer of Land: Obsolete Restrictive Covenants* (Law Com No 201, July 1991), para 3.1. Motivated by similar impulses, the Scottish Law Commission was initially minded to suggest a 'one-off cull' of all burdens created before a prescribed date such as 1900 (see *Draft Discussion Paper on Real Burdens* (1998), para 5.68) or possibly even a rule of automatic extinction for bilateral covenants 40 years after their creation (ibid, para 2.49). The short dateline envisaged in the latter proposal threatened to return the law of covenants to the period when land use covenants were binding upon only the covenanting parties. The Scottish Commission later commuted the proposal to a 'triggered sunset' after 100 years for most categories of real burden, to be activated by the servient owner's service of a 'termination notice' and subject to challenge before the Lands Tribunal (*Report on Real Burdens* (Scot Law Com No 181, October 2000), paras 5.25–5.57).
2   **[Para 13.151]**. See [1992] Conv 2.
3   ECHR Protocol No 1, Art 1 **[para 2.29]**.

PLANNING AND COMPULSORY PURCHASE LAW

13.155 Modern planning control in England and Wales dates from the enactment of the Town and Country Planning Act 1947 and is currently governed by the Town and Country Planning Act 1990 (as most recently amended by the Planning and Compulsory Purchase Act 2004). In many ways this legislation constitutes a socialised replica, on a general scale and in the public domain, of the planning regimes envisaged by networks of privately bargained covenants relating to land use. Nor is it mere metaphor to allege that, through the medium of today's planning legislation, all citizens can now indirectly claim, in some sense, a quantum of 'property' in everyone else's land.[1] Indeed the Planning and Compulsory Purchase Act 2004 requires that every local planning authority prepare, and comply with, a 'statement of community involvement' in the planning process.[2]

1   See D Millichap, 'Real Property and its Regulation: The Community-Rights Rationale for Town Planning', in S Bright and J K Dewar (ed), *Land Law: Themes and Perspectives* (Oxford 1998), p 428.
2   P&CPA 2004, ss 17(1), 18(1)–(2). See also P&CPA 2004, s 6(1).

13.156   The development and use of land are subject to a degree of surveillance in the public interest which has effectively rendered ownership heavily qualified by pervasive notions of civic responsibility.[1] Certain commentators even say that 'some (if not most) sticks' in the estate owner's 'bundle of sticks' are intrinsically 'reserved for communal control and use' and that a 'social welfare orientation' of land use rights 'comports with a community-based sense of justice.'[2] According to this communitarian analysis, the notion of property has much more to do with ideas of *propriety* than of *right*[3]; and private titles ultimately subserve the wider public interest. Ownership is converted into a form of stewardship[4]; rights and duties in respect of land are inseparably fused; and the social responsibility of caring for land becomes a fundamental and inescapable component of real entitlement.[5]

1   [Paras 2.87, 13.10].
2   Eric T Freyfogle, 'Context and Accommodation in Modern Property Law' 41 Stan L Rev 1529 at 1545–1546 (1988–89).
3   [Para 2.6].
4   See W N R Lucy and C Mitchell, 'Replacing Private Property: The Case for Stewardship' [1996] CLJ 566.
5   See Gray, 'Equitable Property' (1994) 47(2) CLP 157 at 188–214.

13.157   State- or community-directed control of land use takes a myriad of forms and is now governed by a vast body of statute law, delegated legislation and Community directives which lies outside the immediate scope of this book. Planning law and the law of compulsory acquisition are therefore described here only in outline form.

PLANNING CONTROL

13.158   Strasbourg jurisprudence has always accepted that, in view of the 'multitude of local factors ... inherent in the choice and implementation of planning policies', the 'margin of appreciation' accorded to national authorities in the planning context is necessarily wide.[1] In England and Wales the process of planning control is governed mainly by the Town and Country Planning Act 1990, whose underlying principle is that any 'development' of land requires planning permission to be granted by the relevant local authority[2] or, on appeal from a refusal of permission, by the relevant Secretary of State.[3]

1   *Buckley v United Kingdom* (1997) 23 EHRR 101 at [75]. See likewise *Connors v United Kingdom* (ECtHR decision, Application No 66746/01, 27 May 2004) at [82], [86].
2   T&CPA 1990, s 57(1).
3   Appeal may, in general, be made only against the *refusal* (as distinct from the *grant*) of planning consent (T&CPA 1990, s 78(1)), a circumstance which many regard as responsible in recent decades for the widespread brutalisation of England's historic town centres through insensitive planning decisions. Appeal also lies in the event of a planning authority's failure to decide on an application within eight weeks (Town and Country Planning (General Development Procedure) Order 1995 (SI 1995/419), art 20) or within 16 weeks in the case of an application involving a mandatory environmental statement (Town and Country Planning (Environmental Impact Assessment) (England and Wales) Regulations 1999 (SI 1999/293), reg 32(2)). See T&CPA 1990, s 70A (as substituted by P&CPA 2004, s 43), 78(2).

A plan-led regulatory process

13.159 The decision-making process pursuant to the Town and Country Planning Act 1990 has been dominated, at least historically, by a hierarchy of structure and local development plans which are intended to provide a 'framework for rational and consistent decision making.'[1] The Planning and Compulsory Purchase Act 2004 is shortly to consolidate these plans in a new unitary system of 'local development documents'[2] to be prepared in general conformity with a centrally co-ordinated 'regional spatial strategy' or (in the case of Greater London) a 'spatial development strategy'.[3] The grant of planning permission has always been heavily influenced by the relevant development plan[4] and the 2004 Act provides that any determination made under the planning Acts 'must be made in accordance with the plan unless material considerations indicate otherwise.'[5] The plan-led nature of such development control has been described as giving rise to an 'environmental contract' between the planning authority and the community that all private development will be regulated 'in a manner consistent with the objectives stated in the plan.'[6] The 2004 Act further emphasises that all persons or bodies who exercise any function in relation to local development plans or regional spatial strategies must do so 'with the objective of contributing to the achievement of sustainable development.'[7]

1   Office of the Deputy Prime Minister, *Planning Policy Guidance Note 12: Development Plans* (PPG12 published 18 January 2000), para 1.1.
2   P&CPA 2004, s 17.
3   P&CPA 2004, ss 1, 19(2), 24(1).
4   See T&CPA 1990, ss 54A, 70(2); *Simpson v Edinburgh Corpn*, 1960 SC 313 at 318–319 per Lord Guest; *City of Edinburgh Council v Secretary of State for Scotland* [1997] 1 WLR 1447 at 1450B–C per Lord Hope of Craighead.
5   P&CPA 2004, s 38(6). See *R v Canterbury CC, ex p Springimage Ltd* (1993) 68 P & CR 171 at 177.
6   *Attorney General (McGarry) v Sligo CC* [1991] 1 IR 99 at 113 per McCarthy J.
7   P&CPA 2004, s 39(2).

The statutory concept of 'development'

13.160 The concept of 'development' in the Town and Country Planning Act 1990 includes[1] the carrying out of building, engineering, mining or other operations in, over or under land[2] and the making of any material change in the use of any buildings or other land.[3]

1   T&CPA 1990, s 55(1).
2   A building operation need not result in a building, although it does not include the erection of a marquee which is intended to be taken down after use (see *Skerritts of Nottingham Ltd v Secretary of State for the Environment, Transport and the Regions and Harrow LBC* [2000] JPL 1025 at 1034–1036).
3   Planning permission for certain kinds of development which have potentially harmful environmental effects must be accompanied by an 'environmental statement' detailing the context and likely impact of the proposed development on environmental amenity (Town and Country Planning (Environmental Impact Assessment) (England and Wales) Regulations 1999, regs 3–9, Schs 1 and 2). See EC Council Directive 85/337 (as amended by EC

Council Directive 97/11). On the importance of environmental statements, see *Grand Duchy of Luxembourg v Linster, Case C-287/98* [2000] ECR I-6917; *R v Rochdale MBC, ex p Tew* [2000] JPL 54. The requirement of an environmental statement cannot be dispensed with retrospectively on the ground that its presence would not have affected the outcome of an application for planning permission (*Berkeley v Secretary of State for the Environment* [2001] 2 AC 603 at 616C–D per Lord Hoffmann). See D Elvin and J Robinson, [2000] JPL 876.

Operational development

13.161   Most types of building work on land, other than marginal works of internal alteration, require the grant of planning permission (and usually, also, of building regulation approval,[1] which effectively monitors the technical quality of the construction and the materials used in it).[2] It is specifically provided, however, that 'development' does *not* include the use of any building or land within the curtilage of a dwelling-house for any purpose incidental to the enjoyment of the dwelling-house[3] or the use of any land for agriculture or forestry.[4] In other cases planning permission must normally be obtained, the legislation now making clear that even demolition comes within the scope of the 'building operations' covered by the requirement of permission.[5] Pursuant to the Planning and Compulsory Purchase Act 2004, permission will also be required for the creation of additional floor space within any building subject to planning control.[6]

1   See Building Regulations 2000 (SI 2000/2531), as amended most recently by Building (Amendment) Regulations 2004 (SI 2004/1465) (fully effective 1 December 2004).
2   *Southwark LBC v Mills* [2001] 1 AC 1 at 9C–F per Lord Hoffmann.
3   T&CPA 1990, s 55(2)(d). This exception does not extend to unreasonable forms of use of domestic land. See e g *Wallington v Secretary of State for Wales* (1990) 62 P & CR 150 at 156 (accommodation of more than 40 dogs); *Croydon LBC v Gladden* (1994) 68 P & CR 300 at 312 (replica Spitfire attached to roof).
4   T&CPA 1990, s 55(2)(e).
5   T&CPA 1990, s 55(1A). See *London County Council v Marks & Spencer Ltd* [1953] AC 535 at 541–542.
6   T&CPA 1990, s 55(2A), as inserted by P&CPA 2004, s 49(1).

13.162   Planning permission is sometimes granted impliedly in a blanket form where a proposed development falls within one of the standard classes of permitted development under the Town and Country Planning (General Permitted Development) Order 1995.[1] In the domestic context such exemptions cover minor works of extension or improvement (e g the construction of small porches, car ports and loft conversions). The Planning and Compulsory Purchase Act 2004 allows local planning authorities to expand local permitted development rights beyond the national categories by 'local development order'.[2]

1   SI 1995/418, as amended. See T&CPA 1990, ss 59–60.
2   See T&CPA 1990, ss 61A–61C, inserted by P&CPA 2004, s 40.

Material changes of use

13.163 Change in the use of land likewise requires planning permission unless the change is non-material. The 1990 Act expressly indicates, moreover, that the conversion of a single dwelling-house for use as two or more dwelling-houses involves a material change of use.[1] However, no relevant change of use arises where the altered use falls within the same 'class' of use as the existing use under a tightly defined canon of residential and business use classes.[2] Thus a bookshop can become a hairdresser's (since both uses fall within Class A1), but not a coffee shop (since this use falls within Class A3). Likewise a family may decide to house an ageing relative (since this change of use is covered by Class C3[3]), but may not convert their home into a hotel (since such a use falls within Class C1).

1   T&CPA 1990, s 55(3)(a).
2   T&CPA 1990, s 55(2)(f); Town and Country Planning (Use Classes) Order 1987 (SI 1987/764).
3   See *R (Hossack) v Kettering BC* [2003] 2 P & CR 444 at [26]–[28] ((household under Class C3 may comprise community care home of up to six persons).

Procedure

13.164 Planning permission may be granted either as *outline* planning permission or as *full* planning permission, and may be subjected to conditions[1] (which regulate the nature or timing of the development) or the requirement of a 'planning contribution'.[2] The grant of planning permission for a development provides no automatic ground for the discharge of any restrictive covenant which stands in the way of the development[3]; nor does it authorise the commission of any nuisance.[4] Development in breach of planning control may be penalised by enforcement proceedings,[5] but operational developments are immune from enforcement once four years have expired since the substantial completion of the operation.[6] The limitation period for enforcement is otherwise normally a period of ten years.[7]

1   T&CPA 1990, s 70(1)(a).
2   See P&CPA 2004, s 46 **[paras 9.141, 13.15]**.
3   **[Para 13.139]**.
4   *Wheeler v J J Saunders Ltd* [1996] Ch 19 at 30C, 36D–F, 38A–B; [1995] CLJ 494 (S Tromans). See also *Ports of Auckland Ltd v Auckland CC* [1999] 1 NZLR 601 at 610–611; *Hawkes Bay Protein Ltd v Davidson* [2003] 1 NZLR 536 at [19].
5   See *R v Wicks* [1998] AC 92. In order to catch unauthorised development at an early stage, the Planning and Compulsory Purchase Act 2004 introduces the possibility of a 'temporary stop notice' (see T&CPA 1990, ss 171E–171H, as inserted by P&CPA 2004, s 52).
6   T&CPA 1990, s 171B(1). See, however, *Sage v Secretary of State for the Environment, Transport and the Regions* [2003] 1 WLR 983; *Wilkie v Redsell* [2003] EWCA Civ 926 at [7]. A wrongful change of use of any building to use as a single dwellinghouse is immune from enforcement proceedings after the end of a period of four years beginning with the date of breach (s 171B(2)). See *Moore v Secretary of State for the Environment* (1998) Times, 18 February.
7   T&CPA 1990, s 171B(3). See, however, *Harborough DC v Wheatcroft & Son Ltd* [1996] EGCS 90.

13.165   A large motivation behind the enactment of the Planning and Compulsory Purchase Act 2004 was the perceived need to speed up the planning process and to increase the predictability of planning decisions. The historic planning process was felt to have become over-heavy with bureaucratic regulation at a time when the country imperatively requires the rapid provision of affordable housing and associated structural regeneration. Accordingly the Act accelerates the handling of 'major infrastructure projects'[1] and requires the identification of 'simplified planning zones' for any area where such an initiative is thought by the local planning authority to be desirable.[2] The Act also finally removes the immunity of the crown from the planning regime.[3]

1   See T&CPA 1990, ss 76A–76B, inserted by P&CPA 2004, s 44 (compulsory referral of application to Secretary of State instead of local planning authority).
2   T&CPA 1990, s 83(1A), as inserted by P&CPA 2004, s 45(2).
3   T&CPA 1990, s 292A; Planning (Listed Buildings and Conservation Areas) Act 1990, s 82A (as inserted by P&CPA 2004, s 79).

Other forms of environmental control

13.166   A vast range of other statutory controls regulates development and change in conservation areas,[1] sites of special scientific interest,[2] areas of outstanding natural beauty,[3] national parks,[4] enterprise zones[5] and urban development areas.[6] Yet more regulation affects such matters as the preservation of trees[7] and hedgerows,[8] the alteration of listed buildings,[9] works affecting scheduled monuments[10] and the control of hazardous waste and environmental pollution.[11] Local planning authorities also have draconian powers to force the sale or compulsory purchase of land which is so deficiently maintained that it adversely affects the amenity of the neighbourhood.[12] In *Miles v Secretary of State for the Environment and the Royal Borough of Kingston upon Thames*,[13] for example, the High Court upheld the compulsory acquisition of a house in 'deplorable condition', in order to arrest a degree of neglect which was causing 'real harm to the character and appearance of the neighbourhood.'[14] The Court disposed of objections based upon the Convention protection of 'family life', 'home' and 'peaceful enjoyment' of possessions,[15] noting that all such protection gave way where 'interference is held to be necessary for the preservation of the environment in the interests of the community.'[16]

1   See Planning (Listed Buildings and Conservation Areas) Act 1990, Part II.
2   Wildlife and Countryside Act 1981, s 28(5)–(6). See *Southern Water Authority v Nature Conservancy Council* [1992] 1 WLR 775; *R v Nature Conservancy Council, ex p London Brick Co Ltd* [1996] Env LR 1. See C P Rodgers, 'Reforming Property Rights for Nature Conservation', in P Jackson and D C Wilde (ed), *Property Law: Current Issues and Debates* (Ashgate 1999), p 48.
3   National Parks and Access to Countryside Act 1949, ss 11, 87–88.
4   Environment Act 1995, s 63; National Parks and Access to Countryside Act 1949, Part II.
5   T&CPA 1990, ss 88–89.
6   Local Government, Planning and Land Act 1980, ss 148–149; T&CPA 1990, s 7(1).
7   T&CPA 1990, Part VIII, ss 197–214D, as amended by P&CPA 2004, ss 85–86. See *Knowles v Chorley BC* [1997] EGCS 141; (1994) 138 Sol Jo 149 (A Samuels). See also *R v Alath Construction Ltd* [1990] 1 WLR 1255 (criminal liability for unauthorised felling of tree). The

making of a tree preservation order does not, in itself, breach an owner's rights under ECHR Art 8 or Protocol No 1, Art 1 (see *R (Brennon) v Bromsgrove DC* [2003] 2 P & CR 430 at [33]–[34]).

8   Environment Act 1995, s 97; Hedgerows Regulations 1997 (SI 1997/1160). See (1997) 141 Sol Jo 550 (I Kinloch); J Holder, (1999) 62 MLR 100.

9   Planning (Listed Buildings and Conservation Areas) Act 1990, ss 7–8.

10   Ancient Monuments and Archaeological Areas Act 1979, ss 2–5.

11   See Planning (Hazardous Substances) Act 1990, ss 4–7; Clean Air Act 1993, Parts I–IV; Pollution Prevention and Control Act 1999, s 2, Sch 1; Pollution Prevention and Control (England and Wales) Regulations 2000 (SI 2000/1973).

12   T&CPA 1990, ss 215–219 (local authority charge for the cost of necessary works of abatement), 226(1)(b) (purchase necessary 'in the interests of the proper planning' of the area). See also Environmental Protection Act 1990, ss 80(1), 81(4), 81A(4); *Stanley v Ealing LBC* (2000) 32 HLR 745 at 749–751 (abatement notice in respect of refuse deposited against front boundary wall of house).

13   [2000] JPL 192 at 199–202.

14   See, however, Land Compensation Act 1973, s 33D(3)–(4), as inserted by P&CPA 2004, s 108(1) (no loss payment for dispossessed owner/occupier).

15   ECHR Art 8, Protocol No 1, Art 1.

16   A local authority's failure to enforce legislation prohibiting unsightly premises does not, however, raise any cause of action in negligence (see *Homburg Canada Inc v Halifax (Regional Municipality)* (2003) 228 DLR (4th) 646 at [14], [21]).

13.167 Various European Convention guarantees now incorporated within the Human Rights Act 1998 have the effect of intensifying the claim to protection for environmental welfare.[1] Article 2 protection of the 'right to life' seems apt to extend to developments which carry a risk of injury to health, particularly where a public authority has made inadequate attempts to inform those affected as to the potential dangers involved.[2] Article 8 protection of the right to respect for privacy and family life has already been invoked in cases of severe environmental pollution which, even in the absence of danger to health, 'may affect individuals' well-being and prevent them from enjoying their homes in such a way as to affect their private and family life adversely.'[3] On the other hand, Convention protection of the 'peaceful enjoyment' of possessions[4] does not remove the state's competence to regulate environmentally injurious activity in response to the fact that 'in today's society the protection of the environment is an increasingly important consideration.'[5]

1   See D Hart, 'The Impact of the European Convention on Human Rights on Planning and Environmental Law' [2000] JPL 117; M DeMerieux, 'Deriving Environmental Rights from the European Convention for the Protection of Human Rights and Fundamental Freedoms' (2001) 21 OJLS 521 **[para 2.64]**.

2   See *Guerra v Italy* (1998) 26 EHRR 357 at [45]–[52], [61]–[62].

3   See *Lopez Ostra v Spain* (1994) 20 EHRR 277 at [51] (emission of noise, fumes and smells from waste treatment plant). See also *Guerra v Italy* (1998) 26 EHRR 357 at [46], [60]; *Anufrijeva v Southwark LBC* [2003] 3 FCR 673 at [18]–[19] per Lord Woolf CJ. Some indication of future developments in this area appears in *Andrews v Reading BC* [2004] EWHC 970 (QB) at [13]–[14] (recognising possibility of ECHR Art 8 claim in respect of excessive traffic noise caused by traffic regulation order).

4   ECHR Protocol No 1, Art 1 **[para 2.29]**.

5   *Fredin v Sweden*, Series A No 192 (1991) at [48]. See also *Guerra v Italy* (1998) 26 EHRR 357 at [43].

COMPULSORY ACQUISITION

13.168   The exercise of eminent domain for supervening community purposes constitutes, without doubt, the most far-reaching form of social intervention in the property relations of individual citizens.[1] The state reserves the power, in the name of all citizens, to call on the individual, in extreme circumstances and in return for just compensation,[2] to yield up some private good for the greater good of the whole community.[3] As Lord Nicholls of Birkenhead explained recently in *Waters v Welsh Development Agency*,[4] compulsory purchase is 'an essential tool in a modern democratic society' in that it 'facilitates planned and orderly development.'[5] But it is 'axiomatic' that '[h]and in hand with the power to acquire land without the owner's consent is an obligation to pay full and fair compensation.' Such compensation is required in order that the economic cost of communally beneficial policies should not be disproportionately concentrated on a few citizens but should be diffused instead amongst the public at large.[6] On these terms the state may therefore be seen as having the right to requisition, for civic purposes, some or all of the 'sticks' in the estate owner's 'bundle'. It might even be more accurate to say that the state has *always* retained for itself a strategic quota of these 'sticks' and that compelling community needs constantly operate as a tacit qualification upon all land ownership. Either way, it is clear that many bodies today enjoy extensive statutory powers of compulsory acquisition which enable the purchase of privately owned land for designated public purposes (ranging from the construction or improvement of highways to the renovation of housing stock).

1   [Para 2.91].
2   See *Belfast Corpn v O D Cars Ltd* [1960] AC 490 at 523 per Lord Radcliffe; *Prest v Secretary of State for Wales* (1982) 81 LGR 193 at 198 per Lord Denning MR.
3   'The power of the Crown to compulsorily acquire land derives from the ancient notion of eminent domain. It is today a draconian – but necessary – power in a complex and collective society' (*Deane v Attorney-General* [1997] 2 NZLR 180 at 191 per Hammond J).
4   [2004] 1 WLR 1304 at [1].
5   Even permanent deprivations of property may be justified under ECHR Protocol No 1, Art 1 **[para 2.29]** (see *James v United Kingdom*, Series A No 98 (1986) **[para 7.337]**; *R (Fuller) v Chief Constable of Dorset Police* [2003] QB 480 at [62]).
6   For Blackstone, writing in 1765, it was inconceivable that 'sacred and inviolable rights of private property' should be postponed to 'public necessity' without 'a full indemnification and equivalent for the injury thereby sustained' (*Bl Comm*, Vol 1, p 135).

Procedure

13.169   The process of compulsory purchase is regulated by statute[1] and involves, in essence, the making of a compulsory purchase order (pursuant to the Acquisition of Land Act 1981) which leads ultimately to a transfer of title subject to compensation for actual loss suffered by the landowner (as assessed under the Land Compensation Act 1961[2]). The Planning and Compulsory Purchase Act 2004 is aimed in part at liberalising the regimes of both compulsory purchase and compensation. Local authorities are given power to acquire land if they think that development, redevelopment or improvement of that land is likely to promote the economic, social or environmental well-being of their area.[3] The statutory procedures of compulsory purchase are made more speedy[4] and the provision of 'loss payments' for those affected by compulsory acquisition is significantly extended.[5]

1   Compulsory Purchase Act 1965. The underlying assumption of Parliament is that the acquiring authority will 'act reasonably in the public interest ... but with due regard to the interests of the person being dispossessed' (*Simpsons Motor Sales (London) Ltd v Hendon Corpn* [1963] Ch 57 at 83 per Upjohn J). See also *Collector of Land Revenue South West District Penang v Kam Gin Paik* [1986] 1 WLR 412 at 416D; *Mallick v Liverpool CC* [2000] JPL 521 at 525–528.

2   Compensation is based on market value, taking no account of the compulsory nature of the acquisition or of the impact on market values of the scheme underlying the acquisition (Land Compensation Act 1961, ss 5–6). See *Point Gourde Quarrying and Transport Co Ltd v Sub-Intendent of Crown Lands* [1947] AC 565 at 572 per Lord MacDermott; *Director of Buildings and Lands v Shun Fung Ironworks Ltd* [1995] 2 AC 111 at 125C–H; *Fletcher Estates (Harlescott) Ltd v Secretary of State for the Environment* [2000] 2 AC 307 at 315B–F; *Waters v Welsh Development Agency* [2004] 1 WLR 1304 at [61]–[63], [138].

3   T&CPA 1990, s 226(1), (1A), as amended by P&CPA 2004, s 99.

4   P&CPA 204, ss 100–102 (amending Acquisition of Land Act 1981).

5   Land Compensation Act 1973, ss 33A–33K, as inserted by P&CPA 2004, ss 106–109.

Privatised utilities

13.170   Potentially more controversial nowadays is the fact that many privatised utility companies, which formerly functioned within the public sector, retain indirectly the substantial economic advantage of the compulsory purchase powers once vested in their predecessors. These companies operate typically in the water, power and communications industries.[1] It is deeply questionable whether powers to expropriate private citizens should be available to such companies for the benefit of their own equity shareholders, but the recent drive towards privatisation rather obscures the fact that the rationale of compulsory acquisition of land has now been fundamentally skewed.[2] With the advent of the privatised utility corporation, it is no longer the case that compulsory acquisition is directed towards exclusively public purposes or that every citizen is equally the beneficiary of the process. The complacency of English law in this regard contrasts with the approach of American courts, which tend to scrutinise with fierce vigilance any proposal that eminent domain be asserted in order to effect a compulsory purchase from one private actor for the benefit of another,[3] thereby compelling the sale to a commercial corporate entity of 'what it could not get through arm's length negotiations.'[4]

1   See e g Water Resources Act 1991, s 154(1); Environment Act 1995, s 2(1)(a)(iv).

2   See Gray and Gray, 'Private Property and Public Propriety', in J McLean (ed), *Property and the Constitution* (1999), pp 36–37.

3   See, for instance, the bitter dissents provoked by the decision of the Supreme Court of Michigan in *Poletown Neighbourhood Council v City of Detroit*, 304 NW2d 455 (1981), which effectively authorised the expropriation of the elderly Polish-American population of a Detroit suburb in order to clear a site for a new assembly plant for General Motors Corporation.

4   See *City of Lansing v Edward Rose Realty, Inc*, 481 NW2d 795 at 798 (Mich App 1992), affd
    502 NW2d 638 at 645–647 (Mich 1993). Compare *James v United Kingdom*, Series A No 98
    (1986) at [40].

REGULATORY TAKINGS

13.171   Much modern environmental regulation involves not the direct acquisition of property by the state, but rather the imposition of substantial
restrictions upon the free enjoyment of estate ownership (eg through planning
or listed building controls or by specific prohibition of certain uses for reasons
of ecological conservation or heritage preservation). This kind of regulatory
intervention leaves title intact in the estate owner's hands, but dramatically
curtails or redefines the ways in which he may exploit his land. One of the large
questions for the future relates to whether such socially directed limitations of
land use merit compensation from public funds.[1] Courts have long been aware
that regulatory impositions may force 'some people alone to bear public
burdens which, in all fairness and justice, should be borne by the public as a
whole.'[2] The ever-present danger is that extensive state intervention may allow
government to 'do by regulation what it cannot do through eminent domain –
ie, take private property without paying for it.'[3]

1   See the pragmatic solution adopted in Sydney, where the impact of heritage preservation law
    (in precluding upward expansion of an historic building) is cushioned under the city's town
    planning code by allowing the disentitled owner to sell the unutilised notional 'transferable
    floor space' (ie development potential) to some other owner not so disentitled (*Uniting Church
    in Australia Property Trust (NSW) v Immer (No 145) Pty Ltd* (1991) 24 NSWLR 510 at
    511B–F (revd on unconnected grounds: (1993) 182 CLR 26)).
2   *Armstrong v United States*, 364 US 40 at 49, 4 L Ed 2d 1554 at 1561 (1960) per Justice Black.
    See likewise *Penn Central Transportation Co v New York City*, 438 US 104 at 124, 57 L Ed 2d
    631 at 648 per Justice Brennan (1978); *Newcrest Mining (WA) Ltd v Commonwealth of
    Australia* (1997) 190 CLR 513 at 639 per Kirby J; *Grape Bay Ltd v Attorney-General of
    Bermuda* [2000] 1 WLR 574 at 583C–D per Lord Hoffmann.
3   *Tahoe-Sierra Preservation Council, Inc v Tahoe Regional Planning Agency*, 228 F3d 998 at 999
    (2000) per Kozinski J. See similarly *Mariner Real Estate Ltd v Nova Scotia (Attorney General)*
    (1999) 177 DLR (4th) 696 at 699 (at stake is the 'policy issue of how minutely government
    may control land without buying it').

Identifying derogations from property

13.172   It is generally accepted throughout the common law world that, at
some point, regulation shades into confiscation and comprises a compensable
'taking' by the state of the essential core of the estate owner's 'bundle of
sticks'.[1] In certain cases regulatory intervention reaches the stage where it
deprives the owner of the 'substance' and 'reality' of proprietorship[2] or of
'everything that made [it] worth having.'[3] The difficulty is that the precise
borderline between regulation and confiscation – the threshold of a compensable 'regulatory taking' – is notoriously elusive.[4] The vital question here is not
about the desirability or statutory competence of environmental regulation, but

rather about who should bear the cost of the environmental protection which the community professes to require.[5] Accordingly, across the common law world, the environmental debate has been transformed into a major struggle about the definition of 'property' and the social limits of ownership.[6]

1   See e g *Belfast Corpn v O D Cars Ltd* [1960] AC 490 at 519–520 per Viscount Simonds, 525 per Lord Radcliffe. See also *Commonwealth of Australia v State of Tasmania* (1983) 158 CLR 1 at 144 per Mason J; *Newcrest Mining (WA) Ltd v Commonwealth of Australia* (1997) 190 CLR 513 at 639 per Kirby J; *Pennsylvania Coal Co v Mahon*, 260 US 393 at 415, 67 L Ed 322 at 326 (1922) per Justice Holmes ('if regulation goes too far it will be recognised as a taking').

2   *Bank of New South Wales v Commonwealth of Australia* (1948) 76 CLR 1 at 349 per Dixon J. See e g *Newcrest Mining (WA) Ltd v Commonwealth of Australia* (1997) 190 CLR 513 at 639 per Kirby J ('rights ... effectively confiscated'), 635 per Gummow J ('effective sterilisation'). In *Newcrest Mining* the High Court of Australia decided by a majority that it was improper to expand a national park for public benefit, thereby frustrating future operations under a privately held mining lease.

3   *Minister of State for the Army v Dalziel* (1944) 68 CLR 261 at 286 per Rich J. See similarly *Commonwealth of Australia v Western Australia* (1999) 196 CLR 392 at [156] per Gummow J; *Mariner Real Estate Ltd v Nova Scotia (Attorney General)* (1999) 177 DLR 696 at 716–717, 727.

4   See *Williamson County Regional Planning Commn v Hamilton Bank of Johnson City*, 473 US 172 at 199, 87 L Ed 2d 126 at 147 (1985) per Justice Blackmun (the 'lawyer's equivalent of the physicist's hunt for the quark'). See also *Trade Practices Commission v Tooth & Co Ltd* (1979) 142 CLR 397 at 415 per Stephen J.

5   See P A Joseph, 'The Environment, Property Rights, and Public Choice Theory' (2003) 20 NZULR 408.

6   See Gray and Gray, 'The Idea of Property in Land', in S Bright and J K Dewar (ed), *Land Law: Themes and Perspectives* (Oxford 1998), pp 43–51.

13.173   Major assumptions relating to the ambit of civic responsibility exert a constant impact upon the definition of 'property' in land.[1] Views inevitably differ as to the intensity of the individual citizen's obligation to contribute gratis towards the environmental welfare enjoyed by the wider community. Some may think that uncompensated regulation is ultimately a form of environmental fascism, in that it concentrates the cost of communal environmental benefits unevenly or randomly on isolated groups of citizens. The 1990s saw a fierce movement in the United States directed towards slaying 'the regulatory monster'[2] and supported by the battle-cry 'no regulation without compensation.' Equally it can be argued that title to land never confers any intrinsic right to inflict avoidable harm on the public interest. On this view the estate owner never has *any* right to exploit his land in an environmentally harmful fashion; and regulatory control merely renders explicit those limitations on user which were always latent qualifications on his title. Analysed in this way, state regulation actually deprives the estate owner of *none* of the 'sticks' in his bundle of rights and thus causes him no net loss.[3] The community is already entitled – has always been entitled – to the benefit of a public-interest forbearance on his part.[4]

1   [Para 2.15].
2   See Laura Underkuffler-Freund, 'Takings and the Nature of Property' 9 Can Jo Law and Juris 161 (1996).
3   In the United States a long line of authority leads back to the proposition of Justice Brandeis

that no derogation from ownership rights – and, *a fortiori*, no compensable taking – occurs if regulatory control merely confirms the prohibition of a 'noxious use' which never fell within the original complement of powers incident to title (*Pennsylvania Coal Co v Mahon*, 260 US 393 at 417, 67 L Ed 322 at 327 (1922)).

4   As one American court has pointed out, 'the question is simply one of basic property ownership rights: within the bundle of rights which property lawyers understand to constitute property, is the right or interest at issue, as a matter of law, owned by the property owner or reserved to the state?' (*Loveladies Harbor, Inc v United States*, 28 F3d 1171 at 1179 (Fed Cir 1994)).

The Lucas decision

13.174   A famous confrontation between competing philosophies emerged in the United States in *Lucas v South Carolina Coastal Council*.[1] Here the petitioner, a property developer, had purchased (for almost $1 million) beach-front property in an ecologically fragile coastal area, intending to construct luxury residences similar to existing (and increasingly valuable) homes in the immediate locality. Two years later – and before he had begun construction – South Carolina enacted state legislation which, for environmental reasons, prevented further development of the land. A state trial court found that the petitioner's land had been rendered valueless by the legislative intervention and the petitioner claimed that he had suffered a 'taking' of private property which, under the Fifth Amendment of the United States Constitution,[2] required the payment of just compensation. The Supreme Court of South Carolina held that where, as here, a regulation was designed 'to prevent serious public harm', such a regulation effected no 'taking' at all and therefore required no payment of compensation by the state.[3]

1   505 US 1003, 120 L Ed 2d 798 (US Supreme Court 1992), on appeal from 404 SE2d 895 (Supreme Court of South Carolina 1991).
2   **[Para 2.27]**.
3   *Lucas v South Carolina Coastal Council*, 404 SE2d 895 at 899 (1991). For a similar issue arising in Canada, see *Mariner Real Estate Ltd v Nova Scotia (Attorney General)* (1998) 165 DLR (4th) 727 at 739–740, reversed by the Court of Appeal of Nova Scotia ((1999) 177 DLR 696 at 727–729 (no compensable expropriation through designation of 'beach')).

13.175   In a highly controversial decision a majority in the Supreme Court of the United States overturned this approach and ruled that the potential for profitable (albeit damaging) development of ecologically sensitive areas was limited merely by 'background principles' of property and nuisance. On this basis, compensation for regulatory control could be denied to the landowner *only if* the control in question duplicated some restriction which already 'inhere[d] in the title itself', with the result that the 'proscribed use interests' were therefore 'not part of [the owner's] title to begin with.'[1] Where, however, a total prohibition of economically productive or beneficial land use 'goes beyond what the relevant background principles would dictate', there is no question: 'compensation must be paid to sustain it.'[2] Significantly, the Supreme Court majority indicated that compensation could not be withheld simply on the basis that a landowner's proposed exploitation of his land was 'inconsistent with the public interest.'[3]

1   505 US 1003 at 1027, 120 L Ed 2d 798 at 820–821 per Justice Scalia. In such cases the estate owner is merely being 'barred from putting land to a use that is proscribed by … "existing rules or understandings"' based on the state law of property and nuisance (505 US 1003 at 1030, 120 L Ed 2d 798 at 822).

2   505 US 1003 at 1030, 120 L Ed 2d 798 at 822. In a powerful dissent Justice Blackmun declined to accept that the petitioner's land had, in fact, lost all economic value. The petitioner could still enjoy 'other attributes of property' such as the right to exclude others and the right to 'picnic, swim, camp in a tent, or live on the property in a movable trailer … Petitioner also retains the right to alienate the land, which would have value for neighbors and for those prepared to enjoy proximity to the ocean without a house' (505 US 1003 at 1044, 120 L Ed 2d 798 at 831). See likewise *Mariner Real Estate Ltd v Nova Scotia (Attorney General)* (1999) 177 DLR (4th) 696 at 706, 728–729.

3   505 US 1003 at 1031, 120 L Ed 2d 798 at 822–823. The Supreme Court later held that a claimant could not be barred from compensation even if he acquired title with knowledge of a pre-existing regulatory limitation on his rights (see *Palazzolo v Rhode Island*, 533 US 606, 150 L Ed 2d 592 (2001)).

13.176 In *Lucas* a majority in the Supreme Court thus regarded the profitable development even of sensitive coastal areas as likely to be permissible under existing rules of property and nuisance,[1] with the consequence that compensation was, in principle, payable to the petitioner.[2] The polarities of philosophy exemplified in the ruling aptly illustrated the way in which 'property' in land is constantly defined and delimited by perceptions of civic responsibility. The landmark decision in *Lucas* reflected an individualist rather than communitarian perspective on property holdings and betrayed little awareness that community obligation – in the form of an inherent duty to avoid environmental degradation – may be a pre-existing and pervasive qualification on a landowner's title.[3]

1   505 US 1003 at 1031, 120 L Ed 2d 798 at 822.

2   The petitioner finally succeeded in obtaining compensation in the state courts (see *Lucas v South Carolina Coastal Council*, 424 SE2d 484 at 486 (1992)).

3   Contrast Greg Alexander's perceptive account of the idea of property as 'propriety' – of property as intimately connected with civic virtue and therefore a 'private basis for the public good' (Gregory S Alexander, *Commodity & Propriety: Competing Visions of Property in American Legal Thought 1776 – 1970* (Univ of Chicago Press 1997)).

13.177 The *Lucas* ruling was widely understood as signalling a strong judicial inclination to stem a tide of uncompensated taking from American citizens under the cover of a mere exercise of regulatory power.[1] Yet even American courts have subsequently realised that to regard all regulatory impositions as compensable 'takings' would 'transform government regulation into a luxury few governments could afford.'[2] The costs of social and economic organisation would become wholly prohibitive.[3] In one of the more recent 'takings' cases in the United States Supreme Court, Justice Stevens pointed to the spectre of a 'tremendous – and tremendously capricious – one-time transfer of wealth from society at large to those individuals who happen to hold title to large tracts of land' in environmentally sensitive locations.[4] There is beginning to be some awareness that 'the purchase of a "bundle of rights" necessarily includes the acquisition of a bundle of limitations.'[5]

1   '[A] State, by ipse dixit, may not transform private property into public property without

compensation' (505 US 1003 at 1031, 120 L Ed 2d 798 at 823). See similarly *Commonwealth of Australia v Western Australia* (1999) 196 CLR 392 at [271]–[285] per Callinan J.

2   *Tahoe-Sierra Preservation Council, Inc v Tahoe Regional Planning Agency*, 535 US 302 at 324, 152 L Ed 2d 517 at 541 (2002) per Justice Stevens. See also *Belfast Corpn v O D Cars Ltd* [1960] AC 490 at 518 per Viscount Simonds; *Florida Rock Industries, Inc v United States* (1999) 45 Fed Cl 21 at 23 per Smith CJ.

3   As Justice Holmes once said, '[g]overnment could hardly go on if, to some extent, values incident to property could not be diminished without paying for every such change in the general law' (*Pennsylvania Coal Co v Mahon*, 260 US 393 at 413, 67 L Ed 322 at 325 (1922)). See likewise *Slattery v Naylor* (1888) 13 App Cas 446 at 449–50 per Lord Hobhouse; *O D Cars Ltd v Belfast Corporation* [1959] NI 62 at 87–88 per Lord MacDermott LCJ; *Belfast Corpn v O D Cars Ltd* [1960] AC 490 at 518 per Viscount Simonds.

4   *Palazzolo v Rhode Island*, 533 US 606 at 645, 150 L Ed 2d 592 at 624–625 (2001).

5   *Gazza v New York State Department of Environmental Conservation*, 679 NE2d 1035 at 1039 (NY 1997). See also *Esplanade Properties, LLC v City of Seattle*, 307 F3d 978 at 985–987 (2002).

The European perspective

13.178   Unlike the 'takings' law of the United States,[1] European law has tended to be generally more receptive to the idea of non-compensable community-oriented constraints on land use.[2] On this side of the Atlantic, the law of environmental regulation resonates with the idea that ownership is intrinsically delimited by community-directed obligation, with the consequence that regulatory intrusions which merely curtail improper or socially undesirable uses of land involve no *taking* of property, let alone any *compensable* taking.[3] Both the common law[4] and European jurisprudence[5] place an implicit emphasis on obligations of civic cohesion – on an interlinked network of socialised duty – as underpinning the reality of land ownership amidst the complex interdependency of modern life. On this analysis the inner meaning of property in land is critically dependent on the communally defined parameters of citizenship. Proprietary rights and proprietary duties are ultimately also social rights and social duties.

1   For a brief, but excellent, survey of American takings law, see David L Callies, *Takings: Land An Introduction and Overview*, 24 Univ of Hawaii L Rev 441 (2002).

2   See *Belfast Corpn v O D Cars Ltd* [1960] AC 490 at 517–518 per Viscount Simonds, 523–524 per Lord Radcliffe; *Grape Bay Ltd v Attorney-General of Bermuda* [2000] 1 WLR 574 at 583B–F per Lord Hoffmann; *Davies v Crawley BC* [2001] EWHC Admin 854 at [115]–[117].

3   See Gray, 'Land Law and Human Rights', in Louise Tee (ed), *Land Law: Issues, Debates, Policy* (Willan Publishing 2002), pp 237–243.

4   See *Re Ellis and Ruislip-Northwood UDC* [1920] 1 KB 343 at 372 per Scrutton LJ.

5   See e g *Hauer v Land Rheinland-Pfalz* [1979] ECR 3727 at [19]–[22].

13.179   A good illustration of the last point can be found in *O'Callaghan v Commissioners of Public Works in Ireland and the Attorney General*.[1] Here the Supreme Court of Ireland flatly rejected the suggestion that public compensation was required in respect of the compulsory preservation of a neolithic fort situated on privately owned farm land. Even though the relevant preservation order inhibited the farmer's gainful activity on the land concerned,

O'Higgins CJ indicated that 'the common good requires that national monuments which are the prized relics of the past should be preserved as part of the history of our people.' The preservation of the fort was therefore 'a requirement of what should be regarded as the common duty of all citizens.'[2]

1   [1985] ILRM 364 at 367–368.
2   For a similar conclusion reached by the German Constitutional Court, see *Rheinland-Pfälzische Denkmalschutzgesetz* Case 100 BVerfGE 226 (1999). See also Art 14(2) of the German *Grundgesetz* [**para 2.92**].

The English perspective

13.180   In England even far-reaching forms of regulatory interference with the enjoyment or exploitation of land are broadly perceived as undeserving of publicly funded cash indemnity.[1] As Lord Hoffmann put it in *Grape Bay Ltd v Attorney-General of Bermuda*,[2] '[t]he give and take of civil society frequently requires that the exercise of private rights should be restricted in the general public interest.'[3] The profitable exploitation of land is 'not in general a matter of right',[4] but merely a privilege granted at the discretion of the state in accordance with socially determined strategies of communally beneficial land use. Thus, for example, only extremely limited rights to compensation are available where an existing planning permission is revoked or modified to the prejudice of the landowner[5] or where an existing use or development of land is ordered to be discontinued.[6] Although in rare (and restrictively defined[7]) circumstances of land use control, a landowner may require his local authority to purchase his interest in any land which has been rendered 'incapable of reasonably beneficial use in its existing state',[8] the courts have shown themselves remarkably slow to find that relevant land has been wholly sterilised by adverse planning outcomes.[9]

1   See e g Planning and Compensation Act 1991, s 31. See also *Westminster Bank Ltd v Minister of Housing and Local Government* [1971] AC 508 at 528D, 529D–F per Lord Reid, 535C per Viscount Dilhorne (no compensation for refusal of planning permission).
2   [2000] 1 WLR 574 at 583C per Lord Hoffmann. See similarly *Wildtree Hotels Ltd v Harrow LBC* [2001] 2 AC 1 at 10A–B; *R (Alconbury Developments Ltd and others) v Secretary of State for the Environment, Transport and the Regions* [2003] 2 AC 295 at [71]–[72].
3   See also *Commonwealth of Australia v State of Tasmania* (1983) 158 CLR 1 at 283 per Deane J; *Cockburn v Minister of Works and Development* [1984] 2 NZLR 466 at 477 per McMullin J; *Luoni v Minister of Works and Development* [1989] 1 NZLR 62 at 65 per Cooke P; *R v Land Use Planning Review Panel, ex p MF Cas Pty Ltd* (Unreported, Supreme Court of Tasmania, 23 October 1998).
4   *R (Alconbury Developments Ltd and others) v Secretary of State for the Environment, Transport and the Regions* [2003] 2 AC 295 at [156] per Lord Clyde.
5   T&CPA 1990, ss 107(1), 108(1). See *Canterbury CC v Colley* [1993] AC 401 at 406F per Lord Oliver of Aylmerton.
6   T&CPA 1990, ss 102(1), 115. Compensation is more readily provided where regulatory activity takes the form of a continuous physical invasion of land, e g through the installation of electricity transmission lines or pylons (see Electricity Act 1989, Sch 4, para 7). Compare *Loretto v Teleprompter Manhattan CATV Corp*, 458 US 419 at 441, 73 L Ed 2d 868 at 886 (1982).
7   See e g *R v Minister of Housing and Local Government, ex p Chichester RDC* [1960] 1 WLR

587 at 589; *Wain v Secretary of State for the Environment* (1981) 44 P & CR 289 at 300; *Cook and Woodham v Winchester CC* (1994) 69 P & CR 99 at 106–107; *R v North West Leicestershire DC and East Midlands International Airport Ltd, ex p Moses* [2000] JPL 1287 at 1299; *Davies v Crawley BC* [2001] EWHC Admin 854 at [99]; *Waltham Forest LBC v Secretary of State for Transport, Local Government and the Regions* [2002] EWCA Civ 330 at [14].

8   T&CPA 1990, s 137(1)–(4). See e g *Gavaghan v Secretary of State for the Environment* (1989) 60 P & CR 515; *Douglas v Berwick-upon-Tweed BC* (Lands Tribunal, 30 July 1985). See also Planning (Listed Buildings and Conservation Areas) Act 1990, s 32(1)–(4); Highways Act 1980, s 246 (but note the restrictive construction in *Owen v Secretary of State for Transport* (Unreported, Court of Appeal, 14 October 1996)).

9   See e g *Whiston v Secretary of State for the Environment* [1989] JPL 178 at 179–180; *Colley v Secretary of State for the Environment and Canterbury CC* (1998) 77 P & CR 190 at 197–198.

A principle of civic reciprocity

13.181   The English stance on these issues gives expression to some deep sense of civic equity: the impact of regulatory control of land use is simply 'part of the burden of common citizenship.'[1] On this view there is little point in the affected landowner invoking the protective force of Magna Carta, not least since there is an increasingly stern reluctance today to view Magna Carta 'as some early Public Works Act compensation statute.'[2] The concept of property is a fusion of right and responsibility[3] and all citizens are exposed, on precisely similar terms, to the risk that overriding public necessity may demand the forgoing of some advantage associated with land; all are equally obliged to conserve and promote the quality of the natural or man-made environment.[4] It has long been recognised that the diffusion of the local or public benefits generated by the state's regulatory activity frequently produces an 'average reciprocity of advantage' for all concerned.[5] In so far as regulatory intervention enhances the quality of life for all in a neighbourhood or protects our common heritage, wildlife or landscape, the individual citizen's proprietary rights can be seen as having been curtailed in exchange for improved civic rights to environmental welfare.[6] The broad mutuality of benefit and burden means, in effect, that a dimension of compensation is already inherent in the very mechanism of regulation.[7]

1   The phrase is that of Justice Frankfurter (*Kimball Laundry Co v United States*, 338 US 1 at 5, 93 L Ed 1765 at 1772 (1949)).

2   *Westco Lagan Ltd v Attorney-General* [2001] 1 NZLR 40 at [42] per McGechan J. See also *Belfast Corpn v O D Cars Ltd* [1960] AC 490 at 519 per Viscount Simonds (legislative attenuation of an owner's user rights 'can be effected without a cry being raised that Magna Carta is dethroned or a sacred principle of liberty infringed').

3   [**Paras 2.27, 13.180**].

4   See Gray and Gray, 'The rhetoric of realty', in J Getzler (ed), *Rationalizing Property, Equity and Trusts: Essays in Honour of Edward Burn* (Butterworths 2003), pp 265–278.

5   *Pennsylvania Coal Co v Mahon*, 260 US 393 at 415, 67 L Ed 322 at 326 (1922) per Justice Holmes.

6   See Frank Michelman, 'Property, Utility and Fairness: Comments on the Ethical Foundations of "Just Compensation" Law' 80 Harv L Rev 1165 at 1225 (1966–67); *Pennsylvania Coal Co v Mahon*, 260 US 393 at 422, 67 L Ed 322 at 329 (1922) per Justice Brandeis; *San Remo Hotel LP v City and County of San Francisco*, 41 P3d 87 at 109 (2002) per Werdegar J.

7   See *Keystone Bituminous Coal Association v DeBenedictis*, 480 US 470 at 491, 94 L Ed 2d 472

at 492 (1987) per Justice Stevens. See also *Tahoe-Sierra Preservation Council, Inc v Tahoe Regional Planning Agency*, 535 US 302, 152 L Ed 2d 517 at 552 (2002) per Justice Stevens.

Strasbourg jurisprudence

13.182   This analysis is broadly consistent with the case law which has evolved over the last 30 years in the construction of the property guarantee of the European Convention on Human Rights.[1] Here, in sharp contrast to its approach to outright *deprivations* of ownership, European jurisprudence expressly preserves the right of the state to 'enforce such laws as it deems necessary to control the use of property in accordance with the general interest.'[2] In *Banér v Sweden*[3] the now defunct European Human Rights Commission endorsed the argument that '[e]veryone must be prepared to accept a certain interference in the public interest without compensation.' It followed that mere regulatory interference with the enjoyment of land carries no 'inherent' right to compensation for the affected landowner,[4] except in those extreme cases where it can be said that no 'fair balance' has been achieved as between the 'general interest of the community' and the 'fundamental rights' of the individual citizen.[5] Accordingly the European Court of Human Rights has frequently confirmed that the 'control of use' proviso covers, in principle at least, most measures of urban planning[6] and environmental conservation.[7]

1   ECHR Protocol No 1, Art 1 **[para 2.29]**.
2   See *R (Fuller) v Chief Constable of Dorset Police* [2003] QB 480 at [62] per Stanley Burnton J.
3   (1989) 60 DR 128 at 140.
4   (1989) 60 DR 128 at 142 (no compensation for imposition of public fishing rights on private landowners as part of national policy directed towards extension of leisure opportunities).
5   See *Tesco Stores Ltd v Secretary of State for the Environment, Transport and the Regions* (2000) 80 P & CR 427 at 429 per Sullivan J; *Booker Aquaculture Ltd v Secretary of State for Scotland* (1998) Times, 24 September; Court of Session: Inner House (Unreported, 12 August 1999). An interference with land rights which lacks 'proportionality' cannot, of course, be deemed 'necessary' in terms of Art 1 of Protocol No 1 or said to subserve the 'general interest' (*Banér v Sweden* (1989) 60 DR 128 at 141).
6   See *Sporrung and Lönnroth v Sweden*, Series A No 52 (1982) at [64]; *Allan Jacobsson v Sweden*, Series A No 163 (1989) at [54], [57]; *Pine Valley Developments Ltd v Ireland*, Series A No 222 (1991) at [59]–[60]; *Katte Klitsche de la Grange v Italy*, Series A No 293-B (1994) at [47]–[48] (1994).
7   See *Denev v Sweden* (1989) 59 DR 127 at 130; *Banér v Sweden* (1989) 60 DR 128 at 140; *Fredin v Sweden*, Series A No 192 (1991) at [47]–[48]; *Matos e Silva, LDA and others v Portugal* (1997) 24 EHRR 573 at [85].

De facto expropriation

13.183   Although regarding regulatory intervention by the state as presumptively non-compensable, the European Court of Human Rights has nevertheless conceded that the distinction between expropriation and mere regulatory control can never be entirely clear-cut. An extreme form of state regulation of land use may constitute 'de facto expropriation' if it sufficiently 'affects the substance of the property ... [that] the measure complained of "can be assimilated to a deprivation of possessions".'[1] Moreover, even the regulation of land use is subject to a criterion of 'proportionality' under which the state may be adjudged to have violated the overarching Convention guarantee of 'peaceful enjoyment' of possessions[2] if the means employed for the furtherance of a relevant social objective was not reasonably proportional to the aim sought to be realised.[3] Whilst a 'wide margin of appreciation' is inevitably enjoyed by states in the implementation of matters of social policy,[4] compensation may be required if the regulatory impact on a landowner's rights has been especially invasive, enduring or debilitating.[5]

1   *Banér v Sweden* (1989) 60 DR 128 at 139–140, citing *Sporrung and Lönnroth v Sweden*, Series A No 52 (1982) at [63]. The regulatory intervention must take away 'all meaningful use of the properties in question' (*Fredin v Sweden*, Series A No 192 (1991) at [42]–[45]). See *Papamichalopoulos v Greece*, Series A No 260-B (1993) at [41]–[46]; *Davies v Crawley BC* [2001] EWHC Admin 854 at [131] per Goldring J. Contrast *Pine Valley Developments Ltd v Ireland*, Series A No 222 (1991) at [56] (land still capable of farming use).

2   **[Para 2.29]**. European jurisprudence has confirmed that certain cases of regulatory intervention may constitute neither a 'deprivation of possessions' nor a 'control of use', but rather a 'third form of interference' which falls under the generic head of interference with the 'peaceful enjoyment of ... possessions' (*Banér v Sweden* (1989) 60 DR 128 at 138–139). See likewise *Katte Klitsche de la Grange v Italy*, Series A No 293-B (1994) at [40]; *Stran Greek Refineries and Stratis Andreadis v Greece*, Series A No 301-B (1994) at [68].

3   *Sporrung and Lönnroth v Sweden*, Series A No 52 (1982) at [73]; *James v United Kingdom*, Series A No 98 (1986) at [50]; *Fredin v Sweden*, Series A No 192 (1991) at [51]; *Air Canada v United Kingdom*, Series A No 316-A (1995) at [36].

4   *Sporrung and Lönnroth v Sweden*, Series A No 52 (1982) at [69]; *Banér v Sweden* (1989) 60 DR 128 at 141; *Case of Mellacher*, Series A No 169 (1989) at [45]; *Fredin v Sweden*, Series A No 192 (1991) at [51].

5   See *Allan Jacobsson v Sweden*, Series A No 163 (1989) at [55]; *Air Canada v United Kingdom*, Series A No 316-A (1995) at [36]; *Pialopoulos v Greece* (2001) 33 EHRR 39 at [56]–[62]; *GL v Italy* (2002) 34 EHRR 41 at [20]–[26].

Exceptional grounds for compensation

13.184   The European Court of Human Rights has accordingly indicated that the 'peaceful enjoyment' clause may be breached by certain kinds of land use control which, even though directed towards perfectly rational regulatory aims, fail to balance fairly the interests of the individual owner and the wider community, thus leaving the landowner uncompensated for his involuntary contribution to public welfare goals.[1] In *Matos e Silva, LDA and others v Portugal*,[2] for example, the applicants' use of their land had been 'incontestably' restricted by a prolonged ban on both new construction and new farming activities. The ban had been imposed in connection with the creation of an aquacultural research station and national nature reserve for migrant birds to be sited on the applicants' portion of the Algarve coast. The Human Rights Court held that, although the intended environmental strategy 'did not lack a reasonable basis', the substantial (and uncompensated) interference with the landowners' rights had contravened the 'peaceful enjoyment' guarantee of Article 1.[3] A similar finding emerged in *Chassagnou v France*,[4] where the regulatory scheme under challenge was aimed at the improved organisation of hunting and the rational management of game stocks. Under new legislation landowners were obliged to surrender to approved municipal hunting associations their exclusive hunting rights over their own lands in return for reciprocal hunting rights over the lands of other association members. In so far as the scheme extinguished, for all practical purposes, the right to prohibit entry by huntsmen belonging to the new associations (and was, of course, both futile and offensive in relation to any landowners opposed to the principle of hunting), the Court held that there had been a clear derogation from the 'peaceful enjoyment of ... possessions' protected by Article 1.[5]

1   In some instances the regulation of land use may have such 'severe economic consequences to the detriment of the property owner' that compensation must be paid (*Banér v Sweden* (1989) 60 DR 128 at 142).

2   (1997) 24 EHRR 573 at [79].

3   (1997) 24 EHRR 573 at [86]–[93].

4   (2000) 29 EHRR 615.

5   (2000) 29 EHRR 615 at [82]–[85].

CHAPTER 14

Regulation of leases and tenancies

THE LEASEHOLD RELATIONSHIP AS A FRAMEWORK OF RIGHTS AND DUTIES

14.1 It was noted in Chapter 7[1] that the term of years has an inherent duality of character as both a *proprietary* and a *contractual* phenomenon. The formation of a leasehold relationship normally involves not merely the conveyance of an estate in land but also the creation of an intricate network of contractual obligations.[2] It is certainly true that a lease or tenancy must, by definition, confer upon the lessee or tenant a right to exclusive possession and a freedom from detailed supervision of his activities on the land.[3] But this does not mean that the relationship between landlord and tenant is *not* usually controlled fairly closely by a range of obligations (both express and implied), the due performance of which requires to be policed throughout the term of the lease.

1 [Paras **7.71, 7.75**].
2 See *National Carriers Ltd v Panalpina (Northern) Ltd* [1981] AC 675 at 705G per Lord Simon of Glaisdale [para **8.80**]; *Southwark LBC v Mills* [2001] Ch 1 at 21H per Schiemann LJ.
3 [Paras **7.131, 7.134**].

The complexity of leasehold regulation

14.2 The regulation of the leasehold nexus – the subject matter of this chapter – is made more complex by a number of factors.

The explosion of protective legislation

14.3 Particularly in the residential sector, the modern tenancy is commonly a vehicle for the delivery of a sophisticated amalgam of consumer utilities of shelter, safety, security and convenience – a role underpinned by a vast body of contemporary statute law. This corpus of legislation has grown both unwieldy and convoluted[1] and there now exists an overwhelming case for the replacement of all landlord and tenant rules by the enactment of a more simple consolidated code of landlord–tenant relations. Moreover, it remains the case that, despite the plethora of legislation, the allocation of burdens in many landlord–tenant relationships is somewhat one-sided. Rules aimed at the protection of vulnerable occupiers – whether these rules be of common law or statutory origin – have not been accorded a particularly liberal application by the courts.[2]

1   See eg Nic Madge, 'It's time to repeal all housing statutes', *Times*, 25 July 2000.
2   See eg *Baxter v Camden LBC (No 2)* [2001] QB 1 at 15F, where Tuckey LJ referred to 'what many might consider to be the harsh way in which tenants are treated by the common law.'

The European dimension

14.4   Recent years have demonstrated the way in which European Community standards and policing mechanisms are beginning to infiltrate the English law of landlord and tenant.[1] Leasehold transactions are not subject to challenge under the Unfair Contract Terms Act 1977,[2] but leasehold covenants (and, more generally, the terms on which rented accommodation is made available) are subject to control by the European-derived Unfair Terms in Consumer Contracts Regulations.[3] Pursuant to these Regulations residential tenancy obligations which operate harshly or oppressively in favour of the landlord may be invalidated as 'unfair' in so far as, 'contrary to the requirement of good faith', they cause a 'significant imbalance in the parties' rights and obligations ... to the detriment of the consumer.'[4] Other leasehold provisions (eg tied-house covenants obliging a tenant publican to purchase beer supplies only from his landlord) may be invalidated as a form of anti-competitive practice prohibited by Article 81 of the Treaty of Rome.[5]

1   See C Bright and S Bright, 'Europe, the Nation State, and Land', in S Bright and J K Dewar (ed), *Land Law: Themes and Perspectives* (OUP 1998), p 356.
2   Unfair Contract Terms Act 1977, s 3, Sch 1, para 1(b). See *Electricity Supply Nominees Ltd v IAF Group Ltd* [1993] 1 WLR 1059 at 1063G–1064B (exclusion of tenant's right to recoup repair costs); *Unchained Growth III plc v Granby Village (Manchester) Management Co Ltd* (1999) *Times*, 4 November (service charge).
3   Unfair Terms in Consumer Contracts Regulations 1999 (SI 1999/2083) (as amended by SI 2001/1186). See Law Commission, *Renting Homes* (Law Com No 284, November 2003), para 1.3; *Newham LBC v Khatun* [2004] EWCA Civ 55 at [83], [88] per Laws LJ.
4   SI 1999/2083, reg 5. See S Bright, 'Winning the battle against unfair contract terms' (2000) 20 *Legal Studies* 331.
5   *Courage Ltd v Crehan* [1999] 2 EGLR 145 at 157K–M (referring the issue to the European Court of Justice); *Courage Ltd v Crehan (Case C-453/99)* [2002] QB 507 at [36]; *Crehan v Inntrepreneur Pub Co CPC* [2004] EWCA Civ 637 at [112]–[120], [146] **[para 15.47]**.

14.5   It is also becoming increasingly clear that the European Convention on Human Rights can impinge heavily on landlord and tenant legislation, even to the extent of causing such legislation to be reformulated by the courts in order to ensure conformity with Convention guarantees.[1] In particular, the Convention right to respect for 'private and family life' and the 'home'[2] is likely to colour the application of residential tenancy law and the legal supervision of

the functions of social landlords. It is even possible that, in certain circumstances, restrictive rules regulating the enforceability of leasehold covenants
may now require modification in the light of the landlord's right to 'peaceful
enjoyment of his possessions.'[3]

1   See eg *Ghaidan v Godin-Mendoza* [2004] 3 WLR 113 at [35], [128]–[129], [144] **[para 14.320]**.
2   ECHR Art 8 **[paras 2.60–2.61]**. See *Pemberton v Southwark LBC* [2000] 1 WLR 1672 at
     1681F–H per Roch LJ, 1684C–D per Clarke LJ.
3   ECHR Protocol No 1, Art 1 **[para 2.29]**. See *PW & Co v Milton Gate Investments Ltd* [2004]
     Ch 142 at [126], [133]–[134], [279(iv)] per Neuberger J **[para 14.306]**.

Public and quasi-public impact of private law enforcement

14.6   In recent years the move towards 'contractualisation' of the lease[1] has
reinforced the idea that residential tenants are entitled to expect their tenancies to
be covered by some implied warranty of habitability or fitness for use.[2] Yet it is also
often the case that an expansive interpretation of contractual and other liability,
particularly as it bears upon hard-pressed public sector landlords (e g local
authorities) and other social landlords (e g housing charities), imposes a financial
burden which threatens the provision of much needed publicly accessible low-cost
accommodation.[3] A dominant influence in recent determinations of landlord
liability has been the recognition that, in the field of housing law, the allocation of
resources must accord with 'democratically determined priorities' and that the
courts should not, of their own motion, increase the fiscal exposure of landlords
in a manner not obviously sanctioned by Parliament.[4]

1   **[Paras 7.80–7.87]**.
2   The likely introduction of a regime of standardised consumer-oriented occupation agreements
     advocated by the Law Commission marks a significant step in this direction. See *Renting
     Homes* (Law Com No 284, November 2003) **[paras 14.349–14.353]**.
3   See e g *Southwark LBC v Mills* [2001] 1 AC 1 at 26D–E, where it emerged that a local housing
     authority with an annual budget of less than £55 million for major housing schemes would
     require £1.271 billion to bring its existing housing stock up to acceptable modern standards.
     Lord Millett referred to the 'intractable' disamenities of a huge stock of pre-war residential
     properties as a 'problem of considerable social importance.' For similar concern as to the
     effects of over-regulation of social housing schemes, see *Bruton v London & Quadrant Housing
     Trust* [2000] 1 AC 406 at 410C–D per Lord Slynn of Hadley, 411C–412B per Lord Jauncey of
     Tullichettle, 414B–D per Lord Hoffmann **[paras 7.85, 7.180]**; *Birmingham CC v Oakley* [2001]
     1 AC 617 at 628F–H per Lord Hoffmann.
4   *Southwark LBC v Mills* [2001] 1 AC 1 at 9H–10A per Lord Hoffmann; *Lee v Leeds CC* [2002]
     1 WLR 1488 at [49] per Tuckey LJ.

Dimension of transferability

14.7   The greater the duration of a tenancy, the more likely it is that the
original parties to the leasehold grant will transfer their respective entitlements
to others, thereby enormously complicating the business of enforcing leasehold
covenants against persons not privy to the initial grant.[1]

1   **[Paras 14.241–14.310]**.

Leasehold covenants are not generally interdependent

14.8 For most of the past century English law has adhered to the general principle that there is no interdependence between the proper performance of covenants by landlord and tenant: breach by the landlord does not justify non-performance by the tenant. This rule contrasts markedly with the historic principle of English contract law that breach of a material term by one contracting party relieves the other contracting party of his obligations.[1] Yet until relatively recently a breach of the landlord's responsibilities under a lease has not usually been considered to release the tenant or entitle him to throw up the lease.[2] The tenant certainly has no general right to withhold rent or service charges in order to bring pressure to bear upon a defaulting landlord.[3] Instead the tenant must seek a remedy in the form of damages, an injunction or a decree of specific performance. By contrast (and subject to certain constraints imposed by law) the landlord normally retains a right to forfeit the lease in the event of misconduct by the tenant.[4] The remedial rights of landlord and tenant have therefore been distributed most unevenly, although the recent infiltration of contractual doctrine into tenancy law has undoubtedly begun to qualify the traditional independence of covenanted obligations.[5]

1   *Kingston v Preston* (1773) 2 Doug 689, 99 ER 437 per Lord Mansfield. See generally W M McGovern, 'Dependent Promises in the History of Leases and Other Contracts' 52 Tulane L Rev 659 (1977–78); J A Humbach, 'The Common-Law Conception of Leasing: Mitigation, Habitability, and Dependence of Covenants' 60 Wash Univ LQ 1213 (1982–83).
2   For partial exceptions to this rule, see *Smith v Marrable* (1843) 11 M & W 5, 152 ER 693 **[para 14.26]**; *Lee-Parker v Izzet* [1971] 1 WLR 1688 **[para 14.60]**.
3   See e g *Amrani v Oniah* [1984] CLY 1974; *Bishop v Moy* [1963] NSWR 468 at 469–470. The tenant who withholds rent is liable to be sued for arrears and may find that his non-payment of rent affords the landlord a ground for forfeiting the lease and recovering possession. For the sad fate of a tenant who retaliated against non-repair by her landlord by withholding service charges, see *Di Palma v Victoria Square Property Co Ltd* [1984] Ch 346; *Di Palma v United Kingdom* (1986) 10 EHRR 149 **[para 14.156]**. The tenant in *Di Palma* was later described as having fallen 'in a black hole' (see *Qazi v Harrow LBC* [2004] 1 AC 983 at [130] per Lord Scott of Foscote).
4   Contrast the law of Ontario, where 'the common law rules respecting the effect of the breach of a material covenant by one party to a contract on the obligation to perform by another party apply to tenancy agreements' (Landlord and Tenant Act (RSO 1980, c 232), s 89). Likewise the Uniform Residential Landlord and Tenant Act adopted in many American jurisdictions specifically allows the tenant to raise a breach of covenant by the landlord as a defence in any action for possession for non-payment of rent (see Uniform Residential Landlord and Tenant Act, 4.105).
5   See e g *Hussein v Mehlman* [1992] 2 EGLR 87 **[paras 7.321, 14.65]**.

EXPRESS OBLIGATIONS OF THE LANDLORD

14.9 Most formal leases contain a wide range of express covenants by the landlord in respect of such matters as repair, insurance, maintenance of the common parts of premises, rights of access and options for renewal. The precise content of these covenants is left to be determined largely by the parties themselves, although the normal balance of bargaining power as between landlord and tenant ensures that the burdens of the leasehold relationship are usually allocated more heavily to the tenant than to the landlord. Where a landlord has undertaken an express obligation, the courts tend to construe the covenant strictly according to its terms.

IMPLIED OBLIGATIONS OF THE LANDLORD

14.10   In the absence of express contrary agreement, the relationship of lessor and lessee imposes certain implied obligations on the landlord.[1] These obligations may vary in accordance with the legal or equitable nature of the lease,[2] but generally include a covenant for quiet enjoyment[3] and a covenant against derogation from grant.[4]

1   These obligations may be modified by specific arrangement between landlord and tenant and if a deed contains an express covenant dealing with a particular matter in respect of the demised premises, 'there is no room for an implied covenant covering the same ground or any part of it' (*Malzy v Eichholz* [1916] 2 KB 308 at 313–314). See likewise *Line v Stephenson* (1838) 4 Bing (NC) 678 at 682–684, 132 ER 950 at 952, affd (1838) 5 Bing (NC) 183 at 186, 132 ER 1075 at 1076; *Miller v Emcer Products Ltd* [1956] Ch 304 at 319; *Western Australia v Ward* (2002) 191 ALR 1 at [499] per McHugh J.
2   Under an equitable lease or contract for a lease **[para 9.60]** there is an implied term, which may be displaced by contrary agreement, that the formal lease when executed should contain 'the usual covenants' (*Propert v Parker* (1832) 3 My & K 280 at 281, 40 ER 107).
3   **[Paras 14.11–14.17]**.
4   **[Paras 14.18–14.19]**.

COVENANT FOR QUIET ENJOYMENT

14.11   There is in every lease (whether legal or equitable[1]) an implied covenant or contractual term[2] that the landlord shall permit the tenant 'quiet enjoyment' of the premises let.[3]

1   See *Hampshire v Wickens* (1878) 7 Ch D 555 at 561.
2   In strict terms a 'covenant' exists only in relation to a lease by deed, but there is an equivalent implied contractual term for quiet enjoyment in tenancies granted otherwise than by deed (see *Budd-Scott v Daniell* [1902] 2 KB 351 at 355–356).
3   *Budd-Scott v Daniell* [1902] 2 KB 351 at 356–357; *Markham v Paget* [1908] 1 Ch 697 at 715–716; *Kenny v Preen* [1963] 1 QB 499 at 511; *Goldsworthy Mining Ltd v Federal Commissioner of Taxation* (1973) 128 CLR 199 at 214 per Mason J; *Western Australia v Ward* (2002) 191 ALR 1 at [499] per McHugh J.

Scope of the covenant

14.12   The covenant for quiet enjoyment has nothing necessarily to do with freedom from acoustic interference,[1] but is rooted historically in the concern to protect the tenant in stable and uninterrupted possession of the demised premises.[2] It is this guarantee which ultimately gives meaning to the tenant's right to exclusive possession.[3] The covenant for quiet enjoyment impliedly warrants that the tenant shall be immune from the exercise of adverse rights over the land.[4] The landlord has a duty, in other words, to ensure that the tenant remains free from any 'substantial interference with the ordinary enjoyment of the premises' during the currency of the lease.[5] Although the landlord's obligation is not absolute, it covers both his own conduct (whether rightful or wrongful) and also the rightful (but not wrongful[6]) acts of any person claiming under him.[7]

1   *Southwark LBC v Mills* [2001] 1 AC 1 at 10B–D per Lord Hoffmann, 22F–G per Lord Millett.
2   See *Jenkins v Jackson* (1888) 40 Ch D 71 at 74 per Kekewich J; *Southwark LBC v Mills* [2001] Ch 1 at 21F–G per Schiemann LJ.
3   [**Para 7.131**]. See *Western Australia v Ward* (2002) 191 ALR 1 at [512] per McHugh J. The covenant for quiet enjoyment has been described as being 'an ordinary incident of a tenancy ... it is of the very essence of the tenancy' (*Kanizaj v Brace* [1954] NZLR 283 at 284 per Gresson J). Breach constitutes 'an invasion of the [claimant's] proprietary right' (*Vasile v Perpetual Trustees WA Ltd* (1987) 10 BPR 18091 at 18096 per Bryson J).
4   See *Hudson v Cripps* [1896] 1 Ch 265 at 268; *Southwark LBC v Mills* [2001] 1 AC 1 at 22G per Lord Millett.
5   *Southwark LBC v Mills* [2001] 1 AC 1 at 10E per Lord Hoffmann. See also Lord Millett at 22G–H ('any substantial interference with the ordinary and lawful enjoyment of the land'). The conduct constituting a breach need not (but usually does) amount to nuisance (*Southwark LBC v Mills*, supra at 23D–E per Lord Millett). The implied covenant extends to 'any acts calculated to interfere with the peace or comfort of the tenant, or his family' (*McCall v Abelesz* [1976] QB 585 at 594E per Lord Denning MR). See also *Kenny v Preen* [1963] 1 QB 499 at 513, 515.
6   See *Malzy v Eichholz* [1916] 2 KB 308 at 315–316 (no breach of landlord's covenant for quiet enjoyment where one tenant complained of acts of nuisance committed, without the landlord's authority or concurrence, by other tenants).
7   *Southwark LBC v Mills* [2001] Ch 1 at 27D per Peter Gibson LJ.

Relevant interference

14.13   Mere temporary inconvenience to the tenant is not, however, enough. There must be a 'serious interference' of a 'grave and permanent nature' with the tenant's proper freedom of action in exercising his right of possession under the lease.[1] Thus, for instance, a landlord may render himself liable where a burst water pipe in premises retained by the landlord causes water to flow into and damage the tenant's premises[2] or where the landlord defaults on his covenant to maintain the weatherproofing of other parts of a block of flats[3] or where the landlord closes off a car park used by tenants of a shopping centre.[4] The covenant is not confined to the prevention of direct and physical injury to land,[5] but covers such intangible disturbances of residential amenity as that caused by the invasion of regular excessive noise from neighbouring land owned by the landlord.[6] Conversely, no breach is committed by a landlord who takes all reasonable precautions to avoid disturbance flowing from the carrying out of covenanted repairs on the demised premises.[7]

1   *Firth v BD Management Ltd* (1990) 73 DLR (4th) 375 at 379. See also *Kenny v Preen* [1963] 1 QB 499 at 511–513; *Shun Cheong Holdings BC Ltd v Gold Ocean City Supermarket Ltd* (2002) 216 DLR (4th) 392 at [9] (British Columbia Court of Appeal).
2   *Anderson v Oppenheimer* (1880) 5 QBD 602 at 607. See also *Martins Camera Corner Pty Ltd v*

Hotel Mayfair Ltd [1976] 2 NSWLR 15 at 24A–C; *Shun Cheong Holdings BC Ltd v Gold Ocean City Supermarket Ltd* (2002) 216 DLR (4th) 392 at [11].

3   *Gordon v Selico Co Ltd* [1985] 2 EGLR 79 at 83D. It is probable that no liability accrues to the landlord in the absence of some wilful or negligent omission or commission by him (see *Anderson v Oppenheimer* (1880) 5 QBD 602 at 607–608; *Booth v Thomas* [1926] Ch 397 at 403, 411).

4   *Todburn Pty Ltd v Taormina International Pty Ltd* (1990) 5 BPR 11173 at 11177. See also *Hawkesbury Nominees Pty Ltd v Battik Pty Ltd* (Federal Court of Australia, 1 March 2000, BPR Casenote 102515) (relocation of exhaust fan with debilitating consequences for tenant's restaurant kitchen); *Vasile v Perpetual Trustees WA Ltd* (1987) 10 BPR 18091 at 18096 (removal of access door).

5   *Southwark LBC v Mills* [2001] 1 AC 1 at 7A–B per Lord Slynn of Hadley, 10G–11C per Lord Hoffmann, 22H–23D per Lord Millett. See also *Caldwell v Valiant Property Management* (1997) 145 DLR (4th) 559 at 566–568.

6   *Southwark LBC v Mills* [2001] 1 AC 1 at 7B per Lord Slynn of Hadley, 11A per Lord Hoffmann. See, however, [2001] Ch 1 at 20E per Schiemann LJ ('It is only at the fringes that difficult things to measure such as noise come into the domain of this covenant').

7   *Goldmile Properties Ltd v Lechouritis* [2003] 2 P & CR 1 at [9]–[10].

Harassment and unlawful eviction

14.14   Any harassment or unlawful eviction of the tenant constitutes a breach of the landlord's implied covenant for quiet enjoyment.[1] The landlord's conduct may give rise to an action in damages or to an injunction on behalf of the tenant,[2] but harassment has not traditionally entitled the tenant to terminate the tenancy.[3] Examples of a breach of the covenant for quiet possession include a changing of the locks,[4] the removal of doors and windows,[5] the removal of the tenant's belongings,[6] the truncation of mains services[7] or central heating[8] in the tenant's home, actual or threatened violence aimed at inducing the departure of the tenant,[9] and the physical replacement of one tenant by another.[10] Even the eviction of a statutorily protected tenant following the issue of a court order for possession, but before its execution by officers of the court, has been held to amount to a breach of the covenant for quiet enjoyment.[11]

1   *Southwark LBC v Mills* [2001] Ch 1 at 21G per Schiemann LJ.
2   See *McCall v Abelesz* [1976] QB 585 at 594G, but compare (1979) 42 MLR 223 at 227–228.
3   There is room here for a doctrine of constructive eviction [**para 14.111**], an argument reinforced by the courts' recognition of a concept of repudiatory breach of leasehold covenants (see *Hussein v Mehlman* [1992] 2 EGLR 87 at 88G). See also A J Bradbrook, (1975–76) 10 Melbourne UL Rev 459 at 466.
4   *Ubhi v Nothey* (1983) LAG Bulletin 105; *Amrani v Oniah* [1984] CLY 1974; *Barnett v Djordjevic* (1984) LAG Bulletin 124.
5   *Lavender v Betts* [1942] 2 All ER 72 at 73H.
6   *Chrysostomou v Georgiou* (1982) LAG Bulletin 33.
7   *Perera v Vandiyar* [1953] 1 WLR 672 at 675–676.
8   *Malloy and Lunt v Alexander* [1982] CLY 1747.
9   *McMillan v Singh* (1985) 17 HLR 120 at 123 (landlord threw tenant's camp bed and suitcase out into garden and threatened to kill him if he tried to return).
10   *McMillan v Singh* (1985) 17 HLR 120 at 122.
11   *Kyriacou v Pandeli* [1980] CLY 1648. Such action by a landlord also gives rise to a liability in damages pursuant to Housing Act 1988, ss 27–28 [**para 14.113**]. See also *Haniff v Robinson* [1993] QB 419 at 428D–E [**para 3.78**]; *Hounslow LBC v Adjei* [2004] 2 All ER 636 at [22].

Remedies

14.15 Although in extreme cases breach of the landlord's covenant to give quiet enjoyment may nowadays entitle the tenant to repudiate his lease,[1] the more usual remedy takes the form of an injunction or award of damages. The tenant's right to damages for breach of this covenant is not prejudiced by the fact that he is himself in breach of some of the terms of the letting. It is well established that the tenant's due payment of rent or performance of other covenants cannot – even by express words – be made a precondition of the tenant's entitlement to quiet enjoyment.[2] The court may award not only general damages for loss suffered,[3] but also aggravated damages for injury to feelings[4] and possibly exemplary or punitive damages[5] in order to 'teach the defendant that a ruthless and cynical disregard of the plaintiff's rights for his own profit is not an appropriate method of proceeding.'[6] In the past awards for wrongful eviction failed to reflect the tenant's true loss,[7] but this deficiency is now amply remedied by the ground of civil liability created by the Housing Act 1988 in respect of unlawful deprivation of occupation rights.[8]

1   [**Para 7.319**]. See *Todburn Pty Ltd v Taormina International Pty Ltd* (1990) 5 BPR 11173 at 11176; *Shun Cheong Holdings BC Ltd v Gold Ocean City Supermarket Ltd* (2002) 216 DLR (4th) 392 at [11]–[14].
2   *Dawson v Dyer* (1833) 5 B & Ad 584 at 588, 110 ER 906 at 907–908; *Edge v Boileau* (1885) 16 QBD 117 at 120; *Khazanchi v Faircharm Investments Ltd* [1998] 1 WLR 1603 at 1625C; *Slater v Hoskins* [1982] 2 NZLR 541 at 551. The equitable doctrine of 'clean hands' has no application to a common law claim for damages (*McMillan v Singh* (1985) 17 HLR 120 at 124).
3   The fundamental objective is to place the claimant so far as possible in the position which he would have occupied in the absence of breach. Damages may thus comprise lost profits or even expenditure which has been thrown away (*Hawkesbury Nominees Pty Ltd v Battik Pty Ltd* (Federal Court of Australia, 1 March 2000, BPR Casenote 102515)).
4   *McMillan v Singh* (1985) 17 HLR 120 at 125; *Ashgar v Armed* (1984) LAG Bulletin 124. Damages may include an element of compensation for the inconvenience and mental distress caused to the tenant or members of his family (*McCall v Abelesz* [1976] QB 585 at 594E–F; *Musumeci v Winadell Pty Ltd* (1994) 34 NSWLR 723 at 752E–F).
5   In strict terms aggravated and exemplary damages are available only where the facts also disclose a cause of action in tort – which they almost certainly will (see *Drane v Evangelou* [1978] 1 WLR 455 at 459C–F; *Ramdath v Daley* (1993) 25 HLR 273 at 277; *Francis v Brown* (1997) 30 HLR 143 at 149–152; *Mehta v Royal Bank of Scotland* [1999] 3 EGLR 153 at 162K–L).
6   *McMillan v Singh* (1985) 17 HLR 120 at 125 per Arnold P (exemplary damages awarded in order to negative the landlord's profit from a re-letting at a higher rent). No principle of 'double jeopardy' precludes the award of exemplary damages where the landlord has already been fined heavily under the Protection from Eviction Act 1977 (*Ashgar v Armed* (1984) LAG Bulletin 124).
7   R Clayton and H Tomlinson, (1986) LAG Bulletin 10. See eg *De Silva v Qureshi* (1984) LAG Bulletin 47 (£500 exemplary damages plus £500 general damages for removal of mains services).
8   Housing Act 1988, ss 27–28 [**paras 14.112–14.114**].

Limitations of the covenant

14.16   Despite its basic protective role in defending the tenant's right to enjoyment of the substance of his tenancy, the implied covenant for quiet enjoyment has severe limitations. The obligation has been narrowly – and unsympathetically – construed.[1] The covenant is 'prospective in its nature' and does not apply to things done before the grant of the tenancy even though they may have continuing consequences for the tenant.[2] Thus defects in rented premises which exist at the commencement of the tenancy cannot be made a matter of complaint. The covenant for quiet enjoyment imposes on the landlord no positive obligation to perform repairs or effect improvements in the demised premises which would not otherwise be his responsibility.[3] Nor can the covenant for quiet enjoyment be 'elevated into a warranty that the land is fit to be used for some special purpose.'[4] The landlord's implied obligation relates only to the subject matter of his grant as identified at the date of that grant. There is no breach if the premises suffer from some inherent defect, since the landlord's covenant is simply not to interfere with the tenant's use and enjoyment of premises which already have that feature.[5] In effect, the tenant takes the premises not only in the physical condition in which he finds them but also 'subject to the uses which the parties must have contemplated would be made of the parts retained by the landlord.'[6]

1   There is, for example, no breach where the tenant suffers discomfort from a malfunctioning of a heating system (*B G Preeco 3 Ltd v Universal Explorations Ltd* (1988) 42 DLR (4th) 673 at 675).

2   *Southwark LBC v Mills* [2001] 1 AC 1 at 11C–D per Lord Hoffmann, 23F–G per Lord Millett. See *Anderson v Oppenheimer* (1880) 5 QBD 602 at 607.

3   See *Duke of Westminster v Guild* [1985] QB 688 at 703F; *Southwark LBC v Mills* [2001] 1 AC 1 at 14C–E per Lord Hoffmann.

4   *Southwark LBC v Mills* [2001] 1 AC 1 at 10F per Lord Hoffmann.

5   *Southwark LBC v Mills* [2001] 1 AC 1 at 23H–24E per Lord Millett. The covenant is 'not a covenant to improve or provide anything' (*Southwark LBC v Mills* [2001] Ch 1 at 21G per Schiemann LJ).

6   *Southwark LBC v Mills* [2001] 1 AC 1 at 11G per Lord Hoffmann.

14.17   In *Southwark LBC v Mills*,[1] for example, a local authority granted lettings of council flats in a jerry-built block where inadequate sound insulation between the flats caused horrendous daily transmission of noise. The House of Lords held unanimously that there had been no breach of the covenant for quiet enjoyment. The House viewed the absence of sound-proofing at the date of grant of the tenancies as an 'inherent structural defect for which the landlord assumed no responsibility.'[2] The noise generated by neighbours was the consequence of perfectly ordinary, reasonable and proper user of neighbouring flats[3] and, in the context of a flat in a building constructed or adapted for multiple occupation, it 'must have been within the contemplation of the prospective tenants that the adjoining flats would be let to residential tenants and that the occupiers would live normally in them.'[4] In the absence of any existing covenant by the council to install sound-proofing, the House of Lords declined to construe the landlord's implied covenant so as to 'extend the operation of the grant.'[5]

1   [2001] 1 AC 1. See [2000] Conv 161 (D Rook).
2   'The council granted and the tenant took a tenancy of that flat. She cannot ... require the council to give her a different flat' ([2001] 1 AC 1 at 12H–13A per Lord Hoffmann). As Lord Millett pointed out, it was simply an 'undesirable feature of the flat' that it had a 'propensity to admit the sounds of the everyday activities of the occupants of adjoining flats' ([2001] 1 AC 1 at 24D).
3   [2001] 1 AC 1 at 7D–E, 13H per Lord Hoffmann.
4   [2001] 1 AC 1 at 25E per Lord Millett (see also Lord Millett at 22D–E). Dissenting in the Court of Appeal, Peter Gibson LJ pointed astutely to the problematic consequences of resting the ability to rely on the covenant for quiet enjoyment on the actual or deemed knowledge of would-be tenants at the date of grant of their tenancies ('Should the prudent would-be tenant insist on inspection by day and night at hours when any noise from neighbours might be expected to be at its most intrusive before taking the tenancy?' ([2001] Ch 1 at 30C)).
5   [2001] 1 AC 1 at 24E per Lord Millett. In the Court of Appeal Schiemann LJ observed that the situation had not 'changed one whit for the worse since the demise' ([2001] Ch 1 at 24G). The Court of Appeal noted that the necessary sound-proofing in the claimant's block would have cost the council some £60,000.

COVENANT AGAINST DEROGATION FROM GRANT

14.18   A landlord has an implied obligation not to 'derogate from his grant.'[1] This obligation has been described as 'a principle which merely embodies in a legal maxim a rule of common honesty.'[2] The landlord may not grant land to the tenant on terms which effectively or substantially negative the utility of the grant.[3] Neither the landlord nor any person claiming under him[4] may engage in conduct which is inconsistent with the purpose for which the lease was granted[5] or renders the demised land materially less fit for that purpose.[6] Most conduct which breaches the landlord's duty to afford quiet enjoyment also comprises a derogation from the leasehold grant,[7] but this is not always or necessarily so.[8] The concept of derogation from grant does not, however, catch any user of the landlord's retained land which was clearly contemplated by both parties at the date of the grant.[9]

1   See generally D W Elliott, (1964) 80 LQR 244; M A Peel, (1965) 81 LQR 28. On the distinction between quiet enjoyment and non-derogation from grant, see *Lend Lease Development Pty Ltd v Zemlicka* (1985) 3 NSWLR 207 at 208G per Kirby P.
2   *Harmer v Jumbil (Nigeria) Tin Areas Ltd* [1921] 1 Ch 200 at 225 per Younger LJ.
3   A grantor 'having given a thing with one hand is not to take away the means of enjoying it with the other' (*Birmingham, Dudley and District Banking Co v Ross* (1888) 38 Ch D 295 at 313 per Bowen LJ). See also *Southwark LBC v Mills* [2001] 1 AC 1 at 23E–F per Lord Millett; *Tram Lease Ltd v Croad* [2003] 2 NZLR 461 at [24] (NZ Court of Appeal).
4   *Aldin v Latimer Clark, Muirhead & Co* [1894] 2 Ch 437 at 447; *Molton Builders Ltd v Westminster CC* (1975) 30 P & CR 182 at 186.
5   The benefit of the landlord's obligation not to derogate from grant may also be claimed by those who take under the tenant (see *Molton Builders Ltd v Westminster CC* (1975) 30 P & CR 182 at 186).
6   *Yankwood Ltd v Havering LBC* [1998] EGCS 75 per Neuberger J. See eg *Tram Lease Ltd v Croad* [2003] 2 NZLR 461 at [31] (demolition of party wall).
7   See *Robinson v Kilvert* (1889) 41 Ch D 88 at 94–98; *Malzy v Eichholz* [1916] 2 KB 308 at 314;

Southwark LBC v Mills [2001] 1 AC 1 at 23E–F per Lord Millett; *Nordern v Blueport Enterprises Ltd* [1996] 3 NZLR 450 at 458; *Tram Lease Ltd v Croad* [2003] 2 NZLR at [28].

8   See e g *Grosvenor Hotel Co v Hamilton* [1894] 2 QB 836 at 840.

9   *Yankwood Ltd v Havering LBC* [1998] EGCS 75 per Neuberger J.

14.19   Failure by a landlord to restrain a nuisance committed by other tenants of his in the common parts of a shopping mall can constitute a derogation from the landlord's grant.[1] A similar derogation may occur where a landlord's failure to police the leasehold covenants undertaken by other tenants within a common development leads to economic interference with the operations of an innocent tenant.[2] Actual physical interference with the tenant's activities need not be shown in order to prove that a derogation has occurred.[3] In *Harmer v Jumbil (Nigeria) Tin Areas Ltd*[4] the Court of Appeal held that the obligation not to derogate had been breached where a landlord, having leased land for the express purpose of storing explosives, allowed his adjoining land to be used for mining operations which endangered the furtherance of the tenant's enterprise.[5] The implied covenant against derogation is likewise breached where a landlord carries out noisy renovations within the same building which render the demised premises unfit for the specialised purposes envisaged by the tenant[6] or which expose the demised premises to unlawful entry by burglars.[7] A landlord similarly derogates from his grant where he lets one floor of a building for commercial purposes and the next floor for use as a brothel,[8] but no derogation occurs merely because the landlord lets adjacent premises to a competing business.[9]

1   *Chartered Trust Plc v Davies* (1997) 76 P & CR 396 at 409. See (1997) 141 Sol Jo 922 (A Bruce).

2   *Prasad v Fairfield CC* (2001) 10 BPR 18747 at [47].

3   *Gordon v Lidcombe Developments Pty Ltd* [1966] 2 NSWR 9; *Telex (Australasia) Pty Ltd v Thomas Cook & Son (Australasia) Pty Ltd* [1970] 2 NSWR 257 at 266; *Aussie Traveller Pty Ltd v Marklea Pty Ltd* [1998] 1 Qd R 1; *Prasad v Fairfield CC* (2001) 10 BPR 18747 at [44]. See e g *Yankwood Ltd v Havering LBC* [1998] EGCS 75 (landlord's failure to control trespass on adjacent land by unauthorised footballers).

4   [1921] 1 Ch 200 at 225.

5   See also *Mount Cook National Park Board v Mount Cook Motels Ltd* [1972] NZLR 481 at 496. Compare *Port v Griffith* [1938] 1 All ER 295 at 299E–300G (although the law reflected in this decision 'has moved on': see *Prasad v Fairfield CC* (2001) 10 BPR 18747 at [47]).

6   *Telex (Australasia) Pty Ltd v Thomas Cook & Son (Australasia) Pty Ltd* [1970] 2 NSWR 257 at 266 (tenant traded in hearing aids and audiometric equipment). See also *Aldin v Latimer Clark, Muirhead & Co* [1894] 2 Ch 437 at 444; *Yankwood Ltd v Havering LBC* [1998] EGCS 75 (permission for noisy activities such as model aircraft flying and motor rallies next to equestrian centre); *Vasile v Perpetual Trustees WA Ltd* (1987) 10 BPR 18091 at 18096 (removal of access door).

7   *Lend Lease Development Pty Ltd v Zemlicka* (1985) 3 NSWLR 207 at 216F–G (Court of Appeal of New South Wales).

8   *Nordern v Blueport Enterprises Ltd* [1996] 3 NZLR 450 at 454–456. Compare *Chartered Trust Plc v Davies* (1997) 76 P & CR 396 at 404 (no derogation by letting of adjacent premises to pawnbroker).

9   *Clark's-Gamble of Canada Ltd v Grant Park Plaza Ltd* (1967) 64 DLR (2d) 570 at 580; *Wilcox v Richardson* (1997) 8 BPR 15491 at 15502. In such cases the tenant should have bargained for a restrictive covenant to protect his interests (see *Browne v Flower* [1911] 1 Ch 219 at 227; *Nordern v Blueport Enterprises Ltd* [1996] 3 NZLR 450 at 455).

OBLIGATIONS IN RESPECT OF FITNESS

14.20 The common law has been sparing in its imposition of implied obligations on the landlord in matters of repair, maintenance and general amenity. It has been said to be a 'fundamental principle' of the common law of landlord and tenant that the landlord gives no implied warranty as to the condition of the demised premises or as to their fitness for the purpose of the letting.[1] There is, for example, no implied covenant that residential premises are fit for human habitation.[2] The broad rule is 'caveat lessee'.[3]

1   *Southwark LBC v Mills* [2001] 1 AC 1 at 7H, 12C–D per Lord Hoffmann. The principle is historic and global (see *Hart v Windsor* (1843) 12 M & W 68 at 86–88, 152 ER 1114 at 1122 per Parke B; *Gott v Gandy* (1853) 2 El & Bl 845 at 847–848, 118 ER 984 at 985; *Duke of Westminster v Guild* [1985] QB 688 at 697D–E per Slade LJ; *J F Hillam Pty Ltd v K L Mooney and P H Hill* (1988) 48 SASR 381 at 388; *Shun Cheong Holdings BC Ltd v Gold Ocean City Supermarket Ltd* (2002) 216 DLR (4th) 392 at [7]).
2   *Southwark LBC v Mills* [2001] 1 AC 1 at 17B per Lord Millett. See P F Smith, 'A Case for Abrogation: The No-Liability for Unfitness Principle' [1998] Conv 189.
3   See *Southwark LBC v Mills* [2001] 1 AC 1 at 12D per Lord Hoffmann; *Baxter v Camden LBC (No 2)* [2001] QB 1 at 15B per Tuckey LJ, 17H per Stuart-Smith LJ.

Assumption of risk by the tenant

14.21 Since historically the leasehold was conceptualised as a conveyance of an estate in land which conferred a right of exclusive possession, the tenant, so long as he was given exclusive possession at the commencement of the lease, had no right thereafter to complain about the fitness of the land for his purpose.[1] He was deemed to assume all risks attached to the condition of the land unless he had reached some contrary agreement with his landlord.[2] The tenant hired at his peril and the landlord gave no implied undertaking as to the physical condition of the land or (in the case of a building) as to its continuing state of repair.[3] In Erle CJ's famous remark, 'fraud apart, there is no law against letting a tumble-down house.'[4] The common law principle was clear: 'the lessee must make his objections to the condition of the premises before taking the lease.'[5]

1   The immunity conferred on the lessor was largely due to the fact that the subject matter of most leases used to be agricultural land rather than residential dwellings (see *Siney v Corporation of Dublin* [1980] IR 400 at 408 per O'Higgins CJ). The courts were always concerned to prevent the extension of lessors' duties under agrarian leases (see e g *Sutton v Temple* (1843) 12 M & W 52 at 65, 152 ER 1108 at 1113 (no liability for cattle killed by lead poisoning in field)).
2   See *Carstairs v Taylor* (1871) LR 6 Ex 217 at 222 per Martin B.
3   The 'take it or leave it' character of the landlord's offer was aptly characterised in *Kiddle v City Business Properties Ltd* [1942] 1 KB 269 at 274–275 per Goddard LJ.
4   *Robbins v Jones* (1863) 15 CB (NS) 221 at 240, 143 ER 768 at 776. See *Anns v Merton LBC* [1978] AC 728 at 768E per Lord Salmon ('The immunity of a landlord who sells or lets a house which is dangerous or unfit for habitation is deeply entrenched in our law'). The exception made for fraud may be important (see e g *Gordon v Selico Co Ltd* [1986] 1 EGLR 71 at 77J, where a vendor of a long lease was held liable in damages for the tort of deceit on the ground that he had fraudulently concealed the existence of dry rot in a flat sold to the claimants).

　　H Tiffany, *Treatise on the Law of Landlord and Tenant* (1912), pp 572–573. See also *Baxter v Camden LBC (No 2)* [2001] QB 1 at 19D–E per Stuart-Smith LJ. At common law there may even be 'situations in which there is no repairing obligation imposed either expressly or impliedly on anyone in relation to a lease' (*Demetriou v Poolaction Ltd* [1991] 1 EGLR 100 at 104D per Stuart-Smith LJ).

14.22　English courts have therefore shown themselves profoundly unwilling to imply at common law any term that a landlord should keep a dwelling in good condition or even in such condition as enables the tenant to perform *his* obligations under the tenancy.[1] In *Southwark LBC v Mills*[2] Lord Millett attributed the unsympathetic stance of the common law to 'the general rule of English law which accords autonomy to contracting parties. In the absence of statutory intervention, the parties are free to let and take a lease of poorly constructed premises and to allocate the cost of putting them in order between themselves as they see fit.' The common law starting point remains the principle – voiced even in modern times – that if the prospective tenant 'wants more he should bargain for it and be prepared to pay the extra rent.'[3] Particularly in relation to cash-strapped social landlords, the courts have felt that the 'limits of permissible judicial creativity' do not permit the fashioning of extra obligations not expressly agreed by the parties.[4]

1　　*Lee v Leeds CC* [2002] 1 WLR 1488 at [62]–[68] per Chadwick LJ.
2　　[2001] 1 AC 1 at 17G.
3　　*Southwark LBC v Mills* [2001] Ch 1 at 20E per Schiemann LJ.
4　　*Southwark LBC v Mills* [2001] 1 AC 1 at 8F per Lord Hoffmann. See similarly *Lee v Leeds CC* [2002] 1 WLR 1488 at [24], [49] per Chadwick LJ.

Piecemeal intervention by statute

14.23　The common law rule, so stated, still applies to most non-residential leases. However, the law could not remain unaffected by the social and economic changes brought about during the 19th century by the emergence of an urbanised proletariat. A myriad of houses 'suitable for ... use ... by members of the working classes'[1] quickly formed in orderly patterns around the factories, textile mills, coal-pits and iron-works of the industrial revolution.[2] This sudden aggregation of residential dwellers in large industrial conurbations[3] inevitably gave an unprecedented prominence to the legal issue of habitability in the residential sector.[4] Gradually the bleaker aspects of the common law rule came to be qualified by a number of exceptions (arising both at common law and by statute) which impose on the landlord various kinds of duty in relation to the physical condition and repair of the premises leased.[5] These sporadic interventions[6] survive in modern law as a piecemeal collection of doctrines and provisions rather than as any particularly coherent code of protection for tenants. Only the grosser emanations of unequal bargaining power have been redressed, with the result that the law in this area is now complex, untidy and deeply unsatisfactory.

1　　This remarkable phrase – no longer present in the statute book – was to recur in legislation dating from the Housing of the Working Classes Act 1885 (see also *Chorley BC v Barratt Developments (North West) Ltd* [1979] 3 All ER 634 at 639a–c; R G Lee, 'The Demise of the Working Classes' [1980] Conv 281).

2   Some of the early industrialists and landowners took care to provide decent housing conditions for the workers, but all too often the new housing took the form of the back-to-back terraces, cellar dwellings or courtyard dwellings which became the slums of the future (see A Briggs, *Victorian Cities* (Harmondsworth, Middx 1968), pp 226–227; J Burnett, *A Social History of Housing 1815–1970* (London 1978), pp 11, 54–56).

3   In 1801 approximately 80 per cent of the population of England and Wales was still 'rural'. By 1851 54 per cent of the population had become urban dwellers and there were already ten urban centres of more than 100,000 inhabitants each, accounting in total for a quarter of the population of the entire country (see J Burnett, op cit, pp 6–7).

4   The full horror of some of the housing supposedly suitable for use by members of the working classes is apparent in the *First Report of the Royal Commission on the Housing of the Working Classes* (PP 1884–85, XXX), pp 11–12 ('privies ... in living rooms' and 'walls ... alive with vermin'). The Commissioners also referred (at p 12) to the curiously modern complaint of 'jerry building'.

5   For a more detailed history of the law in this area, see *Elements of Land Law* (1st edn 1987), pp 901–960.

6   The nature of the interest which even a supposedly enlightened 19th century landlord had in the living conditions of his tenants is apparent in the earnest statement that 'sanitary improvements lead to higher rentals being obtained and to the tenants enjoying better health, and, consequently, being in a better position to pay the said rent' (G H Larmuth, *A Practical Guide to the Law of Landlord and Tenant* (Manchester 1878), p 45).

Modern developments

14.24   In more recent times the Law Commission has recommended that the thrust of the existing law should be reversed by a new statutory principle that all repairing liability should fall upon the landlord in default of an express contractual term allocating that responsibility to the tenant.[1] The Commission has likewise advocated[2] the revival and extension (free of any deadening rental limits) of the implied landlord covenant[3] that a dwelling-house let for a term of less than seven years shall be fit (and kept fit) for habitation. It is also beginning to be realised that the European Convention on Human Rights may have a significant role to play in reshaping the obligations owed by certain landlords towards their tenants. In *Lee v Leeds CC*[4] the Court of Appeal indicated that local authority landlords are obliged to 'take steps to ensure that the condition of a dwelling house which it has let for social housing is such that the tenant's Convention right under article 8 is not infringed.'[5] This duty involves, however, no 'general and unqualified' guarantee of the quality of a local authority's housing stock. The decision whether a tenant's right has been 'infringed' depends, as always in Convention jurisprudence, on the maintenance of a 'fair balance' between the competing needs and resources of the community and of individuals in the light of straitened public finances and the democratic determination of budgetary priorities.[6]

1   *Landlord and Tenant: Responsibility for State and Condition of Property* (Law Com No 238, March 1996), paras 1.5, 7.10.

2   Law Com No 238 (1996), para 8.35. See *Lee v Leeds CC* [2002] 1 WLR 1488 at [22]–[23].

3   See L&TA 1985, s 8 [**para 14.41**].

4   [2002] 1 WLR 1488 at [48] per Chadwick LJ.

5   See ECHR Art 8 (right to respect for 'private and family life' and the 'home' [**para 2.60**]). As

Lord Woolf CJ emphasised recently in *Anufrijeva v Southwark LBC* [2004] 2 WLR 603 at [19], a 'deterioration in the quality of life' can result in an infringement of ECHR Art 8.

6   [2002] 1 WLR 1488 at [49] per Chadwick LJ.

LANDLORD'S COMMON LAW LIABILITY FOR FITNESS OF PREMISES

14.25   At common law the potential liability of the landlord has been steadily, albeit uncertainly, extended by developments in the law of contract and tort.

Implied condition of fitness for human habitation

14.26   A significant exception to the common law principle of *caveat emptor* in landlord–tenant relations was established in 1843 in *Smith v Marrable*.[1] Here the Court of Exchequer held it to be an *implied condition* in the letting of any furnished dwelling-house that the premises should be reasonably fit for habitation at the commencement of the term.[2] Breach of this condition entitles the tenant to quit the letting immediately and without notice.[3]

1   (1843) 11 M & W 5 at 8–9, 152 ER 693 at 694 (infestation by bugs). A further common law exception imposes liability on a lessor who sells a leasehold estate in a house still in the process of construction. The vendor is impliedly taken to warrant the suitability of materials used, the quality of the workmanship and the fitness of the house for habitation (see *Perry v Sharon Development Co Ltd* [1937] 4 All ER 390 at 393A–B; *Siney v Corporation of Dublin* [1980] IR 400 at 408).

2   See also *Wilson v Finch Hatton* (1877) 2 Ex D 336 at 341–342, 344 (defective drains); *Collins v Hopkins* [1923] 2 KB 617 at 628 (recent occupant had contagious illness).

3   *Smith v Marrable* (1843) 11 M & W 5 at 8, 152 ER 693 at 694 per Parke B ('the tenant is at liberty to throw [the demised premises] up'). See similarly *Collins v Barrow* (1831) 1 M & Rob 112 at 114, 174 ER 38 at 39. The tenant is under no obligation to give the landlord an opportunity to remedy the defect (*Wilson v Finch Hatton* (1877) 2 Ex D 336 at 341).

Limited scope

14.27   The implied condition of fitness is extremely limited in scope.[1] It relates only to the condition of the premises at the commencement of the letting.[2] It applies only to a residential tenancy,[3] has no relevance to unfurnished premises[4] and even in relation to furnished premises does not extend to dangerous appliances or furnishings supplied by the landlord.[5] Because the landlord's liability arises *ex contractu*, no person other than the tenant can maintain an action for breach of the implied condition.[6] The restrictiveness of the common law approach was recently, and most supremely, evident in *Lee v Leeds City Council*.[7] Here the Court of Appeal held that to introduce, in the context of local authority tenancies of social housing, some implied term that the landlord should keep the property 'in good condition' would go far beyond the limits of 'permissible judicial creativity'. Even an express obligation on the part of a tenant to use the premises as his or her home implies no correlative common law obligation on the part of the landlord to remedy defects which make the premises unfit for human habitation.[8]

1   The implied condition does not apply to ordinary disrepair which merely renders habitation unpleasant or inconvenient as distinct from impossible (see e g *Maclean v Currie* (1884) Cab & El 361 (cracked plaster)).

2   *Hart v Windsor* (1843) 12 M & W 68 at 85–86, 152 ER 1114 at 1121; *Sarson v Roberts* [1895] 2 QB 395 at 397–398.

3   See *Bradford House Pty Ltd v Leroy Fashion Group Ltd* (1983) 46 ALR 305 at 313. Compare the willingness in the United States to extend a warranty of fitness to commercial leases (see *Davidow v Inwood North Professional Group – Phase 1*, 747 SW2d 373 at 376–377 (Tex 1988)).

4   *Hart v Windsor* (1843) 12 M & W 68 at 87, 152 ER 1114 at 1122; *Lane v Cox* [1897] 1 QB 415 at 417; *Baxter v Camden LBC (No 2)* [2001] QB 1 at 13E. In effect almost all council tenancies and certainly all long (e g 99 year) leases of residential flats are nowadays excluded from the scope of the condition.

5   *Pampris v Thanos* [1968] 1 NSWR 56 at 58 (tenant's wife electrocuted on contact with faulty refrigerator). The landlord may, of course, be liable in negligence (see e g *Parker v South Australian Housing Trust* (1986) 41 SASR 493; *Northern Sandblasting Pty Ltd v Harris* (1997) 188 CLR 313).

6   *Cameron v Young* [1908] AC 176 at 180–181; *Pampris v Thanos* [1968] 1 NSWR 56 at 58.

7   [2002] 1 WLR 1488 at [63] per Chadwick LJ (Tuckey LJ and Sir Murray Stuart-Smith concurring).

8   [2002] 1 WLR 1488 at [67] per Chadwick LJ.

Warranty of habitability

14.28   The common law condition of fitness thus falls far short of the implied 'warranty of habitability' which in other jurisdictions has become a central feature of a modern 'revolution' in the landlord–tenant relationship.[1] In *Javins v First National Realty Corporation*,[2] the symbolic turning-point in this area of law in the United States, Judge Skelly Wright adverted to the contemporary social function of the residential tenancy as a consumer contract for the supply of a 'package of goods and services.' In his view the tenant 'may legitimately expect that the apartment will be fit for habitation for the time period for which it is rented.'[3] The initiative taken in the *Javins* ruling has left a lasting mark on American landlord and tenant law[4] and has entrenched the humane principle that the landlord is contractually liable to supply his residential tenants with decent housing conditions throughout the term of the tenancy. In sharp contrast English common law remains tethered to the limitations of *Smith v Marrable* and has therefore been forced to seek the same goal, somewhat imperfectly, through tortuous and fragmented initiatives of common law and statute.

1   See M A Glendon, 'The Transformation of American Landlord–Tenant Law' 23 Boston Coll L Rev 503 (1982); E H Rabin, 'The Revolution in Residential Landlord–Tenant Law: Causes and Consequences' 69 Cornell L Rev 517 (1983–84).

2   428 F2d 1071 at 1074 (1970).

3   428 F2d 1071 at 1079. Some commentators have even gone so far as to support the warranty of habitability as a device explicitly aimed at 'a significant expropriation or redistribution away from people who are owners of low-income property' (see Duncan Kennedy, 'In favor of the Warranty of Habitability' In brief (May 1987), p 8).

4   See J E Cribbet (1986) U of Ill L Rev 1 at 7. Compare, however, the view that even *Javins* could not resolve the underlying problem of tenant poverty and simply had the effect of raising rents and reducing the supply of low-income housing (Thomas W Merrill and Henry E Smith, 'The Property/Contract Interface' 101 Col L Rev 773 at 820–821 (2001)).

Implied contractual duty of care

14.29   In certain circumstances English courts are willing to imply on the part of the landlord a contractual duty of care, thereby indirectly protecting the amenity enjoyed by tenants.[1] In *Liverpool CC v Irwin*,[2] the House of Lords ruled that a local authority landlord of a high-rise block of flats had a contractual duty to 'take reasonable care to keep in reasonable repair and usability' the common parts and facilities in the block (eg lifts, stairways and rubbish chutes).[3] Such a duty could be implied into the contract of tenancy as a matter of 'necessity'.[4] The maintenance of these facilities could not simply be regarded as 'conveniences provided at discretion: they are essentials of the tenancy without which life in the dwellings, as a tenant, is not possible.'[5] The landlord's obligation of care extends not merely to concealed dangers or traps, but also to defects which are entirely visible and obvious to the tenant.[6]

1   See eg *Dunster v Hollis* [1918] 2 KB 795 at 802 (tenant injured by fall on dilapidated external stairway). See also *Fanjoy v Gaston* (1982) 127 DLR (3d) 163 at 168–169.
2   [1977] AC 239.
3   [1977] AC 239 at 256G per Lord Wilberforce.
4   [1977] AC 239 at 254F. The House of Lords ultimately held that the council had not been shown to be in breach of its contractual obligation of care. It was clear that the council had made considerable efforts, despite the depradations of local vandals, to maintain the efficiency of communal facilities in the flats ([1977] AC 239 at 256G per Lord Wilberforce, 259F–G per Lord Cross of Chelsea, 269C–D per Lord Edmund-Davies). The council's duty was not *absolute*. Lord Salmon (at 263C–G) reached his conclusion 'with some reluctance and doubt', opining that the tenants' counter-claim might well have succeeded if they had pleaded that the landlord was subject to a duty merely to take 'reasonable care'.
5   [1977] AC 239 at 254F–G. As Lord Salmon asked with some force, '[c]an a pregnant woman accompanied by a young child be expected to walk up 15 … storeys in the pitch dark to reach her home? Unless the law … imposes an obligation upon the council at least to use reasonable care to keep the lifts working properly and the staircase lit, the whole transaction becomes inefficacious, futile and absurd' ([1977] AC 239 at 262A–B). See similarly *Dunster v Hollis* [1918] 2 KB 795 at 802 per Lush J.
6   *Dunster v Hollis* [1918] 2 KB 795 at 803.

14.30   The landlord's implied contractual duty of care, although significantly endorsed by the House of Lords, is again somewhat limited in scope. It confers rights only upon the contracting tenant (and not others such as members of his family or associates[1]) and may always be excluded by the simple expedient of express contractual provision.[2] This implied duty of care may also apply more readily to high-rise blocks designed for multiple occupation than to other kinds of tenancy.[3] Moreover the courts can easily stultify the common law duty by adopting an extremely narrow view of the circumstances of 'necessity' or 'business efficacy' which activate the implication of the landlord's obligation.[4]

1   See analogously *Jones v Bartlett* (2000) 205 CLR 166 at [38].
2   *Liverpool CC v Irwin* [1977] AC 239 at 259E, 260C. See eg *Coughlan v The Mayor etc of the City of Limerick* (1977) 111 ILTR 141 at 142.
3   [1977] AC 239 at 254G, 256E–F, 270B–C. See *Duke of Westminster v Guild* [1985] QB 688 at 699B–C; *Gordon v Selico Co Ltd* [1986] 1 EGLR 71L.
4   See eg *O'Leary v LB of Islington* (1983) 9 HLR 81 at 86, 89 (no duty to police the behaviour of other residents on housing estate); *Collins v Northern Ireland Housing Executive* [1984]

17 NIJB, Transcript p 21 (no duty to keep heating system in working order). Carswell J held that the defect in the latter case affected only 'the quality of enjoyment of the facilities supplied, not ... the basic ability to use the accommodation.'

Landlord's liability in negligence

14.31 A landlord's duty towards a tenant is also recognised in the law of negligence. In that the landlord's vulnerability in negligence extends to parties outside the contractual nexus, this form of liability is wider than that imposed by the implied contractual duty of care. Although there is authority, stemming largely from the restrictive and much criticised[1] ruling of the House of Lords in *Cavalier v Pope*,[2] to the effect that a landlord cannot be liable in negligence by reason of the defective nature of the demised premises at the *commencement* of the tenancy,[3] it is clear that liability in negligence can arise in respect of events occurring *after* the commencement date.[4]

1 The decision in *Cavalier v Pope* pre-dates *Donoghue v Stevenson* [1932] AC 562 and has been described as 'conceptually inconsistent with the general principle of liability for negligence' enunciated in that case (see *Parker v South Australian Housing Trust* (1986) 41 SASR 493 at 516 per King CJ).
2 [1906] AC 428 at 430–433. See *Bottomley v Bannister* [1932] 1 KB 458 at 477.
3 See *Robbins v Jones* (1863) 15 CB (NS) 221 at 240, 143 ER 768 at 776; *Bottomley v Bannister* [1932] 1 KB 458 at 477; *Otto v Bolton and Norris* [1936] 2 KB 46 at 54; *Davis v Foots* [1940] 1 KB 116 at 121, 124; *McGowan v Harrison* [1941] IR 331 at 337.
4 It is always possible for one tenant to sue another tenant directly in respect of negligence which has led to a loss of amenity (see *Elfassy v Sylben Investments Ltd* (1979) 91 DLR (3d) 96). However, the defendant may be able to plead successfully that he had no reason to suspect the existence of the problem which caused the damage (see e g *Hawkins v Dhawan* (1987) 19 HLR 232 at 235, where the Court of Appeal held that just as every dog must be 'allowed its first bite', so a tenant's washbasin must be allowed its first flood, even though the overflow escapes to the premises of a neighbouring tenant).

Duty of care

14.32 It is well established that a claim in negligence may lie against a landlord if, by some action or omission on premises retained within his exclusive possession and control,[1] damage is caused to that part of the premises let to the tenant.[2] Liability also extends to personal injury, but is founded, as always, on the showing of a duty of care (and a breach of that duty) by the landlord.[3] If the landlord is not in breach of any duty of care (either express or implied), there can be no liability. In *Ryan v LB of Camden*,[4] for example, the Court of Appeal declined to hold that a local authority was in breach of its duty of care towards a six-month old baby who had suffered severe contact burns after falling on an exposed and uninsulated central heating pipe in a bedroom of a council flat. In the view taken by the Court, the local authority had been under no duty to lag the hot water pipe and was entitled to rely on the child's parents to protect it from the danger presented by the central heating system.[5] In the absence of personal injury or damage to property, the landlord owes no general duty of care to avoid causing mere inconvenience or discomfort to his tenant.[6] The landlord's liability in negligence is, in any event, far from absolute; he is liable only to take reasonable care to ensure the safety of those persons who might reasonably be expected to be affected by his actions or defaults.[7]

1   Problems typically arise where the landlord grants tenancies of flats in a building, whilst retaining for himself exclusive possession over other parts of the building such as the roof or the service ducts.

2   *Cockburn v Smith* [1924] 2 KB 119 at 129; *Duke of Westminster v Guild* [1985] QB 688 at 701C–E. See *Hargroves, Aronson & Co v Hartopp* [1905] 1 KB 472 at 477 (failure to clear a blocked rain-water gutter); *A Prosser & Sons Ltd v Levy* [1955] 1 WLR 1224 at 1233 (overflow of water from basin); *Martins Camera Corner Pty Ltd v Hotel Mayfair Ltd* [1976] 2 NSWLR 15 at 26E (failure to clear blocked down-pipe); *Sharpe v Manchester CC* (1977) 5 HLR 71 at 76 (invasion of cockroaches from service ducts).

3   Prima facie evidence of breach may be provided by the landlord's failure to discharge statutory duties of repair or maintenance (see eg *Gaul v King* (1980) 103 DLR (3d) 233 at 244).

4   (1982) 8 HLR 75.

5   (1982) 8 HLR 75 at 83–84, 87. Contrast the approach of the Supreme Court of New Jersey in *Coleman v Steinberg*, 253 A2d 167 at 170–172 (1969).

6   *Collins v Northern Ireland Housing Executive* [1984] 17 NIJB, Transcript, pp 32–33. The 'neighbour principle' of *Donoghue v Stevenson* does not (oddly) require the landlord to exercise diligence on behalf of one tenant in selecting only civilised tenants to live in neighbouring premises (see *Smith v Scott* [1973] Ch 314 at 322A–B, E–F) or to enforce standards of good neighbourliness generally (see *O'Leary v LB of Islington* (1983) 9 HLR 81 at 88).

7   See eg *Ryan v LB of Camden* (1982) 8 HLR 75 (no liability for unforeseeable injury). See also *McAuliffe v Moloney* [1971] IR 200 at 203.

A duty to protect the tenant from crime?

14.33   English law has shown a marked reluctance to impose on landlords a duty to protect their tenants against the effects of crime committed by persons outside the landlord–tenant relationship.[1] A landlord has, for example, no liability in negligence for malicious damage caused by a third party, unless there was some special relationship between the landlord and the third party or the injury to the claimant is the inevitable and foreseeable result of the landlord's act or omission.[2] Likewise a landlord is burdened by no general duty of reasonable care to prevent trespassing strangers from using his own premises as a 'springboard' for stealing goods from adjoining premises occupied by his tenant.[3] The tenant enjoys, by definition, an exclusive possession of his premises and therefore, in principle, bears sole responsibility for protecting these premises and their occupiers against criminal invasion by third parties.[4] The 'duty to provide police protection' has been described as 'foreign to the history of the landlord–tenant relationship',[5] not least since the imposition of such an 'indeterminate liability owed to an indeterminate class' would create an unprecedented responsibility to control the activities of third persons and tend to discourage tenants from adopting their own measures of self-protection.[6] This approach contrasts strongly with the increasing recognition in the United

States of a duty in the landlord to provide security from criminal attack in respect of both the goods and the person of the residential tenant.[7]

1   A landlord may, of course, be liable in negligence for losses caused by the criminal activity of his agent or employee (see *Lloyd v Grace, Smith & Co* [1912] AC 716 at 731; *Nahhas v Pier House (Cheyne Walk) Management Ltd* (1984) 270 EG 328 at 333 (burglary by porter in block of flats who had extensive criminal record)).

2   *King v Liverpool CC* [1986] 1 WLR 890 at 901B–E, 902B–E (no liability for water damage emanating from vandalised superjacent flat). See also *Smith v Littlewoods Organisation Ltd* [1987] AC 241 at 267F–G per Lord Mackay of Clashfern, 279B per Lord Goff of Chieveley. Compare *Sheppard v Northern Ireland Housing Executive* [1984] 1 NIJB, Transcript, p 4 per Lord Lowry LCJ (liability for landlord's ineffective action to prevent vandalism to soil pipes). See also *Ward v Cannock Chase DC* [1986] Ch 546 at 562G–H, 569F–571C. The landlord's liability for damage emanating from the landlord's adjoining premises may sometimes be more easily founded on the obligation not to derogate from grant (see *Lend Lease Development Pty Ltd v Zemlicka* (1985) 3 NSWLR 207 at 216F–G [**para 14.18**]).

3   *P Perl (Exporters) Ltd v Camden LBC* [1984] 1 QB 342 at 357G–358B, 359C–360C. See also *Smith v Littlewoods Organisation Ltd* [1987] AC 241 at 280A–B; *W D & H O Wills (Australia) Ltd v State Rail Authority of New South Wales* (1998) 43 NSWLR 338 at 360F–G.

4   See *Appah v Parncliffe Investments Ltd* [1964] 1 WLR 1064 at 1067; and compare *Marshall v Rubypoint Ltd* [1997] 1 EGLR 69 at 71J–M [**para 7.146**].

5   *Goldberg v Housing Authority of the City of Newark*, 186 A2d 291 at 296 (1962) per Weintraub CJ.

6   See *W D & H O Wills (Australia) Ltd v State Rail Authority of New South Wales* (1998) 43 NSWLR 338 at 360F–G per Mason P.

7   See eg *Kline v 1500 Massachussetts Ave Apartment Corp*, 439 F2d 477 at 481–485 (1970), where a District Court of Appeals held that, in the context of urban multiple unit apartment dwellings, the landlord, while no 'insurer' of his tenants' safety, 'certainly is no bystander' (landlord, who had notice of repeated criminal assaults on the premises, held liable for injuries suffered by tenant who was assaulted in the common hallway of her apartment house). See also *Trentacost v Brussel*, 412 A2d 436 at 441–443 (1980) (landlord liable both in negligence and on the implied warranty of habitability [**para 14.28**] in respect of mugging of elderly tenant on internal stairway in her apartment block in crime-ridden neighbourhood). The objection to such liability for landlords is, of course, that it merely passes the cost of security measures on to poor tenants by way of increased rents (see *Goldberg v Housing Authority of Newark*, 186 A2d 291 at 298 (1962)). See generally *Elements of Land Law* (1st edn 1987), pp 950–954.

Retreat from Cavalier v Pope

14.34   Strong arguments of principle favour the imposition of negligence liability on a landlord even in respect of defects present in the demised premises at the commencement date of the letting, particularly where the landlord (unlike the tenant) had special means of knowledge of latent defects and concealed dangers.[1] Nevertheless English courts have sternly adhered to the denial of liability enshrined in *Cavalier v Pope*,[2] allowing an exception only where the landlord was also the builder of negligently constructed premises.[3] Even here the landlord's responsibility for negligence depends upon a proven duty of care and its breach and the courts tend to be reluctant to impose such liability on social landlords.[4] Although in broad agreement that the outmoded rule in *Cavalier v Pope* 'must be kept in close confinement',[5] English judges have resisted the trend in other jurisdictions to view the rule as inapplicable to social housing[6] or as simply wrong in general.[7] In *McNerny v LB of Lambeth*[8] the

Court of Appeal took the view that only legislative intervention can finally remove this archaic but obdurate principle.

1   For an extreme instance, see *MacDonald v Sebastian* (1988) 43 DLR (4th) 636 at 637 (arsenic in water supply).

2   [1906] AC 428 at 430–434. See e g *McNerny v LB of Lambeth* (1988) 21 HLR 188 at 192 per Dillon LJ, 195–196 per Taylor LJ; [1989] Conv 216 (P F Smith).

3   See e g *Rimmer v Liverpool CC* [1985] QB 1 at 13G–14F (tenant injured when falling through thin glass panel in inadequately designed flat constructed by local authority landlord). Stephenson LJ (at 14G) distinguished *Cavalier v Pope* as a case relating only to the liability of a 'bare landlord' as distinct from that of a 'builder owner' (see *Gallagher v N. McDowell Ltd* [1961] NI 26 at 44 per Lord MacDermott LCJ). See also *Baxter v Camden LBC (No 2)* [2001] QB 1 at 14H per Tuckey LJ, 19B per Stuart-Smith LJ. Contrast the parallel case in American law, *Becker v IRM Corp*, 213 Cal Rptr 213 (Supreme Court of California 1985). See also *Ward v McMaster* [1985] IR 29 at 42.

4   See *Adams v Rhymney Valley DC* [2000] 3 EGLR 25 (local authority landlord, as designer and builder of housing, not liable in respect of fire causing death of three children when key-operated windows could not be opened (Sedley LJ dissented)).

5   *Rimmer v Liverpool CC* [1985] QB 1 at 9H per Stephenson LJ. See also *Greene v Chelsea BC* [1954] 2 QB 127 at 138 per Denning LJ.

6   *Siney v Corporation of Dublin* [1980] IR 400 at 414–415, 421–422; *Parker v South Australian Housing Trust* (1986) 41 SASR 493 at 544. Compare, however, *McNerny v LB of Lambeth* (1988) 21 HLR 188 at 193 per Dillon LJ.

7   '[A]fter the House of Lords gave its decision in *Donoghue v Stevenson*, the decision in *Cavalier v Pope* seemed difficult, if not impossible, to justify' (*Northern Sandblasting Pty Ltd v Harris* (1997) 188 CLR 313 at 365 per McHugh J). The rule in *Cavalier v Pope* is no longer accepted as good common law in Australia (*Jones v Bartlett* (2000) 205 CLR 166 at [53] per Gleeson CJ, [166] per Gummow and Hayne JJ). See also *Basset Realty Ltd v Lindstrom* (1980) 103 DLR (3d) 654 at 670.

8   (1988) 21 HLR 188 at 193–195 per Dillon LJ, 196 per Taylor LJ.

Landlord's liability for nuisance

14.35   A tenant, being in possession of land, has locus standi to sue for damages and/or an injunction in respect of the tort of nuisance,[1] but the restrictiveness of the law of nuisance often militates against the success of claims. An action in nuisance nevertheless lies where the acts or omissions of the landlord on his own land[2] unduly interfere with the tenant's comfortable and convenient enjoyment of the demised premises.[3] Nuisance by the landlord thus covers such events as the invasion of cockroaches from the service ducts of a block of flats[4] and the wrongful disconnection of water and electricity supplies and interference with washing and toilet facilities.[5]

1   *Inchbald v Robinson* (1869) 4 Ch App 388 at 395–397; *Jones v Chappell* (1875) LR 20 Eq 539 at 543–544. See e g *McCall v Abelesz* [1976] QB 585 at 599F; *Guppys (Bridport) Ltd v Brookling* (1984) 269 EG 846 at 946. Even a tenant who becomes a 'tolerated trespasser' with a right of exclusive possession has standing to sue in nuisance (see *Pemberton v Southwark LBC* [2000] 1 WLR 1672 at 1682H, 1684A–B [**para 7.155**]).

2   No nuisance liability can rest upon a landlord (e g a housing association) which has no occupation of or sufficient degree of control over the premises from which the nuisance allegedly emanates (*Habinteg Housing Association v James* (1994) 27 HLR 299 at 305–306 (no control over remainder of housing estate)).

3   *Thompson-Schwab v Costaki* [1956] 1 WLR 335 at 338. Most nuisances caused or continued by

a landlord also comprise a derogation from the grant to the tenant (*Chartered Trust Plc v Davies* (1997) 76 P & CR 396 at 408 per Henry LJ).

4   *Sharpe v Manchester CC* (1977) 5 HLR 71 at 75–76; *Pemberton v Southwark LBC* [2000] 1 WLR 1672 at 1674H–1675A. See also *Sheppard v Northern Ireland Housing Executive* [1984] 1 NIJB (blocked sewage pipe).

5   *Guppys (Bridport) Ltd v Brookling* (1984) 269 EG 846 at 850–852.

Landlord's liability for nuisance committed by other tenants

14.36   Although not in general liable for a nuisance committed by his tenant,[1] a landlord may nevertheless become liable if – but only if[2] – he has expressly or impliedly authorised his tenant to commit nuisance[3] or has adopted or continued such nuisance.[4] The landlord's liability to one tenant may therefore be founded on acts committed by other tenants in occupation of a different part of the landlord's property.[5] This will be the case where the behaviour complained of has failed to show 'reasonable consideration' for the occupants of adjacent tenants of the same landlord.[6] This form of liability sometimes provides redress in disputes arising between neighbours in a crowded multiple residential context (eg a block of flats),[7] but is less useful in controlling random misbehaviour across the less well defined reaches of a large housing estate. In *Hussain v Lancaster CC*,[8] for instance, H, the owners of a shop and residential property on a council housing estate, were subjected to horrifying racial and other harassment by council tenants and other persons living on the estate. The Court of Appeal declined to hold the council liable in nuisance for failing to exercise its statutory powers as a housing or highway authority to prevent the commission of crime on the estate.[9] In the Court's view, the appalling abuse suffered by H, whilst unquestionably interfering with their enjoyment of their own premises, did not involve the use by the wrongdoing tenants of their own land and therefore fell strictly outside the scope of the tort of nuisance.[10] Moreover, the council could be liable only for conduct which it had specifically authorised or adopted, which was clearly not the case here.[11]

1   *Smith v Scott* [1973] Ch 314 at 321B.
2   For a critical view of this restriction, see [2003] Conv 171 (S Bright).
3   *Southwark LBC v Mills* [2001] 1 AC 1 at 21H–22A per Lord Millett; *Lippiatt v South Gloucestershire CC* [2000] QB 51 at 56G–H. See also *Harris v James* (1876) 35 LT 240 at 241; *Smith v Scott* [1973] Ch 314 at 321C; *Tetley v Chitty* [1986] 1 All ER 663 at 671e–f.
4   *Chartered Trust Plc v Davies* (1997) 76 P & CR 396 at 406–409 (where the Court of Appeal emphasised that the successful operation of both tenanted premises depended vitally on the landlord's special role in discharging the proper management of a shopping mall and its common parts). See *Hussain v Lancaster CC* [2000] QB 1 at 24E–F per Hirst LJ.
5   See eg *Sampson v Hodson-Pressinger* [1981] 3 All ER 710 at 714j (landlord liable for noise penetration between adjacent tenants' properties where he purchased reversion in the knowledge of faulty construction). See [1982] Conv 155; [1982] CLJ 38 (M Owen).
6   *Southwark LBC v Mills* [2001] 1 AC 1 at 16C per Lord Hoffmann. 'The governing principle is good neighbourliness, and this involves reciprocity' ([2001] 1 AC 1 at 20E per Lord Millett). Tenants, just as others, are governed by the 'principle of reasonable user – the principle of give and take as between neighbouring occupiers of land' (*Cambridge Water Co v Eastern Counties Leather Plc* [1994] 2 AC 264 at 299D per Lord Goff of Chieveley) **[para 8.99]**. The criterion turns on that which is 'conveniently done' (*Bamford v Turnley* (1862) 3 B & S 62 at 82, 122 ER 27 at 33 per Bramwell B). See *Southwark LBC v Mills*, supra at 16C–D per Lord Hoffmann, 20F–21E per Lord Millett.

7   The express or implied reservation of a right to enter and repair the demised property may demonstrate that the landlord has retained a 'sufficient basis of control' to enable a nuisance liability to be fastened on him in respect of defects arising on the demised premises (see *Heap v Ind Coope and Allsopp Ltd* [1940] 2 KB 476 at 483; *Mint v Good* [1951] 1 KB 517 at 521, 527–528; *Carter v Murray* [1981] 2 NSWLR 77 at 79F).

8   [2000] QB 1. See Jill Morgan, 'Nuisance and the Unruly Tenant' [2001] CLJ 382.

9   The wrongs inflicted on H must be fought by 'multi-disciplinary co-operation and not by civil suit against one of the relevant agencies' ([2000] QB 1 at 28C–D per Thorpe LJ).

10   [2000] QB 1 at 23F–G.

11   [2000] QB 1 at 24F. A more attractive approach to nuisance liability (as, indeed, to liability for derogation from grant) would be to rest liability not on the landlord's approval of the misconduct, but on whether the landlord was in a position to correct or terminate it (see *Bocchina v Gorn Management Co*, 515 A2d 1179 at 1185 (Md 1986); *Prasad v Fairfield CC* (2001) 10 BPR 18747 at [46]).

Limits of the landlord's liability

14.37   The landlord cannot be vicariously liable in nuisance for conduct which is not in itself nuisance on the part of the tenant.[1] Thus, in *Southwark LBC v Mills*,[2] the House of Lords declined to hold a local authority landlord liable in nuisance to one of its tenants in respect of the noise disturbance caused by adjoining council tenants who were making 'normal use of a residential flat' in the same block.[3] Nor, it has been said, can a landlord be liable in nuisance simply because he grants a letting to a tenant whom he knows to be nuisance-prone.[4] Likewise there are judicial statements to the effect that the landlord bears no liability for a tenant's nuisance merely because he was aware of it and took no steps to prevent it.[5]

1   *Southwark LBC v Mills* [2001] 1 AC 1 at 7A per Lord Slynn of Hadley, 22A–B per Lord Millett.

2   [2001] 1 AC 1 [**para 14.17**].

3   [2001] 1 AC 1 at 15F per Lord Hoffmann. The 'ordinary use of residential premises without more' cannot constitute a nuisance ([2001] 1 AC 1 at 21F–H per Lord Millett). Compare, however, *Toff v McDowell* (1993) 69 P & CR 535 at 546–547. It would be different if one tenant unreasonably installed a television or washing machine 'hard up against a party wall so that noise and vibrations are unnecessarily transmitted to the neighbour's premises' ([2001] 1 AC 1 at 16A).

4   *Smith v Scott* [1973] Ch 314 at 321E–F. See, however, *Page Motors Ltd v Epsom and Ewell BC* (1982) 80 LGR 337 at 347–348.

5   See *Malzy v Eichholz* [1916] 2 KB 308 at 315; *Southwark LBC v Mills* [2001] 1 AC 1 at 22A.

Statutory extensions of the landlord's liability

14.38   It is today too sweeping a proposition to assert that the landlord is *never* obliged to restrain the activities of a tenant who commits a nuisance against an adjacent tenant of the same landlord.[1] Certainly, where the landlord is a public authority (eg a local housing authority), the landlord's failure to halt the offending tenant's nuisance is now likely to be viewed as an infringement of the right to respect for 'private and family life' and the 'home' protected by the European Convention on Human Rights.[2] Moreover, the power of a social landlord to police behaviour in areas of tenanted housing has been greatly reinforced by the insertion of new provisions in the Housing Act 1996 which authorise the issue of injunctions restraining anti-social conduct, unlawful use of rented premises and certain other breaches of a tenancy agreement.[3] In particular, the court may grant an injunction against any person who is engaging, has engaged or threatens to engage in conduct which is capable of causing 'nuisance or annoyance' to a resident or visitor in (or in the neighbourhood of) housing accommodation owned or managed by the relevant landlord or which directly or indirectly interferes with any person employed in connection with that landlord's 'housing management functions'.[4] Local housing authorities, housing action trusts and registered social landlords are also required to prepare, publish and keep under review a 'policy in relation to' and 'procedures for dealing with occurrences' of such behaviour.[5]

1   See *Chartered Trust plc v Davies* (1997) 76 P & CR 396 at 407–408 per Henry LJ ('the law of nuisance has developed since 1917 when *Malzy* was decided').

2   ECHR Art 8. See *Pemberton v Southwark LBC* [2000] 1 WLR 1672 at 1681F–H per Roch LJ, 1684C–D per Clarke LJ. Compare also *Lee v Leeds CC* [2002] 1 WLR 1488 at [48]–[50] per Chadwick LJ.

3   HA 1996, ss 153A–E, as inserted by Anti-social Behaviour Act 2003, s 13(3). See S Bright and C Bakalis, 'Anti-Social Behaviour: Local Authority Responsibility and the Voice of the Victim' [2003] CLJ 305.

4   HA 1996, s 153A. The court may attach to the injunction an exclusion order and/or a power of arrest if of the opinion that the respondent has used or threatened violence or that there is a 'significant risk of harm' to any person employed in connection with the landlord's housing management functions (HA 1996, s 153C). See also the powers conferred on magistrates' courts to issue 'anti-social behaviour orders' pursuant to the Crime and Disorder Act 1998, s 1(4) **[para 3.101]**.

5   HA 1996, s 218A(1)–(4), as inserted by Anti-social Behaviour Act 2003, s 12(1).

Landlord's liability under *Rylands v Fletcher*

14.39 It is possible (although unlikely) that the actions or inactions of a landlord will attract liability under the rule in *Rylands v Fletcher*[1] – a rule which the House of Lords has recently refused to regard as obsolete.[2] The courts have nevertheless declined to accept that a tenant may invoke the rule in *Rylands v Fletcher* in order to make the landlord liable for the tortious acts of other tenants of his who live in the neighbourhood.[3] Noxious neighbours (and the noise created by them) may escape and do damage, but they do not constitute dangerous 'things' likely to do mischief in the sense traditionally required by *Rylands v Fletcher*.

1   (1868) LR 3 HL 330. See e g *Martins Camera Corner Pty Ltd v Hotel Mayfair Ltd* [1976] 2 NSWLR 15 at 27B (damage caused by water overflowing from landlord's premises).

2   *Transco plc v Stockport MBC* [2004] 2 AC 1 at [6]–[8] per Lord Bingham of Cornhill, [43] per Lord Hoffmann, [52] per Lord Hobhouse of Woodborough, [82] per Lord Scott of Foscote, [99] per Lord Walker of Gestingthorpe.

3   *Smith v Scott* [1973] Ch 314 at 321F–G.

LANDLORD'S STATUTORY LIABILITY FOR FITNESS OF PREMISES

14.40   It is widely recognised that, particularly in the area of social housing, many tenants lack the bargaining power to exact an express warranty as to the condition of the premises or the freedom of choice to reject property which may not meet their needs. For this reason Parliament has intervened in various ways 'to protect certain tenants from the bleak laissez-faire of the common law.'[1] A fragmented series of statutory interventions has created a range of potential liabilities for landlords in the context of residential tenancies. The obligations thus imposed are, however, of a partial and imperfect character and have proved deeply unsatisfactory for the purpose of protecting tenants from the impact of poor housing conditions.

1   *Southwark LBC v Mills* [2001] 1 AC 1 at 8C–D per Lord Hoffmann.

Implied terms as to fitness for human habitation

14.41   Section 8(1) of the Landlord and Tenant Act 1985 imposes two implied contractual terms in the letting of a dwelling-house. These terms comprise a condition that the house is 'fit for human habitation at the commencement of the tenancy' and a further undertaking that the house 'will be kept by the landlord fit for human habitation during the tenancy.'[1] The overtly protective intent of this social legislation is underscored by the fact that the implied terms cannot be excluded by express contractual provision.[2]

1   On the original social purpose of section 8(1), which has antecedents extending back to Housing of the Working Classes Act 1890, s 75, see *Summers v Salford Corporation* [1943] AC 283 at 293, 297.
2   L&TA 1985, s 8(1).

14.42   For the purpose of section 8(1), a house is 'unfit for human habitation' only if it is 'not reasonably suitable for occupation' because it suffers one or more of a number of stated defects including its condition of repair, stability, freedom from damp, internal arrangement, natural lighting, ventilation, water supply, drainage, sanitation and cooking facilities.[1] The practical scope of section 8(1) is nowadays disastrously circumscribed.[2] The provision has no application if the property cannot be rendered fit for human habitation at reasonable expense.[3] Judicial construction has added the questionable rider that the landlord's obligation arises only when he is notified of the relevant defect[4] and the statutory rent limits on eligible tenancies[5] now make the section virtually ineffective except in respect of properties which are, in any event, fit only for demolition rather than repair.

1   L&TA 1985, s 10. See e g *Summers v Salford Corporation* [1943] AC 283 at 297–298 (broken sash-cord had the effect of jamming a bedroom window). The criterion of 'unfitness' was not, however, met in *Stanton v Southwick* [1920] 2 KB 642 at 646 (infestation by rats entering house) or in *Wainwright v Leeds CC* (1984) 270 EG 1289 at 1290 (damp penetration).
2   See *Issa v Hackney LBC* [1997] 1 WLR 956 at 964F per Brooke LJ ('completely dead letters'); *Lee v Leeds CC* [2002] 1 WLR 1488 at [3], [6].

3   *Buswell v Goodwin* [1971] 1 WLR 92 at 97A. See J I Reynolds, (1974) 37 MLR 377 at 384, but
     compare M J Robinson, (1976) 39 MLR 43.
4   *Morgan v Liverpool Corporation* [1927] 2 KB 131 at 141, 143, 150–151, 153; *McCarrick v
     Liverpool Corporation* [1947] AC 219 at 229–230.
5   In relation to tenancies granted on or after 6 July 1957, the annual rent limit has long
     remained as £80 in London and £52 elsewhere (L&TA 1985, s 8(4)). Inflation has deprived the
     legislation of any practical application to most tenancies, particularly in London (see
     Southwark LBC v Mills [2001] 1 AC 1 at 8D–E per Lord Hoffmann, 17B–C per Lord Millett)
     and the courts have declined, incongruously, to make good the statutory deficit by any
     broader construction of the landlord's common law liabilities (*McNerny v LB of Lambeth*
     (1988) 21 HLR 188 at 194 per Dillon LJ). There is an overwhelming case for a new statutory
     definition of 'low rent' (see *Quick v Taff Ely BC* [1986] QB 809 at 817B, 821D–E). See also *R v
     Cardiff CC, ex p Cross* (1983) 81 LGR 105 at 116; P F Smith, [1990] Conv 335 at 346–347.

Implied covenant for repair and maintenance

14.43   Pursuant to section 11 of the Landlord and Tenant Act 1985,[1] certain
covenants relating to repair and maintenance are impliedly undertaken by the
landlord in a lease of a dwelling-house for a term of less than seven years.[2] The
landlord must keep in repair the structure and exterior of the dwelling-house.[3]
This obligation extends to the walls (and in some circumstances the roof[4]) of
the demised premises, to drains, gutterings and external pipes, and also to any
steps and flagstones giving access to the house.[5] The landlord also impliedly
covenants[6] to keep in repair and 'proper working order' installations for the
supply of water, gas and electricity, facilities for sanitation,[7] and installations
for space heating and heating water.[8] A breach is instantly committed by any
landlord who cuts off the supply of gas or electricity as a means of harassment
of the tenant.[9]

1   Section 11 cannot normally be excluded by contrary contractual provision (L&TA 1985,
     ss 11(4), 12(1)).
2   See L&TA 1985, s 13(1). The landlord's implied covenant thus has no application to a 99 year
     lease of a residential flat (see e g *Gordon v Selico Co Ltd* [1985] 2 EGLR 79 at 80H–J).
3   L&TA 1985, s 11(1)(a). If the dwelling-house forms part only of a building (e g is a flat), the
     landlord's implied covenant extends to any part of the building's structure or exterior in which
     he has an estate or interest (L&TA 1985, s 11(1A)(a)).
4   *Douglas-Scott v Scorgie* [1984] 1 WLR 716 at 721C–D; [1984] JSWL 228 (M A Jones); [1984]
     Conv 229.
5   *Brown v Liverpool Corporation* [1969] 3 All ER 1345 at 1346I. See, however, *Hopwood v
     Cannock Chase DC* [1975] 1 WLR 373 at 377H–378A, 378C–D (patio in the back-yard);
     McAuley v Bristol CC [1992] QB 134 at 141G (step in back garden); *King v South Northamp-
     tonshire DC* (1992) 64 P & CR 35 at 39 (path outside scope of letting).
6   L&TA 1985, s 11(1)(b)–(c). If the dwelling-house forms part only of a building, the landlord's
     implied covenant extends to any installation which serves the tenant's residence and which is
     owned or controlled by the landlord (e g a boiler) (L&TA 1985, s 11(1A)(b)). See, however,
     L&TA 1985, s 11(1B), (3A).
7   It is irrelevant that the facilities have never been in proper working order. See *Liverpool CC v
     Irwin* [1977] AC 239 at 257E, 264C–D, 270A, C–D (£5 damages for faulty lavatory cistern).
8   See *Taylor v Knowsley BC* (1985) 17 HLR 376.
9   *McCall v Abelesz* [1976] QB 585 at 594C–D.

Requirement of notice

14.44   As in the case of section 8(1) of the Landlord and Tenant Act 1985, no liability arises for the landlord under section 11(1) unless and until he is notified of the relevant defect[1] (on the ground that the tenant in situ is more directly aware of emerging repair needs than the landlord who has handed over possession[2]). Such notice must be reasonable notice[3] and the effect of this extra-statutory requirement[4] is to preclude the tenant from relief under the implied statutory covenants where injury or loss has resulted suddenly from a latent and previously invisible defect.[5]

1   *O'Brien v Robinson* [1973] AC 912 at 926A, 930B. See also *British Telecommunications Plc v Sun Life Assurance Society Plc* [1996] Ch 69 at 74G–H; *Sykes v Harry* [2001] QB 1014 at [21].
2   *Austin v Bonney* [1999] 1 Qd R 114 at 119.
3   *Northern Sandblasting Pty Ltd v Harris* (1997) 188 CLR 313 at 370–371 per Gummow J; *Austin v Bonney* [1999] 1 Qd R 114 at 120, 124. The notice need not come directly from the tenant (*McGreal v Wake* (1984) 269 EG 1254 at 1256; *Dinefwr BC v Jones* (1987) 284 EG 58; *Hall v Howard* (1989) 57 P & CR 226 at 230). See also *Sheldon v West Bromwich Corporation* (1973) 25 P & CR 360 at 363–364.
4   The imposition of a notice requirement has not been thought necessary in relation to similar legislation in other jurisdictions (see e g *Gaul v King* (1980) 103 DLR (3d) 233 at 242).
5   See e g *O'Brien v Robinson* [1973] AC 912 at 915G–926A (collapsing ceiling).

Limited concept of disrepair

14.45   The scope of the landlord's obligations under section 11(1) has also been curtailed by the extremely limited interpretation given by the courts to the concept of 'disrepair'.[1] In *Quick v Taff Ely BC*[2] Dillon LJ indicated that 'disrepair is related to the physical condition of whatever has to be repaired, and not to questions of lack of amenity or inefficiency.'[3] The Court of Appeal thus held the implied statutory covenants substantially inapplicable to a council house where 'very severe condensation' had rendered the living conditions of the tenant and his family 'appalling'.[4] In the absence of evidence of physical damage to the walls or the windows, the landlord authority was held not to be in breach of any implied statutory covenant.[5] Here there was no damage to the tenant's walls, merely lots of mould on them.[6] Relevant disrepair, the Court emphasised, does not include mere loss of amenity,[7] with the result that the statutory obligation imports no duty to eliminate disamenities which were intrinsic features of the accommodation in question. Despite occasional indications that the courts' approach to problems of damp and condensation might have become more realistic,[8] the Court of Appeal took the opportunity in *Lee v Leeds CC*[9] to endorse, in very similar factual circumstances, the correctness of the highly restrictive approach laid down in *Quick v Taff Ely BC*.

1   Under section 11(1) the landlord is under no obligation to do anything at all 'until there exists a condition which calls for repair' (*Quick v Taff Ely BC* [1986] QB 809 at 821F per Lawton LJ).
2   [1986] QB 809 at 818C–D. See [1986] Conv 45 (J E M).
3   This does not preclude the possibility that the statutory obligation to repair may sometimes require the elimination of a design defect (*Stent v Monmouth DC* (1987) 54 P & CR 193 at 209–210; *Lee v Leeds CC* [2002] 1 WLR 1488 at [12]–[13] per Chadwick LJ).

4   [1986] QB 809 at 815A.
5   [1986] QB 809 at 819G.
6   Compare *Stent v Monmouth DC* (1987) 54 P & CR 193 at 206–210 (physical damage caused by defective door).
7   [1986] QB 809 at 817F.
8   Where dampness and condensation are partly caused by defective windows and gutterings, the landlord may be obliged to install extractor fans as part of his responsibilities under section 11 (*Switzer v Law* [1998] CLY 3624 (in addition to general damages of £5,500 for eight years of inconvenience and discomfort)). See also *Welsh v Greenwich LBC* (2000) 81 P & CR 144 at [27]–[28] (express covenant to maintain a dwelling 'in good condition and repair' held to obligate the landlord to provide proper insulation so as to prevent black spot mould growth).
9   *Lee v Leeds CC* [2002] 1 WLR 1488 at [53]–[58]. See P F Smith, 'Disrepair and Unfitness Revisited' [2003] Conv 112.

Statutory objective of repair not improvement

14.46   The ambit of the landlord's statutory duty is further constrained by the way in which the courts have construed the obligation to 'repair' as excluding any liability to enhance the demised premises beyond their condition at the commencement date of the tenancy. The landlord is not obliged to improve the house so that it is a different house from that which the tenant originally took.[1] The net effect of this highly restrictive approach is to make the landlord's implied undertaking inapplicable to inherent design defects in the tenant's housing.[2] The landlord's implied repairing covenant is, in any event, relative to the 'age, character and prospective life of the dwelling-house and the locality in which it is situated.'[3] This means in practice that the repairing obligation is not measured objectively and the statutory standard of repair may tend towards a minimal obligation where the dwelling-house is so severely sub-standard that its expected use is confined to the short-term only.[4]

1   *Quick v Taff Ely BC* [1986] QB 809 at 819E; *Southwark LBC v Mills* [2001] 1 AC 1 at 8B–C per Lord Hoffmann. See eg *Wainwright v Leeds CC* (1984) 270 EG 1289 at 1290 per Dunn LJ (no duty to install new damp course), the parallel to which is now *Eyre v McCracken* (2000) 80 P & CR 220 at 228 (no duty on tenant to install new damp course in pursuance of tenant's express repairing obligation).
2   See eg *McDougall v Easington DC* (1989) 58 P & CR 201 at 207 per Mustill LJ. Nevertheless the landlord may be obligated to make certain *modifications* to the premises, eg by altering the size of water pipes in order to accommodate a later drop in the pressure of the water supply (see *O'Connor v Old Etonian Housing Association* [2002] Ch 295 at [30]–[33]). Compare, however, *Niazi Services Ltd v Van der Loo* [2004] 1 WLR 1254 at [21].
3   L&TA 1985, s 11(3). 'The standard of repair may depend on whether the house is in a South Wales valley or in Grosvenor Square' (*Quick v Taff Ely BC* [1986] QB 809 at 821F per Lawton LJ).
4   Compare *Payne v Haine* (1847) 16 M & W 541 at 545, 153 ER 1304 at 1306; *Proudfoot v Hart* (1890) 25 QBD 42 at 51; *LB of Newham v Patel* (1978) 13 HLR 77 at 83–86. See D Hughes, [1984] JSWL 137 at 148.

Liability under the Human Rights Act 1998

14.47   Article 8 of the European Convention on Human Rights protects the right to respect for 'private and family life' and the 'home'.[1] The Court of

Appeal's deliberations in *Lee v Leeds CC*[2] raised the question whether this Convention right imposes on local authority landlords an independent and positive obligation to maintain their housing stock in sufficiently good condition that no tenant's entitlement under Article 8 is infringed. The Court held, significantly, that the Human Rights Act 1998 has indeed fixed such an obligation on local authority landlords and that the obligation is breached where rented social housing is 'unfit for human habitation or in a state prejudicial to health.'[3] The issue of violation of the Convention right is, however, a matter of fact and degree, due regard being had to 'the needs and resources of the community and of individuals.' The Court concluded that the 'fair balance' required by the European Convention does not involve any 'general and unqualified' guarantee of the quality of a local authority's rental accommodation.[4] Particularly in view of the fiscal priorities and burdens already implicit in regimes of social housing, the Court ruled that the circumstances of interior damp, condensation and mould present in the tenant's home in *Lee v Leeds CC* was not 'sufficiently serious' to constitute a breach of the housing authority's obligation under Article 8.[5]

1   **[Paras 2.60, 14.5]**.
2   [2002] 1 WLR 1488 **[para 14.24]**. See [2003] Conv 80 (M P Thompson).
3   [2002] 1 WLR 1488 at [50] per Chadwick LJ.
4   [2002] 1 WLR 1488 at [49] per Chadwick LJ.
5   [2002] 1 WLR 1488 at [51] (Tuckey LJ and Sir Murray Stuart-Smith concurring).

Liability under the Defective Premises Act 1972

14.48   Section 4(1) of the Defective Premises Act 1972 imposes on the landlord a statutory duty to take reasonable care to prevent personal injury or property damage which may be caused by defects in the state of the demised premises.[1] This duty of care arises only in relation to defects which fall within the landlord's covenanted responsibilities of 'maintenance or repair',[2] although the landlord may be liable in respect of defects introduced into the premises by another tenant.[3] Even in the absence of any repairing obligation under the terms of the tenancy, the landlord is still taken[4] to owe a duty of care within section 4(1) if he has expressly[5] or impliedly[6] reserved for himself 'the right to enter the premises to carry out any description of maintenance or repair.'

1   Any attempt in the contract of tenancy to restrict or exclude the landlord's liability is void (DPA 1972, s 6(3)). Other responsibilities in respect of the safety of furniture and appliances supplied with the tenancy are imposed by Furniture and Furnishing (Fire) (Safety) (Amendment) Regulations 1993 (SI 1993/207).
2   DPA 1972, s 4(3). Such responsibilities include any duties of repair or maintenance impliedly undertaken by the landlord pursuant to L&TA 1985, ss 8(1), 11(1) **[paras 14.41, 14.43]**. See DPA 1972, s 4(5).
3   See e g *Smith v Bradford MC* (1982) 4 HLR 86.
4   DPA 1972, s 4(4).
5   See e g *Hamilton v Martell Securities Ltd* [1984] Ch 266 at 271D–F (express reservation of right to effect repairs in event of tenant's failure to do so).
6   *McAuley v Bristol CC* [1992] QB 134 at 151F–H per Ralph Gibson LJ, 154F per Neill LJ. It has been suggested that under a local authority tenancy the council always has an implied

right to repair any part of its property and to enter demised premises for that purpose (see *Smith v Bradford MC* (1982) 4 HLR 86 at 91–92). Compare, however, *McAuley v Bristol CC*, supra at 149H–150B per Ralph Gibson LJ.

14.49 The landlord's duty of care arises only if he actually knew or if he 'ought in all the circumstances to have known' of the relevant defect.[1] The landlord's duty is not absolute.[2] His statutory duty is owed not to the world at large, but only to 'persons who might reasonably be expected to be affected by defects in the state of the premises.'[3] In relation to such persons, the landlord is obliged to take only 'such care as is reasonable in all the circumstances to see that they are reasonably safe from personal injury or from damage to their property caused by a relevant defect.'[4] It matters not whether the 'relevant defect' was present at the commencement of the tenancy or materialised later.[5] However, the defect must have originated in, or continued because of, an 'act or omission by the landlord' which was a breach of his obligation to repair or maintain or would have been such if he had had the requisite knowledge.[6]

1   DPA 1972, s 4(2). There is no requirement of notification by the tenant (see *Sykes v Harry* [2001] QB 1014 at [21]–[22]). Constructive knowledge of defects may attach to a local authority whose appointed officials fail to detect the relevant defects by inspection (*Clarke v Taff Ely BC* (1980) 10 HLR 44 at 52–53).
2   Cf *Gaul v King* (1980) 103 DLR (3d) 233 at 243 (the legislature did not intend that 'the lessors should be insurers').
3   DPA 1972, s 4(1). See e g *Clarke v Taff Ely BC* (1980) 10 HLR 44 at 53 (tenant's friend injured by collapse of rotten floor whilst standing on table in order to help redecorate ceiling).
4   DPA 1972, s 4(1). See e g *Issitt v LB of Tower Hamlets* (Unreported, Court of Appeal, 6 December 1983) (landlord authority not liable for injury to child where 'any responsible parent' would have put a screw in rather than waiting for the council workman to call round).
5   DPA 1972, s 4(3).
6   DPA 1972, s 4(3). The landlord is not therefore liable in respect of inherent design defects, which by their very nature are not attributable to any failure by him to repair or maintain (see e g *Rimmer v Liverpool CC* [1985] QB 1 at 7D–E). For a shocking demonstration of the narrow application of the 1972 Act, see *McDonagh v Kent AHA* (Unreported, Court of Appeal, 7 October 1985) (no liability where tenant was rendered tetraplegic by fall down steep staircase only partially protected by handrail: absence of part of the handrail no 'defect' within the meaning of the Act).

Liability under the Health and Safety at Work etc Act 1974

14.50 Section 4(2) of the Health and Safety at Work etc Act 1974 imposes a duty to take reasonable care to ensure that all means of access to and egress from the relevant premises, together with any 'plant or substance ... provided for use' on those premises, are 'safe and without risks to health.' The duty bears only upon a person who has control of the relevant premises 'in connection with the carrying on by him of a trade, business or other undertaking (whether for profit or not).'[1] Moreover, the statutory duty relates only to 'non-domestic premises' and only in favour of non-employees.[2] In *Westminster CC v Select Management Ltd*,[3] it was nevertheless held that the statutory duty was fully applicable in respect of the lifts in a block of residential flats managed by the defendant company.[4] This surprising application of the 1974 Act may provide a useful remedy for the residential tenant who finds that the management company which controls the common parts of his block of flats persistently ignores its responsibility in respect of lifts, stairways, and electrical installations in the common parts of the buildings.

1   Health and Safety at Work etc Act 1974, s 4(4).
2   Health and Safety at Work etc Act 1974, s 4(1).
3   [1984] 1 WLR 1058 at 1061E–G. See (1985) 48 MLR 589 (B Barrett); [1986] Conv 45.
4   Taylor J thought that the statutory duty would be raised in favour of workmen who came to repair the lifts or electrical installations ([1984] 1 WLR 1058 at 1061D).

Housing Act control

14.51   A further statutory control over the residential quality of tenanted housing has long been provided by powers conferred on local authorities by the Housing Act 1985. Pursuant to this legislation local authorities have had power, where a dwelling-house is considered to be in a 'state of disrepair'[1] or otherwise 'unfit for human habitation'[2] to issue a repair notice. Ultimately local authorities could make a demolition or a closing order[3] or take steps towards the compulsory purchase of the condemned housing.[4]

1   HA 1985, s 190(1), (1A)–(1B).
2   See HA 1985, s 604(1)–(2).
3   HA 1985, ss 264(1), 265(1).
4   HA 1985, s 300(1).

14.52   Local authority supervision of housing quality is about to be rationalised and intensified by provisions contained in the Housing Bill 2004.[1] Each local housing authority will be required to keep housing conditions in its area 'under review with a view to identifying any action that may need to be taken.'[2] The Housing Bill introduces a new 'Housing Health and Safety Rating System' (HHSRS) which will enable local housing authorities to attach a mathematical rating to each of 29 kinds of residential hazard detailed by regulation.[3] These forms of hazard are grouped in two broad categories according to seriousness. In relation to 'category 1 hazards', the authority has a general *duty* to undertake appropriate enforcement action, which may include the issue of improvement notices,[4] prohibition orders, hazard awareness notices,[5] demolition orders or a declaration that premises are situated in a clearance area.[6] The authority may also take 'emergency remedial action' in order to suppress a defined category 1 hazard.[7] In relation to the less serious 'category 2 hazards', the authority has a *power* (but not a duty) to undertake appropriate enforcement action.[8] Non-compliance with a notice or order may be a criminal offence[9] and, in the case of improvement notices and emergency remedial action, may entitle the authority to execute necessary works itself and recover the cost from the defaulter.[10]

1   HL Bill 71.
2   HB 2004, cl 3(1). The Bill also introduces a mandatory licensing scheme for certain houses in multiple occupation (HB 2004, cls 54–75).
3   HB 2004, cls 1–2 (replacing HA 1985, s 604).

4   See, in relation to the old 'repair notice', *Kenny v Kingston upon Thames Royal LBC* (1985) 274 EG 395 at 397; *White v Barnet LBC* [1990] 2 QB 328 at 337A–B.
5   A 'hazard awareness notice' must specify the remedial action considered practicable and appropriate (HB 2004, cls 27(6)(e), 28(5)(e)).
6   HB 2004, cl 5(1)–(2). The authority, if satisfied that a category 1 hazard exists, will ultimately make a demolition order (HA 1985, s 265, as substituted by HB 2004, cl 45).
7   The local housing authority must be satisfied that the hazard involves 'an imminent risk of serious harm to the health or safety' of any occupier (HB 2004, cl 39(1)).
8   HB 2004, cl 7(1)–(2).
9   HB 2004, cl 29(1), 31(1).
10   See eg HB 2004, cls 30, 41(2), 48(1)(d), Sch 3, paras 3, 8. The expenses (and accrued interest thereon) are a charge on the premises (HB 2004, cl 49(7), Sch 3, para 13).

Intervention in the case of 'statutory nuisance'

14.53   A 'statutory nuisance' arises, within the meaning of section 79(1) of the Environmental Protection Act 1990, where any premises are 'in such a state as to be prejudicial to health or a nuisance.'[1]

1   EPA 1990, s 79(1)(a) (formerly Public Health Act 1936, s 92). See also EPA 1990, s 79(7) (definition of 'prejudicial to health'). A 'statutory nuisance' also includes other forms of disamenity, eg the emission of smoke, fumes, gases or noise from premises 'so as to be prejudicial to health or a nuisance' (EPA 1990, s 79(1)(b)–(c), (g)), and 'any dust, steam, smell or effluvia' or 'accumulation or deposit' which is likewise prejudicial (EPA 1990, s 79(1)(d)–(e)). See *Cunningham v Birmingham CC* (1997) 96 LGR 231 at 236g–237e (objective test).

Restrictive interpretation

14.54   The situations covered include such matters as structural defects in houses, crumbling plaster,[1] the presence of toxic blue asbestos,[2] and blocked drains and lavatories. Disrepair caused by damp can lead to a finding of 'statutory nuisance',[3] but the courts have been deeply reluctant to allow the 'statutory nuisance' jurisdiction to be used as a forum for complaints which are more closely related to design defects in housing than to 'public health' complaints arising from housing conditions.[4] In *R v Bristol CC, ex p Everett*,[5] for example, a Divisional Court held that the legislative history of the 'statutory nuisance' regime indicated that there was no intention that this regime should apply in cases where the sole concern related to the danger that the state of the premises (here an excessively steep staircase) might occasion an accident causing personal injury. However, the mere fact that the landlord is not in breach of any of his obligations as landlord, whether in tort or in contract,[6] constitutes 'persuasive' but by no means 'conclusive' evidence that the landlord is freed of responsibility for a statutory nuisance.[7]

1   *Coventry CC v Quinn* [1981] 1 WLR 1325 at 1328E–F.
2   *R v Camberwell Green Magistrates, ex p Healey* (Unreported, Queen's Bench Divisional Court, 10 October 1984).
3   *Patel v Mehtab* (1980) 5 HLR 78 at 83; *Coventry CC v Quinn* [1981] 1 WLR 1325 at 1329E.
4   *Birmingham CC v Oakley* [2001] 1 AC 617 at 627F–H per Lord Slynn of Hadley, 631B–C per Lord Hoffmann, 637B–C per Lord Millett. See eg *Dover DC v Farrar* (1980) 2 HLR 35 at 38, but compare *GLC v LB of Tower Hamlets* (1983) 15 HLR 54 at 61.

5   [1999] 1 WLR 92 at 102F.
6   See eg L&TA 1985, s 11(1) **[para 14.43]**.
7   *Birmingham DC v Kelly* (1985) 17 HLR 572 at 579–580 per Woolf J. See also *Clayton v Sale UDC* [1926] 1 KB 415 at 426.

Abatement of 'statutory nuisances'

14.55   A tenant's complaint relating to an alleged statutory nuisance may lead either to the service by the local authority of an 'abatement notice'[1] or to an order by a magistrates' court that the nuisance be abated and remedial works executed.[2] The local authority may itself take steps to remove the nuisance at the owner's expense,[3] but a proven statutory nuisance does not, in itself, confer on the aggrieved tenant any cause of action for damages.[4]

1   EPA 1990, s 80(1). An abatement notice cannot be served on the local authority as owner of the premises (*Lee v Leeds CC* [2002] 1 WLR 1488 at [19]).
2   EPA 1990, s 82(2).
3   EPA 1990, s 81(3)–(4). See, however, *Salford CC v McNally* [1976] AC 379 at 390A; *Birmingham DC v Kelly* (1985) 17 HLR 572 at 581 per Woolf J.
4   *Issa v Hackney LBC* [1997] 1 WLR 956 at 961H–962H (although see Brooke LJ's expression of regret at 965G–H).

TENANT'S REMEDIES FOR BREACH OF THE LANDLORD'S REPAIRING COVENANTS

14.56   It has, at least until fairly recently, been a general principle underlying the landlord–tenant relationship in English law that the performance of the parties' respective obligations is not interdependent.[1] For this reason it has not usually been thought wise (and on occasion it has proved disastrous[2]) for the tenant to withhold payment of rent or service charges on the ground of his landlord's patent failure to discharge a duty to repair.[3] The tenant must seek to vindicate his rights through the legitimate channels which the law affords. The remedies open to the tenant include the following.

1   **[Para 14.8]**. See, however, L&TA 1985, s 21A(1), 21B(3), as substituted by CALRA 2002, ss 152–153; L&TA 1987, s 42A(9), as inserted by CALRA 2002, s 156(1) **[paras 14.75, 14.78]**.
2   See eg *Di Palma v Victoria Square Property Co Ltd* [1986] Ch 150 **[para 14.8]**.
3   See now, however, the possibility that a doctrine of repudiatory breach may entitle the tenant both to throw up the tenancy and to sue for breach of the landlord's repairing obligation (*Hussein v Mehlman* [1992] 2 EGLR 87 **[para 14.65]**).

Damages for breach of covenant

14.57   It is of course clear that the tenant may sue the landlord for damages for breach of any repairing covenant expressly or impliedly undertaken by the landlord in the lease.[1] It was reiterated by the Court of Appeal in *Calabar Properties Ltd v Stitcher*[2] that in assessing the tenant's damages for breach of a landlord's repairing covenant, the court starts from the 'fundamental principle' that the purpose of such damages is 'so far as is possible by means of a monetary award, to place the plaintiff in the position which he would have occupied if he had not suffered the wrong complained of.' The object of the award is 'not to punish the landlord but ... to restore the tenant to the position he would have been in had there been no breach.'[3] Damages must therefore be assessed as 'the difference in value to the tenant of the premises.'[4] Where, by reason of the landlord's disrepair, the tenant is forced to sell or sublet the premises, the tenant is entitled to recover the resulting diminution of the sale price or recoverable rent.[5] Where, notwithstanding the landlord's breach, the tenant remains in occupation, the recoverable damages extend only to the loss of comfort and convenience suffered by the tenant in consequence of the disrepair.[6]

1   An action for damages for breach of the landlord's repairing covenant, even if coupled with an application for a mandatory injunction, cannot be registered as a pending land action (see *Regan & Blackburn Ltd v Rogers* [1985] 1 WLR 870 at 875D–E).
2   [1984] 1 WLR 287 at 295G–H per Stephenson LJ.
3   [1984] 1 WLR 287 at 297F. See [1984] Conv 230 (J E M); (1984) LAG Bulletin 51 (N Madge and D Watkinson). See also *Loria v Hammer* [1989] 2 EGLR 249 at 260F–H ([1990] Conv 124 (J E Martin)); *Wallace v Manchester CC* [1998] 3 EGLR 38 at 40B per Morritt LJ.
4   *Hewitt v Rowlands* (1924) 93 LJKB 1080 at 1082 per Bankes LJ. Damages thus cover the difference between the value of the property to the tenant in its condition of disrepair and the value which the property would have had if the landlord had fulfilled his repairing obligation (*Calabar Properties Ltd v Stitcher* [1984] 1 WLR 287 at 296C).
5   *Calabar Properties Ltd v Stitcher* [1984] 1 WLR 287 at 297H–298B.
6   *Wallace v Manchester CC* [1998] 3 EGLR 38 at 42J–43A (total damages of £8,280 for breach of landlord's covenants under L&TA 1985, s 11 [**para 14.43**]). See also *McCoy & Co v Clark* (1982) 13 HLR 87 at 94–96; *Chiodi v De Marney* (1988) 21 HLR 6 at 14–15; *Niazi Services Ltd v Van der Loo* [2004] 1 WLR 1254 at [29].

Order for specific performance

14.58   Although, historically, the remedy of specific performance was not regarded as available for the enforcement of a *tenant's* repairing obligation,[1] the courts have long been prepared in appropriate circumstances to order specific performance of a *landlord's* covenant to repair.[2] Indeed, in the context of residential tenancies, this discretion to award specific performance against the landlord is expressly confirmed by statute.[3] In exceptional circumstances a mandatory injunction compelling repairs may even be made in interlocutory proceedings if the effect of the disrepair is to expose tenants to 'a real risk of damage to health.'[4]

1   *Hill v Barclay* (1810) 16 Ves 402 at 405–406, 33 ER 1037 at 1038; *Regional Properties Ltd v City of London Real Property Co Ltd* (1981) 257 EG 64 at 66. Compare now *Rainbow Estates Ltd v Tokenhold Ltd* [1999] Ch 64 [**para 14.206**].
2   See *Jeune v Queens Cross Properties Ltd* [1974] Ch 97 at 101C–D per Pennycuick V-C. See also *Francis v Cowcliffe* (1977) 33 P & CR 368 at 374–376; *Peninsular Maritime Ltd v Padseal Ltd* (1981) 259 EG 860 at 868.
3   L&TA 1985, s 17(1). See *Parker v Camden LBC* [1986] Ch 162 at 173G–H; *Hi-Lift Elevator Services v Temple* (1994) 70 P & CR 620 at 624–626; (1982) LAG Bulletin 66 at 68 (J Luba).
4   *Parker v Camden LBC* [1986] Ch 162 at 174C, where Donaldson MR pointed out that the

failure of a local authority landlord to repair and restart boilers which supplied heating and hot water made both elderly and very young occupiers of housing on a council estate vulnerable to 'a far from fanciful risk of death.'

Remedies of self-help and set-off

14.59   Further relief in the case of disrepair lies in the form of two similar, but distinct, remedies available to the tenant on a basis of self-help.

Common law right of recoupment

14.60   At common law the tenant has a right of recoupment from future rent in respect of the cost of repairs covenanted, but not executed, by the landlord.[1] The right, of ancient derivation, affords the tenant a significant remedy where the landlord is in breach of any covenant (whether express or implied) to repair the demised premises.[2] In *Lee-Parker v Izzet*[3] Goff J confirmed that the tenant may execute the covenanted repairs himself and then deduct the cost of these repairs from future payments of rent.[4] The tenant who takes advantage of this right has *pro tanto* a defence to any action by the landlord for arrears of rent[5] and also has in the same degree an answer to any claim by the landlord to distrain upon his goods.[6] As a precondition of this abatement of rent, the tenant must first have given the landlord notice of the need for repair[7] and the right of recoupment applies only to such portion of the tenant's expenditure as is reasonable and proper in all the circumstances of the case.[8] The tenant's right may be also be excluded – as happens increasingly frequently – by a covenant in which the tenant undertakes to pay rent 'without any deduction or set-off whatsoever.'[9]

1   See *Mortgage Corpn Ltd v Ubah* (1997) 73 P & CR 500 at 507 per Millett LJ. The set-off is not available in respect of service charges imposed by a manager appointed by the court under the Landlord and Tenant Act 1987 (see *Maunder Taylor v Blaquiere* [2003] 1 WLR 379 at [42], [50] **[para 14.67]**).

2   The remedy can be traced back at least as far as *Taylor v Beal* (1591) Cro Eliz 222, 78 ER 478. See also *Waters v Weigall* (1795) 2 Anst 575 at 576, 145 ER 971. The legitimacy of broad formulations of the common law doctrine has been questioned (see P M Rank, (1976) 40 Conv (NS) 196), but the doctrine seems to have a good common law pedigree (see A Waite, [1981] Conv 199).

3   [1971] 1 WLR 1688 at 1693F–G. See also *Melville v Grapelodge Developments Ltd* (1979) 39 P & CR 179 at 186.

4   See also *Asco Developments Ltd v Gordon* (1978) 248 EG 683 (reduction of existing rent arrears); *Knockholt Proprietary Ltd v Graff* [1975] Qd R 88 at 90G–91A.

5   The tenant's expenditure is regarded *pro tanto* as payment of that rent (*Connaught Restaurants Ltd v Indoor Leisure Ltd* [1994] 1 WLR 501 at 511B per Neill LJ) and therefore as a defence at law to any claim for unpaid rent (*Muscat v Smith* [2003] 1 WLR 2853 at [9] per Sedley LJ).

6   *Lee-Parker v Izzet* [1971] 1 WLR 1688 at 1693A–B, 1695H; *Connaught Restaurants Ltd v Indoor Leisure Ltd* [1994] 1 WLR 501 at 511C per Neill LJ. See generally (1982) LAG Bulletin 66 at 67 (J Luba); A Waite, (1984) LAG Bulletin 66.

7   *Lee-Parker v Izzet* [1971] 1 WLR 1688 at 1693H; *British Anzani (Felixstowe) Ltd v International Marine Management (UK) Ltd* [1979] 2 All ER 1063 at 1070b.

8   *Lee-Parker v Izzet* [1971] 1 WLR 1688 at 1693G, 1695H–1696A. The tenant's right of
     recoupment ranks in registered land as an overriding interest on behalf of a tenant who
     remains 'in actual occupation' of the land (see *Lee-Parker v Izzet* [1971] 1 WLR 1688 at
     1691G) and in unregistered land comprises a non-registrable, non-overreachable right which
     binds all except a purchaser for value without notice.
9   See *Electricity Supply Nominees Ltd v IAF Group Ltd* [1993] 1 WLR 1059 at 1064B–C;
     Debonair Nominees Pty Ltd v J & K Berry Nominees Pty Ltd (2000) 77 SASR 261 at 271;
     Batiste v Lenin (2002) 10 BPR 19441 at [105].

Equitable right of set-off

14.61 In general terms, where a tenant has put up with the damaging
consequences of a landlord's breach (rather than expended his own funds in
remedy of such breach), a right of set-off arises in equity on behalf of the
tenant provided that there exists a 'close reciprocity' in the subject matter of the
parties' cross-claims.[1] Such reciprocity undoubtedly obtains between damages
for breach of a landlord's repairing covenant and the rent payable under the
lease.

1   *Muscat v Smith* [2003] 1 WLR 2853 at [9], [30] per Sedley LJ. A right of set-off is sometimes
     granted by statute (see e g Agricultural Holdings Act 1986, s 17).

14.62 If, instead of paying for necessary repairs which the landlord has
covenanted to carry out, the tenant withholds rent and waits for the landlord to
claim arrears, the tenant is normally entitled in equity to set off his claim for
unliquidated damages for breach of the landlord's covenant against any claim
brought by the landlord for non-payment of rent.[1] This equitable set-off is
justified where (as in the present context) the landlord's claim and the tenant's
cross-claim are sufficiently connected that it becomes unfair that the tenant
should be obliged to pay the landlord's claim without deduction.[2] The tenant's
equitable right can be contractually excluded only by clear words.[3] The equitable set-off may be even more valuable than the common law right to make
deductions from rent, in that it can cover consequential damage flowing from
the landlord's breach.[4]

1   *British Anzani (Felixstowe) Ltd v International Marine Management (UK) Ltd* [1979] 2 All ER
     1063 at 1068d–h, 1074c–d; *Connaught Restaurants Ltd v Indoor Leisure Ltd* [1994] 1 WLR 501
     at 511C. Any other view would discriminate unfairly between the tenant who could find the
     money to effect the repairs and the tenant who was forced by lack of money or access to put
     up with the disadvantageous impact of disrepair (see *Muscat v Smith* [2003] 1 WLR 2853
     at [29] per Sedley LJ).
2   See *Muscat v Smith* [2003] 1 WLR 2853 at [39] per Buxton LJ. See also (1979) LAG Bulletin
     210 at 211 (A Arden). The tenant's right of set-off may also apply so as to restrict the
     landlord's right to distrain on the tenant's goods for rent arrears. It would be 'contrary to
     principle that a landlord should be able to recover more by distress than he can by action'
     (*Eller v Grovecrest Investments Ltd* [1995] QB 272 at 278D per Hoffmann LJ).
3   *Connaught Restaurants Ltd v Indoor Leisure Ltd* [1994] 1 WLR 501 at 509A–C, 510E–G
     (covenant to pay rent 'without any deduction' not sufficiently clear to exclude right of set-off).
     See also *Grant v NZMC Ltd* [1989] 1 NZLR 8 at 13. For an effective exclusion of set-off, see
     Inntrepreneur Beer Supply Co Ltd v Langton [1999] 2 EGLR 145 at 156L–157E.

4   *British Anzani (Felixstowe) Ltd v International Marine Management (UK) Ltd* [1979] 2 All ER
     1063 at 1070a–c, f–g, 1076h–j.

14.63   The tenant's equitable right of set-off may be similarly available against
any successor in title to the landord's reversionary estate.[1] This follows, not so
much on general grounds of fairness,[2] but as a consequence of a venerable rule
relating to the assignment of choses in action. The transferee of the landlord's
reversion sometimes receives a statutory assignment of a chose in action (ie the
transferor's claim for arrears of rent accrued prior to the transfer of the
reversion).[3] The transferee of the reversion must therefore take the assigned
chose in action 'subject to all equities existing at the date of his acquisition',[4]
even though this may mean that he inherits an undetermined abatement of rent
arrears.[5]

1   *Muscat v Smith* [2003] 1 WLR 2853 at [16], [31] per Sedley LJ. Subject always to the terms of
     the assignment, the assignor, to the extent that the disrepair was his fault, may be obligated to
     indemnify the assignee.
2   See Buxton LJ's disobliging reference in *Muscat v Smith* [2003] 1 WLR 2853 at [45] to 'a form
     of palm-tree justice'.
3   LPA 1925, s 141(1) **[para 14.274]**. See *Muscat v Smith* [2003] 1 WLR 2853 at [51] per
     Buxton LJ.
4   See LPA 1925, s 136(1). See *Lotteryking Ltd v AMEC Properties Ltd* [1995] 2 EGLR 13 at 15
     per Lightman J; *Muscat v Smith* [2003] 1 WLR 2853 at [31] per Sedley LJ, [54] per Buxton LJ,
     [56] per Ward LJ. For the root of the doctrine that the assignee of a chose in action takes
     subject to relevant equities, see *Roxburghe v Cox* (1881) 17 Ch D 520 at 526.
5   It is possible that this outcome may constitute a breach of any full title guarantee impliedly
     given by the assignor (see *Muscat v Smith* [2003] 1 WLR 2853 at [25] per Sedley LJ, referring
     to LP(MP)A 1994, s 3).

Statutory 'right to repair' for secure tenants

14.64   'Secure tenants'[1] and 'introductory tenants'[2] whose landlords are local
housing authorities are given a statutory 'right to repair' in respect of certain
kinds of defect in the condition of their accommodation. This 'right to repair'
is currently outlined in a statutory instrument approved under the Housing
Act 1985.[3] The tenant is entitled, on application to the landlord, to have certain
'qualifying' repairs'[4] to his dwelling effected within a prescribed period at the
landlord's expense[5] and, in cases of default by the landlord, to receive compensation.[6]

1   **[Para 14.338]**.
2   **[Para 14.348]**.
3   The Secure Tenants of Local Housing Authorities (Right to Repair) Regulations 1994
     (SI 1994/133), as amended by SI 1994/844 and SI 1997/73. See HA 1985, s 96(1), as substituted
     by LRH&UDA 1993, s 121.
4   A 'qualifying repair' is any repair of a prescribed description 'which the landlord of a secure
     tenant is obliged by a repairing covenant to carry out' (HA 1985, s 96(6)). For the prescribed
     description of repair, see SI 1994/133, reg 4, Sch 1.
5   SI 1994/133, reg 3(1)(a).
6   SI 1994/133, regs 3(1)(b), 7(1). Compensation cannot exceed £50 and the landlord may set off
     any arrears of rent owed by the tenant (SI 1994/133, reg 7(2)–(3)).

Termination for repudiatory breach

14.65 In cases of serious non-repair by the landlord, the most far-reaching remedy available to the tenant is the right to treat the lease as terminated on the ground of breach of a fundamental term.[1] The doctrine of repudiatory breach entitles the aggrieved tenant, at his election, to throw up the lease in its entirety and to sue immediately for damages in respect of the loss caused by the landlord's default in the matter of repair.[2]

1   [**Para 7.321**]. See e g *Hussein v Mehlman* [1992] 2 EGLR 87 at 92C–D; *Bond v Weeks* [1999] 1 Qd R 134 at 140; *Shun Cheong Holdings BC Ltd v Gold Ocean City Supermarket Ltd* (2002) 216 DLR (4th) 392 at [11]–[14].
2   See P F Smith, 'Termination of Tenancies by Tenants: A Just Cause?', in P Jackson and D C Wilde (ed), *The Reform of Property Law* (Ashgate 1997), p 91.

Appointment of receiver

14.66 In the event of continuing default by a landlord in his obligations of repair, tenants may apply to the High Court for the appointment of a receiver to receive the rents due and to manage the demised premises in accordance with the landlord's obligations.[1]

1   Supreme Court Act 1981, s 37(1). See *Hart v Emelkirk Ltd* [1983] 1 WLR 1289 at 1291H; *Daiches v Bluelake Investments Ltd* [1985] 2 EGLR 67 at 70A–D. This remedy may have a limited utility (see e g *Parker v Camden LBC* [1986] Ch 162 at 173B–D, 176E–F, 179A–D (no application to local authority tenancies); *Evans v Clayhope Properties Ltd* [1988] 1 WLR 358 at 363A–F).

Appointment of a manager

14.67 Increasing concern at the plight of long leaseholders in deteriorating mansion blocks led the Nugee Committee in 1985 to propose increased safeguards against the defaults of the neglectful landlord who flagrantly ignores his repairing obligations.[1] The Landlord and Tenant Act 1987 introduced a protective procedure which is more generally effective than the High Court jurisdiction to appoint a receiver. Any tenant of a flat within a building containing two or more flats[2] may apply to a leasehold valuation tribunal for an order appointing a 'manager'[3] to take over the management of the premises.[4] The applicant must first have served a preliminary notice on the defaulting landlord, specifying the matters of complaint and giving him a reasonable time within which to remedy the default.[5] The tribunal may make an order only if satisfied[6] that it is 'just and convenient' to make the order and that the landlord is in breach of his obligations under the tenancy or has made (or proposed) 'unreasonable' service or variable administration charges[7] or has failed to account properly for service charge contributions[8] or has failed to comply with a code of management practice approved by the Secretary of State. The tribunal ultimately has power to make an 'acquisition order' on an application by not less than two-thirds of the qualifying tenants, thereby allowing the tenants to purchase the landlord's interest without his consent.[9] Such an order can be made only if the landlord is in breach (and is likely to continue to be in breach) of his obligations[10] or where two years have elapsed since the appointment of a manager and a more permanent or far-reaching remedy is required.[11]

1   See Report of the Committee of Inquiry on the Management of Privately Owned Blocks of Flats (Chairman: E G Nugee QC, 1985), Vol 1, para 7.2.17.
2   L&TA 1987, s 21(2) (subject to certain qualifications contained in L&TA 1987, s 21(3), (3A)).
3   The manager acts, in a capacity independent of the landlord, as a court-appointed official (see *Maunder Taylor v Blaquiere* [2003] 1 WLR 379 at [41]–[42]).
4   L&TA 1987, s 21(1). The tribunal may, if it thinks fit, appoint a manager to carry out the functions of both a manager and a receiver (L&TA 1987, s 24(1)). A person appointed as manager and receiver normally has power to let vacant parts of the demised premises at a rack rent in discharge of his duty of proper management (*Sparkle Properties Ltd v Residential Developments Ltd* [1998] EGCS 68).
5   L&TA 1987, s 22 (see, however, L&TA 1987, s 22(3)).
6   See L&TA 1987, s 24(2). The leasehold valuation tribunal has a fall-back power where satisfied that other circumstances exist which render it 'just and convenient' for an order to be made (L&TA 1987, s 24(2)(b)).
7   On the meaning of 'unreasonable', see L&TA 1987, s 24(2A), (2B).
8   L&TA 1987, ss 42–42A (as inserted by CALRA 2002, s 156(1)).
9   L&TA 1987, ss 27(4), 28(1), 29(1) (as amended by CALRA 2002, Sch 9, para 9). The qualifying tenants must own not less than two-thirds of the total number of flats contained in the premises (L&TA 1987, s 25(2)(c)).
10 L&TA 1987, s 29(2).
11 L&TA 1987, s 29(3).

14.68   As the Nugee Committee noted in 1985,[1] the solution of many of the problems of multiple leasehold occupation lies ultimately in some form of 'commonhold' ownership – a regime which is now made available, with effect from 27 September 2004, by the provisions of the Commonhold and Leasehold Reform Act 2002.[2] The 2002 Act also confers a more general entitlement on the tenants of flats within a multi-occupied block of flats. Even in the absence of any breach of obligation by the landlord, the tenants of such premises are given a statutory 'right to manage' (or 'RTM') which comprises a power to take over the management of the block through a private company limited by guarantee (a 'RTM company') of which all participating tenants, together with the landlord, are members.[3]

1   Report of the Committee of Inquiry on the Management of Privately Owned Blocks of Flats, Vol 1, para 7.9.11.
2   [**Paras 1.33, 7.356**]. See The Commonhold and Leasehold Reform Act 2002 (Commencement No 4) Order 2004 (SI 2004/1832), art 2.
3   CALRA 2002, ss 71–113.

OTHER STATUTORY OBLIGATIONS OF THE LANDLORD

14.69   Apart from their statutory responsibilities in respect of repair and fitness of premises, landlords (or their agents) are subject to other important obligations imposed by statute. These obligations include the following.

Disclosure of certain information

14.70 The landlord of premises occupied as a dwelling is now statutorily obliged to supply his tenant with certain kinds of information which may prove vital for the effective enforcement of the tenant's rights.

Identity of the landlord

14.71 If the tenant of 'premises occupied as a dwelling' makes a written request for the landlord's name and address *either* to any person who demands or last received rent payable under the tenancy *or* to any agent of the landlord in relation to the tenancy, that person must within 21 days supply the tenant with a written statement of the information requested.[1] In the case of a corporate landlord, the tenant may make a further written request that he be informed of the name and address of every director and of the secretary of the landlord company.[2] Any written demand (e g for rent) which is made to a residential tenant must contain the name and address of the landlord.[3] Furthermore the landlord of every residential tenant must furnish his tenants with written advice of an address in England or Wales at which notices (e g notices of proceedings) may be served[4] and, until such an address is notified to the tenant, no rent or service charge or administration charge otherwise due from the tenant can be treated as due.[5]

1   L&TA 1985, s 1(1). The period of 21 days begins with the date of receipt of the request. Non-compliance is a criminal offence (L&TA 1985, s 1(2)), but only the identity of the immediate landlord need be disclosed (L&TA 1985, s 1(3)).
2   L&TA 1985, s 2(1). The obligations of disclosure imposed by L&TA 1985, ss 1–2, have no reference to business tenancies governed by Part II of the Landlord and Tenant Act 1954 (see L&TA 1985, s 32(1)), but do apply in the case of statutory tenancies under the Rent Act (see L&TA 1985, s 1(3)).
3   L&TA 1987, s 47(1).
4   L&TA 1987, s 48(1). See *Milestate v Clarke* [1994] CLY 2740 (mere indication of landlord company's registered address insufficient notification of address for service under section 48(1)).
5   L&TA 1987, s 48(2), as amended by CALRA 2002, Sch 11, para 11(2). See e g *Milestate v Clarke* [1994] CLY 2740.

Written statement of certain terms of an orally granted assured shorthold tenancy

14.72 In relation to any any assured shorthold tenancy granted on or after 28 February 1997 and not evidenced in writing, the landlord is statutorily obliged to provide the tenant with a written statement of the principal terms of the tenancy.[1]

1   HA 1988, s 20A (e g commencement and term dates, amount and due date of rent, and details of any provision for rent review).

Assignment by the landlord

14.73   In the event of any assignment of the landlord's reversion in respect of tenanted premises which consist of or include a dwelling, the new landlord is statutorily obliged to give the tenant written notice of the assignment and of the landlord's name and address within at most two months of the date of the assignment.[1] In default of such a notice, the former landlord remains expressly liable to the tenant on the covenants of the lease.[2] Where the assignment triggers a right of first refusal under the Landlord and Tenant Act 1987,[3] the new landlord is also required to inform the tenants of their statutory rights.[4]

1   L&TA 1985, s 3(1). This provision catches statutory tenancies and is activated by 'any conveyance other than a mortgage or charge' of the landlord's interest (L&TA 1985, s 3(4)).
2   L&TA 1985, s 3(3A)–(3B).
3   **[Para 7.344]**.
4   L&TA 1985, 3A (as added by HA 1996, s 93).

Provision of rent book

14.74   Where a tenant has a right to occupy premises as a residence in consideration of a rent which is payable weekly, the landlord must provide a 'rent book or other similar document for use in respect of the premises.'[1] Any rent book provided in pursuance of this duty must contain such details as the name and address of the landlord[2] and certain statutorily prescribed information relating to rent and other particulars of the tenancy.[3] Failure to comply with any of these requirements constitutes a criminal offence,[4] but such failure does not invalidate the tenancy or render the rent thereunder irrecoverable.[5] The statutory rules relating to rent books are often ignored by landlords and there is a strong argument for more vigorous enforcement of this branch of the law on behalf of residential tenants.[6]

1   L&TA 1985, s 4(1). This requirement does not apply if the rent includes a payment in respect of board and the value of that board to the tenant forms 'a substantial proportion of the whole rent' (L&TA 1985, s 4(2)).
2   L&TA 1985, s 5(1) (as amended by HA 1988, Sch 17, para 67).
3   L&TA 1985, s 5(2)–(3). See The Rent Book (Forms of Notice) Regulations 1982 (SI 1982/1474), Schedule, as amended by SI 1988/2198, SI 1990/1067 and SI 1993/656. The prescribed information must include details of the tenant's right not to be harassed or unlawfully evicted and of his right (where necessary) to receive help with payment of his rent.
4   L&TA 1985, s 7(1).
5   *Shaw v Groom* [1970] 2 QB 504 at 516E–F, 526B–D; *Lambeth LBC v Udechuku* (1981) 41 P & CR 200 at 208. A tenant is not guilty of participating in any fraud upon the Inland Revenue merely because he suspects that his landlord's refusal to supply a rent book is related to an unwillingness to leave a permanent trace of the rent payments made (see *Chukwu v Iqbal* (Unreported, Court of Appeal, 30 January 1985) per Fox LJ).
6   See D C Hoath, [1978–79] JSWL 3.

Restrictions in respect of service and administration charges

14.75   The Landlord and Tenant Act 1985 imposes certain duties on the landlord in respect of 'service charges'[1] and 'administration charges'[2] which are payable by a residential tenant. Any payments made by way of service charge (plus any income accruing thereon) must be held on trust to defray the costs for which the service charges were payable and otherwise on trust for the contributing tenants for the time being.[3]

1   A 'service charge' is defined as an amount which is payable by a tenant of a dwelling, as part of or in addition to rent, in respect of 'services, repairs, maintenance, improvements or insurance or the landlord's costs of management' and which varies in whole or part according to the relevant costs (L&TA 1985, s 18(1)(a), as amended by CALRA 2002, Sch 9, para 7).

2   An 'administration charge' is defined as an amount levied by a landlord in connection with the grant of approvals under the lease or the provision of information or documents or in respect of any alleged default of the tenant (CALRA 2002, s 158, Sch 11, para 1(1)).

3   L&TA 1987, s 42(2)–(3), as amended by CALRA 2002, Sch 9, para 15. Sums paid as service charges must be held separately in a designated account at a 'relevant financial institution' (L&TA 1987, s 42A(1)–(2), as inserted by CALRA 2002, s 156(1)). A tenant may withhold payment of a service charge if he has reasonable grounds for believing that the payee has failed to comply with the last obligation (L&TA 1987, s 42A(9)). Failure to comply with L&TA 1987, s 42A is also a criminal offence (L&TA 1987, s 42B).

Limitation to reasonable charges

14.76 In determining the amount of a service charge payable for a given period, account may be taken of relevant costs only to the extent that these costs (eg the costs of repairs) were 'reasonably incurred' and the services provided or works carried out were 'of a reasonable standard.'[1] The tenant may refer the issue of reasonableness for determination by a leasehold valuation tribunal either before or after payment of the amount demanded by the landlord.[2] No service charge can normally be based on relevant costs incurred more than 18 months before the presentation of the charge for payment.[3] Where a service charge is payable in advance of any expenditure, the landlord may demand only such amount as is 'reasonable' and must make any necessary adjustment by way of rebate after the relevant costs have been incurred.[4] A broadly similar requirement of reasonableness applies to administration charges imposed under a lease.[5]

1   L&TA 1985, s 19(1). Account must be taken of any grant aid received by the landlord (L&TA 1985, s 20A). Covenanted service charges are not challengeable under the Unfair Contract Terms Act 1977 (*Unchained Growth III plc v Granby Village* (*Manchester*) *Management Co Ltd* (1999) *Times*, 4 November).

2   L&TA 1985, s 27A(1)–(2), as inserted with effect from 30 September 2003 by CALRA 2002, s 155(1) (see SI 2003/1986). The tribunal may, in its discretion, entertain challenges to service charges paid over as long a period as the past twelve years (see *R* (*Daejan Properties Ltd*) *v London Leasehold Valuation Tribunal* [2000] 3 EGLR 44), but it is less than clear that L&TA 1985, s 27A permits the tribunal to entertain a tenant's claim for restitution of overpaid service charges (see N Roberts, [2003] Conv 380).

3   L&TA 1985, s 20B.

4   L&TA 1985, s 19(2). Although it is for the landlord to decide *how* to repair, his decision must be reasonable. The remedy available to a tenant who challenges the need for repair is not an injunction restraining works, but a declaration under the 1985 Act that the cost of the works is unreasonably high (*Hi-Lift Elevator Services v Temple* (1994) 70 P & CR 620 at 625).

5   CALRA 2002, s 158, Sch 11, paras 2–3.

14.77   Pursuant to amendments contained in the Commonhold and Lease-hold Reform Act 2002,[1] the Landlord and Tenant Act 1985 has been refashioned so as to impose extensive requirements of 'consultation' by a landlord in relation to service charges levied in connection with 'qualifying works'. In the absence of appropriate consultation, the tenant's liability to contribute towards such works is normally limited to an amount prescribed by regulation.[2] The 'consultation requirements' envisage that the landlord will provide tenants (or a recognised tenants' association representing them) with details of, and an explanation for, proposed works; will obtain estimates for the works and invite suggestions from tenants of other sources of estimates; and will 'have regard' to observations made by tenants (or their association) in relation to the works or estimates.[3]

1   CALRA 2002, s 151.
2   L&TA 1985, s 20(1), (6)–(7).
3   L&TA 1985, s 20ZA(4)–(5). See Service Charges (Consultation Requirements) (England) Regulations 2003 (SI 2003/1987) (effective 31 October 2003). See also SI 2004/684 (effective 30 March 2004).

14.78   All demands for the payment of a service charge[1] or an administration charge[2] must be accompanied by a written summary of the rights and obligations of residential tenants in relation to such charges. The landlord is also required to supply to each tenant by whom service charges are payable a regular written statement of account detailing the application of these charges in discharge of relevant costs under the lease.[3] The statement must be accompanied by the certificate of a qualified accountant that the statement 'deals fairly' with all relevant matters and is sufficiently supported by accounts, receipts and other documents.[4] Failure to supply the tenant with any of the required documentation not only entitles the tenant to withhold payment of a service charge[5] or administration charge,[6] but may also constitute a criminal offence.[7]

1   L&TA 1985, s 21B(1), as inserted by CALRA 2002, s 153.
2   CALRA 2002, Sch 11, para 4(1).
3   L&TA 1985, s 21(1)–(2), as substituted by CALRA 2002, s 152. The tenant has certain rights, on giving written notice to the landlord, to inspect accounts, receipts and other documents (L&TA 1985, s 22, as substituted by CALRA 2002, s 154).
4   L&TA 1985, s 21(3)(a). The tenant must again be provided with a written summary of his rights and obligations in relation to service charges (L&TA 1985, s 21(3)(b)).
5   L&TA 1985, ss 21A(1)–(2), 21B(3), as substituted by CALRA 2002, ss 152–153.
6   CALRA 2002, Sch 11, para 4(3).
7   L&TA 1985, s 25(1).

Tenants' right to management audit

14.79   The Leasehold Reform, Housing and Urban Development Act 1993 reinforces the tenant's protection through the conferment of a right to join with other tenants who pay a common service charge in requiring that a 'management audit' be carried out on their behalf in relation to the management of the premises.[1] This audit is directed towards ascertaining whether the landlord's obligations and management functions are being discharged in an 'efficient and effective manner' and the extent to which the tenants' service charges are being likewise applied.[2]

1   LRH&UDA 1993, s 76. The auditor must be afforded reasonable facilities for inspection of accounts, receipts and other documents (LRH&UDA 1993, s 79, as amended by CALRA 2002, Sch 9, para 16).
2   LRH&UDA 1993, s 78(1).

EXPRESS OBLIGATIONS OF THE TENANT

14.80   The express terms of leases (both formal and informal) tend to impose extensive liabilities and disabilities on the tenant, ranging from the obligation to pay rent to restrictions on the tenant's freedom to assign or sublet the premises.

Covenant not to assign or sublet

14.81   It is almost invariable in a written lease for the landlord to retain control over future assignment or subletting by his tenant. This control may take an *absolute* form (as in the case of an outright prohibition of any dealing with the tenancy) or a *qualified* form (as where the tenant undertakes not to assign or sublet without the landlord's prior consent).

Absolute covenants not to assign or sublet

14.82   An absolute prohibition of assignment or subletting may be waived by the landlord, but he cannot be compelled to permit a proposed assignment or sublease even if he is acting wholly unreasonably.[1] Covenants against dealings with a tenancy are strictly construed. A covenant against assignment of the tenancy does not, for instance, prohibit subletting or parting with possession (or an assignment of the tenant's beneficial interest in the tenancy).[2] A covenant against assignment or subletting of 'any part of' the demised premises is breached by an assignment or subletting of the whole of the premises,[3] but a covenant which simply relates to the whole is not broken by a transaction in respect of only a part.[4]

1   Assignment without consent is, however, generally permitted to tenants under building leases granted for a term of more than 40 years of which more than seven years remain unexpired (L&TA 1927, s 19(1)(b)).
2   *Burton v Camden LBC* [2000] 2 AC 399 at 409C per Lord Millett.
3   *Field v Barkworth* [1986] 1 WLR 137 at 139F–G, 140E–F.
4   *Wilson v Rosenthal* (1906) 22 TLR 233; *Burton v Camden LBC* [2000] 2 AC 399 at 409C per Lord Millett.

Qualified covenants not to assign or sublet

14.83   If the tenant expressly covenants in a qualified form (ie not to assign or sublet the premises without the landlord's prior consent), there is a statutory implication that such consent shall not be unreasonably withheld.[1] In this context the question of reasonableness is always a question of fact to be decided by the tribunal of fact[2] and must be judged by reference to the circumstances existing and known to the landlord at the time of his refusal.[3] It is generally unreasonable, however, that the landlord should seek to extract some collateral advantage for himself as a precondition of consenting to a proposed assignment or subletting.[4]

1   L&TA 1927, s 19(1). See *Bickel v Duke of Westminster* [1977] QB 517 at 524C–G; *Bocardo SA v S & M Motels Ltd* [1980] 1 WLR 17 at 23F–24G; *Bromley Park Garden Estates Ltd v Moss* [1982] 1 WLR 1019. In the absence of express provision in the lease, no fine or sum of money may be exacted for a licence to assign (LPA 1925, s 144).
2   *Ashworth Fraser Ltd v Gloucester CC* [2001] 1 WLR 2180 at [4], [6] per Lord Bingham of Cornhill, [74] per Lord Rodger of Earlsferry.
3   *International Drilling Fluids Ltd v Louisville Investments (Uxbridge) Ltd* [1986] Ch 513 at 520C; *CIN Properties Ltd v Gill* (1993) 67 P & CR 288 at 310. A landlord who is misled by the tenant as to the circumstances of the application for consent may still be acting unreasonably if disclosure of the full facts would not have justified a refusal (*Storehouse Properties Ltd v Ocobase Ltd* (1998) *Times*, 3 April).
4   See e g *Corunna Bay Holdings Ltd v Robert Gracie Dean Ltd* [2002] 2 NZLR 186 at [19], [53], where a landlord's demand that the proposed assignee enter into a deed of covenant directly with him was regarded as an unreasonable withholding of consent (since it would have extended the assignee's liability beyond his tenure of the term). See similarly *Wallis Fashion Group Ltd v CGU Life Assurance* (2000) 81 P & CR 393 (authorised guarantee agreement) [**para 14.229**].

Reasons for refusal of consent

14.84   On the tenant's service of a written application for consent the landlord is statutorily obliged to supply the consent requested 'within a reasonable time'[1] or, failing this, to provide written reasons for withholding consent or for granting consent only subject to specified conditions.[2] The onus of showing the reasonableness of a refusal of consent lies on the landlord.[3] The landlord is entitled to be protected from having his premises used or occupied in an undesirable way or by an undesirable tenant or assignee, but has no right to refuse consent on grounds 'which have nothing to do with the relationship of landlord and tenant in regard to the subject matter of the lease.'[4] The presence of extensive and longstanding breaches of covenant by the tenant may justify the landlord in refusing to consent to an assignment unless he can be reasonably satisfied that the assignee will remedy the breaches.[5] Consent may also reasonably be withheld on the ground that the assignee is likely to claim protection under the Leasehold Reform Act 1967[6] or to exercise an option to determine the lease which is not available to the would-be assignor.[7] Although the issue of reasonableness depends ultimately on all the circumstances of the case, the House of Lords indicated in *Ashworth Frazer Ltd v Gloucester CC*[8] that a landlord may well be acting entirely properly in refusing consent where he reasonably believes that a proposed assignment will probably – albeit not necessarily – lead to a breach of the covenants of the lease.[9]

1   L&TA 1988, s 1(3)(a) (except, of course, where it is reasonable not to give consent). See *Norwich Union Life Insurance Society v Shopmoor Ltd* [1999] 1 WLR 531 at 545E–G per Scott V-C.

2   L&TA 1988, s 1(3)(b). See *Footwear Corpn Ltd v Amplight Properties Ltd* (1999) 77 P & CR 418 at 426 (oral reasons insufficient).

3   L&TA 1988, s 1(6). The landlord must show that his refusal was reasonable, not that it was right or justified (*Ashworth Fraser Ltd v Gloucester CC* [2001] 1 WLR 2180 at [5] per Lord Bingham of Cornhill). An unreasonable withholding of consent affords no ground for non-payment of rent (*Haberecht v Chapman* (1992) 10 BPR 19063 at 19069).

4   *International Drilling Fluids Ltd v Louisville Investments* (*Uxbridge*) *Ltd* [1986] Ch 513 at 520A per Balcombe LJ. See likewise *Ashworth Frazer Ltd v Gloucester CC* [2001] 1 WLR 2180 at [61] per Lord Rodger of Earlsferry.

5   See *Orlando Investments Ltd v Grosvenor Estate Belgravia* (1990) 59 P & CR 21 at 32–33 (breach of repairing covenants). Refusal of consent is not justified where the breach of a repairing covenant is not extensive or longstanding or is likely to be remedied by the assignee (see *Beale v Worth* [1993] EGCS 135; *Straudley Investments Ltd v Mount Eden Land Ltd* [1997] EGCS 175).

6   See *Norfolk Capital Group Ltd v Kitway Ltd* [1977] QB 506 at 514D, 516A, F–G. Compare, however, *West Layton Ltd v Ford* [1979] QB 593 at 605A–C (fear that Rent Act would come into operation). See also *Leeward Securities Ltd v Lilyheath Properties Ltd* (1983) 17 HLR 35 at 47–49; P F Smith, [1986] 6 RRLR 240.

7   *Olympia & York Canary Wharf Ltd v Oil Property Investment Ltd* (1994) 69 P & CR 43 at 48–50 (early determination of lease would, in days of a slump in market rentals, have cost the landlord a rental loss of £3.6 million and a £6 million reduction in the value of its reversion).

8   [2001] 1 WLR 2180 at [6] per Lord Bingham of Cornhill, [68], [74] per Lord Rodger of Earlsferry. The House of Lords unanimously overturned a contrary decision of the Court of Appeal in *Killick v Second Covent Garden Property Co Ltd* [1973] 1 WLR 658. See [2002] Conv 307 (A Samuels).

9   A landlord may quite reasonably wish to avoid an undesirable outcome which he fears may flow from the proposed assignment, not least where there is a risk of unwelcome and expensive litigation if the apprehended breach eventuates ([2001] 1 WLR 2180 at [6] per Lord Bingham of Cornill, [71] per Lord Rodger of Earlsferry).

Assignment of 'new' tenancies

14.85   Amendments introduced by the Landlord and Tenant (Covenants) Act 1995 confer on landlords a significantly greater degree of control over the assignment of non-residential tenancies granted on or after 1 January 1996.[1] In relation to qualifying leases a landlord and tenant may now enter into an agreement which specifies the circumstances in which the landlord may withhold his licence or consent to any proposed assignment of the demised premises or stipulates the conditions subject to which such a licence may be granted.[2] Thereafter any grant or withholding of consent to assignment need not be objectively 'reasonable', provided it occurs in conformity with the terms of the parties' agreement.[3] The net effect of this change, which has no application to consents for the *subletting* of land, is dramatically to reduce the scope of the courts' power to scrutinise the reasonableness of a landlord's exercise of discretion in granting or withholding consent to dealings with tenanted land.

1   The relevant provisions apply to a 'qualifying lease', ie a 'new' tenancy as defined by L&T(C)A 1995, s 1 [**para 14.224**] other than a residential lease (see L&TA 1927, s 19(1E), as added by L&T(C)A 1995, s 22).

2   The agreement may be made at the date of grant of the lease or at any time prior to the tenant's application for the landlord's licence or consent (L&TA 1927, s 19(1B)(b)). It is highly likely that the landlord will seek to make his consent to assignment conditional on the assignor-tenant's entry into an 'authorised guarantee agreement' **[para 14.227]**.

3   L&TA 1927, s 19(1A) (as added by L&T(C)A 1995, s 22). The circumstances or conditions specified in the agreement must not be framed by reference to a matter which falls to be determined by the landlord or by any other person unless such power of determination is required to be exercised 'reasonably' or the tenant is given an unrestricted right to subject the determination to review by some ascertainable person independent of both landlord and tenant (L&TA 1927, s 19(1C)).

Covenant not to alter the demised premises without consent

14.86   If the tenant expressly covenants not to make improvements or alterations to the demised premises without the landlord's consent, it is again implied by statute that such consent shall not be unreasonably withheld.[1]

1   L&TA 1927, s 19(2).

Other covenants by the tenant

14.87   A covenant by the tenant not to use the premises except for a specified purpose does not constitute a positive undertaking to use the premises for that purpose.[1] No liability attaches to the tenant if under such circumstances he makes no use of the land at all.[2] Although a covenant prohibiting the use of premises otherwise than as a private dwelling-house is breached by short-term lettings to holiday-makers,[3] there is a surprising dearth of authority on the proper construction of prohibitions of use of the demised premises otherwise than as a 'private residence in single occupation.'[4]

1   *Marquis of Bute v Guest* (1846) 15 M & W 160 at 165, 153 ER 804 at 807; *Lacon v Laceby* [1897] WN 39.
2   See *Pulleng v Curran* (1982) 44 P & CR 58 at 68; *Australian Safeway Stores Pty Ltd v Toorak Village Development Pty Ltd* [1974] VR 268 at 273.
3   *Caradon DC v Paton* (2000) Times, 17 May.
4   There are indications that such negative covenants are not inevitably breached by occupation by an unmarried couple or by two or more friends (see *McDonnell v Griffey* [1998] EGCS 70). See also *Segal Securities Ltd v Thoseby* [1963] 1 QB 887 at 894 ('private residence in the occupation of one household only').

IMPLIED OBLIGATIONS OF THE TENANT

14.88   In the absence of contrary stipulation in the lease, certain obligations are imposed on the tenant by implication of law. These include an obligation to pay rent[1] and rates[2] and (where the landlord bears a repairing liability) to allow the landlord to enter and view the premises.[3] The tenant's implied duties are, however, limited in nature and content. The courts are, for instance, slow to imply additional covenants such as a covenant that the tenant should not use the premises for immoral purposes.[4]

1   **[Para 7.91]**.
2   *Squire v C Brewer & Sons Ltd* (Unreported, Court of Appeal, 15 July 1983).
3   *Mint v Good* [1951] 1 KB 517 at 521–522.
4   *Burfort Financial Investments Ltd v Chotard* (1976) 239 EG 891 at 893.

Obligation not to commit waste

14.89   The tenant has an implied duty not to commit waste.[1] The extent of this duty depends on the character of the tenancy concerned.

1   The Law Commission has recommended that the law of waste should (prospectively) cease to apply to tenants holding under a lease and should be replaced by a new implied covenant to 'take proper care' of the demised premises (and of any common parts thereof), to make good any damage wilfully done or caused, and not to carry out any alterations or other works which are likely to destroy or alter the premises to the landlord's detriment (Law Com No 238 (1996), paras 10.33–10.44).

Fixed term of years

14.90   A tenant holding under a fixed term of years is, in the absence of contrary agreement, liable for both voluntary and permissive waste.[1] On this basis a tenant for years is liable for any repair for which his landlord is not expressly or impliedly responsible.[2]

1   *Yellowly v Gower* (1855) 11 Exch 274 at 293–294, 156 ER 833 at 841–842. On the meaning of 'waste', see **[paras 1.133–1.134]**.
2   Compare, however, *Warren v Keen* [1954] 1 QB 15 at 20, where Denning LJ seemed to say that even a tenant for years has no general duty to carry out repairs.

Yearly tenancy

14.91   The liability of a yearly tenant is probably different from that of other periodic tenants.[1] A yearly tenant is liable for voluntary waste,[2] but is liable for permissive waste only if he fails to weatherproof the premises.[3] He is not liable for 'fair wear and tear'.[4]

1   If there is a difference, it is attributable historically to the fact that a tenancy from year to year tended to arise by operation of law **[para 7.251]**, whereas in a tenancy created by the landlord's own act it was the 'landlord's folly' not to restrain the tenant by express provisions as to waste (see *Prior v Hanna* (1988) 43 DLR (4th) 612 at 616).
2   *Marsden v Edward Heyes Ltd* [1927] 2 KB 1 at 6–8.
3   *Wedd v Porter* [1916] 2 KB 91 at 100; but see *Warren v Keen* [1954] 1 QB 15 at 20.
4   *Haskell v Marlow* [1928] 2 KB 45 at 58; *Warren v Keen* [1954] 1 QB 15 at 20. The exception for 'fair wear and tear' exempts the tenant from liability for repairs which are decorative and for remedying parts which wear out or come adrift in the course of reasonable use (*Regis Property Co Ltd v Dudley* [1959] AC 370 at 410 per Lord Denning). The tenant may be liable, however, if further damage flows from fair wear and tear and he takes no remedial action, e g if a missing slate ultimately causes structural decay through water penetration (see *Haskell v Marlow* [1928] 2 KB 45 at 59).

Other periodic tenancies

14.92   The tenant must not damage the premises wilfully or negligently,[1] but it seems that, in the absence of an express contract, periodic tenants other than the yearly tenant have no general duty to put and keep the premises in repair.[2] The only duty of the periodic tenant is to use the premises in a 'husbandlike' or 'tenantlike' manner.[3] As Denning LJ explained in *Warren v Keen*,[4] this means merely that the tenant 'must do the little jobs about the place which a reasonable tenant would do.' He must mend the electric light when it fuses; he must unstop the sink when it is blocked by his waste. If he goes away for any length of time during winter, he must turn off the water and empty the boiler.[5] However, the weekly or monthly tenant bears no liability for disrepair which is caused by 'fair wear and tear or lapse of time.'[6]

1   *Warren v Keen* [1954] 1 QB 15 at 20. See *Prior v Hanna* (1988) 43 DLR (4th) 612 at 618–623 (monthly tenant not liable, in absence of evidence of wilful or negligent damage, when smoking guests caused fire damage).
2   *Warren v Keen* [1954] 1 QB 15 at 20.
3   *Warren v Keen* [1954] 1 QB 15 at 20; *Firstcross Ltd v Teasdale* (1984) 47 P & CR 228 at 233. See also *Bickman v Smith Motors Ltd* [1955] 5 DLR 256 at 257; *Gallo v St Cyr* (1983) 144 DLR (3d) 146 at 148–149, 153.
4   [1954] 1 QB 15 at 20.
5   *Warren v Keen* [1954] 1 QB 15 at 20. See also *Policicchio v Phoenix Assurance Co of Canada* (1978) 79 DLR (3d) 453 at 461. Compare, however, *Wycombe AHA v Barnett* (1984) 264 EG 619 at 621.
6   *Warren v Keen* [1954] 1 QB 15 at 20.

'Usual covenants' in an equitable lease

14.93   Under an equitable lease or a contract for a lease, the obligations impliedly undertaken by the tenant include, in the absence of express agreement, 'the usual covenants'.[1] These covenants comprise[2] undertakings by the tenant to pay rent, to pay tenant's rates and taxes, to keep and deliver up the premises in repair at the end of the term, and to permit the landlord to enter and inspect the premises where the landlord is responsible for any repair. In addition, and in sharp contrast to the law of forfeiture under a legal lease, the landlord under an equitable lease has an *implied* right of re-entry at least in respect of non-payment of rent[3] and probably also nowadays in respect of any breach of covenant.[4]

1   It was held in *Flexman v Corbett* [1930] 1 Ch 672 at 678 that the list of 'usual covenants' is neither fixed nor closed.
2   These, together with the landlord's implied covenant for quiet enjoyment [**para 14.11**], are the 'usual covenants' as classically expounded by Jessel MR in *Hampshire v Wickens* (1878) 7 Ch D 555 at 561 (see *Chester v Buckingham Travel Ltd* [1981] 1 WLR 96 at 99G). It is clear, however, that other covenants may also be 'usual' in particular contexts. The content of the 'usual covenants' turns on the circumstances of each case and is influenced both by the practice of conveyancers in the relevant district (*Flexman v Corbett* [1930] 1 Ch 672 at 678) and by the character of the property concerned. See e g *Chester v Buckingham Travel Ltd* [1981] 1 WLR 96 at 101D–E.
3   *Hodgkinson v Crowe* (1875) 10 Ch App 622 at 626.
4   See *Chester v Buckingham Travel Ltd* [1981] 1 WLR 96 at 105E–F.

Statutory obligations of the tenant

14.94 Statute provides the source for many of the obligations which are imposed on certain categories of tenant. Thus, for example, most of the responsibilities of the 'secure tenant' of local authority housing are laid down in the Housing Act 1985.[1] More generally a tenant may be subject to important rights of entry reserved by statute on behalf of his landlord. In a tenancy governed by section 8 or section 11 of the Landlord and Tenant Act 1985,[2] the landlord, on giving the tenant 24 hours' notice in writing, has a right of entry 'at reasonable times of the day' for the purpose of viewing the condition and state of repair of the demised premises.[3]

1   **[Para 14.340]**.
2   **[Paras 14.41–14.46]**.
3   L&TA 1985, ss 8(2), 11(6).

Unlawful leasehold practices

14.95 Under English law there have been few general restrictions on the kinds of clause or covenant which may be inserted in a tenancy agreement or lease. It has, for instance, been open to the landlord, if he so chooses, to require that the demised premises should be occupied as a private residence for the use of the tenant's family only. (It is fair to record, however, that the courts have tended in this context to accord a wide definition to the term 'family',[1] an extended understanding of 'family' as 'household' having long antecedents both in England and in the United States.[2]) A landlord may also seek to ensure that no children should live in the demised premises[3] or that the tenant should not keep a domestic pet or that the tenant should not be a smoker.[4] The incorporation of Convention protection for 'private and family life' and the 'home' will inevitably make courts much more sensitive to leasehold practices which purport to impose sanctions or disabilities upon various kinds of chosen lifestyle.[5]

1   See *Wrotham Park Settled Estates v Naylor* (1991) 62 P & CR 233 at 237–238, where Hoffmann J declined to find any breach of a family use covenant in a 999 year lease under which a husband and wife occupied the demised premises (comprising several dwellings) with their 'outdoor servants'. Hoffmann J considered this ménage 'to constitute a family provided that they are all subject to one head' (here the husband and wife collectively).
2   See eg *Liskeard Union v Liskeard Waterworks Co* (1881) 7 QBD 505 at 509 (workhouse inmates); *Salter v Lask* [1925] 1 KB 584 at 587; *City of White Plains v Ferraioli*, 313 NE2d 756 at 758–759 (1974); *State of New Jersey v Baker*, 405 A2d 368 at 375 (1979); *City of Santa Barbara v Adamson*, 610 P2d 436 (1980); *Charter Township of Delta v Dinolfo*, 351 NW2d 831 (1984).
3   Compare *Halifax Antiques Ltd v Hildebrand* (1986) 22 DLR (4th) 289; *Québec (Commission des droits de la personne) v Desroches* (1997) 149 DLR (4th) 425 (indirect discrimination against children).
4   See *Salerno v Proprietors of Strata Plan 42724* (1997) 8 BPR 15457 at 15458 (anti-smoker provision held not to be restraint on alienation, although restrictive of the class of persons who might desire to take a lease of the premises).
5   ECHR Art 8 **[para 2.60]**.

Discrimination on grounds of race or sex

14.96   Statute only rarely interferes with the content of leasehold undertakings or with letting practices in general. It is, however, unlawful for a landlord to discriminate on grounds of race or sex either in the 'terms on which he offers ... premises' or in refusing altogether an application for a tenancy.[1] Likewise grounds of race or sex may not be used by a landlord in order to justify the differential provision of access to any benefits or facilities in relation to the premises[2] or to justify the eviction or detrimental treatment of the tenant.[3] However, none of these prohibitions has any application to 'small premises'[4] where the landlord would otherwise be compelled to share accommodation (such as a bathroom or kitchen) with other occupiers.[5] Where the licence or consent of the landlord (or any other person) is required for any assignment or subletting by the tenant, it is likewise unlawful for such licence or consent to be withheld on discriminatory grounds of race or sex.[6] Once again 'small premises' are exempted from the operation of this statutory restraint.[7]

1   Race Relations Act 1976, s 21(1); Sex Discrimination Act 1975, s 30(1). These provisions have no application to an owner-occupier of the premises unless he uses the services of an estate agent or otherwise advertises the vacant accommodation (see Race Relations Act 1976, s 21(3); Sex Discrimination Act 1975, s 30(3)).
2   Race Relations Act 1976, s 21(2)(a); Sex Discrimination Act 1975, s 30(2)(a).
3   Race Relations Act 1976, s 21(2)(b); Sex Discrimination Act 1975, s 30(2)(b).
4   'Small premises' have a statutory definition (see Race Relations Act 1976, s 22(2); Sex Discrimination Act 1975, s 32(2)).
5   Race Relations Act 1976, s 22(1); Sex Discrimination Act 1975, s 32(1).
6   Race Relations Act 1976, s 24(1); Sex Discrimination Act 1975, s 31(1).
7   Race Relations Act 1976, s 24(2); Sex Discrimination Act 1975, s 31(2).

Overseas comparisons

14.97   Past English experience lags somewhat behind that of many overseas jurisdictions, where suspect classifications have been recognised as extending well beyond race and sex. On constitutional and other grounds courts elsewhere have struck down leasehold terms which discriminate against tenants who have children[1] or who are unmarried partners[2] or are single parents, or which discriminate according to other suspect criteria. In *Marina Point Ltd v Wolfson*,[3] for instance, the printed form of lease signed by the tenants, a married couple, contained a clause prohibiting residence in the landlord's apartment complex by children under the age of 18. On the subsequent birth of the tenants' child, the landlord company refused to renew the lease and eventually initiated eviction proceedings. The Supreme Court of California held that the landlord's exclusion of children violated California's Unruh Act which guarantees equal treatment for all citizens 'in all business establishments of every kind whatsoever.'[4] Tobriner J ruled that the Act did not permit a business enterprise to enforce a 'blanket exclusion' of families with minor children, even if children 'as a class' are 'noisier, rowdier, more mischievous and more boisterous than adults.'[5] The Act did not sanction the exclusion of an entire class of individuals from access to facilities 'on the basis of a generalised prediction that the class "as a whole" is more likely to commit misconduct than some other class of the public.'[6] Accordingly the Supreme Court, by a majority,[7] declined to allow the landlord company to recover possession, Tobriner J observing that a society which 'sanctions wholesale discrimination against its children in obtaining housing engages in suspect activity.'[8]

1 See 'Why Johnny can't rent any more – An Examination of laws prohibiting discrimination against families in rental housing' 94 Harv L Rev 1829 (1981); S V MacCallum and A J Bradbrook, (1977–78) 6 Adelaide L Rev 439.
2 See also *Burke v Tralaggan* [1986] EOC 92–161 (refusal to let to unmarried couple held to violate Anti-Discrimination Act 1977, s 48(1)). See G Moens, (1989) 12 Sydney L Rev 195.
3 640 P2d 115 (1982).
4 California Civil Code, 51. In *Halet v Wend Investment Co*, 672 F2d 1305 at 1308–1309 (1982), an adults-only letting policy was also challenged as racially discriminatory, in that it operated with 'greater impact … on blacks and Hispanics because more of those households included minor children.'
5 640 P2d 115 at 124.
6 640 P2d 115 at 125. The Supreme Court did concede, however, that in a different context an age-limited admission policy would be perfectly permissible under the Unruh Act in relation to retirement communities or housing complexes reserved for the elderly (640 P2d 115 at 128). The Court distinguished sharply between the conditions required for meeting such specialised housing needs and the 'wholesale exclusion of children from an apartment complex otherwise open to the general public.'
7 See the interesting dissent of Richardson J (640 P2d 115 at 129–132).
8 640 P2d 115 at 129. Compare, however, *Re Hsuen and Mah* (1987) 31 DLR (4th) 199 at 203–204.

LANDLORD'S REMEDIES FOR BREACH OF COVENANT BY THE TENANT

14.98 The landlord has a number of remedies in respect of a tenant's breach of the covenants contained (either expressly or impliedly) in a lease. These remedies include the following:
– forfeiture of the lease[1]
– distress for unpaid rent[2]
– action for arrears of rent[3]
– damages for breach of covenant[4] and
– injunction or an order for specific performance.[5]

1 **[Paras 14.99–14.189]**.
2 **[Paras 14.193–14.200]**.
3 **[Paras 14.201–14.203]**.
4 **[Paras 14.204]**.
5 **[Paras 14.205–14.207]**.

FORFEITURE OF THE LEASE

14.99 The right to re-enter the demised premises and forfeit the lease or tenancy is the most draconian weapon in the armoury of the landlord whose tenant has committed a breach of covenant.[1] Most written leases contain an ample forfeiture clause which provides, typically, that in the event of any breach by the tenant 'it shall be lawful for the landlord to re-enter upon the demised premises and peaceably to hold and enjoy the demised premises thenceforth as if this lease had not been made and the term hereby granted shall absolutely determine.' As will appear later,[2] the exercise of the landlord's right of re-entry is heavily qualified by the court's discretion to grant relief against forfeiture.[3]

1   The landlord's right of re-entry 'is what gives value and substance to the ... freehold reversion' (*Cowan v Department of Health* [1992] Ch 286 at 295G per Mummery J). Although colloquially a 'remedy' of the landlord, forfeiture does not actually remedy any preceding breach, but 'merely prevents its recurrence and affords relief to the landlord from being saddled with a defaulting tenant' (*Razzaq v Pala* [1997] 1 WLR 1336 at 1343E–F per Lightman J).
2   **[Paras 14.149–14.173]**.
3   This discretion to relieve against forfeiture cannot be evaded by a provision in the tenancy agreement which enables the landlord to terminate the tenancy in the event of breach by giving the tenant a shorter period of notice than would otherwise be required. Such a clause is regarded as the functional equivalent of a forfeiture clause (*Richard Clarke & Co Ltd v Widnall* [1976] 1 WLR 845 at 850F–G). See also *Clays Lane Housing Co-operative Ltd v Patrick* (1985) 49 P & CR 72 at 78–79.

Nature of re-entry

14.100   Notwithstanding the explicit terms of most forfeiture clauses, breach by the tenant does not automatically terminate a lease.[1]

1   **[Para 14.175]**. Where the lease contains a proviso for re-entry, breach renders the lease merely voidable at the option of the landlord (see *Bowser v Colby* (1841) 1 Hare 109 at 133, 66 ER 969 at 979; *Jardine v Attorney General for Newfoundland* [1932] AC 275 at 286). The lease is actually avoided, at the earliest, only upon re-entry (*Shevill v Builders Licensing Board* (1980) 2 BPR 9662 at 9667 per Samuels JA).

The landlord's election

14.101   In the event of breach the landlord must elect either to waive the forfeiture or to enforce it.[1] If he chooses the latter course, the only way in which he may begin to terminate the lease – except in cases covered by some special statutory regime – is by re-entering the demised premises.[2] Re-entry must take the form of some unequivocal act showing the lessor's intention to re-enter for breach of covenant.[3] Re-entry may comprise an actual physical entry upon the demised premises,[4] although the starting of possession proceedings against the tenant is regarded as evidence of an unequivocal election by the landlord[5] and therefore as the equivalent of re-entry.[6] Recognition of this form of notional re-entry is largely attributable to the policy of the law that landlords should not suffer disadvantage by electing for forfeiture through legal process instead of utilising the self-help method of physical re-entry.[7]

1   *Billson v Residential Apartments Ltd* [1992] 1 AC 494 at 534D per Lord Templeman.
2   *Billson v Residential Apartments Ltd* [1992] 1 AC 494 at 534D–E per Lord Templeman. See also *Consolidated Development Pty Ltd v Holt* (1986) 6 NSWLR 607 at 619C–D.
3   *Serjeant v Nash, Field & Co* [1903] 2 KB 304 at 310–311. See also *Jones v Carter* (1846) 15 M

& W 718 at 726, 153 ER 1040 at 1043 per Parke B. The landlord or his agent must 'obtain possession to the physical exclusion of the lessee or anyone properly claiming under him' (*Tattersall's Hotel Penrith Pty Ltd v Permanent Trustee Co of NSW Ltd* (1942) 42 SR (NSW) 104 at 110). Sufficiently unequivocal acts of re-entry include changing the locks (*Eaton Square Properties Ltd v Beveridge* [1993] EGCS 91) or padlocking the doors to the demised premises (*Blue Chip Investments Inc v Hicks* (1985) 18 DLR (4th) 755 at 757) and granting a new lease (*Re AGB Research Plc* [1995] BCC 1091 at 1094F), but not the mere acceptance of rent from some third party (*Cromwell Developments Ltd v Godfrey* [1998] 2 EGLR 62 at 65H–L).

4 The recognition of some person other than the tenant in occupation of the premises can be taken to be the equivalent of re-entry (*Canas Property Co Ltd v KL Television Services Ltd* [1970] 2 QB 433 at 443B per Megaw LJ).

5 *Ivory Gate Ltd v Spetale* [1998] 2 EGLR 43 at 46C per Sir John Vinelott.

6 *Billson v Residential Apartments Ltd* [1992] 1 AC 494 at 534E per Lord Templeman. See also *Canas Property Co Ltd v KL Television Services Ltd* [1970] 2 QB 433 at 440B; *W G Clark (Properties) Ltd v Dupre Properties Ltd* [1992] Ch 297 at 306F; *GS Fashions Ltd v B & Q Plc* [1995] 1 WLR 1088 at 1092F–H. If the defaulting tenant has assigned the term, the proper defendant in possession proceedings is the assignee (see *Canas*, supra at 441E).

7 [**Para 14.166**]. See *W G Clark (Properties) Ltd v Dupre Properties Ltd* [1992] Ch 297 at 307F–G.

Status of lease after re-entry

14.102 A certain provisional quality attaches to forfeiture by re-entry (whether actual or notional),[1] since it often remains to be seen whether the lease will continue to be forfeited or whether, by reason of the tenant's application for relief, the lease 'will be restored as if it had never been forfeited.'[2] The initiation of a possession claim against the tenant does not in itself terminate the lease.[3] The start of possession proceedings is commonly 'taken as forfeiture, but it will be a nullity if the proceedings do not succeed, or there is relief from forfeiture.'[4] It is clear, however, that forfeiture terminates the tenant's obligation to pay rent *stricto sensu*.[5] The tenant becomes thereafter a trespasser[6] whose continuing use and occupation of the premises entitle the landlord to recover mesne profits from the date of actual or notional re-entry.[7]

1 It is sometimes said that a lease is forfeited from the point of re-entry (see *Canas Property Co Ltd v KL Television Services Ltd* [1970] 2 QB 433 at 440A–B per Lord Denning MR), but the reality is that there is 'inevitably a twilight period of some uncertainty' (*GS Fashions Ltd v B & Q Plc* [1995] 1 WLR 1088 at 1093C per Lightman J).

2 *Meadows v Clerical Medical and General Life Assurance Society* [1981] Ch 70 at 75B per Megarry V-C ('The tenancy has a trance-like existence pendente lite; none can assert with assurance whether it is alive or dead ... at least it cannot be said to be dead beyond hope of resurrection'). See *Driscoll v Church Commissioners for England* [1957] 1 QB 330 at 340; *Ivory Gate Ltd v Spetale* [1998] 2 EGLR 43 at 46A–D; *Maryland Estates Ltd v Joseph* [1999] 1 WLR 83 at 91F.

3 *Dendy v Evans* [1910] 1 KB 263 at 267, 270–271; *Ivory Gate Ltd v Spetale* [1998] 2 EGLR 43 at 45G–H, 46C.

4 *Twinsectra Ltd v Hynes* (1995) 71 P & CR 145 at 157 per Aldous LJ. See [1996] Conv 55 (M Pawlowski).

5 *Progressive Mailing House Pty Ltd v Tabali Pty Ltd* (1985) 157 CLR 17 at 39 per Brennan J.

6 In the absence of estoppel (or possibly mistake or misrepresentation emanating from the tenant's actions), the landlord who makes an immediate election to 'take the draconian course of forfeiture' cannot subsequently challenge his own forfeiture by questioning whether breach has occurred (*GS Fashions Ltd v B & Q Plc* [1995] 1 WLR 1088 at 1093G–1094D).

7   *Canas Property Co Ltd v KL Television Services Ltd* [1970] 2 QB 433 at 442D. See also *Capital and City Holdings Ltd v Dean Warburg Ltd* (1989) 58 P & CR 346 at 351.

Purpose of the right of re-entry

14.103   The plain purpose of the landlord's right of re-entry is, in colloquial terms,[1] to provide the landlord with a realistic form of security for the payment of rent due under the lease[2] and to guarantee the landlord an ultimate recovery of the land in the event of other kinds of breach.[3] In other words, the landlord is not relegated to a mere monetary claim in respect of the tenant's breach,[4] but may use the threat of recovery of possession as a lever to enforce compliance with the covenants.[5] Sometimes, however, the landlord's only substantial concern when faced with a defaulting tenant is to ensure the termination of the tenancy and the eviction of the tenant from the premises.

1   See *Razzaq v Pala* [1997] 1 WLR 1336 at 1341F–G per Lightman J.
2   See *Howard v Fanshawe* [1895] 2 Ch 581 at 588; *Richard Clarke & Co Ltd v Widnall* [1976] 1 WLR 845 at 850D–F; *Di Palma v Victoria Square Property Co Ltd* [1984] Ch 346 at 360D; *Jam Factory Pty Ltd v Sunny Paradise Pty Ltd* [1989] VR 584 at 590. The landlord's right to re-enter does not comprise a 'security' in the more technical sense of the Insolvency Act 1986 (see *Razzaq v Pala* [1997] 1 WLR 1336 at 1342H–1343A; *Re Lomax Leisure Ltd* [2000] Ch 502 at 512C–E).
3   See *Re Lomax Leisure Ltd* [2000] Ch 502 at 513E–F, where Neuberger J stressed that, strictly speaking, the right of re-entry is treated in equity as security only for the payment of rent and not as security for the performance of other covenants.
4   As Lord Erskine LC pointed out in *Sanders v Pope* (1806) 12 Ves 282 at 289, 33 ER 108 at 110, the landlord may come 'from time to time against an insolvent estate.'
5   See *Ezekiel v Orakpo* [1977] QB 260 at 268E–269C; *Razzaq v Pala* [1997] 1 WLR 1336 at 1342A–D; *Shevill v Builders Licensing Board* (1980) 2 BPR 9662 at 9667 per Samuels JA.

Right of re-entry as a proprietary right in land

14.104   It is important to realise that a landlord's right of re-entry confers on him a freestanding proprietary interest in the land demised to the tenant.[1]

1   [Para 8.265]. This proprietary right is distinguishable from the landlord's personal right to sue the tenant for arrears of rent, with the result that, in exercise of the proprietary right, the landlord may forfeit the lease even though he has assigned to another the contractual right to recover those same arrears (*Kataria v Safeland plc* (1997) 75 P & CR D30 at D31).

Legal or equitable quality

14.105   If a right of re-entry is exercisable 'over or in respect of a legal term of years absolute', the right of re-entry is itself a *legal* right.[1] This right of re-entry is enforceable against the entire world – even against persons who are not in strict terms bound by the covenants to which the right of re-entry relates.[2] If annexed to an equitable term of years, the right of re-entry is *equitable* only[3] and is binding on some (but not all) third parties.[4] Whether legal or equitable in quality, the right of re-entry need not be exercised immediately at the point when it arises.[5] Except in circumstances of release, abandonment or waiver,[6] the right of re-entry may be exercised at any time within the statutory limitation period of twelve years from the date of the breach which triggers the right.[7]

1   LPA 1925, s 1(2)(e).
2   *Shiloh Spinners Ltd v Harding* [1973] AC 691 at 717C–G per Lord Wilberforce **[para 8.267]**.
3   LPA 1925, s 1(3).
4   **[Paras 8.268, 14.297]**.
5   *Owendale Pty Ltd v Anthony* (1967) 117 CLR 539 at 557.
6   **[Para 14.174]**.
7   Limitation Act 1980, s 15. See *Matthews v Smallwood* [1910] 1 Ch 777 at 786.

Rights of re-entry ultimately underpin the interests of capital

14.106   The right of re-entry comprises the ultimate affirmation of the landlord's proprietary power. Although there are circumstances in which the courts intervene to temper its exercise, there exist 'sound reasons of policy' why the discretion to grant relief against forfeiture should be 'circumscribed and consistently exercised.'[1] As Arden J has observed, in terms hugely indicative of the dominant (if usually unspoken) ideology of commercial landlord–tenant relationships,

> If the courts do not uphold the terms of the lease except in limited situations, there will be a strong disincentive to landlords to invest in property and let it out on lease. By enforcing rights of property, the law promotes the use and availability of this resource within society, and property can be used, as in this case, for commercial purposes which can serve to increase society's prosperity. Not all landlords are large corporations.[2]

1   *Inntrepreneur Pub Co (CPC) Ltd v Langton* [2000] 1 EGLR 34 at 38C–D per Arden J.
2   *Inntrepreneur Pub Co (CPC) Ltd v Langton* [2000] 1 EGLR 34 at 38D.

General conditions for exercise of a right of re-entry

14.107   Under a legal term of years the landlord's right to re-enter and forfeit the lease arises only if the lease itself contains an express proviso for re-entry or if the lease is phrased in such a way that the performance of the tenant's obligations is rendered a condition on which the future subsistence of the lease depends.[1] A right of re-entry cannot be *implied* in a legal lease and, in the absence of an express right of re-entry, a breach of covenant by the tenant gives the landlord at common law a mere right to recover damages or arrears of rent.[2] By curious contrast it seems that a right of re-entry is impliedly contained in every equitable lease, not merely in respect of non-payment of rent,[3] but possibly also in relation to other breaches of covenant by the tenant.[4] Whether the lease be legal or equitable, a right of entry is exercisable only by the person who is currently entitled to the legal reversionary estate or by some other person expressly or impliedly authorised by him.[5]

1   *Doe d Henniker v Watt* (1828) 8 B & C 308 at 315–316, 108 ER 1057 at 1060.
2   *Shevill v Builders Licensing Board* (1980) 2 BPR 9662 at 9667 per Samuels JA. In particular the mere fact of rent arrear gives the landlord no implied entitlement to re-enter against the tenant (see *Lane v Dixon* (1847) 3 CB 776 at 787–791, 136 ER 311 at 315–317; *Doe d Dixon v Roe* (1849) 7 CB 134 at 135, 137 ER 55).
3   A proviso for re-entry in the case of non-payment of rent constitutes one of the 'usual covenants' **[para 14.93]** implied into a contract for a lease (*Hodgkinson v Crowe* (1875) 10 Ch App 622 at 626).
4   *Chester v Buckingham Travel Ltd* [1981] 1 WLR 96 at 105E–G.
5   *Rother District Investments Ltd v Corke* [2004] 2 P & CR 311 at [11]. Re-entry by a transferee of the reversionary estate in advance of his own registration at Land Registry may nevertheless rank as a 'forfeiture by estoppel' which can be fed by subsequent registration, thereupon becoming a full legal forfeiture valid against the world (*Rother District Investments*, supra at [16]).

RESTRICTIONS ON RE-ENTRY UNDER RESIDENTIAL LEASES AND TENANCIES

14.108   In view of the potentially far-reaching consequences of the landlord's right of re-entry, its exercise in the residential sector is subject to certain important restrictions.[1] In the famous words of Coke, 'the law leans against forfeitures.'[2]

1   See, however, *Re R* (*Restraint Order*) [1990] 2 QB 307 at 314A (landlord's right to forfeit not fettered by any restraint order made in respect of the tenant pursuant to drug trafficking legislation).
2   *Co Litt*, pp 201b, 202a; *Duppa v Mayho* (1669) 1 Wms Saund 282 at 287, 85 ER 366 at 375 (Note).

Protection against unlawful eviction

14.109   Under the provisions of the Protection from Eviction Act 1977, it is unlawful to enforce a right of re-entry under a residential lease or tenancy 'otherwise than by proceedings in court while any person is lawfully residing in the premises.'[1] It is therefore dangerous for the landlord to take at face value the blunt wording of the average forfeiture clause.[2] There is in English law a 'basic rule'[3] that possession of residential rented premises cannot be recovered except by court order. This prohibition of eviction without due process of law also applies, in the absence of a right of re-entry, to any premises which have been let as a dwelling. Even though the tenancy has already come to an end, it is unlawful for the owner, otherwise than by court proceedings, to enforce his right to recover possession if the occupier continues to reside in the premises or any part of them.[4] This virtually universal requirement of curial process ensures that, for purposes of the European Convention on Human Rights, the tenant's civil rights and obligations are determined only after a 'fair and public hearing'[5] and due respect is accorded to the tenant's 'private and family life' and 'home'.[6]

1　PEA 1977, s 2 (see also *Billson v Residential Apartments Ltd* [1992] 1 AC 494 at 524D per Nicholls LJ).

2　In the case of tenancies protected under the Rent Act 1977 or the Housing Acts 1985 and 1988, further restrictions are imposed on the landlord's recovery of possession [**paras 14.321, 14.336, 14.342**]. See e g *Antoniades v Villiers* [1990] 1 AC 417 at 461H–462A per Lord Templeman. See also Insolvency Act 1986, s 285(3) (leave of court required before commencement of forfeiture proceedings against bankrupt).

3　*Harrow LBC v Qazi* [2004] 1 AC 983 at [36] per Lord Hope of Craighead.

4　PEA 1977, s 3(1). This provision does not apply to statutorily protected tenancies (see PEA 1977, s 8(1)) and 'excluded' tenancies. A tenancy is 'excluded' if it involves some form of sharing with a resident owner or a member of his family (PEA 1977, s 3A(2)–(3)) or was granted as a 'temporary expedient' to a trespasser (PEA 1977, s 3A(6)) or if it confers a right of occupation for a holiday only (PEA 1977, s 3A(7)(a)) or was granted otherwise than for money or money's worth (PEA 1977, s 3A(7)(b)). Certain kinds of statutorily controlled hostel accommodation are also 'excluded' (PEA 1977, s 3A(8)).

5　ECHR Art 6 [**para 2.65**]. See *Southwark LBC v St Brice* [2002] 1 WLR 1537 at [16] per Kennedy LJ, [34] per Chadwick LJ.

6　ECHR Art 8 [**para 2.60**].

Criminal liability for unlawful eviction

14.110　No matter how heinous the breach committed by the tenant, any re-entry against a residential tenant otherwise than by due execution of a court order for possession gives rise to serious criminal liability under the Protection from Eviction Act 1977.[1] The availability of this criminal sanction demonstrates yet again the age-old concern of the common law to protect actual, even if errant, occupiers of land.[2] Pursuant to section 1(2) of the 1977 Act a criminal offence is committed by any person who unlawfully deprives (or attempts to deprive) a 'residential occupier'[3] of his occupation of premises,[4] 'unless he proves that he believed, and had reasonable cause to believe, that the residential occupier had ceased to reside in the premises.'[5]

1　Even a landlord armed with a possession order has no right to resort to self-help and take possession without the involvement of a bailiff in execution of the order (*Haniff v Robinson* [1993] QB 419 at 428D–E). See also *R v Brennan and Brennan* [1979] Crim LR 603 (landlord without previous convictions used the services of a 'very large man and an alsatian dog' to evict a group of students from their rented premises: 'Loss of liberty should be the usual penalty where landlords used threats or force, in the absence of unusual mitigation').

2　[**Para 3.8**]. Further criminal liability may arise in connection with the offences of using and threatening violence to secure entry to premises under Criminal Law Act 1977, s 6(1) [**para 14.120**]. See A J Ashworth, [1979] JSWL 79–80.

3　This term includes any 'person occupying … premises as a residence, whether under a contract or by virtue of any enactment or rule of law' (PEA 1977, s 1(1)). Protection under section 1 thus extends beyond tenants to include contractual licensees, but does not catch trespassers or casual (ie non-contractual) lodgers or persons whose payments are referable to consumables and services rather than to any right of occupation (see *West Wiltshire CC v Snelgrove* (1998) 30 HLR 57 at 60–62; [1999] Conv 53 (J Morgan)).

4　Section 1(2) applies even where the premises comprise only one room (*Thurrock UDC v Shina* (1972) 23 P & CR 205 at 207).

5　See *R v Yuthiwattana* (1984) 16 HLR 49 at 63–64, where the Court of Appeal emphasised that an unlawful deprivation of occupation must for this purpose have the character of an 'eviction'. A merely temporary 'locking-out' overnight or for a short period of time is more appropriately prosecuted under PEA 1977, s 1(3). See [1981] Conv 377 (M Wasik).

Criminal liability for harassment

14.111   Criminal liability attaches not only to unlawful eviction but also to harassment of a residential tenant. Often only a blurred borderline lies between harassment and 'constructive eviction'.[1] Under section 1(3) of the Protection from Eviction Act 1977, a criminal offence is committed by any person who does 'acts'[2] which are 'calculated to interfere with the peace or comfort of the residential occupier or members of his household', or who persistently[3] withdraws or withholds 'services reasonably required for the occupation of the premises as a residence.'[4] Such is the 'serious stigma' and 'social obloquy' attached to this 'truly criminal offence',[5] that a specific intent is required in the wrongdoer. Criminal liability for harassment arises only if the wrongdoer can be shown to have acted 'with intent to cause the residential occupier ... to give up the occupation of the premises ... or to refrain from exercising any right or pursuing any remedy in respect of the premises.'[6] Section 1(3) is now supplemented by section 1(3A),[7] which, in very similar terms, criminalises acts by a landlord of a residential occupier or by his agent where, even though there is no specific intent, the wrongdoer 'knows, or has reasonable cause to believe' that his conduct is likely to intimidate the occupier.

1   See *Tagro v Cafane* [1991] 1 WLR 378 at 382E–F per Lord Donaldson of Lymington MR.
2   The word 'acts' includes a single act (*R v Evangelos Polycarpou* (1978) 9 HLR 129 at 131), but may not include an omission to act. No offence is committed under PEA 1977, s 1(3) merely because the landlord fails to rectify damage caused by repair work which was itself lawfully undertaken (*R v Ahmad* (1986) 130 Sol Jo 554 at 555). Compare, however, *R v Yuthiwattana* (1984) 16 HLR 49, where a failure to replace a tenant's missing key came within PEA 1977, s 1(3). See also (1986) Legal Action 125.
3   On the importance of 'persistently', see *R v Abrol* (1972) 116 Sol Jo 177.
4   Harassment may comprise the intermittent but persistent withdrawal by the landlord of such services as the domestic supply of water, gas and electricity or may extend to 'more serious threats which are tantamount to the statutory crime of blackmail' (*R v Phekoo* [1981] 1 WLR 1117 at 1126G–H). See also Protection from Harassment Act 1997, ss 1, 2(1), 3(1), 7(2) (criminal offence and actionable civil wrong for a person knowingly and unreasonably to pursue to 'a course of conduct ... which amounts to harassment of another').
5   *R v Phekoo* [1981] 1 WLR 1117 at 1126G per Hollings J.
6   PEA 1977, s 1(3). Thus no offence is committed if the defendant landlord reasonably believed the object of his attentions to be a squatter or trespasser rather than a 'residential occupier' (*R v Phekoo* [1981] 1 WLR 1117 at 1127A–B, 1128D). An intention to cause purely temporary disruption of occupation while repair works are carried out does not amount to an 'intent to cause the residential occupier ... to give up ... occupation', but may nevertheless connote an intent to cause him to 'refrain from exercising' his rights or pursuing any appropriate remedy (see *Schon v Camden LBC* [1986] 2 EGLR 37 at 39F–H).
7   See Housing Act 1988, s 29(2).

Civil liability for wrongful eviction or harassment

14.112   Section 1 of the Protection from Eviction Act 1977 is merely a penal provision and, in itself, creates no statutory cause of action in damages against a landlord.[1] The victim of eviction or harassment may nevertheless find a civil remedy in the law of contract or tort[2] and in this context his rights have been substantially enhanced by the creation of a new statutory tort under the Housing Act 1988.

1   *McCall v Abelesz* [1976] QB 585 at 594C, 597F. It has always been possible for the aggrieved individual to lay an information on oath concerning his eviction before magistrates, which may lead to the issue of a warrant for the arrest of the offending landlord. The landlord may then be granted bail on condition that he reinstates the evicted tenant in possession. The criminal procedure can thus provide by indirect means an immensely practical and potent form of injunction (see (1982) LAG Bulletin, December, p 14).

2   See PEA 1977, s 1(5). In *Drane v Evangelou* [1978] 1 WLR 455 at 461E–F, Lawton LJ observed that '[t]o deprive a man of a roof over his head ... is one of the worst torts which can be committed.' The cases must be 'rare in which eviction ... does not found claims both in contract and in tort' (*Millington v Duffy* (1984) 17 HLR 232 at 235). See also *Caruso v Owen* (1983) LAG Bulletin 106 (£3,000 damages for the tort of wrongful interference with goods where landlord burned research student's PhD notes on bonfire as part of unlawful eviction).

Expropriation of gain

14.113   In language which closely mirrors that of the Protection from Eviction Act 1977, the Housing Act 1988 creates a cause of action in damages[1] for any residential occupier who suffers wrongful eviction or harassment leading to the surrender of occupation of his premises.[2] In order to prevent the landlord from 'profiting from his "Rachmannite" activities',[3] the relevant provisions of the Housing Act 1988 are aimed directly at the expropriation of the notional gain made through the landlord's wrongful conduct. The defaulting landlord is liable to pay damages in respect of the loss of the right of occupation,[4] but may seek to avert an award of damages either in part or in full by reinstating (or making a reasonable offer to reinstate) the occupier in the premises.[5] A landlord also has a statutory defence where he believed on reasonable grounds that the occupier had ceased to reside or that there was reasonable cause to undertake the action or inaction in respect of which complaint is made.[6]

1   The statutory liability is declared to be 'in the nature of a liability in tort' (HA 1988, s 27(4)(a)). Alternatively the evicted occupier may claim a continuing right of occupation in the premises from which he has been ousted (s 27(6)(b)). The occupier's right to elect between compensation and reinstatement arises at trial rather than any earlier date (*Osei-Bonsu v Wandsworth LBC* [1999] 1 WLR 1011 at 1025A–C).

2   HA 1988, s 27(1)–(2). The term 'residential occupier' has the same meaning as in PEA 1977, s 1 (see HA 1988, s 27(9)).

3   *Sampson v Wilson* [1996] Ch 39 at 49E per Sir Thomas Bingham MR. (Rachman was a notorious 'slumlord' of the 1960s.)

4   HA 1988, s 27(3). A landlord is answerable for the acts of his agent (*Mehta v Royal Bank of Scotland* [1999] 3 EGLR 153 at 158G) and section 27(3) imposes a damages liability upon only the landlord and not the agent (*Sampson v Wilson* [1996] Ch 39 at 49C–D).

5   HA 1988, s 27(6)–(7). The mere handing over of a useless key does not suffice for this purpose (see *Tagro v Cafane* [1991] 1 WLR 378 at 383F–G). In so far as it is 'difficult to see how you can reinstate a tenant who does not want to be reinstated', the ousted occupier seems effectively to have an option to take the compensation (*Tagro*, supra at 383F–384B).

6   HA 1988, s 27(8). A local authority landlord's mistaken belief that a joint tenant could validly and unilaterally terminate a tenancy by short notice to quit does not constitute, for present purposes, a reasonably held belief that the other joint tenant had ceased to reside (*Osei-Bonsu v Wandsworth LBC* [1999] 1 WLR 1011 at 1020A–D).

Computation of liability

14.114   The statutory measure of compensation is clearly designed to strip away from the landlord the overall financial benefit otherwise derived from his wrongful actions.[1] Damages are to be assessed as the difference between the value of the landlord's interest had the occupier continued to have the same right of occupation as previously and the value of the landlord's interest freed from any right of occupation.[2] For this purpose the relevant value is the value of the landlord's interest in the 'building' in which the occupier's premises are contained (and not merely in that part of the building which was actually occupied by the claimant).[3] Thus, in *Tagro v Cafane*,[4] a landlord who had wrongfully evicted a monthly tenant from a single room in a house was held liable to pay damages of £31,000.[5] Although the 1988 Act allows the court to reduce the award of damages in the light of any prior misconduct of the former residential occupier (or of any person living with him in the premises),[6] the general effect of the statutory liability is to make any extra-curial eviction of a residential tenant an extremely expensive activity.[7]

1   See *Mehta v Royal Bank of Scotland* [1999] 3 EGLR 153 at 159B–C. It is increasingly recognised in other contexts that loss of a tenancy (particularly a statutorily protected tenancy) represents an extremely significant financial deprivation. See eg *Murray v Lloyd* [1989] 1 WLR 1060 at 1065A–F (damages of £115,000 for loss of statutory tenancy).

2   HA 1988, s 28(1). No damages can be awarded if, because of the continuing occupation of other persons in a house, the eviction complained of has made no difference to the value of the landlord's interest (see *Melville v Bruton* (1996) 29 HLR 319 at 325–326). Nor can the evicted tenant be awarded exemplary damages (*Francis v Brown* (1997) 30 HLR 143 at 149–150).

3   HA 1988, s 28(2). See *Mehta v Royal Bank of Scotland* [1999] 3 EGLR 153 at 160C.

4   [1991] 1 WLR 378 at 387D. See [1991] Conv 297 (C Rodgers); A Clarke, (1992) 45 CLP 81.

5   The claimant also received an additional award in excess of £15,000 in respect of trespass to her personal belongings. Lord Donaldson of Lymington MR accepted that the damages awarded at first instance 'do seem to be high', but was obviously less than overwhelmed by sympathy for a defendant who had shamelessly trashed his tenant's room and its contents. See also *Miller v Eyo* (1999) 31 HLR 306 at 309 (£18,000 award); *Mehta v Royal Bank of Scotland* [1999] 3 EGLR 153 at 160E, 162K (£45,000 for occupier evicted from long-stay hotel in order to facilitate completion of sale of building).

6   HA 1988, s 27(7)(a). See *Regalgrand Ltd v Dickerson and Wade* (1996) 74 P & CR 312 at 317–319; *Osei-Bonsu v Wandsworth LBC* [1999] 1 WLR 1011 at 1021B–E (reduction of damages by two thirds because claimant's violent conduct towards wife precipitated local authority's wrongful termination of joint tenancy).

7   Liability for the statutory tort is in addition to any other tortious or contractual liability, but the claimant cannot recover twice in respect of the same loss (*Mehta v Royal Bank of Scotland* [1999] 3 EGLR 153 at 158H, 162L).

An extra layer of discretionary judgment?

14.115   It is beyond debate that the forced removal of a residential tenant from his premises is bound to interfere 'at least to some extent' with his enjoyment of the right to respect for his 'home' pursuant to Article 8(1) of the European Convention on Human Rights.[1] Article 8(1) is therefore plainly engaged by the decision to make a court order for possession against the tenant.[2] However, a major controversy has been provoked in recent years by the question whether, in every case, an onus lies on the landlord to show that the interference with the tenant's right is objectively justified in terms of the reasons outlined in Article 8(2), ie that the possession order is 'necessary ... in the interests of ... the economic well-being of the country ... or for the protection of the rights and freedoms of others.'[3] Of course, this question is not nearly so pressing in the context of the discretionary grounds for possession which are provided by various statutory schemes within the residential sector.[4] Here the interposition of judicial discretion ensures that the court is compelled, in at least some degree, to address the balance which, under Article 8(2), requires to be maintained between the individual's rights and the wider public interest.[5] Much more difficult are those areas where the landlord, under domestic law and apart from the Human Rights Act 1998, can demonstrate an unqualified mandatory ground for the recovery of possession from the tenant. Here the vital issue is whether, even in such cases, the European Convention has equipped the courts with a novel overlay of discretionary power to decline to make the possession order to which the landlord seems plainly and automatically entitled.[6]

1   *Harrow LBC v Qazi* [2004] 1 AC 983 at [70] per Lord Hope of Craighead, [103] per Lord Millett. See similarly *Lambeth LBC v Howard* (2001) 33 HLR 636 at [30] per Sedley LJ; *Sheffield CC v Smart* [2002] LGR 467 at [26] per Laws LJ. A dwelling is still a 'home' for Convention purposes even though the tenancy has terminated and the former tenant continues in occupation merely as a trespasser (*Qazi*, supra at [11] per Lord Bingham of Cornhill, [68] per Lord Hope of Craighead, [96], [99] per Lord Millett, [148] per Lord Scott of Foscote; *Newham LBC v Kibata* [2003] 3 FCR 724 at [21(5)] per Mummery LJ; *R (on application of Gangera) v Hounslow LBC* [2003] HLR 1028 at [29] per Moses J; *Birmingham CC v Bradney* [2003] EWCA Civ 1783 at [3] per Mummery LJ).

2   *Harrow LBC v Qazi* [2004] 1 AC 983 at [23] per Lord Bingham of Cornhill, [71], [78] per Lord Hope of Craighead. See also *Kay v Lambeth LBC* [2004] EWCA Civ 926 at [91].

3   **[Para 2.60]**. Such an approach would, in effect, require a public sector landlord to demonstrate that the tenant's eviction is not disproportionate to its aim of fair and reasonable management of its housing stock (*Sheffield CC v Smart* [2002] LGR 467 at [29], [37] per Laws LJ).

4   **[Paras 14.322, 14.337, 14.344]**.

5   See *Harrow LBC v Qazi* [2004] 1 AC 983 at [73] per Lord Hope of Craighead; *R (on application of Gangera) v Hounslow LBC* [2003] HLR 1028 at [44] per Moses J.

6   **[Paras 2.62, 2.67]**.

The Qazi decision

14.116 Precisely this issue arose in *Harrow LBC v Qazi*[1] where, under municipal law and apart from Convention rights, a landlord authority was unquestionably entitled to recover possession from an occupier whose tenancy of the premises had been terminated by a notice to quit served on the landlord by his estranged wife. By the narrowest of majorities the House of Lords ruled that, in such circumstances, Article 8 does not authorise some new form of judicial scrutiny as to the appropriateness of the landlord's recovery of possession.[2] In the view taken by the majority,[3] the landlord's entitlement to possession cannot, by reference to Article 8, be deflected by an additional exercise of discretionary judgment based on 'the degree of impact on the tenant's home life of the eviction.'[4] The question of proportionality has already been determined at a collective or 'macro' level by the legislature and cannot, in every case, be reopened at a 'micro' level through an examination of the social merits or demerits of an individual tenant's eviction.[5] As Moses J observed in *R (on application of Gangera) v Hounslow LBC*,[6] Article 8 does not mandate some sort of 'state trial into government housing policy in order to balance ... public and private issues.' In a judgment later endorsed by Lord Millett in the House of Lords,[7] Moses J voiced the fear that any other approach 'would fundamentally transform our law as to enforcement of property rights into one where such rights could only be enforced when the court thinks it justifiable to seek possession and proportionate to make an order.'[8] Thus, where a landlord can plead an automatic and unqualified ground of possession against a tenant, it now seems clear from the House of Lords' ruling in *Qazi* that his entitlement is complete: there is 'nothing further to investigate' in terms of proportionality.[9] Article 8 cannot, in short, be invoked as a defence to possession proceedings.[10]

1   [2004] 1 AC 983 **[paras 2.70–2.73]**. See (2004) 120 LQR 398 (S Bright).

2   The majority in *Qazi* was also anxious to counter the suggestion that Convention guarantees can apply with 'horizontal effect' to the relations of *private* landlords and *private* tenants (see [2004] 1 AC 983 at [108] per Lord Millett, [142]–[143] per Lord Scott of Foscote).

3   On the contrary approach advocated by a forceful minority, see **[para 2.71]**.

4   [2004] 1 AC 983 at [146] per Lord Scott of Foscote.

5   '[T]he "micro" considerations do not arise' (*Hounslow LBC v Adjei* [2004] 2 All ER 636 at [12] per Pumfrey J). See also *Royal Borough of Kensington and Chelsea v O'Sullivan* [2003] HLR 877 at [82] per Waller LJ; *R (on application of Gangera) v Hounslow LBC* [2003] HLR 1028 at [44] per Moses J ('So long as the system as a whole is compatible with the Convention, it is not for the court to arrogate to itself a discretion').

6   [2003] HLR 1028 at [41].

7   [2004] 1 AC 983 at [109]. See also *Hounslow LBC v Adjei* [2004] 2 All ER 636 at [37] per Pumfrey J.

8   [2003] HLR 1028 at [49].

9   [2004] 1 AC 983 at [108] per Lord Millett **[para 2.71]**. For Lord Millett (at [103]) the tenant's eviction was 'plainly necessary to protect the rights of the local authority as landowner ... There was simply no balance to be struck.' The House of Lords left open the possibility that a local housing authority's decision to seek a possession order may be challenged, in cases of alleged unfairness or impropriety, in proceedings for judicial review ([2004] 1 AC 983 at [109] per Lord Millett). See also *Kay v Lambeth LBC* [2004] EWCA Civ 926 at [101]; *Hounslow LBC v Adjei* [2004] 2 All ER 636 at [34].

10   *Harrow LBC v Qazi* [2004] 1 AC 983 at [84] per Lord Hope of Craighead, [144], [149], [152] per Lord Scott of Foscote; *R (on application of Gangera) v Hounslow LBC* [2003] HLR 1028 at [40], [43] per Moses J; *Birmingham CC v McCann* [2003] EWCA Civ 1783 at [28] per Mummery LJ; *Newham LBC v Kibata* [2003] 3 FCR 724 at [11], [25], [39] per Mummery LJ.

Sanctity of proprietary and contractual rights under domestic law

14.117   The *Qazi* ruling was prompted by a certain impatience lest an over-ready resort to Article 8(2) should enable individual tenants to 'resurrect arguments as to necessity and proportionality.'[1] There was certainly a fear that entire statutory schemes could be undermined or disrupted if regard were required to be had, in every case, to the particular merits of the possession being retaken.[2] Regimes of mandatory repossession would, in effect, be converted into regimes of discretionary repossession.[3] Underlying the majority view in *Qazi* was also an extreme reluctance to concede that the guarantees and entitlements provided by the European Convention on Human Rights can ever derogate from proprietary or contractual rights which have otherwise accrued under domestic law.[4] The *Qazi* decision can be seen as a resolute defence of proprietary sovereignty in the face of a much more open-textured form of proprietary morality stemming from a European source. Indeed the minority in *Qazi* condemned the majority view as exhibiting a 'basic fallacy' in that 'it allows domestic notions of title, legal and equitable rights, and interests, to colour the interpretation of article 8(1).'[5] One leading commentator has observed that the decision in *Qazi* is 'somewhat surprising. The idea that legal form trumps substance is alien to the Strasbourg jurisprudence; and Strasbourg cases certainly do not dictate the result.'[6] Although the European Court of Human Rights has mysteriously declared further proceedings in *Qazi* inadmissible,[7] the House of Lords' ruling is extremely difficult to reconcile with the European Court's more recent decision in *Connors v United Kingdom*.[8]

1   *R (on application of Gangera) v Hounslow LBC* [2003] HLR 1028 at [47] per Moses J.
2   See *R (on application of Gangera) v Hounslow LBC* [2003] HLR 1028 at [45] per Moses J. Contrast *Harrow LBC v Qazi* [2004] 1 AC 983 at [25] per Lord Bingham of Cornhill.
3   See *Sheffield CC v Smart* [2002] LGR 467 at [37] per Laws LJ.
4   [2004] 1 AC 983 at [84] per Lord Hope of Craighead, [108]–[109] per Lord Millett, [125], [149], [151]–[152] per Lord Scott of Foscote **[para 2.71]**.
5   [2004] 1 AC 983 at [27] per Lord Steyn (Lord Bingham of Cornhill endorsing this view at [24]).
6   Richard Clayton QC, Key Human Rights Act Cases in the Last Twelve Months (23 June 2004) at [50].
7   Decision of 11 March 2004. See *Kay v Lambeth LBC* [2004] EWCA Civ 926 at [100].
8   Application No 66746/01 (27 May 2004) **[paras 2.73–2.75]**.

RESTRICTIONS ON RE-ENTRY UNDER NON-RESIDENTIAL LEASES AND TENANCIES

14.118   The requirement of legal process does not normally apply to re-entry under non-residential leases.[1] Provided that the landlord first serves any statutory notice which the tenant may be entitled to receive,[2] forfeiture by peaceable re-entry (without any prior warning to the tenant[3]) remains a perfectly viable option in response to a breach of covenant under most leases of business premises.[4]

1   *Kataria v Safeland plc* (1997) 75 P & CR D30 at D31 **[para 14.120]**. Compare, however, Leasehold Property (Repairs) Act 1938, s 1 (re-entry for breach of repairing covenant) **[para 14.134]**. Although a landlord requires the leave of the court before commencing proceedings for forfeiture against a bankrupt (Insolvency Act 1986, s 285(3)), anomalously no leave is required prior to the exercise of the landlord's right of peaceable re-entry (*Razzaq v Pala* [1997] 1 WLR 1336 at 1343F–G). Likewise peaceable re-entry is unfettered by any requirement of court leave during the currency of an interim order pending approval of a voluntary arrangement (Insolvency Act 1986, s 252(1)–(2)). See *Re a Debtor (No 13A-IO-1995)* [1995] 1 WLR 1127 at 1138A.
2   See e g LPA 1925, s 146(1) **[paras 14.129–14.148]**.
3   See *Kataria v Safeland plc* (1997) 75 P & CR D30 at D31.
4   That peaceable re-entry remains available is implicit in the statutory reference to the

enforcement of a right of re-entry 'by action or otherwise' (LPA 1925, s 146(1)). See *Re Riggs. Ex parte Lovell* [1901] 2 KB 16 at 20; *F G Sweeney Ltd v Powerscourt Shopping Centre Ltd* [1984] IR 501 at 504.

Peaceable re-entry

14.119   Peaceable re-entry may be particularly attractive to the landlord under a business tenancy since it avoids the delay, expense and uncertainty associated with court proceedings for possession.[1] An early re-entry by a commercial landlord often forestalls the rapid accumulation of almost certainly unrecoverable rent arrears and thereby serves to prevent unscrupulous tenants from enjoying a 'free ride' in terms of rent and service charges pending a court hearing.[2] There may, moreover, be little purpose in initiating a claim for possession if the defaulting tenant is likely to abandon the tenancy by simply vacating the premises and leaving the key behind.

1   See A Clarke, (1992) 45 CLP 81. It is not open to a landlord to effect a peaceable re-entry against a tenant by means of an agreement with a subtenant under which the latter consents to have the locks changed but otherwise to remain in occupation as a direct tenant of the landlord (see *Ashton v Sobelman* [1987] 1 WLR 177 at 187A–C).
2   See *F G Sweeney Ltd v Powerscourt Shopping Centre Ltd* [1984] IR 501 at 504 per Carroll J.

Conditions of peaceable re-entry

14.120   In spite of the advantages conferred by the self-help remedy of peaceable re-entry, it is still relatively unusual for a landlord under a non-residential lease to re-enter without first starting court proceedings for possession. Peaceable re-entry becomes a realistic option for the commercial landlord only where the demised premises are, at least temporarily, unoccupied by the tenant.[1] Care is needed since in certain circumstances the exercise of the landlord's right of re-entry may give rise to criminal liability.[2] It is an offence under the Criminal Law Act 1977 for any person without lawful authority to use or to threaten violence for the purpose of securing entry into any premises where, to his knowledge, there is someone present who is opposed to the entry.[3] Peaceable re-entry upon commercial premises is usually feasible only out of business hours or at weekends.[4]

1   See M Green, (1983) 80 Law Soc Gaz 328.
2   See *Billson v Residential Apartments Ltd* [1992] 1 AC 494 at 524E per Nicholls LJ, 536G per Lord Templeman.
3   Criminal Law Act 1977, s 6(1). Re-entry is not unlawful where premises are occupied only by the tenant's goods (see *Billson v Residential Apartments Ltd* [1992] 1 AC 494 at 536G per Lord Templeman).
4   See e g *Kataria v Safeland plc* (1997) 75 P & CR D30 (forced entry at 5.00 am).

Modern discouragement of peaceable re-entry

14.121   Forfeiture by physical re-entry, unsanctioned by the court, tends to display a certain surreptitious and lawless aspect. In *Billson v Residential*

Apartments Ltd[1] the tenants of unoccupied premises undertook major works of reconstruction in blatant disregard of the landlord's express reservation of a right of prior written consent to such alterations. As Lord Templeman observed, the landlord, 'perhaps incensed' by this flagrant breach of covenant, 'conceived and carried out a dawn raid which fortunately did not result in bloodshed.'[2] The landlord's agents peaceably re-entered the vacant premises at 6 am, changed the locks and fixed notices announcing that the lease had been forfeited. Four hours later the tenants' workmen broke back into the premises and regained occupation.

1   [1992] 1 AC 494. See [1992] Conv 273 (P F Smith); [1992] CLJ 216 (S Bridge).
2   [1992] 1 AC 494 at 540B.

14.122   Subsequent litigation concerned the question whether there remained in these circumstances any jurisdiction to grant the tenants relief against forfeiture,[1] but both the Court of Appeal and the House of Lords indicated *en passant* their distaste for what Nicholls LJ stigmatised as a 'hole-in-the-corner, self-help route' to the recovery of possession.[2] Nicholls LJ expressed the view that it cannot be right 'to encourage law-abiding citizens to embark on a course which is a sure recipe for violence' and that the policy of the law is 'to discourage self-help when confrontation and a breach of the law are likely to follow.'[3] These thoughts were echoed in the House of Lords, where Lord Templeman referred to 'the civilised method' of determining the lease by the initiation of court proceedings as a course of action far preferable to 'the dubious and dangerous method of determining the lease by re-entering the premises.'[4] In Lord Templeman's view, the courts should not positively encourage any means by which a landlord could 'sneak up on a shop at night, break into the shop, and install new locks so that the tenant loses his lease and can only press his nose against the shop window.'[5] Such sentiments point to a modern shift in emphasis from the endorsement of *peaceable re-entry* to the promotion of *peaceful repossession.*[6]

1   **[Para 14.164]**.
2   [1992] 1 AC 494 at 524G.
3   [1992] 1 AC 494 at 525A–B ('violence is all too likely when the tenant arrives the next day').
4   [1992] 1 AC 494 at 536F (see likewise Lord Oliver of Aylmerton at 543E).
5   [1992] 1 AC 494 at 536G. See the obvious distaste expressed by the Court of Appeal in *Kataria v Safeland plc* (1997) 75 P & CR D30 at D31, where Brooke LJ, although noting that the landlord's behaviour had been described as 'monstrous', concluded that 'whatever view might be taken ... in a court of morals, in this court we are bound to hold that the landlord's conduct was lawful.'
6   See e g *W G Clark (Properties) Ltd v Dupre Properties Ltd* [1992] Ch 297 at 307F–G per Deputy Judge Thomas Morison QC (it 'must be the policy of the law ... to encourage peaceful repossession').

14.123   There is nowadays a widespread apprehension that, although forfeiture by actual re-entry remains lawful at common law, it is 'undesirable to encourage landlords to self-help.'[1] This gathering perception can only be intensified by the statutory assimilation of the European Convention guarantee of the right to a 'fair and public hearing' (and the implicit right of access to adjudication by a court).[2] The clear trend of modern human rights jurisprudence is to castigate the resort to self-help remedies as 'inimical to a society in which the rule of law prevails.'[3] It is highly unlikely that the landlord's remedy of peaceable re-entry without court order can survive much longer as a general feature of the English law of landlord and tenant.

1   *W G Clark* (*Properties*) *Ltd v Dupre Properties Ltd* [1992] Ch 297 at 307F–G. See also *Stear v Scott* [1992] RTR 226 at 232D per Forbes J; *Razzaq v Pala* [1997] 1 WLR 1336 at 1343G; *Kataria v Safeland plc* (1997) 75 P & CR D30 at D31; *R v Bacon* [1977] 2 NSWLR 507 at 513 per Street CJ. For an excellent discussion of the social legitimacy of self-help remedies, see Alison Clarke, (1992) 45 CLP 81.
2   ECHR Art 6 [**para 14.109**].
3   See *Lesapo v North West Agricultural Bank*, 1999 (12) BCLR 1420 (Constitutional Court of South Africa).

Tenant's right to relief against forfeiture

14.124   The most important limitation on the successful exercise of a landlord's right of re-entry lies in the possibility that, in appropriate circumstances, the tenant may obtain relief against forfeiture.[1] Whereas re-entry, either by actual entry or by the initiation of proceedings for possession, has the effect of terminating and avoiding a lease, the granting of relief against forfeiture constitutes a 'revival of the lease'.[2] The consequence of this relief, if granted, is 'to do away with the forfeiture just as if there had never been any.'[3] Relief thus 'involves the coercive re-establishment of the relationship of lessor and lessee which has been effectively sundered at law.'[4]

1   [**Paras 14.149–14.173**].
2   *Billson v Residential Apartments Ltd* [1992] 1 AC 494 at 535C per Lord Templeman.
3   *Shevill v Builders Licensing Board* (1980) 2 BPR 9662 at 9667 per Samuels JA. See *Dendy v Evans* [1910] 1 KB 263 at 267–269 per Cozens-Hardy MR, 270–271 per Farwell LJ ('forfeiture is stopped in limine; so that there is no question of any destruction of an estate which has to be called into existence again').
4   *Stieper v Deviot Pty Ltd* (1977) 2 BPR 9602 at 9610 per Glass JA. Relief will not be granted on condition that the restored lease is immediately surrendered to the landlord: '[t]he object of relief against forfeiture is the continuation of a lease and not its extinction' (*Fuller v Judy Properties Ltd* (1991) 64 P & CR 176 at 184 per Dillon LJ).

PRELIMINARIES TO FORFEITURE

14.125   Certain preliminaries require to be observed in advance of any attempt to forfeit a lease for breach of covenant. The legislation of recent years has been particularly concerned to bolster the protection of residential tenants against oppressive threats or acts of forfeiture by a landlord.

Formal demand for rent

14.126   Where breach comprises the non-payment of rent,[1] the precise operation of forfeiture depends on whether recourse is had to the jurisdiction of the county court or of the High Court.[2] In either case the landlord's right to re-enter must be preceded by a formal demand for rent[3] unless the requirement of formal demand is obviated either by the express terms of the lease[4] or by statute. Section 210 of the Common Law Procedure Act 1852 provides that there is no requirement of formal demand if at least half a year's rent is in arrear and the goods present on the premises and available for distress are insufficient to cover all the arrears due. These conditions are fairly easily met since goods are deemed unavailable for distress if contained in premises which are locked.[5]

1   A maintenance or service charge under a lease may be treated, for relevant purposes, as a form of rent if (but only if) the parties have expressly agreed that the charge should be deemed to be a sum due by way of additional rent (*Escalus Properties Ltd v Robinson* [1996] QB 231 at 243H–244C; *Khar and Khar v Delmounty Ltd* (1996) 75 P & CR 232 at 236–237). See also *Di Palma v Victoria Square Property Co Ltd* [1986] Ch 150 at 158C; *Blatherwick (Services) Ltd v King* [1991] Ch 218 at 224E.
2   A landlord who unnecessarily issues proceedings in the High Court may find that he is penalised in the matter of costs (*CPR Part 55 Practice Direction*, para 1.2). See *Lircata Properties Ltd v Jones* [1967] 1 WLR 1257 at 1261F.
3   The archaic process of formal demand must be made either at an appointed place or on the demised premises and should require that the exact rent owed be paid before sunset on the last date for due payment (see *Duppa v Mayho* (1669) 1 Wms Saund 282 at 287, 85 ER 366 at 374–375 (Note)).
4   Nowadays professionally drafted leases invariably exempt the landlord from making any formal demand for rent.
5   *Doe d Chippendale v Dyson* (1827) Mood & M 77 at 78, 173 ER 1087; *Hammond v Mather* (1862) 3 F & F 151, 176 ER 68. See also County Courts Act 1984, s 139(1).

14.127   The Commonhold and Leasehold Reform Act 2002 has superimposed on these ancient rules a number of further qualifications relating to the forfeiture of certain residential leases on the ground of non-payment of rent. The 2002 Act provides that, where a tenant holds under a 'long lease' of a dwelling (generally a lease granted for a term exceeding 21 years[1]), the tenant is not liable to make any payment of rent[2] unless the landlord first notifies him that rent is due.[3] Furthermore, under a long residential lease of this kind the landlord has no entitlement to exercise a right of re-entry or forfeiture for non-payment of rent or of service or administration charges unless the unpaid amount exceeds a prescribed sum or has been due for more than a prescribed period.[4] The clear purpose of these restrictions is to preclude over-enthusiastic forfeiture for non-payment of small amounts over a short period.

1   CALRA 2002, ss 76–77, 166(9).
2   For this purpose rent excludes most service and administration charges (CALRA 2002, s 166(7)).
3   The landlord must send the tenant a notice in prescribed form specifying a date for payment between 30 and 60 days following the giving of the notice (CALRA 2002, s 166(1)–(6)).
4   CALRA 2002, s 167(1). The prescribed sum cannot itself exceed £500 (CALRA 2002, s 167(2)).

Service of a section 146 notice

14.128   Forfeiture for breach of covenants or conditions other than those relating to the payment of rent is also closely governed by statute.[1] In respect of such covenants and conditions[2] section 146 of the Law of Property Act 1925 lays down a special notice procedure which differs markedly from the rules relating to forfeiture for non-payment of rent.[3] The overall impact of the 'section 146 notice' regime (and of the jurisdiction to provide relief against forfeiture which is triggered by the service of a notice[4]) is to impose certain rudimentary requirements of due process and proportionality upon the divesting of substantial proprietary assets held by way of lease. Apart from several exceptional instances withdrawn from its scope,[5] section 146 is mandatory and cannot be excluded even by express contractual provision.[6] The coverage of the section 146 notice procedure is extensive, catching under-leases and specifically enforceable agreements for a lease[7] (but not agreements for a lease which take effect only as common law periodic tenancies[8]).

1   In rare cases the non-performance of a leasehold covenant may be excused on the ground that the covenant has become incapable of performance, even though the lease itself remains valid (see *Cricklewood Property and Investment Trust Ltd v Leighton's Investment Trust Ltd* [1945] AC 221 at 233–235 per Lord Russell of Killowen; *John Lewis Properties plc v Viscount Chelsea* [1993] 34 EG 116 (covenant to demolish and rebuild frustrated by subsequent listed building status)).

2   Subject to certain limited exceptions detailed in LPA 1925, s 146(9), section 146 is activated by a tenant's bankruptcy if his lease confers on the landlord a right of re-entry in the event of his bankruptcy (see *Cadogan Estates Ltd v McMahon* [2001] 1 AC 378 at 385E–F per Lord Hoffmann).

3   Section 146 does not in general apply to breaches of the covenant to pay rent (LPA 1925, s 146(11)), although see section 146(4) **[para 14.183]**.

4   **[Paras 14.160–14.173]**.

5   See LPA 1925, s 146(8)–(9).

6   LPA 1925, s 146(12). See also *Dream Factory Ltd v Crown Estate Commissioners* (1998) *Times*, 22 October.

7   LPA 1925, s 146(5)(a)) (see *Sport Internationaal Bussum BV v Inter-Footwear Ltd* [1984] 1 WLR 776 at 789H–790B). Section 146 thus covers the case where a tenant's option to renew a lease has been exercised, thereby calling into existence an equitable term capable of specific performance but for the fact that the landlord now seeks forfeiture for breach (see *Beca Developments Pty Ltd v Idameneo* (1989) 4 BPR 9575 at 9576).

8   *Swain v Ayres* (1888) 21 QBD 289 at 293 per Lord Esher MR, 295 per Lindley LJ, 296 per Lopes LJ.

SECTION 146 NOTICES

14.129   Under section 146(1) the landlord may not enforce any right of re-entry or forfeiture, whether by court action or by peaceable re-entry, unless he has first served a valid notice on the tenant and the tenant has failed to comply with its terms within a reasonable period of time.[1] In order to protect residential tenants holding under a 'long lease'[2] from trigger-happy complaints of breach, the Commonhold and Leasehold Reform Act 2002 introduces a further requirement that, prior to service of the statutory notice, the fact of breach must have been established on the landlord's application to a leasehold valuation tribunal, by the tenant's admission or otherwise by some final determination of a court or arbitral tribunal.[3] The interposition of this requirement serves to ensure, at least in the context of certain residential leases, that the tenant's civil rights and obligations are determined only after a 'fair and public hearing' in some independent and impartial forum[4] – an issue which might otherwise have remained highly debatable in cases involving forfeiture by peaceable re-entry.

1 Failure to serve a section 146 notice is liable to be construed as indicating that the landlord lacked an unequivocal intention to forfeit (see e g *Charville Estates Ltd v Unipart Group Ltd* [1997] EGCS 36). In the case of certain kinds of statutorily protected tenancy, the landlord must not only serve a section 146 notice on the defaulting tenant, but also obtain a court order for possession of the premises under the statute concerned (see e g Rent Act 1977, s 98(1) (regulated tenancy) [**para 14.322**]; HA 1985, s 82(1)–(4) (expressly preserving the application of section 146 on the termination of secure tenancies) [**para 14.345**]). Contrast *Artesian Residential Developments Ltd v Beck* [2000] QB 541 at 549A–F (assured tenancy under Housing Act 1988 [**para 14.336**]).

2 For this purpose a 'long lease' is generally a lease granted for a term exceeding 21 years (CALRA 2002, ss 76–77, 169(5)).

3 CALRA 2002, s 168(1)–(2).

4 ECHR Art 6 [**para 2.65**]. See also *Southwark LBC v St Brice* [2002] 1 WLR 1537 [**para 14.343**].

Contents

14.130 A 'section 146 notice' must specify the particular breach of which complaint is made.[1] It must require that the tenant remedy the breach 'if the breach is capable of remedy'[2] and it must normally require that the tenant make compensation in money for the breach.[3] In addition, any notice relating to a breach of the tenant's repairing covenants or to his failure to pay a service or administration charge must make reference to various statutory rights to protection enjoyed by the tenant.[4] Any notice which fails to comply with these requirements of section 146 is rendered invalid[5] and any purported forfeiture based upon an invalid notice is void.[6]

1 LPA 1925, s 146(1)(a). The notice must be sufficiently specific to enable the tenant to provide an effective remedy (*Fletcher v Nokes* [1897] 1 Ch 271 at 273–274). In the case of disrepair by the tenant it is usual to append to the notice a schedule of dilapidations prepared by a builder or surveyor. See also *Adagio Properties Ltd v Ansari* [1998] 2 EGLR 69 at 72D (full particulars of each defect not required).

2 LPA 1925, s 146(1)(b).

3 LPA 1925, s 146(1)(c). The landlord need not demand monetary compensation if he does not want it (*Lock v Pearce* [1893] 2 Ch 271 at 276, 279–280). In *Rugby School (Governors) v Tannahill* [1935] 1 KB 87 at 91 Rugby School was not required to demand that it share by way of compensation in income derived through prostitution.

4 [**Paras 14.136, 14.138**].

5 A section 146 notice is invalid if it omits to require that the tenant remedy a breach of covenant which is 'capable of remedy' in the statutory sense (see e g *Glass v Kencakes Ltd* [1966] 1 QB 611 at 622; *Expert Clothing Service & Sales Ltd v Hillgate House Ltd* [1986] Ch 340 at 362A, 365B; *Savva and Savva v Hussein* (1997) 73 P & CR 150 at 154, 156).

6 *Re Riggs, ex p Lovell* [1901] 2 KB 16 at 20.

Service

14.131   Where section 146 applies, no re-entry may properly be made in the absence of due service of the required notice.¹ A section 146 notice must be served upon the 'lessee',² a term which bears an extended statutory meaning inclusive of an under-lessee and 'any person deriving title under a lessee.'³ The notice should therefore be served upon any subtenant or assignee of the leasehold estate and upon any mortgagee or chargee of whom the lessor is aware. Where the lease has already been assigned (even wrongfully) to a third party, a notice served on the original tenant is insufficient to satisfy the requirement of section 146 and is therefore invalid.⁴ It follows that a landlord who re-enters the demised premises after service of an invalid notice cannot, precisely because he is now in possession, cure the defect by serving a second validating notice on the assignee.⁵ In *Fuller v Judy Properties Ltd*,⁶ however, the Court of Appeal was grudgingly prepared to uphold the validity of a re-entry against the assignee in slightly unusual circumstances where the assignee had received a copy of the original invalid notice and would in no way have benefited from the 'mere token formality' of a return of the keys before service of a second section 146 notice.⁷

1   See e g *Pioneer Quarries (Sydney) Pty Ltd v Permanent Trustee Co of NSW Ltd* (1970) 2 BPR 9562 at 9577 (in respect of the equivalent New South Wales provision). A possession judgment wrongfully obtained without prior service of a section 146 notice may be set aside (see *Jacques v Harrison* (1884) 12 QBD 165 at 167; *Billson v Residential Apartments Ltd* [1992] 1 AC 494 at 542G per Lord Oliver of Aylmerton). Failure to comply with section 146 does not, of course, preclude access to other forms of remedy (e g an action for damages).
2   If there is more than one tenant, the notice must be served on all (*Blewett v Blewett* [1936] 2 All ER 188 at 190).
3   LPA 1925, s 146(5)(b). As to the meaning of service, see LPA 1925, s 196. See also *Van Haarlam v Kasner* (1992) 64 P & CR 214 at 220–222.
4   *Fuller v Judy Properties Ltd* (1991) 64 P & CR 176 at 185 per Stocker LJ. (The sending of a copy of this notice to the assignee is not sufficient service upon the latter.)
5   See e g *Fuller v Judy Properties Ltd* (1991) 64 P & CR 176 at 185, where Stocker LJ confessed to 'considerable doubts whether a landlord in possession can ever serve a valid section 146 notice, since the latter by its terms must presuppose that the tenants are in possession.'
6   (1991) 64 P & CR 176. See [1992] Conv 343 (J E Martin).
7   Dillon LJ held that the second notice was valid ((1991) 64 P & CR 176 at 183). It was in any event clear to all concerned that the tenant's breach (in assigning without consent) was irremediable.

Purpose

14.132   As Slade LJ pointed out in *Expert Clothing Service & Sales Ltd v Hillgate House Ltd*,¹ it is 'an important purpose' of the section 146 procedure 'to give even tenants who have hitherto lacked the will or the means to comply with their obligations one last chance to summon up that will or find the necessary means before the landlord re-enters.'² The landlord may not determine the lease until it is clear that the tenant has failed to comply with the requirements of remedy and compensation contained in the notice.³

1   [1986] Ch 340 at 358A.

2   See also *Savva and Savva v Hussein* (1997) 73 P & CR 150 at 157 per Aldous LJ.
3   *Billson v Residential Apartments Ltd* [1992] 1 AC 494 at 535E per Lord Templeman.

14.133   The precise way in which this inducement operates is itself dependent on whether the breach in question is 'capable of remedy' within the meaning of section 146(1). Where a breach is 'capable of remedy', the real object of the section 146 notice procedure is to afford the tenant two opportunities before the landlord proceeds to enforce his right of re-entry.[1] *First*, the notice gives the tenant the opportunity to remedy his breach 'within a reasonable time' after the service of the notice.[2] *Second*, the notice procedure allows the tenant to apply to the court under section 146 for relief against forfeiture. Where the tenant's breach is not 'capable of remedy', there is clearly no point in providing him with the first of these opportunities[3] and the object of the notice procedure is simply to enable the tenant to throw himself upon the court's discretion to grant relief.[4] The mere fact that a breach is irremediable does not destroy the need to comply with the section 146 notice procedure.[5]

1   *Expert Clothing Service & Sales Ltd v Hillgate House Ltd* [1986] Ch 340 at 351B.
2   LPA 1925, s 146(1).
3   *Expert Clothing Service & Sales Ltd v Hillgate House Ltd* [1986] Ch 340 at 351C.
4   The court always has jurisdiction to grant relief, but it has been described as 'a bold course' to grant relief against forfeiture in the case of a breach which is 'incapable of remedy' (*Dunraven Securities Ltd v Holloway* (1982) 264 EG 709 at 711).
5   See e g *Fuller v Judy Properties Ltd* (1991) 64 P & CR 176 [**para 14.131**].

Forfeiture for breach of repairing covenants

14.134   Forfeiture for breach of a tenant's covenants to repair merits especial attention since further limits on the enforceability of this kind of covenant are contained in the Leasehold Property (Repairs) Act 1938. This Act was introduced in order to counteract a prevalent mischief which enabled an unscrupulous purchaser of the reversion on a long lease to harass the tenant with exaggerated lists of dilapidations, not for the purpose of protecting the landlord's reversion but rather in order to coerce an early surrender of the term.[1]

1   See *National Real Estate and Finance Co Ltd v Hassan* [1939] 2 KB 61 at 78 per Goddard LJ; *Associated British Ports v C H Bailey Plc* [1990] 2 AC 703 at 714E–F per Lord Templeman; [1990] Conv 305 (P F Smith). On the intendment of the legislation, see *Sidnell v Wilson* [1966] 2 QB 67 at 76; *Hamilton v Martell Securities Ltd* [1984] Ch 266 at 278E–F. See generally P F Smith, [1986] Conv 85.

Scope of the Leasehold Property (Repairs) Act 1938

14.135   The Leasehold Property (Repairs) Act 1938 imposes special restrictions on the availability of certain remedies for breach of a tenant's covenant to repair.[1] The Act applies only to leases granted for a term of seven years or more,[2] of which at the relevant time at least three years remain unexpired.[3] The

Act requires in effect that the landlord obtain the sanction of the court before pursuing remedies of forfeiture or damages. The Act does not, however, restrict the landlord's access to other remedies such as a mandatory injunction[4] or an action for a debt due under the lease.[5]

1   For even more specific restrictions on the landlord's remedies for the tenant's default in respect of internal decorative repairs, see LPA 1925, s 147.
2   LP(R)A 1938, s 7(1). A lease of an agricultural holding is excluded.
3   LP(R)A 1938, s 1(1).
4   See *SEDAC Investments Ltd v Tanner* [1982] 1 WLR 1342 at 1349F; *Rainbow Estates Ltd v Tokenhold Ltd* [1999] Ch 64 at 73C–D **[para 14.206]**.
5   See e g *Middlegate Properties Ltd v Gidlow-Jackson* (1977) 34 P & CR 4 at 9 (legal costs and surveyor's fees incurred in preparation of section 146 notice relating to want of repair).

Requirement of court's leave

14.136   Where the landlord seeks either forfeiture of the lease or damages on the basis of a tenant's breach of his covenant or agreement to keep or put the demised premises in repair,[1] the landlord must first serve on the tenant[2] a section 146 notice which makes visible reference to the tenant's rights under the Leasehold Property (Repairs) Act 1938.[3] The tenant is then entitled within 28 days to serve on the landlord a counter-notice claiming the benefit of the 1938 Act.[4] Where a counter-notice is duly served, no proceedings (by action or otherwise) may be taken by the landlord for the purpose of re-entry or recovery of damages unless the court gives leave.[5] The court's leave is available only on the grounds specified in the Act,[6] of which the most important is that the present actuality or imminent likelihood of substantial diminution of the value of the landlord's reversion makes an immediate remedy of the breach impera-tive.[7] The court may also grant leave where 'special circumstances ... render it just and equitable that leave should be given.'[8]

1   The 1938 Act has no application to such covenants as to take out and maintain insurance on the demised premises (*Farimani v Gates* (1984) 271 EG 887 at 888–889) or to clean toilets on the demised premises (*Starrokate Ltd v Burry* (1983) 265 EG 871 at 872).
2   Notice cannot properly be served on the tenant's mortgagee even though in possession (*Smith v Spaul* [2003] QB 983 at [28]–[29]).
3   LP(R)A 1938, s 1(1)–(2). The landlord's notice directed towards forfeiture is invalid unless it indicates 'in characters not less conspicuous than those in any other part of the notice' the tenant's right to serve a counter-notice (LP(R)A 1938, s 1(4)). A section 146 notice relating to the recovery of damages for breach of covenant must be served at least one month before the commencement of the action (LP(R)A 1938, s 1(2)).
4   LP(R)A 1938, s 1(1)–(2).
5   LP(R)A 1938, s 1(3). A landlord's application for the court's leave under section 1(3) is a pending land action within LCA 1972, s 17(1) and is protectable by entry in a registered title (*Selim Ltd v Bickenhall Engineering Ltd* [1981] 1 WLR 1318 at 1323H–1324A).
6   However, in order to obtain leave the landlord need only make out a prima facie case or a bona fide arguable case that at least one of the grounds is satisfied. The standards of proof are 'lowly' (*Land Securities PLC v Receiver for the Metropolitan Police District* [1983] 1 WLR 439 at 444D–E, 445A; [1983] Conv 323 (P F Smith)).
7   LP(R)A 1938, s 1(5)(a).
8   LP(R)A 1938, s 1(5)(e).

Limitations of the Leasehold Property (Repairs) Act 1938

14.137   In spite of its remedial origins, the 1938 Act does not operate entirely satisfactorily.[1] The Act contains one potentially serious trap for the unwary landlord in that the statutory scheme seems to contemplate that the landlord's service of a section 146 notice should precede any actual remedy of the tenant's breach of his repairing covenant.[2] Accordingly it was held in *SEDAC Investments Ltd v Tanner*[3] that the court had no jurisdiction to grant a landlord leave to pursue a claim in damages against the tenant if, in the interests of procuring an immediate remedy,[4] the landlord had already effected the necessary repairs before purporting to serve a section 146 notice on the tenant.[5] This decision threatened to preclude landlords from recovering their expenditure on emergency repairs, but the courts have since attempted to counteract the procedural deficiencies of the 1938 Act by allowing landlords to recover the cost of repairs, not as unliquidated damages in respect of the tenant's breach of covenant, but rather as a claim in debt for a liquidated sum.[6] In so far as the tenant's liability to reimburse the landlord for such works sounds in debt rather than in contractual damages, the landlord's claim requires no judicial sanction under the 1938 Act.[7]

1   The Act 'catches the virtuous in the net which is laid for the sinner' (*Sidnell v Wilson* [1966] 2 QB 67 at 79 per Harman LJ).
2   See *SEDAC Investments Ltd v Tanner* [1982] 1 WLR 1342 at 1347G–H.
3   [1982] 1 WLR 1342 at 1348G–H. See [1983] Conv 72 (P F Smith).
4   There was evidence that the landlord feared that the premises, unless repaired as a matter of urgency, might present a danger of injury to passing pedestrians. He therefore intervened swiftly in order to protect himself from liability ([1982] 1 WLR 1342 at 1344A).
5   The landlord's section 146 notice was invalid because it required a remedy for a breach which had already been remedied by the landlord's emergency action ([1982] 1 WLR 1342 at 1348F–G).
6   See eg *Hamilton v Martell Securities Ltd* [1984] Ch 266 at 281B–C; *Colchester Estates (Cardiff) v Carlton Industries Plc* (1984) 271 EG 778 at 779. See, however, *Swallow Securities Ltd v Brand* (1981) 45 P & CR 328 at 334 per McNeill J, for the criticism that this approach assists a circumvention of the 1938 Act.
7   See similarly *Jervis v Harris* [1996] Ch 195 at 202E–203E per Millett LJ (where there was a leasehold provision entitling the landlord to undertake repairs in default of the tenant).

Forfeiture for non-payment of a service or administration charge

14.138   The Housing Act 1996 imposes special restrictions on forfeiture for non-payment of service or administration charges in respect of premises let as a dwelling. The landlord may not exercise any right of re-entry or forfeiture on this ground unless the tenant's liability to pay the charge in question has been admitted by the tenant or has been established by some final determination of a leasehold valuation tribunal, court or arbitral tribunal.[1] No right of re-entry or forfeiture can be exercised, in any event, until at least 14 days have elapsed since the final determination (if any) of the tenant's liability.[2]

1   HA 1996, s 81(1), as amended by CALRA 2002, s 170(1)–(2). For this purpose exercise of a right of re-entry or forfeiture includes the service of a notice under LPA 1925, s 146 (HA 1996, s 81(4A), as inserted by CALRA 2002, s 170(5)).
2   HA 1996, s 81(2), as substituted by CALRA 2002, s 170(3).

REMEDIABILITY OF BREACH

14.139   The operation of section 146 hinges vitally on the concept of remediability of breach.[1] In the case of a *remediable* breach of covenant, the section 146 notice must give the tenant a reasonable period of time within which to comply with its terms.[2] The reasonableness of the time allowed is intricately linked with the remediability of the breach,[3] but it is generally thought that a period of three months is sufficient.[4] If remedial action is taken and reasonable compensation is paid by the tenant within that time, the landlord is then unable to show that the statutory condition precedent to his ability to enforce the forfeiture has been fulfilled.[5] If, however, compliance with the notice is not forthcoming within that time, the landlord may proceed to enforce the forfeiture either in person or by action,[6] subject only to the tenant's rights to seek relief against forfeiture.[7]

1   [**Para 14.130**].
2   A 'reasonable time' depends ultimately on the facts of the individual case (see *Hick v Raymond & Reid* [1893] AC 22 at 29).
3   See, for example, the conceptual connection made in *Expert Clothing Service & Sales Ltd v Hillgate House Ltd* [1986] Ch 340 at 357B–C.
4   In *Billson v Residential Apartments Ltd* [1992] 1 AC 494 at 508A–E, Browne-Wilkinson V-C considered that an interval of only 14 days between the service of the notice and actual re-entry was a 'reasonable time'. Here the tenants' actions in proceeding with a breach of covenant in total defiance of prior warnings had demonstrated that they 'had no intention to remedy the breach at all.' For the purpose of section 146 a 'reasonable time' has already elapsed if the defaulting tenant, by persisting in breach, makes it 'clear that he is not proposing to remedy the breaches within a reasonable time, or indeed any time.' Compare *Gondal v Dillon Newsagents Ltd* [1998] CLY 3604 (five hours insufficient).
5   *Scala House and District Property Co Ltd v Forbes* [1974] QB 575 at 585B. See also *Pioneer Quarries (Sydney) Pty Ltd v Permanent Trustee Co of NSW Ltd* (1970) 2 BPR 9562 at 9576.
6   *Expert Clothing Service & Sales Ltd v Hillgate House Ltd* [1986] Ch 340 at 362D–E. This seems to have been the basis on which the landlord re-entered in *Billson v Residential Apartments Ltd* [1992] 1 AC 494 [**para 14.121**].
7   [**Paras 14.160–14.173**].

Irremediable breaches of covenant

14.140   Some breaches of covenant by a tenant are *irremediable*[1] and in such cases the section 146 notice need not require that the tenant remedy the breach.[2] It is sufficient merely that the landlord serves a section 146 notice which specifies that the breach has occurred and demands that money compensation be paid by the tenant.[3] After a reasonable interval[4] the landlord is then free to enforce the forfeiture, subject only to the tenant's possible rights to claim relief against the forfeiture.

1   This is expressly envisaged in the terms of LPA 1925, s 146(1). See *Expert Clothing Service & Sales Ltd v Hillgate House Ltd* [1986] Ch 340 at 362E.
2   Such a requirement would be 'pointless' where remedy within a reasonable time is impossible (*Expert Clothing Service & Sales Ltd v Hillgate House Ltd* [1986] Ch 340 at 357A). See also *Rugby School (Governors) v Tannahill* [1935] 1 KB 87 at 91, 94; *Dunraven Securities Ltd v Holloway* (1982) 264 EG 709.

3   It may nevertheless be prudent for the landlord to proceed cautiously by demanding that the tenant's breach be remedied if, in the statutory terminology, it is 'capable of remedy'.

4   Two days are not enough for this purpose (see *Horsey Estate Ltd v Steiger* [1899] 2 QB 79 at 91–92), but fourteen days are sufficient (*Civil Service Co-operative Society Ltd v McGrigor's Trustee* [1923] 2 Ch 347 at 356; *Scala House and District Property Co Ltd v Forbes* [1974] QB 575 at 589B–D).

Concept of capability of remedy

14.141   In view of the 'limited guidance' to be derived from the authorities,[1] it may not be easy to determine whether a particular breach of covenant is of such a character as to be incapable of remedy. There is, of course, a sense in which no breach of covenant can ever truly be remedied.[2] The breach, once committed, cannot be undone or expunged from the record[3] and the case law of the past has tended to adopt this unforgiving approach at least in the context of negative covenants relating to user of the demised premises.[4] However, since section 146(1) clearly contemplates that some breaches *are* 'capable of remedy', this blunt approach cannot be conclusive.[5]

1   *Expert Clothing Service & Sales Ltd v Hillgate House Ltd* [1986] Ch 340 at 351C per Slade LJ.
2   See *Savva and Savva v Hussein* (1997) 73 P & CR 150 at 156 per Aldous LJ.
3   *Expert Clothing Service & Sales Ltd v Hillgate House Ltd* [1986] Ch 340 at 362E–F.
4   See e g *Rugby School (Governors) v Tannahill* [1934] 1 KB 695 at 701–702.
5   *Hoffman v Fineberg* [1949] Ch 245 at 253.

Remediability of damage

14.142   It is widely accepted nowadays that the concept of 'capability of remedy' turns on 'whether the harm that has been done to the landlord by the relevant breach is for practicable purposes capable of being retrieved.'[1] Thus, by a subtle semantic shift, the test of the remediability of a *breach* has become a test of the remediability of the *damage* caused by that breach. As Slade LJ indicated in *Expert Clothing Service & Sales Ltd v Hillgate House Ltd*,[2] the 'ultimate question' is whether the 'harm' suffered by the landlord would be 'effectively remedied' if the tenant were to comply within a reasonable time with a section 146 notice demanding both remedy and compensation. Only if the answer to this question is in the negative may a section 146 notice validly omit any requirement of remedy, thereby opening the way for the landlord to enforce the forfeiture.

1   *Expert Clothing Service & Sales Ltd v Hillgate House Ltd* [1986] Ch 340 at 355B–C. See likewise *Savva and Savva v Hussein* (1997) 73 P & CR 150 at 154 per Staughton LJ.
2   [1986] Ch 340 at 358C–D.

Test based on consequential effects

14.143   The sharp point of the 'remediability' issue has accordingly moved away from judicial assessments of the intrinsic quality of the tenant's acts or defaults towards a consideration of the consequential effect of the tenant's breach as measured in terms of irretrievable long-range damage to the landlord's interests.[1] A breach is 'capable of remedy' within the meaning of the statute if, but only if, the landlord can be restored within a reasonable time to the position he would have been in if no breach had occurred.[2] In this sense, therefore, a breach which has been remedied is 'demonstrated to have been a breach which was ab initio capable of being remedied.'[3] If, however, the effects of the tenant's default cannot be cured either within a reasonable time or at all, then his breach is not 'capable of remedy' in the relevant statutory sense.[4]

1   'The test is one of effect' (*Savva and Savva v Hussein* (1997) 73 P & CR 150 at 157 per Aldous LJ). The 'remediability' issue, thus stated, must be examined at the date of issue of the section 146 notice (*Expert Clothing Service & Sales Ltd v Hillgate House Ltd* [1986] Ch 340 at 362E).

2   *Expert Clothing Service & Sales Ltd v Hillgate House Ltd* [1986] Ch 340 at 362E–F.

3   *Expert Clothing Service & Sales Ltd v Hillgate House Ltd* [1986] Ch 340 at 364E–F. See similarly *Savva and Savva v Hussein* (1997) 73 P & CR 150 at 157 per Aldous LJ.

4   *Expert Clothing Service & Sales Ltd v Hillgate House Ltd* [1986] Ch 340 at 362F.

Remediability of positive covenants

14.144   This pragmatic approach enables some approximate predictions to be made as to the status of certain kinds of breach under section 146(1). A breach of a positive covenant (whether it be a continuing breach or a 'once and for all' breach) will normally be capable of remedy,[1] since such a breach can usually be cured by belated performance of the covenanted action.[2] Thus in *Expert Clothing Service & Sales Ltd v Hillgate House Ltd*[3] the Court of Appeal held that the tenant's breach of a covenant to reconstruct premises within a specified time was 'capable of remedy' by performance out of time, since the landlord would not suffer irretrievable prejudice if the tenant tendered late performance of his covenant and made adequate money compensation for his breach.[4] An effective remedy can be provided for a 'once and for all' breach of covenant if that which ought to have been done can be done within a reasonable time during the subsistence of the term.[5] It may not ultimately be possible to maintain that the breach of a positive covenant is always 'capable of remedy',[6] but it is certainly difficult to think of examples which are not.[7]

1   *Expert Clothing Service & Sales Ltd v Hillgate House Ltd* [1986] Ch 340 at 355B.

2   *Rugby School (Governors) v Tannahill* [1934] 1 KB 695 at 701; *Expert Clothing Service & Sales Ltd v Hillgate House Ltd* [1986] Ch 340 at 355C. See also *Bass Holdings Ltd v Morton Music Ltd* [1988] Ch 493 at 507B per Scott J.

3   [1986] Ch 340.

4   The most substantial damage imposed on the landlord by the tenant's breach flowed from the fact that the reconstructed premises would have commanded a higher rental value. However, as the Court of Appeal indicated (at 356A), this kind of loss was amply compensable in money. The Court further pointed out (at 358A–B) that the landlord would have been entitled to include in the section 146 notice a 'tight timetable' for the fulfilment of the tenant's obligation to reconstruct.

5   *Expert Clothing Service & Sales Ltd v Hillgate House Ltd* [1986] Ch 340 at 362H–363A. See e g *ETS Vehicles Ltd v Fargate Developments Ltd* [1997] NI 25 at 31e–f.

6   See *Expert Clothing Service & Sales Ltd v Hillgate House Ltd* [1986] Ch 340 at 354H–355A,

358F, where Slade LJ hypothesised that irremediability might attach to the breach of a covenant to insure the demised property if the premises had already been burnt down without insurance cover having been obtained.

7   *Expert Clothing Service & Sales Ltd v Hillgate House Ltd* [1986] Ch 340 at 362H–363A. There seems to be no decided English case in which the breach of a positive covenant has been held incapable of remedy (see *Expert Clothing Service*, supra at 358F).

Remediability of negative covenants

14.145   It used to be thought that all breaches of a negative covenant were inherently irremediable by the tenant even though the prohibited user was terminated before the service of the section 146 notice.[1] In *Scala House and District Property Co Ltd v Forbes*,[2] for example, the Court of Appeal seemed to indicate that 'once and for all' breaches of a negative covenant were wholly incapable of remedy. On this basis it was thought impossible to remedy the breach of a covenant prohibiting the assignment or subletting of the demised premises[3] or prohibiting the unconsented alteration of such premises. As Lady Macbeth once declared, 'what's done is done.'[4] Irremediable breach, once proved, was treated as leading almost inexorably to re-entry by the landlord and, almost as inevitably, to the exercise of discretion against any award of relief from forfeiture.[5] In more recent years, however, the courts have moved gradually towards a recognition that the breach of many kinds of negative covenant is indeed 'capable of remedy' within section 146.[6]

1   See *Rugby School (Governors) v Tannahill* [1934] 1 KB 695 at 701; *Scala House and District Property Co Ltd v Forbes* [1974] QB 575 at 588A–B. Compare, however, *Rugby School (Governors) v Tannahill* [1935] 1 KB 87 at 90.
2   [1974] QB 575 at 588D.
3   See also *Expert Clothing Service & Sales Ltd v Hillgate House Ltd* [1986] Ch 340 at 354G, 363A; *Fuller v Judy Properties Ltd* (1991) 64 P & CR 176 at 182.
4   See *Bass Holdings Ltd v Morton Music Ltd* [1988] Ch 493 at 541C per Bingham LJ. The irreversibility of the fact of breach has inspired other literary allusions: see *Savva and Savva v Hussein* (1997) 73 P & CR 150 at 154 per Staughton LJ ('The moving finger writes and cannot be recalled').
5   **[Para 14.172]**.
6   The changing approach was first reflected in the judgment of Bingham LJ in *Bass Holdings Ltd v Morton Music Ltd* [1988] Ch 493 at 541F–H. See also *Hagee (London) Ltd v Cooperative Insurance Society Ltd* (1991) 63 P & CR 362 at 371–372; *Billson v Residential Apartments Ltd* [1992] 1 AC 494 at 508A per Browne-Wilkinson V-C.

Breaches of a continuing nature

14.146   The courts have now affirmed that remedy is normally possible in respect of even negative covenants, provided that the breach does not have a 'once and for all' character but is instead of a *continuing* nature.[1] In such cases the vital determinant is whether the harm inflicted on the landlord can be removed by due compliance on the part of the tenant coupled with appropriate money compensation. The injury caused to the landlord by the tenant's breach can often be retrieved by a simple cesser of the prohibited activity.[2] If such cesser provides an adequate remedy for the landlord and occurs before the service of the section 146 notice, the notice need not demand that remedy be made. At this stage the only issue outstanding will be the payment of compensation for the tenant's breach[3] and the tenant can avert forfeiture simply by paying the required compensation. If cesser has not yet occurred, the section 146 notice must not only demand compensation but also require that cesser occur within such time as is reasonable.

1   It is well established that a breach of a covenant as to user of premises constitutes a continuing breach (see *Cooper v Henderson* (1982) 263 EG 592 at 593).
2   Examples are provided by the breach of such covenants as not to place window boxes in the windows of a residential flat (see *Expert Clothing Service & Sales Ltd v Hillgate House Ltd* [1986] Ch 340 at 362G) or not to use the demised premises for residential purposes (see *Cooper v Henderson* (1982) 263 EG 592 at 594).
3   *Expert Clothing Service & Sales Ltd v Hillgate House Ltd* [1986] Ch 340 at 362H.

Breaches of a 'once and for all nature'

14.147   The courts have now extended this approach to cover many instances of 'once and for all' breach of negative covenants. In *Billson v Residential Apartments Ltd*,[1] Browne-Wilkinson V-C expressed doubt as to whether breach of a covenant against unconsented alteration of the demised premises could, in every instance, be said to be 'irremediable'.[2] This stance was later confirmed in *Savva and Savva v Hussein*,[3] where the Court of Appeal emphasised that, as a matter of general principle, breaches of negative covenants are no less 'capable of remedy' than are breaches of positive covenants, provided that 'the mischief caused by the breach can be removed' by belated compliance with the tenant's covenants.[4]

1   [1992] 1 AC 494 at 508A.
2   See also *W G Clark (Properties) Ltd v Dupre Properties Ltd* [1992] Ch 297 at 309E–F, where Deputy Judge Thomas Morison QC appeared to accept the remediable quality of a breach of the tenant's implied duty not to prejudice his landlord's interests by disclaimer or repudiation.
3   (1997) 73 P & CR 150 at 154 per Staughton LJ. See also Aldous LJ (at 156–157). See (1997) 1 L & TR 70 (J Brown and R Duddridge).
4   *Savva and Savva v Hussein* also concerned unconsented alterations of the demised premises in breach of a negative covenant, but the mischief could be removed by 'restoring the property to the state it was in before the alterations' ((1997) 73 P & CR 150 at 154 per Staughton LJ).

Irremediable breaches

14.148   The issue of remediability depends ultimately on the facts of the particular case, but few breaches of the tenant's leasehold obligations (whether positive or negative in nature) are nowadays incapable of remedy.[1] In relatively rare instances certain kinds of breach nevertheless remain altogether beyond any prospect of effective remedy. It has been accepted, for example, that the breach of a covenant not to assign the leasehold term without the landlord's consent can *never* be remedied,[2] leaving the tenant entirely dependent on the court's discretion to grant relief against forfeiture.[3] There are other cases where the tenant's breach is of such a nature that it cannot be remedied by mere cesser of the offending user and forfeiture therefore becomes virtually inevitable. In the latter category of circumstance even a complete cesser of the prohibited activity does not remove the 'stigma' which the tenant's conduct has caused to attach to the premises.[4] Thus the use of the demised premises in breach of covenant as a brothel cannot be remedied by mere cesser of the immoral user (even if accompanied by the payment of compensation).[5] As O'Connor LJ observed in *Expert Clothing Service & Sales Ltd v Hillgate House Ltd*,[6] 'the taint lingers on and will not dissipate within a reasonable time.' Likewise the involvement of the tenant in any serious criminal activity in relation to the demised premises may constitute a breach incapable of remedy.[7] In *Dunraven Securities Ltd v Holloway*[8] the Court of Appeal regarded as irremediable the conduct of a tenant who had taken a lease of shop premises in Soho supposedly for the sale of old and modern prints, books and objets d'art, but who had instead used the premises as a sex shop.[9] Similarly in *Van Haarlam v Kasner*[10] a tenant's conviction for offences committed under the Official Secrets Acts was held to be an irremediable breach of a leasehold covenant against user of the premises for illegal purposes.[11]

1   'There is ... nothing in the statute, nor in logic, which requires different considerations between a positive and negative covenant, although it may be right to differentiate between particular covenants' (*Savva and Savva v Hussein* (1997) 73 P & CR 150 at 157 per Aldous LJ).
2   *Scala House and District Property Co Ltd v Forbes* [1974] QB 575 at 588D; (1973) 89 LQR 460; [1974] CLJ 54 (D J Hayton). See likewise *Savva and Savva v Hussein* (1997) 73 P & CR 150 at 154 per Staughton LJ.
3   Relief against forfeiture was, in fact, granted in the *Scala House* case with the result, as Staughton LJ pointed out in *Savva and Savva v Hussein* (1997) 73 P & CR 150 at 154, that the supposedly exceptional nature of a covenant against assignment 'may not be of any great consequence.'
4   *Expert Clothing Service & Sales Ltd v Hillgate House Ltd* [1986] Ch 340 at 357D–E.
5   *Rugby School (Governors) v Tannahill* [1935] 1 KB 87 at 90–91, 93–94; *Egerton v Esplanade Hotels, London, Ltd* [1947] 2 All ER 88 at 92A. However, it is possible that such a breach is remediable by a tenant who takes immediate action directed at forfeiture in order to terminate an immoral or illegal user by his subtenant of which he was previously unaware (see e g *Glass v Kencakes Ltd* [1966] 1 QB 611 at 629; *Re Vanek and Bomza* (1977) 74 DLR (3d) 175 at 180; but compare the doubts expressed on this point in *Scala House and District Property Co Ltd v Forbes* [1974] QB 575 at 587B–C). See also *British Petroleum Pension Trust Ltd v Behrendt* (1985) 276 EG 199 at 202, where Purchas LJ declined to regard a breach of a covenant against immoral user as remediable, particularly since the tenant had effectively shut his eyes to the conduct of his subtenant.
6   [1986] Ch 340 at 362G.
7   See *Hoffman v Fineberg* [1949] Ch 245 at 257 (illicit gaming club); *Ali v Booth* (1966) 110 Sol Jo 708 at 709 (conviction of restaurateur under food hygiene regulations); *Kelly v Purvis* (1983) 80 LSG 410 (illegal use of licensed massage parlour as brothel).
8   (1982) 264 EG 709 at 711.
9   See also *British Petroleum Pension Trust Ltd v Behrendt* (1985) 52 P & CR 117 at 124 per Purchas LJ.
10   (1992) 64 P & CR 214 at 223. See [1993] Conv 298 (J Martin).
11   There was evidence that much of the tenant's illegal activity as a spy had been conducted from within his flat.

TENANT'S ACCESS TO RELIEF AGAINST FORFEITURE

14.149   It is clear that from the earliest times courts of equity have asserted the right to relieve against the forfeiture of rights on the ground that such a penalty is disproportionate to the breach upon which the forfeiture is premised[1] and that an insistence on the strict legal right to forfeit is therefore unconscionable.[2] In *Shiloh Spinners Ltd v Harding*[3] the House of Lords confirmed that this inherent equitable jurisdiction extended beyond the granting of relief for non-payment of rent to cover wilful breaches of other forms of covenant.[4] Although equity still 'expects men to carry out their bargains and will not let them buy their way out by uncovenanted payment', Lord Wilberforce emphasised that the courts retain the right 'in appropriate and limited cases' to relieve against forfeiture for breach of covenant or condition 'where the primary object of the bargain is to secure a stated result which can effectively be attained when the matter comes before the court, and where the forfeiture provision is added by way of security for the production of that result.'[5] The European Court of Human Rights has held, furthermore, that the exercise of an orderly discretion to suspend the landlord's right to evict defaulting tenants is not necessarily inconsistent with the Convention guarantee of the property rights of the landlord.[6]

1   See *Billson v Residential Apartments Ltd* [1992] 1 AC 494 at 535B **[para 14.171]**. The tenant who spends £200,000 on the purchase of a 99 year lease of a flat may well have breached the leasehold covenants by keeping a cat or a budgerigar on the premises, but it seems wrong in principle that the entire lease should be rendered forfeitable in the event of trivial misconduct which activates the landlord's right to re-enter. See also *Croydon (Unique) Ltd v Wright* [2001] Ch 318 at 322G, where forfeiture of a 125 year lease would have conferred on the landlord a benefit said to be worth £70,000 as compensation for unpaid rent and costs amounting to £653.

2   See *Tanwar Enterprises Pty Ltd v Cauchi* (2003) 201 ALR 359 at [82], [106] per Kirby J **[para 15.15]**; *Liristis Holdings Pty Ltd v Wallville Pty Ltd* (2001) 10 BPR 18801 at [116].

3   [1973] AC 691. See [1973] CLJ 218 (P B Fairest). See also *1497777 Ontario Inc v Leon's Furniture Ltd* (2003) 232 DLR (4th) 552 at [69]–[70].

4   See *Sanders v Pope* (1806) 12 Ves 282 at 289, 33 ER 108 at 110; *Billson v Residential Apartments Ltd* [1992] 1 AC 494 at 534G–H per Lord Templeman.

5   [1973] AC 691 at 723G–H. See *Sport Internationaal Bussum B V v Inter-Footwear Ltd* [1984] 1 WLR 776 at 783H, 785G. See also J Story, *Commentaries on Equity Jurisprudence* (12th edn 1877), Vol II, p 561.

6   ECHR Protocol No 1, Art 1. See *Spadea and Scalabrino v Italy* (1995) 21 EHRR 482 at [33]–[41] ('fair balance' struck between the interests of the community and the fundamental rights of the landlord).

14.150   Although it remains debatable to what extent legislative intervention has overtaken or extinguished the inherent equitable jurisdiction, it is somewhat rare for a lease ultimately to be forfeited if the tenant's breach is capable of remedy and the purpose of the landlord–tenant relationship is still capable of fulfilment.[1] The aggressively terminal tone of most leasehold forfeiture clauses is seldom borne out against the actuality of the modern jurisdiction to grant relief. It is nowadays a judicially admitted fact that in many leases, no matter how 'diligent or even punctilious a tenant may be in carrying out his obligations', there will 'in practice inevitably be occasions' when the tenant is strictly in breach of some covenant contained in his tenancy.[2] The potential for relief against forfeiture is an ever-present condition of the workability of most leasehold relationships. For this reason alone the right to seek relief is a valuable incident of the landlord–tenant relationship.[3] As such the right to seek relief constitutes a transferable chose in action. It can be passed to a purchaser of the lease; it can vest in the tenant's trustee in bankruptcy[4]; and it can be available to the tenant's mortgagee.[5]

1 'When the landlord can be made whole by the payment of the money, there will rarely be reason to refuse the tenant relief from re-entry or forfeiture' (*Badley v Badley* (1983) 138 DLR (3d) 493 at 502). See also *Platt v Ong* [1972] VR 197 at 198.
2 See *Bass Holdings Ltd v Morton Music Ltd* [1988] Ch 493 at 528F–G per Nicholls LJ.
3 One of a number of joint tenants cannot apply unilaterally for relief against forfeiture (see *Hammersmith and Fulham LBC v Monk* [1992] 1 AC 478 at 490G per Lord Bridge of Harwich; *T M Fairclough & Sons Ltd v Berliner* [1931] 1 Ch 60 at 66).
4 *Howard v Fanshawe* [1895] 2 Ch 581 at 589. The right to seek relief against forfeiture passes to assignees of the original tenant, even though the assignment is itself wrongful because made in breach of covenant (*Old Grovebury Manor Farm Ltd v W Seymour Plant Sales & Hire Ltd (No 2)* [1979] 1 WLR 1397 at 1400F–G; *Re Hurontario Management Services Ltd and Menechella Brothers Ltd* (1983) 146 DLR (3d) 110 at 112). After assignment the original tenant loses any right to apply for relief (see *Re Francini and Canuck Properties Ltd* (1982) 132 DLR (3d) 468 at 471), except in the case of an 'overriding lease' **[para 14.236]**.
5 **[Para 14.186]**.

14.151 The court's powers in matters of relief against forfeiture differ vitally in accordance with whether forfeiture is sought on the ground of non-payment of rent or on the ground of some other breach of covenant.

RELIEF AGAINST FORFEITURE FOR NON-PAYMENT OF RENT

14.152 Notwithstanding the existence of a right in the landlord to forfeit a lease for non-payment of rent, the courts have traditionally restrained the exercise of this right. Since the proviso for re-entry is essentially a security to ensure compliance with the covenant to pay rent,[1] it follows that 'when the rent is paid, the end is obtained; and therefore the landlord shall not be permitted to take advantage of the forfeiture.'[2] Accordingly in the exercise of their equitable jurisdiction the courts have long had power to reinstate the lease, where it just and equitable so to do, provided that the tenant pays all rent owed to and costs incurred by the landlord.[3]

1 **[Para 14.103]**. See *Maryland Estates Ltd v Joseph* [1999] 1 WLR 83 at 87H–88A; *Bland v Ingrams Estates Ltd* [2001] Ch 767 at [70] per Chadwick LJ.
2 *Wadman v Calcraft* (1803) 10 Ves 67 at 69, 32 ER 768 at 769; *Durell v Gread* (1914) 84 CJKB 130 at 132 per Scrutton J; *Silverman v AFCO (UK) Ltd* (1988) 56 P & CR 185 at 189. See also *Baxton v Kara* [1982] 1 NSWLR 604 at 609G–610C; *Badley v Badley* (1983) 138 DLR (3d) 493 at 502; *Shevill v Builders Licensing Board* (1980) 2 BPR 9662 at 9667 per Samuels JA.
3 See *Howard v Fanshawe* [1895] 2 Ch 581 at 592.

Statutory rights to terminate possession proceedings

14.153 The equitable jurisdiction to relieve against forfeiture for non-payment of rent is now supplemented by statute. In possession proceedings brought in the High Court for non-payment of rent,[1] the tenant is entitled, under the Common Law Procedure Act 1852, to have the proceedings stayed if he pays all rent arrears and costs before the date of judgment.[2] Somewhat anomalously this right arises only if at least six months' rent is in arrear.[3] Under the County Courts Act 1984 the tenant has a similar right to the automatic termination of county court possession proceedings on the payment of all rent arrears and costs not less than five days before the trial date.[4]

1   The generally more lenient approach to forfeiture for non-payment of rent applies to the non-payment of a maintenance or service charge only if such a charge is expressly covenanted as a form of additional rent (see *Khar and Khar v Delmounty Ltd* (1996) 75 P & CR 232 at 236–237).
2   CLPA 1852, s 212. For this purpose payment by a third party is not sufficient (*Matthews v Dobbins* [1963] 1 WLR 227 at 229–231).
3   *Standard Pattern Co Ltd v Ivey* [1962] Ch 432 at 438 (but compare (1962) 78 LQR 168 (R E M)). See also *Di Palma v Victoria Square Property Co Ltd* [1984] Ch 346 at 366A–B.
4   CCA 1984, s 138(2). Failure to pay legal costs arising from the service of the landlord's claim leaves a claim in debt outstanding, thereby disentitling the tenant (and his mortgagee) from automatic relief (CCA 1984, s 138(6)). See *Longmint Ltd v Akinlade & Gibbons* [1997] CLY 3292.

Other statutory relief against forfeiture

14.154   The tenant has further access to relief even after the landlord has obtained and enforced a court order for possession.

High Court proceedings

14.155   The High Court has a discretionary power to grant relief where the tenant tenders payment of all arrears and costs subsequently to the granting of a possession order, provided application for relief is made within six months of the execution of the judgment for possession.[1] The High Court's discretion is exercisable notwithstanding physical re-entry by the landlord, provided that the landlord has not yet re-let the premises to a stranger[2] or (if he has done so) that the landlord acted 'unreasonably or precipitously' in granting rights in the premises to third parties.[3] Where relief is granted, the tenant simply continues to hold under the old lease.

1   CLPA 1852, s 210. In strict terms this six-month period of grace is available only where the rent itself is at least six months in arrears (see *Billson v Residential Apartments Ltd* [1992] 1 AC 494 at 529C per Nicholls LJ).
2   *Stanhope v Haworth* (1886) 3 TLR 34.
3   *Silverman v AFCO (UK) Ltd* (1988) 56 P & CR 185 at 192 per Slade LJ. See [1992] Conv 343 (J E Martin).

County court proceedings

14.156   A county court, if satisfied that the landlord is entitled to enforce his right of re-entry, must postpone the execution of any possession order for at least four weeks[1] and has discretion to extend this period further.[2] The tenant[3] has an automatic right to relief if, within the period fixed by the court, he pays 'all the rent in arrear'[4] together with costs due.[5] If the tenant fails to pay within the relevant period, the county court possession order becomes enforceable and, if the order remains unreversed, the tenant is normally thereafter barred from relief.[6] Even now, however, the tenant retains one last opportunity for obtaining relief. Within the six months following the landlord's recovery of possession under the court order, the court has a discretion, on application by the tenant, to grant relief on such terms as it thinks fit.[7] In cases of forfeiture through peaceable re-entry by the landlord, the county court also has power to grant relief provided that application for relief is made within six months of the date of the peaceable re-entry.[8]

1   CCA 1984, s 138(3). See *Croydon (Unique) Ltd v Wright* [2001] Ch 318 at 322D.
2   CCA 1984, s 138(4).
3   The statutory reference to 'lessee' includes an under-lessee and any person deriving title under a lessee (CCA 1984, s 140), with the result that a tenant's mortgagee has the same right to relief as does the tenant himself (see also *Grand Junction Co Ltd v Bates* [1954] 2 QB 160 at 168–169).
4   This phrase includes not merely the rent due at the initiation of the claim, but also the amount accruing in respect of the tenant's continuing use and occupation of the premises prior to the making of the court order (*Maryland Estates Ltd v Joseph* [1999] 1 WLR 83 at 91F–H).
5   CCA 1984, s 138(3), (5).
6   CCA 1984, s 138(7).
7   CCA 1984, s 138(9A). This extension of the relief jurisdiction was intended to prevent any recurrence of the calamitous outcome achieved in *Di Palma v Victoria Square Property Co Ltd* [1986] Ch 150, but see the Court of Appeal's stern refusal in *United Dominions Trust Ltd v Shellpoint Trustees Ltd* [1993] 4 All ER 310 to grant relief where no application was made within the six-month period.
8   CCA 1984, s 139(2).

Assured tenancies under the Housing Act 1988

14.157   An extremely important restriction on the availability of relief against forfeiture has emerged in relation to assured tenancies granted under the Housing Act 1988 (effectively most modern private lettings of residential property).[1] In *Artesian Residential Developments Ltd v Beck*[2] the Court of Appeal held that the Housing Act provides a self-contained and definitive code for the termination of such tenancies which leaves no room for parallel proceedings for forfeiture to be brought by the landlord.[3] In the absence of any claim by the landlord to forfeit by re-entry, the entire range of protection afforded the defaulting tenant by the County Courts Act 1984 becomes inapplicable, thereby disabling the county court from offering *any* form of relief against forfeiture to an assured tenant who faces a temporary difficulty in payment of his rent.[4]

1   **[Paras 14.329–14.337]**.
2   [2000] QB 541 at 549A–F per Hirst LJ (Mantell LJ concurring).
3   See HA 1988, ss 5(1), 7 **[para 14.336]**.
4   The county court judge found it 'repugnant, anomalous, and unjust' that one class of tenant should thus be excluded from the right to relief against forfeiture. Pointing out that the

Housing Act ground of recovery requires only two months' rent default, Judge Nicholas Mitchell thought it 'odd indeed' that an otherwise blameless tenant should find himself 'forfeited and expropriated' as a result of 'a temporary difficulty ... beyond his control' ([2000] QB 541 at 546C–E).

Residual equitable discretion

14.158   In cases where the tenant does not have access to statutory protection against the enforcement of the landlord's right of re-entry, the tenant is relegated to seeking the favourable exercise of the courts' general equitable discretion to grant relief against forfeiture.[1] Thus, for instance, the tenant is thrown back upon the equitable discretion where, in cases falling within the jurisdiction of the High Court, a landlord does not proceed by action but simply exercises a right of peaceable re-entry without a court order.[2] Likewise the equitable jurisdiction is vital where less than six months' rent is in arrear.[3] In such cases the court tends to apply the analogy of the statutory jurisdiction in relief[4] and the tenant can usually avert forfeiture if he pays up all arrears and costs within six months or so of the landlord's resumption of possession.[5] Relief may also be granted if the tenant produces realistic evidence of his ability to pay off arrears of rent during a fixed period within the immediately foreseeable future,[6] but is likely to be withheld if the prospects of full recovery of the arrears are uncertain or speculative.[7] As has been recently emphasised, the discretion to grant relief must be 'based on solid principle' and 'not simply ... exercised in a manner that the court thinks fair on the particular facts before it.'[8]

1   This jurisdiction is preserved by Supreme Court Act 1981, s 38(1).
2   *Howard v Fanshawe* [1895] 2 Ch 581 at 588. See also *Lovelock v Margo* [1963] 2 QB 786 at 788; *Abbey National Building Society v Maybeech Ltd* [1985] Ch 190 at 201F–G.
3   *Billson v Residential Apartments Ltd* [1992] 1 AC 494 at 529C–D per Nicholls LJ.
4   See *Howard v Fanshawe* [1895] 2 Ch 581 at 588–589 per Stirling J.
5   *Thatcher v C H Pearce & Sons (Contractors) Ltd* [1968] 1 WLR 748 at 755G–756A; *Di Palma v Victoria Square Property Co Ltd* [1984] Ch 346 at 366C.
6   *Barton Thompson and Co Ltd v Stapling Machines Co Ltd* [1966] Ch 499 at 510 per Pennycuick J.
7   *Inntrepreneur Pub Co (CPC) Ltd v Langton* [2000] 1 EGLR 34 at 38L–39A per Arden J.
8   *Inntrepreneur Pub Co (CPC) Ltd v Langton* [2000] 1 EGLR 34 at 38C per Arden J.

Indulgence towards the defaulting tenant

14.159   The jurisdiction to relieve against forfeiture is exercised with what often appears at first sight to be an over-indulgent forbearance towards the tenant.[1] It is generally possible for a tenant to stave off the effects of forfeiture by paying up arrears of rent at the last possible moment, a past record of continuous arrears[2] or breaches of other covenants[3] being normally regarded as irrelevant to the question whether discretion should be exercised in his favour.[4] Relief is usually granted if, even by belated payment, the landlord can be put in the same position which he occupied before the question of forfeiture arose.[5]

No matter how 'appalling' the record of the tenant, the courts habitually take the view that re-entry is a mere security for payment of the rent and that if the rent is eventually paid, there is 'nothing that the landlord can currently complain of; he can only complain of the past.'[6] Accordingly relief against forfeiture for non-payment tends to be withheld only in the 'most exceptional' circumstances.[7]

1   See *Ladup Ltd v Williams & Glyn's Bank PLC* [1985] 1 WLR 851 at 860E–F per Warner J.
2   See *Newbolt v Bingham* (1895) 72 LT 852 at 854 per Rigby LJ; *Gill v Lewis* [1956] 2 QB 1 at 11, 14; *Re Brompton Securities Ltd (No 2)* [1988] 3 All ER 677 at 680d–h. A 'desultory' approach to rent payment is not fatal to an application for relief (see *Jam Factory Pty Ltd v Sunny Paradise Pty Ltd* [1989] VR 584 at 591).
3   *Gill v Lewis* [1956] 2 QB 1 at 13; *Pioneer Quarries (Sydney) Pty Ltd v Permanent Trustee Co of NSW Ltd* (1970) 2 BPR 9562 at 9575–9576; *Hayes v Gunbola Pty Ltd* (1986) 4 BPR 9247 at 9253. Other forms of breach may influence against the granting of relief only in very exceptional circumstances where these other breaches have caused irremediable damage to the landlord's interests. See e g *Stieper v Deviot Pty Ltd* (1977) 2 BPR 9602 at 9607 (tenant's disregard of landlord's insurance terms caused 'black mark ... notorious in the insurance world'); *Pioneer Quarries*, supra at 9577 (tenant's immoral use of premises).
4   Relief against forfeiture for non-payment of rent may be conditioned upon an undertaking by the tenant to perform other covenants (see *Public Trustee v Westbrook* [1965] 1 WLR 1160 at 1163F; *Jam Factory Pty Ltd v Sunny Paradise Pty Ltd* [1989] VR 584 at 591).
5   See *Pioneer Quarries (Sydney) Pty Ltd v Permanent Trustee Co of NSW Ltd* (1970) 2 BPR 9562 at 9571–9572.
6   *Bhimji v Salih* (Unreported, Court of Appeal, 4 February 1981) per Brightman LJ. See likewise *Hace Corp Pty Ltd v F Hannan (Properties) Pty Ltd* (1995) 7 BPR 14326 at 14329 per McLelland CJ in Eq. It is sometimes said that relief may be refused only if the tenant's attitude to the lease is such that no reasonable landlord could expect the tenant to honour his obligations in the future (see *Tannous v Cipolla Bros Holdings Pty Ltd* (2001) 10 BPR 18563 at [25]–[27]).
7   *Khar and Khar v Delmounty Ltd* (1996) 75 P & CR 232 at 235 per Lord Woolf MR; *Tannous v Cipolla Bros Holdings Pty Ltd* (2001) 10 BPR 18563 at [25]. See e g *Public Trustee v Westbrook* [1965] 1 WLR 1160 at 1163E (relief refused after no rent was paid for 22 years). See also *Gill v Lewis* [1956] 2 QB 1 at 13–14; *Dalla Costa v Beydoun* (1990) 5 BPR 11379 at 11384. It is not necessarily contrary to the public interest to grant discretionary relief to an insolvent tenant, since the benefit of the valuable property in the lease will inure for the creditors and the landlord should have investigated the creditworthiness of the tenant in the first place (see *Hayes v Gunbola Pty Ltd* (1986) 4 BPR 9247 at 9250–9251). See also *Razzaq v Pala* [1997] 1 WLR 1336 at 1345A–C.

RELIEF AGAINST FORFEITURE FOR BREACHES OTHER THAN NON-PAYMENT OF RENT

14.160   Irrespective of whether the covenant breached by the tenant is or is not 'capable of remedy' within section 146 of the Law of Property Act 1925, there is always a possibility that the court may grant the tenant relief against forfeiture in respect of breaches other than those which involve non-payment of rent. This jurisdiction is confirmed in section 146(2) of the 1925 Act, which provides that where a landlord 'is proceeding, by action or otherwise, to enforce [a] right of re-entry or forfeiture', the tenant may apply for relief against forfeiture, and the court has a discretion to grant or withhold relief as it thinks fit. If the court decides to grant relief, it may do so on such terms as to costs, expenses, damages, compensation or injunctions to restrain future breach or otherwise[1] as it thinks appropriate in the circumstances.[2] The court's discretion is sufficiently broad to enable the court to spare a defaulting tenant from forfeiture of the lease (and the consequent loss of his investment), whilst ordering a sale of the leasehold interest and the recoupment from the sale proceeds of amounts owed to the landlord.[3]

1   Where the breach complained of is a continuing breach, relief can properly be granted only on condition that the breach shall cease (see *Wrotham Park Settled Estates v Naylor* (1991) 62 P & CR 233 at 241 per Hoffmann J). See also *McIvor v Donald* [1984] 2 NZLR 487 at 493 (NZ Court of Appeal) (tenant required to submit to programme for remedy of his defaults).
2   LPA 1925, s 146(2). See, in relation to virtually identical provisions elsewhere, *Platt v Ong* [1972] VR 197 at 201–202; *Dickeson v Lipschitz* [1972] 106 ILTR 1 at 3. Relief from forfeiture may be granted in respect of part only of the demised premises when to do so would produce a 'fair and workable result' (*GMS Syndicate Ltd v Gary Elliott Ltd* [1982] Ch 1 at 12F per Nourse J).
3   *Khar and Khar v Delmounty Ltd* (1996) 75 P & CR 232 at 239–240.

Access to discretionary relief for the tenant

14.161   In *Billson v Residential Apartments Ltd*[1] the House of Lords did much to clarify the availability of the jurisdiction to relieve against forfeiture pursuant to section 146(2). In this context everything turns on the definition of the period during which, for the purpose of section 146(2), it can be said that the landlord 'is proceeding, by action or otherwise, to enforce' his right of re-entry or forfeiture. A number of circumstances can be distinguished,[2] the House of Lords indicating in *Billson* that the tenant enjoys access to the court's merciful discretion in the following interlocking cases.

1   [1992] 1 AC 494 **[para 14.121]**.
2   Each of these circumstances is premised on the assumption that a valid section 146 notice has already been served on the tenant.

Period prior to any possession proceedings

14.162   The section 146(2) jurisdiction becomes available to the tenant as soon as his landlord has served a section 146 notice on him.[1] At this point the landlord is obviously still 'proceeding ... to enforce' his right of re-entry or forfeiture and the tenant may invoke section 146(2) for the purpose of elucidating issues raised by the notice or of 'setting in train the machinery by which the dispute ... can be determined by negotiation or by the court.'[2] The tenant's right to apply for relief is not postponed until forfeiture proceedings are actually instituted by the landlord,[3] but neither is the tenant prejudiced by the fact that he does not apply for relief at this stage.[4] In particular, the tenant's access to relief is not lost merely because he fails to invoke section 146(2) immediately after service of the landlord's notice and the landlord meanwhile takes advantage of his right to make peaceable re-entry.[5]

1   *Billson v Residential Apartments Ltd* [1992] 1 AC 494 at 538E–F, 540D per Lord Templeman.

2   *Billson v Residential Apartments Ltd* [1992] 1 AC 494 at 538H–539B per Lord Templeman.
3   *Pakwood Transport Ltd v 15 Beauchamp Place* (1978) 36 P & CR 112 at 117.
4   *Billson v Residential Apartments Ltd* [1992] 1 AC 494 at 540D per Lord Templeman.
5   *Billson v Residential Apartments Ltd* [1992] 1 AC 494 at 541B per Lord Templeman. As
    Lord Templeman confirmed (at 538F–G), it would be absurd to maintain that when the
    landlord has done no more than serve a section 146 notice it is too early for the tenant to
    apply for relief, but that when the landlord's next step is peaceably to recover possession it is
    then too late for the tenant to make the application (see also *Pakwood Transport Ltd v 15
    Beauchamp Place* (1978) 36 P & CR 112 at 117 per Orr LJ).

Unexecuted judgment for possession

14.163   The tenant still enjoys access to discretionary relief under section 146(2) even where the landlord follows up his section 146 notice by issuing
proceedings and obtaining a court judgment for possession against the tenant,
provided that the landlord has not yet executed this judgment by physical
re-entry.[1] The availability of the court's discretion is cut off only if and when
the landlord regains possession in virtue of a 'final, unappealed and fully
executed judgment.'[2]

1   *Quilter v Mapleson* (1882) 9 QBD 672 at 675–678, as construed by Lord Templeman in *Billson
    v Residential Apartments Ltd* [1992] 1 AC 494 at 537B–F. See also *West v Rogers* (1888) 4 TLR
    229; *Egerton v Jones* [1939] 2 KB 702 at 707–709.
2   *Billson v Residential Apartments Ltd* [1992] 1 AC 494 at 543B–C per Lord Oliver of
    Aylmerton.

Peaceable re-entry without court order

14.164   The *Billson* case itself concerned circumstances where the landlord
elected to forfeit a lease, not by initiating court proceedings and obtaining a
court order for possession but instead by exercising his simple right of
peaceable re-entry upon the demised premises. There is at this point a certain
semantic difficulty in the idea that, having actually succeeded in re-entering, the
landlord is in any real sense still 'proceeding … to enforce his right of re-entry'
within the terms of section 146(2). If by this stage, as Parker LJ argued in the
Court of Appeal in *Billson*,[1] the right of entry has *already been enforced*, it
would seem to follow that the tenant is thereafter excluded from any further
right to relief from forfeiture pursuant to the Law of Property Act 1925.[2]

1   [1992] 1 AC 494 at 519H–520A (see also Browne-Wilkinson V-C, less willingly, at 509B–E).
2   This is why the Court of Appeal was so deeply concerned with the question whether there
    remains outside the Act a more general inherent jurisdiction to relieve in equity [**para 14.187**].

14.165   Although some of the previous case law had long been assumed to
indicate the contrary, the House of Lords ruled in *Billson*'s case that relief
against forfeiture remains available to the tenant even *after* the landlord's
exercise of peaceable re-entry without court order.[1] The semantic difficulty in
coming to this conclusion was averted by reading the present continuous form
of the relevant words in section 146(2) as equivalent to the phrase 'where a

lessor *proceeds*, by action or otherwise, to enforce a right of re-entry or forfeiture.'[2] In Lord Templeman's view, Parliament intended that a tenant should have access to relief under section 146(2) 'whether the landlord has asserted his rights by a writ or by re-entering.'[3] Section 146(2) thus offers the possibility of relief irrespective of the mode of forfeiture elected by the landlord, ie whether by the commencement of proceedings for recovery or by the self-help procedure of peaceable physical re-entry.[4]

1   [1992] 1 AC 494 at 540E–F per Lord Templeman, 543C–E Lord Oliver of Aylmerton. The House of Lords overruled previous authority that peaceable re-entry was in this respect 'to be equiparated with an executed judgment' (see e g *Pakwood Transport Ltd v 15 Beauchamp Place* (1978) 36 P & CR 112). The conclusion in *Billson* had already been reached in respect of similar statutory provisions elsewhere (see e g *Re Rexdale Investments Ltd and Gibson* [1967] 1 OR 251 at 259 per Laskin J; *F G Sweeney Ltd v Powerscourt Shopping Centre Ltd* [1984] IR 501 at 504 per Carroll J).
2   [1992] 1 AC 494 at 536C–D, 537A per Lord Templeman. Lord Oliver of Aylmerton thought (at 543B–D) that a landlord on peaceable re-entry can resist a tenant's allegation of trespass only 'by pointing to the forfeiture clause [in the lease] and pleading his entry under it'. So long as he remains, in this way, dependent on the leasehold provision for re-entry, the landlord is still 'proceeding ... to enforce' it. This description does not cease to be apt 'once he has lawfully set foot on the premises.' Browne-Wilkinson V-C would have shared this view in the Court of Appeal if he had not been constrained by contrary precedent ([1992] 1 AC 494 at 509B–D).
3   [1992] 1 AC 494 at 536B.
4   'So construed, section 146(2) enables the tenant to apply for relief whenever and however the landlord claims that the lease has been determined for breach of covenant' ([1992] 1 AC 494 at 537A per Lord Templeman).

14.166   The ruling in *Billson*'s case has certainly clarified the law relating to peaceable re-entry. As the House of Lords was fully aware, the decision also has two other effects. The mere service of a section 146 notice now clearly carries no implication that a tenant must make an immediate and possibly premature application for relief in the fear that delay might otherwise leave him 'at the mercy of an aggressive landlord' who could then, by actual re-entry, snuff out his access to relief without further warning.[1] Furthermore, the *Billson* decision goes some distance towards ensuring that the self-help remedy of forfeiture by actual re-entry is not rendered visibly more advantageous for landlords than the alternative remedy of forfeiture by legal process. In his dissent in the Court of Appeal, Nicholls LJ observed that to allow access to section 146(2) to be foreclosed by actual re-entry would be 'an incitement to all landlords to re-enter forcibly whenever they can do so.' The courts would in effect be 'granting a charter for forcible entry', thereby encouraging the landlord 'to keep away from court and to pounce on the property, in the evening or at the weekend, and change the locks and then sit back secure in the knowledge that forfeiture is complete.'[2] The House of Lords likewise considered it undesirable and anti-social to attach prejudicial consequences to a landlord's recovery of possession by curial process.[3] The Lords preserved the relief jurisdiction of section 146(2) even after actual re-entry by the landlord without court order, precisely in order to prevent what Lord Templeman called the 'farce' in *Billson* where it was alleged that the forcible re-entry into premises for four hours had irrevocably pre-empted all further statutory rights to relief on the part of the tenants.[4]

1   Lord Templeman noted that, following the contrary decision in the Court of Appeal in *Billson*, there had been 'a proliferation of section 146 notices followed by pressure on tenants to surrender on terms favourable to the landlord.' He observed that the development in the law 'pioneered by the landlords in the present case' would help to avert such coercion ([1992] 1 AC 494 at 540C).
2   [1992] 1 AC 494 at 524D–H.
3   **[Para 14.122]**.
4   [1992] 1 AC 494 at 536H. It is tolerably clear that the House of Lords was scandalised by the 'dawn raid' executed by the landlord's agents in *Billson* (see [1992] 1 AC 494 at 540B **[para 14.121]**).

Circumstances where access to discretionary relief is cut off

14.167   In *Billson*'s case the House of Lords indicated that the tenant's access to discretionary relief under section 146 is finally cut off in only two categories of circumstance.

Final, unappealed and fully executed judgment

14.168   Where the landlord has forfeited the lease by initiating a claim for possession and has both recovered judgment *and entered into possession* pursuant to this judgment, the availability of section 146(2) has finally expired.[1] The tenant's access to section 146(2) is now definitively excluded by the fact that the landlord has obtained possession 'under a final and unassailable judgment.'[2] No longer is the landlord 'proceeding, by action or otherwise, to enforce his right of re-entry or forfeiture.' His possession 'rests now, not upon the exercise of a right under the lease, but upon a judgment of the court.'[3] Moreover, and by way of sharp contrast to the rules concerning forfeiture for non-payment of rent, the court has no jurisdiction here to grant relief during some limited period of six months immediately following the landlord's actual re-entry.[4]

1   *Billson v Residential Apartments Ltd* [1992] 1 AC 494 at 538A–B, 540D–E per Lord Templeman. See also *Rogers v Rice* [1892] 2 Ch 170 at 172 per Lord Coleridge CJ. (There remains of course the possibility that the possession judgment may be successfully appealed or set aside on other grounds.)
2   *Billson v Residential Apartments Ltd* [1992] 1 AC 494 at 542G per Lord Oliver of Aylmerton.
3   *Billson v Residential Apartments Ltd* [1992] 1 AC 494 at 543F per Lord Oliver of Aylmerton ('any attempt by the tenant to raise the lease against him is met by the simple plea of the judgment').
4   *Rogers v Rice* [1892] 2 Ch 170 at 172; *Abbey National Building Society v Maybeech Ltd* [1985] Ch 190 at 198E–G.

Unreasonable delay

14.169   In the absence of a fully executed judgment, the landlord remains vulnerable to an application under section 146,[1] but delay by the tenant in seeking relief will increasingly become relevant to the discretionary decision whether to grant relief and must at some point debar the tenant from relief altogether.[2]

1   [1992] 1 AC 494 at 543E per Lord Oliver of Aylmerton. Contrary authority was distinguished
     in the House of Lords as relating only to the effects of re-entry in pursuance of a final court
     judgment for possession ([1992] 1 AC 494 at 539E–H, 542B–D).
2   [1992] 1 AC 494 at 540E–F per Lord Templeman, 543D–E Lord Oliver of Aylmerton.

Guidelines for the exercise of discretion

14.170   Certain guidelines have emerged in the exercise of the court's discretion to grant relief against forfeiture under section 146(2) of the Law of Property Act 1925. The court is expressly directed to have regard to 'the proceedings and conduct of the parties' and 'all the other circumstances' of the case.[1] The relevant criteria are not very different from those applied in the exercise of the general equitable jurisdiction to relieve against forfeiture.[2] Substantial regard is had, for instance, to the gravity of the breach and the disparity between the value of the premises of which forfeiture is claimed and the extent of the damage caused by the breach. Relief is available only if the landlord's position has not been 'irrevocably damaged' by the breach.[3] Relief is clearly inappropriate if the rights of third parties have intervened, as is the case where the landlord has re-let the property after re-entry.[4] Mere inadvertence on the part of the tenant may not, in itself, constitute a ground for relief,[5] nor is it highly persuasive that the tenant committed the breach through thoughtlessness or because he thought the breach unimportant.[6]

1   LPA 1925, s 146(2). Thus, for instance, relief may be denied if the tenant lacks the financial
     means even belatedly to remedy the relevant breach (*Darlington BC v Denmark Chemists*
     [1993] 02 EG 117 (construction of surgery pursuant to covenant)).
2   See *Shiloh Spinners Ltd v Harding* [1973] AC 691 at 723H–724A per Lord Wilberforce.
3   See *W G Clark (Properties) Ltd v Dupre Properties Ltd* [1992] Ch 297 at 309D–E (where
     Deputy Judge Thomas Morison QC would have been prepared to grant relief).
4   See e g *Fuller v Judy Properties Ltd* (1991) 64 P & CR 176 at 184, where Dillon LJ took the
     view that the replacement tenant ranked as a purchaser of a legal estate without notice of the
     defaulting tenant's 'equity to seek relief against forfeiture.' The Court of Appeal was
     nevertheless prepared to grant relief to the ousted tenant, but only on the basis that the terms
     of relief recognised the priority of the new tenant's term. (The Court exercised discretion by
     placing the old tenant in the position of immediate reversioner on the new lease.) See also
     Khar and Khar v Delmounty Ltd (1996) 75 P & CR 232 at 239–240.
5   *Shiloh Spinners Ltd v Harding* [1973] AC 691 at 722E per Lord Wilberforce.
6   See *Eastern Telegraph Co v Dent* [1899] 1 QB 835 at 839; *Pioneer Quarries (Sydney) Pty Ltd v
     Permanent Trustee Co of NSW Ltd* (1970) 2 BPR 9562 at 9577.

14.171   Certain differences nevertheless exist between the statutory and general equitable jurisdictions in relief. In contrast to the court's general equitable jurisdiction, section 146 is apt to cover 'wilful' breaches of covenant.[1] In *Billson v Residential Apartments Ltd*,[2] for example, the tenants were in gross and deliberate breach, but Mummery J, at first instance, would have been prepared to exercise discretion to relieve against forfeiture.[3] This inclination was founded largely on the fact that the tenants had purchased the lease a year earlier for £280,000 and had already expended perhaps as much as £375,000 in the unconsented renovation of the property. There being no evidence that the value of the landlord's reversion had been diminished by this conduct, it seemed inequitable to refuse relief and to force a compulsory return of such a valuable asset to the landlord.[4] Under section 146(2) the degree of deliberateness or wilfulness of the tenant's breach has nowadays been overtaken in importance by the question of proportionality and the possibility of unjust enrichment of a landlord who has suffered no real damage by reason of the breach.[5]

1   See *W G Clark (Properties) Ltd v Dupre Properties Ltd* [1992] Ch 297 at 309C. Compare e g *Hill v Barclay* (1810) 16 Ves 402 at 405–406, 33 ER 1037 at 1038 per Lord Eldon; *Best and Less (Leasing) Pty Ltd v Darin Nominees Pty Ltd* (1994) 6 BPR 13783 at 13789 (relief precluded by tenant's knowing deception).
2   [1992] 1 AC 494 **[para 14.121]**.
3   (1990) 60 P & CR 392 at 411.
4   Compare the stance of Parker LJ in the Court of Appeal, who thought that to grant relief in the circumstances of *Billson* would have been to permit a lessee in 'deliberate and flagrant' breach to 'buy his way out by uncovenanted payment' and to force the lessor 'to live in neighbourhood with a lessee who had no respect whatever for his contractual obligations' ([1992] 1 AC 494 at 523A–B). The effect of the House of Lords' decision in *Billson* was to remit the application for relief to the High Court ([1992] 1 AC 494 at 540G). The application was ultimately rejected on the ground that the circumstances had changed materially and there was no reliable evidence that the tenant would comply with any conditions imposed by the court (*Billson v Residential Apartments Ltd (No 2)* [1993] EGCS 150 per Deputy Judge Thomas Morison QC).
5   See e g *Billson v Residential Apartments Ltd* [1992] 1 AC 494 at 523F–G per Nicholls LJ, 535B per Lord Templeman. See also *Van Haarlam v Kasner* (1992) 64 P & CR 214 at 226–227, where Harman J thought it disproportionate to add the double penalty of forfeiture of a flat (fairly recently purchased by the tenant for £36,000), where the tenant's illegal user of the flat for purposes of espionage had already caused him to be imprisoned for 10 years.

Irremediable breaches

14.172   Relief is usually (but not always[1]) granted where the tenant's breach has been remedied.[2] Conversely, it is clear that the court will rarely grant relief where the tenant's breach is not 'capable of remedy' in terms of section 146.[3] Although the court is certainly possessed of power to grant relief even in relation to an irremediable breach,[4] the circumstances which made the breach incapable of remedy usually also provide good grounds for refusing relief against forfeiture.[5] Save in exceptional cases,[6] it is the 'established practice' of the court not to grant relief where the breach involves immoral user.[7]

1   See e g *Clifford v Johnson's Personal Representatives* (1979) 251 EG 571 at 573, where the Court of Appeal approved a holding that 'a single man ... unemployed for two years [with] no prospect of work in his field in the area ... does not come within any reasonable ground for relief from forfeiture.' It was also a relevant factor that the granting of relief would have meant that the landlord was saddled with a protected tenant in respect of part of the premises.
2   *Earl Bathurst v Fine* [1974] 1 WLR 905 at 908A.
3   See e g *Dunraven Securities Ltd v Holloway* (1982) 264 EG 709 at 711 **[para 14.148]**.
4   *Scala House and District Property Co Ltd v Forbes* [1974] QB 575 at 589D; *McIvor v Donald* [1984] 2 NZLR 487 at 491. See e g *Fuller v Judy Properties Ltd* (1991) 64 P & CR 176 at 184–186 **[para 14.131]**; *Van Haarlam v Kasner* (1992) 64 P & CR 214 at 226–227 **[para 14.148]**.
5   See *Ali v Booth* (1966) 110 Sol Jo 708 at 709.
6   See e g *Central Estates (Belgravia) Ltd v Woolgar (No 2)* [1972] 1 WLR 1048 at 1053D–1054B.
7   *GMS Syndicate Ltd v Gary Elliott Ltd* [1982] Ch 1 at 10D–E. The same approach may apply to instances of illegal user (see *Jam Factory Pty Ltd v Sunny Paradise Pty Ltd* [1989] VR 584 at 591).

Trivial breaches

14.173   The tenor of the case law suggests that, whereas the wilful transgressor must commonly accept the penalty of flagrant wrongdoing,[1] the transgressor whose breach is unintentional or relatively minor may confidently expect relief against forfeiture.[2] Thus, for example, relief may be granted where a tenant in violation of his covenant has kept a pet on the demised premises, so long as the animal has not interfered with the reasonable enjoyment of other tenants or unduly frustrated the expectations of those other tenants.[3] It would be 'absurd' if a landlord could terminate a tenancy if the tenant's breach comprises some purely trivial conduct such as the keeping of a single goldfish in a bowl or the feeding of a few crumbs of bread to one sparrow or the shaking of a duster out of the window or the placing of paper in a corridor.[4]

1   See also *Shiloh Spinners Ltd v Harding* [1973] AC 691 at 725E–F per Lord Wilberforce.
2   *Re Vanek and Bomza* (1977) 74 DLR (3d) 175 at 180.
3   *Re London Housing Authority and Coulson* (1978) 82 DLR (3d) 754 at 756–758 (two cats); *Re Kay and Parkway Forest Developments* (1982) 133 DLR (3d) 389 at 392–393 (dog).
4   *Re Miller and Zuchek* (1982) 132 DLR (3d) 142 at 149. Such actions would constitute a breach of the covenants commonly found in modern residential leases for terms even as long as 99 or 125 years.

Waiver of breach

14.174   The landlord's exercise of a right of re-entry for breach of the tenant's covenants is subject to the operation of the doctrine of waiver.[1]

1   The doctrine of waiver is based on 'a simple instinct of fairness' (*Oliver Ashworth (Holdings) Ltd v Ballard (Kent) Ltd* [2000] Ch 12 at 27D per Robert Walker LJ).

Principle of waiver of forfeiture

14.175   Even if a lease provides that the tenant's term of years shall be void in the event of a breach of covenant, it is clear that the lease does not ipso facto become void. The tenant is not permitted to take advantage of his own wrong[1] and the landlord retains the right to elect whether to treat the lease as forfeited or as remaining in force.[2] This election need not be made immediately,[3] but once made it cannot be retracted.[4] It is against this background that waiver of forfeiture operates. A landlord is precluded from seeking re-entry (though not in general from recovering damages or arrears[5]) if with knowledge of the tenant's default he does some act which unequivocally indicates his intention to regard the lease as subsisting.[6] Waiver, where it does occur, may be either express or implied; and the legal effect of an act relied on as constituting waiver is to be considered objectively without regard to the motive or intention of the landlord or the actual understanding or belief of the tenant.[7]

1   *Owendale Pty Ltd v Anthony* (1967) 117 CLR 539 at 589.
2   *Expert Clothing Service & Sales Ltd v Hillgate House Ltd* [1986] Ch 340 at 359C per Slade LJ; *Billson v Residential Apartments Ltd* [1992] 1 AC 494 at 534D per Lord Templeman.

3   *Owendale Pty Ltd v Anthony* (1967) 117 CLR 539 at 557–558.
4   *Jones v Carter* (1846) 15 M & W 718 at 726, 153 ER 1040 at 1043 per Parke B. See also *Scarf v Jardine* (1882) 7 App Cas 345 at 360; *Expert Clothing Service & Sales Ltd v Hillgate House Ltd* [1986] Ch 340 at 359C; *Billson v Residential Apartments Ltd* [1992] 1 AC 494 at 534E–F; *GS Fashions Ltd v B & Q Plc* [1995] 1 WLR 1088 at 1093G–1094D.
5   *Stephens v Junior Army and Navy Stores Ltd* [1914] 2 Ch 516 at 523; *Oliver Ashworth (Holdings) Ltd v Ballard (Kent) Ltd* [2000] Ch 12 at 28H–29A.
6   *Matthews v Smallwood* [1910] 1 Ch 777 at 786; *Kammins Ballrooms Co v Zenith Investments* [1971] AC 850 at 883A–B per Lord Diplock; *Oliver Ashworth (Holdings) Ltd v Ballard (Kent) Ltd* [2000] Ch 12 at 28F per Robert Walker LJ.
7   *Central Estates (Belgravia) Ltd v Woolgar (No 2)* [1972] 1 WLR 1048 at 1054D. The doctrine of waiver is therefore 'quite capable in some instances of operating harshly, most particularly where there has been an acceptance of rent by the landlord' (*Expert Clothing Service & Sales Ltd v Hillgate House Ltd* [1986] Ch 340 at 360D per Slade LJ).

Requirements of knowledge and communication

14.176   The operation of waiver requires on the part of the landlord both knowledge of the breach and an active recognition of the continuing existence of the lease. One without the other is ineffective to constitute a waiver of the right to forfeit.[1] The landlord must, at the date of the alleged waiver, have knowledge of the 'basic facts' constituting the tenant's breach[2] (and also of his legal right to forfeit the lease[3]), although his knowledge need not extend to the precise details of the breach concerned.[4] In *Van Haarlam v Kasner*[5] a landlord was held to have waived his right of forfeiture by continuing to demand and accept rent in the face of wide newspaper coverage of the tenant's illegal activities in breach of his leasehold covenants.[6] An operative waiver must unequivocally recognise the continued existence of the lease and this act of recognition must be communicated to the tenant.[7]

1   *Perry v Davis* (1858) 3 CB (NS) 769 at 777, 140 ER 945 at 948.
2   *David Blackstone Ltd v Burnetts (West End) Ltd* [1973] 1 WLR 1487 at 1501E.
3   See *HB Property Developments Ltd v Secretary of State for the Environment* (1999) 78 P & CR 108 at 112–113, 117–118.
4   *Cornillie v Saha and Bradford & Bingley Building Society* (1996) 72 P & CR 147 at 159 (no knowledge of identities of unlawful subtenants). The knowledge required for the purpose of implied waiver is sufficiently present where the landlord or any of his agents or employees is aware of the tenant's breach of covenant (see eg *Metropolitan Properties Co Ltd v Cordery* (1980) 39 P & CR 10 at 16–17, where the knowledge acquired by the landlord's porters in a block of flats was attributed to the landlord). See also *Chrisdell Ltd v Johnson* (1987) 54 P & CR 257 at 264–265; [1988] Conv 139 (J E M).
5   (1992) 64 P & CR 214 at 226.
6   Compare *Official Custodian for Charities v Parway Estates Developments Ltd* [1985] Ch 151 at 162F–163A (disclosure of tenant's breach in the *London Gazette* held not to fix landlord with deemed knowledge).
7   *Cornillie v Saha and Bradford & Bingley Building Society* (1996) 72 P & CR 147 at 157 per Aldous LJ. Thus, for example, it is not enough that a demand for rent is addressed to the tenant's wife (*Trustees of Henry Smith's Charity v Willson* [1983] QB 316 at 332F–333A). See, however, *Oliver Ashworth (Holdings) Ltd v Ballard (Kent) Ltd* [2000] Ch 12 at 30F–G.

Implied waiver by demand for or acceptance of rent

14.177　Although an implied waiver of forfeiture can arise in many kinds of circumstance, it seems that conduct in relation to rent may 'fall into a special category.'[1] An inference of waiver is almost inevitable where a landlord, with actual or constructive knowledge that a breach has occurred, continues unambiguously to demand[2] or to accept[3] any rent[4] which falls due after the breach.[5] In order to spare tenants the 'dilemma of uncertainty' as to their status as tenant or trespasser, there has been 'some attenuation ... in the requirement for elective waiver to be a matter of informed choice.'[6] Thus the mere fact that rent is accepted 'without prejudice' to the right to forfeit[7] or is accepted by reason of clerical error[8] cannot prevent the acceptance from operating as a waiver, thereby assuring the tenant of the continuing force of his lease.[9] Moreover, the act of distraining for rent waives any right to forfeit the lease on the ground of rent arrears accruing before the date of the distress.[10]

1　*Expert Clothing Service & Sales Ltd v Hillgate House Ltd* [1986] Ch 340 at 360D–E per Slade LJ. See also *Oliver Ashworth (Holdings) Ltd v Ballard (Kent) Ltd* [2000] Ch 12 at 30D–G per Robert Walker LJ.

2　*Segal Securities Ltd v Thoseby* [1963] 1 QB 887 at 899; *David Blackstone Ltd v Burnetts (West End) Ltd* [1973] 1 WLR 1487 at 1498E–F; *Welch v Birrane* (1975) 29 P & CR 102 at 112; *Expert Clothing Service & Sales Ltd v Hillgate House Ltd* [1986] Ch 340 at 359C–F.

3　*Croft v Lumley* (1858) 6 HLCas 672 at 713, 10 ER 1459 at 1475; *Davenport v The Queen* (1877) 3 App Cas 115 at 131–132; *Oak Property Co Ltd v Chapman* [1947] KB 886 at 898; *Expert Clothing Service & Sales Ltd v Hillgate House Ltd* [1986] Ch 340 at 359C–D; *Larking v Great Western (Nepean) Gravel Ltd* (1940) 64 CLR 221 at 240; *Owendale Pty Ltd v Anthony* (1967) 117 CLR 539 at 557–558, 588; *Baxton v Kara* [1982] 1 NSWLR 604 at 608. Mere delivery of a cheque to the landlord's office does not import acceptance by the landlord (see *Wong v St Martins Property (Aust) Pty Ltd* (1990) 5 BPR 11334 at 11337).

4　There is no waiver of forfeiture if money is 'received in respect of the tenant's use of the land but not in its quality as rent' (ie as 'mesne profits' paid by a former tenant) (*Larking v Great Western (Nepean) Gravel Ltd* (1940) 64 CLR 221 at 240). See also *Yorkshire Metropolitan Properties Ltd v Co-operative Retail Services Ltd* [1997] EGCS 57 (no waiver by reason of landlord's demand for payment of insurance premium).

5　See *Dendy v Nicholls* (1858) 4 CB (NS) 376 at 385, 140 ER 1130 at 1134; *Oliver Ashworth (Holdings) Ltd v Ballard (Kent) Ltd* [2000] Ch 12 at 29F–30B; *Wong v St Martins Property (Aust) Pty Ltd* (1990) 5 BPR 11334 at 11337. There is no waiver of forfeiture by acceptance of rent accrued due *before* the date of breach (*Re a Debtor (No 13A-10-1995)* [1995] 1 WLR 1127 at 1132E–H; *Endeavour Lodge Motel Ltd v Langford* [1998] 2 NZLR 121 at 127–128).

6　See *Oliver Ashworth (Holdings) Ltd v Ballard (Kent) Ltd* [2000] Ch 12 at 30E–F per Robert Walker LJ.

7　*Segal Securities Ltd v Thoseby* [1963] 1 QB 887 at 897–898; *Central Estates (Belgravia) Ltd v Woolgar (No 2)* [1972] 1 WLR 1048 at 1054E; *Expert Clothing Service & Sales Ltd v Hillgate House Ltd* [1986] Ch 340 at 359D–E.

8　*Central Estates (Belgravia) Ltd v Woolgar (No 2)* [1972] 1 WLR 1048 at 1052F–G, 1055D–F.

9　See, however, *Greenwich LBC v Discreet Selling Estates Ltd* (1990) 61 P & CR 405 at 412 per Staughton LJ.

10　*Doe d Flower v Peck* (1830) 1 B & Ad 428 at 437, 109 ER 847 at 850; *Kirkland v Briancourt* (1890) 6 TLR 441. A request by a landlord that rent arrears (or even current payments for use and occupation) should be deducted at source from statutory benefit payments made to the occupier has been held not to operate as a waiver of a demand for possession (*Northern Ireland Housing Executive v Duffin* [1985] NI 210 at 214B).

Implied waiver on other grounds

14.178 Waiver may also occur, although somewhat less automatically, in other categories of case. In matters not connected directly with the payment of rent, the courts seem to be more 'free to look at *all* the circumstances of the case'[1] in considering whether a landlord's actions are consistent with his avoiding the lease. Waiver may arise where the landlord, with knowledge of a breach giving him a right of re-entry, engages in action so unequivocal as to be consistent only with the continued existence of the landlord–tenant relationship.[2] Such conduct includes, for instance, an agreement by the landlord to grant the tenant a new lease commencing on the normal determination of an existing letting[3] or, in some circumstances, the proffering of a mere negotiating document which contemplates continued contractual relations.[4]

1   *Expert Clothing Service & Sales Ltd v Hillgate House Ltd* [1986] Ch 340 at 360E–F.
2   See e g *Billson v Residential Apartments Ltd* [1992] 1 AC 494 at 508C–D, where Browne-Wilkinson V-C indicated that excessive delay in following up an unproductive section 146 notice by re-entry could lead to an allegation of waiver.
3   See e g *Ward v Day* (1864) 5 B & S 359 at 363, 122 ER 865 at 866.
4   *Expert Clothing Service & Sales Ltd v Hillgate House Ltd* [1986] Ch 340 at 360F–G.

Temporal scope of the waiver

14.179 In the case of a 'once and for all' breach,[1] any proven waiver of forfeiture precludes the landlord from claiming to forfeit the lease on the ground of the particular breach which has occurred,[2] but does not operate as a general waiver in relation to similar breaches in the future.[3] A waiver in respect of a continuing breach of covenant can be withdrawn by the landlord at any time, thereby revitalising his right to claim forfeiture of the lease.[4] In the absence of some plea based upon estoppel, the tenant is not entitled to argue that one prolonged period of waiver gives him any right or expectation that the waiver of a continuing breach should continue indefinitely.[5]

1   Breach of a covenant to insure premises is not a continuing breach (see *Farimani v Gates* (1984) 271 EG 887 at 889; but compare *Larking v Great Western (Nepean) Gravel Ltd* (1940) 64 CLR 221 at 236 per Dixon J).
2   *Farimani v Gates* (1984) 271 EG 887 at 889.
3   LPA 1925, s 148(1). See e g *Billson v Residential Apartments Ltd* [1992] 1 AC 494 at 507A–D per Browne-Wilkinson V-C.
4   *Doe d Ambler v Woodbridge* (1829) 9 B & C 376 at 377–378, 109 ER 140; *Greenwich LBC v Discreet Selling Estates Ltd* (1990) 61 P & CR 405 at 412–413. There is no need to serve a further section 146 notice (*Farimani v Gates* (1984) 271 EG 887 at 888). A landlord's consent to assignment by a tenant who is guilty of a continuing breach does not operate as a waiver (*Straudley Investments Ltd v Mount Eden Land Ltd* [1997] EGCS 175).
5   *Cooper v Henderson* (1982) 263 EG 592 at 594.

EFFECT OF FORFEITURE

14.180 The exercise of the landlord's right of re-entry has a number of important consequences (both actual and potential) for the tenant and for other persons.

Effect on tenant

14.181   The mere fact that a lease or tenancy has become liable to forfeiture does not entitle the landlord to allege trespass by the tenant if the latter remains in occupation. The landlord must convert his right to possession into actual possession by means of re-entry,[1] but once re-entry has occurred the tenant becomes a trespasser.[2] Subject to statutory controls on the recovery of possession[3] and on the use or threat of violence for the purpose of securing entry into the premises,[4] the landlord may now use such force as is reasonably necessary to expel his former tenant, provided that the latter has been requested to leave and has been given a reasonable opportunity of doing so.[5]

1   *Butcher v Butcher* (1827) 7 B & C 399 at 402, 108 ER 772 at 773; *Jones v Chapman* (1849) 2 Exch 803 at 821, 154 ER 717 at 724; *Lows v Telford* (1876) 1 App Cas 414 at 426; *Hegan v Carolan* [1916] 2 IR 27 at 30–31; *Haniotis v Dimitriou* [1983] 1 VR 498 at 500.
2   **[Para 14.102]**. See also *Billson v Residential Apartments Ltd* [1992] 1 AC 494 at 536G–H per Lord Templeman.
3   PEA 1977, ss 1(2), 2–3 **[paras 14.109, 14.111]**. See *Haniff v Robinson* [1993] QB 419 at 428D–E.
4   Criminal Law Act 1977, s 6(1) **[para 14.120]**.
5   *Polkinghorn v Wright* (1845) 8 QB 197 at 206–207, 115 ER 849 at 853; *Haniotis v Dimitriou* [1983] 1 VR 498 at 500. The landlord's right to eject the former tenant is now effectively confined to the context of peaceable re-entry upon non-residential premises **[para 14.119]**.

14.182   Where a tenancy is terminated without sufficient warning to enable the tenant to remove his goods from the premises prior to termination, the tenant has at common law a right of access to the premises for a reasonable time following the termination for the purpose of removing these goods.[1] The landlord has, at common law, no possessory lien over the former tenant's remaining goods for the purpose of securing arrears of rent or any other obligation of the tenant.[2] The former tenant is not entitled to continue to store his goods on the premises and the landlord, on re-entering, may give him notice requiring the removal of these chattels within a reasonable time.[3] If this notice is ignored, the landlord may remove the goods from the premises without incurring any liability in trespass. This is so at least if the goods are carried 'to a convenient distance' and deposited in a 'proper and convenient place' for the use of the tenant[4] and if the landlord does no unnecessary damage.[5] A right of distress damage feasant may be asserted by the landlord where the presence of the tenant's belongings on the premises causes actual damage, although it is possible that the costs of removal may amount to actual damage for this purpose.[6] This latter right is, however, subject to the normal limitation that the remedy of distress may not be claimed in respect of things in actual use by their owner.[7]

1   See *Co Litt*, s 69; *Stodden v Harvey* (1608) Cro Jac 204, 79 ER 178; *Doe v M'Kaeg* (1830) 10 B & C 721 at 723–724; 109 ER 618 at 619; *Martin v King* (1996) 7 BPR 14681 at 14682. The former tenant may require that the landlord deliver his goods to the periphery of the premises (see *Martin v King*, supra at 14683).
2   *Martin v King* (1996) 7 BPR 14681 at 14683 per McLelland CJ in Eq. Forfeiture of the tenancy terminates the landlord's right to distrain for rent **[para 14.196]**.
3   *Haniotis v Dimitriou* [1983] 1 VR 498 at 501–502.

4   *Houghton v Butler* (1791) 4 Term Rep 364 at 365–366, 100 ER 1066 at 1067. See also *Rea v Sheward* (1837) 2 M & W 424 at 426, 150 ER 823 at 824.

5   *Neville v Cooper* (1834) 2 Cr & M 329 at 331, 149 ER 786 at 787. In *Haniotis v Dimitriou* [1983] 1 VR 498 at 502, Brooking J left for future litigation the hypothetical case 'of the Stradivarius put out on to the footpath', suggesting that relevant arguments at that stage would include the contention that such a small object was not 'encumbering' the landlord's premises, or 'doing damage' to him, or that the law will not permit the remedy of self-help where the resulting loss to the tenant is wholly disproportionate to the injury averted by the landlord.

6   *Jamieson's Tow & Salvage Ltd v Murray* [1984] 2 NZLR 144 at 149, but compare *R v Howson* (1966) 55 DLR (2d) 582 at 597.

7   *Jamieson's Tow & Salvage Ltd v Murray* [1984] 2 NZLR 144 at 150 (illegally parked car towed away with driver still sitting resolutely at steering wheel).

Effect on subtenant

14.183   It is trite law that the forfeiture of a head lease necessarily and automatically destroys any sublease created out of the head lease[1] – a principle which flows logically from the derivative nature of the sublease.[2] It is also clear, however, that a subtenant has an independent right under section 146(4) of the Law of Property Act 1925 to seek relief against forfeiture where the landlord is 'proceeding by action or otherwise.'[3] Under this subsection the court has a broad discretion to grant relief on such terms as it thinks fit.[4] In particular the court may invest the subtenant with an entirely new estate[5] in the demised premises on such terms as are deemed appropriate,[6] subject to the proviso that the subtenant may not require a lease to be granted to him for any longer term than he had under his original sublease.[7] Moreover, the court has discretion to grant relief in respect of part only of the premises comprised in the head lease. Thus, absent any express restriction of the landlord's right to re-enter on part only of these premises, the court may grant relief to a tenant in respect of one portion of the premises whilst refusing relief to a subtenant who has been in possession of another part of the premises,[8] or vice versa.

1   *Great Western Railway Co v Smith* (1876) 2 Ch D 235 at 253; *GMS Syndicate Ltd v Gary Elliott Ltd* [1982] Ch 1 at 8C; *Rhodes v Allied Dunbar Pension Services Ltd* [1989] 1 WLR 800 at 809C per Nicholls LJ; *Toronto Harbour Commissioners v THC Parking Inc* (1999) 175 DLR (4th) 536 at 546–547. See generally Stephen Tromans, [1986] Conv 187.

2   See *PW & Co v Milton Gate Investments Ltd* [2004] Ch 142 at [73], [136] per Neuberger J **[para 14.306]**.

3   Section 146(4) relates to forfeiture for breach of *any* covenant (whether or not for non-payment of rent). The right to seek relief pursuant to section 146(4) extends even to an equitable assignee of the sublease (see *High Street Investments Ltd v Bellshore Property Investments Ltd* (1997) 73 P & CR 143 at 147). Section 146(5) gives standing to any person 'deriving title under' a lessee or sublessee, a phrase which (in a similar context) has been understood as comprising 'horizontal' as well as 'vertical' transfers in respect of a leasehold estate (*Croydon (Unique) Ltd v Wright* [2001] Ch 318 at 327F per Sir Christopher Staughton).

4   In *Chatham Empire Theatre (1955) Ltd v Ultrans* [1961] 1 WLR 817 at 820, for instance, relief was granted on condition that the subtenant paid up that proportion of the total arrears of rent which corresponded with his part of the premises comprised within the head lease.

5   The new lease is 'a quite distinct piece of property from the old' (*Cadogan v Dimovic* [1984] 1 WLR 609 at 613H). See also *Official Custodian for Charities v Mackey* [1985] Ch 168 at 183E. In effect the head lessor may be forced into privity of contract with the former

sublessee, but the coercion of such a legal relationship may itself be inequitable if it is unreasonable to saddle the head lessor with a lessee whom he would never willingly have contracted to accept (see *O'Connor v J G Mooney & Co Ltd* [1982] ILRM 373 at 383).

6   LPA 1925, s 146(4).
7   The term of the original sublease is taken to include any extension imposed pursuant to any relevant statutory code (eg Part II of the Landlord and Tenant Act 1954). See *Cadogan v Dimovic* [1984] 1 WLR 609 at 614D–E.
8   *GMS Syndicate Ltd v Gary Elliott Ltd* [1982] Ch 1 at 12E–F, following *Dumpor's Case* (1603) 4 Co Rep 119b, 76 ER 1110. See [1981] Conv 381 (R Griffith).

14.184   The subtenant has an alternative means of obtaining relief from forfeiture in cases where the landlord has proceeded against the head tenant in the county court for non-payment of rent. The subtenant can apply for relief within six months of the landlord's recovery of possession and the court has discretion to grant relief on such terms (eg as to payment of arrears and future leasehold arrangements) as the court thinks fit.[1] Where, however, the landlord has proceeded in the High Court for forfeiture for non-payment of rent, the subtenant, whilst those proceedings are still afoot, can apply to the High Court for relief.[2]

1   CCA 1984, s 138(9C).
2   Supreme Court Act 1981, s 38(1).

Effect on mortgagee

14.185   Forfeiture has a potentially devastating effect on any security enjoyed by a third party who has taken a mortgage (or charge) over the tenant's leasehold estate. For as long as the tenant's estate in the land remains forfeited, the mortgagee is disabled from enforcing his security over the land[1] and (if relief against forfeiture is not granted) the security is rendered valueless. It is therefore important that the mortgagee should be able to obtain relief in respect of the estate to which his security relates.

1   See *Croydon (Unique) Ltd v Wright* [2001] Ch 318 at 325.

Access to statutory relief

14.186   In cases of non-payment of rent by the tenant, a legal mortgagee may seek relief under either section 146(4) of the Law of Property Act 1925[1] or the County Courts Act 1984[2] or the Supreme Court Act 1981.[3] A mortgagee who fails to apply in time is thereafter statutorily barred both in the High Court and in the county court.[4] Where the tenant's breach has taken some form other than non-payment of rent, the right of the legal mortgagee to seek relief is confined to section 146(4) of the Law of Property Act 1925.[5]

1   See *Official Custodian for Charities v Mackey* [1985] Ch 168 at 183B–C; [1985] Conv 50. Relief may also be sought under the Common Law Procedure Act 1852 [**para 14.153**].
2   The legal mortgagee or chargee has access to discretionary relief for a period of up to six months following the landlord's recovery of possession (CCA 1984, ss 138(9C), 140 [**para 14.156**]).

3   Supreme Court Act 1981, s 38(1).
4   See *United Dominions Trust Ltd v Shellpoint Trustees Ltd* [1993] 4 All ER 310 at 319f–g.
5   See *Abbey National Building Society v Maybeech Ltd* [1985] Ch 190 at 198C. The legal
     mortgagee and legal chargee qualify as a persons 'deriving title under a lessee' (LPA 1925,
     s 146(5)(b) [**para 14.131**]).

Inherent equitable jurisdiction to give relief

14.187   A standard difficulty faced by the mortgagee of a leasehold estate is
lack of knowledge that the landlord is proceeding to forfeit the lease which
comprises his security. If the mortgagee is unaware that there has been
peaceable re-entry or that court proceedings have been instituted, he obviously
cannot apply to the court for relief.[1] It has therefore been vital to ascertain
whether, quite apart from statute, the High Court still retains an inherent
equitable jurisdiction to grant relief to the legal mortgagee.[2] Desite suggestions
that this equitable jurisdiction has been extinguished by statutory intervention,[3]
it now seems widely accepted that the High Court's inherent jurisdiction has
survived the enactment of various forms of statutory relief against forfeiture.[4]

1   In the particulars of claim the landlord must state the name and address of any mortgagee
     who, to his knowledge, is entitled to claim relief against forfeiture as an underlessee. The
     mortgagee must also file a copy of the particulars of claim for service on that mortgagee
     (*CPR Part 55 Practice Direction*, para 2.4). Failure to comply with these obligations renders
     the landlord's possession order liable to be set aside (see *Rexhaven Ltd v Nurse* (1995) 28 HLR
     241 at 255–256).
2   If no such jurisdiction exists, there is a danger that a lease containing a forfeiture clause may
     no longer be viewed as an acceptable security for a mortgagee (see (1986) 136 NLJ 254).
3   See e g *Smith v Metropolitan City Properties Ltd* (1986) 277 EG 753 at 754 per Walton J;
     Billson v Residential Apartments Ltd [1992] 1 AC 494 at 516D–E per Browne-Wilkinson V-C,
     522G per Parker LJ. In *Billson's* case the House of Lords found it strictly unnecessary to
     resolve the issue. See [1991] Conv 380 (S Goulding); P F Smith, [1992] Conv 32.
4   See *Abbey National Building Society v Maybeech Ltd* [1985] Ch 190 at 204C per Nicholls J
     ([1985] Conv 50); *Billson v Residential Apartments Ltd* [1992] 1 AC 494 at 528F–529A,
     530A–B per Nicholls LJ; *W G Clark (Properties) Ltd v Dupre Properties Ltd* [1992] Ch 297 at
     309C–G; *Croydon (Unique) Ltd v Wright* [2001] Ch 318 at 325E–F; *Esther Investments Pty Ltd
     v Cherrywood Park Pty Ltd* [1986] WAR 279 at 288 per Burt CJ, 297 per Wallace J, 306 per
     Brinsden J.

Relief against forfeiture for equitable chargee

14.188   More difficult are questions as to the rights to relief enjoyed by an
equitable chargee. It is clear that an equitable chargee of a leasehold estate
cannot claim relief against forfeiture under section 146(4) of the Law of
Property Act 1925[1] and cannot claim any direct relief under the High Court's
inherent jurisdiction.[2] The equitable chargee nevertheless has access to an
indirect form of relief in that the equitable chargor (ie the tenant) has an
implied obligation to take reasonable steps to preserve the chargee's security.
Thus, if a lease has been forfeited for non-payment of rent and the tenant has
failed to seek relief in his own right, the equitable chargee may join the tenant
as a defendant in the forfeiture proceedings and thereby claim relief in the

tenant's shoes.[3] Such relief may be available on terms that the chargee pays all arrears and the costs of re-entry.[4] There is also an even simpler avenue to relief for the equitable chargee. Under the County Courts Act 1984 the equitable chargee would seem to be entitled to seek relief during the six months following the landlord's re-entry as 'a person with an interest under a lease of land derived (whether immediately or otherwise) from the lessee's interest therein.'[5]

1   *Bland v Ingrams Estates Ltd* [2001] Ch 767 at [14] per Nourse LJ, [60] per Chadwick LJ.
2   *Bland v Ingrams Estates Ltd* [2001] Ch 767 at [31] per Nourse LJ, [69] per Chadwick LJ (disapproving *Ladup Ltd v Williams & Glyn's Bank PLC* [1985] 1 WLR 851 at 860H–861A per Warner J).
3   *Bland v Ingrams Estates Ltd* [2001] Ch 767 at [34]–[35] per Nourse LJ, [69]–[73] per Chadwick LJ.
4   *Bland v Ingrams Estates Ltd* [2001] Ch 767 at [74] per Chadwick LJ.
5   CCA 1984, ss 138(9A), (9C), 139(2)–(3). See *Bland v Ingrams Estates Ltd* [2001] Ch 767 at [64], [69] per Chadwick LJ, [83] per Hale LJ. See e g *Croydon (Unique) Ltd v Wright* [2001] Ch 318 at 331G–H, where the Court of Appeal was prepared to allow the holder of a charging order made against a tenant to apply for relief out of time. The court had jurisdiction, not simply to grant the chargee a new lease, but more significantly to restore the original lease for the purpose of enabling the chargee to apply for an order for sale and at least partial recoupment of his debt ([2001] Ch 318 at 329H–330A).

Effect on squatter

14.189   A squatter who has acquired a title by adverse possession against a leaseholder has no sufficient interest in the lease to enable him to apply for relief against its forfeiture.[1]

1   *Tickner v Buzzacott* [1965] Ch 426 at 434.

PROPOSALS FOR REFORM

14.190   The Law Commission has long expressed the view that the existing law of forfeiture is 'unnecessarily complicated, is no longer coherent and may give rise to injustice.'[1] In particular the Commission has pointed to the anomalous way in which the law at present incorporates two almost entirely separate regimes, one relating to forfeiture for non-payment of rent and the other relating to all other cases.[2] Accordingly the Commission has provisionally recommended the statutory introduction of a new 'termination order' scheme for dealing with all cases of tenant default irrespective of the nature of the default.[3] The scheme is intended to apply to all leases and tenancies (other than those to be covered by the new 'occupation agreements' proposed by the Commission in the residential sector[4]). The Commission expects to produce a final report and draft Bill in 2005.[5]

1   *Codification of the Law of Landlord and Tenant: Forfeiture of Tenancies* (Law Com No 142, March 1985), para 1.3. See also *Inntrepreneur Pub Co (CPC) Ltd v Langton* [2000] 1 EGLR 34 at 39C per Arden J.
2   Law Com No 142 (1985), para 3.11.

3   Law Commission, *Termination of Tenancies for Tenant Default* (Law Com CP No 174, January 2004). The current proposals derive in large measure from the recommendations contained in Law Com No 142 (1985).
4   **[Paras 14.349–14.353]**. The 'termination order' scheme would therefore cover commercial tenancies and long residential tenancies granted for a term of 21 years or more.
5   *Law Commission Annual Report 2003/04* (Law Com No 288, HC 642, June 2004), para 7.3.

Process of termination

14.191   Under the Law Commission's proposed scheme, all relevant tenancies would remain in full force until the court made a 'termination order' fixing the date on which the tenancy should end.[1] The landlord could seek a termination order on the ground of 'tenant default', a term sufficiently wide to catch all breaches of express or implied leasehold covenant and the bankruptcy of the tenant.[2] Termination would no longer depend on the inclusion of an express forfeiture clause in the covenants of a lease,[3] but the landlord would, in all cases, be required to serve on the tenant a 'pre-action notice' in prescribed form giving relevant details of the default and indicating the action proposed to be taken in response to the alleged default.[4] Following service of this notice, the tenant would be entitled to refer the notice to the court for the exercise of its 'case management powers'.[5] In the event that the court decided that an order was justified, it would have discretion either to make an 'absolute termination order' ending the tenancy with effect from a stated date or to make a 'remedial order' requiring specified remedial action (including payment of rent arrears) within a certain time scale.[6] Owners of derivative interests (eg subtenants and mortgagees) would be entitled to apply to the court for relief.[7]

1   Law Com CP No 174 (2004), para 1.19.
2   Law Com CP No 174 (2004), paras 4.5–4.12.
3   Law Com CP No 174 (2004), para 4.4.
4   Law Com CP No 174 (2004), paras 5.13–5.15.
5   Law Com CP No 174 (2004), para 5.16.
6   Law Com CP No 174 (2004), paras 6.6–6.21.
7   Law Com CP No 174 (2004), para 7.16.

Unilateral recovery of possession

14.192   In the Law Commission's scheme the doctrines of waiver[1] and peaceable re-entry[2] would be abolished, but the landlord would retain, under strictly controlled conditions, a right to recover possession 'unilaterally' without prior court sanction, thereby suspending the tenant's right to possession pending a court application for relief made by the tenant (or by some owner of a derivative interest).[3] Unilateral recovery of possession would require to be preceded by a pre-action notice indicating that the landlord proposed to take this form of action,[4] but this unilateral form of remedy would be confined to commercial premises and vacant residential premises and would never be exercisable where a tenancy had an unexpired term in excess of 25 years.[5]

1   Law Com CP No 174 (2004), paras 4.27–4.32.

2   Law Com CP No 174 (2004), para 8.9.
3   Law Com CP No 174 (2004), paras 8.10–8.12.
4   Law Com CP No 174 (2004), paras 8.32–8.33.
5   Law Com CP No 174 (2004), paras 8.18, 8.22.

DISTRESS FOR UNPAID RENT

14.193   Distress is an ancient common law remedy which entitles the landlord, in appropriate circumstances, summarily to seize goods found on the demised premises, sell them up and recoup from the proceeds of sale any arrears of rent owed by the tenant.[1] Although sometimes described as an obsolete remedy,[2] distress is not infrequently used, especially by local authority landlords, as a means of recovering arrears of rent from a defaulting tenant.[3]

1   See generally *Distress for Rent* (Law Commission Working Paper No 97, May 1986), Chapter 2. For a critique of the law and practice of distress, see I Loveland, 'Distress for Rent: An Archaic Remedy?' (1990) 17 J Law and Society 363.
2   *Abingdon RDC v O'Gorman* [1968] 2 QB 811 at 819E. See Law Commission, *Landlord and Tenant: Interim Report on Distress for Rent* (Law Com No 5, 1966), para 5 (a 'relic of feudalism').
3   See (1978) LAG Bulletin 57 (A Arden); Law Commission Working Paper No 97 (May 1986), para 3.3. Distress has often seemed preferable to other remedies for commercial arrears in that it provides a faster and less cumbersome form of redress than re-entry, which may rebound on the landlord, leaving him with empty premises and no rent.

Extra-curial nature of distress

14.194   As a remedy founded in self-help, distress is anomalous and controversial. Except in certain limited cases defined by statute,[1] there is no requirement that due process of law or any form of curial adjudication be interposed before the landlord distrains upon his tenant's goods.[2] It is most unlikely that the extra-curial remedy of distress can long survive in the face of the European Convention guarantee of the right to a 'fair and public hearing' (and the implicit right of access to adjudication of relevant issues by a court).[3] Precisely because it is a potentially traumatic remedy, the exercise of distress has always been subject to a number of restrictions, some of which are rooted in statutory provisions of great antiquity.

1   See e g Rent (Agriculture) Act 1976, s 8 (certain agricultural tenancies or occupancies); Rent Act 1977, s 147(1) (protected or statutory tenancy); HA 1988, s 19(1) (assured tenancy); Insolvency Act 1986, s 130 (tenant company in process of being wound up by court).
2   See *Rhodes v Allied Dunbar Pension Services Ltd* [1989] 1 WLR 800 at 803E per Nicholls LJ. It is precisely this absence of legal process which allows a landlord to distrain notwithstanding that an interim order has been made under Insolvency Act 1986, s 252(1)–(2) pending approval of a voluntary arrangement with the tenant's creditors (see *McMullen & Sons Ltd v Cerrone* (1993) 66 P & CR 351 at 357; *Re a Debtor (No 13A-IO-1995)* [1995] 1 WLR 1127 at 1138A). See also A Clarke, (1992) 45 CLP 81.
3   ECHR Art 6 **[para 2.65]**. The remedy of distress is also highly vulnerable to challenge as a violation of the tenant's Convention right to 'peaceful enjoyment' of his possessions (ECHR Protocol No 1, Art 1). See *Tsironis v Greece* (2003) 37 EHRR 183 at [30], [42]. There may also

be a serious interference with the tenant's rights under ECHR Art 8 (*Fuller v Happy Shopper Markets Ltd* [2001] 1 WLR 1681 at [27] per Lightman J) **[para 2.60]**.

General restrictions on the right to distrain

14.195 Distress may be levied only in respect of arrears of rent.[1] No other breach of covenant entitles the landlord to distrain upon the goods of his tenant. Moreover, distress is intrinsically a landlord's remedy, and is therefore available only where there is a tenancy[2] and never where there is merely a licence.[3] The landlord must, at the date of the distress, be possessed of the immediate reversion on the tenancy in relation to which he seeks to distrain. This means, in effect, that distress cannot generally be levied against a subtenant,[4] and a subtenant's goods are in any event exempted by statute from any distress levied by a head landlord against a head tenant.[5]

1   The right to levy distress is limited to six years of rent arrear (Limitation Act 1980, s 19). There is no right to distrain for mesne profits (*Bridges v Smyth* (1829) 5 Bing 410 at 413, 130 ER 1119 at 1120; *Alford v Vickery* (1842) Car & M 280 at 283, 174 ER 507 at 508).
2   The corollary is that an owner who distrains on the goods of one who occupies his premises is estopped from alleging that the occupier is merely a licensee, at least if the other requirements of a lease are also present (see *Ward v Day* (1863) 4 B & S 337 at 357, 122 ER 486 at 493; *Carden v Choudhury* (Unreported, Court of Appeal, 29 February 1984) **[para 7.141]**).
3   *Hancock v Austin* (1863) 14 CB (NS) 634 at 639–640, 143 ER 593 at 596; *Ward v Day* (1863) 4 B & S 337 at 355–357, 122 ER 486 at 493.
4   See *Wade v Marsh* (1625) Lat 211, 82 ER 350.
5   Law of Distress Amendment Act 1908, s 1.

14.196 The landlord's right to distrain arises as soon as any rent is in arrear during the subsistence of the tenancy[1] and the right continues for six months after the termination of the tenancy if the former tenant is still in occupation of the same premises.[2] The remedies of distress and forfeiture are mutually exclusive.[3] Distress is premised on an affirmation of the landlord–tenant relationship,[4] whilst forfeiture marks an unequivocal election by the landlord to terminate that relationship.[5] It follows that distress cannot lawfully be levied where the landlord has already exercised his right to re-enter the demised premises.[6] Recourse to common law distress is likewise excluded if the landlord has already obtained a court judgment for the arrears of rent.[7]

1   This is so even if rent is payable in advance (see *Walsh v Lonsdale* (1882) 21 Ch D 9 at 14–15 **[para 9.64]**). There is no requirement at common law that the landlord should make any further demand for rent before distraining (*Kerby v Harding* (1851) 6 Exch 234 at 240–241, 155 ER 527 at 530), but the tenant may invoke the doctrine of equitable set-off in order to offset overpayments against unpaid rent (*Fuller v Happy Shopper Markets Ltd* [2001] 1 WLR 1681 at [26]–[27]).
2   Landlord and Tenant Act 1709, ss 6, 7.
3   *Bank of Montreal v Woodtown Developments Ltd* (1980) 99 DLR (3d) 739 at 743; *Country Kitchen Ltd v Wabush Enterprises Ltd* (1981) 120 DLR (3d) 358 at 361.
4   *Somerset Investments Pte Ltd v Far East Technology International Ltd* [2004] 3 SLR at [37] per Tay Yong Kwang J.
5   The landlord cannot 'have its cake and eat it too' (*Country Kitchen Ltd v Wabush Enterprises Ltd* (1981) 120 DLR (3d) 358 at 362). The mutually exclusive nature of the remedies

cannot be reversed by express contractual provision (*Re Coopers & Lybrand Ltd and Royal Bank of Canada* (1982) 137 DLR (3d) 356 at 360–361).

6   *Kirkland v Briancourt* (1890) 6 TLR 441. Forfeiture will be established by any 'act so inconsistent with the continuance of the [tenant's] term that [the landlords] were estopped from denying that it was at an end' (*Oastler v Henderson* (1877) 2 QBD 575 at 577). Thus the landlord's right to distrain is lost if he changes the locks on the doors of the demised premises and denies the tenant entry (*Country Kitchen Ltd v Wabush Enterprises Ltd* (1981) 120 DLR (3d) 358 at 363; *Re Coopers & Lybrand Ltd and Royal Bank of Canada* (1982) 137 DLR (3d) 356 at 359), but not if he merely sends a letter demanding payment of existing arrears of rent (*Cameron v Eldorado Properties Ltd* (1981) 113 DLR (3d) 141 at 145).

7   *Chancellor v Webster* (1893) 9 TLR 568 at 569 (even though the judgment debt remains unsatisfied).

Time and manner of lawful distress

14.197   The time and manner of lawful distress are regulated by rather archaic and sometimes irrational rules. The landlord may distrain in person, but it is more normal to employ the services of a bailiff.[1] Distress cannot be levied between sunset and sunrise[2] nor on a Sunday.[3] The distrainor must effect an actual entry upon the tenant's premises[4] and, whatever the nature of the premises, the initial entry must be peaceable and with the tenant's consent.[5] At this stage entry may not be made by breaking an outer door,[6] although inner doors may be broken down once entry has been achieved.[7] Having entered, the distrainor may either remove goods and hold them in a pound pending sale or (as commonly occurs) enter into a 'walking possession' agreement with the tenant under which the distrainor is entitled to return later to remove the goods.[8] Thereafter the distrainor is not entitled to re-enter by force except where, having gained entry peaceably, he is expelled by force or has been deliberately excluded by the tenant.[9] In the absence of express agreement for an unqualified right of re-entry, the distrainor is not simply 'entitled, without notice, to break in at any time of day or night.'[10]

1   A bailiff must have the authority of the landlord (usually in the written form of a warrant of distress). He must also hold a certificate issued by the county court which entitles him to act in this capacity (see Law of Distress (Amendment) Act 1888, s 7). The Distress for Rent Rules 1988 (SI 1988/2050) (as amended most recently by SI 2001/2046 and SI 2003/2141) now provide for general certificates valid for a year and thereafter renewable. County courts display the names of certificated bailiffs (who are often solicitors), and there is a Certificated Bailiffs' Association.

2   *Aldenburgh v Peaple* (1834) 6 C & P 212 at 213, 172 ER 1212; *Tutton v Darke* (1860) 5 H & N 647 at 650, 157 ER 1338 at 1340.

3   *Werth v London & Westminster Loan and Discount Co* (1889) 5 TLR 521 at 522.

4   See *Evans v South Ribble BC* [1992] QB 757 at 764D.

5   *Khazanchi v Faircharm Investments Ltd* [1998] 1 WLR 1603 at 1610E per Morritt LJ; *Evans v South Ribble BC* [1992] QB 757 at 764E per Simon Brown J.

6   *Semayne's Case* (1604) 5 Co Rep 91a at 92b, 77 ER 194 at 198; *Hancock v Austin* (1863) 14 CB (NS) 634 at 640, 143 ER 593 at 596; *Khazanchi v Faircharm Investments Ltd* [1998] 1 WLR 1603 at 1610D–E; *Gordon v Phelan* (1881) 15 ILTR 70 at 72; *Cassidy v Foley* [1904] 2 IR 427 at 428.

7   *Browning v Dann* (1735) Bull NP 81. Entry through an open window is permissible (*Long v Clarke* [1894] 1 QB 119 at 121), but not through a window which, although unlocked, is closed (*Nash v Lucas* (1867) LR 2 QB 590 at 594–595).

8   *Evans v South Ribble BC* [1992] QB 757 at 764E–765D; *Khazanchi v Faircharm Investments Ltd* [1998] 1 WLR 1603 at 1609B–E.
9   *Khazanchi v Faircharm Investments Ltd* [1998] 1 WLR 1603 at 1616B–C per Morritt LJ. Deliberate exclusion covers cases where the tenant, knowing of the distrainor's intended visit, deliberately locks the door or denies entry or goes away from the premises, but does not occur where the tenant 'has no knowledge of an intended visit by the bailiff at any particular time and locks his premises in the ordinary way and goes about his business as normal.'
10 *Khazanchi v Faircharm Investments Ltd* [1998] 1 WLR 1603 at 1616D–E per Morritt LJ.

Exemption for privileged goods

14.198   The process of distraint involves in principle the seizure of any goods found on the demised premises,[1] subject only to certain common law[2] and statutory exceptions in respect of privileged goods. Among the categories of goods immune from seizure are tools of trade,[3] clothes and bedding,[4] perishable foods,[5] tenant's fixtures,[6] the property of lodgers[7] and things in actual use. Things 'in actual use' include articles which are immune from seizure simply on the ground that a breach of the peace would otherwise almost necessarily occur.[8] It is not certain how far the last exemption extends, but it seems that a tenant can effectively resist attempts at distress simply by switching on any kind of electrical apparatus in his home before the landlord or bailiff arrives to carry out the distress (eg television set, radio, refrigerator, washing machine, cooker).[9] Distress can be levied on the goods of innocent strangers which are present on the premises,[10] subject to a right in the true owner to reclaim his property by serving a statutory declaration on the landlord or bailiff.[11]

1   It is unlawful for the landlord to assert any lien over goods of the tenant which already happen to be in the possession of the landlord as bailee (*Finlayson v Taylor* (1983) *Times*, 14 April).
2   At common law coins were always immune from distress unless contained in a closed purse or bag (*East India Co v Skinner* (1695) 1 Botts P L 259; Law Commission Working Paper No 97 (May 1986), para 2.40). See Law of Distress (Amendment) Act 1888, s 4; CCA 1984, s 89(1)(b). Compare, however, the unusual form of purported distress used in *Bank of Montreal v Woodtown Developments Ltd* (1980) 99 DLR (3d) 739 (landlord placed his own representatives in charge of cash register in tenant's shop).
3   Law of Distress (Amendment) Act 1888, s 4; CCA 1984, s 89(1)(a)(i).
4   Law of Distress (Amendment) Act 1888, s 4; CCA 1984, s 89(1)(a)(ii).
5   *Morley v Pincombe* (1848) 2 Exch 101 at 102, 154 ER 423.
6   *Simpson v Hartopp* (1744) Willes 512 at 514–515, 125 ER 1295 at 1296–1297; *Darby v Harris* (1841) 1 QB 895 at 898–899, 113 ER 1374 at 1376; *Crossley Bros Ltd v Lee* [1908] 1 KB 86 at 90–91.
7   See Law of Distress Amendment Act 1908, s 1.
8   *Simpson v Hartopp* (1744) Willes 512 at 516, 125 ER 1295 at 1297; *Storey v Robinson* (1795) 6 Term Rep 138 at 139, 101 ER 476 at 477; *Field v Adames* (1840) 12 Ad & El 649 at 652, 113 ER 960 at 962.
9   See (1978) LAG Bulletin 57 (A Arden).
10 *Juson v Dixon* (1813) 1 M & S 601 at 606–609, 105 ER 225 at 227. A landlord may distrain even on goods which he knows are not the property of the defaulting tenant (*Rhodes v Allied Dunbar Pension Services Ltd* [1989] 1 WLR 800 at 803E–F per Nicholls LJ).
11 Law of Distress Amendment Act 1908, s 1. The owner of the goods may obtain an ex parte interlocutory injunction to restrain sale, even though the required declaration is made through the agency of his solicitor (see *Lawrence Chemical Co Ltd v Rubinstein* [1982] 1 WLR 284 at 291C–E, 292F–H).

Sale

14.199   The landlord or bailiff who levies distress with the intention of selling up the goods seized must give the tenant, or leave at the demised premises, a notice which states the cause for the distress and stipulates the place of sale.[1] No sooner than five days later[2] the goods may be sold – usually by auction – and the landlord may recoup the arrears of rent from the proceeds, returning the balance (if any) minus expenses to the tenant. The landlord is not permitted to purchase the goods himself and there is a duty to obtain the best price possible.[3] It is generally thought that the sale of goods which have been the subject of an illegal distress does not pass a good title to the purchaser.[4]

1   Distress for Rent Act 1689, s 1; Distress for Rent Act 1737, s 9.
2   Distress for Rent Act 1689, s 1.
3   There is a duty, akin to that of a mortgagee exercising his power of sale [**para 15.185**], to use reasonable care in conducting the sale. An independent appraisal of the goods is mandatory only if requested in writing by the tenant (Law of Distress (Amendment) Act 1888, s 5). Compare, however, *Cameron v Eldorado Properties Ltd* (1981) 113 DLR (3d) 141 at 147–149.
4   See the application of the principle *nemo dat quod non habet* in comparable circumstances in *Trustee of Estate of Royal Inns Canada Ltd v Bolus-Revelas-Bolus Ltd* (1982) 136 DLR (3d) 272 at 279.

Proposed abolition of distress

14.200   Some time ago the Law Commission examined the law of distress and, finding it to be 'riddled with inconsistencies, uncertainties, anomalies and archaisms', declared that reform is 'long overdue'.[1] In the opinion of the Commission, the defects in the present law of distress are 'so fundamental and widespread that very little purpose would be served by collecting up the existing principles from the statutes and common law and restating them in modern terms in a codifying statute.'[2] After consultation the Commission confirmed its view that distress for rent is 'wrong in principle' and has no proper place in any modern approach to debt enforcement.[3] The Commission firmly proposed that distress should be abolished in respect of both commercial and residential leases[4] and should not be permitted even as a contractual option for landlord and tenant.[5] The government has finally accepted the Commission's recommendations in so far as residential tenancies are concerned, but seems inclined to retain distress in some modified form as a remedy in the commercial sector.[6] It is anticipated that the government will implement these changes by legislation as soon as parliamentary time allows.[7]

1   *Distress for Rent* (Law Commission Working Paper No 97, May 1986), para 5.1(1).
2   Working Paper No 97, para 5.1(2).
3   Law Commission, *Landlord and Tenant: Distress for Rent* (Law Com No 194, February 1991), para 3.2. See also A Clarke, (1992) 45 CLP 81 at 111–115.
4   Law Com No 194 (1991), para 3.1. See likewise *Report of Committee on the Enforcement of Judgment Debts* (Cmnd 3909, February 1969), para 924. Distress has been abolished in many jurisdictions (see eg Judgments (Enforcement) Act (Northern Ireland) 1969, s 122), and is of doubtful constitutional validity in other jurisdictions (see eg Constitution of Ireland, art 43).
5   Law Com No 194 (1991), para 4.8.

6   *Effective Enforcement* (Cm 5744, March 2003), paras 207–208.
7   See *Law Commission Annual Report 2003/04* (Law Com No 288, HC 642, June 2004), para 3.36.

ACTION FOR ARREARS OF RENT

14.201   In appropriate circumstances a further remedy for the landlord lies in an action for arrears of rent,[1] the Limitation Act restricting the landlord's recovery to a maximum of six years' arrears.[2] There is otherwise no prescriptive right to freedom from the tenant's obligation to pay rent.[3] The Law Commission has proposed that the limitation period for the recovery of rent be reduced to three years from the date when the landlord acquired actual or constructive knowledge of the rent default or ten years from the date of that default, whichever period first expires.[4]

1   See also CALRA 2002, s 166 [**para 14.127**].
2   Limitation Act 1980, s 19. The six-year limitation applies both to an action against the tenant and to an action against any guarantor – even under seal – of the tenant's obligations under the lease (*Romain v Scuba TV Ltd* [1997] QB 887 at 895D–E). A local authority landlord may set off arrears of rent against payment for home loss under the Land Compensation Act 1973 to a tenant whose home is repossessed under a housing improvement scheme (*Khan v Islington LBC* (1999) Times, 6 July).
3   A tenant is entitled on the basis of unjust enrichment to recover from the landlord any overpayment of rent made under a mistake (*Nurdin & Peacock Plc v D B Ramsden & Co Ltd* [1999] 1 WLR 1249 at 1264H, 1274C–D).
4   Law Commission, *Limitation of Actions* (Law Com No 270, July 2001), paras 4.154–4.157.

No duty to mitigate loss

14.202   It is traditionally said that the contractual principle of mitigation of damage has no application, at least in English law, to the relationship of landlord and tenant. The landlord has, supposedly, no duty to mitigate loss by taking steps to re-let premises which have been abandoned by the tenant during the term,[1] even though the tenant has committed breaches which entitle the landlord to re-enter.[2] This view is premised essentially on the theory that a lease confers a proprietary estate on the tenant for a term and that accordingly the landlord need neither concern himself with the tenant's election to under-utilise his own property during this term[3] nor trouble himself to re-enter, where appropriate, on the ground of breach.[4] On this basis the tenant is entirely free, if he wishes, to enjoy his property in absentia and the landlord remains perfectly entitled, notwithstanding the tenant's premature departure, to sue for rent as it continues to accrue.

1   See e g *Boyer v Warbey* [1953] 1 QB 234 at 245–246 per Denning LJ; *Maridakis v Kouvaris* (1975) 5 ALR 197 at 199.
2   Breach by the tenant entitles, but does not oblige, the landlord to re-enter (see *Tall-Bennett & Co Pty Ltd v Sadot Holdings Pty Ltd* (1988) 4 BPR 9522 at 9527–9528 per Young J).
3   See *Brown v RepublicBank First National Midland*, 766 SW2d 203 at 205 (1988) (Supreme Court of Texas). It remains open to the tenant to obtain a sub-tenant or to assign his lease (see *Tall-Bennett & Co Pty Ltd v Sadot Holdings Pty Ltd* (1988) 4 BPR 9522 at 9527).

4   See *Tall-Bennett & Co Pty Ltd v Sadot Holdings Pty Ltd* (1988) 4 BPR 9522 at 9527 per Young
     J).

Gradual move towards the mitigation principle

14.203   Although resistance to any requirement of mitigation is deeply
embedded in the common law of landlord and tenant, it becomes increasingly
debatable whether it can survive the gradual recontractualisation of the leasehold relationship.[1] Courts in other jurisdictions have come to accept in recent
times that the law of leases cannot be permanently or substantially insulated
from exposure to wider aspects of contractual doctrine. It may be only a matter
of time before English law recognises, as it has already done in respect of
frustration,[2] unilateral notices to quit[3] and repudiatory breach[4] that the rapidly
developing 'contract-based' perspective on the leasehold concept requires a
departure from some long cherished features of the 'property-based' analysis.
In the present context such a recognition calls for the acknowledgement of a
principle of mitigation of loss.[5] As the Supreme Court of Texas pointed out in
Brown v RepublicBank First National Midland,[6] this contract-based approach
has the added merit that it 'recognises a public policy element that requires
property to be put to beneficial use.'

1   **[Paras 7.80–7.87]**. See A J Bradbrook, (1977–79) Sydney L Rev 15.
2   *National Carriers Ltd v Panalpina (Northern) Ltd* [1981] AC 675 at 692B–D, 697A **[para 7.323]**.
3   *Hammersmith and Fulham LBC v Monk* [1992] 1 AC 478 at 491E–492A, 492G per
     Lord Browne-Wilkinson **[para 7.299]**.
4   See e g *Hussein v Mehlman* [1992] 2 EGLR 87; *Chartered Trust Plc v Davies* (1997) 76 P & CR
     396 **[para 7.319]**.
5   See the endorsement of a duty of mitigation in *Kendall v Ernest Pestana, Inc*, 709 P2d 837 at
     846 (Cal 1985); *Schneiker v Gordon*, 732 P2d 603 at 610–611 (Colo 1987); *Brown v Repub-
     licBank First National Midland*, 766 SW2d 203 at 205–206 (Tex 1988); *Red Deer College v
     Michaels* (1975) 57 DLR (3d) 386 at 390–391 (Supreme Court of Canada); *Tangye v
     Calmonton Investments Ltd* (1989) 51 DLR (4th) 593 at 602; *Karacominakis v Big Country
     Developments Pty Ltd* (2000) 10 BPR 18235 at [186]–[188] (NSW Court of Appeal).
6   766 SW2d 203 at 205 (1988).

DAMAGES FOR BREACH OF COVENANT

14.204   Damages may be awarded by the court where a landlord proves
breach by the tenant of any covenant other than a covenant respecting payment
of rent.[1] Except where the breach is of a repairing covenant, damages are
assessed on the usual contractual basis. Their purpose is to place the landlord
in the position – in so far as this can be done by means of a monetary award –
in which he would have been if there had been no breach by the tenant.[2]
Damages for breach of a tenant's covenant to keep or put premises in repair
cannot exceed the amount by which the value of the reversion has been
diminished through the breach.[3]

1   The landlord may also, in appropriate cases, recover damages for the tort of waste committed
     by the tenant. The measure of damages is represented by the diminution in the value of the

reversion less a discount which allows for the fact that payment is being made some time before the reversion falls into possession (*Whitham v Kershaw* (1885) 16 QBD 613 at 617).

2   See e g *Costain Property Developments Ltd v Finlay & Co Ltd* (1989) 57 P & CR 345 at 355–358; *Culworth Estates Ltd v Society of Licensed Victuallers* (1991) 62 P & CR 211 at 214–215.

3   L&TA 1927, s 18(1). See *Mather v Barclays Bank plc* [1987] 2 EGLR 254; [1988] Conv 438 (J E M); *Shortlands Investments Ltd v Cargill Plc* (1994) 69 P & CR D9. The landlord is not entitled to damages for mental distress caused by the tenant's breach of his covenant to repair (see e g *Turner v Jatko* (1979) 93 DLR (3d) 314 at 316–317). For restrictions on the landlord's recovery of damages, see Leasehold Property (Repairs) Act 1938, s 1(2) [**para 14.135**].

INJUNCTION AND SPECIFIC PERFORMANCE

14.205   Parties to the leasehold relationship may have access to remedies (such as injunctions and orders for specific performance) which operate more directly *in personam*. In the past the courts have tended to withhold such relief where compensatory damages provided an adequate remedy,[1] but nowadays there are indications that some historic restraints are beginning to be relaxed.

1   See e g *Michael Santarsieri Inc v Unicity Mall Ltd* (2000) 181 DLR (4th) 136 at 143–144 (where the Manitoba Court of Appeal also thought that the tenants' claim for an injunction restraining demolition of their business premises was, in part, motivated by a desire to secure a bargaining advantage in negotiating the terms on which their leases might be terminated).

14.206   It has always been possible in appropriate circumstances for a landlord to seek the discretionary remedy of the injunction for the purpose of restraining breaches of negative covenants contained in the lease.[1] There is venerable authority, however, that a mandatory injunction or order for specific performance should never issue against a tenant to compel the performance of a positive covenant to repair the demised premises.[2] Resistance to the award of such remedies has weakened in recent years.[3] In *Rainbow Estates Ltd v Tokenhold Ltd*[4] Deputy Judge Lawrence Collins QC finally confirmed that, subject to the 'overriding need to avoid injustice or oppression', specific performance should be available against the tenant 'when damages are not an adequate remedy.'[5] Such enforcement will be needed in only rare instances, but may be particularly appropriate where a lease contains no provision for forfeiture or re-entry or for any right of access by the landlord for the purpose of effecting necessary repairs.[6]

1   See e g *Sutton Housing Trust v Lawrence* (1988) 55 P & CR 320 at 324 (covenant against keeping of animals enforceable by injunction against tenant with multiple sclerosis who kept dog for companionship).
2   *Hill v Barclay* (1810) 16 Ves 402 at 405–406, 33 ER 1037 at 1038.
3   See e g *SEDAC Investments Ltd v Tanner* [1982] 1 WLR 1342 at 1349F; [1983] Conv 71.
4   [1999] Ch 64 at 73C–D. See [1998] Conv 163 (P H Kenny); [1999] CLJ 283 (S Bridge).
5   Deputy Judge Lawrence Collins QC added ([1999] Ch 64 at 73E–74A) that the courts must be astute to prevent unscrupulous landlords from perpetrating the sort of mischief at which the Leasehold Property (Repairs) Act 1938 is directed [**para 14.134**].
6   See *Rainbow Estates Ltd v Tokenhold Ltd* [1999] Ch 64 at 74A.

14.207   The refusal of mandatory or *in personam* relief for breaches of leasehold covenants always carries a hint of controversy in so far as it allows a thoroughly cynical landlord or tenant to buy his way out of covenanted obligations undertaken pursuant to an arm's length bargain. In *Co-operative Insurance Society Ltd v Argyll Stores (Holdings) Ltd*,[1] for example, the tenant closed its supermarket, some fifteen years after the commencement of a 35 year lease of premises in a shopping centre, because it was losing money. The closure, in clear breach of the tenant's obligation under the lease to keep the premises open for retail trade during the usual hours of business, threatened the commercial vitality of much of the remainder of the shopping centre. The House of Lords declined to issue a mandatory injunction requiring that the tenant continue to trade on the premises, citing a settled (although not invariable) practice *not* to require a defendant positively to carry on a business.[2] In Lord Hoffmann's view, moreover, the loss inflicted on the tenant through compliance with a mandatory order would cause injustice 'by allowing the plaintiff to enrich himself at the defendant's expense.'[3] The tenant's loss was likely to be far greater than that suffered by his landlord by reason of the breach. In a speech which had the concurrence of the entire House, Lord Hoffmann indicated that the purpose of the law of contract 'is not to punish wrongdoing but to satisfy the expectations of the party entitled to performance.'[4] The decision comes close to endorsing the notion of efficient breach (or even that a contracting party is *entitled* to break his contract on money payment) and has been fiercely criticised.[5]

1   [1998] AC 1; (1998) 61 MLR 421 (A Phang); [1997] CLJ 488 (G H Jones).
2   [1998] AC 1 at 11A–12C. 'Specific performance is traditionally regarded in English law as an exceptional remedy' ([1998] AC 1 at 11E–F per Lord Hoffmann).
3   [1998] AC 1 at 15B.
4   [1998] AC 1 at 15G–16A ('[I]t cannot be in the public interest for the courts to require someone to carry on a business at a loss if there is any plausible alternative by which the other party can be given compensation ... The defendant pays damages, the forensic link between them is severed, they go their separate ways and the wounds of conflict can heal').
5   See e g A M Tettenborn, 'Absolving the Undeserving: Shopping Centres, Specific Performance and the Law of Contract' [1998] Conv 23. Contrast the approach adopted in *Diagnostic X-Ray Services Pty Ltd v Jewel Food Stores Pty Ltd* (2001) 4 VR 632 at [11]–[15] (injunction granted to require tenant to carry on petrol station business).

PRIVITY OF CONTRACT AND PRIVITY OF ESTATE

14.208   The device of the leasehold estate offers an extremely flexible base for the assignment of the tenant's term and the creation of subleases.[1] The enforceability of the covenants in a lease presents little difficulty as between the original landlord and tenant, but becomes increasingly awkward with the emergence of assignees and subtenants who stand remote from the initial contractual relationship. As Lord Templeman pointed out in *City of London Corpn v Fell*,[2] the common law was faced centuries ago with the 'problem of rendering effective the obligations under a lease which might endure for a period of 999 years or more beyond the control of any covenantor.' It simply could not be that the essential covenants of a lease fell away with the disappearance of the original contracting parties, leaving the residue of the leasehold term ungoverned by clear or durable ground rules.[3] It was therefore vital that the law should provide a framework of liability which would ensure the policing of the covenants of the lease in the more distant reaches of the leasehold relationship well beyond the nexus of original lessor and original lessee. This objective came to be achieved largely through reliance on the twin doctrines of *privity of contract* and *privity of estate*, although the operation of these concepts has been dramatically modified – if not indeed displaced – by the Landlord and Tenant (Covenants) Act 1995 and the Contracts (Rights of Third Parties) Act 1999.

1   **[Paras 7.205–7.216]**.
2   [1994] 1 AC 458 at 464H.
3   See *City of London Corpn v Fell* [1994] 1 AC 458 at 465A–B per Lord Templeman.

14.209   The complex of enforcement relationships which arise in the context of leaseholds is controlled by a combination of common law and statutory rules. The precise operation of these rules sometimes depends on whether the lease in question is legal or equitable[1] (although this issue has no significance with regard to leases granted after 1996).[2] *Fig.* 42 contains a representation of a network of leasehold relationships which can serve as a model for further discussion. It is assumed in the following analysis not only that the head lease is legal,[3] but that all subsequent assignments and grants are also legal, being effected (where appropriate) by deed and registered at Land Registry. Accordingly, in terms of *Fig.* 42, L1 creates a 99 year head lease in favour of T1. T1 later assigns his term of years to T2, who grants a five-year lease to a subtenant, ST1. T2 then transfers the residue of his term to T3, while ST1 assigns his underlease to ST2, who finally grants a weekly tenancy to WT. L1 at some stage transfers his freehold reversion to L2.

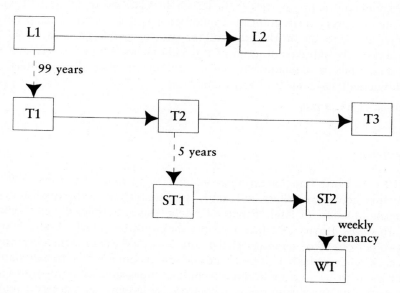

Fig. **42**

1   For the distinction between legal and equitable leases, see [paras 7.217–7.248, 9.42–9.76].
2   [Para 14.249].
3   It matters not for the purposes of exposition whether the lease between L1 and T1 is the head lease. Exactly the same principles, transposed (as it were) one octave down, would apply if L1 were not himself the freeholder but were instead a leaseholder.

The duality of leasehold character

14.210   The framework of legal rules governing the enforcement of leasehold liabilities is premised upon the essential 'duality of character' implicit in the leasehold device.[1] A term of years 'originates in contract',[2] but it also confers on the tenant an estate in the land which, like the reversionary estate held by the landlord, is transferable to third parties. Under a term of years landlord and tenant can therefore be described as standing together in one or other of two distinct kinds of legal relationship, respectively 'privity of contract' and 'privity of estate'.[3]

1   *Progressive Mailing House Pty Ltd v Tabali Pty Ltd* (1985) 157 CLR 17 at 51 per Deane J. See also *Kendall v Ernest Pestana, Inc*, 709 P2d 837 at 843 (Cal 1985).
2   *City of London Corpn v Fell* [1993] QB 589 at 603H per Nourse LJ.
3   *City of London Corpn v Fell* [1993] QB 589 at 604A per Nourse LJ.

Privity of contract

14.211   Privity of contract denotes the ambit of contractual liability within the leasehold framework. In *Fig.* 42 this form of privity clearly obtains between the original contracting parties in the leasehold relationship, L1 and T1, and is replicated on every fresh grant of an inferior leasehold estate. Thus privity of contract also obtains, on the grant of the five-year sublease, between T2 and ST1, and on the subsequent grant of a weekly tenancy, between ST2 and WT. At common law these relationships of contractual privity endure unaffected by the subsequent assignment of any estate.[1]

1   [Paras 14.217–14.223].

Privity of estate

14.212   As Lord Templeman observed in *City of London Corpn v Fell*,[1] the distinction between contract and status is 'fundamental to the English system of leasehold tenure of land.' Privity of estate relates, both legally and semantically, to *status*. Privity of estate describes the condition which obtains between any two persons who, in respect of the same leasehold estate, stand currently vis à vis each other in the position of landlord and tenant.[2] As the title or status of each person 'privy' to a particular leasehold estate is shuffled on by transfers of the superior or inferior interest, each successive assignee can describe himself, both functionally and technically, as holding as either *landlord* or *tenant* in relation to one other identified person.

1   [1994] 1 AC 458 at 466A.
2   Thus, at any given moment, the relationship of privity of estate obtains only as between those who hold their interests in possession.

14.213   Thus, in respect of the head lease depicted in *Fig.* 42, privity of estate potentially involves all who can trace their leasehold status horizontally[1] to the 'estate' comprised within this term of years. Accordingly L1 and T1, prior to any assignment of their respective interests, are conjoined not only in a privity of *contract*, but also in a privity of *estate*,[2] although any transfer of either's estate necessarily terminates the transferor's 'privity' to the estate of the head lease and deflects this form of privity to his transferee.[3] Thus as soon as (say) T1 assigns the whole of his term to T2, a new privity of estate arises, this time between L1 and T2. As Nourse LJ observed in *City of London Corpn v Fell*,[4] an original tenant who has assigned his tenancy 'cannot properly be described as the tenant. He no longer holds the land. It is the assignee who now holds the land. It is he who has the tenancy.' It is now the assignee who is 'privy' to the 'estate' of the leasehold. Equally when L1 transfers the superior reversionary estate to L2, it is L2 who thereafter ranks as the 'landlord'[5] and privity of estate now obtains between L2 and T2.[6] When later T2 assigns to T3, it is L2 and T3 who, at this point, stand in a relationship of privity of estate.[7]

1   See *Croydon (Unique) Ltd v Wright* [2001] Ch 318 at 327F per Sir Christopher Staughton.
2   *Crystalline Investments Ltd v Domgroup Ltd* [2004] 1 SCR 60 at [29] (Supreme Court of Canada).
3   *Karacominakis v Big Country Developments Pty Ltd* (2000) 10 BPR 18235 at [132]; *Liristis Holdings Pty Ltd v Wallville Pty Ltd* (2001) 10 BPR 18801 at [87].
4   [1993] QB 589 at 604C.
5   *Hua Chiao Commercial Bank Ltd v Chiaphua Industries Ltd* [1987] AC 99 at 106G per Lord Oliver of Aylmerton.
6   T2 can also claim to hold as 'landlord' in relation to ST1 as 'tenant', for a new privity of contract and estate has been generated by the five-year sublease.
7   Each of these persons, during the currency of his tenure, can trace his position to one or other side of the notional feudal divide (or 'estate') which separates landlord from tenant.

Different privities of estate

14.214   The versatility of the leasehold device means, of course, that land may be simultaneously subjected to a hierarchy of terms of years, all springing from the grant of a head lease by an owner in fee simple. Privity of estate indicates at any given time the precise allocation of tenancies in the land[1] and it is entirely possible that there may exist concurrently a number of different privities of estate, each referable to a different term of years. Thus, in relation to the 99 year head lease in *Fig.* 42, privity of estate is enjoyed at some time or other by L1, L2, T1, T2 and T3. Privity of estate in relation to the five-year sublease is enjoyed – again at some time or other – by T2, T3, ST1 and ST2. But it is important to realise that ST1 can never be said to be 'privy' to the estate of the head lease granted by L1 to T1,[2] nor WT 'privy' to the estate of the five year sublease – each is 'privy' to a different estate.[3]

1   'A "tenant", both by derivation and by usage, is someone who "holds" land of another' (*City of London Corpn v Fell* [1993] QB 589 at 604B per Nourse LJ).

2   **[Para 14.302]**. See *Amsprop Trading Ltd v Harris Distribution Ltd* [1997] 1 WLR 1025 at
     1029A per Neuberger J.
3   In a quite graphic sense the test of 'privity of estate' turns on whether the party concerned can
     trace his position horizontally to the original landlord–tenant relationship to which it is
     claimed he is 'privy'. ST1 cannot do this in relation to the estate of the head lease between L1
     and T1.

LIABILITY AS BETWEEN L1 AND T1

14.215   In *Fig.* 42, prior to assignment by either, the relationship of L1 and
T1 is straightforwardly contractual. Because they enjoy contractual privity,
each is liable to the other on all the covenants of the lease irrespective of
whether these covenants 'touch and concern' the demised land[1] and irrespective
of whether the lease is legal or equitable.[2] With the exception of covenants
which are illegal or contrary to public policy, even purely personal covenants –
perhaps of an eccentric or capricious character – are fully binding and
enforceable between them.

1   *City of London Corpn v Fell* [1993] QB 589 at 603A per Nourse LJ. 'Touching and concerning'
     covenants are examined shortly **[paras 14.250–14.263]**.
2   See *John Betts & Sons Ltd v Price* (1924) 40 TLR 589 at 590; *Picton-Warlow v Allendale
     Holdings Pty Ltd* [1988] WAR 107 at 109. If L1 and T1 have entered into a specifically
     enforceable contract for a lease **[para 9.46]**, they are bound – perhaps even more obviously –
     by a contractual nexus which at common law endures throughout the entire term.

14.216   If, in the event of an insolvency or bankruptcy affecting T1, the lease
between L1 and T1 is disclaimed by a company liquidator or trustee in
bankruptcy,[1] the disclaimer has the consequence of destroying T1's leasehold
estate in the land.[2] Disclaimer thus accelerates the reversion expectant on the
determination of T1's estate and simultaneously extinguishes all of T1's
liabilities to L1 (together with all of T1's rights against L1).[3] But, although
disclaimer of the lease terminates the rights and obligations of L1 and T1 *inter
se*, it does not terminate obligations already undertaken by some third party
who has guaranteed the performance of T1's covenants under the lease.[4] As
Lord Nicholls of Birkenhead confirmed in *Hindcastle Ltd v Barbara Attenborough Associates Ltd*,[5] L1 remains free to enforce the guarantor's surety covenant.[6] The guarantor's liability to L1 survives the extinguishment of the lease[7]
and is likewise unaffected by the guarantor's loss of any right to be indemnified
by the defaulting T1. The guarantor is similarly liable to L1 on any covenant
which he may have given to take over T1's unexpired term in the event of a
disclaimer of the lease. In such circumstances, as Lord Templeman explained in
Coronation Street Industrial Properties Ltd v Ingall Industries Plc,[8] T1 retires
'mortally wounded' and his guarantor comes in to play as 'the substitute'.

1   On the effect of disclaimer, see **[para 7.318]**.
2   *Hindcastle Ltd v Barbara Attenborough Associates Ltd* [1997] AC 70 at 87F per Lord Nicholls
     of Birkenhead.
3   *Hindcastle Ltd v Barbara Attenborough Associates Ltd* [1997] AC 70 at 87D–E per
     Lord Nicholls; *Scottish Widows Plc v Tripipatkul* [2004] 1 P & CR 461 at [9].

4   *Hindcastle Ltd v Barbara Attenborough Associates Ltd* [1997] AC 70 at 87H–88A per
     Lord Nicholls; *Basch v Stekel* (2000) 81 P & CR D1 at [4]. See Insolvency Act 1986,
     s 178(4)(b).
5   [1997] AC 70 at 88A–C. See [1997] Conv 24 (T Taylor).
6   See similarly *Crystalline Investments Ltd v Domgroup Ltd* [2004] 1 SCR 60 at [42] (Supreme
     Court of Canada).
7   The guarantor's liability even survives the assignment by L1 to L2 of the 'notional reversion'
     on the disclaimed lease, since as between the L2 and the guarantor this reversion can be
     regarded as 'continuing ... despite the termination of the lease, like the Cheshire Cat's grin in
     Lewis Carroll's *Alice*' (*Scottish Widows Plc v Tripipatkul* [2004] 1 P & CR 461 at [10] per
     Pumfrey J).
8   [1989] 1 WLR 304 at 309B–C.

THE PRINCIPLE OF ENDURING CONTRACTUAL LIABILITY

14.217   At common law, in all cases other than those of disclaimer, the intense
contractual nexus between L1 and T1 implicates both in enduring liabilities of
an unexpected order of magnitude. Prior to recent statutory intervention, the
contractual analysis of their relationship was so dominant that, in the absence
of some expressly agreed release, both used to remain fully liable on all the
covenants of the lease for the duration of the whole term – quite irrespective of
assignment by either.[1] The commencement of the lease effectively initiated a
liability on both sides which continued throughout the entire leasehold term.[2]
Given that a term of years can be of extensive duration (e g 125 years or 999
years), the common law liability undertaken by L1 and T1 was so considerable
that it necessitated certain modifications by statute with effect from 1 January
1996.

1   In *City of London Corpn v Fell* [1994] 1 AC 458 at 465E, Lord Templeman attributed this
     principle to 'the sacred character of covenant in English law'.
2   The death of a covenanting party does not exonerate his estate from liability. In order that
     potential claims should not impede the winding up of estates, personal representatives are
     authorised to set aside a 'sufficient fund' to meet possible future liabilities and then distribute
     the remainder of the deceased's estate (TA 1925, s 26(1)).

T1's liability survived assignment of his term

14.218   At common law, in the absence of contrary agreement with L1,[1] T1's
contractual liability on his covenants survived the assignment of his term to T2
(and indeed its further assignment to anyone else).[2] Following assignment,
although L1 and T1 no longer enjoyed any privity of estate,[3] there remained an
enduring privity of contract which preserved the responsibility of T1[4] (and of
any surety of T1[5]) for the due performance of T1's leasehold obligations
throughout the whole term of the lease.[6] In that he became answerable for *any*
breach which occurred (even if committed by assignees), T1 was effectively
rendered an insurer of the lease.[7]

1   It was of course open to L1 and T1 to agree contractually that T1's liability should terminate
     on assignment, but such limitation of liability was unusual – a fact which the Law Commis-
     sion ascribed to the unequal bargaining power of the parties (see *Landlord and Tenant: Privity*

of Contract and Estate (Law Com No 174, November 1988), paras 2.17, 3.3, 3.17). For certain rare statutory exceptions to the general common law rule, see Law of Property Act 1922, Sch 15, para 11 (assignment of perpetually renewable lease); Family Law Act 1996, s 53, Sch 7, para 7 (court-ordered transfer of tenancy between spouses on divorce).

2   *Walker's Case* (1587) 3 Co Rep 22a at 23a, 76 ER 676 at 680; *Baynton v Morgan* (1888) 22 QBD 74 at 82 per Lopes LJ; *Arlesford Trading Co Ltd v Servansingh* [1971] 1 WLR 1080 at 1082G. The common law principle has global acceptance (see also *195 Crown Street Pty Ltd v Hoare* [1969] 1 NSWR 193 at 195; *Francini v Canuck Properties Ltd* (1982) 35 OR (2d) 321 at 323a; *W E Wagener Ltd v Photo Engravers Ltd* [1984] 1 NZLR 412 at 417; *Picton-Warlow v Allendale Holdings Pty Ltd* [1988] WAR 107 at 109.

3   See *Milmo v Carreras* [1946] KB 306 at 310.

4   *Warnford Investments Ltd v Duckworth* [1979] Ch 127 at 138C per Megarry V-C; *Johnsey Estates Ltd v Lewis and Manley (Engineering) Ltd* (1987) 54 P & CR 296 at 300 per Bingham LJ; *W E Wagener Ltd v Photo Engravers Ltd* [1984] 1 NZLR 412 at 424; *Crystalline Investments Ltd v Domgroup Ltd* [2004] 1 SCR 60 at [29]–[31] (Supreme Court of Canada).

5   *Thames Manufacturing Co Ltd v Perrotts (Nichol & Peyton) Ltd* (1984) 271 EG 284 at 287.

6   T1's liability was, of course, discharged *pro tanto* by the performance of his covenants by a guarantor (*Milverton Group Ltd v Warner World Ltd* [1995] 2 EGLR 28 at 29K, 30B–C; [1995] JBL 181 (M Haley)).

7   T1's future contractual liability was cut short if any assignee of his term surrendered the whole of the lease (*Allied London Investments Ltd v Hambro Life Assurance Ltd* (1984) 269 EG 41 at 46). See also *195 Crown Street Pty Ltd v Hoare* [1969] 1 NSWR 193 at 196–197, 200.

Scope of T1's liability

14.219   T1's liability at common law extended not merely to payment of the rent reserved by the lease,[1] but also to all the other covenants contained in the lease.[2] Thus, if T2 or T3 defaulted on any of the leasehold covenants, T1 was ultimately liable on the ground that he had contracted that these covenants would be performed for the duration of the term.[3] A heavy onus of care was imposed on T1 to select a reliable and creditworthy assignee,[4] although almost invariably T1 'had no control over the identity of assignees down the line.'[5] T1's liability was virtually inescapable. In the event of default by (say) T3, T1 had no right to require that L1 first exhaust his remedies against T3.[6] At common law L1 was entitled, if he so wished, to have primary recourse to the liability fastened contractually on T1.[7] T1 had no ground of complaint even if L1, preferring to sue T1, unilaterally granted a release to a third party guarantor of T3's obligations.[8]

1   *Warnford Investments Ltd v Duckworth* [1979] Ch 127 at 138G–139A, 141H–142A.

2   See e g *Thames Manufacturing Co Ltd v Perrotts (Nichol & Peyton) Ltd* (1984) 271 EG 284 at 286–287 (disrepair and breach of covenant to surrender and yield up possession); *Weaver v Mogford* [1988] 31 EG 49 (disrepair).

3   *Warnford Investments Ltd v Duckworth* [1979] Ch 127 at 138H; *Tall-Bennett & Co Pty Ltd v Sadot Holdings Pty Ltd* (1988) 4 BPR 9522 at 9527 per Young J.

4   The mere fact that L1's may have consented to the assignment to T2 did not impliedly release T1 from any continuing liability (*Thames Manufacturing Co Ltd v Perrotts (Nichol & Peyton) Ltd* (1984) 271 EG 284 at 286).

5   *Hindcastle Ltd v Barbara Attenborough Associates Ltd* [1997] AC 70 at 83G per Lord Nicholls of Birkenhead ('He had no opportunity to reject them as financially unsound'). In granting a licence permitting T2 to assign to T3, the landlord owed T1 no duty of care to assess the

creditworthiness of T3 or to take timely measures to enforce the relevant covenants against T3 (see *Norwich Union Life Insurance Society v Low Profile Fashions Ltd* (1992) 64 P & CR 187 at 190–191).

6 *Allied London Investments Ltd v Hambro Life Assurance Ltd* (1984) 270 EG 948 at 950 per Harman J.

7 '[T]he fortunate English landlord has two remedies after an assignment, namely his remedy against the assignee and his remedy against the original tenant' (*City of London Corpn v Fell* [1994] 1 AC 458 at 465A–B per Lord Templeman). See likewise *Norwich Union Life Insurance Society v Low Profile Fashions Ltd* (1992) 64 P & CR 187 at 192 per Beldam LJ. The landlord could not, of course, recover twice for the same breach of covenant: the remedies were alternative not cumulative (*Brett v Cumberland* (1619) Cro Jac 521 at 523, 79 ER 446 at 447).

8 See *Allied London Investments Ltd v Hambro Life Assurance Ltd* (1984) 269 EG 41 at 42–45.

An illusory right to indemnity

14.220   If the defaults of an assignee caused T1 to be made answerable in damages or for arrears of rent, T1 had, at least in theory, certain rights of indemnity. Assignments of the tenant's term commonly contained an express covenant by the assignee to indemnify the assignor against liability for future breaches. Similar rights of restitution arose by statutory implication[1] and by way of quasi-contract.[2] In practice, however, T1's entitlement to indemnity was highly likely to prove ineffective precisely because the defaulting assignee was almost always insolvent and T1 ranked as an unsecured creditor.[3]

1 LPA 1925, s 77. See *Johnsey Estates Ltd v Lewis and Manley (Engineering) Ltd* (1987) 54 P & CR 296 at 298–300.

2 *Moule v Garrett* (1872) LR 7 Ex 101 at 104; *Selous Street Properties Ltd v Oronel Fabrics Ltd* (1984) 270 EG 643 at 747–748. If T1 was made liable for the default not of T2 but of T3, T's right of indemnity was available against T3 directly (see *Moule v Garrett*, supra at 103–104).

3 See *Crystalline Investments Ltd v Domgroup Ltd* [2004] 1 SCR 60 at [32] (Supreme Court of Canada).

L1's liability survived assignment of his reversion

14.221   It also followed from the contractual nature of the initial leasehold commitment that, at common law, L1's liability on the covenants of the lease survived the transfer of his reversion to L2 (or indeed its further transfer),[1] except where the covenants in question clearly imposed liability only on the current owner of the reversionary estate.[2] In practice, given the imbalance of obligation between landlord and tenant, the principle of enduring contractual liability operated less oppressively upon the landlord than on the tenant.

1 *Stuart v Joy* [1904] 1 KB 362 at 367–368. At common law L1's liability not only survived the assignment of his reversion to L2, but could even provide the basis for action against him by an assignee of T1's term of years, e g by T2 or T3 (see *Celsteel Ltd v Alton House Holdings Ltd (No 2)* [1986] 1 WLR 666 at 672G–H; [1987] 1 WLR 291 at 296D–E).

2 *Bath v Bowles* (1905) 93 LT 801 at 805.

Intensification of the contractual principle

14.222   In realistic commercial terms the primary target for enforcement in the event of breaches occurring after assignment is usually the defaulting assignee himself. Nevertheless, with the spate of insolvencies which emerged during the 1980s and early 1990s, it became increasingly common for landlords to have recourse to the ultimate contract-based liability of their original tenant.[1] If L1 (or, in his turn, L2) discovered that an assignee of the leasehold term was bankrupt or insolvent, it was obviously tempting and sometimes relatively easy to enforce a money liability against an attractively solvent T1. For many original tenants such enforcement came as a wholly unanticipated (and financially disastrous) form of liability.[2] The principle of enduring contractual liability often produced harsh consequences. T1, although he had long ago transferred the residue of his term and retained no control over the demised premises,[3] was suddenly confronted with an enforceable demand for arrears of rent unpaid by T2 or T3 or for damages in respect of some other default of which he was wholly innocent. As Lord Nicholls of Birkenhead observed in *Hindcastle Ltd v Barbara Attenborough Associates Ltd*,[4] a 'person of modest means is understandably shocked when out of the blue he receives a rent demand from the landlord of the property he once leased.' The potential impact on T1 was intensified when, during the 1980s, the courts began to hold that T1's liability on his covenants could be increased by subsequent variations of the original leasehold terms agreed between L1 and T2 or T3, over which (of course) T1 had little or no control.[5]

1   The strictly contractual origin of the liability proved beneficial to the tenant in only one respect. In *City of London Corpn v Fell* [1994] 1 AC 458 at 463D–F, the House of Lords declined to hold T1 liable for rent unpaid by an assignee during a *statutory* extension of the latter's term pursuant to Part II of the Landlord and Tenant Act 1954 [**para 14.355**]. Contrast *Herbert Duncan Ltd v Cluttons* [1993] QB 589 at 607C–E (express covenant to pay rent not only during contractual term but also during statutory extension).

2   See e g *RPH Ltd v Mirror Group Newspapers and Mirror Group Holdings* (1992) 65 P & CR 252 at 254–256 (T1 held liable for accrued rent arrears of almost £2 million unpaid by Maxwell Communication Corporation plc). See also Law Com No 174 (1988), paras 3.7–3.8.

3   See e g *Thames Manufacturing Co Ltd v Perrotts (Nichol & Peyton) Ltd* (1984) 271 EG 284 at 286.

4   [1997] AC 70 at 83G.

5   See e g *Selous Street Properties Ltd v Oronel Fabrics Ltd* (1984) 270 EG 643 at 650 (T1 liable for rent arrears of £110,000 on upward rent review negotiated by T2). It is an ironic postscript that the *Selous Street Properties* decision was disapproved by the Court of Appeal just as its reversal by the Landlord and Tenant (Covenants) Act 1995 received the royal assent (see *Friends' Provident Life Office v British Railways Board* [1996] 1 All ER 336 at 348d–e). See Susan Bright, 'Variation of Leases and Tenant Liability', in P Jackson and D C Wilde (ed), *The Reform of Property Law* (Ashgate 1997), p 73.

Attack on the contractual principle

14.223   The enforcement of a continuing contractual liability against original lessees came to be so widely and bitterly criticised[1] that in 1988 the Law Commission advocated a significant reform of the law.[2] The Commission acknowledged the intrinsic unfairness of continuing liability and recognised that landlords were often given excessive protection at the expense of tenants who had long since ceased to have any interest in, or control over, the leasehold property.[3] In the Commission's view the principle of enduring contractual privity unjustifiably duplicated the liability fixed on assignees by privity of estate.[4] The Commission accordingly recommended that the liability of the original tenant on the covenants of his lease (and his corresponding entitlement to the benefits of that lease) should not in general survive assignment of the tenant's term but should instead terminate at this point.[5] The essential thrust of the Commission's proposals was realised in the severe curtailment of contractual privity which was achieved by the Landlord and Tenant (Covenants) Act 1995.[6]

1   See *Hindcastle Ltd v Barbara Attenborough Associates Ltd* [1997] AC 70 at 83H per Lord Nicholls of Birkenhead (referring to a '[m]ounting public concern at this post-assignment state of affairs'). See similarly *RPH Ltd v Mirror Group Newspapers and Mirror Group Holdings* (1992) 65 P & CR 252 at 253 per Nicholls V-C.
2   *Landlord and Tenant: Privity of Contract and Estate* (Law Com No 174, November 1988).
3   *Landlord and Tenant: Privity of Contract and Estate; Duration of Liability of Parties to Leases* (Law Commission Working Paper No 95, March 1986), paras 3.1–3.4.
4   Law Com No 174 (1988), paras 3.5–3.23; Working Paper No 95 (1986), paras 3.17–3.21. See [1989] Conv 145 (H W W).
5   Law Com No 174 (1988), paras 4.3–4.8; Working Paper No 95 (1986), para 6.2.
6   See M Davey, (1996) 59 MLR 78; (1996) 49(1) CLP 95 (A Clarke); S N Bridge, [1996] CLJ 313; P Walter, 'The Landlord and Tenant (Covenants) Act 1995: A Legislative Folly' [1996] Conv 432.

LIABILITY OF LI AND TI UNDER NEW (POST-1995) TENANCIES

14.224   For present purposes the Landlord and Tenant (Covenants) Act 1995 draws a sharp distinction between *new* tenancies and *old* tenancies.[1] A 'new' tenancy comprises any tenancy granted on or after 1 January 1996 (other than a tenancy granted in pursuance of an agreement entered into, or of a court order made, before that date).[2]

1   The 1995 Act 'introduces a new code relating to the enforceability of covenants by landlords and tenants' (*Oceanic Village Ltd v United Attractions Ltd* [2000] Ch 234 at 242F per Neuberger J).
2   L&T(C)A 1995, s 1(3). A tenancy which is the product of an option or right of first refusal granted before 1 January 1996 is treated as an old tenancy irrespective of the date of the exercise of the ancillary right (L&T(C)A 1995, s 1(6)–(7)). In the case of a deemed surrender and regrant by way of variation of a pre-1996 tenancy, the resulting lease is regarded as a 'new' tenancy (L&T(C)A 1995, s 1(5)).

Liability of TI (and his guarantor)

14.225   A pivotal provision of the Landlord and Tenant (Covenants) Act 1995 is the principle (enshrined in section 5) that T1, on assigning the whole of the premises demised to him under a 'new' tenancy, is thereafter released from the 'tenant covenants' contained in the lease and is correspondingly disabled from any further enjoyment of its 'landlord covenants'.[1] Moreover, following the assignment, any guarantor of T1's liability under his tenant covenants is simultaneously released from his surety covenant 'to the same extent' as T1 is released from further liability.[2] The 1995 Act emphasises that T1's release from future liability in no way affects any liability of his which may have arisen from a breach of covenant occurring *before* his release.[3] T1's release does, however, mean that there is no further need for indemnity covenants to be implied in his favour on the assignment of his tenancy to T2.[4]

1   L&T(C)A 1995, s 5(2). T1 is likewise released from, and disabled from taking the benefit of, any covenants entered into under the lease with a third party management company (L&T(C)A 1995, s 12(1)–(3)). An assignment of only part of the demised premises alters T1's rights and liabilities on the landlord and tenant covenants only to the extent that such covenants affect the part of the premises assigned (L&T(C)A 1995, s 5(3)).

2   L&T(C)A 1995, s 24(2). In effect, so long as T1 has remained solvent, T1's guarantor or surety performs the function of a 'quasi tenant who volunteers to be a substitute or twelfth man for the tenant's team' and is 'subject to the same rules and regulations as the player he replaces' (*P & A Swift Investments v Combined English Stores Group Plc* [1989] AC 632 at 638A per Lord Templeman).

3   L&T(C)A 1995, s 24(1). Correspondingly T1 retains the right to sue in respect of any breach of a landlord covenant occurring prior to the date of T1's release (L&T(C)A 1995, s 24(4)).

4   See L&T(C)A 1995, ss 14, 30(2), Sch (abrogating the effect of LPA 1925, s 77(1)(c)–(d)). To the extent that T1 subsequently meets a liability generated by T2 from which T1 is not released, he has the normal restitutionary right to an indemnity from the actual defaulter (see *Moule v Garrett* (1872) LR 7 Ex 101 at 104).

Mandatory operation of statutory release

14.226 The novel principles of the Landlord and Tenant (Covenants) Act 1995 relating to release have mandatory force and cannot be avoided by contrary agreement between the parties.[1] Landlord and tenant are therefore precluded from any private agreement which purports to reinstate the principle of enduring contractual privity. The release provisions of section 5 do not apply, however, where T1's assignment of his term to T2 was an 'excluded assignment' (ie an assignment in breach of covenant or by operation of law)[2] or where the release of T1 is effectively postponed by means of an 'authorised guarantee agreement'.[3]

1   L&T(C)A 1995, s 25(1). See Law Com No 174 (1988), paras 4.57–4.58.

2   L&T(C)A 1995, s 11(1)–(2). The release of T1 may still occur with effect from the next assignment of his term which is not an 'excluded assignment' (L&T(C)A 1995, s 11(2)(b)).

3   L&T(C)A 1995, s 16(1).

Authorised guarantee agreements

14.227 The statutory provision for the release of T1 from liability on his tenant covenants can be partially displaced where L1 and T1 enter into an 'authorised guarantee agreement' under which T1 guarantees the due perform- ance by T2 of the tenant covenants of the lease.[1] The facility of the authorised guarantee agreement constitutes a significant concession to the vested interests of landlords: the agreement has the effect of deferring the release of T1's contractual liability for the duration of his immediate successor's leasehold tenure (and no further).[2]

1   L&T(C)A 1995, s 16(2). See Law Com No 174 (1988), para 4.11.
2   Following the conclusion of the authorised guarantee agreement, T1 and T2 are, in effect, bound jointly and severally by the same covenants (L&T(C)A 1995, s 13(1)). If, however, T1 is subsequently caused to defray a liability incurred by T2, T1 is entitled as guarantor to be indemnified against the principal debtor (see *Duncan Fox & Co v North & South Wales Bank* (1880) 6 App Cas 1); and T1 and T2 are governed by the rules concerning contribution imposed by the Civil Liability (Contribution) Act 1978 (L&T(C)A 1995, s 13(3)).

A parliamentary compromise

14.228   In reality the authorised guarantee agreement represents a smudgy parliamentary compromise between the old principle of enduring contractual liability and the urgent social concern to liberate T1 from post-assignment liability.[1] The principle of the sanctity of covenanted obligations is accorded a limited effect in so far as T1 can be made to bear a continuing liability for the defaults of his immediate successor (T2), but not, for instance, for the defaults of T3.[2] (On a further assignment of the term to T3, there is, of course, nothing to prevent T2 from being caused, consistently with the 1995 Act, to enter into another authorised guarantee agreement under which T2 in his turn warrants the performance of the leasehold covenants by T3.[3]) In this way the common law concept of unqualified liability is transmuted, at each stage, into a principle of time-limited liability at one remove.[4] If a former tenant is compelled, pursuant to an authorised guarantee agreement, to meet a later tenant's 'fixed charge' liability, he is given a compensatory right to call for the grant to himself of an 'overriding lease'.[5] In effect the former tenant is accorded an opportunity to recover the leasehold interest which he had earlier assigned.

1   'In coming to terms with their tenants, the landlords have struck a hard bargain indeed' (S N Bridge, [1996] CLJ 313 at 356).
2   An authorised guarantee agreement cannot be validly constituted by any agreement which purports to impose on T1 a requirement to guarantee the performance of covenants by any person other than T2 or to impose on T1 any liability or restriction in relation to any time after he is released from his authorised guarantee agreement (L&T(C)A 1995, s 16(4)).
3   An authorised guarantee agreement can be validly made only where a tenant would otherwise be 'released from a tenant covenant by virtue of this Act' (L&T(C)A 1995, s 16(1)). The 1995 Act accords an expansive interpretation to the word 'tenant', so that it includes any person 'for the time being' entitled to the leasehold term (L&T(C)A 1995, s 28(1)). T2's assignment of the term to T3 normally effects a statutory release of T2 from the tenant covenants of the tenancy (L&T(C)A 1995, s 5(2)(a), (3)(a)), with the result that T2 is eligible – though probably far from willing – to enter into an authorised guarantee agreement insisted upon by the landlord as a condition of consent to the assignment to T3 (see also L&T(C)A 1995, s 25(3)).
4   T1 is freed from continuing liability in respect of any 'fixed charge' payable under the covenants of the lease unless, within six months of the date on which the charge became due, the landlord serves on T1 a 'problem notice' pursuant to L&T(C)A 1995, s 17. T1 can thus effectively limit his exposure to six months of 'fixed charge' liability **[para 14.235]**.
5   L&T(C)A 1995, s 19(1) **[para 14.236]**. The 'overriding lease' takes effect as a 'new' tenancy under the 1995 Act (L&T(C)A 1995, s 20(1)).

Preconditions of the authorised guarantee agreement

14.229 The availability of the authorised guarantee agreement turns on the fact that most leases expressly require that any assignment of the leasehold term must have the landlord's prior consent. The use of an authorised guarantee agreement is therefore limited by tightly drawn statutory preconditions. An agreement of this kind can be made only where T1's assignment of his term is governed by a leasehold covenant which prohibits assignment except with the consent of his landlord or of some other person.[1] An agreement is an 'authorised guarantee agreement' if consent to T1's assignment was given subject to a 'lawfully imposed' condition that T1 should enter into an authorised guarantee agreement[2] and the agreement was entered into by T1 in pursuance of that condition.[3] Entry into the authorised guarantee agreement becomes, in effect, the price of consent to the assignment, but the courts have emphasised that the landlord is not always or necessarily entitled to insist that T1 should undertake the burden of such an agreement. The statutory proviso that the condition be 'lawfully imposed' has indirectly inserted a requirement that it be 'reasonable' for the landlord to make his consent contingent on entry into an authorised guarantee agreement.[4]

1   L&T(C)A 1995, s 16(3)(a) [**para 14.83**].
2   L&T(C)A 1995, s 16(3)(b).
3   L&T(C)A 1995, s 16(3)(c).
4   *Wallis Fashion Group Ltd v CGU Life Assurance* (2000) 81 P & CR 393 at [24], [28] per Neuberger J. In effect, T1 would be required, in cases of dispute, to 'show that no reasonable landlord could, in the circumstances, require' entry into an authorised guarantee agreement. See L&TA 1927, s 19 [**para 14.83**].

Contents of the authorised guarantee agreement

14.230 Where the statutory preconditions are met, the authorised guarantee agreement may impose on T1 a liability as 'sole or principal debtor' (as distinct from a guarantor) in respect of T2's obligations.[1] The authorised guarantee agreement may also require that, if the term taken by T2 is subsequently disclaimed (e g on T2's insolvency or bankruptcy), T1 should enter into a new tenancy of the demised premises for a term which expires no later than the term of the disclaimed tenancy and on tenant covenants which are no more onerous than those contained in that tenancy.[2]

1   L&T(C)A 1995, s 16(5)(a). Where T1 undertakes the role of guarantor, the rules of law relating to guarantors (and in particular those relating to the release of sureties) are expressly made applicable (L&T(C)A 1995, s 16(8)). Thus, for instance, any material variation of the leasehold obligations subsequently agreed between L1 and T2 has the effect of discharging T1's liability as guarantor (see *Holme v Brunskill* (1878) 3 QBD 495 at 507).
2   L&T(C)A 1995, s 16(5)(c).

T1's liability on varied terms

14.231 Where, following his assignment to T2, T1 bears some continuing liability under his original covenants or pursuant to an authorised guarantee agreement, there is a danger that T1 may be required to meet a heightened liability to the landlord which has been brought about by a variation of the tenant covenants effected after the assignment of his term to T2. Although statutory intervention may have been strictly unnecessary,[1] the Landlord and Tenant (Covenants) Act 1995 seeks to protect T1 from the adverse impact of such alterations of liability. T1 and his guarantor (if any) are relieved of liability to the extent of any amount 'referable to any relevant variation' of the tenant covenants following the assignment.[2] For this purpose a 'relevant variation' is one which the landlord would normally have had, at the time of the variation, an absolute right to refuse or allow.[3]

1 See *Friends' Provident Life Office v British Railways Board* [1996] 1 All ER 336 at 348d–e **[para 14.222]**; *Beegas Nominees Ltd v BHP Petroleum Ltd* [1998] EGCS 60.
2 L&T(C)A 1995, s 18(2)–(3).
3 L&T(C)A 1995, s 18(4). In determining whether the landlord was so entitled, regard must be had to all the circumstances (including the effect of any statutory provision affecting his freedom of action (L&T(C)A 1995, s 18(5)). In effect, T1's immunity applies only in respect of subsequent variations of the leasehold terms which normally lay within the discretion of the landlord, and not in respect of variations (eg a rent review) which were authorised by the original lease.

Liability of L1

14.232 The Landlord and Tenant (Covenants) Act 1995 does not aim for parity between L1 and T1 in the matter of release from post-assignment liability. Contrary to the Law Commission's original recommendation,[1] L1, on assignment to L2 of his reversionary estate in a 'new' tenancy, is *not* afforded an automatic release from liability for the performance of the landlord covenants of the lease. Instead L1 has the opportunity, within certain time limits, to *apply* to T1 for a release from those covenants[2] and will be so released if T1 fails to serve on L1 a written notice of objection within four weeks of L1's initial notice *or* if T1 serves a notice of consent to L1's release *or* if the county court declares, on application by L1, that it is 'reasonable' for L1 to be released.[3] L1's release, where it occurs,[4] is effective from the date of the transfer of the reversion to L2[5] but does not absolve L1 from liability for any breach of covenant committed prior to that date.[6] Nor can L1 apply to be released from covenants which were expressed to be personal to him: such covenants do not constitute 'landlord covenants' for the purpose of the 1995 Act.[7] To this extent it remains possible for landlord and tenant to place a contractual limit on the transmissibility of burdens under a tenancy.

1 See Law Com No 174 (1988), para 4.31.
2 L&T(C)A 1995, s 6(2). An undertaking by T1 in advance to release L1 on assignment is an abuse of the 1995 Act and therefore invalid (L&T(C)A 1995, s 25(1)(a)). Application must be by a notice served either before or within the four weeks following the assignment which informs T1 of the assignment and requests L1's release from the relevant covenants (L&T(C)A 1995, ss 8(1), 27(1)–(2)). Any notice not in the statutorily prescribed form (or in a form 'substantially to the same effect') is declared invalid for the purpose (L&T(C)A 1995, s 27(4)). See Landlord and Tenant (Covenants) Act 1995 (Notices) Regulations 1995 (SI 1995/2964). An assignment of the reversion in only part of the demised premises does not

change L1's position in respect of landlord and tenant covenants relating to that part of the premises outside the scope of the assignment (L&T(C)A 1995, s 6(3)).

3   L&T(C)A 1995, s 8(2). No release of L1 can terminate his liability on landlord covenants relating to residential premises unless and until he gives the tenant written notice of the name and address of L2 (see L&TA 1985, s 3(1), (3A)–(3B) [**para 14.73**]; L&T(C)A 1995, s 26(2)).

4   If L1 either fails in his application for release (or does not apply), he may apply for release on the next assignment of the reversion (L&T(C)A 1995, s 7).

5   L&T(C)A 1995, s 8(3). L1 simultaneously loses the benefit of the tenant covenants which affect the premises to which the assignment relates (L&T(C)A 1995, s 6(2)(b), (3)(b)).

6   L&T(C)A 1995, s 24(1). L1 retains the right to sue in respect of any breach of a tenant covenant occurring prior to the date of L1's release (L&T(C)A 1995, s 24(4)).

7   *BHP Petroleum Great Britain Ltd v Chesterfield Properties Ltd* [2002] Ch 194 at [60].

LIABILITY OF LI AND TI UNDER OLD (PRE-1996) TENANCIES

14.233   The Landlord and Tenant (Covenants) Act 1995 operates rather differently in relation to *pre-1996* tenancies. Here, in the event of assignment of his term, T1 enjoys the benefit of *no* automatic statutory release from his liabilities under the lease. T1 remains responsible, in principle, for the defaults of T2 (and, for that matter, the defaults of subsequent assignees). However, the old common law rule of continuing tenant liability is significantly modified by the introduction of a requirement that L1 give warning to T1 that he is about to be visited with liability for the defaults of T2 (or, as the case may, the defaults of other assignees of the term).

'Problem notice' relating to 'fixed charges'

14.234   The 1995 Act provides that, following his assignment to T2, T1 is no longer to bear any liability for any 'fixed charge' which becomes payable under the covenants of the lease *except* where, within six months of such a charge falling due, the landlord serves on T1 a statutory notice (commonly called a 'problem notice') relating to the relevant breach.[1] An onus is therefore placed on the landlord (whether L1 or L2 or, for that matter, any successor landlord) to serve on T1 (or any guarantor of T1[2]) a notice informing him that the fixed charge is now due and that the landlord intends to recover from T1 the amount specified in the notice (including appropriate interest).[3] For this purpose section 17(6) of the 1995 Act makes it clear that a 'fixed charge' includes rent,[4] service charges[5] and any other liquidated sum by way of tenant liability, but *excludes* claims for unliquidated damages (e g in respect of breach of a repairing covenant).

1   The impulse behind the statutory notice is the need to prevent the unannounced arrival of liability which was the calamitous keynote of the common law in its pre-1996 application [**para 14.222**]. Notice may be served on T1 at his last known place of abode (see L&TA 1927, s 23, as applied by L&T(C)A 1995, s 27(5)).

2   L&T(C)A 1995, s 17(3).

3   L&T(C)A 1995, s 17(2). The landlord's notice must include an explanation of its significance (L&T(C)A 1995, s 27(3)) and any notice not in the statutorily prescribed form (or in a form 'substantially to the same effect') is declared to be ineffective for the purpose of section 17 (L&T(C)A 1995, s 27(4)).

4   An increase of rent may be back-dated, but information to this effect must be contained in a
     further notice served by the landlord (L&T(C)A 1995, s 17(4)).
5   As defined by L&TA 1985, s 18 [**para 14.75**], irrespective of whether the premises comprise a
     dwelling (see L&T(C)A 1995, s 17(6)(b))).

Restriction of T1's liability for 'fixed charges'

14.235   In practice the statutory requirement of the problem notice operates
as an important curtailment of the continuing liability of T1 (and any
guarantor) for 'fixed charges' generated by the breaches of later assignees. T1's
liability extends, at most, to those 'fixed charges' which were incurred during
the six months immediately preceding the service of the notice. If the landlord
altogether fails to serve the appropriate statutory notice, T1 (and his guarantor)
are automatically freed from *any* liability for 'fixed charges'.[1] If the statutory
notice is duly served, no more than six months of 'fixed charge' liability can
accrue before T1 (and his guarantor) are afforded an opportunity to regain
control of the leasehold term which T1 had previously assigned. Such control
arises in the form of an 'overriding lease'.

1   L&T(C)A 1995, s 17(2)–(3).

'Overriding leases'

14.236   If either T1 or his guarantor makes full payment of the amount
demanded under the landlord's problem notice, the payer becomes statutorily
entitled[1] to have the landlord grant him an 'overriding lease' of the premises
demised by the tenancy.[2] This 'overriding lease' takes effect as a statutory
leasehold interposed between the landlord and the defaulting assignee (see *Fig.
43*),[3] thereby compensating T1 (or his guarantor) for his compulsory discharge
of the assignee's liability by the vesting of an intermediate leasehold estate.[4] In
reality T1 (or, as the case may be, his guarantor) takes over as landlord in
relation to the defaulter and becomes able to enforce the covenants of the lease
directly, by way of money remedy, forfeiture or otherwise, against that
defaulter. Notwithstanding the earlier assignment, the person who meets the
liability specified by the problem notice acquires, in the form of an overriding
lease, a commerciable asset which offsets (at least in part) the unwelcome
imposition of liability for somebody else's breach of covenant.

1   A request for an overriding lease is protectable 'as if it were an estate contract' by the entry of
     a notice under the Land Registration Act 2002 [**para 12.90**] or by registration of a Class C(iv)
     charge under the Land Charges Act 1972, but can never comprise an overriding interest in
     registered land (L&T(C)A 1995, s 20(6) [**para 12.172**]).
2   L&T(C)A 1995, s 19(1). See Land Registration (Overriding Leases) Rules 1995 (SI 1995/3154).
     The claim to an overriding lease must be asserted by written application to the landlord at the
     time of the 'qualifying payment' or within 12 months thereafter (L&T(C)A 1995, s 19(5)),
     whereupon the landlord, on pain of liability for a statutory tort (L&T(C)A 1995, s 20(3)),
     must grant and deliver to the claimant an overriding lease 'within a reasonable time'
     (L&T(C)A 1995, s 19(6)). If two or more persons become entitled to the grant of an

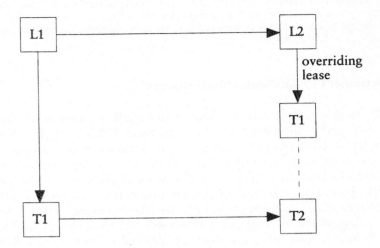

Fig. **43**

overriding lease, priority is given to the first applicant (L&T(C)A 1995, s 19(7)(b)). If two or more requests for an overriding lease are made on the same day, a former tenant takes priority over a guarantor and, as between two former tenants, priority is given to the tenant whose liability commenced earlier (L&T(C)A 1995, s 19(8)). The claimant of an overriding lease may become liable for the landlord's reasonable costs in the event of a withdrawn or abandoned request (L&T(C)A 1995, s 19(9)).

3   The overriding lease is, in effect, a lease of the reversion (L&T(C)A 1995, s 19(2) **[para 7.209]**), although any lease which 'overrides' a tenancy created before 1996 cannot rank as a 'new' tenancy for the purposes of the 1995 Act (L&T(C)A 1995, s 20(1)).

4   The landlord is not obliged to grant an overriding lease if the relevant tenancy has already been determined prior to the payment of the amount demanded by the problem notice or if some other person has already been granted an overriding lease or has a prior right to have one granted to him (L&T(C)A 1995, s 19(7)).

Terms of the 'overriding lease'

14.237   The overriding lease granted under the Landlord and Tenant (Covenants) Act 1995 normally comprises a tenancy of the reversion for a term equal to the remainder of the relevant tenancy plus three days.[1] Subject to any modifications agreed between the landlord and the claimant, the overriding lease contains the same covenants as the overridden tenancy except in so far as such covenants are expressed to be 'personal' covenants[2] or have become 'spent' by the time the overriding lease is granted.[3]

1   L&T(C)A 1995, s 19(2)(a) (or such shorter period as will not wholly displace the landlord's reversionary interest expectant on that tenancy).
2   L&T(C)A 1995, s 19(2)(b), (3).
3   L&T(C)A 1995, s 19(4)(b). The overriding lease is deemed to be authorised as against, and therefore binding upon, any mortgagee or chargee of the landlord's reversion (L&T(C)A 1995, s 20(4)). The grant of the overriding lease cannot constitute a breach of any covenant in the overridden tenancy which restricts subletting or parting with possession of the demised premises (L&T(C)A 1995, s 20(5)).

T1's liability for other charges

14.238 It can be seen that, in relation to 'fixed charges' arising under tenancies granted before 1996, the Landlord and Tenant (Covenants) Act 1995 substantially modifies the old common law rule of unlimited liability. However, the rule of enduring contractual liability continues, with undiminished force, to fix T1 with responsibility for any *unliquidated* liabilities incurred by T2 or T3 (eg for unquantified damage which flows from, say, a failure to perform a covenant to repair).

T1's right to indemnity

14.239 In such circumstances T1, if caused to pay damages for another's breach of covenant, retains a quasi-contractual entitlement to indemnity against the actual defaulter.[1] In reality, however, this right is generally futile. The reason why L1 has sued T1 in the first place (rather than the actual wrongdoer) lies almost certainly in the fact that the defaulting assignee is bankrupt or insolvent,[2] in which case T1's right to indemnity provides only illusory comfort. It may therefore be prudent for an otherwise defenceless assignor of a leasehold term, if possessed of sufficient bargaining power,[3] to reserve an express right of re-entry against his assignee in the event of any breach by the latter for which the assignor is made liable.[4]

1   See *Moule v Garrett* (1872) LR 7 Ex 101 at 104 [**para 14.220**].
2   See eg *Warnford Investments Ltd v Duckworth* [1979] Ch 127.
3   See, however, (1983) 127 Sol Jo 832 (G L Leigh).
4   See eg *Shiloh Spinners Ltd v Harding* [1973] AC 691 [**para 14.297**].

Chains of indemnity covenants

14.240 Even where T1 seeks to pass on the impact of supervening liability by means of a chain of indemnity covenants, this strategy is vulnerable to breakdown if any of the intermediate assignees becomes insolvent or untraceable.[1] T1 cannot enforce the indemnity against assignees further down the chain unless he has obtained an express assignment of the benefit of the particular covenant which it is sought to enforce (and such an assignment is not always forthcoming).[2] The only ray of light for T1 is that if the leasehold obligations taken over by a later assignee are then guaranteed by a solvent stranger, the latter's liability as guarantor is deemed to be prior to that of T1 as the original contractual tenant. In consequence if T1 is sued in respect of the assignee's default, he is entitled to an indemnity from the guarantor.[3]

1   In *RPH Ltd v Mirror Group Newspapers and Mirror Group Holdings* (1992) 65 P & CR 252, there had been successive assignments of the leasehold term to T2, T3 and T4. Of these assignees only T3 was now clearly solvent, but Nicholls V-C rejected an application by T1 that T2 be directed to enforce its right of indemnity against T3. (All the assignees here were parts of the corporate conglomerate controlled by the fraudster Robert Maxwell.)
2   In *RPH Ltd v Mirror Group Newspapers and Mirror Group Holdings* (1992) 65 P & CR 252 at

254–255, Nicholls V-C declined to order the insolvent T2 to assign to T1 the benefit of T3's indemnity covenant. (The only winners were presumably the receivers of L1, also a Maxwell company, whose recovery from the solvent T1 went to diminish the shortfall suffered by the Maxwell pensioners.)

3   See *Becton Dickinson UK Ltd v Zwebner* [1989] QB 208 at 217F–218C; [1989] Conv 292 (P McLoughlin). See also *Kumar v Dunning* [1989] QB 193 at 200A–B per Browne-Wilkinson V-C; *Karacominakis v Big Country Developments Pty Ltd* (2000) 10 BPR 18235 at [242] (NSW Court of Appeal).

RIGHTS AND LIABILITIES OF ASSIGNEES

14.241   Whereas the liability of L1 and T1 *inter se* on the covenants of the lease has rested historically on privity of *contract*, the same principle could never provide a basis for the enforcement of these covenants between those who took an estate from either party by assignment. At common law contracts are not normally enforceable by or against strangers,[1] but to this stark doctrine there arose two outstanding exceptions,[2] namely in the area of freehold restrictive covenants[3] and in respect of those leasehold covenants which were held to be enforceable by reference to the concept of *privity of estate*.[4]

1   See *Rhone v Stephens* [1994] 2 AC 310 at 316H per Lord Templeman.
2   See *Amsprop Trading Ltd v Harris Distribution Ltd* [1997] 1 WLR 1025 at 1028G–H per Neuberger J.
3   See [**paras 9.143–9.153, 13.63–13.116**].
4   See *Cardwell v Walker* [2004] 2 P & CR 122 at [41] per Neuberger J.

The doctrine of privity of estate

14.242   For over four centuries it has been clear that the benefit and burden of the covenants contained in a legal lease may extend beyond those parties who are bound together by contractual privity. This consequence represented a relaxation of the rigours of the common law[1] and flowed from a doctrine of 'privity of estate' which was first spelt out in the historic ruling of the Court of King's Bench in *Spencer's Case*.[2]

1   See *Rhone v Stephens* [1994] 2 AC 310 at 317A per Lord Templeman.
2   (1583) 5 Co Rep 16a at 17b, 77 ER 72 at 75.

Spencer's Case

14.243   *Spencer's Case* held that the benefit and burden of all 'touching and concerning' covenants are annexed at common law to the tenant's term of years and to the corresponding reversionary estate held by the landlord, with the result that every subsequent owner of either legal estate takes his estate with the benefit of, and subject to, the same covenants.[1] It is this doctrinal mechanism of notional attachment to estates which ultimately underpins the extended policing of leasehold covenants. The doctrine of privity of estate effectively imprints the contractual rights and obligations of the original lease upon the respective estates of landlord and tenant so as to bind these estates in the hands of third parties.[2] In this way leasehold covenants (whether positive or negative) run with the landlord's reversion and the tenant's term and therefore affect all assignees who are 'privy' to the estate of the lease.[3]

1   The effect of the doctrine of privity of estate was 'to create rights and obligations which are independent of the parallel obligations of the original human covenantor who and whose heirs may fail and obligations of a corporate covenantor which may be dissolved' (*City of London Corpn v Fell* [1994] 1 AC 458 at 465C per Lord Templeman).

2   See *City of London Corpn v Fell* [1993] QB 589 at 603H–604A per Nourse LJ; *Cardwell v Walker* [2004] 2 P & CR 122 at [41] per Neuberger J; *Picton-Warlow v Allendale Holdings Pty Ltd* [1988] WAR 107 at 110 per Brinsden J.

3   See *Rhone v Stephens* [1994] 2 AC 310 at 317B per Lord Templeman. In *Spencer's Case* the Court was able to draw upon the analogy of the Grantees of Reversions Act 1540, which similarly transmitted to assignees of the reversion the benefit and burden of 'touching and concerning' covenants [**para 14.274**].

Limitations of Spencer's Case

14.244   The doctrine of privity of estate does something which the doctrine of contractual privity is essentially concerned to prevent: it permits the contractual rights and obligations of L1 and T1 to be diffused throughout the leasehold relationships which emerge when either L1 or T1 transfers his estate in the land. By annexing the contractual obligations of L1 and T1 to the estates of both, the common law creates a tenancy which 'is capable of existence as a species of property independently of the contract.'[1] Leasehold covenants thus reach far outside the immediate contractual nexus, becoming enforceable by and against any person who is privy to the leasehold estate. Only two conditions curtail this basis for enforcement, but they are fundamental to the doctrine of privity of estate. *Spencer's Case* applies only as between those who take a *legal* estate in the land[2] and governs only those leasehold covenants which *touch and concern* the demised premises.[3] But if these two conditions are met, the original covenants of every legal lease (whether positive or restrictive in character) are made potentially binding on all assignees of either the term[4] or the reversion.[5]

1   *City of London Corpn v Fell* [1993] QB 589 at 604F–G per Nourse LJ. On the metamorphosis of contract into property, see [**paras 2.52, 7.71, 9.11**].

2   See *Cox v Bishop* (1857) 8 De GM & G 815 at 822–825, 44 ER 604 at 607–608; *Rhone v Stephens* [1994] 2 AC 310 at 316H–317A per Lord Templeman.

3   *Williams v Earle* (1868) LR 3 QB 739 at 749 per Blackburn J. See also *City of London Corpn v Fell* [1994] 1 AC 458 at 464H–465A, G per Lord Templeman; [1993] QB 589 at 603H–604A, 604F–G per Nourse LJ; *Rhone v Stephens* [1994] 2 AC 310 at 317B per Lord Templeman. On the meaning of 'touching and concerning' covenants, see [**paras 14.250–14.263**].

4   See e g *Williams v Bosanquet* (1819) 1 Brod & B 238 at 262–263, 129 ER 714 at 723.

5   See e g *Celsteel Ltd v Alton House Holdings Ltd (No 2)* [1986] 1 WLR 666 at 673A. (Here the application of *Spencer's Case* was simply confirmed by LPA 1925, s 142(1)).

14.245   Irrespective of the nature or duration of the leasehold estate concerned, *Spencer's Case* still provides the linchpin of modern covenant enforcement.[1] Privity of estate has, however, been modified by later statutory developments, some of which, again, distinguish between 'new' (ie post-1995) tenancies and 'old' (ie pre-1996) tenancies.[2]

1   See *Forestview Nominees Pty Ltd v Perpetual Trustees WA Ltd* (1996) 141 ALR 687 at 696 per French J.
2   See L&T(C)A 1995, s 1 **[para 14.224]**.

RIGHTS AND LIABILITIES UNDER NEW (POST-1995) TENANCIES

14.246   It was the historic achievement of the device of privity of estate to cause most leasehold rights and obligations to travel with the estates to which they were attached into the hands of third parties. This extended policing of the leasehold relationship has been adapted, in a simplified form, by the rules which govern tenancies granted on or after 1 January 1996.[1]

1   See the statutory definition of 'new' tenancies (L&T(C)A 1995, s 1(3)–(7) **[para 14.224]**).

Statutory annexation of leasehold covenants

14.247   The Landlord and Tenant (Covenants) Act 1995 provides that the benefit and burden of all landlord and tenant covenants (whether positive or negative) are 'annexed and incident to the whole, and to each and every part, of the premises demised by the tenancy and of the reversion in them.'[1] Thus annexed, the benefit and burden subsequently 'pass on an assignment' of these premises or of the landlord's reversion,[2] provided that the covenants concerned are not 'expressed to be personal to any person.'[3] This statutory confirmation of the transmissibility of leasehold benefits and burdens is more expansive than the rule in *Spencer's Case* in at least two respects.

1   L&T(C)A 1995, s 3(1)(a).
2   L&T(C)A 1995, s 3(1)(b). The 1995 Act thus implements the Law Commission's view that all the terms of a lease should be regarded as 'a single bargain for letting the property' and that, when the interest of one of the parties changes hands, the successor should 'fully take his predecessor's place as landlord or tenant, without distinguishing between different categories of covenant' (Law Com No 174 (1988), para 4.1).
3   L&T(C)A 1995, s 3(6)(a).

Abandonment of the 'touch and concern' criterion

14.248   *Spencer's Case* confers a third party impact only upon those covenants of the lease which 'touch and concern'[1] the demised premises. The 'touch and concern' criterion ensures that covenants of a purely personal character cannot bind the land permanently. The 1995 Act replicates and extends this denial of enduring effect for covenants which are 'merely collateral' to the land.[2] The statutory exception for covenants 'expressed to be personal' neatly avoids the semantic complexity of the 'touch and concern' test[3] and places a new onus on those who draft leasehold covenants to specify expressly those covenants which are *not* intended to run with the land.

1　See *Cardwell v Walker* [2004] 2 P & CR 122 at [41] per Neuberger J ('a somewhat archaic expression').

2　See *Rhone v Stephens* [1994] 2 AC 310 at 317B per Lord Templeman.

3　[Para 14.253]. See *Oceanic Village Ltd v United Attractions Ltd* [2000] Ch 234 at 243G per Neuberger J ('The Act of 1995 makes the law much simpler'). The abandonment of the 'touch and concern' criterion was recommended by the Law Commission, which observed in 1988 that it had become 'hard to discern a clear guiding principle' in some of the case law on 'touching and concerning' covenants (Law Com No 174 (1988), paras 2.23, 4.46).

Covenants run both at law and in equity

14.249　*Spencer's Case* caused covenants to run only at law, with the consequence that privity of estate could not be claimed in relation to an equitable lease and the burden of leasehold covenants could not be enforced against an assignee who took only an equitable estate.[1] The Landlord and Tenant (Covenants) Act 1995 sets aside these restrictive implications of privity of estate. On assignment by either landlord or tenant, the statute accords an enduring force to 'landlord and tenant covenants' which makes no distinction between legal and equitable leases or between legal and equitable assignments of any estate.[2]

1　[Para 14.244].

2　L&T(C)A 1995, s 28(1).

RIGHTS AND LIABILITIES UNDER OLD (PRE-1996) TENANCIES

14.250　Tenancies granted before 1 January 1996 are still governed by *Spencer's Case*,[1] as amended by statutes enacted prior to 1996. Thus privity of estate causes the original leasehold covenants to affect subsequent legal assignees of the reversion and the term in so far as these covenants 'touch and concern' the land demised.

1　(1583) 5 Co Rep 16a, 77 ER 72.

Purpose of the 'touch and concern' requirement

14.251　The 'touch and concern' requirement has no application to the original lessor and lessee, whose relationship is governed by the totality of their contractual stipulations. The 'touch and concern' requirement aims, by contrast, to impose some restriction on the kinds of contractual obligation which may be allowed to benefit and burden third parties who are brought within the ambit of a leasehold relationship by privity of estate. It is not clear that all of the contractual arrangements fixed by L1 and T1 should necessarily have an automatic binding effect on such participants. In so far as privity of estate converts private contracts into potentially long-term arrangements for the governance of land use, the 'touch and concern' test is intended to operate as a silent filtering device for the exclusion of certain categories of covenant which are not integral to the leasehold relationship and are therefore deemed not to deserve such durable impact.[1]

1   'In short, through the exercise of the touch and concern test, the judiciary is vested with power to fix the ambits of private planning' (U Reichman, *Judicial Supervision of Servitudes*, 7 J Legal Stud 139 at 140 (1978)). See also H W R Wade, [1957] CLJ 148 at 149.

14.252   The practical consequence of the 'touch and concern' criterion is that not every covenant contained in a lease is enforceable outside the immediate contractual nexus of lessor and lessee.[1] The professed purpose of the 'touch and concern' test is that such extensive effect should be confined to those covenants which intrinsically affect 'the landlord in his normal capacity as landlord or the tenant in his normal capacity as tenant.'[2] By the application of this test it is thought to withhold long-term effect from leasehold rights and obligations which are of substantially personal or private significance for the parties to the lease.

1   See *Thursby v Plant* (1668) 1 Wms Saund 237 at 239–240, 85 ER 268 at 269.
2   See *Hua Chiao Commercial Bank Ltd v Chiaphua Industries Ltd* [1987] AC 99 at 107B per Lord Oliver of Aylmerton.

Definition of the 'touch and concern' requirement

14.253   Although the overall purpose of the 'touch and concern' requirement is easily identified, more precise definitions of 'touching and concerning' have proved elusive.[1] It is notoriously difficult to propose a definition of 'touching and concerning' which is not flawed by circularity. The ascertainment of 'touching and concerning' quality is ultimately self-determining if guided only by the proposition that 'touching and concerning' covenants are those which affect parties in their generic character as landlord or tenant respectively. As Lord Oliver of Aylmerton put it in *Hua Chiao Commercial Bank Ltd v Chiaphua Industries Ltd*,[2] to ask whether a particular covenant 'affects the landlord qua landlord or the tenant qua tenant is an exercise which begs the question. It does so only if it runs with the reversion or with the land respectively.'[3]

1   *Cardwell v Walker* [2004] 2 P & CR 122 at [46] per Neuberger J. See the similar difficulties inherent in identifying the categories of rights which 'benefit' or 'accommodate' a dominant tenement in the law of easements and restrictive covenants [**paras 8.33–8.46, 9.164–9.169**].
2   [1987] AC 99 at 112F.
3   This vitiating factor probably also afflicts the classic test, articulated in *Mayor of Congleton v Pattison* (1808) 10 East 130 at 135, 103 ER 725 at 727, which defined a covenant as having 'touching and concerning' quality if it 'affected the nature, quality, or value of the thing demised, independently of collateral circumstances; or if it affected the mode of enjoying it.' See also *Rogers v Hosegood* [1900] 2 Ch 388 at 395.

A 'satisfactory working test'

14.254   In *P & A Swift Investments v Combined English Stores Group Plc*,[1] Lord Oliver was later to proffer his own guide to a 'satisfactory working test' for identifying 'touching and concerning' covenants.[2] *First*, such a covenant must benefit only the reversioner for the time being, so that, if separated from the reversion, it ceases to be of benefit to the covenantee. *Second*, the covenant must affect the nature, quality, mode of user or value of the land of the reversioner. *Third*, the covenant must not be expressed to be personal (ie must not have been given only to a specific reversioner or in respect of the obligations only of a specific tenant).[3]

1   [1989] AC 632 at 642E–F. See also *System Floors Ltd v Ruralpride Ltd* [1995] 1 EGLR 48 at 50H; *Cardwell v Walker* [2004] 2 P & CR 122 at [46]–[49]. See J E Adams, '"Touching and Concerning", from *Spencer's Case* to *Swift*' [1989] EG 24 (25 November).
2   **[Para 13.33]**.
3   See also *Lang v Asemo Pty Ltd* [1989] VR 773 at 776.

A peculiar economic interest as estate owner

14.255   Analysed thus, the requirement of 'touch and concern' operates largely to limit the enforcement of leasehold covenants to those promises in whose due performance the respective estate owners under a lease have a peculiar economic interest *qua estate owner*.[1] A 'touching and concerning' covenant is thus demarcated from those other covenants, albeit contained in the same lease, in whose due performance the promisee has no higher or more distinctive economic interest than he would if he were not a party to the lease.[2]

1   See J E Stake, 'Toward an Economic Understanding of Touch and Concern' (1988) Duke LJ 925.
2   'The general principle is, that if the performance of the covenant be beneficial to the reversioner, in respect of the lessor's demand, and to no other person, his assignee may sue upon it; but if it be beneficial to the lessor, without regard to his continuing owner of the estate, it is a mere collateral covenant, upon which the assignee cannot sue' (*Vyvyan v Arthur* (1823) 1 B & C 410 at 417, 107 ER 152 at 155 per Best J).

Application of the 'touch and concern' requirement

14.256   Although an element of inconsistency or artificiality attaches to the definition of 'touching and concerning' covenants, it has not proved difficult to identify most of the leasehold covenants which 'touch and concern' the demised premises.[1]

1   Although a covenant which does not intrinsically 'touch and concern' cannot by agreement between landlord and tenant be made to run with the land, a covenant which would otherwise run can be cut back by the express terms of the lease and made purely personal to the parties (see *Re Robert Stephens & Co Ltd* [1915] 1 Ch 802 at 808; *Re Rakita's Application* [1971] Qd R 59 at 65).

'Touching and concerning' covenants undertaken by a tenant

14.257   Amongst the category of tenant covenants accepted as having 'touching and concerning' quality are positive covenants to pay rent[1] and water charges,[2] to repair the premises[3] or insure them against fire,[4] and to cultivate land in a particular manner.[5] Likewise the 'touch and concern' test has been held to be satisfied by such negative covenants as the tenant's undertaking to use property for domestic purposes only[6] and not to assign or sublet without the lessor's consent.[7]

1   *Parker v Webb* (1693) 3 Salk 5, 91 ER 656; *Kumar v Dunning* [1989] QB 193 at 200F–G per Browne-Wilkinson V-C; *P & A Swift Investments v Combined English Stores Group Plc* [1989] AC 632 at 641F–G per Lord Oliver of Aylmerton; *Karacominakis v Big Country Developments Pty Ltd* (2000) 10 BPR 18235 at [132] (NSW Court of Appeal).
2   *Lambeth LBC v Thomas* (1997) Times, 31 March.
3   *Matures v Westwood* (1598) Cro Eliz 599 at 600, 78 ER 842; *Williams v Earle* (1868) LR 3 QB 739 at 751–752; *Kumar v Dunning* [1989] QB 193 at 200F–G; *P & A Swift Investments v Combined English Stores Group Plc* [1989] AC 632 at 641F–G.
4   *Vernon v Smith* (1821) 5 B & Ald 1 at 6–10, 106 ER 1094 at 1096–1098.
5   *Chapman v Smith* [1907] 2 Ch 97 at 103.
6   *Wilkinson v Rogers* (1864) 2 De GJ & S 62 at 67–70, 46 ER 298 at 300–301.
7   *Williams v Earle* (1868) LR 3 QB 739 at 749–750; *Goldstein v Sanders* [1915] 1 Ch 549 at 556; *Cohen v Popular Restaurants Ltd* [1917] 1 KB 480 at 482; *Burns Philp Hardware Ltd v Howard Chia Pty Ltd* (1986) 8 NSWLR 621 at 640G.

'Touching and concerning' covenants undertaken by a landlord

14.258   'Touching and concerning' covenants by a landlord include covenants to renew the lease,[1] to accept a surrender of the lease,[2] to repair or to insure the demised premises, to supply water to those premises,[3] to give the tenant quiet possession of the premises,[4] and not to develop adjoining land.[5]

1   *Richardson v Sydenham* (1703) 2 Vern 447, 23 ER 885; *Simpson v Clayton* (1838) 4 Bing (NC) 758 at 780, 132 ER 981 at 989; *Woodall v Clifton* [1905] 2 Ch 257 at 279; *Churcher v Danis Hotels Pty Ltd* (1980) 8 BPR 15863 at 15874.
2   *System Floors Ltd v Ruralpride Ltd* [1995] 1 EGLR 48 at 49J–K.
3   *Jourdain v Wilson* (1821) 4 B & Ald 266 at 267, 106 ER 935.
4   *Celsteel Ltd v Alton House Holdings Ltd (No 2)* [1986] 1 WLR 666 at 672H.
5   *Ricketts v Enfield Churchwardens* [1909] 1 Ch 544 at 555.

Purely personal or collateral covenants

14.259   In effect, only covenants which are of a purely personal or collateral nature fall outside the ambit of the classic 'touch and concern' test. Examples of such covenants include a tenant's covenant to perform some personal service for the landlord, a covenant to pay an annual sum to a third party,[1] and a covenant for forfeiture of the lease on the criminal conviction of the tenant or any occupier of the land.[2]

1   *Mayho v Buckhurst* (1617) Cro Jac 438 at 439, 79 ER 374 at 375.
2   *Stevens v Copp* (1868) LR 4 Ex 20 at 24–26 (sed quaere).

Criticism of the 'touch and concern' requirement

14.260   The years preceding the enactment of the Landlord and Tenant (Covenants) Act 1995 saw increasing criticism of the 'touch and concern' requirement in its application to landlord and tenant covenants.[1] The 'touch and concern' test seeks, of course, to identify covenants which are integral (as distinct from merely collateral) to the leasehold relationship, but the precise content of the 'touch and concern' criterion is difficult to pin down. One supporter of the 'touch and concern' test has observed that '[t]he phrase "touch and concern" continues to beguile even astute property specialists into believing that it has some objective meaning.'[2] It has been suggested that the concept ultimately concerns the 'normal expectations of society' as to whether particular benefits or burdens are so closely related to estate ownership 'that the average person would assume that the law would decree that such benefit or burden would accompany the ownership.'[3] On this basis the 'touch and concern' requirement may do little more than impose a trained, but essentially intuitive, judgment as to the kinds of benefit and burden which should be allowed to run indefinitely with land. One commentator has urged an abandonment of the 'rhetoric of touch and concern' on the ground that it merely conceals behind 'a screen of hocus pocus' the exercise of a substantive judicial discretion to terminate certain kinds of privately bargained arrangement respecting the future conduct of estate owners.[4] Other commentators take a contrary view that the operation of this constraint on the long-term private ordering of landholding is conducive to efficient and productive land management.[5]

1   The criticism is not new but merely intensified (see e g *Woodall v Clifton* [1905] 2 Ch 257 at 279 per Romer LJ; *Lyle v Smith* [1909] 2 IR 58 at 76 per Gibson J). The 'touch and concern' requirement is found in many, but not all, common law jurisdictions.
2   Gregory S Alexander, 'Freedom, Coercion, and the Law of Servitudes' 73 Cornell L Rev 883 at 897 (1987–88).
3   L Berger, 'A Policy Analysis of Promises Respecting the Use of Land' 55 Minnesota L Rev 167 at 219–220 (1970–71). See also *Abbott v Bob's U-Drive*, 352 P2d 598 at 604 (Supreme Court of Oregon, 1960).
4   See S F French, 73 Cornell L Rev 928 at 939–940 (1987–88).
5   See U Reichman, 55 S Cal L Rev 1177 at 1233 (1982).

14.261   Whatever the merits of these positions, it emerges painfully clearly that the fundamental problem with the 'touch and concern' requirement stems from the arbitrary or inconsistent outcome of some aspects of its operation.[1] 'Touching and concerning' quality has been attributed, for instance, to a tenant's covenant to retail only the landlord's brand of product on the demised premises[2] but not to the correlative covenant by a landlord to avoid competition with the tenant's business.[3] Just as surprising may be the fact that a covenant not to employ a named individual on business premises has been declared to run with the land,[4] whilst a covenant not to employ a particular class of person on the property does not so run.[5] Other conclusions, even if based faithfully on some criterion of distinctive economic interest vested in the covenantee, seem either perverse or simply contrary to justice. This appears perhaps most markedly in relation to the following kinds of leasehold covenant.

1   See *Grant v Edmondson* [1931] 1 Ch 1 at 28 per Romer LJ ('The established rules … are purely arbitrary, and the distinctions, for the most part, quite illogical'). See likewise *Burns Philp*

Hardware Ltd v Howard Chia Pty Ltd (1986) 8 NSWLR 621 at 641A per Young J; *Auscott Ltd v Panizza* (1988) NSW ConvR 55–395 at 57,665–57,666 per Bryson J.
2   *Clegg v Hands* (1890) 44 Ch D 503 at 518, 522–523 (beer); *Regent Oil Co Ltd v J A Gregory (Hatch End) Ltd* [1966] Ch 402 at 431E–F, 432F (petrol); *Caerns Motor Services Ltd v Texaco Ltd* [1994] 1 WLR 1249 at 1269C–F (petrol).
3   *Thomas v Hayward* (1869) LR 4 Ex 311 at 312.
4   *Lewin v American & Colonial Distributors Ltd* [1945] Ch 225 at 235.
5   *Mayor of Congleton v Pattison* (1808) 10 East 130 at 135–136, 103 ER 725 at 727.

Security deposits

14.262   In *Hua Chiao Commercial Bank Ltd v Chiaphua Industries Ltd*[1] T1 paid a security deposit to L1 at the commencement of the lease, the deposit to be repayable, in the absence of any breach of covenant by T1, at the expiration of the term. At the end of the term (and no breach having occurred) T1 demanded the return of the deposit from L2, who had meanwhile taken an assignment of L1's reversionary estate when L1 went into liquidation. The Judicial Committee of the Privy Council advised that L2 was not bound to pay the deposit sum to T1, thereby relegating T1 to a hopeless claim against the insolvent L1. The Privy Council took the view that such security deposits are merely 'collateral' to the lease and here created only rights *in personam* between T1 and L1.[2] Lord Oliver of Aylmerton agreed that the deposit had provided security for the due performance of T1's obligations during the term, but concluded that not every covenant 'which is related, however obliquely, to some other obligation which touches and concerns the land necessarily takes on from that very relationship, the same character as regards transmissibility to or against successors in title.'[3] In the Privy Council's view it was 'more realistic' to regard the obligation to return the deposit as undertaken by 'the landlord qua payee rather than qua landlord.'[4] This outcome, although perhaps consistent with the idea that T1 had no higher economic interest in the return of his money than any person not a party to the lease, seems both flawed and contrary to normal expectations of transmissible benefit and burden.[5]

1   [1987] AC 99.
2   See also *Eden Park Estates Ltd v Longman* (Unreported, Court of Appeal, 19 May 1980); *Re Dollar Land Corporation Ltd and Solomon* (1963) 39 DLR (2d) 221 at 226.
3   [1987] AC 99 at 112C–D. The obligation to return the deposit was 'bound up with the tenant's covenant only, as it were, at one remove' ([1987] AC 99 at 111D).
4   [1987] AC 99 at 112H–113A.
5   L2 had never, of course, received T1's deposit money ([1987] AC 99 at 113B), but arguably took the risk that transmissible burdens encumbered the estate assigned to it. The Privy Council's conclusion in the *Hua Chiao* case 'was not the only reasonable view which could be taken' (*Ralph Symonds Australia Pty Ltd v Pacific Property Investments Pty Ltd* (1988) 10 BPR 18729 at 18731 per Bryson J).

Options conferred on the tenant

14.263   Allegations of arbitrary outcome may be levelled with even more justification in the context of leasehold options. The 'touching and concerning' category has been held to include a tenant's option to renew his lease,[1] but not a tenant's option to purchase the freehold reversion,[2] nor a tenant's right of pre-emption in respect of the freehold.[3] Here a possible distinction may rest on the basis that whereas an option of renewal can be seen as a matter of peculiar interest to the lessee qua lessee, neither an option of purchase nor a right of pre-emption in respect of the freehold confers any greater benefit on the lessee than on any third party.[4] It is sometimes said that such rights affect the parties not qua lessor and lessee but qua vendor and purchaser, and are therefore truly 'collateral to the relationship of landlord and tenant.'[5] Thus analysed, a freehold option is an 'option in gross',[6] lying 'outside of the terms which regulate the relations between the landlord as landlord and the tenant as tenant.'[7] The reality of the matter is that even the covenant for renewal of a tenant's lease is increasingly regarded as a dubious case for inclusion within the category of 'touching and concerning' covenants.[8] Nowadays courts concede only grudgingly that the benefit of an option of renewal runs automatically with the tenant's term, blaming the disparate treatment of tenants' options on four hundred years of established practice.[9]

1   *Richardson v Sydenham* (1703) 2 Vern 447, 23 ER 885; *Simpson v Clayton* (1838) 4 Bing (NC) 758 at 780, 132 ER 981 at 989; *Mercantile Credits Ltd v Shell Co of Australia Ltd* (1976) 136 CLR 326 at 344 per Gibbs J [**para 14.280**].

2   *Woodall v Clifton* [1905] 2 Ch 257 at 279 per Romer LJ.

3   *Charles Frodsham & Co Ltd v Morris* (1974) 229 EG 961 at 962.

4   A further distinction lies in the fact that the exercise of an option for renewal results in a continuance of the leasehold relationship, whereas the exercise of an option of freehold purchase destroys this relationship (see *Woodall v Clifton* [1905] 2 Ch 257 at 279 per Romer LJ). It may be questioned whether this view is equally tenable nowadays when leasehold enfranchisement and the 'right to buy' have become statutorily entrenched as valuable and integral features of the leasehold relationship [**paras 7.327–7.354**].

5   See *Griffith v Pelton* [1958] Ch 205 at 225; *Davenport Central Service Station Ltd v O'Connell* [1975] 1 NZLR 755 at 757.

6   *Griffith v Pelton* [1958] Ch 205 at 225 per Jenkins LJ.

7   *Re Leeds and Batley Breweries Ltd and Bradbury's Lease* [1920] 2 Ch 548 at 551–552 per Peterson J.

8   See e g *Muller v Trafford* [1901] 1 Ch 54 at 60; *Woodall v Clifton* [1905] 2 Ch 257 at 279. Compare, however, (1981) 125 Sol Jo 816 at 817 (M P Thompson).

9   See e g *Phillips v Mobil Oil Co Ltd* [1989] 1 WLR 888 at 891E per Nicholls LJ. Compare, however, *Alcova Holdings Pty Ltd v Pandarlo Pty Ltd* (1988) 15 NSWLR 53 at 61A–B per Bryson J.

LIABILITY AS BETWEEN L2 AND T1 UNDER NEW (POST-1995) TENANCIES

14.264 Against the background of this discussion of the doctrinal basis for the transmission of leasehold benefits and burdens, it becomes possible to indicate with greater specificity the way in which these benefits and burdens pass to the participants in extended leasehold relationships (see *Fig.* 42[1]). If, during the currency of T1's possession under a term of years, L1 assigns his reversionary estate to L2, the precise effect varies slightly depending on the date of grant of the tenancy. In relation to 'new' tenancies (ie those granted on or after 1 January 1996),[2] the Landlord and Tenant (Covenants) Act 1995 ensures the following consequences.[3]

1   **[Para 14.209]**.
2   See the statutory definition of 'new' tenancies (L&T(C)A 1995, s 1(3)–(7) **[para 14.224]**).
3   The 1995 Act specifically provides that 'new' tenancies are wholly unaffected by LPA 1925, ss 78–79, 141–142 (see L&T(C)A 1995, s 30(4)).

Benefit of T1's 'tenant covenants' passes to L2

14.265   L2, on taking an assignment of L1's reversionary estate, becomes entitled, by force of statute,[1] to the benefit of all 'tenant covenants' (other than those expressed to be 'personal' in character[2]) which relate to the demised premises comprised in the assignment. Although, in the absence of an express assignment of the right to sue, L2 cannot enforce the tenant covenants 'in relation to any time falling before the assignment',[3] L2 acquires, in particular, the following rights.

1   L&T(C)A 1995, s 3(3)(b).
2   L&T(C)A 1995, s 3(6)(a) **[para 14.247]**.
3   L&T(C)A 1995, s 23(1)–(2).

Landlord's right of re-entry under the tenancy

14.266   The 1995 Act provides that the benefit of a landlord's right of re-entry under the tenancy – although not usually expressed as any form of leasehold covenant – is annexed to his reversion and passes with the assignment of that reversion (eg to L2).[1] The 1995 Act explicitly confirms that (in the absence of any waiver or release) the assignee of the reversion is entitled to exercise this right of re-entry in relation to breaches of covenant whether occurring *before* or *after* the date of the assignment.[2] The ultimate sanction within the leasehold relationship is therefore available to L2 even in respect of misconduct which pre-dates his acquisition of the reversionary estate.

1   L&T(C)A 1995, s 4.
2   L&T(C)A 1995, s 23(3).

Surety covenants entered into by T1's guarantor

14.267   L1's remedies for breach by T1 are significantly enhanced if T1 provided a third party guarantor or surety in respect of the due performance of his covenants under the lease. The guarantor will have entered into a surety covenant directly with L1[1] and both are clearly bound in contractual privity. However, when L2 subsequently takes a transfer of L1's reversionary title, L2 cannot claim, as his basis for enforcement against the guarantor, that he has contractual privity with the guarantor or even that the guarantor's covenant is a 'tenant covenant' whose benefit passes to L2 under the Landlord and Tenant (Covenants) Act 1995. In the absence of an express assignment by L1 to L2 of the benefit of the guarantee,[2] it was extremely doubtful for a period during the 1980s whether L2 could enforce the surety covenant against the guarantor.

1 The guarantor's liability, unless modified, is coextensive with that of T1 [**para 14.225**].

2 Such express assignments were relatively uncommon until the ruling in *Pinemain Ltd v Welbeck International Ltd* (1984) 272 EG 1166 at 1169–1171, when the Court of Appeal overturned the prevalent assumption in practice that the benefit of surety covenants ran generally with the reversionary estate. See [1986] Conv 50 (S Murdoch). See also *P & A Swift Investments v Combined English Stores Group Plc* [1989] AC 632 at 635H, 636H.

14.268 The problem was finally resolved in *P & A Swift Investments v Combined English Stores Group Plc*,[1] where the House of Lords explained the guarantor's liability to L2 by reference to the rules governing the enforcement of covenants between *freeholders*[2] rather than on the basis of the rules which regulate *leasehold* covenants. The guarantor in *Swift Investments* was held liable to indemnify L2 in respect of T1's rent default on the ground that, under the general common law of covenants, a surety's covenant in support of a 'touching and concerning' covenant 'must itself be a covenant which touches and concerns the land.'[3] Thus, even in the absence of an express assignment of the guarantee, the benefit of the surety's covenant ran with the L1's reversion in favour of L2.[4] In Lord Templeman's view, T1's guarantor was rendered a 'quasi tenant who volunteers to be a substitute or twelfth man for the tenant's team', with the result that the surety is 'subject to the same rules and regulations as the player he replaces.'[5]

1 [1989] AC 632 [**para 13.33**].

2 See [**paras 13.27–13.36**].

3 [1989] AC 632 at 637H per Lord Templeman. Lord Oliver of Aylmerton reinforced the 'touching and concerning' quality of the surety covenant, noting that the primary obligation of the guarantor was identical to that of the tenant, 'namely that that which is covenanted to be done will be done.' Provided that the other characteristics of a 'touching and concerning' covenant were present and that the covenant was 'connected with something to be done on, to or in relation to the land', Lord Oliver declared that the mere fact that the surety covenant envisaged the payment of a sum of money would not prevent it from running with the landlord's reversion ([1989] AC 632 at 642C–F). See also *Kumar v Dunning* [1989] QB 193 at 200H per Browne-Wilkinson V-C.

4 See also *Amsprop Trading Ltd v Harris Distribution Ltd* [1997] 1 WLR 1025 at 1033H–1034A per Neuberger J.

5 [1989] AC 632 at 638A. See generally P Sparkes, 'Reimbursement of Tenant Substitutes', in P Jackson and D C Wilde (ed), *Contemporary Property Law* (Ashgate 1999), p 342.

14.269 Although far from free of difficulties,[1] the House of Lords' decision in the *Swift Investments* case has certainly clarified the law of surety covenants to the commercial advantage of landlords. In *Coronation Street Industrial Properties Ltd v Ingall Industries Plc*[2] the House of Lords applied a similar approach where T1's guarantor had covenanted to take over the unexpired term of the lease in the event of any disclaimer by a liquidator. In allowing the benefit of this covenant to be claimed by L2, Lord Templeman viewed this particular form of surety covenant as 'touching and concerning' the land 'in equal measure' to a mere covenant for payment as in the *Swift Investments* case. Both types of covenant simply gave 'effect to the surety's obligation to procure compliance with the terms of the old lease.'[3]

1 It is difficult to reconcile *P & A Swift Investments* with the Privy Council's ruling in *Hua Chiao Commercial Bank Ltd v Chiaphua Industries Ltd* [1987] AC 99 [**para 14.262**]. If a *landlord's*

promise to pay money does not run with the landlord's reversion, it seems odd that a stranger's promise of payment should so run. The decision in *Hua Chiao* was expressly based, after all, on the consideration that the promise to repay the tenant's deposit was a money transaction undertaken by the landlord 'qua payee rather than qua landlord' ([1987] AC 99 at 112H–113A per Lord Oliver of Aylmerton).

2   [1989] 1 WLR 304.
3   [1989] 1 WLR 304 at 307E–F.

Burden of L1's 'landlord covenants' passes to L2

14.270 L2, on taking a transfer of L1's reversionary estate under a 'new' tenancy, becomes statutorily bound, as from the date of the assignment, by all the 'landlord covenants' of the tenancy.[1] These 'landlord covenants' (other than covenants expressed to be 'personal' in character[2]) remain fully enforceable by T1.

1   L&T(C)A 1995, s 3(3)(a).
2   L&T(C)A 1995, s 3(6)(a) **[para 14.247]**.

Exceptional covenants

14.271 The 1995 Act indicates that L2 is not affected by any landlord covenants which were not binding on L1 at the date of the assignment or which relate to parts of the demised premises not included in the assignment to L2.[1] For the avoidance of doubt, the 1995 Act also confirms that the statutory transmission of covenanted burdens to L2 cannot involve him in any liability 'in relation to any time falling before the assignment.'[2]

1   L&T(C)A 1995, s 3(3)(a).
2   L&T(C)A 1995, s 23(1).

Burdens which require register entry

14.272 The 1995 Act also provides expressly that the new statutory rule underpinning the transmission of covenanted obligations does not automatically cause L2 to be affected by burdens which independently require some form of register entry.[1] Here the most substantial difficulty arises in relation to landlord covenants which confer on T1 either an option to renew his lease on its expiry or an option to purchase L1's reversionary estate. Such options rank, no less clearly in the leasehold than in the freehold context,[2] as proprietary entitlements vested in T1. Although in registered land T1's option will almost certainly bind L2 as an overriding interest,[3] in unregistered land T1's option must, if it is to bind L2, be protected by the registration against L1 of a Class C(iv) land charge.[4]

1   L&T(C)A 1995, s 3(6)(b).
2   See **[para 9.81]**.
3   LRA 2002, s 29(1), (2)(a)(ii), Sch 3, para 2 **[para 12.160]**. See *Webb v Pollmount Ltd* [1966]

Ch 584 at 603C–D; *Ferrishurst Ltd v Wallcite Ltd* [1999] Ch 355 at 367F–G. Such an option is, of course, best protected by the entry of a 'notice' in the register (LRA 2002, s 32) and imperatively requires such protection if it relates to land outside the current demise contained in a different title number from the reversion on the current lease.

4   **[Para 12.309]**. See J Howell, [1990] Conv 168.

LIABILITY AS BETWEEN L2 AND T1 UNDER OLD (PRE-1996) TENANCIES

14.273   In relation to tenancies granted prior to 1 January 1996, the transmission of covenanted benefits and burdens is still governed by the doctrine of privity of estate (as reinforced by statute law reaching back more than four centuries).

Benefit of T1's covenants passes to L2

14.274   Following the assignment of L1's reversionary estate, L2 undoubtedly takes the benefit of those covenants which, in the older terminology, 'touch and concern' the demised premises. T1's liability to L2, although based essentially on privity of estate, has for centuries been reinforced by a statutory confirmation of the rights of assignees of the landlord's reversion. Under section 141(1) of the Law of Property Act 1925,[1] the assignee of a reversionary estate takes the benefit of the rent reserved by the lease,[2] together with the benefit of every condition (eg of re-entry) and of every covenant entered into by the lessee which has 'reference to the subject-matter' of the lease.[3] All such benefits are statutorily 'annexed and incident to and shall go with the reversionary estate in the land'.[4] This powerful wording effects a statutory transfer from L1 to L2 of the whole benefit of the 'touching and concerning' covenants originally undertaken by T1.[5] In one respect the Law of Property Act 1925 provides for a more extensive transmission of benefit than is allowed by the doctrine of privity of estate. Section 141(1) is equally applicable to an oral tenancy,[6] an equitable lease and a contract for a lease,[7] provided that the covenants in question have 'reference to the subject-matter' of that lease.[8] Whether the lease is legal or equitable, L2 acquires the right (subject to any limitations imposed by the Landlord and Tenant (Covenants) Act 1995[9]) to sue T1 even for breaches committed by later assignees from T1.[10]

1   This provision originates in the Grantees of Reversions Act 1540 (32 Hen VIII, c 34). See *Thursby v Plant* (1668) 1 Wms Saund 237 at 240, 85 ER 268 at 270, for the statement that this statute 'transferred the privity of contract'. In *Bickford v Parson* (1848) 5 CB 920 at 930, 136 ER 1141 at 1145, Wilde CJ observed that the 1540 Act 'annexes, or rather creates, a privity of contract between those who have privity of estate'. See also *Figgins Holdings Pty Ltd v SEAA Enterprises Pty Ltd* (1999) 196 CLR 245 at 267 per Gaudron, Gummow and Callinan JJ.

2   The entitlement to recover arrears of rent thus passes from L1 to L2 (see *Muscat v Smith* [2003] 1 WLR 2853 at [3], [12], [16]).

3   The terminology of 'touching and concerning' and of 'reference to the subject matter of the lease' are merely differing formulations of the same idea. See *Hua Chiao Commercial Bank Ltd v Chiaphua Industries Ltd* [1987] AC 99 at 106H–107A per Lord Oliver of Aylmerton; *Davis v Town Properties Investment Corporation Ltd* [1903] 1 Ch 797 at 805; *Breams Property*

Investment Co Ltd v Stroulger [1948] 2 KB 1 at 7; *Caerns Motor Services Ltd v Texaco Ltd* [1994] 1 WLR 1249 at 1259B; *Dalegrove Pty Ltd v Isles Parking Station Pty Ltd* (1988) 12 NSWLR 546 at 555D.

4   The same outcome follows from LPA 1925, s 78(1) [**para 13.42**], which provides that a covenant 'relating to any land of the covenantee shall be deemed to be made with the covenantee and his successors in title' (see *Caerns Motor Services Ltd v Texaco Ltd* [1994] 1 WLR 1249 at 1267G–H, 1269C–D). See also Contracts (Rights of Third Parties) Act 1999, s 1(1)–(3) [**para 13.43**].

5   See *City and Metropolitan Properties Ltd v Greycroft Ltd* [1987] 1 WLR 1085 at 1087E. A reference in a covenant to the covenantee's 'successors' strengthens the argument that the covenant 'touches and concerns', but is not essential for this purpose (see *Caerns Motor Services Ltd v Texaco Ltd* [1994] 1 WLR 1249 at 1266A–C, 1268E, 1269D).

6   See LPA 1925, s 154. For this purpose a 'covenant' need not be made by deed (see *Weg Motors Ltd v Hales* [1962] Ch 49 at 73).

7   *Rickett v Green* [1910] 1 KB 253 at 259; *Rye v Purcell* [1926] 1 KB 446 at 451–455.

8   See *Manchester Brewery Co v Coombs* [1901] 2 Ch 608 at 617–619.

9   L&T(C)A 1995, s 17 [**para 14.234**].

10 It is irrelevant for this purpose that T1 assigned his term of years to T2 before L1's assignment of the reversionary estate to L2 and that privity of estate never obtained between L2 and T1 (see *Arlesford Trading Co Ltd v Servansingh* [1971] 1 WLR 1080 at 1082F–G).

Exclusive right of action for L2

14.275   The transfer of the reversionary estate to L2 leaves L1 with none of the benefit of T1's leasehold covenants. L2 acquires an exclusive right to sue in respect of all breaches by T1 (whensoever occurring) and may therefore sue T1 in respect of breaches committed prior to the date of assignment[1] (unless these breaches were waived by L1[2]). L2 may even exercise a right of re-entry on the basis of rent arrears which had accrued before the assignment of the reversionary estate.

1   *Arlesford Trading Co Ltd v Servansingh* [1971] 1 WLR 1080 at 1082E–F (right to sue for arrears of rent); *Muscat v Smith* [2003] 1 WLR 2853 at [16]; *London & County (A & D) Ltd v Wilfred Sportsman Ltd* [1971] Ch 764 at 784D.

2   *London & County (A & D) Ltd v Wilfred Sportsman Ltd* [1971] Ch 764 at 783B.

Surety covenants entered into by T1's guarantor

14.276   L2 also takes the benefit of any surety covenant entered into by a third party as guarantor of T1's due performance of his leasehold obligations. This consequence follows not from section 141(1) of the Law of Property Act 1925 (which refers only to covenants undertaken by a *lessee*[1]), but rather from the general common law relating to the benefit of covenants.[2] Although L2 has neither privity of contract nor privity of estate with the guarantor,[3] he can claim the benefit of the guarantee as a matter which (in so far as it relates to a 'touching and concerning' covenant binding on T1) also 'touches and concerns' the reversionary estate which L2 has taken.[4]

1   See *Kumar v Dunning* [1989] QB 193 at 200A–C per Browne-Wilkinson V-C; *P & A Swift Investments v Combined English Stores Group Plc* [1989] AC 632 at 639G per Lord Oliver of Aylmerton.

2   **[Paras 13.33, 14.268]**.
3   See *Kumar v Dunning* [1989] QB 193 at 200A–C per Browne-Wilkinson V-C; *Caerns Motor Services Ltd v Texaco Ltd* [1994] 1 WLR 1249 at 1259G.
4   *P & A Swift Investments v Combined English Stores Group Plc* [1989] AC 632 at 637H per Lord Templeman, 642C–F per Lord Oliver of Aylmerton **[para 14.268]**.

Burden of L1's covenants passes to L2

14.277   The liability of L2 to T1, although founded on privity of estate, also rests now on a slightly broader statutory base. In accordance with section 142(1) of the Law of Property Act 1925, the assignment of L1's reversionary estate to L2 passes to L2 the burden of any obligation imposed by the covenants and conditions entered into by L1[1] in so far as such covenants and conditions have 'reference to the subject-matter of the lease.'[2] T1 is therefore entitled to enforce against L2 all covenants which 'touch and concern' the demised land.[3] Section 142(1) applies indiscriminately to both legal and equitable terms of years.[4] However, as is the general rule with assignees,[5] L2's liability extends only to defaults committed during the period of his possession as assignee of the reversionary estate. L2 cannot therefore be made liable in damages to T1 in respect of any breach committed by L1 prior to the assignment,[6] unless the breach is of a continuing nature (as in the case of a covenant to repair).[7]

1   A 'covenant' within section 142(1) need not be contained in a deed or comprise a covenant under seal. It may even arise outside the document which constitutes the lease (see *Weg Motors Ltd v Hales* [1962] Ch 49 at 73, 76–77; but compare *Eden Park Estates Ltd v Longman* (Unreported, Court of Appeal, 19 May 1980)).
2   The burden of a leasehold covenant can pass to L2 under section 142(1), even though its benefit is expressed to be personal to T1 and does not therefore run with T1's term (*System Floors Ltd v Ruralpride Ltd* [1995] 1 EGLR 48 at 50K–L).
3   After assignment of his term to T2, however, T1 holds no estate in the land and has no standing either to apply for relief against forfeiture of the lease (*Re Francini and Canuck Properties Ltd* (1982) 132 DLR (3d) 468 at 471) or to sue in respect of breaches of the landlord covenants.
4   *Weg Motors Ltd v Hales* [1962] Ch 49 at 73. An equitable lease constitutes an estate contract and, in the case of unregistered land, must be registered by T1 against L1 as a Class C(iv) land charge if the term of years itself is to become binding on L2. Notwithstanding the provision in section 142(1), a failure to register renders the equitable lease statutorily void against L2 if he purchases the legal reversionary estate for money or money's worth (LCA 1972, s 4(6)). See e g *Hollington Bros Ltd v Rhodes* [1951] 2 TLR 691 at 696 **[para 12.287]**. If the reversionary estate is registered at Land Registry, T1's position is much simpler. His equitable lease binds L2 as an overriding interest, provided that T1 is in actual occupation of the land (see LRA 2002, s 29(1), (2)(a)(ii), Sch 3, para 2; *Grace Rymer Investments Ltd v Waite* [1958] Ch 831 at 849–851 **[para 12.160]**).
5   **[Para 14.294]**.
6   *Duncliffe v Caerfelin Properties Ltd* [1989] 2 EGLR 38 at 39M–40B; [1990] Conv 126 (J E Martin). See also D Gordon, [1987] Conv 103 at 105. L2 may, however, be bound by T1's equitable right (originally as against L1) to set-off against L2's claim for assigned rent arrears any damages due to T1 in respect of L1's failure to repair (see *Muscat v Smith* [2003] 1 WLR 2853 at [31] **[para 14.61]**).
7   *Duncliffe v Caerfelin Properties Ltd* [1989] 2 EGLR 38 at 39L–40A. L2 is liable, in effect, for all

extant disrepair, but cannot be made liable in damages to T1 for breaches of the repairing covenant by L1 which occurred prior to the assignment to L2 (see *Muscat v Smith* [2003] 1 WLR 2853 at [12], [43]).

L1 retains the burden of his leasehold obligations

14.278   Although section 142(1) extends the burden of L1's covenants to L2, the transfer of the reversion on a pre-1996 tenancy does not free L1 himself from the burden of his leasehold covenants.[1] In the absence of contrary agreement L1 remains liable throughout the entire term on all the landlord covenants contained in the lease.[2] Irrespective of the assignment to L2, L1 remains vulnerable to an action brought by T1 in respect of defaults committed by L1 while T1 was not in possession.[3]

1   The court would not, however, permit a double recovery against L1 and L2 (see *Muscat v Smith* [2003] 1 WLR 2853 at [20] per Sedley LJ).
2   See e g *Re King, decd* [1963] Ch 459 at 488–489, 497; *Caerns Motor Services Ltd v Texaco Ltd* [1994] 1 WLR 1249 at 1268G–H; *Muscat v Smith* [2003] 1 WLR 2853 at [20]. In this respect there is no longer parity between the continuing liabilities of the original landlord and tenant (see L&T(C)A 1995, s 17 [**para 14.234**]).
3   T1 may bring his action even after he has assigned his term to T2 (*City and Metropolitan Properties Ltd v Greycroft Ltd* [1987] 1 WLR 1085 at 1087F–H), since his right to sue L1 for pre-assignment breaches passes to T2 only by express assignment. L1 may even be sued by T2 or T3 on such covenants as 'touch and concern' the land (*Celsteel Ltd v Alton House Holdings Ltd* (*No 2*) [1986] 1 WLR 666 at 672H). On the danger of a multiplicity of actions against L1, see *City and Metropolitan Properties*, supra at 1087H–1088D; P F Smith, [1990] Conv 335 at 345.

T1's option to purchase L1's reversion

14.279   A tenant's option to purchase his landlord's reversionary estate is not regarded by the common law as a covenant which 'touches and concerns' the demised land.[1] Such an option, if held by T1, cannot therefore burden L2 automatically as the transferee of L1's reversionary estate. The burden of T1's purchase option is not transmissible to L2 by reference to any privity of estate. Where, however, the title to L1's reversion is registered at Land Registry, T1's option binds L2 as an overriding interest if T1 was in actual occupation of the land at the date of the transfer.[2] If L1's reversionary estate was unregistered, the binding effect of T1's option generally depends on whether T1 registered a Class C(iv) land charge against L1 in advance of the transfer of the reversion to L2.[3]

1   [**Para 14.263**].
2   LRA 2002, s 29(1), (2)(a)(ii), Sch 3, para 2; *Webb v Pollmount Ltd* [1966] Ch 584 at 603C–D; *Ferrishurst Ltd v Wallcite Ltd* [1999] Ch 355 at 367F–G [**para 12.160**]. If T1 was not in actual occupation, the survival of his option depends on its protection by the entry of a 'notice' in the register of L1's title [**para 12.89**].
3   See LCA 1972, s 4(6); *Phillips v Mobil Oil Co Ltd* [1989] 1 WLR 888 at 892G [**para 12.309**]. An unprotected option to purchase unregistered land can bind L2 only if L2 is not a purchaser of a legal estate for money or money's worth (e g if he is a mere donee or a purchaser of an equitable estate in the land).

T1's option to renew his lease

14.280 More difficulty attaches to the transmission to L2 of the burden of any option which the head lease may have granted T1 for the renewal of his lease. If L1's reversionary estate comprises a registered title, T1's renewal option ranks as an overriding interest binding on L2, provided that T1 was in actual occupation of the land at the date of the disposition to L2.[1] Where L1's reversion is as yet unregistered, it used to be thought that the burden of L1's covenant to renew T1's lease would automatically run with the land (pursuant to section 142(1)) so as to bind L2.[2] In *Beesly v Hallwood Estates Ltd*,[3] however, Buckley J indicated – to the surprise of many[4] – that T1's option to renew his lease must be registered against L1 as a land charge of Class C(iv)[5] and, if not so registered, is statutorily void against L2 as a purchaser of a legal estate for money or money's worth.[6] The renewal option does not become binding on L2 merely because it 'touches and concerns' the land[7] or even because it is contained in a lease which is itself binding on L2. The renewal option and the lease by which it is granted are distinct proprietary phenomena[8] and the fact that T1's leasehold term is enforceable against L2 in no way implies that L2 is also bound by such incidents (e g as to renewal) as that lease may contain.[9]

---

1   LRA 2002, s 29(1), (2)(a)(ii), Sch 3, para 2 **[para 12.160]**. If not saved as an overriding interest, T1's renewal option binds L2 only if protected by the entry of a 'notice' in the register of L1's title **[para 12.89]**.

2   See e g *Wolstenholme & Cherry's Conveyancing Statutes* (12th edn, London 1932), p 246.

3   [1960] 1 WLR 549 at 557 (affd by the Court of Appeal on different grounds ([1961] Ch 105). See also *Taylors Fashions Ltd v Liverpool Victoria Trustees Co Ltd* [1982] QB 133 (Note) at 142G–143G; *Phillips v Mobil Oil Co Ltd* [1989] 1 WLR 888 at 893F–894E.

4   See e g *Taylors Fashions Ltd v Liverpool Victoria Trustees Co Ltd* [1982] QB 133 (Note) at 138B **[para 10.206]**. Compare the strongly critical view expressed in (1981) 125 Sol Jo 816 at 817–818 (M P Thompson).

5   The option for renewal is effectively put on a par with a lessee's option to purchase the lessor's reversion, in that both rights now constitute estate contracts registrable by the lessee.

6   LCA 1972, s 4(6) **[para 12.282]**. LPA 1925, s 142(1) applies only if and so far as the original lessor has power to bind subsequent holders of the reversion and does not annex the tenant's renewal option so that its burden runs automatically with the reversion free of any requirement of registration (see *Beesly v Hallwood Estates Ltd* [1960] 1 WLR 549 at 557–558 per Buckley J).

7   In unregistered land the 'touching and concerning' quality of the covenant is almost entirely irrelevant to the question of its impact on L2, since L2 will be bound by an unregistered option only if he is someone other than a purchaser for money or money's worth (i e a donee).

8   See e g *Markfaith Investment Ltd v Chiap Hua Flashlights Ltd* [1991] 2 AC 43 at 59A per Lord Templeman ('A covenant to renew at the option of the tenant is not a lease'). Thus the new lease obtained on the tenant's exercise of his renewal option does not impliedly contain the same options (for renewal or freehold purchase) as were included in the old lease (see *Sherwood v Tucker* [1924] 2 Ch 440 at 445–449; *Re Devine and Ferguson* [1947] 1 DLR 76 at 78–81; *Palmer v Ampersand Investments Ltd* (1985) 11 DLR (4th) 295 at 304–307; *Esther Investments Pty Ltd v Cherrywood Park Pty Ltd* [1986] WAR 279 at 284, 303–304). An exception arises where the original renewal covenant expressly provided for a new lease 'on the same terms and conditions in all respects' as the existing lease, in which case the new lease must faithfully replicate the old lease (see *Batchelor v Murphy* [1926] AC 63 at 68–71; *Hill v Hill* [1947] Ch 231 at 242–245).

9   See *Friedman v Barrett, Ex parte Friedman* [1962] Qd R 498 at 509–511. What is protected on

assignment is the tenancy itself 'and not the tenancy with all its incidents' (*Mercantile Credits Ltd v Shell Co of Australia Ltd* (1976) 136 CLR 326 at 347 per Gibbs J; *Re Davies* [1989] 1 Qd R 48 at 51 per McPherson J).

LIABILITY AS BETWEEN L1/L2 AND T2/T3 UNDER NEW (POST-1995) TENANCIES

14.281   For centuries the doctrine of privity of estate has enabled the benefit and burden of the principal covenants of a legal lease to extend beyond the original contracting parties, L1 and T1, to affect their assignees. As between these assignees (say L2 and T2),[1] there clearly exists no contractual privity (even by fiction of statute[2]). Whereas in relation to the enforcement of obligations between L2 and T1 it could at least be said that *one* party was an original contracting party,[3] as between L2 and T2, *neither* is an original covenantor. The impact of leasehold benefits and burdens upon L2 and T2 (or, for that matter, T3) normally turns on whether the lease from which they have taken their respective assignments was granted before 1 January 1996.[4]

1   See *Fig.* 42 [**para 14.209**].
2   Compare the relationship of L2 and T1 under a pre-1996 tenancy pursuant to LPA 1925, ss 141(1), 142(1) [**para 14.274**].
3   [**Para 14.213**].
4   See the statutory definition of 'new' tenancies (L&T(C)A 1995, s 1(3)–(7) [**para 14.224**]).

14.282   Under a head lease granted on or after 1 January 1996 the effects of assignment of T1's term to T2 are governed by the Landlord and Tenant (Covenants) Act 1995 in language which mirrors the statutory consequences which follow L1's transfer of his reversionary estate to L2.[1] The 1995 Act draws no distinction, for present purposes, between legal and equitable leases and nothing turns on the formal or informal character of the assignment to T2 (or indeed to later transferees of the term).[2]

1   [**Para 14.247**].
2   See L&T(C)A 1995, s 28(1) ('tenancy' includes an agreement for a tenancy; and 'assignment' includes equitable assignment).

Benefit of landlord covenants passes to T2 (and later T3)

14.283   The Landlord and Tenant (Covenants) Act 1995 confirms and extends the effect of privity of estate by providing that, with effect from the date of the assignment, T2 becomes entitled to the benefit of all 'landlord covenants' (other than those expressed to be 'personal' in character[1]) which relate to the premises comprised in the assignment to him.[2] The benefit of the same covenants passes to T3 on the further assignment of the leasehold term.

1   L&T(C)A 1995, s 3(6)(a) [**para 14.247**].
2   L&T(C)A 1995, s 3(2)(b).

Options

14.284 T2 receives the benefit of any provision in the lease between L1 and T1 which conferred an option to purchase the reversionary estate or to renew the lease. It is irrelevant, for the purpose of the 1995 Act,[1] whether the option 'touches and concerns' the demised land (provided that it is not expressed to be personal to its original grantee).

1   Contrast the position in relation to options conferred by a pre-1996 tenancy [**para 14.279**].

T1 loses the benefit of landlord covenants

14.285 Under the 1995 Act T1, on assigning his term to T2, ceases to be entitled to the benefit of the 'landlord covenants' of the tenancy.[1] The transfer of his term effectively marks the transfer to T2 of the right to sue in respect of all breaches of landlord covenants other than those occurring prior to the assignment.[2]

1   L&T(C)A 1995, s 5(2)(b), (3)(b).
2   L&T(C)A 1995, s 23(1).

Burden of tenant covenants passes to T2 (and later to T3)

14.286 With effect from the assignment of T1's term to T2, T2 becomes bound by all the 'tenant covenants' of the tenancy.[1] Once again it is irrelevant whether these covenants 'touch and concern' the land so long as they are not expressed to be 'personal' in character.[2]

1   Tenant covenants which are restrictive of the tenant's user of land are automatically enforceable not only against the tenant and the assignees of his term, but also against 'any other person who is the owner or occupier of any demised premises to which the covenant relates even though there is no express provision in the tenancy to that effect' (**L&T(C)A 1995, s 3(5)**).
2   L&T(C)A 1995, s 3(6)(a) [**para 14.247**].

Exceptional covenants

14.287 T2 is unaffected by any tenant covenants which were not binding on T1 at the date of the assignment[1] or which relate to parts of the demised premises not included in the assignment to T2.[2]

1   For example, the landlord may have waived T1's due performance of a particular covenant. The benefit of this waiver or release may be claimed by T2 unless the waiver or release was 'in whatever terms' expressed to be 'personal' to T1 (**L&T(C)A 1995, s 3(4)**).
2   L&T(C)A 1995, s 3(2)(a).

T2 is liable only in respect of his own breaches

14.288 The 1995 Act replicates the effect of the doctrine of privity of estate by providing that assignees of the leasehold term are, in principle, liable only in respect of those breaches of covenant which occur whilst they are owners in possession.[1] Thus the statutory transmission of the burden of tenant covenants to T2 is expressly declared to involve him in no liability 'in relation to any time falling before the assignment.'[2] Likewise the assignment of the leasehold term by T2 to T3 releases T2 from any further liability on the tenant covenants,[3] except in so far as T2 may have entered into an authorised guarantee agreement in respect of the due performance of those covenants by T3.[4]

1   [**Para 14.294**].
2   L&T(C)A 1995, s 23(1).
3   L&T(C)A 1995, s 5(2)(a), (3)(a).
4   L&T(C)A 1995, s 16(1) [**para 14.227**].

Insolvency or bankruptcy of T2

14.289   Any insolvency or bankruptcy affecting T2 has the consequence of terminating T2's liability (but not that of any guarantor of his) if T2's lease is disclaimed by his liquidator or trustee in bankruptcy.[1] As has already been seen, however, T1 (and any guarantor of his) have already been released, on assignment, from further liability on the tenant covenants of the lease,[2] unless T1's liability was preserved by the conclusion of an authorised guarantee agreement under which T1 consented to act as surety for the performance of T2's obligations.[3]

1   [**Para 14.216**].
2   L&T(C)A 1995, ss 5(2), 24(2) [**para 14.225**].
3   [**Para 14.227**]. If made to discharge T2's liability, T1 is, of course, entitled to claim an overriding lease [**para 14.228**].

LIABILITY AS BETWEEN L1/L2 AND T2/T3 UNDER OLD (PRE-1996) TENANCIES

14.290   In relation to pre-1996 tenancies the transmission of benefits and burdens to assignees of the tenant's term is governed by the venerable doctrine of privity of estate.[1] However, *Spencer's Case*[2] applies only to those leasehold covenants which 'touch and concern' the demised premises and only where the relevant parties are privy to a *legal* lease and have acquired a *legal* estate by formal assignment of the tenant's term. If these conditions are fulfilled, the benefit and burden of the leasehold covenants become enforceable as between the assignees of the term and its reversion.

1   [**Para 14.242**].
2   (1583) 5 Co Rep 16a, 77 ER 72.

Benefit of 'touching and concerning' covenants passes to T2

14.291   The benefit of 'touching and concerning' covenants entered into by L1 passes, on the principle of privity of estate, to T2 (and in due course to T3).[1]

The assignees of the term may enforce such covenants against the landlord even though no contractual privity exists between them.

1   See *Fig.* 42 **[para 14.209]**.

14.292   The benefit of a tenant's option to purchase the reversionary estate (or an equivalent right of pre-emption), albeit conferred in a pre-1996 lease, does not 'touch and concern' the demised premises[1] and cannot therefore run with the tenant's term by virtue of the doctrine of privity of estate.[2] The benefit of such rights is, of course, transmissible to T1's successors by express assignment[3] and may even be carried to these successors by force of the recently rediscovered provisions of section 78 of the Law of Property Act 1925.[4]

1   **[Para 14.279]**.
2   Compare the landlord's covenant for renewal of the lease at the tenant's option, the benefit of which has been grudgingly conceded to 'touch and concern' the demised land and thus to run automatically with the tenant's term (see *Phillips v Mobil Oil Co Ltd* [1989] 1 WLR 888 at 891E per Nicholls LJ **[para 14.263]**).
3   *Griffith v Pelton* [1958] Ch 205 at 225–226; *Churcher v Danis Hotels Pty Ltd* (1980) 8 BPR 15863 at 15874; *Esther Investments Pty Ltd v Cherrywood Park Pty Ltd* [1986] WAR 279 at 283, 298; *Re Meewasin Valley Authority and Olfland Land Co Ltd* (1989) 51 DLR (4th) 638 at 639.
4   **[Paras 13.42, 14.304]**. See *Esther Investments Pty Ltd v Cherrywood Park Pty Ltd* [1986] WAR 279 at 299–300 per Brinsden J (on the Western Australian equivalent of section 78). For evidence that section 78 is beginning to come into its own in England, see *Amsprop Trading Ltd v Harris Distribution Ltd* [1997] 1 WLR 1025 at 1033D–G per Neuberger J.

Burden of 'touching and concerning' covenants passes to T2

14.293   The doctrine of privity of estate likewise ensures that the burden of all 'touching and concerning' covenants contained in a pre-1996 legal lease between L1 and T1 passes to T2 (and in due course to T3), provided that each assignment is effected by appropriately formal means.[1]

1   **[Para 14.244]**.

Transient nature of privity of estate

14.294   Since privity of estate denotes the relationship which exists between those who stand *pro tempore* in the shoes of the original lessor and lessee, the liability imposed by *Spencer's Case* is necessarily restricted to the duration of a given tenure in possession. Unlike the common law liability of the original tenant, which is unassignable and therefore coextensive with the leasehold term,[1] the liability of each successive assignee of the term relates only to breaches committed while he is in possession of the land.[2] Thus, in *Fig.* 42,[3] T2 is not liable under *Spencer's Case* in respect of breaches of covenant committed by T1 prior to T2's acquisition of the leasehold term.[4] Nor is T2 liable in respect of breaches committed by T3 after the assignment of the term to the latter,[5] unless – as frequently happens in commercial leases – T2 on taking his own assignment expressly covenanted with the landlord to become liable for the residue of the term.[6]

1   [Para **14.217**].
2   Thus T2, even after the assignment of his term to T3, remains liable in respect of breaches committed whilst he was himself in possession of the land (*Harley v King* (1835) 2 Cr M & R 18 at 22–23, 150 ER 8 at 10). See also *Johnsey Estates Ltd v Lewis and Manley (Engineering) Ltd* (1987) 54 P & CR 296 at 300 per Bingham LJ.
3   [Para **14.209**].
4   *Grescot v Green* (1700) 1 Salk 199, 91 ER 179; *St Saviour's Southwark (Churchwardens) v Smith* (1762) 3 Burr 1271 at 1272–1273, 97 ER 827; *Karacominakis v Big Country Developments Pty Ltd* (2000) 10 BPR 18235 at [133]. A landlord cannot levy distress against T2 in respect of arrears of rent owed by T1 (*Wharfland Ltd v South London Co-operative Building Co Ltd* (1996) Times, 25 April). These results follow even though T2 pays a lower price for the assignment deliberately in view of the prior breach (*Hawkins v Sherman* (1828) 3 C & P 459 at 461, 172 ER 500 at 502). Liability for rent unpaid by T1 and T2 is therefore subject to apportionment between the two with reference to the date of assignment of the term (see *Glass v Patterson* [1902] 2 IR 660 at 676–677).
5   'The assignee is not liable … because once he has assigned over he has ceased to be the owner of the term to which the covenants are annexed' (*City of London Corpn v Fell* [1994] 1 AC 458 at 465G per Lord Templeman). See *Onslow v Corrie* (1817) 2 Madd 330 at 340–341, 56 ER 357 at 360; *Paul v Nurse* (1828) 8 B & C 486 at 488–489, 108 ER 1123 at 1124; *Karacominakis v Big Country Developments Pty Ltd* (2000) 10 BPR 18235 at [133].
6   *J Lyons & Co Ltd v Knowles* [1943] 1 KB 366 at 368–370. See *Estates Gazette Ltd v Benjamin Restaurant Ltd* [1994] 1 WLR 1528 at 1533B (covenant given to landlord by T2 to 'pay the rents reserved by the lease' construed as obligation to pay those rents for the residue of the term). The benefit of this direct covenant cannot pass to the landlord's assignee pursuant to LPA 1925, s 141(1) (which catches only covenants 'contained' in the lease), but can be expressly assigned and must also pass under LPA 1925, s 78(1).

Insolvency or bankruptcy of T2

14.295   The liability of T2 (but not the liability of his guarantor) is terminated, in the event of insolvency or bankruptcy, if the lease is disclaimed by the relevant liquidator or trustee in bankruptcy.[1] The financial catastrophe which overwhelms T2 may also deflect liability back towards T1 because, as the House of Lords indicated in *Hindcastle Ltd v Barbara Attenborough Associates Ltd*,[2] the disclaimer of T2's lease terminates *neither* the enduring contractual liability of T1 as the original covenantor *nor* the contractual liability of any person who guaranteed the performance of T1's covenants. Since the ameliorating impact of the Landlord and Tenant (Covenants) Act 1995 affects only leases granted after 1995, the alarming implications of the *Hindcastle* ruling for original tenants and their guarantors may continue to affect pre-1996 leases for some time to come.

1   [Para **14.216**].
2   [1997] AC 70 at 96D per Lord Nicholls of Birkenhead. See also *Warnford Investments Ltd v Duckworth* [1979] Ch 127 at 138G–139A; *MEPC plc v Scottish Amicable Life Assurance Society* (1993) 67 P & CR 314 at 316; *RA Securities Ltd v Mercantile Credit Co Ltd* [1995] 3 All ER 581 at 585b–d (insolvency); *Mytre Investments Ltd v Reynolds* [1995] 3 All ER 588 at 596j–597a (bankruptcy); *Cromwell Developments Ltd v Godfrey & Wright* (1998) 76 P & CR D14.

Burden of tenant covenants under an equitable lease

14.296 Orthodox doctrine holds that *Spencer's Case*[1] does not apply to an equitable lease[2] and that therefore the burden of an equitable lessee's obligations under a pre-1996 lease does not pass with the assignment of his term to a third party.[3] This being so, it is impossible in *Fig.* 42[4] for either L1 or L2 (as the case may be) to recover rent or any other money remedy for breach of covenant from T2 or T3.[5] This strange result emerges most clearly from the decision of the Divisional Court in *Purchase v Lichfield Brewery Co*.[6] The traditional view goes even further and regards the introduction of any equitable link in an otherwise legal chain of leasehold relationships as similarly having the effect that the burden of the lessee's covenants does not pass.[7] Thus, for instance, an informal or equitable assignment to T2 of a legal lease granted by L1 to T1 does not effectively fasten the burden of T1's leasehold obligations upon T2.[8] The equitable assignee is simply not bound.[9]

1   (1583) 5 Co Rep 16a, 77 ER 72 **[para 14.243]**.
2   The inapplicability of *Spencer's Case* is supposedly premised upon the absence of 'privity of estate' stemming from the lease between L1 and T1. Under an equitable term there simply exists no 'estate' (in the legal sense) to which *anyone* can be 'privy'. Thus, on this reasoning, one of the essential preconditions for enforcement against an assignee of the term is absent, and the issue of liability is now determined by the elementary rule that the benefit but not the burden of a contract is assignable. See *Manchester Brewery Co v Coombs* [1901] 2 Ch 608 at 617–619.
3   See generally R J Smith, 'The Running of Covenants in Equitable Leases and Equitable Assignments of Legal Leases' [1978] CLJ 98.
4   **[Para 14.209]**.
5   Money recovery may be possible from T1 on the basis of his contractual liability **[para 14.233]**. See *Camden v Batterbury* (1860) 7 CB (NS) 864 at 878–880, 141 ER 1055 at 1061.
6   [1915] 1 KB 184 at 187–189.
7   See R J Smith, [1978] CLJ 98 at 113–120.
8   *Moores v Choat* (1839) 8 Sim 508 at 523, 59 ER 202 at 208; *Robinson v Rosher* (1841) 1 Y & C Ch Cas 7 at 11, 62 ER 767 at 768; *Moore v Greg* (1848) 2 Ph 717 at 722–725, 41 ER 1120 at 1122–1123; *Cox v Bishop* (1857) 8 De GM & G 815 at 822–825, 44 ER 604 at 607–608; *Thornton v Thompson* [1930] SASR 310 at 313; *Chronopoulos v Caltex Oil (Australia) Pty Ltd* (1983) 45 ALR 481 at 489; *Tan Soo Leng David v Wee Satku & Kumar Pte Ltd* [1998] 2 SLR 83 at 112F–H.
9   *Friary Holroyd and Healey's Breweries Ltd v Singleton* [1899] 1 Ch 86 at 90; *Hoskins v Dillon* (1950) 67 WN (NSW) 115 at 118; *Quadramain Pty Ltd v Sevastapol Investments Pty Ltd* (1976) 133 CLR 390 at 403 per Gibbs CJ, 405 per Stephen J, 406 per Mason J; *Government Insurance Office (NSW) v K A Reed Services Pty Ltd* [1988] VR 829 at 837.

Availability of non-monetary remedies

14.297 The conventional wisdom of *Purchase v Lichfield Brewery Co* limits only the recovery of *money* remedies against assignees in equity. In appropriate circumstances the owner of the reversionary estate may seek an injunction against any breach by T2 or T3 of a restrictive covenant contained in the equitable head lease[1] and is likewise entitled to re-enter against a defaulting assignee (thereby forfeiting the lease).[2] Both the restrictive covenant and the right of re-entry represent, in their own right, a form of equitable proprietary entitlement which, in relation to other equitable claims on the leasehold estate, must take priority.[3] The availability of a right of re-entry, in particular, may prove an extremely potent stimulus to compliance with the covenants of the lease, whether or not these covenants are technically binding on the assignee.[4]

1   [**Para 14.308**].
2   L1 may well have reserved an express right of re-entry for breach, but in any event it seems that a right of re-entry is implied on behalf of L1 in most, if not all, equitable leases [**para 14.107**].
3   The restrictive covenant is not protectable by register entry (see LRA 2002, s 33(c); LCA 1972, s 2(5)). Likewise, in *Shiloh Spinners Ltd v Harding* [1973] AC 691 at 721D–G [**para 12.319**], the House of Lords decided that an equitable right of re-entry in a lease is not registrable as any kind of land charge.
4   Contrary to *Horsey Estates Ltd v Steiger* [1899] 2 QB 79 at 88–89, there seems to be no fundamental reason why this ground of enforcement should depend on the 'touching and concerning' quality of the covenants reinforced by the right of re-entry.

Alternative approaches

14.298   It is widely accepted that the result generally attributed to *Purchase v Lichfield Brewery Co* is anomalous and inconvenient. For this reason various alternative approaches have been proposed as a means of ensuring the enforceability of the covenants in a pre-1996 equitable lease, although none of these approaches is entirely satisfactory. By far the most radical assault yet mounted on orthodox doctrine occurred in *Boyer v Warbey*,[1] where Denning LJ appeared to suggest that the difference between legal and equitable leases was eliminated by the fusion of law and equity in the Judicature Act 1873. Thus, in Denning LJ's view, there is 'no valid reason nowadays why the doctrine of covenants running with the land – or with the reversion – should not apply equally to agreements under hand as to covenants under seal.' To this the purist is bound to object that, at most, the 1873 Act fused the administration of law and equity[2] and *Boyer v Warbey* has tended to be seen as representing a somewhat maverick view of the issue. It has been suggested in other jurisdictions that 'privity of estate' is not necessarily confined to legal relationships, but may exist even under an equitable lease.[3] If this view were adopted, the authority of *Spencer's Case* would simply transmit the burden of the equitable lessee's covenants to assignees of the term, at least in so far as these covenants 'touched and concerned' the land.

1   [1953] 1 QB 234 at 245–246.
2   [**Para 1.156**].
3   See eg *Dufaur v Kenealy* (1908) 28 NZLR 269 at 295; *De Luxe Confectionery Ltd v Waddington* [1958] NZLR 272 at 278, 283–284.

14.299   Yet another possible avenue of escape from *Purchase v Lichfield Brewery Co* may lie in the principle of novation. It can be argued that a fresh contract (and therefore a new privity of contract) impliedly arises if the assignee from the original equitable lessee goes into possession, pays rent, and is accepted by the reversioner as the current tenant.[1] This possibility was left open in *Purchase v Lichfield Brewery Co* itself, where Lush J appeared to attribute the absence of privity of contract to the fact that the assignees 'never went into possession or were recognised by the landlord.'[2] This approach, although not entirely free of difficulty,[3] may hold the most hopeful key to the resolution of the present dilemma.[4]

1   See R J Smith, [1978] CLJ 98 at 105–106. If novation is to be pleaded successfully as a ground of action against the assignee, it may be prudent to secure a new privity of contract by arranging a tripartite agreement between reversioner, lessee and assignee, which extinguishes all liability on the part of the lessee. See *De Luxe Confectionery Ltd v Waddington* [1958] NZLR 272 at 284; R T Fenton, (1976–77) 7 NZULR 342 at 347, 352.

2   [1915] 1 KB 184 at 188–189. It could even be argued that if specific performance is available in respect of the lease, the doctrine of *Walsh v Lonsdale* **[para 9.66]** subjects the assignee to the same monetary liability as would have existed if a decree of specific performance had been granted and a legal lease had come into effect (see *De Luxe Confectionery Ltd v Waddington* [1958] NZLR 272 at 277).

3   There is a substantial body of case law which denies that novation is possible through a mere entry into possession and payment of rent by the assignee (see *Camden v Batterbury* (1860) 7 CB (NS) 864 at 878–880, 141 ER 1055 at 1061; *Cox v Bishop* (1857) 8 De GM & G 815 at 822–825, 44 ER 604 at 607–608; *Thornton v Thompson* [1930] SASR 310 at 313–314; *Rodenhurst Estates Ltd v W H Barnes Ltd* [1936] 2 All ER 3 at 6). For other difficulties, see R J Smith, [1978] CLJ 98.

4   See eg *Dalegrove Pty Ltd v Isles Parking Station Pty Ltd* (1988) 12 NSWLR 546 at 552F–G per Bryson J.

14.300   A further, and more debatable, approach seeks to fasten liability upon the assignee of the equitable lease on the basis that an implied legal periodic tenancy arises as soon as the assignee enters into possession and pays a periodic rent to the current reversioner.[1] The traditional objection to such an analysis rests on the argument that *Walsh v Lonsdale* excludes the possibility that a legal periodic tenancy may coexist with a specifically enforceable contract for a lease.[2] However, this difficulty presents no obstacle if – as some suggest – this aspect of the ruling in *Walsh v Lonsdale* is applicable only in the 'two-party situation' as between the original lessor and lessee.[3]

1   [Para 7.250].
2   See *Manchester Brewery Co v Coombs* [1901] 2 Ch 608 at 617–618.
3   R J Smith, [1978] CLJ 98 at 108–109. See, in support, *Chronopoulos v Caltex Oil (Australia) Pty Ltd* (1983) 45 ALR 481 at 489.

LIABILITY AS BETWEEN L1/L2 AND ST1/ST2/WT

14.301   The liability of a sublessee on the covenants of a head lease presents different kinds of problem in English law.

Absence of 'privity of estate'

14.302   In *Fig.* 42[1] it is clear that the current subtenant, ST2, and the sub-undertenant, WT, are not 'privy' to the estate of the original head lease.[2] ST2's relationship of privity pertains, not to the head lease created between L1 and T1, but to the sublease granted by T2 to ST1. In principle, therefore, even those covenants of the head lease which 'touch and concern' the land are unenforceable between the head landlord and the holders of inferior estates. The vital element of 'privity of estate' is simply not present.[3] Neither L1 (nor in his turn L2) may recover a money remedy directly from ST1, ST2 or WT (eg arrears of rent or damages for breach of covenant).[4] The appropriate remedy lies in an action against the person who *does* currently stand in a relationship of privity to the estate of head lease, ie ST2's immediate superior, currently T3.[5] Moreover, forfeiture of the head lease has the automatic effect of destroying any sublease.[6]

1   **[Para 14.209]**.
2   *Garry Denning Ltd v Vickers* [1985] 1 NZLR 567 at 570.
3   *Amsprop Trading Ltd v Harris Distribution Ltd* [1997] 1 WLR 1025 at 1029A per Neuberger J.
4   See *Amsprop Trading Ltd v Harris Distribution Ltd* [1997] 1 WLR 1025 at 1032D–E, where Neuberger J turned back a valiant attempt to utilise LPA 1925, s 56(1) **[para 13.39]** in support of a right of action for a head landlord against ST1 and ST2. For the criticism that the immunity thus granted to the sublessee reinforces an unsupportable distinction between the respective positions of assignee of the term and sublessee, see W B Jaccard, 'The Scope of Liability between Landlord and Subtenant' 16 Col Jnl of Law and Soc Prob 364 (1980–81).
5   Where T3 is in arrear with rent it is, however, open to the head landlord to issue a notice under Law of Distress Amendment Act 1908, s 6, requiring ST2 henceforth to make all his payments of rent direct to the head landlord. For reference to the increasing use made of this diversion notice procedure, see [1993] Conv 11 (J E A). See also *Rhodes v Allied Dunbar Pension Services Ltd* [1989] 1 WLR 800 at 805D–F, 808E–H.
6   **[Para 14.183]**.

Statutory intervention

14.303   The Landlord and Tenant (Covenants) Act 1995 does nothing to loosen up the transmissibility to subtenants of the benefit and burden of covenants contained in a head lease, but other statutes may, in part, have achieved such an effect.

Law of Property Act 1925

14.304   It is possible that section 78(1) of the Law of Property Act 1925[1] enables a subtenant of a pre-1996 head lease to claim at least the benefit of covenants contained in that lease.[2]

1   **[Para 13.42]**.
2   See *Caerns Motor Services Ltd v Texaco Ltd* [1994] 1 WLR 1249 at 1269D.

The Contracts (Rights of Third Parties) Act 1999

14.305   In relation to leases arising on or after 11 May 2000, the Contracts (Rights of Third Parties) Act 1999 provides that non-contracting parties may, in their own right, enforce contractual terms if *either* the contract expressly provides that they may *or* the term in question 'purports to confer a benefit' upon them.[1]

1   C(RTP)A 1999, s 1(1)–(3) **[para 13.43]**.

The Human Rights Act 1998

14.306   The Human Rights Act 1998 may indirectly require the modification of certain rules regulating the enforceability of leasehold covenants. It is at least arguable that the traditional doctrine of privity of estate, by limiting the range of enforcement within the leasehold framework, constitutes an infringement of the head landlord's Convention right to 'peaceful enjoyment of his possessions.'[1] In *PW & Co v Milton Gate Investments Ltd*[2] a 25 year lease of an office building gave T1 the right to terminate the lease after 12 years on service of a 'break notice'. Consonantly with common law principle,[3] Neuberger J held that T1's subsequent exercise of this break clause immediately terminated a number of long-term subleases which T1 had created in favour of ST1, thereby triggering a clause in the head lease which obliged T1 to pay to L1 (or his successor, L2) a penalty of some £5 million. Neuberger J held that, as a matter of law, it was impossible for L1 and T1 to contract out of the general rule that termination of a head lease also terminates all derivative leases.[4] He indicated, however, that if (on a contrary view) the subleases had survived the termination of the head lease, L2 and ST1 would have been liable to each other – well outside the scope of privity of estate – on the covenants of those subleases. Any other approach, concluded Neuberger J, would have left the land encumbered for many years by a subtenant from whom no rent was legally recoverable – an outcome which would be 'scarcely "peaceful enjoyment of [L2's] possessions".'[5]

1   ECHR, Protocol No 1, Art 1 **[para 2.29]**.
2   [2004] Ch 142.
3   **[Para 7.278]**.
4   [2004] Ch 142 at [71]–[85], [147], [279(ii)].
5   [2004] Ch 142 at [126], [133]–[134], [279(iv)]. Neuberger J also thought that, pursuant to HRA 1998 s 3, it is possible to accord a 'modern and purposive construction' to LPA 1925, ss 141–142 so as to enable direct enforcement as between head landlord and subtenant of covenants contained in the subtenancy (at [129]–[134]).

Non-monetary remedies

14.307   It should not be overlooked that certain non-monetary remedies may be pursued against under-tenants albeit outside the ambit of privity of estate in relation to the head lease.

Enforcement of restrictive covenants

14.308   Notwithstanding the fact that ST1, ST2 and WT are immune from any direct money recovery on the covenants of the head lease, the head landlord may be able to obtain an injunction restraining holders of inferior estates from breach of any restrictive covenant contained in the head lease, even though these persons are not privy to the head lease. This possibility is a derivative of the principle of *Tulk v Moxhay*,[1] where Lord Cottenham LC effectively converted restrictive covenants into a species of proprietary interest enforceable against all except a purchaser of a legal estate for value without notice.

1   (1848) 2 Ph 774 at 778–779, 41 ER 1143 at 1144–1145 [**para 9.147**].

14.309   Restrictive covenants, in so far as they relate to demised premises to which title is registered, are not capable of protection by the entry of a 'notice' in the register.[1] They are, instead, made automatically binding on any transferee or underlessee by the Land Registration Act 2002 itself.[2] In relation to unregistered land the doctrine of *Tulk v Moxhay* ensures that restrictive covenants contained in a head lease are enforceable by injunction[3] against *any* occupier who takes possession of the demised premises with notice of the covenants.[4] Here the equitable doctrine of notice remains the governing rule, precisely because restrictive covenants between lessor and lessee are never registrable as a Class D(ii) land charge.[5]

1   LRA 2002, s 33(c) [**para 14.297**].
2   LRA 2002, s 29(1), (2)(b) [**para 12.76**]. In relation to post-1995 tenancies, see also L&T(C)A 1995, s 3(5) [**para 14.286**].
3   See the quintessentially Victorian melodrama of *Hall v Ewin* (1888) 37 Ch D 74 at 78–82 (where a sub-underlessee breached a head lease covenant prohibiting 'noisome or offensive trade, business or employment' by holding an exhibition of wild beasts in his back garden). See also *Teape v Douse* (1905) 92 LT 319 at 320; *Northern Ireland Carriers Ltd v Larne Harbour Ltd* [1981] 5 NIJB, Transcript, p 10. The restrictive covenant binds even a licensee who occupies the premises (*Mander v Falcke* [1891] 2 Ch 554 at 557–558).
4   Holders of inferior leasehold estates invariably have notice of restrictive covenants contained in the head lease. Such covenants will almost certainly have been recited in identical terms in the covenants of the sublease. In any event a subtenant has the right, before taking his sublease, to call for the head lease (see *Gosling v Woolf* [1893] 1 QB 39 at 40, (1893) 68 LT 89 at 90) and is therefore affected by its contents (*Teape v Douse* (1905) 92 LT 319 at 320). In relation to post-1995 tenancies, this effect is confirmed by L&T(C)A 1995, s 3(5) [**para 14.286**].
5   LCA 1972, s 2(5) [**para 12.314**].

Remedy of forfeiture

14.310   An under-tenant is also vulnerable to the head lessor's exercise of any right of re-entry which was expressly reserved in the head lease.[1]

1   [Para **8.268**].

STATUTORY REGIMES OF PROTECTION

14.311   Part of the extraordinary complexity of the modern law of landlord and tenant is attributable to the statutory superimposition of special regimes of protection for designated categories of tenant. The following paragraphs contain only a bare summary of these elaborate legislative supplements to the basic law of tenancies. The relevant legislation includes:

- the Rent Act 1977 (protected and statutory tenancies)[1]
- the Housing Act 1988 (assured and shorthold tenancies)[2]
- the Housing Acts 1985 and 1996 (secure tenancies)[3]
- the Landlord and Tenant Act 1954, Part II (business tenancies)[4]
- the Agricultural Holdings Act 1986 (agricultural holdings)[5] and
- the Agricultural Tenancies Act 1995 (farm business tenancies).[6]

1 [Paras 14.312–14.328].
2 [Paras 14.329–14.337].
3 [Paras 14.338–14.348].
4 [Paras 14.354–14.359].
5 [Para 14.361].
6 [Paras 14.362–14.363].

RENT ACT 1977 (PROTECTED AND STATUTORY TENANCIES)

14.312 From their origins in emergency wartime legislation in 1915,[1] successive Rent Acts came to provide the mainstay of the statutory protection enjoyed by residential tenants in the private rented sector during the larger part of the 20th century.[2] This legislation imposed a significant legal control over the relationship between landlords and residential occupiers: the Rent Acts were broadly directed at preventing exploitation of the latter by the former.[3] The operation of the Rent Acts clearly restricted freedom of contract in the housing market and had the effect of inhibiting the exercise by private owners of formerly sacrosanct rights of property.[4] In their most extreme form, Rent Act legislation, by assuring qualifying tenants long-term security of tenure at a 'fair rent', stripped the landlord's rights back to a bare reversion[5] and caused 'an almost permanent alienation from the landlord of the right to get possession of the premises.'[6] Social legislation aimed at the protection of residential security in the rented sector has almost always survived constitutional (or other human rights) challenges.[7] In particular, the jurisprudence of the European Court of Human Rights has long incorporated the premise that legislation in the area of housing and social welfare falls within the 'political sphere'.[8] The Court therefore accords a wide 'margin of appreciation' to the national legislature's assessment of the general domestic interest unless this judgment is 'manifestly without reasonable foundation.'[9] The European Convention provides that no deprivation of property can be justified unless, at the very least, it serves the 'public interest'.[10] However, as Lord Scott of Foscote indicated in *Harrow LBC v Qazi*,[11] social housing legislation is 'well justifiable' on public interest grounds even though its operation diminishes the property rights of landlords.

1 Increase of Rent and Mortgage Interest (War Restrictions) Act 1915. See P Q Watchman, 'The Origin of the 1915 Rent Act' (1980) Law and State (No 5) 20. See also Lord Hoffmann's reference in *Cadogan Estates Ltd v McMahon* [2001] 1 AC 378 at 383F to the Rent Acts as 'a remarkable sequence of enactments which go back to the First World War.'
2 For an extremely good account of this legislation and its effects, see J E Martin, *Residential Security* (London 1989).
3 'The Rent Acts have throughout their history constituted an interference with contract and property rights for a specific purpose – the redress of the balance of advantage enjoyed in a

world of housing shortage by the landlord over those who have to rent their homes' (*Horford Investments Ltd v Lambert* [1976] Ch 39 at 52D–E per Scarman LJ).

4   See *Davis v Johnson* [1979] AC 317 at 348E–G per Lord Scarman.
5   Although 'in the short term interests of residential tenants', the Rent Acts led ultimately to a reduction in the supply of privately rented accommodation. 'There is no simple equation between security of tenure and the public interest' (*Somerset CC v Isaacs* [2002] EWHC 1014 (Admin) at [33] per Stanley Burnton J).
6   *Blake v Attorney-General* [1982] IR 117 at 140 per O'Higgins CJ.
7   See e g *Kilbourn v United Kingdom* (1986) 8 EHRR 81 at 84; *Mellacher v Austria*, Series A No 169 (1989) at [57]; *A & L Investments Ltd v Ontario* (*Minister of Housing*) (1997) 152 DLR (4th) 692 at 701–702. For a notable counter-example, see *Blake v Attorney-General* [1982] IR 117 at 126, 140 (Supreme Court of Ireland).
8   See *Anufrijeva v Southwark LBC* [2004] 2 WLR 603 at [41(5)].
9   *Mellacher v Austria*, Series A No 169 (1989) at [45]; *Jahn and Others v Germany* [2004] ECHR 36 at [80]; *Connors v United Kingdom* (ECtHR decision, Application No 66746/01, 27 May 2004) at [82]. See also *James v United Kingdom*, Series A No 98 (1986) at [46]–[49] **[para 7.337]**; *Poplar Housing and Regeneration Community Association Ltd v Donoghue* [2002] QB 48 at [69] per Lord Woolf CJ.
10   ECHR Protocol No 1, Art 1 **[para 2.29]**. See *Aston Cantlow and Wilmcote with Billesley PCC v Wallbank* [2004] 1 AC 546 at [134] per Lord Scott of Foscote.
11   [2004] 1 AC 983 at [125].

14.313   The importance of the Rent Act has waned dramatically with the decline of the private rented sector.[1] The recent history of the Rent Act is one of creeping obsolescence: relatively few regulated tenants now remain. Successive enactments have cut back the scope of the legislation and the Housing Act 1988 finally provided that no new Rent Act tenancies could be granted on or after 15 January 1989.[2] In practice the private rented sector has been overtaken by the less amply protected 'shorthold tenancy'[3] and observers are left to witness the terminal stages of an idealistic 20th century social experiment in the housing market. The Rent Acts have nevertheless imposed an indelible imprint upon the nature and construction of British housing legislation. The following provides an outline of the protective scheme underpinned by this corpus of legislation.[4]

1   The proportion of households in England and Wales living in private rented accommodation declined from 89 per cent in 1900 to 12 per cent in 2002 (*Social Trends 34* (2004 edn London), p 153 (Table 10.7)).
2   HA 1988, s 34(1).
3   **[Paras 14.331–14.337]**.
4   For a more detailed account of the law in this area, see *Elements of Land Law* (1st edn 1987), pp 961–1044, 1062–1072; Pearl and Gray, *Social Welfare Law* (London 1981), pp 195–227.

Definition of a 'protected tenancy'

14.314   The Rent Act 1977 confirms the existence of a statutory category of 'regulated tenancy', so defined as to include the sub-categories of 'protected tenancy' and 'statutory tenancy'.[1] Section 1 of the 1977 Act defines a 'protected tenancy' as 'a tenancy under which a dwelling-house (which may be a house or part of a house) is let as a separate dwelling'. This definition has mandatory application in that the statutory benefits of a protected tenancy can never be bargained away by the tenant or validly disavowed by declaration or estoppel.[2]

1   RA 1977, s 18(1).
2   *Antoniades v Villiers* [1990] 1 AC 417 at 458D per Lord Templeman. See *Brown v Draper*
     [1944] KB 309 at 313 per Lord Greene MR; *Baxter v Eckersley* [1950] 1 KB 480 at 485. See
     also *Appleton v Aspin* [1988] 1 WLR 410.

Nature of the letting

14.315   A 'protected tenancy' comprises only those forms of occupancy which
have the strict character of a 'tenancy'[1] and can never extend to a licence.[2] The
tenancy may, however, relate to an entire house or a self-contained flat or even
a single bed-sitting room.[3] The accommodation, whatever its nature, must be let
at a rent which can be given a quantifiable money value[4] and must moreover be
let 'as a separate dwelling'. For this reason a tenancy cannot be 'protected'
unless it was intended at its commencement to provide one (and only one) unit
of habitation.[5] The premises claimed as a 'separate dwelling' must be intrinsically capable of sustaining the independent domestic existence of the tenant.[6]

1   **[Para 7.88]**. See *Antoniades v Villiers* [1990] 1 AC 417 at 458D–E per Lord Templeman.
2   Once a tenancy has been found to satisfy the qualifying conditions of section 1 of the 1977
     Act, it is entirely irrelevant whether the tenancy is a periodic tenancy or a fixed term, a legal or
     an equitable tenancy, or a joint tenancy. The Rent Act exemption for furnished tenancies was
     removed in relation to tenancies granted on or after 14 August 1974 (see RA 1974, s 1(1)).
3   See *Antoniades v Villiers* [1990] 1 AC 417 at 459D per Lord Templeman; *Prince v Robinson and
     Robinson* (1998) 76 P & CR D2.
4   See *Barnes v Barratt* [1970] 2 QB 657 at 667E per Sachs LJ; *Montague v Browning* [1954]
     1 WLR 1039 at 1044–1045. There can be no protected tenancy if the tenant pays no rent at all
     or only a 'low rent' (RA 1977, s 5(1)).
5   See *Horford Investments Ltd v Lambert* [1976] Ch 39 at 47G–48D (no protection for house
     already converted into units for multiple residential accommodation). See also *St Catherine's
     College, Oxford v Dorling* [1980] 1 WLR 66 at 70F. It is irrelevant that the protected tenant
     never subsequently 'dwells' in the premises at all, if he sublets the entire unit to a single
     subtenant (see *Horford Investments*, supra at 51A).
6   *Antoniades v Villiers* [1990] 1 AC 417 at 459E per Lord Templeman. See e g *Metropolitan
     Properties Co (FGC) Ltd v Barder* [1968] 1 WLR 286 at 294C per Edmund Davies LJ (tiny
     room inadequate as 'separate dwelling'). See also *Curl v Angelo* [1948] 2 All ER 189 at
     190H–191A; *Hampstead Way Investments Ltd v Lewis-Weare* [1985] 1 WLR 164 at 171H per
     Lord Brandon of Oakwood.

Exclusions from Rent Act protection

14.316   Certain categories of tenancy are expressly excluded from the scope of
the 'protected tenancy'.[1] No tenancy can be a 'protected tenancy' if its purpose
is to confer on the tenant the right to occupy a dwelling-house 'for a holiday'.[2]
The Act also excludes any tenancy under which a dwelling-house is 'bona fide
let at a rent which includes payments in respect of board or attendance.'[3] Nor
can protection be claimed by the tenant of a 'resident landlord'.[4] The primary
purpose of the last exception is plainly to permit a property owner to trade off
some of his domestic privacy in return for the statutory assurance of substantial immunity from any possible claim to protected status on the part of the
intruding tenant.[5]

1   See RA 1977, ss 13–16 (lettings by the Crown, government departments, local authorities, housing associations and housing co-operatives). Also excluded are lettings to students (RA 1977, s 8) or in respect of agricultural holdings (RA 1977, s 10) and licensed premises (RA 1977, s 11).

2   RA 1977, s 9. See *McHale v Daneham* (1979) 123 Sol Jo 86; *Francke v Hakmi* [1984] CLY 1906. The courts have not seemed particularly responsive to the argument that improbable holiday lets should be stigmatised as a 'sham' (see e g *Buchmann v May* [1978] 2 All ER 993 at 998h; *Tetragon Ltd v Shidasb Construction Co Ltd and Darabi* (1981) 7 HLR 113 at 117–118; but compare *R v Rent Officer for LB of Camden, ex p Plant* (1981) 257 EG 713).

3   RA 1977, s 7(1). See *Wilkes v Goodwin* [1923] 2 KB 86 at 110 per Younger LJ. A 'continental breakfast' is sufficient to constitute 'board' (*Otter v Norman* [1989] AC 129 at 146C–E). See, however, *Rita Dale v Adrahill Ltd and Ali Khan* [1982] CLY 1787; *Gavin v Lindsay* 1987 SLT (Sh Ct) 12 at 14–15; *Palser v Grinling* [1948] AC 291 at 310–311, 318 per Viscount Simon.

4   RA 1977, s 12(1). See *Lyons v Caffery* (1983) 266 EG 213 at 214; *Cooper v Tait* (1984) 48 P & CR 460 at 462; *Palmer v McNamara* (1990) 23 HLR 168 at 171.

5   See *Bardrick v Haycock* (1976) 31 P & CR 420 at 424 per Scarman LJ.

The statutory tenancy

14.317   Under the Rent Act a 'protected tenancy' subsists during the contractual period fixed by the terms of the relevant tenancy agreement. When this contractual period comes to an end (either by the effluxion of time or after the service of a notice to quit), it is integral to the Rent Act scheme that the tenancy continues to subsist for an indefinite period, not as a 'protected tenancy' based on the parties' contract, but as a 'statutory tenancy' which derives its legal effect from the Rent Act itself.[1] The former protected tenant thus continues to receive, by statutory extension of his rights, substantially the same protection under the Rent Act.[2] The statutory tenancy created by the Rent Act is a highly anomalous legal phenomenon.[3] It cannot be easily assimilated within the doctrine of estates, for the statutory tenant has no estate or interest known to the common law.[4] All he has is a negatively expressed and largely personal right to be 'free from disturbance'[5] by the landlord unless and until some court of competent jurisdiction makes an order for the recovery of possession on behalf of that landlord.[6] It is for this reason that the statutory tenant is often referred to as having a mere 'status of irremovability'.[7]

1   RA 1977, s 2(1)(a).
2   RA 1977, s 3(1).
3   See *Marcroft Wagons Ltd v Smith* [1951] 2 KB 496 at 501 per Evershed MR ('monstrum horrendum, informe, ingens').
4   *Keeves v Dean* [1924] 1 KB 685 at 690, 697.
5   *Keeves v Dean* [1924] 1 KB 685 at 697 per Lush J.
6   **[Para 14.321]**.
7   *Keeves v Dean* [1924] 1 KB 685 at 686 per Lush J.

Requirement of continuous residential occupation

14.318   A statutory tenancy remains in force only if and so long as the tenant 'occupies the dwelling-house as his residence.'[1] Whether in any given case the tenant can show the required continuity of personal occupation is 'a question of fact and degree.'[2] The Rent Acts have always been concerned with the efficient allocation of private housing as a social resource and it is no purpose of the legislation to confer long-term protection on a tenant who sublets the entire dwelling-house or who cannot show substantial use of the property as a home.[3] A statutory tenancy is not, however, destroyed by short-lived or deliberate absences provided that the tenant retains an *animus revertendi* (or intention to return).[4] Nor is it fatal that the rented premises are used as merely *one* of the tenant's homes,[5] although as the House of Lords held in *Hampstead Way Investments Ltd v Lewis-Weare*,[6] the premises in relation to which a statutory tenancy is claimed must be occupied 'as a complete home in itself.'[7]

1 RA 1977, s 2(1)(a), (3). See *Skinner v Geary* [1931] 2 KB 546 at 564; *Brown v Brash and Ambrose* [1948] 2 KB 247 at 254; *Prince v Robinson and Robinson* (1998) 76 P & CR D2 at D4. A company (if genuinely constituted) cannot for this purpose assert any continuity of personal residence. See *Firstcross Ltd v East West (Export/Import) Ltd* (1981) 41 P & CR 145 at 151–158 (company let). Compare *Hilton v Plustitle Ltd* [1989] 1 WLR 149 at 153F–G, 155D.

2 *Brown v Brash and Ambrose* [1948] 2 KB 247 at 254. See e g *Skinner v Geary* [1931] 2 KB 546 at 562 per Scrutton LJ.

3 *Haskins v Lewis* [1931] 2 KB 1 at 14. See also *Skinner v Geary* [1931] 2 KB 546 at 564 per Scrutton LJ; *Brown v Brash and Ambrose* [1948] 2 KB 247 at 254 per Asquith LJ; *Bevington v Crawford* (1974) 232 EG 191; *Regalian Securities Ltd v Scheuer* (1982) 5 HLR 48 at 56.

4 *Skinner v Geary* [1931] 2 KB 546 at 569. See *Brown v Brash and Ambrose* [1948] 2 KB 247 at 254–255; *Hallwood Estates Ltd v Flack* (1950) 155 EG 408; *Roland House Gardens Ltd v Cravitz* (1975) 29 P & CR 432 at 436; *Brickfield Properties Ltd v Hughes* (1988) 20 HLR 108 at 113–119; *Robert Thackray's Estates Ltd v Kaye* (1989) 21 HLR 160 at 166.

5 *Kavanagh v Lyroudias* [1985] 1 All ER 560 at 562d–e; *Hampstead Way Investments Ltd v Lewis-Weare* [1985] 1 WLR 164 at 168D, 169F.

6 [1985] 1 WLR 164 at 171B. See [1985] Conv 224 (P F Smith).

7 See *Kavanagh v Lyroudias* [1985] 1 All ER 560 at 562g; *Nicholson v Samuel Property Management Ltd* (2002) 217 DLR (4th) 292 at [24].

Transmission on death

14.319 In clear defiance of the contractually agreed duration of the original tenancy, the statutory tenancy, unless terminated by a court or surrendered by the tenant, may then persist throughout a maximum of two or three generations.[1] This potential prolongation of a Rent Act tenancy has proved historically to be one of the most controversial features of the long-term security of tenure conferred upon the statutory tenant, since it effectively deprived the landlord of vacant possession of the rented property for a vast expanse of time.[2]

1 This was certainly true in respect of any Rent Act tenancy held by a tenant who died prior to 15 January 1989. The Housing Act 1988 severely curtails the operation of statutory succession in respect of any Rent Act tenant whose death occurs after this statutory commencement date (HA 1988, s 39, Sch 4).

2 See e g R Street, [1985] Conv 328 (Street was the losing landlord in *Street v Mountford* [1985] AC 809 [**para 7.177**]).

14.320 Where a Rent Act tenant dies on or after 15 January 1989, that tenant's 'surviving spouse' may claim the tenancy by succession if residing in the dwelling-house immediately before the tenant's death.[1] Largely in view of the prohibition of gender-based discrimination contained in the European Convention on Human Rights,[2] the term 'spouse' has now been accorded a Convention-compliant meaning as inclusive of not merely a de iure partner, but also a de facto partner (whether heterosexual or same-sex).[3] In default of any 'surviving spouse',[4] some other 'member of the original tenant's family' may claim the tenancy by succession if this person was residing in the dwelling-house at the time of, and for two years immediately preceding, the tenant's death.[5]

1   RA 1977, Sch 1, para 2. On the death of this spouse there may be a further succession in favour of a member of the family of both the original tenant and the first successor. However, this succession confers only an *assured* tenancy under the Housing Act 1988 and, even then, only if the relevant family member resided with the first successor in the dwelling-house for two years immediately preceding the succession (RA 1977, Sch 1, para 6).
2   ECHR Art 14 [**para 14.5**].
3   *Ghaidan v Godin-Mendoza* [2004] 3 WLR 113 at [35] per Lord Nicholls of Birkenhead, [128]–[129] per Lord Rodger of Earlsferry, [144] per Baroness Hale of Richmond.
4   If there is no surviving spouse, the number of permissible successions (of any sort) is reduced from two to one (HA 1988, Sch 4, paras 3, 7).
5   RA 1977, Sch 1, para 3(1). Much of the controversy surrounding the definition of a 'member of the original tenant's family' has been dispelled by the House of Lords' ruling in *Ghaidan v Godin-Mendoza* [2004] 3 WLR 113 (see generally *Elements of Land Law* (1st edn 1987), pp 1062–1072). Remaining definitional problems revolve around more remote family relationships (see e g *Jones v Whitehill* [1950] 2 KB 204; *Langdon v Horton* [1951] 1 KB 666) and platonic relationships (see e g *Carega Properties SA v Sharratt* [1979] 1 WLR 928).

Security of tenure

14.321   Under a 'regulated' tenancy (whether 'protected' or 'statutory'), the tenant acquires a certain security of tenure. If the tenant is not prepared to vacate his dwelling-house voluntarily, his landlord cannot obtain possession without (i) terminating his contractual tenancy (if such is still in force) and (ii) obtaining a court order for possession, thereby terminating the statutory tenancy which automatically arises at the end of the contractual tenancy. A court will make an order for possession against a protected or statutory tenant only on the grounds specified in the Rent Act 1977. Some of these grounds are discretionary grounds for the recovery of possession; others are mandatory.

Discretionary grounds for possession

14.322   Pursuant to section 98(1) of the Rent Act 1977, no court order for possession can be made unless the court considers it 'reasonable to make such an order',[1] and
EITHER the court is satisfied that 'suitable alternative accommodation' is available for the tenant or will be available for him when the possession order takes effect[2]
OR the circumstances are such as are specified in any of the Cases in Part I of Schedule 15 of the Rent Act 1977.

1   See *Battlespring Ltd v Gates* (1983) 268 EG 355 at 356. See also RA 1977, s 100.
2   RA 1977, s 98(1)(a), Sch 15, Part IV. See *Yewbright Properties Ltd v Stone* (1980) 40 P & CR
     402 at 406–410; *Siddiqui v Rashid* [1980] 1 WLR 1018 at 1023E–F; *Hill v Rochard* [1983]
     1 WLR 478 at 486G.

14.323   The most significant circumstances embraced within the Cases contained in Part I of Schedule 15 include non-payment of rent or other breach of
obligation (Case 1)[1]; commission of 'a nuisance or annoyance' or immoral or
illegal user (Case 2); waste, neglect or default causing the condition of the
dwelling-house to deteriorate (Case 3); damage to furniture (Case 4); assignment or subletting without consent (Case 6); termination of employment to
which a service tenancy is attached (Case 8); and reasonable requirement of the
dwelling-house for residential occupation by the landlord or certain statutorily
specified relatives (Case 9).[2]

1   See *Cadogan Estates Ltd v McMahon* [2001] 1 AC 378 at 386F–387A, 388H (tenant's
     bankruptcy against the background of a right of re-entry for the landlord in the event of
     bankruptcy constitutes a breach of an 'obligation' of the tenancy).
2   See e g *Kidder v Birch* (1983) 46 P & CR 362 at 364. No possession order may be made under
     Case 9 if the court is satisfied that, 'having regard to all the circumstances, including the
     question whether other accommodation is available for the landlord or the tenant, greater
     hardship would be caused by granting the order than by refusing to grant it' (RA 1977,
     Sch 15, Part III, para 1).

Mandatory grounds for possession

14.324   Part II of Schedule 15 of the Rent Act 1977 sets out certain grounds
(Cases 11 to 20) which, if proved, lead automatically to the making of a
possession order against the tenant.[1] These mandatory grounds for the recovery
of possession alike require that the landlord should normally have given written
notice to the tenant *before* the commencement of the tenancy that he might
seek to repossess under a particular Case.[2] Cases 11 to 20 leave virtually no
room for the exercise of discretion. The court may not postpone the giving up
of possession to a date later than 14 days after the making of the order unless
'it appears to the court that exceptional hardship would be caused by requiring
possession to be given up by that date.' Even where 'exceptional hardship' is
present, possession cannot be postponed to a date later than six weeks after the
making of the court order.[3]

1   RA 1977, s 98(2). There is also an automatic ground of recovery for the landlord where the
     dwelling-house is 'overcrowded' within the meaning of the Housing Act 1985 (RA 1977,
     s 101).
2   See *Bradshaw v Baldwin-Wiseman* (1985) 49 P & CR 382 at 385 per Griffiths LJ.
3   HA 1980, s 89(1).

14.325   The most important grounds of mandatory recovery include circumstances where the landlord as the previous owner-occupier requires the
dwelling-house as a residence for himself or a member of his family (Case 11)[1]
or the landlord requires the dwelling-house as a residence on his retirement
from regular employment (Case 12).

1   See *Kennealy v Dunne* [1977] QB 837 at 850A–B, 851B–C; *Tilling v Whiteman* [1980] AC 1 at 18F. Compare *Salter v Beljinac* (2001) 201 DLR (4th) 744 at [21].

Restriction of rents

14.326   The second basic feature of the protection afforded the regulated tenant under the Rent Act 1977 lies in the measure of statutory control exercisable over the rent which may lawfully be charged by the landlord.[1] Under the scheme of the Rent Act the tenant need pay nothing more than an administratively determined 'fair rent'[2] as the price of his or her security of tenure.[3] Historically this restriction of the rent payable served not only to displace the normal operation of market forces but also to cut through the principle of sanctity of contract between landlord and tenant. Determinations of 'fair rent' overrode the rent agreed by the parties, even though in most cases a 'fair rent' in relation to a dwelling-house was considerably less than the rent obtainable on an open and uncontrolled market.[4] Following the commencement of the Housing Act 1988, it became increasingly common for 'fair' rents to be assessed with reference to the market rents chargeable under assured shorthold tenancies of comparable properties.[5] In order to prevent a complete severance of Rent Act security of tenure from its indivisible historic concomitant of fair rent control,[6] maximum limits have now been applied to the increases of 'fair rent' which may be registered.[7]

1   See M J Radin, 'Residential Rent Control' (1986) 15 Philosophy & Public Affairs 350.
2   On the criteria relevant to a determination of 'fair rent', see RA 1977, s 70(1); *Mason v Skilling* [1974] 1 WLR 1437 at 1443B–C per Lord Kilbrandon; *Metropolitan Property Holdings Ltd v Finegold* [1975] 1 WLR 349 at 354A–B.
3   Both landlord and tenant have a statutory right to apply to the local rent officer for registration of a 'fair rent' in respect of any dwelling subject to a regulated tenancy (RA 1977, s 67(1)). Once registered the 'fair rent' cannot normally be varied for a period of two years (RA 1977, s 67(3)).
4   In *Blake v Attorney-General* [1982] IR 117 at 139, the success of the constitutional challenge mounted against the validity of the Irish Rent Act legislation [**para 14.312**] was founded in part on the argument that the rent chargeable under the statutory scheme was 'oppressively uneconomic'. See also 100 Harv L Rev 1067 (1986–87); L L Westray, 62 S Cal L Rev 321 (1988).
5   [**Para 14.335**]. See *R v Secretary of State for the Environment, Transport and the Regions, ex p Spath Holme Ltd* [2001] 2 AC 349 at 379B–E per Lord Bingham of Cornhill.
6   Security of tenure and rent restriction were always viewed as interdependent. In the absence of security of tenure a landlord, although restricted to charging a fair rent, can evict at any time; without effective 'fair rent' control the landlord can likewise rid himself of an unwanted tenant simply by raising the level of the rent (see *Blake v Attorney General* [1982] IR 117 at 141 per O'Higgins CJ).
7   Rent Acts (Maximum Fair Rent) Order 1999 (SI 1999/6), art 2 (pursuant to L&TA 1985, s 31). See *R v Secretary of State for the Environment, Transport and the Regions, ex p Spath Holme Ltd* [2001] 2 AC 349.

Prohibition of unlawful payments by a regulated tenant

14.327   In order to prevent circumventions of the statutory scheme of 'fair rent' restriction, the Rent Act makes it a criminal offence for any person[1] to require or receive a premium or loan as a condition of, or in connection with, the grant, renewal or continuance of a protected tenancy.[2] The court has power to order the repayment of any illicit premium (or 'key money') so paid.[3] The Act also prohibits certain payments made on the assignment of protected tenancies.[4]

1   The ambit of the criminal provision is extensive, for the term 'any person' is wide enough to include such persons as landlords, tenants, agents, middlemen and relatives (see *Farrell v Alexander* [1977] AC 59 at 71E–G, 77B–F, 96A–B).
2   RA 1977, s 119(1).
3   RA 1977, s 125(1).
4   RA 1977, s 120(1), (2).

Restriction of the right to levy distress

14.328   No distress may be levied on the goods of a regulated tenant except by leave of a county court[1] and the court has substantial powers to adjourn, stay, suspend or postpone proceedings.[2]

1   RA 1977, s 147(1).
2   See RA 1977, s 100.

HOUSING ACT 1988 (ASSURED AND SHORTHOLD TENANCIES)

14.329   Most private sector residential tenancies granted on or after 15 January 1989 constitute an 'assured tenancy' governed by the provisions of the Housing Act 1988. The assured tenancy shares some of the features of the Rent Act 'regulated tenancy', which will eventually be phased out of existence if only by the passage of time. In general, however, it was the intention of the 1988 Act to facilitate the creation of a form of tenancy which avoided the non-consensual long-term 'status of irremovability' of the Rent Act tenancy. Particularly in its 'shorthold' form, the assured tenancy sought to regenerate the private rented housing market by guaranteeing the landlord a quick and easy recovery of possession on the expiration of the contractually agreed term.[1] In the result the assured tenancy confers only a heavily curtailed version of the amplitude of rights enjoyed by the Rent Act regulated tenant.

1   See *R v Secretary of State for the Environment, Transport and the Regions, ex p Spath Holme Ltd* [2001] 2 AC 349 at 378H–379A per Lord Bingham of Cornhill.

Definition of an 'assured tenancy'

14.330   The assured tenancy provisions of the Housing Act 1988 apply to 'any tenancy under which a dwelling-house is let as a separate dwelling',[1] this formula importing by analogy the case law relating to the equivalent phrase in the Rent Act 1977.[2] The assured tenant must be an individual and must occupy the dwelling-house 'as his only or principal home.'[3] Under the scheme of the

1988 Act an assured tenancy may be either a periodic tenancy or a 'fixed term tenancy',[4] the latter term including both a tenancy at will and, more significantly, a 'shorthold tenancy' as defined by the Act.

1   HA 1988, s 1(1). Certain categories of tenancy are excluded (HA 1988, Sch 1, Part I), eg tenancies at a low rent, business tenancies, lettings to students, holiday lettings, local authority tenancies and tenancies granted by a resident landlord. Similarly, an assured tenancy cannot comprise a tenancy whose rent exceeds £25,000 per annum (HA 1988, Sch 1, para 2). See *Bankway Properties Ltd v Pensfold-Dunsford* [2001] 1 WLR 1369 at [68]–[70], where the Court of Appeal struck down a rent review clause which purported, wholly unrealistically, to raise the rent to £25,000 per annum **[para 7.180]**.

2   **[Para 14.315].** See generally *Elements of Land Law* (1st edn 1987), pp 970–982. In an age of commercially available fast food it is not essential to the definition of a 'dwelling' that the tenant should have access to cooking facilities (*Uratemp Ventures Ltd v Collins* [2002] 1 AC 301 at [3], [12], [17], [31]). See [2002] Conv 285 (P F Smith); [2002] CLJ (L Tee); Jill Morgan, 'The Changing Meaning of "Dwelling-House"' [2002] CLJ 312.

3   HA 1988, s 1(1)(a)–(b). An assured tenancy may be a joint tenancy provided that each of the joint tenants is an 'individual' and at least one of them occupies the dwelling-house as his 'only or principal home.' A houseboat cannot be a 'dwelling-house' (*Chelsea Yacht & Boat Co Ltd v Pope* [2000] 1 WLR 1941 at 1946C **[para 1.53]**).

4   A 'fixed term tenancy' is defined as including 'any tenancy other than a periodic tenancy' (HA 1988, s 45(1)).

Assured 'shorthold' tenancies

14.331   It is the assured 'shorthold' tenancy which most clearly achieves the statutory objective of prompt and easy recovery of possession for landlords. Under the Housing Act 1988 there has been a progressive diminution of the requirements to be met by the 'shorthold' tenancy.

Tenancies granted before March 1997

14.332   A tenancy granted before March 1997 could comprise an assured 'shorthold' tenancy if granted for a term certain of not less than six months and if the landlord, prior to the entry into the tenancy, served on the tenant a notice in prescribed form stating that the tenancy was to be a shorthold tenancy.[1]

1   HA 1988, s 20(1), (2)(d).

Tenancies granted after February 1997

14.333   The conditions attaching to the shorthold tenancy have been significantly relaxed in relation to tenancies granted since the end of February 1997.[1] The new-style shorthold need not have any minimum term, but may comprise any fixed or periodic tenancy, the 'shorthold' designation now applying automatically to all new private residential tenancies other than those made the subject of a specific opt-out by notice.[2] There need no longer be any prior written notice warning the tenant that he holds under the terms of a recoverable shorthold.

1   See HA 1988, s 19A.
2   HA 1988, Sch 2A, paras 1–2. In a few other exceptional cases a tenancy remains a full assured tenancy, eg an assured tenancy arising for a family member on the death of the spouse of a Rent Act tenant on or after 15 January 1989 (RA 1977, Sch 1, para 6 (as inserted by HA 1988, Sch 4, para 6) **[para 14.320]**).

Terms of the assured tenancy

14.334   An assured tenancy incorporates both terms expressly agreed by the parties and a number of terms implied by statute. The latter include a prohibition on assignment or subletting without the landlord's consent[1] and a term that the tenant shall give the landlord access to the dwelling-house and 'all reasonable facilities' for the execution of any repairs which the landlord is entitled to carry out.[2] An assured periodic tenancy may, on the death of the tenant, devolve upon his or her spouse,[3] provided that the spouse occupied the dwelling-house, immediately before the tenant's death, as his or her 'only or principal home.'[4]

1   HA 1988, s 15(1).
2   HA 1988, s 16.
3   HA 1988, s 17(1), (4) (compare now *Ghaidan v Godin-Mendoza* [2004] 3 WLR 113 **[para 14.320]**). There is no provision for succession by any 'member of the tenant's family', and the devolution under the 1988 Act applies only to an assured tenancy held by a person who was not a joint tenant and had not himself acquired the tenancy by statutory succession (HA 1988, s 17(1)(a), (c)).
4   HA 1988, s 17(1)(b). An assured fixed term tenancy passes on the tenant's death to the appropriate beneficiary under his estate, who ranks as an assured tenant himself only if he fulfils the assured tenancy criteria (the assured tenancy otherwise coming to an end at the expiry of the fixed term).

Market rents

14.335   Unlike the 'fair rent' control in place under the Rent Act 1977, rent levels under an assured tenancy are not in general governed by any statutory scheme of regulation. The rent under a fixed term assured tenancy is subject to no control at all, while in relation to periodic assured tenancies there exists an extremely limited and little used form of rent control, which in practice relegates the shorthold tenant to the mercy of market forces prevailing in the private rental sector. The rent payable under an assured periodic tenancy can be increased on service of a prescribed form of notice,[1] but in this case (and not before) the tenant has a right to refer the rent to a rent assessment committee for a determination of the rent at which the dwelling-house 'might reasonably be expected to be let in the open market by a willing landlord under an assured tenancy.'[2] Under an assured shorthold tenancy granted after February 1997 the tenant is entitled to refer the *initial* rent for consideration by a rent assessment committee,[3] but the rent cannot be varied unless there is a sufficiency of similar dwelling-houses in the locality let on assured tenancies and the rent referred is 'significantly higher' than the rent level which, in this context, the landlord 'might reasonably be expected to be able to obtain.'[4]

1   HA 1988, s 13(2). In the absence of a contrary contractual agreement, no increase is normally
     permissible during the first year of the tenancy (HA 1988, s 13(2)(b)).
2   HA 1988, ss 13(4)(a), 14(1).
3   HA 1988, s 22 (as amended by HA 1996, s 100). The application must be made not later than
     six months after the commencement of the tenancy (HA 1988, s 22(2)(aa)).
4   HA 1988, s 22(3).

Security of tenure

14.336 A landlord may terminate an assured tenancy only by obtaining a
court order for possession on one or other of a number of statutorily specified
grounds.[1] Thus an assured periodic tenancy continues notwithstanding the
landlord's service of a notice to quit[2] and the expiration of a fixed-term tenancy
immediately brings into effect a 'statutory periodic tenancy' on terms similar to
those of the expired tenancy.[3]

1   HA 1988, s 5(1). See *Artesian Residential Developments Ltd v Beck* [2000] QB 541 at 549A–F
     per Hirst LJ (Mantell LJ concurring) [**para 14.157**].
2   HA 1988, s 5(1).
3   HA 1988, s 5(2)–(3). The relevant period is fixed by reference to the rental periods under the
     former fixed-term tenancy (HA 1988, s 5(3)(d)).

14.337 The grounds justifying an order for possession are broadly similar to
those contained in Parts I and II of Schedule 15 to the Rent Act 1977.[1] Some
grounds are *discretionary* and enable the court to order repossession if it
'considers it reasonable to do so.'[2] These grounds are concerned essentially with
cases of breach of covenant by the tenant,[3] but include also the case where
'suitable alternative accommodation' is available for the tenant.[4] Other grounds
are *mandatory*, some requiring that the landlord should have given written
notice to the tenant before the commencement of the tenancy that he might
seek to repossess on a particular ground.[5] Other grounds of mandatory
recovery are even more stringent, necessitating merely that the landlord have an
intention to demolish or carry out substantial works on the property[6] or show
an arrear of weekly or monthly rent payments of at least eight weeks.[7] The
most important mandatory ground of recovery of possession is that dedicated
to the 'shorthold' tenancy.[8] Here, provided that the landlord has served on the
tenant two months' notice in writing of his intention to recover possession,[9] the
landlord's desire to recover his land is self-defining and must result in a court
order for possession against the tenant.[10] In relation, however, to a shorthold
tenancy granted after February 1997, no possession order can take effect earlier
than six months after the beginning of the tenancy,[11] although the landlord
may initiate possession proceedings within this period.

1   [**Para 14.321**].
2   HA 1988, s 7(4). The court has substantial discretion to adjourn proceedings and to stay or
     suspend the execution of a possession order (HA 1988, s 9). See also HA 1985, s 9A, as
     inserted by ASBA 2003, s 16(2) (relating to anti-social behaviour)).
3   See HA 1988, Sch 2, Part II (as amended by HA 1996, ss 148–149), Ground 10 (unpaid rent),
     Ground 11 (persistent delay in payment of rent), Ground 12 (breach of obligation unrelated

to payment of rent), Ground 13 (waste), Ground 14 (nuisance or annoyance), Ground 14A (domestic violence to a partner), Ground 15 (damage to furniture).
4   HA 1988, Sch 2, Part II, Ground 9.
5   See e g HA 1988, Sch 2, Part I, Ground 1 (recovery of home formerly occupied by landlord or now required for occupation by landlord or spouse), Ground 2 (sale by mortgagee under paramount power), Ground 3 (holiday home), Ground 4 (student residence).
6   HA 1988, Sch 2, Part I, Ground 6.
7   HA 1988, Sch 2, Part I, Ground 8 (as amended by HA 1996, s 101). See *Coltrane v Day* [2003] 1 WLR 1379; [2004] Conv 152 (Jill Morgan).
8   HA 1988, s 21 (as amended by HA 1996, ss 98–99).
9   HA 1988, s 21(1)(b).
10   Where a shorthold tenancy is in writing and a notice demanding possession has been duly served, there is provision for an accelerated procedure in the county court under which the judge can order possession without requiring the attendance of the parties (CPR 55.11– 55.19). Postponement of possession is subject to the rigid limits set out in HA 1980, s 89(1) **[para 3.45]**.
11   HA 1988, s 21(5)(a) (as inserted by HA 1996, s 99).

HOUSING ACT 1985 (SECURE TENANCIES)

14.338   After many years of non-regulation the public rented sector was finally subjected by the Housing Act 1980 to some form of protective control. The objective of this enactment (now consolidated in the Housing Act 1985) was 'the social one of giving to tenants in the public housing sector, so far as reasonably practicable, the same kind of protection from being evicted from their homes without good and sufficient cause as had been enjoyed by tenants in the private housing sector for many decades under the Rent Acts.'[1] Accordingly the 1980 and 1985 Acts sought in large measure to assimilate the rights of public and private sector tenants 'in the general interests of social equality and non-discrimination.'[2] The legislation introduced a new legal status for the public sector tenant as a 'secure tenant' and goes some distance towards establishing a 'charter of rights' in the area of public housing. This 'charter of rights' has a significant coverage in terms of the national population, extending in 2003 to some 19 per cent of all households in Britain.[3]

1   *Harrison v Hammersmith and Fulham LBC* [1981] 1 WLR 650 at 661C per Brandon LJ.
2   *Harrison v Hammersmith and Fulham LBC* [1981] 1 WLR 650 at 661D.
3   *Social Trends 34* (2004 edn London), p 153 (Table 10.7). The proportion of households falling within the public housing sector has declined from 34 per cent in 1981, this trend being largely attributable to the exercise by council tenants of their statutory 'right to buy' **[para 7.347]**.

Definition of 'secure tenancy'

14.339   In Part IV of the Housing Act 1985 the 'secure tenancy' effectively provides the broad analogue of the private sector 'regulated tenancy',[1] the 'secure tenant' enjoying a relative permanence of tenure terminable only by court order.[2] A tenancy comprises a 'secure tenancy' where a 'dwelling-house'[3] is 'let as a separate dwelling'[4] and two statutorily prescribed conditions are fulfilled.[5] The 'landlord condition'[6] requires that the dwelling-house must belong to one or other of a number of public or quasi-public bodies.[7] The 'tenant condition'[8] requires that the tenant must be an 'individual'[9] and must occupy the relevant dwelling-house as his 'only or principal home.'[10] In a major departure from the pattern of the Rent Act, the definition of the 'secure tenancy' is specially extended to cover not merely a tenancy in the strict sense but also a licence to occupy a dwelling-house,[11] provided that the licence otherwise fulfils the conditions required of a secure tenancy.[12]

1   It is inevitable that the jurisprudence elaborated under the Rent Act should provide a substantial aid to the construction of the secure tenancy provisions of the Housing Act 1985 (see *Westminster CC v Clarke* [1992] 2 AC 288 at 299B per Lord Templeman).

2   The allocation of public sector housing is effectively entrusted to local housing authorities (see *Runa Begum v Tower Hamlets LBC* [2003] 2 AC 430; *Harrow LBC v Qazi* [2004] 1 AC 983 at [25]) and is subject to challenge in proceedings for judicial review (*Qazi*, supra at [115] per Lord Scott of Foscote). See also *Sharp v Brent LBC* [2003] HLR 65.

3   See HA 1985, s 112(1).

4   HA 1985, s 79(1). On the construction of the equivalent Rent Act provision (imported by analogy), see *Elements of Land Law* (1st edn 1987), pp 970–982. See also *Central YMCA Housing Association Ltd v Saunders* (1990) 23 HLR 212 at 214–216; *Central YMCA Housing Association Ltd & St Giles Hotel Ltd v Goodman* (1991) 24 HLR 109 at 111–113; *Parkins v City of Westminster* (1997) 30 HLR 894 at 900.

5   HA 1985, s 79(1). Certain lettings are expressly excluded from the scope of the 'secure tenancy'. These exceptions include long leases for a term exceeding 21 years (HA 1985, s 115(1), Sch 1, para 1), introductory tenancies (HA 1985, Sch 1, para 1A), tenancies granted in conjunction with some contracts of employment (HA 1985, Sch 1, para 2), and lettings to certain students (HA 1985, Sch 1, para 10). A tenancy granted by a local authority to a homeless person is not a secure tenancy until the local authority has notified the tenant that the tenancy is to be regarded as secure (HA 1985, Sch 1, para 4); *Eastleigh BC v Walsh* [1985] 1 WLR 525 at 530F–H. Likewise no secure tenancy can be claimed in respect of a local authority letting of temporary housing accommodation provided by a third party (HA 1985, Sch 1, para 6; *Tower Hamlets LBC v Miah* [1992] QB 622 at 629B–G).

6   HA 1985, s 80(1).

7   These bodies include a local authority, a new town corporation, a housing action trust, an urban development corporation and certain housing co-operatives. See, however, *R v Plymouth CC and Cornwall CC, ex p Freeman* (1987) 19 HLR 328 at 341–343.

8   HA 1985, s 81. There must be a direct landlord–tenant relationship between the parties. The tenant is not a secure tenant if he holds merely a 'Bruton tenancy' granted by some intermediary (*Kay v Lambeth LBC* [2004] EWCA Civ 926 at [67]).

9   A secure tenancy may be a joint tenancy provided that each of the joint tenants is an 'individual' and at least one of them occupies the dwelling-house as his 'only or principal home.'

10   This residence requirement has been construed on the analogy of the Rent Act [**para 14.318**] so as to allow a person simultaneously to occupy more than one dwelling-house as his home (see *Crawley BC v Sawyer* (1988) 20 HLR 98 at 101–102).

11   HA 1985, s 79(3).

12   A secure tenancy cannot be claimed by a licensee who does not have exclusive possession, ie by a lodger (see *Westminster CC v Clarke* [1992] 2 AC 288 at 300C per Lord Templeman [**para 7.134**]) or by a flat-sharer (*Parkins v City of Westminster* (1997) 30 HLR 894 at 901). A specific statutory provision excludes any person who entered initially as a trespasser (HA 1985, s 79(4)). See *Restormel BC v Buscombe* (1982) 14 HLR 91 at 98–100.

Terms of the secure tenancy

14.340   The terms of a secure tenancy comprise, in part, terms derived from the common law of landlord and tenant and, in part, terms which are stipulated by statute.[1] The residential status conferred by a secure tenancy is essentially personal, non-commerciable and non-transmissible.[2] The Housing Act 1985 thus incorporates a general prohibition of assignment (including release to a joint tenant[3]) except in certain specially designated circumstances.[4] Nor may the secure tenant sublet or part with possession of *part* of the dwelling-house without the written consent of the landlord.[5] If the secure tenant sublets or parts with possession of the *whole* of the dwelling-house, the tenancy ceases to be a secure tenancy and cannot subsequently become a secure tenancy.[6] On satisfaction of certain conditions the 'secure tenant' possesses a statutory 'right to buy' his dwelling.[7] Where this right has not been exercised, a 'spouse'[8] or other 'member of the tenant's family' (on satisfying a 12 month residence qualification) may succeed to the tenancy on the death of the secure tenant.[9]

1   Landlord authorities must supply their tenants annually with up-to-date information which explains 'in simple terms' the express terms of a secure tenancy and the framework of ancillary statutory rights (HA 1985, s 104).
2   See e g *London CC v Bown* (1990) 60 P & CR 42 at 48 (no vesting in tenant's trustee in bankruptcy). See also Insolvency Act 1986, s 283(3A)(d).
3   See *Burton v Camden LBC* [2000] 2 AC 399 at 406D–E per Lord Nicholls of Birkenhead [**para 7.210**].
4   HA 1985, s 91. See HA 1985, ss 91(3)(a), 92 (assignment by way of exchange); assignment pursuant to a property transfer order on divorce (s 91(3)(b)); assignment to a potential successor (s 91(3)(c)). See, however, *Governors of the Peabody Donation Fund v Higgins* [1983] 1 WLR 1091.
5   HA 1985, s 93(1)(b). Such consent must not be unreasonably withheld (HA 1985, s 94(2)).
6   HA 1985, s 93(2). The secure tenant has, however, an unconditional right to allow any persons to reside as 'lodgers' in his dwelling-house (HA 1985, s 93(1)(a)).
7   [**Para 7.349**].
8   See now *Ghaidan v Godin-Mendoza* [2004] 3 WLR 113 [**para 14.320**].
9   HA 1985, ss 87, 113. See, however, *Wandsworth LBC v Michalak* [2003] 1 WLR 617 at [13]–[15], [55] (remote relative not entitled to succeed).

14.341   There is no formal mechanism for the control of rent levels,[1] but the secure tenant is given a statutory 'right to repair' in respect of certain kinds of defect in the condition of his accommodation.[2] The secure tenant may not make any improvement[3] without the written consent of the landlord,[4] but provision is made for an entitlement to compensation at the end of the tenancy for a secure tenant who, with consent, has made an improvement which has materially added to the likely open market price or letting value of the property.[5] The rent payable by an 'improving tenant' (or by his 'qualifying successor'[6]) must not be increased on account of the improvements made except to the extent that the rent increase corresponds to a part of the cost of the improvement which was not borne by the tenant.[7]

1   See HA 1985, s 24(1). A local authority is required to fix rents broadly equivalent to private sector rents in respect of comparable housing stock (HA 1985, s 24(3)–(4), as added by Local Government and Housing Act 1989, s 162).

2   See HA 1985, s 96(1) [**para 14.64**]. A council landlord must account to its tenants in respect of any discount or commission (but not for an administration fee) which it receives in connection with a block insurance policy negotiated on behalf of the tenants (*Williams v Southwark LBC* (2000) Times, 5 April).

3   The term 'improvement' is defined as 'any alteration in, or addition to, a dwelling-house' and includes even such matters as the erection of a wireless or television aerial and the carrying out of external decoration (HA 1985, s 97(2)).

4   HA 1985, s 97(1). The landlord must not unreasonably withhold its consent to any proposed improvement and its consent, if unreasonably withheld, is treated as having been duly given (HA 1985, s 97(3). See also HA 1985, s 98(2), (4)(b)).

5   HA 1985, s 99A (referable to improvements begun after commencement of 1993 Act). See also HA 1985, s 100(1) (discretionary power to reimburse cost of improvements begun on or after 3 October 1980).

6   See HA 1985, s 101(3).

7   HA 1985, s 101(2). The amount of any improvement, repair or other grant obtained by the tenant in connection with the carrying out of the improvement is deemed for this purpose to have been money provided by the tenant (HA 1985, s 101(1)).

Security of tenure

14.342   The Housing Act 1985 imposes strict limitations on the ways in which the status of the secure tenant may be terminated by the landlord.[1] The landlord cannot terminate a secure tenancy otherwise than by obtaining a court order for possession or termination.[2] There is, however, no need for the landlord to show, on a case-by-case basis, that the recovery of possession is necessary or justifiable with reference to Article 8 of the European Convention on Human Rights.[3] Where the landlord does obtain an order for possession, the secure tenancy ends only on the date which is specified in the order for the delivery up of possession.[4]

1   The Housing Act 1985 incorporates significant departures from the common law principles relating to the termination of contractual tenancies (see *Harrison v Hammersmith and Fulham LBC* [1981] 1 WLR 650 at 662A–C). It is always open, however, to the secure tenant to determine his or her tenancy by any of the traditional common law means, eg by notice to quit or surrender [**paras 7.284, 7.305**].

2   HA 1985, s 82(1), (3). The expiration of a fixed-term secure tenancy automatically brings into existence a periodic tenancy of the same dwelling-house on the same terms as under the expired tenancy, the relevant period being ascertainable with reference to the rental periods under the former fixed-term tenancy (HA 1985, s 86(1)–(2)). See *London City Corpn v Bown* (1990) 60 P & CR 42 at 46.

3   *Wandsworth LBC v Michalak* [2003] 1 WLR 617 at [46]–[49], [78]; *Hounslow LBC v Adjei* [2004] 2 All ER 636 at [49]. See also *Harrow LBC v Qazi* [2004] 1 AC 983 [**paras 14.115– 14.117**].

4   HA 1985, s 82(2). A court order is thus not merely a precondition of re-entry but a precondition of the termination of the tenancy itself.

14.343   Where a dwelling-house is held on a secure tenancy, the court cannot entertain proceedings for possession or termination unless the landlord has first served on the tenant a notice in prescribed form specifying the ground on which the proceedings are being brought and giving particulars of that ground.[1] The court may not then make an order for possession of the dwelling-house except on one or more of the Grounds set out in Schedule 2 of the Housing Act 1985.[2] These Grounds fall into three main categories.

1   HA 1985, s 83(1)–(2). See *Torridge DC v Jones* (1985) 18 HLR 107 at 111–115.
2   HA 1985, s 84(1). The Court has an extended discretion to adjourn proceedings, to stay or suspend the execution of a possession order, and to postpone the date of possession, in respect of the Grounds contained in Parts I and III of Schedule 2 (HA 1985, s 85(1)–(2)). See *Pemberton v Southwark LBC* [2000] 1 WLR 1672. The issue of a possession warrant following default by a tenant who holds under a suspended possession order constitutes no violation of the tenant's right to a 'fair and public hearing' under ECHR Art 6 (*Southwark LBC v St Brice* [2002] 1 WLR 1537 at [20], [34]).

Grounds coupled with a requirement of reasonableness

14.344   The court may make a possession order based on any one or more of Grounds 1 to 8 in Part I of Schedule 2, provided that the court 'considers it reasonable to make the order.'[1] These Grounds include such matters as the tenant's failure to pay rent or breach of other covenants,[2] the commission of nuisance or annoyance to other residents or visitors in the locality,[3] domestic violence (or threats thereof) causing one occupant of the dwelling-house to leave,[4] neglect or default by the tenant which causes deterioration in the condition of the dwelling-house or the landlord's furniture,[5] or false statements by the tenant (or some person acting on his instigation) which induced the grant of the tenancy.[6]

1   HA 1985, s 84(2)(a). On the assessment of reasonableness, see *Woodspring DC v Taylor* (1982) 4 HLR 95 at 99.
2   Ground 1. See e g *Lambeth LBC v Thomas* (1997) Times, 31 March (obligation to pay water charge collected by council).
3   Ground 2 (see also HA 1985, s 85A, as inserted by ASBA 2003, s 16(1) (relating to anti-social behaviour)). The relevant actions can be those of the tenant or of some person residing in or visiting the dwelling-house. See also *Northampton BC v Lovatt* (1997) 96 LGR 548; *Sewell v Harlow DC* (Unreported, Court of Appeal, 5 November 1999) (38 cats present in home).
4   Ground 2A (as introduced by HA 1996, s 145). The person driven out must be the tenant or partner of a tenant who, having left, is 'unlikely to return'.
5   Grounds 3 and 4.
6   Ground 5 (as amended by HA 1996, s 146).

14.345   In the event of a secure tenant's breach of covenant under a fixed-term tenancy which is subject to re-entry or forfeiture, the court has no power to order possession in pursuance of the landlord's right of re-entry.[1] The court can only make an order 'terminating the tenancy' on a specified date,[2] at which point a periodic tenancy will automatically arise on the termination of the fixed term.[3] The landlord may elect either to allow this periodic tenancy to continue in force unless or until there is any further breach or to seek both a termination of the fixed term and a simultaneous possession order in respect of the ensuing periodic tenancy.

1   HA 1985, s 82(3).
2   HA 1985, s 82(3). The provisions of LPA 1925, s 146 **[para 14.129]** apply, with the exception of section 146(4) of that Act (see HA 1985, s 82(4)).
3   HA 1985, s 86(1).

Grounds coupled with a requirement of suitable alternative accommodation

14.346   The court may make a possession order based on any one or more of Grounds 9 to 11 in Part II of Schedule 2, provided that the court is 'satisfied that suitable accommodation will be available for the tenant when the order takes effect'.[1] These Grounds include cases of statutory 'overcrowding',[2] demolition or the carrying out of other works on the premises,[3] and conflict with the objects of a charitable landlord.[4]

1   HA 1985, s 84(2)(b), Sch 2, Part IV. See e g *LB of Islington v Metcalfe and Peacock* (1983) LAG Bulletin 105; *Wandsworth LBC v Fadayomi* [1987] 1 WLR 1473.
2   Ground 9.
3   Ground 10.
4   Ground 11.

Grounds coupled with both requirements

14.347   The court may make a possession order based on any one or more of Grounds 12 to 16 in Part III of Schedule 2, provided that the court *both* 'considers it reasonable to make the order' *and* is 'satisfied that suitable accommodation will be available for the tenant when the order takes effect'.[1] These Grounds relate in the main to circumstances in which the premises which are the subject of a secure tenancy have been used or adapted for some special purpose which is no longer relevant in relation to the current tenant.[2] A further Ground of recovery under Part III arises where, following the death of the secure tenant, the accommodation afforded by the dwelling-house is 'more extensive than is reasonably required' by his successor.[3]

1   HA 1985, s 84(2)(c).
2   Such cases arise, for instance, where the dwelling-house was let to an employee and is now required for a new employee (Ground 12) or where the premises have been adapted for disabled living or for some form of specialised or 'special needs' accommodation (Grounds 13, 14, 15).
3   Ground 16. See *Enfield LBC v French* (1985) 49 P & CR 223 at 229–231.

Variant forms of public sector tenancy

14.348   Recent legislation has added two variants upon the model of the secure tenancy, both conferring an inferior security of tenure. Under an innovation contained in the Housing Act 1996, a local housing authority or housing action trust may now elect to grant an 'introductory tenancy' for a probationary period of one year as a prelude to the grant of a secure tenancy.[1] The Anti-social Behaviour Act 2003 also empowers a landlord, in cases of alleged anti-social behaviour or unlawful user of the premises by the tenant, to apply to the county court for a 'demotion order',[2] pursuant to which the tenant will no longer hold a secure tenancy, but will occupy on the terms of a 'demoted tenancy'. A 'demoted tenancy' will normally become a secure tenancy again after a period of one year unless during this period the landlord issues a notice of proceedings for possession.[3]

1   HA 1996, ss 124(1), 125(1) [**para 7.250**]. The Housing Bill 2004 provides a procedure by which the trial period may be extended by six months (HA 1996, ss 125A, 125B, as inserted by HB 2004, cl 156(3)).
2   HA 1985, s 82A(2)–(4), as inserted by ASBA 2003, s 14(2).
3   HA 1996, s 143B, as inserted by ASBA 2003, s 14(5), Sch 1, para 1.

FUTURE REFORM OF THE RESIDENTIAL RENTED SECTOR

14.349   It is fairly obvious that the modern law of residential tenancies incorporates a miasma of statutory regulations which seek, in different ways, to ameliorate the imbalance of power implicit in the contractual relationship of landlord and tenant. The area is now an almost impenetrable forest of legal rules little adapted to the needs of those who require accommodation in the rented sector. The Law Commission is therefore currently engaged in a monumental reformulation and rationalisation of the law of housing tenure.[1] It seems clear that the preferred path for the future involves the introduction of standardised forms of tenure for lettings within the residential rented sector.

1   See Law Commission, *Renting Homes 1: Status and Security* (Consultation Paper No 162, April 2002) and *Renting Homes 2: Co-occupation, Transfer and Succession* (Consultation Paper No 168, September 2002); *Renting Homes* (Law Com No 284, November 2003). The Commission hopes to publish a final report and Bill in 2004 (Law Com No 284 (2003), para 1.2).

A 'consumer approach' to occupation agreements

14.350   The aim of the Law Commission is to integrate consumer law as a component of modern housing law by ensuring that 'the terms of agreements are fairly balanced, rather than having unfairly balanced contracts which have to be overridden by other statutory rules.'[1] A central feature of the Commission's proposals is that reform of housing law should be shaped by the 'consumer approach'.[2] Key features therefore involve the exposure of housing arrangements to the full force of the Unfair Terms in Consumer Contracts Regulations 1999,[3] the prescription of the main structural components of all 'occupation agreements' by regulation,[4] and the comprehensive application of the scheme to 'any contractual agreement (other than an excepted agreement) for the occupation of a dwelling as a home.'[5] The terms of occupation agreements will be required to be 'fair' and 'transparent'[6] and the historic distinction between the lease and the licence will no longer have any significance.[7] The broad result will be the achievement of a 'landlord neutrality'[8] which makes the identity of the landlord (whether public, private or social) irrelevant to the coverage of the scheme. In this way it is hoped to create 'a new social tenancy' for the future.[9]

1   CP No 162 (2002), paras 6.1–6.2. See Law Com No 284 (2003), para 4.2.
2   Law Com No 284 (2003), para 4.1.
3   SI 1999/2083 [**para 14.4**]. See Law Com No 284 (2003), paras 3.3, 4.4, 4.15–4.24.
4   Law Com No 284 (2003), para 3.4.

5   Law Com No 284 (2003), paras 3.4, 6.17.
6   Law Com No 284 (2003), paras 1.3, 3.4.
7   Law Com No 284 (2003), paras 3.12, 3.102, 6.18–6.19 [paras **4.99, 7.81**].
8   Law Com No 284 (2003), paras 3.8, 5.2, 5.15.
9   Law Com No 284 (2003), para 3.8.

Two types of occupation agreement

14.351   The Law Commission envisages the introduction of two basic types of consumer-oriented 'occupation agreement' ('types I and II'), offering different levels of security of tenure and incorporating with clarity and specificity a written description of the rights and obligations of landlords and tenants.[1] Type I agreements will offer extensive security of tenure, will comprise only periodic agreements, and will generally be used by social landlords.[2] Type II agreements (of a fixed term or periodic nature) will normally be used by private landlords and will provide a 'very limited minimum level of security' modelled on the current assured shorthold tenancy.[3]

1   Writing will not be crucial to the creation of the contractual relationship, but the landlord will be required to provide a written statement of the agreement (Law Com No 284 (2003), para 3.22).
2   Law Com No 284 (2003), paras 1.6, 3.7, 5.4.
3   Law Com No 284 (2003), paras 1.6, 3.7, 5.5.

Requirements of due process

14.352   It is integral to the Law Commission's proposed scheme that the principle of due process be retained as a precondition of the recovery of possession from a residential occupier.[1] The Commission therefore envisages a statutory clarification of the procedure of repossession and, furthermore, that even in cases of serious default no possession order should be made in respect of a 'type I' occupation agreement (providing long-term security of tenure) without the interposition of an exercise of discretion by the court.[2] Mandatory orders for possession would be confined to 'type II' occupation agreements.[3]

1   Law Com No 284 (2003), paras 1.18–1.19, 9.6.
2   Law Com No 284 (2003), paras 3.36–3.45, 5.13, 9.46–9.55, 9.81–9.98.
3   Law Com No 284 (2003), paras 3.36, 3.46, 5.14, 9.56–9.60, 9.99–9.100.

Transfer and succession

14.353   The Law Commission also proposes a substantial simplification and modernisation of the complex provisions which, in a number of sectors, regulate the statutory devolution of tenancies on death. In a new 'single and coherent statement of the impact of death on the occupation agreement',[1] the Commission advocates that a surviving spouse or partner should always rank as a 'priority successor' to the occupation agreement held previously by the deceased and that, in addition or in default, certain other members of the family (or a 'carer') should be eligible to be a 'standard successor'.[2]

1   Law Com No 284 (2003), para 14.2.
2   Law Com No 284 (2003), paras 3.76, 14.29–14.47.

LANDLORD AND TENANT ACT 1954, PART II (BUSINESS TENANCIES)

14.354   A certain degree of statutory protection is conferred on commercial tenants by Part II of the Landlord and Tenant Act 1954,[1] as most recently amended by the Regulatory Reform (Business Tenancies) (England and Wales) Order 2003.[2] Except in certain specified cases,[3] this legislation applies to any tenant who occupies premises 'for the purposes of a business carried on by him.'[4] In this context the term 'business' is construed broadly and includes not only the conduct by an individual tenant of some 'trade, profession or employment' but also 'any activity carried on by a body of persons, whether corporate or unincorporate.'[5]

1   See generally M Haley, *The Statutory Regulation of Business Tenancies* (OUP 2000). An agreement to exclude the tenant's exercise of his statutory rights under the 1954 Act is void unless (in the case of a fixed term) the landlord serves a prescribed notice on the tenant prior to the agreement and the tenant makes a declaration that he has received and accepted the consequences of the notice (L&TA 1954, s 38A, as inserted by SI 2003/3096, arts 21–22, Schs 1–2).
2   SI 2003/3096 (effective 1 June 2004). See R Hewitson, 'Reform of Business Tenancies Legislation' [2002] Conv 261. The 2003 Order closely follows *Business Tenancies: A Periodic Review of the Landlord and Tenant Act 1954, Part II* (Law Com No 208, 1992) (see Michael Haley, [1993] Conv 334).
3   No protection is available under Part II of the Landlord and Tenant Act 1954 in respect of agricultural holdings (L&TA 1954, s 43(1)(a)), farm business tenancies (L&TA 1954, s 43(1)(aa)) or mining leases (L&TA 1954, s 43(1)(b)). Likewise the statute does not cover a licensee (*Shell-Mex and BP Ltd v Manchester Garages Ltd* [1971] 1 WLR 612 at 615A–B), a tenant at will [**para 7.273**], a service tenant (L&TA 1954, s 43(2)), or a tenant who is in breach of a leasehold covenant against business user (L&TA 1954, s 23(4)). The 1954 Act does not apply to a fixed term not exceeding 6 months unless there is a provision for renewal beyond six months or the tenant has already been in occupation for 12 months (L&TA 1954, s 43(3)). The Act does not extend to regulated or assured tenancies (see RA 1977, s 24(3); HA 1988, Sch 1, para 4).
4   L&TA 1954, s 23(1), 23(1A) (as inserted by SI 2003/3096, art 13). The business user must exist at the termination of the contractual term (see *Esselte AB & British Sugar plc v Pearl Assurance plc* [1997] 1 WLR 891; [1998] Conv 218 (M Haley)). The tenancy may be legal or equitable, and includes a sublease (L&TA 1954, s 69(1)) and a tenancy by estoppel (*Bell v General Accident, Fire & Life Assurance Corpn Ltd* [1998] 1 EGLR 69 at 72A–B, K).
5   L&TA 1954, s 23(2). See generally M Haley, 'The statutory regulation of business tenancies: private property, public interest and political compromise' (1999) 19 Legal Studies 207.

Continuation of a business tenancy

14.355   The security of tenure offered by Part II of the 1954 Act operates essentially through the statutory prohibition of any termination of an eligible tenancy except in strict accordance with the provisions of the Act.[1] In the absence of a statutorily approved form of termination the tenancy continues in force indefinitely. This 'continuation tenancy' is of uncertain duration and, apart from its legislative status, would be rendered void under the common law requirement of certainty. Subject to the provisions of the 1954 Act, either landlord or tenant may apply to the court for an order for the grant of a new tenancy (whether the subsisting tenancy is a 'continuation tenancy' or still a contractual tenancy).[2]

1   L&TA 1954, s 24(1). This prohibition does not normally prevent a termination brought about by a notice to quit or surrender by the tenant or through forfeiture of a superior letting (L&TA 1954, ss 24(2), 27(2) (as amended by SI 2003/3096, art 25)).
2   L&TA 1954, s 24(1), as amended by SI 2003/3096, art 3. The tenant's statutory rights in respect of renewal constitute 'possessions' for the purpose of ECHR Protocol No 1, Art 1 (see *Shaws (EAL) Ltd v Walbert Pennycook* [2004] EWCA Civ 100 at [31]–[41]).

Termination of a business tenancy

14.356   The procedure by which a business tenancy could be terminated (or replaced by a new tenancy) used to be governed by an elaborate statutory regime of notice and counter-notice. This rather tedious game of serve and volley has been somewhat simplified by the Regulatory Reform (Business Tenancies) (England and Wales) Order 2003.

Procedure for landlord

14.357   The landlord may initiate the termination of an existing business tenancy by serving on the tenant a notice (in prescribed form[1]) not more than twelve months and not less than six months before the termination date specified in the notice.[2] The landlord's notice must indicate whether (and if so on what ground) the landlord is opposed to the grant of a new tenancy and, if the landlord is not opposed, must set out the landlord's proposals as to the terms of the new tenancy.[3] If the landlord signifies his unwillingness to grant a new tenancy, the tenant may, at any time prior to the termination date specified in the landlord's notice, apply to the court for a new tenancy.[4] It is open to the landlord, for his part, to pre-empt the tenant by applying to the court for an order terminating the existing tenancy (provided that he does so before the tenant applies on his own behalf for a new tenancy).[5] In this way the landlord who has a conclusive ground of opposition to the grant of a new tenancy can nip the entire process in the bud.[6]

1.   See The Landlord and Tenant Act 1954, Part 2 (Notices) Regulations 2004 (SI 2004/1005) (effective 1 June 2004).
2   L&TA 1954, s 25(1)–(2). This notice must expire not earlier than the date on which, had the 1954 Act not intervened, the tenancy could have been determined by notice to quit or by the effluxion of time (L&TA 1954, s 25(3)). If the tenant vacates the premises before the contractual term expires, the tenancy ceases to be a business tenancy covered by the 1954 Act, the landlord's notice is irrelevant, and the tenancy simply ends by the effluxion of time on the contractual term date (see *Surrey CC v Single Horse Properties Ltd* [2002] 1 WLR 2106 at [37]–[38]; [2002] Conv 579 (M Haley)). See now L&TA 1954, s 27(1A), as inserted by SI 2003/3096, art 25(1).

3   L&TA 1954, s 25(6)–(8), as inserted by SI 2003/3096, art 4. See The Landlord and Tenant
    Act 1954, Part 2 (Notices) Regulations 2004 (SI 2004/1005), Sch 2.
4   L&TA 1954, ss 24(1), 29A(1) (as inserted by SI 2003/3096, art 10). The parties may, by
    agreement, extend the period within which the tenant can apply to court (L&TA 1954, s 29B).
5   L&TA 1954, s 29(2)(a), (3), as substituted by SI 2003/3096, art 5.
6   L&TA 1954, s 29(4), as substituted by SI 2003/3096, art 5.

Procedure for tenant

14.358   Alternatively the tenant may take the initiative, in advance of any
notice from the landlord, by making a formal request to the landlord for a new
tenancy.[1] The landlord then has two months within which to serve a counter-
notice informing the tenant that the landlord will oppose a court application
for a new tenancy on some specified statutory ground.[2] The tenant may then
apply to the court for a new tenancy.[3]

1   L&TA 1954, s 26. For this purpose the tenant must hold a fixed term and not a periodic
    tenancy (s 26(1)).
2   L&TA 1954, s 26(6).
3   L&TA 1954, s 24(1)(b).

Grant of a new tenancy

14.359   On application by the tenant and in the absence of agreement between
the parties, the court must grant a new tenancy (on such terms as it thinks fit[1])
unless the landlord successfully opposes the grant on at least one of seven
statutorily defined grounds.[2] These grounds are contained in section 30(1) of
the 1954 Act and relate partly to default by the tenant[3] and partly to needs or
circumstances established by the landlord.[4] The tenant is entitled to compensation from the landlord in certain cases where the court fails to order the grant
of a new tenancy.[5] At the termination of his tenancy the tenant may also be
able to obtain compensation in respect of certain valuable improvements
effected in the premises,[6] where due notice had been given to the landlord prior
to the making of the improvements.[7]

1   On renewal the court may not grant a fixed term in excess of 15 years (L&TA 1954, s 33, as
    amended by SI 2003/3096, art 26) and the rent will be an open market rent (L&TA 1954,
    s 34(1)).
2   L&TA 1954, ss 29(1) (as substituted by SI 2003/3096, art 5), 32–35.
3   Such grounds include breach of the tenant's repairing obligation (s 30(1)(a)), persistent delay
    in the payment of rent (s 30(1)(b)) and substantial breaches of other obligations of the tenant
    (s 30(1)(c)).
4   The landlord may establish that he has offered and is willing to provide suitable alternative
    accommodation for the tenant (s 30(1)(d)) or that an intervening merger of interests has made
    the letting of the tenant's part of the premises substantially less valuable in rental terms than
    a letting of the whole (s 30(1)(e)). The landlord may require possession for the purpose of
    demolition or reconstruction or other substantial works on the premises (s 30(1)(f)) or
    demonstrate that he intends to occupy the premises himself (s 30(1)(g)).
5   See L&TA 1954, s 37, as substituted or amended by SI 2003/3096, arts 19–20.
6   L&TA 1927, s 1.

7   L&TA 1927, s 3.

AGRICULTURAL HOLDINGS ACT 1986 AND AGRICULTURAL TENANCIES ACT 1995 (AGRICULTURAL HOLDINGS AND FARM BUSINESS TENANCIES)

14.360   The tenure of agricultural land is now governed by two statutory codes, the Agricultural Holdings Act 1986 and the Agricultural Tenancies Act 1995.[1]

1   See generally C P Rodgers, *Agricultural Law* (London 1998).

The Agricultural Holdings Act 1986

14.361   The Agricultural Holdings Act 1986 confers limited statutory rights on certain categories of agricultural tenant.[1] The Act applies to an 'agricultural holding', so defined as to include the aggregate of land (whether agricultural land or not) comprised in a contract for an agricultural tenancy.[2] The 1986 Act confers limited rights of security of tenure. A fixed-term tenancy for two years or more does not determine automatically with the effluxion of time, but continues in the form of a yearly tenancy unless either party has served written notice of termination not less than one year nor more than two years before the expiration date of the fixed term.[3] A letting for value 'for an interest less than a tenancy from year to year' is, in general, deemed to take effect as a tenancy from year to year.[4] A notice to quit an agricultural holding is normally invalid if it purports to terminate the tenancy before the expiry of twelve months from the end of the then current year of tenancy.[5] On receipt of a notice to quit the tenant may serve a counter-notice on the landlord, the consequence of which is to render the landlord's notice ineffective without a consent given by the Agricultural Land Tribunal on one of a number of statutorily specified grounds.[6] The 1986 Act also provides some protection in respect of the rent payable by a qualifying tenant. Either landlord or tenant may apply, at intervals of not less than three years, for the rent level to be submitted to arbitration.[7]

1   Certain agricultural workers may also enjoy statutory protection in respect of tied dwellings either under the Rent (Agriculture) Act 1976 or HA 1988, s 24, Sch 3 ('assured agricultural occupancies').
2   AHA 1986, s 1(1).
3   AHA 1986, ss 3–4.
4   AHA 1986, s 2(1)–(2) (see *Calcott v J S Bloor* (*Measham*) *Ltd* [1998] 1 WLR 1490). These provisions are sufficiently wide to catch certain contractual licences, but a fixed term letting for more than one year but less than two years simply expires at its term date and enjoys no enhanced security by statute.
5   AHA 1986, s 25(1).
6   AHA 1986, ss 26–27, Sch 3.
7   AHA 1986, ss 12, 84, Sch 2.

The Agricultural Tenancies Act 1995

14.362   The Agricultural Tenancies Act 1995 confers broadly equivalent protection on the holder of a 'farm business tenancy' created on or after

1 September 1995.[1] The concept of 'farm business tenancy' is intended to give a limited recognition to diversified patterns of farming and associated land use. A tenancy constitutes a 'farm business tenancy' if it meets the 'business conditions' imposed by the 1995 Act, together with either the 'agriculture condition' or the 'notice conditions'.[2] The 'business conditions' require that all or part of the land is farmed for the purposes of a trade or business and has been so farmed since the beginning of the tenancy.[3] The 'agriculture condition' envisages that the character of the tenancy must be 'primarily or wholly agricultural'[4] and the 'notice conditions' require that landlord and tenant should have served on each other, at the commencement of the tenancy, a notice indicating that the tenancy of land identified by the notice was intended to be (and to continue to be) a farm business tenancy and that the character of the tenancy was, at that date, 'primarily or wholly agricultural.'[5]

1 The 1995 Act excludes licences and tenancies at will (ATA 1995, s 38(1)).
2 ATA 1995, s 1(1). Certain tenancies are excluded (ATA 1995, s 2).
3 ATA 1995, s 1(2). Continuity of user since commencement is presumed (ATA 1995, s 1(7)).
4 ATA 1995, s 1(3).
5 ATA 1995, s 1(4).

14.363 The 1995 Act lays down rules as to the giving of various notices between landlord and tenant, but does not otherwise (by contrast with the law governing agricultural holdings) provide any statutory mechanism of secure tenure. A fixed-term tenancy for more than two years does not determine automatically with the effluxion of time, but continues in the form of a yearly tenancy unless either party has served written notice of termination between one and two years before the expiration of the fixed term.[1] Any yearly tenancy is terminable by written notice of the same duration.[2] Disputes over the tenant's rights and obligations may ultimately be resolved by recourse to arbitration.[3]

1 ATA 1995, s 5(1).
2 ATA 1995, s 6(1).
3 ATA 1995, ss 12, 28(1).

CHAPTER 15

Regulation of mortgages

THE SIGNIFICANCE OF THE MORTGAGE TRANSACTION

15.1   The mortgage (or charge) over land provides a device by which a loan of money may be secured upon an estate or interest in the borrower's land.[1] If the loan is not repaid in accordance with the contract of loan, the lender's security may be realised through a forced sale of the land, the loan money being recouped from the proceeds. Thus, like so many phenomena of land law,[2] the mortgage represents a conjunction of the *contractual* and the *proprietary*. The mortgage arises from a contract of loan and creates for the lender (or mortgagee) some form of proprietary entitlement in the land of the borrower (or mortgagor).

1   For a description of the types and modes of creation of mortgages and charges, see [**paras 8.232–8.258, 9.102–9.137**].
2   [**Paras 2.52, 7.71, 9.11, 13.63**].

Social and economic significance

15.2   Probably more than any other land law concept discussed so far, the mortgage will come to have a dominating importance for the readers of this book, for the mortgage transaction (and the liabilities which it generates) can underpin almost every feature of the way in which we live our lives. The mortgage provides a method of instalment purchase of the homes of millions, thus combining 'the economic function of a tenancy ... with the ideological function of property.'[1] The mortgage can also play an important demographic role in shaping family size and pattern, an equally significant fiscal role in co-ordinating lifetime savings[2] and the inter-generational transfer of wealth, and even a less readily recognised role as a silent disciplinary force within the workplace. Outside the domestic context the mortgage operates, moreover, as a vital means of injecting capital investment into commercial enterprise. The mortgage of realty provides, in short, one of the most remarkable engines of wealth creation in the modern world.

1   Otto Kahn-Freund, 'Introduction' in K Renner, *The Institutions of Private Law and Their Social Functions* (London and Boston 1949), p 36.

2   Another major, but more subtle, effect of the availability of mortgage finance is to redistribute the application of income over the average family life-cycle. Since the burden of the domestic mortgage commitment shifts housing costs from the later to the earlier stages of the family life-cycle, the phenomenon of home ownership acts 'as an indirect subsidy paid by the young to the old, or, more precisely, forces individual households to subsidise their own old age in their late teens and twenties' (J Kemeny, *The Myth of Home Ownership* (London 1981), p 59). This in turn means that elderly home-owners are better able to survive on minimal pension benefits than are elderly tenants, thereby diminishing (at least on the part of those who favour increased home ownership) any real political incentive to care effectively for the elderly.

Political significance

15.3   Mortgage finance enjoys a certain civic significance not least because the ideology of home ownership has an important political dimension.

Tendency towards preservation of the status quo

15.4   Home ownership, particularly if achieved with the aid of mortgage finance, breeds political conservatism.[1] The enlightened self-interest of the owner-occupier represents a form of political capital for those who are inclined towards the preservation of the status quo. The ready provision of mortgage funds effectively endorses approved patterns of life style and political demeanour. In so far as mortgage finance may be directed towards a variety of ends (whether domestic or entrepreneurial), mortgages bespeak a flexibility of choice and self-determination which are based upon the political philosophy of the right rather than the left. It is, of course, the former influence which has moulded the English law of real property and it came as no surprise when, in *National Provincial Bank Ltd v Ainsworth*,[2] Lord Upjohn declared that

> It has been the policy of the law for over a hundred years to simplify and facilitate transactions in real property. It is of great importance that persons should be able freely and easily to raise money on the security of their property.

1   It was Harold Bellman, one of the leading figures in the early building society movement, who saw clearly that '[t]he man who has something to protect and improve – a stake of some sort in the country – naturally turns his thoughts in the direction of sane, ordered, and perforce economical government. The thrifty man is seldom or never an extremist agitator. To him revolution is anathema; and as in the earliest days Building Societies acted as a stabilising force, so today they stand ... as a "bulwark against Bolshevism and all that Bolshevism stands for"' (Bellman, *The Building Society Movement* (London 1927), pp 53–54).

2   [1965] AC 1175 at 1233G–1234A **[para 2.40]**.

Discrimination against the rented sector

15.5   Much political vigour has been invested in the assertion of owner-occupation as a superior form of tenure to that available in the rented sector.[1]

The policy of encouraging home ownership has effectively stigmatised rented housing as the preserve of the second-class citizen. The renter, instead of enjoying the status of part-owner of housing stock, has often been made the subject of invidious comparisons between the 'owner' and the 'tenant'. The fact that the public sector tenant has been given a statutory right[2] to improve his lot by buying (ie borrowing) and therefore 'owning' his own home further under-lines the negative discrimination against the renter which has so conduced, in recent years, to the running-down of the rented sector.

1   [**Para 7.70**]. For discussion of the 'almost mystical reverence for home-ownership', see J Kemeny, *The Myth of Home Ownership* (London 1981), p 11.
2   [**Paras 7.347–7.354**].

THE HISTORIC DYNAMIC OF THE MORTGAGE RELATIONSHIP

15.6   Two truisms about human experience have influenced the development of the law of mortgage. *First*, those who lend money commercially are more powerfully motivated by the hope of personal gain than by any desire to render useful service to their community. *Second*, borrowers of money have tended to be pictured (at least in the frozen frame of the historic stereotype) as necessitous persons who lack bargaining power and who are therefore especially vulnerable to harsh or unconscionable dealing.[1] As Lord Henley LC declared in *Vernon v Bethell*,[2] 'necessitous men are not, truly speaking, free men, but, to answer a present exigency, will submit to any terms that the crafty may impose upon them.'

1   See *Tanwar Enterprises Pty Ltd v Cauchi* (2003) 201 ALR 359 at [136] per Callinan J.
2   (1762) 2 Eden 110 at 113, 28 ER 838 at 839.

Relaxation of the rules prohibiting usury

15.7   The truisms outlined above both found expression in the medieval canon law's abhorrence of usury and the sin of avarice.[1] The initially inflexible rule of the Church prescribed that no man might lawfully charge money for a loan. To do so was not only contrary to Scripture.[2] It was, in the famous words of R H Tawney,[3] 'contrary to nature, for it is to live without labour; it is to sell time, which belongs to God, for the advantage of wicked men; it is to rob those who use the money lent, and to whom, since they make it profitable, the profits should belong.' As Tawney mischievously pointed out, 'the true descendant of the doctrines of Aquinas is the labour theory of value. The last of the Schoolmen was Karl Marx.'[4]

1   See J T Noonan, *The Scholastic Analysis of Usury* (Cambridge Mass, 1957), pp 11–13; B N Nelson, *The Idea of Usury* (2nd edn Princeton 1969), pp 3–6; S Homer, *A History of Interest Rates* (2nd edn, New Brunswick, NJ 1977), pp 69–72.
2   *Exodus* xxii.25; *Luke* vi.35.
3   *Religion and the Rise of Capitalism* (Harmondsworth 1938), p 55.
4   Op cit, p 48.

15.8 The practice of usury touched on another very sensitive nerve within the medieval scheme of economic ethics. This scheme regarded all commercial intercourse as subordinate in importance to the salvation of the soul; it saw all business life as but one aspect of personal conduct and therefore subject to overriding rules of personal morality. Accordingly the medieval commercial ethic insisted on equity in bargaining and condemned all abuse of superior status or superior bargaining power. Usury was prohibited not least because it was often the most conspicuous kind of extortion practised against the poor and the needy.

15.9 The intellectual and doctrinal assumptions which underlay the proscription of usury were, of course, radically affected by the Protestant Reformation, the arrival of a new age of capitalism and the Calvinist acceptance of the rightness and inevitability of commercial enterprise. But while Luther condemned even the minor fictions by which the canonists had tried to evade the laws against usury, Calvin was later to declare that the charging of interest was not intrinsically unlawful.[1] Indeed, to charge money as the price of a loan was simply to require the debtor to concede some small part of his profit to the creditor with whose capital assistance the gain had been achieved. The Calvinist doctrine held the exaction of interest to be legitimate, provided that the rate of interest did not exceed certain stated limits, provided that the creditor did not require an excessive security and provided always that loans were extended gratis to the poor. The Protestant ethic of thrift, industry and sanctification through one's calling replaced the medieval detestation of usury, first by a qualified tolerance of certain forms of money-lending and finally by the elevation of a new ethic of investment. The lender entered into a community of risk with the borrower, and therefore rightly took his 'fair share of the profits, according to the degree in which God has blessed him by whom the money is used.'[2]

1   J T Noonan, *The Scholastic Analysis of Usury* (Cambridge Mass, 1957), pp 365–367.
2   W Ames, *De Conscientia et eius iure vel Casibus, Libri Quinque* (Amsterdam 1630), Book V, p 289 (Chapter XLIV, xiv, R.1), *De Contracto Usurario*. In his *Essay on Usury*, Bacon pointed out that two things 'are to be reconciled: the one that the tooth of usurie be grinded, that it bite not too much; the other that there be left open a means to invite moneyed men to lend to the merchants for the continuing and quickening of trade' (quoted in *Canada Permanent Trust Co v King Art Developments Ltd* (1985) 12 DLR (4th) 161 at 222 per Laycraft JA).

The historic role of equity

15.10 Over the last three centuries the English law of mortgage has practised a cautious regulation of credit transactions relating to land. In this context the jurisdiction of equity has played a role of pivotal importance.[1] At every stage in the evolution of the law of mortgage since the 17th century, equity has been prepared to intervene on grounds of conscience in the relationship of mortgagor and mortgagee, with the object of preventing any exploitation of the former by the latter. Equity has been particularly conscious of the possibility that the lender of money may abuse his superior bargaining strength and economic capacity by imposing on the borrower oppressive or unconscionable terms of dealing. The balance of legal protection in the mortgage transaction has therefore tended in favour of the mortgagor rather than the mortgagee.

1   Equity was, in effect, beginning to take over the jurisdiction covered by the law against usury, although usury legislation was not finally abolished until 1854 (see Usury Laws Repeal Act 1854).

The modern mortgage transaction

15.11   Although equity's protective influence still overshadows the law of mortgage, the social and commercial role of the mortgage has undoubtedly changed over time. It could scarcely be claimed that the typical mortgage of today – the granting of a legal charge over the family home – falls neatly within the historic stereotype of mortgage as the last resort of those in desperate financial need. The function of the modern domestic mortgage has more to do with family consumption than with the requirements of a rudimentary form of social security. The contemporary borrower is not someone who has fallen upon hard times, but is instead the securely employed and upwardly mobile person whose use of mortgage finance springs from a consciously acquisitive desire to join the 'property-owning democracy'. Similarly, modern corporations often find it more efficient and less expensive to utilise borowed funds than to seek further investment from their shareholders.[1] Nowadays, in both domestic and commercial sectors, mortgage finance generally plays an entirely positive part in the realisation of life chances and the promotion of commercial aspirations. However, notwithstanding these profound alterations in the function of the mortgage, the law of mortgage still maintains its traditional concern to strike down inequitable or unconscionable dealing in the area of credit transactions.[2] In particular, modern legislation relating to the law of mortgage has concentrated on the protection of the residential utility enjoyed by the mortgagor and his family.

1   See *Tanwar Enterprises Pty Ltd v Cauchi* (2003) 201 ALR 359 at [136] per Callinan J.
2   See e g Consumer Credit Act 1974, ss 137–140 [**paras 15.58–15.65**].

THE MORTGAGOR'S EQUITY OF REDEMPTION

15.12   The protective impulse of equity was – and still is – concerned with the safeguarding of the rights retained by the borrower in relation to his land.

A crystalline rule

15.13   The classic form of mortgage prior to the modern era was effected by a conveyance to the mortgagee of the mortgagor's entire estate in his land, subject to a covenant for reconveyance on full repayment of the debt.[1] The mortgagee was technically entitled to possession of the land pending such repayment. Moreover, if the mortgagor failed to redeem the mortgage on the exact date stipulated by the mortgage deed (ie the 'legal date' for repayment), the mortgagee was entitled at common law to retain his security unencumbered by any further interest vested in the mortgagor. Non-payment on the contracted date triggered a permanent forfeiture of the entire mortgaged estate to the mortgagee – the ultimate 'crystalline' rule of property.[2]

1   **[Para 8.238]**.
2   As Carol Rose has said, '[e]arly common law mortgages were very crystalline indeed. They had the look of pawnshop transactions' (C M Rose, 'Crystals and Mud in Property Law' 40 Stan L Rev 577 at 583 (1987–88)). Indeed, this feature of the common law was said by Littleton to explain the etymology of the term 'mortgage': if the debtor 'doth not pay, then the land which he puts in pledge ... is gone from him for ever, and so dead' (*Litt*, s 332).

Intervention of equity

15.14   It was inevitable that the rigour of the common law approach to mortgage would prove unacceptable to the practitioners of equity.[1] From the 17th century the Court of Chancery began to grant significant relief to the mortgagor, notwithstanding that the manner of its intervention was to make the traditional method of mortgage highly fictional in nature. Although the mortgagee was entitled to enjoy physical possession of the land, equity compelled him to account to the mortgagor in respect of any profit derived from the land in excess of the interest due under the contract of loan. There thus ceased to be any material advantage for the mortgagee in the exercise of his right to possess the land and the mortgagor (although he retained no legal title) was commonly left in possession.

1   See *Lavin v Johnson* [2002] EWCA Civ 1138 at [80] per Robert Walker LJ; *Stocks & Enterprises Pty Ltd v McBurney* (1977) 1 BPR 9521 at 9526 per Reynolds JA (NSW Court of Appeal).

Redemption after the due date at law

15.15   Of particular concern to equity was the disproportionate nature of the common law sanction for the mortgagor's failure to repay the mortgage debt on the specified contractual date. Given that the debt might be only a fraction of the market value of the land concerned, the drastic penalty of forfeiture of the mortgagor's entire estate attracted predictable censure.[1] From the 17th century onwards the courts of equity came to regard the mortgagor as being entitled to tender repayment and thus to redeem the mortgage long after the common law date for repayment and reconveyance had passed.[2] The mortgagor could effectively ignore the legal date for repayment, confident that equity would uphold his right to redeem (and compel a reconveyance) at some future date. Only if the Court of Chancery considered it reasonable to grant a decree of 'foreclosure'[3] would the mortgagor's equitable rights finally terminate and the mortgagee be permitted to take a free title to the land. Unless and until such a decree was granted, the mortgagor retained an 'equity to redeem' long past the expiry of his legal right to redeem on the contractually specified date.[4]

1   'On many occasions the law recoils from absolute outcomes, to which logic or the strict letter of the law might seem to point ... [W]here the common law was thought to result in consequences considered extreme and disproportionate, equity would sometimes come to the rescue' (*Tanwar Enterprises Pty Ltd v Cauchi* (2003) 201 ALR 359 at [82] per Kirby J). See also *Stocks & Enterprises Pty Ltd v McBurney* (1977) 1 BPR 9521 at 9526 per Reynolds JA (NSW Court of Appeal).

2   See *Medforth v Blake* [2000] Ch 86 at 101G–H per Scott V-C.

3   **[Para 15.222]**.

4   The contractual date for redemption was thus rendered academic and it became customary to fix this date a mere three or six months after the entry into the contract of loan. It is also likely that the fixing of an early (and effectively fictitious) date for repayment was influenced by the fact that, whereas a certain spiritual opprobrium attached to the charging of interest before the loan was due for repayment, the exaction of interest thereafter was regarded by Church doctrine as a wholly legitimate form of 'compensation' (*interesse*) for failure to restore the principal by the date promised (see R H Tawney, *Religion and the Rise of Capitalism* (Harmondsworth 1938), p 54).

Proprietary character of the 'equity of redemption'

15.16   The mortgagor's continuing right to redeem in equity was known as his 'equity of redemption' and came to symbolise the totality of his rights in the mortgaged land. Indeed equity went to great lengths to protect the borrower's right to restore himself, by the simple act of repayment of the loan money, to the state of unencumbered liberty from which he had fallen with the advent of the mortgage debt.[1] The inviolability in equity of this entitlement to redeem had the effect of inverting the legal relationship of the parties to the mortgage.[2] The mortgagor's 'equity' was soon recognised as a distinct proprietary interest in the land which the mortgagor could sell or mortgage.[3] In this way equity reinforced the perception that, irrespective of the strict legal and contractual position, the mortgagor remained in substance the owner of the mortgaged land – albeit subject to the security created in favour of his creditor.[4]

1   See *Jones v Morgan* [2001] EWCA Civ 995 at [65] per Chadwick LJ.

2   See A W B Simpson, *A History of The Land Law* (2nd edn, Oxford 1986), p 245.

3   See *Casborne v Scarfe* (1738) 1 Atk 603 at 605–606, 26 ER 377 at 379, (1738) 2 Jac & W 194, 37 ER 600; *Latec Investments Ltd v Hotel Terrigal Pty Ltd* (*In Liquidation*) (1965) 113 CLR 265 at 277; *Buhr v Barclays Bank plc* [2001] BPIR 25 at [9] per Arden LJ ([2002] Conv 407 (Lara McMurtry)). The proprietary status of the equity of redemption is so clearly established that it may even be claimed by the crown as bona vacantia (see *Re Sir Thomas Spencer Wells* [1933] Ch 29 at 48, 55, 63).

4   'The mortgagor's equitable right to redeem is, in the eyes of the law, an equitable estate' (*Common Luck Investment Ltd v Cheung Siu Ming* [1999] 2 HKC 719 at 725–726 (HKSAR Final Court of Appeal)).

The modern equity of redemption

15.17   Although the property legislation of 1925 dramatically reformed the mechanics of mortgage creation,[1] the equity of redemption remains as the irreducible entitlement of the modern mortgagor. Under a post-1925 legal mortgage the mortgagor retains his full legal title in the land (subject to the mortgage charge) and the phrase 'equity of redemption' is commonly used as a term synonymous with the mortgagor's estate as burdened by the relevant mortgage or charge. This equity of redemption can even be accorded a money value – effectively the difference, at any given point in time, between the market value of the land and the sum of the mortgage debt currently outstanding.[2] Despite periodic recessions in the property market, increasing value 'appears to be a long-term characteristic of all real property.'[3] The equity of redemption thus embodies the mortgagor's right to capture for himself any capital appreciation which accrues to the mortgaged land.[4]

1 [**Paras 8.242–8.251**].
2 [**Para 8.240**]. For an interesting illustration, see *R v Walls* [2003] 1 WLR 731 at [33] (confiscation order under Drug Trafficking Act 1994 confined to value of offender's equity of redemption).
3 *Palk v Mortgage Services Funding Plc* [1993] Ch 330 at 343H–344A per Sir Michael Kerr.
4 Some sectors of the mortgage market are now beginning to see the introduction of 'shared appreciation' or 'equity participation' mortgages under which, in return for lower interest rates, the mortgagee contracts to take some proportion of the ultimate uplift in the capital value of the land.

Protection of the equity of redemption

15.18 Chancery's traditional concern to protect the mortgagor's equity of redemption gave rise during the 19th century to a 'quaintly labelled'[1] doctrine which insisted that no 'clogs or fetters' should ever be imposed on the exercise of the mortgagor's entitlement to redeem.[2] The right to redeem was (and still is) an 'inseparable incident' of any mortgage[3] and the 'one matter that the mortgagor can insist upon is that, on redemption by payment, he gets back his security.'[4] As Walker LJ declared in *Browne v Ryan*,[5]

> When a transaction appears, or has been declared to be a mortgage ... the mortgagor is entitled to get back his property as free as he gave it, on payment of principal, interest, and costs, and provisions inconsistent with that right cannot be enforced. The equitable rules, 'once a mortgage always a mortgage,' and that the mortgagee cannot impose any 'clog or fetter on the equity of redemption', are merely concise statements of the same rule.

1 *Bannerman Brydone Foster & Co v Murray* [1972] NZLR 411 at 429 per Woodhouse J.
2 '[E]quity regards the mortgaged property as security only for money, and will permit of no attempt to clog, fetter, or impede the borrower's right to redeem and to rescue what was, and still remains in equity, his own' (*Marquess of Northampton v Pollock* (1890) 45 Ch D 190 at 215 per Bowen LJ). See also B Wyman, 21 Harv L Rev 459 (1907–08); G L Williams, (1944) 60 LQR 190.
3 *General Credits Ltd v Wenham* (1989) NSW ConvR 55–492 at p 58,592 per Meagher JA. See also *Re Shankman and Mutual Life Assurance Co of Canada* (1986) 21 DLR (4th) 131 at 134 per Cory JA; *Common Luck Investment Ltd v Cheung Siu Ming* [1999] 2 HKC 719 at 725 (HKSAR Final Court of Appeal).
4 *Cheah v Equiticorp Finance Group Ltd* [1992] 1 AC 472 at 476G per Lord Browne-Wilkinson (JCPC). The mortgagor cannot by contract waive or set aside his equitable right of redemption (see *Municipal Savings & Loan Corp v Wilson* (1982) 127 DLR (3d) 127 at 131). So

long as this equity of redemption remains extant, the mortgagee cannot sue on the mortgagor's personal covenant of payment if the mortgagee has put it out of his power to restore the mortgaged property on repayment (*Palmer v Hendrie* (1859) 27 Beav 349 at 351, 54 ER 136 at 137; *Ellis & Co's Trustee v Dixon-Johnson* [1925] AC 489 at 491; *Cheah*, supra at 476G–H per Lord Browne-Wilkinson).

5   [1901] 2 IR 653 at 676.

Irrelevance of labels

15.19   The significance attached to the mortgagor's equity of redemption is such that, irrespective of the superficial labels applied by the parties themselves, the courts accord the vigilant protection of equity (as nowadays reinforced by statute) to any transaction which is aimed in substance at securing a loan of money upon a borrower's real property.[1] The courts have jurisdiction to determine whether any transaction (no matter in what guise presented or obscured) was intended in reality to operate by way of mortgage.[2] As Harman LJ observed in *Grangeside Properties Ltd v Collingwoods Securities Ltd*,[3] '[o]nce a mortgage, always a mortgage and nothing but a mortgage, has been a principle for centuries.'[4]

1   Extrinsic evidence is admissible to show that a grant, although in terms absolute, was intended to be by way of security only (*Lavin v Johnson* [2002] EWCA Civ 1138 at [80] per Robert Walker LJ).

2   See *Alliance Acceptance Co Ltd v Oakley* (1988) 48 SASR 337 at 341; *Westfield Holdings Ltd v Australian Capital Television Pty Ltd* (1992) 32 NSWLR 194 at 199C; *Nunn v Wily* (2001) 10 BPR 18983 at [107].

3   [1964] 1 WLR 139 at 142–143.

4   'Once a mortgage always a mortgage' has been described as 'merely an expression of the general principle as to fraud in its application to mortgages' (*Last v Rosenfeld* [1972] 2 NSWLR 923 at 931E). See also *Seton v Slade* (1802) 7 Ves 265 at 273, 32 ER 108 at 111.

A test of substance and not of form

15.20   Thus, in a manner not unlike the way in which transactions are tested in the rented sector,[1] the courts examine the inner substance rather than the external form of dealings,[2] in order to ensure that those who borrow money on the security of land actually receive the legal protection promised to mortgagors.[3] The critical question is not whether a particular transaction produces 'the same economic consequences as a mortgage',[4] but whether there was a common intention that it should so operate.[5] In *Lavin v Johnson*,[6] for example, an unregistered estate worth over £400,000 was conveyed for £1 to a transferee who had helped to stave off the transferor's business debts (albeit that the transferee had also received conveyances of other land to the full value of the debts discharged). A majority in the Court of Appeal held that the £1 transfer – although unqualified in its terms – must be taken to have been intended to operate by way of security only. The transfer had closely followed upon, but did not refer to, an earlier agreement that the transferee would reconvey the land for £1 on payment to him of a debt of £270,000 owed by the transferor (effectively as the price for the help given). The transferee therefore took title, not as an absolute owner, but as a mortgagee[7] and was liable not merely to account for a notional rental income in respect of the land,[8] but also to reconvey the land to the transferor.[9]

1   **[Paras 7.173–7.188]**.
2   *Lavin v Johnson* [2002] EWCA Civ 1138 at [80] per Robert Walker LJ.
3   It is also the case that the *lender* of money is deprived of substantial protection unless his advance can be said to be secured by charge. On the increasing importance of subrogation to an existing security, see **[paras 15.98–15.102]**.
4   *Lavin v Johnson* [2002] EWCA Civ 1138 at [82] per Robert Walker LJ.
5   *Lavin v Johnson* [2002] EWCA Civ 1138 at [121] per Sir Martin Nourse.
6   [2002] EWCA Civ 1138.
7   [2002] EWCA Civ 1138 at [111] per Robert Walker LJ, [121] per Sir Martin Nourse.
8   **[Para 15.122]**.
9   Curiously, given the impossibility after 1925 of mortgage by conditional conveyance **[para 8.238]**, the present circumstances must have thrown up a mortgage by long demise pursuant to LPA 1925, s 85(2). See [2003] Conv 326 (C McNall).

TENSIONS IN THE MODERN LAW OF MORTGAGE

15.21   While the law remains alert to strike down inequitable or unconscionable dealing in the area of credit transactions, the modern law of mortgage reflects a greater degree of realism about the inner dynamic of the relationship between lenders and borrowers. The standard mortgage products sold by large institutional lenders no longer resonate with the same oppressive potential as the pawnbroking or moneylending transaction – an apprehension which once shaped much of the law of mortgage. Most domestic borrowers are aggressive consumerists avidly working their way up the ladder of property ownership; most high street lenders tumble over each other in the competition to attract potential mortgagors with the offer of tempting interest rates, lucrative cashbacks and the like. There certainly remains a need for effective consumer protection, particularly within the secondary or 'fringe' lending sector (ie in transactions with finance companies). But, for a number of reasons, today's institutional lenders are not quite the 'hard-hearted mortgagees of the 19th century ... turning out the innocent and grinding the faces of the poor.'[1] The stereotype of the destitute borrower is an image of the past: banks and building societies take care to lend only to people with a relatively sound financial base (ie a reliable income and stable career prospects). The 20th century saw a vast diffusion of wealth and earning capacity,[2] in consequence of which nowadays 'a high proportion of privately owned wealth is invested in the matrimonial home.'[3] Even more to the point is the fact that finance released by second mortgages of family homes has become a significant source of start-up capital for the small business sector, which in this country accounts for some 95 per cent of all businesses and nearly one-third of all employment.[4]

1   *Hanlon v Law Society* [1981] AC 124 at 150E per Lord Denning MR.
2   See *Williams & Glyn's Bank Ltd v Boland* [1981] AC 487 at 508G per Lord Wilberforce **[para 12.195]**; *Barclays Bank Plc v O'Brien* [1994] 1 AC 180 at 188C per Lord Browne-Wilkinson.

3   *Barclays Bank Plc v O'Brien* [1994] 1 AC 180 at 188C per Lord Browne-Wilkinson.
4   *Royal Bank of Scotland plc v Etridge (No 2)* [2002] 2 AC 773 at [34] per Lord Nicholls of Birkenhead.

15.22   Modern mortgage law therefore recognises the need to preserve a balance between the respective claims of lender and borrower. As Lord Bingham of Cornhill declared in *Royal Bank of Scotland plc v Etridge (No 2)*,[1] the law 'must afford both parties a measure of protection.' Earlier, in *Barclays Bank Plc v O'Brien*,[2] Lord Browne-Wilkinson had emphasised the dangers of allowing 'sympathy for the wife who is threatened with the loss of her home at the suit of a rich bank to obscure an important public interest viz, the need to ensure that the wealth currently tied up in the matrimonial home does not become economically sterile.' As Lord Browne-Wilkinson indicated, if the law 'renders vulnerable loans granted on the security of matrimonial homes, institutions will be unwilling to accept such security, thereby reducing the flow of loan capital to business enterprises.' It is essential that a 'law designed to protect the vulnerable' does not choke the availability of loan finance by rendering the matrimonial home 'unacceptable as security to financial institutions.' With this policy consideration in view, one of the potent motivations of the recent law of mortgage has been the realisation that a bank must feel able to advance money on the security of interests in the family home 'in reasonable confidence that, if appropriate procedures have been followed in obtaining the security, it will be enforceable if the need for enforcement arises.'[3]

1   [2002] 2 AC 773 at [2].
2   [1994] 1 AC 180 at 188G–H.
3   *Royal Bank of Scotland plc v Etridge (No 2)* [2002] 2 AC 773 at [2] per Lord Bingham of Cornhill.

PROTECTION FOR THE MORTGAGOR

15.23   Equity has always jealously supervised the mortgage relationship to prevent the lender from abusing his superior bargaining strength by imposing on the borrower oppressive or unconscionable terms. In its most extreme form, the prohibition against 'clogs and fetters'[1] invalidated any clause or condition in a mortgage which tended either to inhibit the realistic possibility of redemption or to prevent the debtor from restoring the unencumbered status of his land by repayment of all moneys owed.[2] Offending terms were liable simply to be struck down as null and void.

1   [Para 15.18].
2   See *Jones v Morgan* [2001] EWCA Civ 995 at [55] per Chadwick LJ.

15.24   The avoidance of formally agreed contractual terms has always represented a remarkable denial of sanctity of contract: the history of the 'clogs and fetters' doctrine provides a fascinating account of the confrontation between the irresistible force of equity and the immovable object of traditional contract doctrine. The fluctuating fortunes of the 'clogs and fetters' prohibition epitomise the resolute opposition of the requirements of conscience and the commercial ethics of late 19th century capitalism. But the threshold of equitable concern in matters of mortgage is high. Equity does not reform mortgage transactions merely on the ground of unreasonableness.[1] The precondition of equitable intervention involves a perception that a challenged mortgage term is 'oppressive or unconscionable' or is 'unfair' or 'morally reprehensible'. Mortgage terms of this kind necessarily comprise some stipulation 'which in the traditional phrase "shocks the conscience of the court", and makes it against equity and good conscience of the stronger party to retain the benefit of a transaction he has unfairly obtained.'[2]

1   See *Knightsbridge Estates Trust Ltd v Byrne* [1939] Ch 441 at 457 **[para 15.37]**.
2   *Alec Lobb* (*Garages*) *Ltd v Total Oil* (*Great Britain*) *Ltd* [1983] 1 WLR 87 at 95C per Deputy Judge Peter Millett QC. See *Jones v Morgan* [2001] EWCA Civ 995 at [35] per Chadwick LJ.

15.25   Although the language of 'clogs and fetters' has recently been condemned as 'archaic' and 'arcane',[1] it is clear that the 'clogs and fetters' rule still survives today as a means of striking down any 'objectionable restriction on the rights of a borrower who has mortgaged his property as security for the debt.'[2] The kinds of mortgage term which have attracted the protective attention of equity have included:

–   exclusion or postponement of the right to redeem[3]
–   unfair advantages or solus ties[4]
–   oppressive interest rates and charges[5] and
–   extortionate credit bargains.[6]

1   *Warnborough Ltd v Garmite Ltd* [2003] EWCA Civ 1544 at [1] per Jonathan Parker LJ. See also *Jones v Morgan* [2001] EWCA Civ 995 at [86] per Lord Phillips of Worth Matravers MR ('an appendix to our law which ... would be better excised').
2   *Warnborough Ltd v Garmite Ltd* [2003] EWCA Civ 1544 at [1], [72] per Jonathan Parker LJ.
3   **[Paras 15.30–15.39]**.
4   **[Paras 15.40–15.47]**.
5   **[Paras 15.48–15.55]**.
6   **[Paras 15.56–15.65]**.

The Financial Services and Markets Act 2000

15.26   Increasingly the protective role of equity has been supplemented in the modern era by various systems of statutory control of credit relationships. The most recent, instituted by the Financial Services and Markets Act 2000, applies with effect from 31 October 2004 to 'regulated mortgage contracts'. The Act of 2000 subjects a large part of the mortgage industry to an extensive regulatory regime administered by the Financial Services Authority as the new single regulator of the banking, credit, securities and insurance sectors. It is one of the 'regulatory objectives' of the Financial Services Authority to secure 'the appropriate degree of protection for consumers.'[1] Accordingly the Authority is empowered to make rules 'for the purpose of protecting the interests of consumers'[2] and to issue these rules in the form of 'rule-making instruments' published in a consolidated version in the *Financial Services Authority Handbook*.[3] One 'module' of one 'Block' of this Handbook is devoted to the conduct of mortgage business[4] and supplies a vast number of rules, principles and guidelines which will increasingly interpenetrate the existing law of mortgage.

1   FS&MA 2000, s 5(1).
2   FS&MA 2000, s 138(1).
3   FS&MA 2000, s 153(1)–(4).
4   *Financial Services Authority Handbook, Mortgages: Conduct of Business* (Release 033, July 2004) (MCOB).

Mandatory authorisation

15.27 Subject to certain exemptions the Financial Services and Markets Act 2000 imposes a 'general prohibition' on any person carrying on an activity regulated by the Act without appropriate authorisation from the Financial Services Authority.[1] In effect, authorisation is required by most mortgage lenders and mortgage administrators who deal with 'regulated mortgage contracts' (including banks, building societies, specialist lenders and mortgage intermediaries).[2] Agreements entered into in breach of the 'general prohibition' are normally unenforceable against the mortgage customer[3] and may give rise not only to criminal liability on the part of the unauthorised mortgage lender[4] but also to a compensation claim on behalf of the mortgage customer.[5]

1   FS&MA 2000, ss 19, 31.
2   FS&MA 2000, s 22(1).
3   FS&MA 2000, s 26(1). If satisfied that it is 'just and equitable in the circumstances of the case', the court has a residual discretion to allow an otherwise unenforceable agreement to be enforced (FS&MA 2000, s 28(3)).
4   FS&MA 2000, s 23(1).
5   FS&MA 2000, ss 26(2), 28(2).

Regulated mortgage contracts

15.28 The *Financial Services Authority Handbook, Mortgages: Conduct of Business* (MCOB) applies to 'regulated mortgage contracts' entered into on or after 31 October 2004.[1] A 'regulated mortgage contract'[2] is a contract under which a loan to an individual or to trustees is secured by a first legal mortgage on land (other than timeshare accommodation) located in the United Kingdom. At least 40 per cent of this land must be used, or intended to be used, as or in connection with a dwelling by the borrower or (in the case of credit provided to trustees) by a trust beneficiary or some 'related person' (ie a member of the immediate family).[3]

1   *FSA Handbook* (Release 033, July 2004): MCOB 1.6.1G. See The Financial Services and Markets Act 2000 (Regulated Activities) (Amendment) (No 1) Order 2003 (SI 2003/1475), art 1(3).
2   See Financial Services and Markets Act 2000 (Regulated Activities) Order 2001 (SI 2001/544) (as amended), art 61.
3   A 'regulated mortgage contract' cannot therefore comprise a second mortgage or an equitable mortgage or any mortgage granted by a company or a mortgage over land used solely for a business purpose.

Required standards of business conduct

15.29 The regulatory regime under the Financial Services and Markets Act 2000 imposes on mortgage lenders and administrators certain standards of conduct. These standards relate to all aspects of mortgage advice, lending and administration and underscore the importance of 'responsible lending policies and practices'[1] and the transparent disclosure of all charges levied in the mortgage context.[2] The overall aim is not only to ensure fair treatment of customers in mortgage payment difficulties, but also to prevent problems which might otherwise arise from misleading interest rate offers, heavy fees for early redemption, hidden charges and the hard selling of endowment mortgages. The duties imposed under the Act of 2000 are not usually capable of contractual variation[3] and the sanctions for breach range from compulsory reference to in-house complaints procedures, to compulsory reference therefrom to the Financial Services Ombudsman, and finally an action in the courts for damages for contravention of Financial Services Authority rules by an authorised person.[4]

1   *FSA Handbook* (Release 033, July 2004): MCOB 11.3.4R. Lenders must be able to show that, before entering into a regulated mortgage contract or making a further advance thereon, they have taken account of the borrower's ability to pay (particularly in the light of his other outgoings) (MCOB 11.3.1R(1)).
2   *FSA Handbook* (Release 033, July 2004): MCOB 5–7. There are, for example, strict requirements relating to the presentation of annual percentage rates of interest (MCOB 10).
3   A firm may not exclude the duties which it owes or the liabilities which it has to a customer under the regulatory system. It may exclude other duties and liabilities 'only if it is reasonable for it to do so' (*FSA Handbook* (Release 033, July 2004): MCOB 2.6.1G, 2.6.2R, 2.6.3R).
4   FS&MA 2000, s 150(1).

CURTAILMENT OF THE RIGHT TO REDEEM

15.30   It is a cardinal principle of the law of mortgage[1] that the mortgagor has a *legal* right to redeem the mortgage on the redemption date fixed by the mortgage deed. Once that date has passed,[2] the mortgagor enjoys an *equitable* right to redeem at any time until his equity of redemption is finally extinguished by sale[3] or foreclosure.[4] It is therefore traditional for equity to direct its sharpest gaze upon any provision which has the effect of negating the mortgagor's equity of redemption.[5] The clearest and most conclusive example of such a provision comprises a mortgage term which potentially deprives the mortgagor of the possibility of removing all liabilities and encumbrances through the simple act of repayment. What is relevant in this context is not the degree of risk that the mortgagor's equity of redemption may be excluded, but rather the fact that there exists any risk at all.

1   See *Van Den Bosch v Australian Provincial Assurance Association Ltd* [1968] 2 NSWR 550 at 552.
2   [Para **15.15**].
3   [Para **15.180**].
4   [Para **15.222**].

5   See P Devonshire, 'The Modern Application of the Rule Against Clogs on the Equity of Redemption' (1997) 5 APLJ 21.

Grant of an option to the mortgagee

15.31   There is venerable authority in *Samuel v Jarrah Timber and Wood Paving Corpn Ltd*[1] that 'a mortgagee can never provide at the time of making the loan for any event or condition on which the equity of redemption shall be discharged.' In the *Jarrah Timber* case the terms of a mortgage had given the mortgagee an option to purchase the mortgaged property outright within twelve months of the date of the loan. The House of Lords declared, albeit reluctantly,[2] that the option was illegal and void in that it excluded the mortgagor's equity of redemption. In effect, the option was invalidated on the doctrinaire basis that any option granted contemporaneously with a mortgage inevitably exposes the mortgagor to the possibility of an involuntary divesting of the mortgaged estate (on exercise of the option) even though the loan has been repaid in full.

1   [1904] AC 323 at 327 per Lord Macnaghten.
2   The House was well aware that the case involved a 'perfectly fair bargain' concluded between two parties 'each of whom was quite sensible of what they were doing' ([1904] AC 323 at 325). See *Warnborough Ltd v Garmite Ltd* [2003] EWCA Civ 1544 at [50] per Jonathan Parker LJ.

Retreat from the 'clogs and fetters' doctrine

15.32   There has been a long and steady retreat from such dogmatic applications of the 'clogs and fetters' doctrine. The historic disfavour of options incorporated within a mortgage[1] was founded on the argument that such options change 'the nature of the transaction from a transfer by way of security to what is essentially a potential transfer on sale, at the option of the mortgagee.'[2] There is always, of course, a danger that this transmutation may have been the result of unfair bargaining by an unscrupulous mortgagee. It is equally possible, as Lord Macnaghten himself recognised in *Samuel v Jarrah Timber and Wood Paving Corpn Ltd*,[3] that an over-ready invocation of the 'clogs and fetters' principle can facilitate the evasion of 'a fair bargain come to between persons dealing at arms' length and negotiating on equal terms.'

1   See also *Harper v Joblin* [1916] NZLR 895 at 915–916; *Baker v Biddle* (1923) 33 CLR 188 at 194, 196–197; *Laurin v Iron Ore Co of Canada* (1978) 82 DLR (3d) 634 at 645. The grant to the mortgagee of a mere right of pre-emption was always less likely to attract equitable censure since such a grant confers on the mortgagee no right to demand a sale (see *Orby v Trigg* (1722) 9 Mod 2, 88 ER 276).
2   P B Fairest, *Mortgages* (2nd edn, London 1980), p 26.
3   [1904] AC 323 at 327.

An inquiry into the substance of the transaction

15.33 In later cases courts have been only too happy to disapply the 'clogs and fetters' principle where a mortgagee is granted an option in some transaction which is separate from, and independent of, the original mortgage.[1] In such circumstances, the argument runs, the mortgagor, once he has obtained the loan which he seeks, is no longer vulnerable to unconscionable dealing by his mortgagee.[2] The essential issue before the court is whether the two documents represent 'in substance a single and undivided contract or two distinct contracts.'[3] Likewise if an option is granted to a vendor in the context of a sale of his land for a price which is left outstanding as a secured loan to the purchaser, there is a 'strong likelihood' that the transaction is genuinely one of sale and purchase rather than one of mortgage.[4] In all instances of challenge the court must examine the 'substance' of the transaction in order to ascertain the 'true nature of the bargain which the parties have made'[5] and whether, in the light of that bargain, there has been unconscionable dealing between mortgagee and mortgagor.

1   See e g *Reeve v Lisle* [1902] AC 461 (option of purchase granted to mortgagee ten days *after* execution of mortgage). See also *Lewis v Frank Love Ltd* [1961] 1 WLR 261 at 271; (1961) 77 LQR 163 (P V Baker); *Jones v Morgan* [2001] EWCA Civ 995 at [69] per Chadwick LJ. In *Bay of Islands Electric Power Board v Buckland* (Unreported, A No 48/1976, 10 July 1978), the Supreme Court of New Zealand even upheld an option granted to the mortgagee in advance of the mortgage which was proved to be a quite separate transaction.

2   For criticism of this logic, see P B Fairest, *Mortgages* (2nd edn, London 1980), pp 27–28. The mere fact that a mortgage and an option are contained in separate documents executed on different days does not necessarily exclude the possibility of a vitiating clog on the equity of redemption (*Re Supreme Court Registrar to Alexander Dawson Inc* [1976] 1 NZLR 615 at 627).

3   *G & C Kreglinger v New Patagonia Meat and Cold Storage Co Ltd* [1914] AC 25 at 39 per Viscount Haldane LC. See similarly *Jones v Morgan* [2001] EWCA Civ 995 at [69] per Chadwick LJ.

4   *Warnborough Ltd v Garmite Ltd* [2003] EWCA Civ 1544 at [76] per Jonathan Parker LJ.

5   *Warnborough Ltd v Garmite Ltd* [2003] EWCA Civ 1544 at [73] per Jonathan Parker LJ. See similarly *Jones v Morgan* [2001] EWCA Civ 995 at [55] per Chadwick LJ.

Equitable doctrine of consolidation

15.34 There is one inhibition on the mortgagor's right to redeem which has never been precluded by the 'clogs and fetters' principle: the equitable doctrine of 'consolidation' has long placed an important limitation on the mortgagor's entitlement to discharge all liability through repayment. Under the doctrine of consolidation, if a mortgagor has charged two different properties under two separate mortgages in respect of distinct debts and these mortgages are both vested in the same mortgagee, the mortgagor is not permitted, where the mortgage money has become due on both mortgages, to redeem one mortgage without also redeeming the other. The mortgagee has a right to consolidate the mortgages, in effect preventing the mortgagor from electing to redeem one mortgage on property which has increased in value, while leaving outstanding the other mortgage on land which, having depreciated in value, no longer affords adequate security. The Law of Property Act 1925 provides that the right to consolidate is available only if expressly reserved by the mortgagee,[1] but the right is commonly so reserved and may be reinforced by entry in the mortgagor's register of title.[2]

1   LPA 1925, s 93(1).
2   LRR 2003, r 110.

Postponement of the date of redemption

15.35   It is possible that a mortgage, instead of excluding altogether the mortgagor's right to redeem, may include a contractual term which *postpones* the earliest date for redemption at law.[1] Such deferment usually has the effect of guaranteeing for the mortgagee a secure investment over a prolonged period at a favourable rate of interest. In some rare circumstances this type of provision may operate so heavily in favour of the mortgagee that the courts will hold it to be invalid and unenforceable.[2] The test is ultimately one of degree as to whether contractual postponement renders the equity of redemption illusory or valueless, in which case it would be unconscionable to uphold the postponement clause in its literal terms.

1   The legal redemption date is customarily, but not invariably, set some three or six months after the date of the mortgage [**para 15.15**].
2   See e g *Fairclough v Swan Brewery Co Ltd* [1912] AC 565 at 570, where the Privy Council invalidated a mortgage term which precluded redemption until six weeks before the expiry of the mortgagor's leasehold term of 17½ years. Here the mortgage had been rendered 'for all practical purposes ... irredeemable', since on redemption the value to the mortgagor of an almost expired lease would have been minimal. '[E]quity will not permit any device or contrivance being part of the mortgage transaction or contemporaneous with it to prevent or impede redemption.'

A more relaxed view in the modern law

15.36   The modern view of contractually retarded redemption is less strict than that adopted a century ago. The borrower has no entitlement either at common law or in equity to insist upon repayment of the principal debt *in advance of* the legal repayment date specified in the mortgage.[1] It may not be unfair that a lender, having taken the trouble to put out his money at an agreed rate of interest, should hold his borrower to a long redemption date.[2] Only infrequently does the court intervene today in support of a mortgagor's claim to redeem earlier than the contracted date. In deference to considerations of mutuality in the parties' bargain,[3] the court may allow early redemption if the mortgagee was equally free under the loan terms to call in the loan money prematurely.[4] Alternatively the court may endorse redemption in advance of the due date if the postponement of the right to repay is in all the circumstances unconscionable or oppressive.[5] In general, however, the earliest permissible redemption may quite validly be postponed until such date as is fixed by the mortgage instrument.

1   See *Brown v Cole* (1845) 14 Sim 427, 60 ER 424; *Stocks & Enterprises Pty Ltd v McBurney* (1977) 1 BPR 9521 at 9526 per Reynolds JA; *Hyde Management Services Pty Ltd v FAI Insurances Ltd* (1979) 144 CLR 541 at 543–544 per Mason J.

2   An express privilege of pre-payment before the contractually stipulated due date can properly be regarded as a 'valuable right' (*Re Cloval Developments Inc and Koledin* (1984) 5 DLR (4th) 190 at 192).

3   See *Stocks & Enterprises Pty Ltd v McBurney* (1977) 1 BPR 9521 at 9526.

4   See *Ex parte Tori* [1977] Qd R 256 at 257D. If the mortgagee demands payment of the mortgage debt or resorts to the security (eg by taking possession), he cannot resist early or premature redemption by the mortgagor (see *Bovill v Endle* [1896] 1 Ch 648 at 650–651; *Re Shankman and Mutual Life Assurance Co of Canada* (1986) 21 DLR (4th) 131 at 134).

5   See *Morgan v Jeffreys* [1910] 1 Ch 620 at 629; *G.A. Investments Pty Ltd v Standard Insurance Co Ltd* [1964] WAR 264 at 266; *Ex parte Tori* [1977] Qd R 256 at 260D.

The Knightsbridge Estates case

15.37 In *Knightsbridge Estates Trust Ltd v Byrne*,[1] for example, the Court of Appeal was confronted with a mortgage term which stipulated that the loan money (amounting to £310,000) should not be repaid before the expiry of 40 years from the granting of the mortgage. The loan had been obtained at an interest rate of 6½ per cent per annum. When interest rates in the market later fell, the Court of Appeal refused to allow the mortgagor to redeem in advance of the legal redemption date and borrow the money more cheaply elsewhere.[2] Sir Wilfred Greene MR made it clear that 'equity does not reform mortgage transactions because they are unreasonable.' Equity is concerned, he said, 'to see two things – one that the essential requirements of a mortgage transaction are observed, and the other that oppressive or unconscionable terms are not enforced.'[3] Thus, in the present case, the postponement of the redemption date could not be challenged on the ground that the length of the postponement was an 'unreasonable' period. The mortgagor had bargained at arm's length for a substantial long-term loan on the most advantageous terms then available. The resulting contract was 'a commercial agreement between two important corporations experienced in such matters' and had 'none of the features of an oppressive bargain where the borrower is at the mercy of an unscrupulous lender.'[4] Equitable intervention was justified only where the contractual right of redemption was rendered 'illusory' by postponement and here the Court was not prepared to view the parties' agreement 'as anything but a proper business transaction.'[5]

1   [1939] Ch 441.

2   The Court of Appeal's decision was affirmed by the House of Lords on a different ground ([1940] AC 613) without any criticism of the lower court's reasoning on the postponement point.

3   [1939] Ch 441 at 457.

4   [1939] Ch 441 at 455.

5   Any other result would have led to the 'highly inequitable' consequence that, whereas the mortgagor would from the outset have had the right to redeem at any time (thereby subjecting the lender to the inconvenience of profitable re-investment), the mortgagee would have had no right to require repayment of the loan otherwise than by the specified contractual instalments (see *Hyde Management Services Pty Ltd v FAI Insurances Ltd* (1979) 144 CLR 541 at 548).

Lock-in provisions in modern mortgages

15.38   The issue of permissible curtailment of redemption is beginning to assume a new, and very contemporary, relevance. Many modern mortgage agreements offer initial periods of attractively low fixed-rate interest payments, but then purport to lock the borrower into the lender's uncompetitive standard variable interest rate for several years thereafter. Such mortgages typically allow early redemption only on the payment of a substantial 'redemption fee'. These penalties for premature redemption – the downside of the allurements offered at the point of sale of the mortgage product – are increasingly vulnerable to attack on grounds of unfairness. Yet it could be argued, in many cases, that mortgage customers quite deliberately play the market, mortgaging or remortgaging with eyes wide open to both the advantageous and the less favourable aspects of the deal. In such circumstances it may be difficult to say that the mortgage terms, even if biased towards the interests of the lender, are intrinsically 'unfair', 'oppressive' or 'unconscionable'. Much may depend on the generosity of the original fixed rate of interest, the duration of the lock-in and the scale or proportionality of the penalty for early redemption.

15.39   Some of the difficulty in this area is now alleviated by the provisions of the *FSA Handbook* (*Mortgages: Conduct of Business*) issued under the Financial Services and Markets Act 2000. In relation to 'regulated mortgage contracts' entered into on or after 31 October 2004, the Handbook requires that all early repayment charges levied on mortgagors must be able to be expressed as a cash value and must comprise a 'reasonable pre-estimate' of the cost incurred by the mortgagee by reason of the premature redemption.[1] This curb on redemption penalties is accompanied, however, by a recognition in the Act of 2000 of 'the general principle that consumers should take responsibility for their decisions.'[2]

1   *FSA Handbook* (Release 033, July 2004): MCOB 12.3.1R. The maximum amount of any early repayment charge must also be disclosed to the mortgage customer in advance of the transaction (MCOB 12.3.4R).
2   FS&MA 2000, s 5(2)(d).

UNFAIR COLLATERAL ADVANTAGES

15.40   Equity always viewed with suspicion any attempt by the mortgagee to stipulate for a 'collateral advantage' which might inhibit or devalue the exercise of the mortgagor's equity of redemption. The sum total of the mortgagee's entitlement is, in principle, restricted to the return of the loan principal (together with interest and costs). The extraction from the mortgagor of some superadded advantage was (and is) inherently dubious.[1] Equity accordingly developed a loose and not always consistent amalgam of rules prohibiting a mortgagee from claiming any 'collateral advantage' in a mortgage transaction which might be deemed unfair or unconscionable.[2]

1   *G & C Kreglinger v New Patagonia Meat and Cold Storage Co Ltd* [1914] AC 25 at 58 per

Lord Parker of Waddington. See also *Bluett v Charmelyn Enterprises Pty Ltd* (1976) 2 BPR 9158 at 9160; *Charmelyn Enterprises Pty Ltd v Klonis* (1981) 2 BPR 9527 at 9535.

2   A 'collateral advantage' has been defined as embracing 'any advantage which the mortgagee obtains as a condition of the mortgagor being able to redeem' (see *Charmelyn Enterprises Pty Ltd v Klonis* (1981) 2 BPR 9527 at 9535 per Reynolds JA (NSW Court of Appeal)).

Modern relaxation of the rule

15.41   It used to be that all collateral advantages bargained for by a mortgagee were rigorously and automatically struck down by the courts.[1] However, modern courts have had less occasion (and probably less desire) to censure the kinds of collateral advantage which would have attracted the displeasure of judges of an earlier era.[2] Distaste for the self-serving preferences of the grasping mortgagee has relaxed into a simple prohibition of those collateral advantages which are excessive and oppressive. The turning-point came in 1914 in *G & C Kreglinger v New Patagonia Meat and Cold Storage Co Ltd*,[3] where the House of Lords declared that 'there is now no rule in equity which precludes a mortgagee ... from stipulating for any collateral advantage.' Such collateral advantages would henceforth be struck down only if they were, in the words of Lord Parker of Waddington, 'either (1) unfair and unconscionable, or (2) in the nature of a penalty clogging the equity of redemption, or (3) inconsistent with or repugnant to the contractual and equitable right to redeem.'

1   'A man shall not have interest for his money, and a collateral advantage besides for the loan of it, or clog the equity of redemption with any by-agreement' (*Jennings v Ward* (1705) 2 Vern 520 at 521, 23 ER 935).
2   See the reference by Lord Mersey in *G & C Kreglinger v New Patagonia Meat and Cold Storage Co Ltd* [1914] AC 25 at 46 to the doctrine of 'clogs and fetters' as being 'like an unruly dog, which, if not securely chained to its own kennel, is prone to wander into places where it ought not to be.'
3   [1914] AC 25 at 61.

15.42   As is suggested by the *Kreglinger* case, the courts' scrutiny of mortgage terms is nowadays governed by a somewhat more flexible test and the older case law requires to be interpreted carefully in the light of the *Kreglinger* criteria. Although few cases in recent decades have turned on the propriety of collateral advantages, the disfavour of oppressive terms and 'clogs' retains a residual strength in contemporary law and has, of course, influenced modern consumer credit legislation.[1] The continuing vitality of the ancient equitable premise was recently evident in *Jones v Morgan*.[2] Here it transpired that M had procured a loan from J, secured on land in which M was interested and which he wished to develop as residential accommodation. As part of a subsequent variation of the loan agreement M undertook to transfer to J, without payment of any price, a one-half interest in the subject land. The Court of Appeal declined, by a majority, to order specific performance of the latter undertaking. Chadwick LJ pointed to the inveterate principle that, upon cesser of the mortgage term by redemption, the mortgagor's estate in the land must be 'unencumbered by any interest created as a term of the mortgage.'[3] A stipulation, agreed as a term of the mortgage, that the mortgagee 'should have a share or interest in the mortgaged property' was therefore an impermissible clog on the mortgagor's equity of redemption and could not be enforced.[4]

1   The old principles may even find a new field of application. Today some mortgage agreements require that the borrower undertake onerous obligations outside the strict scope of the mortgage as a precondition of the grant of the mortgage loan (eg the purchase of expensive home insurance from a commercial associate of the lender). Such requirements are increasingly likely to come under challenge as unfair collateral bargains. See also *FSA Handbook* (Release 033, July 2004): MCOB 12.2.1G(2)(d), 12.5.1R, 12.5.2R.

2   [2001] EWCA Civ 995. See (2001) 75 ALJ 724 (Peter Butt).

3   [2001] EWCA Civ 995 at [65].

4   In *Jones v Morgan* the agreement to transfer a share to J, although made three years after the mortgage, was considered by the majority in the Court of Appeal to have been in substance and in fact 'an integral part of the mortgage transaction' rather than a separate conferment of rights ([2001] EWCA Civ 995 at [67]).

Solus agreements

15.43   Another example of collateral advantage is provided by the 'solus tie' under which a mortgagee, such as a petrol company or a brewery, imposes on the mortgagor a condition that the latter shall deal only in the products manufactured or distributed by the mortgagee. Similar forms of solus tie operate where the mortgagor and mortgagee conduct a common trading concern and the mortgagor is required to refrain from any commercial competition prejudicial to the mortgagee's business. The possibility that a mortgage may confer a collateral advantage on the mortgagee has, in this context, activated the watchful concern of equity. There is, in the solus tie, a scope for coercive bargaining or commercial exploitation by the lender. The 'advance of money with a superadded obligation' has always seemed to offend against 'the settled principles of equity.'[1]

1   *Noakes & Co Ltd v Rice* [1902] AC 24 at 31; *Toohey v Gunther* (1928) 41 CLR 181 at 192.

The old rule of thumb

15.44   The case law in this area is not wholly consistent,[1] but the courts were usually prepared to strike down as void any collateral benefit for a mortgagee which purported to remain in force *after* the redemption of the mortgage.[2] A solus tie not limited to the actual (as distinct from potential) duration of a mortgage was liable to be regarded as invalid, since such a tie – if allowed to remain in force after redemption – could be seen as repugnant to the mortgagor's equity to redeem.[3] The mortgagor would be in a distinctly less favourable position after redemption than before the grant of the mortgage. Full repayment of all money owed would not have the effect of restoring the status quo ante, since the restrictive trading condition would still remain in operation. Conversely the courts generally upheld solus clauses whose force was in terms limited to the actual continuance of the mortgage security,[4] since in these cases there was no danger that redemption of the mortgage would leave the borrower still encumbered by some obligation towards the lender.

1   The difficult case is generally taken to be *Santley v Wilde* [1899] 2 Ch 474, but this decision
    was heavily criticised by the House of Lords in *Noakes & Co Ltd v Rice* [1902] AC 24 at 31–34.
    See also *Bevham Investments Pty Ltd v Belgot Pty Ltd* (1982) 149 CLR 494 at 501.
2   See e g *Noakes & Co Ltd v Rice* [1902] AC 24 at 29, 33; *Bradley v Carritt* [1903] AC 253 at 266.
3   See *Toohey v Gunther* (1928) 41 CLR 181 at 192.
4   *Biggs v Hoddinott* [1898] 2 Ch 307 at 317–318, 321–323.

The qualification imposed by the Kreglinger case

15.45 The distinctions outlined in the older decisions probably remain good
law today, with an important qualification imposed by the decision of the
House of Lords in *G & C Kreglinger v New Patagonia Meat and Cold
Storage Co Ltd.*[1] Here Viscount Haldane LC indicated that although equity
would continue to control any bargain so framed that 'the right to redeem was
cut down',[2] the parties to a mortgage are entirely free to 'stipulate for a
collateral undertaking, outside and clear of the mortgage.'[3] No objection can
be raised against such a collateral advantage, provided that it does not comprise
'remuneration for the use of the money'[4] or constitute any 'part of the
consideration given for the mortgage.'[5] If the collateral advantage is neither a
'part of the mortgage transaction' nor 'one of the terms of the loan',[6] but is
instead 'part of another kind of transaction',[7] it falls completely outside the
ambit of the equitable objection to clogs on the equity of redemption.[8] A
collateral advantage included in a wholly independent transaction may therefore endure even beyond the redemption of the mortgage, provided that the
advantage is not otherwise unconscionable.[9]

1   [1914] AC 25.
2   See *Re Petrol Filling Station, Vauxhall Bridge Road, London* (1969) 20 P & CR 1 at 7 per
    Ungoed-Thomas J; *Yarrangah Pty Ltd v National Australia Bank Ltd* (1999) 9 BPR 17061 at
    17063 per Young J.
3   [1914] AC 25 at 39.
4   *Noakes & Co Ltd v Rice* [1902] AC 24 at 34 per Lord Davey.
5   *De Beers Consolidated Mines Ltd v British South Africa Co* [1912] AC 52 at 67. See *Re Petrol
    Filling Station, Vauxhall Bridge Road, London* (1969) 20 P & CR 1 at 6.
6   *Samuel v Jarrah Timber and Wood Paving Corpn Ltd* [1904] AC 323 at 329 per Lord Lindley.
7   *Re Petrol Filling Station, Vauxhall Bridge Road, London* (1969) 20 P & CR 1 at 9.
8   *Re Petrol Filling Station, Vauxhall Bridge Road, London* (1969) 20 P & CR 1 at 8 per
    Ungoed-Thomas J.
9   *Re Petrol Filling Station, Vauxhall Bridge Road, London* (1969) 20 P & CR 1 at 7 per
    Ungoed-Thomas J.

15.46 Thus it was that in the *Kreglinger* case itself the House of Lords upheld
the validity, even after redemption of the mortgage, of an agreement that the
mortgagor would not sell a specified product to any person other than the
lender so long as the lender was willing to purchase at not less than the best
price offered by any third party. This agreement was regarded as part of a
wholly different transaction from that of the mortgage, even though it was
contained in the same document and even though it may have been 'in the
nature of a collateral bargain the entering into which was a preliminary and
separable condition of the loan.'[1] It is not easy, however, to draw a firm

distinction between, on the one hand, a collateral benefit which although apparently a sine qua non of the mortgage advance is conferred 'outside the security ... [and] in substance independent of it'[2] and, on the other hand, a collateral agreement which is 'part of the consideration given for the mortgage'[3] and which is therefore vulnerable to the censure of equity. It may be for this reason that the more recent legal challenges to solus agreements have tended to be based on a rather different sort of objection.

1　[1914] AC 25 at 39.
2　[1914] AC 25 at 41.
3　*De Beers Consolidated Mines Ltd v British South Africa Co* [1912] AC 52 at 67.

Invalid restraints of trade

15.47　As a matter of contractual doctrine, agreements which operate unreasonably in restraint of trade are void on the ground of public policy. Over the past 40 years solus agreements have been subjected, with varying degrees of success,[1] to challenge on this basis.[2] In general it seems that the courts are prepared to uphold solus agreements which are limited in their stipulated duration to relatively short periods (eg five years), but would not be willing to countenance a tie which extended over a period of 21 years unless such a prolonged tie is founded on a clear case of economic necessity.[3] It is also possible that many solus ties nowadays constitute a form of anti-competitive practice prohibited by Art 81 of the Treaty of Rome.[4]

1　See e g *Shell UK Ltd v Lostock Garage Ltd* [1976] 1 WLR 1187 at 1199C; *Alec Lobb (Garages) Ltd v Total Oil (Great Britain) Ltd* [1985] 1 WLR 173 at 180D; *Irish Shell & BP Ltd v Ryan* [1966] IR 75 at 99; *Continental Oil Co of Ireland Ltd v Moynihan* (1977) 111 ILTR 5 at 9–10.
2　The doctrine against restraint of trade has been held to have no application to restrictive covenants undertaken by persons purchasing or leasing land where those persons had no previous right to trade at all on the land in question. The doctrine applies only where a pre-existing freedom is given up (*Esso Petroleum Co Ltd v Harper's Garage (Stourport) Ltd* [1968] AC 269 at 298B–C, 309A–F, 316F–317A, 325B–F). See also *Quadramain Pty Ltd v Sevastapol Investments Pty Ltd* (1976) 133 CLR 390 at 401; *Stephens v Gulf Oil Canada Ltd* (1976) 65 DLR (3d) 193 at 203–204; *Irish Shell Ltd v Elm Motors Ltd* [1984] IR 200 at 207–213.
3　*Esso Petroleum Co Ltd v Harper's Garage (Stourport) Ltd* [1968] AC 269 at 303E–304B, 320F–321E, 330B, 340C–E. See the reference to a 'rule of thumb' in *Alec Lobb (Garages) Ltd v Total Oil (Great Britain) Ltd* [1985] 1 WLR 173 at 178H–179A; [1985] Conv 141 (P Todd).
4　See *Courage Ltd v Crehan* [1999] 2 EGLR 145 at 157K–M; *Courage Ltd v Crehan (Case C-453/99)* [2002] QB 507 at [36]; *Crehan v Inntrepreneur Pub Co CPC* [2004] EWCA Civ 637 at [112]–[120], [146].

CONTROL OF OPPRESSIVE INTEREST RATES AND CHARGES

15.48　The courts have always claimed an overriding equitable jurisdiction to strike down any mortgage term which operates in an 'oppressive or unconscionable' manner.[1] Although this inherent supervisory function is being steadily superseded by statutory forms of regulation, one of the areas in which judicial intervention may occur clearly involves the rate of interest levied on a mortgage loan.

1   *Knightsbridge Estates Trust Ltd v Byrne* [1939] Ch 441 at 457. Issues of 'unfairness' and 'unconscionability' must be assessed as of the date of the mortgage (see *Charmelyn Enterprises Pty Ltd v Klonis* (1981) 2 BPR 9527 at 9536 per Reynolds JA (NSW Court of Appeal)).

Legality of variable interest rates

15.49   The modern mortgage is a quite remarkable form of transaction. In most cases in this jurisdiction the rate of interest payable by the mortgagor is not fixed throughout the loan period or for any defined portion thereof, but fluctuates in accordance with the rate stipulated from time to time by the mortgagee. The open-ended nature of this contract is little short of astonishing.[1] The borrower generally agrees to pay *any* rate of interest demanded by the lender. There is inevitably some question whether either party is competent to contract on this basis or indeed whether such terms are sufficiently certain to sustain a binding legal relationship.[2]

1   See *Lombard Tricity Finance Ltd v Paton* [1989] 1 All ER 918 at 923b per Staughton LJ.
2   See, however, *ANZ Banking Group (NZ) Ltd v Gibson* [1981] 2 NZLR 513 at 525 (argument of uncertainty dismissed in context of unilaterally variable interest rates in debenture).

15.50   Despite occasional suggestions that an unqualified and unilateral power to vary interest rates may 'savour of being harsh and unconscionable',[1] there have been few legal challenges to the right of mortgagees to adjust interest rates at their sole discretion.[2] Most institutional lenders nowadays reserve the right, on serving notice on their borrowers, to alter from time to time the rate of interest payable on mortgage loans. In the light of this general lending practice, it is widely believed that 'a more robust attitude can now safely be adopted' to the validity of such a power.[3] It has become clear, however, that the mortgagee's discretion in this matter cannot be *entirely* unfettered. In *Paragon Finance plc v Nash*[4] the Court of Appeal held that there is an implied term in every mortgage that the discretion to vary interest rates should not be exercised 'dishonestly, for an improper purpose, capriciously or arbitrarily.'[5] In an interesting transfusion of public law principles into the supposedly private law area of loan finance, the Court expressly imported the analogy of *Wednesbury* unreasonableness, confirming that lenders are subject to an implied term that they should not exercise discretion 'in a way that no reasonable lender, acting reasonably, would do.'[6] Thus, for instance, it would be improper if a lender's decision to raise an interest rate were 'motivated by other than purely commercial considerations.'[7] Legitimate discretion would become unsustainable caprice if, in the examples proffered by Dyson LJ, a bank manager 'did not like the colour of the borrower's hair' or saw a borrower as a 'nuisance' and therefore raised the interest rate in a desire to get rid of him.[8] But if the mortgagee, in the exercise of commercial judgment, increases interest rates in response to genuine market pressures, the decision cannot be stigmatised as dishonest, whimsical or arbitrary.

1   See Wurtzburg and Mills, *Building Society Law* (14th edn, London 1976), p 166.
2   Courts have even been willing to rectify contracts of loan to give effect to the parties' common (but unexpressed) intention that the relevant interest rate should be the lender's current rate at any time (*Westland Savings Bank v Hancock* [1987] 2 NZLR 21 at 29). See also *Barber v Barber* [1987] 1 NZLR 426 at 428, 431, 436.
3   Wurtzburg and Mills, op cit (15th edn 1989), para 6.22. (Compare Wurtzburg and Mills, op cit (14th edn 1976), p 166, which considered it to be 'open to doubt if an unlimited power simply to vary the interest rate at discretion would be legally valid'.)
4   [2002] 1 WLR 685 at [36] (Dyson LJ, Astill and Thorpe LJJ concurring).
5   The implied term is 'necessary in order to give effect to the reasonable expectations of the parties' ([2002] 1 WLR 685 at [36], [42]).
6   [2002] 1 WLR 685 at [41].
7   [2002] 1 WLR 685 at [47].
8   [2002] 1 WLR 685 at [31].

Harsh interest rates

15.51   While the protection of most borrowers rests mainly on the responsible exercise of power by the big institutional lenders, less protection is available for the individual who borrows on mortgage from another individual or from a credit company or other fringe financial institution. In the past the protection of such borrowers has depended on the residual power of the courts to declare void any mortgage term which is 'oppressive' or 'unconscionable'.[1] A dramatic exercise of this power occurred in *Cityland and Property (Holdings) Ltd v Dabrah*,[2] where Goff J held that a capitalised interest rate of 57 per cent was in the circumstances 'unfair and unconscionable',[3] and that the mortgagee was entitled to require only a 'reasonable' rate of interest (which he fixed at 7 per cent per annum).[4] The 'premium' agreed between the parties was unenforceable since it conferred an unconscionable collateral advantage on the mortgagee.[5] *Dabrah*'s case serves as a forceful demonstration that the courts have an inherent equitable power to rewrite the mortgage bargain.

1   An early attempt (long repealed) to restrict mortgage interest rates by statute was contained in the Increase of Rent and Mortgage Interest (War Restrictions) Act 1915 [**para 14.312**].
2   [1968] Ch 166 at 180D. See also *Boote v Brake* [1992] 3 NZLR 136 at 143.
3   See also *Banner v Berridge* (1881) 18 Ch D 254 at 279 per Kay J.
4   In *Dabrah*'s case there was a plain disparity of bargaining power as between mortgagor and mortgagee and there was also a strong suspicion that the mortgagor had agreed to disadvantageous terms only because, as the sitting tenant in the property, he had been threatened with eviction on the expiry of his lease.
5   As Browne-Wilkinson J observed later in *Multiservice Bookbinding Ltd v Marden* [1979] Ch 84 at 110D–E, Goff J treated the words 'unreasonable' and 'unconscionable' as interchangeable (compare *Knightsbridge Estates Trust Ltd v Byrne* [1939] Ch 441 at 457 [**para 15.37**]). However, it 'was unnecessary for [Goff J] to distinguish between the two concepts, since on either test the premium was unenforceable.' See also *Charmelyn Enterprises Pty Ltd v Klonis* (1981) 2 BPR 9527 at 9531 per Waddell J, 9542 per Mahoney JA.

Index-linked interest rates

15.52   It is not unnatural in an age of inflation that the lender should wish to ensure that he is compensated for any fall in the value of money occurring during the term of his loan. For want of such compensation the principal sum, when finally returned, is much less valuable in real terms than at the beginning of the transaction. The obvious means by which a mortgagee can seek to counteract this deleterious effect lies in some index-linking of the capital and interest repayments due under the mortgage. The legality of this protective technique was once, but is no longer, a matter of considerable doubt.[1]

1   See e g Wurtzburg and Mills, op cit (14th edn 1976), pp 167–168; *Nationwide Building Society v Registry of Friendly Societies* [1983] 1 WLR 1226 at 1228B–C.

Challenge based on grounds of public policy

15.53   It used to be asserted that index-linked loans were invalid on grounds of public policy.[1] The force of this argument was convincingly removed by the decision in *Multiservice Bookbinding Ltd v Marden*.[2] Here a mortgage of commercial premises provided that the loan could not be called in by the mortgagee, nor the mortgage redeemed by the mortgagor, within ten years of the date of the grant of the mortgage. Interest was payable at 2 per cent above Minimum Lending Rate on the entire capital sum throughout the duration of the loan. The mortgage included a further provision which stipulated that any repayment of interest or capital should increase or decrease in accordance with alterations in the rate of exchange between the pound sterling and the Swiss franc subsequent to the commencement of the loan. These provisions were plainly designed to ensure that the lender was protected against both domestic inflation and any fall in the value of the pound sterling on the international money market. Ten years after the commencement of the loan period, the mortgagor unsuccessfully claimed that the payment clause contained in the mortgage was void and unenforceable on grounds of public policy.[3] Browne-Wilkinson J treated the 'Swiss franc uplift' provision as a form of index-linking and was clearly moved by the consideration that 'unless lenders can ensure that they are repaid the real value of the money they advanced, and not merely a sum of the same nominal amount but in devalued currency, the availability of loan capital will be much diminished.' This, in Browne-Wilkinson J's view, 'would surely not be in the public interest.'[4]

1   A further challenge on the ground of uncertainty has been dismissed (see *Charmelyn Enterprises Pty Ltd v Klonis* (1981) 2 BPR 9527 at 9529, 9539–9540).
2   [1979] Ch 84. See [1978] CLJ 211 (A J Oakley); (1978) 128 NLJ 1251 (H W Wilkinson); (1979) 42 MLR 338 (W D Bishop and B V Hindley); [1978] Conv 318 (F R Crane). See generally H W Wilkinson, 'Index-Linked Mortgages' [1978] Conv 346.
3   The pound sterling had depreciated relative to the Swiss franc to such an extent that on redemption the mortgagee would, in return for the original loan of £36,000, have received payments of capital and interest amounting to almost £133,000.
4   [1979] Ch 84 at 104G–H. See likewise *Charmelyn Enterprises Pty Ltd v Klonis* (1981) 2 BPR 9527 at 9541 per Mahoney JA (NSW Court of Appeal).

Challenge based on equitable objections

15.54   The mortgagor also claimed that the mortgage terms were 'unconscionable' or 'unreasonable' and therefore unenforceable. Browne-Wilkinson J took the view that the challenge could succeed only if the mortgagor could show 'that the bargain, or some of its terms, was unfair and unconscionable.'[1] Although conceding that these terms had been 'unreasonable',[2] Browne-Wilkinson J was not prepared to stigmatise them as 'unconscionable' or 'oppressive'. The terms had not been 'imposed ... in a morally reprehensible manner ... in a way which affects [the mortgagee's] conscience.'[3] There had been no great inequality of bargaining power; the parties had received the benefit of independent legal advice; and the loan related to commercial premises which had trebled in value during the loan period. Above all, the mortgagee was not 'a professional moneylender' and there was no evidence of 'any sharp practice of any kind' by him. Browne-Wilkinson J refused to regard the 'Swiss franc uplift' element as representing in any sense a 'premium or collateral advantage.' In ensuring that he is repaid the real value of his original advance, the lender 'is not stipulating for anything beyond the repayment of principal.'[4] The overall effect of the *Multiservice Bookbinding* case was therefore a clear confirmation that there is no objection in principle to the index-linking of mortgage commitments.[5]

1   [1979] Ch 84 at 110E ('it is not enough to show that, in the eyes of the court, it was unreasonable').

2   '[I]t was unreasonable both for the debt to be inflation proofed by reference to the Swiss franc and at the same time to provide for a rate of interest two per cent above bank rate ... The defendant made a hard bargain. But the test is not reasonableness'([1979] Ch 84 at 112B–C).

3   [1979] Ch 84 at 110F. Browne-Wilkinson J gave as the classic example of such a bargain the case 'where advantage has been taken of a young, inexperienced or ignorant person to introduce such a term which no sensible well-advised person or party would have accepted.'

4   [1979] Ch 84 at 111C. Similarly, in *Charmelyn Enterprises Pty Ltd v Klonis* (1981) 2 BPR 9527 at 9536, 9541–9542, the Court of Appeal of New South Wales decided that, even in the context of a mortgage of domestic premises, there is in principle nothing unfair or unconscionable in stipulating for protection against inflation. Mahoney JA specifically denied (at 9541) that the indexation clause challenged in *Charmelyn* could be stigmatised as a 'clog on the equity of redemption'.

5   See also *Nationwide Building Society v Registry of Friendly Societies* [1983] 1 WLR 1226 at 1231A–E per Peter Gibson J. There is no intrinsic objection to index-linking even though the process of indexation in a particular case produces a much greater percentage increase in the mortgage sums repayable than is reflected in the inflated value of the mortgaged property (*Charmelyn Enterprises Pty Ltd v Klonis* (1981) 2 BPR 9527 at 9532).

Penal interest rates and charges

15.55   The courts have an inherent power to strike down interest rates and charges which are imposed for penal purposes and not as a genuine estimate of the damage suffered by the mortgagee by reason of the mortgagor's default.[1] Mortgage terms often reserve a right for the mortgagee, on default by the mortgagor, to alter the rate of interest payable and to levy an administration charge in respect of each default which is notified to the borrower. There is certainly some ancient authority that courts may strike down clauses which, on default, increase the interest rate beyond the primary rate normally payable.[2] The modern position is clarified, at least to some extent, by the *FSA Handbook* (*Mortgages: Conduct of Business*) issued under the Financial Services and

Markets Act 2000. The Handbook requires that firms dealing with 'regulated mortgage contracts' entered into on or after 31 October 2004 must ensure that these contracts do not impose, and cannot be used to impose, any charge for arrears other than a charge which is a 'reasonable estimate of the cost of the additional administration required as a result of the customer being in arrears.'[3] The Handbook does not, however, preclude a mortgage term under which the defaulting customer may be transferred from a fixed or discounted interest rate to some other generally applicable standard variable interest rate.[4]

1   See e g *Re 459745 Ontario Ltd and Wideview Holdings Ltd* (1987) 37 DLR (4th) 765 at 767–768 (clause requiring three months' interest on default declared void as penalty).
2   *Holles v Wyse* (1693) 2 Vern 289 at 290, 23 ER 787; *Strode v Parker* (1694) 2 Vern 316 at 317, 23 ER 804 at 805. Curiously, however, courts tended not to interfere if the mortgage agreement merely allowed the mortgagor a reduction or discount from the normal or primary rate if he made punctual payment (see *Sterne v Beck* (1863) 32 LJ Ch 682 at 684–685; *Wallingford v Mutual Society* (1880) 5 App Cas 685 at 702; *Re Jones's Estate* [1914] 1 IR 188 at 192–194).
3   *FSA Handbook* (Release 033, July 2004): MCOB 12.4.1R(1).
4   *FSA Handbook* (Release 033, July 2004): MCOB 12.4.1R(2). See also *C J Belmore Pty Ltd v AGC (General Finance) Ltd* [1976] 1 NSWLR 507 at 509E.

STATUTORY REGULATION OF CREDIT BARGAINS

15.56   Much of the solicitous concern of equity for the interests of borrowers has now been formalised in legislation. Although mortgages are excluded from the scope of the Unfair Contract Terms Act 1977,[1] protection against unfair dealing is provided in several statutory forms.

1   Unfair Contract Terms Act 1977, Sch 1, para 1(b) (see *Cheltenham and Gloucester Building Society v Ebbage* [1994] CLY 3292). The discretionary fixing of mortgage interest rates is not a 'contractual performance' within Unfair Contract Terms Act 1977, s 3(2)(b) (see *Paragon Finance plc v Nash* [2002] 1 WLR 685 at [75]). Nor does a finance company which lends money rank as a 'public authority' within the meaning of Human Rights Act 1998, s 6(1) (*Birmingham Midshires Mortgage Services Ltd v Sabherwal* (2000) 80 P & CR 256 at 264 per Robert Walker LJ).

The Financial Services and Markets Act 2000

15.57   It is one of the principles underpinning the Financial Services and Markets Act 2000 that a firm engaged in mortgage lending or administration must 'pay due regard to the interests of its customers and treat them fairly.'[1] The *FSA Handbook (Mortgages: Conduct of Business)* issued under the Act therefore directs part of its concern to the imposition on the mortgage customer of any charges (including rates of interest) which are 'excessive and contrary to the customer's interest.'[2] The Handbook lays down a positive requirement that firms dealing with 'regulated mortgage contracts' entered into on or after 31 October 2004 must ensure that these contracts do not impose, and cannot be used to impose, 'excessive charges upon a customer.'[3] Little guidance is given as to the meaning of the term 'excessive', save that in determining whether a charge is 'excessive' regard should be had to the 'charges for similar products or services on the market', the degree to which the imposed charges are 'an abuse of the trust that the customer has placed in the firm', and the nature and extent of the disclosure of the charges to the customer.[4]

1   *FSA Handbook* (Release 033, July 2004): MCOB 12.2.1G(1).
2   *FSA Handbook* (Release 033, July 2004): MCOB 12.2.1G(2)(c).
3   *FSA Handbook* (Release 033, July 2004): MCOB 12.5.1R. A similar prohibition of 'excessive' charges applies to the arranging of or advising on a regulated mortgage contract and to the making of further advances on such a contract (MCOB 12.5.2R).
4   *FSA Handbook* (Release 033, July 2004): MCOB 12.5.3G(1)–(3).

The Consumer Credit Act 1974

15.58   The controls imposed by the Financial Services and Markets Act 2000 apply only to 'regulated mortgage contracts' entered into on or after 31 October 2004. Protection for borrowers under other kinds of mortgage (not least those predating 31 October 2004) is generally provided by the Consumer Credit Act 1974, which confers on the court an important power to reopen 'extortionate' credit bargains.[1]

1   The court's power in this respect is not restricted, as is usual under the Consumer Credit Act 1974, to loans of less than £25,000 (see CCA 1974, ss 8(2), 16(7)). See The Consumer Credit (Increase of Monetary Limits) (Amendment) Order 1998 (SI 1998/996). The relevant limitation period for a claim that a bargain is extortionate is 12 years commencing at the date of the agreement (*Rahman v Sterling Credit Ltd* [2001] 1 WLR 496 at 502C).

Scope of the 1974 Act

15.59   Under the Consumer Credit Act 1974 a debtor–creditor agreement secured by a land mortgage ranks as an 'exempt agreement'[1] and not as a 'consumer credit agreement' to be regulated by the general provisions of the Act. However, even 'exempt' agreements are brought within the scope of the specific statutory provision which enables the court to reopen 'extortionate' credit bargains.[2] Thus, regardless of the lender's status or the amount of the loan, a loan agreement secured on land can, in appropriate circumstances, be held to be 'extortionate'. Litigation under the 1974 Act tends to be concerned not with first mortgages of residential premises,[3] but with second mortgages and short-term transactions entered into within the 'fringe' or 'sub-prime' area dominated by non-institutional lenders such as finance or credit companies. It is here that borrowers stand most in need of legal protection, being almost by definition the 'poorer risk' borrowers who cannot obtain loan facilities from one of the institutional lenders.

1   CCA 1974, s 16(2).
2   CCA 1974, ss 16(7), 140.
3   The Consumer Credit Act 1974 does not apply to credit agreements made by a building society or local authority (CCA 1974, s 16(1)).

The court's powers to reopen 'extortionate' credit bargains

15.60 A court which finds a credit bargain 'extortionate' is authorised by section 137(1) of the Consumer Credit Act 1974 to 'reopen the credit agreement so as to do justice between the parties.' Once the Act is invoked by a debtor, the onus is on the creditor to prove that the credit bargain is not 'extortionate'.[1] Unless he can do this, the court may set aside in whole or part any obligation imposed by that bargain on the debtor or may otherwise alter the terms of the agreement.[2] However, recent case law has exposed one significant lacuna in the protection offered by the 1974 Act. In *Paragon Finance plc v Nash*[3] the Court of Appeal ruled that, on strict construction, the 'credit bargain' which is vulnerable to statutory challenge comprises only the terms originally agreed by the parties.[4] It follows therefore that subsequent variations of interest rate pursuant to the agreement are irrelevant to the question whether the 'credit bargain' is extortionate, a conclusion which plainly leaves the legislative regulation of consumer credit wide open to potential abuse.

1   CCA 1974, s 171(7).
2   CCA 1974, s 139. A debtor's trustee in bankruptcy may apply for the setting aside or variation of any 'extortionate' credit transaction which the debtor entered into within the three years preceding the commencement of his bankruptcy (Insolvency Act 1986, s 343(2)).
3   [2002] 1 WLR 685 at [63].
4   See CCA 1974, s 137(2)(b) (confining the 'credit bargain' to the transaction or transactions to be taken into account in computing the total charge for credit).

Meaning of 'extortionate' bargain

15.61 In terms of section 138(1) of the Consumer Credit Act 1974, a credit bargain is 'extortionate if it … requires the debtor or a relative of his to make payments … which are grossly exorbitant, or … otherwise grossly contravenes ordinary principles of fair dealing.'[1] This statutory language has been the subject of some judicial amplification. It has been said that the statutory jurisdiction contemplates 'at least a substantial imbalance in bargaining power of which one party has taken advantage.'[2] Despite some suggestions to the contrary,[3] the term 'extortionate' is now acknowledged as demarcating much the same kind of conduct as is envisaged under the traditional equitable rubric of 'harsh and unconscionable' dealing.[4] It has been pointed out, in any event, that the controlling notion in section 138(1) is that of 'extortionate' rather than merely 'unwise' transactions.[5] The borrower certainly cannot be heard to complain in retrospect that he should have been protected from undertaking an imprudent debt.[6]

1   See *Davies v Directloans Ltd* [1986] 1 WLR 823 at 836G–837B.
2   *Wills v Wood* [1984] CCLR 7 at 15. Compare the reference to abuse of a 'dominant position' in Article 86 of the Treaty of Rome, and see *Matthew v Bobbins* (1981) 41 P & CR 1 at 7.
3   See e g *Davies v Directloans Ltd* [1986] 1 WLR 823 at 831C–E per Deputy Judge Edward Nugee QC.
4   See *Castle Phillips Finance Co Ltd v Khan* [1980] CCLR 1 at 3; *Shahabinia v Gyachi* (Unreported, Court of Appeal, 5 July 1989) per Russell LJ. In the application of statutory consumer credit regimes in other jurisdictions, increasing recourse is now had to North

American concepts of unconscionability (see e g *Prudential Building and Investment Society of Canterbury v Hankins* [1997] 1 NZLR 114 at 124–125).

5   *Wills v Wood* [1984] CCLR 7 at 15; *Paragon Finance plc v Nash* [2002] 1 WLR 685 at [67].

6   *Wills v Wood* [1984] CCLR 7 at 17; *Davies v Directloans Ltd* [1986] 1 WLR 823 at 837H. See also *Williams & Glyn's Bank Ltd v Barnes* [1981] Com LR 205.

15.62 In determining whether a credit bargain is 'extortionate', the court must have regard to such evidence as is adduced concerning 'interest rates prevailing at the time it was made'[1] and to 'any other relevant considerations.'[2] In particular, the court is directed,[3] in relation to the debtor, to have regard to his age, experience, business capacity,[4] state of health, and the degree to which, at the time of making the credit bargain, he was under financial pressure.[5] In relation to the creditor, the court is directed[6] to take account of the degree of risk accepted by him (having regard to the value of any security provided), his relationship with the debtor, and whether or not a colourable cash price was quoted for any goods or services included in the credit bargain.

1   CCA 1974, s 138(2)(a). It was finally recognised in *Davies v Directloans Ltd* [1986] 1 WLR 823 at 835D that only the annual percentage rate of interest (APR), calculable from the HMSO's Consumer Credit Tables, gives any indication of the true rate of interest charged, and that this should be the relevant figure for the purpose of CCA 1974, s 138(2)(a). An APR of 35 per cent could well be expected in a first mortgage granted by a 'fringe' lender to a borrower unable to raise funds from a bank or building society (see *Davies*, supra at 836E).

2   CCA 1974, s 138(2)(c).

3   CCA 1974, s 138(3).

4   The fact that both debtor and creditor are experienced and successful businessmen tends to rebut any allegation that their bargain was 'extortionate' (see *Arrowfield Finance v Kosmider* [1984] CCLR 38 at 49).

5   'Nearly every purchaser who borrows money in order to complete his purchase is under some degree of financial pressure. It is only if the lender takes advantage of the pressure that this factor is ... relevant in considering whether the loan is extortionate' (*Davies v Directloans Ltd* [1986] 1 WLR 823 at 832G).

6   CCA 1974, s 138(4).

Judicial treatment of interest rates

15.63 Notwithstanding the legislative concern to suppress unfair or oppressive dealing in the area of consumer credit, it is difficult to find cases in which the courts have regarded an interest rate as being sufficiently excessive to render a credit bargain 'extortionate'.[1] As the Court of Appeal emphasised in *Paragon Finance plc v Nash*,[2] the statutory threshold for intervention requires that a challenged rate of interest be shown to be not merely exorbitant, but 'grossly exorbitant'. An early landmark in the jurisprudence of the Consumer Credit Act 1974 was *A Ketley Ltd v Scott*.[3] Here, in a decision which was to become an important point of reference, Foster J declined to hold that an annual rate of interest of 48 per cent was 'extortionate' in the statutory sense.[4] The defendants had sought a loan from the claimant company at very short notice for the purpose of completing a purchase of the flat in which they lived. They signed a number of documents in great haste, including a legal charge in respect of a loan for three months at 12 per cent interest. One of the defendants had already charged the property to secure a bank overdraft, but this fact was not disclosed to the claimant in the present transaction. In refusing to grant relief under the 1974 Act, Foster J had regard not only to this element of deceit[5] but also to the fact that the extraordinary nature and urgency of the transaction justified the imposition of a higher rate of interest than that normally charged by banks and building societies. The defendants had known exactly what they were doing and had not been subject to real financial pressure. Although already entitled to a protected tenancy in the property, they simply wished to purchase that property at what was a temporary bargain price.[6]

1 For a rare instance, see *Barcabe Ltd v Edwards* [1983] CCLR 11 at 12, where a county court judge thought it '*prima facie* exorbitant' to lend money at a flat rate of 100 per cent, when similar lenders charged approximately 20 per cent. The APR for the loan in this case was actually 319 per cent, and the court substituted a flat interest rate of 40 per cent (ie an APR of 92 per cent). Likewise, in *Shahabinia v Gyachi* (Unreported, 5 July 1989), the Court of Appeal fixed a reduced interest rate of 30 per cent in respect of three loans where the interest rates had previously stood at 156, 104 and 78 per cent per annum respectively. See also *Castle Phillips Co Ltd v Wilkinson and Wilkinson* [1992] CCLR 83 (20 per cent APR substituted for interest rate 3½ times that of building society).

2 [2002] 1 WLR 685 at [69]. Here, although a couple's monthly mortgage payment was almost doubled, Dyson LJ observed that 'it may be said that [the rates] were high, even unreasonably high, but that is insufficient.'

3 [1980] CCLR 37. See (1980) 130 NLJ 749 (H W Wilkinson).

4 It was later claimed that this decision had laid down a general rule that an interest rate can never be 'extortionate' if it does not exceed 48 per cent. This suggestion was, however, vigorously denied by Dillon LJ in *Castle Phillips Finance Co Ltd v Williams* (Unreported, Court of Appeal, 25 March 1986). The borrower in this case had agreed a bridging loan at 4 per cent per month (ie at an APR of 67.7 per cent), which the Court of Appeal considered quite excessive. Although it did not reopen the transaction, the Court ordered that the conduct of the claimant finance company, which Dillon LJ described as 'dishonest', be referred for further action to the Director General of Fair Trading.

5 Deceit or non-disclosure of all relevant facts tends to be fatal to applications for a reopening of a credit bargain (see eg *First National Securities Ltd v Bertrand* [1980] CCLR 5 at 22; *Premier Finance Co v Gravesande* [1985] CCLR 1 at 7).

6 [1980] CCLR 37 at 43–44. See similarly *Greenbank New Zealand Ltd v Haas* [2000] 3 NZLR 341 at [27]–[28] (high-risk, but potentially hugely profitable, transaction).

The judicial dilemma

15.64 Although no great merit attaches to the conduct of the defendants in *A Ketley Ltd v Scott*, the facts of the case are typical of the sorts of circumstance which feature in section 137 applications. The borrower is often a person of limited means who by reason of misfortune or mismanagement has fallen into financial difficulty. Typically, such a borrower has already exhausted the patience of institutional lenders in connection with existing loans and is on the verge of bankruptcy or repossession. His only remaining hope of averting disaster lies in a further loan or remortgaging arrangement with some 'sub-prime' lender. These circumstances inevitably predetermine the conclusion that the borrower represents an exceedingly poor risk, which in turn justifies the exaction of a high rate of interest. Moreover, since the borrower would be uniformly adjudged a poor risk by the few lenders still prepared to deal with him, even a monstrous rate of interest is not necessarily discordant with the 'interest rates prevailing' at the bottom end of the credit market in relation to borrowers within this risk category. In *Woodstead Finance Ltd v Petrou*,[1] for instance, the defendant had charged her home in order to stave off her husband's bankruptcy. Although Browne-Wilkinson V-C confessed that to his 'untutored eye' the interest rate of 42 per cent per annum appeared 'very harsh', it could not be stigmatised as 'extortionate'. In view of the husband's 'appalling record in relation to payments' and given the 'parlous financial condition' of the couple, the loan arrangement and the rate of interest were 'normal for a risk of this kind.' Thus, somewhat ironically, the more desperate and vulnerable the borrower, the more justified is the imposition of a high interest rate and the less able are the courts to intervene in terms of supposedly protectionist legislation.

1   (1986) Times, 23 January.

Unenforceability of irregular agreements

15.65 So serious is the potential for oppression of borrowers under credit agreements that the Consumer Credit Act 1974 bars the enforcement by the lender of any agreement which fails to comply with strict statutory rules relating to the form, content and execution of credit agreements.[1] Thus even a relatively trivial error on the face of an agreement in the recording of the amount of the credit provided by the lender renders the entire debt irrecoverable.[2] Having particular regard to the 'social mischief' implicit in the exploitation of vulnerable or unsophisticated borrowers, the House of Lords declined in *Wilson v First County Trust Ltd (No 2)*[3] to hold such a drastic penalty for the lender to be incompatible with the fair trial and property guarantees of the European Convention on Human Rights. Indeed, said Lord Nicholls of Birkenhead, it was entirely open to Parliament to decide that, 'severe though this sanction may be, it is an appropriate way of protecting consumers as a matter of social policy.'[4]

1   CCA 1974, ss 61(1), 65(1), 127(3).
2   *Wilson v First County Trust Ltd* [2001] QB 407 at [22], [38].
3   [2004] 1 AC 816 at [68], [75] per Lord Nicholls of Birkenhead, [123] per Lord Hope of Craighead, [169] per Lord Scott of Foscote. See ECHR Art 6 **[para 2.65]**, Protocol No 1, Art 1 **[para 2.29]**.
4   [2004] 1 AC 816 at [75].

The Unfair Terms in Consumer Contracts Regulations

15.66 Further – albeit limited – protection for many borrowers is provided indirectly by the Unfair Terms in Consumer Contracts Regulations 1999,[1] which implement the European Unfair Terms Directive of 1993.[2] These Regulations withdraw binding effect from any 'unfair term', ie any term 'which contrary to the requirement of good faith causes a significant imbalance in the parties' rights and obligations arising under the contract, to the detriment of the consumer.'[3] Although not directly applicable in determining the 'fairness' of the interest rate fixed by a credit agreement,[4] these Regulations provide for a regime of administrative enforcement, principally through the Director General of Fair Trading, in respect of contract terms which prescribe harsh consequences in the event of loan default or otherwise impose unduly preferential terms for the lender.[5]

1　SI 1999/2083.
2　Council Directive (EEC) 93/13 on Unfair Terms in Consumer Contracts (OJ 1993 L95, p 29).
3　Unfair Terms in Consumer Contracts Regulations 1999, reg 5(1). See *Director General of Fair Trading v First National Bank plc* [2002] 1 AC 481 at [54] per Lord Millett.
4　Unfair Terms in Consumer Contracts Regulations 1999, reg 6(2).
5　See *Director General of Fair Trading v First National Bank plc* [2002] 1 AC 481 at [12] per Lord Bingham of Cornhill.

UNDUE INFLUENCE AND MISREPRESENTATION

15.67　Much recent controversy in the law of credit transactions has concerned the degree to which the courts should protect the mortgagor's guarantor or surety from circumstances of exploitation or unfair advantage. The classic problem arises where one family member persuades another to stand surety for the debts of the former (or of the former's company or business) by means of undue influence or by some misrepresentation as to the nature or scale of the surety's liability.[1] For present purposes it matters not whether the surety who signs the contract of guarantee and charges her interest in the family home is a joint owner of the legal title or merely a beneficial co-owner. Nor is the issue essentially different if a beneficial co-owner merely gives a written consent to the postponement of her interest to the rights of the lender.[2] In all cases the question is the same, ie whether the individual concerned can be said to have participated in the transaction 'with her eyes open so far as the basic elements of the transaction are concerned.'[3]

1　See generally Mark Pawlowski and James Brown, *Undue Influence and the Family Home* (Cavendish 2002).
2　See eg *Alliance and Leicester plc v Slayford* [2001] 1 All ER (Comm) 1 at [3].
3　*Royal Bank of Scotland plc v Etridge (No 2)* [2002] 2 AC 773 at [54] per Lord Nicholls of Birkenhead.

15.68　The problem assumes an extra dimension with the question whether a lender (who takes a mortgage over, say, the family home) should be affected by any undue influence or misrepresentation to which he was not an immediate party. Suretyship transactions, under which one person undertakes a liability or disadvantage in connection with a debt owed by another, are necessarily 'tripartite transactions' involving debtor, creditor and guarantor.[1] In this context two distinct issues arise. *First*, does the impropriety entitle the surety to have the transaction set aside as against the debtor? *Second*, does the impropriety entitle the surety to have the mortgage or guarantee set aside as against the lender?[2] Both issues have engaged the attention of the House of Lords on several occasions over the past decade or so.[3] The speech delivered (with the 'unqualified support of all members of the House') by Lord Nicholls of Birkenhead in *Royal Bank of Scotland plc v Etridge* (*No 2*)[4] now serves as an important landmark in the law of mortgage.

1   *Royal Bank of Scotland plc v Etridge* (*No 2*) [2002] 2 AC 773 at [43] per Lord Nicholls of Birkenhead.
2   It is quite feasible that the offending transaction may be set aside as against the wrongdoer, but not as against the lender (see eg *CIBC Mortgages Plc v Pitt* [1994] 1 AC 200).
3   See *Barclays Bank Plc v O'Brien* [1994] 1 AC 180.
4   [2002] 2 AC 773.

Relevant impropriety

15.69   The wrongdoing or impropriety which is relevant for present purposes comprises any conduct which has 'misled' the surety as to the facts of a proposed transaction or has caused her will to be 'overborne or coerced.'[1] It is widely acknowledged today that there is a 'significant overlap' between the categories of misrepresentation and undue influence[2] and there is, accordingly, a tendency to conflate these two kinds of equitable wrong under the overall heading of 'undue influence'.[3] There has long been a general equitable doctrine that the court may set aside, or decline to enforce, any transaction tainted by either form of impropriety.[4]

1   *Royal Bank of Scotland plc v Etridge* (*No 2*) [2002] 2 AC 773 at [3] per Lord Bingham of Cornhill.
2   *UCB Corporate Services Ltd v Williams* [2003] 1 P & CR 168 at [87] per Jonathan Parker LJ.
3   '[U]ndue influence may include fraudulent misrepresentation' (*UCB Corporate Services Ltd v Williams* [2003] 1 P & CR 168 at [87] per Jonathan Parker LJ). See similarly *Royal Bank of Scotland plc v Etridge* (*No 2*) [2002] 2 AC 773 at [33] per Lord Nicholls of Birkenhead.
4   In strict terms it is irrelevant whether, in the absence of impropriety, the vulnerable party would have participated in the transaction in any event (*UCB Corporate Services Ltd v Williams* [2003] 1 P & CR 168 at [89]–[91] per Jonathan Parker LJ).

Misrepresentation

15.70   Financial transactions are voidable on the ground of actual misrepresentation by one party to another. In *Barclays Bank plc v O'Brien*,[1] for example, W joined with H in executing a second mortgage of their jointly owned matrimonial home as security for the bank overdraft of H's company. W was not made aware by the bank of the nature of the relevant documents and signed without reading them, acting throughout in reliance on H's false representation that the security was limited to £60,000 (rather than a total debt of £135,000) and covered merely a short-term borrowing for three weeks while their house was remortgaged. When the overdraft exceeded £154,000, the bank sought possession of the home, only to have its claim to enforce the security rejected by a unanimous House of Lords.

1   [1994] 1 AC 180 [**para 15.81**]. See (1994) 57 MLR 467 (B Fehlberg); [1994] RLR 3 (S M Cretney); [1994] CLJ 21 (M Dixon); (1994) 110 LQR 167 (J R F Lehane); (1995) 15 Legal Studies 35 (G Battersby); [1995] Conv 250 (P Sparkes); (1995) 15 OJLS 119 (S H Goo).

Undue influence

15.71   Undue influence is the form of unacceptable conduct which 'arises out of a relationship between two persons where one has acquired over another a measure of influence, or ascendancy, of which the ascendant person then takes unfair advantage.'[1] Undue influence is exerted when improper means of persuasion are used to procure the complainant's participation in a transaction and the consent procured 'ought not fairly to be treated as the expression of [the complainant's] free will.'[2] Undue influence (like misrepresentation) founds an 'equity' in the complainant (as against the dominant party) to set aside the transaction.[3]

1   *Royal Bank of Scotland plc v Etridge (No 2)* [2002] 2 AC 773 at [8] per Lord Nicholls of Birkenhead. For an account of the nature and various forms of undue influence, see **[paras 12.54–12.59]**.
2   *Royal Bank of Scotland plc v Etridge (No 2)* [2002] 2 AC 773 at [7] per Lord Nicholls of Birkenhead. See likewise *UCB Corporate Services Ltd v Williams* [2003] 1 P & CR 168 at [86] per Jonathan Parker LJ.
3   *Barclays Bank Plc v O'Brien* [1994] 1 AC 180 at 191C–D, 195E per Lord Browne-Wilkinson.

15.72   Undue influence may be *actual* undue influence (as in the case of a transaction brought about by threats or physical coercion). More normally, however, undue influence is *presumed* to have infected a transaction either because of the generic category of relationship in which two persons find themselves (e g solicitor and client)[1] or because of the 'de facto existence of a relationship under which the complainant generally reposed trust and confidence' in the other party.[2] Any of these forms of undue influence may have tainted a transaction of suretyship.

1   **[Para 12.56]**. There is no automatic presumption of undue influence between husband and wife (see *Bank of Montreal v Stuart* [1911] AC 120 at 137; *Barclays Bank plc v O'Brien* [1994] 1 AC 180 at 190A–B per Lord Browne-Wilkinson; *Royal Bank of Scotland plc v Etridge (No 2)* [2002] 2 AC 773 at [19] per Lord Nicholls of Birkenhead). It is not difficult, however, for a wife to establish her title to relief where there is evidence that her husband has taken unfair advantage of his influence over her (*Etridge (No 2)*, supra at [19]).
2   *Barclays Bank plc v O'Brien* [1994] 1 AC 180 at 189G per Lord Browne-Wilkinson.

15.73   In the last-mentioned category of case, as Lord Nicholls of Birkenhead explained in *Royal Bank of Scotland plc v Etridge (No 2)*,[1] an initial evidential onus falls on the complainant to establish that she placed 'trust and confidence' in the principal debtor in relation to the management of her financial affairs. But the presence of this relationship of dependency, when coupled with a transaction which 'calls for explanation', is enough to transfer to the dominant party the onus of showing that undue influence was *not* used to procure the agreement to stand as surety.[2] The greater the disadvantage incurred by the vulnerable party, the 'more cogent must be the explanation before the presumption will be regarded as rebutted.'[3] It is, of course, possible – even likely – that the dominant party can discharge the evidential burden which has shifted to him, thereby dispelling any question of undue influence as an operative factor in procuring the other's co-operation. If, however, the dominant party cannot discharge this onus, the dependent party is entitled 'as of right'[4] to have the transaction set aside as against him.[5]

1   [2002] 2 AC 773 at [13].
2   *Royal Bank of Scotland plc v Etridge (No 2)* [2002] 2 AC 773 at [14] per Lord Nicholls of Birkenhead, [107] per Lord Hobhouse of Woodborough, [156] per Lord Scott of Foscote.
3   *Royal Bank of Scotland plc v Etridge (No 2)* [2002] 2 AC 773 at [24] per Lord Nicholls of Birkenhead.
4   *CIBC Mortgages Plc v Pitt* [1994] 1 AC 200 at 209D per Lord Browne-Wilkinson.
5   See *UCB Corporate Services Ltd v Williams* [2003] 1 P & CR 168 at [87] per Jonathan Parker LJ.

Transactions which call for explanation

15.74   Undue influence is not presumed merely on the basis of a factual relationship of 'trust and confidence' between the parties: 'something more is needed ... something which calls for an explanation.'[1] The challenged transaction must be one which is 'not readily explicable by the relationship between the parties' and cannot be 'accounted for by the ordinary motives of ordinary persons in that relationship.'[2] In *Chater v Mortgage Agency Services Number Two Ltd*,[3] for instance, the Court of Appeal held that a presumption of undue influence was raised by a transaction in which an elderly mother, having transferred her house into the joint names of herself and her adult son, charged the legal estate for a relatively large sum over a 25 year mortgage term. The charge had been intended to raise business finance for the son, but the circumstances posed a predictably severe threat to the mother's entire financial future and disabled her from distributing her modest wealth (as she wished) to other members of her family. Every factual situation is, however, different. For example, the mere fact that a wife guarantees the payment of her husband's business debts is not, 'in the ordinary course', a transaction which, as a class, 'calls for explanation' or raises an inference of undue influence.[4] The fortunes of spouses being inseparably interlinked, nothing could be more normal than that a wife should join in charging the family home for the husband's business purposes: a 'wife's affection and self-interest run hand-in-hand.'[5]

1   *Royal Bank of Scotland plc v Etridge (No 2)* [2002] 2 AC 773 at [24] per Lord Nicholls of Birkenhead.
2   *Royal Bank of Scotland plc v Etridge (No 2)* [2002] 2 AC 773 at [13], [21] per Lord Nicholls of Birkenhead **[para 12.58]**. This additional evidential element has sometimes been labelled, perhaps unhelpfully, as a requirement that 'manifest disadvantage' has been inflicted on the surety (see *National Westminster Bank plc v Morgan* [1985] AC 686 at 704G–H per Lord Scarman), in the sense that the advantage taken of the surety is explicable only on the basis that undue influence was exercised to procure it. The terminology of 'manifest disadvantage' has now fallen into disfavour (see *Etridge (No 2)*, supra at [26]–[29]; *Chater v Mortgage Agency Services Number Two Ltd* [2004] 1 P & CR 28 at [26]–[30]).
3   [2004] 1 P & CR 28 at [39]–[41]. See also *Avon Finance Co Ltd v Bridger* [1985] 2 All ER 281.
4   *Royal Bank of Scotland plc v Etridge (No 2)* [2002] 2 AC 773 at [28]–[30] per Lord Nicholls of Birkenhead.
5   *Royal Bank of Scotland plc v Etridge (No 2)* [2002] 2 AC 773 at [28] per Lord Nicholls of Birkenhead.

Disproving undue influence

15.75 The most usual (but not invariable) means by which the dominant party can rebut any presumption of undue influence is by showing that, prior to the transaction, the dependent party had full access to independent and professional advice.[1] However, the vital question in the context of undue influence is not whether the dependent party understood the implications of what she was doing, but rather whether she was free of pressures which might threaten to overbear her independence of judgment.[2] Proof of outside advice does not, in every case, demonstrate conclusively an absence of undue influence.[3]

1   [**Para 12.59**].
2   *Royal Bank of Scotland plc v Etridge (No 2)* [2002] 2 AC 773 at [20] per Lord Nicholls of Birkenhead; *Niersmans v Pesticcio* [2004] EWCA Civ 372 at [23] per Mummery LJ; *Hammond v Osborn* [2004] EWCA Civ 885 at [39] per Sir Martin Nourse.
3   *Papouis v Gibson-West* [2004] EWHC 396 (Ch) at [5] per Lewison J.

EFFECT OF UNDUE INFLUENCE ON THIRD PARTIES

15.76 If, by one or other means, a surety establishes that her participation in a mortgage charge or contract of guarantee was procured by undue influence or misrepresentation by the primary debtor, the critical issue is usually whether the surety is now entitled to have the transaction set aside, not as against the wrongdoer, but as against the bank or other lender. The surety has, after all, contracted directly with and undertaken obligations directly towards a third party. It is no easy question whether the lender can be restrained from enforcing his legal rights in the light of the primary debtor's improper conduct. In what precise circumstances can the relevant impropriety be held to have reached the conscience of the lender and disabled him from enforcing the security?

Notice and inquiry

15.77 The case law of the past has expressed this crux, not entirely satisfactorily, in terms of the lender being 'put on inquiry'[1] or being fixed by 'constructive notice'[2] of the debtor's improper conduct. Thus, if the lender has notice, actual or constructive, of the undue influence or misrepresentation (and consequentially of the victim's 'equity' to set aside the transaction as against the wrongdoer), the lender takes subject to the 'equity'. The victim is entitled to have the transaction set aside against *both* the wrongdoer *and* the creditor (albeit a purchaser for value).[3] In *Royal Bank of Scotland plc v Etridge (No 2)*[4] the House of Lords adapted and clarified the terminology of 'notice' and 'inquiry' as the basis on which a lender is henceforth to be deemed affected by impropriety in the procuring of a surety's consent. A large part of the impetus towards the *Etridge* resolution of these matters was the desire of the House of Lords to simplify the law and to ensure that, in the interests of the free availability of loan finance, banks should be 'able to have confidence that a wife's signature of the necessary guarantee and charge will be as binding upon her as is the signature of anyone else on documents which he or she may sign.'[5]

1   *Barclays Bank Plc v O'Brien* [1994] 1 AC 180 at 196A per Lord Browne-Wilkinson. Compare *Royal Bank of Scotland plc v Etridge (No 2)* [2002] 2 AC 773 at [44] per Lord Nicholls (referring to the terminology of 'inquiry' as a 'misnomer').

2   Compare *Royal Bank of Scotland plc v Etridge (No 2)* [2002] 2 AC 773 at [39] per Lord Nicholls of Birkenhead ('not a conventional use of the equitable concept of constructive notice').

3   See eg *Barclays Bank Plc v O'Brien* [1994] 1 AC 180 at 191D–E, 195F [**para 15.70**]. The victim of the wrongdoing is entitled to avoid the security in its entirety and not merely that portion covered by any misrepresentation made to her (see *TSB Bank Plc v Camfield* [1995] 1 WLR 430 at 437D–F, 439D–E; (1995) 111 LQR 555 (P Ferguson)).

4   [2002] 2 AC 773. See [2002] Conv 91 (PWK), 174 (M P Thompson), 456 (G Andrews); All ER Rev 2001, pp 254–257 (P J Clarke).

5   [2002] 2 AC 773 at [35] per Lord Nicholls of Birkenhead.

A low threshold for inquiry

15.78   Partly in order to avoid the vagaries of administrative discretion in banking practice, the courts have set an admittedly 'low level for the threshold which must be crossed' before a lender is put on inquiry as to possible impropriety in a transaction of suretyship.[1] The level is set 'much lower' than is required to show that a transaction 'calls for an explanation' which, if not provided, would presumptively indicate the presence of undue influence.[2] In *Royal Bank of Scotland plc v Etridge (No 2)*, Lord Nicholls of Birkenhead confirmed the brightline rule that banks and other lenders are 'put on inquiry' wherever one person offers to stand surety for the debts of:

–   his or her spouse[3]
–   any other person involved in some non-commercial relationship with the surety (whether heterosexual, homosexual or platonic, whether involving cohabitation or not[4]) of which the lender is aware[5]
–   any company in which any of the foregoing persons hold shares (even if the surety is *also* a shareholder).[6]

1   See *Royal Bank of Scotland plc v Etridge (No 2)* [2002] 2 AC 773 at [44] per Lord Nicholls of Birkenhead, [108] per Lord Hobhouse of Woodborough.

2   *Royal Bank of Scotland plc v Etridge (No 2)* [2002] 2 AC 773 at [44] per Lord Nicholls of Birkenhead [**para 15.73**].

3   [2002] 2 AC 773 at [44], [47].

4   See eg *Massey v Midland Bank plc* [1995] 1 All ER 929 at 933c–d.

5   [2002] 2 AC 773 at [47], [87]. Such relationships – eg familial liaisons like that of son and elderly parents – become relevant simply because of their potential to inject a distorting or exploitative pressure of an emotional or other variety into the rational decision of financial issues (see *Barclays Bank plc v O'Brien* [1994] 1 AC 180 at 190G–191B per Lord Browne-Wilkinson). See also *Credit Lyonnais Bank Nederland NV v Burch* [1997] 1 All ER 144 (employee).

6   [2002] 2 AC 773 at [49] per Lord Nicholls (see also Lord Hobhouse of Woodborough at [110]).

15.79   A lender is not, however, put on inquiry as to any equitable wrong where money is advanced to two persons jointly, eg where a joint legal charge over a matrimonial home secures an indebtedness incurred for the joint benefit of husband and wife.[1] Here there is nothing to put the lender on inquiry as to the circumstances in which the relevant signatures were obtained – even if those circumstances involved *actual* undue influence[2] – unless the lender is aware that the loan is being made for the purposes of one party alone 'as distinct from their joint purposes.'[3] In *Chater v Mortgage Agency Services Number Two Ltd*,[4] for example, the Court of Appeal considered that the lender was not put on inquiry by a loan application made jointly by mother and son, ostensibly for joint purposes, even though in reality the transaction had been intended by them to provide a commercial loan to the son alone. The lender was 'not a detective' and the mortgage was 'perfectly reasonably ... accounted for by the ordinary motives of mother and son.'

1   See e g *CIBC Mortgages Plc v Pitt* [1994] 1 AC 200 at 211B–G.
2   As was the case in *CIBC Mortgages Plc v Pitt* [1994] 1 AC 200.
3   *Royal Bank of Scotland plc v Etridge (No 2)* [2002] 2 AC 773 at [48] per Lord Nicholls of Birkenhead.
4   [2004] 1 P & CR 28 at [63]–[68] **[para 15.74]**.

The duty of the lender who is put on inquiry

15.80   Where a lender is 'put on inquiry' – and the bare fact of the lender's knowledge of a relevant relationship between primary debtor and surety is enough – the lender must take 'reasonable steps' to bring home to the surety the risks involved in the transaction of charge or guarantee.[1] The central concern of the House of Lords in *Royal Bank of Scotland plc v Etridge (No 2)* was to specify a 'modest burden for banks and other lenders',[2] necessitating compliance with certain minimum requirements of procedure which are 'clear, simple and practically operable' and which will 'reduce the risk of error, misunderstanding or mishap to an acceptable level.'[3] In this way it was hoped to hold a balance between the competing interests of creditors and sureties.[4] For present purposes the House of Lords drew a distinction between surety transactions entered into prior to the *Etridge* ruling and those entered into thereafter. In the case of post-*Etridge* transactions lenders are required to show that a more exacting schedule of appropriate procedures has been followed in obtaining their security.

1   *Royal Bank of Scotland plc v Etridge (No 2)* [2002] 2 AC 773 at [84] per Lord Nicholls of Birkenhead.
2   [2002] 2 AC 773 at [87] per Lord Nicholls of Birkenhead.
3   [2002] 2 AC 773 at [2] per Lord Bingham of Cornhill.
4   [2002] 2 AC 773 at [37] per Lord Nicholls of Birkenhead.

Pre-*Etridge* transactions

15.81   In *Royal Bank of Scotland plc v Etridge (No 2)*[1] Lord Nicholls of Birkenhead indicated that the duty of lenders in respect of pre-*Etridge* transactions was that described by Lord Browne-Wilkinson in *Barclays Bank plc v*

O'Brien.² On this basis a bank or other lender can 'reasonably be expected' to have taken steps to 'bring home' to the surety the risk which she was running by standing as surety and to have advised her to obtain independent legal advice. The lender will normally satisfy this requirement if it insisted that the wife attend some private meeting (from which the primary debtor was absent) with a representative of the lender at which she was told of the extent of her liability as surety and warned of its implications. As Lord Nicholls confirmed in *Etridge* (*No 2*),³ the lender will ordinarily⁴ be regarded as having discharged its obligations if a solicitor acting for the surety in the transaction gave the lender confirmation that he had brought home to the surety the risks involved in her standing as surety. Subsequent case law has tended, if anything, to intensify the lender's responsibilities. The lender cannot avoid being fixed with constructive notice of a surety's equity by mere reliance on an honest belief that the surety was represented in the transaction by a solicitor.⁵ The lender must have taken active steps, not only to verify that a solicitor was retained, but also that he or she was instructed to give the surety independent advice on the transaction.⁶ Indeed it has been said that the lender, once put on inquiry, must have taken steps 'to ensure, so far as practicable' that the surety was 'properly advised independently by a solicitor.'⁷

1   [2002] 2 AC 773 at [50].
2   [1994] 1 AC 180 at 196G–197A.
3   [2002] 2 AC 773 at [80]. See also *Chater v Mortgage Agency Services Number Two Ltd* [2004] 1 P & CR 28 at [70].
4   See, however, *National Westminster Bank plc v Amin* [2002] 1 FLR 735 at [24] per Lord Scott of Foscote.
5   *UCB Corporate Services Ltd v Williams* [2003] 1 P & CR 168 at [95] per Jonathan Parker LJ.
6   *Yorkshire Bank plc v Tinsley* [2004] 1 WLR 2380 at [29] per Longmore LJ.
7   *First National Bank plc v Achampong* [2004] 1 FCR 18 at [30] per Blackburne J. See [2003] Conv 314 (M P Thompson).

Post-*Etridge* transactions: the *Etridge* protocol

15.82   In respect of all future suretyship transactions the House of Lords took the opportunity in *Royal Bank of Scotland plc v Etridge* (*No 2*) to lay down a protocol which, if faithfully observed, will conclusively ensure that a vulnerable surety is no longer 'able to dispute she is legally bound by the documents once she has signed them',¹ but is relegated instead to a fairly grim battle against the solicitor who advised her.² In spite of the sympathetic understanding of intra-family dynamics evident throughout the speeches of the law lords in *Etridge* (*No 2*), the outcome marks a strengthening, not of the interests of family members, but rather of the titles taken by institutional lenders.

1   [2002] 2 AC 773 at [79(1)] per Lord Nicholls of Birkenhead.
2   [2002] 2 AC 773 at [122] per Lord Hobhouse of Woodborough.

Interposition of an independent adviser

15.83 The vital technique which lies at the heart of the *Etridge* protocol is the interposition of 'some independent person, free from any taint of the relation-ship, or of the consideration of interest which would affect the act' who can put clearly before the surety 'what are the nature and the consequences of the act.'[1] For present purposes, this independent person is the solicitor specifically nominated by the surety to provide her with advice in relation to the surety transaction. The solicitor's principal function is not to comment on the overall commercial wisdom of the transaction, but rather to explain to the surety that 'should it ever become necessary, the bank will rely upon his [or her] involve-ment to counter any suggestion that the [surety] was overborne by [the principal debtor] or that she did not properly understand the implications of the transaction.'[2] Only if it is 'glaringly obvious' that the surety is being 'grievously wronged' should the solicitor veto the transaction or decline to act further.[3]

---

1 See *Re Coomber* [1911] 1 Ch 723 at 730 per Fletcher Moulton LJ, quoted in *Etridge (No 2)* [2002] 2 AC 773 at [60] per Lord Nicholls of Birkenhead (see also Lord Hobhouse of Woodborough at [120]).
2 [2002] 2 AC 773 at [64] per Lord Nicholls of Birkenhead.
3 [2002] 2 AC 773 at [61]–[62] per Lord Nicholls of Birkenhead.

The steps of the protocol

15.84 In *Etridge (No 2)*[1] Lord Nicholls of Birkenhead indicated the following steps as necessary for the protection of lenders in all future suretyship transac-tions, this protection breaking down in the event of non-compliance with any of the successive stages:

- *Direct approach by lender to surety* – The lender must first contact the surety directly, requesting her nomination of a solicitor and informing her that the function of this solicitor will be to ensure that any resulting consent to the transaction cannot later be disputed.
- *Response from surety* – The lender cannot safely proceed unless the surety responds with the nomination of a solicitor (who may, in appropriate cases, also act for the principal debtor and/or the lender).
- *Disclosure* – The lender must then, with the principal debtor's consent, disclose to the nominated solicitor all relevant information in respect of the principal debtor's current financial position and the extent, purpose and terms of the requested loan facility.[2]
- *Face-to-face meeting between surety and solicitor* – The nominated solici-tor must give advice to the surety 'in suitably non-technical language' at a face-to-face meeting at which the principal debtor is not present. The 'core minimum' contents of this advice must:
  - comprise an explanation of relevant documentation and its practi-cal consequences for the surety, ie that she could lose her home or be made bankrupt if the loan goes sour
  - focus on the 'seriousness of the risks involved', the nature and terms

of the proposed loan facility, the amount of her liability under the guarantee and its implications for the finances of both the surety and the principal debtor

—   emphasise the optional nature of the surety's participation – that the decision is 'hers and hers alone'[3] – in the light of the current indebtedness of the principal debtor

—   check whether the surety wishes to proceed and is prepared for the nominated solicitor to send written confirmation to the lender that the solicitor has explained the nature of the documents and their practical implications for the surety.

1   [2002] 2 AC 773 at [65]–[68], [79].
2   Any failure by the primary debtor to consent to the disclosure of this confidential information will cause the *Etridge* protocol to terminate uncompleted, thereby aborting the proposed security transaction ([2002] 2 AC 773 at [67], [79(3)] per Lord Nicholls of Birkenhead).
3   [2002] 2 AC 773 at [65] per Lord Nicholls of Birkenhead.

15.85   A lender who engages in a surety transaction without completing the steps of the *Etridge* protocol is deemed to have notice of any claim the surety may have that the transaction was procured by undue influence or misrepresentation on the part of the debtor.[1] Full compliance with the protocol, as certified in writing by the nominated solicitor, enables the lender to complete the surety transaction, freed from any possible taint of involvement in any impropriety which may have operated between the principal debtor and the surety. For all relevant purposes, the surety's nominated solicitor does not act as an agent for the lender and the lender is not responsible for the content or quality of the advice given to the surety. The net result of *Etridge* (*No 2*) is effectively to diminish the protection afforded to sureties by the ruling in *Barclays Bank plc v O'Brien*[2] and, in the process, to shift the heat from the banks to the solicitors who may or may not have given accurate advice to the surety.[3] There is, unsurprisingly, anecdotal evidence that many high street solicitors are nowadays unwilling to become involved in tendering, inevitably in circumstances of some hazard, advice of the kind envisaged by the House of Lords.

1   [2002] 2 AC 773 at [87] per Lord Nicholls of Birkenhead.
2   [1994] 1 AC 180.
3   See, for instance, the surety's attempt to sue the relevant firm of solicitors in *Etridge v Pritchard Englefield* [1999] PNLR 839 (claim failed only on a matter of causation).

PROTECTION FOR THE MORTGAGEE

15.86   As *Royal Bank of Scotland plc v Etridge* (*No 2*) richly demonstrates, the traditional concern of English law for the vulnerability of mortgagors is counter-balanced by equally important policy considerations which require that legal protection be afforded also to mortgagees. In order that the flow of mortgage finance should be sustained, particularly for purposes of home purchase and commercial investment, it is essential that certain safeguards be maintained on behalf of those who lend money on the security of real property.[1] It is, of course, customary for the lender to investigate the title offered by a borrower before taking a mortgage as security for the loan to be advanced. This investigation normally ensures that the mortgagee takes a sound and reliable security, but the mortgagee is the beneficiary of other significant measures of protection relating to:

– retention of title documents[2]
– substantial immunity from pre-existing equitable interests[3]
– rights of subrogation[4]
– immunity from leases created by the mortgagor[5] and
– the right to immediate possession.[6]

1   See *Multiservice Bookbinding Ltd v Marden* [1979] Ch 84 at 104G–H per Browne-Wilkinson J; *Barclays Bank plc v O'Brien* [1994] 1 AC 180 at 188G–H per Lord Browne-Wilkinson; *Royal Bank of Scotland plc v Etridge (No 2)* [2002] 2 AC 773 at [34]–[35] per Lord Nicholls of Birkenhead **[paras 11.223, 15.22]**.
2   **[Para 15.87]**.
3   **[Paras 15.88–15.97]**.
4   **[Paras 15.98–15.102]**.
5   **[Paras 15.103–15.108]**.
6   **[Paras 15.109–15.125]**.

RETENTION OF TITLE DOCUMENTS

15.87 A lender who, prior to 1 April 1998, took a legal mortgage over an unregistered estate derives important protection from the requirement that the borrower's title documents be deposited with the lender during the currency of the mortgage.[1] This practice of deposit not only limits the capacity of the mortgagor to engage in adverse dealings with the land, but also facilitates any later exercise of the mortgagee's power of sale (in the event that this power becomes exercisable).[2] The chargee of a registered estate used to be protected by the requirement that the chargor's land certificate be retained on deposit by Land Registry during the currency of the charge.[3] With the effective demise of the land certificate,[4] this protection is no longer available, but a similar effect can be achieved if, as is often the case, the chargee requires the chargor to agree in the mortgage deed to apply for a 'restriction' in his own register of title prohibiting any dealing with the registered estate without the chargee's consent.[5]

1   See LPA 1925, s 85(1) **[para 8.255]**. A second mortgagee of unregistered land obviously cannot have the additional security of deposit of the title deeds, but a second mortgage may be protected as a Class C(i) land charge (if the mortgage is legal) and as a Class C(iii) land charge (if the mortgage takes the form of an equitable charge) **[paras 12.301, 12.303]**.
2   **[Para 15.173]**. The mortgagee is, in effect, already equipped with the necessary documents of title for the purpose of dealing with third parties.
3   LRA 1925, s 65.
4   **[Para 6.19]**.
5   **[Para 7.52]**.

SUBSTANTIAL IMMUNITY FROM PRE-EXISTING EQUITABLE INTERESTS

15.88   A significant feature of the modern law of mortgage is the way in which the mortgagee is substantially protected against the possibility that his security may be diminished or defeated by pre-existing equitable interests in the mortgagor's land.

Equitable interests of beneficiaries behind a trust of land

15.89   A mortgage of realty which is subject to an implied trust of land can sometimes present a hazard for the lender of money. The Law of Property Act 1925 provides, of course, no authority for the overreaching of beneficial interests behind such a trust unless the mortgage funds are duly advanced to the relevant land trustees (being at least two in number).[1] Several potential problems emerge in this context.

1   LPA 1925, ss 2(1)(ii), 27(2) [**paras 11.203–11.208**].

Loan money advanced to a sole trustee of land

15.90   It is possible that land legally vested in one person alone is, in reality, held on an implied trust for a number of beneficiaries whose existence in no way appears on the face of the title. A mortgagee who is unaware that the land proffered as security is governed by such a trust will be equally unaware of the need to make payment to at least two trustees.[1] Being excluded from the benefit of statutory overreaching, the mortgagee stands in danger of losing priority to the equitable interests of the trust beneficiaries. In registered land there is a particular risk that the mortgagee may become vulnerable to the adverse claims of beneficiaries who at the material time are 'in actual occupation' of the land.[2] In unregistered land the mortgagee may find that he takes his security subject to beneficial rights of which he is deemed to have constructive notice.[3] The threat posed by pre-existing equitable entitlements is especially acute in a case of mortgage or charge of the family home.

1   [**Paras 12.200–12.201**].
2   LRA 2002, s 29(1), (2)(a)(ii) [**para 12.146**]. See e g *Williams & Glyn's Bank Ltd v Boland* [1981] AC 487 [**para 12.205**]. See also *Hodgson v Marks* [1971] Ch 892 at 932B, 934G, where the real loser was the second defendant, the Cheltenham and Gloucester Building Society, which had advanced loan money to the purchaser (M) [**para 12.178**].
3   See e g *Kingsnorth Finance Co Ltd v Tizard* [1986] 1 WLR 783 at 792H–793A [**para 12.361**].

15.91   In recent years the risks incurred by mortgagees have subsided in consequence of case law developments which mark a significant retreat from the earlier willingness of the courts to protect the interests of trust beneficiaries residing in a family home.[1] By eliminating the theory of the *scintilla temporis*,[2] the unanimous ruling of the House of Lords in *Abbey National Building Society v Cann*[3] ensured that latent equities could never claim priority over an acquisition mortgage of an estate (whether registered or unregistered) held by a sole trustee.[4] If no fragment of time intervenes between the trustee's acquisition of the estate and his disposition of charge to the lender who funds his acquisition, such trust interests as arise can 'only be carved out of [the trustee's] equity of redemption.'[5] The House of Lords also confirmed in *Cann*'s case that potential claims to priority on behalf of trust beneficiaries are barred by any contemporaneous knowledge in the beneficiaries that the legal estate is being mortgaged.[6] Priority is precluded, in effect, by a form of estoppel.[7]

1 These developments are described in some detail in **[paras 12.210–12.221, 12.356–12.362]**.
2 **[Para 15.106]**. For the purpose of this part of its decision, the House of Lords was obliged to overrule *Church of England Building Society v Piskor* [1954] Ch 553 **[para 15.105]**.
3 [1991] 1 AC 56 **[paras 12.217–12.218]**.
4 No *scintilla temporis* arises even on a remortgage (see *Equity & Law Home Loans Ltd v Prestidge* [1992] 1 WLR 137 at 143G–144B, 145D **[para 12.216]**; *Walthamstow Building Society v Davies* (1990) 60 P & CR 99 at 103; *UCB Group Ltd v Hedworth* [2003] EWCA Civ 1717 at [129]).
5 [1991] 1 AC 56 at 102G–H per Lord Jauncey of Tullichettle.
6 In *Cann* the beneficiary who sought priority was 'well aware' that, when her son put together the funds for his purchase of the new joint family home, there was 'a shortfall which would have to be met from somewhere' ([1991] 1 AC 56 at 94B–C per Lord Oliver of Aylmerton). She was therefore taken as having impliedly authorised him to meet this shortfall by mortgage loan and, for this purpose, to create a charge to the lender having priority over her own interest.
7 See likewise *Paddington Building Society v Mendelsohn* (1985) 50 P & CR 244 at 248–249; *Bristol and West Building Society v Henning* [1985] 1 WLR 778 at 782G, 783C. See also LRA 2002, Sch 3, para 2(b) **[para 12.173]**.

15.92 The Land Registration Act 2002 supplies further protection for the lender who unwittingly takes a registered charge from a sole land trustee. Overriding status may be claimed by trust beneficiaries only if their interests were subsisting at the date of disposition of the charge and if their occupation of the land was 'obvious on a reasonably careful inspection of the land at the time of the disposition.'[1] The cumulative effect of modern case law and statute is that the only kind of legal mortgagee now vulnerable to latent trust equities is the lender who takes a *non-acquisition* mortgage of registered or unregistered land from a *sole* trustee in circumstances where the trust beneficiaries were genuinely *unaware* of the transaction in hand.

1 LRA 2002, s 29(1), (2)(a)(ii), Sch 3, para 2(c)(i) **[paras 12.141, 12.177]**.

Loan money advanced to two or more trustees of land

15.93 Where the legal title in land is held by two or more persons, so that a mortgagee must be aware of the existence of a trust of land (although not of its details), he will obviously insist that the mortgage be executed jointly by all the trustees and that they all duly give him a receipt for the loan money.[1] In *City of London Building Society v Flegg*[2] the House of Lords confirmed, after some doubt in the Court of Appeal,[3] that this procedure unfailingly entitles the mortgagee to overreach all beneficial interests existing behind the trust of land (whether he knows of their existence and even though, in other circumstances, these beneficial interests might have constituted overriding interests in registered land).[4] The ruling in *Flegg*'s case conclusively vindicated the orthodox understanding of the overreaching mechanism in the present context.[5] There remains, of course, some question whether the discrepant treatment of trust interests – their fate depending capriciously on the precise number of trustees[6] – constitutes a discriminatory violation of the protection afforded by the European Convention on Human Rights in respect of the 'home' and 'family life' and the 'peaceful enjoyment' of possessions.[7] This is not a question which the courts have been over-eager to address, although in *National Westminster Bank Plc v Malhan*[8] Morritt V-C indicated a tentative view that a Convention-based challenge to the overreaching principle would be unlikely to succeed.

1   The receipt clause is usually incorporated in the mortgage deed.
2   [1988] AC 54 at 73E–G per Lord Templeman, 90E–91D per Lord Oliver of Aylmerton **[para 11.212]**.
3   [1986] Ch 605 at 617C–D, 619H–620A per Dillon LJ **[para 11.212]**.
4   A mortgagee who in good faith advances money to two trustees is statutorily exonerated of any further concern with the propriety or purpose of the mortgage or with the application of the mortgage money (TA 1925, s 17; LPA 1925, s 27(1) **[para 11.218]**).
5   See also *Birmingham Midshires Mortgage Services Ltd v Sabherwal* (2000) 80 P & CR 256 at 260–262 per Robert Walker LJ; *Dearman v Mylocare Ltd* (Unreported, Chancery Division, 26 July 2001) per Neuberger J; *National Westminster Bank Plc v Malhan* [2004] EWHC 847 (Ch) at [52] per Morritt V-C.
6   **[Para 11.218]**.
7   ECHR Art 8 **[para 2.60]**; Protocol No 1, Art 1 **[para 2.29]**. See ECHR Art 14.
8   [2004] EWHC 847 (Ch) at [53].

Loan money advanced to a fraudulent trustee of land

15.94   A further hazard for the mortgagee of land held on trust is raised by the fraudulent disposition of a jointly held legal title. This risk is exemplified in the rare, but not unknown, case where a trustee of land obtains a mortgage advance by procuring the forgery of another joint owner's signature on the document of charge. Even here, however, the degree of danger for the mortgagee is not now so great as was once feared.

15.95   In *First National Securities Ltd v Hegerty*[1] a husband and wife ('H' and 'W' respectively) were joint owners of the legal and equitable estate in a dwelling-house held on a statutory trust. H dishonestly obtained a mortgage advance on the security of this property by forging W's signature on an instrument which purportedly charged the legal estate. H promptly left the country with the loan money and, when he defaulted on the mortgage repayments, the mortgagee brought proceedings for payment and applied ex parte for a charging order under the Charging Orders Act 1979.

1   [1985] QB 850.

15.96   In these circumstances it was clear that the fraudulent instrument of charge had no effect at all on the jointly owned legal title, precisely because the document had not been executed by both legal owners.[1] The mortgagee could not claim to have statutorily overreached the beneficial interests of H and W, since there had been no advance of mortgage money to two trustees. Nor could the forged charge impinge on W's beneficial interest behind the trust: she was wholly uninvolved in the dishonest transaction.[2] The abortive legal charge had, however, severed the spouses' joint tenancy in equity.[3] Accordingly, the Court of Appeal, relying on the 'all estate' clause contained in section 63(1) of the Law of Property Act 1925,[4] held that the forged instrument was effective to create an equitable charge over H's severed beneficial interest in the land.[5] The mortgagee was therefore able to obtain a charging order which conferred locus standi to apply for a court order for sale of the land.[6] A sale (if ordered by the court) would effectively enable a recovery of at least part of the loan money from the cash value of H's share of the proceeds.[7]

1   [1985] QB 850 at 863A per Sir Denys Buckley [**para 11.25**].
2   [1985] QB 850 at 863A. See similarly *Mortgage Corporation v Shaire* [2001] Ch 743 at 747G–H.
3   [1985] QB 850 at 854B per Bingham J, 862G–H per Sir Denys Buckley.
4   Every 'conveyance' is declared by LPA 1925, s 63(1) to be 'effectual to pass all the estate, right, title, interest, claim, and demand which the conveying parties respectively have, in, to, or on the property conveyed, or expressed or intended so to be.'
5   [1985] QB 850 at 862H–863A per Sir Denys Buckley (upholding Bingham J at 854B–C). In according the charge a residual effect against H's severed share, both Bingham J and the Court of Appeal declined to follow *Cedar Holdings Ltd v Green* [1981] Ch 129 at 141E–F, 146C, where the Court of Appeal had reached a contrary view in reluctant deference to an equitable doctrine of conversion which was later discredited by the House of Lords in *Williams & Glyn's Bank Ltd v Boland* [1981] AC 487 at 507F–G [**paras 9.234, 11.173, 12.205**]. See also *Bank of Ireland Home Mortgages Ltd v Bell* [2001] 2 All ER (Comm) 920 at [11]; All ER Rev 2001, p 262 (P J Clarke).
6   [**Para 11.266**].
7   For a similar response to this kind of fraud, see *Bankers Trust Co v Namdar* [1997] EGCS 20; *Mortgage Corporation v Shaire* [2001] Ch 743 at 755H–756A.

Unregistered contractual rights

15.97   A mortgagee who takes merely an equitable security over the mortgagor's land faces special difficulties. Whereas a legal mortgagee may ignore contractual rights which should have been protected by registration in the Register of Land Charges or in the Land Register but were not so protected, an equitable mortgagee is much more vulnerable. An equitable mortgagee of an unregistered estate in land is, for example, bound by an earlier estate contract (even if unregistered[1]), on the basis that 'where the equities are equal, the first in time prevails.'[2] Exactly the same result occurs, albeit for slightly different reasons, where a lender takes an equitable charge over a registered title and is then confronted by claims arising from some earlier (and unprotected) estate contract.[3]

1   The equitable mortgagee cannot, of course, claim the immunity conferred by statute upon a 'purchaser for money or money's worth ... of a legal estate in the land' (LCA 1972, s 4(6) [**para 12.282**]).
2   See eg *McCarthy & Stone Ltd v Julian S Hodge & Co Ltd* [1971] 1 WLR 1547 at 1555D; [1972A] CLJ 34 (P B Fairest).
3   LRA 2002, s 28(1) [**para 12.67**].

RIGHTS OF SUBROGATION

15.98   An increasingly important protection for mortgagees is beginning to appear in the law relating to subrogation. Subrogation is a highly flexible equitable remedy which 'gives effect to a property right which already exists in equity, ie the right to be regarded as chargee of the property in question.'[1] An equity of subrogation arises from conduct of the parties in defined circumstances where it becomes unconscionable for one party to deny the proprietary interest claimed by the other.

1   *Halifax plc v Omar* [2002] 2 P & CR 377 at [81] per Jonathan Parker LJ. See similarly *Boscawen v Bajwa* [1996] 1 WLR 328 at 335D, 342C per Millett LJ.

The classic rationale of subrogation

15.99   The subrogation principle operates classically where one person (A) advances money on the understanding that he is to have security over Greenacre for the money advanced and, for some reason or another,[1] he does not receive the promised security.[2] In this case A may be subrogated to the rights of any other person (B) who previously had security over Greenacre and whose debt has been discharged, in whole or part, by the money advanced by A.[3] In effect, when A's money is used to pay off an existing mortgage over Greenacre,[4] A is normally presumed to 'intend that the mortgage shall be kept alive for his own benefit.'[5] Since the remedy of subrogation is aimed primarily at preventing or reversing the unjust enrichment of the owner of Greenacre,[6] the payer, A, is entitled to the same security as B, the original chargee.[7] Furthermore, if yet another party (C) later advances money in satisfaction of the debt now secured (by reason of subrogation) in favour of A, C is entitled, on a principle of 'sub-subrogation' or 'subrogation at one remove', to take over the security previously enjoyed by A.[8]

1   The reasons for failure to obtain the intended security may be various. See eg *Nottingham Permanent Benefit Building Society v Thurstan* [1903] AC 6 at 10 (mortgagor was a minor); *Filby v Mortgage Express (No 2) Ltd* [2004] EWCA Civ 759 at [9] (mortgagor's signature was forged); *Halifax plc v Omar* [2002] 2 P & CR 377 at [4] (mortgagor never executed legal charge).

2   It makes no difference whether the intended mortgage charge was void or merely voidable (*UCB Group Ltd v Hedworth* [2003] EWCA Civ 1717 at [130]–[132]) or simply never executed at all (*Halifax plc v Omar* [2002] 2 P & CR 377 at [4]).

3   See *Burston Finance Ltd v Speirway Ltd (In liquidation)* [1974] 1 WLR 1648 at 1652B–C per Walton J; *Banque Financière de la Cité v Parc (Battersea) Ltd* [1999] 1 AC 221 at 245C–D per Lord Hutton; *Halifax plc v Omar* [2002] 2 P & CR 377 at [79]–[80] per Jonathan Parker LJ.

4   Subrogation is not available if A does not actually put forward money for the discharge of an existing debt, but merely facilitates the release of money for this purpose by providing a guarantee of its repayment (*Bankers Trust Co v Namdar* [1997] EGCS 20 per Peter Gibson LJ).

5   *Ghana Commercial Bank v Chandiram* [1960] AC 732 at 745 per Lord Jenkins. By means of subrogation, A's relations with the original mortgagor who would otherwise be unjustly enriched are 'regulated *as if* the benefit of the charge had been assigned to him' (*Banque Financière de la Cité v Parc (Battersea) Ltd* [1999] 1 AC 221 at 236F).

6   *Banque Financière de la Cité v Parc (Battersea) Ltd* [1999] 1 AC 221 at 231G–232B per

Lord Hoffmann; *Birmingham Midshires Mortgage Services Ltd v Sabherwal* (2000) 80 P & CR 256 at 264 per Robert Walker LJ; *Cheltenham & Gloucester Plc v Appleyard* [2004] EWCA Civ 291 at [33] per Neuberger LJ; *Filby v Mortgage Express (No 2) Ltd* [2004] EWCA Civ 759 at [62] per May LJ. See similarly *Mutual Trust Co v Creditview Estate Homes Ltd* (1997) 149 DLR (4th) 385 at 389–390; *Armatage Motors Ltd v Royal Trust Corp of Canada* (1997) 149 DLR (4th) 398 at 403.

7   Subrogation is particularly relevant where the practice of remortgaging is widespread (see e g *Halifax Mortgage Services Ltd v Muirhead* (1997) 76 P & CR 418 at 425 per Evans LJ).

8   *UCB Group Ltd v Hedworth* [2003] EWCA Civ 1717 at [137]–[147] per Jonathan Parker LJ. See similarly *Castle Phillips Finance v Piddington* (1995) 70 P & CR 592 at 600 per Peter Gibson LJ.

15.100   In the circumstances outlined above, subrogation in favour of A is not dependent on the knowledge or consent of the owner of Greenacre, since by definition his position is in no way altered.[1] Nor is it any bar to subrogation that A's failure to obtain the intended security was attributable to his own negligence[2] or that A managed to obtain some security (albeit less than that which he had intended to take).[3] However, subrogation can never be allowed to place A in a better position than he would have occupied if he had obtained all the rights for which he bargained.[4] A is entitled only to precisely the same security as the original chargee[5] and the capital sum in respect of which A is subrogated cannot normally be greater than the amount of the secured debt which has been discharged by the payment to B.[6]

1   *Butler v Rice* [1910] Ch 277 at 282–283; *National Guardian Mortgage Corp v Roberts* [1993] NPC 149; *Castle Phillips Finance v Piddington* (1995) 70 P & CR 592 at 599 per Peter Gibson LJ.

2   *Cheltenham & Gloucester Plc v Appleyard* [2004] EWCA Civ 291 at [39] per Neuberger LJ.

3   *Cheltenham & Gloucester Plc v Appleyard* [2004] EWCA Civ 291 at [37], [70] per Neuberger LJ. Subrogation is unavailable, however, if A obtains all the security for which he bargained (per Neuberger LJ at [38]).

4   *Cheltenham & Gloucester Plc v Appleyard* [2004] EWCA Civ 291 at [41] per Neuberger LJ; *Filby v Mortgage Express (No 2) Ltd* [2004] EWCA Civ 759 at [62] per May LJ.

5   *Castle Phillips Finance v Piddington* (1995) 70 P & CR 592 at 602.

6   *Cheltenham & Gloucester Plc v Appleyard* [2004] EWCA Civ 291 at [43] per Neuberger LJ.

Illustrations of subrogation

15.101   A good illustration of subrogation is found in *Boscawen v Bajwa*.[1] Here the Abbey National agreed to advance money to P for his purchase of V's house. For this purpose, the Abbey National paid over the loan money to P's solicitor, S1, intending S1 on the completion date to pay the money to V's solicitor, S2. P was likewise meant, on completion, to execute a legal charge over the house in favour of the Abbey National. Instead, before the completion date, S1 paid the money to S2, who used it (wrongly and in advance of completion) to discharge V's existing mortgage to the Halifax. Completion never did take place; no legal charge was executed in favour of the Abbey National; and S1 became bankrupt. X, who were judgment creditors of V, then attempted to enforce their charging order[2] against the apparently unencumbered estate now held by V. The Court of Appeal held, however, that the Abbey

National could trace its loan money into the payment used to discharge the Halifax mortgage and that S2, in paying off the Halifax, must be taken to have intended to keep the mortgage alive for the benefit of the Abbey National.[3] Accordingly, the Abbey National was entitled, by way of subrogation, to a charge on the eventual proceeds of sale of V's house in priority to the claims of X.[4]

1   [1996] 1 WLR 328. See [1996] CLJ 199 (N H Andrews).
2   **[Para 9.120]**.
3   [1996] 1 WLR 328 at 339G.
4   [1996] 1 WLR 328 at 342B–D.

15.102 A further application of the subrogation principle has proved immensely useful to lenders who fail, perhaps through their own negligence, to ensure that they obtain security for an advance of money which goes to assist a purchase of land. A timely escape from potentially disastrous consequences emerges with the recognition that, pending payment of the purchase money, a vendor enjoys a form of security over the subject matter of the sale, ie an unpaid vendor's lien in the land. Thus, to the extent that a lender's money reaches the vendor, the lender may claim to be subrogated to the unpaid vendor's security.[1] In *Halifax Plc v Omar*,[2] for example, the Court of Appeal was able to hold that the Halifax, having advanced mortgage money to a fraudulent mortgagor, was subrogated to the equitable charge held by a vendor who had received the bulk of the Halifax money.

1   *Nottingham Permanent Benefit Building Society v Thurstan* [1903] AC 6 at 10 per Earl of Halsbury LC, 10 per Lord Shand; *Bank of Ireland Finance Ltd v D J Daly Ltd* [1978] IR 79 at 82. See similarly *Boodle Hatfield & Co v British Films Ltd* (1986) 2 BCC 99,221 at 99,225–99,226 (unsecured advance to client by firm of solicitors in order to facilitate completion of purchase before clearance of client's cheque). Contrast, however, *CID v Cortes* (1987) 4 BPR 9391 at 9393.
2   [2002] 2 P & CR 377 at [84] per Jonathan Parker LJ.

IMMUNITY FROM LEASES CREATED BY THE MORTGAGOR

15.103 A mortgagor, whilst in possession, has a general statutory power to grant certain kinds of lease in respect of the mortgaged land.[1] It is customary, however, for this leasing power to be modified or excluded by the express terms of the mortgage.

1   The mortgagor in possession has the same leasing power as has a mortgagee in possession (LPA 1925, s 99(1)–(2)). Both have statutory authority, if the mortgage was made after 1925, to lease the land for any term not exceeding 50 years (for agricultural or occupation purposes) and for any term not exceeding 999 years (for building purposes) (LPA 1925, s 99(3)). In all cases the lease must normally take effect in possession within twelve months of its date, must reserve 'the best rent that can reasonably be obtained', and must contain a condition of re-entry on the covenanted rent not being paid within a specified time not exceeding 30 days (LPA 1925, s 99(5)–(7)).

Unauthorised leases created by the mortgagor

15.104 It is well established that, although a mortgagee is bound by any lease created prior to his mortgage,[1] he is *not* affected by any lease granted by the mortgagor after the execution of the mortgage (except where the lease was authorised by statute or by the mortgagee himself).[2] For this purpose it matters not whether the lease in question comprises a contractual tenancy[3] or even a statutorily protected tenancy.[4] It is also irrelevant that, subsequent to the grant of the lease, the mortgage is discharged and replaced by a different mortgage.[5] In all these cases the unauthorised lease has been granted in the shadow of, and therefore subject to, a prior mortgage.[6] The lease is therefore liable to be defeated by the assertion of the paramount title already conferred on the mortgagee,[7] leaving the tenant with no remedy except an almost inevitably futile contractual action against the mortgagor landlord. This conclusion has a certain legal inevitability, but still operates unkindly in relation to tenants who are entirely unaware that their landlord has granted a tenancy without authority and has then fallen into arrears with the mortgage payments.[8] In such instances, however, the mortgagee simply has an unqualified right to take possession as against the tenants.

1   There is authority that a legal mortgage of land in lease at the date of mortgage vests in the mortgagee the immediate reversion on the lease (see *Neale v Mackenzie* (1836) 1 M & W 747 at 760–762, 150 ER 635 at 640–641). The mortgagee may therefore be directly liable as reversioner for breaches of the covenant for quiet enjoyment if he demands possession from the tenant on the ground of default by the mortgagor (see D G Barnsley, 'Harassment of Tenants by Mortgagees' [1991] JSWL 220 at 223).

2   *Rogers v Humphreys* (1835) 4 Ad & E 299 at 313, 111 ER 799 at 804; *Dudley and District Benefit Building Society v Emerson* [1949] Ch 707 at 714; *Halifax Building Society v Fanimi* [1997] EWCA Civ 1461; *Hypo-Mortgage Services Ltd v Robinson* (Unreported, Court of Appeal, 7 November 1996); *Carroll v Manek and Bank of India* (2000) 79 P & CR 173 at 185.

3   *Dudley and District Benefit Building Society v Emerson* [1949] Ch 707 at 714.

4   *Quennell v Maltby* [1979] 1 WLR 318 at 323H per Templeman LJ; *Britannia Building Society v Earl* [1990] 1 WLR 422 at 427H–428F per McCowan LJ.

5   See *Walthamstow Building Society v Davies* (1990) 60 P & CR 99 at 103 (no *scintilla temporis*).

6   The only interest with which the mortgagor can transact is his equity of redemption: all his dealings therefore take effect against this entitlement, thereby ensuring priority for the mortgagee's paramount rights.

7   See *Corbett v Plowden* (1884) 25 Ch D 678 at 681 per Earl of Selborne LC; *Holy Spirit Credit Union Ltd v Gurevich* (2000) 187 DLR (4th) 219 at [15].

8   The classic dilemma arises where the mortgagor, in order to help finance his repayments, grants multiple lettings of the mortgaged premises (e g to students). As in *Britannia Building Society v Earl* [1990] 1 WLR 422 at 424B, it is commonly the case that the tenants become aware of the mortgagor's difficulties only on the arrival of notification of possession proceedings or of a notice that a warrant for possession is about to be executed. See D G Barnsley, [1991] JSWL 220.

Tenancies by estoppel

15.105 It used to be thought that the security taken by a mortgagee was inherently vulnerable to any tenancy agreements which might have been granted by the mortgagor before he acquired the legal title offered as security.

In *Church of England Building Society v Piskor*[1] a purchaser, having agreed to buy land, obtained possession of the land before the completion of his purchase. During the interim before completion he granted periodic tenancies to two tenants who assumed possession in advance of the date when the legal estate was conveyed to the purchaser and immediately mortgaged to the lender of the purchase money. When the mortgagee later sought possession of the property on the ground of the mortgagor's default, the Court of Appeal held that the rights of the tenants took priority over the mortgage. The tenancies had been mere 'leases by estoppel' during the period before completion, since the lessor had not yet acquired the legal estate out of which they might be created. However, as soon as the legal estate passed to the mortgagor/lessor on completion, these tenancies automatically became legal tenancies. The rights of the tenants crystallised as legal rights in the instant when the 'estoppel was fed' by the conveyance of the legal estate.[2]

1   [1954] Ch 553.
2   [1954] Ch 553 at 561, 564–565. See also *Universal Permanent Building Society v Cooke* [1952] Ch 95 at 103.

The scintilla temporis

15.106   The internal logic of the decision in *Piskor* depended vitally upon the theory that, where a taking of title is funded by an acquisition mortgage loan, a fragment of time or *scintilla temporis* is interposed between the passing of the legal estate to the mortgagor and the disposition of mortgage in favour of the lender of the purchase money.[1] Notwithstanding that the relevant documents of transfer and charge are executed contemporaneously, the transaction of purchase necessarily involves, in terms of this theory, conveyancing steps which in contemplation of law are regarded as taking place in a defined order. As Lord Oliver of Aylmerton was later to concede, there is 'an attractive legal logic' in the proposition that 'a person cannot charge a legal estate that he does not have.'[2] Accordingly, in *Piskor*'s case, the Court of Appeal held that the metamorphosis of the tenants' rights occurred on the feeding of their estoppel during the *scintilla temporis* between the purchaser/landlord's acquisition of his legal estate and the creation of the building society charge.

1   **[Para 12.217]**.
2   *Abbey National Building Society v Cann* [1991] 1 AC 56 at 92E. Lord Jauncey of Tullichettle likewise noted (at 101F) that 'as a matter of strict legal analysis ... a purchaser of property cannot grant a mortgage over it until the legal estate has vested in him.' See also *Lloyds Bank Plc v Rosset* [1989] Ch 350 at 391H–392B per Mustill LJ.

Repudiation of the scintilla temporis theory

15.107   In *Abbey National Building Society v Cann*[1] the House of Lords conclusively overruled the 'successive steps' analysis[2] of *Piskor* in favour of the 'single transaction' analysis found in analogous areas of law.[3] In a purchase based on mortgage funding, declared Lord Oliver, 'the transactions of acquiring the legal estate and granting the charge are, in law as in reality, one indivisible transaction.'[4] *Piskor's* case 'flies in the face of reality' and the *scintilla temporis* is 'no more than a legal artifice.'[5] In the case of the acquisition mortgage, as Lord Oliver pointed out, the acquisition of the legal estate 'is entirely dependent upon the provision of funds which will have been provided before the conveyance can take effect and which are provided only against an agreement that the estate will be charged to secure them.'[6] The reality is that the purchaser of land who relies upon a building society or bank loan for the completion of his purchase 'never in fact acquires anything but an equity of redemption.' The land 'is, from the very inception, charged with the amount of the loan without which it could never have been transferred at all and it was never intended that it should be otherwise.'[7]

1   [1991] 1 AC 56 [**paras 12.217, 15.91**].
2   The phrase is that of Nicholls LJ in *Lloyds Bank Plc v Rosset* [1989] Ch 350 at 384E.
3   See eg *Re Connolly Brothers Ltd (No 2)* [1912] 2 Ch 25 at 31; *Coventry Permanent Economic Building Society v Jones* [1951] 1 All ER 901 at 903; *Security Trust Co v Royal Bank of Canada* [1976] AC 503 at 519–520.
4   [1991] 1 AC 56 at 92D. Lord Oliver was careful to add that the 'single transaction' analysis obtains 'at least where there is a prior agreement to grant the charge on the legal estate when obtained'.
5   [1991] 1 AC 56 at 92F, 93B. See similarly *Ingram v IRC* [2000] 1 AC 293 at 303F–G per Lord Hoffmann [**para 12.218**]; *Owen v Blathwayt* [2003] 1 P & CR 444 at [61] per Neuberger J.
6   [1991] 1 AC 56 at 92F.
7   [1991] 1 AC 56 at 93A–B. Lord Jauncey of Tullichettle (at 101H, 102A–B) took a similar view of 'the realities of the situation' [**para 12.218**].

15.108   The destruction of the *scintilla temporis* theory in *Cann's* case ensures that the acquisition mortgagor is never able to assert that he held, even momentarily, an unencumbered estate in the land. It is certainly clear that the mortgagor acquires no unencumbered title whereby an estoppel in favour of grantees could be fed to the prejudice of the mortgagee's security.[1]

1   See [1991] 1 AC 56 at 102B per Lord Jauncey of Tullichettle.

THE MORTGAGEE'S RIGHT TO IMMEDIATE POSSESSION

15.109   Of all the protections afforded the legal mortgagee, perhaps the most crucial is the right to take immediate possession of the mortgaged land.

Origin of the legal mortgagee's right to possession

15.110   A legal mortgage confers on the mortgagee a legal estate in the mortgaged land[1] and a charge by way of legal mortgage is statutorily deemed to have an equivalent effect.[2] It is a long established doctrine of mortgage law that, as an incident of this actual or notional estate in the land, the mortgagee has at all times 'an unqualified right to possession of the mortgaged property' (in the absence of any contractual or statutory limitation).[3]

1   LPA 1925, ss 85(1), 86(1) (ie in the case of mortgage by demise or subdemise) [**paras 8.242, 8.251**].
2   LPA 1925, s 87(1) [**para 8.246**].
3   *Mobil Oil Co Ltd v Rawlinson* (1982) 43 P & CR 221 at 223 per Nourse J; *Ashley Guarantee Plc v Zacaria* [1993] 1 WLR 62 at 69B per Nourse LJ; *National Westminster Bank Plc v Skelton (Note)* [1993] 1 WLR 72 at 77A, 81H per Slade LJ. See also LPA 1925, s 95(4). The mortgagee's right to possession, again unless agreed otherwise, is unaffected by a sub-charge (*Credit & Mercantile plc v Marks* [2004] 3 WLR 489 at [54]–[55] per Clarke LJ).

Unqualified nature of the paramount right

15.111   The legal mortgagee's right to possession arises as soon as the mortgage is made (and even in advance of the date fixed for redemption) and is not dependent on any default by the mortgagor.[1] As Harman J graphically pointed out in *Four-Maids Ltd v Dudley Marshall (Properties) Ltd*,[2] the mortgagee 'may go into possession before the ink is dry on the mortgage unless there is something in the contract, express or by implication, whereby he has contracted himself out of that right.'[3] Moreover, a mortgagor who resists his mortgagee's demand for possession automatically becomes a trespasser.[4] If not limited by any relevant contractual or statutory restriction, the mortgagee is entitled to use reasonable force, without the benefit of any court order for possession,[5] in order to remove a wholly blameless mortgagor and there is, amazingly, 'nothing the mortgagor can do about it.'[6]

1   *Four-Maids Ltd v Dudley Marshall (Properties) Ltd* [1957] Ch 317 at 320; *Mobil Oil Co Ltd v Rawlinson* (1982) 43 P & CR 221 at 223–224; *Credit & Mercantile plc v Marks* [2004] 3 WLR 489 at [42] per Clarke LJ. See also *Ropaigealach v Barclays Bank plc* [2000] QB 263 at 284D per Clarke LJ (many mortgagors 'would be astonished to find that a bank which had lent them money to buy a property for them to live in could take possession of it the next day').
2   [1957] Ch 317 at 320. See (1957) 73 LQR 300 (R E M).
3   See also *Alliance Perpetual Building Society v Belrum Investments Ltd* [1957] 1 WLR 720 at 723. It is normally an implied incident of a mortgage of premises where the mortgagor is conducting a business that the mortgagee has power, on exercising his right to possession, to carry on the mortgagor's business (see *Chaplin v Young (No 1)* (1864) 33 Beav 330 at 337–338, 55 ER 395 at 398; *Cook v Thomas* (1876) 24 WR 427 at 428; *County of Gloucester Bank v Rudry Merthyr Steam and House Coal Colliery Co* [1895] 1 Ch 629 at 634, 638; *Mercantile Credits Ltd v Atkins* (1985) 1 NSWLR 670 at 676A–B).
4   *Birch v Wright* (1786) 1 Term Rep 378 at 383, 99 ER 1148 at 1152; *Jolly v Arbuthnot* (1859) 4 De G & J 224 at 236, 45 ER 87 at 92.
5   See *McPhail v Persons, Names Unknown* [1973] Ch 447 at 456D–457B; *Ropaigealach v Barclays Bank plc* [2000] QB 263 [**para 15.145**].
6   *Ropaigealach v Barclays Bank plc* [2000] QB 263 at 284D–E per Clarke LJ.

Exception for land subject to a lease

15.112   A mortgagee's entry into physical occupation is rendered impossible only where the land is subject to a lease which is binding on the mortgagee either because it was created prior to the mortgage or because it was created thereafter with the mortgagee's consent.[1] In such cases, however, the mortgagee may assume 'possession' in the sense of the right to receive the rents and profits due under the lease.[2]

1   See *Rogers v Humphreys* (1835) 4 Ad & E 299 at 313, 111 ER 799 at 804; *Re Ind Coope & Co Ltd* [1911] 2 Ch 223 at 231. The mortgagee himself may grant new leases (see *Chapman v Smith* [1907] 2 Ch 97 at 102), although such lessees are of course subject to the mortgagor's equity of redemption. See also LPA 1925, s 99(2).

2   *Moss v Gallimore* (1779) 1 Doug 279 at 283, 99 ER 182 at 184. See LPA 1925, s 205(1)(xix) **[para 7.21]**. The tenant may be directed to pay his rent henceforth to the mortgagee rather than to the mortgagor (*Horlock v Smith* (1842) 6 Jur 478).

Exclusion of the mortgagee's right to possession

15.113   The mortgagee's inherent right to enter into possession may be negatived either by statutory restrictions[1] or by mortgage terms which expressly or impliedly reserve the right of possession to the mortgagor.[2]

1   **[Para 15.124]**.

2   *Doe d Roylance v Lightfoot* (1841) 8 M & W 553 at 564–565, 151 ER 1158 at 1163. Where the mortgagee's right to possession has been excluded by contract, an injunction may be granted to restrain the mortgagee from wrongfully going into possession (*Doe d Parsley v Day* (1842) 2 QB 147 at 156, 114 ER 58 at 62).

Express exclusion

15.114   It is extremely common nowadays for a bank or building society mortgage expressly to grant the mortgagor a right of possession until default, thereby excluding the mortgagee's right to possession in advance of some default.[1]

1   *Birmingham Citizens Permanent Building Society v Caunt* [1962] Ch 883 at 890 per Russell J.

Implied exclusion

15.115   The mortgagee's right to possession may also be excluded by implication from the terms and attendant circumstances of the mortgage transaction.

Instalment mortgages

15.116   In *Esso Petroleum Co Ltd v Alstonbridge Properties Ltd*[1] Walton J accepted that the court will be particularly ready to find in an instalment mortgage an implied term that the mortgagor is entitled to remain in possession against the mortgagee unless he makes some default in the payment of the instalments. Walton J added, however, that 'there must be something upon which to hang such a conclusion in the mortgage other than the mere fact that it is an instalment mortgage.'[2]

1   [1975] 1 WLR 1474.

2   [1975] 1 WLR 1474 at 1484B. See also *Western Bank Ltd v Schindler* [1977] Ch 1 at 10C–D per Buckley LJ (instalment mortgage made it easier, but not decisively so, to imply a term inhibiting arbitrary repossession by the mortgagee).

Other mortgages

15.117   In relation to mortgages other than instalment mortgages the courts have proved somewhat more reluctant to find that the right to possession has been impliedly reserved to the mortgagor.[1] In *Western Bank Ltd v Schindler*[2] the defendant mortgagor had borrowed £32,000 on the terms of an endowment mortgage which provided that no payment of capital or interest was contractually due until ten years after the date of execution of the mortgage. Notwithstanding the absence of any financial default by the mortgagor, the mortgagee successfully asserted a right to possession, *within* the ten year period, in order to preserve the value of the security.[3] The Court of Appeal thought that the mortgagee's right to possession was not lightly to be held to have been excluded by implication, since only this right could effectively protect the mortgagee's legitimate interest in ensuring that at the redemption date the premises would still represent a good security for a substantial debt of capital and interest. As Scarman LJ pointed out, the only way in which the mortgagee could ultimately guarantee that the property was properly managed and maintained, and the value of the security preserved throughout the loan term, was if the court upheld the mortgagee's claim to possession in the absence of a clear contractual exclusion of that right.[4]

1   See R J Smith, [1979] Conv 266.
2   [1977] Ch 1.
3   [1977] Ch 1 at 16A, 19G, 26F.
4   'So far from implying a term excluding the common law right, I would expect, as a matter of business efficacy, that the mortgagee would in these circumstances require its retention' ([1977] Ch 1 at 17F).

Attornment clauses

15.118   An 'attornment clause', if inserted in a mortgage deed, provides an unusual means of excluding the mortgagee's right to possession. It was once a common practice to insert in deeds of mortgage an attornment clause which had the result of creating a nominal landlord–tenant relationship between the parties to the mortgage.[1] Under an attornment clause the mortgagor holds effectively as a tenant of the mortgagee, the object of the clause being to make available to the mortgagee the additional possessory remedies open to a landlord.[2] There is, however, one respect in which the inclusion of an attornment clause significantly qualifies the mortgagee's right to enter into possession. Precisely because a notional tenancy is created between mortgagor and mortgagee, the latter is required to terminate the tenancy by serving a notice to quit as a necessary preliminary to any exercise of the right to possession.[3] The attornment clause does not, however, confer on the residential mortgagor any of the more specific forms of protection afforded tenants under housing legislation.[4]

1   The rent payable under the tenancy was often a purely nominal rent such as the 2½p stipulated for in *Peckham Mutual Building Society v Registe* (1981) 42 P & CR 186.
2   Historically the attornment clause was used to afford the mortgagee access to the right to levy

distress **[para 14.193]** upon goods and chattels on the mortgaged premises and also to a speedier procedure for the recovery of possession (*Bruton v London & Quadrant Housing Trust* [2000] 1 AC 406 at 416B–C per Lord Hoffmann). See also *Re Tuxedo Savings & Credit Union Ltd and Krusky* (1987) 35 DLR (4th) 211 at 215.

3   *Hinckley and Country Building Society v Henny* [1953] 1 WLR 352 at 355.

4   For example, the mortgagor is not entitled to the minimum period of four weeks' notice to quit generally applicable to residential lettings (*Peckham Mutual Building Society v Registe* (1981) 42 P & CR 186 at 188–189; *Alliance Building Society v Pinwill* [1958] Ch 788 at 792).

No exclusion by reason of mere counterclaim or cross-claim

15.119 The generally paramount quality of the legal mortgagee's right to possession is illustrated by the fact that the mortgagor cannot normally resist an action for possession by claiming an equitable set-off against the mortgagee for an unliquidated sum.[1] This proposition – the so-called '*Mobil Oil* principle'[2] – is often justified on the basis that otherwise the mere allegation of some connected, but perhaps groundless, cross-claim by a mortgagor would have the effect of keeping the mortgagee out of his 'undoubted prima facie right to possession.'[3] Contract and statute apart, the legal mortgagee's right to possession cannot be defeated by a cross-claim on the part of the mortgagor even if it is admitted and for a sum which exceeds the mortgage debt.[4] Under the *Mobil Oil* principle, moreover, it is irrelevant whether the mortgagor is himself the principal debtor of the mortgagee or merely a guarantor of some third party's debt (eg where the mortgagor guarantees the debt of his own trading company).[5] In the latter instance, although the law is undoubted, it has been said to be 'an arresting concept' that a mortgagor could be required to give up possession of his home despite the existence of an unliquidated claim, which is admitted or shown to be likely to succeed, in an amount which either exceeds the sum due from the principal debtor or, when established, enables the debt to be paid in full.[6]

1   In *National Westminster Bank Plc v Skelton (Note)* [1993] 1 WLR 72 at 78C, the Court of Appeal left open the question whether the mortgagee's right to possession is excluded where a mortgagor establishes that he has a claim to a quantified sum by way of equitable set-off.

2   See *Mobil Oil Co Ltd v Rawlinson* (1982) 43 P & CR 221 at 226–227 per Nourse J; *National Westminster Bank Plc v Skelton (Note)* [1993] 1 WLR 72 at 78B per Slade LJ.

3   See *National Westminster Bank Plc v Skelton (Note)* [1993] 1 WLR 72 at 78A–B per Slade LJ.

4   See also *Samuel Keller (Holdings) Ltd v Martins Bank Ltd* [1971] 1 WLR 43 at 47H–48B, 51C–D; *Citibank Trust Ltd v Ayivor* [1987] 1 WLR 1157 at 1161C, 1164A; *Ashley Guarantee Plc v Zacaria* [1993] 1 WLR 62 at 66C–D per Nourse LJ; *National Westminster Bank Plc v Skelton (Note)* [1993] 1 WLR 72 at 77H–78A per Slade LJ.

5   See *National Westminster Bank Plc v Skelton (Note)* [1993] 1 WLR 72 at 78F per Slade LJ; *Ashley Guarantee Plc v Zacaria* [1993] 1 WLR 62 at 69A–B per Nourse LJ.

6   See *Ashley Guarantee Plc v Zacaria* [1993] 1 WLR 62 at 70G–71B per Ralph Gibson LJ, who thought that such circumstances might give rise either to an implied term excluding the mortgagee's immediate right to possession or to a stay under Administration of Justice Act 1970, s 36 **[para 15.154]**, pending trial of the claim to the set-off (see also Woolf LJ at 71C–D, but compare *National Westminster Bank Plc v Skelton (Note)* [1993] 1 WLR 72 at 82B–C per Anthony Lincoln J).

Factors inhibiting actual exercise of the mortgagee's right

15.120   The mortgagee's paramount right to possession has survived in its unqualified form only because a number of factors combine to make it unattractive for a mortgagee to go into possession except in cases of mortgage default (where the recovery of possession is invariably a precursor to the exercise of the mortgagee's power of sale).[1] The principal object of most mortgages is that the mortgagor should remain in possession of the land which forms the subject matter of the security. Large institutional lenders have no interest in physical occupation of mortgaged premises; their real concern is that their borrowers should occupy these premises and discharge their financial obligations to the lenders (and indirectly to the millions of investors who deposit money with such lenders).[2] Indeed, it is not going too far to say that, apart perhaps from the exceptional circumstances typified in *Western Bank Ltd v Schindler*,[3] a mortgagee will never nowadays seek possession unless a default has already occurred. Several factors have conduced to this result.

1   [**Para 15.141**].
2   See *Four-Maids Ltd v Dudley Marshall* (*Properties*) *Ltd* [1957] Ch 317 at 321 per Harman J.
3   [1977] Ch 1 [**para 15.117**].

Mortgagee's strict liability to account

15.121   A mortgagee who goes into possession of the mortgaged property becomes subject to the particularly stringent control of equity in his dealings with the land.[1] If, while in possession, he intercepts the rents and profits drawn from the land[2] in order to ensure the payments due to him under the mortgage, he is liable to account strictly to the mortgagor for any income which he thus receives.[3] Furthermore, the mortgagee may not derive any profit other than the return of the principal and interest stipulated for in the terms of the mortgage.[4]

1   *Robertson v Norris* (1859) 1 Giff 428 at 436, 65 ER 986 at 989.
2   Even in the absence of actual occupation, a mortgagee is treated as having assumed possession if he receives rents and profits in such a manner as to displace the mortgagor from 'the control and dominion' of the land (*Noyes v Pollock* (1885) 32 Ch D 53 at 64 per Bowen LJ). See also *Elders Rural Finance Ltd v Westpac Banking Corporation* (1990) 5 BPR 11790 at 11792–11793.
3   *Lord Trimleston v Hamill* (1810) 1 Ball & B 377 at 385.
4   For instance, a mortgagee in possession may not (even by an express mortgage term) impose any charge for his management of the land, since this would be to usurp the function of a receiver (*Comyns v Comyns* (1871) 5 IR Eq 583 at 587–588).

Liability for 'wilful default'

15.122   The mortgagee's duties are rendered even more onerous by the fact that he is liable on the footing of 'wilful default'.[1] The mortgagee in possession immediately becomes responsible for the physical state of the premises.[2] As Nicholls V-C observed in *Palk v Mortgage Services Funding Plc*,[3] he must 'take reasonable care of the property.'[4] Furthermore the mortgagee cannot simply leave the property empty, perhaps waiting for an improvement in the market, but must let the premises at a 'proper market rent'.[5] He must account to the mortgagor not only in respect of any rents and profits actually received, but also in respect of that income which he would have received if he had managed the property with due diligence.[6] Thus in *White v City of London Brewery Co*[7] a mortgagee who entered into possession and let the mortgaged property as a 'tied' public house (for the benefit of his own brewery business) was held liable to account for the greater rents which he would have received had he let the property as a 'free' house.[8] If the mortgagee himself goes into personal occupation of the property, he is chargeable with the best occupation rent obtainable on the open market in respect of those premises.[9] If the mortgagee takes over possession of an uncompleted building, he must act bona fide and as a provident owner, and must either sell the property or make a genuine effort to complete the building in a proper and economical way.[10]

1   *Downsview Nominees Ltd v First City Corpn Ltd* [1993] AC 295 at 315A–B per Lord Templeman. See *Lord Trimleston v Hamill* (1810) 1 Ball & B 377 at 385; *Sloane v Mahon* (1838) 1 Dr & Wal 189 at 192, 195; *Mobil Oil Co Ltd v Rawlinson* (1982) 43 P & CR 221 at 224; *Medforth v Blake* [2000] Ch 86 at 99B. See also *Kennedy v General Credits Ltd* (1982) 2 BPR 9456 at 9457–9458 per Hope JA (NSW Court of Appeal).
2   See e g *Sterne v Victoria & Grey Trust Co* (1985) 14 DLR (4th) 193 at 203 (liability for negligently caused damage from frozen pipes).
3   [1993] Ch 330 at 338A.
4   In effect the mortgagee 'becomes the manager of the charged property' (*Silven Properties Ltd v Royal Bank of Scotland Plc* [2004] 1 WLR 997 at [13] per Lightman J).
5   [1993] Ch 330 at 338C–D per Nicholls V-C. See likewise *Silven Properties Ltd v Royal Bank of Scotland Plc* [2004] 1 WLR 997 at [13] per Lightman J.
6   See *Chaplin v Young (No 1)* (1864) 33 Beav 330 at 337–338, 55 ER 395 at 398; *Noyes v Pollock* (1885) 32 Ch D 53 at 61; *Elders Rural Finance Ltd v Westpac Banking Corporation* (1990) 5 BPR 11790 at 11793.
7   (1889) 42 Ch D 237 at 245 per Lord Esher MR, 249 per Fry LJ.
8   Similarly, a mortgagee in possession is liable to account for the notional rent of property which he has allowed to remain unoccupied (*Lavin v Johnson* [2002] EWCA Civ 1138 at [111]–[113]) and for due rent which he has failed without good cause to recover from his tenants (*Noyes v Pollock* (1885) 32 Ch D 53 at 61).
9   *Metcalf v Campion* (1828) 1 Mol 238 at 239; *Marriott v Anchor Reversionary Co* (1861) 3 De GF & J 177 at 193, 45 ER 846 at 852. If, however, there is no realistic evidence that the property could have been let out profitably, this rental value may be nil, in which case the mortgagee is not guilty of wilful default (see e g *Fyfe v Smith* [1975] 2 NSWLR 408 at 413F–414A).
10   *Penny v Walker* (1855) 24 LJ Ch 319 at 320–321; *Midland Credit Ltd v Hallad Pty Ltd* (1977) 1 BPR 9570 at 9577–9578 per Hutley JA.

Preference for the appointment of a receiver

15.123   The net result of these stringent rules is that if the mortgagee's primary concern is with the income derived from the mortgaged land, his objectives are in general much better served through the exercise of his statutory power to appoint a receiver[1] than by entry into possession subject to the strict control of equity. The handling of rents and profits by a receiver is not subject to quite the same rigorous surveillance.[2]

1   LPA 1925, s 101(1)(iii) [**para 15.137**].

2   See *Refuge Assurance Co Ltd v Pearlberg* [1938] Ch 687 at 691–692; *Yorkshire Bank Plc v Hall* [1999] 1 WLR 1713 at 1728E per Robert Walker LJ.

Risk of criminal liability

15.124   The mortgagee who exercises a right of physical entry upon mortgaged property may run the risk of criminal liability under the Criminal Law Act 1977. It is an offence for any person without lawful authority to use or to threaten violence for the purpose of securing entry into any premises if, to his knowledge, there is someone present on those premises who is opposed to his entry.[1]

1   Criminal Law Act 1977, s 6(1) [**para 14.120**]. See also Protection from Eviction Act 1977, s 1 [**para 14.111**].

Tacit agreement to allow exclusive possession to the mortgagor

15.125   It is extremely rare in practice for a mortgagee to exercise his right to go into possession while the mortgagor is acting in full compliance with the mortgage terms. There is in general a 'tacit agreement' between mortgagor and mortgagee that possession should be exercised de facto by the mortgagor in all cases except those of actual default.[1] While this tacit consent continues to operate, the mortgagor's possessory status has been described as effectively that of a tenant at sufferance.[2] He is, however, under no duty to account for any rents and profits derived from the land[3] and is liable for waste only if the land ceases by reason of his waste to constitute an adequate security for the mortgage debt.[4] But it should never be forgotten that, although it generally lies dormant, the mortgagee's right to possession is a virtually unqualified entitlement which ultimately provides the platform for a mortgagee's sale with vacant possession in the event of default or otherwise ensures that the property is correctly managed and the value of the security preserved throughout the loan term.

1   See *Moss v Gallimore* (1779) 1 Doug 279 at 283, 99 ER 182 at 184; *Christophers v Sparke* (1820) 2 Jac & W 223 at 235, 37 ER 612 at 617.

2   See *Green v Burns* (1879) 6 LR Ir 173 at 176 per Palles CB; *Fairclough v Marshall* (1878) 4 Ex D 37 at 48; *Heath v Pugh* (1881) 6 QBD 345 at 359 per Lord Selborne LC; *Common Luck Investment Ltd v Cheung Siu Ming* [1999] 2 HKC 719 at 725 (HKSAR Final Court of Appeal).

3   *Campion v Palmer* [1896] 2 IR 445 at 455–456; *Rhodes v Allied Dunbar Pension Services Ltd* [1989] 1 WLR 800 at 807E per Nicholls LJ.

4   *King v Smith* (1843) 2 Hare 239 at 243–244, 67 ER 99 at 101–102; *Harper v Aplin* (1886) 54 LT 383 at 384.

Does the equitable mortgagee have a right to possession?

15.126   Considerable doubt surrounds the question whether an equitable mortgagee or equitable chargee has an inherent right to possession similar to that enjoyed by the legal mortgagee.[1] The latter's right to possession is an incident of an actual or notional legal estate[2] and it therefore seems unlikely that, in the absence of some express conferment by the terms of the mortgage or a court order, a right of possession can be claimed by a mere equitable mortgagee or chargee.[3]

1 For an argument that the equitable mortgagee is entitled to possession, see H W R Wade, (1955) 71 LQR 204 at 207.
2 **[Para 15.110]**.
3 See *Barclays Bank Ltd v Bird* [1954] Ch 274 at 280; *Royal Bank of Canada v Nicholson* (1980) 110 DLR (3d) 763 at 765–766; *Zanzoul v Westpac Banking Corp* (1995) 6 BPR 14142 at 14145. The absence of a right to possession carries the further implication that the equitable mortgagee has no inherent right to receive the rents and profits derived from the land (*Finck v Tranter* [1905] 1 KB 427 at 429; *Vacuum Oil Co Ltd v Ellis* [1914] 1 KB 693 at 703, 708).

15.127 It is sometimes suggested that the doctrine in *Walsh v Lonsdale*,[1] by drawing an analogy between legal and equitable rights, has the indirect effect of conferring a right of possession on the equitable mortgagee.[2] Although this end result would represent an entirely sensible extension of the common law position, judicial authority has tended to reinforce the orthodox view that the equitable mortgagee cannot claim possession as of right.[3] It is clear, however, that even if the equitable mortgagee or chargee has no automatic right of possession, either may apply to the court for an order putting him into possession.[4]

1 **[Para 9.66]**.
2 See *General Finance, Mortgage, and Discount Co v Liberator Benefit Building Society* (1879) 10 Ch D 15 at 24 per Jessel MR; *Antrim County Land, Building, and Investment Co Ltd v Stewart* [1904] 2 IR 357 at 364 per Palles CB; *Mills v Lewis* (1985) 3 BPR 9421 at 9431.1 per Priestley JA.
3 See e g *Ladup Ltd v Williams & Glyn's Bank Plc* [1985] 1 WLR 851 at 855B per Warner J; *Ashley Guarantee Plc v Zacaria* [1993] 1 WLR 62 at 69H per Nourse LJ.
4 The court has power under LPA 1925, s 90(1) to vest a legal estate in the mortgagee sufficient to enable him to assume possession (see *Ladup Ltd v Williams & Glyn's Bank Plc* [1985] 1 WLR 851 at 855B–C). The court also has an inherent jurisdiction to put an equitable mortgagee in possession (see *Re O'Neill* [1967] NI 129 at 135), not least where the mortgage contains an express covenant for entry by the mortgagee in the case of default and the court is willing to grant specific performance of the covenant (see e g *Mills v Lewis* (1985) 3 BPR 9421 at 9431.2 per Priestley JA).

REMEDIES AVAILABLE TO THE LEGAL MORTGAGEE

15.128 In the event of default under a legal mortgage the mortgagee has available a number of remedies which operate directly against the mortgagor.[1] These remedies include:

– action on the mortgagor's personal covenant to repay[2]
– appointment of a receiver[3]
– assertion of the mortgagee's right to possession[4]
– exercise of the mortgagee's power of sale[5] and
– foreclosure.[6]

1 The mortgagee may also have remedies against third parties. If, for instance, the mortgagor of

a leasehold term causes his lease to become forfeit by reason of default, the mortgagee has access to the inherent equitable jurisdiction of the court to grant relief against forfeiture [**para 14.187**].

2   [**Paras 15.133–15.136**].
3   [**Paras 15.137–15.140**].
4   [**Paras 15.141–15.170**].
5   [**Paras 15.171–15.221**].
6   [**Paras 15.222–15.229**].

Constraints of fairness

15.129   The remedies open to the mortgagee are, in general, concurrent and cumulative.[1] The mortgagor has no right to insist that the mortgagee pursue one particular remedy rather than another.[2] Nor is it necessarily an abuse of process that a mortgagee, when met with a defence in respect of one kind of remedy, should elect to have recourse to a different form of remedy.[3] It is increasingly clear, however, that in the exercise of his remedies a mortgagee 'does owe some duties to a mortgagor.'[4] The courts do not find attractive the proposition that the mortgagee may act in a 'cavalier fashion', not least since many mortgagees nowadays carry indemnity insurance against the possibility that the mortgagor may prove unable to discharge his debt in full. Without doubt, as Nicholls V-C pointed out in *Palk v Mortgage Services Funding Plc*,[5] there is 'a legal framework which imposes constraints of fairness on a mortgagee who is exercising his remedies over his security.'[6] It is improbable that a mortgagee remains free, either at law or in equity, 'to exercise his rights in a way that in all likelihood will substantially increase the burden on a borrower or guarantor beyond what otherwise would be the case.'[7]

1   The courts are also slow to imply in an individual voluntary arrangement under the Insolvency Act 1986 any agreement by a mortgagee to abandon his security in respect of the mortgage debt (*Whitehead v Household Mortgage Corpn* [2003] 1 WLR 1173 at [24]–[27]).
2   *Cheah v Equiticorp Finance Group Ltd* [1992] 1 AC 472 at 476F per Lord Browne-Wilkinson.
3   *Alliance and Leicester plc v Slayford* [2001] 1 All ER (Comm) 1 at [20]–[28] per Peter Gibson LJ; All ER Rev 2001, p 257 (P J Clarke); [2002] Conv 53 (M P Thompson) [**para 11.251**]. See also *Wilkinson v West Bromwich Building Society* [2004] EWCA Civ 1063 at [50] per Mummery LJ.
4   *Palk v Mortgage Services Funding Plc* [1993] Ch 330 at 337G per Nicholls V-C.
5   [1993] Ch 330 at 338F–G.
6   See also *Medforth v Blake* [2000] Ch 86 at H-102A per Scott V-C.
7   *Lloyds Bank plc v Cassidy* [2002] EWCA Civ 1427 at [42] per Mance LJ.

The Financial Services and Markets Act 2000

15.130   The responsibilities resting on mortgagees are now reinforced by the Financial Services and Markets Act 2000.[1] This Act institutes a regime which requires mortgage lenders and administrators to 'pay due regard to the interests of customers' under a regulated mortgage contract and to treat these customers 'fairly'.[2] In particular lenders and administrators must deal 'fairly' with any customer who is in arrears on a regulated mortgage contract or has a 'mortgage shortfall debt'.[3]

1   **[Para 15.57]**.

2   *FSA Handbook* (Release 033, July 2004): MCOB 13.2.1G (except where the customer entered into the regulated mortgage contract 'with no intention of meeting his payment obligations' (MCOB 13.2.2G)).

3   Pressure must not be put on a customer through 'excessive telephone calls or correspondence, or by contact at an unreasonable hour' (eg between 9.00pm and 8.00am) (*FSA Handbook* (Release 033, July 2004): MCOB 13.5.3R). Firms which outsource aspects of customer relationships (eg debt collection) remain responsible for the way in which this work is done (MCOB 13.3.8G).

Written policy and procedures

15.131   Every firm burdened by this obligation of fairness must put in place (and operate in accordance with) a 'written policy and procedures' for complying with the objective of fair dealing.[1] This requirement is intended to ensure that firms have addressed the need for 'internal systems to deal fairly with any customer in financial difficulties.'[2] The written policy and procedures should indicate that the eviction of the mortgagor from his home is a last resort, repossession being appropriate 'only where all other reasonable attempts to resolve the position have failed.'[3] It should be the aim of the mortgagee to use 'reasonable efforts' to agree with the mortgagor, as 'an alternative to taking possession of the property', some method of repaying any payment shortfall or mortgage shortfall debt.[4] This may involve an extension of the mortgage term, a switch to a different type of mortgage or a deferment (or possibly a capitalisation) of payments in arrear.[5] The mortgagor should also be given adequate information to understand any proposed restructuring of his obligations.[6]

1   *FSA Handbook* (Release 033, July 2004): MCOB 13.3.1R. Customers can, but need not, be provided with a copy of the 'written policy and procedures' (MCOB 13.3.3G).

2   *FSA Handbook* (Release 033, July 2004): MCOB 13.3.3G.

3   *FSA Handbook* (Release 033, July 2004): MCOB 13.3.2E(1)(f).

4   *FSA Handbook* (Release 033, July 2004): MCOB 13.3.2E(1)(a). Mortgage lenders and administrators are obliged, within 15 business days of becoming aware of a customer's arrears, to supply to that customer details of his default and its cost implications (MCOB 13.4.1R). The customer must then be advised (by at least quarterly written statements) of payments due, the actual payment shortfall, charges incurred and the current overall debt (MCOB 13.5.1R).

5   *FSA Handbook* (Release 033, July 2004): MCOB 13.3.4G(1), 13.3.5G.

6   *FSA Handbook* (Release 033, July 2004): MCOB 13.3.4G(2).

Effect of contravention

15.132   Failure to formulate an appropriate 'written policy and procedures' has evidential significance in that it generates a rebuttable presumption that the mortgage lender or administrator has not dealt 'fairly' with the customer.[1]

1   *FSA Handbook* (Release 033, July 2004): MCOB 13.3.2E(2).

ACTION ON THE MORTGAGOR'S PERSONAL COVENANT TO REPAY

15.133   Since the mortgage transaction is ultimately founded on a contract of loan, the mortgagee has a contractual right to sue the mortgagor on his personal covenant to repay the entire mortgage advance and the accrued interest thereon.[1] This covenant is either an express term of the mortgage agreement or (less usually) an obligation arising presumptively from the mere fact that the mortgagor has accepted the loan.[2]

1   The mortgagee cannot take action on the mortgagor's covenant before the legal redemption date stipulated by the mortgage (*Bolton v Buckenham* [1891] 1 QB 278 at 281–282; *Sinton v Dooley* [1910] 2 IR 162 at 165).

2   *Sutton v Sutton* (1882) 22 Ch D 511 at 515–516 per Jessel MR, 520 per Bowen LJ. This obligation can be implied even in the absence of any express covenant by the mortgagor to repay the whole of the outstanding balance of the loan on a specified date or in a specified event such as default in the payment of instalments (*Wilkinson v West Bromwich Building Society* [2004] EWCA Civ 1063 at [43]–[44] per Mummery LJ).

Effect of mortgagee's exercise of the power of sale

15.134   In cases of serious default the mortgagee may, of course, lean more naturally towards sale of the land and recovery of the mortgage debt from the proceeds.[1] The mere entry of judgment on a claim for possession by the mortgagee in no way releases the mortgagor from further liability on his personal covenant to repay.[2] Even after exercising his power of sale, the mortgagee may still sue on the mortgagor's covenant if the sale does not cover the total mortgage debt.[3] The mortgagor's liability for any shortfall is not diminished in the absence of 'equitable delinquency' in the mortgagee's exercise of the power of sale.[4] However, in suing on a personal covenant for any deficit which remains after the exercise of the power of sale, the mortgagee has no rights superior to those of any other creditor.[5]

1   In practice most institutional lenders are reluctant to increase the (perhaps temporary) financial difficulties of hard-pressed borrowers by suing on the personal covenant for repayment. The remedy of sale is always available if these difficulties cannot be resolved within a reasonable period.

2   *UCB Bank plc v Chandler* (1999) 79 P & CR 270 at 274 per Evans LJ. If, however, a mortgagee, having obtained a money judgment based on the mortgagor's personal covenant, elects to abandon his security and bring bankruptcy proceedings, he cannot thereafter exercise remedies as a secured creditor (*Alliance and Leicester plc v Slayford* [2001] 1 All ER (Comm) 1 at [20] per Peter Gibson LJ).

3   *Rudge v Richens* (1873) LR 8 CP 358 at 361–362; *Gordon Grant & Co Ltd v F L Boos* [1926] AC 781 at 786–787; *Bristol and West plc v Bartlett* [2003] 1 WLR 284 at [3], [17]–[18] per Longmore LJ. In the case of a regulated mortgage contract entered into on or after 31 October 2004, the mortgagee must inform the customer of the 'mortgage shortfall debt' as soon as possible after the sale of the repossessed premises (*FSA Handbook* (Release 033, July 2004): MCOB 13.6.3R(1)).

4   *Scandinavian Pacific Ltd v Burke* (1991) 5 BPR 11846 at 11848–11849 (sale at a gross undervalue). Any claim which the mortgagor may have in respect of a negligently achieved undervalue may be raised as an equitable set-off to any subsisting debt alleged by the mortgagee in a subsequent bankruptcy petition (*Platts v TSB Bank Plc* (1998) Times, 4 March).

5   The mortgagee has 'expended the advantage he had as a secured creditor' and now stands as an unsecured creditor for any balance (see *Scandinavian Pacific Ltd v Burke* (1991) 5 BPR 11846 at 11848, 11851 per Cole J).

Voluntary surrender of mortgaged premises

15.135   Still less is the mortgagor's personal liability terminated by a voluntary surrender of possession to the mortgagee. Contrary to popular mythology, the mortgagor gains no relief from this liability merely because he throws the keys of the premises back at his bank or building society. His indebtedness continues to grow apace unless and until the money owed is fully repaid. The mortgagee is, however, entitled only to simple interest upon any interest left in arrears, unless the mortgage contained an agreement (either expressly or by necessary implication) for the payment of compound interest.[1]

1   *Ex parte Bevan* (1803) 9 Ves 223 at 224, 32 ER 588; *Fergusson v Fyffe* (1841) 8 Cl & F 121 at 141, 8 ER 49 at 57; *Daniell v Sinclair* (1881) 6 App Cas 181 at 189–190; *Domaschenz v Standfield Properties Pty Ltd* (1977) 17 SASR 56 at 61. See *C J Belmore Pty Ltd v AGC (General Finance) Ltd* [1976] 1 NSWLR 507 at 509E–G; *Merlin (Sydney) Pty Ltd v Fintoray Finance Pty Ltd* (1990) 5 BPR 11648 at 116 (express stipulation for compound interest not void as penalty).

Limitation periods

15.136   The recovery of arrears of interest is statute-barred six years after becoming due[1] and the recovery of the mortgage principal is statute-barred after the expiration of twelve years from the date when the right to receive that money accrued.[2] These limitation periods apply even where, before issuing proceedings on the personal covenant, the mortgagee has already exercised his power of sale.[3] In relation, however, to 'regulated mortgage contracts', the Financial Services and Markets Act 2000 has now indirectly reduced the limitation period relevant to the recovery of mortgage principal. The *FSA Handbook* (*Mortgages: Conduct of Business*) requires that the mortgagee must notify the mortgagor within six years of any intention to recover a mortgage shortfall debt.[4]

1   Limitation Act 1980, s 20(5).
2   Limitation Act 1980, s 20(1). The cause of action in respect of the capital debt and interest arises, either expressly or impliedly, on the mortgagor's default in the payment of mortgage instalments and not at some later date when the exercise of the mortgagee's power of sale reveals a calculable shortfall (*Wilkinson v West Bromwich Building Society* [2004] EWCA Civ 1063 at [48]–[50] per Mummery LJ).
3   *Bristol and West plc v Bartlett* [2003] 1 WLR 284 at [35] per Longmore LJ.
4   *FSA Handbook* (Release 033, July 2004): MCOB 13.6.4R(1)–(2).

APPOINTMENT OF A RECEIVER

15.137   The option of appointing a receiver provides the mortgagee with a further remedy for default by his mortgagor.

Preconditions for appointment

15.138 The mortgagee has a statutory power to appoint in writing such person as he thinks fit to act as a receiver in respect of the mortgaged property.[1] This power becomes available in the same circumstances and on the same conditions as those which cause the statutory power of sale to arise and to become exercisable.[2] A receiver cannot therefore be appointed in advance of a legal redemption date stipulated by the mortgage,[3] but appointment is not precluded by the fact that a mortgagee has gone into possession.[4] The receiver is deemed by statute to be the agent of the *mortgagor*.[5] It follows therefore that, unless the mortgage deed otherwise provides, the mortgagor becomes solely liable for any acts or defaults of the receiver even though he has had no hand in his appointment.[6] The mortgagee is not responsible for what the receiver does whilst he is the mortgagor's agent unless the mortgagee directs or interferes with the receiver's activities.[7] But the fact that the receiver functions as the agent of the mortgagor does not, in view of the 'special nature of the agency', preclude the receiver owing a fiduciary duty to both mortgagor and mortgagee.[8]

1 LPA 1925, ss 101(1)(iii), 109(1). A mortgagee has no implied duty to 'act reasonably in an objective sense' in appointing a receiver (*Paul Kennedy Transport Pty Ltd v ANZ Banking Group Ltd* (1993) 6 BPR 13883 at 13887 per Young J).

2 LPA 1925, s 109(1). In registered land the mortgagee must first be registered as the proprietor of a charge over the property (see *Lever Finance Ltd v L N & H M Needleman's Trustee* [1956] Ch 375 at 382).

3 *Twentieth Century Banking Corpn Ltd v Wilkinson* [1977] Ch 99 at 104D.

4 *Refuge Assurance Co Ltd v Pearlberg* [1938] Ch 687 at 693.

5 LPA 1925, s 109(2). The receiver's deemed agency is necessarily terminated by the winding up of a company mortgagor (*Gosling v Gaskell* [1897] AC 575 at 581, 585, 591–592; *Thomas v Todd* [1926] 2 KB 511 at 516–517). In this event, however, the receiver may be able to continue the mortgagor's business on the basis that the mortgagee has entered into possession and given authority to the receiver to act as agent for the *mortgagee* (see *Mercantile Credits Ltd v Atkins* (1985) 1 NSWLR 670 at 679C).

6 LPA 1925, s 109(2). See e g *White v Metcalf* [1903] 2 Ch 567 at 570–572.

7 *American Express International Banking Corp v Hurley* [1985] 3 All ER 564 at 571g.

8 *Silven Properties Ltd v Royal Bank of Scotland Plc* [2004] 1 WLR 997 at [29] per Lightman J.

Functions of the receiver

15.139 The appointment of a receiver may be particularly useful if the mortgagee does not presently wish to realise his security or otherwise undertake the responsibility of going into possession of the mortgaged property.[1] It is the role of the receiver to be active in the protection and preservation of the mortgaged premises.[2] Although managing the security for the benefit of the mortgagee, he owes a fiduciary duty of care to mortgagee, mortgagor and all others interested in the equity of redemption.[3] However, his primary duty in the exercise of his powers of management is to try to bring about a situation in which interest on the secured debt (and ultimately the debt itself) can be paid.[4] The role of the receiver is, accordingly, to collect all the income derived from the mortgaged land and to ensure that from that income there is payment of all sums due by way of rents, rates, taxes, his own commission, insurance premiums, repairs and, of course, interest owed under the mortgage.[5] Any surplus income is payable to the person, usually the mortgagor, who would otherwise have been entitled to the rents and profits of the land.[6] The receiver is also entitled, and sometimes obliged,[7] to exercise a power of sale in the name of the mortgagor.

1   See *Visbord v Federal Commissioner of Taxation* (1943) 68 CLR 354 at 381.
2   *Silven Properties Ltd v Royal Bank of Scotland Plc* [2004] 1 WLR 997 at [23] per Lightman J.
3   *Silven Properties Ltd v Royal Bank of Scotland Plc* [2004] 1 WLR 997 at [27], [29] per Lightman J.
4   *Medforth v Blake* [2000] Ch 86 at 102F–G per Scott V-C; *Silven Properties Ltd v Royal Bank of Scotland Plc* [2004] 1 WLR 997 at [27]–[28] per Lightman J. The receiver's power to manage is not necessarily ancillary to the power of sale, although in many cases it is the function of the receiver to bring the mortgaged property to a state in which a business can be sold as a going concern (*Medforth*, supra at 103A–B).
5   LPA 1925, s 109(8). See *Marshall v Cottingham* [1982] Ch 82.
6   LPA 1925, s 109(8).
7   The receiver's duties of management may sometimes include a duty to sell, e g where a failure to do so would cause loss to both mortgagee and mortgagor (*Silven Properties Ltd v Royal Bank of Scotland Plc* [2004] 1 WLR 997 at [23], [28] per Lightman J).

Standard of duty expected of the receiver

15.140   In *Medforth v Blake*[1] the Court of Appeal significantly clarified the standard of duty expected of the receiver in the management of mortgaged land (and particularly of any business conducted thereon). Scott V-C held that the receiver owes duties to the mortgagor and to anyone else who has an interest in the equity of redemption.[2] These duties are imposed by equity (rather than by the law of tort)[3] and include, but are not necessarily confined to, a duty of good faith.[4] The receiver is not obliged to continue to carry on any business previously conducted by the mortgagor on the mortgaged premises.[5] But if the receiver does decide to carry on the business, he owes a duty to manage the property with 'due diligence'. He must conduct the business with 'reasonable competence',[6] taking 'reasonable steps' to run the business profitably.[7] The receiver can therefore be made liable to the mortgagor (and others) for feats of managerial incompetence which contribute towards the ruination of the commercial enterprise involved.[8] Moreover, if the receiver sells the mortgaged land, he is (like the mortgagee[9]) subject to a non-delegable duty to take reasonable steps to sell at the best price reasonably obtainable.[10] In this respect his level of duty is exactly equivalent to that which binds the selling mortgagee.[11] In particular, as the Court of Appeal confirmed in *Silven Properties Ltd v Royal Bank of Scotland Plc*,[12] the receiver is under no obligation to undertake pre-marketing steps which would improve the value of the security or realise its full potential, but is entitled to sell the property in the condition in which it stands. There is no duty to spend money in order to make the property more attractive or commerciable.

1   [2000] Ch 86 at 102F–H. See (2000) 63 MLR 413 (S Frisby); [2000] CLJ 31 (L S Sealy).
2   See likewise *Raja v Austin Gray (A Firm)* [2003] 1 EGLR 91 at [23], [28] per Clarke LJ; *Silven Properties Ltd v Royal Bank of Scotland Plc* [2004] 1 WLR 997 at [22] per Lightman J.

3   [2000] Ch 86 at 97B–C, 98C, 102D–E (although Scott V-C thought that it matters not 'one jot' whether the receiver's duty is expressed as a common law duty or as a duty in equity ('[t]he result is the same')). See also *Downsview Nominees Ltd v First City Corpn Ltd* [1993] AC 295 at 315A–E, 316D–F per Lord Templeman.

4   The receiver's duties are comparable with, but may not be exactly the same as, the 'particularly onerous duties constructed by courts of equity for mortgagees in possession' ([2000] Ch 86 at 99B per Scott V-C [**para 15.121**]). The receiver's duties are 'not inflexible' and their proper discharge depends on 'the particular facts of the particular case' ([2000] Ch 86 at 102A).

5   [2000] Ch 86 at 93B–C. The receiver may decide to close the business down, having regard to the interests of the mortgagee in obtaining repayment of the secured debt. 'Provided he acts in good faith, he is entitled to sacrifice the interests of the mortgagor in pursuit of that end' ([2000] Ch 86 at 93C).

6   [2000] Ch 86 at 93C.

7   [2000] Ch 86 at 102G–H.

8   [2000] Ch 86 at 93D–F. In *Medforth v Blake* it was alleged that the receiver, in managing the mortgagor's pig-farming business, had failed to obtain freely available discounts from the suppliers of pig-feed. See also *Knight v Lawrence* [1993] BCLC 215 at 224b (receiver liable to mortgagor for failing to activate rent review procedures).

9   [**Paras 15.181–15.198**].

10   *Raja v Austin Gray* (*A Firm*) [2003] 1 EGLR 91 at [34]–[35] per Clarke LJ, [55(4)] per Peter Gibson LJ; *Silven Properties Ltd v Royal Bank of Scotland Plc* [2004] 1 WLR 997 at [22] per Lightman J.

11   [**Paras 15.195–15.198**]. See *Silven Properties Ltd v Royal Bank of Scotland Plc* [2004] 1 WLR 997 at [28] per Lightman J.

12   [2004] 1 WLR 997 at [28]–[29].

ASSERTION OF THE MORTGAGEE'S RIGHT TO POSSESSION

15.141   The mortgagee who exercises his right to take possession of the mortgaged premises is generally concerned not to draw income from the land, but rather, by obtaining vacant possession, to sell on the open market and recoup the outstanding loan money. In reality, therefore, possession is sought almost invariably as a preliminary to the exercise of the mortgagee's power of sale.[1] It follows that a mortgagee hardly ever seeks to go into possession unless and until there is actual default by the mortgagor, since it is only at this point that the mortgagee's statutory power of sale becomes exercisable.[2] Except where the mortgagee's security is threatened by an actual default, the right to possession generally remains unexercised. When the right is exercised, it is usual (but not invariable) practice for the mortgagee to proceed by way of a possession claim in the county court.[3]

1   *Mobil Oil Co Ltd v Rawlinson* (1982) 43 P & CR 221 at 224. See generally Lisa Whitehouse, 'The Right to Possession: The Need for Substantive Reform', in P Jackson and D C Wilde (ed), *The Reform of Property Law* (Ashgate 1997), p 150.

2   [**Para 8.240**].

3   CPR 55.1–55.10. In a possession claim relating to residential property, the mortgagee must, not less than 14 days before the hearing, send a notice to the property addressed to 'the occupiers' which gives details of the parties and the hearing (CPR 55.10(2)–(3)). At the hearing the claimant must produce evidence that the notice has been served (CPR 55.10(4)(b)). The particulars of claim must also give details of the state of the mortgage account and the alleged default (*Part 55 Practice Direction*, para 2.5).

A possible requirement of bona fides?

15.142 The close association between possession and sale has, in the past, raised some question whether the right to possession is indeed an absolute and inherent right of the mortgagee or has instead dwindled into a mere right granted at the discretion of the court. The latter perspective drew considerable support from *Quennell v Maltby*,[1] where Lord Denning MR suggested that 'in modern times equity can step in so as to prevent a mortgagee, or a transferee from him, from getting possession of a house contrary to the justice of the case.' Thus, declared Lord Denning, a mortgagee could be restrained by the court from getting possession 'except where it is sought bona fide and reasonably for the purpose of enforcing the security and then only subject to such conditions as the court thinks fit to impose.'[2] It seems certain, however, that this approach does not represent good law,[3] not least because it renders otiose the protection afforded the mortgagor by section 36 of the Administration of Justice Act 1970.[4] More recent case law has tended to confirm the conventional understanding that, contractual and statutory constraints apart, a mortgagee has an absolute right to possession from the commencement of the mortgage term,[5] regardless of any default or possible counterclaim by the mortgagor.[6]

1   [1979] 1 WLR 318 at 322G–H. See [1979] CLJ 257 (R A Pearce).
2   In *Quennell v Maltby* [1979] 1 WLR 318 at 323C, the Court of Appeal rejected a mortgagee's action for possession which, in Lord Denning's view, had been motivated not by any desire to obtain repayment of the relevant loan money but by the 'ulterior purpose' of recovering possession from two tenants who would otherwise have enjoyed security of tenure under the Rent Act.
3   See *Marquis Cholmondeley v Lord Clinton* (1817) 2 Mer 171 at 359, 35 ER 905 at 976 ('A Court of Equity never interferes to prevent the Mortgagee from assuming the possession'). Maitland pointed out that equity would never interfere with a claim to possession at common law except on terms of payment off of the whole principal, interest and costs, an equity which Maitland described as a 'mock equity', since it required payment in full and implied the termination of the mortgagor–mortgagee relationship (F W Maitland, *Equity* (2nd edn, London 1936), p 186).
4   **[Paras 15.154–15.170]**. See R J Smith, [1979] Conv 266 at 268.
5   See e g *Ropaigealach v Barclays Bank plc* [2000] QB 263 **[para 15.145]**. It is significant that in *Quennell v Maltby* [1979] 1 WLR 318 at 323E, 324F, Bridge and Templeman LJJ found alternative reasons for supporting the result reached by Lord Denning MR.
6   **[Paras 15.109–15.119]**.

An implicit requirement of due legal process?

15.143 Particularly in the residential context the repossession of mortgaged premises necessarily involves highly traumatic consequences. The process runs counter to the instinctive impulse of English land law to protect persons in actual occupation of land.[1] The law therefore imposes various controls on the exercise of the mortgagee's right to possession,[2] but recent developments have exposed a central weakness in the defences supposedly raised around the beleaguered mortgagor.

1   **[Paras 3.8, 12.147]**.

2   See generally, M Haley, 'Mortgage default: possession, relief and judicial discretion' (1997) 17
     Legal Studies 483.

The analogy of the Administration of Justice Act 1970

15.144   Section 36(1) of the Administration of Justice Act 1970 confers on
the court an extensive power to postpone the recovery of possession of
residential premises where any mortgagee 'brings an action in which he claims
possession of the mortgaged property.' The statutory language logically precludes the mortgagor's access to the protective discretion of section 36 in cases
where, without bringing court proceedings, a mortgagee simply asserts his
paramount right to possession by peaceful re-entry. It would seem anomalous,
however, that section 36 should solicitously protect the mortgagor in the
context of court proceedings, whilst leaving him hopelessly vulnerable to an
extra-curial recovery of possession. There was, therefore, a widespread assumption during the 1980s and 1990s that section 36 had impliedly interposed a
requirement of due legal process, thereby displacing the mortgagee's common
law right arbitrarily to enter into possession at any time. It was indeed generally
believed[1] that no responsible mortgagee would ever assume possession without
a court order except, perhaps, where the mortgaged property had already been
vacated by the mortgagor and, correspondingly, that repossession without a
court order would never be enforced whilst a mortgagor and his family were
still living in the premises. A severe challenge to these assumptions emerged in
the fortuitous circumstances of *Ropaigealach v Barclays Bank plc*.[2]

1   See *Ropaigealach v Barclays Bank plc* [2000] QB 263 at 286E.
2   [2000] QB 263. See [1999] CLJ 281 (M Dixon); (1999) 143 Sol Jo 206 (T Grant); [1999] Conv
     263 (A Dunn).

The Ropaigealach case

15.145   In *Ropaigealach v Barclays Bank plc* H and W jointly charged their
home to the bank and subsequently fell into financial difficulties. The bank
notified them at their home address that the house would be sold at auction
three weeks later, but since the property was, at that time, undergoing repair or
refurbishment H and W were temporarily absent and did not receive the
notification. The Court of Appeal held that the bank was entitled to take
possession of the house without first obtaining a court possession order. The
Court rejected, with some obvious reluctance,[1] the argument that section 36 of
the Administration of Justice Act 1970 impliedly imposes a requirement of
prior court order. The Court ruled that the 1970 Act does not abrogate the
unqualified common law entitlement to possession which the mortgagee enjoys
simply by virtue of his actual or notional estate in the land.[2] Since the Act had
not inhibited the mortgagee's right to take possession by self-help, H and W
were denied access to the potentially benign exercise of the court's statutory
discretion to stay or suspend any order for possession of their matrimonial
home.[3]

1   See [2000] QB 263 at 283B per Clarke LJ.
2   'The problem is that the section does not say so. If Parliament had wished so to provide there is no reason why it should not have done so expressly' ([2000] QB 263 at 286H–287A per Clarke LJ). This view had been anticipated some years before by Alison Clarke, [1983] Conv 293 at 296.
3   [2000] QB 263 at 282E–F.

15.146 The ruling in *Ropaigealach* appears to confer a distinct advantage on the mortgagee who enforces his security by the self-help route of peaceable repossession – as distinct from curial process – although similar conclusions have been sternly resisted in other areas of modern land law.[1] In *Ropaigealach* the Court of Appeal even contemplated that, on default by a mortgagor, a mortgagee might exercise his power of sale without actually taking possession, the sale serving to extinguish the mortgagor's equity of redemption[2] and effectively leaving the purchaser to evict the mortgagor as a trespasser. If such an outcome truly represents the law of mortgage, it is likely that Parliament will be required to legislate more forthrightly to protect the interests of residential mortgagors. The outcome in *Ropaigealach* seems particularly strange because it means that various significant forms of protection intended for hard-pressed residential mortgagors (and, where relevant, their families) can be circumvented by a mortgagee who chooses his moment to evict a borrower without first obtaining a court order for possession.[3]

1   See e g *Billson v Residential Apartments Ltd* [1992] 1 AC 494 [**paras 14.121–14.123**]. The equitable mortgagee almost certainly has no automatic right to possession [**para 15.127**].
2   [2000] QB 263 at 268H. See *National and Provincial Building Society v Ahmed* [1995] 2 EGLR 127 at 129J [**para 15.178**].
3   The anomalous nature of this conclusion was conceded in the Court of Appeal ([2000] QB 263 at 283H–284A per Clarke LJ, 287F per Henry LJ).

The human rights dimension

15.147 The mortgagee's inherent right of possession is potentially so draconian that many have questioned whether a crude resort to summary entry on mortgaged property can withstand scrutiny under the European Convention on Human Rights. Repossession almost always entails, in the domestic context, the eviction of a family and the dislocation of a way of life. At first sight the arbitrary and extra-curial enforcement of a mortgagee's paramount right to possession appears inconsistent with the Convention requirement of fair and impartial determination of a person's civil rights and obligations.[1] Further difficulties are posed by the Convention rights to respect for 'private and family life' and the 'home'[2] and 'peaceful enjoyment' of one's possessions.[3] It may indeed be awkward to reconcile summary repossession with the 'fair hearing' guarantee of the Convention, but recent case law has made it seem unlikely that the assumption of possession by a mortgagee pursuant to court order can be challenged by reference to other Convention rights.

1   ECHR Art 6 [**para 2.65**].
2   ECHR Art 8 [**para 2.60**].
3   ECHR Protocol No 1, Art 1 [**para 2.29**].

15.148 In *Wood v United Kingdom*[1] the applicant complained that her right to respect for 'private and family life' and the 'home' had been breached by the repossession of her home when she defaulted on her mortgage payments.[2] The European Human Rights Commission rejected this argument, noting that in so far as the repossession 'constituted an interference with the applicant's home', the interference was 'in accordance with the terms of the loan and domestic law' and was, in the words of ECHR Art 8, 'necessary for the protection of the rights and freedoms of others, namely the lender.'[3] Heavy reliance was placed on this decision in *Harrow LBC v Qazi*,[4] where the House of Lords considered an analogous question relating to the eviction of a former tenant of a local authority. By a bare majority the House decided that ECHR Art 8 cannot be invoked to defeat contractual or proprietary rights to possession which, apart from the Convention, have already crystallised under municipal law. For the majority this carried the implication that no mortgagor may invoke ECHR Art 8 'in order to diminish the contractual and proprietary rights of the mortgagee under the mortgage.'[5]

1   (1997) 24 EHRR CD 69; (1997) 2 EHRLR 685.
2   The mortgagee was a private individual who invested his savings in the making of mortgage loans to a limited number of borrowers selected by his own solicitor. On certain deeply disturbing aspects of the *Wood* litigation, see *Wills v Wood* [1984] CCLR 7 at 11, 17; (1983) LAG Bulletin (September) 9; (1984) Legal Action (April), p 7. See also (1986) 136 NLJ 980.
3   (1997) 24 EHRR CD 69 at 70–71.
4   [2004] 1 AC 983 **[paras 2.70–2.73]**.
5   [2004] 1 AC 983 at [135], [149] per Lord Scott of Foscote (see also Lord Hope of Craighead at [77]).

Regulated mortgage contracts

15.149 Before commencing any action for possession under a regulated mortgage contract entered into on or after 31 October 2004, the mortgage lender or administrator must supply certain information to the mortgagor.[1] The mortgagor must be provided with a 'written update' of details of his default and its cost implications. He must be informed of the need to ascertain whether he will be eligible for local authority accommodation after the repossession. He must also be informed 'clearly' of the 'action that will be taken with regard to repossession.'

1   *FSA Handbook* (Release 033, July 2004): MCOB 13.4.5R.

THE COURT'S INHERENT JURISDICTION TO GRANT RELIEF TO THE MORTGAGOR

15.150 Where a mortgagee's right to possession is asserted (as is still usual) by means of court proceedings, the mortgagor has access to various kinds of discretionary relief. Historically an important source of relief for mortgagors comprised the High Court's inherent equitable jurisdiction to grant a short-term stay of possession proceedings. Irrespective of the nature of the premises concerned (whether domestic or commercial), the exercise of this jurisdiction still offers the possibility of temporary relief for the mortgagor either before or even after the making of a possession order in favour of the mortgagee.

Liberal exercise of a merciful discretion

15.151 The exercise of the inherent jurisdiction has in the past enabled the court to assert some control over the enforcement of the mortgagee's right to possession, largely through the adjournment of proceedings in order to give more time to the mortgagor. The jurisdiction is exercisable by the Masters of the Chancery Division and provides a temporary form of relief which may allow hard-pressed mortgagors to resolve their financial difficulties and repay overdue mortgage money.[1] The court's exercise of discretion in this matter is based on the convention that 'the court has never allowed a mortgagee to enforce his rights under the mortgage in the face of a concrete offer by the mortgagor to redeem.'[2]

1   In the celebrated words of Clauson LJ, 'the facts and the circumstances of the case were brought before the Court, and in proper cases the wind was tempered to the shorn lamb, time being given for payment and so forth' (*Redditch Benefit Building Society v Roberts* [1940] Ch 415 at 420).
2   *Mobil Oil Co Ltd v Rawlinson* (1982) 43 P & CR 221 at 225 per Nourse J.

15.152 In days gone by the court's discretion to temporise was exercised quite liberally, one famous Chancery Master describing his function as being akin to that of a 'social worker rather than a Judge.'[1] It was the task of the Master, if matters were not altogether hopeless, to encourage the borrower to re-organise his finances and to keep his home by paying off mortgage arrears in agreed instalments.[2] It has since been said that the generous approach adopted by Chancery Masters was 'no doubt assisted by the benevolent attitude which the Legislature had by then assumed towards tenants faced with eviction by their landlords.'[3] The analogy drawn – at least tacitly – between the respective positions of the home-owner and the renter was soon to constitute a recurring cross-reference in the law relating to the protection of residential mortgagors.[4]

1   See Master Ball, 'The Chancery Master' (1961) 77 LQR 331 at 351.
2   The lengths to which Chancery Masters were prepared to go appears in Master Ball's frank admission that, if necessary, the Master was generally willing to use 'time and technicality as weapons against a too stony-hearted plaintiff' ((1961) 77 LQR 331 at 351).
3   *Mobil Oil Co Ltd v Rawlinson* (1982) 43 P & CR 221 at 224 per Nourse J.
4   [**Para 15.154**].

Modern restrictions on the inherent jurisdiction

15.153 In more recent times the court's inherent jurisdiction to stay possession proceedings against mortgagors has been exercised much more sparingly.[1] In *Birmingham Citizens Permanent Building Society v Caunt*,[2] Russell J held that the inherent jurisdiction merely empowers the court to adjourn a hearing 'for a short time' in order to 'afford the mortgagor a limited opportunity to find means to pay off the mortgagee or otherwise satisfy him if there was a reasonable prospect of either of those events occurring.'[3] As Russell J indicated, however, it is unlikely that even in these circumstances an adjournment will be granted for a period of more than 28 days.[4]

1   For a description of the judicial reaction against what was seen as excessive indulgence shown towards borrowers, see *Mobil Oil Co Ltd v Rawlinson* (1982) 43 P & CR 221 at 224.
2   [1962] Ch 883 at 891. See (1962) 78 LQR 171 (R E M).
3   See also *London Permanent Benefit Building Society v De Baer* [1969] 1 Ch 321 at 338B–F; *Cheltenham and Gloucester Building Society v Booker* (1997) 73 P & CR 412 at 415–416 (postponement of possession to facilitate private sale under controlled conditions). See [1998] Conv 223 (A Kenny).
4   [1962] Ch 883 at 908. See *Braithwaite v Winwood* [1960] 1 WLR 1257 at 1264–1265.

STATUTORY POWER TO STAY POSSESSION PROCEEDINGS

15.154   The decision in *Birmingham Citizens Permanent Building Society v Caunt* did much to restore to the mortgagee the balance of power which some imagined had been removed by the steady development of the court's inherent jurisdiction.[1] However, the net effect of the tightening-up of the court's inherent jurisdiction was to accentuate the demand for a new statutory form of relief in possession actions relating to the family home. In 1969 the Payne Committee on the Enforcement of Judgment Debts recognised that a succession of governments had 'for some years encouraged the purchase, instead of the renting, of houses by persons of modest means.' The Committee therefore concluded that where a mortgagor, because of financial difficulties, fell into arrears with his mortgage instalments, the courts should be 'empowered, subject to proper safeguards, to extend to the mortgagor the same protection in relation to the continued occupation of the house as would be given to a tenant of a property of a similar rateable value.'[2] In effect the Committee accepted that the expansion of the 'property-owning democracy' had fixed on the government of the day a broad social responsibility to assimilate domestic mortgagors within the same kind of protective legislation as that which benefits residential tenants.[3]

1   'Equity was never and should never be in the hands of the judges a sword to attack any part of the security itself, and the right to possession was an important part of that security' (*Birmingham Citizens Permanent Building Society v Caunt* [1962] Ch 883 at 896). See also *Robertson v Cilia* [1956] 1 WLR 1502 at 1508.
2   *Report of the Committee on Judgment Debts* (Cmnd 3909, February 1969), para 1386(d). See also *Report of the Committee on One-Parent Families* (Cmnd 5629, July 1974), Vol 1, paras 6.116–6.118.
3   See similarly *Hughes v Waite* [1957] 1 WLR 713 at 715 per Harman J.

15.155   The statutory relief proposed by the Payne Committee was almost immediately introduced by section 36 of the Administration of Justice Act 1970.[1]

1   For a critical review of the legal process of repossession, see Lisa Whitehouse, 'The
    Home-owner: Citizen or Consumer?', in S Bright and J K Dewar (ed), *Land Law: Themes and*
    Perspectives (OUP 1998), p 183.

Preconditions for the exercise of the statutory discretion

15.156   Section 36 of the Administration of Justice Act 1970 confers on the
court a far-reaching power 'to stop the mortgagee from taking possession.'[1]
The court has discretion to adjourn possession actions brought by mortgagees
or to postpone the giving of possession in respect of a 'dwelling-house' for such
period or periods 'as the court thinks reasonable.'[2] The term 'dwelling-house'
embraces 'any building or part thereof which is used as a dwelling'[3] and may
include premises some of which are used 'as a shop or office or for business,
trade or professional purposes.'[4] The court's discretion is exercisable in any
claim for possession of residential property in which

> it appears to the court that in the event of its exercising the power the
> mortgagor is likely to be able within a reasonable period to pay any sums
> due under the mortgage or to remedy a default consisting of a breach of
> any other obligation arising under or by virtue of the mortgage.[5]

1   *Ropaigealach v Barclays Bank plc* [2000] QB 263 at 283C–D per Clarke LJ.
2   AJA 1970, s 36(2). A similar power is vested in the county court in respect of any application
    by a local authority mortgagee for a re-vesting of a property which has been purchased by a
    sitting tenant with the assistance of local authority finance (HA 1985, Sch 17, para 1(2)–(3)).
    The county court may adjourn proceedings by the local authority mortgagee or postpone the
    date for execution of the authority's deed for 'such period as the court thinks reasonable' and
    on such terms with regard to mortgage payments as the court thinks fit.
3   AJA 1970, s 39(1). Section 36 thus seems capable of application to an entire office block which
    contains somewhere within it a caretaker's flat (see R J Smith, [1979] Conv 266 at 271). The
    relevant date for determining whether there is a 'dwelling-house' is not the date of execution of
    the mortgage, but the date on which the mortgagee claims possession (*Royal Bank of*
    Scotland plc v Miller [2002] QB 255 at [29] per Dyson LJ).
4   AJA 1970, s 39(2). See e g *Royal Bank of Scotland plc v Miller* [2002] QB 255 (flat above
    nightclub).
5   AJA 1970, s 36(1). The severe restrictions imposed by Housing Act 1980, s 89 on the court's
    exercise of discretion in making possession orders **[para 3.45]** have no application to
    possession actions brought by mortgagees (see HA 1980, s 89(2)(a)).

Mortgagor is not required to repay the entire mortgage debt

15.157   Almost immediately after enactment of the Administration of Justice
Act 1970, a drafting imperfection in section 36 threatened to destroy the
protective import of the provision. In *Halifax Building Society v Clark*[1]
Pennycuick V-C ruled that where (as is frequently the case) a single default in
the payment of mortgage instalments contractually triggered the mortgagor's
immediate liability to repay the entire capital debt,[2] the section 36 discretion
became unavailable in the absence of some realistic prospect that the mortgagor
(or his spouse[3]) could raise this impossibly large sum 'within a reasonable

period.' The legislative defect was eventually remedied by the enactment of section 8(1) of the Administration of Justice Act 1973, which redefines the phrase 'any sums due' in section 36 of the 1970 Act as referring only to such amounts as the mortgagor would have expected to be required to pay if the mortgage had *not* contained a default clause rendering the entire mortgage debt payable.[4] Nowadays, therefore, the court has discretion to adjourn possession proceedings or stay the execution of a possession order if there is any reasonable likelihood that during the interim the mortgagor will be able to find the instalments which have fallen into arrear (and also any other instalments which become due during the period of postponement).[5]

1   [1973] Ch 307 at 313G–H. See (1973) 89 LQR 171 (P V Baker); (1973) 36 MLR 550 (P Jackson); (1973) 37 Conv (NS) 213 (F R Crane). See also *Governor and Company of the Bank of Scotland v Grimes* [1985] QB 1179 at 1190C–F.
2   In effect, the entire principal sum and accrued interest became, for purposes of AJA 1970, s 36(1), the 'sums due under the mortgage.'
3   A spouse who enjoys 'matrimonial home rights' under the Family Law Act 1996 is entitled to tender payment in her own name of any mortgage liability affecting her dwelling-house. Such payments are 'as good as if made ... by the other spouse' (Family Law Act 1996, s 30(3) (formerly Matrimonial Homes Act 1983, s 1(5))).
4   Shortly before the enactment of AJA 1973, s 8, the Court of Appeal declined, in *First Middlesbrough Trading and Mortgage Co Ltd v Cunningham* (1974) 28 P & CR 69 at 74, to adopt the construction applied in *Halifax Building Society v Clark*. For an argument that the ratio of *Cunningham*'s case may still be wider (and therefore more favourable to the mortgagor) than AJA 1973, s 8, see R J Smith, [1979] Conv 266 at 274–275.
5   AJA 1973, s 8(2). See *Peckham Mutual Building Society v Registe* (1981) 42 P & CR 186 at 189.

Social function of the section 36 jurisdiction

15.158   The statutory discretion under section 36 (as amended) provides valuable assistance for many mortgagors who run into temporary financial difficulties, whether by reason of unemployment, short-time working, redundancy or domestic difficulties.[1] Although clearly not all judges agree on the point,[2] it has been said that the Administration of Justice Acts 1970 and 1973 together represent a form of 'social legislation' in which 'Parliament has attempted to give legislative shelter to a wide class of owner-occupiers.'[3] It is consistent with the nature of such legislation that the court's discretion to give relief to domestic mortgagors should be construed liberally.[4] During the last 15 years the statutory discretion has assumed a pivotal importance in relieving the financial crisis otherwise engulfing thousands of innocent mortgagors. Indeed it is fair to say that the scale of the economic recession affecting homeowners during the early 1990s generated a rather more generous judicial approach to section 36.[5]

1   See R J Smith, [1979] Conv 266 at 279–280.
2   See [1983] Conv 80 (P H Kenny).
3   *Centrax Trustees Ltd v Ross* [1979] 2 All ER 952 at 955f per Goulding J.
4   The section 36 jurisdiction applies not only to instalment mortgages but to endowment mortgages (*Governor and Company of the Bank of Scotland v Grimes* [1985] QB 1179 at 1188G, 1190G) and other mortgages repayable at the end of a fixed period (*Royal Bank of Scotland plc v Miller* [2002] QB 255 at [41]–[43]). See [1985] Conv 407 (J E M), but compare

Lord Marples of Wallasey v Holmes (1976) 31 P & CR 94 at 97. Section 36 has no application
to the enforcement of charging orders, but see Charging Orders Act 1979, s 1(5) **[para 9.122]**.
See similarly *Containercare (Ireland) Ltd v Wycherley* [1982] IR 143 at 150.

5   See e g *Target Home Loans Ltd v Clothier* (1992) 25 HLR 48 at 54, where Nolan LJ recognised
that the mortgagor's difficulties were in no way caused by dishonesty, but rather by the fact
that his business had suffered badly as a result of the recession.

No discretion to postpone proceedings indefinitely

15.159 Even if the court is able to exercise discretion in favour of the
mortgagor, there are certain restrictions upon the terms on which it may do so.[1]
The Court of Appeal ruled in *Royal Trust Co of Canada v Markham*[2] that the
court has no jurisdiction to order suspension of possession proceedings *sine
die*.[3] The court must define the period during which the proceedings are
adjourned or any possession order stayed. In any event relief may be granted to
the mortgagor only in respect of such period of time as is 'reasonable'.[4] It may,
however, be reasonable to adjourn proceedings in order to determine, at some
later date, whether there has emerged in the interim any prospect of the
mortgagor being able, within a reasonable period, to pay sums due under the
mortgage.[5]

1   The court normally has no jurisdiction to suspend a possession warrant which has already
been executed by the county court bailiff (*National and Provincial Building Society v Ahmed*
[1995] 2 EGLR 127 at 129F; *Cheltenham and Gloucester Building Society v Obi* (1996) 28 HLR
22 at 24) and may be unwilling to set aside a judgment for the mortgagee entered at a hearing
which the mortgagor failed to attend (*National Counties Building Society v Antonelli* [1995]
NPC 177).

2   [1975] 1 WLR 1416 at 1423C, 1424A–B.

3   See likewise *National Westminster Bank Plc v Skelton (Note)* [1993] 1 WLR 72 at 81A per
Slade LJ; *Cheltenham & Gloucester Building Society v Ensor* (Unreported, Court of Appeal,
13 August 1992) per Dillon LJ. Compare, however, the suggestion in *Western Bank Ltd v
Schindler* [1977] Ch 1 at 14E–G.

4   In 1969 the Payne Committee on the Enforcement of Judgment Debts considered that a
period of six months would be sufficient in most cases (*Report* (Cmnd 3909, 1969), para 1388),
but the period may well be longer or shorter depending on the circumstances (see R J Smith,
[1979] Conv 266 at 278–279).

5   See *Skandia Financial Services Ltd v Greenfield* [1997] CLY 4248, where the court decided to
'wait and see' whether the mortgagor, although currently a student working for qualifications,
could obtain employment which would enable her to pay off the mortgage arrears.

Suspension of possession to facilitate a privately negotiated sale

15.160 It may be reasonable to suspend a warrant for possession against a
mortgagor who is negotiating a private sale of the mortgaged property[1] –
possibly in order to enable him to apply to the High Court for an order for sale
under section 91 of the Law of Property Act 1925[2] – but only if the proposed
sale is likely to produce (possibly in conjunction with independent funding) a
sum sufficient to discharge the entire mortgage debt.[3] There are nevertheless
certain limitations on the leeway which the court can permit the mortgagor. If

the mortgagor is applying for a High Court order under the Law of Property Act 1925, he must do so before the date on which the warrant for possession is due to take effect.[4] There must, moreover, be some firm evidence that a private sale of the mortgaged property is likely to occur within the foreseeable future.[5] It is not enough that the mortgagor has simply expressed an intention to place the property on the market.[6]

1   See *Target Home Loans Ltd v Clothier* (1992) 25 HLR 48 at 54, where Nolan LJ referred to the 'sound commercial sense' of leaving the mortgagors in occupation of the property 'on the basis that they are in a far better position to sell it than the [mortgagee] would be'. An occupied house 'is far more likely to look attractive and to command a buyer than one which has been repossessed by a mortgage company.'

2   [**Para 15.204**]. See M Dixon, (1998) 18 Legal Studies 279.

3   See *Cheltenham and Gloucester plc v Krausz* [1997] 1 WLR 1558 at 1565H–1566A, where the Court of Appeal declined to apply section 36 in order to allow a mortgagor time to make a section 91 application which would inevitably result in a mortgage deficiency ([1998] Conv 223 (A Kenny)).

4   *Cheltenham and Gloucester plc v Krausz* [1997] 1 WLR 1558 at 1567F per Phillips LJ.

5   *Mortgage Service Funding Plc v Steele* (1996) 72 P & CR D40. See also *Target Home Loans Ltd v Clothier* (1992) 25 HLR 48 at 54–55, where there was some evidence from an estate agent that the property was likely to be sold very shortly (although Nolan LJ observed mordantly that he intended 'no disrespect to the estate agency profession' in suggesting that 'they would win by a distance any competition between members of different professions for optimism').

6   *National and Provincial Building Society v Lloyd* [1996] 1 All ER 630 at 639j–640a. In the 'written policy and procedures' required to be formulated by mortgage lenders and administrators under a regulated mortgage contract, there should be an indication of willingness to consider allowing the defaulting mortgagor to 'remain in possession to effect a sale' (*FSA Handbook* (Release 033, July 2004): MCOB 13.3.2E(1)(e)).

Realistic evidence of ability to pay arrears or to remedy any other default

15.161   Before the court's discretion can be exercised in favour of a mortgagor, it must appear to the court that the mortgagor is 'likely to be able within a reasonable period to pay any sums due under the mortgage.'[1]

1   A proposal that money should be raised by a letting of the mortgaged property is unlikely to succeed, not least since such a letting, if unauthorised, constitutes a breach of the mortgage terms (see *Target Home Loans Ltd v Clothier* (1992) 25 HLR 48 at 53). Likewise discretion is unlikely to be exercised in favour of a mortgagor with a 'deplorable' payment record and a history of non-compliance with court orders (see *Abbey National Building Society v Mewton* [1995] CLY 3598).

Rescheduling of arrears

15.162   There is no scope for the exercise of the court's discretion if the mortgagor (or his partner[1]) cannot provide realistic evidence of at least some ability to pay off all the current arrears of mortgage money.[2] Simply to ask for time to pay is not enough to attract the court's discretion.[3] But, as the Court of Appeal indicated in *Cheltenham and Gloucester Building Society v Norgan*,[4] the courts are nowadays prepared, in principle, to reschedule the payment of mortgage arrears using the full remaining term of the mortgage as 'the starting point for calculating a "reasonable period"' for such payment.[5] In effect the courts have shown a new willingness to reconstruct the repayment terms of a mortgage provided that, in all the circumstances, it is reasonable to expect the mortgagee to recoup the arrears over the whole term of the mortgage and the mortgagor appears reasonably able to cope with such a repayment schedule.[6] Section 36 discretion is not available, however, if the mortgagor cannot discharge the arrears by periodic payments[7] and his only prospect of repaying the entire mortgage loan and interest (both accrued and accruing) is from a sale of the mortgaged premises.[8]

1   See Family Law Act 1996, ss 30(3), 36(13) [**para 15.169**].
2   See e g *Williams & Glyn's Bank Ltd v Boland* [1981] AC 487 at 509C–D per Lord Wilberforce; *Peckham Mutual Building Society v Registe* (1981) 42 P & CR 186 at 189; *Town & Country Building Society v Julien* (1991) 24 HLR 312 at 316–318. Evidence of ability to pay must relate to the entirety (and not to a mere part) of the sum currently outstanding (see *Target Home Loans Ltd v Clothier* (1992) 25 HLR 48 at 52 per Nolan LJ).
3   A 'nebulous prospect' of paying off the arrears is not enough (*Cheltenham & Gloucester Building Society v Ensor* (Unreported, Court of Appeal, 13 August 1992)). The courts may postpone possession in order to facilitate a sale of the mortgaged premises, even if the prospect of sale is not immediate: there is a possible leeway of up to perhaps a year (see *Cheltenham and Gloucester Building Society v Johnson* (1996) 28 HLR 885 at 894; *National and Provincial Building Society v Lloyd* [1996] 1 All ER 630 at 637j–638b). See [1998] Conv 125 (M P Thompson).
4   [1996] 1 WLR 343. See [1996] Conv 118 (M P Thompson); (1996) 146 NLJ 252 (H W Wilkinson). The important step taken in *Norgan*'s case was prompted by judicial recognition of the fact that most institutional mortgagees subscribed to the stated policy of the Council of Mortgage Lenders that 'lenders seek to take possession only as a last resort' (see Waite LJ at 349B–F, 353E, Evans LJ at 356F–357B).
5   [1996] 1 WLR 343 at 353D–E per Waite LJ. In *Norgan* the mortgage term still had 12 years to run and there seemed to be sufficient equity to protect the mortgagee's entitlement to repayment of the principal debt in full at the end of that period ([1996] 1 WLR 343 at 352F). Compare cases where the mortgage debt is close to or exceeds the value of the land (see e g *Mortgage Corpn Ltd v Leslie* [1996] CA Transcript 51; *National and Provincial Building Society v Lynd* [1996] NI 47 at 63e–f).
6   See also *Abbey National Building Society v Acharya* [1996] CLY 4979 (8 years outstanding); *Household Mortgage Corpn Plc v Pringle* (1998) 30 HLR 250 at 259–260 (17 years outstanding). It is significant that the *Norgan* ruling has not been followed in Northern Ireland (see *National and Provincial Building Society v Lynd* [1996] NI 47 at 63b–c per Girvan J).
7   For an account of arrangements for Income Support for Mortgage Interest, see J Morgan, 'Mortgages and the Flexible Workforce', in P Jackson and D C Wilde (ed), *Contemporary Property Law* (Ashgate 1999), p 219.
8   *Bristol and West Building Society v Ellis* (1996) 73 P & CR 158 at 161 per Auld LJ; [1998] Conv 125 (M P Thompson). See also Lara McMurtry, [2002] Conv 594.

15.163   The enormously beneficial relaxation of the section 36 discretion initiated by *Norgan*'s case is reflected – and quite deliberately so[1] – in the 'written policy and procedures' which mortgage lenders and administrators are now required to follow in dealing 'fairly' with customers in arrears under a regulated mortgage contract entered into on or after 31 October 2004. The *FSA Handbook* (*Mortgages: Conduct of Business*) issued pursuant to the Financial Services and Markets Act 2000 indicates that the mortgagee should announce its willingness to adopt a 'reasonable approach' to the time over which a payment shortfall should be repaid, having particular regard to 'the need to establish, where feasible, a payment plan which is practical in terms of the circumstances of the customer.'[2] The Financial Services Authority has endorsed the view that, in appropriate cases, 'this will mean that repayments are arranged over the remaining term of the regulated mortgage contract.'[3] This emulation of the *Norgan* ruling underscores the principle that repossession is appropriate 'only where all other reasonable attempts to resolve the position have failed.'[4]

1   See Financial Services Authority, *The Draft Mortgage Sourcebook, including Policy Statement on CP 70* (Consultation Paper 98, June 2001), para 12.3.4.
2   *FSA Handbook* (Release 033, July 2004): MCOB 13.3.2E(1)(c). Failure to articulate this 'reasonable approach' in the lender's 'written policy and procedures' leads to a rebuttable presumption that the customer has not been dealt with 'fairly' (see MCOB 13.3.2E(2); *FSA Reader's Guide: an introduction to the Handbook*, Chapter 6, p 19).
3   *FSA Handbook* (Release 033, July 2004): MCOB 13.3.6G.
4   *FSA Handbook* (Release 033, July 2004): MCOB 13.3.2E(1)(f).

Non-financial breaches

15.164   Where the mortgagor's default lies not in non-payment of money due but in some other form of breach, it is plain that the court's discretion under section 36 can be exercised only where the mortgagor's breach is capable of remedy. In *Britannia Building Society v Earl*,[1] for example, the mortgagor had breached the terms of his mortgage by granting an unauthorised letting of the property to two joint tenants. In holding that the tenants had no independent access to discretionary relief under section 36, the Court of Appeal accepted that the mortgagor's default in this respect could not be remedied save by the departure of the tenants.[2]

1   [1990] 1 WLR 422 [**para 15.104**].
2   [1990] 1 WLR 422 at 430B–C. See also *Royal Bank of Scotland plc v Miller* [2002] QB 255 at [32] per Dyson LJ.

No discretion before mortgage money has become due

15.165   There is some doubt as to whether section 36 of the Administration of Justice Act 1970 can have any application where no mortgage money of any kind has yet become due. In *Western Bank Ltd v Schindler*,[1] two members of the Court of Appeal thought that section 36 must be applicable irrespective of the absence of actual default, since otherwise a blameless mortgagor would be put in a less advantageous position than a defaulting mortgagor who can rely on section 36. Goff LJ was, however, of the view that, on strict construction, section 36 cannot apply where there is no money due or any other default present on the facts of the case.[2] This restrictive approach received some confirmation in *Habib Bank Ltd v Tailor*,[3] where the Court of Appeal ruled that the Administration of Justice Acts had no application to a mortgage given as security for a bank overdraft, under which no money was due unless and until repayment was demanded by the bank.

1   [1977] Ch 1 at 13D–E per Buckley LJ, 19F per Scarman LJ.
2   [1977] Ch 1 at 26E.
3   [1982] 1 WLR 1218 at 1225F.

No discretion available in favour of the mortgagor's tenants

15.166   For the purpose of access to the section 36 discretion, the term 'mortgagor' includes 'any person deriving title under the original mortgagor.'[1] It appears, however, that this extended meaning confers the potential benefit of section 36 merely upon *assignees* from the mortgagor, with the result that the court's discretion is not available to persons who hold as *tenants* of the original mortgagor.[2]

1   AJA 1970, s 39(1).
2   See *Britannia Building Society v Earl* [1990] 1 WLR 422 at 429H–430B per McCowan LJ.

Procedural rights for the mortgagor's spouse or cohabitant

15.167   Statutory intervention has conferred a number of procedural rights on the spouse (and in certain cases the cohabitant) of a mortgagor, for the purpose of enabling this person more effectively to take advantage of the important discretion exercised by the court under section 36 of the Administration of Justice Act 1970. The motive behind these initiatives stems from the disadvantage which is inevitably suffered by a partner who does not know that the mortgagor's financial difficulties are beginning to jeopardise the security of the family home.

No right to be informed of mortgage arrears

15.168   The statutory right[1] of a mortgagor's partner to tender mortgage payments is not of much value to a partner who is unaware that payments have fallen into arrear. In *Hastings and Thanet Building Society v Goddard*[2] the Court of Appeal held that a building society had no obligation to inform the mortgagor's wife of his mortgage default in order that she should have an opportunity to tender payments herself. Russell LJ thought that any contrary view was 'impracticable because a building society can scarcely be expected to keep track of the matrimonial status of its mortgagors.' The Court likewise refused to accept that notice of a mortgagee's possession proceedings should be served on the mortgagor's spouse (where she was not a joint tenant of the property), since her statutory rights of occupation in the matrimonial home were in no way binding on the mortgagee. The decision in *Goddard*'s case, although heavily criticised,[3] remains good at common law. The ruling leads in practice to the unfortunate result that a partner who discovers too late that the mortgagor has allowed substantial arrears to accrue may then find herself precluded from invoking the court's discretion under the Administration of Justice Act. A partial remedy for the shortcomings of the common law has now been provided in legislative form.[4]

1   **[Para 15.157]**.
2   [1970] 1 WLR 1544 at 1548E. See (1971) 35 Conv (NS) 48 (F R Crane).
3   See D A Nevitt and J Levin, 'Social Policy and the Matrimonial Home' (1973) 36 MLR 345 at 349–350; *Report of the Committee on One-Parent Families* (Cmnd 5629, July 1974), Vol 1, para 6.120.
4   For the background to the legislation, see *Third Report on Family Property* (Law Com No 86, June 1978), paras 2.25–2.33.

Right to be joined as a party in possession proceedings

15.169   Pursuant to the Family Law Act 1996, the mortgagor's spouse or partner, if entitled to tender vicarious mortgage payments, is given the right to apply to the court to be joined as a party in any possession proceedings brought by a mortgagee to enforce his security in respect of a dwelling-house.[1] The court must accede to her application if it sees no 'special reason' against it[2] and there is a realistic possibility that she may be able to attract the benevolent exercise of the court's discretion under section 36 of the Administration of Justice Act 1970.[3] This statutory right at least gives the mortgagor's spouse or partner locus standi in possession proceedings to present a case for consideration under section 36,[4] but still fails to tackle the difficulties faced by the person who is entirely unaware that possession proceedings are afoot against the mortgagor. A further compromise solution has been introduced by statute in order to meet these difficulties.

1   FLA 1996, s 55(2) (formerly Matrimonial Homes Act 1983, s 8(2)). The right extends to any cohabitant or former cohabitant of the mortgagor who has obtained an order under FLA 1996, s 36 which confers occupation rights in the quasi-marital home (see FLA 1996, ss 36(13), 55(3)(a)).
2   FLA 1996, s 55(3)(c)(i).
3   FLA 1996, s 55(3)(c)(ii).
4   It has long been recognised that, even if the mortgagor's spouse or partner is unsuccessful in invoking section 36, the mere fact that the possession order is formally entered against her name strengthens her claim to be provided with alternative accommodation by her local housing authority (see *Anglia Building Society v Lewis* (Unreported, Court of Appeal, 29 January 1982) per Dunn LJ).

Right to be served with notice of possession proceedings

15.170   Pursuant again to the Family Law Act 1996, any mortgagee who seeks to enforce his security over land which comprises a dwelling-house is obliged to serve notice of his possession action on any spouse who has protected her 'matrimonial home rights' in that property by entry of the appropriate 'notice' (in registered land) or registration of a Class F land charge (in unregistered land).[1] This requirement affords a further incentive towards the registration of matrimonial home rights, by guaranteeing that a person who duly protects her rights cannot lose her home without at least having an opportunity to be joined and heard as a party in the mortgagee's possession action. This right to notice of possession proceedings clearly imposes a burden of search on any mortgagee who intends to initiate possession proceedings, but in days of increased emphasis on residential security this result is entirely reasonable.

1   FLA 1996, s 56(1)–(2) (formerly Matrimonial Homes Act 1983, s 8(3)). A possession claim in respect of a residential property must include within the particulars of claim whether any register entry has been effected (*CPR Part 55 Practice Direction*, para 2.5(1)).

EXERCISE OF THE POWER OF SALE

15.171   The most usual remedy invoked by the legal mortgagee in the event of serious default by his mortgagor is the exercise of the mortgagee's power of sale. Since vacant possession is almost inevitably an essential condition of a good sale price, the exercise of this power of sale is normally preceded by the mortgagee's recovery of possession of the mortgaged property.

When the power of sale arises

15.172   A mortgagee has no common law power of sale over mortgaged land. A power of sale is sometimes conferred by the express terms of the mortgage deed, but a power of sale is also supplied, in any event, by the Law of Property Act 1925.[1] The 1925 Act draws a firm distinction between the point in time at which the statutory power of sale *arises* and that at which it becomes *exercisable*. Pursuant to section 101 the mortgagee's statutory power *arises* if three conditions are satisfied. *First*, the mortgage in question must have been effected by deed.[2] *Second*, the mortgage money must have become due.[3] Thus the mortgagee's power of sale may arise if the legal date for redemption has passed or if any instalment of the mortgage money has become due under an instalment mortgage.[4] *Third*, the mortgage deed must contain no expression of contrary intention which has the effect of precluding a power of sale in the foregoing circumstances.[5] Section 101 operates as a filter to section 103 of the 1925 Act, which governs the *exercisability* of a power of sale once such power has arisen.[6]

1   The scope of the mortgagee's power of sale and the circumstances of its exercise may be varied or extended by the express terms of the mortgage deed (LPA 1925, s 101(3)).
2   LPA 1925, s 101(1).
3   LPA 1925, s 101(1)(i).
4   *Payne v Cardiff RDC* [1932] 1 KB 241 at 251, 253.
5   LPA 1925, s 101(4).
6   In rare cases a mortgagee's conduct may operate as a waiver of his power of sale (see *Barns v Queensland National Bank Ltd* (1906) 3 CLR 925 at 939–940; *Morton v Suncorp Finance Ltd* (1987) 8 NSWLR 325 at 336A).

When the power of sale becomes exercisable

15.173 Whereas three cumulative conditions must be satisfied in order that the mortgagee's statutory power of sale should *arise*, the power becomes *exercisable* if the mortgagee can show that any one of three conditions specified in section 103 has been met.

The three conditions

15.174 In the absence of an express power of sale conferred by the mortgage instrument itself, the mortgagee may not exercise his statutory power of sale unless and until *either* the mortgagor has been in default for three months following the service upon him of a notice requiring payment of the mortgage money[1] *or* some interest under the mortgage has remained unpaid for two months after becoming due[2] *or* there has been a breach of some mortgage term 'other than and besides a covenant for the payment of mortgage money or interest thereon.'[3]

1   LPA 1925, s 103(i). The notice requirement operates as a crude form of due process for the mortgagor, who is thereby given adequate warning to remedy the default (see *Bevham Investments Pty Ltd v Belgot Pty Ltd* (1982) 149 CLR 494 at 501; *Matich v United Building Society* [1987] 2 NZLR 513 at 517). Money lent on overdraft is prima facie repayable on demand (*Williams & Glyn's Bank Ltd v Barnes* [1981] Com LR 205 **[para 12.204]**).
2   LPA 1925, s 103(ii).
3   LPA 1925, s 103(iii).

A compulsory divesting at the direction of the mortgagee

15.175 If any one of these conditions is satisfied, the mortgagee has statutory authority to proceed with a sale of part or all of the mortgaged land.[1] Unlike the remedy of foreclosure,[2] the exercise of the mortgagee's power of sale requires no sanction or leave of any court.[3] The power of sale authorises, in rather brutal fashion, a compulsory divesting of the mortgagor's title at the direction of the mortgagee.[4] The mortgagee is statutorily clothed with full power to transfer the mortgagor's estate freed from all property rights over which the mortgage had priority, but subject of course to those rights which themselves rank prior to the mortgage.[5] The 1925 Act in effect confers on the mortgagee a power of compulsory sale over a title which does not belong to him at law.[6]

1   LPA 1925, s 101(1)(i). For this purpose the mortgaged property includes fixtures **[para 1.69]**, but in the exercise of his power of sale the mortgagee has no power to sever fixtures from the realty and sell them separately, unless such power is expressly or impliedly conferred by the instrument of mortgage (*Re Yates* (1888) 38 Ch D 112 at 120–121 per Cotton LJ). If the mortgagee wrongly severs and sells fixtures, the property in the fixtures does not revert to the mortgagor but, subject to a damages action for actual loss, the proceeds of the fixtures are treated as proceeds of the realisation of the mortgaged property (see *Re Rogerstone Brick & Stone Co Ltd* [1919] 1 Ch 110 at 124, 127–128; *Re Penning; Ex parte State Bank of South Australia* (1989) 89 ALR 417 at 433).

2   [**Para 15.222**].
3   If the power of sale has arisen but the mortgagor pays the due money before the time of exercise of the power, the court has jurisdiction to restrain sale (see *Lord Waring v London and Manchester Assurance Co Ltd* [1935] Ch 310 at 317; *Morton v Suncorp Finance Ltd* (1987) 8 NSWLR 325 at 335B–C).
4   The mortgagee's sale is not a transaction 'by which the mortgagor, through the medium of an agent, is disposing of his own property. It is one by which his property is being divested from him' (*Forsyth v Blundell* (1973) 129 CLR 477 at 500 per Walsh J). For this reason an enforced sale, conducted under a mortgagee's paramount power, does not constitute a 'disposal' which triggers any liability to repay a 'right to buy' discount on an early sale [**para 7.353**] (see e g *Canterbury City Council v Quine* (1988) 55 P & CR 1 at 3).
5   LPA 1925, s 104(1).
6   LPA 1925, ss 88(1), 89(1).

Premature sale

15.176   Potentially difficult issues emerge if, in the absence of express authority, a mortgagee sells the mortgaged estate either before his statutory power of sale arises or before it becomes exercisable.[1] Where the mortgaged estate (and the mortgagee's charge) are registered at Land Registry, a definitive solution has now been devised by the Land Registration Act 2002. In order to protect the disponee of the mortgaged estate, the proprietor of a registered charge is to be taken to have, subject to any contrary entry in the register, 'the powers of disposition conferred by law on the owner of a legal mortgage.'[2] This statutory formula has the effect that, even though the chargee's sale of the mortgaged estate is premature and improper, 'the title of the disponee cannot be questioned.'[3] The disposition is nevertheless unlawful, with the consequence that the mortgagor, although unable to challenge the title of the disponee, may still sue the mortgagee for damages for the irregular exercise of his power.[4]

1   The court has an inherent jurisdiction to restrain the improper or oppressive exercise of the mortgagee's power of sale (see *Clark v National Mutual Life Association of Australasia Ltd* [1966] NZLR 196 at 197). Equity will therefore intervene in any case of fraud on the power (*Colson v Williams* (1889) 61 LT 71 at 72; *Yarrangah Pty Ltd v National Australia Bank Ltd* (1999) 9 BPR 17061 at [33] per Young J).
2   LRA 2002, s 52(1).
3   LRA 2002, s 52(2).
4   See *Land Registration for the Twenty-First Century: A Conveyancing Revolution* (Law Com No 271, July 2001), para 7.7.

15.177   The equivalent problem in respect of an unregistered mortgage security is rather more complex. If the mortgagee of an unregistered estate purports to sell the estate before his power of sale arises, the transaction transfers to the purchaser merely those rights which the mortgagee enjoyed qua mortgagee and is entirely ineffective to pass the mortgagor's estate.[1] Where the mortgagee sells after his power of sale has arisen but before it becomes exercisable, the purchaser's title is statutorily declared to be unimpeachable,[2] although the sale clearly exposes the selling mortgagee to an action in damages brought by the mortgagor.[3] However, it seems that (unlike the position under the Land Registration Act 2002) the purchaser of the unregistered estate cannot claim any immunity under the statute if at the time of the sale he had actual notice that the power of sale was not exercisable or that there was some other impropriety in the sale.[4] Thus, for example, the purchaser may be prejudicially affected by actual notice that at the date of the sale the mortgagor was not in fact in default of his obligations under the mortgage. It is doubtful that the purchaser can be bound by merely constructive notice of irregularities in the matter of sale,[5] although in *Bailey v Barnes*[6] Stirling J warned that the purchaser must not 'wilfully shut his eyes and abstain from making inquiries which might have led to a knowledge of impropriety or irregularity.'

1   See Law Com No 271 (2001), para 7.8.
2   LPA 1925, s 104(2).
3   LPA 1925, s 104(2).
4   *Lord Waring v London and Manchester Assurance Co Ltd* [1935] Ch 310 at 318. To uphold such a purchaser's title would be 'to convert the provisions of the statute into an instrument of fraud' (*Bailey v Barnes* [1894] 1 Ch 25 at 30 per Stirling J). Likewise a good title may be denied to the purchaser who had actual knowledge of an irregularity in the mortgagee's exercise of an express (as distinct from statutory) power of sale (*Selwyn v Garfit* (1888) 38 Ch D 273 at 280). In default of a good title, the purchaser takes merely a transfer of the mortgage.
5   LPA 1925, s 104(2) seems to release the purchaser from any concern 'to see or inquire' whether the mortgagee has properly exercised his power of sale. Compare, however, the critical view expressed by P B Fairest, *Mortgages* (2nd edn, London 1980), pp 95–96, and see S Robinson, [1989] Conv 412. See also the decision of the Court of Appeal of New Zealand in *Pasquarella v National Australia Finance Ltd* [1987] 1 NZLR 312 at 315–318, which has stimulated the comment that, where the mortgagor is in an irretrievable financial position, the purchaser may not be prejudiced merely by reason of some degree of notice of minor irregularity ([1988] Conv 317 at 319 (H W W)).
6   [1894] 1 Ch 25 at 30.

Effect of sale by the mortgagee

15.178   Where a mortgagee sells under his statutory or express power of sale, his conveyance is effective to vest in the purchaser the mortgagor's full legal estate (whether freehold or leasehold), subject to any rights which themselves rank prior to the mortgage.[1] The transfer otherwise operates to confer on the purchaser a good legal title, enabling him to overreach all interests which are capable of being overreached (eg the selling mortgagee's mortgage and all subsequent mortgages).[2] The purchaser also takes free of any estate contract entered into by the mortgagor during the course of the mortgage term (even though this estate contract may have been protected by register entry).[3] Where the mortgaged estate was registered at Land Registry, the original disposition of charge conferred on the chargee a proprietorship of his registered charge which was patently free of the as yet non-existent estate contract.[4] Subsequent entry of a 'notice' in respect of the estate contract cannot enhance the validity of the estate contract,[5] since it was, inevitably, an interest carved out of and intrinsically subordinated to the chargor's equity of redemption.[6] In effect, all dealings with the mortgaged estate take place in the shadow of the security and therefore concede priority to the rights and powers with which the mortgage has already invested the lender.[7] The Land Registration Act 2002 cannot accord any priority to an interest which, under the general law, it would not otherwise enjoy.[8] The same outcome arises, for similar reasons, in relation to equivalent transactions with an unregistered mortgage security.[9]

1　LPA 1925, s 104(1).

2　LPA 1925, ss 2(1)(iii), 88(1)(b), 89(1). In strict terms the mortgagee's power of sale is exercised at the point of the contract to sell and not at the point of conveyance of the legal estate [**para 15.180**]. It follows that the mortgagor's equity of redemption has already been extinguished by the contract (see *Lord Waring v London and Manchester Assurance Co Ltd* [1935] Ch 310 at 316–318; *National and Provincial Building Society v Ahmed* [1995] 2 EGLR 127 at 129J; *Re Sarlis and Anderson* (1984) 7 DLR (4th) 227 at 233; *Chia v Rennie* (1997) 8 BPR 15601 at 15603).

3　[**Paras 9.23, 12.89, 12.306**].

4　LRA 2002, s 29(1), (2)(a)(i).

5　See LRA 2002, s 32(3) [**para 12.98**].

6　See *Forsyth v Blundell* (1973) 129 CLR 477 at 499 per Walsh J; *Alliance Acceptance Co Ltd v Ellison* (1986) 5 NSWLR 102 at 107D–G; *Vukicevic v Alliance Acceptance Co Ltd* (1987) 9 NSWLR 13 at 15F–16A (NSW Court of Appeal).

7　*Lyus v Prowsa Developments Ltd* [1982] 1 WLR 1044 at 1047G–1048A. See also *James v Registrar-General* (1967) 69 SR (NSW) 361 at 369, 87 WN (Pt 2) 239 at 245; *McKean v Maloney* [1988] 1 Qd R 628 at 635–636.

8　On completion of the mortgagee's sale by registration, his own charge and all entries in the register inferior to it will routinely be cancelled by Land Registry.

9　*Duke v Robson* [1973] 1 WLR 267 at 271D–F, 275B–C; (1973) 37 Conv (NS) 210 (F R Crane).

Mortgagee's duty in relation to the application of proceeds

15.179　On exercising his power of sale the mortgagee is rendered a trustee of the resulting proceeds of sale. The application of these proceeds is governed by section 105 of the Law of Property Act 1925, which directs that the proceeds should be held in trust by the mortgagee, to be applied *first*, in payment of all costs, charges and expenses properly incurred by him in connection with the sale[1]; *second*, in discharge of the mortgage money and interest due under his mortgage[2]; and *third*, in payment of the residue to the subsequent mortgagee or mortgagees (if any) and otherwise to the mortgagor.[3]

1　The mortgagee is not entitled to be reimbursed the costs of defending a third party's action impugning his title to the security or the enforcement or exercise of his rights under the mortgage (see *Parker-Tweedale v Dunbar Bank Plc (No 2)* [1991] Ch 26 at 33D, 47B–F).

2　The selling mortgagee is also liable to account to any subsequent mortgagee or chargee of whom he has notice. See *West London Commercial Bank v Reliance Permanent Building Society* (1885) 29 Ch D 954 at 961–963; *Kerabee Park Pty Ltd v Daley* [1978] 2 NSWLR 222 at 228F.

3　See *FSA Handbook* (Release 033, July 2004): MCOB 13.6.6R.

Mortgagee's general immunity from challenge

15.180　Upon the exercise of the mortgagee's power of sale, the mortgagor's equity of redemption is extinguished[1] and he can bring no complaint against the mortgagee except where it can be shown that the power of sale was exercised in an improper, harsh or oppressive manner. There is, in other words, no general jurisdiction (as in the case of foreclosure[2]) to reopen a mortgagee's sale on grounds of mere hardship, although the sale may in rare circumstances be vitiated by fraud, mistake or other irregularity.[3]

1   Since the statutory power is exercised as soon as the mortgagee contracts to sell the property, the mortgagor is from this point onwards disabled (in the absence of some form of equitable fraud by the mortgagee) from redeeming the mortgage (see also *Holmark Construction Co Pty Ltd v Tsoukaris* (1986) 4 BPR 9131 at 9135). Nor can the mortgagor frustrate the contracted sale by a belated payment of the money due (see *Lord Waring v London and Manchester Assurance Co Ltd* [1935] Ch 310 at 318; *Property & Bloodstock Ltd v Emerton* [1968] Ch 94 at 114F–115B; *Forsyth v Blundell* (1973) 129 CLR 477 at 499).

2   **[Para 15.228]**.

3   **[Para 15.220]**. See e g *McDonald Dure Lumber Co Ltd v Marstone Holdings Ltd* (1976) 66 DLR (3d) 375 (comedy of errors in auctioneer's negligent conduct of sale).

THE DUTY OF THE SELLING MORTGAGEE

15.181   An element of controversy always surrounds the nature of the duties imposed by law on the mortgagee who acts in exercise of his power of sale.

Absence of any statutory standard of fair dealing

15.182   The Law of Property Act 1925 clearly envisages that some exercises of the power of sale may be improper or irregular.[1] It may be a reflection of the latent capitalist emphasis of the 1925 legislation that, except in relation to the application of the proceeds of the sale, this statute does not expressly impose any specific ethical standard or code of conduct on the selling mortgagee.[2] It has been left to the courts to supply an implication that the mortgagee must fulfil certain expectations of equity in his exercise of the power of sale.[3] In the case of regulated mortgage contracts entered into on or after 31 October 2004, these expectations have been reinforced by certain obligations imposed indirectly by the Financial Services and Markets Act 2000.[4]

1   See LPA 1925, s 104(2).

2   Compare e g Victoria's Transfer of Land Act 1958 (No 6399), s 77(1); Queensland's Property Law Act 1974, s 85(1).

3   See *Henry Roach (Petroleum) Pty Ltd v Credit House (Vic) Pty Ltd* [1976] VR 309 at 312.

4   **[Paras 15.130, 15.196]**.

Is the selling mortgagee a trustee for the mortgagor?

15.183   Although a selling mortgagee becomes a trustee of the proceeds of sale, it is commonly said that he is not strictly a trustee for the mortgagor in respect of the power of sale itself.[1] This power is given to him, not for the benefit of another, but 'for his own benefit, to enable him the better to realise his debt.'[2] It is, in one sense, clear that the exercise of the power of sale cannot be a fiduciary exercise,[3] since the mortgagee has 'rights of his own which he is entitled to exercise adversely to the mortgagor.'[4] However, as Cross LJ pointed out in *Cuckmere Brick Co Ltd v Mutual Finance Ltd*,[5] the position of the selling mortgagee is at least 'ambiguous', since it is equally clear that he must 'pay some regard to the interests of the mortgagor when he comes to exercise the power.'

1   *Cuckmere Brick Co Ltd v Mutual Finance Ltd* [1971] Ch 949 at 965F per Salmon LJ; *Bishop v Bonham* [1988] 1 WLR 742 at 753F per Slade LJ; *Raja v Austin Gray (A Firm)* [2003] 1 EGLR 91 at [55(1)] per Peter Gibson LJ; *Corbett v Halifax Building Society* [2003] 1 WLR 964 at [23] per Pumfrey J; *Frost Ltd v Ralph* (1981) 115 DLR (3d) 612 at 622; *Commercial and General Acceptance Ltd v Nixon* (1981) 152 CLR 491 at 494 per Gibbs CJ, 502 per Mason J, 515 per Aickin J. There is, however, some evidence that early 19th century courts were accustomed to enforce trustee-like duties in favour of the mortgagor (see *Marquis Cholmondeley v Lord Clinton* (1817) 2 Mer 171, 35 ER 905; *Robertson v Norris* (1858) 1 Giff 421 at 423–425, 65 ER 983 at 984 per Stuart V-C). See generally *Australia and New Zealand Banking Group Ltd v Comer* (1993) 5 BPR 11748 at 11751–11752 per Young J (who, pointing to *Nash v Eads* (1880) 25 Sol Jo 95, noted a 'definite shift of policy' by 1880).

2   *Warner v Jacob* (1882) 20 Ch D 220 at 224 per Kay J.

3   See Paul Finn, *Fiduciary Obligations* (Sydney 1977), p 10.

4   *Farrar v Farrars Ltd* (1888) 40 Ch D 395 at 411 per Lindley LJ. See also *Sterne v Victoria & Grey Trust Co* (1985) 14 DLR (4th) 193 at 203. The motives of the mortgagee are, moreover, largely irrelevant. It is no objection to the exercise of a power of sale that the mortgagee does not need the money or is delighted to have an opportunity to harm a mortgagor whom he dislikes (*Nash v Eads* (1880) 25 Sol Jo 95; *Belton v Bass, Ratcliffe and Gretton Ltd* [1922] 2 Ch 449 at 465–466; *Artistic Builders Pty Ltd v Elliot & Tuthill (Mortgagees) Pty Ltd* (2002) 10 BPR 19565 at [101]–[102]).

5   [1971] Ch 949 at 969F.

15.184   The law of mortgage therefore holds somewhat inscrutably that, in exercising his power of sale, the mortgagee is entitled to give first, but not exclusive, consideration to his own interests.[1] Increasingly, as Nicholls V-C observed in *Palk v Mortgage Services Funding Plc*,[2] when the mortgagee takes steps to exercise his rights over his security, 'common law and equity alike have set bounds to the extent to which he can look after himself and ignore the mortgagor's interests.' Although the mortgagee is plainly entitled to protect his own interest, he is 'not entitled to conduct himself in a way which unfairly prejudices the mortgagor.'[3] In recent times the courts have so raised the standard of conduct expected of the selling mortgagee that it may now be feasible to maintain, even in the face of the conventional disavowal of trustee status, that the mortgagee's duty to his mortgagor has become 'analogous to a fiduciary duty.'[4] To assert nowadays that the mortgagee can never be a trustee of his power of sale is 'probably [to] overstate the law.'[5]

1   See *Palmer v Barclays Bank Ltd* (1972) 23 P & CR 30 at 35; *Palk v Mortgage Services Funding Plc* [1993] Ch 330 at 337G per Nicholls V-C; *Henry Roach (Petroleum) Pty Ltd v Credit House (Vic) Pty Ltd* [1976] VR 309 at 313.

2   [1993] Ch 330 at 337G.

3   [1993] Ch 330 at 337H. See *Raja v Austin Gray (A Firm)* [2003] 1 EGLR 91 at [57] per Peter Gibson LJ; *Finance Corporation of Australia Ltd v Bentley* (1991) 5 BPR 11833 at 11834 per Kirby P ('Mortgagees are not uncontrolled free agents let loose to pursue exclusively their own interests as they think fit. They are answerable to duties of conscience').

4   Sir Frederick Jordan, *Chapters on Equity in New South Wales*, in *Selected Legal Papers* (Sydney 1983), p 113, cited with approval in the High Court of Australia in *Hospital Products Ltd v United States Surgical Corpn* (1984) 156 CLR 41 at 102 per Mason J. See also

> *Sterne v Victoria & Grey Trust Co* (1985) 14 DLR (4th) 193 at 203 per Rutherford J; *Australia and New Zealand Banking Group Ltd v Comer* (1993) 5 BPR 11748 at 11752 per Young J (conceding that the mortgagee has 'certain residual fiduciary duties').
> 5   *Yarrangah Pty Ltd v National Australia Bank Ltd* (1999) 9 BPR 17061 at [10] per Young J (pointing out that the old cases do not 'all speak with the one voice').

General duty of the selling mortgagee

15.185   There has been much difference of opinion as to the proper balance to be maintained between the respective interests of the mortgagor and the mortgagee. Assessed purely in terms of immediate financial self-interest, the mortgagee's only concern in sale is to obtain with speed and efficiency a sufficient price to cover the amount of the outstanding loan. However, a sale which satisfied only this minimal purpose would almost inevitably inflict grave prejudice on the mortgagor, since any sale at an undervalue erodes the effective value of his equity of redemption. A sale price which is adequate to meet only the costs of the sale and the outstanding mortgage money leaves no surplus at all for the mortgagor.

15.186   The ambiguity of the mortgagee's position was for a long time reflected in the divergent and sometimes inconsistent criteria applied by the courts in determining the propriety of a mortgagee's exercise of his power of sale.[1] It now seems clear, however, that the conduct of the selling mortgagee is to be judged with reference to two criteria, one subjective in nature and the other objective. The mortgagee must always act in good faith; he must also discharge a duty of reasonable care towards his mortgagor. The mortgagor has a valid ground for complaint if either of these criteria has not been met.

1   See *Cuckmere Brick Co Ltd v Mutual Finance Ltd* [1971] Ch 949 at 966B per Salmon LJ. See generally P Devonshire, (1995) 46 NILQ 182.

Subjective criterion of good faith

15.187   There is an elementary requirement of good faith in the exercise of the mortgagee's power of sale. This subjective criterion demands that the mortgagee should not deal 'wilfully and recklessly ... with the property in such a manner that the interests of the mortgagor are sacrificed.'[1] Equity's tradition-ally heavy emphasis on this requirement at first led the courts to deny that mere *carelessness* in the matter of sale could ever be a ground of liability for the mortgagee.[2] Thus it used to be thought that the mortgagee's only obligation to the mortgagor was simply 'not to cheat him.'[3] According to this earlier view, the court would not interfere 'even though the sale be very disadvantageous', unless the sale price was 'so low as in itself to be evidence of fraud' or there was evidence of 'corruption or collusion with the purchaser.'[4]

1   *Kennedy v De Trafford* [1897] AC 180 at 185 per Lord Herschell. See also *Barns v Queensland National Bank Ltd* (1906) 3 CLR 925 at 942–943; *Pendlebury v Colonial Mutual Life Assurance Society Ltd* (1912) 13 CLR 676 at 680, 694, 700.

2   *Pendlebury v Colonial Mutual Life Assurance Society Ltd* (1912) 13 CLR 676 at 700; *British Columbia Land & Investment Agency v Ishitaka* (1911) 45 SCR 302 at 317.
3   *Cuckmere Brick Co Ltd v Mutual Finance Ltd* [1971] Ch 949 at 966B per Salmon LJ.
4   *Warner v Jacob* (1882) 20 Ch D 220 at 224 per Kay J.

15.188   The recent development of the law of mortgage throughout most of the common law world has seen a general rejection of the idea that the subjective requirement of good faith stands alone as the exclusive criterion of the mortgagee's conduct. It now seems clear that his behaviour must also measure up to an objective standard of reasonable care.[1]

1   See *Goldcell Nominees Pty Ltd v Network Finance Ltd* [1983] 2 VR 257 at 262.

Objective criterion of reasonable behaviour

15.189   There have always been isolated statements in the case law that the selling mortgagee should 'behave ... as a reasonable man would behave in the realisation of his own property, so that the mortgagor may receive credit for the fair value of the property sold.'[1] These statements have gathered force over the last 30 years and it has become generally acknowledged that the mortgagee is answerable for carelessness or imprudence in the conduct of the sale.[2] Courts have drawn progressively upon the analogous rule that the mortgagee in possession 'must take reasonable care to maximise his return from the property'[3] and 'must take steps to preserve its value.'[4] Likewise in the exercise of his power of sale the mortgagee cannot act arbitrarily, but 'must exercise reasonable care to sell only at the proper market value.'[5] The injection of this objective criterion of reasonableness has done much to elevate the standard of dealing required of the mortgagee.

1   *McHugh v Union Bank of Canada* [1913] AC 299 at 311 per Lord Moulton. See also *Falkner v Equitable Reversionary Society* (1858) 4 Drew 352 at 355, 62 ER 136 at 137; *Marriott v Anchor Reversionary Co Ltd* (1860) 7 Jur NS 155 at 156–157, 2 Giff 457 at 469, 66 ER 191 at 196–197 (affd 3 De GF & J 177, 45 ER 846).
2   *Holohan v Friends' Provident and Century Life Office* [1966] IR 1 at 21–22, 25.
3   *Palk v Mortgage Services Funding Plc* [1993] Ch 330 at 338A per Nicholls V-C (the mortgagee 'cannot sell hastily at a knock-down price sufficient to pay off his debt'). See likewise *Silven Properties Ltd v Royal Bank of Scotland Plc* [2004] 1 WLR 997 at [19] per Lightman J.
4   See e g *Sterne v Victoria & Grey Trust Co* (1985) 14 DLR (4th) 193 at 203 per Rutherford J.
5   *Palk v Mortgage Services Funding Plc* [1993] Ch 330 at 338B per Nicholls V-C.

Fusion of subjective and objective criteria

15.190   The conduct nowadays expected of the selling mortgagee involves a fusion of subjective and objective elements, and requires that the mortgagee should practise not only good faith but also reasonable diligence. As Salmon LJ said in *Cuckmere Brick Co Ltd v Mutual Finance Ltd*,[1] the mortgagee 'owes both duties.'[2] These two duties interact and coalesce.[3] In the High Court of Australia in *Forsyth v Blundell*,[4] Menzies J likewise expressed the view that to 'take reasonable precautions to obtain a proper price is but part of the duty to act in good faith.'⁵ This blending of concepts ensures that the legitimate primacy of the mortgagee's self-interest is not inconsistent with 'having regard to the interests of others or with taking reasonable care to protect the interests of others.'⁶

1   [1971] Ch 949 at 966C.
2   As long ago as *Farrar v Farrars Ltd* (1888) 40 Ch D 395 at 411, Lindley LJ ruled that the mortgagor had no redress provided the mortgagee 'acts bona fide and takes reasonable precautions to obtain a proper price.' That the mortgagee owes both kinds of duty is now widely recognised (see e g *Freeguard v Royal Bank of Scotland plc* [2002] EWHC 2509 (Ch) at [11]; *Raja v Austin Gray (A Firm)* [2003] 1 EGLR 91 at [55(3)] per Peter Gibson LJ; *Corbett v Halifax Building Society* [2003] 1 WLR 964 at [33] per Pumfrey J; *Bank of Montreal v Allender Investments Ltd* (1984) 4 DLR (4th) 340 at 343; *Suskind v Bank of Nova Scotia* (1984) 10 DLR (4th) 101 at 106, 108).
3   See *Apple Fields Ltd v Damesh Holdings Ltd* [2001] 1 NZLR 194 at [48] per John Hansen J, [2001] 2 NZLR 586 at [40] (NZ Court of Appeal).
4   (1973) 129 CLR 477 at 481.
5   See *Kennedy v De Trafford* [1897] AC 180 at 185 per Lord Herschell (particularly as interpreted by Scott V-C in *Medforth v Blake* [2000] Ch 86 at 101D–F, 103C–D). See also *Sullivan v Darkin* [1986] 1 NZLR 214 at 222 per Somers J. In *Frost Ltd v Ralph* (1981) 115 DLR (3d) 612 at 617, a mortgagee's sale at an undervalue one day after the mortgagor failed to redeem was held to constitute not only a lack of reasonable care on the mortgagee's part, but also strong evidence of mala fides.
6   *Henry Roach (Petroleum) Pty Ltd v Credit House (Vic) Pty Ltd* [1976] VR 309 at 313.

15.191   The precise application of the twin concepts of good faith and reasonable care may depend, to some extent, upon the nature of the remedy sought by the mortgagor. The two tests tend to operate under 'different and mutually exclusive conditions.'¹ The subjective requirement of good faith relates usually to the avoidance of conflicts of interest which lead the court to set aside improperly transacted sales. By contrast the objective requirement of reasonable care more readily generates, in cases of breach, a mere monetary liability in respect of the financial loss caused by the mortgagee's carelessness. Thus, where the mortgagor brings an action against *both* the mortgagee *and* the purchaser for the setting aside of a sale, the court intervenes only if fraud or bad faith is shown to attach to the transaction. Where, however, the mortgagor seeks his remedy solely against the mortgagee and sues only for an accounting between them in respect of the sale price achieved, the court assesses the propriety of the mortgagee's conduct by reference to the rather higher standard represented by the test of reasonable care.

1   See *Sterne v Victoria & Grey Trust Co* (1985) 14 DLR (4th) 193 at 201 per Rutherford J.

MORTGAGEE'S DUTY OF OBJECTIVELY REASONABLE CARE

15.192   The objective requirement of reasonable care has come to exert an impact on much of the mortgagee's conduct in the exercise of his power of sale, most noticeably in relation to the price achieved by the sale. The mortgagee's duty in this respect is non-delegable¹ and the mortgagee is not relieved from responsibility merely because he entrusts the sale of the mortgaged property to an apparently competent or experienced agent or valuer.² It seems also that, although the duty of care may be excluded by contrary agreement between mortgagor and mortgagee,[3] the courts apply such strict construction even to widely drafted exclusion clauses that the rigour of the general duty is virtually inescapable.[4]

1   *Wolff v Vanderzee* (1869) 20 LT 353 at 354; *Tomlin v Luce* (1889) 41 Ch D 573 at 575–576, (1889) 43 Ch D 191 at 194; *Cuckmere Brick Co Ltd v Mutual Finance Ltd* [1971] Ch 949 at 969A–B, 973A. See also *Australia and New Zealand Banking Group Ltd v Bangadilly Pastoral Co Pty Ltd* (1978) 139 CLR 195 at 222 per Aickin J.
2   See *Commercial and General Acceptance Ltd v Nixon* (1981) 152 CLR 491 at 495 per Gibbs CJ, 503 per Mason J, 508 per Aickin J, 521 per Wilson J; *Sterne v Victoria & Grey Trust Co* (1985) 14 DLR (4th) 193 at 204; *McKean v Maloney* [1988] 1 Qd R 628 at 634. The non-delegable responsibility of the mortgagee is unaffected by the probability nowadays that the injured mortgagor has a valid claim in negligence directly against the mortgagee's agent (see *Cuckmere Brick Co Ltd v Mutual Finance Ltd* [1971] Ch 949 at 973C–E; *Commercial and General Acceptance Ltd v Nixon*, supra at 504–505 per Mason J, 516 per Aickin J).
3   *Bishop v Bonham* [1988] 1 WLR 742 at 752A per Slade LJ; *Raja v Lloyds TSB Bank Plc* (2001) 82 P & CR 191 at [20] per Judge LJ.
4   See eg *Bishop v Bonham* [1988] 1 WLR 742 at 753E–F, 754A, where the Court of Appeal declined to hold that an express power of sale authorising the mortgagee to sell 'in such manner and upon such terms and for such consideration ... as you may think fit' gave the mortgagee 'carte blanche' to act as he thought fit in disregard of the duty of care. The mortgagee's exercise of his power was still constrained by the need to act as he thought fit 'within the limits of the duty of reasonable care imposed by the general law.'

Doctrinal basis of the mortgagee's duty

15.193   The doctrinal foundation of the mortgagee's duty of care or diligence has proved to be a matter of some dispute. At one point in his judgment in *Cuckmere Brick Co Ltd v Mutual Finance Ltd*,[1] Salmon LJ seemed to locate the source of the mortgagee's responsibility in some version of the 'neighbour' principle adumbrated by Lord Atkin in *Donoghue v Stevenson*.[2] Salmon LJ also noted, however, that the heightened responsibility of the selling mortgagee flowed from the fact that 'many years before the modern development of the law of negligence, the courts of equity had laid down a doctrine in relation to mortgages which is entirely consonant with the general principles later evolved by the common law.'[3] There have been other suggestions that the mortgagee's duty is essentially contractual in that the mortgagor, knowing at the time of the contract of loan that he remains ultimately liable for any balance undischarged by sale, must be assumed to have conceded the mortgagee's power of sale 'only in the expectation that the mortgagee will use his best efforts to achieve the best price for the security.'[4]

1   [1971] Ch 949 at 966D–E ('The mortgagor is vitally affected by the result of the sale but its preparation and conduct is left entirely in the hands of the mortgagee. The proximity between them could scarcely be closer. Surely they are "neighbours"'). See likewise *Standard Chartered Bank Ltd v Walker* [1982] 1 WLR 1410 at 1415E–G per Lord Denning MR.
2   [1932] AC 562 at 580. See similarly *National Westminster Finance New Zealand Ltd v United Finance & Securities Ltd* [1988] 1 NZLR 226 at 237–238.
3   [1971] Ch 949 at 967D. See eg *Tomlin v Luce* (1889) 43 Ch D 191 at 194–195 per Cotton LJ.
4   *Sterne v Victoria & Grey Trust Co* (1985) 14 DLR (4th) 193 at 203 per Rutherford J. See also *Bishop v Bonham* [1988] 1 WLR 742 at 752A–D per Slade LJ.

15.194   More recent English case law has inclined toward the view that the duty owed by the mortgagee to the mortgagor does not derive from any analogy with tort[1] or contract,[2] but is instead 'recognised in equity as arising out of the particular relationship between them.'[3] Nowadays the more accurate approach seems to be that the mortgagee's conduct falls to be judged with reference to venerable principles of equitable intervention. For this reason the standard expected of the selling mortgagee is perhaps better described in terms of a duty of reasonable diligence rather than a duty of reasonable care.[4] As Knight Bruce V-C held in *Matthie v Edwards*,[5] the mortgagee must 'act in a prudent and business-like manner, with a view to obtain as large a price as may fairly and reasonably, with due diligence and attention, be under the circumstances obtainable.'[6] Thus stated, the mortgagee's responsibility begins closely to resemble Jessel MR's classic definition in *Speight v Gaunt*[7] of the quality of conduct expected of the trustee. The newly intensified equitable perspective on the dealings of mortgagees may indeed have gone some way towards modifying the conventional view that the mortgagee is never a fiduciary of his power of sale.[8]

1   See e g *Parker-Tweedale v Dunbar Bank Plc* [1991] Ch 12 at 18H per Nourse LJ ('both unnecessary and confusing'); *Silven Properties Ltd v Royal Bank of Scotland plc* [2002] EWHC 1976 (Ch) at [112] per Patten J ('a quite different juristic basis'). See also *China and South Sea Bank Ltd v Tan Soon Gin* [1990] 1 AC 536 at 543H–544A per Lord Templeman (the tort of negligence 'has not yet subsumed all torts and does not supplant the principles of equity').

2   A link with the law of contract would confine the mortgagee's duty, within the contractual nexus, to the mortgagor alone (see *Raja v Lloyds TSB Bank Plc* (2001) 82 P & CR 191 at [25]–[27]).

3   *Parker-Tweedale v Dunbar Bank Plc* [1991] Ch 12 at 18H–19A per Nourse LJ. See also *Downsview Nominees Ltd v First City Corpn Ltd* [1993] AC 295 at 315D per Lord Templeman; *AIB Finance Ltd v Debtors* [1998] 2 All ER 929 at 937e per Nourse LJ; *Medforth v Blake* [2000] Ch 86 at 99C–D, 102E per Scott V-C; *Raja v Lloyds TSB Bank Plc* (2001) 82 P & CR 191 at [15]–[18] per Judge LJ; *Freeguard v Royal Bank of Scotland plc* [2002] EWHC 2509 (Ch) at [11]; *Silven Properties Ltd v Royal Bank of Scotland Plc* [2004] 1 WLR 997 at [19].

4   See, however, *Medforth v Blake* [2000] Ch 86 at 102D–E for Scott V-C's view that it ultimately matters little whether the mortgagee's duty is cast in common law or in equity.

5   (1846) 2 Coll 465 at 480, 63 ER 817 at 824 (reversed at (1847) 16 LJ Ch 405 at 409, but without criticism of the principle applied by Knight Bruce V-C).

6   See also *McHugh v Union Bank of Canada* [1913] AC 299 at 311 per Lord Moulton.

7   (1883) 22 Ch D 727 at 739 ('[A] trustee ought to conduct the business of the trust in the same manner that an ordinary prudent man of business would conduct his own').

8   [Para 15.183].

Duty in respect of sale price

15.195   Building society mortgagees were long subject to a statutory duty to take 'reasonable care to ensure' that the price achieved on the exercise of their power of sale is 'the best price that can reasonably be obtained.'[1] Likewise a local authority mortgagee, on exercising its right to vest mortgaged property in itself,[2] must account to the mortgagor for the 'value of the house at the time of the vesting.'[3] This value is statutorily deemed to be the price which the interest vested in the authority would realise if the house, freed of the relevant incumbrance, were 'sold on the open market by a willing vendor.'[4]

1   Building Societies Act 1986, s 13(7), Sch 4, para 1(1)(a), (2). This obligation has now been subsumed (see *Corbett v Halifax Building Society* [2003] 1 WLR 964 at [24]) within the general duty imposed by the courts on all categories of mortgagee (see Building Societies Act 1997, s 12(2)). See also *Reliance Permanent Building Society v Harwood-Stamper* [1944] Ch 362 at 372–374.
2   **[Para 15.156]**.
3   HA 1985, Sch 17, para 3(1)(a).
4   HA 1985, Sch 17, para 3(2).

The general benchmark

15.196   It is also clear nowadays that other kinds of mortgagee owe a similar duty of diligence in respect of the price at which the mortgaged property is ultimately realised. The benchmark of this responsibility was indicated in entirely general terms by the Court of Appeal in *Cuckmere Brick Co Ltd v Mutual Finance Ltd*.[1] Here Salmon LJ described the duty of the selling mortgagee as comprising a responsibility to 'take reasonable precautions to obtain the true market value of the mortgaged property at the date on which he decides to sell it.'[2] This duty, although expressed over the years in varying formulations,[3] comprises essentially an obligation to 'exercise reasonable care to sell only at the proper market value'[4] or to 'obtain the best price reasonably obtainable' at the time of sale.[5] Those who lend under 'regulated mortgage contracts' governed by the Financial Services and Markets Act 2000 are likewise obligated to 'obtain the best price that might reasonably be paid.'[6]

1   [1971] Ch 949 at 968H–969A. The '*Cuckmere* principle' has been described as one of the implied primary obligations of the mortgagee (see *Bishop v Bonham* [1988] 1 WLR 742 at 752A–D per Slade LJ).
2   See similarly *Tse Kwong Lam v Wong Chit Sen* [1983] 1 WLR 1349 at 1356G–H per Lord Templeman ('reasonable precautions to obtain the best price reasonably obtainable at the time of sale'); *China and South Sea Bank Ltd v Tan Soon Gin* [1990] 1 AC 536 at 545D (duty to 'sell for the current market value'); *Freeguard v Royal Bank of Scotland plc* [2002] EWHC 2509 (Ch) at [11]; *Silven Properties Ltd v Royal Bank of Scotland Plc* [2004] 1 WLR 997 at [19].
3   See *Standard Chartered Bank Ltd v Walker* [1982] 1 WLR 1410 at 1415E per Lord Denning MR; *Predeth v Castle Phillips Finance Co Ltd* (1986) 279 EG 1355 at 1356; *Bishop v Bonham* [1988] 1 WLR 742 at 750D–H per Slade LJ; *Michael v Miller* [2004] EWCA Civ 282 at [131] per Jonathan Parker LJ; *Sullivan v Darkin* [1986] 1 NZLR 214 at 218 per Davison CJ; *Hausman v O'Grady* (1988) 42 DLR (4th) 119 at 125 (affd (1989) 57 DLR (4th) 480).
4   *Palk v Mortgage Services Funding Plc* [1993] Ch 330 at 338B per Nicholls V-C. See likewise *Downsview Nominees Ltd v First City Corpn Ltd* [1993] AC 295 at 315C per Lord Templeman; *Yorkshire Bank Plc v Hall* [1999] 1 WLR 1713 at 1728E per Robert Walker LJ; *Medforth v Blake* [2000] Ch 86 at 92E. Compare *Cuckmere Brick Co Ltd v Mutual Finance Ltd* [1971] Ch 949 at 968H–969A, where Salmon LJ preferred not to refer to the concepts of 'proper price' (which was 'perhaps a little nebulous') or 'best price' (which 'might suggest an exceptionally high price').
5   *Raja v Lloyds TSB Bank Plc* (2001) 82 P & CR 191 at [13]–[14] per Judge LJ. See similarly *Apple Fields Ltd v Damesh Holdings Ltd* [2004] 1 NZLR 721 at [22]–[25] per Lord Scott of Foscote.
6   *FSA Handbook* (Release 033, July 2004): MCOB 13.6.1R(2) **[para 15.203]**. The lender is expressly directed, in this context, to take account of 'factors such as market conditions as well as the continuing increase in the amount owed by the customer.'

Perfection is not required

15.197   The mortgagee cannot, of course, be held to any absolute obligation to realise the 'true value'[1] or to obtain the 'best price' of the mortgaged property.[2] 'Perfection is not required' of the mortgagee.[3] His duty is merely to invest reasonable care in the exercise of his power of sale: it is 'the effort rather than the result to which the court looks.'[4] The question whether 'reasonable steps have been taken ... to obtain the best price' must be examined 'in the round ... in practical commercial terms.'[5] It is readily recognised that a forced sale by a mortgagee seldom achieves the 'highest', 'best possible' or even 'market' price.[6] The 'market' for repossessed land is inevitably distorted and cogent evidence is required to rebut the inference that the actual sale price represented the proper price in the circumstances.[7] Provided that the mortgagee exercises an informed judgment as to market conditions and market value, he cannot be faulted if the price achieved is broadly within the correct 'bracket' or falls within an acceptable 'margin of error'.[8] The point remains, however, that the mortgagee is not simply entitled to adopt *any* arrangement or accept *any* price merely because it will see him paid out.[9] He has no right to sacrifice the interest of the mortgagor in the surplus of the proceeds of sale.[10]

1   *Bank of Nova Scotia v Barnard* (1984) 9 DLR (4th) 575 at 586.
2   *Sterne v Victoria & Grey Trust Co* (1985) 14 DLR (4th) 193 at 203.
3   *Hausman v O'Grady* (1988) 42 DLR (4th) 119 at 129 per Anderson J (affd (1989) 57 DLR (4th) 480). In *Cuckmere Brick Co Ltd v Mutual Finance Ltd* [1971] Ch 949 at 969A, Salmon LJ indicated that the mortgagee 'will not be adjudged to be in default unless he is plainly on the wrong side of the line.' See also *Apple Fields Ltd v Damesh Holdings Ltd* [2001] 2 NZLR 586 at [4] (NZ Court of Appeal).
4   *Sterne v Victoria & Grey Trust Co* (1985) 14 DLR (4th) 193 at 203–204 per Rutherford J.
5   *Apple Fields Ltd v Damesh Holdings Ltd* [2004] 1 NZLR 721 at [24] per Lord Scott of Foscote.
6   *Canadian Imperial Bank of Commerce v Whitman* (1985) 12 DLR (4th) 326 at 343. See *Minah v Bank of Ireland* [1995] EGCS 144 (no breach of mortgagee's duty where property sold at £39,000 as against earlier valuations of £45,000 and £40,000).
7   *Hausman v O'Grady* (1988) 42 DLR (4th) 119 at 131–132 (affd (1989) 57 DLR (4th) 480).
8   *Michael v Miller* [2004] EWCA Civ 282 at [138] per Jonathan Parker LJ.
9   *Henry Roach (Petroleum) Pty Ltd v Credit House (Vic) Pty Ltd* [1976] VR 309 at 313. See e g *Frost Ltd v Ralph* (1981) 115 DLR (3d) 612 at 617, 622; *Forsyth v Blundell* (1973) 129 CLR 477 at 510.
10   *Commercial and General Acceptance Ltd v Nixon* (1981) 152 CLR 491 at 494 per Gibbs CJ, 515 per Wilson J. There is inevitably some suspicion that the decisions of both the Court of Appeal and the House of Lords in *Williams & Glyn's Bank Ltd v Boland* [1981] AC 487, [1979] Ch 312 **[para 12.203]** were coloured by the bank mortgagee's ruthless sale for £1,500 of a part of the secured property which was probably worth a sum in the region of £22,500 (see (1978) 36 P & CR 448 at 451).

Examples

15.198   Whether a mortgagee has fulfilled his duty of care is in each case a question of fact,[1] although an aggrieved mortgagor need not discharge the perhaps impossible onus of locating and identifying prospective purchasers who would have been prepared to pay a higher price than the actual purchaser.[2] In *Cuckmere Brick Co Ltd v Mutual Finance Ltd*[3] a mortgagee realised the mortgaged property through a sale by auction. Although informed expressly of a relevant (but fairly complex) planning permission relating to the land, the mortgagee failed to make adequate reference in the auction advertisements to the full extent of the permission.[4] In consequence the land was sold at an undervalue and the Court of Appeal held that the mortgagee was liable in damages to the mortgagor for breach of the duty of care which it owed to the latter.[5] There is, however, no necessary inference of lack of care if, as in *Palmer v Barclays Bank Ltd*,[6] the mortgagee and his agent had never been informed of the availability of any planning permission and were therefore wholly unaware of its existence.[7] Where a mortgagee sells up business premises, there may be a limited duty to pursue a sale of the land together with the business as a going concern, but this duty cannot apply where the mortgagor had already ceased trading before the mortgagee obtained possession.[8]

1   *Apple Fields Ltd v Damesh Holdings Ltd* [2001] 2 NZLR 586 at [50] (NZ Court of Appeal). The content of this duty of care does not vary in proportion to the degree of experience possessed by the mortgagee as vendor. In other words the same standard of care is demanded of the small investor as of the institutional lender (see *Commercial and General Acceptance Ltd v Nixon* (1981) 152 CLR 491 at 503 per Mason J).
2   *McKean v Maloney* [1988] 1 Qd R 628 at 634–635 per McPherson J. The price achieved in a subsequent resale by the mortgagee's purchaser may be of evidential value. See *Hausman v O'Grady* (1988) 42 DLR (4th) 119 at 132, but compare *Parker-Tweedale v Dunbar Bank Plc* [1991] Ch 12.
3   [1971] Ch 949. See (1971) 87 LQR 303.
4   See also *National Westminster Finance New Zealand Ltd v United Finance & Securities Ltd* [1988] 1 NZLR 226 at 237–238 (failure to publicise suitability of property for immediate subdivision).
5   Compare *Bank of Cyprus (London) Ltd v Gill* [1980] 2 Lloyd's Rep 51 at 54. See (1982) 132 NLJ 883 (H W Wilkinson). See also *Predeth v Castle Phillips Finance Co Ltd* (1986) 279 EG 1355 at 1358–1359, where the Court of Appeal held that there had been a want of reasonable care where the mortgagee authorised a 'crash sale' of the mortgaged property.
6   (1972) 23 P & CR 30 at 36.
7   Any serious prospective purchaser would normally discover the existence of the planning permission on requisitioning a local authority search (see *Goldcell Nominees Pty Ltd v Network Finance Ltd* [1983] 2 VR 257 at 277–278).
8   *AIB Finance Ltd v Debtors* [1998] 2 All ER 929 at 936d–j.

Range of the mortgagee's duty of diligence

15.199   The mortgagee's duty of diligence, however defined, is of course fundamentally qualified by the range of persons to whom the duty is owed. The mortgagee's responsibility in respect of the sale price is clearly a duty owed primarily to the mortgagor himself[1] or to any transferee of his equity of redemption.[2] It is well established, however, that second and later mortgagees[3] and any guarantor or surety of the mortgage loan[4] may also claim the benefit of the mortgagee's obligation to strive for a proper market price on sale. Such parties are entitled to an allowance in equity in respect of any financial loss occasioned through proven default by the selling mortgagee.

1   See *Johnson v Ribbins* (1975) 235 EG 757 at 759; *Standard Chartered Bank v Walker* [1982] 1 WLR 1410 at 1415E–G; *Clark v UDC Finance Ltd* [1985] 2 NZLR 636 at 638–639.

2   *Freeguard v Royal Bank of Scotland plc* [2002] EWHC 2509 (Ch) at [12], [14], [17].
3   *Tomlin v Luce* (1889) 41 Ch D 573 at 575–576, (1889) 43 Ch D 191 at 194 per Cotton LJ; *Cuckmere Brick Co Ltd v Mutual Finance Ltd* [1971] Ch 949 at 966G per Salmon LJ; *Raja v Lloyds TSB Bank Plc* (2001) 82 P & CR 191 at [25] per Judge LJ; *Alliance Acceptance Co Ltd v Graham* (1974) 10 SASR 220 at 222; *Suskind v Bank of Nova Scotia* (1984) 10 DLR (4th) 101 at 112; *National Westminster Finance New Zealand Ltd v United Finance & Securities Ltd* [1988] 1 NZLR 226 at 234; *Artistic Builders Pty Ltd v Elliot & Tuthill (Mortgagees) Pty Ltd* (2002) 10 BPR 19565 at [96].
4   'Equity intervenes to protect a surety' (*China and South Sea Bank Ltd v Tan Soon Gin* [1990] 1 AC 536 at 544A per Lord Templeman). See also *Standard Chartered Bank Ltd v Walker* [1982] 1 WLR 1410 at 1415E–G; *American Express International Banking Corpn Ltd v Hurley* [1985] 3 All ER 564 at 571f; *Raja v Lloyds TSB Bank Plc* (2001) 82 P & CR 191 at [25] per Judge LJ; *Clark v UDC Finance Ltd* [1985] 2 NZLR 636 at 638–639. The liability of a guarantor or surety may be reduced pro tanto by the mortgagee's failure to obtain the proper value of the security (*Skipton Building Society v Stott* [2001] QB 261 at [21]).

15.200   There is nevertheless a danger that the matrix of responsibility surrounding the selling mortgagee may become unnecessarily complex and unwieldy, and the courts have therefore set some limit on the multiplication of liabilities. In *Parker-Tweedale v Dunbar Bank Plc*[1] the claimant was a beneficiary under a trust of property which had been held by his wife as sole legal owner and mortgagor. The claimant alleged that the mortgagee, in the exercise of its power of sale, had sold at a price which the purchaser, on resale three weeks later, was able to better by a margin of £125,000. It was conceded that the selling mortgagee had notice at all relevant times of the claimant's interest behind the trust. The Court of Appeal declined to hold that the beneficiary was owed, in respect of the sale price, any independent duty of diligence additional to that already owed by the mortgagee to the mortgagor.[2] The mortgagee's duty arises from a 'particular relationship' with the mortgagor which does not extend to trust beneficiaries holding under the mortgagor.[3] Accordingly, in the view of the Court of Appeal, there was no room for the superimposition of a further duty owed directly to the beneficiary which would enable the beneficiary to sue for the financial loss inflicted on the trust assets.[4]

1   [1991] Ch 12.
2   According to Purchas LJ, the beneficiary's rights are exclusively 'against the mortgagor as trustee upon whom there is a duty to take reasonable care to preserve the assets of the trust' ([1991] Ch 12 at 25A–B). See similarly *Raja v Austin Gray (A Firm)* [2003] 1 EGLR 91 at [55(3)] per Peter Gibson LJ.
3   [1991] Ch 12 at 19D–E per Nourse LJ.
4   [1991] Ch 12 at 19D per Nourse LJ, 23A per Sir Michael Kerr, 25A per Purchas LJ. The Court conceded that a beneficiary might maintain a direct claim against the mortgagee if the trustee/mortgagor unreasonably refused to sue on behalf of the trust or was disabled or disqualified from so acting. Even here the beneficiary would be permitted to sue only in right of the trust and in the room of the trustee ([1991] Ch 12 at 19F–H, 23D–E, 25B–C).

Timing of the sale

15.201   It is settled law that once his power of sale has accrued, the mortgagee is prima facie entitled to exercise it for his own purposes at any time of his own choice and regardless of the wishes of mortgagor.[1] In *Cuckmere Brick Co Ltd v*

Mutual Finance Ltd.[2] Salmon LJ thought that it 'matters not that the moment may be unpropitious and that by waiting a higher price may be obtained.'[3] It was his view that the mortgagee 'has a right to realise his security by turning it into money when he likes.'[4] The mortgagee's general obligation of prudent dealing does not, in effect, extend to the timing of the proposed sale. It is broadly irrelevant that a better price would have been obtained by deferring sale,[5] or by waiting out a protracted slump in the market,[6] or by spending more money on the property prior to sale.[7] The mortgagee has interests of his own which he cannot be required to disregard.

1   *Parker-Tweedale v Dunbar Bank Plc* [1991] Ch 12 at 18B per Nourse LJ; *Silven Properties Ltd v Royal Bank of Scotland plc* [2002] EWHC 1976 (Ch) at [117] per Patten J. A mortgagee who takes possession of a security with a view to selling it must account to the mortgagor for any loss caused by the negligence of the mortgagee (or his agent) in managing the property between the date of taking possession and the date of the sale (*Cuckmere Brick Co Ltd v Mutual Finance Ltd* [1971] Ch 949 at 972G per Cross LJ). See e g *Norwich General Trust v Grierson* [1984] CLY 2306.
2   [1971] Ch 949 at 965G.
3   See similarly *Davey v Durrant* (1857) 1 De G & J 535 at 553, 44 ER 830 at 838; *Warner v Jacob* (1882) 20 Ch D 220 at 224; *Farrar v Farrars Ltd* (1888) 40 Ch D 395 at 398, 411; *Barns v Queensland National Bank Ltd* (1906) 3 CLR 925 at 942; *Tse Kwong Lam v Wong Chit Sen* [1983] 1 WLR 1349 at 1355B, 1359F–G per Lord Templeman; *Predeth v Castle Phillips Finance Co Ltd* (1986) 279 EG 1355 at 1356.
4   Nor has the mortgagor any valid complaint if the mortgagee, by threatening to exercise his statutory power of sale, pressurises the mortgagor into selling the mortgaged property at an unfavourable time (*Page v Barclays Bank Ltd* (Unreported, Court of Appeal, 14 July 1980)).
5   *Hausman v O'Grady* (1988) 42 DLR (4th) 119 at 128, 130 (affd (1989) 57 DLR (4th) 480) ('the mortgagees ... are entitled to recover with reasonable expedition'). However, a mortgagee may be adjudged to have acted carelessly if he fails to expose the property for sale for a reasonable period of time before sale. See *Bank of Nova Scotia v Barnard* (1984) 9 DLR (4th) 575 at 586 (14 days insufficient); *Predeth v Castle Phillips Finance Co Ltd* (1986) 279 EG 1355 at 1356 (uninhabitable property required three months on market).
6   *Sterne v Victoria & Grey Trust Co* (1985) 14 DLR (4th) 193 at 203.
7   *Expo International Pty Ltd v Chant* [1979] 2 NSWLR 820 at 835; *Stoyanovich v National Westminster Finance* (1984) 3 BPR 9310 at 9316.

Unilateral control by mortgagee

15.202 There have been occasional suggestions that the mortgagee's general duty of care in the matter of sale has infiltrated the mortgagee's otherwise unfettered prerogative to determine the timing of sale.[1] The conventional view is, however, that although the mortgagee must sell for the 'current market value', he may 'decide in his own interest if and when he should sell.'[2] The mortgagee is not obliged to wait on a rising market or for a market to recover.[3] It is equally irrelevant that a mortgagee's delay in the matter of sale is accompanied by a catastrophic decline in the value of the security.[4] In the event of default by the mortgagor, the mortgagee 'can sit back and do nothing.'[5] The mortgagee is simply under no duty 'to exercise his power of sale over the mortgaged securities at any particular time or at all.'[6]

1   See e g *Standard Chartered Bank Ltd v Walker* [1982] 1 WLR 1410 at 1415G, where Lord Denning MR thought that the fact that a mortgagee may determine the timing of sale

quite arbitrarily did not necessarily imply that a mortgagee 'can sell at the worst possible time. It is at least arguable that, in choosing the time, he must exercise a reasonable degree of care.'

2   *China and South Sea Bank Ltd v Tan Soon Gin* [1990] 1 AC 536 at 545D per Lord Templeman. See likewise *Palk v Mortgage Services Funding Plc* [1993] Ch 330 at 343A–B per Sir Michael Kerr; *Silven Properties Ltd v Royal Bank of Scotland Plc* [2004] 1 WLR 997 at [15] per Lightman J; *Apple Fields Ltd v Damesh Holdings Ltd* [2001] 2 NZLR 586 at [49] (NZ Court of Appeal).

3   *Bank of Cyprus (London) Ltd v Gill* [1980] 2 Lloyd's Rep 51 at 54 (approving a decision by Lloyd J to this effect). See likewise *Apple Fields Ltd v Damesh Holdings Ltd* [2001] 1 NZLR 194 at [56] per John Hansen J.

4   See e g *China and South Sea Bank Ltd v Tan Soon Gin* [1990] 1 AC 536 (security worthless by time of sale).

5   *Palk v Mortgage Services Funding Plc* [1993] Ch 330 at 337G per Nicholls V-C. See similarly *China and South Sea Bank Ltd v Tan Soon Gin* [1990] 1 AC 536 at 545E–F per Lord Templeman; *Silven Properties Ltd v Royal Bank of Scotland Plc* [2004] 1 WLR 997 at [13] per Lightman J (the mortgagee 'is entitled to remain totally passive').

6   *China and South Sea Bank Ltd v Tan Soon Gin* [1990] 1 AC 536 at 545G–H per Lord Templeman (a requirement to sell at a particular time would mean that '[n]o creditor could carry on the business of lending'). See also *Mailman v Challenge Bank Ltd* (1991) 5 BPR 11721 at 11727; *Apple Fields Ltd v Damesh Holdings Ltd* [2001] 2 NZLR 586 at [49] (NZ Court of Appeal).

15.203   The rigour of this general principle is tempered nowadays by several qualifications. *First*, the mortgagee must never act in bad faith in accelerating or delaying sale.[1] *Second*, the ultimate duty of the selling mortgagee is to ensure that the mortgaged land is fairly and properly exposed to the market. It may therefore be that a mortgagee cannot entirely 'ignore the consequence that a short delay might result in a higher price'[2] but even this proviso can be displaced by circumstances which indicate other reasons for urgency in the matter of sale. *Third*, there is a requirement that, when a dwelling-house held under a regulated mortgage contract is repossessed (whether voluntarily or after legal action), the mortgagee must ensure that steps are taken to 'market the property for sale as soon as possible.'[3] There may nevertheless be legitimate reasons for delaying sale, as for example where a deferred sale avoids an obligation to repay a 'right to buy' discount[4] or enables a title defect to be remedied with beneficial effects for the selling price.[5]

1   *Silven Properties Ltd v Royal Bank of Scotland plc* [2002] EWHC 1976 (Ch) at [115] per Patten J.

2   *Meftah v Lloyds TSB Bank plc* [2001] 2 All ER (Comm) 741 at [9(h)] per Lawrence Collins J. In *Wood v Bank of Nova Scotia* (1979) 10 RPR 156 at 170, affd (1981) 112 DLR (3d) 181, a bank mortgagee was held liable in damages for loss caused by a sale in the middle of the winter where there was no 'overwhelming need to sell the property quickly'. See also *Suskind v Bank of Nova Scotia* (1984) 10 DLR (4th) 101 at 112. See, however, *Silven Properties Ltd v Royal Bank of Scotland Plc* [2004] 1 WLR 997 at [15] per Lightman J.

3   *FSA Handbook* (Release 033, July 2004): MCOB 13.6.1R(1).

4   **[Para 7.351]**.

5   *FSA Handbook* (Release 033, July 2004): MCOB 13.6.2G.

Court's discretion to order sale at request of mortgagor

15.204   The last decade of case law has highlighted one other crucial limitation on the mortgagee's arbitrary control over the date of sale. Pursuant to section 91(2) of the Law of Property Act 1925, the court has a discretion to order sale at the request of either the mortgagor or the mortgagee, notwithstanding that 'any other person dissents.'[1] In appropriate circumstances the court may direct sale 'on such terms as it thinks fit.' It is therefore open to a mortgagor, by invoking section 91(2), to seek to accelerate the sale of the mortgaged property. In practice, however, the scope of this discretion was always curtailed by the court's unwillingness to order a sale contrary to the wishes of a mortgagee in the absence of full security for the repayment of his debt.[2]

1   The discretion conferred by section 91(2) is not dependent on proof of prior breach of duty by the mortgagee. It is 'unfettered', although it must of course be exercised 'judicially' (see *Palk v Mortgage Services Funding Plc* [1993] Ch 330 at 339C, 340A–B per Nicholls V-C, 342A per Sir Michael Kerr).
2   For this purpose security could be achieved by fixing a reserve price for the court-ordered sale sufficient to cover the outstanding debt and costs or by requiring the mortgagor to make a payment into court (see e g *Woolley v Colman* (1882) 21 Ch D 169 at 173).

The Palk decision

15.205   In *Palk v Mortgage Services Funding Plc*,[1] the Court of Appeal was called upon to apply section 91(2) in virtually unprecedented circumstances. Here the defaulting mortgagors, realising that they could no longer cope with mounting arrears of instalments, managed to negotiate a private sale for £283,000, although it was undisputed that the total sum required to redeem the mortgage then amounted to £358,000. The first mortgagee declined to agree to the sale. Instead it proposed simply to let the property on short-term leases until such time as the housing market improved, meanwhile crediting the mortgagors with the rental income. The mortgagors were fully aware that such action would still leave them with an income shortfall which would cause their overall debt to increase by some £30,000 each year. In desperation they sought a court-directed sale of the property in order to stem the indefinite financial haemorrhage to which they were consigned by the mortgagee's proposals. In effect the mortgagee, knowing that it could always sue on the personal covenant to repay, was prepared to speculate, at the expense of the mortgagors, on the future movement of house prices.

1   [1993] Ch 330.

15.206   The Court of Appeal decided that its statutory discretion to order sale was not ousted by the fact that the mortgagors could currently show only a 'negative equity' in the property.[1] Discretion was exercised in favour of sale even though such a sale deprived the mortgagee of its contractual and statutory rights arbitrarily to decide on the disposition of its security[2] and notwithstanding that more than £75,000 of the debt was left unsecured and outstanding.[3] Nicholls V-C led the Court of Appeal in holding that, in the exercise of his rights over his security, 'the mortgagee must act fairly towards the mortgagor.'[4] Here the course on which the mortgagee had embarked was 'likely to be highly prejudicial to [the mortgagor's] financial position as borrower.'[5] It was contrary to 'common fairness' and indeed 'oppressive' to compel the mortgagor to become 'an unwilling risk-taker' in an enterprise in which, short of a dramatic upward surge in the housing market, she was 'bound to suffer financially'.[6] In Nicholls V-C's view, it would be 'manifest unfairness'[7] to saddle the mortgagor with such an unattractive risk in circumstances where her liability was 'open-ended' and she remained personally liable for the ever-increasing deficit.[8] Against this background the Court of Appeal had no doubt that it should direct an immediate sale in order to protect the mortgagor from the burden of the rising debt.[9]

1   [1993] Ch 330 at 340A–B per Nicholls V-C, 343C–D per Sir Michael Kerr.
2   The Court of Appeal regarded section 91(2) as an 'overriding statutory power' which displaced the mortgagee's otherwise unfettered rights to determine the date of sale or decide on lettings ([1993] Ch 330 at 338F–339A per Nicholls V-C, 342H–343C per Sir Michael Kerr).
3   By the date of the Court of Appeal hearing the total mortgage debt in *Palk* had in fact risen to £409,000 (*Times*, 1 August 1992, p 14, col 8). The husband mortgagor had become bankrupt and it was his wife, as co-mortgagor, who claimed the benefit of the section 91(2) discretion.
4   [1993] Ch 330 at 337G.
5   [1993] Ch 330 at 338G–H.
6   [1993] Ch 330 at 339A, F, 340C–D. As Nicholls V-C acutely observed (at 419G), the case revealed, as between mortgagor and mortgagee, a latent 'difference in their attitudes towards taking risks.'
7   [1993] Ch 330 at 340A.
8   [1993] Ch 330 at 340B–D.
9   In effect the mortgagor's liability to continuing mortgage interest was cut to approximately one twelfth of the amounts owed prior to the court-ordered sale. Nicholls V-C pointed out that the mortgagee could still, of course, pursue its preferred policy of speculating on a rising market. It could 'back its own judgment' by purchasing the property itself **[para 15.214]**, in which case the mortgagor would receive an immediate credit for the current market value and the mortgagee would retain the benefit of any future improvement in house prices ([1993] Ch 330 at 339F–H, 340C–D).

15.207   Although the court will direct sale 'only in exceptional circumstances',[1] it seems clear that the discretion available under section 91(2) provides a valuable avenue to relief for certain categories of mortgagor caught in the trap of negative equity.[2] The *Palk* decision throws the mortgagor a lifeline which may enable him or her to escape a calamitous situation in which debts increase exponentially beyond any hope of repayment from the proceeds of an eventual sale.[3]

1   [1993] Ch 330 at 343F per Sir Michael Kerr, who acknowledged (at 344B–C) that the facts in *Palk* were 'extreme and exceptional'. Nicholls V-C stressed (at 340C) that the mortgagee might well have been able to justify a postponement of sale on perfectly valid grounds specific to the particular property (e g pending the outcome of an application for planning permission).
2   It was estimated that at the date of *Palk*'s case more than half a million borrowers in England and Wales were similarly trapped in properties worth less than their current mortgage debt (*Times*, 1 August 1992, p 1, col 6).
3   See e g *Barrett v Halifax Building Society* (1995) 28 HLR 634 at 639–640.

Other preliminaries or modalities of the sale

15.208   In the absence of any restriction in the mortgage deed, the precise arrangements for the sale fall within the mortgagee's sole discretion.[1] Nevertheless the mortgagee's duty to afford reasonable protection for the interests of his mortgagor imposes on him a duty of diligence in relation to certain preliminaries or modalities of the sale. The mortgagee must ensure that the premises are fairly and properly exposed to the market.[2] In organising the sale the mortgagee must act in the same way as would a 'prudent vendor' who wishes to sell property belonging to himself.[3] There is, however, no duty to incur expense in promoting a sale unless it is clear that such further expense is covered by the security.[4] The mortgagee must take care to preserve the value of the security, but is not obliged to improve the premises or to take any pre-marketing steps to increase their value.[5] In particular, he has no duty to explore whether he can unlock any potential increase in value by initiating applications for planning permission or by granting profitable leases. He is, of course, free to undertake such investigation,[6] but equally free to 'pull the plug' at any time and proceed with an immediate sale. In either case, in the absence of some protective provision in the mortgage deed, he owes no responsibility to the mortgagor.[7]

1   *Michael v Miller* [2004] EWCA Civ 282 at [131] per Jonathan Parker LJ.
2   *Silven Properties Ltd v Royal Bank of Scotland Plc* [2004] 1 WLR 997 at [19] per Lightman J.
3   *Commercial and General Acceptance Ltd v Nixon* (1981) 152 CLR 491 at 503 per Mason J. See also *Tse Kwong Lam v Wong Chit Sen* [1983] 1 WLR 1349 at 1359G–H per Lord Templeman. This criterion certainly represents a tightening up of standards when compared with earlier cases (see e g *British Columbia Land & Investment Agency v Ishitaka* (1911) 45 SCR 302 at 317 per Duff J).
4   *Hallifax Property Corp Pty Ltd v GIFC Ltd* (1988) NSW ConvR 55–415 at 57,798.
5   *Silven Properties Ltd v Royal Bank of Scotland Plc* [2004] 1 WLR 997 at [16], [20] per Lightman J.
6   On a cost-benefit basis the mortgagee must act reasonably in incurring expenditure towards this end (*Silven Properties Ltd v Royal Bank of Scotland Plc* [2004] 1 WLR 997 at [17]).
7   *Silven Properties Ltd v Royal Bank of Scotland Plc* [2004] 1 WLR 997 at [17]–[18].

15.209   The mortgagee may have no duty to enhance the security, but certain obligations rest on his shoulders. For example, he must take reasonable steps to ascertain the value of the property before sale.[1] He must inform himself of the market,[2] advertise the property[3] and must make a reasonable effort to bring the proposed sale to the attention of all persons likely to be interested.[4] Where the property holds appeal only for a limited market, the mortgagee must 'seek out that market and take the sale to it.'[5] There is, for example, a want of due care where the mortgagee fails to follow up the possibility of a higher price, knowing that a prospective purchaser is prepared to pay significantly more than an existing offer.[6] Where there are two or more interested potential purchasers, they must be brought into competition with each other so as to obtain the highest price sustainable by the available market.[7] Whether the sale is by public auction or by private treaty, the mortgagee must bring to the notice of interested parties the 'potentiality of the property to be sold.'[8] The mortgagee is under no strict duty to consult either the mortgagor or other mortgagees in the matter of the proposed sale, but a failure to do so may in some circumstances point to a lack of good faith on his part.[9]

1   *Pendlebury v Colonial Mutual Life Assurance Society Ltd* (1912) 13 CLR 676 at 683; *Henry Roach (Petroleum) Pty Ltd v Credit House (Vic) Pty Ltd* [1976] VR 309 at 313; *Frost Ltd v Ralph* (1981) 115 DLR (3d) 612 at 617; *Tse Kwong Lam v Wong Chit Sen* [1983] 1 WLR 1349 at 1357H–1358A. Failure to obtain a second valuation is not necessarily culpable conduct (*Swerus v Central Mortgage Registry of Australia Pty Ltd* (1988) NSW ConvR 55–407 at 57,570), but a single valuation designed to ensure a 'fast sale' is not sufficient (see *Bank of Nova Scotia v Barnard* (1984) 9 DLR (4th) 575 at 586).

2   *Apple Fields Ltd v Damesh Holdings Ltd* [2001] 1 NZLR 194 at [54] per John Hansen J.

3   *National Westminster Finance New Zealand Ltd v United Finance & Securities Ltd* [1988] 1 NZLR 226 at 238. On the importance of advertising in a local newspaper, see *McKean v Maloney* [1988] 1 Qd R 628 at 632–634. However, the courts have rejected the argument that the mortgagor is prejudiced by advertisements which reveal that the sale is a 'mortgagee sale' (*Hallifax Property Corp Pty Ltd v GIFC Ltd* (1988) NSW ConvR 55–415 at 57,799) or that the property 'must sell' (see *Hausman v O'Grady* (1988) 42 DLR (4th) 119 at 127, affd (1989) 57 DLR (4th) 480).

4   *Henry Roach (Petroleum) Pty Ltd v Credit House (Vic) Pty Ltd* [1976] VR 309 at 313. In *Davey v Durrant* (1857) 1 De G & J 535 at 560, 44 ER 830 at 840, Knight Bruce LJ was not prepared to hold that a mortgagee can never accept a fair offer from a private buyer until he has advertised the property for sale.

5   *National Westminster Finance New Zealand Ltd v United Finance & Securities Ltd* [1988] 1 NZLR 226 at 237–238 per Smellie J. See also *Sterne v Victoria & Grey Trust Co* (1985) 14 DLR (4th) 193 at 204 (hobby farm).

6   *Australia and New Zealand Banking Group Ltd v Bangadilly Pastoral Co Pty Ltd* (1978) 139 CLR 195 at 228 per Aickin J.

7   *Forsyth v Blundell* (1973) 129 CLR 477 at 509.

8   *Henry Roach (Petroleum) Pty Ltd v Credit House (Vic) Pty Ltd* [1976] VR 309 at 313; *National Westminster Finance New Zealand Ltd v United Finance & Securities Ltd* [1988] 1 NZLR 226 at 237–238.

9   *Goldcell Nominees Pty Ltd v Network Finance Ltd* [1983] 2 VR 257 at 272, 278. See also *Australia and New Zealand Banking Group Ltd v Bangadilly Pastoral Co Pty Ltd* (1978) 139 CLR 195 at 202 per Jacobs J, 229 per Aickin J.

Sales by auction

15.210   Although the mortgagee may have a duty to seek expert advice as to the method of sale,[1] there is no legal obligation to sell by auction.[2] Indeed sale by public auction rather than by private treaty does not in itself prove the validity of a transaction,[3] particularly since an auction which produces only one bid obviously provides no guarantee that a true market value has been achieved.[4] Where sale by auction occurs, there is a 'central importance' in ensuring that there is competition between prospective purchasers.[5] There is, however, nothing to prevent a mortgagee from accepting the best bid obtainable at an auction, 'even though the auction is badly attended and the bidding exceptionally low', provided that none of these adverse factors is 'due to any fault of the mortgagee.'[6] Equally the mortgagee is under 'no legal duty simpliciter' to accept the highest bid at an auction,[7] particularly if this bid is made by the mortgagor.[8] Nor does the mortgagee commit any breach of his duty of diligence merely because prior to auction he sells the property privately without first informing the mortgagor.[9] In some cases it may be entirely consistent with the discharge of his duty that he should accept a suitably high pre-emptive bid made by a private purchaser who wishes to 'kill' the sale and withdraw the property from auction.[10]

1   *Tse Kwong Lam v Wong Chit Sen* [1983] 1 WLR 1349 at 1357H, 1359G per Lord Templeman. There is, in effect, a duty to consider whether to put the property to auction (see *National Westminster Finance New Zealand Ltd v United Finance & Securities Ltd* [1988] 1 NZLR 226 at 238).

2   *Frost Ltd v Ralph* (1981) 115 DLR (3d) 612 at 624; *Swerus v Central Mortgage Registry of Australia Pty Ltd* (1988) NSW ConvR 55–407 at 57,570.

3   *Tse Kwong Lam v Wong Chit Sen* [1983] 1 WLR 1349 at 1355G.

4   *Tse Kwong Lam v Wong Chit Sen* [1983] 1 WLR 1349 at 1356H–1357A. See also *Australia and New Zealand Banking Group Ltd v Bangadilly Pastoral Co Pty Ltd* (1978) 139 CLR 195 at 227 per Aickin J.

5   *Artistic Builders Pty Ltd v Elliot & Tuthill (Mortgagees) Pty Ltd* (2002) 10 BPR 19565 at [97] per Campbell J (mortgagee guilty of subverting auction process by dissuading interested purchaser from attending).

6   *Cuckmere Brick Co Ltd v Mutual Finance Ltd* [1971] Ch 949 at 965G–H per Salmon LJ. Compare, however, the appalling outcome in *Bank of Montreal v Allender Investments Ltd* (1984) 4 DLR (4th) 340 at 346–348, where a New Brunswick court upheld the sole auction bid of $100 (made by the mortgagee itself) in respect of property which had been valued at $46,000 some three weeks earlier. The mortgagee was permitted to sue the mortgagor for a deficiency of some $45,700, the court holding that the mortgagee could not be faulted, in the absence of other bidders, for buying for a nominal sum at a properly advertised auction.

7   *Stoyanovich v National Westminster Finance* (1984) 3 BPR 9310 at 9315. See also *Payne v Cave* (1789) 3 Term Rep 148 at 149, 100 ER 502 at 503. Compare, however, *Australia and New Zealand Banking Group Ltd v Bangadilly Pastoral Co Pty Ltd* (1978) 139 CLR 195 at 228 per Aickin J.

8   *AGC (Advances) Ltd v McWhirter* (1977) 1 BPR 9454 at 9456; *Stoyanovich v National Westminster Finance* (1984) 3 BPR 9310 at 9315.

9   *Davey v Durrant* (1857) 1 De G & J 535 at 560, 44 ER 830 at 840; *Michael v Miller* [2004] EWCA Civ 282 at [133] per Jonathan Parker LJ; *Goldcell Nominees Pty Ltd v Network Finance Ltd* [1983] 2 VR 257 at 262. However, such a sale may indicate bad faith if the mortgagee had earlier undertaken to consult the mortgagor over any proposal to transact a private sale in advance of the auction (see *Goldcell Nominees Pty Ltd* at 278).

10   *Johnson v Ribbins* (1975) 235 EG 757 at 761.

Advertisements

15.211   Where the mortgagee chooses to sell by public auction, he has a non-delegable duty[1] to ensure that the auction is preceded by appropriate advertisement.[2] The mortgagee may be exposed to a claim in damages for negligence if a relevant newspaper advertisement was carried only once,[3] or allowed only a minimal lead time before the auction date,[4] or was hidden 'in the middle of a mixed grill of auction advertisements' ranging from sales of china and bric-à-brac to old furniture and power tools.[5] The mortgagee may also be chargeable with a want of care if he sells properties of widely differing types and attractions in one block.[6]

1   [Para 15.192].

2   *Pendlebury v Colonial Mutual Life Assurance Society Ltd* (1912) 13 CLR 676 at 683, 696; *Henry Roach (Petroleum) Pty Ltd v Credit House (Vic) Pty Ltd* [1976] VR 309 at 313; *Commercial and General Acceptance Ltd v Nixon* (1981) 152 CLR 491 at 500 per Mason J; *McKean v Maloney* [1988] 1 Qd R 628 at 632–634; (1989) 63 ALJ 556 (P B).

3   *Commercial and General Acceptance Ltd v Nixon* (1981) 152 CLR 491 at 494 per Gibbs CJ, 500–501 per Mason J. It was crucial here that the mortgagee failed to ensure that the advertisement appeared in the Wednesday edition of a daily newspaper which was the normal forum for each week's auction advertisements of real estate (see [1980] Qd R 153 at 156C).

4   *Commercial and General Acceptance Ltd v Nixon* (1981) 152 CLR 491 at 494, 500, [1980] Qd R 153 at 156B–C (two days). See also *Australia and New Zealand Banking Group Ltd v Bangadilly Pastoral Co Pty Ltd* (1978) 139 CLR 195 at 202 per Jacobs J, 229 per Aickin J.

5   *Nixon v Commercial and General Acceptance Ltd* [1980] Qd R 153 at 156C–D.

6   *Aldrich v Canada Permanent Loan & Savings Co* (1897) 24 OAR 193 at 194, 197–198. See also *National Westminster Finance New Zealand Ltd v United Finance & Securities Ltd* [1988] 1 NZLR 226 at 238.

Conduct of the auction

15.212   The mortgagee's duty of diligence also renders him vicariously liable for the actual conduct of the auction sale. The precise date chosen for the day of auction may reflect prejudicially upon the price achieved on sale.[1] A reserve price should be set with the benefit of expert advice,[2] and the auctioneer informed of that price well before the commencement of the auction.[3] In some circumstances it may be a breach of the mortgagee's duty if details of the reserve price are disclosed to an individual prospective purchaser in advance of the auction,[4] or indeed are announced at the auction itself to all the potential bidders collectively.[5] Such disclosure may operate adversely by limiting the number of bidders and may even indicate that a later private sale of the property at a much lower price is not bona fide.[6] On the other hand, the announcement at the outset that there is a reserve price may reduce the chance of an abortive auction and, provided that the amount of this price is not made known until such time as bidding has stopped short, may well conduce to the achieving of the reserve price.[7]

1   See e g *Australia and New Zealand Banking Group Ltd v Bangadilly Pastoral Co Pty Ltd* (1978) 139 CLR 195 at 202 per Jacobs J, 229 per Aickin J (auction two days before Christmas).

2   *Tse Kwong Lam v Wong Chit Sen* [1983] 1 WLR 1349 at 1357H.

3   *Tse Kwong Lam v Wong Chit Sen* [1983] 1 WLR 1349 at 1358A, where Lord Templeman indicated that a want of due care may be present if the auctioneer is not instructed to do more than 'put the property under the hammer.' Such a procedure 'may be appropriate to the sale of second hand furniture but is not necessarily conducive to the attainment of the best price for freehold or leasehold property.'

4   *Goldcell Nominees Pty Ltd v Network Finance Ltd* [1983] 2 VR 257 at 263, 278. See also *Tse Kwong Lam v Wong Chit Sen* [1983] 1 WLR 1349 at 1358C.

5   *Industrial Enterprises Inc v Schelstraete* (1975) 54 DLR (3d) 260 at 274.

6   *Reid v Royal Trust Corpn of Canada* (1985) 20 DLR (4th) 223 at 243.

7   *Reid v Royal Trust Corpn of Canada* (1985) 20 DLR (4th) 223 at 244.

MORTGAGEE'S DUTY OF SUBJECTIVE GOOD FAITH

15.213   The impact of the mortgagee's duty of good faith is nowadays most obviously apparent in the courts' response to cases where there is a potential conflict between the interest of the mortgagee as vendor in obtaining the highest price and some collateral interest of the mortgagee in achieving a lower price for the purchaser. As Jacobs J observed in *Australia and New Zealand Banking Group Ltd v Bangadilly Pastoral Co Pty Ltd*,[1] the requirement of bona fides in a mortgagee 'is concerned with a genuine primary desire to obtain ... the best price obtainable consistently with the right of a mortgagee to realise his security.' This goal is obviously jeopardised where the mortgagee either consciously or unconsciously grants preferment to a conflicting commercial interest on the part of the purchaser. The closer the association between mortgagee and purchaser, the less likely is the court to allow the transaction of sale to stand. The 'legitimate purpose' of the mortgagee's power of sale is to secure repayment of the mortgage money and if the mortgagee 'uses the power for another purpose ... or to serve the purposes of other individuals ... the Court considers that to be a fraud in the exercise of the power.'[2] In such an event the appropriate remedy for the mortgagor is normally rescission of the sale and return of the security. Conflicts of interest affecting the mortgagee tend to arise in two slightly different categories of circumstance.

1   (1978) 139 CLR 195 at 201 (High Court of Australia).
2   *Robertson v Norris* (1858) 1 Giff 421 at 424–425, 65 ER 983 at 984 per Stuart V-C.

Sale to the mortgagee or to his representative

15.214   The first category of case comprises circumstances where any purported sale by the mortgagee is simply void and ineffective. It is settled law, for example, that the mortgagee cannot, in exercise of his power of sale,[1] effect a valid sale either to himself alone or to himself and others.[2] A sale by a person to himself 'is no sale at all',[3] even though the sale price be the full value of the mortgaged property.[4] Precisely the same fate awaits any attempt to sell the mortgaged property to a trustee for the mortgagee,[5] or to the mortgagee's solicitor[6] or other agent.[7]

1   Compare, however, the position in relation to a sale directed by order of the court under LPA 1925, s 91(2). Here the mortgagee may purchase the mortgaged property himself, precisely because the sale is *not* a sale by a mortgagee acting in exercise of his power of sale (see *Palk v Mortgage Services Funding Plc* [1993] Ch 330 at 340D–E). As Nicholls V-C pointed out in *Palk* [**para 15.206**], it may sometimes be entirely proper to allow – even to direct – a sale to the mortgagee. Such a sale may be necessary simply in order to prevent the mortgagee from unfairly saddling the mortgagor with the risk of future fluctuations in the market value of the property ([1993] Ch 330 at 339E–H).
2   *Martinson v Clowes* (1882) 21 Ch D 857 at 860; *Australia and New Zealand Banking Group Ltd v Bangadilly Pastoral Co Pty Ltd* (1978) 139 CLR 195 at 225–227 per Aickin J. It has been questioned whether this strict rule nowadays serves any purpose if the mortgagee is obliged in any event to act reasonably and prudently (see S Robinson, [1989] Conv 336 at 341). If, for instance, there are no external bidders for the property, the rule may seem an unnecessary fetter on the lender's remedy of sale, although application may always be made to the court under LPA 1925, s 91(2) [**para 15.204**]. Some jurisdictions confer on the mortgagee a specific statutory authority to buy in at auction (see e g *Traders Group Ltd v Mason* (1975) 53 DLR (3d) 103 at 117 (New Brunswick)).
3   *Farrar v Farrars Ltd* (1888) 40 Ch D 395 at 409 per Lindley LJ. An important exception to this principle is provided by HA 1985, Sch 17, para 1(1), which allows a local authority mortgagee to vest in itself by deed any house in respect of which it is entitled to exercise a power of sale. This relaxation of the normal rule is subject both to the leave of the county court and to a statutory scheme of compensation and accounting to the mortgagor.

4   *Farrar v Farrars Ltd* (1888) 40 Ch D 395 at 409. On the practice in some parts of the United
      States, under which the mortgagee may purchase in his own name and still sue the mortgagor
      for any deficiency (thereby taking 'both the money and the mud'), see R W M Turner, 21
      Virginia L Rev 600 (1935); R M Washburn, 53 S Cal L Rev 843 (1980). The English practice in
      this respect has been described as 'far fairer to the mortgagor' (see *Canada Permanent
      Trust Co v King Art Developments Ltd* (1985) 12 DLR (4th) 161 at 177 per Moir JA).
5   *Downes v Grazebrook* (1817) 3 Mer 200 at 209, 36 ER 77 at 80; *Australia and New Zealand
      Banking Group Ltd v Bangadilly Pastoral Co Pty Ltd* (1978) 139 CLR 195 at 225 per Aickin J.
6   *Martinson v Clowes* (1882) 21 Ch D 857 at 860.
7   *Downes v Grazebrook* (1817) 3 Mer 200 at 209, 36 ER 77 at 80; *Whitcomb v Minchin* (1820) 5
      Madd 91, 56 ER 830; *Martinson v Clowes* (1882) 21 Ch D 857 at 860.

Sale to an associated person

15.215   A more flexible view is taken of a mortgagee's sale to a less closely
associated person or entity such as an employee or a business acquaintance or a
company in which the mortgagee is himself a shareholder. Such a transaction is
not necessarily ineffective, but the normal onus of proof is reversed and a
burden rests on the mortgagee to demonstrate positively that his 'desire to
obtain the best price was given absolute preference over any desire that an
associate should obtain a good bargain.'[1] The court will scrutinise most
carefully any sale effected by a mortgagee in circumstances which appear to
impeach his bona fides.[2]

1   *Australia and New Zealand Banking Group Ltd v Bangadilly Pastoral Co Pty Ltd* (1978) 139
      CLR 195 at 201 per Jacobs J. See *Tse Kwong Lam v Wong Chit Sen* [1983] 1 WLR 1349 at
      1356G–H per Lord Templeman; *Corbett v Halifax Building Society* [2003] 1 WLR 964 at [28]
      per Pumfrey J.
2   *Goldcell Nominees Pty Ltd v Network Finance Ltd* [1983] 2 VR 257 at 263; *Apple Fields Ltd v
      Damesh Holdings Ltd* [2001] 1 NZLR 194 at [59] per John Hansen J.

15.216   There is, for instance, no hard and fast rule that a mortgagee may not
sell to a company in which he is interested.[1] As Lord Templeman indicated in
Tse Kwong Lam v Wong Chit Sen,[2] the mortgagee and the company seeking to
uphold the transaction 'must show that the sale was in good faith and that the
mortgagee took reasonable precautions to obtain the best price reasonably
obtainable at the time.' In *Tse Kwong Lam*, however, the exercise of the
mortgagee's power of sale had taken the form of a public auction at which the
only bidder was the mortgagee's wife, acting as the representative of the family
company of which both were directors and shareholders.[3] There was no
competitive bidding at the auction; the property was purchased at the reserve
price which had been fixed by the mortgagee and which was, of course, clearly
known to the purchaser; and the purchase was financed from funds provided by
the mortgagee himself. In such circumstances the Privy Council had no doubt
but that the mortgagee had failed to show that 'in all respects he acted fairly to
the borrower and used his best endeavours to obtain the best price reasonably
obtainable for the mortgaged property.'[4]

1   *Farrar v Farrars Ltd* (1888) 40 Ch D 395 at 409–410; *Tse Kwong Lam v Wong Chit Sen* [1983]
      1 WLR 1349 at 1355A; *Australia and New Zealand Banking Group Ltd v Bangadilly*

Pastoral Co Pty Ltd (1978) 139 CLR 195 at 225–226 per Aickin J; *Apple Fields Ltd v Damesh Holdings Ltd* [2004] 1 NZLR 721 at [25] per Lord Scott of Foscote.
2   [1983] 1 WLR 1349. See [1984] Conv 143 (P Jackson).
3   See also *Australia and New Zealand Banking Group Ltd v Bangadilly Pastoral Co Pty Ltd* (1978) 139 CLR 195 (purchase at auction by an associated company controlled by the mortgagee).
4   [1983] 1 WLR 1349 at 1355F–G. 'The close relationship was not fatal but the failure to meet the standard of care required was' (*National Westminster Finance New Zealand Ltd v United Finance & Securities Ltd* [1988] 1 NZLR 226 at 235 per Smellie J).

15.217   The critical question in every case is whether there was an independent bargain between mortgagee and purchaser.[1] It is open to the court to find that no fair bargain has been proved where, for instance, the selling mortgagee appears to have been 'either consciously or unconsciously overborne' by the fact that the purchaser was a business client and acquaintance of some commercial substance in the local community.[2]

1   *Australia and New Zealand Banking Group Ltd v Bangadilly Pastoral Co Pty Ltd* (1978) 139 CLR 195 at 227 per Aickin J.
2   *Goldcell Nominees Pty Ltd v Network Finance Ltd* [1983] 2 VR 257 at 274.

REMEDIES FOR THE MORTGAGOR

15.218   The mortgagor's remedy for the wrongful exercise of the mortgagee's power of sale depends largely on whether the irregularity falls within the category of mere carelessness or is more accurately described in terms of bad faith.[1] In strict theory it is open to the court, in response to either form of irregularity, to set the sale aside.[2] This is particularly the case where a mortgagee has failed to discharge an onus of proof that a sale to an associated person was entirely proper.[3] In other circumstances, however, the modern trend is to reserve the remedy of rescission for instances of equitable fraud, whilst imposing a mere money liability where the mortgagee has failed to adopt 'such means as would be adopted by a prudent man to get the best price that could be obtained' for the land.[4] As Pumfrey J indicated in *Corbett v Halifax Building Society*,[5] 'a completed sale by a mortgagee is not liable to be set aside merely because it takes place at an undervalue.'[6] Impropriety is a prerequisite for rescission of the sale and the completed sale is vulnerable only if the price paid is 'so low as in itself to be evidence of fraud'[7] or if the purchaser has actual knowledge of, or participates in, an impropriety in the exercise of the power.[8]

1   In either case the mortgagor may seek an injunction to restrain the completion of any allegedly improper contract of sale entered into by the mortgagee (*McCambridge v Bank of Ireland* [2002] NI Ch 9 at [6] per Girvan J). Some payment into court may be made a condition of this form of relief, but it is unnecessary to show that the purchaser had any knowledge of the alleged impropriety (see *George v Commercial Union Assurance Co of Australia Ltd* (1977) 1 BPR 9649 at 9652). See also *Pasquarella v National Australia Finance Ltd* [1987] 1 NZLR 312 at 315.
2   *Tse Kwong Lam v Wong Chit Sen* [1983] 1 WLR 1349 at 1359H–1360A per Lord Templeman; *Corbett v Halifax Building Society* [2003] 1 WLR 964 at [40] per Pumfrey J.
3   See *Apple Fields Ltd v Damesh Holdings Ltd* [2001] 2 NZLR 586 at [52] (rescission unless such a remedy is 'inequitable').

4   See *Sterne v Victoria & Grey Trust Co* (1985) 14 DLR (4th) 193 at 201–202 [**para 15.191**]. The limitation period is six years (see *Raja v Lloyds TSB Bank Plc* (2001) 82 P & CR 191 at [27]).

5   [2003] 1 WLR 964 at [26]; [2004] Conv 49 (M P Thompson); All ER Rev 2003, p 266 (P J Clarke).

6   The sale must be 'tainted by some impropriety and not merely an innocent undervalue' ([2003] 1 WLR 964 at [33] per Pumfrey J). See likewise *Property & Bloodstock Ltd v Emerton* [1968] Ch 94 at 113 per Danckwerts LJ.

7   *Warner v Jacob* (1882) 20 Ch D 220 at 224 per Kay J; *Lord Waring v London and Manchester Assurance Co Ltd* [1935] Ch 310 at 319.

8   See *Corbett v Halifax Building Society* [2003] 1 WLR 964 at [26] per Pumfrey J. In *Corbett's* case rescission was refused in circumstances where, unknown to the mortgagee, the mortgaged premises had been purchased at an undervalue by one of its employees who was genuinely and honestly unaware of the undervalue.

Equitable accounting for breach of the mortgagee's duty of care

15.219   The imposition of a money liability therefore represents the more generally appropriate remedy where the mortgagor complains that the selling mortgagee has failed to exercise reasonable care to obtain a proper value for the security.[1] Here the remedy for breach of the mortgagee's equitable duty lies not in the award of common law damages, but in a taking of accounts under which amounts due by mortgagor to mortgagee (and vice versa) can be set off against each and the ultimate balance due can be calculated.[2] As part of this process the mortgagee must account to the mortgagor (and all others interested in the equity of redemption) not just for what the mortgagee actually received on sale, but for what he should have received.[3] The mortgagee is therefore accountable prima facie for the difference between the market value and the actual sale price,[4] but there must in all cases be clear evidence of a causal link between the mortgagee's breach of duty and the shortfall in the price received for the land.[5] A depressed sale price may, for instance, reflect the fact that the mortgagor, by breaching a covenant in the mortgage, has caused the value of the land to decline.[6]

1   It is significant that only a money remedy was sought (and awarded) in *Cuckmere Brick Co Ltd v Mutual Finance Ltd* [1971] Ch 949 at 958B. See *Brutan Investments Pty Ltd v Underwriting and Insurance Ltd* (1980) 58 FLR 289 at 294–295; *Wood v Bank of Nova Scotia* (1981) 112 DLR (3d) 181 at 183.

2   See *Artistic Builders Pty Ltd v Elliot & Tuthill (Mortgagees) Pty Ltd* (2002) 10 BPR 19565 at [119]–[121] per Campbell J.

3   *Silven Properties Ltd v Royal Bank of Scotland Plc* [2004] 1 WLR 997 at [19] per Lightman J. For reference to an equitable 'allowance' or account, see *Standard Chartered Bank Ltd v Walker* [1982] 1 WLR 1410 at 1416B; *General Credits (Finance) Pty Ltd v Stoyakovich* [1975] Qd R 352 at 354B–C. See also *Platts v TSB Bank Plc* (1998) Times, 4 March (negligent undervalue may be subject of equitable set-off to any subsisting debt alleged by the mortgagee).

4   *Sterne v Victoria & Grey Trust Co* (1985) 14 DLR (4th) 193 at 204. The mortgagee's liability is not reduced merely because, if there had been a sale at the correct price, the mortgagee would have been required to account to a second mortgagee for the surplus (*Adamson v Halifax Plc* [2003] 1 WLR 60 at [11]).

5   See e g *Tomlin v Luce* (1889) 43 Ch D 191 at 194; *Cuckmere Brick Co Ltd v Mutual Finance Ltd* [1971] Ch 949 at 966F–967C per Salmon LJ, 977D, 980E–G per Cairns LJ; *Hausman v O'Grady* (1988) 42 DLR (4th) 119 at 132–133, affd (1989) 57 DLR (4th) 480.

6   *Artistic Builders Pty Ltd v Elliot & Tuthill (Mortgagees) Pty Ltd* (2002) 10 BPR 19565 at [119].
     Equally mismanagement by a mortgagee in possession may have had a detrimental impact on
     sale value.

Setting aside the sale because of 'fraud on the power'

15.220   The far-reaching remedy of rescission is more readily available where
a particular exercise of the mortgagee's power of sale goes beyond a case of
mere carelessness and is more akin to equitable fraud or a 'fraud on the
power'.[1] In these circumstances the mortgagee's sale is liable to be set aside
completely, with the result that the mortgagor recovers the equity of redemption of which he has been unjustly deprived.[2] The cases which merit this more
dramatic remedy do not necessarily involve any actual fraud (in the common
law sense) or any actual collusion between the mortgagee and the purchaser,[3]
but comprise instances where the bona fides of the mortgagee has been
irreparably placed in question by evidence of his 'wilful or reckless disregard of
the interests of the mortgagor'[4] or by his transacting in the face of a clear
conflict of interests.[5]

1   *Forsyth v Blundell* (1973) 129 CLR 477 at 496 per Walsh J; *George v Commercial Union
     Assurance Co of Australia Ltd* (1977) 1 BPR 9649 at 9652. See also *Durrett v Washington
     National Insurance Co*, 621 F2d 201 at 204 (1980); *Abramson v Lakewood Bank and Trust Co*,
     647 F2d 547 at 549 (1981).
2   *Tse Kwong Lam v Wong Chit Sen* [1983] 1 WLR 1349 at 1359H–1360A per Lord Templeman.
3   There must be evidence that the purchaser either knew or ought to have known of the
     circumstances giving rise to the impropriety alleged against the mortgagee (see *Forsyth v
     Blundell* (1973) 129 CLR 477 at 497 per Walsh J; *George v Commercial Union Assurance Co of
     Australia Ltd* (1977) 1 BPR 9649 at 9652; *McKean v Maloney* [1988] 1 Qd R 628 at 635).
4   *Forsyth v Blundell* (1973) 129 CLR 477 at 496. See *Brutan Investments Pty Ltd v Underwriting
     and Insurance Ltd* (1980) 58 FLR 289 at 295–296.
5   See e g *Goldcell Nominees Pty Ltd v Network Finance Ltd* [1983] 2 VR 257 at 278–279.

15.221   In *Tse Kwong Lam v Wong Chit Sen*[1] the Privy Council held that
rescission would, 'as a general rule', have been the appropriate remedy in
respect of a sale coloured by a clear conflict of interest. However, Lord Templeman imposed the rider that the complainant will be left to a mere money
remedy if it is 'inequitable as between the borrower and the purchaser for the
sale to be set aside.'[2] In *Tse Kwong Lam* the remedy of rescission was indeed
considered inequitable because of the mortgagor's 'inexcusable delay' in pros-
ecuting his counterclaim.[3] The mortgagor was thus relegated to a money award,
which was measured as the difference between the actual sale price and the best
price reasonably obtainable at the date of sale.[4]

1   [1983] 1 WLR 1349 at 1359H **[para 15.216]**.
2   [1983] 1 WLR 1349 at 1360A. See similarly *Apple Fields Ltd v Damesh Holdings Ltd* [2001] 2
     NZLR 586 at [52] (NZ Court of Appeal).
3   See also *Corbett v Halifax Building Society* [2003] 1 WLR 964 at [43]–[44] per Pumfrey J (delay
     of more than two years in context of rising housing market).
4   [1983] 1 WLR 1360H. The award of HK $950,000 can only have been a fraction of the
     hearing-date value of the land which the mortgagor had effectively hoped to recover through
     an award of rescission.

FORECLOSURE

15.222   Foreclosure is the most draconian remedy open to the mortgagee in the event of default by his mortgagor. An order for foreclosure abrogates the mortgagor's equity of redemption and leaves the entire value of the mortgaged property in the hands of the mortgagee (irrespective of the amount of the mortgage debt). In spite of its theoretical potency, resort to the remedy of foreclosure is now extremely rare in English courts. As Nicholls V-C observed in *Palk v Mortgage Services Funding Plc*,[1] 'foreclosure actions are almost unheard of today and have been so for many years.'

1   [1993] Ch 330 at 336E. See similarly *Habermann v Koehler* (*No 2*) (2000) Times, 22 November (Transcript at [28]) per Robert Walker LJ.

Legal effects of foreclosure

15.223   Unlike the exercise of the statutory power of sale, the drastic remedy of foreclosure requires the interposition of some judicial control and is therefore available only on application to the court.[1] A court order for *foreclosure absolute* vests the mortgagor's entire estate (whether freehold or leasehold) in the mortgagee, without compensation for the mortgagor and subject only to those legal mortgages which have priority to the mortgage in respect of which the foreclosure has been obtained.[2]

1   *Ness v O'Neil* [1916] 1 KB 706 at 709.
2   LPA 1925, ss 88(2), 89(2). (All subsequent mortgage terms or charges are statutorily extinguished by the foreclosure.) An order for foreclosure obtained by a registered chargee is completed by the cancellation of the registered charge and the registration of the former chargee as the sole proprietor of the estate formerly subject to the charge (LRR 2003, r 112).

15.224   Notwithstanding that he has obtained foreclosure absolute, the mortgagee may still sue the mortgagor on his personal covenant to repay,[1] provided the mortgagee retains the mortgaged property in his possession.[2] However, the mortgagee is precluded from such action if, having foreclosed, he then sells the land to a third party.[3] In this event it would be plainly inequitable that the mortgagee should pursue the mortgagor for any deficiency resulting from the sale.[4] The mortgagee who sells following a foreclosure is not subject to the duty of care which binds the mortgagee who exercises a statutory power of sale.[5] It would therefore be grossly unfair to the mortgagor to hold the foreclosing mortgagee to be unaccountable in the matter of the price achieved by the sale yet able to recover from the mortgagor any shortfall which supposedly remains.[6]

1   That is, he may have 'both the money and the mud' (*Canada Permanent Trust Co v King Art Developments Ltd* (1985) 12 DLR (4th) 161 at 173 per Moir JA).
2   *Kinnaird v Trollope* (1888) 39 Ch D 636 at 642. Such action on the mortgagor's covenant gives the mortgagor a new equity of redemption (*Lockhart v Hardy* (1846) 9 Beav 349 at 356, 50 ER 378 at 380; *Palmer v Hendrie* (1859) 27 Beav 349 at 351, 54 ER 136 at 137).
3   *Perry v Barker* (1806) 13 Ves 198 at 205, 33 ER 269 at 272; *Kinnaird v Trollope* (1888) 39 Ch D 636 at 642; *Gordon Grant & Co Ltd v Boos* [1926] AC 781 at 784–787; *Lloyds and Scottish Trust Ltd v Britten* (1982) 44 P & CR 249 at 256–257; *Burnham v Galt* (1869) 16 Gr 417 at 419.

4   The land is no longer available in the mortgagee's hands for valuation (see *Gordon Grant & Co Ltd v Boos* [1926] AC 781 at 785 per Lord Phillimore).
5   **[Paras 15.192–15.198]**.
6   See *Bank of Nova Scotia v Dorval* (1980) 104 DLR (3d) 121 at 125.

Preconditions of foreclosure

15.225   The mortgagee cannot resort to foreclosure until, at the very least, the mortgagor has ceased to have any legal right to redeem the mortgage. Only then does the mortgagor acquire his 'equity' to redeem the mortgage; and it is the possible extinguishment of this equity which is in question in foreclosure proceedings.

15.226   Where a mortgage contains an express proviso for redemption, the mortgagor's legal right to redeem is lost only when he fails to comply with the terms of the proviso.[1] Thus the mortgagor's legal right to redeem clearly ceases once the legal repayment date has already passed.[2] The mortgagor also puts himself in breach of a proviso for redemption if his legal right to redeem was explicitly made conditional on the punctual payment of capital and interest and he has defaulted in this respect.[3] However, even if the mortgage contains no express proviso for redemption, the court can still order a foreclosure if the mortgagor's default is of such a nature as to bar him at law from recovering his property and to justify the court in extinguishing his equity of redemption.[4] A mortgagee may therefore, at least in theory, obtain a foreclosure even though the circumstances fall short of those which would entitle him to exercise his statutory power to sell or to appoint a receiver.[5]

1   *Twentieth Century Banking Corpn Ltd v Wilkinson* [1977] Ch 99 at 105A.
2   **[Para 15.13]**.
3   See e g *Kidderminster Mutual Benefit Building Society v Haddock* [1936] WN 158. Compare the refusal to order foreclosure in *Williams v Morgan* [1906] 1 Ch 804 at 810 (mortgagor's right to redeem at law expressly preserved irrespective of default).
4   *Twentieth Century Banking Corpn Ltd v Wilkinson* [1977] Ch 99 at 105A–C.
5   See *Twentieth Century Banking Corpn Ltd v Wilkinson* [1977] Ch 99 at 104E–F. Ironically, if the mortgagee can show himself entitled to foreclosure, the court has a discretion to direct a sale anyway (LPA 1925, s 91(2)).

Procedure of foreclosure

15.227   Foreclosure proceedings, if they ever occurred, would normally be conducted in the High Court. If the court decides to grant an order for foreclosure, it first makes an order for *foreclosure nisi*. This order directs that accounts be taken and provides that unless the mortgagor repays the mortgage money due within a period stipulated by the court,[1] the mortgage will be foreclosed. If no such payment is forthcoming, the court makes an order for *foreclosure absolute*, which has the effect of transferring the mortgagor's estate to the mortgagee. However, during the interim between the order nisi and the order absolute, it is open to the mortgagor or the mortgagee to apply to the court for an order directing a sale of the property rather than foreclosure.[2] This alternative form of order may be granted in the discretion of the court[3] and has the consequence that at least part of the value of the mortgaged property may be salvaged for the mortgagor.

1   This period is usually six months.
2   LPA 1925, s 91(2).
3   In practice the court will normally direct a sale contrary to the wishes of a mortgagee only if repayment of his debt is fully secured (see *Palk v Mortgage Services Funding Plc* [1993] Ch 330 at 335H per Nicholls V-C).

15.228   Even after the court has made an order for foreclosure absolute, it is possible for the mortgagor to request the court to 'reopen' the order.[1] The court thus has even further discretion to prevent the final destruction of the mortgagor's equity of redemption.[2] The remedy of foreclosure becomes statute-barred twelve years after the date when the relevant mortgage money fell due.[3]

1   A mortgagor's application to reopen an order for foreclosure absolute is registrable as a pending land action, thereby guarding against the possibility that the mortgagee may proceed with a sale of the foreclosed property (see *Re Pacific Savings & Mortgage Corp and Can-Corp Development Ltd* (1982) 135 DLR (3d) 623 at 640).
2   See *Campbell v Holyland* (1877) 7 Ch D 166 at 172–175 per Jessel MR.
3   Limitation Act 1980, s 15(1).

Modern incidence of foreclosure

15.229   Foreclosure is rarely sought today and even more rarely granted.[1] It is usually much more convenient for the mortgagee to appoint a receiver or to exercise his statutory power of sale.[2] Moreover, the court's powers to stay possession proceedings under section 36 of the Administration of Justice Act 1970 extend also to actions for foreclosure.[3] The courts have been increasingly reluctant to grant orders for foreclosure, particularly in the context of rising land values, because an order for foreclosure may have the effect of vesting in the mortgagee a much more valuable property than that over which he originally took his security.

1   The Law Commission proposed some time ago that the remedy of foreclosure be abolished (*Transfer of Land – Land Mortgages* (Law Com No 204, November 1991), para 7.27).
2   *Palk v Mortgage Services Funding Plc* [1993] Ch 330 at 336E–F per Nicholls V-C.
3   AJA 1970, s 36 (as amended by AJA 1973, s 8(2) [**paras 15.154–15.170**]).

REMEDIES AVAILABLE TO THE EQUITABLE MORTGAGEE OR CHARGEE

15.230   The remedies available to an equitable mortgagee differ in some respects from those which are open to a legal mortgagee, largely because the equitable mortgagee does not (even by statutory fiction[1]) take any legal estate or interest in the land offered as security. The equitable nature of the security, although obviously not affecting the mortgagee's ability to sue on the mortgagor's personal covenant to repay, has the following repercussions.

1   [**Para 8.246**].

Exercise of the power of sale

15.231 The statutory power of sale conferred by section 101(1) of the Law of Property Act 1925 is available in respect of any mortgage which has been effected by deed.[1] Thus some equitable mortgagees may have access to the statutory power,[2] but most equitable mortgagees are excluded on the ground that their mortgages were informal.[3] Such mortgagees have no automatic right to sell, but are entitled to apply to the court under section 91 of the Law of Property Act 1925. The court may, in its discretion, direct either that the mortgaged land be sold[4] or that a legal term of years be vested in the mortgagee, thereby converting him into a legal mortgagee for the purpose of entitlement to exercise the statutory power of sale.[5] Equitable chargees likewise have no automatic power of sale, but may nevertheless request the court for an order for sale.[6]

1   **[Para 15.172]**. If the statutory power is available, it is possible that the equitable mortgagee is competent to convey the full *legal* estate of his mortgagor (see *Re White Rose Cottage* [1965] Ch 940 at 951C; but compare *Re Hodson and Howe's Contract* (1887) 35 Ch D 668 at 671, 673). The matter can be put beyond doubt by conferring on the mortgagee an irrevocable power of attorney to convey the mortgagor's legal estate.
2   Sale with vacant possession may prove problematic since it is not clear that an equitable mortgagee has the same right to possession as a legal mortgagee **[para 15.126]**.
3   This exclusion would not, of course, apply where the equitable mortgage was effected by a memorandum of deposit in the form of a deed.
4   LPA 1925, s 91(2).
5   LPA 1925, s 91(7).
6   See *Matthews v Goodday* (1861) 31 LJ Ch 282 at 283; *London County and Westminster Bank Ltd v Tompkins* [1918] 1 KB 515 at 528. See also LPA 1925, s 90(1); *Ladup Ltd v Williams & Glyn's Bank Plc* [1985] 1 WLR 851 at 855B–C.

Appointment of a receiver

15.232 The statutory power to appoint a receiver is available only in respect of mortgages created by deed,[1] but in the absence of such creation the court may be asked to appoint a receiver.[2]

1   LPA 1925, s 101(1)(iii).
2   Supreme Court Act 1981, s 37(1)–(2) (formerly Supreme Court of Judicature (Consolidation) Act 1925, s 45). See *Shakel v Duke of Marlborough* (1819) 4 Madd 463, 56 ER 776.

Foreclosure

15.233 The court has power to order foreclosure of an equitable mortgage or to order a judicial sale in lieu of foreclosure.[1] In the case of an equitable mortgage, however, foreclosure takes the form of a court order that the mortgagor convey the legal title in the mortgaged property into the name of the mortgagee.

1   *James v James* (1873) LR 16 Eq 153 at 154. However, a mere equitable chargee cannot foreclose (see *Tennant v Trenchard* (1869) 4 Ch App 537 at 542; *Ladup Ltd v Williams & Glyn's*

Bank Plc [1985] 1 WLR 851 at 855B; *Croydon (Unique) Ltd v Wright* [2001] Ch 318 at 328D), but can only seek a court order for sale in lieu of foreclosure.

PRIORITY OF MORTGAGES

15.234   There is nothing inherently improper in multiple mortgages of realty,[1] the only limiting factor usually being the capacity for further commercial exploitation of the remaining 'equity' in the land concerned. Difficult questions of priority may arise where the same land has been mortgaged several times over to different mortgagees. If these mortgages remain outstanding and the security eventually proves inadequate to satisfy all due financial claims, some order must be established for giving effect to the respective rights of the mortgagees. The arrangement of priorities ultimately determines the order in which the loans made by various mortgagees are repaid from the available money proceeds of the land.[2] There is, inevitably, a possibility that some mortgagees will be left unpaid.

1   **[Para 8.241]**.
2   Perhaps surprisingly some of the problems disclosed in the law relating to priority have yet to be resolved – which may indicate that, in practice, the more complex issues of priority arise only infrequently.

15.235   The essential issue of priority concerns the preference to be made between the claims of two mortgagees, M1 and M2, who have in that order taken mortgages over the same realty. The rules of priority which determine the sequence in which their claims are met out of the proceeds of sale of the security depend on two key issues: *first*, whether the entitlement over which security has been taken is an estate registered at Land Registry or simply an unregistered estate; and *second*, whether the subject matter of the security is a legal or an equitable interest. A mortgage of an equitable interest generates, of course, only an equitable mortgage, but a mortgage of a legal estate may, in accordance with the precise mode of mortgage employed,[1] produce either a legal or an equitable security.

1   **[Para 8.242]**.

MORTGAGES OF A LEGAL ESTATE IN REGISTERED LAND

15.236   If M1 takes a charge over a legal (ie registered) estate in land, issues of priority will turn on whether his charge is *legal* or *equitable*.

Legal charge over a registered estate

15.237   The only formal method of mortgaging a legal estate in registered land is by way of 'registered charge'.[1] A legal mortgage over a registered estate is completed (ie becomes fully effective) only when the chargee is entered in the

Land Register as the proprietor of the charge.[2] It is possible to create any number of registered charges in respect of the same registered title. However, the Land Registration Act 2002 indicates that, subject to any contrary entry in the individual register, registered charges over the same registered estate rank as between themselves in the order which they are entered in the register (and therefore not necessarily in the order in which they are created).[3]

1   [**Para 8.243**].
2   LRA 2002, s 27(1), (2)(f) [**para 8.244**].
3   LRA 2002, s 48(1); LRR 2003, r 101. It is open to chargees, without the consent of their chargor, to alter the priority of their charges by agreement *inter se* (LRR 2003, r 102(1)). See also *Cheah v Equiticorp Finance Group Ltd* [1992] 1 AC 472 at 477A–D.

15.238   Thus, if M1 has been entered in the Land Register as the registered proprietor of a charge, his charge takes priority over any legal charge of M2 which is subsequently registered against the same registered estate (even if M2's charge was actually created *before* that of M1).[1] The chronological order in which the charges were created is, in fact, irrelevant. Furthermore M1's registered charge takes priority over any equitable charge created in favour of M2 *after* the date of registration of M1's charge. Perhaps less obviously, M1's registered charge also takes priority over any equitable charge which was created earlier than his own but which was not, before the registration of M1's charge, protected by the entry of a 'notice' in the register of the borrower's title[2] or rendered binding as an overriding interest.[3]

1   LRA 2002, ss 29(1), (2)(a)(i), 48(1).
2   LRA 2002, s 29(1), (2)(a)(i).
3   LRA 2002, s 29(1), (2)(a)(ii). It would, of course, be highly unusual – although not impossible (eg in a family situation) – for an equitable chargee to be in 'actual occupation' of the mortgagor's land.

Equitable charge over a registered estate

15.239   It is, of course, possible that the security taken by M1 over a legal estate in registered land may comprise only an *equitable* charge. This result inevitably follows in any case where M1 fails to obtain his own registration as proprietor of a potentially legal charge.[1] Alternatively an equitable charge arises where the chargor has merely *contracted* to charge his land or has created a charge which is expressly equitable.[2] In all of these cases M1's equitable charge is eligible for protection by the entry of a 'notice' in the chargor's register of title.

1   Pending registration of a potentially legal charge, the lender ranks merely as an equitable chargee [**para 9.107**].
2   [**Para 9.109**].

Consequence of protection of M1's charge

15.240   M1's charge, if protected by 'notice', enjoys priority over any legal (ie registered) charge later taken by M2,[1] since all subsequent dispositions for value inevitably have effect subject to existing entries in the register.[2] If not protected by 'notice', M1's charge loses priority to any *legal* charge subsequently registered in the name of M2, unless, unusually, M1's charge is an overriding interest.[3]

1 LRA 2002, s 29(1), (2)(a)(i).
2 LRA 2002, s 29(1), (2)(a)(i).
3 LRA 2002, s 29(1), (2)(a)(i)–(ii).

Competing equitable charges

15.241 M1's equitable charge, whether protected or not, retains priority over any merely *equitable* charge created for M2 subsequent to the date of creation of M1's charge. The special priority rule of the Land Registration Act 2002 is inapplicable (because M2's charge is not the product of a registered disposition of a registered estate[1]). The outcome is governed instead by the 'basic rule' of priority,[2] according to which competing interests rank in the order of their creation. This order of priority remains unaffected by the possibility that M2's equitable charge (although created later) may at some future date be the first to be protected by the entry of a 'notice' in the register.[3]

1 LRA 2002, s 29(1) [**para 12.72**].
2 LRA 2002, s 28(1) [**para 12.67**].
3 This priority will, however, be reversed with the advent of electronic conveyancing. Under the electronic regime the creation and registration of charges will become inseparable events [**para 12.4**], with the consequence that the order of entering charges in the register will also be definitive and conclusive as to priority.

MORTGAGES OF A LEGAL ESTATE IN UNREGISTERED LAND

15.242 As described in Chapter 8,[1] the mortgagee of a legal estate in unregistered land is, in certain circumstances, entitled to the additional security of retention of the title deeds relating to the mortgagor's land. This aspect of mortgage practice in relation to unregistered land is reflected in the way in which priority is accorded as between competing mortgagees. The issue of priority also turns on whether a mortgage is legal[2] or equitable.[3]

1 [**Para 8.255**].
2 [**Para 8.242**]. Most first legal mortgages of an unregistered estate now trigger a compulsory first registration of title [**paras 7.40, 7.242, 8.252**].
3 [**Paras 9.102–9.129**].

Legal mortgage over an unregistered legal estate

15.243 Here the rules of priority depend on whether M1's security is reinforced by custody of the title deeds relating to the land charged.

Mortgage protected by deposit of title deeds

15.244 If M1 takes a legal mortgage protected by a deposit of title documents, his mortgage is unassailable by any competing claim made by a later mortgagee, M2, provided that certain statutory requirements are observed. The mortgage to M1 triggers a compulsory registration of the mortgagor's estate and the consequent entry, in the newly opened register of title, of M1's proprietorship of a charge.[1] In this case the later mortgage in favour of M2 ranks as a disposition of a now registered estate and M1's registered charge inevitably enjoys priority.[2]

1 [Paras 7.40, 8.252–8.253].
2 LRA 2002, s 29(1), (2)(a)(i) [para 12.76].

15.245 If, for some reason, the mortgage to M1 fails to bring about a timely registration of the mortgagor's estate,[1] the mortgagor continues to hold a legal estate, but M1's unregistered charge is relegated to merely equitable effect. For want of registration it lapses as a legal mortgage[2] and takes effect instead as a contract for valuable consideration to create a legal charge.[3] This contract requires registration as an 'estate contract' pursuant to the Land Charges Act 1972.[4] Registration of a land charge of Class C(iv) would therefore guarantee M1 priority over all later mortgages (whether legal or equitable),[5] but a failure to register renders the estate contract void against any subsequent purchaser of the mortgagor's legal estate for money or money's worth (including one who takes a legal mortgage over that estate).[6] The unregistered land charge would, however, take priority over a later equitable charge of the mortgagor's legal estate, since as between competing equitable interests in unregistered land the rule is that the first in time prevails.

1 LRA 2002, s 6(1), (4) [para 7.41] (application for registration required within two months).
2 LRA 2002, s 7(1).
3 LRA 2002, s 7(2)(b) [para 7.43].
4 [Para 12.306].
5 LPA 1925, s 198(1) [para 12.279].
6 LCA 1972, s 4(6) [para 12.282].

Mortgage unaccompanied by deposit of title deeds

15.246 If, on taking his mortgage over an unregistered legal estate, M1 receives no title documents, the mortgage charge does not constitute a 'protected first legal mortgage' and therefore triggers no compulsory registration of either the mortgagor's estate or M1's charge.[1] The priority of M1's mortgage depends vitally on registration under the Land Charges Act 1972.[2] A legal mortgage unaccompanied by a deposit of title documents ranks as a Class C(i) charge (or 'puisne mortgage').[3] In order to achieve priority over M2, M1 must register his mortgage against the borrower's name, in which case the registered land charge acquires an irreversible priority over any later mortgage taken by M2. Failure to secure protection through registration renders M1's mortgage statutorily void against M2 (regardless of whether M2's mortgage is legal or equitable),[4] since M2 ranks for this purpose as 'a purchaser of the land'.[5]

1 LRA 2002, ss 4(1)(g), 6(2)(a) **[para 7.40]**.
2 It is generally assumed nowadays that the registration requirements of the Land Charges Act 1972 take precedence over LPA 1925, s 97 (which seems to indicate that priority as between competing mortgages unprotected by the deposit of title documents depends on the date of land charge registration). If priority were governed by section 97, M1's mortgage (if registered first) would rank ahead of M2's mortgage even if M1 had failed to register by the date on which M2's mortgage was created. Pursuant to section 4(5) of the 1972 Act, however, such failure renders M1's charge void. It is widely believed that the apparently conflicting provision in section 97 cannot have been intended to reactivate a charge which has been statutorily declared 'void', but 'the subject is not one for dogmatism' (R E Megarry, [1940] CLJ 243 at 255–256). See also J Howell, [1993] Conv 22.
3 LCA 1972, s 2(4)(i) **[para 12.301]**.
4 LCA 1972, s 4(5) **[para 12.281]**.
5 A 'purchaser' is defined as any person (including a mortgagee) who, for valuable consideration, takes any interest in or charge on land (LCA 1972, s 17(1)).

Equitable mortgage over an unregistered legal estate

15.247 Here again something depends on whether M1 has protected his security by taking custody of the title deeds relating to the borrower's land.

Mortgage protected by deposit of title deeds

15.248 If M1 takes an equitable mortgage protected by a deposit of title documents,[1] the issue of priority as against M2 depends on the legal or equitable quality of the security taken by M2. Where M2's mortgage is *legal*, the conflicting claims ought to be resolved by an application of the doctrine of notice.[2] Although M1's mortgage is earlier in time, it has the potential to lose priority to M2's legal mortgage if M2 took his mortgage without actual or constructive notice of the earlier incumbrance.[3] If the issue does indeed rest on constructive notice, much may turn on whether the mortgagor's obvious inability to give access to the relevant title deeds can be said to have put M2 on inquiry. However, the case law in this area often seems to have disavowed the strict relevance of constructive notice,[4] focusing instead on whether the later mortgagee, by grossly negligent investigation of the mortgagor's title, has been guilty of postponing conduct.[5] In this respect the courts have tended to treat later legal mortgagees with substantial lenience,[6] postponing claims only where it is clear that the legal mortgagee has acted with extreme imprudence.[7] In spite of the confusion induced by the older case law, the better modern view is that the mortgagor's inability to hand over the title deeds to M2 fixes M2 with notice of the existence of M1's earlier charge.

1 **[Para 9.111]**.
2 See LPA 1925, s 199(1)(ii) **[paras 2.191, 12.345]**.
3 *Brace v Duchess of Marlborough* (1728) 2 P Wms 491 at 493–496, 24 ER 829 at 830–831.
4 See e g *Oliver v Hinton* [1899] 2 Ch 264 at 273 per Lindley MR.

5   See eg *Hewitt v Loosemore* (1851) 9 Hare 449 at 458, 68 ER 586 at 590, where Turner V-C considered that nothing short of 'fraud or gross and wilful negligence' in the later mortgagee would be sufficient to be conceded to an earlier equitable mortgagee.

6   See *Hewitt v Loosemore* (1851) 9 Hare 449 at 456–459, 68 ER 586 at 589–590; *Agra Bank Ltd v Barry* (1874) LR 7 HL 135 at 150–157.

7   See *Oliver v Hinton* [1899] 2 Ch 264 at 274, where Lindley MR indicated that the subsequent purchaser should lose priority only if 'guilty of such gross negligence as would render it unjust to deprive the prior incumbrancer of his priority.'

15.249   Where M1 takes an equitable mortgage protected by a deposit of title documents and M2's later mortgage is likewise *equitable*, M1's security generally overrides that taken by M2. 'Where the equities are equal, the first in time prevails.' The chronological priority of M1's mortgage ensures that M1 must rank ahead of M2, unless M1 has forfeited this privilege by fraud, misrepresentation or gross negligence (eg in failing to retain the deeds securely).[1]

1   See *Taylor v Russell* [1891] 1 Ch 8 at 17.

Mortgage unaccompanied by deposit of title deeds

15.250   If M1 receives no title documents on taking his mortgage, the priority of his mortgage turns on whether it is registered under the Land Charges Act 1972.[1] M1's equitable mortgage constitutes a Class C(iii) charge (or 'general equitable charge')[2] and, if registered, takes priority over any later mortgage (whether legal or equitable) taken by M2. Failure to protect the land charge by registration renders M1's mortgage statutorily void against M2, M2 ranking for this purpose as 'a purchaser of the land'.[3]

1   Again the registration rules of the Land Charges Act 1972 almost certainly take precedence over LPA 1925, s 97 **[para 15.246]**.

2   **[Para 12.303]**.

3   LCA 1972, s 4(5).

PRIORITY OF MORTGAGES OVER AN EQUITABLE INTEREST IN LAND

15.251   A mortgage of an equitable interest in land can itself be equitable only.[1] Where the same equitable interest has been the subject of successive mortgages, it is well settled that the priority accorded to these mortgages is not governed by any rule of registration or even by the chronological order in which the mortgages were created. Instead priority is fixed in accordance with the rather different effects of the rule in *Dearle v Hall*.[2] Equitable interests generally presuppose the existence of a trust of land.[3] Where default by the beneficial owner of a mortgaged equitable interest leads to a sale of the trust land,[4] competing mortgagees of that equitable interest must look to the trustees for repayment of their respective loans out of the proceeds of the sale. It is not therefore unnatural that priority between such mortgagees should turn, in both *registered* and *unregistered* land, on a rule which stipulates that the trustees are normally obliged to pay off the mortgagees in the same order as that in which the trustees received written notification of the mortgages.

1   **[Para 9.103]**.
2   (1823) 3 Russ 1, 38 ER 475. See J de Lacy, [1999] Conv 311. Mortgages of a beneficial interest under a trust of land or strict settlement are incapable of registration under the Land Charges Act 1972 (see LCA 1972, s 2(4)(iii)(b) **[para 12.305]**).
3   **[Para 9.173]**.
4   **[Para 11.248]**.

Service of the notice

15.252   Under the rule in *Dearle v Hall* priority between competing mortgages of an equitable interest is determined essentially by the temporal order in which notice of these mortgages is received by the trustees of the land concerned.[1] The rule applied originally only to mortgages of pure personalty, but its application was extended to mortgages of equitable interests in realty by section 137 of the Law of Property Act 1925. Under the rule, as amended by section 137, notice must be given in writing[2] and the notice must be 'served' on the relevant trustees.[3] It should be noted that, under *Dearle v Hall*, the critical factor concerns the order of *receipt* of notices, not the order in which notices may have been given or sent.[4] It is not even necessary that a notice of mortgage should emanate from the mortgagee himself: it is sufficient if the trustees receive a written notice from some other source.[5] It is important, however, that a notice should be served on all of the relevant trustees in existence at the time, since only such a notice can guarantee priority in every event. A notice given to all the trustees remains effective notwithstanding that the recipients later die or retire without communicating the notice to those trustees who take their place.[6] A notice given to only one trustee protects any mortgage which is created during his trusteeship,[7] but normally ceases to be effective thereafter.[8]

1   LPA 1925, s 137(2) confirms that, in the case of a trust of land, the persons to be served with notice are the trustees **[para 9.204]** and in the context of settled land, notice must be served on the trustees of the strict settlement **[para 9.213]**.
2   LPA 1925, s 137(3).
3   LPA 1925, s 137(2). If the giving of notice proves unduly difficult or cannot be achieved without 'unreasonable cost or delay', the mortgagee may require that a memorandum of the dealing be endorsed on the instrument creating the trust (LPA 1925, s 137(4)). Such endorsement is acceptable as the equivalent of notice.
4   If two or more notices are received simultaneously, priority is governed by the order in which the relevant mortgages were actually created (see *Calisher v Forbes* (1871) 7 Ch App 109 at 113–114).
5   See e g *Ipswich Permanent Money Club Ltd v Arthy* [1920] 2 Ch 257 (notice sent by another mortgagee).
6   See *Re Wasdale* [1899] 1 Ch 163 at 166–167.
7   *Ward v Duncombe* [1893] AC 369 at 382, 395. Priority for such a mortgage is retained even after the termination of the trusteeship of the recipient.
8   Notice given to only one of several trustees becomes ineffective on the recipient's death or retirement unless, in the intervening period, the notice has been communicated to at least one other surviving trustee (see *Timson v Ramsbottom* (1836) 2 Keen 35 at 52–53, 48 ER 541 at 548; *Re Phillips' Trusts* [1903] 1 Ch 183 at 186–187).

An exception to the rule

15.253 There is one exception to the basic rule of priority established in *Dearle v Hall*. No mortgagee can ever secure priority if, at the time of making the loan, he knew (or should have known) of the existence of a prior mortgage created in favour of another creditor.[1] It would clearly be inequitable that, by the mere device of serving notice first, the later mortgagee should steal priority over an earlier mortgage of which he was (or ought to have been) fully aware. In effect, therefore, the rule in *Dearle v Hall* accords priority only to mortgagees who have no actual or constructive knowledge of prior incumbrances. It is irrelevant, however, if knowledge of an earlier mortgage reaches the later mortgagee *after* he takes his own mortgage but *before* he serves his notice on the trustees.[2]

1   *Re Holmes* (1885) 29 Ch D 786 at 788–789.
2   *Mutual Life Assurance Society v Langley* (1886) 32 Ch D 460 at 467–468.

TACKING OF FURTHER ADVANCES

15.254 In some circumstances a prior mortgagee (M1) may be able to gain an enhanced priority by 'tacking' to his own original loan a further loan to the mortgagor which is not made until *after* a second mortgagee (M2) has already taken a security over the same land. The tacking of a further advance effectively increases the loan sum for which M1 may claim priority, thereby diminishing the real value of the security taken by M2.

15.255 M1, the proprietor of a registered charge over a registered estate, is entitled under the Land Registration Act 2002 to make a further advance on the security of his own charge, whilst retaining priority over M2's intervening charge, provided that M1 has not received from M2 notice of the creation of M2's charge.[1] M1 may likewise claim priority over M2's intervening charge if M1's further advance is made in pursuance of an obligation, duly entered in the register before the creation of M2's charge, to make a further advance.[2] Similarly M1 enjoys priority over M2's intervening charge if the parties to the first charge agreed a maximum amount for which M1's charge would be security and that agreement was duly entered in the register at the time of the creation of M2's charge.[3] The 2002 Act specifies, however, that except in these special cases, tacking in relation to a charge over registered land is possible only with the agreement of M2.[4]

1   LRA 2002, s 49(1)–(2); LRR 2003, r 107.
2   LRA 2002, s 49(3); LRR 2003, r 108.
3   LRA 2002, s 49(4); LRR 2003, r 109.
4   LRA 2002, s 49(6).

15.256 In unregistered land M1 has a statutory right[1] to make a further advance in priority to a subsequent mortgage taken by M2 (whether legal or equitable) either by agreement with M2 or if M1 had no notice of M2's mortgage when making the further advance[2] or if (in any event) M1's mortgage imposes an obligation to make further advances.

1   LPA 1925, s 94(1).
2   Registration of the subsequent mortgage will normally constitute sufficient notice to preclude tacking (LPA 1925, s 198(1)). However, if M1's mortgage was expressed to be made for securing further advances, M1 will not be affected by any *deemed* notice under section 198, but only by actual or constructive notice of the subsequent mortgage which arises independently of the fact of registration (LPA 1925, s 94(2)). In practice subsequent mortgagees take care to give the prior mortgagee express notice of their own mortgages, since this effectively prevents tacking.

Index